Weiss Ratings' Investment Research Guide to Exchange-Traded Funds

Weiss Ratings' Investment Research Guide to Exchange-Traded Funds

Fall 2019

GREY HOUSE PUBLISHING

Weiss Ratings
4400 Northcorp Parkway
Palm Beach Gardens, FL 33410
561-627-3300

Independent. Unbiased. Accurate. Trusted.

Published by Grey House Publishing, Inc., located at 4919 Route 22, Amenia, NY 12501; telephone 518-789-8700. Grey House Publishing neither guarantees the accuracy of the data contained herein nor assumes any responsibility for errors, omissions or discrepancies. Grey House Publishing accepts no payment for listing; inclusion in the publication of any organization, agency, institution, publication, service or individual does not imply endorsement of the publisher.

Grey House
Publishing

Edition #10, Fall 2019

ISBN: 978-1-64265-178-2

Contents

Terms and Conditions

This document is prepared strictly for the confidential use of our customer(s). It has been provided to you at your specific request. It is not directed to, or intended for distribution to or use by, any person or entity who is a citizen or resident of or located in any locality, state, country or other jurisdiction where such distribution, publication, availability or use would be contrary to law or regulation or which would subject Weiss Ratings, LLC or its affiliates to any registration or licensing requirement within such jurisdiction.

No part of the analysts' compensation was, is, or will be, directly or indirectly, related to the specific recommendations or views expressed in this research report.

This document is not intended for the direct or indirect solicitation of business. Weiss Ratings, LLC, and its affiliates disclaim any and all liability to any person or entity for any loss or damage caused, in whole or in part, by any error (negligent or otherwise) or other circumstances involved in, resulting from or relating to the procurement, compilation, analysis, interpretation, editing, transcribing, publishing and/or dissemination or transmittal of any information contained herein.

Weiss Ratings, LLC has not taken any steps to ensure that the securities or investment vehicle referred to in this report are suitable for any particular investor. The investment or services contained or referred to in this report may not be suitable for you and it is recommended that you consult an independent investment advisor if you are in doubt about such investments or investment services. Nothing in this report constitutes investment, legal, accounting or tax advice or a representation that any investment or strategy is suitable or appropriate to your individual circumstances or otherwise constitutes a personal recommendation to you.

The ratings and other opinions contained in this document must be construed solely as statements of opinion from Weiss Ratings, LLC, and not statements of fact. Each rating or opinion must be weighed solely as a factor in your choice of an institution and should not be construed as a recommendation to buy, sell or otherwise act with respect to the particular product or company involved.

Past performance should not be taken as an indication or guarantee of future performance, and no representation or warranty, expressed or implied, is made regarding future performance. Information, opinions and estimates contained in this report reflect a judgment at its original date of publication and are subject to change without notice. Weiss Ratings, LLC offers a notification service for rating changes on companies you specify. For more information visit WeissRatings.com or call 1-877-934-7778. The price, value and income from any of the securities or financial instruments mentioned in this report can fall as well as rise.

This document and the information contained herein is copyrighted by Weiss Ratings, LLC. Any copying, displaying, selling, distributing or otherwise delivering of this information or any part of this document to any other person or entity is prohibited without the express written consent of Weiss Ratings, LLC, with the exception of a reviewer or editor who may quote brief passages in connection with a review or a news story.

Date of Data Analyzed: September 30, 2019

Welcome to Weiss Ratings' Investment Research Guide to Exchange-Traded Funds

With investing such a complex subject and the enormous popularity of exchange-traded funds as a simple way to enter the markets it is no surprise that consumers need assistance. It is a complex subject and consumers want unbiased, independent guidance in helping them find a path to investing that is focused on their needs.

This is where Weiss Ratings comes in. We take all the data and process it, daily, to ensure that you receive not only the most up-to-date rating possible but also data that you may not easily find elsewhere. We publish this data in guides, and on our website so that you can feel empowered to make decisions about your investing future. Our focus is on balance and our ratings reflect this. No matter how strong a return has been if the level of risk taken is too high, in our opinion, then the overall rating will be reduced.

Weiss Ratings' Mission Statement

Weiss Ratings' mission is to empower consumers, professionals, and institutions with high quality advisory information for selecting or monitoring a financial services company or financial investment.

In doing so, Weiss Ratings will adhere to the highest ethical standards by maintaining our independent, unbiased outlook and approach for our customers.

Why rely on Weiss Ratings?

Weiss Ratings are fundamentally incomparable to nearly all other ratings available in America today. Here's why …

Complete Independence

We are America's only 100% independent rating agency covering stocks, ETFs, mutual funds, insurance companies, banks, and credit unions; and our independence is grounded in a very critical difference in the way we do business: Unlike most other rating agencies,

- we never accept compensation from any company for its rating;
- we never allow companies to influence our analysis or conclusions (although they are always free to provide us with supplemental data that's not publicly available);
- we reserve the right to publish our ratings based exclusively on publicly available data;
- we never suppress publication of our ratings at a company's request; and
- we are always dedicated to providing our analysis and opinions with complete objectivity.

Dedication to End Users -- Investors and Consumers

Other rating agencies derive most of their revenues from the very same companies that they cover.

In contrast, our primary source of revenues is the end user – investors seeking the best combination of risk and reward, plus consumers seeking the best deals with the most safety.

Unmatched Accuracy and Performance

Our independence and objectivity help explain why the U.S. Government Accountability Office (GAO) concluded that Weiss was first in warning consumers about future insurance company failures three times more often than our closest competitor (A.M. Best) and why, in comparison to S&P or Moody's, there was no contest.

It's the reason why The New York Times wrote "Weiss was the first to warn of dangers and say so unambiguously."

And it's also why The Wall Street Journal was able to report that the Weiss Stock Ratings outperformed all Wall Street investment banks, brokers and independent research organizations in a third-party study of stock ratings.

Broader Coverage

While other rating agencies focus mostly on larger companies that can afford to pay them large fees, Weiss Ratings covers all companies, large or small, as long as they report sufficient data for us to analyze. This allows us to provide far broader coverage, including nearly all U.S.-traded stocks, ETFs and mutual funds plus nearly all U.S. banks, credit unions and insurance companies.

Overall ...

Weiss Ratings gives you more accuracy, more choices, and better wealth-building potential – all with stronger risk protection and safety.

How to Use This Guide

The purpose of the *Weiss Ratings' Investment Research Guide to Exchange-Traded Funds* is to provide investors with a reliable source of investment ratings and analyses on a timely basis. We realize that past performance is an important factor to consider when making the decision to purchase shares in an exchange-traded fund. The ratings and analyses in this Guide can make that evaluation easier when you are considering Exchange-Traded funds. The rating for a particular fund indicates our opinion regarding that fund's past risk-adjusted performance.

When evaluating a specific exchange-traded fund, we recommend you follow these steps:

Step 1 Confirm the fund name and ticker symbol. To ensure you evaluate the correct exchange-traded fund, verify the fund's exact name and ticker symbol as it was given to you in its prospectus or appears on your account statement. Many funds have similar names, so you want to make sure the fund you look up is really the one you are interested in evaluating.

Step 2 Check the fund's Investment Rating. Turn to Section I, the *Weiss Ratings' Investment Research Guide to Exchange-Traded Funds*, and locate the fund you are evaluating. This section contains all Exchange-Traded funds analyzed by Weiss Ratings, including those that did not receive an Investment Rating. All funds are listed in alphabetical order by the name of the fund with the ticker symbol following the name for additional verification. Once you have located your specific fund, the fourth column after the ticker symbol under the Ratings header shows its overall Investment Rating. Turn to *About Weiss Investment Ratings* for information about what this rating means.

Step 3 Analyze the supporting data. In addition to the Weiss Exchange-Traded Fund Rating are some of the various measures we have used in rating the fund. Refer to the Section I introduction to see what each of these factors measures. In most cases, lower rated funds will have a low reward rating and/or a low risk rating (i.e., high volatility). Bear in mind, however, that the Weiss Exchange-Traded Fund Rating is the result of a complex proprietary computer-generated analysis which cannot be reproduced using only the data provided here.

Step 4 When looking to identify an exchange-traded fund that achieves your specific investing goals, we recommend the following:

- **Check the detailed analysis of the BUY rated Exchange-Traded Funds.** If your priority is to invest in only highest rated funds, then this list if for you. Here you will find full analysis of each ETF on the BUY list.

- **Check the detailed analysis of all rated funds with assets over $50 million.** If your priority is the size of an Exchange-Traded Funds, then this list is where you need to look. This list includes detailed analysis of all rated funds with over $50 million in assets.

- **Check the listing of the Largest funds.** If your priority is to stick with large funds because you believe that the size of the fund matters then these funds should be looked at. In this listing of the 100 largest funds you can also be assured that the Weiss Exchange-Traded Fund Rating is just as important as for the smallest fund.

- **Check the listing of the Best One-Year Return BUY Rated Funds.** If you are looking to invest in funds that can provide you with highest total returns over a one-year period, then look at this list. Here you will find all BUY rated funds that are in the top 10% when it comes to providing highest one-year total returns.

- **Check the listing of the Best Low Expense Exchange-Traded Funds.** If your priority is to find an Exchange-Traded Fund that charges the lowest fee, then this list is worth looking at. Here you will find highly rated funds with lowest expense ratios.

- **Check out the Top-Rated Funds by Fund Type.** If you are looking to invest in a particular type of exchange-traded fund turn to our listing of "Buy" rated Exchange-Traded Funds by Fund Type. There you will find the top exchange-traded funds with the highest performance rating in each category.

Step 5 Refer back to Section I. Once you have identified a particular fund that interests you, refer back to Section I, the Index of Exchange-Traded Funds, for a more thorough analysis.

Step 6 Always remember:

- **Read our warnings and cautions.** In order to use Weiss Investment Ratings most effectively, we strongly recommend you consult the Important Warnings and Cautions. These are more than just "standard disclaimers." They are very important factors you should be aware of before using this guide.

- **Stay up to date.** Periodically review the latest Weiss Exchange-Traded Fund Ratings for the funds that you own to make sure they are still in line with your investment goals and level of risk tolerance. You can find more detailed information and receive automated updates on ratings through www.weissratings.com

Data Source: Weiss Ratings
              Morningstar, Inc.

Date of data analyzed: September 30, 2019

About Weiss Investment Ratings

Weiss Investment Ratings of stocks, ETFs and mutual funds are in the same realm as "buy," "sell" and "hold" ratings. They are designed to help investors make more informed decisions with the goal of maximizing gains and minimizing risk. Safety is also an important consideration. The higher the rating, the more likely the investment will be profitable. But when using our investment ratings, you should always remember that, by definition, all investments involve some element of risk.

A   Strong Buy
B   Buy
C   Hold or Avoid
D   Sell
E   Strong Sell

Our **Overall Rating** is measured on a scale from A to E based on each fund's risk and performance. The funds are analyzed using the latest daily data available and the quarterly filings with the SEC. Weiss takes thousands of pieces of fund data and, based on its own model, balances reward against the amount of risk to assign a rating. The results provide a simple and understandable opinion as to whether we think the fund is a BUY, SELL, or HOLD.

Our **Reward Rating** is based on the total return over a period of up to five years, including net asset value and price growth. The total return figure is stated net of the expenses and fees charged by the fund. Based on proprietary modeling the individual components of the risk and reward ratings are calculated and weighted and the final rating is generated.

Our **Risk Rating** includes the risk ratings of component stocks where applicable and also includes the financial stability of the fund, turnover where applicable, together with the level of volatility as measured by the fund's daily returns over a period of up to five years. Funds with greater stability are considered less risky and receive a higher risk rating. Funds with greater volatility are considered riskier, and will receive a lower risk rating. In addition to considering the fund's volatility, the risk rating also considers an assessment of the valuation and quality of a fund's holdings.

In order to help guarantee our objectivity, we reserve the right to publish ratings expressing our opinion of an investment reward and risk based exclusively on publicly available data and our own proprietary standards for safety. But when using our investment ratings, you should always remember that, by definition, all investments involve some element of risk.

Current Weiss Ratings Distribution
of Exchange-Traded Funds

as of September 30, 2019

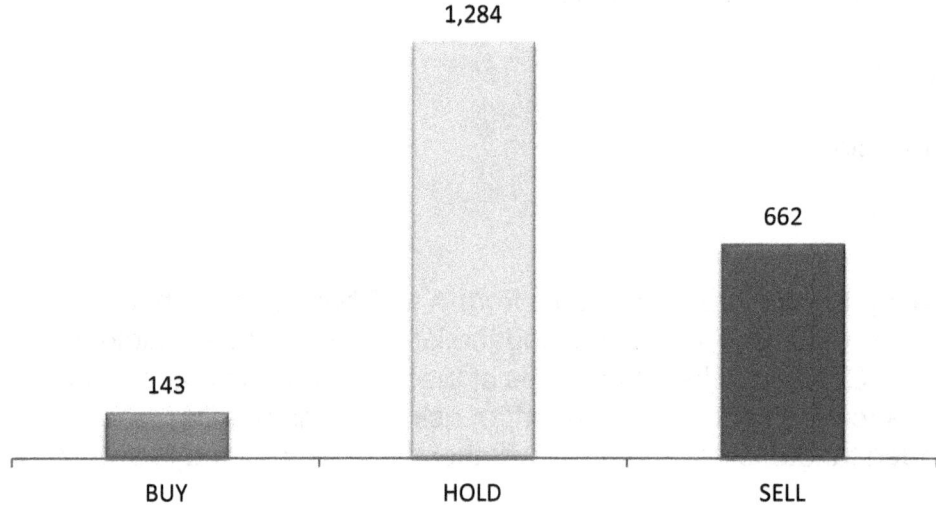

What Our Ratings Mean

Weiss Mutual Funds, Closed-End Funds, and Exchange Traded Funds Ratings represent a completely independent, unbiased opinion of funds—now, and in the future. The funds are analyzed using the latest daily data available and the quarterly filings with the SEC. Weiss takes thousands of pieces of fund data and, based on its own model, balances reward against the amount of risk to assign a rating. The results provide a simple and understandable opinion as to whether we think the fund is a BUY, SELL, or HOLD.

In order to help guarantee our objectivity, we reserve the right to publish ratings expressing our opinion of an investment reward and risk based exclusively on publicly available data and our own proprietary standards for safety. But when using our investment ratings, you should always remember that, by definition, all investments involve some element of risk.

Strong Buy

A   **Excellent.** The fund has an excellent track record for maximizing performance while minimizing risk, thus delivering the best possible combination of total return on investment and reduced volatility. It has made the most of the recent economic environment to maximize risk-adjusted returns compared to other exchange-traded funds. Although even the best funds can decline in a down market, our "A" rating can generally be considered the equivalent of a "Strong Buy".

Buy

B   **Good.** The fund has a good track record for balancing performance with risk. Compared to other exchange-traded funds, it has achieved above-average returns given the level of risk in its underlying investments. Although even good funds can decline in a down market, our "B" rating is considered the equivalent of a "Buy".

Hold or Avoid

C   **Fair.** In the trade-off between performance and risk, the fund has a track record which is about average. It is neither significantly better nor significantly worse than most other funds. With some funds in this category, the total return may be better than average, but this can be misleading if the higher return was achieved with higher than average risk. With other funds, the risk may be lower than average, but the returns are also lower. Although funds can be driven higher or lower by general market trends, our "C" rating can generally be considered the equivalent of a "Hold" or "Avoid."

Sell

D   **Weak.** The fund has underperformed the universe of other funds given the level of risk in its underlying investments, resulting in a weak risk-adjusted performance. Thus, its investment strategy and/or management has not been attuned to capitalize on the recent economic environment. Even weak funds can rise in an up market. However, our "D" rating can generally be considered equivalent to a "Sell."

Strong Sell

E   **Very Weak.** The fund has significantly underperformed most other funds given the level of risk in its underlying investments, resulting in a very weak risk-adjusted performance. Thus, its investment strategy and/or management has done just the opposite of what was needed to maximize returns in the recent economic environment. Even some of the weakest funds can rise in certain market conditions. However, our "E" rating can generally be considered the equivalent of a "Strong Sell."

+   The plus sign is an indication that the fund is in the upper third of the letter grade.

-     The minus sign is an indication that the fund is in the lower third of the letter grade.

U   Unrated. The fund is unrated because it is too new to make a reliable assessment of its risk-adjusted performance. Typically, a fund must be established for at least one year before it is eligible to receive a Weiss Investment Rating.

Important Warnings & Cautions

1. A rating alone cannot tell the whole story. Please read the explanatory information contained here, in the section introductions and in the appendix. It is provided in order to give you an understanding of our rating methodology as well as to paint a more complete picture of an exchange-traded fund's strengths and weaknesses.

2. Investment ratings shown in this directory were current as of the publication date. In the meantime, the rating may have been updated based on more recent data. Weiss Ratings offers a notification service for ratings changes on companies that you specify. For more information visit www.weissratings.com.

3. When deciding to invest in or sell holdings in a specific exchange-traded fund, your decision must be based on a wide variety of factors in addition to the Weiss Exchange-Traded Fund Rating. These include any charges you may incur from switching funds, to what degree it meets your long-term planning needs, and what other choices are available to you. Weiss Ratings recommends that you should always consult an independent financial advisor over your investment decisions.

4. Weiss Exchange-Traded Fund Ratings represent our opinion of an exchange-traded fund's past risk adjusted performance. As such, a high rating means we feel that the exchange-traded fund has at least achieved above-average returns at the same time as it has balanced risk and returns. A high rating is not a guarantee that a fund will continue to perform well, nor is a low rating a prediction of continued weak performance. Any references to "Buy", "Hold", or "Sell" correlate with our opinion of a particular fund and Weiss Exchange-Traded Fund Ratings are not deemed to be a recommendation concerning the purchase or sale of any exchange-traded fund.

5. All funds that have the same Weiss Investment Rating should be considered to be essentially equal from a risk/reward perspective. This is true regardless of any differences in the underlying numbers which might appear to indicate greater strengths.

6. Our rating standards are more consumer-oriented than those used by other rating agencies. We make more conservative assumptions about the amortization of loads and other fees as we attempt to identify those funds that have historically provided superior returns with only little or moderate risk.

7. We are an independent rating agency and do not depend on the cooperation of the managers operating the exchange-traded funds we rate. Our data is obtained from a data aggregator. Data is input daily, as available, into our proprietary models where a complex series of algorithms provide us with ratings based on quantitative analysis. We do not grant exchange-traded fund managers the right to stop or influence publication of the ratings. This policy stems from the fact that this Guide is designed for the information of the consumer.

Mutual Funds vs. Exchange-Traded Funds... Which is Right For You?

Both ETF's and Mutual Funds give you an inexpensive and easy way to diversify your investments and allow you to gain access to different asset classes with a single purchase. Ultimately, you'll need to consider a variety of factors including your tax strategy, the amount of money available to invest, and your overall investment strategy in order to determine which option is right for you.

Mutual Funds

Pros

- Mutual Funds are typically actively managed compared to ETF's which are typically tracking an index. Some of the better fund managers can regularly beat an index, although they will mostly have higher fees associated with them.
- Bigger Universe: There are over 28,000 Mutual Funds vs. less than 2,000 ETF's. You'll have more choices if you choose mutual funds, though the gap is narrowing every year.

Cons

- Mutual funds can only be purchased or sold at the end of the trading day after the market closes and their price is based on Net Asset Value (NAV), the value of fund assets minus liabilities divided by the number of shares.
- Mutual Fund holders can only see the holding of the Funds on a semi-annual basis.
- They are more tax prone- because the buying and selling within the fund by the Portfolio Manager creates more taxable events.
- Higher Minimum Investments

Stock Mutual Funds vs. Bond Mutual Funds

- Primarily, investors purchase stock mutual funds for appreciation or growth from within the companies inside the mutual fund itself. Conversely, bond mutual funds are primarily targeted for income reasons, since the entities inside a bond mutual fund give off income in the form of a coupon payment. Bonds and stocks frequently have an inverse relationship in market cycles, bonds will do well in down markets and stocks will do well in bull markets. For this reason, and for other diversification principles, it's important to have both bond and stock mutual funds in a long term retirement portfolio.
- It's important to note that there are exceptions to this rule, some stocks funds will give off an income in the form of dividend payments and many bond funds seek appreciation as well as income.
- There are risks associated with both bond and stock mutual funds. The risks in stock funds are primarily "market risk" meaning if the overall market is trending lower many stock funds will follow. The risks associated with bond funds are mostly associated with interest rates. In an environment with interest rates rising bond prices will follow and vice versa.

Exchange-Traded Funds (ETFs)

Pros

- ETFs offer much more flexibility. ETFs trade like stocks. They are priced on what Investors believe is Fair Market Value and you can buy and sell shares throughout the day.
- ETFs offer much more transparency, which means that investors can typically see the fund's holdings on a daily basis
- ETFs are more tax efficient than Mutual Funds. Because they are based off an index, there are fewer taxable events. Keep in mind, however, that capital gains and dividends are taxed the same as a Mutual Fund.
- ETFs have a lower expense ratio. In 2016, the average was .23 vs .82 of actively managed funds according to the Investment Company Institute.
- ETFs typically require lower minimum investments. Most of the time you can buy just a single share of the fund.
- You are typically paying a commission on buying and selling an exchange-traded fund. You'll pay a front or back end load when you purchase regular Mutual Funds.

Cons

- Some ETFs have limited choices in their asset class. Mutual Funds typically have more options.
- Given that an ETF trades like a stock, every purchase or sale requires paying a commission.

Section I:
Index of Exchange-Traded Funds

Investment Ratings and analysis of all rated and unrated Exchange-Traded Funds. Funds are listed in alphabetical order.

Section I: Contents

This section contains Weiss Investment Ratings, key rating factors, and summary financial data for over 2,200 Exchange-Traded funds. Funds are listed in alphabetical order.

Left Pages

Fund Name
Describes the fund's assets, regions of investments and investment strategies. Many funds have similar names, so you want to make sure the fund you look up is really the one you are interested in evaluating.

MARKET

Ticker Symbol
An arrangement of characters (usually letters) representing a particular security listed on an exchange or otherwise traded publicly. When a company issues securities to the public marketplace, it selects an available ticker symbol for its securities which investors use to place trade orders. Every listed security has a unique ticker symbol, facilitating the vast array of trade orders that flow through the financial markets every day.

Traded On (Exchange)
The stock exchange on which the fund is listed. The core function of a stock exchange is to ensure fair and orderly trading, as well as efficient dissemination of price information. Exchanges such as: NYSE (New York Stock Exchange), AMEX (American Stock Exchange), NNM (NASDAQ National Market), and NASQ (NASDAQ Small Cap) give companies, governments and other groups a platform to sell securities to the investing public. NASDAQ is abbreviated as NAS.

RATINGS

Overall Rating
The Weiss rating measured on a scale from A to E based on each fund's risk and performance. See the preceding section, "What Our Ratings Mean," for an explanation of each letter grade rating.

Reward Rating

This is based on the total return over a period of up to five years, including net asset value and price growth. The total return figure is stated net of the expenses and fees charged by the fund. Based on proprietary modeling the individual components of the risk and reward ratings are calculated and weighted and the final rating is generated.

Risk Rating

This is includes the risk ratings of component stocks where applicable and also includes the financial stability of the fund, turnover where applicable, together with the level of volatility as measured by the fund's daily returns over a period of up to five years. Funds with greater stability are considered less risky and receive a higher risk rating. Funds with greater volatility are considered riskier, and will receive a lower risk rating. In addition to considering the fund's volatility, the risk rating also considers an assessment of the valuation and quality of a fund's holdings.

Recent Upgrade/Downgrade

An "Up" or "Down" indicates that the Weiss Exchange-Traded Fund rating has changed since the publication of the last print edition. If a fund has had a rating change since June 30, 2019, the change is identified with an "Up" or "Down."

PRICE

Price

The price at which the fund is traded on a regular trading day. Prices in this guide are listed as of September 30, 2019.

52-Week High

The highest price that a fund has achieved during the previous 52 weeks.

52-Week Low

The lowest price that a fund has achieved during the previous 52 weeks.

Open to New Investors

Indicates whether the fund accepts investments from those who are not existing investors. A "Y" in this column identifies that the fund accepts new investors. No data in this column indicates that the fund is closed to new investors. The fund may be closed to new investors because the fund's asset base is getting too large to effectively execute its investing style. Although, the fund may be closed, in most cases, existing investors are able to add to their holdings.

CATEGORY & OBJECTIVE

Category
Identifies funds according to their actual investment styles as measured by their portfolio holdings. This categorization allows investors to spread their money around in a mix of funds with a variety of risk and return characteristics.

Prospectus Objective
Gives a general idea of a fund's overall investment approach and goals.

Right Pages

RETURNS & PERFORMANCE

3-Month Total Return
The rate of return on an investment over three months that includes interest, capital gains, dividends and distributions realized.

6-Month Total Return
The rate of return on an investment over six months that includes interest, capital gains, dividends and distributions realized.

1-Year Total Return
The rate of return on an investment over one year that includes interest, capital gains, dividends and distributions realized.

3-Year Total Return
The rate of return on an investment over three years that includes interest, capital gains, dividends and distributions realized.

5-Year Total Return
The rate of return on an investment over five years that includes interest, capital gains, dividends and distributions realized.

Dividend Yield (TTM)
Trailing twelve months dividends paid out relative to the share price. Expressed as a percentage and measures how much cash flow an investor is getting for each invested dollar. **Trailing Twelve Months (TTM)** is a representation of a fund's financial performance over the most recent 12 months. TTM uses the latest available financial data from a company's interim, quarterly or annual reports.

Expense Ratio

A measure of what it costs an investment company to operate an exchange-traded fund. An expense ratio is determined through an annual calculation, where a fund's operating expenses are divided by the average dollar value of its assets under management. Operating expenses may include money spent on administration and management of the fund, advertising, etc. An expense ratio of 1 percent per annum means that each year 1 percent of the fund's total assets will be used to cover expenses.

3-Year Standard Deviation

A statistical measurement of dispersion about an average, which depicts how widely the returns varied over the past three years. Investors use the standard deviation of historical performance to try to predict the range of returns that are most likely for a given fund. When a fund has a high standard deviation, the predicted range of performance is wide, implying greater volatility. Standard deviation is most appropriate for measuring risk if it is for a fund that is an investor's only holding. The figure cannot be combined for more than one fund because the standard deviation for a portfolio of multiple funds is a function of not only the individual standard deviations, but also of the degree of correlation among the funds' returns. If a fund's returns follow a normal distribution, then approximately 68 percent of the time they will fall within one standard deviation of the mean return for the fund, and 95 percent of the time within two standard deviations.

Effective Duration

Effective duration for all long fixed income positions in a portfolio. This value gives a better estimation of how the price of bonds with embedded options, which are common in many exchange-traded funds, will change as a result of changes in interest rates. Effective duration takes into account expected mortgage prepayment or the likelihood that embedded options will be exercised if a fund holds futures, other derivative securities, or other funds as assets, the aggregate effective duration should include the weighted impact of those exposures.

ASSETS

NAV (Net Asset Value)

A fund's price per share. The value is calculated by dividing the total value of all the securities in the portfolio, less any liabilities, by the number of fund shares outstanding.

Total Assets (MIL)
The total of all assets listed on the institution's balance sheet. This figure primarily consists of loans, investments, and fixed assets. Total Assets are displayed in millions.

ASSET ALLOCATION & TURNOVER

Asset Allocation
Indicates the percentage of assets in each category. Used as an investment strategy that attempts to balance risk versus reward by adjusting the percentage of each asset in an investment portfolio according to the investor's risk tolerance, goals and investment time frame. Allocation percentages may not add up to 100%. Negative values reflect short positions.

%Cash
The percentage of the fund's assets invested in short-term obligations, usually less than 90 days, that provide a return in the form of interest payments. This type of investment generally offers a low return compared to other investments but has a low risk level.

%Stocks
The percentage of the fund's assets invested in stock.

%Bonds
The percentage of the fund's assets invested in bonds. A bond is an unsecured debt security issued by companies, municipalities, states and sovereign governments to raise funds. When a company issues a bond it borrows money from the bondholder to boost the business, in exchange the bondholder receives the principal amount back plus the interest on the determined maturity date.

%Other
The percentage of the fund's assets invested in other financial instruments.

Turnover Ratio
The percentage of an exchange-traded fund or other investment vehicle's holdings that have been replaced with other holdings in a given year. Generally, low turnover ratio is favorable, because high turnover equates to higher brokerage transaction fees, which reduce fund returns.

VALUATION

Premium/Discount 1-Year Average
The annual average premium or discount of the market price to the NAV (Net Asset Value), expressed as a percentage of the NAV. This value provides a year-by-year picture a fund's trading status. A negative number indicates that, on average, the fund's shares sold at a discount to NAV, and a positive number indicates the shares sold at a premium. If the number shown is –10.00, for example, the shares sold at an average 10% discount to NAV during the listed time-period.

Inception Date
The date on which the fund began its operations. The commencement date indicates when a fund began investing in the market. Many investors prefer funds with longer operating histories. Funds with longer histories have longer track records and can thereby provide investors with a more long-standing picture of their performance.

Fund Name	Ticker Symbol	Traded On	Overall Rating	Reward Rating	Risk Rating	Recent Up/ Downgrade	Price as of 9/30/2019	52-Week High	52-Week Low	Open to New Investors	Category & (Prospectus Objective)
AAM S&P 500 High Dividend Value ETF	SPDV	NYSE Arca	C-	D+	C-	Up	26.41	27.51	22.63	Y	US Equity Large Cap Value (Growth & Inc)
AAM S&P Developed Markets High Dividend Value ETF	DMDV	NYSE Arca	U	U	U		24.45	26.44	23.13	Y	Global Equity Large Cap (Equity-Income)
AAM S&P Emerging Markets High Dividend Value ETF	EEMD	NYSE Arca	D	D	D		20.95	24.04	19.86	Y	Global Emerg Mkts Equity (Div Emerg Mkts)
Aberdeen Std Bloomberg All Commod Longer Dated Strat K-1 F	BCD	NYSE Arca	D	D	D		23.60	26.41	22.98	Y	Commodities Broad Basket (Growth & Inc)
● Aberdeen Standard Bloomberg All Commod Strat K-1 Free ETF	BCI	NYSE Arca	D+	D	C-		22.03	24.61	21.46	Y	Commodities Broad Basket (Growth & Inc)
Aberdeen Std Bloomberg WTI Crude Oil Strat K-1 Free ETF	AOIL	NYSE Arca	D	D+	D		24.36	31.18	21.77	Y	Commodities Specified (Natl Res)
★ Aberdeen Standard Physical Palladium Shares ETF	PALL	NYSE Arca	B-	B+	C-	Up	159.19	159.25	99.98	Y	Commodities Specified (Prec Metals)
● Aberdeen Standard Physical Platinum Shares ETF	PPLT	NYSE Arca	D+	D+	D+	Up	83.47	93.15	74.32	Y	Commodities Specified (Prec Metals)
● Aberdeen Standard Physical Prec Metals Basket Shares ETF	GLTR	NYSE Arca	C	C+	C-		72.58	77.41	58.39	Y	Commodities Specified (Prec Metals)
● Aberdeen Standard Physical Silver Shares ETF	SIVR	NYSE Arca	C-	C-	C	Up	16.52	19.03	13.61	Y	Commodities Specified (Prec Metals)
● Aberdeen Standard Physical Swiss Gold Shares ETF	SGOL	NYSE Arca	C+	C+	C+	Up	141.95	149.88	114.76	Y	Commodities Specified (Prec Metals)
AdvisorShares Cornerstone Small Cap ETF	SCAP	NYSE Arca	D+	C-	D		34.57	40.00	30.08	Y	US Equity Small Cap (Small Company)
● AdvisorShares Dorsey Wright ADR ETF	AADR	NYSE Arca	C	C	C-	Up	47.67	53.70	38.43	Y	Global Equity Large Cap (Growth)
AdvisorShares Dorsey Wright Micro-Cap ETF	DWMC	NYSE Arca	D+	D	D+	Up	21.54	24.28	18.04	Y	US Equity Small Cap (Growth)
AdvisorShares Dorsey Wright Short ETF	DWSH	NYSE Arca	D+	D	C-	Up	25.94	32.72	23.13	Y	Multialternative (Growth)
● AdvisorShares DoubleLine Value Equity ETF	DBLV	NYSE Arca	C	C+	C-	Up	69.44	70.92	56.67	Y	US Equity Mid Cap (Growth)
★ AdvisorShares Focused Equity ETF	CWS	NYSE Arca	B	B	C		35.22	35.84	28.12	Y	US Equity Large Cap Blend (Growth)
AdvisorShares FolioBeyond Smart Core Bond ETF	FWDB	NYSE Arca	C	C+	D+	Up	25.84	26.06	24.07	Y	Global Fixed Income (Growth)
AdvisorShares New Tech and Media ETF	FNG	NYSE Arca	D+	C-	D	Up	10.24	22.42	10.23	Y	Technology Sector Equity (Growth & Inc)
● AdvisorShares Newfleet Multi-Sector Income ETF	MINC	NYSE Arca	C	C	D+		48.52	48.66	47.16	Y	US Fixed Income (Income)
AdvisorShares Pacific Asset Enhanced Floating Rate ETF	FLRT	NYSE Arca	C-	C	D		48.89	49.64	46.79	Y	US Fixed Income (Income)
AdvisorShares Pure Cannabis ETF	YOLO	NYSE Arca	U	U	U		14.56	26.24	14.56	Y	Equity Misc (Unaligned)
● AdvisorShares Ranger Equity Bear ETF	HDGE	NYSE Arca	D	D	D		6.58	8.97	6.24	Y	Alternative Misc (Growth)
● AdvisorShares Sage Core Reserves ETF	HOLD	NYSE Arca	C	C	C-	Up	99.74	99.90	99.09	Y	US Fixed Income (Income)
AdvisorShares STAR Global Buy-Write ETF	VEGA	NYSE Arca	C-	C	D		32.55	32.78	27.65	Y	Long/Short Equity (Income)
AdvisorShares Vice ETF	ACT	NAS CM	C+	B	C-	Up	23.64	27.21	21.03	Y	Consumer Goods & Svcs (Growth)
Affinity World Leaders Equity ETF	WLDR	BATS	D+	D	D+	Up	22.23	24.72	19.39	Y	Global Equity Large Cap (Growth & Inc)
AGFIQ Dynamic Hedged U.S. Equity ETF	USHG	NYSE Arca	U	U	U		26.42	26.51	24.48	Y	Long/Short Equity (Growth)
AGFIQ Global Infrastructure ETF	GLIF	NYSE Arca	U	U	U		25.84	26.24	24.69	Y	Infrastructure Sector Equity (World Stock)
AGFIQ Hedged Dividend Income Fund	DIVA	NYSE Arca	C	C	D+	Up	24.23	24.61	23.01	Y	Long/Short Equity (Growth)
● AGFIQ U.S. Market Neutral Anti-Beta Fund	BTAL	NYSE Arca	C	C	C+		23.70	24.63	19.92	Y	Market Neutral (Growth & Inc)
AGFIQ U.S. Market Neutral Momentum Fund	MOM	NYSE Arca	D+	C-	D		24.89	30.48	23.18	Y	Market Neutral (Growth & Inc)
AGFIQ U.S. Market Neutral Size Fund	SIZ	NYSE Arca	D-	D	E		17.41	19.76	16.89	Y	Market Neutral (Growth & Inc)
AGFIQ U.S. Market Neutral Value Fund	CHEP	NYSE Arca	D	D-	D	Up	20.51	23.99	18.64	Y	Market Neutral (Growth & Inc)
● AI Powered Equity ETF	AIEQ	NYSE Arca	C-	C-	C-		26.14	29.46	20.35	Y	US Equity Large Cap Growth (Growth & Inc)
AI Powered International Equity ETF	AIIQ	NYSE Arca	D+	C	D	Up	24.84	25.76	20.05	Y	Global Equity Large Cap (Technology)
● Alerian Energy Infrastructure ETF	ENFR	NYSE Arca	C-	C	C-		20.73	22.66	17.34	Y	Energy Sector Equity (Natl Res)
● Alerian MLP ETF	AMLP	NYSE Arca	C	B-	D+	Up	9.14	10.93	8.32	Y	Energy Sector Equity (Natl Res)
Alpha Architect Freedom 100 Emerging Markets ETF	FRDM	BATS	U	U	U		25.43	26.89	24.10	Y	Global Emerg Mkts Equity (Div Emerg Mkts)
● Alpha Architect International Quantitative Momentum ETF	IMOM	BATS	D+	D+	D+		25.62	28.77	22.43	Y	Global Equity Large Cap (Growth & Inc)
● Alpha Architect International Quantitative Value ETF	IVAL	BATS	D+	D	D+		26.90	30.84	24.27	Y	Global Equity Large Cap (Growth & Inc)
● Alpha Architect U.S. Quantitative Momentum ETF	QMOM	BATS	C	C	D+		30.02	33.70	23.31	Y	US Equity Mid Cap (Growth & Inc)
● Alpha Architect U.S. Quantitative Value ETF	QVAL	BATS	C	C	D+	Up	27.86	30.92	23.89	Y	US Equity Mid Cap (Growth & Inc)
● Alpha Architect Value Momentum Trend ETF	VMOT	BATS	D	D	D+		23.51	28.96	22.87	Y	Long/Short Equity (Growth & Inc)
AlphaClone Alternative Alpha ETF	ALFA	BATS	C	B-	C-		54.30	55.71	39.63	Y	US Equity Large Cap Growth (Growth)
AlphaMark Actively Managed Small Cap ETF	SMCP	NAS CM	D	D	D+		23.22	26.64	19.79	Y	US Equity Small Cap (Small Company)
● ALPS Clean Energy ETF	ACES	BATS	C	C	D+	Up	30.97	32.11	21.36	Y	Energy Sector Equity (Growth & Inc)
● ALPS Disruptive Technologies ETF	DTEC	BATS	C-	C-	C-		29.07	31.11	22.47	Y	Technology Sector Equity (Growth)
ALPS Emerging Sector Dividend Dogs ETF	EDOG	NYSE Arca	C-	C-	D+	Up	20.46	22.89	19.68	Y	Global Emerg Mkts Equity (Div Emerg Mkts)
● ALPS Equal Sector Weight ETF	EQL	NYSE Arca	C	C	D+		75.60	76.51	60.34	Y	US Equity Large Cap Blend (Growth)
● ALPS International Sector Dividend Dogs ETF	IDOG	NYSE Arca	C	C	C-	Up	25.91	26.88	23.10	Y	Global Equity Large Cap (Growth)
● ALPS Medical Breakthroughs ETF	SBIO	NYSE Arca	C-	C-	D+	Down	31.56	38.40	25.86	Y	Healthcare Sector Equity (Health)

★ Expanded analysis of this fund is included in Section II: Analysis of All BUY Rated Funds. ● Expanded analysis of this fund is included in Section III: Analysis of All Rated Funds with Assets over $50 million.

		TOTAL RETURNS & PERFORMANCE							ASSETS		ASSET ALLOCATION & TURNOVER					VALUATION	
3-Month Total Return	6-Month Total Return	1-Year Total Return	3-Year Total Return	5-Year Total Return	Dividend Yield (TTM)	Expense Ratio	3-Yr Std Deviation	Effective Duration	NAV	Total Assets (Mil)	%Cash	%Stocks	%Bonds	%Other	Turnover Ratio	Premium/ Discount 1-Year Avg	Inception Date
1.26	2.12	-0.66			3.25	0.29			26.39	36.9	0	100	0	0		0.05	Nov-17
-2.59	-3.97					0.39			24.36	2.4	1	99	0	0		0.29	Nov-18
-5.67	-6.71	-4.30			4.09	0.5			20.89	3.1	0	100	0	0		0.45	Nov-17
-0.06	-3.24	-8.07			1.56	0.29			23.58	3.5	38	0	44	18		-0.07	Mar-17
-0.05	-2.71	-8.15			1.1	0.25			22.02	154.1	80	20	1	0		-0.03	Mar-17
-7.72	-11.48	-21.14			0	0.39			24.28	3.6	66	20	14	0		-0.18	Mar-17
7.69	20.06	58.02	127.70	110.68	0	0.6	26.26		157.88	236.8	0	0	0	100		-0.62	Jan-10
6.60	5.19	9.49	-14.51	-31.61	0	0.6	17.11		84.88	696.0	0	0	0	100		-0.12	Jan-10
8.28	14.49	25.21	9.18	15.27	0	0.6	11.67		73.14	442.5	0	0	0	100		-0.19	Oct-10
12.98	14.32	18.23	-11.62	-0.24	0	0.3	15.77		16.73	394.1	0	0	0	100	4	-0.33	Jul-09
6.80	14.73	24.62	11.20	19.95	0	0.17	11.18		143.07	1,073	0	0	0	100	11	-0.11	Sep-09
-5.27	-5.55	-13.19	25.35	52.83	0.15	0.9	17.63		34.50	4.7	1	99	0	0		0.00	Jun-12
-4.15	4.81	-10.56	20.65	35.09	0.66	0.88	17.53		47.84	102.9	0	100	0	0		-0.17	Jul-10
-8.96	-3.66	-12.94			0	0.99			21.15	2.1	3	97	0	0		-0.04	Jul-18
4.58	7.06	3.15			0.14	0.99		0.69	25.98	26.6	191	-99	9	0		0.10	Jul-18
1.84	5.40	0.70	23.24	42.98	1.06	0.9	12.82		69.73	59.3	3	97	0	0		-0.31	Oct-11
1.27	7.66	4.63	41.04		0.63	0.68	12.31		35.15	17.6	0	99	1	0		0.40	Sep-16
1.85	4.49	6.77	11.67	19.16	4.61	1.41	3.57	4.35	25.85	5.8	3	26	71	0		-0.08	Jun-11
-19.33	-36.33	-53.79			0	0.86			10.39	10.1	6	94	0	0		-0.55	Jul-17
0.93	2.50	4.39	7.52	12.52	2.94	0.69	0.99	1.62	48.52	72.8	2	0	98	0		-0.07	Mar-13
1.37	2.87	3.39	10.34		4.39	1.14	3.02	0.54	48.88	29.3	3	0	97	0		-0.01	Feb-15
-34.78						0.74				45.9	13	82	10	-5		0.18	Apr-19
2.95	-2.66	-11.69	-31.63	-45.65	0	2.72	16.8	0.69	6.57	179.2	121	-98	76	0		0.05	Jan-11
0.67	1.47	2.76	5.76	6.87	2.31	0.35	0.32	0.68	99.77	107.2	6	0	94	0		0.00	Jan-14
0.34	2.23	1.93	20.42	27.45	0.4	2.06	8.04		32.58	14.7	10	73	17	0		-0.31	Sep-12
-6.26	-7.55	-10.37			1.56	0.75			23.64	12.4	0	100	0	0		-0.09	Dec-17
-1.20	-1.15	-6.45			2.34	0.47				5.6	2	98	0	0	135	-0.23	Jan-18
2.28						0.55			26.39	2.6	21	79	0	0		0.08	May-19
0.48						0.45			25.83	2.6	1	99	0	0		0.08	May-19
3.38	1.89	6.05	9.95		3.58	0.75	6.94		24.27	4.9	51	49	0	0	185	0.00	Jan-15
8.35	11.10	17.84	12.79	20.56	0.36	0.76	11.29		23.66	101.7	102	-2	0	0	341	0.26	Sep-11
1.28	4.61	-0.66	3.22	2.32	0	1.88	11.35		25.02	2.5	107	-7	0	0	384	-0.66	Sep-11
-3.18	-7.14	-10.85	-18.85	-27.43	0	1.71	6.97		17.53	0.88	103	-3	0	0	71	-0.26	Sep-11
1.96	-3.08	-8.92	-14.45	-25.52	0.84	1.12	10.8		20.57	1.0	95	5	0	0	123	-0.65	Sep-11
-1.36	0.05	-2.10			0.61	0.77			26.19	114.6	2	98	0	0		-0.10	Oct-17
-2.30	2.68	2.83			0.68	0.79			24.82	3.7	4	96	0	0		-0.01	Jun-18
-2.82	-3.74	-3.22	-0.01	-17.09	5.05	0.65	16.27		20.71	64.2	0	100	0	0	73	-0.03	Oct-13
-5.38	-6.16	-8.85	-9.19	-28.28	8.43	0.85	16.34		9.15	8,260	0	100	0	0	26	0.00	Aug-10
-4.37						0.49			25.33	12.7	0	100	0	0		0.58	May-19
-2.05	-0.11	-9.15	2.03		1.36	0.59	13.7		25.63	56.4	1	99	0	0	119	0.03	Dec-15
-1.56	-4.11	-10.11	16.89		2.83	0.59	15.15		26.76	80.3	0	100	0	0	30	-0.10	Dec-14
-5.24	1.21	-11.01	22.69		0.05	0.49	18.04		30.02	55.5	0	100	0	0	91	0.00	Dec-15
-1.13	-3.45	-8.16	25.77		1.93	0.49	19.69		27.86	91.9	0	100	0	0	46	0.07	Oct-14
-2.02	-5.48	-18.41			0.52	0.8			23.52	81.2	27	73	0	0	44	-0.01	May-17
2.24	6.60	7.77	52.48	39.40	0.73	0.65	14.18		54.33	21.7	0	100	0	0	197	-0.12	May-12
-2.54	-2.28	-11.73	4.53		0	1.22	16.5		23.18	22.0	1	99	0	0	360	-0.35	Apr-15
3.79	14.35	23.09			1.76	0.65			30.84	87.9	0	100	0	0	9	0.30	Jun-18
-5.37	-1.02	-1.35			0.27	0.5			28.99	68.1	0	100	0	0	33	0.10	Dec-17
-5.28	-3.09	2.90	4.63	-4.21	5.96	0.6	14.14		20.53	30.8	0	100	0	0	85	-0.39	Mar-14
1.50	5.01	5.64	37.79	57.22	2.07	0.28	11.24		75.61	162.6	0	100	0	0	14	-0.02	Jul-09
0.05	0.54	1.22	21.40	12.21	4.42	0.5	11.24		25.94	217.9	1	99	0	0	72	-0.06	Jun-13
-13.84	-12.08	-15.18	26.88		2.48	0.5	26.94		31.60	161.2	0	100	0	0	48	-0.07	Dec-14

Fund Name	Ticker Symbol	Traded On	Overall Rating	Reward Rating	Risk Rating	Recent Up/ Downgrade	Price as of 9/30/2019	52-Week High	52-Week Low	Open to New Investors	Category & (Prospectus Objective)
● ALPS Sector Dividend Dogs ETF	SDOG	NYSE Arca	C	C	C		43.85	46.28	37.25	Y	US Equity Large Cap Value (Income)
● American Century Diversified Corporate Bond ETF	KORP	NYSE Arca	C-	C-	D+	Up	51.34	51.59	47.83	Y	US Fixed Income (Govt Bond - Gen)
American Century Diversified Municipal Bond ETF	TAXF	NYSE Arca	D+	D+	D+		52.88	53.43	49.47	Y	US Muni Fixed Inc (Muni Bond - Natl)
American Century Quality Diversified International ETF	QINT	NYSE Arca	D+	D+	D+		38.29	41.13	33.21	Y	Global Equity Large Cap (Foreign Stock)
American Century STOXX U.S. Quality Value ETF	VALQ	NYSE Arca	C-	C-	D+	Up	40.71	41.17	33.85	Y	US Equity Large Cap Value (Growth & Inc)
American Century U.S. Quality Growth ETF	QGRO	NYSE Arca	D+	C-	D+		40.93	43.07	31.21	Y	US Equity Large Cap Growth (Growth)
● American Customer Satisfaction ETF	ACSI	BATS	C	C+	C-		34.11	34.96	27.89	Y	US Equity Large Cap Blend (Growth & Inc)
American Energy Independence ETF	USAI	NYSE Arca	C	C+	D+	Up	23.48	26.11	19.53	Y	Energy Sector Equity (Natl Res)
Amplify Advanced Battery Metals and Materials ETF	BATT	NYSE Arca	D	D	D-		10.69	15.60	9.94	Y	Natural Resources (Growth & Inc)
Amplify BlackSwan Growth & Treasury Core ETF	SWAN	NYSE Arca	U	U	U		28.50	28.76	24.45	Y	Long/Short Equity (Growth)
Amplify CrowdBureau(R) Peer-to-Peer Lending & Crowdfunding	LEND	NYSE Arca	U	U	U		18.29	29.60	18.05	Y	Financials Sector Equity (Growth & Inc)
★ Amplify CWP Enhanced Dividend Income ETF	DIVO	BATS	B-	B	C	Up	30.48	30.84	25.34	Y	Long/Short Equity (Growth & Inc)
Amplify EASI Tactical Growth ETF	EASI	NYSE Arca	C	C	D+	Up	24.13	26.22	23.15	Y	Aggressive Allocation (Growth)
● Amplify High Income ETF	YYY	NYSE Arca	C	C+	C-		17.80	18.43	15.44	Y	Moderate Allocation (Income)
Amplify International Online Retail ETF	XBUY	NYSE Arca	U	U	U		26.07	29.00	24.77	Y	Consumer Goods & Svcs (Unaligned)
● Amplify Online Retail ETF	IBUY	NAS CM	C	C+	D+		46.76	51.93	37.41	Y	Consumer Goods & Svcs (Growth & Inc)
● Amplify Transformational Data Sharing ETF	BLOK	NYSE Arca	D+	D	C-	Up	17.94	20.39	14.46	Y	Technology Sector Equity (Technology)
● Anfield Capital Diversified Alternatives ETF	DALT	BATS	C-	C-	C-		10.24	10.48	8.53	Y	Multialternative (Growth & Inc)
Anfield Universal Fixed Income ETF	AFIF	BATS	D+	D	C		9.74	10.08	9.57	Y	US Fixed Income (Income)
★ Aptus Behavioral Momentum ETF	BEMO	BATS	B-	B	C	Up	30.48	37.07	28.10	Y	US Equity Large Cap Blend (Growth & Inc)
● Aptus Defined Risk ETF	DRSK	BATS	D+	D+	C-		27.39	28.03	24.82	Y	Long/Short Equity (Growth & Inc)
● Aptus Fortified Value ETF	FTVA	BATS	C-	C-	C-	Up	26.10	29.01	23.23	Y	Long/Short Equity (Growth & Inc)
ARK Fintech Innovation ETF	ARKF	NAS CM	U	U	U		21.49	23.41	20.19	Y	Technology Sector Equity (Growth)
● ARK Genomic Revolution Multi-Sector ETF	ARKG	NYSE Arca	D+	D+	D	Down	29.52	35.25	22.36	Y	Healthcare Sector Equity (Unaligned)
● ARK Industrial Innovation ETF	ARKQ	NYSE Arca	C	C+	D+	Up	31.70	36.56	28.43	Y	Technology Sector Equity (Unaligned)
● ARK Innovation ETF	ARKK	NYSE Arca	C-	C	D+	Down	42.89	49.92	35.34	Y	Technology Sector Equity (Unaligned)
ARK Israel Innovative Technology ETF	IZRL	BATS	D+	D+	D+		20.65	22.61	18.16	Y	Equity Misc (Technology)
● ARK Web x.0 ETF	ARKW	NYSE Arca	C	C+	D+	Down	48.67	58.05	40.89	Y	Technology Sector Equity (Technology)
Arrow Dogs of the World ETF	DOGS	NYSE Arca	D	D	D	Up	43.82	52.58	41.08	Y	Global Equity Large Cap (Growth)
● Arrow Dow Jones Global Yield ETF	GYLD	NYSE Arca	C-	C-	C-	Down	15.96	17.43	14.88	Y	Moderate Allocation (Growth & Inc)
Arrow DWA Country Rotation ETF	DWCR	NAS CM	D	D	D		26.32	28.69	24.70	Y	Global Equity Large Cap (Growth)
Arrow DWA Tactical ETF	DWAT	NAS CM	D+	C-	D		11.26	12.84	9.79	Y	Moderate Allocation (Growth)
Arrow QVM Equity Factor ETF	QVM	NYSE Arca	C	C	C-	Up	28.01	28.83	23.08	Y	US Equity Large Cap Value (Growth)
● Arrow Reserve Capital Management ETF	ARCM	BATS	D+	C	D	Down	100.22	100.73	99.63	Y	US Fixed Income (Growth & Inc)
Aware Ultra-Short Duration Enhanced Income ETF	AWTM	NYSE Arca	U	U	U		50.44	50.46	50.04	Y	US Fixed Income (Growth & Inc)
Barclays ETN+ FI Enhanced Europe 50 ETN Series B	FLEU	NYSE Arca	D+	D	D		137.00	147.03	100.85	Y	Global Equity Large Cap (Growth & Inc)
Barclays ETN+ FI Enhanced Europe 50 ETN Series C	FFEU	NYSE Arca	D+	D	D+		94.64	100.68	68.81	Y	Europe Equity Large Cap (Growth)
● Barclays ETN+ FI Enhanced Global High Yield ETN B	FIYY	NYSE Arca	C-	C-	D+	Up	108.76	110.77	77.47	Y	Global Equity Large Cap (Equity-Income)
Barclays ETN+ S&P VEQTOR™ ETN	VQT	BATS	C-	C-	D+	Down	161.10	172.35	152.50	Y	Long/Short Equity (Growth)
● Barclays ETN+ Select MLP ETN	ATMP	BATS	D+	D	C-	Down	18.36	21.27	16.98	Y	Energy Sector Equity (Growth)
● Barclays ETN+ Shiller Capet ETN	CAPE	NYSE Arca	C	C+	D+		137.41	142.13	106.83	Y	US Equity Large Cap Value (Growth)
Barclays Inverse US Treasury Aggregate ETN	TAPR	BATS	D	E+	D		11.59	32.37	10.13	Y	Trading Tools (Growth & Inc)
Barclays Return on Disability ETN	RODI	BATS	D+	C	E+		86.79	87.52	70.00	Y	US Equity Large Cap Blend (Growth & Inc)
Barclays Women in Leadership ETN	WIL	BATS	C-	C	D		70.69	76.33	53.64	Y	US Equity Large Cap Blend (Equity-Income)
● Barron's 400 ETF	BFOR	NYSE Arca	C-	C-	C-	Up	39.78	44.89	33.40	Y	US Equity Mid Cap (Growth)
BlackRock U.S. Equity Factor Rotation ETF	DYNF	NYSE Arca	U	U	U		26.61	26.93	24.61	Y	US Equity Large Cap Blend (Growth)
● BlueStar Israel Technology ETF	ITEQ	NYSE Arca	C	B-	C-	Down	39.86	42.64	29.60	Y	Technology Sector Equity (Technology)
Brand Value ETF	BVAL	NYSE Arca	C	C+	C-	Up	16.93	17.18	13.71	Y	US Equity Large Cap Value (Growth & Inc)
Breakwave Dry Bulk Shipping ETF	BDRY	NYSE Arca	D	D	D+	Up	19.71	23.15	9.26	Y	Equity Misc (Growth & Inc)
● Cambria Core Equity ETF	CCOR	NYSE Arca	C	C+	C	Up	27.28	28.02	25.11	Y	Long/Short Equity (Growth & Inc)
Cambria Emerging Shareholder Yield ETF	EYLD	BATS	C-	C	D+		30.05	32.20	27.27	Y	Global Emerg Mkts Equity (Div Emerg Mkts)
Cambria Foreign Shareholder Yield ETF	FYLD	BATS	D+	D+	D+	Down	22.35	25.41	20.82	Y	Globa Eq Mid/Small Cap (Foreign Stock)

★Expanded analysis of this fund is included in Section II: Analysis of All BUY Rated Funds. ●Expanded analysis of this fund is included in Section III: Analysis of All Rated Funds with Assets over $50 million.

	TOTAL RETURNS & PERFORMANCE								ASSETS		ASSET ALLOCATION & TURNOVER					VALUATION	
3-Month Total Return	6-Month Total Return	1-Year Total Return	3-Year Total Return	5-Year Total Return	Dividend Yield (TTM)	Expense Ratio	3-Yr Std Deviation	Effective Duration	NAV	Total Assets (MIL)	%Cash	%Stocks	%Bonds	%Other	Turnover Ratio	Premium/ Discount 1-Year Avg	Inception Date
1.26	2.54	-1.33	17.24	42.08	3.49	0.4	14.18		43.86	1,715	0	100	0	0	61	-0.03	Jun-12
1.62	4.80	8.60			2.99	0.29		4.25	51.13	66.6	2	0	98	0	38	0.36	Jan-18
1.85	4.74	8.81			2.57	0.29		6.72	52.82	29.0	0	0	96	4		0.11	Sep-18
-2.06	0.36	-5.01			1.82	0.39			38.29	19.1	0	99	0	0		-0.26	Sep-18
2.61	3.07	1.23			2.51	0.29			40.71	31.6	0	100	0	0	77	-0.01	Jan-18
-1.60	1.66	2.33			0.38	0.29			40.93	24.6	0	100	0	0		-0.16	Sep-18
0.95	3.59	2.23	41.97		1.34	0.66			34.12	58.0	0	100	0	0	72	-0.04	Oct-16
-3.78	-5.46	-5.50			4.51	0.75			23.45	10.6	2	98	0	0	61	0.08	Dec-17
-6.42	-16.97	-30.72			0.97	0.72			10.64	4.8	3	97	0	0	12	0.16	Jun-18
3.28	8.48					0.49			28.31	117.5	0	13	87	0		0.42	Nov-18
-19.72						0.65			19.14	0.96	0	100	0	0		7.70	May-19
2.19	6.67	7.15			5.23	0.49			30.49	19.8	10	90	0	0	151	0.01	Dec-16
-4.20	-0.95	-6.12			0.83	0.76				21.7	0	100	0	0	289	0.04	Jun-18
1.19	4.59	5.92	19.52	22.89	8.77	2.28	9.49	4.98	17.79	236.6	-4	25	79	-9	40	0.06	Jun-12
-4.16	-5.56					0.69			25.97	1.9	0	100	0	0		0.18	Jan-19
-5.50	-5.27	-9.29	69.85		0	0.65	20.87		46.80	238.7	4	96	0	0	17	-0.09	Apr-16
-2.51	0.66	-10.91			1.07	0.7			17.93	102.2	0	100	0	0	44	-0.25	Jan-18
0.35	2.78	1.43			3.59	3.23				74.7	2	64	14	0	50	-0.01	Sep-17
-1.26	-1.73	-0.53			2.57	1				17.7	5	0	93	0		-0.04	Sep-18
-0.41	3.48	-17.04	21.66		0.8	0.81	15.39		30.48	64.0	0	100	0	0	321	-0.01	Jun-16
0.94	5.65	13.23			1.66	0.76			27.38	151.9	1	4	93	0		0.13	Aug-18
-0.55	-2.20	-8.91			0.3	0.79			26.10	63.9	0	100	0	0	51	-0.01	Oct-17
-5.74	-1.28					0.75			21.50	72.0	0	100	0	0		0.12	Feb-19
-14.29	-10.31	-6.97	53.57		0	0.75	32.48		29.55	396.1	0	100	0	0	64	0.03	Oct-14
-6.21	-9.03	-9.31	48.02	68.65	0	0.75	21.94		31.70	150.6	1	99	0	0		-0.02	Sep-14
-10.50	-9.41	-6.47	102.65		0	0.75	27.27		42.93	1,580	0	100	0	0		0.03	Oct-14
-1.00	-6.86	-2.45			2.78	0.49			20.61	19.6	0	100	0	0		0.04	Dec-17
-7.31	-7.72	-5.24	119.24	194.15	0	0.75	21.99		48.65	357.5	0	98	0	1		0.01	Sep-14
-14.79	-7.61	-10.88			2.51	1.64				4.4	1	99	0	0	100	0.00	Jan-18
-0.40	-0.91	-0.88	4.21	-11.37	7.99	0.75	9.34			55.4	0	61	39	0	69	-0.94	May-12
-5.16	-1.65	-6.21			3.11	1.34				14.4	1	99	0	0	146	-0.03	Dec-17
2.43	4.59	-7.03	17.12	24.98	0	1.7	11.12			4.6	11	81	0	5	174	-0.39	Oct-14
1.08	3.39	-0.92	33.16		2.9	0.65	13.54			4.2	0	100	0	0	123	-0.45	Feb-15
0.50	1.16	2.36			2.39	0.42				56.2	30	0	70	0	33	-0.02	Mar-17
0.76	1.75					0.23			50.45	151.4	17	0	81	0		0.03	Jan-19
-4.56	2.54	-2.80	38.73		0	0.76				3.3						-0.63	Nov-16
-4.20	3.40	-0.80			0	1.05				11.4						-0.09	Mar-18
0.37	5.29	5.27			0	0.93				1,133						-0.24	Mar-18
-3.63	-2.55	-7.31	19.54	6.61	0	0.95	9.57			14.2						-0.11	Aug-10
-6.81	-7.64	-5.77	-6.09	-24.39	6.42	0.95	16.18		18.45	359.1						-0.20	Mar-13
-0.45	3.62	2.27	47.63	86.87	0	0.45	13			176.8						-0.03	Oct-12
-31.14	-47.15	-60.97	-35.22	-75.12	0	0.43	42.01			7.0						-0.49	Jul-14
-0.73	2.73	0.35	41.43	64.08	0	0.45	13.32			40.7						-3.97	Sep-14
-2.52	1.57	1.61	25.65	39.51	0	0.45	13.34			40.0						-0.02	Jul-14
-2.31	-2.47	-10.34	26.00	39.08	0.84	0.66	16.9		39.77	143.2	0	100	0	0	88	-0.05	Jun-13
1.48	5.58					0.3			26.60	58.5	0	100	0	0		0.04	Mar-19
1.92	6.09	11.97	58.00		0.26	0.75	13.71		39.92	73.8	0	100	0	0	11	0.04	Nov-15
2.42	6.80	5.77			1.54	0.65			16.92	15.2	0	100	0	0	86	0.03	Jun-17
40.54	111.33	-12.77			0	3.5			19.65	2.0	25	44	0	31		0.08	Mar-18
0.54	1.63	8.41			0.61	1.23			27.24	100.8	2	98	0	0		-0.05	May-17
-4.74	-1.52	0.19	30.16		3.68	0.66	14.1		29.82	28.3	4	96	0	0		0.68	Jul-16
-0.91	-2.21	-6.20	19.91	11.21	5.4	0.59	11.5		22.45	22.5	3	97	0	0		-0.17	Dec-13

Fund Name	Ticker Symbol	Traded On	Overall Rating	Reward Rating	Risk Rating	Recent Up/ Downgrade	Price as of 9/30/2019	52-Week High	52-Week Low	Open to New Investors	Category & (Prospectus Objective)
● Cambria Global Asset Allocation ETF	GAA	BATS	C	C	D+		26.92	27.39	24.59	Y	Cautious Allocation (Asset Allocation)
● Cambria Global Momentum ETF	GMOM	BATS	C-	C-	D+		25.36	26.85	24.22	Y	Moderate Allocation (Growth & Inc)
● Cambria Global Value ETF	GVAL	BATS	C	C	C-	Up	22.36	24.08	20.97	Y	Globa Eq Mid/Small Cap (Div Emerg Mkts)
● Cambria Shareholder Yield ETF	SYLD	BATS	C-	C	D+		36.41	39.44	30.75	Y	US Equity Mid Cap (Growth & Inc)
Cambria Sovereign Bond ETF	SOVB	BATS	C	C	D+	Up	25.06	26.44	23.98	Y	Emerging Mkts Fixed Inc (Corp Bond-High Yld)
● Cambria Tail Risk ETF	TAIL	BATS	D+	D+	D+	Up	20.40	24.70	19.79	Y	Alternative Misc (Growth & Inc)
Cambria Trinity ETF	TRTY	BATS	U	U	U		24.23	24.53	23.39	Y	Flexible Allocation (Growth & Inc)
Cambria Value and Momentum ETF	VAMO	BATS	C-	C-	D+	Up	19.90	25.02	19.41	Y	Long/Short Equity (Growth & Inc)
CBOE Vest S&P 500 Div Aristocrats Target Income Ind ETF	KNG	BATS	C	C	C-	Up	44.14	44.84	36.81	Y	US Equity Large Cap Blend (Growth & Inc)
Change Finance U.S. Large Cap Fossil Fuel Free ETF	CHGX	NYSE Arca	C-	C	D+		21.71	22.29	16.84	Y	US Equity Large Cap Blend (Growth & Inc)
Citigroup ETNs - VelocityShares Daily 4X Long AUD vs. USD	UAUD	NYSE Arca	D-	D	D-		14.26	21.18	14.19	Y	Currency (Growth & Inc)
Citigroup ETNs - VelocityShares Daily 4X Long CHF vs. USD	UCHF	NYSE Arca	D	D	D		18.83	23.42	18.33	Y	Currency (Growth & Inc)
Citigroup ETNs - VelocityShares Daily 4X Long EUR vs. USD	UEUR	NYSE Arca	D-	D	E+		14.73	21.34	14.73	Y	Currency (Growth & Inc)
Citigroup ETNs - VelocityShares Daily 4X Long GBP vs. USD	UGBP	NYSE Arca	D-	D	D-	Down	15.14	22.33	14.06	Y	Currency (Growth & Inc)
Citigroup ETNs - VelocityShares Daily 4X Long JPY vs. USD	UJPY	NYSE Arca	D	D+	D		24.67	27.76	22.12	Y	Currency (Growth & Inc)
Citigroup ETNs - VelocityShares Daily 4X Long USD vs. AUD	DAUD	NYSE Arca	D+	C	D		36.79	37.14	26.56	Y	Currency (Growth & Inc)
Citigroup ETNs - VelocityShares Daily 4X Long USD vs. CHF	DCHF	NYSE Arca	D	D+	E+		29.74	31.26	24.72	Y	Currency (Growth & Inc)
Citigroup ETNs - VelocityShares Daily 4X Long USD vs. EUR	DEUR	NYSE Arca	D+	C	D	Down	38.06	38.06	27.34	Y	Currency (Growth & Inc)
Citigroup ETNs - VelocityShares Daily 4X Long USD vs. GBP	DGBP	NYSE Arca	C-	C	D+	Up	34.63	37.92	24.98	Y	Currency (Growth & Inc)
Citigroup ETNs - VelocityShares Daily 4X Long USD vs. JPY	DJPY	NYSE Arca	D	D	D		23.12	26.45	20.63	Y	Currency (Growth & Inc)
Claymore CEF GS Connect ETN	GCE	NYSE Arca	D+	D	D+		14.88	16.00	12.49	Y	Moderate Allocation (Asset Allocation)
● ClearBridge All Cap Growth ETF	CACG	NAS CM	C	C+	C-	Up	31.66	33.01	25.40	Y	US Equity Large Cap Growth (Growth)
ClearBridge Dividend Strategy ESG ETF	YLDE	NAS CM	C	C+	D	Up	31.32	31.59	25.52	Y	US Equity Large Cap Value (Growth & Inc)
● ClearBridge Large Cap Growth ESG ETF	LRGE	NAS CM	C+	B-	C	Up	34.79	36.31	27.10	Y	US Equity Large Cap Growth (Growth)
● ClearShares OCIO ETF	OCIO	NYSE Arca	C-	C	D+	Up	26.97	27.12	23.77	Y	Moderate Allocation (Growth & Inc)
ClearShares Ultra-Short Maturity ETF	OPER	NYSE Arca	D+	D+	D+	Up	100.06	103.07	100.00	Y	US Fixed Income (Income)
● Cohen & Steers Global Realty Majors ETF	GRI	NYSE Arca	C	C+	D+		48.59	48.83	40.34	Y	Real Estate Sector Equity (Real Estate)
● Columbia Diversified Fixed Income Allocation ETF	DIAL	NYSE Arca	C-	C-	C-		20.80	20.90	18.78	Y	US Fixed Income (Growth & Inc)
Columbia EM Core ex-China ETF	XCEM	NYSE Arca	C	C	D+	Up	25.64	26.93	23.14	Y	Global Emerg Mkts Equity (Div Emerg Mkts)
● Columbia Emerging Markets Consumer ETF	ECON	NYSE Arca	D	D	D+	Down	21.94	23.34	19.79	Y	Global Emerg Mkts Equity (Unaligned)
● Columbia India Consumer ETF	INCO	NYSE Arca	D+	D	D+	Down	41.34	44.75	36.58	Y	India Equity (Unaligned)
Columbia Multi-Sector Municipal Income ETF	MUST	NYSE Arca	U	U	U		21.68	21.90	20.00	Y	US Muni Fixed Inc (Muni Bond - Natl)
Columbia Sustainable Global Equity Income ETF	ESGW	NYSE Arca	D	C	E+	Down	26.33	30.12	22.36	Y	Global Equity Large Cap (Growth & Inc)
Columbia Sustainable International Equity Income ETF	ESGN	NYSE Arca	D	D+	D		24.72	28.90	22.75	Y	Global Equity Large Cap (Growth & Inc)
Columbia Sustainable U.S. Equity Income ETF	ESGS	NYSE Arca	C	C	D+	Up	28.20	30.71	22.87	Y	US Equity Large Cap Value (Growth & Inc)
★ Communication Services Select Sector SPDR® Fund	XLC	NYSE Arca	B-	B	C	Up	49.52	51.72	38.97	Y	Communications Sector Equity (Comm)
★ Consumer Discretionary Select Sector SPDR® Fund	XLY	NYSE Arca	B	B+	C		120.70	124.48	91.98	Y	Consumer Goods & Svcs (Unaligned)
★ Consumer Staples Select Sector SPDR® Fund	XLP	NYSE Arca	B-	B	C	Up	61.42	61.62	48.73	Y	Consumer Goods & Svcs (Unaligned)
Credit Suisse FI Enhanc Europe 50 Exchange Traded Notes (E	FEUL	NYSE Arca	D+	D	D+		90.88	97.00	66.15	Y	Europe Equity Large Cap (Growth & Inc)
● Credit Suisse FI Large Cap Growth Enhanced ETN	FLGE	NYSE Arca	C	C+	D+		276.46	300.04	167.09	Y	US Equity Large Cap Growth (Growth)
Credit Suisse S&P MLP Index ETN	MLPO	NYSE Arca	D+	D	D+		12.97	14.17	12.47	Y	Energy Sector Equity (Growth & Inc)
Credit Suisse X-Links Crude Oil Shares Covered Call ETNs	USOI	NAS CM	D+	D+	D+		19.67	30.61	18.45	Y	Commodities Specified (Natl Res)
Credit Suisse X-Links Gold Shares Covered Call ETN	GLDI	NAS CM	C	C	C-	Up	8.95	9.40	8.06	Y	Commodities Specified (Income)
Credit Suisse X-Links Month Pay 2xLeveraged Alerian MLP In	AMJL	NYSE Arca	D	D	D+		12.02	15.21	11.34	Y	Trading Tools (Growth & Inc)
● Credit Suisse X-Links Month Pay 2xLeveraged Mortg REIT ETN	REML	NYSE Arca	C	C	C-	Up	23.02	26.92	20.20	Y	Trading Tools (Real Estate)
Credit Suisse X-Links Multi-Asset High Income ETN	MLTI	NYSE Arca	D+	D+	D+	Up	27.62	27.64	26.42	Y	Moderate Allocation (Income)
Credit Suisse X-Links Silver Shares Covered Call ETN	SLVO	NAS CM	C-	D+	C-	Up	6.94	7.46	6.31	Y	Commodities Specified (Income)
CSOP FTSE China A50 ETF	AFTY	NYSE Arca	C	C+	C-		16.76	18.10	12.99	Y	Greater China Equity (Pacific Stock)
CSOP MSCI China A International Hedged ETF	CNHX	NYSE Arca	D+	C+	E+		28.11	29.51	21.83	Y	Greater China Equity (Pacific Stock)
C-Tracks ETNs on the Miller/Howard MLP Fundmnt Ind, Ser B	MLPE	NYSE Arca	U	U	U		19.72	21.53	18.81	Y	Energy Sector Equity (Growth & Inc)
● C-Tracks Exch-Traded Notes Miller/Howard MLP Fundmnt Ind	MLPC	NYSE Arca	D	D	D	Down	12.76	15.12	11.82	Y	Energy Sector Equity (Growth)
● C-Tracks Exchange-Traded Notes Miller/Howard Strat Div Rei	DIVC	NYSE Arca	D	C-	E+	Down	34.34	36.39	29.19	Y	US Equity Large Cap Value (Income)

★ Expanded analysis of this fund is included in Section II: Analysis of All BUY Rated Funds. ● Expanded analysis of this fund is included in Section III: Analysis of All Rated Funds with Assets over $50 million.

	TOTAL RETURNS & PERFORMANCE								ASSETS		ASSET ALLOCATION & TURNOVER					VALUATION	
3-Month Total Return	6-Month Total Return	1-Year Total Return	3-Year Total Return	5-Year Total Return	Dividend Yield (TTM)	Expense Ratio	3-Yr Std Deviation	Effective Duration	NAV	Total Assets (MIL)	%Cash	%Stocks	%Bonds	%Other	Turnover Ratio	Premium/ Discount 1-Year Avg	Inception Date
-0.36	2.18	3.42	16.78		3.03	0.34	6.28	7.54	26.89	60.5	6	44	48	2		0.01	Dec-14
1.45	2.51	-2.74	15.03		2.62	0.94	7.49	9.99	25.38	118.0	5	42	50	3		-0.08	Nov-14
-5.40	0.00	-1.19	26.18	14.89	2.75	0.69	14.12		22.40	145.6	1	99	0	0		-0.19	Mar-14
0.63	0.22	-5.68	28.59	44.55	2.15	0.59	16.1		36.35	123.6	1	99	0	0		-0.02	May-13
-2.69	1.10	6.88	5.63		4.49	0.59	8.05		24.93	26.2	5	0	95	0		0.29	Feb-16
1.17	1.91	3.87			1.53	0.59			20.36	66.2	2	4	94	0		0.20	Apr-17
0.12	1.37				2.5	0.48		8.15	24.24	36.4	16	39	44	0		0.23	Sep-18
-3.53	-4.22	-19.49	-12.71		1.33	0.64	9.98		19.85	13.9	14	86	0	0		-0.34	Sep-15
2.82	5.37	8.00			3.53	0.75			44.13	37.5	1	99	0	0		0.03	Mar-18
0.37	4.52	6.93			0.98	0.49			21.70	9.8	0	100	0	0	46	0.12	Oct-17
-14.66	-22.03	-28.42			0	1.5			14.32	1.9						-0.12	Dec-17
-8.90	-7.90	-17.97			0	1.5			18.94	3.0						0.26	Dec-17
-17.56	-16.92	-31.54			0	1.5			14.72	2.0						-0.74	Dec-17
-12.83	-26.12	-28.85			0	1.5			15.19	2.3						-0.31	Dec-17
-1.63	4.76	9.93			0	1.5			24.78	4.0						0.13	Dec-17
15.12	24.22	28.65			0	1.5			36.66	5.7						0.16	Dec-17
8.13	5.72	16.61			0	1.5			29.56	4.7						0.45	Dec-17
19.64	18.05	40.53			0	1.5			38.10	3.7						0.70	Dec-17
11.59	30.04	28.95			0	1.5			34.53	5.5						0.22	Dec-17
0.37	-6.41	-12.55			0	1.5			23.03	3.5						0.08	Dec-17
1.77		-2.46	2.39	3.17	0	0.95	14.28			7.5					0	0.00	Dec-07
-1.12	2.69	1.42			0.57	0.53			31.66	128.2	4	96	0	0	15	0.07	May-17
1.96	7.34	10.57			1.83	0.6			31.23	6.2	5	95	0	0	10	-0.21	May-17
-1.22	3.45	4.07			0.46	0.6			34.75	168.5	2	98	0	0	20	-0.20	May-17
0.30	2.64	1.87			1.14	0.67		4.94	26.97	103.8	7	61	32	0	28	-0.01	Jun-17
0.55	1.15	2.26			2.58	0.2			100.05	30.0	100	0	0	0		0.00	Jul-18
3.48	3.34	15.08	19.11	40.34	2.88	0.55	10.62		48.57	53.4	0	100	0	0	14	-0.15	May-08
2.44	6.45	12.05			3.46	0.28			20.72	176.1	11	0	88	0	140	0.11	Oct-17
-4.15	-0.38	2.19	25.01		2.41	0.16	12.97		25.63	11.5	0	99	0	1	24	0.12	Sep-15
-4.21	-3.67	-0.32	-8.71	-11.24	0.91	0.59	14.19		22.04	239.1	0	100	0	0	61	-0.26	Sep-10
-0.38	-1.73	0.70	15.33	34.98	0.13	0.75	18.24		41.43	111.9	0	100	0	0	15	-0.18	Aug-11
1.63	4.31	10.29				0.23			21.56	25.9	0	0	100	0	48	0.25	Oct-18
0.03	1.51	-2.23	27.71		2.56	0.4	13.26		26.30	15.8	0	100	0	0	67	-0.39	Jun-16
-2.44	-1.85	-6.37	15.95		3.91	0.45	12.03		24.67	4.9	0	100	0	0	82	-0.05	Jun-16
1.43	3.52	0.11	35.41		5.9	0.35	15.05		28.18	4.2	0	100	0	0	61	0.10	Jun-16
-0.41	4.23	1.98			0.92	0.13				5,879	0	100	0	0	7	-0.01	Jun-18
-0.14	4.67	3.80	55.86	92.75	1.3	0.13	14.7			14,001	0	100	0	0	23	-0.01	Dec-98
5.30	10.71	16.67	24.73	54.82	2.55	0.13	11.83			14,061	0	100	0	0	12	-0.02	Dec-98
-4.20	3.48	-0.43			0	1				17.4						-0.28	May-18
-1.33	6.31	-8.97	99.42	162.94	0	0.85	27.91			1,639						-0.06	Jun-14
-4.45			-3.99		7.36	0.95	17.07			30.0						1.48	Dec-14
-2.34	-10.79	-23.76			17.81	0.85				8.3						0.42	Apr-17
2.62	8.81	18.19	5.36	11.23	6.99	0.65	8.94			33.5						-0.11	Jan-13
-13.87			-31.14		19.15	0.85	33.78			9.9						0.45	May-16
1.42	-1.51	5.03	53.14		22.01	0.5	25.33			120.6						0.25	Jul-16
1.68	3.04		17.58		6.24	0.84	8.31			6.9						-0.11	Sep-15
6.84	7.79	11.56	-13.10	-10.25	5.76	0.65	14.1			19.4						-0.13	Apr-13
-5.91	-2.43	12.15	38.93		1.44	0.7	20.24		16.85	12.7	0	100	0	0	20	0.14	Mar-15
-2.07	-1.76	11.93	15.31		2.12	0.79	14.82		28.29	1.4	0	100	0	0	16	-0.77	Oct-15
-6.29					0	0.85	21.24		19.72	--						0.00	Aug-16
-6.46	-5.49	-11.10	-10.02	-43.96	6.22	0.95	17.64		12.76	89.3						0.00	Sep-13
-0.77	-1.13	-5.62	29.50	44.48	0	0.7	17.54		34.34	137.4						0.00	Sep-14

Fund Name	Ticker Symbol	Traded On	Overall Rating	Reward Rating	Risk Rating	Recent Up/ Downgrade	Price as of 9/30/2019	52-Week High	52-Week Low	Open to New Investors	Category & (Prospectus Objective)
Cushing® 30 MLP Index ETN	PPLN	NYSE Arca	D-	D	E	Down	16.10	19.46	14.47	Y	Energy Sector Equity (Income)
Cushing® Energy & MLP ETF	XLEY	NYSE Arca	U	U	U		23.19	26.67	21.18	Y	Energy Sector Equity (Growth & Inc)
Cushing® Energy Supply Chain & MLP ETF	XLSY	NYSE Arca	U	U	U		24.16	26.42	21.94	Y	Energy Sector Equity (Growth & Inc)
Cushing® Transportation & MLP ETF	XLTY	NYSE Arca	U	U	U		24.38	26.31	21.77	Y	Industrials Sector Equity (Growth & Inc)
Cushing® Utility & MLP ETF	XLUY	NYSE Arca	U	U	U		27.37	27.52	23.08	Y	Utilities Sector Equity (Growth & Inc)
● Davis Select Financial ETF	DFNL	NAS CM	C+	B-	C	Up	23.77	24.89	20.12	Y	Financials Sector Equity (Financial)
● Davis Select International ETF	DINT	NAS CM	D+	D	D+	Up	17.40	18.91	14.59	Y	Global Equity Large Cap (Growth)
● Davis Select U.S. Equity ETF	DUSA	NAS CM	C+	B	C	Up	23.85	25.36	19.43	Y	US Equity Large Cap Blend (Growth)
● Davis Select Worldwide ETF	DWLD	NAS CM	C	C	C-	Up	22.86	25.56	19.34	Y	Global Equity Large Cap (World Stock)
DB Agriculture Double Long ETN	DAG	NYSE Arca	E+	D-	E		2.00	2.37	2.00	Y	Trading Tools (Natl Res)
DB Agriculture Double Short ETN	AGATF	NYSE Arca	C	C+	E+		24.46	24.46	24.46	Y	Trading Tools (Natl Res)
DB Agriculture Long ETN	AGF	NYSE Arca	D-	D	E		9.00	12.50	7.20	Y	Commodities Specified (Natl Res)
DB Agriculture Short ETN	ADZ	NYSE Arca	C-	C+	E+		37.00	37.00	37.00	Y	Trading Tools (Natl Res)
DB Base Metals Double Long ETN	BDD	NYSE Arca	D	D	E		7.70	8.18	4.97	Y	Trading Tools (Natl Res)
DB Base Metals Double Short ETN	BOM	NYSE Arca	D+	C	E		7.99	11.86	6.83	Y	Trading Tools (Natl Res)
DB Base Metals Long ETN	BDG	NYSE Arca	U	U	U		16.29	16.29	11.84	Y	Commodities Industrial Metals (Natl Res)
DB Base Metals Short ETN	BOS	NYSE Arca	D+	C	E		19.13	20.75	15.12	Y	Trading Tools (Natl Res)
DB Commodity Double Long ETN	DYY	NYSE Arca	D	D+	E		2.14	3.15	1.83	Y	Trading Tools (Natl Res)
DB Commodity Double Short ETN	DEE	NYSE Arca	D	C-	E		55.00	55.00	55.00	Y	Trading Tools (Natl Res)
DB Commodity Long ETN	DPU	NYSE Arca	D	D+	E		9.15	9.15	9.15	Y	Commodities Broad Basket (Natl Res)
DB Commodity Short ETN	DDP	NYSE Arca	D+	C-	E	Up	46.01	61.00	45.01	Y	Trading Tools (Natl Res)
DB Crude Oil Double Short ETN	DTO	NYSE Arca	D	D	D		59.65	107.47	43.50	Y	Trading Tools (Natl Res)
DB Crude Oil Long ETN	OLO	NYSE Arca	D	D+	E		5.63	7.14	4.23	Y	Commodities Specified (Natl Res)
DB Crude Oil Short ETN	SZO	NYSE Arca	D	D	E		55.69	82.81	51.61	Y	Trading Tools (Natl Res)
● DB Gold Double Long ETN	DGP	NYSE Arca	C	C	C-	Up	29.25	32.59	20.17	Y	Trading Tools (Prec Metals)
DB Gold Double Short ETN	DZZ	NYSE Arca	D	D	D	Down	4.47	6.66	4.01	Y	Trading Tools (Prec Metals)
DB Gold Short ETN	DGZ	NYSE Arca	D	D	D	Down	12.71	15.32	12.03	Y	Trading Tools (Prec Metals)
● Deep Value ETF	DVP	NYSE Arca	C	B-	D	Up	30.63	35.13	27.93	Y	US Equity Mid Cap (Growth & Inc)
Defiance 5G Next Gen Connectivity ETF	FIVG	NYSE Arca	U	U	U		24.47	26.46	22.41	Y	Communications Sector Equity (Growth & Inc)
Defiance NextGen Video Gaming ETF	VIDG	NYSE Arca	D+	D+	D+		23.42	25.55	18.77	Y	Technology Sector Equity (Growth & Inc)
Defiance Quantum ETF	QTUM	NYSE Arca	D+	D+	D+		25.77	26.54	18.83	Y	Technology Sector Equity (Technology)
● DeltaShares S&P 400 Managed Risk ETF	DMRM	NYSE Arca	D	D+	D		51.59	55.88	47.01	Y	US Equity Mid Cap (Growth)
● DeltaShares S&P 500 Managed Risk ETF	DMRL	NYSE Arca	C	C	D+	Up	56.80	58.50	49.51	Y	US Equity Large Cap Blend (Growth)
DeltaShares S&P 600 Managed Risk ETF	DMRS	NYSE Arca	D	D+	D		52.34	58.96	48.97	Y	US Equity Small Cap (Small Company)
● DeltaShares S&P International Managed Risk ETF	DMRI	NYSE Arca	D+	C-	D	Up	48.24	51.19	44.43	Y	Global Equity Large Cap (Foreign Stock)
DeltaShares® S&P EM 100 & Managed Risk ETF	DMRE	NYSE Arca	U	U	U		46.62	51.76	45.32	Y	Global Emerg Mkts Equity (Div Emerg Mkts)
Deutsche Bank FI Enhanced Global High Yield ETN	FIEG	NYSE Arca	D+	C	D	Down	176.00	204.00	106.78	Y	Global Equity Large Cap (Growth & Inc)
● Direxion All Cap Insider Sentiment Shares	KNOW	NYSE Arca	C	C	C-	Up	38.28	41.07	32.19	Y	US Equity Mid Cap (Balanced)
Direxion Auspice Broad Commodity Strategy ETF	COM	NYSE Arca	D+	D+	D+	Up	23.26	25.54	22.78	Y	Commodities Broad Basket (Growth & Inc)
Direxion Daily 20+ Year Treasury Bear 1X Shares	TYBS	NYSE Arca	D	D	D	Down	16.97	22.00	16.56	Y	Trading Tools (Govt Bond - Treasury)
● Direxion Daily 20+ Year Treasury Bear 3X Shares	TMV	NYSE Arca	D	D-	D		10.39	23.66	9.60	Y	Trading Tools (Govt Bond - Treasury)
● Direxion Daily 20+ Year Treasury Bull 3X Shares	TMF	NYSE Arca	C	C	D+	Up	30.63	34.12	15.21	Y	Trading Tools (Govt Bond - Treasury)
Direxion Daily 7-10 Year Treasury Bear 1X Shares	TYNS	NYSE Arca	D	D	E		26.08	29.46	25.62	Y	Trading Tools (Govt Bond - Treasury)
Direxion Daily 7-10 Year Treasury Bear 3X Shares	TYO	NYSE Arca	D	D-	D		10.61	15.88	10.15	Y	Trading Tools (Govt Bond - Treasury)
Direxion Daily 7-10 Year Treasury Bull 3X Shares	TYD	NYSE Arca	C	C	C-	Up	54.03	57.14	37.70	Y	Trading Tools (Govt Bond - Treasury)
● Direxion Daily Aerospace & Defense Bull 3X Sh Direxion Dai	DFEN	NYSE Arca	C	C+	C-	Up	59.81	64.85	24.66	Y	Trading Tools (Unaligned)
Direxion Daily Cnsmr Discret Bear 3XShrs	PASS	NYSE Arca	U	U	U		15.14	31.42	14.31	Y	Trading Tools (Unaligned)
Direxion Daily Cnsmr Discret Bull 3XShrs	WANT	NYSE Arca	U	U	U		31.92	35.91	18.19	Y	Trading Tools (Unaligned)
Direxion Daily Cnsmr Staples Bear 3XShrs	LACK	NYSE Arca	U	U	U		16.58	32.76	16.58	Y	Trading Tools (Unaligned)
Direxion Daily Cnsmr Staples Bull 3XShrs	NEED	NYSE Arca	U	U	U		32.42	32.42	18.30	Y	Trading Tools (Unaligned)
Direxion Daily Communication Services Index Bear 3X Shares	MUTE	NYSE Arca	U	U	U		15.96	25.51	14.44	Y	Trading Tools (Growth & Inc)
Direxion Daily Communication Services Index Bull 3X Shares	TAWK	NYSE Arca	U	U	U		32.22	38.11	24.12	Y	Trading Tools (Growth & Inc)

★ Expanded analysis of this fund is included in Section II: Analysis of All BUY Rated Funds. ● Expanded analysis of this fund is included in Section III: Analysis of All Rated Funds with Assets over $50 million.

3-Month Total Return	6-Month Total Return	1-Year Total Return	3-Year Total Return	5-Year Total Return	Dividend Yield (TTM)	Expense Ratio	3-Yr Std Deviation	Effective Duration	NAV	Total Assets (MIL)	%Cash	%Stocks	%Bonds	%Other	Turnover Ratio	Premium/ Discount 1-Year Avg	Inception Date
-5.63	-7.57	-14.42			4.06	0.95			16.19	4.9						-0.06	Jun-17
-5.38	-7.85					0.65			23.16	2.3	0	100	0	0		-0.02	Dec-18
-3.54	-5.33					0.65			24.14	0.48	0	100	0	0		0.04	Dec-18
-2.18	-3.22					0.65			24.28	0.49	0	100	0	0		0.35	Dec-18
5.19	6.76					0.65			27.29	1.1	0	100	0	0		0.18	Dec-18
0.99	5.43	-0.69			1.79	0.64			23.76	143.8	0	100	0	0	20	-0.04	Jan-17
-3.46	-4.36	-3.51			0.36	0.75			17.38	121.6	0	100	0	0	17	0.26	Mar-18
0.38	3.81	-3.37			1.41	0.63			23.83	200.1	0	100	0	0	28	0.10	Jan-17
-3.42	-3.02	-6.67			1.3	0.64			22.89	219.8	0	100	0	0	36	0.05	Jan-17
-13.02	-11.63	-16.23	-50.47	-59.17	0	0.75	24.69			3.1					0	0.18	Apr-08
13.26	8.56	14.74	75.97	56.31	0	0.75	24.69			0.21					0	-37.78	Apr-08
-6.32	-5.02	-6.98	-26.95	-31.70	0	0.75	12.34			0.64					0	1.15	Apr-08
6.84	5.31	8.91	37.25	33.45	0	0.75	12.35			0.20					0	-6.53	Apr-08
-9.01	-26.90	-23.69	4.40	-29.80	0	0.75	30.32			0.74					0	9.75	Jun-08
8.93	33.23	25.48	-23.32	-8.27	0	0.75	30.46			0.49					0	-17.56	Jun-08
3.68	12.99	11.74	-14.25	-23.44	0	0.75	14.43			0.38					0	-0.10	Jun-08
4.71	16.35	13.86	-8.13	2.29	0	0.75	15.27			0.59					0	-6.91	Jun-08
-7.89	-9.70	-36.31	2.92	-68.21	0	0.75	25.83			0.59					0	4.58	Apr-08
7.86	7.78	34.68	-16.26	87.06	0	0.75	26.78			0.28					0	-19.91	Apr-08
-3.75	-4.38	-18.06	5.42	-39.11	0	0.75	12.9			0.18					0	0.05	Apr-08
4.15	4.56	18.89	-4.97	47.52	0	0.75	13.41			0.35					0	-8.88	Apr-08
10.51	9.03	24.16	-52.60	56.48	0	0.75	55.71			14.6					0	0.19	Jun-08
-5.31	-9.23	-28.94	10.58	-62.21	0	0.75	25.36			3.4					0	4.75	Jun-08
5.45	6.73	20.55	-22.01	64.66	0	0.75	27.86			0.68					0	-6.28	Jun-08
15.74	31.42	50.54	13.35	22.44	0	0.75	21.79			94.2					0	1.26	Feb-08
-14.48	-26.03	-35.24	-19.05	-40.36	0	0.75	21.72			11.8					0	-0.07	Feb-08
-7.16	-13.17	-18.28	-7.33	-18.76	0	0.75	10.84			4.3					0	-0.07	Feb-08
-1.96	-6.07	-10.32	31.68	47.25	2.81	0.59	18.71		30.60	290.7	0	100	0	0	126	0.01	Sep-14
0.82	-1.29					0.3			24.47	112.6	0	100	0	0		0.01	Mar-19
-1.64	-1.17	-7.01			0.67	0.3			23.37	3.5	0	100	0	0		0.07	Jul-18
3.47	6.79	5.32			0.71	0.4			25.69	7.7	0	100	0	0		0.17	Sep-18
-2.00	-0.28	-6.17			1.36	0.45			51.40	92.5	1	55	44	0	435	0.00	Jul-17
-0.36	3.14	0.09			1.74	0.35			56.92	409.8	1	69	30	0	430	-0.03	Jul-17
-1.44	-0.27	-8.95			1.35	0.45			52.50	39.4	1	51	48	0	448	-0.15	Jul-17
-1.51	1.24	-2.27			2.85	0.5			48.27	190.7	1	99	0	0	189	0.34	Jul-17
-6.49						0.6			46.64	42.0						0.13	Mar-19
14.71	10.39	7.19	45.49	50.93	0	0.1	14.89			4.9						-5.29	Oct-13
-1.85	-0.67	-4.54	23.28	46.90	2.38	0.59	15.38		38.27	112.9	0	100	0	0	919	-0.09	Dec-11
0.20	-2.58	-6.25			2.72	0.7			23.24	39.5	86	0	0	14	0	-0.03	Mar-17
-7.64	-12.92	-18.77	-8.78	-29.61	2.43	0.48	11.61		16.97	2.5	109	0	-9	0	27	-0.16	Mar-11
-23.53	-37.16	-50.65	-35.96	-73.74	2.15	1.02	34.38		10.39	124.7	117	0	-17	0	0	-0.10	Apr-09
24.00	48.76	83.13	14.05	78.75	0.95	1.09	36.75	17.32	30.67	280.6	18	0	82	0	1	0.04	Apr-09
-1.98	-5.16	-9.39	-2.69	-15.74	1.43	0.49	5.17		26.10	1.3	105	0	-5	0	0	-0.03	Mar-11
-7.64	-17.83	-30.36	-17.46	-47.05	1.71	1.07	15.7		10.62	11.1	116	0	-16	0	0	-0.18	Apr-09
7.12	19.81	39.98	9.67	42.90	0.99	1.1	15.87	7.63	54.00	21.6	36	0	64	0	0	0.34	Apr-09
15.81	26.73	-4.05			0.58	0.98			59.83	56.8	7	93	0	0	39	-0.01	May-17
-4.26	-20.12					1.08			15.17	1.5	103	0	0	-3		0.33	Nov-18
-1.69	13.60					0.98			31.89	4.8	13	75	0	12		-0.16	Nov-18
-16.60	-27.39					1.06			16.60	0.83	113	-13	0	0		0.12	Nov-18
14.71	29.14					0.97			32.43	4.9	24	76	0	0		-0.20	Nov-18
-3.64	-21.38					1.1			15.97	0.80	104	-4	0	0		-0.11	Jan-19
-4.00	11.00					1.1			32.27	3.2	11	89	0	0		-0.10	Jan-19

Fund Name	Ticker Symbol	Traded On	Overall Rating	Reward Rating	Risk Rating	Recent Up/ Downgrade	Price as of 9/30/2019	52-Week High	52-Week Low	Open to New Investors	Category & (Prospectus Objective)
		MARKET		RATINGS				PRICE			CATEGORY & OBJECTIVE
Direxion Daily CSI 300 China A Share Bear 1X Shares	CHAD	NYSE Arca	D	D	D		30.37	41.12	27.56	Y	Trading Tools (Pacific Stock)
● Direxion Daily CSI 300 China A Share Bull 2X Shares	CHAU	NYSE Arca	D+	D+	D+	Down	20.26	27.64	13.90	Y	Trading Tools (Growth)
Direxion Daily CSI China Internet Bull 2X Shares	CWEB	NYSE Arca	D	D	D		20.59	31.52	17.40	Y	Trading Tools (Technology)
Direxion Daily Energy Bear 3X Shares	ERY	NYSE Arca	D+	D	D		48.15	80.39	29.65	Y	Trading Tools (Natl Res)
● Direxion Daily Energy Bull 3X Shares	ERX	NYSE Arca	D-	D-	D	Down	15.58	40.44	12.78	Y	Trading Tools (Natl Res)
Direxion Daily EURO STOXX 50 (R) Bull 3X Sh Direxion Daily	EUXL	NYSE Arca	D	D+	D		18.70	20.88	11.90	Y	Trading Tools (Europe Stock)
● Direxion Daily Financial Bear 3X Shares	FAZ	NYSE Arca	C+	B-	D+	Up	34.61	41.82	7.64	Y	Trading Tools (Financial)
● Direxion Daily Financial Bull 3X Shares	FAS	NYSE Arca	C	B-	C-		77.64	82.22	37.55	Y	Trading Tools (Financial)
● Direxion Daily FTSE China Bear 3X Shares	YANG	NYSE Arca	D	D-	D		55.28	77.18	39.69	Y	Trading Tools (Pacific Stock)
● Direxion Daily FTSE China Bull 3X Shares	YINN	NYSE Arca	D	D	D	Down	16.48	26.74	14.25	Y	Trading Tools (Pacific Stock)
Direxion Daily FTSE Europe Bull 3X Shares	EURL	NYSE Arca	D+	D	D+		26.36	31.97	18.27	Y	Trading Tools (Europe Stock)
● Direxion Daily Gold Miners Index Bear 3X Shares	DUST	NYSE Arca	D-	E	D-	Down	8.23	39.82	5.69	Y	Trading Tools (Prec Metals)
● Direxion Daily Gold Miners Index Bull 3X Shares	NUGT	NYSE Arca	C-	C	D+	Up	27.86	45.10	12.10	Y	Trading Tools (Prec Metals)
● Direxion Daily Healthcare Bull 3X Shares	CURE	NYSE Arca	C-	C	C-	Down	50.59	67.75	39.11	Y	Trading Tools (Health)
Direxion Daily High Yield Bear 2X Shares	HYDD	NYSE Arca	D	D-	D		15.97	20.91	15.83	Y	Trading Tools (Corp Bond-High Yld)
● Direxion Daily Homebuilders & Supplies Bull 3X Shares	NAIL	NYSE Arca	C	C	D+	Up	64.88	64.88	20.86	Y	Trading Tools (Unaligned)
Direxion Daily Industs Bull 3X Sh Direxion Daily Industs B	DUSL	NYSE Arca	C-	C-	D+	Up	32.41	39.45	16.62	Y	Trading Tools (Unaligned)
Direxion Daily Japan Bull 3X Shares	JPNL	NYSE Arca	D+	D+	D+		55.26	74.71	38.77	Y	Trading Tools (Foreign Stock)
● Direxion Daily Junior Gold Miners Index Bear 3X Shares	JDST	NYSE Arca	D-	E	D-	Down	17.75	85.34	11.99	Y	Trading Tools (Prec Metals)
● Direxion Daily Junior Gold Miners Index Bull 3X Shares	JNUG	NYSE Arca	C	B	D	Up	57.14	100.56	6.23	Y	Trading Tools (Prec Metals)
Direxion Daily Latin America Bull 3X Shares	LBJ	NYSE Arca	D	D	D		18.00	28.86	14.49	Y	Trading Tools (Foreign Stock)
★ Direxion Daily Mid Cap Bear 3X Shares	MIDZ	NYSE Arca	B-	B	D+	Up	50.60	60.93	10.06	Y	Trading Tools (Growth)
Direxion Daily Mid Cap Bull 3X Shares	MIDU	NYSE Arca	C-	C-	D+		41.30	51.75	23.80	Y	Trading Tools (Growth)
● Direxion Daily MSCI Brazil Bull 3X Shares	BRZU	NYSE Arca	D	D+	D		27.42	40.87	18.55	Y	Trading Tools (Foreign Stock)
Direxion Daily MSCI Developed Markets Bear 3X Shares	DPK	NYSE Arca	D+	D	D		12.31	20.08	11.55	Y	Trading Tools (Foreign Stock)
Direxion Daily MSCI Developed Markets Bull 3X Shares	DZK	NYSE Arca	D+	D+	D+	Down	60.61	72.58	42.05	Y	Trading Tools (Foreign Stock)
● Direxion Daily MSCI Emerging Markets Bear 3X Shares	EDZ	NYSE Arca	D	D-	D		47.69	70.95	39.09	Y	Trading Tools (Div Emerg Mkts)
● Direxion Daily MSCI Emerging Markets Bull 3X Shares	EDC	NYSE Arca	D+	D	D+		65.02	88.89	56.33	Y	Trading Tools (Div Emerg Mkts)
Direxion Daily MSCI European Financials Bull 2X Shares	EUFL	NYSE Arca	D	D	D		25.90	34.36	21.87	Y	Trading Tools (Financial)
● Direxion Daily MSCI India Bull 3x Shares	INDL	NYSE Arca	D+	D	D+	Down	61.35	81.14	46.97	Y	Trading Tools (Foreign Stock)
Direxion Daily MSCI Mexico Bull 3X Sh Direxion Daily MSCI	MEXX	NYSE Arca	D	D-	D		9.84	20.47	7.21	Y	Trading Tools (Foreign Stock)
★ Direxion Daily MSCI Real Estate Bear 3X Shares	DRV	NYSE Arca	B	A	D+	Up	26.56	33.23	5.95	Y	Trading Tools (Real Estate)
● Direxion Daily MSCI Real Estate Bull 3X Shares	DRN	NYSE Arca	C	C	C-		30.09	30.45	15.11	Y	Trading Tools (Real Estate)
Direxion Daily Natural Gas Related Bear 3X Shares	GASX	NYSE Arca	C	C	D+	Up	60.57	91.04	16.48		Trading Tools (Natl Res)
Direxion Daily Natural Gas Related Bull 3X Shares	GASL	NYSE Arca	D	D	D	Up	9.11	22.97	3.55	Y	Trading Tools (Natl Res)
Direxion Daily Pharmaceutical & Medical Bull 3X Shares ETF	PILL	NYSE Arca	D	D+	D		12.43	35.73	11.92	Y	Trading Tools (Growth & Inc)
Direxion Daily Regional Banks Bear 3X Shares	WDRW	NYSE Arca	D+	D	D		25.74	56.36	23.97	Y	Trading Tools (Financial)
Direxion Daily Regional Banks Bull 3X Shares	DPST	NYSE Arca	D	D	D	Down	40.02	70.95	26.92	Y	Trading Tools (Financial)
Direxion Daily Retail Bull 3X Shares	RETL	NYSE Arca	D	D	D		22.90	46.71	16.71	Y	Trading Tools (Unaligned)
Direxion Daily Robotics, AI & Automation Ind Bull 3X Share	UBOT	NYSE Arca	D	D	D		10.27	19.79	6.09	Y	Trading Tools (Technology)
Direxion Daily Russia Bear 3X Shares	RUSS	NYSE Arca	D-	E+	D-		10.66	21.65	9.19	Y	Trading Tools (Foreign Stock)
● Direxion Daily Russia Bull 3X Shares	RUSL	NYSE Arca	C	C+	D+		46.44	57.10	28.52	Y	Trading Tools (Foreign Stock)
Direxion Daily S&P 500® Bear 1X Shares	SPDN	NYSE Arca	D	D	D		26.55	34.17	26.29	Y	Trading Tools (Growth)
● Direxion Daily S&P 500® Bear 3X Shares	SPXS	NYSE Arca	D	E+	D		17.15	38.16	16.66	Y	Trading Tools (Growth)
Direxion Daily S&P 500® Bull 2X Shares	SPUU	NYSE Arca	C	C+	D+		57.06	59.04	36.67	Y	Trading Tools (Growth)
● Direxion Daily S&P Biotech Bear 3X Shares	LABD	NYSE Arca	D	E+	D	Up	25.32	59.28	16.49	Y	Trading Tools (Technology)
● Direxion Daily S&P Biotech Bull 3X Shares	LABU	NYSE Arca	D	D	D+	Down	30.90	90.09	25.21	Y	Trading Tools (Technology)
★ Direxion Daily S&P Oil & Gas Exp. & Prod. Bear 3X Shares	DRIP	NYSE Arca	B	A-	D	Up	78.50	119.89	4.94	Y	Trading Tools (Natl Res)
● Direxion Daily S&P Oil & Gas Exp. & Prod. Bull 3X Shares	GUSH	NYSE Arca	E+	E+	D	Down	3.32	43.24	2.78	Y	Trading Tools (Natl Res)
● Direxion Daily S&P500® Bull 3X Shares	SPXL	NYSE Arca	C	C+	D+		52.31	55.74	27.54	Y	Trading Tools (Growth)
● Direxion Daily Semiconductor Bear 3X Shares	SOXS	NYSE Arca	C	C+	D	Up	37.73	53.24	4.39	Y	Trading Tools (Technology)
● Direxion Daily Semiconductor Bull 3X Shares	SOXL	NYSE Arca	C+	B	C-	Up	170.22	200.88	67.08	Y	Trading Tools (Technology)

★ Expanded analysis of this fund is included in Section II: Analysis of All BUY Rated Funds. ● Expanded analysis of this fund is included in Section III: Analysis of All Rated Funds with Assets over $50 million.

	TOTAL RETURNS & PERFORMANCE								ASSETS		ASSET ALLOCATION & TURNOVER					VALUATION	
3-Month Total Return	6-Month Total Return	1-Year Total Return	3-Year Total Return	5-Year Total Return	Dividend Yield (TTM)	Expense Ratio	3-Yr Std Deviation	Effective Duration	NAV	Total Assets (MIL)	%Cash	%Stocks	%Bonds	%Other	Turnover Ratio	Premium/ Discount 1-Year Avg	Inception Date
6.79	8.34	-12.26	-24.07		3.35	0.85	19.34		30.34	21.2	101	-1	0	0	0	0.01	Jun-15
-14.38	-21.11	6.43	11.47		0.72	1.15	40.04		20.33	123.0	59	41	0	0	339	-0.02	Apr-15
-17.98	-30.85	-34.26	-8.40		0.9	1.25			20.64	48.5	51	49	0	0	189	-0.07	Nov-16
15.54	21.96	58.19	-20.80	-43.27	1.22	1.09	63.63		48.18	29.3	109	-9	0	0	0	0.11	Nov-08
-21.94	-33.76	-59.36	-51.54	-82.09	1.8	1.09	61.74		15.59	293.9	42	58	0	0	56	-0.08	Nov-08
-7.19	6.39	-9.69			0.43	1.21			18.70	2.8	50	50	0	0	53	0.01	Jul-17
-7.41	285.80	258.55	10.13	-49.15	0.99	1.07	38.15		34.65	182.7	109	-9	0	0	0	0.07	Nov-08
2.32	19.74	11.47	170.69	217.60	0.82	1	40.94		77.56	1,330	12	88	0	0	73	-0.11	Nov-08
26.18	26.03	-0.76	-60.83	-87.41	0.98	1.08	53.22		55.41	81.9	105	-5	0	0	0	-0.10	Dec-09
-25.94	-34.43	-30.94	-11.29	-35.69	1.36	1.52	56.61		16.50	315.9	52	48	0	0	158	0.02	Dec-09
-8.98	-2.75	-15.92	29.63	-17.78	1.57	1.06	38.18		26.44	25.1	53	47	0	0	54	-0.01	Jan-14
-34.22	-56.53	-78.55	-75.19	-99.40	1.81	1.05	71.17		8.28	431.5	129	-15	0	-15	0	-0.12	Dec-10
14.73	50.30	115.97	-62.74	-84.82	0.4	1.23	76.56		27.85	1,278	14	54	0	32	96	0.08	Dec-10
-10.99	-9.07	-24.51	60.74	105.11	0.85	1.08	40.3		50.62	126.5	29	71	0	0	43	-0.11	Jun-11
-2.19	-6.19	-10.46	-25.19		1.31	0.88			15.97	3.2	110	0	-10	0	0	0.07	Jun-16
38.90	70.85	54.92	152.59		0.27	0.99	58.39		64.82	55.1	22	78	0	0	38	-0.05	Aug-15
-1.68	-0.08	-15.49			1.34	1.07			32.30	3.2					26	-0.03	May-17
4.57	4.02	-25.01	23.38	27.51	0.9	1.29	34.14		55.43	8.3	58	42	0	0	6	-0.04	Jun-13
-40.76	-57.78	-77.06	-81.26	-99.86	2.1	1.09	76.25		17.80	181.4	126	-11	0	-15	0	-0.24	Oct-13
10.75	533.52	668.56	-17.46	-75.27	0.44	1.17	85.63		56.83	698.9	46	42	0	12	116	0.21	Oct-13
-23.76	-23.37	-16.57	-14.08	-73.25	1.38	1.33	71.02		17.99	10.2	95	7	0	-2	56	-0.09	Dec-09
-1.86	358.38	372.08	83.16	-20.43	0.75	1.09	46.59		50.61	3.2	113	-13	0	0	0	-0.17	Jan-09
-5.01	-2.47	-19.28	60.43	118.35	0.83	1.06	45.76		41.28	45.4	26	74	0	0	39	0.00	Jan-09
-17.46	-7.12	49.53	-17.64	-81.25	1.26	1.36	89.89		27.44	424.1	36	64	0	0	133	-0.05	Apr-13
3.77	-3.71	1.17	-46.90	-63.09	2.04	1.08	33.55		12.29	2.9	100	0	0	0	32	-0.07	Dec-08
-6.43	-1.42	-14.72	32.03	-2.01	1.6	1.19	33.79		60.79	12.2	44	56	0	0	30	-0.09	Dec-08
17.45	8.99	-5.42	-57.19	-73.83	1.22	1.09	42.74		47.64	66.5	105	-5	0	0	0	0.01	Dec-08
-19.48	-21.67	-22.38	2.58	-34.25	1.34	1.47	46.19		65.17	181.3	55	45	0	0	136	-0.01	Dec-08
-8.39	-6.01	-20.53	14.62		4.01	1.14	34.9		25.96	6.5					38	-0.29	Jul-16
-20.49	-21.55	-5.51	6.14	-28.47	0.93	1.38	49.85		61.39	85.9	59	41	0	0	59	-0.21	Mar-10
-11.65	-13.96	-50.98			1.94	1.27			9.86	13.3	61	39	0	0	140	0.13	May-17
-20.11	285.85	179.40	120.24	-33.05	0.95	1.1	36.88		26.55	16.0	105	-5	0	0	0	-0.02	Jul-09
19.94	19.23	45.11	30.49	134.47	1.63	1.04	39.54		30.09	52.7	29	71	0	0	149	0.00	Jul-09
45.94	123.73	245.10	138.47		0.53	1.09	85.42		60.85	4.6	115	-15	0	0	0	-0.03	Dec-15
-58.05	12.23	-57.80	-81.18	-99.91	0	1.04	77.92		9.10	28.0	59	41	0	0	44	0.09	Jul-10
-32.80	-47.50	-64.40			1.56	0.99			12.44	14.3	45	59	-2	-2	152	-0.13	Nov-17
-4.37	-14.96	-1.65	-76.18		1.9	1.07	70.66		25.74	1.3	106	-6	0	0	0	-0.03	Aug-15
-9.25	-7.00	-38.52	23.00		1.77	1	73.98		40.00	20.0	28	72	0	0	76	-0.05	Aug-15
-4.97	-24.16	-50.51	-44.06	32.82	1.25	0.99	54		22.87	13.7	25	75	0	0	81	0.02	Jul-10
-19.75	-10.38	-47.74			0.47	1.49			10.32	19.1	50	50	0	0	75	0.01	Apr-18
13.06	-23.87	-32.91	-78.76	-96.49	1.84	1.12	48.2		10.66	25.0	116	-15	0	-1	0	0.04	May-11
-16.16	17.95	8.71	38.74	-62.56	1.96	1.36	56.75		46.48	68.2	72	29	0	-1	93	0.02	May-11
-0.44	-3.42	-2.17	-28.95		1.87	0.49	12.1		26.56	19.9	106	-6	0	0	0	-0.01	Jun-16
-3.94	-14.13	-17.76	-71.50	-86.39	1.72	1.08	35.52		17.18	482.7	114	-14	0	0	1	0.03	Nov-08
0.48	7.27	1.76	87.35	134.89	1.62	0.64	24.4		57.02	10.4	-6	106	0	0	59	-0.08	May-14
43.35	38.57	0.69	-85.06		1.32	1.11	82.14		25.39	93.5	106	-6	0	0	0	0.05	May-15
-39.49	-47.97	-65.07	-36.07		0.82	1.12	80.38		30.89	471.5	40	60	0	0	510	-0.07	May-15
31.66	741.59	1,399.15	299.54		0.61	1.07	94.29		78.61	39.8	107	-7	0	0	0	-0.06	May-15
-52.85	-71.32	-91.82	-92.33		1.77	1.17	88.3		3.30	194.6	47	53	0	0	119	0.21	May-15
-0.54	8.69	-3.52	126.98	195.95	0.96	1.02	36.87		52.31	941.9	4	96	0	0	95	-0.08	Nov-08
-20.34	518.80	292.37	-48.65	-90.52	2	1.08	67.83		37.69	214.3	124	-24	0	0	0	0.05	Mar-10
6.50	15.59	10.17	275.19	585.65	0.61	0.99	67.33		170.23	604.3	-7	107	0	0	101	-0.03	Mar-10

Fund Name	Ticker Symbol	Traded On	Overall Rating	Reward Rating	Risk Rating	Recent Up/ Downgrade	Price as of 9/30/2019	52-Week High	52-Week Low	Open to New Investors	Category & (Prospectus Objective)
★ Direxion Daily Small Cap Bear 3X Shares	TZA	NYSE Arca	B-	B	D+	Up	46.99	55.00	8.48	Y	Trading Tools (Small Company)
Direxion Daily Small Cap Bull 2X Shares	SMLL	NYSE Arca	D+	C-	D		44.49	57.25	32.10	Y	Trading Tools (Small Company)
● Direxion Daily Small Cap Bull 3X Shares	TNA	NYSE Arca	D+	C-	D+	Down	55.67	85.79	35.43	Y	Trading Tools (Small Company)
Direxion Daily South Korea Bull 3X Shares	KORU	NYSE Arca	D-	D-	D	Down	18.81	39.28	14.42	Y	Trading Tools (Pacific Stock)
● Direxion Daily Technology Bear 3X Shares	TECS	NYSE Arca	D-	E+	D-		10.85	35.20	10.52	Y	Trading Tools (Technology)
● Direxion Daily Technology Bull 3X Shares	TECL	NYSE Arca	C	B-	D+		166.79	187.10	68.96	Y	Trading Tools (Technology)
Direxion Daily Total Bond Market Bear 1X Shares	SAGG	NYSE Arca	D+	D	D+	Up	29.54	32.50	29.42	Y	Trading Tools (Govt Bond - Treasury)
Direxion Daily Transportation Bull 3X Shares	TPOR	NYSE Arca	D+	D+	D+		24.40	39.11	16.14	Y	Trading Tools (Utility)
Direxion Daily Utilities Bull 3X Shares	UTSL	NYSE Arca	C	C+	C		47.34	47.75	24.69	Y	Trading Tools (Utility)
Direxion FTSE Russell International Over US ETF	RWIU	NYSE Arca	U	U	U		50.88	54.09	47.83	Y	Global Equity Large Cap (Growth)
Direxion FTSE Russell US Over International ETF	RWUI	NYSE Arca	U	U	U		59.13	60.22	50.53	Y	US Equity Large Cap Blend (Growth)
Direxion MSCI Cyclicals Over Defensives ETF	RWCD	NYSE Arca	U	U	U		61.24	63.24	50.55	Y	Consumer Goods & Svcs (Growth)
Direxion MSCI Defensives Over Cyclicals ETF	RWDC	NYSE Arca	U	U	U		50.73	52.53	48.78	Y	Consumer Goods & Svcs (Growth)
Direxion MSCI Developed Over Emerging Markets ETF	RWDE	NYSE Arca	U	U	U		55.30	55.64	50.04	Y	Global Equity Large Cap (Growth)
Direxion MSCI Emerging Over Developed Markets ETF	RWED	NYSE Arca	U	U	U		48.02	54.80	45.83	Y	Global Emerg Mkts Equity (Div Emerg Mkts)
● Direxion NASDAQ-100® Equal Weighted Index Shares	QQQE	NYSE Arca	C	C+	C-		49.41	51.83	38.25	Y	US Equity Large Cap Growth (Growth)
Direxion Russell 1000® Growth Over Value ETF	RWGV	NYSE Arca	U	U	U		59.50	61.67	49.97	Y	US Equity Large Cap Growth (Growth)
Direxion Russell 1000® Value Over Growth ETF	RWVG	NYSE Arca	U	U	U		54.79	55.25	50.44	Y	US Equity Large Cap Value (Growth)
Direxion Russell Large Over Small Cap ETF	RWLS	NYSE Arca	U	U	U		59.37	59.93	50.50	Y	US Equity Large Cap Blend (Growth)
Direxion Russell Small Over Large Cap ETF	RWSL	NYSE Arca	U	U	U		50.72	55.76	48.14	Y	US Equity Small Cap (Growth)
● Direxion Zacks MLP High Income Index Shares	ZMLP	NYSE Arca	C	C+	D	Up	12.55	15.73	11.78	Y	Energy Sector Equity (Income)
Distillate U.S. Fundamental Stability & Value ETF	DSTL	NYSE Arca	U	U	U		27.86	28.19	22.36	Y	US Equity Large Cap Blend (Income)
★ Eaton Vance Global Income Builder NextShares™	EVGBC	NAS CM	B-	C	B+	Up	9.73	10.58	8.62	Y	Moderate Allocation (Income)
Eaton Vance Stock NextShares™	EVSTC	NAS CM	C	B	D		14.65	14.85	10.97	Y	US Equity Large Cap Blend (Growth)
★ Eaton Vance TABS 5-to-15 Year Ladder Muni Bond NextShares™	EVLMC	NAS CM	B-	C+	B		10.47	10.57	9.78	Y	US Muni Fixed Inc (Muni Bond - Natl)
● ELEMENTS Dogs of the Dow - Dow Jones High Yld Select 10 To	DOD	NYSE Arca	D+	C	E+	Down	25.65	26.78	21.22	Y	US Equity Large Cap Value (Growth)
ELEMENTS Linked to SPECTRUM Large Cap U.S. Sector Momentum	EEH	NYSE Arca	C-	C+	E+	Up	21.84	22.00	17.84	Y	US Equity Large Cap Blend (Growth)
ELEMENTS - MLCX Biofuels Ind (Exchange Series) - Total Ret	FUE	NYSE Arca	D-	D-	D-		5.70	6.56	4.93	Y	Commodities Specified (Natl Res)
ELEMENTS Linked to the MLCX Grains Index - Total Return	GRU	NYSE Arca	D	D	D		3.09	3.50	2.83	Y	Commodities Specified (Natl Res)
ELEMENTS - Morningstar Wide Moat Focus Total Ret Ind	WMW	NYSE Arca	D+	C	E+	Down	34.90	37.79	28.59	Y	US Equity Large Cap Blend (Growth)
● ELEMENTS - Rogers Intl Commod Ind - Agriculture Total Ret	RJA	NYSE Arca	D	D-	D		5.25	5.94	4.97	Y	Commodities Specified (Natl Res)
ELEMENTS - Rogers Intl Commodity Ind - Energy Total Ret	RJN	NYSE Arca	D+	C-	D+		2.75	3.61	2.45	Y	Commodities Specified (Natl Res)
ELEMENTS - Rogers Intl Commodity Ind - Metals Total Ret	RJZ	NYSE Arca	D+	C	D	Up	8.17	8.54	7.56	Y	Commodities Specified (Natl Res)
● ELEMENTS - Rogers Intl Commodity Ind - Total Ret	RJI	NYSE Arca	C-	D+	C-		5.08	5.76	4.87	Y	Commodities Broad Basket (Natl Res)
● EMQQ The Emerging Markets Internet & Ecommerce ETF	EMQQ	NYSE Arca	C-	C-	C-		31.20	35.27	26.09	Y	Global Emerg Mkts Equity (Div Emerg Mkts)
EquityCompass Risk Manager ETF	ERM	NYSE Arca	D+	D+	D+		20.36	23.55	18.96	Y	US Equity Large Cap Blend (Growth)
EquityCompass Tactical Risk Manager ETF	TERM	NYSE Arca	D	D	D		17.77	23.55	16.64	Y	US Equity Large Cap Blend (Growth)
● ERShares Entrepreneur 30 ETF	ENTR	NYSE Arca	C+	B	C-	Up	16.84	18.72	13.02	Y	US Equity Large Cap Growth (Growth & Inc)
ERShares Non-US Small Cap Fund	ERSX	NYSE Arca	U	U	U		16.24	17.36	15.15	Y	Globa Eq Mid/Small Cap (Small Company)
● ETFMG Alternative Harvest ETF	MJ	NYSE Arca	D+	D+	D	Down	20.76	42.48	20.76	Y	Misc (Unaligned)
ETFMG Drone Economy Strategy ETF	IFLY	NYSE Arca	C-	C	D+		36.03	39.06	28.19	Y	Globa Eq Mid/Small Cap (Growth & Inc)
● ETFMG Prime Cyber Security ETF	HACK	NYSE Arca	C	C	C		37.40	41.82	31.73	Y	Technology Sector Equity (Growth)
● ETFMG Prime Junior Silver ETF	SILJ	NYSE Arca	C-	C-	D+	Up	9.46	11.39	6.80	Y	Prec Metals (Prec Metals)
★ ETFMG Prime Mobile Payments ETF	IPAY	NYSE Arca	B	B+	C		46.61	50.00	32.45	Y	Equity Misc (Growth & Inc)
● ETFMG Video Game Tech ETF	GAMR	NYSE Arca	C-	D+	C-		41.53	47.60	37.44	Y	Technology Sector Equity (Technology)
● Etho Climate Leadership U.S. ETF	ETHO	NYSE Arca	C	C+	D+		39.58	40.20	30.11	Y	US Equity Mid Cap (Growth & Inc)
ETRACS 2xMonthly Pay Leveraged Preferred Stock Index ETN	PFFL	NYSE Arca	D+	D+	C-		25.54	25.74	20.90	Y	Trading Tools (Growth)
ETRACS 2xMonthly Pay Leveraged US Small Cap High Div ETN	SMHB	NYSE Arca	U	U	U		17.35	22.88	14.35	Y	Trading Tools (Equity-Income)
EventShares U.S. Policy Alpha ETF	PLCY	BATS	D+	D	D+		21.57	23.00	18.32	Y	Long/Short Equity (Growth & Inc)
● Fidelity® Corporate Bond ETF	FCOR	NYSE Arca	C	B-	C-		53.00	53.63	47.14	Y	US Fixed Income (Corp Bond - Gen)
● Fidelity® Dividend ETF for Rising Rates	FDRR	NYSE Arca	C	C	C-		32.26	32.81	27.18	Y	US Equity Large Cap Value (Growth & Inc)
● Fidelity® High Dividend ETF	FDVV	NYSE Arca	C	C	C-		30.20	30.83	26.00	Y	US Equity Large Cap Value (Growth & Inc)

★Expanded analysis of this fund is included in Section II: Analysis of All BUY Rated Funds. ● Expanded analysis of this fund is included in Section III: Analysis of All Rated Funds with Assets over $50 million.

	TOTAL RETURNS & PERFORMANCE								ASSETS		ASSET ALLOCATION & TURNOVER					VALUATION	
3-Month Total Return	6-Month Total Return	1-Year Total Return	3-Year Total Return	5-Year Total Return	Dividend Yield (TTM)	Expense Ratio	3-Yr Std Deviation	Effective Duration	NAV	Total Assets (MIL)	%Cash	%Stocks	%Bonds	%Other	Turnover Ratio	Premium/ Discount 1-Year Avg	Inception Date
4.02	392.40	438.26	77.22	-32.80	0.82	1.11	51.52		46.93	346.9	115	-15	0	0	0	0.06	Nov-08
-6.79	-5.91	-20.61	39.53	81.43	0.96	0.79	34.56		44.48	3.0	-2	102	0	0	119	-0.29	Jul-14
-11.46	-11.46	-34.59	40.26	86.23	0.54	1.14	51.89		55.71	724.2	26	74	0	0	51	-0.09	Nov-08
-19.49	-31.94	-51.83	-36.51	-50.23	1.01	1.28	57.31		18.84	39.6	71	29	0	0	96	0.12	Apr-13
-9.39	-29.05	-39.04	-88.32	-96.06	1.74	1.1	42.05		10.86	53.2	116	-16	0	0	0	0.07	Dec-08
0.80	15.55	-1.30	245.84	459.17	0.3	1.08	46.94		166.84	750.8	4	96	0	0	41	-0.04	Dec-08
-1.39	-3.69	-6.06	-1.99	-10.48	1.92	0.49	3.37		29.55	3.0	83	0	-5	22	0	-0.06	Mar-11
-7.96	-13.97	-36.76			1.14	0.98			24.40	3.7	71	29	0	0	0	0.00	May-17
28.54	39.90	82.68			1.48	1.07			47.29	14.2	32	68	0	0	44	0.11	May-17
-3.83	-2.59					0.55			50.90	14.0	6	94	0	0		0.02	Jan-19
1.90	6.42					0.46			59.07	14.8	1	99	0	0		0.09	Jan-19
1.36	10.04					0.45			61.19	22.9	2	98	0	0		-0.02	Jan-19
-1.47	-2.26					0.45			50.71	13.9	7	93	0	0		0.04	Jan-19
1.13	4.53					0.52			55.29	15.2	5	95	0	0		-0.02	Jan-19
-8.42	-9.32					0.58			47.97	13.2	5	95	0	0		0.05	Jan-19
-1.66	1.99	5.36	48.47	76.36	0.77	0.35	14.77		49.42	210.0	0	100	0	0	27	-0.04	Mar-12
0.16	5.01					0.46			59.48	28.3	1	99	0	0		0.03	Jan-19
0.57	3.12					0.46			54.75	31.5	3	97	0	0		0.08	Jan-19
2.10	7.16					0.46			59.34	16.3	0	100	0	0		0.05	Jan-19
-4.43	-4.62					0.47			50.67	15.2	7	93	0	0		0.09	Jan-19
-4.71	-2.77	-9.71	-8.10	-49.84	12.77	0.65	17.9		12.53	51.4	0	100	0	0	115	0.00	Jan-14
1.42	5.47					0.39			27.86	43.9	0	100	0	0		0.01	Oct-18
0.31	3.76	3.06	23.56		11.33	0.86	8.56		9.73	6.1	2	56	40	0	102	0.00	Mar-16
1.38	7.64	7.76	45.61		1.8	0.65	11.63		14.65	6.6	0	100	0	0	90	0.00	Feb-16
1.32	3.61	8.40	8.58		2.18	0.35	4.35	4.53	10.47	7.3	2	0	98	0	78	0.00	Mar-16
0.00	0.76	4.79	41.47	69.08	0	0.75	14.35			51.0					0	0.00	Nov-07
3.75	6.08	20.97	33.83	48.53	0	0.75	13.22			4.6					0	0.00	Aug-07
-12.58	-7.38	-8.00	-33.73	-31.51	0	0.75	11.28			0.97					0	0.00	Feb-08
-9.37	-2.75	-9.24	-19.48	-31.30	0	0.75	17.86			4.2					0	0.00	Feb-08
0.00	-0.29	4.02	48.00	64.23	0	0.75	14.76			33.5					0	0.00	Oct-07
-6.72	-6.40	-9.51	-16.23	-25.60	0	0.75	9.45			104.5					0	0.00	Oct-07
-1.56	-7.67	-20.88	13.00	-56.40	0	0.75	23.86			19.7					0	0.00	Oct-07
4.09	2.03	5.49	6.03	-2.70	0	0.75	11.04			12.9					0	0.00	Oct-07
-1.81	-4.29	-10.00	2.60	-31.78	0	0.75	9.43			368.2						0.00	Oct-07
-3.77	-6.58	-1.60	17.91		0	0.86	21.93		31.33	360.2	0	100	0	0	33	-0.12	Nov-14
-0.03	1.02	-11.18			2.45	0.65			20.35	21.4	0	100	0	0	121	-0.02	Apr-17
-0.05	1.00	-22.80			2.06	1.5			17.78	30.2	0	100	0	0	120	-0.10	Apr-17
-4.91	-3.10	-6.47			0.16	0.49			16.84	72.4	1	99	0	0		-0.06	Nov-17
-4.03	-3.69					0.75			16.17	25.9						0.36	Dec-18
-31.93	-40.12	-43.79	-11.92		4.66	0.75	40.3			801.0	0	100	0	0	97	0.13	Dec-15
2.22	5.39	-7.05	37.92		0.84	0.75	17.66		35.92	37.7	3	97	0	0	42	-0.21	Mar-16
-6.18	-7.14	-5.06	35.23		0.22	0.6	15.98		37.46	1,427	1	99	0	0	41	-0.07	Nov-14
11.81	8.66	10.71	-37.91	-0.42	1.52	0.69	31.05		9.45	100.1	0	100	0	0	36	0.01	Nov-12
-1.15	7.07	9.11	88.23		0.1	0.75	14.76		46.60	743.2	1	99	0	0	16	0.03	Jul-15
-2.78	-6.16	-11.40	32.42		1.56	0.75	17.8		41.50	83.0	1	99	0	0	42	-0.22	Mar-16
0.65	5.59	6.86	51.23		0.84	0.45	13.7		39.58	53.4	1	99	0	0	19	0.03	Nov-15
5.35	9.15	14.07			9.82	0.85			25.60	29.4						0.02	Sep-18
1.30	-19.09					0.85			17.35	48.6						-0.29	Nov-18
-2.06	0.97	-6.01			0.12	0.86			21.54	17.2	0	100	0	0	214	0.02	Oct-17
2.94	7.97	12.93	13.91	24.11	3.23	0.36	4.13	7.49	52.82	132.0	3	0	94	0	81	0.19	Oct-14
1.20	2.90	3.18	38.86		3.54	0.29	11.68		32.28	343.7	0	100	0	0	35	-0.05	Sep-16
2.06	2.00	2.67	33.84		4.22	0.29	11.07		30.16	395.1	0	100	0	0	50	0.09	Sep-16

Fund Name	Ticker Symbol	Traded On	Overall Rating	Reward Rating	Risk Rating	Recent Up/ Downgrade	Price as of 9/30/2019	52-Week High	52-Week Low	Open to New Investors	Category & (Prospectus Objective)
● Fidelity® High Yield Factor ETF	FDHY	NYSE Arca	C-	C-	C-	Up	52.70	53.05	47.35	Y	US Fixed Income (Corp Bond-High Yld)
Fidelity® International High Dividend ETF	FIDI	NYSE Arca	D	D	C-		20.19	22.15	18.75	Y	Global Equity Large Cap (Equity-Income)
Fidelity® International Value Factor ETF	FIVA	NYSE Arca	D	D	D+		21.22	22.79	19.24	Y	Global Equity Large Cap (Growth & Inc)
● Fidelity® Limited Term Bond ETF	FLTB	NYSE Arca	C	C+	C-		50.94	51.20	49.01	Y	US Fixed Income (Income)
● Fidelity® Low Duration Bond Factor ETF	FLDR	NYSE Arca	C-	C-	C-	Up	50.72	50.84	49.79	Y	US Fixed Income (Growth & Inc)
● Fidelity® Low Volatility Factor ETF	FDLO	NYSE Arca	C	C	C-		36.72	37.11	28.31	Y	US Equity Large Cap Blend (Growth & Inc)
● Fidelity® Momentum Factor ETF	FDMO	NYSE Arca	C	C	C-		35.00	36.62	27.72	Y	US Equity Large Cap Growth (Growth & Inc)
★ Fidelity® MSCI Communication Services Index ETF	FCOM	NYSE Arca	B-	B	C	Up	33.07	35.04	26.75	Y	Communications Sector Equity (Comm)
● Fidelity® MSCI Consumer Discretionary Index ETF	FDIS	NYSE Arca	C+	B-	C-	Up	45.75	47.66	35.51	Y	Consumer Goods & Svcs (Unaligned)
★ Fidelity® MSCI Consumer Staples Index ETF	FSTA	NYSE Arca	B-	B	C	Up	36.61	36.73	29.30	Y	Consumer Goods & Svcs (Unaligned)
● Fidelity® MSCI Energy Index ETF	FENY	NYSE Arca	D+	D+	D		15.74	21.82	14.63	Y	Energy Sector Equity (Natl Res)
● Fidelity® MSCI Financials Index ETF	FNCL	NYSE Arca	C+	C+	C+	Up	40.66	41.70	32.43	Y	Financials Sector Equity (Financial)
● Fidelity® MSCI Health Care Index ETF	FHLC	NYSE Arca	C+	C+	C+		43.37	46.93	38.80	Y	Healthcare Sector Equity (Health)
● Fidelity® MSCI Industrials Index ETF	FIDU	NYSE Arca	C	C+	C-		39.86	40.69	30.66	Y	Industrials Sector Equity (Unaligned)
★ Fidelity® MSCI Information Technology Index ETF	FTEC	NYSE Arca	B-	B	C+	Down	63.77	66.03	45.74	Y	Technology Sector Equity (Technology)
● Fidelity® MSCI Materials Index ETF	FMAT	NYSE Arca	C+	B-	C	Up	32.33	33.91	26.67	Y	Natural Resources (Natl Res)
● Fidelity® MSCI Real Estate Index ETF	FREL	NYSE Arca	C+	B-	C+		27.90	28.11	21.52	Y	Real Estate Sector Equity (Real Estate)
★ Fidelity® MSCI Utilities Index ETF	FUTY	NYSE Arca	B-	B	C+	Down	42.49	42.60	33.93	Y	Utilities Sector Equity (Utility)
● Fidelity® NASDAQ Composite Index® Tracking Stock Fund	ONEQ	NAS CM	C	C+	C-		314.01	327.50	243.03	Y	US Equity Large Cap Growth (Growth)
● Fidelity® Quality Factor ETF	FQAL	NYSE Arca	C	C	C-		35.04	35.80	28.26	Y	US Equity Large Cap Blend (Growth & Inc)
Fidelity® Small-Mid Factor ETF	FSMD	NYSE Arca	U	U	U		25.00	25.67	23.76	Y	US Equity Mid Cap (Growth)
Fidelity® Targeted Emerging Markets Factor ETF	FDEM	BATS	U	U	U		23.83	25.49	22.82	Y	Global Emerg Mkts Equity (Div Emerg Mkts)
Fidelity® Targeted International Factor ETF	FDEV	BATS	U	U	U		25.68	26.16	24.63	Y	Global Equity Large Cap (World Stock)
● Fidelity® Total Bond ETF	FBND	NYSE Arca	C+	C+	C+	Up	51.70	52.16	47.95	Y	US Fixed Income (Income)
● Fidelity® Value Factor ETF	FVAL	NYSE Arca	C	C	C-		34.35	35.11	28.19	Y	US Equity Large Cap Value (Growth & Inc)
Fieldstone UVA Unconstrained Medium-Term Fixed Income ETF	FFIU	NYSE Arca	C-	C-	D+	Up	25.54	25.74	23.99	Y	US Fixed Income (Income)
★ Financial Select Sector SPDR® Fund	XLF	NYSE Arca	B-	C+	B-	Up	28.00	28.69	22.31	Y	Financials Sector Equity (Financial)
First Trust Alternative Absolute Return Strategy ETF	FAAR	NAS CM	D	D	D+	Down	26.19	28.84	26.19	Y	Commodities Broad Basket (Growth & Inc)
First Trust Asia Pacific Ex-Japan AlphaDEX® Fund	FPA	NAS CM	D	D	D+	Down	27.47	31.40	25.99	Y	Asia ex-Japan Equity (Pacific Stock)
First Trust Australia AlphaDEX® Fund	FAUS	NYSE Arca	D+	C	E+	Up	31.09	33.02	26.66	Y	Equity Misc (Foreign Stock)
● First Trust BICK Index Fund	BICK	NAS CM	D+	D	C-	Down	25.36	27.92	23.64	Y	Global Emerg Mkts Equity (Foreign Stock)
★ First Trust Brazil AlphaDEX® Fund	FBZ	NAS CM	B-	B	C-	Up	15.82	17.29	11.39	Y	Latin America Equity (Foreign Stock)
● First Trust BuyWrite Income ETF	FTHI	NAS CM	C	C	C-		22.49	23.32	19.24	Y	Long/Short Equity (Income)
● First Trust California Municipal High Income ETF	FCAL	NAS CM	C	C	C-	Up	53.25	53.78	49.04	Y	US Muni Fixed Inc (Muni Bond - Natl)
First Trust Canada AlphaDEX® Fund	FCAN	NAS CM	D	D+	D	Down	23.34	25.64	19.57	Y	Equity Misc (Foreign Stock)
★ First Trust Capital Strength ETF	FTCS	NAS CM	B-	B-	C+	Up	56.78	57.95	45.20	Y	US Equity Large Cap Blend (Growth)
First Trust CEF Income Opportunity ETF	FCEF	NAS CM	C	C	D+	Up	22.23	22.33	18.07	Y	Moderate Allocation (Income)
First Trust China AlphaDEX® Fund	FCA	NAS CM	D+	C-	D+	Down	23.93	28.92	22.44	Y	Greater China Equity (Pacific Stock)
● First Trust Chindia ETF	FNI	NYSE Arca	C-	C-	C-		34.35	38.48	29.74	Y	Equity Misc (Pacific Stock)
● First Trust Cloud Computing ETF	SKYY	NAS CM	C	C	C	Down	56.42	60.91	45.37	Y	Technology Sector Equity (Technology)
● First Trust Consumer Discretionary AlphaDEX® Fund	FXD	NYSE Arca	C	C	C-		42.05	44.45	34.86	Y	Consumer Goods & Svcs (Unaligned)
● First Trust Consumer Staples AlphaDEX® Fund	FXG	NYSE Arca	C	B-	C-		48.32	48.81	40.68	Y	Consumer Goods & Svcs (Unaligned)
First Trust Developed International Equity Select ETF	RNDM	NAS CM	C-	C	D+	Up	49.90	51.65	44.31	Y	Global Equity Large Cap (Equity-Income)
● First Trust Developed Markets Ex-US AlphaDEX® Fund	FDT	NAS CM	C-	D+	C		52.34	59.64	47.63	Y	Global Equity Large Cap (Foreign Stock)
First Trust Developed Mkts ex-US Small Cap AlphaDEX® Fund	FDTS	NAS CM	D+	D	D+	Up	35.24	41.67	32.03	Y	Globa Eq Mid/Small Cap (Foreign Stock)
● First Trust Dorsey Wright DALI 1 ETF	DALI	NAS CM	D+	D	D+		19.89	21.03	16.00	Y	Aggressive Allocation (Growth & Inc)
● First Trust Dorsey Wright Dynamic Focus 5 ETF	FVC	NAS CM	C-	C	C-	Down	26.43	28.70	21.74	Y	US Equity Mid Cap (Growth & Inc)
● First Trust Dorsey Wright Focus 5 ETF	FV	NAS CM	C	C	C+		29.59	31.38	23.41	Y	US Equity Large Cap Growth (Growth & Inc)
● First Trust Dorsey Wright International Focus 5 ETF	IFV	NAS CM	C	D+	C+		19.03	20.34	16.87	Y	Global Equity Large Cap (Growth & Inc)
First Trust Dorsey Wright Momentum & Dividend ETF	DDIV	NAS CM	C	C+	C		26.09	26.25	19.63	Y	US Equity Mid Cap (World Stock)
● First Trust Dorsey Wright Momentum & Low Volatility ETF	DVOL	NAS CM	C	C	B-		22.82	22.91	17.33	Y	US Equity Large Cap Blend (Growth & Inc)
First Trust Dorsey Wright Momentum & Value ETF	DVLU	NAS CM	C	C	C-		18.46	19.53	14.57	Y	US Equity Mid Cap (Growth & Inc)

★ Expanded analysis of this fund is included in Section II: Analysis of All BUY Rated Funds. ● Expanded analysis of this fund is included in Section III: Analysis of All Rated Funds with Assets over $50 million.

			TOTAL RETURNS & PERFORMANCE						ASSETS		ASSET ALLOCATION & TURNOVER					VALUATION	
3-Month Total Return	6-Month Total Return	1-Year Total Return	3-Year Total Return	5-Year Total Return	Dividend Yield (TTM)	Expense Ratio	3-Yr Std Deviation	Effective Duration	NAV	Total Assets (MIL)	%Cash	%Stocks	%Bonds	%Other	Turnover Ratio	Premium/ Discount 1-Year Avg	Inception Date
2.12	5.61	9.24			4.7	0.45			52.38	73.3	7	0	92	0		0.60	Jun-18
-0.58	-1.12	-4.90			4.74	0.39			20.11	42.2	1	99	0	0	42	0.42	Jan-18
-1.98	-1.00	-3.43			4.01	0.39			21.11	12.7	0	100	0	0	65	0.26	Jan-18
1.15	3.18	6.29	7.18	12.23	2.73	0.36	1.52	2.60	50.92	129.9	1	0	97	0	113	0.05	Oct-14
0.97	2.26	4.02			2.63	0.15		0.93	50.67	127.9	2	0	96	0		0.14	Jun-18
2.63	7.85	10.68	53.09		1.57	0.29	10.09		36.69	297.2	0	100	0	0	36	0.00	Sep-16
-1.83	3.15	-0.20	42.56		1.2	0.29	12.42		34.98	138.2	0	100	0	0	133	0.03	Sep-16
-0.85	2.67	6.28	22.65	49.48	1.04	0.08	13.93		33.06	434.7	0	100	0	0	82	0.05	Oct-13
-0.33	3.80	2.20	51.10	84.19	1.2	0.08	14.51		45.80	721.3	0	100	0	0	25	-0.02	Oct-13
5.47	9.73	15.62	24.08	53.86	2.5	0.08	11.65		36.59	634.8	0	100	0	0	30	0.05	Oct-13
-7.81	-12.58	-24.44	-13.25	-29.83	3.58	0.08	21.63		15.74	420.4	0	100	0	0	6	0.00	Oct-13
0.90	7.21	3.36	50.45	68.19	2.37	0.08	17.16		40.68	988.5	0	100	0	0	5	-0.03	Oct-13
-3.74	-1.95	-5.37	32.25	56.63	2.2	0.08	13.83		43.39	1,443	0	100	0	0	5	0.01	Oct-13
0.45	3.15	0.52	39.18	62.92	1.78	0.08	16.77		39.86	436.5	0	100	0	0	5	-0.02	Oct-13
1.11	6.63	7.13	80.60	129.18	1.17	0.08	15.8		63.75	2,556	0	100	0	0	18	-0.03	Oct-13
-1.57	2.17	-2.34	24.60	30.65	2.01	0.08	15.67		32.34	192.4	0	100	0	0	12	-0.02	Oct-13
7.65	9.25	20.96	29.13		3.23	0.08	12.37		27.88	952.0	0	100	0	0	10	0.06	Feb-15
9.15	13.20	25.93	47.17	83.80	2.66	0.08	10.27		42.46	896.0	0	100	0	0	7	0.03	Oct-13
-0.79	3.15	1.04	55.25	91.02	1.1	0.21	14.44		314.40	2,028	13	87	0	0	10	-0.01	Sep-03
0.57	3.35	2.56	44.18		1.65	0.29	11.57		35.02	148.8	0	100	0	0	29	0.00	Sep-16
-0.56	1.34					0.29			25.01	7.5	0	100	0	0	2	0.03	Feb-19
-3.84	-3.02					0.45			23.76	9.5	1	99	0	0		0.28	Feb-19
0.00	2.55					0.39			25.58	10.2	0	100	0	0		0.18	Feb-19
2.00	5.40	9.80	10.40	19.22	2.92	0.36	2.98	5.25	51.61	774.3	3	0	96	0	91	0.22	Oct-14
0.59	2.96	0.10	42.65		2	0.29	13.52		34.29	152.6	0	100	0	0	31	-0.04	Sep-16
1.94	4.81	8.16			2.91	0.46			25.55	47.3	3	0	94	-1	49	0.05	Aug-17
0.92	7.59	3.54	53.43	63.90	2.01	0.13	17.24			22,702	0	100	0	0	3	-0.03	Dec-98
-1.82	-2.02	-8.75	-7.08		0.39	0.95	5.79		26.19	45.8	83	0	0	17	0	0.13	May-16
-6.82	-9.38	-9.88	-0.25	6.70	2.86	0.8	15.09		27.66	29.0	1	99	0	0	88	-0.51	Apr-11
-1.41	0.69	-0.55	16.01	28.50	3.21	0.8	12.35		31.05	1.6	1	99	0	0	80	-0.04	Feb-12
-5.15	-7.20	-1.57	16.39	12.13	1.57	0.64	14.25		25.61	116.5	0	100	0	0	65	-0.32	Apr-10
0.69	9.67	45.70	53.07	26.59	2.77	0.8	27.51		15.89	108.9	0	100	0	0	128	-0.29	Apr-11
0.67	5.04	1.02	24.06	40.30	4.28	0.85	9.68		22.43	80.2	1	99	0	0	239	0.02	Jan-14
2.30	5.38	9.91			2.8	0.5		6.11	53.20	50.5	7	0	93	0	69	0.13	Jun-17
-1.34	0.81	-7.97	0.61	-30.19	1.24	0.8	15.09		23.27	4.7	0	100	0	0	88	-0.23	Feb-12
0.15	4.42	3.86	46.96	74.18	1.39	0.6	11.38		56.74	2,863	0	100	0	0	117	0.01	Jul-06
1.97	5.66	5.79	29.35		5.21	2.96	10.62	2.56	22.22	37.9	-1	48	49	-3	15	-0.06	Sep-16
-7.09	-10.01	-9.56	27.73	28.62	3.59	0.8	18.96		24.08	9.6	1	99	0	0	97	0.01	Apr-11
-6.03	-9.25	0.47	18.03	25.54	0.76	0.59	17.68		34.29	92.6	0	100	0	0	22	-0.02	May-07
-3.11	-3.22	0.82	68.03	115.13	1.06	0.6	13.42		56.39	2,168	0	100	0	0	7	0.04	Jul-11
-1.70	-0.63	-1.61	22.80	38.43	1.03	0.64	14.76		42.04	323.7	0	100	0	0	97	-0.02	May-07
5.78	6.34	5.18	9.32	35.82	1.48	0.64	12.24		48.32	372.1	0	100	0	0	90	0.00	May-07
-0.98	1.67	1.43			2.74	0.65			49.66	27.3	1	99	0	0	52	0.22	Jun-17
-2.99	-3.40	-10.21	12.58	17.16	2.23	0.8	13.5		52.34	680.5	1	99	0	0	109	-0.09	Apr-11
-3.04	-5.16	-13.76	6.43	10.77	1.74	0.8	14.2		35.38	8.8	1	99	0	0	142	-0.32	Feb-12
-3.24	-1.87	-5.02			0.26	0.91			19.86	70.5	0	100	0	0	34	-0.03	May-18
-1.83	-1.29	-7.03	26.70		0.76	0.89	13.91		26.46	468.3	40	60	0	0	42	-0.11	Mar-16
-3.04	-2.41	-3.49	31.51	50.82	0.32	0.89	15.45		29.63	2,350	0	100	0	0	44	-0.04	Mar-14
-3.35	-0.99	-4.35	13.94	11.82	1.93	1.03	14.36		19.06	453.7	0	100	0	0	0	-0.08	Jul-14
4.78	8.88	6.82	27.88	49.69	2.76	0.6	12.28		26.07	41.7	1	99	0	0	297	0.08	Mar-14
6.04	12.00	16.09			1.21	0.6			22.81	131.2	0	100	0	0	0	-0.01	Sep-18
1.22	4.15	-2.86			1.76	0.6			18.52	19.5	1	99	0	0	0	0.04	Sep-18

Fund Name	Ticker Symbol	Traded On	Overall Rating	Reward Rating	Risk Rating	Recent Up/Downgrade	Price as of 9/30/2019	52-Week High	52-Week Low	Open to New Investors	Category & (Prospectus Objective)
● First Trust Dorsey Wright People's Portfolio ETF	DWPP	NAS CM	C	C	C-		31.08	31.82	24.51	Y	Long/Short Equity (Growth & Inc)
★ First Trust Dow 30 Equal Weight ETF	EDOW	NYSE Arca	B-	B	C	Up	24.52	25.12	20.09	Y	US Equity Large Cap Value (Growth & Inc)
● First Trust Dow Jones Global Select Dividend Index Fund	FGD	NYSE Arca	C	D+	C+	Up	22.93	25.14	21.06	Y	Global Equity Large Cap (World Stock)
First Trust Dow Jones International Internet ETF	FDNI	NAS CM	U	U	U		22.05	27.18	15.67	Y	Technology Sector Equity (Technology)
● First Trust Dow Jones Internet Index Fund	FDN	NYSE Arca	C+	B	C		134.64	151.35	107.21	Y	Technology Sector Equity (Technology)
● First Trust Dow Jones Select MicroCap Index Fund	FDM	NYSE Arca	C-	C	C-	Up	45.70	50.54	38.71	Y	US Equity Small Cap (Growth)
● First Trust Emerging Markets AlphaDEX® Fund	FEM	NAS CM	C	C	C+		23.54	25.79	22.37	Y	Global Emerg Mkts Equity (Div Emerg Mkts)
First Trust Emerging Markets Equity Select ETF	RNEM	NAS CM	C-	C	D+	Up	49.08	52.82	45.46	Y	Global Emerg Mkts Equity (Equity-Income)
● First Trust Emerging Markets Local Currency Bond ETF	FEMB	NAS CM	C	C	C-	Up	38.05	39.95	35.97	Y	Emerging Mkts Fixed Inc (Div Emerg Mkts)
● First Trust Emerging Markets Small Cap AlphaDEX® Fund	FEMS	NAS CM	C-	C-	C-		34.07	36.82	31.64	Y	Global Emerg Mkts Equity (Div Emerg Mkts)
● First Trust Energy AlphaDEX® Fund	FXN	NYSE Arca	C-	C	D	Up	9.81	18.18	8.94	Y	Energy Sector Equity (Natl Res)
● First Trust Enhanced Short Maturity ETF	FTSM	NAS CM	C	C	C+		60.07	60.19	59.79	Y	US Fixed Income (Income)
● First Trust Europe AlphaDEX® Fund	FEP	NAS CM	C-	C-	C-		34.37	38.17	30.01	Y	Europe Equity Large Cap (Foreign Stock)
First Trust Eurozone AlphaDEX® ETF	FEUZ	NAS CM	C-	D+	C-		37.82	41.88	33.28	Y	Europe Equity Large Cap (Income)
● First Trust Financials AlphaDEX® Fund	FXO	NYSE Arca	C	C	C+		31.81	32.72	25.49	Y	Financials Sector Equity (Financial)
● First Trust FTSE EPRA/NAREIT Dev Mkts Real Estate Ind Fund	FFR	NYSE Arca	C	C	D+		49.58	49.58	40.92	Y	Real Estate Sector Equity (Real Estate)
● First Trust Germany AlphaDEX® Fund	FGM	NAS CM	D+	D	C-	Down	39.93	46.52	36.33	Y	Europe Equity Large Cap (Europe Stock)
First Trust Global Engineering and Construction ETF	FLM	NYSE Arca	D+	D	D+	Up	47.07	56.72	43.16	Y	Industrials Sector Equity (Unaligned)
● First Trust Global Tactical Commodity Strategy Fund	FTGC	NAS CM	D	D	D+		18.15	20.24	17.70	Y	Commodities Broad Basket (Growth & Inc)
● First Trust Global Wind Energy ETF	FAN	NYSE Arca	C	C	C-		13.16	13.73	11.09	Y	Utilities Sector Equity (Natl Res)
● First Trust Health Care AlphaDEX® Fund	FXH	NYSE Arca	C	C	C		74.02	84.57	64.01	Y	Healthcare Sector Equity (Health)
First Trust Hedged BuyWrite Income ETF	FTLB	NAS CM	C	C	D+		22.32	22.89	19.51	Y	Long/Short Equity (Income)
First Trust Hong Kong AlphaDEX® Fund	FHK	NAS CM	D	D	D	Down	31.72	38.34	30.29	Y	Greater China Equity (Pacific Stock)
● First Trust Horizon Managed Volatility Developed Intl ETF	HDMV	NYSE Arca	C	C	C-		33.28	34.35	29.97	Y	Global Equity Large Cap (Growth)
● First Trust Horizon Managed Volatility Domestic ETF	HUSV	NYSE Arca	C	C	C-		27.54	27.65	21.11	Y	US Equity Large Cap Blend (Growth)
First Trust India NIFTY 50 Equal Weight ETF	NFTY	NAS CM	D	D	D+	Down	34.47	38.50	31.25	Y	India Equity (Growth)
● First Trust Industrials/Producer Durables AlphaDEX® Fund	FXR	NYSE Arca	C+	C+	C+	Up	41.82	43.36	32.01	Y	Industrials Sector Equity (Unaligned)
First Trust Indxx Global Agriculture ETF	FTAG	NAS CM	D+	C-	D	Up	22.77	26.26	21.29	Y	Commodities Specified (Unaligned)
First Trust Indxx Global Natural Resources Income ETF	FTRI	NAS CM	D+	C	D	Down	11.45	12.84	10.60	Y	Natural Resources (Natl Res)
First Trust Indxx Innovative Transaction & Process ETF	LEGR	NAS CM	C-	C-	D+	Up	29.35	31.01	24.47	Y	Technology Sector Equity (Growth & Inc)
● First Trust IndXX NextG ETF	NXTG	NAS CM	C	C	C-	Up	50.33	51.53	41.69	Y	Technology Sector Equity (Technology)
● First Trust Inst Preferred Securities & Income ETF	FPEI	NYSE Arca	C-	C-	C-		19.62	19.74	18.05	Y	US Fixed Income (Growth & Inc)
First Trust International Equity Opportunities ETF	FPXI	NAS CM	C	B	D+	Up	36.35	38.70	29.75	Y	Global Equity Large Cap (World Stock)
First Trust IPOX Europe Equity Opportunities ETF	FPXE	NAS CM	U	U	U		19.71	20.66	16.44	Y	Europe Equity Large Cap (Europe Stock)
● First Trust Japan AlphaDEX® Fund	FJP	NAS CM	D	D	D+	Down	47.87	57.97	44.61	Y	Japan Equity (Pacific Stock)
● First Trust Large Cap Core AlphaDEX® Fund	FEX	NAS CM	C	C	C-		60.90	62.91	48.95	Y	US Equity Large Cap Blend (Growth)
● First Trust Large Cap Growth AlphaDEX® Fund	FTC	NAS CM	C	C	C-		69.98	72.64	53.12	Y	US Equity Large Cap Growth (Growth)
First Trust Large Cap US Equity Select ETF	RNLC	NAS CM	C	C	D+	Up	23.20	23.63	18.51	Y	US Equity Large Cap Blend (Equity-Income)
● First Trust Large Cap Value AlphaDEX® Fund	FTA	NAS CM	C-	C-	C-	Down	51.57	54.36	43.92	Y	US Equity Large Cap Value (Growth)
● First Trust Latin America AlphaDEX® Fund	FLN	NAS CM	C	C+	C-		20.42	21.76	17.71	Y	Latin America Equity (Foreign Stock)
First Trust Long Duration Opportunities ETF	LGOV	NYSE Arca	U	U	U		28.12	28.68	25.12	Y	US Fixed Income (Income)
● First Trust Long/Short Equity ETF	FTLS	NYSE Arca	C	C+	C-		41.00	41.27	35.84	Y	Long/Short Equity (Growth)
● First Trust Low Duration Opportunities ETF	LMBS	NAS CM	C+	C	C+	Up	51.99	52.09	50.81	Y	US Fixed Income (Govt Bond - Mortgage)
First Trust Low Duration Strategic Focus ETF	LDSF	NAS CM	U	U	U		20.55	20.59	20.21	Y	US Fixed Income (Growth & Inc)
First Trust Lunt U.S. Factor Rotation ETF	FCTR	BATS	C-	D+	C-	Up	21.80	22.29	16.74	Y	US Equity Large Cap Blend (Growth)
● First Trust Managed Futures Strategy Fund	FMF	NYSE Arca	D	D	D+		44.56	50.71	43.28	Y	Alternative Misc (Growth & Inc)
● First Trust Managed Municipal ETF	FMB	NAS CM	C+	C+	C+		55.56	56.20	51.54	Y	US Muni Fixed Inc (Growth & Inc)
● First Trust Materials AlphaDEX® Fund	FXZ	NYSE Arca	C-	C	C-		37.24	41.59	31.50	Y	Natural Resources (Unaligned)
First Trust Mega Cap AlphaDEX® Fund	FMK	NAS CM	C	C+	C-		36.11	37.47	30.39	Y	US Equity Large Cap Blend (Growth)
● First Trust Mid Cap Core AlphaDEX® Fund	FNX	NAS CM	C-	C	C-	Down	67.54	70.98	54.08	Y	US Equity Mid Cap (Growth)
● First Trust Mid Cap Growth AlphaDEX® Fund	FNY	NAS CM	C	C	C-		44.75	47.28	33.42	Y	US Equity Mid Cap (Growth)
First Trust Mid Cap US Equity Select ETF	RNMC	NAS CM	C-	C	D+	Up	22.23	22.64	17.65	Y	US Equity Mid Cap (Equity-Income)

★Expanded analysis of this fund is included in Section II: Analysis of All BUY Rated Funds. ● Expanded analysis of this fund is included in Section III: Analysis of All Rated Funds with Assets over $50 million.

		TOTAL RETURNS & PERFORMANCE							ASSETS		ASSET ALLOCATION & TURNOVER					VALUATION	
3-Month Total Return	6-Month Total Return	1-Year Total Return	3-Year Total Return	5-Year Total Return	Dividend Yield (TTM)	Expense Ratio	3-Yr Std Deviation	Effective Duration	NAV	Total Assets (MIL)	%Cash	%Stocks	%Bonds	%Other	Turnover Ratio	Premium/ Discount 1-Year Avg	Inception Date
0.01	3.80	3.65	36.46	41.40	1.26	0.6	12.59		31.09	54.4	0	100	0	0	32	0.01	Aug-12
0.60	3.35	5.19			1.77	0.5			24.51	49.0	0	100	0	0	16	-0.01	Aug-17
0.64	0.87	-3.00	13.08	10.76	6.14	0.58	11.31		22.90	532.3	0	100	0	0	31	0.15	Nov-07
-3.34	-4.58					0.65			21.02	4.2	0	100	0	0		4.51	Nov-18
-7.24	-4.57	-4.23	65.02	125.28	0	0.52	17.09		134.63	8,058	0	100	0	0		0.00	Jun-06
1.33	1.80	-8.06	30.39	65.47	1.72	0.6	18.72		45.65	139.5	1	99	0	0	75	-0.01	Sep-05
-4.16	-3.06	-2.43	26.50	17.16	3.61	0.8	15.19		23.73	584.9	2	98	0	0	103	0.07	Apr-11
-4.17	-2.37	2.91			3.1	0.75			49.00	9.8	2	98	0	0	69	0.47	Jun-17
-1.21	2.70	9.30	5.30		5.07	0.85	9.2	5.34	37.94	142.3	7	0	93	0	61	0.18	Nov-14
-1.54	-1.90	-1.37	18.10	13.87	4.35	0.8	16.87		34.43	132.6	2	98	0	0	126	-0.58	Feb-12
-13.84	-24.47	-43.88	-33.86	-58.28	1.82	0.63	27.65		9.82	101.6	0	100	0	0	99	-0.05	May-07
0.41	1.17	2.38	5.87	7.20	2.45	0.4	0.23	0.37	60.06	4,892	33	0	65	0	45	0.02	Aug-14
-2.18	-0.53	-7.92	23.72	26.33	2.32	0.8	14.62		34.42	514.6	1	99	0	0	99	-0.11	Apr-11
-1.83	0.33	-8.21	22.56		1.75	0.8	15.03		37.84	49.2	4	96	0	0	90	0.04	Oct-14
0.40	3.98	1.89	38.50	60.10	2	0.63	14.44		31.79	1,796	0	100	0	0	81	-0.02	May-07
4.64	4.37	13.85	18.53	40.71	2.89	0.6	10.68		49.44	56.4	0	99	0	1	9	-0.04	Aug-07
-4.09	-2.19	-12.38	13.44	25.59	2.4	0.8	15.97		39.93	125.8	0	100	0	0	81	0.02	Feb-12
-6.34	-6.15	-15.49	1.58	7.85	1.89	0.7	14.47		47.04	9.4	0	100	0	0	16	-0.10	Oct-08
-2.13	-3.61	-8.89	-10.35	-36.84	0.6	0.95	7.26		18.13	164.2	85	0	0	15	0	-0.09	Oct-13
-1.59	1.44	8.52	11.04	35.35	2.34	0.6	14.96		13.13	75.5	0	96	0	4	22	-0.01	Jun-08
-5.01	-3.65	-12.43	21.68	34.02	0	0.63	16.01		74.02	1,051	0	100	0	0	123	-0.01	May-07
0.62	4.20	0.64	19.56	30.65	2.96	0.85	8.74		22.30	8.9	2	98	0	0	219	-0.13	Jan-14
-10.66	-15.57	-7.63	0.43	3.37	3.88	0.8	15.27		31.86	3.2	1	99	0	0	66	-0.40	Feb-12
-0.68	1.95	2.71	21.20		2.86	0.8	9.32		33.21	132.8	1	99	0	0	99	0.44	Aug-16
3.67	10.21	16.17	45.04		1.45	0.7	9.37		27.50	243.4	0	100	0	0	147	0.10	Aug-16
-8.74	-9.61	-1.02	9.37	8.58	1.01	0.8	14.81		33.86	3.4	0	100	0	0	156	0.20	Feb-12
-1.45	3.29	-0.01	45.30	51.28	0.99	0.62	18.54		41.81	307.3	0	100	0	0	79	-0.04	May-07
-3.98	-0.74	-10.01	12.55	-54.53	2.96	0.7	15.02		22.87	3.2	0	100	0	0	30	-0.44	Mar-10
-5.46	-4.50	-5.09	22.73	-34.28	6.08	0.7	12.36		11.47	7.5	0	100	0	0	50	0.15	Mar-10
-2.71	0.50	-1.17			2.21	0.65			29.32	41.0	4	96	0	0	53	-0.14	Jan-18
1.41	2.15	2.35	26.11	46.70	0.48	0.7	13.86		50.26	196.0	0	100	0	0	80	-0.05	Feb-11
2.63	6.28	8.58			5.29	0.85		3.72	19.63	212.9	3	0	55	0		0.27	Aug-17
0.29	3.70	4.46	36.96		0.83	0.7	14.21		36.39	30.9	0	100	0	0	83	-0.09	Nov-14
-3.00	3.45	1.34				0.7			19.66	2.0	0	100	0	0		0.10	Oct-18
-2.30	-4.24	-15.73	1.28	11.08	1.97	0.8	11.76		47.56	80.8	0	100	0	0	90	-0.17	Apr-11
-0.90	1.79	-1.04	35.31	51.68	1.42	0.61	13.68		60.92	1,328	0	100	0	0	102	-0.02	May-07
-1.14	3.69	-0.17	40.80	68.31	0.6	0.61	13.99		69.93	1,031	0	100	0	0	132	0.03	May-07
1.26	4.31	3.02			1.73	0.6			23.15	18.5	1	100	0	0	28	-0.12	Jun-17
-1.05	-0.44	-2.62	28.13	35.26	2.17	0.61	15.21		51.54	1,103	0	100	0	0	96	0.00	May-07
-1.63	2.82	12.84	32.11	14.04	2.75	0.8	21.33		20.37	113.0	1	99	0	0	158	-0.17	Apr-11
4.06	9.67					0.65		11.02	28.15	11.3	18	0	82	0		-0.01	Jan-19
1.35	4.41	2.31	26.97	45.22	1.03	1.59	7.86		40.96	227.3	35	65	0	0	249	0.02	Sep-14
1.00	2.51	4.65	7.43		2.55	0.68	0.82	2.29	51.87	3,551	5	0	95	0	331	0.12	Nov-14
1.05	2.46					0.86		2.03	20.51	55.4	12	0	88	0		0.08	Jan-19
0.13	4.07	6.15			1.13	0.65			21.78	47.9	0	100	0	0		0.02	Jul-18
1.29	-0.53	-10.31	-5.66	-7.96	1.41	0.95	5.75		44.49	9.0	85	15	0	0	0	0.33	Aug-13
1.95	4.54	9.00	11.26	25.20	2.51	0.5	3.72	5.81	55.46	1,065	4	0	96	0	42	0.14	May-14
-3.59	-3.01	-8.80	13.24	26.82	1.62	0.64	18.81		37.25	121.1	0	100	0	0	82	-0.02	May-07
0.51	3.70	-2.12	37.86	49.60	1.38	0.7	12.31		36.07	23.4	0	100	0	0	156	-0.01	May-11
-2.13	-0.02	-3.81	31.72	43.59	1.12	0.62	16.35		67.48	843.4	0	100	0	0	114	-0.01	May-07
-2.02	2.57	-2.18	45.76	67.39	0.1	0.7	16.62		44.73	290.7	0	100	0	0	144	-0.01	Apr-11
0.54	3.42	1.37			1.7	0.6			22.17	13.3	-9	109	0	0	42	0.13	Jun-17

Fund Name	Ticker Symbol	Traded On	Overall Rating	Reward Rating	Risk Rating	Recent Up/ Downgrade	Price as of 9/30/2019	52-Week High	52-Week Low	Open to New Investors	Category & (Prospectus Objective)
● First Trust Mid Cap Value AlphaDEX® Fund	FNK	NAS CM	D+	C-	D+		33.62	36.67	29.15	Y	US Equity Small Cap (Growth)
● First Trust Morningstar Dividend Leaders Index Fund	FDL	NYSE Arca	C+	C+	C		31.04	31.57	25.99	Y	US Equity Large Cap Value (Growth & Inc)
● First Trust Multi Cap Growth AlphaDEX® Fund	FAD	NAS CM	C	C	D+		73.30	76.90	56.57	Y	US Equity Mid Cap (Growth)
● First Trust Multi Cap Value AlphaDEX® Fund	FAB	NAS CM	D+	C-	D+		53.40	57.35	45.89	Y	US Equity Mid Cap (Growth)
● First Trust Multi-Asset Diversified Income Index Fund	MDIV	NAS CM	C	C	C-		18.43	18.75	16.21	Y	Moderate Allocation (Income)
First Trust Municipal CEF Income Opportunity ETF	MCEF	NAS CM	C	C	D+	Up	19.45	19.71	17.01	Y	US Muni Fixed Inc (Income)
● First Trust Municipal High Income ETF	FMHI	NAS CM	C-	C-	D+	Up	53.25	53.60	49.43	Y	US Muni Fixed Inc (Muni Bond - Natl)
● First Trust Nasdaq Artificial Intelligence & Robotics ETF	ROBT	NAS CM	C-	C-	C-		31.61	33.88	24.55	Y	Technology Sector Equity (Technology)
★ First Trust Nasdaq Bank ETF	FTXO	NAS CM	B-	B	C	Up	25.59	28.52	21.01	Y	Financials Sector Equity (Financial)
● First Trust NASDAQ Cybersecurity ETF	CIBR	NYSE Arca	C	C	C	Down	27.66	30.70	21.94	Y	Technology Sector Equity (Technology)
★ First Trust Nasdaq Food & Beverage ETF	FTXG	NAS CM	B-	B	C	Up	21.25	21.45	17.50	Y	Consumer Goods & Svcs (Unaligned)
First Trust NASDAQ Global Auto Index Fund	CARZ	NAS CM	D+	D	D+		32.12	36.60	29.51	Y	Consumer Goods & Svcs (Unaligned)
First Trust Nasdaq Oil & Gas ETF	FTXN	NAS CM	C	C	D+	Up	16.08	26.00	14.82	Y	Energy Sector Equity (Natl Res)
First Trust Nasdaq Pharmaceuticals ETF	FTXH	NAS CM	C+	B-	C-	Up	20.36	23.69	18.25	Y	Healthcare Sector Equity (Health)
★ First Trust Nasdaq Retail ETF	FTXD	NAS CM	B-	B	C	Up	23.36	24.79	19.60	Y	Consumer Goods & Svcs (Unaligned)
★ First Trust Nasdaq Semiconductor ETF	FTXL	NAS CM	B-	B+	C	Up	34.70	35.94	23.92	Y	Technology Sector Equity (Technology)
★ First Trust NASDAQ Technology Dividend Index Fund	TDIV	NAS CM	B-	B	C	Up	40.11	41.12	31.20	Y	Technology Sector Equity (Technology)
★ First Trust Nasdaq Transportation ETF	FTXR	NAS CM	B-	B	C	Up	23.08	25.40	20.86	Y	Industrials Sector Equity (Unaligned)
● First Trust NASDAQ® ABA Community Bank Index Fund	QABA	NAS CM	C-	C-	C-	Up	47.89	53.74	41.05	Y	Financials Sector Equity (Financial)
● First Trust NASDAQ® Clean Edge® Green Energy Index Fund	QCLN	NAS CM	C	B-	D+		21.41	22.53	16.31	Y	Technology Sector Equity (Technology)
First Trust NASDAQ® Clean Edge® Smart Grid Infrastr Ind Fu	GRID	NAS CM	C	C	D+	Up	49.59	50.68	37.28	Y	Equity Misc (Utility)
● First Trust NASDAQ-100 Equal Weighted Index Fund	QQEW	NAS CM	C	C+	C-	Down	66.35	69.62	51.19	Y	US Equity Large Cap Growth (Growth)
● First Trust NASDAQ-100 Ex-Technology Sector Index Fund	QQXT	NAS CM	C	C	D+		53.39	55.77	43.14	Y	US Equity Large Cap Growth (Growth)
● First Trust NASDAQ-100-Technology Sector Index Fund	QTEC	NAS CM	C+	B-	C		87.53	92.25	63.38	Y	Technology Sector Equity (Technology)
● First Trust Natural Gas ETF	FCG	NYSE Arca	D+	C	D	Up	11.46	23.18	10.66	Y	Energy Sector Equity (Natl Res)
● First Trust North American Energy Infrastructure Fund	EMLP	NYSE Arca	C+	C+	C+	Up	25.59	25.93	20.55	Y	Energy Sector Equity (Utility)
● First Trust NYSE Arca Biotechnology Index Fund	FBT	NYSE Arca	C	C	D+		123.77	157.53	114.50	Y	Healthcare Sector Equity (Health)
★ First Trust Preferred Securities and Income ETF	FPE	NYSE Arca	B-	B-	C+		19.73	19.84	17.82	Y	US Fixed Income (Income)
● First Trust RBA American Industrial RenaissanceTM ETF	AIRR	NAS CM	C	C+	C-	Up	26.86	27.74	20.46	Y	Industrials Sector Equity (Growth & Inc)
● First Trust Rising Dividend Achievers ETF	RDVY	NAS CM	C+	C+	C+		31.85	32.57	24.76	Y	US Equity Large Cap Value (Income)
First Trust RiverFront Dynamic Asia Pacific ETF	RFAP	NAS CM	D+	D	D+		50.23	57.55	46.26	Y	Asia Equity (Growth)
● First Trust RiverFront Dynamic Developed International ETF	RFDI	NAS CM	C-	D+	C-		55.69	61.99	49.45	Y	Global Equity Large Cap (Growth)
● First Trust RiverFront Dynamic Emerging Markets ETF	RFEM	NAS CM	D+	D	D+		57.79	65.11	54.25	Y	Global Emerg Mkts Equity (Div Emerg Mkts)
First Trust RiverFront Dynamic Europe ETF	RFEU	NAS CM	D+	D+	D+	Down	57.65	63.50	50.49	Y	Europe Equity Large Cap (Growth)
First Trust S&P International Dividend Aristocrats ETF	FID	NAS CM	C	C	D+	Up	17.17	17.42	15.33	Y	Global Equity Large Cap (Multi-Asset Global)
● First Trust S&P REIT Index Fund	FRI	NYSE Arca	C	C+	C-		26.62	26.64	20.79	Y	Real Estate Sector Equity (Real Estate)
● First Trust Senior Loan Fund	FTSL	NAS CM	C	C	C+	Down	47.41	48.15	45.42	Y	US Fixed Income (Income)
First Trust Short Duration Managed Municipal ETF	FSMB	NYSE Arca	U	U	U		20.49	20.58	20.14	Y	US Muni Fixed Inc (Muni Bond - Natl)
● First Trust Small Cap Core AlphaDEX® Fund	FYX	NAS CM	C-	C-	C-		60.07	68.02	50.98	Y	US Equity Small Cap (Small Company)
● First Trust Small Cap Growth AlphaDEX® Fund	FYC	NAS CM	C-	C	C-	Down	43.87	51.51	37.33	Y	US Equity Small Cap (Small Company)
First Trust Small Cap US Equity Select ETF	RNSC	NAS CM	D+	D+	D+	Up	20.83	22.98	17.89	Y	US Equity Small Cap (Equity-Income)
● First Trust Small Cap Value AlphaDEX® Fund	FYT	NAS CM	C-	D+	C-	Up	34.63	38.38	29.75	Y	US Equity Small Cap (Small Company)
First Trust SMID Cap Rising Dividend Achievers ETF	SDVY	NAS CM	D+	D	D+	Up	20.30	22.75	16.85	Y	US Equity Mid Cap (Growth & Inc)
First Trust South Korea AlphaDEX® Fund	FKO	NAS CM	D	D	D		19.70	25.86	18.50	Y	Equity Misc (Pacific Stock)
● First Trust SSI Strategic Convertible Securities ETF	FCVT	NAS CM	C	C+	C-		31.20	32.22	26.47	Y	Convertibles (Convertible Bond)
● First Trust STOXX® European Select Dividend Index Fund	FDD	NYSE Arca	C	C	C+		12.74	13.32	11.69	Y	Europe Equity Large Cap (Europe Stock)
● First Trust Strategic Income ETF	FDIV	NAS CM	C	C+	D+		50.81	51.84	45.32	Y	Cautious Allocation (Income)
● First Trust Switzerland AlphaDEX® Fund	FSZ	NAS CM	C-	C	C-		48.65	51.43	42.24	Y	Europe Equity Large Cap (Europe Stock)
● First Trust Tactical High Yield ETF	HYLS	NAS CM	C+	C+	C+	Down	48.24	48.50	44.51	Y	US Fixed Income (Corp Bond-High Yld)
● First Trust TCW Opportunistic Fixed Income ETF	FIXD	NAS CM	C	C	C+		52.66	53.21	48.40	Y	US Fixed Income (Growth & Inc)
● First Trust TCW Unconstrained Plus Bond ETF	UCON	NYSE Arca	C-	C-	C-	Up	25.78	25.91	24.78	Y	Fixed Income Misc (Multisector Bond)
● First Trust Technology AlphaDEX® Fund	FXL	NYSE Arca	C+	C+	C+	Down	65.15	71.30	48.15	Y	Technology Sector Equity (Technology)

★ Expanded analysis of this fund is included in Section II: Analysis of All BUY Rated Funds. ● Expanded analysis of this fund is included in Section III: Analysis of All Rated Funds with Assets over $50 million.

			TOTAL RETURNS & PERFORMANCE						ASSETS		ASSET ALLOCATION & TURNOVER					VALUATION	
3-Month Total Return	6-Month Total Return	1-Year Total Return	3-Year Total Return	5-Year Total Return	Dividend Yield (TTM)	Expense Ratio	3-Yr Std Deviation	Effective Duration	NAV	Total Assets (MIL)	%Cash	%Stocks	%Bonds	%Other	Turnover Ratio	Premium/ Discount 1-Year Avg	Inception Date
-2.62	-3.45	-6.39	18.45	23.69	1.81	0.7	17.7		33.55	52.0	0	100	0	0	113	0.03	Apr-11
2.22	4.24	8.00	26.79	59.21	3.93	0.45	11.19		31.02	1,678	0	100	0	0	39	0.01	Mar-06
-2.38	1.49	-3.77	40.25	67.13	0.38	0.69	15.21		73.26	179.5	0	100	0	0	130	0.01	May-07
-1.21	-1.70	-4.93	23.05	29.78	1.94	0.71	16.6		53.24	82.5	0	100	0	0	96	-0.13	May-07
1.04	2.55	5.63	16.95	17.65	6.08	0.71	8.17	1.90	18.43	716.0	2	60	19	0	84	0.07	Aug-12
3.23	6.95	14.30	8.39		3.06	2.37	6.5	5.12	19.44	10.7	-3	0	107	0	11	-0.13	Sep-16
2.38	5.44	9.76			3.37	0.55		6.04	53.05	71.6	3	0	97	0	71	0.25	Nov-17
-5.52	-1.78	-1.37			0.44	0.65			31.51	61.4	0	100	0	0	67	0.20	Feb-18
0.78	3.52	-4.17	35.51		3.78	0.6	23.03		25.59	139.5	1	99	0	0	87	-0.04	Sep-16
-3.44	-2.46	-1.46	40.46		0.22	0.6	16.18		27.63	979.6	0	100	0	0	56	0.07	Jul-15
4.67	7.72	11.75	10.21		1.32	0.6	11.25		21.36	5.3	0	100	0	0	108	-0.28	Sep-16
-2.84	-2.37	-9.25	3.87	-3.46	3.22	0.7	14.9		32.04	17.6	0	100	0	0	16	-0.02	May-11
-8.22	-14.97	-35.08	-18.78		3.28	0.6	25.24		16.00	8.8	1	99	0	0	126	-0.15	Sep-16
-4.77	-5.38	-12.85	6.22		0.75	0.6	15.79		20.28	7.1	0	100	0	0	107	-0.03	Sep-16
4.67	4.63	-3.24	21.80		1.25	0.6	14.46		23.33	8.2	0	100	0	0	127	-0.12	Sep-16
5.15	7.17	15.07	71.58		0.95	0.6	24.55		34.70	31.2	0	100	0	0	94	0.05	Sep-16
1.93	4.53	7.01	47.14	71.05	2.41	0.5	14.05		40.09	1,011	1	99	0	0	27	0.02	Aug-12
-2.86	-1.87	-7.57	17.52		1.53	0.6	18.17		23.17	2.3	1	99	0	0	108	0.13	Sep-16
-0.33	1.82	-7.28	21.44	54.13	2.31	0.6	22.02		47.71	145.5	0	100	0	0	11	0.00	Jun-09
0.28	5.01	9.02	44.91	20.32	1.24	0.6	16.76		21.38	113.3	0	100	0	0	45	-0.01	Feb-07
2.45	13.07	5.23	31.26	50.85	1.25	0.7	16.83		49.51	27.2	0	100	0	0	60	-0.06	Nov-09
-1.73	1.86	5.07	47.35	74.18	0.55	0.6	14.78		66.33	673.3	0	100	0	0	27	-0.02	Apr-06
-2.98	0.37	1.29	33.47	49.48	0.42	0.6	14.05		53.43	93.5	0	100	0	0	26	0.05	Feb-07
0.27	4.23	11.22	76.17	129.53	0.75	0.57	17.87		87.52	2,481	0	100	0	0	21	-0.02	Apr-06
-20.61	-33.76	-48.63	-54.65	-85.45	2.12	0.6	26.95		11.45	75.5	1	99	0	0	47	0.02	May-07
2.69	4.97	12.44	13.76	15.04	3.82	0.95	10.6		25.54	2,600	4	96	0	0	35	0.01	Jun-12
-12.35	-18.01	-21.31	24.27	37.02	0	0.57	24.35		123.89	1,641	0	100	0	0	37	-0.02	Jun-06
2.96	6.32	9.47	19.68	38.94	5.55	0.85	4.42	3.70	19.71	4,425	3	0	36	0		0.12	Feb-13
0.98	7.52	-2.64	31.60	50.71	0.21	0.7	21.52		26.76	66.9	0	100	0	0	35	0.06	Mar-14
1.81	5.45	2.57	50.38	68.61	1.67	0.5	15.94		31.82	832.2	0	100	0	0	40	0.04	Jan-14
-1.55	-1.59	-9.90	3.66		2.53	0.83	11.34		50.13	27.6	0	100	0	0		-0.20	Apr-16
-2.28	-0.49	-7.50	14.37		2.67	0.83	12.21		55.65	256.0	0	100	0	0		-0.19	Apr-16
-5.46	-6.29	-4.60	12.13		2.35	0.95	15.12		58.22	81.5	1	99	0	0		-0.12	Jun-16
-2.76	-0.04	-6.43	20.06		2.98	0.83	13.38		57.69	37.5	0	100	0	0		-0.14	Apr-16
1.03	3.49	3.38	14.09	7.41	3.69	0.6	9.87		17.11	19.7	1	99	0	0	196	0.41	Aug-13
7.60	7.93	18.22	20.37	55.90	2.6	0.5	12.96		26.60	184.8	0	100	0	0	10	0.03	May-07
1.38	2.56	3.32	10.58	18.02	4.57	0.87	3.03	0.40	47.38	1,606	4	0	96	0	88	-0.05	May-13
0.68	1.92					0.45		2.33	20.44	19.4	5	0	95	0	66	-0.07	Nov-18
-2.26	-3.07	-10.61	24.06	42.34	1.1	0.66	18.52		60.08	567.8	0	100	0	0	117	-0.02	May-07
-6.01	-5.32	-14.50	30.56	63.05	0.12	0.7	18.39		43.90	245.8	0	100	0	0	152	-0.02	Apr-11
0.17	-0.60	-6.36			1.94	0.6			20.78	7.3	0	100	0	0	52	0.18	Jun-17
0.41	-2.30	-8.38	17.12	25.31	1.75	0.76	20.06		34.58	55.3	0	100	0	0	120	0.06	Apr-11
-0.59	1.03	-1.92			1.68	0.6			20.37	7.1	0	100	0	0	72	0.01	Nov-17
-8.77	-13.51	-21.00	-15.45	-21.50	1.62	0.8	18.52		20.13	3.0	0	98	0	2	73	-1.01	Apr-11
-1.21	2.69	3.30	28.46		1.58	0.95	8.74	2.18	31.12	191.4	1	3	0	1	71	-0.06	Nov-15
2.80	2.95	2.88	22.76	18.83	5.16	0.57	11.34		12.75	293.8	0	100	0	0	35	-0.05	Aug-07
1.74	3.98	7.92	15.24	27.02	4.17	0.87	5.71	3.62	50.81	88.9	3	37	50	0	113	-0.01	Aug-14
-4.31	1.77	-2.21	25.31	37.54	2.23	0.8	12.37		48.70	131.5	0	100	0	0	65	-0.08	Feb-12
1.52	3.40	6.44	16.71	25.49	5.38	1.16	4.04	1.87	48.14	1,394	-2	0	102	0	52	0.01	Feb-13
2.40	5.90	10.65			2.76	0.55		5.91	52.56	906.6	4	0	96	0	358	0.09	Feb-17
0.93	3.24	5.67			3.12	0.75		1.80	25.76	209.9	7	0	92	0	70	0.04	Jun-18
-3.60	0.27	3.77	79.51	111.61	0.53	0.63	18.46		65.14	2,215	0	100	0	0	91	0.01	May-07

Fund Name	Ticker Symbol	Traded On	Overall Rating	Reward Rating	Risk Rating	Recent Up/ Downgrade	Price as of 9/30/2019	52-Week High	52-Week Low	Open to New Investors	Category & (Prospectus Objective)
First Trust Total US Market AlphaDEX ETF	TUSA	NAS CM	C-	C	D+	Down	33.59	36.09	28.10	Y	US Equity Mid Cap (Growth)
First Trust Ultra Short Duration Municipal ETF	FUMB	NYSE Arca	U	U	U		20.10	20.14	20.02	Y	US Muni Fixed Inc (Muni Bond - Natl)
First Trust United Kingdom AlphaDEX® Fund	FKU	NAS CM	D+	D+	D+		35.58	38.45	31.21	Y	Equity Misc (Europe Stock)
First Trust US Equity Dividend Select ETF	RNDV	NAS CM	C-	C	D	Up	22.31	22.62	18.70	Y	US Equity Large Cap Value (Equity-Income)
● First Trust US Equity Opportunities ETF	FPX	NYSE Arca	C	B-	C-		75.83	81.43	57.83	Y	US Equity Large Cap Growth (Growth)
★ First Trust Utilities AlphaDEX® Fund	FXU	NYSE Arca	B-	B-	C+	Up	29.65	29.95	25.97	Y	Utilities Sector Equity (Utility)
First Trust Value Line® 100 Exchange-Traded Fund	FVL	NYSE Arca	C-	C	D+		22.32	23.11	17.84	Y	US Equity Mid Cap (Growth)
● First Trust Value Line® Dividend Index Fund	FVD	NYSE Arca	C+	C+	C+	Down	34.87	35.03	27.80	Y	US Equity Large Cap Value (Growth & Inc)
★ First Trust Water ETF	FIW	NYSE Arca	B-	B	C	Up	56.11	56.69	41.46	Y	Industrials Sector Equity (Natl Res)
FLAG-Forensic Accounting Long-Short ETF	FLAG	NYSE Arca	D+	C-	D	Up	38.18	42.35	34.01	Y	US Equity Large Cap Value (Growth & Inc)
FlexShares Core Select Bond Fund	BNDC	NYSE Arca	C	C	D+	Up	25.68	25.93	23.61	Y	US Fixed Income (Multisector Bond)
● FlexShares Credit-Scored US Corporate Bond Index Fund	SKOR	NAS CM	C	C+	D+		52.30	52.77	48.38	Y	US Fixed Income (Corp Bond - Gen)
FlexShares Credit-Scored US Long Corporate Bond Index Fund	LKOR	BATS	C	B	D+		57.55	58.96	47.27	Y	US Fixed Income (Corp Bond - Gen)
FlexShares Curr Hedg Morningstar DM ex-US Factor Tilt Ind	TLDH	NYSE Arca	D+	C	D		27.75	28.60	23.84	Y	Global Equity Large Cap (Foreign Stock)
FlexShares Curr Hedg Morningstar EM Factor Tilt Ind Fund	TLEH	NYSE Arca	D	D	D	Down	26.65	29.84	25.64	Y	Global Emerg Mkts Equity (Div Emerg Mkts)
FlexShares Disciplined Duration MBS Index Fund	MBSD	NAS CM	C	C	D+		23.57	23.66	22.69	Y	US Fixed Income (Income)
● FlexShares Global Quality Real Estate Index Fund	GQRE	NYSE Arca	C	C	C-		65.17	65.50	53.78	Y	Real Estate Sector Equity (Real Estate)
● FlexShares iBoxx 3-Year Target Duration TIPS Index Fund	TDTT	NYSE Arca	C	C	C-		24.59	24.76	23.71	Y	US Fixed Income (Govt Bond - Treasury)
● FlexShares iBoxx 5-Year Target Duration TIPS Index Fund	TDTF	NYSE Arca	C	C+	C-		25.53	25.87	23.80	Y	US Fixed Income (Govt Bond - Treasury)
● FlexShares Intl Quality Dividend Defensive Ind Fund	IQDE	NYSE Arca	D+	D+	C-	Down	21.20	22.94	19.98	Y	Global Equity Large Cap (World Stock)
FlexShares Intl Quality Dividend Dynamic Ind Fund	IQDY	NYSE Arca	D+	D+	D+	Down	23.92	25.61	21.17	Y	Global Equity Large Cap (World Stock)
● FlexShares International Quality Dividend Index Fund	IQDF	NYSE Arca	C	D+	C+		22.28	24.11	20.28	Y	Global Equity Large Cap (World Stock)
● FlexShares Morningstar Dev Mkts ex-US Factor Tilt Ind Fund	TLTD	NYSE Arca	C-	C-	C-		60.24	65.55	53.42	Y	Global Equity Large Cap (Foreign Stock)
● FlexShares Morningstar Emerg Mkts Factor Tilt Ind Fund	TLTE	NYSE Arca	D+	D	C-	Down	48.23	55.13	46.27	Y	Global Emerg Mkts Equity (Div Emerg Mkts)
● FlexShares Morningstar Global Upstream Natl Resources Ind	GUNR	NYSE Arca	C	C	C+		31.15	34.18	28.13	Y	Natural Resources (Natl Res)
● FlexShares Morningstar US Market Factors Tilt Index Fund	TILT	BATS	C	C	C-		117.01	119.77	94.13	Y	US Equity Large Cap Blend (Growth)
● FlexShares Quality Dividend Defensive Index Fund	QDEF	NYSE Arca	C	C+	C-		45.72	46.96	37.31	Y	US Equity Large Cap Value (Income)
● FlexShares Quality Dividend Dynamic Index Fund	QDYN	NYSE Arca	C	C	D+		44.30	45.61	36.30	Y	US Equity Large Cap Value (Income)
● FlexShares Quality Dividend Index Fund	QDF	NYSE Arca	C	C+	C-		45.44	47.57	37.39	Y	US Equity Large Cap Value (Income)
● FlexShares Ready Access Variable Income Fund	RAVI	NYSE Arca	C	C	C-		75.83	75.92	74.89	Y	US Fixed Income (Income)
FlexShares Real Assets Allocation Index Fund	ASET	NAS CM	C	C	D+		29.82	30.04	24.97	Y	Global Equity Large Cap (Asset Allocation)
● FlexShares STOXX Global Broad Infrastructure Index Fund	NFRA	NYSE Arca	C	C+	C-		51.74	52.12	42.10	Y	Infrastructure Sector Equity (Utility)
● FlexShares STOXX Global ESG Impact Index Fund	ESGG	BATS	C	C	D+		99.37	100.93	80.43	Y	Global Equity Large Cap (Growth & Inc)
● FlexShares STOXX US ESG Impact Index Fund	ESG	BATS	C	C+	C-		70.93	72.43	56.27	Y	US Equity Large Cap Blend (Growth & Inc)
● FlexShares US Quality Large Cap Index Fund	QLC	BATS	C	C	C-		34.01	35.98	28.41	Y	US Equity Large Cap Value (Growth)
● FlexShares® High Yield Value-Scored Bond Index Fund	HYGV	NYSE Arca	D+	D+	C-		48.42	49.91	44.70	Y	US Fixed Income (Corp Bond-High Yld)
● FormulaFolios Hedged Growth ETF	FFHG	BATS	D+	D+	C-		25.96	29.50	24.91	Y	Long/Short Equity (Growth)
● FormulaFolios Smart Growth ETF	FFSG	BATS	C-	D+	C-	Up	26.54	26.97	21.78	Y	Aggressive Allocation (Growth)
● FormulaFolios Tactical Growth ETF	FFTG	BATS	C-	C-	C-	Up	26.33	27.12	21.11	Y	Moderate Allocation (Growth)
● FormulaFolios Tactical Income ETF	FFTI	BATS	C	C	C-	Up	25.01	25.21	22.89	Y	US Fixed Income (Multisector Bond)
Franklin FTSE Asia ex Japan ETF	FLAX	NYSE Arca	D+	D	C-	Up	20.57	22.68	19.21	Y	Asia ex-Japan Equity (Foreign Stock)
Franklin FTSE Australia ETF	FLAU	NYSE Arca	C-	C-	D+	Up	25.46	26.15	21.16	Y	Equity Misc (Foreign Stock)
Franklin FTSE Brazil ETF	FLBR	NYSE Arca	D+	C-	D+		26.12	29.17	21.06	Y	Latin America Equity (Foreign Stock)
Franklin FTSE Canada ETF	FLCA	NYSE Arca	C	C	C-	Up	25.69	25.92	20.45	Y	Equity Misc (Foreign Stock)
Franklin FTSE China ETF	FLCH	NYSE Arca	D	D	D+		21.79	25.23	19.75	Y	Greater China Equity (Foreign Stock)
● Franklin FTSE Europe ETF	FLEE	NYSE Arca	D+	D+	D+		23.47	24.42	20.33	Y	Europe Equity Large Cap (Foreign Stock)
Franklin FTSE Europe Hedged ETF	FLEH	NYSE Arca	D	C-	E+	Down	24.18	25.03	19.90	Y	Europe Equity Large Cap (Foreign Stock)
Franklin FTSE France ETF	FLFR	NYSE Arca	D+	C-	D	Up	24.94	25.56	20.80	Y	Global Equity Large Cap (Foreign Stock)
Franklin FTSE Germany ETF	FLGR	NYSE Arca	D	D	D+		20.93	22.88	18.78	Y	Global Equity Large Cap (Foreign Stock)
Franklin FTSE Hong Kong ETF	FLHK	NYSE Arca	D	D+	D	Down	23.68	27.91	22.05	Y	Greater China Equity (Foreign Stock)
Franklin FTSE India ETF	FLIN	NYSE Arca	D	D	C-	Down	22.14	24.06	19.56	Y	India Equity (Foreign Stock)
Franklin FTSE Italy ETF	FLIY	NYSE Arca	D+	C-	D	Up	23.13	24.03	19.63	Y	Equity Misc (Foreign Stock)

★ Expanded analysis of this fund is included in Section II: Analysis of All BUY Rated Funds. ● Expanded analysis of this fund is included in Section III: Analysis of All Rated Funds with Assets over $50 million.

			TOTAL RETURNS & PERFORMANCE						ASSETS		ASSET ALLOCATION & TURNOVER					VALUATION	
3-Month Total Return	6-Month Total Return	1-Year Total Return	3-Year Total Return	5-Year Total Return	Dividend Yield (TTM)	Expense Ratio	3-Yr Std Deviation	Effective Duration	NAV	Total Assets (MIL.)	%Cash	%Stocks	%Bonds	%Other	Turnover Ratio	Premium/ Discount 1-Year Avg	Inception Date
-1.67	-0.15	-4.89	32.05	38.95	1.2	0.7	15.16		33.57	16.8	1	99	0	0	110	0.13	Dec-06
0.29	0.84					0.35		0.56	20.06	20.1	12	0	83	5	145	-0.04	Nov-18
-1.65	-2.02	-3.54	14.67	8.63	3.23	0.8	14.42		35.62	8.9	2	97	0	2	107	0.09	Feb-12
1.83	2.92	2.45			2.78	0.5			22.31	5.6	1	99	0	0	98	-0.02	Jun-17
-3.03	1.12	3.22	42.66	66.35	0.69	0.59	14.01		75.82	1,243	0	100	0	0	57	0.00	Apr-06
4.44	6.10	10.34	24.70	52.98	2.49	0.63	8.71		29.63	1,308	0	100	0	0	60	-0.01	May-07
-0.23	4.94	-2.44	10.41	21.90	0.91	0.7	14.29		22.30	39.9	0	100	0	0	424	0.00	Jun-03
3.61	7.87	12.99	38.14	75.14	2.2	0.7	9.81		34.85	7,866	0	100	0	0	58	0.03	Aug-03
2.35	9.21	11.80	52.97	87.06	0.67	0.55	14.99		56.12	468.6	0	100	0	0	11	0.03	May-07
0.03	-1.96	-7.73	16.06	34.36	2.03	1.52	16.79		38.25	9.6	0	100	0	0		-0.22	Jan-13
2.35	5.82	9.95			2.9	0.35		5.80	25.64	23.1	2	0	96	0	53	0.02	Nov-16
1.81	5.56	10.41	9.86		3.01	0.22	3.03	4.81	52.38	94.3	0	0	96	0	76	0.04	Nov-14
5.63	14.20	20.81	19.01		3.81	0.22	7.98	14.05	57.67	17.3	0	0	100	0	93	-0.45	Sep-15
1.44	2.51	-0.69	29.51		2.93	0.44	10.44		27.64	8.3	1	99	0	0	34	0.13	Nov-15
-4.37	-6.73	-2.65	11.45		2.92	0.64	11.6		26.65	5.3	2	98	0	0	49	0.08	Nov-15
1.40	3.30	6.61	4.33	9.54	3.55	0.2	1.95	2.91	23.57	34.2	5	0	95	0	160	0.09	Sep-14
3.41	3.37	9.84	18.28	45.37	2.77	0.45	10.86		65.14	368.0	1	99	0	1	61	0.15	Nov-13
0.39	2.49	4.45	5.06	6.12	1.8	0.18	1.57		24.56	1,190	0	0	100	0	85	0.01	Sep-11
0.87	4.05	7.25	6.70	10.78	1.74	0.18	2.86		25.48	558.0	0	0	100	0	65	0.02	Sep-11
-2.97	-1.87	-2.93	7.98	2.37	5.28	0.47	10.76		21.15	76.1	1	99	0	0	69	-0.05	Apr-13
-2.32	-1.16	-1.39	15.59	11.03	4.78	0.47	12.68		23.91	45.4	1	99	0	0	75	-0.18	Apr-13
-2.65	-1.04	-2.83	13.09	5.00	5.08	0.47	11.62		22.27	739.4	1	99	0	0	71	-0.03	Apr-13
-1.33	0.26	-4.53	17.33	16.04	3.03	0.39	11.42		60.31	928.7	1	99	0	0	34	-0.28	Sep-12
-6.09	-7.00	-4.43	11.53	7.34	2.99	0.59	13.48		48.66	399.0	0	100	0	0	49	-0.40	Sep-12
-5.41	-4.36	-5.12	23.00	8.53	3.54	0.46	12.75		31.10	5,432	0	100	0	0	30	0.00	Sep-11
-0.03	2.58	-0.08	36.41	56.95	1.79	0.25	13.78		116.98	1,427	1	99	0	0	15	-0.01	Sep-11
1.68	2.71	4.30	37.97	63.50	2.41	0.37	11.33		45.68	440.8	2	98	0	0	94	0.07	Dec-12
0.58	1.54	0.23	33.98	48.53	2.66	0.37	13.91		44.31	51.0	1	99	0	0	77	-0.01	Dec-12
1.10	1.57	-0.24	32.43	54.69	2.6	0.37	12.7		45.43	1,667	1	99	0	0	76	0.01	Dec-12
0.69	1.63	3.05	6.09	7.70	2.61	0.25	0.41	0.57	75.84	267.3	11	0	85	0	131	0.00	Oct-12
1.82	3.53	9.96	20.06		2.55	0.57	9.79		29.76	11.2	0	99	0	0	5	-0.01	Nov-15
2.06	5.56	13.27	25.07	32.28	2.37	0.47	9.63		51.65	1,428	1	99	0	0		0.06	Oct-13
0.25	4.48	1.83	36.69		2.03	0.42	11.35		98.99	84.1	1	99	0	0	78	0.26	Jul-16
1.05	5.34	4.10	46.83		1.55	0.32	12.1		70.89	51.4	1	99	0	0	78	0.05	Jul-16
0.47	1.15	-3.05	33.84		2.11	0.32	12.9		33.99	51.0	0	100	0	0	94	0.01	Sep-15
1.21	3.71	5.41			9.42	0.37		3.28	48.28	55.5	0	0	99	0	18	0.07	Jul-18
-4.20	-5.28	-10.52			0.58	1.19				64.9	-12	112	0	0	666	-0.11	Jun-17
-0.28	1.77	-0.07			1.58	0.7				55.7	1	99	0	0	0	0.06	Oct-17
5.31	9.90	7.47			1.4	1.02				59.2	11	79	1	0	92	0.03	Oct-17
2.40	5.81	7.05			3.19	1.04		5.22		242.5	3	0	91	0	135	-0.02	Jun-17
-5.19	-6.05	-3.56			2.42	0.19			20.63	16.5	1	99	0	0	7	0.09	Feb-18
-1.20	4.64	6.38			4.68	0.09			25.31	11.4	0	100	0	0	5	0.09	Nov-17
-5.30	1.34	29.00			3.44	0.19			26.04	15.6	0	99	0	0	40	-0.05	Nov-17
1.86	5.98	4.55			2.69	0.09			25.62	5.1	0	100	0	0	7	0.13	Nov-17
-5.55	-9.85	-3.74			1.46	0.19			21.92	39.5	0	100	0	0	7	0.15	Nov-17
-2.00	1.45	-0.71			2.51	0.09			23.51	65.8	0	100	0	0	6	-0.05	Nov-17
1.84	6.73	10.17			2.88	0.09			24.26	4.9	1	99	0	0	27	0.31	Nov-17
-1.54	4.46	-0.65			1.84	0.09			24.89	3.7	0	100	0	0	6	0.18	Nov-17
-4.21	2.02	-6.78			2.29	0.09			20.92	4.2	0	100	0	0	11	0.13	Nov-17
-11.15	-12.29	-3.11			2.35	0.09			23.65	17.7	0	100	0	0	5	0.38	Nov-17
-5.79	-5.69	2.53			1.42	0.19			21.95	15.4	0	100	0	0	8	0.42	Feb-18
0.52	2.04	4.48			3.28	0.09			23.13	11.6	0	100	0	0	17	0.18	Nov-17

Fund Name	Ticker Symbol	Traded On	Overall Rating	Reward Rating	Risk Rating	Recent Up/ Downgrade	Price as of 9/30/2019	52-Week High	52-Week Low	Open to New Investors	Category & (Prospectus Objective)
● Franklin FTSE Japan ETF	FLJP	NYSE Arca	D+	D	C-	Up	24.94	26.94	21.71	Y	Japan Equity (Foreign Stock)
Franklin FTSE Japan Hedged ETF	FLJH	NYSE Arca	D	D	D		23.85	27.30	20.49	Y	Japan Equity (Foreign Stock)
Franklin FTSE Latin America ETF	FLLA	NYSE Arca	U	U	U		26.10	28.42	24.08	Y	Latin America Equity (Growth)
Franklin FTSE Mexico ETF	FLMX	NYSE Arca	D	D	D		21.78	26.33	19.44	Y	Global Equity Large Cap (Foreign Stock)
Franklin FTSE Russia ETF	FLRU	NYSE Arca	C-	C	D+		26.60	27.91	20.51	Y	Equity Misc (Foreign Stock)
Franklin FTSE Saudi Arabia ETF	FLSA	NYSE Arca	U	U	U		25.77	30.29	24.73	Y	Equity Misc (Growth)
Franklin FTSE South Africa ETF	FLZA	NYSE Arca	U	U	U		24.56	29.55	23.55	Y	Africa Equity (Growth)
Franklin FTSE South Korea ETF	FLKR	NYSE Arca	D	D	D		19.59	23.61	17.69	Y	Equity Misc (Foreign Stock)
Franklin FTSE Switzerland ETF	FLSW	NYSE Arca	D+	C	D		25.69	25.95	20.61	Y	Equity Misc (Foreign Stock)
Franklin FTSE Taiwan ETF	FLTW	NYSE Arca	D	D+	D		25.86	26.06	21.81	Y	Greater China Equity (Foreign Stock)
Franklin FTSE United Kingdom ETF	FLGB	NYSE Arca	D+	D	C-	Up	23.43	25.03	21.00	Y	Global Equity Large Cap (Foreign Stock)
Franklin Liberty High Yield Corporate ETF	FLHY	BATS	D+	C-	D	Up	25.84	25.99	23.70	Y	US Fixed Income (Corp Bond-High Yld)
Franklin Liberty Intermediate Municipal Opportunities ETF	FLMI	NYSE Arca	D+	C-	D		25.57	25.90	24.05	Y	US Muni Fixed Inc (Muni Bond - Natl)
Franklin Liberty International Aggregate Bond ETF	FLIA	BATS	D+	C-	D		25.75	26.19	23.82	Y	Global Fixed Income (Growth & Inc)
Franklin Liberty International Opportunities ETF	FLIO	NYSE Arca	D+	C-	D	Up	26.51	28.14	23.46	Y	Global Equity Large Cap (Foreign Stock)
● Franklin Liberty Investment Grade Corporate ETF	FLCO	NYSE Arca	C	C	D+	Up	25.61	25.90	22.86	Y	US Fixed Income (Corp Bond - Gen)
Franklin Liberty Municipal Bond ETF	FLMB	NYSE Arca	C-	C-	C-		26.11	26.52	23.77	Y	US Muni Fixed Inc (Muni Bond - Natl)
● Franklin Liberty Senior Loan ETF	FLBL	BATS	D+	C-	D+	Up	25.00	25.35	24.26	Y	US Fixed Income (Income)
● Franklin Liberty U.S. Low Volatility ETF	FLLV	NYSE Arca	C	C	D+		36.61	37.08	27.74	Y	US Equity Large Cap Blend (Growth)
● Franklin LibertyQ Emerging Markets ETF	FLQE	NYSE Arca	C-	C-	D+		28.94	30.62	27.40	Y	Global Emerg Mkts Equity (Growth & Inc)
Franklin LibertyQ Global Dividend ETF	FLQD	NYSE Arca	C	C+	D	Up	29.11	29.69	24.68	Y	Global Equity Large Cap (Growth & Inc)
Franklin LibertyQ Global Equity ETF	FLQG	NYSE Arca	C-	C	D	Down	31.62	31.81	26.42	Y	Global Equity Large Cap (Growth & Inc)
Franklin LibertyQ International Equity Hedged ETF	FLQH	NYSE Arca	C	C+	D+	Up	26.18	26.23	21.67	Y	Global Equity Large Cap (Growth & Inc)
● Franklin LibertyQ U.S. Equity ETF	FLQL	BATS	C	C	C-		33.03	33.24	26.18	Y	US Equity Large Cap Blend (Growth & Inc)
Franklin LibertyQ U.S. Mid Cap Equity ETF	FLQM	BATS	C	C	D+	Up	31.48	32.18	24.95	Y	US Equity Mid Cap (Growth & Inc)
Franklin LibertyQ U.S. Small Cap Equity ETF	FLQS	BATS	C-	C-	D+		27.78	29.81	23.78	Y	US Equity Small Cap (Small Company)
Fundamental Income Net Lease Real Estate ETF	NETL	NYSE Arca	U	U	U		27.56	27.77	24.38	Y	Real Estate Sector Equity (Real Estate)
Gabelli Media Mogul NextShares	MOGLC	NAS CM	C	C+	C-	Up	10.93	100.04	9.46	Y	Communications Sector Equity (Unaligned)
Gabelli Pet Parents'™ NextShares™	PETZC	NAS CM	U	U	U		9.48	9.57	8.94	Y	Equity Misc (Growth)
Gadsden Dynamic Growth ETF	GDG	NYSE Arca	U	U	U		24.55	25.36	24.09	Y	Market Neutral (World Stock)
Gadsden Dynamic Multi-Asset ETF New	GDMA	NYSE Arca	U	U	U		25.84	26.14	24.05	Y	Cautious Allocation (Growth & Inc)
● Global X Adaptive U.S. Factor ETF	AUSF	NYSE Arca	C-	D+	C-		25.10	25.31	21.22	Y	US Equity Large Cap Value (Growth)
Global X Autonomous & Electric Vehicles ETF	DRIV	NAS CM	D+	D+	C-		13.14	14.85	11.39	Y	Global Equity Large Cap (Unaligned)
Global X Cloud Computing ETF Global X Cloud Computing ETF	CLOU	NAS CM	U	U	U		14.65	16.88	14.44	Y	Technology Sector Equity (Technology)
● Global X Conscious Companies ETF	KRMA	NAS CM	C	C	C-		22.16	22.47	17.71	Y	US Equity Large Cap Blend (Growth & Inc)
Global X Copper Miners ETF	COPX	NYSE Arca	D	D	D	Down	17.11	23.49	15.85	Y	Natural Resources (Natl Res)
Global X E-commerce ETF	EBIZ	NAS CM	U	U	U		17.19	19.13	13.89	Y	Consumer Goods & Svcs (Growth & Inc)
Global X Fertilizers/Potash ETF	SOIL	NYSE Arca	D+	D+	D+		8.70	10.88	8.31	Y	Natural Resources (Unaligned)
● Global X FinTech ETF	FINX	NAS CM	C+	B-	C		28.77	31.23	20.71	Y	Technology Sector Equity (Technology)
Global X Founder-Run Companies ETF	BOSS	BATS	D+	C-	D	Down	18.71	20.94	15.57	Y	US Equity Mid Cap (Growth & Inc)
Global X FTSE Nordic Region ETF	GXF	NYSE Arca	D+	D+	D+	Down	20.39	22.74	19.24	Y	Equity Misc (Europe Stock)
Global X FTSE Southeast Asia ETF	ASEA	NYSE Arca	C-	C	D+		15.58	16.98	14.66	Y	Asia ex-Japan Equity (Foreign Stock)
Global X Future Analytics Tech ETF	AIQ	NAS CM	C	C	C-	Up	15.97	17.15	12.25	Y	Technology Sector Equity (Technology)
Global X Genomics & Biotechnology ETF	GNOM	NAS CM	U	U	U		12.51	15.37	12.42	Y	Healthcare Sector Equity (Unaligned)
Global X Gold Explorers ETF	GOEX	NYSE Arca	C	C	C-	Up	24.22	28.60	17.60	Y	Prec Metals (Prec Metals)
● Global X Guru™ Index ETF	GURU	NYSE Arca	C	C+	D+		33.22	34.56	26.14	Y	US Equity Large Cap Growth (Income)
Global X Health & Wellness Thematic ETF	BFIT	NAS CM	C	C	D+		20.13	20.52	16.81	Y	Globa Eq Mid/Small Cap (Health)
● Global X Internet of Things ETF	SNSR	NAS CM	C	C+	C-	Up	20.40	20.76	15.40	Y	Technology Sector Equity (Technology)
● Global X Lithium & Battery Tech ETF	LIT	NYSE Arca	D	D	D	Down	24.37	33.25	22.61	Y	Natural Resources (Unaligned)
Global X Longevity Thematic ETF	LNGR	NAS CM	C	C	D+		21.26	22.60	18.13	Y	Healthcare Sector Equity (Unaligned)
● Global X Millennials Thematic ETF	MILN	NAS CM	C+	B-	C	Up	24.82	26.14	18.58	Y	US Equity Large Cap Growth (Growth & Inc)
● Global X MLP & Energy Infrastructure ETF	MLPX	NYSE Arca	C	C+	C-		12.30	13.70	10.40	Y	Energy Sector Equity (Growth & Inc)

★ Expanded analysis of this fund is included in Section II: Analysis of All BUY Rated Funds. ● Expanded analysis of this fund is included in Section III: Analysis of All Rated Funds with Assets over $50 million.

	TOTAL RETURNS & PERFORMANCE								ASSETS		ASSET ALLOCATION & TURNOVER					VALUATION	
3-Month Total Return	6-Month Total Return	1-Year Total Return	3-Year Total Return	5-Year Total Return	Dividend Yield (TTM)	Expense Ratio	3-Yr Std Deviation	Effective Duration	NAV	Total Assets (MIL)	%Cash	%Stocks	%Bonds	%Other	Turnover Ratio	Premium/ Discount 1-Year Avg	Inception Date
1.47	2.51	-5.21			2.15	0.09			24.75	207.9	0	100	0	0	4	-0.09	Nov-17
1.72	0.63	-8.20			5.28	0.09			23.62	4.7	0	100	0	0	20	-0.18	Nov-17
-5.00	-1.24					0.19			25.99	2.6	0	99	0	0	4	0.41	Oct-18
-3.38	-2.27	-14.77			3.18	0.19			21.71	4.3	0	100	0	0	10	0.02	Nov-17
-3.37	12.96	16.44			2.93	0.19			26.61	17.3	0	100	0	0	32	-0.26	Feb-18
-7.81	-7.79					0.39			25.60	2.6	0	100	0	0	12	0.55	Oct-18
-12.50	-9.65					0.19			24.55	2.5	0	100	0	0	7	0.08	Oct-18
-5.12	-8.54	-15.44			2.19	0.09			19.63	13.7	0	100	0	0	5	-0.33	Nov-17
0.27	8.13	11.28			1.18	0.09			25.63	7.7	0	100	0	0	14	-0.11	Feb-18
0.86	3.83	-2.60			0.97	0.19			25.73	15.4	0	100	0	0	9	-0.31	Nov-17
-2.49	-2.63	-2.52			3.63	0.09			23.41	28.1	1	99	0	0	10	-0.02	Nov-17
1.23	4.04	7.83			5.95	0.4			25.73	30.9	0	0	99	0	24	0.24	May-18
1.07	3.50	7.81			2.36	0.3			25.54	8.9	0	0	100	0	36	0.07	Aug-17
0.62	5.01	7.34			1.49	0.25			25.70	5.1	4	0	96	0	50	0.41	May-18
-3.31	-1.48	-3.10			1.65	0.6			26.57	9.3	1	99	0	0	21	0.07	Jan-17
2.51	7.75	12.18	16.56		2.9	0.35		7.83	25.57	232.7	2	0	96	0	22	0.07	Oct-16
1.63	4.53	11.09			2.04	0.3			26.10	27.4	4	0	96	0	21	0.20	Aug-17
1.01	2.20	2.89			4.09	0.45			24.89	57.3	9	0	91	0	11	0.27	May-18
2.41	8.64	13.34	52.71		1.27	0.29	10.55		36.59	56.7	1	99	0	0	47	0.07	Sep-16
-3.52	-2.41	-1.96	12.01		3.72	0.45	11.15		29.00	336.4	0	100	0	0	52	-0.05	Jun-16
0.36	4.42	7.15	23.85		3.41	0.45	9.82		29.12	17.5	0	100	0	0	26	-0.29	Jun-16
0.76	2.76	4.23	31.02		2.99	0.35	10.23		31.56	18.9	0	100	0	0	35	-0.08	Jun-16
1.91	5.17	7.19	26.10		0.71	0.4	7.83		26.01	10.4	0	100	0	0	39	0.18	Jun-16
2.55	5.19	7.19			1.75	0.15			32.99	1,217	0	100	0	0	18	0.07	Apr-17
0.71	3.30	5.54			1.28	0.3			31.45	14.2	0	100	0	0	23	0.00	Apr-17
0.80	0.38	-4.86			1.45	0.35			27.75	20.8	0	100	0	0	22	-0.03	Apr-17
6.52	10.68					0.6				24.8	0	100	0	0		0.07	Mar-19
12.10	-3.78	4.29			0	0.91				5.0	0	99	0	0	19	0.07	Dec-16
5.33	-7.80					0.96				0.95	0	100	0	0	59	0.00	Jun-18
0.79	-1.61					0.88		24.40	24.57	21.5	18	60	22	0		0.01	Nov-18
1.73	3.96					0.71		17.17	25.82	29.7	3	49	49	0		0.07	Nov-18
2.13	4.59	4.73			3.97	0.27			25.07	175.5	0	100	0	0	29	0.13	Aug-18
-2.45	-2.13	-7.98			3.33	0.68			13.13	12.5	0	100	0	0	24	-0.03	Apr-18
-8.31						0.68			14.67	461.3	0	100	0	0		-0.04	Apr-19
0.50	4.27	6.32	48.90		2.27	0.43	12.69		22.07	73.9	0	100	0	0	36	0.10	Jul-16
-18.09	-23.13	-20.24	8.17	-29.30	4.08	0.65	31.32		17.11	45.3	0	100	0	0	17	-0.22	Apr-10
-7.25	-3.86					0.68			17.14	2.6	0	100	0	0		0.02	Nov-18
-6.87	-6.67	-17.86	7.64	-9.52	2.76	0.69	14.79		8.67	10.0	0	100	0	0	28	-0.06	May-11
-2.40	2.74	0.85	88.44		0.01	0.68	18.18		28.80	404.6	0	100	0	0	21	-0.01	Sep-16
-6.35	-6.73	-6.91			0.37	0.45			18.73	3.7	0	100	0	0	25	-0.03	Feb-17
-4.34	-1.99	-4.86	13.44	1.15	5.93	0.58	13		20.47	18.6	0	100	0	0	7	-0.30	Aug-09
-7.13	-0.41	0.39	22.01	7.77	4.59	0.65	12.15		15.63	23.4	0	100	0	0	12	-0.13	Feb-11
-3.45	-0.10	1.28			0.75	0.68			15.91	39.0	0	100	0	0	8	0.00	May-18
-17.84						0.68			12.43	14.3	0	100	0	0		0.21	Apr-19
5.39	17.66	30.70	-10.58	52.46	0.06	0.65	26.28		24.40	43.0	0	100	0	0	20	-0.41	Nov-10
-1.56	2.85	3.07	43.77	33.03	0.64	0.75	14.44		33.23	56.5	0	100	0	0	113	0.06	Jun-12
1.51	2.73	3.88	33.70		0.81	0.5	12.18		20.11	19.1	0	100	0	0	21	0.27	May-16
1.49	10.14	2.57	35.09		1.39	0.68	18.13		20.37	95.7	0	100	0	0	17	-0.02	Sep-16
-6.49	-14.65	-23.57	9.15	8.86	3.68	0.75	19.61		24.48	457.1	0	100	0	0	16	-0.26	Jul-10
-0.79	-0.82	-4.14	32.81		0.85	0.5	15.23		21.23	21.2	0	100	0	0	14	0.21	May-16
-0.56	3.93	5.93	58.63		0.4	0.5	13.99		24.84	75.8	0	100	0	0	11	0.03	May-16
-4.03	-5.05	-4.86	-5.19	-20.74	5.78	0.45	17.46		12.28	593.9	0	100	0	0	26	-0.36	Aug-13

Fund Name	Ticker Symbol	Traded On	Overall Rating	Reward Rating	Risk Rating	Recent Up/ Downgrade	Price as of 9/30/2019	52-Week High	52-Week Low	Open to New Investors	Category & (Prospectus Objective)
● Global X MLP ETF	MLPA	NYSE Arca	C	B-	D+	Up	8.38	9.84	7.33	Y	Energy Sector Equity (Utility)
● Global X MSCI Argentina ETF	ARGT	NYSE Arca	C-	C	D		22.81	33.89	21.88	Y	Equity Misc (Foreign Stock)
Global X MSCI China Consumer Staples ETF	CHIS	NYSE Arca	U	U	U		20.09	21.00	14.36	Y	Greater China Equity (Growth & Inc)
Global X MSCI China Health Care ETF	CHIH	NYSE Arca	U	U	U		15.68	18.39	12.62	Y	Greater China Equity (Health)
Global X MSCI China Information Technology ETF	CHIK	NYSE Arca	U	U	U		16.93	19.55	13.45	Y	Greater China Equity (Technology)
Global X MSCI China Large-Cap 50 ETF	CHIL	NYSE Arca	U	U	U		26.62	30.21	23.41	Y	Greater China Equity (Growth & Inc)
Global X MSCI China Real Estate ETF	CHIR	NYSE Arca	U	U	U		15.84	19.78	14.36	Y	Greater China Equity (Real Estate)
Global X MSCI China Utilities ETF	CHIU	NYSE Arca	U	U	U		14.93	16.07	14.11	Y	Greater China Equity (Utility)
● Global X MSCI Colombia ETF	GXG	NYSE Arca	D+	D+	C-	Down	8.95	10.24	7.75	Y	Equity Misc (Foreign Stock)
● Global X MSCI Greece ETF	GREK	NYSE Arca	C+	B	C	Up	9.33	9.95	6.79	Y	Europe Equity Mid/Small Cap (Foreign Stock)
Global X MSCI Nigeria ETF	NGE	NYSE Arca	D	D	D		13.34	18.53	12.40	Y	Equity Misc (Foreign Stock)
● Global X MSCI Norway ETF	NORW	NYSE Arca	C-	C-	C-		11.62	15.32	10.83	Y	Equity Misc (Europe Stock)
Global X MSCI Pakistan ETF	PAK	NYSE Arca	E+	E+	E+	Down	6.21	10.60	5.51	Y	Equity Misc (Foreign Stock)
Global X MSCI Portugal ETF	PGAL	NYSE Arca	D+	D	D+	Down	10.12	12.04	9.66	Y	Equity Misc (Foreign Stock)
Global X MSCI SuperDividend® EAFE ETF	EFAS	NAS CM	D+	D	C-		15.60	17.14	14.50	Y	Global Equity Large Cap (Equity-Income)
Global X MSCI SuperDividend® Emerging Markets ETF	SDEM	NYSE Arca	D+	D+	D+		12.62	14.58	12.14	Y	Global Emerg Mkts Equity (Div Emerg Mkts)
Global X Next Emerging & Frontier ETF	EMFM	NYSE Arca	D+	D+	D+	Down	19.98	21.50	19.54	Y	Global Emerg Mkts Equity (Foreign Stock)
● Global X Robotics & Artificial Intelligence ETF	BOTZ	NAS CM	C-	D+	C		20.02	23.10	16.06	Y	Equity Misc (Technology)
Global X Russell 2000 Covered Call ETF	RYLD	BATS	U	U	U		24.84	25.90	24.04	Y	Alternative Misc (Growth & Inc)
● Global X S&P 500® Catholic Values ETF	CATH	NAS CM	C	C+	C-		36.46	36.95	29.28	Y	US Equity Large Cap Blend (Growth & Inc)
Global X S&P 500® Quality Dividend ETF	QDIV	BATS	C-	C-	D+	Up	25.31	26.10	21.03	Y	US Equity Large Cap Value (Equity-Income)
Global X Scientific Beta Asia ex-Japan ETF	SCIX	NYSE Arca	D+	C	D	Down	23.69	25.50	21.67	Y	Asia ex-Japan Equity (Pacific Stock)
Global X Scientific Beta Europe ETF	SCID	NYSE Arca	D+	C-	D		24.03	27.13	21.70	Y	Europe Equity Large Cap (Europe Stock)
Global X Scientific Beta Japan ETF	SCIJ	NYSE Arca	D	D	D	Down	27.41	31.05	25.22	Y	Japan Equity (Pacific Stock)
● Global X Scientific Beta US ETF	SCIU	NYSE Arca	C	C+	D+		33.70	33.86	27.01	Y	US Equity Large Cap Blend (Growth)
● Global X Silver Miners ETF	SIL	NYSE Arca	D+	C-	D	Up	28.11	32.22	21.98	Y	Prec Metals (Prec Metals)
● Global X Social Media ETF	SOCL	NAS CM	C	C	C-		31.93	34.60	26.60	Y	Technology Sector Equity (Technology)
Global X SuperDividend® Alternatives ETF	ALTY	NAS CM	C	C	C-		14.96	15.17	12.93	Y	Aggressive Allocation (Growth & Inc)
★ Global X SuperDividend® REIT ETF	SRET	NAS CM	B-	B-	C+	Up	15.04	15.24	13.25	Y	Real Estate Sector Equity (Real Estate)
● Global X SuperDividend™ ETF	SDIV	NYSE Arca	D	D	C-	Down	16.97	20.27	15.85	Y	Globa Eq Mid/Small Cap (Equity-Income)
● Global X SuperDividend™ U.S. ETF	DIV	NYSE Arca	C	C	C+		23.57	25.33	21.69	Y	US Equity Mid Cap (Income)
● Global X SuperIncome™ Preferred ETF	SPFF	NYSE Arca	C	C	C-	Up	11.74	11.86	10.92	Y	US Fixed Income (Equity-Income)
Global X TargetIncome™ 5 ETF	TFIV	BATS	D	D+	D		24.34	25.01	22.54	Y	Allocation Misc (Income)
Global X TargetIncome™ Plus 2 ETF	TFLT	BATS	D	D+	E+		24.49	25.03	22.74	Y	Cautious Allocation (Income)
● Global X U.S. Infrastructure Development ETF	PAVE	BATS	C	C	C-	Up	16.17	17.23	12.79	Y	Infrastructure Sector Equity (Utility)
● Global X U.S. Preferred ETF	PFFD	BATS	C	C-	C+	Up	25.09	25.09	22.14	Y	US Fixed Income (Growth & Inc)
● Global X Uranium ETF	URA	NYSE Arca	D	D	D		11.00	13.58	10.01	Y	Natural Resources (Unaligned)
Global X YieldCo & Renewable Energy Income ETF	YLCO	NAS CM	C+	B	C-		13.80	13.88	11.12	Y	Globa Eq Mid/Small Cap (Growth & Inc)
● Goldman Sachs Access High Yield Corporate Bond ETF	GHYB	NYSE Arca	C-	C-	C-		49.35	49.58	45.28	Y	US Fixed Income (Corp Bond-High Yld)
Goldman Sachs Access Inflation Protected USD Bond ETF	GTIP	BATS	U	U	U		52.45	53.26	49.05	Y	US Fixed Income (Income)
● Goldman Sachs Access Investment Grade Corporate Bond ETF	GIGB	NYSE Arca	C	C	C-	Up	52.41	52.95	46.80	Y	Canada Fixed Income (Corp Bond - Gen)
● Goldman Sachs Access Treasury 0-1 Year ETF	GBIL	NYSE Arca	C	C	C+		100.38	100.40	100.00	Y	US Fixed Income (Govt Bond - Treasury)
Goldman Sachs Access Ultra Short Bond ETF	GSST	BATS	U	U	U		50.50	50.51	50.02	Y	US Fixed Income (Multisector Bond)
● Goldman Sachs ActiveBeta® Emerging Markets Equity ETF	GEM	NYSE Arca	C	C	C+		31.36	33.75	28.94	Y	Global Emerg Mkts Equity (Div Emerg Mkts)
● Goldman Sachs ActiveBeta® Europe Equity ETF	GSEU	NYSE Arca	C-	C	D+		29.15	30.70	25.60	Y	Europe Equity Large Cap (Europe Stock)
● Goldman Sachs ActiveBeta® International Equity ETF	GSIE	NYSE Arca	C	C	C+		28.29	29.60	24.56	Y	Global Equity Large Cap (Foreign Stock)
Goldman Sachs ActiveBeta® Japan Equity ETF	GSJY	NYSE Arca	C-	C	D+		31.98	34.45	27.89	Y	Japan Equity (Pacific Stock)
● Goldman Sachs ActiveBeta® U.S. Large Cap Equity ETF	GSLC	NYSE Arca	C+	C+	C+		59.89	60.73	47.19	Y	US Equity Large Cap Blend (Growth)
● Goldman Sachs ActiveBeta® U.S. Small Cap Equity ETF	GSSC	NYSE Arca	D+	C-	D+	Up	43.79	47.65	36.76	Y	US Equity Small Cap (Growth)
● Goldman Sachs Equal Weight U.S. Large Cap Equity ETF	GSEW	BATS	C-	C-	C-		47.34	48.16	37.41	Y	US Equity Large Cap Blend (Growth & Inc)
● Goldman Sachs Hedge Industry VIP ETF	GVIP	NYSE Arca	C	C	D+		55.67	60.03	46.00	Y	US Equity Large Cap Blend (Growth & Inc)
● Goldman Sachs JUST U.S. Large Cap Equity ETF	JUST	NYSE Arca	C-	C	D+	Up	42.65	43.44	33.79	Y	US Equity Large Cap Blend (Growth & Inc)

★ Expanded analysis of this fund is included in Section II: Analysis of All BUY Rated Funds. ● Expanded analysis of this fund is included in Section III: Analysis of All Rated Funds with Assets over $50 million.

		TOTAL RETURNS & PERFORMANCE							ASSETS		ASSET ALLOCATION & TURNOVER					VALUATION	
3-Month Total Return	6-Month Total Return	1-Year Total Return	3-Year Total Return	5-Year Total Return	Dividend Yield (TTM)	Expense Ratio	3-Yr Std Deviation	Effective Duration	NAV	Total Assets (MIL)	%Cash	%Stocks	%Bonds	%Other	Turnover Ratio	Premium/ Discount 1-Year Avg	Inception Date
-3.16	-2.54	-6.77	-8.46	-28.46	8.66	0.45	17.14		8.38	961.0	0	100	0	0	30	0.05	Apr-12
-29.79	-17.52	-12.45	-0.97	15.41	2.44	0.59	30.36		22.86	60.0	0	100	0	0	34	-0.18	Mar-11
-1.56	5.71					0.65			20.11	2.0	0	100	0	0		0.57	Dec-18
1.35	-7.68					0.65			15.72	2.4	0	100	0	0		0.54	Dec-18
2.27	-7.92					0.65			17.05	1.7	0	100	0	0		0.06	Dec-18
-5.20	-7.99					0.29			26.60	2.7	0	100	0	0		0.26	Dec-18
-11.25	-16.00					0.65			15.85	1.6	0	100	0	0		0.41	Dec-18
-3.12	-3.60					0.65			14.87	1.5	0	100	0	0		0.70	Dec-18
-5.09	-7.18	-6.49	2.57	-43.51	4.35	0.61	19.95		8.95	68.3	0	99	0	0	39	-0.42	Feb-09
-3.00	14.09	15.88	40.13	-44.18	2.23	0.59	22.72		9.36	336.0	0	100	0	0	16	-0.26	Dec-11
-6.90	-16.58	-19.55	-15.72	-72.56	12.54	0.88	22.21		13.22	35.2	-2	102	0	0	63	0.80	Apr-13
-5.81	-5.30	-17.58	20.06	-8.56	7.75	0.5	14.93		11.67	76.4	0	100	0	0	10	-0.36	Nov-10
-3.45	-25.09	-37.85	-52.31		9.64	0.87	21.57		6.14	39.0	3	97	0	0	44	1.13	Apr-15
-4.25	-4.64	-9.84	17.87	-9.03	7.67	0.57	14.53		10.12	21.3	0	100	0	0	21	-0.17	Nov-13
-0.10	0.05	-2.04			6.64	0.55			15.62	18.0	0	100	0	0	53	0.20	Nov-16
-5.93	-8.94	-2.06	5.22		6.83	0.67	14.4		12.69	17.1	0	100	0	0	80	-0.22	Mar-15
-5.81	-1.93	-3.60	7.43	-10.82	4.95	0.55	13.03		19.91	17.9	0	100	0	0	15	-0.04	Nov-13
-5.50	-1.59	-11.62	34.19		1.97	0.68	21.62		19.91	1,418	0	100	0	0	29	-0.11	Sep-16
-0.64						0.6			24.79	7.4	3	97	0	0		0.16	Apr-19
0.91	4.42	3.03	44.97		2.23	0.29	12.41		36.43	265.9	0	100	0	0	4	0.15	Apr-16
0.67	1.77	1.13			2.83	0.2			25.28	8.8	0	100	0	0	1	-0.41	Jul-18
-5.42	-3.14	1.24	16.33		6.54	0.38	10.64		23.73	2.4	0	100	0	0	43	-0.37	May-15
-1.35	0.52	-4.18	19.33		7.5	0.38	12.58		24.03	4.8	0	100	0	0	45	-0.17	May-15
1.22	-0.52	-8.66	10.97		3.1	0.39	10.41		27.21	2.7	0	100	0	0	43	-0.27	May-15
1.90	6.07	4.88	37.62		2.71	0.19	11.46		33.70	99.4	0	100	0	0	39	0.04	May-15
8.44	8.34	19.18	-33.49	-5.97	1.42	0.65	24.6		28.25	505.5	0	100	0	0	26	-0.07	Apr-10
-1.80	-1.17	0.75	29.74	72.90	0	0.65	18.64		32.06	126.6	0	100	0	0	21	-0.23	Nov-11
1.93	4.34	6.79	21.70		7.05	3.48	10.28	7.43	14.93	29.9	1	79	20	-1	18	0.09	Jul-15
3.39	3.22	7.88	25.84		7.9	0.59	12.02		14.99	324.5	0	100	0	0	42	0.18	Mar-15
1.11	-3.12	-8.29	-0.21	2.45	9.4	0.58	12.18		16.99	922.7	0	100	0	0	59	0.00	Jun-11
6.75	2.08	0.52	15.65	14.01	7.35	0.45	9.65		23.57	528.0	0	100	0	0	33	0.01	Mar-13
2.55	3.68	5.55	7.28	11.81	6.39	0.58	4.25		11.74	197.8	0	5	0	0	105	0.13	Jul-12
2.38	3.89	4.62			5.94	0.8		3.81	24.32	1.2	3	21	57	0	16	0.00	Jul-18
1.68	3.72	4.39			5.19	0.8		4.40	24.47	1.2	3	6	72	0	11	0.02	Jul-18
-1.58	1.59	-4.85			1.05	0.47			16.19	136.0	0	100	0	0	7	-0.01	Mar-17
3.97	6.33	10.66			5.5	0.23			25.06	527.6	0	3	0	0	43	0.23	Sep-17
-8.80	-12.35	-16.73	-5.45	-48.52	1.4	0.69	32.13		11.08	194.9	0	100	0	0	54	-0.68	Nov-10
2.73	7.86	19.03	35.96		3.46	0.65	10.39		13.74	24.0	0	97	0	3	34	0.08	May-15
1.07	3.51	6.73			5.65	0.34			49.38	76.5	1	0	99	0	69	-0.23	Sep-17
1.54	4.49	7.90				0.12			52.32	7.8						0.03	Oct-18
2.95	7.96	13.03			3.24	0.14			52.39	489.8	0	0	97	0	22	0.05	Jun-17
0.54	1.21	2.41	4.44		2.16	0.12	0.25		100.36	3,301	38	0	62	0		0.01	Sep-16
0.78						0.16			50.49	17.7	1	0	100	0		0.02	Apr-19
-3.87	-2.77	-0.96	19.19		2.74	0.45	13.41		31.48	1,731	0	100	0	0	28	0.04	Sep-15
-2.04	1.54	-0.92	22.11		3.77	0.25	12.46		29.22	19.0	0	100	0	0	23	-0.05	Mar-16
-1.25	1.76	-1.21	21.92		2.93	0.25	10.88		28.25	1,576	0	100	0	0	16	0.12	Nov-15
1.59	2.83	-3.89	21.09		2.93	0.25	9.76		31.75	25.4	0	100	0	0	23	-0.10	Mar-16
1.46	5.16	3.66	45.11		1.64	0.09	12.12		59.92	6,819	0	100	0	0	16	0.00	Sep-15
-1.09	0.20	-6.41			1.25	0.2			43.82	96.4	0	100	0	0	27	0.08	Jun-17
0.51	4.40	4.19			1.58	0.09			47.30	177.4	0	100	0	0	34	0.01	Sep-17
-5.48	-2.69	-3.45	43.44		1	0.45			55.61	80.6	0	100	0	0	1	0.01	Nov-16
0.92	5.03	3.09			2.03	0.2			42.63	131.1	0	100	0	0	2	0.01	Jun-18

Fund Name	Ticker Symbol	Traded On	Overall Rating	Reward Rating	Risk Rating	Recent Up/ Downgrade	Price as of 9/30/2019	52-Week High	52-Week Low	Open to New Investors	Category & (Prospectus Objective)
Goldman Sachs Motif Data-Driven World ETF	GDAT	NYSE Arca	U	U	U		51.67	54.03	47.90	Y	Technology Sector Equity (Growth & Inc)
Goldman Sachs Motif Finance Reimagined ETF	GFIN	NYSE Arca	U	U	U		54.61	58.21	50.42	Y	Financials Sector Equity (Growth & Inc)
Goldman Sachs Motif Human Evolution ETF	GDNA	NYSE Arca	U	U	U		48.93	52.68	46.98	Y	Healthcare Sector Equity (Growth & Inc)
Goldman Sachs Motif Manufacturing Revolution ETF	GMAN	NYSE Arca	U	U	U		49.91	52.10	45.67	Y	Industrials Sector Equity (Growth & Inc)
Goldman Sachs Motif New Age Consumer ETF	GBUY	NYSE Arca	U	U	U		52.27	54.72	48.96	Y	Consumer Goods & Svcs (Growth & Inc)
● GraniteShares Bloomberg Commod Broad Strategy No K-1 ETF	COMB	NYSE Arca	D+	D	C-	Up	23.52	26.31	22.97	Y	Commodities Broad Basket (Growth & Inc)
● GraniteShares Gold Trust	BAR	NYSE Arca	D-	D-	D-		14.71	133.77	12.67	Y	Commodities Specified (Prec Metals)
GraniteShares HIPS US High Income ETF	HIPS	NYSE Arca	C	C	D+		16.73	17.75	14.45	Y	Aggressive Allocation (Income)
GraniteShares Platinum Trust	PLTM	NYSE Arca	E+	D-	E+		8.77	87.16	7.83	Y	Commodities Specified (Growth & Inc)
GraniteShares S&P GSCI Commodity Broad Strategy No K-1 ETF	COMG	NYSE Arca	D+	D+	D+	Up	20.98	31.88	19.37	Y	Commodities Broad Basket (Growth & Inc)
★ Grayscale Bitcoin Trust	GBTC	OTC BB	B	A+	D+	Up	10.59	17.08	3.84	Y	Trading Tools (Growth & Inc)
Grayscale Ethereum Classic Trust	ETCG	OTC BB	D	D	D-		8.90	45.88	5.05	Y	Trading Tools (Growth & Inc)
Grayscale Ethereum Trust (ETH)	ETHE	OTC BB	U	U	U		21.71	580.00	21.71	Y	Trading Tools (Growth & Inc)
● GS Connect S&P GSCI Enhanced Commodity Total Return ETN	GSC	NYSE Arca	D+	D+	D+		21.83	30.97	17.93	Y	Commodities Broad Basket (Natl Res)
Hartford Global Impact NextShares Fund	HFGIC	NAS CM	C	D+	B-	Up	19.78	100.10	16.60	Y	Globa Eq Mid/Small Cap (Growth)
● Hartford Multifactor Developed Markets (ex-US) ETF	RODM	NYSE Arca	C	C	C+		27.88	29.04	25.02	Y	Global Equity Large Cap (Foreign Stock)
● Hartford Multifactor Emerging Markets ETF	ROAM	NYSE Arca	C-	C	C-		22.04	24.39	21.30	Y	Global Emerg Mkts Equity (Div Emerg Mkts)
Hartford Multifactor Global Small Cap ETF	ROGS	NYSE Arca	C-	C-	D+		28.50	31.66	25.82	Y	Globa Eq Mid/Small Cap (Small Company)
Hartford Multifactor Low Volatility Intl Equity ETF	LVIN	BATS	D+	C	D	Up	26.83	27.59	23.92	Y	Global Equity Large Cap (Growth & Inc)
Hartford Multifactor Low Volatility US Equity ETF	LVUS	BATS	C-	C	D	Up	30.85	31.14	24.10	Y	US Equity Large Cap Blend (Growth & Inc)
Hartford Multifactor REIT ETF	RORE	NYSE Arca	C	C+	C-		16.36	16.43	13.29	Y	Real Estate Sector Equity (Real Estate)
● Hartford Multifactor US Equity ETF	ROUS	NYSE Arca	C	C	C-		32.22	33.06	26.23	Y	US Equity Large Cap Blend (Growth)
● Hartford Municipal Opportunities ETF	HMOP	NYSE Arca	C-	C-	D+		41.91	42.47	39.08	Y	US Muni Fixed Inc (Growth & Inc)
Hartford Schroders Tax-Aware Bond ETF	HTAB	NYSE Arca	C-	C-	D+	Up	21.06	21.24	19.64	Y	US Muni Fixed Inc (Growth & Inc)
● Hartford Short Duration ETF	HSRT	BATS	C-	C-	D+	Up	40.83	41.02	39.56	Y	US Fixed Income (Growth & Inc)
● Hartford Total Return Bond ETF	HTRB	NYSE Arca	C-	C-	D+	Up	41.47	41.94	38.34	Y	US Fixed Income (Income)
● High Yield ETF	HYLD	NYSE Arca	C	C	C-		33.88	36.72	33.65	Y	US Fixed Income (Income)
● Highland/iBoxx Senior Loan ETF	SNLN	NAS CM	C	C	C+		17.45	18.27	17.10	Y	US Fixed Income (Income)
Hull Tactical US ETF	HTUS	NYSE Arca	C	C	D+		25.54	27.75	20.79	Y	Long/Short Equity (Growth)
IM DBi Managed Futures Strategy ETF	DBMF	NYSE Arca	U	U	U		27.70	28.37	24.84	Y	Global Macro (Growth & Inc)
Impact Shares NAACP Minority Empowerment ETF	NACP	NYSE Arca	C-	C-	D	Up	21.44	21.99	17.06	Y	US Equity Large Cap Blend (Growth & Inc)
Impact Shares Sustainable Dev Goals Global Equity ETF	SDGA	NYSE Arca	D+	C-	D		20.67	21.02	17.53	Y	US Equity Large Cap Value (Growth)
Impact Shares YWCA Women's Empowerment ETF	WOMN	NYSE Arca	C-	C-	C-		20.96	21.35	16.65	Y	US Equity Large Cap Blend (Growth & Inc)
● Industrial Select Sector SPDR® Fund	XLI	NYSE Arca	C+	C+	C+		77.63	79.60	60.34	Y	Industrials Sector Equity (Unaligned)
● InfraCap MLP ETF	AMZA	NYSE Arca	C	C+	D+	Up	4.93	7.64	4.57	Y	Energy Sector Equity (Growth & Inc)
InfraCap REIT Preferred ETF	PFFR	NYSE Arca	C	C	C-	Up	25.28	25.28	21.65	Y	US Fixed Income (Real Estate)
Innovation a® Global ETF	INAG	NYSE Arca	U	U	U		27.17	27.65	25.72	Y	Global Equity Large Cap (World Stock)
Innovation a® Trade War ETF	TWAR	NYSE Arca	U	U	U		27.31	27.73	25.83	Y	Global Equity Large Cap (Unaligned)
Innovation a® United States ETF	INAU	NYSE Arca	U	U	U		27.49	28.02	25.69	Y	US Equity Large Cap Blend (Growth)
★ Innovation Shares NextGen Protocol ETF	KOIN	NYSE Arca	B-	B	C	Up	26.81	28.37	20.71	Y	Technology Sector Equity (Unaligned)
Innovation Shares NextGen Vehicles and Technology ETF	EKAR	NYSE Arca	D	D	D		19.84	24.00	18.17	Y	Technology Sector Equity (Technology)
● Innovator IBD® 50 ETF	FFTY	NYSE	C	C+	C		32.27	38.07	25.43	Y	US Equity Mid Cap (Growth)
Innovator IBD® Breakout Opportunities ETF	BOUT	NYSE Arca	C	C+	C-		19.58	24.42	16.35	Y	US Equity Mid Cap (Growth)
Innovator IBD® ETF Leaders ETF	LDRS	NYSE Arca	D	D	D+		21.99	25.25	20.21	Y	Global Equity Large Cap (Growth & Inc)
Innovator Loup Frontier Tech ETF	LOUP	NYSE Arca	D+	C-	D+	Up	22.77	26.46	19.08	Y	Technology Sector Equity (Technology)
● Innovator Lunt Low Vol/High Beta Tactical ETF	LVHB	BATS	C	C	C-		36.82	37.03	28.29	Y	US Equity Large Cap Blend (Growth & Inc)
Innovator MSCI EAFE Power Buffer ETF - July	IJUL	NYSE Arca	U	U	U		23.10	23.30	22.40	Y	Alternative Misc (Growth & Inc)
Innovator MSCI Emerging Markets Power Buffer ETF - July	EJUL	NYSE Arca	U	U	U		24.79	25.38	24.14	Y	Alternative Misc (Growth & Inc)
Innovator S&P 500 Buffer ETF - April New	BAPR	BATS	U	U	U		26.25	27.43	24.52	Y	Alternative Misc (Growth & Inc)
● Innovator S&P 500 Buffer ETF – July	BJUL	BATS	D+	D+	C-		26.15	26.40	22.50	Y	Long/Short Equity (Growth)
Innovator S&P 500 Buffer ETF - June	BJUN	BATS	U	U	U		27.02	27.20	25.38	Y	Alternative Misc (Growth & Inc)
Innovator S&P 500 Buffer ETF - October	BOCT	BATS	U	U	U		24.87	25.48	21.34	Y	Long/Short Equity (Growth)

★ Expanded analysis of this fund is included in Section II: Analysis of All BUY Rated Funds. ● Expanded analysis of this fund is included in Section III: Analysis of All Rated Funds with Assets over $50 million.

3-Month Total Return	6-Month Total Return	1-Year Total Return	3-Year Total Return	5-Year Total Return	Dividend Yield (TTM)	Expense Ratio	3-Yr Std Deviation	Effective Duration	NAV	Total Assets (MIL)	%Cash	%Stocks	%Bonds	%Other	Turnover Ratio	Premium/ Discount 1-Year Avg	Inception Date
-0.69	0.25					0.5			51.61	10.3	0	100	0	0		0.10	Mar-19
-2.83	4.97					0.5			54.62	10.9	0	100	0	0		0.07	Mar-19
-6.30	-2.33					0.5			48.92	8.6	0	100	0	0		0.14	Mar-19
-1.08	2.01					0.5			49.86	6.2	0	100	0	0		0.08	Mar-19
-2.02	0.06					0.5			52.20	5.2	0	100	0	0		0.13	Mar-19
-1.15	-3.86	-8.15			0.94	0.25			23.53	67.1	100	0	0	0		-0.09	May-17
6.80	14.72	-87.53			0	0.17			14.80	611.8	0	0	0	100		-0.11	Aug-17
1.42	1.25	1.89	18.19		7.72	1.3	13.07		16.72	8.4	-1	94	7	0	112	0.07	Jan-15
6.61	5.23	-89.03			0	0.5			8.92	5.8	0	0	0	100		0.09	Jan-18
-4.06	-6.75	-18.42			20.57	0.35			20.99	6.3	100	0	0	0		-0.13	May-17
-24.56	93.87	20.39	1,154.20	1,795.68	0	2	98.93		7.86	1,925	-55	0	0	155		24.90	Sep-13
-38.55	-2.92	-59.08			0	3			4.40	39.3						128.88	Apr-17
-40.62					0	2.5			16.53	66.5						147.53	Dec-17
2.93		-17.81	1.87	-51.48	0	1.25	20.65			98.3					0	0.00	Jul-07
	12.00	1.02			1.3	0.69				5.3	13	87	0	0	79	0.00	Dec-17
-1.74	-0.25	-1.65	21.70		2.45	0.29	9.55		27.76	2,336	0	100	0	0	47	0.15	Feb-15
-6.60	-4.65	-1.70	9.52		2.73	0.44	13.1		22.20	68.8	0	100	0	0	25	-0.24	Feb-15
-2.61	-3.13	-6.78	20.75		2.84	0.39	11.67		28.56	17.1	1	99	0	0	41	-0.11	Mar-15
-1.44	1.71	0.76			2.57	0.29			26.84	5.4	0	100	0	0	35	-0.07	May-17
2.80	7.96	9.69			1.93	0.21			30.83	7.7	0	100	0	0	26	0.33	May-17
7.55	6.50	13.06	26.46		4.56	0.45			16.36	18.0	0	100	0	0	35	0.07	Oct-16
1.61	3.93	-0.23	39.12		2.03	0.19	13.67		32.20	307.5	1	99	0	0	36	0.08	Feb-15
1.56	4.10	9.07			2.43	0.29			41.92	144.6	2	0	98	0	32	0.06	Dec-17
1.19	3.63	8.94			2.44	0.39			21.05	30.5	1	0	94	0	165	0.03	Apr-18
1.14	2.94	5.52			3.38	0.29			40.82	114.3	4	0	95	0	28	0.05	May-18
2.45	6.03	10.27			3.16	0.29			41.45	601.0	5	0	94	0	54	0.11	Sep-17
0.03	1.36	0.16	20.30	0.57	7.51	1.25	3.68		34.11	139.9	6	0	94	0	74	-0.41	Nov-10
0.53	1.48	0.52	8.07	12.26	5.18	0.55	3.18		17.44	261.6	22	0	78	0	186	0.02	Nov-12
2.23	4.14	2.05	21.03		0.83	0.97	9.79		25.63	47.4	12	88	0	0	1,320	-0.21	Jun-15
7.72						0.85			27.66	22.1	-21	25	96	0		0.12	May-19
0.94	4.17	5.00			1.4	0.76			21.46	2.1	-1	101	0	0		-0.10	Jul-18
-0.01	3.85	6.12			2.26	0.76			20.55	1.0	3	97	0	0		0.37	Sep-18
0.92	4.48	4.65			1.4	0.76			20.95	6.3	1	99	0	0		0.10	Aug-18
0.49	2.16	0.14	40.89	61.57	2.02	0.13	16.76			9,810	0	100	0	0	6	-0.02	Dec-98
-7.84	-10.98	-22.41	-21.61	-52.86	21.38	2.4	22.04		4.91	370.4	-32	132	0	0	255	0.02	Oct-14
3.60	5.55	10.95			5.62	0.45			25.18	32.7	4	1	0	1	70	0.23	Feb-17
-0.77						0.81			27.11	4.1	0	100	0	0		0.12	Jun-19
-0.30						0.81			27.25	4.1	0	100	0	0		0.11	Jun-19
0.17						0.81			27.46	4.1	0	100	0	0		0.12	Jun-19
-1.97	1.93	0.72			0.8	0.95			26.81	10.1	0	100	0	0		-0.15	Jan-18
-2.42	-5.41	-14.33			3.17	0.95			19.74	1.5	0	100	0	0		-0.03	Feb-18
-6.97	-4.47	-15.17	37.42		0	0.8	20.1		32.27	337.2	0	100	0	0	719	-0.04	Apr-15
-7.50	-3.75	-19.84			0.2	0.8			19.59	8.8	0	100	0	0		0.01	Sep-18
2.87	2.86	-12.15			1.09	1.08		12.35	21.95	14.3	1	84	15	0		-0.09	Dec-17
-6.66	-7.02	-13.95			0	0.7			22.75	10.2	0	100	0	0		-0.01	Jul-18
5.24	11.32	19.78	46.03		1.89	0.52			36.81	136.2	0	100	0	0	667	-0.03	Oct-16
-0.69						0.85			23.08	46.7	2	98	0	0		0.29	Jun-19
-2.81						0.89			24.81	34.7	5	95	0	0		0.06	Jun-19
1.21	4.49					0.79			26.30	39.4						0.24	Mar-19
1.00	2.52	1.97			0	0.79			26.21	76.0	4	96	0	0		0.09	Aug-18
1.25						0.79			27.04	4.7	4	96	0	0		0.02	May-19
-0.62	1.77	0.90			0	0.79			24.89	187.3	0	100	0	0		0.05	Sep-18

Fund Name	Ticker Symbol	Traded On	Overall Rating	Reward Rating	Risk Rating	Recent Up/ Downgrade	Price as of 9/30/2019	52-Week High	52-Week Low	Open to New Investors	Category & (Prospectus Objective)
Innovator S&P 500 Buffer ETF January	BJAN	BATS	U	U	U		29.14	29.32	24.80	Y	Alternative Misc (Growth)
Innovator S&P 500 Power Buffer ETF - April New	PAPR	BATS	U	U	U		26.00	26.12	24.70	Y	Alternative Misc (Growth & Inc)
● Innovator S&P 500 Power Buffer ETF — July	PJUL	BATS	D+	D+	C-		26.08	26.21	23.30	Y	Long/Short Equity (Growth)
Innovator S&P 500 Power Buffer ETF - New	PJUN	BATS	U	U	U		26.48	26.55	25.41	Y	Alternative Misc (Growth & Inc)
Innovator S&P 500 Power Buffer ETF - October	POCT	BATS	U	U	U		24.89	25.45	22.21	Y	Long/Short Equity (Growth)
Innovator S&P 500 Power Buffer ETF January	PJAN	BATS	U	U	U		27.79	27.84	24.98	Y	Alternative Misc (Growth)
Innovator S&P 500 Ultra Buffer ETF - April New	UAPR	BATS	U	U	U		25.97	26.05	24.73	Y	Alternative Misc (Growth & Inc)
Innovator S&P 500 Ultra Buffer ETF — July	UJUL	BATS	D+	D+	D+		26.06	26.19	23.62	Y	Long/Short Equity (Growth)
Innovator S&P 500 Ultra Buffer ETF - June	UJUN	BATS	U	U	U		26.39	26.50	25.41	Y	Alternative Misc (Growth & Inc)
Innovator S&P 500 Ultra Buffer ETF - October	UOCT	BATS	U	U	U		24.90	25.37	22.72	Y	Long/Short Equity (Growth)
Innovator S&P 500 Ultra Buffer ETF January	UJAN	BATS	U	U	U		27.40	27.45	24.98	Y	Alternative Misc (Growth)
Innovator S&P Investment Grade Preferred ETF	EPRF	BATS	C	C+	D+	Up	24.26	24.38	20.89	Y	US Fixed Income (Corp Bond - High Quality)
InsightShares LGBT Employment Equality ETF	PRID	NYSE Arca	C-	C	D	Up	27.43	28.02	21.72	Y	US Equity Large Cap Blend (Growth & Inc)
InsightShares Patriotic Employers ETF	HONR	NYSE Arca	D+	C	E+	Up	26.32	26.64	20.44	Y	US Equity Large Cap Value (Growth & Inc)
● Inspire 100 ETF	BIBL	NYSE Arca	C-	C-	C-		27.91	28.33	22.55	Y	US Equity Large Cap Blend (Growth & Inc)
● Inspire Corporate Bond Impact ETF	IBD	NYSE Arca	C	C	C-	Up	25.68	25.98	24.16	Y	US Fixed Income (Corp Bond - Gen)
● Inspire Global Hope ETF	BLES	NYSE Arca	C	C	C-		27.76	28.95	23.44	Y	Global Equity Large Cap (Growth)
● Inspire Small/Mid Cap Impact ETF	ISMD	NYSE Arca	C-	D+	C-		26.33	29.18	21.59	Y	US Equity Mid Cap (Growth)
● Invesco 1-30 Laddered Treasury ETF	PLW	NAS CM	C	C	C+		35.57	36.39	30.35	Y	US Fixed Income (Govt Bond - Treasury)
● Invesco Active U.S. Real Estate Fund	PSR	NYSE Arca	C+	B-	C-	Up	95.80	96.82	73.52	Y	Real Estate Sector Equity (Real Estate)
★ Invesco Aerospace & Defense ETF	PPA	NYSE Arca	B	B+	C	Up	67.70	69.48	46.46	Y	Industrials Sector Equity (Unaligned)
Invesco Balanced Multi-Asset Allocation ETF	PSMB	BATS	C	C	C-	Up	14.03	14.21	12.21	Y	Moderate Allocation (Asset Allocation)
Invesco BLDRS Asia 50 ADR Index Fund	ADRA	NAS CM	C	B-	C-	Up	31.32	32.78	27.79	Y	Asia Equity (Pacific Stock)
Invesco BLDRS Developed Markets 100 ADR Index Fund	ADRD	NAS CM	C	C	C-	Up	21.08	22.46	18.89	Y	Global Equity Large Cap (Foreign Stock)
● Invesco BLDRS Emerging Markets 50 ADR Index Fund	ADRE	NAS CM	C	B-	D+	Up	38.42	42.47	34.99	Y	Global Emerg Mkts Equity (Div Emerg Mkts)
Invesco BLDRS Europe Select ADR Index Fund	ADRU	NAS CM	C	C	C-	Up	20.35	21.79	18.42	Y	Europe Equity Large Cap (Europe Stock)
● Invesco BRIC ETF	EEB	NYSE Arca	C	C	D+		35.04	37.82	31.24	Y	Global Emerg Mkts Equity (Growth)
Invesco BulletShares (R) 2021 USD Emerg Mkts Debt ETF	BSAE	NYSE Arca	U	U	U		25.53	25.61	24.85	Y	Emerging Mkts Fixed Inc (Div Emerg Mkts)
Invesco BulletShares (R) 2022 USD Emerg Mkts Debt ETF	BSBE	NYSE Arca	U	U	U		25.96	26.02	24.76	Y	Emerging Mkts Fixed Inc (Div Emerg Mkts)
Invesco BulletShares (R) 2023 USD Emerg Mkts Debt ETF	BSCE	NYSE Arca	U	U	U		26.24	26.32	24.61	Y	Emerging Mkts Fixed Inc (Div Emerg Mkts)
Invesco BulletShares (R) 2024 Emerging Markets Debt ETF	BSDE	NYSE Arca	U	U	U		26.55	26.61	24.61	Y	Emerging Mkts Fixed Inc (Div Emerg Mkts)
● Invesco BulletShares 2019 Corporate Bond ETF	BSCJ	NYSE Arca	C	C	C+		21.08	21.14	21.02	Y	US Fixed Income (Corp Bond - Gen)
● Invesco BulletShares 2019 High Yield Corporate Bond ETF	BSJJ	NYSE Arca	C+	C	C+		23.92	24.27	23.46	Y	US Fixed Income (Corp Bond-High Yld)
● Invesco BulletShares 2020 Corporate Bond ETF	BSCK	NYSE Arca	C	C	C+		21.30	21.35	20.97	Y	US Fixed Income (Corp Bond - Gen)
● Invesco BulletShares 2020 High Yield Corporate Bond ETF	BSJK	NYSE Arca	C+	C	C+		23.95	24.35	23.23	Y	US Fixed Income (Corp Bond-High Yld)
● Invesco BulletShares 2021 Corporate Bond ETF	BSCL	NYSE Arca	C+	C	C+	Up	21.26	21.30	20.62	Y	US Fixed Income (Corp Bond - Gen)
● Invesco BulletShares 2021 High Yield Corporate Bond ETF	BSJL	NYSE Arca	C+	C	C+		24.63	24.89	23.39	Y	US Fixed Income (Corp Bond-High Yld)
● Invesco BulletShares 2022 Corporate Bond ETF	BSCM	NYSE Arca	C+	C+	C+		21.49	21.56	20.47	Y	US Fixed Income (Corp Bond - Gen)
● Invesco BulletShares 2022 High Yield Corporate Bond ETF	BSJM	NYSE Arca	C+	C	C+		24.37	24.68	22.88	Y	US Fixed Income (Corp Bond-High Yld)
● Invesco BulletShares 2023 Corporate Bond ETF	BSCN	NYSE Arca	C+	C+	C+		21.29	21.40	20.00	Y	US Fixed Income (Corp Bond - Gen)
● Invesco BulletShares 2023 High Yield Corporate Bond ETF	BSJN	NYSE Arca	C	C	C-		26.07	26.29	24.23	Y	US Fixed Income (Corp Bond-High Yld)
● Invesco BulletShares 2024 Corporate Bond ETF	BSCO	NYSE Arca	C+	C+	C+		21.43	21.54	19.77	Y	US Fixed Income (Corp Bond - Gen)
● Invesco BulletShares 2024 High Yield Corporate Bond ETF	BSJO	NYSE Arca	C	C	C-		25.22	25.42	23.03	Y	US Fixed Income (Corp Bond-High Yld)
● Invesco BulletShares 2025 Corporate Bond ETF	BSCP	NYSE Arca	C+	C+	C+		21.37	21.51	19.40	Y	US Fixed Income (Corp Bond - Gen)
● Invesco BulletShares 2025 High Yield Corporate Bond ETF	BSJP	NYSE Arca	C-	C-	C-		24.53	24.73	21.97	Y	US Fixed Income (Corp Bond-High Yld)
● Invesco BulletShares 2026 Corporate Bond ETF	BSCQ	NYSE Arca	C	C	C-		20.45	20.67	18.38	Y	US Fixed Income (Corp Bond - Gen)
● Invesco BulletShares 2026 High Yield Corporate Bond ETF	BSJQ	NYSE Arca	D+	D+	D+		25.80	25.96	23.02	Y	US Fixed Income (Corp Bond-High Yld)
● Invesco BulletShares 2027 Corporate Bond ETF	BSCR	NYSE Arca	C-	C-	C-		20.87	21.12	18.58	Y	US Fixed Income (Corp Bond - Gen)
Invesco BulletShares 2028 Corporate Bond ETF	BSCS	NYSE Arca	D+	D+	C-		21.96	22.22	19.39	Y	US Fixed Income (Corp Bond - Gen)
● Invesco BuyBack Achievers ETF	PKW	NAS CM	C	B-	C	Down	62.58	64.22	49.25	Y	US Equity Large Cap Blend (Unaligned)
● Invesco California AMT-Free Municipal Bond ETF	PWZ	NYSE Arca	C	C+	C-		27.35	27.69	25.05	Y	US Muni Fixed Inc (Muni Bond - Single State)
● Invesco CEF Income Composite ETF	PCEF	NYSE Arca	C+	C+	C+		22.61	22.85	19.45	Y	Cautious Allocation (Income)

★ Expanded analysis of this fund is included in Section II: Analysis of All BUY Rated Funds. ● Expanded analysis of this fund is included in Section III: Analysis of All Rated Funds with Assets over $50 million.

		TOTAL RETURNS & PERFORMANCE							ASSETS		ASSET ALLOCATION & TURNOVER					VALUATION	
3-Month Total Return	6-Month Total Return	1-Year Total Return	3-Year Total Return	5-Year Total Return	Dividend Yield (TTM)	Expense Ratio	3-Yr Std Deviation	Effective Duration	NAV	Total Assets (MIL)	%Cash	%Stocks	%Bonds	%Other	Turnover Ratio	Premium/ Discount 1-Year Avg	Inception Date
0.71	3.80					0.79				22.6	4	96	0	0		-0.02	Dec-18
1.08	3.77					0.79			26.07	132.9						0.22	Mar-19
0.92	2.36	1.91			0	0.79			26.11	105.7	4	96	0	0		0.20	Aug-18
1.02						0.79			26.50	18.6						0.09	May-19
-0.85	1.44	1.44			0	0.79			24.88	263.1	0	100	0	0		0.29	Sep-18
0.96	2.96					0.79			27.83	65.4	9	91	0	0		0.17	Dec-18
1.12	3.36					0.79			26.00	18.8						0.12	Mar-19
0.94	3.30	1.98			0	0.79			26.11	37.9	3	97	0	0	0	0.07	Aug-18
0.95						0.79			26.44	2.0	5	95	0	0		-0.03	May-19
-0.24	1.85	1.03			0	0.79			24.88	108.2	0	100	0	0		0.23	Sep-18
0.93	2.75					0.79			27.42	30.2	10	90	0	0		0.15	Dec-18
3.84	6.01	11.64	13.74		4.99	0.47	6.4		24.21	19.4	0	0	0	0	58	0.20	May-16
0.67	5.03	3.07			1.54	0.65			27.41	2.7	0	100	0	0	3	-0.29	Jan-18
1.76	7.46	7.43			1.48	0.65			26.31	1.3	0	100	0	0	18	-0.14	Jan-18
-0.28	0.94	-0.35			1.13	0.35				76.6	1	99	0	0		0.12	Oct-17
1.45	4.30	8.21			2.46	0.61				128.3	5	0	95	0		0.28	Jul-17
-1.45	0.56	0.86			2.1	0.61				150.0	1	99	0	0		0.19	Feb-17
-1.19	-0.90	-6.69			1.24	0.61				93.5	1	99	0	0		-0.07	Feb-17
5.08	10.28	17.34	9.06	24.11	1.93	0.25	7.27	11.09	35.54	170.6	0	0	100	0		0.08	Oct-07
7.73	9.45	22.09	29.28	67.90	2.48	0.35	11.96		95.84	115.0	0	100	0	0	92	0.07	Nov-08
5.27	15.27	11.04	80.30	126.50	0.95	0.59	16.7		67.71	1,087	0	100	0	0	15	0.00	Oct-05
0.89	4.05	5.69			2.73	0.4		6.12	14.04	4.2	1	60	39	0	26	0.18	Feb-17
-1.33	-2.06	-3.41	16.33	19.92	2.51	0.3	13.94		30.71	16.9	1	99	0	0		-0.13	Nov-02
-2.53	-0.71	-2.65	16.04	5.40	3.85	0.3	11.36		21.06	30.5	1	99	0	0	3	-0.12	Nov-02
-4.77	-6.24	-3.75	16.96	11.68	1.64	0.3	16.76		38.53	125.2	1	99	0	0	10	-0.14	Nov-02
-3.57	-1.81	-2.63	15.54	2.82	3.81	0.3	12.06		20.46	10.2	1	99	0	0	2	-0.41	Nov-02
-7.04	-5.92	2.16	26.74	17.76	2.82	0.64	15.05		35.07	57.9	0	100	0	0		-0.03	Sep-06
1.21	3.15	6.76				0.29		1.82	25.54	10.2	1	0	99	0		0.09	Oct-18
1.39	4.28	8.63				0.29		2.60	25.95	10.4	1	0	99	0		0.10	Oct-18
1.80	5.13	9.93				0.29		3.38	26.24	10.5	1	0	99	0		0.11	Oct-18
2.10	5.75	11.27				0.29		3.99	26.48	10.6	0	0	100	0		0.27	Oct-18
0.58	1.25	2.63	5.09	11.14	2.27	0.1	0.71	0.23	21.10	1,010	99	0	1	0	3	0.02	Mar-12
0.70	1.47	2.88	12.97	17.37	4.09	0.42	1.58	0.17	23.95	768.8	63	0	37	0	25	-0.12	Sep-13
0.77	1.80	3.85	5.42	13.41	2.49	0.1	1.3	0.93	21.28	1,810	1	0	98	0	1	0.16	Mar-12
0.46	1.47	2.94	13.95	18.57	4.62	0.42	2.13	0.75	23.89	1,161	7	0	93	0	27	0.13	Sep-13
0.96	2.48	5.37	6.50	15.93	2.71	0.1	1.79	1.79	21.21	1,664	0	0	100	0	3	0.23	Jul-13
0.77	2.12	4.50	15.85	27.00	5.16	0.42	2.77	1.41	24.55	879.0	6	0	94	0	14	0.14	Sep-14
1.18	3.21	7.23	7.76	18.70	2.87	0.1	2.44	2.73	21.43	1,414	1	0	99	0	0	0.24	Jul-13
0.57	2.36	4.21	14.69	27.30	5.48	0.42	3.5	1.67	24.31	547.1	4	0	96	0	17	0.14	Sep-14
1.56	3.74	8.45	9.12	21.85	3.02	0.1	2.92	3.49	21.22	859.5	1	0	98	0	0	0.28	Sep-14
0.77	2.77	4.63	15.38		5.64	0.42	3.9	2.08	25.94	249.0	1	0	98	0	6	0.14	Oct-15
1.64	5.23	10.26	10.69	23.94	3.22	0.1	3.44	4.37	21.35	608.3	0	0	100	0	2	0.27	Sep-14
0.82	3.80	6.80	16.05		5.44	0.42	4.22	2.39	25.11	97.9	1	0	99	0	8	0.21	Sep-16
1.97	5.76	11.71	11.08		3.23	0.1	4.02	5.14	21.31	316.4	0	0	99	0	1	0.25	Oct-15
1.39	4.42	6.48			5.71	0.42		3.33	24.46	75.8	0	0	100	0	9	0.11	Sep-17
2.41	6.76	13.14	11.36		3.24	0.1	4.38	6.03	20.41	134.7	0	0	100	0	0	0.26	Sep-16
1.72	5.08	9.07			5.71	0.42		3.58	25.74	25.7	0	0	100	0	0	0.11	Aug-18
2.67	7.43	13.94			3.43	0.1		6.65	20.81	74.9	0	0	99	0	0	0.26	Sep-17
2.82	8.51	13.83				0.1		7.25	21.90	42.7	1	0	98	0	0	0.25	Aug-19
-0.69	4.17	4.43	36.67	50.36	1.37	0.62	15.14		62.59	1,127	0	100	0	0	76	-0.03	Dec-06
2.34	5.20	9.81	11.24	23.40	2.45	0.28	4.35	8.86	27.34	348.5	1	0	99	0		-0.03	Oct-07
1.37	5.07	6.61	23.22	36.45	7.23	2.25	8.32	4.00	22.58	765.6	-2	29	68	-5		0.06	Feb-10

Fund Name	Ticker Symbol	Traded On	Overall Rating	Reward Rating	Risk Rating	Recent Up/ Downgrade	Price as of 9/30/2019	52-Week High	52-Week Low	Open to New Investors	Category & (Prospectus Objective)
Invesco China Real Estate ETF	TAO	NYSE Arca	C-	C-	C-	Down	24.71	30.80	23.45	Y	Greater China Equity (Real Estate)
● Invesco China Small Cap ETF	HAO	NYSE Arca	D+	D+	C-	Down	23.70	27.79	21.99	Y	Greater China Equity (Pacific Stock)
● Invesco China Technology ETF	CQQQ	NYSE Arca	D+	D+	C-	Down	45.76	51.96	37.92	Y	Greater China Equity (Technology)
● Invesco Cleantech™ ETF	PZD	NYSE Arca	C	C	D+		44.61	46.01	35.15	Y	Industrials Sector Equity (Technology)
Invesco Conservative Multi-Asset Allocation ETF	PSMC	BATS	C	C	D+	Up	13.00	13.23	11.98	Y	Cautious Allocation (Asset Allocation)
Invesco Corporate Income Defensive ETF	IHYD	NYSE Arca	D+	D+	D+		25.87	25.92	24.29	Y	US Fixed Income (Corp Bond-High Yld)
Invesco Corporate Income Value ETF	IHYV	NYSE Arca	D	D+	D		24.68	25.06	23.12	Y	US Fixed Income (Corp Bond-High Yld)
● Invesco CurrencyShares® Australian Dollar Trust	FXA	NYSE Arca	D	D	C-		67.51	73.59	67.25	Y	Currency (Worldwide Bond)
● Invesco CurrencyShares® British Pound Sterling Trust	FXB	NYSE Arca	D	D	C-	Down	119.25	129.05	116.66	Y	Currency (Worldwide Bond)
● Invesco CurrencyShares® Canadian Dollar Trust	FXC	NYSE Arca	C-	D+	C-	Up	74.51	77.02	72.20	Y	Currency (Worldwide Bond)
Invesco CurrencyShares® Chinese Renminbi Trust	FXCH	NYSE Arca	D	D	D	Up	68.13	73.15	67.85	Y	Currency (Growth & Inc)
● Invesco CurrencyShares® Euro Currency Trust	FXE	NYSE Arca	D	D	C-	Down	103.56	110.99	103.56	Y	Currency (Worldwide Bond)
● Invesco CurrencyShares® Japanese Yen Trust	FXY	NYSE Arca	C	C	C	Up	87.95	90.37	83.60	Y	Currency (Worldwide Bond)
Invesco CurrencyShares® Singapore Dollar Trust	FXSG	NYSE Arca	D+	C-	D	Up	70.89	72.95	70.40	Y	Currency (Growth & Inc)
Invesco CurrencyShares® Swedish Krona Trust	FXS	NYSE Arca	D	D-	D		94.03	106.50	94.03	Y	Currency (Worldwide Bond)
● Invesco CurrencyShares® Swiss Franc Trust	FXF	NYSE Arca	D+	D+	C-	Up	92.62	95.74	90.99	Y	Currency (Worldwide Bond)
● Invesco DB Agriculture Fund	DBA	NYSE Arca	D	D-	D		15.86	17.77	14.84	Y	Commodities Specified (Natl Res)
● Invesco DB Base Metals Fund	DBB	NYSE Arca	D	D	D+	Down	14.77	17.30	14.45	Y	Commodities Specified (Prec Metals)
● Invesco DB Commodity Index Tracking Fund	DBC	NYSE Arca	D+	D+	C-	Down	15.04	18.54	14.39	Y	Commodities Broad Basket (Natl Res)
● Invesco DB Energy Fund	DBE	NYSE Arca	C-	D+	C-		13.38	18.74	12.16	Y	Commodities Specified (Natl Res)
Invesco DB G10 Currency Harvest Fund	DBV	NYSE Arca	C-	C	D+	Up	24.48	24.99	23.15	Y	Currency (Growth & Inc)
● Invesco DB Gold Fund	DGL	NYSE Arca	C	C	C-	Up	44.96	47.45	37.34	Y	Commodities Specified (Prec Metals)
● Invesco DB Oil Fund	DBO	NYSE Arca	C-	D+	C-		9.46	14.02	8.12	Y	Commodities Specified (Natl Res)
● Invesco DB Precious Metals Fund	DBP	NYSE Arca	C	C	C-	Up	40.98	43.96	34.26	Y	Commodities Specified (Prec Metals)
Invesco DB Silver Fund	DBS	NYSE Arca	D+	C-	D+	Up	24.90	28.58	21.03	Y	Commodities Specified (Prec Metals)
Invesco DB US Dollar Index Bearish Fund	UDN	NYSE Arca	D	D	C-		20.20	21.55	20.20	Y	Currency (Growth & Inc)
● Invesco DB US Dollar Index Bullish Fund	UUP	NYSE Arca	C+	C	C+		27.10	27.10	25.19	Y	Currency (Growth & Inc)
● Invesco Defensive Equity ETF	DEF	NYSE Arca	C	B-	C-	Down	54.20	54.45	41.71	Y	US Equity Large Cap Blend (Growth)
● Invesco Dividend Achievers™ ETF	PFM	NAS CM	C+	B-	C	Up	29.56	29.84	23.52	Y	US Equity Large Cap Value (Equity-Income)
★ Invesco Dow Jones Industrial Average Dividend ETF	DJD	NYSE Arca	B-	B	C	Up	37.23	38.05	31.25	Y	US Equity Large Cap Value (Growth & Inc)
● Invesco DWA Basic Materials Momentum ETF	PYZ	NAS CM	C-	C	C	Up	58.19	69.15	50.28	Y	Natural Resources (Unaligned)
★ Invesco DWA Consumer Cyclicals Momentum ETF	PEZ	NAS CM	B-	B	C	Up	52.75	59.29	43.46	Y	Consumer Goods & Svcs (Unaligned)
★ Invesco DWA Consumer Staples Momentum ETF	PSL	NAS CM	B-	B	C	Up	72.10	75.95	62.43	Y	Consumer Goods & Svcs (Unaligned)
● Invesco DWA Developed Markets Momentum ETF	PIZ	NAS CM	C-	C-	C-		26.38	27.60	22.12	Y	Global Equity Large Cap (Foreign Stock)
● Invesco DWA Emerging Markets Momentum ETF	PIE	NAS CM	C-	C-	C-		17.50	18.16	15.34	Y	Global Emerg Mkts Equity (Div Emerg Mkts)
Invesco DWA Energy Momentum ETF	PXI	NAS CM	D	D+	D		26.04	45.54	23.86	Y	Energy Sector Equity (Natl Res)
★ Invesco DWA Financial Momentum ETF	PFI	NAS CM	B	B+	C	Up	37.43	38.84	27.13	Y	Financials Sector Equity (Financial)
● Invesco DWA Healthcare Momentum ETF	PTH	NAS CM	C	C	C-		78.22	97.20	64.96	Y	Healthcare Sector Equity (Health)
★ Invesco DWA Industrials Momentum ETF	PRN	NAS CM	B	B	C	Up	65.57	69.69	47.61	Y	Industrials Sector Equity (Unaligned)
★ Invesco DWA Momentum ETF	PDP	NAS CM	B-	B-	C+	Up	60.90	63.22	45.29	Y	US Equity Mid Cap (Growth)
● Invesco DWA NASDAQ Momentum ETF	DWAQ	NAS CM	C-	C	D+		107.72	123.33	80.71	Y	US Equity Mid Cap (Growth)
● Invesco DWA SmallCap Momentum ETF	DWAS	NAS CM	C-	C	C-	Down	50.04	56.36	40.08	Y	US Equity Small Cap (Small Company)
Invesco DWA Tactical Multi-Asset Income ETF	DWIN	NAS CM	C	C	D+	Up	25.65	25.89	23.61	Y	Cautious Allocation (Multi-Asset Global)
● Invesco DWA Tactical Sector Rotation ETF	DWTR	NAS CM	C	C	D+		31.38	32.98	22.70	Y	US Equity Mid Cap (Growth & Inc)
● Invesco DWA Technology Momentum ETF	PTF	NAS CM	C	B-	D+	Down	68.59	80.31	48.33	Y	Technology Sector Equity (Technology)
★ Invesco DWA Utilities Momentum ETF	PUI	NAS CM	B-	B	C+		35.02	35.16	28.07	Y	Utilities Sector Equity (Utility)
● Invesco Dynamic Biotechnology & Genome ETF	PBE	NYSE Arca	C	C+	D+		47.37	58.75	43.44	Y	Healthcare Sector Equity (Health)
★ Invesco Dynamic Building & Construction ETF	PKB	NYSE Arca	B	B+	C	Up	32.64	32.64	22.38	Y	Industrials Sector Equity (Unaligned)
Invesco Dynamic Energy Exploration & Production ETF	PXE	NYSE Arca	C	C+	D	Up	15.14	28.22	13.58	Y	Energy Sector Equity (Natl Res)
★ Invesco Dynamic Food & Beverage ETF	PBJ	NYSE Arca	B-	B	C	Up	35.18	35.65	28.60	Y	Consumer Goods & Svcs (Unaligned)
● Invesco Dynamic Large Cap Growth ETF	PWB	NYSE Arca	C+	B-	C	Up	48.34	50.26	38.42	Y	US Equity Large Cap Growth (Growth)
● Invesco Dynamic Large Cap Value ETF	PWV	NYSE Arca	C	C+	C		38.33	39.10	30.83	Y	US Equity Large Cap Value (Growth)

★ Expanded analysis of this fund is included in Section II: Analysis of All BUY Rated Funds.   ● Expanded analysis of this fund is included in Section III: Analysis of All Rated Funds with Assets over $50 million.

	TOTAL RETURNS & PERFORMANCE								ASSETS		ASSET ALLOCATION & TURNOVER					VALUATION	
3-Month Total Return	6-Month Total Return	1-Year Total Return	3-Year Total Return	5-Year Total Return	Dividend Yield (TTM)	Expense Ratio	3-Yr Std Deviation	Effective Duration	NAV	Total Assets (MIL)	%Cash	%Stocks	%Bonds	%Other	Turnover Ratio	Premium/ Discount 1-Year Avg	Inception Date
-13.38	-18.69	0.35	28.20	51.81	7.65	0.7	20.23		24.79	48.6	0	100	0	0		-0.05	Dec-07
-7.30	-11.37	-6.16	9.41	9.85	5.01	0.75	17.25		23.85	54.9	0	100	0	0		-0.25	Jan-08
-0.92	-8.32	-3.87	16.66	37.90	0.37	0.7	23.09		45.91	498.1	0	100	0	0		-0.02	Dec-09
-2.90	4.35	3.84	37.63	59.60	0.46	0.68	15.99		44.53	191.5	0	100	0	0	21	0.12	Oct-06
1.53	4.29	7.22			5.12	0.39		5.22	12.97	3.9	2	20	70	0	38	0.15	Feb-17
1.45	3.84	7.10			4.43	0.23		2.63	25.73	12.9	1	0	99	0		0.23	Jul-18
0.63	3.00	4.80			6.54	0.23		4.06	24.60	12.3	0	0	100	0		0.07	Jul-18
-3.15	-5.10	-6.24	-9.67	-18.48	0.82	0.4	7.96		67.44	97.8	100	0	0	0	0	-0.12	Jun-06
-2.60	-6.27	-5.54	-5.81	-24.97	0	0.4	8.12		119.49	155.3	100	0	0	0	0	-0.13	Jun-06
-0.85	1.29	-1.62	0.03	-15.25	0.76	0.4	6.98		74.54	115.5	100	0	0	0	0	-0.08	Jun-06
-4.06	-6.09	-4.00	-7.38	-14.82	0	0.4	5.51		68.37	3.4	100	0	0	0		-0.16	Sep-11
-3.92	-3.23	-6.89	-5.31	-16.58	0	0.4	6.37		103.56	253.7	100	0	0	0	0	-0.07	Dec-05
0.10	2.63	4.56	-7.70	-0.96	0	0.4	7.8		88.02	220.0	100	0	0	0	0	-0.03	Feb-07
-1.84	-1.64	-0.41	-0.78	-7.90	0.75	0.4	4.15		71.13	3.6	100	0	0	0		-0.24	Feb-13
-5.53	-6.52	-11.04	-17.11	-31.63	0	0.4	9.18		94.04	14.1	100	0	0	0	0	-0.07	Jun-06
-1.54	-0.54	-3.17	-6.10	-9.06	0	0.4	6.5		92.72	143.7	100	0	0	0	0	-0.07	Jun-06
-4.23	-4.34	-5.82	-19.95	-37.52	1.13	0.85	9.48		15.86	383.9	41	0	8	50		-0.07	Jan-07
-3.60	-13.05	-10.47	7.20	-10.45	0	0.75	15.12		14.82	118.6	48	0	4	48	0	-0.14	Jan-07
-4.65	-6.57	-16.90	1.13	-34.23	1.26	0.85	12.14		15.01	1,405	45	0	6	44	0	-0.13	Feb-06
-7.19	-10.49	-26.87	9.16	-49.20	1.56	0.75	21.17		13.34	56.0	34	0	15	50		-0.15	Jan-07
0.24	-0.43	2.19	-0.68	-3.41	1.13	0.75	5.64		24.49	24.5	100	0	0	0	0	-0.07	Sep-06
5.61	13.13	21.75	6.95	12.73	1.29	0.75	10.94		44.77	170.1	47	0	3	0	0	0.01	Jan-07
-8.06	-11.84	-30.93	7.15	-64.31	1.43	0.75	25.38		9.41	250.4	50	0	1	49		-0.17	Jan-07
6.75	12.71	20.40	2.01	8.10	1.1	0.75	11.68		40.78	130.5	48	0	1	10		-0.03	Jan-07
11.55	10.80	14.50	-16.57	-10.57	1.31	0.75	16.96		24.78	14.9	49	0	0	51		-0.09	Jan-07
-2.73	-2.44	-4.72	-7.21	-18.38	1.31	0.75	5.68		20.21	36.4	100	0	0	0		0.00	Feb-07
3.53	4.12	8.21	11.10	19.85	1.02	0.75	5.75		27.09	330.5	89	0	11	0		-0.03	Feb-07
1.68	7.50	9.78	46.59	62.01	1.13	0.59	10.97		54.18	254.6	0	100	0	0	136	0.03	Dec-06
3.12	7.18	9.06	39.15	60.16	1.93	0.54	10.91		29.55	307.3	0	100	0	0	13	0.05	Sep-05
0.57	2.64	5.46	47.98		2.75	0.07	11.22		37.22	81.9	0	100	0	0	20	0.11	Dec-15
-3.77	-2.49	-14.29	3.59	14.67	1.4	0.6	19.28		58.21	55.3	0	100	0	0	89	-0.13	Oct-06
-5.60	-4.30	-10.71	26.13	35.50	0.1	0.6	17.22		52.80	31.7	0	100	0	0		-0.02	Oct-06
-0.11	2.06	1.60	31.14	63.06	0.53	0.6	9.74		72.08	205.4	0	100	0	0		-0.02	Oct-06
-2.40	2.61	-2.62	16.41	16.89	1.34	0.8	12.76		26.44	201.0	0	100	0	0	94	-0.15	Dec-07
-0.55	4.03	0.74	16.17	3.52	2.35	0.9	13.56		17.59	162.7	0	100	0	0	163	-0.34	Dec-07
-12.54	-19.38	-40.61	-35.19	-50.91	2.25	0.6	28.23		25.99	35.1	1	99	0	0		-0.06	Oct-06
-0.12	11.15	11.21	27.03	42.63	1.09	0.6	14		37.36	65.4	0	100	0	0		-0.05	Oct-06
-11.49	-0.89	-19.47	48.62	60.51	0	0.6	25		78.25	140.8	0	100	0	0		-0.08	Oct-06
-2.06	5.76	2.98	37.24	50.48	0.43	0.6	16.06		65.55	131.1	0	100	0	0		-0.15	Oct-06
0.39	6.77	2.86	45.18	60.78	0.26	0.62	13.66		60.92	1,706	0	100	0	0	82	-0.02	Mar-07
-9.63	-2.14	-6.15	40.34	65.77	0	0.6	18.89		107.69	59.2	0	100	0	0		0.12	May-03
-7.82	-1.21	-11.11	31.02	44.32	0.03	0.6	19.37		50.05	302.8	0	100	0	0		-0.08	Jul-12
1.99	4.91	8.86	7.51		5.8	0.61	5.08	6.67	25.60	42.2	5	0	75	0		0.02	Mar-16
0.28	6.02	0.86	26.80		0.56	0.75	15.7		31.40	65.9	0	100	0	0		-0.15	Oct-15
-6.79	0.49	5.49	65.89	105.27	0	0.6	21.01		68.58	312.0	0	100	0	0		-0.09	Oct-06
8.36	10.27	24.66	46.47	81.91	1.56	0.6	10.86		34.99	297.4	0	100	0	0		0.09	Oct-05
-11.92	-14.14	-19.36	14.03	5.51	0	0.57	22.44		47.42	213.4	0	100	0	0	117	-0.05	Jun-05
5.13	16.67	10.82	27.84	62.31	0.42	0.6	19.16		32.66	112.7	0	100	0	0	148	-0.04	Oct-05
-12.34	-21.89	-44.58	-26.46	-46.79	1.7	0.63	28.65		15.11	27.2	0	100	0	0	110	-0.10	Oct-05
4.90	6.88	10.38	10.93	33.30	1.09	0.63	11.28		35.17	73.9	0	100	0	0	122	-0.02	Jun-05
-0.59	1.28	0.53	56.20	86.40	0.86	0.55	12.81		48.36	752.0	0	100	0	0		-0.02	Mar-05
3.64	7.91	4.96	29.91	42.87	2.27	0.55	12.97		38.34	945.1	0	100	0	0		-0.02	Mar-05

Fund Name	Ticker Symbol	Traded On	Overall Rating	Reward Rating	Risk Rating	Recent Up/ Downgrade	Price as of 9/30/2019	52-Week High	52-Week Low	Open to New Investors	Category & (Prospectus Objective)
★ Invesco Dynamic Leisure and Entertainment ETF	PEJ	NYSE Arca	B-	B	C	Up	42.55	46.42	38.07	Y	Consumer Goods & Svcs (Unaligned)
● Invesco Dynamic Market ETF	PWC	NYSE Arca	C	C	C-	Up	94.91	106.09	83.08	Y	US Equity Mid Cap (Growth)
Invesco Dynamic Media ETF	PBS	NYSE Arca	C+	B	C-	Up	31.38	35.15	26.83	Y	Consumer Goods & Svcs (Comm)
● Invesco Dynamic Networking ETF	PXQ	NYSE Arca	C+	B	C	Up	56.33	63.15	45.28	Y	Technology Sector Equity (Technology)
Invesco Dynamic Oil & Gas Services ETF	PXJ	NYSE Arca	D+	C-	D	Up	4.74	10.49	4.45	Y	Energy Sector Equity (Natl Res)
● Invesco Dynamic Pharmaceuticals ETF	PJP	NYSE Arca	C	C+	C-	Up	56.66	72.73	55.49	Y	Healthcare Sector Equity (Health)
★ Invesco Dynamic Retail ETF	PMR	NYSE Arca	B-	B	C-	Up	39.23	41.04	31.76	Y	Consumer Goods & Svcs (Unaligned)
★ Invesco Dynamic Semiconductors ETF	PSI	NYSE Arca	B-	B	C-	Up	57.81	60.29	41.12	Y	Technology Sector Equity (Technology)
● Invesco Dynamic Software ETF	PSJ	NYSE Arca	C+	B	C	Down	93.08	104.07	68.31	Y	Technology Sector Equity (Technology)
Invesco Emerging Markets Debt Defensive ETF	IEMD	NYSE Arca	D	D+	D		25.90	26.01	24.83	Y	Emerging Mkts Fixed Inc (Div Emerg Mkts)
Invesco Emerging Markets Debt Value ETF	IEMV	NYSE Arca	D	D+	D		26.77	26.98	24.62	Y	Emerging Mkts Fixed Inc (Div Emerg Mkts)
Invesco Emerging Markets Revenue ETF	REEM	BATS	D	D+	D		23.46	26.60	22.48	Y	Global Emerg Mkts Equity (Div Emerg Mkts)
● Invesco Emerging Markets Sovereign Debt ETF	PCY	NYSE Arca	C+	B-	C+		29.15	30.00	25.56	Y	Emerging Mkts Fixed Inc (Worldwide Bond)
Invesco Emerging Markets Ultra Dividend Revenue ETF	REDV	NYSE Arca	D	D	D		22.34	25.31	21.73	Y	Global Emerg Mkts Equity (Div Emerg Mkts)
Invesco ESG Revenue ETF	ESGL	NYSE Arca	C-	C	D		31.95	32.59	26.60	Y	US Equity Large Cap Value (Growth & Inc)
● Invesco Financial Preferred ETF	PGF	NYSE Arca	C+	C+	C+		18.78	18.86	17.04	Y	US Fixed Income (Financial)
● Invesco Frontier Markets ETF	FRN	NYSE Arca	C-	C	C-		13.63	14.79	12.00	Y	Global Emerg Mkts Equity (Div Emerg Mkts)
● Invesco FTSE International Low Beta Equal Weight ETF	IDLB	NAS CM	C-	C-	C-		27.43	29.45	25.28	Y	Global Equity Large Cap (Growth & Inc)
● Invesco FTSE RAFI Developed Markets ex-U.S. ETF	PXF	NYSE Arca	C	D+	C+	Up	39.65	43.34	36.29	Y	Global Equity Large Cap (Foreign Stock)
● Invesco FTSE RAFI Developed Markets ex-U.S. Small-Mid ETF	PDN	NYSE Arca	D+	D+	C-	Down	29.47	32.71	26.23	Y	Globa Eq Mid/Small Cap (Foreign Stock)
● Invesco FTSE RAFI Emerging Markets ETF	PXH	NYSE Arca	C	C	C+		20.08	22.18	19.25	Y	Global Emerg Mkts Equity (Div Emerg Mkts)
● Invesco FTSE RAFI US 1000 ETF	PRF	NYSE Arca	C+	C	C+	Up	117.86	119.73	95.78	Y	US Equity Large Cap Value (Growth)
● Invesco FTSE RAFI US 1500 Small-Mid ETF	PRFZ	NAS CM	C-	C-	C-		126.92	140.77	107.24	Y	US Equity Small Cap (Growth)
● Invesco Fundamental High Yield® Corporate Bond ETF	PHB	NYSE Arca	C+	C+	C+		19.03	19.16	17.49	Y	US Fixed Income (Corp Bond-High Yld)
● Invesco Fundamental Investment Grade Corporate Bond ETF	PFIG	NYSE Arca	C	C+	C-		26.19	26.38	24.40	Y	US Fixed Income (Corp Bond - Gen)
Invesco Global Clean Energy ETF	PBD	NYSE Arca	C	C	D+	Up	12.17	12.77	9.75	Y	Equity Misc (Natl Res)
Invesco Global ESG Revenue ETF	ESGF	NYSE Arca	C-	C-	D+	Up	29.13	30.72	25.72	Y	Global Equity Large Cap (Growth & Inc)
● Invesco Global Listed Private Equity ETF	PSP	NYSE Arca	C	C	C+		11.82	12.34	9.72	Y	Financials Sector Equity (Growth)
Invesco Global Revenue ETF	RGLB	BATS	D+	C-	D	Up	25.60	27.29	22.97	Y	Global Equity Large Cap (Growth & Inc)
● Invesco Global Short Term High Yield Bond ETF	PGHY	NYSE Arca	C	C	C-		22.91	23.36	22.65	Y	Global Fixed Income (Worldwide Bond)
● Invesco Global Water ETF	PIO	NAS CM	C	C+	C-		27.88	28.36	22.13	Y	Equity Misc (Natl Res)
● Invesco Golden Dragon China ETF	PGJ	NAS CM	C	C+	D+	Up	35.61	42.73	30.68	Y	Greater China Equity (Pacific Stock)
Invesco Growth Multi-Asset Allocation ETF	PSMG	BATS	C-	C	D	Down	14.53	14.73	12.35	Y	Aggressive Allocation (Asset Allocation)
● Invesco High Yield Equity Dividend Achievers™ ETF	PEY	NAS CM	C	C	C	Down	18.31	18.58	15.14	Y	US Equity Mid Cap (Growth & Inc)
● Invesco India ETF	PIN	NYSE Arca	D+	D+	C-	Down	24.22	25.96	21.45	Y	India Equity (Foreign Stock)
● Invesco Insider Sentiment ETF	NFO	NYSE Arca	C	B-	D+		70.14	70.91	53.28	Y	US Equity Mid Cap (Growth)
● Invesco International BuyBack Achievers™ ETF	IPKW	NAS CM	D+	D+	C-	Down	30.99	34.44	28.19	Y	Global Equity Large Cap (Growth)
● Invesco International Corporate Bond ETF	PICB	NYSE Arca	C	C	C-	Up	26.20	26.70	24.84	Y	Global Fixed Income (Worldwide Bond)
● Invesco International Dividend Achievers ETF	PID	NAS CM	C	C	C+	Down	16.04	16.80	13.74	Y	Global Equity Large Cap (Foreign Stock)
Invesco International Revenue ETF	REFA	BATS	D	D+	D		24.20	26.65	22.51	Y	Global Equity Large Cap (Growth & Inc)
Invesco International Ultra Dividend Revenue ETF	RIDV	NYSE Arca	D	D	E+		22.80	24.77	21.22	Y	Global Equity Large Cap (Foreign Stock)
● Invesco Investment Grade Defensive ETF	IIGD	NYSE Arca	D+	D+	D+		26.30	26.41	24.88	Y	US Fixed Income (Corp Bond - Gen)
Invesco Investment Grade Value ETF	IIGV	NYSE Arca	D+	D+	D+		27.13	27.41	24.57	Y	US Fixed Income (Corp Bond - Gen)
★ Invesco KBW Bank ETF	KBWB	NAS CM	B-	B	C	Up	51.52	55.36	41.50		Financials Sector Equity (Financial)
● Invesco KBW High Dividend Yield Financial ETF	KBWD	NAS CM	C	C	D+		20.88	22.70	18.90		Financials Sector Equity (Financial)
● Invesco KBW Premium Yield Equity REIT ETF	KBWY	NAS CM	C	C+	D+	Up	31.23	33.29	26.11		Real Estate Sector Equity (Real Estate)
★ Invesco KBW Property & Casualty Insurance ETF	KBWP	NAS CM	B	B	C+	Up	73.94	74.04	53.39		Financials Sector Equity (Growth)
● Invesco KBW Regional Banking ETF	KBWR	NAS CM	C-	C	D+	Up	49.78	56.50	42.37		Financials Sector Equity (Financial)
Invesco LadderRite 0-5 Year Corporate Bond ETF	LDRI	NAS CM	C	C	D+		25.30	25.38	24.08		US Fixed Income (Corp Bond - Gen)
Invesco Moderately Conservative Multi-Asset Allocation ETF	PSMM	BATS	C	C	D+	Up	13.74	13.89	12.11	Y	Cautious Allocation (Asset Allocation)
Invesco MSCI Emerging Markets Equal Country Weight ETF	EWEM	NYSE Arca	D+	D+	D+	Down	30.04	32.71	29.02	Y	Global Emerg Mkts Equity (Growth)
● Invesco MSCI Global Timber ETF	CUT	NYSE Arca	D+	D+	C-	Down	26.02	32.03	23.21	Y	Natural Resources (Natl Res)

★ Expanded analysis of this fund is included in Section II: Analysis of All BUY Rated Funds. ● Expanded analysis of this fund is included in Section III: Analysis of All Rated Funds with Assets over $50 million.

	TOTAL RETURNS & PERFORMANCE								ASSETS		ASSET ALLOCATION & TURNOVER					VALUATION	
3-Month Total Return	6-Month Total Return	1-Year Total Return	3-Year Total Return	5-Year Total Return	Dividend Yield (TTM)	Expense Ratio	3-Yr Std Deviation	Effective Duration	NAV	Total Assets (Mil)	%Cash	%Stocks	%Bonds	%Other	Turnover Ratio	Premium/ Discount 1-Year Avg	Inception Date
-2.13	-1.33	-7.99	22.06	34.66	0.42	0.63	13.41		42.56	55.3	0	100	0	0	207	0.02	Jun-05
-4.29	-2.13	-9.59	30.65	44.03	0.96	0.59	13.31		94.85	147.0	0	100	0	0	240	-0.05	May-03
-6.66	-4.16	-3.44	24.79	33.06	0.4	0.63	15.53		31.38	48.6	0	100	0	0	103	0.01	Jun-05
-4.56	-5.21	-0.46	43.83	81.98	1.09	0.63	17.08		56.35	62.0	0	100	0	0	98	-0.02	Jun-05
-22.61	-35.14	-53.29	-56.42	-79.19	0.65	0.63	34.85		4.75	11.9	1	99	0	0	81	-0.04	Oct-05
-6.40	-12.66	-20.77	-5.57	0.80	1.24	0.56	17.54		56.71	354.4	0	100	0	0	81	-0.07	Jun-05
6.70	4.82	-2.78	15.38	25.92	0.68	0.63	16.8		39.18	7.8	1	99	0	0	148	-0.04	Oct-05
4.12	7.04	9.89	80.11	168.39	0.69	0.58	24.78		57.85	179.3	0	100	0	0	98	-0.05	Jun-05
-3.95	0.97	8.18	91.93	167.51	0	0.58	17.87		93.06	493.2	0	100	0	0	157	0.01	Jun-05
1.36	3.57	6.83			3.31	0.29		2.69	25.75	25.8	0	0	100	0		0.30	Jul-18
2.63	6.60	12.57			4.21	0.29		5.16	26.67	40.0	0	0	100	0		0.39	Jul-18
-6.81	-7.12	-4.72			2.89	0.46			23.44	14.1	0	100	0	0	67	0.46	Jul-17
1.12	6.58	13.66	10.44	31.19	4.85	0.5	6.97	9.33	29.21	3,566	0	0	100	0	54	-0.06	Oct-07
-6.35	-7.22	-1.20			5.31	0.46			22.25	3.3	0	100	0	0	88	0.52	Aug-18
1.64	3.05	0.94	39.09		2.43	0.4			31.93	24.0	0	100	0	0	34	0.04	Oct-16
2.96	4.79	9.43	15.94	37.62	5.32	0.62	4.72	3.41	18.74	1,543	0	1	0	0	21	0.07	Dec-06
-5.21	-0.36	5.55	27.70	-2.56	1.72	0.7	12.96		13.81	57.9	0	100	0	0		-0.23	Jun-08
-1.85	-1.01	-3.77	16.09		3.15	0.45	10.32		27.47	57.7	0	100	0	0	50	-0.35	Nov-15
-1.83	-0.73	-4.77	19.63	11.53	4.05	0.45	11.99		39.64	1,205	0	100	0	0	10	-0.03	Jun-07
-1.71	-0.94	-7.50	13.79	22.52	2.54	0.49	11.65		29.44	315.0	0	100	0	0	21	-0.20	Sep-07
-6.46	-5.02	-1.79	24.12	16.35	3.56	0.5	14.64		20.03	1,212	0	100	0	0	16	0.02	Sep-07
0.96	3.72	1.12	33.88	50.73	2.05	0.39	13.08		117.82	5,337	0	100	0	0	10	-0.03	Dec-05
-0.63	-1.08	-8.47	25.09	46.10	1.25	0.39	17.05		127.03	1,963	0	100	0	0	24	-0.03	Sep-06
1.28	3.82	6.89	14.68	23.82	4.12	0.5	3.55	3.20	19.03	753.6	1	0	99	0		-0.12	Nov-07
1.79	5.21	9.56	9.38	17.60	2.92	0.22	2.77	4.48	26.19	89.1	1	0	99	0		0.06	Sep-11
-3.54	1.43	3.91	15.81	4.01	1.98	0.75	14.98		12.19	47.9	-1	96	0	4	46	-0.34	Jun-07
-0.84	1.05	-2.66	26.30		2.68	0.45			29.00	23.2	0	100	0	0	28	0.25	Oct-16
-0.12	4.92	-1.27	32.57	46.33	3.26	1.78	13.91		11.81	205.0	6	86	0	7	64	-0.10	Oct-06
-1.89	-0.44	-3.74			2.58	0.43			25.60	12.8	0	100	0	0	24	-0.11	Jul-17
0.02	1.35	3.26	11.27	23.92	5.29	0.35	1.74	1.15	22.89	231.2	10	0	90	0	42	0.00	Jun-13
-0.10	3.70	9.93	31.07	33.17	1.49	0.75	12.33		27.94	188.6	0	100	0	0	34	-0.26	Jun-07
-6.61	-13.91	-6.67	12.48	28.65	0.2	0.7	24.38		35.75	171.6	0	100	0	0	36	-0.16	Dec-04
0.55	3.78	4.71			2.44	0.39		6.66	14.51	4.4	1	79	20	0	21	0.12	Feb-17
1.85	3.68	6.43	28.88	77.84	3.8	0.53	12.37		18.31	876.3	0	100	0	0	50	-0.01	Dec-04
-4.94	-5.09	1.83	19.68	16.84	1.14	0.82	15.86		24.22	135.6	0	100	0	0	27	-0.20	Mar-08
1.12	6.87	6.57	46.60	63.56	0.84	0.66	11.3		70.14	70.2	0	100	0	0	116	-0.01	Sep-06
-2.52	-1.77	-7.12	16.36	38.44	3.02	0.55	13.56		30.97	148.7	0	100	0	0	121	-0.19	Feb-14
-1.07	1.04	2.92	3.30	-0.62	1.52	0.5	7.08	7.01	26.26	109.0	1	0	97	0	12	-0.21	Jun-10
-1.25	2.75	5.20	22.35	5.73	3.86	0.54	11.51		16.06	719.6	0	100	0	0	47	-0.08	Sep-05
-2.30	-1.39	-6.32			3.12	0.42			24.14	12.1	0	100	0	0	21	-0.06	Jul-17
-3.24	-1.38	-4.10			3.81	0.42			22.82	2.3	0	100	0	0	81	0.08	Aug-18
1.57	4.20	7.96			2.85	0.13		3.58	26.21	70.8	0	0	100	0		0.18	Jul-18
2.42	7.33	12.25			3.42	0.13		6.16	27.03	39.2	-1	0	101	0		0.29	Jul-18
1.73	5.27	-2.16	49.98	55.78	2.56	0.35	22.75		51.51	535.7	0	100	0	0		-0.04	Nov-11
-0.86	-0.85	0.19	22.58	29.45	8.76	2.42	15.49		20.85	281.5	-1	101	0	0		0.00	Dec-10
6.48	4.17	0.21	7.45	40.53	6.16	0.35	19.31		31.26	331.4	0	100	0	0		-0.01	Dec-10
4.56	19.12	20.07	56.60	111.54	1.95	0.35	11.4		73.82	118.1	0	100	0	0		0.03	Dec-10
-1.11	0.24	-7.54	21.13	51.54	2.55	0.35	23.69		49.63	64.5	0	100	0	0		0.07	Nov-11
0.95	2.79	5.65	7.48	11.29	2.54	0.22	1.31		25.31	10.1	6	0	94	0		-0.28	Sep-14
1.33	4.46	6.97			2.65	0.39		5.52	13.71	5.5	1	40	53	0	32	0.18	Feb-17
-6.62	-4.64	-2.72	12.00	0.01	2.7	0.7	13.15		30.07	12.0	0	100	0	0	51	-0.01	Dec-10
-4.75	-7.03	-16.01	12.27	24.77	3.17	0.55	16.53		26.03	126.2	0	100	0	0		-0.12	Nov-07

Fund Name	Ticker Symbol	Traded On	Overall Rating	Reward Rating	Risk Rating	Recent Up/Downgrade	Price as of 9/30/2019	52-Week High	52-Week Low	Open to New Investors	Category & (Prospectus Objective)
Invesco Multi-Factor Core Fixed Income ETF	IMFC	NYSE Arca	D	D+	D		26.34	26.54	24.68	Y	US Fixed Income (Multisector Bond)
Invesco Multi-Factor Core Plus fixed Income ETF	IMFP	NYSE Arca	D	D+	D		26.48	26.66	24.70	Y	US Fixed Income (Multisector Bond)
Invesco Multi-Factor Defensive Core Fixed Income ETF	IMFD	BATS	U	U	U		25.67	25.83	25.16	Y	US Fixed Income (Growth & Inc)
Invesco Multi-Factor Income ETF	IMFI	BATS	U	U	U		26.23	26.40	25.03	Y	US Fixed Income (Income)
Invesco NASDAQ Internet ETF	PNQI	NAS CM	C+	B	C-	Up	130.06	144.17	102.97	Y	Technology Sector Equity (Technology)
Invesco National AMT-Free Municipal Bond ETF	PZA	NYSE Arca	C+	C+	C+		26.54	26.84	24.38	Y	US Muni Fixed Inc (Muni Bond - Natl)
Invesco New York AMT-Free Municipal Bond ETF	PZT	NYSE Arca	C	C+	C-		25.44	25.78	23.24	Y	US Muni Fixed Inc (Muni Bond - Single State)
Invesco Optimum Yield Div Commod Strategy No K-1 ETF	PDBC	NAS CM	D+	D+	C-	Down	15.62	19.39	14.98	Y	Commodities Broad Basket (Growth)
Invesco Preferred ETF	PGX	NYSE Arca	C+	B-	C+	Down	15.02	15.03	13.18	Y	US Fixed Income (Growth & Inc)
Invesco PureBeta 0-5 Yr US TIPS ETF	PBTP	BATS	D+	C-	D	Up	24.83	25.22	24.30	Y	US Fixed Income (Income)
Invesco PureBeta FTSE Developed ex-North America ETF	PBDM	BATS	D	D	E		23.51	24.41	21.02	Y	Global Equity Large Cap (Foreign Stock)
Invesco PureBeta FTSE Emerging Markets ETF	PBEE	BATS	D	D+	E		22.91	25.03	21.37	Y	Global Emerg Mkts Equity (Div Emerg Mkts)
Invesco PureBeta MSCI USA ETF	PBUS	BATS	D+	C	D		29.59	30.20	23.49	Y	US Equity Large Cap Blend (Growth & Inc)
Invesco PureBeta MSCI USA Small Cap ETF	PBSM	BATS	D	D	D		26.56	29.50	22.37	Y	US Equity Small Cap (Small Company)
Invesco PureBeta US Aggregate Bond ETF	PBND	BATS	C-	C-	D+	Up	25.76	26.03	23.65	Y	US Fixed Income (Growth & Inc)
★ Invesco QQQ Trust	QQQ	NAS CM	B-	B-	B-		188.81	195.29	143.50	Y	US Equity Large Cap Growth (Growth)
Invesco RAFI™ Strategic Developed ex-US ETF	ISDX	NAS CM	D+	D+	C-		24.57	27.06	22.25	Y	Global Equity Large Cap (Growth)
Invesco RAFI™ Strategic Developed ex-US Small Company ETF	ISDS	NAS CM	D	D	E		22.72	25.72	20.49	Y	Globa Eq Mid/Small Cap (Small Company)
Invesco RAFI™ Strategic Emerging Markets ETF	ISEM	NAS CM	D	D	D+		24.16	27.21	23.33	Y	Global Emerg Mkts Equity (Div Emerg Mkts)
Invesco RAFI™ Strategic US ETF	IUS	NAS CM	C-	D+	C-		25.53	26.08	21.65	Y	US Equity Large Cap Blend (Growth)
Invesco RAFI™ Strategic US Small Company ETF	IUSS	NAS CM	D+	D+	D+		23.26	24.89	19.40	Y	US Equity Small Cap (Small Company)
Invesco Raymond James SB-1 Equity ETF	RYJ	NYSE Arca	D+	C-	D+	Down	42.56	48.36	34.27	Y	US Equity Mid Cap (Growth)
Invesco Russell 1000 Enhanced Equal Weight ETF	USEQ	BATS	C-	C	D+	Up	28.51	28.91	22.78	Y	US Equity Large Cap Value (Growth & Inc)
Invesco Russell 1000 Equal Weight ETF	EQAL	NYSE Arca	C	C	C-		32.07	33.16	26.31		US Equity Mid Cap (Growth)
Invesco Russell 1000 Low Beta Equal Weight ETF	USLB	NAS CM	C	C	D+		33.59	33.88	27.11		US Equity Mid Cap (Growth & Inc)
Invesco Russell 1000® Dynamic Multifactor ETF	OMFL	BATS	C-	C	C-		31.03	31.97	23.84	Y	US Equity Large Cap Blend (Growth)
Invesco Russell 1000® Low Volatility Factor ETF	OVOL	BATS	C-	C	D	Up	29.86	30.04	23.37	Y	US Equity Large Cap Blend (Growth & Inc)
Invesco Russell 1000® Momentum Factor ETF	OMOM	BATS	D+	C	D	Up	28.92	29.36	22.70	Y	US Equity Large Cap Growth (Growth & Inc)
Invesco Russell 1000® Quality Factor ETF	OQAL	BATS	D+	C	D-	Up	29.13	29.79	23.22	Y	US Equity Large Cap Blend (Growth & Inc)
Invesco Russell 1000® Size Factor ETF	OSIZ	BATS	D	C-	E+		27.83	28.86	22.28	Y	US Equity Large Cap Blend (Growth & Inc)
Invesco Russell 1000® Value Factor ETF	OVLU	BATS	D+	C-	D	Up	27.30	27.79	22.51	Y	US Equity Large Cap Value (Growth & Inc)
Invesco Russell 1000® Yield Factor ETF	OYLD	BATS	C-	C	D	Up	27.37	27.68	22.83	Y	US Equity Large Cap Blend (Growth & Inc)
Invesco Russell 2000® Dynamic Multifactor ETF	OMFS	BATS	D	D	D+		26.99	28.30	22.06	Y	US Equity Small Cap (Growth)
Invesco S&P 100 Equal Weight ETF	EQWL	NYSE Arca	C	C+	D+		57.16	58.22	45.99	Y	US Equity Large Cap Blend (Growth)
Invesco S&P 500 BuyWrite ETF	PBP	NYSE Arca	C	C	C-		21.65	22.76	19.12	Y	Long/Short Equity (Growth)
Invesco S&P 500 GARP ETF	SPGP	NYSE Arca	C	C+	C-		56.42	58.76	42.07	Y	US Equity Large Cap Growth (Growth)
Invesco S&P 500 Minimum Variance ETF	SPMV	BATS	C-	C	D	Up	30.70	30.83	24.28	Y	US Equity Large Cap Blend (Growth & Inc)
Invesco S&P 500 Minimum Variance ETF	RWL	NYSE Arca	C	C	C-		53.95	55.06	44.16	Y	US Equity Large Cap Value (Growth)
Invesco S&P 500 Value with Momentum ETF	SPVM	NYSE Arca	C	C	D+		40.09	41.21	32.62	Y	US Equity Large Cap Value (Growth)
Invesco S&P 500® Downside Hedged ETF	PHDG	NYSE Arca	C-	C-	C-	Down	27.44	29.81	26.00	Y	Long/Short Equity (Growth & Inc)
Invesco S&P 500® Enhanced Value ETF	SPVU	NYSE Arca	C	C+	D+		35.10	36.28	29.09	Y	US Equity Large Cap Value (Growth)
Invesco S&P 500® Equal Weight Communication Services ETF	EWCO	NYSE Arca	U	U	U		24.89	26.36	21.95	Y	Communications Sector Equity (Comm)
Invesco S&P 500® Equal Weight Consumer Discretionary ETF	RCD	NYSE Arca	C	C	D+		104.48	109.19	84.82	Y	Consumer Goods & Svcs (Unaligned)
★ Invesco S&P 500® Equal Weight Consumer Staples ETF	RHS	NYSE Arca	B-	B	C	Up	140.40	140.40	112.22	Y	Consumer Goods & Svcs (Unaligned)
Invesco S&P 500® Equal Weight Energy ETF	RYE	NYSE Arca	C-	C	D	Up	44.38	63.78	40.29	Y	Energy Sector Equity (Natl Res)
Invesco S&P 500® Equal Weight ETF	RSP	NYSE Arca	C	C	C+	Down	108.08	110.18	86.19	Y	US Equity Large Cap Blend (Growth)
Invesco S&P 500® Equal Weight Financials ETF	RYF	NYSE Arca	C	C	C-		43.65	45.22	34.13	Y	Financials Sector Equity (Financial)
Invesco S&P 500® Equal Weight Health Care ETF	RYH	NYSE Arca	C	C	C-		195.97	206.12	165.92	Y	Healthcare Sector Equity (Health)
Invesco S&P 500® Equal Weight Industrials ETF	RGI	NYSE Arca	C	C+	C-		126.46	129.26	96.98	Y	Industrials Sector Equity (Unaligned)
Invesco S&P 500® Equal Weight Materials ETF	RTM	NYSE Arca	C+	B	C	Up	108.95	111.94	88.78	Y	Natural Resources (Unaligned)
★ Invesco S&P 500® Equal Weight Real Estate ETF	EWRE	NYSE Arca	B-	B	C	Up	31.84	31.94	24.98	Y	Real Estate Sector Equity (Real Estate)
Invesco S&P 500® Equal Weight Technology ETF	RYT	NYSE Arca	C	C+	C-	Down	178.82	188.04	131.48	Y	Technology Sector Equity (Technology)

★ Expanded analysis of this fund is included in Section II: Analysis of All BUY Rated Funds. ● Expanded analysis of this fund is included in Section III: Analysis of All Rated Funds with Assets over $50 million.

3-Month Total Return	6-Month Total Return	1-Year Total Return	3-Year Total Return	5-Year Total Return	Dividend Yield (TTM)	Expense Ratio	3-Yr Std Deviation	Effective Duration	NAV	Total Assets (MIL)	%Cash	%Stocks	%Bonds	%Other	Turnover Ratio	Premium/ Discount 1-Year Avg	Inception Date
1.84	4.52	8.91			3.08	0.12		4.06	26.26	26.3	0	0	100	0		0.04	Jul-18
2.17	5.33	9.87			3.63	0.16		4.60	26.40	52.8	0	0	100	0		0.11	Jul-18
0.90	2.50					0.12		2.20	25.68	20.5	0	0	100	0		-0.02	Dec-18
1.52	4.23					0.16		3.52	26.24	42.0	0	0	100	0		-0.01	Dec-18
-6.49	-5.03	-2.91	48.44	94.35	0	0.62	18.83		130.01	520.1	0	100	0	0		0.01	Jun-08
2.17	4.96	9.94	11.51	24.08	2.87	0.28	3.95	8.55	26.50	2,020	1	0	99	0		-0.01	Oct-07
2.15	5.10	10.23	11.00	22.18	2.75	0.28	3.91	7.98	25.41	80.0	4	0	96	0		-0.07	Oct-07
-4.99	-7.03	-17.63	-0.16		0.97	0.58	12.48		15.59	1,540	32	0	46	22		-0.09	Nov-14
3.78	5.71	11.31	17.38	38.44	5.41	0.52	5.74	3.85	14.98	5,481	0	1	0	0		0.07	Jan-08
0.23	1.86	3.27			1.97	0.07		2.63	24.81	7.4	0	0	100	0	19	0.12	Sep-17
-1.93	0.62	-2.40			3.27	0.07			23.45	2.3	0	100	0	0	7	0.79	Sep-17
-5.20	-4.25	0.40			2.61	0.14			22.91	2.3	0	100	0	0	16	0.25	Sep-17
0.53	4.41	3.49			1.57	0.04			29.60	3.0	0	100	0	0		-0.03	Sep-17
-1.94	-0.45	-4.24			1.24	0.06			26.55	2.7	1	99	0	0		0.12	Sep-17
2.32	5.89	10.37			2.72	0.05		5.61	25.74	25.7	0	0	98	0		0.04	Sep-17
-0.03	4.06	2.31	63.28	103.88	0.82	0.2	14.9		188.77	74,717	0	100	0	0		-0.02	Mar-99
-1.47	0.48	-1.92			2.73	0.23			24.59	241.0	0	100	0	0		0.14	Sep-18
-3.32	-3.20	-10.08			1.86	0.35			22.56	14.7	0	100	0	0		-0.30	Sep-18
-6.28	-7.46	-6.52			2.64	0.35			24.14	25.3	0	100	0	0		-0.14	Sep-18
0.83	4.28	2.66			2.03	0.19			25.53	120.0	0	100	0	0		-0.91	Sep-18
-1.17	0.84	-4.73			1.15	0.23			23.21	25.5	0	100	0	0		-0.19	Sep-18
-5.80	-4.03	-10.42	19.96	33.90	1.23	0.82	18.41		42.53	152.0	0	100	0	0		0.04	May-06
0.56	3.34	2.52			2.08	0.29			28.52	17.1	0	100	0	0		-0.08	Jul-17
-1.76	-0.54	-1.64	27.90		1.52	0.2	13.51		32.05	570.5	0	100	0	0		0.03	Dec-14
2.22	5.48	4.32	33.30		1.74	0.35	11.36		33.60	109.2	0	100	0	0		-0.15	Nov-15
4.05	7.66	8.62			1.5	0.29			31.00	1,084	0	100	0	0	138	0.09	Nov-17
2.82	7.34	9.08			1.79	0.19			29.72	7.4	0	100	0	0	8	0.27	Nov-17
0.90	5.30	1.13			1.34	0.19			28.84	5.8	0	100	0	0	33	-0.30	Nov-17
0.51	3.05	2.24			1.34	0.19			29.10	5.8	0	100	0	0	22	0.04	Nov-17
-1.69	1.62	0.83			1.23	0.19			27.81	5.6	0	100	0	0	21	0.07	Nov-17
1.39	4.15	2.51			2.14	0.19			27.29	6.8	0	100	0	0	28	-0.06	Nov-17
2.23	4.51	6.66			3.01	0.19			27.37	6.8	0	100	0	0	17	-0.21	Nov-17
0.62	2.94	-1.33			1.46	0.39			26.91	13.5	1	99	0	0	189	0.15	Nov-17
0.88	4.21	3.78	45.71	65.42	2.11	0.25	12.1		57.16	60.0	0	100	0	0		-0.13	Dec-06
-0.13	3.21	-1.67	20.34	30.54	1.48	0.49	7.93		21.65	291.2	0	100	0	0	15	0.10	Dec-07
-0.32	4.88	4.22	71.63	89.08	0.98	0.35	14.41		56.40	253.8	0	100	0	0		-0.10	Jun-11
2.79	8.07	8.81			1.53	0.1			30.67	1.5	0	100	0	0		-0.29	Jul-17
0.99	4.31	1.37	37.17	55.72	1.93	0.39	13.37		53.97	1.5	0	100	0	0	19	-0.01	Feb-08
-0.39	4.46	5.30	37.37	53.88	2.57	0.39	12.93		40.10	54.1	0	100	0	0		0.08	Jun-11
-3.11	-1.91	-6.44	20.81	9.37	1.65	0.39	9.49		27.33	21.9	9	91	0	0	542	-0.06	Dec-12
0.40	4.14	1.72	43.20		2.44	0.13	16.32		35.08	64.9	0	100	0	0		0.11	Oct-15
-2.81	3.18					0.4			24.90	29.9	0	100	0	0		-0.03	Nov-18
-0.33	0.21	0.43	25.83	41.69	1.74	0.4	15.41		104.46	83.6	0	100	0	0		0.02	Nov-06
5.44	8.57	12.35	22.17	60.64	2.29	0.4	11.93		140.32	477.1	0	100	0	0		-0.04	Nov-06
-8.20	-12.54	-27.75	-21.10	-38.22	2.34	0.4	25.36		44.41	126.6	0	100	0	0	31	-0.01	Nov-06
0.05	3.09	3.17	35.91	56.80	1.87	0.2	13.17		108.05	15,852	0	100	0	0		-0.03	Apr-03
-0.05	9.32	3.61	47.20	66.41	2.16	0.4	17.25		43.64	255.3	0	100	0	0		-0.02	Nov-06
-3.71	-0.88	-4.38	28.18	57.17	0.61	0.4	15.05		196.04	695.9	0	100	0	0		-0.03	Nov-06
0.27	3.80	1.66	41.16	62.34	1.52	0.4	17.24		126.41	189.6	0	100	0	0		-0.04	Nov-06
-0.93	2.54	1.69	32.18	44.64	2	0.4	15.36		109.05	141.8	0	100	0	0		-0.02	Nov-06
7.34	8.01	20.96	27.41		2.68	0.4	12.59		31.87	46.2	0	100	0	0		0.06	Aug-15
-0.78	3.56	7.56	74.33	126.79	0.99	0.4	16.05		178.86	1,654	0	100	0	0		-0.01	Nov-06

Fund Name	Ticker Symbol	Traded On	Overall Rating	Reward Rating	Risk Rating	Recent Up/ Downgrade	Price as of 9/30/2019	52-Week High	52-Week Low	Open to New Investors	Category & (Prospectus Objective)
★ Invesco S&P 500® Equal Weight Utilities ETF	RYU	NYSE Arca	B-	B	C		106.64	107.12	86.44	Y	Utilities Sector Equity (Utility)
● Invesco S&P 500® ex-Rate Sensitive Low Volatility ETF	XRLV	NYSE Arca	C+	B-	C-		39.42	39.69	30.55		US Equity Large Cap Blend (Growth)
● Invesco S&P 500® High Beta ETF	SPHB	NYSE Arca	C	C	C+		41.34	45.16	32.76		US Equity Large Cap Blend (Growth)
● Invesco S&P 500® High Dividend Low Volatility ETF	SPHD	NYSE Arca	C	C	C	Down	42.63	43.31	36.52		US Equity Large Cap Value (Income)
★ Invesco S&P 500® Low Volatility ETF	SPLV	NYSE Arca	B	B	A-	Down	57.90	57.96	44.55		US Equity Large Cap Value (Growth)
● Invesco S&P 500® Momentum ETF	SPMO	NYSE Arca	C+	B-	C	Up	40.59	41.76	31.20		US Equity Large Cap Growth (Growth)
● Invesco S&P 500® Pure Growth ETF	RPG	NYSE Arca	C	C+	C-	Down	118.43	122.44	93.15	Y	US Equity Large Cap Growth (Growth)
● Invesco S&P 500® Pure Value ETF	RPV	NYSE Arca	C	C	C+		64.84	68.97	53.85	Y	US Equity Large Cap Value (Growth)
★ Invesco S&P 500® Quality ETF	SPHQ	NYSE Arca	B-	B-	C+	Up	33.54	34.13	25.94	Y	US Equity Large Cap Blend (Growth)
● Invesco S&P 500® Top 50 ETF	XLG	NYSE Arca	C+	B-	C	Up	212.44	217.27	167.99	Y	US Equity Large Cap Blend (Growth)
● Invesco S&P Emerging Markets Low Volatility ETF	EELV	NYSE Arca	C	C	C-	Up	22.74	24.92	22.22		Global Emerg Mkts Equity (Div Emerg Mkts)
Invesco S&P Emerging Markets Momentum ETF	EEMO	NYSE Arca	C-	C	D+		16.03	18.68	14.71		Global Emerg Mkts Equity (Div Emerg Mkts)
Invesco S&P Financials Revenue ETF	RWW	NYSE Arca	C	C+	C-		68.21	70.24	54.38	Y	Financials Sector Equity (Financial)
Invesco S&P Global Dividend Opportunities Index ETF	LVL	NYSE Arca	C	C+	D+	Down	11.84	11.96	9.93	Y	Global Equity Large Cap (World Stock)
● Invesco S&P Global Water Index ETF	CGW	NYSE Arca	C	B-	C-		38.26	38.26	29.76	Y	Equity Misc (Natl Res)
● Invesco S&P High Income Infrastructure ETF	GHII	NYSE Arca	C	C	D+		27.21	27.53	22.90	Y	Infrastructure Sector Equity (Equity-Income)
Invesco S&P Intl Dev High Div Low Vol ETF	IDHD	BATS	C-	C	D+		27.70	28.77	25.19	Y	Global Equity Large Cap (World Stock)
● Invesco S&P International Developed Low Volatility ETF	IDLV	NYSE Arca	C+	C+	C+	Up	34.16	34.43	29.12		Global Equity Large Cap (Foreign Stock)
Invesco S&P International Developed Momentum ETF	IDMO	NYSE Arca	C-	C	D	Up	26.38	27.42	21.95		Global Equity Large Cap (Growth)
Invesco S&P International Developed Quality ETF	IDHQ	NYSE Arca	C	C	C-	Up	23.60	24.07	19.90		Global Equity Large Cap (Foreign Stock)
● Invesco S&P MidCap 400 Revenue ETF	RWK	NYSE Arca	C-	C-	C-	Down	59.54	62.82	48.52	Y	US Equity Mid Cap (Growth)
● Invesco S&P MidCap 400® Equal Weight ETF	EWMC	NYSE Arca	C-	C-	D+		63.31	67.70	52.58	Y	US Equity Mid Cap (Growth)
● Invesco S&P MidCap 400® Pure Growth ETF	RFG	NYSE Arca	C-	C-	D+	Up	141.36	163.24	124.17	Y	US Equity Mid Cap (Growth)
● Invesco S&P MidCap 400® Pure Value ETF	RFV	NYSE Arca	C-	C-	C-	Up	63.81	71.62	53.74	Y	US Equity Small Cap (Growth)
● Invesco S&P MidCap Low Volatility ETF	XMLV	NYSE Arca	C+	C+	C+	Down	52.61	52.71	42.36		US Equity Mid Cap (Income)
● Invesco S&P MidCap Momentum ETF	XMMO	NYSE Arca	C	C+	C-	Down	58.27	60.28	41.61	Y	US Equity Mid Cap (Growth)
Invesco S&P MidCap Quality ETF	XMHQ	NYSE Arca	C	C+	D	Up	49.86	51.80	40.08	Y	US Equity Mid Cap (Growth)
● Invesco S&P MidCap Value with Momentum ETF	XMVM	NYSE Arca	C	C	D+		32.37	33.12	26.32	Y	US Equity Mid Cap (Growth)
● Invesco S&P SmallCap 600 Revenue ETF	RWJ	NYSE Arca	D+	D	C-	Down	63.73	74.25	54.53	Y	US Equity Small Cap (Small Company)
Invesco S&P SmallCap 600® Equal Weight ETF	EWSC	NYSE Arca	D+	C-	D+		53.25	60.04	45.30	Y	US Equity Small Cap (Growth)
● Invesco S&P SmallCap 600® Pure Growth ETF	RZG	NYSE Arca	C-	C-	D+	Up	106.66	131.68	98.06	Y	US Equity Small Cap (Small Company)
● Invesco S&P SmallCap 600® Pure Value ETF	RZV	NYSE Arca	D+	D+	D+		64.11	75.60	55.11	Y	US Equity Small Cap (Small Company)
Invesco S&P SmallCap Consumer Discretionary ETF	PSCD	NAS CM	C-	C	D+	Up	60.22	67.60	51.80		Consumer Goods & Svcs (Unaligned)
Invesco S&P SmallCap Consumer Staples ETF	PSCC	NAS CM	C	B-	C-	Up	74.40	82.78	66.72		Consumer Goods & Svcs (Unaligned)
Invesco S&P SmallCap Energy ETF	PSCE	NAS CM	D+	C-	D	Up	7.04	16.56	6.63		Energy Sector Equity (Natl Res)
● Invesco S&P SmallCap Financials ETF	PSCF	NAS CM	C	C	C-		54.37	56.75	46.25		Financials Sector Equity (Financial)
● Invesco S&P SmallCap Health Care ETF	PSCH	NAS CM	C	C	C-	Up	113.47	138.29	100.46		Healthcare Sector Equity (Health)
Invesco S&P SmallCap High Dividend Low Volatility ETF	XSHD	BATS	C-	C	D+	Up	24.03	25.75	21.23	Y	US Equity Small Cap (Small Company)
● Invesco S&P SmallCap Industrials ETF	PSCI	NAS CM	C	C	D+	Up	67.16	71.96	52.49		Industrials Sector Equity (Unaligned)
● Invesco S&P SmallCap Information Technology ETF	PSCT	NAS CM	C	C	C-		85.80	88.72	64.05		Technology Sector Equity (Technology)
● Invesco S&P SmallCap Low Volatility ETF	XSLV	NYSE Arca	C	C	C+		48.89	49.75	40.81		US Equity Small Cap (Income)
Invesco S&P SmallCap Materials ETF	PSCM	NAS CM	C	B-	C-	Up	44.66	54.61	37.59		Natural Resources (Unaligned)
● Invesco S&P SmallCap Momentum ETF	XSMO	NYSE Arca	C	C	D+		37.27	39.03	28.65	Y	US Equity Small Cap (Growth)
Invesco S&P SmallCap Quality ETF	XSHQ	BATS	D+	C-	D		27.42	30.03	23.57	Y	US Equity Small Cap (Small Company)
● Invesco S&P SmallCap Utilities & Comm Services ETF	PSCU	NAS CM	C+	B-	C-	Up	52.72	58.05	46.95		Utilities Sector Equity (Utility)
● Invesco S&P SmallCap Value with Momentum ETF	XSVM	NYSE Arca	C-	C-	D+	Up	30.53	32.29	25.28	Y	US Equity Small Cap (Growth)
● Invesco S&P Spin-Off ETF	CSD	NYSE Arca	C	C+	C-	Up	46.44	54.88	39.90	Y	US Equity Mid Cap (Growth)
● Invesco S&P Ultra Dividend Revenue ETF	RDIV	NYSE Arca	C	C+	C-		37.69	39.32	32.38	Y	US Equity Large Cap Value (Growth)
● Invesco Senior Loan ETF	BKLN	NYSE Arca	C+	C	B	Down	22.59	23.21	21.59	Y	US Fixed Income (Income)
Invesco Shipping ETF	SEA	NYSE Arca	D	D	D+		8.81	10.32	7.88	Y	Industrials Sector Equity (Unaligned)
★ Invesco Solar ETF	TAN	NYSE Arca	B-	B	C	Up	29.37	32.30	17.70	Y	Technology Sector Equity (Natl Res)
★ Invesco Taxable Municipal Bond ETF	BAB	NYSE Arca	B-	B-	C+	Up	32.40	33.08	28.54	Y	US Fixed Income (Muni Bond - Natl)

★ Expanded analysis of this fund is included in Section II: Analysis of All BUY Rated Funds. ● Expanded analysis of this fund is included in Section III: Analysis of All Rated Funds with Assets over $50 million.

		TOTAL RETURNS & PERFORMANCE							ASSETS		ASSET ALLOCATION & TURNOVER					VALUATION	
3-Month Total Return	6-Month Total Return	1-Year Total Return	3-Year Total Return	5-Year Total Return	Dividend Yield (TTM)	Expense Ratio	3-Yr Std Deviation	Effective Duration	NAV	Total Assets (MIL)	%Cash	%Stocks	%Bonds	%Other	Turnover Ratio	Premium/ Discount 1-Year Avg	Inception Date
8.99	12.44	25.20	44.00	74.37	2.45	0.4	9.29		106.66	400.0	0	100	0	0		0.01	Nov-06
1.78	8.21	10.73	49.68		1.68	0.25	11.03		39.45	169.6	0	100	0	0		0.05	Apr-15
-4.20	-1.93	-6.94	31.72	36.38	1.4	0.25	19.67		41.32	126.0	0	100	0	0		-0.01	May-11
2.51	1.66	7.26	23.33	68.69	4.11	0.3	11.3		42.61	3,507	0	100	0	0		0.01	Oct-12
5.34	11.05	19.75	48.88	86.14	2	0.25	9.02		57.89	12,816	0	100	0	0		-0.01	May-11
-0.04	3.40	0.69	55.39		1.3	0.13	12.85		40.56	71.0	0	100	0	0		0.02	Oct-15
-1.32	1.64	-0.68	43.16	60.96	0.78	0.35	13.62		118.42	2,653	0	100	0	0		-0.02	Mar-06
-0.20	2.18	-3.15	30.62	37.73	2.46	0.35	16.36		64.87	908.4	0	100	0	0		-0.01	Mar-06
0.86	4.02	3.62	40.54	72.42	1.56	0.15	12.03		33.53	1,492	0	100	0	0	73	-0.03	Dec-05
0.63	4.20	2.89	47.10	71.92	1.8	0.2	12.2		212.29	828.1	0	100	0	0	8	0.02	May-05
-5.17	-3.18	-4.27	14.74	-0.17	4.89	0.29	11.07		22.80	329.5	0	100	0	0	125	0.03	Jan-12
-3.49	0.96	-1.12	24.26	-0.78	2.39	0.3	12.73		16.09	7.2	0	100	0	0	140	-0.44	Feb-12
-0.26	6.87	2.81	48.02	55.82	1.8	0.45	17.32		68.17	34.1	0	100	0	0	12	0.06	Nov-08
0.63	5.56	10.80	30.62	16.05	3.4	0.64	8.9		11.80	29.3	0	100	0	0		-0.27	Jun-07
1.92	7.18	11.82	31.11	52.96	1.74	0.62	11.61		38.20	670.9	0	100	0	0		0.00	May-07
2.73	4.86	8.83	20.81		4.05	0.45	11.49		27.26	61.3	0	100	0	0	45	-0.07	Feb-15
-0.19	3.36	6.16			4.5	0.3			27.68	12.5	0	100	0	0	65	0.80	Nov-16
1.58	5.82	8.98	24.89	29.79	3.48	0.25	8.8		34.09	935.6	0	100	0	0	65	0.03	Jan-12
-0.36	2.78	-1.24	15.45	5.75	2.82	0.25	12.49		26.44	2.6	0	100	0	0	123	-0.26	Feb-12
-0.92	3.48	3.03	23.50	35.60	2.53	0.29	11.25		23.45	39.9	0	100	0	0	54	0.11	Jun-07
-2.13	-0.88	-3.44	22.78	41.09	1.12	0.39	18.6		59.52	336.4	0	100	0	0	33	-0.05	Feb-08
-1.82	-1.45	-5.06	23.82	39.01	1.33	0.4	16.64		63.33	85.5	0	100	0	0		-0.07	Dec-10
-4.65	-7.13	-12.78	15.58	21.51	0.74	0.35	16.19		141.41	381.8	0	100	0	0		0.07	Mar-06
-4.29	-4.62	-9.02	19.79	36.15	1.51	0.35	22.18		63.83	153.2	0	100	0	0		-0.06	Mar-06
3.00	6.46	11.66	44.06	96.53	1.93	0.25	9.93		52.62	3,373	0	100	0	0		0.01	Feb-13
-0.93	2.24	8.14	85.52	98.98	0.43	0.39	17.16		58.26	559.3	0	100	0	0		-0.01	Mar-05
0.01	0.72	-0.60	27.57	45.99	1.3	0.25	13.99		49.87	24.9	0	100	0	0		0.15	Dec-06
-1.24	2.77	6.29	21.09	41.86	2.27	0.39	14.15		32.31	50.1	0	100	0	0		-0.09	Mar-05
0.98	-3.75	-12.87	10.99	31.01	1.21	0.39	21.98		63.76	369.9	0	100	0	0	39	-0.04	Feb-08
-0.38	-2.18	-10.30	23.27	34.03	1.07	0.4	19.39		53.31	29.3	1	99	0	0		-0.28	Dec-10
-4.19	-6.15	-18.46	21.75	47.70	0.67	0.35	19.46		106.70	202.7	0	100	0	0		-0.10	Mar-06
2.65	-3.65	-14.12	5.91	17.57	1.22	0.35	24.23		64.14	182.8	0	100	0	0		0.00	Mar-06
1.27	-1.30	-10.21	27.99	45.42	0.99	0.29	18.41		60.12	21.0	2	98	0	0		-0.04	Apr-10
2.56	-0.69	-7.77	18.70	60.08	1.79	0.29	16.21		74.40	48.4	0	100	0	0		0.03	Apr-10
-22.80	-36.63	-56.72	-61.60	-83.00	0.03	0.29	38.02		7.00	20.0	0	100	0	0		0.04	Apr-10
1.08	3.67	0.78	32.85	69.35	3	0.29	17.25		54.26	122.1	0	100	0	0		-0.04	Apr-10
-4.05	-1.82	-17.89	53.33	113.97	0	0.29	21.24		113.51	454.0	0	100	0	0		-0.09	Apr-10
2.44	0.60	-1.93			4.95	0.3			23.97	26.4	0	100	0	0		0.08	Nov-16
0.68	5.63	-6.01	38.27	71.48	0.63	0.29	20.68		67.20	57.1	0	100	0	0		-0.11	Apr-10
2.32	5.21	3.99	36.99	98.11	0.27	0.29	19.17		86.11	305.7	1	99	0	0		-0.16	Apr-10
2.38	4.67	3.29	35.64	84.34	2.61	0.25	14.28		48.91	2,159	1	99	0	0		-0.01	Feb-13
-3.13	-7.02	-17.15	13.64	11.00	1.03	0.29	26.62		44.60	15.6	0	100	0	0		0.02	Apr-10
-0.58	2.46	-4.27	44.83	65.03	0.43	0.39	17.46		37.27	80.1	1	99	0	0		-0.03	Mar-05
0.67	1.84	-7.35			1.12	0.29			27.42	4.1	1	99	0	0		0.03	Apr-17
3.12	-1.11	-5.60	28.66	84.71	2.07	0.29	13.34		52.74	50.1	0	100	0	0		-0.02	Apr-10
4.33	2.41	-3.17	24.07	45.92	1.69	0.39	19.16		30.54	74.8	1	99	0	0		-0.18	Mar-05
-7.30	-9.59	-14.16	11.86	12.04	0.91	0.62	17.49		46.45	118.4	0	100	0	0	49	-0.03	Dec-06
1.01	0.56	0.69	30.82	65.09	3.61	0.39	14.9		37.70	1,621	0	100	0	0	122	-0.02	Sep-13
0.92	2.14	2.67	10.71	14.55	5.1	0.65	3.06		22.62	4,961	13	0	87	0	74	-0.19	Mar-11
-3.49	1.40	-12.01	-13.31	-43.09	2.94	0.66	19.49		8.82	44.1	0	100	0	0		-0.23	Jun-10
3.11	24.61	42.71	57.30	-17.32	0.44	0.7	25.43		29.46	438.6	0	100	0	0	54	-0.08	Apr-08
4.18	9.22	15.29	16.61	34.23	3.79	0.28	5.25	8.66	32.29	1,306	1	0	99	0		0.21	Nov-09

Fund Name	Ticker Symbol	Traded On	Overall Rating	Reward Rating	Risk Rating	Recent Up/ Downgrade	Price as of 9/30/2019	52-Week High	52-Week Low	Open to New Investors	Category & (Prospectus Objective)
● Invesco Total Return Bond ETF	GTO	NYSE Arca	C+	B-	C-	Up	54.27	54.87	50.00	Y	US Fixed Income (Corp Bond - Gen)
● Invesco Treasury Collateral ETF	CLTL	NYSE Arca	C-	C	C-		105.58	105.76	105.37	Y	US Fixed Income (Govt Bond - Treasury)
● Invesco Ultra Short Duration ETF	GSY	NYSE Arca	C	C	C+		50.41	50.47	50.04	Y	US Fixed Income (Income)
● Invesco Variable Rate Investment Grade ETF	VRIG	NAS CM	C	C	C-	Up	24.89	25.12	24.60	Y	US Fixed Income (Income)
● Invesco Variable Rate Preferred ETF	VRP	NYSE Arca	C+	C+	C+	Down	25.42	25.49	22.45	Y	US Fixed Income (Growth & Inc)
● Invesco VRDO Tax-Free Weekly ETF	PVI	NYSE Arca	C-	C	C-		24.91	24.99	24.87	Y	US Muni Fixed Inc (Muni Bond - Natl)
★ Invesco Water Resources ETF	PHO	NAS CM	B-	B	C		36.60	37.05	26.56	Y	Industrials Sector Equity (Utility)
● Invesco WilderHill Clean Energy ETF	PBW	NYSE Arca	C+	B	C-	Up	29.17	31.46	20.12	Y	Technology Sector Equity (Natl Res)
● Invesco Zacks Mid-Cap ETF	CZA	NYSE Arca	C	C+	C-		72.82	73.51	56.31	Y	US Equity Mid Cap (Growth)
● Invesco Zacks Multi-Asset Income ETF	CVY	NYSE Arca	C	C	C-		22.28	22.88	18.31	Y	Aggressive Allocation (Multi-Asset Global)
iPath® Asian & Gulf Currency Revaluation ETN	PGDDF	OTC BB	D-	D	E		38.29	40.10	38.29	Y	Currency (Worldwide Bond)
iPath® Bloomberg Agriculture Subindex Total Return(SM) ETN	JJATF	OTC BB	D-	D-	D		24.41	28.41	23.21	Y	Commodities Specified (Natl Res)
iPath® Bloomberg Aluminum Subindex Total Return(SM) ETN	JJUFF	NYSE Arca	D-	D	E	Down	15.20	43.63	15.14	Y	Commodities Specified (Natl Res)
iPath® Bloomberg Cocoa Subindex Total Return(SM) ETN	NIB	NYSE Arca	D+	D+	D		28.04	30.33	22.95	Y	Commodities Specified (Natl Res)
iPath® Bloomberg Coffee Subindex Total Return(SM) ETN	JJOFF	OTC BB	D-	D-	E+	Up	9.30	13.94	8.37	Y	Commodities Specified (Natl Res)
● iPath® Bloomberg Commodity Index Total Return(SM) ETN	DJP	NYSE Arca	D	D	D+		21.80	24.59	21.13	Y	Commodities Broad Basket (Natl Res)
iPath® Bloomberg Copper Subindex Total Return(SM) ETN	JJCTF	OTC BB	D+	D	D+		28.18	32.88	27.30	Y	Commodities Specified (Natl Res)
iPath® Bloomberg Cotton Subindex Total Return(SM) ETN	BALTF	OTC BB	E+	D-	E	Down	40.80	54.25	37.21	Y	Commodities Specified (Natl Res)
iPath® Bloomberg Energy Subindex Total Return(SM) ETN	JJETF	OTC BB	D	D+	D		5.94	46.11	5.10	Y	Commodities Specified (Natl Res)
iPath® Bloomberg Grains Subindex Total Return(SM) ETN	JJGTF	OTC BB	D	D	D	Up	21.30	24.48	19.27	Y	Commodities Specified (Natl Res)
iPath® Bloomberg Indust Metals Subind Total Ret(SM) ETN	JJMTF	OTC BB	D	D+	D		25.80	44.44	23.84	Y	Commodities Specified (Natl Res)
iPath® Bloomberg Lead Subindex Total Return(SM) ETN	LD	NYSE Arca	D	D+	D	Up	46.60	49.87	40.30	Y	Commodities Specified (Natl Res)
iPath® Bloomberg Livestock Subindex Total Return(SM) ETN	COWTF	NYSE Arca	D-	D	E	Down	21.37	25.79	18.92	Y	Commodities Specified (Natl Res)
iPath® Bloomberg Natural Gas Subindex Total Return(SM) ETN			U	U	U		0.02	0.30	0.00	Y	Commodities Energy (Natl Res)
iPath® Bloomberg Nickel Subindex Total Return(SM) ETN	JJNTF	OTC BB	C+	B	D+	Up	21.06	22.55	12.35	Y	Commodities Specified (Natl Res)
iPath® Bloomberg Platinum Subindex Total Return(SM) ETN			D+	D+	D+	Up	40.71	40.71	18.68	Y	Commodities Specified (Prec Metals)
iPath® Bloomberg Precious Metals Subind Total Ret(SM) ETN	JJPFF	NYSE Arca	D	C	E	Up	48.00	59.06	48.00	Y	Commodities Specified (Prec Metals)
iPath® Bloomberg Softs Subindex Total Return(SM) ETN	JJSSF	NYSE Arca	E+	D-	E		22.94	42.13	21.99	Y	Commodities Specified (Natl Res)
iPath® Bloomberg Sugar Subindex Total Return(SM) ETN	SGGFF	OTC BB	D	D	D	Up	20.34	25.65	18.65	Y	Commodities Specified (Natl Res)
iPath® Bloomberg Tin Subindex Total Return(SM) ETN	JJTFF	NYSE Arca	D-	D	E	Down	48.42	48.42	48.42	Y	Commodities Specified (Natl Res)
iPath® CBOE S&P 500 BuyWrite Index(SM) ETN	BWVTF	OTC BB	D+	C	E+		81.00	81.50	72.55	Y	US Equity Large Cap Blend (Growth)
iPath® EUR/USD Exchange Rate ETN	EROTF	OTC BB	D-	D	E		34.75	45.01	34.75	Y	Currency (Worldwide Bond)
iPath® GBP/USD Exchange Rate ETN	GBBEF	OTC BB	D	D	D		31.90	33.55	27.72	Y	Currency (Worldwide Bond)
iPath® GEMS Asia 8 ETN	AYTEF	OTC BB	D+	C	E+	Up	39.50	42.16	39.50	Y	Currency (Worldwide Bond)
iPath® GEMS Index ETN	JEMTF	OTC BB	D	C-	E		29.20	29.20	29.20	Y	Currency (Worldwide Bond)
iPath® Global Carbon ETN	GRNTF	OTC BB	C+	B+	D	Down	33.67	42.30	17.90	Y	Commodities Specified (Natl Res)
iPath® Inverse S&P 500 VIX Short-Term Futures™ ETN	XXVFF	OTC BB	D+	C	E+		37.00	37.00	37.00	Y	Alternative Misc (Growth)
iPath® JPY/USD Exchange Rate ETN	JYNFF	OTC BB	D	C	E+		52.02	52.02	52.02	Y	Currency (Worldwide Bond)
iPath® Long Enhanced MSCI EAFE® Index ETN	MFLAF	OTC BB	D	C	E+		194.36	194.36	194.36	Y	Trading Tools (Foreign Stock)
iPath® Long Enhanced MSCI Emerging Markets Index ETN	EMLBF	OTC BB	D	D+	E		80.80	80.80	80.80	Y	Trading Tools (Foreign Stock)
iPath® Long Extended Russell 1000® TR Index ETN	ROLAF	OTC BB	D+	C+	E+	Down	228.79	228.79	228.79	Y	Trading Tools (Growth & Inc)
iPath® Long Extended Russell 2000® TR Index ETN	RTLAF	OTC BB	D	C-	E		209.90	209.90	209.90	Y	Trading Tools (Small Company)
iPath® Long Extended S&P 500® TR Index ETN	SFLAF	OTC BB	D+	C+	E+	Down	230.00	245.01	230.00	Y	Trading Tools (Growth & Inc)
● iPath® MSCI India Index(SM) ETN	INPTF	OTC BB	D+	D+	D+	Down	82.30	89.00	69.81	Y	India Equity (Foreign Stock)
iPath® Optimized Currency Carry ETN	ICITF	OTC BB	D	C-	E		33.52	37.90	33.52	Y	Currency (Worldwide Bond)
● iPath® Pure Beta Broad Commodity ETN	BCM	NYSE Arca	D+	D+	D+		27.21	30.49	25.68	Y	Commodities Broad Basket (Natl Res)
iPath® Pure Beta Crude Oil ETN	OLEM	NYSE Arca	D	D+	D		16.52	23.25	13.93	Y	Commodities Specified (Natl Res)
iPath® S&P 500 Dynamic VIX ETN	XVZ	BATS	D	D	D-	Up	18.51	21.31	17.53	Y	Alternative Misc (Growth)
● iPath® S&P GSCI® Crude Oil Total Return Index ETN	OILNF	NYSE Arca	D	C-	E		9.26	9.49	9.16	Y	Commodities Specified (Natl Res)
iPath® S&P GSCI® Total Return Index ETN	GSP	NYSE Arca	C-	D+	C-		14.16	18.31	12.78	Y	Commodities Broad Basket (Natl Res)
iPath® S&P MLP ETN	IMLP	BATS	D+	D	C-		15.78	18.73	14.10	Y	Energy Sector Equity (Income)
iPath® Series B Bloomberg Agriculture Subind Total Ret ETN	JJA	NYSE Arca	D	D	D		42.40	47.76	40.19	Y	Commodities Specified (Growth & Inc)

★ Expanded analysis of this fund is included in Section II: Analysis of All BUY Rated Funds. ● Expanded analysis of this fund is included in Section III: Analysis of All Rated Funds with Assets over $50 million.

	TOTAL RETURNS & PERFORMANCE								ASSETS		ASSET ALLOCATION & TURNOVER					VALUATION	
3-Month Total Return	6-Month Total Return	1-Year Total Return	3-Year Total Return	5-Year Total Return	Dividend Yield (TTM)	Expense Ratio	3-Yr Std Deviation	Effective Duration	NAV	Total Assets (Mil.)	%Cash	%Stocks	%Bonds	%Other	Turnover Ratio	Premium/ Discount 1-Year Avg	Inception Date
2.64	6.65	10.61	16.06		2.91	0.51	3.04	5.66	54.26	116.7	4	0	94	0		0.01	Feb-16
0.53	1.22	2.46			2.3	0.08			105.57	551.1	40	0	60	0		0.02	Jan-17
0.67	1.64	3.13	7.27	10.17	2.71	0.25	0.28	0.46	50.40	2,535	28	0	71	0		0.01	Feb-08
0.80	1.68	2.57	8.08		3.22	0.3	0.76	-0.05	24.91	393.6	3	0	94	0	26	-0.09	Sep-16
3.17	5.93	7.56	15.78	31.37	5.28	0.5	5.19		25.38	1,543	0	0	62	0		-0.20	May-14
0.25	0.58	1.24	2.74	2.61	1.24	0.25	0.11	0.00	24.93	57.3	5	0	96	0	0	-0.06	Nov-07
2.61	7.19	16.20	51.08	54.08	0.47	0.6	13.55		36.63	1,017	0	100	0	0	31	0.00	Dec-05
-2.64	8.35	19.14	58.08	4.29	1.47	0.7	19.76		29.14	179.8	0	100	0	0	40	-0.01	Mar-05
0.91	5.47	7.97	42.98	63.02	1.03	0.76	12.51		72.79	276.6	0	100	0	0		0.03	Apr-07
1.22	3.56	4.34	29.54	16.31	3.31	0.97	12.91	4.82	22.32	209.8	0	82	8	-1		-0.15	Sep-06
-0.79		1.37	-1.42		1.22	0.89	1.67			0.37						-17.51	Feb-08
-7.90	-5.78	-10.13	-32.41	-38.56	0	0.75	14.54			5.9					0	22.72	Oct-07
-4.12	-11.19	-21.09	-0.93	-25.06	0	0.75	18.59			0.72					0	0.39	Jun-08
-2.49	8.10	25.45	-18.77	-34.14	0	0.75	31.79			17.0					0	0.05	Jun-08
-15.32	1.51	-16.99	-58.26	-74.47	0	0.75	26.1			42.9					0	80.95	Jun-08
-0.66	-3.92	-9.04	-6.68	-36.02	0	0.7	9.2			589.0					0	-0.08	Jun-06
-3.75	-12.27	-7.49	12.94	-21.91	0	0.75	21.12			19.8					0	13.78	Oct-07
-9.04	-22.27	-23.73	-12.58	-3.86	0	0.75	19.81			3.1					0	0.22	Jun-08
-2.77	-10.41	-26.83	-2.44	-65.99	0	0.75	25.51			0.53					0	1.50	Oct-07
-8.62	-3.89	-10.11	-25.92	-37.34	0	0.75	18.69			32.4					0	26.61	Oct-07
3.97	-5.67	-3.20	17.63	-12.12	0	0.75	17.88			3.6					0	0.07	Oct-07
10.09	3.58	3.53	-3.09	-6.02	0	0.75	24.07			0.53					0	3.01	Jun-08
-2.17	-13.28	-9.22	15.98	-34.33	0	0.75	18.76			5.5					0	0.00	Oct-07
320.00	200.59	1.13	-78.17	-92.72	0	0.75	147.78			1.1					0	-52.15	Oct-07
45.92	36.06	43.03	66.08	-1.70	0	0.75	36.26			7.1					0	79.67	Oct-07
13.19	10.10	13.52	-13.80	-34.25	0	0.75	19.99			2.6					0	140.97	Jun-08
10.43	17.19	25.97	3.50	11.11	0	0.75	13.03			2.9					0	-15.02	Jun-08
-11.07	-10.50	-11.64	-51.38	-51.42	0	0.75	18.84			0.59					0	2.09	Jun-08
-9.60	-13.23	-1.59	-60.71	-52.10	0	0.75	26.7			18.6					0	29.80	Jun-08
-15.32	-25.45	-13.57	-15.20	-15.69	0	0.75	15.27			0.91					0	8.47	Jun-08
-0.72	2.75	-2.68	20.43	29.65	0	0.75	8.46			3.6					0	-2.05	May-07
-3.71	-2.97	-6.56	-5.56	-17.83	0	0.4	6.68			1.3					0	3.26	May-07
-2.63	-6.49	-5.70	-5.66	-25.40	0	0.4	8.58			1.7					0	-6.99	May-07
-1.31	-0.19	2.84	3.36	-0.27	2.36	0.89	4			0.43					0	3.06	Apr-08
-3.16	-0.26	3.19	-0.20	-6.58	8.08	0.89	7.72			0.30	-97	0	0	197		14.43	Feb-08
-6.01	16.94	18.15	488.63	369.75	0	0.75	55.72			8.4					0	0.86	Jun-08
0.30	0.68	1.43	2.15	1.29	0	0.89	0.19			0.16						-4.22	Jul-10
0.04	2.73	5.15	-8.44	-1.70	0	0.4	8.18			0.22					0	2.58	May-07
-2.61	1.57	-4.00	28.13	18.56	0	0.8	18.44			0.48						8.07	Nov-10
-10.88	-11.09	-7.55	30.53	10.27	0	0.8	28.84			0.54						-27.08	Nov-10
1.69	4.65	2.50	62.20	96.06	0	0.5	17.33			1.3						-23.47	Nov-10
-2.47	-3.37	-13.03	36.53	74.10	0	0.5	26.32			1.4						-8.24	Nov-10
0.22	5.22	3.07	63.63	99.53	0	0.35	17.1			0.65						-20.74	Nov-10
-5.09	-4.86	5.10	20.66	18.29	0.3	0.89	18.04			98.4					0	-1.39	Dec-06
-0.54	-2.80	0.43	2.89	-1.35	0	0.65	5.49			0.59					0	-11.34	Jan-08
-0.67	-2.46	-8.26	3.91	-24.88	0	0.6	9.8			53.7						-0.10	Apr-11
-5.12	-9.13	-27.37	5.66	-58.28	0	0.75	26.29			2.2						0.02	Apr-11
3.23	2.71	-3.36	-35.69	-39.91	0	0.95	12			5.8						0.09	Aug-11
-5.96	-10.72	-31.76	9.94	-71.53	2.53	0.75	37.97			220.5					0	49.19	Aug-06
-3.57	-6.81	-20.17	4.76	-51.55	0	0.75	17.99			23.7					0	-0.17	Jun-06
-4.74	-5.92	-9.22	-5.94	-37.25	7.52	0.8	17.75			27.5						0.08	Jan-13
-6.77	-4.85	-8.53			0	0.45				6.8						-0.06	Jan-18

Fund Name	Ticker Symbol	Traded On	Overall Rating	Reward Rating	Risk Rating	Recent Up/ Downgrade	Price as of 9/30/2019	52-Week High	52-Week Low	Open to New Investors	Category & (Prospectus Objective)
iPath® Series B Bloomberg Aluminum SubInd Total Ret ETN	JJU	NYSE Arca	D	D	D		39.05	52.30	39.05	Y	Commodities Specified (Growth & Inc)
● iPath® Series B Bloomberg Coffee Subindex Total Return ETN	JO	NYSE Arca	D	D	D-	Up	33.43	46.23	30.92	Y	Commodities Broad Basket (Growth & Inc)
iPath® Series B Bloomberg Copper Subindex Total Return ETN	JJC	NYSE Arca	D	D	D		39.81	45.84	39.12	Y	Commodities Specified (Growth & Inc)
iPath® Series B Bloomberg Cotton Subindex Total Return ETN	BAL	NYSE Arca	D	D	D		37.06	49.93	35.13	Y	Commodities Specified (Growth & Inc)
iPath® Series B Bloomberg Energy Subindex Total Return ETN	JJE	NYSE Arca	D-	D	E		43.88	57.32	41.44	Y	Commodities Specified (Growth & Inc)
iPath® Series B Bloomberg Grains Subindex Total Return ETN	JJG	NYSE Arca	D	D	D		44.57	50.05	40.97	Y	Commodities Specified (Growth & Inc)
iPath® Ser B Bloomberg Indust Metals SubInd Total Ret ETN	JJM	NYSE Arca	D	D	D	Up	43.95	46.56	40.59	Y	Commodities Specified (Growth & Inc)
iPath® Series B Bloomberg Livestock SubInd Total Ret ETN	COW	NYSE Arca	D	D	D	Down	45.75	54.18	40.92	Y	Commodities Specified (Growth & Inc)
iPath® Ser B Bloomberg Natl Gas SubInd Total RetSM ETN	GAZ	NYSE Arca	D	D	D-		30.70	63.89	28.55	Y	Commodities Specified (Natl Res)
iPath® Series B Bloomberg Nickel Subindex Total Return ETN	JJN	NYSE Arca	D+	C-	D	Up	69.25	72.57	42.71	Y	Commodities Specified (Growth & Inc)
iPath® Series B Bloomberg Platinum SubInd Total Ret ETN	PGM	NYSE Arca	D	C-	E		43.50	48.23	38.76	Y	Commodities Specified (Growth & Inc)
iPath® Ser B Bloomberg Prec Metals SubInd Total Ret ETN	JJP	NYSE Arca	D+	C	D	Up	52.84	56.80	43.38	Y	Commodities Specified (Growth & Inc)
iPath® Series B Bloomberg Softs Subindex Total Return ETN	JJS	NYSE Arca	D	D	D-		37.06	47.56	35.23	Y	Commodities Broad Basket (Growth & Inc)
iPath® Series B Bloomberg Sugar Subindex Total Return ETN	SGG	NYSE Arca	D	D+	D		39.76	47.98	36.89	Y	Commodities Specified (Growth & Inc)
iPath® Series B Bloomberg Tin Subindex Total Return ETN	JJT	NYSE Arca	D	D	D		40.97	54.91	40.47	Y	Commodities Specified (Growth & Inc)
iPath® Series B S&P 500® VIX Mid-Term Futures™ ETN	VXZB	BATS	D	C-	E		17.95	22.68	17.17	Y	Alternative Misc (Growth & Inc)
● iPath® Series B S&P 500® VIX Short-Term Futures™ ETN	VXX	BATS	D	D	D		23.74	49.43	21.54	Y	Alternative Misc (Growth & Inc)
● iPath® Series B S&P GSCI® Crude Oil Total Return Index ETN	OIL	NYSE Arca	D-	D-	D	Down	11.11	79.07	10.65	Y	Commodities Specified (Natl Res)
iPath® US Treasury 10-year Bear ETN	DTYS	BATS	D	D-	D	Down	10.24	25.60	7.83	Y	Trading Tools (Govt Bond - Treasury)
iPath® US Treasury 10-year Bull ETN	DTYL	BATS	D+	C	E+	Up	86.82	89.18	72.62	Y	Trading Tools (Govt Bond - Treasury)
iPath® US Treasury 2-year Bear ETN	DTUS	BATS	D	D+	E	Down	32.74	42.67	30.18	Y	Trading Tools (Govt Bond - Treasury)
iPath® US Treasury 2-year Bull ETN	DTUL	BATS	D	C	E+		64.37	66.62	54.73	Y	Trading Tools (Govt Bond - Treasury)
iPath® US Treasury 5-year Bear ETN	DFVS	BATS	D	D	D		25.12	39.50	22.56	Y	Trading Tools (Govt Bond - Treasury)
iPath® US Treasury 5-year Bull ETN	DFVL	BATS	D+	C	E+		73.71	75.70	60.34	Y	Trading Tools (Govt Bond - Treasury)
iPath® US Treasury Flattener ETN	FLAT	BATS	C	C+	E+	Up	70.35	70.69	62.81	Y	Trading Tools (Govt Bond - Treasury)
iPath® US Treasury Long Bond Bear ETN	DLBS	BATS	D	E+	D		7.91	23.79	6.11	Y	Trading Tools (Govt Bond - Treasury)
iPath® US Treasury Long Bond Bull ETN	DLBLF	NAS CM	D+	C	E+		75.08	75.08	75.08	Y	Trading Tools (Govt Bond - Treasury)
iPath® US Treasury Steepener ETN	STPP	BATS	D	D-	D		25.59	31.00	25.30	Y	Trading Tools (Govt Bond - Treasury)
IQ 50 Percent Hedged FTSE Europe ETF	HFXE	NYSE Arca	C-	C	D	Down	19.63	19.96	16.85	Y	Europe Equity Large Cap (Europe Stock)
● IQ 50 Percent Hedged FTSE International ETF	HFXI	NYSE Arca	C	C	C-		20.34	21.10	17.88	Y	Global Equity Large Cap (World Stock)
IQ 50 Percent Hedged FTSE Japan ETF	HFXJ	NYSE Arca	D+	C-	D	Down	20.53	22.63	18.21	Y	Japan Equity (Pacific Stock)
IQ 500 International ETF	IQIN	NYSE Arca	U	U	U		26.69	27.85	24.54	Y	Global Equity Large Cap (Foreign Stock)
● IQ Chaikin U.S. Large Cap ETF	CLRG	NAS CM	D+	D+	D+		24.97	27.28	20.41	Y	US Equity Large Cap Blend (Growth & Inc)
● IQ Chaikin U.S. Small Cap ETF	CSML	NAS CM	D+	D+	C-	Up	25.13	27.90	21.19	Y	US Equity Small Cap (Small Company)
● IQ Enhanced Core Bond U.S. ETF	AGGE	NYSE Arca	C	C	C-	Up	19.38	19.51	18.31	Y	US Fixed Income (Income)
● IQ Enhanced Core Plus Bond U.S. ETF	AGGP	NYSE Arca	C	C	C-	Up	19.70	19.84	18.74	Y	US Fixed Income (Income)
IQ Global Agribusiness Small Cap ETF	CROP	NYSE Arca	C-	C-	D+	Up	31.72	33.43	29.00	Y	Consumer Goods & Svcs (Unaligned)
● IQ Global Resources ETF	GRES	NYSE Arca	C-	C	D+		26.52	27.96	25.05	Y	Natural Resources (World Stock)
IQ Hedge Event-Driven Tracker ETF	QED	NYSE Arca	C-	C	D	Down	21.47	21.62	19.51	Y	Market Neutral (Growth & Inc)
IQ Hedge Long/Short Tracker ETF	QLS	NYSE Arca	C-	C	D		22.09	22.33	19.49	Y	Long/Short Equity (Growth & Inc)
IQ Hedge Macro Tracker ETF	MCRO	NYSE Arca	C-	C	D	Up	26.13	26.38	24.90	Y	Cautious Allocation (Growth)
IQ Hedge Market Neutral Tracker ETF	QMN	NYSE Arca	C-	C	D+	Up	26.53	26.59	24.98	Y	Market Neutral (Growth & Inc)
● IQ Hedge Multi-Strategy Tracker ETF	QAI	NYSE Arca	C	C	C-		30.42	30.69	28.81	Y	Multialternative (Growth)
IQ Leaders GTAA Tracker ETF	QGTA	NYSE Arca	C	C	D+	Up	24.08	24.39	21.58	Y	Moderate Allocation (Growth & Inc)
● IQ MacKay Shields Municipal Insured ETF	MMIN	NYSE Arca	C-	C-	C-	Up	26.38	26.67	24.32	Y	US Muni Fixed Inc (Muni Bond - Natl)
IQ MacKay Shields Municipal Intermediate ETF	MMIT	NYSE Arca	C-	C-	D+	Up	26.33	26.61	24.44	Y	US Muni Fixed Inc (Muni Bond - Natl)
● IQ Merger Arbitrage ETF	MNA	NYSE Arca	C	C	C		32.05	32.31	31.26	Y	Market Neutral (Growth)
● IQ Real Return ETF	CPI	NYSE Arca	C-	C	D+		27.95	28.16	26.47	Y	Moderate Allocation (Growth & Inc)
IQ S&P High Yield Low Volatility Bond ETF	HYLV	NYSE Arca	C	C	C-	Up	25.32	25.44	23.07	Y	US Fixed Income (Corp Bond-High Yld)
IQ Short Duration Enhanced Core Bond U.S. ETF	SDAG	NYSE Arca	U	U	U		25.68	25.79	25.04	Y	US Fixed Income (Income)
● IQ U.S. Real Estate Small Cap ETF	ROOF	NYSE Arca	C	C	D+		25.62	25.82	21.68	Y	Real Estate Sector Equity (Real Estate)
● iShares 0-5 Year High Yield Corporate Bond ETF	SHYG	NYSE Arca	C+	C	C+		46.49	46.94	43.90	Y	US Fixed Income (Corp Bond-High Yld)

★ Expanded analysis of this fund is included in Section II: Analysis of All BUY Rated Funds. ● Expanded analysis of this fund is included in Section III: Analysis of All Rated Funds with Assets over $50 million.

		TOTAL RETURNS & PERFORMANCE							ASSETS		ASSET ALLOCATION & TURNOVER					VALUATION	
3-Month Total Return	6-Month Total Return	1-Year Total Return	3-Year Total Return	5-Year Total Return	Dividend Yield (TTM)	Expense Ratio	3-Yr Std Deviation	Effective Duration	NAV	Total Assets (MIL)	%Cash	%Stocks	%Bonds	%Other	Turnover Ratio	Premium/ Discount 1-Year Avg	Inception Date
-3.58	-9.88	-18.90			0	0.45				4.0						0.00	Jan-18
-12.16	1.31	-13.37			0	0.45				72.9						-0.10	Jan-18
-3.28	-10.94	-6.44			0	0.45				13.1						-0.07	Jan-18
-8.17	-20.47	-21.74			0	0.45				11.1						-0.09	Jan-18
-2.07	-8.05	-21.79			0	0.45				3.8						0.81	Jan-18
-7.34	-3.17	-8.43			0	0.45				21.2						0.00	Jan-18
3.62	-4.99	-2.62			0	0.45				4.8						-0.09	Jan-18
-1.87	-11.87	-8.02			0	0.45				8.5						-0.10	Jan-18
3.03	-16.67	-24.32			0	0.45				3.4						-0.12	Mar-17
40.34	32.04	38.18			0	0.45				8.7						0.08	Jan-18
11.55	8.97	12.09			0	0.45				3.9						0.02	Jan-18
9.61	15.79	23.85			0	0.45				5.1						0.04	Jan-18
-9.45	-8.89	-9.74			0	0.45				4.0						-0.12	Jan-18
-7.95	-11.00	-0.96			0	0.45				20.0						-0.11	Jan-18
-14.03	-23.54	-12.17			0	0.45				3.8						-0.03	Jan-18
13.16	11.94	16.69			0	0.89				21.5						-2.24	Jan-18
-0.29	-14.63	-7.47			0	0.89				989.7						0.35	Jan-18
-80.98	-81.78	-85.31			0	0.75				81.5						-0.11	Nov-16
-20.60	-42.46	-57.81	-15.74	-61.41	0	0.75	44.72			22.7						-0.22	Aug-10
3.49	10.39	21.40	4.54	23.67	0	0.75	9.02			5.5						0.23	Aug-10
0.12	-10.86	-21.08	12.94	-12.98	0	0.75	14.32			2.2						0.32	Aug-10
0.39	7.75	18.44	-2.81	8.93	0	0.75	8.5			5.4						-2.97	Aug-10
-6.09	-20.44	-33.78	3.09	-34.88	0	0.75	22.16			3.4						-0.42	Jul-11
2.69	10.74	24.01	2.33	24.41	0	0.75	9.93			5.2						-2.25	Jul-11
4.16	5.76	9.04	10.01	19.05	0	0.75	4.95			4.8						-0.77	Aug-10
-35.91	-51.73	-63.81	-38.48	-70.69	0	0.75	45.97			5.6						-0.26	Aug-10
5.59	11.42	20.73	8.30	28.03	0	0.75	8.67			0.67						-7.25	Aug-10
-9.09	-11.27	-15.58	-16.08	-30.94	0	0.75	10.01			4.1						0.05	Aug-10
-0.26	3.85	3.56	27.15		3.58	0.3	11.07		19.67	8.9	-3	103	0	0		-0.24	Jul-15
-0.24	2.67	0.60	26.38		4.46	0.2	10.31		20.31	199.0	0	100	0	0		0.02	Jul-15
1.57	1.52	-6.74	25.63		3	0.3	11.41		20.46	5.1	-1	101	0	0		-0.52	Jul-15
-1.47	-0.19					0.25			26.61	91.8	0	100	0	0		0.07	Dec-18
0.72	4.83	-2.51			2.11	0.25			24.93	228.1	0	100	0	0		-0.14	Dec-17
0.62	0.41	-8.45			1.4	0.35			25.12	229.8	0	100	0	0		-0.01	May-17
1.79	4.51	7.52	2.86		2.6	0.28	3.17	5.55	19.38	64.0	2	0	97	0		-0.03	May-16
1.82	4.38	6.07	5.96		2.84	0.33	2.86	5.55	19.71	114.3	2	0	96	0		-0.09	May-16
-3.80	-2.23	1.25	2.68	30.64	0.89	0.76	10.69		31.72	7.9	0	100	0	0		-0.19	Mar-11
-3.03	-3.70	-2.15	3.74	1.42	0.73	0.77	8.95		26.57	143.5	0	91	0	0		-0.24	Oct-09
0.29	2.23	3.75	15.16		4.03	0.78	4.89	2.91	21.46	4.3	4	10	78	1		0.02	Mar-15
0.61	4.00	3.91	19.82		4.32	0.67	5.91	6.73	22.05	4.4	8	60	26	2	95	-0.04	Mar-15
-0.86	-0.25	0.47	4.55	3.37	1.07	0.69	4.21	2.32	26.12	5.2	23	30	45	2		-0.02	Jun-09
0.18	1.67	2.38	4.52	6.38	0	0.67	2.28	3.38	26.51	14.6	28	19	51	1		0.00	Oct-12
-0.27	0.95	0.96	5.82	7.13	1.8	0.8	3.7	3.66	30.44	826.4	22	28	47	2		-0.04	Mar-09
-0.30	2.21	2.62	19.72		2.92	0.37	7.58	5.82	24.10	28.9	1	51	33	3		-0.07	Sep-15
1.79	4.38	9.55			2.51	0.31			26.34	56.6	2	0	98	0		0.08	Oct-17
1.78	4.20	9.43			2.57	0.31			26.29	46.0	5	0	95	0		0.16	Oct-17
1.46	0.20	1.10	10.24	17.88	0	0.77	3.17	0.39	32.04	882.6	1	84	0	0		0.06	Nov-09
0.20	1.17	1.06	6.23	8.48	1.24	0.44	2.9		27.97	55.9	42	11	42	3		-0.08	Oct-09
1.70	4.63	8.27			4.38	0.4			25.23	65.6	0	0	100	0		0.10	Feb-17
1.05	2.91					0.29		2.55	25.68	11.6	1	0	97	0		-0.01	Dec-18
5.17	4.55	6.11	11.81	37.87	6.17	0.7	15.17		25.59	66.5	-1	100	0	0		0.02	Jun-11
0.60	2.55	4.21	16.10	22.51	5.55	0.3	3.06		46.32	3,224	4	0	96	0	35	0.22	Oct-13

Fund Name	Ticker Symbol	Traded On	Overall Rating	Reward Rating	Risk Rating	Recent Up/ Downgrade	Price as of 9/30/2019	52-Week High	52-Week Low	Open to New Investors	Category & (Prospectus Objective)
● iShares 0-5 Year Investment Grade Corporate Bond ETF	SLQD	NAS CM	C+	C+	C+	Up	51.14	51.24	49.20	Y	US Fixed Income (Corp Bond - Gen)
● iShares 0-5 Year TIPS Bond ETF	STIP	NYSE Arca	C	C	C+		100.17	100.65	97.69	Y	US Fixed Income (Govt Bond - Treasury)
● iShares 10-20 Year Treasury Bond ETF	TLH	NYSE Arca	C	C	C+		149.48	152.94	125.72	Y	US Fixed Income (Govt Bond - Treasury)
● iShares 1-3 Year International Treasury Bond ETF	ISHG	NAS CM	D	D	D+		77.68	81.56	77.68	Y	Global Fixed Income (Worldwide Bond)
● iShares 1-3 Year Treasury Bond ETF	SHY	NAS CM	C	C	C+		84.82	85.10	82.85	Y	US Fixed Income (Govt Bond - Treasury)
● iShares 20+ Year Treasury Bond ETF	TLT	NAS CM	C+	C	B-	Up	143.08	147.80	112.00	Y	US Fixed Income (Govt Bond - Treasury)
● iShares 3-7 Year Treasury Bond ETF	IEI	NAS CM	C	C	C+		126.80	128.02	118.21	Y	US Fixed Income (Govt Bond - Treasury)
● iShares 7-10 Year Treasury Bond ETF	IEF	NAS CM	C+	C	B-	Up	112.47	114.25	99.72	Y	US Fixed Income (Govt Bond - Treasury)
● iShares Aaa - A Rated Corporate Bond ETF	QLTA	NYSE Arca	C	C+	C-		54.81	55.45	49.32	Y	US Fixed Income (Corp Bond - High Quality)
iShares Adaptive Currency Hedged MSCI EAFE ETF	DEFA	BATS	C-	C	D		27.67	28.79	24.15	Y	Global Equity Large Cap (Foreign Stock)
● iShares Agency Bond ETF	AGZ	NYSE Arca	C	C	C-		116.54	117.35	109.93	Y	US Fixed Income (Govt Bond - Gen)
● iShares Asia 50 ETF	AIA	NAS CM	C-	C-	C-		58.63	64.26	53.23	Y	Asia ex-Japan Equity (Pacific Stock)
iShares Asia/Pacific Dividend ETF	DVYA	NYSE Arca	C-	C	D+		42.93	44.69	39.35	Y	Asia Equity (Pacific Stock)
iShares Bloomberg Roll Select Broad Commodity ETF	CMDY	NYSE Arca	D	D	D	Down	44.11	50.26	43.18	Y	Commodities Broad Basket (Growth & Inc)
● iShares Broad USD High Yield Corporate Bond ETF	USHY	BATS	D	D	D+		40.95	48.77	39.80	Y	US Fixed Income (Corp Bond-High Yld)
● iShares Broad USD Investment Grade Corporate Bond ETF	USIG	NAS CM	D	D	D		58.28	58.86	52.37	Y	US Fixed Income (Income)
● iShares California Muni Bond ETF	CMF	NYSE Arca	C+	C+	C+	Up	61.28	61.99	56.95	Y	US Muni Fixed Inc (Muni Bond - Single State)
● iShares China Large-Cap ETF	FXI	NYSE Arca	C-	D+	C	Down	39.80	45.85	37.67	Y	Greater China Equity (Pacific Stock)
● iShares CMBS ETF	CMBS	NYSE Arca	C	C+	C-		53.47	54.19	49.03	Y	US Fixed Income (Growth)
★ iShares Cohen & Steers REIT ETF	ICF	BATS	B-	B+	C	Up	120.02	121.41	92.00	Y	Real Estate Sector Equity (Real Estate)
● iShares Commodities Select Strategy ETF	COMT	NAS CM	C-	C-	C	Down	31.54	39.93	29.85	Y	Commodities Broad Basket (Growth & Inc)
● iShares Convertible Bond ETF	ICVT	BATS	C	C	C-		58.14	61.42	50.03	Y	Convertibles (Convertible Bond)
● iShares Core 10+ Year USD Bond ETF	ILTB	NYSE Arca	C	B-	C-		69.36	71.13	57.00	Y	US Fixed Income (Growth)
● iShares Core 1-5 Year USD Bond ETF	ISTB	NAS CM	C+	C	C+	Up	50.49	50.67	48.64	Y	US Fixed Income (Multisector Bond)
● iShares Core 5-10 Year USD Bond ETF	IMTB	NYSE Arca	C	C	C-	Up	50.75	51.08	46.97	Y	US Fixed Income (Income)
● iShares Core Aggressive Allocation ETF	AOA	NYSE Arca	C	C	C-		54.92	55.45	47.04	Y	Aggressive Allocation (Asset Allocation)
● iShares Core Conservative Allocation ETF	AOK	NYSE Arca	C	C+	C-		35.66	35.73	32.37	Y	Cautious Allocation (Asset Allocation)
● iShares Core Dividend Growth ETF	DGRO	NYSE Arca	C+	C+	C+		39.14	39.54	31.18	Y	US Equity Large Cap Value (Equity-Income)
● iShares Core Growth Allocation ETF	AOR	NYSE Arca	C	C	C-		46.06	46.22	40.34	Y	Moderate Allocation (Asset Allocation)
★ iShares Core High Dividend ETF	HDV	NYSE Arca	B-	B	C	Up	94.16	95.92	80.00	Y	US Equity Large Cap Value (Equity-Income)
★ iShares Core International Aggregate Bond ETF	IAGG	BATS	B-	B-	C+	Up	55.79	56.14	51.69	Y	Global Fixed Income (Worldwide Bond)
● iShares Core Moderate Allocation ETF	AOM	NYSE Arca	C+	C+	C+	Up	39.29	39.31	35.24	Y	Cautious Allocation (Asset Allocation)
● iShares Core MSCI EAFE ETF	IEFA	BATS	C	C	B		61.07	64.19	53.06	Y	Global Equity Large Cap (Growth & Inc)
● iShares Core MSCI Emerging Markets ETF	IEMG	NYSE Arca	C	C-	C+		49.02	53.71	45.85	Y	Global Emerg Mkts Equity (Div Emerg Mkts)
● iShares Core MSCI Europe ETF	IEUR	NYSE Arca	C	C	C+		45.74	47.98	40.03	Y	Europe Equity Large Cap (Europe Stock)
● iShares Core MSCI International Developed Markets ETF	IDEV	NYSE Arca	C	C-	C+	Up	54.62	56.99	47.08	Y	Global Equity Large Cap (Foreign Stock)
● iShares Core MSCI Pacific ETF	IPAC	NYSE Arca	C	C	C-	Up	56.20	59.12	49.08	Y	Asia Equity (Pacific Stock)
● iShares Core MSCI Total International Stock ETF	IXUS	NAS CM	C	C	C+		57.76	60.45	50.85	Y	Global Equity Large Cap (Foreign Stock)
★ iShares Core S&P 500 ETF	IVV	NYSE Arca	B-	C+	B		298.52	303.77	236.09	Y	US Equity Large Cap Blend (Growth)
● iShares Core S&P Mid-Cap ETF	IJH	NYSE Arca	C	C	C+		193.23	199.76	156.48	Y	US Equity Mid Cap (Growth)
● iShares Core S&P Small-Cap ETF	IJR	NYSE Arca	C	C-	C		77.84	85.94	65.14	Y	US Equity Small Cap (Small Company)
● iShares Core S&P Total U.S. Stock Market ETF	ITOT	NYSE Arca	C+	C+	C+		67.07	68.57	53.25	Y	US Equity Large Cap Blend (Growth)
● iShares Core S&P U.S. Growth ETF	IUSG	NAS CM	C+	C+	C+	Down	62.87	64.70	49.22	Y	US Equity Large Cap Growth (Growth)
● iShares Core Total USD Bond Market ETF	IUSB	NAS CM	C+	C+	C+		52.41	52.80	48.37	Y	US Fixed Income (Corp Bond - Gen)
★ iShares Core U.S. Aggregate Bond ETF	AGG	NYSE Arca	B-	C+	B		113.17	114.13	104.01	Y	US Fixed Income (Corp Bond - Gen)
● iShares Core U.S. REIT ETF	USRT	NYSE Arca	C+	C+	C+	Up	55.55	55.60	43.17	Y	Real Estate Sector Equity (Real Estate)
iShares Currency Hedged JPX-Nikkei 400 ETF	HJPX	NYSE Arca	D	C-	E+		28.27	31.34	24.76	Y	Japan Equity (Growth)
● iShares Currency Hedged MSCI ACWI ex U.S. ETF	HAWX	NYSE Arca	C	C	D+		26.96	27.36	23.30	Y	Global Equity Large Cap (Growth & Inc)
iShares Currency Hedged MSCI Australia ETF	HAUD	NYSE Arca	C	B	D		26.85	26.95	21.90	Y	Equity Misc (Foreign Stock)
iShares Currency Hedged MSCI Canada ETF	HEWC	NYSE Arca	C	C+	C-		26.98	27.24	22.32	Y	Equity Misc (Foreign Stock)
● iShares Currency Hedged MSCI EAFE ETF	HEFA	BATS	C	C	C+		29.94	30.19	25.29	Y	Global Equity Large Cap (Foreign Stock)
iShares Currency Hedged MSCI EAFE Small-Cap ETF	HSCZ	NYSE Arca	C-	C	D+		29.13	31.43	24.63	Y	Globa Eq Mid/Small Cap (Small Company)

★ Expanded analysis of this fund is included in Section II: Analysis of All BUY Rated Funds. ● Expanded analysis of this fund is included in Section III: Analysis of All Rated Funds with Assets over $50 million.

3-Month Total Return	6-Month Total Return	1-Year Total Return	3-Year Total Return	5-Year Total Return	Dividend Yield (TTM)	Expense Ratio	3-Yr Std Deviation	Effective Duration	NAV	Total Assets (MIL)	%Cash	%Stocks	%Bonds	%Other	Turnover Ratio	Premium/ Discount 1-Year Avg	Inception Date
1.07	3.23	6.00	7.92	12.38	2.82	0.06	1.36		51.07	1,915	2	0	95	0	15	0.12	Oct-13
0.40	2.04	3.38	4.91	5.97	2	0.06	1.13		100.06	2,306	0	0	100	0	40	0.04	Dec-10
5.27	11.23	19.35	9.98	25.83	2.18	0.15	7.52	12.46	149.38	1,165	1	0	99	0	45	0.13	Jan-07
-2.52	-1.44	-2.64	-4.36	-10.55	1.84	0.35	5.72		77.73	66.1	5	0	95	0	47	-0.08	Jan-09
0.63	2.26	4.26	4.22	5.98	2.11	0.15	1.03	1.85	84.79	17,773	5	0	95	0	62	0.04	Jul-02
8.68	16.08	25.73	12.48	37.15	2.24	0.15	11.86	18.35	142.89	18,504	0	0	100	0	17	0.16	Jul-02
1.45	4.59	8.82	5.69	12.75	2.08	0.15	2.99		126.74	9,126	0	0	100	0	41	0.05	Jan-07
2.95	7.60	14.01	7.03	18.93	2.21	0.15	5.28	7.63	112.45	18,869	0	0	100	0	63	0.07	Jul-02
2.83	7.34	12.18	11.64	22.50	3.01	0.15	4.08		54.68	429.3	0	0	97	0	15	0.21	Feb-12
-0.46	2.38	1.14	27.21		3.01	0.34	10.17		27.66	8.3	1	99	0	0	8	-0.08	Jan-16
1.82	4.23	7.89	7.05	12.61	2.37	0.2	2.39		116.48	582.4	1	0	99	0	69	0.10	Nov-08
-4.07	-4.00	-3.41	26.71	41.78	2.49	0.5	15.79		59.03	1,033	0	100	0	0	10	-0.07	Nov-07
-0.64	1.68	4.09	8.60	5.79	6.09	0.49	10.13		42.85	32.1	1	99	0	0	46	-0.01	Feb-12
-1.69	-4.68	-9.48			1.72	0.28			44.12	26.5	100	0	0	0	0	0.27	Apr-18
1.07	3.94	-11.50			6.06	0.22			40.70	2,552	0	0	100	0	15	0.42	Oct-17
3.07	7.84	12.81	-43.39	-38.38	3.39	0.06	4.04	7.22	58.19	3,788	2	0	96	0	27	0.13	Jan-07
1.55	4.06	7.93	8.27	17.19	2.1	0.25	3.58	6.18	61.14	1,367	0	0	100	0	32	0.16	Oct-07
-6.17	-9.67	-4.68	15.49	19.41	2.13	0.74	17.43		40.08	4,275	0	100	0	0	14	-0.05	Oct-04
2.00	5.51	10.34	9.04	17.76	2.68	0.25	3.19		53.37	397.6	0	0	99	0	13	0.15	Feb-12
7.27	9.29	23.93	26.09	67.53	2.34	0.34	12.4		119.97	2,417	0	100	0	0	17	-0.02	Jan-01
-3.78	-5.59	-12.02	13.62		9.84	0.48	11.02		31.55	517.5	67	30	2	0	167	-0.18	Oct-14
-2.73	0.50	2.06	32.97		3.45	0.2	9.36	1.83	58.10	398.0	0	0	0	0	29	0.19	Jun-15
6.34	14.07	21.53	17.83	37.56	3.52	0.06	8.27		69.29	315.3	1	0	99	0	10	0.23	Dec-09
0.86	2.87	5.98	7.02	11.90	2.75	0.06	1.43	2.54	50.43	2,809	1	0	98	0	107	0.11	Oct-12
1.73	4.89	9.83	10.13		3.05	0.06			50.66	86.1	1	0	98	0	481	0.28	Nov-16
0.00	2.96	2.56	27.36	40.07	2.27	0.25	9.06		54.89	955.1	1	79	20	0	4	0.03	Nov-08
0.93	4.64	7.27	15.99	24.44	2.73	0.25	4.08		35.64	568.5	1	29	69	0	3	0.03	Nov-08
2.36	6.70	7.90	51.93	78.06	2.29	0.08	11.65		39.13	8,645	0	100	0	0	26	0.02	Jun-14
0.57	3.65	4.45	22.85	34.37	2.44	0.25	6.94	2.34	46.01	1,339	1	58	40	0	4	0.04	Nov-08
0.12	1.70	7.01	28.45	50.78	3.33	0.08	10.95		94.14	7,409	0	100	0	0	57	-0.01	Mar-11
2.93	6.43	11.63	13.16		4.16	0.09	2.84		55.66	1,790	-1	0	100	0	11	0.23	Nov-15
1.15	4.31	6.35	18.33	27.70	2.55	0.25	4.93		39.26	1,133	2	39	60	0	4	0.03	Nov-08
-1.45	1.40	-1.64	21.25	21.62	3.2	0.07	11.19		60.95	65,004	1	99	0	0	3	0.00	Oct-12
-5.10	-4.89	-2.23	17.40	11.91	2.74	0.14	13.81		49.24	54,218	0	100	0	0	6	-0.02	Oct-12
-2.07	1.28	-1.30	21.54	17.10	3.41	0.09	12.63		45.75	3,193	0	100	0	0	4	-0.01	Jun-14
-1.23	1.67	-1.03			2.9	0.05			54.49	1,545	1	99	0	0	5	-0.04	Mar-17
-0.37	1.55	-1.83	21.37	30.33	2.85	0.09	10.16		55.96	1,058	1	99	0	0	5	0.04	Jun-14
-2.25	0.00	-1.61	20.19	18.23	2.82	0.09	11.48		57.62	16,192	1	99	0	0	6	0.09	Oct-12
0.91	4.84	3.84	45.65	69.14	2.06	0.04	12.18		298.48	186,488	0	100	0	0	5	-0.01	May-00
-0.43	1.52	-1.79	30.64	54.71	1.5	0.07	15.32		193.14	49,539	0	100	0	0	17	-0.01	May-00
-0.36	0.37	-8.02	25.20	55.48	1.44	0.07	18.05		77.87	44,003	1	99	0	0	14	0.00	May-00
0.40	4.05	2.68	43.46	67.01	1.98	0.03	12.55		67.10	22,811	0	100	0	0	6	-0.04	Jan-04
-0.12	4.08	2.58	54.05	83.28	1.42	0.04	12.44		62.91	6,832	0	100	0	0	31	-0.01	Jul-00
2.18	5.59	10.07	9.75	18.78	2.99	0.06	3.11		52.34	3,988	1	0	98	0	253	0.14	Jun-14
2.36	5.78	10.35	8.90	17.24	2.71	0.05	3.35	5.29	113.13	66,025	1	0	98	0	146	0.06	Sep-03
8.00	8.87	19.45	24.45	60.06	2.85	0.08	12.84		55.55	1,669	1	99	0	0	11	-0.02	May-07
3.23	0.90	-7.77	32.23		1.58	0.48	14.6		28.39	2.8	1	99	0	0	5	0.11	Sep-15
0.19	2.55	3.24	29.75		2.47	0.35	9.46		26.97	72.8	1	99	0	0	7	0.01	Jun-15
2.35	10.55	15.45	39.67		5.02	0.5	8.39		26.92	1.3	1	99	0	0	12	-0.74	Jun-15
1.78	4.12	6.80	23.59		2.31	0.5	9.33		26.95	39.1	0	100	0	0	10	-0.06	Jun-15
1.33	4.52	4.12	33.69	42.61	3	0.35	10.02		29.96	2,938	1	99	0	0	7	-0.01	Jan-14
1.60	2.84	-1.22	32.31		2.68	0.42	10.78		29.16	29.2	1	99	0	1	10	0.03	Jun-15

Fund Name	Ticker Symbol	Traded On	Overall Rating	Reward Rating	Risk Rating	Recent Up/ Downgrade	Price as of 9/30/2019	52-Week High	52-Week Low	Open to New Investors	Category & (Prospectus Objective)
● iShares Currency Hedged MSCI Emerging Markets ETF	HEEM	BATS	C-	C	C-		24.62	26.35	22.74	Y	Global Emerg Mkts Equity (Div Emerg Mkts)
● iShares Currency Hedged MSCI Eurozone ETF	HEZU	NYSE Arca	C	C	C+		30.92	31.03	25.39	Y	Europe Equity Large Cap (Europe Stock)
● iShares Currency Hedged MSCI Germany ETF	HEWG	NAS CM	C	C	C+		27.13	28.03	22.95	Y	Equity Misc (Foreign Stock)
iShares Currency Hedged MSCI Italy ETF	HEWI	NYSE Arca	C	C+	D	Up	17.64	17.65	14.28	Y	Equity Misc (Foreign Stock)
● iShares Currency Hedged MSCI Japan ETF	HEWJ	NYSE Arca	C	C-	C		31.16	34.61	27.38	Y	Japan Equity (Pacific Stock)
iShares Currency Hedged MSCI Mexico ETF	HEWW	NYSE Arca	D	D	D	Up	16.19	19.46	14.62	Y	Equity Misc (Foreign Stock)
iShares Currency Hedged MSCI South Korea ETF	HEWY	NYSE Arca	D	D	D	Down	25.15	29.04	23.21	Y	Equity Misc (Foreign Stock)
iShares Currency Hedged MSCI Spain ETF	HEWP	NYSE Arca	C-	C-	D+		21.80	22.52	19.49	Y	Equity Misc (Foreign Stock)
iShares Currency Hedged MSCI Switzerland ETF	HEWL	NYSE Arca	C	C+	D	Down	29.82	29.89	23.30	Y	Equity Misc (Foreign Stock)
iShares Currency Hedged MSCI United Kingdom ETF	HEWU	NYSE Arca	C	C	C-		24.02	24.69	21.25	Y	Equity Misc (Foreign Stock)
iShares Cybersecurity and Tech ETF	IHAK	NYSE Arca	U	U	U		24.74	27.42	24.45	Y	Technology Sector Equity (Technology)
● iShares Dow Jones U.S. ETF	IYY	NYSE Arca	C	C+	C-		147.54	150.59	116.74	Y	US Equity Large Cap Blend (Growth)
iShares Edge High Yield Defensive Bond ETF	HYDB	BATS	C-	C	D+	Up	50.60	50.64	45.60	Y	US Fixed Income (Corp Bond-High Yld)
● iShares Edge Investment Grade Enhanced Bond ETF	IGEB	BATS	C	C	C-	Up	52.76	53.08	46.87	Y	US Fixed Income (Corp Bond - Gen)
● iShares Edge MSCI Intl Momentum Factor ETF	IMTM	NYSE Arca	C	C	C-	Up	29.38	30.71	24.83	Y	Global Equity Large Cap (World Stock)
● iShares Edge MSCI Intl Quality Factor ETF	IQLT	NYSE Arca	C+	C+	C+	Up	29.68	30.57	24.90	Y	Global Equity Large Cap (World Stock)
iShares Edge MSCI Intl Size Factor ETF	ISZE	NYSE Arca	D+	C	D		26.16	27.56	22.98	Y	Global Equity Large Cap (Growth)
● iShares Edge MSCI Intl Value Factor ETF	IVLU	NYSE Arca	C-	D	C		22.79	25.50	21.17	Y	Global Equity Large Cap (Foreign Stock)
● iShares Edge MSCI Min Vol EAFE ETF	EFAV	BATS	C+	C+	C+	Up	73.28	73.75	65.01	Y	Global Equity Large Cap (Foreign Stock)
● iShares Edge MSCI Min Vol Emerging Markets ETF	EEMV	BATS	C	C	C+		57.09	60.02	53.54	Y	Global Emerg Mkts Equity (Div Emerg Mkts)
iShares Edge MSCI Min Vol Europe ETF	EUMV	NYSE Arca	C	C+	C-		25.43	25.94	22.37	Y	Europe Equity Large Cap (Growth)
★ iShares Edge MSCI Min Vol Global ETF	ACWV	BATS	B-	B-	C+		94.75	95.06	78.32	Y	Global Equity Large Cap (World Stock)
iShares Edge MSCI Min Vol Japan ETF	JPMV	NYSE Arca	C-	C	D+		68.08	68.94	61.00	Y	Japan Equity (Pacific Stock)
★ iShares Edge MSCI Min Vol USA ETF	USMV	BATS	B	B	A-	Down	64.10	64.69	49.77	Y	US Equity Large Cap Blend (Growth)
● iShares Edge MSCI Min Vol USA Small-Cap ETF	SMMV	BATS	C	C	C+		34.33	34.72	27.82	Y	US Equity Small Cap (Small Company)
● iShares Edge MSCI Multifactor Emerging Markets ETF	EMGF	BATS	D+	D+	C-	Down	40.88	43.96	37.92	Y	Global Emerg Mkts Equity (Div Emerg Mkts)
● iShares Edge MSCI Multifactor Global ETF	ACWF	NYSE Arca	C	C	C-	Up	29.00	30.77	24.98	Y	Global Equity Large Cap (Growth & Inc)
● iShares Edge MSCI Multifactor Intl ETF	INTF	NYSE Arca	C	C-	C+		25.50	28.22	22.95	Y	Global Equity Large Cap (Growth & Inc)
● iShares Edge MSCI Multifactor Intl Small-Cap ETF	ISCF	NYSE Arca	C-	C-	C-		28.58	31.52	24.74	Y	Globa Eq Mid/Small Cap (Small Company)
● iShares Edge MSCI Multifactor USA ETF	LRGF	NYSE Arca	C	C	C+		31.92	33.76	26.57	Y	US Equity Large Cap Value (Growth & Inc)
iShares Edge MSCI Multifactor USA Mid-Cap ETF			U	U	U		26.60	27.47	25.29	Y	US Equity Mid Cap (Growth)
● iShares Edge MSCI Multifactor USA Small-Cap ETF	SMLF	NYSE Arca	C-	C-	C-		39.89	43.15	33.54	Y	US Equity Small Cap (Small Company)
★ iShares Edge MSCI USA Momentum Factor ETF	MTUM	BATS	B-	B	C+	Up	119.25	123.04	92.80	Y	US Equity Large Cap Growth (Growth)
● iShares Edge MSCI USA Quality Factor ETF	QUAL	BATS	C+	C+	C+		92.40	94.10	71.91	Y	US Equity Large Cap Blend (Growth)
● iShares Edge MSCI USA Size Factor ETF	SIZE	NYSE Arca	C	C	C-		90.78	93.23	72.15	Y	US Equity Large Cap Blend (Growth)
● iShares Edge MSCI USA Value Factor ETF	VLUE	BATS	C	C	C		82.04	88.78	68.64	Y	US Equity Large Cap Value (Growth)
● iShares Edge U.S. Fixed Income Balanced Risk ETF	FIBR	BATS	C	C+	D+		101.32	101.63	94.77	Y	Fixed Income Misc (Income)
● iShares Emerging Markets Dividend ETF	DVYE	NYSE Arca	C	C	C+	Down	37.42	42.09	36.59	Y	Global Emerg Mkts Equity (Div Emerg Mkts)
● iShares Emerging Markets High Yield Bond ETF	EMHY	BATS	C	C+	C-		46.49	48.10	44.09	Y	Emerging Mkts Fixed Inc (Corp Bond-High Yld)
iShares Emerging Markets Infrastructure ETF	EMIF	NAS CM	C-	C	D+	Up	27.87	30.44	26.56	Y	Global Emerg Mkts Equity (Div Emerg Mkts)
● iShares ESG 1-5 Year USD Corporate Bond ETF	SUSB	NAS CM	C	C	C-	Up	25.45	25.53	24.33	Y	US Fixed Income (Corp Bond - Gen)
● iShares ESG MSCI EM ETF	ESGE	NAS CM	C	C	C		32.53	35.40	29.80	Y	Global Emerg Mkts Equity (Div Emerg Mkts)
iShares ESG MSCI USA Leaders ETF	SUSL	NAS CM	U	U	U		51.47	52.10	47.15	Y	US Equity Large Cap Blend (Unaligned)
iShares ESG U.S. Aggregate Bond ETF	EAGG	NYSE Arca	U	U	U		54.19	54.65	50.94	Y	US Fixed Income (Growth)
● iShares ESG USD Corporate Bond ETF	SUSC	NAS CM	C	C	C-	Up	26.29	26.68	23.63	Y	US Fixed Income (Corp Bond - Gen)
iShares Europe Developed Real Estate ETF	IFEU	NAS CM	D+	D+	D+		37.45	38.64	34.06	Y	Real Estate Sector Equity (Real Estate)
● iShares Europe ETF	IEV	NYSE Arca	C	C	C+		43.27	45.05	37.89	Y	Europe Equity Large Cap (Europe Stock)
★ iShares Evolved U.S. Consumer Staples ETF	IECS	BATS	B-	B	C	Up	28.01	28.24	22.54	Y	Consumer Goods & Svcs (Unaligned)
iShares Evolved U.S. Discretionary Spending ETF	IEDI	BATS	C	C+	C-	Up	29.96	30.43	22.91	Y	Consumer Goods & Svcs (Unaligned)
iShares Evolved U.S. Financials ETF	IEFN	BATS	D+	C-	D	Up	24.38	25.19	19.24	Y	Financials Sector Equity (Financial)
iShares Evolved U.S. Healthcare Staples ETF	IEHS	BATS	C	C	D+	Up	28.60	29.92	24.54	Y	Healthcare Sector Equity (Health)
iShares Evolved U.S. Innovative Healthcare ETF	IEIH	BATS	C	C+	C-	Up	24.21	27.41	22.22	Y	Healthcare Sector Equity (Health)

★Expanded analysis of this fund is included in Section II: Analysis of All BUY Rated Funds. ●Expanded analysis of this fund is included in Section III: Analysis of All Rated Funds with Assets over $50 million.

		TOTAL RETURNS & PERFORMANCE							ASSETS		ASSET ALLOCATION & TURNOVER					VALUATION	
3-Month Total Return	6-Month Total Return	1-Year Total Return	3-Year Total Return	5-Year Total Return	Dividend Yield (TTM)	Expense Ratio	3-Yr Std Deviation	Effective Duration	NAV	Total Assets (MIL)	%Cash	%Stocks	%Bonds	%Other	Turnover Ratio	Premium/ Discount 1-Year Avg	Inception Date
-3.90	-3.60	-0.67	19.15	21.04	2.44	0.67	12.15		24.64	179.9	1	99	0	0	7	-0.05	Sep-14
2.14	6.39	7.07	35.33	44.87	2.91	0.5	12.13		30.92	748.3	1	99	0	0	11	-0.02	Jul-14
-0.27	5.66	1.35	21.85	36.40	2.68	0.53	12.74		27.12	161.4	1	99	0	0	11	-0.01	Jan-14
5.03	6.19	15.57	55.64		5.36	0.47	16.88		17.65	1.8	0	100	0	0	11	-0.06	Jun-15
2.70	1.32	-7.84	32.65	35.55	2.04	0.48	14.41		31.22	337.2	1	99	0	0	9	0.03	Jan-14
-1.05	-2.27	-14.18	-16.78		2.8	0.5	13		16.23	0.81	1	99	0	0	23	-0.15	Jun-15
-2.07	-3.38	-8.04	14.70		1.39	0.59	14.94		25.22	2.5	0	100	0	0	11	-0.20	Jun-15
0.17	1.50	6.77	28.30		3.56	0.5	14.48		21.83	10.9	0	100	0	0	11	-0.21	Jun-15
2.52	9.61	16.02	47.03		1.94	0.5	10.06		29.82	7.5	1	99	0	0	14	-0.20	Jun-15
-0.18	3.67	4.50	22.95		4.42	0.47	10.23		24.05	45.7	1	99	0	0	17	-0.04	Jun-15
-4.19						0.47			24.69	3.7	0	100	0	0		0.19	Jun-19
0.56	4.26	3.14	43.65	65.70	1.86	0.2	12.38		147.53	1,195	0	100	0	0	5	-0.01	Jun-00
2.11	4.99	7.59			5.77	0.35			50.27	27.6	3	0	97	0	59	0.37	Jul-17
3.18	8.69	14.03			3.51				52.51	89.3	1	0	98	0	63	0.28	Jul-17
-1.17	3.45	-1.69	19.53		2.33	0.3	11.34		29.32	181.8	0	100	0	0	105	0.08	Jan-15
-1.95	2.78	2.85	25.56		2.26	0.3	11.03		29.66	815.6	1	99	0	0	29	0.11	Jan-15
-1.47	0.45	-1.70	17.71		2.78	0.3	10.78		26.13	5.2	1	99	0	0	26	-0.23	Jun-15
-2.02	-3.15	-7.10	15.81		3.44	0.3	11.84		22.77	316.5	1	99	0	0	20	0.05	Jun-15
0.70	3.22	3.94	19.67	36.06	2.95	0.2	8.52		73.11	11,982	1	99	0	0	22	0.06	Oct-11
-3.25	-2.80	-1.07	14.74	8.77	2.6	0.25	10.04		57.07	5,439	0	100	0	0	22	-0.04	Oct-11
0.19	4.30	4.54	21.03	25.08	3.2	0.25	10.6		25.52	24.2	1	99	0	0	23	-0.04	Jun-14
2.59	6.83	10.18	33.43	59.78	2.13	0.2	7.95		94.60	5,477	1	99	0	0	23	0.06	Oct-11
3.51	3.18	0.52	18.06	44.34	1.44	0.3	8		67.73	33.9	1	99	0	0	23	-0.04	Jun-14
3.81	9.64	14.68	49.72	89.73	1.84	0.15	9.12		64.07	35,010	0	100	0	0	21	-0.05	Oct-11
2.86	6.64	7.39	46.69		1.5	0.2	9.87		34.26	325.5	0	100	0	0	48	0.16	Sep-16
-3.05	-3.80	-2.71	15.92		2.88	0.45	13.87		40.99	418.1	1	99	0	0	39	0.07	Dec-15
-1.49	-0.29	-3.09	28.45		2.22	0.35	12.56		29.03	111.8	0	100	0	0	43	0.01	Apr-15
-2.96	-2.09	-6.28	16.82		3.17	0.3	12.12		25.51	1,069	1	99	0	0	44	0.04	Apr-15
-1.78	0.19	-6.49	19.87		2.27	0.4	12.22		28.62	83.0	1	99	0	1	45	0.05	Apr-15
0.39	2.50	-2.00	35.44		3.02	0.2	13.21		31.93	962.8	0	100	0	0	45	-0.02	Apr-15
-1.73						0.25			26.59	2.7	0	100	0	0	1	0.00	Jun-19
-1.00	-1.07	-6.18	29.68		1.29	0.3	16.67		39.87	271.1	0	100	0	0	45	0.09	Apr-15
-0.14	6.68	1.28	60.39	98.99	1.46	0.15	12.49		119.21	10,222	0	100	0	0	138	0.00	Apr-13
0.54	4.16	3.73	44.68	72.38	1.72	0.15	12.38		92.36	11,734	0	100	0	0	41	0.00	Jul-13
-0.44	2.75	5.05	37.80	64.52	1.59	0.15	12.96		90.81	390.5	0	100	0	0	30	0.06	Apr-13
1.18	2.44	-4.14	35.32	48.06	2.77	0.15	15.06		82.05	3,520	0	100	0	0	35	-0.01	Apr-13
1.10	3.86	8.07	10.24		3.52	0.25	2.61		101.24	141.7	-23	0	121	0	633	0.10	Feb-15
-6.75	-4.10	1.64	23.06	7.89	6.35	0.49	12.42		37.42	606.1	1	99	0	0	69	0.03	Feb-12
-1.54	2.14	8.36	10.03	25.38	7.06	0.5	6.81		46.43	332.0	1	0	99	0	19	0.34	Apr-12
-2.54	-0.24	1.80	0.47	-4.83	2.77	0.75	12.13		28.31	22.6	1	99	0	0	25	-0.50	Jun-09
1.19	3.40	6.81			2.83	0.12			25.38	129.4	3	0	94	0	29	0.29	Jul-17
-4.82	-4.28	-0.31	20.32		2.1	0.25	14		32.58	684.2	0	100	0	0	45	0.15	Jun-16
1.75						0.1			51.42	1,589	0	100	0	0		0.08	May-19
2.33	5.82					0.1			54.08	86.5	10	0	90	0	99	0.20	Oct-18
3.06	8.14	13.07			3.18	0.18			26.32	60.5	1	0	97	0	20	0.32	Jul-17
3.47	0.41	1.25	13.89	27.48	4.24	0.48	13.51		37.55	26.3	1	94	0	5	13	-0.22	Nov-07
-2.05	1.35	-0.84	20.20	11.96	3.27	0.59	12.51		43.33	1,623	1	99	0	0	7	-0.12	Jul-00
4.08	9.72	16.10			2.55	0.18			27.98	8.4	0	100	0	0	9	0.04	Mar-18
3.07	7.03	7.10			1.48	0.18			29.94	7.5	1	99	0	0	11	-0.01	Mar-18
0.62	6.71	2.27			2.18	0.18			24.37	4.9	0	100	0	0	10	-0.15	Mar-18
-1.94	1.49	-2.92			1.49	0.18			28.59	7.1	0	100	0	0	12	-0.01	Mar-18
-5.37	-6.19	-9.51			1.56	0.18			24.21	4.8	0	100	0	0	8	0.10	Mar-18

Fund Name	Ticker Symbol	Traded On	Overall Rating	Reward Rating	Risk Rating	Recent Up/ Downgrade	Price as of 9/30/2019	52-Week High	52-Week Low	Open to New Investors	Category & (Prospectus Objective)
		MARKET		RATINGS				PRICE			CATEGORY & OBJECTIVE
iShares Evolved U.S. Media and Entertainment ETF	IEME	BATS	C	C	D+	Up	26.62	28.70	21.99	Y	Communications Sector Equity (Unaligned)
iShares Evolved U.S. Technology ETF	IETC	BATS	C	C+	C-	Up	29.29	30.73	21.55	Y	Technology Sector Equity (Technology)
● iShares Expanded Tech Sector ETF	IGM	NYSE Arca	C+	B	C		217.02	228.47	159.35	Y	Technology Sector Equity (Technology)
★ iShares Expanded Tech-Software Sector ETF	IGV	BATS	B-	B	C		211.88	230.04	159.19	Y	Technology Sector Equity (Technology)
● iShares Exponential Technologies ETF	XT	NAS CM	C+	C	C+		38.66	39.71	31.56	Y	Equity Misc (Technology)
● iShares Fallen Angels USD Bond ETF	FALN	NAS CM	C	C+	C-		26.77	26.99	24.12	Y	US Fixed Income (Corp Bond-High Yld)
● iShares Floating Rate Bond ETF	FLOT	BATS	C	C	C+		50.97	50.98	50.22	Y	US Fixed Income (Worldwide Bond)
iShares Focused Value Factor ETF	FOVL	NYSE Arca	U	U	U		49.02	51.58	45.05	Y	US Equity Large Cap Value (Growth)
iShares Genomics Immunology and Healthcare ETF	IDNA	NYSE Arca	U	U	U		24.50	27.71	24.48	Y	Healthcare Sector Equity (Unaligned)
● iShares Global 100 ETF	IOO	NYSE Arca	C	C+	C	Down	49.45	49.89	40.41	Y	Global Equity Large Cap (World Stock)
● iShares Global Clean Energy ETF	ICLN	NAS CM	C+	B-	C		10.90	11.39	7.91	Y	Utilities Sector Equity (Natl Res)
● iShares Global Comm Services ETF	IXP	NYSE Arca	C	C+	C		57.28	60.35	48.09	Y	Communications Sector Equity (Comm)
● iShares Global Consumer Discretionary ETF	RXI	NYSE Arca	C	C+	C-		119.88	122.34	94.89	Y	Consumer Goods & Svcs (Unaligned)
● iShares Global Consumer Staples ETF	KXI	NYSE Arca	C	C	C-		54.82	55.27	44.53	Y	Consumer Goods & Svcs (Unaligned)
● iShares Global Energy ETF	IXC	NYSE Arca	C-	C-	C-		30.56	38.52	27.97	Y	Energy Sector Equity (Natl Res)
● iShares Global Financials ETF	IXG	NYSE Arca	C	C	C-	Up	64.05	66.25	54.20	Y	Financials Sector Equity (Financial)
iShares Global Green Bond ETF	BGRN	NAS CM	U	U	U		55.63	56.18	50.70	Y	Global Fixed Income (Worldwide Bond)
● iShares Global Healthcare ETF	IXJ	NYSE Arca	C+	C+	C+	Up	61.09	63.41	53.92	Y	Healthcare Sector Equity (Health)
● iShares Global Industrials ETF	EXI	NYSE Arca	C	C	C-		91.33	94.16	73.93	Y	Industrials Sector Equity (World Stock)
● iShares Global Infrastructure ETF	IGF	NAS CM	C+	C+	C+	Down	46.47	46.97	38.21	Y	Infrastructure Sector Equity (Utility)
● iShares Global Materials ETF	MXI	NYSE Arca	C	C	C-		62.72	68.02	54.93	Y	Natural Resources (Natl Res)
● iShares Global REIT ETF	REET	NYSE Arca	C+	C	C+		28.08	28.09	22.86	Y	Real Estate Sector Equity (Real Estate)
★ iShares Global Tech ETF	IXN	NYSE Arca	B-	B	C	Up	184.97	188.59	134.75	Y	Technology Sector Equity (Technology)
● iShares Global Timber & Forestry ETF	WOOD	NAS CM	D+	D+	D+	Down	58.64	75.21	52.98	Y	Natural Resources (Natl Res)
● iShares Global Utilities ETF	JXI	NYSE Arca	C+	B	C	Down	58.35	58.45	48.15	Y	Utilities Sector Equity (Utility)
● iShares GNMA Bond ETF	GNMA	NAS CM	C	C	C-		50.31	50.45	47.32	Y	US Fixed Income (Govt Bond - Mortgage)
iShares Gold Strategy ETF	IAUF	BATS	C-	C	D+	Up	55.96	59.14	45.72	Y	Commodities Specified (Growth & Inc)
● iShares Gold Trust	IAU	NYSE Arca	C+	C+	C+	Up	14.10	14.88	11.39	Y	Commodities Specified (Prec Metals)
● iShares Government/Credit Bond ETF	GBF	NYSE Arca	C	C+	D+		119.02	120.25	108.16	Y	US Fixed Income (Income)
iShares iBonds 2021 Term High Yield and Income ETF	IBHA	BATS	U	U	U		25.04	25.19	24.76	Y	US Fixed Income (Corp Bond-High Yld)
iShares iBonds 2022 Term High Yield and Income ETF	IBHB	BATS	U	U	U		24.79	25.28	24.49	Y	US Fixed Income (Corp Bond-High Yld)
iShares iBonds 2023 Term High Yield and Income ETF	IBHC	BATS	U	U	U		24.86	25.29	24.52	Y	US Fixed Income (Corp Bond-High Yld)
iShares iBonds 2024 Term High Yield and Income ETF	IBHD	BATS	U	U	U		25.35	25.51	24.69	Y	US Fixed Income (Corp Bond-High Yld)
iShares iBonds 2025 Term High Yield and Income ETF	IBHE	BATS	U	U	U		25.29	25.45	24.55	Y	US Fixed Income (Corp Bond-High Yld)
● iShares iBonds Dec 2019 Term Corporate ETF	IBDK	NYSE Arca	C	C	C+		24.85	24.87	24.73	Y	US Fixed Income (Corp Bond - Gen)
● iShares iBonds Dec 2020 Term Corporate ETF	IBDL	NYSE Arca	C	C	C+		25.37	25.38	24.92	Y	US Fixed Income (Corp Bond - Gen)
● iShares iBonds Dec 2021 Term Corporate ETF	IBDM	NYSE Arca	C+	C	C+	Up	25.00	25.02	24.16	Y	US Fixed Income (Corp Bond - Gen)
● iShares iBonds Dec 2021 Term Muni Bond ETF	IBMJ	NYSE Arca	C	C	C-		25.78	25.89	25.19	Y	US Muni Fixed Inc (Muni Bond - Natl)
● iShares iBonds Dec 2022 Term Corporate ETF	IBDN	NYSE Arca	C+	C+	C+		25.32	25.39	24.10	Y	US Fixed Income (Corp Bond - Gen)
● iShares iBonds Dec 2022 Term Muni Bond ETF	IBMK	NYSE Arca	C	C	C-		26.14	26.33	25.21	Y	US Muni Fixed Inc (Muni Bond - Natl)
● iShares iBonds Dec 2023 Term Corporate ETF	IBDO	NYSE Arca	C+	C+	C+		25.60	25.69	23.99	Y	US Fixed Income (Corp Bond - Gen)
● iShares iBonds Dec 2023 Term Muni Bond ETF	IBML	BATS	C	C	C-	Up	25.76	26.04	24.60	Y	US Muni Fixed Inc (Muni Bond - Natl)
● iShares iBonds Dec 2024 Term Corporate ETF	IBDP	NYSE Arca	C	C+	C-		25.69	25.80	23.69	Y	US Fixed Income (Corp Bond - Gen)
● iShares iBonds Dec 2024 Term Muni Bond ETF	IBMM	BATS	C-	C-	C-		26.32	26.67	24.83	Y	US Muni Fixed Inc (Growth & Inc)
● iShares iBonds Dec 2025 Term Corporate ETF	IBDQ	NYSE Arca	C	B-	C-		25.88	26.02	23.51	Y	US Fixed Income (Corp Bond - Gen)
iShares iBonds Dec 2025 Term Muni Bond ETF	IBMN	BATS	U	U	U		27.08	27.50	25.85	Y	US Muni Fixed Inc (Muni Bond - Natl)
● iShares iBonds Dec 2026 Term Corporate ETF	IBDR	NYSE Arca	C	C	C+		25.47	25.68	22.85	Y	US Fixed Income (Corp Bond - Gen)
iShares iBonds Dec 2026 Term Muni Bond ETF	IBMO	BATS	U	U	U		25.92	26.29	24.98	Y	US Muni Fixed Inc (Muni Bond - Natl)
● iShares iBonds Dec 2027 Term Corporate ETF	IBDS	NYSE Arca	C-	C-	C-		25.92	26.19	23.05	Y	US Fixed Income (Corp Bond - Gen)
iShares iBonds Dec 2027 Term Muni Bond ETF	IBMP	BATS	U	U	U		26.01	26.39	25.00	Y	US Muni Fixed Inc (Muni Bond - Natl)
● iShares iBonds Dec 2028 Term Corporate ETF	IBDT	NYSE Arca	D+	D+	C-		27.75	28.06	24.64	Y	US Fixed Income (Corp Bond - Gen)
iShares iBonds Dec 2028 Term Muni Bond ETF	IBMQ	BATS	U	U	U		26.18	26.56	25.07	Y	US Muni Fixed Inc (Muni Bond - Natl)

★ Expanded analysis of this fund is included in Section II: Analysis of All BUY Rated Funds.　● Expanded analysis of this fund is included in Section III: Analysis of All Rated Funds with Assets over $50 million.

3-Month Total Return	6-Month Total Return	1-Year Total Return	3-Year Total Return	5-Year Total Return	Dividend Yield (TTM)	Expense Ratio	3-Yr Std Deviation	Effective Duration	NAV	Total Assets (MIL)	%Cash	%Stocks	%Bonds	%Other	Turnover Ratio	Premium/Discount 1-Year Avg	Inception Date
-4.08	0.63	-2.30			0.99	0.18			26.62	5.3	1	99	0	0	10	0.13	Mar-18
-0.19	5.08	4.88			1.15	0.18			29.26	16.1	0	100	0	0	7	0.07	Mar-18
-0.65	3.97	4.08	78.67	134.34	0.52	0.46	16.07		217.05	1,639	0	100	0	0	8	-0.03	Mar-01
-4.47	-0.82	3.81	87.15	152.65	0.13	0.46	16.32		211.87	2,553	0	100	0	0	18	-0.02	Jul-01
-0.84	1.38	1.09	52.55		1.43	0.47	13.74		38.68	2,508	0	100	0	0	21	-0.10	Mar-15
1.39	4.18	5.92	20.05		5.66	0.25	4.84		26.54	134.0	2	1	97	0	29	0.43	Jun-16
0.72	1.85	2.80	6.94	8.05	2.88	0.2	0.5		50.93	9,885	4	0	94	0	17	0.02	Jun-11
-1.42	-0.44					0.25			49.04	31.9	0	100	0	0		-0.04	Mar-19
-10.43						0.47			24.45	22.0	0	100	0	0		0.20	Jun-19
0.48	4.35	3.14	41.81	46.44	2.19	0.4	11.14		49.50	1,995	0	100	0	0	9	-0.08	Dec-00
2.35	11.63	29.82	29.67	17.48	1.68	0.46	16.68		10.88	357.9	1	99	0	0	42	0.13	Jun-08
-0.43	2.38	2.19	3.80	10.37	3.07	0.46	12.95		57.32	255.1	0	100	0	0	79	-0.05	Nov-01
0.17	5.31	1.40	40.35	61.23	1.57	0.46	13.37		119.72	215.5	0	100	0	0	30	-0.06	Sep-06
3.94	7.31	11.78	18.54	41.46	2.4	0.46	10.64		54.76	856.9	1	99	0	0	7	0.01	Sep-06
-5.99	-8.34	-16.72	2.99	-16.55	3.98	0.46	17.56		30.60	858.5	0	100	0	0	6	-0.12	Nov-01
-1.05	3.49	-0.37	35.23	30.12	2.8	0.46	14.56		63.88	261.9	1	99	0	0	7	-0.03	Nov-01
2.75	6.98					0.2		7.71	55.41	30.5	0	0	99	0		0.27	Nov-18
-1.62	0.37	-1.68	27.52	38.24	1.93	0.46	12.1		61.05	1,908	0	100	0	0	8	0.02	Nov-01
-0.79	2.24	-0.90	30.63	44.69	1.88	0.46	13.92		91.27	187.1	0	100	0	0	5	-0.03	Sep-06
1.00	5.45	13.63	23.16	28.26	3.18	0.46	10.26		46.44	3,241	0	100	0	0	19	0.09	Dec-07
-4.38	-1.43	-3.72	26.87	20.61	3.84	0.46	13.8		62.77	182.0	0	100	0	0	11	-0.14	Sep-06
6.00	6.99	16.51	19.28	46.76	3.72	0.14	11.14		28.00	1,767	1	98	0	1	9	-0.01	Jul-14
1.31	7.26	6.06	72.17	116.09	1.03	0.46	15.06		184.56	2,805	0	100	0	0	17	-0.03	Nov-01
-3.19	-8.49	-19.77	24.42	31.63	3.3	0.46	19.18		58.46	217.5	1	100	0	0	18	-0.12	Jun-08
7.18	10.45	22.62	37.03	46.72	3.04	0.46	10.3		58.32	387.8	0	100	0	0	8	0.02	Sep-06
1.18	3.50	7.40	6.10	11.75	2.7	0.15	2.4		50.28	173.5	8	0	92	0	834	0.05	Feb-12
5.79	13.77	23.03			0.67	0.25			55.85	8.4	77	0	0	23	13	0.09	Jun-18
6.78	14.68	24.57	11.48	20.57	0	0.25	11.17		14.20	16,353	0	0	0	100	0	-0.10	Jan-05
2.72	6.62	11.26	9.25	17.79	2.52	0.2	3.78		118.83	202.0	1	0	98	0	24	0.08	Jan-07
0.90						0.35		1.32	24.98	12.5	1	0	99	0		0.10	May-19
-0.02						0.35		1.60	24.73	9.9	2	0	98	0		0.14	May-19
0.21						0.35		2.20	24.78	12.4	1	0	99	0		0.14	May-19
1.19						0.35		2.30	25.28	12.6	1	0	99	0		0.10	May-19
1.31						0.35		3.05	25.20	12.6	0	0	100	0		0.09	May-19
0.57	1.21	2.64	5.38		2.26	0.1	0.66		24.87	677.7	99	0	0	0	5	0.05	Mar-15
0.77	1.83	3.92	5.75		2.52	0.1	1.29		25.33	1,236	4	0	95	0	5	0.15	Dec-14
0.96	2.53	5.40	6.68		2.68	0.1	1.79		24.94	1,279	0	0	99	0	6	0.21	Mar-15
0.31	1.24	3.37	3.02		1.42	0.18	2.48		25.76	293.6	0	0	100	0	0	0.05	Sep-15
1.19	3.42	7.22	8.05		2.87	0.1	2.41		25.28	998.4	1	0	97	0	2	0.18	Mar-15
0.35	1.57	4.42	3.56		1.53	0.18	3.12		26.10	321.1	0	0	100	0	0	0.07	Sep-15
1.46	4.29	8.69	9.42		3.03	0.1	2.88	3.39	25.53	824.5	0	0	97	0	8	0.22	Mar-15
0.42	1.93	5.58			1.7	0.18			25.72	201.9	0	0	100	0	0	0.11	Apr-17
1.65	5.32	10.20	10.94		3.21	0.1	3.37		25.61	596.7	0	0	97	0	6	0.27	Mar-15
0.58	2.43	7.15			1.83	0.18			26.30	93.4	0	0	100	0	0	0.09	Mar-18
1.92	6.21	11.83	12.03		3.29	0.1	3.87		25.80	492.9	1	0	98	0	5	0.22	Mar-15
0.88	3.02					0.18			27.04	39.2	1	0	99	0		0.09	Nov-18
2.36	7.31	13.10	11.66		3.34	0.1	4.36		25.36	353.8	0	0	97	0	3	0.31	Sep-16
1.33	4.22					0.18			25.87	14.2	1	0	99	0		0.12	Apr-19
2.61	8.02	13.88			3.41	0.1			25.82	227.2	0	0	99	0	5	0.36	Sep-17
1.55						0.18			25.98	13.0	1	0	99	0		0.11	Apr-19
2.86	8.57	14.70			3.71	0.1			27.63	106.4	0	0	98	0	0	0.47	Sep-18
1.93						0.18			26.15	23.5	1	0	99	0		0.13	Apr-19

Fund Name	Ticker Symbol	Traded On	Overall Rating	Reward Rating	Risk Rating	Recent Up/ Downgrade	Price as of 9/30/2019	52-Week High	52-Week Low	Open to New Investors	Category & (Prospectus Objective)
● iShares iBonds Mar 2020 Term Corporate ETF	IBDC	NYSE Arca	C	C	C-		26.15	26.15	25.85	Y	US Fixed Income (Corp Bond - Gen)
● iShares iBonds Mar 2020 Term Corporate ex-Financials ETF	IBCD	NYSE Arca	C	C	C-	Up	24.61	24.62	24.32	Y	US Fixed Income (Corp Bond - High Quality)
● iShares iBonds Mar 2023 Term Corporate ETF	IBDD	NYSE Arca	C	C+	D+		26.86	26.97	25.36	Y	US Fixed Income (Corp Bond - Gen)
iShares iBonds Mar 2023 Term Corporate ex-Financials ETF	IBCE	NYSE Arca	C	C+	D+	Up	24.61	24.68	23.34	Y	US Fixed Income (Corp Bond - High Quality)
● iShares iBonds Sep 2020 Term Muni Bond ETF	IBMI	NYSE Arca	C	C	C-	Up	25.53	25.61	25.17	Y	US Muni Fixed Inc (Muni Bond - Natl)
★ iShares iBoxx $ High Yield Corporate Bond ETF	HYG	NYSE Arca	B	C+	A		87.17	87.61	79.63	Y	US Fixed Income (Corp Bond-High Yld)
iShares iBoxx $ High Yield ex Oil & Gas Corporate Bond ETF	HYXE	NAS CM	C	C+	D+	Up	51.94	51.94	47.38	Y	US Fixed Income (Corp Bond-High Yld)
★ iShares iBoxx $ Investment Grade Corporate Bond ETF	LQD	NYSE Arca	B-	B-	B		127.48	129.10	111.35	Y	US Fixed Income (Corp Bond - Gen)
● iShares India 50 ETF	INDY	NAS CM	C	C-	C+	Down	36.70	39.47	31.33	Y	India Equity (Foreign Stock)
iShares Inflation Hedged Corporate Bond ETF	LQDI	BATS	D+	C-	D	Up	26.31	26.84	23.74	Y	US Fixed Income (Corp Bond - Gen)
● iShares Interest Rate Hedged Corporate Bond ETF	LQDH	NYSE Arca	C	C	C-		92.97	97.25	90.21	Y	US Fixed Income (Growth & Inc)
● iShares Interest Rate Hedged Emerging Markets Bond ETF	EMBH	NYSE Arca	C-	C	D+	Down	24.32	25.84	24.08	Y	Emerging Mkts Fixed Inc (Growth & Inc)
● iShares Interest Rate Hedged High Yield Bond ETF	HYGH	NYSE Arca	C	C	C-		88.20	92.71	84.17	Y	US Fixed Income (Corp Bond-High Yld)
● iShares Interest Rate Hedged Long-Term Corporate Bond ETF	IGBH	NYSE Arca	C	C	C-		24.11	26.37	23.80	Y	US Fixed Income (Growth & Inc)
● iShares Intermediate Government/Credit Bond ETF	GVI	BATS	C	C	C-		113.22	113.96	106.45	Y	US Fixed Income (Income)
● iShares Intermediate-Term Corporate Bond ETF	IGIB	NAS CM	D	D	D		57.92	58.42	52.01	Y	US Fixed Income (Growth & Inc)
● iShares International Developed Property ETF	WPS	NYSE Arca	C	C	C-		38.50	39.08	34.00	Y	Real Estate Sector Equity (Real Estate)
● iShares International Developed Real Estate ETF	IFGL	NAS CM	C	C	C-	Down	29.67	30.55	26.69	Y	Real Estate Sector Equity (Real Estate)
● iShares International Dividend Growth ETF	IGRO	BATS	C	C	D+	Up	55.36	56.34	48.08	Y	Global Equity Large Cap (Equity-Income)
iShares International High Yield Bond ETF	HYXU	BATS	C	C	C-	Up	49.96	52.57	47.72	Y	Global Fixed Income (Corp Bond-High Yld)
iShares International Preferred Stock ETF	IPFF	BATS	D+	D	C-	Up	15.08	17.80	14.14	Y	US Fixed Income (Growth & Inc)
● iShares International Select Dividend ETF	IDV	BATS	C	C	C+		30.74	32.63	27.96	Y	Global Equity Large Cap (Foreign Stock)
● iShares International Treasury Bond ETF	IGOV	NAS CM	C	C	C+		50.47	51.68	47.13	Y	Global Fixed Income (Worldwide Bond)
● iShares J.P. Morgan EM Corporate Bond ETF	CEMB	BATS	C	B-	C-		51.19	51.29	47.04	Y	Emerging Mkts Fixed Inc (Income)
● iShares J.P. Morgan EM Local Currency Bond ETF	LEMB	NYSE Arca	C-	C-	C		44.21	46.98	42.53	Y	Emerging Mkts Fixed Inc (Worldwide Bond)
★ iShares J.P. Morgan USD Emerging Markets Bond ETF	EMB	NAS CM	B-	B-	B-		113.35	115.59	102.36	Y	Emerging Mkts Fixed Inc (Div Emerg Mkts)
● iShares JPX-Nikkei 400 ETF	JPXN	NYSE Arca	C-	C-	C-		61.12	65.34	52.64	Y	Japan Equity (Pacific Stock)
● iShares Latin America 40 ETF	ILF	NYSE Arca	C	C	C		31.58	35.55	29.20	Y	Latin America Equity (Growth)
★ iShares Long-Term Corporate Bond ETF	IGLB	NYSE Arca	B-	B	C+		66.63	67.97	55.17	Y	US Fixed Income (Growth & Inc)
● iShares MBS ETF	MBB	NAS CM	C+	C+	C+	Up	108.30	108.50	101.79	Y	US Fixed Income (Govt Bond - Mortgage)
● iShares Micro-Cap ETF	IWC	NYSE Arca	C-	D+	C-		88.15	104.35	77.77	Y	US Equity Small Cap (Growth)
● iShares Morningstar Large-Cap ETF	JKD	NYSE Arca	C	C+	C		167.94	170.80	133.93	Y	US Equity Large Cap Blend (Growth)
● iShares Morningstar Large-Cap Growth ETF	JKE	NYSE Arca	C+	B-	C	Up	191.45	198.74	147.58	Y	US Equity Large Cap Growth (Growth)
● iShares Morningstar Large-Cap Value ETF	JKF	NYSE Arca	C	C+	C-		110.45	111.53	91.27	Y	US Equity Large Cap Value (Growth)
● iShares Morningstar Mid-Cap ETF	JKG	NYSE Arca	C	C	D+		197.77	200.59	152.72	Y	US Equity Mid Cap (Growth)
● iShares Morningstar Mid-Cap Growth ETF	JKH	NYSE Arca	C	C+	C-	Down	243.43	259.55	180.97	Y	US Equity Mid Cap (Growth)
● iShares Morningstar Mid-Cap Value ETF	JKI	NAS CM	C	C	D+		160.99	162.69	132.21	Y	US Equity Mid Cap (Growth)
● iShares Morningstar Multi-Asset Income ETF	IYLD	BATS	C	C+	C-		24.97	25.17	23.02	Y	Cautious Allocation (Multi-Asset Global)
● iShares Morningstar Small-Cap ETF	JKJ	NYSE Arca	C-	C	D+		175.07	179.26	139.81	Y	US Equity Small Cap (Small Company)
● iShares Morningstar Small-Cap Growth ETF	JKK	NYSE Arca	C-	C	D+	Down	194.66	210.36	154.61	Y	US Equity Small Cap (Small Company)
● iShares Morningstar Small-Cap Value ETF	JKL	NYSE Arca	D+	D+	D+		133.73	152.91	117.04	Y	US Equity Small Cap (Small Company)
● iShares Mortgage Real Estate Capped ETF	REM	BATS	C	C+	C	Down	42.13	44.37	38.44	Y	Real Estate Sector Equity (Real Estate)
★ iShares MSCI ACWI ETF	ACWI	NAS CM	B-	C	B		73.75	75.05	61.18	Y	Global Equity Large Cap (World Stock)
● iShares MSCI ACWI ex U.S. ETF	ACWX	NAS CM	C	C	C+		46.05	47.84	40.69	Y	Global Equity Large Cap (Foreign Stock)
● iShares MSCI ACWI Low Carbon Target ETF	CRBN	NYSE Arca	C	C	D+		120.16	122.22	99.00	Y	Global Equity Large Cap (World Stock)
● iShares MSCI All Country Asia ex Japan ETF	AAXJ	NAS CM	C	C-	C+		66.32	73.40	61.12	Y	Asia ex-Japan Equity (Pacific Stock)
iShares MSCI Argentina and Global Exposure ETF	AGT	BATS	C-	C	D	Up	19.62	28.99	18.45	Y	Equity Misc (Foreign Stock)
● iShares MSCI Australia ETF	EWA	NYSE Arca	C+	B-	C+		22.25	22.81	18.42	Y	Australia & New Zealand Equity (Pacific Stock)
● iShares MSCI Austria Capped ETF	EWO	NYSE Arca	D+	D+	C-	Down	19.26	22.99	17.50	Y	Europe Equity Mid/Small Cap (Europe Stock)
iShares MSCI Belgium Capped ETF	EWK	NYSE Arca	D+	D+	C-	Down	18.88	19.44	16.01	Y	Equity Misc (Europe Stock)
● iShares MSCI Brazil Capped ETF	EWZ	NYSE Arca	C	C+	C		42.13	46.73	33.71	Y	Latin America Equity (Foreign Stock)
★ iShares MSCI Brazil Small-Cap ETF	EWZS	NAS CM	B	B+	C	Up	17.21	18.65	11.78	Y	Latin America Equity (Foreign Stock)

★Expanded analysis of this fund is included in Section II: Analysis of All BUY Rated Funds. ● Expanded analysis of this fund is included in Section III: Analysis of All Rated Funds with Assets over $50 million.

									ASSETS		ASSET ALLOCATION & TURNOVER					VALUATION	
3-Month Total Return	6-Month Total Return	1-Year Total Return	3-Year Total Return	5-Year Total Return	Dividend Yield (TTM)	Expense Ratio	3-Yr Std Deviation	Effective Duration	NAV	Total Assets (MIL)	%Cash	%Stocks	%Bonds	%Other	Turnover Ratio	Premium/ Discount 1-Year Avg	Inception Date
0.58	1.37	2.99	5.45	12.03	2.32	0.1	0.84		26.10	152.7	57	0	43	0	5	0.09	Jul-13
0.59	1.36	2.90	4.72	10.85	2	0.1	0.86		24.60	79.9	62	0	38	0	5	0.07	Apr-13
1.25	3.65	7.64	8.14	19.03	2.85	0.1	2.62		26.82	79.1	2	0	96	0	3	0.13	Jul-13
1.21	3.46	7.33	6.82	17.82	2.67	0.1	2.67		24.60	25.8	1	0	99	0	5	0.03	Apr-13
0.24	0.85	2.37	2.54	7.67	1.23	0.18	1.78		25.54	341.0	0	0	100	0	0	0.04	Aug-14
0.97	3.80	6.14	17.19	23.69	5.29	0.49	4.23	3.37	86.89	17,978	1	0	99	0	14	0.15	Apr-07
1.77	4.68	8.29	18.84		5.75	0.5	4		51.68	18.1	2	0	98	0	24	0.43	Jun-16
3.37	9.70	14,99	14.75	26.90	3.35	0.15	5.13	9.11	127.23	36,121	0	0	97	0	10	0.09	Jul-02
-5.54	-3.20	7.88	25.59	27.36	0.98	0.94	16.14		36.62	749.0	0	100	0	0	24	0.03	Nov-09
1.08	5.98	8.52			3.46	0.19		9.11	26.25	7.9	12	0	85	0	0	0.09	May-18
-1.12	0.82	0.79	11.61	10.83	3.34	0.25	3.75		93.01	125.6	1	0	96	0	2	-0.05	May-14
-2.84	-1.80	-0.84	9.69		5.3	0.48	5.72		24.33	7.3	6	0	94	0	0	-0.01	Jul-15
0.02	0.88	1.00	17.57	18.28	6.01	0.53	5.06		88.21	119.1	3	0	97	0	0	-0.04	May-14
-2.31	-0.62	-2.53	13.88		3.99	0.16	5.86		24.17	61.6	11	0	89	0	5	-0.06	Jul-15
1.43	4.16	8.01	6.80	12.68	2.26	0.2	2.38		113.16	1,997	1	0	98	0	21	0.05	Jan-07
2.58	7.51	13.34	-43.00	-39.30	3.65	0.06	3.37		57.82	8,297	0	0	96	0	86	0.08	Jan-07
1.65	1.17	9.19	17.84	30.41	4.22	0.48	10.33		38.58	123.5	1	98	0	1	9	-0.11	Jul-07
1.14	0.45	9.02	17.99	26.61	4.92	0.48	10.66		29.73	383.5	1	98	0	2	8	-0.11	Nov-07
-0.49	3.30	1.28	20.15		2.88	0.22	11.41		55.11	74.4	1	99	0	0	34	0.30	May-16
-2.67	0.04	-1.26	9.52	3.88	3.89	0.4	7.77		49.82	39.9	1	0	99	0	31	0.22	Apr-12
-1.41	-1.64	-12.81	4.66	-20.26	4.78	0.55	10.77	2.87	14.94	45.6	9	0	0	3	34	-0.27	Nov-11
0.84	2.21	-0.09	19.50	11.25	5.9	0.49	11.32		30.75	4,251	1	99	0	0	35	-0.03	Jun-07
-0.47	3.13	5.22	1.32	3.09	0.3	0.35	6.67		50.37	916.7	5	0	95	0	10	0.06	Jan-09
1.69	5.42	10.88	14.55	24.86	4.42	0.5	3.66		51.09	155.8	1	0	97	0	16	0.38	Apr-12
-3.87	0.54	6.77	0.34	-3.82	3.35	0.3	10.36	5.09	44.42	550.8	2	0	98	0	51	0.12	Oct-11
0.89	5.85	11.53	12.24	28.19	5.45	0.39	6.12	7.41	113.24	14,869	0	0	100	0	15	0.30	Dec-07
1.64	2.55	-5.14	17.90	30.23	1.56	0.48	10.51		60.49	99.8	1	99	0	0	11	-0.19	Oct-01
-7.33	-5.13	3.15	21.80	-0.87	2.95	0.48	22.36		31.57	1,476	0	100	0	0	20	-0.07	Oct-01
5.73	13.80	20.05	19.85	36.16	3.92	0.06	7.58		66.44	1,734	2	0	98	0	24	0.21	Dec-09
1.43	3.64	7.86	6.69	13.41	2.77	0.07	2.52	3.15	108.28	18,818	1	0	99	0	343	0.03	Mar-07
-5.57	-5.21	-14.71	16.52	36.85	1.16	0.6	18.02		88.14	784.5	0	100	0	0	25	-0.02	Aug-05
1.39	5.41	1.77	39.78	64.48	2.47	0.2	12.18		167.94	814.5	0	100	0	0	38	0.00	Jun-04
-1.06	3.61	3.17	61.08	86.73	0.57	0.25	13.19		191.37	1,139	0	100	0	0	23	-0.01	Jun-04
2.50	5.03	5.48	35.92	52.39	2.76	0.25	12.16		110.44	508.0	0	100	0	0	24	0.00	Jun-04
1.75	4.43	6.19	34.21	56.35	1.39	0.25	13.88		197.73	711.8	0	100	0	0	60	0.05	Jun-04
-3.96	2.57	4.19	51.68	70.84	0.24	0.3	14.51		243.40	596.3	0	100	0	0	30	0.03	Jun-04
2.05	3.29	2.15	28.20	52.20	2.46	0.3	14		160.66	473.9	0	100	0	0	35	0.02	Jun-04
-0.37	3.17	6.52	14.73	23.87	5.21	0.59	5.8		24.97	382.0	1	36	58	0	50	0.06	Apr-12
0.21	2.88	-0.25	26.17	47.95	1.3	0.25	16.16		175.14	236.4	0	100	0	0	67	0.09	Jun-04
-4.90	-2.93	-6.98	37.80	62.28	0.26	0.3	17.34		194.72	214.2	0	100	0	0	55	-0.06	Jun-04
-2.01	-3.46	-10.12	9.96	27.90	2.46	0.3	18.17		133.70	387.7	0	100	0	0	48	0.04	Jun-04
2.17	1.16	5.99	31.92	48.16	8.84	0.48	12.76		42.11	1,297	2	98	0	0	25	-0.01	May-07
-0.63	2.44	1.34	33.15	41.16	2.1	0.32	11.33		73.73	10,677	0	100	0	0	11	0.00	Mar-08
-2.39	-0.04	-1.31	19.83	15.85	2.54	0.32	11.5		45.96	3,916	1	99	0	0	15	-0.05	Mar-08
-0.39	3.11	2.24	32.45		2.24	0.2	11.32		120.05	480.2	0	100	0	0	14	0.02	Dec-14
-5.38	-6.37	-3.94	17.87	19.49	2.01	0.69	14.55		66.56	3,661	0	100	0	0	17	-0.09	Aug-08
-29.72	-17.28	-12.24			1.26	0.59			19.62	8.8	0	100	0	0	42	-0.19	Apr-17
-1.11	4.64	6.51	23.92	17.83	5.36	0.47	11.09		22.18	1,544	1	99	0	0	3	0.04	Mar-96
-3.54	-1.68	-12.54	29.04	36.19	4.04	0.47	16.59		19.30	56.0	2	98	0	0	19	-0.22	Mar-96
2.27	3.44	0.53	8.71	30.78	2.35	0.47	14.48		18.87	48.3	0	98	0	2	13	-0.09	Mar-96
-5.15	1.27	28.28	34.50	11.95	2.64	0.59	28.48		41.92	8,411	1	99	0	0	30	-0.12	Jul-00
1.24	11.54	53.12	67.66	22.24	3.48	0.59	30.24		17.14	115.7	0	100	0	0	67	-0.16	Sep-10

Fund Name	Ticker Symbol	Traded On	Overall Rating	Reward Rating	Risk Rating	Recent Up/ Downgrade	Price as of 9/30/2019	52-Week High	52-Week Low	Open to New Investors	Category & (Prospectus Objective)
● iShares MSCI BRIC ETF	BKF	NYSE Arca	C-	C	C-	Down	40.45	44.29	36.50	Y	Global Emerg Mkts Equity (Foreign Stock)
● iShares MSCI Canada ETF	EWC	NYSE Arca	C+	C+	B-	Up	28.90	29.16	23.10	Y	Canadian Equity Large Cap (Foreign Stock)
● iShares MSCI Chile Capped ETF	ECH	BATS	D	D	D	Down	37.44	47.51	34.44	Y	Equity Misc (Foreign Stock)
● iShares MSCI China A ETF	CNYA	BATS	C	C	C-	Up	27.71	31.33	22.38	Y	Greater China Equity (Pacific Stock)
● iShares MSCI China ETF	MCHI	NAS CM	C	C-	C		56.08	65.03	51.00	Y	Greater China Equity (Pacific Stock)
iShares MSCI China Small-Cap ETF	ECNS	NYSE Arca	D	D	D+	Down	38.70	47.43	37.63	Y	Greater China Equity (Pacific Stock)
iShares MSCI Colombia ETF	ICOL	NYSE Arca	D+	D+	C-		12.69	14.19	10.81	Y	Equity Misc (Foreign Stock)
iShares MSCI Denmark ETF	EDEN	BATS	D+	C-	D+	Down	60.83	64.67	55.52	Y	Equity Misc (Europe Stock)
● iShares MSCI EAFE ESG Optimized ETF	ESGD	NAS CM	C	C	C+		64.12	66.33	55.20	Y	Global Equity Large Cap (Growth & Inc)
● iShares MSCI EAFE ETF	EFA	NYSE Arca	C	C	B		65.21	68.07	56.89	Y	Global Equity Large Cap (Foreign Stock)
● iShares MSCI EAFE Growth ETF	EFG	BATS	C+	C	C+	Up	80.51	82.17	66.77	Y	Global Equity Large Cap (Foreign Stock)
● iShares MSCI EAFE Small-Cap ETF	SCZ	NAS CM	C	C-	C+		57.23	62.49	49.58	Y	Globa Eq Mid/Small Cap (Small Company)
● iShares MSCI EAFE Value ETF	EFV	BATS	C-	D+	C+	Down	47.37	52.00	43.66	Y	Global Equity Large Cap (Foreign Stock)
● iShares MSCI Emerging Markets Asia ETF	EEMA	NAS CM	D+	D+	C-	Down	63.74	70.17	58.61	Y	Asia ex-Japan Equity (Pacific Stock)
● iShares MSCI Emerging Markets ETF	EEM	NYSE Arca	C	C-	C+		40.87	44.59	38.00	Y	Global Emerg Mkts Equity (Div Emerg Mkts)
iShares MSCI Emerging Markets ex China ETF	EMXC	NAS CM	C-	C-	D+	Up	47.70	50.47	44.67	Y	Global Emerg Mkts Equity (Div Emerg Mkts)
● iShares MSCI Emerging Markets Small-Cap ETF	EEMS	NYSE Arca	D+	D	C-	Down	42.11	46.29	39.95	Y	Global Emerg Mkts Equity (Div Emerg Mkts)
● iShares MSCI Europe Financials ETF	EUFN	NAS CM	D+	D	C	Down	17.60	20.14	16.08	Y	Financials Sector Equity (Financial)
● iShares MSCI Europe Small-Cap ETF	IEUS	NAS CM	D+	D+	C-	Down	48.74	55.55	43.21	Y	Europe Equity Large Cap (Small Company)
● iShares MSCI Eurozone ETF	EZU	BATS	C	C-	C+		38.89	41.01	33.85	Y	Europe Equity Large Cap (Europe Stock)
iShares MSCI Finland ETF	EFNL	BATS	D+	C-	D+	Down	36.38	41.09	34.19	Y	Equity Misc (Europe Stock)
● iShares MSCI France ETF	EWQ	NYSE Arca	C	C	C+		30.14	31.36	25.56	Y	Europe Equity Large Cap (Europe Stock)
● iShares MSCI Frontier 100 ETF	FM	NYSE Arca	C	C	C		28.14	30.49	26.01	Y	Global Emerg Mkts Equity (Div Emerg Mkts)
● iShares MSCI Germany ETF	EWG	NYSE Arca	C-	D+	C		26.91	29.90	24.44	Y	Europe Equity Large Cap (Europe Stock)
iShares MSCI Germany Small-Cap ETF	EWGS	BATS	C-	C-	D+		53.03	60.36	46.49	Y	Equity Misc (Europe Stock)
iShares MSCI Global Agriculture Producers ETF	VEGI	NYSE Arca	C	C	C-	Up	27.47	30.12	24.90	Y	Natural Resources (Unaligned)
iShares MSCI Global Energy Producers ETF	FILL	NYSE Arca	C-	C-	C-	Up	18.80	24.30	17.42	Y	Energy Sector Equity (Natl Res)
● iShares MSCI Global Gold Miners ETF	RING	NAS CM	C	C	C-	Up	21.53	24.66	14.21	Y	Prec Metals (Prec Metals)
● iShares MSCI Global Impact ETF	SDG	NAS CM	C	C	D+	Up	58.38	60.34	51.40	Y	Global Equity Large Cap (Growth & Inc)
● iShares MSCI Global Metals & Mining Producers ETF	PICK	BATS	C	C-	C		26.62	32.95	24.56	Y	Prec Metals (Prec Metals)
● iShares MSCI Global Silver Miners ETF	SLVP	BATS	C-	C-	D+	Up	9.67	11.35	7.32	Y	Prec Metals (Prec Metals)
● iShares MSCI Hong Kong ETF	EWH	NYSE Arca	C	C-	B-	Down	22.70	27.14	21.26	Y	Greater China Equity (Pacific Stock)
● iShares MSCI India ETF	INDA	BATS	C	D+	B-	Down	33.57	36.38	29.30	Y	India Equity (Pacific Stock)
● iShares MSCI India Small-Cap ETF	SMIN	BATS	D	D	D+	Down	35.16	40.98	32.20	Y	India Equity (Small Company)
● iShares MSCI Indonesia ETF	EIDO	NYSE Arca	C-	C	D+		24.47	27.69	20.88	Y	Asia ex-Japan Equity (Pacific Stock)
● iShares MSCI Ireland ETF	EIRL	NYSE Arca	D+	D+	D+	Down	40.96	44.70	36.16	Y	Equity Misc (Europe Stock)
● iShares MSCI Israel Capped ETF	EIS	NYSE Arca	C	C	C-	Up	54.60	56.84	46.52	Y	Equity Misc (Foreign Stock)
● iShares MSCI Italy Capped ETF	EWI	NYSE Arca	C	C	C+		27.57	28.59	23.28	Y	Europe Equity Large Cap (Europe Stock)
iShares MSCI Japan Equal Weighted ETF	EWJE	NAS CM	U	U	U		34.34	34.89	32.30	Y	Japan Equity (Pacific Stock)
● iShares MSCI Japan ETF	EWJ	NYSE Arca	C	C-	C+		56.74	60.64	49.12	Y	Japan Equity (Pacific Stock)
● iShares MSCI Japan Small-Cap ETF	SCJ	NYSE Arca	C-	C-	C-		71.84	78.48	61.80	Y	Japan Equity (Pacific Stock)
iShares MSCI Japan Value ETF	EWJV	NAS CM	U	U	U		25.09	25.37	22.98	Y	Japan Equity (Pacific Stock)
● iShares MSCI KLD 400 Social ETF	DSI	NYSE Arca	C	C+	C		110.91	113.26	87.24	Y	US Equity Large Cap Blend (Growth)
● iShares MSCI Kokusai ETF	TOK	NYSE Arca	C	C	D+		68.45	69.26	55.44	Y	Global Equity Large Cap (World Stock)
● iShares MSCI Malaysia ETF	EWM	NYSE Arca	D+	D	C-	Down	27.85	32.50	27.64	Y	Asia ex-Japan Equity (Pacific Stock)
● iShares MSCI Mexico Capped ETF	EWW	NYSE Arca	D	D	C-		42.72	51.61	37.76	Y	Mexico Equity (Foreign Stock)
● iShares MSCI Netherlands ETF	EWN	NYSE Arca	C+	C	C+	Up	31.36	31.98	25.35	Y	Europe Equity Large Cap (Europe Stock)
● iShares MSCI New Zealand ETF	ENZL	NAS CM	C+	B	C-	Down	51.87	55.85	43.93	Y	Australia & New Zealand Equity (Pacific Stock)
iShares MSCI Norway ETF	ENOR	BATS	C-	C-	C-		23.28	29.46	21.79	Y	Equity Misc (Europe Stock)
● iShares MSCI Pacific ex Japan ETF	EPP	NYSE Arca	C	C	C+	Down	44.73	47.91	39.46	Y	Asia ex-Japan Equity (Pacific Stock)
● iShares MSCI Peru ETF	EPU	NYSE Arca	C-	C-	C-		35.06	40.04	32.84	Y	Equity Misc (Foreign Stock)
● iShares MSCI Philippines ETF	EPHE	NYSE Arca	D+	D	D+		33.45	37.08	28.20	Y	Asia ex-Japan Equity (Pacific Stock)

★ Expanded analysis of this fund is included in Section II: Analysis of All BUY Rated Funds. ● Expanded analysis of this fund is included in Section III: Analysis of All Rated Funds with Assets over $50 million.

			TOTAL RETURNS & PERFORMANCE						ASSETS		ASSET ALLOCATION & TURNOVER					VALUATION	
3-Month Total Return	6-Month Total Return	1-Year Total Return	3-Year Total Return	5-Year Total Return	Dividend Yield (TTM)	Expense Ratio	3-Yr Std Deviation	Effective Duration	NAV	Total Assets (MIL)	%Cash	%Stocks	%Bonds	%Other	Turnover Ratio	Premium/ Discount 1-Year Avg	Inception Date
-5.33	-5.95	2.77	26.42	22.16	2.17	0.67	15.36		40.65	162.6	1	99	0	0	22	-0.22	Nov-07
0.90	4.37	2.02	20.35	5.64	2.29	0.47	13.3		28.90	2,717	0	100	0	0	3	-0.07	Mar-96
-8.37	-13.05	-16.37	7.75	-1.67	2.17	0.59	22.56		37.41	376.0	0	100	0	0	54	-0.22	Nov-07
-5.76	-7.75	9.04	14.04		0.65	0.65	18.24		27.65	163.2	0	100	0	0	44	0.48	Jun-16
-5.68	-9.99	-4.18	22.99	30.66	1.56	0.59	19.42		56.38	3,687	0	100	0	0	14	0.05	Mar-11
-8.12	-14.64	-11.47	-1.15	-1.90	6.2	0.59	14.99		38.43	21.1	1	99	0	0	63	0.49	Sep-10
-4.17	-6.73	-6.97	2.27	-43.21	3.12	0.61	18.99		12.61	25.2	0	100	0	0	26	0.06	Jun-13
-3.51	-2.20	-3.41	17.29	35.40	2.87	0.53	13.57		60.86	33.5	2	98	0	0	13	-0.08	Jan-12
-0.91	2.34	-0.41	21.90		2.65	0.2	11.17		63.97	1,030	1	99	0	0	24	0.17	Jun-16
-1.58	1.43	-1.22	20.52	18.06	3.1	0.31	11.09		65.05	58,937	1	99	0	0	4	-0.08	Aug-01
-0.98	4.27	1.99	24.24	30.06	1.72	0.4	11.45		80.31	3,951	1	99	0	0	22	0.00	Aug-05
-1.33	-0.08	-5.80	18.62	34.71	2.83	0.39	12.12		57.11	9,332	1	99	0	1	10	-0.05	Dec-07
-2.27	-1.56	-4.68	15.58	5.03	4.25	0.38	11.78		47.30	5,222	1	99	0	0	21	-0.07	Aug-05
-4.30	-5.56	-4.10	18.71	20.62	2.02	0.5	14.66		64.03	429.0	0	100	0	0	33	-0.08	Feb-12
-5.27	-5.01	-2.46	16.95	9.92	2.19	0.67	14.03		40.96	25,089	0	100	0	0	16	-0.04	Apr-03
-4.85	-2.26	-1.24			2.37	0.49			47.65	28.6	0	100	0	0	9	0.31	Jul-17
-5.34	-6.65	-5.34	4.32	-1.06	2.69	0.67	12.96		42.34	196.9	0	100	0	0	39	-0.31	Aug-11
-3.56	-1.26	-7.91	17.13	-7.73	5.57	0.48	17.4		17.60	610.9	1	99	0	0	5	-0.13	Jan-10
-3.09	-1.34	-8.03	18.03	32.63	4.49	0.4	14.18		48.92	134.5	0	98	0	1	17	-0.29	Nov-07
-2.03	2.54	-2.26	22.55	16.62	3.12	0.47	14.15		38.92	5,409	1	99	0	0	5	-0.09	Jul-00
-3.43	-3.47	-7.60	17.66	30.25	4.17	0.53	13.69		36.54	27.4	1	99	0	0	11	-0.10	Jan-12
-1.72	3.82	-1.46	34.31	30.25	2.83	0.47	13.95		30.12	1,247	0	100	0	0	4	0.01	Mar-96
-3.12	1.63	4.83	24.47	-5.93	3.9	0.81	11.66		28.49	488.5	1	99	0	0	35	-0.34	Sep-12
-4.47	1.53	-7.74	10.25	10.15	2.74	0.47	14.66		26.92	2,019	1	99	0	0	6	-0.01	Mar-96
-5.02	-1.64	-9.24	28.42	60.78	3.19	0.59	17.21		53.16	37.2	0	100	0	0	14	-0.21	Jan-12
-3.39	-1.83	-5.40	22.16	16.47	2.01	0.39	12.96		27.57	26.2	0	100	0	0	25	-0.43	Jan-12
-6.76	-9.72	-18.92	7.89	-13.68	3.34	0.39	17.44		18.87	49.1	0	100	0	0	5	-0.09	Jan-12
7.73	26.52	52.94	1.16	25.56	0.86	0.39	26.13		21.72	309.5	0	100	0	0	4	-0.25	Jan-12
0.44	-0.97	2.50	25.46		1.8	0.49	11.2		58.29	61.2	0	100	0	0	36	0.30	Apr-16
-12.45	-14.16	-12.66	28.39	-6.30	6.34	0.39	21.78		26.72	203.1	1	99	0	0	14	-0.27	Jan-12
4.66	8.66	18.60	-28.81	3.26	0.88	0.39	26.58		9.64	92.5	0	100	0	0	19	0.25	Jan-12
-12.19	-13.16	-2.47	15.71	31.34	3.15	0.48	15.45		22.83	1,562	1	99	0	0	7	-0.20	Mar-96
-5.70	-5.05	4.11	17.67	15.81	1.75	0.68	16.32		33.39	5,052	0	100	0	0	10	0.11	Feb-12
-10.17	-13.42	-3.74	0.04	17.73	0.61	0.77	22.04		34.86	282.4	0	100	0	0	49	0.20	Feb-12
-6.08	-3.32	8.78	-1.43	-3.21	1.87	0.59	16.23		24.55	448.1	0	100	0	0	7	-0.20	May-10
-2.99	-1.34	-7.35	11.83	29.92	1.65	0.47	12.32		40.81	57.1	0	97	0	3	20	0.01	May-10
-0.10	0.24	-1.78	17.83	16.62	0.45	0.59	15.74		54.63	117.5	0	100	0	0	6	-0.05	Mar-08
0.36	1.92	4.84	39.13	4.22	4.48	0.47	19.52		27.54	233.4	0	100	0	0	10	-0.07	Mar-96
1.75	1.94					0.15			34.13	6.8	0	100	0	0		0.31	Mar-19
1.49	3.01	-4.82	18.55	29.80	1.59	0.47	10.42		56.24	11,507	1	99	0	0	4	-0.12	Mar-96
1.98	1.80	-6.07	18.40	45.28	2.41	0.47	11.31		71.25	106.9	1	99	0	0	9	-0.18	Dec-07
0.97	1.25					0.15			24.88	7.5	0	100	0	0		0.37	Mar-19
0.94	4.62	5.16	44.05	65.18	1.5	0.25	12.26		110.88	1,558	0	100	0	0	13	-0.02	Nov-06
-0.20	3.50	2.42	36.06	45.76	2.2	0.25	11.53		68.21	143.2	1	99	0	0	4	-0.04	Dec-07
-6.94	-4.60	-10.67	1.18	-24.35	3.68	0.47	11.83		27.85	401.1	1	99	0	0	63	-0.06	Mar-96
-3.02	-2.24	-15.06	-6.03	-29.60	2.94	0.47	22.24		42.66	678.4	0	100	0	0	7	-0.12	Mar-96
0.70	6.42	6.55	34.91	46.58	2.75	0.47	13.83		31.35	144.2	0	100	0	0	14	-0.07	Mar-96
-2.08	0.91	10.26	26.04	65.82	3.06	0.47	13.48		52.05	161.3	1	99	0	0	14	-0.10	Sep-10
-5.83	-5.42	-17.70	19.56	-8.86	3.43	0.53	15		23.38	23.4	0	100	0	0	13	-0.21	Jan-12
-5.23	-1.79	3.13	21.40	20.10	4.49	0.48	11.51		44.75	2,282	0	100	0	0	6	-0.05	Oct-01
-6.02	-9.45	-3.63	13.66	12.70	2.36	0.59	13.88		34.92	165.9	0	100	0	0	11	0.03	Jun-09
-5.99	-0.40	13.16	-7.01	-8.88	0.76	0.59	14.24		33.74	222.7	0	100	0	0	8	-0.08	Sep-10

Fund Name	Ticker Symbol	Traded On	Overall Rating	Reward Rating	Risk Rating	Recent Up/ Downgrade	Price as of 9/30/2019	52-Week High	52-Week Low	Open to New Investors	Category & (Prospectus Objective)
● iShares MSCI Poland ETF	EPOL	NYSE Arca	D+	D	C	Down	20.64	24.40	20.01	Y	Europe Equity Mid/Small Cap (Europe Stock)
● iShares MSCI Qatar ETF	QAT	NAS CM	C-	C	D+		17.56	19.86	16.29	Y	Equity Misc (Foreign Stock)
★ iShares MSCI Russia Capped ETF	ERUS	NYSE Arca	B	B	C+		38.90	40.76	30.59	Y	Equity Misc (Foreign Stock)
● iShares MSCI Saudi Arabia ETF	KSA	NYSE Arca	C	C-	C+	Down	30.48	35.65	27.31	Y	Equity Misc (Growth)
● iShares MSCI Singapore Capped ETF	EWS	NYSE Arca	C	C	C+		23.20	25.34	21.69	Y	Asia ex-Japan Equity (Pacific Stock)
● iShares MSCI South Africa ETF	EZA	NYSE Arca	D+	D	D+	Down	47.45	58.17	45.52	Y	Equity Misc (Foreign Stock)
● iShares MSCI South Korea Capped ETF	EWY	NYSE Arca	D	D	D+	Down	56.34	67.95	51.18	Y	Korea Equity (Pacific Stock)
● iShares MSCI Spain Capped ETF	EWP	NYSE Arca	C-	D+	C	Down	27.84	30.05	26.11	Y	Europe Equity Large Cap (Europe Stock)
● iShares MSCI Sweden ETF	EWD	NYSE Arca	C-	D+	C+	Down	29.45	32.72	26.79	Y	Europe Equity Large Cap (Europe Stock)
★ iShares MSCI Switzerland ETF	EWL	NYSE Arca	B-	B	C+	Down	37.70	38.11	30.43	Y	Europe Equity Large Cap (Europe Stock)
● iShares MSCI Taiwan Capped ETF	EWT	NYSE Arca	C	C	B		36.36	37.83	30.30	Y	Greater China Equity (Pacific Stock)
● iShares MSCI Thailand Capped ETF	THD	NYSE Arca	C+	C+	C+	Up	88.70	96.22	81.75	Y	Thailand Equity (Pacific Stock)
● iShares MSCI Turkey ETF	TUR	NAS CM	D	D+	D		26.72	28.97	20.24	Y	Equity Misc (Foreign Stock)
iShares MSCI UAE ETF	UAE	NAS CM	D+	D	C-	Up	13.54	15.71	13.14	Y	Equity Misc (Foreign Stock)
● iShares MSCI United Kingdom ETF	EWU	NYSE Arca	C	C-	C+		31.43	34.09	28.56	Y	UK Equity Large Cap (Europe Stock)
● iShares MSCI United Kingdom Small-Cap ETF	EWUS	BATS	D+	D+	D+		37.58	41.97	32.68	Y	Equity Misc (Europe Stock)
● iShares MSCI USA Equal Weighted ETF	EUSA	NYSE Arca	C	C	C-		59.64	60.88	47.02	Y	US Equity Large Cap Blend (Growth)
● iShares MSCI USA ESG Optimized ETF	ESGU	NAS CM	C	C	C-		65.37	66.45	51.48	Y	US Equity Large Cap Blend (Growth & Inc)
● iShares MSCI USA ESG Select ETF	SUSA	NYSE Arca	C	C+	C		123.61	125.51	96.94	Y	US Equity Large Cap Blend (Growth)
● iShares MSCI USA Small-Cap ESG Optimized ETF	ESML	BATS	D+	D	C-		26.70	27.89	21.37	Y	US Equity Small Cap (Growth & Inc)
● iShares MSCI World ETF	URTH	NYSE Arca	C	C	C-		91.78	93.05	75.04	Y	Global Equity Large Cap (World Stock)
● iShares Nasdaq Biotechnology ETF	IBB	NAS CM	C	C	C		99.50	121.26	89.61	Y	Healthcare Sector Equity (Technology)
● iShares National Muni Bond ETF	MUB	NYSE Arca	C+	C+	C+		114.10	115.35	106.42	Y	US Muni Fixed Inc (Muni Bond - Natl)
● iShares New York Muni Bond ETF	NYF	NYSE Arca	C	C+	C-		57.22	57.88	53.49	Y	US Muni Fixed Inc (Muni Bond - Single State)
● iShares North American Natural Resources ETF	IGE	BATS	D+	D+	D+	Up	29.08	36.70	25.63	Y	Natural Resources (Natl Res)
● iShares North American Tech-Multimedia Networking ETF	IGN	NYSE Arca	C	B-	C-	Up	53.19	60.69	44.15	Y	Technology Sector Equity (Technology)
★ iShares PHLX Semiconductor ETF	SOXX	NAS CM	B-	B+	C	Up	211.41	220.43	145.00	Y	Technology Sector Equity (Technology)
★ iShares Preferred and Income Securities ETF	PFF	NAS CM	B	C+	A-	Up	37.53	37.53	33.41	Y	US Fixed Income (Growth & Inc)
★ iShares Residential Real Estate Capped ETF	REZ	NYSE Arca	B-	B	C	Up	79.47	80.58	59.92	Y	Real Estate Sector Equity (Real Estate)
iShares Robotics and Artificial Intelligence ETF	IRBO	NYSE Arca	C-	C-	C-	Up	24.45	26.00	19.24	Y	Technology Sector Equity (Technology)
● iShares Russell 1000 ETF	IWB	NYSE Arca	C+	C+	C+		164.54	167.98	129.86	Y	US Equity Large Cap Blend (Growth)
● iShares Russell 1000 Growth ETF	IWF	NYSE Arca	C+	B-	C+	Down	159.63	164.18	121.77	Y	US Equity Large Cap Growth (Growth)
iShares Russell 1000 Pure U.S. Revenue ETF	AMCA	NAS CM	C-	C-	C-	Up	28.78	29.11	23.45	Y	US Equity Large Cap Blend (Growth & Inc)
● iShares Russell 1000 Value ETF	IWD	NYSE Arca	C+	C	C+	Up	128.26	130.25	104.79	Y	US Equity Large Cap Value (Growth)
● iShares Russell 2000 ETF	IWM	NYSE Arca	C	C-	C+		151.34	166.33	125.88	Y	US Equity Small Cap (Small Company)
● iShares Russell 2000 Growth ETF	IWO	NYSE Arca	C	C	C+		192.73	211.73	156.33	Y	US Equity Small Cap (Growth)
iShares Russell 2500 ETF	SMMD	BATS	C-	C-	D+		44.53	47.17	36.00	Y	US Equity Small Cap (Growth & Inc)
● iShares Russell Mid-Cap ETF	IWR	NYSE Arca	D	D	D	Up	55.95	57.42	43.70	Y	US Equity Mid Cap (Growth)
● iShares Russell Mid-Cap Growth ETF	IWP	NYSE Arca	C+	C+	C+	Down	141.35	148.30	106.03	Y	US Equity Mid Cap (Growth)
● iShares Russell Mid-Cap Value ETF	IWS	NYSE Arca	C	C	C+		89.70	91.13	72.26	Y	US Equity Mid Cap (Growth)
● iShares Russell Top 200 ETF	IWL	NYSE Arca	C	C+	C-		68.93	70.25	54.65	Y	US Equity Large Cap Blend (Growth)
● iShares Russell Top 200 Growth ETF	IWY	NYSE Arca	C+	B	C	Up	87.06	89.05	66.58	Y	US Equity Large Cap Growth (Growth)
● iShares Russell Top 200 Value ETF	IWX	NYSE Arca	C	C	C-		54.78	55.72	44.99	Y	US Equity Large Cap Value (Growth)
● iShares S&P 100 ETF	OEF	NYSE Arca	C+	C+	C+		131.49	134.09	104.34	Y	US Equity Large Cap Blend (Growth)
● iShares S&P 500 Growth ETF	IVW	NYSE Arca	C+	C+	C+	Down	180.03	185.08	140.58	Y	US Equity Large Cap Growth (Growth)
● iShares S&P 500 Value ETF	IVE	NYSE Arca	C+	C	C+	Up	119.14	120.88	95.36	Y	US Equity Large Cap Value (Growth)
● iShares S&P GSCI Commodity-Indexed Trust	GSG	NYSE Arca	C-	D+	C-		15.05	18.72	13.86	Y	Commodities Broad Basket (Unaligned)
● iShares S&P Mid-Cap 400 Growth ETF	IJK	NYSE Arca	C	C	C-		223.86	231.08	179.90	Y	US Equity Mid Cap (Growth)
● iShares S&P Mid-Cap 400 Value ETF	IJJ	NYSE Arca	C	C-	C+		159.90	166.59	130.36	Y	US Equity Mid Cap (Growth)
● iShares S&P Small-Cap 600 Growth ETF	IJT	NAS CM	C	C	C-		178.38	198.92	151.48	Y	US Equity Small Cap (Small Company)
● iShares S&P Small-Cap 600 Value ETF	IJS	NYSE Arca	C	C-	C	Up	150.19	164.59	124.11	Y	US Equity Small Cap (Small Company)
● iShares Select Dividend ETF	DVY	NAS CM	C	C	C+	Down	101.95	103.22	85.20	Y	US Equity Large Cap Value (Equity-Income)

★ Expanded analysis of this fund is included in Section II: Analysis of All BUY Rated Funds.   ● Expanded analysis of this fund is included in Section III: Analysis of All Rated Funds with Assets over $50 million.

			TOTAL RETURNS & PERFORMANCE							ASSETS		ASSET ALLOCATION & TURNOVER					VALUATION	
3-Month Total Return	6-Month Total Return	1-Year Total Return	3-Year Total Return	5-Year Total Return	Dividend Yield (TTM)	Expense Ratio	3-Yr Std Deviation	Effective Duration	NAV	Total Assets (MIL)	%Cash	%Stocks	%Bonds	%Other	Turnover Ratio	Premium/ Discount 1-Year Avg	Inception Date
-12.60	-10.70	-11.98	20.80	-18.22	1.71	0.63	20.78		20.67	268.8	0	100	0	0	7	-0.06	May-10
-1.81	-0.31	5.08	4.94	-17.08	4.24	0.59	17.47		17.82	55.2	0	100	0	0	58	-0.45	Apr-14
-2.57	13.06	17.20	52.80	41.18	5.2	0.59	18.63		38.98	658.8	0	100	0	0	32	-0.23	Nov-10
-8.28	-7.79	3.33	61.21		2.45	0.74	16.59		30.35	722.4	0	100	0	0	20	0.29	Sep-15
-7.44	-1.50	-0.93	21.75	4.76	3.87	0.47	15.93		23.13	507.7	1	99	0	0	26	0.02	Mar-96
-13.44	-10.20	-7.40	-6.81	-12.96	5.01	0.59	20.91		47.53	356.5	0	100	0	0	15	-0.17	Feb-03
-5.27	-8.47	-15.56	3.76	4.18	1.39	0.59	18.68		56.71	4,092	0	100	0	0	18	-0.10	May-00
-4.13	-2.49	-3.10	14.70	-13.65	3.29	0.47	17.03		27.84	860.3	0	100	0	0	21	-0.12	Mar-96
-5.49	-1.70	-7.20	12.85	9.17	3.28	0.53	15.36		29.42	207.4	2	98	0	0	5	-0.06	Mar-96
0.39	8.14	10.47	31.85	31.05	1.99	0.47	11.52		37.65	1,026	1	99	0	0	9	0.03	Mar-96
1.48	4.22	-1.53	26.59	35.05	2.75	0.59	13.2		36.24	2,801	1	99	0	0	12	-0.28	Jun-00
-7.02	2.07	-3.43	32.05	21.19	2.29	0.59	15.04		89.30	451.0	0	100	0	0	10	0.00	Mar-08
5.60	10.94	15.54	-22.53	-36.83	2.5	0.59	34.7		26.77	348.0	0	100	0	0	7	0.00	Mar-08
1.24	-1.69	-6.57	-8.23	-30.41	3.98	0.59	11.69		13.80	44.8	0	100	0	0	33	-0.03	Apr-14
-2.98	-3.26	-3.23	12.73	0.68	4.59	0.47	12.4		31.51	2,083	1	99	0	0	5	-0.07	Mar-96
-1.25	-3.06	-7.65	13.74	15.45	2.8	0.59	15.11		37.65	64.0	1	97	0	2	20	-0.37	Jan-12
0.10	3.39	2.85	36.34	56.21	1.55	0.15	13.38		59.61	318.9	0	100	0	0	23	0.00	May-10
0.63	4.59	3.62			1.47	0.15			65.41	1,151	0	100	0	0	28	0.11	Dec-16
1.01	4.14	4.69	42.61	64.69	1.63	0.25	12.62		123.57	1,032	0	100	0	0	21	0.02	Jan-05
-1.34	0.48	-3.11			1.15	0.17			26.64	61.3	0	100	0	0	15	0.15	Apr-18
0.01	3.51	1.99	34.89	44.87	2.15	0.24	11.3		91.71	678.6	1	100	0	0	3	0.06	Jan-12
-9.18	-10.92	-17.55	3.92	11.77	0.15	0.47	21.14		99.57	6,626	0	100	0	0	18	-0.04	Feb-01
1.48	3.89	8.35	8.63	17.07	2.46	0.07	3.41	5.93	114.04	14,198	1	0	99	0	10	0.05	Sep-07
1.31	3.53	7.95	7.88	16.46	2.3	0.25	3.31		57.09	439.6	3	0	97	0	19	0.23	Oct-07
-4.60	-6.07	-17.83	-9.59	-25.70	2.84	0.46	19.12		29.07	555.3	0	100	0	0	12	-0.02	Oct-01
-3.35	-7.38	-1.50	32.02	62.20	0.38	0.46	18.03		53.19	79.8	0	100	0	0	29	-0.03	Jul-01
4.41	9.82	15.51	94.03	167.08	1.22	0.46	22.4		211.58	1,756	0	100	0	0	26	-0.01	Jul-01
2.99	4.83	7.35	12.53	26.69	5.56	0.46	5.1	2.77	37.45	16,568	1	6	0	0	28	0.17	Mar-07
9.90	14.18	31.54	35.93	86.80	2.63	0.48	13.84		79.43	575.9	1	99	0	0	10	0.04	May-07
-3.22	-2.00	-2.35			0.65	0.47			24.32	48.6	0	100	0	0	35	0.31	Jun-18
0.61	4.42	3.46	44.44	66.86	1.84	0.15	12.31		164.54	20,403	0	100	0	0	6	-0.03	May-00
0.48	4.85	3.26	58.83	88.51	1.06	0.19	13.29		159.66	44,890	0	100	0	0	12	-0.04	May-00
2.33	4.99	4.10			2.4	0.15			28.79	5.8	0	100	0	0	12	0.07	Aug-17
0.72	3.92	3.53	30.39	46.12	2.35	0.19	12.32		128.29	39,502	0	100	0	0	17	-0.03	May-00
-2.60	-1.44	-7.67	26.69	50.52	1.29	0.19	17.2		151.42	43,616	0	100	0	0	22	-0.05	May-00
-4.42	-2.30	-8.24	32.42	57.76	0.72	0.24	17.47		192.86	8,746	0	100	0	0	35	-0.06	Jul-00
-1.73	0.40	-3.21			1.5	0.15			44.48	33.4	0	100	0	0	12	0.03	Jul-17
-0.21	3.25	3.43	-66.23	-61.10	1.43	0.19	13.41		55.96	20,009	0	100	0	0	11	-0.01	Jul-01
-1.55	3.20	5.49	49.10	70.41	0.6	0.24	14.37		141.37	10,758	0	100	0	0	20	-0.01	Jul-01
0.67	3.13	1.73	24.65	44.23	1.99	0.24	13.36		89.70	10,979	0	100	0	0	25	-0.01	Jul-01
0.91	4.85	3.45	48.19	71.12	1.9	0.15	12.07		68.90	251.5	0	100	0	0	5	0.02	Sep-09
0.85	5.38	2.84	62.16	95.24	1.19	0.2	13.23		87.09	1,489	0	100	0	0	15	0.01	Sep-09
0.74	4.31	4.39	33.16	46.96	2.51	0.2	12.05		54.76	460.0	0	100	0	0	14	0.04	Sep-09
1.04	4.88	3.10	45.55	67.46	2.03	0.2	12.21		131.45	5,120	0	100	0	0	7	-0.03	Oct-00
-0.10	4.15	2.77	54.21	83.88	1.37	0.18	12.32		180.03	23,323	0	100	0	0	27	-0.03	May-00
2.03	5.49	4.97	34.66	50.84	2.3	0.18	13.18		119.11	15,747	0	100	0	0	31	-0.01	May-00
-4.38	-7.16	-18.71	1.55	-48.99	0	0.75	14.8		15.03	725.8	73	0	27	0	0	-0.11	Jul-06
-1.04	1.70	-1.96	32.33	58.23	1.06	0.24	14.49		223.95	7,301	0	100	0	0	50	-0.02	Jul-00
0.05	1.10	-2.02	26.63	47.03	1.74	0.25	16.64		159.91	6,316	0	100	0	0	44	-0.03	Jul-00
-2.13	-0.47	-9.27	33.78	69.21	0.99	0.25	17.55		178.54	5,133	0	100	0	0	45	-0.07	Jul-00
1.27	1.02	-7.19	25.98	52.88	1.54	0.25	18.98		150.32	6,374	0	100	0	0	38	-0.03	Jul-00
3.18	4.62	5.69	31.52	64.33	3.4	0.39	11.03		101.98	17,744	0	100	0	0	21	-0.02	Nov-03

Fund Name	Ticker Symbol	Traded On	Overall Rating	Reward Rating	Risk Rating	Recent Up/ Downgrade	Price as of 9/30/2019	52-Week High	52-Week Low	Open to New Investors	Category & (Prospectus Objective)
iShares Self-Driving EV and Tech ETF	IDRV	NYSE Arca	U	U	U		24.17	25.93	21.90	Y	Industrials Sector Equity (Unaligned)
● iShares Short Maturity Bond ETF	NEAR	BATS	C	C	C+		50.34	50.35	49.82	Y	US Fixed Income (Income)
● iShares Short Maturity Municipal Bond ETF	MEAR	BATS	C	C	C-	Up	50.14	50.30	49.74	Y	US Muni Fixed Inc (Muni Bond - Natl)
● iShares Short Treasury Bond ETF	SHV	NAS CM	C	C	C+		110.62	110.67	110.21	Y	US Fixed Income (Govt Bond - Treasury)
● iShares Short-Term Corporate Bond ETF	IGSB	NAS CM	D-	D-	D	Down	53.67	53.82	51.35	Y	US Fixed Income (Growth & Inc)
● iShares Short-Term National Muni Bond ETF	SUB	NYSE Arca	C	C	C-		106.54	107.20	104.30	Y	US Muni Fixed Inc (Muni Bond - Natl)
● iShares Silver Trust	SLV	NYSE Arca	C-	C-	C	Up	15.92	18.34	13.15	Y	Commodities Specified (Prec Metals)
● iShares TIPS Bond ETF	TIP	NYSE Arca	C+	C+	C+	Up	116.29	118.10	108.28	Y	US Fixed Income (Govt Bond - Treasury)
★ iShares Transportation Average ETF	IYT	BATS	B-	B	C	Up	186.14	205.13	155.39	Y	Industrials Sector Equity (Unaligned)
● iShares Treasury Floating Rate Bond ETF	TFLO	NYSE Arca	C	C	C-	Up	50.28	50.38	50.20	Y	US Fixed Income (Govt Bond - Treasury)
★ iShares U.S. Aerospace & Defense ETF	ITA	BATS	B-	B	C	Up	224.70	231.12	162.03	Y	Industrials Sector Equity (Growth)
★ iShares U.S. Broker-Dealers & Securities Exchanges ETF	IAI	NYSE Arca	B-	B	C	Up	64.31	66.75	52.67	Y	Financials Sector Equity (Financial)
● iShares U.S. Consumer Goods ETF	IYK	NYSE Arca	C+	B	C	Up	126.49	126.90	102.26	Y	Consumer Goods & Svcs (Unaligned)
● iShares U.S. Consumer Services ETF	IYC	NYSE Arca	C+	B	C		217.39	226.85	168.12	Y	Consumer Goods & Svcs (Unaligned)
iShares U.S. Dividend and Buyback ETF	DIVB	BATS	C-	C	D+	Up	28.22	28.62	22.41	Y	US Equity Large Cap Blend (Growth & Inc)
● iShares U.S. Energy ETF	IYE	NYSE Arca	D+	D+	D+		31.76	43.05	29.27	Y	Energy Sector Equity (Natl Res)
★ iShares U.S. Financial Services ETF	IYG	NYSE Arca	B	B	C	Up	136.43	140.99	105.05	Y	Financials Sector Equity (Financial)
● iShares U.S. Financials ETF	IYF	NYSE Arca	C+	C+	C+		128.73	130.38	100.04	Y	Financials Sector Equity (Financial)
● iShares U.S. Healthcare ETF	IYH	NYSE Arca	C	B-	C	Down	189.05	204.02	170.02	Y	Healthcare Sector Equity (Health)
★ iShares U.S. Healthcare Providers ETF	IHF	NYSE Arca	B-	B	C	Up	161.70	201.83	151.11	Y	Healthcare Sector Equity (Health)
★ iShares U.S. Home Construction ETF	ITB	BATS	B-	B+	C	Up	43.31	43.31	28.55	Y	Consumer Goods & Svcs (Real Estate)
● iShares U.S. Industrials ETF	IYJ	BATS	C	C+	C-		158.82	161.62	120.07	Y	Industrials Sector Equity (Unaligned)
iShares U.S. Infrastructure ETF	IFRA	BATS	D+	C-	D+		27.70	27.99	22.00	Y	Infrastructure Sector Equity (Utility)
● iShares U.S. Insurance ETF	IAK	NYSE Arca	C+	B	C	Up	72.04	72.90	54.51	Y	Financials Sector Equity (Financial)
★ iShares U.S. Medical Devices ETF	IHI	NYSE Arca	B	B+	C+	Up	247.24	251.72	183.66	Y	Healthcare Sector Equity (Health)
● iShares U.S. Oil & Gas Exploration & Production ETF	IEO	BATS	C	B-	D	Up	51.00	78.42	46.40	Y	Energy Sector Equity (Natl Res)
● iShares U.S. Oil Equipment & Services ETF	IEZ	NYSE Arca	D+	C	D	Up	17.61	36.99	16.32	Y	Energy Sector Equity (Natl Res)
● iShares U.S. Pharmaceuticals ETF	IHE	NYSE Arca	C+	B-	C-	Up	139.85	167.62	132.01	Y	Healthcare Sector Equity (Health)
★ iShares U.S. Real Estate ETF	IYR	NYSE Arca	B-	B-	B-		93.54	94.09	72.00	Y	Real Estate Sector Equity (Real Estate)
★ iShares U.S. Regional Banks ETF	IAT	NYSE Arca	B-	B	C		46.56	49.96	37.63	Y	Financials Sector Equity (Financial)
★ iShares U.S. Technology ETF	IYW	NYSE Arca	B	B+	C+	Up	204.21	211.51	148.42	Y	Technology Sector Equity (Technology)
★ iShares U.S. Telecommunications ETF	IYZ	BATS	B-	B	C	Up	29.20	31.04	24.71	Y	Communications Sector Equity (Comm)
● iShares U.S. Treasury Bond ETF	GOVT	BATS	C+	C	B		26.33	26.63	24.07	Y	US Fixed Income (Govt Bond - Treasury)
★ iShares U.S. Utilities ETF	IDU	NYSE Arca	B-	B	C		162.85	163.32	130.66	Y	Utilities Sector Equity (Utility)
● iShares Ultra Short-Term Bond ETF	ICSH	BATS	C	C	C+		50.39	50.42	50.00	Y	US Fixed Income (Income)
● iShares US & Intl High Yield Corp Bond ETF	GHYG	BATS	C	C+	C-		48.79	49.41	45.07	Y	Global Fixed Income (Corp Bond-High Yld)
● iShares Yield Optimized Bond ETF	BYLD	NYSE Arca	C	B-	C-		25.59	25.76	23.53	Y	US Fixed Income (Income)
Ivy Focused Energy NextShares	IVENC	NAS CM	C	C+	D	Up	10.90	19.77	10.52		Energy Sector Equity (Unaligned)
★ Ivy Focused Growth NextShares™	IVFGC	NAS CM	B	A-	C	Up	20.54	34.01	20.54		US Equity Large Cap Growth (Growth)
Ivy Focused Value NextShares™	IVFVC	NAS CM	C+	B	C-	Up	18.30	23.95	17.78		US Equity Large Cap Value (Growth & Inc)
● Janus Henderson Mortgage-Backed Securities ETF	JMBS	NYSE Arca	D+	D+	C-		52.45	52.49	49.20	Y	US Fixed Income (Convertible Bond)
● Janus Henderson Short Duration Income ETF	VNLA	NYSE Arca	C	C	C+		50.03	50.14	49.00	Y	US Fixed Income (Multisector Bond)
Janus Henderson Small Cap Growth Alpha ETF	JSML	NAS CM	C	C	D+		42.01	44.61	33.68	Y	US Equity Small Cap (Growth)
● Janus Henderson Small/Mid Cap Growth Alpha ETF	JSMD	NAS CM	C	C+	D+		43.77	46.38	34.41	Y	US Equity Mid Cap (Growth)
John Hancock Multifactor Consumer Discretionary ETF	JHMC	NYSE Arca	C	C+	C-		33.67	34.68	26.49	Y	Consumer Goods & Svcs (Growth & Inc)
★ John Hancock Multifactor Consumer Staples ETF	JHMS	NYSE Arca	B-	B	C	Up	29.14	29.17	23.55	Y	Consumer Goods & Svcs (Unaligned)
● John Hancock Multifactor Developed International ETF	JHMD	NYSE Arca	C-	C-	C-		27.83	29.49	24.81	Y	Global Equity Large Cap (Foreign Stock)
John Hancock Multifactor Emerging Markets ETF	JHEM	NYSE Arca	U	U	U		24.43	26.41	22.41	Y	Global Emerg Mkts Equity (Div Emerg Mkts)
John Hancock Multifactor Energy ETF	JHME	NYSE Arca	D+	D+	D	Up	23.10	33.64	21.16	Y	Energy Sector Equity (Unaligned)
John Hancock Multifactor Financials ETF	JHMF	NYSE Arca	C	C+	D+		38.47	39.51	29.33	Y	Financials Sector Equity (Financial)
John Hancock Multifactor Health Care ETF	JHMH	NYSE Arca	C	C+	C-		32.98	36.25	29.55	Y	Healthcare Sector Equity (Health)
John Hancock Multifactor Industrials ETF	JHMI	NYSE Arca	C	C+	D+		37.62	38.03	28.59	Y	Industrials Sector Equity (Unaligned)

★ Expanded analysis of this fund is included in Section II: Analysis of All BUY Rated Funds. ● Expanded analysis of this fund is included in Section III: Analysis of All Rated Funds with Assets over $50 million.

		TOTAL RETURNS & PERFORMANCE							ASSETS		ASSET ALLOCATION & TURNOVER					VALUATION	
3-Month Total Return	6-Month Total Return	1-Year Total Return	3-Year Total Return	5-Year Total Return	Dividend Yield (TTM)	Expense Ratio	3-Yr Std Deviation	Effective Duration	NAV	Total Assets (MIL.)	%Cash	%Stocks	%Bonds	%Other	Turnover Ratio	Premium/ Discount 1-Year Avg	Inception Date
-0.33						0.47			24.11	26.5	0	100	0	0		0.14	Apr-19
0.71	1.64	3.06	6.51	8.50	2.65	0.25	0.35	0.47	50.35	6,847	14	0	85	0	48	0.00	Sep-13
0.33	1.07	2.07	3.97		1.57	0.25	0.48		50.10	207.9	11	0	89	0	221	0.04	Mar-15
0.53	1.40	2.42	4.36	4.71	2.22	0.15	0.26	0.39	110.61	21,314	36	0	64	0	73	0.02	Jan-07
1.25	3.48	6.78	-45.73	-44.22	3.06	0.06	1.34		53.64	12,902	2	0	95	0	80	0.07	Jan-07
0.31	1.29	3.36	4.09	5.43	1.61	0.07	1.18	2.13	106.42	2,474	4	0	96	0	24	0.09	Nov-08
12.93	14.21	18.00	-12.16	-1.25	0	0.5	15.78		16.14	6,617	0	0	0	100		-0.34	Apr-06
1.56	4.51	7.12	6.38	11.26	1.85	0.19	3.28	7.68	116.02	20,420	0	0	100	0	21	0.06	Dec-03
-1.09	-2.05	-7.99	32.74	33.95	1.31	0.42	19.21		186.17	512.0	0	100	0	0	17	-0.01	Oct-03
0.45	1.01	2.08	4.50	4.91	2.12	0.15	0.2		50.27	532.9	1	0	99	0	17	0.03	Feb-14
6.17	10.75	4.60	79.77	125.14	0.9	0.42	17.02		224.77	5,496	0	100	0	0	38	-0.02	May-06
1.22	7.61	4.94	62.54	79.31	1.63	0.42	16.39		64.32	238.0	0	100	0	0	27	-0.01	May-06
4.05	6.85	8.78	19.06	44.54	2.21	0.42	11.76		126.46	480.6	0	100	0	0	4	0.03	Jun-00
-0.67	5.72	3.93	52.09	86.02	0.83	0.42	14.11		217.41	945.7	0	100	0	0	15	-0.01	Jun-00
1.40	5.67	4.75			2.08	0.25			28.22	9.9	0	100	0	0	31	-0.01	Nov-17
-7.13	-10.38	-23.01	-11.58	-28.05	3.29	0.42	21.19		31.75	619.1	0	100	0	0	6	-0.02	Jun-00
1.19	10.20	3.91	62.69	73.07	1.75	0.42	17.8		136.30	1,193	0	100	0	0	4	-0.01	Jun-00
2.11	8.03	7.97	50.62	69.26	1.78	0.42	13.56		128.63	1,601	0	100	0	0	8	-0.01	May-00
-3.33	-1.94	-5.29	31.40	53.51	2.02	0.43	13.52		189.02	1,994	0	100	0	0	6	0.00	Jun-00
-5.16	-3.67	-15.67	36.57	61.78	4.36	0.43	16.58		161.69	808.4	0	100	0	0	48	0.00	May-06
12.86	22.50	23.78	59.45	98.79	0.52	0.42	19.08		43.30	1,264	0	100	0	0	17	-0.02	May-06
0.14	3.31	2.54	44.75	71.98	1.31	0.42	15.68		158.81	905.2	0	100	0	0	5	-0.02	Jun-00
1.46	5.08	5.24			2.48	0.4			27.68	6.9	0	100	0	0	43	0.02	Apr-18
0.96	12.36	11.44	44.24	70.18	1.84	0.43	13.46		72.02	111.6	0	100	0	0	17	-0.07	May-06
2.12	7.24	9.05	72.08	156.02	0.3	0.43	15.35		247.43	4,268	0	100	0	0	36	0.01	May-06
-8.90	-12.62	-32.59	-13.73	-35.64	2.08	0.42	25.81		50.99	206.5	0	100	0	0	12	-0.02	May-06
-18.59	-31.42	-50.19	-52.51	-69.87	2.43	0.42	35.6		17.61	81.9	0	100	0	0	35	0.01	May-06
-7.70	-8.71	-14.45	-2.76	7.56	1.48	0.42	15.33		139.81	307.6	0	100	0	0	51	0.01	May-06
7.40	9.00	20.99	29.09	62.70	2.59	0.42	12.06		93.46	5,005	1	99	0	0	11	0.01	Jun-00
1.26	5.58	-1.86	40.65	56.93	2.63	0.42	22.82		46.55	391.0	0	100	0	0	10	-0.04	May-06
1.91	6.14	6.04	76.29	117.12	0.8	0.42	16.02		204.27	4,126	0	100	0	0	19	-0.01	May-00
-0.55	-1.91	0.29	-2.18	12.13	1.69	0.42	14.65		29.21	496.5	0	100	0	0	35	-0.05	May-00
2.62	5.91	10.53	6.52	14.33	1.98	0.15	3.94		26.31	13,877	3	0	97	0	27	0.02	Feb-12
9.00	12.11	25.32	44.87	80.39	2.56	0.42	10.39		162.86	952.8	0	100	0	0	6	-0.01	Jun-00
0.70	1.58	3.16	6.78	7.98	2.67	0.08	0.28	0.42	50.39	2,129	50	0	49	0	32	0.02	Dec-13
0.06	2.56	4.31	15.53	19.73	5.51	0.4	4.58		48.73	175.4	1	0	99	0	20	0.22	Apr-12
1.69	5.85	10.46	13.19	20.68	4.05	0.2	3.25		25.58	126.6	2	0	97	0	48	0.01	Apr-14
-14.99	-22.22	-40.32			0.07	0.95				4.9	4	96	0	0	29	0.00	Oct-16
1.20	9.19	9.82			0.17	0.78				14.3	2	98	0	0	29	0.00	Oct-16
-6.78	-8.67	-12.10			3.6	0.78				8.4	1	99	0	0	186	0.00	Oct-16
1.50	3.83	8.16			2.65	0.35			52.40	144.1	2	0	98	0	91	0.03	Sep-18
0.96	2.23	4.04			2.75	0.35			50.03	1,031	10	0	87	0	22	0.02	Nov-16
-4.62	0.19	-5.88	43.90		0.47	0.35	18.2		41.81	35.6	0	100	0	0	84	0.01	Feb-16
-3.63	-0.04	-3.45	49.61		0.43	0.35	17.06		43.73	96.3	0	100	0	0	79	0.00	Feb-16
0.28	3.49	3.26	36.74		1.22	0.4	13.6		33.69	39.7	5	95	0	0	42	-0.05	Sep-15
5.11	8.17	12.01	21.11		2.6	0.4	11.28		29.14	30.3	5	95	0	0	14	0.02	Mar-16
-1.79	0.29	-2.85			2.35	0.45			27.88	501.8	2	98	0	0	17	-0.07	Dec-16
-5.18	-4.84	-1.73			0.88	0.55			24.39	787.8	2	98	0	0	3	0.10	Sep-18
-7.87	-13.22	-28.64	-13.95		2.5	0.4	23.48		23.09	20.1	0	100	0	0	25	0.15	Mar-16
0.55	7.83	5.34	52.83		1.69	0.4	16.1		38.44	44.6	0	100	0	0	9	-0.05	Sep-15
-3.89	-1.88	-6.60	27.46		2.47	0.4	14.31		33.01	47.9	1	99	0	0	21	0.01	Sep-15
1.02	3.92	3.12	46.20		1.72	0.4	16.27		37.60	26.3	1	99	0	0	49	-0.07	Mar-16

Fund Name	Ticker Symbol	Traded On	Overall Rating	Reward Rating	Risk Rating	Recent Up/ Downgrade	Price as of 9/30/2019	52-Week High	52-Week Low	Open to New Investors	Category & (Prospectus Objective)
● John Hancock Multifactor Large Cap ETF	JHML	NYSE Arca	C	C	C-		38.43	38.92	30.10	Y	US Equity Large Cap Blend (Growth)
John Hancock Multifactor Materials ETF	JHMA	NYSE Arca	C	C	D	Up	32.87	34.52	26.95	Y	Natural Resources (Growth & Inc)
John Hancock Multifactor Media and Communications ETF	JHCS	NYSE Arca	U	U	U		26.42	27.86	24.78	Y	Communications Sector Equity (Growth & Inc)
● John Hancock Multifactor Mid Cap ETF	JHMM	NYSE Arca	C	C	C+		36.82	37.48	28.59	Y	US Equity Mid Cap (Growth)
● John Hancock Multifactor Small Cap ETF	JHSC	NYSE Arca	D+	D	C-		26.15	27.70	21.34	Y	US Equity Small Cap (Small Company)
● John Hancock Multifactor Technology ETF	JHMT	NYSE Arca	C	B-	C-		50.01	52.66	36.84	Y	Technology Sector Equity (Technology)
John Hancock Multifactor Utilities ETF	JHMU	NYSE Arca	C+	B	C		34.71	34.82	27.55	Y	Utilities Sector Equity (Utility)
● JPMorgan Alerian MLP Index ETN	AMJ	NYSE Arca	D	D	C-	Down	23.27	28.14	21.22	Y	Energy Sector Equity (Unaligned)
JPMorgan BetaBuilders 1-5 Year U.S. Aggregate Bond ETF	BBSA	BATS	U	U	U		25.53	25.68	25.09	Y	US Fixed Income (Growth & Inc)
● JPMorgan BetaBuilders Canada ETF	BBCA	BATS	C	C-	C+		25.02	25.41	19.94	Y	Canadian Equity Large Cap (Growth)
● JPMorgan BetaBuilders Developed Asia ex-Japan ETF	BBAX	BATS	C	D+	C+		24.71	26.74	22.06	Y	Asia ex-Japan Equity (Growth)
● JPMorgan BetaBuilders Europe ETF	BBEU	BATS	C	D+	C+	Up	23.52	24.55	20.77	Y	Europe Equity Large Cap (Europe Stock)
● JPMorgan BetaBuilders Japan ETF	BBJP	BATS	C-	D	C	Up	23.74	25.13	20.43	Y	Japan Equity (Pacific Stock)
● JPMorgan BetaBuilders MSCI U.S. REIT ETF	BBRE	BATS	C	C	C-	Up	90.07	90.29	69.49	Y	Real Estate Sector Equity (Real Estate)
JPMorgan BetaBuilders U.S. Equity ETF	BBUS	BATS	U	U	U		53.48	54.48	49.50	Y	US Equity Large Cap Blend (Growth & Inc)
JPMorgan Core Plus Bond ETF	JCPB	BATS	U	U	U		53.37	53.74	51.02	Y	US Fixed Income (Income)
JPMorgan Corporate Bond Research Enhanced ETF	JIGB	NYSE Arca	U	U	U		55.49	56.26	50.38	Y	US Fixed Income (Income)
● JPMorgan Diversified Alternative ETF	JPHF	NYSE Arca	D+	D+	C-		24.95	25.09	23.72	Y	Multialternative (Asset Allocation)
● JPMorgan Diversified Return Emerging Markets Equity ETF	JPEM	NYSE Arca	C	C	C-	Up	52.45	56.56	49.44	Y	Global Emerg Mkts Equity (Div Emerg Mkts)
JPMorgan Diversified Return Europe Equity ETF	JPEU	NYSE Arca	C-	C-	D+		55.26	58.46	49.14	Y	Europe Equity Large Cap (Europe Stock)
● JPMorgan Diversified Return Global Equity ETF	JPGE	NYSE Arca	C	C	C-		59.26	61.42	52.65	Y	Global Equity Large Cap (Growth & Inc)
● JPMorgan Diversified Return International Equity ETF	JPIN	NYSE Arca	C	C-	C+		53.17	58.41	49.33	Y	Global Equity Large Cap (Growth & Inc)
● JPMorgan Diversified Return U.S. Equity ETF	JPUS	NYSE Arca	C	C	C-		75.92	76.66	61.37	Y	US Equity Large Cap Blend (Growth & Inc)
● JPMorgan Diversified Return U.S. Mid Cap Equity ETF	JPME	NYSE Arca	C	C	D+		66.81	67.86	54.16	Y	US Equity Mid Cap (Growth)
● JPMorgan Diversified Return U.S. Small Cap Equity ETF	JPSE	NYSE Arca	C	C-	C+		30.30	32.29	25.38	Y	US Equity Small Cap (Small Company)
JPMorgan Event Driven ETF	JPED	NYSE Arca	D	D+	D		25.46	26.50	22.61	Y	Long/Short Equity (Growth & Inc)
● JPMorgan Global Bond Opportunities ETF	JPGB	BATS	C	C	C-	Up	51.12	51.53	47.26	Y	US Fixed Income (Worldwide Bond)
● JPMorgan High Yield Research Enhanced ETF	JPHY	BATS	C	C	C-		51.33	51.83	47.14	Y	US Fixed Income (Corp Bond-High Yld)
JPMorgan Long/Short ETF	JPLS	NYSE Arca	D	D	D+		21.99	22.73	21.15	Y	Long/Short Equity (Growth & Inc)
● JPMorgan Managed Futures Strategy ETF	JPMF	NYSE Arca	D+	C-	D+		25.46	26.00	22.97	Y	Alternative Misc (Growth & Inc)
JPMorgan Municipal ETF	JMUB	BATS	U	U	U		54.17	54.83	51.30	Y	US Muni Fixed Inc (Income)
JPMorgan U.S. Aggregate Bond ETF	JAGG	NYSE Arca	U	U	U		26.82	27.09	25.19	Y	US Fixed Income (Growth)
JPMorgan U.S. Dividend ETF	JDIV	NYSE Arca	C-	C-	D+	Up	26.93	27.11	22.29	Y	US Equity Large Cap Value (Growth & Inc)
● JPMorgan U.S. Minimum Volatility ETF	JMIN	NYSE Arca	C-	C	C-		30.19	30.28	23.72	Y	US Equity Large Cap Blend (Growth & Inc)
● JPMorgan U.S. Momentum Factor ETF	JMOM	NYSE Arca	C-	C	D+	Up	28.87	29.79	22.40	Y	US Equity Large Cap Growth (Growth & Inc)
● JPMorgan U.S. Quality Factor ETF	JQUA	NYSE Arca	C	C	C-	Up	29.39	29.78	23.43	Y	US Equity Large Cap Blend (Growth & Inc)
● JPMorgan U.S. Value Factor ETF	JVAL	NYSE Arca	C-	C-	C-	Up	26.74	27.33	21.96	Y	US Equity Large Cap Value (Growth & Inc)
● JPMorgan Ultra-Short Income ETF	JPST	BATS	C	C	C+		50.43	50.52	50.09	Y	US Fixed Income (Growth & Inc)
JPMorgan Ultra-Short Municipal Income ETF	JMST	BATS	U	U	U		50.42	50.59	50.27	Y	US Muni Fixed Inc (Muni Bond - Natl)
● JPMorgan USD Emerging Markets Sovereign Bond ETF	JPMB	NYSE Arca	C-	C-	D+	Up	50.61	51.48	44.79	Y	Emerging Mkts Fixed Inc (Div Emerg Mkts)
KFA Large Cap Quality Dividend Index ETF	KLCD	NYSE Arca	U	U	U		26.36	26.49	24.89	Y	US Equity Large Cap Value (Growth & Inc)
KFA Small Cap Quality Dividend Index ETF	KSCD	NYSE Arca	U	U	U		25.66	25.93	24.39	Y	US Equity Small Cap (Small Company)
● Knowledge Leaders Developed World ETF	KLDW	NYSE Arca	C-	C	C-		33.74	35.01	27.85	Y	Global Equity Large Cap (Growth & Inc)
● KraneShares Bosera MSCI China A ETF	KBA	NYSE Arca	C	C	C		29.96	34.06	24.20	Y	Greater China Equity (Pacific Stock)
KraneShares CCBS China Corp High Yield Bond USD Ind ETF	KCCB	NYSE Arca	D	D+	D		40.61	41.05	39.17	Y	Emerging Mkts Fixed Inc (Corp Bond-High Yld)
KraneShares CICC China Leaders 100 Index ETF	KFYP	NYSE Arca	C-	C	D+	Down	26.63	31.10	21.05	Y	Greater China Equity (Growth & Inc)
● KraneShares CSI China Internet ETF	KWEB	NYSE Arca	C-	C-	D+	Up	41.33	49.64	36.20	Y	Greater China Equity (Pacific Stock)
KraneShares E Fund China Commercial Paper ETF	KCNY	NYSE Arca	D+	C-	D+		32.00	34.58	31.81	Y	Emerging Mkts Fixed Inc (Foreign Stock)
KraneShares Electric Vehicles & Future Mobility Ind ETF	KARS	NYSE Arca	D+	D	D+	Up	20.57	22.59	17.23	Y	Industrials Sector Equity (Unaligned)
KraneShares Emerging Markets Healthcare Index ETF	KMED	NYSE Arca	D	D	D		20.24	24.69	18.37	Y	Global Emerg Mkts Equity (Health)
KraneShares FTSE Emerg Mkts Consumer Technology Ind ETF	KEMQ	NYSE Arca	D	D	D+		21.62	23.66	18.43	Y	Global Emerg Mkts Equity (Growth & Inc)
KraneShares MSCI All China Health Care Index ETF	KURE	NYSE Arca	D	D	D		21.05	23.82	16.42	Y	Greater China Equity (Health)

★ Expanded analysis of this fund is included in Section II: Analysis of All BUY Rated Funds. ● Expanded analysis of this fund is included in Section III: Analysis of All Rated Funds with Assets over $50 million.

		TOTAL RETURNS & PERFORMANCE							ASSETS		ASSET ALLOCATION & TURNOVER					VALUATION	
3-Month Total Return	6-Month Total Return	1-Year Total Return	3-Year Total Return	5-Year Total Return	Dividend Yield (TTM)	Expense Ratio	3-Yr Std Deviation	Effective Duration	NAV	Total Assets (MIL)	%Cash	%Stocks	%Bonds	%Other	Turnover Ratio	Premium/ Discount 1-Year Avg	Inception Date
1.01	4.97	4.01	43.11		1.54	0.34	12.48		38.43	903.2	1	99	0	0	6	0.01	Sep-15
-0.32	2.27	-1.94	26.22		1.81	0.4	16.17		32.87	20.7	3	97	0	0	46	0.02	Mar-16
-1.23	5.05					0.4			26.42	21.1	0	100	0	0	0	0.00	Mar-19
0.09	3.75	2.64	37.44		1.19	0.44	13.76		36.79	1,377	3	97	0	0	13	0.05	Sep-15
-1.21	0.17	-4.67			0.86	0.5			26.13	518.7	7	93	0	0	33	0.04	Nov-17
-0.15	3.58	6.17	68.30		0.95	0.4	16.24		50.00	57.5	3	97	0	0	27	-0.05	Sep-15
8.62	12.31	25.42	46.86		2.11	0.4	10.1		34.69	39.2	0	100	0	0	19	0.03	Mar-16
-4.71	-6.15	-10.75	-9.22	-37.86	7.71	0.85	17.45		23.27	2,770						0.02	Apr-09
0.80	2.74					0.05			25.51	37.0	0	0	99	0		0.09	Mar-19
1.30	4.49	3.29			2.39	0.19			24.98	3,794	0	100	0	0		0.03	Aug-18
-5.24	-1.49	4.02			4.06	0.19			24.61	1,393	0	100	0	0		0.18	Aug-18
-1.96	1.24	-0.68			3.3	0.09			23.52	3,749	0	100	0	0		0.17	Jun-18
2.42	3.00	-4.48			0.58	0.19			23.66	4,135	0	100	0	0		-0.06	Jun-18
7.90	8.82	19.38			2.07	0.11			90.15	640.0	0	100	0	0	5	-0.01	Jun-18
0.81	4.68					0.02			53.44	34.7	0	100	0	0		0.06	Mar-19
2.15	5.38					0.4		5.34	53.04	31.8	13	0	86	0		0.53	Jan-19
2.65	7.96					0.14		7.68	55.39	29.1	0	0	100	0		0.19	Dec-18
1.54	0.12	0.44	-0.10		0	0.85	4.54		25.05	106.4	34	51	2	14	145	-0.22	Sep-16
-4.53	-1.78	0.07	18.59		2.88	0.45	12		52.70	342.5	0	100	0	0	53	0.09	Jan-15
-1.61	0.43	-2.09	17.36		3.07	0.38	12.54		55.34	16.6	1	99	0	0	51	-0.05	Dec-15
-0.38	0.73	-0.69	20.87	35.79	2.74	0.38	10.24		59.33	142.4	0	100	0	0	29	-0.07	Jun-14
-2.18	-2.83	-5.54	11.43		3.21	0.38	10.91		53.19	1,378	0	100	0	0	28	-0.11	Nov-14
1.38	3.86	3.97	37.22		1.95	0.19	11.44		75.90	804.5	0	100	0	0	32	0.02	Sep-15
0.33	2.45	1.40	32.24		1.6	0.24	12.38		66.76	180.2	0	100	0	0	35	0.04	May-16
-1.61	-0.26	-4.62			1.25	0.29			30.29	131.8	1	99	0	0	30	0.04	Nov-16
-0.85	-0.93	0.35			3.27	0.85			25.37	29.2	11	69	20	0		0.35	Nov-17
1.49	4.70	7.76			5.31	0.55		4.30	51.02	193.9	7	0	90	0	73	0.08	Apr-17
1.01	3.85	7.42	17.18		4.94	0.24	4.08	3.51	51.17	163.7	4	0	96	0	23	0.20	Sep-16
0.64	-0.09	-2.40			0	0.69			21.90	25.2	27	64	9	0		0.19	Jan-18
4.01	5.18	5.78			0.65	0.59			25.38	50.8	94	0	-1	7		-0.13	Dec-17
1.64	4.16					0.24		5.79	54.17	37.9	9	0	91	0		-0.01	Oct-18
2.19	5.47					0.07		5.64	26.74	228.6	0	0	99	0		0.12	Dec-18
2.53	3.57	6.35			3.24	0.12			26.91	36.3	0	100	0	0		-0.01	Nov-17
3.62	8.42	12.58			1.72	0.12			30.16	104.1	0	100	0	0		-0.06	Nov-17
-0.41	4.35	1.85			1.04	0.12			28.84	95.2	0	100	0	0		0.07	Nov-17
1.41	4.05	5.49			1.73	0.12			29.37	105.7	0	100	0	0		-0.02	Nov-17
0.54	2.77	1.86			2.38	0.12			26.71	64.1	0	100	0	0		0.06	Nov-17
0.50	1.45	3.00			2.65	0.18		0.48	50.40	8,810	22	0	74	0	43	0.06	May-17
0.24	0.88					0.18		0.70	50.39	128.5	18	0	82	0		0.08	Oct-18
1.97	7.20	13.64			4.64	0.39		7.35	50.50	65.6	1	0	99	0	28	0.30	Jan-18
3.62						0.41			26.33	52.7	0	100	0	0		0.06	Jun-19
1.62						0.51			25.63	25.6	0	100	0	0		0.11	Jun-19
-0.08	1.78	-2.32	26.66		0.85	0.75	12.01		33.70	133.1	0	100	0	0	18	-0.05	Jul-15
-5.74	-5.86	8.18	11.58	22.58	1.71	0.6	18.72		30.01	550.7	0	100	0	0	106	-0.01	Mar-14
0.41	1.85	6.95			4.92	0.69			40.50	12.2	3	0	86	0		0.51	Jun-18
-9.99	-9.11	0.47	26.66	35.16	2.28	0.7	18.46		26.12	3.9	1	99	0	0	181	-0.71	Jul-13
-7.27	-13.88	-11.96	5.83	29.55	0.04	0.76	25.72		41.42	1,551	0	100	0	0	70	0.01	Jul-13
-3.42	-4.68	-0.65	3.38		5.85	0.59	5.43		32.05	17.6	76	0	24	0	0	-0.02	Dec-14
0.24	-2.96	-4.50			1.2	0.7			20.61	24.7	0	100	0	0	74	0.35	Jan-18
-4.95	-10.12	-17.44			0.01	0.79			20.33	1.0						-0.10	Aug-18
-3.93	-6.49	-0.18			0	0.8			21.73	21.7	0	100	0	0	119	-0.23	Oct-17
1.83	-6.87	-4.78			0.17	0.65			21.13	15.8	4	96	0	0	71	0.04	Jan-18

Fund Name	Ticker Symbol	Traded On	Overall Rating	Reward Rating	Risk Rating	Recent Up/Downgrade	Price as of 9/30/2019	52-Week High	52-Week Low	Open to New Investors	Category & (Prospectus Objective)
KraneShares MSCI All China Index ETF	KALL	NYSE Arca	D+	C-	D		23.46	27.10	20.42	Y	Global Emerg Mkts Equity (Div Emerg Mkts)
KraneShares MSCI China Environment Index ETF	KGRN	NYSE Arca	D	D	D		17.27	20.86	16.66	Y	Greater China Equity (Pacific Stock)
KraneShares MSCI Emerging Markets ex China Index ETF	KEMX	NYSE Arca	U	U	U		24.56	25.63	23.13	Y	Global Emerg Mkts Equity (Div Emerg Mkts)
KraneShares MSCI One Belt One Road Index ETF	OBOR	NYSE Arca	D+	D+	D+	Up	22.52	24.54	21.26	Y	Infrastructure Sector Equity (Growth & Inc)
LeaderSharesTM AlphaFactor® US Core Equity ETF	LSAF	NYSE Arca	U	U	U		24.92	25.45	19.87	Y	US Equity Large Cap Blend (Growth)
Legg Mason Emerg Mkts Low Volatility High Dividend ETF	LVHE	BATS	C-	C	D+		25.72	27.88	24.85	Y	Global Emerg Mkts Equity (Div Emerg Mkts)
Legg Mason Global Infrastructure ETF	INFR	NAS CM	C	C	C-	Up	31.04	31.56	25.73	Y	Infrastructure Sector Equity (Unaligned)
● Legg Mason International Low Volatility High Dividend ETF	LVHI	BATS	C-	C	D+		26.73	27.11	24.04	Y	Global Equity Large Cap (Growth & Inc)
● Legg Mason Low Volatility High Dividend ETF	LVHD	NAS CM	C	C+	C		33.59	33.59	27.85	Y	US Equity Large Cap Value (Income)
Legg Mason Small-Cap Quality Value ETF	SQLV	NAS CM	D+	D+	D+	Up	26.02	29.94	23.02	Y	US Equity Small Cap (Small Company)
LHA Market State Tactical U.S. Equity ETF	MSUS	BATS	D	D	D		24.40	26.45	21.12	Y	Long/Short Equity (Growth & Inc)
Loncar Cancer Immunotherapy ETF	CNCR	NAS CM	D+	D+	D	Up	18.76	24.69	17.21	Y	Healthcare Sector Equity (Health)
Loncar China BioPharma ETF	CHNA	NAS CM	D	D	D+		21.80	25.43	17.93	Y	Greater China Equity (Health)
● Main Sector Rotation ETF	SECT	BATS	C-	C-	C-		29.09	29.40	23.31	Y	US Equity Large Cap Blend (Growth & Inc)
Market Vectors® Chinese Renminbi/USD ETN	CNY	NYSE Arca	D+	C-	D+	Up	43.75	45.99	42.10	Y	Currency (Worldwide Bond)
Market Vectors® Double Long Euro ETN	URR	NYSE Arca	D	D-	D	Up	36.00	41.01	12.26	Y	Trading Tools (Worldwide Bond)
Market Vectors® Double Short Euro ETN	DRR	NYSE Arca	C+	B-	D+	Up	67.48	67.48	53.86	Y	Trading Tools (Worldwide Bond)
Market Vectors® Indian Rupee/USD ETN	INR	NYSE Arca	D	C	E+	Down	90.00	94.00	36.99	Y	Currency (Worldwide Bond)
★ Materials Select Sector SPDR® Fund	XLB	NYSE Arca	B-	B	C	Up	58.20	59.46	47.34	Y	Natural Resources (Natl Res)
Metaurus U.S. Equity Cumulative Dividends Fund-Series 2027	IDIV	NYSE Arca	D+	D+	D+	Up	11.48	13.50	11.33	Y	US Equity Large Cap Blend (Equity-Income)
Metaurus U.S. Equity Ex-Dividend Fund-Series 2027	XDIV	NYSE Arca	D+	C-	D	Up	61.50	62.37	46.12	Y	US Equity Large Cap Blend (Growth)
MFAM Small-Cap Growth ETF	MFMS	BATS	U	U	U		22.50	24.90	18.11	Y	US Equity Small Cap (Small Company)
MicroSectors™ FANG+™ Index -2X Inverse Leveraged ETN	FNGZ	NYSE Arca	D+	D	D		45.20	77.98	39.24	Y	Trading Tools (Technology)
MicroSectors™ FANG+™ Index 2X Leveraged ETN	FNGO	NYSE Arca	D	D	D		37.27	51.96	26.94	Y	Trading Tools (Technology)
MicroSectors™ FANG+™ Index -3X Inverse Leveraged ETN	FNGD	NYSE Arca	D	D	D		20.85	51.89	17.63	Y	Trading Tools (Growth & Inc)
● MicroSectors™ FANG+™ Index 3X Leveraged ETN	FNGU	NYSE Arca	D	D	D		33.55	65.43	22.61	Y	Trading Tools (Growth & Inc)
MicroSectors™ FANG+™ Index Inverse ETN	GNAF	NYSE Arca	D+	D	D+		49.93	63.69	45.86	Y	Trading Tools (Technology)
MicroSectors™ U.S. Big Banks Ind -2X Inverse Leveraged ETN	BNKZ	NYSE Arca	U	U	U		41.47	53.19	40.02	Y	Trading Tools (Growth & Inc)
MicroSectors™ U.S. Big Banks Index 2X Leveraged ETNs	BNKO	NYSE Arca	U	U	U		55.07	58.40	43.96	Y	Trading Tools (Growth & Inc)
MicroSectors™ U.S. Big Banks Ind -3X Inverse Leveraged ETN	BNKD	NYSE Arca	U	U	U		36.58	54.42	34.70	Y	Trading Tools (Growth & Inc)
MicroSectors™ U.S. Big Banks Index 3X Leveraged ETNs	BNKU	NYSE Arca	U	U	U		55.64	61.98	39.93	Y	Trading Tools (Growth & Inc)
MicroSectors™ U.S. Big Banks Index Inverse ETNs	KNAB	NYSE Arca	U	U	U		46.06	51.86	45.23	Y	Trading Tools (Growth & Inc)
MicroSectors™ U.S. Big Oil Ind -2X Inverse Leveraged ETNs	NRGZ	NYSE Arca	U	U	U		51.08	62.35	43.67	Y	Trading Tools (Growth & Inc)
MicroSectors™ U.S. Big Oil Index 2X Leveraged ETNs	NRGO	NYSE Arca	U	U	U		44.28	56.73	36.95	Y	Trading Tools (Growth & Inc)
MicroSectors™ U.S. Big Oil Ind -3X Inverse Leveraged ETNs	NRGD	NYSE Arca	U	U	U		49.80	67.67	40.66	Y	Trading Tools (Growth & Inc)
MicroSectors™ U.S. Big Oil Index 3X Leveraged ETNs	NRGU	NYSE Arca	U	U	U		39.98	60.23	30.67	Y	Trading Tools (Growth & Inc)
MicroSectors™ U.S. Big Oil Index Inverse ETNs	YGRN	NYSE Arca	U	U	U		51.16	56.41	46.79	Y	Trading Tools (Growth & Inc)
● Motley Fool 100 Index ETF	TMFC	BATS	C	C+	C	Up	22.46	23.23	17.54	Y	US Equity Large Cap Growth (Growth & Inc)
Nationwide Maximum Div Emerg Mkts Core Equity ETF	MXDE	NYSE Arca	D	D	D		21.85	22.93	20.64	Y	Global Emerg Mkts Equity (Div Emerg Mkts)
● Nationwide Maximum Diversification U.S. Core Equity ETF	MXDU	NYSE Arca	C-	C-	D+	Up	29.43	29.83	23.92	Y	US Equity Large Cap Blend (Growth)
● Nationwide Risk-Based International Equity ETF	RBIN	NYSE Arca	D	D+	D	Up	25.23	26.05	22.56	Y	Global Equity Large Cap (Foreign Stock)
● Nationwide Risk-Based U.S. Equity ETF	RBUS	NYSE Arca	D+	C-	D	Up	29.82	29.85	23.93	Y	US Equity Large Cap Blend (Growth)
Natixis Loomis Sayles Short Duration Income ETF	LSST	NYSE Arca	D+	C-	D	Up	25.26	25.36	24.54	Y	US Fixed Income (Corp Bond - Gen)
Natixis Seeyond International Minimum Volatility ETF	MVIN	NYSE Arca	C	C	D+	Up	44.26	44.60	38.46	Y	Global Equity Large Cap (Growth)
Nuveen Enhanced Yield 1-5 Year U.S. Aggregate Bond ETF	NUSA	NYSE Arca	C-	C	D+		25.05	25.12	24.12	Y	US Fixed Income (Income)
● Nuveen Enhanced Yield U.S. Aggregate Bond ETF	NUAG	NYSE Arca	C	C	C-	Up	24.89	25.09	22.81	Y	US Fixed Income (Corp Bond - Gen)
● Nuveen ESG Emerging Markets Equity ETF	NUEM	BATS	D+	D+	D+	Up	24.90	27.10	23.23	Y	Global Emerg Mkts Equity (Div Emerg Mkts)
● Nuveen ESG International Developed Markets Equity ETF	NUDM	BATS	C-	C	D+	Up	25.84	26.35	22.15	Y	Global Equity Large Cap (World Stock)
Nuveen ESG Large-Cap ETF	NULC	BATS	U	U	U		27.51	27.71	25.75	Y	US Equity Large Cap Growth (Growth)
● Nuveen ESG Large-Cap Growth ETF	NULG	BATS	C	C+	C		38.09	38.78	29.07	Y	US Equity Large Cap Growth (Growth)
● Nuveen ESG Large-Cap Value ETF	NULV	BATS	C	C+	C		31.25	31.38	25.77	Y	US Equity Large Cap Value (Growth)
● Nuveen ESG Mid-Cap Growth ETF	NUMG	BATS	C	C+	D+		32.73	34.60	25.46	Y	US Equity Mid Cap (Growth)

★ Expanded analysis of this fund is included in Section II: Analysis of All BUY Rated Funds. ● Expanded analysis of this fund is included in Section III: Analysis of All Rated Funds with Assets over $50 million.

		TOTAL RETURNS & PERFORMANCE							ASSETS		ASSET ALLOCATION & TURNOVER					VALUATION	
3-Month Total Return	6-Month Total Return	1-Year Total Return	3-Year Total Return	5-Year Total Return	Dividend Yield (TTM)	Expense Ratio	3-Yr Std Deviation	Effective Duration	NAV	Total Assets (MIL.)	%Cash	%Stocks	%Bonds	%Other	Turnover Ratio	Premium/ Discount 1-Year Avg	Inception Date
-5.86	-9.74	0.24	11.86		1.84	0.49	16.79		23.43	7.0	0	100	0	0	62	0.92	Feb-15
-7.44	-15.12	-9.37			2.06	0.8			17.40	3.5	1	99	0	0	147	0.13	Oct-17
-4.09						0.49			24.33	2.4	1	99	0	0		0.80	Apr-19
-5.73	-4.22	-2.16			2.69	0.79			22.69	18.2	1	100	0	0	72	-0.33	Sep-17
-0.59	2.75	-0.22				0.75				89.7	1	99	0	0		0.09	Oct-18
-3.06	-0.93	-2.33			3.36	0.5			25.68	6.2	1	99	0	0	27	0.56	Nov-16
3.15	6.69	17.57			3.34	0.4			31.25	21.9	1	99	0	0	45	-0.22	Dec-16
2.26	4.42	7.24	26.69		4.17	0.4	8.61		26.60	51.1	2	98	0	0	41	0.36	Jul-16
4.73	6.40	12.82	32.98		2.66	0.27	9.06		33.56	790.2	1	99	0	0	44	0.03	Dec-15
-1.30	-4.39	-11.28			1.89	0.6			25.85	11.6	0	100	0	0	87	0.05	Jul-17
0.92	2.57	-6.49			0.27	1.18			24.37	5.5	13	87	0	0	2	-0.22	Apr-18
-12.69	-12.02	-24.25	-26.27		0	0.79	29.46		18.71	32.7	0	100	0	0	78	0.00	Oct-15
-1.79	-8.18	-4.97			0	0.79			21.83	6.5	0	100	0	0		0.48	Aug-18
-0.18	3.57	1.16			1.49	0.83				507.0	13	87	0	0	61	0.08	Sep-17
-2.81	-4.46	-0.27	3.11	0.71	0	0.55	5.44			7.6					0	-0.70	Mar-08
-7.83	-7.66	-16.12	-17.86	-39.78	0	0.65	13.9			2.9					0	25.19	May-08
8.56	9.05	20.91	19.80	46.13	0	0.65	13.54			12.5					0	-0.87	May-08
-0.70	1.51	12.17	11.41	16.62	0	0.55	7.01			2.2					0	8.50	Mar-08
-1.56	3.65	0.83	28.34	28.82	2.06	0.13	14.24			4,245	0	100	0	0	17	-0.01	Dec-98
-3.64	-1.75	-3.81			0	0.87			11.47	23.5	1	54	45	0	20	0.61	Feb-18
1.57	6.17	4.73			0	0.58			61.72	24.7	50	50	0	0	0	-0.15	Feb-18
-6.78	-3.17					0.85			22.48	68.0	3	97	0	0		0.08	Oct-18
-0.85	-0.56	-6.34			0	0.95			45.17	45.2						1.29	Aug-18
-5.52	-11.19	-26.30			0	0.95			37.29	37.3						-1.01	Aug-18
-3.53	-5.13	-21.00			0	0.95			20.92	20.9						-0.19	Jan-18
-10.59	-20.52	-45.42			0	0.95			33.94	108.6						-0.02	Jan-18
0.36	1.26	1.39			0	0.95			49.92	49.9						0.37	Aug-18
-8.02	-15.80					0.95			41.53	20.8						-0.02	Apr-19
2.98	8.53					0.95			54.99	27.5						0.00	Apr-19
-13.43	-25.17					0.95			36.66	18.3						-0.04	Apr-19
2.18	8.87					0.95			55.53	27.8						0.00	Apr-19
-3.46	-7.20					0.95			46.09	23.0						0.00	Apr-19
4.52						0.95			51.14	51.1						-0.07	Apr-19
-9.75						0.95			44.23	44.2						0.07	Apr-19
4.68						0.95			49.88	49.9						-0.11	Apr-19
-16.28						0.95			39.92	39.9						0.09	Apr-19
2.96						0.95			51.20	51.2						-0.04	Apr-19
-0.32	4.06	1.65			0.51	0.5			22.46	184.8	0	100	0	0	10	-0.08	Jan-18
-3.70	-2.95	-2.83			1.32	0.64			21.85	26.2	0	100	0	0		-0.09	Mar-18
0.81	4.51	1.51			1.43	0.34			29.41	105.9	0	100	0	0		-0.22	Sep-17
0.31	1.11	-0.13			2.64	0.42			25.22	119.2	0	100	0	0		0.05	Sep-17
3.01	8.46	9.62			2.01	0.3			29.81	117.0	0	100	0	0		-0.03	Sep-17
0.86	2.58	5.06			2.74	0.38		1.79	25.26	30.3	3	0	95	0	167	0.02	Dec-17
1.35	5.33	5.32	27.30		2.49	0.55			44.16	26.5	2	98	0	0	135	0.13	Oct-16
1.04	3.05	6.07			2.79	0.2		2.60	25.00	30.0	1	0	97	0	36	0.12	Mar-17
2.60	6.37	10.20	9.23		3.51	0.2	3.44	5.99	24.84	243.5	0	0	99	0	167	-0.10	Sep-16
-5.98	-6.32	-3.51			1.98	0.45			24.67	54.3	0	100	0	0	65	0.77	Jun-17
-0.31	4.73	0.49			2.14	0.4			25.66	61.6	1	100	0	0	56	0.26	Jun-17
1.84						0.2			27.50	5.5	0	100	0	0		0.04	Jun-19
1.39	6.69	5.23			0.61	0.35			38.04	79.9	0	100	0	0	65	0.07	Dec-16
2.68	5.33	6.89			1.8	0.35			31.22	82.7	0	100	0	0	59	0.05	Dec-16
-3.69	2.98	1.02			0.17	0.4			32.69	52.3	0	100	0	0	60	0.10	Dec-16

Fund Name	Ticker Symbol	Traded On	Overall Rating	Reward Rating	Risk Rating	Recent Up/ Downgrade	Price as of 9/30/2019	52-Week High	52-Week Low	Open to New Investors	Category & (Prospectus Objective)
● Nuveen ESG Mid-Cap Value ETF	NUMV	BATS	C	C	C-	Up	29.04	29.26	23.56	Y	US Equity Mid Cap (Growth)
● Nuveen ESG Small-Cap ETF	NUSC	BATS	C-	C-	C-	Down	29.28	31.28	24.25	Y	US Equity Small Cap (Small Company)
● Nuveen ESG U.S. Aggregate Bond ETF	NUBD	NYSE Arca	C-	C-	C-		25.72	26.00	23.73	Y	US Fixed Income (Growth & Inc)
★ Nuveen Short-Term REIT ETF	NURE	BATS	B-	B	C	Up	30.76	30.90	24.37	Y	Real Estate Sector Equity (Real Estate)
Opus Small Cap Value Plus ETF	OSCV	NYSE Arca	D+	D+	D+		25.84	26.10	20.79	Y	US Equity Small Cap (Growth)
O'Shares FTSE Europe Quality Dividend ETF	OEUR	NYSE Arca	C	C	D+	Up	23.91	24.45	21.31	Y	Europe Equity Large Cap (Europe Stock)
● O'Shares FTSE Russell Small Cap Quality Dividend ETF	OUSM	NYSE Arca	C	C	C-	Up	27.88	28.38	22.48	Y	US Equity Small Cap (Small Company)
● O'Shares FTSE U.S. Quality Dividend ETF	OUSA	NYSE Arca	C	C+	C		34.75	35.07	28.55	Y	US Equity Large Cap Value (Growth)
O'Shares Global Internet Giants ETF	OGIG	NYSE Arca	C-	C	C-	Up	23.41	26.46	17.77	Y	Technology Sector Equity (Growth & Inc)
★ Pacer Benchmark Data & Infrastructure Real Estate SCTR ETF	SRVR	NYSE Arca	B-	B+	C-	Up	32.20	32.66	22.35	Y	Real Estate Sector Equity (Growth & Inc)
★ Pacer Benchmark Industrial Real Estate SCTR ETF	INDS	NYSE Arca	B	B+	C	Up	32.41	32.61	23.10	Y	Real Estate Sector Equity (Real Estate)
Pacer Benchmark Retail Real Estate SCTR ETF	RTL	NYSE Arca	C+	B	D+	Up	28.40	28.63	23.88	Y	Real Estate Sector Equity (Growth & Inc)
Pacer Cash Cows Fund of Funds ETF	HERD	NAS CM	U	U	U		24.19	24.74	22.86	Y	Global Equity Large Cap (Growth & Inc)
Pacer CFRA-Stovall Equal Weight Seasonal Rotation ETF	SZNE	NYSE Arca	C-	D+	C-	Up	28.97	29.29	21.90	Y	US Equity Large Cap Blend (Growth & Inc)
Pacer Developed Markets International Cash Cows 100 ETF	ICOW	BATS	D+	D+	D+		25.29	27.75	23.28	Y	Global Equity Large Cap (Growth & Inc)
Pacer Emerging Markets Cash Cows 100 ETF	ECOW	NAS CM	U	U	U		23.90	25.25	22.74	Y	Global Emerg Mkts Equity (Div Emerg Mkts)
● Pacer Global Cash Cows Dividend ETF	GCOW	BATS	C	C	C-		29.69	31.52	26.95	Y	Global Equity Large Cap (Growth & Inc)
Pacer Military Times Best Employers ETF	VETS	NAS CM	C	C	D+	Up	29.78	30.26	23.81	Y	US Equity Large Cap Blend (Growth & Inc)
Pacer Trendpilot Fund of Funds ETF	TRND	NAS CM	U	U	U		25.07	25.49	23.60	Y	Global Equity Large Cap (Growth & Inc)
Pacer Trendpilot International ETF	PTIN	NYSE Arca	U	U	U		25.13	25.76	23.83	Y	Global Equity Large Cap (Foreign Stock)
● Pacer Trendpilot™ 100 ETF	PTNQ	BATS	C+	B-	C	Up	35.92	37.17	31.83	Y	US Equity Large Cap Growth (Growth)
● Pacer Trendpilot™ European Index ETF	PTEU	BATS	C-	C-	C-		26.40	27.08	24.59	Y	Europe Equity Large Cap (Growth & Inc)
● Pacer Trendpilot™ US Large Cap ETF	PTLC	BATS	C+	C	C+		31.07	31.58	28.51	Y	US Equity Large Cap Blend (Growth)
● Pacer Trendpilot™ US Mid Cap ETF	PTMC	BATS	C-	C-	C-		29.18	33.09	27.72	Y	US Equity Mid Cap (Growth)
● Pacer US Cash Cows 100 ETF	COWZ	BATS	C-	C-	C-		28.79	30.88	24.24	Y	US Equity Large Cap Blend (Growth & Inc)
Pacer US Cash Cows Growth ETF	BUL	NYSE Arca	U	U	U		24.41	25.28	23.12	Y	US Equity Large Cap Growth (Growth)
Pacer US Export Leaders ETF	PEXL	NYSE Arca	D	D+	D		25.97	26.63	19.60	Y	US Equity Mid Cap (Growth)
Pacer US Small Cap Cash Cows 100 ETF	CALF	BATS	D+	D	C-	Up	24.65	28.33	21.63	Y	US Equity Small Cap (Small Company)
● Pacer WealthShield ETF	PWS	BATS	D+	D	C-		22.95	26.83	22.02	Y	Moderate Allocation (Growth & Inc)
Pacific Global US Equity Income ETF	USDY	NYSE Arca	U	U	U		26.76	27.19	24.77	Y	US Equity Large Cap Value (Growth & Inc)
● Perth Mint Physical Gold ETF	AAAU	NYSE Arca	D+	D+	C-		14.72	15.52	11.86	Y	Commodities Specified (Prec Metals)
PGIM Active High Yield Bond ETF	PHYL	NYSE Arca	U	U	U		41.18	41.40	37.63	Y	US Fixed Income (Corp Bond-High Yld)
PGIM QMA Strategic Alpha International Equity ETF	PQIN	NYSE Arca	U	U	U		51.39	52.87	47.32	Y	Global Equity Large Cap (Growth)
PGIM QMA Strategic Alpha Large-Cap Core ETF	PQLC	NYSE Arca	U	U	U		53.15	53.81	44.00	Y	US Equity Large Cap Blend (Growth)
PGIM QMA Strategic Alpha Small-Cap Growth ETF	PQSG	NYSE Arca	U	U	U		48.84	53.00	44.45	Y	US Equity Small Cap (Small Company)
PGIM QMA Strategic Alpha Small-Cap Value ETF	PQSV	NYSE Arca	U	U	U		49.46	51.30	44.49	Y	US Equity Small Cap (Small Company)
● PGIM Ultra Short Bond ETF	PULS	NYSE Arca	C	C-	C+	Up	50.19	50.19	49.89	Y	US Fixed Income (Growth & Inc)
Pickens Morningstar® Renewable Energy™ Response ETF	RENW	NYSE Arca	D	D	D		20.31	27.20	17.88	Y	Energy Sector Equity (Natl Res)
● PIMCO 0-5 Year High Yield Corp Bond Ind ETF	HYS	NYSE Arca	C+	C	C+		99.76	100.83	94.14	Y	US Fixed Income (Corp Bond-High Yld)
● PIMCO 1-3 Year U.S. Treasury Index Exchange-Traded Fund	TUZ	NYSE Arca	C	C	D+	Up	50.93	51.08	49.70	Y	US Fixed Income (Govt Bond - Treasury)
● PIMCO 1-5 Year U.S. TIPS Index Exchange-Traded Fund	STPZ	NYSE Arca	C	C	C-		52.42	52.67	50.72	Y	US Fixed Income (Govt Bond - Treasury)
● PIMCO 15+ Year U.S. TIPS Index Exchange-Traded Fund	LTPZ	NYSE Arca	C	C+	C-		73.53	76.75	60.38	Y	US Fixed Income (Govt Bond - Treasury)
● PIMCO 25+ Year Zero Coupon U.S. Treasury Ind ETF	ZROZ	NYSE Arca	C	C	C-		144.61	151.72	100.48	Y	US Fixed Income (Govt Bond - Treasury)
● PIMCO Active Bond Exchange-Traded Fund	BOND	NYSE Arca	C+	B-	C+		108.90	109.60	100.83	Y	US Fixed Income (Income)
● PIMCO Broad U.S. TIPS Index Exchange-Traded Fund	TIPZ	NYSE Arca	C	C+	D+		60.04	61.03	55.39	Y	US Fixed Income (Govt Bond - Treasury)
● PIMCO Enhanced Low Duration Active Exchange-Traded Fund	LDUR	NYSE Arca	C	C	C-		100.35	100.53	98.55	Y	US Fixed Income (Income)
● PIMCO Enhanced Short Maturity Active Exchange-Traded Fund	MINT	NYSE Arca	C	C	C+		101.73	101.76	100.95	Y	US Fixed Income (Income)
● PIMCO Intermediate Muni Bond Active ETF	MUNI	NYSE Arca	C	C+	C-		55.30	55.79	51.81	Y	US Muni Fixed Inc (Muni Bond - Natl)
★ PIMCO Investment Grade Corp Bond Ind ETF	CORP	NYSE Arca	B-	B-	C+	Up	109.72	110.62	97.96	Y	US Fixed Income (Corp Bond - High Quality)
● PIMCO RAFI Dynamic Multi-Factor Emerg Mkts Equity ETF	MFEM	NYSE Arca	C-	D+	C-	Up	22.93	24.23	21.67	Y	Global Emerg Mkts Equity (Div Emerg Mkts)
● PIMCO RAFI Dynamic Multi-Factor International Equity ETF	MFDX	NYSE Arca	D+	D	D+	Up	24.81	25.76	21.85	Y	Global Equity Large Cap (Growth & Inc)
● PIMCO RAFI Dynamic Multi-Factor U.S. Equity ETF	MFUS	NYSE Arca	C-	C-	C-	Up	30.03	30.13	24.14	Y	US Equity Large Cap Blend (Growth & Inc)

★ Expanded analysis of this fund is included in Section II: Analysis of All BUY Rated Funds.   ● Expanded analysis of this fund is included in Section III: Analysis of All Rated Funds with Assets over $50 million.

3-Month Total Return	6-Month Total Return	1-Year Total Return	3-Year Total Return	5-Year Total Return	Dividend Yield (TTM)	Expense Ratio	3-Yr Std Deviation	Effective Duration	NAV	Total Assets (MIL)	%Cash	%Stocks	%Bonds	%Other	Turnover Ratio	Premium/Discount 1-Year Avg	Inception Date
1.31	4.78	5.33			2.1	0.4			28.99	58.0	5	95	0	0	69	0.03	Dec-16
-1.57	0.56	-2.74			0.9	0.4			29.23	154.9	0	100	0	0	54	0.07	Dec-16
2.25	5.57	10.09			2.61	0.2		5.43	25.73	61.8	2	0	98	0	27	0.10	Sep-17
6.78	9.04	18.62			3.27	0.35			30.73	55.3	8	92	0	0	16	0.03	Dec-16
2.69	7.03	3.53			1.93	0.79			25.82	42.6	0	100	0	0		0.14	Jul-18
-0.33	3.20	3.17	14.54		3.83	0.48	11.77		24.00	25.2	1	99	0	0	35	-0.34	Aug-15
1.58	5.98	1.28			2.12	0.48			27.87	100.5	0	100	0	0	52	0.01	Dec-16
2.10	4.55	8.43	37.03		2.49	0.48	10.46		34.75	538.6	0	100	0	0	15	0.02	Jul-15
-7.58	-4.06	-0.17			0	0.48			23.40	45.6	0	100	0	0	55	-0.11	Jun-18
9.44	14.95	26.28			1.63	0.6			32.15	120.6	0	100	0	0	27	0.02	May-18
3.99	13.04	32.75			1.88	0.6			32.36	24.3	0	100	0	0	36	0.13	May-18
8.34	1.16	9.51			3.65	0.6			28.36	2.8	0	100	0	0	60	0.03	May-18
-0.21						0.74			24.14	2.4	0	100	0	0		0.44	May-19
0.81	5.74	11.52			0.97	0.6			28.95	37.6	0	100	0	0	262	-0.03	Jul-18
-1.96	-3.61	-4.91			3.37	0.65			25.26	32.8	0	100	0	0	80	0.13	Jun-17
-3.93						0.7			23.91	3.6	0	100	0	0		-0.33	May-19
-1.54	-1.46	-0.11	19.56		4.35	0.6	11.07		29.70	209.4	0	100	0	0	74	0.07	Feb-16
2.29	8.79	10.11			1.71	0.6			29.80	3.0	0	100	0	0	9	-0.03	Apr-18
-0.63						0.78			25.02	11.3	0	100	0	0		0.11	May-19
-1.24						0.65			25.03	73.8	0	100	0	0		0.53	May-19
-0.14	4.00	-0.18	58.00		0.41	0.65	12.93		35.94	569.6	0	100	0	0	107	0.06	Jun-15
-1.93	2.16	1.33	14.25		1.77	0.65	12.5		26.36	123.9	0	100	0	0	396	-0.04	Dec-15
0.73	4.53	-0.58	38.16		0.92	0.6	10.1		31.07	2,646	0	100	0	0	162	0.01	Jun-15
-0.35	-3.96	-11.02	16.90		0.94	0.6	10.07		29.16	635.6	0	100	0	0	405	0.01	Jun-15
-0.22	-0.85	-4.56			1.91	0.49			28.83	239.3	0	100	0	0	122	0.03	Dec-16
-0.81						0.6			24.43	2.4	0	100	0	0		0.03	May-19
0.67	2.37	2.70			0.54	0.6			25.98	1.3	0	100	0	0	55	-0.08	Jul-18
3.86	-2.71	-11.96			1.32	0.59			24.64	41.9	0	100	0	0	123	0.13	Jun-17
-5.78	-5.18	-13.15			1.57	0.6			22.94	98.6	0	0	100	0	542	-0.03	Dec-17
1.75	4.29					0.29			26.77	29.4	0	100	0	0		0.07	Feb-19
6.77	14.70	24.64			0	0.18			14.82	164.5	0	0	0	100		-0.10	Jul-18
1.15	4.64	8.09			5.88	0.53		3.80	40.97	27.7	2	0	98	1		0.64	Sep-18
-1.31	1.08					0.29			51.01	35.7	1	100	0	0		0.40	Dec-18
0.86	5.02					0.17			53.11	10.6	0	100	0	0		-0.15	Oct-18
-3.32	-3.03					0.29			48.81	9.8	0	100	0	0		-0.05	Nov-18
0.37	1.95					0.29			49.41	9.9	1	99	0	0		-0.02	Nov-18
0.72	1.49	2.90			2.69	0.15		0.20	50.19	647.4	20	0	79	1	145	0.01	Apr-18
-8.47	-10.63	-22.21			0.56	0.65			20.35	3.1	1	99	0	0		0.02	Feb-18
0.33	2.16	3.90	16.61	23.67	4.95	0.56	3.34	1.61	99.88	1,618	0	0	96	4	27	-0.24	Jun-11
0.59	2.20	4.19	4.15	5.84	2.03	0.16	0.99	1.87	50.92	51.0	1	0	99	0	54	-0.01	Jun-09
0.28	2.07	3.50	4.23	5.26	1.25	0.2	1.32	2.93	52.42	727.1	0	0	100	0	36	0.00	Aug-09
6.96	12.58	16.65	11.08	24.13	1.45	0.2	9.55	21.42	73.53	247.8	0	0	100	0	6	0.02	Sep-09
13.75	24.85	38.09	16.04	52.83	2.16	0.15	18.34	27.48	144.52	349.7	0	0	100	0	21	0.12	Oct-09
2.02	5.25	9.94	11.34	19.94	3.4	0.76	3.05	4.79	108.77	2,712	-6	0	105	0	155	0.03	Feb-12
1.82	4.99	7.78	6.48	11.79	1.23	0.21	3.53	7.96	60.02	52.8	1	0	99	0	9	0.02	Sep-09
0.90	2.12	3.86	7.25	12.49	3.06	1.02	0.69	1.33	100.33	409.4	-28	0	120	7	1,613	0.05	Jan-14
0.68	1.54	2.87	6.80	8.97	2.7	0.42	0.3	0.24	101.75	12,788	14	0	83	0	72	-0.01	Nov-09
1.32	3.60	7.91	8.35	15.89	2.51	0.35	3.04	4.61	55.18	337.1	6	0	94	0	39	0.12	Nov-09
3.38	8.68	13.35	13.93	25.35	3.29	0.2	4.2	7.12	109.71	650.6	-8	0	105	0	27	-0.05	Sep-10
-4.87	-2.55	-2.07			3.3	0.49			23.04	546.5	1	99	0	0	43	-0.06	Aug-17
-0.16	1.33	-1.92			2.93	0.39			24.72	47.5	11	89	0	0	24	0.17	Aug-17
2.63	5.88	2.20			1.95	0.29			29.99	135.6	7	93	0	0	40	0.09	Aug-17

Fund Name	Ticker Symbol	Traded On	Overall Rating	Reward Rating	Risk Rating	Recent Up/ Downgrade	Price as of 9/30/2019	52-Week High	52-Week Low	Open to New Investors	Category & (Prospectus Objective)
● PIMCO Short Term Muni Bond Active ETF	SMMU	NYSE Arca	C	C	C-		50.65	50.98	49.50	Y	US Muni Fixed Inc (Muni Bond - Natl)
Point Bridge GOP Stock Tracker ETF	MAGA	BATS	D	D+	D		27.44	28.54	22.04	Y	US Equity Large Cap Blend (Growth & Inc)
PortfolioPlus Developed Markets ETF	PPDM	NYSE Arca	D	D	D		22.25	23.20	18.91	Y	Trading Tools (Growth)
PortfolioPlus Emerging Markets ETF	PPEM	NYSE Arca	D	D+	D		19.98	22.39	18.57	Y	Trading Tools (Div Emerg Mkts)
PortfolioPlus S&P 500® ETF	PPLC	NYSE Arca	C	C+	D+		40.41	41.22	30.45	Y	Trading Tools (Growth)
PortfolioPlus S&P® Mid Cap ETF	PPMC	NYSE Arca	D	D	D		24.92	27.84	20.00	Y	Trading Tools (Growth)
PortfolioPlus S&P® Small Cap ETF	PPSC	NYSE Arca	D+	C-	D	Down	35.29	41.45	28.77	Y	Trading Tools (Small Company)
● PPTY – U.S. Diversified Real Estate ETF	PPTY	NYSE Arca	C	C	C-	Up	32.66	32.69	24.89	Y	Real Estate Sector Equity (Real Estate)
Premise Capital Frontier Advantage Div Tactical ETF	TCTL	BATS	C-	C	D+		31.03	31.21	28.53	Y	Flexible Allocation (Growth & Inc)
● Principal Active Global Dividend Income ETF	GDVD	BATS	C	C	D+	Up	28.08	28.37	23.59	Y	Global Equity Large Cap (Growth & Inc)
● Principal Active Income ETF	YLD	NYSE Arca	C	C	C-		40.20	41.05	37.39	Y	Cautious Allocation (Income)
Principal Contrarian Value Index ETF	PVAL	NAS CM	D+	D+	D+	Up	26.97	27.20	22.19	Y	US Equity Large Cap Value (Growth & Inc)
Principal Healthcare Innovators Index ETF	BTEC	NAS CM	D+	C-	D		31.22	36.79	25.07	Y	Healthcare Sector Equity (Health)
● Principal Investment Grade Corporate Active ETF	IG	NYSE Arca	D+	C-	D		26.81	27.12	23.97	Y	US Fixed Income (Corp Bond - Gen)
Principal Millennials Index ETF	GENY	NAS CM	C-	C	D	Down	37.87	39.58	30.03	Y	Global Equity Large Cap (Growth & Inc)
Principal Price Setters Index ETF	PSET	NAS CM	C	B-	C-		38.43	38.83	30.51	Y	US Equity Large Cap Growth (Growth & Inc)
Principal Shareholder Yield Index ETF	PY	NAS CM	C-	C	D+		32.17	33.73	27.03	Y	US Equity Mid Cap (Growth & Inc)
● Principal Spectrum Preferred Securities Active ETF	PREF	BATS	C	C	D+	Up	99.55	99.55	89.67	Y	US Fixed Income (Equity-Income)
Principal Sustainable Momentum Index ETF	PMOM	NAS CM	D	D+	D		28.05	30.06	23.01	Y	US Equity Large Cap Blend (Growth & Inc)
● Principal U.S. Mega-Cap Multi-Factor Index ETF	USMC	NAS CM	C+	C+	C+	Up	29.38	29.73	23.78	Y	US Equity Large Cap Blend (Growth & Inc)
● Principal U.S. Small-Cap Multi-Factor Index ETF	PSC	NAS CM	C-	D+	C-	Up	30.73	34.90	26.04	Y	US Equity Small Cap (Small Company)
Principal Ultra-Short Active Income ETF	USI	NYSE Arca	U	U	U		25.07	25.10	25.00	Y	US Fixed Income (Income)
Procure Space ETF	UFO	NYSE Arca	U	U	U		25.85	26.94	24.12	Y	Industrials Sector Equity (Unaligned)
ProShares Decline of the Retail Store ETF	EMTY	NYSE Arca	C	C-	C-	Up	36.39	43.51	30.00	Y	Trading Tools (Unaligned)
● ProShares DJ Brookfield Global Infrastructure ETF	TOLZ	NYSE Arca	C	B-	C-		45.55	46.15	37.16	Y	Infrastructure Sector Equity (Utility)
ProShares Equities for Rising Rates ETF	EQRR	NAS CM	C-	C	D+	Up	39.30	50.29	35.75	Y	US Equity Large Cap Value (Growth & Inc)
ProShares Global Listed Private Equity ETF	PEX	BATS	C	C	D+	Up	34.60	36.17	29.48	Y	Financials Sector Equity (Growth)
ProShares Hedge Replication ETF	HDG	NYSE Arca	C-	C	D+		45.32	45.73	42.69	Y	Multialternative (Growth)
● ProShares High Yield—Interest Rate Hedged	HYHG	BATS	C	C	D+		64.55	68.33	61.54	Y	Fixed Income Misc (Income)
ProShares Inflation Expectations ETF	RINF	NYSE Arca	D+	D+	D+	Up	25.35	30.08	24.98	Y	Fixed Income Misc (Govt Bond - Treasury)
● ProShares Investment Grade—Interest Rate Hedged	IGHG	BATS	C	C	C-		74.55	75.82	70.32	Y	Fixed Income Misc (Worldwide Bond)
ProShares K-1 Free Crude Oil Strategy ETF	OILK	BATS	D+	D+	D+		19.62	28.66	16.55	Y	Commodities Specified (Natl Res)
● ProShares Large Cap Core Plus	CSM	BATS	C	C	C-		70.93	72.35	57.18	Y	US Equity Large Cap Blend (Growth)
ProShares Long Online/Short Stores ETF	CLIX	NYSE Arca	C	C+	D+	Up	47.15	55.40	39.59	Y	Long/Short Equity (Growth & Inc)
ProShares Managed Futures Strategy ETF	FUT	BATS	C-	C	D+	Up	39.88	41.01	39.25	Y	Alternative Misc (Growth & Inc)
ProShares Merger ETF	MRGR	BATS	C	C+	D+	Up	37.64	37.82	35.99	Y	Market Neutral (Growth)
ProShares Morningstar Alternatives Solution ETF	ALTS	BATS	D+	C	D		37.57	37.90	36.03	Y	Multialternative (Growth & Inc)
● ProShares MSCI EAFE Dividend Growers ETF	EFAD	BATS	C-	C	C-		37.32	38.23	32.66	Y	Global Equity Large Cap (Equity-Income)
ProShares MSCI Emerging Markets Dividend Growers ETF	EMDV	BATS	C-	C	D+	Down	55.73	59.66	49.57	Y	Global Emerg Mkts Equity (Div Emerg Mkts)
ProShares MSCI Europe Dividend Growers ETF	EUDV	BATS	C-	C-	D+	Up	40.30	41.80	35.69	Y	Europe Equity Large Cap (Growth & Inc)
ProShares Online Retail ETF	ONLN	BATS	C	C+	D+	Up	33.76	40.16	27.71	Y	Consumer Goods & Svcs (Growth)
ProShares Pet Care ETF	PAWZ	BATS	U	U	U		39.74	43.26	36.08	Y	Equity Misc (Unaligned)
ProShares RAFI® Long/Short	RALS	NYSE Arca	D	D	D+		34.86	37.73	34.26	Y	Market Neutral (Growth)
● ProShares Russell 2000 Dividend Growers ETF	SMDV	BATS	C	C	C-		59.36	60.75	51.72	Y	US Equity Small Cap (Growth)
● ProShares S&P 500 Dividend Aristocrats ETF	NOBL	BATS	C+	C+	C+		71.58	72.24	57.62	Y	US Equity Large Cap Blend (Growth)
ProShares S&P 500® Bond ETF	SPXB	NYSE Arca	C-	C-	D+	Up	87.64	88.82	78.16	Y	US Fixed Income (Corp Bond - Gen)
ProShares S&P 500® ex-Energy ETF	SPXE	NYSE Arca	C	C+	D		63.21	64.19	49.98	Y	US Equity Large Cap Blend (Growth & Inc)
ProShares S&P 500® ex-Financials ETF	SPXN	NYSE Arca	C	C+	D	Up	61.32	62.51	48.75	Y	US Equity Large Cap Blend (Growth & Inc)
ProShares S&P 500® ex-Health Care ETF	SPXV	NYSE Arca	C-	C+	E+	Down	62.52	63.56	48.72	Y	US Equity Large Cap Blend (Growth & Inc)
ProShares S&P 500® ex-Technology ETF	SPXT	NYSE Arca	C	C+	D	Up	55.59	56.46	45.42	Y	US Equity Large Cap Blend (Growth & Inc)
● ProShares S&P MidCap 400 Dividend Aristocrats ETF	REGL	BATS	C	C	C-		58.08	59.54	49.63	Y	US Equity Mid Cap (Growth)
● ProShares Short 20+ Year Treasury	TBF	NYSE Arca	D	D	D	Down	18.77	24.42	18.29	Y	Trading Tools (Govt Bond - Treasury)

★ Expanded analysis of this fund is included in Section II: Analysis of All BUY Rated Funds. ● Expanded analysis of this fund is included in Section III: Analysis of All Rated Funds with Assets over $50 million.

		TOTAL RETURNS & PERFORMANCE							ASSETS		ASSET ALLOCATION & TURNOVER					VALUATION	
3-Month Total Return	6-Month Total Return	1-Year Total Return	3-Year Total Return	5-Year Total Return	Dividend Yield (TTM)	Expense Ratio	3-Yr Std Deviation	Effective Duration	NAV	Total Assets (MIL)	%Cash	%Stocks	%Bonds	%Other	Turnover Ratio	Premium/ Discount 1-Year Avg	Inception Date
0.52	1.56	3.66	5.03	6.90	1.88	0.35	1.22	1.86	50.57	114.3	15	0	85	0	49	0.08	Feb-10
-0.44	2.90	-1.67			1.82	0.72			27.43	15.8	0	100	0	0	37	0.01	Sep-17
-2.16	0.51	-3.71			3.7	0.52			22.28	1.1	2	98	0	0	22	-0.14	Feb-18
-7.81	-6.29	-0.35			5.28	0.58			20.01	1.0	1	99	0	0	22	0.01	Feb-18
0.80	5.76	4.60	56.97		2.87	0.36	15.46		40.39	24.2	-2	102	0	0	30	-0.46	Jan-15
-0.99	1.22	-3.47			4.56	0.45			24.96	1.2	0	100	0	0	18	-0.14	Feb-18
-1.03	-0.50	-11.68	33.35		1.51	0.43	22.29		35.26	7.1	1	98	0	0	235	0.06	Jan-15
7.01	9.42	21.13			2.29	0.53			32.65	124.1	0	100	0	0		-0.01	Mar-18
0.38	2.58	1.25	30.27		0.83	0.91			31.03	45.0	1	84	15	0	195	-0.03	Oct-16
0.99	4.40	2.89			3.07	0.58			27.89	729.4	1	99	0	0	32	0.40	May-17
1.49	3.23	4.89	16.85		5.7	0.49	5.19	3.59	40.10	271.6	3	20	66	0	32	0.44	Jul-15
-0.12	3.54	0.12			1.46	0.29			26.82	5.4	0	100	0	0	47	-0.38	Oct-17
-11.60	-11.97	-16.02	16.66		0	0.42	25.52		30.53	48.8	0	100	0	0	35	0.35	Aug-16
3.11	8.56	13.80			3.7	0.26		7.80	26.74	123.0	2	0	97	0	93	0.36	Apr-18
-1.93	1.37	-0.92	55.42		0.46	0.45	14.67		37.83	20.8	0	100	0	0	82	-0.08	Aug-16
0.81	6.33	10.64	52.48		1.22	0.29	11.64		38.36	19.2	1	99	0	0	40	-0.48	Mar-16
0.33	3.01	-2.22	33.39		2.25	0.29	16.62		32.17	11.3	0	100	0	0	49	-0.24	Mar-16
3.34	7.07	10.19			5	0.55		5.03	99.03	84.2	2	0	83	0	28	0.52	Jul-17
-1.24	0.18	-5.42			1.12	0.29			28.09	5.6	0	100	0	0	103	-0.77	Oct-17
0.68	4.36	5.51			2.23	0.12			29.35	1,431	0	100	0	0	27	0.11	Oct-17
-2.41	-1.94	-10.56	25.76		1.33	0.38	17.3		30.63	370.7	0	100	0	0	82	0.10	Sep-16
0.68						0.18		0.44	25.06	12.5	14	0	86	0	0	0.03	Apr-19
-2.05						0.75			25.84	12.3	0	100	0	0		0.19	Apr-19
-4.92	7.28	20.64			0.7	0.65			36.41	12.7	200	-100	0	0		-0.01	Nov-17
2.03	5.41	12.74	21.81	23.87	3.07	0.46	9.93		45.53	113.4	0	99	0	0	14	0.08	Mar-14
-4.70	-5.81	-19.09			2.32	0.35			39.37	3.1	0	100	0	0	89	-0.14	Jul-17
1.63	6.49	1.16	23.40	40.65	5.09	3.13	11.83		34.56	19.7	3	88	0	8	25	-0.09	Feb-13
-0.44	0.51	0.68	7.49	10.25	1.09	0.95	4.56		45.30	30.6	67	33	0	0	106	-0.16	Jul-11
-0.49	0.38	0.01	15.72	12.22	6.35	0.5	5.74		64.40	117.5	57	0	43	0	49	0.04	May-13
-4.18	-7.22	-12.13	-2.62	-16.98	2.11	0.3	8.2		25.19	49.1	-142	0	242	0	120	0.01	Jan-12
-0.01	2.30	2.32	12.16	12.19	3.89	0.3	4.84		74.55	287.0	102	0	-6	0	22	0.01	Nov-13
-8.17	-12.30	-30.00	0.34		1.43	0.65	27.78		19.56	8.8	0	0	0	100		-0.16	Sep-16
0.20	3.06	-0.39	40.35	61.63	1.51	0.45	12.47		70.89	762.0	0	100	0	0	52	0.03	Jul-09
-13.83	-9.12	-0.55			0	0.65			47.18	34.7	50	50	0	0	53	-0.02	Nov-17
0.96	0.77	-0.37	0.78		1.84	0.75	4.34		39.87	2.6	134	-5	0	-29	2,398	-0.09	Feb-16
0.79	1.43	4.27	6.99	6.26	0.23	0.75	2.32		37.69	5.7	25	85	0	-9	314	0.12	Dec-12
0.91	1.74	0.45	3.77	3.32	1.84	0.95	3.66		37.58	6.8	39	60	6	-5	67	-0.07	Oct-14
-0.10	2.15	-0.20	14.20	9.99	2.05	0.5	10.94		37.31	122.4	1	99	0	0	31	-0.07	Aug-14
-4.33	-3.63	4.11	20.43		1.87	0.6	12.58		55.74	21.5	0	100	0	0	79	-0.05	Jan-16
-0.22	2.22	-1.55	14.88		2.24	0.55	12.28		40.33	7.9	1	99	0	0	28	-0.19	Sep-15
-11.85	-12.78	-11.47			0	0.58			33.73	21.9	0	100	0	0	46	0.04	Jul-18
-7.16	-1.29					0.5			39.64	51.5	0	100	0	0	42	0.06	Nov-18
0.80	0.01	-1.04	-5.51	-9.81	2.03	0.95	3.26		34.86	6.6	100	0	0	0	30	-0.02	Dec-10
0.94	2.72	4.02	31.60		2.06	0.4	12.77		59.30	730.0	0	100	0	0	26	0.04	Feb-15
2.98	5.83	8.99	40.36	72.96	1.97	0.35	11.64		71.56	5,510	0	100	0	0	20	-0.02	Oct-13
3.11	8.48	13.75			3.57	0.15			87.56	28.5	1	0	99	0	29	0.15	May-18
1.21	5.57	5.15	48.59		1.56	0.27	11.98		63.19	7.9	0	100	0	0	6	-0.01	Sep-15
0.60	4.11	3.09	43.78		1.51	0.27	12.12		61.27	2.1	0	100	0	0	6	-0.28	Sep-15
1.48	5.70	4.99	46.78		1.67	0.27	12.53		62.50	1.6	0	100	0	0	6	0.09	Sep-15
0.58	3.84	2.49	35.42		1.78	0.27	12.1		55.57	3.3	0	100	0	0	22	-0.31	Sep-15
-0.20	3.26	4.83	32.16		1.89	0.4	11.62		58.07	711.9	0	100	0	0	32	0.03	Feb-15
-7.85	-13.11	-18.83	-8.96	-29.63	1.82	0.92	11.5		18.78	258.2	139	0	13	-52	0	-0.13	Aug-09

Fund Name	Ticker Symbol	Traded On	Overall Rating	Reward Rating	Risk Rating	Recent Up/ Downgrade	Price as of 9/30/2019	52-Week High	52-Week Low	Open to New Investors	Category & (Prospectus Objective)
ProShares Short 7-10 Year Treasury	TBX	NYSE Arca	D+	D	D+		26.18	29.76	25.84	Y	Trading Tools (Govt Bond - Treasury)
ProShares Short Basic Materials	SBM	NYSE Arca	D+	D	D		18.43	22.08	17.59	Y	Trading Tools (Unaligned)
● ProShares Short Dow30	DOG	NYSE Arca	D	D-	D		52.46	65.91	51.97	Y	Trading Tools (Growth)
ProShares Short Euro	EUFX	NYSE Arca	C	C+	D+		46.73	46.73	42.12	Y	Trading Tools (Income)
ProShares Short Financials	SEF	NYSE Arca	D	D	D		20.65	26.98	20.51	Y	Trading Tools (Financial)
ProShares Short FTSE China 50	YXI	NYSE Arca	C-	D+	D+	Up	20.08	21.84	17.78	Y	Trading Tools (Pacific Stock)
● ProShares Short High Yield	SJB	NYSE Arca	D	D	D+		21.13	24.12	21.10	Y	Trading Tools (Corp Bond-High Yld)
ProShares Short MidCap400	MYY	NYSE Arca	D+	D	D	Up	42.51	53.51	41.83	Y	Trading Tools (Growth)
ProShares Short MSCI EAFE	EFZ	NYSE Arca	C-	D+	D+	Up	26.18	30.59	25.55	Y	Trading Tools (Foreign Stock)
● ProShares Short MSCI Emerging Markets	EUM	NYSE Arca	C-	D+	D+	Up	19.14	21.51	17.79	Y	Trading Tools (Div Emerg Mkts)
ProShares Short Oil & Gas	DDG	NYSE Arca	C-	C-	D+		25.91	29.53	20.67	Y	Trading Tools (Natl Res)
● ProShares Short QQQ	PSQ	NYSE Arca	D	D-	D-		27.74	37.20	27.04	Y	Trading Tools (Growth)
ProShares Short Real Estate	REK	NYSE Arca	D	D	D		12.95	17.18	12.90	Y	Trading Tools (Real Estate)
● ProShares Short Russell2000	RWM	NYSE Arca	D+	D	D		40.63	49.87	38.23	Y	Trading Tools (Small Company)
● ProShares Short S&P500	SH	NYSE Arca	D	D	D		26.13	33.59	25.89	Y	Trading Tools (Growth)
ProShares Short SmallCap600	SBB	NYSE Arca	D+	D	D		32.32	39.49	30.33	Y	Trading Tools (Small Company)
ProShares Short Term USD Emerging Markets Bond ETF	EMSH	BATS	C-	C	D	Down	75.29	76.62	73.00		Emerging Mkts Fixed Inc (Div Emerg Mkts)
● ProShares Short VIX Short-Term Futures ETF	SVXY	NYSE Arca	C	C	D+		53.41	59.50	41.30	Y	Alternative Misc (Growth)
ProShares Ultra 20+ Year Treasury	UBT	NYSE Arca	C	C	C-		105.45	112.83	65.19	Y	Trading Tools (Govt Bond - Treasury)
● ProShares Ultra 7-10 Year Treasury	UST	NYSE Arca	C	C	C-	Up	64.75	67.13	51.24	Y	Trading Tools (Govt Bond - Treasury)
ProShares Ultra Basic Materials	UYM	NYSE Arca	C+	B-	C	Up	55.95	68.66	42.31	Y	Trading Tools (Unaligned)
● ProShares Ultra Bloomberg Crude Oil	UCO	NYSE Arca	D+	D	D+		16.22	38.61	12.43	Y	Trading Tools (Natl Res)
ProShares Ultra Bloomberg Natural Gas	BOIL	NYSE Arca	E+	E+	D-		12.87	71.96	11.36	Y	Trading Tools (Natl Res)
ProShares Ultra Communication Services Select Sector	XCOM	NYSE Arca	U	U	U		47.12	51.99	38.21	Y	Trading Tools (Comm)
ProShares Ultra Consumer Goods	UGE	NYSE Arca	C	C	D+		47.87	47.95	31.84	Y	Trading Tools (Unaligned)
ProShares Ultra Consumer Services	UCC	NYSE Arca	C	B-	C-	Down	107.91	121.02	68.00	Y	Trading Tools (Unaligned)
● ProShares Ultra Dow30	DDM	NYSE Arca	C+	B-	C		49.59	51.35	33.20	Y	Trading Tools (Growth)
ProShares Ultra Euro	ULE	NYSE Arca	D	D-	D		13.17	15.64	13.17	Y	Trading Tools (Worldwide Bond)
● ProShares Ultra Financials	UYG	NYSE Arca	C	C+	C-		46.90	48.06	29.07	Y	Trading Tools (Financial)
ProShares Ultra FTSE China 50	XPP	NYSE Arca	D+	D	D+	Down	54.92	76.55	51.40	Y	Trading Tools (Pacific Stock)
ProShares Ultra FTSE Europe	UPV	NYSE Arca	D+	D+	D+	Down	46.45	53.22	36.85	Y	Trading Tools (Europe Stock)
● ProShares Ultra Gold	UGL	NYSE Arca	C	C	C	Up	46.94	52.55	32.56	Y	Trading Tools (Prec Metals)
● ProShares Ultra Health Care	RXL	NYSE Arca	C	C+	C-		98.21	117.11	80.30	Y	Trading Tools (Health)
ProShares Ultra High Yield	UJB	NYSE Arca	C	C+	D		71.06	72.83	58.33	Y	Trading Tools (Corp Bond-High Yld)
ProShares Ultra Industrials	UXI	NYSE Arca	C	C+	D+		78.57	81.83	46.66	Y	Trading Tools (Unaligned)
● ProShares Ultra MidCap400	MVV	NYSE Arca	C-	C	C-	Down	39.95	44.78	27.06	Y	Trading Tools (Growth)
ProShares Ultra MSCI Brazil Capped	UBR	NYSE Arca	D+	C-	D	Down	70.72	90.23	50.15	Y	Trading Tools (Foreign Stock)
ProShares Ultra MSCI EAFE	EFO	NYSE Arca	D+	D+	D+	Down	37.28	41.11	28.88	Y	Trading Tools (Foreign Stock)
ProShares Ultra MSCI Emerging Markets	EET	NYSE Arca	D+	D	D+	Down	64.94	79.37	57.30	Y	Trading Tools (Div Emerg Mkts)
ProShares Ultra MSCI Japan	EZJ	NYSE Arca	D	D+	D	Down	34.57	42.90	28.10	Y	Trading Tools (Pacific Stock)
● ProShares Ultra Nasdaq Biotechnology	BIB	NAS CM	D+	D+	D+		42.53	68.95	36.42	Y	Trading Tools (Technology)
● ProShares Ultra Oil & Gas	DIG	NYSE Arca	D	D+	D		23.63	45.75	20.84	Y	Trading Tools (Natl Res)
● ProShares Ultra QQQ	QLD	NYSE Arca	C+	B-	C	Up	96.73	104.48	58.52	Y	Trading Tools (Growth)
● ProShares Ultra Real Estate	URE	NYSE Arca	C	C+	C-		87.44	88.11	52.35	Y	Trading Tools (Real Estate)
● ProShares Ultra Russell2000	UWM	NYSE Arca	C-	C-	C-		64.47	82.19	46.50	Y	Trading Tools (Small Company)
● ProShares Ultra S&P500	SSO	NYSE Arca	C	C+	C		128.45	133.28	81.81	Y	Trading Tools (Growth)
★ ProShares Ultra Semiconductors	USD	NYSE Arca	B-	B	C	Up	45.01	52.31	25.73	Y	Trading Tools (Technology)
● ProShares Ultra Silver	AGQ	NYSE Arca	C-	C-	D+	Up	29.48	39.66	21.75	Y	Trading Tools (Prec Metals)
ProShares Ultra SmallCap600	SAA	NYSE Arca	D+	C-	D		94.69	121.81	69.10	Y	Trading Tools (Small Company)
● ProShares Ultra Technology	ROM	NYSE Arca	C+	B	C	Up	123.27	133.94	68.54	Y	Trading Tools (Technology)
ProShares Ultra Telecommunications	LTL	NYSE Arca	D+	C	D	Up	39.76	45.20	30.18	Y	Trading Tools (Comm)
★ ProShares Ultra Utilities	UPW	NYSE Arca	B-	B	D+	Up	70.29	70.64	45.19	Y	Trading Tools (Utility)

★ Expanded analysis of this fund is included in Section II: Analysis of All BUY Rated Funds.   ● Expanded analysis of this fund is included in Section III: Analysis of All Rated Funds with Assets over $50 million.

		TOTAL RETURNS & PERFORMANCE							ASSETS		ASSET ALLOCATION & TURNOVER					VALUATION	
3-Month Total Return	6-Month Total Return	1-Year Total Return	3-Year Total Return	5-Year Total Return	Dividend Yield (TTM)	Expense Ratio	3-Yr Std Deviation	Effective Duration	NAV	Total Assets (MIL)	%Cash	%Stocks	%Bonds	%Other	Turnover Ratio	Premium/ Discount 1-Year Avg	Inception Date
-2.27	-5.56	-9.67	-2.49	-14.70	1.58	0.95	5.13		26.19	20.3	143	0	12	-54	0	-0.06	Apr-11
2.95	-0.67	4.30	-21.69	-27.48	0.66	0.95	15.52		18.40	2.8	200	0	0	-100		0.14	Mar-10
-0.98	-2.54	-2.14	-35.38	-46.44	1.53	0.95	12.17		52.48	240.0	146	-58	12	0	0	0.02	Jun-06
4.17	4.50	10.02	10.00	20.60	0	0.97	6.42			18.7	100	0	0	0		-0.05	Jun-12
-1.89	-6.80	-6.73	-34.13	-45.86	1.25	0.95	13.33		20.69	21.2	149	-55	10	-4		0.01	Jun-08
8.72	11.11	3.32	-20.01	-37.37	1.03	0.95	18.13		20.07	7.0	200	-100	0	0		-0.08	Mar-10
-0.98	-2.77	-4.66	-14.05	-23.20	1.28	0.95	4.42		21.15	108.9	155	0	6	-61		-0.01	Mar-11
0.50	-1.12	2.11	-23.49	-39.44	1.34	0.95	15.46		42.54	14.6	200	-100	0	0	77,384	-0.05	Jun-06
1.66	-0.43	2.65	-16.01	-21.39	1.32	0.95	11.25		26.16	36.0	153	-27	9	-35		-0.03	Oct-07
6.23	5.99	1.64	-18.29	-25.10	1.66	0.95	14.7		19.14	75.6	154	-61	7	0	0	-0.02	Oct-07
6.98	12.28	26.67	5.19	10.27	0.76	0.95	21.49		26.03	2.0	200	0	0	-100		-0.10	Jun-08
-0.01	-3.63	-3.60	-40.36	-55.65	1.64	0.95	14.47		27.73	570.3	147	-58	12	0		0.01	Jun-06
-6.59	-7.62	-16.38	-22.84	-43.11	1.43	0.95	11.6		12.96	7.8	200	0	0	-100		0.06	Mar-10
2.59	1.63	7.63	-22.82	-40.44	1.39	0.95	17.21		40.60	327.5	149	-60	11	0	0	0.02	Jan-07
-0.54	-3.54	-2.44	-29.67	-42.59	1.64	0.89	12.06		26.14	1,957	145	-56	11	0		0.02	Jun-06
0.20	-0.43	7.80	-25.74	-44.72	1.14	0.95	18.03		32.35	3.8	200	-100	0	0	0	-0.01	Jan-07
-0.37	1.93	4.96	7.05	18.76	3.52	0.5	2.2		75.52	7.6	0	0	100	0	40	-0.19	Nov-13
-4.86	-0.32	-11.02	45.19	40.91	0	1.38	64.14			336.2	150	-50	0	0		-0.19	Oct-11
16.71	32.02	51.89	14.14	60.16	1.24	0.95	23.93		105.23	50.0	-97	0	71	126	48	0.25	Jan-10
5.15	13.43	25.74	6.17	27.64	1.48	0.95	10.48		64.74	51.8	-100	0	57	143	188	0.10	Jan-10
-7.23	-2.13	-16.55	29.38	11.88	1.37	0.95	31.46		55.94	43.4	-100	102	0	98	38	-0.15	Jan-07
-14.14	-23.73	-54.44	-18.14	-94.28	0	0.95	54			301.6	-100	0	0	200	0	-0.20	Nov-08
2.60	-34.78	-57.24	-81.05	-98.10	0	1.31	69.35			24.8	-100	0	0	200		0.51	Oct-11
-1.74	5.78					0.95			47.16	1.2	-100	37	0	163		-0.05	Jan-19
6.90	11.41	12.31	26.64	76.85	0.98	0.95	23.52		47.97	7.2	-100	89	0	111		-0.10	Jan-07
-4.38	7.25	-0.85	98.99	179.74	0.19	0.95	28.76		108.09	21.6	-100	74	0	126	9	-0.11	Jan-07
1.24	4.59	-0.53	113.70	161.26	0.57	0.95	25.09		49.60	347.2	-100	83	0	117	35	-0.02	Jun-06
-7.13	-6.99	-15.03	-17.73	-39.00	0	1.01	12.66			5.3	100	0	0	0	0	0.02	Nov-08
2.86	13.77	9.82	99.06	133.14	1.05	0.95	27.5		46.92	779.3	-100	200	0	1	10	-0.10	Jan-07
-17.11	-22.53	-17.01	7.21	4.97	4.55	0.95	37.42		54.86	27.4	-100	200	0	0		0.04	Jun-09
-5.48	-0.61	-8.70	27.08	4.61	0.71	0.95	25.44		46.59	4.7	-99	180	0	20	0	-0.05	Apr-10
15.19	31.32	49.40	9.60	18.48	0	0.95	22.5			109.3	-100	138	0	63	0	0.07	Dec-08
-7.70	-6.26	-15.77	51.03	89.95	0.34	0.95	27.2		98.28	98.3	-100	98	0	102	11	-0.09	Jan-07
1.86	5.71	9.62	28.58	39.77	2.87	1.27	9.16	3.37	71.10	5.3	-100	0	38	162	12	0.39	Apr-11
-1.16	3.85	-1.90	82.29	139.89	0.68	0.95	31.53		78.53	19.6	-100	103	0	97	5	-0.07	Jan-07
-2.51	-0.12	-10.10	47.30	91.18	0.68	0.95	30.58		39.95	134.8	-100	200	0	0	31	0.07	Jun-06
-10.62	-2.09	42.19	19.92	-38.84	0.74	0.95	58.34		70.86	6.5	-101	201	0	0	0	-0.33	Apr-10
-3.99	-0.40	-8.86	24.40	9.56	0.49	0.95	22.5		37.32	4.7	-99	199	0	0	145	-0.32	Jun-09
-12.74	-13.59	-11.89	12.31	-7.54	1.45	0.95	30.46		64.97	34.1	-100	200	0	0	163	0.03	Jun-09
3.50	3.65	-15.53	20.26	33.39	0.27	0.95	22.82		34.67	5.2	-99	198	0	1		-0.03	Jun-09
-18.80	-23.36	-37.93	-12.20	-15.59	0	0.95	41.97		42.58	172.4	-100	182	0	18	31	-0.08	Apr-10
-15.56	-24.78	-45.85	-35.10	-63.42	2.7	0.95	42.27		23.60	71.4	-101	107	0	93	14	0.02	Jan-07
-1.75	4.82	-4.07	123.98	220.23	0.15	0.95	30.2		96.74	1,848	-100	200	0	0	7	-0.02	Jun-06
14.08	16.03	38.30	46.61	117.83	1.09	0.95	24.46		87.56	151.8	-100	103	0	97	6	-0.09	Jan-07
-6.73	-5.92	-20.84	37.40	77.90	0.68	0.95	34.5		64.56	155.0	-100	200	0	0	41	-0.08	Jan-07
0.32	6.86	0.74	83.91	130.79	0.56	0.9	24.47		128.49	2,345	-100	200	0	0	5	-0.06	Jun-06
4.51	4.28	0.81	123.66	254.14	0.97	0.95	43.16		45.07	69.9	-99	83	0	117	38	-0.14	Jan-07
30.63	28.82	32.53	-35.62	-32.02	0	0.95	31.28			216.0	-100	163	0	37	0	-0.14	Dec-08
-2.51	-2.72	-21.86	44.15	104.62	0.45	0.95	36.24		94.76	23.7	-100	200	0	0	18	-0.09	Jan-07
1.74	8.52	2.16	159.88	262.39	0.23	0.95	32.56		123.31	345.3	-100	101	0	99	14	-0.04	Jan-07
-2.57	-6.51	-6.02	-19.93	-4.29	2.08	0.95	29.41		39.75	0.99	-100	79	0	122	221	-0.67	Mar-08
17.58	24.51	49.25	85.97	169.34	0.65	0.95	20.88		70.27	35.1	-100	101	0	98	5	0.11	Jan-07

Fund Name	Ticker Symbol	Traded On	Overall Rating	Reward Rating	Risk Rating	Recent Up/ Downgrade	Price as of 9/30/2019	52-Week High	52-Week Low	Open to New Investors	Category & (Prospectus Objective)
● ProShares Ultra VIX Short-Term Futures ETF	UVXY	NYSE Arca	D	D	D		26.04	88.08	23.61	Y	Alternative Misc (Growth)
ProShares Ultra Yen	YCL	NYSE Arca	D+	D+	D+	Up	57.08	60.52	53.53	Y	Trading Tools (Worldwide Bond)
● ProShares UltraPro 3x Crude Oil ETF	OILU	NYSE Arca	D	D	D+		15.62	73.04	12.37	Y	Trading Tools (Growth & Inc)
● ProShares UltraPro 3x Short Crude Oil ETF	OILD	NYSE Arca	D	D-	D		16.80	59.09	11.91	Y	Trading Tools (Growth & Inc)
ProShares UltraPro Communication Services Select Sector	UCOM	NYSE Arca	U	U	U		49.57	58.58	37.25	Y	Trading Tools (Comm)
● ProShares UltraPro Dow30	UDOW	NYSE Arca	C+	B-	C-	Up	105.16	113.73	59.11	Y	Trading Tools (Growth)
ProShares UltraPro Financial Select Sector	FINU	NYSE Arca	C	C	D+	Up	86.73	99.67	47.72	Y	Trading Tools (Financial)
ProShares UltraPro MidCap400	UMDD	NYSE Arca	C-	C-	D+		102.97	129.90	59.31	Y	Trading Tools (Growth)
ProShares UltraPro Nasdaq Biotechnology	UBIO	NAS CM	D+	D+	D+	Up	18.93	43.40	16.09	Y	Trading Tools (Technology)
● ProShares UltraPro QQQ	TQQQ	NAS CM	C	C+	C-		61.63	71.55	30.39	Y	Trading Tools (Growth)
● ProShares UltraPro Russell2000	URTY	NYSE Arca	D+	C-	D+	Down	65.83	100.94	41.91	Y	Trading Tools (Small Company)
● ProShares UltraPro S&P500	UPRO	NYSE Arca	C	C+	C-		55.27	58.94	29.00	Y	Trading Tools (Growth)
ProShares UltraPro Short 20+ Year Treasury	TTT	NYSE Arca	D	D-	D		14.59	32.97	13.45	Y	Trading Tools (Govt Bond - Treasury)
ProShares UltraPro Short Comm Services Select Sector	SCOM	NYSE Arca	U	U	U		26.20	42.47	23.64	Y	Trading Tools (Comm)
● ProShares UltraPro Short Dow30	SDOW	NYSE Arca	C	C	D+		46.16	61.56	13.45	Y	Trading Tools (Growth)
ProShares UltraPro Short Financial Select Sector	FINZ	NYSE Arca	D	E+	D		5.70	12.91	5.50	Y	Trading Tools (Financial)
ProShares UltraPro Short MidCap400	SMDD	NYSE Arca	D	D	D		7.62	16.18	7.31	Y	Trading Tools (Growth)
ProShares UltraPro Short Nasdaq Biotechnology	ZBIO	NAS CM	D	D-	D		16.83	28.33	12.14	Y	Trading Tools (Technology)
● ProShares UltraPro Short QQQ	SQQQ	NAS CM	C	C-	D+		32.51	47.29	9.71	Y	Trading Tools (Growth)
● ProShares UltraPro Short Russell2000	SRTY	NYSE Arca	D+	D	D	Up	24.16	48.34	21.62	Y	Trading Tools (Small Company)
● ProShares UltraPro Short S&P500	SPXU	NYSE Arca	D	E+	D		25.98	57.55	25.26	Y	Trading Tools (Growth)
● ProShares UltraShort 20+ Year Treasury	TBT	NYSE Arca	D	D-	D		24.36	41.62	23.13	Y	Trading Tools (Govt Bond - Treasury)
● ProShares UltraShort 7-10 Year Treasury	PST	NYSE Arca	D	D	D	Down	18.49	23.88	17.97	Y	Trading Tools (Govt Bond - Treasury)
ProShares UltraShort Australian Dollar	CROC	NYSE Arca	C	C	D+		60.42	60.92	50.70	Y	Trading Tools (Income)
ProShares UltraShort Basic Materials	SMN	NYSE Arca	D+	D	D		26.56	39.32	25.06	Y	Trading Tools (Unaligned)
● ProShares UltraShort Bloomberg Crude Oil	SCO	NYSE Arca	D+	D	D	Up	16.24	33.13	12.52	Y	Trading Tools (Natl Res)
ProShares UltraShort Bloomberg Natural Gas	KOLD	NYSE Arca	D+	D	D+		29.47	35.37	11.00	Y	Trading Tools (Natl Res)
ProShares UltraShort Communication Services Select Sector	YCOM	NYSE Arca	U	U	U		30.69	41.70	28.51	Y	Trading Tools (Comm)
ProShares UltraShort Consumer Goods	SZK	NYSE Arca	D	D	D		12.17	19.55	12.17	Y	Trading Tools (Unaligned)
ProShares UltraShort Consumer Services	SCC	NYSE Arca	D	D-	D-		14.45	25.29	13.25	Y	Trading Tools (Unaligned)
● ProShares UltraShort Dow30	DXD	NYSE Arca	D	D-	D-		25.55	40.95	25.08	Y	Trading Tools (Growth)
● ProShares UltraShort Euro	EUO	NYSE Arca	C+	C+	C-		28.03	28.03	23.39	Y	Trading Tools (Worldwide Bond)
ProShares UltraShort Financials	SKF	NYSE Arca	D	D-	D		15.91	27.57	15.65	Y	Trading Tools (Financial)
ProShares UltraShort FTSE China 50	FXP	NYSE Arca	D	D	D		68.24	84.08	54.56	Y	Trading Tools (Pacific Stock)
ProShares UltraShort FTSE Europe	EPV	NYSE Arca	D+	D	D		31.40	43.90	29.57	Y	Trading Tools (Europe Stock)
ProShares UltraShort Gold	GLL	NYSE Arca	D	D-	D	Down	56.01	84.31	50.42	Y	Trading Tools (Prec Metals)
ProShares UltraShort Health Care	RXD	NYSE Arca	D	D-	D		22.51	29.66	20.76	Y	Trading Tools (Health)
ProShares UltraShort Industrials	SIJ	NYSE Arca	D	D-	D		12.37	23.04	11.97	Y	Trading Tools (Unaligned)
ProShares UltraShort MidCap400	MZZ	NYSE Arca	D+	D	D	Up	16.06	25.98	15.61	Y	Trading Tools (Growth)
ProShares UltraShort MSCI Brazil Capped	BZQ	NYSE Arca	D	D-	D		24.54	52.26	20.78	Y	Trading Tools (Foreign Stock)
ProShares UltraShort MSCI EAFE	EFU	NYSE Arca	D+	D	D		23.42	32.08	22.40	Y	Trading Tools (Foreign Stock)
ProShares UltraShort MSCI Emerging Markets	EEV	NYSE Arca	D	D	D		44.71	57.72	39.03	Y	Trading Tools (Div Emerg Mkts)
ProShares UltraShort MSCI Japan	EWV	NYSE Arca	D+	D	D		26.85	36.47	24.75	Y	Trading Tools (Pacific Stock)
ProShares UltraShort Nasdaq Biotechnology	BIS	NAS CM	D+	D+	D	Up	20.02	27.27	15.77	Y	Trading Tools (Technology)
ProShares UltraShort Oil & Gas	DUG	NYSE Arca	C-	D+	D+	Up	43.42	57.58	28.25	Y	Trading Tools (Natl Res)
● ProShares UltraShort QQQ	QID	NYSE Arca	D	E+	D-		30.03	55.66	28.74	Y	Trading Tools (Growth)
ProShares UltraShort Real Estate	SRS	NYSE Arca	D	D-	D		18.85	33.51	18.72	Y	Trading Tools (Real Estate)
● ProShares UltraShort Russell2000	TWM	NYSE Arca	D+	D	D	Up	15.19	23.50	14.04	Y	Trading Tools (Small Company)
● ProShares UltraShort S&P500	SDS	NYSE Arca	D	D-	D		29.50	49.43	28.97	Y	Trading Tools (Growth)
ProShares UltraShort Semiconductors	SSG	NYSE Arca	D+	D	D	Down	21.20	32.41	12.66	Y	Trading Tools (Technology)
ProShares UltraShort Silver	ZSL	NYSE Arca	D+	D	D	Down	29.60	45.45	22.85	Y	Trading Tools (Prec Metals)
ProShares UltraShort SmallCap600	SDD	NYSE Arca	D+	D	D	Up	13.14	20.11	11.96	Y	Trading Tools (Small Company)

★ Expanded analysis of this fund is included in Section II: Analysis of All BUY Rated Funds. ● Expanded analysis of this fund is included in Section III: Analysis of All Rated Funds with Assets over $50 million.

		TOTAL RETURNS & PERFORMANCE							ASSETS		ASSET ALLOCATION & TURNOVER					VALUATION	
3-Month Total Return	6-Month Total Return	1-Year Total Return	3-Year Total Return	5-Year Total Return	Dividend Yield (TTM)	Expense Ratio	3-Yr Std Deviation	Effective Duration	NAV	Total Assets (MIL)	%Cash	%Stocks	%Bonds	%Other	Turnover Ratio	Premium/ Discount 1-Year Avg	Inception Date
-5.54	-27.75	-24.83	-91.94	-99.81	0	1.65	87.06			597.1	-50	150	0	0		0.50	Oct-11
-0.31	3.85	6.07	-23.10	-15.65	0	1.01	15.46			2.9	100	0	0	0	0	-0.01	Nov-08
-26.45	-40.82	-75.78			0	0.49				79.4	-200	0	0	300		-0.32	Mar-17
-19.15	-18.98	3.03			0	0.49				71.1	400	0	0	-300		0.33	Mar-17
-4.11	5.54					0.95			49.60	1.2	-199	299	0	0	6	-0.05	Jan-19
0.85	5.20	-5.11	185.08	261.02	0.64	0.95	38.05		105.01	409.5	-200	300	0	0	2	-0.05	Feb-10
-1.59	15.38	-6.98	139.89	159.82	1.15	0.95	53.57		86.64	23.8	-200	77	0	224	21	-0.20	Jul-12
-4.79	-2.27	-19.18	61.44	122.02	0.78	0.95	45.79		102.97	23.2	-200	300	0	0	41	-0.22	Feb-10
-28.03	-35.41	-56.02	-34.69		0	0.95	62.42		18.97	19.9	-201	94	0	206	32	-0.08	Jun-15
-4.11	4.33	-13.86	187.38	349.80	0.1	0.95	45.84		61.59	3,631	-200	300	0	0	15	-0.12	Feb-10
-11.31	-11.29	-34.42	41.20	89.86	0.26	0.95	51.84		65.90	82.4	-200	300	0	0	24	-0.07	Feb-10
-0.53	8.55	-3.89	127.13	198.87	0.52	0.92	36.89		55.27	1,288	-200	300	0	0	15	-0.10	Jun-09
-23.64	-36.98	-49.98	-34.22	-72.20	2.01	0.95	33.92		14.62	28.9	227	0	13	-141		-0.30	Mar-12
-3.69	-18.10					0.95			26.25	0.66	400	-300	0	0		-0.18	Jan-19
-5.00	-10.89	236.24	-10.44	-53.74	2.38	0.95	35.43		46.23	253.5	251	-164	12	0		0.02	Feb-10
-5.48	-22.94	-20.96	-80.93	-90.51	1.3	0.95	48.93		5.72	1.7	400	0	0	-300		0.42	Jul-12
-1.37	-8.09	-5.62	-63.60	-84.02	1.19	0.95	46.56		7.64	3.2	400	-300	0	0	0	-0.23	Feb-10
28.34	27.99	28.73	-60.06		0.3	0.95	64.94		16.82	4.2	400	0	0	-300		0.19	Jun-15
-3.05	-15.56	200.09	-37.00	-77.68	2.94	0.95	41.69		32.52	1,129	234	-147	12	0		0.08	Feb-10
4.47	-1.46	7.10	-65.05	-86.35	1.73	0.95	51.42		24.12	69.1	251	-163	11	0		0.11	Feb-10
-3.82	-13.83	-17.13	-71.06	-85.81	2.18	0.91	35.54		25.99	652.3	260	-172	12	0	0	0.09	Jun-09
-15.84	-25.62	-35.75	-21.08	-53.99	2.36	0.9	22.79		24.41	639.8	178	0	15	-93		-0.26	Apr-08
-4.83	-11.40	-19.54	-6.30	-27.75	1.86	0.95	10.32		18.50	52.7	200	0	6	-106	0	-0.14	Apr-08
6.35	11.31	14.46	21.09	31.70	0	1.03	16.1			9.1	100	0	0	0		-0.07	Jul-12
4.89	-3.36	3.12	-44.70	-55.40	0.63	0.95	30.8		26.59	5.9	299	0	0	-199	0	0.21	Jan-07
-6.75	-4.30	19.88	-61.53	-0.08	0	0.95	57.57			94.9	300	0	0	-200	0	0.19	Nov-08
-12.93	26.72	-17.44	-23.68	79.48	0	1.54	78.28			8.1	300	0	0	-200		-0.49	Oct-11
-1.40	-10.65					0.95			30.73	0.77	301	-201	0	0		-0.12	Jan-19
-7.90	-12.41	-16.16	-32.54	-60.21	1.59	0.95	23.65		12.18	2.0	300	-15	0	-185	73	0.00	Jan-07
2.33	-10.26	-11.99	-60.84	-77.85	2.61	0.95	27.23		14.46	0.90	300	-3	0	-197		0.01	Jan-07
-2.76	-6.49	-8.17	-61.06	-73.92	1.77	0.95	23.98		25.58	174.0	204	-115	12	0	0	0.02	Jul-06
7.89	8.14	18.62	16.91	39.15	0	0.95	12.79			135.9	100	0	0	0	0	-0.06	Nov-08
-4.63	-14.54	-16.51	-59.64	-73.77	0.93	0.95	26.35		15.93	30.2	208	-95	10	-23		0.08	Jan-07
17.12	21.21	1.46	-43.24	-69.38	0.96	0.95	35.78		68.25	37.7	212	-122	10	0	0	-0.06	Nov-07
4.14	-2.38	0.33	-37.65	-48.24	0.97	0.95	24.93		31.32	13.7	202	-113	11	0		-0.01	Jun-09
-14.39	-25.71	-35.64	-22.20	-44.13	0	0.95	22			22.5	300	-114	0	-86	0	-0.04	Dec-08
6.68	3.49	7.13	-47.81	-69.24	1.33	0.95	26.51		22.53	2.5	300	-6	0	-194		-0.08	Jan-07
-1.36	-7.75	-10.81	-57.99	-75.32	1.4	0.95	31.07		12.38	2.3	300	0	0	-200		0.02	Jan-07
-0.01	-3.93	-0.02	-45.56	-67.03	1.5	0.95	30.95		16.08	3.3	300	-200	0	0		-0.09	Jul-06
4.32	-10.95	-52.28	-75.01	-86.66	1.66	0.95	52.38		24.56	27.9	180	-93	13	0		-0.03	Jun-09
2.67	-2.26	1.75	-33.19	-44.90	0.89	0.95	22.38		23.38	2.0	301	-201	0	0	0	0.01	Oct-07
11.84	10.36	-1.59	-39.99	-53.44	1.14	0.95	28.89		44.71	19.6	213	-123	10	0	25	-0.01	Oct-07
-4.94	-6.53	7.64	-34.28	-58.52	0.26	0.95	22.78		26.64	6.0	301	-201	0	0	27	-0.06	Nov-07
19.48	21.28	28.10	-35.32	-67.17	1.54	0.95	43.2		20.00	24.7	202	-113	11	0		0.04	Apr-10
12.96	23.05	51.02	-0.85	-3.67	0.66	0.95	43.27		43.39	15.9	218	-128	10	0	0	0.05	Jan-07
-1.12	-9.16	-12.79	-68.01	-83.07	2.46	0.95	28.39		30.04	321.2	192	-105	13	0	0	0.03	Jul-06
-13.28	-15.67	-32.30	-43.99	-70.58	1.87	0.95	22.96		18.83	17.8	190	-102	13	0		0.03	Jan-07
3.96	0.88	9.48	-46.12	-69.40	1.38	0.95	34.33		15.19	98.1	216	-122	6	0	0	0.02	Jan-07
-1.92	-8.43	-8.80	-53.75	-70.07	1.83	0.89	23.91		29.51	1,021	195	-107	11	0		0.04	Jul-06
-10.55	-16.45	39.17	-56.02	-82.61	1.66	0.95	43.82		21.22	11.0	301	0	0	-201	0	0.28	Jan-07
-28.61	-29.12	-33.93	-0.46	-48.07	0	1.62	29.4			15.4	300	-105	0	-95	0	0.12	Dec-08
-0.70	-3.01	10.50	-49.51	-73.23	1.22	0.95	35.93		13.16	2.9	300	-200	0	0	16	-0.06	Jan-07

Fund Name	Ticker Symbol	Traded On	Overall Rating	Reward Rating	Risk Rating	Recent Up/ Downgrade	Price as of 9/30/2019	52-Week High	52-Week Low	Open to New Investors	Category & (Prospectus Objective)
ProShares UltraShort Technology	REW	NYSE Arca	D+	D	D	Down	16.52	22.44	9.61	Y	Trading Tools (Technology)
ProShares UltraShort Utilities	SDP	NYSE Arca	D	D-	D-		14.68	24.04	14.65	Y	Trading Tools (Utility)
ProShares UltraShort Yen	YCS	NYSE Arca	C-	D+	D+		74.69	79.20	70.52	Y	Trading Tools (Worldwide Bond)
ProShares VIX Mid-Term Futures ETF	VIXM	NYSE Arca	D	D	D		23.67	27.29	20.53	Y	Alternative Misc (Growth)
● ProShares VIX Short-Term Futures ETF	VIXY	NYSE Arca	D-	E+	D		19.52	40.68	17.70	Y	Alternative Misc (Growth)
QRAFT AI-Enhanced U.S. Large Cap ETF	QRFT	NYSE Arca	U	U	U		26.28	26.95	23.91	Y	US Equity Large Cap Blend (Growth)
QRAFT AI-Enhanced U.S. Large Cap Momentum ETF	AMOM	NYSE Arca	U	U	U		26.23	26.93	23.99	Y	US Equity Large Cap Blend (Growth)
Quadratic Interest Rate Vol & Inflation Hedge ETF New	IVOL	NYSE Arca	U	U	U		25.41	26.33	25.01	Y	Fixed Income Misc (Growth)
Reality Shares Divcon Dividend Defender ETF	DFND	BATS	C	C+	C-		30.27	30.40	25.91	Y	Long/Short Equity (Income)
Reality Shares Divcon Dividend Guard ETF	GARD	BATS	C-	C	D	Up	24.56	26.12	22.56	Y	Long/Short Equity (Income)
Reality Shares Divcon Leaders Dividend ETF	LEAD	BATS	C	C+	C-		35.47	36.15	27.76	Y	US Equity Large Cap Growth (Growth & Inc)
● Reality Shares DIVS ETF	DIVY	NYSE Arca	C-	C-	D+		26.11	27.12	24.84	Y	Multialternative (Growth)
Reality Shares Fundstrat DQM Long ETF	DQML	NYSE Arca	U	U	U		26.19	27.03	22.05	Y	US Equity Large Cap Blend (Growth)
Reality Shares Nasdaq NexGen Economy China ETF	BCNA	NAS CM	D	D+	D		19.93	26.17	17.68	Y	Greater China Equity (Growth)
● Reality Shares Nasdaq NexGen Economy ETF	BLCN	NAS CM	C-	C-	D+	Up	23.05	24.04	18.83	Y	Technology Sector Equity (Growth)
Renaissance International IPO ETF	IPOS	NYSE Arca	D+	C	D		21.58	22.49	18.10	Y	Globa Eq Mid/Small Cap (Foreign Stock)
Renaissance IPO ETF	IPO	NYSE Arca	C-	C-	D+	Down	28.17	33.49	21.70	Y	US Equity Mid Cap (Growth)
Reverse Cap Weighted U.S. Large Cap ETF	RVRS	BATS	D+	C-	D+		16.75	17.17	13.59	Y	US Equity Large Cap Blend (Growth & Inc)
● RiverFront Dynamic Core Income ETF	RFCI	NYSE Arca	C	C+	C-	Up	25.24	25.49	23.48	Y	US Fixed Income (Income)
RiverFront Dynamic Unconstrained Income ETF	RFUN	NYSE Arca	C	C+	D+	Up	25.38	25.50	23.55	Y	Fixed Income Misc (Income)
● RiverFront Dynamic US Dividend Advantage ETF	RFDA	NYSE Arca	C	C	C-		32.73	33.34	26.47	Y	US Equity Large Cap Blend (Growth & Inc)
● RiverFront Dynamic US Flex-Cap ETF	RFFC	NYSE Arca	C	C	C-		32.98	36.06	27.40	Y	US Equity Large Cap Blend (Growth)
● RiverFront Strategic Income Fund	RIGS	NYSE Arca	C	C	C-		24.84	24.94	23.90	Y	Global Fixed Income (Income)
Robo Global® Healthcare Technology and Innovation ETF	HTEC	NYSE Arca	U	U	U		23.51	25.41	23.29	Y	Healthcare Sector Equity (Health)
● Robo Global® Robotics and Automation Index ETF	ROBO	NAS CM	C	C-	C		38.35	42.10	30.86	Y	Globa Eq Mid/Small Cap (Growth)
Roundhill BITKRAFT Esports & Digital Entertainment ETF	NERD	NYSE Arca	U	U	U		15.22	15.88	14.44	Y	Consumer Goods & Svcs (Unaligned)
RYZZ Managed Futures Strategy Plus ETF	RYZZ	NYSE Arca	U	U	U		23.26	25.90	23.07	Y	Global Macro (Growth & Inc)
Saba Closed-End Funds ETF	CEFS	BATS	C	C	C-		20.05	20.55	16.83	Y	Long/Short Credit (Growth & Inc)
Sage ESG Intermediate Credit ETF	GUDB	BATS	D+	C-	D	Up	51.18	51.49	47.92	Y	US Fixed Income (Growth & Inc)
Salt High truBeta™ US Market ETF	SLT	BATS	C-	C-	D+	Up	25.14	26.94	18.98	Y	US Equity Large Cap Blend (Growth & Inc)
Salt Low truBeta US Market ETF	LSLT	BATS	U	U	U		28.12	28.15	25.01	Y	US Equity Large Cap Blend (Growth & Inc)
● Schwab 1000 ETF	SCHK	NYSE Arca	C	C	C+		29.16	29.75	23.02	Y	US Equity Large Cap Blend (Growth & Inc)
● Schwab Emerging Markets Equity ETF™	SCHE	NYSE Arca	C	C	C+		25.13	26.96	22.96	Y	Global Emerg Mkts Equity (Div Emerg Mkts)
● Schwab Fundamental Emerg Mkts Large Company Ind ETF	FNDE	NYSE Arca	C	C	C+		27.38	29.15	25.30	Y	Global Emerg Mkts Equity (Div Emerg Mkts)
● Schwab Fundamental International Large Company Index ETF	FNDF	NYSE Arca	C	C-	C+		27.57	30.01	24.38	Y	Global Equity Large Cap (World Stock)
● Schwab Fundamental International Small Company Index ETF	FNDC	NYSE Arca	C-	D+	C	Down	30.73	34.66	27.19	Y	Globa Eq Mid/Small Cap (World Stock)
● Schwab Fundamental U.S. Broad Market Index ETF	FNDB	NYSE Arca	C	C	C-		39.13	39.77	31.73	Y	US Equity Large Cap Value (Growth & Inc)
● Schwab Fundamental U.S. Large Company Index ETF	FNDX	NYSE Arca	C+	C	C+	Up	39.55	40.14	32.01	Y	US Equity Large Cap Value (Growth & Inc)
● Schwab Fundamental U.S. Small Company Index ETF	FNDA	NYSE Arca	C	C	C+		37.76	40.37	31.04	Y	US Equity Small Cap (Small Company)
● Schwab Intermediate-Term U.S. Treasury ETF™	SCHR	NYSE Arca	C	C	C+		55.56	56.19	51.34	Y	US Fixed Income (Govt Bond - Treasury)
● Schwab International Equity ETF™	SCHF	NYSE Arca	C	C	B		31.86	33.62	27.44	Y	Global Equity Large Cap (Foreign Stock)
● Schwab International Small-Cap Equity ETF™	SCHC	NYSE Arca	C	D+	C+		31.80	35.86	27.92	Y	Globa Eq Mid/Small Cap (Small Company)
● Schwab Short-Term U.S. Treasury ETF™	SCHO	NYSE Arca	C	C	C+		50.59	50.77	49.42	Y	US Fixed Income (Govt Bond - Treasury)
● Schwab U.S. Aggregate Bond ETF™	SCHZ	NYSE Arca	C+	C+	C+	Up	53.85	54.32	49.51	Y	US Fixed Income (Multisector Bond)
● Schwab U.S. Broad Market ETF™	SCHB	NYSE Arca	C+	C+	C+		71.02	72.55	56.21	Y	US Equity Large Cap Blend (Growth)
★ Schwab U.S. Dividend Equity ETF™	SCHD	NYSE Arca	B-	B	C	Up	54.78	55.76	44.23	Y	US Equity Large Cap Value (Equity-Income)
● Schwab U.S. Large-Cap ETF™	SCHX	NYSE Arca	C+	C+	C+		70.93	72.27	56.03	Y	US Equity Large Cap Blend (Growth)
● Schwab U.S. Large-Cap Growth ETF™	SCHG	NYSE Arca	C+	B-	C+	Down	84.01	86.17	64.30	Y	US Equity Large Cap Growth (Growth)
● Schwab U.S. Large-Cap Value ETF™	SCHV	NYSE Arca	C+	C	C+		56.73	57.50	46.58	Y	US Equity Large Cap Value (Growth)
● Schwab U.S. Mid-Cap ETF™	SCHM	NYSE Arca	C	C	C+	Down	56.54	58.44	45.02	Y	US Equity Mid Cap (Growth)
● Schwab U.S. REIT ETF™	SCHH	NYSE Arca	C+	C+	C	Up	47.17	47.21	37.04	Y	Real Estate Sector Equity (Real Estate)
● Schwab U.S. Small-Cap ETF™	SCHA	NYSE Arca	C	C	C+		69.73	75.26	57.06	Y	US Equity Small Cap (Small Company)

★ Expanded analysis of this fund is included in Section II: Analysis of All BUY Rated Funds. ● Expanded analysis of this fund is included in Section III: Analysis of All Rated Funds with Assets over $50 million.

	TOTAL RETURNS & PERFORMANCE								ASSETS		ASSET ALLOCATION & TURNOVER					VALUATION	
3-Month Total Return	6-Month Total Return	1-Year Total Return	3-Year Total Return	5-Year Total Return	Dividend Yield (TTM)	Expense Ratio	3-Yr Std Deviation	Effective Duration	NAV	Total Assets (MIL)	%Cash	%Stocks	%Bonds	%Other	Turnover Ratio	Premium/ Discount 1-Year Avg	Inception Date
-5.51	-14.25	56.18	-49.94	-73.73	1.56	0.95	30.41		16.53	5.0	300	-200	0	0		0.09	Jan-07
-15.79	-21.47	-37.09	-55.85	-76.24	0.88	0.95	20.37		14.70	3.5	301	0	0	-201	45	0.09	Jan-07
0.25	-3.53	-5.39	22.73	-1.69	0	0.95	16.35			41.0	100	0	0	0	0	-0.05	Nov-08
13.15	11.88	16.34	-47.69	-62.62	0	0.87	26.63			44.9	0	100	0	0		0.16	Jan-11
-0.27	-14.61	-7.56	-82.38	-95.17	0	0.87	58.83			299.4	0	100	0	0		0.35	Jan-11
0.49						0.75			26.27	3.3	0	100	0	0		0.02	May-19
1.07						0.75			26.24	3.3	0	100	0	0		-0.04	May-19
-1.08						0.99		7.48	25.30	61.4	10	0	90	0		0.30	May-19
1.91	5.28	6.95	33.97		0.85	1.21	7.05		30.18	6.0	41	56	3	0	37	-0.06	Jan-16
0.80	2.11	-4.88	19.22		0.85	1.29	10.67		24.56	13.5	0	100	0	0	309	0.01	Jan-16
0.94	4.62	4.75	45.87		1.4	0.43	13.36		35.48	35.5	0	100	0	0	0	-0.02	Jan-16
-0.83	-1.05	-2.25	9.89		0.92	0.85	5.18		26.20	65.6	13	6	85	-4	0	-0.15	Dec-14
-0.59	2.16					0.69			26.20	2.6	0	100	0	0	0	-0.07	Oct-18
-7.92	-19.07	-3.88				0.45	0.76		20.22	2.0	0	100	0	0		-0.35	Jun-18
-1.41	0.96	-1.11			1.55	0.68			23.11	65.9	1	99	0	0		-0.29	Jan-18
-0.32	3.36	0.93	18.48	18.81	4.58	0.8	12.3		21.56	2.2	1	99	0	0	107	0.03	Oct-14
-10.80	-8.60	-6.10	34.62	29.87	0.07	0.6	19.05		28.21	42.3	0	100	0	0	192	0.04	Oct-13
-1.34	0.23	0.59			0.96	0.29			16.75	9.2	0	100	0	0	36	-0.04	Oct-17
2.21	5.28	9.30	8.35		2.79	0.53	3.1		25.29	135.3	15	0	84	0	15	-0.01	Jun-16
1.22	3.26	5.52	13.96		4.94	0.52	3.72		25.42	16.5	14	0	86	0	51	-0.31	Jun-16
1.15	1.66	0.31	34.04		2.03	0.52	13.3		32.72	129.2	0	100	0	0	96	0.02	Jun-16
-1.45	-0.44	-6.92	31.95		1.51	0.52	14.82		32.99	125.3	0	100	0	0	152	-0.06	Jun-16
0.97	2.40	4.81	11.15	22.74	4.17	0.48	1.74		24.70	161.8	14	0	87	0	35	0.19	Oct-13
-5.86						0.68			23.45	2.9	0	100	0	0		0.24	Jun-19
-5.72	-3.19	-8.78	36.10	49.65	0.32	0.95	20.16		38.22	1,225	0	100	0	0	29	-0.15	Oct-13
-3.84						0.25			15.15	9.9	0	100	0	0		0.29	Jun-19
-4.92	-7.82					0.99			23.18	42.3	40	60	0	0		0.08	Mar-19
0.36	4.62	9.14			8.62	2.56		4.55	20.04	43.1	-8	4	100	-1	44	0.23	Mar-17
1.70	4.66	8.75			2.77	0.35		3.92		17.9	1	0	97	0	65	0.01	Oct-17
-3.04	-2.41	-1.50			0.26	0.29			25.12	13.2	0	100	0	0	145	0.05	May-18
4.40	9.71					0			28.12	7.7	0	100	0	0		0.03	Mar-19
0.67	4.57	3.57			1.74	0.05			29.17	846.1	0	100	0	0		-0.02	Oct-17
-4.81	-3.67	0.92	19.21	13.60	3.16	0.13	13.42		25.12	5,899	1	99	0	0	18	0.19	Jan-10
-5.77	-2.03	-1.57	25.59	18.59	3.55	0.39	13.7		27.39	2,495	0	99	0	0	33	-0.03	Aug-13
-1.82	-0.56	-4.30	19.68	14.48	4	0.25	11.7		27.48	4,425	0	100	0	0	14	0.07	Aug-13
-2.22	-1.59	-8.14	13.14	27.44	2.99	0.39	11.54		30.75	1,950	0	100	0	0	25	0.00	Aug-13
1.06	3.86	1.06	35.32	53.38	2.19	0.25	13.04		39.13	285.7	0	100	0	0	11	-0.01	Aug-13
1.11	4.11	1.54	36.02	53.74	2.2	0.25	12.85		39.54	5,431	0	100	0	0	11	-0.01	Aug-13
0.18	0.80	-4.83	26.90	48.28	1.55	0.25	16.31		37.78	3,479	0	100	0	0	23	-0.04	Aug-13
1.78	5.06	9.93	6.10	14.16	2.31	0.06	3.47	5.19	55.57	4,790	0	0	100	0	41	0.03	Aug-10
-1.39	1.38	-1.59	20.74	18.50	3.54	0.06	11.25		31.76	18,690	0	100	0	0	5	0.10	Nov-09
-2.95	-1.79	-8.28	12.00	16.89	2.81	0.12	12.26		31.83	2,234	0	99	0	0	16	0.04	Jan-10
0.66	2.13	4.36	4.42	6.28	2.22	0.06	1.03	1.93	50.59	5,899	0	0	100	0	65	0.02	Aug-10
2.38	5.78	10.32	8.71	17.03	2.76	0.04	3.36	5.51	53.82	6,986	3	0	97	0	71	0.02	Jul-11
0.43	4.09	2.76	43.58	66.27	1.88	0.03	12.54		71.00	15,109	0	100	0	0	4	-0.01	Nov-09
3.30	5.31	6.42	41.48	66.81	3.04	0.06	12.24		54.77	10,335	0	100	0	0	23	-0.03	Oct-11
0.74	4.63	3.72	45.58	68.42	1.9	0.03	12.26		70.92	18,300	0	100	0	0	3	-0.01	Nov-09
0.34	5.09	3.46	56.47	83.39	1.15	0.04	13.1		84.02	8,108	0	100	0	0	5	-0.03	Dec-09
1.13	3.92	3.86	35.28	54.46	2.82	0.04	12.09		56.75	6,563	0	100	0	0	8	-0.03	Dec-09
-1.13	1.58	-0.19	35.69	59.34	1.49	0.04	14.35		56.52	6,327	0	100	0	0	13	0.00	Jan-11
7.01	7.46	17.41	20.43	57.88	2.69	0.07	12.78		47.14	6,022	0	100	0	0	7	0.01	Jan-11
-2.50	-0.80	-5.88	26.29	47.65	1.51	0.04	16.66		69.72	8,199	0	100	0	0	9	-0.01	Nov-09

Fund Name	Ticker Symbol	Traded On	Overall Rating	Reward Rating	Risk Rating	Recent Up/ Downgrade	Price as of 9/30/2019	52-Week High	52-Week Low	Open to New Investors	Category & (Prospectus Objective)
● Schwab U.S. TIPS ETF™	SCHP	NYSE Arca	C+	C+	C+	Up	56.76	57.71	52.79	Y	US Fixed Income (Govt Bond - Treasury)
Sit Rising Rate ETF	RISE	NYSE Arca	D	D	D+		22.63	25.49	22.06	Y	Fixed Income Misc (Govt Bond - Treasury)
SoFi 50 ETF	SFYF	NYSE Arca	U	U	U		18.96	20.61	18.41	Y	US Equity Large Cap Growth (Growth)
SoFi Gig Economy ETF	GIGE	NAS CM	U	U	U		18.03	20.29	17.86	Y	Global Equity Large Cap (Growth & Inc)
SoFi Next 500 ETF	SFYX	NYSE Arca	U	U	U		9.91	10.37	9.42	Y	US Equity Large Cap Blend (Growth)
SoFi Select 500 ETF	SFY	NYSE Arca	U	U	U		10.31	10.54	9.47	Y	US Equity Large Cap Growth (Growth)
● SPDR S&P® North American Natural Resources ETF	NANR	NYSE Arca	C-	C	C-		31.40	34.85	27.82	Y	Natural Resources (Natl Res)
● SPDR® Blackstone / GSO Senior Loan ETF	SRLN	NYSE Arca	C+	C	C+		46.32	47.23	44.46	Y	US Fixed Income (Income)
● SPDR® Bloomberg Barclays 1-10 Year TIPS ETF	TIPX	NYSE Arca	C	C	C-		19.57	19.76	18.75	Y	US Fixed Income (Govt Bond - Treasury)
● SPDR® Bloomberg Barclays 1-3 Month T-Bill ETF	BIL	NYSE Arca	C	C	B-		91.59	91.62	91.37	Y	US Fixed Income (Govt Bond - Treasury)
● SPDR® Bloomberg Barclays Convertible Securities ETF	CWB	NYSE Arca	C+	C	C+		52.45	54.19	45.13	Y	Convertibles (Convertible Bond)
● SPDR® Bloomberg Barclays Emerging Markets Local Bond ETF	EBND	NYSE Arca	C	C	C+		27.21	28.15	25.85	Y	Emerging Mkts Fixed Inc (Worldwide Bond)
★ SPDR® Bloomberg Barclays High Yield Bond ETF	JNK	NYSE Arca	A+	A+	A		108.74	109.46	32.95	Y	US Fixed Income (Corp Bond-High Yld)
● SPDR® Bloomberg Barclays International Corporate Bond ETF	IBND	NYSE Arca	C	C	C-	Up	33.30	34.34	32.28	Y	Global Fixed Income (Worldwide Bond)
● SPDR® Bloomberg Barclays International Treasury Bond ETF	BWX	NYSE Arca	C	C	C+		28.70	29.35	26.76	Y	Global Fixed Income (Worldwide Bond)
● SPDR® Bloomberg Barclays Investm Grade Floating Rate ETF	FLRN	NYSE Arca	C	C	C+		30.76	30.76	30.32	Y	US Fixed Income (Corp Bond-High Yld)
★ SPDR® Bloomberg Barclays Short Term High Yield Bond ETF	SJNK	NYSE Arca	B-	C	B	Down	27.01	27.52	25.68	Y	US Fixed Income (Corp Bond-High Yld)
● SPDR® Bloomberg Barclays Short Term Intl Treasury Bond ETF	BWZ	NYSE Arca	D+	D+	C-		30.29	31.16	30.28	Y	Global Fixed Income (Worldwide Bond)
● SPDR® Dorsey Wright Fixed Income Allocation ETF	DWFI	NAS CM	C-	C	C-	Up	23.55	23.86	22.07	Y	Cautious Allocation (Growth & Inc)
● SPDR® DoubleLine Short Duration Total Return Tactical ETF	STOT	BATS	C	C	C-	Up	49.67	49.77	48.39	Y	US Fixed Income (Income)
● SPDR® DoubleLine Total Return Tactical ETF	TOTL	NYSE Arca	C+	C+	C+		49.23	49.65	46.68	Y	US Fixed Income (Growth & Inc)
● SPDR® DoubleLine® Emerging Markets Fixed Income ETF	EMTL	BATS	C	B-	D+		50.68	51.43	47.34	Y	Emerging Mkts Fixed Inc (Income)
● SPDR® Dow Jones Global Real Estate ETF	RWO	NYSE Arca	C+	C	C+	Up	51.86	51.88	42.86	Y	Real Estate Sector Equity (Real Estate)
★ SPDR® Dow Jones Industrial Average ETF	DIA	NYSE Arca	B	B	C+	Up	269.18	273.60	218.10	Y	US Equity Large Cap Value (Growth)
● SPDR® Dow Jones International Real Estate ETF	RWX	NYSE Arca	C+	C	C+	Up	39.52	39.66	34.74	Y	Real Estate Sector Equity (Real Estate)
● SPDR® Dow Jones REIT ETF	RWR	NYSE Arca	C+	C+	C	Up	104.57	104.74	82.76	Y	Real Estate Sector Equity (Real Estate)
● SPDR® EURO STOXX 50 ETF	FEZ	NYSE Arca	C	C	C+		37.74	38.89	32.08	Y	Europe Equity Large Cap (Europe Stock)
SPDR® EURO STOXX Small Cap ETF	SMEZ	NYSE Arca	C-	C	D+		56.28	59.56	49.23	Y	Europe Equity Large Cap (Europe Stock)
● SPDR® FactSet Innovative Technology ETF	XITK	NYSE Arca	C	C	D+		99.83	112.48	76.98	Y	Technology Sector Equity (Technology)
● SPDR® FTSE Intl Govt Inflation-Protected Bond ETF	WIP	NYSE Arca	C	C+	C-	Up	54.71	55.72	51.61	Y	Global Fixed Income (Worldwide Bond)
● SPDR® Global Dow ETF	DGT	NYSE Arca	C	C	D+		83.40	86.69	72.28	Y	Global Equity Large Cap (World Stock)
● SPDR® Gold MiniShares	GLDM	NYSE Arca	C	D+	C+	Up	14.70	15.51	11.89	Y	Commodities Specified (Prec Metals)
● SPDR® Gold Shares	GLD	NYSE Arca	C+	C+	C+	Up	138.87	146.66	112.54	Y	Commodities Specified (Prec Metals)
SPDR® Kensho Clean Power ETF	CNRG	NYSE Arca	U	U	U		39.09	41.25	28.57	Y	Energy Sector Equity (Natl Res)
SPDR® Kensho Final Frontiers ETF	ROKT	NYSE Arca	U	U	U		35.61	36.59	25.14	Y	Industrials Sector Equity (Growth & Inc)
★ SPDR® MFS Systematic Core Equity ETF	SYE	NYSE Arca	B-	B	C	Up	82.41	84.40	66.60	Y	US Equity Large Cap Value (Growth)
★ SPDR® MFS Systematic Growth Equity ETF	SYG	NYSE Arca	B-	B	C	Up	81.40	87.51	66.16	Y	US Equity Large Cap Growth (Growth)
SPDR® MFS Systematic Value Equity ETF	SYV	NYSE Arca	C	C+	C-		67.14	69.90	56.35	Y	US Equity Large Cap Value (Growth)
● SPDR® MSCI ACWI ex-US ETF	CWI	NYSE Arca	C	C	C+		24.04	37.42	22.70	Y	Global Equity Large Cap (Foreign Stock)
● SPDR® MSCI ACWI Low Carbon Target ETF	LOWC	NYSE Arca	C	C	D+		92.15	93.67	75.73	Y	Global Equity Large Cap (World Stock)
● SPDR® MSCI EAFE Fossil Fuel Free ETF	EFAX	NYSE Arca	C-	C-	D+	Up	67.83	70.26	58.71	Y	Global Equity Large Cap (Growth & Inc)
● SPDR® MSCI EAFE StrategicFactors ETF	QEFA	NYSE Arca	C	C	C-		63.05	64.34	54.70	Y	Global Equity Large Cap (World Stock)
● SPDR® MSCI Emerging Markets Fossil Fuel Free ETF	EEMX	NYSE Arca	D+	D+	D+		59.81	64.86	55.74	Y	Global Emerg Mkts Equity (Growth & Inc)
● SPDR® MSCI Emerging Markets StrategicFactors ETF	QEMM	NYSE Arca	C-	C	D+		57.36	60.98	52.90	Y	Global Emerg Mkts Equity (World Stock)
● SPDR® MSCI USA StrategicFactors ETF	QUS	NYSE Arca	C	B-	C-	Down	88.76	89.27	69.01	Y	US Equity Large Cap Blend (Growth & Inc)
SPDR® MSCI World StrategicFactors ETF	QWLD	NYSE Arca	C	C+	D+		80.79	81.19	65.50	Y	Global Equity Large Cap (World Stock)
● SPDR® Nuveen Bloomberg Barclays Municipal Bond ETF	TFI	NYSE Arca	C+	C+	C+		50.69	51.39	46.65	Y	US Muni Fixed Inc (Muni Bond - Natl)
● SPDR® Nuveen Bloomberg Barclays Short Term Muni Bond ETF	SHM	NYSE Arca	C	C	C+		48.99	49.36	47.43	Y	US Muni Fixed Inc (Muni Bond - Natl)
● SPDR® Nuveen S&P High Yield Municipal Bond ETF	HYMB	NYSE Arca	C	B-	C-	Down	59.37	59.62	55.29	Y	US Muni Fixed Inc (Muni Bond - Natl)
● SPDR® NYSE Technology ETF	XNTK	NYSE Arca	C	B-	C-		72.75	94.96	54.51	Y	Technology Sector Equity (Technology)
● SPDR® Portfolio Aggregate Bond ETF	SPAB	NYSE Arca	C+	C+	C+	Up	29.64	29.86	27.25	Y	US Fixed Income (Multisector Bond)
● SPDR® Portfolio Corporate Bond ETF	SPBO	NYSE Arca	C	B-	D+		33.83	34.21	30.11	Y	US Fixed Income (Growth)

★ Expanded analysis of this fund is included in Section II: Analysis of All BUY Rated Funds.   ● Expanded analysis of this fund is included in Section III: Analysis of All Rated Funds with Assets over $50 million.

| | | TOTAL RETURNS & PERFORMANCE | | | | | | | ASSETS | | ASSET ALLOCATION & TURNOVER | | | | | VALUATION | |
3-Month Total Return	6-Month Total Return	1-Year Total Return	3-Year Total Return	5-Year Total Return	Dividend Yield (TTM)	Expense Ratio	3-Yr Std Deviation	Effective Duration	NAV	Total Assets (MIL)	%Cash	%Stocks	%Bonds	%Other	Turnover Ratio	Premium/ Discount 1-Year Avg	Inception Date
1.53	4.53	7.23	6.57	11.63	1.86	0.05	3.28	7.48	56.65	8,441	0	0	100	0	17	0.02	Aug-10
-0.79	-4.97	-10.08	0.22		0	1	5.66		22.61	6.2	385	0	-285	0		-0.03	Feb-15
-7.70						0.29			18.95	5.7	0	100	0	0		0.09	May-19
-9.63						0.59			18.02	7.2	1	99	0	0		0.18	May-19
-2.29						0			9.91	6.9	0	100	0	0		0.12	Apr-19
0.32						0			10.30	55.6	0	100	0	0		0.06	Apr-19
-2.97	-2.78	-6.63	1.51		2.05	0.35	15.79			717.6	0	100	0	0	20	-0.04	Dec-15
1.39	2.97	3.23	12.45	17.14	5.53	0.7	2.83			2,237	12	0	88	0	124	-0.11	Apr-13
0.84	3.47	5.88	5.70	9.54	2.59	0.15	2.32	5.23		340.0	0	0	100	0	20	0.03	May-13
0.50	1.08	2.18	4.11	4.06	2.16	0.14	0.22	0.08	91.58	8,603	100	0	0	0	635	0.01	May-07
-1.57	0.36	2.66	29.26	40.72	5.3	0.4	9.71	2.77		4,055	0	4	0	1	36	0.04	Apr-09
-0.93	3.17	8.87	5.71	1.08	3.85	0.3	8.55	6.41		847.7	1	0	99	0	43	0.20	Feb-11
1.01	3.54	218.82	252.02	262.72	5.59	0.4	4.53	3.08		10,168	1	0	99	0	44	0.09	Nov-07
-2.16	0.34	0.06	1.16	-4.11	0.48	0.5	6.83	5.74		165.7	0	0	99	0	16	0.15	May-10
0.29	3.89	6.68	2.02	3.59	1.17	0.35	6.53	8.87		1,119	0	0	100	0	18	-0.07	Oct-07
0.72	1.59	2.81	7.16	8.44	2.86	0.15	0.5	0.13		3,820	5	0	93	0	19	-0.01	Nov-11
0.34	1.85	3.47	15.66	19.16	5.69	0.4	3.3	1.62		3,301	2	0	97	0	65	0.11	Mar-12
-1.99	-0.80	-1.22	-2.77	-9.15	1.32	0.35	5.53	1.87		302.2	1	0	99	0	66	0.02	Jan-09
1.26	3.86	4.66	4.04		4.26	0.6	5	8.09		114.8	0	0	99	0	104	-0.01	Jun-16
0.72	2.30	4.56	5.87		2.67	0.45	1.09	1.30		128.8	20	0	80	0	62	0.16	Apr-16
1.32	4.04	7.70	8.40		3.41	0.55	2.3	3.28		3,360	2	0	97	0	47	0.23	Feb-15
0.09	4.09	9.02	14.21		3.98	0.65	3.28	4.80		68.3	4	0	96	0	37	0.21	Apr-16
4.94	5.29	13.50	16.13	38.68	3.12	0.5	10.69			2,220	0	100	0	0	11	-0.02	May-08
0.97	3.30	3.70	56.62	76.57	2.15	0.17	12.38			21,223	0	100	0	0	2	0.00	Jan-98
2.29	2.61	8.73	12.07	18.86	4.79	0.59	10.33			2,093	0	99	0	1	15	-0.17	Dec-06
6.97	7.38	17.29	19.97	56.96	3.21	0.25	12.75			2,744	0	100	0	0	9	0.00	Apr-01
-1.76	4.45	0.99	25.03	9.87	2.87	0.29	14.57			2,050	0	100	0	0	7	-0.09	Oct-02
-2.96	1.23	-2.34	27.61	24.97	3.14	0.46	14.52			16.9	0	100	0	0	61	-0.27	Jun-14
-7.32	-6.52	-1.37	65.63		0.1	0.45	19.31			59.9	0	100	0	0	43	0.00	Jan-16
0.47	3.69	7.76	5.85	3.84	1.75	0.5	7.04	12.33		450.1	0	0	99	0	37	-0.02	Mar-08
-1.81	0.73	-0.73	31.58	33.91	2.91	0.5	11.76			89.7	0	100	0	0	11	-0.16	Sep-00
6.80	14.72	24.66			0	0.18			14.82	1,051	0	0	0	100		-0.10	Jun-18
6.74	14.60	24.39	10.97	19.68	0	0.4	11.17		140.00	43,959	0	0	0	100	0	-0.11	Nov-04
1.63	16.57					0.45				8.8	0	100	0	0	24	-0.46	Oct-18
6.22	18.36					0.45				6.8	0	100	0	0	17	-0.36	Oct-18
0.10	1.74	2.03	43.54	69.34	1.67	0.6	12.64			35.4	1	99	0	0	65	-0.05	Jan-14
-4.69	-1.23	-4.79	35.60	63.61	1.13	0.61	14.24			37.4	1	99	0	0	77	-0.01	Jan-14
1.09	1.33	-0.23	36.95	55.67	2.27	0.6	12.31			34.2	1	99	0	0	53	0.04	Jan-14
-34.62	-32.97	-33.52	-19.33	-21.77	2.92	0.3	11.47			1,683	0	100	0	0	3	-0.09	Jan-07
-0.47	2.93	1.97	32.01		2.2	0.2	11.32			82.8	0	100	0	0	17	0.13	Nov-14
-0.70	2.58	-0.20	23.71		2.87	0.2				84.2	0	100	0	0	5	0.07	Oct-16
-0.30	2.73	2.09	22.74	25.72	3.16	0.3	9.92			320.5	1	99	0	0	6	0.09	Jun-14
-5.20	-4.80	-2.47	16.59		2.11	0.3				68.7	0	99	0	0	8	-0.11	Oct-16
-3.14	-2.73	-0.51	15.12	8.23	2.97	0.3	11.96			268.9	1	99	0	0	30	-0.03	Jun-14
1.69	6.11	7.70	47.89		1.85	0.15	11.17			471.0	0	100	0	0	18	0.05	Apr-15
0.99	4.58	4.87	35.70	52.53	2.24	0.3	10.12			24.2	0	100	0	0	18	0.06	Jun-14
1.55	4.03	9.04	8.33	18.62	2.16	0.23	4.13	6.16		2,957	0	0	100	0	22	-0.13	Sep-07
0.33	1.47	3.94	3.88	5.93	1.37	0.2	1.82	2.78		3,599	0	0	100	0	35	-0.04	Oct-07
2.47	5.41	9.41	11.89	27.90	3.96	0.35	4.1	6.26		889.6	0	0	100	0	18	0.03	Apr-11
-2.49	-0.33	0.00	61.90	103.96	0.61	0.35	16.79			363.6	0	100	0	0	10	0.01	Sep-00
2.32	5.77	10.33	8.78	17.68	2.93	0.04	3.37	5.72		4,694	4	0	96	0	82	0.06	May-07
3.07	8.19	13.31	14.01	23.91	3.53	0.06	4.06	7.90		87.7	0	0	98	0	29	0.21	Apr-11

Fund Name	Ticker Symbol	Traded On	Overall Rating	Reward Rating	Risk Rating	Recent Up/ Downgrade	Price as of 9/30/2019	52-Week High	52-Week Low	Open to New Investors	Category & (Prospectus Objective)
● SPDR® Portfolio Developed World ex-US ETF	SPDW	NYSE Arca	C	C	C+		29.36	30.85	25.64	Y	Global Equity Large Cap (Foreign Stock)
● SPDR® Portfolio Emerging Markets ETF	SPEM	NYSE Arca	C	C	C+		34.28	36.86	31.29	Y	Global Emerg Mkts Equity (Div Emerg Mkts)
● SPDR® Portfolio Europe ETF	SPEU	NYSE Arca	C	C	C-		33.25	34.78	28.95	Y	Europe Equity Large Cap (Europe Stock)
● SPDR® Portfolio High Yield Bond ETF	SPHY	NYSE Arca	C	C+	C-		26.18	26.22	24.47	Y	US Fixed Income (Corp Bond-High Yld)
● SPDR® Portfolio Intermediate Term Corporate Bond ETF	SPIB	NYSE Arca	C+	C+	C+		35.28	35.46	32.78	Y	US Fixed Income (Corp Bond - Gen)
● SPDR® Portfolio Intermediate Term Treasury ETF	SPTI	NYSE Arca	C+	C	C+	Up	31.27	61.86	30.88	Y	US Fixed Income (Govt Bond - Treasury)
● SPDR® Portfolio Large Cap ETF	SPLG	NYSE Arca	C+	C+	C+		34.85	35.57	27.32	Y	US Equity Large Cap Blend (Growth & Inc)
★ SPDR® Portfolio Long Term Corporate Bond ETF	SPLB	NYSE Arca	B	B	C+	Up	30.09	30.71	24.89	Y	US Fixed Income (Corp Bond - Gen)
● SPDR® Portfolio Long Term Treasury ETF	SPTL	NYSE Arca	C	C	C+		41.03	42.38	32.31	Y	US Fixed Income (Govt Bond - Treasury)
● SPDR® Portfolio Mid Cap ETF	SPMD	NYSE Arca	C	C	C+		33.89	35.82	27.71	Y	US Equity Mid Cap (Growth)
● SPDR® Portfolio Mortgage Backed Bond ETF	SPMB	NYSE Arca	C	C+	C-		26.27	26.34	24.78	Y	US Fixed Income (Govt Bond - Mortgage)
● SPDR® Portfolio MSCI Global Stock Market ETF	SPGM	NYSE Arca	C	C	C-		39.91	81.46	37.90	Y	Global Equity Large Cap (World Stock)
● SPDR® Portfolio S&P 500 Growth ETF	SPYG	NYSE Arca	C+	C+	C+	Down	38.89	39.97	30.33	Y	US Equity Large Cap Growth (Growth)
● SPDR® Portfolio S&P 500 High Dividend ETF	SPYD	NYSE Arca	C	C	C+	Down	37.98	38.85	32.59	Y	US Equity Large Cap Value (Growth & Inc)
● SPDR® Portfolio S&P 500 Value ETF	SPYV	NYSE Arca	C+	C	C+	Up	31.96	32.44	25.59	Y	US Equity Large Cap Value (Growth)
● SPDR® Portfolio Short Term Corporate Bond ETF	SPSB	NYSE Arca	C+	C	C+	Up	30.85	30.89	29.99	Y	US Fixed Income (Corp Bond - Gen)
● SPDR® Portfolio Short Term Treasury ETF	SPTS	NYSE Arca	C	C	C+		30.02	30.11	29.34	Y	US Fixed Income (Govt Bond - Treasury)
● SPDR® Portfolio Small Cap ETF	SPSM	NYSE Arca	C	C	C+		30.00	32.82	24.83	Y	US Equity Small Cap (Growth)
● SPDR® Portfolio TIPS ETF	SPIP	NYSE Arca	C	C+	C-		28.52	56.80	28.24	Y	US Fixed Income (Govt Bond - Treasury)
● SPDR® Portfolio Total Stock Market ETF	SPTM	NYSE Arca	C+	C+	C+		36.74	37.53	28.90	Y	US Equity Large Cap Blend (Growth)
● SPDR® Russell 1000 Low Volatility Focus ETF	ONEV	NYSE Arca	C	C+	C-		81.55	82.36	64.20	Y	US Equity Mid Cap (Growth & Inc)
● SPDR® Russell 1000 Momentum Focus ETF	ONEO	NYSE Arca	C-	C	D	Down	73.55	76.15	59.44	Y	US Equity Mid Cap (Growth & Inc)
● SPDR® Russell 1000® Yield Focus ETF	ONEY	NYSE Arca	C	C	D+		70.70	72.88	59.15	Y	US Equity Mid Cap (Growth & Inc)
● SPDR® S&P 1500 Momentum Tilt ETF	MMTM	NYSE Arca	C	C+	D+		129.84	131.53	100.85	Y	US Equity Large Cap Blend (Growth)
SPDR® S&P 1500 Value Tilt ETF	VLU	NYSE Arca	C-	C	D		105.05	108.00	86.88	Y	US Equity Large Cap Value (Growth)
● SPDR® S&P 400 Mid Cap Growth ETF	MDYG	NYSE Arca	D	D	D	Up	53.72	55.46	43.09	Y	US Equity Mid Cap (Growth)
● SPDR® S&P 400 Mid Cap Value ETF	MDYV	NYSE Arca	D	D	D		51.32	53.44	41.80	Y	US Equity Mid Cap (Growth)
SPDR® S&P 500 Buyback ETF	SPYB	NYSE Arca	C	C	D+		67.30	68.88	53.41	Y	US Equity Large Cap Value (Growth)
★ SPDR® S&P 500 ETF	SPY	NYSE Arca	B-	C+	B		296.77	302.01	234.34	Y	US Equity Large Cap Blend (Growth)
● SPDR® S&P 500 Fossil Fuel Reserves Free ETF	SPYX	NYSE Arca	C	C+	C-		72.65	73.80	57.18	Y	US Equity Large Cap Blend (Growth & Inc)
● SPDR® S&P 600 Small Cap ETF	SLY	NYSE Arca	D	D	D		67.21	74.30	56.32	Y	US Equity Small Cap (Small Company)
● SPDR® S&P 600 Small Cap Growth ETF	SLYG	NYSE Arca	D-	D-	D		59.59	66.43	50.63	Y	US Equity Small Cap (Small Company)
● SPDR® S&P 600 Small Cap Value ETF	SLYV	NYSE Arca	D	D+	D		61.26	67.25	50.73	Y	US Equity Small Cap (Small Company)
● SPDR® S&P Bank ETF	KBE	NYSE Arca	C	C	C+		43.16	47.44	35.17	Y	Financials Sector Equity (Financial)
● SPDR® S&P Biotech ETF	XBI	NYSE Arca	C-	C-	C	Down	76.25	94.90	65.42	Y	Healthcare Sector Equity (Health)
SPDR® S&P Capital Markets ETF	KCE	NYSE Arca	C	C	D+	Up	54.75	57.96	44.84	Y	Financials Sector Equity (Financial)
● SPDR® S&P China ETF	GXC	NYSE Arca	C	C-	C		90.26	104.47	82.09	Y	Greater China Equity (Pacific Stock)
● SPDR® S&P Dividend ETF	SDY	NYSE Arca	C+	C	C+		102.60	103.80	84.76	Y	US Equity Large Cap Value (Growth & Inc)
● SPDR® S&P Emerging Asia Pacific ETF	GMF	NYSE Arca	C-	C-	C-		93.45	101.85	84.71	Y	Asia ex-Japan Equity (Pacific Stock)
● SPDR® S&P Emerging Markets Dividend ETF	EDIV	NYSE Arca	C	C	C-		29.84	33.14	27.94	Y	Global Emerg Mkts Equity (Div Emerg Mkts)
● SPDR® S&P Emerging Markets Small Cap ETF	EWX	NYSE Arca	C	D+	C	Up	43.44	45.72	40.07	Y	Global Emerg Mkts Equity (Div Emerg Mkts)
● SPDR® S&P Global Dividend ETF	WDIV	NYSE Arca	C	C	C-		67.52	68.57	60.00	Y	Global Equity Large Cap (Growth & Inc)
● SPDR® S&P Global Infrastructure ETF	GII	NYSE Arca	C	C+	C-	Down	53.40	53.92	43.84	Y	Infrastructure Sector Equity (Utility)
● SPDR® S&P Global Natural Resources ETF	GNR	NYSE Arca	C	C-	C+		43.07	51.00	39.53	Y	Natural Resources (Natl Res)
● SPDR® S&P Health Care Equipment ETF	XHE	NYSE Arca	C	C	C-		78.07	86.98	64.44	Y	Healthcare Sector Equity (Health)
● SPDR® S&P Health Care Services ETF	XHS	NYSE Arca	C	C	D+	Up	62.30	76.46	59.72	Y	Healthcare Sector Equity (Health)
★ SPDR® S&P Homebuilders ETF	XHB	NYSE Arca	B-	B	C	Up	44.08	44.08	30.74	Y	Consumer Goods & Svcs (Real Estate)
★ SPDR® S&P Insurance ETF	KIE	NYSE Arca	B-	B-	C+		35.23	35.33	26.73	Y	Financials Sector Equity (Financial)
● SPDR® S&P International Dividend ETF	DWX	NYSE Arca	C+	C+	C+	Up	38.95	39.99	33.98	Y	Global Equity Large Cap (Foreign Stock)
● SPDR® S&P International Small Cap ETF	GWX	NYSE Arca	D+	D	C	Down	29.39	34.40	26.70	Y	Globa Eq Mid/Small Cap (Foreign Stock)
SPDR® S&P Internet ETF	XWEB	NYSE Arca	C-	C	D+	Down	78.82	96.57	70.86	Y	Technology Sector Equity (Technology)
SPDR® S&P Kensho Future Security ETF	FITE	NYSE Arca	C	C	D+	Up	37.21	39.06	27.42	Y	Technology Sector Equity (Technology)

★ Expanded analysis of this fund is included in Section II: Analysis of All BUY Rated Funds. ● Expanded analysis of this fund is included in Section III: Analysis of All Rated Funds with Assets over $50 million.

	TOTAL RETURNS & PERFORMANCE								ASSETS		ASSET ALLOCATION & TURNOVER					VALUATION	
3-Month Total Return	6-Month Total Return	1-Year Total Return	3-Year Total Return	5-Year Total Return	Dividend Yield (TTM)	Expense Ratio	3-Yr Std Deviation	Effective Duration	NAV	Total Assets (MIL)	%Cash	%Stocks	%Bonds	%Other	Turnover Ratio	Premium/ Discount 1-Year Avg	Inception Date
-0.62	1.56	-1.54	20.68	18.55	2.93	0.04	11.2			4,809	0	100	0	0	3	0.02	Apr-07
-3.53	-3.23	1.56	20.90	14.52	2.38	0.11	13.41			2,599	2	98	0	0	10	0.05	Mar-07
-2.31	2.01	2.55	21.65	7.33	3.5	0.09	12.42			186.5	1	99	0	0	5	-0.09	Oct-02
1.16	3.59	8.00	12.99	24.53	5.2	0.15	3.55	2.95		78.3	1	0	99	0	75	0.09	Jun-12
1.74	5.17	9.47	10.54	19.19	3.13	0.07	2.65	4.29		4,860	0	0	97	0	24	0.02	Feb-09
-49.09	-47.46	-45.02	-46.25	-43.34	2.11	0.06	3.06	5.22		912.6	0	0	100	0	24	0.06	May-07
0.07	4.12	3.49	44.84	65.23	1.9	0.03	12.33			2,977	0	100	0	0	5	0.00	Nov-05
5.56	13.97	19.98	20.21	39.59	3.86	0.07	7.71	14.58		641.1	1	0	99	0	18	0.13	Mar-09
8.40	15.72	25.35	12.40	38.02	2.39	0.06	11.46	18.47		1,944	0	0	100	0	12	0.14	May-07
-0.93	0.69	-4.16	30.05	45.54	1.65	0.05	15.98			1,677	0	100	0	0	8	0.01	Nov-05
1.31	3.56	7.76	6.43	13.55	3.32	0.06	2.5	2.38		624.4	8	0	92	0	245	0.13	Jan-09
-50.41	-48.99	-49.77	-34.21	-29.70	2.03	0.09	11.43			167.9	0	100	0	0	4	0.01	Feb-12
-0.57	3.68	2.36	53.77	80.80	1.41	0.04	12.3			5,099	0	100	0	0	21	0.00	Sep-00
0.95	1.43	5.60	27.07		4.46	0.07	12.38			1,870	0	100	0	0	28	0.01	Oct-15
1.53	5.01	4.58	34.27	48.62	2.47	0.04	13.14			3,671	0	100	0	0	30	-0.01	Sep-00
0.94	2.52	5.06	7.37	10.83	2.79	0.07	1	1.80		6,084	2	0	96	0	46	0.06	Dec-09
0.64	2.12	4.37	3.48	7.04	2.34	0.06	1.31	1.92		1,656	0	0	100	0	52	0.03	Nov-11
-2.33	-1.47	-7.16	28.05	49.99	1.73	0.05	17.29			1,392	0	100	0	0	14	-0.02	Jul-13
-49.05	-47.51	-46.15	-46.63	-43.55	2.5	0.12	3.5	8.48		1,656	0	0	100	0	14	0.03	May-07
-0.14	3.62	2.64	43.47	64.09	1.72	0.03	12.59			3,735	0	100	0	0	4	-0.04	Oct-00
1.09	6.35	8.38	41.52		1.81	0.2	11.76			562.6	0	100	0	0	33	0.02	Dec-15
-0.09	2.35	-2.04	30.35		1.61	0.2	13.22			431.7	0	100	0	0	40	-0.02	Dec-15
-0.17	1.97	0.86	30.20		3.29	0.2	13.69			427.4	0	100	0	0	42	0.06	Dec-15
0.44	4.70	1.81	46.96	68.87	1.55	0.12	12.4			51.9	0	100	0	0	58	0.09	Oct-12
0.62	2.93	-0.33	36.32	51.19	2.33	0.13	13.36			18.9	0	100	0	0	13	0.01	Oct-12
-1.65	1.10	-2.45	-56.05	-48.09	1.26	0.15	14.48			1,643	0	100	0	0	38	0.01	Nov-05
-0.63	0.46	-2.55	-36.91	-27.62	1.92	0.15	16.62			1,390	0	100	0	0	35	0.01	Nov-05
-0.78	3.16	2.13	41.78		1.43	0.35	15.2			20.2	0	100	0	0	72	-0.01	Feb-15
0.38	4.26	3.28	44.59	65.58	1.85	0.09	12.15			273,532	0	100	0	0	2	-0.05	Jan-93
0.64	4.75	3.81	46.69		1.67	0.2	12.24			388.4	0	100	0	0	6	0.01	Nov-15
-0.53	0.20	-9.53	-34.87	-20.24	1.42	0.15	18.04			1,261	1	99	0	0	11	-0.01	Nov-05
-2.07	-0.61	-9.32	-66.54	-58.19	1.11	0.15	17.54			1,885	1	99	0	0	37	-0.01	Sep-00
1.23	0.98	7.96	-27.18	-12.59	1.8	0.15	18.94			2,186	0	100	0	0	34	-0.01	Sep-00
-0.32	2.10	-4.28	36.95	48.58	2.39	0.35	23.35			1,577	0	100	0	0	24	0.01	Nov-05
-13.44	-15.48	-19.11	15.88	49.47	0.02	0.35	27.19			3,672	0	100	0	0	45	-0.04	Jan-06
-1.45	1.44	-0.03	44.86	28.22	2.42	0.35	17.02			36.9	0	100	0	0	24	0.01	Nov-05
-5.50	-10.01	-4.61	21.79	31.08	2.18	0.59	18.84			1,123	1	99	0	0	3	-0.08	Mar-07
1.57	3.21	7.17	34.85	69.45	2.45	0.35	11.18			18,915	0	100	0	0	20	-0.02	Nov-05
-3.88	-5.22	-1.51	21.95	25.68	2.19	0.49	13.96			440.3	0	100	0	0	5	0.03	Mar-07
-6.92	-3.47	1.27	21.98	0.00	4.17	0.49	13.91			410.8	0	100	0	0	55	-0.14	Feb-11
-2.45	-2.54	0.13	11.08	3.70	3.01	0.65	12.09			522.0	1	98	0	0	24	-0.10	May-08
0.82	3.02	4.15	20.13	28.92	4.54	0.4	10.09			276.7	0	100	0	0	39	0.05	May-13
0.92	5.37	13.61	23.38	28.20	3.14	0.4	10.24			399.9	0	100	0	0	21	0.08	Jan-07
-6.25	-6.36	-11.43	20.75	3.25	3.84	0.4	14.82			1,045	0	100	0	0	19	-0.08	Sep-10
-5.78	-3.77	-11.00	50.57	127.61	0.11	0.35	17.6			566.5	-1	101	0	0	32	-0.01	Jan-11
-7.07	-4.11	-18.58	12.87	24.33	0.34	0.35	18.72			82.3	3	97	0	0	35	-0.02	Sep-11
3.83	12.36	15.00	31.93	52.98	1	0.35	17.38			680.8	0	100	0	0	32	-0.01	Jan-06
2.48	12.92	12.57	50.04	83.05	1.68	0.35	12.84			898.7	0	100	0	0	21	-0.03	Nov-05
0.06	4.46	7.62	22.47	6.72	4.34	0.45	8.9			781.6	0	100	0	0	47	-0.14	Feb-08
-1.72	-2.55	-10.79	7.95	19.61	3.92	0.4	12.1			786.8	1	99	0	0	29	-0.14	Apr-07
-12.92	-13.07	-17.38	47.65		0.48	0.35	19.17			23.7	3	97	0	0	85	-0.05	Jun-16
-1.07	4.25	4.94			1.58	0.46				15.3	0	100	0	0	28	-0.07	Dec-17

Fund Name	Ticker Symbol	Traded On	Overall Rating	Reward Rating	Risk Rating	Recent Up/ Downgrade	Price as of 9/30/2019	52-Week High	52-Week Low	Open to New Investors	Category & (Prospectus Objective)
SPDR® S&P Kensho Intelligent Structures ETF	SIMS	NYSE Arca	C	C+	D+	Up	29.88	30.93	23.29	Y	Infrastructure Sector Equity (Technology)
SPDR® S&P Kensho New Economies Composite ETF	KOMP	NYSE Arca	U	U	U		33.16	34.39	25.94	Y	US Equity Mid Cap (Technology)
SPDR® S&P Kensho Smart Mobility ETF	HAIL	NYSE Arca	D	D+	D		26.42	30.80	22.36	Y	Industrials Sector Equity (Technology)
● SPDR® S&P Metals and Mining ETF	XME	NYSE Arca	C	C	D	Up	25.45	34.49	24.40	Y	Natural Resources (Natl Res)
● SPDR® S&P MidCap 400 ETF	MDY	NYSE Arca	C	C	C+		352.47	364.55	284.96	Y	US Equity Mid Cap (Growth)
● SPDR® S&P Oil & Gas Equipment & Services ETF	XES	NYSE Arca	D+	D+	D	Up	7.24	17.45	6.85	Y	Energy Sector Equity (Natl Res)
● SPDR® S&P Oil & Gas Exploration & Production ETF	XOP	NYSE Arca	D	D	D		22.36	44.57	20.60	Y	Energy Sector Equity (Natl Res)
● SPDR® S&P Pharmaceuticals ETF	XPH	NYSE Arca	C	C	D+	Up	35.59	47.26	34.77	Y	Healthcare Sector Equity (Health)
● SPDR® S&P Regional Banking ETF	KRE	NYSE Arca	C	C	C	Up	52.79	60.15	44.22	Y	Financials Sector Equity (Financial)
● SPDR® S&P Retail ETF	XRT	NYSE Arca	D+	D+	D+	Down	42.43	50.72	37.81	Y	Consumer Goods & Svcs (Unaligned)
★ SPDR® S&P Semiconductor ETF	XSD	NYSE Arca	B-	B	C-		89.82	94.32	60.13	Y	Technology Sector Equity (Technology)
● SPDR® S&P Software & Services ETF	XSW	NYSE Arca	C	C	C-	Down	93.36	101.79	70.06	Y	Technology Sector Equity (Technology)
SPDR® S&P Technology Hardware ETF	XTH	NYSE Arca	C	B-	D+	Up	75.45	79.51	57.48	Y	Technology Sector Equity (Technology)
● SPDR® S&P Telecom ETF	XTL	NYSE Arca	C	C+	C-	Up	67.13	75.71	58.72	Y	Communications Sector Equity (Comm)
● SPDR® S&P Transportation ETF	XTN	NYSE Arca	C	C	C-	Up	61.03	66.70	50.73	Y	Industrials Sector Equity (Utility)
SPDR® Solactive Canada ETF	ZCAN	NYSE Arca	C	C+	D+	Up	60.35	60.83	48.13	Y	Equity Misc (Foreign Stock)
SPDR® Solactive Germany ETF	ZDEU	NYSE Arca	D+	D+	D+		54.84	60.62	50.04	Y	Equity Misc (Europe Stock)
SPDR® Solactive Hong Kong ETF	ZHOK	NYSE Arca	D	D	D+		58.76	69.12	54.02	Y	Greater China Equity (Pacific Stock)
SPDR® Solactive Japan ETF	ZJPN	NYSE Arca	C-	C-	D+	Up	74.96	80.65	64.75	Y	Japan Equity (Pacific Stock)
SPDR® Solactive United Kingdom ETF	ZGBR	NYSE Arca	C-	C-	D+		48.45	52.28	43.78	Y	Equity Misc (Foreign Stock)
SPDR® SSGA Fixed Income Sector Rotation ETF	FISR	NYSE Arca	U	U	U		31.51	31.63	30.06	Y	US Fixed Income (Growth & Inc)
● SPDR® SSGA Gender Diversity Index ETF	SHE	NYSE Arca	C+	B-	C	Up	73.47	76.68	60.07	Y	US Equity Large Cap Blend (Growth & Inc)
● SPDR® SSgA Global Allocation ETF	GAL	NYSE Arca	C	C	D+		38.59	38.98	33.88	Y	Moderate Allocation (Growth)
● SPDR® SSgA Income Allocation ETF	INKM	NYSE Arca	C	C+	C-		33.76	34.02	30.39	Y	Moderate Allocation (Income)
● SPDR® SSgA Multi-Asset Real Return ETF	RLY	NYSE Arca	C-	C-	C-		24.74	26.72	22.58	Y	Moderate Allocation (Growth & Inc)
SPDR® SSGA U.S. Sector Rotation ETF	XLSR	NYSE Arca	U	U	U		31.12	31.58	28.68	Y	US Equity Large Cap Blend (Growth)
● SPDR® SSgA Ultra Short Term Bond ETF	ULST	NYSE Arca	C	C	C-		40.43	40.45	40.10	Y	US Fixed Income (Growth & Inc)
★ SPDR® SSGA US Large Cap Low Volatility Index ETF	LGLV	NYSE Arca	B	B	C+	Up	111.48	112.40	84.44	Y	US Equity Large Cap Blend (Income)
● SPDR® SSGA US Small Cap Low Volatility Index ETF	SMLV	NYSE Arca	C	C	C-		95.07	96.95	79.55	Y	US Equity Small Cap (Income)
● SPDR® Wells Fargo Preferred Stock ETF	PSK	NYSE Arca	C+	B-	C+		44.16	44.19	38.67	Y	US Fixed Income (Growth & Inc)
● Sprott Gold Miners ETF	SGDM	NYSE Arca	C	C	C-	Up	22.90	26.40	14.90	Y	Prec Metals (Prec Metals)
● Sprott Junior Gold Miners ETF	SGDJ	NYSE Arca	C-	C-	C-	Up	30.64	36.25	21.48	Y	Prec Metals (Prec Metals)
● Strategy Shares EcoLogical Strategy ETF	HECO	NYSE Arca	C	C+	C-		41.19	44.31	38.80	Y	Equity Misc (Growth)
Strategy Shares Nasdaq 7 HandI™ Index ETF	HNDL	NAS CM	C-	C-	C-	Up	24.15	24.41	21.80	Y	Cautious Allocation (Growth & Inc)
● Strategy Shares US Market Rotation Strategy ETF	HUSE	NYSE Arca	C-	C-	C-		33.60	40.86	32.94	Y	US Equity Large Cap Blend (Growth)
Syntax Stratified LargeCap ETF	SSPY	NYSE Arca	U	U	U		48.08	48.55	41.75	Y	US Equity Large Cap Blend (Growth)
Teucrium Agricultural Fund	TAGS	NYSE Arca	D	D-	D	Up	18.93	21.06	17.92	Y	Commodities Specified (Unaligned)
● Teucrium Corn Fund	CORN	NYSE Arca	D	D	D		15.18	17.41	14.30	Y	Commodities Specified (Unaligned)
Teucrium Soybean	SOYB	NYSE Arca	D	D	D		15.51	16.82	14.35	Y	Commodities Specified (Unaligned)
Teucrium Sugar	CANE	NYSE Arca	D-	D-	D-		6.67	8.07	6.30	Y	Commodities Specified (Unaligned)
● Teucrium Wheat	WEAT	NYSE Arca	D	D	D	Up	5.30	6.43	4.88	Y	Commodities Specified (Unaligned)
The 3D Printing ETF	PRNT	BATS	D+	D+	D+	Up	20.62	26.10	19.04	Y	Technology Sector Equity (Technology)
The Acquirers Fund ETF	ZIG	NYSE Arca	U	U	U		24.76	26.00	22.57	Y	US Equity Large Cap Blend (Growth)
The Hoya Capital Housing ETF	HOMZ	NYSE Arca	U	U	U		28.44	28.44	24.96	Y	Real Estate Sector Equity (Real Estate)
The Long-Term Care ETF	OLD	NAS CM	C+	B	C-	Up	30.91	31.26	24.38	Y	Real Estate Sector Equity (Health)
The Obesity ETF	SLIM	NAS CM	C-	C	D+		33.73	38.04	29.88	Y	Healthcare Sector Equity (Health)
The Organics ETF	ORG	NAS CM	D	D	D	Down	24.94	31.60	23.36	Y	Consumer Goods & Svcs (Growth & Inc)
★ The Real Estate Select Sector SPDR Fund	XLRE	NYSE Arca	B	B+	C	Up	39.34	40.10	29.81	Y	Real Estate Sector Equity (Real Estate)
TigerShares China-U.S. Internet Titans ETF	TTTN	NAS CM	U	U	U		22.49	30.08	20.46	Y	Technology Sector Equity (Technology)
Timothy Plan High Dividend Stock ETF	TPHD	NYSE Arca	U	U	U		25.54	25.54	23.29	Y	US Equity Large Cap Value (Equity-Income)
Timothy Plan US Large Cap Core ETF			U	U	U		25.55	25.89	23.58	Y	US Equity Large Cap Blend (Growth)
Tortoise Cloud Infrastructure Fund	TCLD	BATS	U	U	U		26.50	28.14	25.26	Y	Technology Sector Equity (Growth & Inc)

★ Expanded analysis of this fund is included in Section II: Analysis of All BUY Rated Funds. ● Expanded analysis of this fund is included in Section III: Analysis of All Rated Funds with Assets over $50 million.

		TOTAL RETURNS & PERFORMANCE								ASSETS	ASSET ALLOCATION & TURNOVER					VALUATION	
3-Month Total Return	6-Month Total Return	1-Year Total Return	3-Year Total Return	5-Year Total Return	Dividend Yield (TTM)	Expense Ratio	3-Yr Std Deviation	Effective Duration	NAV	Total Assets (MIL)	%Cash	%Stocks	%Bonds	%Other	Turnover Ratio	Premium/ Discount 1-Year Avg	Inception Date
-2.37	4.89	-2.81			0.74	0.46				9.0	0	100	0	0	22	-0.25	Dec-17
-1.26	5.46					0.2				73.0	0	100	0	0	98	0.07	Oct-18
-6.43	-5.87	-10.92			2.55	0.46				6.6	0	100	0	0	36	-0.58	Dec-17
-8.62	-13.58	-23.34	2.16	-23.23	2.66	0.35	27.66			415.0	0	100	0	0	28	-0.05	Jun-06
-0.49	1.42	-1.94	29.80	53.08	1.38	0.24	15.28		352.30	19,100	0	100	0	0	17	0.00	May-95
-24.61	-36.36	-56.34	-60.30	-80.57	1.28	0.35	40.8			128.7	0	100	0	0	34	0.00	Jun-06
-17.11	-27.35	-47.91	-39.88	-65.45	1.41	0.35	30.39			1,726	0	100	0	0	37	0.03	Jun-06
-10.35	-13.15	-22.68	-16.85	-21.72	1.62	0.35	20.28			183.5	0	100	0	0	42	-0.01	Jun-06
-0.68	1.75	-7.53	32.76	53.85	2.34	0.35	24.27			1,968	0	100	0	0	27	-0.04	Jun-06
-0.58	-6.49	-15.74	0.91	5.20	1.59	0.35	18.7			265.3	2	99	0	0	45	-0.03	Jun-06
3.07	11.35	19.16	72.03	152.33	0.66	0.35	22.91			337.0	0	100	0	0	32	0.00	Jan-06
-4.73	-2.98	3.28	68.42	120.05	0.22	0.35	16.11			214.6	0	100	0	0	47	-0.06	Sep-11
-1.23	0.05	-1.55	39.95		0.71	0.35	20.02			3.8	3	97	0	0	40	-0.06	Jun-16
-2.00	-6.38	-9.90	6.89	30.76	1.01	0.35	15.15			53.7	-3	103	0	0	35	-0.05	Jan-11
-0.51	-0.65	-7.71	32.28	36.91	1.21	0.35	20.98			123.3	0	100	0	0	18	-0.05	Jan-11
1.20	4.94	3.79	23.03	14.02	2.59	0.14	12.73			21.1	0	100	0	0	29	-0.09	Jun-14
-4.39	1.71	-6.95	13.78	15.53	2.94	0.14	14.26			8.2	0	100	0	0	28	-0.07	Jun-14
-10.97	-11.99	-1.41			2.03	0.14				7.4	1	99	0	0	0	0.07	Sep-18
2.59	3.94	-3.50	18.34	35.86	2.59	0.14	9.95			7.4	0	100	0	0	53	-0.11	Jun-14
-2.40	-2.45	-2.35	14.04	4.08	4.98	0.14	12.37			10.9	0	100	0	0	50	-0.04	Jun-14
1.95						0.5		7.06		16.4	14	0	85	0		0.00	Apr-19
-1.11	2.95	1.96	37.34		1.91	0.2	11.59			271.5	0	100	0	0	53	0.06	Mar-16
0.72	2.99	2.75	22.52	28.11	2.74	0.35	8.24	5.50		260.0	9	60	28	0	71	-0.02	Apr-12
2.14	4.99	9.20	19.55	27.59	4.86	0.5	6.01	9.35		127.6	3	36	51	0	71	0.01	Apr-12
-1.23	-0.95	-4.38	8.08	-3.33	2.84	0.5	9.43	9.53		101.1	9	55	30	4	28	-0.06	Apr-12
0.61						0.7				29.2	0	100	0	0		0.07	Apr-19
0.66	1.49	2.81	6.18	7.60	2.53	0.2	0.29	0.26		212.2	7	0	93	0	100	0.04	Oct-13
2.74	10.85	16.96	52.52	83.95	1.81	0.12	9.74			881.9	0	100	0	0	32	0.11	Feb-13
2.29	4.39	2.16	33.30	66.05	2.81	0.12	14.6			267.9	0	100	0	0	34	0.00	Feb-13
3.90	6.16	11.24	15.44	34.91	5.8	0.45	6.18			936.5	1	3	0	1	35	0.11	Sep-09
8.33	23.74	47.77	-3.65	19.52	0.38	0.5	27.6		22.95	180.2	0	100	0	0	82	-0.09	Jul-14
3.83	14.76	28.05	-23.57		0	0.5	27.29		30.82	57.0	0	100	0	0	37	-0.30	Mar-15
-1.01	1.53	-5.17	30.02	46.59	0.27	1.07	9.3		41.14	64.8	26	71	0	3		-0.07	Jun-12
2.02	5.94	7.73			6.82	1.2		5.29	24.13	20.5	11	19	59	3		0.08	Jan-18
-4.47	-4.55	-15.19	6.74	20.11	0.17	1.2	9.47		33.55	72.1	8	86	0	6		-0.12	Jul-12
0.76	3.69					0.3			48.06	58.9						0.05	Jan-19
-4.37	-3.62	-6.76	-30.13	-38.13	0	1	11.48		19.00	1.4	-2	0	0	102		0.02	Mar-12
-5.65	-1.12	-6.13	-18.63	-33.36	0	1.11	12.16		15.22	91.0	-3	0	0	103		-0.09	Jun-10
-0.01	-2.80	-3.31	-16.30	-19.41	0	1.15	13.5		15.51	27.9	-2	0	0	102		-0.06	Sep-11
-5.96	-9.78	-2.99	-54.61	-48.84	0	1	19.44		6.65	10.1	-1	0	0	101		0.01	Sep-11
-5.88	-0.68	-15.31	-26.11	-51.17	0	1	22.4		5.31	50.5	-2	0	0	102		-0.03	Sep-11
-11.69	-7.61	-17.95	-7.10		0	0.66	24.25		20.76	36.3	0	100	0	0		0.07	Jul-16
-3.88						0.94			24.72	11.7	23	77	0	0		0.13	May-19
7.37	12.22					0.45			28.36	7.1	0	100	0	0		0.08	Mar-19
7.92	11.67	18.86	25.73		1.92	0.35	14.76		30.68	30.7	0	100	0	0	38	0.46	Jun-16
-2.53	-0.42	-10.32	39.59		0.66	0.35	15.08		33.75	10.1	0	100	0	0	67	-0.18	Jun-16
-1.80	-7.09	-19.72	4.62		2.06	0.35	13.78		24.94	7.5	1	99	0	0	52	-0.05	Jun-16
7.73	10.35	25.33	33.59		2.89	0.13	12.22			3,902	0	100	0	0	7	-0.03	Oct-15
-5.79	-8.21					0.59			26.22	8.0	0	100	0	0		-5.64	Nov-18
2.36						0.52			25.50	72.7	0	100	0	0		-0.10	Apr-19
0.35						0.52			25.52	79.1	1	99	0	0		0.09	Apr-19
-1.94	-1.38					0.4			26.57	4.0	0	100	0	0		0.94	Jan-19

Fund Name	Ticker Symbol	Traded On	MARKET Overall Rating	RATINGS Reward Rating	Risk Rating	Recent Up/ Downgrade	PRICE Price as of 9/30/2019	52-Week High	52-Week Low	Open to New Investors	CATEGORY & OBJECTIVE Category & (Prospectus Objective)
Tortoise Digital Payments Infrastructure Fund	TPAY	BATS	U	U	U		31.05	32.56	26.94	Y	Technology Sector Equity (Growth & Inc)
Tortoise Global Water ESG Fund	TBLU	BATS	C	C	D+	Up	31.15	31.36	25.07	Y	Natural Resources (Unaligned)
● Tortoise North American Pipeline Fund	TPYP	NYSE Arca	C	C+	C-		23.40	24.58	19.22	Y	Energy Sector Equity (Unaligned)
TrimTabs All Cap International Free-Cash-Flow ETF	TTAI	BATS	D+	C-	D	Up	25.84	26.93	21.86	Y	Global Equity Large Cap (Growth & Inc)
● TrimTabs All Cap U.S. Free-Cash-Flow ETF	TTAC	BATS	C	C	D+		37.16	38.32	29.75	Y	US Equity Large Cap Blend (Growth & Inc)
U.S. Global GO GOLD and Precious Metal Miners ETF	GOAU	NYSE Arca	C	C	D+	Up	15.28	17.98	10.05	Y	Commodities Specified (Prec Metals)
U.S. Global Jets ETF	JETS	NYSE Arca	C+	B-	C-	Up	29.35	32.93	26.83	Y	Industrials Sector Equity (Growth)
UBS AG FI Enhanced Europe 50 ETN	FIEE	NYSE Arca	D+	C-	D+	Down	160.75	171.06	116.52	Y	Europe Equity Large Cap (Europe Stock)
● UBS AG FI Enhanced Global High Yield ETN	FIHD	NYSE Arca	C	C	C-		183.30	186.08	129.64	Y	Global Equity Large Cap (Convertible Bond)
● UBS AG FI Enhanced Large Cap Growth ETN	FBGX	NYSE Arca	C	C+	D+		277.32	301.54	167.50	Y	US Equity Large Cap Growth (Growth)
UBS ETRACS - ProShares Daily 3x Inverse Crude ETN	WTID	NYSE Arca	D	D-	D		6.03	21.15	4.27	Y	Trading Tools (Natl Res)
UBS ETRACS - ProShares Daily 3x Long Crude ETN	WTIU	NYSE Arca	D	D	D		10.04	46.94	7.91	Y	Trading Tools (Natl Res)
UBS ETRACS 2×Lev Long ETRACS Wells Fargo® Bus Dev Co Ind E	LBDC	NYSE Arca	C-	C	D	Down	14.71	16.06	10.88	Y	Trading Tools (Growth & Inc)
● UBS ETRACS 2xLeveraged Long Wells Fargo Bus Dev Co Ind ETN	BDCL	NYSE Arca	C	C	C-		14.70	16.03	11.01	Y	Trading Tools (Growth)
● UBS ETRACS 2xMonth Leveraged Alerian MLP Infrastr Ind ETN	MLPQ	NYSE Arca	D	D	D+		24.65	36.91	21.00	Y	Trading Tools (Growth & Inc)
UBS ETRACS 2xMonthly Leveraged S&P MLP Index ETN Series B	MLPZ	NYSE Arca	D	D	D+	Down	28.86	43.25	24.14	Y	Trading Tools (Growth & Inc)
● UBS ETRACS Alerian MLP Index ETN	AMU	NYSE Arca	D	D	C-	Down	14.67	17.68	13.39	Y	Energy Sector Equity (Income)
UBS ETRACS Alerian MLP Index ETN Series B	AMUB	NYSE Arca	D-	D	E	Down	14.69	17.47	13.34	Y	Energy Sector Equity (Growth & Inc)
● UBS ETRACS Alerian MLP Infrastructure Index ETN	MLPI	NYSE Arca	D	D	C-	Down	20.85	24.70	18.86	Y	Energy Sector Equity (Natl Res)
UBS ETRACS Alerian MLP Infrastructure Index ETN Series B	MLPB	NYSE Arca	D-	D	E	Down	20.87	23.86	18.88	Y	Energy Sector Equity (Utility)
UBS ETRACS Alerian Natural Gas MLP Index ETN	MLPG	NYSE Arca	D	D	D+		20.48	25.23	18.95	Y	Energy Sector Equity (Natl Res)
● UBS ETRACS Bloomberg Commodity Index Total Return ETN	DJCI	NYSE Arca	D	D	D+		14.53	16.16	13.96	Y	Commodities Broad Basket (Natl Res)
UBS ETRACS CMCI Agriculture Total Return ETN	UAG	NYSE Arca	D	D	D		15.20	16.74	14.26	Y	Commodities Specified (Natl Res)
UBS ETRACS CMCI Food Total Return ETN	FUD	NYSE Arca	D	D	D		15.71	17.40	14.59	Y	Commodities Specified (Natl Res)
UBS ETRACS CMCI Gold Total Return ETN	UBG	NYSE Arca	C-	C	D	Up	37.12	39.20	30.08	Y	Commodities Specified (Prec Metals)
UBS ETRACS CMCI Silver Total Return ETN	USV	NYSE Arca	D+	C-	D	Up	21.35	24.56	17.25	Y	Commodities Specified (Prec Metals)
● UBS ETRACS CMCI Total Return ETN	UCI	NYSE Arca	D+	D+	C-	Down	14.05	15.85	13.50	Y	Commodities Broad Basket (Natl Res)
● UBS ETRACS - Wells Fargo Business Dev Company Ind ETN	BDCS	NYSE Arca	C	C	C-		20.16	20.67	17.15	Y	Financials Sector Equity (Growth)
● UBS ETRACS Monthly Pay 2xLeveraged Closed-End Fund ETN	CEFL	NYSE Arca	C+	C+	C+		14.12	15.90	11.05	Y	Trading Tools (Growth & Inc)
UBS ETRACS Monthly Pay 2xLeveraged Div High Income ETN	DVHL	NYSE Arca	C	C	C-		17.59	19.72	14.60	Y	Trading Tools (Income)
UBS ETRACS Month Pay 2xLeveraged Dow Jones Select Div Ind	DVYL	NYSE Arca	C	C	D+		71.35	74.27	51.35	Y	Trading Tools (Equity-Income)
● UBS ETRACS Monthly Pay 2xLeveraged Mortgage REIT ETN	MORL	NYSE Arca	C	C	C+		13.80	15.70	11.70	Y	Trading Tools (Real Estate)
● UBS ETRACS Monthly Pay 2xLeveraged Mortg REIT ETN Ser B	MRRL	NYSE Arca	C	C	C+		13.13	15.46	11.53	Y	Trading Tools (Real Estate)
UBS ETRACS Monthly Pay 2xLeveraged MSCI US REIT Index ETN	LRET	NYSE Arca	C	C	D+		29.70	29.74	18.85	Y	Trading Tools (Real Estate)
UBS ETRACS Monthly Pay 2xLeveraged S&P Dividend ETN	SDYL	NYSE Arca	C	C	D+		92.80	93.71	64.58	Y	Trading Tools (Equity-Income)
UBS ETRACS Monthly Pay 2xLeveraged US High Div Low Vol ETN	HDLV	NYSE Arca	C	C	D+		28.05	28.85	20.61	Y	Trading Tools (Growth & Inc)
UBS ETRACS Month Pay 2xLeveraged US Small Cap High Div ETN	SMHD	NYSE Arca	D	D	D		11.94	17.89	10.19	Y	Trading Tools (Growth)
UBS ETRACS Month Pay 2xLeveraged Wells Fargo MLP Ex-Energy	LMLP	NYSE Arca	C	B	D+		17.38	17.93	9.55	Y	Trading Tools (Income)
UBS ETRACS Month Reset 2xLeveraged ISE Exclusively Homebui	HOML	NYSE Arca	C	C+	D+	Up	58.43	58.43	20.45	Y	Trading Tools (Real Estate)
UBS ETRACS NYSE® Pickens Core Midstream™ Index ETN	PYPE	NYSE Arca	D	D	E		21.61	24.37	18.69	Y	Energy Sector Equity (Growth)
UBS ETRACS S&P GSCI Crude Oil Total Return Index ETN	OILX	NYSE Arca	D+	D+	D+	Up	32.41	45.07	26.60	Y	Commodities Specified (Growth & Inc)
UBS ETRACS UBS Bloomberg Const Matur Commod Ind (CMCI) Tot	UCIB	NYSE Arca	D	D+	E		14.04	15.23	13.54	Y	Commodities Broad Basket (Growth & Inc)
UBS ETRACS Wells Fargo® Business Dev Company Ind ETN	BDCZ	NYSE Arca	C	C	D+		20.14	20.86	16.97	Y	Financials Sector Equity (Growth & Inc)
United States 12 Month Natural Gas Fund, LP	UNL	NYSE Arca	D	D	D		8.84	11.67	8.45	Y	Commodities Specified (Natl Res)
● United States 12 Month Oil Fund, LP	USL	NYSE Arca	C-	C-	C-		20.18	28.28	17.20	Y	Commodities Specified (Natl Res)
United States 3x Oil Fund	USOU	NYSE Arca	D	D	D+		18.93	91.11	15.10	Y	Trading Tools (Growth & Inc)
United States 3x Short Oil Fund	USOD	NYSE Arca	D	D	D		8.50	15.27	3.07	Y	Trading Tools (Growth & Inc)
● United States Brent Oil Fund, LP	BNO	NYSE Arca	C-	C-	C-		18.15	24.21	14.70	Y	Commodities Specified (Natl Res)
● United States Commodity Index Fund, LP	USCI	NYSE Arca	D	D	D		35.83	43.11	34.69	Y	Commodities Broad Basket (Natl Res)
United States Copper Index Fund, LP	CPER	NYSE Arca	D	D	D+	Down	16.13	18.57	15.85	Y	Commodities Specified (Prec Metals)
United States Gasoline Fund, LP	UGA	NYSE Arca	D+	C-	D+	Down	29.18	36.91	22.18	Y	Commodities Specified (Natl Res)
● United States Natural Gas Fund, LP	UNG	NYSE Arca	D-	D-	D	Down	19.93	39.32	18.10	Y	Commodities Specified (Natl Res)

★ Expanded analysis of this fund is included in Section II: Analysis of All BUY Rated Funds. ● Expanded analysis of this fund is included in Section III: Analysis of All Rated Funds with Assets over $50 million.

3-Month Total Return	6-Month Total Return	1-Year Total Return	3-Year Total Return	5-Year Total Return	Dividend Yield (TTM)	Expense Ratio	3-Yr Std Deviation	Effective Duration	NAV	Total Assets (MIL)	%Cash	%Stocks	%Bonds	%Other	Turnover Ratio	Premium/ Discount 1-Year Avg	Inception Date
0.76	9.70					0.4			30.66	6.1	0	100	0	0		1.33	Jan-19
2.56	9.25	12.16			1.7	0.4			31.11	7.8	0	100	0	0	36	0.30	Feb-17
-1.18	-0.61	3.16	11.57		4.17	0.4	14.42		23.37	343.6	0	100	0	0	16	0.03	Jun-15
-2.24	3.31	-2.48			0.79	0.59			25.84	12.3	0	100	0	0	43	0.21	Jun-17
-1.17	3.39	-1.72	49.01		0.52	0.59	13.44		37.14	122.6	1	99	0	0	49	-0.01	Sep-16
11.22	21.16	46.77			0.35	0.6			15.36	33.0	0	100	0	0	130	-0.03	Jun-17
-3.61	-0.45	-7.40	31.22		0.51	0.6	21.94		29.38	49.9	0	100	0	0	33	-0.04	Apr-15
-4.19	3.51	-0.02	33.57		0	0.95	24.96		161.09	24.2						-0.24	Feb-16
0.72	5.75	5.48	44.93		0	0.8	20.02		183.11	1,628						-0.06	Feb-16
0.16	7.97	-7.80	102.99	174.80	0	0.85	28.06		277.12	1,200						-0.05	Jun-14
-11.05	-10.79	13.71			0	1.85			6.12	4.3						0.30	Jan-17
-33.65	-46.55	-78.05			0	1.45			9.88	10.9						-0.34	Jan-17
5.77	10.68	7.74	27.32		15.51	0.85	26.23		14.68	5.9						0.04	Oct-15
5.77	10.68	7.74	27.32	40.95	15.51	0.85	26.23		14.68	191.1						0.06	May-11
-11.40	-13.60	-22.61	-30.11		17.83	0.85	33.17		24.57	69.3						0.20	Feb-16
-9.47	-13.41	-23.76	-24.64		17.64	0.95	33.32		28.77	24.7						0.25	Feb-16
-5.22	-6.20	-10.71	-8.98	-37.64	7.75	0.8	16.9		14.66	319.5						-0.05	Jul-12
-5.22	-6.20	-5.89	-8.98		7.75	0.8	16.9		14.66	5.9						1.11	Oct-15
-5.43	-6.26	-9.32	-10.26	-36.18	7.53	0.85	16.82		20.85	1,114						-0.06	Apr-10
-5.43	-6.26	-9.32	-10.26		7.53	0.85	16.82		20.85	8.3						1.59	Oct-15
-6.68	-9.74	-11.48	-0.37	-31.90	7.91	0.85	17.35		20.45	5.1						0.09	Jul-10
-1.30	-4.23	-8.84	-6.25	-33.86	0	0.5	8.46		14.51	50.6					0	-0.02	Oct-09
-5.09	-4.05	-4.65	-25.64	-26.54	0	0.65	12.29		15.21	2.0					0	-0.14	Apr-08
-4.05	-3.78	-3.73	-20.65	-27.07	0	0.65	11.07		15.69	3.1					0	0.06	Apr-08
5.85	13.84	23.44	9.10	16.89	0	0.3	11.33		36.93	4.6					0	0.13	Apr-08
12.34	12.14	16.64	-16.24	-8.98	0	0.4	18.02		21.17	2.1					0	0.10	Apr-08
-3.10	-6.37	-9.57	4.17	-26.24	0	0.55	10.16		14.06	66.5					0	-0.18	Apr-08
3.06	5.82	6.34	17.80	26.30	8.53	0.85	13.21		20.13	87.6						-0.02	Apr-11
-0.01	5.63	5.44	29.01	31.76	17.1	0.5	18.94		14.21	237.7						-0.09	Dec-13
0.04	1.45	1.33	17.53	31.22	14.31	0.85	16.6		17.56	20.5						0.02	Nov-13
4.60	5.50	4.72	57.21	141.07	7.58	0.35	21.98		71.33	36.7						-0.05	May-12
2.38	-0.46	3.90	52.02	84.68	21.9	0.4	25.6		13.08	395.7						4.80	Oct-12
2.38	-0.46	3.90	52.02		21.9	0.4	25.51		13.08	189.7						0.02	Oct-15
14.49	15.24	32.67	29.66		7.04	0.85	25.71		29.67	4.2						0.00	May-15
2.63	4.54	9.21	65.68	159.17	5.36	0.3	22.38		92.53	16.2						-0.21	May-12
4.05	3.32	19.57	19.48	77.28	10.36	0.85	22.13		28.03	18.6						-0.05	Sep-14
4.99	-12.14	-24.14	0.20		22.71	0.85	32.99		11.34	40.7						9.71	Feb-15
9.39	25.21	15.48	131.76	54.47	12.11	0.85	34.92		17.34	26.5						-0.07	Jun-14
43.20	67.67	69.70	150.00		0	0.85	45.19		58.38	2.9						-0.82	Mar-15
-5.20	-7.82	-9.93			1.91	0.85			21.57	21.6						0.11	Aug-18
-8.04	-11.95	-29.03	2.79		0		27.95		32.28	3.2						0.18	Feb-16
-3.10	-6.37	-9.57	4.17		0	0.55	10.16		14.06	5.6						0.44	Oct-15
3.06	5.82	6.34	17.90		8.53	0.85	13.21		20.13	8.1						-0.27	Oct-15
-1.67	-16.26	-7.76	-12.79	-50.00	0	0.9	19.1		8.84	4.0	35	0	17	47		0.17	Nov-09
-8.50	-12.17	-27.85	7.50	-51.45	0	0.82	24.85		20.16	51.4	34	0	17	48	50	-0.21	Dec-07
-34.39	-47.19	-78.66			0	1.51			18.64	15.8	27	0	0	73		-0.21	Jul-17
-10.75	-11.31	12.99			0	1.65			8.66	7.1						0.28	Jul-17
-5.89	-7.79	-24.32	24.05	-51.76	0	0.9	25.74		18.09	76.9	33	0	18	49		-0.21	Jun-10
-2.43	-8.29	-16.43	-13.66	-34.81	0	1.03	8.57		35.83	249.0	39	0	11	49		-0.14	Aug-10
-3.93	-11.63	-7.59	11.16	-21.20	0	0.8	19.06		16.16	7.3	39	0	12	49		-0.09	Nov-11
-7.91	-2.10	-20.95	4.98	-46.76	0	0.75	29.29		29.11	30.6	34	0	17	48	0	-0.10	Feb-08
2.32	-16.32	-22.06	-40.14	-76.90	0	1.28	38.7		19.93	256.8	28	0	24	48		0.31	Apr-07

Fund Name	Ticker Symbol	Traded On	Overall Rating	Reward Rating	Risk Rating	Recent Up/ Downgrade	Price as of 9/30/2019	52-Week High	52-Week Low	Open to New Investors	Category & (Prospectus Objective)
● United States Oil Fund, LP	USO	NYSE Arca	D+	D+	D+	Down	11.34	16.08	9.29	Y	Commodities Specified (Natl Res)
USCF SummerHaven Dynamic Commodity Strategy No K-1 Fund	SDCI	NYSE Arca	D	D	D		17.82	21.67	17.33	Y	Commodities Broad Basket (Growth & Inc)
USCF SummerHaven SHPEI Index Fund	BUY	NYSE Arca	D	D	D		19.29	27.41	17.28	Y	US Equity Large Cap Blend (Growth & Inc)
USCF SummerHaven SHPEN Index Fund	BUYN	NYSE Arca	D-	D	E+		14.67	28.07	13.05	Y	Natural Resources (Growth & Inc)
★ Utilities Select Sector SPDR® Fund	XLU	NYSE Arca	B	B	B-		64.74	64.93	51.56	Y	Utilities Sector Equity (Utility)
Validea Market Legends ETF	VALX	NAS CM	D+	D+	D+		24.85	29.41	22.87	Y	US Equity Small Cap (Growth & Inc)
● VanEck Merk Gold Trust	OUNZ	NYSE Arca	C	C+	C-	Up	14.42	15.23	11.66	Y	Commodities Specified (Prec Metals)
● VanEck Vectors Africa Index ETF	AFK	NYSE Arca	D	D	D+	Down	19.95	22.55	19.22	Y	Equity Misc (Growth)
● VanEck Vectors Agribusiness ETF	MOO	NYSE Arca	C+	B-	C-	Up	65.86	67.52	54.16	Y	Natural Resources (Unaligned)
★ VanEck Vectors AMT-Free Intermediate Municipal Index ETF	ITM	BATS	B	B	C+		50.31	51.11	45.90	Y	US Muni Fixed Inc (Muni Bond - Natl)
● VanEck Vectors AMT-Free Long Municipal Index ETF	MLN	BATS	C	B-	C-		21.15	21.46	18.91	Y	US Muni Fixed Inc (Muni Bond - Natl)
● VanEck Vectors AMT-Free Short Municipal Index ETF	SMB	BATS	C	C	C-		17.70	17.88	17.09	Y	US Muni Fixed Inc (Muni Bond - Natl)
★ VanEck Vectors BDC Income ETF	BIZD	NYSE Arca	B-	B	C	Up	16.86	16.99	14.04	Y	Financials Sector Equity (Income)
● VanEck Vectors Biotech ETF	BBH	NAS CM	C	C	D+		117.98	135.09	103.76	Y	Healthcare Sector Equity (Unaligned)
● VanEck Vectors Brazil Small-Cap ETF	BRF	NYSE Arca	C+	B	C-	Up	23.19	25.57	16.67	Y	Latin America Equity (Growth)
● VanEck Vectors CEF Municipal Income ETF	XMPT	BATS	C	C+	C-		27.60	27.96	23.37	Y	US Muni Fixed Inc (Muni Bond - Natl)
VanEck Vectors ChinaAMC China Bond ETF	CBON	NYSE Arca	C-	C-	D+	Up	21.81	23.21	21.64	Y	Emerging Mkts Fixed Inc (Govt Bond - Gen)
● VanEck Vectors ChinaAMC CSI 300 ETF	PEK	NYSE Arca	C-	C-	D+		38.53	43.99	31.34	Y	Greater China Equity (Pacific Stock)
VanEck Vectors ChinaAMC SME-ChiNext ETF	CNXT	NYSE Arca	D	D	D		26.22	30.80	20.35	Y	Greater China Equity (Pacific Stock)
VanEck Vectors Coal ETF	KOL	NYSE Arca	D	D	D	Down	10.87	15.65	10.57	Y	Equity Misc (Natl Res)
VanEck Vectors Egypt Index ETF	EGPT	NYSE Arca	D+	D+	D+		30.94	33.72	26.91	Y	Equity Misc (Growth)
VanEck Vectors Emerging Markets Aggregate Bond ETF	EMAG	NYSE Arca	C	B-	D+		21.52	21.76	19.81	Y	Emerging Mkts Fixed Inc (Income)
● VanEck Vectors Emerging Markets High Yield Bond ETF	HYEM	NYSE Arca	C	C	C-	Down	23.18	23.93	22.23	Y	Emerging Mkts Fixed Inc (Corp Bond-High Yld)
★ VanEck Vectors Environmental Services ETF	EVX	NYSE Arca	B-	B	C	Up	104.43	105.32	78.68	Y	Industrials Sector Equity (Unaligned)
● VanEck Vectors Fallen Angel High Yield Bond ETF	ANGL	NYSE Arca	C+	C+	C+	Down	29.32	29.57	26.29	Y	US Fixed Income (Corp Bond-High Yld)
VanEck Vectors Gaming ETF	BJK	NYSE Arca	C-	C-	D+	Up	36.44	39.96	31.53	Y	Consumer Goods & Svcs (Unaligned)
● VanEck Vectors Gold Miners ETF	GDX	NYSE Arca	C	C	C-	Up	26.71	30.95	18.39	Y	Prec Metals (Prec Metals)
VanEck Vectors Green Bond ETF	GRNB	NYSE Arca	C-	C	D+		26.67	27.08	25.14	Y	Global Fixed Income (Growth & Inc)
VanEck Vectors High Income Infrastructure MLP ETF	YMLI	NYSE Arca	C	B-	D	Up	10.82	13.67	10.16	Y	Energy Sector Equity (Utility)
VanEck Vectors High Income MLP ETF	YMLP	NYSE Arca	C	C+	D+	Up	18.44	22.20	16.27	Y	Energy Sector Equity (Natl Res)
★ VanEck Vectors High-Yield Municipal Index ETF	HYD	BATS	B	B	C+		64.43	64.90	60.28	Y	US Muni Fixed Inc (Muni Bond - Natl)
● VanEck Vectors India Small-Cap Index ETF	SCIF	NYSE Arca	D-	D-	D	Down	32.60	44.62	29.73	Y	India Equity (Small Company)
VanEck Vectors Indonesia Index ETF	IDX	NYSE Arca	C-	C	C-		21.70	24.12	18.81	Y	Equity Misc (Growth)
● VanEck Vectors International High Yield Bond ETF	IHY	NYSE Arca	C	C+	C-		24.46	24.93	23.30	Y	Global Fixed Income (Corp Bond-High Yld)
● VanEck Vectors Investment Grade Floating Rate ETF	FLTR	NYSE Arca	C	C	C+		25.24	25.28	24.68	Y	US Fixed Income (Income)
● VanEck Vectors Israel ETF	ISRA	NYSE Arca	C	C	D+		32.89	33.90	26.75	Y	Equity Misc (Growth)
★ VanEck Vectors J.P. Morgan EM Local Currency Bond ETF	EMLC	NYSE Arca	B-	B	C+		33.00	35.17	32.12	Y	Emerging Mkts Fixed Inc (Div Emerg Mkts)
● VanEck Vectors Junior Gold Miners ETF	GDXJ	NYSE Arca	C	C	C-	Up	36.26	42.74	26.17	Y	Prec Metals (Prec Metals)
● VanEck Vectors Low Carbon Energy ETF	SMOG	NYSE Arca	C	C+	C-		64.01	67.90	51.82	Y	Equity Misc (Natl Res)
VanEck Vectors Morningstar Durable Dividend ETF	DURA	NYSE Arca	U	U	U		28.25	28.67	23.91	Y	US Equity Large Cap Value (Growth & Inc)
VanEck Vectors Morningstar Global Wide Moat ETF	GOAT	NYSE Arca	U	U	U		29.03	29.19	24.22	Y	Global Equity Large Cap (World Stock)
● VanEck Vectors Morningstar International Moat ETF	MOTI	NYSE Arca	D+	D+	D+	Down	30.50	33.10	27.71	Y	Global Equity Large Cap (Foreign Stock)
● VanEck Vectors Morningstar Wide Moat ETF	MOAT	NYSE Arca	C+	C+	C		50.15	50.75	38.89	Y	US Equity Large Cap Blend (Growth)
● VanEck Vectors Mortgage REIT Income ETF	MORT	NYSE Arca	C	C+	C		23.28	23.77	21.00	Y	Real Estate Sector Equity (Real Estate)
VanEck Vectors Municipal Allocation ETF	MAAX	BATS	U	U	U		25.63	25.91	25.05	Y	US Muni Fixed Inc (Muni Bond - Natl)
● VanEck Vectors Natural Resources ETF	HAP	NYSE Arca	C	C	D+	Up	35.20	38.05	30.80	Y	Natural Resources (Natl Res)
VanEck Vectors Oil Refiners ETF	CRAK	NYSE Arca	C-	C-	D+		28.26	36.07	25.27	Y	Energy Sector Equity (Unaligned)
● VanEck Vectors Oil Services ETF	OIH	NYSE Arca	D+	C-	D	Up	11.75	26.02	10.89	Y	Energy Sector Equity (Natl Res)
● VanEck Vectors Pharmaceutical ETF	PPH	NAS CM	C	C+	C-	Up	56.99	64.52	52.66	Y	Healthcare Sector Equity (Health)
● VanEck Vectors Preferred Securities ex Financials ETF	PFXF	NYSE Arca	C+	C+	C+		20.30	20.30	17.35	Y	US Fixed Income (Income)
● VanEck Vectors Rare Earth/Strategic Metals ETF	REMX	NYSE Arca	D	D	D		12.63	20.28	11.95	Y	Prec Metals (Natl Res)
VanEck Vectors Real Asset Allocation ETF	RAAX	NYSE Arca	D+	D+	D+		25.28	26.13	24.12	Y	Moderate Allocation (Growth & Inc)

★ Expanded analysis of this fund is included in Section II: Analysis of All BUY Rated Funds. ● Expanded analysis of this fund is included in Section III: Analysis of All Rated Funds with Assets over $50 million.

			TOTAL RETURNS & PERFORMANCE						ASSETS		ASSET ALLOCATION & TURNOVER					VALUATION	
3-Month Total Return	6-Month Total Return	1-Year Total Return	3-Year Total Return	5-Year Total Return	Dividend Yield (TTM)	Expense Ratio	3-Yr Std Deviation	Effective Duration	NAV	Total Assets (MIL)	%Cash	%Stocks	%Bonds	%Other	Turnover Ratio	Premium/ Discount 1-Year Avg	Inception Date
-8.01	-11.89	-29.07	2.49	-66.96	0	0.73	27.9		11.28	1,427	27	0	22	52	0	-0.09	Apr-06
-2.32	-8.04	-15.92			1.08	0.6			17.87	5.4	70	0	12	18		-0.05	May-18
-2.59	-5.21	-17.87			0.59	0.8			19.26	27.9	1	99	0	0		0.00	Dec-17
-18.10	-24.17	-35.02			0.3	0.8			14.64	0.73	0	100	0	0		-0.14	Dec-17
9.52	13.71	27.07	45.74	81.83	2.88	0.13	10.65			11,403	0	100	0	0	5	-0.01	Dec-98
-4.73	-7.74	-13.17	5.18		1.51	0.79	17.53		25.00	20.0	1	99	0	0	122	0.01	Dec-14
6.75	14.66	24.41	10.99	19.70	0	0.4	11.15		14.54	171.5	0	0	0	100		-0.15	May-14
-8.86	-7.90	-4.99	3.84	-27.54	1.66	0.78	14.73		20.26	52.7	0	100	0	0	23	-0.82	Jul-08
-1.81	4.55	1.84	39.01	41.41	1.46	0.54	11.78		65.87	691.7	0	100	0	0	16	-0.14	Aug-07
1.65	4.43	10.15	119.13	140.24	2.22	0.24	4.54	6.19	50.39	1,892	1	0	99	0	7	-0.11	Dec-07
2.44	5.82	11.68	11.32	26.15	2.82	0.24	5.36	8.01	21.14	192.4	0	0	100	0	22	-0.08	Jan-08
0.43	1.75	4.59	4.92	7.20	1.57	0.2	1.93	3.02	17.73	197.7	0	0	100	0	33	-0.11	Feb-08
3.56	7.01	8.86	24.16	34.98	9.45	9.62	13.31		16.83	221.3	1	98	0	2	13	-0.08	Feb-13
-9.17	-8.72	-12.29	3.81	15.02	0.47	0.35	20.38		118.04	318.3	0	100	0	0	30	-0.07	Dec-11
-2.18	6.78	43.52	54.14	11.75	2.48	0.6	27.47		23.30	82.7	0	100	0	0	45	-0.17	May-09
3.75	8.04	17.07	10.68	37.19	4.16	1.86	8.03	7.94	27.60	160.1	-5	0	107	-1	13	0.00	Jul-11
-2.98	-4.13	1.05	0.74		3.65	0.5	5.7	2.49	21.80	4.4	0	0	100	0	22	-0.16	Nov-14
-6.27	-8.97	7.83	11.73	37.59	0.75	0.6	19.38		38.86	62.2	0	100	0	0	34	-0.07	Oct-10
-1.52	-13.06	4.92	-19.25	-9.53	0	0.65	22.81		26.41	27.7	0	100	0	0	36	-0.02	Jul-14
-18.36	-20.73	-25.87	4.12	-23.06	7.54	0.6	21.47		10.93	37.7	0	100	0	0	24	-0.36	Jan-08
-1.08	-5.55	2.74	-14.76	-53.40	1.53	0.98	27.63		31.09	33.4	0	100	0	0	41	-0.48	Feb-10
0.72	4.93	10.00	12.24	14.69	4.72	0.35	5.4	5.65	21.44	15.0	1	0	99	0	25	-0.01	May-11
-0.98	2.35	7.27	12.46	24.60	6.16	0.4	5.01	3.52	23.17	305.8	1	0	99	0	27	0.25	May-12
1.34	7.28	9.05	52.67	71.96	0.31	0.56	13.58		104.25	36.5	0	100	0	0	24	0.10	Oct-06
1.34	4.46	6.37	19.62	41.06	5.44	0.35	4.92	5.75	29.23	1,166	0	1	97	0	29	-0.05	Apr-12
-3.73	-3.37	-5.13	10.62	2.36	3.09	0.66	19.01		36.61	23.8	0	100	0	0	31	-0.12	Jan-08
7.96	21.71	45.52	3.30	29.34	0.39	0.53	24.92		26.84	11,268	0	100	0	0	15	-0.10	May-06
-0.12	3.65	4.91			1.31	0.2		4.57	26.61	26.6	0	0	99	0	28	0.03	Mar-17
-6.40	-9.21	-13.64	-9.93	-30.23	8.6	0.83	16.98		10.84	13.6	0	100	0	0	52	0.29	Feb-13
-3.91	-3.43	-8.78	-7.02	-64.57	9.45	0.84	16.24		18.50	36.4	0	100	0	0	34	-0.13	Mar-12
2.18	4.91	7.68	127.72	161.80	4.17	0.35	4.75	6.22	64.43	3,054	1	0	99	0	22	-0.06	Feb-09
-15.68	-27.08	-17.95	-28.97	-22.51	0.15	0.83	26.33		32.36	125.4	1	49	0	49	39	-0.09	Aug-10
-6.71	-4.21	6.90	-1.90	-4.00	2.18	0.57	16.04		21.81	39.3	0	100	0	0	14	-0.21	Jan-09
-0.38	2.44	5.23	14.00	18.61	4.83	0.4	4.81	3.32	24.51	102.9	0	0	99	0	32	-0.26	Apr-12
0.87	1.98	3.01	8.65	9.79	3.15	0.14	1.08	0.05	25.26	477.4	0	0	98	0	30	-0.06	Apr-11
1.01	3.13	0.05	22.29	15.51	0.63	0.6	14.2		32.85	54.2	0	100	0	0	23	0.06	Jun-13
-2.80	1.85	7.90	108.53	94.33	6.44	0.3	10.08	5.23	33.27	4,798	1	0	99	0	36	-0.18	Jul-10
8.35	18.03	34.31	-12.32	15.73	0.37	0.54	27.31		36.59	4,180	0	100	0	0	28	-0.30	Nov-09
-3.31	0.50	9.77	24.20	15.41	0.53	0.63	16.61		63.95	88.5	0	100	0	0	31	-0.19	May-07
0.93	4.74					0.29			28.24	18.4	1	99	0	0		0.03	Oct-18
1.44	5.41					0.52			28.97	5.8	1	99	0	0		0.19	Oct-18
-2.05	-3.38	-4.21	20.17		3.46	0.57	13.1		30.57	82.6	0	100	0	0	112	-0.01	Jul-15
3.51	6.27	9.22	53.44	75.22	1.47	0.49	13.86		50.13	2,486	0	100	0	0	56	0.00	Apr-12
2.19	1.51	5.22	30.92	47.36	7.22	0.42	12.95		23.31	197.0	0	100	0	0	35	-0.02	Aug-11
2.10						0.36		6.49	25.62	2.6	1	0	99	0		0.01	May-19
-4.18	-2.51	-4.22	18.93	8.76	2.6	0.5	13.04		35.25	65.2	0	100	0	0	23	-0.14	Aug-08
1.18	-3.45	-18.82	52.21		1.82	0.6	17.63		28.22	15.5	0	100	0	0	31	-0.20	Aug-15
-21.02	-33.78	-52.83	-57.17	-72.74	2.54	0.35	35.88		11.76	597.9	0	100	0	0	22	0.00	Dec-11
-3.21	-5.49	-9.78	4.86	-0.38	1.95	0.36	15.33		56.93	141.7	0	100	0	0	18	-0.02	Dec-11
4.10	6.47	11.22	17.07	32.79	5.32	0.41	6.5		20.25	706.6	0	8	0	3	31	0.14	Jul-12
-16.78	-21.18	-29.83	-6.77	-45.45	13.28	0.59	28.02		12.69	178.6	0	100	0	0	68	-0.18	Oct-10
-0.66	-0.19	-0.22			0.55	0.64			25.25	30.3	42	30	3	25		0.10	Apr-18

Fund Name	Ticker Symbol	Traded On	Overall Rating	Reward Rating	Risk Rating	Recent Up/ Downgrade	Price as of 9/30/2019	52-Week High	52-Week Low	Open to New Investors	Category & (Prospectus Objective)
★ VanEck Vectors Retail ETF	RTH	NYSE Arca	B-	B+	C	Up	114.47	116.89	87.33	Y	Consumer Goods & Svcs (Unaligned)
★ VanEck Vectors Russia ETF	RSX	NYSE Arca	B	B	B-		22.81	24.12	18.44	Y	Equity Misc (Growth)
VanEck Vectors Russia Small-Cap ETF	RSXJ	NYSE Arca	C	C+	D+	Up	34.05	35.27	26.88	Y	Equity Misc (Growth)
★ VanEck Vectors Semiconductor ETF	SMH	NYSE Arca	B-	B	C	Up	119.13	123.31	80.96	Y	Technology Sector Equity (Technology)
● VanEck Vectors Short High-Yield Municipal Index ETF	SHYD	BATS	C	C+	C-		25.18	25.37	23.89	Y	US Muni Fixed Inc (Muni Bond - Natl)
● VanEck Vectors Steel ETF	SLX	NYSE Arca	C	B-	D+	Up	33.90	46.56	30.97	Y	Natural Resources (Unaligned)
VanEck Vectors Unconventional Oil & Gas ETF	FRAK	NYSE Arca	C-	C	D	Up	10.41	17.62	9.60	Y	Energy Sector Equity (Natl Res)
VanEck Vectors Uranium+Nuclear Energy ETF	NLR	NYSE Arca	C-	C	D+	Down	49.84	53.81	47.98	Y	Utilities Sector Equity (Natl Res)
● VanEck Vectors Vietnam ETF	VNM	NYSE Arca	C-	C-	C	Down	16.31	17.18	14.48	Y	Asia ex-Japan Equity (Growth)
● VanEck Vectors® NDR CMG Long/Flat Allocation ETF	LFEQ	NYSE Arca	C-	C-	C-		28.03	28.40	23.52	Y	US Equity Large Cap Blend (Growth & Inc)
VanEck Vectors® Video Gaming and eSports ETF	ESPO	NYSE Arca	U	U	U		33.79	34.94	26.21	Y	Technology Sector Equity (Technology)
★ Vanguard Communication Services Index Fund ETF Shares	VOX	NYSE Arca	B-	B	C	Up	86.70	91.54	69.56	Y	Communications Sector Equity (Comm)
● Vanguard Consumer Discretionary Index Fund ETF Shares	VCR	NYSE Arca	C	B-	C-		180.12	186.75	139.59	Y	Consumer Goods & Svcs (Unaligned)
★ Vanguard Consumer Staples Index Fund ETF Shares	VDC	NYSE Arca	B-	B	C	Up	156.56	157.18	125.78	Y	Consumer Goods & Svcs (Unaligned)
★ Vanguard Dividend Appreciation Index Fund ETF Shares	VIG	NYSE Arca	B-	B	C+		119.58	120.84	92.08	Y	US Equity Large Cap Blend (Equity-Income)
★ Vanguard Emerg Mkts Govt Bond Ind Fund ETF Shares	VWOB	NAS CM	B-	B	C+		80.60	81.56	73.40	Y	Emerging Mkts Fixed Inc (Govt Bond - Gen)
● Vanguard Energy Index Fund ETF Shares	VDE	NYSE Arca	D+	D+	D		78.02	107.80	72.37	Y	Energy Sector Equity (Natl Res)
● Vanguard ESG International Stock ETF	VSGX	BATS	D+	D+	C-		49.28	50.77	43.28	Y	Global Equity Large Cap (Foreign Stock)
● Vanguard ESG U.S. Stock ETF	ESGV	BATS	C-	D+	C-		51.91	53.06	40.33	Y	US Equity Large Cap Blend (Growth & Inc)
● Vanguard Extended Duration Treasury Index Fund ETF Shares	EDV	NYSE Arca	C	C	C+		141.30	148.21	101.75	Y	US Fixed Income (Govt Bond - Treasury)
● Vanguard Extended Market Index Fund ETF Shares	VXF	NYSE Arca	C	C	C+		116.33	121.78	93.42	Y	US Equity Mid Cap (Growth)
● Vanguard FTSE All-World ex-US Index Fund ETF Shares	VEU	NYSE Arca	C	C	B		49.90	52.19	44.23	Y	Global Equity Large Cap (Foreign Stock)
● Vanguard FTSE All-World ex-US Small-Cap Ind Fund ETF Shares	VSS	NYSE Arca	C	D+	C+		101.95	112.28	91.12	Y	Globa Eq Mid/Small Cap (Foreign Stock)
● Vanguard FTSE Developed Markets Index Fund ETF Shares	VEA	NYSE Arca	C	C	B		41.08	43.38	35.84	Y	Global Equity Large Cap (Foreign Stock)
● Vanguard FTSE Emerging Markets Index Fund ETF Shares	VWO	NYSE Arca	C	C	C+		40.26	44.01	36.68	Y	Global Emerg Mkts Equity (Div Emerg Mkts)
● Vanguard FTSE Europe Index Fund ETF Shares	VGK	NYSE Arca	C	C	B-		53.61	56.26	46.99	Y	Europe Equity Large Cap (Europe Stock)
● Vanguard FTSE Pacific Index Fund ETF Shares	VPL	NYSE Arca	C	C-	C+		66.05	71.30	58.71	Y	Asia Equity (Pacific Stock)
● Vanguard Global ex-U.S. Real Estate Index Fund ETF Shares	VNQI	NAS CM	C	C	C+		58.59	60.15	51.24	Y	Real Estate Sector Equity (Real Estate)
★ Vanguard Growth Index Fund ETF Shares	VUG	NYSE Arca	B-	B-	C+	Up	166.28	170.26	124.85	Y	US Equity Large Cap Growth (Growth)
● Vanguard Health Care Index Fund ETF Shares	VHT	NYSE Arca	C+	C+	C+		167.68	180.89	149.65	Y	Healthcare Sector Equity (Health)
● Vanguard High Dividend Yield Index Fund ETF Shares	VYM	NYSE Arca	C+	C	C+		88.73	89.75	73.71	Y	US Equity Large Cap Value (Equity-Income)
● Vanguard Industrials Index Fund ETF Shares	VIS	NYSE Arca	C+	C+	C+	Up	146.07	149.32	112.87	Y	Industrials Sector Equity (Unaligned)
★ Vanguard Information Technology Index Fund ETF Shares	VGT	NYSE Arca	B-	B	C+	Down	215.55	223.32	154.81	Y	Technology Sector Equity (Unaligned)
● Vanguard Intermediate-Term Bond Index Fund ETF Shares	BIV	NYSE Arca	C+	C+	C+	Up	88.00	88.95	79.35	Y	US Fixed Income (Income)
● Vanguard Intermediate-Term Corp Bond Ind Fund ETF Shares	VCIT	NAS CM	C+	B-	C+		91.24	92.09	82.02	Y	US Fixed Income (Corp Bond - Gen)
● Vanguard Intermediate-Term Treasury Index Fund ETF Shares	VGIT	NAS CM	C	C	C+		66.67	67.41	61.57	Y	US Fixed Income (Govt Bond - Gen)
● Vanguard Intl Dividend Appreciation Ind Fund ETF Shares	VIGI	NAS CM	C	C	C-		66.57	68.88	55.63	Y	Global Equity Large Cap (Foreign Stock)
● Vanguard Intl High Dividend Yield Ind Fund ETF Shares	VYMI	NAS CM	C	C	C+	Up	59.39	63.23	54.56	Y	Global Equity Large Cap (Foreign Stock)
● Vanguard Large-Cap Index Fund ETF Shares	VV	NYSE Arca	C+	C+	C+		136.33	138.83	107.63	Y	US Equity Large Cap Blend (Growth)
● Vanguard Long-Term Bond Index Fund ETF Shares	BLV	NYSE Arca	C+	C+	C+		102.67	105.49	83.53	Y	US Fixed Income (Income)
★ Vanguard Long-Term Corporate Bond Index Fund ETF Shares	VCLT	NAS CM	B-	B	C+		101.14	103.47	83.50	Y	US Fixed Income (Corp Bond - Gen)
● Vanguard Long-Term Treasury Index Fund ETF Shares	VGLT	NAS CM	C	C	C+		87.74	90.55	69.06	Y	US Fixed Income (Govt Bond - Gen)
● Vanguard Materials Index Fund ETF Shares	VAW	NYSE Arca	C	C	C	Up	126.38	132.39	104.05	Y	Natural Resources (Unaligned)
★ Vanguard Mega Cap Growth Index Fund ETF Shares	MGK	NYSE Arca	B-	B	C+	Up	132.66	135.16	99.52	Y	US Equity Large Cap Growth (Growth)
● Vanguard Mega Cap Index Fund ETF Shares	MGC	NYSE Arca	C	C+	C-		103.11	104.52	81.34	Y	US Equity Large Cap Blend (Growth)
● Vanguard Mega Cap Value Index Fund ETF Shares	MGV	NYSE Arca	C+	C+	C+		81.44	82.19	67.32	Y	US Equity Large Cap Value (Growth & Inc)
● Vanguard Mid-Cap Growth Index Fund ETF Shares	VOT	NYSE Arca	C+	C+	C+		148.11	154.00	111.81	Y	US Equity Mid Cap (Growth)
● Vanguard Mid-Cap Index Fund ETF Shares	VO	NYSE Arca	C+	C	C+		167.60	171.52	129.93	Y	US Equity Mid Cap (Growth)
● Vanguard Mid-Cap Value Index Fund ETF Shares	VOE	NYSE Arca	C	C	C+		113.00	114.13	90.18	Y	US Equity Mid Cap (Growth)
● Vanguard Mortgage-Backed Securities Index Fund ETF Shares	VMBS	NAS CM	C+	C+	C+	Up	53.26	53.32	50.20	Y	US Fixed Income (Govt Bond - Mortgage)
★ Vanguard Real Estate Index Fund ETF Shares	VNQ	NYSE Arca	B-	C+	B-	Up	93.25	93.92	71.74	Y	Real Estate Sector Equity (Real Estate)
● Vanguard Russell 1000 Growth Index Fund ETF Shares	VONG	NAS CM	C	B-	C-		164.16	168.75	124.90	Y	US Equity Large Cap Growth (Growth)

★ Expanded analysis of this fund is included in Section II: Analysis of All BUY Rated Funds. ● Expanded analysis of this fund is included in Section III: Analysis of All Rated Funds with Assets over $50 million.

		TOTAL RETURNS & PERFORMANCE							ASSETS		ASSET ALLOCATION & TURNOVER					VALUATION	
3-Month Total Return	6-Month Total Return	1-Year Total Return	3-Year Total Return	5-Year Total Return	Dividend Yield (TTM)	Expense Ratio	3-Yr Std Deviation	Effective Duration	NAV	Total Assets (MIL)	%Cash	%Stocks	%Bonds	%Other	Turnover Ratio	Premium/ Discount 1-Year Avg	Inception Date
4.23	8.23	3.87	53.35	98.97	0.86	0.35	15.28		114.49	71.2	0	100	0	0	16	-0.01	Dec-11
-4.39	8.96	10.85	36.52	24.12	4.23	0.65	17.73		22.84	1,173	0	100	0	0	20	-0.24	Apr-07
-1.98	10.92	9.98	19.18	32.65	3.57	0.76	17.71		34.11	33.5	0	98	0	2	49	-0.37	Apr-11
5.11	9.35	13.83	78.97	156.51	1.37	0.35	21.52		119.14	1,361	0	100	0	0	23	0.05	Dec-11
1.37	3.47	6.68	9.44	15.62	3.19	0.35	3.16	4.33	25.14	236.3	0	0	100	0	22	0.08	Jan-14
-14.15	-17.93	-21.86	20.72	-6.55	6.43	0.56	25.15		33.91	50.9	0	100	0	0	16	-0.03	Oct-06
-13.40	-19.58	-39.81	-41.11	-62.26	0.85	0.54	27.72		10.40	18.7	0	100	0	0	17	-0.12	Feb-12
-2.34	-4.02	-1.45	15.33	17.50	3.88	0.6	9.23		49.87	23.3	0	100	0	0	32	-0.21	Aug-07
1.10	-1.96	-0.69	12.82	-17.54	0.87	0.68	15.49		16.46	467.4	0	100	0	0	49	0.21	Aug-09
0.75	4.55	-0.06			0.94	0.6			28.02	65.9	0	100	0	0	28	0.04	Oct-17
0.56	5.48					0.55			33.74	38.8	0	100	0	0		0.23	Oct-18
-0.80	2.55	0.67	-1.30	16.25	0.93	0.1	13.36		86.69	2,134	1	99	0	0	84	-0.01	Sep-04
-0.93	2.93	0.28	47.58	77.45	1.13	0.1	14.83		180.10	3,378	1	99	0	0	28	-0.01	Jan-04
4.96	9.03	14.38	23.11	52.68	2.51	0.1	11.45		156.51	6,131	0	100	0	0	8	0.00	Jan-04
3.05	8.48	9.16	50.41	71.36	1.77	0.06	11.55		119.50	47,776	0	100	0	0	16	-0.01	Apr-06
1.00	5.65	11.47	13.66	28.84	4.54	0.3	4.72	7.60	80.41	1,789	0	0	99	0	25	0.36	May-13
-7.07	-11.95	-23.94	-12.31	-29.87	3.46	0.1	21.76		77.99	3,558	1	99	0	0	5	-0.02	Sep-04
-1.36	2.38	-0.69			2.04	0.15			49.11	437.1	3	97	0	0		0.34	Sep-18
0.87	5.21	4.55			1.17	0.12			51.83	631.0	0	100	0	0		0.07	Sep-18
12.12	22.37	35.05	15.85	50.69	2.33	0.07	16.63	24.40	140.55	2,912	0	0	100	0	18	0.55	Dec-07
-2.12	0.19	-2.95	32.94	52.77	1.26	0.07	15.32		116.34	69,318	3	97	0	0	10	0.01	Dec-01
-1.59	0.01	-1.18	20.06	17.10	3.07	0.09	11.51		49.88	37,889	1	99	0	0	6	0.00	Mar-07
-2.78	-1.94	-6.21	12.08	15.34	2.93	0.12	11.97		102.15	6,368	5	94	0	1	15	-0.04	Apr-09
-1.28	1.02	-2.12	20.08	20.87	3.13	0.05	11.44		41.00	114,321	3	97	0	0	3	0.05	Jul-07
-4.73	-4.16	1.25	16.73	11.87	2.82	0.12	13.34		40.42	83,541	3	96	0	1	11	0.04	Mar-05
-2.01	1.16	-1.34	21.30	15.54	3.54	0.09	12.5		53.57	18,214	1	99	0	0	6	-0.02	Mar-05
-0.81	-0.12	-4.38	18.18	27.92	2.86	0.09	11.4		65.87	6,577	1	99	0	0	4	-0.15	Mar-05
-0.65	-1.05	8.46	18.95	30.75	3.76	0.12	11.36		58.60	6,511	2	97	0	1	7	0.05	Nov-10
1.03	5.65	4.25	53.67	80.40	1.06	0.04	13.27		166.35	92,060	0	100	0	0	11	-0.03	Jan-04
-4.54	-2.76	-5.92	31.23	54.03	2.1	0.1	13.84		167.63	10,016	0	100	0	0	6	0.00	Jan-04
1.53	3.85	4.59	34.72	55.87	3.16	0.06	11.4		88.71	34,794	0	100	0	0	13	0.01	Nov-06
0.15	2.95	0.00	38.54	59.26	1.75	0.1	16.89		146.16	3,738	0	100	0	0	4	-0.03	Sep-04
0.03	5.51	6.46	83.56	128.70	1.26	0.1	15.93		215.48	23,769	1	99	0	0	7	-0.02	Jan-04
2.37	6.20	12.60	9.54	20.43	2.74	0.07	4.08	6.34	87.87	34,291	1	0	98	0	53	0.07	Apr-07
2.40	6.81	12.99	12.77	25.80	3.42	0.07	3.98	6.18	91.04	26,893	1	0	96	0	65	0.18	Nov-09
1.58	4.97	9.80	6.04	14.62	2.22	0.07	3.46	5.22	66.67	7,468	1	0	100	0	31	0.04	Nov-09
-2.09	2.91	4.50	23.21		1.45	0.25	11.52		66.41	1,430	1	99	0	0	36	0.17	Feb-16
-2.39	0.51	-1.37	18.59		4.43	0.32	11.36		59.28	1,362	0	100	0	0	10	0.16	Feb-16
0.28	4.18	3.31	44.96	65.42	1.88	0.04	12.2		136.30	23,362	1	99	0	0	4	-0.01	Jan-04
6.79	13.51	22.64	17.27	36.99	3.33	0.07	8.9	15.82	102.60	12,668	0	0	100	0	38	0.12	Apr-07
5.58	12.86	19.93	20.12	39.51	3.88	0.07	7.73	14.36	100.93	4,732	0	0	99	0	48	0.22	Nov-09
7.85	13.97	24.58	12.31	38.06	2.36	0.07	11.57	18.09	87.68	3,325	1	0	99	0	19	0.08	Nov-09
-2.20	3.08	-2.96	24.08	27.23	2.01	0.1	15.67		126.35	2,403	0	100	0	0	5	-0.01	Jan-04
0.71	5.07	2.88	55.40	80.04	0.47	0.07	13.35		132.63	4,508	0	100	0	0	9	-0.01	Dec-07
0.44	4.35	3.27	47.01	67.62	1.47	0.07	12.07		103.09	2,130	0	100	0	0	4	-0.01	Dec-07
0.13	3.57	3.17	39.27	56.84	2.07	0.07	12.03		81.43	2,659	0	100	0	0	8	0.01	Dec-07
-2.08	2.32	4.39	41.58	59.78	0.75	0.07	13.54		148.14	14,142	1	99	0	0	25	-0.02	Aug-06
-0.07	3.76	3.91	35.57	57.62	1.4	0.04	13.3		167.60	105,404	1	99	0	0	16	0.01	Jan-04
1.01	4.14	2.02	28.55	49.05	2.12	0.07	13.75		113.02	19,610	0	100	0	0	17	-0.01	Aug-06
1.37	3.43	7.42	6.58	13.72	2.9	0.07	2.41	3.67	53.21	11,416	7	0	93	0	279	0.08	Nov-09
7.64	9.27	20.97	22.70	60.39	3.12	0.12	12.88		93.26	69,465	1	99	0	0	24	-0.01	Sep-04
-0.23	4.13	2.59	58.04	85.03	0.88	0.12	13.29		164.07	5,959	0	100	0	0	15	0.01	Sep-10

Fund Name	Ticker Symbol	Traded On	Overall Rating	Reward Rating	Risk Rating	Recent Up/ Downgrade	Price as of 9/30/2019	52-Week High	52-Week Low	Open to New Investors	Category & (Prospectus Objective)
● Vanguard Russell 1000 Index Fund ETF Shares	VONE	NAS CM	C	C+	C-		136.03	138.93	107.21	Y	US Equity Large Cap Blend (Growth)
● Vanguard Russell 1000 Value Index Fund ETF Shares	VONV	NAS CM	C	C	C-		112.44	114.18	91.61	Y	US Equity Large Cap Value (Growth & Inc)
● Vanguard Russell 2000 Growth Index Fund ETF Shares	VTWG	NAS CM	C-	C	D+	Down	140.10	153.71	114.04	Y	US Equity Small Cap (Small Company)
● Vanguard Russell 2000 Index Fund ETF Shares	VTWO	NAS CM	C	C-	C+		121.70	133.46	101.52	Y	US Equity Small Cap (Small Company)
● Vanguard Russell 2000 Value Index Fund ETF Shares	VTWV	NAS CM	C-	C-	C-	Up	104.61	114.43	88.80	Y	US Equity Small Cap (Small Company)
● Vanguard Russell 3000 Index Fund ETF Shares	VTHR	NAS CM	C	C+	C-		135.18	138.05	106.85	Y	US Equity Large Cap Blend (Growth)
★ Vanguard S&P 500 ETF	VOO	NYSE Arca	B-	C+	B		272.60	277.38	215.07	Y	US Equity Large Cap Blend (Growth)
● Vanguard S&P 500 Growth Index Fund ETF Shares	VOOG	NYSE Arca	C+	C+	C+	Up	161.66	166.22	125.87	Y	US Equity Large Cap Growth (Growth & Inc)
● Vanguard S&P 500 Value Index Fund ETF Shares	VOOV	NYSE Arca	C	C	C-		114.96	116.66	92.00	Y	US Equity Large Cap Value (Growth & Inc)
● Vanguard S&P Mid-Cap 400 Growth Index Fund ETF Shares	IVOG	NYSE Arca	C-	C	D+	Down	139.41	143.38	111.15	Y	US Equity Mid Cap (Growth & Inc)
● Vanguard S&P Mid-Cap 400 Index Fund ETF Shares	IVOO	NYSE Arca	C-	C	C-	Down	130.51	134.94	105.39	Y	US Equity Mid Cap (Growth & Inc)
● Vanguard S&P Mid-Cap 400 Value Index Fund ETF Shares	IVOV	NYSE Arca	C-	C	C-	Down	123.38	128.20	99.28	Y	US Equity Mid Cap (Growth & Inc)
● Vanguard S&P Small-Cap 600 Growth Index Fund ETF Shares	VIOG	NYSE Arca	C-	C	D+		153.42	170.64	129.95	Y	US Equity Small Cap (Growth & Inc)
● Vanguard S&P Small-Cap 600 Index Fund ETF Shares	VIOO	NYSE Arca	C-	C	C-		142.63	157.23	118.22	Y	US Equity Small Cap (Growth & Inc)
● Vanguard S&P Small-Cap 600 Value Index Fund ETF Shares	VIOV	NYSE Arca	C-	C-	D+		129.65	141.95	107.15	Y	US Equity Small Cap (Growth & Inc)
● Vanguard Short-Term Bond Index Fund ETF Shares	BSV	NYSE Arca	C+	C	C+	Up	80.79	81.16	77.67	Y	US Fixed Income (Income)
● Vanguard Short-Term Corporate Bond Index Fund ETF Shares	VCSH	NAS CM	C+	C+	C+		81.05	81.29	77.54	Y	US Fixed Income (Corp Bond - Gen)
● Vanguard Sh-Term Inflation-Prot Securities Ind ETF Shares	VTIP	NAS CM	C	C	C+		49.05	49.64	47.71	Y	US Fixed Income (Govt Bond - Treasury)
● Vanguard Short-Term Treasury Index Fund ETF Shares	VGSH	NAS CM	C	C	C+		60.93	61.15	59.55	Y	US Fixed Income (Govt Bond - Gen)
● Vanguard Small-Cap Growth Index Fund ETF Shares	VBK	NYSE Arca	C+	C	C+		182.04	191.90	140.03	Y	US Equity Small Cap (Small Company)
● Vanguard Tax-Exempt Bond Index Fund ETF Shares	VTEB	NYSE Arca	C+	C+	C+		53.62	54.17	49.85	Y	US Muni Fixed Inc (Muni Bond - Natl)
★ Vanguard Total Bond Market Index Fund ETF Shares	BND	NAS CM	B-	C+	B		84.43	85.16	77.49	Y	US Fixed Income (Income)
● Vanguard Total Corporate Bond ETF ETF Shares	VTC	NAS CM	C-	C-	C-		88.46	89.51	79.04	Y	US Fixed Income (Corp Bond - Gen)
★ Vanguard Total International Bond Index Fund ETF Shares	BNDX	NAS CM	B-	B-	C+	Up	58.83	59.22	54.09	Y	Global Fixed Income (Worldwide Bond)
● Vanguard Total International Stock Index Fund ETF Shares	VXUS	NAS CM	C	C	C+		51.66	54.09	45.72	Y	Global Equity Large Cap (Foreign Stock)
● Vanguard Total World Bond ETF	BNDW	NAS CM	D+	D+	C-		80.43	81.08	74.05	Y	Global Fixed Income (Worldwide Bond)
● Vanguard Total World Stock Index Fund ETF Shares	VT	NYSE Arca	C	C	C+		74.82	76.53	62.33	Y	Global Equity Large Cap (World Stock)
Vanguard U.S. Liquidity Factor ETF ETF Shares	VFLQ	BATS	D+	C-	D+	Up	82.60	84.79	65.86	Y	US Equity Mid Cap (Growth)
● Vanguard U.S. Minimum Volatility ETF ETF Shares	VFMV	BATS	C-	C	D+	Up	89.25	90.11	70.84	Y	US Equity Mid Cap (Growth)
Vanguard U.S. Momentum Factor ETF ETF Shares	VFMO	BATS	D+	D+	D+		80.79	86.13	63.67	Y	US Equity Mid Cap (Growth)
● Vanguard U.S. Multifactor ETF Shares	VFMF	BATS	D	D	D+		75.64	82.00	63.72	Y	US Equity Mid Cap (Growth)
Vanguard U.S. Quality Factor ETF ETF Shares	VFQY	BATS	D	D	D+	Down	79.61	85.13	65.83	Y	US Equity Mid Cap (Growth)
● Vanguard U.S. Value Factor ETF ETF Shares	VFVA	BATS	D	D	C-		72.24	80.01	60.57	Y	US Equity Mid Cap (Growth)
★ Vanguard Utilities Index Fund ETF Shares	VPU	NYSE Arca	B	B	C+		143.65	144.54	114.71	Y	Utilities Sector Equity (Utility)
● Vanguard Value Index Fund ETF Shares	VTV	NYSE Arca	C+	C	C+		111.62	113.17	92.30	Y	US Equity Large Cap Value (Growth)
VelocityShares 1x Daily Inverse VSTOXX Futures ETN	EXIV	BATS	C	C-	D+	Up	33.41	41.50	20.26	Y	Alternative Misc (Growth & Inc)
VelocityShares 1x Long VSTOXX Futures ETN	EVIX	BATS	D-	D-	D-	Down	5.22	13.15	4.83	Y	Alternative Misc (Growth & Inc)
VelocityShares 3x Inverse Crude Oil ETN - S&P GSCI® Crude	DWTIF	OTC BB	D	E+	D		11.30	39.00	9.10	Y	Trading Tools (Natl Res)
● VelocityShares 3x Inv Crude Oil ETNs - S&P GSCI® Crude Oil	DWT	NYSE Arca	D	D-	D		5.52	19.42	3.91	Y	Trading Tools (Growth & Inc)
VelocityShares 3x Inverse Gold ETN - S&P GSCI® Gold Ind ER	DGLD	NAS CM	D	D-	D	Down	30.96	58.39	26.45	Y	Trading Tools (Prec Metals)
● VelocityShares 3x Inverse Natl Gas ETN - S&P GSCI® Natl Ga	DGAZ	NYSE Arca	C+	B	D	Down	136.05	337.40	47.88	Y	Trading Tools (Natl Res)
VelocityShares 3x Inverse Silver ETN - S&P GSCI® Silver In	DSLV	NAS CM	D	D-	D	Down	18.92	38.40	13.10	Y	Trading Tools (Prec Metals)
VelocityShares 3x Long Crude Oil ETN - S&P GSCI® Crude Oil			D	D-	D		24.62			Y	Trading Tools (Natl Res)
● VelocityShares 3x Long Crude Oil ETNs - S&P GSCI® Crude Oi	UWT	NYSE Arca	D	D	D		10.37	49.34	8.22	Y	Trading Tools (Growth & Inc)
★ VelocityShares 3x Long Gold ETN - S&P GSCI® Gold Ind ER	UGLD	NAS CM	B	A-	C-	Up	132.67	157.03	77.90	Y	Trading Tools (Prec Metals)
● VelocityShares 3x Long Natl Gas ETN - S&P GSCI® Natl Gas I	UGAZ	NYSE Arca	E+	E	D-		14.59	253.10	11.64	Y	Trading Tools (Natl Res)
★ VelocityShares 3x Long Silver ETN - S&P GSCI® Silver Ind E	USLV	NAS CM	B	A-	D+	Up	83.51	132.23	54.70	Y	Trading Tools (Prec Metals)
● VelocityShares Daily 2x VIX Short-Term ETN	TVIX	NAS CM	D	D-	D		13.60	78.72	12.14	Y	Alternative Misc (Growth)
● VelocityShares Daily Inverse VIX Medium-Term ETN	ZIV	NAS CM	C-	D+	C-	Down	65.66	80.87	59.10	Y	Alternative Misc (Growth)
VelocityShares Long LIBOR ETN	ULBR	NYSE Arca	D	D	D		21.75	40.76	18.48	Y	Trading Tools (Growth & Inc)
VelocityShares Short LIBOR ETN	DLBR	NYSE Arca	C	C	D+	Up	26.21	29.30	16.42	Y	Trading Tools (Growth & Inc)
● VelocityShares VIX Short-Term ETN	VIIX	NAS CM	D-	E+	D		10.02	20.87	9.10	Y	Alternative Misc (Growth)

★ Expanded analysis of this fund is included in Section II: Analysis of All BUY Rated Funds. ● Expanded analysis of this fund is included in Section III: Analysis of All Rated Funds with Assets over $50 million.

	TOTAL RETURNS & PERFORMANCE								ASSETS		ASSET ALLOCATION & TURNOVER					VALUATION	
3-Month Total Return	6-Month Total Return	1-Year Total Return	3-Year Total Return	5-Year Total Return	Dividend Yield (TTM)	Expense Ratio	3-Yr Std Deviation	Effective Duration	NAV	Total Assets (MIL)	%Cash	%Stocks	%Bonds	%Other	Turnover Ratio	Premium/ Discount 1-Year Avg	Inception Date
0.11	3.94	3.00	43.84	63.68	1.76	0.12	12.31		136.02	3,567	0	100	0	0	9	0.00	Sep-10
1.06	3.73	3.37	30.38	44.28	2.39	0.12	12.33		112.36	3,934	0	100	0	0	16	0.00	Sep-10
-4.56	-2.64	-8.54	31.84	53.94	0.72	0.2	17.47		140.13	746.0	3	97	0	0	35	-0.01	Sep-10
-2.57	-1.53	-7.72	26.70	48.12	1.31	0.15	17.2		121.75	2,397	2	98	0	0	19	-0.06	Sep-10
-0.55	-0.53	-7.10	20.78	40.75	1.77	0.2	17.66		104.02	414.0	1	99	0	0	30	0.06	Sep-10
-0.08	3.56	2.18	42.46	62.35	1.75	0.15	12.53		134.94	1,354	0	100	0	0	14	0.03	Sep-10
0.92	4.85	3.87	45.66	69.21	1.99	0.03	12.18		272.60	493,907	0	100	0	0	4	-0.03	Sep-10
-0.58	3.69	2.29	53.56	80.62	1.23	0.15	12.33		161.68	2,765	0	100	0	0	18	-0.02	Sep-10
1.54	5.02	4.50	34.11	48.47	2.32	0.15	13.17		114.93	1,120	0	100	0	0	20	-0.01	Sep-10
-1.63	1.13	-2.46	31.75	55.34	0.86	0.2	14.49		139.45	942.0	1	99	0	0	43	-0.02	Sep-10
-1.11	0.84	-2.48	29.53	51.07	1.44	0.15	15.31		130.50	2,162	1	99	0	0	12	-0.02	Sep-10
-0.60	0.47	-2.56	26.11	44.49	1.59	0.2	16.64		123.35	912.2	1	99	0	0	36	0.00	Sep-10
-2.29	-0.62	-10.68	33.80	66.66	1.02	0.2	17.56		153.37	387.3	1	99	0	0	37	-0.05	Sep-10
-0.49	0.25	-8.18	30.37	59.56	1.17	0.15	18.05		142.69	2,260	2	98	0	0	13	-0.02	Sep-10
1.21	0.98	-7.13	26.20	51.12	1.62	0.2	18.97		129.71	429.2	1	99	0	0	34	0.01	Sep-10
0.94	2.77	6.00	5.94	9.84	2.23	0.07	1.53	2.67	80.80	48,183	1	0	99	0	48	0.04	Apr-07
1.11	3.13	6.66	8.43	14.06	2.84	0.07	1.57	2.64	80.98	30,932	0	0	97	0	56	0.09	Nov-09
0.38	2.03	3.45	4.89	6.20	1.97	0.06	1.15	2.67	49.03	31,193	0	0	100	0	25	0.07	Oct-12
0.57	1.98	4.35	4.41	6.43	2.26	0.07	1.02	1.92	60.93	7,935	0	0	100	0	67	0.03	Nov-09
-2.75	0.58	-0.88	41.57	61.72	0.62	0.07	16.07		182.10	23,785	2	98	0	0	22	-0.02	Jan-04
1.56	3.90	8.54	9.32		2.31	0.08	3.43	5.22	53.56	6,149	1	0	99	0	22	0.07	Aug-15
2.43	5.50	10.59	8.92	17.29	2.74	0.04	3.44	6.20	84.41	241,309	2	0	98	0	54	0.05	Apr-07
2.81	8.00	13.07			3.36	0.07		7.48	88.44	212.3	1	0	97	0	4	0.06	Nov-17
3.06	6.06	11.36	12.93	24.95	2.85	0.09	2.74	8.41	58.72	140,100	0	0	99	0	22	0.16	May-13
-2.07	1.10	-1.60	19.35	18.16	3.05	0.09	11.51		51.53	384,493	2	97	0	0	3	0.11	Jan-11
2.62	6.12	11.02			2.79	0.09		7.13	80.44	172.9	1	0	98	0		0.05	Sep-18
-0.35	1.92	0.61	31.49	39.32	2.35	0.09	11.46		74.79	16,872	1	99	0	0	9	-0.04	Jun-08
-0.46	3.00	1.18			1.41	0.13			82.56	39.2	0	100	0	0	20	0.01	Feb-18
3.56	8.79	8.19			2.49	0.13			89.21	69.1	0	100	0	0	5	0.02	Feb-18
-2.52	1.94	-5.30			1.08	0.13			80.76	30.3	0	100	0	0	53	0.02	Feb-18
-0.66	0.43	-6.23			1.68	0.18			75.62	79.4	0	100	0	0	64	-0.01	Feb-18
-0.32	-0.17	-5.14			1.42	0.13			79.59	19.9	0	100	0	0	25	0.06	Feb-18
-0.48	-0.97	-7.26			2.17	0.13			72.19	55.9	0	100	0	0	16	0.06	Feb-18
9.08	12.37	25.87	47.41	84.91	2.81	0.1	10.3		143.61	5,717	0	100	0	0	4	-0.01	Jan-04
0.53	3.72	3.14	38.50	58.22	2.51	0.04	12.22		111.60	82,529	0	100	0	0	8	-0.01	Jan-04
-13.15	6.63	-7.68			0	1.35			33.59	13.4						0.32	May-17
-5.35	-28.37	-38.67			0	1.35			5.15	2.1						0.17	May-17
-10.19	-9.91	15.92	-82.68	-63.23	0	1.35	90.2		11.44	3.6						0.50	Feb-12
-10.22	-9.98	15.75			0	1.5			5.60	255.1						0.26	Dec-16
-16.15	-32.61	-46.48	-29.36	-58.22	0	1.35	32.29		31.37	20.5						-0.02	Oct-11
-19.85	31.47	-60.35	340.60	598.38	0	1.65	121.65		135.49	231.6						-0.85	Feb-12
-35.02	-36.34	-45.27	-7.16	-70.72	0	1.65	47.63		19.17	33.9						-0.03	Oct-11
-34.34	-47.16	-78.53	-58.78	-99.61	0	1.35	81.93		10.11	25.1						78.57	Feb-12
-34.37	-47.20	-78.56			0	1.5			10.23	305.4						-0.33	Dec-16
14.59	38.67	67.91	916.04	940.29	0	1.35	33.25		130.76	169.5						0.05	Oct-11
-5.05	-51.52	-80.93	-95.97	-99.92	0	1.65	97.03		14.64	540.3						0.87	Feb-12
29.16	25.22	30.35	275.82	194.18	0	1.65	52.64		82.34	278.7						0.02	Oct-11
-21.10	-47.05	-49.07	-92.95	-99.85	0	1.65	105.01		12.97	1,066						1.79	Nov-10
-11.80	-11.60	-17.75	51.39	54.14	0	1.35	27.97		66.25	75.4						-0.18	Nov-10
-5.95	-28.41	-43.71			0	1.5			22.21	6.6						-0.44	Aug-17
2.58	27.24	59.42			0	1.5			26.20	5.6						-0.03	Aug-17
-4.78	-18.44	-11.52	-82.95	-95.46	0	0.89	58.88		9.88	23.0						0.34	Nov-10

Fund Name	Ticker Symbol	Traded On	Overall Rating	Reward Rating	Risk Rating	Recent Up/ Downgrade	Price as of 9/30/2019	52-Week High	52-Week Low	Open to New Investors	Category & (Prospectus Objective)
★ Vesper U.S. Large Cap Short-Term Reversal Strategy ETF	UTRN	NYSE Arca	B-	B	C		26.31	26.71	20.20	Y	US Equity Large Cap Blend (Growth & Inc)
● VictoryShares Developed Enhanced Volatility Wtd ETF	CIZ	NAS CM	C-	C-	C-		31.33	34.13	29.68	Y	Global Equity Large Cap (Income)
● VictoryShares Dividend Accelerator ETF	VSDA	NAS CM	C	C+	C-		34.07	34.66	26.21	Y	US Equity Large Cap Value (Equity-Income)
VictoryShares Emerging Market High Div Volatility Wtd ETF	CEY	NAS CM	D+	C-	D+		22.49	25.11	21.58	Y	Global Emerg Mkts Equity (Div Emerg Mkts)
VictoryShares Emerging Market Volatility Wtd ETF	CEZ	NAS CM	C-	C	D		24.60	27.12	23.56	Y	Global Emerg Mkts Equity (Div Emerg Mkts)
● VictoryShares International High Div Volatility Wtd ETF	CID	NAS CM	C-	C-	D+		31.77	33.74	29.45	Y	Global Equity Large Cap (Foreign Stock)
● VictoryShares International Volatility Wtd ETF	CIL	NAS CM	D+	C	D	Down	37.30	40.21	33.54	Y	Global Equity Large Cap (Foreign Stock)
● VictoryShares US 500 Enhanced Volatility Wtd ETF	CFO	NAS CM	C-	C	C-		49.34	51.62	41.40	Y	US Equity Large Cap Blend (Income)
● VictoryShares US 500 Volatility Wtd ETF	CFA	NAS CM	C	C	C-		52.93	53.83	41.41	Y	US Equity Large Cap Blend (Income)
● VictoryShares US Discovery Enhanced Volatility Wtd ETF	CSF	NAS CM	D	D	D+	Down	36.29	47.82	35.33	Y	US Equity Small Cap (Income)
● VictoryShares US EQ Income Enhanced Volatility Wtd ETF	CDC	NAS CM	C	C	C-		46.53	47.77	40.65	Y	US Equity Large Cap Value (Income)
● VictoryShares US Large Cap High Div Volatility Wtd ETF	CDL	NAS CM	C	C	C-		48.02	48.20	39.56	Y	US Equity Large Cap Value (Growth)
● VictoryShares US Multi-Factor Minimum Volatility ETF	VSMV	NAS CM	C	B-	C-	Up	31.94	31.99	25.31	Y	US Equity Large Cap Blend (Growth & Inc)
● VictoryShares US Small Cap High Div Volatility Wtd ETF	CSB	NAS CM	C	C	C-	Up	44.43	46.64	38.78	Y	US Equity Small Cap (Small Company)
VictoryShares US Small Cap Volatility Wtd ETF	CSA	NAS CM	C-	C	D+		46.20	49.14	39.16	Y	US Equity Small Cap (Small Company)
● VictoryShares USAA Core Intermediate-Term Bond ETF	UITB	NYSE Arca	C-	C-	C-		52.12	52.75	47.60	Y	US Fixed Income (Income)
● VictoryShares USAA Core Short-Term Bond ETF	USTB	NYSE Arca	C-	C-	D+	Up	50.63	50.81	49.24	Y	US Fixed Income (Income)
● VictoryShares USAA MSCI Emerg Mkts Value Momentum ETF	UEVM	NYSE Arca	D	D	D		42.09	46.24	39.95	Y	Global Emerg Mkts Equity (Div Emerg Mkts)
● VictoryShares USAA MSCI International Value Momentum ETF	UIVM	NYSE Arca	D	D	D+		44.59	49.09	40.20	Y	Global Equity Large Cap (Growth & Inc)
● VictoryShares USAA MSCI USA Small Cap Value Momentum ETF	USVM	NYSE Arca	D	D	D+		50.22	54.99	42.68	Y	US Equity Small Cap (Small Company)
● VictoryShares USAA MSCI USA Value Momentum ETF	ULVM	NYSE Arca	D+	D+	D+		51.28	53.73	42.49	Y	US Equity Large Cap Blend (Growth & Inc)
● Vident Core U.S. Bond Strategy ETF™	VBND	NYSE Arca	C	C+	C-		50.83	51.26	46.86	Y	US Fixed Income (Growth & Inc)
● Vident Core U.S. Equity Fund™	VUSE	NYSE Arca	C-	C-	C-		30.98	34.24	26.41	Y	US Equity Mid Cap (Growth & Inc)
● Vident International Equity Fund™	VIDI	NYSE Arca	D+	D+	C-	Down	23.41	25.56	22.04	Y	Global Equity Large Cap (Foreign Stock)
Virtus Glovista Emerging Markets ETF	EMEM	NYSE Arca	D+	C-	D	Up	21.71	23.34	20.49	Y	Global Emerg Mkts Equity (Div Emerg Mkts)
● Virtus InfraCap U.S. Preferred Stock ETF	PFFA	NYSE Arca	C-	C-	C-	Up	26.34	26.43	21.26	Y	US Fixed Income (Income)
Virtus LifeSci Biotech Clinical Trials ETF	BBC	NYSE Arca	D+	C-	D+	Down	23.82	33.77	20.92	Y	Healthcare Sector Equity (Technology)
Virtus LifeSci Biotech Products ETF	BBP	NYSE Arca	D+	D+	D+		35.86	46.30	31.99	Y	Healthcare Sector Equity (Technology)
Virtus Newfleet Dynamic Credit ETF	BLHY	NYSE Arca	C-	C	D+		23.75	24.57	22.92	Y	US Fixed Income (Growth & Inc)
Virtus Newfleet Multi-Sector Bond ETF	NFLT	NYSE Arca	C	C+	D+		24.56	24.62	23.27	Y	US Fixed Income (Income)
Virtus Private Credit ETF	VPC	NYSE Arca	U	U	U		24.91	26.31	24.65	Y	Financials Sector Equity (Growth & Inc)
Virtus Real Asset Income ETF	VRAI	NYSE Arca	U	U	U		24.77	26.20	23.17	Y	US Equity Large Cap Blend (Real Estate)
★ Virtus Reaves Utilities ETF	UTES	NYSE Arca	B-	B	C+	Up	41.83	41.83	32.64	Y	Utilities Sector Equity (Utility)
Virtus Seix Senior Loan ETF	SEIX	NYSE Arca	U	U	U		24.75	25.08	24.75	Y	US Fixed Income (Income)
Virtus WMC Global Factor Opportunities ETF	VGFO	NYSE Arca	D	C-	E+		26.00	27.43	21.46	Y	Global Equity Large Cap (Growth & Inc)
● WBI BullBear Global Income ETF	WBII	NYSE Arca	C	B-	C-		25.56	25.76	23.26	Y	US Fixed Income (Income)
★ WBI BullBear Quality 1000 ETF	WBIL	NYSE Arca	B-	B	C	Up	26.68	28.27	24.58	Y	US Equity Large Cap Blend (Growth & Inc)
WBI BullBear Quality 2000 ETF	WBID	NYSE Arca	C-	C-	C-	Up	19.46	23.93	18.89	Y	US Equity Mid Cap (Growth & Inc)
★ WBI BullBear Rising Income 1000 ETF	WBIE	NYSE Arca	B	B	C	Up	27.19	28.12	24.97	Y	US Equity Large Cap Growth (Growth & Inc)
★ WBI BullBear Rising Income 2000 ETF	WBIA	NYSE Arca	B-	B	C	Up	21.53	24.32	20.43	Y	US Equity Mid Cap (Growth & Inc)
WBI BullBear Trend Switch US 3000 Total Return ETF	WBIT	NYSE Arca	U	U	U		20.97	21.34	20.23	Y	Flexible Allocation (Growth)
● WBI BullBear Value 1000 ETF	WBIF	NYSE Arca	C	C	C-	Up	26.86	30.79	26.31	Y	US Equity Large Cap Blend (Growth & Inc)
WBI BullBear Value 2000 ETF	WBIB	NYSE Arca	C-	C	C-	Up	22.10	23.59	20.84	Y	US Equity Mid Cap (Growth & Inc)
● WBI BullBear Yield 1000 ETF	WBIG	NYSE Arca	C	C	C	Up	23.78	26.94	22.95	Y	US Equity Large Cap Blend (Growth & Inc)
WBI BullBear Yield 2000 ETF	WBIC	NYSE Arca	D+	D+	D+	Up	18.05	22.51	17.64	Y	US Equity Mid Cap (Growth & Inc)
● WBI Power Factor™ High Dividend ETF	WBIY	NYSE Arca	C	B-	D+	Up	24.44	26.96	21.81	Y	US Equity Large Cap Value (Equity-Income)
Western Asset Short Duration Income ETF	WINC	NAS CM	U	U	U		25.80	26.02	25.02	Y	US Fixed Income (Income)
Western Asset Total Return ETF	WBND	NAS CM	U	U	U		27.38	27.49	24.68	Y	US Fixed Income (Growth & Inc)
WisdomTree 90/60 U.S. Balanced Fund	NTSX	NYSE Arca	D+	D+	C-		27.89	28.07	21.56	Y	US Equity Large Cap Blend (Balanced)
WisdomTree Asia Pacific ex-Japan Fund	AXJL	NYSE Arca	C-	C	D+	Down	64.23	69.16	59.78	Y	Asia ex-Japan Equity (Pacific Stock)
WisdomTree Balanced Income Fund	WBAL	NYSE Arca	D+	C-	D	Up	24.81	25.05	22.10	Y	Moderate Allocation (Balanced)
WisdomTree Bloomberg U.S. Dollar Bullish Fund	USDU	NYSE Arca	C	C	C-		28.18	28.18	26.38	Y	Currency (Growth & Inc)

★ Expanded analysis of this fund is included in Section II: Analysis of All BUY Rated Funds. ● Expanded analysis of this fund is included in Section III: Analysis of All Rated Funds with Assets over $50 million.

TOTAL RETURNS & PERFORMANCE · ASSETS · ASSET ALLOCATION & TURNOVER · VALUATION

3-Month Total Return	6-Month Total Return	1-Year Total Return	3-Year Total Return	5-Year Total Return	Dividend Yield (TTM)	Expense Ratio	3-Yr Std Deviation	Effective Duration	NAV	Total Assets (MIL)	%Cash	%Stocks	%Bonds	%Other	Turnover Ratio	Premium/ Discount 1-Year Avg	Inception Date
1.58	2.05	7.07			0.58	0.75			26.27	31.5	0	100	0	0		0.08	Sep-18
-1.89	0.24	-5.17	13.24	0.37	3.01	0.45	9.53		31.41	95.8	0	100	0	0	154	-0.29	Sep-14
3.32	7.80	11.47			1.42	0.35			34.04	131.0	0	100	0	0	62	-0.05	Apr-17
-6.38	-4.04	-0.15			5.41	0.5			22.46	42.7	1	99	0	0	103	0.19	Oct-17
-4.57	-3.48	-0.57	11.71		2.3	0.5	11.73		24.80	44.6	0	100	0	0	103	-0.69	Mar-16
-1.51	0.00	0.28	12.68		5.01	0.45	10.2		31.66	88.7	0	100	0	0	76	0.44	Aug-15
-1.73	0.37	-2.57	19.02		2.89	0.45	10.77		37.35	84.0	0	100	0	0	53	0.33	Aug-15
0.54	4.91	-2.90	33.25	55.28	1.5	0.35	12.02		49.33	754.8	0	100	0	0	116	-0.04	Jul-14
0.54	4.90	3.98	42.71	66.62	1.39	0.35	12.96		52.93	770.2	0	100	0	0	46	0.00	Jul-14
-3.79	-8.63	-22.78	5.03	12.67	1.79	0.35	15.64		36.26	65.3	73	27	0	0	398	0.07	Jul-14
2.23	4.95	1.45	28.66	57.84	3.07	0.35	10.7		46.52	662.9	1	99	0	0	143	-0.04	Jul-14
2.24	4.95	7.52	36.36		2.98	0.35	11.44		48.02	343.3	1	99	0	0	66	0.06	Jul-15
3.37	8.92	7.93			2.09	0.35			31.90	154.7	0	100	0	0	34	0.16	Jun-17
0.91	1.51	-1.45	32.71		3.22	0.35	15.76		44.35	90.9	1	99	0	0	83	0.19	Jul-15
0.33	1.75	-4.42	29.96		1.47	0.35	17.26		46.01	27.6	0	100	0	0	62	-0.09	Jul-15
2.51	6.66	11.58			2.98	0.4		6.17	52.06	322.8	2	0	95	0	10	0.06	Oct-17
0.92	2.47	5.15			2.67	0.35		1.69	50.56	83.4	7	0	93	0	22	0.10	Oct-17
-6.24	-6.40	-6.66			2.21	0.45			42.01	172.2	1	99	0	0	58	0.25	Oct-17
-2.05	-1.70	-6.15			2.82	0.35			44.40	337.4	1	99	0	0	65	0.20	Oct-17
-1.48	-1.52	-6.79			2	0.25			50.19	105.4	1	99	0	0	17	0.08	Oct-17
-0.17	1.96	-2.44			1.85	0.2			51.25	479.2	0	100	0	0	84	0.14	Oct-17
2.32	5.66	10.68	7.43		3.08	0.43	3.46		50.86	473.0	9	0	91	0	324	-0.10	Oct-14
-1.82	-0.88	-8.13	20.39	32.43	1.62	0.5	15.98		30.97	498.6	0	100	0	0	63	-0.03	Jan-14
-3.72	-3.04	-5.58	15.34	8.17	2.89	0.61	13.14		23.45	586.3	0	100	0	0	66	-0.10	Oct-13
-5.51	-2.84	-0.49			5.12	0.67			21.82	6.5	1	99	0	0		-0.09	Nov-17
4.99	8.83	13.80			8.67	2.13			26.31	75.0	-18	9	-8	0		0.40	May-18
-18.33	-16.26	-29.35	6.59		0	0.79	31.5		23.86	21.5	0	100	0	0	65	-0.13	Dec-14
-13.20	-19.69	-19.00	7.98		0	0.79	26.83		35.91	25.1	2	98	0	0	32	-0.03	Dec-14
0.86	1.87	2.34			5.75	0.68			23.88	10.8	20	0	80	0	82	-0.45	Dec-16
1.29	3.98	6.32	11.23		4.61	0.81	2.64		24.57	24.6	2	0	96	0	82	-0.17	Aug-15
1.19	3.24				7.64			0.44	24.91	206.7	1	65	33	0		0.07	Feb-19
-0.43	-2.07					0.55			24.72	244.7	1	99	0	0		0.14	Feb-19
8.78	13.41	26.63	48.62		1.82	0.49	10.42		41.70	27.1	4	96	0	0	28	0.12	Sep-15
0.82						0.57			24.80	6.2	2	0	98	0	544	-0.02	Apr-19
-1.43	1.80	-0.82			1.85	0.49			25.89	5.2	1	99	0	0	80	0.20	Oct-17
2.50	5.92	10.59	10.87	16.76	3.62	1.28	3.63	5.19	25.60	108.8	2	0	98	0	686	-0.13	Aug-14
-2.31	0.95	-5.07	27.81	12.09	0.66	1.07	11.51		26.69	53.4	1	99	0	0	477	-0.06	Aug-14
-3.18	-7.02	-17.87	-4.28	-16.87	0.96	1.06	13.26		19.48	6.8	15	85	0	0	828	-0.08	Aug-14
1.19	4.08	-2.18	28.90	16.87	0.9	1.05	10.79		27.19	58.5	1	99	0	0	512	-0.05	Aug-14
-1.07	-0.70	-10.44	1.11	-9.81	0.85	1.08	14.46		21.54	7.5	11	89	0	0	718	-0.02	Aug-14
2.82						0.68		3.09	20.99	37.3	2	0	98	0	126	-0.03	May-19
-1.60	-4.11	-11.87	26.35	15.86	1.07	1.05	11.34		26.82	57.7	1	99	0	0	567	-0.03	Aug-14
-5.38	-0.41	-5.26	2.19	-4.27	0.79	1.06	12.93		22.12	7.7	23	77	0	0	640	-0.03	Aug-14
-1.26	-2.84	-9.66	24.97	3.59	2.16	1.04	10.75		23.77	82.0	1	99	0	0	610	-0.13	Aug-14
-4.89	-7.45	-17.39	-7.82	-20.57	2.73	1.06	11.34		18.06	9.9	15	85	0	0	762	-0.10	Aug-14
0.35	0.24	-3.51			4.89	0.7			24.47	93.0	1	99	0	0	163	-0.05	Dec-16
0.37	3.34					0.29		2.85	25.70	25.7	2	0	96	0	54	0.15	Feb-19
2.75	7.14	13.74				0.47		4.60	27.28	43.6	6	0	94	0	18	0.23	Oct-18
2.22	7.74	9.39			1.1	0.2			27.87	39.0	0	60	39	0	11	0.06	Aug-18
-4.35	-2.81	-1.19	18.56	15.18	3.86	0.48	11.72		64.52	29.0	0	100	0	0	21	-0.38	Jun-06
1.18	3.77	6.26			3.57	0.35		6.13	24.77	3.7	4	60	36	0	3	0.15	Dec-17
2.90	3.36	6.15	8.47	18.17	0.85	0.5	5.43	0.02	28.22	45.2	96	0	4	0	0	-0.02	Dec-13

Fund Name	Ticker Symbol	Traded On	Overall Rating	Reward Rating	Risk Rating	Recent Up/ Downgrade	Price as of 9/30/2019	52-Week High	52-Week Low	Open to New Investors	Category & (Prospectus Objective)
WisdomTree CBOE Russell 2000 PutWrite Strategy Fund	RPUT	BATS	D	D	D	Up	19.58	26.27	17.24	Y	Long/Short Equity (Growth & Inc)
● WisdomTree CBOE S&P 500 PutWrite Strategy Fund	PUTW	NYSE Arca	C-	C-	C-		27.63	30.73	24.52	Y	Long/Short Equity (Growth)
● WisdomTree China ex-State-Owned Enterprises Fund	CXSE	NAS CM	C-	C-	C-		71.09	82.08	58.75	Y	Greater China Equity (Pacific Stock)
WisdomTree Chinese Yuan Strategy Fund	CYB	NYSE Arca	D+	C-	D+		24.77	26.27	24.62	Y	Currency (Worldwide Bond)
● WisdomTree Continuous Commodity Index Fund	GCC	NYSE Arca	D	D	D+		17.54	18.76	16.84	Y	Commodities Broad Basket (Natl Res)
WisdomTree Dynamic Bearish U.S. Equity Fund	DYB	BATS	D	D	D		22.01	26.33	21.39	Y	Alternative Misc (Equity-Income)
● WisdomTree Dynamic Currency Hedged Intl Equity Fund	DDWM	BATS	C	C	C-		28.82	29.62	25.36	Y	Global Equity Large Cap (Foreign Stock)
WisdomTree Dynamic Curr Hedg Intl Quality Div Growth Fund	DHDG	BATS	C-	C	D+		24.32	24.93	19.80	Y	Global Equity Large Cap (World Stock)
WisdomTree Dynamic Currency Hedg Intl SmallCap Equity Fund	DDLS	BATS	C-	C-	C-		29.97	32.21	26.31	Y	Globa Eq Mid/Small Cap (Small Company)
WisdomTree Dynamic Long/Short U.S. Equity Fund	DYLS	BATS	D+	D	D+		27.79	35.37	26.68	Y	Long/Short Equity (Equity-Income)
WisdomTree Emerging Currency Strategy Fund	CEW	NYSE Arca	C-	C	D+	Up	18.33	18.93	17.92	Y	Currency (Worldwide Bond)
WisdomTree Emerging Markets Consumer Growth Fund	EMCG	NAS CM	C-	C-	D+		21.39	23.20	19.02	Y	Global Emerg Mkts Equity (Div Emerg Mkts)
WisdomTree Emerging Markets Corporate Bond Fund	EMCB	NAS CM	C	B-	D+		72.94	73.49	67.08	Y	Emerging Mkts Fixed Inc (Div Emerg Mkts)
● WisdomTree Emerging Markets Dividend Fund	DVEM	BATS	C-	C	D+		29.97	32.62	28.00	Y	Global Emerg Mkts Equity (Div Emerg Mkts)
● WisdomTree Emerg Mkts ex-State-Owned Enterprises Fund	XSOE	NYSE Arca	C	C-	C	Up	27.65	30.16	24.50	Y	Global Emerg Mkts Equity (Div Emerg Mkts)
● WisdomTree Emerging Markets High Dividend Fund	DEM	NYSE Arca	C	C	C+		41.31	45.25	39.27	Y	Global Emerg Mkts Equity (Div Emerg Mkts)
● WisdomTree Emerging Markets Local Debt Fund	ELD	NYSE Arca	C	C+	C-	Up	34.41	36.25	32.28	Y	Emerging Mkts Fixed Inc (Income)
WisdomTree Emerging Markets Multifactor Fund	EMMF	NYSE Arca	D	D	D+		21.57	24.79	21.29	Y	Global Emerg Mkts Equity (Div Emerg Mkts)
● WisdomTree Emerging Markets Quality Dividend Growth Fund	DGRE	NAS CM	C-	C-	C-		23.44	25.68	21.16	Y	Global Emerg Mkts Equity (Div Emerg Mkts)
● WisdomTree Emerging Markets SmallCap Dividend Fund	DGS	NYSE Arca	C	C	C	Up	44.30	48.79	40.12	Y	Global Emerg Mkts Equity (Div Emerg Mkts)
● WisdomTree Europe Hedged Equity Fund	HEDJ	NYSE Arca	C	C	C+		67.29	68.03	54.71	Y	Europe Equity Large Cap (Foreign Stock)
● WisdomTree Europe Hedged SmallCap Equity Fund	EUSC	NYSE Arca	C	C	D+	Up	30.33	31.54	25.52	Y	Europe Equity Large Cap (Small Company)
WisdomTree Europe Multifactor Fund	EUMF	BATS	C-	C	D+	Up	28.56	29.84	24.83	Y	Europe Equity Large Cap (Foreign Stock)
WisdomTree Europe Quality Dividend Growth Fund	EUDG	NYSE Arca	C	C	D+	Up	25.14	26.29	21.53	Y	Europe Equity Large Cap (Growth)
● WisdomTree Europe SmallCap Dividend Fund	DFE	NYSE Arca	D+	D	C-	Down	55.91	63.45	51.32	Y	Europe Equity Large Cap (Europe Stock)
● WisdomTree Floating Rate Treasury Fund	USFR	NYSE Arca	C	C	C+		25.05	25.14	25.04	Y	US Fixed Income (Govt Bond - Treasury)
WisdomTree Germany Hedged Equity Fund	DXGE	NAS CM	C-	C	D+		29.68	30.80	25.70	Y	Europe Equity Large Cap (Europe Stock)
WisdomTree Global ex-Mexico Equity Fund	XMX	NYSE Arca	D+	C	E+	Down	29.78	30.75	24.90	Y	Global Equity Large Cap (World Stock)
● WisdomTree Global ex-U.S. Quality Dividend Growth Fund	DNL	NYSE Arca	C	C	C-		58.22	59.24	47.65	Y	Global Equity Large Cap (Foreign Stock)
● WisdomTree Global ex-US Real Estate Fund	DRW	NYSE Arca	C-	C	D+	Down	29.27	32.57	27.14	Y	Real Estate Sector Equity (Real Estate)
● WisdomTree Global High Dividend Fund	DEW	NYSE Arca	C	C	D+		46.00	47.09	40.24	Y	Global Equity Large Cap (Equity-Income)
WisdomTree ICBCCS S&P China 500 Fund	WCHN	NYSE Arca	D+	D+	D+		26.07	30.49	22.70	Y	Greater China Equity (Pacific Stock)
● WisdomTree India Earnings Fund	EPI	NYSE Arca	C-	D	C	Down	23.85	26.71	21.83	Y	India Equity (Foreign Stock)
WisdomTree India ex-State-Owned Enterprises Fund	IXSE	NYSE Arca	U	U	U		24.28	25.30	22.42	Y	India Equity (Pacific Stock)
● WisdomTree Interest Rate Hedged High Yield Bond Fund	HYZD	NAS CM	C	C	C-		23.01	24.26	22.16	Y	Fixed Income Misc (Corp Bond-High Yld)
● WisdomTree Interest Rate Hedged U.S. Aggregate Bond Fund	AGZD	NAS CM	C	C	D+		47.80	48.00	47.23	Y	Fixed Income Misc (Growth & Inc)
● WisdomTree International Dividend ex-Financials Fund	DOO	NYSE Arca	C	C	C-	Up	40.38	42.06	36.91	Y	Global Equity Large Cap (Foreign Stock)
● WisdomTree International Equity Fund	DWM	NYSE Arca	C-	C-	C-		49.72	53.25	44.98	Y	Global Equity Large Cap (Foreign Stock)
● WisdomTree Intl Hedged Quality Dividend Growth Fund	IHDG	NYSE Arca	C	C+	C-		33.62	33.71	26.92	Y	Global Equity Large Cap (Growth)
● WisdomTree International High Dividend Fund	DTH	NYSE Arca	C-	C-	C-		39.02	41.71	36.10	Y	Global Equity Large Cap (Foreign Stock)
● WisdomTree International LargeCap Dividend Fund	DOL	NYSE Arca	C	C	C-	Up	45.95	48.29	41.44	Y	Global Equity Large Cap (Foreign Stock)
● WisdomTree International MidCap Dividend Fund	DIM	NYSE Arca	C-	D+	C-		60.31	65.57	54.86	Y	Globa Eq Mid/Small Cap (Foreign Stock)
WisdomTree International Multifactor Fund	DWMF	NYSE Arca	D+	D+	D+		24.90	25.56	22.06	Y	Global Equity Large Cap (Foreign Stock)
● WisdomTree International Quality Dividend Growth Fund	IQDG	BATS	C-	C	C-		28.79	29.78	24.23	Y	Global Equity Large Cap (Growth & Inc)
● WisdomTree International SmallCap Dividend Fund	DLS	NYSE Arca	C-	D	C		63.52	71.35	58.00	Y	Globa Eq Mid/Small Cap (Foreign Stock)
● WisdomTree Japan Hedged Equity Fund	DXJ	NYSE Arca	D+	D	C-	Down	50.46	58.69	44.87	Y	Japan Equity (Pacific Stock)
● WisdomTree Japan Hedged SmallCap Equity Fund	DXJS	NAS CM	D+	D+	C-	Down	39.35	45.59	35.05	Y	Japan Equity (Pacific Stock)
WisdomTree Japan Multifactor Fund	JAMF	BATS	D	D	E	Down	25.14	29.51	23.15	Y	Japan Equity (Pacific Stock)
● WisdomTree Japan SmallCap Dividend Fund	DFJ	NYSE Arca	D+	D+	C-	Down	68.77	77.64	60.90	Y	Japan Equity (Pacific Stock)
● WisdomTree Managed Futures Strategy Fund	WTMF	NYSE Arca	D+	D+	C-		38.06	41.16	37.68	Y	Alternative Misc (Growth & Inc)
WisdomTree Middle East Dividend Fund	GULF	NAS CM	C-	C-	D+	Down	19.62	21.78	18.42	Y	Equity Misc (Div Emerg Mkts)
WisdomTree Modern Tech Platforms Fund	PLAT	NYSE Arca	U	U	U		25.13	27.18	25.01	Y	Global Equity Large Cap (Technology)

★ Expanded analysis of this fund is included in Section II: Analysis of All BUY Rated Funds. ● Expanded analysis of this fund is included in Section III: Analysis of All Rated Funds with Assets over $50 million.

	TOTAL RETURNS & PERFORMANCE								ASSETS		ASSET ALLOCATION & TURNOVER					VALUATION	
3-Month Total Return	6-Month Total Return	1-Year Total Return	3-Year Total Return	5-Year Total Return	Dividend Yield (TTM)	Expense Ratio	3-Yr Std Deviation	Effective Duration	NAV	Total Assets (MIL)	%Cash	%Stocks	%Bonds	%Other	Turnover Ratio	Premium/ Discount 1-Year Avg	Inception Date
-2.09	3.07	-8.45			2.56	0.43			19.55	0.98	103	-3	0	0	0	0.03	Feb-18
-0.21	2.34	-4.25	14.67		0.85	0.38	7.91		27.69	210.4	102	-2	0	0	0	-0.10	Feb-16
-4.50	-8.95	1.17	41.13	47.32	1.22	0.32	21.34		71.44	126.8	0	100	0	0	35	-0.05	Sep-12
-3.23	-4.39	-0.25	3.28	0.20	1.16	0.45	5.56	0.02	25.00	26.2	96	0	4	0	0	-0.31	May-08
-1.51	-3.16	-3.69	-10.02	-29.25	0	0.75	6.16		17.56	114.1	50	0	1	48		-0.10	Jan-08
1.78	-3.78	-16.11	-11.17		0	0.48	5.8		22.01	5.5	101	0	0	-1	249	-0.07	Dec-15
-0.26	2.43	1.14	25.94		3.56	0.35	9.86		28.82	256.5	0	100	0	0	26	0.10	Jan-16
0.68	3.35	3.46	33.01		1.59	0.48			24.27	29.1	0	100	0	0	6	0.12	Nov-16
0.16	1.15	-3.14	22.33		3.06	0.43	10.23		29.76	37.2	0	100	0	0	55	0.51	Jan-16
0.43	-5.36	-19.37	4.70		2.25	0.48	12.1		27.81	43.1	0	100	0	0	184	-0.14	Dec-15
-2.68	-0.89	2.24	2.75	-5.07	1.84	0.55	6.57	0.02	18.34	20.2	96	0	4	0	0	-0.11	May-09
-3.22	-2.18	3.48	3.28	-1.91	3.32	0.32	14.42		21.41	37.5	0	100	0	0	88	0.35	Sep-13
1.19	4.86	10.33	15.03	19.11	4.18	0.6	3.87	4.33	73.01	36.5	0	0	99	0	132	-0.16	Mar-12
-4.20	-2.98	-1.61	20.89		3.67	0.32	12.89		29.80	50.7	0	100	0	0	26	0.29	Apr-16
-3.64	-3.78	-0.06	23.77		2.13	0.32	15.16		27.57	452.2	0	100	0	0	24	0.21	Dec-14
-5.34	-2.80	-1.21	26.09	7.38	4.86	0.63	12.56		41.38	2,098	0	100	0	0	44	0.01	Jul-07
-1.55	3.08	10.68	5.96	-0.26	5.18	0.55	9.27	5.00	34.57	190.2	7	0	93	0	44	-0.06	Aug-10
-6.02	-6.70	-9.22			2.97	0.48			21.76	23.9	0	100	0	0	133	0.12	Aug-18
-3.61	-3.80	0.80	12.20	6.00	2.84	0.32	12.93		23.60	66.1	0	100	0	0	81	0.02	Aug-13
-4.71	-4.30	0.29	19.44	13.25	4.1	0.63	13.76		44.27	1,589	0	100	0	0	40	0.02	Oct-07
1.00	5.90	7.64	33.91	47.08	1.71	0.58	12.22		67.32	3,383	0	100	0	0	18	-0.06	Dec-09
0.19	2.64	2.90	34.01		2.93	0.58	12.31		30.40	83.6	0	100	0	0	37	-0.18	Mar-15
1.08	2.51	1.42	28.83		2.24	0.43	12		28.59	12.9	0	100	0	0	109	-0.27	Jan-16
-2.94	1.15	0.44	21.15	21.70	2.75	0.58	12.68		25.14	36.5	0	100	0	0	42	-0.24	May-14
-3.97	-2.63	-8.39	12.73	27.31	3.91	0.58	13.63		56.10	518.9	0	100	0	0	52	-0.24	Jun-06
0.44	0.99	2.04	4.67	4.92	2.16	0.15	0.19	0.02	25.05	1,659	0	0	100	0	170	0.02	Feb-14
-0.21	5.31	1.19	23.04	41.63	2.72	0.48	12.58		29.73	41.6	0	100	0	0	16	-0.05	Oct-13
-0.17	3.21	1.87			4.6	0.2			29.79	3.0	0	100	0	0	18	-0.23	Feb-17
0.60	4.89	3.71	26.49	28.63	2.02	0.58	11.88		58.18	75.6	0	100	0	0	60	-0.02	Jun-06
-2.93	-4.56	6.29	24.86	38.28	6.49	0.58	12.74		29.30	101.1	0	99	0	1	17	-0.15	Jun-07
0.05	1.22	2.35	20.85	20.49	3.88	0.58	10.23		46.08	89.9	0	100	0	0	19	-0.10	Jun-06
-5.99	-8.86	1.39			1.88	0.55			26.27	17.1	0	100	0	0	28	0.30	Dec-17
-8.29	-9.40	-0.29	13.76	13.95	1.2	0.85	17.25		23.79	1,213	0	100	0	0	37	0.00	Feb-08
-2.10	-2.27					0.58			24.10	2.4	0	100	0	0		0.40	Apr-19
0.38	1.04	1.08	15.39	20.99	5.57	0.43	3.57	-0.09	23.15	238.4	73	0	27	0	60	-0.34	Dec-13
0.80	1.62	2.61	7.52	7.22	2.9	0.23	0.97	0.12	47.74	81.2	101	0	-1	0	81	0.05	Dec-13
-1.35	-0.14	0.23	17.17	6.36	4.29	0.58	10.83		40.35	155.4	0	100	0	0	41	-0.19	Jun-06
-2.44	-0.36	-2.97	17.48	13.97	3.68	0.48	11.11		49.75	788.5	0	100	0	0	15	-0.12	Jun-06
1.40	4.83	5.61	31.70	51.95	1.57	0.58	10.55		33.48	473.7	0	100	0	0	56	0.03	May-14
-2.79	-1.18	-2.24	16.31	6.67	4.5	0.58	11.31		39.11	234.6	0	100	0	0	24	-0.21	Jun-06
-2.17	0.37	-1.39	18.32	10.63	3.69	0.48	11.11		45.92	397.2	0	100	0	0	14	-0.03	Jun-06
-2.58	-1.33	-4.65	17.81	23.93	3.51	0.58	11.38		60.37	256.6	0	100	0	0	28	-0.20	Jun-06
0.13	1.37	1.94			2.87	0.38			24.79	27.3	0	100	0	0	114	0.27	Aug-18
-1.65	0.86	-0.59	19.33		2.18	0.38	12.58		28.72	94.8	0	100	0	0	55	0.21	Apr-16
-2.24	-2.24	-7.52	14.63	26.23	3.47	0.58	11.51		63.58	1,574	0	100	0	0	35	-0.13	Jun-06
0.62	-1.22	-12.08	26.66	23.13	1.85	0.48	15.1		50.08	2,539	0	100	0	0	23	-0.14	Jun-06
1.14	-2.00	-12.38	32.91	48.52	1.14	0.58	14.41		39.10	58.6	0	100	0	0	38	-0.23	Jun-13
0.29	-3.02	-12.84	13.17		3.19	0.43	11.23		24.89	1.2	0	100	0	0	104	0.15	Jan-16
1.03	-0.11	-9.54	17.88	44.74	2.1	0.58	11.34		68.17	426.1	0	100	0	0	42	-0.21	Jun-06
0.85	-2.20	-3.57	-6.35	-9.64	3.66	0.65	4.48		38.05	207.4	112	0	39	-51	0	-0.04	Jan-11
-3.04	-1.34	6.20	28.33	-0.61	3.74	0.88	9.79		19.68	19.7	0	100	0	0	30	-0.06	Jul-08
-4.15						0.45			25.09	2.5	0	100	0	0		0.12	May-19

Fund Name	Ticker Symbol	Traded On	Overall Rating	Reward Rating	Risk Rating	Recent Up/ Downgrade	Price as of 9/30/2019	52-Week High	52-Week Low	Open to New Investors	Category & (Prospectus Objective)
WisdomTree Negative Duration High Yield Bond Fund	HYND	NAS CM	C-	D+	C-		18.40	21.79	18.02	Y	Fixed Income Misc (Govt Bond - Treasury)
WisdomTree Negative Duration U.S. Aggregate Bond Fund	AGND	NAS CM	D+	D+	D+		40.72	44.41	40.23	Y	Fixed Income Misc (Growth)
WisdomTree U.S. Corporate Bond Fund	WFIG	BATS	C	B-	D+	Up	52.14	52.72	47.00	Y	US Fixed Income (Corp Bond - Gen)
● WisdomTree U.S. Dividend ex-Financials Fund	DTN	NYSE Arca	C	C	C-		87.43	91.27	73.26	Y	US Equity Large Cap Value (Growth & Inc)
● WisdomTree U.S. Earnings 500 Fund	EPS	NYSE Arca	C	C+	C-		33.54	34.14	26.55	Y	US Equity Large Cap Blend (Growth & Inc)
● WisdomTree U.S. High Dividend Fund	DHS	NYSE Arca	C	C	C-		74.48	74.68	62.15	Y	US Equity Large Cap Value (Growth & Inc)
WisdomTree U.S. High Yield Corporate Bond Fund	WFHY	BATS	C	C+	D+	Up	51.55	51.95	46.78	Y	US Fixed Income (Corp Bond-High Yld)
● WisdomTree U.S. LargeCap Dividend Fund	DLN	NYSE Arca	C	C+	C-		99.07	99.66	79.69	Y	US Equity Large Cap Value (Growth & Inc)
● WisdomTree U.S. MidCap Dividend Fund	DON	NYSE Arca	C	C	C+		36.31	36.88	29.98	Y	US Equity Mid Cap (Growth & Inc)
● WisdomTree U.S. MidCap Earnings Fund	EZM	NYSE Arca	C-	C-	C-	Down	39.44	41.26	32.31	Y	US Equity Mid Cap (Growth & Inc)
● WisdomTree U.S. Multifactor Fund	USMF	BATS	C	C	C-	Up	30.34	30.91	24.84	Y	US Equity Large Cap Blend (Growth & Inc)
● WisdomTree U.S. Quality Dividend Growth Fund	DGRW	NAS CM	C+	C+	C+		45.09	45.42	36.09	Y	US Equity Large Cap Blend (Growth & Inc)
WisdomTree U.S. Quality Shareholder Yield Fund	QSY	NYSE Arca	C	C	D+	Up	87.43	89.39	69.78	Y	US Equity Large Cap Value (Growth & Inc)
WisdomTree U.S. Short-Term Corporate Bond Fund	SFIG	BATS	C	C	D+	Up	50.68	50.80	48.67	Y	US Fixed Income (Corp Bond - Gen)
WisdomTree U.S. Short-Term High Yield Corporate Bond Fund	SFHY	BATS	C	C	D+	Up	50.13	50.90	47.78	Y	US Fixed Income (Corp Bond-High Yld)
● WisdomTree U.S. SmallCap Dividend Fund	DES	NYSE Arca	C	C-	C+		27.37	29.36	23.32	Y	US Equity Small Cap (Small Company)
● WisdomTree U.S. SmallCap Earnings Fund	EES	NYSE Arca	C-	C-	C-		35.60	39.39	30.28	Y	US Equity Small Cap (Small Company)
● WisdomTree U.S. SmallCap Quality Dividend Growth Fund	DGRS	NAS CM	C-	C	D+		35.58	37.24	29.46	Y	US Equity Small Cap (Small Company)
● WisdomTree U.S. Total Dividend Fund	DTD	NYSE Arca	C	C	C-		99.11	99.68	79.60	Y	US Equity Large Cap Value (Growth & Inc)
● WisdomTree U.S. Total Earnings Fund	EXT	NYSE Arca	C	C	D+		33.90	34.53	26.85	Y	US Equity Large Cap Blend (Growth & Inc)
WisdomTree Yield Enhanced Global Aggregate Bond Fund	GLBY	NYSE Arca	U	U	U		27.68	27.99	25.15	Y	Global Fixed Income (Growth)
● WisdomTree Yield Enhanced U.S. Aggregate Bond Fund	AGGY	NYSE Arca	C+	C+	C+		52.28	52.89	47.36	Y	US Fixed Income (Growth & Inc)
● WisdomTree Yield Enhanc U.S. Short-Term Aggreg Bond Fund	SHAG	BATS	C	C	C-	Up	50.38	50.66	48.47	Y	US Fixed Income (Growth & Inc)
Xtrackers Barclays International Corporate Bond Hedged ETF	IFIX	BATS	C-	C	D	Up	53.20	53.53	49.29	Y	Global Fixed Income (Income)
Xtrackers Barclays International Treasury Bond Hedged ETF	IGVT	BATS	C-	C	D	Up	53.18	53.49	48.63	Y	Global Fixed Income (Income)
Xtrackers Emerging Markets Bond - Interest Rate Hedged ETF	EMIH	BATS	C	C	C-	Up	23.51	24.72	22.60	Y	Fixed Income Misc (Govt Bond - Treasury)
Xtrackers Eurozone Equity ETF	EURZ	BATS	D+	C-	D+		21.73	23.35	18.89	Y	Europe Equity Large Cap (Europe Stock)
★ Xtrackers FTSE Developed ex US Comprehensive Factor ETF	DEEF	NYSE Arca	C-	C-	C-		27.03	28.70	24.42	Y	Global Equity Large Cap (Foreign Stock)
Xtrackers FTSE Emerging Comprehensive Factor ETF	DEMG	NYSE Arca	D	D+	D	Down	23.09	25.36	22.45	Y	Global Emerg Mkts Equity (Div Emerg Mkts)
● Xtrackers Harvest CSI 300 China A-Shares ETF	ASHR	NYSE Arca	C	C	C		27.09	30.79	21.51	Y	Greater China Equity (Pacific Stock)
Xtrackers Harvest CSI 500 China-A Shares Small Cap ETF	ASHS	NYSE Arca	D	D	D		25.32	32.39	21.21	Y	Greater China Equity (Pacific Stock)
● Xtrackers High Beta High Yield Bond ETF	HYUP	NYSE Arca	D+	C-	D		48.43	49.35	44.26	Y	US Fixed Income (Corp Bond-High Yld)
Xtrackers High Yield Corp Bond - Interest Rate Hedged ETF	HYIH	BATS	C	C	D+		21.92	23.41	20.96	Y	Fixed Income Misc (Corp Bond-High Yld)
● Xtrackers International Real Estate ETF	HAUZ	NYSE Arca	C	C	C-		28.74	29.14	24.80	Y	Asia ex-Japan Equity (Pacific Stock)
Xtrackers Investment Grade Bond - Interest Rate Hedged ETF	IGIH	BATS	C-	C	D		23.28	23.96	22.47	Y	Fixed Income Misc (Corp Bond - Gen)
Xtrackers Japan JPX-Nikkei 400 Equity ETF	JPN	NYSE Arca	C-	C-	C-		27.50	29.60	23.94	Y	Japan Equity (Growth & Inc)
● Xtrackers Low Beta High Yield Bond ETF	HYDW	NYSE Arca	C-	C-	D+	Up	50.58	50.61	46.81	Y	US Fixed Income (Corp Bond-High Yld)
Xtrackers MSCI [Latin America Pacific Alliance] ETF	PACA	NYSE Arca	U	U	U		24.76	27.90	23.06	Y	Latin America Equity (Foreign Stock)
Xtrackers MSCI ACWI ex USA ESG Leaders Equity ETF	ACSG	NYSE Arca	U	U	U		26.16	26.96	24.65	Y	Global Equity Large Cap (Foreign Stock)
Xtrackers MSCI All China Equity ETF	CN	NYSE Arca	D+	C-	D+	Down	31.72	36.62	27.72	Y	Greater China Equity (Pacific Stock)
● Xtrackers MSCI All World ex U.S. Hedged Equity ETF	DBAW	NYSE Arca	C	C	D+		27.61	28.14	23.68	Y	Global Equity Large Cap (World Stock)
Xtrackers MSCI All World ex US High Div Yield Hedg Eq ETF	HDAW	NYSE Arca	C	C	D+	Up	24.26	25.20	21.92	Y	Global Equity Large Cap (Growth & Inc)
Xtrackers MSCI China A Inclusion Equity ETF	ASHX	NYSE Arca	C-	C-	D+		19.32	21.93	15.60	Y	Greater China Equity (Pacific Stock)
Xtrackers MSCI EAFE ESG Leaders Equity ETF	EASG	NYSE Arca	D	D+	D		25.09	30.69	21.59	Y	Global Equity Large Cap (Foreign Stock)
● Xtrackers MSCI EAFE Hedged Equity ETF	DBEF	NYSE Arca	C+	C	C+		32.34	32.47	27.10	Y	Global Equity Large Cap (World Stock)
● Xtrackers MSCI EAFE High Dividend Yield Equity ETF	HDEF	NYSE Arca	C	C	C+	Up	22.71	23.45	20.25	Y	Global Equity Large Cap (Growth & Inc)
Xtrackers MSCI Emerging Markets ESG Leaders Equity ETF	EMSG	NYSE Arca	U	U	U		24.98	27.25	23.36	Y	Global Emerg Mkts Equity (Div Emerg Mkts)
● Xtrackers MSCI Europe Hedged Equity ETF	DBEU	NYSE Arca	C+	C	C+		29.83	29.83	24.49	Y	Europe Equity Large Cap (Europe Stock)
Xtrackers MSCI Eurozone Hedged Equity ETF	DBEZ	NYSE Arca	C	C	C-		31.48	31.53	25.66	Y	Europe Equity Large Cap (Europe Stock)
Xtrackers MSCI Germany Hedged Equity ETF	DBGR	NYSE Arca	C-	C	D+		26.67	27.45	22.54	Y	Equity Misc (Foreign Stock)
● Xtrackers MSCI Japan Hedged Equity ETF	DBJP	NYSE Arca	C	C-	C		39.82	45.08	35.24	Y	Japan Equity (Pacific Stock)
Xtrackers MSCI South Korea Hedged Equity ETF	DBKO	NYSE Arca	D	D	D		25.87	28.95	23.83	Y	Equity Misc (Pacific Stock)

★ Expanded analysis of this fund is included in Section II: Analysis of All BUY Rated Funds. ● Expanded analysis of this fund is included in Section III: Analysis of All Rated Funds with Assets over $50 million.

3-Month Total Return	6-Month Total Return	1-Year Total Return	3-Year Total Return	5-Year Total Return	Dividend Yield (TTM)	Expense Ratio	3-Yr Std Deviation	Effective Duration	NAV	Total Assets (MIL)	%Cash	%Stocks	%Bonds	%Other	Turnover Ratio	Premium/ Discount 1-Year Avg	Inception Date
-3.07	-5.47	-9.20	10.61	4.21	6.09	0.48	7.18	-6.83	18.52	25.9	101	0	-1	0	98	-0.63	Dec-13
-1.69	-2.87	-4.38	3.79	-2.52	3.13	0.28	3.94	-4.72	40.76	24.5	126	0	-26	0	169	-0.07	Dec-13
2.79	7.70	12.06	12.47		3.09	0.18	4.1	6.94	52.06	10.4	0	0	100	0	22	0.13	Apr-16
2.11	3.01	-0.30	23.61	43.16	3.38	0.38	12.68		87.39	799.6	0	100	0	0	32	0.01	Jun-06
1.63	5.12	4.53	46.29	63.27	1.86	0.08	12.79		33.52	300.0	0	100	0	0	14	0.03	Feb-07
2.92	3.84	6.75	24.03	50.40	3.39	0.38	11.02		74.46	930.7	0	100	0	0	20	-0.01	Jun-06
0.97	3.90	7.70	17.72		5.27	0.38	4.32	3.25	51.42	25.7	0	0	100	0	14	-0.10	Apr-16
2.24	5.45	6.33	39.40	61.45	2.61	0.28	11.48		99.06	2,189	0	100	0	0	11	0.00	Jun-06
0.64	1.68	1.22	28.63	59.78	2.33	0.38	13.58		36.29	3,939	0	100	0	0	27	0.00	Jun-06
-1.27	-0.38	-2.21	29.02	46.95	1.41	0.38	16.45		39.46	1,123	0	100	0	0	36	0.02	Feb-07
0.76	4.72	0.95			1.53	0.28			30.35	118.4	0	100	0	0	179	0.04	Jun-17
3.18	4.98	3.95	49.24	74.19	2.22	0.28	12.48		45.11	2,892	0	100	0	0	29	-0.01	May-13
0.66	2.34	2.19	44.93	56.83	1.59	0.38	14.43		87.37	43.7	0	100	0	0	54	-0.11	Feb-07
1.08	2.84	5.81	7.49		2.46	0.18	1.33	2.16	50.65	10.1	0	0	100	0	28	-0.05	Apr-16
0.47	2.27	4.58	14.69		5.36	0.38	2.94	1.66	50.08	20.0	0	0	100	0	18	0.10	Apr-16
1.96	-0.22	-3.97	19.19	48.24	2.84	0.38	16.78		27.36	2,089	0	100	0	0	26	-0.01	Jun-06
-0.35	-2.04	-7.90	30.67	51.70	1.47	0.38	19.34		35.65	798.6	0	100	0	0	45	0.04	Feb-07
0.69	2.10	-1.91	23.79	50.97	2.61	0.38	17.91		35.55	120.9	0	100	0	0	42	0.10	Jul-13
2.13	5.01	5.80	37.46	61.18	2.57	0.28	11.65		99.07	718.3	0	100	0	0	11	-0.01	Jun-06
1.23	4.48	3.49	44.23	61.24	2.05	0.28	13.06		33.89	86.4	0	100	0	0	22	-0.01	Feb-07
3.35	7.78					0.2			27.67	2.8	1	0	98	0		0.09	Dec-18
2.83	7.12	11.92	11.00		3.1	0.12	3.88	6.47	52.27	914.6	1	0	98	0	82	0.00	Jul-15
1.10	3.22	6.48			2.79	0.12		2.68	50.40	90.7	3	0	96	0	177	0.09	May-17
1.71	4.68	8.93	13.83		2.2	0.3		5.74	53.13	5.3	4	0	95	0	28	0.19	Oct-16
2.96	6.33	10.31	11.63		1.15	0.25		8.46	53.07	10.6	2	0	98	0	31	0.15	Oct-16
-0.43	1.84	3.79	13.54		4.11	0.45	4.88	0.04	23.56	16.5	96	0	4	0	31	-0.06	Mar-15
-2.02	2.48	-2.29	24.45		2.69	0.09	15.38		21.72	5.4	0	100	0	0	14	0.02	Aug-15
-1.05	-0.12	-2.27	16.81		3.49	0.24	10.31		27.02	73.0	0	100	0	0	45	-0.14	Nov-15
-4.76	-3.44	-3.93	4.91		5.45	0.5	12.24		23.14	3.5	0	100	0	0	74	-0.28	Apr-16
-6.12	-8.24	8.48	13.59	41.29	1.06	0.65	19.14		27.14	1,656	0	100	0	0	81	0.17	Nov-13
-6.76	-18.81	0.15	-26.73	-17.42	0	0.65	20.66		25.37	48.2	0	100	0	0	16	0.18	May-14
0.44	3.62	5.51			6.84	0.2		3.66	48.42	150.1	1	0	99	0		-0.18	Jan-18
0.29	0.59	0.61	15.86		6.19	0.35	5.3	-1.18	21.90	8.8	95	0	5	0	19	0.27	Mar-15
0.41	0.97	4.70	28.75	33.56	2.05	0.1	9.94		28.73	117.8	1	99	0	1	43	0.05	Oct-13
0.00	2.04	1.66	9.34		4.74	0.25	3.81	-0.03	23.33	7.0	96	0	3	0	25	0.05	Mar-15
1.74	2.71	-5.00	18.39		1.84	0.09	10.62		27.33	27.3	-1	100	1	0	149	-0.12	Jun-15
1.40	3.76	7.55			4.53	0.2		2.42	50.52	146.5	1	0	99	0		-0.08	Jan-18
-5.26	-6.53					0.45			24.65	2.5	0	100	0	0		0.40	Oct-18
-1.76	1.07					0.16			26.11	7.8	1	99	0	0		0.80	Dec-18
-5.79	-10.44	-0.33	17.87	48.44	1.86	0.5	18.16		31.89	36.7	2	98	0	0	102	-0.07	Apr-14
0.07	2.47	2.77	28.76	33.08	3.21	0.4	9.43		27.61	102.2	3	97	0	0	13	-0.10	Jan-14
-1.55	1.05	1.42	14.47		4.68	0.2	10.3		24.29	31.6	0	100	0	0	30	-0.10	Aug-15
-5.72	-7.78	8.71	6.87		0.88	0.6	18.28		19.43	15.5	0	100	0	0	180	0.15	Oct-15
-0.67	3.47	0.25			2.66	0.14			24.94	7.5	0	100	0	0		0.68	Sep-18
1.15	4.67	3.87	33.24	40.57	3.95	0.35	9.79		32.29	4,958	3	97	0	0	5	-0.04	Jun-11
-0.53	1.66	2.20	13.66		5.27	0.2	10.69		22.67	335.6	0	100	0	0	20	0.06	Aug-15
-5.10	-4.87					0.2			24.91	7.5	2	98	0	0		0.09	Dec-18
1.70	6.52	7.71	33.61	43.78	3.28	0.45	10.12		29.82	829.0	2	98	0	0	7	0.03	Oct-13
2.20	6.83	6.58	35.95		3.06	0.45	11.96		31.54	23.7	4	97	-1	0	5	-0.12	Dec-14
-0.07	6.10	1.34	21.66	36.22	2.33	0.45	12.68		26.76	17.4	4	97	-1	0	11	-0.06	Jun-11
1.75	1.09	-7.91	31.98	30.82	3.78	0.45	13.21		39.52	367.6	5	96	-1	0	15	-0.09	Jun-11
-1.65	-2.54	-7.82	13.96	16.00	2.84	0.58	14.5		26.12	5.2	2	101	-3	0	49	-0.88	Jan-14

Fund Name	MARKET		RATINGS				PRICE				CATEGORY & OBJECTIVE
	Ticker Symbol	Traded On	Overall Rating	Reward Rating	Risk Rating	Recent Up/ Downgrade	Price as of 9/30/2019	52-Week High	52-Week Low	Open to New Investors	Category & (Prospectus Objective)
Xtrackers MSCI USA ESG Leaders Equity ETF	USSG	NYSE Arca	U	U	U		27.07	27.40	24.91	Y	US Equity Large Cap Blend (Growth)
● Xtrackers Municipal Infrastructure Revenue Bond ETF	RVNU	NYSE Arca	C	B-	D+		28.27	28.61	25.58	Y	US Muni Fixed Inc (Muni Bond - Natl)
● Xtrackers Russell 1000 Comprehensive Factor ETF	DEUS	NYSE Arca	C	C	C-		34.49	34.81	27.13	Y	US Equity Mid Cap (Growth & Inc)
● Xtrackers Russell 1000 US QARP ETF	QARP	NYSE Arca	C-	C	D+	Up	27.54	28.07	22.66	Y	US Equity Large Cap Blend (Growth & Inc)
Xtrackers Russell 2000 Comprehensive Factor ETF	DESC	NYSE Arca	D+	C-	D	Up	33.34	36.59	28.41	Y	US Equity Small Cap (Growth & Inc)
Xtrackers S&P 500 ESG ETF			U	U	U		25.64	26.10	24.54	Y	US Equity Large Cap Blend (Growth & Inc)
Xtrackers Short Duration High Yield Bond ETF	SHYL	NYSE Arca	C-	C-	D+	Up	48.89	49.81	46.49	Y	US Fixed Income (Corp Bond-High Yld)
● Xtrackers USD High Yield Corporate Bond ETF	HYLB	NYSE Arca	C	C	C+		50.08	50.40	45.99	Y	US Fixed Income (Corp Bond-High Yld)

★ Expanded analysis of this fund is included in Section II: Analysis of All BUY Rated Funds. ● Expanded analysis of this fund is included in Section III: Analysis of All Rated Funds with Assets over $50 million.

3-Month Total Return	6-Month Total Return	1-Year Total Return	3-Year Total Return	5-Year Total Return	Dividend Yield (TTM)	Expense Ratio	3-Yr Std Deviation	Effective Duration	NAV	Total Assets (MIL)	%Cash	%Stocks	%Bonds	%Other	Turnover Ratio	Premium/ Discount 1-Year Avg	Inception Date
					TOTAL RETURNS & PERFORMANCE					**ASSETS**			**ASSET ALLOCATION & TURNOVER**			**VALUATION**	
1.75	6.64					0.1			27.04	1,482	0	100	0	0		0.07	Mar-19
2.42	5.67	11.13	11.30	26.69	2.66	0.15	4.87	9.79	28.22	73.4	0	0	100	0	25	0.09	Jun-13
1.61	5.84	4.58	37.83		1.67	0.17	12.08		34.47	208.5	1	99	0	0	45	0.01	Nov-15
1.53	3.77	2.22			1.81	0.19			27.51	112.8	3	97	0	0		-0.05	Apr-18
-0.07	0.49	-6.91	26.48		1.62	0.3	16.6		33.32	10.0	1	99	0	0	60	-0.02	Jun-16
0.61						0.11			25.61	79.4	0	100	0	0		0.12	Jun-19
0.46	2.02	4.02			5.85	0.2		1.87	48.94	22.0	4	0	96	0		-0.19	Jan-18
0.89	3.42	6.22			5.82	0.15		3.09	50.10	3,391	1	0	99	0		-0.18	Dec-16

110

Section II:
Analysis of All BUY-Rated Funds

Detailed analysis of all BUY-Rated funds. Funds are listed in alphabetical order.

Section II: Contents

This section contains an expanded analysis of all BUY-Rated funds, with current and historical Weiss Investment Ratings, key rating factors, summary financial data and performance charts. Funds are listed in alphabetical order.

TOP ROW

Fund Name
Describes the fund's assets, regions of investments and investment strategies. Many funds have similar names, so you want to make sure the fund you look up is really the one you are interested in evaluating.

Overall Rating
The Weiss rating measured on a scale from A to E based on each fund's risk and performance. See the preceding section, "What Our Ratings Mean," for an explanation of each letter grade rating.

BUY-HOLD-SELL Recommendation
Funds that are rated in the A or B range are, in our opinion, a potential BUY. Funds in the C range will indicate a HOLD status. Funds in the D or E range will indicate a SELL status.

Ticker Symbol
An arrangement of characters (usually letters) representing a particular security listed on an exchange or otherwise traded publicly. When a company issues securities to the public marketplace, it selects an available ticker symbol for its securities which investors use to place trade orders. Every listed security has a unique ticker symbol, facilitating the vast array of trade orders that flow through the financial markets every day.

Traded On (Exchange)
The stock exchange on which the fund is listed. The core function of a stock exchange is to ensure fair and orderly trading, as well as efficient dissemination of price information. Exchanges such as: NYSE (New York Stock Exchange), AMEX (American Stock Exchange), NNM (NASDAQ National Market), and NASQ (NASDAQ Small Cap) give companies, governments and other groups a platform to sell securities to the investing public. NASDAQ is abbreviated as NAS.

NAV (Net Asset Value)

A fund's price per share. The value is calculated by dividing the total value of all the securities in the portfolio, less any liabilities, by the number of fund shares outstanding.

Total Assets ($)

The total of all assets listed on the institution's balance sheet. This figure primarily consists of loans, investments, and fixed assets. Total Assets are displayed in dollars.

Dividend Yield (TTM)

Trailing twelve months dividends paid out relative to the share price. Expressed as a percentage and measures how much cash flow an investor is getting for each invested dollar. **Trailing Twelve Months (TTM)** is a representation of a fund's financial performance over the most recent 12 months. TTM uses the latest available financial data from a company's interim, quarterly or annual reports.

Turnover Ratio

The percentage of an exchange-traded fund or other investment vehicle's holdings that have been replaced with other holdings in a given year. Generally, low turnover ratio is favorable, because high turnover equates to higher brokerage transaction fees, which reduce fund returns.

Expense Ratio

A measure of what it costs an investment company to operate an exchange-traded fund. An expense ratio is determined through an annual calculation, where a fund's operating expenses are divided by the average dollar value of its assets under management. Operating expenses may include money spent on administration and management of the fund, advertising, etc. An expense ratio of 1 percent per annum means that each year 1 percent of the fund's total assets will be used to cover expenses.

LEFT COLUMN

Ratings

Reward Rating

This is based on the total return over a period of up to five years, including net asset value and price growth. The total return figure is stated net of the expenses and fees charged by the fund.   Based on proprietary modeling the individual components of the risk and reward ratings are calculated and weighted and the final rating is generated.

Risk Rating

This is includes the risk ratings of component stocks where applicable and also includes the financial stability of the fund, turnover where applicable, together with the level of volatility as measured by the fund's daily returns over a period of up to five years. Funds with greater stability are considered less risky and receive a higher risk rating. Funds with greater volatility are considered riskier, and will receive a lower risk rating. In addition to considering the fund's volatility, the risk rating also considers an assessment of the valuation and quality of a fund's holdings.

Recent Upgrade/Downgrade

An "Up" or "Down" indicates that the Weiss Exchange-Traded Fund rating has changed since the publication of the last print edition. If a fund has had a rating change since June 30, 2019, the change is identified with an "Up" or "Down."

Fund Information

Fund Type

Describes the fund's assets, regions of investments and investment strategies.

Category

Identifies funds according to their actual investment styles as measured by their portfolio holdings. This categorization allows investors to spread their money around in a mix of funds with a variety of risk and return characteristics.

Sub-Category

A subdivision of funds, usually with common characteristics as the category.

Prospectus Objective

Gives a general idea of a fund's overall investment approach and goals.

Inception Date

The date on which the fund began its operations. The commencement date indicates when a fund began investing in the market. Many investors prefer funds with longer operating histories. Funds with longer histories have longer track records and can thereby provide investors with a more long-standing picture of their performance.

Open to New Investments

Indicates whether the fund accepts investments from those who are not existing investors. A "Y" in this column identifies that the fund accepts new investors. No data in this column indicates that the fund is closed to new investors. The fund may be closed to new investors because the fund's asset base is getting too large to effectively execute its investing style. Although, the fund may be closed, in most cases, existing investors are able to add to their holdings.

Prices

Price
The price at which the fund is traded on a regular trading day. Prices in this guide are listed as of September 30, 2019.

52-Week High
The highest price that a fund has achieved during the previous 52 weeks.

52-Week Low
The lowest price that a fund has achieved during the previous 52 weeks.

Total Returns (%)

3-Month Total Return
The rate of return on an investment over three months that includes interest, capital gains, dividends and distributions realized.

6-Month Total Return
The rate of return on an investment over six months that includes interest, capital gains, dividends and distributions realized.

1-Year Total Return
The rate of return on an investment over one year that includes interest, capital gains, dividends and distributions realized.

3-Year Total Return
The rate of return on an investment over three years that includes interest, capital gains, dividends and distributions realized.

5-Year Total Return
The rate of return on an investment over five years that includes interest, capital gains, dividends and distributions realized.

3-Year Standard Deviation
A statistical measurement of dispersion about an average, which depicts how widely the returns varied over the past three years. Investors use the standard deviation of historical performance to try to predict the range of returns that are most likely for a given fund. When a fund has a high standard deviation, the predicted range of performance is wide, implying greater volatility. Standard deviation is most appropriate for measuring risk if it is for a fund that is an investor's only holding. The figure cannot be combined for more than one fund because the standard deviation for a portfolio of multiple funds is a function of not only the individual standard

deviations, but also of the degree of correlation among the funds' returns. If a fund's returns follow a normal distribution, then approximately 68 percent of the time they will fall within one standard deviation of the mean return for the fund, and 95 percent of the time within two standard deviations.

Effective Duration

Effective duration for all long fixed income positions in a portfolio. This value gives a better estimation of how the price of bonds with embedded options, which are common in many exchange-traded funds, will change as a result of changes in interest rates. Effective duration takes into account expected mortgage prepayment or the likelihood that embedded options will be exercised if a fund holds futures, other derivative securities, or other funds as assets, the aggregate effective duration should include the weighted impact of those exposures.

Valuation

Premium/Discount 1-Year Average

The annual average premium or discount of the market price to the NAV (Net Asset Value), expressed as a percentage of the NAV. This value provides a year-by-year picture a fund's trading status. A negative number indicates that, on average, the fund's shares sold at a discount to NAV, and a positive number indicates the shares sold at a premium. If the number shown is –10.00, for example, the shares sold at an average 10% discount to NAV during the listed time-period.

Company Information

Provider
The legal company that issues the fund.

Manager/Tenure (Years)
The name of the manager and the number of years spent managing the fund.

Website
The company's web address.

Address
The company's street address.

Phone Number
The company's phone number.

RIGHT COLUMN

Performance Chart
A graphical representation of the fund's total returns over the past year.

Ratings History

Indicates the fund's Overall, Risk and Reward Ratings for the previous four years. Ratings are listed as of September 30, 2019 (Q3-19), December 31, 2018 (Q4-18), December 31, 2017 (Q4-17), December 31, 2016 (Q4-16), and December 31, 2015 (Q4-15).

Overall Rating
The Weiss rating measured on a scale from A to E based on each fund's risk and performance. See the preceding section, "What Our Ratings Mean," for an explanation of each letter grade rating.

Risk Rating
This is includes the risk ratings of component stocks where applicable and also includes the financial stability of the fund, turnover where applicable, together with the level of volatility as measured by the fund's daily returns over a period of up to five years. Funds with greater stability are considered less risky and receive a higher risk rating. Funds with greater volatility are considered riskier, and will receive a lower risk rating. In addition to considering the fund's volatility, the risk rating also considers an assessment of the valuation and quality of a fund's holdings.

Reward Rating
This is based on the total return over a period of up to five years, including net asset value and price growth. The total return figure is stated net of the expenses and fees charged by the fund. Based on proprietary modeling the individual components of the risk and reward ratings are calculated and weighted and the final rating is generated.

Asset & Performance History
Indicates the fund's NAV (Net Asset Value) and 1-Year Total Return for the previous 6 years.

NAV (Net Asset Value)
A fund's price per share. The value is calculated by dividing the total value of all the securities in the portfolio, less any liabilities, by the number of fund shares outstanding.

1-Year Total Return

The rate of return on an investment over one year that includes interest, capital gains, dividends and distributions realized.

Total Assets ($)

The total of all assets listed on the institution's balance sheet. This figure primarily consists of loans, investments, and fixed assets. Total Assets are displayed in dollars.

Asset Allocation

Indicates the percentage of assets in each category. Used as an investment strategy that attempts to balance risk versus reward by adjusting the percentage of each asset in an investment portfolio according to the investor's risk tolerance, goals and investment time frame. Allocation percentages may not add up to 100%. Negative values reflect short positions.

%Cash

The percentage of the fund's assets invested in short-term obligations, usually less than 90 days, that provide a return in the form of interest payments. This type of investment generally offers a low return compared to other investments but has a low risk level.

%Stocks

The percentage of the fund's assets invested in stock.

%US Stocks

The percentage of the fund's assets invested in U.S. stock.

%Bonds

The percentage of the fund's assets invested in bonds. A bond is an unsecured debt security issued by companies, municipalities, states and sovereign governments to raise funds. When a company issues a bond it borrows money from the bondholder to boost the business, in exchange the bondholder receives the principal amount back plus the interest on the determined maturity date.

%US Bonds

The percentage of the fund's assets invested in U.S. bonds.

%Other

The percentage of the fund's assets invested in other financial instruments.

Services Offered
Services offered by the fund provider. Such services can include:

Systematic Withdrawal Plan
A plan offered by exchange-traded funds that pays specific amounts to shareholders at predetermined intervals.

Institutional Only
This indicates if the fund is offered to institutional clients only (pension funds, mutual funds, money managers, insurance companies, investment banks, commercial trusts, endowment funds, hedge funds, and some hedge fund investors).

Phone Exchange
This indicates that investors can move money between different funds within the same fund family over the phone.

Wire Redemption
This indicates whether or not investors can redeem electronically.

Qualified Investment
Under a qualified plan, an investor may invest in the variable annuity with pretax dollars through an employee pension plan, such as a 401(k) or 403(b). Money builds up on a tax-deferred basis, and when the qualified investor makes a withdrawal or annuitizes, all contributions received are taxable income.

Investment Strategy
A set of rules, behaviors or procedures, designed to guide an investor's selection of an investment portfolio. Individuals have different profit objectives, and their individual skills make different tactics and strategies appropriate.

Top Holdings
The highest amount of publicly traded assets held by a fund. These publicly traded assets may include company stock, mutual funds or other investment vehicles.

Aberdeen Standard Physical Palladium Shares ETF   B-   BUY

Ticker	Traded On	NAV	Total Assets ($)	Dividend Yield (TTM)	Turnover Ratio	Expense Ratio
PALL	NYSE Arca	157.88	$236,820,588	0		0.6

Ratings
Reward	B+
Risk	C-
Recent Upgrade/Downgrade	Up

Fund Information
Fund Type	Exchange Traded Funds
Category	Commodities Specified
Sub-Category	Commodities Precious Metals
Prospectus Objective	Prec Metals
Inception Date	Jan-10
Open to New Investments	Y

Prices
Price (as of 9/30/2019)	159.19
52-Week High	159.25
52-Week Low	99.98

Total Returns (%)
3-Month	6-Month	1-Year	3-Year	5-Year
7.69	20.06	58.02	127.70	110.68

3-Year Standard Deviation	26.26
Effective Duration	

Valuation
Premium/Discount (1-Year Average)	-0.62

Company Information
Provider	Aberdeen Standard Investments
Manager/Tenure	Management Team (9)
Website	http://www.aberdeenstandardetfs.us
Address	Aberdeen Standard Investments 405 Lexington Avenue New York NY 10174 United States
Phone Number	212-918-4954

PERFORMANCE

Ratings History
Date	Overall Rating	Risk Rating	Reward Rating
Q3-19	B-	C-	B+
Q4-18	B-	C-	B+
Q4-17	B	C	A
Q4-16	D+	C-	D+
Q4-15	D	D	D

Asset & Performance History
Date	NAV	1-Year Total Return
2018	119.66	18.88
2017	100.65	55.27
2016	64.82	22.84
2015	52.77	-31.86
2014	77.44	11.56
2013	69.42	1.1

Total Assets: $236,820,588
Asset Allocation
Asset	%
Cash	0%
Stocks	0%
US Stocks	0%
Bonds	0%
US Bonds	0%
Other	100%

Services Offered:

Investment Strategy: The investment seeks to reflect the performance of the price of physical palladium, less the expenses of the Trust's operations.
The fund is designed for investors who want a cost-effective and convenient way to invest in palladium with minimal credit risk. **Top Holdings:** Physical Palladium Bullion Physical Gold Bullion

AdvisorShares Focused Equity ETF   B   BUY

Ticker	Traded On	NAV	Total Assets ($)	Dividend Yield (TTM)	Turnover Ratio	Expense Ratio
CWS	NYSE Arca	35.15	$17,576,922	0.63		0.68

Ratings
Reward	B
Risk	C
Recent Upgrade/Downgrade	Up

Fund Information
Fund Type	Exchange Traded Funds
Category	US Equity Large Cap Blend
Sub-Category	Mid-Cap Growth
Prospectus Objective	Growth
Inception Date	Sep-16
Open to New Investments	Y

Prices
Price (as of 9/30/2019)	35.22
52-Week High	35.84
52-Week Low	28.12

Total Returns (%)
3-Month	6-Month	1-Year	3-Year	5-Year
1.27	7.66	4.63	41.04	

3-Year Standard Deviation	12.31
Effective Duration	

Valuation
Premium/Discount (1-Year Average)	0.40

Company Information
Provider	AdvisorShares
Manager/Tenure	Edward J Elfenbein (3)
Website	http://www.advisorshares.com
Address	AdvisorShares 2 Bethesda Metro Center, Suite 1330 Bethesda MD 20814 United States
Phone Number	877-843-3831

PERFORMANCE

Ratings History
Date	Overall Rating	Risk Rating	Reward Rating
Q3-19	B	C	B
Q4-18	B-	C	B
Q4-17	D	B	C-
Q4-16	U		
Q4-15			

Asset & Performance History
Date	NAV	1-Year Total Return
2018	28.68	-7.38
2017	31.21	20.66
2016	25.94	
2015		
2014		
2013		

Total Assets: $17,576,922
Asset Allocation
Asset	%
Cash	0%
Stocks	99%
US Stocks	99%
Bonds	1%
US Bonds	1%
Other	0%

Services Offered:

Investment Strategy: The investment seeks long-term capital appreciation. The fund seeks to achieve its investment objective by investing primarily in a focused group of U.S. exchange listed equity securities, including common and preferred stock and American Depositary Receipts. It will invest at least 80% of its net assets (plus any borrowings for investment purposes) in equity securities. The Advisor may use a variety of methods for security selection and will seek to focus on firms that are fundamentally sound and have shown consistency in their financial results and high earnings quality. **Top Holdings:** Moody's Corporation The Hershey Co Fiserv Inc Stryker Corp Danaher Corp

Amplify CWP Enhanced Dividend Income ETF   B-   BUY

Ticker	Traded On	NAV	Total Assets ($)	Dividend Yield (TTM)	Turnover Ratio	Expense Ratio
DIVO	BATS	30.49	$19,821,585	5.23	151	0.49

Ratings

Reward	B
Risk	C
Recent Upgrade/Downgrade	Up

Fund Information

Fund Type	Exchange Traded Funds
Category	Long/Short Equity
Sub-Category	Large Blend
Prospectus Objective	Growth & Inc
Inception Date	Dec-16
Open to New Investments	Y

Prices

Price (as of 9/30/2019)	30.48
52-Week High	30.84
52-Week Low	25.34

Total Returns (%)

3-Month	6-Month	1-Year	3-Year	5-Year
2.19	6.67	7.15		

3-Year Standard Deviation	
Effective Duration	

Valuation

Premium/Discount (1-Year Average)	0.01

Company Information

Provider	Amplifyetfs
Manager/Tenure	Anand Desai (2), Dustin Lewellyn (2), Kevin G. Simpson (2), 2 others
Website	http://www.amplifyetfs.com
Address	3250 Lacey Road, Suite 130 Downers Grove Downers Grove IL 60515 United States
Phone Number	630-487-2530

PERFORMANCE

Ratings History

Date	Overall Rating	Risk Rating	Reward Rating
Q3-19	B-	C	B
Q4-18	B-	C	B
Q4-17	D	A-	D+
Q4-16			
Q4-15			

Asset & Performance History

Date	NAV	1-Year Total Return
2018	26.85	-2.47
2017	28.93	21.3
2016	24.84	
2015		
2014		
2013		

Total Assets: $19,821,585

Asset Allocation

Asset	%
Cash	10%
Stocks	90%
US Stocks	90%
Bonds	0%
US Bonds	0%
Other	0%

Services Offered:

Investment Strategy: The investment seeks to provide current income as its primary investment objective and to provide capital appreciation as its secondary investment objective. Under normal circumstances, the fund invests at least 80% of its total assets in dividend-paying U.S. exchange-traded equity securities ("Equity Securities") and will opportunistically utilize an "option strategy" consisting of writing (selling) U.S. exchange-traded covered call options on such Equity Securities. The fund is non-diversified. **Top Holdings:** McDonald's Corp The Home Depot Inc Walmart Inc The Walt Disney Co Apple Inc

Aptus Behavioral Momentum ETF   B-   BUY

Ticker	Traded On	NAV	Total Assets ($)	Dividend Yield (TTM)	Turnover Ratio	Expense Ratio
BEMO	BATS	30.48	$64,004,703	0.8	321	0.81

Ratings

Reward	B
Risk	C
Recent Upgrade/Downgrade	Up

Fund Information

Fund Type	Exchange Traded Funds
Category	US Equity Large Cap Blend
Sub-Category	Large Growth
Prospectus Objective	Growth & Inc
Inception Date	Jun-16
Open to New Investments	Y

Prices

Price (as of 9/30/2019)	30.48
52-Week High	37.07
52-Week Low	28.10

Total Returns (%)

3-Month	6-Month	1-Year	3-Year	5-Year
-0.41	3.48	-17.04	21.66	

3-Year Standard Deviation	15.39
Effective Duration	

Valuation

Premium/Discount (1-Year Average)	-0.01

Company Information

Provider	Aptus Capital Advisors
Manager/Tenure	John D. Gardner (2), Beckham D. Wyrick (2)
Website	
Address	407 Johnson Avenue, Fairhope, Alabama 36532 United States
Phone Number	

PERFORMANCE

Ratings History

Date	Overall Rating	Risk Rating	Reward Rating
Q3-19	B-	C	B
Q4-18	B-	C	B
Q4-17	D+	B	C
Q4-16	U		
Q4-15			

Asset & Performance History

Date	NAV	1-Year Total Return
2018	28.26	-5.88
2017	30.28	17.28
2016	25.9	
2015		
2014		
2013		

Total Assets: $64,004,703

Asset Allocation

Asset	%
Cash	0%
Stocks	100%
US Stocks	100%
Bonds	0%
US Bonds	0%
Other	0%

Services Offered:

Investment Strategy: The investment seeks to track the performance, before fees and expenses, of the Aptus Behavioral Momentum Index. The index uses an objective, rules-based methodology to implement a systematic trend-following strategy that directs 100% of its exposure to either equity exposure or treasure exposure. The fund invests at least 80% of its total assets in the component securities of the index. The fund generally may invest up to 20% of its total assets (exclusive of any collateral held from securities lending) in securities or other investments not included in the index, but which the Adviser believes will help the fund track the index. **Top Holdings:** Ball Corp Veeva Systems Inc Class A Tyson Foods Inc Class A Edwards Lifesciences Corp TransDigm Group Inc

Communication Services Select Sector SPDR® Fund

B- **BUY**

Ticker	Traded On	NAV	Total Assets ($)	Dividend Yield (TTM)	Turnover Ratio	Expense Ratio
XLC	NYSE Arca		$5,878,517,060	0.92	7	0.13

Ratings
Reward	B
Risk	C
Recent Upgrade/Downgrade	Up

Fund Information
Fund Type	Exchange Traded Funds
Category	Communications Sector Equity
Sub-Category	Communications
Prospectus Objective	Comm
Inception Date	Jun-18
Open to New Investments	Y

Prices
Price (as of 9/30/2019)	49.52
52-Week High	51.72
52-Week Low	38.97

Total Returns (%)
3-Month	6-Month	1-Year	3-Year	5-Year
-0.41	4.23	1.98		

3-Year Standard Deviation	
Effective Duration	

Valuation
Premium/Discount (1-Year Average)	-0.01

Company Information
Provider	SPDR State Street Global Advisors
Manager/Tenure	Michael J. Feehily (1), Kala O'Donnell (1), Karl A. Schneider (1)
Website	http://www.spdrs.com
Address	SPDR State Street Global Advisors State Street Financial Center, 1 Lincoln Street Boston MA 02111-2900 United States
Phone Number	617-786-3000

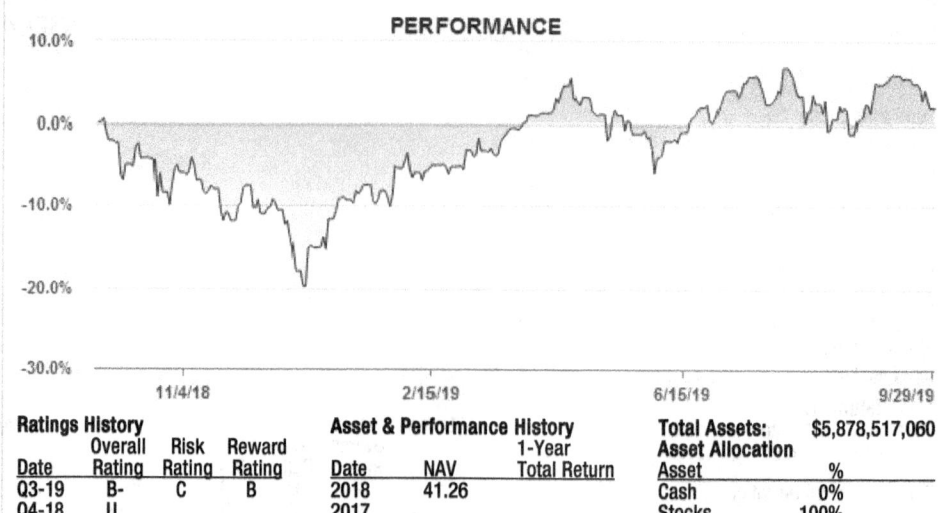

PERFORMANCE

Ratings History
Date	Overall Rating	Risk Rating	Reward Rating
Q3-19	B-	C	B
Q4-18	U		
Q4-17			
Q4-16			
Q4-15			

Asset & Performance History
Date	NAV	1-Year Total Return
2018	41.26	
2017		
2016		
2015		
2014		
2013		

Total Assets: $5,878,517,060

Asset Allocation
Asset	%
Cash	0%
Stocks	100%
US Stocks	100%
Bonds	0%
US Bonds	0%
Other	0%

Services Offered:

Investment Strategy: The investment seeks to correspond generally to the price and yield performance of publicly traded equity securities of companies in the Communication Services Select Sector Index. Normally, the fund generally invests substantially all, but at least 95%, of its total assets in the securities comprising the index. The index includes companies that have been identified as Communication Services companies by the GICS®, including securities of companies from the following industries: diversified telecommunication services; wireless telecommunication services; media; entertainment; and interactive media & services. The fund is non-diversified.
Top Holdings: Facebook Inc A Alphabet Inc Class C Alphabet Inc A Activision Blizzard Inc AT&T Inc

---

Consumer Discretionary Select Sector SPDR® Fund

B **BUY**

Ticker	Traded On	NAV	Total Assets ($)	Dividend Yield (TTM)	Turnover Ratio	Expense Ratio
XLY	NYSE Arca		$14,000,727,254	1.3	23	0.13

Ratings
Reward	B+
Risk	C
Recent Upgrade/Downgrade	

Fund Information
Fund Type	Exchange Traded Funds
Category	Consumer Goods & Svcs
Sub-Category	Consumer Cyclical
Prospectus Objective	Unaligned
Inception Date	Dec-98
Open to New Investments	Y

Prices
Price (as of 9/30/2019)	120.70
52-Week High	124.48
52-Week Low	91.98

Total Returns (%)
3-Month	6-Month	1-Year	3-Year	5-Year
-0.14	4.67	3.80	55.86	92.75

3-Year Standard Deviation	14.7
Effective Duration	

Valuation
Premium/Discount (1-Year Average)	-0.01

Company Information
Provider	SPDR State Street Global Advisors
Manager/Tenure	Michael J. Feehily (8), Karl A. Schneider (4), Kala O'Donnell (2)
Website	http://www.spdrs.com
Address	SPDR State Street Global Advisors State Street Financial Center, 1 Lincoln Street Boston MA 02111-2900 United States
Phone Number	617-786-3000

PERFORMANCE

Ratings History
Date	Overall Rating	Risk Rating	Reward Rating
Q3-19	B	C	B+
Q4-18	B-	C	B
Q4-17	B	A	B
Q4-16	B	B	B
Q4-15	B	A-	B

Asset & Performance History
Date	NAV	1-Year Total Return
2018	98.99	1.66
2017	98.6	22.76
2016	81.36	5.79
2015	78.2	9.92
2014	72.18	9.49
2013	66.84	42.74

Total Assets: $14,000,727,254

Asset Allocation
Asset	%
Cash	0%
Stocks	100%
US Stocks	99%
Bonds	0%
US Bonds	0%
Other	0%

Services Offered: Dividend Investment Plan, CashInvestment Plan

Investment Strategy: The investment seeks investment results that, before expenses, correspond to the price and yield performance of publicly traded equity securities of companies in the Consumer Discretionary Select Sector Index. The fund employs a replication strategy. It generally invests substantially all, but at least 95%, of its total assets in the securities comprising the index. The index includes securities of companies from the following industries: retail; hotels, restaurants and leisure; textiles, apparel and luxury goods; household durables; automobiles; auto components; distributors; leisure products; and diversified consumer services. It is non-diversified. **Top Holdings:** Amazon.com Inc The Home Depot Inc McDonald's Corp Starbucks Corp Nike Inc B

Consumer Staples Select Sector SPDR® Fund   B-   BUY

Ticker	Traded On	NAV	Total Assets ($)	Dividend Yield (TTM)	Turnover Ratio	Expense Ratio
XLP	NYSE Arca		$14,061,058,297	2.55	12	0.13

Ratings
Reward	B
Risk	C
Recent Upgrade/Downgrade	Up

Fund Information
Fund Type	Exchange Traded Funds
Category	Consumer Goods & Svcs
Sub-Category	Consumer Defensive
Prospectus Objective	Unaligned
Inception Date	Dec-98
Open to New Investments	Y

Prices
Price (as of 9/30/2019)	61.42
52-Week High	61.62
52-Week Low	48.73

Total Returns (%)
3-Month	6-Month	1-Year	3-Year	5-Year
5.30	10.71	16.67	24.73	54.82

3-Year Standard Deviation	11.83
Effective Duration	

Valuation
Premium/Discount (1-Year Average)	-0.02

Company Information
Provider	SPDR State Street Global Advisors
Manager/Tenure	Michael J. Feehily (8), Karl A. Schneider (4), David Chin (2)
Website	http://www.spdrs.com
Address	SPDR State Street Global Advisors State Street Financial Center, 1 Lincoln Street Boston MA 02111-2900 United States
Phone Number	617-786-3000

PERFORMANCE

Ratings History
Date	Overall Rating	Risk Rating	Reward Rating
Q3-19	B-	C	B
Q4-18	C+	C	B
Q4-17	B	A	C+
Q4-16	B-	C+	B
Q4-15	B	B-	B

Asset & Performance History
Date	NAV	1-Year Total Return
2018	50.78	-8.01
2017	56.86	12.9
2016	51.72	4.34
2015	50.49	6.84
2014	48.51	15.86
2013	42.95	26.27

Total Assets: $14,061,058,297

Asset Allocation
Asset	%
Cash	0%
Stocks	100%
US Stocks	100%
Bonds	0%
US Bonds	0%
Other	0%

Services Offered: Dividend Investment Plan, CashInvestment Plan

Investment Strategy: The investment seeks to provide investment results that, before expenses, correspond generally to the price and yield performance of publicly traded equity securities of companies in the Consumer Staples Select Sector Index. In seeking to track the performance of the index, the fund employs a replication strategy. It generally invests substantially all, but at least 95%, of its total assets in the securities comprising the index. The index includes securities of companies from the following industries: food and staples retailing; household products; food products; beverages; tobacco; and personal products. The fund is non-diversified. **Top Holdings:** Procter & Gamble Co   Coca-Cola Co   PepsiCo Inc   Walmart Inc   Costco Wholesale Corp

---

Direxion Daily Mid Cap Bear 3X Shares   B-   BUY

Ticker	Traded On	NAV	Total Assets ($)	Dividend Yield (TTM)	Turnover Ratio	Expense Ratio
MIDZ	NYSE Arca	50.61	$3,178,871	0.75	0	1.09

Ratings
Reward	B
Risk	D+
Recent Upgrade/Downgrade	Up

Fund Information
Fund Type	Exchange Traded Funds
Category	Trading Tools
Sub-Category	Trading--Inverse Equity
Prospectus Objective	Growth
Inception Date	Jan-09
Open to New Investments	Y

Prices
Price (as of 9/30/2019)	50.60
52-Week High	60.93
52-Week Low	10.06

Total Returns (%)
3-Month	6-Month	1-Year	3-Year	5-Year
-1.86	358.38	372.08	83.16	-20.43

3-Year Standard Deviation	46.59
Effective Duration	

Valuation
Premium/Discount (1-Year Average)	-0.17

Company Information
Provider	Direxion Funds
Manager/Tenure	Paul Brigandi (10), Tony Ng (4)
Website	http://www.direxionfunds.com
Address	Direxion Funds 1301 Avenue Of The Americas (6th Avenue) New York NY 10019 United States
Phone Number	646-572-3390

PERFORMANCE

Ratings History
Date	Overall Rating	Risk Rating	Reward Rating
Q3-19	B-	D+	B
Q4-18	D	D	D-
Q4-17	E+	E+	E+
Q4-16	D	D-	E+
Q4-15	D-	E+	E+

Asset & Performance History
Date	NAV	1-Year Total Return
2018	17.53	29.73
2017	13.53	-38.41
2016	21.97	-51.38
2015	45.19	-8.07
2014	49.16	-32.73
2013	73.08	-62.93

Total Assets: $3,178,871

Asset Allocation
Asset	%
Cash	113%
Stocks	-13%
US Stocks	-13%
Bonds	0%
US Bonds	0%
Other	0%

Services Offered:

Investment Strategy: The investment seeks daily investment results, before fees and expenses, of 300% of the inverse (or opposite) of the daily performance of the S&P MidCap® 400 Index. The fund, under normal circumstances, invests in swap agreements, futures contracts, short positions or other financial instruments that, in combination, provide inverse (opposite) or short leveraged exposure to the index equal to at least 80% of the fund's net assets (plus borrowing for investment purposes). The index measures the performance of 400 mid-sized companies in the United States. The fund is non-diversified. **Top Holdings:** S&P Mid Cap 400 Index Swa   S&P Mid Cap 400 Index Swa   S&P Mid Cap 400 Index Swa   S&P Mid Cap 400 Index Swa   S&P Mid Cap 400 Index Swa

Direxion Daily MSCI Real Estate Bear 3X Shares   B   BUY

Ticker	Traded On	NAV	Total Assets ($)	Dividend Yield (TTM)	Turnover Ratio	Expense Ratio
DRV	NYSE Arca	26.55	$15,966,751	0.95	0	1.1

Ratings
Reward   A
Risk   D+
Recent Upgrade/Downgrade   Up

Fund Information
Fund Type   Exchange Traded Funds
Category   Trading Tools
Sub-Category   Trading--Inverse Equity
Prospectus Objective   Real Estate
Inception Date   Jul-09
Open to New Investments   Y

Prices
Price (as of 9/30/2019)   26.56
52-Week High   33.23
52-Week Low   5.95

Total Returns (%)

3-Month	6-Month	1-Year	3-Year	5-Year
-20.11	285.85	179.40	120.24	-33.05

3-Year Standard Deviation   36.88
Effective Duration

Valuation
Premium/Discount (1-Year Average)   -0.02

Company Information
Provider   Direxion Funds
Manager/Tenure   Paul Brigandi (10), Tony Ng (4)
Website   http://www.direxionfunds.com
Address   Direxion Funds 1301 Avenue Of The
                 Americas (6th Avenue) New York NY
                 10019 United States
Phone Number   646-572-3390

PERFORMANCE

Ratings History

Date	Overall Rating	Risk Rating	Reward Rating
Q3-19	B	D+	A
Q4-18	D	D	D-
Q4-17	D-	D-	D-
Q4-16	D	D-	D-
Q4-15	D-	E+	E+

Asset & Performance History

Date	NAV	1-Year Total Return
2018	10.95	4.97
2017	10.48	-17.22
2016	12.66	-35.34
2015	19.58	-24.77
2014	26.03	-59.56
2013	64.37	-22.22

Total Assets: $15,966,751

Asset Allocation

Asset	%
Cash	105%
Stocks	-5%
US Stocks	-5%
Bonds	0%
US Bonds	0%
Other	0%

Services Offered:

Investment Strategy: The investment seeks daily investment results, before fees and expenses, of 300% of the inverse of the daily performance of the MSCI US IMI Real Estate 25/50 Index. The fund invests in swap agreements, futures contracts, short positions or other financial instruments that, in combination, provide inverse or short leveraged exposure to the index equal to at least 80% of its net assets (plus borrowing for investment purposes). The index is designed to measure the performance of the large-, mid- and small-capitalization segments of the U.S. equity universe that are classified in the real estate sector as per the GICS. The fund is non-diversified. **Top Holdings:** Msci Us Reit Index Swap   Msci Us Reit Index Swap   Msci Us Reit Index Swap   Msci Us Reit Index Swap   Goldman Finl Sq Trsry Ins

Direxion Daily S&P Oil & Gas Exp. & Prod. Bear 3X Shares   B   BUY

Ticker	Traded On	NAV	Total Assets ($)	Dividend Yield (TTM)	Turnover Ratio	Expense Ratio
DRIP	NYSE Arca	78.61	$39,757,962	0.61	0	1.07

Ratings
Reward   A-
Risk   D
Recent Upgrade/Downgrade   Up

Fund Information
Fund Type   Exchange Traded Funds
Category   Trading Tools
Sub-Category   Trading--Inverse Equity
Prospectus Objective   Natl Res
Inception Date   May-15
Open to New Investments   Y

Prices
Price (as of 9/30/2019)   78.50
52-Week High   119.89
52-Week Low   4.94

Total Returns (%)

3-Month	6-Month	1-Year	3-Year	5-Year
31.66	741.59	1,399.15	299.54	

3-Year Standard Deviation   94.29
Effective Duration

Valuation
Premium/Discount (1-Year Average)   -0.06

Company Information
Provider   Direxion Funds
Manager/Tenure   Paul Brigandi (4), Tony Ng (4)
Website   http://www.direxionfunds.com
Address   Direxion Funds 1301 Avenue Of The
                 Americas (6th Avenue) New York NY
                 10019 United States
Phone Number   646-572-3390

PERFORMANCE

Ratings History

Date	Overall Rating	Risk Rating	Reward Rating
Q3-19	B	D	A-
Q4-18	D	D	D-
Q4-17	D-	D-	D-
Q4-16	D	D-	D-
Q4-15	U		

Asset & Performance History

Date	NAV	1-Year Total Return
2018	17.54	49.1
2017	11.87	-9.04
2016	13.05	-87.56
2015	104.96	
2014		
2013		

Total Assets: $39,757,962

Asset Allocation

Asset	%
Cash	107%
Stocks	-7%
US Stocks	-7%
Bonds	0%
US Bonds	0%
Other	0%

Services Offered:

Investment Strategy: The investment seeks daily investment results, of 300% of the inverse (or opposite) of the daily performance of the S&P Oil & Gas Exploration & Production Select Industry Index. The fund invests in swap agreements, futures contracts, short positions or other financial instruments that, in combination, provide inverse (opposite) or short leveraged exposure to the index equal to at least 80% of the fund's net assets (plus borrowing for investment purposes). The index is designed to measure the performance of a sub-industry or group of sub-industries determined based on the Global Industry Classification Standards ("GICS"). The fund is non-diversified. **Top Holdings:** S&P Oil & Gas Exploration   S&P Oil & Gas Exploration   S&P Oil & Gas Exploration   Goldman Finl Sq Trsry Ins   S&P Oil & Gas Exploration

Direxion Daily Small Cap Bear 3X Shares　　　　　　　　　　　B-　　BUY

Ticker	Traded On	NAV	Total Assets ($)	Dividend Yield (TTM)	Turnover Ratio	Expense Ratio
TZA	NYSE Arca	46.93	$346,854,638	0.82	0	1.11

Ratings

Reward	B
Risk	D+
Recent Upgrade/Downgrade	Up

Fund Information

Fund Type	Exchange Traded Funds
Category	Trading Tools
Sub-Category	Trading--Inverse Equity
Prospectus Objective	Small Company
Inception Date	Nov-08
Open to New Investments	Y

Prices

Price (as of 9/30/2019)	46.99
52-Week High	55.00
52-Week Low	8.48

Total Returns (%)

3-Month	6-Month	1-Year	3-Year	5-Year
4.02	392.40	438.26	77.22	-32.80

3-Year Standard Deviation	51.52
Effective Duration	

Valuation

Premium/Discount (1-Year Average)	0.06

Company Information

Provider	Direxion Funds
Manager/Tenure	Paul Brigandi (10), Tony Ng (4)
Website	http://www.direxionfunds.com
Address	Direxion Funds 1301 Avenue Of The Americas (6th Avenue) New York NY 10019 United States
Phone Number	646-572-3390

PERFORMANCE

Ratings History

Date	Overall Rating	Risk Rating	Reward Rating
Q3-19	B-	D+	B
Q4-18	D	D	D-
Q4-17	E+	E+	E+
Q4-16	D	D-	E+
Q4-15	D-	E+	E+

Asset & Performance History

Date	NAV	1-Year Total Return
2018	15.2	24.79
2017	12.28	-38.35
2016	19.92	-55.53
2015	44.8	-6.82
2014	48.08	-29.12
2013	67.84	-68.61

Total Assets: $346,854,638

Asset Allocation

Asset	%
Cash	115%
Stocks	-15%
US Stocks	-15%
Bonds	0%
US Bonds	0%
Other	0%

Services Offered:

Investment Strategy: The investment seeks daily investment results, before fees and expenses, of 300% of the inverse (or opposite) of the daily performance of the Russell 2000® Index. The fund invests in swap agreements, futures contracts, short positions or other financial instruments that, in combination, provide inverse (opposite) or short leveraged exposure to the index equal to at least 80% of the fund's net assets (plus borrowing for investment purposes). The index measures the performance of approximately 2,000 small-capitalization companies in the Russell 3000® Index, based on a combination of their market capitalization and current index membership. It is non-diversified. **Top Holdings:** Russ 2000 Indx Small Swap　Russ 2000 Indx Small Swap　Russ 2000 Indx Small Swap　Russ 2000 Indx Small Swap　Russ 2000 Indx Small Swap

Eaton Vance Global Income Builder NextShares™　　　　　　　B-　　BUY

Ticker	Traded On	NAV	Total Assets ($)	Dividend Yield (TTM)	Turnover Ratio	Expense Ratio
EVGBC	NAS CM	9.73	$6,083,878	11.33	102	0.86

Ratings

Reward	C
Risk	B+
Recent Upgrade/Downgrade	Up

Fund Information

Fund Type	Exchange Traded Funds
Category	Moderate Allocation
Sub-Category	World Allocation
Prospectus Objective	Income
Inception Date	Mar-16
Open to New Investments	Y

Prices

Price (as of 9/30/2019)	9.73
52-Week High	10.58
52-Week Low	8.62

Total Returns (%)

3-Month	6-Month	1-Year	3-Year	5-Year
0.31	3.76	3.06	23.56	

3-Year Standard Deviation	8.56
Effective Duration	

Valuation

Premium/Discount (1-Year Average)	0.00

Company Information

Provider	Eaton Vance
Manager/Tenure	Michael A. Allison (3), John H. Croft (3), Christopher M. Dyer (3), 1 other
Website	
Address	P.O. Boc 43027 Providence RI 02940-3027 United States
Phone Number	

PERFORMANCE

Ratings History

Date	Overall Rating	Risk Rating	Reward Rating
Q3-19	B-	B+	C
Q4-18	D+	D	C-
Q4-17	D+	A-	C-
Q4-16	U		
Q4-15			

Asset & Performance History

Date	NAV	1-Year Total Return
2018	8.87	-8.2
2017	11.26	16.47
2016	10.23	
2015		
2014		
2013		

Total Assets: $6,083,878

Asset Allocation

Asset	%
Cash	2%
Stocks	56%
US Stocks	31%
Bonds	40%
US Bonds	25%
Other	0%

Services Offered:

Investment Strategy: The investment seeks to achieve total return for its investors.
The fund seeks to invest in common stocks, preferred stocks and other hybrid securities and fixed and floating-rate securities and other debt ("income instruments") of U.S. and foreign issuers. Under normal market conditions, the fund will invest (i) at least 30% of its net assets in securities or other instruments issued by issuers located outside of the United States, which may include emerging market countries; and (ii) in issuers located in at least five different countries (including the United States). **Top Holdings:** Amazon.com Inc　Alphabet Inc Class C　Microsoft Corp　SPDR® S&P 500 ETF　The Walt Disney Co

Eaton Vance TABS 5-to-15 Year Laddered Municipal Bond NextShares™   B-   BUY

Ticker	Traded On	NAV	Total Assets ($)	Dividend Yield (TTM)	Turnover Ratio	Expense Ratio
EVLMC	NAS CM	10.47	$7,328,396	2.18	78	0.35

Ratings
Reward	C+
Risk	B
Recent Upgrade/Downgrade	

Fund Information
Fund Type	Exchange Traded Funds
Category	US Muni Fixed Inc
Sub-Category	Muni National Interm
Prospectus Objective	Muni Bond - Natl
Inception Date	Mar-16
Open to New Investments	Y

Prices
Price (as of 9/30/2019)	10.47
52-Week High	10.57
52-Week Low	9.78

Total Returns (%)
3-Month	6-Month	1-Year	3-Year	5-Year
1.32	3.61	8.40	8.58	

3-Year Standard Deviation	4.35
Effective Duration	4.53

Valuation
Premium/Discount (1-Year Average)	0.00

Company Information
Provider	Eaton Vance
Manager/Tenure	Brian C. Barney (3), James H. Evans (3), Christopher J. Harshman (3)
Website	
Address	P.O. Boc 43027 Providence RI 02940-3027 United States
Phone Number	

PERFORMANCE

Ratings History
Date	Overall Rating	Risk Rating	Reward Rating
Q3-19	B-	B	C+
Q4-18	C-	C-	D+
Q4-17	D+	B-	D+
Q4-16	U		
Q4-15			

Asset & Performance History
Date	NAV	1-Year Total Return
2018	10	0.5
2017	10.17	6.42
2016	9.76	
2015		
2014		
2013		

Total Assets: $7,328,396
Asset Allocation
Asset	%
Cash	2%
Stocks	0%
US Stocks	0%
Bonds	98%
US Bonds	98%
Other	0%

Services Offered:

Investment Strategy: The investment seeks current income exempt from regular federal income tax. Under normal market conditions, the fund invests at least 80% of its net assets (plus any borrowings for investment purposes) in municipal obligations with final maturities of between five and fifteen years, the interest on which is exempt from regular federal income tax (the "80% Policy"). **Top Holdings:** TENNERGY CORP TENN GAS REV 5% KENTUCKY INC KY PUB ENERGY AUTH GAS SUPLLY REV 2.61% DISTRICT COLUMBIA 5% METROPOLITAN TRANSN AUTH N Y REV 2.31% TEXAS ST 1.52%

ETFMG Prime Mobile Payments ETF   B   BUY

Ticker	Traded On	NAV	Total Assets ($)	Dividend Yield (TTM)	Turnover Ratio	Expense Ratio
IPAY	NYSE Arca	46.60	$743,193,432	0.1	16	0.75

Ratings
Reward	B+
Risk	C
Recent Upgrade/Downgrade	

Fund Information
Fund Type	Exchange Traded Funds
Category	Equity Misc
Sub-Category	Miscellaneous Sector
Prospectus Objective	Growth & Inc
Inception Date	Jul-15
Open to New Investments	Y

Prices
Price (as of 9/30/2019)	46.61
52-Week High	50.00
52-Week Low	32.45

Total Returns (%)
3-Month	6-Month	1-Year	3-Year	5-Year
-1.15	7.07	9.11	88.23	

3-Year Standard Deviation	14.76
Effective Duration	

Valuation
Premium/Discount (1-Year Average)	0.03

Company Information
Provider	ETFMG
Manager/Tenure	Samuel R. Masucci (1), Devin Ryder (1), Donal Bishnoi (0), 1 other
Website	http://www.etfmg.com
Address	ETFMG 30 Maple Street, Suite 2 NJ United States
Phone Number	

PERFORMANCE

Ratings History
Date	Overall Rating	Risk Rating	Reward Rating
Q3-19	B	C	B+
Q4-18	B-	C+	B
Q4-17	C	B	B-
Q4-16	D	C	B-
Q4-15	U		

Asset & Performance History
Date	NAV	1-Year Total Return
2018	35.02	1.33
2017	34.8	36.87
2016	25.43	3.42
2015	24.55	
2014		
2013		

Total Assets: $743,193,432
Asset Allocation
Asset	%
Cash	1%
Stocks	99%
US Stocks	70%
Bonds	0%
US Bonds	0%
Other	0%

Services Offered:

Investment Strategy: The investment seeks to provide investment results that correspond generally to the Prime Mobile Payments Index. The fund invests at least 80% of its total assets in the component securities of the index and in ADRs and GDRs based on the component securities in the index. The index tracks the performance of the exchange-listed equity securities of companies across the globe that (i) engage in providing payment processing services or applications, (ii) provide payment solutions, (iii) build or provide payment industry architecture, infrastructure or software, or (iv) provide services as a credit card network. The fund is non-diversified. **Top Holdings:** Fidelity National Information Services Inc Fiserv Inc Mastercard Inc A Visa Inc Class A American Express Co

Fidelity® MSCI Communication Services Index ETF   B-   BUY

Ticker	Traded On	NAV	Total Assets ($)	Dividend Yield (TTM)	Turnover Ratio	Expense Ratio
FCOM	NYSE Arca	33.06	$434,732,600	1.04	82	0.08

Ratings
Reward	B
Risk	C
Recent Upgrade/Downgrade	Up

Fund Information
Fund Type	Exchange Traded Funds
Category	Communications Sector Equity
Sub-Category	Communications
Prospectus Objective	Comm
Inception Date	Oct-13
Open to New Investments	Y

Prices
Price (as of 9/30/2019)	33.07
52-Week High	35.04
52-Week Low	26.75

Total Returns (%)
3-Month	6-Month	1-Year	3-Year	5-Year
-0.85	2.67	6.28	22.65	49.48

3-Year Standard Deviation	13.93
Effective Duration	

Valuation
Premium/Discount (1-Year Average)	0.05

Company Information
Provider	Fidelity Investments
Manager/Tenure	Jennifer Hsui (5), Greg Savage (5), Alan Mason (3), 2 others
Website	http://www.institutional.fidelity.com
Address	Fidelity Investments 82 Devonshire Street Boston MA 2109 United States
Phone Number	617-563-7000

PERFORMANCE

Ratings History
Date	Overall Rating	Risk Rating	Reward Rating
Q3-19	B-	C	B
Q4-18	C+	C-	B
Q4-17	B-	B	C
Q4-16	B-	C-	B
Q4-15	C-	C	B-

Asset & Performance History
Date	NAV	1-Year Total Return
2018	28.43	-5.44
2017	30.88	-0.53
2016	32.08	23.17
2015	26.68	3.26
2014	26.6	6.39
2013	25.69	

Total Assets: $434,732,600
Asset Allocation
Asset	%
Cash	0%
Stocks	100%
US Stocks	99%
Bonds	0%
US Bonds	0%
Other	0%

Services Offered:

Investment Strategy: The investment seeks to provide investment returns that correspond, before fees and expenses, generally to the performance of the MSCI USA IMI Communication Services 25/50 Index. The fund invests at least 80% of assets in securities included in the fund's underlying index. The fund's underlying index is the MSCI USA IMI Communication Services 25/50 Index, which represents the performance of the communication services sector in the U.S. equity market. It may or may not hold all of the securities in the MSCI USA IMI Communication Services 25/50 Index. The fund is non-diversified. **Top Holdings:** Facebook Inc A Alphabet Inc Class C Alphabet Inc A The Walt Disney Co Comcast Corp Class A

Fidelity® MSCI Consumer Staples Index ETF   B-   BUY

Ticker	Traded On	NAV	Total Assets ($)	Dividend Yield (TTM)	Turnover Ratio	Expense Ratio
FSTA	NYSE Arca	36.59	$634,819,232	2.5	30	0.08

Ratings
Reward	B
Risk	C
Recent Upgrade/Downgrade	Up

Fund Information
Fund Type	Exchange Traded Funds
Category	Consumer Goods & Svcs
Sub-Category	Consumer Defensive
Prospectus Objective	Unaligned
Inception Date	Oct-13
Open to New Investments	Y

Prices
Price (as of 9/30/2019)	36.61
52-Week High	36.73
52-Week Low	29.30

Total Returns (%)
3-Month	6-Month	1-Year	3-Year	5-Year
5.47	9.73	15.62	24.08	53.86

3-Year Standard Deviation	11.65
Effective Duration	

Valuation
Premium/Discount (1-Year Average)	0.05

Company Information
Provider	Fidelity Investments
Manager/Tenure	Jennifer Hsui (5), Greg Savage (5), Alan Mason (3), 2 others
Website	http://www.institutional.fidelity.com
Address	Fidelity Investments 82 Devonshire Street Boston MA 2109 United States
Phone Number	617-563-7000

PERFORMANCE

Ratings History
Date	Overall Rating	Risk Rating	Reward Rating
Q3-19	B-	C	B
Q4-18	C+	C	B
Q4-17	B	A-	C+
Q4-16	B-	C	B
Q4-15	C-	B-	B

Asset & Performance History
Date	NAV	1-Year Total Return
2018	30.52	-8.29
2017	34.26	12.5
2016	31.21	5.9
2015	30.21	5.65
2014	29.45	15.75
2013	26.06	

Total Assets: $634,819,232
Asset Allocation
Asset	%
Cash	0%
Stocks	100%
US Stocks	100%
Bonds	0%
US Bonds	0%
Other	0%

Services Offered:

Investment Strategy: The investment seeks to provide investment returns that correspond, before fees and expenses, generally to the performance of the MSCI USA IMI Consumer Staples Index. The fund invests at least 80% of assets in securities included in the fund's underlying index. The fund's underlying index is the MSCI USA IMI Consumer Staples Index, which represents the performance of the consumer staples sector in the U.S. equity market. It may or may not hold all of the securities in the MSCI USA IMI Consumer Staples Index. The fund is non-diversified. **Top Holdings:** Procter & Gamble Co Coca-Cola Co PepsiCo Inc Walmart Inc Costco Wholesale Corp

Fidelity® MSCI Information Technology Index ETF B- BUY

Ticker	Traded On	NAV	Total Assets ($)	Dividend Yield (TTM)	Turnover Ratio	Expense Ratio
FTEC	NYSE Arca	63.75	$2,556,289,555	1.17	18	0.08

Ratings
Reward B
Risk C+
Recent Upgrade/Downgrade Down

Fund Information
Fund Type Exchange Traded Funds
Category Technology Sector Equity
Sub-Category Technology
Prospectus Objective Technology
Inception Date Oct-13
Open to New Investments Y

Prices
Price (as of 9/30/2019) 63.77
52-Week High 66.03
52-Week Low 45.74

Total Returns (%)

3-Month	6-Month	1-Year	3-Year	5-Year
1.11	6.63	7.13	80.60	129.18

3-Year Standard Deviation 15.8
Effective Duration

Valuation
Premium/Discount (1-Year Average) -0.03

Company Information
Provider Fidelity Investments
Manager/Tenure Jennifer Hsui (5), Greg Savage (5), Alan Mason (3), 2 others
Website http://www.institutional.fidelity.com
Address Fidelity Investments 82 Devonshire Street Boston MA 2109 United States
Phone Number 617-563-7000

PERFORMANCE

Ratings History

Date	Overall Rating	Risk Rating	Reward Rating
Q3-19	B-	C+	B
Q4-18	C+	C+	C+
Q4-17	A-	B	A+
Q4-16	B-	C+	B
Q4-15	C-	B-	C

Asset & Performance History

Date	NAV	1-Year Total Return
2018	49.33	-0.17
2017	49.96	37.07
2016	36.83	13.78
2015	32.81	5.03
2014	31.64	18.15
2013	27.09	

Total Assets: $2,556,289,555

Asset Allocation

Asset	%
Cash	0%
Stocks	100%
US Stocks	99%
Bonds	0%
US Bonds	0%
Other	0%

Services Offered:

Investment Strategy: The investment seeks to provide investment returns that correspond, before fees and expenses, generally to the performance of the MSCI USA IMI Information Technology Index. The fund invests at least 80% of assets in securities included in the fund's underlying index. The fund's underlying index is the MSCI USA IMI Information Technology Index, which represents the performance of the information technology sector in the U.S. equity market. It may or may not hold all of the securities in the MSCI USA IMI Information Technology Index. The fund is non-diversified. **Top Holdings:** Microsoft Corp Apple Inc Visa Inc Class A Mastercard Inc A Intel Corp

Fidelity® MSCI Utilities Index ETF B- BUY

Ticker	Traded On	NAV	Total Assets ($)	Dividend Yield (TTM)	Turnover Ratio	Expense Ratio
FUTY	NYSE Arca	42.46	$895,970,050	2.66	7	0.08

Ratings
Reward B
Risk C+
Recent Upgrade/Downgrade Down

Fund Information
Fund Type Exchange Traded Funds
Category Utilities Sector Equity
Sub-Category Utilities
Prospectus Objective Utility
Inception Date Oct-13
Open to New Investments Y

Prices
Price (as of 9/30/2019) 42.49
52-Week High 42.60
52-Week Low 33.93

Total Returns (%)

3-Month	6-Month	1-Year	3-Year	5-Year
9.15	13.20	25.93	47.17	83.80

3-Year Standard Deviation 10.27
Effective Duration

Valuation
Premium/Discount (1-Year Average) 0.03

Company Information
Provider Fidelity Investments
Manager/Tenure Jennifer Hsui (5), Greg Savage (5), Alan Mason (3), 2 others
Website http://www.institutional.fidelity.com
Address Fidelity Investments 82 Devonshire Street Boston MA 2109 United States
Phone Number 617-563-7000

PERFORMANCE

Ratings History

Date	Overall Rating	Risk Rating	Reward Rating
Q3-19	B-	C+	B
Q4-18	B-	C+	B-
Q4-17	B	B	B
Q4-16	B-	C+	B
Q4-15	C-	C	B

Asset & Performance History

Date	NAV	1-Year Total Return
2018	34.86	4.4
2017	34.47	12.32
2016	31.61	17.44
2015	27.83	-4.79
2014	30.52	26.83
2013	24.87	

Total Assets: $895,970,050

Asset Allocation

Asset	%
Cash	0%
Stocks	100%
US Stocks	100%
Bonds	0%
US Bonds	0%
Other	0%

Services Offered:

Investment Strategy: The investment seeks to provide investment returns that correspond, before fees and expenses, generally to the performance of the MSCI USA IMI Utilities Index. The fund invests at least 80% of assets in securities included in the fund's underlying index. The fund's underlying index is the MSCI USA IMI Utilities Index, which represents the performance of the utilities sector in the U.S. equity market. It may or may not hold all of the securities in the MSCI USA IMI Utilities Index. The fund is non-diversified. **Top Holdings:** NextEra Energy Inc Duke Energy Corp Dominion Energy Inc Southern Co Exelon Corp

Financial Select Sector SPDR® Fund   B-   BUY

Ticker	Traded On	NAV	Total Assets ($)	Dividend Yield (TTM)	Turnover Ratio	Expense Ratio
XLF	NYSE Arca		$22,702,093,451	2.01	3	0.13

Ratings
Reward   C+
Risk   B-
Recent Upgrade/Downgrade   Up

Fund Information
Fund Type   Exchange Traded Funds
Category   Financials Sector Equity
Sub-Category   Financial
Prospectus Objective   Financial
Inception Date   Dec-98
Open to New Investments   Y

Prices
Price (as of 9/30/2019)   28.00
52-Week High   28.69
52-Week Low   22.31

Total Returns (%)

3-Month	6-Month	1-Year	3-Year	5-Year
0.92	7.59	3.54	53.43	63.90

3-Year Standard Deviation   17.24
Effective Duration

Valuation
Premium/Discount (1-Year Average)   -0.03

Company Information
Provider   SPDR State Street Global Advisors
Manager/Tenure   Michael J. Feehily (8), Karl A. Schneider (4), Melissa Kapitulik (2)
Website   http://www.spdrs.com
Address   SPDR State Street Global Advisors State Street Financial Center, 1 Lincoln Street Boston MA 02111-2900 United States
Phone Number   617-786-3000

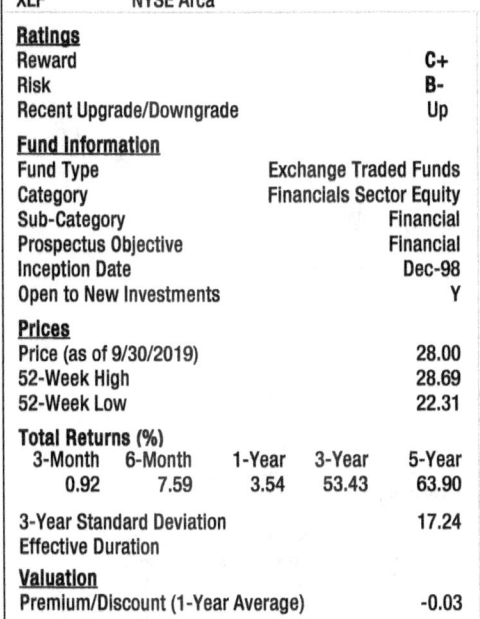

PERFORMANCE

Ratings History

Date	Overall Rating	Risk Rating	Reward Rating
Q3-19	B-	B-	C+
Q4-18	C+	C+	C
Q4-17	A-	B	A
Q4-16	B	C+	B
Q4-15	B	A	B

Asset & Performance History

Date	NAV	1-Year Total Return
2018	23.82	-13.08
2017	27.92	22.02
2016	23.26	21.15
2015	19.36	-1.6
2014	20.06	15.02
2013	17.74	35.36

Total Assets: $22,702,093,451

Asset Allocation

Asset	%
Cash	0%
Stocks	100%
US Stocks	98%
Bonds	0%
US Bonds	0%
Other	0%

Services Offered: Dividend Investment Plan, CashInvestment Plan

Investment Strategy: The investment seeks investment results that, before expenses, correspond generally to the price and yield performance of publicly traded equity securities of companies in the Financial Select Sector Index. The fund generally invests substantially all, but at least 95%, of its total assets in the securities comprising the index. The index includes securities of companies from the following industries: diversified financial services; insurance; banks; capital markets; mortgage real estate investment trusts ("REITs"); consumer finance; and thrifts and mortgage finance. The fund is non-diversified. **Top Holdings:** Berkshire Hathaway Inc B   JPMorgan Chase & Co   Bank of America Corporation   Wells Fargo & Co   Citigroup Inc

First Trust Brazil AlphaDEX® Fund   B-   BUY

Ticker	Traded On	NAV	Total Assets ($)	Dividend Yield (TTM)	Turnover Ratio	Expense Ratio
FBZ	NAS CM	15.89	$108,875,991	2.77	128	0.8

Ratings
Reward   B
Risk   C-
Recent Upgrade/Downgrade   Up

Fund Information
Fund Type   Exchange Traded Funds
Category   Latin America Equity
Sub-Category   Latin America Stock
Prospectus Objective   Foreign Stock
Inception Date   Apr-11
Open to New Investments   Y

Prices
Price (as of 9/30/2019)   15.82
52-Week High   17.29
52-Week Low   11.39

Total Returns (%)

3-Month	6-Month	1-Year	3-Year	5-Year
0.69	9.67	45.70	53.07	26.59

3-Year Standard Deviation   27.51
Effective Duration

Valuation
Premium/Discount (1-Year Average)   -0.29

Company Information
Provider   First Trust
Manager/Tenure   Jon C. Erickson (8), Daniel J. Lindquist (8), David G. McGarel (8), 3 others
Website   http://www.ftportfolios.com/
Address   First Trust 120 E. Liberty Drive, Suite 400 Wheaton IL 60187 United States
Phone Number   800-621-1675

PERFORMANCE

Ratings History

Date	Overall Rating	Risk Rating	Reward Rating
Q3-19	B-	C-	B
Q4-18	C	C-	C
Q4-17	C	C-	C
Q4-16	D+	D+	D+
Q4-15	D-	D-	D-

Asset & Performance History

Date	NAV	1-Year Total Return
2018	13.37	-1.12
2017	15.51	21.01
2016	13.93	59.84
2015	8.87	-41.76
2014	15.65	-16.42
2013	19.45	-14.69

Total Assets: $108,875,991

Asset Allocation

Asset	%
Cash	0%
Stocks	100%
US Stocks	0%
Bonds	0%
US Bonds	0%
Other	0%

Services Offered:

Investment Strategy: The investment seeks investment results that correspond generally to the price and yield (before the fund's fees and expenses) of an equity index called the NASDAQ AlphaDEX® Brazil Index. The fund will normally invest at least 90% of its net assets (including investment borrowings) in the common stocks and depositary receipts that comprise the index. The index is designed to select stocks from the NASDAQ Brazil Index (the "base index") that may generate positive alpha, or risk-adjusted returns, relative to traditional indices through the use of the AlphaDEX® selection methodology. **Top Holdings:** JBS SA   Centrais Eletricas Brasileiras SA Participating Preferred   Sul America SA   Telefonica Brasil SA Participating Preferred   Cia Paranaense De Energia Copel Participating Preferred

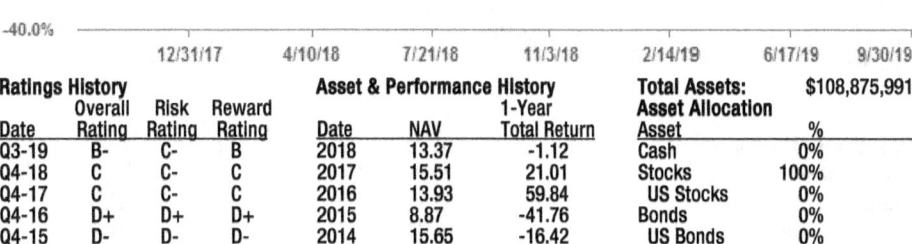

First Trust Capital Strength ETF

B- BUY

Ticker	Traded On	NAV	Total Assets ($)	Dividend Yield (TTM)	Turnover Ratio	Expense Ratio
FTCS	NAS CM	56.74	$2,862,573,537	1.39	117	0.6

Ratings
Reward   B-
Risk   C+
Recent Upgrade/Downgrade   Up

Fund Information
Fund Type   Exchange Traded Funds
Category   US Equity Large Cap Blend
Sub-Category   Large Blend
Prospectus Objective   Growth
Inception Date   Jul-06
Open to New Investments   Y

Prices
Price (as of 9/30/2019)   56.78
52-Week High   57.95
52-Week Low   45.20

Total Returns (%)

3-Month	6-Month	1-Year	3-Year	5-Year
0.15	4.42	3.86	46.96	74.18

3-Year Standard Deviation   11.38
Effective Duration

Valuation
Premium/Discount (1-Year Average)   0.01

Company Information
Provider   First Trust
Manager/Tenure   Jon C. Erickson (13), Daniel J. Lindquist (13), David G. McGarel (13), 3 others
Website   http://www.ftportfolios.com/
Address   First Trust 120 E. Liberty Drive, Suite 400 Wheaton IL 60187 United States
Phone Number   800-621-1675

PERFORMANCE

Ratings History

Date	Overall Rating	Risk Rating	Reward Rating
Q3-19	B-	C+	B-
Q4-18	C	C+	C
Q4-17	B	B	B
Q4-16	C+	C	B
Q4-15	C	C	C

Asset & Performance History

Date	NAV	1-Year Total Return
2018	48.28	-4.09
2017	50.95	26.48
2016	40.79	8.57
2015	38.12	1.63
2014	38.08	15.44
2013	33.69	35.9

Total Assets: $2,862,573,537
Asset Allocation

Asset	%
Cash	0%
Stocks	100%
US Stocks	98%
Bonds	0%
US Bonds	0%
Other	0%

Services Offered:

Investment Strategy: The investment seeks investment results that correspond generally to the price and yield (before the fund's fees and expenses) of an equity index called the Capital Strength Index(SM). The fund will normally invest at least 90% of its net assets (including investment borrowings) in the common stocks and real estate investment trusts ("REITs") that comprise the index. The index seeks to provide exposure to well-capitalized companies with strong market positions that have the potential to provide their stockholders with a greater degree of stability and performance over time. **Top Holdings:** Amgen Inc   American Tower Corp   Zoetis Inc Class A   S&P Global Inc   Moody's Corporation

First Trust Dow 30 Equal Weight ETF

B- BUY

Ticker	Traded On	NAV	Total Assets ($)	Dividend Yield (TTM)	Turnover Ratio	Expense Ratio
EDOW	NYSE Arca	24.51	$49,012,843	1.77	16	0.5

Ratings
Reward   B
Risk   C
Recent Upgrade/Downgrade   Up

Fund Information
Fund Type   Exchange Traded Funds
Category   US Equity Large Cap Value
Sub-Category   Large Value
Prospectus Objective   Growth & Inc
Inception Date   Aug-17
Open to New Investments   Y

Prices
Price (as of 9/30/2019)   24.52
52-Week High   25.12
52-Week Low   20.09

Total Returns (%)

3-Month	6-Month	1-Year	3-Year	5-Year
0.60	3.35	5.19		

3-Year Standard Deviation
Effective Duration

Valuation
Premium/Discount (1-Year Average)   -0.01

Company Information
Provider   First Trust
Manager/Tenure   Jon C. Erickson (2), Daniel J. Lindquist (2), David G. McGarel (2), 3 others
Website   http://www.ftportfolios.com/
Address   First Trust 120 E. Liberty Drive, Suite 400 Wheaton IL 60187 United States
Phone Number   800-621-1675

PERFORMANCE

Ratings History

Date	Overall Rating	Risk Rating	Reward Rating
Q3-19	B-	C	B
Q4-18	B-	C	B
Q4-17	U		
Q4-16			
Q4-15			

Asset & Performance History

Date	NAV	1-Year Total Return
2018	21.43	-0.89
2017	22	
2016		
2015		
2014		
2013		

Total Assets: $49,012,843
Asset Allocation

Asset	%
Cash	0%
Stocks	100%
US Stocks	100%
Bonds	0%
US Bonds	0%
Other	0%

Services Offered:

Investment Strategy: The investment seeks investment results that correspond generally to the price and yield of an equity index called the Dow Jones Industrial Average Equal Weight Index. The fund will normally invest at least 90% of its net assets (including investment borrowings) in the common stocks that comprise the index. The index is the equal weight version of the Dow Jones Industrial Average (the "DJIA"). The DJIA is composed of 30 securities issued by blue-chip U.S. companies covering all industries, with the exception of transportation and utilities. The fund is non-diversified. **Top Holdings:** The Home Depot Inc   Procter & Gamble Co   Apple Inc   McDonald's Corp   Coca-Cola Co

First Trust Nasdaq Bank ETF   B-   BUY

Ticker	Traded On	NAV	Total Assets ($)	Dividend Yield (TTM)	Turnover Ratio	Expense Ratio
FTXO	NAS CM	25.59	$139,476,462	3.78	87	0.6

Ratings
Reward   B
Risk   C
Recent Upgrade/Downgrade   Up

Fund Information
Fund Type   Exchange Traded Funds
Category   Financials Sector Equity
Sub-Category   Financial
Prospectus Objective   Financial
Inception Date   Sep-16
Open to New Investments   Y

Prices
Price (as of 9/30/2019)   25.59
52-Week High   28.52
52-Week Low   21.01

Total Returns (%)

3-Month	6-Month	1-Year	3-Year	5-Year
0.78	3.52	-4.17	35.51	

3-Year Standard Deviation   23.03
Effective Duration

Valuation
Premium/Discount (1-Year Average)   -0.04

Company Information
Provider   First Trust
Manager/Tenure   Jon C. Erickson (3), Daniel J. Lindquist (3), David G. McGarel (3), 3 others
Website   http://www.ftportfolios.com/
Address   First Trust 120 E. Liberty Drive, Suite 400 Wheaton IL 60187 United States
Phone Number   800-621-1675

PERFORMANCE

Ratings History

Date	Overall Rating	Risk Rating	Reward Rating
Q3-19	B-	C	B
Q4-18	B-	C	B
Q4-17	D	B	C
Q4-16	U		
Q4-15			

Asset & Performance History

Date	NAV	1-Year Total Return
2018	22.28	-21.57
2017	29.32	13.95
2016	26.02	
2015		
2014		
2013		

Total Assets: $139,476,462
Asset Allocation

Asset	%
Cash	1%
Stocks	99%
US Stocks	99%
Bonds	0%
US Bonds	0%
Other	0%

Services Offered:

Investment Strategy: The investment seeks investment results that correspond generally to the price and yield (before the fund's fees and expenses) of an equity index called the Nasdaq US Smart Banks Index. The fund will normally invest at least 90% of its net assets (including investment borrowings) in the common stocks and depository receipts that comprise the underlying index. The index is designed to provide exposure to U.S. companies comprising the banking sector that have been selected based upon their liquidity and weighted based upon their cumulative score on three investing factors: volatility, value and growth. The fund is non-diversified.
Top Holdings: US Bancorp   JPMorgan Chase & Co   Citigroup Inc   PNC Financial Services Group Inc   Fifth Third Bancorp

First Trust Nasdaq Food & Beverage ETF   B-   BUY

Ticker	Traded On	NAV	Total Assets ($)	Dividend Yield (TTM)	Turnover Ratio	Expense Ratio
FTXG	NAS CM	21.36	$5,338,945	1.32	108	0.6

Ratings
Reward   B
Risk   C
Recent Upgrade/Downgrade   Up

Fund Information
Fund Type   Exchange Traded Funds
Category   Consumer Goods & Svcs
Sub-Category   Consumer Defensive
Prospectus Objective   Unaligned
Inception Date   Sep-16
Open to New Investments   Y

Prices
Price (as of 9/30/2019)   21.25
52-Week High   21.45
52-Week Low   17.50

Total Returns (%)

3-Month	6-Month	1-Year	3-Year	5-Year
4.67	7.72	11.75	10.21	

3-Year Standard Deviation   11.25
Effective Duration

Valuation
Premium/Discount (1-Year Average)   -0.28

Company Information
Provider   First Trust
Manager/Tenure   Jon C. Erickson (3), Daniel J. Lindquist (3), David G. McGarel (3), 3 others
Website   http://www.ftportfolios.com/
Address   First Trust 120 E. Liberty Drive, Suite 400 Wheaton IL 60187 United States
Phone Number   800-621-1675

PERFORMANCE

Ratings History

Date	Overall Rating	Risk Rating	Reward Rating
Q3-19	B-	C	B
Q4-18	B-	C	B
Q4-17	D	B	D+
Q4-16	U		
Q4-15			

Asset & Performance History

Date	NAV	1-Year Total Return
2018	18.05	-12.38
2017	20.87	6.09
2016	19.99	
2015		
2014		
2013		

Total Assets: $5,338,945
Asset Allocation

Asset	%
Cash	0%
Stocks	100%
US Stocks	98%
Bonds	0%
US Bonds	0%
Other	0%

Services Offered:

Investment Strategy: The investment seeks investment results that correspond generally to the price and yield (before the fund's fees and expenses) of an equity index called the Nasdaq US Smart Food & Beverage Index. The fund will normally invest at least 90% of its net assets (including investment borrowings) in the common stocks and depository receipts that comprise the underlying index. The index is designed to provide exposure to U.S. companies comprising the food and beverage sector that have been selected based upon their liquidity and weighted based upon their cumulative score on three investing factors: volatility, value and growth. The fund is non-diversified. **Top Holdings:** Tyson Foods Inc Class A   The Hershey Co   Mondelez International Inc Class A   PepsiCo Inc   Archer-Daniels Midland Co

First Trust Nasdaq Retail ETF

B-   **BUY**

Ticker	Traded On	NAV	Total Assets ($)	Dividend Yield (TTM)	Turnover Ratio	Expense Ratio
FTXD	NAS CM	23.33	$8,165,061	1.25	127	0.6

Ratings
Reward	B
Risk	C
Recent Upgrade/Downgrade	Up

Fund Information
Fund Type	Exchange Traded Funds
Category	Consumer Goods & Svcs
Sub-Category	Consumer Cyclical
Prospectus Objective	Unaligned
Inception Date	Sep-16
Open to New Investments	Y

Prices
Price (as of 9/30/2019)	23.36
52-Week High	24.79
52-Week Low	19.60

Total Returns (%)
3-Month	6-Month	1-Year	3-Year	5-Year
4.67	4.63	-3.24	21.80	

3-Year Standard Deviation	14.46
Effective Duration	

Valuation
Premium/Discount (1-Year Average)	-0.12

Company Information
Provider	First Trust
Manager/Tenure	Jon C. Erickson (3), Daniel J. Lindquist (3), David G. McGarel (3), 3 others
Website	http://www.ftportfolios.com/
Address	First Trust 120 E. Liberty Drive, Suite 400 Wheaton IL 60187 United States
Phone Number	800-621-1675

PERFORMANCE

Ratings History
Date	Overall Rating	Risk Rating	Reward Rating
Q3-19	B-	C	B
Q4-18	B-	C	B
Q4-17	D	B+	D+
Q4-16	U		
Q4-15			

Asset & Performance History
Date	NAV	1-Year Total Return
2018	20.86	-2.06
2017	21.48	9.43
2016	19.98	
2015		
2014		
2013		

Total Assets: $8,165,061
Asset Allocation
Asset	%
Cash	0%
Stocks	100%
US Stocks	100%
Bonds	0%
US Bonds	0%
Other	0%

Services Offered:

Investment Strategy: The investment seeks investment results that correspond generally to the price and yield (before the fund's fees and expenses) of the Nasdaq US Smart Retail Index. The fund will normally invest at least 90% of its net assets (including investment borrowings) in the common stocks and depository receipts that comprise the index. The index is designed to provide exposure to U.S. companies comprising the retail sector that have been selected based upon their liquidity and weighted based upon their cumulative score on three investing factors: volatility, value and growth. It is non-diversified. **Top Holdings:** Target Corp AutoZone Inc Walmart Inc The Home Depot Inc H&R Block Inc

---

First Trust Nasdaq Semiconductor ETF

B-   **BUY**

Ticker	Traded On	NAV	Total Assets ($)	Dividend Yield (TTM)	Turnover Ratio	Expense Ratio
FTXL	NAS CM	34.70	$31,233,638	0.95	94	0.6

Ratings
Reward	B+
Risk	C
Recent Upgrade/Downgrade	Up

Fund Information
Fund Type	Exchange Traded Funds
Category	Technology Sector Equity
Sub-Category	Technology
Prospectus Objective	Technology
Inception Date	Sep-16
Open to New Investments	Y

Prices
Price (as of 9/30/2019)	34.70
52-Week High	35.94
52-Week Low	23.92

Total Returns (%)
3-Month	6-Month	1-Year	3-Year	5-Year
5.15	7.17	15.07	71.58	

3-Year Standard Deviation	24.55
Effective Duration	

Valuation
Premium/Discount (1-Year Average)	0.05

Company Information
Provider	First Trust
Manager/Tenure	Jon C. Erickson (3), Daniel J. Lindquist (3), David G. McGarel (3), 3 others
Website	http://www.ftportfolios.com/
Address	First Trust 120 E. Liberty Drive, Suite 400 Wheaton IL 60187 United States
Phone Number	800-621-1675

PERFORMANCE

Ratings History
Date	Overall Rating	Risk Rating	Reward Rating
Q3-19	B-	C	B+
Q4-18	C+	C-	B
Q4-17	D	B+	C
Q4-16	U		
Q4-15			

Asset & Performance History
Date	NAV	1-Year Total Return
2018	25.87	-13.51
2017	30.09	31.87
2016	22.94	
2015		
2014		
2013		

Total Assets: $31,233,638
Asset Allocation
Asset	%
Cash	0%
Stocks	100%
US Stocks	98%
Bonds	0%
US Bonds	0%
Other	0%

Services Offered:

Investment Strategy: The investment seeks investment results that correspond generally to the price and yield (before the fund's fees and expenses) of the Nasdaq US Smart Semiconductor Index. The fund invests at least 90% of its net assets (including investment borrowings) in the common stocks and depository receipts that comprise the index. The index is designed to provide exposure to U.S. companies comprising the semiconductor sector that have been selected based upon their liquidity and weighted based upon their cumulative score on three investing factors: volatility, value and growth. It is non-diversified. **Top Holdings:** Texas Instruments Inc Analog Devices Inc Intel Corp InterDigital Inc KLA Corp

First Trust NASDAQ Technology Dividend Index Fund   B-   BUY

Ticker	Traded On	NAV	Total Assets ($)	Dividend Yield (TTM)	Turnover Ratio	Expense Ratio
TDIV	NAS CM	40.09	$1,010,555,716	2.41	27	0.5

Ratings
Reward   B
Risk   C
Recent Upgrade/Downgrade   Up

Fund Information
Fund Type   Exchange Traded Funds
Category   Technology Sector Equity
Sub-Category   Technology
Prospectus Objective   Technology
Inception Date   Aug-12
Open to New Investments   Y

Prices
Price (as of 9/30/2019)   40.11
52-Week High   41.12
52-Week Low   31.20

PERFORMANCE

Total Returns (%)

3-Month	6-Month	1-Year	3-Year	5-Year
1.93	4.53	7.01	47.14	71.05

3-Year Standard Deviation   14.05
Effective Duration

Valuation
Premium/Discount (1-Year Average)   0.02

Company Information
Provider   First Trust
Manager/Tenure   Jon C. Erickson (7), Daniel J. Lindquist
                    (7), David G. McGarel (7), 3 others
Website   http://www.ftportfolios.com/
Address   First Trust 120 E. Liberty Drive, Suite
                    400 Wheaton IL 60187 United States
Phone Number   800-621-1675

Ratings History

Date	Overall Rating	Risk Rating	Reward Rating
Q3-19	B-	C	B
Q4-18	C+	C	B
Q4-17	B	B-	B+
Q4-16	B	C	B+
Q4-15	B	B-	B

Asset & Performance History

Date	NAV	1-Year Total Return
2018	33.16	-3.04
2017	35.15	21.92
2016	29.55	19.64
2015	25.35	-5.98
2014	27.64	15.54
2013	24.63	30.38

Total Assets: $1,010,555,716
Asset Allocation

Asset	%
Cash	1%
Stocks	99%
US Stocks	82%
Bonds	0%
US Bonds	0%
Other	0%

Services Offered:

Investment Strategy: The investment seeks investment results that correspond generally to the price and yield (before the fund's fees and expenses) of an equity index called the NASDAQ Technology Dividend IndexSM. The fund will normally invest at least 90% of its net assets (including investment borrowings) in the common stocks and depositary receipts that comprise the index. The index is owned and was developed by Nasdaq, Inc. (the "index provider"). The index includes up to 100 technology and telecommunications companies that pay a regular or common dividend. The fund is non-diversified. **Top Holdings:** Apple Inc Microsoft Corp Intel Corp International Business Machines Corp Cisco Systems Inc

---

First Trust Nasdaq Transportation ETF   B-   BUY

Ticker	Traded On	NAV	Total Assets ($)	Dividend Yield (TTM)	Turnover Ratio	Expense Ratio
FTXR	NAS CM	23.17	$2,317,402	1.53	108	0.6

Ratings
Reward   B
Risk   C
Recent Upgrade/Downgrade   Up

Fund Information
Fund Type   Exchange Traded Funds
Category   Industrials Sector Equity
Sub-Category   Industrials
Prospectus Objective   Unaligned
Inception Date   Sep-16
Open to New Investments   Y

Prices
Price (as of 9/30/2019)   23.08
52-Week High   25.40
52-Week Low   20.86

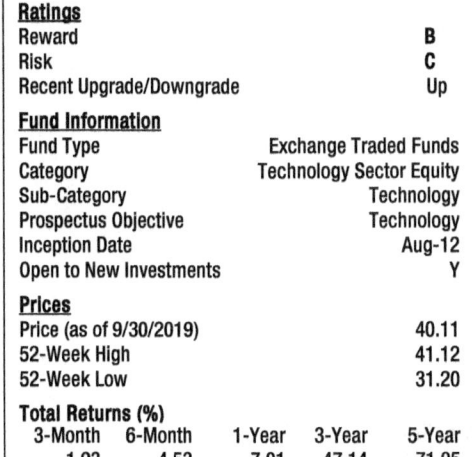

PERFORMANCE

Total Returns (%)

3-Month	6-Month	1-Year	3-Year	5-Year
-2.86	-1.87	-7.57	17.52	

3-Year Standard Deviation   18.17
Effective Duration

Valuation
Premium/Discount (1-Year Average)   0.13

Company Information
Provider   First Trust
Manager/Tenure   Jon C. Erickson (3), Daniel J. Lindquist
                    (3), David G. McGarel (3), 3 others
Website   http://www.ftportfolios.com/
Address   First Trust 120 E. Liberty Drive, Suite
                    400 Wheaton IL 60187 United States
Phone Number   800-621-1675

Ratings History

Date	Overall Rating	Risk Rating	Reward Rating
Q3-19	B-	C	B
Q4-18	B-	C	B
Q4-17	D	B+	C-
Q4-16	U		
Q4-15			

Asset & Performance History

Date	NAV	1-Year Total Return
2018	21.65	-15
2017	25.87	15.63
2016	22.66	
2015		
2014		
2013		

Total Assets: $2,317,402
Asset Allocation

Asset	%
Cash	1%
Stocks	99%
US Stocks	99%
Bonds	0%
US Bonds	0%
Other	0%

Services Offered:

Investment Strategy: The investment seeks investment results that correspond generally to the price and yield (before the fund's fees and expenses) of the Nasdaq US Smart Transportation Index. The fund invests at least 90% of its net assets (including investment borrowings) in the common stocks and depository receipts that comprise the index. The index is designed to provide exposure to U.S. companies comprising the transportation sector that have been selected based upon their liquidity and weighted based upon their cumulative score on three investing factors: volatility, value and growth. It is non-diversified. **Top Holdings:** General Motors Co United Airlines Holdings Inc Ford Motor Co Genuine Parts Co Norfolk Southern Corp

First Trust Preferred Securities and Income ETF

B- **BUY**

Ticker	Traded On	NAV	Total Assets ($)	Dividend Yield (TTM)	Turnover Ratio	Expense Ratio
FPE	NYSE Arca	19.71	$4,424,785,872	5.55		0.85

Ratings
Reward	B-
Risk	C+
Recent Upgrade/Downgrade	

Fund Information
Fund Type	Exchange Traded Funds
Category	US Fixed Income
Sub-Category	Preferred Stock
Prospectus Objective	Income
Inception Date	Feb-13
Open to New Investments	Y

Prices
Price (as of 9/30/2019)	19.73
52-Week High	19.84
52-Week Low	17.82

Total Returns (%)
3-Month	6-Month	1-Year	3-Year	5-Year
2.96	6.32	9.47	19.68	38.94

3-Year Standard Deviation	4.42
Effective Duration	3.70

Valuation
Premium/Discount (1-Year Average)	0.12

Company Information
Provider	First Trust
Manager/Tenure	Scott T. Fleming (6), Robert Wolf (6)
Website	http://www.ftportfolios.com/
Address	First Trust 120 E. Liberty Drive, Suite 400 Wheaton IL 60187 United States
Phone Number	800-621-1675

PERFORMANCE

Ratings History	Overall Rating	Risk Rating	Reward Rating
Date			
Q3-19	B-	C+	B-
Q4-18	C	C+	D+
Q4-17	B	A-	C+
Q4-16	C	C+	C
Q4-15	C	C+	C

Asset & Performance History		1-Year
Date	NAV	Total Return
2018	17.98	-4.68
2017	19.99	11.35
2016	18.95	6.46
2015	18.89	6.21
2014	18.79	10.91
2013	17.98	

Total Assets: $4,424,785,872
Asset Allocation
Asset	%
Cash	3%
Stocks	0%
US Stocks	0%
Bonds	36%
US Bonds	20%
Other	0%

Services Offered:

Investment Strategy: The investment seeks total return and to provide current income. Under normal market conditions, the fund invests at least 80% of its net assets (including investment borrowings) in preferred securities ("Preferred Securities") and income-producing debt securities ("Income Securities"). The fund invests in securities that are traded over-the-counter or listed on an exchange. **Top Holdings:** EMERA INCORPORATED 6.75% Enel - Societa per Azioni 8.75% GMAC Capital Trust I Pfd Secs 2011-15.2.40 Gtd Series 2 Catlin Insurance Company Ltd. 5.28% BHP Billiton Finance (USA) Limited 1.69%

First Trust Utilities AlphaDEX® Fund

B- **BUY**

Ticker	Traded On	NAV	Total Assets ($)	Dividend Yield (TTM)	Turnover Ratio	Expense Ratio
FXU	NYSE Arca	29.63	$1,308,227,487	2.49	60	0.63

Ratings
Reward	B-
Risk	C+
Recent Upgrade/Downgrade	Up

Fund Information
Fund Type	Exchange Traded Funds
Category	Utilities Sector Equity
Sub-Category	Utilities
Prospectus Objective	Utility
Inception Date	May-07
Open to New Investments	Y

Prices
Price (as of 9/30/2019)	29.65
52-Week High	29.95
52-Week Low	25.97

Total Returns (%)
3-Month	6-Month	1-Year	3-Year	5-Year
4.44	6.10	10.34	24.70	52.98

3-Year Standard Deviation	8.71
Effective Duration	

Valuation
Premium/Discount (1-Year Average)	-0.01

Company Information
Provider	First Trust
Manager/Tenure	Jon C. Erickson (12), Daniel J. Lindquist (12), David G. McGarel (12), 3 others
Website	http://www.ftportfolios.com/
Address	First Trust 120 E. Liberty Drive, Suite 400 Wheaton IL 60187 United States
Phone Number	800-621-1675

PERFORMANCE

Ratings History	Overall Rating	Risk Rating	Reward Rating
Date			
Q3-19	B-	C+	B-
Q4-18	B	C+	B+
Q4-17	C+	B	C
Q4-16	B-	C	B
Q4-15	B-	C	B

Asset & Performance History		1-Year
Date	NAV	Total Return
2018	26.8	5.59
2017	26	0.93
2016	26.73	22.54
2015	22.4	-6.42
2014	24.87	25.5
2013	20.27	17.6

Total Assets: $1,308,227,487
Asset Allocation
Asset	%
Cash	0%
Stocks	100%
US Stocks	100%
Bonds	0%
US Bonds	0%
Other	0%

Services Offered:

Investment Strategy: The investment seeks investment results that correspond generally to the price and yield (before the fund's fees and expenses) of an equity index called the StrataQuant® Utilities Index. The fund will normally invest at least 90% of its net assets (including investment borrowings) in common stocks that comprise the index. The index is a modified equal-dollar weighted index designed by IDI to objectively identify and select stocks from the Russell 1000® Index in the utilities sector that may generate positive alpha relative to traditional passive-style indices through the use of the AlphaDEX® selection methodology. **Top Holdings:** Vistra Energy Corp AT&T Inc PPL Corp National Fuel Gas Co Telephone and Data Systems Inc

First Trust Water ETF   B-   BUY

Ticker	Traded On	NAV	Total Assets ($)	Dividend Yield (TTM)	Turnover Ratio	Expense Ratio
FIW	NYSE Arca	56.12	$468,607,744	0.67	11	0.55

Ratings
Reward   B
Risk   C
Recent Upgrade/Downgrade   Up

Fund Information
Fund Type   Exchange Traded Funds
Category   Industrials Sector Equity
Sub-Category   Miscellaneous Sector
Prospectus Objective   Natl Res
Inception Date   May-07
Open to New Investments   Y

Prices
Price (as of 9/30/2019)   56.11
52-Week High   56.69
52-Week Low   41.46

Total Returns (%)

3-Month	6-Month	1-Year	3-Year	5-Year
2.35	9.21	11.80	52.97	87.06

3-Year Standard Deviation   14.99
Effective Duration

Valuation
Premium/Discount (1-Year Average)   0.03

Company Information
Provider   First Trust
Manager/Tenure   Jon C. Erickson (12), Daniel J. Lindquist (12), David G. McGarel (12), 3 others
Website   http://www.ftportfolios.com/
Address   First Trust 120 E. Liberty Drive, Suite 400 Wheaton IL 60187 United States
Phone Number   800-621-1675

PERFORMANCE

Ratings History

Date	Overall Rating	Risk Rating	Reward Rating
Q3-19	B-	C	B
Q4-18	C+	C	B
Q4-17	B+	C+	A
Q4-16	C+	C-	B
Q4-15	B-	C+	B-

Asset & Performance History

Date	NAV	1-Year Total Return
2018	43.96	-8.88
2017	48.58	24.25
2016	39.6	32.21
2015	30.12	-9.81
2014	33.65	0.35
2013	33.78	30.91

Total Assets: $468,607,744

Asset Allocation

Asset	%
Cash	0%
Stocks	100%
US Stocks	98%
Bonds	0%
US Bonds	0%
Other	0%

Services Offered:

Investment Strategy: The investment seeks investment results that correspond generally to the price and yield (before the fund's fees and expenses) of an equity index called the ISE Clean Edge Water Index. The fund will normally invest at least 90% of its net assets (including investment borrowings) in the common stocks and depositary receipts that comprise the index. The index is designed to track the performance of small, mid and large capitalization companies that derive a substantial portion of their revenues from the potable water and wastewater industry, according to Clean Edge. **Top Holdings:** IDEXX Laboratories Inc   American Water Works Co Inc   Ecolab Inc   Tetra Tech Inc   IDEX Corp

Global X SuperDividend® REIT ETF   B-   BUY

Ticker	Traded On	NAV	Total Assets ($)	Dividend Yield (TTM)	Turnover Ratio	Expense Ratio
SRET	NAS CM	14.99	$324,475,083	7.9	42	0.59

Ratings
Reward   B-
Risk   C+
Recent Upgrade/Downgrade   Up

Fund Information
Fund Type   Exchange Traded Funds
Category   Real Estate Sector Equity
Sub-Category   Real Estate
Prospectus Objective   Real Estate
Inception Date   Mar-15
Open to New Investments   Y

Prices
Price (as of 9/30/2019)   15.04
52-Week High   15.24
52-Week Low   13.25

Total Returns (%)

3-Month	6-Month	1-Year	3-Year	5-Year
3.39	3.22	7.88	25.84	

3-Year Standard Deviation   12.02
Effective Duration

Valuation
Premium/Discount (1-Year Average)   0.18

Company Information
Provider   Global X Funds
Manager/Tenure   Chang Kim (4), Nam To (1), Wayne Xie (0), 1 other
Website   http://www.globalxfunds.com
Address   Global X Funds 600 Lexington Avenue, 20th Floor New York NY 10022 United States
Phone Number   888-493-8631

PERFORMANCE

Ratings History

Date	Overall Rating	Risk Rating	Reward Rating
Q3-19	B-	C+	B-
Q4-18	C+	C	B
Q4-17	C+	B-	C+
Q4-16	D+	C-	B-
Q4-15	U		

Asset & Performance History

Date	NAV	1-Year Total Return
2018	13.59	-5.14
2017	15.5	17.8
2016	14.3	23.72
2015	12.55	
2014		
2013		

Total Assets: $324,475,083

Asset Allocation

Asset	%
Cash	0%
Stocks	100%
US Stocks	87%
Bonds	0%
US Bonds	0%
Other	0%

Services Offered:

Investment Strategy: The investment seeks investment results that correspond generally to the price and yield performance, before fees and expenses, of the Solactive Global SuperDividend® REIT Index. The fund invests at least 80% of its total assets in the securities of the underlying index and in American Depositary Receipts ("ADRs") and Global Depositary Receipts ("GDRs") based on the securities in the underlying index. The underlying index tracks the performance of REITs that rank among the highest yielding REITs globally, as determined by Solactive AG, the provider of the underlying index. **Top Holdings:** Independence Realty Trust Inc   VEREIT Inc Class A   Stockland Corp Ltd   Arbor Realty Trust Inc   Starwood Property Trust Inc

Grayscale Bitcoin Trust

B   **BUY**

Ticker	Traded On	NAV	Total Assets ($)	Dividend Yield (TTM)	Turnover Ratio	Expense Ratio
GBTC	OTC BB	7.86	$1,924,721,609	0		2

Ratings

Reward	A+
Risk	D+
Recent Upgrade/Downgrade	Up

Fund Information

Fund Type	Exchange Traded Funds
Category	Trading Tools
Sub-Category	Trading--Miscellaneous
Prospectus Objective	Growth & Inc
Inception Date	Sep-13
Open to New Investments	Y

Prices

Price (as of 9/30/2019)	10.59
52-Week High	17.08
52-Week Low	3.84

Total Returns (%)

3-Month	6-Month	1-Year	3-Year	5-Year
-24.56	93.87	20.39	1,154.20	1,795.68

3-Year Standard Deviation	98.93
Effective Duration	

Valuation

Premium/Discount (1-Year Average)	24.90

Company Information

Provider	Grayscale
Manager/Tenure	Management Team (6)
Website	http://grayscale.co/bitcoin-investment-trust/#overview
Address	Grayscale 636 Avenue of the Americas New York New York 10011 United States
Phone Number	212-668-5920

PERFORMANCE

Ratings History

Date	Overall Rating	Risk Rating	Reward Rating
Q3-19	B	D+	A+
Q4-18	D+	D+	C-
Q4-17	B+	C	A+
Q4-16	D+	D+	D+
Q4-15			

Asset & Performance History

Date	NAV	1-Year Total Return
2018	3.72	-74.61
2017	14.65	1,391.43
2016	0.98	119.87
2015	0.45	33.36
2014	0.33	-59.95
2013	0.84	

Total Assets: $1,924,721,609

Asset Allocation

Asset	%
Cash	-55%
Stocks	0%
US Stocks	0%
Bonds	0%
US Bonds	0%
Other	155%

Services Offered:

Investment Strategy: The investment objective of the Trust is for the NAV per Share to track the Bitcoin Market Price per Share, less the Trust's liabilities (including estimated accrued expenses). **Top Holdings:** Bitcoin

Innovation Shares NextGen Protocol ETF

B-   **BUY**

Ticker	Traded On	NAV	Total Assets ($)	Dividend Yield (TTM)	Turnover Ratio	Expense Ratio
KOIN	NYSE Arca	26.81	$10,052,402	0.8		0.95

Ratings

Reward	B
Risk	C
Recent Upgrade/Downgrade	Up

Fund Information

Fund Type	Exchange Traded Funds
Category	Technology Sector Equity
Sub-Category	Technology
Prospectus Objective	Unaligned
Inception Date	Jan-18
Open to New Investments	Y

Prices

Price (as of 9/30/2019)	26.81
52-Week High	28.37
52-Week Low	20.71

Total Returns (%)

3-Month	6-Month	1-Year	3-Year	5-Year
-1.97	1.93	0.72		

3-Year Standard Deviation	
Effective Duration	

Valuation

Premium/Discount (1-Year Average)	-0.15

Company Information

Provider	Innovation Shares
Manager/Tenure	Anand Desai (1), Dustin Lewellyn (1), Ernesto Tong (1)
Website	http://www.innovationshares.com
Address	Innovation Shares 10900 Hefner Pointe Drive, Suite 207 Oklahoma City OK 73120 United States
Phone Number	833-466-6383

PERFORMANCE

Ratings History

Date	Overall Rating	Risk Rating	Reward Rating
Q3-19	B-	C	B
Q4-18	U		
Q4-17			
Q4-16			
Q4-15			

Asset & Performance History

Date	NAV	1-Year Total Return
2018	21.96	
2017		
2016		
2015		
2014		
2013		

Total Assets: $10,052,402

Asset Allocation

Asset	%
Cash	0%
Stocks	100%
US Stocks	68%
Bonds	0%
US Bonds	0%
Other	0%

Services Offered:

Investment Strategy: The investment seeks to provide investment results that, before fees and expenses, track the performance of the Innovation Labs Blockchain Innovators Index (the "index"). The fund will normally invest at least 80% of its total assets in securities of the index. The index was designed by the fund's index creator, to measure the performance of a diversified group of publicly-listed companies that use, or are involved in, blockchain ("Blockchain Innovators"). **Top Holdings:** Taiwan Semiconductor Manufacturing Co Ltd ADR Visa Inc Class A Mastercard Inc A NVIDIA Corp Intel Corp

Invesco Aerospace & Defense ETF   B   BUY

Ticker	Traded On	NAV	Total Assets ($)	Dividend Yield (TTM)	Turnover Ratio	Expense Ratio
PPA	NYSE Arca	67.71	$1,086,711,186	0.95	15	0.59

Ratings

Reward	B+
Risk	C
Recent Upgrade/Downgrade	Up

Fund Information

Fund Type	Exchange Traded Funds
Category	Industrials Sector Equity
Sub-Category	Industrials
Prospectus Objective	Unaligned
Inception Date	Oct-05
Open to New Investments	Y

Prices

Price (as of 9/30/2019)	67.70
52-Week High	69.48
52-Week Low	46.46

Total Returns (%)

3-Month	6-Month	1-Year	3-Year	5-Year
5.27	15.27	11.04	80.30	126.50

3-Year Standard Deviation	16.7
Effective Duration	

Valuation

Premium/Discount (1-Year Average)	0.00

Company Information

Provider	Invesco
Manager/Tenure	Peter Hubbard (12), Michael Jeanette (11), Tony Seisser (5)
Website	http://www.invesco.com/us
Address	Invesco 11 Greenway Plaza, Ste. 2500 Houston TX 77046 United States
Phone Number	800-659-1005

PERFORMANCE

Ratings History

Date	Overall Rating	Risk Rating	Reward Rating
Q3-19	B	C	B+
Q4-18	B-	C+	B
Q4-17	B+	B-	A+
Q4-16	B	C+	B+
Q4-15	B	B	B

Asset & Performance History

Date	NAV	1-Year Total Return
2018	49.5	-7.35
2017	53.87	30.02
2016	41.74	19.2
2015	35.66	4.23
2014	34.7	12.74
2013	30.98	49.81

Total Assets: $1,086,711,186

Asset Allocation

Asset	%
Cash	0%
Stocks	100%
US Stocks	98%
Bonds	0%
US Bonds	0%
Other	0%

Services Offered:

Investment Strategy: The investment seeks to track the investment results (before fees and expenses) of the SPADE® Defense Index. The fund generally will invest at least 90% of its total assets in the securities that comprise the underlying index. The underlying index is composed of common stocks of companies that are engaged principally in the development, manufacture, operation and support of U.S. defense, military, homeland security and space operations. The fund is non-diversified. **Top Holdings:** L3Harris Technologies Inc Lockheed Martin Corp United Technologies Corp Boeing Co Honeywell International Inc

---

Invesco Dow Jones Industrial Average Dividend ETF   B-   BUY

Ticker	Traded On	NAV	Total Assets ($)	Dividend Yield (TTM)	Turnover Ratio	Expense Ratio
DJD	NYSE Arca	37.22	$81,876,769	2.75	20	0.07

Ratings

Reward	B
Risk	C
Recent Upgrade/Downgrade	Up

Fund Information

Fund Type	Exchange Traded Funds
Category	US Equity Large Cap Value
Sub-Category	Large Value
Prospectus Objective	Growth & Inc
Inception Date	Dec-15
Open to New Investments	Y

Prices

Price (as of 9/30/2019)	37.23
52-Week High	38.05
52-Week Low	31.25

Total Returns (%)

3-Month	6-Month	1-Year	3-Year	5-Year
0.57	2.64	5.46	47.98	

3-Year Standard Deviation	11.22
Effective Duration	

Valuation

Premium/Discount (1-Year Average)	0.11

Company Information

Provider	Invesco
Manager/Tenure	Peter Hubbard (1), Michael Jeanette (1), Tony Seisser (1)
Website	http://www.invesco.com/us
Address	Invesco 11 Greenway Plaza, Ste. 2500 Houston TX 77046 United States
Phone Number	800-659-1005

PERFORMANCE

Ratings History

Date	Overall Rating	Risk Rating	Reward Rating
Q3-19	B-	C	B
Q4-18	C+	C	B
Q4-17	C-	B+	C
Q4-16	D-	C	B
Q4-15			

Asset & Performance History

Date	NAV	1-Year Total Return
2018	33.17	0.11
2017	34.02	21.75
2016	28.82	16.26
2015	25.3	
2014		
2013		

Total Assets: $81,876,769

Asset Allocation

Asset	%
Cash	0%
Stocks	100%
US Stocks	100%
Bonds	0%
US Bonds	0%
Other	0%

Services Offered:

Investment Strategy: The investment seeks to track the investment results (before fees and expenses) of the Dow Jones Industrial Average Yield Weighted (the "underlying index"). The fund will generally invest at least 90% of its total assets in the securities that comprise the underlying index. The underlying index is designed to provide exposure to dividend-paying equity securities of companies included in the Dow Jones Industrial Average™, which is a price-weighted index of 30 U.S. companies that meet certain size, listing and liquidity requirements. The fund is non-diversified. **Top Holdings:** International Business Machines Corp Verizon Communications Inc Coca-Cola Co Chevron Corp The Home Depot Inc

Invesco DWA Consumer Cyclicals Momentum ETF   B-   BUY

Ticker	Traded On	NAV	Total Assets ($)	Dividend Yield (TTM)	Turnover Ratio	Expense Ratio
PEZ	NAS CM	52.80	$31,681,391	0.1		0.6

Ratings
Reward   B
Risk   C
Recent Upgrade/Downgrade   Up

Fund Information
Fund Type   Exchange Traded Funds
Category   Consumer Goods & Svcs
Sub-Category   Consumer Cyclical
Prospectus Objective   Unaligned
Inception Date   Oct-06
Open to New Investments   Y

Prices
Price (as of 9/30/2019)   52.75
52-Week High   59.29
52-Week Low   43.46

Total Returns (%)

3-Month	6-Month	1-Year	3-Year	5-Year
-5.60	-4.30	-10.71	26.13	35.50

3-Year Standard Deviation   17.22
Effective Duration

Valuation
Premium/Discount (1-Year Average)   -0.02

Company Information
Provider   Invesco
Manager/Tenure   Peter Hubbard (12), Michael Jeanette (11), Tony Seisser (5)
Website   http://www.invesco.com/us
Address   Invesco 11 Greenway Plaza, Ste. 2500 Houston TX 77046 United States
Phone Number   800-659-1005

PERFORMANCE

Ratings History

Date	Overall Rating	Risk Rating	Reward Rating
Q3-19	B-	C	B
Q4-18	C+	C-	B
Q4-17	C+	B-	C+
Q4-16	B-	C	B
Q4-15	B	B-	B+

Asset & Performance History

Date	NAV	1-Year Total Return
2018	46.82	-6.3
2017	50.15	19.33
2016	42.21	-3.31
2015	44.02	-0.7
2014	44.6	8.07
2013	41.33	39.87

Total Assets: $31,681,391

Asset Allocation

Asset	%
Cash	0%
Stocks	100%
US Stocks	97%
Bonds	0%
US Bonds	0%
Other	0%

Services Offered:

Investment Strategy: The investment seeks to track the investment results (before fees and expenses) of the Dorsey Wright® Consumer Cyclicals Technical Leaders Index (the "underlying index"). The fund generally will invest at least 90% of its total assets in the securities that comprise the underlying index. The underlying index is composed of at least 30 securities of companies in the consumer discretionary (or cyclicals) sector that have powerful relative strength or "momentum" characteristics. **Top Holdings:** O'Reilly Automotive Inc   The Trade Desk Inc A   Nike Inc B   IAC/InterActiveCorp   Live Nation Entertainment Inc

---

Invesco DWA Consumer Staples Momentum ETF   B-   BUY

Ticker	Traded On	NAV	Total Assets ($)	Dividend Yield (TTM)	Turnover Ratio	Expense Ratio
PSL	NAS CM	72.08	$205,430,503	0.53		0.6

Ratings
Reward   B
Risk   C
Recent Upgrade/Downgrade   Up

Fund Information
Fund Type   Exchange Traded Funds
Category   Consumer Goods & Svcs
Sub-Category   Consumer Defensive
Prospectus Objective   Unaligned
Inception Date   Oct-06
Open to New Investments   Y

Prices
Price (as of 9/30/2019)   72.10
52-Week High   75.95
52-Week Low   62.43

Total Returns (%)

3-Month	6-Month	1-Year	3-Year	5-Year
-0.11	2.06	1.60	31.14	63.06

3-Year Standard Deviation   9.74
Effective Duration

Valuation
Premium/Discount (1-Year Average)   -0.02

Company Information
Provider   Invesco
Manager/Tenure   Peter Hubbard (12), Michael Jeanette (11), Tony Seisser (5)
Website   http://www.invesco.com/us
Address   Invesco 11 Greenway Plaza, Ste. 2500 Houston TX 77046 United States
Phone Number   800-659-1005

PERFORMANCE

Ratings History

Date	Overall Rating	Risk Rating	Reward Rating
Q3-19	B-	C	B
Q4-18	B-	C	B
Q4-17	B	B	B
Q4-16	B	C+	B
Q4-15	B+	B	A

Asset & Performance History

Date	NAV	1-Year Total Return
2018	65.44	1.51
2017	64.93	21.4
2016	53.68	-3.49
2015	56.77	13.48
2014	50.64	15.77
2013	44.19	34.53

Total Assets: $205,430,503

Asset Allocation

Asset	%
Cash	0%
Stocks	100%
US Stocks	100%
Bonds	0%
US Bonds	0%
Other	0%

Services Offered:

Investment Strategy: The investment seeks to track the investment results (before fees and expenses) of the Dorsey Wright® Consumer Staples Technical Leaders Index (the "underlying index"). The fund generally will invest at least 90% of its total assets in the securities that comprise the underlying index. The underlying index is composed of at least 30 securities of companies in the consumer staples sector that have powerful relative strength or "momentum" characteristics. **Top Holdings:** Tyson Foods Inc Class A   Boston Beer Co Inc Class A   Church & Dwight Co Inc   Chegg Inc   Constellation Brands Inc A

Invesco DWA Financial Momentum ETF   B   BUY

Ticker	Traded On	NAV	Total Assets ($)	Dividend Yield (TTM)	Turnover Ratio	Expense Ratio
PFI	NAS CM	37.36	$65,382,803	1.09		0.6

Ratings
Reward   B+
Risk   C
Recent Upgrade/Downgrade   Up

Fund Information
Fund Type   Exchange Traded Funds
Category   Financials Sector Equity
Sub-Category   Financial
Prospectus Objective   Financial
Inception Date   Oct-06
Open to New Investments Y

Prices
Price (as of 9/30/2019)   37.43
52-Week High   38.84
52-Week Low   27.13

Total Returns (%)

3-Month	6-Month	1-Year	3-Year	5-Year
-0.12	11.15	11.21	27.03	42.63

3-Year Standard Deviation   14
Effective Duration

Valuation
Premium/Discount (1-Year Average)   -0.05

Company Information
Provider   Invesco
Manager/Tenure   Peter Hubbard (12), Michael Jeanette (11), Tony Seisser (5)
Website   http://www.invesco.com/us
Address   Invesco 11 Greenway Plaza, Ste. 2500 Houston TX 77046 United States
Phone Number   800-659-1005

PERFORMANCE

Ratings History

Date	Overall Rating	Risk Rating	Reward Rating
Q3-19	B	C	B+
Q4-18	C	C-	C
Q4-17	B	B+	C+
Q4-16	C	C-	B-
Q4-15	B-	C	B

Asset & Performance History

Date	NAV	1-Year Total Return
2018	28.67	-16.66
2017	35	14.82
2016	30.6	2.16
2015	30.61	1.13
2014	30.71	6.22
2013	29.24	40.25

Total Assets: $65,382,803
Asset Allocation

Asset	%
Cash	0%
Stocks	100%
US Stocks	97%
Bonds	0%
US Bonds	0%
Other	0%

Services Offered:

Investment Strategy: The investment seeks to track the investment results (before fees and expenses) of the Dorsey Wright® Financials Technical Leaders Index (the "underlying index"). The fund generally will invest at least 90% of its total assets in the securities that comprise the underlying index. The underlying index is composed of at least 30 securities of companies in the financials sector that have powerful relative strength or "momentum" characteristics. **Top Holdings:** MarketAxess Holdings Inc Crown Castle International Corp Mastercard Inc A Extra Space Storage Inc UDR Inc

Invesco DWA Industrials Momentum ETF   B   BUY

Ticker	Traded On	NAV	Total Assets ($)	Dividend Yield (TTM)	Turnover Ratio	Expense Ratio
PRN	NAS CM	65.55	$131,102,482	0.43		0.6

Ratings
Reward   B
Risk   C
Recent Upgrade/Downgrade   Up

Fund Information
Fund Type   Exchange Traded Funds
Category   Industrials Sector Equity
Sub-Category   Industrials
Prospectus Objective   Unaligned
Inception Date   Oct-06
Open to New Investments Y

Prices
Price (as of 9/30/2019)   65.57
52-Week High   69.69
52-Week Low   47.61

Total Returns (%)

3-Month	6-Month	1-Year	3-Year	5-Year
-2.06	5.76	2.98	37.24	50.48

3-Year Standard Deviation   16.06
Effective Duration

Valuation
Premium/Discount (1-Year Average)   -0.15

Company Information
Provider   Invesco
Manager/Tenure   Peter Hubbard (12), Michael Jeanette (11), Tony Seisser (5)
Website   http://www.invesco.com/us
Address   Invesco 11 Greenway Plaza, Ste. 2500 Houston TX 77046 United States
Phone Number   800-659-1005

PERFORMANCE

Ratings History

Date	Overall Rating	Risk Rating	Reward Rating
Q3-19	B	C	B
Q4-18	C	C-	C
Q4-17	B	B	B+
Q4-16	C	C-	B-
Q4-15	C+	C	B-

Asset & Performance History

Date	NAV	1-Year Total Return
2018	51.22	-15.54
2017	60.81	22.48
2016	49.97	13.05
2015	44.46	-5.7
2014	47.35	-0.42
2013	47.72	48.82

Total Assets: $131,102,482
Asset Allocation

Asset	%
Cash	0%
Stocks	100%
US Stocks	100%
Bonds	0%
US Bonds	0%
Other	0%

Services Offered:

Investment Strategy: The investment seeks to track the investment results (before fees and expenses) of the Dorsey Wright® Industrials Technical Leaders Index (the "underlying index"). The fund generally will invest at least 90% of its total assets in the securities that comprise the underlying index. The underlying index is composed of at least 30 securities of companies in the industrials sector that have powerful relative strength or "momentum" characteristics. **Top Holdings:** Heico Corp TransDigm Group Inc Sherwin-Williams Co Lockheed Martin Corp Fair Isaac Corp

Invesco DWA Momentum ETF   B-   BUY

Ticker	Traded On	NAV	Total Assets ($)	Dividend Yield (TTM)	Turnover Ratio	Expense Ratio
PDP	NAS CM	60.92	$1,705,890,370	0.26	82	0.62

Ratings
Reward	B-
Risk	C+
Recent Upgrade/Downgrade	Up

Fund Information
Fund Type	Exchange Traded Funds
Category	US Equity Mid Cap
Sub-Category	Mid-Cap Growth
Prospectus Objective	Growth
Inception Date	Mar-07
Open to New Investments	Y

Prices
Price (as of 9/30/2019)	60.90
52-Week High	63.22
52-Week Low	45.29

Total Returns (%)
3-Month	6-Month	1-Year	3-Year	5-Year
0.39	6.77	2.86	45.18	60.78

3-Year Standard Deviation	13.66
Effective Duration	

Valuation
Premium/Discount (1-Year Average)	-0.02

Company Information
Provider	Invesco
Manager/Tenure	Peter Hubbard (12), Michael Jeanette (11), Tony Seisser (5)
Website	http://www.invesco.com/us
Address	Invesco 11 Greenway Plaza, Ste. 2500 Houston TX 77046 United States
Phone Number	800-659-1005

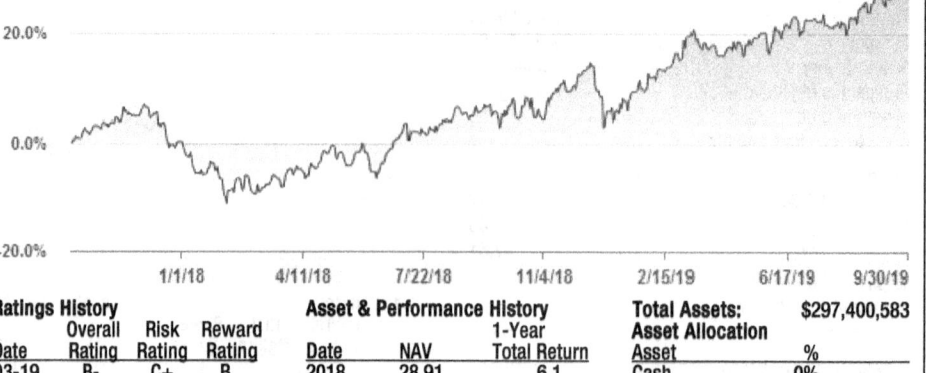

PERFORMANCE

Ratings History
Date	Overall Rating	Risk Rating	Reward Rating
Q3-19	B-	C+	B-
Q4-18	C	C+	C
Q4-17	B	B+	B-
Q4-16	C+	C+	C+
Q4-15	C+	B-	C+

Asset & Performance History
Date	NAV	1-Year Total Return
2018	48.49	-5.88
2017	51.61	23.36
2016	41.96	2.17
2015	41.4	1.3
2014	41.02	12.12
2013	36.64	31.79

Total Assets: $1,705,890,370
Asset Allocation
Asset	%
Cash	0%
Stocks	100%
US Stocks	100%
Bonds	0%
US Bonds	0%
Other	0%

Services Offered:

Investment Strategy: The investment seeks to track the investment results (before fees and expenses) of the Dorsey Wright® Technical Leaders Index. The fund generally will invest at least 90% of its total assets in securities that comprise the underlying index. The underlying index is composed of approximately 100 securities from an eligible universe of approximately 1,000 securities of the largest constituents by market capitalization within the NASDAQ US Benchmark Index. **Top Holdings:** American Tower Corp Apple Inc Ball Corp O'Reilly Automotive Inc Mastercard Inc A

Invesco DWA Utilities Momentum ETF   B-   BUY

Ticker	Traded On	NAV	Total Assets ($)	Dividend Yield (TTM)	Turnover Ratio	Expense Ratio
PUI	NAS CM	34.99	$297,400,583	1.56		0.6

Ratings
Reward	B
Risk	C+
Recent Upgrade/Downgrade	

Fund Information
Fund Type	Exchange Traded Funds
Category	Utilities Sector Equity
Sub-Category	Utilities
Prospectus Objective	Utility
Inception Date	Oct-05
Open to New Investments	Y

Prices
Price (as of 9/30/2019)	35.02
52-Week High	35.16
52-Week Low	28.07

Total Returns (%)
3-Month	6-Month	1-Year	3-Year	5-Year
8.36	10.27	24.66	46.47	81.91

3-Year Standard Deviation	10.86
Effective Duration	

Valuation
Premium/Discount (1-Year Average)	0.09

Company Information
Provider	Invesco
Manager/Tenure	Peter Hubbard (12), Michael Jeanette (11), Tony Seisser (5)
Website	http://www.invesco.com/us
Address	Invesco 11 Greenway Plaza, Ste. 2500 Houston TX 77046 United States
Phone Number	800-659-1005

PERFORMANCE

Ratings History
Date	Overall Rating	Risk Rating	Reward Rating
Q3-19	B-	C+	B
Q4-18	B	C+	B
Q4-17	B-	B	B-
Q4-16	B-	C	B
Q4-15	B	C+	B

Asset & Performance History
Date	NAV	1-Year Total Return
2018	28.91	6.1
2017	27.79	11.64
2016	25.63	19.07
2015	22.25	-2.98
2014	23.61	16.92
2013	20.64	21.93

Total Assets: $297,400,583
Asset Allocation
Asset	%
Cash	0%
Stocks	100%
US Stocks	100%
Bonds	0%
US Bonds	0%
Other	0%

Services Offered:

Investment Strategy: The investment seeks to track the investment results (before fees and expenses) of the Dorsey Wright® Utilities Technical Leaders Index (the "underlying index"). The fund generally will invest at least 90% of its total assets in the securities that comprise the underlying index. The underlying index is composed of at least 30 securities of companies in the utilities sector that have powerful relative strength or "momentum" characteristics. **Top Holdings:** WEC Energy Group Inc NextEra Energy Inc CMS Energy Corp Entergy Corp Atmos Energy Corp

Invesco Dynamic Building & Construction ETF   B   BUY

Ticker	Traded On	NAV	Total Assets ($)	Dividend Yield (TTM)	Turnover Ratio	Expense Ratio
PKB	NYSE Arca	32.66	$112,691,705	0.42	148	0.6

Ratings
Reward	B+
Risk	C
Recent Upgrade/Downgrade	Up

Fund Information
Fund Type	Exchange Traded Funds
Category	Industrials Sector Equity
Sub-Category	Industrials
Prospectus Objective	Unaligned
Inception Date	Oct-05
Open to New Investments	Y

Prices
Price (as of 9/30/2019)	32.64
52-Week High	32.64
52-Week Low	22.38

Total Returns (%)
3-Month	6-Month	1-Year	3-Year	5-Year
5.13	16.67	10.82	27.84	62.31

3-Year Standard Deviation	19.16
Effective Duration	

Valuation
Premium/Discount (1-Year Average)	-0.04

Company Information
Provider	Invesco
Manager/Tenure	Peter Hubbard (12), Michael Jeanette (11), Tony Seisser (5)
Website	http://www.invesco.com/us
Address	Invesco 11 Greenway Plaza, Ste. 2500 Houston TX 77046 United States
Phone Number	800-659-1005

PERFORMANCE

Ratings History
Date	Overall Rating	Risk Rating	Reward Rating
Q3-19	B	C	B+
Q4-18	C+	C-	B
Q4-17	A-	B+	A
Q4-16	B-	C	B
Q4-15	B+	B-	A-

Asset & Performance History
Date	NAV	1-Year Total Return
2018	23.83	-30.87
2017	34.64	24.43
2016	27.89	17.71
2015	23.77	10.42
2014	21.55	-3.57
2013	22.37	28.93

Total Assets: $112,691,705
Asset Allocation
Asset	%
Cash	0%
Stocks	100%
US Stocks	100%
Bonds	0%
US Bonds	0%
Other	0%

Services Offered:

Investment Strategy: The investment seeks to track the investment results (before fees and expenses) of the Dynamic Building & Construction IntellidexSM Index. The fund generally will invest at least 90% of its total assets in the securities that comprise the underlying intellidex. The underlying intellidex was composed of common stocks of U.S. building and construction companies. These companies are engaged primarily in providing construction and related engineering services for building and remodeling residential properties, commercial or industrial buildings, etc. It is non-diversified. **Top Holdings:** Martin Marietta Materials Inc The Home Depot Inc Jacobs Engineering Group Inc NVR Inc Johnson Controls International PLC

Invesco Dynamic Food & Beverage ETF   B-   BUY

Ticker	Traded On	NAV	Total Assets ($)	Dividend Yield (TTM)	Turnover Ratio	Expense Ratio
PBJ	NYSE Arca	35.17	$73,851,139	1.09	122	0.63

Ratings
Reward	B
Risk	C
Recent Upgrade/Downgrade	Up

Fund Information
Fund Type	Exchange Traded Funds
Category	Consumer Goods & Svcs
Sub-Category	Consumer Defensive
Prospectus Objective	Unaligned
Inception Date	Jun-05
Open to New Investments	Y

Prices
Price (as of 9/30/2019)	35.18
52-Week High	35.65
52-Week Low	28.60

Total Returns (%)
3-Month	6-Month	1-Year	3-Year	5-Year
4.90	6.88	10.38	10.93	33.30

3-Year Standard Deviation	11.28
Effective Duration	

Valuation
Premium/Discount (1-Year Average)	-0.02

Company Information
Provider	Invesco
Manager/Tenure	Peter Hubbard (12), Michael Jeanette (11), Tony Seisser (5)
Website	http://www.invesco.com/us
Address	Invesco 11 Greenway Plaza, Ste. 2500 Houston TX 77046 United States
Phone Number	800-659-1005

PERFORMANCE

Ratings History
Date	Overall Rating	Risk Rating	Reward Rating
Q3-19	B-	C	B
Q4-18	B-	C	B
Q4-17	B-	B	C
Q4-16	B	C+	B
Q4-15	B	B	B+

Asset & Performance History
Date	NAV	1-Year Total Return
2018	29.8	-10.77
2017	33.84	1.57
2016	33.56	5.91
2015	32.19	6.82
2014	30.51	17.37
2013	26.36	33.38

Total Assets: $73,851,139
Asset Allocation
Asset	%
Cash	0%
Stocks	100%
US Stocks	94%
Bonds	0%
US Bonds	0%
Other	0%

Services Offered:

Investment Strategy: The investment seeks to track the investment results (before fees and expenses) of the Dynamic Food & Beverage IntellidexSM Index. The fund generally will invest at least 90% of its total assets in the securities that comprise the underlying intellidex. The underlying intellidex was composed of common stocks of U.S. food and beverage companies. These companies are engaged principally in the manufacture, sale or distribution of food and beverage products, agricultural products and products related to the development of new food technologies. The fund is non-diversified. **Top Holdings:** Starbucks Corp The Hershey Co Tyson Foods Inc Class A Yum Brands Inc Coca-Cola Co

Invesco Dynamic Leisure and Entertainment ETF   B-   BUY

Ticker	Traded On	NAV	Total Assets ($)	Dividend Yield (TTM)	Turnover Ratio	Expense Ratio
PEJ	NYSE Arca	42.56	$55,323,979	0.42	207	0.63

Ratings
Reward   B
Risk   C
Recent Upgrade/Downgrade   Up

Fund Information
Fund Type   Exchange Traded Funds
Category   Consumer Goods & Svcs
Sub-Category   Consumer Cyclical
Prospectus Objective   Unaligned
Inception Date   Jun-05
Open to New Investments   Y

Prices
Price (as of 9/30/2019)   42.55
52-Week High   46.42
52-Week Low   38.07

Total Returns (%)

3-Month	6-Month	1-Year	3-Year	5-Year
-2.13	-1.33	-7.99	22.06	34.66

3-Year Standard Deviation   13.41
Effective Duration

Valuation
Premium/Discount (1-Year Average)   0.02

Company Information
Provider   Invesco
Manager/Tenure   Peter Hubbard (12), Michael Jeanette (11), Tony Seisser (5)
Website   http://www.invesco.com/us
Address   Invesco 11 Greenway Plaza, Ste. 2500 Houston TX 77046 United States
Phone Number   800-659-1005

PERFORMANCE

Ratings History

Date	Overall Rating	Risk Rating	Reward Rating
Q3-19	B-	C	B
Q4-18	C+	C-	B
Q4-17	B	B+	B-
Q4-16	C	C	C
Q4-15	B	B-	B+

Asset & Performance History

Date	NAV	1-Year Total Return
2018	39.86	-8.93
2017	44.08	10.88
2016	40.04	9.7
2015	36.77	3.71
2014	35.63	5.13
2013	34.07	49.21

Total Assets: $55,323,979
Asset Allocation

Asset	%
Cash	0%
Stocks	100%
US Stocks	92%
Bonds	0%
US Bonds	0%
Other	0%

Services Offered:

Investment Strategy: The investment seeks to track the investment results (before fees and expenses) of the Dynamic Leisure & Entertainment IntellidexSM Index. The fund generally will invest at least 90% of its total assets in the securities that comprise the underlying intellidex. The underlying intellidex was composed of common stocks of U.S. leisure and entertainment companies. These companies are engaged principally in the design, production or distribution of goods or services in the leisure and entertainment industries. The fund is non-diversified. **Top Holdings:** Starbucks Corp   Chipotle Mexican Grill Inc Class A   Yum Brands Inc   Expedia Group Inc   The Walt Disney Co

Invesco Dynamic Retail ETF   B-   BUY

Ticker	Traded On	NAV	Total Assets ($)	Dividend Yield (TTM)	Turnover Ratio	Expense Ratio
PMR	NYSE Arca	39.18	$7,836,911	0.68	148	0.63

Ratings
Reward   B
Risk   C-
Recent Upgrade/Downgrade   Up

Fund Information
Fund Type   Exchange Traded Funds
Category   Consumer Goods & Svcs
Sub-Category   Consumer Cyclical
Prospectus Objective   Unaligned
Inception Date   Oct-05
Open to New Investments   Y

Prices
Price (as of 9/30/2019)   39.23
52-Week High   41.04
52-Week Low   31.76

Total Returns (%)

3-Month	6-Month	1-Year	3-Year	5-Year
6.70	4.82	-2.78	15.38	25.92

3-Year Standard Deviation   16.8
Effective Duration

Valuation
Premium/Discount (1-Year Average)   -0.04

Company Information
Provider   Invesco
Manager/Tenure   Peter Hubbard (12), Michael Jeanette (11), Tony Seisser (5)
Website   http://www.invesco.com/us
Address   Invesco 11 Greenway Plaza, Ste. 2500 Houston TX 77046 United States
Phone Number   800-659-1005

PERFORMANCE

Ratings History

Date	Overall Rating	Risk Rating	Reward Rating
Q3-19	B-	C-	B
Q4-18	C+	C-	B
Q4-17	C-	C+	D+
Q4-16	B-	C	B
Q4-15	B	B-	B

Asset & Performance History

Date	NAV	1-Year Total Return
2018	33.77	-7.82
2017	37.07	4.24
2016	35.98	-1.76
2015	36.96	-4.02
2014	38.81	12.26
2013	34.93	39.42

Total Assets: $7,836,911
Asset Allocation

Asset	%
Cash	1%
Stocks	99%
US Stocks	99%
Bonds	0%
US Bonds	0%
Other	0%

Services Offered:

Investment Strategy: The investment seeks to track the investment results (before fees and expenses) of the Dynamic Retail IntellidexSM Index. The fund generally will invest at least 90% of its total assets in the securities that comprise the underlying intellidex. The underlying intellidex was composed of common stocks of U.S. retailers. These companies are engaged principally in operating general merchandise stores such as department stores, discount stores, warehouse clubs and superstores; specialty stores, including apparel, electronics, accessories and footwear stores; and home improvement and home furnishings stores. It is non-diversified. **Top Holdings:** Target Corp   Costco Wholesale Corp   Lululemon Athletica Inc   Walmart Inc   eBay Inc

Invesco Dynamic Semiconductors ETF   B-   BUY

Ticker	Traded On	NAV	Total Assets ($)	Dividend Yield (TTM)	Turnover Ratio	Expense Ratio
PSI	NYSE Arca	57.85	$179,338,358	0.69	98	0.58

Ratings
Reward	B
Risk	C-
Recent Upgrade/Downgrade	Up

Fund Information
Fund Type	Exchange Traded Funds
Category	Technology Sector Equity
Sub-Category	Technology
Prospectus Objective	Technology
Inception Date	Jun-05
Open to New Investments	Y

Prices
Price (as of 9/30/2019)	57.81
52-Week High	60.29
52-Week Low	41.12

Total Returns (%)
3-Month	6-Month	1-Year	3-Year	5-Year
4.12	7.04	9.89	80.11	168.39

3-Year Standard Deviation	24.78
Effective Duration	

Valuation
Premium/Discount (1-Year Average)	-0.05

Company Information
Provider	Invesco
Manager/Tenure	Peter Hubbard (12), Michael Jeanette (11), Tony Seisser (5)
Website	http://www.invesco.com/us
Address	Invesco 11 Greenway Plaza, Ste. 2500 Houston TX 77046 United States
Phone Number	800-659-1005

PERFORMANCE

Ratings History
Date	Overall Rating	Risk Rating	Reward Rating
Q3-19	B-	C-	B
Q4-18	C+	C-	B
Q4-17	A-	B	A+
Q4-16	C	C	C+
Q4-15	B	B-	B

Asset & Performance History
Date	NAV	1-Year Total Return
2018	44.46	-11.19
2017	50.44	40.03
2016	36.1	44.44
2015	25.18	-0.78
2014	25.42	36.98
2013	18.9	31.57

Total Assets: $179,338,358

Asset Allocation
Asset	%
Cash	0%
Stocks	100%
US Stocks	94%
Bonds	0%
US Bonds	0%
Other	0%

Services Offered:

Investment Strategy: The investment seeks to track the investment results (before fees and expenses) of the Dynamic Semiconductor IntellidexSM Index. The fund generally will invest at least 90% of its total assets in the securities that comprise the underlying intellidex. The underlying intellidex was composed of common stocks of U.S. semiconductor companies. These companies are principally engaged in the manufacture of semiconductors. The fund is non-diversified. **Top Holdings:** Micron Technology Inc Applied Materials Inc Texas Instruments Inc Qualcomm Inc NXP Semiconductors NV

Invesco KBW Bank ETF   B-   BUY

Ticker	Traded On	NAV	Total Assets ($)	Dividend Yield (TTM)	Turnover Ratio	Expense Ratio
KBWB	NAS CM	51.51	$535,714,958	2.56		0.35

Ratings
Reward	B
Risk	C
Recent Upgrade/Downgrade	Up

Fund Information
Fund Type	Exchange Traded Funds
Category	Financials Sector Equity
Sub-Category	Financial
Prospectus Objective	Financial
Inception Date	Nov-11
Open to New Investments	

Prices
Price (as of 9/30/2019)	51.52
52-Week High	55.36
52-Week Low	41.50

Total Returns (%)
3-Month	6-Month	1-Year	3-Year	5-Year
1.73	5.27	-2.16	49.98	55.78

3-Year Standard Deviation	22.75
Effective Duration	

Valuation
Premium/Discount (1-Year Average)	-0.04

Company Information
Provider	Invesco
Manager/Tenure	Peter Hubbard (7), Michael Jeanette (7), Tony Seisser (5)
Website	http://www.invesco.com/us
Address	Invesco 11 Greenway Plaza, Ste. 2500 Houston TX 77046 United States
Phone Number	800-659-1005

PERFORMANCE

Ratings History
Date	Overall Rating	Risk Rating	Reward Rating
Q3-19	B-	C	B
Q4-18	B-	C	B
Q4-17	B+	B-	A
Q4-16	B	C	B+
Q4-15	A-	A-	B+

Asset & Performance History
Date	NAV	1-Year Total Return
2018	44.12	-17.95
2017	54.98	18.15
2016	47.21	28.03
2015	37.57	0.13
2014	38.1	8.97
2013	35.51	37.25

Total Assets: $535,714,958

Asset Allocation
Asset	%
Cash	0%
Stocks	100%
US Stocks	100%
Bonds	0%
US Bonds	0%
Other	0%

Services Offered:

Investment Strategy: The investment seeks to track the investment results (before fees and expenses) of the KBW Nasdaq Bank Index (the "underlying index"). The fund generally will invest at least 90% of its total assets in the securities that comprise the underlying index. The underlying index is a modified-market capitalization-weighted index of companies primarily engaged in U.S. banking activities, as determined by the index provider. The underlying index is designed to track the performance of large national U.S. money centers, regional banks, and thrift institutions that are publicly traded in the U.S. The fund is non-diversified. **Top Holdings:** US Bancorp Wells Fargo & Co JPMorgan Chase & Co Citigroup Inc Bank of America Corporation

Invesco KBW Property & Casualty Insurance ETF

B **BUY**

Ticker	Traded On	NAV	Total Assets ($)	Dividend Yield (TTM)	Turnover Ratio	Expense Ratio
KBWP	NAS CM	73.82	$118,108,142	1.95		0.35

Ratings
Reward	B
Risk	C+
Recent Upgrade/Downgrade	Up

Fund Information
Fund Type	Exchange Traded Funds
Category	Financials Sector Equity
Sub-Category	Financial
Prospectus Objective	Growth
Inception Date	Dec-10
Open to New Investments	

Prices
Price (as of 9/30/2019)	73.94
52-Week High	74.04
52-Week Low	53.39

Total Returns (%)
3-Month	6-Month	1-Year	3-Year	5-Year
4.56	19.12	20.07	56.60	111.54

3-Year Standard Deviation	11.4
Effective Duration	

Valuation
Premium/Discount (1-Year Average)	0.03

Company Information
Provider	Invesco
Manager/Tenure	Peter Hubbard (8), Michael Jeanette (8), Tony Seisser (5)
Website	http://www.invesco.com/us
Address	Invesco 11 Greenway Plaza, Ste. 2500 Houston TX 77046 United States
Phone Number	800-659-1005

PERFORMANCE

Ratings History
Date	Overall Rating	Risk Rating	Reward Rating
Q3-19	B	C+	B
Q4-18	B-	C	B
Q4-17	B+	A	B
Q4-16	B	B	A-
Q4-15	B	C	A-

Asset & Performance History
Date	NAV	1-Year Total Return
2018	56.92	-2.24
2017	59.42	8.96
2016	55.59	19.09
2015	47.76	14.24
2014	42.4	11.25
2013	39.22	33.88

Total Assets: $118,108,142
Asset Allocation
Asset	%
Cash	0%
Stocks	100%
US Stocks	92%
Bonds	0%
US Bonds	0%
Other	0%

Services Offered:

Investment Strategy: The investment seeks to track the investment results (before fees and expenses) of the KBW Nasdaq Property & Casualty Index (the "underlying index"). The fund generally will invest at least 90% of its total assets in the securities that comprise the underlying index. The underlying index is a modified-market capitalization-weighted index of companies primarily engaged in U.S. property and casualty insurance activities, as determined by the index provider. The fund is non-diversified. **Top Holdings:** Chubb Ltd Allstate Corp American International Group Inc The Travelers Companies Inc Progressive Corp

Invesco QQQ Trust

B- **BUY**

Ticker	Traded On	NAV	Total Assets ($)	Dividend Yield (TTM)	Turnover Ratio	Expense Ratio
QQQ	NAS CM	188.77	$74,717,022,394	0.82		0.2

Ratings
Reward	B-
Risk	B-
Recent Upgrade/Downgrade	

Fund Information
Fund Type	Exchange Traded Funds
Category	US Equity Large Cap Growth
Sub-Category	Large Growth
Prospectus Objective	Growth
Inception Date	Mar-99
Open to New Investments	Y

Prices
Price (as of 9/30/2019)	188.81
52-Week High	195.29
52-Week Low	143.50

Total Returns (%)
3-Month	6-Month	1-Year	3-Year	5-Year
-0.03	4.06	2.31	63.28	103.88

3-Year Standard Deviation	14.9
Effective Duration	

Valuation
Premium/Discount (1-Year Average)	-0.02

Company Information
Provider	Invesco
Manager/Tenure	Management Team (20)
Website	http://www.invesco.com/us
Address	Invesco 11 Greenway Plaza, Ste. 2500 Houston TX 77046 United States
Phone Number	800-659-1005

PERFORMANCE

Ratings History
Date	Overall Rating	Risk Rating	Reward Rating
Q3-19	B-	B-	B-
Q4-18	B-	B	C+
Q4-17	A-	B	A-
Q4-16	B+	B	A-
Q4-15	B	A-	B

Asset & Performance History
Date	NAV	1-Year Total Return
2018	154.14	-0.14
2017	155.68	32.7
2016	118.39	7.01
2015	111.87	9.54
2014	103.17	19.11
2013	87.94	36.6

Total Assets: $74,717,022,394
Asset Allocation
Asset	%
Cash	0%
Stocks	100%
US Stocks	97%
Bonds	0%
US Bonds	0%
Other	0%

Services Offered: Dividend Investment Plan, Cash Investment Plan

Investment Strategy: The investment seeks investment results that generally correspond to the price and yield performance of the index. To maintain the correspondence between the composition and weights of the securities in the trust (the "securities") and the stocks in the Nasdaq-100 Index®, the adviser adjusts the securities from time to time to conform to periodic changes in the identity and/or relative weights of index securities. The composition and weighting of the securities portion of a portfolio deposit are also adjusted to conform to changes in the index. **Top Holdings:** Microsoft Corp Apple Inc Amazon.com Inc Facebook Inc A Alphabet Inc Class C

Invesco S&P 500® Equal Weight Consumer Staples ETF   B-   BUY

Ticker	Traded On	NAV	Total Assets ($)	Dividend Yield (TTM)	Turnover Ratio	Expense Ratio
RHS	NYSE Arca	140.32	$477,075,458	2.29		0.4

Ratings
Reward	B
Risk	C
Recent Upgrade/Downgrade	Up

Fund Information
Fund Type	Exchange Traded Funds
Category	Consumer Goods & Svcs
Sub-Category	Consumer Defensive
Prospectus Objective	Unaligned
Inception Date	Nov-06
Open to New Investments	Y

Prices
Price (as of 9/30/2019)	140.40
52-Week High	140.40
52-Week Low	112.22

Total Returns (%)
3-Month	6-Month	1-Year	3-Year	5-Year
5.44	8.57	12.35	22.17	60.64

3-Year Standard Deviation	11.93
Effective Duration	

Valuation
Premium/Discount (1-Year Average)	-0.04

Company Information
Provider	Invesco
Manager/Tenure	Peter Hubbard (1), Michael Jeanette (1), Tony Seisser (1)
Website	http://www.invesco.com/us
Address	Invesco 11 Greenway Plaza, Ste. 2500 Houston TX 77046 United States
Phone Number	800-659-1005

PERFORMANCE

Ratings History
Date	Overall Rating	Risk Rating	Reward Rating
Q3-19	B-	C	B
Q4-18	C+	C	B
Q4-17	B	A-	C+
Q4-16	C	C	C+
Q4-15	B	C	B+

Asset & Performance History
Date	NAV	1-Year Total Return
2018	116.47	-10.72
2017	133.52	13.6
2016	119.44	4.3
2015	115.93	13.1
2014	104.45	17.92
2013	90.22	32.55

Total Assets: $477,075,458
Asset Allocation
Asset	%
Cash	0%
Stocks	100%
US Stocks	100%
Bonds	0%
US Bonds	0%
Other	0%

Services Offered:

Investment Strategy: The investment seeks to track the investment results (before fees and expenses) of the S&P 500® Equal Weight Consumer Staples Index (the "underlying index"). The fund generally will invest at least 90% of its total assets in the securities that comprise the underlying index. The underlying index is composed of all of the components of the S&P 500® Consumer Staples Index, an index that contains the common stocks of all companies included in the S&P 500® Index that are classified as members of the consumer staples sector, as defined according to the Global Industry Classification Standard ("GICS"). The fund is non-diversified. **Top Holdings:** The Hershey Co Lamb Weston Holdings Inc Tyson Foods Inc Class A Costco Wholesale Corp The Estee Lauder Companies Inc Class A

Invesco S&P 500® Equal Weight Real Estate ETF   B-   BUY

Ticker	Traded On	NAV	Total Assets ($)	Dividend Yield (TTM)	Turnover Ratio	Expense Ratio
EWRE	NYSE Arca	31.87	$46,216,355	2.68		0.4

Ratings
Reward	B
Risk	C
Recent Upgrade/Downgrade	Up

Fund Information
Fund Type	Exchange Traded Funds
Category	Real Estate Sector Equity
Sub-Category	Real Estate
Prospectus Objective	Real Estate
Inception Date	Aug-15
Open to New Investments	Y

Prices
Price (as of 9/30/2019)	31.84
52-Week High	31.94
52-Week Low	24.98

Total Returns (%)
3-Month	6-Month	1-Year	3-Year	5-Year
7.34	8.01	20.96	27.41	

3-Year Standard Deviation	12.59
Effective Duration	

Valuation
Premium/Discount (1-Year Average)	0.06

Company Information
Provider	Invesco
Manager/Tenure	Peter Hubbard (1), Michael Jeanette (1), Tony Seisser (1)
Website	http://www.invesco.com/us
Address	Invesco 11 Greenway Plaza, Ste. 2500 Houston TX 77046 United States
Phone Number	800-659-1005

PERFORMANCE

Ratings History
Date	Overall Rating	Risk Rating	Reward Rating
Q3-19	B-	C	B
Q4-18	C+	C-	B-
Q4-17	C	B	C
Q4-16	D	C	B
Q4-15	U		

Asset & Performance History
Date	NAV	1-Year Total Return
2018	25.88	-4.12
2017	27.74	8.82
2016	26.33	2.09
2015	25.81	
2014		
2013		

Total Assets: $46,216,355
Asset Allocation
Asset	%
Cash	0%
Stocks	100%
US Stocks	100%
Bonds	0%
US Bonds	0%
Other	0%

Services Offered:

Investment Strategy: The investment seeks to track the investment results (before fees and expenses) of the S&P 500® Equal Weight Real Estate Index (the "underlying index"). The fund generally will invest at least 90% of its total assets in the securities that comprise the underlying index. The underlying index is composed of all of the components of the S&P 500® Real Estate Index, an index that contains the common stocks of all companies included in the S&P 500® Index that are classified as members of the real estate sector, as defined according to the Global Industry Classification Standard ("GICS"). The fund is non-diversified. **Top Holdings:** SBA Communications Corp Extra Space Storage Inc Ventas Inc Equinix Inc Welltower Inc

Invesco S&P 500® Equal Weight Utilities ETF

B- **BUY**

Ticker	Traded On	NAV	Total Assets ($)	Dividend Yield (TTM)	Turnover Ratio	Expense Ratio
RYU	NYSE Arca	106.66	$399,956,465	2.45		0.4

Ratings
Reward	B
Risk	C
Recent Upgrade/Downgrade	

Fund Information
Fund Type	Exchange Traded Funds
Category	Utilities Sector Equity
Sub-Category	Utilities
Prospectus Objective	Utility
Inception Date	Nov-06
Open to New Investments	Y

Prices
Price (as of 9/30/2019)	106.64
52-Week High	107.12
52-Week Low	86.44

Total Returns (%)
3-Month	6-Month	1-Year	3-Year	5-Year
8.99	12.44	25.20	44.00	74.37

3-Year Standard Deviation	9.29
Effective Duration	

Valuation
Premium/Discount (1-Year Average)	0.01

Company Information
Provider	Invesco
Manager/Tenure	Peter Hubbard (1), Michael Jeanette (1), Tony Seisser (1)
Website	http://www.invesco.com/us
Address	Invesco 11 Greenway Plaza, Ste. 2500 Houston TX 77046 United States
Phone Number	800-659-1005

PERFORMANCE

Ratings History
Date	Overall Rating	Risk Rating	Reward Rating
Q3-19	B-	C	B
Q4-18	B-	C	B
Q4-17	B	B	B
Q4-16	C	C	C+
Q4-15	B-	C	B

Asset & Performance History
Date	NAV	1-Year Total Return
2018	88.83	6.95
2017	85.81	9.01
2016	80.8	14.67
2015	72.37	-4.02
2014	78.58	28.03
2013	63.32	13.33

Total Assets: $399,956,465

Asset Allocation
Asset	%
Cash	0%
Stocks	100%
US Stocks	100%
Bonds	0%
US Bonds	0%
Other	0%

Services Offered:

Investment Strategy: The investment seeks to track the investment results (before fees and expenses) of the S&P 500® Equal Weight Utilities Plus Index. The fund generally will invest at least 90% of its total assets in the securities that comprise the underlying index. The underlying index is composed of all of the components of the S&P 500® Utilities Plus Index, an index that contains the common stocks of all companies included in the S&P 500® Index that are classified as members of the utilities sector, as defined according to the Global Industry Classification Standard ("GICS"). It is non-diversified. **Top Holdings:** Edison International WEC Energy Group Inc Entergy Corp American Water Works Co Inc CMS Energy Corp

Invesco S&P 500® Low Volatility ETF

B **BUY**

Ticker	Traded On	NAV	Total Assets ($)	Dividend Yield (TTM)	Turnover Ratio	Expense Ratio
SPLV	NYSE Arca	57.89	$12,815,868,642	2		0.25

Ratings
Reward	B
Risk	A-
Recent Upgrade/Downgrade	Down

Fund Information
Fund Type	Exchange Traded Funds
Category	US Equity Large Cap Value
Sub-Category	Large Blend
Prospectus Objective	Growth
Inception Date	May-11
Open to New Investments	

Prices
Price (as of 9/30/2019)	57.90
52-Week High	57.96
52-Week Low	44.55

Total Returns (%)
3-Month	6-Month	1-Year	3-Year	5-Year
5.34	11.05	19.75	48.88	86.14

3-Year Standard Deviation	9.02
Effective Duration	

Valuation
Premium/Discount (1-Year Average)	-0.01

Company Information
Provider	Invesco
Manager/Tenure	Peter Hubbard (8), Michael Jeanette (8), Tony Seisser (5)
Website	http://www.invesco.com/us
Address	Invesco 11 Greenway Plaza, Ste. 2500 Houston TX 77046 United States
Phone Number	800-659-1005

PERFORMANCE

Ratings History
Date	Overall Rating	Risk Rating	Reward Rating
Q3-19	B	A-	B
Q4-18	B	A	C
Q4-17	B+	A+	B
Q4-16	C	C+	C
Q4-15	B-	C+	B

Asset & Performance History
Date	NAV	1-Year Total Return
2018	46.64	0.03
2017	47.63	17.07
2016	41.57	10.09
2015	38.56	4.06
2014	37.93	17.18
2013	33.16	23.24

Total Assets: $12,815,868,642

Asset Allocation
Asset	%
Cash	0%
Stocks	100%
US Stocks	99%
Bonds	0%
US Bonds	0%
Other	0%

Services Offered:

Investment Strategy: The investment seeks to track the investment results (before fees and expenses) of the S&P 500® Low Volatility Index (the "underlying index"). The fund generally will invest at least 90% of its total assets in the securities that comprise the underlying index. Strictly in accordance with its guidelines and mandated procedures, the index provider selects 100 securities from the S&P 500® Index for inclusion in the underlying index that have the lowest realized volatility over the past 12 months as determined by S&P DJI. **Top Holdings:** Republic Services Inc Class A Waste Management Inc Duke Energy Corp WEC Energy Group Inc Evergy Inc

Invesco S&P 500® Quality ETF   B-   BUY

Ticker	Traded On	NAV	Total Assets ($)	Dividend Yield (TTM)	Turnover Ratio	Expense Ratio
SPHQ	NYSE Arca	33.53	$1,491,871,394	1.56	73	0.15

Ratings
Reward   B-
Risk   C+
Recent Upgrade/Downgrade   Up

Fund Information
Fund Type   Exchange Traded Funds
Category   US Equity Large Cap Blend
Sub-Category   Large Blend
Prospectus Objective   Growth
Inception Date   Dec-05
Open to New Investments   Y

Prices
Price (as of 9/30/2019)   33.54
52-Week High   34.13
52-Week Low   25.94

Total Returns (%)

3-Month	6-Month	1-Year	3-Year	5-Year
0.86	4.02	3.62	40.54	72.42

3-Year Standard Deviation   12.03
Effective Duration

Valuation
Premium/Discount (1-Year Average)   -0.03

Company Information
Provider   Invesco
Manager/Tenure   Peter Hubbard (12), Michael Jeanette (11), Tony Seisser (5)
Website   http://www.invesco.com/us
Address   Invesco 11 Greenway Plaza, Ste. 2500 Houston TX 77046 United States
Phone Number   800-659-1005

PERFORMANCE

Ratings History

Date	Overall Rating	Risk Rating	Reward Rating
Q3-19	B-	C+	B-
Q4-18	C+	C+	C
Q4-17	B	B+	B
Q4-16	B-	C+	B
Q4-15	C+	C+	B-

Asset & Performance History

Date	NAV	1-Year Total Return
2018	27.8	-6.98
2017	30.41	19.12
2016	25.95	14.17
2015	23.12	1.66
2014	23.27	16.09
2013	20.4	32.04

Total Assets: $1,491,871,394

Asset Allocation

Asset	%
Cash	0%
Stocks	100%
US Stocks	100%
Bonds	0%
US Bonds	0%
Other	0%

Services Offered:

Investment Strategy: The investment seeks to track the investment results (before fees and expenses) of the S&P 500® Quality Index. The fund generally will invest at least 90% of its total assets in the securities that comprise the underlying index. In selecting constituent securities for the underlying index, the index provider calculates the quality score of each security in the S&P 500® Index, then selects the 100 stocks with the highest quality score for inclusion in the underlying index. **Top Holdings:** Apple Inc Microsoft Corp Mastercard Inc A Visa Inc Class A Johnson & Johnson

---

Invesco Solar ETF   B-   BUY

Ticker	Traded On	NAV	Total Assets ($)	Dividend Yield (TTM)	Turnover Ratio	Expense Ratio
TAN	NYSE Arca	29.46	$438,590,825	0.44	54	0.7

Ratings
Reward   B
Risk   C
Recent Upgrade/Downgrade   Up

Fund Information
Fund Type   Exchange Traded Funds
Category   Technology Sector Equity
Sub-Category   Miscellaneous Sector
Prospectus Objective   Natl Res
Inception Date   Apr-08
Open to New Investments   Y

Prices
Price (as of 9/30/2019)   29.37
52-Week High   32.30
52-Week Low   17.70

Total Returns (%)

3-Month	6-Month	1-Year	3-Year	5-Year
3.11	24.61	42.71	57.30	-17.32

3-Year Standard Deviation   25.43
Effective Duration

Valuation
Premium/Discount (1-Year Average)   -0.08

Company Information
Provider   Invesco
Manager/Tenure   Peter Hubbard (1), Michael Jeanette (1), Tony Seisser (1)
Website   http://www.invesco.com/us
Address   Invesco 11 Greenway Plaza, Ste. 2500 Houston TX 77046 United States
Phone Number   800-659-1005

PERFORMANCE

Ratings History

Date	Overall Rating	Risk Rating	Reward Rating
Q3-19	B-	C	B
Q4-18	D+	D	D+
Q4-17	C-	D+	C-
Q4-16	D	D-	D
Q4-15	C	C-	C

Asset & Performance History

Date	NAV	1-Year Total Return
2018	18.61	-25.76
2017	25.07	53.1
2016	16.55	-42.7
2015	30.61	-9.37
2014	34.3	-0.71
2013	35.2	129.94

Total Assets: $438,590,825

Asset Allocation

Asset	%
Cash	0%
Stocks	100%
US Stocks	46%
Bonds	0%
US Bonds	0%
Other	0%

Services Offered:

Investment Strategy: The investment seeks to track the investment results (before fees and expenses) of the MAC Global Solar Energy Index (the "underlying index"). The fund will invest at least 90% of its total assets in the securities (including ADRs and GDRs) that comprise the underlying index. The underlying index is designed to provide exposure to companies listed on exchanges in developed markets that derive a significant amount of their revenues from the following business segments of the solar industry: solar power equipment producers including ancillary or enabling products; etc. The fund is non-diversified. **Top Holdings:** SolarEdge Technologies Inc Enphase Energy Inc First Solar Inc Xinyi Solar Holdings Ltd SunPower Corp

Invesco Taxable Municipal Bond ETF   B-   BUY

Ticker	Traded On	NAV	Total Assets ($)	Dividend Yield (TTM)	Turnover Ratio	Expense Ratio
BAB	NYSE Arca	32.29	$1,306,278,460	3.79		0.28

Ratings
Reward   B-
Risk   C+
Recent Upgrade/Downgrade   Up

Fund Information
Fund Type   Exchange Traded Funds
Category   US Fixed Income
Sub-Category   Long-Term Bond
Prospectus Objective   Muni Bond - Natl
Inception Date   Nov-09
Open to New Investments   Y

Prices
Price (as of 9/30/2019)   32.40
52-Week High   33.08
52-Week Low   28.54

Total Returns (%)

3-Month	6-Month	1-Year	3-Year	5-Year
4.18	9.22	15.29	16.61	34.23

3-Year Standard Deviation   5.25
Effective Duration   8.66

Valuation
Premium/Discount (1-Year Average)   0.21

Company Information
Provider   Invesco
Manager/Tenure   Philip Fang (9), Peter Hubbard (9),
                  Jeffrey W. Kernagis (9), 2 others
Website   http://www.invesco.com/us
Address   Invesco 11 Greenway Plaza, Ste. 2500
                  Houston TX 77046 United States
Phone Number   800-659-1005

PERFORMANCE

Ratings History

Date	Overall Rating	Risk Rating	Reward Rating
Q3-19	B-	C+	B-
Q4-18	C	C+	C-
Q4-17	B	A-	C+
Q4-16	C	C+	C
Q4-15	C	C-	C

Asset & Performance History

Date	NAV	1-Year Total Return
2018	29.51	0.63
2017	30.59	8.2
2016	29.44	5.27
2015	29.13	0.91
2014	30.23	15.69
2013	27.41	-5.09

Total Assets: $1,306,278,460
Asset Allocation

Asset	%
Cash	1%
Stocks	0%
US Stocks	0%
Bonds	99%
US Bonds	99%
Other	0%

Services Offered:

Investment Strategy: The investment seeks to track the investment results (before fees and expenses) of the ICE BofAML US Taxable Municipal Securities Plus Index (the "underlying index"). The fund generally will invest at least 80% of its total assets in taxable municipal securities that comprise the underlying index. The underlying index is designed to track the performance of U.S. dollar-denominated taxable municipal debt publicly issued by U.S. states and territories, and their political subdivisions, in the U.S. market. **Top Holdings:** CALIFORNIA ST 7.6% UNIVERSITY CALIF REVS 4.13% CALIFORNIA ST 7.3% COMMONWEALTH FING AUTH PA REV 3.66% AMERICAN MUN PWR OHIO INC REV 8.08%

Invesco Water Resources ETF   B-   BUY

Ticker	Traded On	NAV	Total Assets ($)	Dividend Yield (TTM)	Turnover Ratio	Expense Ratio
PHO	NAS CM	36.63	$1,016,561,922	0.47	31	0.6

Ratings
Reward   B
Risk   C
Recent Upgrade/Downgrade

Fund Information
Fund Type   Exchange Traded Funds
Category   Industrials Sector Equity
Sub-Category   Miscellaneous Sector
Prospectus Objective   Utility
Inception Date   Dec-05
Open to New Investments   Y

Prices
Price (as of 9/30/2019)   36.60
52-Week High   37.05
52-Week Low   26.56

Total Returns (%)

3-Month	6-Month	1-Year	3-Year	5-Year
2.61	7.19	16.20	51.08	54.08

3-Year Standard Deviation   13.55
Effective Duration

Valuation
Premium/Discount (1-Year Average)   0.00

Company Information
Provider   Invesco
Manager/Tenure   Peter Hubbard (12), Michael Jeanette
                  (11), Tony Seisser (5)
Website   http://www.invesco.com/us
Address   Invesco 11 Greenway Plaza, Ste. 2500
                  Houston TX 77046 United States
Phone Number   800-659-1005

PERFORMANCE

Ratings History

Date	Overall Rating	Risk Rating	Reward Rating
Q3-19	B-	C	B
Q4-18	B-	C	B
Q4-17	C+	C	B-
Q4-16	B-	C	B
Q4-15	B-	C+	B

Asset & Performance History

Date	NAV	1-Year Total Return
2018	28.24	-6.26
2017	30.26	23.55
2016	24.58	13.86
2015	21.69	-15.2
2014	25.76	-1.1
2013	26.2	26.97

Total Assets: $1,016,561,922
Asset Allocation

Asset	%
Cash	0%
Stocks	100%
US Stocks	97%
Bonds	0%
US Bonds	0%
Other	0%

Services Offered:

Investment Strategy: The investment seeks to track the investment results (before fees and expenses) of the NASDAQ OMX US Water IndexSM (the "underlying index"). The fund generally will invest at least 90% of its total assets in the securities that comprise the underlying index. The underlying index seeks to track the performance of U.S. exchange-listed companies that create products designed to conserve and purify water for homes, businesses and industries. The underlying index may include common stocks, ordinary shares, American depositary receipts ("ADRs"), shares of beneficial interest and tracking stocks. The fund is non-diversified. **Top Holdings:** Ecolab Inc American Water Works Co Inc Danaher Corp Roper Technologies Inc Waters Corp

iShares Cohen & Steers REIT ETF   B-   BUY

Ticker	Traded On	NAV		Total Assets ($)	Dividend Yield (TTM)	Turnover Ratio	Expense Ratio
ICF	BATS	119.97		$2,417,428,968	2.34	17	0.34

Ratings

Reward	B+
Risk	C
Recent Upgrade/Downgrade	Up

Fund Information

Fund Type	Exchange Traded Funds
Category	Real Estate Sector Equity
Sub-Category	Real Estate
Prospectus Objective	Real Estate
Inception Date	Jan-01
Open to New Investments	Y

Prices

Price (as of 9/30/2019)	120.02
52-Week High	121.41
52-Week Low	92.00

Total Returns (%)

3-Month	6-Month	1-Year	3-Year	5-Year
7.27	9.29	23.93	26.09	67.53

3-Year Standard Deviation	12.4
Effective Duration	

Valuation

Premium/Discount (1-Year Average)	-0.02

Company Information

Provider	iShares
Manager/Tenure	Greg Savage (11), Jennifer Hsui (7), Alan Mason (3), 2 others
Website	http://www.ishares.com
Address	iShares 400 Howard Street San Francisco CA 94105 United States
Phone Number	800-474-2737

PERFORMANCE

Ratings History

Date	Overall Rating	Risk Rating	Reward Rating
Q3-19	B-	C	B+
Q4-18	B-	C	B
Q4-17	B-	B	C+
Q4-16	B-	C	B
Q4-15	B	C+	B+

Asset & Performance History

Date	NAV	1-Year Total Return
2018	95.71	-2.45
2017	101.27	4.95
2016	99.55	4.57
2015	99.21	5.96
2014	96.87	34.07
2013	74.66	-1.8

Total Assets: $2,417,428,968

Asset Allocation

Asset	%
Cash	0%
Stocks	100%
US Stocks	100%
Bonds	0%
US Bonds	0%
Other	0%

Services Offered: CashInvestment Plan

Investment Strategy: The investment seeks to track the investment results of the Cohen & Steers Realty Majors Index, which consists of REITs. The fund generally invests at least 90% of its assets in securities of the underlying index and in depositary receipts representing securities of the underlying index. The objective of the underlying index is to represent relatively large and liquid REITs that may benefit from future consolidation and securitization of the U.S. real estate industry. The fund is non-diversified. **Top Holdings:** American Tower Corp   Prologis Inc   Equinix Inc   Simon Property Group Inc   Public Storage

iShares Core High Dividend ETF   B-   BUY

Ticker	Traded On	NAV		Total Assets ($)	Dividend Yield (TTM)	Turnover Ratio	Expense Ratio
HDV	NYSE Arca	94.14		$7,408,950,088	3.33	57	0.08

Ratings

Reward	B
Risk	C
Recent Upgrade/Downgrade	Up

Fund Information

Fund Type	Exchange Traded Funds
Category	US Equity Large Cap Value
Sub-Category	Large Value
Prospectus Objective	Equity-Income
Inception Date	Mar-11
Open to New Investments	Y

Prices

Price (as of 9/30/2019)	94.16
52-Week High	95.92
52-Week Low	80.00

Total Returns (%)

3-Month	6-Month	1-Year	3-Year	5-Year
0.12	1.70	7.01	28.45	50.78

3-Year Standard Deviation	10.95
Effective Duration	

Valuation

Premium/Discount (1-Year Average)	-0.01

Company Information

Provider	iShares
Manager/Tenure	Greg Savage (8), Jennifer Hsui (7), Alan Mason (3), 2 others
Website	http://www.ishares.com
Address	iShares 400 Howard Street San Francisco CA 94105 United States
Phone Number	800-474-2737

PERFORMANCE

Ratings History

Date	Overall Rating	Risk Rating	Reward Rating
Q3-19	B-	C	B
Q4-18	B-	C	B
Q4-17	B	B	B-
Q4-16	B-	C	B
Q4-15	B-	C	B

Asset & Performance History

Date	NAV	1-Year Total Return
2018	84.33	-2.92
2017	90.04	13.35
2016	82.2	15.78
2015	73.41	-0.26
2014	76.54	12.54
2013	70.26	23.6

Total Assets: $7,408,950,088

Asset Allocation

Asset	%
Cash	0%
Stocks	100%
US Stocks	100%
Bonds	0%
US Bonds	0%
Other	0%

Services Offered:

Investment Strategy: The investment seeks to track the investment results of the Morningstar® Dividend Yield Focus IndexSM composed of relatively high dividend paying U.S. equities. The fund generally will invest at least 90% of its assets in the component securities of the underlying index and may invest up to 10% of its assets in certain futures, options and swap contracts, cash and cash equivalents. The underlying index is comprised of qualified income paying securities that are screened for superior company quality and financial health as determined by Morningstar, Inc.'s ("Morningstar" or the "index provider") proprietary index methodology. The fund is non-diversified. **Top Holdings:** Exxon Mobil Corp   Verizon Communications Inc   Johnson & Johnson   Chevron Corp   Procter & Gamble Co

iShares Core International Aggregate Bond ETF

B- **BUY**

Ticker	Traded On	NAV	Total Assets ($)	Dividend Yield (TTM)	Turnover Ratio	Expense Ratio
IAGG	BATS	55.66	$1,789,511,884	4.16	11	0.09

Ratings
Reward   B-
Risk   C+
Recent Upgrade/Downgrade   Up

Fund Information
Fund Type   Exchange Traded Funds
Category   Global Fixed Income
Sub-Category   World Bond-USD Hedged
Prospectus Objective   Worldwide Bond
Inception Date   Nov-15
Open to New Investments   Y

Prices
Price (as of 9/30/2019)   55.79
52-Week High   56.14
52-Week Low   51.69

Total Returns (%)

3-Month	6-Month	1-Year	3-Year	5-Year
2.93	6.43	11.63	13.16	

3-Year Standard Deviation   2.84
Effective Duration

Valuation
Premium/Discount (1-Year Average)   0.23

Company Information
Provider   iShares
Manager/Tenure Scott Radell (3), Sid Swaminathan (1)
Website   http://www.ishares.com
Address   iShares 400 Howard Street San
                Francisco CA 94105 United States
Phone Number   800-474-2737

PERFORMANCE

Ratings History

Date	Overall Rating	Risk Rating	Reward Rating
Q3-19	B-	C+	B-
Q4-18	C-	C-	C
Q4-17	C	B+	D+
Q4-16	D	C+	D
Q4-15			

Asset & Performance History

Date	NAV	1-Year Total Return
2018	52.03	2.92
2017	52.1	2.51
2016	51.72	4.98
2015	50.04	
2014		
2013		

Total Assets: $1,789,511,884
Asset Allocation

Asset	%
Cash	-1%
Stocks	0%
US Stocks	0%
Bonds	100%
US Bonds	3%
Other	0%

Services Offered:

Investment Strategy: The investment seeks to track the investment results of the Bloomberg Barclays Global Aggregate ex USD 10% Issuer Capped (Hedged) Index composed of global non-U.S. dollar-denominated investment-grade bonds that mitigates exposure to fluctuations between the value of the component currencies and the U.S. dollar. The fund generally will invest at least 90% of its assets in the component securities and other instruments of the underlying index. The index measures the performance of the global investment-grade bond market. The fund is non-diversified. **Top Holdings:** France (Republic Of) 0% Japan (Government Of) 0.1% Germany (Federal Republic Of) 2.25% Italy (Republic Of) 0.65% Japan (Government Of) 0.6%

---

iShares Core S&P 500 ETF

B- **BUY**

Ticker	Traded On	NAV	Total Assets ($)	Dividend Yield (TTM)	Turnover Ratio	Expense Ratio
IVV	NYSE Arca	298.48	$186,488,000,000	2.06	5	0.04

Ratings
Reward   C+
Risk   B
Recent Upgrade/Downgrade

Fund Information
Fund Type   Exchange Traded Funds
Category   US Equity Large Cap Blend
Sub-Category   Large Blend
Prospectus Objective   Growth
Inception Date   May-00
Open to New Investments   Y

Prices
Price (as of 9/30/2019)   298.52
52-Week High   303.77
52-Week Low   236.09

Total Returns (%)

3-Month	6-Month	1-Year	3-Year	5-Year
0.91	4.84	3.84	45.65	69.14

3-Year Standard Deviation   12.18
Effective Duration

Valuation
Premium/Discount (1-Year Average)   -0.01

Company Information
Provider   iShares
Manager/Tenure Greg Savage (11), Jennifer Hsui (7),
                Alan Mason (3), 2 others
Website   http://www.ishares.com
Address   iShares 400 Howard Street San
                Francisco CA 94105 United States
Phone Number   800-474-2737

PERFORMANCE

Ratings History

Date	Overall Rating	Risk Rating	Reward Rating
Q3-19	B-	B	C+
Q4-18	C+	B	C
Q4-17	B	B	B
Q4-16	B	B	B
Q4-15	C+	C+	C

Asset & Performance History

Date	NAV	1-Year Total Return
2018	251.4	-4.54
2017	268.5	21.79
2016	224.64	11.89
2015	205.02	1.33
2014	206.94	13.62
2013	185.62	32.3

Total Assets: $186,488,000,000
Asset Allocation

Asset	%
Cash	0%
Stocks	100%
US Stocks	99%
Bonds	0%
US Bonds	0%
Other	0%

Services Offered: CashInvestment Plan

Investment Strategy: The investment seeks to track the investment results of the S&P 500 (the "underlying index"), which measures the performance of the large-capitalization sector of the U.S. equity market. The fund generally invests at least 90% of its assets in securities of the underlying index and in depositary receipts representing securities of the underlying index. It may invest the remainder of its assets in certain futures, options and swap contracts, cash and cash equivalents, as well as in securities not included in the underlying index, but which the advisor believes will help the fund track the underlying index. **Top Holdings:** Microsoft Corp Apple Inc Amazon.com Inc Facebook Inc A Berkshire Hathaway Inc B

---

iShares Core U.S. Aggregate Bond ETF

B- **BUY**

Ticker	Traded On	NAV		Total Assets ($)	Dividend Yield (TTM)	Turnover Ratio	Expense Ratio
AGG	NYSE Arca	113.13		$66,025,267,982	2.71	146	0.05

Ratings
Reward	C+
Risk	B
Recent Upgrade/Downgrade	

Fund Information
Fund Type	Exchange Traded Funds
Category	US Fixed Income
Sub-Category	Intermediate Core Bond
Prospectus Objective	Corp Bond - Gen
Inception Date	Sep-03
Open to New Investments	Y

Prices
Price (as of 9/30/2019)	113.17
52-Week High	114.13
52-Week Low	104.01

Total Returns (%)
3-Month	6-Month	1-Year	3-Year	5-Year
2.36	5.78	10.35	8.90	17.24

3-Year Standard Deviation	3.35
Effective Duration	5.29

Valuation
Premium/Discount (1-Year Average)	0.06

Company Information
Provider	iShares
Manager/Tenure	Scott Radell (9), James Mauro (8)
Website	http://www.ishares.com
Address	iShares 400 Howard Street San Francisco CA 94105 United States
Phone Number	800-474-2737

PERFORMANCE

Ratings History

Date	Overall Rating	Risk Rating	Reward Rating
Q3-19	B-	B	C+
Q4-18	C	C+	D+
Q4-17	B-	A-	C
Q4-16	C	B-	C
Q4-15	C	C+	C

Asset & Performance History

Date	NAV	1-Year Total Return
2018	106.27	-0.04
2017	109.26	3.58
2016	108.02	2.55
2015	107.82	0.47
2014	109.93	6.03
2013	106.21	-2.14

Total Assets: $66,025,267,982

Asset Allocation

Asset	%
Cash	1%
Stocks	0%
US Stocks	0%
Bonds	98%
US Bonds	92%
Other	0%

Services Offered: Dividend Investment Plan, CashInvestment Plan

Investment Strategy: The investment seeks to track the investment results of the Bloomberg Barclays U.S. Aggregate Bond Index. The index measures the performance of the total U.S. investment-grade bond market. The fund generally invests at least 90% of its net assets in component securities of its underlying index and in investments that have economic characteristics that are substantially identical to the economic characteristics of the component securities of its underlying index. **Top Holdings:** Fnma Pass-Thru I 3% Gnma2 30yr 2017 Production Gnma2 30yr 2017 Production Fgold 30yr 2016 Production Gnma2 30yr 2016 Production

---

iShares Edge MSCI Min Vol Global ETF

B- **BUY**

Ticker	Traded On	NAV		Total Assets ($)	Dividend Yield (TTM)	Turnover Ratio	Expense Ratio
ACWV	BATS	94.60		$5,477,341,032	2.13	23	0.2

Ratings
Reward	B-
Risk	C+
Recent Upgrade/Downgrade	

Fund Information
Fund Type	Exchange Traded Funds
Category	Global Equity Large Cap
Sub-Category	World Large Stock
Prospectus Objective	World Stock
Inception Date	Oct-11
Open to New Investments	Y

Prices
Price (as of 9/30/2019)	94.75
52-Week High	95.06
52-Week Low	78.32

Total Returns (%)
3-Month	6-Month	1-Year	3-Year	5-Year
2.59	6.83	10.18	33.43	59.78

3-Year Standard Deviation	7.95
Effective Duration	

Valuation
Premium/Discount (1-Year Average)	0.06

Company Information
Provider	iShares
Manager/Tenure	Diane Hsiung (7), Greg Savage (7), Jennifer Hsui (6), 3 others
Website	http://www.ishares.com
Address	iShares 400 Howard Street San Francisco CA 94105 United States
Phone Number	800-474-2737

PERFORMANCE

Ratings History

Date	Overall Rating	Risk Rating	Reward Rating
Q3-19	B-	C+	B-
Q4-18	C	C+	C
Q4-17	B	B+	B-
Q4-16	C	C+	C
Q4-15	C	C+	C

Asset & Performance History

Date	NAV	1-Year Total Return
2018	81.21	-1.34
2017	84.21	18.17
2016	72.76	7.7
2015	69.28	3.04
2014	68.77	11.12
2013	63.31	17.27

Total Assets: $5,477,341,032

Asset Allocation

Asset	%
Cash	1%
Stocks	99%
US Stocks	52%
Bonds	0%
US Bonds	0%
Other	0%

Services Offered:

Investment Strategy: The investment seeks to track the investment results of the MSCI ACWI Minimum Volatility (USD) Index. The fund generally will invest at least 90% of its assets in the component securities of the underlying index and in investments that have economic characteristics that are substantially identical to the component securities of the underlying index. The index measures the combined performance of equity securities in both developed and emerging markets that, in the aggregate, have lower volatility relative to the broader developed and emerging markets. **Top Holdings:** Waste Management Inc Nestle SA Consolidated Edison Inc Motorola Solutions Inc McDonald's Corp

iShares Edge MSCI Min Vol USA ETF

B **BUY**

Ticker	Traded On	NAV	Total Assets ($)	Dividend Yield (TTM)	Turnover Ratio	Expense Ratio
USMV	BATS	64.07	$35,009,523,106	1.84	21	0.15

Ratings

Reward	B
Risk	A-
Recent Upgrade/Downgrade	Down

Fund Information

Fund Type	Exchange Traded Funds
Category	US Equity Large Cap Blend
Sub-Category	Large Blend
Prospectus Objective	Growth
Inception Date	Oct-11
Open to New Investments	Y

Prices

Price (as of 9/30/2019)	64.10
52-Week High	64.69
52-Week Low	49.77

Total Returns (%)

3-Month	6-Month	1-Year	3-Year	5-Year
3.81	9.64	14.68	49.72	89.73

3-Year Standard Deviation	9.12
Effective Duration	

Valuation

Premium/Discount (1-Year Average)	-0.05

Company Information

Provider	iShares
Manager/Tenure	Diane Hsiung (7), Greg Savage (7), Jennifer Hsui (6), 3 others
Website	http://www.ishares.com
Address	iShares 400 Howard Street San Francisco CA 94105 United States
Phone Number	800-474-2737

PERFORMANCE

Ratings History

Date	Overall Rating	Risk Rating	Reward Rating
Q3-19	B	A-	B
Q4-18	B	A	C
Q4-17	B+	A+	B-
Q4-16	C	C+	C
Q4-15	B-	C+	B-

Asset & Performance History

Date	NAV	1-Year Total Return
2018	52.39	1.35
2017	52.77	18.97
2016	45.19	10.49
2015	41.82	5.5
2014	40.46	16.33
2013	35.48	25.1

Total Assets: $35,009,523,106

Asset Allocation

Asset	%
Cash	0%
Stocks	100%
US Stocks	98%
Bonds	0%
US Bonds	0%
Other	0%

Services Offered:

Investment Strategy: The investment seeks the investment results of the MSCI USA Minimum Volatility (USD) Index. The fund will invest at least 90% of its assets in the component securities of the index and may invest up to 10% of its assets in certain futures, options and swap contracts, cash and cash equivalents. The index measures the performance of large and mid-capitalization equity securities listed on stock exchanges in the U.S. that, in the aggregate, have lower volatility relative to the broader U.S. equity market. **Top Holdings:** Newmont Goldcorp Corp Coca-Cola Co Waste Management Inc Visa Inc Class A McDonald's Corp

iShares Edge MSCI USA Momentum Factor ETF

B- **BUY**

Ticker	Traded On	NAV	Total Assets ($)	Dividend Yield (TTM)	Turnover Ratio	Expense Ratio
MTUM	BATS	119.21	$10,221,977,219	1.46	138	0.15

Ratings

Reward	B
Risk	C+
Recent Upgrade/Downgrade	Up

Fund Information

Fund Type	Exchange Traded Funds
Category	US Equity Large Cap Growth
Sub-Category	Large Growth
Prospectus Objective	Growth
Inception Date	Apr-13
Open to New Investments	Y

Prices

Price (as of 9/30/2019)	119.25
52-Week High	123.04
52-Week Low	92.80

Total Returns (%)

3-Month	6-Month	1-Year	3-Year	5-Year
-0.14	6.68	1.28	60.39	98.99

3-Year Standard Deviation	12.49
Effective Duration	

Valuation

Premium/Discount (1-Year Average)	0.00

Company Information

Provider	iShares
Manager/Tenure	Diane Hsiung (6), Jennifer Hsui (6), Greg Savage (6), 3 others
Website	http://www.ishares.com
Address	iShares 400 Howard Street San Francisco CA 94105 United States
Phone Number	800-474-2737

PERFORMANCE

Ratings History

Date	Overall Rating	Risk Rating	Reward Rating
Q3-19	B-	C+	B
Q4-18	C+	C+	C+
Q4-17	A	A	A
Q4-16	B-	B-	B-
Q4-15	C	B-	C+

Asset & Performance History

Date	NAV	1-Year Total Return
2018	100.06	-1.76
2017	103.07	37.6
2016	75.76	4.89
2015	73.27	9.12
2014	67.92	14.47
2013	59.98	

Total Assets: $10,221,977,219

Asset Allocation

Asset	%
Cash	0%
Stocks	100%
US Stocks	99%
Bonds	0%
US Bonds	0%
Other	0%

Services Offered:

Investment Strategy: The investment seeks to track the investment results of the MSCI USA Momentum Index. The fund generally will invest at least 90% of its assets in the component securities of the underlying index and may invest up to 10% of its assets in certain futures, options and swap contracts, cash and cash equivalents. The index consists of stocks exhibiting relatively higher momentum characteristics than the traditional market capitalization-weighted parent index, the MSCI USA Index, which includes U.S. large- and mid-capitalization stocks. **Top Holdings:** Procter & Gamble Co Mastercard Inc A Visa Inc Class A Microsoft Corp The Walt Disney Co

iShares Evolved U.S. Consumer Staples ETF   B-   BUY

Ticker	Traded On	NAV	Total Assets ($)	Dividend Yield (TTM)	Turnover Ratio	Expense Ratio
IECS	BATS	27.98	$8,395,305	2.55	9	0.18

Ratings

Reward	B
Risk	C
Recent Upgrade/Downgrade	Up

Fund Information

Fund Type	Exchange Traded Funds
Category	Consumer Goods & Svcs
Sub-Category	Consumer Defensive
Prospectus Objective	Unaligned
Inception Date	Mar-18
Open to New Investments	Y

Prices

Price (as of 9/30/2019)	28.01
52-Week High	28.24
52-Week Low	22.54

Total Returns (%)

3-Month	6-Month	1-Year	3-Year	5-Year
4.08	9.72	16.10		

3-Year Standard Deviation	
Effective Duration	

Valuation

Premium/Discount (1-Year Average)	0.04

Company Information

Provider	iShares
Manager/Tenure	Travis Cooke (1), Jeff Shen (1)
Website	http://www.ishares.com
Address	iShares 400 Howard Street San Francisco CA 94105 United States
Phone Number	800-474-2737

PERFORMANCE

Ratings History

Date	Overall Rating	Risk Rating	Reward Rating
Q3-19	B-	C	B
Q4-18	U		
Q4-17			
Q4-16			
Q4-15			

Asset & Performance History

Date	NAV	1-Year Total Return
2018	23.09	
2017		
2016		
2015		
2014		
2013		

Total Assets: $8,395,305

Asset Allocation

Asset	%
Cash	0%
Stocks	100%
US Stocks	99%
Bonds	0%
US Bonds	0%
Other	0%

Services Offered:

Investment Strategy: The investment seeks to provide access to U.S. companies with consumer staples exposure, as classified using a proprietary classification system. The fund seeks to achieve its investment objective by investing, under normal circumstances, at least 80% of its net assets in U.S. listed common stock of large-, mid- and small-capitalization consumer staples companies. It will hold common stock of those companies that fall into the Consumer Staples Evolved Sector which have economic characteristics that have been historically correlated with companies traditionally defined as consumer staples companies. The fund is non-diversified. **Top Holdings:** Coca-Cola Co   PepsiCo Inc   Procter & Gamble Co   McDonald's Corp   Mondelez International Inc Class A

---

iShares Expanded Tech-Software Sector ETF   B-   BUY

Ticker	Traded On	NAV	Total Assets ($)	Dividend Yield (TTM)	Turnover Ratio	Expense Ratio
IGV	BATS	211.87	$2,553,069,125	0.13	18	0.46

Ratings

Reward	B
Risk	C
Recent Upgrade/Downgrade	

Fund Information

Fund Type	Exchange Traded Funds
Category	Technology Sector Equity
Sub-Category	Technology
Prospectus Objective	Technology
Inception Date	Jul-01
Open to New Investments	Y

Prices

Price (as of 9/30/2019)	211.88
52-Week High	230.04
52-Week Low	159.19

Total Returns (%)

3-Month	6-Month	1-Year	3-Year	5-Year
-4.47	-0.82	3.81	87.15	152.65

3-Year Standard Deviation	16.32
Effective Duration	

Valuation

Premium/Discount (1-Year Average)	-0.02

Company Information

Provider	iShares
Manager/Tenure	Greg Savage (11), Jennifer Hsui (6), Alan Mason (3), 2 others
Website	http://www.ishares.com
Address	iShares 400 Howard Street San Francisco CA 94105 United States
Phone Number	800-474-2737

PERFORMANCE

Ratings History

Date	Overall Rating	Risk Rating	Reward Rating
Q3-19	B-	C	B
Q4-18	C+	C	B-
Q4-17	A-	B+	A+
Q4-16	B-	C	B
Q4-15	B-	C	B

Asset & Performance History

Date	NAV	1-Year Total Return
2018	173.45	12.43
2017	154.52	42.16
2016	108.81	5.86
2015	103.7	11.96
2014	92.83	13.39
2013	82.12	30.59

Total Assets: $2,553,069,125

Asset Allocation

Asset	%
Cash	0%
Stocks	100%
US Stocks	98%
Bonds	0%
US Bonds	0%
Other	0%

Services Offered: CashInvestment Plan

Investment Strategy: The investment seeks to track the investment results of the S&P North American Expanded Technology Software IndexTM. The fund generally invests at least 90% of its assets in securities of the underlying index and in depositary receipts representing securities of the underlying index. The index measures the performance of U.S.-traded stocks from the software industry and select companies from the interactive home entertainment and interactive media and services industries in the U.S. and Canada. The fund is non-diversified. **Top Holdings:** Salesforce.com Inc   Microsoft Corp   Adobe Inc   Oracle Corp   Intuit Inc

iShares Global Tech ETF — B- BUY

Ticker	Traded On	NAV	Total Assets ($)	Dividend Yield (TTM)	Turnover Ratio	Expense Ratio
IXN	NYSE Arca	184.56	$2,805,382,882	1.03	17	0.46

Ratings
Reward	B
Risk	C
Recent Upgrade/Downgrade	Up

Fund Information
Fund Type	Exchange Traded Funds
Category	Technology Sector Equity
Sub-Category	Technology
Prospectus Objective	Technology
Inception Date	Nov-01
Open to New Investments	Y

Prices
Price (as of 9/30/2019)	184.97
52-Week High	188.59
52-Week Low	134.75

Total Returns (%)
3-Month	6-Month	1-Year	3-Year	5-Year
1.31	7.26	6.06	72.17	116.09

3-Year Standard Deviation	15.06
Effective Duration	

Valuation
Premium/Discount (1-Year Average)	-0.03

Company Information
Provider	iShares
Manager/Tenure	Greg Savage (11), Jennifer Hsui (7), Alan Mason (3), 2 others
Website	http://www.ishares.com
Address	iShares 400 Howard Street San Francisco CA 94105 United States
Phone Number	800-474-2737

PERFORMANCE

Ratings History
Date	Overall Rating	Risk Rating	Reward Rating
Q3-19	B-	C	B
Q4-18	C+	C+	C+
Q4-17	A-	B	A+
Q4-16	C	C	C+
Q4-15	C+	C	C+

Asset & Performance History
Date	NAV	1-Year Total Return
2018	144.24	-5.13
2017	153.38	40.77
2016	110.04	13.69
2015	97.85	4.37
2014	94.8	15.43
2013	83.1	25.03

Total Assets: $2,805,382,882

Asset Allocation
Asset	%
Cash	0%
Stocks	100%
US Stocks	79%
Bonds	0%
US Bonds	0%
Other	0%

Services Offered: CashInvestment Plan

Investment Strategy: The investment seeks to track the investment results of the S&P Global 1200 Information Technology IndexTM. The fund generally invests at least 90% of its assets in securities of the index and in depositary receipts representing securities of the index. It may invest the remainder of its assets in certain futures, options and swap contracts, cash and cash equivalents, as well as in securities not included in the index. The index measures the performance of companies that the index provider deems to be part of the information technology sector of the economy and that the index provider believes are important to global markets. It is non-diversified.

Top Holdings: Microsoft Corp Apple Inc Visa Inc Class A Mastercard Inc A Intel Corp

iShares iBoxx $ High Yield Corporate Bond ETF — B BUY

Ticker	Traded On	NAV	Total Assets ($)	Dividend Yield (TTM)	Turnover Ratio	Expense Ratio
HYG	NYSE Arca	86.89	$17,978,406,784	5.29	14	0.49

Ratings
Reward	C+
Risk	A
Recent Upgrade/Downgrade	

Fund Information
Fund Type	Exchange Traded Funds
Category	US Fixed Income
Sub-Category	High Yield Bond
Prospectus Objective	Corp Bond-High Yld
Inception Date	Apr-07
Open to New Investments	Y

Prices
Price (as of 9/30/2019)	87.17
52-Week High	87.61
52-Week Low	79.63

Total Returns (%)
3-Month	6-Month	1-Year	3-Year	5-Year
0.97	3.80	6.14	17.19	23.69

3-Year Standard Deviation	4.23
Effective Duration	3.37

Valuation
Premium/Discount (1-Year Average)	0.15

Company Information
Provider	iShares
Manager/Tenure	Scott Radell (9), James Mauro (8)
Website	http://www.ishares.com
Address	iShares 400 Howard Street San Francisco CA 94105 United States
Phone Number	800-474-2737

PERFORMANCE

Ratings History
Date	Overall Rating	Risk Rating	Reward Rating
Q3-19	B	A	C+
Q4-18	C+	A-	C-
Q4-17	B-	B	C+
Q4-16	C+	B	C
Q4-15	C	C	C-

Asset & Performance History
Date	NAV	1-Year Total Return
2018	80.9	-1.93
2017	86.97	6.08
2016	86.26	13.92
2015	79.97	-5.54
2014	89.43	2
2013	92.62	5.89

Total Assets: $17,978,406,784

Asset Allocation
Asset	%
Cash	1%
Stocks	0%
US Stocks	0%
Bonds	99%
US Bonds	84%
Other	0%

Services Offered:

Investment Strategy: The investment seeks to track the investment results of the Markit iBoxx® USD Liquid High Yield Index (the "underlying index"). The underlying index is a rules-based index consisting of U.S. dollar-denominated, high yield corporate bonds for sale in the U.S. The fund generally will invest at least 90% of its assets in the component securities of the underlying index and may invest up to 10% of its assets in certain futures, options and swap contracts, cash and cash equivalents, as well as in securities not included in the underlying index. **Top Holdings:** ALTICE FRANCE S.A 7.38% Sprint Corporation 7.88% TransDigm, Inc. 6.25% CCO Holdings, LLC/ CCO Holdings Capital Corp. 5.13% Bausch Health Companies Inc 6.13%

iShares iBoxx $ Investment Grade Corporate Bond ETF   B-   BUY

Ticker	Traded On	NAV	Total Assets ($)	Dividend Yield (TTM)	Turnover Ratio	Expense Ratio
LQD	NYSE Arca	127.23	$36,120,663,153	3.35	10	0.15

Ratings

Reward	B-
Risk	B
Recent Upgrade/Downgrade	

Fund Information

Fund Type	Exchange Traded Funds
Category	US Fixed Income
Sub-Category	Corporate Bond
Prospectus Objective	Corp Bond - Gen
Inception Date	Jul-02
Open to New Investments	Y

Prices

Price (as of 9/30/2019)	127.48
52-Week High	129.10
52-Week Low	111.35

Total Returns (%)

3-Month	6-Month	1-Year	3-Year	5-Year
3.37	9.70	14.99	14.75	26.90

3-Year Standard Deviation	5.13
Effective Duration	9.11

Valuation

Premium/Discount (1-Year Average)	0.09

Company Information

Provider	iShares
Manager/Tenure	Scott Radell (9), James Mauro (8)
Website	http://www.ishares.com
Address	iShares 400 Howard Street San Francisco CA 94105 United States
Phone Number	800-474-2737

PERFORMANCE

Ratings History

Date	Overall Rating	Risk Rating	Reward Rating
Q3-19	B-	B	B-
Q4-18	C	C+	D+
Q4-17	B-	B+	C
Q4-16	B-	B+	C
Q4-15	C	C	C

Asset & Performance History

Date	NAV	1-Year Total Return
2018	112.69	-3.75
2017	121.39	7.15
2016	116.91	5.97
2015	114.01	-1.07
2014	119.2	8.56
2013	113.62	-2.49

Total Assets: $36,120,663,153

Asset Allocation

Asset	%
Cash	0%
Stocks	0%
US Stocks	0%
Bonds	97%
US Bonds	85%
Other	0%

Services Offered:

Investment Strategy: The investment seeks to track the investment results of the Markit iBoxx® USD Liquid Investment Grade Index. The fund generally invests at least 90% of its assets in component securities of the underlying index and at least 95% of its assets in investment-grade corporate bonds. The underlying index is designed to provide a broad representation of the U.S. dollar-denominated liquid investment-grade corporate bond market. **Top Holdings:** GE Capital International Funding Company Unlimited Company 4.42% Anheuser-Busch Companies LLC / Anheuser-Busch InBev Worldwide Inc 4.9% CVS Health Corp 4.3% CVS Health Corp 5.05% Verizon Communications Inc. 4.33%

---

iShares J.P. Morgan USD Emerging Markets Bond ETF   B-   BUY

Ticker	Traded On	NAV	Total Assets ($)	Dividend Yield (TTM)	Turnover Ratio	Expense Ratio
EMB	NAS CM	113.24	$14,869,014,222	5.45	15	0.39

Ratings

Reward	B-
Risk	B-
Recent Upgrade/Downgrade	

Fund Information

Fund Type	Exchange Traded Funds
Category	Emerging Mkts Fixed Inc
Sub-Category	Emerging Markets Bond
Prospectus Objective	Div Emerg Mkts
Inception Date	Dec-07
Open to New Investments	Y

Prices

Price (as of 9/30/2019)	113.35
52-Week High	115.59
52-Week Low	102.36

Total Returns (%)

3-Month	6-Month	1-Year	3-Year	5-Year
0.89	5.85	11.53	12.24	28.19

3-Year Standard Deviation	6.12
Effective Duration	7.41

Valuation

Premium/Discount (1-Year Average)	0.30

Company Information

Provider	iShares
Manager/Tenure	Scott Radell (9), James Mauro (8)
Website	http://www.ishares.com
Address	iShares 400 Howard Street San Francisco CA 94105 United States
Phone Number	800-474-2737

PERFORMANCE

Ratings History

Date	Overall Rating	Risk Rating	Reward Rating
Q3-19	B-	B-	B-
Q4-18	C-	C	D+
Q4-17	B	B+	C+
Q4-16	C	C+	C
Q4-15	C	C	C-

Asset & Performance History

Date	NAV	1-Year Total Return
2018	103.17	-5.67
2017	115.53	9.97
2016	110	9.41
2015	105.44	0.43
2014	110.03	6.69
2013	107.84	-7.42

Total Assets: $14,869,014,222

Asset Allocation

Asset	%
Cash	0%
Stocks	0%
US Stocks	0%
Bonds	100%
US Bonds	0%
Other	0%

Services Offered:

Investment Strategy: The investment seeks to track the investment results of the J.P. Morgan EMBI® Global Core Index composed of U.S. dollar-denominated, emerging market bonds. The fund generally will invest at least 90% of its assets in the component securities of the underlying index and may invest up to 10% of its assets in certain futures, options and swap contracts, cash and cash equivalents, as well as in securities not included in the underlying index. The index is a broad, diverse U.S. dollar-denominated emerging markets debt benchmark that tracks the total return of actively traded external debt instruments in emerging market countries. **Top Holdings:** Uruguay (Republic of) 5.1% State of Kuwait 3.5% The Republic of Peru 5.63% Russian Federation 5.25% The Republic of Peru 8.75%

iShares Long-Term Corporate Bond ETF

B-   **BUY**

Ticker	Traded On	NAV	Total Assets ($)	Dividend Yield (TTM)	Turnover Ratio	Expense Ratio
IGLB	NYSE Arca	66.44	$1,734,119,069	3.92	24	0.06

Ratings
Reward B
Risk C+
Recent Upgrade/Downgrade

Fund Information
Fund Type Exchange Traded Funds
Category US Fixed Income
Sub-Category Long-Term Bond
Prospectus Objective Growth & Inc
Inception Date Dec-09
Open to New Investments Y

Prices
Price (as of 9/30/2019) 66.63
52-Week High 67.97
52-Week Low 55.17

Total Returns (%)

3-Month	6-Month	1-Year	3-Year	5-Year
5.73	13.80	20.05	19.85	36.16

3-Year Standard Deviation 7.58
Effective Duration

Valuation
Premium/Discount (1-Year Average) 0.21

Company Information
Provider iShares
Manager/Tenure Scott Radell (9), James Mauro (8)
Website http://www.ishares.com
Address iShares 400 Howard Street San
Francisco CA 94105 United States
Phone Number 800-474-2737

PERFORMANCE

Ratings History

Date	Overall Rating	Risk Rating	Reward Rating
Q3-19	B-	C+	B
Q4-18	D+	C-	D+
Q4-17	B-	B	B-
Q4-16	C	C+	C
Q4-15	C	C	C-

Asset & Performance History

Date	NAV	1-Year Total Return
2018	56.08	-7.17
2017	63.15	11.67
2016	58.7	9.91
2015	55.66	-4.75
2014	61.03	15.54
2013	55.12	-7.05

Total Assets: $1,734,119,069
Asset Allocation

Asset	%
Cash	2%
Stocks	0%
US Stocks	0%
Bonds	98%
US Bonds	82%
Other	0%

Services Offered:

Investment Strategy: The investment seeks to track the investment results of the ICE BofAML 10+ Year US Corporate Index. The fund generally will invest at least 90% of its assets in the component securities of the underlying index and may invest up to 10% of its assets in certain futures, options and swap contracts, cash and cash equivalents. The underlying index measures the performance of investment-grade corporate bonds of both U.S. and non-U.S. issuers that are U.S. dollar-denominated and publicly issued in the U.S. domestic market and have a remaining maturity of greater than or equal to ten years. **Top Holdings:** GE Capital International Funding Company Unlimited Company 4.42% Anheuser-Busch Companies LLC / Anheuser-Busch InBev Worldwide Inc 4.9% Goldman Sachs Group, Inc. 6.75% CVS Health Corp 5.05% Anheuser-Busch Companies LLC / Anheuser-Busch InBev Worldwide Inc 4.7%

iShares MSCI ACWI ETF

B-   **BUY**

Ticker	Traded On	NAV	Total Assets ($)	Dividend Yield (TTM)	Turnover Ratio	Expense Ratio
ACWI	NAS CM	73.73	$10,676,806,408	2.1	11	0.32

Ratings
Reward C
Risk B
Recent Upgrade/Downgrade

Fund Information
Fund Type Exchange Traded Funds
Category Global Equity Large Cap
Sub-Category World Large Stock
Prospectus Objective World Stock
Inception Date Mar-08
Open to New Investments Y

Prices
Price (as of 9/30/2019) 73.75
52-Week High 75.05
52-Week Low 61.18

Total Returns (%)

3-Month	6-Month	1-Year	3-Year	5-Year
-0.63	2.44	1.34	33.15	41.16

3-Year Standard Deviation 11.33
Effective Duration

Valuation
Premium/Discount (1-Year Average) 0.00

Company Information
Provider iShares
Manager/Tenure Diane Hsiung (11), Greg Savage (11), Jennifer Hsui (6), 3 others
Website http://www.ishares.com
Address iShares 400 Howard Street San
Francisco CA 94105 United States
Phone Number 800-474-2737

PERFORMANCE

Ratings History

Date	Overall Rating	Risk Rating	Reward Rating
Q3-19	B-	B	C
Q4-18	C	C+	C-
Q4-17	B-	C+	B-
Q4-16	C	C+	C
Q4-15	C	C+	C

Asset & Performance History

Date	NAV	1-Year Total Return
2018	64.19	-9.21
2017	72.15	24.34
2016	59.22	8.21
2015	55.96	-2.38
2014	58.75	4.64
2013	57.41	22.9

Total Assets: $10,676,806,408
Asset Allocation

Asset	%
Cash	0%
Stocks	100%
US Stocks	55%
Bonds	0%
US Bonds	0%
Other	0%

Services Offered:

Investment Strategy: The investment seeks to track the investment results of the MSCI ACWI composed of large- and mid-capitalization developed and emerging market equities. The fund generally will invest at least 90% of its assets in the component securities of the underlying index and in investments that have economic characteristics that are substantially identical to the component securities of the underlying index. The index is a free float-adjusted market capitalization index designed to measure the combined equity market performance of developed and emerging markets countries. **Top Holdings:** Microsoft Corp Apple Inc Amazon.com Inc iShares MSCI India ETF Facebook Inc A

iShares MSCI Brazil Small-Cap ETF   B   BUY

Ticker	Traded On	NAV	Total Assets ($)	Dividend Yield (TTM)	Turnover Ratio	Expense Ratio
EWZS	NAS CM	17.14	$115,705,325	3.48	67	0.59

Ratings
Reward   B+
Risk   C
Recent Upgrade/Downgrade   Up

Fund Information
Fund Type   Exchange Traded Funds
Category   Latin America Equity
Sub-Category   Latin America Stock
Prospectus Objective   Foreign Stock
Inception Date   Sep-10
Open to New Investments   Y

Prices
Price (as of 9/30/2019)   17.21
52-Week High   18.65
52-Week Low   11.78

Total Returns (%)

3-Month	6-Month	1-Year	3-Year	5-Year
1.24	11.54	53.12	67.66	22.24

3-Year Standard Deviation   30.24
Effective Duration

Valuation
Premium/Discount (1-Year Average)   -0.16

Company Information
Provider   iShares
Manager/Tenure   Diane Hsiung (9), Greg Savage (9), Jennifer Hsui (6), 3 others
Website   http://www.ishares.com
Address   iShares 400 Howard Street San Francisco CA 94105 United States
Phone Number   800-474-2737

PERFORMANCE

Ratings History

Date	Overall Rating	Risk Rating	Reward Rating
Q3-19	B	C	B+
Q4-18	C-	D+	C
Q4-17	C	D+	C+
Q4-16	D+	D+	D+
Q4-15	E+	D-	E+

Asset & Performance History

Date	NAV	1-Year Total Return
2018	14.36	-7.17
2017	16.28	51.13
2016	11.19	64.81
2015	7.06	-49.35
2014	14.37	-25.77
2013	19.85	-26.52

Total Assets: $115,705,325

Asset Allocation

Asset	%
Cash	0%
Stocks	100%
US Stocks	0%
Bonds	0%
US Bonds	0%
Other	0%

Services Offered:

Investment Strategy: The investment seeks to track the investment results of the MSCI Brazil Small Cap Index. The fund generally will invest at least 90% of its assets in the component securities of the underlying index and in investments that have economic characteristics that are substantially identical to the component securities of the underlying index. The index is a free float-adjusted market capitalization-weighted index designed to measure the performance of equity securities in the bottom 14% by market capitalization of equity securities listed on stock exchanges in Brazil. **Top Holdings:** Azul SA Participating Preferred Totvs SA Estacio Participacoes SA Via Varejo SA CVC Brasil Operadora e Agencia de Viagens SA

---

iShares MSCI Russia Capped ETF   B   BUY

Ticker	Traded On	NAV	Total Assets ($)	Dividend Yield (TTM)	Turnover Ratio	Expense Ratio
ERUS	NYSE Arca	38.98	$658,807,248	5.2	32	0.59

Ratings
Reward   B
Risk   C+
Recent Upgrade/Downgrade

Fund Information
Fund Type   Exchange Traded Funds
Category   Equity Misc
Sub-Category   Miscellaneous Region
Prospectus Objective   Foreign Stock
Inception Date   Nov-10
Open to New Investments   Y

Prices
Price (as of 9/30/2019)   38.90
52-Week High   40.76
52-Week Low   30.59

Total Returns (%)

3-Month	6-Month	1-Year	3-Year	5-Year
-2.57	13.06	17.20	52.80	41.18

3-Year Standard Deviation   18.63
Effective Duration

Valuation
Premium/Discount (1-Year Average)   -0.23

Company Information
Provider   iShares
Manager/Tenure   Diane Hsiung (8), Greg Savage (8), Jennifer Hsui (6), 3 others
Website   http://www.ishares.com
Address   iShares 400 Howard Street San Francisco CA 94105 United States
Phone Number   800-474-2737

PERFORMANCE

Ratings History

Date	Overall Rating	Risk Rating	Reward Rating
Q3-19	B	C+	B
Q4-18	C+	C+	C+
Q4-17	B	C	A-
Q4-16	C-	D+	C-
Q4-15	D	D	D

Asset & Performance History

Date	NAV	1-Year Total Return
2018	30.96	-3.66
2017	33.61	4.5
2016	33.42	53.94
2015	22.28	3.36
2014	22.38	-44.95
2013	43.12	-3.21

Total Assets: $658,807,248

Asset Allocation

Asset	%
Cash	0%
Stocks	100%
US Stocks	0%
Bonds	0%
US Bonds	0%
Other	0%

Services Offered:

Investment Strategy: The investment seeks to track the investment results of the MSCI Russia 25/50 Index. The fund generally will invest at least 90% of its assets in the component securities of the underlying index and in investments that have economic characteristics that are substantially identical to the component securities of the underlying index. The index is designed to measure the performance of equity securities listed on stock exchanges in Russia. The fund is non-diversified. **Top Holdings:** Gazprom PJSC PJSC Lukoil Sberbank of Russia PJSC Mining and Metallurgical Company NORILSK NICKEL PJSC Tatneft PJSC

iShares MSCI Switzerland ETF
B-   **BUY**

Ticker	Traded On	NAV	Total Assets ($)	Dividend Yield (TTM)	Turnover Ratio	Expense Ratio
EWL	NYSE Arca	37.65	$1,026,046,515	1.99	9	0.47

Ratings
Reward   B
Risk   C+
Recent Upgrade/Downgrade   Down

Fund Information
Fund Type   Exchange Traded Funds
Category   Europe Equity Large Cap
Sub-Category   Miscellaneous Region
Prospectus Objective   Europe Stock
Inception Date   Mar-96
Open to New Investments   Y

Prices
Price (as of 9/30/2019)   37.70
52-Week High   38.11
52-Week Low   30.43

Total Returns (%)

3-Month	6-Month	1-Year	3-Year	5-Year
0.39	8.14	10.47	31.85	31.05

3-Year Standard Deviation   11.52
Effective Duration

Valuation
Premium/Discount (1-Year Average)   0.03

Company Information
Provider   iShares
Manager/Tenure   Diane Hsiung (11), Greg Savage (11), Jennifer Hsui (6), 3 others
Website   http://www.ishares.com
Address   iShares 400 Howard Street San Francisco CA 94105 United States
Phone Number   800-474-2737

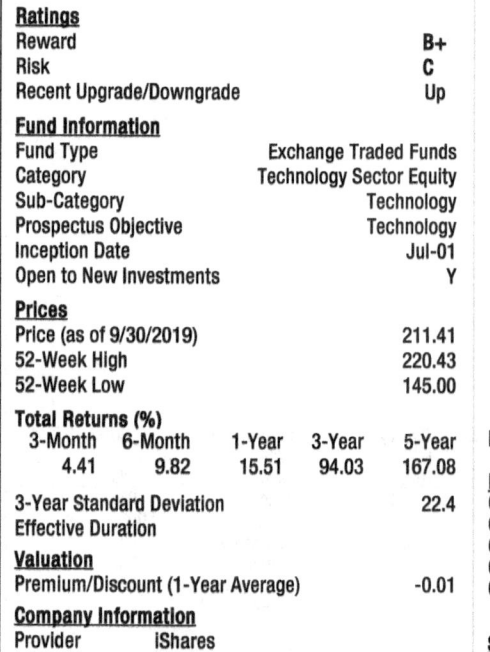

PERFORMANCE

Ratings History

Date	Overall Rating	Risk Rating	Reward Rating
Q3-19	B-	C+	B
Q4-18	C	C+	D+
Q4-17	B-	B	C+
Q4-16	C-	C-	C-
Q4-15	C	C+	C

Asset & Performance History

Date	NAV	1-Year Total Return
2018	31.35	-9.77
2017	35.62	23.36
2016	29.49	-3.04
2015	31.24	0.51
2014	31.82	-0.81
2013	32.82	26.47

Total Assets: $1,026,046,515

Asset Allocation

Asset	%
Cash	1%
Stocks	99%
US Stocks	0%
Bonds	0%
US Bonds	0%
Other	0%

Services Offered: CashInvestment Plan

Investment Strategy: The investment seeks to track the investment results of the MSCI Switzerland 25/50 Index. The fund will at all times invest at least 80% of its assets in the securities of its underlying index and in depositary receipts representing securities in its underlying index. The underlying index is a free float-adjusted market capitalization-weighted index with a capping methodology applied to issuer weights so that no single issuer of a component exceeds 25% of the underlying index weight, and all issuers with a weight above 5% do not cumulatively exceed 50% of the underlying index weight. The fund is non-diversified. **Top Holdings:** Nestle SA Novartis AG Roche Holding AG Dividend Right Cert. Zurich Insurance Group AG UBS Group AG

---

iShares PHLX Semiconductor ETF
B-   **BUY**

Ticker	Traded On	NAV	Total Assets ($)	Dividend Yield (TTM)	Turnover Ratio	Expense Ratio
SOXX	NAS CM	211.58	$1,756,106,182	1.22	26	0.46

Ratings
Reward   B+
Risk   C
Recent Upgrade/Downgrade   Up

Fund Information
Fund Type   Exchange Traded Funds
Category   Technology Sector Equity
Sub-Category   Technology
Prospectus Objective   Technology
Inception Date   Jul-01
Open to New Investments   Y

Prices
Price (as of 9/30/2019)   211.41
52-Week High   220.43
52-Week Low   145.00

Total Returns (%)

3-Month	6-Month	1-Year	3-Year	5-Year
4.41	9.82	15.51	94.03	167.08

3-Year Standard Deviation   22.4
Effective Duration

Valuation
Premium/Discount (1-Year Average)   -0.01

Company Information
Provider   iShares
Manager/Tenure   Greg Savage (11), Jennifer Hsui (6), Alan Mason (3), 2 others
Website   http://www.ishares.com
Address   iShares 400 Howard Street San Francisco CA 94105 United States
Phone Number   800-474-2737

PERFORMANCE

Ratings History

Date	Overall Rating	Risk Rating	Reward Rating
Q3-19	B-	C	B+
Q4-18	B-	C-	B
Q4-17	A-	B	A+
Q4-16	C	C	C
Q4-15	B	B-	B

Asset & Performance History

Date	NAV	1-Year Total Return
2018	156.88	-6.47
2017	169.77	39.82
2016	122.66	38.4
2015	89.76	-2.06
2014	92.86	29.89
2013	72.66	41.25

Total Assets: $1,756,106,182

Asset Allocation

Asset	%
Cash	0%
Stocks	100%
US Stocks	86%
Bonds	0%
US Bonds	0%
Other	0%

Services Offered: CashInvestment Plan

Investment Strategy: The investment seeks to track the investment results of the PHLX Semiconductor Sector Index composed of U.S. equities in the semiconductor sector. The fund generally invests at least 90% of its assets in securities of the underlying index and in depositary receipts representing securities of the underlying index. The underlying index measures the performance of U.S.-traded securities of companies engaged in the semiconductor business. The fund is non-diversified. **Top Holdings:** NVIDIA Corp Texas Instruments Inc Qualcomm Inc Broadcom Inc Intel Corp

iShares Preferred and Income Securities ETF   B   BUY

Ticker	Traded On	NAV	Total Assets ($)	Dividend Yield (TTM)	Turnover Ratio	Expense Ratio
PFF	NAS CM	37.45	$16,567,857,761	5.56	28	0.46

Ratings
Reward	C+
Risk	A-
Recent Upgrade/Downgrade	Up

Fund Information
Fund Type	Exchange Traded Funds
Category	US Fixed Income
Sub-Category	Preferred Stock
Prospectus Objective	Growth & Inc
Inception Date	Mar-07
Open to New Investments	Y

Prices
Price (as of 9/30/2019)	37.53
52-Week High	37.53
52-Week Low	33.41

Total Returns (%)
3-Month	6-Month	1-Year	3-Year	5-Year
2.99	4.83	7.35	12.53	26.69

3-Year Standard Deviation	5.1
Effective Duration	2.77

Valuation
Premium/Discount (1-Year Average)	0.17

Company Information
Provider	iShares
Manager/Tenure	Greg Savage (11), Jennifer Hsui (7), Alan Mason (3), 2 others
Website	http://www.ishares.com
Address	iShares 400 Howard Street San Francisco CA 94105 United States
Phone Number	800-474-2737

PERFORMANCE

Ratings History
Date	Overall Rating	Risk Rating	Reward Rating
Q3-19	B	A-	C+
Q4-18	C-	C	D+
Q4-17	B	A	C+
Q4-16	C	C	C
Q4-15	C+	C+	C+

Asset & Performance History
Date	NAV	1-Year Total Return
2018	34.26	-4.77
2017	38.16	8.32
2016	37.22	1.25
2015	38.88	4.61
2014	39.34	13.44
2013	36.95	-0.59

Total Assets: $16,567,857,761
Asset Allocation
Asset	%
Cash	1%
Stocks	6%
US Stocks	5%
Bonds	0%
US Bonds	0%
Other	0%

Services Offered:

Investment Strategy: The investment seeks to track the investment results of the ICE Exchange-Listed Preferred & Hybrid Securities Transition Index, which measures the performance of a select group of exchange-listed, U.S. dollar-denominated preferred securities, hybrid securities and convertible preferred securities listed on the NYSE or NASDAQ. The fund may invest at least 80% of its assets in the component securities of the index and may invest up to 20% of its assets in certain futures, options and swap contracts, cash and cash equivalents, as well as in securities not included in the index, but which the advisor believes will help the fund track the index. **Top Holdings:** Becton, Dickinson and Co Pfd   GMAC Capital Trust I Pfd Secs 2011-15.2.40 Gtd Series 2   Citigroup Capital XIII Floating Rate Trust Pfd Secs Registered 2010-30.10.4   Sempra Energy 6% PRF CONVERT 15/01/2021 USD 100   Crown Castle International Corp Cum Conv Pfd Registered Shs Series -A-

iShares Residential Real Estate Capped ETF   B-   BUY

Ticker	Traded On	NAV	Total Assets ($)	Dividend Yield (TTM)	Turnover Ratio	Expense Ratio
REZ	NYSE Arca	79.43	$575,853,900	2.63	10	0.48

Ratings
Reward	B
Risk	C
Recent Upgrade/Downgrade	Up

Fund Information
Fund Type	Exchange Traded Funds
Category	Real Estate Sector Equity
Sub-Category	Real Estate
Prospectus Objective	Real Estate
Inception Date	May-07
Open to New Investments	Y

Prices
Price (as of 9/30/2019)	79.47
52-Week High	80.58
52-Week Low	59.92

Total Returns (%)
3-Month	6-Month	1-Year	3-Year	5-Year
9.90	14.18	31.54	35.93	86.80

3-Year Standard Deviation	13.84
Effective Duration	

Valuation
Premium/Discount (1-Year Average)	0.04

Company Information
Provider	iShares
Manager/Tenure	Greg Savage (11), Jennifer Hsui (7), Alan Mason (3), 2 others
Website	http://www.ishares.com
Address	iShares 400 Howard Street San Francisco CA 94105 United States
Phone Number	800-474-2737

PERFORMANCE

Ratings History
Date	Overall Rating	Risk Rating	Reward Rating
Q3-19	B-	C	B
Q4-18	C+	C	B
Q4-17	C+	B	C
Q4-16	B-	C	B
Q4-15	B	C+	B+

Asset & Performance History
Date	NAV	1-Year Total Return
2018	62.39	4.09
2017	62.2	3.82
2016	62.02	3.29
2015	63.39	11.32
2014	58.88	35.02
2013	45.14	-3.53

Total Assets: $575,853,900
Asset Allocation
Asset	%
Cash	1%
Stocks	99%
US Stocks	99%
Bonds	0%
US Bonds	0%
Other	0%

Services Offered:

Investment Strategy: The investment seeks to track the investment results of the FTSE NAREIT All Residential Capped Index composed of U.S. residential, healthcare and self-storage real estate equities. The fund generally will invest at least 90% of its assets in the component securities of the underlying index and may invest up to 10% of its assets in certain futures, options and swap contracts, cash and cash equivalents. The underlying index measures the performance of the residential apartments, manufactured homes, healthcare and self-storage real estate sectors of the U.S. equity market. The fund is non-diversified. **Top Holdings:** Public Storage Welltower Inc Equity Residential AvalonBay Communities Inc Ventas Inc

iShares Transportation Average ETF   B-   BUY

Ticker	Traded On	NAV	Total Assets ($)	Dividend Yield (TTM)	Turnover Ratio	Expense Ratio
IYT	BATS	186.17	$511,968,947	1.31	17	0.42

Ratings
Reward   B
Risk   C
Recent Upgrade/Downgrade   Up

Fund Information
Fund Type   Exchange Traded Funds
Category   Industrials Sector Equity
Sub-Category   Industrials
Prospectus Objective   Unaligned
Inception Date   Oct-03
Open to New Investments   Y

Prices
Price (as of 9/30/2019)   186.14
52-Week High   205.13
52-Week Low   155.39

Total Returns (%)

3-Month	6-Month	1-Year	3-Year	5-Year
-1.09	-2.05	-7.99	32.74	33.95

3-Year Standard Deviation   19.21
Effective Duration

Valuation
Premium/Discount (1-Year Average)   -0.01

Company Information
Provider   iShares
Manager/Tenure   Greg Savage (11), Jennifer Hsui (7),
                  Alan Mason (3), 2 others
Website   http://www.ishares.com
Address   iShares 400 Howard Street San
                  Francisco CA 94105 United States
Phone Number   800-474-2737

PERFORMANCE

Ratings History

Date	Overall Rating	Risk Rating	Reward Rating
Q3-19	B-	C	B
Q4-18	B	C	B+
Q4-17	C+	C+	B-
Q4-16	B-	C	B
Q4-15	B	B-	B+

Asset & Performance History

Date	NAV	1-Year Total Return
2018	164.99	-12.82
2017	191.53	18.93
2016	162.7	22.05
2015	134.74	-16.88
2014	164.04	25.32
2013	131.91	41.18

Total Assets: $511,968,947
Asset Allocation

Asset	%
Cash	0%
Stocks	100%
US Stocks	100%
Bonds	0%
US Bonds	0%
Other	0%

Services Offered: CashInvestment Plan

Investment Strategy: The investment seeks to track the investment results of the Dow Jones Transportation Average Index composed of U.S. equities in the transportation sector. The fund generally invests at least 90% of its assets in securities of the underlying index and in depositary receipts representing securities of the underlying index. The underlying index measures the performance of large, well-known companies within the transportation sector of the U.S. equity market. The fund is non-diversified. **Top Holdings:** Norfolk Southern Corp Union Pacific Corp FedEx Corp Kansas City Southern United Parcel Service Inc Class B

iShares U.S. Aerospace & Defense ETF   B-   BUY

Ticker	Traded On	NAV	Total Assets ($)	Dividend Yield (TTM)	Turnover Ratio	Expense Ratio
ITA	BATS	224.77	$5,495,533,072	0.9	38	0.42

Ratings
Reward   B
Risk   C
Recent Upgrade/Downgrade   Up

Fund Information
Fund Type   Exchange Traded Funds
Category   Industrials Sector Equity
Sub-Category   Industrials
Prospectus Objective   Growth
Inception Date   May-06
Open to New Investments   Y

Prices
Price (as of 9/30/2019)   224.70
52-Week High   231.12
52-Week Low   162.03

Total Returns (%)

3-Month	6-Month	1-Year	3-Year	5-Year
6.17	10.75	4.60	79.77	125.14

3-Year Standard Deviation   17.02
Effective Duration

Valuation
Premium/Discount (1-Year Average)   -0.02

Company Information
Provider   iShares
Manager/Tenure   Greg Savage (11), Jennifer Hsui (7),
                  Alan Mason (3), 2 others
Website   http://www.ishares.com
Address   iShares 400 Howard Street San
                  Francisco CA 94105 United States
Phone Number   800-474-2737

PERFORMANCE

Ratings History

Date	Overall Rating	Risk Rating	Reward Rating
Q3-19	B-	C	B
Q4-18	B-	C+	B
Q4-17	A-	B-	A+
Q4-16	B	C+	B+
Q4-15	B	B	B

Asset & Performance History

Date	NAV	1-Year Total Return
2018	172.98	-7.15
2017	188.14	35.17
2016	140.62	20.4
2015	118.16	4.03
2014	114.76	9.85
2013	105.79	57.07

Total Assets: $5,495,533,072
Asset Allocation

Asset	%
Cash	0%
Stocks	100%
US Stocks	100%
Bonds	0%
US Bonds	0%
Other	0%

Services Offered:

Investment Strategy: The investment seeks to track the investment results of the Dow Jones U.S. Select Aerospace & Defense Index composed of U.S. equities in the aerospace and defense sector. The fund generally invests at least 90% of its assets in securities of the underlying index and in depositary receipts representing securities of the underlying index. The underlying index measures the performance of the aerospace and defense sector of the U.S. equity market. Aerospace companies in the index include manufacturers, assemblers and distributors of aircraft and aircraft parts. The fund is non-diversified. **Top Holdings:** Boeing Co United Technologies Corp L3Harris Technologies Inc Lockheed Martin Corp Northrop Grumman Corp

iShares U.S. Broker-Dealers & Securities Exchanges ETF   B-   BUY

Ticker	Traded On	NAV	Total Assets ($)	Dividend Yield (TTM)	Turnover Ratio	Expense Ratio
IAI	NYSE Arca	64.32	$237,990,584	1.63	27	0.42

Ratings
Reward   B
Risk   C
Recent Upgrade/Downgrade   Up

Fund Information
Fund Type   Exchange Traded Funds
Category   Financials Sector Equity
Sub-Category   Financial
Prospectus Objective   Financial
Inception Date   May-06
Open to New Investments   Y

Prices
Price (as of 9/30/2019)   64.31
52-Week High   66.75
52-Week Low   52.67

Total Returns (%)

3-Month	6-Month	1-Year	3-Year	5-Year
1.22	7.61	4.94	62.54	79.31

3-Year Standard Deviation   16.39
Effective Duration

Valuation
Premium/Discount (1-Year Average)   -0.01

Company Information
Provider   iShares
Manager/Tenure   Greg Savage (11), Jennifer Hsui (7), Alan Mason (3), 2 others
Website   http://www.ishares.com
Address   iShares 400 Howard Street San Francisco CA 94105 United States
Phone Number   800-474-2737

PERFORMANCE

Ratings History

Date	Overall Rating	Risk Rating	Reward Rating
Q3-19	B-	C	B
Q4-18	B-	C	B
Q4-17	A-	B	A
Q4-16	B-	C	B
Q4-15	B	B+	B

Asset & Performance History

Date	NAV	1-Year Total Return
2018	56.08	-9.29
2017	62.72	28.78
2016	49.47	21.73
2015	41.38	-1.59
2014	42.6	11.6
2013	38.63	65.61

Total Assets: $237,990,584
Asset Allocation

Asset	%
Cash	0%
Stocks	100%
US Stocks	100%
Bonds	0%
US Bonds	0%
Other	0%

Services Offered:

Investment Strategy: The investment seeks to track the investment results of the Dow Jones U.S. Select Investment Services Index composed of U.S. equities in the investment services sector. The fund generally invests at least 90% of its assets in securities of the underlying index and in depositary receipts representing securities of the underlying index. The underlying index measures the performance of the investment services sector of the U.S. equity market. The fund may invest the remainder of its assets in certain futures, options and swap contracts, cash and cash equivalents. It is non-diversified. **Top Holdings:** CME Group Inc Class A   Goldman Sachs Group Inc   Morgan Stanley   MarketAxess Holdings Inc   Cboe Global Markets Inc

---

iShares U.S. Financial Services ETF   B   BUY

Ticker	Traded On	NAV	Total Assets ($)	Dividend Yield (TTM)	Turnover Ratio	Expense Ratio
IYG	NYSE Arca	136.30	$1,192,667,118	1.75	4	0.42

Ratings
Reward   B
Risk   C
Recent Upgrade/Downgrade   Up

Fund Information
Fund Type   Exchange Traded Funds
Category   Financials Sector Equity
Sub-Category   Financial
Prospectus Objective   Financial
Inception Date   Jun-00
Open to New Investments   Y

Prices
Price (as of 9/30/2019)   136.43
52-Week High   140.99
52-Week Low   105.05

Total Returns (%)

3-Month	6-Month	1-Year	3-Year	5-Year
1.19	10.20	3.91	62.69	73.07

3-Year Standard Deviation   17.8
Effective Duration

Valuation
Premium/Discount (1-Year Average)   -0.01

Company Information
Provider   iShares
Manager/Tenure   Greg Savage (11), Jennifer Hsui (7), Alan Mason (3), 2 others
Website   http://www.ishares.com
Address   iShares 400 Howard Street San Francisco CA 94105 United States
Phone Number   800-474-2737

PERFORMANCE

Ratings History

Date	Overall Rating	Risk Rating	Reward Rating
Q3-19	B	C	B
Q4-18	B-	C+	B
Q4-17	B+	B	A
Q4-16	B-	C	B
Q4-15	B+	B	B+

Asset & Performance History

Date	NAV	1-Year Total Return
2018	112.32	-12.44
2017	130.36	24.41
2016	106.23	19.88
2015	89.97	-0.71
2014	91.82	10.93
2013	83.76	42.83

Total Assets: $1,192,667,118
Asset Allocation

Asset	%
Cash	0%
Stocks	100%
US Stocks	100%
Bonds	0%
US Bonds	0%
Other	0%

Services Offered: CashInvestment Plan

Investment Strategy: The investment seeks to track the investment results of the Dow Jones U.S. Financial Services Index composed of U.S. equities in the financial services sector. The fund generally invests at least 90% of its assets in securities of the underlying index and in depositary receipts representing securities of the underlying index. The underlying index measures the performance of the financial services sector of the U.S. equity market. The fund is non-diversified. **Top Holdings:** JPMorgan Chase & Co   Visa Inc Class A   Mastercard Inc A   Bank of America Corporation   Wells Fargo & Co

iShares U.S. Healthcare Providers ETF

B-   **BUY**

Ticker	Traded On	NAV	Total Assets ($)	Dividend Yield (TTM)	Turnover Ratio	Expense Ratio
IHF	NYSE Arca	161.69	$808,431,460	4.36	48	0.43

Ratings
Reward   B
Risk   C
Recent Upgrade/Downgrade   Up

Fund Information
Fund Type	Exchange Traded Funds
Category	Healthcare Sector Equity
Sub-Category	Health
Prospectus Objective	Health
Inception Date	May-06
Open to New Investments	Y

Prices
Price (as of 9/30/2019)	161.70
52-Week High	201.83
52-Week Low	151.11

Total Returns (%)
3-Month	6-Month	1-Year	3-Year	5-Year
-5.16	-3.67	-15.67	36.57	61.78

3-Year Standard Deviation   16.58
Effective Duration

Valuation
Premium/Discount (1-Year Average)   0.00

Company Information
Provider	iShares
Manager/Tenure	Greg Savage (11), Jennifer Hsui (7), Alan Mason (3), 2 others
Website	http://www.ishares.com
Address	iShares 400 Howard Street San Francisco CA 94105 United States
Phone Number	800-474-2737

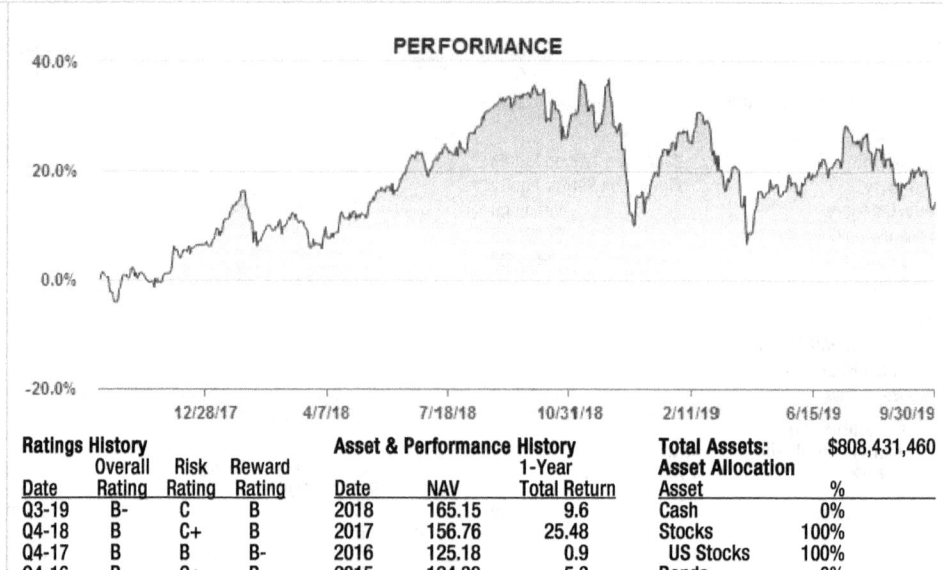

PERFORMANCE

Ratings History
Date	Overall Rating	Risk Rating	Reward Rating
Q3-19	B-	C	B
Q4-18	B	C+	B
Q4-17	B	B	B-
Q4-16	B-	C+	B
Q4-15	B+	B	B+

Asset & Performance History
Date	NAV	1-Year Total Return
2018	165.15	9.6
2017	156.76	25.48
2016	125.18	0.9
2015	124.38	5.3
2014	118.35	27.21
2013	93.22	36.71

Total Assets: $808,431,460
Asset Allocation
Asset	%
Cash	0%
Stocks	100%
US Stocks	100%
Bonds	0%
US Bonds	0%
Other	0%

Services Offered:

Investment Strategy: The investment seeks to track the investment results of the Dow Jones U.S. Select Health Care Providers Index composed of U.S. equities in the healthcare providers sector. The fund generally invests at least 90% of its assets in securities of the underlying index and in depositary receipts representing securities of the underlying index. The underlying index measures the performance of the healthcare providers sector of the U.S. equity market. The fund may invest the remainder of its assets in certain futures, options and swap contracts, cash and cash equivalents. It is non-diversified. **Top Holdings:** UnitedHealth Group Inc   Anthem Inc   CVS Health Corp Humana Inc   Laboratory Corp of America Holdings

iShares U.S. Home Construction ETF

B-   **BUY**

Ticker	Traded On	NAV	Total Assets ($)	Dividend Yield (TTM)	Turnover Ratio	Expense Ratio
ITB	BATS	43.30	$1,264,482,688	0.52	17	0.42

Ratings
Reward   B+
Risk   C
Recent Upgrade/Downgrade   Up

Fund Information
Fund Type	Exchange Traded Funds
Category	Consumer Goods & Svcs
Sub-Category	Consumer Cyclical
Prospectus Objective	Real Estate
Inception Date	May-06
Open to New Investments	Y

Prices
Price (as of 9/30/2019)	43.31
52-Week High	43.31
52-Week Low	28.55

Total Returns (%)
3-Month	6-Month	1-Year	3-Year	5-Year
12.86	22.50	23.78	59.45	98.79

3-Year Standard Deviation   19.08
Effective Duration

Valuation
Premium/Discount (1-Year Average)   -0.02

Company Information
Provider	iShares
Manager/Tenure	Greg Savage (11), Jennifer Hsui (7), Alan Mason (3), 2 others
Website	http://www.ishares.com
Address	iShares 400 Howard Street San Francisco CA 94105 United States
Phone Number	800-474-2737

PERFORMANCE

Ratings History
Date	Overall Rating	Risk Rating	Reward Rating
Q3-19	B-	C	B+
Q4-18	C	D+	B-
Q4-17	A-	B	A+
Q4-16	B-	C	B
Q4-15	B	B	B+

Asset & Performance History
Date	NAV	1-Year Total Return
2018	29.99	-30.96
2017	43.68	59.44
2016	27.49	1.8
2015	27.12	4.98
2014	25.92	4.68
2013	24.85	17.81

Total Assets: $1,264,482,688
Asset Allocation
Asset	%
Cash	0%
Stocks	100%
US Stocks	100%
Bonds	0%
US Bonds	0%
Other	0%

Services Offered:

Investment Strategy: The investment seeks to track the investment results of the Dow Jones U.S. Select Home Construction Index composed of U.S. equities in the home construction sector. The fund generally invests at least 90% of its assets in securities of the underlying index and in depositary receipts representing securities of the underlying index. The underlying index measures the performance of the home construction sector of the U.S. equity market. The fund may invest the remainder of its assets in certain futures, options and swap contracts, cash and cash equivalents. It is non-diversified. **Top Holdings:** D.R. Horton Inc   Lennar Corp   NVR Inc   PulteGroup Inc Lowe's Companies Inc

iShares U.S. Medical Devices ETF   B   BUY

Ticker	Traded On	NAV	Total Assets ($)	Dividend Yield (TTM)	Turnover Ratio	Expense Ratio
IHI	NYSE Arca	247.43	$4,268,157,193	0.3	36	0.43

Ratings
Reward	B+
Risk	C+
Recent Upgrade/Downgrade	Up

Fund Information
Fund Type	Exchange Traded Funds
Category	Healthcare Sector Equity
Sub-Category	Health
Prospectus Objective	Health
Inception Date	May-06
Open to New Investments	Y

Prices
Price (as of 9/30/2019)	247.24
52-Week High	251.72
52-Week Low	183.66

Total Returns (%)
3-Month	6-Month	1-Year	3-Year	5-Year
2.12	7.24	9.05	72.08	156.02

3-Year Standard Deviation   15.35
Effective Duration

Valuation
Premium/Discount (1-Year Average)   0.01

Company Information
Provider	iShares
Manager/Tenure	Greg Savage (11), Jennifer Hsui (7), Alan Mason (3), 2 others
Website	http://www.ishares.com
Address	iShares 400 Howard Street San Francisco CA 94105 United States
Phone Number	800-474-2737

PERFORMANCE

Ratings History
Date	Overall Rating	Risk Rating	Reward Rating
Q3-19	B	C+	B+
Q4-18	B-	C	B
Q4-17	B+	A-	B+
Q4-16	B-	C+	B
Q4-15	C	C	C

Asset & Performance History
Date	NAV	1-Year Total Return
2018	199.77	15.46
2017	173.46	30.93
2016	132.99	9.18
2015	122.47	9.68
2014	113.11	22.64
2013	92.87	37.75

Total Assets: $4,268,157,193
Asset Allocation
Asset	%
Cash	0%
Stocks	100%
US Stocks	100%
Bonds	0%
US Bonds	0%
Other	0%

Services Offered:

Investment Strategy: The investment seeks to track the investment results of the Dow Jones U.S. Select Medical Equipment Index composed of U.S. equities in the medical devices sector. The fund generally invests at least 90% of its assets in securities of the underlying index and in depositary receipts representing securities of the underlying index. The underlying index includes medical equipment companies, including manufacturers and distributors of medical devices such as magnetic resonance imaging (MRI) scanners, prosthetics, pacemakers, X-ray machines, and other non-disposable medical devices. The fund is non-diversified. **Top Holdings:** Abbott Laboratories   Medtronic PLC   Thermo Fisher Scientific Inc   Danaher Corp   Edwards Lifesciences Corp

---

iShares U.S. Real Estate ETF   B-   BUY

Ticker	Traded On	NAV	Total Assets ($)	Dividend Yield (TTM)	Turnover Ratio	Expense Ratio
IYR	NYSE Arca	93.46	$5,004,518,221	2.59	11	0.42

Ratings
Reward	B-
Risk	B-
Recent Upgrade/Downgrade	

Fund Information
Fund Type	Exchange Traded Funds
Category	Real Estate Sector Equity
Sub-Category	Real Estate
Prospectus Objective	Real Estate
Inception Date	Jun-00
Open to New Investments	Y

Prices
Price (as of 9/30/2019)	93.54
52-Week High	94.09
52-Week Low	72.00

Total Returns (%)
3-Month	6-Month	1-Year	3-Year	5-Year
7.40	9.00	20.99	29.09	62.70

3-Year Standard Deviation   12.06
Effective Duration

Valuation
Premium/Discount (1-Year Average)   0.01

Company Information
Provider	iShares
Manager/Tenure	Greg Savage (11), Jennifer Hsui (7), Alan Mason (3), 2 others
Website	http://www.ishares.com
Address	iShares 400 Howard Street San Francisco CA 94105 United States
Phone Number	800-474-2737

PERFORMANCE

Ratings History
Date	Overall Rating	Risk Rating	Reward Rating
Q3-19	B-	B-	B-
Q4-18	C+	B	C
Q4-17	B	B	B-
Q4-16	C+	B-	C+
Q4-15	C+	B-	C+

Asset & Performance History
Date	NAV	1-Year Total Return
2018	74.91	-4.28
2017	80.97	9.37
2016	76.88	7
2015	75.04	1.61
2014	76.81	26.61
2013	63.09	1.04

Total Assets: $5,004,518,221
Asset Allocation
Asset	%
Cash	1%
Stocks	99%
US Stocks	99%
Bonds	0%
US Bonds	0%
Other	0%

Services Offered: CashInvestment Plan

Investment Strategy: The investment seeks to track the investment results of the Dow Jones U.S. Real Estate Index. The fund generally invests at least 90% of its assets in securities of the underlying index and in depositary receipts representing securities of the underlying index. The underlying fund measures the performance of the real estate sector of the U.S. equity market and may include large-, mid- or small-capitalization companies. **Top Holdings:** American Tower Corp   Crown Castle International Corp   Prologis Inc   Equinix Inc   Simon Property Group Inc

iShares U.S. Regional Banks ETF   B-   BUY

Ticker	Traded On	NAV	Total Assets ($)	Dividend Yield (TTM)	Turnover Ratio	Expense Ratio
IAT	NYSE Arca	46.55	$391,011,051	2.63	10	0.42

Ratings
Reward	B
Risk	C
Recent Upgrade/Downgrade	Up

Fund Information
Fund Type	Exchange Traded Funds
Category	Financials Sector Equity
Sub-Category	Financial
Prospectus Objective	Financial
Inception Date	May-06
Open to New Investments	Y

Prices
Price (as of 9/30/2019)	46.56
52-Week High	49.96
52-Week Low	37.63

Total Returns (%)
3-Month	6-Month	1-Year	3-Year	5-Year
1.26	5.58	-1.86	40.65	56.93

3-Year Standard Deviation	22.82
Effective Duration	

Valuation
Premium/Discount (1-Year Average)	-0.04

Company Information
Provider	iShares
Manager/Tenure	Greg Savage (11), Jennifer Hsui (7), Alan Mason (3), 2 others
Website	http://www.ishares.com
Address	iShares 400 Howard Street San Francisco CA 94105 United States
Phone Number	800-474-2737

PERFORMANCE

Ratings History
Date	Overall Rating	Risk Rating	Reward Rating
Q3-19	B-	C	B
Q4-18	B-	C	B
Q4-17	B+	B-	A
Q4-16	B	C+	B+
Q4-15	B+	B+	B+

Asset & Performance History
Date	NAV	1-Year Total Return
2018	39.86	-17.38
2017	49.29	10.53
2016	45.33	32.18
2015	34.96	1.73
2014	34.97	7.58
2013	33.06	37.59

Total Assets: $391,011,051
Asset Allocation
Asset	%
Cash	0%
Stocks	100%
US Stocks	99%
Bonds	0%
US Bonds	0%
Other	0%

Services Offered:

Investment Strategy: The investment seeks to track the investment results of the Dow Jones U.S. Select Regional Banks Index. The fund generally invests at least 90% of its assets in securities of the index and in depositary receipts representing securities of the index. The underlying index measures the performance of the regional bank sector of the U.S. equity market and is a subset of the Dow Jones U.S. Bank Index. The fund is non-diversified. **Top Holdings:** US Bancorp PNC Financial Services Group Inc BB&T Corp SunTrust Banks Inc M&T Bank Corp

iShares U.S. Technology ETF   B   BUY

Ticker	Traded On	NAV	Total Assets ($)	Dividend Yield (TTM)	Turnover Ratio	Expense Ratio
IYW	NYSE Arca	204.27	$4,126,232,299	0.8	19	0.42

Ratings
Reward	B+
Risk	C+
Recent Upgrade/Downgrade	Up

Fund Information
Fund Type	Exchange Traded Funds
Category	Technology Sector Equity
Sub-Category	Technology
Prospectus Objective	Technology
Inception Date	May-00
Open to New Investments	Y

Prices
Price (as of 9/30/2019)	204.21
52-Week High	211.51
52-Week Low	148.42

Total Returns (%)
3-Month	6-Month	1-Year	3-Year	5-Year
1.91	6.14	6.04	76.29	117.12

3-Year Standard Deviation	16.02
Effective Duration	

Valuation
Premium/Discount (1-Year Average)	-0.01

Company Information
Provider	iShares
Manager/Tenure	Greg Savage (11), Jennifer Hsui (7), Alan Mason (3), 2 others
Website	http://www.ishares.com
Address	iShares 400 Howard Street San Francisco CA 94105 United States
Phone Number	800-474-2737

PERFORMANCE

Ratings History
Date	Overall Rating	Risk Rating	Reward Rating
Q3-19	B	C+	B+
Q4-18	B-	C	B
Q4-17	A-	B	A+
Q4-16	B	C+	A-
Q4-15	B	B	B

Asset & Performance History
Date	NAV	1-Year Total Return
2018	159.77	-0.96
2017	162.67	36.58
2016	120.2	13.68
2015	107.02	3.66
2014	104.42	19.49
2013	88.43	26.47

Total Assets: $4,126,232,299
Asset Allocation
Asset	%
Cash	0%
Stocks	100%
US Stocks	99%
Bonds	0%
US Bonds	0%
Other	0%

Services Offered: CashInvestment Plan

Investment Strategy: The investment seeks to track the investment results of the Dow Jones U.S. Technology Capped Index. The fund generally invests at least 90% of its assets in securities of the underlying index and in depositary receipts representing securities of the underlying index. The underlying index measures the performance of U.S. companies in the technology sector. The fund is non-diversified. **Top Holdings:** Microsoft Corp Apple Inc Alphabet Inc Class C Alphabet Inc A Facebook Inc A

iShares U.S. Telecommunications ETF   B-   BUY

Ticker	Traded On	NAV		Total Assets ($)	Dividend Yield (TTM)	Turnover Ratio	Expense Ratio
IYZ	BATS	29.21		$496,515,441	1.69	35	0.42

Ratings
Reward   B
Risk   C
Recent Upgrade/Downgrade   Up

Fund Information
Fund Type   Exchange Traded Funds
Category   Communications Sector Equity
Sub-Category   Communications
Prospectus Objective   Comm
Inception Date   May-00
Open to New Investments   Y

Prices
Price (as of 9/30/2019)   29.20
52-Week High   31.04
52-Week Low   24.71

Total Returns (%)

3-Month	6-Month	1-Year	3-Year	5-Year
-0.55	-1.91	0.29	-2.18	12.13

3-Year Standard Deviation   14.65
Effective Duration

Valuation
Premium/Discount (1-Year Average)   -0.05

Company Information
Provider   iShares
Manager/Tenure   Greg Savage (11), Jennifer Hsui (7),
                 Alan Mason (3), 2 others
Website   http://www.ishares.com
Address   iShares 400 Howard Street San
                 Francisco CA 94105 United States
Phone Number   800-474-2737

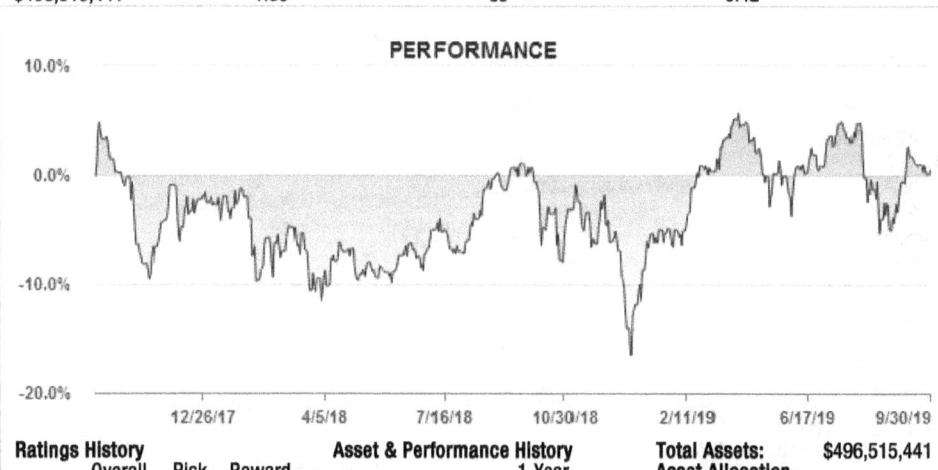

PERFORMANCE

Ratings History

Date	Overall Rating	Risk Rating	Reward Rating
Q3-19	B-	C	B
Q4-18	C+	C-	B
Q4-17	C-	C-	D+
Q4-16	C	D+	B-
Q4-15	C+	C	B-

Asset & Performance History

Date	NAV	1-Year Total Return
2018	26.34	-8.54
2017	29.39	-11.58
2016	34.38	22.14
2015	28.84	0.47
2014	29.26	0.51
2013	29.76	26.24

Total Assets: $496,515,441

Asset Allocation

Asset	%
Cash	0%
Stocks	100%
US Stocks	96%
Bonds	0%
US Bonds	0%
Other	0%

Services Offered: CashInvestment Plan

Investment Strategy: The investment seeks to track the investment results of the Dow Jones U.S. Select Telecommunications Index. The fund generally invests at least 90% of its assets in securities of the underlying index and in depositary receipts representing securities of the underlying index. The underlying index measures the performance of the telecommunications sector of the U.S. equity market and may include large-, mid- or small-capitalization companies. The fund is non-diversified. **Top Holdings:** Verizon Communications Inc   Cisco Systems Inc   Motorola Solutions Inc   AT&T Inc   T-Mobile US Inc

---

iShares U.S. Utilities ETF   B-   BUY

Ticker	Traded On	NAV		Total Assets ($)	Dividend Yield (TTM)	Turnover Ratio	Expense Ratio
IDU	NYSE Arca	162.86		$952,751,372	2.56	6	0.42

Ratings
Reward   B
Risk   C
Recent Upgrade/Downgrade

Fund Information
Fund Type   Exchange Traded Funds
Category   Utilities Sector Equity
Sub-Category   Utilities
Prospectus Objective   Utility
Inception Date   Jun-00
Open to New Investments   Y

Prices
Price (as of 9/30/2019)   162.85
52-Week High   163.32
52-Week Low   130.66

Total Returns (%)

3-Month	6-Month	1-Year	3-Year	5-Year
9.00	12.11	25.32	44.87	80.39

3-Year Standard Deviation   10.39
Effective Duration

Valuation
Premium/Discount (1-Year Average)   -0.01

Company Information
Provider   iShares
Manager/Tenure   Greg Savage (11), Jennifer Hsui (7),
                 Alan Mason (3), 2 others
Website   http://www.ishares.com
Address   iShares 400 Howard Street San
                 Francisco CA 94105 United States
Phone Number   800-474-2737

PERFORMANCE

Ratings History

Date	Overall Rating	Risk Rating	Reward Rating
Q3-19	B-	C	B
Q4-18	B-	C+	B-
Q4-17	B	B	B
Q4-16	B-	C+	B
Q4-15	B-	C+	B

Asset & Performance History

Date	NAV	1-Year Total Return
2018	134.18	3.91
2017	132.88	11.95
2016	121.83	16.51
2015	107.87	-4.97
2014	118.4	27.43
2013	95.84	14.69

Total Assets: $952,751,372

Asset Allocation

Asset	%
Cash	0%
Stocks	100%
US Stocks	100%
Bonds	0%
US Bonds	0%
Other	0%

Services Offered: CashInvestment Plan

Investment Strategy: The investment seeks to track the investment results of the Dow Jones U.S. Utilities Index. The fund generally invests at least 90% of its assets in securities of the underlying index and in depositary receipts representing securities of the underlying index. The underlying index measures the performance of the utilities sector of the U.S. equity market and may include large-, mid- or small-capitalization companies. The fund is non-diversified. **Top Holdings:** NextEra Energy Inc   Duke Energy Corp   Dominion Energy Inc   Southern Co   Exelon Corp

Ivy Focused Growth NextShares™   B   BUY

Ticker	Traded On	NAV	Total Assets ($)	Dividend Yield (TTM)	Turnover Ratio	Expense Ratio
IVFGC	NAS CM		$14,338,503	0.17	29	0.78

Ratings

Reward	A-
Risk	C
Recent Upgrade/Downgrade	Up

Fund Information

Fund Type	Exchange Traded Funds
Category	US Equity Large Cap Growth
Sub-Category	Large Growth
Prospectus Objective	Growth
Inception Date	Oct-16
Open to New Investments	

Prices

Price (as of 9/30/2019)	20.54
52-Week High	34.01
52-Week Low	20.54

Total Returns (%)

3-Month	6-Month	1-Year	3-Year	5-Year
1.20	9.19	9.82		

3-Year Standard Deviation	
Effective Duration	

Valuation

Premium/Discount (1-Year Average)	0.00

Company Information

Provider	Ivy Funds
Manager/Tenure	Bradley M. Klapmeyer (2)
Website	http://www.ivyfunds.com
Address	Ivy Funds Inc 6300 Lamar Ave
	Overland Park KS 66202 United States
Phone Number	

PERFORMANCE

Ratings History

Date	Overall Rating	Risk Rating	Reward Rating
Q3-19	B	C	A-
Q4-18	B	C+	B+
Q4-17	D	A-	D+
Q4-16	U		
Q4-15			

Asset & Performance History

Date	NAV	1-Year Total Return
2018	26.09	5.18
2017	26.09	30.17
2016	20.13	
2015		
2014		
2013		

Total Assets: $14,338,503

Asset Allocation

Asset	%
Cash	2%
Stocks	98%
US Stocks	98%
Bonds	0%
US Bonds	0%
Other	0%

Services Offered:

Investment Strategy: The investment seeks to provide growth of capital. The fund seeks to achieve its objective by investing primarily in a portfolio of common stocks issued by large-capitalization, growth-oriented companies with above-average levels of profitability and that the fund's investment manager, believes have the ability to sustain growth over the long term. Although it primarily invests in securities issued by large capitalization companies, it may invest in securities issued by companies of any size. Growth-oriented companies are those whose earnings IICO believes are likely to grow faster than the economy. The fund is non-diversified. **Top Holdings:** Microsoft Corp Alphabet Inc Class C Mastercard Inc A PayPal Holdings Inc Amazon.com Inc

---

John Hancock Multifactor Consumer Staples ETF   B-   BUY

Ticker	Traded On	NAV	Total Assets ($)	Dividend Yield (TTM)	Turnover Ratio	Expense Ratio
JHMS	NYSE Arca	29.14	$30,301,743	2.6	14	0.4

Ratings

Reward	B
Risk	C
Recent Upgrade/Downgrade	Up

Fund Information

Fund Type	Exchange Traded Funds
Category	Consumer Goods & Svcs
Sub-Category	Consumer Defensive
Prospectus Objective	Unaligned
Inception Date	Mar-16
Open to New Investments	Y

Prices

Price (as of 9/30/2019)	29.14
52-Week High	29.17
52-Week Low	23.55

Total Returns (%)

3-Month	6-Month	1-Year	3-Year	5-Year
5.11	8.17	12.01	21.11	

3-Year Standard Deviation	11.28
Effective Duration	

Valuation

Premium/Discount (1-Year Average)	0.02

Company Information

Provider	John Hancock
Manager/Tenure	Joel P. Schneider (3), Lukas J. Smart (3), Joseph F. Hohn (1)
Website	http://jhinvestments.com
Address	601 Congress Street, Boston MA 02210 United States
Phone Number	800-225-5913

PERFORMANCE

Ratings History

Date	Overall Rating	Risk Rating	Reward Rating
Q3-19	B-	C	B
Q4-18	C+	C-	B-
Q4-17	D+	B-	D+
Q4-16	U		
Q4-15			

Asset & Performance History

Date	NAV	1-Year Total Return
2018	24.57	-8.47
2017	27.66	11.92
2016	25.12	
2015		
2014		
2013		

Total Assets: $30,301,743

Asset Allocation

Asset	%
Cash	5%
Stocks	95%
US Stocks	95%
Bonds	0%
US Bonds	0%
Other	0%

Services Offered:

Investment Strategy: The investment seeks to provide investment results that closely correspond, before fees and expenses, to the performance of the John Hancock Dimensional Consumer Staples Index (the index). The fund normally invests at least 80% of its net assets (plus any borrowings for investment purposes) in securities that compose the fund's index. The index is designed to comprise securities in the consumer staples sector within the U.S. Universe whose market capitalizations are larger than that of the 1001st largest U.S. company at the time of reconstitution. The fund is non-diversified. **Top Holdings:** PepsiCo Inc Coca-Cola Co Walmart Inc Procter & Gamble Co General Mills Inc

Materials Select Sector SPDR® Fund   B-   BUY

Ticker	Traded On	NAV	Total Assets ($)	Dividend Yield (TTM)	Turnover Ratio	Expense Ratio
XLB	NYSE Arca		$4,245,101,675	2.06	17	0.13

Ratings
Reward	B
Risk	C
Recent Upgrade/Downgrade	Up

Fund Information
Fund Type	Exchange Traded Funds
Category	Natural Resources
Sub-Category	Natural Resources
Prospectus Objective	Natl Res
Inception Date	Dec-98
Open to New Investments	Y

Prices
Price (as of 9/30/2019)	58.20
52-Week High	59.46
52-Week Low	47.34

Total Returns (%)
3-Month	6-Month	1-Year	3-Year	5-Year
-1.56	3.65	0.83	28.34	28.82

3-Year Standard Deviation	14.24
Effective Duration	

Valuation
Premium/Discount (1-Year Average)	-0.01

Company Information
Provider	SPDR State Street Global Advisors
Manager/Tenure	Michael J. Feehily (8), Karl A. Schneider (4), Ted Janowsky (2)
Website	http://www.spdrs.com
Address	SPDR State Street Global Advisors State Street Financial Center, 1 Lincoln Street Boston MA 02111-2900 United States
Phone Number	617-786-3000

PERFORMANCE

Ratings History
Date	Overall Rating	Risk Rating	Reward Rating
Q3-19	B-	C	B
Q4-18	C	C-	B-
Q4-17	B	C	B
Q4-16	C+	C	B
Q4-15	B	B-	B

Asset & Performance History
Date	NAV	1-Year Total Return
2018	50.53	-14.77
2017	60.48	23.95
2016	49.68	16.6
2015	43.46	-8.6
2014	48.59	7.31
2013	46.17	25.81

Total Assets: $4,245,101,675

Asset Allocation
Asset	%
Cash	0%
Stocks	100%
US Stocks	82%
Bonds	0%
US Bonds	0%
Other	0%

Services Offered: Dividend Investment Plan, CashInvestment Plan

Investment Strategy: The investment seeks to provide investment results that, before expenses, correspond generally to the price and yield performance of publicly traded equity securities of companies in the Materials Select Sector Index. In seeking to track the performance of the index, the fund employs a replication strategy. It generally invests substantially all, but at least 95%, of its total assets in the securities comprising the index. The index includes securities of companies from the following industries: chemicals; metals and mining; paper and forest products; containers and packaging; and construction materials. The fund is non-diversified. **Top Holdings:** Linde PLC Ecolab Inc DuPont de Nemours Inc Air Products & Chemicals Inc Sherwin-Williams Co

Nuveen Short-Term REIT ETF   B-   BUY

Ticker	Traded On	NAV	Total Assets ($)	Dividend Yield (TTM)	Turnover Ratio	Expense Ratio
NURE	BATS	30.73	$55,308,575	3.27	16	0.35

Ratings
Reward	B
Risk	C
Recent Upgrade/Downgrade	Up

Fund Information
Fund Type	Exchange Traded Funds
Category	Real Estate Sector Equity
Sub-Category	Real Estate
Prospectus Objective	Real Estate
Inception Date	Dec-16
Open to New Investments	Y

Prices
Price (as of 9/30/2019)	30.76
52-Week High	30.90
52-Week Low	24.37

Total Returns (%)
3-Month	6-Month	1-Year	3-Year	5-Year
6.78	9.04	18.62		

3-Year Standard Deviation	
Effective Duration	

Valuation
Premium/Discount (1-Year Average)	0.03

Company Information
Provider	Nuveen
Manager/Tenure	Philip James(Jim) Campagna (2), Lei Liao (2)
Website	http://www.nuveen.com
Address	Nuveen Investment Trust John Nuveen & Co. Inc. Chicago IL 60606 United States
Phone Number	312-917-8146

PERFORMANCE

Ratings History
Date	Overall Rating	Risk Rating	Reward Rating
Q3-19	B-	C	B
Q4-18	B-	C	B
Q4-17	D-	B+	D+
Q4-16			
Q4-15			

Asset & Performance History
Date	NAV	1-Year Total Return
2018	25.05	-2.09
2017	26.35	7.07
2016	25.49	
2015		
2014		
2013		

Total Assets: $55,308,575

Asset Allocation
Asset	%
Cash	8%
Stocks	92%
US Stocks	92%
Bonds	0%
US Bonds	0%
Other	0%

Services Offered:

Investment Strategy: The investment seeks to track the investment results of the Dow Jones U.S. Select Short-Term REIT Index. The fund invests at least 80% of the sum of its net assets and the amount of any borrowings for investment purposes in REITs. The index is a subset of the Dow Jones U.S. Select REIT Index, which generally includes equity REITs traded on a national securities exchange in the U.S. that derive at least 75% of their total revenue from the ownership and operation of real estate assets and that have a minimum total market capitalization of $200 million at the time of their inclusion. It is non-diversified. **Top Holdings:** Invitation Homes Inc Sun Communities Inc Extra Space Storage Inc Equity Lifestyle Properties Inc Public Storage

Pacer Benchmark Data & Infrastructure Real Estate SCTR ETF   B-   BUY

Ticker	Traded On	NAV	Total Assets ($)	Dividend Yield (TTM)	Turnover Ratio	Expense Ratio
SRVR	NYSE Arca	32.15	$120,576,022	1.63	27	0.6

Ratings
Reward	B+
Risk	C-
Recent Upgrade/Downgrade	Up

Fund Information
Fund Type	Exchange Traded Funds
Category	Real Estate Sector Equity
Sub-Category	Real Estate
Prospectus Objective	Growth & Inc
Inception Date	May-18
Open to New Investments	Y

Prices
Price (as of 9/30/2019)	32.20
52-Week High	32.66
52-Week Low	22.35

Total Returns (%)
3-Month	6-Month	1-Year	3-Year	5-Year
9.44	14.95	26.28		

3-Year Standard Deviation
Effective Duration

Valuation
Premium/Discount (1-Year Average)	0.02

Company Information
Provider	Pacer
Manager/Tenure	Bruce Kavanaugh (1), Michael Mack (1)
Website	http://www.paceretfs.com
Address	Pacer 16 Industrial Blvd, Suite 201 Paoli PA 19301 United States
Phone Number	

PERFORMANCE

Ratings History
Date	Overall Rating	Risk Rating	Reward Rating
Q3-19	B-	C-	B+
Q4-18	U		
Q4-17			
Q4-16			
Q4-15			

Asset & Performance History
Date	NAV	1-Year Total Return
2018	23.42	
2017		
2016		
2015		
2014		
2013		

Total Assets: $120,576,022
Asset Allocation
Asset	%
Cash	0%
Stocks	100%
US Stocks	95%
Bonds	0%
US Bonds	0%
Other	0%

Services Offered:

Investment Strategy: The investment seeks to track the total return performance, before fees and expenses, of the Pacer Benchmark Data & Infrastructure Real Estate SCTR Index (the "index"). Under normal circumstances, at least 80% of the fund's total assets (exclusive of collateral held from securities lending) will be invested in the component securities of the index. The index is generally composed of the U.S.-listed equity securities of companies that derive at least 85% of their earnings or revenues from real estate operations in the data and infrastructure real estate sectors ("Eligible Companies"). The fund is non-diversified. **Top Holdings:** Equinix Inc Crown Castle International Corp American Tower Corp CyrusOne Inc SBA Communications Corp

Pacer Benchmark Industrial Real Estate SCTR ETF   B   BUY

Ticker	Traded On	NAV	Total Assets ($)	Dividend Yield (TTM)	Turnover Ratio	Expense Ratio
INDS	NYSE Arca	32.36	$24,271,017	1.88	36	0.6

Ratings
Reward	B+
Risk	C
Recent Upgrade/Downgrade	Up

Fund Information
Fund Type	Exchange Traded Funds
Category	Real Estate Sector Equity
Sub-Category	Real Estate
Prospectus Objective	Real Estate
Inception Date	May-18
Open to New Investments	Y

Prices
Price (as of 9/30/2019)	32.41
52-Week High	32.61
52-Week Low	23.10

Total Returns (%)
3-Month	6-Month	1-Year	3-Year	5-Year
3.99	13.04	32.75		

3-Year Standard Deviation
Effective Duration

Valuation
Premium/Discount (1-Year Average)	0.13

Company Information
Provider	Pacer
Manager/Tenure	Bruce Kavanaugh (1), Michael Mack (1)
Website	http://www.paceretfs.com
Address	Pacer 16 Industrial Blvd, Suite 201 Paoli PA 19301 United States
Phone Number	

PERFORMANCE

Ratings History
Date	Overall Rating	Risk Rating	Reward Rating
Q3-19	B	C	B+
Q4-18	U		
Q4-17			
Q4-16			
Q4-15			

Asset & Performance History
Date	NAV	1-Year Total Return
2018	24.03	
2017		
2016		
2015		
2014		
2013		

Total Assets: $24,271,017
Asset Allocation
Asset	%
Cash	0%
Stocks	100%
US Stocks	100%
Bonds	0%
US Bonds	0%
Other	0%

Services Offered:

Investment Strategy: The investment seeks to track the total return performance, before fees and expenses, of the Benchmark Industrial Real Estate SCTR Index (the "index"). Under normal circumstances, at least 80% of the fund's total assets (exclusive of collateral held from securities lending) will be invested in the component securities of the index. The index was developed by Benchmark Investments, LLC, the index provider (the "index provider"), and measures the performance of the industrial real estate sector of the U.S. equity market, which includes warehouse and self-storage real estate sub-sectors. The fund is non-diversified. **Top Holdings:** Prologis Inc Duke Realty Corp Liberty Property Trust Innovative Industrial Properties Inc Registered Shs Rexford Industrial Realty Inc

PIMCO Investment Grade Corporate Bond Index Exchange-Traded Fund

B-   BUY

Ticker	Traded On	NAV	Total Assets ($)	Dividend Yield (TTM)	Turnover Ratio	Expense Ratio
CORP	NYSE Arca	109.71	$650,574,809	3.29	27	0.2

Ratings
Reward	B-
Risk	C+
Recent Upgrade/Downgrade	Up

Fund Information
Fund Type	Exchange Traded Funds
Category	US Fixed Income
Sub-Category	Corporate Bond
Prospectus Objective	Corp Bond - High Quality
Inception Date	Sep-10
Open to New Investments	Y

Prices
Price (as of 9/30/2019)	109.72
52-Week High	110.62
52-Week Low	97.96

Total Returns (%)
3-Month	6-Month	1-Year	3-Year	5-Year
3.38	8.68	13.35	13.93	25.35

3-Year Standard Deviation	4.2
Effective Duration	7.12

Valuation
Premium/Discount (1-Year Average)	-0.05

Company Information
Provider	PIMCO
Manager/Tenure	Matthew P. Dorsten (3), Mitchell Handa (0), Graham A. Rennison (0)
Website	http://www.pimco.com
Address	PIMCO 840 Newport Center Drive, Suite 100 Newport Beach CA 92660 United States
Phone Number	866-746-2602

PERFORMANCE

Ratings History

Date	Overall Rating	Risk Rating	Reward Rating
Q3-19	B-	C+	B-
Q4-18	C-	C-	D+
Q4-17	B-	B+	C
Q4-16	C	C-	C
Q4-15	C	C-	C

Asset & Performance History

Date	NAV	1-Year Total Return
2018	99.11	-2.7
2017	105.43	6.38
2016	102.24	6.17
2015	99.11	-0.46
2014	102.66	7.43
2013	99.02	-1.62

Total Assets: $650,574,809

Asset Allocation

Asset	%
Cash	-8%
Stocks	0%
US Stocks	0%
Bonds	105%
US Bonds	81%
Other	0%

Services Offered:

Investment Strategy: The investment seeks to provide total return that closely corresponds, before fees and expenses, to the total return of the ICE BofAML US Corporate Index. The fund invests at least 80% of its total assets (exclusive of collateral held from securities lending) in the component securities of the ICE BofAML US Corporate Index (the "underlying index"). The underlying index is an unmanaged index comprised of U.S. dollar denominated investment grade corporate debt securities publicly issued in the U.S. domestic market with at least one year remaining term to final maturity. **Top Holdings:** Cdx Ig32 10y Ice Fin Fut Us 2yr Cbt 12/31/19 Cdx Ig32 5y Ice Fin Fut Us 30yr Cbt 12/19/19 Fin Fut Us Ultra 30yr Cbt 12/19/19

ProShares Ultra Semiconductors

B-   BUY

Ticker	Traded On	NAV	Total Assets ($)	Dividend Yield (TTM)	Turnover Ratio	Expense Ratio
USD	NYSE Arca	45.07	$69,863,329	0.97	38	0.95

Ratings
Reward	B
Risk	C
Recent Upgrade/Downgrade	Up

Fund Information
Fund Type	Exchange Traded Funds
Category	Trading Tools
Sub-Category	Trading--Leveraged Equity
Prospectus Objective	Technology
Inception Date	Jan-07
Open to New Investments	Y

Prices
Price (as of 9/30/2019)	45.01
52-Week High	52.31
52-Week Low	25.73

Total Returns (%)
3-Month	6-Month	1-Year	3-Year	5-Year
4.51	4.28	0.81	123.66	254.14

3-Year Standard Deviation	43.16
Effective Duration	

Valuation
Premium/Discount (1-Year Average)	-0.14

Company Information
Provider	ProShares
Manager/Tenure	Michael Neches (6), Tarak Davé (1)
Website	http://www.proshares.com
Address	ProShares 7501 Wisconsin Avenue, Suite 1000 Bethesda MD 20814 United States
Phone Number	866-776-5125

PERFORMANCE

Ratings History

Date	Overall Rating	Risk Rating	Reward Rating
Q3-19	B-	C	B
Q4-18	C	C-	C
Q4-17	B	C	A-
Q4-16	C+	C-	B
Q4-15	C	C	C+

Asset & Performance History

Date	NAV	1-Year Total Return
2018	29.77	-26.27
2017	40.68	80.92
2016	22.58	58.14
2015	14.36	-8.32
2014	15.73	78.02
2013	8.92	77.91

Total Assets: $69,863,329

Asset Allocation

Asset	%
Cash	-99%
Stocks	83%
US Stocks	81%
Bonds	0%
US Bonds	0%
Other	117%

Services Offered:

Investment Strategy: The investment seeks daily investment results that correspond to two times (2x) the daily performance of the Dow Jones U.S. SemiconductorsSM Index. The fund invests in financial instruments that ProShare Advisors believes, in combination, should produce daily returns consistent with the fund's investment objective. The index measures the performance of certain companies in the semiconductor sub-sector of the U.S. equity market. Component companies are engaged in the production of semiconductors and other integrated chips, as well as other related products such as semiconductor capital equipment and mother-boards. The fund is non-diversified. **Top Holdings:** Dj U.S. Semiconductors Index Swap Societe Generale Dj U.S. Semiconductors Index Swap Ubs Ag Intel Corp Texas Instruments Inc Broadcom Inc

ProShares Ultra Utilities

B- **BUY**

Ticker	Traded On	NAV	Total Assets ($)	Dividend Yield (TTM)	Turnover Ratio	Expense Ratio
UPW	NYSE Arca	70.27	$35,137,019	0.65	5	0.95

Ratings
Reward	B
Risk	D+
Recent Upgrade/Downgrade	Up

Fund Information
Fund Type	Exchange Traded Funds
Category	Trading Tools
Sub-Category	Trading--Leveraged Equity
Prospectus Objective	Utility
Inception Date	Jan-07
Open to New Investments	Y

Prices
Price (as of 9/30/2019)	70.29
52-Week High	70.64
52-Week Low	45.19

Total Returns (%)
3-Month	6-Month	1-Year	3-Year	5-Year
17.58	24.51	49.25	85.97	169.34

3-Year Standard Deviation	20.88
Effective Duration	

Valuation
Premium/Discount (1-Year Average)	0.11

Company Information
Provider	ProShares
Manager/Tenure	Michael Neches (6), Tarak Davé (1)
Website	http://www.proshares.com
Address	ProShares 7501 Wisconsin Avenue, Suite 1000 Bethesda MD 20814 United States
Phone Number	866-776-5125

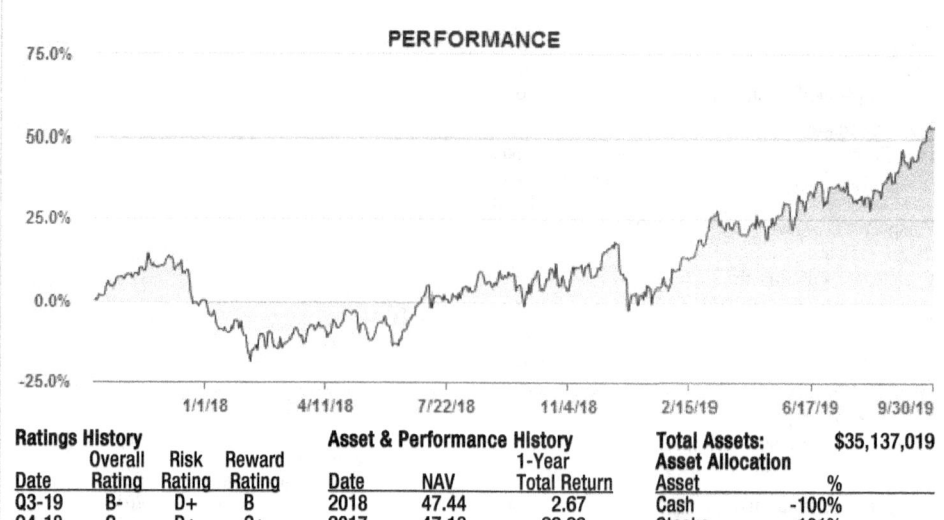

PERFORMANCE

Ratings History
Date	Overall Rating	Risk Rating	Reward Rating
Q3-19	B-	D+	B
Q4-18	C	D+	C+
Q4-17	B	C+	A-
Q4-16	C	C-	C+
Q4-15	C	C-	C+

Asset & Performance History
Date	NAV	1-Year Total Return
2018	47.44	2.67
2017	47.18	22.29
2016	39.17	31.27
2015	30.33	-13.01
2014	35.67	58.61
2013	22.94	28.61

Total Assets: $35,137,019
Asset Allocation
Asset	%
Cash	-100%
Stocks	101%
US Stocks	101%
Bonds	0%
US Bonds	0%
Other	98%

Services Offered:

Investment Strategy: The investment seeks daily investment results, before fees and expenses, that correspond to two times (2x) the daily performance of the Dow Jones U.S. UtilitiesSM Index. The fund invests in financial instruments that ProShare Advisors believes, in combination, should produce daily returns consistent with the fund's investment objective. The index measures the performance of certain companies in the utilities sector of the U.S. equity market. Component companies include, among others, electric utilities, gas utilities, multi-utilities and water utilities. The fund is non-diversified. **Top Holdings:** Ishares U.S. Utilities (Idu) Swap Bank Of America Na Dj U.S. Utilities Index Swap Societe Generale   Dj U.S. Utilities Index Swap Credit Suisse International   Dj U.S. Utilities Index Swap Ubs Ag   Dj U.S. Utilities Index Swap Bank Of America Na

---

Schwab U.S. Dividend Equity ETF™

B- **BUY**

Ticker	Traded On	NAV	Total Assets ($)	Dividend Yield (TTM)	Turnover Ratio	Expense Ratio
SCHD	NYSE Arca	54.77	$10,335,299,640	3.04	23	0.06

Ratings
Reward	B
Risk	C
Recent Upgrade/Downgrade	Up

Fund Information
Fund Type	Exchange Traded Funds
Category	US Equity Large Cap Value
Sub-Category	Large Value
Prospectus Objective	Equity-Income
Inception Date	Oct-11
Open to New Investments	Y

Prices
Price (as of 9/30/2019)	54.78
52-Week High	55.76
52-Week Low	44.23

Total Returns (%)
3-Month	6-Month	1-Year	3-Year	5-Year
3.30	5.31	6.42	41.48	66.81

3-Year Standard Deviation	12.24
Effective Duration	

Valuation
Premium/Discount (1-Year Average)	-0.03

Company Information
Provider	Schwab ETFs
Manager/Tenure	Ferian Juwono (7), Christopher Bliss (2), Sabya Sinha (2), 1 other
Website	http://www.schwabfunds.com
Address	Schwab ETFs United States
Phone Number	800-435-4000

PERFORMANCE

Ratings History
Date	Overall Rating	Risk Rating	Reward Rating
Q3-19	B-	C	B
Q4-18	B-	C	B
Q4-17	B	B	B
Q4-16	B-	C	B
Q4-15	C+	C+	C+

Asset & Performance History
Date	NAV	1-Year Total Return
2018	46.98	-5.46
2017	51.13	20.67
2016	43.52	16.23
2015	38.58	-0.21
2014	39.83	11.66
2013	36.65	32.9

Total Assets: $10,335,299,640
Asset Allocation
Asset	%
Cash	0%
Stocks	100%
US Stocks	100%
Bonds	0%
US Bonds	0%
Other	0%

Services Offered:

Investment Strategy: The investment seeks to track as closely as possible, before fees and expenses, the total return of the Dow Jones U.S. Dividend 100™ Index. To pursue its goal, the fund generally invests in stocks that are included in the index. The fund invests at least 90% of its net assets in stocks that are included in the index. The index is designed to measure the performance of high dividend yielding stocks issued by U.S. companies that have a record of consistently paying dividends, selected for fundamental strength relative to their peers, based on financial ratios. **Top Holdings:** The Home Depot Inc   Procter & Gamble Co   Coca-Cola Co   PepsiCo Inc   Intel Corp

SPDR® Bloomberg Barclays High Yield Bond ETF　　　　　　　　　　A+　　BUY

Ticker	Traded On	NAV	Total Assets ($)	Dividend Yield (TTM)	Turnover Ratio	Expense Ratio
JNK	NYSE Arca		$10,167,617,070	5.59	44	0.4

Ratings
Reward　　　　　　　　　　　　　　　A+
Risk　　　　　　　　　　　　　　　　A
Recent Upgrade/Downgrade

Fund Information
Fund Type　　　　　　　Exchange Traded Funds
Category　　　　　　　　　US Fixed Income
Sub-Category　　　　　　　High Yield Bond
Prospectus Objective　　　Corp Bond-High Yld
Inception Date　　　　　　　Nov-07
Open to New Investments　　　Y

Prices
Price (as of 9/30/2019)　　　　108.74
52-Week High　　　　　　　　109.46
52-Week Low　　　　　　　　　32.95

Total Returns (%)

3-Month	6-Month	1-Year	3-Year	5-Year
1.01	3.54	218.82	252.02	262.72

3-Year Standard Deviation　　　　　4.53
Effective Duration　　　　　　　　3.08

Valuation
Premium/Discount (1-Year Average)　　0.09

Company Information
Provider　　　　SPDR State Street Global Advisors
Manager/Tenure　Michael J. Brunell (11), Kyle Kelly (6),
　　　　　　　　Bradley J. Sullivan (3)
Website　　　　http://www.spdrs.com
Address　　　　SPDR State Street Global Advisors
　　　　　　　　State Street Financial Center, 1
　　　　　　　　Lincoln Street Boston MA 02111-2900
　　　　　　　　United States
Phone Number　617-786-3000

PERFORMANCE

Ratings History

Date	Overall Rating	Risk Rating	Reward Rating
Q3-19	A+	A	A+
Q4-18	C+	B+	C-
Q4-17	C+	B	C+
Q4-16	C+	B-	C
Q4-15	C-	C-	C-

Asset & Performance History

Date	NAV	1-Year Total Return
2018	33.55	-3.17
2017	36.64	6
2016	36.37	14.74
2015	33.75	-7.21
2014	38.62	1.15
2013	40.42	5.89

Total Assets: $10,167,617,070
Asset Allocation

Asset	%
Cash	1%
Stocks	0%
US Stocks	0%
Bonds	99%
US Bonds	81%
Other	0%

Services Offered:

Investment Strategy: The investment seeks to provide investment results that correspond generally to the price and yield performance of the Bloomberg Barclays High Yield Very Liquid Index. The fund generally invests substantially all, but at least 80%, of its total assets in the securities comprising the index or in securities that the Adviser determines have economic characteristics that are substantially identical to the economic characteristics of the securities that comprise the index. The index is designed to measure the performance of publicly issued U.S. dollar denominated high yield corporate bonds with above-average liquidity. The fund is non-diversified. **Top Holdings:** ALTICE FRANCE S.A 7.38% Sprint Corporation 7.88% TransDigm, Inc. 6.25% CCO Holdings, LLC/ CCO Holdings Capital Corp. 5.12% Diamond Sports Group LLC / Diamond Sports Finance Co 5.38%

SPDR® Bloomberg Barclays Short Term High Yield Bond ETF　　　　B-　　BUY

Ticker	Traded On	NAV	Total Assets ($)	Dividend Yield (TTM)	Turnover Ratio	Expense Ratio
SJNK	NYSE Arca		$3,300,549,760	5.69	65	0.4

Ratings
Reward　　　　　　　　　　　　　　　C
Risk　　　　　　　　　　　　　　　　B
Recent Upgrade/Downgrade　　　　　Down

Fund Information
Fund Type　　　　　　　Exchange Traded Funds
Category　　　　　　　　　US Fixed Income
Sub-Category　　　　　　　High Yield Bond
Prospectus Objective　　　Corp Bond-High Yld
Inception Date　　　　　　　Mar-12
Open to New Investments　　　Y

Prices
Price (as of 9/30/2019)　　　　27.01
52-Week High　　　　　　　　27.52
52-Week Low　　　　　　　　　25.68

Total Returns (%)

3-Month	6-Month	1-Year	3-Year	5-Year
0.34	1.85	3.47	15.66	19.16

3-Year Standard Deviation　　　　　3.3
Effective Duration　　　　　　　　1.62

Valuation
Premium/Discount (1-Year Average)　　0.11

Company Information
Provider　　　　SPDR State Street Global Advisors
Manager/Tenure　Michael J. Brunell (7), Kyle Kelly (6),
　　　　　　　　Bradley J. Sullivan (3)
Website　　　　http://www.spdrs.com
Address　　　　SPDR State Street Global Advisors
　　　　　　　　State Street Financial Center, 1
　　　　　　　　Lincoln Street Boston MA 02111-2900
　　　　　　　　United States
Phone Number　617-786-3000

PERFORMANCE

Ratings History

Date	Overall Rating	Risk Rating	Reward Rating
Q3-19	B-	B	C
Q4-18	C+	B	C
Q4-17	C+	B-	C+
Q4-16	C	C+	C
Q4-15	C	C+	C-

Asset & Performance History

Date	NAV	1-Year Total Return
2018	25.98	-0.25
2017	27.51	4.85
2016	27.62	14.27
2015	25.62	-6.56
2014	28.93	-0.73
2013	30.7	6.85

Total Assets: $3,300,549,760
Asset Allocation

Asset	%
Cash	2%
Stocks	0%
US Stocks	0%
Bonds	97%
US Bonds	83%
Other	0%

Services Offered:

Investment Strategy: The investment seeks to provide investment results that correspond generally to the price and yield performance of the Bloomberg Barclays US High Yield 350mn Cash Pay 0-5 Yr 2% Capped Index. The fund generally invests substantially all, but at least 80%, of its total assets in the securities comprising the index or in securities that the Adviser determines have economic characteristics that are substantially identical to the economic characteristics of the securities that comprise the index. The index is designed to measure the performance of short-term publicly issued U.S. dollar-denominated high yield corporate bonds. It is non-diversified. **Top Holdings:** Sprint Corporation 7.88% Reynolds Group Issuer LLC. 5.75% Community Health Systems Incorporated 6.25% Nielsen Finance LLC/Nielsen Finance Co 5% Tenet Healthcare Corporation 8.12%

SPDR® Dow Jones Industrial Average ETF   B   BUY

Ticker	Traded On	NAV	Total Assets ($)	Dividend Yield (TTM)	Turnover Ratio	Expense Ratio
DIA	NYSE Arca		$21,222,816,446	2.15	2	0.17

Ratings
Reward	B
Risk	C+
Recent Upgrade/Downgrade	Up

Fund Information
Fund Type	Exchange Traded Funds
Category	US Equity Large Cap Value
Sub-Category	Large Value
Prospectus Objective	Growth
Inception Date	Jan-98
Open to New Investments	Y

Prices
Price (as of 9/30/2019)	269.18
52-Week High	273.60
52-Week Low	218.10

Total Returns (%)
3-Month	6-Month	1-Year	3-Year	5-Year
0.97	3.30	3.70	56.62	76.57

3-Year Standard Deviation	12.38
Effective Duration	

Valuation
Premium/Discount (1-Year Average)	0.00

Company Information
Provider	SPDR State Street Global Advisors
Manager/Tenure	Management Team (21)
Website	http://www.spdrs.com
Address	SPDR State Street Global Advisors State Street Financial Center, 1 Lincoln Street Boston MA 02111-2900 United States
Phone Number	617-786-3000

PERFORMANCE

Ratings History
Date	Overall Rating	Risk Rating	Reward Rating
Q3-19	B	C+	B
Q4-18	B-	C+	B
Q4-17	B+	B	A-
Q4-16	B-	C	B
Q4-15	B	B	B

Asset & Performance History
Date	NAV	1-Year Total Return
2018	233.16	-3.6
2017	246.98	27.97
2016	197.36	15.42
2015	174	0.09
2014	177.91	9.87
2013	165.4	29.41

Total Assets: $21,222,816,446
Asset Allocation
Asset	%
Cash	0%
Stocks	100%
US Stocks	100%
Bonds	0%
US Bonds	0%
Other	0%

Services Offered: Dividend Investment Plan, CashInvestment Plan

Investment Strategy: O investimento destina-se a fornecer os resultados do investimento que, antes das despesas, geralmente corresponde ao preço de desempenho produtivo e do Dow Jones Industrial Average (DJIA). O fundo tem a carteira e dinheiro, e não está activa "administrado" pelos métodos tradicionais. **Top Holdings:** Boeing Co   UnitedHealth Group Inc   The Home Depot Inc   McDonald's Corp   Apple Inc

SPDR® MFS Systematic Core Equity ETF   B-   BUY

Ticker	Traded On	NAV	Total Assets ($)	Dividend Yield (TTM)	Turnover Ratio	Expense Ratio
SYE	NYSE Arca		$35,421,104	1.67	65	0.6

Ratings
Reward	B
Risk	C
Recent Upgrade/Downgrade	Up

Fund Information
Fund Type	Exchange Traded Funds
Category	US Equity Large Cap Value
Sub-Category	Large Blend
Prospectus Objective	Growth
Inception Date	Jan-14
Open to New Investments	Y

Prices
Price (as of 9/30/2019)	82.41
52-Week High	84.40
52-Week Low	66.60

Total Returns (%)
3-Month	6-Month	1-Year	3-Year	5-Year
0.10	1.74	2.03	43.54	69.34

3-Year Standard Deviation	12.64
Effective Duration	

Valuation
Premium/Discount (1-Year Average)	-0.05

Company Information
Provider	SPDR State Street Global Advisors
Manager/Tenure	Matthew W. Krummell (5)
Website	http://www.spdrs.com
Address	SPDR State Street Global Advisors State Street Financial Center, 1 Lincoln Street Boston MA 02111-2900 United States
Phone Number	617-786-3000

PERFORMANCE

Ratings History
Date	Overall Rating	Risk Rating	Reward Rating
Q3-19	B-	C	B
Q4-18	C+	C	B
Q4-17	B	B	B
Q4-16	C	D+	B-
Q4-15	D+	C	C+

Asset & Performance History
Date	NAV	1-Year Total Return
2018	70.91	-2.93
2017	74.2	21.17
2016	62.76	10.16
2015	57.97	4.68
2014	56.87	18.15
2013		

Total Assets: $35,421,104
Asset Allocation
Asset	%
Cash	1%
Stocks	99%
US Stocks	99%
Bonds	0%
US Bonds	0%
Other	0%

Services Offered:

Investment Strategy: The investment seeks capital appreciation. Under normal circumstances, the fund invests at least 80% of its net assets (plus the amount of borrowings for investment purposes) in equity securities. Equity securities in which the fund invests include common stocks, preferred stocks, and securities convertible into stocks. In selecting securities for the fund, the Sub-Adviser utilizes a bottom-up approach to buying and selling investments for the fund. **Top Holdings:** Microsoft Corp   Apple Inc   Johnson & Johnson   Intel Corp   Citigroup Inc

SPDR® MFS Systematic Growth Equity ETF   B-   BUY

Ticker	Traded On	NAV	Total Assets ($)	Dividend Yield (TTM)	Turnover Ratio	Expense Ratio
SYG	NYSE Arca		$37,434,853	1.13	77	0.61

Ratings
Reward	B
Risk	C
Recent Upgrade/Downgrade	Up

Fund Information
Fund Type	Exchange Traded Funds
Category	US Equity Large Cap Growth
Sub-Category	Large Growth
Prospectus Objective	Growth
Inception Date	Jan-14
Open to New Investments	Y

Prices
Price (as of 9/30/2019)	81.40
52-Week High	87.51
52-Week Low	66.16

Total Returns (%)

3-Month	6-Month	1-Year	3-Year	5-Year
-4.69	-1.23	-4.79	35.60	63.61

3-Year Standard Deviation	14.24
Effective Duration	

Valuation
Premium/Discount (1-Year Average)	-0.01

Company Information
Provider	SPDR State Street Global Advisors
Manager/Tenure	Matthew W. Krummell (5)
Website	http://www.spdrs.com
Address	SPDR State Street Global Advisors
	State Street Financial Center, 1
	Lincoln Street Boston MA 02111-2900
	United States
Phone Number	617-786-3000

PERFORMANCE

Ratings History

Date	Overall Rating	Risk Rating	Reward Rating
Q3-19	B-	C	B
Q4-18	C+	C-	B
Q4-17	B	B	B
Q4-16	C	C-	B-
Q4-15	D+	C	C+

Asset & Performance History

Date	NAV	1-Year Total Return
2018	71.15	-8.11
2017	79.33	27.85
2016	62.65	5.24
2015	60.13	7.98
2014	57.4	19.84
2013		

Total Assets: $37,434,853

Asset Allocation

Asset	%
Cash	1%
Stocks	99%
US Stocks	95%
Bonds	0%
US Bonds	0%
Other	0%

Services Offered:

Investment Strategy: The investment seeks capital appreciation. Under normal circumstances, the fund invests at least 80% of its net assets (plus the amount of borrowings for investment purposes) in equity securities. Equity securities in which the fund invests include common stocks, preferred stocks, and securities convertible into stocks. In selecting securities for the fund, the Sub-Adviser utilizes a bottom-up approach to buying and selling investments for the fund. **Top Holdings:** Apple Inc Amazon.com Inc Microsoft Corp Starbucks Corp PayPal Holdings Inc

---

SPDR® Portfolio Long Term Corporate Bond ETF   B   BUY

Ticker	Traded On	NAV	Total Assets ($)	Dividend Yield (TTM)	Turnover Ratio	Expense Ratio
SPLB	NYSE Arca		$641,085,661	3.86	18	0.07

Ratings
Reward	B
Risk	C+
Recent Upgrade/Downgrade	Up

Fund Information
Fund Type	Exchange Traded Funds
Category	US Fixed Income
Sub-Category	Long-Term Bond
Prospectus Objective	Corp Bond - Gen
Inception Date	Mar-09
Open to New Investments	Y

Prices
Price (as of 9/30/2019)	30.09
52-Week High	30.71
52-Week Low	24.89

Total Returns (%)

3-Month	6-Month	1-Year	3-Year	5-Year
5.56	13.97	19.98	20.21	39.59

3-Year Standard Deviation	7.71
Effective Duration	14.58

Valuation
Premium/Discount (1-Year Average)	0.13

Company Information
Provider	SPDR State Street Global Advisors
Manager/Tenure	Kyle Kelly (6), Christopher DiStefano (4), Frank Miethe (2)
Website	http://www.spdrs.com
Address	SPDR State Street Global Advisors
	State Street Financial Center, 1
	Lincoln Street Boston MA 02111-2900
	United States
Phone Number	617-786-3000

PERFORMANCE

Ratings History

Date	Overall Rating	Risk Rating	Reward Rating
Q3-19	B	C+	B
Q4-18	C-	C	D+
Q4-17	B	B	B-
Q4-16	C	C-	C
Q4-15	C	C	C-

Asset & Performance History

Date	NAV	1-Year Total Return
2018	25.3	-7.43
2017	28.55	11.79
2016	26.54	10.87
2015	24.96	-4.53
2014	27.34	15.61
2013	24.71	-5.9

Total Assets: $641,085,661

Asset Allocation

Asset	%
Cash	1%
Stocks	0%
US Stocks	0%
Bonds	99%
US Bonds	89%
Other	0%

Services Offered:

Investment Strategy: The investment seeks to provide investment results that, before fees and expenses, correspond generally to the price and yield performance of the Bloomberg Barclays U.S. Long Term Corporate Bond Index. The fund generally invests substantially all, but at least 80%, of its total assets in the securities comprising the index or in securities that the Adviser determines have economic characteristics that are substantially identical to the economic characteristics of the securities that comprise the index. The index is designed to measure the performance of U.S. corporate bonds that have a maturity of greater than or equal to 10 years. The fund is non-diversified. **Top Holdings:** Anheuser-Busch Companies LLC / Anheuser-Busch InBev Worldwide Inc 4.9% CVS Health Corp 5.05% Verizon Communications Inc. 4.02% GE Capital International Funding Company Unlimited Company 4.42% Goldman Sachs Group, Inc. 6.75%

SPDR® S&P 500 ETF

B-   **BUY**

Ticker	Traded On	NAV	Total Assets ($)	Dividend Yield (TTM)	Turnover Ratio	Expense Ratio
SPY	NYSE Arca		$273,532,000,000	1.85	2	0.09

Ratings

Reward	C+
Risk	B
Recent Upgrade/Downgrade	

Fund Information

Fund Type	Exchange Traded Funds
Category	US Equity Large Cap Blend
Sub-Category	Large Blend
Prospectus Objective	Growth
Inception Date	Jan-93
Open to New Investments	Y

Prices

Price (as of 9/30/2019)	296.77
52-Week High	302.01
52-Week Low	234.34

Total Returns (%)

3-Month	6-Month	1-Year	3-Year	5-Year
0.38	4.26	3.28	44.59	65.58

3-Year Standard Deviation	12.15
Effective Duration	

Valuation

Premium/Discount (1-Year Average)	-0.05

Company Information

Provider	SPDR State Street Global Advisors
Manager/Tenure	Management Team (26)
Website	http://www.spdrs.com
Address	SPDR State Street Global Advisors
	State Street Financial Center, 1
	Lincoln Street Boston MA 02111-2900
	United States
Phone Number	617-786-3000

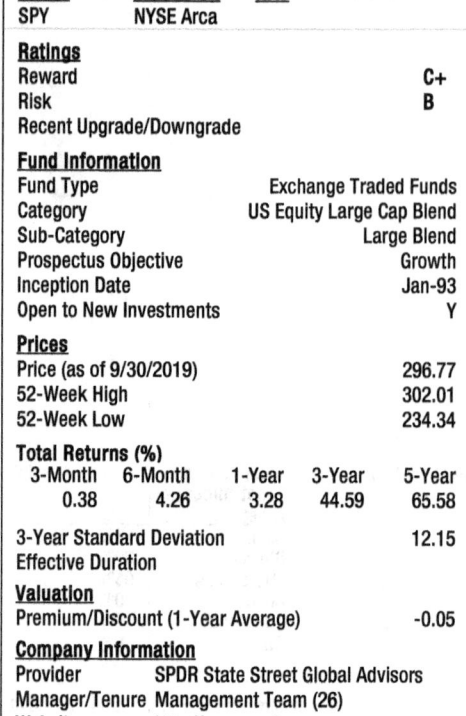

PERFORMANCE

Ratings History

Date	Overall Rating	Risk Rating	Reward Rating
Q3-19	B-	B	C+
Q4-18	C+	B	C
Q4-17	B	B	B
Q4-16	B	B	B
Q4-15	C+	B-	C

Asset & Performance History

Date	NAV	1-Year Total Return
2018	249.92	-4.44
2017	266.55	21.69
2016	223.28	11.25
2015	204.02	1.34
2014	205.5	13.53
2013	184.54	32.21

Total Assets: $273,532,000,000

Asset Allocation

Asset	%
Cash	0%
Stocks	100%
US Stocks	99%
Bonds	0%
US Bonds	0%
Other	0%

Services Offered: Dividend Investment Plan, CashInvestment Plan

Investment Strategy: The investment seeks to provide investment results that, before expenses, generally correspond to the price and yield performance of the S&P 500 Index. The Trust holds the Portfolio and cash and is not actively "managed" by traditional methods. To maintain the correspondence between the composition and weightings of Portfolio Securities and component stocks of the S&P 500 Index ("Index Securities"), the Trustee adjusts the Portfolio from time to time to conform to periodic changes in the identity and/or relative weightings of Index Securities. **Top Holdings:** Microsoft Corp Apple Inc Amazon.com Inc Facebook Inc A Berkshire Hathaway Inc B

SPDR® S&P Homebuilders ETF

B-   **BUY**

Ticker	Traded On	NAV	Total Assets ($)	Dividend Yield (TTM)	Turnover Ratio	Expense Ratio
XHB	NYSE Arca		$680,805,782	1	32	0.35

Ratings

Reward	B
Risk	C
Recent Upgrade/Downgrade	Up

Fund Information

Fund Type	Exchange Traded Funds
Category	Consumer Goods & Svcs
Sub-Category	Consumer Cyclical
Prospectus Objective	Real Estate
Inception Date	Jan-06
Open to New Investments	Y

Prices

Price (as of 9/30/2019)	44.08
52-Week High	44.08
52-Week Low	30.74

Total Returns (%)

3-Month	6-Month	1-Year	3-Year	5-Year
3.83	12.36	15.00	31.93	52.98

3-Year Standard Deviation	17.38
Effective Duration	

Valuation

Premium/Discount (1-Year Average)	-0.01

Company Information

Provider	SPDR State Street Global Advisors
Manager/Tenure	Michael J. Feehily (7), Karl A. Schneider (4), Raymond V. Donofrio (2)
Website	http://www.spdrs.com
Address	SPDR State Street Global Advisors
	State Street Financial Center, 1
	Lincoln Street Boston MA 02111-2900
	United States
Phone Number	617-786-3000

PERFORMANCE

Ratings History

Date	Overall Rating	Risk Rating	Reward Rating
Q3-19	B-	C	B
Q4-18	C	D+	B-
Q4-17	B+	C	A-
Q4-16	B-	C	B
Q4-15	B+	B	A-

Asset & Performance History

Date	NAV	1-Year Total Return
2018	32.52	-25.64
2017	44.22	31.65
2016	33.86	-0.28
2015	34.17	0.59
2014	34.13	3.15
2013	33.27	25.5

Total Assets: $680,805,782

Asset Allocation

Asset	%
Cash	0%
Stocks	100%
US Stocks	100%
Bonds	0%
US Bonds	0%
Other	0%

Services Offered: Dividend Investment Plan, CashInvestment Plan

Investment Strategy: The investment seeks to provide investment results that, before fees and expenses, correspond generally to the total return performance of an index derived from the homebuilding segment of a U.S. total market composite index. In seeking to track the performance of the S&P Homebuilders Select Industry Index (the "index"), the fund employs a sampling strategy. It generally invests substantially all, but at least 80%, of its total assets in the securities comprising the index. The index represents the homebuilders segment of the S&P Total Market Index ("S&P TMI"). The fund is non-diversified. **Top Holdings:** Lowe's Companies Inc The Home Depot Inc D.R. Horton Inc Williams-Sonoma Inc Johnson Controls International PLC

SPDR® S&P Insurance ETF   B-   BUY

Ticker	Traded On	NAV	Total Assets ($)	Dividend Yield (TTM)	Turnover Ratio	Expense Ratio
KIE	NYSE Arca		$898,731,202	1.68	21	0.35

Ratings
Reward   B-
Risk   C+
Recent Upgrade/Downgrade

Fund Information
Fund Type   Exchange Traded Funds
Category   Financials Sector Equity
Sub-Category   Financial
Prospectus Objective   Financial
Inception Date   Nov-05
Open to New Investments   Y

Prices
Price (as of 9/30/2019)   35.23
52-Week High   35.33
52-Week Low   26.73

Total Returns (%)

3-Month	6-Month	1-Year	3-Year	5-Year
2.48	12.92	12.57	50.04	83.05

3-Year Standard Deviation   12.84
Effective Duration

Valuation
Premium/Discount (1-Year Average)   -0.03

Company Information
Provider   SPDR State Street Global Advisors
Manager/Tenure   Michael J. Feehily (7), Karl A. Schneider (4), Raymond V. Donofrio (2)
Website   http://www.spdrs.com
Address   SPDR State Street Global Advisors State Street Financial Center, 1 Lincoln Street Boston MA 02111-2900 United States
Phone Number   617-786-3000

PERFORMANCE

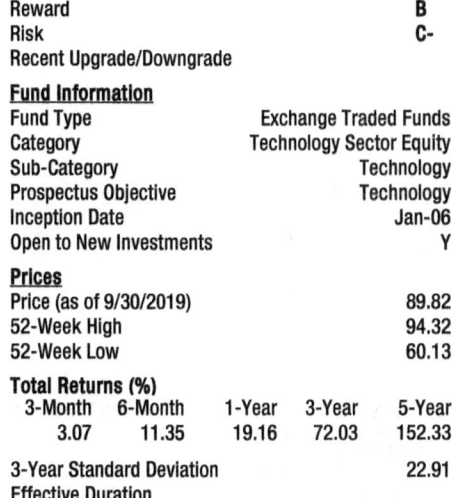

Ratings History

Date	Overall Rating	Risk Rating	Reward Rating
Q3-19	B-	C+	B-
Q4-18	C	C+	C
Q4-17	B+	A-	B
Q4-16	C	C	C
Q4-15	B+	B-	A

Asset & Performance History

Date	NAV	1-Year Total Return
2018	28.4	-5.86
2017	30.7	12.89
2016	27.63	19.97
2015	23.17	6.01
2014	22.22	7.61
2013	21.04	45.57

Total Assets: $898,731,202
Asset Allocation

Asset	%
Cash	0%
Stocks	100%
US Stocks	97%
Bonds	0%
US Bonds	0%
Other	0%

Services Offered: Dividend Investment Plan, CashInvestment Plan

Investment Strategy: The investment seeks to provide investment results that, before fees and expenses, correspond generally to the total return performance of an index that tracks the performance of publicly traded companies in the insurance industry. In seeking to track the performance of the S&P Insurance Select Industry Index (the "index"), the fund employs a sampling strategy. It generally invests substantially all, but at least 80%, of its total assets in the securities comprising the index. The index represents the insurance segment of the S&P Total Market Index ("S&P TMI"). The fund is non-diversified. **Top Holdings:** Assurant Inc   Brown & Brown Inc   Arch Capital Group Ltd   First American Financial Corp   Fidelity National Financial Inc

SPDR® S&P Semiconductor ETF   B-   BUY

Ticker	Traded On	NAV	Total Assets ($)	Dividend Yield (TTM)	Turnover Ratio	Expense Ratio
XSD	NYSE Arca		$336,968,345	0.66	32	0.35

Ratings
Reward   B
Risk   C-
Recent Upgrade/Downgrade

Fund Information
Fund Type   Exchange Traded Funds
Category   Technology Sector Equity
Sub-Category   Technology
Prospectus Objective   Technology
Inception Date   Jan-06
Open to New Investments   Y

Prices
Price (as of 9/30/2019)   89.82
52-Week High   94.32
52-Week Low   60.13

Total Returns (%)

3-Month	6-Month	1-Year	3-Year	5-Year
3.07	11.35	19.16	72.03	152.33

3-Year Standard Deviation   22.91
Effective Duration

Valuation
Premium/Discount (1-Year Average)   0.00

Company Information
Provider   SPDR State Street Global Advisors
Manager/Tenure   Michael J. Feehily (7), Karl A. Schneider (4), Kala O'Donnell (2)
Website   http://www.spdrs.com
Address   SPDR State Street Global Advisors State Street Financial Center, 1 Lincoln Street Boston MA 02111-2900 United States
Phone Number   617-786-3000

PERFORMANCE

Ratings History

Date	Overall Rating	Risk Rating	Reward Rating
Q3-19	B-	C-	B
Q4-18	C	C-	B-
Q4-17	A-	B	A+
Q4-16	C	C-	C
Q4-15	C	C	C+

Asset & Performance History

Date	NAV	1-Year Total Return
2018	64.74	-6.25
2017	69.79	25.23
2016	56.08	29.08
2015	43.71	10.29
2014	39.86	30.97
2013	30.59	36.31

Total Assets: $336,968,345
Asset Allocation

Asset	%
Cash	0%
Stocks	100%
US Stocks	97%
Bonds	0%
US Bonds	0%
Other	0%

Services Offered: Dividend Investment Plan, CashInvestment Plan

Investment Strategy: The investment seeks to provide investment results that, before fees and expenses, correspond generally to the total return performance of an index derived from the semiconductor segment of a U.S. total market composite index. In seeking to track the performance of the S&P Semiconductor Select Industry Index (the "index"), the fund employs a sampling strategy. It generally invests substantially all, but at least 80%, of its total assets in the securities comprising the index. The index represents the semiconductors segment of the S&P Total Market Index ("S&P TMI"). The fund is non-diversified. **Top Holdings:** Lattice Semiconductor Corp   Micron Technology Inc   Cirrus Logic Inc   Inphi Corp   Monolithic Power Systems Inc

SPDR® SSGA US Large Cap Low Volatility Index ETF

B   **BUY**

Ticker	Traded On	NAV	Total Assets ($)	Dividend Yield (TTM)	Turnover Ratio	Expense Ratio
LGLV	NYSE Arca		$881,915,966	1.81	32	0.12

Ratings
Reward	B
Risk	C+
Recent Upgrade/Downgrade	Up

Fund Information
Fund Type	Exchange Traded Funds
Category	US Equity Large Cap Blend
Sub-Category	Large Blend
Prospectus Objective	Income
Inception Date	Feb-13
Open to New Investments	Y

Prices
Price (as of 9/30/2019)	111.48
52-Week High	112.40
52-Week Low	84.44

Total Returns (%)
3-Month	6-Month	1-Year	3-Year	5-Year
2.74	10.85	16.96	52.52	83.95

3-Year Standard Deviation	9.74
Effective Duration	

Valuation
Premium/Discount (1-Year Average)	0.11

Company Information
Provider	SPDR State Street Global Advisors
Manager/Tenure	Michael J. Feehily (6), Karl A. Schneider (4), Juan Acevedo (0)
Website	http://www.spdrs.com
Address	SPDR State Street Global Advisors State Street Financial Center, 1 Lincoln Street Boston MA 02111-2900 United States
Phone Number	617-786-3000

PERFORMANCE

Ratings History
Date	Overall Rating	Risk Rating	Reward Rating
Q3-19	B	C+	B
Q4-18	C	C-	C
Q4-17	B+	A+	B-
Q4-16	C	C-	B-
Q4-15	C	C-	C

Asset & Performance History
Date	NAV	1-Year Total Return
2018	88.93	0.54
2017	90.27	17.82
2016	80.05	11.25
2015	73.84	2.36
2014	74.34	16.65
2013	68.38	

Total Assets: $881,915,966
Asset Allocation
Asset	%
Cash	0%
Stocks	100%
US Stocks	97%
Bonds	0%
US Bonds	0%
Other	0%

Services Offered:

Investment Strategy: The investment seeks to provide investment results that, before fees and expenses, correspond generally to the total return performance of the SSGA US Large Cap Low Volatility Index. The fund generally invests substantially all, but at least 80%, of its total assets in the securities comprising the index. The index is designed to measure the performance of the stocks of U.S. large capitalization companies that exhibit low volatility. Volatility is a statistical measurement of the magnitude of movements in a stock's price over time. The fund is non-diversified. **Top Holdings:** Republic Services Inc Class A Chubb Ltd Berkshire Hathaway Inc B CME Group Inc Class A Marsh & McLennan Companies Inc

The Real Estate Select Sector SPDR Fund

B   **BUY**

Ticker	Traded On	NAV	Total Assets ($)	Dividend Yield (TTM)	Turnover Ratio	Expense Ratio
XLRE	NYSE Arca		$3,901,982,260	2.89	7	0.13

Ratings
Reward	B+
Risk	C
Recent Upgrade/Downgrade	Up

Fund Information
Fund Type	Exchange Traded Funds
Category	Real Estate Sector Equity
Sub-Category	Real Estate
Prospectus Objective	Real Estate
Inception Date	Oct-15
Open to New Investments	Y

Prices
Price (as of 9/30/2019)	39.34
52-Week High	40.10
52-Week Low	29.81

Total Returns (%)
3-Month	6-Month	1-Year	3-Year	5-Year
7.73	10.35	25.33	33.59	

3-Year Standard Deviation	12.22
Effective Duration	

Valuation
Premium/Discount (1-Year Average)	-0.03

Company Information
Provider	SPDR State Street Global Advisors
Manager/Tenure	Michael J. Feehily (3), Karl A. Schneider (3), Amy Cheng (2)
Website	http://www.spdrs.com
Address	SPDR State Street Global Advisors State Street Financial Center, 1 Lincoln Street Boston MA 02111-2900 United States
Phone Number	617-786-3000

PERFORMANCE

Ratings History
Date	Overall Rating	Risk Rating	Reward Rating
Q3-19	B	C	B+
Q4-18	B-	C	B
Q4-17	C	B-	C
Q4-16	D	C	B
Q4-15			

Asset & Performance History
Date	NAV	1-Year Total Return
2018	31	-2.27
2017	32.92	10.66
2016	30.74	3.17
2015	31.04	
2014		
2013		

Total Assets: $3,901,982,260
Asset Allocation
Asset	%
Cash	0%
Stocks	100%
US Stocks	100%
Bonds	0%
US Bonds	0%
Other	0%

Services Offered:

Investment Strategy: The investment seeks to provide investment results that, before expenses, correspond generally to the price and yield performance of publicly traded equity securities of companies in the Real Estate Select Sector Index (the "index"). Under normal market conditions, the fund generally invests substantially all, but at least 95%, of its total assets in the securities comprising the index. The index includes securities of companies from the following industries: real estate management and development and REITs, excluding mortgage REITs. The fund is non-diversified. **Top Holdings:** American Tower Corp Crown Castle International Corp Prologis Inc Equinix Inc Simon Property Group Inc

Utilities Select Sector SPDR® Fund   B   BUY

Ticker	Traded On	NAV	Total Assets ($)	Dividend Yield (TTM)	Turnover Ratio	Expense Ratio
XLU	NYSE Arca		$11,403,280,323	2.88	5	0.13

Ratings
Reward   B
Risk   B-
Recent Upgrade/Downgrade

Fund Information
Fund Type	Exchange Traded Funds
Category	Utilities Sector Equity
Sub-Category	Utilities
Prospectus Objective	Utility
Inception Date	Dec-98
Open to New Investments	Y

Prices
Price (as of 9/30/2019)	64.74
52-Week High	64.93
52-Week Low	51.56

Total Returns (%)
3-Month	6-Month	1-Year	3-Year	5-Year
9.52	13.71	27.07	45.74	81.83

3-Year Standard Deviation   10.65
Effective Duration

Valuation
Premium/Discount (1-Year Average)   -0.01

Company Information
Provider	SPDR State Street Global Advisors
Manager/Tenure	Michael J. Feehily (8), Karl A. Schneider (4), Dwayne Hancock (2)
Website	http://www.spdrs.com
Address	SPDR State Street Global Advisors State Street Financial Center, 1 Lincoln Street Boston MA 02111-2900 United States
Phone Number	617-786-3000

PERFORMANCE

Ratings History

Date	Overall Rating	Risk Rating	Reward Rating
Q3-19	B	B-	B
Q4-18	B	B	B-
Q4-17	B	B	B
Q4-16	B	C+	B
Q4-15	B	C+	B

Asset & Performance History

Date	NAV	1-Year Total Return
2018	52.92	4.01
2017	52.65	11.94
2016	48.58	15.4
2015	43.29	-4.85
2014	47.2	28.65
2013	37.98	13.01

Total Assets: $11,403,280,323

Asset Allocation

Asset	%
Cash	0%
Stocks	100%
US Stocks	100%
Bonds	0%
US Bonds	0%
Other	0%

Services Offered: Dividend Investment Plan, CashInvestment Plan

Investment Strategy: The investment seeks to provide investment results that, before expenses, correspond generally to the price and yield performance of publicly traded equity securities of companies in the Utilities Select Sector Index. In seeking to track the performance of the index, the fund employs a replication strategy. It generally invests substantially all, but at least 95%, of its total assets in the securities comprising the index. The index includes securities of companies from the following industries: electric utilities; water utilities; multi-utilities; independent power and renewable electricity producers; and gas utilities. The fund is non-diversified. **Top Holdings:** NextEra Energy Inc   Duke Energy Corp   Dominion Energy Inc   Southern Co   Exelon Corp

---

VanEck Vectors AMT-Free Intermediate Municipal Index ETF   B   BUY

Ticker	Traded On	NAV	Total Assets ($)	Dividend Yield (TTM)	Turnover Ratio	Expense Ratio
ITM	BATS	50.39	$1,892,265,445	2.22	7	0.24

Ratings
Reward   B
Risk   C+
Recent Upgrade/Downgrade

Fund Information
Fund Type	Exchange Traded Funds
Category	US Muni Fixed Inc
Sub-Category	Muni National Long
Prospectus Objective	Muni Bond - Natl
Inception Date	Dec-07
Open to New Investments	Y

Prices
Price (as of 9/30/2019)	50.31
52-Week High	51.11
52-Week Low	45.90

Total Returns (%)
3-Month	6-Month	1-Year	3-Year	5-Year
1.65	4.43	10.15	119.13	140.24

3-Year Standard Deviation   4.54
Effective Duration   6.19

Valuation
Premium/Discount (1-Year Average)   -0.11

Company Information
Provider	VanEck
Manager/Tenure	James T. Colby (11)
Website	http://www.vaneck.com
Address	Van Eck Associates Corporation 666 Third Avenue New York NY 10017 United States
Phone Number	800-826-1115

PERFORMANCE

Ratings History

Date	Overall Rating	Risk Rating	Reward Rating
Q3-19	B	C+	B
Q4-18	B	C+	A
Q4-17	B-	B	C
Q4-16	C	C+	C
Q4-15	C	C+	C

Asset & Performance History

Date	NAV	1-Year Total Return
2018	47.44	100.88
2017	24.13	6.21
2016	23.23	-0.56
2015	23.88	3.64
2014	23.58	8.97
2013	22.18	-3.51

Total Assets: $1,892,265,445

Asset Allocation

Asset	%
Cash	1%
Stocks	0%
US Stocks	0%
Bonds	99%
US Bonds	99%
Other	0%

Services Offered:

Investment Strategy: The investment seeks to replicate as closely as possible, before fees and expenses, the price and yield performance of the Bloomberg Barclays AMT-Free Intermediate Continuous Municipal Index. The fund normally invests at least 80% of its total assets in fixed income securities that comprise the index. The index is comprised of publicly traded municipal bonds that cover the U.S. dollar denominated intermediate term tax-exempt bond market. **Top Holdings:** NEW YORK ST DORM AUTH ST PERS INCOME TAX REV 5%   MARYLAND ST 5%   CALIFORNIA ST 5%   GEORGIA ST 5%   SALES TAX ASSET RECEIVABLE CORP N Y 5%

VanEck Vectors BDC Income ETF B- BUY

Ticker	Traded On	NAV	Total Assets ($)	Dividend Yield (TTM)	Turnover Ratio	Expense Ratio
BIZD	NYSE Arca	16.83	$221,327,099	9.45	13	9.62

Ratings
Reward B
Risk C
Recent Upgrade/Downgrade Up

Fund Information
Fund Type Exchange Traded Funds
Category Financials Sector Equity
Sub-Category Financial
Prospectus Objective Income
Inception Date Feb-13
Open to New Investments Y

Prices
Price (as of 9/30/2019) 16.86
52-Week High 16.99
52-Week Low 14.04

Total Returns (%)

3-Month	6-Month	1-Year	3-Year	5-Year
3.56	7.01	8.86	24.16	34.98

3-Year Standard Deviation 13.31
Effective Duration

Valuation
Premium/Discount (1-Year Average) -0.08

Company Information
Provider VanEck
Manager/Tenure Hao-Hung (Peter) Liao (6), Guo Hua (Jason) Jin (1)
Website http://www.vaneck.com
Address Van Eck Associates Corporation 666 Third Avenue New York NY 10017 United States
Phone Number 800-826-1115

PERFORMANCE

Ratings History

Date	Overall Rating	Risk Rating	Reward Rating
Q3-19	B-	C	B
Q4-18	C+	C-	B
Q4-17	C	C+	C
Q4-16	C	C-	C+
Q4-15	D+	C-	D+

Asset & Performance History

Date	NAV	1-Year Total Return
2018	14.22	-5.53
2017	16.57	0.04
2016	18.03	25.35
2015	15.73	-4.45
2014	17.92	-7.29
2013	20.9	

Total Assets: $221,327,099
Asset Allocation

Asset	%
Cash	1%
Stocks	98%
US Stocks	98%
Bonds	0%
US Bonds	0%
Other	2%

Services Offered:

Investment Strategy: The investment seeks to replicate as closely as possible, before fees and expenses, the price and yield performance of the MVIS® US Business Development Companies Index. The fund normally invests at least 80% of its total assets in securities that comprise the fund's benchmark index. The index is comprised of BDCs. BDCs are vehicles whose principal business is to invest in, lend capital to or provide services to privately-held companies or thinly traded U.S. public companies. **Top Holdings:** Ares Capital Corp FS KKR Capital Corp Main Street Capital Corp Prospect Capital Corp Hercules Capital Inc

VanEck Vectors Environmental Services ETF B- BUY

Ticker	Traded On	NAV	Total Assets ($)	Dividend Yield (TTM)	Turnover Ratio	Expense Ratio
EVX	NYSE Arca	104.25	$36,488,590	0.31	24	0.56

Ratings
Reward B
Risk C
Recent Upgrade/Downgrade Up

Fund Information
Fund Type Exchange Traded Funds
Category Industrials Sector Equity
Sub-Category Industrials
Prospectus Objective Unaligned
Inception Date Oct-06
Open to New Investments Y

Prices
Price (as of 9/30/2019) 104.43
52-Week High 105.32
52-Week Low 78.68

Total Returns (%)

3-Month	6-Month	1-Year	3-Year	5-Year
1.34	7.28	9.05	52.67	71.96

3-Year Standard Deviation 13.58
Effective Duration

Valuation
Premium/Discount (1-Year Average) 0.10

Company Information
Provider VanEck
Manager/Tenure Hao-Hung (Peter) Liao (12), Guo Hua (Jason) Jin (1)
Website http://www.vaneck.com
Address Van Eck Associates Corporation 666 Third Avenue New York NY 10017 United States
Phone Number 800-826-1115

PERFORMANCE

Ratings History

Date	Overall Rating	Risk Rating	Reward Rating
Q3-19	B-	C	B
Q4-18	B-	C	B
Q4-17	B	C+	A-
Q4-16	C+	C-	B
Q4-15	B	B-	B

Asset & Performance History

Date	NAV	1-Year Total Return
2018	83.47	-3.12
2017	86.5	15.77
2016	75.42	29.99
2015	58.42	-10.31
2014	65.91	2.56
2013	65.29	28.72

Total Assets: $36,488,590
Asset Allocation

Asset	%
Cash	0%
Stocks	100%
US Stocks	88%
Bonds	0%
US Bonds	0%
Other	0%

Services Offered:

Investment Strategy: The investment seeks to replicate as closely as possible, before fees and expenses, the price and yield performance of the NYSE® Arca Environmental Services IndexTM. The fund normally invests at least 80% of its total assets in common stocks and ADRs of companies involved in the environmental services industry. The index is designed to measure the performance of widely held, highly capitalized companies engaged in business activities that may benefit from the global increase in demand for consumer waste disposal, removal and storage of industrial by-products, and the management of associated resources. It is non-diversified. **Top Holdings:** Steris PLC Waste Management Inc Republic Services Inc Class A Waste Connections Inc Cantel Medical Corp

VanEck Vectors High-Yield Municipal Index ETF　　B　　BUY

Ticker	Traded On	NAV	Total Assets ($)	Dividend Yield (TTM)	Turnover Ratio	Expense Ratio
HYD	BATS	64.43	$3,053,594,109	4.17	22	0.35

Ratings
Reward	B
Risk	C+
Recent Upgrade/Downgrade	

Fund Information
Fund Type	Exchange Traded Funds
Category	US Muni Fixed Inc
Sub-Category	High Yield Muni
Prospectus Objective	Muni Bond - Natl
Inception Date	Feb-09
Open to New Investments	Y

Prices
Price (as of 9/30/2019)	64.43
52-Week High	64.90
52-Week Low	60.28

Total Returns (%)
3-Month	6-Month	1-Year	3-Year	5-Year
2.18	4.91	7.68	127.72	161.80

3-Year Standard Deviation	4.75
Effective Duration	6.22

Valuation
Premium/Discount (1-Year Average)	-0.06

Company Information
Provider	VanEck
Manager/Tenure	James T. Colby (10)
Website	http://www.vaneck.com
Address	Van Eck Associates Corporation 666 Third Avenue New York NY 10017 United States
Phone Number	800-826-1115

PERFORMANCE

Ratings History
Date	Overall Rating	Risk Rating	Reward Rating
Q3-19	B	C+	B
Q4-18	B+	C+	A
Q4-17	B	A	C+
Q4-16	C	C+	C
Q4-15	C+	C+	C

Asset & Performance History
Date	NAV	1-Year Total Return
2018	61.23	103.45
2017	31.31	10.49
2016	29.59	0.4
2015	30.78	4.81
2014	30.82	13.82
2013	28.49	-8.13

Total Assets: $3,053,594,109
Asset Allocation
Asset	%
Cash	1%
Stocks	0%
US Stocks	0%
Bonds	99%
US Bonds	94%
Other	0%

Services Offered:

Investment Strategy: The investment seeks to replicate as closely as possible, before fees and expenses, the price and yield performance of the Bloomberg Barclays Municipal Custom High Yield Composite Index. The fund normally invests at least 80% of its total assets in securities that comprise the benchmark index. The index is comprised of publicly traded municipal bonds that cover the U.S. dollar denominated high yield long-term tax-exempt bond market. **Top Holdings:** PUERTO RICO SALES TAX FING CORP SALES TAX REV 5%　NEW YORK LIBERTY DEV CORP LIBERTY REV 5%　PUBLIC FIN AUTH WIS LTD OBLIG PILOT REV 7%　BUCKEYE OHIO TOB SETTLEMENT FING AUTH 5.88%　BUCKEYE OHIO TOB SETTLEMENT FING AUTH 5.12%

VanEck Vectors J.P. Morgan EM Local Currency Bond ETF　　B-　　BUY

Ticker	Traded On	NAV	Total Assets ($)	Dividend Yield (TTM)	Turnover Ratio	Expense Ratio
EMLC	NYSE Arca	33.27	$4,797,671,392	6.44	36	0.3

Ratings
Reward	B
Risk	C+
Recent Upgrade/Downgrade	

Fund Information
Fund Type	Exchange Traded Funds
Category	Emerging Mkts Fixed Inc
Sub-Category	Emerging-Markets Local-Currency Bond
Prospectus Objective	Div Emerg Mkts
Inception Date	Jul-10
Open to New Investments	Y

Prices
Price (as of 9/30/2019)	33.00
52-Week High	35.17
52-Week Low	32.12

Total Returns (%)
3-Month	6-Month	1-Year	3-Year	5-Year
-2.80	1.85	7.90	108.53	94.33

3-Year Standard Deviation	10.08
Effective Duration	5.23

Valuation
Premium/Discount (1-Year Average)	-0.18

Company Information
Provider	VanEck
Manager/Tenure	Francis G. Rodilosso (7)
Website	http://www.vaneck.com
Address	Van Eck Associates Corporation 666 Third Avenue New York NY 10017 United States
Phone Number	800-826-1115

PERFORMANCE

Ratings History
Date	Overall Rating	Risk Rating	Reward Rating
Q3-19	B-	C+	B
Q4-18	B	C+	A
Q4-17	C	C	C
Q4-16	D+	D+	D
Q4-15	D	D	D

Asset & Performance History
Date	NAV	1-Year Total Return
2018	32.96	83.81
2017	18.96	13.98
2016	17.56	8.76
2015	17	-14.63
2014	21.06	-5.62
2013	23.57	-8.76

Total Assets: $4,797,671,392
Asset Allocation
Asset	%
Cash	1%
Stocks	0%
US Stocks	0%
Bonds	99%
US Bonds	0%
Other	0%

Services Offered:

Investment Strategy: The investment seeks to replicate as closely as possible, before fees and expenses, the price and yield performance of the J.P. Morgan GBI-EM Global Core Index. The fund normally invests at least 80% of its total assets in securities that comprise the fund's benchmark index. The index is comprised of bonds issued by emerging market governments and denominated in the local currency of the issuer. It may concentrate its investments in a particular industry or group of industries to the extent that the index concentrates in an industry or group of industries. The fund is non-diversified. **Top Holdings:** Brazil (Federative Republic) 10%　Dominican Republic 8.9%　Philippines (Republic Of) 6.25%　Uruguay (Republic of) 9.88%　Brazil (Federative Republic) 10%

VanEck Vectors Retail ETF

B- **BUY**

Ticker	Traded On	NAV	Total Assets ($)	Dividend Yield (TTM)	Turnover Ratio	Expense Ratio
RTH	NYSE Arca	114.49	$71,156,086	0.86	16	0.35

Ratings

Reward	B+
Risk	C
Recent Upgrade/Downgrade	Up

Fund Information

Fund Type	Exchange Traded Funds
Category	Consumer Goods & Svcs
Sub-Category	Consumer Cyclical
Prospectus Objective	Unaligned
Inception Date	Dec-11
Open to New Investments	Y

Prices

Price (as of 9/30/2019)	114.47
52-Week High	116.89
52-Week Low	87.33

Total Returns (%)

3-Month	6-Month	1-Year	3-Year	5-Year
4.23	8.23	3.87	53.35	98.97

3-Year Standard Deviation	15.28
Effective Duration	

Valuation

Premium/Discount (1-Year Average)	-0.01

Company Information

Provider	VanEck
Manager/Tenure	Hao-Hung (Peter) Liao (7), Guo Hua (Jason) Jin (1)
Website	http://www.vaneck.com
Address	Van Eck Associates Corporation 666 Third Avenue New York NY 10017 United States
Phone Number	800-826-1115

PERFORMANCE

Ratings History

Date	Overall Rating	Risk Rating	Reward Rating
Q3-19	B-	C	B+
Q4-18	C+	C-	B
Q4-17	B+	A	B
Q4-16	C+	C-	B
Q4-15	B	C+	B+

Asset & Performance History

Date	NAV	1-Year Total Return
2018	93.97	3.76
2017	91.31	22.22
2016	75.88	-0.6
2015	77.71	10.84
2014	71.7	18.31
2013	60.85	40.48

Total Assets: $71,156,086

Asset Allocation

Asset	%
Cash	0%
Stocks	100%
US Stocks	98%
Bonds	0%
US Bonds	0%
Other	0%

Services Offered:

Investment Strategy: The investment seeks to replicate as closely as possible, before fees and expenses, the price and yield performance of the MVIS® US Listed Retail 25 Index. The fund normally invests at least 80% of its total assets in securities that comprise the fund's benchmark index. To be initially eligible for the index, companies must generate at least 50% of their revenues from retail. Retail includes companies engaged primarily in retail distribution; wholesalers; online, direct mail and TV retailers; multi-line retailers; specialty retailers; and food and other staples retailers. The fund is non-diversified. **Top Holdings:** Amazon.com Inc The Home Depot Inc Walmart Inc Lowe's Companies Inc Costco Wholesale Corp

---

VanEck Vectors Russia ETF

B **BUY**

Ticker	Traded On	NAV	Total Assets ($)	Dividend Yield (TTM)	Turnover Ratio	Expense Ratio
RSX	NYSE Arca	22.84	$1,172,717,557	4.23	20	0.65

Ratings

Reward	B
Risk	B-
Recent Upgrade/Downgrade	

Fund Information

Fund Type	Exchange Traded Funds
Category	Equity Misc
Sub-Category	Miscellaneous Region
Prospectus Objective	Growth
Inception Date	Apr-07
Open to New Investments	Y

Prices

Price (as of 9/30/2019)	22.81
52-Week High	24.12
52-Week Low	18.44

Total Returns (%)

3-Month	6-Month	1-Year	3-Year	5-Year
-4.39	8.96	10.85	36.52	24.12

3-Year Standard Deviation	17.73
Effective Duration	

Valuation

Premium/Discount (1-Year Average)	-0.24

Company Information

Provider	VanEck
Manager/Tenure	Hao-Hung (Peter) Liao (12), Guo Hua (Jason) Jin (1)
Website	http://www.vaneck.com
Address	Van Eck Associates Corporation 666 Third Avenue New York NY 10017 United States
Phone Number	800-826-1115

PERFORMANCE

Ratings History

Date	Overall Rating	Risk Rating	Reward Rating
Q3-19	B	B-	B
Q4-18	C	C	C
Q4-17	B-	C	B
Q4-16	C-	D+	C-
Q4-15	D	D	D

Asset & Performance History

Date	NAV	1-Year Total Return
2018	18.79	-6.02
2017	21.14	4.57
2016	21.09	45.91
2015	14.69	0.31
2014	15.17	-44.9
2013	28.69	-0.63

Total Assets: $1,172,717,557

Asset Allocation

Asset	%
Cash	0%
Stocks	100%
US Stocks	0%
Bonds	0%
US Bonds	0%
Other	0%

Services Offered: Automatic Investment Plan, Retirement Investment

Investment Strategy: The investment seeks to replicate as closely as possible, before fees and expenses, the price and yield performance of the MVIS® Russia Index. The fund normally invests at least 80% of its total assets in securities that comprise the fund's benchmark index. The index includes securities, which may include depositary receipts, of Russian companies. A company is generally considered to be a Russian company if it is incorporated in Russia or is incorporated outside of Russia but has at least 50% of its revenues/related assets in Russia. Such companies may include medium-capitalization companies. It is non-diversified. **Top Holdings:** Gazprom PJSC ADR Sberbank of Russia PJSC ADR PJSC Lukoil ADR Tatneft PJSC ADR Mining and Metallurgical Company NORILSK NICKEL PJSC ADR

VanEck Vectors Semiconductor ETF

B-   BUY

Ticker	Traded On	NAV	Total Assets ($)	Dividend Yield (TTM)	Turnover Ratio	Expense Ratio
SMH	NYSE Arca	119.14	$1,360,736,581	1.37	23	0.35

Ratings

Reward	B
Risk	C
Recent Upgrade/Downgrade	Up

Fund Information

Fund Type	Exchange Traded Funds
Category	Technology Sector Equity
Sub-Category	Technology
Prospectus Objective	Technology
Inception Date	Dec-11
Open to New Investments	Y

Prices

Price (as of 9/30/2019)	119.13
52-Week High	123.31
52-Week Low	80.96

Total Returns (%)

3-Month	6-Month	1-Year	3-Year	5-Year
5.11	9.35	13.83	78.97	156.51

3-Year Standard Deviation	21.52
Effective Duration	

Valuation

Premium/Discount (1-Year Average)	0.05

Company Information

Provider	VanEck
Manager/Tenure	Hao-Hung (Peter) Liao (7), Guo Hua (Jason) Jin (1)
Website	http://www.vaneck.com
Address	Van Eck Associates Corporation 666 Third Avenue New York NY 10017 United States
Phone Number	800-826-1115

PERFORMANCE

Ratings History

Date	Overall Rating	Risk Rating	Reward Rating
Q3-19	B-	C	B
Q4-18	C+	C	B
Q4-17	B+	C+	A+
Q4-16	C+	C	C+
Q4-15	B	B	B

Asset & Performance History

Date	NAV	1-Year Total Return
2018	87.33	-9.46
2017	97.77	38.31
2016	71.68	35.4
2015	53.36	-0.11
2014	54.56	29.99
2013	42.45	33.7

Total Assets: $1,360,736,581

Asset Allocation

Asset	%
Cash	0%
Stocks	100%
US Stocks	74%
Bonds	0%
US Bonds	0%
Other	0%

Services Offered:

Investment Strategy: The investment seeks to replicate as closely as possible, before fees and expenses, the price and yield performance of the MVIS® US Listed Semiconductor 25 Index. The fund normally invests at least 80% of its total assets in securities that comprise the fund's benchmark index. The index includes common stocks and depositary receipts of U.S. exchange-listed companies in the semiconductor industry. Such companies may include medium-capitalization companies and foreign companies that are listed on a U.S. exchange. The fund is non-diversified. **Top Holdings:** Taiwan Semiconductor Manufacturing Co Ltd ADR   Intel Corp   Texas Instruments Inc   Micron Technology Inc   NVIDIA Corp

Vanguard Communication Services Index Fund ETF Shares

B-   BUY

Ticker	Traded On	NAV	Total Assets ($)	Dividend Yield (TTM)	Turnover Ratio	Expense Ratio
VOX	NYSE Arca	86.69	$2,134,380,301	0.93	84	0.1

Ratings

Reward	B
Risk	C
Recent Upgrade/Downgrade	Up

Fund Information

Fund Type	Exchange Traded Funds
Category	Communications Sector Equity
Sub-Category	Communications
Prospectus Objective	Comm
Inception Date	Sep-04
Open to New Investments	Y

Prices

Price (as of 9/30/2019)	86.70
52-Week High	91.54
52-Week Low	69.56

Total Returns (%)

3-Month	6-Month	1-Year	3-Year	5-Year
-0.80	2.55	0.67	-1.30	16.25

3-Year Standard Deviation	13.36
Effective Duration	

Valuation

Premium/Discount (1-Year Average)	-0.01

Company Information

Provider	Vanguard
Manager/Tenure	Walter Nejman (3), Awais Khan (1)
Website	http://www.vanguard.com
Address	Vanguard 100 Vanguard Boulevard Malvern PA 19355 United States
Phone Number	877-662-7447

PERFORMANCE

Ratings History

Date	Overall Rating	Risk Rating	Reward Rating
Q3-19	B-	C	B
Q4-18	C+	C-	B
Q4-17	C	C+	C
Q4-16	B-	C	B
Q4-15	C+	C	B-

Asset & Performance History

Date	NAV	1-Year Total Return
2018	73.75	-16.95
2017	90.96	-5.32
2016	100	22.3
2015	83.94	2.72
2014	84.73	3.98
2013	83.66	24.31

Total Assets: $2,134,380,301

Asset Allocation

Asset	%
Cash	1%
Stocks	99%
US Stocks	97%
Bonds	0%
US Bonds	0%
Other	0%

Services Offered:

Investment Strategy: The investment seeks to track the performance of a benchmark index. The fund employs an indexing investment approach designed to track the performance of the MSCI US Investable Market Index (IMI)/Communication Services 25/50, an index made up of stocks of large, mid-size, and small U.S. companies within the communication services sector, as classified under the GICS. The Advisor attempts to replicate the target index by seeking to invest all, or substantially all, of its assets in the stocks that make up the index, in order to hold each stock in approximately the same proportion as its weighting in the index. It is non-diversified. **Top Holdings:** Facebook Inc A   Alphabet Inc Class C   Alphabet Inc A   Verizon Communications Inc   AT&T Inc

Vanguard Consumer Staples Index Fund ETF Shares

B- BUY

Ticker	Traded On	NAV	Total Assets ($)	Dividend Yield (TTM)	Turnover Ratio	Expense Ratio
VDC	NYSE Arca	156.51	$6,131,467,784	2.51	8	0.1

Ratings

Reward	B
Risk	C
Recent Upgrade/Downgrade	Up

Fund Information

Fund Type	Exchange Traded Funds
Category	Consumer Goods & Svcs
Sub-Category	Consumer Defensive
Prospectus Objective	Unaligned
Inception Date	Jan-04
Open to New Investments	Y

Prices

Price (as of 9/30/2019)	156.56
52-Week High	157.18
52-Week Low	125.78

Total Returns (%)

3-Month	6-Month	1-Year	3-Year	5-Year
4.96	9.03	14.38	23.11	52.68

3-Year Standard Deviation	11.45
Effective Duration	

Valuation

Premium/Discount (1-Year Average)	0.00

Company Information

Provider	Vanguard
Manager/Tenure	Michael A. Johnson (8), Awais Khan (1)
Website	http://www.vanguard.com
Address	Vanguard 100 Vanguard Boulevard Malvern PA 19355 United States
Phone Number	877-662-7447

PERFORMANCE

Ratings History

Date	Overall Rating	Risk Rating	Reward Rating
Q3-19	B-	C	B
Q4-18	C+	C	B
Q4-17	B	A-	C+
Q4-16	B-	C+	B
Q4-15	B	C+	B

Asset & Performance History

Date	NAV	1-Year Total Return
2018	130.63	-8.12
2017	145.97	11.38
2016	133.98	5.6
2015	129.05	6
2014	125	15.78
2013	110.04	27.99

Total Assets: $6,131,467,784

Asset Allocation

Asset	%
Cash	0%
Stocks	100%
US Stocks	99%
Bonds	0%
US Bonds	0%
Other	0%

Services Offered:

Investment Strategy: The investment seeks to track the performance of a benchmark index. The fund employs an indexing investment approach designed to track the performance of the MSCI US Investable Market Index/Consumer Staples 25/50, an index made up of stocks of large, mid-size, and small U.S. companies within the consumer staples sector, as classified under the Global Industry Classification Standard. The Advisor attempts to replicate the target index by seeking to invest all, or substantially all, of its assets in the stocks that make up the index, in order to hold each stock in approximately the same proportion as its weighting in the index. The fund is non-diversified. **Top Holdings:** Procter & Gamble Co Coca-Cola Co PepsiCo Inc Walmart Inc Philip Morris International Inc

Vanguard Dividend Appreciation Index Fund ETF Shares

B- BUY

Ticker	Traded On	NAV	Total Assets ($)	Dividend Yield (TTM)	Turnover Ratio	Expense Ratio
VIG	NYSE Arca	119.50	$47,775,778,497	1.77	16	0.06

Ratings

Reward	B
Risk	C+
Recent Upgrade/Downgrade	

Fund Information

Fund Type	Exchange Traded Funds
Category	US Equity Large Cap Blend
Sub-Category	Large Blend
Prospectus Objective	Equity-Income
Inception Date	Apr-06
Open to New Investments	Y

Prices

Price (as of 9/30/2019)	119.58
52-Week High	120.84
52-Week Low	92.08

Total Returns (%)

3-Month	6-Month	1-Year	3-Year	5-Year
3.05	8.48	9.16	50.41	71.36

3-Year Standard Deviation	11.55
Effective Duration	

Valuation

Premium/Discount (1-Year Average)	-0.01

Company Information

Provider	Vanguard
Manager/Tenure	Walter Nejman (3), Gerard C. O'Reilly (3)
Website	http://www.vanguard.com
Address	Vanguard 100 Vanguard Boulevard Malvern PA 19355 United States
Phone Number	877-662-7447

PERFORMANCE

Ratings History

Date	Overall Rating	Risk Rating	Reward Rating
Q3-19	B-	C+	B
Q4-18	C+	C+	C
Q4-17	B	B+	B
Q4-16	B-	C+	B-
Q4-15	C+	C+	C+

Asset & Performance History

Date	NAV	1-Year Total Return
2018	96.92	-3.01
2017	101.93	22.06
2016	85.1	11.17
2015	77.78	-1.94
2014	81.18	10.05
2013	75.27	28.98

Total Assets: $47,775,778,497

Asset Allocation

Asset	%
Cash	0%
Stocks	100%
US Stocks	99%
Bonds	0%
US Bonds	0%
Other	0%

Services Offered:

Investment Strategy: The investment seeks to track the performance of a benchmark index that measures the investment return of common stocks of companies that have a record of increasing dividends over time. The fund employs an indexing investment approach designed to track the performance of the Nasdaq US Dividend Achievers Select Index, which consists of common stocks of companies that have a record of increasing dividends over time. The adviser attempts to replicate the target index by investing all, or substantially all, of its assets in the stocks that make up the index, holding each stock in approximately the same proportion as its weighting in the index. **Top Holdings:** Microsoft Corp Visa Inc Class A Procter & Gamble Co Walmart Inc Comcast Corp Class A

Vanguard Emerging Markets Government Bond Index Fund ETF Shares   B-   BUY

Ticker	Traded On	NAV	Total Assets ($)	Dividend Yield (TTM)	Turnover Ratio	Expense Ratio
VWOB	NAS CM	80.41	$1,789,228,125	4.54	25	0.3

Ratings
Reward   B
Risk   C+
Recent Upgrade/Downgrade

Fund Information
Fund Type   Exchange Traded Funds
Category   Emerging Mkts Fixed Inc
Sub-Category   Emerging Markets Bond
Prospectus Objective   Govt Bond - Gen
Inception Date   May-13
Open to New Investments   Y

Prices
Price (as of 9/30/2019)   80.60
52-Week High   81.56
52-Week Low   73.40

Total Returns (%)

3-Month	6-Month	1-Year	3-Year	5-Year
1.00	5.65	11.47	13.66	28.84

3-Year Standard Deviation   4.72
Effective Duration   7.60

Valuation
Premium/Discount (1-Year Average)   0.36

Company Information
Provider   Vanguard
Manager/Tenure   Joshua C. Barrickman (6)
Website   http://www.vanguard.com
Address   Vanguard 100 Vanguard Boulevard
                    Malvern PA 19355 United States
Phone Number   877-662-7447

PERFORMANCE

Ratings History

Date	Overall Rating	Risk Rating	Reward Rating
Q3-19	B-	C+	B
Q4-18	C	C+	C-
Q4-17	B	A	C+
Q4-16	C	C-	C
Q4-15	D+	C-	D+

Asset & Performance History

Date	NAV	1-Year Total Return
2018	74.28	-2.89
2017	79.97	8.48
2016	77.24	9.8
2015	73.69	1.58
2014	76.1	5.12
2013	75.63	

Total Assets: $1,789,228,125
Asset Allocation

Asset	%
Cash	0%
Stocks	0%
US Stocks	0%
Bonds	99%
US Bonds	0%
Other	0%

Services Offered:

Investment Strategy: The investment seeks to track the performance of a benchmark index that measures the investment return of U.S. dollar-denominated bonds issued by governments and government-related issuers in emerging market countries. The fund employs an indexing investment approach designed to track the performance of the Bloomberg Barclays USD Emerging Markets Government RIC Capped Index. All of the fund's investments will be selected through the sampling process, and under normal circumstances at least 80% of the fund's assets will be invested in bonds included in the index. It is non-diversified. **Top Holdings:** Qatar St 5.1% State of Qatar 4.82% Saudi Arabia (Kingdom Of) 4.5% Petrobras Global Finance B.V. 6% Petroleos Mexicanos 6.5%

Vanguard Growth Index Fund ETF Shares   B-   BUY

Ticker	Traded On	NAV	Total Assets ($)	Dividend Yield (TTM)	Turnover Ratio	Expense Ratio
VUG	NYSE Arca	166.35	$92,059,629,583	1.06	11	0.04

Ratings
Reward   B-
Risk   C+
Recent Upgrade/Downgrade   Up

Fund Information
Fund Type   Exchange Traded Funds
Category   US Equity Large Cap Growth
Sub-Category   Large Growth
Prospectus Objective   Growth
Inception Date   Jan-04
Open to New Investments   Y

Prices
Price (as of 9/30/2019)   166.28
52-Week High   170.26
52-Week Low   124.85

Total Returns (%)

3-Month	6-Month	1-Year	3-Year	5-Year
1.03	5.65	4.25	53.67	80.40

3-Year Standard Deviation   13.27
Effective Duration

Valuation
Premium/Discount (1-Year Average)   -0.03

Company Information
Provider   Vanguard
Manager/Tenure   Gerard C. O'Reilly (24), Walter Nejman
                    (3)
Website   http://www.vanguard.com
Address   Vanguard 100 Vanguard Boulevard
                    Malvern PA 19355 United States
Phone Number   877-662-7447

PERFORMANCE

Ratings History

Date	Overall Rating	Risk Rating	Reward Rating
Q3-19	B-	C+	B-
Q4-18	C	C+	C
Q4-17	B+	A-	B
Q4-16	B-	C+	B-
Q4-15	C+	C+	C+

Asset & Performance History

Date	NAV	1-Year Total Return
2018	133.04	-4.16
2017	140.55	27.7
2016	111.33	5.76
2015	106.4	3.31
2014	104.33	13.61
2013	92.99	32.37

Total Assets: $92,059,629,583
Asset Allocation

Asset	%
Cash	0%
Stocks	100%
US Stocks	99%
Bonds	0%
US Bonds	0%
Other	0%

Services Offered:

Investment Strategy: The investment seeks to track the performance of a benchmark index that measures the investment return of the CRSP US Large Cap Growth Index. The fund employs an indexing investment approach designed to track the performance of index, a broadly diversified index predominantly made up of growth stocks of large U.S. companies. The advisor attempts to replicate the target index by investing all, or substantially all, of its assets in the stocks that make up the index, holding each stock in approximately the same proportion as its weighting in the index. The fund is non-diversified. **Top Holdings:** Microsoft Corp Apple Inc Amazon.com Inc Facebook Inc A Alphabet Inc A

Vanguard Information Technology Index Fund ETF Shares

B-   BUY

Ticker	Traded On	NAV	Total Assets ($)	Dividend Yield (TTM)	Turnover Ratio	Expense Ratio
VGT	NYSE Arca	215.48	$23,769,348,271	1.26	7	0.1

Ratings
Reward   B
Risk   C+
Recent Upgrade/Downgrade   Down

Fund Information
Fund Type   Exchange Traded Funds
Category   Technology Sector Equity
Sub-Category   Technology
Prospectus Objective   Unaligned
Inception Date   Jan-04
Open to New Investments   Y

Prices
Price (as of 9/30/2019)   215.55
52-Week High   223.32
52-Week Low   154.81

Total Returns (%)

3-Month	6-Month	1-Year	3-Year	5-Year
0.03	5.51	6.46	83.56	128.70

3-Year Standard Deviation   15.93
Effective Duration

Valuation
Premium/Discount (1-Year Average)   -0.02

Company Information
Provider   Vanguard
Manager/Tenure   Walter Nejman (3), Michael A.
                               Johnson (1)
Website   http://www.vanguard.com
Address   Vanguard 100 Vanguard Boulevard
                               Malvern PA 19355 United States
Phone Number   877-662-7447

PERFORMANCE

Ratings History

Date	Overall Rating	Risk Rating	Reward Rating
Q3-19	B-	C+	B
Q4-18	C+	C+	C+
Q4-17	A-	B	A+
Q4-16	C+	C+	C+
Q4-15	B-	B-	B-

Asset & Performance History

Date	NAV	1-Year Total Return
2018	165.24	1.53
2017	164.64	36.62
2016	121.44	13.22
2015	108.27	5.02
2014	104.48	18.01
2013	89.52	30.91

Total Assets: $23,769,348,271
Asset Allocation

Asset	%
Cash	1%
Stocks	99%
US Stocks	99%
Bonds	0%
US Bonds	0%
Other	0%

Services Offered:

Investment Strategy: The investment seeks to track the performance of a benchmark index. The fund employs an indexing investment approach designed to track the performance of the MSCI US Investable Market Index/Information Technology 25/50, an index made up of stocks of large, mid-size, and small U.S. companies within the information technology sector, as classified under the Global Industry Classification Standard. The Advisor attempts to replicate the target index by seeking to invest all, or substantially all, of its assets in the stocks that make up the index, in order to hold each stock in approximately the same proportion as its weighting in the index. It is non-diversified. **Top Holdings:** Apple Inc   Microsoft Corp   Visa Inc Class A   Mastercard Inc A   Cisco Systems Inc

Vanguard Long-Term Corporate Bond Index Fund ETF Shares

B-   BUY

Ticker	Traded On	NAV	Total Assets ($)	Dividend Yield (TTM)	Turnover Ratio	Expense Ratio
VCLT	NAS CM	100.93	$4,732,399,516	3.88	48	0.07

Ratings
Reward   B
Risk   C+
Recent Upgrade/Downgrade

Fund Information
Fund Type   Exchange Traded Funds
Category   US Fixed Income
Sub-Category   Long-Term Bond
Prospectus Objective   Corp Bond - Gen
Inception Date   Nov-09
Open to New Investments   Y

Prices
Price (as of 9/30/2019)   101.14
52-Week High   103.47
52-Week Low   83.50

Total Returns (%)

3-Month	6-Month	1-Year	3-Year	5-Year
5.58	12.86	19.93	20.12	39.51

3-Year Standard Deviation   7.73
Effective Duration   14.36

Valuation
Premium/Discount (1-Year Average)   0.22

Company Information
Provider   Vanguard
Manager/Tenure   Joshua C. Barrickman (9)
Website   http://www.vanguard.com
Address   Vanguard 100 Vanguard Boulevard
                               Malvern PA 19355 United States
Phone Number   877-662-7447

PERFORMANCE

Ratings History

Date	Overall Rating	Risk Rating	Reward Rating
Q3-19	B-	C+	B
Q4-18	C-	C	D+
Q4-17	B-	B	B-
Q4-16	C	C+	C
Q4-15	C	C	C

Asset & Performance History

Date	NAV	1-Year Total Return
2018	84.83	-7.21
2017	95.55	12.48
2016	88.62	10.6
2015	83.65	-4.62
2014	91.71	16.74
2013	82.13	-5.92

Total Assets: $4,732,399,516
Asset Allocation

Asset	%
Cash	0%
Stocks	0%
US Stocks	0%
Bonds	99%
US Bonds	89%
Other	0%

Services Offered:

Investment Strategy: The investment seeks to track the performance of a market-weighted corporate bond index with a long-term dollar-weighted average maturity. The fund employs an indexing investment approach designed to track the performance of the Bloomberg Barclays U.S. 10+ Year Corporate Bond Index. This index includes U.S. dollar-denominated, investment-grade, fixed-rate, taxable securities issued by industrial, utility, and financial companies, with maturities greater than 10 years. Under normal circumstances, at least 80% of the fund's assets will be invested in bonds included in the index. **Top Holdings:** Anheuser-Busch Companies LLC / Anheuser-Busch InBev Worldwide Inc 4.9%   GE Capital International Funding Company Unlimited Company 4.42%   CVS Health Corp 5.05%   Goldman Sachs Group, Inc. 6.75%   Anheuser-Busch Companies LLC / Anheuser-Busch InBev Worldwide Inc 4.7%

Vanguard Mega Cap Growth Index Fund ETF Shares   B-   BUY

Ticker	Traded On	NAV	Total Assets ($)	Dividend Yield (TTM)	Turnover Ratio	Expense Ratio
MGK	NYSE Arca	132.63	$4,508,122,602	0.47	9	0.07

Ratings

Reward	B
Risk	C+
Recent Upgrade/Downgrade	Up

Fund Information

Fund Type	Exchange Traded Funds
Category	US Equity Large Cap Growth
Sub-Category	Large Growth
Prospectus Objective	Growth
Inception Date	Dec-07
Open to New Investments	Y

Prices

Price (as of 9/30/2019)	132.66
52-Week High	135.16
52-Week Low	99.52

Total Returns (%)

3-Month	6-Month	1-Year	3-Year	5-Year
0.71	5.07	2.88	55.40	80.04

3-Year Standard Deviation	13.35
Effective Duration	

Valuation

Premium/Discount (1-Year Average)	-0.01

Company Information

Provider	Vanguard
Manager/Tenure	Gerard C. O'Reilly (4), Michael A. Johnson (3)
Website	http://www.vanguard.com
Address	Vanguard 100 Vanguard Boulevard Malvern PA 19355 United States
Phone Number	877-662-7447

PERFORMANCE

Ratings History

Date	Overall Rating	Risk Rating	Reward Rating
Q3-19	B-	C+	B
Q4-18	C	C+	C
Q4-17	B	B	B
Q4-16	C+	C-	B-
Q4-15	C+	B-	C+

Asset & Performance History

Date	NAV	1-Year Total Return
2018	106.03	-3.67
2017	111.2	29.26
2016	87.02	6.03
2015	83.07	3.71
2014	81.24	13.65
2013	72.42	32.48

Total Assets: $4,508,122,602

Asset Allocation

Asset	%
Cash	0%
Stocks	100%
US Stocks	99%
Bonds	0%
US Bonds	0%
Other	0%

Services Offered:

Investment Strategy: The investment seeks to track the performance of the CRSP US Mega Cap Growth Index. The fund employs an indexing investment approach designed to track the performance of the index. The index is a float-adjusted, market-capitalization-weighted index designed to measure equity market performance of mega-capitalization growth stocks in the United States. The Advisor attempts to replicate the target index by investing all, or substantially all, of its assets in the stocks that make up the index, holding each stock in approximately the same proportion as its weighting in the index. The fund is non-diversified. **Top Holdings:** Microsoft Corp Apple Inc Amazon.com Inc Facebook Inc A Alphabet Inc A

Vanguard Real Estate Index Fund ETF Shares   B-   BUY

Ticker	Traded On	NAV	Total Assets ($)	Dividend Yield (TTM)	Turnover Ratio	Expense Ratio
VNQ	NYSE Arca	93.26	$69,464,761,255	3.12	24	0.12

Ratings

Reward	C+
Risk	B-
Recent Upgrade/Downgrade	Up

Fund Information

Fund Type	Exchange Traded Funds
Category	Real Estate Sector Equity
Sub-Category	Real Estate
Prospectus Objective	Real Estate
Inception Date	Sep-04
Open to New Investments	Y

Prices

Price (as of 9/30/2019)	93.25
52-Week High	93.92
52-Week Low	71.74

Total Returns (%)

3-Month	6-Month	1-Year	3-Year	5-Year
7.64	9.27	20.97	22.70	60.39

3-Year Standard Deviation	12.88
Effective Duration	

Valuation

Premium/Discount (1-Year Average)	-0.01

Company Information

Provider	Vanguard
Manager/Tenure	Gerard C. O'Reilly (23), Walter Nejman (3)
Website	http://www.vanguard.com
Address	Vanguard 100 Vanguard Boulevard Malvern PA 19355 United States
Phone Number	877-662-7447

PERFORMANCE

Ratings History

Date	Overall Rating	Risk Rating	Reward Rating
Q3-19	B-	B-	C+
Q4-18	C+	B	C
Q4-17	B-	B	C+
Q4-16	C+	B-	C+
Q4-15	C+	B-	C+

Asset & Performance History

Date	NAV	1-Year Total Return
2018	74.44	-6.13
2017	82.94	6.31
2016	82.46	6.32
2015	79.72	2.36
2014	81.03	30.29
2013	64.62	2.41

Total Assets: $69,464,761,255

Asset Allocation

Asset	%
Cash	1%
Stocks	99%
US Stocks	99%
Bonds	0%
US Bonds	0%
Other	0%

Services Offered:

Investment Strategy: The investment seeks to provide a high level of income and moderate long-term capital appreciation by tracking the performance of the MSCI US Investable Market Real Estate 25/50 Index that measures the performance of publicly traded equity REITs and other real estate-related investments. The advisor attempts to track the index by investing all, or substantially all, of its assets-either directly or indirectly through a wholly owned subsidiary, which is itself a registered investment company-in the stocks that make up the index, holding each stock in approximately the same proportion as its weighting in the index. The fund is non-diversified. **Top Holdings:** Vanguard Real Estate II Index American Tower Corp Crown Castle International Corp Prologis Inc Simon Property Group Inc

Vanguard S&P 500 ETF   B-   BUY

Ticker	Traded On	NAV	Total Assets ($)	Dividend Yield (TTM)	Turnover Ratio	Expense Ratio
VOO	NYSE Arca	272.60	$493,907,000,000	1.99	4	0.03

Ratings
Reward   C+
Risk   B
Recent Upgrade/Downgrade

Fund Information
Fund Type	Exchange Traded Funds
Category	US Equity Large Cap Blend
Sub-Category	Large Blend
Prospectus Objective	Growth
Inception Date	Sep-10
Open to New Investments	Y

Prices
Price (as of 9/30/2019)	272.60
52-Week High	277.38
52-Week Low	215.07

Total Returns (%)
3-Month	6-Month	1-Year	3-Year	5-Year
0.92	4.85	3.87	45.66	69.21

3-Year Standard Deviation	12.18
Effective Duration	

Valuation
Premium/Discount (1-Year Average)	-0.03

Company Information
Provider	Vanguard
Manager/Tenure	Donald M. Butler (3), Michelle Louie (1)
Website	http://www.vanguard.com
Address	Vanguard 100 Vanguard Boulevard Malvern PA 19355 United States
Phone Number	877-662-7447

PERFORMANCE

Ratings History

Date	Overall Rating	Risk Rating	Reward Rating
Q3-19	B-	B	C+
Q4-18	C+	B	C
Q4-17	B	B	B
Q4-16	B-	C+	B
Q4-15	C+	C+	C

Asset & Performance History

Date	NAV	1-Year Total Return
2018	227.72	-5.23
2017	244.94	21.84
2016	205	11.39
2015	187.05	1.35
2014	188.45	13.63
2013	169.07	32.33

Total Assets: $493,907,000,000

Asset Allocation

Asset	%
Cash	0%
Stocks	100%
US Stocks	99%
Bonds	0%
US Bonds	0%
Other	0%

Services Offered:

Investment Strategy: The investment seeks to track the performance of a benchmark index that measures the investment return of large-capitalization stocks. The fund employs an indexing investment approach designed to track the performance of the Standard & Poor's 500 Index, a widely recognized benchmark of U.S. stock market performance that is dominated by the stocks of large U.S. companies. The advisor attempts to replicate the target index by investing all, or substantially all, of its assets in the stocks that make up the index, holding each stock in approximately the same proportion as its weighting in the index. **Top Holdings:** Microsoft Corp   Apple Inc   Amazon.com Inc   Facebook Inc A   Berkshire Hathaway Inc B

Vanguard Total Bond Market Index Fund ETF Shares   B-   BUY

Ticker	Traded On	NAV	Total Assets ($)	Dividend Yield (TTM)	Turnover Ratio	Expense Ratio
BND	NAS CM	84.41	$241,309,000,000	2.74	54	0.04

Ratings
Reward   C+
Risk   B
Recent Upgrade/Downgrade

Fund Information
Fund Type	Exchange Traded Funds
Category	US Fixed Income
Sub-Category	Intermediate Core Bond
Prospectus Objective	Income
Inception Date	Apr-07
Open to New Investments	Y

Prices
Price (as of 9/30/2019)	84.43
52-Week High	85.16
52-Week Low	77.49

Total Returns (%)
3-Month	6-Month	1-Year	3-Year	5-Year
2.43	5.50	10.59	8.92	17.29

3-Year Standard Deviation	3.44
Effective Duration	6.20

Valuation
Premium/Discount (1-Year Average)	0.05

Company Information
Provider	Vanguard
Manager/Tenure	Joshua C. Barrickman (6)
Website	http://www.vanguard.com
Address	Vanguard 100 Vanguard Boulevard Malvern PA 19355 United States
Phone Number	877-662-7447

PERFORMANCE

Ratings History

Date	Overall Rating	Risk Rating	Reward Rating
Q3-19	B-	B	C+
Q4-18	C	C+	D+
Q4-17	B-	A-	C
Q4-16	C	C+	C
Q4-15	C	C+	C

Asset & Performance History

Date	NAV	1-Year Total Return
2018	79.01	-0.23
2017	81.46	3.62
2016	80.64	2.5
2015	80.58	0.38
2014	82.33	5.95
2013	79.91	-2.14

Total Assets: $241,309,000,000

Asset Allocation

Asset	%
Cash	2%
Stocks	0%
US Stocks	0%
Bonds	98%
US Bonds	90%
Other	0%

Services Offered:

Investment Strategy: The investment seeks the performance of Bloomberg Barclays U.S. Aggregate Float Adjusted Index. Bloomberg Barclays U.S. Aggregate Float Adjusted Index represents a wide spectrum of public, investment-grade, taxable, fixed income securities in the United States-including government, corporate, and international dollar-denominated bonds, as well as mortgage-backed and asset-backed securities-all with maturities of more than 1 year. All of its investments will be selected through the sampling process, and at least 80% of its assets will be invested in bonds held in the index. **Top Holdings:** United States Treasury Notes 2.38% Federal National Mortgage Association 3.5%   United States Treasury Notes 2.88%   United States Treasury Notes 2.12%   United States Treasury Notes 2.12%

Vanguard Total International Bond Index Fund ETF Shares   B-   BUY

Ticker	Traded On	NAV	Total Assets ($)	Dividend Yield (TTM)	Turnover Ratio	Expense Ratio
BNDX	NAS CM	58.72	$140,100,000,000	2.85	22	0.09

Ratings
Reward	B-
Risk	C+
Recent Upgrade/Downgrade	Up

Fund Information
Fund Type	Exchange Traded Funds
Category	Global Fixed Income
Sub-Category	World Bond-USD Hedged
Prospectus Objective	Worldwide Bond
Inception Date	May-13
Open to New Investments	Y

Prices
Price (as of 9/30/2019)	58.83
52-Week High	59.22
52-Week Low	54.09

Total Returns (%)

3-Month	6-Month	1-Year	3-Year	5-Year
3.06	6.06	11.36	12.93	24.95

3-Year Standard Deviation	2.74
Effective Duration	8.41

Valuation
Premium/Discount (1-Year Average)	0.16

Company Information
Provider	Vanguard
Manager/Tenure	Joshua C. Barrickman (6)
Website	http://www.vanguard.com
Address	Vanguard 100 Vanguard Boulevard Malvern PA 19355 United States
Phone Number	877-662-7447

PERFORMANCE

Ratings History

Date	Overall Rating	Risk Rating	Reward Rating
Q3-19	B-	C+	B-
Q4-18	C	C+	C
Q4-17	B	A	C
Q4-16	C	C+	C
Q4-15	C	C+	C-

Asset & Performance History

Date	NAV	1-Year Total Return
2018	54.14	2.96
2017	54.19	2.28
2016	54.11	4.82
2015	52.68	1.07
2014	52.97	8.83
2013	49.45	

Total Assets: $140,100,000,000

Asset Allocation

Asset	%
Cash	0%
Stocks	0%
US Stocks	0%
Bonds	99%
US Bonds	3%
Other	0%

Services Offered:

Investment Strategy: The investment seeks to track the performance of a benchmark index that measures the investment return of non-U.S. dollar-denominated investment-grade bonds. The fund employs an indexing investment approach designed to track the performance of the Bloomberg Barclays Global Aggregate ex-USD Float Adjusted RIC Capped Index (USD Hedged). This index provides a broad-based measure of the global, investment-grade, fixed-rate debt markets. It is non-diversified. **Top Holdings:** Germany (Federal Republic Of) 0.25% France(Govt Of) 1.75%   Italy (Republic Of) 2.45%   Italy (Republic Of) 2.1%   France(Govt Of) 0.75%

Vanguard Utilities Index Fund ETF Shares   B   BUY

Ticker	Traded On	NAV	Total Assets ($)	Dividend Yield (TTM)	Turnover Ratio	Expense Ratio
VPU	NYSE Arca	143.61	$5,716,549,067	2.81	4	0.1

Ratings
Reward	B
Risk	C+
Recent Upgrade/Downgrade	

Fund Information
Fund Type	Exchange Traded Funds
Category	Utilities Sector Equity
Sub-Category	Utilities
Prospectus Objective	Utility
Inception Date	Jan-04
Open to New Investments	Y

Prices
Price (as of 9/30/2019)	143.65
52-Week High	144.54
52-Week Low	114.71

Total Returns (%)

3-Month	6-Month	1-Year	3-Year	5-Year
9.08	12.37	25.87	47.41	84.91

3-Year Standard Deviation	10.3
Effective Duration	

Valuation
Premium/Discount (1-Year Average)	-0.01

Company Information
Provider	Vanguard
Manager/Tenure	Michael A. Johnson (4), Awais Khan (1)
Website	http://www.vanguard.com
Address	Vanguard 100 Vanguard Boulevard Malvern PA 19355 United States
Phone Number	877-662-7447

PERFORMANCE

Ratings History

Date	Overall Rating	Risk Rating	Reward Rating
Q3-19	B	C+	B
Q4-18	B-	C+	B-
Q4-17	B	B	B
Q4-16	B-	C+	B
Q4-15	B-	C+	B

Asset & Performance History

Date	NAV	1-Year Total Return
2018	117.5	4.09
2017	116.57	11.94
2016	106.94	16.84
2015	93.93	-4.83
2014	102.36	26.92
2013	83.33	14.93

Total Assets: $5,716,549,067

Asset Allocation

Asset	%
Cash	0%
Stocks	100%
US Stocks	100%
Bonds	0%
US Bonds	0%
Other	0%

Services Offered:

Investment Strategy: The investment seeks to track the performance of a benchmark index. The fund employs an indexing investment approach designed to track the performance of the MSCI US Investable Market Index (IMI)/Utilities 25/50, an index made up of stocks of large, mid-size, and small U.S. companies within the utilities sector, as classified under the Global Industry Classification Standard (GICS). The Advisor attempts to replicate the target index by seeking to invest all, or substantially all, of its assets in the stocks that make up the index, in order to hold each stock in approximately the same proportion as its weighting in the index. The fund is non-diversified.
Top Holdings: NextEra Energy Inc Duke Energy Corp Dominion Energy Inc Southern Co Exelon Corp

VelocityShares 3x Long Gold ETN Linked to the S&P GSCI® Gold Index ER   B   BUY

Ticker	Traded On	NAV	Total Assets ($)	Dividend Yield (TTM)	Turnover Ratio	Expense Ratio
UGLD	NAS CM	130.76	$169,540,817	0		1.35

Ratings

Reward	A-
Risk	C-
Recent Upgrade/Downgrade	Up

Fund Information

Fund Type	Exchange Traded Funds
Category	Trading Tools
Sub-Category	Trading--Leveraged Commodities
Prospectus Objective	Prec Metals
Inception Date	Oct-11
Open to New Investments	Y

Prices

Price (as of 9/30/2019)	132.67
52-Week High	157.03
52-Week Low	77.90

Total Returns (%)

3-Month	6-Month	1-Year	3-Year	5-Year
14.59	38.67	67.91	916.04	940.29

3-Year Standard Deviation	33.25
Effective Duration	

Valuation

Premium/Discount (1-Year Average)	0.05

Company Information

Provider	Credit Suisse AG
Manager/Tenure	Management Team (7)
Website	
Address	Kilmore House Park Lane Dublin Ireland
Phone Number	

PERFORMANCE

Ratings History

Date	Overall Rating	Risk Rating	Reward Rating
Q3-19	B	C-	A-
Q4-18	B	D+	A-
Q4-17	D+	D	C-
Q4-16	D	D	D+
Q4-15	E+	D-	E+

Asset & Performance History

Date	NAV	1-Year Total Return
2018	94.74	742.64
2017	11.24	28.67
2016	8.36	15.48
2015	7.37	-34.6
2014	11.27	-11.95
2013	12.8	-69.52

Total Assets: $169,540,817

Asset Allocation

Asset	%
Cash	%
Stocks	%
US Stocks	%
Bonds	%
US Bonds	%
Other	%

Services Offered:

Investment Strategy: The investment seeks to replicate, net of expenses, three times the S&P GSCI Gold index ER. The index comprises futures contracts on a single commodity. The fluctuations in the values of it are intended generally to correlate with changes in the price of gold in global markets. **Top Holdings:**

VelocityShares 3x Long Silver ETN Linked to the S&P GSCI® Silver Index ER   B   BUY

Ticker	Traded On	NAV	Total Assets ($)	Dividend Yield (TTM)	Turnover Ratio	Expense Ratio
USLV	NAS CM	82.34	$278,667,025	0		1.65

Ratings

Reward	A-
Risk	D+
Recent Upgrade/Downgrade	Up

Fund Information

Fund Type	Exchange Traded Funds
Category	Trading Tools
Sub-Category	Trading--Leveraged Commodities
Prospectus Objective	Prec Metals
Inception Date	Oct-11
Open to New Investments	Y

Prices

Price (as of 9/30/2019)	83.51
52-Week High	132.23
52-Week Low	54.70

Total Returns (%)

3-Month	6-Month	1-Year	3-Year	5-Year
29.16	25.22	30.35	275.82	194.18

3-Year Standard Deviation	52.64
Effective Duration	

Valuation

Premium/Discount (1-Year Average)	0.02

Company Information

Provider	Credit Suisse AG
Manager/Tenure	Management Team (7)
Website	
Address	Kilmore House Park Lane Dublin Ireland
Phone Number	

PERFORMANCE

Ratings History

Date	Overall Rating	Risk Rating	Reward Rating
Q3-19	B	D+	A-
Q4-18	B-	D+	A-
Q4-17	D-	D-	D-
Q4-16	D	D-	D
Q4-15	E	E+	E

Asset & Performance History

Date	NAV	1-Year Total Return
2018	74.1	521.72
2017	11.92	-4.04
2016	11.44	21.31
2015	9.76	-47.55
2014	18.61	-58.52
2013	44.87	-82.54

Total Assets: $278,667,025

Asset Allocation

Asset	%
Cash	%
Stocks	%
US Stocks	%
Bonds	%
US Bonds	%
Other	%

Services Offered:

Investment Strategy: The investment seeks to replicate, net of expenses, three times the S&P GSCI Silver index ER. The index comprises futures contracts on a single commodity. The fluctuations in the values of it are intended generally to correlate with changes in the price of silver in global markets. **Top Holdings:**

Vesper U.S. Large Cap Short-Term Reversal Strategy ETF   B-   BUY

Ticker	Traded On	NAV	Total Assets ($)	Dividend Yield (TTM)	Turnover Ratio	Expense Ratio
UTRN	NYSE Arca	26.27	$31,522,329	0.58		0.75

Ratings

Reward	B
Risk	C
Recent Upgrade/Downgrade	

Fund Information

Fund Type	Exchange Traded Funds
Category	US Equity Large Cap Blend
Sub-Category	Large Blend
Prospectus Objective	Growth & Inc
Inception Date	Sep-18
Open to New Investments	Y

Prices

Price (as of 9/30/2019)	26.31
52-Week High	26.71
52-Week Low	20.20

Total Returns (%)

3-Month	6-Month	1-Year	3-Year	5-Year
1.58	2.05	7.07		

3-Year Standard Deviation	
Effective Duration	

Valuation

Premium/Discount (1-Year Average)	0.08

Company Information

Provider	Exchange Traded Concepts
Manager/Tenure	Andrew Serowik (1), Travis E. Trampe (1)
Website	
Address	10900 Hefner Pointe Drive, Suite 207, Oklahoma City, Oklahoma 73120 Oklahoma City United States
Phone Number	

PERFORMANCE

Ratings History

Date	Overall Rating	Risk Rating	Reward Rating
Q3-19	B-	C	B
Q4-18	U		
Q4-17			
Q4-16			
Q4-15			

Asset & Performance History

Date	NAV	1-Year Total Return
2018	21.36	
2017		
2016		
2015		
2014		
2013		

Total Assets: $31,522,329

Asset Allocation

Asset	%
Cash	0%
Stocks	100%
US Stocks	96%
Bonds	0%
US Bonds	0%
Other	0%

Services Offered:

Investment Strategy: The investment seeks to provide investment results that, before fees and expenses, correspond generally to the total return performance of the Vesper U.S. Large Cap Short-Term Reversal Index (the "index"). The fund will normally invest at least 80% of its total assets in securities of the index. The index is designed to measure the performance of a portfolio of 25 stocks selected from the S&P 500 that Vesper Capital Management, LLC believes will most likely benefit from the "short-term reversal" effect, as determined by applying a proprietary algorithm ("Chow's Ratio" or "Algorithm"). **Top Holdings:** Eaton Corp PLC General Dynamics Corp Roper Technologies Inc Emerson Electric Co FLIR Systems Inc

---

Virtus Reaves Utilities ETF   B-   BUY

Ticker	Traded On	NAV	Total Assets ($)	Dividend Yield (TTM)	Turnover Ratio	Expense Ratio
UTES	NYSE Arca	41.70	$27,107,007	1.82	28	0.49

Ratings

Reward	B
Risk	C+
Recent Upgrade/Downgrade	Up

Fund Information

Fund Type	Exchange Traded Funds
Category	Utilities Sector Equity
Sub-Category	Utilities
Prospectus Objective	Utility
Inception Date	Sep-15
Open to New Investments	Y

Prices

Price (as of 9/30/2019)	41.83
52-Week High	41.83
52-Week Low	32.64

Total Returns (%)

3-Month	6-Month	1-Year	3-Year	5-Year
8.78	13.41	26.63	48.62	

3-Year Standard Deviation	10.42
Effective Duration	

Valuation

Premium/Discount (1-Year Average)	0.12

Company Information

Provider	Virtus
Manager/Tenure	John P. Bartlett (4), Joseph (Jay) Rhame (4)
Website	http://www.virtus.com
Address	Virtus Opportunities Trust 101 Munson Street Greenfield MA 1301 United States
Phone Number	800-243-1574

PERFORMANCE

Ratings History

Date	Overall Rating	Risk Rating	Reward Rating
Q3-19	B-	C+	B
Q4-18	B	C+	B
Q4-17	C	B	C
Q4-16	D	C+	B
Q4-15			

Asset & Performance History

Date	NAV	1-Year Total Return
2018	33.58	5.42
2017	32.53	12.86
2016	29.48	14.83
2015	26.36	
2014		
2013		

Total Assets: $27,107,007

Asset Allocation

Asset	%
Cash	4%
Stocks	96%
US Stocks	93%
Bonds	0%
US Bonds	0%
Other	0%

Services Offered:

Investment Strategy: The investment seeks to provide total return through a combination of capital appreciation and income. The fund invests not less than 80% of its net assets (plus the amount of any borrowings for investment purposes) in equity securities of companies in the Utility Sector ("Utility Sector Companies"). The manager considers a company to be a "Utility Sector Company" if at least 50% of the company's assets or customers are committed to, or at least 50% of the company's revenues, gross income or profits derive from, the provision of products, services or equipment for the generation or distribution of electricity, gas or water. The fund is non-diversified. **Top Holdings:** NextEra Energy Inc Sempra Energy NextEra Energy Partners LP DTE Energy Co NiSource Inc

WBI BullBear Quality 1000 ETF   B-   BUY

Ticker	Traded On	NAV	Total Assets ($)	Dividend Yield (TTM)	Turnover Ratio	Expense Ratio
WBIL	NYSE Arca	26.69	$53,388,923	0.66	477	1.07

Ratings

Reward	B
Risk	C
Recent Upgrade/Downgrade	Up

Fund Information

Fund Type	Exchange Traded Funds
Category	US Equity Large Cap Blend
Sub-Category	Large Blend
Prospectus Objective	Growth & Inc
Inception Date	Aug-14
Open to New Investments	Y

Prices

Price (as of 9/30/2019)	26.68
52-Week High	28.27
52-Week Low	24.58

Total Returns (%)

3-Month	6-Month	1-Year	3-Year	5-Year
-2.31	0.95	-5.07	27.81	12.09

3-Year Standard Deviation	11.51
Effective Duration	

Valuation

Premium/Discount (1-Year Average)	-0.06

Company Information

Provider	WBI Investments
Manager/Tenure	Donald R. Schreiber (5), Steven Van Solkema (0)
Website	http://www.wbishares.com
Address	34 Sycamore Ave Suite 1-E Little Silver NJ 07739 United States
Phone Number	732-842-4920

PERFORMANCE

Ratings History

Date	Overall Rating	Risk Rating	Reward Rating
Q3-19	B-	C	B
Q4-18	C	C-	C
Q4-17	C+	C+	C+
Q4-16	C	C	B
Q4-15	D-	B-	B

Asset & Performance History

Date	NAV	1-Year Total Return
2018	24.63	-9.39
2017	27.41	19
2016	23.24	4.05
2015	22.42	-7.14
2014	24.19	
2013		

Total Assets: $53,388,923

Asset Allocation

Asset	%
Cash	1%
Stocks	99%
US Stocks	99%
Bonds	0%
US Bonds	0%
Other	0%

Services Offered:

Investment Strategy: The investment seeks long-term capital appreciation and the potential for current income, while also seeking to protect principal during unfavorable market conditions. The fund will seek to invest in the equity securities of large capitalization domestic and foreign companies that WBI Investments, Inc., the sub-advisor ("Sub-Advisor") to the fund and an affiliate of Millington Securities Inc., the advisor ("Advisor"), believes display an attractive financial condition and prospects for ongoing financial stability, and in other tactical investment opportunities. It may invest up to 50% of its net assets in the securities of issuers in emerging markets. **Top Holdings:** Target Corp Texas Instruments Inc PayPal Holdings Inc Hormel Foods Corp S&P Global Inc

---

WBI BullBear Rising Income 1000 ETF   B   BUY

Ticker	Traded On	NAV	Total Assets ($)	Dividend Yield (TTM)	Turnover Ratio	Expense Ratio
WBIE	NYSE Arca	27.19	$58,463,232	0.9	512	1.05

Ratings

Reward	B
Risk	C
Recent Upgrade/Downgrade	Up

Fund Information

Fund Type	Exchange Traded Funds
Category	US Equity Large Cap Growth
Sub-Category	Large Growth
Prospectus Objective	Growth & Inc
Inception Date	Aug-14
Open to New Investments	Y

Prices

Price (as of 9/30/2019)	27.19
52-Week High	28.12
52-Week Low	24.97

Total Returns (%)

3-Month	6-Month	1-Year	3-Year	5-Year
1.19	4.08	-2.18	28.90	16.87

3-Year Standard Deviation	10.79
Effective Duration	

Valuation

Premium/Discount (1-Year Average)	-0.05

Company Information

Provider	WBI Investments
Manager/Tenure	Donald R. Schreiber (5), Steven Van Solkema (0)
Website	http://www.wbishares.com
Address	34 Sycamore Ave Suite 1-E Little Silver NJ 07739 United States
Phone Number	732-842-4920

PERFORMANCE

Ratings History

Date	Overall Rating	Risk Rating	Reward Rating
Q3-19	B	C	B
Q4-18	C	C	C
Q4-17	C+	C+	C
Q4-16	C	C	B
Q4-15	D-	B-	B

Asset & Performance History

Date	NAV	1-Year Total Return
2018	24.99	-2.86
2017	25.97	16.55
2016	22.4	-2.67
2015	23.04	-7.29
2014	25.09	
2013		

Total Assets: $58,463,232

Asset Allocation

Asset	%
Cash	1%
Stocks	99%
US Stocks	99%
Bonds	0%
US Bonds	0%
Other	0%

Services Offered:

Investment Strategy: The investment seeks long-term capital appreciation and the potential for current income, while also seeking to protect principal during unfavorable market conditions. The fund will seek to invest in the equity securities of large capitalization domestic and foreign companies. These securities will be selected on the basis of the Sub-Advisor's proprietary selection process ("Selection Process"). Cash and cash equivalents are some of the investment opportunities evaluated by the Selection Process. It may invest up to 50% of its net assets in the securities of issuers in emerging markets. **Top Holdings:** Tyson Foods Inc Class A Motorola Solutions Inc Northrop Grumman Corp Amgen Inc NextEra Energy Inc

---

WBI BullBear Rising Income 2000 ETF   B-   BUY

Ticker	Traded On	NAV	Total Assets ($)	Dividend Yield (TTM)	Turnover Ratio	Expense Ratio
WBIA	NYSE Arca	21.54	$7,539,709	0.85	718	1.08

Ratings
Reward	B
Risk	C
Recent Upgrade/Downgrade	Up

Fund Information
Fund Type	Exchange Traded Funds
Category	US Equity Mid Cap
Sub-Category	Mid-Cap Blend
Prospectus Objective	Growth & Inc
Inception Date	Aug-14
Open to New Investments	Y

Prices
Price (as of 9/30/2019)	21.53
52-Week High	24.32
52-Week Low	20.43

Total Returns (%)
3-Month	6-Month	1-Year	3-Year	5-Year
-1.07	-0.70	-10.44	1.11	-9.81

3-Year Standard Deviation	14.46
Effective Duration	

Valuation
Premium/Discount (1-Year Average)	-0.02

Company Information
Provider	WBI Investments
Manager/Tenure	Donald R. Schreiber (5), Steven Van Solkema (0)
Website	http://www.wbishares.com
Address	34 Sycamore Ave Suite 1-E Little Silver NJ 07739 United States
Phone Number	732-842-4920

PERFORMANCE

Ratings History
Date	Overall Rating	Risk Rating	Reward Rating
Q3-19	B-	C	B
Q4-18	D+	D+	D+
Q4-17	C	C	C
Q4-16	C	C	C
Q4-15	D-	C+	C+

Asset & Performance History
Date	NAV	1-Year Total Return
2018	21.17	-14.69
2017	25.03	8.31
2016	23.26	2.39
2015	22.61	-9.32
2014	25.02	
2013		

Total Assets: $7,539,709
Asset Allocation
Asset	%
Cash	11%
Stocks	89%
US Stocks	89%
Bonds	0%
US Bonds	0%
Other	0%

Services Offered:

Investment Strategy: The investment seeks long-term capital appreciation and the potential for current income, while also seeking to protect principal during unfavorable market conditions. The fund will seek to invest in the equity securities of small-capitalization and mid-capitalization domestic and foreign companies. These securities will be selected on the basis of the Sub-Advisor's proprietary selection process ("Selection Process"). Cash and cash equivalents are some of the investment opportunities evaluated by the Selection Process. It may invest up to 50% of its net assets in the securities of issuers in emerging markets. **Top Holdings:** M.D.C. Holdings Inc Aaron's Inc Hubbell Inc Amdocs Ltd Casey's General Stores Inc

Section III:
Analysis of All Rated Funds with Assets over 50 Million

Detailed analysis of all rated funds with assets over 50 million. Funds are listed in order by asset size.

Section III: Contents

This section contains an expanded analysis of all rated funds with assets over 50 million, with current and historical Weiss Investment Ratings, key rating factors, summary financial data and performance charts. Funds are listed in order by asset size.

TOP ROW

Fund Name
Describes the fund's assets, regions of investments and investment strategies. Many funds have similar names, so you want to make sure the fund you look up is really the one you are interested in evaluating.

Overall Rating
The Weiss rating measured on a scale from A to E based on each fund's risk and performance. See the preceding section, "What Our Ratings Mean," for an explanation of each letter grade rating.

BUY-HOLD-SELL Recommendation
Funds that are rated in the A or B range are, in our opinion, a potential BUY. Funds in the C range will indicate a HOLD status. Funds in the D or E range will indicate a SELL status.

Ticker Symbol
An arrangement of characters (usually letters) representing a particular security listed on an exchange or otherwise traded publicly. When a company issues securities to the public marketplace, it selects an available ticker symbol for its securities which investors use to place trade orders. Every listed security has a unique ticker symbol, facilitating the vast array of trade orders that flow through the financial markets every day.

Traded On (Exchange)
The stock exchange on which the fund is listed. The core function of a stock exchange is to ensure fair and orderly trading, as well as efficient dissemination of price information. Exchanges such as: NYSE (New York Stock Exchange), AMEX (American Stock Exchange), NNM (NASDAQ National Market), and NASQ (NASDAQ Small Cap) give companies, governments and other groups a platform to sell securities to the investing public. NASDAQ is abbreviated as NAS.

NAV (Net Asset Value)

A fund's price per share. The value is calculated by dividing the total value of all the securities in the portfolio, less any liabilities, by the number of fund shares outstanding.

Total Assets ($)

The total of all assets listed on the institution's balance sheet. This figure primarily consists of loans, investments, and fixed assets. Total Assets are displayed in dollars.

Dividend Yield (TTM)

Trailing twelve months dividends paid out relative to the share price. Expressed as a percentage and measures how much cash flow an investor is getting for each invested dollar. **Trailing Twelve Months (TTM)** is a representation of a fund's financial performance over the most recent 12 months. TTM uses the latest available financial data from a company's interim, quarterly or annual reports.

Turnover Ratio

The percentage of an exchange-traded fund or other investment vehicle's holdings that have been replaced with other holdings in a given year. Generally, low turnover ratio is favorable, because high turnover equates to higher brokerage transaction fees, which reduce fund returns.

Expense Ratio

A measure of what it costs an investment company to operate an exchange-traded fund. An expense ratio is determined through an annual calculation, where a fund's operating expenses are divided by the average dollar value of its assets under management. Operating expenses may include money spent on administration and management of the fund, advertising, etc. An expense ratio of 1 percent per annum means that each year 1 percent of the fund's total assets will be used to cover expenses.

LEFT COLUMN

Ratings

Reward Rating

This is based on the total return over a period of up to five years, including net asset value and price growth. The total return figure is stated net of the expenses and fees charged by the fund. Based on proprietary modeling the individual components of the risk and reward ratings are calculated and weighted and the final rating is generated.

Risk Rating
This is includes the risk ratings of component stocks where applicable and also includes the financial stability of the fund, turnover where applicable, together with the level of volatility as measured by the fund's daily returns over a period of up to five years. Funds with greater stability are considered less risky and receive a higher risk rating. Funds with greater volatility are considered riskier, and will receive a lower risk rating. In addition to considering the fund's volatility, the risk rating also considers an assessment of the valuation and quality of a fund's holdings.

Recent Upgrade/Downgrade
An "Up" or "Down" indicates that the Weiss Exchange-Traded Fund rating has changed since the publication of the last print edition. If a fund has had a rating change since June 30, 2019, the change is identified with an "Up" or "Down."

Fund Information

Fund Type
Describes the fund's assets, regions of investments and investment strategies.

Category
Identifies funds according to their actual investment styles as measured by their portfolio holdings. This categorization allows investors to spread their money around in a mix of funds with a variety of risk and return characteristics.

Sub-Category
A subdivision of funds, usually with common characteristics as the category.

Prospectus Objective
Gives a general idea of a fund's overall investment approach and goals.

Inception Date
The date on which the fund began its operations. The commencement date indicates when a fund began investing in the market. Many investors prefer funds with longer operating histories. Funds with longer histories have longer track records and can thereby provide investors with a more long-standing picture of their performance.

Open to New Investments
Indicates whether the fund accepts investments from those who are not existing investors. A "Y" in this column identifies that the fund accepts new investors. No data in this column indicates that the fund is closed to new investors. The fund may be closed to new investors because the fund's asset base is getting too large to effectively execute its investing style. Although, the fund may be closed, in most cases, existing investors are able to add to their holdings.

Prices

Price
The price at which the fund is traded on a regular trading day. Prices in this guide are listed as of September 30, 2019.

52-Week High
The highest price that a fund has achieved during the previous 52 weeks.

52-Week Low
The lowest price that a fund has achieved during the previous 52 weeks.

Total Returns (%)

3-Month Total Return
The rate of return on an investment over three months that includes interest, capital gains, dividends and distributions realized.

6-Month Total Return
The rate of return on an investment over six months that includes interest, capital gains, dividends and distributions realized.

1-Year Total Return
The rate of return on an investment over one year that includes interest, capital gains, dividends and distributions realized.

3-Year Total Return
The rate of return on an investment over three years that includes interest, capital gains, dividends and distributions realized.

5-Year Total Return
The rate of return on an investment over five years that includes interest, capital gains, dividends and distributions realized.

3-Year Standard Deviation
A statistical measurement of dispersion about an average, which depicts how widely the returns varied over the past three years. Investors use the standard deviation of historical performance to try to predict the range of returns that are most likely for a given fund. When a fund has a high standard deviation, the predicted range of performance is wide, implying greater volatility. Standard deviation is most appropriate for measuring risk if it is for a fund that is an investor's only holding. The figure cannot be combined for more than one fund because the standard deviation

for a portfolio of multiple funds is a function of not only the individual standard deviations, but also of the degree of correlation among the funds' returns. If a fund's returns follow a normal distribution, then approximately 68 percent of the time they will fall within one standard deviation of the mean return for the fund, and 95 percent of the time within two standard deviations.

Effective Duration

Effective duration for all long fixed income positions in a portfolio. This value gives a better estimation of how the price of bonds with embedded options, which are common in many exchange-traded funds, will change as a result of changes in interest rates. Effective duration takes into account expected mortgage prepayment or the likelihood that embedded options will be exercised if a fund holds futures, other derivative securities, or other funds as assets, the aggregate effective duration should include the weighted impact of those exposures.

Valuation

Premium/Discount 1-Year Average

The annual average premium or discount of the market price to the NAV (Net Asset Value), expressed as a percentage of the NAV. This value provides a year-by-year picture a fund's trading status. A negative number indicates that, on average, the fund's shares sold at a discount to NAV, and a positive number indicates the shares sold at a premium. If the number shown is –10.00, for example, the shares sold at an average 10% discount to NAV during the listed time-period.

Company Information

Provider
The legal company that issues the fund.

Manager/Tenure (Years)
The name of the manager and the number of years spent managing the fund.

Website
The company's web address.

Address
The company's street address.

Phone Number
The company's phone number.

RIGHT COLUMN

Performance Chart
A graphical representation of the fund's total returns over the past year.

Ratings History

Indicates the fund's Overall, Risk and Reward Ratings for the previous four years. Ratings are listed as of September 30, 2019 (Q3-19), December 31, 2018 (Q4-18), December 31, 2017 (Q4-17), December 31, 2016 (Q4-16), and December 31, 2015 (Q4-15).

Overall Rating
The Weiss rating measured on a scale from A to E based on each fund's risk and performance. See the preceding section, "What Our Ratings Mean," for an explanation of each letter grade rating.

Risk Rating
This is includes the risk ratings of component stocks where applicable and also includes the financial stability of the fund, turnover where applicable, together with the level of volatility as measured by the fund's daily returns over a period of up to five years. Funds with greater stability are considered less risky and receive a higher risk rating. Funds with greater volatility are considered riskier, and will receive a lower risk rating. In addition to considering the fund's volatility, the risk rating also considers an assessment of the valuation and quality of a fund's holdings.

Reward Rating
This is based on the total return over a period of up to five years, including net asset value and price growth. The total return figure is stated net of the expenses and fees charged by the fund. Based on proprietary modeling the individual components of the risk and reward ratings are calculated and weighted and the final rating is generated.

Asset & Performance History
Indicates the fund's NAV (Net Asset Value) and 1-Year Total Return for the previous 6 years.

NAV (Net Asset Value)
A fund's price per share. The value is calculated by dividing the total value of all the securities in the portfolio, less any liabilities, by the number of fund shares outstanding.

1-Year Total Return
The rate of return on an investment over one year that includes interest, capital gains, dividends and distributions realized.

Total Assets ($)
The total of all assets listed on the institution's balance sheet. This figure primarily consists of loans, investments, and fixed assets. Total Assets are displayed in dollars.

Asset Allocation
Indicates the percentage of assets in each category. Used as an investment strategy that attempts to balance risk versus reward by adjusting the percentage of each asset in an investment portfolio according to the investor's risk tolerance, goals and investment time frame. Allocation percentages may not add up to 100%. Negative values reflect short positions.

%Cash
The percentage of the fund's assets invested in short-term obligations, usually less than 90 days, that provide a return in the form of interest payments. This type of investment generally offers a low return compared to other investments but has a low risk level.

%Stocks
The percentage of the fund's assets invested in stock.

%US Stocks
The percentage of the fund's assets invested in U.S. stock.

%Bonds
The percentage of the fund's assets invested in bonds. A bond is an unsecured debt security issued by companies, municipalities, states and sovereign governments to raise funds. When a company issues a bond it borrows money from the bondholder to boost the business, in exchange the bondholder receives the principal amount back plus the interest on the determined maturity date.

%US Bonds
The percentage of the fund's assets invested in U.S. bonds.

%Other
The percentage of the fund's assets invested in other financial instruments.

Services Offered
Services offered by the fund provider. Such services can include:

Systematic Withdrawal Plan
A plan offered by exchange-traded funds that pays specific amounts to shareholders at predetermined intervals.

Institutional Only
This indicates if the fund is offered to institutional clients only (pension funds, mutual funds, money managers, insurance companies, investment banks, commercial trusts, endowment funds, hedge funds, and some hedge fund investors).

Phone Exchange
This indicates that investors can move money between different funds within the same fund family over the phone.

Wire Redemption
This indicates whether or not investors can redeem electronically.

Qualified Investment
Under a qualified plan, an investor may invest in the variable annuity with pretax dollars through an employee pension plan, such as a 401(k) or 403(b). Money builds up on a tax-deferred basis, and when the qualified investor makes a withdrawal or annuitizes, all contributions received are taxable income.

Investment Strategy
A set of rules, behaviors or procedures, designed to guide an investor's selection of an investment portfolio. Individuals have different profit objectives, and their individual skills make different tactics and strategies appropriate.

Top Holdings
The highest amount of publicly traded assets held by a fund. These publicly traded assets may include company stock, mutual funds or other investment vehicles.

Vanguard S&P 500 ETF   B-   BUY

Ticker	Traded On	NAV	Total Assets ($)	Dividend Yield (TTM)	Turnover Ratio	Expense Ratio
VOO	NYSE Arca	272.60	$493,907,000,000	1.99	4	0.03

Ratings
Reward   C+
Risk   B
Recent Upgrade/Downgrade

Fund Information
Fund Type	Exchange Traded Funds
Category	US Equity Large Cap Blend
Sub-Category	Large Blend
Prospectus Objective	Growth
Inception Date	Sep-10
Open to New Investments	Y

Prices
Price (as of 9/30/2019)	272.60
52-Week High	277.38
52-Week Low	215.07

Total Returns (%)

3-Month	6-Month	1-Year	3-Year	5-Year
0.92	4.85	3.87	45.66	69.21

3-Year Standard Deviation	12.18
Effective Duration	

Valuation
Premium/Discount (1-Year Average)	-0.03

Company Information
Provider	Vanguard
Manager/Tenure	Donald M. Butler (3), Michelle Louie (1)
Website	http://www.vanguard.com
Address	Vanguard 100 Vanguard Boulevard Malvern PA 19355 United States
Phone Number	877-662-7447

PERFORMANCE

Ratings History

Date	Overall Rating	Risk Rating	Reward Rating
Q3-19	B-	B	C+
Q4-18	C+	B	C
Q4-17	B	B	B
Q4-16	B-	C+	B
Q4-15	C+	C+	C

Asset & Performance History

Date	NAV	1-Year Total Return
2018	227.72	-5.23
2017	244.94	21.84
2016	205	11.39
2015	187.05	1.35
2014	188.45	13.63
2013	169.07	32.33

Total Assets: $493,907,000,000
Asset Allocation

Asset	%
Cash	0%
Stocks	100%
US Stocks	99%
Bonds	0%
US Bonds	0%
Other	0%

Services Offered:

Investment Strategy: The investment seeks to track the performance of a benchmark index that measures the investment return of large-capitalization stocks. The fund employs an indexing investment approach designed to track the performance of the Standard & Poor's 500 Index, a widely recognized benchmark of U.S. stock market performance that is dominated by the stocks of large U.S. companies. The advisor attempts to replicate the target index by investing all, or substantially all, of its assets in the stocks that make up the index, holding each stock in approximately the same proportion as its weighting in the index. **Top Holdings:** Microsoft Corp Apple Inc Amazon.com Inc Facebook Inc A Berkshire Hathaway Inc B

Vanguard Total International Stock Index Fund ETF Shares   C   HOLD

Ticker	Traded On	NAV	Total Assets ($)	Dividend Yield (TTM)	Turnover Ratio	Expense Ratio
VXUS	NAS CM	51.53	$384,493,000,000	3.05	3	0.09

Ratings
Reward   C
Risk   C+
Recent Upgrade/Downgrade

Fund Information
Fund Type	Exchange Traded Funds
Category	Global Equity Large Cap
Sub-Category	Foreign Large Blend
Prospectus Objective	Foreign Stock
Inception Date	Jan-11
Open to New Investments	Y

Prices
Price (as of 9/30/2019)	51.66
52-Week High	54.09
52-Week Low	45.72

Total Returns (%)

3-Month	6-Month	1-Year	3-Year	5-Year
-2.07	1.10	-1.60	19.35	18.16

3-Year Standard Deviation	11.51
Effective Duration	

Valuation
Premium/Discount (1-Year Average)	0.11

Company Information
Provider	Vanguard
Manager/Tenure	Michael Perre (11), Christine D. Franquin (1)
Website	http://www.vanguard.com
Address	Vanguard 100 Vanguard Boulevard Malvern PA 19355 United States
Phone Number	877-662-7447

PERFORMANCE

Ratings History

Date	Overall Rating	Risk Rating	Reward Rating
Q3-19	C	C+	C
Q4-18	C-	C	D+
Q4-17	B-	B-	B-
Q4-16	C-	C	D+
Q4-15	C	C+	C-

Asset & Performance History

Date	NAV	1-Year Total Return
2018	46.97	-14.79
2017	56.75	27.67
2016	45.81	3.75
2015	45.08	-4.28
2014	48.36	-4.16
2013	52.09	15.15

Total Assets: $384,493,000,000
Asset Allocation

Asset	%
Cash	2%
Stocks	97%
US Stocks	1%
Bonds	0%
US Bonds	0%
Other	0%

Services Offered:

Investment Strategy: The investment seeks to track the performance of a benchmark index that measures the investment return of stocks issued by companies located in developed and emerging markets, excluding the United States. The fund employs an indexing investment approach designed to track the performance of the FTSE Global All Cap ex US Index, a float-adjusted market-capitalization-weighted index designed to measure equity market performance of companies located in developed and emerging markets, excluding the United States. It invests all, or substantially all, of its assets in the common stocks included in its target index. **Top Holdings:** Nestle SA Tencent Holdings Ltd Alibaba Group Holding Ltd ADR Novartis AG Taiwan Semiconductor Manufacturing Co Ltd

SPDR® S&P 500 ETF   B-   BUY

Ticker	Traded On	NAV	Total Assets ($)	Dividend Yield (TTM)	Turnover Ratio	Expense Ratio
SPY	NYSE Arca		$273,532,000,000	1.85	2	0.09

Ratings
Reward   C+
Risk   B
Recent Upgrade/Downgrade

Fund Information
Fund Type	Exchange Traded Funds
Category	US Equity Large Cap Blend
Sub-Category	Large Blend
Prospectus Objective	Growth
Inception Date	Jan-93
Open to New Investments	Y

Prices
Price (as of 9/30/2019)	296.77
52-Week High	302.01
52-Week Low	234.34

Total Returns (%)
3-Month	6-Month	1-Year	3-Year	5-Year
0.38	4.26	3.28	44.59	65.58

3-Year Standard Deviation	12.15
Effective Duration	

Valuation
Premium/Discount (1-Year Average)	-0.05

Company Information
Provider	SPDR State Street Global Advisors
Manager/Tenure	Management Team (26)
Website	http://www.spdrs.com
Address	SPDR State Street Global Advisors
	State Street Financial Center, 1
	Lincoln Street Boston MA 02111-2900
	United States
Phone Number	617-786-3000

PERFORMANCE

Ratings History

Date	Overall Rating	Risk Rating	Reward Rating
Q3-19	B-	B	C+
Q4-18	C+	B	C
Q4-17	B	B	B
Q4-16	B	B	B
Q4-15	C+	B-	C

Asset & Performance History

Date	NAV	1-Year Total Return
2018	249.92	-4.44
2017	266.55	21.69
2016	223.28	11.25
2015	204.02	1.34
2014	205.5	13.53
2013	184.54	32.21

Total Assets: $273,532,000,000

Asset Allocation

Asset	%
Cash	0%
Stocks	100%
US Stocks	99%
Bonds	0%
US Bonds	0%
Other	0%

Services Offered: Dividend Investment Plan, CashInvestment Plan

Investment Strategy: The investment seeks to provide investment results that, before expenses, generally correspond to the price and yield performance of the S&P 500 Index. The Trust holds the Portfolio and cash and is not actively "managed" by traditional methods. To maintain the correspondence between the composition and weightings of Portfolio Securities and component stocks of the S&P 500 Index ("Index Securities"), the Trustee adjusts the Portfolio from time to time to conform to periodic changes in the identity and/or relative weightings of Index Securities. **Top Holdings:** Microsoft Corp   Apple Inc   Amazon.com Inc   Facebook Inc A   Berkshire Hathaway Inc B

Vanguard Total Bond Market Index Fund ETF Shares   B-   BUY

Ticker	Traded On	NAV	Total Assets ($)	Dividend Yield (TTM)	Turnover Ratio	Expense Ratio
BND	NAS CM	84.41	$241,309,000,000	2.74	54	0.04

Ratings
Reward   C+
Risk   B
Recent Upgrade/Downgrade

Fund Information
Fund Type	Exchange Traded Funds
Category	US Fixed Income
Sub-Category	Intermediate Core Bond
Prospectus Objective	Income
Inception Date	Apr-07
Open to New Investments	Y

Prices
Price (as of 9/30/2019)	84.43
52-Week High	85.16
52-Week Low	77.49

Total Returns (%)
3-Month	6-Month	1-Year	3-Year	5-Year
2.43	5.50	10.59	8.92	17.29

3-Year Standard Deviation	3.44
Effective Duration	6.20

Valuation
Premium/Discount (1-Year Average)	0.05

Company Information
Provider	Vanguard
Manager/Tenure	Joshua C. Barrickman (6)
Website	http://www.vanguard.com
Address	Vanguard 100 Vanguard Boulevard
	Malvern PA 19355 United States
Phone Number	877-662-7447

PERFORMANCE

Ratings History

Date	Overall Rating	Risk Rating	Reward Rating
Q3-19	B-	B	C+
Q4-18	C	C+	D+
Q4-17	B-	A-	C
Q4-16	C	C+	C
Q4-15	C	C+	C

Asset & Performance History

Date	NAV	1-Year Total Return
2018	79.01	-0.23
2017	81.46	3.62
2016	80.64	2.5
2015	80.58	0.38
2014	82.33	5.95
2013	79.91	-2.14

Total Assets: $241,309,000,000

Asset Allocation

Asset	%
Cash	2%
Stocks	0%
US Stocks	0%
Bonds	98%
US Bonds	90%
Other	0%

Services Offered:

Investment Strategy: The investment seeks the performance of Bloomberg Barclays U.S. Aggregate Float Adjusted Index. Bloomberg Barclays U.S. Aggregate Float Adjusted Index represents a wide spectrum of public, investment-grade, taxable, fixed income securities in the United States-including government, corporate, and international dollar-denominated bonds, as well as mortgage-backed and asset-backed securities-all with maturities of more than 1 year. All of its investments will be selected through the sampling process, and at least 80% of its assets will be invested in bonds held in the index. **Top Holdings:** United States Treasury Notes 2.38% Federal National Mortgage Association 3.5%   United States Treasury Notes 2.88%   United States Treasury Notes 2.12%   United States Treasury Notes 2.12%

iShares Core S&P 500 ETF   B-   BUY

Ticker	Traded On	NAV	Total Assets ($)	Dividend Yield (TTM)	Turnover Ratio	Expense Ratio
IVV	NYSE Arca	298.48	$186,488,000,000	2.06	5	0.04

Ratings
Reward   C+
Risk   B
Recent Upgrade/Downgrade

Fund Information
Fund Type   Exchange Traded Funds
Category   US Equity Large Cap Blend
Sub-Category   Large Blend
Prospectus Objective   Growth
Inception Date   May-00
Open to New Investments   Y

Prices
Price (as of 9/30/2019)   298.52
52-Week High   303.77
52-Week Low   236.09

Total Returns (%)

3-Month	6-Month	1-Year	3-Year	5-Year
0.91	4.84	3.84	45.65	69.14

3-Year Standard Deviation   12.18
Effective Duration

Valuation
Premium/Discount (1-Year Average)   -0.01

Company Information
Provider   iShares
Manager/Tenure   Greg Savage (11), Jennifer Hsui (7),
                 Alan Mason (3), 2 others
Website   http://www.ishares.com
Address   iShares 400 Howard Street San
                            Francisco CA 94105 United States
Phone Number   800-474-2737

PERFORMANCE

Ratings History

Date	Overall Rating	Risk Rating	Reward Rating
Q3-19	B-	B	C+
Q4-18	C+	B	C
Q4-17	B	B	B
Q4-16	B	B	B
Q4-15	C+	C+	C

Asset & Performance History

Date	NAV	1-Year Total Return
2018	251.4	-4.54
2017	268.5	21.79
2016	224.64	11.89
2015	205.02	1.33
2014	206.94	13.62
2013	185.62	32.3

Total Assets: $186,488,000,000
Asset Allocation

Asset	%
Cash	0%
Stocks	100%
US Stocks	99%
Bonds	0%
US Bonds	0%
Other	0%

Services Offered: CashInvestment Plan

Investment Strategy: The investment seeks to track the investment results of the S&P 500 (the "underlying index"), which measures the performance of the large-capitalization sector of the U.S. equity market. The fund generally invests at least 90% of its assets in securities of the underlying index and in depositary receipts representing securities of the underlying index. It may invest the remainder of its assets in certain futures, options and swap contracts, cash and cash equivalents, as well as in securities not included in the underlying index, but which the advisor believes will help the fund track the underlying index. **Top Holdings:** Microsoft Corp   Apple Inc   Amazon.com Inc   Facebook Inc A   Berkshire Hathaway Inc B

Vanguard Total International Bond Index Fund ETF Shares   B-   BUY

Ticker	Traded On	NAV	Total Assets ($)	Dividend Yield (TTM)	Turnover Ratio	Expense Ratio
BNDX	NAS CM	58.72	$140,100,000,000	2.85	22	0.09

Ratings
Reward   B-
Risk   C+
Recent Upgrade/Downgrade   Up

Fund Information
Fund Type   Exchange Traded Funds
Category   Global Fixed Income
Sub-Category   World Bond-USD Hedged
Prospectus Objective   Worldwide Bond
Inception Date   May-13
Open to New Investments   Y

Prices
Price (as of 9/30/2019)   58.83
52-Week High   59.22
52-Week Low   54.09

Total Returns (%)

3-Month	6-Month	1-Year	3-Year	5-Year
3.06	6.06	11.36	12.93	24.95

3-Year Standard Deviation   2.74
Effective Duration   8.41

Valuation
Premium/Discount (1-Year Average)   0.16

Company Information
Provider   Vanguard
Manager/Tenure   Joshua C. Barrickman (6)
Website   http://www.vanguard.com
Address   Vanguard 100 Vanguard Boulevard
                           Malvern PA 19355 United States
Phone Number   877-662-7447

PERFORMANCE

Ratings History

Date	Overall Rating	Risk Rating	Reward Rating
Q3-19	B-	C+	B-
Q4-18	C	C+	C
Q4-17	B	A	C
Q4-16	C	C+	C
Q4-15	C	C+	C-

Asset & Performance History

Date	NAV	1-Year Total Return
2018	54.14	2.96
2017	54.19	2.28
2016	54.11	4.82
2015	52.68	1.07
2014	52.97	8.83
2013	49.45	

Total Assets: $140,100,000,000
Asset Allocation

Asset	%
Cash	0%
Stocks	0%
US Stocks	0%
Bonds	99%
US Bonds	3%
Other	0%

Services Offered:

Investment Strategy: The investment seeks to track the performance of a benchmark index that measures the investment return of non-U.S. dollar-denominated investment-grade bonds. The fund employs an indexing investment approach designed to track the performance of the Bloomberg Barclays Global Aggregate ex-USD Float Adjusted RIC Capped Index (USD Hedged). This index provides a broad-based measure of the global, investment-grade, fixed-rate debt markets. It is non-diversified. **Top Holdings:** Germany (Federal Republic Of) 0.25%   France(Govt Of) 1.75%   Italy (Republic Of) 2.45%   Italy (Republic Of) 2.1%   France(Govt Of) 0.75%

Vanguard FTSE Developed Markets Index Fund ETF Shares   C   HOLD

Ticker	Traded On	NAV	Total Assets ($)	Dividend Yield (TTM)	Turnover Ratio	Expense Ratio
VEA	NYSE Arca	41.00	$114,321,000,000	3.13	3	0.05

Ratings
Reward   C
Risk   B
Recent Upgrade/Downgrade

Fund Information
Fund Type   Exchange Traded Funds
Category   Global Equity Large Cap
Sub-Category   Foreign Large Blend
Prospectus Objective   Foreign Stock
Inception Date   Jul-07
Open to New Investments   Y

Prices
Price (as of 9/30/2019)   41.08
52-Week High   43.38
52-Week Low   35.84

Total Returns (%)

3-Month	6-Month	1-Year	3-Year	5-Year
-1.28	1.02	-2.12	20.08	20.87

3-Year Standard Deviation   11.44
Effective Duration

Valuation
Premium/Discount (1-Year Average)   0.05

Company Information
Provider   Vanguard
Manager/Tenure Christine D. Franquin (6), Michael Perre (1)
Website   http://www.vanguard.com
Address   Vanguard 100 Vanguard Boulevard Malvern PA 19355 United States
Phone Number   877-662-7447

PERFORMANCE

Ratings History

Date	Overall Rating	Risk Rating	Reward Rating
Q3-19	C	B	C
Q4-18	C-	C	D+
Q4-17	B	B	B-
Q4-16	C-	C	D+
Q4-15	C	C	C-

Asset & Performance History

Date	NAV	1-Year Total Return
2018	37.02	-14.88
2017	44.83	26.77
2016	36.51	1.28
2015	36.75	-0.21
2014	37.85	-5.7
2013	41.53	22.12

Total Assets: $114,321,000,000
Asset Allocation

Asset	%
Cash	3%
Stocks	97%
US Stocks	1%
Bonds	0%
US Bonds	0%
Other	0%

Services Offered:

Investment Strategy: The investment seeks to track the performance of the FTSE Developed All Cap ex US Index. The fund employs an indexing investment approach designed to track the performance of the FTSE Developed All Cap ex US Index, a market-capitalization-weighted index that is made up of approximately 3,885 common stocks of large-, mid-, and small-cap companies located in Canada and the major markets of Europe and the Pacific region. The adviser attempts to replicate the target index by investing all, or substantially all, of its assets in the stocks that make up the index, holding each stock in approximately the same proportion as its weighting in the index. **Top Holdings:** Nestle SA Novartis AG Roche Holding AG Dividend Right Cert. Samsung Electronics Co Ltd HSBC Holdings PLC

Vanguard Mid-Cap Index Fund ETF Shares   C+   HOLD

Ticker	Traded On	NAV	Total Assets ($)	Dividend Yield (TTM)	Turnover Ratio	Expense Ratio
VO	NYSE Arca	167.60	$105,404,000,000	1.4	16	0.04

Ratings
Reward   C
Risk   C+
Recent Upgrade/Downgrade

Fund Information
Fund Type   Exchange Traded Funds
Category   US Equity Mid Cap
Sub-Category   Mid-Cap Blend
Prospectus Objective   Growth
Inception Date   Jan-04
Open to New Investments   Y

Prices
Price (as of 9/30/2019)   167.60
52-Week High   171.52
52-Week Low   129.93

Total Returns (%)

3-Month	6-Month	1-Year	3-Year	5-Year
-0.07	3.76	3.91	35.57	57.62

3-Year Standard Deviation   13.3
Effective Duration

Valuation
Premium/Discount (1-Year Average)   0.01

Company Information
Provider   Vanguard
Manager/Tenure Donald M. Butler (21), Michael A. Johnson (3)
Website   http://www.vanguard.com
Address   Vanguard 100 Vanguard Boulevard Malvern PA 19355 United States
Phone Number   877-662-7447

PERFORMANCE

Ratings History

Date	Overall Rating	Risk Rating	Reward Rating
Q3-19	C+	C+	C
Q4-18	C	C+	C-
Q4-17	B-	B-	B-
Q4-16	B-	C+	B
Q4-15	C	C+	C

Asset & Performance History

Date	NAV	1-Year Total Return
2018	136.84	-10.02
2017	154.65	19.57
2016	131.55	10.85
2015	120.07	-1.33
2014	123.5	13.75
2013	109.96	35.14

Total Assets: $105,404,000,000
Asset Allocation

Asset	%
Cash	1%
Stocks	99%
US Stocks	97%
Bonds	0%
US Bonds	0%
Other	0%

Services Offered:

Investment Strategy: The investment seeks to track the performance of a benchmark index that measures the investment return of mid-capitalization stocks. The fund employs an indexing investment approach designed to track the performance of the CRSP US Mid Cap Index, a broadly diversified index of stocks of mid-size U.S. companies. The advisor attempts to replicate the target index by investing all, or substantially all, of its assets in the stocks that make up the index, holding each stock in approximately the same proportion as its weighting in the index. **Top Holdings:** Twitter Inc Newmont Goldcorp Corp Fiserv Inc Advanced Micro Devices Inc Xilinx Inc

Vanguard Growth Index Fund ETF Shares   B-   BUY

Ticker	Traded On	NAV	Total Assets ($)	Dividend Yield (TTM)	Turnover Ratio	Expense Ratio
VUG	NYSE Arca	166.35	$92,059,629,583	1.06	11	0.04

Ratings
Reward   B-
Risk   C+
Recent Upgrade/Downgrade   Up

Fund Information
Fund Type   Exchange Traded Funds
Category   US Equity Large Cap Growth
Sub-Category   Large Growth
Prospectus Objective   Growth
Inception Date   Jan-04
Open to New Investments   Y

Prices
Price (as of 9/30/2019)   166.28
52-Week High   170.26
52-Week Low   124.85

Total Returns (%)

3-Month	6-Month	1-Year	3-Year	5-Year
1.03	5.65	4.25	53.67	80.40

3-Year Standard Deviation   13.27
Effective Duration

Valuation
Premium/Discount (1-Year Average)   -0.03

Company Information
Provider   Vanguard
Manager/Tenure   Gerard C. O'Reilly (24), Walter Nejman (3)
Website   http://www.vanguard.com
Address   Vanguard 100 Vanguard Boulevard Malvern PA 19355 United States
Phone Number   877-662-7447

PERFORMANCE

Ratings History

Date	Overall Rating	Risk Rating	Reward Rating
Q3-19	B-	C+	B-
Q4-18	C	C+	C
Q4-17	B+	A-	B
Q4-16	B-	C+	B-
Q4-15	C+	C+	C+

Asset & Performance History

Date	NAV	1-Year Total Return
2018	133.04	-4.16
2017	140.55	27.7
2016	111.33	5.76
2015	106.4	3.31
2014	104.33	13.61
2013	92.99	32.37

Total Assets: $92,059,629,583
Asset Allocation

Asset	%
Cash	0%
Stocks	100%
US Stocks	99%
Bonds	0%
US Bonds	0%
Other	0%

Services Offered:

Investment Strategy: The investment seeks to track the performance of a benchmark index that measures the investment return of the CRSP US Large Cap Growth Index. The fund employs an indexing investment approach designed to track the performance of index, a broadly diversified index predominantly made up of growth stocks of large U.S. companies. The advisor attempts to replicate the target index by investing all, or substantially all, of its assets in the stocks that make up the index, holding each stock in approximately the same proportion as its weighting in the index. The fund is non-diversified. **Top Holdings:** Microsoft Corp Apple Inc Amazon.com Inc Facebook Inc A Alphabet Inc A

Vanguard FTSE Emerging Markets Index Fund ETF Shares   C   HOLD

Ticker	Traded On	NAV	Total Assets ($)	Dividend Yield (TTM)	Turnover Ratio	Expense Ratio
VWO	NYSE Arca	40.42	$83,541,079,440	2.82	11	0.12

Ratings
Reward   C
Risk   C+
Recent Upgrade/Downgrade

Fund Information
Fund Type   Exchange Traded Funds
Category   Global Emerg Mkts Equity
Sub-Category   Diversified Emerging Mkts
Prospectus Objective   Div Emerg Mkts
Inception Date   Mar-05
Open to New Investments   Y

Prices
Price (as of 9/30/2019)   40.26
52-Week High   44.01
52-Week Low   36.68

Total Returns (%)

3-Month	6-Month	1-Year	3-Year	5-Year
-4.73	-4.16	1.25	16.73	11.87

3-Year Standard Deviation   13.34
Effective Duration

Valuation
Premium/Discount (1-Year Average)   0.04

Company Information
Provider   Vanguard
Manager/Tenure   Michael Perre (11), Jeffrey D. Miller (3)
Website   http://www.vanguard.com
Address   Vanguard 100 Vanguard Boulevard Malvern PA 19355 United States
Phone Number   877-662-7447

PERFORMANCE

Ratings History

Date	Overall Rating	Risk Rating	Reward Rating
Q3-19	C	C+	C
Q4-18	C-	C-	C-
Q4-17	C+	C	B-
Q4-16	C-	C	D+
Q4-15	C-	C-	C-

Asset & Performance History

Date	NAV	1-Year Total Return
2018	38.03	-14.9
2017	45.9	30.96
2016	35.8	11.86
2015	32.86	-15.34
2014	39.98	0.59
2013	40.83	-5

Total Assets: $83,541,079,440
Asset Allocation

Asset	%
Cash	3%
Stocks	96%
US Stocks	0%
Bonds	0%
US Bonds	0%
Other	1%

Services Offered:

Investment Strategy: The investment seeks to track the performance of a benchmark index that measures the investment return of stocks issued by companies located in emerging market countries. The fund employs an indexing investment approach designed to track the performance of the FTSE Emerging Markets All Cap China A Inclusion Index. It invests by sampling the index, meaning that it holds a broadly diversified collection of securities that, in the aggregate, approximates the index in terms of key characteristics. **Top Holdings:** Tencent Holdings Ltd Alibaba Group Holding Ltd ADR Taiwan Semiconductor Manufacturing Co Ltd Naspers Ltd Class N Taiwan Semiconductor Manufacturing Co Ltd ADR

Vanguard Value Index Fund ETF Shares C+ HOLD

Ticker	Traded On	NAV	Total Assets ($)	Dividend Yield (TTM)	Turnover Ratio	Expense Ratio
VTV	NYSE Arca	111.60	$82,528,677,938	2.51	8	0.04

Ratings
Reward C
Risk C+
Recent Upgrade/Downgrade

Fund Information
Fund Type Exchange Traded Funds
Category US Equity Large Cap Value
Sub-Category Large Value
Prospectus Objective Growth
Inception Date Jan-04
Open to New Investments Y

Prices
Price (as of 9/30/2019) 111.62
52-Week High 113.17
52-Week Low 92.30

Total Returns (%)

3-Month	6-Month	1-Year	3-Year	5-Year
0.53	3.72	3.14	38.50	58.22

3-Year Standard Deviation 12.22
Effective Duration

Valuation
Premium/Discount (1-Year Average) -0.01

Company Information
Provider Vanguard
Manager/Tenure Gerard C. O'Reilly (24), Walter Nejman (3)
Website http://www.vanguard.com
Address Vanguard 100 Vanguard Boulevard Malvern PA 19355 United States
Phone Number 877-662-7447

PERFORMANCE

Ratings History

Date	Overall Rating	Risk Rating	Reward Rating
Q3-19	C+	C+	C
Q4-18	C	C+	C
Q4-17	B	B+	B
Q4-16	B-	C+	B
Q4-15	C+	C+	C

Asset & Performance History

Date	NAV	1-Year Total Return
2018	97.02	-6.17
2017	106.14	17.35
2016	92.87	16.21
2015	81.56	-0.88
2014	84.45	13.18
2013	76.34	33.03

Total Assets: $82,528,677,938

Asset Allocation

Asset	%
Cash	0%
Stocks	100%
US Stocks	99%
Bonds	0%
US Bonds	0%
Other	0%

Services Offered:

Investment Strategy: The investment seeks to track the performance of a benchmark index that measures the investment return of large-capitalization value stocks. The fund employs an indexing investment approach designed to track the performance of the CRSP US Large Cap Value Index, a broadly diversified index predominantly made up of value stocks of large U.S. companies. The advisor attempts to replicate the target index by investing all, or substantially all, of its assets in the stocks that make up the index, holding each stock in approximately the same proportion as its weighting in the index. **Top Holdings:** Berkshire Hathaway Inc B JPMorgan Chase & Co Johnson & Johnson Exxon Mobil Corp Procter & Gamble Co

---

Invesco QQQ Trust B- BUY

Ticker	Traded On	NAV	Total Assets ($)	Dividend Yield (TTM)	Turnover Ratio	Expense Ratio
QQQ	NAS CM	188.77	$74,717,022,394	0.82		0.2

Ratings
Reward B-
Risk B-
Recent Upgrade/Downgrade

Fund Information
Fund Type Exchange Traded Funds
Category US Equity Large Cap Growth
Sub-Category Large Growth
Prospectus Objective Growth
Inception Date Mar-99
Open to New Investments Y

Prices
Price (as of 9/30/2019) 188.81
52-Week High 195.29
52-Week Low 143.50

Total Returns (%)

3-Month	6-Month	1-Year	3-Year	5-Year
-0.03	4.06	2.31	63.28	103.88

3-Year Standard Deviation 14.9
Effective Duration

Valuation
Premium/Discount (1-Year Average) -0.02

Company Information
Provider Invesco
Manager/Tenure Management Team (20)
Website http://www.invesco.com/us
Address Invesco 11 Greenway Plaza, Ste. 2500 Houston TX 77046 United States
Phone Number 800-659-1005

PERFORMANCE

Ratings History

Date	Overall Rating	Risk Rating	Reward Rating
Q3-19	B-	B-	B-
Q4-18	B-	B	C+
Q4-17	A-	B	A-
Q4-16	B+	B	A-
Q4-15	B	A-	B

Asset & Performance History

Date	NAV	1-Year Total Return
2018	154.14	-0.14
2017	155.68	32.7
2016	118.39	7.01
2015	111.87	9.54
2014	103.17	19.11
2013	87.94	36.6

Total Assets: $74,717,022,394

Asset Allocation

Asset	%
Cash	0%
Stocks	100%
US Stocks	97%
Bonds	0%
US Bonds	0%
Other	0%

Services Offered: Dividend Investment Plan, Cash Investment Plan

Investment Strategy: The investment seeks investment results that generally correspond to the price and yield performance of the index. To maintain the correspondence between the composition and weights of the securities in the trust (the "securities") and the stocks in the Nasdaq-100 Index®, the adviser adjusts the securities from time to time to conform to periodic changes in the identity and/or relative weights of index securities. The composition and weighting of the securities portion of a portfolio deposit are also adjusted to conform to changes in the index. **Top Holdings:** Microsoft Corp Apple Inc Amazon.com Inc Facebook Inc A Alphabet Inc Class C

Vanguard Real Estate Index Fund ETF Shares
B-   BUY

Ticker	Traded On	NAV	Total Assets ($)	Dividend Yield (TTM)	Turnover Ratio	Expense Ratio
VNQ	NYSE Arca	93.26	$69,464,761,255	3.12	24	0.12

Ratings

Reward	C+
Risk	B-
Recent Upgrade/Downgrade	Up

Fund Information

Fund Type	Exchange Traded Funds
Category	Real Estate Sector Equity
Sub-Category	Real Estate
Prospectus Objective	Real Estate
Inception Date	Sep-04
Open to New Investments	Y

Prices

Price (as of 9/30/2019)	93.25
52-Week High	93.92
52-Week Low	71.74

Total Returns (%)

3-Month	6-Month	1-Year	3-Year	5-Year
7.64	9.27	20.97	22.70	60.39

3-Year Standard Deviation	12.88
Effective Duration	

Valuation

Premium/Discount (1-Year Average)	-0.01

Company Information

Provider	Vanguard
Manager/Tenure	Gerard C. O'Reilly (23), Walter Nejman (3)
Website	http://www.vanguard.com
Address	Vanguard 100 Vanguard Boulevard Malvern PA 19355 United States
Phone Number	877-662-7447

PERFORMANCE

Ratings History

Date	Overall Rating	Risk Rating	Reward Rating
Q3-19	B-	B-	C+
Q4-18	C+	B	C
Q4-17	B-	B	C+
Q4-16	C+	B-	C+
Q4-15	C+	B-	C+

Asset & Performance History

Date	NAV	1-Year Total Return
2018	74.44	-6.13
2017	82.94	6.31
2016	82.46	6.32
2015	79.72	2.36
2014	81.03	30.29
2013	64.62	2.41

Total Assets: $69,464,761,255

Asset Allocation

Asset	%
Cash	1%
Stocks	99%
US Stocks	99%
Bonds	0%
US Bonds	0%
Other	0%

Services Offered:

Investment Strategy: The investment seeks to provide a high level of income and moderate long-term capital appreciation by tracking the performance of the MSCI US Investable Market Real Estate 25/50 Index that measures the performance of publicly traded equity REITs and other real estate-related investments. The advisor attempts to track the index by investing all, or substantially all, of its assets-either directly or indirectly through a wholly owned subsidiary, which is itself a registered investment company-in the stocks that make up the index, holding each stock in approximately the same proportion as its weighting in the index. The fund is non-diversified. **Top Holdings:** Vanguard Real Estate II Index   American Tower Corp   Crown Castle International Corp   Prologis Inc   Simon Property Group Inc

---

Vanguard Extended Market Index Fund ETF Shares
C   HOLD

Ticker	Traded On	NAV	Total Assets ($)	Dividend Yield (TTM)	Turnover Ratio	Expense Ratio
VXF	NYSE Arca	116.34	$69,318,209,474	1.26	10	0.07

Ratings

Reward	C
Risk	C+
Recent Upgrade/Downgrade	

Fund Information

Fund Type	Exchange Traded Funds
Category	US Equity Mid Cap
Sub-Category	Mid-Cap Blend
Prospectus Objective	Growth
Inception Date	Dec-01
Open to New Investments	Y

Prices

Price (as of 9/30/2019)	116.33
52-Week High	121.78
52-Week Low	93.42

Total Returns (%)

3-Month	6-Month	1-Year	3-Year	5-Year
-2.12	0.19	-2.95	32.94	52.77

3-Year Standard Deviation	15.32
Effective Duration	

Valuation

Premium/Discount (1-Year Average)	0.01

Company Information

Provider	Vanguard
Manager/Tenure	Donald M. Butler (21), William A. Coleman (1)
Website	http://www.vanguard.com
Address	Vanguard 100 Vanguard Boulevard Malvern PA 19355 United States
Phone Number	877-662-7447

PERFORMANCE

Ratings History

Date	Overall Rating	Risk Rating	Reward Rating
Q3-19	C	C+	C
Q4-18	C	C+	C-
Q4-17	B	B	B
Q4-16	B-	C+	B-
Q4-15	C	C+	C

Asset & Performance History

Date	NAV	1-Year Total Return
2018	98.85	-10.2
2017	111.72	18.44
2016	95.86	15.67
2015	83.8	-3.26
2014	87.79	7.54
2013	82.71	38.37

Total Assets: $69,318,209,474

Asset Allocation

Asset	%
Cash	3%
Stocks	97%
US Stocks	96%
Bonds	0%
US Bonds	0%
Other	0%

Services Offered:

Investment Strategy: The investment seeks to track a benchmark index that measures the investment return of small- and mid-capitalization stocks. The fund employs an indexing investment approach designed to track the performance of S&P Completion Index, a broadly diversified index of stocks of small and mid-size U.S. companies. It invests by sampling the index, meaning that it holds a broadly diversified collection of securities that, in the aggregate, approximates the full index in terms of key characteristics. These characteristics include industry weightings and market capitalization, as well as certain financial measures, such as price/earnings ratio and dividend yield. **Top Holdings:** ServiceNow Inc   Worldpay Inc Class A   Tesla Inc   Workday Inc Class A   Square Inc A

iShares Core U.S. Aggregate Bond ETF　　　　　　　　　　　　　　B-　　BUY

Ticker	Traded On	NAV	Total Assets ($)	Dividend Yield (TTM)	Turnover Ratio	Expense Ratio
AGG	NYSE Arca	113.13	$66,025,267,982	2.71	146	0.05

Ratings
Reward　　　　　　　　　　　　　　C+
Risk　　　　　　　　　　　　　　　B
Recent Upgrade/Downgrade

Fund Information
Fund Type　　　　　　　Exchange Traded Funds
Category　　　　　　　　US Fixed Income
Sub-Category　　　　　Intermediate Core Bond
Prospectus Objective　Corp Bond - Gen
Inception Date　　　　　Sep-03
Open to New Investments　Y

Prices
Price (as of 9/30/2019)　113.17
52-Week High　　　　　　114.13
52-Week Low　　　　　　104.01

Total Returns (%)

3-Month	6-Month	1-Year	3-Year	5-Year
2.36	5.78	10.35	8.90	17.24

3-Year Standard Deviation　　　3.35
Effective Duration　　　　　　　5.29

Valuation
Premium/Discount (1-Year Average)　0.06

Company Information
Provider　　　　iShares
Manager/Tenure　Scott Radell (9), James Mauro (8)
Website　　　　　http://www.ishares.com
Address　　　　　iShares 400 Howard Street San
　　　　　　　　　Francisco CA 94105 United States
Phone Number　　800-474-2737

PERFORMANCE

Ratings History

Date	Overall Rating	Risk Rating	Reward Rating
Q3-19	B-	B	C+
Q4-18	C	C+	D+
Q4-17	B-	A-	C
Q4-16	C	B-	C
Q4-15	C	C+	C

Asset & Performance History

Date	NAV	1-Year Total Return
2018	106.27	-0.04
2017	109.26	3.58
2016	108.02	2.55
2015	107.82	0.47
2014	109.93	6.03
2013	106.21	-2.14

Total Assets: $66,025,267,982
Asset Allocation

Asset	%
Cash	1%
Stocks	0%
US Stocks	0%
Bonds	98%
US Bonds	92%
Other	0%

Services Offered: Dividend Investment Plan, CashInvestment Plan

Investment Strategy: The investment seeks to track the investment results of the Bloomberg Barclays U.S. Aggregate Bond Index. The index measures the performance of the total U.S. investment-grade bond market. The fund generally invests at least 90% of its net assets in component securities of its underlying index and in investments that have economic characteristics that are substantially identical to the economic characteristics of the component securities of its underlying index. **Top Holdings:** Fnma Pass-Thru I 3%　Gnma2 30yr 2017 Production　Gnma2 30yr 2017 Production　Fgold 30yr 2016 Production　Gnma2 30yr 2016 Production

---

iShares Core MSCI EAFE ETF　　　　　　　　　　　　　　　　　C　　HOLD

Ticker	Traded On	NAV	Total Assets ($)	Dividend Yield (TTM)	Turnover Ratio	Expense Ratio
IEFA	BATS	60.95	$65,004,347,694	3.2	3	0.07

Ratings
Reward　　　　　　　　　　　　　　C
Risk　　　　　　　　　　　　　　　B
Recent Upgrade/Downgrade

Fund Information
Fund Type　　　　　　　Exchange Traded Funds
Category　　　　　　　　Global Equity Large Cap
Sub-Category　　　　　Foreign Large Blend
Prospectus Objective　Growth & Inc
Inception Date　　　　　Oct-12
Open to New Investments　Y

Prices
Price (as of 9/30/2019)　61.07
52-Week High　　　　　　64.19
52-Week Low　　　　　　53.06

Total Returns (%)

3-Month	6-Month	1-Year	3-Year	5-Year
-1.45	1.40	-1.64	21.25	21.62

3-Year Standard Deviation　　　11.19
Effective Duration

Valuation
Premium/Discount (1-Year Average)　0.00

Company Information
Provider　　　　iShares
Manager/Tenure　Diane Hsiung (6), Jennifer Hsui (6),
　　　　　　　　　Greg Savage (6), 3 others
Website　　　　　http://www.ishares.com
Address　　　　　iShares 400 Howard Street San
　　　　　　　　　Francisco CA 94105 United States
Phone Number　　800-474-2737

PERFORMANCE

Ratings History

Date	Overall Rating	Risk Rating	Reward Rating
Q3-19	C	B	C
Q4-18	C-	C	D+
Q4-17	B	B	B
Q4-16	C-	C	D+
Q4-15	C	C+	D+

Asset & Performance History

Date	NAV	1-Year Total Return
2018	55.05	-14.2
2017	66.21	26.42
2016	53.8	1.36
2015	54.67	0.52
2014	55.73	-4.82
2013	60.26	23.73

Total Assets: $65,004,347,694
Asset Allocation

Asset	%
Cash	1%
Stocks	99%
US Stocks	2%
Bonds	0%
US Bonds	0%
Other	0%

Services Offered:

Investment Strategy: The investment seeks to track the investment results of the MSCI EAFE IMI Index composed of large-, mid- and small-capitalization developed market equities, excluding the U.S. and Canada. The fund generally will invest at least 90% of its assets in the component securities of the underlying index and in investments that have economic characteristics that are substantially identical to the component securities of the underlying index. The index is designed to measure large-, mid- and small-capitalization equity market performance and includes stocks from Europe, Australasia and the Far East. **Top Holdings:** Nestle SA　Novartis AG　Roche Holding AG Dividend Right Cert.　Toyota Motor Corp　HSBC Holdings PLC

iShares MSCI EAFE ETF
C   HOLD

Ticker	Traded On	NAV	Total Assets ($)	Dividend Yield (TTM)	Turnover Ratio	Expense Ratio
EFA	NYSE Arca	65.05	$58,936,928,030	3.1	4	0.31

Ratings
Reward	C
Risk	B
Recent Upgrade/Downgrade	

Fund Information
Fund Type	Exchange Traded Funds
Category	Global Equity Large Cap
Sub-Category	Foreign Large Blend
Prospectus Objective	Foreign Stock
Inception Date	Aug-01
Open to New Investments	Y

Prices
Price (as of 9/30/2019)	65.21
52-Week High	68.07
52-Week Low	56.89

Total Returns (%)
3-Month	6-Month	1-Year	3-Year	5-Year
-1.58	1.43	-1.22	20.52	18.06

3-Year Standard Deviation	11.09
Effective Duration	

Valuation
Premium/Discount (1-Year Average)	-0.08

Company Information
Provider	iShares
Manager/Tenure	Diane Hsiung (11), Greg Savage (11), Jennifer Hsui (6), 3 others
Website	http://www.ishares.com
Address	iShares 400 Howard Street San Francisco CA 94105 United States
Phone Number	800-474-2737

PERFORMANCE

Ratings History
Date	Overall Rating	Risk Rating	Reward Rating
Q3-19	C	B	C
Q4-18	C-	C	D+
Q4-17	B	B	B
Q4-16	D+	C-	D
Q4-15	C	C	C-

Asset & Performance History
Date	NAV	1-Year Total Return
2018	58.91	-13.82
2017	70.49	24.94
2016	57.95	0.96
2015	59.18	-0.9
2014	61.26	-5.04
2013	66.75	22.62

Total Assets: $58,936,928,030
Asset Allocation
Asset	%
Cash	1%
Stocks	99%
US Stocks	2%
Bonds	0%
US Bonds	0%
Other	0%

Services Offered: CashInvestment Plan

Investment Strategy: The investment seeks to track the investment results of the MSCI EAFE Index composed of large- and mid-capitalization developed market equities, excluding the U.S. and Canada. The fund generally invests at least 90% of its assets in securities of the underlying index and in depositary receipts representing securities of the underlying index. The index measures the equity market performance of developed markets outside of the U.S. and Canada. The underlying index may include large- or mid-capitalization companies. **Top Holdings:** Nestle SA Novartis AG Roche Holding AG Dividend Right Cert. Toyota Motor Corp HSBC Holdings PLC

iShares Core MSCI Emerging Markets ETF
C   HOLD

Ticker	Traded On	NAV	Total Assets ($)	Dividend Yield (TTM)	Turnover Ratio	Expense Ratio
IEMG	NYSE Arca	49.24	$54,218,068,966	2.74	6	0.14

Ratings
Reward	C-
Risk	C+
Recent Upgrade/Downgrade	

Fund Information
Fund Type	Exchange Traded Funds
Category	Global Emerg Mkts Equity
Sub-Category	Diversified Emerging Mkts
Prospectus Objective	Div Emerg Mkts
Inception Date	Oct-12
Open to New Investments	Y

Prices
Price (as of 9/30/2019)	49.02
52-Week High	53.71
52-Week Low	45.85

Total Returns (%)
3-Month	6-Month	1-Year	3-Year	5-Year
-5.10	-4.89	-2.23	17.40	11.91

3-Year Standard Deviation	13.81
Effective Duration	

Valuation
Premium/Discount (1-Year Average)	-0.02

Company Information
Provider	iShares
Manager/Tenure	Diane Hsiung (6), Jennifer Hsui (6), Greg Savage (6), 3 others
Website	http://www.ishares.com
Address	iShares 400 Howard Street San Francisco CA 94105 United States
Phone Number	800-474-2737

PERFORMANCE

Ratings History
Date	Overall Rating	Risk Rating	Reward Rating
Q3-19	C	C+	C-
Q4-18	C-	C-	C-
Q4-17	B-	C	B
Q4-16	D+	C-	D+
Q4-15	D+	D+	D+

Asset & Performance History
Date	NAV	1-Year Total Return
2018	47.21	-14.69
2017	56.82	36.77
2016	42.58	9.97
2015	39.62	-13.85
2014	47.06	-2.03
2013	49.14	-2.16

Total Assets: $54,218,068,966
Asset Allocation
Asset	%
Cash	0%
Stocks	100%
US Stocks	0%
Bonds	0%
US Bonds	0%
Other	0%

Services Offered:

Investment Strategy: The investment seeks to track the investment results of the MSCI Emerging Markets Investable Market Index. The fund generally will invest at least 90% of its assets in the component securities of the underlying index and in investments that have economic characteristics that are substantially identical to the component securities of the underlying index. The index is designed to measure large-, mid- and small-cap equity market performance in the global emerging markets. **Top Holdings:** Alibaba Group Holding Ltd ADR Tencent Holdings Ltd Taiwan Semiconductor Manufacturing Co Ltd Samsung Electronics Co Ltd Naspers Ltd Class N

iShares Core S&P Mid-Cap ETF

C   HOLD

Ticker	Traded On	NAV	Total Assets ($)	Dividend Yield (TTM)	Turnover Ratio	Expense Ratio
IJH	NYSE Arca	193.14	$49,539,370,776	1.5	17	0.07

Ratings
Reward   C
Risk   C+
Recent Upgrade/Downgrade

Fund Information
Fund Type	Exchange Traded Funds
Category	US Equity Mid Cap
Sub-Category	Mid-Cap Blend
Prospectus Objective	Growth
Inception Date	May-00
Open to New Investments	Y

Prices
Price (as of 9/30/2019)	193.23
52-Week High	199.76
52-Week Low	156.48

Total Returns (%)
3-Month	6-Month	1-Year	3-Year	5-Year
-0.43	1.52	-1.79	30.64	54.71

3-Year Standard Deviation	15.32
Effective Duration	

Valuation
Premium/Discount (1-Year Average)	-0.01

Company Information
Provider	iShares
Manager/Tenure	Greg Savage (11), Jennifer Hsui (7), Alan Mason (3), 2 others
Website	http://www.ishares.com
Address	iShares 400 Howard Street San Francisco CA 94105 United States
Phone Number	800-474-2737

PERFORMANCE

Ratings History
Date	Overall Rating	Risk Rating	Reward Rating
Q3-19	C	C+	C
Q4-18	C	C+	C-
Q4-17	B	B	B
Q4-16	B	C+	B
Q4-15	C	C+	C

Asset & Performance History
Date	NAV	1-Year Total Return
2018	166.03	-11.14
2017	189.67	16.18
2016	165.35	20.63
2015	139.44	-2.22
2014	144.77	9.63
2013	133.87	33.4

Total Assets: $49,539,370,776

Asset Allocation
Asset	%
Cash	0%
Stocks	100%
US Stocks	100%
Bonds	0%
US Bonds	0%
Other	0%

Services Offered: CashInvestment Plan

Investment Strategy: The investment seeks to track the investment results of the S&P MidCap 400® (the "underlying index"), which measures the performance of the mid-capitalization sector of the U.S. equity market. The fund generally invests at least 90% of its assets in securities of the underlying index and in depositary receipts representing securities of the underlying index. It may invest the remainder of its assets in certain futures, options and swap contracts, cash and cash equivalents, as well as in securities not included in the underlying index, but which the advisor believes will help the fund track the underlying index. **Top Holdings:** Steris PLC NVR Inc Teledyne Technologies Inc Zebra Technologies Corp Alleghany Corp

---

Vanguard Short-Term Bond Index Fund ETF Shares

C+   HOLD

Ticker	Traded On	NAV	Total Assets ($)	Dividend Yield (TTM)	Turnover Ratio	Expense Ratio
BSV	NYSE Arca	80.80	$48,182,601,252	2.23	48	0.07

Ratings
Reward   C
Risk   C+
Recent Upgrade/Downgrade   Up

Fund Information
Fund Type	Exchange Traded Funds
Category	US Fixed Income
Sub-Category	Short-Term Bond
Prospectus Objective	Income
Inception Date	Apr-07
Open to New Investments	Y

Prices
Price (as of 9/30/2019)	80.79
52-Week High	81.16
52-Week Low	77.67

Total Returns (%)
3-Month	6-Month	1-Year	3-Year	5-Year
0.94	2.77	6.00	5.94	9.84

3-Year Standard Deviation	1.53
Effective Duration	2.67

Valuation
Premium/Discount (1-Year Average)	0.04

Company Information
Provider	Vanguard
Manager/Tenure	Joshua C. Barrickman (6)
Website	http://www.vanguard.com
Address	Vanguard 100 Vanguard Boulevard Malvern PA 19355 United States
Phone Number	877-662-7447

PERFORMANCE

Ratings History
Date	Overall Rating	Risk Rating	Reward Rating
Q3-19	C+	C+	C
Q4-18	C	C+	D+
Q4-17	C	B	C
Q4-16	C	C+	C
Q4-15	C	C+	C

Asset & Performance History
Date	NAV	1-Year Total Return
2018	78.47	1.22
2017	79.09	1.2
2016	79.44	1.41
2015	79.49	0.92
2014	79.87	1.32
2013	79.89	0.17

Total Assets: $48,182,601,252

Asset Allocation
Asset	%
Cash	1%
Stocks	0%
US Stocks	0%
Bonds	99%
US Bonds	88%
Other	0%

Services Offered:

Investment Strategy: The investment seeks to track the performance of Bloomberg Barclays U.S. 1-5 Year Government/Credit Float Adjusted Index. Bloomberg Barclays U.S. 1-5 Year Government/Credit Float Adjusted Index includes all medium and larger issues of U.S. government, investment-grade corporate, and investment-grade international dollar-denominated bonds that have maturities between 1 and 5 years and are publicly issued. All of its investments will be selected through the sampling process, and at least 80% of its assets will be invested in bonds held in the index. **Top Holdings:** United States Treasury Notes 1.25% United States Treasury Notes 1.25% United States Treasury Notes 1.38% United States Treasury Notes 1.12% United States Treasury Notes 1.62%

Vanguard Dividend Appreciation Index Fund ETF Shares

B- **BUY**

Ticker	Traded On	NAV	Total Assets ($)	Dividend Yield (TTM)	Turnover Ratio	Expense Ratio
VIG	NYSE Arca	119.50	$47,775,778,497	1.77	16	0.06

Ratings
Reward	B
Risk	C+
Recent Upgrade/Downgrade	

Fund Information
Fund Type	Exchange Traded Funds
Category	US Equity Large Cap Blend
Sub-Category	Large Blend
Prospectus Objective	Equity-Income
Inception Date	Apr-06
Open to New Investments	Y

Prices
Price (as of 9/30/2019)	119.58
52-Week High	120.84
52-Week Low	92.08

Total Returns (%)
3-Month	6-Month	1-Year	3-Year	5-Year
3.05	8.48	9.16	50.41	71.36

3-Year Standard Deviation	11.55
Effective Duration	

Valuation
Premium/Discount (1-Year Average)	-0.01

Company Information
Provider	Vanguard
Manager/Tenure	Walter Nejman (3), Gerard C. O'Reilly (3)
Website	http://www.vanguard.com
Address	Vanguard 100 Vanguard Boulevard Malvern PA 19355 United States
Phone Number	877-662-7447

PERFORMANCE

Ratings History
Date	Overall Rating	Risk Rating	Reward Rating
Q3-19	B-	C+	B
Q4-18	C+	C+	C
Q4-17	B	B+	B
Q4-16	B-	C+	B-
Q4-15	C+	C+	C+

Asset & Performance History
Date	NAV	1-Year Total Return
2018	96.92	-3.01
2017	101.93	22.06
2016	85.1	11.17
2015	77.78	-1.94
2014	81.18	10.05
2013	75.27	28.98

Total Assets: $47,775,778,497
Asset Allocation
Asset	%
Cash	0%
Stocks	100%
US Stocks	99%
Bonds	0%
US Bonds	0%
Other	0%

Services Offered:

Investment Strategy: The investment seeks to track the performance of a benchmark index that measures the investment return of common stocks of companies that have a record of increasing dividends over time. The fund employs an indexing investment approach designed to track the performance of the Nasdaq US Dividend Achievers Select Index, which consists of common stocks of companies that have a record of increasing dividends over time. The adviser attempts to replicate the target index by investing all, or substantially all, of its assets in the stocks that make up the index, holding each stock in approximately the same proportion as its weighting in the index. **Top Holdings:** Microsoft Corp Visa Inc Class A Procter & Gamble Co Walmart Inc Comcast Corp Class A

---

iShares Russell 1000 Growth ETF

C+ **HOLD**

Ticker	Traded On	NAV	Total Assets ($)	Dividend Yield (TTM)	Turnover Ratio	Expense Ratio
IWF	NYSE Arca	159.66	$44,889,616,923	1.06	12	0.19

Ratings
Reward	B-
Risk	C+
Recent Upgrade/Downgrade	Down

Fund Information
Fund Type	Exchange Traded Funds
Category	US Equity Large Cap Growth
Sub-Category	Large Growth
Prospectus Objective	Growth
Inception Date	May-00
Open to New Investments	Y

Prices
Price (as of 9/30/2019)	159.63
52-Week High	164.18
52-Week Low	121.77

Total Returns (%)
3-Month	6-Month	1-Year	3-Year	5-Year
0.48	4.85	3.26	58.83	88.51

3-Year Standard Deviation	13.29
Effective Duration	

Valuation
Premium/Discount (1-Year Average)	-0.04

Company Information
Provider	iShares
Manager/Tenure	Greg Savage (11), Jennifer Hsui (7), Alan Mason (3), 2 others
Website	http://www.ishares.com
Address	iShares 400 Howard Street San Francisco CA 94105 United States
Phone Number	800-474-2737

PERFORMANCE

Ratings History
Date	Overall Rating	Risk Rating	Reward Rating
Q3-19	C+	C+	B-
Q4-18	C	C+	C
Q4-17	B+	B+	B+
Q4-16	B-	C+	B
Q4-15	C+	C+	C+

Asset & Performance History
Date	NAV	1-Year Total Return
2018	130.78	-1.69
2017	134.58	29.95
2016	104.82	6.91
2015	99.49	5.47
2014	95.64	12.84
2013	85.93	33.19

Total Assets: $44,889,616,923
Asset Allocation
Asset	%
Cash	0%
Stocks	100%
US Stocks	100%
Bonds	0%
US Bonds	0%
Other	0%

Services Offered: CashInvestment Plan

Investment Strategy: The investment seeks to track the investment results of the Russell 1000® Growth Index, which measures the performance of large- and mid-capitalization growth sectors of the U.S. equity market. The fund generally invests at least 90% of its assets in securities of the underlying index and in depositary receipts representing securities of the underlying index. It may invest the remainder of its assets in certain futures, options and swap contracts, cash and cash equivalents, as well as in securities not included in the underlying index, but which the advisor believes will help the fund track the underlying index. **Top Holdings:** Microsoft Corp Apple Inc Amazon.com Inc Facebook Inc A Alphabet Inc Class C

iShares Core S&P Small-Cap ETF   C   HOLD

Ticker	Traded On	NAV	Total Assets ($)	Dividend Yield (TTM)	Turnover Ratio	Expense Ratio
IJR	NYSE Arca	77.87	$44,003,173,451	1.44	14	0.07

Ratings
Reward   C-
Risk   C
Recent Upgrade/Downgrade

Fund Information
Fund Type   Exchange Traded Funds
Category   US Equity Small Cap
Sub-Category   Small Blend
Prospectus Objective   Small Company
Inception Date   May-00
Open to New Investments   Y

Prices
Price (as of 9/30/2019)   77.84
52-Week High   85.94
52-Week Low   65.14

Total Returns (%)

3-Month	6-Month	1-Year	3-Year	5-Year
-0.36	0.37	-8.02	25.20	55.48

3-Year Standard Deviation   18.05
Effective Duration

Valuation
Premium/Discount (1-Year Average)   0.00

Company Information
Provider   iShares
Manager/Tenure   Greg Savage (11), Jennifer Hsui (7), Alan Mason (3), 2 others
Website   http://www.ishares.com
Address   iShares 400 Howard Street San Francisco CA 94105 United States
Phone Number   800-474-2737

PERFORMANCE

Ratings History

Date	Overall Rating	Risk Rating	Reward Rating
Q3-19	C	C	C-
Q4-18	C	B-	C-
Q4-17	A-	B	A
Q4-16	B	C+	B+
Q4-15	C+	C+	C

Asset & Performance History

Date	NAV	1-Year Total Return
2018	69.35	-12.23
2017	76.79	13.19
2016	68.72	26.49
2015	55.07	-1.99
2014	57	5.66
2013	54.63	41.36

Total Assets: $44,003,173,451
Asset Allocation

Asset	%
Cash	1%
Stocks	99%
US Stocks	98%
Bonds	0%
US Bonds	0%
Other	0%

Services Offered: CashInvestment Plan

Investment Strategy: The investment seeks to track the investment results of the S&P SmallCap 600 (the "underlying index"), which measures the performance of the small-capitalization sector of the U.S. equity market. The fund generally invests at least 90% of its assets in securities of the underlying index and in depositary receipts representing securities of the underlying index. It may invest the remainder of its assets in certain futures, options and swap contracts, cash and cash equivalents, as well as in securities not included in the underlying index, but which the advisor believes will help the fund track the underlying index. **Top Holdings:** Mercury Systems Inc Selective Insurance Group Inc FirstCash Inc Repligen Corp FTI Consulting Inc

SPDR® Gold Shares   C+   HOLD

Ticker	Traded On	NAV	Total Assets ($)	Dividend Yield (TTM)	Turnover Ratio	Expense Ratio
GLD	NYSE Arca	140.00	$43,959,000,424	0	0	0.4

Ratings
Reward   C+
Risk   C+
Recent Upgrade/Downgrade   Up

Fund Information
Fund Type   Exchange Traded Funds
Category   Commodities Specified
Sub-Category   Commodities Precious Metals
Prospectus Objective   Prec Metals
Inception Date   Nov-04
Open to New Investments   Y

Prices
Price (as of 9/30/2019)   138.87
52-Week High   146.66
52-Week Low   112.54

Total Returns (%)

3-Month	6-Month	1-Year	3-Year	5-Year
6.74	14.60	24.39	10.97	19.68

3-Year Standard Deviation   11.17
Effective Duration

Valuation
Premium/Discount (1-Year Average)   -0.11

Company Information
Provider   SPDR State Street Global Advisors
Manager/Tenure   Management Team (14)
Website   http://www.spdrs.com
Address   SPDR State Street Global Advisors State Street Financial Center, 1 Lincoln Street Boston MA 02111-2900 United States
Phone Number   617-786-3000

PERFORMANCE

Ratings History

Date	Overall Rating	Risk Rating	Reward Rating
Q3-19	C+	C+	C+
Q4-18	D+	C-	D
Q4-17	C-	C-	C-
Q4-16	C-	D+	C-
Q4-15	D	D	D

Asset & Performance History

Date	NAV	1-Year Total Return
2018	121.16	-1.54
2017	123.06	11.41
2016	110.45	8.68
2015	101.62	-11.78
2014	115.2	-0.58
2013	115.87	-28.09

Total Assets: $43,959,000,424
Asset Allocation

Asset	%
Cash	0%
Stocks	0%
US Stocks	0%
Bonds	0%
US Bonds	0%
Other	100%

Services Offered:
Investment Strategy:
Top Holdings: Gold Trust

iShares Russell 2000 ETF

C   HOLD

Ticker	Traded On	NAV		Total Assets ($)	Dividend Yield (TTM)	Turnover Ratio	Expense Ratio
IWM	NYSE Arca	151.42		$43,616,497,360	1.29	22	0.19

Ratings
Reward	C-
Risk	C+
Recent Upgrade/Downgrade	

Fund Information
Fund Type	Exchange Traded Funds
Category	US Equity Small Cap
Sub-Category	Small Blend
Prospectus Objective	Small Company
Inception Date	May-00
Open to New Investments	Y

Prices
Price (as of 9/30/2019)	151.34
52-Week High	166.33
52-Week Low	125.88

Total Returns (%)

3-Month	6-Month	1-Year	3-Year	5-Year
-2.60	-1.44	-7.67	26.69	50.52

3-Year Standard Deviation	17.2
Effective Duration	

Valuation
Premium/Discount (1-Year Average)	-0.05

Company Information
Provider	iShares
Manager/Tenure	Greg Savage (11), Jennifer Hsui (7), Alan Mason (3), 2 others
Website	http://www.ishares.com
Address	iShares 400 Howard Street San Francisco CA 94105 United States
Phone Number	800-474-2737

PERFORMANCE

Ratings History

Date	Overall Rating	Risk Rating	Reward Rating
Q3-19	C	C+	C-
Q4-18	C	B-	C-
Q4-17	B+	B	A-
Q4-16	B-	C+	B
Q4-15	C	C	C

Asset & Performance History

Date	NAV	1-Year Total Return
2018	134.01	-11.02
2017	152.44	14.65
2016	134.75	21.36
2015	112.76	-4.33
2014	119.6	4.94
2013	115.44	38.85

Total Assets: $43,616,497,360

Asset Allocation

Asset	%
Cash	0%
Stocks	100%
US Stocks	99%
Bonds	0%
US Bonds	0%
Other	0%

Services Offered: CashInvestment Plan

Investment Strategy: The investment seeks to track the investment results of the Russell 2000® Index, which measures the performance of the small-capitalization sector of the U.S. equity market. The Fund generally invests at least 90% of its assets in securities of the underlying index and in depositary receipts representing securities of the underlying index. It may invest the remainder of its assets in certain futures, options and swap contracts, cash and cash equivalents, as well as in securities not included in the underlying index, but which the advisor believes will help the fund track the underlying index. **Top Holdings:** NovoCure Ltd Haemonetics Corp Science Applications International Corp Portland General Electric Co Trex Co Inc

iShares Russell 1000 Value ETF

C+   HOLD

Ticker	Traded On	NAV		Total Assets ($)	Dividend Yield (TTM)	Turnover Ratio	Expense Ratio
IWD	NYSE Arca	128.29		$39,501,656,911	2.35	17	0.19

Ratings
Reward	C
Risk	C+
Recent Upgrade/Downgrade	Up

Fund Information
Fund Type	Exchange Traded Funds
Category	US Equity Large Cap Value
Sub-Category	Large Value
Prospectus Objective	Growth
Inception Date	May-00
Open to New Investments	Y

Prices
Price (as of 9/30/2019)	128.26
52-Week High	130.25
52-Week Low	104.79

Total Returns (%)

3-Month	6-Month	1-Year	3-Year	5-Year
0.72	3.92	3.53	30.39	46.12

3-Year Standard Deviation	12.32
Effective Duration	

Valuation
Premium/Discount (1-Year Average)	-0.03

Company Information
Provider	iShares
Manager/Tenure	Greg Savage (11), Jennifer Hsui (7), Alan Mason (3), 2 others
Website	http://www.ishares.com
Address	iShares 400 Howard Street San Francisco CA 94105 United States
Phone Number	800-474-2737

PERFORMANCE

Ratings History

Date	Overall Rating	Risk Rating	Reward Rating
Q3-19	C+	C+	C
Q4-18	C+	B	C
Q4-17	B-	B	B-
Q4-16	B	B-	B
Q4-15	C+	C+	C

Asset & Performance History

Date	NAV	1-Year Total Return
2018	110.94	-8.39
2017	124.19	13.46
2016	111.88	17.09
2015	97.87	-3.94
2014	104.39	13.2
2013	94.13	32.17

Total Assets: $39,501,656,911

Asset Allocation

Asset	%
Cash	0%
Stocks	100%
US Stocks	98%
Bonds	0%
US Bonds	0%
Other	0%

Services Offered: CashInvestment Plan

Investment Strategy: The investment seeks to track the investment results of the Russell 1000® Value Index (the "underlying index"), which measures the performance of large- and mid- capitalization value sectors of the U.S. equity market. The fund generally invests at least 90% of its assets in securities of the underlying index and in depositary receipts representing securities of the underlying index. It may invest the remainder of its assets in certain futures, options and swap contracts, cash and cash equivalents, as well as in securities not included in the underlying index, but which the advisor believes will help the fund track the underlying index. **Top Holdings:** Berkshire Hathaway Inc B JPMorgan Chase & Co Exxon Mobil Corp Johnson & Johnson Procter & Gamble Co

Vanguard FTSE All-World ex-US Index Fund ETF Shares   C   HOLD

Ticker	Traded On	NAV	Total Assets ($)	Dividend Yield (TTM)	Turnover Ratio	Expense Ratio
VEU	NYSE Arca	49.88	$37,889,032,762	3.07	6	0.09

Ratings
Reward   C
Risk   B
Recent Upgrade/Downgrade

Fund Information
Fund Type   Exchange Traded Funds
Category   Global Equity Large Cap
Sub-Category   Foreign Large Blend
Prospectus Objective   Foreign Stock
Inception Date   Mar-07
Open to New Investments   Y

Prices
Price (as of 9/30/2019)   49.90
52-Week High   52.19
52-Week Low   44.23

Total Returns (%)

3-Month	6-Month	1-Year	3-Year	5-Year
-1.59	0.01	-1.18	20.06	17.10

3-Year Standard Deviation   11.51
Effective Duration

Valuation
Premium/Discount (1-Year Average)   0.00

Company Information
Provider   Vanguard
Manager/Tenure   Christine D. Franquin (3), Justin E.
                    Hales (3)
Website   http://www.vanguard.com
Address   Vanguard 100 Vanguard Boulevard
                    Malvern PA 19355 United States
Phone Number   877-662-7447

PERFORMANCE

Ratings History

Date	Overall Rating	Risk Rating	Reward Rating
Q3-19	C	B	C
Q4-18	C-	C	D+
Q4-17	B-	B-	B-
Q4-16	C-	C	D+
Q4-15	C	C+	C-

Asset & Performance History

Date	NAV	1-Year Total Return
2018	45.44	-14.32
2017	54.64	27.44
2016	44.16	3.81
2015	43.45	-4.67
2014	46.85	-4.04
2013	50.46	14.49

Total Assets: $37,889,032,762
Asset Allocation

Asset	%
Cash	1%
Stocks	99%
US Stocks	1%
Bonds	0%
US Bonds	0%
Other	0%

Services Offered:

Investment Strategy: The investment seeks to track the performance of a benchmark index that measures the investment return of stocks of companies located in developed and emerging markets outside of the United States. The fund employs an indexing investment approach designed to track the performance of the FTSE All-World ex US Index. The advisor attempts to replicate the target index by investing all, or substantially all, of its assets in the stocks that make up the index, holding each stock in approximately the same proportion as its weighting in the index. **Top Holdings:** Nestle SA Tencent Holdings Ltd Alibaba Group Holding Ltd ADR Novartis AG Roche Holding AG Dividend Right Cert.

---

iShares iBoxx $ Investment Grade Corporate Bond ETF   B-   BUY

Ticker	Traded On	NAV	Total Assets ($)	Dividend Yield (TTM)	Turnover Ratio	Expense Ratio
LQD	NYSE Arca	127.23	$36,120,663,153	3.35	10	0.15

Ratings
Reward   B-
Risk   B
Recent Upgrade/Downgrade

Fund Information
Fund Type   Exchange Traded Funds
Category   US Fixed Income
Sub-Category   Corporate Bond
Prospectus Objective   Corp Bond - Gen
Inception Date   Jul-02
Open to New Investments   Y

Prices
Price (as of 9/30/2019)   127.48
52-Week High   129.10
52-Week Low   111.35

Total Returns (%)

3-Month	6-Month	1-Year	3-Year	5-Year
3.37	9.70	14.99	14.75	26.90

3-Year Standard Deviation   5.13
Effective Duration   9.11

Valuation
Premium/Discount (1-Year Average)   0.09

Company Information
Provider   iShares
Manager/Tenure   Scott Radell (9), James Mauro (8)
Website   http://www.ishares.com
Address   iShares 400 Howard Street San
                    Francisco CA 94105 United States
Phone Number   800-474-2737

PERFORMANCE

Ratings History

Date	Overall Rating	Risk Rating	Reward Rating
Q3-19	B-	B	B-
Q4-18	C	C+	D+
Q4-17	B-	B+	C
Q4-16	B-	B+	C
Q4-15	C	C	C

Asset & Performance History

Date	NAV	1-Year Total Return
2018	112.69	-3.75
2017	121.39	7.15
2016	116.91	5.97
2015	114.01	-1.07
2014	119.2	8.56
2013	113.62	-2.49

Total Assets: $36,120,663,153
Asset Allocation

Asset	%
Cash	0%
Stocks	0%
US Stocks	0%
Bonds	97%
US Bonds	85%
Other	0%

Services Offered:

Investment Strategy: The investment seeks to track the investment results of the Markit iBoxx® USD Liquid Investment Grade Index. The fund generally invests at least 90% of its assets in component securities of the underlying index and at least 95% of its assets in investment-grade corporate bonds. The underlying index is designed to provide a broad representation of the U.S. dollar-denominated liquid investment-grade corporate bond market. **Top Holdings:** GE Capital International Funding Company Unlimited Company 4.42% Anheuser-Busch Companies LLC / Anheuser-Busch InBev Worldwide Inc 4.9% CVS Health Corp 4.3% CVS Health Corp 5.05% Verizon Communications Inc. 4.33%

iShares Edge MSCI Min Vol USA ETF

B **BUY**

Ticker	Traded On	NAV	Total Assets ($)	Dividend Yield (TTM)	Turnover Ratio	Expense Ratio
USMV	BATS	64.07	$35,009,523,106	1.84	21	0.15

Ratings

Reward	B
Risk	A-
Recent Upgrade/Downgrade	Down

Fund Information

Fund Type	Exchange Traded Funds
Category	US Equity Large Cap Blend
Sub-Category	Large Blend
Prospectus Objective	Growth
Inception Date	Oct-11
Open to New Investments	Y

Prices

Price (as of 9/30/2019)	64.10
52-Week High	64.69
52-Week Low	49.77

Total Returns (%)

3-Month	6-Month	1-Year	3-Year	5-Year
3.81	9.64	14.68	49.72	89.73

3-Year Standard Deviation	9.12
Effective Duration	

Valuation

Premium/Discount (1-Year Average)	-0.05

Company Information

Provider	iShares
Manager/Tenure	Diane Hsiung (7), Greg Savage (7), Jennifer Hsui (6), 3 others
Website	http://www.ishares.com
Address	iShares 400 Howard Street San Francisco CA 94105 United States
Phone Number	800-474-2737

PERFORMANCE

Ratings History

Date	Overall Rating	Risk Rating	Reward Rating
Q3-19	B	A-	B
Q4-18	B	A	C
Q4-17	B+	A+	B-
Q4-16	C	C+	C
Q4-15	B-	C+	B-

Asset & Performance History

Date	NAV	1-Year Total Return
2018	52.39	1.35
2017	52.77	18.97
2016	45.19	10.49
2015	41.82	5.5
2014	40.46	16.33
2013	35.48	25.1

Total Assets: $35,009,523,106

Asset Allocation

Asset	%
Cash	0%
Stocks	100%
US Stocks	98%
Bonds	0%
US Bonds	0%
Other	0%

Services Offered:

Investment Strategy: The investment seeks the investment results of the MSCI USA Minimum Volatility (USD) Index. The fund will invest at least 90% of its assets in the component securities of the index and may invest up to 10% of its assets in certain futures, options and swap contracts, cash and cash equivalents. The index measures the performance of large and mid-capitalization equity securities listed on stock exchanges in the U.S. that, in the aggregate, have lower volatility relative to the broader U.S. equity market. **Top Holdings:** Newmont Goldcorp Corp Coca-Cola Co Waste Management Inc Visa Inc Class A McDonald's Corp

Vanguard High Dividend Yield Index Fund ETF Shares

C+ **HOLD**

Ticker	Traded On	NAV	Total Assets ($)	Dividend Yield (TTM)	Turnover Ratio	Expense Ratio
VYM	NYSE Arca	88.71	$34,794,213,478	3.16	13	0.06

Ratings

Reward	C
Risk	C+
Recent Upgrade/Downgrade	

Fund Information

Fund Type	Exchange Traded Funds
Category	US Equity Large Cap Value
Sub-Category	Large Value
Prospectus Objective	Equity-Income
Inception Date	Nov-06
Open to New Investments	Y

Prices

Price (as of 9/30/2019)	88.73
52-Week High	89.75
52-Week Low	73.71

Total Returns (%)

3-Month	6-Month	1-Year	3-Year	5-Year
1.53	3.85	4.59	34.72	55.87

3-Year Standard Deviation	11.4
Effective Duration	

Valuation

Premium/Discount (1-Year Average)	0.01

Company Information

Provider	Vanguard
Manager/Tenure	William A. Coleman (3), Gerard C. O'Reilly (3)
Website	http://www.vanguard.com
Address	Vanguard 100 Vanguard Boulevard Malvern PA 19355 United States
Phone Number	877-662-7447

PERFORMANCE

Ratings History

Date	Overall Rating	Risk Rating	Reward Rating
Q3-19	C+	C+	C
Q4-18	C	C+	C
Q4-17	B	B+	B-
Q4-16	B-	C+	B
Q4-15	C+	C+	C+

Asset & Performance History

Date	NAV	1-Year Total Return
2018	77.33	-6.59
2017	85.53	16.47
2016	75.68	16.19
2015	66.77	0.33
2014	68.73	13.47
2013	62.33	30.26

Total Assets: $34,794,213,478

Asset Allocation

Asset	%
Cash	0%
Stocks	100%
US Stocks	98%
Bonds	0%
US Bonds	0%
Other	0%

Services Offered:

Investment Strategy: The investment seeks to track the performance of a benchmark index that measures the investment return of common stocks of companies that are characterized by high dividend yield. The fund employs an indexing investment approach designed to track the performance of the FTSE High Dividend Yield Index, which consists of common stocks of companies that pay dividends that generally are higher than average. The adviser attempts to replicate the target index by investing all, or substantially all, of its assets in the stocks that make up the index, holding each stock in approximately the same proportion as its weighting in the index. **Top Holdings:** JPMorgan Chase & Co Johnson & Johnson Exxon Mobil Corp Procter & Gamble Co AT&T Inc

Vanguard Intermediate-Term Bond Index Fund ETF Shares   C+   HOLD

Ticker	Traded On	NAV	Total Assets ($)	Dividend Yield (TTM)	Turnover Ratio	Expense Ratio
BIV	NYSE Arca	87.87	$34,291,306,124	2.74	53	0.07

Ratings
Reward	C+
Risk	C+
Recent Upgrade/Downgrade	Up

Fund Information
Fund Type	Exchange Traded Funds
Category	US Fixed Income
Sub-Category	Intermediate Core Bond
Prospectus Objective	Income
Inception Date	Apr-07
Open to New Investments	Y

Prices
Price (as of 9/30/2019)	88.00
52-Week High	88.95
52-Week Low	79.35

Total Returns (%)
3-Month	6-Month	1-Year	3-Year	5-Year
2.37	6.20	12.60	9.54	20.43

3-Year Standard Deviation	4.08
Effective Duration	6.34

Valuation
Premium/Discount (1-Year Average)	0.07

Company Information
Provider	Vanguard
Manager/Tenure	Joshua C. Barrickman (11)
Website	http://www.vanguard.com
Address	Vanguard 100 Vanguard Boulevard Malvern PA 19355 United States
Phone Number	877-662-7447

PERFORMANCE

Ratings History
Date	Overall Rating	Risk Rating	Reward Rating
Q3-19	C+	C+	C+
Q4-18	C-	C	D
Q4-17	B-	B+	C
Q4-16	C	C+	C
Q4-15	C	C+	C

Asset & Performance History
Date	NAV	1-Year Total Return
2018	81.07	-0.33
2017	83.73	3.76
2016	82.86	2.43
2015	82.95	1.22
2014	84.41	6.99
2013	81.65	-3.43

Total Assets: $34,291,306,124
Asset Allocation
Asset	%
Cash	1%
Stocks	0%
US Stocks	0%
Bonds	98%
US Bonds	89%
Other	0%

Services Offered:

Investment Strategy: The investment seeks the performance of the Bloomberg Barclays U.S. 5-10 Year Government/Credit Float Adjusted Index. Bloomberg Barclays U.S. 5-10 Year Government/Credit Float Adjusted Index includes all medium and larger issues of U.S. government, investment-grade corporate and investment-grade international dollar-denominated bonds that have maturities between 5 and 10 years and are publicly issued. All of its investments will be selected through the sampling process, and at least 80% of its assets will be invested in bonds held in the index. **Top Holdings:** United States Treasury Notes 2.38% United States Treasury Notes 3.12% United States Treasury Notes 1.62% United States Treasury Notes 2.25% United States Treasury Notes 2.62%

Vanguard Short-Term Inflation-Protected Securities Index Fund ETF Shares   C   HOLD

Ticker	Traded On	NAV	Total Assets ($)	Dividend Yield (TTM)	Turnover Ratio	Expense Ratio
VTIP	NAS CM	49.03	$31,192,501,537	1.97	25	0.06

Ratings
Reward	C
Risk	C+
Recent Upgrade/Downgrade	

Fund Information
Fund Type	Exchange Traded Funds
Category	US Fixed Income
Sub-Category	Inflation-Protected Bond
Prospectus Objective	Govt Bond - Treasury
Inception Date	Oct-12
Open to New Investments	Y

Prices
Price (as of 9/30/2019)	49.05
52-Week High	49.64
52-Week Low	47.71

Total Returns (%)
3-Month	6-Month	1-Year	3-Year	5-Year
0.38	2.03	3.45	4.89	6.20

3-Year Standard Deviation	1.15
Effective Duration	2.67

Valuation
Premium/Discount (1-Year Average)	0.07

Company Information
Provider	Vanguard
Manager/Tenure	Joshua C. Barrickman (6)
Website	http://www.vanguard.com
Address	Vanguard 100 Vanguard Boulevard Malvern PA 19355 United States
Phone Number	877-662-7447

PERFORMANCE

Ratings History
Date	Overall Rating	Risk Rating	Reward Rating
Q3-19	C	C+	C
Q4-18	C	C+	C-
Q4-17	C	B-	C
Q4-16	C	C+	C
Q4-15	D+	C	D

Asset & Performance History
Date	NAV	1-Year Total Return
2018	47.82	0.45
2017	48.77	0.77
2016	49.11	2.75
2015	48.18	-0.14
2014	48.25	-1.16
2013	49.22	-1.55

Total Assets: $31,192,501,537
Asset Allocation
Asset	%
Cash	0%
Stocks	0%
US Stocks	0%
Bonds	100%
US Bonds	100%
Other	0%

Services Offered:

Investment Strategy: The investment seeks to track the performance of the Bloomberg Barclays U.S. Treasury Inflation-Protected Securities (TIPS) 0-5 Year Index. The index is a market-capitalization-weighted index that includes all inflation-protected public obligations issued by the U.S. Treasury with remaining maturities of less than 5 years. The manager attempts to replicate the target index by investing all, or substantially all, of its assets in the securities that make up the index, holding each security in approximately the same proportion as its weighting in the index. **Top Holdings:** United States Treasury Notes 0.12% United States Treasury Notes 0.12% United States Treasury Notes 0.12% United States Treasury Notes 0.62% United States Treasury Notes 0.62%

Vanguard Short-Term Corporate Bond Index Fund ETF Shares

C+ HOLD

Ticker	Traded On	NAV	Total Assets ($)	Dividend Yield (TTM)	Turnover Ratio	Expense Ratio
VCSH	NAS CM	80.98	$30,932,432,651	2.84	56	0.07

Ratings
Reward   C+
Risk   C+
Recent Upgrade/Downgrade

Fund Information
Fund Type   Exchange Traded Funds
Category   US Fixed Income
Sub-Category   Short-Term Bond
Prospectus Objective   Corp Bond - Gen
Inception Date   Nov-09
Open to New Investments Y

Prices
Price (as of 9/30/2019) 81.05
52-Week High   81.29
52-Week Low   77.54

Total Returns (%)

3-Month	6-Month	1-Year	3-Year	5-Year
1.11	3.13	6.66	8.43	14.06

3-Year Standard Deviation   1.57
Effective Duration   2.64

Valuation
Premium/Discount (1-Year Average)   0.09

Company Information
Provider   Vanguard
Manager/Tenure   Joshua C. Barrickman (9)
Website   http://www.vanguard.com
Address   Vanguard 100 Vanguard Boulevard
                 Malvern PA 19355 United States
Phone Number   877-662-7447

PERFORMANCE

Ratings History

Date	Overall Rating	Risk Rating	Reward Rating
Q3-19	C+	C+	C+
Q4-18	C	C+	C
Q4-17	B	A+	C
Q4-16	C	C+	C
Q4-15	C	C+	C

Asset & Performance History

Date	NAV	1-Year Total Return
2018	77.83	0.77
2017	79.3	2.42
2016	79.16	2.65
2015	78.76	1.24
2014	79.41	1.95
2013	79.46	1.37

Total Assets: $30,932,432,651
Asset Allocation

Asset	%
Cash	0%
Stocks	0%
US Stocks	0%
Bonds	97%
US Bonds	81%
Other	0%

Services Offered:

Investment Strategy: The investment seeks to track the performance of a market-weighted corporate bond index with a short-term dollar-weighted average maturity. The fund employs an indexing investment approach designed to track the performance of the Bloomberg Barclays U.S. 1-5 Year Corporate Bond Index. This index includes U.S. dollar-denominated, investment-grade, fixed-rate, taxable securities issued by industrial, utility, and financial companies, with maturities between 1 and 5 years. Under normal circumstances, at least 80% of the fund's assets will be invested in bonds included in the index. **Top Holdings:** United States Treasury Notes 1.75% Bank of America Corporation 3% CVS Health Corp 3.7% United States Treasury Notes 1.75% GE Capital International Funding Company Unlimited Company 2.34%

Vanguard Intermediate-Term Corporate Bond Index Fund ETF Shares

C+ HOLD

Ticker	Traded On	NAV	Total Assets ($)	Dividend Yield (TTM)	Turnover Ratio	Expense Ratio
VCIT	NAS CM	91.04	$26,893,491,612	3.42	65	0.07

Ratings
Reward   B-
Risk   C+
Recent Upgrade/Downgrade

Fund Information
Fund Type   Exchange Traded Funds
Category   US Fixed Income
Sub-Category   Corporate Bond
Prospectus Objective   Corp Bond - Gen
Inception Date   Nov-09
Open to New Investments Y

Prices
Price (as of 9/30/2019) 91.24
52-Week High   92.09
52-Week Low   82.02

Total Returns (%)

3-Month	6-Month	1-Year	3-Year	5-Year
2.40	6.81	12.99	12.77	25.80

3-Year Standard Deviation   3.98
Effective Duration   6.18

Valuation
Premium/Discount (1-Year Average)   0.18

Company Information
Provider   Vanguard
Manager/Tenure   Joshua C. Barrickman (9)
Website   http://www.vanguard.com
Address   Vanguard 100 Vanguard Boulevard
                 Malvern PA 19355 United States
Phone Number   877-662-7447

PERFORMANCE

Ratings History

Date	Overall Rating	Risk Rating	Reward Rating
Q3-19	C+	C+	B-
Q4-18	C	C+	D+
Q4-17	B	A	C
Q4-16	C	C+	C
Q4-15	C	C+	C

Asset & Performance History

Date	NAV	1-Year Total Return
2018	82.49	-1.96
2017	87.21	5.56
2016	85.37	5.27
2015	83.74	0.87
2014	85.78	7.46
2013	82.55	-1.8

Total Assets: $26,893,491,612
Asset Allocation

Asset	%
Cash	1%
Stocks	0%
US Stocks	0%
Bonds	96%
US Bonds	86%
Other	0%

Services Offered:

Investment Strategy: The investment seeks to track the performance of a market-weighted corporate bond index with an intermediate-term dollar-weighted average maturity. The fund employs an indexing investment approach designed to track the performance of the Bloomberg Barclays U.S. 5-10 Year Corporate Bond Index. This index includes U.S. dollar-denominated, investment-grade, fixed-rate, taxable securities issued by industrial, utility, and financial companies, with maturities between 5 and 10 years. Under normal circumstances, at least 80% of the fund's assets will be invested in bonds included in the index. **Top Holdings:** CVS Health Corp 4.3% Anheuser-Busch InBev Worldwide Inc. 4.75% Bank of America Corporation 3.42% Verizon Communications Inc. 4.33% United States Treasury Notes 2.38%

iShares MSCI Emerging Markets ETF   C   HOLD

Ticker	Traded On	NAV	Total Assets ($)	Dividend Yield (TTM)	Turnover Ratio	Expense Ratio
EEM	NYSE Arca	40.96	$25,088,820,690	2.19	16	0.67

Ratings
Reward   C-
Risk   C+
Recent Upgrade/Downgrade

Fund Information
Fund Type	Exchange Traded Funds
Category	Global Emerg Mkts Equity
Sub-Category	Diversified Emerging Mkts
Prospectus Objective	Div Emerg Mkts
Inception Date	Apr-03
Open to New Investments	Y

Prices
Price (as of 9/30/2019)	40.87
52-Week High	44.59
52-Week Low	38.00

Total Returns (%)
3-Month	6-Month	1-Year	3-Year	5-Year
-5.27	-5.01	-2.46	16.95	9.92

3-Year Standard Deviation   14.03
Effective Duration

Valuation
Premium/Discount (1-Year Average)   -0.04

Company Information
Provider	iShares
Manager/Tenure	Diane Hsiung (11), Greg Savage (11), Jennifer Hsui (6), 3 others
Website	http://www.ishares.com
Address	iShares 400 Howard Street San Francisco CA 94105 United States
Phone Number	800-474-2737

PERFORMANCE

Ratings History

Date	Overall Rating	Risk Rating	Reward Rating
Q3-19	C	C+	C-
Q4-18	C-	C-	C-
Q4-17	B-	C	B
Q4-16	D+	C-	D+
Q4-15	D+	D+	D+

Asset & Performance History

Date	NAV	1-Year Total Return
2018	39.17	-14.98
2017	47.07	36.42
2016	35.19	10.51
2015	32.46	-15.41
2014	39.26	-2.82
2013	41.3	-3.13

Total Assets: $25,088,820,690

Asset Allocation

Asset	%
Cash	0%
Stocks	100%
US Stocks	0%
Bonds	0%
US Bonds	0%
Other	0%

Services Offered: Dividend Investment Plan, CashInvestment Plan

Investment Strategy: The investment seeks to track the investment results of the MSCI Emerging Markets Index. The fund generally invests at least 90% of its assets in the securities of its underlying index and in depositary receipts representing securities in its underlying index. The index is designed to measure equity market performance in the global emerging markets. It may invest the remainder of its assets in other securities, including securities not in the underlying index, but which BFA believes will help the fund track the index, and in other investments, including futures contracts, options on futures contracts, other types of options and swaps related to its index. **Top Holdings:** Alibaba Group Holding Ltd ADR   Tencent Holdings Ltd   Taiwan Semiconductor Manufacturing Co Ltd   Samsung Electronics Co Ltd   Naspers Ltd Class N

Vanguard Small-Cap Growth Index Fund ETF Shares   C+   HOLD

Ticker	Traded On	NAV	Total Assets ($)	Dividend Yield (TTM)	Turnover Ratio	Expense Ratio
VBK	NYSE Arca	182.10	$23,784,828,458	0.62	22	0.07

Ratings
Reward   C
Risk   C+
Recent Upgrade/Downgrade

Fund Information
Fund Type	Exchange Traded Funds
Category	US Equity Small Cap
Sub-Category	Small Growth
Prospectus Objective	Small Company
Inception Date	Jan-04
Open to New Investments	Y

Prices
Price (as of 9/30/2019)	182.04
52-Week High	191.90
52-Week Low	140.03

Total Returns (%)
3-Month	6-Month	1-Year	3-Year	5-Year
-2.75	0.58	-0.88	41.57	61.72

3-Year Standard Deviation   16.07
Effective Duration

Valuation
Premium/Discount (1-Year Average)   -0.02

Company Information
Provider	Vanguard
Manager/Tenure	Gerard C. O'Reilly (14), William A. Coleman (3)
Website	http://www.vanguard.com
Address	Vanguard 100 Vanguard Boulevard Malvern PA 19355 United States
Phone Number	877-662-7447

PERFORMANCE

Ratings History

Date	Overall Rating	Risk Rating	Reward Rating
Q3-19	C+	C+	C
Q4-18	C	C+	C-
Q4-17	B	B	B
Q4-16	C+	C+	C+
Q4-15	C+	C+	C

Asset & Performance History

Date	NAV	1-Year Total Return
2018	148.73	-6.82
2017	160.81	22.19
2016	133.07	10.19
2015	121.53	-2.5
2014	125.88	4.02
2013	122.23	38.18

Total Assets: $23,784,828,458

Asset Allocation

Asset	%
Cash	2%
Stocks	98%
US Stocks	98%
Bonds	0%
US Bonds	0%
Other	0%

Services Offered:

Investment Strategy: The investment seeks to track the performance of a benchmark index that measures the investment return of small-capitalization growth stocks. The fund employs an indexing investment approach designed to track the performance of the CRSP US Small Cap Growth Index, a broadly diversified index of growth stocks of small U.S. companies. The advisor attempts to replicate the target index by investing all, or substantially all, of its assets in the stocks that make up the index, holding each stock in approximately the same proportion as its weighting in the index. **Top Holdings:** MarketAxess Holdings Inc   Burlington Stores Inc   Zebra Technologies Corp   Sun Communities Inc   Teledyne Technologies Inc

Vanguard Information Technology Index Fund ETF Shares
B-   BUY

Ticker	Traded On	NAV	Total Assets ($)	Dividend Yield (TTM)	Turnover Ratio	Expense Ratio
VGT	NYSE Arca	215.48	$23,769,348,271	1.26	7	0.1

Ratings
Reward	B
Risk	C+
Recent Upgrade/Downgrade	Down

Fund Information
Fund Type	Exchange Traded Funds
Category	Technology Sector Equity
Sub-Category	Technology
Prospectus Objective	Unaligned
Inception Date	Jan-04
Open to New Investments	Y

Prices
Price (as of 9/30/2019)	215.55
52-Week High	223.32
52-Week Low	154.81

Total Returns (%)
3-Month	6-Month	1-Year	3-Year	5-Year
0.03	5.51	6.46	83.56	128.70

3-Year Standard Deviation	15.93
Effective Duration	

Valuation
Premium/Discount (1-Year Average)	-0.02

Company Information
Provider	Vanguard
Manager/Tenure	Walter Nejman (3), Michael A. Johnson (1)
Website	http://www.vanguard.com
Address	Vanguard 100 Vanguard Boulevard Malvern PA 19355 United States
Phone Number	877-662-7447

PERFORMANCE

Ratings History

Date	Overall Rating	Risk Rating	Reward Rating
Q3-19	B-	C+	B
Q4-18	C+	C+	C+
Q4-17	A-	B	A+
Q4-16	C+	C+	C+
Q4-15	B-	B-	B-

Asset & Performance History

Date	NAV	1-Year Total Return
2018	165.24	1.53
2017	164.64	36.62
2016	121.44	13.22
2015	108.27	5.02
2014	104.48	18.01
2013	89.52	30.91

Total Assets: $23,769,348,271

Asset Allocation

Asset	%
Cash	1%
Stocks	99%
US Stocks	99%
Bonds	0%
US Bonds	0%
Other	0%

Services Offered:

Investment Strategy: The investment seeks to track the performance of a benchmark index. The fund employs an indexing investment approach designed to track the performance of the MSCI US Investable Market Index/Information Technology 25/50, an index made up of stocks of large, mid-size, and small U.S. companies within the information technology sector, as classified under the Global Industry Classification Standard. The Advisor attempts to replicate the target index by seeking to invest all, or substantially all, of its assets in the stocks that make up the index, in order to hold each stock in approximately the same proportion as its weighting in the index. It is non-diversified. **Top Holdings:** Apple Inc Microsoft Corp Visa Inc Class A Mastercard Inc A Cisco Systems Inc

---

Vanguard Large-Cap Index Fund ETF Shares
C+   HOLD

Ticker	Traded On	NAV	Total Assets ($)	Dividend Yield (TTM)	Turnover Ratio	Expense Ratio
VV	NYSE Arca	136.30	$23,361,578,260	1.88	4	0.04

Ratings
Reward	C+
Risk	C+
Recent Upgrade/Downgrade	

Fund Information
Fund Type	Exchange Traded Funds
Category	US Equity Large Cap Blend
Sub-Category	Large Blend
Prospectus Objective	Growth
Inception Date	Jan-04
Open to New Investments	Y

Prices
Price (as of 9/30/2019)	136.33
52-Week High	138.83
52-Week Low	107.63

Total Returns (%)
3-Month	6-Month	1-Year	3-Year	5-Year
0.28	4.18	3.31	44.96	65.42

3-Year Standard Deviation	12.2
Effective Duration	

Valuation
Premium/Discount (1-Year Average)	-0.01

Company Information
Provider	Vanguard
Manager/Tenure	Michael A. Johnson (3), Walter Nejman (3)
Website	http://www.vanguard.com
Address	Vanguard 100 Vanguard Boulevard Malvern PA 19355 United States
Phone Number	877-662-7447

PERFORMANCE

Ratings History

Date	Overall Rating	Risk Rating	Reward Rating
Q3-19	C+	C+	C+
Q4-18	C	C+	C
Q4-17	B	B	B
Q4-16	B-	C+	B
Q4-15	C+	C+	C

Asset & Performance History

Date	NAV	1-Year Total Return
2018	113.79	-5.25
2017	122.49	22.1
2016	102.27	11.13
2015	93.52	1.07
2014	94.36	13.39
2013	84.76	32.64

Total Assets: $23,361,578,260

Asset Allocation

Asset	%
Cash	1%
Stocks	99%
US Stocks	99%
Bonds	0%
US Bonds	0%
Other	0%

Services Offered:

Investment Strategy: The investment seeks to track the performance of the CRSP US Large Cap Index that measures the investment return of large-capitalization stocks. The fund employs an indexing investment approach designed to track the performance of the CRSP US Large Cap Index, a broadly diversified index of large U.S. companies representing approximately the top 85% of the U.S. market capitalization. The advisor attempts to replicate the target index by investing all, or substantially all, of its assets in the stocks that make up the index, holding each stock in approximately the same proportion as its weighting in the index. **Top Holdings:** Microsoft Corp Apple Inc Amazon.com Inc Facebook Inc A Berkshire Hathaway Inc B

iShares S&P 500 Growth ETF   C+   HOLD

Ticker	Traded On	NAV	Total Assets ($)	Dividend Yield (TTM)	Turnover Ratio	Expense Ratio
IVW	NYSE Arca	180.03	$23,322,516,752	1.37	27	0.18

Ratings
Reward	C+
Risk	C+
Recent Upgrade/Downgrade	Down

Fund Information
Fund Type	Exchange Traded Funds
Category	US Equity Large Cap Growth
Sub-Category	Large Growth
Prospectus Objective	Growth
Inception Date	May-00
Open to New Investments	Y

Prices
Price (as of 9/30/2019)	180.03
52-Week High	185.08
52-Week Low	140.58

Total Returns (%)
3-Month	6-Month	1-Year	3-Year	5-Year
-0.10	4.15	2.77	54.21	83.88

3-Year Standard Deviation	12.32
Effective Duration	

Valuation
Premium/Discount (1-Year Average)	-0.03

Company Information
Provider	iShares
Manager/Tenure	Greg Savage (11), Jennifer Hsui (7), Alan Mason (3), 2 others
Website	http://www.ishares.com
Address	iShares 400 Howard Street San Francisco CA 94105 United States
Phone Number	800-474-2737

PERFORMANCE

Ratings History

Date	Overall Rating	Risk Rating	Reward Rating
Q3-19	C+	C+	C+
Q4-18	C	C+	C
Q4-17	B	B+	B
Q4-16	B-	C+	B
Q4-15	C+	B-	C+

Asset & Performance History

Date	NAV	1-Year Total Return
2018	150.56	-0.17
2017	152.63	27.19
2016	121.7	6.73
2015	115.8	5.33
2014	111.64	14.66
2013	98.76	32.47

Total Assets: $23,322,516,752

Asset Allocation

Asset	%
Cash	0%
Stocks	100%
US Stocks	99%
Bonds	0%
US Bonds	0%
Other	0%

Services Offered: CashInvestment Plan

Investment Strategy: The investment seeks to track the investment results of the S&P 500 Growth IndexTM, which measures the performance of the large-capitalization growth sector of the U.S. equity market. The fund generally invests at least 90% of its assets in securities of the underlying index and in depositary receipts representing securities of the underlying index. It may invest the remainder of its assets in certain futures, options and swap contracts, cash and cash equivalents, as well as in securities not included in the underlying index, but which BFA believes will help the fund track the underlying index. **Top Holdings:** Microsoft Corp Amazon.com Inc Facebook Inc A Alphabet Inc Class C Alphabet Inc A

---

iShares Core S&P Total U.S. Stock Market ETF   C+   HOLD

Ticker	Traded On	NAV	Total Assets ($)	Dividend Yield (TTM)	Turnover Ratio	Expense Ratio
ITOT	NYSE Arca	67.10	$22,811,257,911	1.98	6	0.03

Ratings
Reward	C+
Risk	C+
Recent Upgrade/Downgrade	

Fund Information
Fund Type	Exchange Traded Funds
Category	US Equity Large Cap Blend
Sub-Category	Large Blend
Prospectus Objective	Growth
Inception Date	Jan-04
Open to New Investments	Y

Prices
Price (as of 9/30/2019)	67.07
52-Week High	68.57
52-Week Low	53.25

Total Returns (%)
3-Month	6-Month	1-Year	3-Year	5-Year
0.40	4.05	2.68	43.46	67.01

3-Year Standard Deviation	12.55
Effective Duration	

Valuation
Premium/Discount (1-Year Average)	-0.04

Company Information
Provider	iShares
Manager/Tenure	Greg Savage (11), Jennifer Hsui (7), Alan Mason (3), 2 others
Website	http://www.ishares.com
Address	iShares 400 Howard Street San Francisco CA 94105 United States
Phone Number	800-474-2737

PERFORMANCE

Ratings History

Date	Overall Rating	Risk Rating	Reward Rating
Q3-19	C+	C+	C+
Q4-18	C	C+	C
Q4-17	B	B	B
Q4-16	B-	C+	B
Q4-15	C+	C+	C

Asset & Performance History

Date	NAV	1-Year Total Return
2018	56.69	-5.36
2017	61.04	21.22
2016	51.27	12.59
2015	46.42	0.96
2014	46.91	13
2013	42.26	32.66

Total Assets: $22,811,257,911

Asset Allocation

Asset	%
Cash	0%
Stocks	100%
US Stocks	99%
Bonds	0%
US Bonds	0%
Other	0%

Services Offered: CashInvestment Plan

Investment Strategy: The investment seeks to track the investment results of the S&P Total Market Index™ (TMI), which is comprised of the common equities included in the S&P 500® and the S&P Completion Index™. The fund generally invests at least 90% of its assets in securities of the underlying index and in depositary receipts representing securities of the underlying index. It may invest the remainder of its assets in certain futures, options and swap contracts, cash and cash equivalents, including shares of money market funds advised by BFA or its affiliates, as well as in securities not included in the underlying index. **Top Holdings:** Microsoft Corp Apple Inc Amazon.com Inc Facebook Inc A Berkshire Hathaway Inc B

Financial Select Sector SPDR® Fund
B- BUY

Ticker	Traded On	NAV	Total Assets ($)	Dividend Yield (TTM)	Turnover Ratio	Expense Ratio
XLF	NYSE Arca		$22,702,093,451	2.01	3	0.13

Ratings
Reward	C+
Risk	B-
Recent Upgrade/Downgrade	Up

Fund Information
Fund Type	Exchange Traded Funds
Category	Financials Sector Equity
Sub-Category	Financial
Prospectus Objective	Financial
Inception Date	Dec-98
Open to New Investments	Y

Prices
Price (as of 9/30/2019)	28.00
52-Week High	28.69
52-Week Low	22.31

Total Returns (%)
3-Month	6-Month	1-Year	3-Year	5-Year
0.92	7.59	3.54	53.43	63.90

3-Year Standard Deviation	17.24
Effective Duration	

Valuation
Premium/Discount (1-Year Average)	-0.03

Company Information
Provider	SPDR State Street Global Advisors
Manager/Tenure	Michael J. Feehily (8), Karl A. Schneider (4), Melissa Kapitulik (2)
Website	http://www.spdrs.com
Address	SPDR State Street Global Advisors State Street Financial Center, 1 Lincoln Street Boston MA 02111-2900 United States
Phone Number	617-786-3000

PERFORMANCE

Ratings History
Date	Overall Rating	Risk Rating	Reward Rating
Q3-19	B-	B-	C+
Q4-18	C+	C+	C
Q4-17	A-	B	A
Q4-16	B	C+	B
Q4-15	B	A	B

Asset & Performance History
Date	NAV	1-Year Total Return
2018	23.82	-13.08
2017	27.92	22.02
2016	23.26	21.15
2015	19.36	-1.6
2014	20.06	15.02
2013	17.74	35.36

Total Assets: $22,702,093,451
Asset Allocation
Asset	%
Cash	0%
Stocks	100%
US Stocks	98%
Bonds	0%
US Bonds	0%
Other	0%

Services Offered: Dividend Investment Plan, CashInvestment Plan

Investment Strategy: The investment seeks investment results that, before expenses, correspond generally to the price and yield performance of publicly traded equity securities of companies in the Financial Select Sector Index. The fund generally invests substantially all, but at least 95%, of its total assets in the securities comprising the index. The index includes securities of companies from the following industries: diversified financial services; insurance; banks; capital markets; mortgage real estate investment trusts ("REITs"); consumer finance; and thrifts and mortgage finance. The fund is non-diversified. **Top Holdings:** Berkshire Hathaway Inc B JPMorgan Chase & Co Bank of America Corporation Wells Fargo & Co Citigroup Inc

---

iShares Short Treasury Bond ETF
C HOLD

Ticker	Traded On	NAV	Total Assets ($)	Dividend Yield (TTM)	Turnover Ratio	Expense Ratio
SHV	NAS CM	110.61	$21,313,597,501	2.22	73	0.15

Ratings
Reward	C
Risk	C+
Recent Upgrade/Downgrade	

Fund Information
Fund Type	Exchange Traded Funds
Category	US Fixed Income
Sub-Category	Ultrashort Bond
Prospectus Objective	Govt Bond - Treasury
Inception Date	Jan-07
Open to New Investments	Y

Prices
Price (as of 9/30/2019)	110.62
52-Week High	110.67
52-Week Low	110.21

Total Returns (%)
3-Month	6-Month	1-Year	3-Year	5-Year
0.53	1.40	2.42	4.36	4.71

3-Year Standard Deviation	0.26
Effective Duration	0.39

Valuation
Premium/Discount (1-Year Average)	0.02

Company Information
Provider	iShares
Manager/Tenure	Scott Radell (9), James Mauro (8)
Website	http://www.ishares.com
Address	iShares 400 Howard Street San Francisco CA 94105 United States
Phone Number	800-474-2737

PERFORMANCE

Ratings History
Date	Overall Rating	Risk Rating	Reward Rating
Q3-19	C	C+	C
Q4-18	C	C+	C-
Q4-17	C	C+	C-
Q4-16	C	C+	C-
Q4-15	C	C+	C-

Asset & Performance History
Date	NAV	1-Year Total Return
2018	110.29	1.74
2017	110.21	0.65
2016	110.29	0.42
2015	110.19	0
2014	110.23	0
2013	110.23	0.01

Total Assets: $21,313,597,501
Asset Allocation
Asset	%
Cash	36%
Stocks	0%
US Stocks	0%
Bonds	64%
US Bonds	64%
Other	0%

Services Offered:

Investment Strategy: The investment seeks to track the investment results of the ICE U.S. Treasury Short Bond Index. The fund generally invests at least 90% of its assets in the bonds of the underlying index and at least 95% of its assets in U.S. government bonds. The index measures the performance of public obligations of the U.S. Treasury that have a remaining maturity of equal to or greater than one month and less than one year. It may invest up to 10% of its assets in U.S. government bonds not included in the underlying index, but which BFA believes will help the fund track the underlying index. **Top Holdings:** United States Treasury Notes 1.5% United States Treasury Notes 2.13% United States Treasury Notes 3.5% United States Treasury Notes 1.38% United States Treasury Notes 3.63%

SPDR® Dow Jones Industrial Average ETF   B   BUY

Ticker	Traded On	NAV	Total Assets ($)	Dividend Yield (TTM)	Turnover Ratio	Expense Ratio
DIA	NYSE Arca		$21,222,816,446	2.15	2	0.17

Ratings
Reward	B
Risk	C+
Recent Upgrade/Downgrade	Up

Fund Information
Fund Type	Exchange Traded Funds
Category	US Equity Large Cap Value
Sub-Category	Large Value
Prospectus Objective	Growth
Inception Date	Jan-98
Open to New Investments	Y

Prices
Price (as of 9/30/2019)	269.18
52-Week High	273.60
52-Week Low	218.10

Total Returns (%)
3-Month	6-Month	1-Year	3-Year	5-Year
0.97	3.30	3.70	56.62	76.57

3-Year Standard Deviation	12.38
Effective Duration	

Valuation
Premium/Discount (1-Year Average)	0.00

Company Information
Provider	SPDR State Street Global Advisors
Manager/Tenure	Management Team (21)
Website	http://www.spdrs.com
Address	SPDR State Street Global Advisors State Street Financial Center, 1 Lincoln Street Boston MA 02111-2900 United States
Phone Number	617-786-3000

PERFORMANCE

Ratings History
Date	Overall Rating	Risk Rating	Reward Rating
Q3-19	B	C+	B
Q4-18	B-	C+	B
Q4-17	B+	B	A-
Q4-16	B-	C	B
Q4-15	B	B	B

Asset & Performance History
Date	NAV	1-Year Total Return
2018	233.16	-3.6
2017	246.98	27.97
2016	197.36	15.42
2015	174	0.09
2014	177.91	9.87
2013	165.4	29.41

Total Assets: $21,222,816,446
Asset Allocation
Asset	%
Cash	0%
Stocks	100%
US Stocks	100%
Bonds	0%
US Bonds	0%
Other	0%

Services Offered: Dividend Investment Plan, CashInvestment Plan

Investment Strategy: O investimento destina-se a fornecer os resultados do investimento que, antes das despesas, geralmente corresponde ao preço de desempenho produtivo e do Dow Jones Industrial Average (DJIA). O fundo tem a carteira e dinheiro, e não está activa "administrado" pelos métodos tradicionais. **Top Holdings:** Boeing Co UnitedHealth Group Inc The Home Depot Inc McDonald's Corp Apple Inc

---

iShares TIPS Bond ETF   C+   HOLD

Ticker	Traded On	NAV	Total Assets ($)	Dividend Yield (TTM)	Turnover Ratio	Expense Ratio
TIP	NYSE Arca	116.02	$20,420,246,366	1.85	21	0.19

Ratings
Reward	C+
Risk	C+
Recent Upgrade/Downgrade	Up

Fund Information
Fund Type	Exchange Traded Funds
Category	US Fixed Income
Sub-Category	Inflation-Protected Bond
Prospectus Objective	Govt Bond - Treasury
Inception Date	Dec-03
Open to New Investments	Y

Prices
Price (as of 9/30/2019)	116.29
52-Week High	118.10
52-Week Low	108.28

Total Returns (%)
3-Month	6-Month	1-Year	3-Year	5-Year
1.56	4.51	7.12	6.38	11.26

3-Year Standard Deviation	3.28
Effective Duration	7.68

Valuation
Premium/Discount (1-Year Average)	0.06

Company Information
Provider	iShares
Manager/Tenure	Scott Radell (9), James Mauro (8)
Website	http://www.ishares.com
Address	iShares 400 Howard Street San Francisco CA 94105 United States
Phone Number	800-474-2737

PERFORMANCE

Ratings History
Date	Overall Rating	Risk Rating	Reward Rating
Q3-19	C+	C+	C+
Q4-18	C-	C	D
Q4-17	C	B-	C
Q4-16	C	C+	C
Q4-15	D+	C	D+

Asset & Performance History
Date	NAV	1-Year Total Return
2018	109.46	-1.43
2017	114.04	2.91
2016	113.13	4.55
2015	109.77	-1.58
2014	111.91	3.49
2013	109.91	-8.65

Total Assets: $20,420,246,366
Asset Allocation
Asset	%
Cash	0%
Stocks	0%
US Stocks	0%
Bonds	100%
US Bonds	100%
Other	0%

Services Offered: Dividend Investment Plan

Investment Strategy: The investment seeks to track the investment results of Bloomberg Barclays U.S. Treasury Inflation Protected Securities (TIPS) Index (Series-L) which composed of inflation-protected U.S. Treasury bonds. The fund generally invests at least 90% of its assets in the bonds of the underlying index and at least 95% of its assets in U.S. government bonds. It may invest up to 10% of its assets in U.S. government bonds not included in the underlying index, but which BFA believes will help the fund track the underlying index. It also may invest up to 5% of its assets in repurchase agreements collateralized by U.S. government obligations and in cash and cash equivalents. **Top Holdings:** United States Treasury Notes 0.13% United States Treasury Notes 0.63% United States Treasury Notes 0.13% United States Treasury Notes 0.13% United States Treasury Notes 0.38%

iShares Russell 1000 ETF   C+   HOLD

Ticker	Traded On	NAV	Total Assets ($)	Dividend Yield (TTM)	Turnover Ratio	Expense Ratio
IWB	NYSE Arca	164.54	$20,402,837,983	1.84	6	0.15

Ratings
Reward   C+
Risk   C+
Recent Upgrade/Downgrade

Fund Information
Fund Type   Exchange Traded Funds
Category   US Equity Large Cap Blend
Sub-Category   Large Blend
Prospectus Objective   Growth
Inception Date   May-00
Open to New Investments   Y

Prices
Price (as of 9/30/2019)   164.54
52-Week High   167.98
52-Week Low   129.86

PERFORMANCE

Total Returns (%)

3-Month	6-Month	1-Year	3-Year	5-Year
0.61	4.42	3.46	44.44	66.86

3-Year Standard Deviation   12.31
Effective Duration

Valuation
Premium/Discount (1-Year Average)   -0.03

Company Information
Provider   iShares
Manager/Tenure   Greg Savage (11), Jennifer Hsui (7),
                  Alan Mason (3), 2 others
Website   http://www.ishares.com
Address   iShares 400 Howard Street San
                  Francisco CA 94105 United States
Phone Number   800-474-2737

Ratings History

Date	Overall Rating	Risk Rating	Reward Rating
Q3-19	C+	C+	C+
Q4-18	C	C+	C
Q4-17	B	B	B
Q4-16	B-	C+	B
Q4-15	C+	C+	C

Asset & Performance History

Date	NAV	1-Year Total Return
2018	138.54	-4.9
2017	148.5	21.52
2016	124.37	11.91
2015	113.35	0.82
2014	114.63	13.08
2013	103.17	32.93

Total Assets: $20,402,837,983

Asset Allocation

Asset	%
Cash	0%
Stocks	100%
US Stocks	99%
Bonds	0%
US Bonds	0%
Other	0%

Services Offered: CashInvestment Plan

Investment Strategy: The investment seeks to track the investment results of the Russell 1000® Index, which measures the performance of large- and mid- capitalization sectors of the U.S. equity market. The fund generally invests at least 90% of its assets in securities of the underlying index and in depositary receipts representing securities of the underlying index. It may invest the remainder of its assets in certain futures, options and swap contracts, cash and cash equivalents, as well as in securities not included in the underlying index, but which the advisor believes will help the fund track the underlying index. **Top Holdings:** Microsoft Corp Apple Inc Amazon.com Inc Facebook Inc A Berkshire Hathaway Inc B

---

iShares Russell Mid-Cap ETF   D   SELL

Ticker	Traded On	NAV	Total Assets ($)	Dividend Yield (TTM)	Turnover Ratio	Expense Ratio
IWR	NYSE Arca	55.96	$20,009,202,336	1.43	11	0.19

Ratings
Reward   D
Risk   D
Recent Upgrade/Downgrade   Up

Fund Information
Fund Type   Exchange Traded Funds
Category   US Equity Mid Cap
Sub-Category   Mid-Cap Blend
Prospectus Objective   Growth
Inception Date   Jul-01
Open to New Investments   Y

Prices
Price (as of 9/30/2019)   55.95
52-Week High   57.42
52-Week Low   43.70

PERFORMANCE

Total Returns (%)

3-Month	6-Month	1-Year	3-Year	5-Year
-0.21	3.25	3.43	-66.23	-61.10

3-Year Standard Deviation   13.41
Effective Duration

Valuation
Premium/Discount (1-Year Average)   -0.01

Company Information
Provider   iShares
Manager/Tenure   Greg Savage (11), Jennifer Hsui (7),
                  Alan Mason (3), 2 others
Website   http://www.ishares.com
Address   iShares 400 Howard Street San
                  Francisco CA 94105 United States
Phone Number   800-474-2737

Ratings History

Date	Overall Rating	Risk Rating	Reward Rating
Q3-19	D	D	D
Q4-18	E+	D	E
Q4-17	B	B	B
Q4-16	B-	C+	B-
Q4-15	C	C+	C

Asset & Performance History

Date	NAV	1-Year Total Return
2018	46.46	-77.28
2017	208.15	18.32
2016	178.78	13.57
2015	160.27	-2.57
2014	167.06	13.03
2013	150.02	34.49

Total Assets: $20,009,202,336

Asset Allocation

Asset	%
Cash	0%
Stocks	100%
US Stocks	99%
Bonds	0%
US Bonds	0%
Other	0%

Services Offered: CashInvestment Plan

Investment Strategy: The investment seeks to track the investment results of the Russell Midcap Index, which measures the performance of the mid-capitalization sector of the U.S. equity market. The fund generally invests at least 90% of its assets in securities of the underlying index and in depositary receipts representing securities of the underlying index. It may invest the remainder of its assets in certain futures, options and swap contracts, cash and cash equivalents, as well as in securities not included in the underlying index, but which the advisor believes will help the fund track the underlying index. **Top Holdings:** Fiserv Inc L3Harris Technologies Inc Dollar General Corp Sempra Energy Welltower Inc

Vanguard Mid-Cap Value Index Fund ETF Shares   C   HOLD

Ticker	Traded On	NAV	Total Assets ($)	Dividend Yield (TTM)	Turnover Ratio	Expense Ratio
VOE	NYSE Arca	113.02	$19,610,088,120	2.12	17	0.07

Ratings
Reward	C
Risk	C+
Recent Upgrade/Downgrade	

Fund Information
Fund Type	Exchange Traded Funds
Category	US Equity Mid Cap
Sub-Category	Mid-Cap Value
Prospectus Objective	Growth
Inception Date	Aug-06
Open to New Investments	Y

Prices
Price (as of 9/30/2019)	113.00
52-Week High	114.13
52-Week Low	90.18

Total Returns (%)
3-Month	6-Month	1-Year	3-Year	5-Year
1.01	4.14	2.02	28.55	49.05

3-Year Standard Deviation	13.75
Effective Duration	

Valuation
Premium/Discount (1-Year Average)	-0.01

Company Information
Provider	Vanguard
Manager/Tenure	Donald M. Butler (13), Michael A. Johnson (3)
Website	http://www.vanguard.com
Address	Vanguard 100 Vanguard Boulevard Malvern PA 19355 United States
Phone Number	877-662-7447

PERFORMANCE

Ratings History

Date	Overall Rating	Risk Rating	Reward Rating
Q3-19	C	C+	C
Q4-18	C	C+	C-
Q4-17	B	B+	B
Q4-16	B	C+	B
Q4-15	C	C+	C

Asset & Performance History

Date	NAV	1-Year Total Return
2018	94.43	-13.13
2017	111.47	17.34
2016	97.12	14.81
2015	85.99	-1.8
2014	89.39	13.98
2013	79.73	37.65

Total Assets: $19,610,088,120
Asset Allocation

Asset	%
Cash	0%
Stocks	100%
US Stocks	97%
Bonds	0%
US Bonds	0%
Other	0%

Services Offered:

Investment Strategy: The investment seeks to track the performance of the CRSP US Mid Cap Value Index that measures the investment return of mid-capitalization value stocks. The fund employs an indexing investment approach designed to track the performance of the CRSP US Mid Cap Value Index, a broadly diversified index of value stocks of mid-size U.S. companies. The advisor attempts to replicate the target index by investing all, or substantially all, of its assets in the stocks that make up the index, holding each stock in approximately the same proportion as its weighting in the index. **Top Holdings:** Newmont Goldcorp Corp Motorola Solutions Inc WEC Energy Group Inc Willis Towers Watson PLC Eversource Energy

SPDR® S&P MidCap 400 ETF   C   HOLD

Ticker	Traded On	NAV	Total Assets ($)	Dividend Yield (TTM)	Turnover Ratio	Expense Ratio
MDY	NYSE Arca	352.30	$19,100,390,590	1.38	17	0.24

Ratings
Reward	C
Risk	C+
Recent Upgrade/Downgrade	

Fund Information
Fund Type	Exchange Traded Funds
Category	US Equity Mid Cap
Sub-Category	Mid-Cap Blend
Prospectus Objective	Growth
Inception Date	May-95
Open to New Investments	Y

Prices
Price (as of 9/30/2019)	352.47
52-Week High	364.55
52-Week Low	284.96

Total Returns (%)
3-Month	6-Month	1-Year	3-Year	5-Year
-0.49	1.42	-1.94	29.80	53.08

3-Year Standard Deviation	15.28
Effective Duration	

Valuation
Premium/Discount (1-Year Average)	0.00

Company Information
Provider	SPDR State Street Global Advisors
Manager/Tenure	Management Team (24)
Website	http://www.spdrs.com
Address	SPDR State Street Global Advisors State Street Financial Center, 1 Lincoln Street Boston MA 02111-2900 United States
Phone Number	617-786-3000

PERFORMANCE

Ratings History

Date	Overall Rating	Risk Rating	Reward Rating
Q3-19	C	C+	C
Q4-18	C	C+	C-
Q4-17	B	B	B
Q4-16	B	C+	B
Q4-15	C	C+	C

Asset & Performance History

Date	NAV	1-Year Total Return
2018	302.54	-11.27
2017	345.24	15.88
2016	301.68	20.33
2015	254.27	-2.4
2014	263.93	9.41
2013	244.1	33.08

Total Assets: $19,100,390,590
Asset Allocation

Asset	%
Cash	0%
Stocks	100%
US Stocks	100%
Bonds	0%
US Bonds	0%
Other	0%

Services Offered: Dividend Investment Plan, CashInvestment Plan

Investment Strategy: The investment seeks to provide investment results that, before expenses, generally correspond to the price and yield performance of the S&P MidCap 400 Index. The Trust holds the Portfolio and cash and is not actively "managed" by traditional methods. To maintain the correspondence between the composition and weightings of Portfolio Securities and component stocks of the S&P MidCap 400 Index, the Trustee adjusts the Portfolio from time to time to conform to periodic changes in the identity and/or relative weightings of Index Securities. **Top Holdings:** IDEX Corp Steris PLC Leidos Holdings Inc Zebra Technologies Corp NVR Inc

SPDR® S&P Dividend ETF

C+ **HOLD**

Ticker	Traded On	NAV	Total Assets ($)	Dividend Yield (TTM)	Turnover Ratio	Expense Ratio
SDY	NYSE Arca		$18,915,038,333	2.45	20	0.35

Ratings
Reward	C
Risk	C+
Recent Upgrade/Downgrade	

Fund Information
Fund Type	Exchange Traded Funds
Category	US Equity Large Cap Value
Sub-Category	Large Value
Prospectus Objective	Growth & Inc
Inception Date	Nov-05
Open to New Investments	Y

Prices
Price (as of 9/30/2019)	102.60
52-Week High	103.80
52-Week Low	84.76

Total Returns (%)
3-Month	6-Month	1-Year	3-Year	5-Year
1.57	3.21	7.17	34.85	69.45

3-Year Standard Deviation	11.18
Effective Duration	

Valuation
Premium/Discount (1-Year Average)	-0.02

Company Information
Provider	SPDR State Street Global Advisors
Manager/Tenure	Michael J. Feehily (7), Karl A. Schneider (4), Emiliano Rabinovich (2)
Website	http://www.spdrs.com
Address	SPDR State Street Global Advisors State Street Financial Center, 1 Lincoln Street Boston MA 02111-2900 United States
Phone Number	617-786-3000

PERFORMANCE

Ratings History
Date	Overall Rating	Risk Rating	Reward Rating
Q3-19	C+	C+	C
Q4-18	C	C+	C
Q4-17	B	A-	B
Q4-16	B-	C+	B
Q4-15	C+	C+	C

Asset & Performance History
Date	NAV	1-Year Total Return
2018	89.47	-2.71
2017	94.42	14.17
2016	85.46	19.21
2015	73.55	-0.69
2014	78.76	13.79
2013	72.58	30.08

Total Assets: $18,915,038,333
Asset Allocation
Asset	%
Cash	0%
Stocks	100%
US Stocks	98%
Bonds	0%
US Bonds	0%
Other	0%

Services Offered: Dividend Investment Plan, CashInvestment Plan

Investment Strategy: The investment seeks to provide investment results that, before fees and expenses, correspond generally to the total return performance of the S&P High Yield Dividend Aristocrats Index. The fund generally invests substantially all, but at least 80%, of its total assets in the securities comprising the index. The index is designed to measure the performance of the highest dividend yielding S&P Composite 1500® Index constituents that have followed a managed-dividends policy of consistently increasing dividends every year for at least 20 consecutive years. The fund is non-diversified. **Top Holdings:** AT&T Inc AbbVie Inc International Business Machines Corp Realty Income Corp National Retail Properties Inc

iShares 7-10 Year Treasury Bond ETF

C+ **HOLD**

Ticker	Traded On	NAV	Total Assets ($)	Dividend Yield (TTM)	Turnover Ratio	Expense Ratio
IEF	NAS CM	112.45	$18,869,346,030	2.21	63	0.15

Ratings
Reward	C
Risk	B-
Recent Upgrade/Downgrade	Up

Fund Information
Fund Type	Exchange Traded Funds
Category	US Fixed Income
Sub-Category	Long Government
Prospectus Objective	Govt Bond - Treasury
Inception Date	Jul-02
Open to New Investments	Y

Prices
Price (as of 9/30/2019)	112.47
52-Week High	114.25
52-Week Low	99.72

Total Returns (%)
3-Month	6-Month	1-Year	3-Year	5-Year
2.95	7.60	14.01	7.03	18.93

3-Year Standard Deviation	5.28
Effective Duration	7.63

Valuation
Premium/Discount (1-Year Average)	0.07

Company Information
Provider	iShares
Manager/Tenure	Scott Radell (9), James Mauro (8)
Website	http://www.ishares.com
Address	iShares 400 Howard Street San Francisco CA 94105 United States
Phone Number	800-474-2737

PERFORMANCE

Ratings History
Date	Overall Rating	Risk Rating	Reward Rating
Q3-19	C+	B-	C
Q4-18	D+	C	D
Q4-17	C	C	C-
Q4-16	C	C+	C
Q4-15	C	C+	C

Asset & Performance History
Date	NAV	1-Year Total Return
2018	104.02	0.82
2017	105.56	2.46
2016	104.9	0.99
2015	105.68	1.54
2014	106.04	8.91
2013	99.42	-6.11

Total Assets: $18,869,346,030
Asset Allocation
Asset	%
Cash	0%
Stocks	0%
US Stocks	0%
Bonds	100%
US Bonds	100%
Other	0%

Services Offered:

Investment Strategy: The investment seeks to track the investment results of the ICE U.S. Treasury 7-10 Year Bond Index. The fund generally invests at least 90% of its assets in the bonds of the underlying index and at least 95% of its assets in U.S. government bonds. The underlying index measures the performance of public obligations of the U.S. Treasury that have a remaining maturity of greater than or equal to seven years and less than ten years. **Top Holdings:** United States Treasury Notes 2.38% United States Treasury Notes 2.25% United States Treasury Notes 3.13% United States Treasury Notes 2.88% United States Treasury Notes 2.75%

iShares MBS ETF　　　　　　　　　　　　　　　　　　　C+　HOLD

Ticker	Traded On	NAV	Total Assets ($)	Dividend Yield (TTM)	Turnover Ratio	Expense Ratio
MBB	NAS CM	108.28	$18,818,484,089	2.77	343	0.07

Ratings
Reward	C+
Risk	C+
Recent Upgrade/Downgrade	Up

Fund Information
Fund Type	Exchange Traded Funds
Category	US Fixed Income
Sub-Category	Intermediate Government
Prospectus Objective	Govt Bond - Mortgage
Inception Date	Mar-07
Open to New Investments	Y

Prices
Price (as of 9/30/2019)	108.30
52-Week High	108.50
52-Week Low	101.79

Total Returns (%)
3-Month	6-Month	1-Year	3-Year	5-Year
1.43	3.64	7.86	6.69	13.41

3-Year Standard Deviation	2.52
Effective Duration	3.15

Valuation
Premium/Discount (1-Year Average)	0.03

Company Information
Provider	iShares
Manager/Tenure	Scott Radell (9), James Mauro (8)
Website	http://www.ishares.com
Address	iShares 400 Howard Street San Francisco CA 94105 United States
Phone Number	800-474-2737

PERFORMANCE

Ratings History
Date	Overall Rating	Risk Rating	Reward Rating
Q3-19	C+	C+	C+
Q4-18	C-	C+	D+
Q4-17	B-	B+	C
Q4-16	C	C+	C
Q4-15	C	C+	C

Asset & Performance History
Date	NAV	1-Year Total Return
2018	104.6	0.81
2017	106.55	2.37
2016	106.42	1.28
2015	107.77	1.27
2014	109.24	6.15
2013	104.71	-1.91

Total Assets: $18,818,484,089

Asset Allocation
Asset	%
Cash	1%
Stocks	0%
US Stocks	0%
Bonds	99%
US Bonds	99%
Other	0%

Services Offered:

Investment Strategy: The investment seeks to track the investment results of the Bloomberg Barclays U.S. MBS Index. The fund seeks to track the performance of the underlying index by investing at least 90% of its assets in the securities of the underlying index and in investments that provide substantially similar exposure to securities in the underlying index. The index measures the performance of investment-grade mortgage-backed pass-through securities ("MBS") issued or guaranteed by U.S. government agencies. **Top Holdings:** Gnma2 30yr 2017 Production Gnma2 30yr 2017 Production Fgold 30yr 2017 Production Fnma Pass-Thru I 4% Federal National Mortgage Association 3%

Schwab International Equity ETF™　　　　　　　　　　　C　HOLD

Ticker	Traded On	NAV	Total Assets ($)	Dividend Yield (TTM)	Turnover Ratio	Expense Ratio
SCHF	NYSE Arca	31.76	$18,689,758,017	3.54	5	0.06

Ratings
Reward	C
Risk	B
Recent Upgrade/Downgrade	

Fund Information
Fund Type	Exchange Traded Funds
Category	Global Equity Large Cap
Sub-Category	Foreign Large Blend
Prospectus Objective	Foreign Stock
Inception Date	Nov-09
Open to New Investments	Y

Prices
Price (as of 9/30/2019)	31.86
52-Week High	33.62
52-Week Low	27.44

Total Returns (%)
3-Month	6-Month	1-Year	3-Year	5-Year
-1.39	1.38	-1.59	20.74	18.50

3-Year Standard Deviation	11.25
Effective Duration	

Valuation
Premium/Discount (1-Year Average)	0.10

Company Information
Provider	Schwab ETFs
Manager/Tenure	Chuck Craig (6), Christopher Bliss (2), Jane Qin (2), 1 other
Website	http://www.schwabfunds.com
Address	Schwab ETFs United States
Phone Number	800-435-4000

PERFORMANCE

Ratings History
Date	Overall Rating	Risk Rating	Reward Rating
Q3-19	C	B	C
Q4-18	C-	C	D+
Q4-17	B	B	B
Q4-16	D+	C	D+
Q4-15	C	C+	C-

Asset & Performance History
Date	NAV	1-Year Total Return
2018	28.36	-14.39
2017	34.11	25.88
2016	27.75	2.88
2015	27.67	-2.43
2014	29.01	-4.44
2013	31.23	20.02

Total Assets: $18,689,758,017

Asset Allocation
Asset	%
Cash	0%
Stocks	100%
US Stocks	1%
Bonds	0%
US Bonds	0%
Other	0%

Services Offered:

Investment Strategy: The investment seeks to track as closely as possible, before fees and expenses, the total return of the FTSE Developed ex US Index. The fund will invest at least 90% of its net assets in stocks, including depositary receipts representing securities of the index; such depositary receipts may be in the form of American Depositary Receipts, Global Depositary Receipts and European Depositary Receipts. The index is comprised of large and mid capitalization companies in developed countries outside the United States, as defined by the index provider. The index defines the large and mid capitalization universe as approximately the top 90% of the eligible universe. **Top Holdings:** Nestle SA Novartis AG Roche Holding AG Dividend Right Cert. Samsung Electronics Co Ltd Toyota Motor Corp

iShares 20+ Year Treasury Bond ETF

C+   HOLD

Ticker	Traded On	NAV	Total Assets ($)	Dividend Yield (TTM)	Turnover Ratio	Expense Ratio
TLT	NAS CM	142.89	$18,504,098,874	2.24	17	0.15

Ratings

Reward	C
Risk	B-
Recent Upgrade/Downgrade	Up

Fund Information

Fund Type	Exchange Traded Funds
Category	US Fixed Income
Sub-Category	Long Government
Prospectus Objective	Govt Bond - Treasury
Inception Date	Jul-02
Open to New Investments	Y

Prices

Price (as of 9/30/2019)	143.08
52-Week High	147.80
52-Week Low	112.00

Total Returns (%)

3-Month	6-Month	1-Year	3-Year	5-Year
8.68	16.08	25.73	12.48	37.15

3-Year Standard Deviation	11.86
Effective Duration	18.35

Valuation

Premium/Discount (1-Year Average)	0.16

Company Information

Provider	iShares
Manager/Tenure	Scott Radell (9), James Mauro (8)
Website	http://www.ishares.com
Address	iShares 400 Howard Street San Francisco CA 94105 United States
Phone Number	800-474-2737

PERFORMANCE

Ratings History

Date	Overall Rating	Risk Rating	Reward Rating
Q3-19	C+	B-	C
Q4-18	D+	C-	D
Q4-17	C	C	C
Q4-16	C+	B	C
Q4-15	C	C-	C

Asset & Performance History

Date	NAV	1-Year Total Return
2018	121.01	-2.07
2017	126.94	8.69
2016	119.49	1.36
2015	120.73	-1.64
2014	125.9	27.35
2013	101.8	-13.91

Total Assets: $18,504,098,874

Asset Allocation

Asset	%
Cash	0%
Stocks	0%
US Stocks	0%
Bonds	100%
US Bonds	100%
Other	0%

Services Offered:

Investment Strategy: The investment seeks to track the investment results of the ICE U.S. Treasury 20+ Year Bond Index (the "underlying index"). The fund generally invests at least 90% of its assets in the bonds of the underlying index and at least 95% of its assets in U.S. government bonds. The underlying index measures the performance of public obligations of the U.S. Treasury that have a remaining maturity greater than or equal to twenty years. **Top Holdings:** United States Treasury Bonds 2.5% United States Treasury Bonds 2.5% United States Treasury Bonds 3% United States Treasury Bonds 3.13% United States Treasury Bonds 2.88%

Schwab U.S. Large-Cap ETF™

C+   HOLD

Ticker	Traded On	NAV	Total Assets ($)	Dividend Yield (TTM)	Turnover Ratio	Expense Ratio
SCHX	NYSE Arca	70.92	$18,300,168,522	1.9	3	0.03

Ratings

Reward	C+
Risk	C+
Recent Upgrade/Downgrade	

Fund Information

Fund Type	Exchange Traded Funds
Category	US Equity Large Cap Blend
Sub-Category	Large Blend
Prospectus Objective	Growth
Inception Date	Nov-09
Open to New Investments	Y

Prices

Price (as of 9/30/2019)	70.93
52-Week High	72.27
52-Week Low	56.03

Total Returns (%)

3-Month	6-Month	1-Year	3-Year	5-Year
0.74	4.63	3.72	45.58	68.42

3-Year Standard Deviation	12.26
Effective Duration	

Valuation

Premium/Discount (1-Year Average)	-0.01

Company Information

Provider	Schwab ETFs
Manager/Tenure	Ferian Juwono (9), Christopher Bliss (2), Sabya Sinha (2), 1 other
Website	http://www.schwabfunds.com
Address	Schwab ETFs United States
Phone Number	800-435-4000

PERFORMANCE

Ratings History

Date	Overall Rating	Risk Rating	Reward Rating
Q3-19	C+	C+	C+
Q4-18	C	C+	C
Q4-17	B	B	B
Q4-16	B-	C+	B
Q4-15	C+	C+	C

Asset & Performance History

Date	NAV	1-Year Total Return
2018	59.63	-4.52
2017	63.7	21.98
2016	53.21	11.77
2015	48.57	1.01
2014	49.06	13.33
2013	44.09	32.54

Total Assets: $18,300,168,522

Asset Allocation

Asset	%
Cash	0%
Stocks	100%
US Stocks	99%
Bonds	0%
US Bonds	0%
Other	0%

Services Offered:

Investment Strategy: The investment seeks to track as closely as possible, before fees and expenses, the total return of the Dow Jones U.S. Large-Cap Total Stock Market Index. To pursue its goal, the fund generally invests in stocks that are included in the Dow Jones U.S. Large-Cap Total Stock Market Index. The index includes the large-cap portion of the Dow Jones U.S. Total Stock Market Index actually available to investors in the marketplace. The Dow Jones U.S. Large-Cap Total Stock Market Index includes the components ranked 1-750 by full market capitalization. The index is a float-adjusted market capitalization weighted index. **Top Holdings:** Microsoft Corp Apple Inc Amazon.com Inc Facebook Inc A Berkshire Hathaway Inc B

Vanguard FTSE Europe Index Fund ETF Shares   C   HOLD

Ticker	Traded On	NAV	Total Assets ($)	Dividend Yield (TTM)	Turnover Ratio	Expense Ratio
VGK	NYSE Arca	53.57	$18,213,709,427	3.54	6	0.09

Ratings
Reward   C
Risk   B-
Recent Upgrade/Downgrade

Fund Information
Fund Type   Exchange Traded Funds
Category   Europe Equity Large Cap
Sub-Category   Europe Stock
Prospectus Objective   Europe Stock
Inception Date   Mar-05
Open to New Investments   Y

Prices
Price (as of 9/30/2019)   53.61
52-Week High   56.26
52-Week Low   46.99

Total Returns (%)

3-Month	6-Month	1-Year	3-Year	5-Year
-2.01	1.16	-1.34	21.30	15.54

3-Year Standard Deviation   12.5
Effective Duration

Valuation
Premium/Discount (1-Year Average)   -0.02

Company Information
Provider   Vanguard
Manager/Tenure   Christine D. Franquin (3), Justin E. Hales (3)
Website   http://www.vanguard.com
Address   Vanguard 100 Vanguard Boulevard Malvern PA 19355 United States
Phone Number   877-662-7447

PERFORMANCE

Ratings History

Date	Overall Rating	Risk Rating	Reward Rating
Q3-19	C	B-	C+
Q4-18	C-	C-	D+
Q4-17	B-	B	B-
Q4-16	D	C-	D
Q4-15	C-	C-	C-

Asset & Performance History

Date	NAV	1-Year Total Return
2018	48.43	-15.27
2017	59.17	27.56
2016	47.93	-2.25
2015	49.98	-1.87
2014	52.48	-6.55
2013	58.54	24.93

Total Assets: $18,213,709,427
Asset Allocation

Asset	%
Cash	1%
Stocks	99%
US Stocks	2%
Bonds	0%
US Bonds	0%
Other	0%

Services Offered:

Investment Strategy: The investment seeks to track the performance of a benchmark index that measures the investment return of stocks issued by companies located in the major markets of Europe. The fund employs an indexing investment approach by investing all, or substantially all, of its assets in the common stocks included in the FTSE Developed Europe All Cap Index. The index is a market-capitalization-weighted index. **Top Holdings:** Nestle SA   Novartis AG   Roche Holding AG Dividend Right Cert.   HSBC Holdings PLC   Royal Dutch Shell PLC Class A

---

iShares iBoxx $ High Yield Corporate Bond ETF   B   BUY

Ticker	Traded On	NAV	Total Assets ($)	Dividend Yield (TTM)	Turnover Ratio	Expense Ratio
HYG	NYSE Arca	86.89	$17,978,406,784	5.29	14	0.49

Ratings
Reward   C+
Risk   A
Recent Upgrade/Downgrade

Fund Information
Fund Type   Exchange Traded Funds
Category   US Fixed Income
Sub-Category   High Yield Bond
Prospectus Objective   Corp Bond-High Yld
Inception Date   Apr-07
Open to New Investments   Y

Prices
Price (as of 9/30/2019)   87.17
52-Week High   87.61
52-Week Low   79.63

Total Returns (%)

3-Month	6-Month	1-Year	3-Year	5-Year
0.97	3.80	6.14	17.19	23.69

3-Year Standard Deviation   4.23
Effective Duration   3.37

Valuation
Premium/Discount (1-Year Average)   0.15

Company Information
Provider   iShares
Manager/Tenure   Scott Radell (9), James Mauro (8)
Website   http://www.ishares.com
Address   iShares 400 Howard Street San Francisco CA 94105 United States
Phone Number   800-474-2737

PERFORMANCE

Ratings History

Date	Overall Rating	Risk Rating	Reward Rating
Q3-19	B	A	C+
Q4-18	C+	A-	C-
Q4-17	B-	B	C+
Q4-16	C+	B	C
Q4-15	C	C	C-

Asset & Performance History

Date	NAV	1-Year Total Return
2018	80.9	-1.93
2017	86.97	6.08
2016	86.26	13.92
2015	79.97	-5.54
2014	89.43	2
2013	92.62	5.89

Total Assets: $17,978,406,784
Asset Allocation

Asset	%
Cash	1%
Stocks	0%
US Stocks	0%
Bonds	99%
US Bonds	84%
Other	0%

Services Offered:

Investment Strategy: The investment seeks to track the investment results of the Markit iBoxx® USD Liquid High Yield Index (the "underlying index"). The underlying index is a rules-based index consisting of U.S. dollar-denominated, high yield corporate bonds for sale in the U.S. The fund generally will invest at least 90% of its assets in the component securities of the underlying index and may invest up to 10% of its assets in certain futures, options and swap contracts, cash and cash equivalents, as well as in securities not included in the underlying index. **Top Holdings:**   ALTICE FRANCE S.A 7.38%   Sprint Corporation 7.88%   TransDigm, Inc. 6.25%   CCO Holdings, LLC/ CCO Holdings Capital Corp. 5.13%   Bausch Health Companies Inc 6.13%

iShares 1-3 Year Treasury Bond ETF

C   HOLD

Ticker	Traded On	NAV	Total Assets ($)	Dividend Yield (TTM)	Turnover Ratio	Expense Ratio
SHY	NAS CM	84.79	$17,772,615,677	2.11	62	0.15

Ratings

Reward	C
Risk	C+
Recent Upgrade/Downgrade	

Fund Information

Fund Type	Exchange Traded Funds
Category	US Fixed Income
Sub-Category	Short Government
Prospectus Objective	Govt Bond - Treasury
Inception Date	Jul-02
Open to New Investments	Y

Prices

Price (as of 9/30/2019)	84.82
52-Week High	85.10
52-Week Low	82.85

Total Returns (%)

3-Month	6-Month	1-Year	3-Year	5-Year
0.63	2.26	4.26	4.22	5.98

3-Year Standard Deviation	1.03
Effective Duration	1.85

Valuation

Premium/Discount (1-Year Average)	0.04

Company Information

Provider	iShares
Manager/Tenure	Scott Radell (9), James Mauro (8)
Website	http://www.ishares.com
Address	iShares 400 Howard Street San Francisco CA 94105 United States
Phone Number	800-474-2737

PERFORMANCE

Ratings History

Date	Overall Rating	Risk Rating	Reward Rating
Q3-19	C	C+	C
Q4-18	C	C+	C-
Q4-17	C	C	C-
Q4-16	C	C+	C
Q4-15	C	C+	C

Asset & Performance History

Date	NAV	1-Year Total Return
2018	83.6	1.45
2017	83.84	0.27
2016	84.43	0.74
2015	84.4	0.42
2014	84.49	0.48
2013	84.39	0.22

Total Assets: $17,772,615,677

Asset Allocation

Asset	%
Cash	5%
Stocks	0%
US Stocks	0%
Bonds	95%
US Bonds	95%
Other	0%

Services Offered:

Investment Strategy: The investment seeks to track the investment results of the ICE U.S. Treasury 1-3 Year Bond Index (the "underlying index"). The fund generally invests at least 90% of its assets in the bonds of the underlying index and at least 95% of its assets in U.S. government bonds. The underlying index measures the performance of public obligations of the U.S. Treasury that have a remaining maturity of greater than or equal to one year and less than three years. **Top Holdings:** United States Treasury Notes 2.25% United States Treasury Notes 1.88% United States Treasury Notes 2.13% United States Treasury Notes 2.5% United States Treasury Notes 2.5%

---

iShares Select Dividend ETF

C   HOLD

Ticker	Traded On	NAV	Total Assets ($)	Dividend Yield (TTM)	Turnover Ratio	Expense Ratio
DVY	NAS CM	101.98	$17,744,238,254	3.4	21	0.39

Ratings

Reward	C
Risk	C+
Recent Upgrade/Downgrade	Down

Fund Information

Fund Type	Exchange Traded Funds
Category	US Equity Large Cap Value
Sub-Category	Large Value
Prospectus Objective	Equity-Income
Inception Date	Nov-03
Open to New Investments	Y

Prices

Price (as of 9/30/2019)	101.95
52-Week High	103.22
52-Week Low	85.20

Total Returns (%)

3-Month	6-Month	1-Year	3-Year	5-Year
3.18	4.62	5.69	31.52	64.33

3-Year Standard Deviation	11.03
Effective Duration	

Valuation

Premium/Discount (1-Year Average)	-0.02

Company Information

Provider	iShares
Manager/Tenure	Greg Savage (11), Jennifer Hsui (7), Alan Mason (3), 2 others
Website	http://www.ishares.com
Address	iShares 400 Howard Street San Francisco CA 94105 United States
Phone Number	800-474-2737

PERFORMANCE

Ratings History

Date	Overall Rating	Risk Rating	Reward Rating
Q3-19	C	C+	C
Q4-18	C	C+	C
Q4-17	B	B	B
Q4-16	B	C+	B
Q4-15	C+	C+	C

Asset & Performance History

Date	NAV	1-Year Total Return
2018	89.29	-6.3
2017	98.52	14.95
2016	88.44	21.45
2015	75.16	-2.02
2014	79.38	14.89
2013	71.31	28.71

Total Assets: $17,744,238,254

Asset Allocation

Asset	%
Cash	0%
Stocks	100%
US Stocks	97%
Bonds	0%
US Bonds	0%
Other	0%

Services Offered: CashInvestment Plan

Investment Strategy: The investment seeks to track the investment results of the Dow Jones U.S. Select Dividend Index composed of relatively high dividend paying U.S. equities. The fund generally invests at least 90% of its assets in securities of the underlying index and in depositary receipts representing securities of the underlying index. The underlying index measures the performance of the U.S.'s leading stocks by dividend yield. **Top Holdings:** AT&T Inc Ford Motor Co Qualcomm Inc ONEOK Inc Dominion Energy Inc

Vanguard Total World Stock Index Fund ETF Shares   C   HOLD

Ticker	Traded On	NAV	Total Assets ($)	Dividend Yield (TTM)	Turnover Ratio	Expense Ratio
VT	NYSE Arca	74.79	$16,872,110,485	2.35	9	0.09

Ratings
Reward   C
Risk   C+
Recent Upgrade/Downgrade

Fund Information
Fund Type   Exchange Traded Funds
Category   Global Equity Large Cap
Sub-Category   World Large Stock
Prospectus Objective   World Stock
Inception Date   Jun-08
Open to New Investments   Y

Prices
Price (as of 9/30/2019)   74.82
52-Week High   76.53
52-Week Low   62.33

Total Returns (%)

3-Month	6-Month	1-Year	3-Year	5-Year
-0.35	1.92	0.61	31.49	39.32

3-Year Standard Deviation   11.46
Effective Duration

Valuation
Premium/Discount (1-Year Average)   -0.04

Company Information
Provider   Vanguard
Manager/Tenure   Christine D. Franquin (6), Scott E. Geiger (1)
Website   http://www.vanguard.com
Address   Vanguard 100 Vanguard Boulevard Malvern PA 19355 United States
Phone Number   877-662-7447

PERFORMANCE

Ratings History

Date	Overall Rating	Risk Rating	Reward Rating
Q3-19	C	C+	C
Q4-18	C	C+	C-
Q4-17	B-	C+	B-
Q4-16	C	C+	C
Q4-15	C	C+	C

Asset & Performance History

Date	NAV	1-Year Total Return
2018	64.99	-10.27
2017	74.15	24.3
2016	61.06	8.05
2015	57.54	-1.88
2014	60.05	3.97
2013	59.16	22.97

Total Assets: $16,872,110,485
Asset Allocation

Asset	%
Cash	1%
Stocks	99%
US Stocks	55%
Bonds	0%
US Bonds	0%
Other	0%

Services Offered:

Investment Strategy: The investment seeks to track the performance of a benchmark index that measures the investment return of stocks of companies located in developed and emerging markets around the world. The fund employs an indexing investment approach designed to track the performance of the FTSE Global All Cap Index. The advisor attempts to sample the target index by investing all, or substantially all, of its assets in common stocks in the index and by holding a representative sample of securities that resembles the full index in terms of key risk factors and other characteristics. **Top Holdings:** Microsoft Corp Apple Inc Amazon.com Inc Facebook Inc A JPMorgan Chase & Co

---

iShares Preferred and Income Securities ETF   B   BUY

Ticker	Traded On	NAV	Total Assets ($)	Dividend Yield (TTM)	Turnover Ratio	Expense Ratio
PFF	NAS CM	37.45	$16,567,857,761	5.56	28	0.46

Ratings
Reward   C+
Risk   A-
Recent Upgrade/Downgrade   Up

Fund Information
Fund Type   Exchange Traded Funds
Category   US Fixed Income
Sub-Category   Preferred Stock
Prospectus Objective   Growth & Inc
Inception Date   Mar-07
Open to New Investments   Y

Prices
Price (as of 9/30/2019)   37.53
52-Week High   37.53
52-Week Low   33.41

Total Returns (%)

3-Month	6-Month	1-Year	3-Year	5-Year
2.99	4.83	7.35	12.53	26.69

3-Year Standard Deviation   5.1
Effective Duration   2.77

Valuation
Premium/Discount (1-Year Average)   0.17

Company Information
Provider   iShares
Manager/Tenure   Greg Savage (11), Jennifer Hsui (7), Alan Mason (3), 2 others
Website   http://www.ishares.com
Address   iShares 400 Howard Street San Francisco CA 94105 United States
Phone Number   800-474-2737

PERFORMANCE

Ratings History

Date	Overall Rating	Risk Rating	Reward Rating
Q3-19	B	A-	C+
Q4-18	C-	C	D+
Q4-17	B	A	C+
Q4-16	C	C	C
Q4-15	C+	C+	C+

Asset & Performance History

Date	NAV	1-Year Total Return
2018	34.26	-4.77
2017	38.16	8.32
2016	37.22	1.25
2015	38.88	4.61
2014	39.34	13.44
2013	36.95	-0.59

Total Assets: $16,567,857,761
Asset Allocation

Asset	%
Cash	1%
Stocks	6%
US Stocks	5%
Bonds	0%
US Bonds	0%
Other	0%

Services Offered:

Investment Strategy: The investment seeks to track the investment results of the ICE Exchange-Listed Preferred & Hybrid Securities Transition Index, which measures the performance of a select group of exchange-listed, U.S. dollar-denominated preferred securities, hybrid securities and convertible preferred securities listed on the NYSE or NASDAQ. The fund may invest at least 80% of its assets in the component securities of the index and may invest up to 20% of its assets in certain futures, options and swap contracts, cash and cash equivalents, as well as in securities not included in the index, but which the advisor believes will help the fund track the index. **Top Holdings:** Becton, Dickinson and Co Pfd GMAC Capital Trust I Pfd Secs 2011-15.2.40 Gtd Series 2 Citigroup Capital XIII Floating Rate Trust Pfd Secs Registered 2010-30.10.4 Sempra Energy 6% PRF CONVERT 15/01/2021 USD 100 Crown Castle International Corp Cum Conv Pfd Registered Shs Series -A-

iShares Gold Trust   C+   HOLD

Ticker	Traded On	NAV	Total Assets ($)	Dividend Yield (TTM)	Turnover Ratio	Expense Ratio
IAU	NYSE Arca	14.20	$16,352,798,380	0	0	0.25

Ratings
Reward   C+
Risk   C+
Recent Upgrade/Downgrade   Up

Fund Information
Fund Type   Exchange Traded Funds
Category   Commodities Specified
Sub-Category   Commodities Precious Metals
Prospectus Objective   Prec Metals
Inception Date   Jan-05
Open to New Investments Y

Prices
Price (as of 9/30/2019)   14.10
52-Week High   14.88
52-Week Low   11.39

Total Returns (%)

3-Month	6-Month	1-Year	3-Year	5-Year
6.78	14.68	24.57	11.48	20.57

3-Year Standard Deviation   11.17
Effective Duration

Valuation
Premium/Discount (1-Year Average)   -0.10

Company Information
Provider   iShares
Manager/Tenure   Management Team (14)
Website   http://www.ishares.com
Address   iShares 400 Howard Street San
                  Francisco CA 94105 United States
Phone Number   800-474-2737

PERFORMANCE

Ratings History				Asset & Performance History			Total Assets:	$16,352,798,380
Date	Overall Rating	Risk Rating	Reward Rating	Date	NAV	1-Year Total Return	Asset Allocation	
							Asset	%
Q3-19	C+	C+	C+	2018	12.28	-1.37	Cash	0%
Q4-18	D+	C-	D+	2017	12.45	11.55	Stocks	0%
Q4-17	C-	C-	C-	2016	11.16	8.87	US Stocks	0%
Q4-16	C-	D+	C-	2015	10.25	-11.71	Bonds	0%
Q4-15	D	D	D	2014	11.61	-0.42	US Bonds	0%
				2013	11.66	-27.93	Other	100%

Services Offered:

Investment Strategy: The investment seeks to reflect generally the performance of the price of gold. The Trust seeks to reflect such performance before payment of the Trust's expenses and liabilities. It is not actively managed. The Trust does not engage in any activities designed to obtain a profit from, or to ameliorate losses caused by, changes in the price of gold. The advisor intends to constitute a simple and cost-effective means of making an investment similar to an investment in gold. An investment in physical gold requires expensive and sometimes complicated arrangements in connection with the assay, transportation, warehousing and insurance of the metal. **Top Holdings:** Gold

---

iShares Core MSCI Total International Stock ETF   C   HOLD

Ticker	Traded On	NAV	Total Assets ($)	Dividend Yield (TTM)	Turnover Ratio	Expense Ratio
IXUS	NAS CM	57.62	$16,191,978,589	2.82	6	0.09

Ratings
Reward   C
Risk   C+
Recent Upgrade/Downgrade

Fund Information
Fund Type   Exchange Traded Funds
Category   Global Equity Large Cap
Sub-Category   Foreign Large Blend
Prospectus Objective   Foreign Stock
Inception Date   Oct-12
Open to New Investments Y

Prices
Price (as of 9/30/2019)   57.76
52-Week High   60.45
52-Week Low   50.85

Total Returns (%)

3-Month	6-Month	1-Year	3-Year	5-Year
-2.25	0.00	-1.61	20.19	18.23

3-Year Standard Deviation   11.48
Effective Duration

Valuation
Premium/Discount (1-Year Average)   0.09

Company Information
Provider   iShares
Manager/Tenure   Diane Hsiung (6), Jennifer Hsui (6),
                  Greg Savage (6), 3 others
Website   http://www.ishares.com
Address   iShares 400 Howard Street San
                  Francisco CA 94105 United States
Phone Number   800-474-2737

PERFORMANCE

Ratings History				Asset & Performance History			Total Assets:	$16,191,978,589
Date	Overall Rating	Risk Rating	Reward Rating	Date	NAV	1-Year Total Return	Asset Allocation	
							Asset	%
Q3-19	C	C+	C	2018	52.49	-14.55	Cash	1%
Q4-18	C-	C	D+	2017	63.15	28.07	Stocks	99%
Q4-17	B	B-	B	2016	50.57	4.65	US Stocks	1%
Q4-16	C-	C	D+	2015	49.59	-4.61	Bonds	0%
Q4-15	C	C+	D+	2014	53.36	-3.96	US Bonds	0%
				2013	57.13	15.84	Other	0%

Services Offered:

Investment Strategy: The investment seeks to track the investment results of the MSCI ACWI ex USA IMI composed of large-, mid- and small-capitalization non-U.S. equities. The fund generally will invest at least 90% of its assets in the component securities of the underlying index and in investments that have economic characteristics that are substantially identical to the component securities of the underlying index. The index is a free float-adjusted market capitalization index designed to measure the combined equity market performance of developed and emerging markets countries, excluding the United States. **Top Holdings:** Nestle SA Alibaba Group Holding Ltd ADR Tencent Holdings Ltd Taiwan Semiconductor Manufacturing Co Ltd Novartis AG

Invesco S&P 500® Equal Weight ETF   C   HOLD

Ticker	Traded On	NAV	Total Assets ($)	Dividend Yield (TTM)	Turnover Ratio	Expense Ratio
RSP	NYSE Arca	108.05	$15,851,591,660	1.87		0.2

Ratings

Reward	C
Risk	C+
Recent Upgrade/Downgrade	Down

Fund Information

Fund Type	Exchange Traded Funds
Category	US Equity Large Cap Blend
Sub-Category	Large Blend
Prospectus Objective	Growth
Inception Date	Apr-03
Open to New Investments	Y

Prices

Price (as of 9/30/2019)	108.08
52-Week High	110.18
52-Week Low	86.19

Total Returns (%)

3-Month	6-Month	1-Year	3-Year	5-Year
0.05	3.09	3.17	35.91	56.80

3-Year Standard Deviation	13.17
Effective Duration	

Valuation

Premium/Discount (1-Year Average)	-0.03

Company Information

Provider	Invesco
Manager/Tenure	Peter Hubbard (1), Michael Jeanette (1), Tony Seisser (1)
Website	http://www.invesco.com/us
Address	Invesco 11 Greenway Plaza, Ste. 2500 Houston TX 77046 United States
Phone Number	800-659-1005

PERFORMANCE

Ratings History

Date	Overall Rating	Risk Rating	Reward Rating
Q3-19	C	C+	C
Q4-18	C	C+	C-
Q4-17	B-	B-	B-
Q4-16	B-	C+	B
Q4-15	C	C+	C

Asset & Performance History

Date	NAV	1-Year Total Return
2018	91.39	-7.76
2017	100.96	18.68
2016	86.57	13.97
2015	76.69	-2.57
2014	80.03	14.01
2013	71.26	35.59

Total Assets: $15,851,591,660

Asset Allocation

Asset	%
Cash	0%
Stocks	100%
US Stocks	98%
Bonds	0%
US Bonds	0%
Other	0%

Services Offered: Dividend Investment Plan

Investment Strategy: The investment seeks to track the investment results (before fees and expenses) of the S&P 500® Equal Weight Index (the "underlying index"). The fund generally will invest at least 90% of its total assets in the securities that comprise the underlying index. Strictly in accordance with its guidelines and mandated procedures, the index provider compiles, maintains and calculates the underlying index, which is an equal-weighted version of the S&P 500® Index. The fund is non-diversified. **Top Holdings:** Western Digital Corp Micron Technology Inc Allergan PLC KLA Corp Ball Corp

---

iShares S&P 500 Value ETF   C+   HOLD

Ticker	Traded On	NAV	Total Assets ($)	Dividend Yield (TTM)	Turnover Ratio	Expense Ratio
IVE	NYSE Arca	119.11	$15,746,796,122	2.3	31	0.18

Ratings

Reward	C
Risk	C+
Recent Upgrade/Downgrade	Up

Fund Information

Fund Type	Exchange Traded Funds
Category	US Equity Large Cap Value
Sub-Category	Large Value
Prospectus Objective	Growth
Inception Date	May-00
Open to New Investments	Y

Prices

Price (as of 9/30/2019)	119.14
52-Week High	120.88
52-Week Low	95.36

Total Returns (%)

3-Month	6-Month	1-Year	3-Year	5-Year
2.03	5.49	4.97	34.66	50.84

3-Year Standard Deviation	13.18
Effective Duration	

Valuation

Premium/Discount (1-Year Average)	-0.01

Company Information

Provider	iShares
Manager/Tenure	Greg Savage (11), Jennifer Hsui (7), Alan Mason (3), 2 others
Website	http://www.ishares.com
Address	iShares 400 Howard Street San Francisco CA 94105 United States
Phone Number	800-474-2737

PERFORMANCE

Ratings History

Date	Overall Rating	Risk Rating	Reward Rating
Q3-19	C+	C+	C
Q4-18	C	C+	C
Q4-17	B	B	B-
Q4-16	B-	C+	B
Q4-15	C+	C+	C

Asset & Performance History

Date	NAV	1-Year Total Return
2018	101.11	-9.09
2017	114.08	15.19
2016	101.29	17.16
2015	88.56	-3.23
2014	93.75	12.14
2013	85.46	31.69

Total Assets: $15,746,796,122

Asset Allocation

Asset	%
Cash	0%
Stocks	100%
US Stocks	98%
Bonds	0%
US Bonds	0%
Other	0%

Services Offered: CashInvestment Plan

Investment Strategy: The investment seeks to track the investment results of the S&P 500 Value IndexTM, which measures the performance of the large-capitalization value sector of the U.S. equity market. The fund generally invests at least 90% of its assets in securities of the underlying index and in depositary receipts representing securities of the underlying index. It may invest the remainder of its assets in certain futures, options and swap contracts, cash and cash equivalents, as well as in securities not included in the underlying index, but which the advisor believes will help the fund track the underlying index. **Top Holdings:** Apple Inc JPMorgan Chase & Co AT&T Inc Bank of America Corporation Chevron Corp

Schwab U.S. Broad Market ETF™

C+   **HOLD**

Ticker	Traded On	NAV	Total Assets ($)	Dividend Yield (TTM)	Turnover Ratio	Expense Ratio
SCHB	NYSE Arca	71.00	$15,109,055,577	1.88	4	0.03

Ratings
Reward	C+
Risk	C+
Recent Upgrade/Downgrade	

Fund Information
Fund Type	Exchange Traded Funds
Category	US Equity Large Cap Blend
Sub-Category	Large Blend
Prospectus Objective	Growth
Inception Date	Nov-09
Open to New Investments	Y

Prices
Price (as of 9/30/2019)	71.02
52-Week High	72.55
52-Week Low	56.21

Total Returns (%)
3-Month	6-Month	1-Year	3-Year	5-Year
0.43	4.09	2.76	43.58	66.27

3-Year Standard Deviation	12.54
Effective Duration	

Valuation
Premium/Discount (1-Year Average)	-0.01

Company Information
Provider	Schwab ETFs
Manager/Tenure	Ferian Juwono (9), Christopher Bliss (2), Sabya Sinha (2), 1 other
Website	http://www.schwabfunds.com
Address	Schwab ETFs United States
Phone Number	800-435-4000

PERFORMANCE

Ratings History
Date	Overall Rating	Risk Rating	Reward Rating
Q3-19	C+	C+	C+
Q4-18	C	C+	C
Q4-17	B	B	B
Q4-16	B-	C+	B
Q4-15	C+	C+	C

Asset & Performance History
Date	NAV	1-Year Total Return
2018	59.9	-5.24
2017	64.45	21.29
2016	54.13	12.54
2015	49.04	0.45
2014	49.79	12.67
2013	44.99	33.37

Total Assets: $15,109,055,577

Asset Allocation
Asset	%
Cash	0%
Stocks	100%
US Stocks	99%
Bonds	0%
US Bonds	0%
Other	0%

Services Offered:

Investment Strategy: The investment seeks to track as closely as possible, before fees and expenses, the total return of the Dow Jones U.S. Broad Stock Market Index. To pursue its goal, the fund generally invests in stocks that are included in the index. The fund will invest at least 90% of its net assets in these stocks. The index includes the largest 2,500 publicly traded U.S. companies for which pricing information is readily available. The index is a float-adjusted market capitalization weighted index that reflects the shares of securities actually available to investors in the marketplace. **Top Holdings:** Microsoft Corp Apple Inc Amazon.com Inc Facebook Inc A Berkshire Hathaway Inc B

---

iShares J.P. Morgan USD Emerging Markets Bond ETF

B-   **BUY**

Ticker	Traded On	NAV	Total Assets ($)	Dividend Yield (TTM)	Turnover Ratio	Expense Ratio
EMB	NAS CM	113.24	$14,869,014,222	5.45	15	0.39

Ratings
Reward	B-
Risk	B-
Recent Upgrade/Downgrade	

Fund Information
Fund Type	Exchange Traded Funds
Category	Emerging Mkts Fixed Inc
Sub-Category	Emerging Markets Bond
Prospectus Objective	Div Emerg Mkts
Inception Date	Dec-07
Open to New Investments	Y

Prices
Price (as of 9/30/2019)	113.35
52-Week High	115.59
52-Week Low	102.36

Total Returns (%)
3-Month	6-Month	1-Year	3-Year	5-Year
0.89	5.85	11.53	12.24	28.19

3-Year Standard Deviation	6.12
Effective Duration	7.41

Valuation
Premium/Discount (1-Year Average)	0.30

Company Information
Provider	iShares
Manager/Tenure	Scott Radell (9), James Mauro (8)
Website	http://www.ishares.com
Address	iShares 400 Howard Street San Francisco CA 94105 United States
Phone Number	800-474-2737

PERFORMANCE

Ratings History
Date	Overall Rating	Risk Rating	Reward Rating
Q3-19	B-	B-	B-
Q4-18	C-	C	D+
Q4-17	B	B+	C+
Q4-16	C	C+	C
Q4-15	C	C	C-

Asset & Performance History
Date	NAV	1-Year Total Return
2018	103.17	-5.67
2017	115.53	9.97
2016	110	9.41
2015	105.44	0.43
2014	110.03	6.69
2013	107.84	-7.42

Total Assets: $14,869,014,222

Asset Allocation
Asset	%
Cash	0%
Stocks	0%
US Stocks	0%
Bonds	100%
US Bonds	0%
Other	0%

Services Offered:

Investment Strategy: The investment seeks to track the investment results of the J.P. Morgan EMBI® Global Core Index composed of U.S. dollar-denominated, emerging market bonds. The fund generally will invest at least 90% of its assets in the component securities of the underlying index and may invest up to 10% of its assets in certain futures, options and swap contracts, cash and cash equivalents, as well as in securities not included in the underlying index. The index is a broad, diverse U.S. dollar-denominated emerging markets debt benchmark that tracks the total return of actively traded external debt instruments in emerging market countries. **Top Holdings:** Uruguay (Republic of) 5.1% State of Kuwait 3.5% The Republic of Peru 5.63% Russian Federation 5.25% The Republic of Peru 8.75%

iShares National Muni Bond ETF

C+   HOLD

Ticker	Traded On	NAV	Total Assets ($)	Dividend Yield (TTM)	Turnover Ratio	Expense Ratio
MUB	NYSE Arca	114.04	$14,198,103,722	2.46	10	0.07

Ratings
Reward	C+
Risk	C+
Recent Upgrade/Downgrade	

Fund Information
Fund Type	Exchange Traded Funds
Category	US Muni Fixed Inc
Sub-Category	Muni National Interm
Prospectus Objective	Muni Bond - Natl
Inception Date	Sep-07
Open to New Investments	Y

Prices
Price (as of 9/30/2019)	114.10
52-Week High	115.35
52-Week Low	106.42

Total Returns (%)
3-Month	6-Month	1-Year	3-Year	5-Year
1.48	3.89	8.35	8.63	17.07

3-Year Standard Deviation	3.41
Effective Duration	5.93

Valuation
Premium/Discount (1-Year Average)	0.05

Company Information
Provider	iShares
Manager/Tenure	Scott Radell (9), James Mauro (8)
Website	http://www.ishares.com
Address	iShares 400 Howard Street San Francisco CA 94105 United States
Phone Number	800-474-2737

PERFORMANCE

Ratings History
Date	Overall Rating	Risk Rating	Reward Rating
Q3-19	C+	C+	C+
Q4-18	C	C+	C-
Q4-17	B-	B+	C
Q4-16	C	C+	C
Q4-15	C+	C+	C

Asset & Performance History
Date	NAV	1-Year Total Return
2018	108.73	0.86
2017	110.5	4.42
2016	108.06	0.05
2015	110.34	2.99
2014	109.88	8.61
2013	104.01	-3.26

Total Assets: $14,198,103,722

Asset Allocation
Asset	%
Cash	1%
Stocks	0%
US Stocks	0%
Bonds	99%
US Bonds	99%
Other	0%

Services Offered:

Investment Strategy: The investment seeks to track the investment results of the S&P National AMT-Free Municipal Bond Index™. The fund generally will invest at least 90% of its assets in the component securities of the underlying index and may invest up to 10% of its assets in certain futures, options and swap contracts, cash and cash equivalents. The index measures the performance of the investment-grade segment of the U.S. municipal bond market. **Top Holdings:** NEW YORK N Y CITY TRANSITIONAL FIN AUTH BLDG AID REV 5.25% SAN FRANCISCO CALIF CITY & CNTY PUB UTILS COMMN WASTEWATER REV 4% UNIVERSITY CALIF REVS 5% CALIFORNIA ST 5% ORANGE CNTY CALIF LOC TRANSN AUTH SALES TAX REV 5%

Vanguard Mid-Cap Growth Index Fund ETF Shares

C+   HOLD

Ticker	Traded On	NAV	Total Assets ($)	Dividend Yield (TTM)	Turnover Ratio	Expense Ratio
VOT	NYSE Arca	148.14	$14,142,167,703	0.75	25	0.07

Ratings
Reward	C+
Risk	C+
Recent Upgrade/Downgrade	

Fund Information
Fund Type	Exchange Traded Funds
Category	US Equity Mid Cap
Sub-Category	Mid-Cap Growth
Prospectus Objective	Growth
Inception Date	Aug-06
Open to New Investments	Y

Prices
Price (as of 9/30/2019)	148.11
52-Week High	154.00
52-Week Low	111.81

Total Returns (%)
3-Month	6-Month	1-Year	3-Year	5-Year
-2.08	2.32	4.39	41.58	59.78

3-Year Standard Deviation	13.54
Effective Duration	

Valuation
Premium/Discount (1-Year Average)	-0.02

Company Information
Provider	Vanguard
Manager/Tenure	Donald M. Butler (6), Michael A. Johnson (3)
Website	http://www.vanguard.com
Address	Vanguard 100 Vanguard Boulevard Malvern PA 19355 United States
Phone Number	877-662-7447

PERFORMANCE

Ratings History
Date	Overall Rating	Risk Rating	Reward Rating
Q3-19	C+	C+	C+
Q4-18	C	C+	C
Q4-17	B-	C+	B
Q4-16	C	C-	B-
Q4-15	C+	C+	C

Asset & Performance History
Date	NAV	1-Year Total Return
2018	118.43	-6.5
2017	127.67	22.18
2016	105.6	6.46
2015	99.75	-0.99
2014	101.57	13.49
2013	90.2	32.22

Total Assets: $14,142,167,703

Asset Allocation
Asset	%
Cash	1%
Stocks	99%
US Stocks	98%
Bonds	0%
US Bonds	0%
Other	0%

Services Offered:

Investment Strategy: The investment seeks to track the performance of the CRSP US Mid Cap Growth Index that measures the investment return of mid-capitalization growth stocks. The fund employs an indexing investment approach designed to track the performance of the CRSP US Mid Cap Growth Index, a broadly diversified index of growth stocks of mid-size U.S. companies. The advisor attempts to replicate the target index by investing all, or substantially all, of its assets in the stocks that make up the index, holding each stock in approximately the same proportion as its weighting in the index. **Top Holdings:** Twitter Inc Fiserv Inc Advanced Micro Devices Inc Xilinx Inc ONEOK Inc

Consumer Staples Select Sector SPDR® Fund
B- **BUY**

Ticker	Traded On	NAV	Total Assets ($)	Dividend Yield (TTM)	Turnover Ratio	Expense Ratio
XLP	NYSE Arca		$14,061,058,297	2.55	12	0.13

Ratings
Reward — B
Risk — C
Recent Upgrade/Downgrade — Up

Fund Information
Fund Type	Exchange Traded Funds
Category	Consumer Goods & Svcs
Sub-Category	Consumer Defensive
Prospectus Objective	Unaligned
Inception Date	Dec-98
Open to New Investments	Y

Prices
Price (as of 9/30/2019)	61.42
52-Week High	61.62
52-Week Low	48.73

Total Returns (%)
3-Month	6-Month	1-Year	3-Year	5-Year
5.30	10.71	16.67	24.73	54.82

3-Year Standard Deviation — 11.83
Effective Duration —

Valuation
Premium/Discount (1-Year Average) — -0.02

Company Information
Provider	SPDR State Street Global Advisors
Manager/Tenure	Michael J. Feehily (8), Karl A. Schneider (4), David Chin (2)
Website	http://www.spdrs.com
Address	SPDR State Street Global Advisors State Street Financial Center, 1 Lincoln Street Boston MA 02111-2900 United States
Phone Number	617-786-3000

PERFORMANCE

Ratings History
Date	Overall Rating	Risk Rating	Reward Rating
Q3-19	B-	C	B
Q4-18	C+	C	B
Q4-17	B	A	C+
Q4-16	B-	C+	B
Q4-15	B	B-	B

Asset & Performance History
Date	NAV	1-Year Total Return
2018	50.78	-8.01
2017	56.86	12.9
2016	51.72	4.34
2015	50.49	6.84
2014	48.51	15.86
2013	42.95	26.27

Total Assets: $14,061,058,297
Asset Allocation
Asset	%
Cash	0%
Stocks	100%
US Stocks	100%
Bonds	0%
US Bonds	0%
Other	0%

Services Offered: Dividend Investment Plan, CashInvestment Plan

Investment Strategy: The investment seeks to provide investment results that, before expenses, correspond generally to the price and yield performance of publicly traded equity securities of companies in the Consumer Staples Select Sector Index. In seeking to track the performance of the index, the fund employs a replication strategy. It generally invests substantially all, but at least 95%, of its total assets in the securities comprising the index. The index includes securities of companies from the following industries: food and staples retailing; household products; food products; beverages; tobacco; and personal products. The fund is non-diversified. **Top Holdings:** Procter & Gamble Co Coca-Cola Co PepsiCo Inc Walmart Inc Costco Wholesale Corp

Consumer Discretionary Select Sector SPDR® Fund
B **BUY**

Ticker	Traded On	NAV	Total Assets ($)	Dividend Yield (TTM)	Turnover Ratio	Expense Ratio
XLY	NYSE Arca		$14,000,727,254	1.3	23	0.13

Ratings
Reward — B+
Risk — C
Recent Upgrade/Downgrade —

Fund Information
Fund Type	Exchange Traded Funds
Category	Consumer Goods & Svcs
Sub-Category	Consumer Cyclical
Prospectus Objective	Unaligned
Inception Date	Dec-98
Open to New Investments	Y

Prices
Price (as of 9/30/2019)	120.70
52-Week High	124.48
52-Week Low	91.98

Total Returns (%)
3-Month	6-Month	1-Year	3-Year	5-Year
-0.14	4.67	3.80	55.86	92.75

3-Year Standard Deviation — 14.7
Effective Duration —

Valuation
Premium/Discount (1-Year Average) — -0.01

Company Information
Provider	SPDR State Street Global Advisors
Manager/Tenure	Michael J. Feehily (8), Karl A. Schneider (4), Kala O'Donnell (2)
Website	http://www.spdrs.com
Address	SPDR State Street Global Advisors State Street Financial Center, 1 Lincoln Street Boston MA 02111-2900 United States
Phone Number	617-786-3000

PERFORMANCE

Ratings History
Date	Overall Rating	Risk Rating	Reward Rating
Q3-19	B	C	B+
Q4-18	B-	C	B
Q4-17	B	A	B
Q4-16	B	B	B
Q4-15	B	A-	B

Asset & Performance History
Date	NAV	1-Year Total Return
2018	98.99	1.66
2017	98.6	22.76
2016	81.36	5.79
2015	78.2	9.92
2014	72.18	9.49
2013	66.84	42.74

Total Assets: $14,000,727,254
Asset Allocation
Asset	%
Cash	0%
Stocks	100%
US Stocks	99%
Bonds	0%
US Bonds	0%
Other	0%

Services Offered: Dividend Investment Plan, CashInvestment Plan

Investment Strategy: The investment seeks investment results that, before expenses, correspond to the price and yield performance of publicly traded equity securities of companies in the Consumer Discretionary Select Sector Index. The fund employs a replication strategy. It generally invests substantially all, but at least 95%, of its total assets in the securities comprising the index. The index includes securities of companies from the following industries: retail; hotels, restaurants and leisure; textiles, apparel and luxury goods; household durables; automobiles; auto components; distributors; leisure products; and diversified consumer services. It is non-diversified. **Top Holdings:** Amazon.com Inc The Home Depot Inc McDonald's Corp Starbucks Corp Nike Inc B

iShares U.S. Treasury Bond ETF

C+ HOLD

Ticker	Traded On	NAV	Total Assets ($)	Dividend Yield (TTM)	Turnover Ratio	Expense Ratio
GOVT	BATS	26.31	$13,876,878,327	1.98	27	0.15

Ratings
Reward | C
Risk | B
Recent Upgrade/Downgrade |

Fund Information
Fund Type	Exchange Traded Funds
Category	US Fixed Income
Sub-Category	Intermediate Government
Prospectus Objective	Govt Bond - Treasury
Inception Date	Feb-12
Open to New Investments	Y

Prices
Price (as of 9/30/2019)	26.33
52-Week High	26.63
52-Week Low	24.07

Total Returns (%)
3-Month	6-Month	1-Year	3-Year	5-Year
2.62	5.91	10.53	6.52	14.33

3-Year Standard Deviation | 3.94
Effective Duration |

Valuation
Premium/Discount (1-Year Average) | 0.02

Company Information
Provider	iShares
Manager/Tenure	James Mauro (7), Scott Radell (7)
Website	http://www.ishares.com
Address	iShares 400 Howard Street San Francisco CA 94105 United States
Phone Number	800-474-2737

PERFORMANCE

Ratings History
Date	Overall Rating	Risk Rating	Reward Rating
Q3-19	C+	B	C
Q4-18	C-	C	D
Q4-17	C	C	C
Q4-16	C	C+	C
Q4-15	C	C+	C

Asset & Performance History
Date	NAV	1-Year Total Return
2018	24.78	0.74
2017	25.09	2.04
2016	24.94	0.92
2015	25.05	0.76
2014	25.17	4.98
2013	24.26	-2.84

Total Assets: $13,876,878,327
Asset Allocation
Asset	%
Cash	3%
Stocks	0%
US Stocks	0%
Bonds	97%
US Bonds	97%
Other	0%

Services Offered:

Investment Strategy: The investment seeks to track the investment results of the ICE U.S. Treasury Core Bond Index (the "underlying index"). The fund generally will invest at least 90% of its assets in the component securities of the underlying index and may invest up to 10% of its assets in certain futures, options and swap contracts, cash and cash equivalents, as well as in securities not included in the underlying index, but which the advisor believes will help the fund track the index. The underlying index measures the performance of public obligations of the U.S. Treasury that have a remaining maturity greater than one year and less than or equal to thirty years. **Top Holdings:** United States Treasury Notes 2.38% United States Treasury Notes 2.25% United States Treasury Bonds 2.88% United States Treasury Notes 2.25% United States Treasury Notes 2.25%

iShares Short-Term Corporate Bond ETF

D- SELL

Ticker	Traded On	NAV	Total Assets ($)	Dividend Yield (TTM)	Turnover Ratio	Expense Ratio
IGSB	NAS CM	53.64	$12,902,358,215	3.06	80	0.06

Ratings
Reward | D-
Risk | D
Recent Upgrade/Downgrade | Down

Fund Information
Fund Type	Exchange Traded Funds
Category	US Fixed Income
Sub-Category	Short-Term Bond
Prospectus Objective	Growth & Inc
Inception Date	Jan-07
Open to New Investments	Y

Prices
Price (as of 9/30/2019)	53.67
52-Week High	53.82
52-Week Low	51.35

Total Returns (%)
3-Month	6-Month	1-Year	3-Year	5-Year
1.25	3.48	6.78	-45.73	-44.22

3-Year Standard Deviation | 1.34
Effective Duration |

Valuation
Premium/Discount (1-Year Average) | 0.07

Company Information
Provider	iShares
Manager/Tenure	Scott Radell (9), James Mauro (8)
Website	http://www.ishares.com
Address	iShares 400 Howard Street San Francisco CA 94105 United States
Phone Number	800-474-2737

PERFORMANCE

Ratings History
Date	Overall Rating	Risk Rating	Reward Rating
Q3-19	D-	D	D-
Q4-18	E+	D-	E+
Q4-17	B-	B+	C
Q4-16	C	C+	C
Q4-15	C	C+	C

Asset & Performance History
Date	NAV	1-Year Total Return
2018	51.67	-49.33
2017	104.51	1.26
2016	104.77	1.77
2015	104.45	0.7
2014	104.95	0.73
2013	105.16	1.03

Total Assets: $12,902,358,215
Asset Allocation
Asset	%
Cash	2%
Stocks	0%
US Stocks	0%
Bonds	95%
US Bonds	71%
Other	0%

Services Offered:

Investment Strategy: The investment seeks to track the investment results of the ICE BofAML 1-5 Year US Corporate Index. The fund generally invests at least 90% of its assets in securities of the underlying index. The underlying index measures the performance of investment-grade corporate bonds of both U.S. and non-U.S. issuers that are U.S. dollar-denominated and publicly issued in the U.S. domestic market and have a remaining maturity of greater than or equal to one year and less than five years. **Top Holdings:** B.A.T. Capital Corporation 2.76% GE Capital International Funding Company Unlimited Company 2.34% CVS Health Corp 3.7% Shire Acquisitions Investments Ireland DAC 2.4% Bank of America Corporation 3%

Invesco S&P 500® Low Volatility ETF   B   BUY

Ticker	Traded On	NAV	Total Assets ($)	Dividend Yield (TTM)	Turnover Ratio	Expense Ratio
SPLV	NYSE Arca	57.89	$12,815,868,642	2		0.25

Ratings
Reward   B
Risk   A-
Recent Upgrade/Downgrade   Down

Fund Information
Fund Type   Exchange Traded Funds
Category   US Equity Large Cap Value
Sub-Category   Large Blend
Prospectus Objective   Growth
Inception Date   May-11
Open to New Investments

Prices
Price (as of 9/30/2019)   57.90
52-Week High   57.96
52-Week Low   44.55

Total Returns (%)

3-Month	6-Month	1-Year	3-Year	5-Year
5.34	11.05	19.75	48.88	86.14

3-Year Standard Deviation   9.02
Effective Duration

Valuation
Premium/Discount (1-Year Average)   -0.01

Company Information
Provider   Invesco
Manager/Tenure   Peter Hubbard (8), Michael Jeanette (8), Tony Seisser (5)
Website   http://www.invesco.com/us
Address   Invesco 11 Greenway Plaza, Ste. 2500 Houston TX 77046 United States
Phone Number   800-659-1005

PERFORMANCE

Ratings History

Date	Overall Rating	Risk Rating	Reward Rating
Q3-19	B	A-	B
Q4-18	B	A	C
Q4-17	B+	A+	B
Q4-16	C	C+	C
Q4-15	B-	C+	B

Asset & Performance History

Date	NAV	1-Year Total Return
2018	46.64	0.03
2017	47.63	17.07
2016	41.57	10.09
2015	38.56	4.06
2014	37.93	17.18
2013	33.16	23.24

Total Assets: $12,815,868,642
Asset Allocation

Asset	%
Cash	0%
Stocks	100%
US Stocks	99%
Bonds	0%
US Bonds	0%
Other	0%

Services Offered:

Investment Strategy: The investment seeks to track the investment results (before fees and expenses) of the S&P 500® Low Volatility Index (the "underlying index"). The fund generally will invest at least 90% of its total assets in the securities that comprise the underlying index. Strictly in accordance with its guidelines and mandated procedures, the index provider selects 100 securities from the S&P 500® Index for inclusion in the underlying index that have the lowest realized volatility over the past 12 months as determined by S&P DJI. **Top Holdings:** Republic Services Inc Class A   Waste Management Inc   Duke Energy Corp   WEC Energy Group Inc   Evergy Inc

---

PIMCO Enhanced Short Maturity Active Exchange-Traded Fund   C   HOLD

Ticker	Traded On	NAV	Total Assets ($)	Dividend Yield (TTM)	Turnover Ratio	Expense Ratio
MINT	NYSE Arca	101.75	$12,787,717,510	2.7	72	0.42

Ratings
Reward   C
Risk   C+
Recent Upgrade/Downgrade

Fund Information
Fund Type   Exchange Traded Funds
Category   US Fixed Income
Sub-Category   Ultrashort Bond
Prospectus Objective   Income
Inception Date   Nov-09
Open to New Investments   Y

Prices
Price (as of 9/30/2019)   101.73
52-Week High   101.76
52-Week Low   100.95

Total Returns (%)

3-Month	6-Month	1-Year	3-Year	5-Year
0.68	1.54	2.87	6.80	8.97

3-Year Standard Deviation   0.3
Effective Duration   0.24

Valuation
Premium/Discount (1-Year Average)   -0.01

Company Information
Provider   PIMCO
Manager/Tenure   Jerome M. Schneider (9)
Website   http://www.pimco.com
Address   PIMCO 840 Newport Center Drive, Suite 100 Newport Beach CA 92660 United States
Phone Number   866-746-2602

PERFORMANCE

Ratings History

Date	Overall Rating	Risk Rating	Reward Rating
Q3-19	C	C+	C
Q4-18	C	C+	C
Q4-17	B-	A-	C
Q4-16	C	C+	C
Q4-15	C	C+	C

Asset & Performance History

Date	NAV	1-Year Total Return
2018	100.96	1.71
2017	101.57	1.89
2016	101.3	2.01
2015	100.67	0.52
2014	101.03	0.53
2013	101.3	0.71

Total Assets: $12,787,717,510
Asset Allocation

Asset	%
Cash	14%
Stocks	0%
US Stocks	0%
Bonds	83%
US Bonds	60%
Other	0%

Services Offered:

Investment Strategy: The investment seeks maximum current income, consistent with preservation of capital and daily liquidity. The fund invests at least 80% of its net assets in a diversified portfolio of Fixed Income Instruments of varying maturities, which may be represented by forwards. "Fixed Income Instruments" include bonds, debt securities and other similar instruments issued by various U.S. and non-U.S. public- or private-sector entities. The average portfolio duration of this fund will vary based on PIMCO's market forecasts and will normally not exceed one year. **Top Holdings:** Broadcom Corporation/Broadcom Cayman Finance Ltd 2.38%   Federal Home Loan Mortgage Corporation 2.8%   PNC Bank, National Association 2.71%   Hertz Fleet Lease Funding Lp 2.67%   NTT Finance Corp 2.86%

Vanguard Long-Term Bond Index Fund ETF Shares   C+   HOLD

Ticker	Traded On	NAV	Total Assets ($)	Dividend Yield (TTM)	Turnover Ratio	Expense Ratio
BLV	NYSE Arca	102.60	$12,667,523,830	3.33	38	0.07

Ratings
Reward   C+
Risk   C+
Recent Upgrade/Downgrade

Fund Information
Fund Type	Exchange Traded Funds
Category	US Fixed Income
Sub-Category	Long-Term Bond
Prospectus Objective	Income
Inception Date	Apr-07
Open to New Investments	Y

Prices
Price (as of 9/30/2019)	102.67
52-Week High	105.49
52-Week Low	83.53

Total Returns (%)
3-Month	6-Month	1-Year	3-Year	5-Year
6.79	13.51	22.64	17.27	36.99

3-Year Standard Deviation	8.9
Effective Duration	15.82

Valuation
Premium/Discount (1-Year Average)	0.12

Company Information
Provider	Vanguard
Manager/Tenure	Joshua C. Barrickman (6)
Website	http://www.vanguard.com
Address	Vanguard 100 Vanguard Boulevard Malvern PA 19355 United States
Phone Number	877-662-7447

PERFORMANCE

Ratings History

Date	Overall Rating	Risk Rating	Reward Rating
Q3-19	C+	C+	C+
Q4-18	D+	C	D
Q4-17	B-	B	C+
Q4-16	C	C+	C
Q4-15	C	C-	C

Asset & Performance History

Date	NAV	1-Year Total Return
2018	87.08	-4.75
2017	94.91	10.99
2016	88.86	6.37
2015	86.8	-3.44
2014	93.73	19.88
2013	81.45	-9.02

Total Assets: $12,667,523,830
Asset Allocation

Asset	%
Cash	0%
Stocks	0%
US Stocks	0%
Bonds	100%
US Bonds	91%
Other	0%

Services Offered:

Investment Strategy: The investment seeks to track the performance of the Bloomberg Barclays U.S. Long Government/Credit Float Adjusted Index. Bloomberg Barclays U.S. Long Government/Credit Float Adjusted Index includes all medium and larger issues of U.S. government, investment-grade corporate, and investment-grade international dollar-denominated bonds that have maturities of greater than 10 years and are publicly issued. All of its investments will be selected through the sampling process, and at least 80% of the fund's assets will be invested in bonds held in the index. **Top Holdings:** United States Treasury Bonds 2.88% United States Treasury Bonds 3% United States Treasury Bonds 3% United States Treasury Bonds 3.38% United States Treasury Bonds 3%

---

iShares Edge MSCI Min Vol EAFE ETF   C+   HOLD

Ticker	Traded On	NAV	Total Assets ($)	Dividend Yield (TTM)	Turnover Ratio	Expense Ratio
EFAV	BATS	73.11	$11,981,925,642	2.95	22	0.2

Ratings
Reward   C+
Risk   C+
Recent Upgrade/Downgrade   Up

Fund Information
Fund Type	Exchange Traded Funds
Category	Global Equity Large Cap
Sub-Category	Foreign Large Blend
Prospectus Objective	Foreign Stock
Inception Date	Oct-11
Open to New Investments	Y

Prices
Price (as of 9/30/2019)	73.28
52-Week High	73.75
52-Week Low	65.01

Total Returns (%)
3-Month	6-Month	1-Year	3-Year	5-Year
0.70	3.22	3.94	19.67	36.06

3-Year Standard Deviation	8.52
Effective Duration	

Valuation
Premium/Discount (1-Year Average)	0.06

Company Information
Provider	iShares
Manager/Tenure	Diane Hsiung (7), Greg Savage (7), Jennifer Hsui (6), 3 others
Website	http://www.ishares.com
Address	iShares 400 Howard Street San Francisco CA 94105 United States
Phone Number	800-474-2737

PERFORMANCE

Ratings History

Date	Overall Rating	Risk Rating	Reward Rating
Q3-19	C+	C+	C+
Q4-18	C	C	C-
Q4-17	B	B	B-
Q4-16	C	C	C
Q4-15	C+	C+	C

Asset & Performance History

Date	NAV	1-Year Total Return
2018	66.6	-5.8
2017	72.98	21.56
2016	61.57	-1.85
2015	65.16	7.83
2014	61.92	4.6
2013	61.27	16.51

Total Assets: $11,981,925,642
Asset Allocation

Asset	%
Cash	1%
Stocks	99%
US Stocks	2%
Bonds	0%
US Bonds	0%
Other	0%

Services Offered:

Investment Strategy: The investment seeks the investment results of the MSCI EAFE Minimum Volatility (USD) Index composed of developed market equities that, in the aggregate, have lower volatility characteristics relative to the broader developed equity markets, excluding the U.S. and Canada. The fund generally will invest at least 90% of its assets in the component securities of the index and in investments that have economic characteristics that are substantially identical to the component securities of the index. The index measures the performance of international equity securities that in the aggregate have lower volatility relative to the MSCI EAFE Index. **Top Holdings:** Nestle SA Roche Holding AG Dividend Right Cert. Novartis AG NTT DOCOMO Inc Swisscom AG

iShares Edge MSCI USA Quality Factor ETF

C+   HOLD

Ticker	Traded On	NAV	Total Assets ($)	Dividend Yield (TTM)	Turnover Ratio	Expense Ratio
QUAL	BATS	92.36	$11,733,843,496	1.72	41	0.15

Ratings
Reward   C+
Risk   C+
Recent Upgrade/Downgrade

Fund Information
Fund Type	Exchange Traded Funds
Category	US Equity Large Cap Blend
Sub-Category	Large Blend
Prospectus Objective	Growth
Inception Date	Jul-13
Open to New Investments	Y

Prices
Price (as of 9/30/2019)	92.40
52-Week High	94.10
52-Week Low	71.91

Total Returns (%)
3-Month	6-Month	1-Year	3-Year	5-Year
0.54	4.16	3.73	44.68	72.38

3-Year Standard Deviation   12.38
Effective Duration

Valuation
Premium/Discount (1-Year Average)   0.00

Company Information
Provider	iShares
Manager/Tenure	Diane Hsiung (6), Jennifer Hsui (6), Greg Savage (6), 3 others
Website	http://www.ishares.com
Address	iShares 400 Howard Street San Francisco CA 94105 United States
Phone Number	800-474-2737

PERFORMANCE

Ratings History
Date	Overall Rating	Risk Rating	Reward Rating
Q3-19	C+	C+	C+
Q4-18	C	C+	C
Q4-17	B	B+	B
Q4-16	B	C+	B
Q4-15	C	C	C

Asset & Performance History
Date	NAV	1-Year Total Return
2018	76.65	-5.77
2017	82.86	22.26
2016	69.07	9.17
2015	64.56	5.56
2014	62.18	11.61
2013	56.5	

Total Assets: $11,733,843,496

Asset Allocation
Asset	%
Cash	0%
Stocks	100%
US Stocks	100%
Bonds	0%
US Bonds	0%
Other	0%

Services Offered:

Investment Strategy: The investment seeks to track the investment results of the MSCI USA Sector Neutral Quality Index composed of U.S. large- and mid-capitalization stocks with quality characteristics as identified through certain fundamental metrics. The fund generally will invest at least 90% of its assets in the component securities of the underlying index and may invest up to 10% of its assets in certain futures, options and swap contracts, cash and cash equivalents. The index is based on a traditional market capitalization-weighted parent index, the MSCI USA Index. **Top Holdings:** Apple Inc Johnson & Johnson Mastercard Inc A Facebook Inc A Visa Inc Class A

---

iShares MSCI Japan ETF

C   HOLD

Ticker	Traded On	NAV	Total Assets ($)	Dividend Yield (TTM)	Turnover Ratio	Expense Ratio
EWJ	NYSE Arca	56.24	$11,507,052,351	1.59	4	0.47

Ratings
Reward   C-
Risk   C+
Recent Upgrade/Downgrade

Fund Information
Fund Type	Exchange Traded Funds
Category	Japan Equity
Sub-Category	Japan Stock
Prospectus Objective	Pacific Stock
Inception Date	Mar-96
Open to New Investments	Y

Prices
Price (as of 9/30/2019)	56.74
52-Week High	60.64
52-Week Low	49.12

Total Returns (%)
3-Month	6-Month	1-Year	3-Year	5-Year
1.49	3.01	-4.82	18.55	29.80

3-Year Standard Deviation   10.42
Effective Duration

Valuation
Premium/Discount (1-Year Average)   -0.12

Company Information
Provider	iShares
Manager/Tenure	Diane Hsiung (11), Greg Savage (11), Jennifer Hsui (6), 3 others
Website	http://www.ishares.com
Address	iShares 400 Howard Street San Francisco CA 94105 United States
Phone Number	800-474-2737

PERFORMANCE

Ratings History
Date	Overall Rating	Risk Rating	Reward Rating
Q3-19	C	C+	C-
Q4-18	C	C+	D+
Q4-17	B+	B	A-
Q4-16	B-	C+	B-
Q4-15	B-	B+	C

Asset & Performance History
Date	NAV	1-Year Total Return
2018	51.2	-13.17
2017	59.89	23.55
2016	49.11	1.95
2015	49.12	9.33
2014	45.48	-4.42
2013	48.2	26.47

Total Assets: $11,507,052,351

Asset Allocation
Asset	%
Cash	1%
Stocks	99%
US Stocks	0%
Bonds	0%
US Bonds	0%
Other	0%

Services Offered: CashInvestment Plan

Investment Strategy: The investment seeks to track the investment results of the MSCI Japan Index. The fund will at all times invest at least 90% of its assets in the securities of its underlying index and in depositary receipts representing securities in its underlying index. The underlying index consists of stocks traded primarily on the Tokyo Stock Exchange. It may include large- or mid-capitalization companies. **Top Holdings:** Toyota Motor Corp SoftBank Group Corp Sony Corp Mitsubishi UFJ Financial Group Inc Keyence Corp

Vanguard Mortgage-Backed Securities Index Fund ETF Shares   C+   HOLD

Ticker	Traded On	NAV	Total Assets ($)	Dividend Yield (TTM)	Turnover Ratio	Expense Ratio
VMBS	NAS CM	53.21	$11,415,733,919	2.9	279	0.07

Ratings
Reward	C+
Risk	C+
Recent Upgrade/Downgrade	Up

Fund Information
Fund Type	Exchange Traded Funds
Category	US Fixed Income
Sub-Category	Intermediate Government
Prospectus Objective	Govt Bond - Mortgage
Inception Date	Nov-09
Open to New Investments	Y

Prices
Price (as of 9/30/2019)	53.26
52-Week High	53.32
52-Week Low	50.20

Total Returns (%)
3-Month	6-Month	1-Year	3-Year	5-Year
1.37	3.43	7.42	6.58	13.72

3-Year Standard Deviation	2.41
Effective Duration	3.67

Valuation
Premium/Discount (1-Year Average)	0.08

Company Information
Provider	Vanguard
Manager/Tenure	William D. Baird (9), Joshua C. Barrickman (6)
Website	http://www.vanguard.com
Address	Vanguard 100 Vanguard Boulevard Malvern PA 19355 United States
Phone Number	877-662-7447

PERFORMANCE

Ratings History
Date	Overall Rating	Risk Rating	Reward Rating
Q3-19	C+	C+	C+
Q4-18	C	C+	D+
Q4-17	B-	A-	C
Q4-16	C	C+	C
Q4-15	C	C+	C

Asset & Performance History
Date	NAV	1-Year Total Return
2018	51.39	0.71
2017	52.44	2.45
2016	52.34	1.07
2015	52.68	1.42
2014	52.98	5.81
2013	51.04	-1.27

Total Assets: $11,415,733,919
Asset Allocation
Asset	%
Cash	7%
Stocks	0%
US Stocks	0%
Bonds	93%
US Bonds	93%
Other	0%

Services Offered:

Investment Strategy: The investment seeks to track the performance of a market-weighted mortgage-backed securities index. The fund employs an indexing investment approach designed to track the performance of the Bloomberg Barclays U.S. MBS Float Adjusted Index. This index covers U.S. agency mortgage-backed pass-through securities. To be included in the index, pool aggregates must have at least $250 million currently outstanding and a weighted average maturity of at least 1 year. All of the fund's investments will be selected through the sampling process, and under normal circumstances, at least 80% of the fund's assets will be invested in bonds included in the index. **Top Holdings:** Government National Mortgage Association 3.5% Federal National Mortgage Association 3.5% Federal Home Loan Mortgage Corporation 3% Federal National Mortgage Association 4% Federal Home Loan Mortgage Corporation 4%

Utilities Select Sector SPDR® Fund   B   BUY

Ticker	Traded On	NAV	Total Assets ($)	Dividend Yield (TTM)	Turnover Ratio	Expense Ratio
XLU	NYSE Arca		$11,403,280,323	2.88	5	0.13

Ratings
Reward	B
Risk	B-
Recent Upgrade/Downgrade	

Fund Information
Fund Type	Exchange Traded Funds
Category	Utilities Sector Equity
Sub-Category	Utilities
Prospectus Objective	Utility
Inception Date	Dec-98
Open to New Investments	Y

Prices
Price (as of 9/30/2019)	64.74
52-Week High	64.93
52-Week Low	51.56

Total Returns (%)
3-Month	6-Month	1-Year	3-Year	5-Year
9.52	13.71	27.07	45.74	81.83

3-Year Standard Deviation	10.65
Effective Duration	

Valuation
Premium/Discount (1-Year Average)	-0.01

Company Information
Provider	SPDR State Street Global Advisors
Manager/Tenure	Michael J. Feehily (8), Karl A. Schneider (4), Dwayne Hancock (2)
Website	http://www.spdrs.com
Address	SPDR State Street Global Advisors State Street Financial Center, 1 Lincoln Street Boston MA 02111-2900 United States
Phone Number	617-786-3000

PERFORMANCE

Ratings History
Date	Overall Rating	Risk Rating	Reward Rating
Q3-19	B	B-	B
Q4-18	B	B	B-
Q4-17	B	B	B
Q4-16	B	C+	B
Q4-15	B	C+	B

Asset & Performance History
Date	NAV	1-Year Total Return
2018	52.92	4.01
2017	52.65	11.94
2016	48.58	15.4
2015	43.29	-4.85
2014	47.2	28.65
2013	37.98	13.01

Total Assets: $11,403,280,323
Asset Allocation
Asset	%
Cash	0%
Stocks	100%
US Stocks	100%
Bonds	0%
US Bonds	0%
Other	0%

Services Offered: Dividend Investment Plan, CashInvestment Plan

Investment Strategy: The investment seeks to provide investment results that, before expenses, correspond generally to the price and yield performance of publicly traded equity securities of companies in the Utilities Select Sector Index. In seeking to track the performance of the index, the fund employs a replication strategy. It generally invests substantially all, but at least 95%, of its total assets in the securities comprising the index. The index includes securities of companies from the following industries: electric utilities; water utilities; multi-utilities; independent power and renewable electricity producers; and gas utilities. The fund is non-diversified. **Top Holdings:** NextEra Energy Inc Duke Energy Corp Dominion Energy Inc Southern Co Exelon Corp

VanEck Vectors Gold Miners ETF   C   HOLD

Ticker	Traded On	NAV	Total Assets ($)	Dividend Yield (TTM)	Turnover Ratio	Expense Ratio
GDX	NYSE Arca	26.84	$11,268,185,766	0.39	15	0.53

Ratings
Reward   C
Risk   C-
Recent Upgrade/Downgrade   Up

Fund Information
Fund Type   Exchange Traded Funds
Category   Prec Metals
Sub-Category   Equity Precious Metals
Prospectus Objective   Prec Metals
Inception Date   May-06
Open to New Investments   Y

Prices
Price (as of 9/30/2019)   26.71
52-Week High   30.95
52-Week Low   18.39

Total Returns (%)

3-Month	6-Month	1-Year	3-Year	5-Year
7.96	21.71	45.52	3.30	29.34

3-Year Standard Deviation   24.92
Effective Duration

Valuation
Premium/Discount (1-Year Average)   -0.10

Company Information
Provider   VanEck
Manager/Tenure Hao-Hung (Peter) Liao (13), Guo Hua
                (Jason) Jin (1)
Website   http://www.vaneck.com
Address   Van Eck Associates Corporation 666
                Third Avenue New York NY 10017
                United States
Phone Number   800-826-1115

PERFORMANCE

Ratings History

Date	Overall Rating	Risk Rating	Reward Rating
Q3-19	C	C-	C
Q4-18	D+	D	C-
Q4-17	C-	D	C
Q4-16	C-	D	C
Q4-15	D+	D+	C-

Asset & Performance History

Date	NAV	1-Year Total Return
2018	21.07	-8.85
2017	23.25	12.02
2016	20.92	52.91
2015	13.72	-24.92
2014	18.43	-12.3
2013	21.16	-53.88

Total Assets: $11,268,185,766
Asset Allocation

Asset	%
Cash	0%
Stocks	100%
US Stocks	17%
Bonds	0%
US Bonds	0%
Other	0%

Services Offered:

Investment Strategy: The investment seeks to replicate as closely as possible, before fees and expenses, the price and yield performance of the NYSE® Arca Gold Miners Index®. The fund normally invests at least 80% of its total assets in common stocks and depositary receipts of companies involved in the gold mining industry. The index is a modified market-capitalization weighted index primarily comprised of publicly traded companies involved in the mining for gold and silver. The fund is non-diversified. **Top Holdings:** Barrick Gold Corp Newmont Goldcorp Corp Newcrest Mining Ltd Franco-Nevada Corp Agnico Eagle Mines Ltd

---

iShares Russell Mid-Cap Value ETF   C   HOLD

Ticker	Traded On	NAV	Total Assets ($)	Dividend Yield (TTM)	Turnover Ratio	Expense Ratio
IWS	NYSE Arca	89.70	$10,978,739,032	1.99	25	0.24

Ratings
Reward   C
Risk   C+
Recent Upgrade/Downgrade

Fund Information
Fund Type   Exchange Traded Funds
Category   US Equity Mid Cap
Sub-Category   Mid-Cap Value
Prospectus Objective   Growth
Inception Date   Jul-01
Open to New Investments   Y

Prices
Price (as of 9/30/2019)   89.70
52-Week High   91.13
52-Week Low   72.26

Total Returns (%)

3-Month	6-Month	1-Year	3-Year	5-Year
0.67	3.13	1.73	24.65	44.23

3-Year Standard Deviation   13.36
Effective Duration

Valuation
Premium/Discount (1-Year Average)   -0.01

Company Information
Provider   iShares
Manager/Tenure Greg Savage (11), Jennifer Hsui (7),
                Alan Mason (3), 2 others
Website   http://www.ishares.com
Address   iShares 400 Howard Street San
                Francisco CA 94105 United States
Phone Number   800-474-2737

PERFORMANCE

Ratings History

Date	Overall Rating	Risk Rating	Reward Rating
Q3-19	C	C+	C
Q4-18	C	C+	C-
Q4-17	B	B	B-
Q4-16	B-	C+	B
Q4-15	C	C+	C

Asset & Performance History

Date	NAV	1-Year Total Return
2018	76.34	-12.36
2017	89.09	13.09
2016	80.41	19.69
2015	68.7	-4.93
2014	73.77	14.49
2013	65.66	33.1

Total Assets: $10,978,739,032
Asset Allocation

Asset	%
Cash	0%
Stocks	100%
US Stocks	98%
Bonds	0%
US Bonds	0%
Other	0%

Services Offered: CashInvestment Plan

Investment Strategy: The investment seeks to track the investment results of the Russell Midcap Value Index, which measures the performance of the mid-capitalization value sector of the U.S. equity market. The fund generally invests at least 90% of its assets in securities of the underlying index and in depositary receipts representing securities of the underlying index. It may invest the remainder of its assets in certain futures, options and swap contracts, cash and cash equivalents, as well as in securities not included in the underlying index, but which the advisor believes will help the fund track the underlying index. **Top Holdings:** Sempra Energy Welltower Inc Xcel Energy Inc Newmont Goldcorp Corp Equity Residential

iShares Russell Mid-Cap Growth ETF   C+   HOLD

Ticker	Traded On	NAV	Total Assets ($)	Dividend Yield (TTM)	Turnover Ratio	Expense Ratio
IWP	NYSE Arca	141.37	$10,758,451,708	0.6	20	0.24

Ratings
Reward	C+
Risk	C+
Recent Upgrade/Downgrade	Down

Fund Information
Fund Type	Exchange Traded Funds
Category	US Equity Mid Cap
Sub-Category	Mid-Cap Growth
Prospectus Objective	Growth
Inception Date	Jul-01
Open to New Investments	Y

Prices
Price (as of 9/30/2019)	141.35
52-Week High	148.30
52-Week Low	106.03

Total Returns (%)
3-Month	6-Month	1-Year	3-Year	5-Year
-1.55	3.20	5.49	49.10	70.41

3-Year Standard Deviation	14.37
Effective Duration	

Valuation
Premium/Discount (1-Year Average)	-0.01

Company Information
Provider	iShares
Manager/Tenure	Greg Savage (11), Jennifer Hsui (7), Alan Mason (3), 2 others
Website	http://www.ishares.com
Address	iShares 400 Howard Street San Francisco CA 94105 United States
Phone Number	800-474-2737

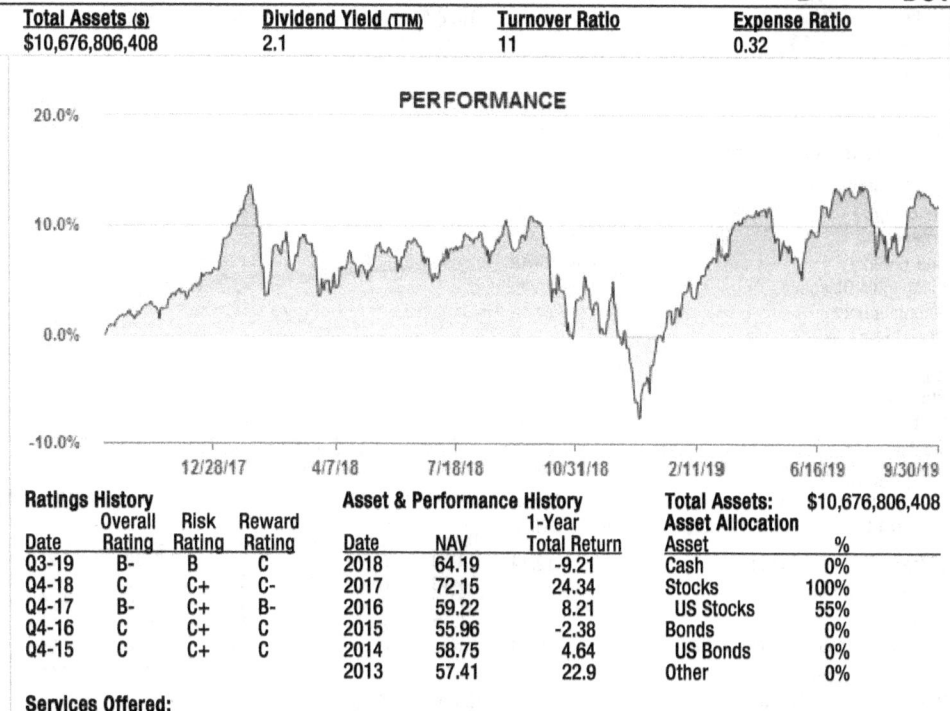

PERFORMANCE

Ratings History
Date	Overall Rating	Risk Rating	Reward Rating
Q3-19	C+	C+	C+
Q4-18	C	C+	C-
Q4-17	B	B-	B
Q4-16	C+	C+	B-
Q4-15	C	C+	C

Asset & Performance History
Date	NAV	1-Year Total Return
2018	113.63	-4.94
2017	120.65	24.98
2016	97.36	7.14
2015	91.96	-0.38
2014	93.21	11.68
2013	84.35	35.43

Total Assets: $10,758,451,708
Asset Allocation
Asset	%
Cash	0%
Stocks	100%
US Stocks	99%
Bonds	0%
US Bonds	0%
Other	0%

Services Offered: CashInvestment Plan

Investment Strategy: The investment seeks to track the investment results of the Russell Midcap Growth Index, which measures the performance of the mid-capitalization growth sector of the U.S. equity market. The fund generally invests at least 90% of its assets in securities of the underlying index and in depositary receipts representing securities of the underlying index. It may invest the remainder of its assets in certain futures, options and swap contracts, cash and cash equivalents, as well as in securities not included in the underlying index, but which the advisor believes will help the fund track the underlying index. **Top Holdings:** Fiserv Inc Dollar General Corp Twitter Inc Advanced Micro Devices Inc O'Reilly Automotive Inc

---

iShares MSCI ACWI ETF   B-   BUY

Ticker	Traded On	NAV	Total Assets ($)	Dividend Yield (TTM)	Turnover Ratio	Expense Ratio
ACWI	NAS CM	73.73	$10,676,806,408	2.1	11	0.32

Ratings
Reward	C
Risk	B
Recent Upgrade/Downgrade	

Fund Information
Fund Type	Exchange Traded Funds
Category	Global Equity Large Cap
Sub-Category	World Large Stock
Prospectus Objective	World Stock
Inception Date	Mar-08
Open to New Investments	Y

Prices
Price (as of 9/30/2019)	73.75
52-Week High	75.05
52-Week Low	61.18

Total Returns (%)
3-Month	6-Month	1-Year	3-Year	5-Year
-0.63	2.44	1.34	33.15	41.16

3-Year Standard Deviation	11.33
Effective Duration	

Valuation
Premium/Discount (1-Year Average)	0.00

Company Information
Provider	iShares
Manager/Tenure	Diane Hsiung (11), Greg Savage (11), Jennifer Hsui (6), 3 others
Website	http://www.ishares.com
Address	iShares 400 Howard Street San Francisco CA 94105 United States
Phone Number	800-474-2737

PERFORMANCE

Ratings History
Date	Overall Rating	Risk Rating	Reward Rating
Q3-19	B-	B	C
Q4-18	C	C+	C-
Q4-17	B-	C+	B-
Q4-16	C	C+	C
Q4-15	C	C+	C

Asset & Performance History
Date	NAV	1-Year Total Return
2018	64.19	-9.21
2017	72.15	24.34
2016	59.22	8.21
2015	55.96	-2.38
2014	58.75	4.64
2013	57.41	22.9

Total Assets: $10,676,806,408
Asset Allocation
Asset	%
Cash	0%
Stocks	100%
US Stocks	55%
Bonds	0%
US Bonds	0%
Other	0%

Services Offered:

Investment Strategy: The investment seeks to track the investment results of the MSCI ACWI composed of large- and mid-capitalization developed and emerging market equities. The fund generally will invest at least 90% of its assets in the component securities of the underlying index and in investments that have economic characteristics that are substantially identical to the component securities of the underlying index. The index is a free float-adjusted market capitalization index designed to measure the combined equity market performance of developed and emerging markets countries. **Top Holdings:** Microsoft Corp Apple Inc Amazon.com Inc iShares MSCI India ETF Facebook Inc A

Schwab U.S. Dividend Equity ETF™   B-   BUY

Ticker	Traded On	NAV	Total Assets ($)	Dividend Yield (TTM)	Turnover Ratio	Expense Ratio
SCHD	NYSE Arca	54.77	$10,335,299,640	3.04	23	0.06

Ratings

Reward	B
Risk	C
Recent Upgrade/Downgrade	Up

Fund Information

Fund Type	Exchange Traded Funds
Category	US Equity Large Cap Value
Sub-Category	Large Value
Prospectus Objective	Equity-Income
Inception Date	Oct-11
Open to New Investments	Y

Prices

Price (as of 9/30/2019)	54.78
52-Week High	55.76
52-Week Low	44.23

Total Returns (%)

3-Month	6-Month	1-Year	3-Year	5-Year
3.30	5.31	6.42	41.48	66.81

3-Year Standard Deviation	12.24
Effective Duration	

Valuation

Premium/Discount (1-Year Average)	-0.03

Company Information

Provider	Schwab ETFs
Manager/Tenure	Ferian Juwono (7), Christopher Bliss (2), Sabya Sinha (2), 1 other
Website	http://www.schwabfunds.com
Address	Schwab ETFs United States
Phone Number	800-435-4000

PERFORMANCE

Ratings History

Date	Overall Rating	Risk Rating	Reward Rating
Q3-19	B-	C	B
Q4-18	B-	C	B
Q4-17	B	B	B
Q4-16	B-	C	B
Q4-15	C+	C+	C+

Asset & Performance History

Date	NAV	1-Year Total Return
2018	46.98	-5.46
2017	51.13	20.67
2016	43.52	16.23
2015	38.58	-0.21
2014	39.83	11.66
2013	36.65	32.9

Total Assets: $10,335,299,640

Asset Allocation

Asset	%
Cash	0%
Stocks	100%
US Stocks	100%
Bonds	0%
US Bonds	0%
Other	0%

Services Offered:

Investment Strategy: The investment seeks to track as closely as possible, before fees and expenses, the total return of the Dow Jones U.S. Dividend 100™ Index. To pursue its goal, the fund generally invests in stocks that are included in the index. The fund invests at least 90% of its net assets in stocks that are included in the index. The index is designed to measure the performance of high dividend yielding stocks issued by U.S. companies that have a record of consistently paying dividends, selected for fundamental strength relative to their peers, based on financial ratios. **Top Holdings:** The Home Depot Inc   Procter & Gamble Co   Coca-Cola Co   PepsiCo Inc   Intel Corp

iShares Edge MSCI USA Momentum Factor ETF   B-   BUY

Ticker	Traded On	NAV	Total Assets ($)	Dividend Yield (TTM)	Turnover Ratio	Expense Ratio
MTUM	BATS	119.21	$10,221,977,219	1.46	138	0.15

Ratings

Reward	B
Risk	C+
Recent Upgrade/Downgrade	Up

Fund Information

Fund Type	Exchange Traded Funds
Category	US Equity Large Cap Growth
Sub-Category	Large Growth
Prospectus Objective	Growth
Inception Date	Apr-13
Open to New Investments	Y

Prices

Price (as of 9/30/2019)	119.25
52-Week High	123.04
52-Week Low	92.80

Total Returns (%)

3-Month	6-Month	1-Year	3-Year	5-Year
-0.14	6.68	1.28	60.39	98.99

3-Year Standard Deviation	12.49
Effective Duration	

Valuation

Premium/Discount (1-Year Average)	0.00

Company Information

Provider	iShares
Manager/Tenure	Diane Hsiung (6), Jennifer Hsui (6), Greg Savage (6), 3 others
Website	http://www.ishares.com
Address	iShares 400 Howard Street San Francisco CA 94105 United States
Phone Number	800-474-2737

PERFORMANCE

Ratings History

Date	Overall Rating	Risk Rating	Reward Rating
Q3-19	B-	C+	B
Q4-18	C+	C+	C+
Q4-17	A	A	A
Q4-16	B-	B-	B-
Q4-15	C	B-	C+

Asset & Performance History

Date	NAV	1-Year Total Return
2018	100.06	-1.76
2017	103.07	37.6
2016	75.76	4.89
2015	73.27	9.12
2014	67.92	14.47
2013	59.98	

Total Assets: $10,221,977,219

Asset Allocation

Asset	%
Cash	0%
Stocks	100%
US Stocks	99%
Bonds	0%
US Bonds	0%
Other	0%

Services Offered:

Investment Strategy: The investment seeks to track the investment results of the MSCI USA Momentum Index. The fund generally will invest at least 90% of its assets in the component securities of the underlying index and may invest up to 10% of its assets in certain futures, options and swap contracts, cash and cash equivalents. The index consists of stocks exhibiting relatively higher momentum characteristics than the traditional market capitalization-weighted parent index, the MSCI USA Index, which includes U.S. large- and mid-capitalization stocks. **Top Holdings:** Procter & Gamble Co   Mastercard Inc A   Visa Inc Class A   Microsoft Corp   The Walt Disney Co

SPDR® Bloomberg Barclays High Yield Bond ETF   A+   BUY

Ticker	Traded On	NAV	Total Assets ($)	Dividend Yield (TTM)	Turnover Ratio	Expense Ratio
JNK	NYSE Arca		$10,167,617,070	5.59	44	0.4

Ratings
Reward   A+
Risk   A
Recent Upgrade/Downgrade

Fund Information
Fund Type	Exchange Traded Funds
Category	US Fixed Income
Sub-Category	High Yield Bond
Prospectus Objective	Corp Bond-High Yld
Inception Date	Nov-07
Open to New Investments	Y

Prices
Price (as of 9/30/2019)	108.74
52-Week High	109.46
52-Week Low	32.95

Total Returns (%)
3-Month	6-Month	1-Year	3-Year	5-Year
1.01	3.54	218.82	252.02	262.72

3-Year Standard Deviation	4.53
Effective Duration	3.08

Valuation
Premium/Discount (1-Year Average)	0.09

Company Information
Provider	SPDR State Street Global Advisors
Manager/Tenure	Michael J. Brunell (11), Kyle Kelly (6), Bradley J. Sullivan (3)
Website	http://www.spdrs.com
Address	SPDR State Street Global Advisors State Street Financial Center, 1 Lincoln Street Boston MA 02111-2900 United States
Phone Number	617-786-3000

PERFORMANCE

Ratings History
Date	Overall Rating	Risk Rating	Reward Rating
Q3-19	A+	A	A+
Q4-18	C+	B+	C-
Q4-17	C+	B	C+
Q4-16	C+	B-	C
Q4-15	C-	C-	C-

Asset & Performance History
Date	NAV	1-Year Total Return
2018	33.55	-3.17
2017	36.64	6
2016	36.37	14.74
2015	33.75	-7.21
2014	38.62	1.15
2013	40.42	5.89

Total Assets: $10,167,617,070
Asset Allocation
Asset	%
Cash	1%
Stocks	0%
US Stocks	0%
Bonds	99%
US Bonds	81%
Other	0%

Services Offered:

Investment Strategy: The investment seeks to provide investment results that correspond generally to the price and yield performance of the Bloomberg Barclays High Yield Very Liquid Index. The fund generally invests substantially all, but at least 80%, of its total assets in the securities comprising the index or in securities that the Adviser determines have economic characteristics that are substantially identical to the economic characteristics of the securities that comprise the index. The index is designed to measure the performance of publicly issued U.S. dollar denominated high yield corporate bonds with above-average liquidity. The fund is non-diversified. **Top Holdings:** ALTICE FRANCE S.A 7.38% Sprint Corporation 7.88% TransDigm, Inc. 6.25% CCO Holdings, LLC/ CCO Holdings Capital Corp. 5.12% Diamond Sports Group LLC / Diamond Sports Finance Co 5.38%

Vanguard Health Care Index Fund ETF Shares   C+   HOLD

Ticker	Traded On	NAV	Total Assets ($)	Dividend Yield (TTM)	Turnover Ratio	Expense Ratio
VHT	NYSE Arca	167.63	$10,016,250,966	2.1	6	0.1

Ratings
Reward   C+
Risk   C+
Recent Upgrade/Downgrade

Fund Information
Fund Type	Exchange Traded Funds
Category	Healthcare Sector Equity
Sub-Category	Health
Prospectus Objective	Health
Inception Date	Jan-04
Open to New Investments	Y

Prices
Price (as of 9/30/2019)	167.68
52-Week High	180.89
52-Week Low	149.65

Total Returns (%)
3-Month	6-Month	1-Year	3-Year	5-Year
-4.54	-2.76	-5.92	31.23	54.03

3-Year Standard Deviation	13.84
Effective Duration	

Valuation
Premium/Discount (1-Year Average)	0.00

Company Information
Provider	Vanguard
Manager/Tenure	Walter Nejman (3), Michelle Louie (1)
Website	http://www.vanguard.com
Address	Vanguard 100 Vanguard Boulevard Malvern PA 19355 United States
Phone Number	877-662-7447

PERFORMANCE

Ratings History
Date	Overall Rating	Risk Rating	Reward Rating
Q3-19	C+	C+	C+
Q4-18	C+	C+	C+
Q4-17	B	B	B-
Q4-16	C+	C+	C+
Q4-15	B	B-	B

Asset & Performance History
Date	NAV	1-Year Total Return
2018	158.2	4.02
2017	154.1	23.84
2016	126.65	-3.82
2015	132.91	7.21
2014	125.5	25.37
2013	101.1	42.66

Total Assets: $10,016,250,966
Asset Allocation
Asset	%
Cash	0%
Stocks	100%
US Stocks	99%
Bonds	0%
US Bonds	0%
Other	0%

Services Offered:

Investment Strategy: The investment seeks to track the performance of a benchmark index. The fund employs an indexing investment approach designed to track the performance of the MSCI US Investable Market Index (IMI)/Health Care 25/50, an index made up of stocks of large, mid-size, and small U.S. companies within the health care sector, as classified under the Global Industry Classification Standard (GICS). The Advisor attempts to replicate the target index by seeking to invest all, or substantially all, of its assets in the stocks that make up the index, in order to hold each stock in approximately the same proportion as its weighting in the index. The fund is non-diversified. **Top Holdings:** Johnson & Johnson UnitedHealth Group Inc Merck & Co Inc Pfizer Inc Abbott Laboratories

iShares Floating Rate Bond ETF   C   HOLD

Ticker	Traded On	NAV	Total Assets ($)	Dividend Yield (TTM)	Turnover Ratio	Expense Ratio
FLOT	BATS	50.93	$9,885,363,856	2.88	17	0.2

Ratings
Reward   C
Risk   C+
Recent Upgrade/Downgrade

Fund Information
Fund Type   Exchange Traded Funds
Category   US Fixed Income
Sub-Category   Ultrashort Bond
Prospectus Objective   Worldwide Bond
Inception Date   Jun-11
Open to New Investments   Y

Prices
Price (as of 9/30/2019)   50.97
52-Week High   50.98
52-Week Low   50.22

Total Returns (%)

3-Month	6-Month	1-Year	3-Year	5-Year
0.72	1.85	2.80	6.94	8.05

3-Year Standard Deviation   0.5
Effective Duration

Valuation
Premium/Discount (1-Year Average)   0.02

Company Information
Provider   iShares
Manager/Tenure   James Mauro (8), Scott Radell (8)
Website   http://www.ishares.com
Address   iShares 400 Howard Street San
                      Francisco CA 94105 United States
Phone Number   800-474-2737

PERFORMANCE

Ratings History

Date	Overall Rating	Risk Rating	Reward Rating
Q3-19	C	C+	C
Q4-18	C	C+	C
Q4-17	B-	A-	C
Q4-16	C	C+	C
Q4-15	C	C+	C

Asset & Performance History

Date	NAV	1-Year Total Return
2018	50.42	1.56
2017	50.84	1.82
2016	50.66	1.54
2015	50.38	0.11
2014	50.59	0.3
2013	50.66	1.11

Total Assets: $9,885,363,856
Asset Allocation

Asset	%
Cash	4%
Stocks	0%
US Stocks	0%
Bonds	94%
US Bonds	57%
Other	0%

Services Offered:

Investment Strategy: The investment seeks to track the investment results of the Bloomberg Barclays US Floating Rate Note < 5 Years Index (the "underlying index"), which measures the performance of U.S. dollar-denominated, investment-grade floating rate notes. The fund generally will invest at least 90% of its assets in the component securities of the underlying index and may invest up to 10% of its assets in certain futures, options and swap contracts, cash and cash equivalents, as well as in securities not included in the underlying index, but which BFA believes will help the fund track the underlying index. **Top Holdings:** United States Treasury Notes 2% Morgan Stanley 3.46% Morgan Stanley 3.21% Inter-American Development Bank 2.37% Goldman Sachs Group, Inc. 2.9%

Industrial Select Sector SPDR® Fund   C+   HOLD

Ticker	Traded On	NAV	Total Assets ($)	Dividend Yield (TTM)	Turnover Ratio	Expense Ratio
XLI	NYSE Arca		$9,810,132,320	2.02	6	0.13

Ratings
Reward   C+
Risk   C+
Recent Upgrade/Downgrade

Fund Information
Fund Type   Exchange Traded Funds
Category   Industrials Sector Equity
Sub-Category   Industrials
Prospectus Objective   Unaligned
Inception Date   Dec-98
Open to New Investments   Y

Prices
Price (as of 9/30/2019)   77.63
52-Week High   79.60
52-Week Low   60.34

Total Returns (%)

3-Month	6-Month	1-Year	3-Year	5-Year
0.49	2.16	0.14	40.89	61.57

3-Year Standard Deviation   16.76
Effective Duration

Valuation
Premium/Discount (1-Year Average)   -0.02

Company Information
Provider   SPDR State Street Global Advisors
Manager/Tenure   Michael J. Feehily (8), Karl A.
                      Schneider (4), Emiliano Rabinovich (2)
Website   http://www.spdrs.com
Address   SPDR State Street Global Advisors
                      State Street Financial Center, 1
                      Lincoln Street Boston MA 02111-2900
                      United States
Phone Number   617-786-3000

PERFORMANCE

Ratings History

Date	Overall Rating	Risk Rating	Reward Rating
Q3-19	C+	C+	C+
Q4-18	C	C+	C
Q4-17	B	B-	B+
Q4-16	B	B-	B
Q4-15	B-	B	C+

Asset & Performance History

Date	NAV	1-Year Total Return
2018	64.43	-13.09
2017	75.58	23.84
2016	62.2	19.53
2015	53.03	-4.27
2014	56.58	10.44
2013	52.22	40.44

Total Assets: $9,810,132,320
Asset Allocation

Asset	%
Cash	0%
Stocks	100%
US Stocks	100%
Bonds	0%
US Bonds	0%
Other	0%

Services Offered: Dividend Investment Plan, CashInvestment Plan

Investment Strategy: The investment seeks to provide investment results that, before expenses, correspond generally to the price and yield performance of publicly traded equity securities of companies in the Industrial Select Sector Index. Under normal market conditions, the fund generally invests substantially all, but at least 95%, of its total assets in the securities comprising the index. The index includes securities of companies from the following industries: aerospace and defense; industrial conglomerates; marine; transportation infrastructure; machinery; road and rail; air freight and logistics; commercial services and supplies; etc. It is non-diversified. **Top Holdings:** Boeing Co Honeywell International Inc Union Pacific Corp United Technologies Corp Lockheed Martin Corp

iShares MSCI EAFE Small-Cap ETF   C   HOLD

Ticker	Traded On	NAV	Total Assets ($)	Dividend Yield (TTM)	Turnover Ratio	Expense Ratio
SCZ	NAS CM	57.11	$9,332,302,409	2.83	10	0.39

Ratings
Reward   C-
Risk   C+
Recent Upgrade/Downgrade

Fund Information
Fund Type	Exchange Traded Funds
Category	Globa Eq Mid/Small Cap
Sub-Category	Foreign Small/Mid Blend
Prospectus Objective	Small Company
Inception Date	Dec-07
Open to New Investments	Y

Prices
Price (as of 9/30/2019)	57.23
52-Week High	62.49
52-Week Low	49.58

Total Returns (%)
3-Month	6-Month	1-Year	3-Year	5-Year
-1.33	-0.08	-5.80	18.62	34.71

3-Year Standard Deviation	12.12
Effective Duration	

Valuation
Premium/Discount (1-Year Average)	-0.05

Company Information
Provider	iShares
Manager/Tenure	Diane Hsiung (11), Greg Savage (11), Jennifer Hsui (6), 3 others
Website	http://www.ishares.com
Address	iShares 400 Howard Street San Francisco CA 94105 United States
Phone Number	800-474-2737

PERFORMANCE

Ratings History

Date	Overall Rating	Risk Rating	Reward Rating
Q3-19	C	C+	C-
Q4-18	C-	C-	D+
Q4-17	A-	A-	A-
Q4-16	C	C+	C
Q4-15	C	C+	C

Asset & Performance History

Date	NAV	1-Year Total Return
2018	51.79	-17.64
2017	64.6	32.51
2016	50	2.42
2015	50.21	9.16
2014	46.93	-5.01
2013	50.66	29.21

Total Assets: $9,332,302,409
Asset Allocation

Asset	%
Cash	1%
Stocks	99%
US Stocks	2%
Bonds	0%
US Bonds	0%
Other	1%

Services Offered:

Investment Strategy: The investment seeks to track the investment results of the MSCI EAFE Small Cap Index composed of small-capitalization developed market equities, excluding the U.S. and Canada. The fund generally will invest at least 90% of its assets in the component securities of the underlying index and in investments that have economic characteristics that are substantially identical to the component securities of the underlying index. The index represents the small-capitalization segment of the MSCI EAFE IMI Index. **Top Holdings:** LEG Immobilien AG   Galapagos NV   Logitech International SA   Rightmove PLC   Scout24 AG

---

iShares 3-7 Year Treasury Bond ETF   C   HOLD

Ticker	Traded On	NAV	Total Assets ($)	Dividend Yield (TTM)	Turnover Ratio	Expense Ratio
IEI	NAS CM	126.74	$9,125,536,663	2.08	41	0.15

Ratings
Reward   C
Risk   C+
Recent Upgrade/Downgrade

Fund Information
Fund Type	Exchange Traded Funds
Category	US Fixed Income
Sub-Category	Intermediate Government
Prospectus Objective	Govt Bond - Treasury
Inception Date	Jan-07
Open to New Investments	Y

Prices
Price (as of 9/30/2019)	126.80
52-Week High	128.02
52-Week Low	118.21

Total Returns (%)
3-Month	6-Month	1-Year	3-Year	5-Year
1.45	4.59	8.82	5.69	12.75

3-Year Standard Deviation	2.99
Effective Duration	

Valuation
Premium/Discount (1-Year Average)	0.05

Company Information
Provider	iShares
Manager/Tenure	Scott Radell (9), James Mauro (8)
Website	http://www.ishares.com
Address	iShares 400 Howard Street San Francisco CA 94105 United States
Phone Number	800-474-2737

PERFORMANCE

Ratings History

Date	Overall Rating	Risk Rating	Reward Rating
Q3-19	C	C+	C
Q4-18	C-	C	D
Q4-17	C	C	C
Q4-16	C	C+	C
Q4-15	C	C+	C

Asset & Performance History

Date	NAV	1-Year Total Return
2018	121.36	1.35
2017	122.13	1.18
2016	122.52	1.21
2015	122.63	1.67
2014	122.29	3.14
2013	120.04	-1.95

Total Assets: $9,125,536,663
Asset Allocation

Asset	%
Cash	0%
Stocks	0%
US Stocks	0%
Bonds	100%
US Bonds	100%
Other	0%

Services Offered:

Investment Strategy: The investment seeks to track the investment results of the ICE U.S. Treasury 3-7 Year Bond Index (the "underlying index"). The fund generally invests at least 90% of its assets in the bonds of the underlying index and at least 95% of its assets in U.S. government bonds. The underlying index measures the performance of public obligations of the U.S. Treasury that have a remaining maturity of greater than or equal to three years and less than seven years. **Top Holdings:** United States Treasury Notes 2.38%   United States Treasury Notes 2.25%   United States Treasury Notes 2%   United States Treasury Notes 1.75%   United States Treasury Notes 2.5%

JPMorgan Ultra-Short Income ETF   C   HOLD

Ticker	Traded On	NAV	Total Assets ($)	Dividend Yield (TTM)	Turnover Ratio	Expense Ratio
JPST	BATS	50.40	$8,809,766,279	2.65	43	0.18

Ratings
Reward   C
Risk   C+
Recent Upgrade/Downgrade

Fund Information
Fund Type   Exchange Traded Funds
Category   US Fixed Income
Sub-Category   Ultrashort Bond
Prospectus Objective   Growth & Inc
Inception Date   May-17
Open to New Investments   Y

Prices
Price (as of 9/30/2019)   50.43
52-Week High   50.52
52-Week Low   50.09

Total Returns (%)
3-Month	6-Month	1-Year	3-Year	5-Year
0.50	1.45	3.00		

3-Year Standard Deviation
Effective Duration   0.48

Valuation
Premium/Discount (1-Year Average)   0.06

Company Information
Provider   JPMorgan
Manager/Tenure   Cecilia Junker (2), David N. Martucci
                 (2), James McNerny (2), 1 other
Website
Address   JPMorgan One Beacon Street Boston
                 MA 02108 United States
Phone Number

PERFORMANCE

Ratings History

Date	Overall Rating	Risk Rating	Reward Rating
Q3-19	C	C+	C
Q4-18	C	C+	D+
Q4-17	U		
Q4-16			
Q4-15			

Asset & Performance History

Date	NAV	1-Year Total Return
2018	50.09	2.19
2017	50.04	
2016		
2015		
2014		
2013		

Total Assets: $8,809,766,279
Asset Allocation

Asset	%
Cash	22%
Stocks	0%
US Stocks	0%
Bonds	74%
US Bonds	49%
Other	0%

Services Offered:

Investment Strategy: The investment seeks to provide current income while seeking to maintain a low volatility of principal. Under normal circumstances, the fund seeks to achieve its investment objective by investing at least 80% of its Assets in investment grade, U.S. dollar denominated short-term fixed, variable and floating rate debt. "Assets" means net assets, plus the amount of borrowings for investment purposes. As part of its principal investment strategy, it may invest in corporate securities, asset-backed securities, mortgage-backed and mortgage-related securities, and high quality money market instruments such as commercial paper and certificates of deposit. **Top Holdings:** United States Treasury Notes 1.5% United States Treasury Notes 1.62% United States Treasury Notes 1.62% Bank of Montreal 2.68% Macquarie Bank Limited 2.62%

iShares Russell 2000 Growth ETF   C   HOLD

Ticker	Traded On	NAV	Total Assets ($)	Dividend Yield (TTM)	Turnover Ratio	Expense Ratio
IWO	NYSE Arca	192.86	$8,746,132,582	0.72	35	0.24

Ratings
Reward   C
Risk   C+
Recent Upgrade/Downgrade

Fund Information
Fund Type   Exchange Traded Funds
Category   US Equity Small Cap
Sub-Category   Small Growth
Prospectus Objective   Growth
Inception Date   Jul-00
Open to New Investments   Y

Prices
Price (as of 9/30/2019)   192.73
52-Week High   211.73
52-Week Low   156.33

Total Returns (%)
3-Month	6-Month	1-Year	3-Year	5-Year
-4.42	-2.30	-8.24	32.42	57.76

3-Year Standard Deviation   17.47
Effective Duration

Valuation
Premium/Discount (1-Year Average)   -0.06

Company Information
Provider   iShares
Manager/Tenure   Greg Savage (11), Jennifer Hsui (7),
                 Alan Mason (3), 2 others
Website   http://www.ishares.com
Address   iShares 400 Howard Street San
                 Francisco CA 94105 United States
Phone Number   800-474-2737

PERFORMANCE

Ratings History

Date	Overall Rating	Risk Rating	Reward Rating
Q3-19	C	C+	C
Q4-18	C	C+	C-
Q4-17	B+	B	A-
Q4-16	B-	C+	B-
Q4-15	C+	C+	C+

Asset & Performance History

Date	NAV	1-Year Total Return
2018	168.12	-9.33
2017	186.64	22.24
2016	153.9	11.47
2015	139.51	-1.18
2014	142.4	5.72
2013	135.7	43.43

Total Assets: $8,746,132,582
Asset Allocation

Asset	%
Cash	0%
Stocks	100%
US Stocks	99%
Bonds	0%
US Bonds	0%
Other	0%

Services Offered: CashInvestment Plan

Investment Strategy: The investment seeks to track the investment results of the Russell 2000 Growth Index, which measures the performance of the small-capitalization growth sector of the U.S. equity market. The fund generally invests at least 90% of its assets in securities of the underlying index and in depositary receipts representing securities of the underlying index. It may invest the remainder of its assets in certain futures, options and swap contracts, cash and cash equivalents, as well as in securities not included in the underlying index, but which the advisor believes will help the fund track the underlying index. **Top Holdings:** NovoCure Ltd Haemonetics Corp Science Applications International Corp Trex Co Inc Maximus Inc

iShares Core Dividend Growth ETF   C+   HOLD

Ticker	Traded On	NAV	Total Assets ($)	Dividend Yield (TTM)	Turnover Ratio	Expense Ratio
DGRO	NYSE Arca	39.13	$8,645,152,893	2.29	26	0.08

Ratings
Reward	C+
Risk	C+
Recent Upgrade/Downgrade	

Fund Information
Fund Type	Exchange Traded Funds
Category	US Equity Large Cap Value
Sub-Category	Large Value
Prospectus Objective	Equity-Income
Inception Date	Jun-14
Open to New Investments	Y

Prices
Price (as of 9/30/2019)	39.14
52-Week High	39.54
52-Week Low	31.18

Total Returns (%)
3-Month	6-Month	1-Year	3-Year	5-Year
2.36	6.70	7.90	51.93	78.06

3-Year Standard Deviation	11.65
Effective Duration	

Valuation
Premium/Discount (1-Year Average)	0.02

Company Information
Provider	iShares
Manager/Tenure	Jennifer Hsui (5), Greg Savage (5), Alan Mason (3), 2 others
Website	http://www.ishares.com
Address	iShares 400 Howard Street San Francisco CA 94105 United States
Phone Number	800-474-2737

PERFORMANCE

Ratings History

Date	Overall Rating	Risk Rating	Reward Rating
Q3-19	C+	C+	C+
Q4-18	C	C+	C
Q4-17	B	B	B
Q4-16	C	C+	C+
Q4-15	D	C-	D+

Asset & Performance History

Date	NAV	1-Year Total Return
2018	33.16	-2.24
2017	34.72	22.83
2016	28.89	15.27
2015	25.67	-0.62
2014	26.49	
2013		

Total Assets: $8,645,152,893
Asset Allocation

Asset	%
Cash	0%
Stocks	100%
US Stocks	98%
Bonds	0%
US Bonds	0%
Other	0%

Services Offered:

Investment Strategy: The investment seeks to track the investment results of the Morningstar® US Dividend Growth IndexSM. The fund generally will invest at least 90% of its assets in the component securities of the underlying index. The underlying index is a subset of the Morningstar® US Market IndexSM, which is a diversified broad market index that represents approximately 97% of the market capitalization of publicly-traded U.S. stocks.
Top Holdings: Apple Inc Microsoft Corp Verizon Communications Inc JPMorgan Chase & Co Chevron Corp

---

SPDR® Bloomberg Barclays 1-3 Month T-Bill ETF   C   HOLD

Ticker	Traded On	NAV	Total Assets ($)	Dividend Yield (TTM)	Turnover Ratio	Expense Ratio
BIL	NYSE Arca	91.58	$8,603,062,974	2.16	635	0.14

Ratings
Reward	C
Risk	B-
Recent Upgrade/Downgrade	

Fund Information
Fund Type	Exchange Traded Funds
Category	US Fixed Income
Sub-Category	Ultrashort Bond
Prospectus Objective	Govt Bond - Treasury
Inception Date	May-07
Open to New Investments	Y

Prices
Price (as of 9/30/2019)	91.59
52-Week High	91.62
52-Week Low	91.37

Total Returns (%)
3-Month	6-Month	1-Year	3-Year	5-Year
0.50	1.08	2.18	4.11	4.06

3-Year Standard Deviation	0.22
Effective Duration	0.08

Valuation
Premium/Discount (1-Year Average)	0.01

Company Information
Provider	SPDR State Street Global Advisors
Manager/Tenure	Todd Bean (12), Sean Lussier (2)
Website	http://www.spdrs.com
Address	SPDR State Street Global Advisors State Street Financial Center, 1 Lincoln Street Boston MA 02111-2900 United States
Phone Number	617-786-3000

PERFORMANCE

Ratings History

Date	Overall Rating	Risk Rating	Reward Rating
Q3-19	C	B-	C
Q4-18	C	C+	C-
Q4-17	C	C+	C-
Q4-16	C-	C	D+
Q4-15	D+	C	D

Asset & Performance History

Date	NAV	1-Year Total Return
2018	91.44	1.51
2017	91.42	0.68
2016	91.42	0.12
2015	91.37	-0.1
2014	91.47	-0.09
2013	91.56	-0.07

Total Assets: $8,603,062,974
Asset Allocation

Asset	%
Cash	100%
Stocks	0%
US Stocks	0%
Bonds	0%
US Bonds	0%
Other	0%

Services Offered:

Investment Strategy: The investment seeks to provide investment results that correspond generally to the price and yield performance of the Bloomberg Barclays 1-3 Month U.S. Treasury Bill Index. The fund invests substantially all, but at least 80%, of its total assets in the securities comprising the index or in securities that the Adviser determines have economic characteristics that are substantially identical to the economic characteristics of the securities that comprise the index. The index measures the performance of public obligations of the U.S. Treasury that have a remaining maturity of greater than or equal to 1 month and less than 3 months. It is non-diversified.
Top Holdings: United States Treasury Bills 0.01% Ssi Us Gov Money Market Class State Street Inst Us Gov

Schwab U.S. TIPS ETF™   C+   HOLD

Ticker	Traded On	NAV	Total Assets ($)	Dividend Yield (TTM)	Turnover Ratio	Expense Ratio
SCHP	NYSE Arca	56.65	$8,441,107,343	1.86	17	0.05

Ratings
Reward	C+
Risk	C+
Recent Upgrade/Downgrade	Up

Fund Information
Fund Type	Exchange Traded Funds
Category	US Fixed Income
Sub-Category	Inflation-Protected Bond
Prospectus Objective	Govt Bond - Treasury
Inception Date	Aug-10
Open to New Investments	Y

Prices
Price (as of 9/30/2019)	56.76
52-Week High	57.71
52-Week Low	52.79

Total Returns (%)
3-Month	6-Month	1-Year	3-Year	5-Year
1.53	4.53	7.23	6.57	11.63

3-Year Standard Deviation	3.28
Effective Duration	7.48

Valuation
Premium/Discount (1-Year Average)	0.02

Company Information
Provider	Schwab ETFs
Manager/Tenure	Matthew Hastings (9), Mark R. McKissick (2)
Website	http://www.schwabfunds.com
Address	Schwab ETFs United States
Phone Number	800-435-4000

PERFORMANCE

Ratings History
Date	Overall Rating	Risk Rating	Reward Rating
Q3-19	C+	C+	C+
Q4-18	C-	C	D+
Q4-17	C	B-	C
Q4-16	C	C+	C
Q4-15	D+	C-	D+

Asset & Performance History
Date	NAV	1-Year Total Return
2018	53.27	-1.31
2017	55.39	3.06
2016	54.84	4.59
2015	53.15	-1.5
2014	54.11	3.56
2013	52.92	-8.66

Total Assets: $8,441,107,343
Asset Allocation
Asset	%
Cash	0%
Stocks	0%
US Stocks	0%
Bonds	100%
US Bonds	100%
Other	0%

Services Offered:

Investment Strategy: The investment seeks to track as closely as possible, before fees and expenses, the total return of the Bloomberg Barclays US Treasury Inflation-Linked Bond Index (Series-L). The fund will invest at least 90% of its net assets in securities included in the index. The index includes all publicly-issued U.S. Treasury Inflation-Protected Securities (TIPS) that have at least one year remaining to maturity, are rated investment grade and have $500 million or more of outstanding face value. The TIPS in the index must be denominated in U.S. dollars and must be fixed-rate and non-convertible. **Top Holdings:** United States Treasury Notes 0.12% United States Treasury Notes 0.62% United States Treasury Notes 0.62% United States Treasury Notes 0.12% United States Treasury Notes 0.38%

iShares MSCI Brazil Capped ETF   C   HOLD

Ticker	Traded On	NAV	Total Assets ($)	Dividend Yield (TTM)	Turnover Ratio	Expense Ratio
EWZ	NYSE Arca	41.92	$8,411,112,858	2.64	30	0.59

Ratings
Reward	C+
Risk	C
Recent Upgrade/Downgrade	

Fund Information
Fund Type	Exchange Traded Funds
Category	Latin America Equity
Sub-Category	Latin America Stock
Prospectus Objective	Foreign Stock
Inception Date	Jul-00
Open to New Investments	Y

Prices
Price (as of 9/30/2019)	42.13
52-Week High	46.73
52-Week Low	33.71

Total Returns (%)
3-Month	6-Month	1-Year	3-Year	5-Year
-5.15	1.27	28.28	34.50	11.95

3-Year Standard Deviation	28.48
Effective Duration	

Valuation
Premium/Discount (1-Year Average)	-0.12

Company Information
Provider	iShares
Manager/Tenure	Diane Hsiung (11), Greg Savage (11), Jennifer Hsui (6), 3 others
Website	http://www.ishares.com
Address	iShares 400 Howard Street San Francisco CA 94105 United States
Phone Number	800-474-2737

PERFORMANCE

Ratings History
Date	Overall Rating	Risk Rating	Reward Rating
Q3-19	C	C	C+
Q4-18	C	C-	C
Q4-17	C	C-	C
Q4-16	D+	D+	D+
Q4-15	D-	D-	D-

Asset & Performance History
Date	NAV	1-Year Total Return
2018	38.32	-1.78
2017	40.26	21.9
2016	33.66	63.91
2015	20.95	-41.28
2014	36.76	-14.5
2013	44.38	-17

Total Assets: $8,411,112,858
Asset Allocation
Asset	%
Cash	1%
Stocks	99%
US Stocks	0%
Bonds	0%
US Bonds	0%
Other	0%

Services Offered: CashInvestment Plan

Investment Strategy: The investment seeks to track the investment results of the MSCI Brazil 25/50 Index. The fund invests at least 95% of its assets in the securities of its underlying index and in depositary receipts representing securities in its underlying index. The index, consists of stocks traded primarily on B3 (the largest Brazilian exchange), is a free float-adjusted market capitalization-weighted index with a capping methodology applied to issuer weights so that no single issuer of a component exceeds 25% of the underlying index weight, and all issuers with weight above 5% do not cumulatively exceed 50% of the underlying index weight. The fund is non-diversified. **Top Holdings:** Itau Unibanco Holding SA Participating Preferred Vale SA Bank Bradesco SA Participating Preferred Petroleo Brasileiro SA Petrobras Participating Preferred Petroleo Brasileiro SA Petrobras

iShares Intermediate-Term Corporate Bond ETF   D   SELL

Ticker	Traded On	NAV	Total Assets ($)	Dividend Yield (TTM)	Turnover Ratio	Expense Ratio
IGIB	NAS CM	57.82	$8,296,577,194	3.65	86	0.06

Ratings
Reward   D
Risk   D
Recent Upgrade/Downgrade

Fund Information
Fund Type   Exchange Traded Funds
Category   US Fixed Income
Sub-Category   Corporate Bond
Prospectus Objective   Growth & Inc
Inception Date   Jan-07
Open to New Investments   Y

Prices
Price (as of 9/30/2019)   57.92
52-Week High   58.42
52-Week Low   52.01

Total Returns (%)

3-Month	6-Month	1-Year	3-Year	5-Year
2.58	7.51	13.34	-43.00	-39.30

3-Year Standard Deviation   3.37
Effective Duration

Valuation
Premium/Discount (1-Year Average)   0.08

Company Information
Provider   iShares
Manager/Tenure   Scott Radell (9), James Mauro (8)
Website   http://www.ishares.com
Address   iShares 400 Howard Street San
                       Francisco CA 94105 United States
Phone Number   800-474-2737

PERFORMANCE

Ratings History

Date	Overall Rating	Risk Rating	Reward Rating
Q3-19	D	D	D
Q4-18	D-	D-	E+
Q4-17	B	A	C
Q4-16	C	C+	C
Q4-15	C	C+	C

Asset & Performance History

Date	NAV	1-Year Total Return
2018	52.49	-50.25
2017	109.15	3.3
2016	108.14	3.37
2015	107.18	0.68
2014	109.12	3.88
2013	107.65	-0.38

Total Assets: $8,296,577,194
Asset Allocation

Asset	%
Cash	0%
Stocks	0%
US Stocks	0%
Bonds	96%
US Bonds	75%
Other	0%

Services Offered:

Investment Strategy: The investment seeks to track the investment results of the ICE BofAML 5-10 Year US Corporate Index. The fund generally invests at least 90% of its assets in securities of the underlying index. The index measures the performance of investment-grade corporate bonds of both U.S. and non-U.S. issuers that are U.S. dollar-denominated and publicly issued in the U.S. domestic market and have a remaining maturity of greater than or equal to five years and less than ten years. The fund may invest the remainder of its assets in certain futures, options and swap contracts, cash and cash equivalents. **Top Holdings:** CVS Health Corp 4.3%   CVS Health Corp 4.1%   Petroleos Mexicanos 6.5%   Anheuser-Busch Companies LLC / Anheuser-Busch InBev Worldwide Inc 3.65%   HSBC Holdings plc 4.3%

Alerian MLP ETF   C   HOLD

Ticker	Traded On	NAV	Total Assets ($)	Dividend Yield (TTM)	Turnover Ratio	Expense Ratio
AMLP	NYSE Arca	9.15	$8,259,879,130	8.43	26	0.85

Ratings
Reward   B-
Risk   D+
Recent Upgrade/Downgrade   Up

Fund Information
Fund Type   Exchange Traded Funds
Category   Energy Sector Equity
Sub-Category   Energy Limited Partnership
Prospectus Objective   Natl Res
Inception Date   Aug-10
Open to New Investments   Y

Prices
Price (as of 9/30/2019)   9.14
52-Week High   10.93
52-Week Low   8.32

Total Returns (%)

3-Month	6-Month	1-Year	3-Year	5-Year
-5.38	-6.16	-8.85	-9.19	-28.28

3-Year Standard Deviation   16.34
Effective Duration

Valuation
Premium/Discount (1-Year Average)   0.00

Company Information
Provider   ALPS
Manager/Tenure   Ryan Mischker (4), Andrew Hicks (3)
Website   http://www.alpsfunds.com
Address   ALPS 1290 Broadway, Suite 1100
                       Denver CO 80203 United States
Phone Number   866-759-5679

PERFORMANCE

Ratings History

Date	Overall Rating	Risk Rating	Reward Rating
Q3-19	C	D+	B-
Q4-18	C	D	B-
Q4-17	D	D	D
Q4-16	D	D	D
Q4-15	B-	C	B

Asset & Performance History

Date	NAV	1-Year Total Return
2018	8.75	-12.71
2017	10.82	-7.92
2016	12.64	15.75
2015	11.99	-25.91
2014	17.49	4.82
2013	17.76	18.2

Total Assets: $8,259,879,130
Asset Allocation

Asset	%
Cash	0%
Stocks	100%
US Stocks	100%
Bonds	0%
US Bonds	0%
Other	0%

Services Offered:

Investment Strategy: The investment seeks investment results that correspond (before fees and expenses) generally to the price and yield performance of its underlying index, the Alerian MLP Infrastructure Index. The fund will normally invest at least 90% of its total assets in securities that comprise the underlying index. The underlying index is comprised of energy infrastructure MLPs that earn a majority of their cash flow from the transportation, storage and processing of energy commodities. It is non-diversified. **Top Holdings:** Magellan Midstream Partners LP   Enterprise Products Partners LP   Energy Transfer LP   MPLX LP Partnership Units   Plains All American Pipeline LP

Schwab U.S. Small-Cap ETF™   C   HOLD

Ticker	Traded On	NAV	Total Assets ($)	Dividend Yield (TTM)	Turnover Ratio	Expense Ratio
SCHA	NYSE Arca	69.72	$8,198,730,951	1.51	9	0.04

Ratings
Reward   C
Risk   C+
Recent Upgrade/Downgrade

Fund Information
Fund Type   Exchange Traded Funds
Category   US Equity Small Cap
Sub-Category   Small Blend
Prospectus Objective   Small Company
Inception Date   Nov-09
Open to New Investments   Y

Prices
Price (as of 9/30/2019)   69.73
52-Week High   75.26
52-Week Low   57.06

Total Returns (%)

3-Month	6-Month	1-Year	3-Year	5-Year
-2.50	-0.80	-5.88	26.29	47.65

3-Year Standard Deviation   16.66
Effective Duration

Valuation
Premium/Discount (1-Year Average)   -0.01

Company Information
Provider   Schwab ETFs
Manager/Tenure   Ferian Juwono (9), Christopher Bliss
                      (2), Sabya Sinha (2), 1 other
Website   http://www.schwabfunds.com
Address   Schwab ETFs United States
Phone Number   800-435-4000

PERFORMANCE

Ratings History

Date	Overall Rating	Risk Rating	Reward Rating
Q3-19	C	C+	C
Q4-18	C	C+	C-
Q4-17	B	B	B+
Q4-16	B-	C+	B
Q4-15	C	C+	C

Asset & Performance History

Date	NAV	1-Year Total Return
2018	60.69	-11.75
2017	69.74	15.41
2016	61.42	19.88
2015	52.07	-4.23
2014	55.14	6.53
2013	52.53	39.58

Total Assets: $8,198,730,951
Asset Allocation

Asset	%
Cash	0%
Stocks	100%
US Stocks	99%
Bonds	0%
US Bonds	0%
Other	0%

Services Offered:

Investment Strategy: The investment seeks to track as closely as possible, before fees and expenses, the total return of the Dow Jones U.S. Small-Cap Total Stock Market Index. To pursue its goal, the fund generally invests in stocks that are included in the index. The fund will invest at least 90% of its net assets in these stocks. The index includes the small-cap portion of the Dow Jones U.S. Total Stock Market Index actually available to investors in the marketplace. The Dow Jones U.S. Small-Cap Total Stock Market Index includes the components ranked 751-2500 by full market capitalization. The index is a float-adjusted market capitalization weighted index. **Top Holdings:** Amcor PLC Ordinary Shares   Exact Sciences Corp   Twilio Inc A   Okta Inc A   Roku Inc Class A

Schwab U.S. Large-Cap Growth ETF™   C+   HOLD

Ticker	Traded On	NAV	Total Assets ($)	Dividend Yield (TTM)	Turnover Ratio	Expense Ratio
SCHG	NYSE Arca	84.02	$8,108,352,932	1.15	5	0.04

Ratings
Reward   B-
Risk   C+
Recent Upgrade/Downgrade   Down

Fund Information
Fund Type   Exchange Traded Funds
Category   US Equity Large Cap Growth
Sub-Category   Large Growth
Prospectus Objective   Growth
Inception Date   Dec-09
Open to New Investments   Y

Prices
Price (as of 9/30/2019)   84.01
52-Week High   86.17
52-Week Low   64.30

Total Returns (%)

3-Month	6-Month	1-Year	3-Year	5-Year
0.34	5.09	3.46	56.47	83.39

3-Year Standard Deviation   13.1
Effective Duration

Valuation
Premium/Discount (1-Year Average)   -0.03

Company Information
Provider   Schwab ETFs
Manager/Tenure   Ferian Juwono (9), Christopher Bliss
                      (2), Sabya Sinha (2), 1 other
Website   http://www.schwabfunds.com
Address   Schwab ETFs United States
Phone Number   800-435-4000

PERFORMANCE

Ratings History

Date	Overall Rating	Risk Rating	Reward Rating
Q3-19	C+	C+	B-
Q4-18	C	C+	C
Q4-17	B	B	B
Q4-16	B-	C+	B
Q4-15	C+	B-	C+

Asset & Performance History

Date	NAV	1-Year Total Return
2018	68.89	-1.34
2017	70.66	28.05
2016	55.79	6.75
2015	52.82	3.25
2014	51.77	15.73
2013	45.25	33.96

Total Assets: $8,108,352,932
Asset Allocation

Asset	%
Cash	0%
Stocks	100%
US Stocks	99%
Bonds	0%
US Bonds	0%
Other	0%

Services Offered:

Investment Strategy: The investment seeks to track as closely as possible, before fees and expenses, the total return of the Dow Jones U.S. Large-Cap Growth Total Stock Market Index. To pursue its goal, the fund generally invests in stocks that are included in the Dow Jones U.S. Large-Cap Growth Total Stock Market Index. The index includes the large-cap growth portion of the Dow Jones U.S. Total Stock Market Index actually available to investors in the marketplace. The index includes the components ranked 1-750 by full market capitalization and that are classified as "growth" based on a number of factors. The fund is non-diversified. **Top Holdings:** Microsoft Corp   Apple Inc   Amazon.com Inc   Facebook Inc A   Berkshire Hathaway Inc B

First Trust Dow Jones Internet Index Fund   C+   HOLD

Ticker	Traded On	NAV	Total Assets ($)	Dividend Yield (TTM)	Turnover Ratio	Expense Ratio
FDN	NYSE Arca	134.63	$8,057,558,263	0		0.52

Ratings
Reward   B
Risk   C
Recent Upgrade/Downgrade

Fund Information
Fund Type   Exchange Traded Funds
Category   Technology Sector Equity
Sub-Category   Technology
Prospectus Objective   Technology
Inception Date   Jun-06
Open to New Investments   Y

Prices
Price (as of 9/30/2019)   134.64
52-Week High   151.35
52-Week Low   107.21

Total Returns (%)

3-Month	6-Month	1-Year	3-Year	5-Year
-7.24	-4.57	-4.23	65.02	125.28

3-Year Standard Deviation   17.09
Effective Duration

Valuation
Premium/Discount (1-Year Average)   0.00

Company Information
Provider   First Trust
Manager/Tenure   Jon C. Erickson (13), Daniel J.
                  Lindquist (13), David G. McGarel (13),
                  3 others
Website   http://www.ftportfolios.com/
Address   First Trust 120 E. Liberty Drive, Suite
                  400 Wheaton IL 60187 United States
Phone Number   800-621-1675

PERFORMANCE

Ratings History

Date	Overall Rating	Risk Rating	Reward Rating
Q3-19	C+	C	B
Q4-18	C+	C-	B
Q4-17	A-	B	A
Q4-16	B-	C	B
Q4-15	B	C	B+

Asset & Performance History

Date	NAV	1-Year Total Return
2018	116.65	6.22
2017	109.81	37.62
2016	79.79	6.91
2015	74.63	21.76
2014	61.29	2.42
2013	59.84	53.39

Total Assets: $8,057,558,263
Asset Allocation

Asset	%
Cash	0%
Stocks	100%
US Stocks	100%
Bonds	0%
US Bonds	0%
Other	0%

Services Offered:

Investment Strategy: The investment seeks investment results that correspond generally to the price and yield (before the fund's fees and expenses) of an equity index called the Dow Jones Internet Composite Index (SM) (the "index"). The fund will normally invest at least 90% of its net assets (including investment borrowings) in the common stocks that comprise the index. The index is designed to measure the performance of the largest and most actively traded securities issued by U.S. companies in the Internet industry. The index is a composite of its two sub-indices, the Dow Jones Internet Commerce Index and the Dow Jones Internet Services Index. It is non-diversified. **Top Holdings:** Amazon.com Inc Facebook Inc A Salesforce.com Inc Alphabet Inc Class C Alphabet Inc A

Vanguard Short-Term Treasury Index Fund ETF Shares   C   HOLD

Ticker	Traded On	NAV	Total Assets ($)	Dividend Yield (TTM)	Turnover Ratio	Expense Ratio
VGSH	NAS CM	60.93	$7,935,172,439	2.26	67	0.07

Ratings
Reward   C
Risk   C+
Recent Upgrade/Downgrade

Fund Information
Fund Type   Exchange Traded Funds
Category   US Fixed Income
Sub-Category   Short Government
Prospectus Objective   Govt Bond - Gen
Inception Date   Nov-09
Open to New Investments   Y

Prices
Price (as of 9/30/2019)   60.93
52-Week High   61.15
52-Week Low   59.55

Total Returns (%)

3-Month	6-Month	1-Year	3-Year	5-Year
0.57	1.98	4.35	4.41	6.43

3-Year Standard Deviation   1.02
Effective Duration   1.92

Valuation
Premium/Discount (1-Year Average)   0.03

Company Information
Provider   Vanguard
Manager/Tenure   Joshua C. Barrickman (6)
Website   http://www.vanguard.com
Address   Vanguard 100 Vanguard Boulevard
                  Malvern PA 19355 United States
Phone Number   877-662-7447

PERFORMANCE

Ratings History

Date	Overall Rating	Risk Rating	Reward Rating
Q3-19	C	C+	C
Q4-18	C	C+	C-
Q4-17	C	C+	C
Q4-16	C	C-	C
Q4-15	C	C+	C

Asset & Performance History

Date	NAV	1-Year Total Return
2018	60.03	1.41
2017	60.27	0.36
2016	60.7	0.78
2015	60.73	0.5
2014	60.85	0.52
2013	60.81	0.25

Total Assets: $7,935,172,439
Asset Allocation

Asset	%
Cash	0%
Stocks	0%
US Stocks	0%
Bonds	100%
US Bonds	100%
Other	0%

Services Offered:

Investment Strategy: The investment seeks to track the performance of a market-weighted government bond index with a short-term dollar-weighted average maturity. The fund employs an indexing investment approach designed to track the performance of the Bloomberg Barclays US Treasury 1-3 Year Bond Index. This index includes fixed income securities issued by the U.S. Treasury (not including inflation-protected securities), all with maturities between 1 and 3 years. At least 80% of the fund's assets will be invested in bonds included in the index. **Top Holdings:** United States Treasury Notes 1.25% United States Treasury Notes 2.62% United States Treasury Notes 1.75% United States Treasury Notes 1.38% United States Treasury Notes 2.25%

First Trust Value Line® Dividend Index Fund
C+   HOLD

Ticker	Traded On	NAV	Total Assets ($)	Dividend Yield (TTM)	Turnover Ratio	Expense Ratio
FVD	NYSE Arca	34.85	$7,865,609,721	2.2	58	0.7

Ratings
Reward	C+
Risk	C+
Recent Upgrade/Downgrade	Down

Fund Information
Fund Type	Exchange Traded Funds
Category	US Equity Large Cap Value
Sub-Category	Large Value
Prospectus Objective	Growth & Inc
Inception Date	Aug-03
Open to New Investments	Y

Prices
Price (as of 9/30/2019)	34.87
52-Week High	35.03
52-Week Low	27.80

Total Returns (%)
3-Month	6-Month	1-Year	3-Year	5-Year
3.61	7.87	12.99	38.14	75.14

3-Year Standard Deviation	9.81
Effective Duration	

Valuation
Premium/Discount (1-Year Average)	0.03

Company Information
Provider	First Trust
Manager/Tenure	Jon C. Erickson (16), David G. McGarel (16), Roger F. Testin (16), 3 others
Website	http://www.ftportfolios.com/
Address	First Trust 120 E. Liberty Drive, Suite 400 Wheaton IL 60187 United States
Phone Number	800-621-1675

PERFORMANCE

Ratings History

Date	Overall Rating	Risk Rating	Reward Rating
Q3-19	C+	C+	C+
Q4-18	C	C+	C
Q4-17	B	A+	B-
Q4-16	B	C+	B
Q4-15	B-	C+	B-

Asset & Performance History

Date	NAV	1-Year Total Return
2018	29.07	-3.45
2017	30.84	12.48
2016	28.02	19.95
2015	23.86	1.24
2014	24.13	15.95
2013	21.36	26.6

Total Assets: $7,865,609,721
Asset Allocation

Asset	%
Cash	0%
Stocks	100%
US Stocks	86%
Bonds	0%
US Bonds	0%
Other	0%

Services Offered:

Investment Strategy: The investment seeks investment results that correspond generally to the price and yield (before the fund's fees and expenses) of an equity index called the Value Line® Dividend Index. The fund will normally invest at least 90% of its net assets (including investment borrowings) in the common stocks and depositary receipts that comprise the index. The index seeks to measure the performance of the securities ranked #1 or #2 according to the index provider's proprietary Value Line® Safety™ Ranking System (the "Safety Ranking System") that are also still expected to provide above-average dividend yield. **Top Holdings:** Lowe's Companies Inc Rockwell Automation Inc Hubbell Inc Honeywell International Inc Cummins Inc

---

Vanguard Intermediate-Term Treasury Index Fund ETF Shares
C   HOLD

Ticker	Traded On	NAV	Total Assets ($)	Dividend Yield (TTM)	Turnover Ratio	Expense Ratio
VGIT	NAS CM	66.67	$7,467,688,065	2.22	31	0.07

Ratings
Reward	C
Risk	C+
Recent Upgrade/Downgrade	

Fund Information
Fund Type	Exchange Traded Funds
Category	US Fixed Income
Sub-Category	Intermediate Government
Prospectus Objective	Govt Bond - Gen
Inception Date	Nov-09
Open to New Investments	Y

Prices
Price (as of 9/30/2019)	66.67
52-Week High	67.41
52-Week Low	61.57

Total Returns (%)
3-Month	6-Month	1-Year	3-Year	5-Year
1.58	4.97	9.80	6.04	14.62

3-Year Standard Deviation	3.46
Effective Duration	5.22

Valuation
Premium/Discount (1-Year Average)	0.04

Company Information
Provider	Vanguard
Manager/Tenure	Joshua C. Barrickman (6)
Website	http://www.vanguard.com
Address	Vanguard 100 Vanguard Boulevard Malvern PA 19355 United States
Phone Number	877-662-7447

PERFORMANCE

Ratings History

Date	Overall Rating	Risk Rating	Reward Rating
Q3-19	C	C+	C
Q4-18	C-	C	D
Q4-17	C	C	C
Q4-16	C	C+	C
Q4-15	C	C-	C

Asset & Performance History

Date	NAV	1-Year Total Return
2018	63.26	1.08
2017	63.9	1.62
2016	63.95	0.99
2015	64.29	1.63
2014	64.33	4.22
2013	62.69	-2.73

Total Assets: $7,467,688,065
Asset Allocation

Asset	%
Cash	0%
Stocks	0%
US Stocks	0%
Bonds	100%
US Bonds	100%
Other	0%

Services Offered:

Investment Strategy: The investment seeks to track the performance of a market-weighted government bond index with an intermediate-term dollar-weighted average maturity. The fund employs an indexing investment approach designed to track the performance of the Bloomberg Barclays US Treasury 3-10 Year Bond Index. This index includes fixed income securities issued by the U.S. Treasury (not including inflation-protected bonds), with maturities between 3 and 10 years. At least 80% of the fund's assets will be invested in bonds included in the index. **Top Holdings:** United States Treasury Notes 2.38% United States Treasury Notes 2.5% United States Treasury Notes 2% United States Treasury Notes 1.62% United States Treasury Notes 2.75%

iShares Core High Dividend ETF   B-   BUY

Ticker	Traded On	NAV	Total Assets ($)	Dividend Yield (TTM)	Turnover Ratio	Expense Ratio
HDV	NYSE Arca	94.14	$7,408,950,088	3.33	57	0.08

Ratings
Reward	B
Risk	C
Recent Upgrade/Downgrade	Up

Fund Information
Fund Type	Exchange Traded Funds
Category	US Equity Large Cap Value
Sub-Category	Large Value
Prospectus Objective	Equity-Income
Inception Date	Mar-11
Open to New Investments	Y

Prices
Price (as of 9/30/2019)	94.16
52-Week High	95.92
52-Week Low	80.00

Total Returns (%)
3-Month	6-Month	1-Year	3-Year	5-Year
0.12	1.70	7.01	28.45	50.78

3-Year Standard Deviation	10.95
Effective Duration	

Valuation
Premium/Discount (1-Year Average)	-0.01

Company Information
Provider	iShares
Manager/Tenure	Greg Savage (8), Jennifer Hsui (7), Alan Mason (3), 2 others
Website	http://www.ishares.com
Address	iShares 400 Howard Street San Francisco CA 94105 United States
Phone Number	800-474-2737

PERFORMANCE

Ratings History
Date	Overall Rating	Risk Rating	Reward Rating
Q3-19	B-	C	B
Q4-18	B-	C	B
Q4-17	B	B	B-
Q4-16	B-	C	B
Q4-15	B-	C	B

Asset & Performance History
Date	NAV	1-Year Total Return
2018	84.33	-2.92
2017	90.04	13.35
2016	82.2	15.78
2015	73.41	-0.26
2014	76.54	12.54
2013	70.26	23.6

Total Assets: $7,408,950,088
Asset Allocation
Asset	%
Cash	0%
Stocks	100%
US Stocks	100%
Bonds	0%
US Bonds	0%
Other	0%

Services Offered:

Investment Strategy: The investment seeks to track the investment results of the Morningstar® Dividend Yield Focus IndexSM composed of relatively high dividend paying U.S. equities. The fund generally will invest at least 90% of its assets in the component securities of the underlying index and may invest up to 10% of its assets in certain futures, options and swap contracts, cash and cash equivalents. The underlying index is comprised of qualified income paying securities that are screened for superior company quality and financial health as determined by Morningstar, Inc.'s ("Morningstar" or the "index provider") proprietary index methodology. The fund is non-diversified. **Top Holdings:** Exxon Mobil Corp   Verizon Communications Inc   Johnson & Johnson   Chevron Corp   Procter & Gamble Co

---

iShares S&P Mid-Cap 400 Growth ETF   C   HOLD

Ticker	Traded On	NAV	Total Assets ($)	Dividend Yield (TTM)	Turnover Ratio	Expense Ratio
IJK	NYSE Arca	223.95	$7,300,734,554	1.06	50	0.24

Ratings
Reward	C
Risk	C-
Recent Upgrade/Downgrade	

Fund Information
Fund Type	Exchange Traded Funds
Category	US Equity Mid Cap
Sub-Category	Mid-Cap Growth
Prospectus Objective	Growth
Inception Date	Jul-00
Open to New Investments	Y

Prices
Price (as of 9/30/2019)	223.86
52-Week High	231.08
52-Week Low	179.90

Total Returns (%)
3-Month	6-Month	1-Year	3-Year	5-Year
-1.04	1.70	-1.96	32.33	58.23

3-Year Standard Deviation	14.49
Effective Duration	

Valuation
Premium/Discount (1-Year Average)	-0.02

Company Information
Provider	iShares
Manager/Tenure	Greg Savage (11), Jennifer Hsui (7), Alan Mason (3), 2 others
Website	http://www.ishares.com
Address	iShares 400 Howard Street San Francisco CA 94105 United States
Phone Number	800-474-2737

PERFORMANCE

Ratings History
Date	Overall Rating	Risk Rating	Reward Rating
Q3-19	C	C-	C
Q4-18	C	C+	C-
Q4-17	B+	B+	B
Q4-16	B-	C+	B
Q4-15	C+	C+	C+

Asset & Performance History
Date	NAV	1-Year Total Return
2018	191.2	-10.53
2017	215.84	19.65
2016	182.19	14.51
2015	161.03	1.8
2014	159.9	7.39
2013	150.28	32.51

Total Assets: $7,300,734,554
Asset Allocation
Asset	%
Cash	0%
Stocks	100%
US Stocks	100%
Bonds	0%
US Bonds	0%
Other	0%

Services Offered: CashInvestment Plan

Investment Strategy: The investment seeks to track the investment results of the S&P MidCap 400 Growth IndexTM, which measures the performance of the mid-capitalization growth sector of the U.S. equity market. The fund generally invests at least 90% of its assets in securities of the underlying index and in depositary receipts representing securities of the underlying index. It may invest the remainder of its assets in certain futures, options and swap contracts, cash and cash equivalents, as well as in securities not included in the underlying index, but which the advisor believes will help the fund track the underlying index. **Top Holdings:** Steris PLC   Zebra Technologies Corp   West Pharmaceutical Services Inc   FactSet Research Systems Inc   Fair Isaac Corp

Schwab U.S. Aggregate Bond ETF™   C+   HOLD

Ticker	Traded On	NAV	Total Assets ($)	Dividend Yield (TTM)	Turnover Ratio	Expense Ratio
SCHZ	NYSE Arca	53.82	$6,986,128,717	2.76	71	0.04

Ratings
Reward   C+
Risk   C+
Recent Upgrade/Downgrade   Up

Fund Information
Fund Type   Exchange Traded Funds
Category   US Fixed Income
Sub-Category   Intermediate Core Bond
Prospectus Objective   Multisector Bond
Inception Date   Jul-11
Open to New Investments   Y

Prices
Price (as of 9/30/2019)   53.85
52-Week High   54.32
52-Week Low   49.51

Total Returns (%)

3-Month	6-Month	1-Year	3-Year	5-Year
2.38	5.78	10.32	8.71	17.03

3-Year Standard Deviation   3.36
Effective Duration   5.51

Valuation
Premium/Discount (1-Year Average)   0.02

Company Information
Provider   Schwab ETFs
Manager/Tenure   Matthew Hastings (8), Steven Hung (8), Alfonso Portillo (8), 1 other
Website   http://www.schwabfunds.com
Address   Schwab ETFs United States
Phone Number   800-435-4000

PERFORMANCE

Ratings History

Date	Overall Rating	Risk Rating	Reward Rating
Q3-19	C+	C+	C+
Q4-18	C-	C+	D+
Q4-17	B-	B+	C
Q4-16	C	C+	C
Q4-15	C	C+	C

Asset & Performance History

Date	NAV	1-Year Total Return
2018	50.59	-0.09
2017	52.07	3.56
2016	51.55	2.49
2015	51.41	0.55
2014	52.2	5.97
2013	50.28	-2.18

Total Assets: $6,986,128,717

Asset Allocation

Asset	%
Cash	3%
Stocks	0%
US Stocks	0%
Bonds	97%
US Bonds	90%
Other	0%

Services Offered:

Investment Strategy: The investment seeks to track as closely as possible, before fees and expenses, the total return of the Bloomberg Barclays US Aggregate Bond Index. The fund will invest at least 90% of its net assets in securities included in the index. The index is a broad-based benchmark measuring the performance of the U.S. investment grade, taxable bond market, including U.S. Treasuries, government-related and corporate bonds, mortgage pass-through securities, commercial mortgage-backed securities, and asset-backed securities that are publicly available for sale in the United States. **Top Holdings:** United States Treasury Notes 2.75% United States Treasury Notes 2.5% United States Treasury Notes 2% United States Treasury Notes 2.38% United States Treasury Notes 2.25%

---

iShares Short Maturity Bond ETF   C   HOLD

Ticker	Traded On	NAV	Total Assets ($)	Dividend Yield (TTM)	Turnover Ratio	Expense Ratio
NEAR	BATS	50.35	$6,847,060,142	2.65	48	0.25

Ratings
Reward   C
Risk   C+
Recent Upgrade/Downgrade

Fund Information
Fund Type   Exchange Traded Funds
Category   US Fixed Income
Sub-Category   Ultrashort Bond
Prospectus Objective   Income
Inception Date   Sep-13
Open to New Investments   Y

Prices
Price (as of 9/30/2019)   50.34
52-Week High   50.35
52-Week Low   49.82

Total Returns (%)

3-Month	6-Month	1-Year	3-Year	5-Year
0.71	1.64	3.06	6.51	8.50

3-Year Standard Deviation   0.35
Effective Duration   0.47

Valuation
Premium/Discount (1-Year Average)   0.00

Company Information
Provider   iShares
Manager/Tenure   Thomas F. Musmanno (6), Scott Radell (6)
Website   http://www.ishares.com
Address   iShares 400 Howard Street San Francisco CA 94105 United States
Phone Number   800-474-2737

PERFORMANCE

Ratings History

Date	Overall Rating	Risk Rating	Reward Rating
Q3-19	C	C+	C
Q4-18	C	C+	C
Q4-17	B-	A-	C
Q4-16	C	C+	C
Q4-15	C-	C+	D+

Asset & Performance History

Date	NAV	1-Year Total Return
2018	49.87	1.71
2017	50.14	1.55
2016	50.13	1.41
2015	49.96	0.69
2014	50.04	0.75
2013	50.09	

Total Assets: $6,847,060,142

Asset Allocation

Asset	%
Cash	14%
Stocks	0%
US Stocks	0%
Bonds	85%
US Bonds	69%
Other	0%

Services Offered:

Investment Strategy: The investment seeks to maximize current income. The fund seeks to achieve its investment objective by investing, under normal circumstances, at least 80% of its net assets in a portfolio of U.S. dollar-denominated investment-grade fixed-income securities. Under normal circumstances, the effective duration of its portfolio is expected to be one year or less, as calculated by the management team. It is an actively managed exchange-traded fund ("ETF") that does not seek to replicate the performance of a specified index. **Top Holdings:** Charter Communications Operating, LLC/Charter Communications Operating Capi B.A.T. Capital Corporation 2.3% Allergan Funding SCS 3% CVS Health Corp 2.8% AbbVie Inc. 2.5%

iShares Core S&P U.S. Growth ETF　　　　　　　　　　　　　C+　　HOLD

Ticker	Traded On	NAV	Total Assets ($)	Dividend Yield (TTM)	Turnover Ratio	Expense Ratio
IUSG	NAS CM	62.91	$6,831,778,291	1.42	31	0.04

Ratings
Reward	C+
Risk	C+
Recent Upgrade/Downgrade	Down

Fund Information
Fund Type	Exchange Traded Funds
Category	US Equity Large Cap Growth
Sub-Category	Large Growth
Prospectus Objective	Growth
Inception Date	Jul-00
Open to New Investments	Y

Prices
Price (as of 9/30/2019)	62.87
52-Week High	64.70
52-Week Low	49.22

Total Returns (%)
3-Month	6-Month	1-Year	3-Year	5-Year
-0.12	4.08	2.58	54.05	83.28

3-Year Standard Deviation	12.44
Effective Duration	

Valuation
Premium/Discount (1-Year Average)	-0.01

Company Information
Provider	iShares
Manager/Tenure	Greg Savage (11), Jennifer Hsui (7), Alan Mason (3), 2 others
Website	http://www.ishares.com
Address	iShares 400 Howard Street San Francisco CA 94105 United States
Phone Number	800-474-2737

PERFORMANCE

Ratings History
Date	Overall Rating	Risk Rating	Reward Rating
Q3-19	C+	C+	C+
Q4-18	C	C+	C
Q4-17	B	B	B
Q4-16	B-	C+	B
Q4-15	C	C	C+

Asset & Performance History
Date	NAV	1-Year Total Return
2018	52.64	-0.79
2017	53.72	26.93
2016	42.91	7.39
2015	40.57	5.05
2014	39.13	12.3
2013	35.28	33.93

Total Assets: $6,831,778,291
Asset Allocation
Asset	%
Cash	0%
Stocks	100%
US Stocks	99%
Bonds	0%
US Bonds	0%
Other	0%

Services Offered: CashInvestment Plan

Investment Strategy: The investment seeks to track the investment results of the S&P 900 Growth Index (the "underlying index"). The fund generally invests at least 90% of its assets in securities of the underlying index and in depositary receipts representing securities of the underlying index. The underlying index measures the performance of the large- and mid- capitalization growth sector of the U.S. equity market. **Top Holdings:** Microsoft Corp　Amazon.com Inc　Facebook Inc A　Alphabet Inc Class C　Alphabet Inc A

Goldman Sachs ActiveBeta® U.S. Large Cap Equity ETF　　　　C+　　HOLD

Ticker	Traded On	NAV	Total Assets ($)	Dividend Yield (TTM)	Turnover Ratio	Expense Ratio
GSLC	NYSE Arca	59.92	$6,818,618,127	1.64	16	0.09

Ratings
Reward	C+
Risk	C+
Recent Upgrade/Downgrade	

Fund Information
Fund Type	Exchange Traded Funds
Category	US Equity Large Cap Blend
Sub-Category	Large Blend
Prospectus Objective	Growth
Inception Date	Sep-15
Open to New Investments	Y

Prices
Price (as of 9/30/2019)	59.89
52-Week High	60.73
52-Week Low	47.19

Total Returns (%)
3-Month	6-Month	1-Year	3-Year	5-Year
1.46	5.16	3.66	45.11	

3-Year Standard Deviation	12.12
Effective Duration	

Valuation
Premium/Discount (1-Year Average)	0.00

Company Information
Provider	Goldman Sachs
Manager/Tenure	Raj Garigipati (4), Jamie McGregor (3)
Website	http://www.gsamfunds.com
Address	Goldman Sachs 200 West Stree New York NY 10282 United States
Phone Number	800-526-7384

PERFORMANCE

Ratings History
Date	Overall Rating	Risk Rating	Reward Rating
Q3-19	C+	C+	C+
Q4-18	C	C+	C
Q4-17	C	B	C+
Q4-16	D	C+	D+
Q4-15			

Asset & Performance History
Date	NAV	1-Year Total Return
2018	50.26	-4.01
2017	53.31	22.52
2016	44.32	8.1
2015	41.5	
2014		
2013		

Total Assets: $6,818,618,127
Asset Allocation
Asset	%
Cash	0%
Stocks	100%
US Stocks	99%
Bonds	0%
US Bonds	0%
Other	0%

Services Offered:

Investment Strategy: The investment seeks to provide investment results that closely correspond, before fees and expenses, to the performance of the Goldman Sachs ActiveBeta® U.S. Large Cap Equity Index. The fund seeks to achieve its investment objective by investing at least 80% of its assets (exclusive of collateral held from securities lending) in securities included in its underlying index, in depositary receipts representing securities included in its underlying index and in underlying stocks in respect of depositary receipts included in its underlying index. The index is designed to deliver exposure to equity securities of large capitalization U.S. issuers. **Top Holdings:** Microsoft Corp　Apple Inc　Amazon.com Inc　Facebook Inc A　Johnson & Johnson

iShares Nasdaq Biotechnology ETF

C   HOLD

Ticker	Traded On	NAV	Total Assets ($)	Dividend Yield (TTM)	Turnover Ratio	Expense Ratio
IBB	NAS CM	99.57	$6,626,188,823	0.15	18	0.47

Ratings
Reward	C
Risk	C
Recent Upgrade/Downgrade	

Fund Information
Fund Type	Exchange Traded Funds
Category	Healthcare Sector Equity
Sub-Category	Health
Prospectus Objective	Technology
Inception Date	Feb-01
Open to New Investments	Y

Prices
Price (as of 9/30/2019)	99.50
52-Week High	121.26
52-Week Low	89.61

Total Returns (%)
3-Month	6-Month	1-Year	3-Year	5-Year
-9.18	-10.92	-17.55	3.92	11.77

3-Year Standard Deviation	21.14
Effective Duration	

Valuation
Premium/Discount (1-Year Average)	-0.04

Company Information
Provider	iShares
Manager/Tenure	Greg Savage (11), Jennifer Hsui (7), Alan Mason (3), 2 others
Website	http://www.ishares.com
Address	iShares 400 Howard Street San Francisco CA 94105 United States
Phone Number	800-474-2737

PERFORMANCE

Ratings History
Date	Overall Rating	Risk Rating	Reward Rating
Q3-19	C	C	C
Q4-18	C	C-	C
Q4-17	C	C	C-
Q4-16	C	D+	C+
Q4-15	B	C+	B

Asset & Performance History
Date	NAV	1-Year Total Return
2018	96.83	-9.13
2017	106.75	21.2
2016	88.35	-21.53
2015	112.81	11.46
2014	101.23	34.12
2013	75.6	65.47

Total Assets: $6,626,188,823

Asset Allocation
Asset	%
Cash	0%
Stocks	100%
US Stocks	94%
Bonds	0%
US Bonds	0%
Other	0%

Services Offered: Dividend Investment Plan

Investment Strategy: The investment seeks to track the investment results of the NASDAQ Biotechnology Index, which contains securities of companies listed on NASDAQ that are classified according to the Industry Classification Benchmark as either biotechnology or pharmaceuticals and that also meet other eligibility criteria determined by Nasdaq, Inc. The fund generally invests at least 90% of its assets in securities of the index and in depositary receipts representing securities of the index. It may invest the remainder of its assets in certain futures, options and swap contracts, cash and cash equivalents. It is non-diversified. **Top Holdings:** Amgen Inc Celgene Corp Gilead Sciences Inc Vertex Pharmaceuticals Inc Illumina Inc

---

iShares Silver Trust

C-   HOLD

Ticker	Traded On	NAV	Total Assets ($)	Dividend Yield (TTM)	Turnover Ratio	Expense Ratio
SLV	NYSE Arca	16.14	$6,617,148,290	0		0.5

Ratings
Reward	C-
Risk	C
Recent Upgrade/Downgrade	Up

Fund Information
Fund Type	Exchange Traded Funds
Category	Commodities Specified
Sub-Category	Commodities Precious Metals
Prospectus Objective	Prec Metals
Inception Date	Apr-06
Open to New Investments	Y

Prices
Price (as of 9/30/2019)	15.92
52-Week High	18.34
52-Week Low	13.15

Total Returns (%)
3-Month	6-Month	1-Year	3-Year	5-Year
12.93	14.21	18.00	-12.16	-1.25

3-Year Standard Deviation	15.78
Effective Duration	

Valuation
Premium/Discount (1-Year Average)	-0.34

Company Information
Provider	iShares
Manager/Tenure	Management Team (13)
Website	http://www.ishares.com
Address	iShares 400 Howard Street San Francisco CA 94105 United States
Phone Number	800-474-2737

PERFORMANCE

Ratings History
Date	Overall Rating	Risk Rating	Reward Rating
Q3-19	C-	C	C-
Q4-18	D	D	D-
Q4-17	D+	D+	D+
Q4-16	D+	D	C-
Q4-15	D-	E+	D-

Asset & Performance History
Date	NAV	1-Year Total Return
2018	14.52	-8.76
2017	15.91	3.31
2016	15.4	16.93
2015	13.17	-13.86
2014	15.29	-18.54
2013	18.77	-35.22

Total Assets: $6,617,148,290

Asset Allocation
Asset	%
Cash	0%
Stocks	0%
US Stocks	0%
Bonds	0%
US Bonds	0%
Other	100%

Services Offered:

Investment Strategy: The investment seeks to reflect generally the performance of the price of silver. The Trust seeks to reflect such performance before payment of the Trust's expenses and liabilities. It is not actively managed. The Trust does not engage in any activities designed to obtain a profit from, or to ameliorate losses caused by, changes in the price of silver. **Top Holdings:** Silver

Vanguard FTSE Pacific Index Fund ETF Shares

C HOLD

Ticker	Traded On	NAV	Total Assets ($)	Dividend Yield (TTM)	Turnover Ratio	Expense Ratio
VPL	NYSE Arca	65.87	$6,576,514,553	2.86	4	0.09

Ratings
Reward	C-
Risk	C+
Recent Upgrade/Downgrade	

Fund Information
Fund Type	Exchange Traded Funds
Category	Asia Equity
Sub-Category	Diversified Pacific/Asia
Prospectus Objective	Pacific Stock
Inception Date	Mar-05
Open to New Investments	Y

Prices
Price (as of 9/30/2019)	66.05
52-Week High	71.30
52-Week Low	58.71

Total Returns (%)
3-Month	6-Month	1-Year	3-Year	5-Year
-0.81	-0.12	-4.38	18.18	27.92

3-Year Standard Deviation	11.4
Effective Duration	

Valuation
Premium/Discount (1-Year Average)	-0.15

Company Information
Provider	Vanguard
Manager/Tenure	Jeffrey D. Miller (3), Michael Perre (3)
Website	http://www.vanguard.com
Address	Vanguard 100 Vanguard Boulevard Malvern PA 19355 United States
Phone Number	877-662-7447

PERFORMANCE

Ratings History
Date	Overall Rating	Risk Rating	Reward Rating
Q3-19	C	C+	C-
Q4-18	C-	C	D+
Q4-17	B	B	B
Q4-16	C	C+	C
Q4-15	C	C+	C

Asset & Performance History
Date	NAV	1-Year Total Return
2018	60.72	-14.08
2017	72.74	28.82
2016	58.11	4.79
2015	56.68	2.42
2014	56.66	-4.57
2013	60.92	17.55

Total Assets: $6,576,514,553

Asset Allocation
Asset	%
Cash	1%
Stocks	99%
US Stocks	0%
Bonds	0%
US Bonds	0%
Other	0%

Services Offered:

Investment Strategy: The investment seeks to track the performance of a benchmark index that measures the investment return of stocks issued by companies located in the major markets of the Pacific region. The fund employs an indexing investment approach by investing all, or substantially all, of its assets in the common stocks included in the FTSE Developed Asia Pacific All Cap Index. The FTSE Developed Asia Pacific All Cap Index is a market-capitalization-weighted index. **Top Holdings:** Samsung Electronics Co Ltd Toyota Motor Corp AIA Group Ltd Commonwealth Bk Of Australia SoftBank Group Corp

---

Schwab U.S. Large-Cap Value ETF™

C+ HOLD

Ticker	Traded On	NAV	Total Assets ($)	Dividend Yield (TTM)	Turnover Ratio	Expense Ratio
SCHV	NYSE Arca	56.75	$6,562,779,193	2.82	8	0.04

Ratings
Reward	C
Risk	C+
Recent Upgrade/Downgrade	

Fund Information
Fund Type	Exchange Traded Funds
Category	US Equity Large Cap Value
Sub-Category	Large Value
Prospectus Objective	Growth
Inception Date	Dec-09
Open to New Investments	Y

Prices
Price (as of 9/30/2019)	56.73
52-Week High	57.50
52-Week Low	46.58

Total Returns (%)
3-Month	6-Month	1-Year	3-Year	5-Year
1.13	3.92	3.86	35.28	54.46

3-Year Standard Deviation	12.09
Effective Duration	

Valuation
Premium/Discount (1-Year Average)	-0.03

Company Information
Provider	Schwab ETFs
Manager/Tenure	Ferian Juwono (9), Christopher Bliss (2), Sabya Sinha (2), 1 other
Website	http://www.schwabfunds.com
Address	Schwab ETFs United States
Phone Number	800-435-4000

PERFORMANCE

Ratings History
Date	Overall Rating	Risk Rating	Reward Rating
Q3-19	C+	C+	C
Q4-18	C	C+	C
Q4-17	B-	B	B-
Q4-16	B-	C+	B
Q4-15	C+	C+	C

Asset & Performance History
Date	NAV	1-Year Total Return
2018	49.27	-7.23
2017	54.61	16.64
2016	48.05	16.42
2015	42.44	-1.08
2014	44.07	10.96
2013	40.7	30.98

Total Assets: $6,562,779,193

Asset Allocation
Asset	%
Cash	0%
Stocks	100%
US Stocks	99%
Bonds	0%
US Bonds	0%
Other	0%

Services Offered:

Investment Strategy: The investment seeks to track as closely as possible, before fees and expenses, the total return of the Dow Jones U.S. Large-Cap Value Total Stock Market Index. To pursue its goal, the fund generally invests in stocks that are included in the Dow Jones U.S. Large-Cap Value Total Stock Market Index. The index includes the large-cap value portion of the Dow Jones U.S. Total Stock Market Index actually available to investors in the marketplace. The Dow Jones U.S. Large-Cap Value Total Stock Market Index includes the components ranked 1-750 by full market capitalization and that are classified as "value" based on a number of factors. **Top Holdings:** JPMorgan Chase & Co Johnson & Johnson Procter & Gamble Co Exxon Mobil Corp AT&T Inc

Vanguard Global ex-U.S. Real Estate Index Fund ETF Shares

C   HOLD

Ticker	Traded On	NAV	Total Assets ($)	Dividend Yield (TTM)	Turnover Ratio	Expense Ratio
VNQI	NAS CM	58.60	$6,510,704,479	3.76	7	0.12

Ratings
Reward	C
Risk	C+
Recent Upgrade/Downgrade	

Fund Information
Fund Type	Exchange Traded Funds
Category	Real Estate Sector Equity
Sub-Category	Global Real Estate
Prospectus Objective	Real Estate
Inception Date	Nov-10
Open to New Investments	Y

Prices
Price (as of 9/30/2019)	58.59
52-Week High	60.15
52-Week Low	51.24

Total Returns (%)
3-Month	6-Month	1-Year	3-Year	5-Year
-0.65	-1.05	8.46	18.95	30.75

3-Year Standard Deviation	11.36
Effective Duration	

Valuation
Premium/Discount (1-Year Average)	0.05

Company Information
Provider	Vanguard
Manager/Tenure	Justin E. Hales (4), Michael Perre (4)
Website	http://www.vanguard.com
Address	Vanguard 100 Vanguard Boulevard Malvern PA 19355 United States
Phone Number	877-662-7447

PERFORMANCE

Ratings History
Date	Overall Rating	Risk Rating	Reward Rating
Q3-19	C	C+	C
Q4-18	C-	C	D+
Q4-17	B-	B	B-
Q4-16	C	C	C
Q4-15	C	C+	C

Asset & Performance History
Date	NAV	1-Year Total Return
2018	52.13	-9.96
2017	60.53	27.22
2016	49.75	0.47
2015	51.41	-1.33
2014	53.57	2.64
2013	54.31	3.33

Total Assets: $6,510,704,479

Asset Allocation
Asset	%
Cash	2%
Stocks	97%
US Stocks	0%
Bonds	0%
US Bonds	0%
Other	1%

Services Offered:

Investment Strategy: The investment seeks to track the performance of a benchmark index. The fund employs an indexing investment approach designed to track the performance of the S&P Global ex-U.S. Property Index, a float-adjusted, market-capitalization-weighted index that measures the equity market performance of international real estate stocks in both developed and emerging markets. The index is composed of stocks of publicly traded equity real estate investment trusts (known as REITs) and certain real estate management and development companies (REMDs). **Top Holdings:** Vonovia SE Mitsubishi Estate Co Ltd Sun Hung Kai Properties Ltd Link Real Estate Investment Trust Mitsui Fudosan Co Ltd

---

iShares S&P Small-Cap 600 Value ETF

C   HOLD

Ticker	Traded On	NAV	Total Assets ($)	Dividend Yield (TTM)	Turnover Ratio	Expense Ratio
IJS	NYSE Arca	150.32	$6,373,624,017	1.54	38	0.25

Ratings
Reward	C-
Risk	C
Recent Upgrade/Downgrade	Up

Fund Information
Fund Type	Exchange Traded Funds
Category	US Equity Small Cap
Sub-Category	Small Value
Prospectus Objective	Small Company
Inception Date	Jul-00
Open to New Investments	Y

Prices
Price (as of 9/30/2019)	150.19
52-Week High	164.59
52-Week Low	124.11

Total Returns (%)
3-Month	6-Month	1-Year	3-Year	5-Year
1.27	1.02	-7.19	25.98	52.88

3-Year Standard Deviation	18.98
Effective Duration	

Valuation
Premium/Discount (1-Year Average)	-0.03

Company Information
Provider	iShares
Manager/Tenure	Greg Savage (11), Jennifer Hsui (7), Alan Mason (3), 2 others
Website	http://www.ishares.com
Address	iShares 400 Howard Street San Francisco CA 94105 United States
Phone Number	800-474-2737

PERFORMANCE

Ratings History
Date	Overall Rating	Risk Rating	Reward Rating
Q3-19	C	C	C-
Q4-18	C	C+	C-
Q4-17	B+	B	A-
Q4-16	B	C+	B+
Q4-15	C	C+	C

Asset & Performance History
Date	NAV	1-Year Total Return
2018	131.84	-12.79
2017	153.49	11.35
2016	139.93	31.17
2015	108.16	-6.84
2014	117.87	7.27
2013	111.49	39.71

Total Assets: $6,373,624,017

Asset Allocation
Asset	%
Cash	0%
Stocks	100%
US Stocks	98%
Bonds	0%
US Bonds	0%
Other	0%

Services Offered: CashInvestment Plan

Investment Strategy: The investment seeks to track the investment results of the S&P SmallCap 600 Value IndexTM, which measures the performance of the small-capitalization value sector of the U.S. equity market. The fund generally invests at least 90% of its assets in securities of the underlying index and in depositary receipts representing securities of the underlying index. It may invest the remainder of its assets in certain futures, options and swap contracts, cash and cash equivalents, as well as in securities not included in the underlying index, but which the advisor believes will help the fund track the underlying index. **Top Holdings:** TopBuild Corp Darling Ingredients Inc South Jersey Industries Inc SkyWest Inc Lithia Motors Inc Class A

Vanguard FTSE All-World ex-US Small-Cap Index Fund ETF Shares   C   HOLD

Ticker	Traded On	NAV	Total Assets ($)	Dividend Yield (TTM)	Turnover Ratio	Expense Ratio
VSS	NYSE Arca	102.15	$6,367,675,318	2.93	15	0.12

Ratings

Reward	D+
Risk	C+
Recent Upgrade/Downgrade	

Fund Information

Fund Type	Exchange Traded Funds
Category	Globa Eq Mid/Small Cap
Sub-Category	Foreign Small/Mid Blend
Prospectus Objective	Foreign Stock
Inception Date	Apr-09
Open to New Investments	Y

Prices

Price (as of 9/30/2019)	101.95
52-Week High	112.28
52-Week Low	91.12

Total Returns (%)

3-Month	6-Month	1-Year	3-Year	5-Year
-2.78	-1.94	-6.21	12.08	15.34

3-Year Standard Deviation	11.97
Effective Duration	

Valuation

Premium/Discount (1-Year Average)	-0.04

Company Information

Provider	Vanguard
Manager/Tenure	Jeffrey D. Miller (4), Michael Perre (3)
Website	http://www.vanguard.com
Address	Vanguard 100 Vanguard Boulevard Malvern PA 19355 United States
Phone Number	877-662-7447

PERFORMANCE

Ratings History

Date	Overall Rating	Risk Rating	Reward Rating
Q3-19	C	C+	D+
Q4-18	D+	C-	D+
Q4-17	B	B	B
Q4-16	C-	C-	C-
Q4-15	C	C+	C-

Asset & Performance History

Date	NAV	1-Year Total Return
2018	93.76	-19.03
2017	118.89	30.34
2016	94.01	3.45
2015	92.75	-0.2
2014	95.38	-4.66
2013	102.61	17.72

Total Assets: $6,367,675,318

Asset Allocation

Asset	%
Cash	5%
Stocks	94%
US Stocks	1%
Bonds	0%
US Bonds	0%
Other	1%

Services Offered:

Investment Strategy: The investment seeks to track the performance of a benchmark index that measures the investment return of stocks of international small-cap companies. The fund employs an indexing investment approach designed to track the performance of the FTSE Global Small Cap ex US Index. The advisor attempts to sample the target index by investing all, or substantially all, of its assets in common stocks in the index and by holding a representative sample of securities that resembles the full index in terms of key risk factors and other characteristics. **Top Holdings:** Open Text Corp Emera Inc Gildan Activewear Inc Kirkland Lake Gold Ltd CCL Industries Inc B- Non-Voting

---

Schwab U.S. Mid-Cap ETF™   C   HOLD

Ticker	Traded On	NAV	Total Assets ($)	Dividend Yield (TTM)	Turnover Ratio	Expense Ratio
SCHM	NYSE Arca	56.52	$6,326,875,721	1.49	13	0.04

Ratings

Reward	C
Risk	C+
Recent Upgrade/Downgrade	Down

Fund Information

Fund Type	Exchange Traded Funds
Category	US Equity Mid Cap
Sub-Category	Mid-Cap Blend
Prospectus Objective	Growth
Inception Date	Jan-11
Open to New Investments	Y

Prices

Price (as of 9/30/2019)	56.54
52-Week High	58.44
52-Week Low	45.02

Total Returns (%)

3-Month	6-Month	1-Year	3-Year	5-Year
-1.13	1.58	-0.19	35.69	59.34

3-Year Standard Deviation	14.35
Effective Duration	

Valuation

Premium/Discount (1-Year Average)	0.00

Company Information

Provider	Schwab ETFs
Manager/Tenure	Ferian Juwono (8), Christopher Bliss (2), Sabya Sinha (2), 1 other
Website	http://www.schwabfunds.com
Address	Schwab ETFs United States
Phone Number	800-435-4000

PERFORMANCE

Ratings History

Date	Overall Rating	Risk Rating	Reward Rating
Q3-19	C	C+	
Q4-18	C	C+	C-
Q4-17	B	B+	B
Q4-16	B-	C+	B
Q4-15	C	C+	C

Asset & Performance History

Date	NAV	1-Year Total Return
2018	47.94	-8.68
2017	53.23	19.89
2016	45.12	14.43
2015	40.06	-0.01
2014	40.66	10.23
2013	37.45	36.36

Total Assets: $6,326,875,721

Asset Allocation

Asset	%
Cash	0%
Stocks	100%
US Stocks	99%
Bonds	0%
US Bonds	0%
Other	0%

Services Offered:

Investment Strategy: The investment seeks to track as closely as possible, before fees and expenses, the total return of the Dow Jones U.S. Mid-Cap Total Stock Market Index. The fund will invest at least 90% of its net assets in securities that are included in the index. The index includes the mid-cap portion of the Dow Jones U.S. Total Stock Market Index actually available to investors in the marketplace. The Dow Jones U.S. Mid-Cap Total Stock Market Index includes the components ranked 501-1000 by full market capitalization. The index is a float-adjusted market capitalization weighted index. **Top Holdings:** Veeva Systems Inc Class A Cadence Design Systems Inc Keysight Technologies Inc CDW Corp Arthur J. Gallagher & Co

iShares S&P Mid-Cap 400 Value ETF
C   HOLD

Ticker	Traded On	NAV	Total Assets ($)	Dividend Yield (TTM)	Turnover Ratio	Expense Ratio
IJJ	NYSE Arca	159.91	$6,316,383,144	1.74	44	0.25

Ratings
Reward	C-
Risk	C+
Recent Upgrade/Downgrade	

Fund Information
Fund Type	Exchange Traded Funds
Category	US Equity Mid Cap
Sub-Category	Mid-Cap Value
Prospectus Objective	Growth
Inception Date	Jul-00
Open to New Investments	Y

Prices
Price (as of 9/30/2019)	159.90
52-Week High	166.59
52-Week Low	130.36

Total Returns (%)
3-Month	6-Month	1-Year	3-Year	5-Year
0.05	1.10	-2.02	26.63	47.03

3-Year Standard Deviation	16.64
Effective Duration	

Valuation
Premium/Discount (1-Year Average)	-0.03

Company Information
Provider	iShares
Manager/Tenure	Greg Savage (11), Jennifer Hsui (7), Alan Mason (3), 2 others
Website	http://www.ishares.com
Address	iShares 400 Howard Street San Francisco CA 94105 United States
Phone Number	800-474-2737

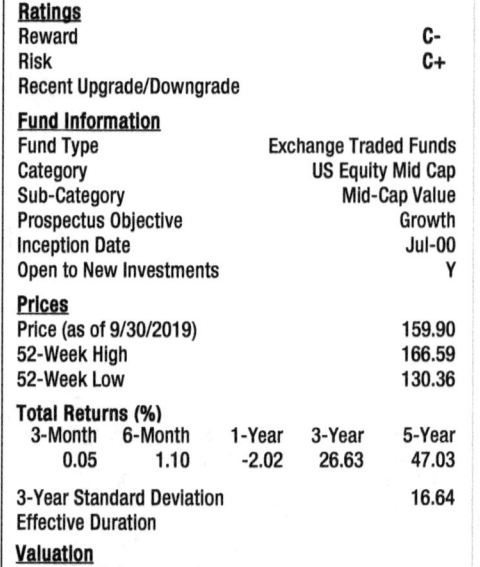

PERFORMANCE

Ratings History
Date	Overall Rating	Risk Rating	Reward Rating
Q3-19	C	C+	C-
Q4-18	C	C+	C-
Q4-17	B	B	B
Q4-16	B	C+	B
Q4-15	C	C-	C

Asset & Performance History
Date	NAV	1-Year Total Return
2018	138.26	-12.07
2017	160.08	12.05
2016	145.17	26.2
2015	117.15	-6.8
2014	127.9	11.87
2013	116.27	33.97

Total Assets: $6,316,383,144
Asset Allocation
Asset	%
Cash	0%
Stocks	100%
US Stocks	100%
Bonds	0%
US Bonds	0%
Other	0%

Services Offered: CashInvestment Plan

Investment Strategy: The investment seeks to track the investment results of the S&P MidCap 400 Value IndexTM, which measures the performance of the mid-capitalization value sector of the U.S. equity market. The fund generally invests at least 90% of its assets in securities of the underlying index and in depositary receipts representing securities of the underlying index. It may invest the remainder of its assets in certain futures, options and swap contracts, cash and cash equivalents, as well as in securities not included in the underlying index, but which the advisor believes will help the fund track the underlying index. **Top Holdings:** Alleghany Corp   WR Berkley Corp   Reinsurance Group of America Inc   RenaissanceRe Holdings Ltd   Kilroy Realty Corp

---

Vanguard Tax-Exempt Bond Index Fund ETF Shares
C+   HOLD

Ticker	Traded On	NAV	Total Assets ($)	Dividend Yield (TTM)	Turnover Ratio	Expense Ratio
VTEB	NYSE Arca	53.56	$6,149,145,444	2.31	22	0.08

Ratings
Reward	C+
Risk	C+
Recent Upgrade/Downgrade	

Fund Information
Fund Type	Exchange Traded Funds
Category	US Muni Fixed Inc
Sub-Category	Muni National Interm
Prospectus Objective	Muni Bond - Natl
Inception Date	Aug-15
Open to New Investments	Y

Prices
Price (as of 9/30/2019)	53.62
52-Week High	54.17
52-Week Low	49.85

Total Returns (%)
3-Month	6-Month	1-Year	3-Year	5-Year
1.56	3.90	8.54	9.32	

3-Year Standard Deviation	3.43
Effective Duration	5.22

Valuation
Premium/Discount (1-Year Average)	0.07

Company Information
Provider	Vanguard
Manager/Tenure	Adam M. Ferguson (4)
Website	http://www.vanguard.com
Address	Vanguard 100 Vanguard Boulevard Malvern PA 19355 United States
Phone Number	877-662-7447

PERFORMANCE

Ratings History
Date	Overall Rating	Risk Rating	Reward Rating
Q3-19	C+	C+	C+
Q4-18	C	C+	C-
Q4-17	C	B	C
Q4-16	D	C	D+
Q4-15	U		

Asset & Performance History
Date	NAV	1-Year Total Return
2018	50.91	0.9
2017	51.61	4.98
2016	50.15	0.27
2015	50.81	
2014		
2013		

Total Assets: $6,149,145,444
Asset Allocation
Asset	%
Cash	1%
Stocks	0%
US Stocks	0%
Bonds	99%
US Bonds	99%
Other	0%

Services Offered:

Investment Strategy: The investment seeks to track the Standard & Poor's National AMT-Free Municipal Bond Index, which measures the performance of the investment-grade segment of the U.S. municipal bond market. This index includes municipal bonds from issuers that are primarily state or local governments or agencies whose interest is exempt from U.S. federal income taxes and the federal alternative minimum tax (AMT). All of the fund's investments will be selected through the sampling process, and at least 80% of the fund's assets will be invested in securities held in the index. **Top Holdings:** CALIFORNIA ST 5%   SAN JACINTO TEX CMNTY COLLEGE DIST 5% NEW YORK N Y CITY MUN WTR FIN AUTH WTR & SWR SYS REV 5%   TEXAS ST 5%   MASSACHUSETTS ST WTR RES AUTH 5%

Vanguard Consumer Staples Index Fund ETF Shares

B-   BUY

Ticker	Traded On	NAV	Total Assets ($)	Dividend Yield (TTM)	Turnover Ratio	Expense Ratio
VDC	NYSE Arca	156.51	$6,131,467,784	2.51	8	0.1

Ratings
Reward	B
Risk	C
Recent Upgrade/Downgrade	Up

Fund Information
Fund Type	Exchange Traded Funds
Category	Consumer Goods & Svcs
Sub-Category	Consumer Defensive
Prospectus Objective	Unaligned
Inception Date	Jan-04
Open to New Investments	Y

Prices
Price (as of 9/30/2019)	156.56
52-Week High	157.18
52-Week Low	125.78

Total Returns (%)
3-Month	6-Month	1-Year	3-Year	5-Year
4.96	9.03	14.38	23.11	52.68

3-Year Standard Deviation	11.45
Effective Duration	

Valuation
Premium/Discount (1-Year Average)	0.00

Company Information
Provider	Vanguard
Manager/Tenure	Michael A. Johnson (8), Awais Khan (1)
Website	http://www.vanguard.com
Address	Vanguard 100 Vanguard Boulevard Malvern PA 19355 United States
Phone Number	877-662-7447

Ratings History
Date	Overall Rating	Risk Rating	Reward Rating
Q3-19	B-	C	B
Q4-18	C+	C	B
Q4-17	B	A-	C+
Q4-16	B-	C+	B
Q4-15	B	C+	B

Asset & Performance History
Date	NAV	1-Year Total Return
2018	130.63	-8.12
2017	145.97	11.38
2016	133.98	5.6
2015	129.05	6
2014	125	15.78
2013	110.04	27.99

Total Assets: $6,131,467,784

Asset Allocation
Asset	%
Cash	0%
Stocks	100%
US Stocks	99%
Bonds	0%
US Bonds	0%
Other	0%

Services Offered:

Investment Strategy: The investment seeks to track the performance of a benchmark index. The fund employs an indexing investment approach designed to track the performance of the MSCI US Investable Market Index/Consumer Staples 25/50, an index made up of stocks of large, mid-size, and small U.S. companies within the consumer staples sector, as classified under the Global Industry Classification Standard. The Advisor attempts to replicate the target index by seeking to invest all, or substantially all, of its assets in the stocks that make up the index, in order to hold each stock in approximately the same proportion as its weighting in the index. The fund is non-diversified. **Top Holdings:** Procter & Gamble Co Coca-Cola Co PepsiCo Inc Walmart Inc Philip Morris International Inc

---

SPDR® Portfolio Short Term Corporate Bond ETF

C+   HOLD

Ticker	Traded On	NAV	Total Assets ($)	Dividend Yield (TTM)	Turnover Ratio	Expense Ratio
SPSB	NYSE Arca		$6,083,667,709	2.79	46	0.07

Ratings
Reward	C
Risk	C+
Recent Upgrade/Downgrade	Up

Fund Information
Fund Type	Exchange Traded Funds
Category	US Fixed Income
Sub-Category	Short-Term Bond
Prospectus Objective	Corp Bond - Gen
Inception Date	Dec-09
Open to New Investments	Y

Prices
Price (as of 9/30/2019)	30.85
52-Week High	30.89
52-Week Low	29.99

Total Returns (%)
3-Month	6-Month	1-Year	3-Year	5-Year
0.94	2.52	5.06	7.37	10.83

3-Year Standard Deviation	1
Effective Duration	1.80

Valuation
Premium/Discount (1-Year Average)	0.06

Company Information
Provider	SPDR State Street Global Advisors
Manager/Tenure	Kyle Kelly (6), Christopher DiStefano (4), Frank Miethe (2)
Website	http://www.spdrs.com
Address	SPDR State Street Global Advisors State Street Financial Center, 1 Lincoln Street Boston MA 02111-2900 United States
Phone Number	617-786-3000

Ratings History
Date	Overall Rating	Risk Rating	Reward Rating
Q3-19	C+	C+	C
Q4-18	C	C+	C
Q4-17	B	A+	C
Q4-16	C	C+	C
Q4-15	C	C+	C

Asset & Performance History
Date	NAV	1-Year Total Return
2018	30.13	1.46
2017	30.4	1.43
2016	30.47	2.1
2015	30.34	0.8
2014	30.53	0.87
2013	30.65	1.37

Total Assets: $6,083,667,709

Asset Allocation
Asset	%
Cash	2%
Stocks	0%
US Stocks	0%
Bonds	96%
US Bonds	78%
Other	0%

Services Offered:

Investment Strategy: The investment seeks to provide investment results that, before fees and expenses, correspond generally to the price and yield performance of the Bloomberg Barclays U.S. 1-3 Year Corporate Bond Index. The fund generally invests substantially all, but at least 80%, of its total assets in the securities comprising the index or in securities that the Adviser determines have economic characteristics that are substantially identical to the economic characteristics of the securities that comprise the index. The index is designed to measure the performance of the short term U.S. corporate bond market. The fund is non-diversified. **Top Holdings:** GE Capital International Funding Company Unlimited Company 2.34% Oracle Corporation 1.9% Goldman Sachs Group, Inc. 5.25% Morgan Stanley 2.62% Wells Fargo & Company 2.62%

Schwab U.S. REIT ETF™   C+   HOLD

Ticker	Traded On	NAV	Total Assets ($)	Dividend Yield (TTM)	Turnover Ratio	Expense Ratio
SCHH	NYSE Arca	47.14	$6,022,260,873	2.69	7	0.07

Ratings
Reward   C+
Risk   C
Recent Upgrade/Downgrade   Up

Fund Information
Fund Type   Exchange Traded Funds
Category   Real Estate Sector Equity
Sub-Category   Real Estate
Prospectus Objective   Real Estate
Inception Date   Jan-11
Open to New Investments   Y

Prices
Price (as of 9/30/2019)   47.17
52-Week High   47.21
52-Week Low   37.04

Total Returns (%)

3-Month	6-Month	1-Year	3-Year	5-Year
7.01	7.46	17.41	20.43	57.88

3-Year Standard Deviation   12.78
Effective Duration

Valuation
Premium/Discount (1-Year Average)   0.01

Company Information
Provider   Schwab ETFs
Manager/Tenure Ferian Juwono (8), Christopher Bliss (2), Sabya Sinha (2), 1 other
Website   http://www.schwabfunds.com
Address   Schwab ETFs United States
Phone Number   800-435-4000

PERFORMANCE

Ratings History

Date	Overall Rating	Risk Rating	Reward Rating
Q3-19	C+	C	C+
Q4-18	C	C	C
Q4-17	B-	B+	C+
Q4-16	C+	C	C+
Q4-15	C+	C+	B-

Asset & Performance History

Date	NAV	1-Year Total Return
2018	38.49	-4.2
2017	41.59	5.08
2016	41	6.42
2015	39.62	4.35
2014	38.94	31.92
2013	30.23	1.11

Total Assets: $6,022,260,873
Asset Allocation

Asset	%
Cash	0%
Stocks	100%
US Stocks	100%
Bonds	0%
US Bonds	0%
Other	0%

Services Offered:

Investment Strategy: The investment seeks to track as closely as possible, before fees and expenses, the total return of the Dow Jones U.S. Select REIT IndexTM. The fund invests at least 90% of its net assets (including, for this purpose, any borrowings for investment purposes) in securities included in the index. It will generally give the same weight to a given security as the index does. The index is a float-adjusted market capitalization weighted index comprised of real estate investment trusts ("REITs"). The fund may invest up to 10% of its net assets in securities not included in its index. **Top Holdings:** Prologis Inc Simon Property Group Inc Public Storage Welltower Inc Equity Residential

---

Vanguard Russell 1000 Growth Index Fund ETF Shares   C   HOLD

Ticker	Traded On	NAV	Total Assets ($)	Dividend Yield (TTM)	Turnover Ratio	Expense Ratio
VONG	NAS CM	164.07	$5,959,383,864	0.88	15	0.12

Ratings
Reward   B-
Risk   C-
Recent Upgrade/Downgrade

Fund Information
Fund Type   Exchange Traded Funds
Category   US Equity Large Cap Growth
Sub-Category   Large Growth
Prospectus Objective   Growth
Inception Date   Sep-10
Open to New Investments   Y

Prices
Price (as of 9/30/2019)   164.16
52-Week High   168.75
52-Week Low   124.90

Total Returns (%)

3-Month	6-Month	1-Year	3-Year	5-Year
-0.23	4.13	2.59	58.04	85.03

3-Year Standard Deviation   13.29
Effective Duration

Valuation
Premium/Discount (1-Year Average)   0.01

Company Information
Provider   Vanguard
Manager/Tenure Michael A. Johnson (9), Walter Nejman (3)
Website   http://www.vanguard.com
Address   Vanguard 100 Vanguard Boulevard Malvern PA 19355 United States
Phone Number   877-662-7447

PERFORMANCE

Ratings History

Date	Overall Rating	Risk Rating	Reward Rating
Q3-19	C	C-	B-
Q4-18	C	C+	C
Q4-17	B+	B+	B+
Q4-16	C+	C-	B
Q4-15	C	C	C+

Asset & Performance History

Date	NAV	1-Year Total Return
2018	132.98	-2.56
2017	137.93	29.89
2016	107.44	6.58
2015	101.97	5.52
2014	98.07	12.93
2013	88.15	33.28

Total Assets: $5,959,383,864
Asset Allocation

Asset	%
Cash	0%
Stocks	100%
US Stocks	100%
Bonds	0%
US Bonds	0%
Other	0%

Services Offered:

Investment Strategy: The investment seeks to track the performance of a benchmark index that measures the investment return of large-capitalization growth stocks in the United States. The fund employs an indexing investment approach designed to track the performance of the Russell 1000® Growth Index. The index is designed to measure the performance of large-capitalization growth stocks in the United States. The Advisor attempts to replicate the target index by investing all, or substantially all, of its assets in the stocks that make up the index, holding each stock in approximately the same proportion as its weighting in the index. **Top Holdings:** Microsoft Corp Apple Inc Amazon.com Inc Facebook Inc A Alphabet Inc Class C

Schwab Emerging Markets Equity ETF™　　　　　　　　　　C　　HOLD

Ticker	Traded On	NAV	Total Assets ($)	Dividend Yield (TTM)	Turnover Ratio	Expense Ratio
SCHE	NYSE Arca	25.12	$5,898,809,282	3.16	18	0.13

Ratings
Reward　　　　　　　　　　　　　　　　C
Risk　　　　　　　　　　　　　　　　　C+
Recent Upgrade/Downgrade

Fund Information
Fund Type　　　　　　　Exchange Traded Funds
Category　　　　　　　Global Emerg Mkts Equity
Sub-Category　　　　Diversified Emerging Mkts
Prospectus Objective　　　　Div Emerg Mkts
Inception Date　　　　　　　　　　Jan-10
Open to New Investments　　　　　　　Y

Prices
Price (as of 9/30/2019)　　　　　　25.13
52-Week High　　　　　　　　　　26.96
52-Week Low　　　　　　　　　　22.96

Total Returns (%)

3-Month	6-Month	1-Year	3-Year	5-Year
-4.81	-3.67	0.92	19.21	13.60

3-Year Standard Deviation　　　　13.42
Effective Duration

Valuation
Premium/Discount (1-Year Average)　　0.19

Company Information
Provider　　　　Schwab ETFs
Manager/Tenure　Chuck Craig (6), Christopher Bliss (2), Jane Qin (2), 1 other
Website　　　　http://www.schwabfunds.com
Address　　　　Schwab ETFs United States
Phone Number　800-435-4000

PERFORMANCE

Ratings History

Date	Overall Rating	Risk Rating	Reward Rating
Q3-19	C	C+	C
Q4-18	C-	C	C-
Q4-17	B-	C	B
Q4-16	C-	C	D+
Q4-15	C-	C-	C-

Asset & Performance History

Date	NAV	1-Year Total Return
2018	23.54	-13.31
2017	27.88	32.08
2016	21.62	12.9
2015	19.59	-15.8
2014	23.85	1.1
2013	24.27	-3.83

Total Assets: $5,898,809,282
Asset Allocation

Asset	%
Cash	1%
Stocks	99%
US Stocks	0%
Bonds	0%
US Bonds	0%
Other	0%

Services Offered:

Investment Strategy: The investment seeks to track as closely as possible, before fees and expenses, the total return of the FTSE Emerging Index. The fund will invest at least 90% of its net assets (including, for this purpose, any borrowings for investment purposes) in these stocks, including depositary receipts representing securities of the index; such depositary receipts may be in the form of ADRs, GDRs and EDRs. It generally invests in stocks that are included in the FTSE Emerging Index. The index is comprised of large and mid capitalization companies in emerging market countries, as defined by the index provider. **Top Holdings:** Tencent Holdings Ltd Alibaba Group Holding Ltd ADR Taiwan Semiconductor Manufacturing Co Ltd Naspers Ltd Class N China Construction Bank Corp Class H

Schwab Short-Term U.S. Treasury ETF™　　　　　　　　　　C　　HOLD

Ticker	Traded On	NAV	Total Assets ($)	Dividend Yield (TTM)	Turnover Ratio	Expense Ratio
SCHO	NYSE Arca	50.59	$5,898,531,064	2.22	65	0.06

Ratings
Reward　　　　　　　　　　　　　　　　C
Risk　　　　　　　　　　　　　　　　　C+
Recent Upgrade/Downgrade

Fund Information
Fund Type　　　　　　　Exchange Traded Funds
Category　　　　　　　　　US Fixed Income
Sub-Category　　　　　　Short Government
Prospectus Objective　　Govt Bond - Treasury
Inception Date　　　　　　　　　　Aug-10
Open to New Investments　　　　　　　Y

Prices
Price (as of 9/30/2019)　　　　　　50.59
52-Week High　　　　　　　　　　50.77
52-Week Low　　　　　　　　　　49.42

Total Returns (%)

3-Month	6-Month	1-Year	3-Year	5-Year
0.66	2.13	4.36	4.42	6.28

3-Year Standard Deviation　　　　1.03
Effective Duration　　　　　　　　1.93

Valuation
Premium/Discount (1-Year Average)　　0.02

Company Information
Provider　　　　Schwab ETFs
Manager/Tenure　Matthew Hastings (9), Mark R. McKissick (2)
Website　　　　http://www.schwabfunds.com
Address　　　　Schwab ETFs United States
Phone Number　800-435-4000

PERFORMANCE

Ratings History

Date	Overall Rating	Risk Rating	Reward Rating
Q3-19	C	C+	C
Q4-18	C	C+	C-
Q4-17	C	C	C-
Q4-16	C	C+	C
Q4-15	C	C+	C

Asset & Performance History

Date	NAV	1-Year Total Return
2018	49.88	1.49
2017	50.03	0.35
2016	50.41	0.78
2015	50.43	0.43
2014	50.55	0.54
2013	50.51	0.25

Total Assets: $5,898,531,064
Asset Allocation

Asset	%
Cash	0%
Stocks	0%
US Stocks	0%
Bonds	100%
US Bonds	100%
Other	0%

Services Offered:

Investment Strategy: The investment seeks to track as closely as possible, before fees and expenses, the total return of the Bloomberg Barclays US Treasury 1-3 Year Index. The fund will invest at least 90% of its net assets (including, for this purpose, any borrowings for investment purposes) in securities included in the index. The index includes all publicly-issued U.S. Treasury securities that have a remaining maturity of greater than or equal to one year and less than three years, are rated investment grade, and have $300 million or more of outstanding face value. The securities in the index must be denominated in U.S. dollars and must be fixed-rate and non-convertible. **Top Holdings:** United States Treasury Notes 2.88% United States Treasury Notes 2.75% United States Treasury Notes 1.75% United States Treasury Notes 2.62% United States Treasury Notes 1.12%

Communication Services Select Sector SPDR® Fund   B-   BUY

Ticker	Traded On	NAV	Total Assets ($)	Dividend Yield (TTM)	Turnover Ratio	Expense Ratio
XLC	NYSE Arca		$5,878,517,060	0.92	7	0.13

Ratings
Reward   B
Risk   C
Recent Upgrade/Downgrade   Up

Fund Information
Fund Type   Exchange Traded Funds
Category   Communications Sector Equity
Sub-Category   Communications
Prospectus Objective   Comm
Inception Date   Jun-18
Open to New Investments   Y

Prices
Price (as of 9/30/2019)   49.52
52-Week High   51.72
52-Week Low   38.97

Total Returns (%)

3-Month	6-Month	1-Year	3-Year	5-Year
-0.41	4.23	1.98		

3-Year Standard Deviation
Effective Duration

Valuation
Premium/Discount (1-Year Average)   -0.01

Company Information
Provider   SPDR State Street Global Advisors
Manager/Tenure   Michael J. Feehily (1), Kala O'Donnell (1), Karl A. Schneider (1)
Website   http://www.spdrs.com
Address   SPDR State Street Global Advisors
                  State Street Financial Center, 1
                  Lincoln Street Boston MA 02111-2900
                  United States
Phone Number   617-786-3000

PERFORMANCE

Ratings History

Date	Overall Rating	Risk Rating	Reward Rating
Q3-19	B-	C	B
Q4-18	U		
Q4-17			
Q4-16			
Q4-15			

Asset & Performance History

Date	NAV	1-Year Total Return
2018	41.26	
2017		
2016		
2015		
2014		
2013		

Total Assets: $5,878,517,060

Asset Allocation

Asset	%
Cash	0%
Stocks	100%
US Stocks	100%
Bonds	0%
US Bonds	0%
Other	0%

Services Offered:

Investment Strategy: The investment seeks to correspond generally to the price and yield performance of publicly traded equity securities of companies in the Communication Services Select Sector Index. Normally, the fund generally invests substantially all, but at least 95%, of its total assets in the securities comprising the index. The index includes companies that have been identified as Communication Services companies by the GICS®, including securities of companies from the following industries: diversified telecommunication services; wireless telecommunication services; media; entertainment; and interactive media & services. The fund is non-diversified.
Top Holdings: Facebook Inc A Alphabet Inc Class C Alphabet Inc A Activision Blizzard Inc AT&T Inc

Vanguard Utilities Index Fund ETF Shares   B   BUY

Ticker	Traded On	NAV	Total Assets ($)	Dividend Yield (TTM)	Turnover Ratio	Expense Ratio
VPU	NYSE Arca	143.61	$5,716,549,067	2.81	4	0.1

Ratings
Reward   B
Risk   C+
Recent Upgrade/Downgrade

Fund Information
Fund Type   Exchange Traded Funds
Category   Utilities Sector Equity
Sub-Category   Utilities
Prospectus Objective   Utility
Inception Date   Jan-04
Open to New Investments   Y

Prices
Price (as of 9/30/2019)   143.65
52-Week High   144.54
52-Week Low   114.71

Total Returns (%)

3-Month	6-Month	1-Year	3-Year	5-Year
9.08	12.37	25.87	47.41	84.91

3-Year Standard Deviation   10.3
Effective Duration

Valuation
Premium/Discount (1-Year Average)   -0.01

Company Information
Provider   Vanguard
Manager/Tenure   Michael A. Johnson (4), Awais Khan (1)
Website   http://www.vanguard.com
Address   Vanguard 100 Vanguard Boulevard
                  Malvern PA 19355 United States
Phone Number   877-662-7447

PERFORMANCE

Ratings History

Date	Overall Rating	Risk Rating	Reward Rating
Q3-19	B	C+	B
Q4-18	B-	C+	B-
Q4-17	B	B	B
Q4-16	B-	C+	B
Q4-15	B-	C+	B

Asset & Performance History

Date	NAV	1-Year Total Return
2018	117.5	4.09
2017	116.57	11.94
2016	106.94	16.84
2015	93.93	-4.83
2014	102.36	26.92
2013	83.33	14.93

Total Assets: $5,716,549,067

Asset Allocation

Asset	%
Cash	0%
Stocks	100%
US Stocks	100%
Bonds	0%
US Bonds	0%
Other	0%

Services Offered:

Investment Strategy: The investment seeks to track the performance of a benchmark index. The fund employs an indexing investment approach designed to track the performance of the MSCI US Investable Market Index (IMI)/Utilities 25/50, an index made up of stocks of large, mid-size, and small U.S. companies within the utilities sector, as classified under the Global Industry Classification Standard (GICS). The Advisor attempts to replicate the target index by seeking to invest all, or substantially all, of its assets in the stocks that make up the index, in order to hold each stock in approximately the same proportion as its weighting in the index. The fund is non-diversified.
Top Holdings: NextEra Energy Inc Duke Energy Corp Dominion Energy Inc Southern Co Exelon Corp

ProShares S&P 500 Dividend Aristocrats ETF   C+   HOLD

Ticker	Traded On	NAV	Total Assets ($)	Dividend Yield (TTM)	Turnover Ratio	Expense Ratio
NOBL	BATS	71.56	$5,509,945,499	1.97	20	0.35

Ratings
Reward   C+
Risk   C+
Recent Upgrade/Downgrade

Fund Information
Fund Type   Exchange Traded Funds
Category   US Equity Large Cap Blend
Sub-Category   Large Blend
Prospectus Objective   Growth
Inception Date   Oct-13
Open to New Investments   Y

Prices
Price (as of 9/30/2019)   71.58
52-Week High   72.24
52-Week Low   57.62

Total Returns (%)

3-Month	6-Month	1-Year	3-Year	5-Year
2.98	5.83	8.99	40.36	72.96

3-Year Standard Deviation   11.64
Effective Duration

Valuation
Premium/Discount (1-Year Average)   -0.02

Company Information
Provider   ProShares
Manager/Tenure   Michael Neches (5), Devin Sullivan (1)
Website   http://www.proshares.com
Address   ProShares 7501 Wisconsin Avenue, Suite 1000 Bethesda MD 20814 United States
Phone Number   866-776-5125

PERFORMANCE

Ratings History

Date	Overall Rating	Risk Rating	Reward Rating
Q3-19	C+	C+	C+
Q4-18	C	C+	C
Q4-17	B	B	B
Q4-16	C+	C+	C+
Q4-15	C-	C+	C

Asset & Performance History

Date	NAV	1-Year Total Return
2018	60.53	-3.17
2017	63.96	21.22
2016	53.75	11.42
2015	49.28	0.46
2014	50.06	15.38
2013	44.13	

Total Assets: $5,509,945,499

Asset Allocation

Asset	%
Cash	0%
Stocks	100%
US Stocks	96%
Bonds	0%
US Bonds	0%
Other	0%

Services Offered:

Investment Strategy: The investment seeks investment results, before fees and expenses, that track the performance of the S&P 500® Dividend Aristocrats® Index (the "index"). The fund will invest at least 80% of its total assets in component securities (i.e., securities of the index and comparable securities that have economic characteristics that are substantially identical to the economic characteristics of the securities of the index). The index contains a minimum of 40 stocks, which are equally weighted, and no single sector is allowed to comprise more than 30% of the index weight. **Top Holdings:** Target Corp Lowe's Companies Inc S&P Global Inc Procter & Gamble Co Brown-Forman Corp Class B

---

iShares U.S. Aerospace & Defense ETF   B-   BUY

Ticker	Traded On	NAV	Total Assets ($)	Dividend Yield (TTM)	Turnover Ratio	Expense Ratio
ITA	BATS	224.77	$5,495,533,072	0.9	38	0.42

Ratings
Reward   B
Risk   C
Recent Upgrade/Downgrade   Up

Fund Information
Fund Type   Exchange Traded Funds
Category   Industrials Sector Equity
Sub-Category   Industrials
Prospectus Objective   Growth
Inception Date   May-06
Open to New Investments   Y

Prices
Price (as of 9/30/2019)   224.70
52-Week High   231.12
52-Week Low   162.03

Total Returns (%)

3-Month	6-Month	1-Year	3-Year	5-Year
6.17	10.75	4.60	79.77	125.14

3-Year Standard Deviation   17.02
Effective Duration

Valuation
Premium/Discount (1-Year Average)   -0.02

Company Information
Provider   iShares
Manager/Tenure   Greg Savage (11), Jennifer Hsui (7), Alan Mason (3), 2 others
Website   http://www.ishares.com
Address   iShares 400 Howard Street San Francisco CA 94105 United States
Phone Number   800-474-2737

PERFORMANCE

Ratings History

Date	Overall Rating	Risk Rating	Reward Rating
Q3-19	B-	C	B
Q4-18	B-	C+	B
Q4-17	A-	B-	A+
Q4-16	B	C+	B+
Q4-15	B	B	B

Asset & Performance History

Date	NAV	1-Year Total Return
2018	172.98	-7.15
2017	188.14	35.17
2016	140.62	20.4
2015	118.16	4.03
2014	114.76	9.85
2013	105.79	57.07

Total Assets: $5,495,533,072

Asset Allocation

Asset	%
Cash	0%
Stocks	100%
US Stocks	100%
Bonds	0%
US Bonds	0%
Other	0%

Services Offered:

Investment Strategy: The investment seeks to track the investment results of the Dow Jones U.S. Select Aerospace & Defense Index composed of U.S. equities in the aerospace and defense sector. The fund generally invests at least 90% of its assets in securities of the underlying index and in depositary receipts representing securities of the underlying index. The underlying index measures the performance of the aerospace and defense sector of the U.S. equity market. Aerospace companies in the index include manufacturers, assemblers and distributors of aircraft and aircraft parts. The fund is non-diversified. **Top Holdings:** Boeing Co United Technologies Corp L3Harris Technologies Inc Lockheed Martin Corp Northrop Grumman Corp

Invesco Preferred ETF   C+   HOLD

Ticker	Traded On	NAV	Total Assets ($)	Dividend Yield (TTM)	Turnover Ratio	Expense Ratio
PGX	NYSE Arca	14.98	$5,481,147,974	5.41		0.52

Ratings
Reward   B-
Risk   C+
Recent Upgrade/Downgrade   Down

Fund Information
Fund Type   Exchange Traded Funds
Category   US Fixed Income
Sub-Category   Preferred Stock
Prospectus Objective   Growth & Inc
Inception Date   Jan-08
Open to New Investments   Y

Prices
Price (as of 9/30/2019)   15.02
52-Week High   15.03
52-Week Low   13.18

Total Returns (%)

3-Month	6-Month	1-Year	3-Year	5-Year
3.78	5.71	11.31	17.38	38.44

3-Year Standard Deviation   5.74
Effective Duration   3.85

Valuation
Premium/Discount (1-Year Average)   0.07

Company Information
Provider   Invesco
Manager/Tenure   Philip Fang (11), Peter Hubbard (11),
                  Jeffrey W. Kernagis (11), 2 others
Website   http://www.invesco.com/us
Address   Invesco 11 Greenway Plaza, Ste. 2500
                  Houston TX 77046 United States
Phone Number   800-659-1005

PERFORMANCE

Ratings History

Date	Overall Rating	Risk Rating	Reward Rating
Q3-19	C+	C+	B-
Q4-18	C-	C	D+
Q4-17	B	A	C+
Q4-16	C	C+	C
Q4-15	B-	C+	B-

Asset & Performance History

Date	NAV	1-Year Total Return
2018	13.49	-4.24
2017	14.92	10.84
2016	14.24	1.19
2015	14.91	8.07
2014	14.64	15.28
2013	13.5	-1.82

Total Assets: $5,481,147,974
Asset Allocation

Asset	%
Cash	0%
Stocks	1%
US Stocks	1%
Bonds	0%
US Bonds	0%
Other	0%

Services Offered:

Investment Strategy: The investment seeks to track the investment results (before fees and expenses) of the ICE BofAML Core Plus Fixed Rate Preferred Securities Index (the "underlying index"). The fund generally will invest at least 80% of its total assets in fixed rate U.S. dollar-denominated preferred securities that comprise the underlying index. The underlying index is a market capitalization-weighted index designed to reflect the total return performance of the fixed rate U.S. dollar-denominated preferred securities market. It is non-diversified. **Top Holdings:** Citigroup Inc Deposit Shs Repr 1/1000th 6 7/8 % Non-Cum Perp Pfd Shs Series Deutsche Bank Conting Cp-8 05 PC Tr Pfd Secs 08-Without Fixed Maturity Pfd PNC Financial Services Group Inc Perpetual Preferred Share class-P JPMorgan Chase & Co Pfd Wells Fargo & Co Deposit Shs Repr 1/1000th 5.85 % Non-Cum Perp Pfd Shs -A-

iShares Edge MSCI Min Vol Global ETF   B-   BUY

Ticker	Traded On	NAV	Total Assets ($)	Dividend Yield (TTM)	Turnover Ratio	Expense Ratio
ACWV	BATS	94.60	$5,477,341,032	2.13	23	0.2

Ratings
Reward   B-
Risk   C+
Recent Upgrade/Downgrade

Fund Information
Fund Type   Exchange Traded Funds
Category   Global Equity Large Cap
Sub-Category   World Large Stock
Prospectus Objective   World Stock
Inception Date   Oct-11
Open to New Investments   Y

Prices
Price (as of 9/30/2019)   94.75
52-Week High   95.06
52-Week Low   78.32

Total Returns (%)

3-Month	6-Month	1-Year	3-Year	5-Year
2.59	6.83	10.18	33.43	59.78

3-Year Standard Deviation   7.95
Effective Duration

Valuation
Premium/Discount (1-Year Average)   0.06

Company Information
Provider   iShares
Manager/Tenure   Diane Hsiung (7), Greg Savage (7),
                  Jennifer Hsui (6), 3 others
Website   http://www.ishares.com
Address   iShares 400 Howard Street San
                  Francisco CA 94105 United States
Phone Number   800-474-2737

PERFORMANCE

Ratings History

Date	Overall Rating	Risk Rating	Reward Rating
Q3-19	B-	C+	B-
Q4-18	C	C+	C
Q4-17	B	B+	B-
Q4-16	C	C+	C
Q4-15	C	C+	C

Asset & Performance History

Date	NAV	1-Year Total Return
2018	81.21	-1.34
2017	84.21	18.17
2016	72.76	7.7
2015	69.28	3.04
2014	68.77	11.12
2013	63.31	17.27

Total Assets: $5,477,341,032
Asset Allocation

Asset	%
Cash	1%
Stocks	99%
US Stocks	52%
Bonds	0%
US Bonds	0%
Other	0%

Services Offered:

Investment Strategy: The investment seeks to track the investment results of the MSCI ACWI Minimum Volatility (USD) Index. The fund generally will invest at least 90% of its assets in the component securities of the underlying index and in investments that have economic characteristics that are substantially identical to the component securities of the underlying index. The index measures the combined performance of equity securities in both developed and emerging markets that, in the aggregate, have lower volatility relative to the broader developed and emerging markets. **Top Holdings:** Waste Management Inc Nestle SA Consolidated Edison Inc Motorola Solutions Inc McDonald's Corp

iShares Edge MSCI Min Vol Emerging Markets ETF   C   HOLD

Ticker	Traded On	NAV	Total Assets ($)	Dividend Yield (TTM)	Turnover Ratio	Expense Ratio
EEMV	BATS	57.07	$5,438,844,109	2.6	22	0.25

Ratings
Reward	C
Risk	C+
Recent Upgrade/Downgrade	

Fund Information
Fund Type	Exchange Traded Funds
Category	Global Emerg Mkts Equity
Sub-Category	Diversified Emerging Mkts
Prospectus Objective	Div Emerg Mkts
Inception Date	Oct-11
Open to New Investments	Y

Prices
Price (as of 9/30/2019)	57.09
52-Week High	60.02
52-Week Low	53.54

Total Returns (%)
3-Month	6-Month	1-Year	3-Year	5-Year
-3.25	-2.80	-1.07	14.74	8.77

3-Year Standard Deviation	10.04
Effective Duration	

Valuation
Premium/Discount (1-Year Average)	-0.04

Company Information
Provider	iShares
Manager/Tenure	Diane Hsiung (7), Greg Savage (7), Jennifer Hsui (6), 3 others
Website	http://www.ishares.com
Address	iShares 400 Howard Street San Francisco CA 94105 United States
Phone Number	800-474-2737

PERFORMANCE

Ratings History
Date	Overall Rating	Risk Rating	Reward Rating
Q3-19	C	C+	C
Q4-18	C	C+	D+
Q4-17	C+	C	C+
Q4-16	D+	C-	D
Q4-15	C-	C-	C-

Asset & Performance History
Date	NAV	1-Year Total Return
2018	55.73	-6.07
2017	60.78	26.32
2016	49.3	3.72
2015	48.85	-12.12
2014	56.91	0.87
2013	57.95	-0.28

Total Assets: $5,438,844,109

Asset Allocation
Asset	%
Cash	0%
Stocks	100%
US Stocks	0%
Bonds	0%
US Bonds	0%
Other	0%

Services Offered:

Investment Strategy: The investment seeks to track the investment results of the MSCI Emerging Markets Minimum Volatility (USD) Index. The fund generally will invest at least 90% of its assets in the component securities of the underlying index and in investments that have economic characteristics that are substantially identical to the component securities of the underlying index. The index measures the performance of equity securities in global emerging markets that, in the aggregate, have lower volatility relative to the broader global emerging markets.
Top Holdings: PT Bank Central Asia Tbk   Guangdong Investment Ltd   Taiwan Cooperative Financial Holding Co Ltd   First Financial Holding Co Ltd   Chunghwa Telecom Co Ltd

---

FlexShares Morningstar Global Upstream Natural Resources Index Fund   C   HOLD

Ticker	Traded On	NAV	Total Assets ($)	Dividend Yield (TTM)	Turnover Ratio	Expense Ratio
GUNR	NYSE Arca	31.10	$5,432,429,903	3.54	30	0.46

Ratings
Reward	C
Risk	C+
Recent Upgrade/Downgrade	

Fund Information
Fund Type	Exchange Traded Funds
Category	Natural Resources
Sub-Category	Natural Resources
Prospectus Objective	Natl Res
Inception Date	Sep-11
Open to New Investments	Y

Prices
Price (as of 9/30/2019)	31.15
52-Week High	34.18
52-Week Low	28.13

Total Returns (%)
3-Month	6-Month	1-Year	3-Year	5-Year
-5.41	-4.36	-5.12	23.00	8.53

3-Year Standard Deviation	12.75
Effective Duration	

Valuation
Premium/Discount (1-Year Average)	0.00

Company Information
Provider	Flexshares Trust
Manager/Tenure	Robert Anstine (5), Brendan Sullivan (3)
Website	http://www.flexshares.com
Address	50 South LaSalle Street Chicago, Illinois 60603 Chicago Illinois 60603 United States
Phone Number	855-353-9383

PERFORMANCE

Ratings History
Date	Overall Rating	Risk Rating	Reward Rating
Q3-19	C	C+	C
Q4-18	C	C+	C
Q4-17	C+	C	C+
Q4-16	C-	D+	C-
Q4-15	D	D	D

Asset & Performance History
Date	NAV	1-Year Total Return
2018	29.36	-9.21
2017	33.31	18.45
2016	28.75	30.91
2015	22.38	-24.47
2014	30.93	-7.43
2013	34.33	-0.45

Total Assets: $5,432,429,903

Asset Allocation
Asset	%
Cash	0%
Stocks	100%
US Stocks	35%
Bonds	0%
US Bonds	0%
Other	0%

Services Offered:

Investment Strategy: The investment seeks investment results that correspond generally to the price and yield performance, before fees and expenses, of the Morningstar® Global Upstream Natural Resources IndexSM. The fund will invest at least 80% of its total assets (exclusive of collateral held from securities lending) in the securities of the index and in ADRs and GDRs based on the securities in the index. The index reflects the performance of a selection of equity securities that are traded in or are issued by companies domiciled in global developed or emerging markets, as determined by the index provider pursuant to its index methodology. It is non-diversified.
Top Holdings: Exxon Mobil Corp   Nutrien Ltd   BHP Group Ltd   Chevron Corp   Tyson Foods Inc Class A

Schwab Fundamental U.S. Large Company Index ETF   C+   HOLD

Ticker	Traded On	NAV	Total Assets ($)	Dividend Yield (TTM)	Turnover Ratio	Expense Ratio
FNDX	NYSE Arca	39.54	$5,431,161,858	2.2	11	0.25

Ratings
Reward	C
Risk	C+
Recent Upgrade/Downgrade	Up

Fund Information
Fund Type	Exchange Traded Funds
Category	US Equity Large Cap Value
Sub-Category	Large Value
Prospectus Objective	Growth & Inc
Inception Date	Aug-13
Open to New Investments	Y

Prices
Price (as of 9/30/2019)	39.55
52-Week High	40.14
52-Week Low	32.01

Total Returns (%)
3-Month	6-Month	1-Year	3-Year	5-Year
1.11	4.11	1.54	36.02	53.74

3-Year Standard Deviation	12.85
Effective Duration	

Valuation
Premium/Discount (1-Year Average)	-0.01

Company Information
Provider	Schwab ETFs
Manager/Tenure	Christopher Bliss (2), Ferian Juwono (2), Sabya Sinha (2), 1 other
Website	http://www.schwabfunds.com
Address	Schwab ETFs United States
Phone Number	800-435-4000

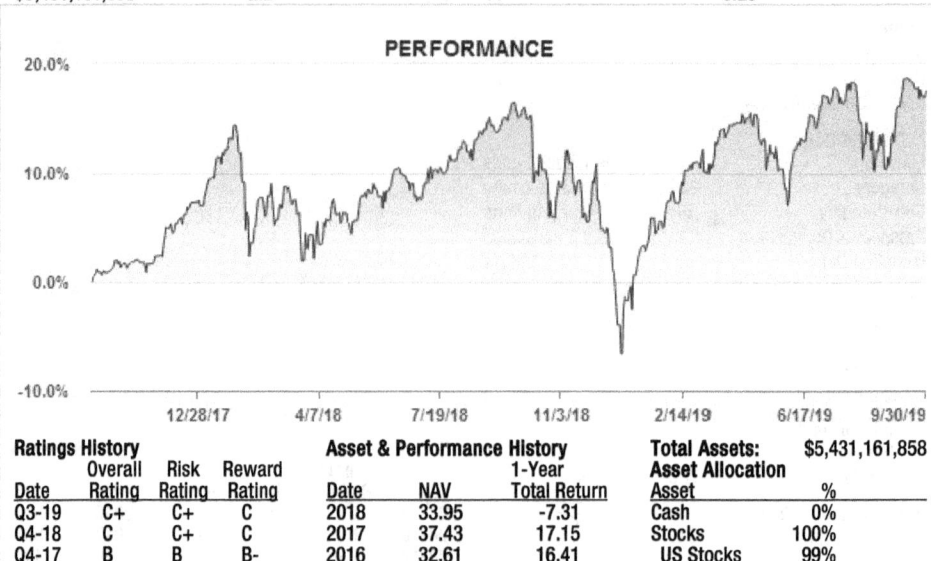

Ratings History
Date	Overall Rating	Risk Rating	Reward Rating
Q3-19	C+	C+	C
Q4-18	C	C+	C
Q4-17	B	B	B-
Q4-16	B-	C+	B
Q4-15	C-	C+	C-

Asset & Performance History
Date	NAV	1-Year Total Return
2018	33.95	-7.31
2017	37.43	17.15
2016	32.61	16.41
2015	28.62	-2.92
2014	30.08	12.29
2013	27.24	

Total Assets: $5,431,161,858
Asset Allocation
Asset	%
Cash	0%
Stocks	100%
US Stocks	99%
Bonds	0%
US Bonds	0%
Other	0%

Services Offered:

Investment Strategy: The investment seeks to track as closely as possible, before fees and expenses, the total return of the Russell RAFI™ US Large Company Index. The fund normally will invest at least 90% of its net assets (including, for this purpose, any borrowings for investment purposes) in stocks included in the index. The index measures the performance of the large company size segment by fundamental overall company scores (scores), which are created using as the universe the U.S. companies in the FTSE Global Total Cap Index (the parent index). It may invest up to 10% of its net assets in securities not included in the index. **Top Holdings:** Apple Inc   Exxon Mobil Corp   AT&T Inc   Microsoft Corp   Chevron Corp

---

iShares MSCI Eurozone ETF   C   HOLD

Ticker	Traded On	NAV	Total Assets ($)	Dividend Yield (TTM)	Turnover Ratio	Expense Ratio
EZU	BATS	38.92	$5,409,227,905	3.12	5	0.47

Ratings
Reward	C-
Risk	C+
Recent Upgrade/Downgrade	

Fund Information
Fund Type	Exchange Traded Funds
Category	Europe Equity Large Cap
Sub-Category	Europe Stock
Prospectus Objective	Europe Stock
Inception Date	Jul-00
Open to New Investments	Y

Prices
Price (as of 9/30/2019)	38.89
52-Week High	41.01
52-Week Low	33.85

Total Returns (%)
3-Month	6-Month	1-Year	3-Year	5-Year
-2.03	2.54	-2.26	22.55	16.62

3-Year Standard Deviation	14.15
Effective Duration	

Valuation
Premium/Discount (1-Year Average)	-0.09

Company Information
Provider	iShares
Manager/Tenure	Diane Hsiung (11), Greg Savage (11), Jennifer Hsui (6), 3 others
Website	http://www.ishares.com
Address	iShares 400 Howard Street San Francisco CA 94105 United States
Phone Number	800-474-2737

Ratings History
Date	Overall Rating	Risk Rating	Reward Rating
Q3-19	C	C+	C-
Q4-18	D+	D+	D+
Q4-17	B	B	B
Q4-16	D	C-	D
Q4-15	C	B	C-

Asset & Performance History
Date	NAV	1-Year Total Return
2018	35.07	-16.97
2017	43.52	27.92
2016	34.71	1.29
2015	35.35	-1.62
2014	36.64	-8.5
2013	41.11	28.75

Total Assets: $5,409,227,905
Asset Allocation
Asset	%
Cash	1%
Stocks	99%
US Stocks	3%
Bonds	0%
US Bonds	0%
Other	0%

Services Offered: CashInvestment Plan

Investment Strategy: The investment seeks to track the investment results of the MSCI EMU Index composed of large- and mid-capitalization equities from developed market countries that use the euro as their official currency. The fund generally invests at least 95% of its assets in the securities of its underlying index and in depositary receipts representing securities in its underlying index. The index consists of stocks from the following 10 developed market countries: Austria, Belgium, Finland, France, Germany, Ireland, Italy, the Netherlands, Portugal and Spain. **Top Holdings:** Total SA   SAP SE   LVMH Moet Hennessy Louis Vuitton SE   Sanofi SA   ASML Holding NV

Invesco FTSE RAFI US 1000 ETF   C+   HOLD

Ticker	Traded On	NAV	Total Assets ($)	Dividend Yield (TTM)	Turnover Ratio	Expense Ratio
PRF	NYSE Arca	117.82	$5,337,126,301	2.05	10	0.39

Ratings
Reward	C
Risk	C+
Recent Upgrade/Downgrade	Up

Fund Information
Fund Type	Exchange Traded Funds
Category	US Equity Large Cap Value
Sub-Category	Large Value
Prospectus Objective	Growth
Inception Date	Dec-05
Open to New Investments	Y

Prices
Price (as of 9/30/2019)	117.86
52-Week High	119.73
52-Week Low	95.78

Total Returns (%)
3-Month	6-Month	1-Year	3-Year	5-Year
0.96	3.72	1.12	33.88	50.73

3-Year Standard Deviation	13.08
Effective Duration	

Valuation
Premium/Discount (1-Year Average)	-0.03

Company Information
Provider	Invesco
Manager/Tenure	Peter Hubbard (12), Michael Jeanette (11), Tony Seisser (4)
Website	http://www.invesco.com/us
Address	Invesco 11 Greenway Plaza, Ste. 2500 Houston TX 77046 United States
Phone Number	800-659-1005

PERFORMANCE

Ratings History
Date	Overall Rating	Risk Rating	Reward Rating
Q3-19	C+	C+	C
Q4-18	C	C+	C
Q4-17	B	B	B
Q4-16	B-	C+	B
Q4-15	C+	C+	C

Asset & Performance History
Date	NAV	1-Year Total Return
2018	101.56	-8.56
2017	113.42	15.94
2016	99.46	17.18
2015	86.84	-2.83
2014	91.38	12.2
2013	82.89	35.13

Total Assets: $5,337,126,301
Asset Allocation
Asset	%
Cash	0%
Stocks	100%
US Stocks	98%
Bonds	0%
US Bonds	0%
Other	0%

Services Offered:

Investment Strategy: The investment seeks to track the investment results (before fees and expenses) of the FTSE RAFI™ US 1000 Index (the "underlying index"). The fund generally will invest at least 90% of its total assets in common stocks that comprise the underlying index. The underlying index is composed of 1,000 common stocks that FTSE International Limited and Research Affiliates LLC strictly in accordance with their guidelines and mandated procedures, include to track the performance of the largest U.S. companies based on the following four fundamental measures: book value, cash flow, sales and dividends. **Top Holdings:** Apple Inc AT&T Inc Exxon Mobil Corp Berkshire Hathaway Inc B Microsoft Corp

iShares MSCI EAFE Value ETF   C-   HOLD

Ticker	Traded On	NAV	Total Assets ($)	Dividend Yield (TTM)	Turnover Ratio	Expense Ratio
EFV	BATS	47.30	$5,222,464,038	4.25	21	0.38

Ratings
Reward	D+
Risk	C+
Recent Upgrade/Downgrade	Down

Fund Information
Fund Type	Exchange Traded Funds
Category	Global Equity Large Cap
Sub-Category	Foreign Large Value
Prospectus Objective	Foreign Stock
Inception Date	Aug-05
Open to New Investments	Y

Prices
Price (as of 9/30/2019)	47.37
52-Week High	52.00
52-Week Low	43.66

Total Returns (%)
3-Month	6-Month	1-Year	3-Year	5-Year
-2.27	-1.56	-4.68	15.58	5.03

3-Year Standard Deviation	11.78
Effective Duration	

Valuation
Premium/Discount (1-Year Average)	-0.07

Company Information
Provider	iShares
Manager/Tenure	Diane Hsiung (11), Greg Savage (11), Jennifer Hsui (6), 3 others
Website	http://www.ishares.com
Address	iShares 400 Howard Street San Francisco CA 94105 United States
Phone Number	800-474-2737

PERFORMANCE

Ratings History
Date	Overall Rating	Risk Rating	Reward Rating
Q3-19	C-	C+	D+
Q4-18	D+	C-	D+
Q4-17	C+	C	C+
Q4-16	D+	C-	D
Q4-15	C	C+	C-

Asset & Performance History
Date	NAV	1-Year Total Return
2018	45.23	-14.87
2017	55.37	21.22
2016	47.4	4.86
2015	46.75	-5.88
2014	51.3	-5.65
2013	56.82	22.6

Total Assets: $5,222,464,038
Asset Allocation
Asset	%
Cash	1%
Stocks	99%
US Stocks	1%
Bonds	0%
US Bonds	0%
Other	0%

Services Offered:

Investment Strategy: The investment seeks to track the investment results of the MSCI EAFE Value Index composed of developed market equities, excluding the U.S. and Canada, that exhibit value characteristics. The fund generally invests at least 90% of its assets in securities of the underlying index and in depositary receipts representing securities of the underlying index. The underlying index is a subset of the MSCI EAFE Index. Constituents of the underlying index include securities from Europe, Australasia and the Far East. **Top Holdings:** Toyota Motor Corp HSBC Holdings PLC BP PLC Royal Dutch Shell PLC Class A Total SA

iShares S&P Small-Cap 600 Growth ETF

C   **HOLD**

Ticker	Traded On	NAV	Total Assets ($)	Dividend Yield (TTM)	Turnover Ratio	Expense Ratio
IJT	NAS CM	178.54	$5,133,125,632	0.99	45	0.25

Ratings
Reward	C
Risk	C-
Recent Upgrade/Downgrade	

Fund Information
Fund Type	Exchange Traded Funds
Category	US Equity Small Cap
Sub-Category	Small Growth
Prospectus Objective	Small Company
Inception Date	Jul-00
Open to New Investments	Y

Prices
Price (as of 9/30/2019)	178.38
52-Week High	198.92
52-Week Low	151.48

Total Returns (%)
3-Month	6-Month	1-Year	3-Year	5-Year
-2.13	-0.47	-9.27	33.78	69.21

3-Year Standard Deviation	17.55
Effective Duration	

Valuation
Premium/Discount (1-Year Average)	-0.07

Company Information
Provider	iShares
Manager/Tenure	Greg Savage (11), Jennifer Hsui (7), Alan Mason (3), 2 others
Website	http://www.ishares.com
Address	iShares 400 Howard Street San Francisco CA 94105 United States
Phone Number	800-474-2737

PERFORMANCE

Ratings History
Date	Overall Rating	Risk Rating	Reward Rating
Q3-19	C	C-	C
Q4-18	C	C+	C
Q4-17	A-	B+	A
Q4-16	B	C+	B+
Q4-15	C+	C+	C+

Asset & Performance History
Date	NAV	1-Year Total Return
2018	161.56	-4.28
2017	170.2	14.57
2016	149.91	22
2015	124.3	2.64
2014	122.44	3.71
2013	119	42.62

Total Assets: $5,133,125,632

Asset Allocation
Asset	%
Cash	0%
Stocks	100%
US Stocks	98%
Bonds	0%
US Bonds	0%
Other	0%

Services Offered: CashInvestment Plan

Investment Strategy: The investment seeks to track the investment results of the S&P SmallCap 600 Growth IndexTM, which measures the performance of the small-capitalization growth sector of the U.S. equity market. The fund generally invests at least 90% of its assets in securities of the underlying index and in depositary receipts representing securities of the underlying index. It may invest the remainder of its assets in certain futures, options and swap contracts, cash and cash equivalents, as well as in securities not included in the underlying index, but which the advisor believes will help the fund track the underlying index. **Top Holdings:** FirstCash Inc Repligen Corp Aerojet Rocketdyne Holdings Inc Strategic Education Inc Exponent Inc

---

iShares S&P 100 ETF

C+   **HOLD**

Ticker	Traded On	NAV	Total Assets ($)	Dividend Yield (TTM)	Turnover Ratio	Expense Ratio
OEF	NYSE Arca	131.45	$5,120,145,419	2.03	7	0.2

Ratings
Reward	C+
Risk	C+
Recent Upgrade/Downgrade	

Fund Information
Fund Type	Exchange Traded Funds
Category	US Equity Large Cap Blend
Sub-Category	Large Blend
Prospectus Objective	Growth
Inception Date	Oct-00
Open to New Investments	Y

Prices
Price (as of 9/30/2019)	131.49
52-Week High	134.09
52-Week Low	104.34

Total Returns (%)
3-Month	6-Month	1-Year	3-Year	5-Year
1.04	4.88	3.10	45.55	67.46

3-Year Standard Deviation	12.21
Effective Duration	

Valuation
Premium/Discount (1-Year Average)	-0.03

Company Information
Provider	iShares
Manager/Tenure	Greg Savage (11), Jennifer Hsui (7), Alan Mason (3), 2 others
Website	http://www.ishares.com
Address	iShares 400 Howard Street San Francisco CA 94105 United States
Phone Number	800-474-2737

PERFORMANCE

Ratings History
Date	Overall Rating	Risk Rating	Reward Rating
Q3-19	C+	C+	C+
Q4-18	C	C+	C
Q4-17	B	B+	B
Q4-16	B-	C+	B
Q4-15	C+	B-	C+

Asset & Performance History
Date	NAV	1-Year Total Return
2018	111.47	-4.05
2017	118.47	21.76
2016	99.21	11.16
2015	91.2	2.49
2014	90.9	12.49
2013	82.36	30.05

Total Assets: $5,120,145,419

Asset Allocation
Asset	%
Cash	0%
Stocks	100%
US Stocks	100%
Bonds	0%
US Bonds	0%
Other	0%

Services Offered: CashInvestment Plan

Investment Strategy: The investment seeks to track the investment results of the S&P 100®, which measures the performance of the large-capitalization sector of the U.S. equity market. The fund generally invests at least 90% of its assets in securities of the underlying index and in depositary receipts representing securities of the underlying index. It may invest the remainder of its assets in certain futures, options and swap contracts, cash and cash equivalents, including shares of money market funds advised by BFA or its affiliates, as well as in securities not included in the underlying index, but which the advisor believes will help the fund track the underlying index. **Top Holdings:** Microsoft Corp Apple Inc Amazon.com Inc Facebook Inc A Berkshire Hathaway Inc B

SPDR® Portfolio S&P 500 Growth ETF

C+   HOLD

Ticker	Traded On	NAV	Total Assets ($)	Dividend Yield (TTM)	Turnover Ratio	Expense Ratio
SPYG	NYSE Arca		$5,098,734,031	1.41	21	0.04

Ratings
Reward	C+
Risk	C+
Recent Upgrade/Downgrade	Down

Fund Information
Fund Type	Exchange Traded Funds
Category	US Equity Large Cap Growth
Sub-Category	Large Growth
Prospectus Objective	Growth
Inception Date	Sep-00
Open to New Investments	Y

Prices
Price (as of 9/30/2019)	38.89
52-Week High	39.97
52-Week Low	30.33

Total Returns (%)
3-Month	6-Month	1-Year	3-Year	5-Year
-0.57	3.68	2.36	53.77	80.80

3-Year Standard Deviation	12.3
Effective Duration	

Valuation
Premium/Discount (1-Year Average)	0.00

Company Information
Provider	SPDR State Street Global Advisors
Manager/Tenure	Michael J. Feehily (7), Karl A. Schneider (4), Mark Krivitsky (2)
Website	http://www.spdrs.com
Address	SPDR State Street Global Advisors State Street Financial Center, 1 Lincoln Street Boston MA 02111-2900 United States
Phone Number	617-786-3000

PERFORMANCE

Ratings History
Date	Overall Rating	Risk Rating	Reward Rating
Q3-19	C+	C+	C+
Q4-18	C	C+	C
Q4-17	B	B+	B
Q4-16	C+	C-	B
Q4-15	C	C	C+

Asset & Performance History
Date	NAV	1-Year Total Return
2018	32.48	-0.02
2017	32.95	27.19
2016	26.3	6.27
2015	25.04	5.36
2014	24.14	14.63
2013	21.36	32.41

Total Assets: $5,098,734,031
Asset Allocation
Asset	%
Cash	0%
Stocks	100%
US Stocks	99%
Bonds	0%
US Bonds	0%
Other	0%

Services Offered: Dividend Investment Plan, Cash Investment Plan

Investment Strategy: The investment seeks to provide investment results that, before fees and expenses, correspond generally to the total return performance of the S&P 500 Growth Index that tracks the performance of large capitalization exchange traded U.S. equity securities exhibiting "growth" characteristics. The fund generally invests substantially all, but at least 80%, of its total assets in the securities comprising the index. The index measures the performance of the large-capitalization growth segment of the U.S. equity market. It is non-diversified. **Top Holdings:** Microsoft Corp Amazon.com Inc Facebook Inc A Alphabet Inc Class C Alphabet Inc A

iShares MSCI India ETF

C   HOLD

Ticker	Traded On	NAV	Total Assets ($)	Dividend Yield (TTM)	Turnover Ratio	Expense Ratio
INDA	BATS	33.39	$5,051,688,150	1.75	10	0.68

Ratings
Reward	D+
Risk	B-
Recent Upgrade/Downgrade	Down

Fund Information
Fund Type	Exchange Traded Funds
Category	India Equity
Sub-Category	India Equity
Prospectus Objective	Pacific Stock
Inception Date	Feb-12
Open to New Investments	Y

Prices
Price (as of 9/30/2019)	33.57
52-Week High	36.38
52-Week Low	29.30

Total Returns (%)
3-Month	6-Month	1-Year	3-Year	5-Year
-5.70	-5.05	4.11	17.67	15.81

3-Year Standard Deviation	16.32
Effective Duration	

Valuation
Premium/Discount (1-Year Average)	0.11

Company Information
Provider	iShares
Manager/Tenure	Diane Hsiung (7), Greg Savage (7), Jennifer Hsui (6), 3 others
Website	http://www.ishares.com
Address	iShares 400 Howard Street San Francisco CA 94105 United States
Phone Number	800-474-2737

PERFORMANCE

Ratings History
Date	Overall Rating	Risk Rating	Reward Rating
Q3-19	C	B-	D+
Q4-18	C-	C-	D+
Q4-17	B-	C	B
Q4-16	C	C	C
Q4-15	C	C+	C

Asset & Performance History
Date	NAV	1-Year Total Return
2018	33.16	-7.44
2017	36.17	36.19
2016	26.86	-2.23
2015	27.72	-6.62
2014	30.03	23.31
2013	24.51	-4.23

Total Assets: $5,051,688,150
Asset Allocation
Asset	%
Cash	0%
Stocks	100%
US Stocks	0%
Bonds	0%
US Bonds	0%
Other	0%

Services Offered:

Investment Strategy: The investment seeks to track the investment results of the MSCI India Index composed of Indian equities. The fund generally will collectively invest at least 90% of its assets in the component securities of the index and in investments that have economic characteristics that are substantially identical to the component securities of the index. The index measures the performance of equity securities of companies whose market capitalization, as calculated by the index provider, represents the top 85% of companies in the Indian securities market. The fund is non-diversified. **Top Holdings:** Reliance Industries Ltd Housing Development Finance Corp Ltd Infosys Ltd Tata Consultancy Services Ltd Axis Bank Ltd

iShares U.S. Real Estate ETF

B- **BUY**

Ticker	Traded On	NAV	Total Assets ($)	Dividend Yield (TTM)	Turnover Ratio	Expense Ratio
IYR	NYSE Arca	93.46	$5,004,518,221	2.59	11	0.42

Ratings
Reward   B-
Risk   B-
Recent Upgrade/Downgrade

Fund Information
Fund Type	Exchange Traded Funds
Category	Real Estate Sector Equity
Sub-Category	Real Estate
Prospectus Objective	Real Estate
Inception Date	Jun-00
Open to New Investments	Y

Prices
Price (as of 9/30/2019)	93.54
52-Week High	94.09
52-Week Low	72.00

Total Returns (%)
3-Month	6-Month	1-Year	3-Year	5-Year
7.40	9.00	20.99	29.09	62.70

3-Year Standard Deviation   12.06
Effective Duration

Valuation
Premium/Discount (1-Year Average)   0.01

Company Information
Provider	iShares
Manager/Tenure	Greg Savage (11), Jennifer Hsui (7), Alan Mason (3), 2 others
Website	http://www.ishares.com
Address	iShares 400 Howard Street San Francisco CA 94105 United States
Phone Number	800-474-2737

PERFORMANCE

Ratings History
Date	Overall Rating	Risk Rating	Reward Rating
Q3-19	B-	B-	B-
Q4-18	C+	B	C
Q4-17	B	B	B-
Q4-16	C+	B-	C+
Q4-15	C+	B-	C+

Asset & Performance History
Date	NAV	1-Year Total Return
2018	74.91	-4.28
2017	80.97	9.37
2016	76.88	7
2015	75.04	1.61
2014	76.81	26.61
2013	63.09	1.04

Total Assets: $5,004,518,221
Asset Allocation
Asset	%
Cash	1%
Stocks	99%
US Stocks	99%
Bonds	0%
US Bonds	0%
Other	0%

Services Offered: CashInvestment Plan

Investment Strategy: The investment seeks to track the investment results of the Dow Jones U.S. Real Estate Index. The fund generally invests at least 90% of its assets in securities of the underlying index and in depositary receipts representing securities of the underlying index. The underlying fund measures the performance of the real estate sector of the U.S. equity market and may include large-, mid- or small-capitalization companies. **Top Holdings:** American Tower Corp Crown Castle International Corp Prologis Inc Equinix Inc Simon Property Group Inc

---

Invesco Senior Loan ETF

C+ **HOLD**

Ticker	Traded On	NAV	Total Assets ($)	Dividend Yield (TTM)	Turnover Ratio	Expense Ratio
BKLN	NYSE Arca	22.62	$4,960,924,513	5.1	74	0.65

Ratings
Reward   C
Risk   B
Recent Upgrade/Downgrade   Down

Fund Information
Fund Type	Exchange Traded Funds
Category	US Fixed Income
Sub-Category	Bank Loan
Prospectus Objective	Income
Inception Date	Mar-11
Open to New Investments	Y

Prices
Price (as of 9/30/2019)	22.59
52-Week High	23.21
52-Week Low	21.59

Total Returns (%)
3-Month	6-Month	1-Year	3-Year	5-Year
0.92	2.14	2.67	10.71	14.55

3-Year Standard Deviation   3.06
Effective Duration

Valuation
Premium/Discount (1-Year Average)   -0.19

Company Information
Provider	Invesco
Manager/Tenure	Scott Baskind (8), Philip Fang (8), Peter Hubbard (8), 4 others
Website	http://www.invesco.com/us
Address	Invesco 11 Greenway Plaza, Ste. 2500 Houston TX 77046 United States
Phone Number	800-659-1005

PERFORMANCE

Ratings History
Date	Overall Rating	Risk Rating	Reward Rating
Q3-19	C+	B	C
Q4-18	C	B	C-
Q4-17	C+	B	C
Q4-16	B-	B	C
Q4-15	C	C+	C-

Asset & Performance History
Date	NAV	1-Year Total Return
2018	21.97	-0.55
2017	23.06	2.38
2016	23.32	8.89
2015	22.43	-2.85
2014	24.01	0.69
2013	24.82	4.32

Total Assets: $4,960,924,513
Asset Allocation
Asset	%
Cash	13%
Stocks	0%
US Stocks	0%
Bonds	87%
US Bonds	59%
Other	0%

Services Offered:

Investment Strategy: The investment seeks to track the investment results (before fees and expenses) of the S&P/LSTA U.S. Leveraged Loan 100 Index (the "underlying index"). The fund generally will invest at least 80% of its total assets in senior loans that comprise the underlying index. The Adviser and the fund's sub-adviser define senior loans to include loans referred to as leveraged loans, bank loans and/or floating rate loans. Banks and other lending institutions generally issue senior loans to corporations, partnerships or other entities ("borrowers"). These borrowers operate in a variety of industries and geographic regions, including foreign countries. **Top Holdings:** Financial & Risk US Holdings, Inc. 09/18/25 BURGER KING 2/17 COV-LITE 02/16/24 CENTURYLINK, INC. 01/31/2025 Charter Communications Operating 04/13/25 Grifols Worldwide 01/31/25

Xtrackers MSCI EAFE Hedged Equity ETF   C+   HOLD

Ticker	Traded On	NAV	Total Assets ($)	Dividend Yield (TTM)	Turnover Ratio	Expense Ratio
DBEF	NYSE Arca	32.29	$4,958,409,741	3.95	5	0.35

Ratings
Reward   C
Risk   C+
Recent Upgrade/Downgrade

Fund Information
Fund Type   Exchange Traded Funds
Category   Global Equity Large Cap
Sub-Category   Foreign Large Blend
Prospectus Objective   World Stock
Inception Date   Jun-11
Open to New Investments   Y

Prices
Price (as of 9/30/2019)   32.34
52-Week High   32.47
52-Week Low   27.10

Total Returns (%)

3-Month	6-Month	1-Year	3-Year	5-Year
1.15	4.67	3.87	33.24	40.57

3-Year Standard Deviation   9.79
Effective Duration

Valuation
Premium/Discount (1-Year Average)   -0.04

Company Information
Provider   DWS
Manager/Tenure   Patrick Dwyer (2), Bryan Richards (2),
                    Shlomo Bassous (1)
Website   http://dws.com
Address   DWS 210 West 10th Street Kansas
                    City MO 64105-1614 United States
Phone Number

PERFORMANCE

Ratings History

Date	Overall Rating	Risk Rating	Reward Rating
Q3-19	C+	C+	C
Q4-18	C	C+	C-
Q4-17	B	B	B
Q4-16	C+	C+	C
Q4-15	C	C+	C

Asset & Performance History

Date	NAV	1-Year Total Return
2018	28.03	-9.43
2017	31.84	16.59
2016	28.15	5.74
2015	27.38	4.5
2014	27.11	5.26
2013	27.07	25.9

Total Assets: $4,958,409,741
Asset Allocation

Asset	%
Cash	3%
Stocks	97%
US Stocks	2%
Bonds	0%
US Bonds	0%
Other	0%

Services Offered:

Investment Strategy: The investment seeks investment results that correspond generally to the performance, before fees and expenses, of the MSCI EAFE US Dollar Hedged Index. The fund, using a "passive" or indexing investment approach, seeks investment results that correspond generally to the performance, before fees and expenses, of the underlying index, which is designed to track developed market performance while mitigating exposure to fluctuations between the value of the U.S. dollar and the currencies of the countries included in the underlying index. It will invest at least 80% of its total assets in component securities of the underlying index. **Top Holdings:** Nestle SA Roche Holding AG Dividend Right Cert. Novartis AG Toyota Motor Corp HSBC Holdings PLC

First Trust Enhanced Short Maturity ETF   C   HOLD

Ticker	Traded On	NAV	Total Assets ($)	Dividend Yield (TTM)	Turnover Ratio	Expense Ratio
FTSM	NAS CM	60.06	$4,891,955,557	2.45	45	0.4

Ratings
Reward   C
Risk   C+
Recent Upgrade/Downgrade

Fund Information
Fund Type   Exchange Traded Funds
Category   US Fixed Income
Sub-Category   Ultrashort Bond
Prospectus Objective   Income
Inception Date   Aug-14
Open to New Investments   Y

Prices
Price (as of 9/30/2019)   60.07
52-Week High   60.19
52-Week Low   59.79

Total Returns (%)

3-Month	6-Month	1-Year	3-Year	5-Year
0.41	1.17	2.38	5.87	7.20

3-Year Standard Deviation   0.23
Effective Duration   0.37

Valuation
Premium/Discount (1-Year Average)   0.02

Company Information
Provider   First Trust
Manager/Tenure   Jeremiah Charles (5), Todd W. Larson
                    (5), James W. Snyder (5), 2 others
Website   http://www.ftportfolios.com/
Address   First Trust 120 E. Liberty Drive, Suite
                    400 Wheaton IL 60187 United States
Phone Number   800-621-1675

PERFORMANCE

Ratings History

Date	Overall Rating	Risk Rating	Reward Rating
Q3-19	C	C+	C
Q4-18	C	C+	C
Q4-17	C+	B+	C
Q4-16	C	C+	C
Q4-15	D-	C+	D+

Asset & Performance History

Date	NAV	1-Year Total Return
2018	59.83	1.85
2017	60.01	1.53
2016	59.92	1.3
2015	59.86	0.33
2014	59.95	
2013		

Total Assets: $4,891,955,557
Asset Allocation

Asset	%
Cash	33%
Stocks	0%
US Stocks	0%
Bonds	65%
US Bonds	52%
Other	0%

Services Offered:

Investment Strategy: The investment seeks current income, consistent with preservation of capital and daily liquidity. Under normal market conditions, the Advisor intends to achieve its investment objective by investing at least 80% of its net assets in a portfolio of U.S. dollar-denominated fixed- and variable-rate debt securities. Normally the fund's portfolio is expected to have an average duration of less than one year and an average maturity of less than three years. It is non-diversified. **Top Holdings:** United States Treasury Notes 1.75% United States Treasury Notes 1.38% United States Treasury Notes 1.5% Towd Point Mortgage Trust 2.75% OSCAR US Funding Trust V 2.99%

SPDR® Portfolio Intermediate Term Corporate Bond ETF   C+   HOLD

Ticker	Traded On	NAV	Total Assets ($)	Dividend Yield (TTM)	Turnover Ratio	Expense Ratio
SPIB	NYSE Arca		$4,860,112,961	3.13	24	0.07

Ratings
Reward   C+
Risk   C+
Recent Upgrade/Downgrade

Fund Information
Fund Type   Exchange Traded Funds
Category   US Fixed Income
Sub-Category   Corporate Bond
Prospectus Objective   Corp Bond - Gen
Inception Date   Feb-09
Open to New Investments   Y

Prices
Price (as of 9/30/2019)   35.28
52-Week High   35.46
52-Week Low   32.78

Total Returns (%)

3-Month	6-Month	1-Year	3-Year	5-Year
1.74	5.17	9.47	10.54	19.19

3-Year Standard Deviation   2.65
Effective Duration   4.29

Valuation
Premium/Discount (1-Year Average)   0.02

Company Information
Provider   SPDR State Street Global Advisors
Manager/Tenure   Kyle Kelly (6), Christopher DiStefano (4), Frank Miethe (2)
Website   http://www.spdrs.com
Address   SPDR State Street Global Advisors State Street Financial Center, 1 Lincoln Street Boston MA 02111-2900 United States
Phone Number   617-786-3000

PERFORMANCE

Ratings History

Date	Overall Rating	Risk Rating	Reward Rating
Q3-19	C+	C+	C+
Q4-18	C	C+	C-
Q4-17	B	A	C
Q4-16	C	C+	C
Q4-15	C	C+	C

Asset & Performance History

Date	NAV	1-Year Total Return
2018	33.06	-0.35
2017	34.2	3.48
2016	33.87	4.01
2015	33.43	0.91
2014	34.01	4.12
2013	33.54	-0.19

Total Assets: $4,860,112,961
Asset Allocation

Asset	%
Cash	0%
Stocks	0%
US Stocks	0%
Bonds	97%
US Bonds	84%
Other	0%

Services Offered:

Investment Strategy: The investment seeks to provide investment results that correspond generally to the price and yield performance of the Bloomberg Barclays U.S. Intermediate Corporate Bond Index. The fund invests substantially all, but at least 80%, of its total assets in the securities comprising the index or in securities that the Adviser determines have economic characteristics that are substantially identical to the economic characteristics of the securities that comprise the index. The index is designed to measure the performance of U.S. corporate bonds that have a maturity of greater than or equal to 1 year and less than 10 years. It is non-diversified. **Top Holdings:** Dominion Energy Inc 2.72% Oracle Corporation 2.5% CVS Health Corp 4.3% BB&T Corporation 2.75% AbbVie Inc. 3.6%

SPDR® Portfolio Developed World ex-US ETF   C   HOLD

Ticker	Traded On	NAV	Total Assets ($)	Dividend Yield (TTM)	Turnover Ratio	Expense Ratio
SPDW	NYSE Arca		$4,808,906,698	2.93	3	0.04

Ratings
Reward   C
Risk   C+
Recent Upgrade/Downgrade

Fund Information
Fund Type   Exchange Traded Funds
Category   Global Equity Large Cap
Sub-Category   Foreign Large Blend
Prospectus Objective   Foreign Stock
Inception Date   Apr-07
Open to New Investments   Y

Prices
Price (as of 9/30/2019)   29.36
52-Week High   30.85
52-Week Low   25.64

Total Returns (%)

3-Month	6-Month	1-Year	3-Year	5-Year
-0.62	1.56	-1.54	20.68	18.55

3-Year Standard Deviation   11.2
Effective Duration

Valuation
Premium/Discount (1-Year Average)   0.02

Company Information
Provider   SPDR State Street Global Advisors
Manager/Tenure   Michael J. Feehily (8), Karl A. Schneider (4), Kala O'Donnell (2)
Website   http://www.spdrs.com
Address   SPDR State Street Global Advisors State Street Financial Center, 1 Lincoln Street Boston MA 02111-2900 United States
Phone Number   617-786-3000

PERFORMANCE

Ratings History

Date	Overall Rating	Risk Rating	Reward Rating
Q3-19	C	C+	C
Q4-18	C-	C	D+
Q4-17	B	B	B
Q4-16	C-	C	D+
Q4-15	C	C+	C-

Asset & Performance History

Date	NAV	1-Year Total Return
2018	26.47	-14.23
2017	31.73	25.55
2016	25.78	1.85
2015	25.86	-1.79
2014	27.03	-4.04
2013	29.1	19.52

Total Assets: $4,808,906,698
Asset Allocation

Asset	%
Cash	0%
Stocks	100%
US Stocks	2%
Bonds	0%
US Bonds	0%
Other	0%

Services Offered:

Investment Strategy: The investment seeks investment results that, before fees and expenses, correspond generally to the total return performance of the S&P Developed Ex-U.S. BMI Index. The fund generally invests substantially all, but at least 80%, of its total assets in the securities comprising the index and in depositary receipts based on securities comprising the index. The index is a market capitalization weighted index designed to define and measure the investable universe of publicly traded companies domiciled in developed countries outside the United States. The fund is non-diversified. **Top Holdings:** Nestle SA Novartis AG Roche Holding AG Dividend Right Cert. Samsung Electronics Co Ltd GDR Toyota Motor Corp

VanEck Vectors J.P. Morgan EM Local Currency Bond ETF   B-   BUY

Ticker	Traded On	NAV	Total Assets ($)	Dividend Yield (TTM)	Turnover Ratio	Expense Ratio
EMLC	NYSE Arca	33.27	$4,797,671,392	6.44	36	0.3

Ratings
Reward	B
Risk	C+
Recent Upgrade/Downgrade	

Fund Information
Fund Type	Exchange Traded Funds
Category	Emerging Mkts Fixed Inc
Sub-Category	Emerging-Markets Local-Currency Bond
Prospectus Objective	Div Emerg Mkts
Inception Date	Jul-10
Open to New Investments	Y

Prices
Price (as of 9/30/2019)	33.00
52-Week High	35.17
52-Week Low	32.12

Total Returns (%)
3-Month	6-Month	1-Year	3-Year	5-Year
-2.80	1.85	7.90	108.53	94.33

3-Year Standard Deviation	10.08
Effective Duration	5.23

Valuation
Premium/Discount (1-Year Average)	-0.18

Company Information
Provider	VanEck
Manager/Tenure	Francis G. Rodilosso (7)
Website	http://www.vaneck.com
Address	Van Eck Associates Corporation 666 Third Avenue New York NY 10017 United States
Phone Number	800-826-1115

PERFORMANCE

Ratings History
Date	Overall Rating	Risk Rating	Reward Rating
Q3-19	B-	C+	B
Q4-18	B	C+	A
Q4-17	C	C	C
Q4-16	D+	D+	D
Q4-15	D	D	D

Asset & Performance History
Date	NAV	1-Year Total Return
2018	32.96	83.81
2017	18.96	13.98
2016	17.56	8.76
2015	17	-14.63
2014	21.06	-5.62
2013	23.57	-8.76

Total Assets: $4,797,671,392
Asset Allocation
Asset	%
Cash	1%
Stocks	0%
US Stocks	0%
Bonds	99%
US Bonds	0%
Other	0%

Services Offered:

Investment Strategy: The investment seeks to replicate as closely as possible, before fees and expenses, the price and yield performance of the J.P. Morgan GBI-EM Global Core Index. The fund normally invests at least 80% of its total assets in securities that comprise the fund's benchmark index. The index is comprised of bonds issued by emerging market governments and denominated in the local currency of the issuer. It may concentrate its investments in a particular industry or group of industries to the extent that the index concentrates in an industry or group of industries. The fund is non-diversified. **Top Holdings:** Brazil (Federative Republic) 10% Dominican Republic 8.9% Philippines (Republic Of) 6.25% Uruguay (Republic of) 9.88% Brazil (Federative Republic) 10%

Schwab Intermediate-Term U.S. Treasury ETF™   C   HOLD

Ticker	Traded On	NAV	Total Assets ($)	Dividend Yield (TTM)	Turnover Ratio	Expense Ratio
SCHR	NYSE Arca	55.57	$4,789,912,973	2.31	41	0.06

Ratings
Reward	C
Risk	C+
Recent Upgrade/Downgrade	

Fund Information
Fund Type	Exchange Traded Funds
Category	US Fixed Income
Sub-Category	Intermediate Government
Prospectus Objective	Govt Bond - Treasury
Inception Date	Aug-10
Open to New Investments	Y

Prices
Price (as of 9/30/2019)	55.56
52-Week High	56.19
52-Week Low	51.34

Total Returns (%)
3-Month	6-Month	1-Year	3-Year	5-Year
1.78	5.06	9.93	6.10	14.16

3-Year Standard Deviation	3.47
Effective Duration	5.19

Valuation
Premium/Discount (1-Year Average)	0.03

Company Information
Provider	Schwab ETFs
Manager/Tenure	Matthew Hastings (9), Mark R. McKissick (2)
Website	http://www.schwabfunds.com
Address	Schwab ETFs United States
Phone Number	800-435-4000

PERFORMANCE

Ratings History
Date	Overall Rating	Risk Rating	Reward Rating
Q3-19	C	C+	C
Q4-18	C-	C	D
Q4-17	C	C	C
Q4-16	C	C-	C
Q4-15	C	C-	C

Asset & Performance History
Date	NAV	1-Year Total Return
2018	52.89	1.28
2017	53.35	1.63
2016	53.41	1.16
2015	53.55	1.61
2014	53.52	4.26
2013	52.08	-2.85

Total Assets: $4,789,912,973
Asset Allocation
Asset	%
Cash	0%
Stocks	0%
US Stocks	0%
Bonds	100%
US Bonds	100%
Other	0%

Services Offered:

Investment Strategy: The investment seeks to track as closely as possible, before fees and expenses, the total return of the Bloomberg Barclays US Treasury 3-10 Year Index. The fund will invest at least 90% of its net assets (including, for this purpose, any borrowings for investment purposes) in securities included in the index. The index includes all publicly-issued U.S. Treasury securities that have a remaining maturity of greater than or equal to three years and less than ten years, are rated investment grade, and have $300 million or more of outstanding face value. The securities in the index must be denominated in U.S. dollars and must be fixed-rate and non-convertible. **Top Holdings:** United States Treasury Notes 2.88% United States Treasury Notes 3.12% United States Treasury Notes 2.88% United States Treasury Notes 2% United States Treasury Notes 2.25%

Vanguard Long-Term Corporate Bond Index Fund ETF Shares   B-   BUY

Ticker	Traded On	NAV	Total Assets ($)	Dividend Yield (TTM)	Turnover Ratio	Expense Ratio
VCLT	NAS CM	100.93	$4,732,399,516	3.88	48	0.07

Ratings
Reward	B
Risk	C+
Recent Upgrade/Downgrade	

Fund Information
Fund Type	Exchange Traded Funds
Category	US Fixed Income
Sub-Category	Long-Term Bond
Prospectus Objective	Corp Bond - Gen
Inception Date	Nov-09
Open to New Investments	Y

Prices
Price (as of 9/30/2019)	101.14
52-Week High	103.47
52-Week Low	83.50

Total Returns (%)
3-Month	6-Month	1-Year	3-Year	5-Year
5.58	12.86	19.93	20.12	39.51

3-Year Standard Deviation	7.73
Effective Duration	14.36

Valuation
Premium/Discount (1-Year Average)	0.22

Company Information
Provider	Vanguard
Manager/Tenure	Joshua C. Barrickman (9)
Website	http://www.vanguard.com
Address	Vanguard 100 Vanguard Boulevard
	Malvern PA 19355 United States
Phone Number	877-662-7447

PERFORMANCE

Ratings History
Date	Overall Rating	Risk Rating	Reward Rating
Q3-19	B-	C+	B
Q4-18	C-	C	D+
Q4-17	B-	B	B-
Q4-16	C	C+	C
Q4-15	C	C	C

Asset & Performance History
Date	NAV	1-Year Total Return
2018	84.83	-7.21
2017	95.55	12.48
2016	88.62	10.6
2015	83.65	-4.62
2014	91.71	16.74
2013	82.13	-5.92

Total Assets: $4,732,399,516
Asset Allocation
Asset	%
Cash	0%
Stocks	0%
US Stocks	0%
Bonds	99%
US Bonds	89%
Other	0%

Services Offered:

Investment Strategy: The investment seeks to track the performance of a market-weighted corporate bond index with a long-term dollar-weighted average maturity. The fund employs an indexing investment approach designed to track the performance of the Bloomberg Barclays U.S. 10+ Year Corporate Bond Index. This index includes U.S. dollar-denominated, investment-grade, fixed-rate, taxable securities issued by industrial, utility, and financial companies, with maturities greater than 10 years. Under normal circumstances, at least 80% of the fund's assets will be invested in bonds included in the index. **Top Holdings:** Anheuser-Busch Companies LLC / Anheuser-Busch InBev Worldwide Inc 4.9%   GE Capital International Funding Company Unlimited Company 4.42%   CVS Health Corp 5.05%   Goldman Sachs Group, Inc. 6.75%   Anheuser-Busch Companies LLC / Anheuser-Busch InBev Worldwide Inc 4.7%

SPDR® Portfolio Aggregate Bond ETF   C+   HOLD

Ticker	Traded On	NAV	Total Assets ($)	Dividend Yield (TTM)	Turnover Ratio	Expense Ratio
SPAB	NYSE Arca		$4,694,132,394	2.93	82	0.04

Ratings
Reward	C+
Risk	C+
Recent Upgrade/Downgrade	Up

Fund Information
Fund Type	Exchange Traded Funds
Category	US Fixed Income
Sub-Category	Intermediate Core Bond
Prospectus Objective	Multisector Bond
Inception Date	May-07
Open to New Investments	Y

Prices
Price (as of 9/30/2019)	29.64
52-Week High	29.86
52-Week Low	27.25

Total Returns (%)
3-Month	6-Month	1-Year	3-Year	5-Year
2.32	5.77	10.33	8.78	17.68

3-Year Standard Deviation	3.37
Effective Duration	5.72

Valuation
Premium/Discount (1-Year Average)	0.06

Company Information
Provider	SPDR State Street Global Advisors
Manager/Tenure	Marc DiCosimo (5), Michael Przygoda (4), Nicholas Fischer (0)
Website	http://www.spdrs.com
Address	SPDR State Street Global Advisors
	State Street Financial Center, 1
	Lincoln Street Boston MA 02111-2900
	United States
Phone Number	617-786-3000

PERFORMANCE

Ratings History
Date	Overall Rating	Risk Rating	Reward Rating
Q3-19	C+	C+	C+
Q4-18	C-	C+	D+
Q4-17	B-	B+	C
Q4-16	C	C-	C
Q4-15	C	C-	C

Asset & Performance History
Date	NAV	1-Year Total Return
2018	27.83	-0.13
2017	28.7	3.27
2016	28.48	2.5
2015	28.49	0.49
2014	29.08	5.84
2013	28.16	-2.07

Total Assets: $4,694,132,394
Asset Allocation
Asset	%
Cash	4%
Stocks	0%
US Stocks	0%
Bonds	96%
US Bonds	89%
Other	0%

Services Offered:

Investment Strategy: The investment seeks to provide investment results that, before fees and expenses, correspond generally to the price and yield performance of the Bloomberg Barclays U.S. Aggregate Bond Index. The fund generally invests substantially all, but at least 80%, of its total assets in the securities comprising the index or in securities that the Adviser determines have economic characteristics that are substantially identical to the economic characteristics of the securities that comprise the index. The index is designed to measure the performance of the U.S. dollar denominated investment grade bond market. The fund is non-diversified. **Top Holdings:** United States Treasury Bonds 4.62%   United States Treasury Notes 2.62%   United States Treasury Notes 2.62%   United States Treasury Bonds 2.88%   United States Treasury Notes 1.75%

Vanguard Mega Cap Growth Index Fund ETF Shares   B-   BUY

Ticker	Traded On	NAV	Total Assets ($)	Dividend Yield (TTM)	Turnover Ratio	Expense Ratio
MGK	NYSE Arca	132.63	$4,508,122,602	0.47	9	0.07

Ratings
Reward	B
Risk	C+
Recent Upgrade/Downgrade	Up

Fund Information
Fund Type	Exchange Traded Funds
Category	US Equity Large Cap Growth
Sub-Category	Large Growth
Prospectus Objective	Growth
Inception Date	Dec-07
Open to New Investments	Y

Prices
Price (as of 9/30/2019)	132.66
52-Week High	135.16
52-Week Low	99.52

Total Returns (%)
3-Month	6-Month	1-Year	3-Year	5-Year
0.71	5.07	2.88	55.40	80.04

3-Year Standard Deviation	13.35
Effective Duration	

Valuation
Premium/Discount (1-Year Average)	-0.01

Company Information
Provider	Vanguard
Manager/Tenure	Gerard C. O'Reilly (4), Michael A. Johnson (3)
Website	http://www.vanguard.com
Address	Vanguard 100 Vanguard Boulevard Malvern PA 19355 United States
Phone Number	877-662-7447

PERFORMANCE

Ratings History
Date	Overall Rating	Risk Rating	Reward Rating
Q3-19	B-	C+	B
Q4-18	C	C+	C
Q4-17	B	B	B
Q4-16	C+	C-	B-
Q4-15	C+	B-	C+

Asset & Performance History
Date	NAV	1-Year Total Return
2018	106.03	-3.67
2017	111.2	29.26
2016	87.02	6.03
2015	83.07	3.71
2014	81.24	13.65
2013	72.42	32.48

Total Assets: $4,508,122,602

Asset Allocation
Asset	%
Cash	0%
Stocks	100%
US Stocks	99%
Bonds	0%
US Bonds	0%
Other	0%

Services Offered:

Investment Strategy: The investment seeks to track the performance of the CRSP US Mega Cap Growth Index. The fund employs an indexing investment approach designed to track the performance of the index. The index is a float-adjusted, market-capitalization-weighted index designed to measure equity market performance of mega-capitalization growth stocks in the United States. The Advisor attempts to replicate the target index by investing all, or substantially all, of its assets in the stocks that make up the index, holding each stock in approximately the same proportion as its weighting in the index. The fund is non-diversified. **Top Holdings:** Microsoft Corp Apple Inc Amazon.com Inc Facebook Inc A Alphabet Inc A

First Trust Preferred Securities and Income ETF   B-   BUY

Ticker	Traded On	NAV	Total Assets ($)	Dividend Yield (TTM)	Turnover Ratio	Expense Ratio
FPE	NYSE Arca	19.71	$4,424,785,872	5.55		0.85

Ratings
Reward	B-
Risk	C+
Recent Upgrade/Downgrade	

Fund Information
Fund Type	Exchange Traded Funds
Category	US Fixed Income
Sub-Category	Preferred Stock
Prospectus Objective	Income
Inception Date	Feb-13
Open to New Investments	Y

Prices
Price (as of 9/30/2019)	19.73
52-Week High	19.84
52-Week Low	17.82

Total Returns (%)
3-Month	6-Month	1-Year	3-Year	5-Year
2.96	6.32	9.47	19.68	38.94

3-Year Standard Deviation	4.42
Effective Duration	3.70

Valuation
Premium/Discount (1-Year Average)	0.12

Company Information
Provider	First Trust
Manager/Tenure	Scott T. Fleming (6), Robert Wolf (6)
Website	http://www.ftportfolios.com/
Address	First Trust 120 E. Liberty Drive, Suite 400 Wheaton IL 60187 United States
Phone Number	800-621-1675

PERFORMANCE

Ratings History
Date	Overall Rating	Risk Rating	Reward Rating
Q3-19	B-	C+	B-
Q4-18	C	C+	D+
Q4-17	B	A-	C+
Q4-16	C	C+	C
Q4-15	C	C+	C

Asset & Performance History
Date	NAV	1-Year Total Return
2018	17.98	-4.68
2017	19.99	11.35
2016	18.95	6.46
2015	18.89	6.21
2014	18.79	10.91
2013	17.98	

Total Assets: $4,424,785,872

Asset Allocation
Asset	%
Cash	3%
Stocks	0%
US Stocks	0%
Bonds	36%
US Bonds	20%
Other	0%

Services Offered:

Investment Strategy: The investment seeks total return and to provide current income. Under normal market conditions, the fund invests at least 80% of its net assets (including investment borrowings) in preferred securities ("Preferred Securities") and income-producing debt securities ("Income Securities"). The fund invests in securities that are traded over-the-counter or listed on an exchange. **Top Holdings:** EMERA INCORPORATED 6.75% Enel - Societa per Azioni 8.75% GMAC Capital Trust I Pfd Secs 2011-15.2.40 Gtd Series 2 Catlin Insurance Company Ltd. 5.28% BHP Billiton Finance (USA) Limited 1.69%

Schwab Fundamental International Large Company Index ETF   C   HOLD

Ticker	Traded On	NAV	Total Assets ($)	Dividend Yield (TTM)	Turnover Ratio	Expense Ratio
FNDF	NYSE Arca	27.48	$4,424,532,285	4	14	0.25

Ratings
Reward   C-
Risk   C+
Recent Upgrade/Downgrade

Fund Information
Fund Type   Exchange Traded Funds
Category   Global Equity Large Cap
Sub-Category   Foreign Large Value
Prospectus Objective   World Stock
Inception Date   Aug-13
Open to New Investments   Y

Prices
Price (as of 9/30/2019)   27.57
52-Week High   30.01
52-Week Low   24.38

Total Returns (%)

3-Month	6-Month	1-Year	3-Year	5-Year
-1.82	-0.56	-4.30	19.68	14.48

3-Year Standard Deviation   11.7
Effective Duration

Valuation
Premium/Discount (1-Year Average)   0.07

Company Information
Provider   Schwab ETFs
Manager/Tenure   Chuck Craig (6), Jane Qin (6),
          Christopher Bliss (2), 1 other
Website   http://www.schwabfunds.com
Address   Schwab ETFs United States
Phone Number   800-435-4000

PERFORMANCE

Ratings History

Date	Overall Rating	Risk Rating	Reward Rating
Q3-19	C	C+	C-
Q4-18	C-	C-	D+
Q4-17	B-	C	B
Q4-16	C-	C-	D+
Q4-15	C-	C+	D

Asset & Performance History

Date	NAV	1-Year Total Return
2018	25.24	-14.18
2017	30.4	23.85
2016	25.13	7.7
2015	23.9	-5.14
2014	25.73	-5.04
2013	27.59	

Total Assets: $4,424,532,285
Asset Allocation

Asset	%
Cash	0%
Stocks	100%
US Stocks	1%
Bonds	0%
US Bonds	0%
Other	0%

Services Offered:

Investment Strategy: The investment seeks to track as closely as possible, before fees and expenses, the total return of the Russell RAFI™ Developed ex US Large Company Index. The fund will invest at least 90% of its net assets in stocks included in the index, including depositary receipts representing securities of the index; which may be in the form of American Depositary Receipts, Global Depositary Receipts and European Depositary Receipts. The index measures the performance of the large company size segment by fundamental overall company scores, which are created using as the universe the developed ex U.S. companies in the FTSE Global Total Cap Index (the parent index). **Top Holdings:** Toyota Motor Corp Samsung Electronics Co Ltd BP PLC Nestle SA Total SA

iShares China Large-Cap ETF   C-   HOLD

Ticker	Traded On	NAV	Total Assets ($)	Dividend Yield (TTM)	Turnover Ratio	Expense Ratio
FXI	NYSE Arca	40.08	$4,274,750,041	2.13	14	0.74

Ratings
Reward   D+
Risk   C
Recent Upgrade/Downgrade   Down

Fund Information
Fund Type   Exchange Traded Funds
Category   Greater China Equity
Sub-Category   China Region
Prospectus Objective   Pacific Stock
Inception Date   Oct-04
Open to New Investments   Y

Prices
Price (as of 9/30/2019)   39.80
52-Week High   45.85
52-Week Low   37.67

Total Returns (%)

3-Month	6-Month	1-Year	3-Year	5-Year
-6.17	-9.67	-4.68	15.49	19.41

3-Year Standard Deviation   17.43
Effective Duration

Valuation
Premium/Discount (1-Year Average)   -0.05

Company Information
Provider   iShares
Manager/Tenure   Diane Hsiung (11), Greg Savage (11),
          Jennifer Hsui (6), 3 others
Website   http://www.ishares.com
Address   iShares 400 Howard Street San
          Francisco CA 94105 United States
Phone Number   800-474-2737

PERFORMANCE

Ratings History

Date	Overall Rating	Risk Rating	Reward Rating
Q3-19	C-	C	D+
Q4-18	C-	C	C-
Q4-17	B	C	A-
Q4-16	C-	C-	C
Q4-15	C	C	C

Asset & Performance History

Date	NAV	1-Year Total Return
2018	39.47	-12.4
2017	46.18	34.47
2016	35.17	1.74
2015	35.52	-11.9
2014	41.41	12.02
2013	37.98	-1.2

Total Assets: $4,274,750,041
Asset Allocation

Asset	%
Cash	0%
Stocks	100%
US Stocks	0%
Bonds	0%
US Bonds	0%
Other	0%

Services Offered: Dividend Investment Plan, CashInvestment Plan

Investment Strategy: The investment seeks to track the investment results of the FTSE China 50 Index composed of large-capitalization Chinese equities that trade on the Hong Kong Stock Exchange. The fund generally invests at least 90% of its assets in securities of the underlying index and in depositary receipts representing securities of the underlying index. The index designed to measure the performance of the largest companies in the Chinese equity market that trade on the Stock Exchange of Hong Kong ("SEHK") and are available to international investors, as determined by FTSE International Limited (the "Index Provider" or "FTSE"). The fund is non-diversified. **Top Holdings:** Tencent Holdings Ltd China Construction Bank Corp Class H Ping An Insurance (Group) Co. of China Ltd Class H Industrial And Commercial Bank Of China Ltd Class H China Mobile Ltd

iShares U.S. Medical Devices ETF   B   BUY

Ticker	Traded On	NAV	Total Assets ($)	Dividend Yield (TTM)	Turnover Ratio	Expense Ratio
IHI	NYSE Arca	247.43	$4,268,157,193	0.3	36	0.43

Ratings
Reward	B+
Risk	C+
Recent Upgrade/Downgrade	Up

Fund Information
Fund Type	Exchange Traded Funds
Category	Healthcare Sector Equity
Sub-Category	Health
Prospectus Objective	Health
Inception Date	May-06
Open to New Investments	Y

Prices
Price (as of 9/30/2019)	247.24
52-Week High	251.72
52-Week Low	183.66

Total Returns (%)
3-Month	6-Month	1-Year	3-Year	5-Year
2.12	7.24	9.05	72.08	156.02

3-Year Standard Deviation	15.35
Effective Duration	

Valuation
Premium/Discount (1-Year Average)	0.01

Company Information
Provider	iShares
Manager/Tenure	Greg Savage (11), Jennifer Hsui (7), Alan Mason (3), 2 others
Website	http://www.ishares.com
Address	iShares 400 Howard Street San Francisco CA 94105 United States
Phone Number	800-474-2737

PERFORMANCE

Ratings History
Date	Overall Rating	Risk Rating	Reward Rating
Q3-19	B	C+	B+
Q4-18	B-	C	B
Q4-17	B+	A-	B+
Q4-16	B-	C+	B
Q4-15	C	C	C

Asset & Performance History
Date	NAV	1-Year Total Return
2018	199.77	15.46
2017	173.46	30.93
2016	132.99	9.18
2015	122.47	9.68
2014	113.11	22.64
2013	92.87	37.75

Total Assets: $4,268,157,193

Asset Allocation
Asset	%
Cash	0%
Stocks	100%
US Stocks	100%
Bonds	0%
US Bonds	0%
Other	0%

Services Offered:

Investment Strategy: The investment seeks to track the investment results of the Dow Jones U.S. Select Medical Equipment Index composed of U.S. equities in the medical devices sector. The fund generally invests at least 90% of its assets in securities of the underlying index and in depositary receipts representing securities of the underlying index. The underlying index includes medical equipment companies, including manufacturers and distributors of medical devices such as magnetic resonance imaging (MRI) scanners, prosthetics, pacemakers, X-ray machines, and other non-disposable medical devices. The fund is non-diversified. **Top Holdings:** Abbott Laboratories Medtronic PLC Thermo Fisher Scientific Inc Danaher Corp Edwards Lifesciences Corp

---

iShares International Select Dividend ETF   C   HOLD

Ticker	Traded On	NAV	Total Assets ($)	Dividend Yield (TTM)	Turnover Ratio	Expense Ratio
IDV	BATS	30.75	$4,250,616,372	5.9	35	0.49

Ratings
Reward	C
Risk	C+
Recent Upgrade/Downgrade	

Fund Information
Fund Type	Exchange Traded Funds
Category	Global Equity Large Cap
Sub-Category	Foreign Large Value
Prospectus Objective	Foreign Stock
Inception Date	Jun-07
Open to New Investments	Y

Prices
Price (as of 9/30/2019)	30.74
52-Week High	32.63
52-Week Low	27.96

Total Returns (%)
3-Month	6-Month	1-Year	3-Year	5-Year
0.84	2.21	-0.09	19.50	11.25

3-Year Standard Deviation	11.32
Effective Duration	

Valuation
Premium/Discount (1-Year Average)	-0.03

Company Information
Provider	iShares
Manager/Tenure	Greg Savage (11), Jennifer Hsui (7), Alan Mason (3), 2 others
Website	http://www.ishares.com
Address	iShares 400 Howard Street San Francisco CA 94105 United States
Phone Number	800-474-2737

PERFORMANCE

Ratings History
Date	Overall Rating	Risk Rating	Reward Rating
Q3-19	C	C+	C
Q4-18	C	C+	D+
Q4-17	C+	C+	C+
Q4-16	D+	D+	D+
Q4-15	C-	D+	C

Asset & Performance History
Date	NAV	1-Year Total Return
2018	28.76	-10.49
2017	33.91	19.58
2016	29.71	7.71
2015	28.92	-10.91
2014	34.02	-4.89
2013	37.75	20.01

Total Assets: $4,250,616,372

Asset Allocation
Asset	%
Cash	1%
Stocks	99%
US Stocks	0%
Bonds	0%
US Bonds	0%
Other	0%

Services Offered:

Investment Strategy: The investment seeks to track the investment results of the Dow Jones EPAC Select Dividend Index composed of relatively high dividend paying equities in non-U.S. developed markets. The fund generally will invest at least 90% of its assets in the component securities of the underlying index and in investments that have economic characteristics that are substantially identical to the component securities of the underlying index. The underlying index measures the performance of high dividend-paying companies in the EPAC (Europe, Pacific, Asia and Canada) region. **Top Holdings:** British American Tobacco PLC Commonwealth Bank of Australia Azimut Holding SPA Royal Dutch Shell PLC Class A Wesfarmers Ltd

Materials Select Sector SPDR® Fund   B-   BUY

Ticker	Traded On	NAV	Total Assets ($)	Dividend Yield (TTM)	Turnover Ratio	Expense Ratio
XLB	NYSE Arca		$4,245,101,675	2.06	17	0.13

Ratings
Reward   B
Risk   C
Recent Upgrade/Downgrade   Up

Fund Information
Fund Type   Exchange Traded Funds
Category   Natural Resources
Sub-Category   Natural Resources
Prospectus Objective   Natl Res
Inception Date   Dec-98
Open to New Investments Y

Prices
Price (as of 9/30/2019)   58.20
52-Week High   59.46
52-Week Low   47.34

Total Returns (%)

3-Month	6-Month	1-Year	3-Year	5-Year
-1.56	3.65	0.83	28.34	28.82

3-Year Standard Deviation   14.24
Effective Duration

Valuation
Premium/Discount (1-Year Average)   -0.01

Company Information
Provider   SPDR State Street Global Advisors
Manager/Tenure   Michael J. Feehily (8), Karl A.
                  Schneider (4), Ted Janowsky (2)
Website   http://www.spdrs.com
Address   SPDR State Street Global Advisors
                  State Street Financial Center, 1
                  Lincoln Street Boston MA 02111-2900
                  United States
Phone Number   617-786-3000

PERFORMANCE

Ratings History

Date	Overall Rating	Risk Rating	Reward Rating
Q3-19	B-	C	B
Q4-18	C	C-	B-
Q4-17	B	C	B
Q4-16	C+	C	B
Q4-15	B	B-	B

Asset & Performance History

Date	NAV	1-Year Total Return
2018	50.53	-14.77
2017	60.48	23.95
2016	49.68	16.6
2015	43.46	-8.6
2014	48.59	7.31
2013	46.17	25.81

Total Assets: $4,245,101,675
Asset Allocation

Asset	%
Cash	0%
Stocks	100%
US Stocks	82%
Bonds	0%
US Bonds	0%
Other	0%

Services Offered: Dividend Investment Plan, CashInvestment Plan

Investment Strategy: The investment seeks to provide investment results that, before expenses, correspond generally to the price and yield performance of publicly traded equity securities of companies in the Materials Select Sector Index. In seeking to track the performance of the index, the fund employs a replication strategy. It generally invests substantially all, but at least 95%, of its total assets in the securities comprising the index. The index includes securities of companies from the following industries: chemicals; metals and mining; paper and forest products; containers and packaging; and construction materials. The fund is non-diversified. **Top Holdings:** Linde PLC Ecolab Inc DuPont de Nemours Inc Air Products & Chemicals Inc Sherwin-Williams Co

VanEck Vectors Junior Gold Miners ETF   C   HOLD

Ticker	Traded On	NAV	Total Assets ($)	Dividend Yield (TTM)	Turnover Ratio	Expense Ratio
GDXJ	NYSE Arca	36.59	$4,179,981,598	0.37	28	0.54

Ratings
Reward   C
Risk   C-
Recent Upgrade/Downgrade   Up

Fund Information
Fund Type   Exchange Traded Funds
Category   Prec Metals
Sub-Category   Equity Precious Metals
Prospectus Objective   Prec Metals
Inception Date   Nov-09
Open to New Investments Y

Prices
Price (as of 9/30/2019)   36.26
52-Week High   42.74
52-Week Low   26.17

Total Returns (%)

3-Month	6-Month	1-Year	3-Year	5-Year
8.35	18.03	34.31	-12.32	15.73

3-Year Standard Deviation   27.31
Effective Duration

Valuation
Premium/Discount (1-Year Average)   -0.30

Company Information
Provider   VanEck
Manager/Tenure   Hao-Hung (Peter) Liao (9), Guo Hua
                  (Jason) Jin (1)
Website   http://www.vaneck.com
Address   Van Eck Associates Corporation 666
                  Third Avenue New York NY 10017
                  United States
Phone Number   800-826-1115

PERFORMANCE

Ratings History

Date	Overall Rating	Risk Rating	Reward Rating
Q3-19	C	C-	C
Q4-18	D	D	D+
Q4-17	C-	D	C
Q4-16	C-	D+	C
Q4-15	D-	D-	D-

Asset & Performance History

Date	NAV	1-Year Total Return
2018	30.11	-11.47
2017	34.21	7.88
2016	31.72	73.83
2015	19.22	-19.47
2014	24.04	-21.57
2013	30.9	-60.94

Total Assets: $4,179,981,598
Asset Allocation

Asset	%
Cash	0%
Stocks	100%
US Stocks	2%
Bonds	0%
US Bonds	0%
Other	0%

Services Offered:

Investment Strategy: The investment seeks to replicate as closely as possible, before fees and expenses, the price and yield performance of the MVIS® Global Junior Gold Miners Index. The fund normally invests at least 80% of its total assets in securities that comprise the index. The index includes companies that generate at least 50% of their revenues from gold and/or silver mining/royalties/streaming or have mining projects with the potential to generate at least 50% of their revenues from gold and/or silver when developed. It is non-diversified. **Top Holdings:** Kinross Gold Corp Evolution Mining Ltd Northern Star Resources Ltd Gold Fields Ltd ADR Pan American Silver Corp

JPMorgan BetaBuilders Japan ETF   C-   HOLD

Ticker	Traded On	NAV	Total Assets ($)	Dividend Yield (TTM)	Turnover Ratio	Expense Ratio
BBJP	BATS	23.66	$4,135,357,152	0.58		0.19

Ratings
Reward	D
Risk	C
Recent Upgrade/Downgrade	Up

Fund Information
Fund Type	Exchange Traded Funds
Category	Japan Equity
Sub-Category	Japan Stock
Prospectus Objective	Pacific Stock
Inception Date	Jun-18
Open to New Investments	Y

Prices
Price (as of 9/30/2019)	23.74
52-Week High	25.13
52-Week Low	20.43

Total Returns (%)
3-Month	6-Month	1-Year	3-Year	5-Year
2.42	3.00	-4.48		

3-Year Standard Deviation	
Effective Duration	

Valuation
Premium/Discount (1-Year Average)	-0.06

Company Information
Provider	JPMorgan
Manager/Tenure	Nicholas D'Eramo (1), Oliver Furby (1), Alex Hamilton (1), 1 other
Website	http://www.jpmorganfunds.com
Address	JPMorgan 270 Park Avenue New York NY 10017-2070 United States
Phone Number	800-480-4111

PERFORMANCE

Ratings History
Date	Overall Rating	Risk Rating	Reward Rating
Q3-19	C-	C	D
Q4-18	U		
Q4-17			
Q4-16			
Q4-15			

Asset & Performance History
Date	NAV	1-Year Total Return
2018	21.17	
2017		
2016		
2015		
2014		
2013		

Total Assets: $4,135,357,152

Asset Allocation
Asset	%
Cash	0%
Stocks	100%
US Stocks	0%
Bonds	0%
US Bonds	0%
Other	0%

Services Offered:

Investment Strategy: The investment seeks investment results that closely correspond, before fees and expenses, to the performance of the Morningstar® Japan Target Market Exposure IndexSM. The fund will invest at least 80% of its assets in securities included in the underlying index. The underlying index is a free float adjusted market capitalization weighted index which consists of stocks traded primarily on the Tokyo Stock Exchange or the Nagoya Stock Exchange. The fund may invest up to 20% of its assets in exchange-traded futures and forward foreign currency contracts to seek performance that corresponds to the underlying index. **Top Holdings:** Toyota Motor Corp SoftBank Group Corp Sony Corp Mitsubishi UFJ Financial Group Inc Keyence Corp

iShares U.S. Technology ETF   B   BUY

Ticker	Traded On	NAV	Total Assets ($)	Dividend Yield (TTM)	Turnover Ratio	Expense Ratio
IYW	NYSE Arca	204.27	$4,126,232,299	0.8	19	0.42

Ratings
Reward	B+
Risk	C+
Recent Upgrade/Downgrade	Up

Fund Information
Fund Type	Exchange Traded Funds
Category	Technology Sector Equity
Sub-Category	Technology
Prospectus Objective	Technology
Inception Date	May-00
Open to New Investments	Y

Prices
Price (as of 9/30/2019)	204.21
52-Week High	211.51
52-Week Low	148.42

Total Returns (%)
3-Month	6-Month	1-Year	3-Year	5-Year
1.91	6.14	6.04	76.29	117.12

3-Year Standard Deviation	16.02
Effective Duration	

Valuation
Premium/Discount (1-Year Average)	-0.01

Company Information
Provider	iShares
Manager/Tenure	Greg Savage (11), Jennifer Hsui (7), Alan Mason (3), 2 others
Website	http://www.ishares.com
Address	iShares 400 Howard Street San Francisco CA 94105 United States
Phone Number	800-474-2737

PERFORMANCE

Ratings History
Date	Overall Rating	Risk Rating	Reward Rating
Q3-19	B	C+	B+
Q4-18	B-	C	B
Q4-17	A-	B	A+
Q4-16	B	C+	A-
Q4-15	B	B	B

Asset & Performance History
Date	NAV	1-Year Total Return
2018	159.77	-0.96
2017	162.67	36.58
2016	120.2	13.68
2015	107.02	3.66
2014	104.42	19.49
2013	88.43	26.47

Total Assets: $4,126,232,299

Asset Allocation
Asset	%
Cash	0%
Stocks	100%
US Stocks	99%
Bonds	0%
US Bonds	0%
Other	0%

Services Offered: CashInvestment Plan

Investment Strategy: The investment seeks to track the investment results of the Dow Jones U.S. Technology Capped Index. The fund generally invests at least 90% of its assets in securities of the underlying index and in depositary receipts representing securities of the underlying index. The underlying index measures the performance of U.S. companies in the technology sector. The fund is non-diversified. **Top Holdings:** Microsoft Corp Apple Inc Alphabet Inc Class C Alphabet Inc A Facebook Inc A

iShares MSCI South Korea Capped ETF   D   SELL

Ticker	Traded On	NAV	Total Assets ($)	Dividend Yield (TTM)	Turnover Ratio	Expense Ratio
EWY	NYSE Arca	56.71	$4,091,578,860	1.39	18	0.59

Ratings
Reward   D
Risk   D+
Recent Upgrade/Downgrade   Down

Fund Information
Fund Type   Exchange Traded Funds
Category   Korea Equity
Sub-Category   Miscellaneous Region
Prospectus Objective   Pacific Stock
Inception Date   May-00
Open to New Investments   Y

Prices
Price (as of 9/30/2019)   56.34
52-Week High   67.95
52-Week Low   51.18

Total Returns (%)

3-Month	6-Month	1-Year	3-Year	5-Year
-5.27	-8.47	-15.56	3.76	4.18

3-Year Standard Deviation   18.68
Effective Duration

Valuation
Premium/Discount (1-Year Average) -0.10

Company Information
Provider   iShares
Manager/Tenure   Diane Hsiung (11), Greg Savage (11),
                     Jennifer Hsui (6), 3 others
Website   http://www.ishares.com
Address   iShares 400 Howard Street San
                     Francisco CA 94105 United States
Phone Number   800-474-2737

PERFORMANCE

Ratings History				Asset & Performance History			Total Assets:	$4,091,578,860
Date	Overall Rating	Risk Rating	Reward Rating	Date	NAV	1-Year Total Return	Asset Allocation Asset	%
Q3-19	D	D+	D	2018	58.86	-20.3	Cash	0%
Q4-18	D+	D+	C-	2017	74.86	44.4	Stocks	100%
Q4-17	B	C	A	2016	53.38	7.12	US Stocks	0%
Q4-16	D+	C-	D+	2015	50.43	-6.72	Bonds	0%
Q4-15	D	D	D	2014	55.36	-11.9	US Bonds	0%
				2013	63.6	3.49	Other	0%

Services Offered: CashInvestment Plan

Investment Strategy: The investment seeks to track the investment results of the MSCI Korea 25/50 Index. The fund will at all times invest at least 80% of its assets in the securities of its underlying index and in depositary receipts representing securities in its underlying index. The underlying index is a free float-adjusted market capitalization-weighted index with a capping methodology applied to issuer weights so that no single issuer of a component exceeds 25% of the underlying index weight, and all issuers with a weight above 5% do not cumulatively exceed 50% of the underlying index weight. The fund is non-diversified. **Top Holdings:** Samsung Electronics Co Ltd SK Hynix Inc NAVER Corp Hyundai Motor Co Shinhan Financial Group Co Ltd

---

SPDR® Bloomberg Barclays Convertible Securities ETF   C+   HOLD

Ticker	Traded On	NAV	Total Assets ($)	Dividend Yield (TTM)	Turnover Ratio	Expense Ratio
CWB	NYSE Arca		$4,054,618,873	5.3	36	0.4

Ratings
Reward   C
Risk   C+
Recent Upgrade/Downgrade

Fund Information
Fund Type   Exchange Traded Funds
Category   Convertibles
Sub-Category   Convertibles
Prospectus Objective   Convertible Bond
Inception Date   Apr-09
Open to New Investments   Y

Prices
Price (as of 9/30/2019)   52.45
52-Week High   54.19
52-Week Low   45.13

Total Returns (%)

3-Month	6-Month	1-Year	3-Year	5-Year
-1.57	0.36	2.66	29.26	40.72

3-Year Standard Deviation   9.71
Effective Duration   2.77

Valuation
Premium/Discount (1-Year Average)   0.04

Company Information
Provider   SPDR State Street Global Advisors
Manager/Tenure   Michael J. Brunell (10), Christopher
                     DiStefano (3)
Website   http://www.spdrs.com
Address   SPDR State Street Global Advisors
                     State Street Financial Center, 1
                     Lincoln Street Boston MA 02111-2900
                     United States
Phone Number   617-786-3000

PERFORMANCE

Ratings History				Asset & Performance History			Total Assets:	$4,054,618,873
Date	Overall Rating	Risk Rating	Reward Rating	Date	NAV	1-Year Total Return	Asset Allocation Asset	%
Q3-19	C+	C+	C	2018	46.68	-2.31	Cash	0%
Q4-18	C	C+	C-	2017	50.67	14.54	Stocks	4%
Q4-17	B-	B-	B-	2016	45.5	10.83	US Stocks	4%
Q4-16	C+	C+	C+	2015	43.16	-0.6	Bonds	0%
Q4-15	C	C+	C	2014	46.66	7.5	US Bonds	0%
				2013	46.61	20.79	Other	1%

Services Offered:

Investment Strategy: The investment seeks to provide investment results that, before fees and expenses, correspond generally to the price and yield performance of the Bloomberg Barclays U.S. Convertible Liquid Bond Index. The fund generally invests substantially all, but at least 80%, of its total assets in the securities comprising the index or in securities that the Adviser determines have economic characteristics that are substantially identical to the economic characteristics of the securities that comprise the index. The index is designed to represent the market of U.S. convertible securities, such as convertible bonds and convertible preferred stock. It is non-diversified. **Top Holdings:** Wells Fargo & Co 7 1/2 % Non Cum Perp Conv Pfd Shs -A- Series -L- Bank of America Corporation 7 1/4 % Non-Cum Perp Conv Pfd Shs Series -L- Becton, Dickinson and Co Pfd Microchip Technology Incorporated 1.62% Advanced Micro Devices, Inc. 2.12%

iShares Core Total USD Bond Market ETF   C+   HOLD

Ticker	Traded On	NAV	Total Assets ($)	Dividend Yield (TTM)	Turnover Ratio	Expense Ratio
IUSB	NAS CM	52.34	$3,987,962,586	2.99	253	0.06

Ratings
Reward	C+
Risk	C+
Recent Upgrade/Downgrade	

Fund Information
Fund Type	Exchange Traded Funds
Category	US Fixed Income
Sub-Category	Intermediate Core-Plus Bond
Prospectus Objective	Corp Bond - Gen
Inception Date	Jun-14
Open to New Investments	Y

Prices
Price (as of 9/30/2019)	52.41
52-Week High	52.80
52-Week Low	48.37

Total Returns (%)
3-Month	6-Month	1-Year	3-Year	5-Year
2.18	5.59	10.07	9.75	18.78

3-Year Standard Deviation	3.11
Effective Duration	

Valuation
Premium/Discount (1-Year Average)	0.14

Company Information
Provider	iShares
Manager/Tenure	James Mauro (5), Scott Radell (5)
Website	http://www.ishares.com
Address	iShares 400 Howard Street San Francisco CA 94105 United States
Phone Number	800-474-2737

PERFORMANCE

Ratings History
Date	Overall Rating	Risk Rating	Reward Rating
Q3-19	C+	C+	C+
Q4-18	C	C+	D+
Q4-17	B	A	C
Q4-16	C-	C-	C-
Q4-15	D	D+	D+

Asset & Performance History
Date	NAV	1-Year Total Return
2018	49.14	-0.37
2017	50.82	4
2016	50.11	3.77
2015	49.54	0.46
2014	50.27	
2013		

Total Assets: $3,987,962,586
Asset Allocation
Asset	%
Cash	1%
Stocks	0%
US Stocks	0%
Bonds	98%
US Bonds	83%
Other	0%

Services Offered:

Investment Strategy: The investment seeks to track the investment results of the Bloomberg Barclays U.S. Universal Index. The fund generally will invest at least 90% of its assets in the component securities of the underlying index and may invest up to 10% of its assets in certain futures, options and swap contracts, cash and cash equivalents, including shares of money market funds advised by BFA or its affiliates, as well as in securities not included in the underlying index, but which BFA believes will help the fund track the underlying index. The index measures the performance of U.S. dollar-denominated taxable bonds that are rated either investment-grade or high yield. **Top Holdings:** United States Treasury Notes 2.5% United States Treasury Notes 2.63% United States Treasury Notes 2% Gnma2 30yr 2017 Production United States Treasury Notes 2.25%

iShares MSCI EAFE Growth ETF   C+   HOLD

Ticker	Traded On	NAV	Total Assets ($)	Dividend Yield (TTM)	Turnover Ratio	Expense Ratio
EFG	BATS	80.31	$3,951,038,230	1.72	22	0.4

Ratings
Reward	C
Risk	C+
Recent Upgrade/Downgrade	Up

Fund Information
Fund Type	Exchange Traded Funds
Category	Global Equity Large Cap
Sub-Category	Foreign Large Growth
Prospectus Objective	Foreign Stock
Inception Date	Aug-05
Open to New Investments	Y

Prices
Price (as of 9/30/2019)	80.51
52-Week High	82.17
52-Week Low	66.77

Total Returns (%)
3-Month	6-Month	1-Year	3-Year	5-Year
-0.98	4.27	1.99	24.24	30.06

3-Year Standard Deviation	11.45
Effective Duration	

Valuation
Premium/Discount (1-Year Average)	0.00

Company Information
Provider	iShares
Manager/Tenure	Diane Hsiung (11), Greg Savage (11), Jennifer Hsui (6), 3 others
Website	http://www.ishares.com
Address	iShares 400 Howard Street San Francisco CA 94105 United States
Phone Number	800-474-2737

PERFORMANCE

Ratings History
Date	Overall Rating	Risk Rating	Reward Rating
Q3-19	C+	C+	C
Q4-18	C-	C	D+
Q4-17	B	B	B
Q4-16	C-	C	C-
Q4-15	C	C+	C

Asset & Performance History
Date	NAV	1-Year Total Return
2018	69.02	-13.01
2017	80.78	28.49
2016	63.91	-3.33
2015	67.54	3.74
2014	66.19	-4.64
2013	70.96	22.15

Total Assets: $3,951,038,230
Asset Allocation
Asset	%
Cash	1%
Stocks	99%
US Stocks	3%
Bonds	0%
US Bonds	0%
Other	0%

Services Offered:

Investment Strategy: The investment seeks to track the investment results of the MSCI EAFE Growth Index composed of developed market equities, excluding the U.S. and Canada, that exhibit growth characteristics. The fund generally invests at least 90% of its assets in securities of the underlying index and in depositary receipts representing securities of the underlying index. The index is a subset of the MSCI EAFE Index. Constituents of the underlying index include securities of companies located in Europe, Australasia and the Far East. **Top Holdings:** Nestle SA Roche Holding AG Dividend Right Cert. Novartis AG SAP SE AIA Group Ltd

WisdomTree U.S. MidCap Dividend Fund

C   HOLD

Ticker	Traded On	NAV	Total Assets (s)	Dividend Yield (TTM)	Turnover Ratio	Expense Ratio
DON	NYSE Arca	36.29	$3,939,416,439	2.33	27	0.38

Ratings

Reward	C
Risk	C+
Recent Upgrade/Downgrade	

Fund Information

Fund Type	Exchange Traded Funds
Category	US Equity Mid Cap
Sub-Category	Mid-Cap Value
Prospectus Objective	Growth & Inc
Inception Date	Jun-06
Open to New Investments	Y

Prices

Price (as of 9/30/2019)	36.31
52-Week High	36.88
52-Week Low	29.98

Total Returns (%)

3-Month	6-Month	1-Year	3-Year	5-Year
0.64	1.68	1.22	28.63	59.78

3-Year Standard Deviation	13.58
Effective Duration	

Valuation

Premium/Discount (1-Year Average)	0.00

Company Information

Provider	WisdomTree
Manager/Tenure	Richard A. Brown (11), Thomas J. Durante (11), Karen Q. Wong (11)
Website	http://www.wisdomtree.com
Address	WisdomTree 245 Park Avenue, 35th floor New York NY 10167 United States
Phone Number	866-909-9473

PERFORMANCE

Ratings History

Date	Overall Rating	Risk Rating	Reward Rating
Q3-19	C	C+	C
Q4-18	C	C+	C-
Q4-17	B	B+	B
Q4-16	B	C+	B
Q4-15	C	C-	C

Asset & Performance History

Date	NAV	1-Year Total Return
2018	31.61	-8.27
2017	35.27	14.86
2016	31.45	20.29
2015	26.84	-0.97
2014	27.88	15.27
2013	24.85	32.98

Total Assets: $3,939,416,439

Asset Allocation

Asset	%
Cash	0%
Stocks	100%
US Stocks	100%
Bonds	0%
US Bonds	0%
Other	0%

Services Offered:

Investment Strategy: The investment seeks to track the price and yield performance, before fees and expenses, of the WisdomTree U.S. MidCap Dividend Index. Under normal circumstances, at least 95% of the fund's total assets (exclusive of collateral held from securities lending) will be invested in component securities of the index and investments that have economic characteristics that are substantially identical to the economic characteristics of such component securities. The index is a fundamentally weighted index that is comprised of the mid-capitalization segment of the U.S. dividend-paying market. The fund is non-diversified. **Top Holdings:** Targa Resources Corp Coty Inc Class A Campbell Soup Co Hasbro Inc The Western Union Co

Vanguard Russell 1000 Value Index Fund ETF Shares

C   HOLD

Ticker	Traded On	NAV	Total Assets (s)	Dividend Yield (TTM)	Turnover Ratio	Expense Ratio
VONV	NAS CM	112.36	$3,933,833,425	2.39	16	0.12

Ratings

Reward	C
Risk	C-
Recent Upgrade/Downgrade	

Fund Information

Fund Type	Exchange Traded Funds
Category	US Equity Large Cap Value
Sub-Category	Large Value
Prospectus Objective	Growth & Inc
Inception Date	Sep-10
Open to New Investments	Y

Prices

Price (as of 9/30/2019)	112.44
52-Week High	114.18
52-Week Low	91.61

Total Returns (%)

3-Month	6-Month	1-Year	3-Year	5-Year
1.06	3.73	3.37	30.38	44.28

3-Year Standard Deviation	12.33
Effective Duration	

Valuation

Premium/Discount (1-Year Average)	0.00

Company Information

Provider	Vanguard
Manager/Tenure	Michael A. Johnson (9), Walter Nejman (3)
Website	http://www.vanguard.com
Address	Vanguard 100 Vanguard Boulevard Malvern PA 19355 United States
Phone Number	877-662-7447

PERFORMANCE

Ratings History

Date	Overall Rating	Risk Rating	Reward Rating
Q3-19	C	C-	C
Q4-18	C	C-	C
Q4-17	B	B	B-
Q4-16	C+	C-	B
Q4-15	C	C	C

Asset & Performance History

Date	NAV	1-Year Total Return
2018	96.34	-9.05
2017	108.44	13.84
2016	97.71	16.42
2015	85.64	-3.89
2014	91.22	13.3
2013	82.27	32.31

Total Assets: $3,933,833,425

Asset Allocation

Asset	%
Cash	0%
Stocks	100%
US Stocks	98%
Bonds	0%
US Bonds	0%
Other	0%

Services Offered:

Investment Strategy: The investment seeks to track the performance of a benchmark index that measures the investment return of large-capitalization value stocks in the United States. The fund employs an indexing investment approach designed to track the performance of the Russell 1000® Value Index. The index is designed to measure the performance of large-capitalization value stocks in the United States. The Advisor attempts to replicate the target index by investing all, or substantially all, of its assets in the stocks that make up the index, holding each stock in approximately the same proportion as its weighting in the index. **Top Holdings:** Berkshire Hathaway Inc B JPMorgan Chase & Co Exxon Mobil Corp Johnson & Johnson Procter & Gamble Co

iShares MSCI ACWI ex U.S. ETF   C   HOLD

Ticker	Traded On	NAV	Total Assets ($)	Dividend Yield (TTM)	Turnover Ratio	Expense Ratio
ACWX	NAS CM	45.96	$3,915,934,381	2.54	15	0.32

Ratings
Reward   C
Risk   C+
Recent Upgrade/Downgrade

Fund Information
Fund Type   Exchange Traded Funds
Category   Global Equity Large Cap
Sub-Category   Foreign Large Blend
Prospectus Objective   Foreign Stock
Inception Date   Mar-08
Open to New Investments   Y

Prices
Price (as of 9/30/2019)   46.05
52-Week High   47.84
52-Week Low   40.69

Total Returns (%)

3-Month	6-Month	1-Year	3-Year	5-Year
-2.39	-0.04	-1.31	19.83	15.85

3-Year Standard Deviation   11.5
Effective Duration

Valuation
Premium/Discount (1-Year Average)   -0.05

Company Information
Provider   iShares
Manager/Tenure   Diane Hsiung (11), Greg Savage (11),
                   Jennifer Hsui (6), 3 others
Website   http://www.ishares.com
Address   iShares 400 Howard Street San
                   Francisco CA 94105 United States
Phone Number   800-474-2737

PERFORMANCE

Ratings History

Date	Overall Rating	Risk Rating	Reward Rating
Q3-19	C	C+	C
Q4-18	C-	C	D+
Q4-17	B-	B-	B-
Q4-16	D+	C-	D
Q4-15	C	C+	C-

Asset & Performance History

Date	NAV	1-Year Total Return
2018	41.96	-14.08
2017	50.04	27.04
2016	40.4	4.32
2015	39.82	-5.72
2014	43.21	-3.96
2013	46.35	15.21

Total Assets: $3,915,934,381
Asset Allocation

Asset	%
Cash	1%
Stocks	99%
US Stocks	1%
Bonds	0%
US Bonds	0%
Other	0%

Services Offered:

Investment Strategy: The investment seeks to track the investment results of the MSCI ACWI ex USA Index composed of large- and mid-capitalization non-U.S. equities. The fund generally will invest at least 90% of its assets in the component securities of the underlying index and in investments that have economic characteristics that are substantially identical to the component securities of the underlying index. The index is a free float-adjusted market capitalization-weighted index designed to measure the combined equity market performance of developed and emerging markets countries, excluding the United States. **Top Holdings:** iShares MSCI India ETF Nestle SA Alibaba Group Holding Ltd ADR Tencent Holdings Ltd Taiwan Semiconductor Manufacturing Co Ltd

---

The Real Estate Select Sector SPDR Fund   B   BUY

Ticker	Traded On	NAV	Total Assets ($)	Dividend Yield (TTM)	Turnover Ratio	Expense Ratio
XLRE	NYSE Arca		$3,901,982,260	2.89	7	0.13

Ratings
Reward   B+
Risk   C
Recent Upgrade/Downgrade   Up

Fund Information
Fund Type   Exchange Traded Funds
Category   Real Estate Sector Equity
Sub-Category   Real Estate
Prospectus Objective   Real Estate
Inception Date   Oct-15
Open to New Investments   Y

Prices
Price (as of 9/30/2019)   39.34
52-Week High   40.10
52-Week Low   29.81

Total Returns (%)

3-Month	6-Month	1-Year	3-Year	5-Year
7.73	10.35	25.33	33.59	

3-Year Standard Deviation   12.22
Effective Duration

Valuation
Premium/Discount (1-Year Average)   -0.03

Company Information
Provider   SPDR State Street Global Advisors
Manager/Tenure   Michael J. Feehily (3), Karl A.
                   Schneider (3), Amy Cheng (2)
Website   http://www.spdrs.com
Address   SPDR State Street Global Advisors
                   State Street Financial Center, 1
                   Lincoln Street Boston MA 02111-2900
                   United States
Phone Number   617-786-3000

PERFORMANCE

Ratings History

Date	Overall Rating	Risk Rating	Reward Rating
Q3-19	B	C	B+
Q4-18	B-	C	B
Q4-17	C	B-	C
Q4-16	D	C	B
Q4-15			

Asset & Performance History

Date	NAV	1-Year Total Return
2018	31	-2.27
2017	32.92	10.66
2016	30.74	3.17
2015	31.04	
2014		
2013		

Total Assets: $3,901,982,260
Asset Allocation

Asset	%
Cash	0%
Stocks	100%
US Stocks	100%
Bonds	0%
US Bonds	0%
Other	0%

Services Offered:

Investment Strategy: The investment seeks to provide investment results that, before expenses, correspond generally to the price and yield performance of publicly traded equity securities of companies in the Real Estate Select Sector Index (the "index"). Under normal market conditions, the fund generally invests substantially all, but at least 95%, of its total assets in the securities comprising the index. The index includes securities of companies from the following industries: real estate management and development and REITs, excluding mortgage REITs. The fund is non-diversified. **Top Holdings:** American Tower Corp Crown Castle International Corp Prologis Inc Equinix Inc Simon Property Group Inc

SPDR® Bloomberg Barclays Investment Grade Floating Rate ETF   C   HOLD

Ticker	Traded On	NAV	Total Assets ($)	Dividend Yield (TTM)	Turnover Ratio	Expense Ratio
FLRN	NYSE Arca		$3,820,300,570	2.86	19	0.15

Ratings
Reward   C
Risk   C+
Recent Upgrade/Downgrade

Fund Information
Fund Type	Exchange Traded Funds
Category	US Fixed Income
Sub-Category	Ultrashort Bond
Prospectus Objective	Corp Bond-High Yld
Inception Date	Nov-11
Open to New Investments	Y

Prices
Price (as of 9/30/2019)	30.76
52-Week High	30.76
52-Week Low	30.32

Total Returns (%)
3-Month	6-Month	1-Year	3-Year	5-Year
0.72	1.59	2.81	7.16	8.44

3-Year Standard Deviation	0.5
Effective Duration	0.13

Valuation
Premium/Discount (1-Year Average)	-0.01

Company Information
Provider	SPDR State Street Global Advisors
Manager/Tenure	Christopher DiStefano (5), Kyle Kelly (4), Frank Miethe (1)
Website	http://www.spdrs.com
Address	SPDR State Street Global Advisors State Street Financial Center, 1 Lincoln Street Boston MA 02111-2900 United States
Phone Number	617-786-3000

PERFORMANCE

Ratings History				Asset & Performance History			Total Assets:	$3,820,300,570
	Overall	Risk	Reward			1-Year	**Asset Allocation**	
Date	Rating	Rating	Rating	Date	NAV	Total Return	Asset	%
Q3-19	C	C+	C	2018	30.41	1.58	Cash	5%
Q4-18	C	C+	C	2017	30.65	1.74	Stocks	0%
Q4-17	B-	A-	C	2016	30.55	1.59	US Stocks	0%
Q4-16	C	C-	C	2015	30.4	0.2	Bonds	93%
Q4-15	C	C-	C	2014	30.52	0.39	US Bonds	54%
				2013	30.57	1.1	Other	0%

Services Offered:

Investment Strategy: The investment seeks to provide investment results that, before fees and expenses, correspond generally to the price and yield performance of the Bloomberg Barclays U.S. Dollar Floating Rate Note < 5 Years Index. The fund generally invests substantially all, but at least 80%, of its total assets in the securities comprising the index or in securities that the Adviser determines have economic characteristics that are substantially identical to the economic characteristics of the securities that comprise the index. The index is designed to measure the performance of U.S. dollar-denominated, investment grade floating rate notes. The fund is non-diversified. **Top Holdings:** Morgan Stanley 3.46% AT&T Inc 3.27% Asian Development Bank 2.42% Morgan Stanley 3.68% Kommunalbanken AS 2.48%

JPMorgan BetaBuilders Canada ETF   C   HOLD

Ticker	Traded On	NAV	Total Assets ($)	Dividend Yield (TTM)	Turnover Ratio	Expense Ratio
BBCA	BATS	24.98	$3,794,213,106	2.39		0.19

Ratings
Reward   C-
Risk   C+
Recent Upgrade/Downgrade

Fund Information
Fund Type	Exchange Traded Funds
Category	Canadian Equity Large Cap
Sub-Category	Miscellaneous Region
Prospectus Objective	Growth
Inception Date	Aug-18
Open to New Investments	Y

Prices
Price (as of 9/30/2019)	25.02
52-Week High	25.41
52-Week Low	19.94

Total Returns (%)
3-Month	6-Month	1-Year	3-Year	5-Year
1.30	4.49	3.29		

3-Year Standard Deviation	
Effective Duration	

Valuation
Premium/Discount (1-Year Average)	0.03

Company Information
Provider	JPMorgan
Manager/Tenure	Nicholas D'Eramo (1), Oliver Furby (1), Alex Hamilton (1), 1 other
Website	http://www.jpmorganfunds.com
Address	JPMorgan 270 Park Avenue New York NY 10017-2070 United States
Phone Number	800-480-4111

PERFORMANCE

Ratings History				Asset & Performance History			Total Assets:	$3,794,213,106
	Overall	Risk	Reward			1-Year	**Asset Allocation**	
Date	Rating	Rating	Rating	Date	NAV	Total Return	Asset	%
Q3-19	C	C+	C-	2018	20.73		Cash	0%
Q4-18	U			2017			Stocks	100%
Q4-17				2016			US Stocks	0%
Q4-16				2015			Bonds	0%
Q4-15				2014			US Bonds	0%
				2013			Other	0%

Services Offered:

Investment Strategy: The investment seeks investment results that closely correspond, before fees and expenses, to the performance of the Morningstar® Canada Target Market Exposure IndexSM. The fund will invest at least 80% of its assets in securities included in the underlying index. The underlying index is a free float adjusted market capitalization weighted index which consists of stocks traded primarily on the Toronto Stock Exchange. The fund may invest up to 20% of its assets in exchange-traded futures and forward foreign currency contracts to seek performance that corresponds to the underlying index. **Top Holdings:** Royal Bank of Canada The Toronto-Dominion Bank Enbridge Inc Canadian National Railway Co Bank of Nova Scotia

iShares Broad USD Investment Grade Corporate Bond ETF   D   SELL

Ticker	Traded On	NAV	Total Assets ($)	Dividend Yield (TTM)	Turnover Ratio	Expense Ratio
USIG	NAS CM	58.19	$3,788,261,705	3.39	27	0.06

Ratings
Reward   D
Risk   D
Recent Upgrade/Downgrade

Fund Information
Fund Type   Exchange Traded Funds
Category   US Fixed Income
Sub-Category   Corporate Bond
Prospectus Objective   Income
Inception Date   Jan-07
Open to New Investments   Y

Prices
Price (as of 9/30/2019)   58.28
52-Week High   58.86
52-Week Low   52.37

Total Returns (%)

3-Month	6-Month	1-Year	3-Year	5-Year
3.07	7.84	12.81	-43.39	-38.38

3-Year Standard Deviation   4.04
Effective Duration   7.22

Valuation
Premium/Discount (1-Year Average)   0.13

Company Information
Provider   iShares
Manager/Tenure   Scott Radell (9), James Mauro (8)
Website   http://www.ishares.com
Address   iShares 400 Howard Street San
                    Francisco CA 94105 United States
Phone Number   800-474-2737

PERFORMANCE

Ratings History

Date	Overall Rating	Risk Rating	Reward Rating
Q3-19	D	D	D
Q4-18	D-	D-	E+
Q4-17	B-	B+	C
Q4-16	C	C-	C
Q4-15	C	C-	C

Asset & Performance History

Date	NAV	1-Year Total Return
2018	52.81	-51.2
2017	111.96	5.74
2016	108.91	5.45
2015	106.52	-0.97
2014	111.02	7.37
2013	106.93	-2.33

Total Assets: $3,788,261,705
Asset Allocation

Asset	%
Cash	2%
Stocks	0%
US Stocks	0%
Bonds	96%
US Bonds	76%
Other	0%

Services Offered:

Investment Strategy: The investment seeks to track the investment results of the ICE BofAML US Corporate Index (the "underlying index"). The fund generally invests at least 90% of its assets in securities of the underlying index. It may invest the remainder of its assets in certain futures, options and swap contracts, cash and cash equivalents, as well as in securities not included in the underlying index. The underlying index measures the performance of investment-grade corporate bonds of both U.S. and non-U.S. issuers that are U.S. dollar-denominated and publicly issued in the U.S. domestic market. **Top Holdings:** GE Capital International Funding Company Unlimited Company 4.42% Bank of America Corporation 3% CVS Health Corp 4.3% CVS Health Corp 5.05% Anheuser-Busch InBev Worldwide Inc. 4.75%

JPMorgan BetaBuilders Europe ETF   C   HOLD

Ticker	Traded On	NAV	Total Assets ($)	Dividend Yield (TTM)	Turnover Ratio	Expense Ratio
BBEU	BATS	23.52	$3,749,010,843	3.3		0.09

Ratings
Reward   D+
Risk   C+
Recent Upgrade/Downgrade   Up

Fund Information
Fund Type   Exchange Traded Funds
Category   Europe Equity Large Cap
Sub-Category   Europe Stock
Prospectus Objective   Europe Stock
Inception Date   Jun-18
Open to New Investments   Y

Prices
Price (as of 9/30/2019)   23.52
52-Week High   24.55
52-Week Low   20.77

Total Returns (%)

3-Month	6-Month	1-Year	3-Year	5-Year
-1.96	1.24	-0.68		

3-Year Standard Deviation
Effective Duration

Valuation
Premium/Discount (1-Year Average)   0.17

Company Information
Provider   JPMorgan
Manager/Tenure   Nicholas D'Eramo (1), Oliver Furby (1),
                 Alex Hamilton (1), 1 other
Website   http://www.jpmorganfunds.com
Address   JPMorgan 270 Park Avenue New York
                    NY 10017-2070 United States
Phone Number   800-480-4111

PERFORMANCE

Ratings History

Date	Overall Rating	Risk Rating	Reward Rating
Q3-19	C	C+	D+
Q4-18	U		
Q4-17			
Q4-16			
Q4-15			

Asset & Performance History

Date	NAV	1-Year Total Return
2018	21.35	
2017		
2016		
2015		
2014		
2013		

Total Assets: $3,749,010,843
Asset Allocation

Asset	%
Cash	0%
Stocks	100%
US Stocks	2%
Bonds	0%
US Bonds	0%
Other	0%

Services Offered:

Investment Strategy: The investment seeks investment results that closely correspond, before fees and expenses, to the performance of the Morningstar® Developed Europe Target Market Exposure IndexSM. The fund will invest at least 80% of its assets in securities included in the underlying index. The underlying index is a free float adjusted market capitalization-weighted index which consists of equity securities from developed European countries or regions, including: Austria, Belgium, Denmark, Finland, France, Germany, Ireland, Italy, the Netherlands, Norway, Portugal, Spain, Sweden, Switzerland and the United Kingdom. **Top Holdings:** Nestle SA Novartis AG Roche Holding AG Dividend Right Cert. HSBC Holdings PLC SAP SE

Vanguard Industrials Index Fund ETF Shares   C+   HOLD

Ticker	Traded On	NAV	Total Assets ($)	Dividend Yield (TTM)	Turnover Ratio	Expense Ratio
VIS	NYSE Arca	146.16	$3,737,735,997	1.75	4	0.1

Ratings
Reward	C+
Risk	C+
Recent Upgrade/Downgrade	Up

Fund Information
Fund Type	Exchange Traded Funds
Category	Industrials Sector Equity
Sub-Category	Industrials
Prospectus Objective	Unaligned
Inception Date	Sep-04
Open to New Investments	Y

Prices
Price (as of 9/30/2019)	146.07
52-Week High	149.32
52-Week Low	112.87

Total Returns (%)
3-Month	6-Month	1-Year	3-Year	5-Year
0.15	2.95	0.00	38.54	59.26

3-Year Standard Deviation	16.89
Effective Duration	

Valuation
Premium/Discount (1-Year Average)	-0.03

Company Information
Provider	Vanguard
Manager/Tenure	Walter Nejman (3), Michelle Louie (1)
Website	http://www.vanguard.com
Address	Vanguard 100 Vanguard Boulevard Malvern PA 19355 United States
Phone Number	877-662-7447

PERFORMANCE

Ratings History
Date	Overall Rating	Risk Rating	Reward Rating
Q3-19	C+	C+	C+
Q4-18	C	C+	C
Q4-17	B	B-	B+
Q4-16	B-	C	B
Q4-15	C	C	C+

Asset & Performance History
Date	NAV	1-Year Total Return
2018	119.21	-14.8
2017	142.27	21.38
2016	119.15	20.04
2015	100.94	-3.58
2014	106.81	8.5
2013	99.99	41.93

Total Assets: $3,737,735,997
Asset Allocation
Asset	%
Cash	0%
Stocks	100%
US Stocks	99%
Bonds	0%
US Bonds	0%
Other	0%

Services Offered:

Investment Strategy: The investment seeks to track the performance of a benchmark index. The fund employs an indexing investment approach designed to track the performance of the MSCI US Investable Market Index (IMI)/Industrials 25/50, an index made up of stocks of large, mid-size, and small U.S. companies within the industrials sector, as classified under the Global Industry Classification Standard (GICS). The Advisor attempts to replicate the target index by seeking to invest all, or substantially all, of its assets in the stocks that make up the index, in order to hold each stock in approximately the same proportion as its weighting in the index. The fund is non-diversified. **Top Holdings:** Boeing Co   Union Pacific Corp   Honeywell International Inc   United Technologies Corp   3M Co

---

SPDR® Portfolio Total Stock Market ETF   C+   HOLD

Ticker	Traded On	NAV	Total Assets ($)	Dividend Yield (TTM)	Turnover Ratio	Expense Ratio
SPTM	NYSE Arca		$3,735,344,555	1.72	4	0.03

Ratings
Reward	C+
Risk	C+
Recent Upgrade/Downgrade	

Fund Information
Fund Type	Exchange Traded Funds
Category	US Equity Large Cap Blend
Sub-Category	Large Blend
Prospectus Objective	Growth
Inception Date	Oct-00
Open to New Investments	Y

Prices
Price (as of 9/30/2019)	36.74
52-Week High	37.53
52-Week Low	28.90

Total Returns (%)
3-Month	6-Month	1-Year	3-Year	5-Year
-0.14	3.62	2.64	43.47	64.09

3-Year Standard Deviation	12.59
Effective Duration	

Valuation
Premium/Discount (1-Year Average)	-0.04

Company Information
Provider	SPDR State Street Global Advisors
Manager/Tenure	Michael J. Feehily (7), Karl A. Schneider (4), Kathleen Morgan (0)
Website	http://www.spdrs.com
Address	SPDR State Street Global Advisors State Street Financial Center, 1 Lincoln Street Boston MA 02111-2900 United States
Phone Number	617-786-3000

PERFORMANCE

Ratings History
Date	Overall Rating	Risk Rating	Reward Rating
Q3-19	C+	C+	C+
Q4-18	C	C+	C
Q4-17	B	B	B
Q4-16	C+	C-	B
Q4-15	C	C-	C

Asset & Performance History
Date	NAV	1-Year Total Return
2018	30.87	-5.25
2017	33.15	21.14
2016	27.86	12.25
2015	25.2	0.45
2014	25.57	12.48
2013	23.23	33.29

Total Assets: $3,735,344,555
Asset Allocation
Asset	%
Cash	0%
Stocks	100%
US Stocks	99%
Bonds	0%
US Bonds	0%
Other	0%

Services Offered: Dividend Investment Plan, CashInvestment Plan

Investment Strategy: The investment seeks to provide investment results that, before fees and expenses, correspond generally to the total return performance of the SSGA Total Stock Market Index that tracks a broad universe of exchange traded U.S. equity securities. The fund generally invests substantially all, but at least 80%, of its total assets in the securities comprising the index. It may invest in equity securities that are not included in the index (including common stock, preferred stock, depositary receipts and shares of other investment companies), cash and cash equivalents or money market instruments. The fund is non-diversified. **Top Holdings:** Microsoft Corp   Apple Inc   Amazon.com Inc   Facebook Inc A   JPMorgan Chase & Co

iShares MSCI China ETF   C   HOLD

Ticker	Traded On	NAV	Total Assets ($)	Dividend Yield (TTM)	Turnover Ratio	Expense Ratio
MCHI	NAS CM	56.38	$3,687,093,600	1.56	14	0.59

Ratings
Reward   C-
Risk   C
Recent Upgrade/Downgrade

Fund Information
Fund Type   Exchange Traded Funds
Category   Greater China Equity
Sub-Category   China Region
Prospectus Objective   Pacific Stock
Inception Date   Mar-11
Open to New Investments   Y

Prices
Price (as of 9/30/2019)   56.08
52-Week High   65.03
52-Week Low   51.00

Total Returns (%)

3-Month	6-Month	1-Year	3-Year	5-Year
-5.68	-9.99	-4.18	22.99	30.66

3-Year Standard Deviation   19.42
Effective Duration

Valuation
Premium/Discount (1-Year Average)   0.05

Company Information
Provider   iShares
Manager/Tenure   Diane Hsiung (8), Greg Savage (8), Jennifer Hsui (6), 3 others
Website   http://www.ishares.com
Address   iShares 400 Howard Street San Francisco CA 94105 United States
Phone Number   800-474-2737

PERFORMANCE

Ratings History

Date	Overall Rating	Risk Rating	Reward Rating
Q3-19	C	C	C-
Q4-18	C-	D+	C-
Q4-17	B+	C	A
Q4-16	C	C-	C
Q4-15	C	C	C

Asset & Performance History

Date	NAV	1-Year Total Return
2018	52.96	-19.18
2017	66.48	53.02
2016	44.16	0.4
2015	44.73	-8.25
2014	49.95	7.46
2013	47.67	3.11

Total Assets: $3,687,093,600
Asset Allocation

Asset	%
Cash	0%
Stocks	100%
US Stocks	1%
Bonds	0%
US Bonds	0%
Other	0%

Services Offered:

Investment Strategy: The investment seeks to track the investment results of the MSCI China Index. The fund generally will invest at least 90% of its assets in the component securities of the underlying index and in investments that have economic characteristics that are substantially identical to the component securities of the underlying index. The index is a free float-adjusted market capitalization-weighted index designed to measure the performance of equity securities in the top 85% in market capitalization of the Chinese equity securities markets, as represented by the H-Shares and B-Shares markets. The fund is non-diversified. **Top Holdings:** Alibaba Group Holding Ltd ADR   Tencent Holdings Ltd   China Construction Bank Corp Class H   Ping An Insurance (Group) Co. of China Ltd Class H   China Mobile Ltd

SPDR® S&P Biotech ETF   C-   HOLD

Ticker	Traded On	NAV	Total Assets ($)	Dividend Yield (TTM)	Turnover Ratio	Expense Ratio
XBI	NYSE Arca		$3,671,641,402	0.02	45	0.35

Ratings
Reward   C-
Risk   C
Recent Upgrade/Downgrade   Down

Fund Information
Fund Type   Exchange Traded Funds
Category   Healthcare Sector Equity
Sub-Category   Health
Prospectus Objective   Health
Inception Date   Jan-06
Open to New Investments   Y

Prices
Price (as of 9/30/2019)   76.25
52-Week High   94.90
52-Week Low   65.42

Total Returns (%)

3-Month	6-Month	1-Year	3-Year	5-Year
-13.44	-15.48	-19.11	15.88	49.47

3-Year Standard Deviation   27.19
Effective Duration

Valuation
Premium/Discount (1-Year Average)   -0.04

Company Information
Provider   SPDR State Street Global Advisors
Manager/Tenure   Michael J. Feehily (7), Karl A. Schneider (4), Raymond V. Donofrio (2)
Website   http://www.spdrs.com
Address   SPDR State Street Global Advisors State Street Financial Center, 1 Lincoln Street Boston MA 02111-2900 United States
Phone Number   617-786-3000

PERFORMANCE

Ratings History

Date	Overall Rating	Risk Rating	Reward Rating
Q3-19	C-	C	C-
Q4-18	C-	C	C-
Q4-17	B-	C	B
Q4-16	C-	D+	C
Q4-15	B-	C+	B

Asset & Performance History

Date	NAV	1-Year Total Return
2018	72.03	-14.9
2017	84.83	43.69
2016	59.19	-15.45
2015	70.2	13.6
2014	62.13	44.66
2013	43.48	48.5

Total Assets: $3,671,641,402
Asset Allocation

Asset	%
Cash	0%
Stocks	100%
US Stocks	100%
Bonds	0%
US Bonds	0%
Other	0%

Services Offered: Dividend Investment Plan, CashInvestment Plan

Investment Strategy: The investment seeks to provide investment results that, before fees and expenses, correspond generally to the total return performance of the S&P Biotechnology Select Industry Index derived from the biotechnology segment of a U.S. total market composite index. In seeking to track the performance of the S&P Biotechnology Select Industry Index (the "index"), the fund employs a sampling strategy. It generally invests substantially all, but at least 80%, of its total assets in the securities comprising the index. The index represents the biotechnology segment of the S&P Total Market Index ("S&P TMI"). The fund is non-diversified. **Top Holdings:** Genomic Health Inc   Invitae Corp   Amgen Inc   Neurocrine Biosciences Inc   Alnylam Pharmaceuticals Inc

SPDR® Portfolio S&P 500 Value ETF

C+   HOLD

Ticker	Traded On	NAV	Total Assets ($)	Dividend Yield (TTM)	Turnover Ratio	Expense Ratio
SPYV	NYSE Arca		$3,671,121,099	2.47	30	0.04

Ratings

Reward	C
Risk	C+
Recent Upgrade/Downgrade	Up

Fund Information

Fund Type	Exchange Traded Funds
Category	US Equity Large Cap Value
Sub-Category	Large Value
Prospectus Objective	Growth
Inception Date	Sep-00
Open to New Investments	Y

Prices

Price (as of 9/30/2019)	31.96
52-Week High	32.44
52-Week Low	25.59

Total Returns (%)

3-Month	6-Month	1-Year	3-Year	5-Year
1.53	5.01	4.58	34.27	48.62

3-Year Standard Deviation	13.14
Effective Duration	

Valuation

Premium/Discount (1-Year Average)	-0.01

Company Information

Provider	SPDR State Street Global Advisors
Manager/Tenure	Michael J. Feehily (7), Karl A. Schneider (4), Mark Krivitsky (1)
Website	http://www.spdrs.com
Address	SPDR State Street Global Advisors State Street Financial Center, 1 Lincoln Street Boston MA 02111-2900 United States
Phone Number	617-786-3000

PERFORMANCE

Ratings History

Date	Overall Rating	Risk Rating	Reward Rating
Q3-19	C+	C+	C
Q4-18	C	C+	C
Q4-17	B	B	B-
Q4-16	C+	C-	B
Q4-15	C	C-	C

Asset & Performance History

Date	NAV	1-Year Total Return
2018	27.15	-8.92
2017	30.65	15.18
2016	27.39	16.54
2015	23.97	-3.2
2014	25.4	12.1
2013	23.17	31.63

Total Assets: $3,671,121,099

Asset Allocation

Asset	%
Cash	0%
Stocks	100%
US Stocks	99%
Bonds	0%
US Bonds	0%
Other	0%

Services Offered: Dividend Investment Plan, CashInvestment Plan

Investment Strategy: The investment seeks to provide investment results that, before fees and expenses, correspond generally to the total return performance of the S&P 500 Value Index that tracks the performance of large capitalization exchange traded U.S. equity securities exhibiting "value" characteristics. The fund employs a sampling strategy in seeking to track the performance of the S&P 500 Value Index. It generally invests substantially all, but at least 80%, of its total assets in the securities comprising the index. The index measures the performance of the large-capitalization value segment of the U.S. equity market. The fund is non-diversified. **Top Holdings:** Apple Inc   JPMorgan Chase & Co   AT&T Inc   Bank of America Corporation   Chevron Corp

iShares MSCI All Country Asia ex Japan ETF

C   HOLD

Ticker	Traded On	NAV	Total Assets ($)	Dividend Yield (TTM)	Turnover Ratio	Expense Ratio
AAXJ	NAS CM	66.56	$3,660,798,976	2.01	17	0.69

Ratings

Reward	C-
Risk	C+
Recent Upgrade/Downgrade	

Fund Information

Fund Type	Exchange Traded Funds
Category	Asia ex-Japan Equity
Sub-Category	Pacific/Asia ex-Japan Stk
Prospectus Objective	Pacific Stock
Inception Date	Aug-08
Open to New Investments	Y

Prices

Price (as of 9/30/2019)	66.32
52-Week High	73.40
52-Week Low	61.12

Total Returns (%)

3-Month	6-Month	1-Year	3-Year	5-Year
-5.38	-6.37	-3.94	17.87	19.49

3-Year Standard Deviation	14.55
Effective Duration	

Valuation

Premium/Discount (1-Year Average)	-0.09

Company Information

Provider	iShares
Manager/Tenure	Diane Hsiung (11), Greg Savage (11), Jennifer Hsui (6), 3 others
Website	http://www.ishares.com
Address	iShares 400 Howard Street San Francisco CA 94105 United States
Phone Number	800-474-2737

PERFORMANCE

Ratings History

Date	Overall Rating	Risk Rating	Reward Rating
Q3-19	C	C+	C-
Q4-18	C-	C-	C-
Q4-17	B	C+	A-
Q4-16	C-	C	D+
Q4-15	C-	C	C-

Asset & Performance History

Date	NAV	1-Year Total Return
2018	63.65	-14.81
2017	76.23	40.51
2016	55.38	4.83
2015	53.77	-9.85
2014	61.03	3.92
2013	59.79	2.47

Total Assets: $3,660,798,976

Asset Allocation

Asset	%
Cash	0%
Stocks	100%
US Stocks	0%
Bonds	0%
US Bonds	0%
Other	0%

Services Offered:

Investment Strategy: The investment seeks to track the investment results of the MSCI AC Asia ex Japan Index. The fund will invest at least 90% of its assets in the component securities of the index and in investments that have economic characteristics that are substantially identical to the component securities of the index. The index is a free float-adjusted market capitalization index designed to measure equity market performance of securities from the following 11 developed, emerging and frontier market countries or regions: China, Hong Kong, India, Indonesia, Malaysia, Pakistan, the Philippines, Singapore, South Korea, Taiwan and Thailand. **Top Holdings:** Alibaba Group Holding Ltd ADR   Tencent Holdings Ltd   Taiwan Semiconductor Manufacturing Co Ltd   Samsung Electronics Co Ltd   AIA Group Ltd

ProShares UltraPro QQQ   C   HOLD

Ticker	Traded On	NAV	Total Assets ($)	Dividend Yield (TTM)	Turnover Ratio	Expense Ratio
TQQQ	NAS CM	61.59	$3,630,970,416	0.1	15	0.95

Ratings

Reward	C+
Risk	C-
Recent Upgrade/Downgrade	

Fund Information

Fund Type	Exchange Traded Funds
Category	Trading Tools
Sub-Category	Trading--Leveraged Equity
Prospectus Objective	Growth
Inception Date	Feb-10
Open to New Investments	Y

Prices

Price (as of 9/30/2019)	61.63
52-Week High	71.55
52-Week Low	30.39

Total Returns (%)

3-Month	6-Month	1-Year	3-Year	5-Year
-4.11	4.33	-13.86	187.38	349.80

3-Year Standard Deviation	45.84
Effective Duration	

Valuation

Premium/Discount (1-Year Average)	-0.12

Company Information

Provider	ProShares
Manager/Tenure	Michael Neches (6), Devin Sullivan (1)
Website	http://www.proshares.com
Address	ProShares 7501 Wisconsin Avenue, Suite 1000 Bethesda MD 20814 United States
Phone Number	866-776-5125

PERFORMANCE

Ratings History

Date	Overall Rating	Risk Rating	Reward Rating
Q3-19	C	C-	C+
Q4-18	C	C-	C
Q4-17	B	C	A
Q4-16	C+	C-	B-
Q4-15	B-	C+	B-

Asset & Performance History

Date	NAV	1-Year Total Return
2018	37.08	-19.64
2017	46.2	118.64
2016	21.13	11.04
2015	19.03	17.41
2014	16.21	56.81
2013	10.34	139.98

Total Assets: $3,630,970,416

Asset Allocation

Asset	%
Cash	-200%
Stocks	300%
US Stocks	293%
Bonds	0%
US Bonds	0%
Other	0%

Services Offered:

Investment Strategy: The investment seeks daily investment results, before fees and expenses, that correspond to three times (3x) the daily performance of the NASDAQ-100 Index®. The fund invests in financial instruments that ProShare Advisors believes, in combination, should produce daily returns consistent with the fund's investment objective. The index includes 100 of the largest domestic and international non-financial companies listed on The Nasdaq Stock Market based on market capitalization. The fund is non-diversified. **Top Holdings:** Nasdaq 100 Index Swap Citibank, N.A. Nasdaq 100 Index Swap Bnp Paribas Nasdaq 100 Index Swap Goldman Sachs International Nasdaq 100 Index Swap Ubs Ag Nasdaq 100 Index Swap Societe Generale

SPDR® Nuveen Bloomberg Barclays Short Term Municipal Bond ETF   C   HOLD

Ticker	Traded On	NAV	Total Assets ($)	Dividend Yield (TTM)	Turnover Ratio	Expense Ratio
SHM	NYSE Arca		$3,599,238,955	1.37	35	0.2

Ratings

Reward	C
Risk	C+
Recent Upgrade/Downgrade	

Fund Information

Fund Type	Exchange Traded Funds
Category	US Muni Fixed Inc
Sub-Category	Muni National Short
Prospectus Objective	Muni Bond - Natl
Inception Date	Oct-07
Open to New Investments	Y

Prices

Price (as of 9/30/2019)	48.99
52-Week High	49.36
52-Week Low	47.43

Total Returns (%)

3-Month	6-Month	1-Year	3-Year	5-Year
0.33	1.47	3.94	3.88	5.93

3-Year Standard Deviation	1.82
Effective Duration	2.78

Valuation

Premium/Discount (1-Year Average)	-0.04

Company Information

Provider	SPDR State Street Global Advisors
Manager/Tenure	Timothy T. Ryan (11), Steven M. Hlavin (9)
Website	http://www.spdrs.com
Address	SPDR State Street Global Advisors State Street Financial Center, 1 Lincoln Street Boston MA 02111-2900 United States
Phone Number	617-786-3000

PERFORMANCE

Ratings History

Date	Overall Rating	Risk Rating	Reward Rating
Q3-19	C	C+	C
Q4-18	C-	C	D+
Q4-17	C	C	C
Q4-16	C	C	C-
Q4-15	C	C+	C

Asset & Performance History

Date	NAV	1-Year Total Return
2018	48.05	1.38
2017	47.99	1.17
2016	47.89	-0.46
2015	48.59	1.11
2014	48.49	0.91
2013	48.5	0.89

Total Assets: $3,599,238,955

Asset Allocation

Asset	%
Cash	0%
Stocks	0%
US Stocks	0%
Bonds	100%
US Bonds	100%
Other	0%

Services Offered:

Investment Strategy: The investment seeks to provide investment results that, before fees and expenses, correspond generally to the price and yield performance of the Bloomberg Barclays Managed Money Municipal Short Term Index. The fund invests substantially all, but at least 80%, of its total assets in the securities comprising the index or in securities that the Sub-Adviser determines have economic characteristics that are substantially identical to the economic characteristics of the securities that comprise the index. The index tracks the short term tax exempt municipal bond market and provides income that is exempt from federal income taxes. The fund is non-diversified. **Top Holdings:** CONNECTICUT ST HEALTH & EDL FACS AUTH REV 5% SAN ANTONIO TEX WTR REV 2.62% SAN DIEGO CNTY CALIF WTR AUTH WTR REV 5% BAY AREA TOLL AUTH CALIF TOLL BRDG REV 2.25% CALIFORNIA ST 5%

Vanguard Russell 1000 Index Fund ETF Shares

C   HOLD

Ticker	Traded On	NAV	Total Assets ($)	Dividend Yield (TTM)	Turnover Ratio	Expense Ratio
VONE	NAS CM	136.02	$3,566,773,504	1.76	9	0.12

Ratings

Reward	C+
Risk	C-
Recent Upgrade/Downgrade	

Fund Information

Fund Type	Exchange Traded Funds
Category	US Equity Large Cap Blend
Sub-Category	Large Blend
Prospectus Objective	Growth
Inception Date	Sep-10
Open to New Investments	Y

Prices

Price (as of 9/30/2019)	136.03
52-Week High	138.93
52-Week Low	107.21

Total Returns (%)

3-Month	6-Month	1-Year	3-Year	5-Year
0.11	3.94	3.00	43.84	63.68

3-Year Standard Deviation	12.31
Effective Duration	

Valuation

Premium/Discount (1-Year Average)	0.00

Company Information

Provider	Vanguard
Manager/Tenure	Michael A. Johnson (3), Walter Nejman (3)
Website	http://www.vanguard.com
Address	Vanguard 100 Vanguard Boulevard Malvern PA 19355 United States
Phone Number	877-662-7447

PERFORMANCE

Ratings History

Date	Overall Rating	Risk Rating	Reward Rating
Q3-19	C	C-	C+
Q4-18	C	C-	C
Q4-17	B	B	B
Q4-16	C+	C-	B
Q4-15	C	C	C

Asset & Performance History

Date	NAV	1-Year Total Return
2018	113.4	-5.7
2017	122.43	21.61
2016	102.57	11.24
2015	93.62	0.81
2014	94.61	13.1
2013	85.12	32.92

Total Assets: $3,566,773,504

Asset Allocation

Asset	%
Cash	0%
Stocks	100%
US Stocks	99%
Bonds	0%
US Bonds	0%
Other	0%

Services Offered:

Investment Strategy: The investment seeks to track the performance of a benchmark index that measures the investment return of large-capitalization stocks in the United States. The fund employs an indexing investment approach designed to track the performance of the Russell 1000® Index. The index is designed to measure the performance of large-capitalization stocks in the United States. The Advisor attempts to replicate the target index by investing all, or substantially all, of its assets in the stocks that make up the index, holding each stock in approximately the same proportion as its weighting in the index. **Top Holdings:** Microsoft Corp Apple Inc Amazon.com Inc Facebook Inc A Berkshire Hathaway Inc B

Invesco Emerging Markets Sovereign Debt ETF

C+   HOLD

Ticker	Traded On	NAV	Total Assets ($)	Dividend Yield (TTM)	Turnover Ratio	Expense Ratio
PCY	NYSE Arca	29.21	$3,566,211,395	4.85	54	0.5

Ratings

Reward	B-
Risk	C+
Recent Upgrade/Downgrade	

Fund Information

Fund Type	Exchange Traded Funds
Category	Emerging Mkts Fixed Inc
Sub-Category	Emerging Markets Bond
Prospectus Objective	Worldwide Bond
Inception Date	Oct-07
Open to New Investments	Y

Prices

Price (as of 9/30/2019)	29.15
52-Week High	30.00
52-Week Low	25.56

Total Returns (%)

3-Month	6-Month	1-Year	3-Year	5-Year
1.12	6.58	13.66	10.44	31.19

3-Year Standard Deviation	6.97
Effective Duration	9.33

Valuation

Premium/Discount (1-Year Average)	-0.06

Company Information

Provider	Invesco
Manager/Tenure	Philip Fang (11), Peter Hubbard (11), Jeffrey W. Kernagis (11), 2 others
Website	http://www.invesco.com/us
Address	Invesco 11 Greenway Plaza, Ste. 2500 Houston TX 77046 United States
Phone Number	800-659-1005

PERFORMANCE

Ratings History

Date	Overall Rating	Risk Rating	Reward Rating
Q3-19	C+	C+	B-
Q4-18	C-	C	D
Q4-17	B	A	C+
Q4-16	C+	C+	C
Q4-15	C	C	C

Asset & Performance History

Date	NAV	1-Year Total Return
2018	26.38	-6.14
2017	29.49	9.43
2016	28.28	8.99
2015	27.31	1.98
2014	28.24	9.18
2013	27.07	-9.78

Total Assets: $3,566,211,395

Asset Allocation

Asset	%
Cash	0%
Stocks	0%
US Stocks	0%
Bonds	100%
US Bonds	0%
Other	0%

Services Offered:

Investment Strategy: The investment seeks to track the investment results (before fees and expenses) of the DBIQ Emerging Market USD Liquid Balanced Index (the "underlying index"). The fund generally will invest at least 80% of its total assets in U.S. dollar-denominated government bonds from emerging market countries that comprise the underlying index. The underlying index measures potential returns of a theoretical portfolio of liquid emerging market U.S. dollar-denominated government bonds. **Top Holdings:** Trinidad & Tobago 4.5% Croatia (Republic Of) 6% Trinidad & Tobago 4.38% Croatia (Republic Of) 5.5% Republika Slovenija 5.25%

Vanguard Energy Index Fund ETF Shares   D+   SELL

Ticker	Traded On	NAV	Total Assets ($)	Dividend Yield (TTM)	Turnover Ratio	Expense Ratio
VDE	NYSE Arca	77.99	$3,558,312,891	3.46	5	0.1

Ratings
Reward	D+
Risk	D
Recent Upgrade/Downgrade	

Fund Information
Fund Type	Exchange Traded Funds
Category	Energy Sector Equity
Sub-Category	Equity Energy
Prospectus Objective	Natl Res
Inception Date	Sep-04
Open to New Investments	Y

Prices
Price (as of 9/30/2019)	78.02
52-Week High	107.80
52-Week Low	72.37

Total Returns (%)
3-Month	6-Month	1-Year	3-Year	5-Year
-7.07	-11.95	-23.94	-12.31	-29.87

3-Year Standard Deviation	21.76
Effective Duration	

Valuation
Premium/Discount (1-Year Average)	-0.02

Company Information
Provider	Vanguard
Manager/Tenure	William A. Coleman (3), Awais Khan (1)
Website	http://www.vanguard.com
Address	Vanguard 100 Vanguard Boulevard Malvern PA 19355 United States
Phone Number	877-662-7447

PERFORMANCE

Ratings History
Date	Overall Rating	Risk Rating	Reward Rating
Q3-19	D+	D	D+
Q4-18	C	C-	C
Q4-17	C-	C	D+
Q4-16	C-	D	C
Q4-15	C	C	C

Asset & Performance History
Date	NAV	1-Year Total Return
2018	76.75	-20.3
2017	98.92	-2.3
2016	104.54	29.99
2015	83.16	-23.21
2014	111.66	-9.91
2013	126.44	25.77

Total Assets: $3,558,312,891
Asset Allocation
Asset	%
Cash	1%
Stocks	99%
US Stocks	98%
Bonds	0%
US Bonds	0%
Other	0%

Services Offered:
Investment Strategy: The investment seeks to track the performance of a benchmark index. The fund employs an indexing investment approach designed to track the performance of the MSCI US Investable Market Index (IMI)/Energy 25/50, an index made up of stocks of large, mid-size, and small U.S. companies within the energy sector, as classified under the Global Industry Classification Standard (GICS). The Advisor attempts to replicate the target index by seeking to invest all, or substantially all, of its assets in the stocks that make up the index, in order to hold each stock in approximately the same proportion as its weighting in the index. The fund is non-diversified.
Top Holdings: Exxon Mobil Corp Chevron Corp ConocoPhillips Schlumberger Ltd EOG Resources Inc

First Trust Low Duration Opportunities ETF   C+   HOLD

Ticker	Traded On	NAV	Total Assets ($)	Dividend Yield (TTM)	Turnover Ratio	Expense Ratio
LMBS	NAS CM	51.87	$3,550,826,651	2.55	331	0.68

Ratings
Reward	C
Risk	C+
Recent Upgrade/Downgrade	Up

Fund Information
Fund Type	Exchange Traded Funds
Category	US Fixed Income
Sub-Category	Short-Term Bond
Prospectus Objective	Govt Bond - Mortgage
Inception Date	Nov-14
Open to New Investments	Y

Prices
Price (as of 9/30/2019)	51.99
52-Week High	52.09
52-Week Low	50.81

Total Returns (%)
3-Month	6-Month	1-Year	3-Year	5-Year
1.00	2.51	4.65	7.43	

3-Year Standard Deviation	0.82
Effective Duration	2.29

Valuation
Premium/Discount (1-Year Average)	0.12

Company Information
Provider	First Trust
Manager/Tenure	Jeremiah Charles (4), James W. Snyder (4)
Website	http://www.ftportfolios.com/
Address	First Trust 120 E. Liberty Drive, Suite 400 Wheaton IL 60187 United States
Phone Number	800-621-1675

PERFORMANCE

Ratings History
Date	Overall Rating	Risk Rating	Reward Rating
Q3-19	C+	C+	C
Q4-18	C	C+	C
Q4-17	B-	A	C
Q4-16	C	C+	C-
Q4-15	U		

Asset & Performance History
Date	NAV	1-Year Total Return
2018	50.97	1.24
2017	51.64	1.76
2016	52.14	6.84
2015	50.22	2.37
2014	50.57	
2013		

Total Assets: $3,550,826,651
Asset Allocation
Asset	%
Cash	5%
Stocks	0%
US Stocks	0%
Bonds	95%
US Bonds	95%
Other	0%

Services Offered:
Investment Strategy: The investment seeks to generate current income with a secondary objective of capital appreciation. Under normal market conditions, the fund will seek to achieve its investment objectives by investing at least 80% of its net assets (including investment borrowings) in mortgage-related debt securities and other mortgage-related instruments (collectively, "Mortgage-Related Investments"). The advisor normally expects to invest in Mortgage-Related Investments tied to residential and commercial mortgages. It is non-diversified. **Top Holdings:** Us 5yr Note (Cbt) Dec19 US 10 Year Ultra Future Dec19 Federal National Mortgage Association 2.5% Federal National Mortgage Association 5% Federal National Mortgage Association 4%

iShares Edge MSCI USA Value Factor ETF   C   HOLD

Ticker	Traded On	NAV	Total Assets ($)	Dividend Yield (TTM)	Turnover Ratio	Expense Ratio
VLUE	BATS	82.05	$3,519,766,929	2.77	35	0.15

Ratings
Reward   C
Risk   C
Recent Upgrade/Downgrade

Fund Information
Fund Type   Exchange Traded Funds
Category   US Equity Large Cap Value
Sub-Category   Large Value
Prospectus Objective   Growth
Inception Date   Apr-13
Open to New Investments   Y

Prices
Price (as of 9/30/2019)   82.04
52-Week High   88.78
52-Week Low   68.64

Total Returns (%)

3-Month	6-Month	1-Year	3-Year	5-Year
1.18	2.44	-4.14	35.32	48.06

3-Year Standard Deviation   15.06
Effective Duration

Valuation
Premium/Discount (1-Year Average)   -0.01

Company Information
Provider   iShares
Manager/Tenure   Diane Hsiung (6), Jennifer Hsui (6),
                    Greg Savage (6), 3 others
Website   http://www.ishares.com
Address   iShares 400 Howard Street San
                    Francisco CA 94105 United States
Phone Number   800-474-2737

PERFORMANCE

Ratings History

Date	Overall Rating	Risk Rating	Reward Rating
Q3-19	C	C	C
Q4-18	C	C	C
Q4-17	B	B	B
Q4-16	B-	C	B
Q4-15	C	C	C

Asset & Performance History

Date	NAV	1-Year Total Return
2018	72.47	-11.18
2017	83.58	21.96
2016	70.15	15.68
2015	62.03	-3.54
2014	65.83	12.29
2013	59.63	

Total Assets: $3,519,766,929
Asset Allocation

Asset	%
Cash	0%
Stocks	100%
US Stocks	99%
Bonds	0%
US Bonds	0%
Other	0%

Services Offered:

Investment Strategy: The investment seeks to track the investment results of the MSCI USA Enhanced Value Index composed of U.S. large- and mid-capitalization stocks with value characteristics and relatively lower valuations. The fund generally will invest at least 90% of its assets in the component securities of the underlying index and may invest up to 10% of its assets in certain futures, options and swap contracts, cash and cash equivalents. The index is based on a traditional market capitalization-weighted parent index, the MSCI USA Index (the "parent index"). The parent index includes U.S. large- and mid- capitalization stocks. **Top Holdings:** AT&T Inc   Intel Corp   International Business Machines Corp   Micron Technology Inc   Bank of America Corporation

---

Invesco S&P 500® High Dividend Low Volatility ETF   C   HOLD

Ticker	Traded On	NAV	Total Assets ($)	Dividend Yield (TTM)	Turnover Ratio	Expense Ratio
SPHD	NYSE Arca	42.61	$3,506,649,796	4.11		0.3

Ratings
Reward   C
Risk   C
Recent Upgrade/Downgrade   Down

Fund Information
Fund Type   Exchange Traded Funds
Category   US Equity Large Cap Value
Sub-Category   Large Value
Prospectus Objective   Income
Inception Date   Oct-12
Open to New Investments

Prices
Price (as of 9/30/2019)   42.63
52-Week High   43.31
52-Week Low   36.52

Total Returns (%)

3-Month	6-Month	1-Year	3-Year	5-Year
2.51	1.66	7.26	23.33	68.69

3-Year Standard Deviation   11.3
Effective Duration

Valuation
Premium/Discount (1-Year Average)   0.01

Company Information
Provider   Invesco
Manager/Tenure   Peter Hubbard (6), Michael Jeanette
                    (6), Tony Seisser (5)
Website   http://www.invesco.com/us
Address   Invesco 11 Greenway Plaza, Ste. 2500
                    Houston TX 77046 United States
Phone Number   800-659-1005

PERFORMANCE

Ratings History

Date	Overall Rating	Risk Rating	Reward Rating
Q3-19	C	C	C
Q4-18	C	C+	C
Q4-17	B+	A+	B
Q4-16	B-	C+	B
Q4-15	C+	C+	C+

Asset & Performance History

Date	NAV	1-Year Total Return
2018	38.18	-6.12
2017	42.4	11.93
2016	39.14	22.3
2015	33.32	5.2
2014	32.82	19.83
2013	28.37	20.84

Total Assets: $3,506,649,796
Asset Allocation

Asset	%
Cash	0%
Stocks	100%
US Stocks	100%
Bonds	0%
US Bonds	0%
Other	0%

Services Offered:

Investment Strategy: The investment seeks to track the investment results (before fees and expenses) of the S&P 500® Low Volatility High Dividend Index (the "underlying index"). The fund generally will invest at least 90% of its total assets in the securities that comprise the underlying index. The index provider compiles, maintains and calculates the underlying index, which is composed of 50 securities in the S&P 500® Index that historically have provided high dividend yields with lower volatility. **Top Holdings:** Iron Mountain Inc   AT&T Inc   Altria Group Inc Kimco Realty Corp   Macerich Co

---

Schwab Fundamental U.S. Small Company Index ETF   C   HOLD

Ticker	Traded On	NAV	Total Assets ($)	Dividend Yield (TTM)	Turnover Ratio	Expense Ratio
FNDA	NYSE Arca	37.78	$3,479,476,042	1.55	23	0.25

Ratings
Reward	C
Risk	C+
Recent Upgrade/Downgrade	

Fund Information
Fund Type	Exchange Traded Funds
Category	US Equity Small Cap
Sub-Category	Small Blend
Prospectus Objective	Small Company
Inception Date	Aug-13
Open to New Investments	Y

Prices
Price (as of 9/30/2019)	37.76
52-Week High	40.37
52-Week Low	31.04

Total Returns (%)
3-Month	6-Month	1-Year	3-Year	5-Year
0.18	0.80	-4.83	26.90	48.28

3-Year Standard Deviation	16.31
Effective Duration	

Valuation
Premium/Discount (1-Year Average)	-0.04

Company Information
Provider	Schwab ETFs
Manager/Tenure	Christopher Bliss (2), Ferian Juwono (2), Sabya Sinha (2), 1 other
Website	http://www.schwabfunds.com
Address	Schwab ETFs United States
Phone Number	800-435-4000

PERFORMANCE

Ratings History
Date	Overall Rating	Risk Rating	Reward Rating
Q3-19	C	C+	C
Q4-18	C	C+	C-
Q4-17	B	B	B+
Q4-16	B-	C+	B
Q4-15	C-	C+	D+

Asset & Performance History
Date	NAV	1-Year Total Return
2018	32.84	-12.09
2017	37.9	13.06
2016	34.05	23.47
2015	27.94	-5.04
2014	29.81	7.78
2013	27.96	

Total Assets: $3,479,476,042
Asset Allocation
Asset	%
Cash	0%
Stocks	100%
US Stocks	97%
Bonds	0%
US Bonds	0%
Other	0%

Services Offered:

Investment Strategy: The investment seeks to track as closely as possible, before fees and expenses, the total return of the Russell RAFI™ US Small Company Index. The fund normally will invest at least 90% of its net assets (including, for this purpose, any borrowings for investment purposes) in stocks included in the index. The index measures the performance of the small company size segment by fundamental overall company scores (scores), which are created using as the universe the U.S. companies in the FTSE Global Total Cap Index (the parent index). It may invest up to 10% of its net assets in securities not included in the index. **Top Holdings:** Avon Products Inc Alaska Air Group Inc JetBlue Airways Corp Genpact Ltd Teledyne Technologies Inc

---

Xtrackers USD High Yield Corporate Bond ETF   C   HOLD

Ticker	Traded On	NAV	Total Assets ($)	Dividend Yield (TTM)	Turnover Ratio	Expense Ratio
HYLB	NYSE Arca	50.10	$3,391,468,207	5.82		0.15

Ratings
Reward	C
Risk	C+
Recent Upgrade/Downgrade	

Fund Information
Fund Type	Exchange Traded Funds
Category	US Fixed Income
Sub-Category	High Yield Bond
Prospectus Objective	Corp Bond-High Yld
Inception Date	Dec-16
Open to New Investments	Y

Prices
Price (as of 9/30/2019)	50.08
52-Week High	50.40
52-Week Low	45.99

Total Returns (%)
3-Month	6-Month	1-Year	3-Year	5-Year
0.89	3.42	6.22		

3-Year Standard Deviation	
Effective Duration	3.09

Valuation
Premium/Discount (1-Year Average)	-0.18

Company Information
Provider	DWS
Manager/Tenure	Alexander Bridgeforth (2), Tanuj Dora (2), Brandon Matsui (2), 1 other
Website	http://dws.com
Address	DWS 210 West 10th Street Kansas City MO 64105-1614 United States
Phone Number	

PERFORMANCE

Ratings History
Date	Overall Rating	Risk Rating	Reward Rating
Q3-19	C	C+	C
Q4-18	C-	C+	D+
Q4-17	D	A	D+
Q4-16			
Q4-15			

Asset & Performance History
Date	NAV	1-Year Total Return
2018	46.79	-2.07
2017	50.48	5.96
2016	50.47	
2015		
2014		
2013		

Total Assets: $3,391,468,207
Asset Allocation
Asset	%
Cash	1%
Stocks	0%
US Stocks	0%
Bonds	99%
US Bonds	83%
Other	0%

Services Offered:

Investment Strategy: The investment seeks investment results that correspond generally to the performance, before fees and expenses, of the Solactive USD High Yield Corporates Total Market Index (the "underlying index"). The fund will normally invest at least 80% of its net assets, plus the amount of any borrowings for investment purposes, in high yield corporate bonds. The index comprised of U.S. dollar-denominated high yield corporate bonds. It will concentrate its investments (i.e., hold 25% or more of its total assets) in a particular industry or group of industries to the extent that its underlying index is concentrated. The fund is non-diversified. **Top Holdings:** ALTICE FRANCE S.A 7.38% Sprint Corporation 7.88% TransDigm, Inc. 6.25% Teva Pharmaceutical Finance Netherlands III B.V. 2.2% Bausch Health Companies Inc 6.12%

WisdomTree Europe Hedged Equity Fund   C   HOLD

Ticker	Traded On	NAV	Total Assets ($)	Dividend Yield (TTM)	Turnover Ratio	Expense Ratio
HEDJ	NYSE Arca	67.32	$3,382,724,212	1.71	18	0.58

Ratings
Reward	C
Risk	C+
Recent Upgrade/Downgrade	

Fund Information
Fund Type	Exchange Traded Funds
Category	Europe Equity Large Cap
Sub-Category	Europe Stock
Prospectus Objective	Foreign Stock
Inception Date	Dec-09
Open to New Investments	Y

Prices
Price (as of 9/30/2019)	67.29
52-Week High	68.03
52-Week Low	54.71

Total Returns (%)
3-Month	6-Month	1-Year	3-Year	5-Year
1.00	5.90	7.64	33.91	47.08

3-Year Standard Deviation	12.22
Effective Duration	

Valuation
Premium/Discount (1-Year Average)	-0.06

Company Information
Provider	WisdomTree
Manager/Tenure	Richard A. Brown (9), Thomas J. Durante (9), Karen Q. Wong (9)
Website	http://www.wisdomtree.com
Address	WisdomTree 245 Park Avenue, 35th floor New York NY 10167 United States
Phone Number	866-909-9473

PERFORMANCE

Ratings History
Date	Overall Rating	Risk Rating	Reward Rating
Q3-19	C	C+	C
Q4-18	C-	C	D+
Q4-17	B	B	B
Q4-16	C+	C	C+
Q4-15	B-	B+	C

Asset & Performance History
Date	NAV	1-Year Total Return
2018	56.6	-9.26
2017	63.91	13.89
2016	57.55	9.3
2015	54.25	5.86
2014	56.03	6.54
2013	55.64	21.5

Total Assets: $3,382,724,212
Asset Allocation
Asset	%
Cash	0%
Stocks	100%
US Stocks	5%
Bonds	0%
US Bonds	0%
Other	0%

Services Offered:

Investment Strategy: The investment seeks to track the price and yield performance, before fees and expenses, of the WisdomTree Europe Hedged Equity Index. The fund invests at least 95% of its total assets (exclusive of collateral held from securities lending) in component securities of the index and investments that have economic characteristics that are substantially identical to the economic characteristics of such component securities. The index provides exposure to European equity securities, particularly shares of European exporters, while at the same time neutralizing exposure to fluctuations between the value of the U.S. dollar and the euro. The fund is non-diversified. **Top Holdings:** Anheuser-Busch InBev SA/NV Banco Santander SA Unilever NV Sanofi SA LVMH Moet Hennessy Louis Vuitton SE

Vanguard Consumer Discretionary Index Fund ETF Shares   C   HOLD

Ticker	Traded On	NAV	Total Assets ($)	Dividend Yield (TTM)	Turnover Ratio	Expense Ratio
VCR	NYSE Arca	180.10	$3,377,757,228	1.13	28	0.1

Ratings
Reward	B-
Risk	C-
Recent Upgrade/Downgrade	

Fund Information
Fund Type	Exchange Traded Funds
Category	Consumer Goods & Svcs
Sub-Category	Consumer Cyclical
Prospectus Objective	Unaligned
Inception Date	Jan-04
Open to New Investments	Y

Prices
Price (as of 9/30/2019)	180.12
52-Week High	186.75
52-Week Low	139.59

Total Returns (%)
3-Month	6-Month	1-Year	3-Year	5-Year
-0.93	2.93	0.28	47.58	77.45

3-Year Standard Deviation	14.83
Effective Duration	

Valuation
Premium/Discount (1-Year Average)	-0.01

Company Information
Provider	Vanguard
Manager/Tenure	Michael A. Johnson (8), Awais Khan (1)
Website	http://www.vanguard.com
Address	Vanguard 100 Vanguard Boulevard Malvern PA 19355 United States
Phone Number	877-662-7447

PERFORMANCE

Ratings History
Date	Overall Rating	Risk Rating	Reward Rating
Q3-19	C	C-	B-
Q4-18	C	C-	C
Q4-17	B	A-	B
Q4-16	C+	C-	B
Q4-15	B-	B-	B-

Asset & Performance History
Date	NAV	1-Year Total Return
2018	149.05	-3.19
2017	155.87	22.67
2016	128.56	6.64
2015	122.54	6.35
2014	116.77	9.39
2013	108.08	43.56

Total Assets: $3,377,757,228
Asset Allocation
Asset	%
Cash	1%
Stocks	99%
US Stocks	97%
Bonds	0%
US Bonds	0%
Other	0%

Services Offered:

Investment Strategy: The investment seeks to track the performance of a benchmark index. The fund employs an indexing investment approach designed to track the performance of the MSCI US Investable Market Index/Consumer Discretionary 25/50, an index made up of stocks of large, mid-size, and small U.S. companies within the consumer discretionary sector, as classified under the Global Industry Classification Standard. The Advisor attempts to replicate the target index by seeking to invest all, or substantially all, of its assets in the stocks that make up the index, in order to hold each stock in approximately the same proportion as its weighting in the index. It is non-diversified. **Top Holdings:** Amazon.com Inc The Home Depot Inc McDonald's Corp Starbucks Corp Nike Inc B

Invesco S&P MidCap Low Volatility ETF　　　　　C+　HOLD

Ticker	Traded On	NAV	Total Assets ($)	Dividend Yield (TTM)	Turnover Ratio	Expense Ratio
XMLV	NYSE Arca	52.62	$3,372,933,406	1.93		0.25

Ratings
Reward　　C+
Risk　　C+
Recent Upgrade/Downgrade　　Down

Fund Information
Fund Type　　Exchange Traded Funds
Category　　US Equity Mid Cap
Sub-Category　　Mid-Cap Value
Prospectus Objective　　Income
Inception Date　　Feb-13
Open to New Investments

Prices
Price (as of 9/30/2019)　　52.61
52-Week High　　52.71
52-Week Low　　42.36

Total Returns (%)

3-Month	6-Month	1-Year	3-Year	5-Year
3.00	6.46	11.66	44.06	96.53

3-Year Standard Deviation　　9.93
Effective Duration

Valuation
Premium/Discount (1-Year Average)　　0.01

Company Information
Provider　　Invesco
Manager/Tenure　　Peter Hubbard (6), Michael Jeanette (6), Tony Seisser (5)
Website　　http://www.invesco.com/us
Address　　Invesco 11 Greenway Plaza, Ste. 2500 Houston TX 77046 United States
Phone Number　　800-659-1005

PERFORMANCE

Ratings History

Date	Overall Rating	Risk Rating	Reward Rating
Q3-19	C+	C+	C+
Q4-18	C	C+	C
Q4-17	B+	A+	B
Q4-16	B	C+	B
Q4-15	C	C	B

Asset & Performance History

Date	NAV	1-Year Total Return
2018	44.38	-0.19
2017	45.4	13.79
2016	40.6	21.6
2015	33.99	5.51
2014	32.82	18.04
2013	28.39	

Total Assets: $3,372,933,406
Asset Allocation

Asset	%
Cash	0%
Stocks	100%
US Stocks	100%
Bonds	0%
US Bonds	0%
Other	0%

Services Offered:

Investment Strategy: The investment seeks to track the investment results (before fees and expenses) of the S&P MidCap 400® Low Volatility Index (the "underlying index"). The fund generally will invest at least 90% of its total assets in the securities that comprise the underlying index. Strictly in accordance with its procedures and mandated guidelines, the index provider selects for inclusion in the underlying index the 80 securities that it has determined have the lowest volatility over the past 12 months out of the 400 medium capitalization securities that are contained in the S&P MidCap 400® Index. **Top Holdings:** Hawaiian Electric Industries Inc　WR Berkley Corp NorthWestern Corp　Idacorp Inc　OGE Energy Corp

---

SPDR® DoubleLine Total Return Tactical ETF　　　　　C+　HOLD

Ticker	Traded On	NAV	Total Assets ($)	Dividend Yield (TTM)	Turnover Ratio	Expense Ratio
TOTL	NYSE Arca		$3,360,314,149	3.41	47	0.55

Ratings
Reward　　C+
Risk　　C+
Recent Upgrade/Downgrade

Fund Information
Fund Type　　Exchange Traded Funds
Category　　US Fixed Income
Sub-Category　　Intermediate Core-Plus Bond
Prospectus Objective　　Growth & Inc
Inception Date　　Feb-15
Open to New Investments　　Y

Prices
Price (as of 9/30/2019)　　49.23
52-Week High　　49.65
52-Week Low　　46.68

Total Returns (%)

3-Month	6-Month	1-Year	3-Year	5-Year
1.32	4.04	7.70	8.40	

3-Year Standard Deviation　　2.3
Effective Duration　　3.28

Valuation
Premium/Discount (1-Year Average)　　0.23

Company Information
Provider　　SPDR State Street Global Advisors
Manager/Tenure　　Philip A. Barach (4), Jeffrey E. Gundlach (4), Jeffrey J. Sherman (4)
Website　　http://www.spdrs.com
Address　　SPDR State Street Global Advisors State Street Financial Center, 1 Lincoln Street Boston MA 02111-2900 United States
Phone Number　　617-786-3000

PERFORMANCE

Ratings History

Date	Overall Rating	Risk Rating	Reward Rating
Q3-19	C+	C+	C+
Q4-18	C	C+	C-
Q4-17	C+	B+	C
Q4-16	C-	C+	D+
Q4-15	U		

Asset & Performance History

Date	NAV	1-Year Total Return
2018	47.19	0.3
2017	48.67	3.42
2016	48.48	3.02
2015	48.58	
2014		
2013		

Total Assets: $3,360,314,149
Asset Allocation

Asset	%
Cash	2%
Stocks	0%
US Stocks	0%
Bonds	97%
US Bonds	88%
Other	0%

Services Offered:

Investment Strategy: The investment seeks to maximize total return. Under normal circumstances, the Sub-Adviser will invest at least 80% of the fund's net assets in a portfolio of fixed income securities of any credit quality. The fund may invest up to 25% of its net assets in corporate high yield securities (commonly known as "junk bonds"). It may invest up to 15% of its net assets in securities denominated in foreign currencies, and may invest beyond this limit in U.S. dollar-denominated securities of foreign issuers. The fund is non-diversified. **Top Holdings:** United States Treasury Bills 0.01%　United States Treasury Bills 0.01%　United States Treasury Bills 0%　United States Treasury Notes 2.38%　United States Treasury Notes 2.12%

Vanguard Long-Term Treasury Index Fund ETF Shares

C HOLD

Ticker	Traded On	NAV	Total Assets ($)	Dividend Yield (TTM)	Turnover Ratio	Expense Ratio
VGLT	NAS CM	87.68	$3,325,082,973	2.36	19	0.07

Ratings
Reward   C
Risk   C+
Recent Upgrade/Downgrade

Fund Information
Fund Type   Exchange Traded Funds
Category   US Fixed Income
Sub-Category   Long Government
Prospectus Objective   Govt Bond - Gen
Inception Date   Nov-09
Open to New Investments   Y

Prices
Price (as of 9/30/2019)   87.74
52-Week High   90.55
52-Week Low   69.06

Total Returns (%)

3-Month	6-Month	1-Year	3-Year	5-Year
7.85	13.97	24.58	12.31	38.06

3-Year Standard Deviation   11.57
Effective Duration   18.09

Valuation
Premium/Discount (1-Year Average)   0.08

Company Information
Provider   Vanguard
Manager/Tenure   Joshua C. Barrickman (6)
Website   http://www.vanguard.com
Address   Vanguard 100 Vanguard Boulevard
                      Malvern PA 19355 United States
Phone Number   877-662-7447

PERFORMANCE

Ratings History

Date	Overall Rating	Risk Rating	Reward Rating
Q3-19	C	C+	C
Q4-18	D+	C-	D
Q4-17	C	C	C
Q4-16	C	C-	C
Q4-15	C	C-	C

Asset & Performance History

Date	NAV	1-Year Total Return
2018	74.39	-1.93
2017	77.99	8.77
2016	73.67	1.39
2015	74.52	-1.35
2014	77.62	25.04
2013	63.96	-12.73

Total Assets: $3,325,082,973
Asset Allocation

Asset	%
Cash	1%
Stocks	0%
US Stocks	0%
Bonds	99%
US Bonds	99%
Other	0%

Services Offered:

Investment Strategy: The investment seeks to track the performance of a market-weighted government bond index with a long-term dollar-weighted average maturity. The fund employs an indexing investment approach designed to track the performance of the Bloomberg Barclays US Long Treasury Bond Index. This index includes fixed income securities issued by the U.S. Treasury (not including inflation-protected bonds), with maturities greater than 10 years. Under normal circumstances, at least 80% of the fund's assets will be invested in bonds included in the index. **Top Holdings:** United States Treasury Bonds 3.38% United States Treasury Bonds 3% United States Treasury Bonds 3% United States Treasury Bonds 3.75% United States Treasury Bonds 2.88%

Goldman Sachs Access Treasury 0-1 Year ETF

C HOLD

Ticker	Traded On	NAV	Total Assets ($)	Dividend Yield (TTM)	Turnover Ratio	Expense Ratio
GBIL	NYSE Arca	100.36	$3,300,798,020	2.16		0.12

Ratings
Reward   C
Risk   C+
Recent Upgrade/Downgrade

Fund Information
Fund Type   Exchange Traded Funds
Category   US Fixed Income
Sub-Category   Ultrashort Bond
Prospectus Objective   Govt Bond - Treasury
Inception Date   Sep-16
Open to New Investments   Y

Prices
Price (as of 9/30/2019)   100.38
52-Week High   100.40
52-Week Low   100.00

Total Returns (%)

3-Month	6-Month	1-Year	3-Year	5-Year
0.54	1.21	2.41	4.44	

3-Year Standard Deviation   0.25
Effective Duration

Valuation
Premium/Discount (1-Year Average)   0.01

Company Information
Provider   Goldman Sachs
Manager/Tenure   Dave Fishman (3), Jason Singer (1),
                      David Westbrook (1)
Website   http://www.gsamfunds.com
Address   Goldman Sachs 200 West Stree New
                      York NY 10282 United States
Phone Number   800-526-7384

PERFORMANCE

Ratings History

Date	Overall Rating	Risk Rating	Reward Rating
Q3-19	C	C+	C
Q4-18	C	C+	C-
Q4-17	D	C+	D+
Q4-16	U		
Q4-15			

Asset & Performance History

Date	NAV	1-Year Total Return
2018	100.03	1.58
2017	99.97	0.7
2016	100	
2015		
2014		
2013		

Total Assets: $3,300,798,020
Asset Allocation

Asset	%
Cash	38%
Stocks	0%
US Stocks	0%
Bonds	62%
US Bonds	62%
Other	0%

Services Offered:

Investment Strategy: The investment seeks to provide investment results that closely correspond, before fees and expenses, to the performance of the FTSE US Treasury 0-1 Year Composite Select Index. The fund seeks to achieve its investment objective by investing at least 80% of its assets (exclusive of collateral held from securities lending) in securities included in its underlying index. The index is designed to measure the performance of U.S. Treasury Securities with a maximum remaining maturity of 12 months. The investment adviser uses a representative sampling strategy to manage the fund. **Top Holdings:** United States Treasury Bills 0% United States Treasury Notes 1.5% United States Treasury Bills 0% United States Treasury Bills 0% United States Treasury Notes 1.38%

SPDR® Bloomberg Barclays Short Term High Yield Bond ETF　　B-　BUY

Ticker	Traded On	NAV	Total Assets ($)	Dividend Yield (TTM)	Turnover Ratio	Expense Ratio
SJNK	NYSE Arca		$3,300,549,760	5.69	65	0.4

Ratings
Reward	C
Risk	B
Recent Upgrade/Downgrade	Down

Fund Information
Fund Type	Exchange Traded Funds
Category	US Fixed Income
Sub-Category	High Yield Bond
Prospectus Objective	Corp Bond-High Yld
Inception Date	Mar-12
Open to New Investments	Y

Prices
Price (as of 9/30/2019)	27.01
52-Week High	27.52
52-Week Low	25.68

Total Returns (%)
3-Month	6-Month	1-Year	3-Year	5-Year
0.34	1.85	3.47	15.66	19.16

3-Year Standard Deviation	3.3
Effective Duration	1.62

Valuation
Premium/Discount (1-Year Average)	0.11

Company Information
Provider	SPDR State Street Global Advisors
Manager/Tenure	Michael J. Brunell (7), Kyle Kelly (6), Bradley J. Sullivan (3)
Website	http://www.spdrs.com
Address	SPDR State Street Global Advisors State Street Financial Center, 1 Lincoln Street Boston MA 02111-2900 United States
Phone Number	617-786-3000

PERFORMANCE

Ratings History
Date	Overall Rating	Risk Rating	Reward Rating
Q3-19	B-	B	C
Q4-18	C+	B	C
Q4-17	C+	B-	C+
Q4-16	C	C+	C
Q4-15	C	C+	C-

Asset & Performance History
Date	NAV	1-Year Total Return
2018	25.98	-0.25
2017	27.51	4.85
2016	27.62	14.27
2015	25.62	-6.56
2014	28.93	-0.73
2013	30.7	6.85

Total Assets: $3,300,549,760
Asset Allocation
Asset	%
Cash	2%
Stocks	0%
US Stocks	0%
Bonds	97%
US Bonds	83%
Other	0%

Services Offered:

Investment Strategy: The investment seeks to provide investment results that correspond generally to the price and yield performance of the Bloomberg Barclays US High Yield 350mn Cash Pay 0-5 Yr 2% Capped Index. The fund generally invests substantially all, but at least 80%, of its total assets in the securities comprising the index or in securities that the Adviser determines have economic characteristics that are substantially identical to the economic characteristics of the securities that comprise the index. The index is designed to measure the performance of short-term publicly issued U.S. dollar-denominated high yield corporate bonds. It is non-diversified.
Top Holdings: Sprint Corporation 7.88% Reynolds Group Issuer LLC. 5.75% Community Health Systems Incorporated 6.25% Nielsen Finance LLC/Nielsen Finance Co 5% Tenet Healthcare Corporation 8.12%

iShares Global Infrastructure ETF　　C+　HOLD

Ticker	Traded On	NAV	Total Assets ($)	Dividend Yield (TTM)	Turnover Ratio	Expense Ratio
IGF	NAS CM	46.44	$3,241,307,227	3.18	19	0.46

Ratings
Reward	C+
Risk	C+
Recent Upgrade/Downgrade	Down

Fund Information
Fund Type	Exchange Traded Funds
Category	Infrastructure Sector Equity
Sub-Category	Infrastructure
Prospectus Objective	Utility
Inception Date	Dec-07
Open to New Investments	Y

Prices
Price (as of 9/30/2019)	46.47
52-Week High	46.97
52-Week Low	38.21

Total Returns (%)
3-Month	6-Month	1-Year	3-Year	5-Year
1.00	5.45	13.63	23.16	28.26

3-Year Standard Deviation	10.26
Effective Duration	

Valuation
Premium/Discount (1-Year Average)	0.09

Company Information
Provider	iShares
Manager/Tenure	Greg Savage (11), Jennifer Hsui (7), Alan Mason (3), 2 others
Website	http://www.ishares.com
Address	iShares 400 Howard Street San Francisco CA 94105 United States
Phone Number	800-474-2737

PERFORMANCE

Ratings History
Date	Overall Rating	Risk Rating	Reward Rating
Q3-19	C+	C+	C+
Q4-18	C	C	C-
Q4-17	C+	C+	C+
Q4-16	C	C	C
Q4-15	C	C+	C

Asset & Performance History
Date	NAV	1-Year Total Return
2018	39.31	-10.19
2017	45.27	19.25
2016	39.11	11.54
2015	36.1	-11.97
2014	42.28	12.14
2013	38.82	13.99

Total Assets: $3,241,307,227
Asset Allocation
Asset	%
Cash	0%
Stocks	100%
US Stocks	40%
Bonds	0%
US Bonds	0%
Other	0%

Services Offered:

Investment Strategy: The investment seeks to track the S&P Global Infrastructure IndexTM. The fund generally invests at least 90% of its assets in the component securities of the index and in investments that have economic characteristics that are substantially identical to the component securities and may invest up to 10% of its assets in certain futures, options and swap contracts, cash and cash equivalents. The index is designed to track performance of the stocks of large infrastructure companies in developed or emerging markets that must be domiciled in developed markets, or whose stocks are listed on developed market exchanges around the world.
Top Holdings: Transurban Group NextEra Energy Inc Aena SME SA Enbridge Inc Atlantia SpA

iShares 0-5 Year High Yield Corporate Bond ETF — C+ HOLD

Ticker	Traded On	NAV	Total Assets ($)	Dividend Yield (TTM)	Turnover Ratio	Expense Ratio
SHYG	NYSE Arca	46.32	$3,223,769,921	5.55	35	0.3

Ratings
Reward   C
Risk   C+
Recent Upgrade/Downgrade

Fund Information
Fund Type	Exchange Traded Funds
Category	US Fixed Income
Sub-Category	High Yield Bond
Prospectus Objective	Corp Bond-High Yld
Inception Date	Oct-13
Open to New Investments	Y

Prices
Price (as of 9/30/2019)	46.49
52-Week High	46.94
52-Week Low	43.90

Total Returns (%)
3-Month	6-Month	1-Year	3-Year	5-Year
0.60	2.55	4.21	16.10	22.51

3-Year Standard Deviation   3.06
Effective Duration

Valuation
Premium/Discount (1-Year Average)   0.22

Company Information
Provider	iShares
Manager/Tenure	James Mauro (5), Scott Radell (5)
Website	http://www.ishares.com
Address	iShares 400 Howard Street San Francisco CA 94105 United States
Phone Number	800-474-2737

PERFORMANCE

Ratings History
Date	Overall Rating	Risk Rating	Reward Rating
Q3-19	C+	C+	C
Q4-18	C	C+	C
Q4-17	B-	B	C+
Q4-16	C	C+	C
Q4-15	C-	C+	D

Asset & Performance History
Date	NAV	1-Year Total Return
2018	44.54	0.43
2017	46.93	5.4
2016	47.02	12.3
2015	44.33	-3.73
2014	48.35	0.5
2013	50.18	

Total Assets: $3,223,769,921
Asset Allocation
Asset	%
Cash	4%
Stocks	0%
US Stocks	0%
Bonds	96%
US Bonds	81%
Other	0%

Services Offered:

Investment Strategy: The investment seeks to track the investment results of the Markit iBoxx® USD Liquid High Yield 0-5 Index composed of U.S. dollar-denominated, high yield corporate bonds with remaining maturities of less than five years. The fund generally invests at least 90% of its assets in the component securities of the index and may invest up to 10% of its assets in certain futures, options and swap contracts, cash and cash equivalents. The index is designed to reflect the performance of U.S. dollar-denominated high yield corporate debt. **Top Holdings:** Sprint Corporation 7.88% Tenet Healthcare Corporation 8.13% Community Health Systems Incorporated 6.25% Teva Pharmaceutical Finance Netherlands III B.V. 2.2% Reynolds Group Issuer LLC. 5.75%

---

iShares Core MSCI Europe ETF — C HOLD

Ticker	Traded On	NAV	Total Assets ($)	Dividend Yield (TTM)	Turnover Ratio	Expense Ratio
IEUR	NYSE Arca	45.75	$3,193,068,003	3.41	4	0.09

Ratings
Reward   C
Risk   C+
Recent Upgrade/Downgrade

Fund Information
Fund Type	Exchange Traded Funds
Category	Europe Equity Large Cap
Sub-Category	Europe Stock
Prospectus Objective	Europe Stock
Inception Date	Jun-14
Open to New Investments	Y

Prices
Price (as of 9/30/2019)	45.74
52-Week High	47.98
52-Week Low	40.03

Total Returns (%)
3-Month	6-Month	1-Year	3-Year	5-Year
-2.07	1.28	-1.30	21.54	17.10

3-Year Standard Deviation   12.63
Effective Duration

Valuation
Premium/Discount (1-Year Average)   -0.01

Company Information
Provider	iShares
Manager/Tenure	Diane Hsiung (5), Jennifer Hsui (5), Greg Savage (5), 3 others
Website	http://www.ishares.com
Address	iShares 400 Howard Street San Francisco CA 94105 United States
Phone Number	800-474-2737

PERFORMANCE

Ratings History
Date	Overall Rating	Risk Rating	Reward Rating
Q3-19	C	C+	C
Q4-18	D+	C-	D+
Q4-17	B	B	B
Q4-16	D+	C-	D
Q4-15	D	C+	D

Asset & Performance History
Date	NAV	1-Year Total Return
2018	41.27	-15.24
2017	50.34	26.85
2016	40.79	-0.41
2015	42.27	-1.14
2014	43.87	
2013		

Total Assets: $3,193,068,003
Asset Allocation
Asset	%
Cash	0%
Stocks	100%
US Stocks	2%
Bonds	0%
US Bonds	0%
Other	0%

Services Offered:

Investment Strategy: The investment seeks to track the investment results of the MSCI Europe IMI. The fund generally will invest at least 90% of its assets in the component securities of the underlying index and in investments that have economic characteristics that are substantially identical to the component securities of the underlying index. The index is a free float-adjusted market capitalization-weighted index which consists of securities from the following 15 developed market countries or regions: Austria, Belgium, Denmark, Finland, France, Germany, Ireland, Italy, the Netherlands, Norway, Portugal, Spain, Sweden, Switzerland and the United Kingdom. **Top Holdings:** Nestle SA Novartis AG Roche Holding AG Dividend Right Cert. HSBC Holdings PLC BP PLC

VanEck Vectors High-Yield Municipal Index ETF   B   BUY

Ticker	Traded On	NAV	Total Assets ($)	Dividend Yield (TTM)	Turnover Ratio	Expense Ratio
HYD	BATS	64.43	$3,053,594,109	4.17	22	0.35

Ratings

Reward	B
Risk	C+
Recent Upgrade/Downgrade	

Fund Information

Fund Type	Exchange Traded Funds
Category	US Muni Fixed Inc
Sub-Category	High Yield Muni
Prospectus Objective	Muni Bond - Natl
Inception Date	Feb-09
Open to New Investments	Y

Prices

Price (as of 9/30/2019)	64.43
52-Week High	64.90
52-Week Low	60.28

Total Returns (%)

3-Month	6-Month	1-Year	3-Year	5-Year
2.18	4.91	7.68	127.72	161.80

3-Year Standard Deviation	4.75
Effective Duration	6.22

Valuation

Premium/Discount (1-Year Average)	-0.06

Company Information

Provider	VanEck
Manager/Tenure	James T. Colby (10)
Website	http://www.vaneck.com
Address	Van Eck Associates Corporation 666 Third Avenue New York NY 10017 United States
Phone Number	800-826-1115

PERFORMANCE

Ratings History

Date	Overall Rating	Risk Rating	Reward Rating
Q3-19	B	C+	B
Q4-18	B+	C+	A
Q4-17	B	A	C+
Q4-16	C	C+	C
Q4-15	C+	C+	C

Asset & Performance History

Date	NAV	1-Year Total Return
2018	61.23	103.45
2017	31.31	10.49
2016	29.59	0.4
2015	30.78	4.81
2014	30.82	13.82
2013	28.49	-8.13

Total Assets: $3,053,594,109

Asset Allocation

Asset	%
Cash	1%
Stocks	0%
US Stocks	0%
Bonds	99%
US Bonds	94%
Other	0%

Services Offered:

Investment Strategy: The investment seeks to replicate as closely as possible, before fees and expenses, the price and yield performance of the Bloomberg Barclays Municipal Custom High Yield Composite Index. The fund normally invests at least 80% of its total assets in securities that comprise the benchmark index. The index is comprised of publicly traded municipal bonds that cover the U.S. dollar denominated high yield long-term tax-exempt bond market. **Top Holdings:** PUERTO RICO SALES TAX FING CORP SALES TAX REV 5% NEW YORK LIBERTY DEV CORP LIBERTY REV 5% PUBLIC FIN AUTH WIS LTD OBLIG PILOT REV 7% BUCKEYE OHIO TOB SETTLEMENT FING AUTH 5.88% BUCKEYE OHIO TOB SETTLEMENT FING AUTH 5.12%

SPDR® Portfolio Large Cap ETF   C+   HOLD

Ticker	Traded On	NAV	Total Assets ($)	Dividend Yield (TTM)	Turnover Ratio	Expense Ratio
SPLG	NYSE Arca		$2,977,252,856	1.9	5	0.03

Ratings

Reward	C+
Risk	C+
Recent Upgrade/Downgrade	

Fund Information

Fund Type	Exchange Traded Funds
Category	US Equity Large Cap Blend
Sub-Category	Large Blend
Prospectus Objective	Growth & Inc
Inception Date	Nov-05
Open to New Investments	Y

Prices

Price (as of 9/30/2019)	34.85
52-Week High	35.57
52-Week Low	27.32

Total Returns (%)

3-Month	6-Month	1-Year	3-Year	5-Year
0.07	4.12	3.49	44.84	65.23

3-Year Standard Deviation	12.33
Effective Duration	

Valuation

Premium/Discount (1-Year Average)	0.00

Company Information

Provider	SPDR State Street Global Advisors
Manager/Tenure	Michael J. Feehily (7), Karl A. Schneider (4), John Law (0)
Website	http://www.spdrs.com
Address	SPDR State Street Global Advisors State Street Financial Center, 1 Lincoln Street Boston MA 02111-2900 United States
Phone Number	617-786-3000

PERFORMANCE

Ratings History

Date	Overall Rating	Risk Rating	Reward Rating
Q3-19	C+	C+	C+
Q4-18	C	C+	C
Q4-17	B	B	B
Q4-16	C+	D+	B
Q4-15	C	C-	C

Asset & Performance History

Date	NAV	1-Year Total Return
2018	29.2	-4.7
2017	31.27	21.6
2016	26.2	11.49
2015	23.89	0.84
2014	24.16	13.13
2013	21.76	32.78

Total Assets: $2,977,252,856

Asset Allocation

Asset	%
Cash	0%
Stocks	100%
US Stocks	100%
Bonds	0%
US Bonds	0%
Other	0%

Services Offered: Dividend Investment Plan, CashInvestment Plan

Investment Strategy: The investment seeks to provide investment results that, before fees and expenses, correspond generally to the total return performance of the SSGA Large Cap Index. The fund generally invests substantially all, but at least 80%, of its total assets in the securities comprising the index. The index is designed to measure the performance of the large-capitalization segment of the U.S. equity market. The fund may purchase a subset of the securities in the index in an effort to hold a portfolio of securities with generally the same risk and return characteristics of the index. It is non-diversified. **Top Holdings:** Microsoft Corp Apple Inc Amazon.com Inc Facebook Inc A JPMorgan Chase & Co

SPDR® Nuveen Bloomberg Barclays Municipal Bond ETF

C+ HOLD

Ticker	Traded On	NAV	Total Assets ($)	Dividend Yield (TTM)	Turnover Ratio	Expense Ratio
TFI	NYSE Arca		$2,957,205,189	2.16	22	0.23

Ratings
Reward	C+
Risk	C+
Recent Upgrade/Downgrade	

Fund Information
Fund Type	Exchange Traded Funds
Category	US Muni Fixed Inc
Sub-Category	Muni National Long
Prospectus Objective	Muni Bond - Natl
Inception Date	Sep-07
Open to New Investments	Y

Prices
Price (as of 9/30/2019)	50.69
52-Week High	51.39
52-Week Low	46.65

Total Returns (%)
3-Month	6-Month	1-Year	3-Year	5-Year
1.55	4.03	9.04	8.33	18.62

3-Year Standard Deviation	4.13
Effective Duration	6.16

Valuation
Premium/Discount (1-Year Average)	-0.13

Company Information
Provider	SPDR State Street Global Advisors
Manager/Tenure	Timothy T. Ryan (12), Steven M. Hlavin (9)
Website	http://www.spdrs.com
Address	SPDR State Street Global Advisors State Street Financial Center, 1 Lincoln Street Boston MA 02111-2900 United States
Phone Number	617-786-3000

PERFORMANCE

Ratings History

Date	Overall Rating	Risk Rating	Reward Rating
Q3-19	C+	C+	C+
Q4-18	C	C	D+
Q4-17	B-	B	C
Q4-16	C	C+	C
Q4-15	C+	C+	C

Asset & Performance History

Date	NAV	1-Year Total Return
2018	48.14	0.43
2017	49.03	5.4
2016	47.46	-0.24
2015	48.65	3.33
2014	48.24	9.24
2013	45.24	-3.59

Total Assets: $2,957,205,189

Asset Allocation

Asset	%
Cash	0%
Stocks	0%
US Stocks	0%
Bonds	100%
US Bonds	100%
Other	0%

Services Offered:

Investment Strategy: The investment seeks investment results that correspond generally to the price and yield performance of the Bloomberg Barclays Municipal Managed Money 1-25 Years Index. The fund invests substantially all, but at least 80%, of its total assets in the securities comprising the index or in securities that the Sub-Adviser determines have economic characteristics that are substantially identical to the economic characteristics of the securities that comprise the index. The index is designed to track the U.S. fully tax-exempt bond market. It is non-diversified. **Top Holdings:** NEW YORK N Y 3% BAY AREA TOLL AUTH CALIF TOLL BRDG REV 2.62% PENNSYLVANIA ST 5% NEW YORK ST URBAN DEV CORP REV 5% NEW YORK N Y CITY TRANSITIONAL FIN AUTH REV 5%

iShares Currency Hedged MSCI EAFE ETF

C HOLD

Ticker	Traded On	NAV	Total Assets ($)	Dividend Yield (TTM)	Turnover Ratio	Expense Ratio
HEFA	BATS	29.96	$2,937,964,279	3	7	0.35

Ratings
Reward	C
Risk	C+
Recent Upgrade/Downgrade	

Fund Information
Fund Type	Exchange Traded Funds
Category	Global Equity Large Cap
Sub-Category	Foreign Large Blend
Prospectus Objective	Foreign Stock
Inception Date	Jan-14
Open to New Investments	Y

Prices
Price (as of 9/30/2019)	29.94
52-Week High	30.19
52-Week Low	25.29

Total Returns (%)
3-Month	6-Month	1-Year	3-Year	5-Year
1.33	4.52	4.12	33.69	42.61

3-Year Standard Deviation	10.02
Effective Duration	

Valuation
Premium/Discount (1-Year Average)	-0.01

Company Information
Provider	iShares
Manager/Tenure	Diane Hsiung (5), Jennifer Hsui (5), Orlando Montalvo (5), 2 others
Website	http://www.ishares.com
Address	iShares 400 Howard Street San Francisco CA 94105 United States
Phone Number	800-474-2737

PERFORMANCE

Ratings History

Date	Overall Rating	Risk Rating	Reward Rating
Q3-19	C	C+	C
Q4-18	C	C+	C-
Q4-17	B	B	B
Q4-16	C	C+	C
Q4-15	D+	C+	C-

Asset & Performance History

Date	NAV	1-Year Total Return
2018	25.82	-9.69
2017	29.68	16.69
2016	26.11	6.57
2015	25.35	4.44
2014	25.1	
2013		

Total Assets: $2,937,964,279

Asset Allocation

Asset	%
Cash	1%
Stocks	99%
US Stocks	2%
Bonds	0%
US Bonds	0%
Other	0%

Services Offered:

Investment Strategy: The investment seeks to track the investment results of the MSCI EAFE® 100% Hedged to USD Index. The fund generally will invest at least 90% of its assets in the component securities (including indirect investments through the underlying fund) and other instruments of the underlying index and in investments that have economic characteristics that are substantially identical to the component securities of the underlying index. The index is composed of large- and mid-capitalization equities in Europe, Australasia, and the Far East while mitigating exposure to fluctuations between the value of the component currencies and the U.S. dollar. **Top Holdings:** Nestle SA Novartis AG Roche Holding AG Dividend Right Cert. Toyota Motor Corp HSBC Holdings PLC

Vanguard Extended Duration Treasury Index Fund ETF Shares   C   HOLD

Ticker	Traded On	NAV	Total Assets ($)	Dividend Yield (TTM)	Turnover Ratio	Expense Ratio
EDV	NYSE Arca	140.55	$2,911,971,005	2.33	18	0.07

Ratings
Reward   C
Risk   C+
Recent Upgrade/Downgrade

Fund Information
Fund Type   Exchange Traded Funds
Category   US Fixed Income
Sub-Category   Long Government
Prospectus Objective   Govt Bond - Treasury
Inception Date   Dec-07
Open to New Investments   Y

Prices
Price (as of 9/30/2019)   141.30
52-Week High   148.21
52-Week Low   101.75

Total Returns (%)

3-Month	6-Month	1-Year	3-Year	5-Year
12.12	22.37	35.05	15.85	50.69

3-Year Standard Deviation   16.63
Effective Duration   24.40

Valuation
Premium/Discount (1-Year Average)   0.55

Company Information
Provider   Vanguard
Manager/Tenure   William D. Baird (6), Joshua C. Barrickman (6)
Website   http://www.vanguard.com
Address   Vanguard 100 Vanguard Boulevard Malvern PA 19355 United States
Phone Number   877-662-7447

PERFORMANCE

Ratings History

Date	Overall Rating	Risk Rating	Reward Rating
Q3-19	C	C+	C
Q4-18	D+	C-	D
Q4-17	C	C	C
Q4-16	C	C-	C
Q4-15	C	D+	C

Asset & Performance History

Date	NAV	1-Year Total Return
2018	112.21	-3.77
2017	120.15	13.72
2016	109.1	1.6
2015	113.04	-4.44
2014	123.28	45.63
2013	87.72	-20.94

Total Assets: $2,911,971,005
Asset Allocation

Asset	%
Cash	0%
Stocks	0%
US Stocks	0%
Bonds	100%
US Bonds	100%
Other	0%

Services Offered:

Investment Strategy: The investment seeks to track the performance of an index of extended-duration zero-coupon U.S. Treasury securities. The fund employs an indexing investment approach designed to track the performance of the Bloomberg Barclays U.S. Treasury STRIPS 20-30 Year Equal Par Bond Index. This index includes zero-coupon U.S. Treasury securities (Treasury STRIPS), which are backed by the full faith and credit of the U.S. government, with maturities ranging from 20 to 30 years. The fund invests by sampling the index. At least 80% of the fund's assets will be invested in U.S. Treasury securities held in the index. **Top Holdings:** U.S. Treasury Security Stripped Interest Security 0% U.S. Treasury Bond Stripped Principal Payment 0% U.S. Treasury Security Stripped Interest Security 0% U.S. Treasury Bond Stripped Principal Payment 0% U.S. Treasury Bond Stripped Principal Payment 0%

WisdomTree U.S. Quality Dividend Growth Fund   C+   HOLD

Ticker	Traded On	NAV	Total Assets ($)	Dividend Yield (TTM)	Turnover Ratio	Expense Ratio
DGRW	NAS CM	45.11	$2,891,807,255	2.22	29	0.28

Ratings
Reward   C+
Risk   C+
Recent Upgrade/Downgrade

Fund Information
Fund Type   Exchange Traded Funds
Category   US Equity Large Cap Blend
Sub-Category   Large Blend
Prospectus Objective   Growth & Inc
Inception Date   May-13
Open to New Investments   Y

Prices
Price (as of 9/30/2019)   45.09
52-Week High   45.42
52-Week Low   36.09

Total Returns (%)

3-Month	6-Month	1-Year	3-Year	5-Year
3.18	4.98	3.95	49.24	74.19

3-Year Standard Deviation   12.48
Effective Duration

Valuation
Premium/Discount (1-Year Average)   -0.01

Company Information
Provider   WisdomTree
Manager/Tenure   Richard A. Brown (6), Thomas J. Durante (6), Karen Q. Wong (6)
Website   http://www.wisdomtree.com
Address   WisdomTree 245 Park Avenue, 35th floor New York NY 10167 United States
Phone Number   866-909-9473

PERFORMANCE

Ratings History

Date	Overall Rating	Risk Rating	Reward Rating
Q3-19	C+	C+	C+
Q4-18	C	C+	C
Q4-17	B	B	B
Q4-16	B-	C+	B
Q4-15	C	C+	C+

Asset & Performance History

Date	NAV	1-Year Total Return
2018	38.33	-5.22
2017	41.37	26.94
2016	33.22	11.61
2015	30.34	-0.01
2014	31	13.55
2013	27.83	

Total Assets: $2,891,807,255
Asset Allocation

Asset	%
Cash	0%
Stocks	100%
US Stocks	100%
Bonds	0%
US Bonds	0%
Other	0%

Services Offered:

Investment Strategy: The investment seeks to track the price and yield performance, before fees and expenses, of the WisdomTree U.S. Quality Dividend Growth Index. Under normal circumstances, at least 80% of the fund's total assets (exclusive of collateral held from securities lending) will be invested in component securities of the index and investments that have economic characteristics that are substantially identical to the economic characteristics of such component securities. The index is a fundamentally weighted index that consists of dividend-paying U.S. common stocks with growth characteristics. The fund is non-diversified. **Top Holdings:** Microsoft Corp Apple Inc Verizon Communications Inc Exxon Mobil Corp Procter & Gamble Co

First Trust Capital Strength ETF
B-   **BUY**

Ticker	Traded On	NAV
FTCS	NAS CM	56.74

Total Assets ($)	Dividend Yield (TTM)	Turnover Ratio	Expense Ratio
$2,862,573,537	1.39	117	0.6

Ratings
Reward	B-
Risk	C+
Recent Upgrade/Downgrade	Up

Fund Information
Fund Type	Exchange Traded Funds
Category	US Equity Large Cap Blend
Sub-Category	Large Blend
Prospectus Objective	Growth
Inception Date	Jul-06
Open to New Investments	Y

Prices
Price (as of 9/30/2019)	56.78
52-Week High	57.95
52-Week Low	45.20

Total Returns (%)
3-Month	6-Month	1-Year	3-Year	5-Year
0.15	4.42	3.86	46.96	74.18

3-Year Standard Deviation	11.38
Effective Duration	

Valuation
Premium/Discount (1-Year Average)	0.01

Company Information
Provider	First Trust
Manager/Tenure	Jon C. Erickson (13), Daniel J. Lindquist (13), David G. McGarel (13), 3 others
Website	http://www.ftportfolios.com/
Address	First Trust 120 E. Liberty Drive, Suite 400 Wheaton IL 60187 United States
Phone Number	800-621-1675

PERFORMANCE

Ratings History
Date	Overall Rating	Risk Rating	Reward Rating
Q3-19	B-	C+	B-
Q4-18	C	C+	C
Q4-17	B	B	B
Q4-16	C+	C	B
Q4-15	C	C	C

Asset & Performance History
Date	NAV	1-Year Total Return
2018	48.28	-4.09
2017	50.95	26.48
2016	40.79	8.57
2015	38.12	1.63
2014	38.08	15.44
2013	33.69	35.9

Total Assets: $2,862,573,537
Asset Allocation
Asset	%
Cash	0%
Stocks	100%
US Stocks	98%
Bonds	0%
US Bonds	0%
Other	0%

Services Offered:

Investment Strategy: The investment seeks investment results that correspond generally to the price and yield (before the fund's fees and expenses) of an equity index called the Capital Strength Index(SM). The fund will normally invest at least 90% of its net assets (including investment borrowings) in the common stocks and real estate investment trusts ("REITs") that comprise the index. The index seeks to provide exposure to well-capitalized companies with strong market positions that have the potential to provide their stockholders with a greater degree of stability and performance over time. **Top Holdings:** Amgen Inc American Tower Corp Zoetis Inc Class A S&P Global Inc Moody's Corporation

---

iShares Core 1-5 Year USD Bond ETF
C+   **HOLD**

Ticker	Traded On	NAV
ISTB	NAS CM	50.43

Total Assets ($)	Dividend Yield (TTM)	Turnover Ratio	Expense Ratio
$2,808,844,972	2.75	107	0.06

Ratings
Reward	C
Risk	C+
Recent Upgrade/Downgrade	Up

Fund Information
Fund Type	Exchange Traded Funds
Category	US Fixed Income
Sub-Category	Short-Term Bond
Prospectus Objective	Multisector Bond
Inception Date	Oct-12
Open to New Investments	Y

Prices
Price (as of 9/30/2019)	50.49
52-Week High	50.67
52-Week Low	48.64

Total Returns (%)
3-Month	6-Month	1-Year	3-Year	5-Year
0.86	2.87	5.98	7.02	11.90

3-Year Standard Deviation	1.43
Effective Duration	2.54

Valuation
Premium/Discount (1-Year Average)	0.11

Company Information
Provider	iShares
Manager/Tenure	James Mauro (6), Scott Radell (6)
Website	http://www.ishares.com
Address	iShares 400 Howard Street San Francisco CA 94105 United States
Phone Number	800-474-2737

PERFORMANCE

Ratings History
Date	Overall Rating	Risk Rating	Reward Rating
Q3-19	C+	C+	C
Q4-18	C	C+	C-
Q4-17	B	A+	C
Q4-16	C	C-	C
Q4-15	C	C-	C

Asset & Performance History
Date	NAV	1-Year Total Return
2018	49.03	1.18
2017	49.72	1.73
2016	49.84	2.64
2015	49.48	0.83
2014	49.85	1.06
2013	49.85	0.12

Total Assets: $2,808,844,972
Asset Allocation
Asset	%
Cash	1%
Stocks	0%
US Stocks	0%
Bonds	98%
US Bonds	78%
Other	0%

Services Offered:

Investment Strategy: The investment seeks to track the investment results of the Bloomberg Barclays U.S. Universal 1-5 Year Index, which measures the performance of U.S. dollar-denominated taxable bonds that are rated either investment-grade or high yield with remaining effective maturities between one and five years. The fund invests at least 90% of its assets in the component securities of the index and in investments that have economic characteristics that are substantially identical to the component securities and may invest up to 10% of its assets in certain futures, options and swap contracts, cash and cash equivalents, as well as in securities not included in the index. **Top Holdings:** United States Treasury Notes 1.38% United States Treasury Notes 1.38% United States Treasury Notes 2.13% United States Treasury Notes 2% United States Treasury Notes 2.13%

---

iShares Global Tech ETF   B-   BUY

Ticker	Traded On	NAV	Total Assets ($)	Dividend Yield (TTM)	Turnover Ratio	Expense Ratio
IXN	NYSE Arca	184.56	$2,805,382,882	1.03	17	0.46

Ratings
Reward	B
Risk	C
Recent Upgrade/Downgrade	Up

Fund Information
Fund Type	Exchange Traded Funds
Category	Technology Sector Equity
Sub-Category	Technology
Prospectus Objective	Technology
Inception Date	Nov-01
Open to New Investments	Y

Prices
Price (as of 9/30/2019)	184.97
52-Week High	188.59
52-Week Low	134.75

Total Returns (%)
3-Month	6-Month	1-Year	3-Year	5-Year
1.31	7.26	6.06	72.17	116.09

3-Year Standard Deviation	15.06
Effective Duration	

Valuation
Premium/Discount (1-Year Average)	-0.03

Company Information
Provider	iShares
Manager/Tenure	Greg Savage (11), Jennifer Hsui (7), Alan Mason (3), 2 others
Website	http://www.ishares.com
Address	iShares 400 Howard Street San Francisco CA 94105 United States
Phone Number	800-474-2737

PERFORMANCE

Ratings History
Date	Overall Rating	Risk Rating	Reward Rating
Q3-19	B-	C	B
Q4-18	C+	C+	C+
Q4-17	A-	B	A+
Q4-16	C	C	C+
Q4-15	C+	C	C+

Asset & Performance History
Date	NAV	1-Year Total Return
2018	144.24	-5.13
2017	153.38	40.77
2016	110.04	13.69
2015	97.85	4.37
2014	94.8	15.43
2013	83.1	25.03

Total Assets: $2,805,382,882
Asset Allocation
Asset	%
Cash	0%
Stocks	100%
US Stocks	79%
Bonds	0%
US Bonds	0%
Other	0%

Services Offered: CashInvestment Plan

Investment Strategy: The investment seeks to track the investment results of the S&P Global 1200 Information Technology IndexTM. The fund generally invests at least 90% of its assets in securities of the index and in depositary receipts representing securities of the index. It may invest the remainder of its assets in certain futures, options and swap contracts, cash and cash equivalents, as well as in securities not included in the index. The index measures the performance of companies that the index provider deems to be part of the information technology sector of the economy and that the index provider believes are important to global markets. It is non-diversified.
Top Holdings: Microsoft Corp Apple Inc Visa Inc Class A Mastercard Inc A Intel Corp

iShares MSCI Taiwan Capped ETF   C   HOLD

Ticker	Traded On	NAV	Total Assets ($)	Dividend Yield (TTM)	Turnover Ratio	Expense Ratio
EWT	NYSE Arca	36.24	$2,801,336,579	2.75	12	0.59

Ratings
Reward	C
Risk	B
Recent Upgrade/Downgrade	

Fund Information
Fund Type	Exchange Traded Funds
Category	Greater China Equity
Sub-Category	China Region
Prospectus Objective	Pacific Stock
Inception Date	Jun-00
Open to New Investments	Y

Prices
Price (as of 9/30/2019)	36.36
52-Week High	37.83
52-Week Low	30.30

Total Returns (%)
3-Month	6-Month	1-Year	3-Year	5-Year
1.48	4.22	-1.53	26.59	35.05

3-Year Standard Deviation	13.2
Effective Duration	

Valuation
Premium/Discount (1-Year Average)	-0.28

Company Information
Provider	iShares
Manager/Tenure	Diane Hsiung (11), Greg Savage (11), Jennifer Hsui (6), 3 others
Website	http://www.ishares.com
Address	iShares 400 Howard Street San Francisco CA 94105 United States
Phone Number	800-474-2737

PERFORMANCE

Ratings History
Date	Overall Rating	Risk Rating	Reward Rating
Q3-19	C	B	C
Q4-18	C-	C	D+
Q4-17	C+	C+	C+
Q4-16	B-	C	B
Q4-15	C	C+	C-

Asset & Performance History
Date	NAV	1-Year Total Return
2018	31.74	-9.59
2017	36.22	25.51
2016	29.69	17.33
2015	25.9	-12.27
2014	30.44	8.72
2013	28.56	8.57

Total Assets: $2,801,336,579
Asset Allocation
Asset	%
Cash	1%
Stocks	99%
US Stocks	0%
Bonds	0%
US Bonds	0%
Other	0%

Services Offered: CashInvestment Plan

Investment Strategy: The investment seeks to track the investment results of the MSCI Taiwan 25/50 Index. The fund will at all times invest at least 80% of its assets in the securities of its underlying index and in depositary receipts representing securities in its underlying index. The index is designed to measure the performance of the large- and mid-cap segments of the Taiwanese market. A capping methodology is applied that limits the weight of any single component to a maximum of 25% of the underlying index. The fund is non-diversified. **Top Holdings:** Taiwan Semiconductor Manufacturing Co Ltd Hon Hai Precision Industry Co Ltd MediaTek Inc Formosa Plastics Corp Largan Precision Co Ltd

JPMorgan Alerian MLP Index ETN

D   SELL

Ticker	Traded On	NAV	Total Assets ($)	Dividend Yield (TTM)	Turnover Ratio	Expense Ratio
AMJ	NYSE Arca	23.27	$2,769,725,000	7.71		0.85

Ratings
Reward	D
Risk	C-
Recent Upgrade/Downgrade	Down

Fund Information
Fund Type	Exchange Traded Funds
Category	Energy Sector Equity
Sub-Category	Energy Limited Partnership
Prospectus Objective	Unaligned
Inception Date	Apr-09
Open to New Investments	Y

Prices
Price (as of 9/30/2019)	23.27
52-Week High	28.14
52-Week Low	21.22

Total Returns (%)
3-Month	6-Month	1-Year	3-Year	5-Year
-4.71	-6.15	-10.75	-9.22	-37.86

3-Year Standard Deviation	17.45
Effective Duration	

Valuation
Premium/Discount (1-Year Average)	0.02

Company Information
Provider	JPMorgan
Manager/Tenure	No Manager (10)
Website	http://www.jpmorganfunds.com
Address	JPMorgan 270 Park Avenue New York NY 10017-2070 United States
Phone Number	800-480-4111

PERFORMANCE

Ratings History
Date	Overall Rating	Risk Rating	Reward Rating
Q3-19	D	C-	D
Q4-18	D+	C-	D+
Q4-17	D	D	D
Q4-16	D	D	D
Q4-15	D+	D	D+

Asset & Performance History
Date	NAV	1-Year Total Return
2018	22.26	-13.19
2017	27.48	-7.07
2016	31.58	17.15
2015	28.96	-32.94
2014	45.92	3.76
2013	46.35	28.5

Total Assets: $2,769,725,000
Asset Allocation
Asset	%
Cash	%
Stocks	%
US Stocks	%
Bonds	%
US Bonds	%
Other	%

Services Offered:

Investment Strategy: The investment seeks to replicate, net of expenses, the Alerian MLP Index. The index tracks the performance of midstream energy Master Limited Partnerships. **Top Holdings:**

Vanguard S&P 500 Growth Index Fund ETF Shares

C+   HOLD

Ticker	Traded On	NAV	Total Assets ($)	Dividend Yield (TTM)	Turnover Ratio	Expense Ratio
VOOG	NYSE Arca	161.68	$2,764,728,000	1.23	18	0.15

Ratings
Reward	C+
Risk	C+
Recent Upgrade/Downgrade	Up

Fund Information
Fund Type	Exchange Traded Funds
Category	US Equity Large Cap Growth
Sub-Category	Large Growth
Prospectus Objective	Growth & Inc
Inception Date	Sep-10
Open to New Investments	Y

Prices
Price (as of 9/30/2019)	161.66
52-Week High	166.22
52-Week Low	125.87

Total Returns (%)
3-Month	6-Month	1-Year	3-Year	5-Year
-0.58	3.69	2.29	53.56	80.62

3-Year Standard Deviation	12.33
Effective Duration	

Valuation
Premium/Discount (1-Year Average)	-0.02

Company Information
Provider	Vanguard
Manager/Tenure	Donald M. Butler (3), Michelle Louie (1)
Website	http://www.vanguard.com
Address	Vanguard 100 Vanguard Boulevard Malvern PA 19355 United States
Phone Number	877-662-7447

PERFORMANCE

Ratings History
Date	Overall Rating	Risk Rating	Reward Rating
Q3-19	C+	C+	C+
Q4-18	C	C-	C
Q4-17	B	B+	B
Q4-16	C+	C-	B
Q4-15	C	C	C+

Asset & Performance History
Date	NAV	1-Year Total Return
2018	133.7	-1.11
2017	136.87	27.08
2016	109.13	6.27
2015	103.78	5.38
2014	100.03	14.72
2013	88.37	32.57

Total Assets: $2,764,728,000
Asset Allocation
Asset	%
Cash	0%
Stocks	100%
US Stocks	99%
Bonds	0%
US Bonds	0%
Other	0%

Services Offered:

Investment Strategy: The investment seeks to track the performance of a benchmark index that measures the investment return of large-capitalization growth stocks in the United States. The fund employs an indexing investment approach designed to track the performance of the S&P 500® Growth Index, which represents the growth companies, as determined by the index sponsor, of the S&P 500 Index. The index measures the performance of large-capitalization growth stocks in the United States. **Top Holdings:** Microsoft Corp Amazon.com Inc Facebook Inc A Alphabet Inc Class C Alphabet Inc A

SPDR® Dow Jones REIT ETF   C+   HOLD

Ticker	Traded On	NAV	Total Assets ($)	Dividend Yield (TTM)	Turnover Ratio	Expense Ratio
RWR	NYSE Arca		$2,743,718,105	3.21	9	0.25

Ratings
Reward	C+
Risk	C
Recent Upgrade/Downgrade	Up

Fund Information
Fund Type	Exchange Traded Funds
Category	Real Estate Sector Equity
Sub-Category	Real Estate
Prospectus Objective	Real Estate
Inception Date	Apr-01
Open to New Investments	Y

Prices
Price (as of 9/30/2019)	104.57
52-Week High	104.74
52-Week Low	82.76

Total Returns (%)
3-Month	6-Month	1-Year	3-Year	5-Year
6.97	7.38	17.29	19.97	56.96

3-Year Standard Deviation	12.75
Effective Duration	

Valuation
Premium/Discount (1-Year Average)	0.00

Company Information
Provider	SPDR State Street Global Advisors
Manager/Tenure	Michael J. Feehily (6), Karl A. Schneider (4), Daniel TenPas (2)
Website	http://www.spdrs.com
Address	SPDR State Street Global Advisors State Street Financial Center, 1 Lincoln Street Boston MA 02111-2900 United States
Phone Number	617-786-3000

PERFORMANCE

Ratings History

Date	Overall Rating	Risk Rating	Reward Rating
Q3-19	C+	C	C+
Q4-18	C	C	C
Q4-17	B-	B+	C+
Q4-16	C+	C	C+
Q4-15	C+	C+	B-

Asset & Performance History

Date	NAV	1-Year Total Return
2018	86.04	-4.3
2017	93.64	3.49
2016	93.27	4.07
2015	91.59	4.17
2014	90.82	31.66
2013	71.29	0.95

Total Assets: $2,743,718,105

Asset Allocation

Asset	%
Cash	0%
Stocks	100%
US Stocks	100%
Bonds	0%
US Bonds	0%
Other	0%

Services Offered:

Investment Strategy: The investment seeks to provide investment results that, before fees and expenses, correspond generally to the total return performance of the Dow Jones U.S. Select REIT Index. The fund generally invests substantially all, but at least 80%, of its total assets in the securities comprising the index. The index is designed to provide a measure of real estate securities that serve as proxies for direct real estate investing, in part by excluding securities whose value is not always closely tied to the value of the underlying real estate. The fund is non-diversified. **Top Holdings:** Prologis Inc Simon Property Group Inc Public Storage Welltower Inc Equity Residential

iShares MSCI Canada ETF   C+   HOLD

Ticker	Traded On	NAV	Total Assets ($)	Dividend Yield (TTM)	Turnover Ratio	Expense Ratio
EWC	NYSE Arca	28.90	$2,716,852,069	2.29	3	0.47

Ratings
Reward	C+
Risk	B-
Recent Upgrade/Downgrade	Up

Fund Information
Fund Type	Exchange Traded Funds
Category	Canadian Equity Large Cap
Sub-Category	Miscellaneous Region
Prospectus Objective	Foreign Stock
Inception Date	Mar-96
Open to New Investments	Y

Prices
Price (as of 9/30/2019)	28.90
52-Week High	29.16
52-Week Low	23.10

Total Returns (%)
3-Month	6-Month	1-Year	3-Year	5-Year
0.90	4.37	2.02	20.35	5.64

3-Year Standard Deviation	13.3
Effective Duration	

Valuation
Premium/Discount (1-Year Average)	-0.07

Company Information
Provider	iShares
Manager/Tenure	Diane Hsiung (11), Greg Savage (11), Jennifer Hsui (6), 3 others
Website	http://www.ishares.com
Address	iShares 400 Howard Street San Francisco CA 94105 United States
Phone Number	800-474-2737

PERFORMANCE

Ratings History

Date	Overall Rating	Risk Rating	Reward Rating
Q3-19	C+	B-	C+
Q4-18	C	C	C
Q4-17	C	C	C+
Q4-16	C	C-	C
Q4-15	C-	D+	C

Asset & Performance History

Date	NAV	1-Year Total Return
2018	24	-17.21
2017	29.71	15.97
2016	26.16	24.32
2015	21.42	-24.29
2014	28.9	1.36
2013	29.12	5.4

Total Assets: $2,716,852,069

Asset Allocation

Asset	%
Cash	0%
Stocks	100%
US Stocks	0%
Bonds	0%
US Bonds	0%
Other	0%

Services Offered: CashInvestment Plan

Investment Strategy: The investment seeks to track the investment results of the MSCI Canada Custom Capped Index. The fund will at all times invest at least 90% of its assets in the securities of its underlying index and in depositary receipts representing securities in its underlying index. The underlying index is designed to measure broad-based equity performance in Canada. The underlying index uses a capping methodology to limit the weight of any single component to a maximum of 25% of the underlying index. The underlying index may include large- or mid-capitalization companies. **Top Holdings:** Royal Bank of Canada The Toronto-Dominion Bank Enbridge Inc Bank of Nova Scotia Canadian National Railway Co

PIMCO Active Bond Exchange-Traded Fund   C+   HOLD

Ticker	Traded On	NAV	Total Assets ($)	Dividend Yield (TTM)	Turnover Ratio	Expense Ratio
BOND	NYSE Arca	108.77	$2,711,581,715	3.4	155	0.76

Ratings
Reward   B-
Risk   C+
Recent Upgrade/Downgrade

Fund Information
Fund Type   Exchange Traded Funds
Category   US Fixed Income
Sub-Category   Intermediate Core-Plus Bond
Prospectus Objective   Income
Inception Date   Feb-12
Open to New Investments   Y

Prices
Price (as of 9/30/2019)   108.90
52-Week High   109.60
52-Week Low   100.83

Total Returns (%)

3-Month	6-Month	1-Year	3-Year	5-Year
2.02	5.25	9.94	11.34	19.94

3-Year Standard Deviation   3.05
Effective Duration   4.79

Valuation
Premium/Discount (1-Year Average)   0.03

Company Information
Provider   PIMCO
Manager/Tenure   David Braun (2), Daniel Herbert
                  Hyman (2), Jerome M. Schneider (2)
Website   http://www.pimco.com
Address   PIMCO 840 Newport Center Drive,
                  Suite 100 Newport Beach CA 92660
                  United States
Phone Number   866-746-2602

PERFORMANCE

Ratings History

Date	Overall Rating	Risk Rating	Reward Rating
Q3-19	C+	C+	B-
Q4-18	C	C+	D+
Q4-17	B-	A-	C
Q4-16	C	C-	C
Q4-15	C	C+	C

Asset & Performance History

Date	NAV	1-Year Total Return
2018	102.65	0.16
2017	106.09	4.75
2016	104.22	2.92
2015	103.95	0.73
2014	107.45	6.86
2013	104.72	-1.17

Total Assets: $2,711,581,715
Asset Allocation

Asset	%
Cash	-6%
Stocks	0%
US Stocks	0%
Bonds	105%
US Bonds	95%
Other	0%

Services Offered:

Investment Strategy: The investment seeks current income and long-term capital appreciation, consistent with prudent investment management. The fund normally invests at least 80% of its assets in a diversified portfolio of Fixed Income Instruments of varying maturities, which may be represented by forwards or derivatives such as options, futures contracts, or swap agreement. It invests primarily in investment grade debt securities, but may invest up to 30% of its total assets in high yield securities, as rated by Moody's, S&P or Fitch, or, if unrated, as determined by PIMCO. **Top Holdings:** Federal Home Loan Mortgage Corporation 4% Fin Fut Us Ultra 30yr Cbt 12/19/19 United States Treasury Bonds 2.88% Federal Home Loan Mortgage Corporation 3.5% Federal Home Loan Mortgage Corporation 3.5%

Vanguard Mega Cap Value Index Fund ETF Shares   C+   HOLD

Ticker	Traded On	NAV	Total Assets ($)	Dividend Yield (TTM)	Turnover Ratio	Expense Ratio
MGV	NYSE Arca	81.43	$2,658,850,162	2.07	8	0.07

Ratings
Reward   C+
Risk   C+
Recent Upgrade/Downgrade

Fund Information
Fund Type   Exchange Traded Funds
Category   US Equity Large Cap Value
Sub-Category   Large Value
Prospectus Objective   Growth & Inc
Inception Date   Dec-07
Open to New Investments   Y

Prices
Price (as of 9/30/2019)   81.44
52-Week High   82.19
52-Week Low   67.32

Total Returns (%)

3-Month	6-Month	1-Year	3-Year	5-Year
0.13	3.57	3.17	39.27	56.84

3-Year Standard Deviation   12.03
Effective Duration

Valuation
Premium/Discount (1-Year Average)   0.01

Company Information
Provider   Vanguard
Manager/Tenure   Gerard C. O'Reilly (4), Michael A.
                  Johnson (3)
Website   http://www.vanguard.com
Address   Vanguard 100 Vanguard Boulevard
                  Malvern PA 19355 United States
Phone Number   877-662-7447

PERFORMANCE

Ratings History

Date	Overall Rating	Risk Rating	Reward Rating
Q3-19	C+	C+	C+
Q4-18	C	C+	C
Q4-17	B	B+	B
Q4-16	C+	C	B
Q4-15	C	C	C+

Asset & Performance History

Date	NAV	1-Year Total Return
2018	70.76	-4.87
2017	76.32	17
2016	67	15.9
2015	59.02	-0.18
2014	60.67	12.96
2013	54.97	32.12

Total Assets: $2,658,850,162
Asset Allocation

Asset	%
Cash	0%
Stocks	100%
US Stocks	99%
Bonds	0%
US Bonds	0%
Other	0%

Services Offered:

Investment Strategy: The investment seeks the performance of a benchmark index. The fund employs an indexing investment approach designed to track the performance of the CRSP US Mega Cap Value Index. The index is a float-adjusted, market-capitalization-weighted index designed to measure equity market performance of mega-capitalization value stocks in the United States. The Advisor attempts to replicate the target index by investing all, or substantially all, of its assets in the stocks that make up the index, holding each stock in approximately the same proportion as its weighting in the index. **Top Holdings:** Berkshire Hathaway Inc B JPMorgan Chase & Co Johnson & Johnson Exxon Mobil Corp Procter & Gamble Co

Invesco S&P 500® Pure Growth ETF   C   HOLD

Ticker	Traded On	NAV	Total Assets ($)	Dividend Yield (TTM)	Turnover Ratio	Expense Ratio
RPG	NYSE Arca	118.42	$2,652,619,425	0.78		0.35

Ratings
Reward	C+
Risk	C-
Recent Upgrade/Downgrade	Down

Fund Information
Fund Type	Exchange Traded Funds
Category	US Equity Large Cap Growth
Sub-Category	Large Growth
Prospectus Objective	Growth
Inception Date	Mar-06
Open to New Investments	Y

Prices
Price (as of 9/30/2019)	118.43
52-Week High	122.44
52-Week Low	93.15

Total Returns (%)
3-Month	6-Month	1-Year	3-Year	5-Year
-1.32	1.64	-0.68	43.16	60.96

3-Year Standard Deviation	13.62
Effective Duration	

Valuation
Premium/Discount (1-Year Average)	-0.02

Company Information
Provider	Invesco
Manager/Tenure	Peter Hubbard (1), Michael Jeanette (1), Tony Seisser (1)
Website	http://www.invesco.com/us
Address	Invesco 11 Greenway Plaza, Ste. 2500 Houston TX 77046 United States
Phone Number	800-659-1005

PERFORMANCE

Ratings History
Date	Overall Rating	Risk Rating	Reward Rating
Q3-19	C	C-	C+
Q4-18	C	C+	C
Q4-17	B+	A-	B+
Q4-16	C	C-	B-
Q4-15	C+	C+	C

Asset & Performance History
Date	NAV	1-Year Total Return
2018	99.58	-4.58
2017	104.82	26.39
2016	83.51	3.53
2015	80.75	2.32
2014	79.48	13.88
2013	70.27	43.29

Total Assets: $2,652,619,425

Asset Allocation
Asset	%
Cash	0%
Stocks	100%
US Stocks	100%
Bonds	0%
US Bonds	0%
Other	0%

Services Offered:

Investment Strategy: The investment seeks to track the investment results (before fees and expenses) of the S&P 500® Pure Growth Index (the "underlying index"). The fund generally will invest at least 90% of its total assets in the securities that comprise the underlying index. The underlying index is composed of a subset of securities from the S&P 500® Index that exhibit strong growth characteristics as measured using the following three factors: three-year sales per share growth, the three-year ratio of earnings per share change to price per share, and momentum (the 12-month percentage change in price). The fund is non-diversified. **Top Holdings:** Keysight Technologies Inc   Thermo Fisher Scientific Inc   Salesforce.com Inc   CSX Corp   Autodesk Inc

---

Pacer Trendpilot™ US Large Cap ETF   C+   HOLD

Ticker	Traded On	NAV	Total Assets ($)	Dividend Yield (TTM)	Turnover Ratio	Expense Ratio
PTLC	BATS	31.07	$2,645,749,083	0.92	162	0.6

Ratings
Reward	C
Risk	C+
Recent Upgrade/Downgrade	

Fund Information
Fund Type	Exchange Traded Funds
Category	US Equity Large Cap Blend
Sub-Category	Large Blend
Prospectus Objective	Growth
Inception Date	Jun-15
Open to New Investments	Y

Prices
Price (as of 9/30/2019)	31.07
52-Week High	31.58
52-Week Low	28.51

Total Returns (%)
3-Month	6-Month	1-Year	3-Year	5-Year
0.73	4.53	-0.58	38.16	

3-Year Standard Deviation	10.1
Effective Duration	

Valuation
Premium/Discount (1-Year Average)	0.01

Company Information
Provider	Pacer
Manager/Tenure	Bruce Kavanaugh (4), Michael Mack (4)
Website	http://www.paceretfs.com
Address	Pacer 16 Industrial Blvd, Suite 201 Paoli PA 19301 United States
Phone Number	

PERFORMANCE

Ratings History
Date	Overall Rating	Risk Rating	Reward Rating
Q3-19	C+	C+	C
Q4-18	C	C+	C-
Q4-17	C	B-	C+
Q4-16	D	C-	D+
Q4-15	U		

Asset & Performance History
Date	NAV	1-Year Total Return
2018	28.76	1.67
2017	28.57	21
2016	23.84	4.07
2015	23.04	
2014		
2013		

Total Assets: $2,645,749,083

Asset Allocation
Asset	%
Cash	0%
Stocks	100%
US Stocks	99%
Bonds	0%
US Bonds	0%
Other	0%

Services Offered:

Investment Strategy: The investment seeks to track the total return performance, before fees and expenses, of the Pacer Trendpilot US Large Cap Index. The fund invests at least 80% of its total assets (exclusive of collateral held from securities lending) in the component securities of the index. The index uses an objective, rules-based methodology to implement a systematic trend-following strategy that directs exposure (i) 100% to the S&P 500® Index, (ii) 50% to the S&P 500 and 50% to 3-Month U.S. Treasury bills, or (iii) 100% to 3-Month U.S. Treasury bills, depending on the relative performance of the S&P 500 and its 200-business day historical simple moving average. **Top Holdings:** Microsoft Corp   Apple Inc   Amazon.com Inc   Facebook Inc A   Berkshire Hathaway Inc B

First Trust North American Energy Infrastructure Fund   C+   HOLD

Ticker	Traded On	NAV	Total Assets ($)	Dividend Yield (TTM)	Turnover Ratio	Expense Ratio
EMLP	NYSE Arca	25.54	$2,600,386,397	3.82	35	0.95

Ratings
Reward	C+
Risk	C+
Recent Upgrade/Downgrade	Up

Fund Information
Fund Type	Exchange Traded Funds
Category	Energy Sector Equity
Sub-Category	Energy Limited Partnership
Prospectus Objective	Utility
Inception Date	Jun-12
Open to New Investments	Y

Prices
Price (as of 9/30/2019)	25.59
52-Week High	25.93
52-Week Low	20.55

Total Returns (%)
3-Month	6-Month	1-Year	3-Year	5-Year
2.69	4.97	12.44	13.76	15.04

3-Year Standard Deviation	10.6
Effective Duration	

Valuation
Premium/Discount (1-Year Average)	0.01

Company Information
Provider	First Trust
Manager/Tenure	James J. Murchie (7), Eva Pao (7), John K. Tysseland (3)
Website	http://www.ftportfolios.com/
Address	First Trust 120 E. Liberty Drive, Suite 400 Wheaton IL 60187 United States
Phone Number	800-621-1675

PERFORMANCE

Ratings History
Date	Overall Rating	Risk Rating	Reward Rating
Q3-19	C+	C+	C+
Q4-18	C	C+	C
Q4-17	C	C-	C
Q4-16	C	C-	C
Q4-15	C	C	C

Asset & Performance History
Date	NAV	1-Year Total Return
2018	21.44	-8.52
2017	24.51	1.06
2016	25.19	29.66
2015	20.18	-25.2
2014	28.08	23.63
2013	23.47	16.9

Total Assets: $2,600,386,397
Asset Allocation
Asset	%
Cash	4%
Stocks	96%
US Stocks	78%
Bonds	0%
US Bonds	0%
Other	0%

Services Offered:

Investment Strategy: The investment seeks total return. The fund invests at least 80% of its net assets in equity securities of companies deemed by the sub-advisor to be engaged in the energy infrastructure sector. These companies principally include publicly-traded MLPs and limited liability companies taxed as partnerships, MLP affiliates, pipeline companies, utilities, and other companies that derive the majority of their revenues from operating or providing services in support of infrastructure assets such as pipelines, power transmission and petroleum and natural gas storage in the petroleum, natural gas and power generation industries. It is non-diversified. **Top Holdings:** TC Energy Corp   Enterprise Products Partners LP   Kinder Morgan Inc Class P   NextEra Energy Inc   NextEra Energy Partners LP

SPDR® Portfolio Emerging Markets ETF   C   HOLD

Ticker	Traded On	NAV	Total Assets ($)	Dividend Yield (TTM)	Turnover Ratio	Expense Ratio
SPEM	NYSE Arca		$2,599,479,029	2.38	10	0.11

Ratings
Reward	C
Risk	C+
Recent Upgrade/Downgrade	

Fund Information
Fund Type	Exchange Traded Funds
Category	Global Emerg Mkts Equity
Sub-Category	Diversified Emerging Mkts
Prospectus Objective	Div Emerg Mkts
Inception Date	Mar-07
Open to New Investments	Y

Prices
Price (as of 9/30/2019)	34.28
52-Week High	36.86
52-Week Low	31.29

Total Returns (%)
3-Month	6-Month	1-Year	3-Year	5-Year
-3.53	-3.23	1.56	20.90	14.52

3-Year Standard Deviation	13.41
Effective Duration	

Valuation
Premium/Discount (1-Year Average)	0.05

Company Information
Provider	SPDR State Street Global Advisors
Manager/Tenure	Michael J. Feehily (8), Karl A. Schneider (4), Dwayne Hancock (2)
Website	http://www.spdrs.com
Address	SPDR State Street Global Advisors State Street Financial Center, 1 Lincoln Street Boston MA 02111-2900 United States
Phone Number	617-786-3000

PERFORMANCE

Ratings History
Date	Overall Rating	Risk Rating	Reward Rating
Q3-19	C	C+	C
Q4-18	C-	C	C-
Q4-17	B-	C	B
Q4-16	D+	C-	D+
Q4-15	C-	C-	C-

Asset & Performance History
Date	NAV	1-Year Total Return
2018	32.43	-13.06
2017	38.15	34.48
2016	28.71	11.03
2015	26.23	-15.21
2014	31.62	1.24
2013	31.93	-1.67

Total Assets: $2,599,479,029
Asset Allocation
Asset	%
Cash	2%
Stocks	98%
US Stocks	0%
Bonds	0%
US Bonds	0%
Other	0%

Services Offered:

Investment Strategy: The investment seeks investment results that, before fees and expenses, correspond generally to the total return performance of the S&P Emerging BMI Index. The fund generally invests substantially all, but at least 80%, of its total assets in the securities comprising the index and in depositary receipts based on securities comprising the index. The index is a market capitalization weighted index designed to define and measure the investable universe of publicly traded companies domiciled in emerging markets. The fund is non-diversified. **Top Holdings:** Tencent Holdings Ltd   Alibaba Group Holding Ltd ADR   Taiwan Semiconductor Manufacturing Co Ltd   Naspers Ltd Class N   China Construction Bank Corp Class H

Fidelity® MSCI Information Technology Index ETF   B-   BUY

Ticker	Traded On	NAV	Total Assets ($)	Dividend Yield (TTM)	Turnover Ratio	Expense Ratio
FTEC	NYSE Arca	63.75	$2,556,289,555	1.17	18	0.08

Ratings
Reward	B
Risk	C+
Recent Upgrade/Downgrade	Down

Fund Information
Fund Type	Exchange Traded Funds
Category	Technology Sector Equity
Sub-Category	Technology
Prospectus Objective	Technology
Inception Date	Oct-13
Open to New Investments	Y

Prices
Price (as of 9/30/2019)	63.77
52-Week High	66.03
52-Week Low	45.74

Total Returns (%)
3-Month	6-Month	1-Year	3-Year	5-Year
1.11	6.63	7.13	80.60	129.18

3-Year Standard Deviation	15.8
Effective Duration	

Valuation
Premium/Discount (1-Year Average)	-0.03

Company Information
Provider	Fidelity Investments
Manager/Tenure	Jennifer Hsui (5), Greg Savage (5), Alan Mason (3), 2 others
Website	http://www.institutional.fidelity.com
Address	Fidelity Investments 82 Devonshire Street Boston MA 2109 United States
Phone Number	617-563-7000

PERFORMANCE

Ratings History
Date	Overall Rating	Risk Rating	Reward Rating
Q3-19	B-	C+	B
Q4-18	C+	C+	C+
Q4-17	A-	B	A+
Q4-16	B-	C+	B
Q4-15	C-	B-	C

Asset & Performance History
Date	NAV	1-Year Total Return
2018	49.33	-0.17
2017	49.96	37.07
2016	36.83	13.78
2015	32.81	5.03
2014	31.64	18.15
2013	27.09	

Total Assets: $2,556,289,555
Asset Allocation
Asset	%
Cash	0%
Stocks	100%
US Stocks	99%
Bonds	0%
US Bonds	0%
Other	0%

Services Offered:

Investment Strategy: The investment seeks to provide investment returns that correspond, before fees and expenses, generally to the performance of the MSCI USA IMI Information Technology Index. The fund invests at least 80% of assets in securities included in the fund's underlying index. The fund's underlying index is the MSCI USA IMI Information Technology Index, which represents the performance of the information technology sector in the U.S. equity market. It may or may not hold all of the securities in the MSCI USA IMI Information Technology Index. The fund is non-diversified. **Top Holdings:** Microsoft Corp Apple Inc Visa Inc Class A Mastercard Inc A Intel Corp

---

iShares Expanded Tech-Software Sector ETF   B-   BUY

Ticker	Traded On	NAV	Total Assets ($)	Dividend Yield (TTM)	Turnover Ratio	Expense Ratio
IGV	BATS	211.87	$2,553,069,125	0.13	18	0.46

Ratings
Reward	B
Risk	C
Recent Upgrade/Downgrade	

Fund Information
Fund Type	Exchange Traded Funds
Category	Technology Sector Equity
Sub-Category	Technology
Prospectus Objective	Technology
Inception Date	Jul-01
Open to New Investments	Y

Prices
Price (as of 9/30/2019)	211.88
52-Week High	230.04
52-Week Low	159.19

Total Returns (%)
3-Month	6-Month	1-Year	3-Year	5-Year
-4.47	-0.82	3.81	87.15	152.65

3-Year Standard Deviation	16.32
Effective Duration	

Valuation
Premium/Discount (1-Year Average)	-0.02

Company Information
Provider	iShares
Manager/Tenure	Greg Savage (11), Jennifer Hsui (6), Alan Mason (3), 2 others
Website	http://www.ishares.com
Address	iShares 400 Howard Street San Francisco CA 94105 United States
Phone Number	800-474-2737

PERFORMANCE

Ratings History
Date	Overall Rating	Risk Rating	Reward Rating
Q3-19	B-	C	B
Q4-18	C+	C	B-
Q4-17	A-	B+	A+
Q4-16	B-	C	B
Q4-15	B-	C	B

Asset & Performance History
Date	NAV	1-Year Total Return
2018	173.45	12.43
2017	154.52	42.16
2016	108.81	5.86
2015	103.7	11.96
2014	92.83	13.39
2013	82.12	30.59

Total Assets: $2,553,069,125
Asset Allocation
Asset	%
Cash	0%
Stocks	100%
US Stocks	98%
Bonds	0%
US Bonds	0%
Other	0%

Services Offered: CashInvestment Plan

Investment Strategy: The investment seeks to track the investment results of the S&P North American Expanded Technology Software Index™. The fund generally invests at least 90% of its assets in securities of the underlying index and in depositary receipts representing securities of the underlying index. The index measures the performance of U.S.-traded stocks from the software industry and select companies from the interactive home entertainment and interactive media and services industries in the U.S. and Canada. The fund is non-diversified. **Top Holdings:** Salesforce.com Inc Microsoft Corp Adobe Inc Oracle Corp Intuit Inc

iShares Broad USD High Yield Corporate Bond ETF

D   SELL

Ticker	Traded On	NAV	Total Assets ($)	Dividend Yield (TTM)	Turnover Ratio	Expense Ratio
USHY	BATS	40.70	$2,551,853,446	6.06	15	0.22

Ratings

Reward	D
Risk	D+
Recent Upgrade/Downgrade	

Fund Information

Fund Type	Exchange Traded Funds
Category	US Fixed Income
Sub-Category	High Yield Bond
Prospectus Objective	Corp Bond-High Yld
Inception Date	Oct-17
Open to New Investments	Y

Prices

Price (as of 9/30/2019)	40.95
52-Week High	48.77
52-Week Low	39.80

Total Returns (%)

3-Month	6-Month	1-Year	3-Year	5-Year
1.07	3.94	-11.50		

3-Year Standard Deviation	
Effective Duration	

Valuation

Premium/Discount (1-Year Average)	0.42

Company Information

Provider	iShares
Manager/Tenure	James Mauro (1), Scott Radell (1)
Website	http://www.ishares.com
Address	iShares 400 Howard Street San Francisco CA 94105 United States
Phone Number	800-474-2737

PERFORMANCE

Ratings History

Date	Overall Rating	Risk Rating	Reward Rating
Q3-19	D	D+	D
Q4-18	D+	C-	D
Q4-17	U		
Q4-16			
Q4-15			

Asset & Performance History

Date	NAV	1-Year Total Return
2018	45.56	-2.54
2017	49.63	
2016		
2015		
2014		
2013		

Total Assets: $2,551,853,446

Asset Allocation

Asset	%
Cash	0%
Stocks	0%
US Stocks	0%
Bonds	100%
US Bonds	85%
Other	0%

Services Offered:

Investment Strategy: The investment seeks to track the investment results of the ICE BofAML US High Yield Constrained Index. The fund generally will invest at least 90% of its assets in the component securities of the underlying index and may invest up to 10% of its assets in certain futures, options and swap contracts, cash and cash equivalents, including shares of money market funds advised by BFA or its affiliates, as well as in securities not included in the underlying index. The underlying index is designed to provide a broad representation of the U.S. dollar-denominated high yield corporate bond market. The fund is non-diversified. **Top Holdings:** ALTICE FRANCE S.A 7.38% Sprint Corporation 7.88% TransDigm, Inc. 6.25% CCO Holdings, LLC/ CCO Holdings Capital Corp. 5.13% Community Health Systems Incorporated 6.25%

WisdomTree Japan Hedged Equity Fund

D+   SELL

Ticker	Traded On	NAV	Total Assets ($)	Dividend Yield (TTM)	Turnover Ratio	Expense Ratio
DXJ	NYSE Arca	50.08	$2,538,903,810	1.85	23	0.48

Ratings

Reward	D
Risk	C-
Recent Upgrade/Downgrade	Down

Fund Information

Fund Type	Exchange Traded Funds
Category	Japan Equity
Sub-Category	Japan Stock
Prospectus Objective	Pacific Stock
Inception Date	Jun-06
Open to New Investments	Y

Prices

Price (as of 9/30/2019)	50.46
52-Week High	58.69
52-Week Low	44.87

Total Returns (%)

3-Month	6-Month	1-Year	3-Year	5-Year
0.62	-1.22	-12.08	26.66	23.13

3-Year Standard Deviation	15.1
Effective Duration	

Valuation

Premium/Discount (1-Year Average)	-0.14

Company Information

Provider	WisdomTree
Manager/Tenure	Richard A. Brown (11), Thomas J. Durante (11), Karen Q. Wong (11)
Website	http://www.wisdomtree.com
Address	WisdomTree 245 Park Avenue, 35th floor New York NY 10167 United States
Phone Number	866-909-9473

PERFORMANCE

Ratings History

Date	Overall Rating	Risk Rating	Reward Rating
Q3-19	D+	C-	D
Q4-18	C-	C	D+
Q4-17	B	C+	A-
Q4-16	C	C	C-
Q4-15	B	B+	C+

Asset & Performance History

Date	NAV	1-Year Total Return
2018	46.95	-18.8
2017	59.32	22.25
2016	49.75	0.07
2015	50.8	8.15
2014	49.73	10.47
2013	50.24	41.85

Total Assets: $2,538,903,810

Asset Allocation

Asset	%
Cash	0%
Stocks	100%
US Stocks	0%
Bonds	0%
US Bonds	0%
Other	0%

Services Offered:

Investment Strategy: The investment seeks to track the price and yield performance, before fees and expenses, of the WisdomTree Japan Hedged Equity Index. Under normal circumstances, at least 95% of the fund's total assets (exclusive of collateral held from securities lending) will be invested in component securities of the index and investments that have economic characteristics that are substantially identical to the economic characteristics of such component securities. The index is designed to provide exposure to Japanese equity markets while at the same time neutralizing exposure to fluctuations of the Japanese yen relative to the U.S. dollar. The fund is non-diversified. **Top Holdings:** Toyota Motor Corp Mitsubishi UFJ Financial Group Inc Japan Tobacco Inc Sumitomo Mitsui Financial Group Inc Nissan Motor Co Ltd

Invesco Ultra Short Duration ETF   C   HOLD

Ticker	Traded On	NAV	Total Assets ($)	Dividend Yield (TTM)	Turnover Ratio	Expense Ratio
GSY	NYSE Arca	50.40	$2,535,219,685	2.71		0.25

Ratings
Reward	C
Risk	C+
Recent Upgrade/Downgrade	

Fund Information
Fund Type	Exchange Traded Funds
Category	US Fixed Income
Sub-Category	Ultrashort Bond
Prospectus Objective	Income
Inception Date	Feb-08
Open to New Investments	Y

Prices
Price (as of 9/30/2019)	50.41
52-Week High	50.47
52-Week Low	50.04

Total Returns (%)
3-Month	6-Month	1-Year	3-Year	5-Year
0.67	1.64	3.13	7.27	10.17

3-Year Standard Deviation	0.28
Effective Duration	0.46

Valuation
Premium/Discount (1-Year Average)	0.01

Company Information
Provider	Invesco
Manager/Tenure	Laurie F. Brignac (1), Joseph S. Madrid (1), Marques Mercier (1)
Website	http://www.invesco.com/us
Address	Invesco 11 Greenway Plaza, Ste. 2500 Houston TX 77046 United States
Phone Number	800-659-1005

PERFORMANCE

Ratings History
Date	Overall Rating	Risk Rating	Reward Rating
Q3-19	C	C+	C
Q4-18	C	C+	C
Q4-17	B-	A	C
Q4-16	C	C+	C
Q4-15	C	C+	C

Asset & Performance History
Date	NAV	1-Year Total Return
2018	50.07	2.16
2017	50.14	1.91
2016	50.09	1.68
2015	49.85	1.03
2014	49.92	0.78
2013	50.17	1.38

Total Assets: $2,535,219,685
Asset Allocation
Asset	%
Cash	28%
Stocks	0%
US Stocks	0%
Bonds	71%
US Bonds	56%
Other	0%

Services Offered:

Investment Strategy: The investment seeks maximum current income, consistent with preservation of capital and daily liquidity. The fund will invest at least 80% of its net assets in fixed income securities and in ETFs and closed-end funds that invest substantially all of their assets in fixed income securities. It uses a low duration strategy to seek to outperform the ICE BofAML US Treasury Bill Index in addition to providing returns in excess of those available in U.S. Treasury bills, government repurchase agreements, and money market funds, while seeking to provide preservation of capital and daily liquidity. The fund is non-diversified. **Top Holdings:** Verizon Communications Inc. 2.7%   Comcast Corporation 2.76%   Federal Home Loan Banks 2.45%   Hertz Vehicle Financing Llc 2.73%   Morgan Stanley 3.13%

iShares Exponential Technologies ETF   C+   HOLD

Ticker	Traded On	NAV	Total Assets ($)	Dividend Yield (TTM)	Turnover Ratio	Expense Ratio
XT	NAS CM	38.68	$2,508,150,356	1.43	21	0.47

Ratings
Reward	C
Risk	C+
Recent Upgrade/Downgrade	

Fund Information
Fund Type	Exchange Traded Funds
Category	Equity Misc
Sub-Category	Miscellaneous Sector
Prospectus Objective	Technology
Inception Date	Mar-15
Open to New Investments	Y

Prices
Price (as of 9/30/2019)	38.66
52-Week High	39.71
52-Week Low	31.56

Total Returns (%)
3-Month	6-Month	1-Year	3-Year	5-Year
-0.84	1.38	1.09	52.55	

3-Year Standard Deviation	13.74
Effective Duration	

Valuation
Premium/Discount (1-Year Average)	-0.10

Company Information
Provider	iShares
Manager/Tenure	Diane Hsiung (4), Jennifer Hsui (4), Greg Savage (4), 3 others
Website	http://www.ishares.com
Address	iShares 400 Howard Street San Francisco CA 94105 United States
Phone Number	800-474-2737

PERFORMANCE

Ratings History
Date	Overall Rating	Risk Rating	Reward Rating
Q3-19	C+	C+	C
Q4-18	C	C+	C
Q4-17	B-	B-	B-
Q4-16	D+	C-	C-
Q4-15	U		

Asset & Performance History
Date	NAV	1-Year Total Return
2018	33.32	-4.67
2017	35.41	33.7
2016	26.76	9.03
2015	24.9	
2014		
2013		

Total Assets: $2,508,150,356
Asset Allocation
Asset	%
Cash	0%
Stocks	100%
US Stocks	58%
Bonds	0%
US Bonds	0%
Other	0%

Services Offered:

Investment Strategy: The investment seeks to track the investment results of the Morningstar® Exponential Technologies IndexSM which composed of stocks of developed and emerging market companies that create or use exponential technologies. The fund generally will invest at least 90% of its assets in the component securities of the underlying index and in investments that have economic characteristics that are substantially identical to the component securities of the underlying index. The underlying index is a subset of the Morningstar US Market Index and the Morningstar Global Markets ex-US Index family. **Top Holdings:** ASM International NV   Cypress Semiconductor Corp   ams AG   London Stock Exchange Group PLC   MercadoLibre Inc

Schwab Fundamental Emerging Markets Large Company Index ETF

C   HOLD

Ticker	Traded On	NAV	Total Assets ($)	Dividend Yield (TTM)	Turnover Ratio	Expense Ratio
FNDE	NYSE Arca	27.39	$2,494,872,200	3.55	33	0.39

Ratings
Reward	C
Risk	C+
Recent Upgrade/Downgrade	

Fund Information
Fund Type	Exchange Traded Funds
Category	Global Emerg Mkts Equity
Sub-Category	Diversified Emerging Mkts
Prospectus Objective	Div Emerg Mkts
Inception Date	Aug-13
Open to New Investments	Y

Prices
Price (as of 9/30/2019)	27.38
52-Week High	29.15
52-Week Low	25.30

Total Returns (%)
3-Month	6-Month	1-Year	3-Year	5-Year
-5.77	-2.03	-1.57	25.59	18.59

3-Year Standard Deviation	13.7
Effective Duration	

Valuation
Premium/Discount (1-Year Average)	-0.03

Company Information
Provider	Schwab ETFs
Manager/Tenure	Chuck Craig (6), Jane Qin (6), Christopher Bliss (2), 1 other
Website	http://www.schwabfunds.com
Address	Schwab ETFs United States
Phone Number	800-435-4000

PERFORMANCE

Ratings History
Date	Overall Rating	Risk Rating	Reward Rating
Q3-19	C	C+	C
Q4-18	C	C	C-
Q4-17	B	C	B+
Q4-16	C-	C-	C-
Q4-15	D	D	D

Asset & Performance History
Date	NAV	1-Year Total Return
2018	25.87	-10.01
2017	29.61	26.18
2016	23.96	32.3
2015	18.41	-19.11
2014	23.22	-11.09
2013	26.47	

Total Assets: $2,494,872,200

Asset Allocation
Asset	%
Cash	0%
Stocks	99%
US Stocks	0%
Bonds	0%
US Bonds	0%
Other	0%

Services Offered:

Investment Strategy: The investment seeks to track as closely as possible, before fees and expenses, the total return of the Russell RAFI™ Emerging Markets Large Company Index. The fund will invest at least 80% of its net assets in stocks included in the index, including depositary receipts representing securities of the index; which may be in the form of American Depositary Receipts, Global Depositary Receipts and European Depositary Receipts. The index measures the performance of the large company size segment by fundamental overall company scores, which are created using as the universe the emerging markets companies in the FTSE Global Total Cap Index (the parent index). **Top Holdings:** Gazprom PJSC Taiwan Semiconductor Manufacturing Co Ltd   PJSC Lukoil   China Construction Bank Corp Class H   Hon Hai Precision Industry Co Ltd

---

VanEck Vectors Morningstar Wide Moat ETF

C+   HOLD

Ticker	Traded On	NAV	Total Assets ($)	Dividend Yield (TTM)	Turnover Ratio	Expense Ratio
MOAT	NYSE Arca	50.13	$2,486,375,067	1.47	56	0.49

Ratings
Reward	C+
Risk	C
Recent Upgrade/Downgrade	

Fund Information
Fund Type	Exchange Traded Funds
Category	US Equity Large Cap Blend
Sub-Category	Large Blend
Prospectus Objective	Growth
Inception Date	Apr-12
Open to New Investments	Y

Prices
Price (as of 9/30/2019)	50.15
52-Week High	50.75
52-Week Low	38.89

Total Returns (%)
3-Month	6-Month	1-Year	3-Year	5-Year
3.51	6.27	9.22	53.44	75.22

3-Year Standard Deviation	13.86
Effective Duration	

Valuation
Premium/Discount (1-Year Average)	0.00

Company Information
Provider	VanEck
Manager/Tenure	Hao-Hung (Peter) Liao (7), Guo Hua (Jason) Jin (1)
Website	http://www.vaneck.com
Address	Van Eck Associates Corporation 666 Third Avenue New York NY 10017 United States
Phone Number	800-826-1115

PERFORMANCE

Ratings History
Date	Overall Rating	Risk Rating	Reward Rating
Q3-19	C+	C	C+
Q4-18	C	C	C
Q4-17	B	B-	B
Q4-16	C+	C-	B
Q4-15	B-	C	B

Asset & Performance History
Date	NAV	1-Year Total Return
2018	41.14	-1.39
2017	42.42	23.19
2016	34.8	21.73
2015	28.92	-4.85
2014	31.06	9.25
2013	28.81	30.88

Total Assets: $2,486,375,067

Asset Allocation
Asset	%
Cash	0%
Stocks	100%
US Stocks	100%
Bonds	0%
US Bonds	0%
Other	0%

Services Offered:

Investment Strategy: The investment seeks to replicate as closely as possible, before fees and expenses, the price and yield performance of the Morningstar® Wide Moat Focus IndexSM. The fund normally invests at least 80% of its total assets in securities that comprise the fund's benchmark index. The index is comprised of securities issued by companies that Morningstar, Inc. ("Morningstar") determines to have sustainable competitive advantages based on a proprietary methodology that considers quantitative and qualitative factors ("wide moat companies"). The fund is non-diversified. **Top Holdings:** KLA Corp Applied Materials Inc Kellogg Co The Western Union Co Facebook Inc A

First Trust NASDAQ-100-Technology Sector Index Fund   C+   HOLD

Ticker	Traded On	NAV	Total Assets ($)	Dividend Yield (TTM)	Turnover Ratio	Expense Ratio
QTEC	NAS CM	87.52	$2,481,150,183	0.75	21	0.57

Ratings
Reward   B-
Risk   C
Recent Upgrade/Downgrade

Fund Information
Fund Type	Exchange Traded Funds
Category	Technology Sector Equity
Sub-Category	Technology
Prospectus Objective	Technology
Inception Date	Apr-06
Open to New Investments	Y

Prices
Price (as of 9/30/2019)	87.53
52-Week High	92.25
52-Week Low	63.38

PERFORMANCE

Total Returns (%)

3-Month	6-Month	1-Year	3-Year	5-Year
0.27	4.23	11.22	76.17	129.53

3-Year Standard Deviation   17.87
Effective Duration

Valuation
Premium/Discount (1-Year Average)   -0.02

Company Information
Provider	First Trust
Manager/Tenure	Jon C. Erickson (13), Daniel J. Lindquist (13), David G. McGarel (13), 3 others
Website	http://www.ftportfolios.com/
Address	First Trust 120 E. Liberty Drive, Suite 400 Wheaton IL 60187 United States
Phone Number	800-621-1675

Ratings History

Date	Overall Rating	Risk Rating	Reward Rating
Q3-19	C+	C	B-
Q4-18	C	C	C+
Q4-17	A-	B	A+
Q4-16	C+	C	C+
Q4-15	C	C	C+

Asset & Performance History

Date	NAV	1-Year Total Return
2018	67.97	-4.71
2017	71.92	37.85
2016	52.62	25.29
2015	42.64	-1.38
2014	43.67	24.81
2013	35.43	38.13

Total Assets: $2,481,150,183
Asset Allocation

Asset	%
Cash	0%
Stocks	100%
US Stocks	89%
Bonds	0%
US Bonds	0%
Other	0%

Services Offered:

Investment Strategy: The investment seeks investment results that correspond generally to the price and yield (before the fund's fees and expenses) of an equity index called the NASDAQ-100 Technology Sector IndexSM. The fund will normally invest at least 90% of its net assets (including investment borrowings) in the common stocks and depositary receipts that comprise the index. The index is an equal-weighted index composed of the securities comprising the NASDAQ-100 Index® that are classified as "technology" according to the Industry Classification Benchmark classification system. **Top Holdings:** Western Digital Corp   Micron Technology Inc   KLA Corp   Lam Research Corp   Symantec Corp

---

iShares Short-Term National Muni Bond ETF   C   HOLD

Ticker	Traded On	NAV	Total Assets ($)	Dividend Yield (TTM)	Turnover Ratio	Expense Ratio
SUB	NYSE Arca	106.42	$2,474,264,504	1.61	24	0.07

Ratings
Reward   C
Risk   C-
Recent Upgrade/Downgrade

Fund Information
Fund Type	Exchange Traded Funds
Category	US Muni Fixed Inc
Sub-Category	Muni National Short
Prospectus Objective	Muni Bond - Natl
Inception Date	Nov-08
Open to New Investments	Y

Prices
Price (as of 9/30/2019)	106.54
52-Week High	107.20
52-Week Low	104.30

PERFORMANCE

Total Returns (%)

3-Month	6-Month	1-Year	3-Year	5-Year
0.31	1.29	3.36	4.09	5.43

3-Year Standard Deviation   1.18
Effective Duration   2.13

Valuation
Premium/Discount (1-Year Average)   0.09

Company Information
Provider	iShares
Manager/Tenure	Scott Radell (9), James Mauro (8)
Website	http://www.ishares.com
Address	iShares 400 Howard Street San Francisco CA 94105 United States
Phone Number	800-474-2737

Ratings History

Date	Overall Rating	Risk Rating	Reward Rating
Q3-19	C	C-	C
Q4-18	C	C	C-
Q4-17	C	C	C
Q4-16	C-	C-	C
Q4-15	C	C-	C

Asset & Performance History

Date	NAV	1-Year Total Return
2018	105.05	1.56
2017	104.81	0.77
2016	104.86	-0.03
2015	105.68	0.64
2014	105.81	0.56
2013	106.01	0.7

Total Assets: $2,474,264,504
Asset Allocation

Asset	%
Cash	4%
Stocks	0%
US Stocks	0%
Bonds	96%
US Bonds	96%
Other	0%

Services Offered:

Investment Strategy: The investment seeks to track the investment results of the S&P Short Term National AMT-Free Municipal Bond IndexTM. The fund generally will invest at least 90% of its assets in the component securities of the underlying index and may invest up to 10% of its assets in certain futures, options and swap contracts, cash and cash equivalents. The index measures the performance of the short-term investment-grade segment of the U.S. municipal bond market. **Top Holdings:** ILLINOIS ST 5%   HONOLULU HAWAII CITY & CNTY WASTEWTR SYS REV 5%   MASSACHUSETTS ST 5%   NEW YORK ST DORM AUTH SALES TAX REV ST SUPPORTED DEBT 5%   NEW JERSEY ST TPK AUTH TPK REV 5%

iShares Cohen & Steers REIT ETF   B-   BUY

Ticker	Traded On	NAV	Total Assets ($)	Dividend Yield (TTM)	Turnover Ratio	Expense Ratio
ICF	BATS	119.97	$2,417,428,968	2.34	17	0.34

Ratings
Reward   B+
Risk   C
Recent Upgrade/Downgrade   Up

Fund Information
Fund Type   Exchange Traded Funds
Category   Real Estate Sector Equity
Sub-Category   Real Estate
Prospectus Objective   Real Estate
Inception Date   Jan-01
Open to New Investments Y

Prices
Price (as of 9/30/2019)   120.02
52-Week High   121.41
52-Week Low   92.00

Total Returns (%)

3-Month	6-Month	1-Year	3-Year	5-Year
7.27	9.29	23.93	26.09	67.53

3-Year Standard Deviation   12.4
Effective Duration

Valuation
Premium/Discount (1-Year Average)   -0.02

Company Information
Provider   iShares
Manager/Tenure   Greg Savage (11), Jennifer Hsui (7), Alan Mason (3), 2 others
Website   http://www.ishares.com
Address   iShares 400 Howard Street San Francisco CA 94105 United States
Phone Number   800-474-2737

PERFORMANCE

Ratings History

Date	Overall Rating	Risk Rating	Reward Rating
Q3-19	B-	C	B+
Q4-18	B-	C	B
Q4-17	B-	B	C+
Q4-16	B-	C	B
Q4-15	B	C+	B+

Asset & Performance History

Date	NAV	1-Year Total Return
2018	95.71	-2.45
2017	101.27	4.95
2016	99.55	4.57
2015	99.21	5.96
2014	96.87	34.07
2013	74.66	-1.8

Total Assets: $2,417,428,968

Asset Allocation

Asset	%
Cash	0%
Stocks	100%
US Stocks	100%
Bonds	0%
US Bonds	0%
Other	0%

Services Offered: CashInvestment Plan

Investment Strategy: The investment seeks to track the investment results of the Cohen & Steers Realty Majors Index, which consists of REITs. The fund generally invests at least 90% of its assets in securities of the underlying index and in depositary receipts representing securities of the underlying index. The objective of the underlying index is to represent relatively large and liquid REITs that may benefit from future consolidation and securitization of the U.S. real estate industry. The fund is non-diversified. **Top Holdings:** American Tower Corp Prologis Inc Equinix Inc Simon Property Group Inc Public Storage

Vanguard Materials Index Fund ETF Shares   C   HOLD

Ticker	Traded On	NAV	Total Assets ($)	Dividend Yield (TTM)	Turnover Ratio	Expense Ratio
VAW	NYSE Arca	126.35	$2,402,666,964	2.01	5	0.1

Ratings
Reward   C
Risk   C
Recent Upgrade/Downgrade   Up

Fund Information
Fund Type   Exchange Traded Funds
Category   Natural Resources
Sub-Category   Natural Resources
Prospectus Objective   Unaligned
Inception Date   Jan-04
Open to New Investments Y

Prices
Price (as of 9/30/2019)   126.38
52-Week High   132.39
52-Week Low   104.05

Total Returns (%)

3-Month	6-Month	1-Year	3-Year	5-Year
-2.20	3.08	-2.96	24.08	27.23

3-Year Standard Deviation   15.67
Effective Duration

Valuation
Premium/Discount (1-Year Average)   -0.01

Company Information
Provider   Vanguard
Manager/Tenure   William A. Coleman (4), Michelle Louie (1)
Website   http://www.vanguard.com
Address   Vanguard 100 Vanguard Boulevard Malvern PA 19355 United States
Phone Number   877-662-7447

PERFORMANCE

Ratings History

Date	Overall Rating	Risk Rating	Reward Rating
Q3-19	C	C	C
Q4-18	C	C	C
Q4-17	B	C+	B+
Q4-16	C	C-	B-
Q4-15	C	C	C

Asset & Performance History

Date	NAV	1-Year Total Return
2018	109.91	-18.07
2017	136.55	23.04
2016	112.41	21.47
2015	94.23	-10.11
2014	107.36	5.9
2013	103.18	24.91

Total Assets: $2,402,666,964

Asset Allocation

Asset	%
Cash	0%
Stocks	100%
US Stocks	85%
Bonds	0%
US Bonds	0%
Other	0%

Services Offered:

Investment Strategy: The investment seeks to track the performance of a benchmark index. The fund employs an indexing investment approach designed to track the performance of the MSCI US Investable Market Index (IMI)/Materials 25/50, an index made up of stocks of large, mid-size, and small U.S. companies within the materials sector, as classified under the Global Industry Classification Standard (GICS). The Advisor attempts to replicate the target index by seeking to invest all, or substantially all, of its assets in the stocks that make up the index, in order to hold each stock in approximately the same proportion as its weighting in the index. The fund is non-diversified. **Top Holdings:** Linde PLC DuPont de Nemours Inc Ecolab Inc Air Products & Chemicals Inc Sherwin-Williams Co

Vanguard Russell 2000 Index Fund ETF Shares   C   HOLD

Ticker	Traded On	NAV	Total Assets ($)	Dividend Yield (TTM)	Turnover Ratio	Expense Ratio
VTWO	NAS CM	121.75	$2,397,060,324	1.31	19	0.15

Ratings
Reward   C-
Risk   C+
Recent Upgrade/Downgrade

Fund Information
Fund Type	Exchange Traded Funds
Category	US Equity Small Cap
Sub-Category	Small Blend
Prospectus Objective	Small Company
Inception Date	Sep-10
Open to New Investments	Y

Prices
Price (as of 9/30/2019)	121.70
52-Week High	133.46
52-Week Low	101.52

Total Returns (%)
3-Month	6-Month	1-Year	3-Year	5-Year
-2.57	-1.53	-7.72	26.70	48.12

3-Year Standard Deviation	17.2
Effective Duration	

Valuation
Premium/Discount (1-Year Average)	-0.06

Company Information
Provider	Vanguard
Manager/Tenure	Walter Nejman (4), Michael A. Johnson (3)
Website	http://www.vanguard.com
Address	Vanguard 100 Vanguard Boulevard Malvern PA 19355 United States
Phone Number	877-662-7447

PERFORMANCE

Ratings History

Date	Overall Rating	Risk Rating	Reward Rating
Q3-19	C	C+	C-
Q4-18	C	C+	C-
Q4-17	B+	B	A-
Q4-16	C+	C-	B
Q4-15	C	C-	C

Asset & Performance History

Date	NAV	1-Year Total Return
2018	106.72	-11.68
2017	122.3	15.17
2016	107.96	20.42
2015	90.23	-4.41
2014	95.55	4.92
2013	92.09	38.81

Total Assets: $2,397,060,324
Asset Allocation

Asset	%
Cash	2%
Stocks	98%
US Stocks	97%
Bonds	0%
US Bonds	0%
Other	0%

Services Offered:

Investment Strategy: The investment seeks to track the performance of a benchmark index that measures the investment return of small-capitalization stocks in the United States. The fund employs an indexing investment approach designed to track the performance of the Russell 2000® Index. The index is designed to measure the performance of small-capitalization stocks in the United States. The advisor attempts to replicate the target index by investing all, or substantially all, of its assets in the stocks that make up the index, holding each stock in approximately the same proportion as its weighting in the index. **Top Holdings:** NovoCure Ltd Haemonetics Corp HealthEquity Inc Chegg Inc Science Applications International Corp

---

First Trust Dorsey Wright Focus 5 ETF   C   HOLD

Ticker	Traded On	NAV	Total Assets ($)	Dividend Yield (TTM)	Turnover Ratio	Expense Ratio
FV	NAS CM	29.63	$2,349,672,700	0.32	44	0.89

Ratings
Reward   C
Risk   C+
Recent Upgrade/Downgrade

Fund Information
Fund Type	Exchange Traded Funds
Category	US Equity Large Cap Growth
Sub-Category	Large Growth
Prospectus Objective	Growth & Inc
Inception Date	Mar-14
Open to New Investments	Y

Prices
Price (as of 9/30/2019)	29.59
52-Week High	31.38
52-Week Low	23.41

Total Returns (%)
3-Month	6-Month	1-Year	3-Year	5-Year
-3.04	-2.41	-3.49	31.51	50.82

3-Year Standard Deviation	15.45
Effective Duration	

Valuation
Premium/Discount (1-Year Average)	-0.04

Company Information
Provider	First Trust
Manager/Tenure	Jon C. Erickson (5), Daniel J. Lindquist (5), David G. McGarel (5), 3 others
Website	http://www.ftportfolios.com/
Address	First Trust 120 E. Liberty Drive, Suite 400 Wheaton IL 60187 United States
Phone Number	800-621-1675

PERFORMANCE

Ratings History

Date	Overall Rating	Risk Rating	Reward Rating
Q3-19	C	C+	C
Q4-18	C-	C	C-
Q4-17	B	C+	B
Q4-16	C	C+	C-
Q4-15	D	C+	C

Asset & Performance History

Date	NAV	1-Year Total Return
2018	25.31	-8.06
2017	27.57	19.84
2016	23.16	-0.34
2015	23.47	6.81
2014	22	
2013		

Total Assets: $2,349,672,700
Asset Allocation

Asset	%
Cash	0%
Stocks	100%
US Stocks	97%
Bonds	0%
US Bonds	0%
Other	0%

Services Offered:

Investment Strategy: The investment seeks investment results that correspond generally to the price and yield (before the fund's fees and expenses) of an index called the Dorsey Wright Focus Five Index (the "index"). The fund will normally invest at least 90% of its net assets (including investment borrowings) in the exchange-traded funds ("ETFs") that comprise the index. The index is designed to provide targeted exposure to the five First Trust sector-based ETFs that the index provider believes offer the greatest potential to outperform the other ETFs in the selection universe and that satisfy certain trading volume and liquidity requirements. The fund is non-diversified. **Top Holdings:** First Trust Utilities AlphaDEX® ETF First Trust Technology AlphaDEX® ETF First Trust NASDAQ-100-Tech Sector ETF First Trust Dow Jones Internet ETF First Trust NYSE Arca Biotech ETF

ProShares Ultra S&P500   C   HOLD

Ticker	Traded On	NAV	Total Assets ($)	Dividend Yield (TTM)	Turnover Ratio	Expense Ratio
SSO	NYSE Arca	128.49	$2,344,886,532	0.56	5	0.9

Ratings
Reward   C+
Risk   C
Recent Upgrade/Downgrade

Fund Information
Fund Type   Exchange Traded Funds
Category   Trading Tools
Sub-Category   Trading--Leveraged Equity
Prospectus Objective   Growth
Inception Date   Jun-06
Open to New Investments   Y

Prices
Price (as of 9/30/2019)   128.45
52-Week High   133.28
52-Week Low   81.81

Total Returns (%)

3-Month	6-Month	1-Year	3-Year	5-Year
0.32	6.86	0.74	83.91	130.79

3-Year Standard Deviation   24.47
Effective Duration

Valuation
Premium/Discount (1-Year Average)   -0.06

Company Information
Provider   ProShares
Manager/Tenure   Michael Neches (6), Devin Sullivan (1)
Website   http://www.proshares.com
Address   ProShares 7501 Wisconsin Avenue, Suite 1000 Bethesda MD 20814 United States
Phone Number   866-776-5125

PERFORMANCE

Ratings History

Date	Overall Rating	Risk Rating	Reward Rating
Q3-19	C	C	C+
Q4-18	C	C+	C
Q4-17	B+	C+	A+
Q4-16	B	C+	B+
Q4-15	B-	B+	C

Asset & Performance History

Date	NAV	1-Year Total Return
2018	92.74	-14.43
2017	109.1	44.2
2016	75.99	21.24
2015	63.03	-1.09
2014	64.12	25.63
2013	51.21	70.45

Total Assets: $2,344,886,532
Asset Allocation

Asset	%
Cash	-100%
Stocks	200%
US Stocks	198%
Bonds	0%
US Bonds	0%
Other	0%

Services Offered:

Investment Strategy: The investment seeks daily investment results, before fees and expenses, that correspond to two times (2x) the daily performance of the S&P 500® Index. The fund invests in financial instruments that ProShare Advisors believes, in combination, should produce daily returns consistent with the fund's investment objective. The index is a measure of large-cap U.S. stock market performance. It is a float-adjusted, market capitalization-weighted index of 500 U.S. operating companies and real estate investment trusts selected through a process that factors in criteria such as liquidity, price, market capitalization and financial viability. The fund is non-diversified. **Top Holdings:** Spdr S&P 500 (Spy) Swap Goldman Sachs International   S&P 500 Index Swap Ubs Ag S&P 500 Index Swap Societe Generale   S&P 500 Index Swap Goldman Sachs International   S&P 500 Index Swap Bank Of America Na

---

Hartford Multifactor Developed Markets (ex-US) ETF   C   HOLD

Ticker	Traded On	NAV	Total Assets ($)	Dividend Yield (TTM)	Turnover Ratio	Expense Ratio
RODM	NYSE Arca	27.76	$2,335,701,190	2.45	47	0.29

Ratings
Reward   C
Risk   C+
Recent Upgrade/Downgrade

Fund Information
Fund Type   Exchange Traded Funds
Category   Global Equity Large Cap
Sub-Category   Foreign Large Blend
Prospectus Objective   Foreign Stock
Inception Date   Feb-15
Open to New Investments   Y

Prices
Price (as of 9/30/2019)   27.88
52-Week High   29.04
52-Week Low   25.02

Total Returns (%)

3-Month	6-Month	1-Year	3-Year	5-Year
-1.74	-0.25	-1.65	21.70	

3-Year Standard Deviation   9.55
Effective Duration

Valuation
Premium/Discount (1-Year Average)   0.15

Company Information
Provider   Hartford Funds
Manager/Tenure   Richard A. Brown (4), Thomas J. Durante (4), Karen Q. Wong (4)
Website   http://www.hartfordfunds.com
Address   690 Lee Road Wayne PA 19087 United States
Phone Number   800-456-7526

PERFORMANCE

Ratings History

Date	Overall Rating	Risk Rating	Reward Rating
Q3-19	C	C+	C
Q4-18	C	C+	D+
Q4-17	C+	B-	C+
Q4-16	D+	D+	D+
Q4-15	U		

Asset & Performance History

Date	NAV	1-Year Total Return
2018	25.77	-9.73
2017	29.1	25.76
2016	23.69	3.22
2015	23.69	
2014		
2013		

Total Assets: $2,335,701,190
Asset Allocation

Asset	%
Cash	0%
Stocks	100%
US Stocks	2%
Bonds	0%
US Bonds	0%
Other	0%

Services Offered:

Investment Strategy: The investment seeks to provide investment results that, before fees and expenses, correspond to the total return performance of the Hartford Risk-Optimized Multifactor Developed Markets (ex-US) Index. The fund generally invests at least 80% of its assets in securities included in the index and in depositary receipts representing securities included in the index. The index is designed to address risks and opportunities within developed international economies outside the U.S. **Top Holdings:** Swiss Life Holding AG   Wesfarmers Ltd Merck KGaA   Zurich Insurance Group AG   Smith & Nephew PLC

iShares 0-5 Year TIPS Bond ETF   C   HOLD

Ticker	Traded On	NAV	Total Assets ($)	Dividend Yield (TTM)	Turnover Ratio	Expense Ratio
STIP	NYSE Arca	100.06	$2,306,402,433	2	40	0.06

Ratings
Reward   C
Risk   C+
Recent Upgrade/Downgrade

Fund Information
Fund Type   Exchange Traded Funds
Category   US Fixed Income
Sub-Category   Inflation-Protected Bond
Prospectus Objective   Govt Bond - Treasury
Inception Date   Dec-10
Open to New Investments   Y

Prices
Price (as of 9/30/2019)   100.17
52-Week High   100.65
52-Week Low   97.69

Total Returns (%)

3-Month	6-Month	1-Year	3-Year	5-Year
0.40	2.04	3.38	4.91	5.97

3-Year Standard Deviation   1.13
Effective Duration

Valuation
Premium/Discount (1-Year Average)   0.04

Company Information
Provider   iShares
Manager/Tenure   Scott Radell (8), James Mauro (8)
Website   http://www.ishares.com
Address   iShares 400 Howard Street San Francisco CA 94105 United States
Phone Number   800-474-2737

PERFORMANCE

Ratings History

Date	Overall Rating	Risk Rating	Reward Rating
Q3-19	C	C+	C
Q4-18	C	C+	C-
Q4-17	C	B-	C
Q4-16	C	C-	C
Q4-15	D+	C-	D

Asset & Performance History

Date	NAV	1-Year Total Return
2018	97.99	0.49
2017	99.88	0.68
2016	100.67	2.77
2015	98.83	-0.1
2014	98.93	-1.28
2013	100.94	-1.73

Total Assets: $2,306,402,433
Asset Allocation

Asset	%
Cash	0%
Stocks	0%
US Stocks	0%
Bonds	100%
US Bonds	100%
Other	0%

Services Offered:

Investment Strategy: The investment seeks to track the investment results of the Bloomberg Barclays U.S. Treasury Inflation-Protected Securities (TIPS) 0-5 Years Index (Series-L). The fund generally will invest at least 90% of its assets in the component securities of the underlying index and may invest up to 10% of its assets in certain futures, options and swap contracts, cash and cash equivalents. The index measures the performance of the inflation-protected public obligations of the U.S. Treasury, commonly known as "TIPS," that have a remaining maturity of less than five years. **Top Holdings:** United States Treasury Notes 0.63% United States Treasury Notes 0.13% United States Treasury Notes 0.13% United States Treasury Notes 1.25% United States Treasury Notes 0.13%

---

iShares MSCI Pacific ex Japan ETF   C   HOLD

Ticker	Traded On	NAV	Total Assets ($)	Dividend Yield (TTM)	Turnover Ratio	Expense Ratio
EPP	NYSE Arca	44.75	$2,282,000,836	4.49	6	0.48

Ratings
Reward   C
Risk   C+
Recent Upgrade/Downgrade   Down

Fund Information
Fund Type   Exchange Traded Funds
Category   Asia ex-Japan Equity
Sub-Category   Pacific/Asia ex-Japan Stk
Prospectus Objective   Pacific Stock
Inception Date   Oct-01
Open to New Investments   Y

Prices
Price (as of 9/30/2019)   44.73
52-Week High   47.91
52-Week Low   39.46

Total Returns (%)

3-Month	6-Month	1-Year	3-Year	5-Year
-5.23	-1.79	3.13	21.40	20.10

3-Year Standard Deviation   11.51
Effective Duration

Valuation
Premium/Discount (1-Year Average)   -0.05

Company Information
Provider   iShares
Manager/Tenure   Diane Hsiung (11), Greg Savage (11), Jennifer Hsui (6), 3 others
Website   http://www.ishares.com
Address   iShares 400 Howard Street San Francisco CA 94105 United States
Phone Number   800-474-2737

PERFORMANCE

Ratings History

Date	Overall Rating	Risk Rating	Reward Rating
Q3-19	C	C+	C
Q4-18	C-	C	D+
Q4-17	B-	C	B
Q4-16	D+	C-	D+
Q4-15	C-	D+	C-

Asset & Performance History

Date	NAV	1-Year Total Return
2018	40.85	-10.68
2017	47.94	25.43
2016	39.89	7.38
2015	38.64	-8.88
2014	44.38	-0.85
2013	46.68	5.03

Total Assets: $2,282,000,836
Asset Allocation

Asset	%
Cash	0%
Stocks	100%
US Stocks	1%
Bonds	0%
US Bonds	0%
Other	0%

Services Offered: CashInvestment Plan

Investment Strategy: The investment seeks to track the investment results of the MSCI Pacific ex Japan Index. The fund normally invests at least 95% of its total assets in the securities of its underlying index and in depositary receipts representing securities in its underlying index. It will at all times invest at least 90% of its total assets in such securities. The underlying index consists of stocks from the following four countries or regions: Australia, Hong Kong, New Zealand and Singapore. It may include large- or mid-capitalization companies. **Top Holdings:** AIA Group Ltd Commonwealth Bank of Australia CSL Ltd BHP Group Ltd Westpac Banking Corp

Vanguard S&P Small-Cap 600 Index Fund ETF Shares

C- HOLD

Ticker	Traded On	NAV	Total Assets ($)	Dividend Yield (TTM)	Turnover Ratio	Expense Ratio
VIOO	NYSE Arca	142.69	$2,260,147,578	1.17	13	0.15

Ratings
Reward C
Risk C-
Recent Upgrade/Downgrade

Fund Information
Fund Type	Exchange Traded Funds
Category	US Equity Small Cap
Sub-Category	Small Blend
Prospectus Objective	Growth & Inc
Inception Date	Sep-10
Open to New Investments	Y

Prices
Price (as of 9/30/2019)	142.63
52-Week High	157.23
52-Week Low	118.22

Total Returns (%)
3-Month	6-Month	1-Year	3-Year	5-Year
-0.49	0.25	-8.18	30.37	59.56

3-Year Standard Deviation 18.05
Effective Duration

Valuation
Premium/Discount (1-Year Average) -0.02

Company Information
Provider	Vanguard
Manager/Tenure	William A. Coleman (5), Donald M. Butler (3)
Website	http://www.vanguard.com
Address	Vanguard 100 Vanguard Boulevard Malvern PA 19355 United States
Phone Number	877-662-7447

PERFORMANCE

Ratings History
Date	Overall Rating	Risk Rating	Reward Rating
Q3-19	C-	C-	C
Q4-18	C-	C-	C-
Q4-17	A-	B	A
Q4-16	C	C-	C
Q4-15	C	D+	C

Asset & Performance History
Date	NAV	1-Year Total Return
2018	125.8	-9.08
2017	139.31	13.69
2016	124.31	25.28
2015	99.25	-2.04
2014	102.6	5.6
2013	98.19	41.04

Total Assets: $2,260,147,578
Asset Allocation
Asset	%
Cash	2%
Stocks	98%
US Stocks	97%
Bonds	0%
US Bonds	0%
Other	0%

Services Offered:

Investment Strategy: The investment seeks to track the performance of a benchmark index that measures the investment return of small-capitalization stocks in the United States. The fund employs an indexing investment approach designed to track the performance of the S&P SmallCap 600® Index. The Advisor attempts to replicate the target index by investing all, or substantially all, of its assets in the stocks that make up the index, holding each stock in approximately the same proportion as its weighting in the index. **Top Holdings:** Mercury Systems Inc Selective Insurance Group Inc FirstCash Inc Repligen Corp FTI Consulting Inc

---

SPDR® Blackstone / GSO Senior Loan ETF

C+ HOLD

Ticker	Traded On	NAV	Total Assets ($)	Dividend Yield (TTM)	Turnover Ratio	Expense Ratio
SRLN	NYSE Arca		$2,236,907,010	5.53	124	0.7

Ratings
Reward C
Risk C+
Recent Upgrade/Downgrade

Fund Information
Fund Type	Exchange Traded Funds
Category	US Fixed Income
Sub-Category	Bank Loan
Prospectus Objective	Income
Inception Date	Apr-13
Open to New Investments	Y

Prices
Price (as of 9/30/2019)	46.32
52-Week High	47.23
52-Week Low	44.46

Total Returns (%)
3-Month	6-Month	1-Year	3-Year	5-Year
1.39	2.97	3.23	12.45	17.14

3-Year Standard Deviation 2.83
Effective Duration

Valuation
Premium/Discount (1-Year Average) -0.11

Company Information
Provider	SPDR State Street Global Advisors
Manager/Tenure	Gordon McKemie (4), Daniel T. McMullen (4)
Website	http://www.spdrs.com
Address	SPDR State Street Global Advisors State Street Financial Center, 1 Lincoln Street Boston MA 02111-2900 United States
Phone Number	617-786-3000

PERFORMANCE

Ratings History
Date	Overall Rating	Risk Rating	Reward Rating
Q3-19	C+	C+	C
Q4-18	C	C+	C-
Q4-17	B-	B	C
Q4-16	C	C+	C
Q4-15	C	C+	C

Asset & Performance History
Date	NAV	1-Year Total Return
2018	44.92	-0.25
2017	47.22	3.6
2016	47.43	6.85
2015	46.19	-0.85
2014	48.6	0.89
2013	49.93	

Total Assets: $2,236,907,010
Asset Allocation
Asset	%
Cash	12%
Stocks	0%
US Stocks	0%
Bonds	88%
US Bonds	64%
Other	0%

Services Offered:

Investment Strategy: The investment seeks to provide current income consistent with the preservation of capital. The fund seeks to outperform the Markit iBoxx USD Liquid Leveraged Loan Index and the S&P/LSTA U.S. Leveraged Loan 100 Index by normally investing at least 80% of its net assets (plus any borrowings for investment purposes) in Senior Loans. For purposes of this 80% test, "Senior Loans" are first lien senior secured floating rate bank loans. **Top Holdings:** CENTURYLINK ESCROW LLC TERM LOAN B ENTERPRISE MERGER SUB INC INITIAL TERM LOANS UNIVISION COMMUNICATIONS 2017 REPLACEMENT REPRICED NEW DUN + BRADSTREET CORP TERM LOAN SCIENTIFIC GAMES INTL INC TERM B 5

Schwab International Small-Cap Equity ETF™   C   HOLD

Ticker	Traded On	NAV	Total Assets ($)	Dividend Yield (TTM)	Turnover Ratio	Expense Ratio
SCHC	NYSE Arca	31.83	$2,234,378,316	2.81	16	0.12

Ratings
Reward	D+
Risk	C+
Recent Upgrade/Downgrade	

Fund Information
Fund Type	Exchange Traded Funds
Category	Globa Eq Mid/Small Cap
Sub-Category	Foreign Small/Mid Blend
Prospectus Objective	Small Company
Inception Date	Jan-10
Open to New Investments	Y

Prices
Price (as of 9/30/2019)	31.80
52-Week High	35.86
52-Week Low	27.92

Total Returns (%)
3-Month	6-Month	1-Year	3-Year	5-Year
-2.95	-1.79	-8.28	12.00	16.89

3-Year Standard Deviation	12.26
Effective Duration	

Valuation
Premium/Discount (1-Year Average)	0.04

Company Information
Provider	Schwab ETFs
Manager/Tenure	Chuck Craig (6), Christopher Bliss (2), Jane Qin (2), 1 other
Website	http://www.schwabfunds.com
Address	Schwab ETFs United States
Phone Number	800-435-4000

PERFORMANCE

Ratings History
Date	Overall Rating	Risk Rating	Reward Rating
Q3-19	C	C+	D+
Q4-18	D+	C-	D+
Q4-17	B	B	B+
Q4-16	C	C	C-
Q4-15	C	C+	C-

Asset & Performance History
Date	NAV	1-Year Total Return
2018	29.11	-18.64
2017	36.65	29.36
2016	29.13	3.16
2015	28.81	1.85
2014	28.96	-5.82
2013	31.55	21.91

Total Assets: $2,234,378,316
Asset Allocation
Asset	%
Cash	0%
Stocks	99%
US Stocks	1%
Bonds	0%
US Bonds	0%
Other	0%

Services Offered:

Investment Strategy: The investment seeks to track as closely as possible, before fees and expenses, the total return of the FTSE Developed Small Cap ex US Liquid Index. The fund will invest at least 90% of its net assets in stocks, including depositary receipts representing securities of the index; such depositary receipts may be in the form of American Depositary Receipts, Global Depositary Receipts and European Depositary Receipts. The index is comprised of small capitalization companies in developed countries outside the United States. **Top Holdings:** Open Text Corp   Emera, Inc.   Kirkland Lake Gold Ltd   Gildan Activewear, Inc. Class A   CAE Inc

---

SPDR® Dow Jones Global Real Estate ETF   C+   HOLD

Ticker	Traded On	NAV	Total Assets ($)	Dividend Yield (TTM)	Turnover Ratio	Expense Ratio
RWO	NYSE Arca		$2,219,748,572	3.12	11	0.5

Ratings
Reward	C
Risk	C+
Recent Upgrade/Downgrade	Up

Fund Information
Fund Type	Exchange Traded Funds
Category	Real Estate Sector Equity
Sub-Category	Global Real Estate
Prospectus Objective	Real Estate
Inception Date	May-08
Open to New Investments	Y

Prices
Price (as of 9/30/2019)	51.86
52-Week High	51.88
52-Week Low	42.86

Total Returns (%)
3-Month	6-Month	1-Year	3-Year	5-Year
4.94	5.29	13.50	16.13	38.68

3-Year Standard Deviation	10.69
Effective Duration	

Valuation
Premium/Discount (1-Year Average)	-0.02

Company Information
Provider	SPDR State Street Global Advisors
Manager/Tenure	Michael J. Feehily (6), Karl A. Schneider (4), Keith Richardson (2)
Website	http://www.spdrs.com
Address	SPDR State Street Global Advisors State Street Financial Center, 1 Lincoln Street Boston MA 02111-2900 United States
Phone Number	617-786-3000

PERFORMANCE

Ratings History
Date	Overall Rating	Risk Rating	Reward Rating
Q3-19	C+	C+	C
Q4-18	C	C+	C-
Q4-17	B-	B	C+
Q4-16	C	C+	C
Q4-15	C+	C+	C

Asset & Performance History
Date	NAV	1-Year Total Return
2018	44.25	-6.06
2017	48.89	7.78
2016	46.87	1.85
2015	46.79	0.96
2014	47.74	19.13
2013	41.38	2.85

Total Assets: $2,219,748,572
Asset Allocation
Asset	%
Cash	0%
Stocks	100%
US Stocks	58%
Bonds	0%
US Bonds	0%
Other	0%

Services Offered:

Investment Strategy: The investment seeks to provide investment results that, before fees and expenses, correspond generally to the total return performance of the Dow Jones Global Select Real Estate Securities Indexsm based upon the global real estate market. The fund generally invests substantially all, but at least 80%, of its total assets in the securities comprising the index and in depositary receipts based on securities comprising the index. The index is a float-adjusted market capitalization index designed to measure the performance of publicly traded global real estate securities. The fund is non-diversified. **Top Holdings:** Prologis Inc   Simon Property Group Inc   Public Storage   Welltower Inc   Equity Residential

First Trust Technology AlphaDEX® Fund

C+   **HOLD**

Ticker	Traded On	NAV	Total Assets ($)	Dividend Yield (TTM)	Turnover Ratio	Expense Ratio
FXL	NYSE Arca	65.14	$2,215,241,812	0.53	91	0.63

Ratings

Reward	C+
Risk	C+
Recent Upgrade/Downgrade	Down

Fund Information

Fund Type	Exchange Traded Funds
Category	Technology Sector Equity
Sub-Category	Technology
Prospectus Objective	Technology
Inception Date	May-07
Open to New Investments	Y

Prices

Price (as of 9/30/2019)	65.15
52-Week High	71.30
52-Week Low	48.15

Total Returns (%)

3-Month	6-Month	1-Year	3-Year	5-Year
-3.60	0.27	3.77	79.51	111.61

3-Year Standard Deviation	18.46
Effective Duration	

Valuation

Premium/Discount (1-Year Average)	0.01

Company Information

Provider	First Trust
Manager/Tenure	Jon C. Erickson (12), Daniel J. Lindquist (12), David G. McGarel (12), 3 others
Website	http://www.ftportfolios.com/
Address	First Trust 120 E. Liberty Drive, Suite 400 Wheaton IL 60187 United States
Phone Number	800-621-1675

PERFORMANCE

Ratings History				Asset & Performance History			Total Assets:	$2,215,241,812
Date	Overall Rating	Risk Rating	Reward Rating	Date	NAV	1-Year Total Return	Asset Allocation Asset	%
Q3-19	C+	C+	C+	2018	52.52	2.57	Cash	0%
Q4-18	C	C+	C	2017	51.31	35.79	Stocks	100%
Q4-17	B+	C+	A+	2016	37.9	15.42	US Stocks	98%
Q4-16	B	C+	A-	2015	33.23	-3.3	Bonds	0%
Q4-15	C+	C+	C	2014	34.49	16.37	US Bonds	0%
				2013	29.83	37.74	Other	0%

Services Offered:

Investment Strategy: The investment seeks investment results that correspond generally to the price and yield (before the fund's fees and expenses) of an equity index called the StrataQuant® Technology Index. The fund will normally invest at least 90% of its net assets (including investment borrowings) in common stocks that comprise the index. The index is a modified equal-dollar weighted index designed by IDI to objectively identify and select stocks from the Russell 1000® Index in the technology sector that may generate positive alpha relative to traditional passive-style indices through the use of the AlphaDEX® selection methodology. **Top Holdings:** Alteryx Inc Class A   Match Group Inc   Switch Inc Class A   Avalara Inc   Micron Technology Inc

---

WisdomTree U.S. LargeCap Dividend Fund

C   **HOLD**

Ticker	Traded On	NAV	Total Assets ($)	Dividend Yield (TTM)	Turnover Ratio	Expense Ratio
DLN	NYSE Arca	99.06	$2,189,144,246	2.61	11	0.28

Ratings

Reward	C+
Risk	C-
Recent Upgrade/Downgrade	

Fund Information

Fund Type	Exchange Traded Funds
Category	US Equity Large Cap Value
Sub-Category	Large Value
Prospectus Objective	Growth & Inc
Inception Date	Jun-06
Open to New Investments	Y

Prices

Price (as of 9/30/2019)	99.07
52-Week High	99.66
52-Week Low	79.69

Total Returns (%)

3-Month	6-Month	1-Year	3-Year	5-Year
2.24	5.45	6.33	39.40	61.45

3-Year Standard Deviation	11.48
Effective Duration	

Valuation

Premium/Discount (1-Year Average)	0.00

Company Information

Provider	WisdomTree
Manager/Tenure	Richard A. Brown (11), Thomas J. Durante (11), Karen Q. Wong (11)
Website	http://www.wisdomtree.com
Address	WisdomTree 245 Park Avenue, 35th floor New York NY 10167 United States
Phone Number	866-909-9473

PERFORMANCE

Ratings History				Asset & Performance History			Total Assets:	$2,189,144,246
Date	Overall Rating	Risk Rating	Reward Rating	Date	NAV	1-Year Total Return	Asset Allocation Asset	%
Q3-19	C	C-	C+	2018	84.39	-5.77	Cash	0%
Q4-18	C	C-	C	2017	92.03	18.21	Stocks	100%
Q4-17	B-	B	B-	2016	79.83	15.38	US Stocks	100%
Q4-16	C+	C-	B	2015	71.16	-1.26	Bonds	0%
Q4-15	C	C	C	2014	74.08	14.07	US Bonds	0%
				2013	66.57	27.35	Other	0%

Services Offered:

Investment Strategy: The investment seeks to track the price and yield performance, before fees and expenses, of the WisdomTree U.S. LargeCap Dividend Index. Under normal circumstances, at least 95% of the fund's total assets (exclusive of collateral held from securities lending) will be invested in component securities of the index and investments that have economic characteristics that are substantially identical to the economic characteristics of such component securities. The index is a fundamentally weighted index that is comprised of the large-capitalization segment of the U.S. dividend-paying market. The fund is non-diversified. **Top Holdings:** Microsoft Corp   Apple Inc   AT&T Inc   Exxon Mobil Corp   JPMorgan Chase & Co

SPDR® S&P 600 Small Cap Value ETF   D   SELL

Ticker	Traded On	NAV	Total Assets ($)	Dividend Yield (TTM)	Turnover Ratio	Expense Ratio
SLYV	NYSE Arca		$2,186,057,622	1.8	34	0.15

Ratings
Reward   D+
Risk   D
Recent Upgrade/Downgrade

Fund Information
Fund Type	Exchange Traded Funds
Category	US Equity Small Cap
Sub-Category	Small Value
Prospectus Objective	Small Company
Inception Date	Sep-00
Open to New Investments	Y

Prices
Price (as of 9/30/2019)	61.26
52-Week High	67.25
52-Week Low	50.73

Total Returns (%)
3-Month	6-Month	1-Year	3-Year	5-Year
1.23	0.98	7.96	-27.18	-12.59

3-Year Standard Deviation	18.94
Effective Duration	

Valuation
Premium/Discount (1-Year Average)	-0.01

Company Information
Provider	SPDR State Street Global Advisors
Manager/Tenure	Michael J. Feehily (7), Karl A. Schneider (4), David Chin (0)
Website	http://www.spdrs.com
Address	SPDR State Street Global Advisors State Street Financial Center, 1 Lincoln Street Boston MA 02111-2900 United States
Phone Number	617-786-3000

PERFORMANCE

Ratings History

Date	Overall Rating	Risk Rating	Reward Rating
Q3-19	D	D	D+
Q4-18	D-	D	D-
Q4-17	B+	B	A-
Q4-16	C	C-	C
Q4-15	C	C-	C

Asset & Performance History

Date	NAV	1-Year Total Return
2018	53.81	-56.68
2017	125.58	11.5
2016	119.03	30.15
2015	92.91	-6.65
2014	106.08	7.31
2013	106.38	39.65

Total Assets: $2,186,057,622

Asset Allocation

Asset	%
Cash	0%
Stocks	100%
US Stocks	98%
Bonds	0%
US Bonds	0%
Other	0%

Services Offered: Dividend Investment Plan, CashInvestment Plan

Investment Strategy: The investment seeks to provide investment results that, before fees and expenses, correspond generally to the total return performance of the S&P SmallCap 600 Value Index. The fund generally invests substantially all, but at least 80%, of its total assets in the securities comprising the index. The index measures the performance of the small-capitalization value segment of the U.S. equity market. It may purchase a subset of the securities in the index in an effort to hold a portfolio of securities with generally the same risk and return characteristics of the index. The fund is non-diversified. **Top Holdings:** TopBuild Corp Darling Ingredients Inc South Jersey Industries Inc SkyWest Inc Lithia Motors Inc Class A

First Trust Cloud Computing ETF   C   HOLD

Ticker	Traded On	NAV	Total Assets ($)	Dividend Yield (TTM)	Turnover Ratio	Expense Ratio
SKYY	NAS CM	56.39	$2,168,197,623	1.06	7	0.6

Ratings
Reward   C
Risk   C
Recent Upgrade/Downgrade   Down

Fund Information
Fund Type	Exchange Traded Funds
Category	Technology Sector Equity
Sub-Category	Technology
Prospectus Objective	Technology
Inception Date	Jul-11
Open to New Investments	Y

Prices
Price (as of 9/30/2019)	56.42
52-Week High	60.91
52-Week Low	45.37

Total Returns (%)
3-Month	6-Month	1-Year	3-Year	5-Year
-3.11	-3.22	0.82	68.03	115.13

3-Year Standard Deviation	13.42
Effective Duration	

Valuation
Premium/Discount (1-Year Average)	0.04

Company Information
Provider	First Trust
Manager/Tenure	Jon C. Erickson (8), Daniel J. Lindquist (8), David G. McGarel (8), 3 others
Website	http://www.ftportfolios.com/
Address	First Trust 120 E. Liberty Drive, Suite 400 Wheaton IL 60187 United States
Phone Number	800-621-1675

PERFORMANCE

Ratings History

Date	Overall Rating	Risk Rating	Reward Rating
Q3-19	C	C	C
Q4-18	C+	C-	B
Q4-17	A-	B	A
Q4-16	C-	C-	C-
Q4-15	C+	C	B

Asset & Performance History

Date	NAV	1-Year Total Return
2018	48.25	5.62
2017	45.84	33.38
2016	34.47	15.41
2015	29.98	5.88
2014	28.43	7.42
2013	26.51	33.35

Total Assets: $2,168,197,623

Asset Allocation

Asset	%
Cash	0%
Stocks	100%
US Stocks	93%
Bonds	0%
US Bonds	0%
Other	0%

Services Offered:

Investment Strategy: The investment seeks investment results that correspond generally to the price and yield, before the fund's fees and expenses, of an equity index called the ISE Cloud ComputingTM Index. The fund will normally invest at least 90% of its net assets (including investment borrowings) in the common stocks and depositary receipts that comprise the index. The index is designed to provide a benchmark for investors interested in tracking companies involved in the cloud computing industry. **Top Holdings:** Microsoft Corp Alphabet Inc A MongoDB Inc Class A Oracle Corp CenturyLink Inc

Vanguard S&P Mid-Cap 400 Index Fund ETF Shares | C- HOLD

Ticker	Traded On	NAV	Total Assets ($)	Dividend Yield (TTM)	Turnover Ratio	Expense Ratio
IVOO	NYSE Arca	130.50	$2,162,426,089	1.44	12	0.15

Ratings
Reward	C
Risk	C-
Recent Upgrade/Downgrade	Down

Fund Information
Fund Type	Exchange Traded Funds
Category	US Equity Mid Cap
Sub-Category	Mid-Cap Blend
Prospectus Objective	Growth & Inc
Inception Date	Sep-10
Open to New Investments	Y

Prices
Price (as of 9/30/2019)	130.51
52-Week High	134.94
52-Week Low	105.39

Total Returns (%)
3-Month	6-Month	1-Year	3-Year	5-Year
-1.11	0.84	-2.48	29.53	51.07

3-Year Standard Deviation	15.31
Effective Duration	

Valuation
Premium/Discount (1-Year Average)	-0.02

Company Information
Provider	Vanguard
Manager/Tenure	William A. Coleman (3), Awais Khan (1)
Website	http://www.vanguard.com
Address	Vanguard 100 Vanguard Boulevard Malvern PA 19355 United States
Phone Number	877-662-7447

PERFORMANCE

Ratings History
Date	Overall Rating	Risk Rating	Reward Rating
Q3-19	C-	C-	C
Q4-18	C-	C-	C-
Q4-17	B	B	B
Q4-16	C+	C-	B
Q4-15	C	C-	C

Asset & Performance History
Date	NAV	1-Year Total Return
2018	110.81	-12.09
2017	127.79	16.26
2016	111.48	19.8
2015	93.82	-2.29
2014	97.41	9.64
2013	89.96	33.3

Total Assets: $2,162,426,089
Asset Allocation
Asset	%
Cash	1%
Stocks	99%
US Stocks	99%
Bonds	0%
US Bonds	0%
Other	0%

Services Offered:

Investment Strategy: The investment seeks to track the performance of a benchmark index that measures the investment return of mid-capitalization stocks in the United States. The fund employs an indexing investment approach designed to track the performance of the S&P MidCap 400® Index. The index measures the performance of mid-capitalization stocks in the United States. The Advisor attempts to replicate the target index by investing all, or substantially all, of its assets in the stocks that make up the index, holding each stock in approximately the same proportion as its weighting in the index. **Top Holdings:** IDEX Corp Steris PLC Leidos Holdings Inc Zebra Technologies Corp NVR Inc

---

Invesco S&P SmallCap Low Volatility ETF | C HOLD

Ticker	Traded On	NAV	Total Assets ($)	Dividend Yield (TTM)	Turnover Ratio	Expense Ratio
XSLV	NYSE Arca	48.91	$2,159,446,882	2.61		0.25

Ratings
Reward	C
Risk	C+
Recent Upgrade/Downgrade	

Fund Information
Fund Type	Exchange Traded Funds
Category	US Equity Small Cap
Sub-Category	Small Value
Prospectus Objective	Income
Inception Date	Feb-13
Open to New Investments	

Prices
Price (as of 9/30/2019)	48.89
52-Week High	49.75
52-Week Low	40.81

Total Returns (%)
3-Month	6-Month	1-Year	3-Year	5-Year
2.38	4.67	3.29	35.64	84.34

3-Year Standard Deviation	14.28
Effective Duration	

Valuation
Premium/Discount (1-Year Average)	-0.01

Company Information
Provider	Invesco
Manager/Tenure	Peter Hubbard (6), Michael Jeanette (6), Tony Seisser (5)
Website	http://www.invesco.com/us
Address	Invesco 11 Greenway Plaza, Ste. 2500 Houston TX 77046 United States
Phone Number	800-659-1005

PERFORMANCE

Ratings History
Date	Overall Rating	Risk Rating	Reward Rating
Q3-19	C	C+	C
Q4-18	C	C+	C-
Q4-17	A	A	A
Q4-16	B	C+	A
Q4-15	C	C-	C+

Asset & Performance History
Date	NAV	1-Year Total Return
2018	42.64	-5.33
2017	46.23	8.68
2016	43.35	31.34
2015	33.72	2.77
2014	33.55	10.8
2013	31.04	

Total Assets: $2,159,446,882
Asset Allocation
Asset	%
Cash	1%
Stocks	99%
US Stocks	99%
Bonds	0%
US Bonds	0%
Other	0%

Services Offered:

Investment Strategy: The investment seeks to track the investment results (before fees and expenses) of the S&P SmallCap 600® Low Volatility Index (the "underlying index"). The fund generally will invest at least 90% of its total assets in the securities that comprise the underlying index. Strictly in accordance with its procedures and mandated guidelines, S&P DJI selects for inclusion in the underlying index the 120 securities that it has determined have the lowest volatility over the past 12 months out of the 600 small-capitalization securities that are contained in the S&P SmallCap 600® Index. **Top Holdings:** Redwood Trust Inc Granite Point Mortgage Trust Inc Apollo Commercial Real Estate Finance Inc New York Mortgage Trust Inc American States Water Co

---

Vanguard Communication Services Index Fund ETF Shares   B-   BUY

Ticker	Traded On	NAV	Total Assets ($)	Dividend Yield (TTM)	Turnover Ratio	Expense Ratio
VOX	NYSE Arca	86.69	$2,134,380,301	0.93	84	0.1

Ratings
Reward   B
Risk   C
Recent Upgrade/Downgrade   Up

Fund Information
Fund Type   Exchange Traded Funds
Category   Communications Sector Equity
Sub-Category   Communications
Prospectus Objective   Comm
Inception Date   Sep-04
Open to New Investments   Y

Prices
Price (as of 9/30/2019)   86.70
52-Week High   91.54
52-Week Low   69.56

Total Returns (%)

3-Month	6-Month	1-Year	3-Year	5-Year
-0.80	2.55	0.67	-1.30	16.25

3-Year Standard Deviation   13.36
Effective Duration

Valuation
Premium/Discount (1-Year Average)   -0.01

Company Information
Provider   Vanguard
Manager/Tenure   Walter Nejman (3), Awais Khan (1)
Website   http://www.vanguard.com
Address   Vanguard 100 Vanguard Boulevard
                  Malvern PA 19355 United States
Phone Number   877-662-7447

PERFORMANCE

Ratings History

Date	Overall Rating	Risk Rating	Reward Rating
Q3-19	B-	C	B
Q4-18	C+	C-	B
Q4-17	C	C+	C
Q4-16	B-	C	B
Q4-15	C+	C	B-

Asset & Performance History

Date	NAV	1-Year Total Return
2018	73.75	-16.95
2017	90.96	-5.32
2016	100	22.3
2015	83.94	2.72
2014	84.73	3.98
2013	83.66	24.31

Total Assets: $2,134,380,301
Asset Allocation

Asset	%
Cash	1%
Stocks	99%
US Stocks	97%
Bonds	0%
US Bonds	0%
Other	0%

Services Offered:

Investment Strategy: The investment seeks to track the performance of a benchmark index. The fund employs an indexing investment approach designed to track the performance of the MSCI US Investable Market Index (IMI)/Communication Services 25/50, an index made up of stocks of large, mid-size, and small U.S. companies within the communication services sector, as classified under the GICS. The Advisor attempts to replicate the target index by seeking to invest all, or substantially all, of its assets in the stocks that make up the index, in order to hold each stock in approximately the same proportion as its weighting in the index. It is non-diversified. **Top Holdings:** Facebook Inc A   Alphabet Inc Class C   Alphabet Inc A   Verizon Communications Inc   AT&T Inc

Vanguard Mega Cap Index Fund ETF Shares   C   HOLD

Ticker	Traded On	NAV	Total Assets ($)	Dividend Yield (TTM)	Turnover Ratio	Expense Ratio
MGC	NYSE Arca	103.09	$2,129,779,744	1.47	4	0.07

Ratings
Reward   C+
Risk   C-
Recent Upgrade/Downgrade

Fund Information
Fund Type   Exchange Traded Funds
Category   US Equity Large Cap Blend
Sub-Category   Large Blend
Prospectus Objective   Growth
Inception Date   Dec-07
Open to New Investments   Y

Prices
Price (as of 9/30/2019)   103.11
52-Week High   104.52
52-Week Low   81.34

Total Returns (%)

3-Month	6-Month	1-Year	3-Year	5-Year
0.44	4.35	3.27	47.01	67.62

3-Year Standard Deviation   12.07
Effective Duration

Valuation
Premium/Discount (1-Year Average)   -0.01

Company Information
Provider   Vanguard
Manager/Tenure   Michael A. Johnson (3), Gerard C.
                  O'Reilly (3)
Website   http://www.vanguard.com
Address   Vanguard 100 Vanguard Boulevard
                  Malvern PA 19355 United States
Phone Number   877-662-7447

PERFORMANCE

Ratings History

Date	Overall Rating	Risk Rating	Reward Rating
Q3-19	C	C-	C+
Q4-18	C	C-	C
Q4-17	B	B	B
Q4-16	C+	C-	B
Q4-15	C	C	C

Asset & Performance History

Date	NAV	1-Year Total Return
2018	86.03	-4.24
2017	91.67	22.59
2016	76.27	11.23
2015	69.77	1.53
2014	70.17	13.26
2013	63.13	32.1

Total Assets: $2,129,779,744
Asset Allocation

Asset	%
Cash	0%
Stocks	100%
US Stocks	99%
Bonds	0%
US Bonds	0%
Other	0%

Services Offered:

Investment Strategy: The investment seeks to track the performance of a benchmark index that measures the investment return of large-capitalization stocks in the United States. The fund employs an indexing investment approach designed to track the performance of the CRSP US Mega Cap Index. The index is a float-adjusted, market-capitalization-weighted index designed to measure equity market performance of mega-capitalization stocks in the United States. The Advisor attempts to replicate the target index by investing all, or substantially all, of its assets in the stocks that make up the index, holding each stock in approximately the same proportion as its weighting in the index. **Top Holdings:** Microsoft Corp   Apple Inc   Amazon.com Inc   Facebook Inc A   Berkshire Hathaway Inc B

iShares Ultra Short-Term Bond ETF   C   HOLD

Ticker	Traded On	NAV	Total Assets ($)	Dividend Yield (TTM)	Turnover Ratio	Expense Ratio
ICSH	BATS	50.39	$2,128,840,201	2.67	32	0.08

Ratings

Reward	C
Risk	C+
Recent Upgrade/Downgrade	

Fund Information

Fund Type	Exchange Traded Funds
Category	US Fixed Income
Sub-Category	Ultrashort Bond
Prospectus Objective	Income
Inception Date	Dec-13
Open to New Investments	Y

Prices

Price (as of 9/30/2019)	50.39
52-Week High	50.42
52-Week Low	50.00

Total Returns (%)

3-Month	6-Month	1-Year	3-Year	5-Year
0.70	1.58	3.16	6.78	7.98

3-Year Standard Deviation	0.28
Effective Duration	0.42

Valuation

Premium/Discount (1-Year Average)	0.02

Company Information

Provider	iShares
Manager/Tenure	Richard Mejzak (5), Scott Radell (5)
Website	http://www.ishares.com
Address	iShares 400 Howard Street San Francisco CA 94105 United States
Phone Number	800-474-2737

PERFORMANCE

Ratings History

Date	Overall Rating	Risk Rating	Reward Rating
Q3-19	C	C+	C
Q4-18	C	C+	C
Q4-17	B-	A-	C
Q4-16	C-	D+	C
Q4-15	D+	D+	D+

Asset & Performance History

Date	NAV	1-Year Total Return
2018	50.05	2.26
2017	50.03	1.53
2016	49.95	1.18
2015	49.8	0.17
2014	49.98	0.43
2013	49.99	

Total Assets: $2,128,840,201

Asset Allocation

Asset	%
Cash	50%
Stocks	0%
US Stocks	0%
Bonds	49%
US Bonds	28%
Other	0%

Services Offered:

Investment Strategy: The investment seeks to provide current income consistent with preservation of capital. The fund seeks to achieve its investment objective by investing, under normal circumstances, at least 80% of its net assets in a portfolio of U.S. dollar-denominated investment-grade fixed- and floating-rate debt securities that are rated BBB- or higher by S&P Global Ratings and/or Fitch Ratings, Inc. ("Fitch"), or Baa3 or higher by Moody's Investors Service, Inc. ("Moody's"), or, if unrated, determined by BFA to be of equivalent quality. **Top Holdings:** Verizon Communications Inc. 2.7% Tencent Holdings Limited 2.88% BRANCH BANKING & TRUST CO 2.1% American Honda Finance Corporation 2.2% International Business Machines Corporation 2.58%

WisdomTree Emerging Markets High Dividend Fund   C   HOLD

Ticker	Traded On	NAV	Total Assets ($)	Dividend Yield (TTM)	Turnover Ratio	Expense Ratio
DEM	NYSE Arca	41.38	$2,098,081,982	4.86	44	0.63

Ratings

Reward	C
Risk	C+
Recent Upgrade/Downgrade	

Fund Information

Fund Type	Exchange Traded Funds
Category	Global Emerg Mkts Equity
Sub-Category	Diversified Emerging Mkts
Prospectus Objective	Div Emerg Mkts
Inception Date	Jul-07
Open to New Investments	Y

Prices

Price (as of 9/30/2019)	41.31
52-Week High	45.25
52-Week Low	39.27

Total Returns (%)

3-Month	6-Month	1-Year	3-Year	5-Year
-5.34	-2.80	-1.21	26.09	7.38

3-Year Standard Deviation	12.56
Effective Duration	

Valuation

Premium/Discount (1-Year Average)	0.01

Company Information

Provider	WisdomTree
Manager/Tenure	Richard A. Brown (11), Thomas J. Durante (11), Karen Q. Wong (11)
Website	http://www.wisdomtree.com
Address	WisdomTree 245 Park Avenue, 35th floor New York NY 10167 United States
Phone Number	866-909-9473

PERFORMANCE

Ratings History

Date	Overall Rating	Risk Rating	Reward Rating
Q3-19	C	C+	C
Q4-18	C	C+	C-
Q4-17	C+	C	C+
Q4-16	D+	D+	D+
Q4-15	D	D	D

Asset & Performance History

Date	NAV	1-Year Total Return
2018	40.24	-7.3
2017	45.26	24.88
2016	37.68	22.53
2015	31.9	-21.95
2014	42.77	-11.58
2013	50.75	-5.61

Total Assets: $2,098,081,982

Asset Allocation

Asset	%
Cash	0%
Stocks	100%
US Stocks	0%
Bonds	0%
US Bonds	0%
Other	0%

Services Offered:

Investment Strategy: The investment seeks to track the price and yield performance, before fees and expenses, of the WisdomTree Emerging Markets High Dividend Index. Under normal circumstances, at least 95% of the fund's total assets (exclusive of collateral held from securities lending) will be invested in component securities of the index and investments that have economic characteristics that are substantially identical to the economic characteristics of such component securities. The index is a fundamentally weighted index that is comprised of the highest dividend-yielding common stocks selected from the WisdomTree Emerging Markets Dividend Index. The fund is non-diversified. **Top Holdings:** Gazprom PJSC ADR Mining and Metallurgical Company NORILSK NICKEL PJSC ADR PJSC Lukoil ADR Tatneft PJSC ADR China Construction Bank Corp Class H

SPDR® Dow Jones International Real Estate ETF   C+   HOLD

Ticker	Traded On	NAV	Total Assets ($)	Dividend Yield (TTM)	Turnover Ratio	Expense Ratio
RWX	NYSE Arca		$2,093,102,124	4.79	15	0.59

Ratings
Reward   C
Risk   C+
Recent Upgrade/Downgrade   Up

Fund Information
Fund Type   Exchange Traded Funds
Category   Real Estate Sector Equity
Sub-Category   Global Real Estate
Prospectus Objective   Real Estate
Inception Date   Dec-06
Open to New Investments   Y

Prices
Price (as of 9/30/2019)   39.52
52-Week High   39.66
52-Week Low   34.74

Total Returns (%)

3-Month	6-Month	1-Year	3-Year	5-Year
2.29	2.61	8.73	12.07	18.86

3-Year Standard Deviation   10.33
Effective Duration

Valuation
Premium/Discount (1-Year Average)   -0.17

Company Information
Provider   SPDR State Street Global Advisors
Manager/Tenure   Michael J. Feehily (6), Karl A.
      Schneider (4), Keith Richardson (2)
Website   http://www.spdrs.com
Address   SPDR State Street Global Advisors
      State Street Financial Center, 1
      Lincoln Street Boston MA 02111-2900
      United States
Phone Number   617-786-3000

PERFORMANCE

Ratings History

Date	Overall Rating	Risk Rating	Reward Rating
Q3-19	C+	C+	C
Q4-18	C-	C-	D+
Q4-17	C+	B-	C
Q4-16	C-	C-	D+
Q4-15	C	C+	C

Asset & Performance History

Date	NAV	1-Year Total Return
2018	35.42	-8.37
2017	40.63	15.26
2016	36.28	-1.53
2015	39.34	-3.29
2014	41.83	5.84
2013	40.87	5.07

Total Assets: $2,093,102,124
Asset Allocation

Asset	%
Cash	0%
Stocks	99%
US Stocks	0%
Bonds	0%
US Bonds	0%
Other	1%

Services Offered:

Investment Strategy: The investment seeks to provide investment results, before fees and expenses, correspond generally to the total return performance of the Dow Jones Global ex-U.S. Select Real Estate Securities Indexsm. The fund generally invests substantially all, but at least 80%, of its total assets in the securities comprising the index and in depositary receipts based on securities comprising the index. The index is a float-adjusted market capitalization index designed to measure the performance of publicly traded real estate securities in countries excluding the United States. The fund is non-diversified. **Top Holdings:** Mitsui Fudosan Co Ltd   Link Real Estate Investment Trust   Goodman Group   Scentre Group   Deutsche Wohnen SE

WisdomTree U.S. SmallCap Dividend Fund   C   HOLD

Ticker	Traded On	NAV	Total Assets ($)	Dividend Yield (TTM)	Turnover Ratio	Expense Ratio
DES	NYSE Arca	27.36	$2,088,721,783	2.84	26	0.38

Ratings
Reward   C-
Risk   C+
Recent Upgrade/Downgrade

Fund Information
Fund Type   Exchange Traded Funds
Category   US Equity Small Cap
Sub-Category   Small Value
Prospectus Objective   Small Company
Inception Date   Jun-06
Open to New Investments   Y

Prices
Price (as of 9/30/2019)   27.37
52-Week High   29.36
52-Week Low   23.32

Total Returns (%)

3-Month	6-Month	1-Year	3-Year	5-Year
1.96	-0.22	-3.97	19.19	48.24

3-Year Standard Deviation   16.78
Effective Duration

Valuation
Premium/Discount (1-Year Average)   -0.01

Company Information
Provider   WisdomTree
Manager/Tenure   Richard A. Brown (11), Thomas J.
      Durante (11), Karen Q. Wong (11)
Website   http://www.wisdomtree.com
Address   WisdomTree 245 Park Avenue, 35th
      floor New York NY 10167 United
      States
Phone Number   866-909-9473

PERFORMANCE

Ratings History

Date	Overall Rating	Risk Rating	Reward Rating
Q3-19	C	C+	C-
Q4-18	C	C+	C-
Q4-17	B+	B	A-
Q4-16	C	C-	C
Q4-15	C	C-	C

Asset & Performance History

Date	NAV	1-Year Total Return
2018	24.53	-12.75
2017	29.02	8.68
2016	27.54	31.05
2015	21.67	-5.53
2014	23.63	7.54
2013	22.59	36.85

Total Assets: $2,088,721,783
Asset Allocation

Asset	%
Cash	0%
Stocks	100%
US Stocks	100%
Bonds	0%
US Bonds	0%
Other	0%

Services Offered:

Investment Strategy: The investment seeks to track the price and yield performance, before fees and expenses, of the WisdomTree U.S. SmallCap Dividend Index. Under normal circumstances, at least 95% of the fund's total assets (exclusive of collateral held from securities lending) will be invested in component securities of the index and investments that have economic characteristics that are substantially identical to the economic characteristics of such component securities. The index is a fundamentally weighted index measuring the performance of the small-capitalization segment of the U.S. dividend-paying market. The fund is non-diversified. **Top Holdings:** Vector Group Ltd   TerraForm Power Inc Class A   Pattern Energy Group Inc Class A   Covanta Holding Corp   Cogent Communications Holdings Inc

iShares MSCI United Kingdom ETF

C   HOLD

Ticker	Traded On	NAV	Total Assets ($)	Dividend Yield (TTM)	Turnover Ratio	Expense Ratio
EWU	NYSE Arca	31.51	$2,083,141,057	4.59	5	0.47

Ratings
Reward	C-
Risk	C+
Recent Upgrade/Downgrade	

Fund Information
Fund Type	Exchange Traded Funds
Category	UK Equity Large Cap
Sub-Category	Miscellaneous Region
Prospectus Objective	Europe Stock
Inception Date	Mar-96
Open to New Investments	Y

Prices
Price (as of 9/30/2019)	31.43
52-Week High	34.09
52-Week Low	28.56

Total Returns (%)
3-Month	6-Month	1-Year	3-Year	5-Year
-2.98	-3.26	-3.23	12.73	0.68

3-Year Standard Deviation	12.4
Effective Duration	

Valuation
Premium/Discount (1-Year Average)	-0.07

Company Information
Provider	iShares
Manager/Tenure	Diane Hsiung (11), Greg Savage (11), Jennifer Hsui (6), 3 others
Website	http://www.ishares.com
Address	iShares 400 Howard Street San Francisco CA 94105 United States
Phone Number	800-474-2737

PERFORMANCE

Ratings History
Date	Overall Rating	Risk Rating	Reward Rating
Q3-19	C	C+	C-
Q4-18	C-	C-	D+
Q4-17	C+	B-	C
Q4-16	D+	D+	D+
Q4-15	C	B-	C-

Asset & Performance History
Date	NAV	1-Year Total Return
2018	29.48	-14.6
2017	36.12	21.7
2016	30.92	-0.61
2015	32.32	-7.98
2014	36.48	-5.86
2013	41.48	20

Total Assets: $2,083,141,057

Asset Allocation
Asset	%
Cash	1%
Stocks	99%
US Stocks	2%
Bonds	0%
US Bonds	0%
Other	0%

Services Offered: CashInvestment Plan

Investment Strategy: The investment seeks to track the investment results of the MSCI United Kingdom Index. The fund will at all times invest at least 90% of its assets in the securities of its underlying index and in depositary receipts representing securities in its underlying index. The underlying index consists of stocks traded primarily on the London Stock Exchange. The underlying index may include large- or mid-capitalization companies. The fund is non-diversified. **Top Holdings:** HSBC Holdings PLC BP PLC Royal Dutch Shell PLC Class A AstraZeneca PLC GlaxoSmithKline PLC

SPDR® EURO STOXX 50 ETF

C   HOLD

Ticker	Traded On	NAV	Total Assets ($)	Dividend Yield (TTM)	Turnover Ratio	Expense Ratio
FEZ	NYSE Arca		$2,050,306,191	2.87	7	0.29

Ratings
Reward	C
Risk	C+
Recent Upgrade/Downgrade	

Fund Information
Fund Type	Exchange Traded Funds
Category	Europe Equity Large Cap
Sub-Category	Europe Stock
Prospectus Objective	Europe Stock
Inception Date	Oct-02
Open to New Investments	Y

Prices
Price (as of 9/30/2019)	37.74
52-Week High	38.89
52-Week Low	32.08

Total Returns (%)
3-Month	6-Month	1-Year	3-Year	5-Year
-1.76	4.45	0.99	25.03	9.87

3-Year Standard Deviation	14.57
Effective Duration	

Valuation
Premium/Discount (1-Year Average)	-0.09

Company Information
Provider	SPDR State Street Global Advisors
Manager/Tenure	Michael J. Feehily (8), Karl A. Schneider (4), Mark Krivitsky (2)
Website	http://www.spdrs.com
Address	SPDR State Street Global Advisors State Street Financial Center, 1 Lincoln Street Boston MA 02111-2900 United States
Phone Number	617-786-3000

PERFORMANCE

Ratings History
Date	Overall Rating	Risk Rating	Reward Rating
Q3-19	C	C+	C
Q4-18	C-	D+	C-
Q4-17	B-	C	B
Q4-16	D+	D+	D
Q4-15	C+	B	C

Asset & Performance History
Date	NAV	1-Year Total Return
2018	33.3	-16.05
2017	40.85	24.39
2016	33.68	-1.31
2015	34.58	-4.25
2014	37.13	-8.36
2013	41.88	27.42

Total Assets: $2,050,306,191

Asset Allocation
Asset	%
Cash	0%
Stocks	100%
US Stocks	2%
Bonds	0%
US Bonds	0%
Other	0%

Services Offered: Dividend Investment Plan

Investment Strategy: The investment seeks investment results that, before fees and expenses, correspond generally to the total return performance of the EURO STOXX 50® Index. The fund employs a sampling strategy, which means that the fund is not required to purchase all of the securities represented in the index. It generally invests substantially all, but at least 80%, of its total assets in the securities comprising the index. The index is designed to represent the performance of some of the largest companies across components of the 19 EURO STOXX Supersector Indexes. The EURO STOXX Supersector Indexes are subsets of the EURO STOXX Index. It is non-diversified. **Top Holdings:** Total SA SAP SE LVMH Moet Hennessy Louis Vuitton SE Linde PLC Sanofi SA

Fidelity® NASDAQ Composite Index® Tracking Stock Fund   C   HOLD

Ticker	Traded On	NAV	Total Assets ($)	Dividend Yield (TTM)	Turnover Ratio	Expense Ratio
ONEQ	NAS CM	314.40	$2,027,871,436	1.1	10	0.21

Ratings
Reward   C+
Risk   C-
Recent Upgrade/Downgrade

Fund Information
Fund Type   Exchange Traded Funds
Category   US Equity Large Cap Growth
Sub-Category   Large Growth
Prospectus Objective   Growth
Inception Date   Sep-03
Open to New Investments   Y

Prices
Price (as of 9/30/2019)   314.01
52-Week High   327.50
52-Week Low   243.03

Total Returns (%)

3-Month	6-Month	1-Year	3-Year	5-Year
-0.79	3.15	1.04	55.25	91.02

3-Year Standard Deviation   14.44
Effective Duration

Valuation
Premium/Discount (1-Year Average)   -0.01

Company Information
Provider   Fidelity Investments
Manager/Tenure Louis Bottari (10), Peter Matthew (7),
                Deane Gyllenhaal (5), 3 others
Website   http://www.institutional.fidelity.com
Address   Fidelity Investments 82 Devonshire
                 Street Boston MA 2109 United States
Phone Number   617-563-7000

PERFORMANCE

Ratings History

Date	Overall Rating	Risk Rating	Reward Rating
Q3-19	C	C-	C+
Q4-18	C	C-	C
Q4-17	B+	B	A-
Q4-16	C	C-	C
Q4-15	C	C	C+

Asset & Performance History

Date	NAV	1-Year Total Return
2018	259.98	-3.06
2017	270.86	29.22
2016	211.52	8.92
2015	196.5	6.88
2014	185.79	14.59
2013	164.19	39.67

Total Assets: $2,027,871,436
Asset Allocation

Asset	%
Cash	13%
Stocks	87%
US Stocks	83%
Bonds	0%
US Bonds	0%
Other	0%

Services Offered:

Investment Strategy: The investment seeks to provide investment returns that closely correspond to the price and yield performance of the Nasdaq Composite Index ®. The fund normally invests at least 80% of assets in common stocks included in the index. It uses statistical sampling techniques that take into account such factors as capitalization, industry exposures, dividend yield, price/earnings (P/E) ratio, price/book (P/B) ratio, and earnings growth to create a portfolio of securities listed in the Nasdaq Composite Index ® that have a similar investment profile to the entire index. **Top Holdings:** E-mini NASDAQ 100 Futures Sept19 Microsoft Corp Apple Inc Amazon.com Inc Facebook Inc A

Invesco National AMT-Free Municipal Bond ETF   C+   HOLD

Ticker	Traded On	NAV	Total Assets ($)	Dividend Yield (TTM)	Turnover Ratio	Expense Ratio
PZA	NYSE Arca	26.50	$2,019,517,646	2.87		0.28

Ratings
Reward   C+
Risk   C+
Recent Upgrade/Downgrade

Fund Information
Fund Type   Exchange Traded Funds
Category   US Muni Fixed Inc
Sub-Category   Muni National Long
Prospectus Objective   Muni Bond - Natl
Inception Date   Oct-07
Open to New Investments   Y

Prices
Price (as of 9/30/2019)   26.54
52-Week High   26.84
52-Week Low   24.38

Total Returns (%)

3-Month	6-Month	1-Year	3-Year	5-Year
2.17	4.96	9.94	11.51	24.08

3-Year Standard Deviation   3.95
Effective Duration   8.55

Valuation
Premium/Discount (1-Year Average)   -0.01

Company Information
Provider   Invesco
Manager/Tenure Philip Fang (11), Peter Hubbard (11),
                Jeffrey W. Kernagis (11), 2 others
Website   http://www.invesco.com/us
Address   Invesco 11 Greenway Plaza, Ste. 2500
                 Houston TX 77046 United States
Phone Number   800-659-1005

PERFORMANCE

Ratings History

Date	Overall Rating	Risk Rating	Reward Rating
Q3-19	C+	C+	C+
Q4-18	C	C+	C-
Q4-17	B-	B+	C
Q4-16	C	C+	C
Q4-15	C+	C+	C+

Asset & Performance History

Date	NAV	1-Year Total Return
2018	25.02	0.22
2017	25.77	6.61
2016	24.93	1.26
2015	25.4	4.02
2014	25.32	14.16
2013	23.11	-6.4

Total Assets: $2,019,517,646
Asset Allocation

Asset	%
Cash	1%
Stocks	0%
US Stocks	0%
Bonds	99%
US Bonds	98%
Other	0%

Services Offered:

Investment Strategy: The investment seeks to track the investment results (before fees and expenses) of the ICE BofAML National Long-Term Core Plus Municipal Securities Index (the "underlying index"). The fund generally will invest at least 80% of its total assets in municipal securities that comprise the underlying index and that also are exempt from the federal alternative minimum tax ("AMT"). The underlying index is composed of U.S. dollar-denominated, investment grade, tax-exempt debt publicly issued by U.S. states and territories or their political subdivisions, in the U.S. domestic market with a term of at least 15 years remaining to final maturity. **Top Holdings:** CALIFORNIA ST 0.97% ALASKA HSG FIN CORP HOME MTG REV 1.38% CHICAGO ILL WASTEWATER TRANSMISSION REV 5% ARAPAHOE CNTY COLO SCH DIST NO 006 LITTLETON 5.5% HILLSBOROUGH CNTY FLA AVIATION AUTH REV 5%

iShares MSCI Germany ETF

C- HOLD

Ticker	Traded On	NAV	Total Assets ($)	Dividend Yield (TTM)	Turnover Ratio	Expense Ratio
EWG	NYSE Arca	26.92	$2,019,003,295	2.74	6	0.47

Ratings

Reward	D+
Risk	C
Recent Upgrade/Downgrade	

Fund Information

Fund Type	Exchange Traded Funds
Category	Europe Equity Large Cap
Sub-Category	Miscellaneous Region
Prospectus Objective	Europe Stock
Inception Date	Mar-96
Open to New Investments	Y

Prices

Price (as of 9/30/2019)	26.91
52-Week High	29.90
52-Week Low	24.44

Total Returns (%)

3-Month	6-Month	1-Year	3-Year	5-Year
-4.47	1.53	-7.74	10.25	10.15

3-Year Standard Deviation	14.66
Effective Duration	

Valuation

Premium/Discount (1-Year Average)	-0.01

Company Information

Provider	iShares
Manager/Tenure	Diane Hsiung (11), Greg Savage (11), Jennifer Hsui (6), 3 others
Website	http://www.ishares.com
Address	iShares 400 Howard Street San Francisco CA 94105 United States
Phone Number	800-474-2737

PERFORMANCE

Ratings History

Date	Overall Rating	Risk Rating	Reward Rating
Q3-19	C-	C	D+
Q4-18	D+	C-	C-
Q4-17	B	B-	A-
Q4-16	D+	D+	D+
Q4-15	C	B	C-

Asset & Performance History

Date	NAV	1-Year Total Return
2018	25.17	-22.29
2017	33.18	27.44
2016	26.61	2.58
2015	26.58	-2.06
2014	27.61	-10.49
2013	31.47	31.18

Total Assets: $2,019,003,295

Asset Allocation

Asset	%
Cash	1%
Stocks	99%
US Stocks	2%
Bonds	0%
US Bonds	0%
Other	0%

Services Offered: CashInvestment Plan

Investment Strategy: The investment seeks to track the investment results of the MSCI Germany Index. The fund will at all times invest at least 80% of its assets in the securities of its underlying index and in depositary receipts representing securities in its underlying index. The underlying index consists of stocks traded primarily on the Frankfurt Stock Exchange. It may include large- or mid-capitalization companies. The fund is non-diversified. **Top Holdings:** SAP SE Allianz SE Siemens AG Bayer AG Basf SE

---

iShares Intermediate Government/Credit Bond ETF

C HOLD

Ticker	Traded On	NAV	Total Assets ($)	Dividend Yield (TTM)	Turnover Ratio	Expense Ratio
GVI	BATS	113.16	$1,997,305,535	2.26	21	0.2

Ratings

Reward	C
Risk	C-
Recent Upgrade/Downgrade	

Fund Information

Fund Type	Exchange Traded Funds
Category	US Fixed Income
Sub-Category	Intermediate Core Bond
Prospectus Objective	Income
Inception Date	Jan-07
Open to New Investments	Y

Prices

Price (as of 9/30/2019)	113.22
52-Week High	113.96
52-Week Low	106.45

Total Returns (%)

3-Month	6-Month	1-Year	3-Year	5-Year
1.43	4.16	8.01	6.80	12.68

3-Year Standard Deviation	2.38
Effective Duration	

Valuation

Premium/Discount (1-Year Average)	0.05

Company Information

Provider	iShares
Manager/Tenure	Scott Radell (9), James Mauro (8)
Website	http://www.ishares.com
Address	iShares 400 Howard Street San Francisco CA 94105 United States
Phone Number	800-474-2737

PERFORMANCE

Ratings History

Date	Overall Rating	Risk Rating	Reward Rating
Q3-19	C	C-	C
Q4-18	C	C+	D+
Q4-17	C+	B	C
Q4-16	C	C-	C
Q4-15	C	C-	C

Asset & Performance History

Date	NAV	1-Year Total Return
2018	108.15	0.7
2017	109.76	1.76
2016	109.72	1.89
2015	109.57	0.85
2014	110.54	2.93
2013	109.25	-1.04

Total Assets: $1,997,305,535

Asset Allocation

Asset	%
Cash	1%
Stocks	0%
US Stocks	0%
Bonds	98%
US Bonds	89%
Other	0%

Services Offered:

Investment Strategy: The investment seeks to track the investment results of the Bloomberg Barclays U.S. Intermediate Government/Credit Bond Index. The fund generally invests at least 90% of its assets in securities of the underlying index. The index measures the performance of U.S. dollar-denominated U.S. Treasury bonds, government-related bonds (i.e., U.S. and non-U.S. agencies, sovereign, supranational and local authority debt) and investment-grade U.S. corporate bonds that have a remaining maturity of greater than one year and less than ten years. **Top Holdings:** United States Treasury Notes 2.75% United States Treasury Notes 2.13% United States Treasury Notes 1.38% United States Treasury Notes 2.13% United States Treasury Notes 2%

iShares Global 100 ETF

C   HOLD

Ticker	Traded On	NAV		Total Assets ($)	Dividend Yield (TTM)	Turnover Ratio	Expense Ratio
100	NYSE Arca	49.50		$1,994,682,907	2.19	9	0.4

Ratings
Reward	C+
Risk	C
Recent Upgrade/Downgrade	Down

Fund Information
Fund Type	Exchange Traded Funds
Category	Global Equity Large Cap
Sub-Category	World Large Stock
Prospectus Objective	World Stock
Inception Date	Dec-00
Open to New Investments	Y

Prices
Price (as of 9/30/2019)	49.45
52-Week High	49.89
52-Week Low	40.41

Total Returns (%)
3-Month	6-Month	1-Year	3-Year	5-Year
0.48	4.35	3.14	41.81	46.44

3-Year Standard Deviation	11.14
Effective Duration	

Valuation
Premium/Discount (1-Year Average)	-0.08

Company Information
Provider	iShares
Manager/Tenure	Greg Savage (11), Jennifer Hsui (7), Alan Mason (3), 2 others
Website	http://www.ishares.com
Address	iShares 400 Howard Street San Francisco CA 94105 United States
Phone Number	800-474-2737

PERFORMANCE

Ratings History
Date	Overall Rating	Risk Rating	Reward Rating
Q3-19	C	C	C+
Q4-18	C	C+	C
Q4-17	B-	B-	B-
Q4-16	C	C-	C+
Q4-15	C	C	C

Asset & Performance History
Date	NAV	1-Year Total Return
2018	42.49	-6.19
2017	46.4	23.39
2016	38.49	8.76
2015	36.41	-1.94
2014	38.17	2.46
2013	38.54	24.62

Total Assets: $1,994,682,907

Asset Allocation
Asset	%
Cash	0%
Stocks	100%
US Stocks	66%
Bonds	0%
US Bonds	0%
Other	0%

Services Offered: CashInvestment Plan

Investment Strategy: The investment seeks to track the investment results of the S&P Global 100TM (the "underlying index"), which is designed to measure the performance of the stocks of 100 large-capitalization global companies. The fund generally invests at least 90% of its assets in securities of the underlying index and in depositary receipts representing securities of the underlying index. It may invest the remainder of its assets in certain futures, options and swap contracts, cash and cash equivalents, as well as in securities not included in the underlying index, but which the advisor believes will help the fund track the underlying index. **Top Holdings:** Microsoft Corp Apple Inc Amazon.com Inc JPMorgan Chase & Co Nestle SA

---

iShares U.S. Healthcare ETF

C   HOLD

Ticker	Traded On	NAV		Total Assets ($)	Dividend Yield (TTM)	Turnover Ratio	Expense Ratio
IYH	NYSE Arca	189.02		$1,994,200,781	2.02	6	0.43

Ratings
Reward	B-
Risk	C
Recent Upgrade/Downgrade	Down

Fund Information
Fund Type	Exchange Traded Funds
Category	Healthcare Sector Equity
Sub-Category	Health
Prospectus Objective	Health
Inception Date	Jun-00
Open to New Investments	Y

Prices
Price (as of 9/30/2019)	189.05
52-Week High	204.02
52-Week Low	170.02

Total Returns (%)
3-Month	6-Month	1-Year	3-Year	5-Year
-3.33	-1.94	-5.29	31.40	53.51

3-Year Standard Deviation	13.52
Effective Duration	

Valuation
Premium/Discount (1-Year Average)	0.00

Company Information
Provider	iShares
Manager/Tenure	Greg Savage (11), Jennifer Hsui (7), Alan Mason (3), 2 others
Website	http://www.ishares.com
Address	iShares 400 Howard Street San Francisco CA 94105 United States
Phone Number	800-474-2737

PERFORMANCE

Ratings History
Date	Overall Rating	Risk Rating	Reward Rating
Q3-19	C	C	B-
Q4-18	C+	C	C+
Q4-17	B	B	B-
Q4-16	B-	C	B
Q4-15	B-	B-	B

Asset & Performance History
Date	NAV	1-Year Total Return
2018	180.79	5.02
2017	174.12	22.3
2016	144	-2.81
2015	150.07	6.13
2014	144.24	25.17
2013	116.54	41.28

Total Assets: $1,994,200,781

Asset Allocation
Asset	%
Cash	0%
Stocks	100%
US Stocks	100%
Bonds	0%
US Bonds	0%
Other	0%

Services Offered: CashInvestment Plan

Investment Strategy: The investment seeks to track the investment results of the Dow Jones U.S. Health Care Index composed of U.S. equities in the healthcare sector. The fund generally invests at least 90% of its assets in securities of the underlying index and in depositary receipts representing securities of the underlying index. The underlying index measures the performance of the healthcare sector of the U.S. equity market. The fund is non-diversified. **Top Holdings:** Johnson & Johnson Merck & Co Inc UnitedHealth Group Inc Pfizer Inc Abbott Laboratories

SPDR® S&P Regional Banking ETF   C   HOLD

Ticker	Traded On	NAV	Total Assets ($)	Dividend Yield (TTM)	Turnover Ratio	Expense Ratio
KRE	NYSE Arca		$1,968,397,966	2.34	27	0.35

Ratings
Reward   C
Risk   C
Recent Upgrade/Downgrade   Up

Fund Information
Fund Type   Exchange Traded Funds
Category   Financials Sector Equity
Sub-Category   Financial
Prospectus Objective   Financial
Inception Date   Jun-06
Open to New Investments   Y

Prices
Price (as of 9/30/2019)   52.79
52-Week High   60.15
52-Week Low   44.22

Total Returns (%)

3-Month	6-Month	1-Year	3-Year	5-Year
-0.68	1.75	-7.53	32.76	53.85

3-Year Standard Deviation   24.27
Effective Duration

Valuation
Premium/Discount (1-Year Average)   -0.04

Company Information
Provider   SPDR State Street Global Advisors
Manager/Tenure   Michael J. Feehily (7), Karl A. Schneider (4), Kala O'Donnell (0)
Website   http://www.spdrs.com
Address   SPDR State Street Global Advisors State Street Financial Center, 1 Lincoln Street Boston MA 02111-2900 United States
Phone Number   617-786-3000

PERFORMANCE

Ratings History

Date	Overall Rating	Risk Rating	Reward Rating
Q3-19	C	C	C
Q4-18	C	C	C
Q4-17	B+	C+	A
Q4-16	C	C	C
Q4-15	B+	A-	B

Asset & Performance History

Date	NAV	1-Year Total Return
2018	46.78	-18.97
2017	58.83	7.52
2016	55.53	33.02
2015	41.94	4.9
2014	40.71	1.95
2013	40.57	47.34

Total Assets: $1,968,397,966
Asset Allocation

Asset	%
Cash	0%
Stocks	100%
US Stocks	98%
Bonds	0%
US Bonds	0%
Other	0%

Services Offered:

Investment Strategy: The investment seeks to provide investment results that, before fees and expenses, correspond generally to the total return performance of an index derived from the regional banking segment of the U.S. banking industry. In seeking to track the performance of the S&P Regional Banks Select Industry Index (the "index"), the fund employs a sampling strategy. It generally invests substantially all, but at least 80%, of its total assets in the securities comprising the index. The index represents the regional banks segment of the S&P Total Market Index ("S&P TMI"). The fund is non-diversified. **Top Holdings:** Synovus Financial Corp Signature Bank Regions Financial Corp Huntington Bancshares Inc KeyCorp

---

Invesco FTSE RAFI US 1500 Small-Mid ETF   C-   HOLD

Ticker	Traded On	NAV	Total Assets ($)	Dividend Yield (TTM)	Turnover Ratio	Expense Ratio
PRFZ	NAS CM	127.03	$1,962,604,219	1.25	24	0.39

Ratings
Reward   C-
Risk   C-
Recent Upgrade/Downgrade

Fund Information
Fund Type   Exchange Traded Funds
Category   US Equity Small Cap
Sub-Category   Small Blend
Prospectus Objective   Growth
Inception Date   Sep-06
Open to New Investments   Y

Prices
Price (as of 9/30/2019)   126.92
52-Week High   140.77
52-Week Low   107.24

Total Returns (%)

3-Month	6-Month	1-Year	3-Year	5-Year
-0.63	-1.08	-8.47	25.09	46.10

3-Year Standard Deviation   17.05
Effective Duration

Valuation
Premium/Discount (1-Year Average)   -0.03

Company Information
Provider   Invesco
Manager/Tenure   Peter Hubbard (12), Michael Jeanette (11), Tony Seisser (4)
Website   http://www.invesco.com/us
Address   Invesco 11 Greenway Plaza, Ste. 2500 Houston TX 77046 United States
Phone Number   800-659-1005

PERFORMANCE

Ratings History

Date	Overall Rating	Risk Rating	Reward Rating
Q3-19	C-	C-	C-
Q4-18	C-	C-	C-
Q4-17	B+	B	A-
Q4-16	C+	C-	B
Q4-15	C	C-	C

Asset & Performance History

Date	NAV	1-Year Total Return
2018	113.68	-11.39
2017	129.88	13.95
2016	115.14	24.42
2015	93.84	-5.7
2014	100.86	4.47
2013	97.66	41.8

Total Assets: $1,962,604,219
Asset Allocation

Asset	%
Cash	0%
Stocks	100%
US Stocks	97%
Bonds	0%
US Bonds	0%
Other	0%

Services Offered:

Investment Strategy: The investment seeks to track the investment results (before fees and expenses) of the FTSE RAFI™ US Mid Small 1500 Index. The fund generally will invest at least 90% of its total assets in the securities that comprise the underlying index. The underlying index is composed of 1,500 common stocks that the index provider strictly in accordance with its guidelines and mandated procedures, include to track the performance of small- and medium-sized U.S. companies based on the following four fundamental measures of firm size: book value, cash flow, sales and dividends. **Top Holdings:** FTI Consulting Inc Generac Holdings Inc Copart Inc West Pharmaceutical Services Inc Summit Materials Inc A

ProShares Short S&P500　　　　　　　　　　　　　　　　　　　　D　　SELL

Ticker	Traded On	NAV	Total Assets ($)	Dividend Yield (TTM)	Turnover Ratio	Expense Ratio
SH	NYSE Arca	26.14	$1,957,319,984	1.64		0.89

Ratings
Reward	D
Risk	D
Recent Upgrade/Downgrade	

Fund Information
Fund Type	Exchange Traded Funds
Category	Trading Tools
Sub-Category	Trading--Inverse Equity
Prospectus Objective	Growth
Inception Date	Jun-06
Open to New Investments	Y

Prices
Price (as of 9/30/2019)	26.13
52-Week High	33.59
52-Week Low	25.89

Total Returns (%)
3-Month	6-Month	1-Year	3-Year	5-Year
-0.54	-3.54	-2.44	-29.67	-42.59

3-Year Standard Deviation	12.06
Effective Duration	

Valuation
Premium/Discount (1-Year Average)	0.02

Company Information
Provider	ProShares
Manager/Tenure	Michael Neches (6), Devin Sullivan (1)
Website	http://www.proshares.com
Address	ProShares 7501 Wisconsin Avenue, Suite 1000 Bethesda MD 20814 United States
Phone Number	866-776-5125

PERFORMANCE

Ratings History
Date	Overall Rating	Risk Rating	Reward Rating
Q3-19	D	D	D
Q4-18	D	D	D
Q4-17	D-	D	D-
Q4-16	D	D	D
Q4-15	D	D-	D

Asset & Performance History
Date	NAV	1-Year Total Return
2018	31.36	4.86
2017	30.23	-17.33
2016	36.59	-12.38
2015	41.76	-4.17
2014	43.58	-13.66
2013	50.48	-25.8

Total Assets: $1,957,319,984
Asset Allocation
Asset	%
Cash	145%
Stocks	-56%
US Stocks	-55%
Bonds	11%
US Bonds	11%
Other	0%

Services Offered:

Investment Strategy: The investment seeks daily investment results that correspond to the inverse (-1x) of the daily performance of the S&P 500® Index. The fund invests in financial instruments that ProShare Advisors believes, in combination, should produce daily returns consistent with the fund's investment objective. The index is a measure of large-cap U.S. stock market performance. It is a float-adjusted, market capitalization-weighted index of 500 U.S. operating companies and real estate investment trusts selected through a process that factors in criteria such as liquidity, price, market capitalization and financial viability. The fund is non-diversified. **Top Holdings:** S&P 500 Index Swap Societe Generale S&P 500 Index Swap Credit Suisse International S&P 500 Index Swap Ubs Ag S&P 500 Index Swap Bank Of America Na E-mini S&P 500 Sept19

Schwab Fundamental International Small Company Index ETF　　　　　　　C-　　HOLD

Ticker	Traded On	NAV	Total Assets ($)	Dividend Yield (TTM)	Turnover Ratio	Expense Ratio
FNDC	NYSE Arca	30.75	$1,949,678,402	2.99	25	0.39

Ratings
Reward	D+
Risk	C
Recent Upgrade/Downgrade	Down

Fund Information
Fund Type	Exchange Traded Funds
Category	Globa Eq Mid/Small Cap
Sub-Category	Foreign Small/Mid Blend
Prospectus Objective	World Stock
Inception Date	Aug-13
Open to New Investments	Y

Prices
Price (as of 9/30/2019)	30.73
52-Week High	34.66
52-Week Low	27.19

Total Returns (%)
3-Month	6-Month	1-Year	3-Year	5-Year
-2.22	-1.59	-8.14	13.14	27.44

3-Year Standard Deviation	11.54
Effective Duration	

Valuation
Premium/Discount (1-Year Average)	0.00

Company Information
Provider	Schwab ETFs
Manager/Tenure	Chuck Craig (6), Jane Qin (6), Christopher Bliss (2), 1 other
Website	http://www.schwabfunds.com
Address	Schwab ETFs United States
Phone Number	800-435-4000

PERFORMANCE

Ratings History
Date	Overall Rating	Risk Rating	Reward Rating
Q3-19	C-	C	D+
Q4-18	C-	C-	D+
Q4-17	B+	B+	A-
Q4-16	C	C-	C+
Q4-15	D+	C-	D

Asset & Performance History
Date	NAV	1-Year Total Return
2018	28.46	-18.76
2017	35.94	29
2016	28.4	8.88
2015	26.6	5.12
2014	25.64	-4.06
2013	27.16	

Total Assets: $1,949,678,402
Asset Allocation
Asset	%
Cash	0%
Stocks	100%
US Stocks	1%
Bonds	0%
US Bonds	0%
Other	0%

Services Offered:

Investment Strategy: The investment seeks to track as closely as possible, before fees and expenses, the total return of the Russell RAFI™ Developed ex US Small Company Index. The fund will invest at least 90% of its net assets in stocks included in the index, including depositary receipts representing securities of the index, which may be in the form of American Depositary Receipts, Global Depositary Receipts and European Depositary Receipts. The index measures the performance of the small company size segment by fundamental overall company scores, which are created using as the universe the developed ex U.S. companies in the FTSE Global Total Cap Index (the parent index). **Top Holdings:** Msci Eafe Sep19 Ifus 20190920 Hitachi Chemical Co Ltd Westjet Airlines Ltd Altice Europe NV Shs series -A- Hitachi High-Technologies Corp

SPDR® Portfolio Long Term Treasury ETF

C   HOLD

Ticker	Traded On	NAV	Total Assets ($)	Dividend Yield (TTM)	Turnover Ratio	Expense Ratio
SPTL	NYSE Arca		$1,944,081,486	2.39	12	0.06

Ratings

Reward	C
Risk	C+
Recent Upgrade/Downgrade	

Fund Information

Fund Type	Exchange Traded Funds
Category	US Fixed Income
Sub-Category	Long Government
Prospectus Objective	Govt Bond - Treasury
Inception Date	May-07
Open to New Investments	Y

Prices

Price (as of 9/30/2019)	41.03
52-Week High	42.38
52-Week Low	32.31

Total Returns (%)

3-Month	6-Month	1-Year	3-Year	5-Year
8.40	15.72	25.35	12.40	38.02

3-Year Standard Deviation	11.46
Effective Duration	18.47

Valuation

Premium/Discount (1-Year Average)	0.14

Company Information

Provider	SPDR State Street Global Advisors
Manager/Tenure	Joanna Madden (4), Cynthia Moy (2), Orhan Imer (1)
Website	http://www.spdrs.com
Address	SPDR State Street Global Advisors State Street Financial Center, 1 Lincoln Street Boston MA 02111-2900 United States
Phone Number	617-786-3000

PERFORMANCE

Ratings History

Date	Overall Rating	Risk Rating	Reward Rating
Q3-19	C	C+	C
Q4-18	D+	C-	D
Q4-17	C	C	C
Q4-16	C	C-	C
Q4-15	C	C-	C

Asset & Performance History

Date	NAV	1-Year Total Return
2018	34.87	-1.88
2017	36.53	8.13
2016	34.58	1.12
2015	34.97	-1.32
2014	36.35	24.87
2013	29.95	-12.75

Total Assets: $1,944,081,486

Asset Allocation

Asset	%
Cash	0%
Stocks	0%
US Stocks	0%
Bonds	100%
US Bonds	100%
Other	0%

Services Offered:

Investment Strategy: The investment seeks to provide investment results that correspond generally to the price and yield performance of the Bloomberg Barclays Long U.S. Treasury Index. The fund generally invests substantially all, but at least 80%, of its total assets in the securities comprising the index or in securities that the adviser determines have economic characteristics that are substantially identical to the economic characteristics of the securities that comprise the index. The index is designed to measure the performance of public obligations of the U.S. Treasury that have a remaining maturity of 10 years or more. The fund is non-diversified. **Top Holdings:** United States Treasury Bonds 3.38%   United States Treasury Bonds 3%   United States Treasury Bonds 2.88% United States Treasury Bonds 3.62%   United States Treasury Bonds 3.75%

Grayscale Bitcoin Trust

B   BUY

Ticker	Traded On	NAV	Total Assets ($)	Dividend Yield (TTM)	Turnover Ratio	Expense Ratio
GBTC	OTC BB	7.86	$1,924,721,609	0		2

Ratings

Reward	A+
Risk	D+
Recent Upgrade/Downgrade	Up

Fund Information

Fund Type	Exchange Traded Funds
Category	Trading Tools
Sub-Category	Trading--Miscellaneous
Prospectus Objective	Growth & Inc
Inception Date	Sep-13
Open to New Investments	Y

Prices

Price (as of 9/30/2019)	10.59
52-Week High	17.08
52-Week Low	3.84

Total Returns (%)

3-Month	6-Month	1-Year	3-Year	5-Year
-24.56	93.87	20.39	1,154.20	1,795.68

3-Year Standard Deviation	98.93
Effective Duration	

Valuation

Premium/Discount (1-Year Average)	24.90

Company Information

Provider	Grayscale
Manager/Tenure	Management Team (6)
Website	http://grayscale.co/bitcoin-investment-trust/#overview
Address	Grayscale 636 Avenue of the Americas New York New York 10011 United States
Phone Number	212-668-5920

PERFORMANCE

Ratings History

Date	Overall Rating	Risk Rating	Reward Rating
Q3-19	B	D+	A+
Q4-18	D+	D+	C-
Q4-17	B+	C	A+
Q4-16	D+	D+	D+
Q4-15			

Asset & Performance History

Date	NAV	1-Year Total Return
2018	3.72	-74.61
2017	14.65	1,391.43
2016	0.98	119.87
2015	0.45	33.36
2014	0.33	-59.95
2013	0.84	

Total Assets: $1,924,721,609

Asset Allocation

Asset	%
Cash	-55%
Stocks	0%
US Stocks	0%
Bonds	0%
US Bonds	0%
Other	155%

Services Offered:

Investment Strategy: The investment objective of the Trust is for the NAV per Share to track the Bitcoin Market Price per Share, less the Trust's liabilities (including estimated accrued expenses). **Top Holdings:** Bitcoin

iShares 0-5 Year Investment Grade Corporate Bond ETF   C+   HOLD

Ticker	Traded On	NAV	Total Assets ($)	Dividend Yield (TTM)	Turnover Ratio	Expense Ratio
SLQD	NAS CM	51.07	$1,915,140,924	2.82	15	0.06

Ratings
Reward	C+
Risk	C+
Recent Upgrade/Downgrade	Up

Fund Information
Fund Type	Exchange Traded Funds
Category	US Fixed Income
Sub-Category	Short-Term Bond
Prospectus Objective	Corp Bond - Gen
Inception Date	Oct-13
Open to New Investments	Y

Prices
Price (as of 9/30/2019)	51.14
52-Week High	51.24
52-Week Low	49.20

Total Returns (%)
3-Month	6-Month	1-Year	3-Year	5-Year
1.07	3.23	6.00	7.92	12.38

3-Year Standard Deviation	1.36
Effective Duration	

Valuation
Premium/Discount (1-Year Average)	0.12

Company Information
Provider	iShares
Manager/Tenure	James Mauro (5), Scott Radell (5)
Website	http://www.ishares.com
Address	iShares 400 Howard Street San Francisco CA 94105 United States
Phone Number	800-474-2737

PERFORMANCE

Ratings History
Date	Overall Rating	Risk Rating	Reward Rating
Q3-19	C+	C+	C+
Q4-18	C	C+	C
Q4-17	B	A+	C
Q4-16	C-	C-	C-
Q4-15	C-	C-	D+

Asset & Performance History
Date	NAV	1-Year Total Return
2018	49.48	1.15
2017	50.18	2.13
2016	50.11	2.14
2015	49.95	1.11
2014	50.11	1.36
2013	50.05	

Total Assets: $1,915,140,924
Asset Allocation
Asset	%
Cash	2%
Stocks	0%
US Stocks	0%
Bonds	95%
US Bonds	79%
Other	0%

Services Offered:

Investment Strategy: The investment seeks to track the investment results of the Markit iBoxx® USD Liquid Investment Grade 0-5 Index composed of U.S. dollar-denominated, investment-grade corporate bonds with remaining maturities of less than five years. The fund generally will invest at least 90% of its assets in the component securities of the underlying index and may invest up to 10% of its assets in certain futures, options and swap contracts, cash and cash equivalents. The index is designed to reflect the performance of U.S. dollar-denominated investment-grade corporate debt. **Top Holdings:** Bank of America Corporation 3% CVS Health Corp 3.7% GE Capital International Funding Company Unlimited Company 2.34% Morgan Stanley 3.13% Verizon Communications Inc. 5.15%

---

iShares Global Healthcare ETF   C+   HOLD

Ticker	Traded On	NAV	Total Assets ($)	Dividend Yield (TTM)	Turnover Ratio	Expense Ratio
IXJ	NYSE Arca	61.05	$1,907,943,189	1.93	8	0.46

Ratings
Reward	C+
Risk	C+
Recent Upgrade/Downgrade	Up

Fund Information
Fund Type	Exchange Traded Funds
Category	Healthcare Sector Equity
Sub-Category	Health
Prospectus Objective	Health
Inception Date	Nov-01
Open to New Investments	Y

Prices
Price (as of 9/30/2019)	61.09
52-Week High	63.41
52-Week Low	53.92

Total Returns (%)
3-Month	6-Month	1-Year	3-Year	5-Year
-1.62	0.37	-1.68	27.52	38.24

3-Year Standard Deviation	12.1
Effective Duration	

Valuation
Premium/Discount (1-Year Average)	0.02

Company Information
Provider	iShares
Manager/Tenure	Greg Savage (11), Jennifer Hsui (7), Alan Mason (3), 2 others
Website	http://www.ishares.com
Address	iShares 400 Howard Street San Francisco CA 94105 United States
Phone Number	800-474-2737

PERFORMANCE

Ratings History
Date	Overall Rating	Risk Rating	Reward Rating
Q3-19	C+	C+	C+
Q4-18	C	C	C
Q4-17	B-	B	C+
Q4-16	C	C-	C
Q4-15	B-	C+	B-

Asset & Performance History
Date	NAV	1-Year Total Return
2018	56.69	2.24
2017	56.29	20.34
2016	47.48	-6.18
2015	51.47	5.91
2014	49.96	17.65
2013	43.07	36.15

Total Assets: $1,907,943,189
Asset Allocation
Asset	%
Cash	0%
Stocks	100%
US Stocks	68%
Bonds	0%
US Bonds	0%
Other	0%

Services Offered: CashInvestment Plan

Investment Strategy: The investment seeks to track the S&P Global 1200 Health Care IndexTM. The fund generally invests at least 90% of its assets in securities of the underlying index and in depositary receipts representing securities of the underlying index. It may invest the remainder of its assets in certain futures, options and swap contracts, cash and cash equivalents, as well as in securities not included in the underlying index. The index measures the performance of companies that the index provider deems to be a part of the healthcare sector of the economy and that the index provider believes are important to global markets. **Top Holdings:** Johnson & Johnson Novartis AG Merck & Co Inc UnitedHealth Group Inc Pfizer Inc

VanEck Vectors AMT-Free Intermediate Municipal Index ETF　　　　　　B　　BUY

Ticker	Traded On	NAV	Total Assets ($)	Dividend Yield (TTM)	Turnover Ratio	Expense Ratio
ITM	BATS	50.39	$1,892,265,445	2.22	7	0.24

Ratings
Reward　　　　　　　　　　　　　　　　　B
Risk　　　　　　　　　　　　　　　　　　C+
Recent Upgrade/Downgrade

Fund Information
Fund Type	Exchange Traded Funds
Category	US Muni Fixed Inc
Sub-Category	Muni National Long
Prospectus Objective	Muni Bond - Natl
Inception Date	Dec-07
Open to New Investments	Y

Prices
Price (as of 9/30/2019)	50.31
52-Week High	51.11
52-Week Low	45.90

Total Returns (%)
3-Month	6-Month	1-Year	3-Year	5-Year
1.65	4.43	10.15	119.13	140.24

3-Year Standard Deviation　　　　　　4.54
Effective Duration　　　　　　　　　　6.19

Valuation
Premium/Discount (1-Year Average)　　-0.11

Company Information
Provider	VanEck
Manager/Tenure	James T. Colby (11)
Website	http://www.vaneck.com
Address	Van Eck Associates Corporation 666 Third Avenue New York NY 10017 United States
Phone Number	800-826-1115

PERFORMANCE

Ratings History
Date	Overall Rating	Risk Rating	Reward Rating
Q3-19	B	C+	B
Q4-18	B	C+	A
Q4-17	B-	B	C
Q4-16	C	C+	C
Q4-15	C	C+	C

Asset & Performance History
Date	NAV	1-Year Total Return
2018	47.44	100.88
2017	24.13	6.21
2016	23.23	-0.56
2015	23.88	3.64
2014	23.58	8.97
2013	22.18	-3.51

Total Assets: $1,892,265,445

Asset Allocation
Asset	%
Cash	1%
Stocks	0%
US Stocks	0%
Bonds	99%
US Bonds	99%
Other	0%

Services Offered:

Investment Strategy: The investment seeks to replicate as closely as possible, before fees and expenses, the price and yield performance of the Bloomberg Barclays AMT-Free Intermediate Continuous Municipal Index. The fund normally invests at least 80% of its total assets in fixed income securities that comprise the index. The index is comprised of publicly traded municipal bonds that cover the U.S. dollar denominated intermediate term tax-exempt bond market. **Top Holdings:** NEW YORK ST DORM AUTH ST PERS INCOME TAX REV 5% MARYLAND ST 5% CALIFORNIA ST 5% GEORGIA ST 5% SALES TAX ASSET RECEIVABLE CORP N Y 5%

SPDR® S&P 600 Small Cap Growth ETF　　　　　　　　　　　　　D-　　SELL

Ticker	Traded On	NAV	Total Assets ($)	Dividend Yield (TTM)	Turnover Ratio	Expense Ratio
SLYG	NYSE Arca		$1,884,938,959	1.11	37	0.15

Ratings
Reward　　　　　　　　　　　　　　　　　D-
Risk　　　　　　　　　　　　　　　　　　D
Recent Upgrade/Downgrade

Fund Information
Fund Type	Exchange Traded Funds
Category	US Equity Small Cap
Sub-Category	Small Growth
Prospectus Objective	Small Company
Inception Date	Sep-00
Open to New Investments	Y

Prices
Price (as of 9/30/2019)	59.59
52-Week High	66.43
52-Week Low	50.63

Total Returns (%)
3-Month	6-Month	1-Year	3-Year	5-Year
-2.07	-0.61	-9.32	-66.54	-58.19

3-Year Standard Deviation　　　　　　17.54
Effective Duration

Valuation
Premium/Discount (1-Year Average)　　-0.01

Company Information
Provider	SPDR State Street Global Advisors
Manager/Tenure	Michael J. Feehily (7), Karl A. Schneider (4), David Chin (0)
Website	http://www.spdrs.com
Address	SPDR State Street Global Advisors State Street Financial Center, 1 Lincoln Street Boston MA 02111-2900 United States
Phone Number	617-786-3000

PERFORMANCE

Ratings History
Date	Overall Rating	Risk Rating	Reward Rating
Q3-19	D-	D	D-
Q4-18	D-	D	E+
Q4-17	A-	B+	A
Q4-16	C	C-	C
Q4-15	C	C-	C+

Asset & Performance History
Date	NAV	1-Year Total Return
2018	53.98	-76.02
2017	227.39	14.57
2016	208.01	20.8
2015	172.55	2.77
2014	177.57	3.73
2013	178.89	42.45

Total Assets: $1,884,938,959

Asset Allocation
Asset	%
Cash	1%
Stocks	99%
US Stocks	98%
Bonds	0%
US Bonds	0%
Other	0%

Services Offered: Dividend Investment Plan, CashInvestment Plan

Investment Strategy: The investment seeks to provide investment results that, before fees and expenses, correspond generally to the total return performance of the S&P SmallCap 600 Growth Index. The fund generally invests substantially all, but at least 80%, of its total assets in the securities comprising the index. The index measures the performance of the small-capitalization growth segment of the U.S. equity market. It may purchase a subset of the securities in the index in an effort to hold a portfolio of securities with generally the same risk and return characteristics as the index. The fund is non-diversified. **Top Holdings:** FirstCash Inc Repligen Corp Aerojet Rocketdyne Holdings Inc Strategic Education Inc Exponent Inc

SPDR® Portfolio S&P 500 High Dividend ETF

C   HOLD

Ticker	Traded On	NAV	Total Assets ($)	Dividend Yield (TTM)	Turnover Ratio	Expense Ratio
SPYD	NYSE Arca		$1,869,626,440	4.46	28	0.07

Ratings
Reward	C
Risk	C+
Recent Upgrade/Downgrade	Down

Fund Information
Fund Type	Exchange Traded Funds
Category	US Equity Large Cap Value
Sub-Category	Large Value
Prospectus Objective	Growth & Inc
Inception Date	Oct-15
Open to New Investments	Y

Prices
Price (as of 9/30/2019)	37.98
52-Week High	38.85
52-Week Low	32.59

Total Returns (%)
3-Month	6-Month	1-Year	3-Year	5-Year
0.95	1.43	5.60	27.07	

3-Year Standard Deviation	12.38
Effective Duration	

Valuation
Premium/Discount (1-Year Average)	0.01

Company Information
Provider	SPDR State Street Global Advisors
Manager/Tenure	Michael J. Feehily (3), Karl A. Schneider (3), John Law (0)
Website	http://www.spdrs.com
Address	SPDR State Street Global Advisors State Street Financial Center, 1 Lincoln Street Boston MA 02111-2900 United States
Phone Number	617-786-3000

PERFORMANCE

Ratings History
Date	Overall Rating	Risk Rating	Reward Rating
Q3-19	C	C+	C
Q4-18	C	C+	C-
Q4-17	C	B+	C-
Q4-16	D	C-	D+
Q4-15			

Asset & Performance History
Date	NAV	1-Year Total Return
2018	34.05	-4.77
2017	37.39	12.58
2016	34.83	24.74
2015	29.19	
2014		
2013		

Total Assets: $1,869,626,440

Asset Allocation
Asset	%
Cash	0%
Stocks	100%
US Stocks	99%
Bonds	0%
US Bonds	0%
Other	0%

Services Offered:

Investment Strategy: The investment seeks to track the performance of the S&P 500 High Dividend Index. Under normal market conditions, the fund generally invests substantially all, but at least 80%, of its total assets in the securities comprising the index. The index is designed to measure the performance of 80 high dividend-yielding companies within the S&P 500® Index. The S&P 500 Index focuses on the large capitalization U.S. equity market, including common stock and real estate investment trusts ("REITs"). The fund is non-diversified. **Top Holdings:** Newell Brands Inc Crown Castle International Corp Campbell Soup Co HCP Inc Ventas Inc

ProShares Ultra QQQ

C+   HOLD

Ticker	Traded On	NAV	Total Assets ($)	Dividend Yield (TTM)	Turnover Ratio	Expense Ratio
QLD	NYSE Arca	96.74	$1,847,643,980	0.15	7	0.95

Ratings
Reward	B-
Risk	C
Recent Upgrade/Downgrade	Up

Fund Information
Fund Type	Exchange Traded Funds
Category	Trading Tools
Sub-Category	Trading--Leveraged Equity
Prospectus Objective	Growth
Inception Date	Jun-06
Open to New Investments	Y

Prices
Price (as of 9/30/2019)	96.73
52-Week High	104.48
52-Week Low	58.52

Total Returns (%)
3-Month	6-Month	1-Year	3-Year	5-Year
-1.75	4.82	-4.07	123.98	220.23

3-Year Standard Deviation	30.2
Effective Duration	

Valuation
Premium/Discount (1-Year Average)	-0.02

Company Information
Provider	ProShares
Manager/Tenure	Michael Neches (6), Devin Sullivan (1)
Website	http://www.proshares.com
Address	ProShares 7501 Wisconsin Avenue, Suite 1000 Bethesda MD 20814 United States
Phone Number	866-776-5125

PERFORMANCE

Ratings History
Date	Overall Rating	Risk Rating	Reward Rating
Q3-19	C+	C	B-
Q4-18	C	C	C
Q4-17	A-	B-	A+
Q4-16	C+	C	B-
Q4-15	B-	C+	B-

Asset & Performance History
Date	NAV	1-Year Total Return
2018	67.1	-8.37
2017	73.28	70.53
2016	42.98	10
2015	39.17	14.74
2014	34.17	37.52
2013	24.9	81.83

Total Assets: $1,847,643,980

Asset Allocation
Asset	%
Cash	-100%
Stocks	200%
US Stocks	195%
Bonds	0%
US Bonds	0%
Other	0%

Services Offered:

Investment Strategy: The investment seeks daily investment results, before fees and expenses, that correspond to two times (2x) the daily performance of the NASDAQ-100 Index®. The fund invests in financial instruments that ProShare Advisors believes, in combination, should produce daily returns consistent with the fund's investment objective. The index includes 100 of the largest domestic and international non-financial companies listed on The Nasdaq Stock Market based on market capitalization. The fund is non-diversified. **Top Holdings:** Nasdaq 100 Index Swap Societe Generale Powershares Qqq (Qqq) Swap Goldman Sachs International Nasdaq 100 Index Swap Ubs Ag Nasdaq 100 Index Swap Credit Suisse International Nasdaq 100 Index Swap Goldman Sachs International

Invesco BulletShares 2020 Corporate Bond ETF

C   HOLD

Ticker	Traded On	NAV	Total Assets ($)	Dividend Yield (TTM)	Turnover Ratio	Expense Ratio
BSCK	NYSE Arca	21.28	$1,809,960,751	2.49	1	0.1

Ratings
Reward	C
Risk	C+
Recent Upgrade/Downgrade	

Fund Information
Fund Type	Exchange Traded Funds
Category	US Fixed Income
Sub-Category	Short-Term Bond
Prospectus Objective	Corp Bond - Gen
Inception Date	Mar-12
Open to New Investments	Y

Prices
Price (as of 9/30/2019)	21.30
52-Week High	21.35
52-Week Low	20.97

Total Returns (%)
3-Month	6-Month	1-Year	3-Year	5-Year
0.77	1.80	3.85	5.42	13.41

3-Year Standard Deviation	1.3
Effective Duration	0.93

Valuation
Premium/Discount (1-Year Average)	0.16

Company Information
Provider	Invesco
Manager/Tenure	Jeremy Neisewander (3), Peter Hubbard (1), Jeffrey W. Kernagis (1), 1 other
Website	http://www.invesco.com/us
Address	Invesco 11 Greenway Plaza, Ste. 2500 Houston TX 77046 United States
Phone Number	800-659-1005

PERFORMANCE

Ratings History
Date	Overall Rating	Risk Rating	Reward Rating
Q3-19	C	C+	C
Q4-18	C	C+	C
Q4-17	B	A+	C
Q4-16	C	C+	C
Q4-15	C+	C+	C

Asset & Performance History
Date	NAV	1-Year Total Return
2018	21.02	1.14
2017	21.24	2.21
2016	21.17	3.86
2015	20.84	1.83
2014	20.97	5.02
2013	20.49	-0.72

Total Assets: $1,809,960,751

Asset Allocation
Asset	%
Cash	1%
Stocks	0%
US Stocks	0%
Bonds	98%
US Bonds	85%
Other	0%

Services Offered:

Investment Strategy: The investment seeks to track the investment results (before fees and expenses) of the Nasdaq BulletShares® USD Corporate Bond 2020 Index (the "underlying index"). The fund generally will invest at least 80% of its total assets in securities that comprise the underlying index. The underlying index seeks to measure the performance of a portfolio of U.S. dollar-denominated investment grade corporate bonds with maturities or, in some cases, "effective maturities" in the year 2020 (collectively, "2020 Bonds"). The fund is non-diversified. **Top Holdings:** GE Capital International Funding Company Unlimited Company 2.34% JPMorgan Chase & Co. 2.25% AbbVie Inc. 2.5% Allergan Funding SCS 3% HP Inc 3.6%

First Trust Financials AlphaDEX® Fund

C   HOLD

Ticker	Traded On	NAV	Total Assets ($)	Dividend Yield (TTM)	Turnover Ratio	Expense Ratio
FXO	NYSE Arca	31.79	$1,795,906,013	2	81	0.63

Ratings
Reward	C
Risk	C+
Recent Upgrade/Downgrade	

Fund Information
Fund Type	Exchange Traded Funds
Category	Financials Sector Equity
Sub-Category	Financial
Prospectus Objective	Financial
Inception Date	May-07
Open to New Investments	Y

Prices
Price (as of 9/30/2019)	31.81
52-Week High	32.72
52-Week Low	25.49

Total Returns (%)
3-Month	6-Month	1-Year	3-Year	5-Year
0.40	3.98	1.89	38.50	60.10

3-Year Standard Deviation	14.44
Effective Duration	

Valuation
Premium/Discount (1-Year Average)	-0.02

Company Information
Provider	First Trust
Manager/Tenure	Jon C. Erickson (12), Daniel J. Lindquist (12), David G. McGarel (12), 3 others
Website	http://www.ftportfolios.com/
Address	First Trust 120 E. Liberty Drive, Suite 400 Wheaton IL 60187 United States
Phone Number	800-621-1675

PERFORMANCE

Ratings History
Date	Overall Rating	Risk Rating	Reward Rating
Q3-19	C	C+	C
Q4-18	C	C+	C-
Q4-17	B+	B+	B
Q4-16	B	C+	B
Q4-15	B-	C+	B

Asset & Performance History
Date	NAV	1-Year Total Return
2018	27.01	-11.65
2017	31.3	17.93
2016	27	18.15
2015	23.19	1.19
2014	23.26	8.7
2013	21.74	40.43

Total Assets: $1,795,906,013

Asset Allocation
Asset	%
Cash	0%
Stocks	100%
US Stocks	99%
Bonds	0%
US Bonds	0%
Other	0%

Services Offered:

Investment Strategy: The investment seeks investment results that correspond generally to the price and yield (before the fund's fees and expenses) of an equity index called the StrataQuant® Financials Index. The fund will normally invest at least 90% of its net assets (including investment borrowings) in common stocks that comprise the index. The index is a modified equal-dollar weighted index designed by IDI to objectively identify and select stocks from the Russell 1000® Index in the financial services sector that may generate positive alpha relative to traditional passive-style indices through the use of the AlphaDEX® selection methodology. **Top Holdings:** MarketAxess Holdings Inc Fair Isaac Corp OneMain Holdings Inc Santander Consumer USA Holdings Inc First American Financial Corp

iShares Core International Aggregate Bond ETF   B-   BUY

Ticker	Traded On	NAV	Total Assets ($)	Dividend Yield (TTM)	Turnover Ratio	Expense Ratio
IAGG	BATS	55.66	$1,789,511,884	4.16	11	0.09

Ratings
Reward	B-
Risk	C+
Recent Upgrade/Downgrade	Up

Fund Information
Fund Type	Exchange Traded Funds
Category	Global Fixed Income
Sub-Category	World Bond-USD Hedged
Prospectus Objective	Worldwide Bond
Inception Date	Nov-15
Open to New Investments	Y

Prices
Price (as of 9/30/2019)	55.79
52-Week High	56.14
52-Week Low	51.69

Total Returns (%)
3-Month	6-Month	1-Year	3-Year	5-Year
2.93	6.43	11.63	13.16	

3-Year Standard Deviation	2.84
Effective Duration	

Valuation
Premium/Discount (1-Year Average)	0.23

Company Information
Provider	iShares
Manager/Tenure	Scott Radell (3), Sid Swaminathan (1)
Website	http://www.ishares.com
Address	iShares 400 Howard Street San Francisco CA 94105 United States
Phone Number	800-474-2737

Ratings History
Date	Overall Rating	Risk Rating	Reward Rating
Q3-19	B-	C+	B-
Q4-18	C-	C-	C
Q4-17	C	B+	D+
Q4-16	D	C+	D
Q4-15			

Asset & Performance History
Date	NAV	1-Year Total Return
2018	52.03	2.92
2017	52.1	2.51
2016	51.72	4.98
2015	50.04	
2014		
2013		

Total Assets: $1,789,511,884
Asset Allocation
Asset	%
Cash	-1%
Stocks	0%
US Stocks	0%
Bonds	100%
US Bonds	3%
Other	0%

Services Offered:

Investment Strategy: The investment seeks to track the investment results of the Bloomberg Barclays Global Aggregate ex USD 10% Issuer Capped (Hedged) Index composed of global non-U.S. dollar-denominated investment-grade bonds that mitigates exposure to fluctuations between the value of the component currencies and the U.S. dollar. The fund generally will invest at least 90% of its assets in the component securities and other instruments of the underlying index. The index measures the performance of the global investment-grade bond market. The fund is non-diversified. **Top Holdings:** France (Republic Of) 0% Japan (Government Of) 0.1% Germany (Federal Republic Of) 2.25% Italy (Republic Of) 0.65% Japan (Government Of) 0.6%

Vanguard Emerging Markets Government Bond Index Fund ETF Shares   B-   BUY

Ticker	Traded On	NAV	Total Assets ($)	Dividend Yield (TTM)	Turnover Ratio	Expense Ratio
VWOB	NAS CM	80.41	$1,789,228,125	4.54	25	0.3

Ratings
Reward	B
Risk	C+
Recent Upgrade/Downgrade	

Fund Information
Fund Type	Exchange Traded Funds
Category	Emerging Mkts Fixed Inc
Sub-Category	Emerging Markets Bond
Prospectus Objective	Govt Bond - Gen
Inception Date	May-13
Open to New Investments	Y

Prices
Price (as of 9/30/2019)	80.60
52-Week High	81.56
52-Week Low	73.40

Total Returns (%)
3-Month	6-Month	1-Year	3-Year	5-Year
1.00	5.65	11.47	13.66	28.84

3-Year Standard Deviation	4.72
Effective Duration	7.60

Valuation
Premium/Discount (1-Year Average)	0.36

Company Information
Provider	Vanguard
Manager/Tenure	Joshua C. Barrickman (6)
Website	http://www.vanguard.com
Address	Vanguard 100 Vanguard Boulevard Malvern PA 19355 United States
Phone Number	877-662-7447

Ratings History
Date	Overall Rating	Risk Rating	Reward Rating
Q3-19	B-	C+	B
Q4-18	C	C+	C-
Q4-17	B	A	C+
Q4-16	C	C-	C
Q4-15	D+	C-	D+

Asset & Performance History
Date	NAV	1-Year Total Return
2018	74.28	-2.89
2017	79.97	8.48
2016	77.24	9.8
2015	73.69	1.58
2014	76.1	5.12
2013	75.63	

Total Assets: $1,789,228,125
Asset Allocation
Asset	%
Cash	0%
Stocks	0%
US Stocks	0%
Bonds	99%
US Bonds	0%
Other	0%

Services Offered:

Investment Strategy: The investment seeks to track the performance of a benchmark index that measures the investment return of U.S. dollar-denominated bonds issued by governments and government-related issuers in emerging market countries. The fund employs an indexing investment approach designed to track the performance of the Bloomberg Barclays USD Emerging Markets Government RIC Capped Index. All of the fund's investments will be selected through the sampling process, and under normal circumstances at least 80% of the fund's assets will be invested in bonds included in the index. It is non-diversified. **Top Holdings:** Qatar St 5.1% State of Qatar 4.82% Saudi Arabia (Kingdom Of) 4.5% Petrobras Global Finance B.V. 6% Petroleos Mexicanos 6.5%

iShares Global REIT ETF

C+   **HOLD**

Ticker	Traded On	NAV		Total Assets ($)	Dividend Yield (TTM)	Turnover Ratio	Expense Ratio
REET	NYSE Arca	28.00		$1,766,711,232	3.72	9	0.14

Ratings
Reward	C
Risk	C+
Recent Upgrade/Downgrade	

Fund Information
Fund Type	Exchange Traded Funds
Category	Real Estate Sector Equity
Sub-Category	Real Estate
Prospectus Objective	Real Estate
Inception Date	Jul-14
Open to New Investments	Y

Prices
Price (as of 9/30/2019)	28.08
52-Week High	28.09
52-Week Low	22.86

Total Returns (%)
3-Month	6-Month	1-Year	3-Year	5-Year
6.00	6.99	16.51	19.28	46.76

3-Year Standard Deviation	11.14
Effective Duration	

Valuation
Premium/Discount (1-Year Average)	-0.01

Company Information
Provider	iShares
Manager/Tenure	Jennifer Hsui (5), Greg Savage (5), Alan Mason (3), 2 others
Website	http://www.ishares.com
Address	iShares 400 Howard Street San Francisco CA 94105 United States
Phone Number	800-474-2737

PERFORMANCE

Ratings History
Date	Overall Rating	Risk Rating	Reward Rating
Q3-19	C+	C+	C
Q4-18	C	C+	C
Q4-17	B-	B	C+
Q4-16	C	C-	C
Q4-15	D	D+	D+

Asset & Performance History
Date	NAV	1-Year Total Return
2018	23.5	-4.89
2017	26.08	7.57
2016	25.21	6.19
2015	25.01	0.24
2014	25.86	
2013		

Total Assets: $1,766,711,232

Asset Allocation
Asset	%
Cash	1%
Stocks	98%
US Stocks	66%
Bonds	0%
US Bonds	0%
Other	1%

Services Offered:

Investment Strategy: The investment seeks to track the investment results of the FTSE EPRA/NAREIT Global REITs Index. The index is designed to track the performance of publicly-listed real estate investment trusts ("REITs") (or their local equivalents) in both developed and emerging markets. The fund generally will invest at least 90% of its assets in the component securities of the underlying index and in investments that have economic characteristics that are substantially identical to the component securities of the underlying index and may invest up to 10% of its assets in certain futures, options and swap contracts, cash and cash equivalents. **Top Holdings:** Prologis Inc Simon Property Group Inc Public Storage Welltower Inc Equity Residential

iShares PHLX Semiconductor ETF

B-   **BUY**

Ticker	Traded On	NAV		Total Assets ($)	Dividend Yield (TTM)	Turnover Ratio	Expense Ratio
SOXX	NAS CM	211.58		$1,756,106,182	1.22	26	0.46

Ratings
Reward	B+
Risk	C
Recent Upgrade/Downgrade	Up

Fund Information
Fund Type	Exchange Traded Funds
Category	Technology Sector Equity
Sub-Category	Technology
Prospectus Objective	Technology
Inception Date	Jul-01
Open to New Investments	Y

Prices
Price (as of 9/30/2019)	211.41
52-Week High	220.43
52-Week Low	145.00

Total Returns (%)
3-Month	6-Month	1-Year	3-Year	5-Year
4.41	9.82	15.51	94.03	167.08

3-Year Standard Deviation	22.4
Effective Duration	

Valuation
Premium/Discount (1-Year Average)	-0.01

Company Information
Provider	iShares
Manager/Tenure	Greg Savage (11), Jennifer Hsui (6), Alan Mason (3), 2 others
Website	http://www.ishares.com
Address	iShares 400 Howard Street San Francisco CA 94105 United States
Phone Number	800-474-2737

PERFORMANCE

Ratings History
Date	Overall Rating	Risk Rating	Reward Rating
Q3-19	B-	C	B+
Q4-18	B-	C-	B
Q4-17	A-	B	A+
Q4-16	C	C	C
Q4-15	B	B-	B

Asset & Performance History
Date	NAV	1-Year Total Return
2018	156.88	-6.47
2017	169.77	39.82
2016	122.66	38.4
2015	89.76	-2.06
2014	92.86	29.89
2013	72.66	41.25

Total Assets: $1,756,106,182

Asset Allocation
Asset	%
Cash	0%
Stocks	100%
US Stocks	86%
Bonds	0%
US Bonds	0%
Other	0%

Services Offered: CashInvestment Plan

Investment Strategy: The investment seeks to track the investment results of the PHLX Semiconductor Sector Index composed of U.S. equities in the semiconductor sector. The fund generally invests at least 90% of its assets in securities of the underlying index and in depositary receipts representing securities of the underlying index. The underlying index measures the performance of U.S.-traded securities of companies engaged in the semiconductor business. The fund is non-diversified. **Top Holdings:** NVIDIA Corp Texas Instruments Inc Qualcomm Inc Broadcom Inc Intel Corp

iShares Long-Term Corporate Bond ETF   B-   BUY

Ticker	Traded On	NAV	Total Assets ($)	Dividend Yield (TTM)	Turnover Ratio	Expense Ratio
IGLB	NYSE Arca	66.44	$1,734,119,069	3.92	24	0.06

Ratings
Reward   B
Risk   C+
Recent Upgrade/Downgrade

Fund Information
Fund Type   Exchange Traded Funds
Category   US Fixed Income
Sub-Category   Long-Term Bond
Prospectus Objective   Growth & Inc
Inception Date   Dec-09
Open to New Investments   Y

Prices
Price (as of 9/30/2019)   66.63
52-Week High   67.97
52-Week Low   55.17

Total Returns (%)

3-Month	6-Month	1-Year	3-Year	5-Year
5.73	13.80	20.05	19.85	36.16

3-Year Standard Deviation   7.58
Effective Duration

Valuation
Premium/Discount (1-Year Average)   0.21

Company Information
Provider   iShares
Manager/Tenure   Scott Radell (9), James Mauro (8)
Website   http://www.ishares.com
Address   iShares 400 Howard Street San
                    Francisco CA 94105 United States
Phone Number   800-474-2737

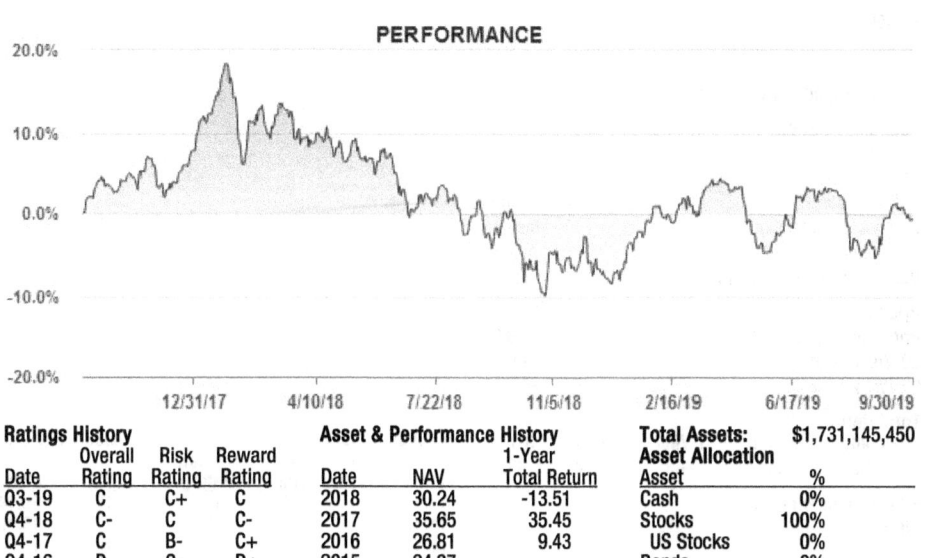

PERFORMANCE

Ratings History

Date	Overall Rating	Risk Rating	Reward Rating
Q3-19	B-	C+	B
Q4-18	D+	C-	D+
Q4-17	B-	B	B-
Q4-16	C	C+	C
Q4-15	C	C	C-

Asset & Performance History

Date	NAV	1-Year Total Return
2018	56.08	-7.17
2017	63.15	11.67
2016	58.7	9.91
2015	55.66	-4.75
2014	61.03	15.54
2013	55.12	-7.05

Total Assets: $1,734,119,069
Asset Allocation

Asset	%
Cash	2%
Stocks	0%
US Stocks	0%
Bonds	98%
US Bonds	82%
Other	0%

Services Offered:

Investment Strategy: The investment seeks to track the investment results of the ICE BofAML 10+ Year US Corporate Index. The fund generally will invest at least 90% of its assets in the component securities of the underlying index and may invest up to 10% of its assets in certain futures, options and swap contracts, cash and cash equivalents. The underlying index measures the performance of investment-grade corporate bonds of both U.S. and non-U.S. issuers that are U.S. dollar-denominated and publicly issued in the U.S. domestic market and have a remaining maturity of greater than or equal to ten years. **Top Holdings:** GE Capital International Funding Company Unlimited Company 4.42% Anheuser-Busch Companies LLC / Anheuser-Busch InBev Worldwide Inc 4.9% Goldman Sachs Group, Inc. 6.75% CVS Health Corp 5.05% Anheuser-Busch Companies LLC / Anheuser-Busch InBev Worldwide Inc 4.7%

Goldman Sachs ActiveBeta® Emerging Markets Equity ETF   C   HOLD

Ticker	Traded On	NAV	Total Assets ($)	Dividend Yield (TTM)	Turnover Ratio	Expense Ratio
GEM	NYSE Arca	31.48	$1,731,145,450	2.74	28	0.45

Ratings
Reward   C
Risk   C+
Recent Upgrade/Downgrade

Fund Information
Fund Type   Exchange Traded Funds
Category   Global Emerg Mkts Equity
Sub-Category   Diversified Emerging Mkts
Prospectus Objective   Div Emerg Mkts
Inception Date   Sep-15
Open to New Investments   Y

Prices
Price (as of 9/30/2019)   31.36
52-Week High   33.75
52-Week Low   28.94

Total Returns (%)

3-Month	6-Month	1-Year	3-Year	5-Year
-3.87	-2.77	-0.96	19.19	

3-Year Standard Deviation   13.41
Effective Duration

Valuation
Premium/Discount (1-Year Average)   0.04

Company Information
Provider   Goldman Sachs
Manager/Tenure   Raj Garigipati (4), Jamie McGregor (3)
Website   http://www.gsamfunds.com
Address   Goldman Sachs 200 West Stree New
                    York NY 10282 United States
Phone Number   800-526-7384

PERFORMANCE

Ratings History

Date	Overall Rating	Risk Rating	Reward Rating
Q3-19	C	C+	C
Q4-18	C-	C	C-
Q4-17	C	B-	C+
Q4-16	D	C-	D+
Q4-15			

Asset & Performance History

Date	NAV	1-Year Total Return
2018	30.24	-13.51
2017	35.65	35.45
2016	26.81	9.43
2015	24.97	
2014		
2013		

Total Assets: $1,731,145,450
Asset Allocation

Asset	%
Cash	0%
Stocks	100%
US Stocks	0%
Bonds	0%
US Bonds	0%
Other	0%

Services Offered:

Investment Strategy: The investment seeks to provide investment results that closely correspond, before fees and expenses, to the performance of the Goldman Sachs ActiveBeta® Emerging Markets Equity Index. The fund invests at least 80% of its assets (exclusive of collateral held from securities lending) in securities included in its underlying index, in depositary receipts representing securities included in its underlying index and in underlying stocks in respect of depositary receipts included in its underlying index. The index is designed to deliver exposure to equity securities of emerging market issuers. **Top Holdings:** Tencent Holdings Ltd Alibaba Group Holding Ltd ADR Taiwan Semiconductor Manufacturing Co Ltd Samsung Electronics Co Ltd Ping An Insurance (Group) Co. of China Ltd Class H

SPDR® S&P Oil & Gas Exploration & Production ETF

D   **SELL**

Ticker	Traded On	NAV	Total Assets ($)	Dividend Yield (TTM)	Turnover Ratio	Expense Ratio
XOP	NYSE Arca		$1,725,791,179	1.41	37	0.35

Ratings
Reward   D
Risk   D
Recent Upgrade/Downgrade

Fund Information
Fund Type   Exchange Traded Funds
Category   Energy Sector Equity
Sub-Category   Equity Energy
Prospectus Objective   Natl Res
Inception Date   Jun-06
Open to New Investments   Y

Prices
Price (as of 9/30/2019)   22.36
52-Week High   44.57
52-Week Low   20.60

Total Returns (%)

3-Month	6-Month	1-Year	3-Year	5-Year
-17.11	-27.35	-47.91	-39.88	-65.45

3-Year Standard Deviation   30.39
Effective Duration

Valuation
Premium/Discount (1-Year Average)   0.03

Company Information
Provider   SPDR State Street Global Advisors
Manager/Tenure   Michael J. Feehily (7), Karl A. Schneider (4), Olga Winner (2)
Website   http://www.spdrs.com
Address   SPDR State Street Global Advisors State Street Financial Center, 1 Lincoln Street Boston MA 02111-2900 United States
Phone Number   617-786-3000

PERFORMANCE

Ratings History

Date	Overall Rating	Risk Rating	Reward Rating
Q3-19	D	D	D
Q4-18	D+	D+	C-
Q4-17	D	D	D
Q4-16	D+	D	D+
Q4-15	D	D	D

Asset & Performance History

Date	NAV	1-Year Total Return
2018	26.54	-28.21
2017	37.25	-9.31
2016	41.43	42.4
2015	30.23	-35.73
2014	47.85	-29.44
2013	68.53	27.92

Total Assets: $1,725,791,179
Asset Allocation

Asset	%
Cash	0%
Stocks	100%
US Stocks	99%
Bonds	0%
US Bonds	0%
Other	0%

Services Offered:

Investment Strategy: The investment seeks to provide investment results that, before fees and expenses, correspond generally to the total return performance of an index derived from the oil and gas exploration and production segment of a U.S. total market composite index. In seeking to track the performance of the S&P Oil & Gas Exploration & Production Select Industry Index, the fund employs a sampling strategy. It generally invests substantially all, but at least 80%, of its total assets in the securities comprising the index. The index represents the oil and gas exploration and production segment of the S&P Total Market Index ("S&P TMI"). The fund is non-diversified. **Top Holdings:** Phillips 66   Noble Energy Inc   HollyFrontier Corp   Hess Corp   Parsley Energy Inc A

ALPS Sector Dividend Dogs ETF

C   **HOLD**

Ticker	Traded On	NAV	Total Assets ($)	Dividend Yield (TTM)	Turnover Ratio	Expense Ratio
SDOG	NYSE Arca	43.86	$1,715,257,592	3.49	61	0.4

Ratings
Reward   C
Risk   C
Recent Upgrade/Downgrade

Fund Information
Fund Type   Exchange Traded Funds
Category   US Equity Large Cap Value
Sub-Category   Large Value
Prospectus Objective   Income
Inception Date   Jun-12
Open to New Investments   Y

Prices
Price (as of 9/30/2019)   43.85
52-Week High   46.28
52-Week Low   37.25

Total Returns (%)

3-Month	6-Month	1-Year	3-Year	5-Year
1.26	2.54	-1.33	17.24	42.08

3-Year Standard Deviation   14.18
Effective Duration

Valuation
Premium/Discount (1-Year Average)   -0.03

Company Information
Provider   ALPS
Manager/Tenure   Ryan Mischker (4), Andrew Hicks (3)
Website   http://www.alpsfunds.com
Address   ALPS 1290 Broadway, Suite 1100 Denver CO 80203 United States
Phone Number   866-759-5679

PERFORMANCE

Ratings History

Date	Overall Rating	Risk Rating	Reward Rating
Q3-19	C	C	C
Q4-18	C	C	C
Q4-17	B	B	B-
Q4-16	B-	C	B
Q4-15	C	C+	C

Asset & Performance History

Date	NAV	1-Year Total Return
2018	39.14	-11.29
2017	45.76	12.68
2016	42.02	22.37
2015	35.54	-3.23
2014	38.05	14.98
2013	34.25	34.29

Total Assets: $1,715,257,592
Asset Allocation

Asset	%
Cash	0%
Stocks	100%
US Stocks	98%
Bonds	0%
US Bonds	0%
Other	0%

Services Offered:

Investment Strategy: The investment seeks investment results that replicate as closely as possible, before fees and expenses, the performance of the S-Network® Sector Dividend Dogs Index. The underlying index generally consists of 50 stocks on each annual reconstitution date, which is the third Friday of December each year. The underlying index's stocks must be constituents of the S&P 500 Index, the leading benchmark index for U.S. large capitalization stocks. The underlying index methodology selects the five stocks in ten of the eleven GICS sectors that make up the S&P 500 which offer the highest dividend yields as of the last business day of November. **Top Holdings:** Western Digital Corp   Edison International   United Parcel Service Inc Class B   Newell Brands Inc   Qualcomm Inc

Invesco DWA Momentum ETF   B-   BUY

Ticker	Traded On	NAV	Total Assets ($)	Dividend Yield (TTM)	Turnover Ratio	Expense Ratio
PDP	NAS CM	60.92	$1,705,890,370	0.26	82	0.62

Ratings
Reward	B-
Risk	C+
Recent Upgrade/Downgrade	Up

Fund Information
Fund Type	Exchange Traded Funds
Category	US Equity Mid Cap
Sub-Category	Mid-Cap Growth
Prospectus Objective	Growth
Inception Date	Mar-07
Open to New Investments	Y

Prices
Price (as of 9/30/2019)	60.90
52-Week High	63.22
52-Week Low	45.29

Total Returns (%)
3-Month	6-Month	1-Year	3-Year	5-Year
0.39	6.77	2.86	45.18	60.78

3-Year Standard Deviation	13.66
Effective Duration	

Valuation
Premium/Discount (1-Year Average)	-0.02

Company Information
Provider	Invesco
Manager/Tenure	Peter Hubbard (12), Michael Jeanette (11), Tony Seisser (5)
Website	http://www.invesco.com/us
Address	Invesco 11 Greenway Plaza, Ste. 2500 Houston TX 77046 United States
Phone Number	800-659-1005

PERFORMANCE

Ratings History
Date	Overall Rating	Risk Rating	Reward Rating
Q3-19	B-	C+	B-
Q4-18	C	C+	C
Q4-17	B	B+	B
Q4-16	C+	C+	C+
Q4-15	C+	B-	C+

Asset & Performance History
Date	NAV	1-Year Total Return
2018	48.49	-5.88
2017	51.61	23.36
2016	41.96	2.17
2015	41.4	1.3
2014	41.02	12.12
2013	36.64	31.79

Total Assets: $1,705,890,370
Asset Allocation
Asset	%
Cash	0%
Stocks	100%
US Stocks	100%
Bonds	0%
US Bonds	0%
Other	0%

Services Offered:

Investment Strategy: The investment seeks to track the investment results (before fees and expenses) of the Dorsey Wright® Technical Leaders Index. The fund generally will invest at least 90% of its total assets in securities that comprise the underlying index. The underlying index is composed of approximately 100 securities from an eligible universe of approximately 1,000 securities of the largest constituents by market capitalization within the NASDAQ US Benchmark Index. **Top Holdings:** American Tower Corp Apple Inc Ball Corp O'Reilly Automotive Inc Mastercard Inc A

SPDR® MSCI ACWI ex-US ETF   C   HOLD

Ticker	Traded On	NAV	Total Assets ($)	Dividend Yield (TTM)	Turnover Ratio	Expense Ratio
CWI	NYSE Arca		$1,683,107,623	2.92	3	0.3

Ratings
Reward	C
Risk	C+
Recent Upgrade/Downgrade	

Fund Information
Fund Type	Exchange Traded Funds
Category	Global Equity Large Cap
Sub-Category	Foreign Large Blend
Prospectus Objective	Foreign Stock
Inception Date	Jan-07
Open to New Investments	Y

Prices
Price (as of 9/30/2019)	24.04
52-Week High	37.42
52-Week Low	22.70

Total Returns (%)
3-Month	6-Month	1-Year	3-Year	5-Year
-34.62	-32.97	-33.52	-19.33	-21.77

3-Year Standard Deviation	11.47
Effective Duration	

Valuation
Premium/Discount (1-Year Average)	-0.09

Company Information
Provider	SPDR State Street Global Advisors
Manager/Tenure	Michael J. Feehily (8), Karl A. Schneider (4), Michael Finocchi (2)
Website	http://www.spdrs.com
Address	SPDR State Street Global Advisors State Street Financial Center, 1 Lincoln Street Boston MA 02111-2900 United States
Phone Number	617-786-3000

PERFORMANCE

Ratings History
Date	Overall Rating	Risk Rating	Reward Rating
Q3-19	C	C+	C
Q4-18	C-	C	D+
Q4-17	B-	B-	B-
Q4-16	C-	C	D+
Q4-15	C	C+	C-

Asset & Performance History
Date	NAV	1-Year Total Return
2018	32.73	-14.03
2017	39.08	26.95
2016	31.54	3.68
2015	30.92	-5.26
2014	33.45	-2.7
2013	35.42	14.91

Total Assets: $1,683,107,623
Asset Allocation
Asset	%
Cash	0%
Stocks	100%
US Stocks	1%
Bonds	0%
US Bonds	0%
Other	0%

Services Offered:

Investment Strategy: The investment seeks investment results that, before fees and expenses, correspond generally to the total return performance of the MSCI All Country World Index ex USA Index. The fund generally invests substantially all, but at least 80%, of its total assets in the securities comprising the index and in depositary receipts based on securities comprising the index. The index is a free float-adjusted market capitalization index that is designed to measure the combined equity market performance of large- and mid-cap securities in developed and emerging market countries excluding the United States. The fund is non-diversified. **Top Holdings:** Nestle SA Tencent Holdings Ltd Alibaba Group Holding Ltd ADR Novartis AG Taiwan Semiconductor Manufacturing Co Ltd ADR

First Trust Morningstar Dividend Leaders Index Fund   C+   HOLD

Ticker	Traded On	NAV	Total Assets ($)	Dividend Yield (TTM)	Turnover Ratio	Expense Ratio
FDL	NYSE Arca	31.02	$1,678,221,278	3.93	39	0.45

Ratings
Reward   C+
Risk   C
Recent Upgrade/Downgrade

Fund Information
Fund Type   Exchange Traded Funds
Category   US Equity Large Cap Value
Sub-Category   Large Value
Prospectus Objective   Growth & Inc
Inception Date   Mar-06
Open to New Investments   Y

Prices
Price (as of 9/30/2019)   31.04
52-Week High   31.57
52-Week Low   25.99

Total Returns (%)

3-Month	6-Month	1-Year	3-Year	5-Year
2.22	4.24	8.00	26.79	59.21

3-Year Standard Deviation   11.19
Effective Duration

Valuation
Premium/Discount (1-Year Average)   0.01

Company Information
Provider   First Trust
Manager/Tenure   Jon C. Erickson (13), Daniel J. Lindquist (13), David G. McGarel (13), 3 others
Website   http://www.ftportfolios.com/
Address   First Trust 120 E. Liberty Drive, Suite 400 Wheaton IL 60187 United States
Phone Number   800-621-1675

PERFORMANCE

Ratings History

Date	Overall Rating	Risk Rating	Reward Rating
Q3-19	C+	C	C+
Q4-18	C	C	C
Q4-17	B	A	B-
Q4-16	B	C	B
Q4-15	B-	C	B

Asset & Performance History

Date	NAV	1-Year Total Return
2018	27.24	-5.86
2017	30.06	11.97
2016	27.74	20.68
2015	23.69	2.71
2014	23.94	12.94
2013	21.93	22.76

Total Assets: $1,678,221,278
Asset Allocation

Asset	%
Cash	0%
Stocks	100%
US Stocks	99%
Bonds	0%
US Bonds	0%
Other	0%

Services Offered:

Investment Strategy: The investment seeks investment results that correspond generally to the price and yield (before the fund's fees and expenses) of an equity index called the Morningstar® Dividend Leaders IndexSM. The fund will normally invest at least 90% of its net assets (including investment borrowings) in the common stocks that comprise the index. The index is designed to measure the performance of the 100 highest-yielding stocks that have a consistent record of dividend payment and have the ability to sustain their dividend payments. It is non-diversified. **Top Holdings:** AT&T Inc   Exxon Mobil Corp   Verizon Communications Inc   Chevron Corp   Wells Fargo & Co

SPDR® Portfolio Mid Cap ETF   C   HOLD

Ticker	Traded On	NAV	Total Assets ($)	Dividend Yield (TTM)	Turnover Ratio	Expense Ratio
SPMD	NYSE Arca		$1,677,274,281	1.65	8	0.05

Ratings
Reward   C
Risk   C+
Recent Upgrade/Downgrade

Fund Information
Fund Type   Exchange Traded Funds
Category   US Equity Mid Cap
Sub-Category   Mid-Cap Blend
Prospectus Objective   Growth
Inception Date   Nov-05
Open to New Investments   Y

Prices
Price (as of 9/30/2019)   33.89
52-Week High   35.82
52-Week Low   27.71

Total Returns (%)

3-Month	6-Month	1-Year	3-Year	5-Year
-0.93	0.69	-4.16	30.05	45.54

3-Year Standard Deviation   15.98
Effective Duration

Valuation
Premium/Discount (1-Year Average)   0.01

Company Information
Provider   SPDR State Street Global Advisors
Manager/Tenure   Michael J. Feehily (7), Karl A. Schneider (4), Mark Krivitsky (2)
Website   http://www.spdrs.com
Address   SPDR State Street Global Advisors State Street Financial Center, 1 Lincoln Street Boston MA 02111-2900 United States
Phone Number   617-786-3000

PERFORMANCE

Ratings History

Date	Overall Rating	Risk Rating	Reward Rating
Q3-19	C	C+	C
Q4-18	C	C+	C-
Q4-17	B	B	B
Q4-16	C	D+	B-
Q4-15	C	D+	C

Asset & Performance History

Date	NAV	1-Year Total Return
2018	29.43	-10.28
2017	33.35	15.27
2016	29.53	17.69
2015	25.56	-3.4
2014	27.87	7.39
2013	27.46	38.13

Total Assets: $1,677,274,281
Asset Allocation

Asset	%
Cash	0%
Stocks	100%
US Stocks	99%
Bonds	0%
US Bonds	0%
Other	0%

Services Offered: Dividend Investment Plan, CashInvestment Plan

Investment Strategy: The investment seeks to provide investment results that, before fees and expenses, correspond generally to the total return performance of the S&P 1000 Index. The fund generally invests substantially all, but at least 80%, of its total assets in the securities comprising the index. The index measures the performance of the small- and mid-capitalization segments of the U.S. equity market. The fund is non-diversified. **Top Holdings:** Steris PLC   NVR Inc   Teledyne Technologies Inc   Zebra Technologies Corp   Alleghany Corp

iShares Core U.S. REIT ETF   C+   HOLD

Ticker	Traded On	NAV	Total Assets ($)	Dividend Yield (TTM)	Turnover Ratio	Expense Ratio
USRT	NYSE Arca	55.55	$1,669,359,079	2.85	11	0.08

Ratings

Reward	C+
Risk	C+
Recent Upgrade/Downgrade	Up

Fund Information

Fund Type	Exchange Traded Funds
Category	Real Estate Sector Equity
Sub-Category	Real Estate
Prospectus Objective	Real Estate
Inception Date	May-07
Open to New Investments	Y

Prices

Price (as of 9/30/2019)	55.55
52-Week High	55.60
52-Week Low	43.17

Total Returns (%)

3-Month	6-Month	1-Year	3-Year	5-Year
8.00	8.87	19.45	24.45	60.06

3-Year Standard Deviation	12.84
Effective Duration	

Valuation

Premium/Discount (1-Year Average)	-0.02

Company Information

Provider	iShares
Manager/Tenure	Greg Savage (11), Jennifer Hsui (7), Alan Mason (3), 2 others
Website	http://www.ishares.com
Address	iShares 400 Howard Street San Francisco CA 94105 United States
Phone Number	800-474-2737

PERFORMANCE

Ratings History

Date	Overall Rating	Risk Rating	Reward Rating
Q3-19	C+	C+	C+
Q4-18	C	C+	C
Q4-17	B	B+	C+
Q4-16	C+	C-	B
Q4-15	B-	C	B

Asset & Performance History

Date	NAV	1-Year Total Return
2018	44.86	-4.55
2017	49.59	5.16
2016	48.81	8.08
2015	46.98	3.86
2014	46.93	28.15
2013	38.02	-1.06

Total Assets: $1,669,359,079

Asset Allocation

Asset	%
Cash	1%
Stocks	99%
US Stocks	99%
Bonds	0%
US Bonds	0%
Other	0%

Services Offered:

Investment Strategy: The investment seeks to track the investment results of the FTSE NAREIT Equity REITs Index composed of U.S. real estate equities. The fund generally will invest at least 90% of its assets in the component securities of the underlying index and may invest up to 10% of its assets in certain futures, options and swap contracts, cash and cash equivalents. The index measures the performance of U.S. listed equity real estate investment trusts ("REITs"), excluding infrastructure REITs, mortgage REITs, and timber REITs. **Top Holdings:** Prologis Inc Equinix Inc Simon Property Group Inc Public Storage Welltower Inc

FlexShares Quality Dividend Index Fund   C   HOLD

Ticker	Traded On	NAV	Total Assets ($)	Dividend Yield (TTM)	Turnover Ratio	Expense Ratio
QDF	NYSE Arca	45.43	$1,667,277,750	2.6	76	0.37

Ratings

Reward	C+
Risk	C-
Recent Upgrade/Downgrade	

Fund Information

Fund Type	Exchange Traded Funds
Category	US Equity Large Cap Value
Sub-Category	Large Value
Prospectus Objective	Income
Inception Date	Dec-12
Open to New Investments	Y

Prices

Price (as of 9/30/2019)	45.44
52-Week High	47.57
52-Week Low	37.39

Total Returns (%)

3-Month	6-Month	1-Year	3-Year	5-Year
1.10	1.57	-0.24	32.43	54.69

3-Year Standard Deviation	12.7
Effective Duration	

Valuation

Premium/Discount (1-Year Average)	0.01

Company Information

Provider	Flexshares Trust
Manager/Tenure	Robert Anstine (5), Brendan Sullivan (3)
Website	http://www.flexshares.com
Address	50 South LaSalle Street Chicago, Illinois 60603 Chicago Illinois 60603 United States
Phone Number	855-353-9383

PERFORMANCE

Ratings History

Date	Overall Rating	Risk Rating	Reward Rating
Q3-19	C	C-	C+
Q4-18	C	C+	C
Q4-17	B	B+	B-
Q4-16	C+	C-	B
Q4-15	C	C	C

Asset & Performance History

Date	NAV	1-Year Total Return
2018	39.78	-9.13
2017	44.97	17.15
2016	39.49	17.16
2015	34.81	-0.94
2014	36.19	12
2013	33.22	35.65

Total Assets: $1,667,277,750

Asset Allocation

Asset	%
Cash	1%
Stocks	99%
US Stocks	98%
Bonds	0%
US Bonds	0%
Other	0%

Services Offered:

Investment Strategy: The investment seeks investment results that correspond generally to the price and yield performance, before fees and expenses, of the Northern Trust Quality Dividend IndexSM. Under normal circumstances, the fund will invest at least 80% of its total assets (exclusive of collateral held from securities lending) in the securities of the underlying index. The underlying index is designed to provide exposure to a high-quality, income-oriented portfolio of U.S. equity securities, with an emphasis on long-term capital growth and a targeted overall volatility similar to that of the Northern Trust 1250 IndexSM. **Top Holdings:** Microsoft Corp PepsiCo Inc The Home Depot Inc Johnson & Johnson Apple Inc

Invesco BulletShares 2021 Corporate Bond ETF

C+   HOLD

Ticker	Traded On	NAV	Total Assets ($)	Dividend Yield (TTM)	Turnover Ratio	Expense Ratio
BSCL	NYSE Arca	21.21	$1,663,570,645	2.71	3	0.1

Ratings
Reward	C
Risk	C+
Recent Upgrade/Downgrade	Up

Fund Information
Fund Type	Exchange Traded Funds
Category	US Fixed Income
Sub-Category	Target Maturity
Prospectus Objective	Corp Bond - Gen
Inception Date	Jul-13
Open to New Investments	Y

Prices
Price (as of 9/30/2019)	21.26
52-Week High	21.30
52-Week Low	20.62

Total Returns (%)
3-Month	6-Month	1-Year	3-Year	5-Year
0.96	2.48	5.37	6.50	15.93

3-Year Standard Deviation	1.79
Effective Duration	1.79

Valuation
Premium/Discount (1-Year Average)	0.23

Company Information
Provider	Invesco
Manager/Tenure	Jeremy Neisewander (3), Peter Hubbard (1), Jeffrey W. Kernagis (1), 1 other
Website	http://www.invesco.com/us
Address	Invesco 11 Greenway Plaza, Ste. 2500 Houston TX 77046 United States
Phone Number	800-659-1005

PERFORMANCE

Ratings History
Date	Overall Rating	Risk Rating	Reward Rating
Q3-19	C+	C+	C
Q4-18	C	C+	C-
Q4-17	B	A	C
Q4-16	C	C+	C
Q4-15	C-	C-	D+

Asset & Performance History
Date	NAV	1-Year Total Return
2018	20.69	0.66
2017	21.07	2.81
2016	20.95	5.01
2015	20.44	0.99
2014	20.78	7.15
2013	19.94	

Total Assets: $1,663,570,645
Asset Allocation
Asset	%
Cash	0%
Stocks	0%
US Stocks	0%
Bonds	100%
US Bonds	78%
Other	0%

Services Offered:

Investment Strategy: The investment seeks to track the investment results (before fees and expenses) of the Nasdaq BulletShares® USD Corporate Bond 2021 Index (the "underlying index"). The fund generally will invest at least 80% of its total assets in securities that comprise the underlying index. The underlying index seeks to measure the performance of a portfolio of U.S. dollar-denominated investment grade corporate bonds with maturities or, in some cases, "effective maturities" in the year 2021 (collectively, "2021 Bonds"). The fund is non-diversified. **Top Holdings:** Anheuser-Busch InBev Finance Inc. 2.65% Oracle Corporation 1.9% Goldman Sachs Group, Inc. 5.25% Deutsche Bank AG New York Branch 4.25% Shire Acquisitions Investments Ireland DAC 2.4%

WisdomTree Floating Rate Treasury Fund

C   HOLD

Ticker	Traded On	NAV	Total Assets ($)	Dividend Yield (TTM)	Turnover Ratio	Expense Ratio
USFR	NYSE Arca	25.05	$1,658,617,873	2.16	170	0.15

Ratings
Reward	C
Risk	C+
Recent Upgrade/Downgrade	

Fund Information
Fund Type	Exchange Traded Funds
Category	US Fixed Income
Sub-Category	Short Government
Prospectus Objective	Govt Bond - Treasury
Inception Date	Feb-14
Open to New Investments	Y

Prices
Price (as of 9/30/2019)	25.05
52-Week High	25.14
52-Week Low	25.04

Total Returns (%)
3-Month	6-Month	1-Year	3-Year	5-Year
0.44	0.99	2.04	4.67	4.92

3-Year Standard Deviation	0.19
Effective Duration	0.02

Valuation
Premium/Discount (1-Year Average)	0.02

Company Information
Provider	WisdomTree
Manager/Tenure	Paul L. Benson (3), Stephanie Shu (3)
Website	http://www.wisdomtree.com
Address	WisdomTree 245 Park Avenue, 35th floor New York NY 10167 United States
Phone Number	866-909-9473

PERFORMANCE

Ratings History
Date	Overall Rating	Risk Rating	Reward Rating
Q3-19	C	C+	C
Q4-18	C	C+	C-
Q4-17	C	B-	C-
Q4-16	C-	D+	C-
Q4-15	D	D+	D

Asset & Performance History
Date	NAV	1-Year Total Return
2018	25.07	1.81
2017	25.04	1.03
2016	25.04	0.58
2015	24.96	-0.07
2014	24.98	
2013		

Total Assets: $1,658,617,873
Asset Allocation
Asset	%
Cash	0%
Stocks	0%
US Stocks	0%
Bonds	100%
US Bonds	100%
Other	0%

Services Offered:

Investment Strategy: The investment seeks to track the price and yield performance, before fees and expenses, of the Bloomberg U.S. Treasury Floating Rate Bond Index (the "index"). The fund invests at least 80% of its total assets (exclusive of collateral held from securities lending) in the component securities of the index and investments that have economic characteristics that are substantially identical to the economic characteristics of such component securities. The index is designed to measure the performance of floating rate public obligations of the U.S. Treasury. The fund is non-diversified. **Top Holdings:** United States Treasury Notes 2.1% United States Treasury Notes 2.07% United States Treasury Notes 2% United States Treasury Notes 2.18%

SPDR® Portfolio Short Term Treasury ETF   C   HOLD

Ticker	Traded On	NAV	Total Assets ($)	Dividend Yield (TTM)	Turnover Ratio	Expense Ratio
SPTS	NYSE Arca		$1,656,360,898	2.34	52	0.06

Ratings
Reward   C
Risk   C+
Recent Upgrade/Downgrade

Fund Information
Fund Type   Exchange Traded Funds
Category   US Fixed Income
Sub-Category   Short Government
Prospectus Objective   Govt Bond - Treasury
Inception Date   Nov-11
Open to New Investments   Y

Prices
Price (as of 9/30/2019)   30.02
52-Week High   30.11
52-Week Low   29.34

Total Returns (%)

3-Month	6-Month	1-Year	3-Year	5-Year
0.64	2.12	4.37	3.48	7.04

3-Year Standard Deviation   1.31
Effective Duration   1.92

Valuation
Premium/Discount (1-Year Average)   0.03

Company Information
Provider   SPDR State Street Global Advisors
Manager/Tenure   Joanna Madden (4), Cynthia Moy (2),
                 Orhan Imer (1)
Website   http://www.spdrs.com
Address   SPDR State Street Global Advisors
                 State Street Financial Center, 1
                 Lincoln Street Boston MA 02111-2900
                 United States
Phone Number   617-786-3000

PERFORMANCE

Ratings History

Date	Overall Rating	Risk Rating	Reward Rating
Q3-19	C	C+	C
Q4-18	C-	C	D+
Q4-17	C	C	C
Q4-16	C	C-	C
Q4-15	C	C-	C

Asset & Performance History

Date	NAV	1-Year Total Return
2018	29.58	1.07
2017	29.87	0.42
2016	30.06	0.89
2015	30.07	0.81
2014	30.07	1.09
2013	29.95	-0.26

Total Assets: $1,656,360,898
Asset Allocation

Asset	%
Cash	0%
Stocks	0%
US Stocks	0%
Bonds	100%
US Bonds	100%
Other	0%

Services Offered:

Investment Strategy: The investment seeks to provide investment results that correspond generally to the price and yield performance of the Bloomberg Barclays 1-3 Year U.S. Treasury Index. The fund invests at least 80%, of its total assets in the securities comprising the index or in securities that the Adviser determines have economic characteristics that are substantially identical to the economic characteristics of the securities that comprise the index. The index is designed to measure the performance of short term (1-3 years) public obligations of the U.S. Treasury. The fund is non-diversified. **Top Holdings:** United States Treasury Notes 1.75% United States Treasury Notes 2.25% United States Treasury Notes 2.25% United States Treasury Notes 2.62% United States Treasury Notes 1.75%

SPDR® Portfolio TIPS ETF   C   HOLD

Ticker	Traded On	NAV	Total Assets ($)	Dividend Yield (TTM)	Turnover Ratio	Expense Ratio
SPIP	NYSE Arca		$1,656,275,698	2.5	14	0.12

Ratings
Reward   C+
Risk   C-
Recent Upgrade/Downgrade

Fund Information
Fund Type   Exchange Traded Funds
Category   US Fixed Income
Sub-Category   Inflation-Protected Bond
Prospectus Objective   Govt Bond - Treasury
Inception Date   May-07
Open to New Investments   Y

Prices
Price (as of 9/30/2019)   28.52
52-Week High   56.80
52-Week Low   28.24

Total Returns (%)

3-Month	6-Month	1-Year	3-Year	5-Year
-49.05	-47.51	-46.15	-46.63	-43.55

3-Year Standard Deviation   3.5
Effective Duration   8.48

Valuation
Premium/Discount (1-Year Average)   0.03

Company Information
Provider   SPDR State Street Global Advisors
Manager/Tenure   Cynthia Moy (4), James Kramer (2),
                 Orhan Imer (1)
Website   http://www.spdrs.com
Address   SPDR State Street Global Advisors
                 State Street Financial Center, 1
                 Lincoln Street Boston MA 02111-2900
                 United States
Phone Number   617-786-3000

PERFORMANCE

Ratings History

Date	Overall Rating	Risk Rating	Reward Rating
Q3-19	C	C-	C+
Q4-18	C-	C	D
Q4-17	C	C+	C
Q4-16	C-	C-	C
Q4-15	D+	C-	D+

Asset & Performance History

Date	NAV	1-Year Total Return
2018	53.89	-1.61
2017	56.3	2.38
2016	56.25	4.6
2015	54.73	-1.86
2014	55.85	4.25
2013	54.45	-9.42

Total Assets: $1,656,275,698
Asset Allocation

Asset	%
Cash	0%
Stocks	0%
US Stocks	0%
Bonds	100%
US Bonds	100%
Other	0%

Services Offered:

Investment Strategy: The investment seeks to provide investment results that correspond generally to the price and yield performance of the Bloomberg Barclays U.S. Government Inflation-Linked Bond Index. The fund generally invests substantially all, but at least 80%, of its total assets in the securities comprising the index or in securities that the adviser determines have economic characteristics that are substantially identical to the economic characteristics of the securities that comprise the index. The index is designed to measure the performance of the inflation protected public obligations of the U.S. Treasury, commonly known as "TIPS." It is non-diversified. **Top Holdings:** United States Treasury Notes 0.12% United States Treasury Notes 0.62% United States Treasury Notes 0.62% United States Treasury Notes 0.12% United States Treasury Notes 0.25%

Xtrackers Harvest CSI 300 China A-Shares ETF   C   HOLD

Ticker	Traded On	NAV	Total Assets ($)	Dividend Yield (TTM)	Turnover Ratio	Expense Ratio
ASHR	NYSE Arca	27.14	$1,655,659,443	1.06	81	0.65

Ratings

Reward	C
Risk	C
Recent Upgrade/Downgrade	

Fund Information

Fund Type	Exchange Traded Funds
Category	Greater China Equity
Sub-Category	China Region
Prospectus Objective	Pacific Stock
Inception Date	Nov-13
Open to New Investments	Y

Prices

Price (as of 9/30/2019)	27.09
52-Week High	30.79
52-Week Low	21.51

Total Returns (%)

3-Month	6-Month	1-Year	3-Year	5-Year
-6.12	-8.24	8.48	13.59	41.29

3-Year Standard Deviation	19.14
Effective Duration	

Valuation

Premium/Discount (1-Year Average)	0.17

Company Information

Provider	DWS
Manager/Tenure	Tom Chan (0), Kevin Sung (0)
Website	http://dws.com
Address	DWS 210 West 10th Street Kansas City MO 64105-1614 United States
Phone Number	

PERFORMANCE

Ratings History

Date	Overall Rating	Risk Rating	Reward Rating
Q3-19	C	C	C
Q4-18	D	D	D
Q4-17	B	C	A-
Q4-16	C-	D+	C
Q4-15	D+	C	C

Asset & Performance History

Date	NAV	1-Year Total Return
2018	22	-28.18
2017	30.96	31.8
2016	23.69	-15.06
2015	28.09	0.07
2014	36.54	49.69
2013	24.48	

Total Assets: $1,655,659,443

Asset Allocation

Asset	%
Cash	0%
Stocks	100%
US Stocks	0%
Bonds	0%
US Bonds	0%
Other	0%

Services Offered:

Investment Strategy: The investment seeks investment results that correspond generally to the performance, before fees and expenses, of the CSI 300 Index. The fund will normally invest at least 80% of its total assets in securities of issuers that comprise the underlying index. The underlying index is designed to reflect the price fluctuation and performance of the China A-Share market and is composed of the 300 largest and most liquid stocks in the China A-Share market. The underlying index includes small-cap, mid-cap, and large-cap stocks. **Top Holdings:** Ping An Insurance (Group) Co. of China Ltd Kweichow Moutai Co Ltd China Merchants Bank Co Ltd Wuliangye Yibin Co Ltd Gree Electric Appliances Inc of Zhuhai

---

Invesco S&P 500® Equal Weight Technology ETF   C   HOLD

Ticker	Traded On	NAV	Total Assets ($)	Dividend Yield (TTM)	Turnover Ratio	Expense Ratio
RYT	NYSE Arca	178.86	$1,654,488,104	0.99		0.4

Ratings

Reward	C+
Risk	C-
Recent Upgrade/Downgrade	Down

Fund Information

Fund Type	Exchange Traded Funds
Category	Technology Sector Equity
Sub-Category	Technology
Prospectus Objective	Technology
Inception Date	Nov-06
Open to New Investments	Y

Prices

Price (as of 9/30/2019)	178.82
52-Week High	188.04
52-Week Low	131.48

Total Returns (%)

3-Month	6-Month	1-Year	3-Year	5-Year
-0.78	3.56	7.56	74.33	126.79

3-Year Standard Deviation	16.05
Effective Duration	

Valuation

Premium/Discount (1-Year Average)	-0.01

Company Information

Provider	Invesco
Manager/Tenure	Peter Hubbard (1), Michael Jeanette (1), Tony Seisser (1)
Website	http://www.invesco.com/us
Address	Invesco 11 Greenway Plaza, Ste. 2500 Houston TX 77046 United States
Phone Number	800-659-1005

PERFORMANCE

Ratings History

Date	Overall Rating	Risk Rating	Reward Rating
Q3-19	C	C-	C+
Q4-18	C	C+	C
Q4-17	A-	B	A+
Q4-16	C+	C+	B-
Q4-15	C+	C+	C

Asset & Performance History

Date	NAV	1-Year Total Return
2018	140.89	-0.57
2017	142.97	32.8
2016	108.47	18.57
2015	92.33	2.95
2014	90.76	19.2
2013	77.06	40.17

Total Assets: $1,654,488,104

Asset Allocation

Asset	%
Cash	0%
Stocks	100%
US Stocks	99%
Bonds	0%
US Bonds	0%
Other	0%

Services Offered:

Investment Strategy: The investment seeks to track the investment results (before fees and expenses) of the S&P 500® Equal Weight Information Technology Index (the "underlying index"). The fund generally will invest at least 90% of its total assets in the securities that comprise the underlying index. The underlying index is composed of all of the components of the S&P 500® Information Technology Index, an index that contains the common stocks of all companies included in the S&P 500® Index that are classified as members of the information technology services sector, as defined according to the Global Industry Classification Standard ("GICS"). The fund is non-diversified. **Top Holdings:** Western Digital Corp Micron Technology Inc KLA Corp Symantec Corp Fiserv Inc

SPDR® S&P 400 Mid Cap Growth ETF   D   SELL

Ticker	Traded On	NAV	Total Assets ($)	Dividend Yield (TTM)	Turnover Ratio	Expense Ratio
MDYG	NYSE Arca		$1,643,147,370	1.26	38	0.15

Ratings
Reward	D
Risk	D
Recent Upgrade/Downgrade	Up

Fund Information
Fund Type	Exchange Traded Funds
Category	US Equity Mid Cap
Sub-Category	Mid-Cap Growth
Prospectus Objective	Growth
Inception Date	Nov-05
Open to New Investments	Y

Prices
Price (as of 9/30/2019)	53.72
52-Week High	55.46
52-Week Low	43.09

Total Returns (%)

3-Month	6-Month	1-Year	3-Year	5-Year
-1.65	1.10	-2.45	-56.05	-48.09

3-Year Standard Deviation	14.48
Effective Duration	

Valuation
Premium/Discount (1-Year Average)	0.01

Company Information
Provider	SPDR State Street Global Advisors
Manager/Tenure	Michael J. Feehily (7), Karl A. Schneider (4), Juan Acevedo (0)
Website	http://www.spdrs.com
Address	SPDR State Street Global Advisors State Street Financial Center, 1 Lincoln Street Boston MA 02111-2900 United States
Phone Number	617-786-3000

PERFORMANCE

Ratings History

Date	Overall Rating	Risk Rating	Reward Rating
Q3-19	D	D	D
Q4-18	D-	D	E+
Q4-17	B+	B+	B+
Q4-16	C+	C-	B
Q4-15	C	C-	C+

Asset & Performance History

Date	NAV	1-Year Total Return
2018	45.84	-70.14
2017	155.44	19.73
2016	132.81	13.84
2015	117.43	1.96
2014	118.05	7.38
2013	111.71	32.45

Total Assets: $1,643,147,370

Asset Allocation

Asset	%
Cash	0%
Stocks	100%
US Stocks	100%
Bonds	0%
US Bonds	0%
Other	0%

Services Offered: Dividend Investment Plan, CashInvestment Plan

Investment Strategy: The investment seeks to provide investment results that, before fees and expenses, correspond generally to the total return performance of the S&P MidCap 400 Growth Index that tracks the performance of medium capitalization exchange traded U.S. equity securities exhibiting "growth" characteristics. The fund generally invests substantially all, but at least 80%, of its total assets in the securities comprising the index. The index measures the performance of the mid-capitalization growth segment of the U.S. equity market. The fund is non-diversified. **Top Holdings:** Steris PLC Zebra Technologies Corp West Pharmaceutical Services Inc FactSet Research Systems Inc Fair Isaac Corp

First Trust NYSE Arca Biotechnology Index Fund   C   HOLD

Ticker	Traded On	NAV	Total Assets ($)	Dividend Yield (TTM)	Turnover Ratio	Expense Ratio
FBT	NYSE Arca	123.89	$1,641,485,115	0	37	0.57

Ratings
Reward	C
Risk	D+
Recent Upgrade/Downgrade	

Fund Information
Fund Type	Exchange Traded Funds
Category	Healthcare Sector Equity
Sub-Category	Health
Prospectus Objective	Health
Inception Date	Jun-06
Open to New Investments	Y

Prices
Price (as of 9/30/2019)	123.77
52-Week High	157.53
52-Week Low	114.50

Total Returns (%)

3-Month	6-Month	1-Year	3-Year	5-Year
-12.35	-18.01	-21.31	24.27	37.02

3-Year Standard Deviation	24.35
Effective Duration	

Valuation
Premium/Discount (1-Year Average)	-0.02

Company Information
Provider	First Trust
Manager/Tenure	Jon C. Erickson (13), Daniel J. Lindquist (13), David G. McGarel (13), 3 others
Website	http://www.ftportfolios.com/
Address	First Trust 120 E. Liberty Drive, Suite 400 Wheaton IL 60187 United States
Phone Number	800-621-1675

PERFORMANCE

Ratings History

Date	Overall Rating	Risk Rating	Reward Rating
Q3-19	C	D+	C
Q4-18	C	D+	C
Q4-17	B	C+	B
Q4-16	C	D+	C
Q4-15	C+	C	B-

Asset & Performance History

Date	NAV	1-Year Total Return
2018	124.25	-0.2
2017	124.51	36.98
2016	90.89	-19.6
2015	113.05	10.96
2014	101.99	47.63
2013	69.12	50.09

Total Assets: $1,641,485,115

Asset Allocation

Asset	%
Cash	0%
Stocks	100%
US Stocks	97%
Bonds	0%
US Bonds	0%
Other	0%

Services Offered:

Investment Strategy: The investment seeks investment results that correspond generally to the price and yield (before the fund's fees and expenses) of an equity index called the NYSE Arca Biotechnology IndexSM. The fund will normally invest at least 90% of its net assets (including investment borrowings) in the common stocks and depositary receipts that comprise the index. The index is an equal-dollar weighted index designed to measure the performance of a cross section of small, mid and large capitalization companies in the biotechnology industry that are primarily involved in the use of biological processes to develop products or provide services. **Top Holdings:** Amgen Inc Neurocrine Biosciences Inc ACADIA Pharmaceuticals Inc United Therapeutics Corp Alnylam Pharmaceuticals Inc

Credit Suisse FI Large Cap Growth Enhanced ETN

C   HOLD

Ticker	Traded On	NAV	Total Assets ($)	Dividend Yield (TTM)	Turnover Ratio	Expense Ratio
FLGE	NYSE Arca		$1,639,348,973	0		0.85

Ratings

Reward	C+
Risk	D+
Recent Upgrade/Downgrade	

Fund Information

Fund Type	Exchange Traded Funds
Category	US Equity Large Cap Growth
Sub-Category	Large Growth
Prospectus Objective	Growth
Inception Date	Jun-14
Open to New Investments	Y

Prices

Price (as of 9/30/2019)	276.46
52-Week High	300.04
52-Week Low	167.09

Total Returns (%)

3-Month	6-Month	1-Year	3-Year	5-Year
-1.33	6.31	-8.97	99.42	162.94

3-Year Standard Deviation	27.91
Effective Duration	

Valuation

Premium/Discount (1-Year Average)	-0.06

Company Information

Provider	Credit Suisse AG
Manager/Tenure	Not Disclosed (5)
Website	
Address	Kilmore House Park Lane Dublin Ireland
Phone Number	

PERFORMANCE

Ratings History

Date	Overall Rating	Risk Rating	Reward Rating
Q3-19	C	D+	C+
Q4-18	C-	D+	C
Q4-17	A	B	A+
Q4-16	C	C-	C+
Q4-15	D	D+	D

Asset & Performance History

Date	NAV	1-Year Total Return
2018	188.35	-16.81
2017	226.42	62.43
2016	138.96	11.77
2015	123.56	8.95
2014	113.4	
2013		

Total Assets: $1,639,348,973

Asset Allocation

Asset	%
Cash	%
Stocks	%
US Stocks	%
Bonds	%
US Bonds	%
Other	%

Services Offered:

Investment Strategy: The investment seeks a leveraged return linked to the performance of the Russell 1000® Growth Index Total Return (the "index"), an index that seeks to track the performance of the large-cap growth segment of the U.S. equity market.
The ETNs are subject to a leverage factor of 2.0, but the effective leverage will vary with changes in the Closing Indicative Value of the ETNs since the previous Rebalance Event. **Top Holdings:**

---

iShares Expanded Tech Sector ETF

C+   HOLD

Ticker	Traded On	NAV	Total Assets ($)	Dividend Yield (TTM)	Turnover Ratio	Expense Ratio
IGM	NYSE Arca	217.05	$1,638,695,393	0.52	8	0.46

Ratings

Reward	B
Risk	C
Recent Upgrade/Downgrade	

Fund Information

Fund Type	Exchange Traded Funds
Category	Technology Sector Equity
Sub-Category	Technology
Prospectus Objective	Technology
Inception Date	Mar-01
Open to New Investments	Y

Prices

Price (as of 9/30/2019)	217.02
52-Week High	228.47
52-Week Low	159.35

Total Returns (%)

3-Month	6-Month	1-Year	3-Year	5-Year
-0.65	3.97	4.08	78.67	134.34

3-Year Standard Deviation	16.07
Effective Duration	

Valuation

Premium/Discount (1-Year Average)	-0.03

Company Information

Provider	iShares
Manager/Tenure	Greg Savage (11), Jennifer Hsui (6), Alan Mason (3), 2 others
Website	http://www.ishares.com
Address	iShares 400 Howard Street San Francisco CA 94105 United States
Phone Number	800-474-2737

PERFORMANCE

Ratings History

Date	Overall Rating	Risk Rating	Reward Rating
Q3-19	C+	C	B
Q4-18	C	C	C+
Q4-17	A-	B	A+
Q4-16	C	C	C+
Q4-15	C+	C	B-

Asset & Performance History

Date	NAV	1-Year Total Return
2018	172.02	2.53
2017	168.64	37.11
2016	123.78	13.03
2015	110.57	9.41
2014	101.89	14.74
2013	89.61	33.94

Total Assets: $1,638,695,393

Asset Allocation

Asset	%
Cash	0%
Stocks	100%
US Stocks	99%
Bonds	0%
US Bonds	0%
Other	0%

Services Offered: CashInvestment Plan

Investment Strategy: The investment seeks to track the investment results of an index composed of North American equities in the technology sector and select North American equities from communication services and consumer discretionary sectors. The fund invests at least 90% of its assets in securities of the index and in depositary receipts representing securities of the index. The index measures the performance of U.S.-traded stocks from the technology sector and select technology-related companies from the communication services and consumer discretionary sectors in the U.S. and Canada. The fund is non-diversified. **Top Holdings:** Apple Inc Microsoft Corp Amazon.com Inc Facebook Inc A Alphabet Inc Class C

UBS AG FI Enhanced Global High Yield ETN   C   HOLD

Ticker	Traded On	NAV	Total Assets ($)	Dividend Yield (TTM)	Turnover Ratio	Expense Ratio
FIHD	NYSE Arca	183.11	$1,627,889,683	0		0.8

Ratings
Reward   C
Risk   C-
Recent Upgrade/Downgrade

Fund Information
Fund Type   Exchange Traded Funds
Category   Global Equity Large Cap
Sub-Category   World Large Stock
Prospectus Objective   Convertible Bond
Inception Date   Feb-16
Open to New Investments   Y

Prices
Price (as of 9/30/2019)   183.30
52-Week High   186.08
52-Week Low   129.64

Total Returns (%)

3-Month	6-Month	1-Year	3-Year	5-Year
0.72	5.75	5.48	44.93	

3-Year Standard Deviation   20.02
Effective Duration

Valuation
Premium/Discount (1-Year Average)   -0.06

Company Information
Provider   UBS Group AG
Manager/Tenure   No Manager (3)
Website   http://www.ubs.com
Address   Bahnhofstrasse 45 Zürich 8098
                      Switzerland
Phone Number   412-037-1952

PERFORMANCE

Ratings History

Date	Overall Rating	Risk Rating	Reward Rating
Q3-19	C	C-	C
Q4-18	C-	C-	D+
Q4-17	C-	B	C
Q4-16	U		
Q4-15			

Asset & Performance History

Date	NAV	1-Year Total Return
2018	141.86	-17.41
2017	171.78	37.38
2016	125.18	
2015		
2014		
2013		

Total Assets: $1,627,889,683
Asset Allocation

Asset	%
Cash	%
Stocks	%
US Stocks	%
Bonds	%
US Bonds	%
Other	%

Services Offered:

Investment Strategy: The investment seeks a return linked to the MSCI World High Dividend Yield USD Gross Total Return Index.
 The ETN is a series of FI Enhanced ETNs. The Securities are senior unsecured debt securities issued by UBS AG. The Securities are designed to provide a two times leveraged long exposure to the performance of the index compounded on a quarterly basis, reduced by the Accrued Fees. The index is designed to track the performance of large- and mid-cap stocks (excluding REITS) across 23 developed markets countries tracked by the MSCI World Index with higher than average dividend yields that are potentially both sustainable and persistent. **Top Holdings:**

---

iShares Europe ETF   C   HOLD

Ticker	Traded On	NAV	Total Assets ($)	Dividend Yield (TTM)	Turnover Ratio	Expense Ratio
IEV	NYSE Arca	43.33	$1,622,814,193	3.27	7	0.59

Ratings
Reward   C
Risk   C+
Recent Upgrade/Downgrade

Fund Information
Fund Type   Exchange Traded Funds
Category   Europe Equity Large Cap
Sub-Category   Europe Stock
Prospectus Objective   Europe Stock
Inception Date   Jul-00
Open to New Investments   Y

Prices
Price (as of 9/30/2019)   43.27
52-Week High   45.05
52-Week Low   37.89

Total Returns (%)

3-Month	6-Month	1-Year	3-Year	5-Year
-2.05	1.35	-0.84	20.20	11.96

3-Year Standard Deviation   12.51
Effective Duration

Valuation
Premium/Discount (1-Year Average)   -0.12

Company Information
Provider   iShares
Manager/Tenure   Greg Savage (11), Jennifer Hsui (7),
                      Alan Mason (3), 2 others
Website   http://www.ishares.com
Address   iShares 400 Howard Street San
                      Francisco CA 94105 United States
Phone Number   800-474-2737

PERFORMANCE

Ratings History

Date	Overall Rating	Risk Rating	Reward Rating
Q3-19	C	C+	C
Q4-18	D+	C-	D+
Q4-17	B-	B-	B-
Q4-16	D	C-	D
Q4-15	C	C+	C-

Asset & Performance History

Date	NAV	1-Year Total Return
2018	39.15	-15.01
2017	47.5	24.94
2016	38.98	-0.45
2015	40.37	-3.36
2014	42.84	-6.07
2013	47.16	25.17

Total Assets: $1,622,814,193
Asset Allocation

Asset	%
Cash	1%
Stocks	99%
US Stocks	2%
Bonds	0%
US Bonds	0%
Other	0%

Services Offered: CashInvestment Plan

Investment Strategy: The investment seeks to track the investment results of the S&P Europe 350TM, which measures the performance of the stocks of leading companies in the following countries: Austria, Belgium, Denmark, Finland, France, Germany, Ireland, Italy, Luxembourg, the Netherlands, Norway, Portugal, Spain, Sweden, Switzerland and the United Kingdom. The fund generally invests at least 90% of its assets in securities of the index and in depositary receipts representing securities of the index. It may invest the remainder of its assets in certain futures, options and swap contracts, cash and cash equivalents, as well as in securities not included in the index.
Top Holdings: Nestle SA   Novartis AG   Roche Holding AG Dividend Right Cert.   HSBC Holdings PLC   SAP SE

Invesco S&P Ultra Dividend Revenue ETF

C   HOLD

Ticker	Traded On	NAV	Total Assets ($)	Dividend Yield (TTM)	Turnover Ratio	Expense Ratio
RDIV	NYSE Arca	37.70	$1,620,981,776	3.61	122	0.39

Ratings
Reward	C+
Risk	C-
Recent Upgrade/Downgrade	

Fund Information
Fund Type	Exchange Traded Funds
Category	US Equity Large Cap Value
Sub-Category	Large Value
Prospectus Objective	Growth
Inception Date	Sep-13
Open to New Investments	Y

Prices
Price (as of 9/30/2019)	37.69
52-Week High	39.32
52-Week Low	32.38

Total Returns (%)
3-Month	6-Month	1-Year	3-Year	5-Year
1.01	0.56	0.69	30.82	65.09

3-Year Standard Deviation	14.9
Effective Duration	

Valuation
Premium/Discount (1-Year Average)	-0.02

Company Information
Provider	Invesco
Manager/Tenure	Peter Hubbard (0), Michael Jeanette (0), Tony Seisser (0)
Website	http://www.invesco.com/us
Address	Invesco 11 Greenway Plaza, Ste. 2500 Houston TX 77046 United States
Phone Number	800-659-1005

PERFORMANCE

Ratings History
Date	Overall Rating	Risk Rating	Reward Rating
Q3-19	C	C-	C+
Q4-18	C	C	C
Q4-17	B	B	B+
Q4-16	C	D+	B-
Q4-15	C-	C	B

Asset & Performance History
Date	NAV	1-Year Total Return
2018	33.53	-4.47
2017	36.51	11.49
2016	34.24	28.5
2015	27.56	-5.21
2014	30.34	21.4
2013	25.87	

Total Assets: $1,620,981,776

Asset Allocation
Asset	%
Cash	0%
Stocks	100%
US Stocks	100%
Bonds	0%
US Bonds	0%
Other	0%

Services Offered:

Investment Strategy: The investment seeks to track the investment results (before fees and expenses) of the S&P 900® Dividend Revenue-Weighted Index (the "underlying index"). The fund generally will invest at least 90% of its total assets in the securities that comprise the underlying index. The underlying index is constructed using a rules-based methodology that selects components from the S&P 900® Index (the "parent index"), which combines the S&P 500® Index and S&P MidCap® 400 Index to form an investable benchmark for the large- and mid-cap universe of the U.S. equity market. The fund is non-diversified. **Top Holdings:** Verizon Communications Inc AbbVie Inc Cardinal Health Inc Exxon Mobil Corp General Motors Co

---

PIMCO 0-5 Year High Yield Corporate Bond Index Exchange-Traded Fund

C+   HOLD

Ticker	Traded On	NAV	Total Assets ($)	Dividend Yield (TTM)	Turnover Ratio	Expense Ratio
HYS	NYSE Arca	99.88	$1,618,048,087	4.95	27	0.56

Ratings
Reward	C
Risk	C+
Recent Upgrade/Downgrade	

Fund Information
Fund Type	Exchange Traded Funds
Category	US Fixed Income
Sub-Category	High Yield Bond
Prospectus Objective	Corp Bond-High Yld
Inception Date	Jun-11
Open to New Investments	Y

Prices
Price (as of 9/30/2019)	99.76
52-Week High	100.83
52-Week Low	94.14

Total Returns (%)
3-Month	6-Month	1-Year	3-Year	5-Year
0.33	2.16	3.90	16.61	23.67

3-Year Standard Deviation	3.34
Effective Duration	1.61

Valuation
Premium/Discount (1-Year Average)	-0.24

Company Information
Provider	PIMCO
Manager/Tenure	Matthew P. Dorsten (3), Mitchell Handa (0), Graham A. Rennison (0)
Website	http://www.pimco.com
Address	PIMCO 840 Newport Center Drive, Suite 100 Newport Beach CA 92660 United States
Phone Number	866-746-2602

PERFORMANCE

Ratings History
Date	Overall Rating	Risk Rating	Reward Rating
Q3-19	C+	C+	C
Q4-18	C	C+	C-
Q4-17	B-	B	C+
Q4-16	C+	C+	C
Q4-15	C	C+	C-

Asset & Performance History
Date	NAV	1-Year Total Return
2018	95.44	-0.55
2017	100.64	5.83
2016	99.93	14.61
2015	92.02	-4.7
2014	101.36	0.49
2013	106.26	8.26

Total Assets: $1,618,048,087

Asset Allocation
Asset	%
Cash	0%
Stocks	0%
US Stocks	0%
Bonds	96%
US Bonds	80%
Other	4%

Services Offered:

Investment Strategy: The investment seeks to provide total return that closely corresponds, before fees and expenses, to the total return of the ICE BofAML 0-5 Year US High Yield Constrained Index. The fund invests under normal circumstances at least 80% of its total assets (exclusive of collateral held from securities lending) in the component securities of the ICE BofAML 0-5 Year US High Yield Constrained Index. The underlying index is an unmanaged index comprised of U.S. dollar denominated below investment grade corporate debt securities publicly issued in the U.S. domestic market with remaining maturities of less than 5 years. **Top Holdings:** Cdx Hy32 5y Ice Fin Fut Us 5yr Cbt 12/31/19 Fin Fut Us 2yr Cbt 12/31/19 Trs Iboxhy/3ml Indx 12/20/19 Jpm Sprint Corporation 7.88%

First Trust Senior Loan Fund   C   HOLD

Ticker	Traded On	NAV	Total Assets ($)	Dividend Yield (TTM)	Turnover Ratio	Expense Ratio
FTSL	NAS CM	47.38	$1,606,244,000	4.57	88	0.87

Ratings
Reward	C
Risk	C+
Recent Upgrade/Downgrade	Down

Fund Information
Fund Type	Exchange Traded Funds
Category	US Fixed Income
Sub-Category	Bank Loan
Prospectus Objective	Income
Inception Date	May-13
Open to New Investments	Y

Prices
Price (as of 9/30/2019)	47.41
52-Week High	48.15
52-Week Low	45.42

Total Returns (%)
3-Month	6-Month	1-Year	3-Year	5-Year
1.38	2.56	3.32	10.58	18.02

3-Year Standard Deviation	3.03
Effective Duration	0.40

Valuation
Premium/Discount (1-Year Average)	-0.05

Company Information
Provider	First Trust
Manager/Tenure	Scott D. Fries (6), William Housey (6)
Website	http://www.ftportfolios.com/
Address	First Trust 120 E. Liberty Drive, Suite 400 Wheaton IL 60187 United States
Phone Number	800-621-1675

PERFORMANCE

Ratings History
Date	Overall Rating	Risk Rating	Reward Rating
Q3-19	C	C+	C
Q4-18	C	C+	C-
Q4-17	B-	B	C
Q4-16	C	C-	C
Q4-15	C	C-	C

Asset & Performance History
Date	NAV	1-Year Total Return
2018	45.73	-0.83
2017	48.04	2.85
2016	48.43	7.09
2015	46.95	0.31
2014	48.62	1.9
2013	49.5	

Total Assets: $1,606,244,000

Asset Allocation
Asset	%
Cash	4%
Stocks	0%
US Stocks	0%
Bonds	96%
US Bonds	89%
Other	0%

Services Offered:

Investment Strategy: The investment seeks to provide high current income; the fund's secondary investment objective is the preservation of capital. Under normal market conditions, the fund seeks to outperform each of the primary index and secondary index by investing at least 80% of its net assets in first lien senior floating rate bank loans. The S&P/LSTA U.S. Leveraged Loan 100 Index (the "primary index") is a market value-weighted index designed to measure the performance of the largest segment of the U.S. syndicated leveraged loan market. The Markit iBoxx USD Liquid Leveraged Loan Index (the "secondary index") selects the 100 most liquid Senior Loans in the market. **Top Holdings:** Valeant Pharma Vrxcn TI 06/02/25   Hub International Ltd Hbgcn TI 04/25/25 Reynolds Group Holdings Reynol 02/05/23   Alixpartners Llp Alixpa TI 04/04/24   First Trust Enhanced Short Maturity ETF

iShares U.S. Financials ETF   C+   HOLD

Ticker	Traded On	NAV	Total Assets ($)	Dividend Yield (TTM)	Turnover Ratio	Expense Ratio
IYF	NYSE Arca	128.63	$1,601,476,067	1.78	8	0.42

Ratings
Reward	C+
Risk	C+
Recent Upgrade/Downgrade	

Fund Information
Fund Type	Exchange Traded Funds
Category	Financials Sector Equity
Sub-Category	Financial
Prospectus Objective	Financial
Inception Date	May-00
Open to New Investments	Y

Prices
Price (as of 9/30/2019)	128.73
52-Week High	130.38
52-Week Low	100.04

Total Returns (%)
3-Month	6-Month	1-Year	3-Year	5-Year
2.11	8.03	7.97	50.62	69.26

3-Year Standard Deviation	13.56
Effective Duration	

Valuation
Premium/Discount (1-Year Average)	-0.01

Company Information
Provider	iShares
Manager/Tenure	Greg Savage (11), Jennifer Hsui (7), Alan Mason (3), 2 others
Website	http://www.ishares.com
Address	iShares 400 Howard Street San Francisco CA 94105 United States
Phone Number	800-474-2737

PERFORMANCE

Ratings History
Date	Overall Rating	Risk Rating	Reward Rating
Q3-19	C+	C+	C+
Q4-18	C	C+	C
Q4-17	B+	B	A-
Q4-16	B-	C+	B
Q4-15	B-	B-	B-

Asset & Performance History
Date	NAV	1-Year Total Return
2018	106.38	-9.25
2017	119.29	19.54
2016	101.38	16.81
2015	88.41	-0.3
2014	90.16	14.11
2013	80.17	33.59

Total Assets: $1,601,476,067

Asset Allocation
Asset	%
Cash	0%
Stocks	100%
US Stocks	98%
Bonds	0%
US Bonds	0%
Other	0%

Services Offered: CashInvestment Plan

Investment Strategy: The investment seeks to track the investment results of the Dow Jones U.S. Financials Capped Index composed of U.S. equities in the financial sector. The fund generally invests at least 90% of its assets in securities of the underlying index and in depositary receipts representing securities of the underlying index. The underlying index measures the performance of U.S. companies in the financial sector. **Top Holdings:** Berkshire Hathaway Inc B   JPMorgan Chase & Co   Visa Inc Class A   Mastercard Inc A   Bank of America Corporation

WisdomTree Emerging Markets SmallCap Dividend Fund   C   HOLD

Ticker	Traded On	NAV	Total Assets ($)	Dividend Yield (TTM)	Turnover Ratio	Expense Ratio
DGS	NYSE Arca	44.27	$1,589,174,994	4.1	40	0.63

Ratings

Reward	C
Risk	C
Recent Upgrade/Downgrade	Up

Fund Information

Fund Type	Exchange Traded Funds
Category	Global Emerg Mkts Equity
Sub-Category	Diversified Emerging Mkts
Prospectus Objective	Div Emerg Mkts
Inception Date	Oct-07
Open to New Investments	Y

Prices

Price (as of 9/30/2019)	44.30
52-Week High	48.79
52-Week Low	40.12

Total Returns (%)

3-Month	6-Month	1-Year	3-Year	5-Year
-4.71	-4.30	0.29	19.44	13.25

3-Year Standard Deviation	13.76
Effective Duration	

Valuation

Premium/Discount (1-Year Average)	0.02

Company Information

Provider	WisdomTree
Manager/Tenure	Richard A. Brown (11), Thomas J. Durante (11), Karen Q. Wong (11)
Website	http://www.wisdomtree.com
Address	WisdomTree 245 Park Avenue, 35th floor New York NY 10167 United States
Phone Number	866-909-9473

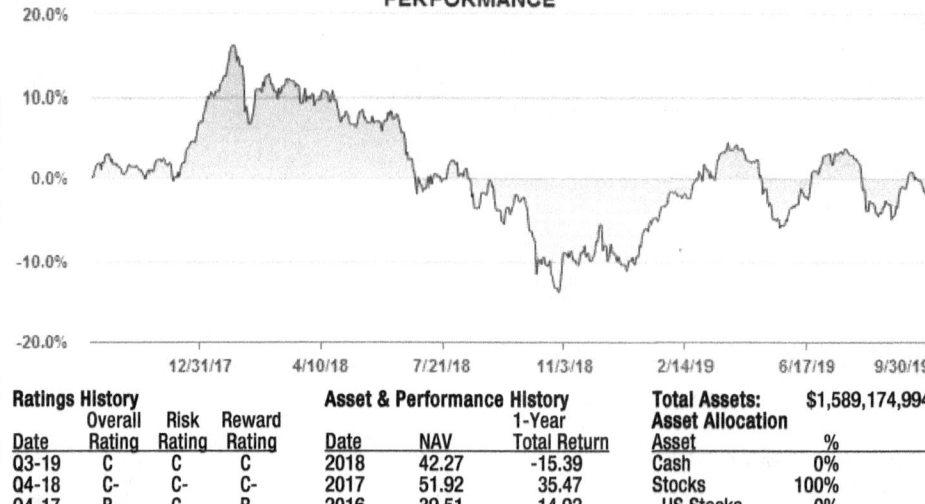

PERFORMANCE

Ratings History

Date	Overall Rating	Risk Rating	Reward Rating
Q3-19	C	C	C
Q4-18	C-	C	C-
Q4-17	B-	C	B
Q4-16	C-	C	D+
Q4-15	D	D+	D

Asset & Performance History

Date	NAV	1-Year Total Return
2018	42.27	-15.39
2017	51.92	35.47
2016	39.51	14.92
2015	35.56	-15.94
2014	43.56	-1.96
2013	45.77	-2.56

Total Assets: $1,589,174,994

Asset Allocation

Asset	%
Cash	0%
Stocks	100%
US Stocks	0%
Bonds	0%
US Bonds	0%
Other	0%

Services Offered:

Investment Strategy: The investment seeks to track the price and yield performance, before fees and expenses, of the WisdomTree Emerging Markets SmallCap Dividend Index. Under normal circumstances, at least 95% of the fund's total assets (exclusive of collateral held from securities lending) will be invested in component securities of the index and investments that have economic characteristics that are substantially identical to the economic characteristics of such component securities. The index is a fundamentally weighted index that is comprised of small cap common stocks selected from the WisdomTree Emerging Markets Dividend Index. The fund is non-diversified. **Top Holdings:** Transmissora Alianca de Energia Eletrica SA Unit Guangzhou R&F Properties Co Ltd Class H Qualicorp Consultoria E Corretora De Seguros SA WisdomTree Emerging Markets High Div ETF Moneta Money Bank AS

ARK Innovation ETF   C-   HOLD

Ticker	Traded On	NAV	Total Assets ($)	Dividend Yield (TTM)	Turnover Ratio	Expense Ratio
ARKK	NYSE Arca	42.93	$1,579,767,169	0		0.75

Ratings

Reward	C
Risk	D+
Recent Upgrade/Downgrade	Down

Fund Information

Fund Type	Exchange Traded Funds
Category	Technology Sector Equity
Sub-Category	Technology
Prospectus Objective	Unaligned
Inception Date	Oct-14
Open to New Investments	Y

Prices

Price (as of 9/30/2019)	42.89
52-Week High	49.92
52-Week Low	35.34

Total Returns (%)

3-Month	6-Month	1-Year	3-Year	5-Year
-10.50	-9.41	-6.47	102.65	

3-Year Standard Deviation	27.27
Effective Duration	

Valuation

Premium/Discount (1-Year Average)	0.03

Company Information

Provider	ARK ETF Trust
Manager/Tenure	Catherine D. Wood (4)
Website	http://www.ark-funds.com
Address	ARK ETF Trust 155 West 19th Street, 5th Floor New York New York 10011 United States
Phone Number	212-426-7040

PERFORMANCE

Ratings History

Date	Overall Rating	Risk Rating	Reward Rating
Q3-19	C-	D+	C
Q4-18	C-	D+	C
Q4-17	B-	C+	B
Q4-16	D+	D+	C-
Q4-15	U		

Asset & Performance History

Date	NAV	1-Year Total Return
2018	37.18	0.56
2017	37.05	87.38
2016	20.03	-1.95
2015	20.43	3.75
2014	20.13	
2013		

Total Assets: $1,579,767,169

Asset Allocation

Asset	%
Cash	0%
Stocks	100%
US Stocks	84%
Bonds	0%
US Bonds	0%
Other	0%

Services Offered:

Investment Strategy: The investment seeks long-term growth of capital. The fund is an actively-managed exchange-traded fund ("ETF") that will invest under normal circumstances primarily (at least 65% of its assets) in domestic and foreign equity securities of companies that are relevant to the fund's investment theme of disruptive innovation. Its investments in foreign equity securities will be in both developed and emerging markets. It may invest in foreign securities (including investments in American Depositary Receipts ("ADRs") and Global Depositary Receipts ("GDRs")) and securities listed on local foreign exchanges. The fund is non-diversified. **Top Holdings:** Tesla Inc Stratasys Ltd Invitae Corp Illumina Inc Square Inc A

SPDR® S&P Bank ETF   C   HOLD

Ticker	Traded On	NAV	Total Assets ($)	Dividend Yield (TTM)	Turnover Ratio	Expense Ratio
KBE	NYSE Arca		$1,577,157,606	2.39	24	0.35

Ratings
Reward   C
Risk   C+
Recent Upgrade/Downgrade

Fund Information
Fund Type   Exchange Traded Funds
Category   Financials Sector Equity
Sub-Category   Financial
Prospectus Objective   Financial
Inception Date   Nov-05
Open to New Investments   Y

Prices
Price (as of 9/30/2019)   43.16
52-Week High   47.44
52-Week Low   35.17

Total Returns (%)

3-Month	6-Month	1-Year	3-Year	5-Year
-0.32	2.10	-4.28	36.95	48.58

3-Year Standard Deviation   23.35
Effective Duration

Valuation
Premium/Discount (1-Year Average)   0.01

Company Information
Provider   SPDR State Street Global Advisors
Manager/Tenure   Michael J. Feehily (7), Karl A. Schneider (4), Melissa Kapitulik (0)
Website   http://www.spdrs.com
Address   SPDR State Street Global Advisors State Street Financial Center, 1 Lincoln Street Boston MA 02111-2900 United States
Phone Number   617-786-3000

PERFORMANCE

Ratings History

Date	Overall Rating	Risk Rating	Reward Rating
Q3-19	C	C+	C
Q4-18	C-	C	C-
Q4-17	B+	C+	A
Q4-16	B-	C	B
Q4-15	B	B-	B

Asset & Performance History

Date	NAV	1-Year Total Return
2018	37.34	-19.58
2017	47.31	10.35
2016	43.49	29.17
2015	33.85	2.64
2014	33.54	2.67
2013	33.18	41.53

Total Assets: $1,577,157,606
Asset Allocation

Asset	%
Cash	0%
Stocks	100%
US Stocks	98%
Bonds	0%
US Bonds	0%
Other	0%

Services Offered: Dividend Investment Plan, CashInvestment Plan

Investment Strategy: The investment seeks to provide investment results that, before fees and expenses, correspond generally to the total return performance of the S&P Banks Select Industry Index. The fund generally invests substantially all, but at least 80%, of its total assets in the securities comprising the index. The index tracks the performance of publicly traded national money centers and leading regional banks. It may invest in equity securities that are not included in the index, cash and cash equivalents or money market instruments, such as repurchase agreements and money market funds. The fund is non-diversified. **Top Holdings:** New York Community Bancorp Inc First Horizon National Corp Synovus Financial Corp Wells Fargo & Co Northern Trust Corp

Goldman Sachs ActiveBeta® International Equity ETF   C   HOLD

Ticker	Traded On	NAV	Total Assets ($)	Dividend Yield (TTM)	Turnover Ratio	Expense Ratio
GSIE	NYSE Arca	28.25	$1,576,252,149	2.93	16	0.25

Ratings
Reward   C
Risk   C+
Recent Upgrade/Downgrade

Fund Information
Fund Type   Exchange Traded Funds
Category   Global Equity Large Cap
Sub-Category   Foreign Large Blend
Prospectus Objective   Foreign Stock
Inception Date   Nov-15
Open to New Investments   Y

Prices
Price (as of 9/30/2019)   28.29
52-Week High   29.60
52-Week Low   24.56

Total Returns (%)

3-Month	6-Month	1-Year	3-Year	5-Year
-1.25	1.76	-1.21	21.92	

3-Year Standard Deviation   10.88
Effective Duration

Valuation
Premium/Discount (1-Year Average)   0.12

Company Information
Provider   Goldman Sachs
Manager/Tenure   Raj Garigipati (3), Jamie McGregor (3)
Website   http://www.gsamfunds.com
Address   Goldman Sachs 200 West Stree New York NY 10282 United States
Phone Number   800-526-7384

PERFORMANCE

Ratings History

Date	Overall Rating	Risk Rating	Reward Rating
Q3-19	C	C+	C
Q4-18	C-	C	D+
Q4-17	C	B+	C
Q4-16	D	C-	D
Q4-15			

Asset & Performance History

Date	NAV	1-Year Total Return
2018	25.42	-12.92
2017	29.91	26.01
2016	24.38	0.48
2015	24.49	
2014		
2013		

Total Assets: $1,576,252,149
Asset Allocation

Asset	%
Cash	0%
Stocks	100%
US Stocks	2%
Bonds	0%
US Bonds	0%
Other	0%

Services Offered:

Investment Strategy: The investment seeks to provide investment results that closely correspond, before fees and expenses, to the performance of the Goldman Sachs ActiveBeta® International Equity Index. The fund invests at least 80% of its assets (exclusive of collateral held from securities lending) in securities included in its underlying index, in depositary receipts representing securities included in its underlying index and in underlying stocks in respect of depositary receipts included in its underlying index. The index is designed to deliver exposure to equity securities of developed market issuers outside of the United States. **Top Holdings:** Nestle SA Roche Holding AG Dividend Right Cert. Novartis AG LVMH Moet Hennessy Louis Vuitton SE adidas AG

WisdomTree International SmallCap Dividend Fund

C- HOLD

Ticker	Traded On	NAV	Total Assets ($)	Dividend Yield (TTM)	Turnover Ratio	Expense Ratio
DLS	NYSE Arca	63.58	$1,573,656,755	3.47	35	0.58

Ratings
Reward **D**
Risk **C**
Recent Upgrade/Downgrade

Fund Information
Fund Type	Exchange Traded Funds
Category	Globa Eq Mid/Small Cap
Sub-Category	Foreign Small/Mid Value
Prospectus Objective	Foreign Stock
Inception Date	Jun-06
Open to New Investments	Y

Prices
Price (as of 9/30/2019)	63.52
52-Week High	71.35
52-Week Low	58.00

Total Returns (%)
3-Month	6-Month	1-Year	3-Year	5-Year
-2.24	-2.24	-7.52	14.63	26.23

3-Year Standard Deviation	11.51
Effective Duration	

Valuation
Premium/Discount (1-Year Average)	-0.13

Company Information
Provider	WisdomTree
Manager/Tenure	Richard A. Brown (11), Thomas J. Durante (11), Karen Q. Wong (11)
Website	http://www.wisdomtree.com
Address	WisdomTree 245 Park Avenue, 35th floor New York NY 10167 United States
Phone Number	866-909-9473

PERFORMANCE

Ratings History
Date	Overall Rating	Risk Rating	Reward Rating
Q3-19	C-	C	D
Q4-18	C-	C-	D+
Q4-17	B+	B+	A-
Q4-16	C	C-	C
Q4-15	C-	C-	C-

Asset & Performance History
Date	NAV	1-Year Total Return
2018	60.53	-18.69
2017	76.83	30.95
2016	60.45	7
2015	58.39	6.94
2014	56.06	-7.11
2013	62.35	27.4

Total Assets: $1,573,656,755

Asset Allocation
Asset	%
Cash	0%
Stocks	100%
US Stocks	0%
Bonds	0%
US Bonds	0%
Other	0%

Services Offered:

Investment Strategy: The investment seeks to track the price and yield performance, before fees and expenses, of the WisdomTree International SmallCap Dividend Index. Under normal circumstances, at least 95% of the fund's total assets (exclusive of collateral held from securities lending) will be invested in component securities of the index and investments that have economic characteristics that are substantially identical to the economic characteristics of such component securities. The index is comprised of the small-capitalization segment of the dividend-paying market in the industrialized world outside the U.S. and Canada. The fund is non-diversified. **Top Holdings:** Royal Mail PLC Bpost SA de Droit Public WisdomTree Europe SmallCap Dividend ETF freenet AG The Navigator Co SA

---

iShares MSCI Hong Kong ETF

C HOLD

Ticker	Traded On	NAV	Total Assets ($)	Dividend Yield (TTM)	Turnover Ratio	Expense Ratio
EWH	NYSE Arca	22.83	$1,561,895,901	3.15	7	0.48

Ratings
Reward **C-**
Risk **B-**
Recent Upgrade/Downgrade **Down**

Fund Information
Fund Type	Exchange Traded Funds
Category	Greater China Equity
Sub-Category	China Region
Prospectus Objective	Pacific Stock
Inception Date	Mar-96
Open to New Investments	Y

Prices
Price (as of 9/30/2019)	22.70
52-Week High	27.14
52-Week Low	21.26

Total Returns (%)
3-Month	6-Month	1-Year	3-Year	5-Year
-12.19	-13.16	-2.47	15.71	31.34

3-Year Standard Deviation	15.45
Effective Duration	

Valuation
Premium/Discount (1-Year Average)	-0.20

Company Information
Provider	iShares
Manager/Tenure	Diane Hsiung (11), Greg Savage (11), Jennifer Hsui (6), 3 others
Website	http://www.ishares.com
Address	iShares 400 Howard Street San Francisco CA 94105 United States
Phone Number	800-474-2737

PERFORMANCE

Ratings History
Date	Overall Rating	Risk Rating	Reward Rating
Q3-19	C	B-	C-
Q4-18	C-	C	D+
Q4-17	B	B-	B+
Q4-16	B-	C	B-
Q4-15	C+	B	C

Asset & Performance History
Date	NAV	1-Year Total Return
2018	22.72	-8.26
2017	25.46	35.58
2016	19.64	1.75
2015	19.9	-1.4
2014	20.67	4.58
2013	20.47	10.44

Total Assets: $1,561,895,901

Asset Allocation
Asset	%
Cash	1%
Stocks	99%
US Stocks	2%
Bonds	0%
US Bonds	0%
Other	0%

Services Offered: CashInvestment Plan

Investment Strategy: The investment seeks to track the investment results of the MSCI Hong Kong Index. The fund will at all times invest at least 80% of its assets in the securities of its underlying index and in depositary receipts representing securities in its underlying index. The underlying index consists of stocks traded primarily on the Stock Exchange of Hong Kong Limited (SEHK). It may include large- or mid-capitalization companies. The fund is non-diversified. **Top Holdings:** AIA Group Ltd Hong Kong Exchanges and Clearing Ltd Link Real Estate Investment Trust CK Hutchison Holdings Ltd Sun Hung Kai Properties Ltd

iShares MSCI KLD 400 Social ETF   C   HOLD

Ticker	Traded On	NAV	Total Assets ($)	Dividend Yield (TTM)	Turnover Ratio	Expense Ratio
DSI	NYSE Arca	110.88	$1,557,817,828	1.5	13	0.25

Ratings
Reward   C+
Risk   C
Recent Upgrade/Downgrade

Fund Information
Fund Type   Exchange Traded Funds
Category   US Equity Large Cap Blend
Sub-Category   Large Blend
Prospectus Objective   Growth
Inception Date   Nov-06
Open to New Investments   Y

Prices
Price (as of 9/30/2019)   110.91
52-Week High   113.26
52-Week Low   87.24

Total Returns (%)

3-Month	6-Month	1-Year	3-Year	5-Year
0.94	4.62	5.16	44.05	65.18

3-Year Standard Deviation   12.26
Effective Duration

Valuation
Premium/Discount (1-Year Average)   -0.02

Company Information
Provider   iShares
Manager/Tenure   Greg Savage (11), Jennifer Hsui (7),
                    Alan Mason (3), 2 others
Website   http://www.ishares.com
Address   iShares 400 Howard Street San
                    Francisco CA 94105 United States
Phone Number   800-474-2737

PERFORMANCE

Ratings History

Date	Overall Rating	Risk Rating	Reward Rating
Q3-19	C	C	C+
Q4-18	C	C-	C
Q4-17	B	B	B
Q4-16	C+	C-	B
Q4-15	C	C	C

Asset & Performance History

Date	NAV	1-Year Total Return
2018	92.98	-3.8
2017	98.14	20.96
2016	82.25	10.34
2015	75.72	0.46
2014	76.48	12.14
2013	69.09	35.49

Total Assets: $1,557,817,828
Asset Allocation

Asset	%
Cash	0%
Stocks	100%
US Stocks	98%
Bonds	0%
US Bonds	0%
Other	0%

Services Offered:

Investment Strategy: The investment seeks to track the investment results of the MSCI KLD 400 Social Index composed of U.S. companies that have positive environmental, social and governance characteristics. The fund generally invests at least 90% of its assets in securities of the underlying index and in depositary receipts representing securities of the underlying index. The underlying index is a free float-adjusted market capitalization index designed to target U.S. companies that have positive environmental, social and governance ("ESG") characteristics. **Top Holdings:** Microsoft Corp Facebook Inc A Alphabet Inc Class C Alphabet Inc A Visa Inc Class A

KraneShares CSI China Internet ETF   C-   HOLD

Ticker	Traded On	NAV	Total Assets ($)	Dividend Yield (TTM)	Turnover Ratio	Expense Ratio
KWEB	NYSE Arca	41.42	$1,551,265,151	0.04	70	0.76

Ratings
Reward   C-
Risk   D+
Recent Upgrade/Downgrade   Up

Fund Information
Fund Type   Exchange Traded Funds
Category   Greater China Equity
Sub-Category   China Region
Prospectus Objective   Pacific Stock
Inception Date   Jul-13
Open to New Investments   Y

Prices
Price (as of 9/30/2019)   41.33
52-Week High   49.64
52-Week Low   36.20

Total Returns (%)

3-Month	6-Month	1-Year	3-Year	5-Year
-7.27	-13.88	-11.96	5.83	29.55

3-Year Standard Deviation   25.72
Effective Duration

Valuation
Premium/Discount (1-Year Average)   0.01

Company Information
Provider   KraneShares
Manager/Tenure   Mark Schlarbaum (3), Jonathan
                    Shelon (1)
Website   http://www.kraneshares.com
Address   1350 Avenue of the Americas Second
                    Floor New York NY 10019 United
                    States
Phone Number   855-857-2638

PERFORMANCE

Ratings History

Date	Overall Rating	Risk Rating	Reward Rating
Q3-19	C-	D+	C-
Q4-18	C-	D	C
Q4-17	B+	C	A+
Q4-16	D+	D+	D+
Q4-15	C	C	C

Asset & Performance History

Date	NAV	1-Year Total Return
2018	37.67	-33.51
2017	58.56	69.25
2016	34.77	-8.41
2015	38.43	17.82
2014	32.68	-0.61
2013	33.15	

Total Assets: $1,551,265,151
Asset Allocation

Asset	%
Cash	0%
Stocks	100%
US Stocks	0%
Bonds	0%
US Bonds	0%
Other	0%

Services Offered:

Investment Strategy: The investment seeks to provide investment results that, before fees and expenses, correspond generally to the price and yield performance of the CSI Overseas China Internet Index. The fund invests at least 80% of its total assets in equity securities of the index and in depositary receipts representing such securities. The index is designed to measure the equity market performance of the investable universe of publicly traded China-based companies whose primary business or businesses are in the Internet and Internet-related sectors, and are listed outside of Mainland China, as determined by the index provider. The fund is non-diversified. **Top Holdings:** Alibaba Group Holding Ltd ADR Tencent Holdings Ltd Meituan Dianping Baidu Inc ADR JD.com Inc ADR

iShares Core MSCI International Developed Markets ETF   C   HOLD

Ticker	Traded On	NAV	Total Assets ($)	Dividend Yield (TTM)	Turnover Ratio	Expense Ratio
IDEV	NYSE Arca	54.49	$1,544,793,207	2.9	5	0.05

Ratings
Reward   C-
Risk   C+
Recent Upgrade/Downgrade   Up

Fund Information
Fund Type   Exchange Traded Funds
Category   Global Equity Large Cap
Sub-Category   Foreign Large Blend
Prospectus Objective   Foreign Stock
Inception Date   Mar-17
Open to New Investments Y

Prices
Price (as of 9/30/2019)   54.62
52-Week High   56.99
52-Week Low   47.08

Total Returns (%)

3-Month	6-Month	1-Year	3-Year	5-Year
-1.23	1.67	-1.03		

3-Year Standard Deviation
Effective Duration

Valuation
Premium/Discount (1-Year Average)   -0.04

Company Information
Provider   iShares
Manager/Tenure   Diane Hsiung (2), Jennifer Hsui (2),
                  Alan Mason (2), 3 others
Website   http://www.ishares.com
Address   iShares 400 Howard Street San
                  Francisco CA 94105 United States
Phone Number   800-474-2737

PERFORMANCE

Ratings History

Date	Overall Rating	Risk Rating	Reward Rating
Q3-19	C	C+	C-
Q4-18	D	D+	D
Q4-17	U		
Q4-16			
Q4-15			

Asset & Performance History

Date	NAV	1-Year Total Return
2018	48.84	-14.31
2017	58.65	
2016		
2015		
2014		
2013		

Total Assets: $1,544,793,207
Asset Allocation

Asset	%
Cash	1%
Stocks	99%
US Stocks	2%
Bonds	0%
US Bonds	0%
Other	0%

Services Offered:

Investment Strategy: The investment seeks to track the investment results of the MSCI World ex USA Investable Market Index. The fund generally will invest at least 90% of its assets in the component securities of the underlying index and in investments that have economic characteristics that are substantially identical to the component securities of the underlying index. The underlying index is free float adjusted, market cap weighted, and is designed to measure large-, mid- and small-capitalization equity market performance and includes stocks from North America, Europe, Australasia and the Far East. The fund is non-diversified. **Top Holdings:** Nestle SA Novartis AG Roche Holding AG Dividend Right Cert. Toyota Motor Corp HSBC Holdings PLC

iShares MSCI Australia ETF   C+   HOLD

Ticker	Traded On	NAV	Total Assets ($)	Dividend Yield (TTM)	Turnover Ratio	Expense Ratio
EWA	NYSE Arca	22.18	$1,543,816,728	5.36	3	0.47

Ratings
Reward   B-
Risk   C+
Recent Upgrade/Downgrade

Fund Information
Fund Type   Exchange Traded Funds
Category   Australia & New Zealand Equity
Sub-Category   Miscellaneous Region
Prospectus Objective   Pacific Stock
Inception Date   Mar-96
Open to New Investments Y

Prices
Price (as of 9/30/2019)   22.25
52-Week High   22.81
52-Week Low   18.42

Total Returns (%)

3-Month	6-Month	1-Year	3-Year	5-Year
-1.11	4.64	6.51	23.92	17.83

3-Year Standard Deviation   11.09
Effective Duration

Valuation
Premium/Discount (1-Year Average)   0.04

Company Information
Provider   iShares
Manager/Tenure   Diane Hsiung (11), Greg Savage (11),
                  Jennifer Hsui (6), 3 others
Website   http://www.ishares.com
Address   iShares 400 Howard Street San
                  Francisco CA 94105 United States
Phone Number   800-474-2737

PERFORMANCE

Ratings History

Date	Overall Rating	Risk Rating	Reward Rating
Q3-19	C+	C+	B-
Q4-18	C-	C	C-
Q4-17	C+	C	B-
Q4-16	D+	D+	C-
Q4-15	D	D	D+

Asset & Performance History

Date	NAV	1-Year Total Return
2018	19.25	-12.31
2017	23.25	19.55
2016	20.36	11.04
2015	19.09	-10.31
2014	22.41	-3.79
2013	24.42	3.74

Total Assets: $1,543,816,728
Asset Allocation

Asset	%
Cash	1%
Stocks	99%
US Stocks	0%
Bonds	0%
US Bonds	0%
Other	0%

Services Offered: CashInvestment Plan

Investment Strategy: The investment seeks to track the investment results of the MSCI Australia Index composed of Australian equities. The fund generally invests at least 90% of its assets in the securities of its underlying index and in depositary receipts representing securities in its underlying index. The underlying index consists of stocks traded primarily on the Australian Stock Exchange. It may include large- or mid-capitalization companies. The fund is non-diversified. **Top Holdings:** Commonwealth Bank of Australia CSL Ltd BHP Group Ltd Westpac Banking Corp National Australia Bank Ltd

Invesco Financial Preferred ETF   C+   HOLD

Ticker	Traded On	NAV	Total Assets ($)	Dividend Yield (TTM)	Turnover Ratio	Expense Ratio
PGF	NYSE Arca	18.74	$1,543,108,208	5.32	21	0.62

Ratings
Reward   C+
Risk   C+
Recent Upgrade/Downgrade

Fund Information
Fund Type   Exchange Traded Funds
Category   US Fixed Income
Sub-Category   Preferred Stock
Prospectus Objective   Financial
Inception Date   Dec-06
Open to New Investments   Y

Prices
Price (as of 9/30/2019)   18.78
52-Week High   18.86
52-Week Low   17.04

Total Returns (%)

3-Month	6-Month	1-Year	3-Year	5-Year
2.96	4.79	9.43	15.94	37.62

3-Year Standard Deviation   4.72
Effective Duration   3.41

Valuation
Premium/Discount (1-Year Average)   0.07

Company Information
Provider   Invesco
Manager/Tenure   Peter Hubbard (12), Jeffrey W. Kernagis (12), Gary Jones (6), 2 others
Website   http://www.invesco.com/us
Address   Invesco 11 Greenway Plaza, Ste. 2500 Houston TX 77046 United States
Phone Number   800-659-1005

PERFORMANCE

Ratings History

Date	Overall Rating	Risk Rating	Reward Rating
Q3-19	C+	C+	C+
Q4-18	C	C+	C-
Q4-17	B	A	C+
Q4-16	C	C+	C
Q4-15	B-	C+	B-

Asset & Performance History

Date	NAV	1-Year Total Return
2018	17.38	-2.71
2017	18.87	10.62
2016	17.99	1.2
2015	18.82	9.2
2014	18.25	14.02
2013	17	-0.88

Total Assets: $1,543,108,208
Asset Allocation

Asset	%
Cash	0%
Stocks	1%
US Stocks	1%
Bonds	0%
US Bonds	0%
Other	0%

Services Offered:

Investment Strategy: The investment seeks to track the investment results (before fees and expenses) of the Wells Fargo® Hybrid and Preferred Securities Financial Index. The fund generally will invest at least 90% of its total assets in the securities that comprise the underlying index. The underlying index is a market capitalization weighted index designed to track the performance of preferred securities and securities that the index provider believes are functionally equivalent to preferred securities, including, but not limited to, depositary preferred securities, perpetual subordinated debt and certain capital securities. It is non-diversified. **Top Holdings:** JPMorgan Chase & Co Pfd Wells Fargo & Co Deposit Shs Repr 1/1000th 5.85 % Non-Cum Perp Pfd Shs -A- PNC Financial Services Group Inc Perpetual Preferred Share class-P JPMorgan Chase & Co Deposit Shs Repr 1/40th 6.15 % Non-Cum Pfd Shs Series - JPMorgan Chase & Co 6% PRF PERPETUAL USD 25 - Dep rep 1/400 Ser EE

Invesco Variable Rate Preferred ETF   C+   HOLD

Ticker	Traded On	NAV	Total Assets ($)	Dividend Yield (TTM)	Turnover Ratio	Expense Ratio
VRP	NYSE Arca	25.38	$1,543,064,227	5.28		0.5

Ratings
Reward   C+
Risk   C+
Recent Upgrade/Downgrade   Down

Fund Information
Fund Type   Exchange Traded Funds
Category   US Fixed Income
Sub-Category   Preferred Stock
Prospectus Objective   Growth & Inc
Inception Date   May-14
Open to New Investments   Y

Prices
Price (as of 9/30/2019)   25.42
52-Week High   25.49
52-Week Low   22.45

Total Returns (%)

3-Month	6-Month	1-Year	3-Year	5-Year
3.17	5.93	7.56	15.78	31.37

3-Year Standard Deviation   5.19
Effective Duration

Valuation
Premium/Discount (1-Year Average)   -0.20

Company Information
Provider   Invesco
Manager/Tenure   Philip Fang (5), Peter Hubbard (5), Gary Jones (5), 2 others
Website   http://www.invesco.com/us
Address   Invesco 11 Greenway Plaza, Ste. 2500 Houston TX 77046 United States
Phone Number   800-659-1005

PERFORMANCE

Ratings History

Date	Overall Rating	Risk Rating	Reward Rating
Q3-19	C+	C+	C+
Q4-18	C	C+	D+
Q4-17	B	A+	C
Q4-16	C	C+	C
Q4-15	D	C+	D+

Asset & Performance History

Date	NAV	1-Year Total Return
2018	23.05	-5.69
2017	25.66	9.7
2016	24.51	6.8
2015	24.16	2.99
2014	24.65	
2013		

Total Assets: $1,543,064,227
Asset Allocation

Asset	%
Cash	0%
Stocks	0%
US Stocks	0%
Bonds	62%
US Bonds	58%
Other	0%

Services Offered:

Investment Strategy: The investment seeks to track the investment results (before fees and expenses) of the Wells Fargo® Hybrid and Preferred Securities Floating and Variable Rate Index. The fund will invest at least 90% of its total assets in the securities that comprise the underlying index. The underlying index is a market capitalization-weighted index designed to track the performance of preferred stock, as well as certain types of hybrid securities that are functionally equivalent to preferred stocks, that are issued by U.S.-based or foreign issuers and that pay a floating or variable rate dividend or coupon. It is non-diversified. **Top Holdings:** General Electric Company 5% JPMorgan Chase & Co. 5.74% Wells Fargo & Company 6.18% GMAC Capital Trust I Pfd Secs 2011-15.2.40 Gtd Series 2 Wachovia Capital Trust III 5.57%

Invesco Optimum Yield Diversified Commodity Strategy No K-1 ETF   D+   SELL

Ticker	Traded On	NAV		Total Assets ($)	Dividend Yield (TTM)	Turnover Ratio	Expense Ratio
PDBC	NAS CM	15.59		$1,540,109,798	0.97		0.58

Ratings
Reward   D+
Risk   C-
Recent Upgrade/Downgrade   Down

Fund Information
Fund Type   Exchange Traded Funds
Category   Commodities Broad Basket
Sub-Category   Commodities Broad Basket
Prospectus Objective   Growth
Inception Date   Nov-14
Open to New Investments   Y

Prices
Price (as of 9/30/2019)   15.62
52-Week High   19.39
52-Week Low   14.98

Total Returns (%)

3-Month	6-Month	1-Year	3-Year	5-Year
-4.99	-7.03	-17.63	-0.16	

3-Year Standard Deviation   12.48
Effective Duration

Valuation
Premium/Discount (1-Year Average)   -0.09

Company Information
Provider   Invesco
Manager/Tenure   Peter Hubbard (4), Theodore
                    Samulowitz (4), David Hemming (3)
Website   http://www.invesco.com/us
Address   Invesco 11 Greenway Plaza, Ste. 2500
                    Houston TX 77046 United States
Phone Number   800-659-1005

PERFORMANCE

Ratings History

Date	Overall Rating	Risk Rating	Reward Rating
Q3-19	D+	C-	D+
Q4-18	C-	C	C-
Q4-17	C	C	C
Q4-16	D	D	D+
Q4-15	U		

Asset & Performance History

Date	NAV	1-Year Total Return
2018	15.02	-13.19
2017	17.48	5.27
2016	17.27	18.76
2015	15.5	-27.02
2014	21.24	
2013		

Total Assets: $1,540,109,798
Asset Allocation

Asset	%
Cash	32%
Stocks	0%
US Stocks	0%
Bonds	46%
US Bonds	46%
Other	22%

Services Offered:

Investment Strategy: The investment seeks long term capital appreciation. The fund is an actively managed exchange-traded fund ("ETF") that seeks to achieve its investment objective by investing in a combination of financial instruments that are economically linked to the world's most heavily traded commodities. Commodities are assets that have tangible properties, such as oil, agricultural produce or raw metals. **Top Holdings:** United States Treasury Bills 0%   PowerShares NXQ   United States Treasury Bills 0%   US Treasury Bill   Ny Harb Ulsd Fut Jun16

Invesco S&P 500® Quality ETF   B-   BUY

Ticker	Traded On	NAV		Total Assets ($)	Dividend Yield (TTM)	Turnover Ratio	Expense Ratio
SPHQ	NYSE Arca	33.53		$1,491,871,394	1.56	73	0.15

Ratings
Reward   B-
Risk   C+
Recent Upgrade/Downgrade   Up

Fund Information
Fund Type   Exchange Traded Funds
Category   US Equity Large Cap Blend
Sub-Category   Large Blend
Prospectus Objective   Growth
Inception Date   Dec-05
Open to New Investments   Y

Prices
Price (as of 9/30/2019)   33.54
52-Week High   34.13
52-Week Low   25.94

Total Returns (%)

3-Month	6-Month	1-Year	3-Year	5-Year
0.86	4.02	3.62	40.54	72.42

3-Year Standard Deviation   12.03
Effective Duration

Valuation
Premium/Discount (1-Year Average)   -0.03

Company Information
Provider   Invesco
Manager/Tenure   Peter Hubbard (12), Michael Jeanette
                    (11), Tony Seisser (5)
Website   http://www.invesco.com/us
Address   Invesco 11 Greenway Plaza, Ste. 2500
                    Houston TX 77046 United States
Phone Number   800-659-1005

PERFORMANCE

Ratings History

Date	Overall Rating	Risk Rating	Reward Rating
Q3-19	B-	C+	B-
Q4-18	C+	C+	C
Q4-17	B	B+	B
Q4-16	B-	C+	B
Q4-15	C+	C+	B-

Asset & Performance History

Date	NAV	1-Year Total Return
2018	27.8	-6.98
2017	30.41	19.12
2016	25.95	14.17
2015	23.12	1.66
2014	23.27	16.09
2013	20.4	32.04

Total Assets: $1,491,871,394
Asset Allocation

Asset	%
Cash	0%
Stocks	100%
US Stocks	100%
Bonds	0%
US Bonds	0%
Other	0%

Services Offered:

Investment Strategy: The investment seeks to track the investment results (before fees and expenses) of the S&P 500® Quality Index. The fund generally will invest at least 90% of its total assets in the securities that comprise the underlying index. In selecting constituent securities for the underlying index, the index provider calculates the quality score of each security in the S&P 500® Index, then selects the 100 stocks with the highest quality score for inclusion in the underlying index. **Top Holdings:** Apple Inc   Microsoft Corp   Mastercard Inc A   Visa Inc Class A   Johnson & Johnson

iShares Russell Top 200 Growth ETF

C+   HOLD

Ticker	Traded On	NAV	Total Assets ($)	Dividend Yield (TTM)	Turnover Ratio	Expense Ratio
IWY	NYSE Arca	87.09	$1,489,218,989	1.19	15	0.2

Ratings
Reward	B
Risk	C
Recent Upgrade/Downgrade	Up

Fund Information
Fund Type	Exchange Traded Funds
Category	US Equity Large Cap Growth
Sub-Category	Large Growth
Prospectus Objective	Growth
Inception Date	Sep-09
Open to New Investments	Y

Prices
Price (as of 9/30/2019)	87.06
52-Week High	89.05
52-Week Low	66.58

Total Returns (%)
3-Month	6-Month	1-Year	3-Year	5-Year
0.85	5.38	2.84	62.16	95.24

3-Year Standard Deviation	13.23
Effective Duration	

Valuation
Premium/Discount (1-Year Average)	0.01

Company Information
Provider	iShares
Manager/Tenure	Greg Savage (10), Jennifer Hsui (7), Alan Mason (3), 2 others
Website	http://www.ishares.com
Address	iShares 400 Howard Street San Francisco CA 94105 United States
Phone Number	800-474-2737

PERFORMANCE

Ratings History
Date	Overall Rating	Risk Rating	Reward Rating
Q3-19	C+	C	B
Q4-18	C	C	C+
Q4-17	B+	B+	A-
Q4-16	B-	C	B
Q4-15	C+	C	B-

Asset & Performance History
Date	NAV	1-Year Total Return
2018	71.62	-0.76
2017	73.05	31.62
2016	56.27	6.76
2015	53.53	7.95
2014	50.4	13.34
2013	45.14	32.34

Total Assets: $1,489,218,989
Asset Allocation
Asset	%
Cash	0%
Stocks	100%
US Stocks	100%
Bonds	0%
US Bonds	0%
Other	0%

Services Offered:

Investment Strategy: The investment seeks to track the investment results of the Russell Top 200 Growth Index, which measures the performance of the largest capitalization growth sector of the U.S. equity market. The fund generally will invest at least 90% of its assets in the component securities of the underlying index and may invest up to 10% of its assets in certain futures, options and swap contracts, cash and cash equivalents, as well as in securities not included in the underlying index, but which the advisor believes will help the fund track the underlying index. **Top Holdings:** Microsoft Corp   Apple Inc   Amazon.com Inc   Facebook Inc A   Visa Inc Class A

---

iShares Latin America 40 ETF

C   HOLD

Ticker	Traded On	NAV	Total Assets ($)	Dividend Yield (TTM)	Turnover Ratio	Expense Ratio
ILF	NYSE Arca	31.57	$1,475,946,427	2.95	20	0.48

Ratings
Reward	C
Risk	C
Recent Upgrade/Downgrade	

Fund Information
Fund Type	Exchange Traded Funds
Category	Latin America Equity
Sub-Category	Latin America Stock
Prospectus Objective	Growth
Inception Date	Oct-01
Open to New Investments	Y

Prices
Price (as of 9/30/2019)	31.58
52-Week High	35.55
52-Week Low	29.20

Total Returns (%)
3-Month	6-Month	1-Year	3-Year	5-Year
-7.33	-5.13	3.15	21.80	-0.87

3-Year Standard Deviation	22.36
Effective Duration	

Valuation
Premium/Discount (1-Year Average)	-0.07

Company Information
Provider	iShares
Manager/Tenure	Greg Savage (11), Jennifer Hsui (7), Alan Mason (3), 2 others
Website	http://www.ishares.com
Address	iShares 400 Howard Street San Francisco CA 94105 United States
Phone Number	800-474-2737

PERFORMANCE

Ratings History
Date	Overall Rating	Risk Rating	Reward Rating
Q3-19	C	C	C
Q4-18	C	C	C
Q4-17	C	C	C
Q4-16	D+	D+	C-
Q4-15	D	D	D

Asset & Performance History
Date	NAV	1-Year Total Return
2018	30.86	-6.71
2017	34.16	25.84
2016	27.68	31.95
2015	21.33	-31.42
2014	31.97	-11.46
2013	36.88	-12.52

Total Assets: $1,475,946,427
Asset Allocation
Asset	%
Cash	0%
Stocks	100%
US Stocks	1%
Bonds	0%
US Bonds	0%
Other	0%

Services Offered: CashInvestment Plan

Investment Strategy: The investment seeks to track the investment results of the S&P Latin America 40TM composed of 40 of the largest Latin American equities. The fund generally invests at least 90% of its assets in securities of the underlying index and in depositary receipts representing securities of the underlying index. It seeks to track the investment results of the S&P Latin America 40TM (the "underlying index"), which is comprised of selected equities trading on the exchanges of five Latin American countries. The fund is non-diversified. **Top Holdings:** Itau Unibanco Holding SA ADR   Vale SA ADR   Bank Bradesco SA ADR   Petroleo Brasileiro SA Petrobras ADR   B3 SA - Brasil Bolsa Balcao

Fidelity® MSCI Health Care Index ETF   C+   HOLD

Ticker	Traded On	NAV	Total Assets ($)	Dividend Yield (TTM)	Turnover Ratio	Expense Ratio
FHLC	NYSE Arca	43.39	$1,442,563,086	2.2	5	0.08

Ratings
Reward   C+
Risk   C+
Recent Upgrade/Downgrade

Fund Information
Fund Type	Exchange Traded Funds
Category	Healthcare Sector Equity
Sub-Category	Health
Prospectus Objective	Health
Inception Date	Oct-13
Open to New Investments	Y

Prices
Price (as of 9/30/2019)	43.37
52-Week High	46.93
52-Week Low	38.80

Total Returns (%)
3-Month	6-Month	1-Year	3-Year	5-Year
-3.74	-1.95	-5.37	32.25	56.63

3-Year Standard Deviation   13.83
Effective Duration

Valuation
Premium/Discount (1-Year Average)   0.01

Company Information
Provider	Fidelity Investments
Manager/Tenure	Jennifer Hsui (5), Greg Savage (5), Alan Mason (3), 2 others
Website	http://www.institutional.fidelity.com
Address	Fidelity Investments 82 Devonshire Street Boston MA 2109 United States
Phone Number	617-563-7000

PERFORMANCE

Ratings History

Date	Overall Rating	Risk Rating	Reward Rating
Q3-19	C+	C+	C+
Q4-18	C+	C	C+
Q4-17	B	B	B-
Q4-16	C+	C+	C+
Q4-15	C-	B-	C+

Asset & Performance History

Date	NAV	1-Year Total Return
2018	41.31	5.52
2017	39.98	23.3
2016	32.89	-3.31
2015	34.5	7.05
2014	32.88	25.22
2013	26.55	

Total Assets: $1,442,563,086
Asset Allocation

Asset	%
Cash	0%
Stocks	100%
US Stocks	100%
Bonds	0%
US Bonds	0%
Other	0%

Services Offered:

Investment Strategy: The investment seeks to provide investment returns that correspond, before fees and expenses, generally to the performance of the MSCI USA IMI Health Care Index. The fund invests at least 80% of assets in securities included in the fund's underlying index. The fund's underlying index is the MSCI USA IMI Health Care Index, which represents the performance of the health care sector in the U.S. equity market. It may or may not hold all of the securities in the MSCI USA IMI Health Care Index. The fund is non-diversified. **Top Holdings:** Johnson & Johnson Merck & Co Inc UnitedHealth Group Inc Pfizer Inc Abbott Laboratories

---

Principal U.S. Mega-Cap Multi-Factor Index ETF   C+   HOLD

Ticker	Traded On	NAV	Total Assets ($)	Dividend Yield (TTM)	Turnover Ratio	Expense Ratio
USMC	NAS CM	29.35	$1,430,657,344	2.23	27	0.12

Ratings
Reward   C+
Risk   C+
Recent Upgrade/Downgrade   Up

Fund Information
Fund Type	Exchange Traded Funds
Category	US Equity Large Cap Blend
Sub-Category	Large Blend
Prospectus Objective	Growth & Inc
Inception Date	Oct-17
Open to New Investments	Y

Prices
Price (as of 9/30/2019)	29.38
52-Week High	29.73
52-Week Low	23.78

Total Returns (%)
3-Month	6-Month	1-Year	3-Year	5-Year
0.68	4.36	5.51		

3-Year Standard Deviation
Effective Duration

Valuation
Premium/Discount (1-Year Average)   0.11

Company Information
Provider	Principal Funds
Manager/Tenure	Paul S. Kim (1), Mark R. Nebelung (1), Jeffrey A. Schwarte (1)
Website	http://www.principalfunds.com
Address	Principal Funds 430 W 7th St, Ste 219971 Kansas City MO 64105-1407 United States
Phone Number	800-787-1621

PERFORMANCE

Ratings History

Date	Overall Rating	Risk Rating	Reward Rating
Q3-19	C+	C+	C+
Q4-18	C-	C-	C
Q4-17	U		
Q4-16			
Q4-15			

Asset & Performance History

Date	NAV	1-Year Total Return
2018	25.11	-1.76
2017	26.13	
2016		
2015		
2014		
2013		

Total Assets: $1,430,657,344
Asset Allocation

Asset	%
Cash	0%
Stocks	100%
US Stocks	100%
Bonds	0%
US Bonds	0%
Other	0%

Services Offered:

Investment Strategy: The investment seeks to provide investment results that closely correspond, before expenses, to the performance of the Nasdaq U.S. Mega Cap Select Leaders Index (the "index"). Under normal circumstances, the fund invests at least 80% of its net assets, plus any borrowings for investment purposes, in equity securities that compose the index at the time of purchase. The index uses a quantitative model designed to identify equity securities of companies in the Nasdaq US 500 Large Cap Index (the "parent index") that have the largest market capitalizations, with higher weights given to less volatile securities. **Top Holdings:** Microsoft Corp Apple Inc The Walt Disney Co Walmart Inc Procter & Gamble Co

---

Vanguard International Dividend Appreciation Index Fund ETF Shares   C   HOLD

Ticker	Traded On	NAV	Total Assets ($)	Dividend Yield (TTM)	Turnover Ratio	Expense Ratio
VIGI	NAS CM	66.41	$1,429,709,042	1.45	36	0.25

Ratings
Reward   C
Risk   C-
Recent Upgrade/Downgrade

Fund Information
Fund Type   Exchange Traded Funds
Category   Global Equity Large Cap
Sub-Category   Foreign Large Growth
Prospectus Objective   Foreign Stock
Inception Date   Feb-16
Open to New Investments   Y

Prices
Price (as of 9/30/2019)   66.57
52-Week High   68.88
52-Week Low   55.63

Total Returns (%)
3-Month	6-Month	1-Year	3-Year	5-Year
-2.09	2.91	4.50	23.21	

3-Year Standard Deviation   11.52
Effective Duration

Valuation
Premium/Discount (1-Year Average)   0.17

Company Information
Provider   Vanguard
Manager/Tenure   Justin E. Hales (3), Michael Perre (3)
Website   http://www.vanguard.com
Address   Vanguard 100 Vanguard Boulevard
                   Malvern PA 19355 United States
Phone Number   877-662-7447

PERFORMANCE

Ratings History
Date	Overall Rating	Risk Rating	Reward Rating
Q3-19	C	C-	C
Q4-18	D+	C-	D+
Q4-17	C-	B-	C
Q4-16	U		
Q4-15			

Asset & Performance History
Date	NAV	1-Year Total Return
2018	57.31	-11.8
2017	66.19	27.72
2016	52.77	
2015		
2014		
2013		

Total Assets: $1,429,709,042

Asset Allocation
Asset	%
Cash	1%
Stocks	99%
US Stocks	1%
Bonds	0%
US Bonds	0%
Other	0%

Services Offered:
Investment Strategy: The investment seeks to track the performance of Nasdaq International Dividend Achievers Select Index that measures the investment return of non-U.S. companies that have a history of increasing dividends. The index focuses on high-quality companies located in developed and emerging markets, excluding the U.S., that have both the ability and the commitment to grow their dividends over time. The manager attempts to replicate the target index by investing all, or substantially all, of its assets in the broadly diversified collection of securities that make up the index, holding each stock in approximately the same proportion as its weighting in the index. **Top Holdings:** Nestle SA Tencent Holdings Ltd Novartis AG Samsung Electronics Co Ltd LVMH Moet Hennessy Louis Vuitton SE

FlexShares STOXX Global Broad Infrastructure Index Fund   C   HOLD

Ticker	Traded On	NAV	Total Assets ($)	Dividend Yield (TTM)	Turnover Ratio	Expense Ratio
NFRA	NYSE Arca	51.65	$1,428,166,226	2.37		0.47

Ratings
Reward   C+
Risk   C-
Recent Upgrade/Downgrade

Fund Information
Fund Type   Exchange Traded Funds
Category   Infrastructure Sector Equity
Sub-Category   Infrastructure
Prospectus Objective   Utility
Inception Date   Oct-13
Open to New Investments   Y

Prices
Price (as of 9/30/2019)   51.74
52-Week High   52.12
52-Week Low   42.10

Total Returns (%)
3-Month	6-Month	1-Year	3-Year	5-Year
2.06	5.56	13.27	25.07	32.28

3-Year Standard Deviation   9.63
Effective Duration

Valuation
Premium/Discount (1-Year Average)   0.06

Company Information
Provider   Flexshares Trust
Manager/Tenure   Robert Anstine (5), Brendan Sullivan (3)
Website   http://www.flexshares.com
Address   50 South LaSalle Street Chicago,
                   Illinois 60603 Chicago Illinois 60603
                   United States
Phone Number   855-353-9383

PERFORMANCE

Ratings History
Date	Overall Rating	Risk Rating	Reward Rating
Q3-19	C	C-	C+
Q4-18	C-	C-	C-
Q4-17	C+	B-	C+
Q4-16	C-	C-	C-
Q4-15	C-	C-	D+

Asset & Performance History
Date	NAV	1-Year Total Return
2018	43.67	-7.92
2017	48.83	16.05
2016	43.3	8.49
2015	41.1	-6.86
2014	45.17	10.28
2013	42.21	

Total Assets: $1,428,166,226

Asset Allocation
Asset	%
Cash	1%
Stocks	99%
US Stocks	40%
Bonds	0%
US Bonds	0%
Other	0%

Services Offered:
Investment Strategy: The investment seeks investment results that correspond generally to the price and yield performance, before fees and expenses, of the STOXX® Global Broad Infrastructure Index. The fund will invest at least 80% of its total assets (exclusive of collateral held from securities lending) in the securities of the underlying index and in ADRs and GDRs based on the securities in the underlying index. The underlying index reflects the performance of a selection of equity securities of infrastructure-related companies that are domiciled or traded in developed and emerging markets around the world (including the U.S.). The fund is non-diversified. **Top Holdings:** AT&T Inc Verizon Communications Inc Canadian National Railway Co Comcast Corp Class A Enbridge Inc

FlexShares Morningstar US Market Factors Tilt Index Fund

C   HOLD

Ticker	Traded On	NAV	Total Assets ($)	Dividend Yield (TTM)	Turnover Ratio	Expense Ratio
TILT	BATS	116.98	$1,427,197,659	1.79	15	0.25

Ratings
Reward C
Risk .... C-
Recent Upgrade/Downgrade

Fund Information
Fund Type	Exchange Traded Funds
Category	US Equity Large Cap Blend
Sub-Category	Large Blend
Prospectus Objective	Growth
Inception Date	Sep-11
Open to New Investments	Y

Prices
Price (as of 9/30/2019)	117.01
52-Week High	119.77
52-Week Low	94.13

Total Returns (%)
3-Month	6-Month	1-Year	3-Year	5-Year
-0.03	2.58	-0.08	36.41	56.95

3-Year Standard Deviation 13.78
Effective Duration

Valuation
Premium/Discount (1-Year Average) .... -0.01

Company Information
Provider	Flexshares Trust
Manager/Tenure	Robert Anstine (5), Brendan Sullivan (3)
Website	http://www.flexshares.com
Address	50 South LaSalle Street Chicago, Illinois 60603 Chicago Illinois 60603 United States
Phone Number	855-353-9383

PERFORMANCE

Ratings History
Date	Overall Rating	Risk Rating	Reward Rating
Q3-19	C	C-	C
Q4-18	C-	C-	C-
Q4-17	B	B	B
Q4-16	D+	D+	D+
Q4-15	C	C-	C

Asset & Performance History
Date	NAV	1-Year Total Return
2018	100.18	-8.51
2017	111.48	17.84
2016	96.18	16.97
2015	83.63	-2.1
2014	87.09	9.92
2013	80.27	35.75

Total Assets: $1,427,197,659
Asset Allocation
Asset	%
Cash	1%
Stocks	99%
US Stocks	98%
Bonds	0%
US Bonds	0%
Other	0%

Services Offered:

Investment Strategy: The investment seeks investment results that correspond generally to the price and yield performance, before fees and expenses, of the Morningstar® US Market Factor Tilt IndexSM. The fund will invest at least 80% of its total assets (exclusive of collateral held from securities lending) in the securities of the underlying index. The underlying index reflects the performance of a selection of U.S. equity securities that is designed to provide broad exposure to the overall U.S. equities market, with increased exposure (or a "tilt") to small-capitalization stocks and value stocks. It may also invest up to 20% of its assets in cash and cash equivalents. **Top Holdings:** Microsoft Corp Apple Inc Amazon.com Inc Berkshire Hathaway Inc B JPMorgan Chase & Co

---

ETFMG Prime Cyber Security ETF

C   HOLD

Ticker	Traded On	NAV	Total Assets ($)	Dividend Yield (TTM)	Turnover Ratio	Expense Ratio
HACK	NYSE Arca	37.46	$1,427,177,058	0.22	41	0.6

Ratings
Reward C
Risk C
Recent Upgrade/Downgrade

Fund Information
Fund Type	Exchange Traded Funds
Category	Technology Sector Equity
Sub-Category	Technology
Prospectus Objective	Growth
Inception Date	Nov-14
Open to New Investments	Y

Prices
Price (as of 9/30/2019)	37.40
52-Week High	41.82
52-Week Low	31.73

Total Returns (%)
3-Month	6-Month	1-Year	3-Year	5-Year
-6.18	-7.14	-5.06	35.23	

3-Year Standard Deviation 15.98
Effective Duration

Valuation
Premium/Discount (1-Year Average) .... -0.07

Company Information
Provider	ETFMG
Manager/Tenure	Samuel R. Masucci (1), Devin Ryder (1), Donal Bishnoi (0), 1 other
Website	http://www.etfmg.com
Address	ETFMG 30 Maple Street, Suite 2 NJ United States
Phone Number	

PERFORMANCE

Ratings History
Date	Overall Rating	Risk Rating	Reward Rating
Q3-19	C	C	C
Q4-18	C	C	C
Q4-17	C	C	C
Q4-16	C-	C-	C
Q4-15	U		

Asset & Performance History
Date	NAV	1-Year Total Return
2018	33.85	7.06
2017	31.68	19.6
2016	26.49	2.6
2015	25.98	-1.66
2014	26.42	
2013		

Total Assets: $1,427,177,058
Asset Allocation
Asset	%
Cash	1%
Stocks	99%
US Stocks	85%
Bonds	0%
US Bonds	0%
Other	0%

Services Offered:

Investment Strategy: The investment seeks investment results that, before fees and expenses, correspond generally to the price and yield performance of the Prime Cyber Defense Index. The fund invests at least 80% of its total assets in the component securities of the index and in ADRs and GDRs based on the component securities in the index. The index tracks the performance of the exchange-listed equity securities of companies across the globe that (i) engage in providing cybersecurity applications or services as a vital component of its overall business or (ii) provide hardware or software for cybersecurity activities as a vital component of its overall business. **Top Holdings:** Symantec Corp SailPoint Technologies Holdings Inc Avast PLC Akamai Technologies Inc CACI International Inc Class A

United States Oil Fund, LP   D+   SELL

Ticker	Traded On	NAV	Total Assets ($)	Dividend Yield (TTM)	Turnover Ratio	Expense Ratio
USO	NYSE Arca	11.28	$1,426,846,401	0	0	0.73

Ratings
Reward	D+
Risk	D+
Recent Upgrade/Downgrade	Down

Fund Information
Fund Type	Exchange Traded Funds
Category	Commodities Specified
Sub-Category	Commodities Energy
Prospectus Objective	Natl Res
Inception Date	Apr-06
Open to New Investments	Y

Prices
Price (as of 9/30/2019)	11.34
52-Week High	16.08
52-Week Low	9.29

Total Returns (%)
3-Month	6-Month	1-Year	3-Year	5-Year
-8.01	-11.89	-29.07	2.49	-66.96

3-Year Standard Deviation	27.9
Effective Duration	

Valuation
Premium/Discount (1-Year Average)	-0.09

Company Information
Provider	USCF Investments
Manager/Tenure	Management Team (13)
Website	http://www.uscfinvestments.com
Address	USCF 1290 Broadway, Suite 1100
	Denver CO 80203 United States
Phone Number	

PERFORMANCE

Ratings History
Date	Overall Rating	Risk Rating	Reward Rating
Q3-19	D+	D+	D+
Q4-18	D+	D+	D+
Q4-17	D	D	D+
Q4-16	D-	D-	D-
Q4-15	D-	D-	D-

Asset & Performance History
Date	NAV	1-Year Total Return
2018	9.59	-20.64
2017	12.08	3.18
2016	11.71	6.17
2015	11.02	-45.29
2014	20.15	-42.79
2013	35.23	5.41

Total Assets: $1,426,846,401

Asset Allocation
Asset	%
Cash	27%
Stocks	0%
US Stocks	0%
Bonds	22%
US Bonds	22%
Other	52%

Services Offered:

Investment Strategy: The investment seeks the daily changes in percentage terms of its shares' per share net asset value ("NAV") to reflect the daily changes in percentage terms of the spot price of light, sweet crude oil delivered to Cushing, Oklahoma, as measured by the daily changes in the price of a specified short-term futures contract on light, sweet crude oil called the "Benchmark Oil Futures Contract," less USO's expenses.
USO seeks to achieve its investment objective by investing primarily in futures contracts for light, sweet crude oil, other types of crude oil, diesel-heating oil, gasoline, natural gas, and other petroleum-based fuels. **Top Holdings:** Future Contract On Wti Crude Future Oct19   United States Treasury Bills   United States Treasury Bills   United States Treasury Bills   United States Treasury Bills

---

Global X Robotics & Artificial Intelligence ETF   C-   HOLD

Ticker	Traded On	NAV	Total Assets ($)	Dividend Yield (TTM)	Turnover Ratio	Expense Ratio
BOTZ	NAS CM	19.91	$1,418,479,050	1.97	29	0.68

Ratings
Reward	D+
Risk	C
Recent Upgrade/Downgrade	

Fund Information
Fund Type	Exchange Traded Funds
Category	Equity Misc
Sub-Category	Miscellaneous Sector
Prospectus Objective	Technology
Inception Date	Sep-16
Open to New Investments	Y

Prices
Price (as of 9/30/2019)	20.02
52-Week High	23.10
52-Week Low	16.06

Total Returns (%)
3-Month	6-Month	1-Year	3-Year	5-Year
-5.50	-1.59	-11.62	34.19	

3-Year Standard Deviation	21.62
Effective Duration	

Valuation
Premium/Discount (1-Year Average)	-0.11

Company Information
Provider	Global X Funds
Manager/Tenure	Chang Kim (3), Nam To (1), Wayne Xie (0), 1 other
Website	http://www.globalxfunds.com
Address	Global X Funds 600 Lexington Avenue, 20th Floor New York NY 10022 United States
Phone Number	888-493-8631

PERFORMANCE

Ratings History
Date	Overall Rating	Risk Rating	Reward Rating
Q3-19	C-	C	D+
Q4-18	D+	D+	D+
Q4-17	D	B	C
Q4-16	U		
Q4-15			

Asset & Performance History
Date	NAV	1-Year Total Return
2018	16.87	-27.79
2017	23.7	58.53
2016	14.95	
2015		
2014		
2013		

Total Assets: $1,418,479,050

Asset Allocation
Asset	%
Cash	0%
Stocks	100%
US Stocks	31%
Bonds	0%
US Bonds	0%
Other	0%

Services Offered:

Investment Strategy: The investment seeks to provide investment results that correspond generally to the price and yield performance, before fees and expenses, of the Indxx Global Robotics & Artificial Intelligence Thematic Index. The fund invests at least 80% of its total assets in the securities of the underlying index. The underlying index is designed to provide exposure to exchange-listed companies in developed markets that are involved in the development of robotics and/or artificial intelligence as defined by Indxx, the provider of the underlying index. The fund is non-diversified. **Top Holdings:** NVIDIA Corp   Keyence Corp   Intuitive Surgical Inc   ABB Ltd   Fanuc Corp

Invesco BulletShares 2022 Corporate Bond ETF   C+   HOLD

Ticker	Traded On	NAV	Total Assets ($)	Dividend Yield (TTM)	Turnover Ratio	Expense Ratio
BSCM	NYSE Arca	21.43	$1,414,327,885	2.87	0	0.1

Ratings
Reward   C+
Risk   C+
Recent Upgrade/Downgrade

Fund Information
Fund Type   Exchange Traded Funds
Category   US Fixed Income
Sub-Category   Target Maturity
Prospectus Objective   Corp Bond - Gen
Inception Date   Jul-13
Open to New Investments   Y

Prices
Price (as of 9/30/2019)   21.49
52-Week High   21.56
52-Week Low   20.47

Total Returns (%)

3-Month	6-Month	1-Year	3-Year	5-Year
1.18	3.21	7.23	7.76	18.70

3-Year Standard Deviation   2.44
Effective Duration   2.73

Valuation
Premium/Discount (1-Year Average)   0.24

Company Information
Provider   Invesco
Manager/Tenure   Jeremy Neisewander (3), Peter Hubbard (1), Jeffrey W. Kernagis (1), 1 other
Website   http://www.invesco.com/us
Address   Invesco 11 Greenway Plaza, Ste. 2500 Houston TX 77046 United States
Phone Number   800-659-1005

PERFORMANCE

Ratings History

Date	Overall Rating	Risk Rating	Reward Rating
Q3-19	C+	C+	C+
Q4-18	C	C+	C-
Q4-17	B	A	C
Q4-16	C	C-	C
Q4-15	C-	C-	D+

Asset & Performance History

Date	NAV	1-Year Total Return
2018	20.56	0.03
2017	21.12	3.63
2016	20.86	5.8
2015	20.23	0.57
2014	20.67	7.74
2013	19.79	

Total Assets: $1,414,327,885

Asset Allocation

Asset	%
Cash	1%
Stocks	0%
US Stocks	0%
Bonds	99%
US Bonds	84%
Other	0%

Services Offered:

Investment Strategy: The investment seeks to track the investment results (before fees and expenses) of the Nasdaq BulletShares® USD Corporate Bond 2022 Index (the "underlying index"). The fund generally will invest at least 80% of its total assets in securities that comprise the underlying index. The underlying index seeks to measure the performance of a portfolio of U.S. dollar-denominated investment grade corporate bonds with maturities or, in some cases, "effective maturities" in the year 2022 (collectively, "2022 Bonds"). The fund is non-diversified. **Top Holdings:** Goldman Sachs Group, Inc. 5.75%   Wells Fargo & Company 2.62%   Broadcom Corporation/Broadcom Cayman Finance Ltd 3%   JPMorgan Chase & Co. 4.5%   Barclays Bank plc 7.62%

Invesco DB Commodity Index Tracking Fund   D+   SELL

Ticker	Traded On	NAV	Total Assets ($)	Dividend Yield (TTM)	Turnover Ratio	Expense Ratio
DBC	NYSE Arca	15.01	$1,405,359,103	1.26	0	0.85

Ratings
Reward   D+
Risk   C-
Recent Upgrade/Downgrade   Down

Fund Information
Fund Type   Exchange Traded Funds
Category   Commodities Broad Basket
Sub-Category   Commodities Broad Basket
Prospectus Objective   Natl Res
Inception Date   Feb-06
Open to New Investments   Y

Prices
Price (as of 9/30/2019)   15.04
52-Week High   18.54
52-Week Low   14.39

Total Returns (%)

3-Month	6-Month	1-Year	3-Year	5-Year
-4.65	-6.57	-16.90	1.13	-34.23

3-Year Standard Deviation   12.14
Effective Duration

Valuation
Premium/Discount (1-Year Average)   -0.13

Company Information
Provider   Invesco
Manager/Tenure   Management Team (13)
Website   http://www.invesco.com/us
Address   Invesco 11 Greenway Plaza, Ste. 2500 Houston TX 77046 United States
Phone Number   800-659-1005

PERFORMANCE

Ratings History

Date	Overall Rating	Risk Rating	Reward Rating
Q3-19	D+	C-	D+
Q4-18	C	C	C-
Q4-17	C-	D+	C
Q4-16	D	D	D
Q4-15	D-	D-	D-

Asset & Performance History

Date	NAV	1-Year Total Return
2018	14.44	-12.02
2017	16.63	4.82
2016	15.83	19.12
2015	13.35	-27.41
2014	18.4	-28.18
2013	25.62	-7.57

Total Assets: $1,405,359,103

Asset Allocation

Asset	%
Cash	45%
Stocks	0%
US Stocks	0%
Bonds	6%
US Bonds	6%
Other	44%

Services Offered:

Investment Strategy: The investment seeks to track changes, whether positive or negative, in the level of the DBIQ Optimum Yield Diversified Commodity Index Excess Return™.
The fund pursues its investment objective by investing in a portfolio of exchange-traded futures on Light Sweet Crude Oil (WTI), Heating Oil, RBOB Gasoline, Natural Gas, Brent Crude, Gold, Silver, Aluminum, Zinc, Copper Grade A, Corn, Wheat, Soybeans, and Sugar. The index is composed of notional amounts of each of these commodities. **Top Holdings:** United States Treasury Bills 0%   Invesco Treasury Collateral ETF   Gasoline Rbob Fut Jan20   Ny Harb Ulsd Fut Jun20   Wti Crude Future Mar20

First Trust Tactical High Yield ETF

C+ HOLD

Ticker	Traded On	NAV
HYLS	NAS CM	48.14

Total Assets ($)	Dividend Yield (TTM)	Turnover Ratio	Expense Ratio
$1,393,754,656	5.38	52	1.16

Ratings
Reward	C+
Risk	C+
Recent Upgrade/Downgrade	Down

Fund Information
Fund Type	Exchange Traded Funds
Category	US Fixed Income
Sub-Category	High Yield Bond
Prospectus Objective	Corp Bond-High Yld
Inception Date	Feb-13
Open to New Investments	Y

Prices
Price (as of 9/30/2019)	48.24
52-Week High	48.50
52-Week Low	44.51

Total Returns (%)
3-Month	6-Month	1-Year	3-Year	5-Year
1.52	3.40	6.44	16.71	25.49

3-Year Standard Deviation	4.04
Effective Duration	1.87

Valuation
Premium/Discount (1-Year Average)	0.01

Company Information
Provider	First Trust
Manager/Tenure	Scott D. Fries (6), William Housey (6), Orlando Purpura (3)
Website	http://www.ftportfolios.com/
Address	First Trust 120 E. Liberty Drive, Suite 400 Wheaton IL 60187 United States
Phone Number	800-621-1675

PERFORMANCE

Ratings History
Date	Overall Rating	Risk Rating	Reward Rating
Q3-19	C+	C+	C+
Q4-18	C	C+	C-
Q4-17	B	A-	C+
Q4-16	C	C+	C
Q4-15	C	C-	C

Asset & Performance History
Date	NAV	1-Year Total Return
2018	45.07	-1.79
2017	48.48	6.08
2016	48.28	8.55
2015	46.95	-0.15
2014	49.83	2.42
2013	51.43	

Total Assets: $1,393,754,656
Asset Allocation
Asset	%
Cash	-2%
Stocks	0%
US Stocks	0%
Bonds	102%
US Bonds	93%
Other	0%

Services Offered:

Investment Strategy: The investment seeks current income; capital appreciation is the secondary objective. Under normal market conditions, the fund invests at least 80% of its net assets (including investment borrowings) in high yield debt securities that are rated below investment grade at the time of purchase or unrated securities deemed by the fund's advisor to be of comparable quality. **Top Holdings:** Tenet Healthcare Corporation 8.12% Gray Television, Inc. 5.88% Stars Group Holdings Bv Tsgicn Ti 07/10/25 MPH Acquisition Holdings LLC 7.12% Bausch Health Companies Inc 6.12%

JPMorgan BetaBuilders Developed Asia ex-Japan ETF

C HOLD

Ticker	Traded On	NAV
BBAX	BATS	24.61

Total Assets ($)	Dividend Yield (TTM)	Turnover Ratio	Expense Ratio
$1,392,738,278	4.06		0.19

Ratings
Reward	D+
Risk	C+
Recent Upgrade/Downgrade	

Fund Information
Fund Type	Exchange Traded Funds
Category	Asia ex-Japan Equity
Sub-Category	Pacific/Asia ex-Japan Stk
Prospectus Objective	Growth
Inception Date	Aug-18
Open to New Investments	Y

Prices
Price (as of 9/30/2019)	24.71
52-Week High	26.74
52-Week Low	22.06

Total Returns (%)
3-Month	6-Month	1-Year	3-Year	5-Year
-5.24	-1.49	4.02		

3-Year Standard Deviation	
Effective Duration	

Valuation
Premium/Discount (1-Year Average)	0.18

Company Information
Provider	JPMorgan
Manager/Tenure	Nicholas D'Eramo (1), Oliver Furby (1), Alex Hamilton (1), 1 other
Website	http://www.jpmorganfunds.com
Address	JPMorgan 270 Park Avenue New York NY 10017-2070 United States
Phone Number	800-480-4111

PERFORMANCE

Ratings History
Date	Overall Rating	Risk Rating	Reward Rating
Q3-19	C	C+	D+
Q4-18	U		
Q4-17			
Q4-16			
Q4-15			

Asset & Performance History
Date	NAV	1-Year Total Return
2018	22.74	
2017		
2016		
2015		
2014		
2013		

Total Assets: $1,392,738,278
Asset Allocation
Asset	%
Cash	0%
Stocks	100%
US Stocks	1%
Bonds	0%
US Bonds	0%
Other	0%

Services Offered:

Investment Strategy: The investment seeks investment results that closely correspond, before fees and expenses, to the performance of the Morningstar® Developed Asia Pacific ex-Japan Target Market Exposure IndexSM. The fund will invest at least 80% of its assets in securities included in the underlying index. The underlying index targets 85% of the stocks traded on the primary exchanges in each country or region by market capitalization, and primarily includes large- and mid-capitalization companies. **Top Holdings:** AIA Group Ltd Commonwealth Bank of Australia CSL Ltd BHP Group Ltd Westpac Banking Corp

SPDR® Portfolio Small Cap ETF   C   HOLD

Ticker	Traded On	NAV	Total Assets ($)	Dividend Yield (TTM)	Turnover Ratio	Expense Ratio
SPSM	NYSE Arca		$1,391,720,672	1.73	14	0.05

Ratings
Reward   C
Risk   C+
Recent Upgrade/Downgrade

Fund Information
Fund Type   Exchange Traded Funds
Category   US Equity Small Cap
Sub-Category   Small Blend
Prospectus Objective   Growth
Inception Date   Jul-13
Open to New Investments   Y

Prices
Price (as of 9/30/2019)   30.00
52-Week High   32.82
52-Week Low   24.83

Total Returns (%)

3-Month	6-Month	1-Year	3-Year	5-Year
-2.33	-1.47	-7.16	28.05	49.99

3-Year Standard Deviation   17.29
Effective Duration

Valuation
Premium/Discount (1-Year Average)   -0.02

Company Information
Provider   SPDR State Street Global Advisors
Manager/Tenure   Michael J. Feehily (6), Karl A.
                    Schneider (4), Teddy Wong (2)
Website   http://www.spdrs.com
Address   SPDR State Street Global Advisors
                    State Street Financial Center, 1
                    Lincoln Street Boston MA 02111-2900
                    United States
Phone Number   617-786-3000

PERFORMANCE

Ratings History

Date	Overall Rating	Risk Rating	Reward Rating
Q3-19	C	C+	C
Q4-18	C	C+	C-
Q4-17	B+	B	A-
Q4-16	C+	C-	B
Q4-15	C-	D+	C-

Asset & Performance History

Date	NAV	1-Year Total Return
2018	26.37	-11.07
2017	30.14	15.39
2016	26.54	21.47
2015	22.21	-4.34
2014	23.76	4.95
2013	23.03	

Total Assets: $1,391,720,672
Asset Allocation

Asset	%
Cash	0%
Stocks	100%
US Stocks	99%
Bonds	0%
US Bonds	0%
Other	0%

Services Offered:

Investment Strategy: The investment seeks to provide investment results that, before fees and expenses, correspond generally to the total return performance of the SSGA Small Cap Index that tracks the performance of small capitalization exchange traded U.S. equity securities. The fund generally invests substantially all, but at least 80%, of its total assets in the securities comprising the index. It may purchase a subset of the securities in the index in an effort to hold a portfolio of securities with generally the same risk and return characteristics of the index. The fund is non-diversified. **Top Holdings:** Roku Inc Class A Coupa Software Inc Chemed Corp Cable One Inc Casey's General Stores Inc

SPDR® S&P 400 Mid Cap Value ETF   D   SELL

Ticker	Traded On	NAV	Total Assets ($)	Dividend Yield (TTM)	Turnover Ratio	Expense Ratio
MDYV	NYSE Arca		$1,390,123,685	1.92	35	0.15

Ratings
Reward   D
Risk   D
Recent Upgrade/Downgrade

Fund Information
Fund Type   Exchange Traded Funds
Category   US Equity Mid Cap
Sub-Category   Mid-Cap Value
Prospectus Objective   Growth
Inception Date   Nov-05
Open to New Investments   Y

Prices
Price (as of 9/30/2019)   51.32
52-Week High   53.44
52-Week Low   41.80

Total Returns (%)

3-Month	6-Month	1-Year	3-Year	5-Year
-0.63	0.46	-2.55	-36.91	-27.62

3-Year Standard Deviation   16.62
Effective Duration

Valuation
Premium/Discount (1-Year Average)   0.01

Company Information
Provider   SPDR State Street Global Advisors
Manager/Tenure   Michael J. Feehily (7), Karl A.
                    Schneider (4), Juan Acevedo (0)
Website   http://www.spdrs.com
Address   SPDR State Street Global Advisors
                    State Street Financial Center, 1
                    Lincoln Street Boston MA 02111-2900
                    United States
Phone Number   617-786-3000

PERFORMANCE

Ratings History

Date	Overall Rating	Risk Rating	Reward Rating
Q3-19	D	D	D
Q4-18	D-	D	D-
Q4-17	B	B	B
Q4-16	C-	C-	C-
Q4-15	C	D+	C

Asset & Performance History

Date	NAV	1-Year Total Return
2018	44.34	-55.97
2017	102.83	12.17
2016	94.05	25.58
2015	75.95	-6.72
2014	84.92	11.82
2013	79.08	33.86

Total Assets: $1,390,123,685
Asset Allocation

Asset	%
Cash	0%
Stocks	100%
US Stocks	100%
Bonds	0%
US Bonds	0%
Other	0%

Services Offered: Dividend Investment Plan, CashInvestment Plan

Investment Strategy: The investment seeks to provide investment results that, before fees and expenses, correspond generally to the total return performance of the S&P MidCap 400 Value Index. The fund generally invests substantially all, but at least 80%, of its total assets in the securities comprising the index. The index measures the performance of the mid-capitalization value segment of the U.S. equity market. It may purchase a subset of the securities in the index in an effort to hold a portfolio of securities with generally the same risk and return characteristics of the index. The fund is non-diversified. **Top Holdings:** Alleghany Corp WR Berkley Corp Reinsurance Group of America Inc RenaissanceRe Holdings Ltd Kilroy Realty Corp

JPMorgan Diversified Return International Equity ETF　　　　　C　　HOLD

Ticker	Traded On	NAV	Total Assets ($)	Dividend Yield (TTM)	Turnover Ratio	Expense Ratio
JPIN	NYSE Arca	53.19	$1,377,548,578	3.21	28	0.38

Ratings
Reward　　　　　　　　　　　　　　C-
Risk　　　　　　　　　　　　　　C+
Recent Upgrade/Downgrade

Fund Information
Fund Type　　　　　　　Exchange Traded Funds
Category　　　　　　　　Global Equity Large Cap
Sub-Category　　　　　　Foreign Large Blend
Prospectus Objective　　　Growth & Inc
Inception Date　　　　　　Nov-14
Open to New Investments　　Y

Prices
Price (as of 9/30/2019)　　　53.17
52-Week High　　　　　　　58.41
52-Week Low　　　　　　　49.33

Total Returns (%)

3-Month	6-Month	1-Year	3-Year	5-Year
-2.18	-2.83	-5.54	11.43	

3-Year Standard Deviation　　10.91
Effective Duration

Valuation
Premium/Discount (1-Year Average)　　-0.11

Company Information
Provider　　　JPMorgan
Manager/Tenure　Kartik Aiyar (2), Wei (Victor) Li (2), Yazann Romahi (2), 1 other
Website　　　http://www.jpmorganfunds.com
Address　　　JPMorgan 270 Park Avenue New York NY 10017-2070 United States
Phone Number　800-480-4111

PERFORMANCE

Ratings History

Date	Overall Rating	Risk Rating	Reward Rating
Q3-19	C	C+	C-
Q4-18	C-	C	D+
Q4-17	C+	B-	C+
Q4-16	D+	C-	D+
Q4-15	U		

Asset & Performance History

Date	NAV	1-Year Total Return
2018	51.07	-12.5
2017	59.84	25.25
2016	48.8	0.91
2015	49.17	2.93
2014	48.81	
2013		

Total Assets: $1,377,548,578
Asset Allocation

Asset	%
Cash	0%
Stocks	100%
US Stocks	2%
Bonds	0%
US Bonds	0%
Other	0%

Services Offered:

Investment Strategy: The investment seeks investment results that closely correspond, before fees and expenses, to the performance of the JP Morgan Diversified Factor International Equity Index. The fund will invest at least 80% of its net assets in securities included in the underlying index. The underlying index is comprised of equity securities across developed global markets (excluding North America) selected to represent a diversified set of factor characteristics: value, price momentum and quality. **Top Holdings:** Capcom Co Ltd　AstraZeneca PLC　Hikma Pharmaceuticals PLC　Rentokil Initial PLC　Smith & Nephew PLC

John Hancock Multifactor Mid Cap ETF　　　　　　　　　C　　HOLD

Ticker	Traded On	NAV	Total Assets ($)	Dividend Yield (TTM)	Turnover Ratio	Expense Ratio
JHMM	NYSE Arca	36.79	$1,376,714,447	1.19	13	0.44

Ratings
Reward　　　　　　　　　　　　　　C
Risk　　　　　　　　　　　　　　C+
Recent Upgrade/Downgrade

Fund Information
Fund Type　　　　　　　Exchange Traded Funds
Category　　　　　　　　US Equity Mid Cap
Sub-Category　　　　　　Mid-Cap Blend
Prospectus Objective　　　Growth
Inception Date　　　　　　Sep-15
Open to New Investments　　Y

Prices
Price (as of 9/30/2019)　　　36.82
52-Week High　　　　　　　37.48
52-Week Low　　　　　　　28.59

Total Returns (%)

3-Month	6-Month	1-Year	3-Year	5-Year
0.09	3.75	2.64	37.44	

3-Year Standard Deviation　　13.76
Effective Duration

Valuation
Premium/Discount (1-Year Average)　　0.05

Company Information
Provider　　　John Hancock
Manager/Tenure　Joel P. Schneider (4), Lukas J. Smart (4), Joseph F. Hohn (1)
Website　　　http://jhinvestments.com
Address　　　601 Congress Street, Boston MA 02210 United States
Phone Number　800-225-5913

PERFORMANCE

Ratings History

Date	Overall Rating	Risk Rating	Reward Rating
Q3-19	C	C+	C
Q4-18	C	C+	C-
Q4-17	C	B	C+
Q4-16	D	D+	D+
Q4-15			

Asset & Performance History

Date	NAV	1-Year Total Return
2018	30.44	-9.62
2017	34.14	20.06
2016	28.7	14.02
2015	25.47	
2014		
2013		

Total Assets: $1,376,714,447
Asset Allocation

Asset	%
Cash	3%
Stocks	97%
US Stocks	95%
Bonds	0%
US Bonds	0%
Other	0%

Services Offered:

Investment Strategy: The investment seeks to provide investment results that closely correspond, before fees and expenses, to the performance of the John Hancock Dimensional Mid Cap Index. The fund normally invests at least 80% of its net assets (plus any borrowings for investment purposes) in securities that compose the fund's index. The index is designed to comprise a subset of securities in the U.S. Universe issued by companies whose market capitalizations are between the 200th and 951st largest U.S. company at the time of reconstitution. **Top Holdings:** L3Harris Technologies Inc　United Airlines Holdings Inc　Xcel Energy Inc　Amphenol Corp Class A　Republic Services Inc Class A

iShares California Muni Bond ETF
C+   HOLD

Ticker	Traded On	NAV	Total Assets ($)	Dividend Yield (TTM)	Turnover Ratio	Expense Ratio
CMF	NYSE Arca	61.14	$1,366,524,628	2.1	32	0.25

Ratings
Reward	C+
Risk	C+
Recent Upgrade/Downgrade	Up

Fund Information
Fund Type	Exchange Traded Funds
Category	US Muni Fixed Inc
Sub-Category	Muni California Long
Prospectus Objective	Muni Bond - Single State
Inception Date	Oct-07
Open to New Investments	Y

Prices
Price (as of 9/30/2019)	61.28
52-Week High	61.99
52-Week Low	56.95

Total Returns (%)
3-Month	6-Month	1-Year	3-Year	5-Year
1.55	4.06	7.93	8.27	17.19

3-Year Standard Deviation	3.58
Effective Duration	6.18

Valuation
Premium/Discount (1-Year Average)	0.16

Company Information
Provider	iShares
Manager/Tenure	Scott Radell (9), James Mauro (8)
Website	http://www.ishares.com
Address	iShares 400 Howard Street San Francisco CA 94105 United States
Phone Number	800-474-2737

PERFORMANCE

Ratings History
Date	Overall Rating	Risk Rating	Reward Rating
Q3-19	C+	C+	C+
Q4-18	C	C+	C-
Q4-17	B-	B+	C
Q4-16	C	C-	C
Q4-15	C	C-	C+

Asset & Performance History
Date	NAV	1-Year Total Return
2018	58.22	0.68
2017	59.1	4.67
2016	57.57	-0.2
2015	58.94	3.3
2014	58.55	9.99
2013	54.78	-1.93

Total Assets: $1,366,524,628
Asset Allocation
Asset	%
Cash	0%
Stocks	0%
US Stocks	0%
Bonds	100%
US Bonds	100%
Other	0%

Services Offered:

Investment Strategy: The investment seeks to track the investment results of the S&P California AMT-Free Municipal Bond IndexTM. The index measures the performance of the investment-grade segment of the California municipal bond market. The fund generally will invest at least 90% of its assets in the component securities of the index and may invest up to 10% of its assets in certain futures, options and swap contracts, cash and cash equivalents, including shares of money market funds advised by BFA or its affiliates, as well as in securities not included in the index, but which BFA believes will help the fund track the index. It is non-diversified. **Top Holdings:** LOS ANGELES CNTY CALIF MET TRANSN AUTH SALES TAX REV 5% CALIFORNIA ST DEPT WTR RES PWR SUPPLY REV 5% LOS ANGELES CALIF DEPT WTR & PWR WTRWKS REV 5% SAN JOAQUIN HILLS CALIF TRANSN CORRIDOR AGY TOLL RD REV 5% UNIVERSITY CALIF REVS 5%

Vanguard International High Dividend Yield Index Fund ETF Shares
C   HOLD

Ticker	Traded On	NAV	Total Assets ($)	Dividend Yield (TTM)	Turnover Ratio	Expense Ratio
VYMI	NAS CM	59.28	$1,361,927,628	4.43	10	0.32

Ratings
Reward	C
Risk	C+
Recent Upgrade/Downgrade	Up

Fund Information
Fund Type	Exchange Traded Funds
Category	Global Equity Large Cap
Sub-Category	Foreign Large Value
Prospectus Objective	Foreign Stock
Inception Date	Feb-16
Open to New Investments	Y

Prices
Price (as of 9/30/2019)	59.39
52-Week High	63.23
52-Week Low	54.56

Total Returns (%)
3-Month	6-Month	1-Year	3-Year	5-Year
-2.39	0.51	-1.37	18.59	

3-Year Standard Deviation	11.36
Effective Duration	

Valuation
Premium/Discount (1-Year Average)	0.16

Company Information
Provider	Vanguard
Manager/Tenure	Justin E. Hales (3), Michael Perre (3)
Website	http://www.vanguard.com
Address	Vanguard 100 Vanguard Boulevard Malvern PA 19355 United States
Phone Number	877-662-7447

PERFORMANCE

Ratings History
Date	Overall Rating	Risk Rating	Reward Rating
Q3-19	C	C+	C
Q4-18	C-	C	D+
Q4-17	C-	B+	C
Q4-16	U		
Q4-15			

Asset & Performance History
Date	NAV	1-Year Total Return
2018	56.03	-12.75
2017	66.78	22.55
2016	56.44	
2015		
2014		
2013		

Total Assets: $1,361,927,628
Asset Allocation
Asset	%
Cash	0%
Stocks	100%
US Stocks	1%
Bonds	0%
US Bonds	0%
Other	0%

Services Offered:

Investment Strategy: The investment seeks to track the performance of FTSE All-World ex US High Dividend Yield Index that measures the investment return of non-U.S. companies that are characterized by high dividend yield. The fund invests by sampling the index, meaning that it holds a broadly diversified collection of securities that, in the aggregate, approximates the full index in terms of key characteristics. The index focuses on companies located in developed and emerging markets, excluding the United States, that are forecasted to have above-average dividend yields. **Top Holdings:** Taiwan Semiconductor Manufacturing Co Ltd HSBC Holdings PLC Toyota Motor Corp Royal Dutch Shell PLC Class A BP PLC

VanEck Vectors Semiconductor ETF   B-   BUY

Ticker	Traded On	NAV	Total Assets ($)	Dividend Yield (TTM)	Turnover Ratio	Expense Ratio
SMH	NYSE Arca	119.14	$1,360,736,581	1.37	23	0.35

Ratings
Reward	B
Risk	C
Recent Upgrade/Downgrade	Up

Fund Information
Fund Type	Exchange Traded Funds
Category	Technology Sector Equity
Sub-Category	Technology
Prospectus Objective	Technology
Inception Date	Dec-11
Open to New Investments	Y

Prices
Price (as of 9/30/2019)	119.13
52-Week High	123.31
52-Week Low	80.96

Total Returns (%)

3-Month	6-Month	1-Year	3-Year	5-Year
5.11	9.35	13.83	78.97	156.51

3-Year Standard Deviation	21.52
Effective Duration	

Valuation
Premium/Discount (1-Year Average)	0.05

Company Information
Provider	VanEck
Manager/Tenure	Hao-Hung (Peter) Liao (7), Guo Hua (Jason) Jin (1)
Website	http://www.vaneck.com
Address	Van Eck Associates Corporation 666 Third Avenue New York NY 10017 United States
Phone Number	800-826-1115

PERFORMANCE

Ratings History

Date	Overall Rating	Risk Rating	Reward Rating
Q3-19	B-	C	B
Q4-18	C+	C	B
Q4-17	B+	C+	A+
Q4-16	C+	C	C+
Q4-15	B	B	B

Asset & Performance History

Date	NAV	1-Year Total Return
2018	87.33	-9.46
2017	97.77	38.31
2016	71.68	35.4
2015	53.36	-0.11
2014	54.56	29.99
2013	42.45	33.7

Total Assets: $1,360,736,581

Asset Allocation

Asset	%
Cash	0%
Stocks	100%
US Stocks	74%
Bonds	0%
US Bonds	0%
Other	0%

Services Offered:

Investment Strategy: The investment seeks to replicate as closely as possible, before fees and expenses, the price and yield performance of the MVIS® US Listed Semiconductor 25 Index. The fund normally invests at least 80% of its total assets in securities that comprise the fund's benchmark index. The index includes common stocks and depositary receipts of U.S. exchange-listed companies in the semiconductor industry. Such companies may include medium-capitalization companies and foreign companies that are listed on a U.S. exchange. The fund is non-diversified. **Top Holdings:** Taiwan Semiconductor Manufacturing Co Ltd ADR Intel Corp Texas Instruments Inc Micron Technology Inc NVIDIA Corp

---

Vanguard Russell 3000 Index Fund ETF Shares   C   HOLD

Ticker	Traded On	NAV	Total Assets ($)	Dividend Yield (TTM)	Turnover Ratio	Expense Ratio
VTHR	NAS CM	134.94	$1,354,136,232	1.75	14	0.15

Ratings
Reward	C+
Risk	C-
Recent Upgrade/Downgrade	

Fund Information
Fund Type	Exchange Traded Funds
Category	US Equity Large Cap Blend
Sub-Category	Large Blend
Prospectus Objective	Growth
Inception Date	Sep-10
Open to New Investments	Y

Prices
Price (as of 9/30/2019)	135.18
52-Week High	138.05
52-Week Low	106.85

Total Returns (%)

3-Month	6-Month	1-Year	3-Year	5-Year
-0.08	3.56	2.18	42.46	62.35

3-Year Standard Deviation	12.53
Effective Duration	

Valuation
Premium/Discount (1-Year Average)	0.03

Company Information
Provider	Vanguard
Manager/Tenure	Michael A. Johnson (3), Walter Nejman (3)
Website	http://www.vanguard.com
Address	Vanguard 100 Vanguard Boulevard Malvern PA 19355 United States
Phone Number	877-662-7447

PERFORMANCE

Ratings History

Date	Overall Rating	Risk Rating	Reward Rating
Q3-19	C	C-	C+
Q4-18	C-	D+	C
Q4-17	B	B	B
Q4-16	C+	C-	B
Q4-15	C	C-	C

Asset & Performance History

Date	NAV	1-Year Total Return
2018	112.92	-6.15
2017	122.41	21.06
2016	102.99	11.92
2015	93.33	0.35
2014	94.71	12.41
2013	85.72	33.34

Total Assets: $1,354,136,232

Asset Allocation

Asset	%
Cash	0%
Stocks	100%
US Stocks	99%
Bonds	0%
US Bonds	0%
Other	0%

Services Offered:

Investment Strategy: The investment seeks to track the performance of a benchmark index that measures the investment return of the broad U.S. stock market. The fund employs an indexing investment approach designed to track the performance of the Russell 3000® Index, which represents approximately 98% of the U.S. equity market and comprises the 3,000 largest companies in the United States. The Advisor attempts to replicate the target index by investing all, or substantially all, of its assets in the stocks that make up the index, holding each stock in approximately the same proportion as its weighting in the index. **Top Holdings:** Microsoft Corp Apple Inc Amazon.com Inc Facebook Inc A Berkshire Hathaway Inc B

iShares Core Growth Allocation ETF

C   HOLD

Ticker	Traded On	NAV	Total Assets ($)	Dividend Yield (TTM)	Turnover Ratio	Expense Ratio
AOR	NYSE Arca	46.01	$1,338,881,392	2.44	4	0.25

Ratings
Reward   C
Risk   C-
Recent Upgrade/Downgrade

Fund Information
Fund Type   Exchange Traded Funds
Category   Moderate Allocation
Sub-Category   Allocation--50% to 70% Equity
Prospectus Objective   Asset Allocation
Inception Date   Nov-08
Open to New Investments   Y

Prices
Price (as of 9/30/2019)   46.06
52-Week High   46.22
52-Week Low   40.34

Total Returns (%)

3-Month	6-Month	1-Year	3-Year	5-Year
0.57	3.65	4.45	22.85	34.37

3-Year Standard Deviation   6.94
Effective Duration   2.34

Valuation
Premium/Discount (1-Year Average)   0.04

Company Information
Provider   iShares
Manager/Tenure Diane Hsiung (10), Greg Savage (10),
                Jennifer Hsui (6), 3 others
Website   http://www.ishares.com
Address   iShares 400 Howard Street San
                Francisco CA 94105 United States
Phone Number   800-474-2737

PERFORMANCE

Ratings History

Date	Overall Rating	Risk Rating	Reward Rating
Q3-19	C	C-	C
Q4-18	C	C+	C-
Q4-17	B	A-	C+
Q4-16	C	C-	C
Q4-15	C	C-	C

Asset & Performance History

Date	NAV	1-Year Total Return
2018	41.25	-5.83
2017	44.86	15.87
2016	40.5	6.66
2015	38.81	-1.07
2014	40.05	6.21
2013	38.51	15.92

Total Assets: $1,338,881,392
Asset Allocation

Asset	%
Cash	1%
Stocks	58%
US Stocks	32%
Bonds	40%
US Bonds	29%
Other	0%

Services Offered:

Investment Strategy: The investment seeks to track the investment results of the S&P Target Risk Growth Index composed of a portfolio of underlying equity and fixed income funds intended to represent a growth allocation target risk strategy. The fund is a fund of funds and seeks its investment objective by investing primarily in other iShares Underlying Funds that themselves seek investment results corresponding to their own respective underlying indexes. It generally will invest at least 90% of its assets in the component securities of the underlying index. The index measures the performance of the S&P Dow Jones Indices LLC proprietary allocation model. **Top Holdings:** Microsoft Corp Apple Inc Amazon.com Inc Facebook Inc A Berkshire Hathaway Inc B

Direxion Daily Financial Bull 3X Shares

C   HOLD

Ticker	Traded On	NAV	Total Assets ($)	Dividend Yield (TTM)	Turnover Ratio	Expense Ratio
FAS	NYSE Arca	77.56	$1,330,063,689	0.82	73	1

Ratings
Reward   B-
Risk   C-
Recent Upgrade/Downgrade

Fund Information
Fund Type   Exchange Traded Funds
Category   Trading Tools
Sub-Category   Trading--Leveraged Equity
Prospectus Objective   Financial
Inception Date   Nov-08
Open to New Investments   Y

Prices
Price (as of 9/30/2019)   77.64
52-Week High   82.22
52-Week Low   37.55

Total Returns (%)

3-Month	6-Month	1-Year	3-Year	5-Year
2.32	19.74	11.47	170.69	217.60

3-Year Standard Deviation   40.94
Effective Duration

Valuation
Premium/Discount (1-Year Average)   -0.11

Company Information
Provider   Direxion Funds
Manager/Tenure Paul Brigandi (10), Tony Ng (4)
Website   http://www.direxionfunds.com
Address   Direxion Funds 1301 Avenue Of The
                Americas (6th Avenue) New York NY
                10019 United States
Phone Number   646-572-3390

PERFORMANCE

Ratings History

Date	Overall Rating	Risk Rating	Reward Rating
Q3-19	C	C-	B-
Q4-18	C	C-	C
Q4-17	B	C-	A-
Q4-16	C	D+	B-
Q4-15	A	B+	A+

Asset & Performance History

Date	NAV	1-Year Total Return
2018	44.8	-33.59
2017	68.17	66.94
2016	40.88	40.62
2015	29.07	-8.49
2014	31.77	40.57
2013	22.6	125.93

Total Assets: $1,330,063,689
Asset Allocation

Asset	%
Cash	12%
Stocks	88%
US Stocks	87%
Bonds	0%
US Bonds	0%
Other	0%

Services Offered:

Investment Strategy: The investment seeks daily investment results, before fees and expenses, of 300% of the daily performance of the Russell 1000® Financial Services Index. The fund invests at least 80% of its net assets (plus borrowing for investment purposes) in financial instruments and securities of the index, ETFs that track the index and other financial instruments that provide daily leveraged exposure to the index or ETFs that track the index. The index is a subset of the Russell 1000® Index that measures the performance of the securities classified in the financial services sector of the large-capitalization U.S. equity market. It is non-diversified. **Top Holdings:** Russ 1000 Finan Indx Swap Berkshire Hathaway Inc B Russ 1000 Finan Indx Swap JPMorgan Chase & Co Visa Inc Class A

First Trust Large Cap Core AlphaDEX® Fund   C   HOLD

Ticker	Traded On	NAV	Total Assets ($)	Dividend Yield (TTM)	Turnover Ratio	Expense Ratio
FEX	NAS CM	60.92	$1,327,973,606	1.42	102	0.61

Ratings
Reward   C
Risk   C-
Recent Upgrade/Downgrade

Fund Information
Fund Type   Exchange Traded Funds
Category   US Equity Large Cap Blend
Sub-Category   Large Blend
Prospectus Objective   Growth
Inception Date   May-07
Open to New Investments   Y

Prices
Price (as of 9/30/2019)   60.90
52-Week High   62.91
52-Week Low   48.95

Total Returns (%)
3-Month	6-Month	1-Year	3-Year	5-Year
-0.90	1.79	-1.04	35.31	51.68

3-Year Standard Deviation   13.68
Effective Duration

Valuation
Premium/Discount (1-Year Average)   -0.02

Company Information
Provider   First Trust
Manager/Tenure   Jon C. Erickson (12), Daniel J.
                 Lindquist (12), David G. McGarel (12),
                 3 others
Website   http://www.ftportfolios.com/
Address   First Trust 120 E. Liberty Drive, Suite
                 400 Wheaton IL 60187 United States
Phone Number   800-621-1675

PERFORMANCE

Ratings History
Date	Overall Rating	Risk Rating	Reward Rating
Q3-19	C	C-	C
Q4-18	C	C+	C-
Q4-17	B-	B-	B
Q4-16	B-	C+	B-
Q4-15	C	C+	C

Asset & Performance History
Date	NAV	1-Year Total Return
2018	52.13	-9.81
2017	58.51	21.52
2016	48.7	14.11
2015	43.26	-3.88
2014	45.59	12.33
2013	41.13	35.78

Total Assets: $1,327,973,606
Asset Allocation
Asset	%
Cash	0%
Stocks	100%
US Stocks	99%
Bonds	0%
US Bonds	0%
Other	0%

Services Offered:

Investment Strategy: The investment seeks investment results that correspond generally to the price and yield (before the fund's fees and expenses) of an equity index called the Nasdaq AlphaDEX® Large Cap Core Index. The fund will normally invest at least 90% of its net assets (including investment borrowings) in common stocks that comprise the index. The index is designed to select stocks from the NASDAQ US 500 Large Cap Index (the "base index") that may generate positive alpha, or risk-adjusted returns, relative to traditional indices through the use of the AlphaDEX® selection methodology. **Top Holdings:** Altice USA Inc Class A   Starbucks Corp   Micron Technology Inc   Ball Corp   DexCom Inc

First Trust Utilities AlphaDEX® Fund   B-   BUY

Ticker	Traded On	NAV	Total Assets ($)	Dividend Yield (TTM)	Turnover Ratio	Expense Ratio
FXU	NYSE Arca	29.63	$1,308,227,487	2.49	60	0.63

Ratings
Reward   B-
Risk   C+
Recent Upgrade/Downgrade   Up

Fund Information
Fund Type   Exchange Traded Funds
Category   Utilities Sector Equity
Sub-Category   Utilities
Prospectus Objective   Utility
Inception Date   May-07
Open to New Investments   Y

Prices
Price (as of 9/30/2019)   29.65
52-Week High   29.95
52-Week Low   25.97

Total Returns (%)
3-Month	6-Month	1-Year	3-Year	5-Year
4.44	6.10	10.34	24.70	52.98

3-Year Standard Deviation   8.71
Effective Duration

Valuation
Premium/Discount (1-Year Average)   -0.01

Company Information
Provider   First Trust
Manager/Tenure   Jon C. Erickson (12), Daniel J.
                 Lindquist (12), David G. McGarel (12),
                 3 others
Website   http://www.ftportfolios.com/
Address   First Trust 120 E. Liberty Drive, Suite
                 400 Wheaton IL 60187 United States
Phone Number   800-621-1675

PERFORMANCE

Ratings History
Date	Overall Rating	Risk Rating	Reward Rating
Q3-19	B-	C+	B-
Q4-18	B	C+	B+
Q4-17	C+	B	C
Q4-16	B-	C	B
Q4-15	B-	C	B

Asset & Performance History
Date	NAV	1-Year Total Return
2018	26.8	5.59
2017	26	0.93
2016	26.73	22.54
2015	22.4	-6.42
2014	24.87	25.5
2013	20.27	17.6

Total Assets: $1,308,227,487
Asset Allocation
Asset	%
Cash	0%
Stocks	100%
US Stocks	100%
Bonds	0%
US Bonds	0%
Other	0%

Services Offered:

Investment Strategy: The investment seeks investment results that correspond generally to the price and yield (before the fund's fees and expenses) of an equity index called the StrataQuant® Utilities Index. The fund will normally invest at least 90% of its net assets (including investment borrowings) in common stocks that comprise the index. The index is a modified equal-dollar weighted index designed by IDI to objectively identify and select stocks from the Russell 1000® Index in the utilities sector that may generate positive alpha relative to traditional passive-style indices through the use of the AlphaDEX® selection methodology. **Top Holdings:** Vistra Energy Corp   AT&T Inc   PPL Corp   National Fuel Gas Co   Telephone and Data Systems Inc

Invesco Taxable Municipal Bond ETF   B-   BUY

Ticker	Traded On	NAV	Total Assets ($)	Dividend Yield (TTM)	Turnover Ratio	Expense Ratio
BAB	NYSE Arca	32.29	$1,306,278,460	3.79		0.28

Ratings
Reward   B-
Risk   C+
Recent Upgrade/Downgrade   Up

Fund Information
Fund Type   Exchange Traded Funds
Category   US Fixed Income
Sub-Category   Long-Term Bond
Prospectus Objective   Muni Bond - Natl
Inception Date   Nov-09
Open to New Investments   Y

Prices
Price (as of 9/30/2019)   32.40
52-Week High   33.08
52-Week Low   28.54

Total Returns (%)

3-Month	6-Month	1-Year	3-Year	5-Year
4.18	9.22	15.29	16.61	34.23

3-Year Standard Deviation   5.25
Effective Duration   8.66

Valuation
Premium/Discount (1-Year Average)   0.21

Company Information
Provider   Invesco
Manager/Tenure   Philip Fang (9), Peter Hubbard (9),
                  Jeffrey W. Kernagis (9), 2 others
Website   http://www.invesco.com/us
Address   Invesco 11 Greenway Plaza, Ste. 2500
                  Houston TX 77046 United States
Phone Number   800-659-1005

PERFORMANCE

Ratings History

Date	Overall Rating	Risk Rating	Reward Rating
Q3-19	B-	C+	B-
Q4-18	C	C+	C-
Q4-17	B	A-	C+
Q4-16	C	C+	C
Q4-15	C	C-	C

Asset & Performance History

Date	NAV	1-Year Total Return
2018	29.51	0.63
2017	30.59	8.2
2016	29.44	5.27
2015	29.13	0.91
2014	30.23	15.69
2013	27.41	-5.09

Total Assets: $1,306,278,460
Asset Allocation

Asset	%
Cash	1%
Stocks	0%
US Stocks	0%
Bonds	99%
US Bonds	99%
Other	0%

Services Offered:

Investment Strategy: The investment seeks to track the investment results (before fees and expenses) of the ICE BofAML US Taxable Municipal Securities Plus Index (the "underlying index"). The fund generally will invest at least 80% of its total assets in taxable municipal securities that comprise the underlying index. The underlying index is designed to track the performance of U.S. dollar-denominated taxable municipal debt publicly issued by U.S. states and territories, and their political subdivisions, in the U.S. market. **Top Holdings:** CALIFORNIA ST 7.6% UNIVERSITY CALIF REVS 4.13% CALIFORNIA ST 7.3% COMMONWEALTH FING AUTH PA REV 3.66% AMERICAN MUN PWR OHIO INC REV 8.08%

---

iShares Mortgage Real Estate Capped ETF   C   HOLD

Ticker	Traded On	NAV	Total Assets ($)	Dividend Yield (TTM)	Turnover Ratio	Expense Ratio
REM	BATS	42.11	$1,297,041,071	8.84	25	0.48

Ratings
Reward   C+
Risk   C
Recent Upgrade/Downgrade   Down

Fund Information
Fund Type   Exchange Traded Funds
Category   Real Estate Sector Equity
Sub-Category   Real Estate
Prospectus Objective   Real Estate
Inception Date   May-07
Open to New Investments   Y

Prices
Price (as of 9/30/2019)   42.13
52-Week High   44.37
52-Week Low   38.44

Total Returns (%)

3-Month	6-Month	1-Year	3-Year	5-Year
2.17	1.16	5.99	31.92	48.16

3-Year Standard Deviation   12.76
Effective Duration

Valuation
Premium/Discount (1-Year Average)   -0.01

Company Information
Provider   iShares
Manager/Tenure   Greg Savage (11), Jennifer Hsui (7),
                  Alan Mason (3), 2 others
Website   http://www.ishares.com
Address   iShares 400 Howard Street San
                  Francisco CA 94105 United States
Phone Number   800-474-2737

PERFORMANCE

Ratings History

Date	Overall Rating	Risk Rating	Reward Rating
Q3-19	C	C	C+
Q4-18	B-	C	B
Q4-17	B-	C+	B-
Q4-16	C	C-	B-
Q4-15	C	C	B-

Asset & Performance History

Date	NAV	1-Year Total Return
2018	39.96	-2.95
2017	45.21	18.56
2016	42.06	21.96
2015	38.24	-9.31
2014	46.88	16.69
2013	46.16	-2.46

Total Assets: $1,297,041,071
Asset Allocation

Asset	%
Cash	2%
Stocks	98%
US Stocks	98%
Bonds	0%
US Bonds	0%
Other	0%

Services Offered:

Investment Strategy: The investment seeks to track the investment results of the FTSE NAREIT All Mortgage Capped Index composed of U.S. real estate investment trusts ("REITs") that hold U.S. residential and commercial mortgages. The fund generally will invest at least 90% of its assets in the component securities of the underlying index and may invest up to 10% of its assets in certain futures, options and swap contracts, cash and cash equivalents. The underlying index measures the performance of the residential and commercial mortgage real estate, mortgage finance and savings associations sectors of the U.S. equity market. The fund is non-diversified. **Top Holdings:** Annaly Capital Management Inc AGNC Investment Corp Starwood Property Trust Inc New Residential Investment Corp Two Harbors Investment Corp

---

ProShares UltraPro S&P500   C   HOLD

Ticker	Traded On	NAV	Total Assets ($)	Dividend Yield (TTM)	Turnover Ratio	Expense Ratio
UPRO	NYSE Arca	55.27	$1,287,851,715	0.52	15	0.92

Ratings
Reward   C+
Risk   C-
Recent Upgrade/Downgrade

Fund Information
Fund Type   Exchange Traded Funds
Category   Trading Tools
Sub-Category   Trading--Leveraged Equity
Prospectus Objective   Growth
Inception Date   Jun-09
Open to New Investments   Y

Prices
Price (as of 9/30/2019)   55.27
52-Week High   58.94
52-Week Low   29.00

Total Returns (%)

3-Month	6-Month	1-Year	3-Year	5-Year
-0.53	8.55	-3.89	127.13	198.87

3-Year Standard Deviation   36.89
Effective Duration

Valuation
Premium/Discount (1-Year Average)   -0.10

Company Information
Provider   ProShares
Manager/Tenure   Michael Neches (6), Devin Sullivan (1)
Website   http://www.proshares.com
Address   ProShares 7501 Wisconsin Avenue,
                      Suite 1000 Bethesda MD 20814
                      United States
Phone Number   866-776-5125

PERFORMANCE

Ratings History				Asset & Performance History			Total Assets:	$1,287,851,715
Date	Overall Rating	Risk Rating	Reward Rating	Date	NAV	1-Year Total Return	Asset Allocation Asset	%
Q3-19	C	C-	C+	2018	34.73	-24.91	Cash	-200%
Q4-18	C	C	C	2017	46.5	71.26	Stocks	300%
Q4-17	B+	C	A+	2016	27.15	30.1	US Stocks	297%
Q4-16	C	C	C	2015	20.9	-5.04	Bonds	0%
Q4-15	C+	B	C	2014	22.08	38	US Bonds	0%
				2013	16.04	118.55	Other	0%

Services Offered:

Investment Strategy: The investment seeks daily investment results, before fees and expenses, that correspond to three times (3x) the daily performance of the S&P 500® Index. The fund invests in financial instruments that ProShare Advisors believes, in combination, should produce daily returns consistent with the fund's investment objective. The index is a measure of large-cap U.S. stock market performance. The fund is non-diversified. **Top Holdings:** S&P 500 Index Swap Ubs Ag   S&P 500 Index Swap Societe Generale   S&P 500 Index Swap Goldman Sachs International   S&P 500 Index Swap Bnp Paribas   S&P 500 Index Swap Bank Of America Na

---

iShares iBonds Dec 2021 Term Corporate ETF   C+   HOLD

Ticker	Traded On	NAV	Total Assets ($)	Dividend Yield (TTM)	Turnover Ratio	Expense Ratio
IBDM	NYSE Arca	24.94	$1,279,367,085	2.68	6	0.1

Ratings
Reward   C
Risk   C+
Recent Upgrade/Downgrade   Up

Fund Information
Fund Type   Exchange Traded Funds
Category   US Fixed Income
Sub-Category   Target Maturity
Prospectus Objective   Corp Bond - Gen
Inception Date   Mar-15
Open to New Investments   Y

Prices
Price (as of 9/30/2019)   25.00
52-Week High   25.02
52-Week Low   24.16

Total Returns (%)

3-Month	6-Month	1-Year	3-Year	5-Year
0.96	2.53	5.40	6.68	

3-Year Standard Deviation   1.79
Effective Duration

Valuation
Premium/Discount (1-Year Average)   0.21

Company Information
Provider   iShares
Manager/Tenure   James Mauro (4), Scott Radell (4)
Website   http://www.ishares.com
Address   iShares 400 Howard Street San
                      Francisco CA 94105 United States
Phone Number   800-474-2737

PERFORMANCE

Ratings History				Asset & Performance History			Total Assets:	$1,279,367,085
Date	Overall Rating	Risk Rating	Reward Rating	Date	NAV	1-Year Total Return	Asset Allocation Asset	%
Q3-19	C+	C+	C	2018	24.3	0.81	Cash	0%
Q4-18	C	C+	C-	2017	24.74	2.97	Stocks	0%
Q4-17	C+	B+	C	2016	24.58	4.41	US Stocks	0%
Q4-16	D+	C-	D+	2015	24.13		Bonds	99%
Q4-15	U			2014			US Bonds	78%
				2013			Other	0%

Services Offered:

Investment Strategy: The investment seeks to track the investment results of the Bloomberg Barclays December 2021 Maturity Corporate Index which composed of U.S. dollar-denominated, investment-grade corporate bonds maturing in 2021. The fund generally will invest at least 90% of its assets in the component securities of the underlying index. The underlying index is composed of U.S. dollar-denominated, taxable, investment-grade corporate bonds scheduled to mature after December 31, 2020 and before December 16, 2021. **Top Holdings:** Dell International L.L.C. and EMC Corporation 4.42%   Oracle Corporation 1.9%   Morgan Stanley 5.5%   Goldman Sachs Group, Inc. 5.25%   Citigroup Inc. 2.7%

Direxion Daily Gold Miners Index Bull 3X Shares   C-   HOLD

Ticker	Traded On	NAV	Total Assets ($)	Dividend Yield (TTM)	Turnover Ratio	Expense Ratio
NUGT	NYSE Arca	27.85	$1,277,742,177	0.4	96	1.23

Ratings
Reward	C
Risk	D+
Recent Upgrade/Downgrade	Up

Fund Information
Fund Type	Exchange Traded Funds
Category	Trading Tools
Sub-Category	Trading--Leveraged Equity
Prospectus Objective	Prec Metals
Inception Date	Dec-10
Open to New Investments	Y

Prices
Price (as of 9/30/2019)	27.86
52-Week High	45.10
52-Week Low	12.10

Total Returns (%)
3-Month	6-Month	1-Year	3-Year	5-Year
14.73	50.30	115.97	-62.74	-84.82

3-Year Standard Deviation	76.56
Effective Duration	

Valuation
Premium/Discount (1-Year Average)	0.08

Company Information
Provider	Direxion Funds
Manager/Tenure	Paul Brigandi (8), Tony Ng (4)
Website	http://www.direxionfunds.com
Address	Direxion Funds 1301 Avenue Of The Americas (6th Avenue) New York NY 10019 United States
Phone Number	646-572-3390

PERFORMANCE

Ratings History
Date	Overall Rating	Risk Rating	Reward Rating
Q3-19	C-	D+	C
Q4-18	E+	D-	E+
Q4-17	D	D-	D
Q4-16	D	D-	D
Q4-15	E+	E+	E

Asset & Performance History
Date	NAV	1-Year Total Return
2018	17.45	-44.78
2017	31.76	3.25
2016	30.76	57.83
2015	19.49	-78.09
2014	88.96	-59.53
2013	219.84	-95

Total Assets: $1,277,742,177
Asset Allocation
Asset	%
Cash	14%
Stocks	54%
US Stocks	9%
Bonds	0%
US Bonds	0%
Other	32%

Services Offered:

Investment Strategy: The investment seeks daily investment results, before fees and expenses, of 300% of the daily performance of the NYSE Arca Gold Miners Index. The fund invests at least 80% of its net assets (plus borrowing for investment purposes) in financial instruments, such as swap agreements, and securities of the index, ETFs that track the index and other financial instruments that provide daily leveraged exposure to the index or ETFs that track the index. The index is a comprised of publicly traded companies that operate globally in both developed and emerging markets, and are involved primarily in mining for gold and, in mining for silver. It is non-diversified. **Top Holdings:** VanEck Vectors Gold Miners ETF Ve Vectors Gld Miners Ve Vectors Gld Miners Ve Vectors Gld Miners Ve Vectors Gld Miners

iShares U.S. Home Construction ETF   B-   BUY

Ticker	Traded On	NAV	Total Assets ($)	Dividend Yield (TTM)	Turnover Ratio	Expense Ratio
ITB	BATS	43.30	$1,264,482,688	0.52	17	0.42

Ratings
Reward	B+
Risk	C
Recent Upgrade/Downgrade	Up

Fund Information
Fund Type	Exchange Traded Funds
Category	Consumer Goods & Svcs
Sub-Category	Consumer Cyclical
Prospectus Objective	Real Estate
Inception Date	May-06
Open to New Investments	Y

Prices
Price (as of 9/30/2019)	43.31
52-Week High	43.31
52-Week Low	28.55

Total Returns (%)
3-Month	6-Month	1-Year	3-Year	5-Year
12.86	22.50	23.78	59.45	98.79

3-Year Standard Deviation	19.08
Effective Duration	

Valuation
Premium/Discount (1-Year Average)	-0.02

Company Information
Provider	iShares
Manager/Tenure	Greg Savage (11), Jennifer Hsui (7), Alan Mason (3), 2 others
Website	http://www.ishares.com
Address	iShares 400 Howard Street San Francisco CA 94105 United States
Phone Number	800-474-2737

PERFORMANCE

Ratings History
Date	Overall Rating	Risk Rating	Reward Rating
Q3-19	B-	C	B+
Q4-18	C	D+	B-
Q4-17	A-	B	A+
Q4-16	B-	C	B
Q4-15	B	B	B+

Asset & Performance History
Date	NAV	1-Year Total Return
2018	29.99	-30.96
2017	43.68	59.44
2016	27.49	1.8
2015	27.12	4.98
2014	25.92	4.68
2013	24.85	17.81

Total Assets: $1,264,482,688
Asset Allocation
Asset	%
Cash	0%
Stocks	100%
US Stocks	100%
Bonds	0%
US Bonds	0%
Other	0%

Services Offered:

Investment Strategy: The investment seeks to track the investment results of the Dow Jones U.S. Select Home Construction Index composed of U.S. equities in the home construction sector. The fund generally invests at least 90% of its assets in securities of the underlying index and in depositary receipts representing securities of the underlying index. The underlying index measures the performance of the home construction sector of the U.S. equity market. The fund may invest the remainder of its assets in certain futures, options and swap contracts, cash and cash equivalents. It is non-diversified. **Top Holdings:** D.R. Horton Inc Lennar Corp NVR Inc PulteGroup Inc Lowe's Companies Inc

SPDR® S&P 600 Small Cap ETF   D   SELL

Ticker	Traded On	NAV	Total Assets ($)	Dividend Yield (TTM)	Turnover Ratio	Expense Ratio
SLY	NYSE Arca		$1,261,412,289	1.42	11	0.15

Ratings
Reward	D
Risk	D
Recent Upgrade/Downgrade	

Fund Information
Fund Type	Exchange Traded Funds
Category	US Equity Small Cap
Sub-Category	Small Blend
Prospectus Objective	Small Company
Inception Date	Nov-05
Open to New Investments	Y

Prices
Price (as of 9/30/2019)	67.21
52-Week High	74.30
52-Week Low	56.32

Total Returns (%)
3-Month	6-Month	1-Year	3-Year	5-Year
-0.53	0.20	-9.53	-34.87	-20.24

3-Year Standard Deviation	18.04
Effective Duration	

Valuation
Premium/Discount (1-Year Average)	-0.01

Company Information
Provider	SPDR State Street Global Advisors
Manager/Tenure	Michael J. Feehily (7), Karl A. Schneider (4), Mark Krivitsky (2)
Website	http://www.spdrs.com
Address	SPDR State Street Global Advisors State Street Financial Center, 1 Lincoln Street Boston MA 02111-2900 United States
Phone Number	617-786-3000

PERFORMANCE

Ratings History
Date	Overall Rating	Risk Rating	Reward Rating
Q3-19	D	D	D
Q4-18	D-	D	D-
Q4-17	A-	B	A
Q4-16	C	C-	C
Q4-15	C	C-	C

Asset & Performance History
Date	NAV	1-Year Total Return
2018	59.95	-54.24
2017	132.86	13.16
2016	120.58	25.32
2015	98.91	-1.99
2014	104.63	5.59
2013	102.73	41.02

Total Assets: $1,261,412,289
Asset Allocation
Asset	%
Cash	1%
Stocks	99%
US Stocks	98%
Bonds	0%
US Bonds	0%
Other	0%

Services Offered: Dividend Investment Plan, CashInvestment Plan

Investment Strategy: The investment seeks to provide investment results that, before fees and expenses, correspond generally to the total return performance of the S&P SmallCap 600 Index. The fund generally invests substantially all, but at least 80%, of its total assets in the securities comprising the index. The index measures the performance of the small-capitalization segment of the U.S. equity market. It may purchase a subset of the securities in the index in an effort to hold a portfolio of securities with generally the same risk and return characteristics of the index. The fund is non-diversified. **Top Holdings:** Mercury Systems Inc Selective Insurance Group Inc FirstCash Inc Repligen Corp FTI Consulting Inc

iShares MSCI France ETF   C   HOLD

Ticker	Traded On	NAV	Total Assets ($)	Dividend Yield (TTM)	Turnover Ratio	Expense Ratio
EWQ	NYSE Arca	30.12	$1,246,953,067	2.83	4	0.47

Ratings
Reward	C
Risk	C+
Recent Upgrade/Downgrade	

Fund Information
Fund Type	Exchange Traded Funds
Category	Europe Equity Large Cap
Sub-Category	Miscellaneous Region
Prospectus Objective	Europe Stock
Inception Date	Mar-96
Open to New Investments	Y

Prices
Price (as of 9/30/2019)	30.14
52-Week High	31.36
52-Week Low	25.56

Total Returns (%)
3-Month	6-Month	1-Year	3-Year	5-Year
-1.72	3.82	-1.46	34.31	30.25

3-Year Standard Deviation	13.95
Effective Duration	

Valuation
Premium/Discount (1-Year Average)	0.01

Company Information
Provider	iShares
Manager/Tenure	Diane Hsiung (11), Greg Savage (11), Jennifer Hsui (6), 3 others
Website	http://www.ishares.com
Address	iShares 400 Howard Street San Francisco CA 94105 United States
Phone Number	800-474-2737

PERFORMANCE

Ratings History
Date	Overall Rating	Risk Rating	Reward Rating
Q3-19	C	C+	C
Q4-18	C-	C-	C-
Q4-17	B	C+	A-
Q4-16	D+	C-	D
Q4-15	C	C+	C

Asset & Performance History
Date	NAV	1-Year Total Return
2018	26.6	-12.68
2017	31.25	28.83
2016	24.75	4.97
2015	24.27	-0.16
2014	24.81	-9.91
2013	28.37	26.35

Total Assets: $1,246,953,067
Asset Allocation
Asset	%
Cash	0%
Stocks	100%
US Stocks	1%
Bonds	0%
US Bonds	0%
Other	0%

Services Offered: CashInvestment Plan

Investment Strategy: The investment seeks to track the investment results of the MSCI France Index. The fund will at all times invest at least 80% of its assets in the securities of its underlying index and in depositary receipts representing securities in its underlying index. The underlying index consists of stocks traded primarily on the Paris Stock Exchange. It may include large- or mid-capitalization companies. The fund is non-diversified. **Top Holdings:** Total SA LVMH Moet Hennessy Louis Vuitton SE Sanofi SA Airbus SE L'Oreal SA

First Trust US Equity Opportunities ETF

C   HOLD

Ticker	Traded On	NAV	Total Assets ($)	Dividend Yield (TTM)	Turnover Ratio	Expense Ratio
FPX	NYSE Arca	75.82	$1,243,405,077	0.69	57	0.59

Ratings

Reward	B-
Risk	C-
Recent Upgrade/Downgrade	

Fund Information

Fund Type	Exchange Traded Funds
Category	US Equity Large Cap Growth
Sub-Category	Large Growth
Prospectus Objective	Growth
Inception Date	Apr-06
Open to New Investments	Y

Prices

Price (as of 9/30/2019)	75.83
52-Week High	81.43
52-Week Low	57.83

Total Returns (%)

3-Month	6-Month	1-Year	3-Year	5-Year
-3.03	1.12	3.22	42.66	66.35

3-Year Standard Deviation	14.01
Effective Duration	

Valuation

Premium/Discount (1-Year Average)	0.00

Company Information

Provider	First Trust
Manager/Tenure	Jon C. Erickson (13), Daniel J. Lindquist (13), David G. McGarel (13), 3 others
Website	http://www.ftportfolios.com/
Address	First Trust 120 E. Liberty Drive, Suite 400 Wheaton IL 60187 United States
Phone Number	800-621-1675

PERFORMANCE

Ratings History

Date	Overall Rating	Risk Rating	Reward Rating
Q3-19	C	C-	B-
Q4-18	C	C	C
Q4-17	B	B-	A-
Q4-16	C+	C	B
Q4-15	C+	C+	B-

Asset & Performance History

Date	NAV	1-Year Total Return
2018	62.07	-8.23
2017	68.17	26.96
2016	54.1	6.7
2015	51.11	2.18
2014	50.32	11.9
2013	45.34	47.98

Total Assets: $1,243,405,077

Asset Allocation

Asset	%
Cash	0%
Stocks	100%
US Stocks	94%
Bonds	0%
US Bonds	0%
Other	0%

Services Offered:

Investment Strategy: The investment seeks investment results that correspond generally to the price and yield (before the fund's fees and expenses) of an equity index called the IPOX®-100 U.S. Index. The fund will normally invest at least 90% of its net assets (including investment borrowings) in the common stocks that comprise the index. The index seeks to measure the performance of the equity securities of the 100 largest and typically most liquid initial public offerings ("IPOs") (including spin-offs and equity carve-outs) of U.S. companies. It is non-diversified. **Top Holdings:** PayPal Holdings Inc   Stryker Corp   Thermo Fisher Scientific Inc   Verizon Communications Inc   Fidelity National Information Services Inc

iShares iBonds Dec 2020 Term Corporate ETF

C   HOLD

Ticker	Traded On	NAV	Total Assets ($)	Dividend Yield (TTM)	Turnover Ratio	Expense Ratio
IBDL	NYSE Arca	25.33	$1,235,963,685	2.52	5	0.1

Ratings

Reward	C
Risk	C+
Recent Upgrade/Downgrade	

Fund Information

Fund Type	Exchange Traded Funds
Category	US Fixed Income
Sub-Category	Short-Term Bond
Prospectus Objective	Corp Bond - Gen
Inception Date	Dec-14
Open to New Investments	Y

Prices

Price (as of 9/30/2019)	25.37
52-Week High	25.38
52-Week Low	24.92

Total Returns (%)

3-Month	6-Month	1-Year	3-Year	5-Year
0.77	1.83	3.92	5.75	

3-Year Standard Deviation	1.29
Effective Duration	

Valuation

Premium/Discount (1-Year Average)	0.15

Company Information

Provider	iShares
Manager/Tenure	James Mauro (4), Scott Radell (4)
Website	http://www.ishares.com
Address	iShares 400 Howard Street San Francisco CA 94105 United States
Phone Number	800-474-2737

PERFORMANCE

Ratings History

Date	Overall Rating	Risk Rating	Reward Rating
Q3-19	C	C+	C
Q4-18	C	C+	C
Q4-17	B-	A-	C
Q4-16	C-	C-	D+
Q4-15	U		

Asset & Performance History

Date	NAV	1-Year Total Return
2018	24.97	1.17
2017	25.27	2.53
2016	25.15	3.69
2015	24.81	1.76
2014	24.98	
2013		

Total Assets: $1,235,963,685

Asset Allocation

Asset	%
Cash	4%
Stocks	0%
US Stocks	0%
Bonds	95%
US Bonds	79%
Other	0%

Services Offered:

Investment Strategy: The investment seeks to track the investment results of the Bloomberg Barclays December 2020 Maturity Corporate Index (the "underlying index"). The fund generally will invest at least 90% of its assets in the component securities of the underlying index. The underlying index is composed of U.S. dollar-denominated, taxable, investment-grade corporate bonds scheduled to mature after December 31, 2019 and before December 16, 2020. **Top Holdings:** GE Capital International Funding Company Unlimited Company 2.34%   CVS Health Corp 2.8%   Visa Inc 2.2%   AbbVie Inc. 2.5%   Wells Fargo & Company 2.6%

Robo Global® Robotics and Automation Index ETF   C   HOLD

Ticker	Traded On	NAV	Total Assets ($)	Dividend Yield (TTM)	Turnover Ratio	Expense Ratio
ROBO	NAS CM	38.22	$1,224,946,141	0.32	29	0.95

Ratings
Reward	C-
Risk	C
Recent Upgrade/Downgrade	

Fund Information
Fund Type	Exchange Traded Funds
Category	Globa Eq Mid/Small Cap
Sub-Category	World Small/Mid Stock
Prospectus Objective	Growth
Inception Date	Oct-13
Open to New Investments	Y

Prices
Price (as of 9/30/2019)	38.35
52-Week High	42.10
52-Week Low	30.86

Total Returns (%)
3-Month	6-Month	1-Year	3-Year	5-Year
-5.72	-3.19	-8.78	36.10	49.65

3-Year Standard Deviation	20.16
Effective Duration	

Valuation
Premium/Discount (1-Year Average)	-0.15

Company Information
Provider	Robo Global
Manager/Tenure	Denise M. Krisko (4), Rafael Zayas (1)
Website	http://www.roboglobaletfs.com
Address	Robo Global United States
Phone Number	

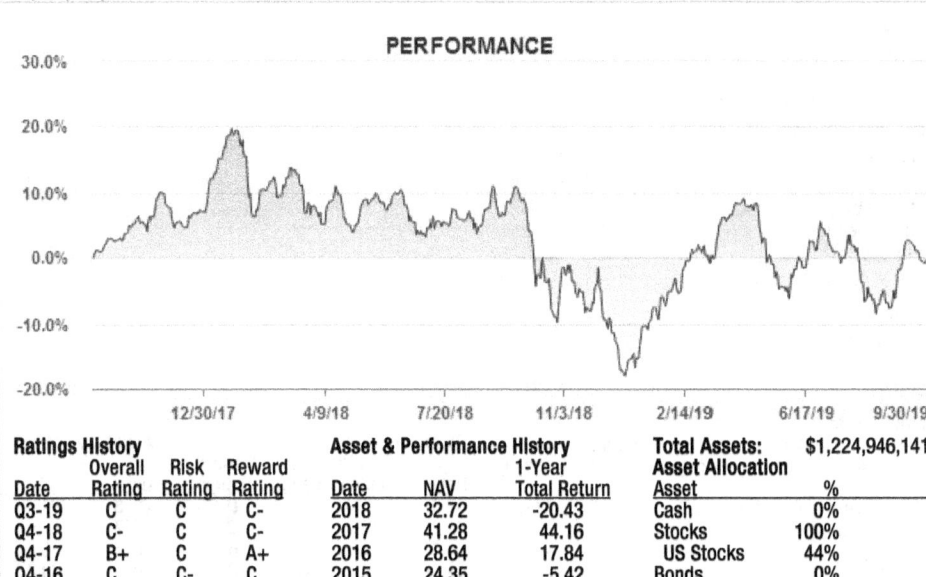

PERFORMANCE

Ratings History
Date	Overall Rating	Risk Rating	Reward Rating
Q3-19	C	C	C-
Q4-18	C-	C	C-
Q4-17	B+	C	A+
Q4-16	C	C-	C
Q4-15	D	C-	D

Asset & Performance History
Date	NAV	1-Year Total Return
2018	32.72	-20.43
2017	41.28	44.16
2016	28.64	17.84
2015	24.35	-5.42
2014	25.82	-4.12
2013	27.01	

Total Assets: $1,224,946,141
Asset Allocation
Asset	%
Cash	0%
Stocks	100%
US Stocks	44%
Bonds	0%
US Bonds	0%
Other	0%

Services Offered:

Investment Strategy: The investment seeks to provide investment results that, before fees and expenses, correspond generally to the price and yield performance of the ROBO Global® Robotics and Automation Index. The fund will normally invest at least 80% of its total assets in securities of the index or in depositary receipts representing securities of the index. The index is designed to measure the performance of robotics-related and/or automation-related companies. The fund may invest up to 20% of its assets in investments that are not included in the index, but which the Adviser and Sub-Adviser believe will help it track the index. It is non-diversified. **Top Holdings:** Hiwin Technologies Corp   NVIDIA Corp   YASKAWA Electric Corp   Nabtesco Corp   Harmonic Drive Systems Inc

Franklin LibertyQ U.S. Equity ETF   C   HOLD

Ticker	Traded On	NAV	Total Assets ($)	Dividend Yield (TTM)	Turnover Ratio	Expense Ratio
FLQL	BATS	32.99	$1,217,449,348	1.75	18	0.15

Ratings
Reward	C
Risk	C-
Recent Upgrade/Downgrade	

Fund Information
Fund Type	Exchange Traded Funds
Category	US Equity Large Cap Blend
Sub-Category	Large Blend
Prospectus Objective	Growth & Inc
Inception Date	Apr-17
Open to New Investments	Y

Prices
Price (as of 9/30/2019)	33.03
52-Week High	33.24
52-Week Low	26.18

Total Returns (%)
3-Month	6-Month	1-Year	3-Year	5-Year
2.55	5.19	7.19		

3-Year Standard Deviation	
Effective Duration	

Valuation
Premium/Discount (1-Year Average)	0.07

Company Information
Provider	Franklin Templeton Investments
Manager/Tenure	Dina Ting (2), Louis Hsu (1)
Website	http://www.franklintempleton.com
Address	Franklin Templeton Investments One Franklin Parkway, Building 970, 1st Floor San Mateo CA 94403 United States
Phone Number	650-312-2000

PERFORMANCE

Ratings History
Date	Overall Rating	Risk Rating	Reward Rating
Q3-19	C	C-	C
Q4-18	C-	C-	D+
Q4-17	U		
Q4-16			
Q4-15			

Asset & Performance History
Date	NAV	1-Year Total Return
2018	27.69	-1.97
2017	28.74	
2016		
2015		
2014		
2013		

Total Assets: $1,217,449,348
Asset Allocation
Asset	%
Cash	0%
Stocks	100%
US Stocks	100%
Bonds	0%
US Bonds	0%
Other	0%

Services Offered:

Investment Strategy: The investment seeks to provide investment results that closely correspond, before fees and expenses, to the performance of the LibertyQ U.S. Large Cap Equity Index (the U.S. Large Cap underlying index). Under normal market conditions, the fund invests at least 80% of its assets in the component securities of the U.S. Large Cap underlying index. The U.S. Large Cap underlying index is based on the Russell 1000® Index using a methodology developed with Franklin Templeton to reflect Franklin Templeton's desired investment strategy. **Top Holdings:** Amgen Inc   Costco Wholesale Corp   Target Corp   The Home Depot Inc   Apple Inc

WisdomTree India Earnings Fund   C-   HOLD

Ticker	Traded On	NAV	Total Assets ($)	Dividend Yield (TTM)	Turnover Ratio	Expense Ratio
EPI	NYSE Arca	23.79	$1,213,183,316	1.2	37	0.85

Ratings
Reward   D
Risk   C
Recent Upgrade/Downgrade   Down

Fund Information
Fund Type   Exchange Traded Funds
Category   India Equity
Sub-Category   India Equity
Prospectus Objective Foreign Stock
Inception Date   Feb-08
Open to New Investments   Y

Prices
Price (as of 9/30/2019)   23.85
52-Week High   26.71
52-Week Low   21.83

Total Returns (%)

3-Month	6-Month	1-Year	3-Year	5-Year
-8.29	-9.40	-0.29	13.76	13.95

3-Year Standard Deviation   17.25
Effective Duration

Valuation
Premium/Discount (1-Year Average)   0.00

Company Information
Provider   WisdomTree
Manager/Tenure   Richard A. Brown (11), Thomas J. Durante (11), Karen Q. Wong (11)
Website   http://www.wisdomtree.com
Address   WisdomTree 245 Park Avenue, 35th floor New York NY 10167 United States
Phone Number   866-909-9473

PERFORMANCE

Ratings History

Date	Overall Rating	Risk Rating	Reward Rating
Q3-19	C-	C	D
Q4-18	C-	C-	C-
Q4-17	B-	C	B
Q4-16	C	C	C+
Q4-15	C	C	C-

Asset & Performance History

Date	NAV	1-Year Total Return
2018	24.76	-10.44
2017	27.97	39.01
2016	20.31	2.26
2015	20.07	-8.68
2014	22.23	29.75
2013	17.32	-8.74

Total Assets: $1,213,183,316
Asset Allocation

Asset	%
Cash	0%
Stocks	100%
US Stocks	0%
Bonds	0%
US Bonds	0%
Other	0%

Services Offered:

Investment Strategy: The investment seeks to track the price and yield performance, before fees and expenses, of the WisdomTree India Earnings Index. Under normal circumstances, at least 95% of the fund's total assets (exclusive of collateral held from securities lending) will be invested in component securities of the index and investments that have economic characteristics that are substantially identical to the economic characteristics of such component securities. The index is comprised of companies incorporated and traded in India that are profitable and that are eligible to be purchased by foreign investors as of the annual index screening date. It is non-diversified. **Top Holdings:** Housing Development Finance Corp Ltd Reliance Industries Ltd Infosys Ltd Tata Consultancy Services Ltd ICICI Bank Ltd

---

Invesco FTSE RAFI Emerging Markets ETF   C   HOLD

Ticker	Traded On	NAV	Total Assets ($)	Dividend Yield (TTM)	Turnover Ratio	Expense Ratio
PXH	NYSE Arca	20.03	$1,211,857,305	3.56	16	0.5

Ratings
Reward   C
Risk   C+
Recent Upgrade/Downgrade

Fund Information
Fund Type   Exchange Traded Funds
Category   Global Emerg Mkts Equity
Sub-Category   Diversified Emerging Mkts
Prospectus Objective Div Emerg Mkts
Inception Date   Sep-07
Open to New Investments

Prices
Price (as of 9/30/2019)   20.08
52-Week High   22.18
52-Week Low   19.25

Total Returns (%)

3-Month	6-Month	1-Year	3-Year	5-Year
-6.46	-5.02	-1.79	24.12	16.35

3-Year Standard Deviation   14.64
Effective Duration

Valuation
Premium/Discount (1-Year Average)   0.02

Company Information
Provider   Invesco
Manager/Tenure   Peter Hubbard (12), Michael Jeanette (4), Tony Seisser (4)
Website   http://www.invesco.com/us
Address   Invesco 11 Greenway Plaza, Ste. 2500 Houston TX 77046 United States
Phone Number   800-659-1005

PERFORMANCE

Ratings History

Date	Overall Rating	Risk Rating	Reward Rating
Q3-19	C	C+	C
Q4-18	C	C	C-
Q4-17	B-	C	B
Q4-16	C-	C-	C-
Q4-15	D	D	D

Asset & Performance History

Date	NAV	1-Year Total Return
2018	19.83	-8.12
2017	22.27	25.69
2016	18.23	32.43
2015	14.06	-22.68
2014	18.75	-4.91
2013	20.29	-7.65

Total Assets: $1,211,857,305
Asset Allocation

Asset	%
Cash	0%
Stocks	100%
US Stocks	0%
Bonds	0%
US Bonds	0%
Other	0%

Services Offered:

Investment Strategy: The investment seeks to track the investment results (before fees and expenses) of the FTSE RAFITM Emerging Index (the "underlying index"). The fund generally will invest at least 90% of its total assets in the securities that comprise the underlying index, as well as ADRs and GDRs that represent securities in the underlying index. The underlying index is designed to track the performance of securities of companies domiciled in emerging market countries with the highest ranking cumulative score ("Fundamental Value"), selected from the constituents of the FTSE Emerging All Cap Index, as determined by the index provider. **Top Holdings:** China Construction Bank Corp Class H Taiwan Semiconductor Manufacturing Co Ltd Industrial And Commercial Bank Of China Ltd Class H Gazprom PJSC ADR PJSC Lukoil ADR

Invesco FTSE RAFI Developed Markets ex-U.S. ETF   C   HOLD

Ticker	Traded On	NAV	Total Assets ($)	Dividend Yield (TTM)	Turnover Ratio	Expense Ratio
PXF	NYSE Arca	39.64	$1,204,957,363	4.05	10	0.45

Ratings
Reward   D+
Risk   C+
Recent Upgrade/Downgrade   Up

Fund Information
Fund Type	Exchange Traded Funds
Category	Global Equity Large Cap
Sub-Category	Foreign Large Value
Prospectus Objective	Foreign Stock
Inception Date	Jun-07
Open to New Investments	

Prices
Price (as of 9/30/2019)	39.65
52-Week High	43.34
52-Week Low	36.29

Total Returns (%)

3-Month	6-Month	1-Year	3-Year	5-Year
-1.83	-0.73	-4.77	19.63	11.53

3-Year Standard Deviation   11.99
Effective Duration

Valuation
Premium/Discount (1-Year Average)   -0.03

Company Information
Provider	Invesco
Manager/Tenure	Peter Hubbard (12), Michael Jeanette (4), Tony Seisser (4)
Website	http://www.invesco.com/us
Address	Invesco 11 Greenway Plaza, Ste. 2500 Houston TX 77046 United States
Phone Number	800-659-1005

PERFORMANCE

Ratings History

Date	Overall Rating	Risk Rating	Reward Rating
Q3-19	C	C+	D+
Q4-18	C-	C-	D+
Q4-17	C+	C	B-
Q4-16	D+	C-	D+
Q4-15	C	C+	C-

Asset & Performance History

Date	NAV	1-Year Total Return
2018	37.51	-15.12
2017	45.55	24.77
2016	37.59	6.5
2015	36.5	-4.83
2014	39.46	-6.19
2013	43.63	23.44

Total Assets: $1,204,957,363
Asset Allocation

Asset	%
Cash	0%
Stocks	100%
US Stocks	1%
Bonds	0%
US Bonds	0%
Other	0%

Services Offered:

Investment Strategy: The investment seeks to track the investment results (before fees and expenses) of the FTSE RAFI TM Developed ex U.S. 1000 Index (the "underlying index"). The fund generally will invest at least 90% of its total assets in the securities that comprise the underlying index, as well as American depositary receipts ("ADRs") and global depositary receipts ("GDRs") that represent securities in the underlying index. The underlying index is comprised of companies originating in countries that are classified as "developed" within the country classification definition of FTSE, excluding the United States. **Top Holdings:** Toyota Motor Corp   BP PLC   Nestle SA   Royal Dutch Shell PLC Class A   Total SA

UBS AG FI Enhanced Large Cap Growth ETN   C   HOLD

Ticker	Traded On	NAV	Total Assets ($)	Dividend Yield (TTM)	Turnover Ratio	Expense Ratio
FBGX	NYSE Arca	277.12	$1,199,941,724	0		0.85

Ratings
Reward   C+
Risk   D+
Recent Upgrade/Downgrade

Fund Information
Fund Type	Exchange Traded Funds
Category	US Equity Large Cap Growth
Sub-Category	Large Growth
Prospectus Objective	Growth
Inception Date	Jun-14
Open to New Investments	Y

Prices
Price (as of 9/30/2019)	277.32
52-Week High	301.54
52-Week Low	167.50

Total Returns (%)

3-Month	6-Month	1-Year	3-Year	5-Year
0.16	7.97	-7.80	102.99	174.80

3-Year Standard Deviation   28.06
Effective Duration

Valuation
Premium/Discount (1-Year Average)   -0.05

Company Information
Provider	UBS Group AG
Manager/Tenure	No Manager (5)
Website	http://www.ubs.com
Address	Bahnhofstrasse 45 Zürich 8098 Switzerland
Phone Number	412-037-1952

PERFORMANCE

Ratings History

Date	Overall Rating	Risk Rating	Reward Rating
Q3-19	C	D+	C+
Q4-18	C-	D+	C
Q4-17	A	B	A+
Q4-16	C	D+	C+
Q4-15	D	C-	D

Asset & Performance History

Date	NAV	1-Year Total Return
2018	191.23	-15.29
2017	225.75	62.42
2016	138.55	12.24
2015	123.44	8.88
2014	113.36	
2013		

Total Assets: $1,199,941,724
Asset Allocation

Asset	%
Cash	%
Stocks	%
US Stocks	%
Bonds	%
US Bonds	%
Other	%

Services Offered:

Investment Strategy: The investment seeks a return linked to the Russell 1000® Growth Total Return Index (the "index").

The UBS AG FI Enhanced Large Cap Growth ETN due June 19, 2024 (the "Securities") are a series of FI Enhanced ETNs. The level of the index reflects both the price performance of the index constituent Securities and the reinvestment of dividends on the index constituent securities. The Securities are two times leveraged with respect to the index and, as a result, may benefit from two times any positive, but will be exposed to two times any negative, quarterly performance of the index. **Top Holdings:**

iShares Dow Jones U.S. ETF

C   HOLD

Ticker	Traded On	NAV	Total Assets ($)	Dividend Yield (TTM)	Turnover Ratio	Expense Ratio
IYY	NYSE Arca	147.53	$1,194,975,620	1.86	5	0.2

Ratings

Reward	C+
Risk	C-
Recent Upgrade/Downgrade	

Fund Information

Fund Type	Exchange Traded Funds
Category	US Equity Large Cap Blend
Sub-Category	Large Blend
Prospectus Objective	Growth
Inception Date	Jun-00
Open to New Investments	Y

Prices

Price (as of 9/30/2019)	147.54
52-Week High	150.59
52-Week Low	116.74

Total Returns (%)

3-Month	6-Month	1-Year	3-Year	5-Year
0.56	4.26	3.14	43.65	65.70

3-Year Standard Deviation	12.38
Effective Duration	

Valuation

Premium/Discount (1-Year Average)	-0.01

Company Information

Provider	iShares
Manager/Tenure	Greg Savage (11), Jennifer Hsui (7), Alan Mason (3), 2 others
Website	http://www.ishares.com
Address	iShares 400 Howard Street San Francisco CA 94105 United States
Phone Number	800-474-2737

PERFORMANCE

Ratings History

Date	Overall Rating	Risk Rating	Reward Rating
Q3-19	C	C-	C+
Q4-18	C	C-	C
Q4-17	B	B	B
Q4-16	C+	C-	B
Q4-15	C	C	C

Asset & Performance History

Date	NAV	1-Year Total Return
2018	124.41	-5.22
2017	133.54	21.23
2016	112.07	12.03
2015	101.95	0.51
2014	103.43	12.74
2013	93.33	32.64

Total Assets: $1,194,975,620

Asset Allocation

Asset	%
Cash	0%
Stocks	100%
US Stocks	99%
Bonds	0%
US Bonds	0%
Other	0%

Services Offered: CashInvestment Plan

Investment Strategy: The investment seeks to track the investment results of the Dow Jones U.S. Index composed of U.S. equities. The fund generally invests at least 90% of its assets in securities of the underlying index and in depositary receipts representing securities of the underlying index. The underlying index aims to consistently represent the top 95% of U.S. companies based on a float-adjusted market capitalization, excluding the very smallest and least liquid stocks. **Top Holdings:** Microsoft Corp Apple Inc Amazon.com Inc Facebook Inc A Berkshire Hathaway Inc B

---

iShares U.S. Financial Services ETF

B   BUY

Ticker	Traded On	NAV	Total Assets ($)	Dividend Yield (TTM)	Turnover Ratio	Expense Ratio
IYG	NYSE Arca	136.30	$1,192,667,118	1.75	4	0.42

Ratings

Reward	B
Risk	C
Recent Upgrade/Downgrade	Up

Fund Information

Fund Type	Exchange Traded Funds
Category	Financials Sector Equity
Sub-Category	Financial
Prospectus Objective	Financial
Inception Date	Jun-00
Open to New Investments	Y

Prices

Price (as of 9/30/2019)	136.43
52-Week High	140.99
52-Week Low	105.05

Total Returns (%)

3-Month	6-Month	1-Year	3-Year	5-Year
1.19	10.20	3.91	62.69	73.07

3-Year Standard Deviation	17.8
Effective Duration	

Valuation

Premium/Discount (1-Year Average)	-0.01

Company Information

Provider	iShares
Manager/Tenure	Greg Savage (11), Jennifer Hsui (7), Alan Mason (3), 2 others
Website	http://www.ishares.com
Address	iShares 400 Howard Street San Francisco CA 94105 United States
Phone Number	800-474-2737

PERFORMANCE

Ratings History

Date	Overall Rating	Risk Rating	Reward Rating
Q3-19	B	C	B
Q4-18	B-	C+	B
Q4-17	B+	B	A
Q4-16	B-	C	B
Q4-15	B+	B	B+

Asset & Performance History

Date	NAV	1-Year Total Return
2018	112.32	-12.44
2017	130.36	24.41
2016	106.23	19.88
2015	89.97	-0.71
2014	91.82	10.93
2013	83.76	42.83

Total Assets: $1,192,667,118

Asset Allocation

Asset	%
Cash	0%
Stocks	100%
US Stocks	100%
Bonds	0%
US Bonds	0%
Other	0%

Services Offered: CashInvestment Plan

Investment Strategy: The investment seeks to track the investment results of the Dow Jones U.S. Financial Services Index composed of U.S. equities in the financial services sector. The fund generally invests at least 90% of its assets in securities of the underlying index and in depositary receipts representing securities of the underlying index. The underlying index measures the performance of the financial services sector of the U.S. equity market. The fund is non-diversified. **Top Holdings:** JPMorgan Chase & Co Visa Inc Class A Mastercard Inc A Bank of America Corporation Wells Fargo & Co

FlexShares iBoxx 3-Year Target Duration TIPS Index Fund   C   HOLD

Ticker	Traded On	NAV	Total Assets ($)	Dividend Yield (TTM)	Turnover Ratio	Expense Ratio
TDTT	NYSE Arca	24.56	$1,190,157,955	1.8	85	0.18

Ratings
Reward   C
Risk   C-
Recent Upgrade/Downgrade

Fund Information
Fund Type   Exchange Traded Funds
Category   US Fixed Income
Sub-Category   Inflation-Protected Bond
Prospectus Objective   Govt Bond - Treasury
Inception Date   Sep-11
Open to New Investments   Y

Prices
Price (as of 9/30/2019)   24.59
52-Week High   24.76
52-Week Low   23.71

Total Returns (%)

3-Month	6-Month	1-Year	3-Year	5-Year
0.39	2.49	4.45	5.06	6.12

3-Year Standard Deviation   1.57
Effective Duration

Valuation
Premium/Discount (1-Year Average)   0.01

Company Information
Provider   Flexshares Trust
Manager/Tenure   Michael R. Chico (8), Brandon P.
                 Ferguson (8), Daniel J. Personette (8)
Website   http://www.flexshares.com
Address   50 South LaSalle Street Chicago,
                 Illinois 60603 Chicago Illinois 60603
                 United States
Phone Number   855-353-9383

PERFORMANCE

Ratings History

Date	Overall Rating	Risk Rating	Reward Rating
Q3-19	C	C-	C
Q4-18	C-	C	D+
Q4-17	C	C+	C
Q4-16	C	C-	C
Q4-15	D+	C	D

Asset & Performance History

Date	NAV	1-Year Total Return
2018	23.82	0.12
2017	24.38	0.51
2016	24.71	2.92
2015	24.25	-0.14
2014	24.28	-1.63
2013	24.89	-1.98

Total Assets: $1,190,157,955
Asset Allocation

Asset	%
Cash	0%
Stocks	0%
US Stocks	0%
Bonds	100%
US Bonds	100%
Other	0%

Services Offered:

Investment Strategy: The investment seeks to provide investment results that, before fees and expenses, correspond generally to the price and yield performance of the iBoxx 3-Year Target Duration TIPS Index. Under normal circumstances, the fund will invest at least 80% of its total assets (exclusive of collateral held from securities lending) in the securities of the underlying index. The underlying index reflects the performance of a selection of inflation protected public obligations of the U.S. Treasury, commonly known as "TIPS," with a targeted average modified adjusted duration, as defined by the underlying index, of approximately three years. The fund is non-diversified. **Top Holdings:** United States Treasury Notes 0.62% United States Treasury Notes 0.62% United States Treasury Notes 0.38% United States Treasury Notes 0.12% United States Treasury Notes 0.5%

VanEck Vectors Russia ETF   B   BUY

Ticker	Traded On	NAV	Total Assets ($)	Dividend Yield (TTM)	Turnover Ratio	Expense Ratio
RSX	NYSE Arca	22.84	$1,172,717,557	4.23	20	0.65

Ratings
Reward   B
Risk   B-
Recent Upgrade/Downgrade

Fund Information
Fund Type   Exchange Traded Funds
Category   Equity Misc
Sub-Category   Miscellaneous Region
Prospectus Objective   Growth
Inception Date   Apr-07
Open to New Investments   Y

Prices
Price (as of 9/30/2019)   22.81
52-Week High   24.12
52-Week Low   18.44

Total Returns (%)

3-Month	6-Month	1-Year	3-Year	5-Year
-4.39	8.96	10.85	36.52	24.12

3-Year Standard Deviation   17.73
Effective Duration

Valuation
Premium/Discount (1-Year Average)   -0.24

Company Information
Provider   VanEck
Manager/Tenure   Hao-Hung (Peter) Liao (12), Guo Hua
                 (Jason) Jin (1)
Website   http://www.vaneck.com
Address   Van Eck Associates Corporation 666
                 Third Avenue New York NY 10017
                 United States
Phone Number   800-826-1115

PERFORMANCE

Ratings History

Date	Overall Rating	Risk Rating	Reward Rating
Q3-19	B	B-	B
Q4-18	C	C	C
Q4-17	B-	C	B
Q4-16	C-	D+	C-
Q4-15	D	D	D

Asset & Performance History

Date	NAV	1-Year Total Return
2018	18.79	-6.02
2017	21.14	4.57
2016	21.09	45.91
2015	14.69	0.31
2014	15.17	-44.9
2013	28.69	-0.63

Total Assets: $1,172,717,557
Asset Allocation

Asset	%
Cash	0%
Stocks	100%
US Stocks	0%
Bonds	0%
US Bonds	0%
Other	0%

Services Offered: Automatic Investment Plan, Retirement Investment

Investment Strategy: The investment seeks to replicate as closely as possible, before fees and expenses, the price and yield performance of the MVIS® Russia Index. The fund normally invests at least 80% of its total assets in securities that comprise the fund's benchmark index. The index includes securities, which may include depositary receipts, of Russian companies. A company is generally considered to be a Russian company if it is incorporated in Russia or is incorporated outside of Russia but has at least 50% of its revenues/related assets in Russia. Such companies may include medium-capitalization companies. It is non-diversified. **Top Holdings:** Gazprom PJSC ADR Sberbank of Russia PJSC ADR PJSC Lukoil ADR Tatneft PJSC ADR Mining and Metallurgical Company NORILSK NICKEL PJSC ADR

VanEck Vectors Fallen Angel High Yield Bond ETF   C+   HOLD

Ticker	Traded On	NAV	Total Assets ($)	Dividend Yield (TTM)	Turnover Ratio	Expense Ratio
ANGL	NYSE Arca	29.23	$1,166,143,481	5.44	29	0.35

Ratings
Reward   C+
Risk   C+
Recent Upgrade/Downgrade   Down

Fund Information
Fund Type	Exchange Traded Funds
Category	US Fixed Income
Sub-Category	High Yield Bond
Prospectus Objective	Corp Bond-High Yld
Inception Date	Apr-12
Open to New Investments	Y

Prices
Price (as of 9/30/2019)	29.32
52-Week High	29.57
52-Week Low	26.29

Total Returns (%)
3-Month	6-Month	1-Year	3-Year	5-Year
1.34	4.46	6.37	19.62	41.06

3-Year Standard Deviation   4.92
Effective Duration   5.75

Valuation
Premium/Discount (1-Year Average)   -0.05

Company Information
Provider	VanEck
Manager/Tenure	Francis G. Rodilosso (7)
Website	http://www.vaneck.com
Address	Van Eck Associates Corporation 666 Third Avenue New York NY 10017 United States
Phone Number	800-826-1115

PERFORMANCE

Ratings History
Date	Overall Rating	Risk Rating	Reward Rating
Q3-19	C+	C+	C+
Q4-18	C	C+	C-
Q4-17	B-	B-	B-
Q4-16	B-	C+	B
Q4-15	C	C-	C

Asset & Performance History
Date	NAV	1-Year Total Return
2018	26.87	-5.43
2017	29.88	9.33
2016	28.73	25.34
2015	24.36	-3.89
2014	26.74	6.04
2013	26.89	6.88

Total Assets: $1,166,143,481
Asset Allocation
Asset	%
Cash	0%
Stocks	1%
US Stocks	0%
Bonds	97%
US Bonds	80%
Other	0%

Services Offered:

Investment Strategy: The investment seeks to replicate as closely as possible, before fees and expenses, the price and yield performance of the ICE BofAML US Fallen Angel High Yield Index (the "Fallen Angel Index"). The fund normally invests at least 80% of its total assets in securities that comprise the fund's benchmark index. The index is comprised of below investment grade corporate bonds denominated in U.S. dollars that were rated investment grade at the time of issuance. **Top Holdings:** Sprint Capital Corporation 6.88% Sprint Capital Corporation 8.75% Intesa Sanpaolo S.p.A. 5.02% FREEPORT-MCMORAN INC 3.88% FREEPORT-MCMORAN INC 3.55%

---

iShares 10-20 Year Treasury Bond ETF   C   HOLD

Ticker	Traded On	NAV	Total Assets ($)	Dividend Yield (TTM)	Turnover Ratio	Expense Ratio
TLH	NYSE Arca	149.38	$1,165,202,161	2.18	45	0.15

Ratings
Reward   C
Risk   C+
Recent Upgrade/Downgrade

Fund Information
Fund Type	Exchange Traded Funds
Category	US Fixed Income
Sub-Category	Long Government
Prospectus Objective	Govt Bond - Treasury
Inception Date	Jan-07
Open to New Investments	Y

Prices
Price (as of 9/30/2019)	149.48
52-Week High	152.94
52-Week Low	125.72

Total Returns (%)
3-Month	6-Month	1-Year	3-Year	5-Year
5.27	11.23	19.35	9.98	25.83

3-Year Standard Deviation   7.52
Effective Duration   12.46

Valuation
Premium/Discount (1-Year Average)   0.13

Company Information
Provider	iShares
Manager/Tenure	Scott Radell (9), James Mauro (8)
Website	http://www.ishares.com
Address	iShares 400 Howard Street San Francisco CA 94105 United States
Phone Number	800-474-2737

PERFORMANCE

Ratings History
Date	Overall Rating	Risk Rating	Reward Rating
Q3-19	C	C+	C
Q4-18	D	C-	D
Q4-17	C	C	C
Q4-16	C	C-	C
Q4-15	C	C-	C

Asset & Performance History
Date	NAV	1-Year Total Return
2018	132.92	-0.1
2017	136.05	4.05
2016	133.17	0.9
2015	134.37	1.27
2014	135.49	14.42
2013	121.06	-8.48

Total Assets: $1,165,202,161
Asset Allocation
Asset	%
Cash	1%
Stocks	0%
US Stocks	0%
Bonds	99%
US Bonds	99%
Other	0%

Services Offered:

Investment Strategy: The investment seeks to track the investment results of the ICE U.S. Treasury 10-20 Year Bond Index. The fund generally invests at least 90% of its assets in the bonds of its underlying index and at least 95% of its assets in U.S. government bonds. It seeks to track the investment results of the underlying index which measures the performance of public obligations of the U.S. Treasury that have a remaining maturity of greater than or equal to ten years and less than twenty years. **Top Holdings:** United States Treasury Bonds 4.38% United States Treasury Bonds 4.5% United States Treasury Bonds 4.25% United States Treasury Bonds 6.25% United States Treasury Bonds 4.5%

Invesco BulletShares 2020 High Yield Corporate Bond ETF   C+   HOLD

Ticker	Traded On	NAV	Total Assets ($)	Dividend Yield (TTM)	Turnover Ratio	Expense Ratio
BSJK	NYSE Arca	23.89	$1,160,972,132	4.62	27	0.42

Ratings
Reward	C
Risk	C+
Recent Upgrade/Downgrade	

Fund Information
Fund Type	Exchange Traded Funds
Category	US Fixed Income
Sub-Category	High Yield Bond
Prospectus Objective	Corp Bond-High Yld
Inception Date	Sep-13
Open to New Investments	Y

Prices
Price (as of 9/30/2019)	23.95
52-Week High	24.35
52-Week Low	23.23

Total Returns (%)
3-Month	6-Month	1-Year	3-Year	5-Year
0.46	1.47	2.94	13.95	18.57

3-Year Standard Deviation	2.13
Effective Duration	0.75

Valuation
Premium/Discount (1-Year Average)	0.13

Company Information
Provider	Invesco
Manager/Tenure	Jeremy Neisewander (3), Peter Hubbard (1), Jeffrey W. Kernagis (1), 1 other
Website	http://www.invesco.com/us
Address	Invesco 11 Greenway Plaza, Ste. 2500 Houston TX 77046 United States
Phone Number	800-659-1005

PERFORMANCE

Ratings History
Date	Overall Rating	Risk Rating	Reward Rating
Q3-19	C+	C+	C
Q4-18	C	C+	C
Q4-17	C+	B-	C+
Q4-16	C	C+	C
Q4-15	D+	C-	D

Asset & Performance History
Date	NAV	1-Year Total Return
2018	23.46	0.46
2017	24.49	5.88
2016	24.24	13.11
2015	22.58	-5.34
2014	25.11	2.41
2013	25.66	

Total Assets: $1,160,972,132
Asset Allocation
Asset	%
Cash	7%
Stocks	0%
US Stocks	0%
Bonds	93%
US Bonds	88%
Other	0%

Services Offered:

Investment Strategy: The investment seeks to track the investment results (before fees and expenses) of the Nasdaq BulletShares® USD High Yield Corporate Bond 2020 Index (the "underlying index"). The fund generally will invest at least 80% of its total assets in securities that comprise the underlying index. The underlying index seeks to measure the performance of a portfolio of U.S. dollar-denominated high yield corporate bonds (commonly known as "junk bonds") with maturities or, in some cases, "effective maturities" in the year 2020 (collectively, "2020 Bonds"). The fund is non-diversified. **Top Holdings:** Reynolds Group Issuer LLC. 5.75% EMC Corporation 2.65% CSC Holdings, LLC 10.88% Tenet Healthcare Corporation 6% Navient Corporation 8%

---

iShares MSCI USA ESG Optimized ETF   C   HOLD

Ticker	Traded On	NAV	Total Assets ($)	Dividend Yield (TTM)	Turnover Ratio	Expense Ratio
ESGU	NAS CM	65.41	$1,151,294,667	1.47	28	0.15

Ratings
Reward	C
Risk	C-
Recent Upgrade/Downgrade	

Fund Information
Fund Type	Exchange Traded Funds
Category	US Equity Large Cap Blend
Sub-Category	Large Blend
Prospectus Objective	Growth & Inc
Inception Date	Dec-16
Open to New Investments	Y

Prices
Price (as of 9/30/2019)	65.37
52-Week High	66.45
52-Week Low	51.48

Total Returns (%)
3-Month	6-Month	1-Year	3-Year	5-Year
0.63	4.59	3.62		

3-Year Standard Deviation	
Effective Duration	

Valuation
Premium/Discount (1-Year Average)	0.11

Company Information
Provider	iShares
Manager/Tenure	Diane Hsiung (2), Jennifer Hsui (2), Alan Mason (2), 3 others
Website	http://www.ishares.com
Address	iShares 400 Howard Street San Francisco CA 94105 United States
Phone Number	800-474-2737

PERFORMANCE

Ratings History
Date	Overall Rating	Risk Rating	Reward Rating
Q3-19	C	C-	C
Q4-18	C-	C-	D+
Q4-17	D	A	D+
Q4-16			
Q4-15			

Asset & Performance History
Date	NAV	1-Year Total Return
2018	54.78	-4.13
2017	58.12	21.25
2016	48.88	
2015		
2014		
2013		

Total Assets: $1,151,294,667
Asset Allocation
Asset	%
Cash	0%
Stocks	100%
US Stocks	99%
Bonds	0%
US Bonds	0%
Other	0%

Services Offered:

Investment Strategy: The investment seeks to track the investment results of the MSCI USA Extended ESG Focus Index. The fund generally will invest at least 90% of its assets in the component securities of the underlying index and may invest up to 10% of its assets in certain futures, options and swap contracts, cash and cash equivalents. The underlying index is an optimized equity index designed to reflect the equity performance of U.S. companies that have favorable environmental, social and governance ("ESG") characteristics, while exhibiting risk and return characteristics similar to those of the MSCI USA Index. The fund is non-diversified. **Top Holdings:** Microsoft Corp Apple Inc Amazon.com Inc Facebook Inc A Alphabet Inc Class C

iShares Morningstar Large-Cap Growth ETF   C+   HOLD

Ticker	Traded On	NAV	Total Assets ($)	Dividend Yield (TTM)	Turnover Ratio	Expense Ratio
JKE	NYSE Arca	191.37	$1,138,621,932	0.57	23	0.25

Ratings

Reward	B-
Risk	C
Recent Upgrade/Downgrade	Up

Fund Information

Fund Type	Exchange Traded Funds
Category	US Equity Large Cap Growth
Sub-Category	Large Growth
Prospectus Objective	Growth
Inception Date	Jun-04
Open to New Investments	Y

Prices

Price (as of 9/30/2019)	191.45
52-Week High	198.74
52-Week Low	147.58

Total Returns (%)

3-Month	6-Month	1-Year	3-Year	5-Year
-1.06	3.61	3.17	61.08	86.73

3-Year Standard Deviation	13.19
Effective Duration	

Valuation

Premium/Discount (1-Year Average)	-0.01

Company Information

Provider	iShares
Manager/Tenure	Greg Savage (11), Jennifer Hsui (7), Alan Mason (3), 2 others
Website	http://www.ishares.com
Address	iShares 400 Howard Street San Francisco CA 94105 United States
Phone Number	800-474-2737

PERFORMANCE

Ratings History

Date	Overall Rating	Risk Rating	Reward Rating
Q3-19	C+	C	B-
Q4-18	C	C	C
Q4-17	B+	A-	B+
Q4-16	C+	C	B-
Q4-15	C+	C	B-

Asset & Performance History

Date	NAV	1-Year Total Return
2018	158.44	2.08
2017	156.38	30.61
2016	120.9	1.56
2015	120.19	7.44
2014	112.99	14.07
2013	99.96	32.06

Total Assets: $1,138,621,932

Asset Allocation

Asset	%
Cash	0%
Stocks	100%
US Stocks	98%
Bonds	0%
US Bonds	0%
Other	0%

Services Offered:

Investment Strategy: The investment seeks to track the investment results of the Morningstar® Large Growth IndexSM composed of large-capitalization U.S. equities that exhibit growth characteristics. The fund generally invests at least 90% of its assets in securities of the underlying index and in depositary receipts representing securities of the underlying index. The underlying index measures the performance of stocks issued by large-capitalization companies that have exhibited above-average "growth" characteristics as determined by Morningstar, Inc.'s ("Morningstar" or the "index provider") proprietary index methodology. **Top Holdings:** Microsoft Corp   Amazon.com Inc   Facebook Inc A   Alphabet Inc Class C   Visa Inc Class A

Barclays ETN+ FI Enhanced Global High Yield ETN B   C-   HOLD

Ticker	Traded On	NAV	Total Assets ($)	Dividend Yield (TTM)	Turnover Ratio	Expense Ratio
FIYY	NYSE Arca		$1,133,327,278	0		0.93

Ratings

Reward	C-
Risk	D+
Recent Upgrade/Downgrade	Up

Fund Information

Fund Type	Exchange Traded Funds
Category	Global Equity Large Cap
Sub-Category	World Large Stock
Prospectus Objective	Equity-Income
Inception Date	Mar-18
Open to New Investments	Y

Prices

Price (as of 9/30/2019)	108.76
52-Week High	110.77
52-Week Low	77.47

Total Returns (%)

3-Month	6-Month	1-Year	3-Year	5-Year
0.37	5.29	5.27		

3-Year Standard Deviation	
Effective Duration	

Valuation

Premium/Discount (1-Year Average)	-0.24

Company Information

Provider	Milleis Investissements Funds
Manager/Tenure	No Manager (1)
Website	
Address	2-4, rue Eugène Ruppert L-2453 Luxembourg Luxembourg L-2453 Luxembourg
Phone Number	

PERFORMANCE

Ratings History

Date	Overall Rating	Risk Rating	Reward Rating
Q3-19	C-	D+	C-
Q4-18	U		
Q4-17			
Q4-16			
Q4-15			

Asset & Performance History

Date	NAV	1-Year Total Return
2018	83.7	
2017		
2016		
2015		
2014		
2013		

Total Assets: $1,133,327,278

Asset Allocation

Asset	%
Cash	%
Stocks	%
US Stocks	%
Bonds	%
US Bonds	%
Other	%

Services Offered:

Investment Strategy: The investment seeks return linked to a quarterly rebalanced leveraged participation in the performance of the MSCI World High Dividend Yield USD Gross Total Return Index (the "index").
At inception the ETN is designed to target two times the performance of the index. A quarterly rebalancing event or a loss rebalancing event will aim to reset the leveraged exposure to the index to approximately two. The index is designed to track the performance of large and mid cap stocks (excluding REITS) across 23 developed markets countries tracked by the MSCI World Index with higher than average dividend yields that are potentially both sustainable and persistent. **Top Holdings:**

iShares Core Moderate Allocation ETF   C+   HOLD

Ticker	Traded On	NAV	Total Assets ($)	Dividend Yield (TTM)	Turnover Ratio	Expense Ratio
AOM	NYSE Arca	39.26	$1,132,519,191	2.55	4	0.25

Ratings
Reward	C+
Risk	C+
Recent Upgrade/Downgrade	Up

Fund Information
Fund Type	Exchange Traded Funds
Category	Cautious Allocation
Sub-Category	Allocation--30% to 50% Equity
Prospectus Objective	Asset Allocation
Inception Date	Nov-08
Open to New Investments	Y

Prices
Price (as of 9/30/2019)	39.29
52-Week High	39.31
52-Week Low	35.24

Total Returns (%)
3-Month	6-Month	1-Year	3-Year	5-Year
1.15	4.31	6.35	18.33	27.70

3-Year Standard Deviation	4.93
Effective Duration	

Valuation
Premium/Discount (1-Year Average)	0.03

Company Information
Provider	iShares
Manager/Tenure	Diane Hsiung (10), Greg Savage (10), Jennifer Hsui (6), 3 others
Website	http://www.ishares.com
Address	iShares 400 Howard Street San Francisco CA 94105 United States
Phone Number	800-474-2737

PERFORMANCE

Ratings History
Date	Overall Rating	Risk Rating	Reward Rating
Q3-19	C+	C+	C+
Q4-18	C	C+	C-
Q4-17	B	A-	C+
Q4-16	C	C-	C
Q4-15	C	C-	C

Asset & Performance History
Date	NAV	1-Year Total Return
2018	35.69	-3.85
2017	38.04	11.69
2016	35.21	5.67
2015	34.04	-1.18
2014	35.12	4.44
2013	34.33	10.41

Total Assets: $1,132,519,191
Asset Allocation
Asset	%
Cash	2%
Stocks	39%
US Stocks	21%
Bonds	60%
US Bonds	43%
Other	0%

Services Offered:

Investment Strategy: The investment seeks to track the investment results of the S&P Target Risk Moderate Index composed of a portfolio of underlying equity and fixed income funds intended to represent a moderate target risk allocation strategy. The fund is a fund of funds and seeks its investment objective by investing primarily in other iShares Underlying Funds that themselves seek investment results corresponding to their own respective underlying indexes. It generally will invest at least 90% of its assets in the component securities of the underlying index. The index measures the performance of the S&P Dow Jones Indices LLC proprietary allocation model. **Top Holdings:** Microsoft Corp Apple Inc United States Treasury Notes 2.5% United States Treasury Notes 2.63% Amazon.com Inc

ProShares UltraPro Short QQQ   C   HOLD

Ticker	Traded On	NAV	Total Assets ($)	Dividend Yield (TTM)	Turnover Ratio	Expense Ratio
SQQQ	NAS CM	32.52	$1,129,233,101	2.94		0.95

Ratings
Reward	C-
Risk	D+
Recent Upgrade/Downgrade	

Fund Information
Fund Type	Exchange Traded Funds
Category	Trading Tools
Sub-Category	Trading--Inverse Equity
Prospectus Objective	Growth
Inception Date	Feb-10
Open to New Investments	Y

Prices
Price (as of 9/30/2019)	32.51
52-Week High	47.29
52-Week Low	9.71

Total Returns (%)
3-Month	6-Month	1-Year	3-Year	5-Year
-3.05	-15.56	200.09	-37.00	-77.68

3-Year Standard Deviation	41.69
Effective Duration	

Valuation
Premium/Discount (1-Year Average)	0.08

Company Information
Provider	ProShares
Manager/Tenure	Michael Neches (6), Devin Sullivan (1)
Website	http://www.proshares.com
Address	ProShares 7501 Wisconsin Avenue, Suite 1000 Bethesda MD 20814 United States
Phone Number	866-776-5125

PERFORMANCE

Ratings History
Date	Overall Rating	Risk Rating	Reward Rating
Q3-19	C	D+	C-
Q4-18	D	D-	E+
Q4-17	E+	E+	E
Q4-16	D-	E+	E+
Q4-15	D-	E+	E+

Asset & Performance History
Date	NAV	1-Year Total Return
2018	16.75	-20.93
2017	21.55	-58.75
2016	52.32	-30.05
2015	74.8	-37.47
2014	119.64	-47.89
2013	229.6	-64.65

Total Assets: $1,129,233,101
Asset Allocation
Asset	%
Cash	234%
Stocks	-147%
US Stocks	-143%
Bonds	12%
US Bonds	12%
Other	0%

Services Offered:

Investment Strategy: The investment seeks daily investment results, before fees and expenses, that correspond to three times the inverse (-3x) of the daily performance of the NASDAQ-100 Index®. The fund invests in financial instruments that ProShare Advisors believes, in combination, should produce daily returns consistent with the fund's investment objective. The index includes 100 of the largest domestic and international non-financial companies listed on The Nasdaq Stock Market based on market capitalization. The fund is non-diversified. **Top Holdings:** Nasdaq 100 Index Swap Societe Generale Nasdaq 100 Index Swap Citibank, N.A. Nasdaq 100 Index Swap Bank Of America, Na Nasdaq 100 Index Swap Bnp Paribas Nasdaq 100 Index Swap Ubs Ag

Invesco BuyBack Achievers ETF

C   HOLD

Ticker	Traded On	NAV	Total Assets ($)	Dividend Yield (TTM)	Turnover Ratio	Expense Ratio
PKW	NAS CM	62.59	$1,126,692,094	1.37	76	0.62

Ratings
Reward	B-
Risk	C
Recent Upgrade/Downgrade	Down

Fund Information
Fund Type	Exchange Traded Funds
Category	US Equity Large Cap Blend
Sub-Category	Large Blend
Prospectus Objective	Unaligned
Inception Date	Dec-06
Open to New Investments	Y

Prices
Price (as of 9/30/2019)	62.58
52-Week High	64.22
52-Week Low	49.25

Total Returns (%)
3-Month	6-Month	1-Year	3-Year	5-Year
-0.69	4.17	4.43	36.67	50.36

3-Year Standard Deviation	15.14
Effective Duration	

Valuation
Premium/Discount (1-Year Average)	-0.03

Company Information
Provider	Invesco
Manager/Tenure	Peter Hubbard (12), Michael Jeanette (11), Tony Seisser (5)
Website	http://www.invesco.com/us
Address	Invesco 11 Greenway Plaza, Ste. 2500 Houston TX 77046 United States
Phone Number	800-659-1005

PERFORMANCE

Ratings History
Date	Overall Rating	Risk Rating	Reward Rating
Q3-19	C	C	B-
Q4-18	C	C	C
Q4-17	B	B	B-
Q4-16	C+	C-	B-
Q4-15	C+	B-	C+

Asset & Performance History
Date	NAV	1-Year Total Return
2018	52.2	-10.42
2017	58.98	17.8
2016	50.41	12.81
2015	45.44	-4.31
2014	48.02	12.77
2013	43.04	45.58

Total Assets: $1,126,692,094

Asset Allocation
Asset	%
Cash	0%
Stocks	100%
US Stocks	100%
Bonds	0%
US Bonds	0%
Other	0%

Services Offered:

Investment Strategy: The investment seeks to track the investment results (before fees and expenses) of the NASDAQ US BuyBack Achievers™ Index. The fund generally will invest at least 90% of its total assets in the securities that comprise the underlying index. The NASDAQ includes common stocks in the underlying index pursuant to a proprietary selection methodology that identifies a universe of "BuyBack Achievers ™". **Top Holdings:** Apple Inc Amgen Inc Starbucks Corp Oracle Corp Citigroup Inc

---

SPDR® S&P China ETF

C   HOLD

Ticker	Traded On	NAV	Total Assets ($)	Dividend Yield (TTM)	Turnover Ratio	Expense Ratio
GXC	NYSE Arca		$1,122,940,077	2.18	3	0.59

Ratings
Reward	C-
Risk	C
Recent Upgrade/Downgrade	

Fund Information
Fund Type	Exchange Traded Funds
Category	Greater China Equity
Sub-Category	China Region
Prospectus Objective	Pacific Stock
Inception Date	Mar-07
Open to New Investments	Y

Prices
Price (as of 9/30/2019)	90.26
52-Week High	104.47
52-Week Low	82.09

Total Returns (%)
3-Month	6-Month	1-Year	3-Year	5-Year
-5.50	-10.01	-4.61	21.79	31.08

3-Year Standard Deviation	18.84
Effective Duration	

Valuation
Premium/Discount (1-Year Average)	-0.08

Company Information
Provider	SPDR State Street Global Advisors
Manager/Tenure	Michael J. Feehily (8), Juan Acevedo (2), Thomas Coleman (2)
Website	http://www.spdrs.com
Address	SPDR State Street Global Advisors State Street Financial Center, 1 Lincoln Street Boston MA 02111-2900 United States
Phone Number	617-786-3000

PERFORMANCE

Ratings History
Date	Overall Rating	Risk Rating	Reward Rating
Q3-19	C	C	C-
Q4-18	C-	C-	C-
Q4-17	B+	C+	A
Q4-16	C	C	C
Q4-15	C	C+	C

Asset & Performance History
Date	NAV	1-Year Total Return
2018	85.71	-18.67
2017	107.37	50.5
2016	72.73	0
2015	73.79	-4.56
2014	79.41	5.03
2013	77.29	9.33

Total Assets: $1,122,940,077

Asset Allocation
Asset	%
Cash	1%
Stocks	99%
US Stocks	1%
Bonds	0%
US Bonds	0%
Other	0%

Services Offered:

Investment Strategy: The investment seeks investment results that, before fees and expenses, correspond generally to the total return performance of the S&P China BMI Index. The fund generally invests substantially all, but at least 80%, of its total assets in the securities comprising the index and in depositary receipts based on securities comprising the index. The index is a market capitalization weighted index designed to define and measure the investable universe of publicly traded companies domiciled in China available to foreign investors. The fund is non-diversified. **Top Holdings:** Tencent Holdings Ltd Alibaba Group Holding Ltd ADR China Construction Bank Corp Class H Ping An Insurance (Group) Co. of China Ltd Class H Industrial And Commercial Bank Of China Ltd Class H

WisdomTree U.S. MidCap Earnings Fund   C-   HOLD

Ticker	Traded On	NAV	Total Assets ($)	Dividend Yield (TTM)	Turnover Ratio	Expense Ratio
EZM	NYSE Arca	39.46	$1,122,672,397	1.41	36	0.38

Ratings

Reward	C-
Risk	C-
Recent Upgrade/Downgrade	Down

Fund Information

Fund Type	Exchange Traded Funds
Category	US Equity Mid Cap
Sub-Category	Mid-Cap Blend
Prospectus Objective	Growth & Inc
Inception Date	Feb-07
Open to New Investments	Y

Prices

Price (as of 9/30/2019)	39.44
52-Week High	41.26
52-Week Low	32.31

Total Returns (%)

3-Month	6-Month	1-Year	3-Year	5-Year
-1.27	-0.38	-2.21	29.02	46.95

3-Year Standard Deviation	16.45
Effective Duration	

Valuation

Premium/Discount (1-Year Average)	0.02

Company Information

Provider	WisdomTree
Manager/Tenure	Richard A. Brown (11), Thomas J. Durante (11), Karen Q. Wong (11)
Website	http://www.wisdomtree.com
Address	WisdomTree 245 Park Avenue, 35th floor New York NY 10167 United States
Phone Number	866-909-9473

PERFORMANCE

Ratings History

Date	Overall Rating	Risk Rating	Reward Rating
Q3-19	C-	C-	C-
Q4-18	C-	C-	C-
Q4-17	B	B	B
Q4-16	C+	C-	B
Q4-15	C	C-	C

Asset & Performance History

Date	NAV	1-Year Total Return
2018	34.26	-12.28
2017	39.63	17.2
2016	34.22	19.71
2015	29.07	-4.63
2014	30.86	8.43
2013	28.8	40.19

Total Assets: $1,122,672,397

Asset Allocation

Asset	%
Cash	0%
Stocks	100%
US Stocks	100%
Bonds	0%
US Bonds	0%
Other	0%

Services Offered:

Investment Strategy: The investment seeks to track the price and yield performance, before fees and expenses, of the WisdomTree U.S. MidCap Index. Under normal circumstances, at least 95% of the fund's total assets (exclusive of collateral held from securities lending) will be invested in component securities of the index and investments that have economic characteristics that are substantially identical to the economic characteristics of such component securities. The index is a fundamentally weighted index that is comprised of earnings-generating companies within the mid-capitalization segment of the U.S. stock market. The fund is non-diversified. **Top Holdings:** PulteGroup Inc Huntsman Corp Reliance Steel & Aluminum Co Santander Consumer USA Holdings Inc GrafTech International Ltd

---

Vanguard S&P 500 Value Index Fund ETF Shares   C   HOLD

Ticker	Traded On	NAV	Total Assets ($)	Dividend Yield (TTM)	Turnover Ratio	Expense Ratio
VOOV	NYSE Arca	114.93	$1,120,353,430	2.32	20	0.15

Ratings

Reward	C
Risk	C-
Recent Upgrade/Downgrade	

Fund Information

Fund Type	Exchange Traded Funds
Category	US Equity Large Cap Value
Sub-Category	Large Value
Prospectus Objective	Growth & Inc
Inception Date	Sep-10
Open to New Investments	Y

Prices

Price (as of 9/30/2019)	114.96
52-Week High	116.66
52-Week Low	92.00

Total Returns (%)

3-Month	6-Month	1-Year	3-Year	5-Year
1.54	5.02	4.50	34.11	48.47

3-Year Standard Deviation	13.17
Effective Duration	

Valuation

Premium/Discount (1-Year Average)	-0.01

Company Information

Provider	Vanguard
Manager/Tenure	Donald M. Butler (3), Michelle Louie (1)
Website	http://www.vanguard.com
Address	Vanguard 100 Vanguard Boulevard Malvern PA 19355 United States
Phone Number	877-662-7447

PERFORMANCE

Ratings History

Date	Overall Rating	Risk Rating	Reward Rating
Q3-19	C	C-	C
Q4-18	C	C-	C
Q4-17	B	B	B-
Q4-16	C+	C-	B
Q4-15	C	C-	C

Asset & Performance History

Date	NAV	1-Year Total Return
2018	96.77	-9.77
2017	109.88	15.47
2016	97.54	16.55
2015	85.24	-3.22
2014	90.14	12.17
2013	82.02	31.78

Total Assets: $1,120,353,430

Asset Allocation

Asset	%
Cash	0%
Stocks	100%
US Stocks	99%
Bonds	0%
US Bonds	0%
Other	0%

Services Offered:

Investment Strategy: The investment seeks to track the performance of a benchmark index that measures the investment return of large-capitalization value stocks in the United States. The fund employs an indexing investment approach designed to track the performance of the S&P 500® Value Index, which represents the value companies, as determined by the index sponsor, of the S&P 500 Index. The index measures the performance of large-capitalization value stocks in the United States. **Top Holdings:** Apple Inc JPMorgan Chase & Co Bank of America Corporation AT&T Inc UnitedHealth Group Inc

SPDR® Bloomberg Barclays International Treasury Bond ETF

C   HOLD

Ticker	Traded On	NAV	Total Assets ($)	Dividend Yield (TTM)	Turnover Ratio	Expense Ratio
BWX	NYSE Arca		$1,119,355,167	1.17	18	0.35

Ratings

Reward	C
Risk	C+
Recent Upgrade/Downgrade	

Fund Information

Fund Type	Exchange Traded Funds
Category	Global Fixed Income
Sub-Category	World Bond
Prospectus Objective	Worldwide Bond
Inception Date	Oct-07
Open to New Investments	Y

Prices

Price (as of 9/30/2019)	28.70
52-Week High	29.35
52-Week Low	26.76

Total Returns (%)

3-Month	6-Month	1-Year	3-Year	5-Year
0.29	3.89	6.68	2.02	3.59

3-Year Standard Deviation	6.53
Effective Duration	8.87

Valuation

Premium/Discount (1-Year Average)	-0.07

Company Information

Provider	SPDR State Street Global Advisors
Manager/Tenure	Joanna Madden (4), James Kramer (2), Orhan Imer (1)
Website	http://www.spdrs.com
Address	SPDR State Street Global Advisors State Street Financial Center, 1 Lincoln Street Boston MA 02111-2900 United States
Phone Number	617-786-3000

Ratings History

Date	Overall Rating	Risk Rating	Reward Rating
Q3-19	C	C+	C
Q4-18	C-	C	D+
Q4-17	C	C	C
Q4-16	D+	C-	D+
Q4-15	D	D+	D

Asset & Performance History

Date	NAV	1-Year Total Return
2018	27.53	-2.16
2017	28.47	10.14
2016	25.96	0.57
2015	25.7	-6.99
2014	27.63	-2.48
2013	28.82	-3.66

Total Assets: $1,119,355,167

Asset Allocation

Asset	%
Cash	0%
Stocks	0%
US Stocks	0%
Bonds	100%
US Bonds	0%
Other	0%

Services Offered:

Investment Strategy: The investment seeks to provide investment results that, before fees and expenses, correspond generally to the price and yield performance of the Bloomberg Barclays Global Treasury ex-US Capped Index. The fund generally invests substantially all, but at least 80%, of its total assets in the securities comprising the index or in securities that the Adviser determines have economic characteristics that are substantially identical to the economic characteristics of the securities that comprise the index. The index is designed to track the fixed-rate local currency sovereign debt of investment grade countries outside the United States. The fund is non-diversified. **Top Holdings:** The Republic of Korea 2% Denmark (Kingdom Of) 4.5% Indonesia Government Sr Unsecured 05/28 6.125 China (People's Republic Of) 3.29% Netherlands (Kingdom of) 4%

UBS ETRACS Alerian MLP Infrastructure Index ETN

D   SELL

Ticker	Traded On	NAV	Total Assets ($)	Dividend Yield (TTM)	Turnover Ratio	Expense Ratio
MLPI	NYSE Arca	20.85	$1,114,352,325	7.53		0.85

Ratings

Reward	D
Risk	C-
Recent Upgrade/Downgrade	Down

Fund Information

Fund Type	Exchange Traded Funds
Category	Energy Sector Equity
Sub-Category	Energy Limited Partnership
Prospectus Objective	Natl Res
Inception Date	Apr-10
Open to New Investments	Y

Prices

Price (as of 9/30/2019)	20.85
52-Week High	24.70
52-Week Low	18.86

Total Returns (%)

3-Month	6-Month	1-Year	3-Year	5-Year
-5.43	-6.26	-9.32	-10.26	-36.18

3-Year Standard Deviation	16.82
Effective Duration	

Valuation

Premium/Discount (1-Year Average)	-0.06

Company Information

Provider	UBS Group AG
Manager/Tenure	No Manager (9)
Website	http://www.ubs.com
Address	Bahnhofstrasse 45 Zürich 8098 Switzerland
Phone Number	412-037-1952

Ratings History

Date	Overall Rating	Risk Rating	Reward Rating
Q3-19	D	C-	D
Q4-18	D+	D+	D+
Q4-17	D	D	D
Q4-16	D	D	D+
Q4-15	D+	D+	C-

Asset & Performance History

Date	NAV	1-Year Total Return
2018	19.83	-12.4
2017	24.23	-9.08
2016	28.47	17.39
2015	26.13	-31.91
2014	40.52	6.86
2013	39.64	27.78

Total Assets: $1,114,352,325

Asset Allocation

Asset	%
Cash	%
Stocks	%
US Stocks	%
Bonds	%
US Bonds	%
Other	%

Services Offered:

Investment Strategy: The investment seeks to replicate, net of expenses, the Alerian MLP Infrastructure Index. The index provides exposure to the infrastructure component of the Master Limited Partnership asset class. Its constituents each earn at least 50% of their EBITDA from assets that are not directly exposed to changes in commodity prices. The index is a composite of 25 energy infrastructure MLPs. **Top Holdings:**

First Trust Large Cap Value AlphaDEX® Fund　　　　　　　　　C-　　HOLD

Ticker	Traded On	NAV	Total Assets ($)	Dividend Yield (TTM)	Turnover Ratio	Expense Ratio
FTA	NAS CM	51.54	$1,102,930,896	2.17	96	0.61

Ratings
Reward	C-
Risk	C-
Recent Upgrade/Downgrade	Down

Fund Information
Fund Type	Exchange Traded Funds
Category	US Equity Large Cap Value
Sub-Category	Large Value
Prospectus Objective	Growth
Inception Date	May-07
Open to New Investments	Y

Prices
Price (as of 9/30/2019)	51.57
52-Week High	54.36
52-Week Low	43.92

Total Returns (%)
3-Month	6-Month	1-Year	3-Year	5-Year
-1.05	-0.44	-2.62	28.13	35.26

3-Year Standard Deviation	15.21
Effective Duration	

Valuation
Premium/Discount (1-Year Average)	0.00

Company Information
Provider	First Trust
Manager/Tenure	Jon C. Erickson (12), Daniel J. Lindquist (12), David G. McGarel (12), 3 others
Website	http://www.ftportfolios.com/
Address	First Trust 120 E. Liberty Drive, Suite 400 Wheaton IL 60187 United States
Phone Number	800-621-1675

PERFORMANCE

Ratings History

Date	Overall Rating	Risk Rating	Reward Rating
Q3-19	C-	C-	C-
Q4-18	C-	C-	C-
Q4-17	B	B-	B
Q4-16	C	C-	B-
Q4-15	C	C+	C

Asset & Performance History

Date	NAV	1-Year Total Return
2018	46.21	-13.58
2017	54.59	18.45
2016	46.84	23.92
2015	38.45	-10.28
2014	43.7	10.87
2013	40.14	33.94

Total Assets: $1,102,930,896

Asset Allocation

Asset	%
Cash	0%
Stocks	100%
US Stocks	98%
Bonds	0%
US Bonds	0%
Other	0%

Services Offered:

Investment Strategy: The investment seeks investment results that correspond generally to the price and yield (before the fund's fees and expenses) of an equity index called the Nasdaq AlphaDEX® Large Cap Value Index. The fund will normally invest at least 90% of its net assets (including investment borrowings) in common stocks that comprise the index. The index is designed to select value stocks from the NASDAQ US 500 Large Cap Index (the "base index") that may generate positive alpha, or risk-adjusted returns, relative to traditional indices through the use of the AlphaDEX® selection methodology. **Top Holdings:** Micron Technology Inc　D.R. Horton Inc　The Kroger Co　Lennar Corp　Phillips 66

Invesco Aerospace & Defense ETF　　　　　　　　　　　　　B　　BUY

Ticker	Traded On	NAV	Total Assets ($)	Dividend Yield (TTM)	Turnover Ratio	Expense Ratio
PPA	NYSE Arca	67.71	$1,086,711,186	0.95	15	0.59

Ratings
Reward	B+
Risk	C
Recent Upgrade/Downgrade	Up

Fund Information
Fund Type	Exchange Traded Funds
Category	Industrials Sector Equity
Sub-Category	Industrials
Prospectus Objective	Unaligned
Inception Date	Oct-05
Open to New Investments	Y

Prices
Price (as of 9/30/2019)	67.70
52-Week High	69.48
52-Week Low	46.46

Total Returns (%)
3-Month	6-Month	1-Year	3-Year	5-Year
5.27	15.27	11.04	80.30	126.50

3-Year Standard Deviation	16.7
Effective Duration	

Valuation
Premium/Discount (1-Year Average)	0.00

Company Information
Provider	Invesco
Manager/Tenure	Peter Hubbard (12), Michael Jeanette (11), Tony Seisser (5)
Website	http://www.invesco.com/us
Address	Invesco 11 Greenway Plaza, Ste. 2500 Houston TX 77046 United States
Phone Number	800-659-1005

PERFORMANCE

Ratings History

Date	Overall Rating	Risk Rating	Reward Rating
Q3-19	B	C	B+
Q4-18	B-	C+	B
Q4-17	B+	B-	A+
Q4-16	B	C+	B+
Q4-15	B	B	B

Asset & Performance History

Date	NAV	1-Year Total Return
2018	49.5	-7.35
2017	53.87	30.02
2016	41.74	19.2
2015	35.66	4.23
2014	34.7	12.74
2013	30.98	49.81

Total Assets: $1,086,711,186

Asset Allocation

Asset	%
Cash	0%
Stocks	100%
US Stocks	98%
Bonds	0%
US Bonds	0%
Other	0%

Services Offered:

Investment Strategy: The investment seeks to track the investment results (before fees and expenses) of the SPADE® Defense Index. The fund generally will invest at least 90% of its total assets in the securities that comprise the underlying index. The underlying index is composed of common stocks of companies that are engaged principally in the development, manufacture, operation and support of U.S. defense, military, homeland security and space operations. The fund is non-diversified. **Top Holdings:** L3Harris Technologies Inc　Lockheed Martin Corp　United Technologies Corp　Boeing Co　Honeywell International Inc

Invesco Russell 1000® Dynamic Multifactor ETF   C-   HOLD

Ticker	Traded On	NAV	Total Assets ($)	Dividend Yield (TTM)	Turnover Ratio	Expense Ratio
OMFL	BATS	31.00	$1,083,591,723	1.5	138	0.29

Ratings
Reward   C
Risk   C-
Recent Upgrade/Downgrade

Fund Information
Fund Type   Exchange Traded Funds
Category   US Equity Large Cap Blend
Sub-Category   Large Blend
Prospectus Objective   Growth
Inception Date   Nov-17
Open to New Investments   Y

Prices
Price (as of 9/30/2019)   31.03
52-Week High   31.97
52-Week Low   23.84

Total Returns (%)

3-Month	6-Month	1-Year	3-Year	5-Year
4.05	7.66	8.62		

3-Year Standard Deviation
Effective Duration

Valuation
Premium/Discount (1-Year Average)   0.09

Company Information
Provider   Invesco
Manager/Tenure   Peter Hubbard (0), Michael Jeanette
                  (0), Tony Seisser (0)
Website   http://www.invesco.com/us
Address   Invesco 11 Greenway Plaza, Ste. 2500
                  Houston TX 77046 United States
Phone Number   800-659-1005

PERFORMANCE

Ratings History

Date	Overall Rating	Risk Rating	Reward Rating
Q3-19	C-	C-	C
Q4-18	C-	C-	C-
Q4-17	U		
Q4-16			
Q4-15			

Asset & Performance History

Date	NAV	1-Year Total Return
2018	25.09	-2.3
2017	26.02	
2016		
2015		
2014		
2013		

Total Assets: $1,083,591,723
Asset Allocation

Asset	%
Cash	0%
Stocks	100%
US Stocks	98%
Bonds	0%
US Bonds	0%
Other	0%

Services Offered:

Investment Strategy: The investment seeks to provide investment results that correspond generally, before fees and expenses, to the performance of the Russell 1000 OFI Dynamic Multifactor Index. Under normal circumstances, the fund will invest at least 80% of its net assets, plus any borrowings for investment purposes, in securities of companies included in the underlying index. The underlying index is constructed using a rules-based methodology by selecting equity securities from the Russell 1000 Index (the "parent index"), which measures the performance of the 1,000 largest-capitalization companies in the United States. **Top Holdings:** Fiserv Inc   L3Harris Technologies Inc   Crown Holdings Inc   CDW Corp   The AES Corp

---

Aberdeen Standard Physical Swiss Gold Shares ETF   C+   HOLD

Ticker	Traded On	NAV	Total Assets ($)	Dividend Yield (TTM)	Turnover Ratio	Expense Ratio
SGOL	NYSE Arca	143.07	$1,073,002,061	0	11	0.17

Ratings
Reward   C+
Risk   C+
Recent Upgrade/Downgrade   Up

Fund Information
Fund Type   Exchange Traded Funds
Category   Commodities Specified
Sub-Category   Commodities Precious Metals
Prospectus Objective   Prec Metals
Inception Date   Sep-09
Open to New Investments   Y

Prices
Price (as of 9/30/2019)   141.95
52-Week High   149.88
52-Week Low   114.76

Total Returns (%)

3-Month	6-Month	1-Year	3-Year	5-Year
6.80	14.73	24.62	11.20	19.95

3-Year Standard Deviation   11.18
Effective Duration

Valuation
Premium/Discount (1-Year Average)   -0.11

Company Information
Provider   Aberdeen Standard Investments
Manager/Tenure   Management Team (10)
Website   http://www.aberdeenstandardetfs.us
Address   Aberdeen Standard Investments 405
                  Lexington Avenue New York NY 10174
                  United States
Phone Number   212-918-4954

PERFORMANCE

Ratings History

Date	Overall Rating	Risk Rating	Reward Rating
Q3-19	C+	C+	C+
Q4-18	D+	C-	D
Q4-17	C-	C-	C-
Q4-16	C-	D+	C-
Q4-15	D	D	D

Asset & Performance History

Date	NAV	1-Year Total Return
2018	123.61	-1.51
2017	125.51	11.41
2016	112.65	8.69
2015	103.64	-11.76
2014	117.46	-0.57
2013	118.14	-28.07

Total Assets: $1,073,002,061
Asset Allocation

Asset	%
Cash	0%
Stocks	0%
US Stocks	0%
Bonds	0%
US Bonds	0%
Other	100%

Services Offered:

Investment Strategy: The investment seeks to reflect the performance of the price of gold bullion, less the Trust's expenses.
The Shares are intended to constitute a simple and cost-effective means of making an investment similar to an investment in gold. An investment in physical gold requires expensive and sometimes complicated arrangements in connection with the assay, transportation, warehousing and insurance of the metal. Although the Shares are not the exact equivalent of an investment in gold, they provide investors with an alternative that allows a level of participation in the gold market through the securities market. **Top Holdings:** Physical Gold Bullion

iShares Edge MSCI Multifactor Intl ETF   C   HOLD

Ticker	Traded On	NAV	Total Assets ($)	Dividend Yield (TTM)	Turnover Ratio	Expense Ratio
INTF	NYSE Arca	25.51	$1,068,760,672	3.17	44	0.3

Ratings
Reward   C-
Risk   C+
Recent Upgrade/Downgrade

Fund Information
Fund Type   Exchange Traded Funds
Category   Global Equity Large Cap
Sub-Category   Foreign Large Blend
Prospectus Objective   Growth & Inc
Inception Date   Apr-15
Open to New Investments   Y

Prices
Price (as of 9/30/2019)   25.50
52-Week High   28.22
52-Week Low   22.95

Total Returns (%)

3-Month	6-Month	1-Year	3-Year	5-Year
-2.96	-2.09	-6.28	16.82	

3-Year Standard Deviation   12.12
Effective Duration

Valuation
Premium/Discount (1-Year Average)   0.04

Company Information
Provider   iShares
Manager/Tenure   Diane Hsiung (4), Jennifer Hsui (4),
     Greg Savage (4), 3 others
Website   http://www.ishares.com
Address   iShares 400 Howard Street San
     Francisco CA 94105 United States
Phone Number   800-474-2737

PERFORMANCE

Ratings History

Date	Overall Rating	Risk Rating	Reward Rating
Q3-19	C	C+	C-
Q4-18	C-	C	D+
Q4-17	B-	B-	C+
Q4-16	D+	D+	D+
Q4-15	U		

Asset & Performance History

Date	NAV	1-Year Total Return
2018	23.77	-15.66
2017	28.86	28.15
2016	23.3	-0.2
2015	23.74	
2014		
2013		

Total Assets: $1,068,760,672

Asset Allocation

Asset	%
Cash	1%
Stocks	99%
US Stocks	4%
Bonds	0%
US Bonds	0%
Other	0%

Services Offered:

Investment Strategy: The investment seeks to track the investment results of the MSCI World ex USA Diversified Multiple-Factor Index. The fund generally will invest at least 90% of its assets in the component securities of the underlying index and in investments that have economic characteristics that are substantially identical to the component securities of the underlying index. The index is designed to select equity securities from the MSCI World ex USA Index (the "parent index") that have high exposure to four investment style factors: value, quality, momentum and low size, while maintaining a level of risk similar to that of the parent index. **Top Holdings:** Roche Holding AG Dividend Right Cert. Woolworths Group Ltd Hitachi Ltd Rio Tinto PLC Koninklijke Ahold Delhaize NV

VelocityShares Daily 2x VIX Short-Term ETN   D   SELL

Ticker	Traded On	NAV	Total Assets ($)	Dividend Yield (TTM)	Turnover Ratio	Expense Ratio
TVIX	NAS CM	12.97	$1,066,022,300	0		1.65

Ratings
Reward   D-
Risk   D
Recent Upgrade/Downgrade

Fund Information
Fund Type   Exchange Traded Funds
Category   Alternative Misc
Sub-Category   Volatility
Prospectus Objective   Growth
Inception Date   Nov-10
Open to New Investments   Y

Prices
Price (as of 9/30/2019)   13.60
52-Week High   78.72
52-Week Low   12.14

Total Returns (%)

3-Month	6-Month	1-Year	3-Year	5-Year
-21.10	-47.05	-49.07	-92.95	-99.85

3-Year Standard Deviation   105.01
Effective Duration

Valuation
Premium/Discount (1-Year Average)   1.79

Company Information
Provider   Credit Suisse AG
Manager/Tenure   Management Team (8)
Website
Address   Kilmore House Park Lane Dublin
     Ireland
Phone Number

PERFORMANCE

Ratings History

Date	Overall Rating	Risk Rating	Reward Rating
Q3-19	D	D	D-
Q4-18	C-	D	C
Q4-17	E	E	E-
Q4-16	E+	D-	E-
Q4-15	E	E+	E

Asset & Performance History

Date	NAV	1-Year Total Return
2018	70.65	1,151.86
2017	5.64	-94.05
2016	94.4	-93.98
2015	1,540.00	-77.68
2014	6,900.00	-62.13
2013	18,225.00	-91.68

Total Assets: $1,066,022,300

Asset Allocation

Asset	%
Cash	%
Stocks	%
US Stocks	%
Bonds	%
US Bonds	%
Other	%

Services Offered:

Investment Strategy: The investment seeks to replicate, net of expenses, the returns of twice (2x) the daily performance of the S&P 500 VIX Short-Term Futures Index.
The index was designed to provide investors with exposure to one or more maturities of futures contracts on the VIX, which reflects implied volatility of the S&P 500 Index at various points along the volatility forward curve. The ETNs are linked to a multiple (2x) of the daily return of the index and do not represent an investment in the VIX. **Top Holdings:**

First Trust Managed Municipal ETF   C+   HOLD

Ticker	Traded On	NAV	Total Assets ($)	Dividend Yield (TTM)	Turnover Ratio	Expense Ratio
FMB	NAS CM	55.46	$1,064,863,196	2.51	42	0.5

Ratings
Reward   C+
Risk   C+
Recent Upgrade/Downgrade

Fund Information
Fund Type   Exchange Traded Funds
Category   US Muni Fixed Inc
Sub-Category   Muni National Interm
Prospectus Objective   Growth & Inc
Inception Date   May-14
Open to New Investments   Y

Prices
Price (as of 9/30/2019)   55.56
52-Week High   56.20
52-Week Low   51.54

Total Returns (%)

3-Month	6-Month	1-Year	3-Year	5-Year
1.95	4.54	9.00	11.26	25.20

3-Year Standard Deviation   3.72
Effective Duration   5.81

Valuation
Premium/Discount (1-Year Average)   0.14

Company Information
Provider   First Trust
Manager/Tenure   J. Thomas Futrell (5), Johnathan N. Wilhelm (5)
Website   http://www.ftportfolios.com/
Address   First Trust 120 E. Liberty Drive, Suite 400 Wheaton IL 60187 United States
Phone Number   800-621-1675

PERFORMANCE

Ratings History

Date	Overall Rating	Risk Rating	Reward Rating
Q3-19	C+	C+	C+
Q4-18	C-	C-	C
Q4-17	B	A	C
Q4-16	C	C-	C
Q4-15	D	D+	C-

Asset & Performance History

Date	NAV	1-Year Total Return
2018	52.54	0.88
2017	53.44	7.4
2016	51.03	1.44
2015	51.75	3.84
2014	51.4	
2013		

Total Assets: $1,064,863,196

Asset Allocation

Asset	%
Cash	4%
Stocks	0%
US Stocks	0%
Bonds	96%
US Bonds	96%
Other	0%

Services Offered:

Investment Strategy: The investment seeks to generate current income that is exempt from regular federal income taxes and its secondary objective is long term capital appreciation. Under normal market conditions, the fund seeks to achieve its investment objectives by investing at least 80% of its net assets (including investment borrowings) in municipal debt securities that pay interest that is exempt from regular federal income taxes (collectively, "Municipal Securities"). **Top Holdings:** CAPITAL CITY ECONOMIC DEV AUTH CONN PKG & ENERGY FEE REV 1.51% NEW YORK N Y CITY TRANSITIONAL FIN AUTH REV 1.45% COLORADO SPRINGS COLO UTILS REV 1.39% US 10 Year Ultra Future Sept19 ORANGE CNTY FLA HEALTH FACS AUTH REV 5%

---

iShares Core MSCI Pacific ETF   C   HOLD

Ticker	Traded On	NAV	Total Assets ($)	Dividend Yield (TTM)	Turnover Ratio	Expense Ratio
IPAC	NYSE Arca	55.96	$1,057,596,522	2.85	5	0.09

Ratings
Reward   C
Risk   C-
Recent Upgrade/Downgrade   Up

Fund Information
Fund Type   Exchange Traded Funds
Category   Asia Equity
Sub-Category   Diversified Pacific/Asia
Prospectus Objective   Pacific Stock
Inception Date   Jun-14
Open to New Investments   Y

Prices
Price (as of 9/30/2019)   56.20
52-Week High   59.12
52-Week Low   49.08

Total Returns (%)

3-Month	6-Month	1-Year	3-Year	5-Year
-0.37	1.55	-1.83	21.37	30.33

3-Year Standard Deviation   10.16
Effective Duration

Valuation
Premium/Discount (1-Year Average)   0.04

Company Information
Provider   iShares
Manager/Tenure   Diane Hsiung (5), Jennifer Hsui (5), Greg Savage (5), 3 others
Website   http://www.ishares.com/
Address   iShares 400 Howard Street San Francisco CA 94105 United States
Phone Number   800-474-2737

PERFORMANCE

Ratings History

Date	Overall Rating	Risk Rating	Reward Rating
Q3-19	C	C-	C
Q4-18	D+	C-	D+
Q4-17	B+	B	A-
Q4-16	C	C-	C
Q4-15	D	C+	D

Asset & Performance History

Date	NAV	1-Year Total Return
2018	50.95	-12.37
2017	59.75	25.83
2016	48.97	4.54
2015	48.11	3.35
2014	47.72	
2013		

Total Assets: $1,057,596,522

Asset Allocation

Asset	%
Cash	1%
Stocks	99%
US Stocks	0%
Bonds	0%
US Bonds	0%
Other	0%

Services Offered:

Investment Strategy: The investment seeks to track the investment results of the MSCI Pacific IMI (the "underlying index"). The fund generally will invest at least 90% of its assets in the component securities of the underlying index and in investments that have economic characteristics that are substantially identical to the component securities of the underlying index. The index is a free float-adjusted market capitalization-weighted index which consists of securities from the following five countries or regions: Australia, Hong Kong, Japan, New Zealand and Singapore. **Top Holdings:** Toyota Motor Corp AIA Group Ltd Commonwealth Bank of Australia SoftBank Group Corp Sony Corp

First Trust Health Care AlphaDEX® Fund   C   HOLD

Ticker	Traded On	NAV	Total Assets ($)	Dividend Yield (TTM)	Turnover Ratio	Expense Ratio
FXH	NYSE Arca	74.02	$1,051,098,055	0	123	0.63

Ratings
Reward   C
Risk   C
Recent Upgrade/Downgrade

Fund Information
Fund Type   Exchange Traded Funds
Category   Healthcare Sector Equity
Sub-Category   Health
Prospectus Objective   Health
Inception Date   May-07
Open to New Investments   Y

Prices
Price (as of 9/30/2019)   74.02
52-Week High   84.57
52-Week Low   64.01

Total Returns (%)

3-Month	6-Month	1-Year	3-Year	5-Year
-5.01	-3.65	-12.43	21.68	34.02

3-Year Standard Deviation   16.01
Effective Duration

Valuation
Premium/Discount (1-Year Average) -0.01

Company Information
Provider   First Trust
Manager/Tenure Jon C. Erickson (12), Daniel J.
                Lindquist (12), David G. McGarel (12),
                3 others
Website   http://www.ftportfolios.com/
Address   First Trust 120 E. Liberty Drive, Suite
                400 Wheaton IL 60187 United States
Phone Number   800-621-1675

PERFORMANCE

Ratings History

Date	Overall Rating	Risk Rating	Reward Rating
Q3-19	C	C	C
Q4-18	C	C+	C
Q4-17	C+	B-	C+
Q4-16	C	C	C
Q4-15	B-	C+	B-

Asset & Performance History

Date	NAV	1-Year Total Return
2018	68.89	-1.26
2017	69.77	21.78
2016	57.29	-5.19
2015	60.43	0.23
2014	60.29	25.39
2013	48.08	47.46

Total Assets: $1,051,098,055
Asset Allocation

Asset	%
Cash	0%
Stocks	100%
US Stocks	98%
Bonds	0%
US Bonds	0%
Other	0%

Services Offered:

Investment Strategy: The investment seeks investment results that correspond generally to the price and yield (before the fund's fees and expenses) of an equity index called the StrataQuant® Health Care Index. The fund will normally invest at least 90% of its net assets (including investment borrowings) in common stocks that comprise the index. The index is a modified equal-dollar weighted index designed by IDI to objectively identify and select stocks from the Russell 1000® Index in the health care sector that may generate positive alpha relative to traditional passive-style indices through the use of the AlphaDEX® selection methodology. **Top Holdings:** Insulet Corp   DexCom Inc   Universal Health Services Inc Class B   Mylan NV   Steris PLC

SPDR® Gold MiniShares   C   HOLD

Ticker	Traded On	NAV	Total Assets ($)	Dividend Yield (TTM)	Turnover Ratio	Expense Ratio
GLDM	NYSE Arca	14.82	$1,050,703,325	0		0.18

Ratings
Reward   D+
Risk   C+
Recent Upgrade/Downgrade   Up

Fund Information
Fund Type   Exchange Traded Funds
Category   Commodities Specified
Sub-Category   Commodities Precious Metals
Prospectus Objective   Prec Metals
Inception Date   Jun-18
Open to New Investments   Y

Prices
Price (as of 9/30/2019)   14.70
52-Week High   15.51
52-Week Low   11.89

Total Returns (%)

3-Month	6-Month	1-Year	3-Year	5-Year
6.80	14.72	24.66		

3-Year Standard Deviation
Effective Duration

Valuation
Premium/Discount (1-Year Average) -0.10

Company Information
Provider   SPDR State Street Global Advisors
Manager/Tenure Management Team (1)
Website   http://www.spdrs.com
Address   SPDR State Street Global Advisors
                State Street Financial Center, 1
                Lincoln Street Boston MA 02111-2900
                United States
Phone Number   617-786-3000

PERFORMANCE

Ratings History

Date	Overall Rating	Risk Rating	Reward Rating
Q3-19	C	C+	D+
Q4-18	U		
Q4-17			
Q4-16			
Q4-15			

Asset & Performance History

Date	NAV	1-Year Total Return
2018	12.8	
2017		
2016		
2015		
2014		
2013		

Total Assets: $1,050,703,325
Asset Allocation

Asset	%
Cash	0%
Stocks	0%
US Stocks	0%
Bonds	0%
US Bonds	0%
Other	100%

Services Offered:

Investment Strategy: The investment seeks to reflect the performance of the price of gold bullion, less the expenses of operations.
The Shares are designed for investors who want a cost-effective and convenient way to invest in gold. Advantages of investing in the Shares include ease and flexibility of investment and expenses. **Top Holdings:** Gold Trust

SPDR® S&P Global Natural Resources ETF

C   HOLD

Ticker	Traded On	NAV	Total Assets ($)	Dividend Yield (TTM)	Turnover Ratio	Expense Ratio
GNR	NYSE Arca		$1,044,870,305	3.84	19	0.4

Ratings
Reward	C-
Risk	C+
Recent Upgrade/Downgrade	

Fund Information
Fund Type	Exchange Traded Funds
Category	Natural Resources
Sub-Category	Natural Resources
Prospectus Objective	Natl Res
Inception Date	Sep-10
Open to New Investments	Y

Prices
Price (as of 9/30/2019)	43.07
52-Week High	51.00
52-Week Low	39.53

Total Returns (%)
3-Month	6-Month	1-Year	3-Year	5-Year
-6.25	-6.36	-11.43	20.75	3.25

3-Year Standard Deviation	14.82
Effective Duration	

Valuation
Premium/Discount (1-Year Average)	-0.08

Company Information
Provider	SPDR State Street Global Advisors
Manager/Tenure	Michael J. Feehily (8), Karl A. Schneider (4), David Chin (2)
Website	http://www.spdrs.com
Address	SPDR State Street Global Advisors State Street Financial Center, 1 Lincoln Street Boston MA 02111-2900 United States
Phone Number	617-786-3000

PERFORMANCE

Ratings History
Date	Overall Rating	Risk Rating	Reward Rating
Q3-19	C	C+	C-
Q4-18	C	C+	C
Q4-17	C+	C	B-
Q4-16	C-	D+	C-
Q4-15	D	D	D

Asset & Performance History
Date	NAV	1-Year Total Return
2018	41.25	-13.11
2017	49.04	22.16
2016	41.22	31.35
2015	32.08	-24.31
2014	44.09	-10.15
2013	50.22	0.96

Total Assets: $1,044,870,305

Asset Allocation
Asset	%
Cash	0%
Stocks	100%
US Stocks	30%
Bonds	0%
US Bonds	0%
Other	0%

Services Offered:

Investment Strategy: The investment seeks investment results that, before fees and expenses, correspond generally to the total return performance of the S&P Global Natural Resources Index. The fund generally invests substantially all, but at least 80%, of its total assets in the securities comprising the index and in depositary receipts based on securities comprising the index. The index is comprised of 90 of the largest U.S. and foreign publicly traded companies, based on market capitalization, in natural resources and commodities businesses that meet certain investability requirements. The fund is non-diversified. **Top Holdings:** Nutrien Ltd BHP Group Ltd Exxon Mobil Corp Total SA BP PLC

---

iShares Asia 50 ETF

C-   HOLD

Ticker	Traded On	NAV	Total Assets ($)	Dividend Yield (TTM)	Turnover Ratio	Expense Ratio
AIA	NAS CM	59.03	$1,032,945,899	2.49	10	0.5

Ratings
Reward	C-
Risk	C-
Recent Upgrade/Downgrade	

Fund Information
Fund Type	Exchange Traded Funds
Category	Asia ex-Japan Equity
Sub-Category	Pacific/Asia ex-Japan Stk
Prospectus Objective	Pacific Stock
Inception Date	Nov-07
Open to New Investments	Y

Prices
Price (as of 9/30/2019)	58.63
52-Week High	64.26
52-Week Low	53.23

Total Returns (%)
3-Month	6-Month	1-Year	3-Year	5-Year
-4.07	-4.00	-3.41	26.71	41.78

3-Year Standard Deviation	15.79
Effective Duration	

Valuation
Premium/Discount (1-Year Average)	-0.07

Company Information
Provider	iShares
Manager/Tenure	Greg Savage (11), Jennifer Hsui (7), Alan Mason (3), 2 others
Website	http://www.ishares.com
Address	iShares 400 Howard Street San Francisco CA 94105 United States
Phone Number	800-474-2737

PERFORMANCE

Ratings History
Date	Overall Rating	Risk Rating	Reward Rating
Q3-19	C-	C-	C-
Q4-18	C-	C-	C-
Q4-17	B+	C+	A
Q4-16	C	C-	C
Q4-15	C	C-	C

Asset & Performance History
Date	NAV	1-Year Total Return
2018	55.43	-13.94
2017	65.98	43.51
2016	46.68	11.82
2015	42.72	-6.45
2014	46.93	1.07
2013	47.48	2.64

Total Assets: $1,032,945,899

Asset Allocation
Asset	%
Cash	0%
Stocks	100%
US Stocks	0%
Bonds	0%
US Bonds	0%
Other	0%

Services Offered:

Investment Strategy: The investment seeks to track the S&P Asia 50TM, which is a total float-adjusted, market capitalization-weighted index that is designed to measure the performance of the 51 leading companies listed in four Asian countries or regions: Hong Kong, Singapore, South Korea and Taiwan. The fund generally will invest at least 90% of its assets in the component securities of the index and in investments that have economic characteristics that are substantially identical to the component securities and may invest up to 10% of its assets in certain futures, options and swap contracts, cash and cash equivalents. It is non-diversified. **Top Holdings:** Tencent Holdings Ltd Samsung Electronics Co Ltd Taiwan Semiconductor Manufacturing Co Ltd AIA Group Ltd China Construction Bank Corp Class H

iShares MSCI USA ESG Select ETF   C   HOLD

Ticker	Traded On	NAV	Total Assets ($)	Dividend Yield (TTM)	Turnover Ratio	Expense Ratio
SUSA	NYSE Arca	123.57	$1,031,845,370	1.63	21	0.25

Ratings
Reward   C+
Risk   C
Recent Upgrade/Downgrade

Fund Information
Fund Type	Exchange Traded Funds
Category	US Equity Large Cap Blend
Sub-Category	Large Blend
Prospectus Objective	Growth
Inception Date	Jan-05
Open to New Investments	Y

Prices
Price (as of 9/30/2019)	123.61
52-Week High	125.51
52-Week Low	96.94

Total Returns (%)
3-Month	6-Month	1-Year	3-Year	5-Year
1.01	4.14	4.69	42.61	64.69

3-Year Standard Deviation   12.62
Effective Duration

Valuation
Premium/Discount (1-Year Average)   0.02

Company Information
Provider	iShares
Manager/Tenure	Greg Savage (11), Jennifer Hsui (7), Alan Mason (3), 2 others
Website	http://www.ishares.com
Address	iShares 400 Howard Street San Francisco CA 94105 United States
Phone Number	800-474-2737

PERFORMANCE

Ratings History

Date	Overall Rating	Risk Rating	Reward Rating
Q3-19	C	C	C+
Q4-18	C	C	C
Q4-17	B-	B-	B
Q4-16	C+	C	B
Q4-15	C	C	C+

Asset & Performance History

Date	NAV	1-Year Total Return
2018	103.16	-5.56
2017	110.99	22.52
2016	91.95	12.24
2015	83.25	-1.88
2014	86.06	13.49
2013	76.79	30.86

Total Assets: $1,031,845,370

Asset Allocation

Asset	%
Cash	0%
Stocks	100%
US Stocks	99%
Bonds	0%
US Bonds	0%
Other	0%

Services Offered:

Investment Strategy: The investment seeks to track the investment results of the MSCI USA Extended ESG Select Index composed of U.S. companies that have positive environmental, social and governance characteristics as identified by the index provider. The fund generally invests at least 90% of its assets in securities of the underlying index and in depositary receipts representing securities of the underlying index. The underlying index is an optimized index designed to maximize exposure to favorable environmental, social and governance ("ESG") characteristics, while exhibiting risk and return characteristics similar to the MSCI USA Index. **Top Holdings:** Microsoft Corp Ecolab Inc Apple Inc Accenture PLC Class A Alphabet Inc A

First Trust Large Cap Growth AlphaDEX® Fund   C   HOLD

Ticker	Traded On	NAV	Total Assets ($)	Dividend Yield (TTM)	Turnover Ratio	Expense Ratio
FTC	NAS CM	69.93	$1,031,495,699	0.6	132	0.61

Ratings
Reward   C
Risk   C-
Recent Upgrade/Downgrade

Fund Information
Fund Type	Exchange Traded Funds
Category	US Equity Large Cap Growth
Sub-Category	Large Growth
Prospectus Objective	Growth
Inception Date	May-07
Open to New Investments	Y

Prices
Price (as of 9/30/2019)	69.98
52-Week High	72.64
52-Week Low	53.12

Total Returns (%)
3-Month	6-Month	1-Year	3-Year	5-Year
-1.14	3.69	-0.17	40.80	68.31

3-Year Standard Deviation   13.99
Effective Duration

Valuation
Premium/Discount (1-Year Average)   0.03

Company Information
Provider	First Trust
Manager/Tenure	Jon C. Erickson (12), Daniel J. Lindquist (12), David G. McGarel (12), 3 others
Website	http://www.ftportfolios.com/
Address	First Trust 120 E. Liberty Drive, Suite 400 Wheaton IL 60187 United States
Phone Number	800-621-1675

PERFORMANCE

Ratings History

Date	Overall Rating	Risk Rating	Reward Rating
Q3-19	C	C-	C
Q4-18	C	C+	C-
Q4-17	B+	A	B
Q4-16	C	C-	C+
Q4-15	B	C+	B

Asset & Performance History

Date	NAV	1-Year Total Return
2018	57.26	-5.98
2017	61.1	25.18
2016	49.02	2.55
2015	48.21	4.28
2014	46.47	14.46
2013	40.92	37.71

Total Assets: $1,031,495,699

Asset Allocation

Asset	%
Cash	0%
Stocks	100%
US Stocks	100%
Bonds	0%
US Bonds	0%
Other	0%

Services Offered:

Investment Strategy: The investment seeks investment results that correspond generally to the price and yield (before the fund's fees and expenses) of an equity index called the Nasdaq AlphaDEX® Large Cap Growth Index. The fund will normally invest at least 90% of its net assets (including investment borrowings) in common stocks that comprise the index. The index is designed to select growth stocks from the NASDAQ US 500 Large Cap Index (the "base index") that may generate positive alpha, or risk-adjusted returns, relative to traditional indices through the use of the AlphaDEX® selection methodology. **Top Holdings:** Altice USA Inc Class A Starbucks Corp TransDigm Group Inc Chipotle Mexican Grill Inc Class A Ball Corp

Janus Henderson Short Duration Income ETF   C   HOLD

Ticker	Traded On	NAV	Total Assets ($)	Dividend Yield (TTM)	Turnover Ratio	Expense Ratio
VNLA	NYSE Arca	50.03	$1,030,660,337	2.75	22	0.35

Ratings
Reward   C
Risk   C+
Recent Upgrade/Downgrade

Fund Information
Fund Type   Exchange Traded Funds
Category   US Fixed Income
Sub-Category   Ultrashort Bond
Prospectus Objective   Multisector Bond
Inception Date   Nov-16
Open to New Investments   Y

Prices
Price (as of 9/30/2019)   50.03
52-Week High   50.14
52-Week Low   49.00

Total Returns (%)

3-Month	6-Month	1-Year	3-Year	5-Year
0.96	2.23	4.04		

3-Year Standard Deviation
Effective Duration

Valuation
Premium/Discount (1-Year Average)   0.02

Company Information
Provider   Janus Henderson
Manager/Tenure   Nick Maroutsos (2), Daniel Siluk (2), Jason England (0)
Website   http://janushenderson.com
Address   Janus 151 Detroit Street Denver CO 80206 United States
Phone Number   877-335-2687

PERFORMANCE

Ratings History

Date	Overall Rating	Risk Rating	Reward Rating
Q3-19	C	C+	C
Q4-18	C	C+	D+
Q4-17	D	A	D+
Q4-16	U		
Q4-15			

Asset & Performance History

Date	NAV	1-Year Total Return
2018	49.05	1.57
2017	50.1	2.07
2016	49.97	
2015		
2014		
2013		

Total Assets: $1,030,660,337
Asset Allocation

Asset	%
Cash	10%
Stocks	0%
US Stocks	0%
Bonds	87%
US Bonds	39%
Other	0%

Services Offered:

Investment Strategy: The investment seeks to provide a steady income stream with capital preservation across various market cycles and consistently outperform the FTSE 3-Month US Treasury Bill Index by a moderate amount through various market cycles while at the same time providing low volatility. The fund normally invests at least 80% of its net assets in a portfolio of fixed income instruments of varying maturities. It may invest up to 20% in asset-backed securities that are rated investment grade or of similar quality as determined by Janus Capital. The average portfolio duration of the fund generally will be within 0-2 years of the index. **Top Holdings:** Australia 3 Year Bond Sept19 Us 5yr Note (Cbt) Dec19 Xcbt 20191231 B49209959 Cds Usd P F 1.00000 1649209959_fee Ccpcdx B68827605 Cds Usd P F 1.00000 1668827605_fee Ccpcdx B49209959 Cds Usd R V 03mevent 1649209959_pro Ccpcdx

iShares MSCI EAFE ESG Optimized ETF   C   HOLD

Ticker	Traded On	NAV	Total Assets ($)	Dividend Yield (TTM)	Turnover Ratio	Expense Ratio
ESGD	NAS CM	63.97	$1,029,987,526	2.65	24	0.2

Ratings
Reward   C
Risk   C+
Recent Upgrade/Downgrade

Fund Information
Fund Type   Exchange Traded Funds
Category   Global Equity Large Cap
Sub-Category   Foreign Large Blend
Prospectus Objective   Growth & Inc
Inception Date   Jun-16
Open to New Investments   Y

Prices
Price (as of 9/30/2019)   64.12
52-Week High   66.33
52-Week Low   55.20

Total Returns (%)

3-Month	6-Month	1-Year	3-Year	5-Year
-0.91	2.34	-0.41	21.90	

3-Year Standard Deviation   11.17
Effective Duration

Valuation
Premium/Discount (1-Year Average)   0.17

Company Information
Provider   iShares
Manager/Tenure   Diane Hsiung (3), Jennifer Hsui (3), Alan Mason (3), 3 others
Website   http://www.ishares.com
Address   iShares 400 Howard Street San Francisco CA 94105 United States
Phone Number   800-474-2737

PERFORMANCE

Ratings History

Date	Overall Rating	Risk Rating	Reward Rating
Q3-19	C	C+	C
Q4-18	D+	C-	D+
Q4-17	D	B	C
Q4-16	U		
Q4-15			

Asset & Performance History

Date	NAV	1-Year Total Return
2018	57.19	-13.62
2017	67.86	25.21
2016	55.72	
2015		
2014		
2013		

Total Assets: $1,029,987,526
Asset Allocation

Asset	%
Cash	1%
Stocks	99%
US Stocks	2%
Bonds	0%
US Bonds	0%
Other	0%

Services Offered:

Investment Strategy: The investment seeks to track the investment results of the MSCI EAFE Extended ESG Focus Index. The fund generally will invest at least 90% of its assets in the component securities of the underlying index and in investments that have economic characteristics that are substantially identical to the component securities of the underlying index. The underlying index is composed of large- and mid-capitalization developed market equities, excluding the U.S. and Canada that have positive environmental, social and governance characteristics as identified by the index provider. **Top Holdings:** Nestle SA Roche Holding AG Dividend Right Cert. BP PLC Toyota Motor Corp SAP SE

iShares MSCI Switzerland ETF   B-   BUY

Ticker	Traded On	NAV	Total Assets ($)	Dividend Yield (TTM)	Turnover Ratio	Expense Ratio
EWL	NYSE Arca	37.65	$1,026,046,515	1.99	9	0.47

Ratings
Reward	B
Risk	C+
Recent Upgrade/Downgrade	Down

Fund Information
Fund Type	Exchange Traded Funds
Category	Europe Equity Large Cap
Sub-Category	Miscellaneous Region
Prospectus Objective	Europe Stock
Inception Date	Mar-96
Open to New Investments	Y

Prices
Price (as of 9/30/2019)	37.70
52-Week High	38.11
52-Week Low	30.43

Total Returns (%)
3-Month	6-Month	1-Year	3-Year	5-Year
0.39	8.14	10.47	31.85	31.05

3-Year Standard Deviation	11.52
Effective Duration	

Valuation
Premium/Discount (1-Year Average)	0.03

Company Information
Provider	iShares
Manager/Tenure	Diane Hsiung (11), Greg Savage (11), Jennifer Hsui (6), 3 others
Website	http://www.ishares.com
Address	iShares 400 Howard Street San Francisco CA 94105 United States
Phone Number	800-474-2737

PERFORMANCE

Ratings History

Date	Overall Rating	Risk Rating	Reward Rating
Q3-19	B-	C+	B
Q4-18	C	C+	D+
Q4-17	B-	B	C+
Q4-16	C-	C-	C-
Q4-15	C	C+	C

Asset & Performance History

Date	NAV	1-Year Total Return
2018	31.35	-9.77
2017	35.62	23.36
2016	29.49	-3.04
2015	31.24	0.51
2014	31.82	-0.81
2013	32.82	26.47

Total Assets: $1,026,046,515
Asset Allocation

Asset	%
Cash	1%
Stocks	99%
US Stocks	0%
Bonds	0%
US Bonds	0%
Other	0%

Services Offered: CashInvestment Plan

Investment Strategy: The investment seeks to track the investment results of the MSCI Switzerland 25/50 Index. The fund will at all times invest at least 80% of its assets in the securities of its underlying index and in depositary receipts representing securities in its underlying index. The underlying index is a free float-adjusted market capitalization-weighted index with a capping methodology applied to issuer weights so that no single issuer of a component exceeds 25% of the underlying index weight, and all issuers with a weight above 5% do not cumulatively exceed 50% of the underlying index weight. The fund is non-diversified. **Top Holdings:** Nestle SA Novartis AG Roche Holding AG Dividend Right Cert. Zurich Insurance Group AG UBS Group AG

ProShares UltraShort S&P500   D   SELL

Ticker	Traded On	NAV	Total Assets ($)	Dividend Yield (TTM)	Turnover Ratio	Expense Ratio
SDS	NYSE Arca	29.51	$1,020,955,892	1.83		0.89

Ratings
Reward	D-
Risk	D
Recent Upgrade/Downgrade	

Fund Information
Fund Type	Exchange Traded Funds
Category	Trading Tools
Sub-Category	Trading--Inverse Equity
Prospectus Objective	Growth
Inception Date	Jul-06
Open to New Investments	Y

Prices
Price (as of 9/30/2019)	29.50
52-Week High	49.43
52-Week Low	28.97

Total Returns (%)
3-Month	6-Month	1-Year	3-Year	5-Year
-1.92	-8.43	-8.80	-53.75	-70.07

3-Year Standard Deviation	23.91
Effective Duration	

Valuation
Premium/Discount (1-Year Average)	0.04

Company Information
Provider	ProShares
Manager/Tenure	Michael Neches (6), Devin Sullivan (1)
Website	http://www.proshares.com
Address	ProShares 7501 Wisconsin Avenue, Suite 1000 Bethesda MD 20814 United States
Phone Number	866-776-5125

PERFORMANCE

Ratings History

Date	Overall Rating	Risk Rating	Reward Rating
Q3-19	D	D	D-
Q4-18	D	D-	D-
Q4-17	D-	D-	E+
Q4-16	D	D-	D-
Q4-15	D	E+	D-

Asset & Performance History

Date	NAV	1-Year Total Return
2018	42.97	5.86
2017	41.18	-31.94
2016	60.56	-24.03
2015	79.72	-9.61
2014	88.2	-25.73
2013	118.76	-45.16

Total Assets: $1,020,955,892
Asset Allocation

Asset	%
Cash	195%
Stocks	-107%
US Stocks	-105%
Bonds	11%
US Bonds	11%
Other	0%

Services Offered:

Investment Strategy: The investment seeks daily investment results, before fees and expenses, that correspond to two times the inverse (-2x) of the daily performance of the S&P 500® Index. The fund invests in financial instruments that ProShare Advisors believes, in combination, should produce daily returns consistent with the fund's investment objective. The index is a measure of large-cap U.S. stock market performance. The fund is non-diversified. **Top Holdings:** S&P 500 Index Swap Societe Generale S&P 500 Index Swap Ubs Ag S&P 500 Index Swap Bnp Paribas S&P 500 Index Swap Citibank Na S&P 500 Index Swap Goldman Sachs International

Invesco Water Resources ETF   B-   BUY

Ticker	Traded On	NAV	Total Assets ($)	Dividend Yield (TTM)	Turnover Ratio	Expense Ratio
PHO	NAS CM	36.63	$1,016,561,922	0.47	31	0.6

Ratings
Reward   B
Risk   C
Recent Upgrade/Downgrade

Fund Information
Fund Type   Exchange Traded Funds
Category   Industrials Sector Equity
Sub-Category   Miscellaneous Sector
Prospectus Objective   Utility
Inception Date   Dec-05
Open to New Investments   Y

Prices
Price (as of 9/30/2019)   36.60
52-Week High   37.05
52-Week Low   26.56

Total Returns (%)

3-Month	6-Month	1-Year	3-Year	5-Year
2.61	7.19	16.20	51.08	54.08

3-Year Standard Deviation   13.55
Effective Duration

Valuation
Premium/Discount (1-Year Average)   0.00

Company Information
Provider   Invesco
Manager/Tenure   Peter Hubbard (12), Michael Jeanette
                      (11), Tony Seisser (5)
Website   http://www.invesco.com/us
Address   Invesco 11 Greenway Plaza, Ste. 2500
                      Houston TX 77046 United States
Phone Number   800-659-1005

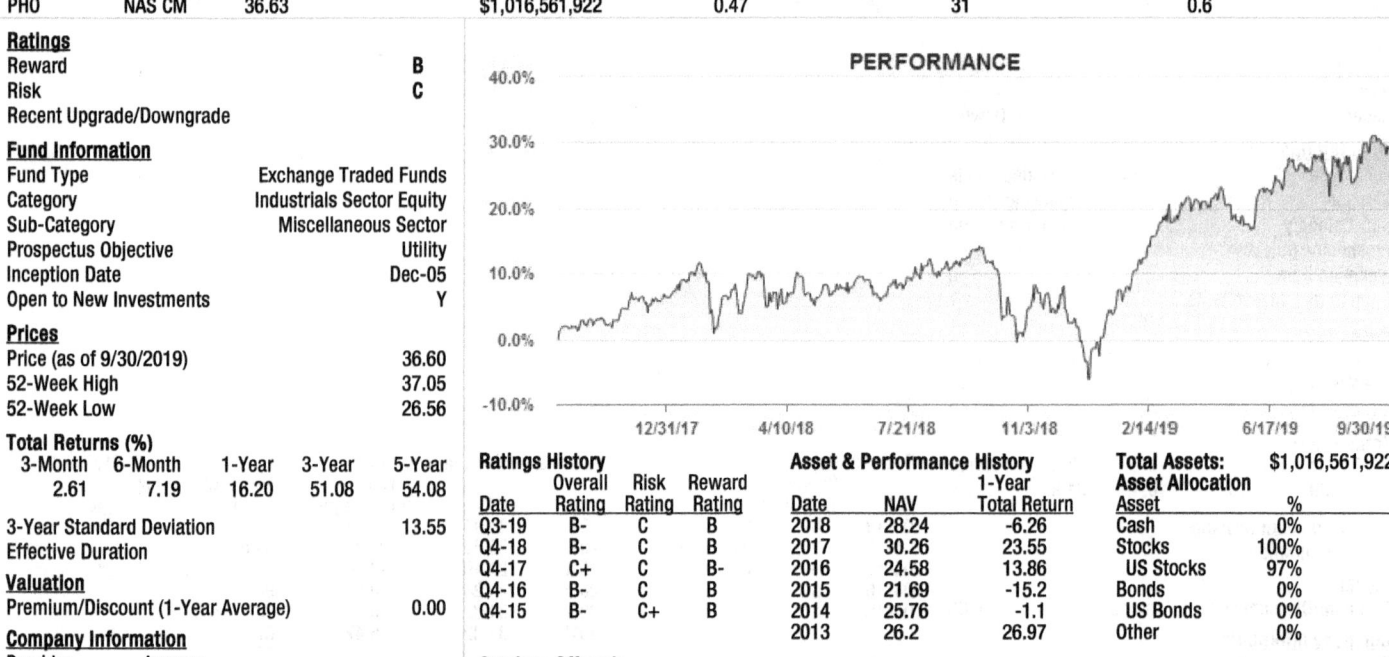

PERFORMANCE

Ratings History

Date	Overall Rating	Risk Rating	Reward Rating
Q3-19	B-	C	B
Q4-18	B-	C	B
Q4-17	C+	C	B-
Q4-16	B-	C	B
Q4-15	B-	C+	B

Asset & Performance History

Date	NAV	1-Year Total Return
2018	28.24	-6.26
2017	30.26	23.55
2016	24.58	13.86
2015	21.69	-15.2
2014	25.76	-1.1
2013	26.2	26.97

Total Assets: $1,016,561,922
Asset Allocation

Asset	%
Cash	0%
Stocks	100%
US Stocks	97%
Bonds	0%
US Bonds	0%
Other	0%

Services Offered:

Investment Strategy: The investment seeks to track the investment results (before fees and expenses) of the NASDAQ OMX US Water IndexSM (the "underlying index"). The fund generally will invest at least 90% of its total assets in the securities that comprise the underlying index. The underlying index seeks to track the performance of U.S. exchange-listed companies that create products designed to conserve and purify water for homes, businesses and industries. The underlying index may include common stocks, ordinary shares, American depositary receipts ("ADRs"), shares of beneficial interest and tracking stocks. The fund is non-diversified. **Top Holdings:** Ecolab Inc American Water Works Co Inc Danaher Corp Roper Technologies Inc Waters Corp

---

First Trust NASDAQ Technology Dividend Index Fund   B-   BUY

Ticker	Traded On	NAV	Total Assets ($)	Dividend Yield (TTM)	Turnover Ratio	Expense Ratio
TDIV	NAS CM	40.09	$1,010,555,716	2.41	27	0.5

Ratings
Reward   B
Risk   C
Recent Upgrade/Downgrade   Up

Fund Information
Fund Type   Exchange Traded Funds
Category   Technology Sector Equity
Sub-Category   Technology
Prospectus Objective   Technology
Inception Date   Aug-12
Open to New Investments   Y

Prices
Price (as of 9/30/2019)   40.11
52-Week High   41.12
52-Week Low   31.20

Total Returns (%)

3-Month	6-Month	1-Year	3-Year	5-Year
1.93	4.53	7.01	47.14	71.05

3-Year Standard Deviation   14.05
Effective Duration

Valuation
Premium/Discount (1-Year Average)   0.02

Company Information
Provider   First Trust
Manager/Tenure   Jon C. Erickson (7), Daniel J. Lindquist
                      (7), David G. McGarel (7), 3 others
Website   http://www.ftportfolios.com/
Address   First Trust 120 E. Liberty Drive, Suite
                      400 Wheaton IL 60187 United States
Phone Number   800-621-1675

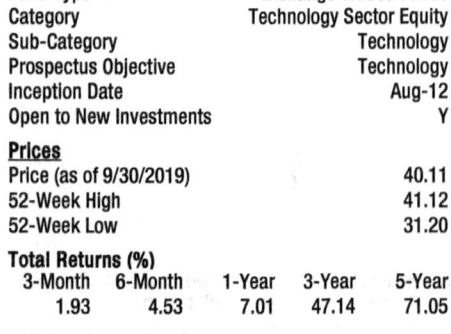

PERFORMANCE

Ratings History

Date	Overall Rating	Risk Rating	Reward Rating
Q3-19	B-	C	B
Q4-18	C+	C	B
Q4-17	B	B-	B+
Q4-16	B	C	B+
Q4-15	B	B-	B

Asset & Performance History

Date	NAV	1-Year Total Return
2018	33.16	-3.04
2017	35.15	21.92
2016	29.55	19.64
2015	25.35	-5.98
2014	27.64	15.54
2013	24.63	30.38

Total Assets: $1,010,555,716
Asset Allocation

Asset	%
Cash	1%
Stocks	99%
US Stocks	82%
Bonds	0%
US Bonds	0%
Other	0%

Services Offered:

Investment Strategy: The investment seeks investment results that correspond generally to the price and yield (before the fund's fees and expenses) of an equity index called the NASDAQ Technology Dividend IndexSM. The fund will normally invest at least 90% of its net assets (including investment borrowings) in the common stocks and depositary receipts that comprise the index. The index is owned and was developed by Nasdaq, Inc. (the "index provider"). The index includes up to 100 technology and telecommunications companies that pay a regular or common dividend. The fund is non-diversified. **Top Holdings:** Apple Inc Microsoft Corp Intel Corp International Business Machines Corp Cisco Systems Inc

Invesco BulletShares 2019 Corporate Bond ETF   C   HOLD

Ticker	Traded On	NAV	Total Assets ($)	Dividend Yield (TTM)	Turnover Ratio	Expense Ratio
BSCJ	NYSE Arca	21.10	$1,009,590,662	2.27	3	0.1

Ratings
Reward	C
Risk	C+
Recent Upgrade/Downgrade	

Fund Information
Fund Type	Exchange Traded Funds
Category	US Fixed Income
Sub-Category	Target Maturity
Prospectus Objective	Corp Bond - Gen
Inception Date	Mar-12
Open to New Investments	Y

Prices
Price (as of 9/30/2019)	21.08
52-Week High	21.14
52-Week Low	21.02

Total Returns (%)
3-Month	6-Month	1-Year	3-Year	5-Year
0.58	1.25	2.63	5.09	11.14

3-Year Standard Deviation	0.71
Effective Duration	0.23

Valuation
Premium/Discount (1-Year Average)	0.02

Company Information
Provider	Invesco
Manager/Tenure	Jeremy Neisewander (3), Peter Hubbard (1), Jeffrey W. Kernagis (1), 1 other
Website	http://www.invesco.com/us
Address	Invesco 11 Greenway Plaza, Ste. 2500 Houston TX 77046 United States
Phone Number	800-659-1005

PERFORMANCE

Chart Y-axis: 6.0%, 4.0%, 2.0%, 0.0%, -2.0%
Chart X-axis: 10/12/17, 1/20/18, 4/30/18, 8/10/18, 11/24/18, 3/7/19, 6/17/19, 9/30/19

Ratings History
Date	Overall Rating	Risk Rating	Reward Rating
Q3-19	C	C+	C
Q4-18	C	C+	C
Q4-17	B	A+	C
Q4-16	C	C+	C
Q4-15	C	C-	C

Asset & Performance History
Date	NAV	1-Year Total Return
2018	21.01	1.71
2017	21.06	1.53
2016	21.08	3.14
2015	20.82	1.6
2014	20.91	3.91
2013	20.56	-0.1

Total Assets: $1,009,590,662
Asset Allocation
Asset	%
Cash	99%
Stocks	0%
US Stocks	0%
Bonds	1%
US Bonds	1%
Other	0%

Services Offered:

Investment Strategy: The investment seeks to track the investment results (before fees and expenses) of the Nasdaq BulletShares® USD Corporate Bond 2019 Index (the "underlying index"). The fund generally will invest at least 80% of its total assets in securities that comprise the underlying index. The underlying index seeks to measure the performance of a portfolio of U.S. dollar-denominated investment grade corporate bonds with maturities or, in some cases, "effective maturities" in the year 2019 (collectively, "2019 Bonds"). The fund is non-diversified. **Top Holdings:** Wells Fargo Bank, National Association 2.15% Goldman Sachs Group, Inc. 2.3% Kinder Morgan, Inc. 3.05% Costco Wholesale Corporation 1.7% Becton, Dickinson and Company 2.68%

iShares iBonds Dec 2022 Term Corporate ETF   C+   HOLD

Ticker	Traded On	NAV	Total Assets ($)	Dividend Yield (TTM)	Turnover Ratio	Expense Ratio
IBDN	NYSE Arca	25.28	$998,409,239	2.87	2	0.1

Ratings
Reward	C+
Risk	C+
Recent Upgrade/Downgrade	

Fund Information
Fund Type	Exchange Traded Funds
Category	US Fixed Income
Sub-Category	Target Maturity
Prospectus Objective	Corp Bond - Gen
Inception Date	Mar-15
Open to New Investments	Y

Prices
Price (as of 9/30/2019)	25.32
52-Week High	25.39
52-Week Low	24.10

Total Returns (%)
3-Month	6-Month	1-Year	3-Year	5-Year
1.19	3.42	7.22	8.05	

3-Year Standard Deviation	2.41
Effective Duration	

Valuation
Premium/Discount (1-Year Average)	0.18

Company Information
Provider	iShares
Manager/Tenure	James Mauro (4), Scott Radell (4)
Website	http://www.ishares.com
Address	iShares 400 Howard Street San Francisco CA 94105 United States
Phone Number	800-474-2737

PERFORMANCE

Chart Y-axis: 7.5%, 5.0%, 2.5%, 0.0%, -2.5%, -5.0%
Chart X-axis: 12/28/17, 4/7/18, 7/18/18, 10/31/18, 2/11/19, 6/16/19, 9/30/19

Ratings History
Date	Overall Rating	Risk Rating	Reward Rating
Q3-19	C+	C+	C+
Q4-18	C	C+	C-
Q4-17	B-	A-	C
Q4-16	D+	C-	D+
Q4-15	U		

Asset & Performance History
Date	NAV	1-Year Total Return
2018	24.22	0.08
2017	24.9	3.76
2016	24.62	5.45
2015	24.02	
2014		
2013		

Total Assets: $998,409,239
Asset Allocation
Asset	%
Cash	1%
Stocks	0%
US Stocks	0%
Bonds	97%
US Bonds	83%
Other	0%

Services Offered:

Investment Strategy: The investment seeks to track the investment results of the Bloomberg Barclays December 2022 Maturity Corporate Index which composed of U.S. dollar-denominated, investment-grade corporate bonds maturing in 2022. The fund generally will invest at least 90% of its assets in the component securities of the underlying index. The underlying index is composed of U.S. dollar-denominated, taxable, investment-grade corporate bonds scheduled to mature after December 31, 2021 and before December 16, 2022. **Top Holdings:** Goldman Sachs Group, Inc. 5.75% Goldman Sachs Group, Inc. 3% Wells Fargo & Company 2.63% Morgan Stanley 2.75% Broadcom Corporation/Broadcom Cayman Finance Ltd 3%

iPath® Series B S&P 500® VIX Short-Term Futures™ ETN   D   SELL

Ticker	Traded On	NAV	Total Assets ($)	Dividend Yield (TTM)	Turnover Ratio	Expense Ratio
VXX	BATS		$989,706,216	0		0.89

Ratings
Reward   D
Risk   D
Recent Upgrade/Downgrade

Fund Information
Fund Type   Exchange Traded Funds
Category   Alternative Misc
Sub-Category   Volatility
Prospectus Objective   Growth & Inc
Inception Date   Jan-18
Open to New Investments   Y

Prices
Price (as of 9/30/2019)   23.74
52-Week High   49.43
52-Week Low   21.54

Total Returns (%)

3-Month	6-Month	1-Year	3-Year	5-Year
-0.29	-14.63	-7.47		

3-Year Standard Deviation
Effective Duration

Valuation
Premium/Discount (1-Year Average)   0.35

Company Information
Provider   Milleis Investissements Funds
Manager/Tenure   No Manager (1)
Website
Address   2-4, rue Eugène Ruppert L-2453
                      Luxembourg Luxembourg L-2453
                      Luxembourg
Phone Number

PERFORMANCE

Ratings History

Date	Overall Rating	Risk Rating	Reward Rating
Q3-19	D	D	D
Q4-18	U		
Q4-17			
Q4-16			
Q4-15			

Asset & Performance History

Date	NAV	1-Year Total Return
2018	48.83	
2017		
2016		
2015		
2014		
2013		

Total Assets: $989,706,216
Asset Allocation

Asset	%
Cash	%
Stocks	%
US Stocks	%
Bonds	%
US Bonds	%
Other	%

Services Offered:

Investment Strategy: The investment seeks return linked to the performance of the S&P 500® VIX Short-Term Futures Index TR.
The ETN offers exposure to futures contracts of specified maturities on the VIX index and not direct exposure to the VIX index or its spot level. The index is designed to provide investors with exposure to one or more maturities of futures contracts on the CBOE Volatility Index®. **Top Holdings:**

Fidelity® MSCI Financials Index ETF   C+   HOLD

Ticker	Traded On	NAV	Total Assets ($)	Dividend Yield (TTM)	Turnover Ratio	Expense Ratio
FNCL	NYSE Arca	40.68	$988,507,088	2.37	5	0.08

Ratings
Reward   C+
Risk   C+
Recent Upgrade/Downgrade   Up

Fund Information
Fund Type   Exchange Traded Funds
Category   Financials Sector Equity
Sub-Category   Financial
Prospectus Objective   Financial
Inception Date   Oct-13
Open to New Investments   Y

Prices
Price (as of 9/30/2019)   40.66
52-Week High   41.70
52-Week Low   32.43

Total Returns (%)

3-Month	6-Month	1-Year	3-Year	5-Year
0.90	7.21	3.36	50.45	68.19

3-Year Standard Deviation   17.16
Effective Duration

Valuation
Premium/Discount (1-Year Average)   -0.03

Company Information
Provider   Fidelity Investments
Manager/Tenure   Jennifer Hsui (5), Greg Savage (5),
                      Alan Mason (3), 2 others
Website   http://www.institutional.fidelity.com
Address   Fidelity Investments 82 Devonshire
                      Street Boston MA 2109 United States
Phone Number   617-563-7000

PERFORMANCE

Ratings History

Date	Overall Rating	Risk Rating	Reward Rating
Q3-19	C+	C+	C+
Q4-18	C	C+	C
Q4-17	A-	B	A
Q4-16	C+	C+	B-
Q4-15	C-	B-	C

Asset & Performance History

Date	NAV	1-Year Total Return
2018	34.54	-13.36
2017	40.72	19.97
2016	34.54	24.72
2015	28.3	-0.62
2014	29.1	13.97
2013	26.01	

Total Assets: $988,507,088
Asset Allocation

Asset	%
Cash	0%
Stocks	100%
US Stocks	98%
Bonds	0%
US Bonds	0%
Other	0%

Services Offered:

Investment Strategy: The investment seeks to provide investment returns that correspond, before fees and expenses, generally to the performance of the MSCI USA IMI Financials Index. The fund invests at least 80% of assets in securities included in the fund's underlying index. The fund's underlying index is the MSCI USA IMI Financials Index, which represents the performance of the financial sector in the U.S. equity market. It may or may not hold all of the securities in the MSCI USA IMI Financials Index. The fund is non-diversified. **Top Holdings:**
JPMorgan Chase & Co   Berkshire Hathaway Inc B   Bank of America Corporation   Wells Fargo & Co   Citigroup Inc

First Trust NASDAQ Cybersecurity ETF

C   **HOLD**

Ticker	Traded On	NAV	Total Assets ($)	Dividend Yield (TTM)	Turnover Ratio	Expense Ratio
CIBR	NAS CM	27.63	$979,649,796	0.22	56	0.6

Ratings
Reward	C
Risk	C
Recent Upgrade/Downgrade	Down

Fund Information
Fund Type	Exchange Traded Funds
Category	Technology Sector Equity
Sub-Category	Technology
Prospectus Objective	Technology
Inception Date	Jul-15
Open to New Investments	Y

Prices
Price (as of 9/30/2019)	27.66
52-Week High	30.70
52-Week Low	21.94

Total Returns (%)
3-Month	6-Month	1-Year	3-Year	5-Year
-3.44	-2.46	-1.46	40.46	

3-Year Standard Deviation	16.18
Effective Duration	

Valuation
Premium/Discount (1-Year Average)	0.07

Company Information
Provider	First Trust
Manager/Tenure	Jon C. Erickson (4), Daniel J. Lindquist (4), David G. McGarel (4), 3 others
Website	http://www.ftportfolios.com/
Address	First Trust 120 E. Liberty Drive, Suite 400 Wheaton IL 60187 United States
Phone Number	800-621-1675

PERFORMANCE

Ratings History

Date	Overall Rating	Risk Rating	Reward Rating
Q3-19	C	C	C
Q4-18	C	C-	C+
Q4-17	C	B-	C+
Q4-16	D	D+	C+
Q4-15	U		

Asset & Performance History

Date	NAV	1-Year Total Return
2018	23.44	1.91
2017	23.05	18.32
2016	19.5	10.88
2015	17.74	
2014		
2013		

Total Assets: $979,649,796

Asset Allocation
Asset	%
Cash	0%
Stocks	100%
US Stocks	88%
Bonds	0%
US Bonds	0%
Other	0%

Services Offered:

Investment Strategy: The investment seeks investment results that correspond generally to the price and yield (before the fund's fees and expenses) of an equity index called the Nasdaq CTA Cybersecurity IndexSM (the "index"). The fund will normally invest at least 90% of its net assets (including investment borrowings) in the common stocks and depositary receipts that comprise the index. The index includes securities of companies classified as "cyber security" companies by the CTA. The fund is non-diversified. **Top Holdings:** Okta Inc A Raytheon Co Palo Alto Networks Inc Splunk Inc Cisco Systems Inc

---

iShares Edge MSCI Multifactor USA ETF

C   **HOLD**

Ticker	Traded On	NAV	Total Assets ($)	Dividend Yield (TTM)	Turnover Ratio	Expense Ratio
LRGF	NYSE Arca	31.93	$962,779,243	3.02	45	0.2

Ratings
Reward	C
Risk	C+
Recent Upgrade/Downgrade	

Fund Information
Fund Type	Exchange Traded Funds
Category	US Equity Large Cap Value
Sub-Category	Large Value
Prospectus Objective	Growth & Inc
Inception Date	Apr-15
Open to New Investments	Y

Prices
Price (as of 9/30/2019)	31.92
52-Week High	33.76
52-Week Low	26.57

Total Returns (%)
3-Month	6-Month	1-Year	3-Year	5-Year
0.39	2.50	-2.00	35.44	

3-Year Standard Deviation	13.21
Effective Duration	

Valuation
Premium/Discount (1-Year Average)	-0.02

Company Information
Provider	iShares
Manager/Tenure	Diane Hsiung (4), Jennifer Hsui (4), Greg Savage (4), 3 others
Website	http://www.ishares.com
Address	iShares 400 Howard Street San Francisco CA 94105 United States
Phone Number	800-474-2737

PERFORMANCE

Ratings History

Date	Overall Rating	Risk Rating	Reward Rating
Q3-19	C	C+	C
Q4-18	C	C+	C
Q4-17	B-	B	C+
Q4-16	D+	C-	C-
Q4-15	U		

Asset & Performance History

Date	NAV	1-Year Total Return
2018	27.83	-10.96
2017	31.81	21.25
2016	26.71	13.39
2015	23.95	
2014		
2013		

Total Assets: $962,779,243

Asset Allocation
Asset	%
Cash	0%
Stocks	100%
US Stocks	98%
Bonds	0%
US Bonds	0%
Other	0%

Services Offered:

Investment Strategy: The investment seeks to track the investment results of the MSCI USA Diversified Multiple-Factor Index. The fund generally will invest at least 90% of its assets in the component securities of the underlying index and may invest up to 10% of its assets in certain futures, options and swap contracts, cash and cash equivalents. The underlying index is designed to select equity securities from the MSCI USA Index (the "parent index") that have high exposure to four investment style factors: value, quality, momentum and low size, while maintaining a level of risk similar to that of the parent index. **Top Holdings:** Intel Corp AT&T Inc Intuit Inc Anthem Inc Target Corp

Global X MLP ETF   C   HOLD

Ticker	Traded On	NAV	Total Assets ($)	Dividend Yield (TTM)	Turnover Ratio	Expense Ratio
MLPA	NYSE Arca	8.38	$960,978,120	8.66	30	0.45

Ratings

Reward	B-
Risk	D+
Recent Upgrade/Downgrade	Up

Fund Information

Fund Type	Exchange Traded Funds
Category	Energy Sector Equity
Sub-Category	Energy Limited Partnership
Prospectus Objective	Utility
Inception Date	Apr-12
Open to New Investments	Y

Prices

Price (as of 9/30/2019)	8.38
52-Week High	9.84
52-Week Low	7.33

Total Returns (%)

3-Month	6-Month	1-Year	3-Year	5-Year
-3.16	-2.54	-6.77	-8.46	-28.46

3-Year Standard Deviation	17.14
Effective Duration	

Valuation

Premium/Discount (1-Year Average)	0.05

Company Information

Provider	Global X Funds
Manager/Tenure	Chang Kim (5), Nam To (1), Wayne Xie (0), 1 other
Website	http://www.globalxfunds.com
Address	Global X Funds 600 Lexington Avenue, 20th Floor New York NY 10022 United States
Phone Number	888-493-8631

PERFORMANCE

Ratings History

Date	Overall Rating	Risk Rating	Reward Rating
Q3-19	C	D+	B-
Q4-18	C	D	B-
Q4-17	D	D	D
Q4-16	D	D	D
Q4-15	B-	C	B

Asset & Performance History

Date	NAV	1-Year Total Return
2018	7.68	-15.47
2017	9.85	-8.5
2016	11.58	21.12
2015	10.36	-30.13
2014	15.92	4.15
2013	16.16	17.82

Total Assets: $960,978,120

Asset Allocation

Asset	%
Cash	0%
Stocks	100%
US Stocks	100%
Bonds	0%
US Bonds	0%
Other	0%

Services Offered:

Investment Strategy: The investment seeks to provide investment results that correspond generally to the price and yield performance, before fees and expenses, of the Solactive MLP Infrastructure Index ("underlying index"). The fund invests at least 80% of its net assets in the securities of the underlying index. Moreover, at least 80% of the fund's net assets will be invested in securities that have economic characteristics of the Master Limited Partnership ("MLP") asset class. The underlying index is intended to give investors a means of tracking the performance of the energy infrastructure MLP asset class in the United States. The fund is non-diversified. **Top Holdings:** Enterprise Products Partners LP Energy Transfer LP Magellan Midstream Partners LP Plains All American Pipeline LP MPLX LP Partnership Units

---

iShares Core Aggressive Allocation ETF   C   HOLD

Ticker	Traded On	NAV	Total Assets ($)	Dividend Yield (TTM)	Turnover Ratio	Expense Ratio
AOA	NYSE Arca	54.89	$955,052,071	2.27	4	0.25

Ratings

Reward	C
Risk	C-
Recent Upgrade/Downgrade	

Fund Information

Fund Type	Exchange Traded Funds
Category	Aggressive Allocation
Sub-Category	Allocation--70% to 85% Equity
Prospectus Objective	Asset Allocation
Inception Date	Nov-08
Open to New Investments	Y

Prices

Price (as of 9/30/2019)	54.92
52-Week High	55.45
52-Week Low	47.04

Total Returns (%)

3-Month	6-Month	1-Year	3-Year	5-Year
0.00	2.96	2.56	27.36	40.07

3-Year Standard Deviation	9.06
Effective Duration	

Valuation

Premium/Discount (1-Year Average)	0.03

Company Information

Provider	iShares
Manager/Tenure	Diane Hsiung (10), Greg Savage (10), Jennifer Hsui (6), 3 others
Website	http://www.ishares.com
Address	iShares 400 Howard Street San Francisco CA 94105 United States
Phone Number	800-474-2737

PERFORMANCE

Ratings History

Date	Overall Rating	Risk Rating	Reward Rating
Q3-19	C	C-	C
Q4-18	C	C+	C-
Q4-17	B-	B	B-
Q4-16	C	C-	C
Q4-15	C	C-	C

Asset & Performance History

Date	NAV	1-Year Total Return
2018	48.56	-7.76
2017	53.83	20.03
2016	47.18	7.62
2015	44.86	-0.98
2014	46.26	6.01
2013	44.59	22.4

Total Assets: $955,052,071

Asset Allocation

Asset	%
Cash	1%
Stocks	79%
US Stocks	43%
Bonds	20%
US Bonds	15%
Other	0%

Services Offered:

Investment Strategy: The investment seeks to track the investment results of the S&P Target Risk Aggressive Index composed of a portfolio of underlying equity and fixed income funds intended to represent an aggressive target risk allocation strategy. The fund is a fund of funds and seeks its investment objective by investing primarily in other iShares Underlying Funds that themselves seek investment results corresponding to their own respective underlying indexes. It generally will invest at least 90% of its assets in the component securities of the underlying index. The index measures the performance of the S&P Dow Jones Indices LLC proprietary allocation model. **Top Holdings:** Microsoft Corp Apple Inc Amazon.com Inc Facebook Inc A Berkshire Hathaway Inc B

iShares U.S. Utilities ETF   B-   BUY

Ticker	Traded On	NAV	Total Assets ($)	Dividend Yield (TTM)	Turnover Ratio	Expense Ratio
IDU	NYSE Arca	162.86	$952,751,372	2.56	6	0.42

Ratings

Reward	B
Risk	C
Recent Upgrade/Downgrade	

Fund Information

Fund Type	Exchange Traded Funds
Category	Utilities Sector Equity
Sub-Category	Utilities
Prospectus Objective	Utility
Inception Date	Jun-00
Open to New Investments	Y

Prices

Price (as of 9/30/2019)	162.85
52-Week High	163.32
52-Week Low	130.66

Total Returns (%)

3-Month	6-Month	1-Year	3-Year	5-Year
9.00	12.11	25.32	44.87	80.39

3-Year Standard Deviation	10.39
Effective Duration	

Valuation

Premium/Discount (1-Year Average)	-0.01

Company Information

Provider	iShares
Manager/Tenure	Greg Savage (11), Jennifer Hsui (7), Alan Mason (3), 2 others
Website	http://www.ishares.com
Address	iShares 400 Howard Street San Francisco CA 94105 United States
Phone Number	800-474-2737

PERFORMANCE

Ratings History

Date	Overall Rating	Risk Rating	Reward Rating
Q3-19	B-	C	B
Q4-18	B-	C+	B-
Q4-17	B	B	B
Q4-16	B-	C+	B
Q4-15	B-	C+	B

Asset & Performance History

Date	NAV	1-Year Total Return
2018	134.18	3.91
2017	132.88	11.95
2016	121.83	16.51
2015	107.87	-4.97
2014	118.4	27.43
2013	95.84	14.69

Total Assets: $952,751,372
Asset Allocation

Asset	%
Cash	0%
Stocks	100%
US Stocks	100%
Bonds	0%
US Bonds	0%
Other	0%

Services Offered: CashInvestment Plan

Investment Strategy: The investment seeks to track the investment results of the Dow Jones U.S. Utilities Index. The fund generally invests at least 90% of its assets in securities of the underlying index and in depositary receipts representing securities of the underlying index. The underlying index measures the performance of the utilities sector of the U.S. equity market and may include large-, mid- or small-capitalization companies. The fund is non-diversified. **Top Holdings:** NextEra Energy Inc Duke Energy Corp Dominion Energy Inc Southern Co Exelon Corp

---

Fidelity® MSCI Real Estate Index ETF   C+   HOLD

Ticker	Traded On	NAV	Total Assets ($)	Dividend Yield (TTM)	Turnover Ratio	Expense Ratio
FREL	NYSE Arca	27.88	$952,020,479	3.23	10	0.08

Ratings

Reward	B-
Risk	C+
Recent Upgrade/Downgrade	

Fund Information

Fund Type	Exchange Traded Funds
Category	Real Estate Sector Equity
Sub-Category	Real Estate
Prospectus Objective	Real Estate
Inception Date	Feb-15
Open to New Investments	Y

Prices

Price (as of 9/30/2019)	27.90
52-Week High	28.11
52-Week Low	21.52

Total Returns (%)

3-Month	6-Month	1-Year	3-Year	5-Year
7.65	9.25	20.96	29.13	

3-Year Standard Deviation	12.37
Effective Duration	

Valuation

Premium/Discount (1-Year Average)	0.06

Company Information

Provider	Fidelity Investments
Manager/Tenure	Jennifer Hsui (4), Greg Savage (4), Alan Mason (3), 2 others
Website	http://www.institutional.fidelity.com
Address	Fidelity Investments 82 Devonshire Street Boston MA 2109 United States
Phone Number	617-563-7000

PERFORMANCE

Ratings History

Date	Overall Rating	Risk Rating	Reward Rating
Q3-19	C+	C+	B-
Q4-18	C	C+	C
Q4-17	B-	B	C
Q4-16	C-	C	C
Q4-15	U		

Asset & Performance History

Date	NAV	1-Year Total Return
2018	22.37	-4.49
2017	24.68	8.91
2016	23.42	8.06
2015	22.55	
2014		
2013		

Total Assets: $952,020,479
Asset Allocation

Asset	%
Cash	0%
Stocks	100%
US Stocks	100%
Bonds	0%
US Bonds	0%
Other	0%

Services Offered:

Investment Strategy: The investment seeks to provide investment returns that correspond, before fees and expenses, generally to the performance of the MSCI USA IMI Real Estate Index. The fund invests at least 80% of assets in securities included in the fund's underlying index. The fund's underlying index is the MSCI USA IMI Real Estate Index, which represents the performance of the real estate sector in the U.S. equity market. It may or may not hold all of the securities in the MSCI USA IMI Real Estate Index. **Top Holdings:** American Tower Corp Crown Castle International Corp Prologis Inc Equinix Inc Simon Property Group Inc

iShares U.S. Consumer Services ETF

C+   HOLD

Ticker	Traded On	NAV	Total Assets ($)	Dividend Yield (TTM)	Turnover Ratio	Expense Ratio
IYC	NYSE Arca	217.41	$945,715,716	0.83	15	0.42

Ratings
Reward	B
Risk	C
Recent Upgrade/Downgrade	

Fund Information
Fund Type	Exchange Traded Funds
Category	Consumer Goods & Svcs
Sub-Category	Consumer Cyclical
Prospectus Objective	Unaligned
Inception Date	Jun-00
Open to New Investments	Y

Prices
Price (as of 9/30/2019)	217.39
52-Week High	226.85
52-Week Low	168.12

Total Returns (%)
3-Month	6-Month	1-Year	3-Year	5-Year
-0.67	5.72	3.93	52.09	86.02

3-Year Standard Deviation	14.11
Effective Duration	

Valuation
Premium/Discount (1-Year Average)	-0.01

Company Information
Provider	iShares
Manager/Tenure	Greg Savage (11), Jennifer Hsui (7), Alan Mason (3), 2 others
Website	http://www.ishares.com
Address	iShares 400 Howard Street San Francisco CA 94105 United States
Phone Number	800-474-2737

PERFORMANCE

Ratings History

Date	Overall Rating	Risk Rating	Reward Rating
Q3-19	C+	C	B
Q4-18	C	C	C+
Q4-17	B	A-	B-
Q4-16	C+	C	B
Q4-15	C+	C	B-

Asset & Performance History

Date	NAV	1-Year Total Return
2018	180.89	1.79
2017	179.19	19.88
2016	150.97	5.52
2015	144.68	6.18
2014	137.68	14.04
2013	121.76	41.48

Total Assets: $945,715,716
Asset Allocation

Asset	%
Cash	0%
Stocks	100%
US Stocks	99%
Bonds	0%
US Bonds	0%
Other	0%

Services Offered: Cash Investment Plan

Investment Strategy: The investment seeks to track the investment results of the Dow Jones U.S. Consumer Services Capped Index. The fund generally invests at least 90% of its assets in securities of the underlying index and in depositary receipts representing securities of the underlying index. The underlying index measures the performance of domestic equities in the consumer services industry. **Top Holdings:** Amazon.com Inc The Walt Disney Co The Home Depot Inc Comcast Corp Class A McDonald's Corp

Invesco Dynamic Large Cap Value ETF

C   HOLD

Ticker	Traded On	NAV	Total Assets ($)	Dividend Yield (TTM)	Turnover Ratio	Expense Ratio
PWV	NYSE Arca	38.34	$945,057,661	2.27		0.55

Ratings
Reward	C+
Risk	C
Recent Upgrade/Downgrade	

Fund Information
Fund Type	Exchange Traded Funds
Category	US Equity Large Cap Value
Sub-Category	Large Value
Prospectus Objective	Growth
Inception Date	Mar-05
Open to New Investments	Y

Prices
Price (as of 9/30/2019)	38.33
52-Week High	39.10
52-Week Low	30.83

Total Returns (%)
3-Month	6-Month	1-Year	3-Year	5-Year
3.64	7.91	4.96	29.91	42.87

3-Year Standard Deviation	12.97
Effective Duration	

Valuation
Premium/Discount (1-Year Average)	-0.02

Company Information
Provider	Invesco
Manager/Tenure	Peter Hubbard (12), Michael Jeanette (11), Tony Seisser (5)
Website	http://www.invesco.com/us
Address	Invesco 11 Greenway Plaza, Ste. 2500 Houston TX 77046 United States
Phone Number	800-659-1005

PERFORMANCE

Ratings History

Date	Overall Rating	Risk Rating	Reward Rating
Q3-19	C	C	C+
Q4-18	C	C	C
Q4-17	B	B	B
Q4-16	C+	C-	B
Q4-15	B-	B-	C+

Asset & Performance History

Date	NAV	1-Year Total Return
2018	32.65	-13.93
2017	38.76	16.99
2016	33.67	18.68
2015	29.09	-4.68
2014	31.25	12.26
2013	28.39	32.65

Total Assets: $945,057,661
Asset Allocation

Asset	%
Cash	0%
Stocks	100%
US Stocks	99%
Bonds	0%
US Bonds	0%
Other	0%

Services Offered:

Investment Strategy: The investment seeks to track the investment results (before fees and expenses) of the Dynamic Large Cap Value IntellidexSM Index. The fund generally will invest at least 90% of its total assets in the securities that comprise the underlying intellidex. The underlying intellidex is composed of large-capitalization U.S. value stocks that the Intellidex Provider includes principally on the basis of their capital appreciation potential. **Top Holdings:** Amgen Inc Apple Inc Medtronic PLC Walmart Inc NextEra Energy Inc

Invesco S&P 500 Revenue ETF   C   BUY

Ticker	Traded On	NAV	Total Assets ($)	Dividend Yield (TTM)	Turnover Ratio	Expense Ratio
RWL	NYSE Arca	53.97	$944,608,862	1.93	19	0.39

Ratings
Reward   C
Risk   C-
Recent Upgrade/Downgrade

Fund Information
Fund Type   Exchange Traded Funds
Category   US Equity Large Cap Value
Sub-Category   Large Value
Prospectus Objective   Growth
Inception Date   Feb-08
Open to New Investments   Y

Prices
Price (as of 9/30/2019)   53.95
52-Week High   55.06
52-Week Low   44.16

Total Returns (%)

3-Month	6-Month	1-Year	3-Year	5-Year
0.99	4.31	1.37	37.17	55.72

3-Year Standard Deviation   13.37
Effective Duration

Valuation
Premium/Discount (1-Year Average)   -0.01

Company Information
Provider   Invesco
Manager/Tenure Peter Hubbard (0), Michael Jeanette (0), Tony Seisser (0)
Website   http://www.invesco.com/us
Address   Invesco 11 Greenway Plaza, Ste. 2500 Houston TX 77046 United States
Phone Number   800-659-1005

PERFORMANCE

Ratings History

Date	Overall Rating	Risk Rating	Reward Rating
Q3-19	C	C-	C
Q4-18	C	C-	C
Q4-17	B-	B-	B
Q4-16	B-	C+	B
Q4-15	C+	C+	C

Asset & Performance History

Date	NAV	1-Year Total Return
2018	46.51	-7.57
2017	51.25	19.88
2016	43.49	12.23
2015	39.45	-1.2
2014	40.71	13.38
2013	36.45	37.63

Total Assets: $944,608,862

Asset Allocation

Asset	%
Cash	0%
Stocks	100%
US Stocks	99%
Bonds	0%
US Bonds	0%
Other	0%

Services Offered:

Investment Strategy: The investment seeks to track the investment results (before fees and expenses) of the S&P 500® Revenue-Weighted Index (the "underlying index"). The fund generally will invest at least 90% of its total assets in the securities that comprise the underlying index. The underlying index is constructed using a rules-based methodology that re-weights the constituent securities of the S&P 500® Index ("the "parent index") according to the revenue earned by the companies in the parent index, subject to a maximum 5% per company weighting. The fund is non-diversified. **Top Holdings:** Walmart Inc Apple Inc Exxon Mobil Corp Berkshire Hathaway Inc B CVS Health Corp

---

Vanguard S&P Mid-Cap 400 Growth Index Fund ETF Shares   C-   HOLD

Ticker	Traded On	NAV	Total Assets ($)	Dividend Yield (TTM)	Turnover Ratio	Expense Ratio
IVOG	NYSE Arca	139.45	$941,983,313	0.86	43	0.2

Ratings
Reward   C
Risk   D+
Recent Upgrade/Downgrade   Down

Fund Information
Fund Type   Exchange Traded Funds
Category   US Equity Mid Cap
Sub-Category   Mid-Cap Growth
Prospectus Objective   Growth & Inc
Inception Date   Sep-10
Open to New Investments   Y

Prices
Price (as of 9/30/2019)   139.41
52-Week High   143.38
52-Week Low   111.15

Total Returns (%)

3-Month	6-Month	1-Year	3-Year	5-Year
-1.63	1.13	-2.46	31.75	55.34

3-Year Standard Deviation   14.49
Effective Duration

Valuation
Premium/Discount (1-Year Average)   -0.02

Company Information
Provider   Vanguard
Manager/Tenure William A. Coleman (3), Awais Khan (1)
Website   http://www.vanguard.com
Address   Vanguard 100 Vanguard Boulevard Malvern PA 19355 United States
Phone Number   877-662-7447

PERFORMANCE

Ratings History

Date	Overall Rating	Risk Rating	Reward Rating
Q3-19	C-	D+	C
Q4-18	C-	C-	C-
Q4-17	B+	B+	B
Q4-16	C+	C-	B
Q4-15	C	C-	C

Asset & Performance History

Date	NAV	1-Year Total Return
2018	116.59	-11.53
2017	133.06	19.97
2016	112.17	13.77
2015	98.92	1.85
2014	98.14	7.37
2013	92.13	32.49

Total Assets: $941,983,313

Asset Allocation

Asset	%
Cash	1%
Stocks	99%
US Stocks	99%
Bonds	0%
US Bonds	0%
Other	0%

Services Offered:

Investment Strategy: The investment seeks to track the performance of a benchmark index that measures the investment return of mid-capitalization growth stocks in the United States. The fund employs an indexing investment approach designed to track the performance of the S&P MidCap 400® Growth Index, which represents the growth companies, as determined by the index sponsor, of the S&P MidCap 400 Index. The Advisor attempts to replicate the target index by investing all, or substantially all, of its assets in the stocks that make up the index, holding each stock in approximately the same proportion as its weighting in the index. **Top Holdings:** IDEX Corp Steris PLC Leidos Holdings Inc Zebra Technologies Corp Trimble Inc

Direxion Daily S&P500® Bull 3X Shares

C   HOLD

Ticker	Traded On	NAV		Total Assets ($)	Dividend Yield (TTM)	Turnover Ratio	Expense Ratio
SPXL	NYSE Arca	52.31		$941,880,079	0.96	95	1.02

Ratings
Reward   C+
Risk   D+
Recent Upgrade/Downgrade

Fund Information
Fund Type   Exchange Traded Funds
Category   Trading Tools
Sub-Category   Trading--Leveraged Equity
Prospectus Objective   Growth
Inception Date   Nov-08
Open to New Investments   Y

Prices
Price (as of 9/30/2019)   52.31
52-Week High   55.74
52-Week Low   27.54

Total Returns (%)

3-Month	6-Month	1-Year	3-Year	5-Year
-0.54	8.69	-3.52	126.98	195.95

3-Year Standard Deviation   36.87
Effective Duration

Valuation
Premium/Discount (1-Year Average)   -0.08

Company Information
Provider   Direxion Funds
Manager/Tenure   Paul Brigandi (10), Tony Ng (4)
Website   http://www.direxionfunds.com
Address   Direxion Funds 1301 Avenue Of The
                    Americas (6th Avenue) New York NY
                    10019 United States
Phone Number   646-572-3390

PERFORMANCE

Ratings History

Date	Overall Rating	Risk Rating	Reward Rating
Q3-19	C	D+	C+
Q4-18	C	C	C
Q4-17	B+	C	A+
Q4-16	C	C	C
Q4-15	C	C+	C

Asset & Performance History

Date	NAV	1-Year Total Return
2018	32.86	-24.86
2017	44.12	70.88
2016	26.84	29.37
2015	20.74	-5.47
2014	21.95	37.82
2013	15.92	117.94

Total Assets: $941,880,079
Asset Allocation

Asset	%
Cash	4%
Stocks	96%
US Stocks	95%
Bonds	0%
US Bonds	0%
Other	0%

Services Offered:

Investment Strategy: The investment seeks daily investment results, before fees and expenses, of 300% of the daily performance of the S&P 500® Index. The fund, under normal circumstances, invests at least 80% of its net assets (plus borrowing for investment purposes) in financial instruments, such as swap agreements, and securities of the index, exchange-traded funds ("ETFs") that track the index and other financial instruments that provide daily leveraged exposure to the index or ETFs that track the index. The index is a float-adjusted, market capitalization-weighted index. The fund is non-diversified. **Top Holdings:** iShares Core S&P 500 ETF   S&P 500 Index Swap   S&P 500 Index Swap   S&P 500 Index Swap   S&P 500 Index Swap

---

SPDR® Wells Fargo Preferred Stock ETF

C+   HOLD

Ticker	Traded On	NAV		Total Assets ($)	Dividend Yield (TTM)	Turnover Ratio	Expense Ratio
PSK	NYSE Arca			$936,522,234	5.8	35	0.45

Ratings
Reward   B-
Risk   C+
Recent Upgrade/Downgrade

Fund Information
Fund Type   Exchange Traded Funds
Category   US Fixed Income
Sub-Category   Preferred Stock
Prospectus Objective   Growth & Inc
Inception Date   Sep-09
Open to New Investments   Y

Prices
Price (as of 9/30/2019)   44.16
52-Week High   44.19
52-Week Low   38.67

Total Returns (%)

3-Month	6-Month	1-Year	3-Year	5-Year
3.90	6.16	11.24	15.44	34.91

3-Year Standard Deviation   6.18
Effective Duration

Valuation
Premium/Discount (1-Year Average)   0.11

Company Information
Provider   SPDR State Street Global Advisors
Manager/Tenure   Michael J. Feehily (7), Karl A.
                    Schneider (4), Amy Scofield (2)
Website   http://www.spdrs.com
Address   SPDR State Street Global Advisors
                    State Street Financial Center, 1
                    Lincoln Street Boston MA 02111-2900
                    United States
Phone Number   617-786-3000

PERFORMANCE

Ratings History

Date	Overall Rating	Risk Rating	Reward Rating
Q3-19	C+	C+	B-
Q4-18	D+	C-	D+
Q4-17	B	A	C+
Q4-16	C	C-	C
Q4-15	C+	C+	C+

Asset & Performance History

Date	NAV	1-Year Total Return
2018	39.55	-4.58
2017	44.05	10.5
2016	41.97	-0.48
2015	44.61	8.17
2014	43.54	16.49
2013	39.56	-5.35

Total Assets: $936,522,234
Asset Allocation

Asset	%
Cash	1%
Stocks	3%
US Stocks	1%
Bonds	0%
US Bonds	0%
Other	1%

Services Offered:

Investment Strategy: The investment seeks to provide investment results that, before fees and expenses, correspond generally to the total return performance of an index. In seeking to track the performance of Wells Fargo Hybrid and Preferred Securities Aggregate Index (the "index"), the fund employs a sampling strategy. It generally invests substantially all, but at least 80%, of its total assets in the securities comprising the index. The index is a modified market capitalization weighted index designed to measure the performance of non-convertible preferred stock and securities that are functionally equivalent to preferred stock. The fund is non-diversified. **Top Holdings:** Citigroup Capital XIII Floating Rate Trust Pfd Secs Registered 2010-30.10.4   PNC Financial Services Group Inc Perpetual Preferred Share class-P   HSBC Holdings PLC ADR   AT&T Inc 0%   US Bancorp Shs Repr 1/1000th Non Cum Perp Pfd Shs Series-F

Invesco S&P International Developed Low Volatility ETF   C+   HOLD

Ticker	Traded On	NAV	Total Assets ($)	Dividend Yield (TTM)	Turnover Ratio	Expense Ratio
IDLV	NYSE Arca	34.09	$935,638,656	3.48	65	0.25

Ratings
Reward	C+
Risk	C+
Recent Upgrade/Downgrade	Up

Fund Information
Fund Type	Exchange Traded Funds
Category	Global Equity Large Cap
Sub-Category	Foreign Large Blend
Prospectus Objective	Foreign Stock
Inception Date	Jan-12
Open to New Investments	

Prices
Price (as of 9/30/2019)	34.16
52-Week High	34.43
52-Week Low	29.12

Total Returns (%)
3-Month	6-Month	1-Year	3-Year	5-Year
1.58	5.82	8.98	24.89	29.79

3-Year Standard Deviation	8.8
Effective Duration	

Valuation
Premium/Discount (1-Year Average)	0.03

Company Information
Provider	Invesco
Manager/Tenure	Peter Hubbard (7), Michael Jeanette (4), Tony Seisser (4)
Website	http://www.invesco.com/us
Address	Invesco 11 Greenway Plaza, Ste. 2500 Houston TX 77046 United States
Phone Number	800-659-1005

PERFORMANCE

Ratings History

Date	Overall Rating	Risk Rating	Reward Rating
Q3-19	C+	C+	C+
Q4-18	C	C+	D+
Q4-17	B-	B-	C+
Q4-16	C-	C	C-
Q4-15	C-	C-	C-

Asset & Performance History

Date	NAV	1-Year Total Return
2018	29.89	-7.91
2017	33.68	21.9
2016	28.5	3.29
2015	28.67	-3.97
2014	31.01	1.66
2013	31.47	15.92

Total Assets: $935,638,656

Asset Allocation

Asset	%
Cash	0%
Stocks	100%
US Stocks	0%
Bonds	0%
US Bonds	0%
Other	0%

Services Offered:

Investment Strategy: The investment seeks to track the investment results (before fees and expenses) of the S&P BMI International Developed Low VolatilityTM Index (the "underlying index"). The fund will invest at least 90% of its total assets in the securities of companies that comprise the underlying index. S&P Dow Jones Indices ("S&P DJI" or the "index provider") compiles, maintains and calculates the underlying index, which is designed to measure the performance of 200 of the least volatile stocks of the S&P Developed ex-U.S. & South Korea LargeMidCap Index.
Top Holdings: Innogy SE   National Bank of Canada   MORI TRUST Sogo Reit Inc   TELUS Corp   Orix Jreit Inc

---

WisdomTree U.S. High Dividend Fund   C   HOLD

Ticker	Traded On	NAV	Total Assets ($)	Dividend Yield (TTM)	Turnover Ratio	Expense Ratio
DHS	NYSE Arca	74.46	$930,731,417	3.39	20	0.38

Ratings
Reward	C
Risk	C-
Recent Upgrade/Downgrade	

Fund Information
Fund Type	Exchange Traded Funds
Category	US Equity Large Cap Value
Sub-Category	Large Value
Prospectus Objective	Growth & Inc
Inception Date	Jun-06
Open to New Investments	Y

Prices
Price (as of 9/30/2019)	74.48
52-Week High	74.68
52-Week Low	62.15

Total Returns (%)
3-Month	6-Month	1-Year	3-Year	5-Year
2.92	3.84	6.75	24.03	50.40

3-Year Standard Deviation	11.02
Effective Duration	

Valuation
Premium/Discount (1-Year Average)	-0.01

Company Information
Provider	WisdomTree
Manager/Tenure	Richard A. Brown (11), Thomas J. Durante (11), Karen Q. Wong (11)
Website	http://www.wisdomtree.com
Address	WisdomTree 245 Park Avenue, 35th floor New York NY 10167 United States
Phone Number	866-909-9473

PERFORMANCE

Ratings History

Date	Overall Rating	Risk Rating	Reward Rating
Q3-19	C	C-	C
Q4-18	C	C-	C
Q4-17	B	B+	B-
Q4-16	C+	C-	B-
Q4-15	C	C	C+

Asset & Performance History

Date	NAV	1-Year Total Return
2018	65.18	-7.25
2017	72.8	11.68
2016	67.27	17.85
2015	59.05	-0.6
2014	61.52	15.12
2013	55.1	24.44

Total Assets: $930,731,417

Asset Allocation

Asset	%
Cash	0%
Stocks	100%
US Stocks	100%
Bonds	0%
US Bonds	0%
Other	0%

Services Offered:

Investment Strategy: The investment seeks to track the price and yield performance, before fees and expenses, of the WisdomTree U.S. High Dividend Index. Under normal circumstances, at least 95% of the fund's total assets (exclusive of collateral held from securities lending) will be invested in component securities of the index and investments that have economic characteristics that are substantially identical to the economic characteristics of such component securities. The index is a fundamentally weighted index that is comprised of companies with high dividend yields selected from the WisdomTree U.S. Dividend Index. The fund is non-diversified. **Top Holdings:** AT&T Inc   Exxon Mobil Corp   Verizon Communications Inc   Procter & Gamble Co   Chevron Corp

FlexShares Morningstar Developed Markets ex-US Factor Tilt Index Fund — C- HOLD

Ticker	Traded On	NAV	Total Assets ($)	Dividend Yield (TTM)	Turnover Ratio	Expense Ratio
TLTD	NYSE Arca	60.31	$928,730,707	3.03	34	0.39

Ratings
Reward   C-
Risk   C-
Recent Upgrade/Downgrade

Fund Information
Fund Type	Exchange Traded Funds
Category	Global Equity Large Cap
Sub-Category	Foreign Large Value
Prospectus Objective	Foreign Stock
Inception Date	Sep-12
Open to New Investments	Y

Prices
Price (as of 9/30/2019)	60.24
52-Week High	65.55
52-Week Low	53.42

Total Returns (%)
3-Month	6-Month	1-Year	3-Year	5-Year
-1.33	0.26	-4.53	17.33	16.04

3-Year Standard Deviation   11.42
Effective Duration

Valuation
Premium/Discount (1-Year Average)   -0.28

Company Information
Provider	Flexshares Trust
Manager/Tenure	Robert Anstine (5), Brendan Sullivan (3)
Website	http://www.flexshares.com
Address	50 South LaSalle Street Chicago, Illinois 60603 Chicago Illinois 60603 United States
Phone Number	855-353-9383

PERFORMANCE

Ratings History
Date	Overall Rating	Risk Rating	Reward Rating
Q3-19	C-	C-	C-
Q4-18	D+	C-	D+
Q4-17	B-	C+	B
Q4-16	C-	C-	C-
Q4-15	C-	C-	D+

Asset & Performance History
Date	NAV	1-Year Total Return
2018	55.62	-17.24
2017	69.08	25.92
2016	56.46	5.4
2015	55.19	-2.03
2014	57.78	-4.61
2013	62.45	21.96

Total Assets: $928,730,707
Asset Allocation
Asset	%
Cash	1%
Stocks	99%
US Stocks	1%
Bonds	0%
US Bonds	0%
Other	0%

Services Offered:

Investment Strategy: The investment seeks investment results that correspond generally to the price and yield performance, before fees and expenses, of the Morningstar® Developed Markets ex-US Factor Tilt IndexSM. The fund will invest at least 80% of its total assets (exclusive of collateral held from securities lending) in the securities of the index and in American ADRs and GDRs based on the securities in the index. The underlying index reflects the performance of a selection of equity securities designed to provide broad exposure to the global developed equities markets, excluding the U.S., with increased exposure (or a "tilt") to small-capitalization stocks and value stocks.
Top Holdings: Nestle SA   Toyota Motor Corp   HSBC Holdings PLC   Novartis AG   BP PLC

Global X SuperDividend™ ETF — D SELL

Ticker	Traded On	NAV	Total Assets ($)	Dividend Yield (TTM)	Turnover Ratio	Expense Ratio
SDIV	NYSE Arca	16.99	$922,689,051	9.4	59	0.58

Ratings
Reward   D
Risk   C-
Recent Upgrade/Downgrade   Down

Fund Information
Fund Type	Exchange Traded Funds
Category	Globa Eq Mid/Small Cap
Sub-Category	World Small/Mid Stock
Prospectus Objective	Equity-Income
Inception Date	Jun-11
Open to New Investments	Y

Prices
Price (as of 9/30/2019)	16.97
52-Week High	20.27
52-Week Low	15.85

Total Returns (%)
3-Month	6-Month	1-Year	3-Year	5-Year
1.11	-3.12	-8.29	-0.21	2.45

3-Year Standard Deviation   12.18
Effective Duration

Valuation
Premium/Discount (1-Year Average)   0.00

Company Information
Provider	Global X Funds
Manager/Tenure	Chang Kim (5), Nam To (1), Wayne Xie (0), 1 other
Website	http://www.globalxfunds.com
Address	Global X Funds 600 Lexington Avenue, 20th Floor New York NY 10022 United States
Phone Number	888-493-8631

PERFORMANCE

Ratings History
Date	Overall Rating	Risk Rating	Reward Rating
Q3-19	D	C-	D
Q4-18	C-	C	C-
Q4-17	C+	C+	C+
Q4-16	C	C	C-
Q4-15	C	C	C-

Asset & Performance History
Date	NAV	1-Year Total Return
2018	17.2	-15.36
2017	21.81	11.54
2016	20.91	13.16
2015	19.84	-8.54
2014	23.19	5.78
2013	23.3	14.73

Total Assets: $922,689,051
Asset Allocation
Asset	%
Cash	0%
Stocks	100%
US Stocks	46%
Bonds	0%
US Bonds	0%
Other	0%

Services Offered: Retirement Investment

Investment Strategy: The investment seeks investment results that correspond generally to the price and yield performance, before fees and expenses, of the Solactive Global SuperDividend® Index. The fund invests at least 80% of its total assets in the securities of the underlying index and in American Depositary Receipts ("ADRs") and Global Depositary Receipts ("GDRs") based on the securities in the underlying index. The underlying index tracks the performance of 100 equally-weighted companies that rank among the highest dividend yielding equity securities in the world, including emerging market countries. **Top Holdings:** Pattern Energy Group Inc Class A Jasmine International PCL DR   Sabra Health Care REIT Inc   Ship Finance International Ltd   Genworth Mortgage Insurance Australia Ltd

iShares International Treasury Bond ETF   C   HOLD

Ticker	Traded On	NAV	Total Assets ($)	Dividend Yield (TTM)	Turnover Ratio	Expense Ratio
IGOV	NAS CM	50.37	$916,673,414	0.3	10	0.35

Ratings
Reward   C
Risk   C+
Recent Upgrade/Downgrade

Fund Information
Fund Type   Exchange Traded Funds
Category   Global Fixed Income
Sub-Category   World Bond
Prospectus Objective   Worldwide Bond
Inception Date   Jan-09
Open to New Investments   Y

Prices
Price (as of 9/30/2019)   50.47
52-Week High   51.68
52-Week Low   47.13

Total Returns (%)

3-Month	6-Month	1-Year	3-Year	5-Year
-0.47	3.13	5.22	1.32	3.09

3-Year Standard Deviation   6.67
Effective Duration

Valuation
Premium/Discount (1-Year Average)   0.06

Company Information
Provider   iShares
Manager/Tenure   Scott Radell (9), James Mauro (8)
Website   http://www.ishares.com
Address   iShares 400 Howard Street San
                   Francisco CA 94105 United States
Phone Number   800-474-2737

PERFORMANCE

Ratings History

Date	Overall Rating	Risk Rating	Reward Rating
Q3-19	C	C+	C
Q4-18	D+	C-	D+
Q4-17	C	C+	C
Q4-16	D+	C-	D+
Q4-15	D	D+	D

Asset & Performance History

Date	NAV	1-Year Total Return
2018	48.35	-2.68
2017	49.84	10.9
2016	45.01	1.22
2015	44.77	-6.89
2014	48.14	-2.43
2013	49.95	-1.55

Total Assets: $916,673,414

Asset Allocation

Asset	%
Cash	5%
Stocks	0%
US Stocks	0%
Bonds	95%
US Bonds	0%
Other	0%

Services Offered:

Investment Strategy: The investment seeks to track the investment results of the S&P International Sovereign Ex-U.S. Bond Index. The fund generally will invest at least 90% of its assets in the component securities of the underlying index and may invest up to 10% of its assets in certain futures, options and swap contracts, cash and cash equivalents. The underlying index is a broad, diverse, market value-weighted index designed to measure the performance of bonds denominated in local currencies and issued by foreign governments in developed market countries outside the U.S. The fund is non-diversified. **Top Holdings:** Denmark (Kingdom Of) 4.5% Portugal (Republic Of) 5.65% Portugal (Republic Of) 4.95% Ireland (Republic Of) 5.4% Ireland (Republic Of) 2%

WisdomTree Yield Enhanced U.S. Aggregate Bond Fund   C+   HOLD

Ticker	Traded On	NAV	Total Assets ($)	Dividend Yield (TTM)	Turnover Ratio	Expense Ratio
AGGY	NYSE Arca	52.27	$914,638,577	3.1	82	0.12

Ratings
Reward   C+
Risk   C+
Recent Upgrade/Downgrade

Fund Information
Fund Type   Exchange Traded Funds
Category   US Fixed Income
Sub-Category   Intermediate Core Bond
Prospectus Objective   Growth & Inc
Inception Date   Jul-15
Open to New Investments   Y

Prices
Price (as of 9/30/2019)   52.28
52-Week High   52.89
52-Week Low   47.36

Total Returns (%)

3-Month	6-Month	1-Year	3-Year	5-Year
2.83	7.12	11.92	11.00	

3-Year Standard Deviation   3.88
Effective Duration   6.47

Valuation
Premium/Discount (1-Year Average)   0.00

Company Information
Provider   WisdomTree
Manager/Tenure   Paul L. Benson (3), Stephanie Shu (3)
Website   http://www.wisdomtree.com
Address   WisdomTree 245 Park Avenue, 35th
                   floor New York NY 10167 United
                   States
Phone Number   866-909-9473

PERFORMANCE

Ratings History

Date	Overall Rating	Risk Rating	Reward Rating
Q3-19	C+	C+	C+
Q4-18	D+	C-	D+
Q4-17	C	B	C
Q4-16	D	C-	D+
Q4-15	U		

Asset & Performance History

Date	NAV	1-Year Total Return
2018	48.15	-1.72
2017	50.66	5.21
2016	49.52	4.1
2015	49.08	
2014		
2013		

Total Assets: $914,638,577

Asset Allocation

Asset	%
Cash	1%
Stocks	0%
US Stocks	0%
Bonds	98%
US Bonds	90%
Other	0%

Services Offered:

Investment Strategy: The investment seeks to track the price and yield performance, before fees and expenses, of the Bloomberg Barclays U.S. Aggregate Enhanced Yield Index (the "index"). Under normal circumstances, the fund will invest at least 80% of its total asset in component securities of the index and investments that have economic characteristics that are substantially identical to the economic characteristics of such component securities. The index is designed to broadly capture the U.S. investment grade, fixed income securities market while seeking to enhance yield within desired risk parameters and constraints. The fund is non-diversified. **Top Holdings:** United States Treasury Notes 1.75% United States Treasury Notes 1.13% United States Treasury Notes 2% United States Treasury Bonds 3% United States Treasury Bonds 3.13%

SPDR® Portfolio Intermediate Term Treasury ETF

C+   HOLD

Ticker	Traded On	NAV	Total Assets ($)	Dividend Yield (TTM)	Turnover Ratio	Expense Ratio
SPTI	NYSE Arca		$912,580,887	2.11	24	0.06

Ratings
Reward	C
Risk	C+
Recent Upgrade/Downgrade	Up

Fund Information
Fund Type	Exchange Traded Funds
Category	US Fixed Income
Sub-Category	Intermediate Government
Prospectus Objective	Govt Bond - Treasury
Inception Date	May-07
Open to New Investments	Y

Prices
Price (as of 9/30/2019)	31.27
52-Week High	61.86
52-Week Low	30.88

Total Returns (%)
3-Month	6-Month	1-Year	3-Year	5-Year
-49.09	-47.46	-45.02	-46.25	-43.34

3-Year Standard Deviation	3.06
Effective Duration	5.22

Valuation
Premium/Discount (1-Year Average)	0.06

Company Information
Provider	SPDR State Street Global Advisors
Manager/Tenure	Joanna Madden (4), Cynthia Moy (2), Orhan Imer (1)
Website	http://www.spdrs.com
Address	SPDR State Street Global Advisors State Street Financial Center, 1 Lincoln Street Boston MA 02111-2900 United States
Phone Number	617-786-3000

PERFORMANCE

Ratings History
Date	Overall Rating	Risk Rating	Reward Rating
Q3-19	C+	C+	C
Q4-18	D+	C-	D+
Q4-17	C	C	C
Q4-16	C-	C-	C
Q4-15	C	C-	C

Asset & Performance History
Date	NAV	1-Year Total Return
2018	59.38	1.94
2017	59.43	0.85
2016	59.67	0.91
2015	59.83	1.07
2014	59.89	2.45
2013	59.08	-1.45

Total Assets: $912,580,887
Asset Allocation
Asset	%
Cash	0%
Stocks	0%
US Stocks	0%
Bonds	100%
US Bonds	100%
Other	0%

Services Offered:

Investment Strategy: The investment seeks to provide investment results that correspond generally to the price and yield performance of the Bloomberg Barclays 3-10 Year U.S. Treasury Index. The fund generally invests substantially all, but at least 80%, of its total assets in the securities comprising the index or in securities that the Adviser determines have economic characteristics that are substantially identical to the economic characteristics of the securities that comprise the index. The index is designed to measure the performance of intermediate term (3-10 years) public obligations of the U.S. Treasury. It is non-diversified. **Top Holdings:** United States Treasury Notes 2% United States Treasury Notes 3.12% United States Treasury Notes 2.88% United States Treasury Notes 2.88% United States Treasury Notes 2.62%

Vanguard S&P Mid-Cap 400 Value Index Fund ETF Shares

C-   HOLD

Ticker	Traded On	NAV	Total Assets ($)	Dividend Yield (TTM)	Turnover Ratio	Expense Ratio
IVOV	NYSE Arca	123.35	$912,222,330	1.59	36	0.2

Ratings
Reward	C
Risk	C-
Recent Upgrade/Downgrade	Down

Fund Information
Fund Type	Exchange Traded Funds
Category	US Equity Mid Cap
Sub-Category	Mid-Cap Value
Prospectus Objective	Growth & Inc
Inception Date	Sep-10
Open to New Investments	Y

Prices
Price (as of 9/30/2019)	123.38
52-Week High	128.20
52-Week Low	99.28

Total Returns (%)
3-Month	6-Month	1-Year	3-Year	5-Year
-0.60	0.47	-2.56	26.11	44.49

3-Year Standard Deviation	16.64
Effective Duration	

Valuation
Premium/Discount (1-Year Average)	0.00

Company Information
Provider	Vanguard
Manager/Tenure	William A. Coleman (3), Awais Khan (1)
Website	http://www.vanguard.com
Address	Vanguard 100 Vanguard Boulevard Malvern PA 19355 United States
Phone Number	877-662-7447

PERFORMANCE

Ratings History
Date	Overall Rating	Risk Rating	Reward Rating
Q3-19	C-	C-	C
Q4-18	C-	D+	C-
Q4-17	B	B	B
Q4-16	C-	C-	C-
Q4-15	C	D+	C

Asset & Performance History
Date	NAV	1-Year Total Return
2018	105.18	-12.75
2017	121.62	12.23
2016	110.15	25.52
2015	88.4	-6.77
2014	96.41	11.86
2013	87.45	33.93

Total Assets: $912,222,330
Asset Allocation
Asset	%
Cash	1%
Stocks	99%
US Stocks	99%
Bonds	0%
US Bonds	0%
Other	0%

Services Offered:

Investment Strategy: The investment seeks to track the performance of a benchmark index that measures the investment return of mid-capitalization value stocks in the United States. The fund employs an indexing investment approach designed to track the performance of the S&P MidCap 400® Value Index, which represents the value companies, as determined by the index sponsor, of the S&P MidCap 400 Index. The Advisor attempts to replicate the target index by investing all, or substantially all, of its assets in the stocks that make up the index, holding each stock in approximately the same proportion as its weighting in the index. **Top Holdings:** WR Berkley Corp Alleghany Corp Reinsurance Group of America Inc Kilroy Realty Corp RenaissanceRe Holdings Ltd

Invesco S&P 500® Pure Value ETF   C   HOLD

Ticker	Traded On	NAV	Total Assets ($)	Dividend Yield (TTM)	Turnover Ratio	Expense Ratio
RPV	NYSE Arca	64.87	$908,402,640	2.46		0.35

Ratings
Reward   C
Risk   C+
Recent Upgrade/Downgrade

Fund Information
Fund Type	Exchange Traded Funds
Category	US Equity Large Cap Value
Sub-Category	Large Value
Prospectus Objective	Growth
Inception Date	Mar-06
Open to New Investments	Y

Prices
Price (as of 9/30/2019)	64.84
52-Week High	68.97
52-Week Low	53.85

Total Returns (%)
3-Month	6-Month	1-Year	3-Year	5-Year
-0.20	2.18	-3.15	30.62	37.73

3-Year Standard Deviation	16.36
Effective Duration	

Valuation
Premium/Discount (1-Year Average)	-0.01

Company Information
Provider	Invesco
Manager/Tenure	Peter Hubbard (1), Michael Jeanette (1), Tony Seisser (1)
Website	http://www.invesco.com/us
Address	Invesco 11 Greenway Plaza, Ste. 2500 Houston TX 77046 United States
Phone Number	800-659-1005

PERFORMANCE

Ratings History
Date	Overall Rating	Risk Rating	Reward Rating
Q3-19	C	C+	C
Q4-18	C	C+	C
Q4-17	B-	B-	B
Q4-16	C	C-	B-
Q4-15	C+	B-	C

Asset & Performance History
Date	NAV	1-Year Total Return
2018	56.82	-12.26
2017	66.22	17.65
2016	57.55	18.79
2015	49.24	-8.29
2014	54.93	12.26
2013	49.72	47.46

Total Assets: $908,402,640
Asset Allocation
Asset	%
Cash	0%
Stocks	100%
US Stocks	97%
Bonds	0%
US Bonds	0%
Other	0%

Services Offered:

Investment Strategy: The investment seeks to track the investment results (before fees and expenses) of the S&P 500® Pure Value Index (the "underlying index"). The fund generally will invest at least 90% of its total assets in the securities that comprise the underlying index. The underlying index is composed of a subset of securities from the S&P 500® Index that exhibit strong value characteristics as measured using the following three factors: book value to price ratio, earnings to price ratio, and sales to price ratio. The fund is non-diversified. **Top Holdings:** Ford Motor Co   Tyson Foods Inc Class A   MetLife Inc   Baker Hughes, a GE Co Class A   Lennar Corp

---

First Trust TCW Opportunistic Fixed Income ETF   C   HOLD

Ticker	Traded On	NAV	Total Assets ($)	Dividend Yield (TTM)	Turnover Ratio	Expense Ratio
FIXD	NAS CM	52.56	$906,597,402	2.76	358	0.55

Ratings
Reward   C
Risk   C+
Recent Upgrade/Downgrade

Fund Information
Fund Type	Exchange Traded Funds
Category	US Fixed Income
Sub-Category	Intermediate Core-Plus Bond
Prospectus Objective	Growth & Inc
Inception Date	Feb-17
Open to New Investments	Y

Prices
Price (as of 9/30/2019)	52.66
52-Week High	53.21
52-Week Low	48.40

Total Returns (%)
3-Month	6-Month	1-Year	3-Year	5-Year
2.40	5.90	10.65		

3-Year Standard Deviation	
Effective Duration	5.91

Valuation
Premium/Discount (1-Year Average)	0.09

Company Information
Provider	First Trust
Manager/Tenure	Stephen M. Kane (2), Laird R. Landmann (2), Tad Rivelle (2), 1 other
Website	http://www.ftportfolios.com/
Address	First Trust 120 E. Liberty Drive, Suite 400 Wheaton IL 60187 United States
Phone Number	800-621-1675

PERFORMANCE

Ratings History
Date	Overall Rating	Risk Rating	Reward Rating
Q3-19	C	C+	C
Q4-18	D+	C-	D
Q4-17	U		
Q4-16			
Q4-15			

Asset & Performance History
Date	NAV	1-Year Total Return
2018	49.37	0.69
2017	50.66	
2016		
2015		
2014		
2013		

Total Assets: $906,597,402
Asset Allocation
Asset	%
Cash	4%
Stocks	0%
US Stocks	0%
Bonds	96%
US Bonds	92%
Other	0%

Services Offered:

Investment Strategy: The investment seeks to maximize long-term total return. The fund pursues its objective by investing at least 80% of its net assets (including investment borrowings) in fixed income securities. It may invest up to 35% of its net assets in corporate, non-U.S. and non-agency debt and other securities rated below investment grade by one or more nationally recognized statistical rating organization ("NRSRO"), or, if unrated, judged to be of comparable quality by the Sub-Advisor. The fund is non-diversified. **Top Holdings:** United States Treasury Notes 1.75%   Us 5yr Note (Cbt) Dec19   Us 2yr Note (Cbt) Dec19   United States Treasury Notes 1.75%   United States Treasury Bonds 2.25%

iShares U.S. Industrials ETF

C   HOLD

Ticker	Traded On	NAV	Total Assets ($)	Dividend Yield (TTM)	Turnover Ratio	Expense Ratio
IYJ	BATS	158.81	$905,219,803	1.31	5	0.42

Ratings
Reward   C+
Risk   C-
Recent Upgrade/Downgrade

Fund Information
Fund Type   Exchange Traded Funds
Category   Industrials Sector Equity
Sub-Category   Industrials
Prospectus Objective   Unaligned
Inception Date   Jun-00
Open to New Investments   Y

Prices
Price (as of 9/30/2019)   158.82
52-Week High   161.62
52-Week Low   120.07

Total Returns (%)

3-Month	6-Month	1-Year	3-Year	5-Year
0.14	3.31	2.54	44.75	71.98

3-Year Standard Deviation   15.68
Effective Duration

Valuation
Premium/Discount (1-Year Average)   -0.02

Company Information
Provider   iShares
Manager/Tenure   Greg Savage (11), Jennifer Hsui (7),
                  Alan Mason (3), 2 others
Website   http://www.ishares.com
Address   iShares 400 Howard Street San
                  Francisco CA 94105 United States
Phone Number   800-474-2737

PERFORMANCE

Ratings History

Date	Overall Rating	Risk Rating	Reward Rating
Q3-19	C	C-	C+
Q4-18	C	C+	C
Q4-17	B	B-	A-
Q4-16	B-	C	B
Q4-15	C	C	C

Asset & Performance History

Date	NAV	1-Year Total Return
2018	128.56	-11.59
2017	147.29	23.96
2016	120.51	18.94
2015	102.82	-2.09
2014	106.62	6.85
2013	101.28	39.92

Total Assets: $905,219,803
Asset Allocation

Asset	%
Cash	0%
Stocks	100%
US Stocks	99%
Bonds	0%
US Bonds	0%
Other	0%

Services Offered: CashInvestment Plan

Investment Strategy: The investment seeks to track the investment results of the Dow Jones U.S. Industrials Index composed of U.S. equities in the industrials sector. The fund generally invests at least 90% of its assets in securities of the underlying index and in depositary receipts representing securities of the underlying index. The underlying index measures the performance of the industrials sector of the U.S. equity market. **Top Holdings:** Boeing Co   PayPal Holdings Inc   Accenture PLC Class A   Honeywell International Inc   Union Pacific Corp

---

John Hancock Multifactor Large Cap ETF

C   HOLD

Ticker	Traded On	NAV	Total Assets ($)	Dividend Yield (TTM)	Turnover Ratio	Expense Ratio
JHML	NYSE Arca	38.43	$903,157,582	1.54	6	0.34

Ratings
Reward   C
Risk   C-
Recent Upgrade/Downgrade

Fund Information
Fund Type   Exchange Traded Funds
Category   US Equity Large Cap Blend
Sub-Category   Large Blend
Prospectus Objective   Growth
Inception Date   Sep-15
Open to New Investments   Y

Prices
Price (as of 9/30/2019)   38.43
52-Week High   38.92
52-Week Low   30.10

Total Returns (%)

3-Month	6-Month	1-Year	3-Year	5-Year
1.01	4.97	4.01	43.11	

3-Year Standard Deviation   12.48
Effective Duration

Valuation
Premium/Discount (1-Year Average)   0.01

Company Information
Provider   John Hancock
Manager/Tenure   Joel P. Schneider (4), Lukas J. Smart
                  (4), Joseph F. Hohn (1)
Website   http://jhinvestments.com
Address   601 Congress Street, Boston MA
                  02210 United States
Phone Number   800-225-5913

PERFORMANCE

Ratings History

Date	Overall Rating	Risk Rating	Reward Rating
Q3-19	C	C-	C
Q4-18	C-	C-	C-
Q4-17	C	B	C+
Q4-16	D	C-	D+
Q4-15			

Asset & Performance History

Date	NAV	1-Year Total Return
2018	32.02	-6.33
2017	34.72	21.24
2016	29.07	12.67
2015	26.17	
2014		
2013		

Total Assets: $903,157,582
Asset Allocation

Asset	%
Cash	1%
Stocks	99%
US Stocks	98%
Bonds	0%
US Bonds	0%
Other	0%

Services Offered:

Investment Strategy: The investment seeks to provide investment results that closely correspond, before fees and expenses, to the performance of the John Hancock Dimensional Large Cap Index. The fund normally invests at least 80% of its net assets (plus any borrowings for investment purposes) in securities that compose the fund's index. The index is designed to comprise a subset of securities in the U.S. Universe issued by companies whose market capitalizations are larger than that of the 801st largest U.S. company at the time of reconstitution. **Top Holdings:** Apple Inc   Microsoft Corp   Amazon.com Inc   Alphabet Inc A   JPMorgan Chase & Co

SPDR® S&P Insurance ETF   B-   BUY

Ticker	Traded On	NAV	Total Assets ($)	Dividend Yield (TTM)	Turnover Ratio	Expense Ratio
KIE	NYSE Arca		$898,731,202	1.68	21	0.35

Ratings

Reward	B-
Risk	C+
Recent Upgrade/Downgrade	

Fund Information

Fund Type	Exchange Traded Funds
Category	Financials Sector Equity
Sub-Category	Financial
Prospectus Objective	Financial
Inception Date	Nov-05
Open to New Investments	Y

Prices

Price (as of 9/30/2019)	35.23
52-Week High	35.33
52-Week Low	26.73

Total Returns (%)

3-Month	6-Month	1-Year	3-Year	5-Year
2.48	12.92	12.57	50.04	83.05

3-Year Standard Deviation	12.84
Effective Duration	

Valuation

Premium/Discount (1-Year Average)	-0.03

Company Information

Provider	SPDR State Street Global Advisors
Manager/Tenure	Michael J. Feehily (7), Karl A. Schneider (4), Raymond V. Donofrio (2)
Website	http://www.spdrs.com
Address	SPDR State Street Global Advisors State Street Financial Center, 1 Lincoln Street Boston MA 02111-2900 United States
Phone Number	617-786-3000

PERFORMANCE

Ratings History

Date	Overall Rating	Risk Rating	Reward Rating
Q3-19	B-	C+	B-
Q4-18	C	C+	C
Q4-17	B+	A-	B
Q4-16	C	C	C
Q4-15	B+	B-	A

Asset & Performance History

Date	NAV	1-Year Total Return
2018	28.4	-5.86
2017	30.7	12.89
2016	27.63	19.97
2015	23.17	6.01
2014	22.22	7.61
2013	21.04	45.57

Total Assets: $898,731,202

Asset Allocation

Asset	%
Cash	0%
Stocks	100%
US Stocks	97%
Bonds	0%
US Bonds	0%
Other	0%

Services Offered: Dividend Investment Plan, CashInvestment Plan

Investment Strategy: The investment seeks to provide investment results that, before fees and expenses, correspond generally to the total return performance of an index that tracks the performance of publicly traded companies in the insurance industry. In seeking to track the performance of the S&P Insurance Select Industry Index (the "index"), the fund employs a sampling strategy. It generally invests substantially all, but at least 80%, of its total assets in the securities comprising the index. The index represents the insurance segment of the S&P Total Market Index ("S&P TMI"). The fund is non-diversified. **Top Holdings:** Assurant Inc Brown & Brown Inc Arch Capital Group Ltd First American Financial Corp Fidelity National Financial Inc

Fidelity® MSCI Utilities Index ETF   B-   BUY

Ticker	Traded On	NAV	Total Assets ($)	Dividend Yield (TTM)	Turnover Ratio	Expense Ratio
FUTY	NYSE Arca	42.46	$895,970,050	2.66	7	0.08

Ratings

Reward	B
Risk	C+
Recent Upgrade/Downgrade	Down

Fund Information

Fund Type	Exchange Traded Funds
Category	Utilities Sector Equity
Sub-Category	Utilities
Prospectus Objective	Utility
Inception Date	Oct-13
Open to New Investments	Y

Prices

Price (as of 9/30/2019)	42.49
52-Week High	42.60
52-Week Low	33.93

Total Returns (%)

3-Month	6-Month	1-Year	3-Year	5-Year
9.15	13.20	25.93	47.17	83.80

3-Year Standard Deviation	10.27
Effective Duration	

Valuation

Premium/Discount (1-Year Average)	0.03

Company Information

Provider	Fidelity Investments
Manager/Tenure	Jennifer Hsui (5), Greg Savage (5), Alan Mason (3), 2 others
Website	http://www.institutional.fidelity.com
Address	Fidelity Investments 82 Devonshire Street Boston MA 2109 United States
Phone Number	617-563-7000

PERFORMANCE

Ratings History

Date	Overall Rating	Risk Rating	Reward Rating
Q3-19	B-	C+	B
Q4-18	B-	C+	B-
Q4-17	B	B	B
Q4-16	B-	C+	B
Q4-15	C-	C	B

Asset & Performance History

Date	NAV	1-Year Total Return
2018	34.86	4.4
2017	34.47	12.32
2016	31.61	17.44
2015	27.83	-4.79
2014	30.52	26.83
2013	24.87	

Total Assets: $895,970,050

Asset Allocation

Asset	%
Cash	0%
Stocks	100%
US Stocks	100%
Bonds	0%
US Bonds	0%
Other	0%

Services Offered:

Investment Strategy: The investment seeks to provide investment returns that correspond, before fees and expenses, generally to the performance of the MSCI USA IMI Utilities Index. The fund invests at least 80% of assets in securities included in the fund's underlying index. The fund's underlying index is the MSCI USA IMI Utilities Index, which represents the performance of the utilities sector in the U.S. equity market. It may or may not hold all of the securities in the MSCI USA IMI Utilities Index. The fund is non-diversified. **Top Holdings:** NextEra Energy Inc Duke Energy Corp Dominion Energy Inc Southern Co Exelon Corp

SPDR® Nuveen S&P High Yield Municipal Bond ETF

C **HOLD**

Ticker	Traded On	NAV	Total Assets ($)	Dividend Yield (TTM)	Turnover Ratio	Expense Ratio
HYMB	NYSE Arca		$889,594,048	3.96	18	0.35

Ratings
Reward   B-
Risk   C-
Recent Upgrade/Downgrade   Down

Fund Information
Fund Type   Exchange Traded Funds
Category   US Muni Fixed Inc
Sub-Category   High Yield Muni
Prospectus Objective   Muni Bond - Natl
Inception Date   Apr-11
Open to New Investments Y

Prices
Price (as of 9/30/2019) 59.37
52-Week High   59.62
52-Week Low   55.29

Total Returns (%)

3-Month	6-Month	1-Year	3-Year	5-Year
2.47	5.41	9.41	11.89	27.90

3-Year Standard Deviation   4.1
Effective Duration   6.26

Valuation
Premium/Discount (1-Year Average)   0.03

Company Information
Provider   SPDR State Street Global Advisors
Manager/Tenure Steven M. Hlavin (8), Timothy T. Ryan (8)
Website   http://www.spdrs.com
Address   SPDR State Street Global Advisors
            State Street Financial Center, 1
            Lincoln Street Boston MA 02111-2900
            United States
Phone Number 617-786-3000

PERFORMANCE

Ratings History

Date	Overall Rating	Risk Rating	Reward Rating
Q3-19	C	C-	B-
Q4-18	C	C+	C
Q4-17	C+	B+	C
Q4-16	C	C-	C
Q4-15	C	C-	C

Asset & Performance History

Date	NAV	1-Year Total Return
2018	55.83	3.8
2017	56	3.51
2016	55.96	2.17
2015	56.96	3.7
2014	57.48	16.44
2013	51.71	-7

Total Assets: $889,594,048
Asset Allocation

Asset	%
Cash	0%
Stocks	0%
US Stocks	0%
Bonds	100%
US Bonds	89%
Other	0%

Services Offered:

Investment Strategy: The investment seeks to provide investment results that correspond generally to the price and yield performance of the Bloomberg Barclays Municipal Yield Index. The fund invests substantially all, but at least 80%, of its total assets in the securities comprising the index and in securities that the Sub-Adviser determines have economic characteristics that are substantially identical to the economic characteristics of the securities that comprise the index. The index measures the performance of USD-denominated high-yield municipal bonds issued by U.S. states, the District of Columbia, U.S. territories and local governments or agencies. It is non-diversified. **Top Holdings:** PUERTO RICO SALES TAX FING CORP SALES TAX REV 5%   PUERTO RICO SALES TAX FING CORP SALES TAX REV 4.75%   GOLDEN ST TOB SECURITIZATION CORP CALIF TOB SETTLEMENT REV 5%   BUCKEYE OHIO TOB SETTLEMENT FING AUTH 5.88%   BUCKEYE OHIO TOB SETTLEMENT FING AUTH 5.75%

IQ Merger Arbitrage ETF

C **HOLD**

Ticker	Traded On	NAV	Total Assets ($)	Dividend Yield (TTM)	Turnover Ratio	Expense Ratio
MNA	NYSE Arca	32.04	$882,563,955	0		0.77

Ratings
Reward   C
Risk   C
Recent Upgrade/Downgrade

Fund Information
Fund Type   Exchange Traded Funds
Category   Market Neutral
Sub-Category   Market Neutral
Prospectus Objective   Growth
Inception Date   Nov-09
Open to New Investments Y

Prices
Price (as of 9/30/2019) 32.05
52-Week High   32.31
52-Week Low   31.26

Total Returns (%)

3-Month	6-Month	1-Year	3-Year	5-Year
1.46	0.20	1.10	10.24	17.88

3-Year Standard Deviation   3.17
Effective Duration   0.39

Valuation
Premium/Discount (1-Year Average)   0.06

Company Information
Provider   IndexIQ
Manager/Tenure Greg Barrato (8), James Harrison (1)
Website   http://www.indexiq.com
Address   IndexIQ 800 Westchester Avenue,
            Suite N-611 Rye Brook NY 10573
            United States
Phone Number 888-934-0777

PERFORMANCE

Ratings History

Date	Overall Rating	Risk Rating	Reward Rating
Q3-19	C	C	C
Q4-18	C+	C	C+
Q4-17	C+	B	C
Q4-16	C	C-	C+
Q4-15	C	C	C

Asset & Performance History

Date	NAV	1-Year Total Return
2018	31.68	2.08
2017	31.03	5.86
2016	29.31	4.86
2015	28.01	1.27
2014	27.9	5.28
2013	26.5	7.65

Total Assets: $882,563,955
Asset Allocation

Asset	%
Cash	1%
Stocks	84%
US Stocks	76%
Bonds	0%
US Bonds	0%
Other	0%

Services Offered:

Investment Strategy: The investment seeks investment results that correspond generally to the price and yield performance of its underlying index, the IQ Merger Arbitrage Index. The fund invests at least 80% of its net assets, plus the amount of any borrowings for investment purposes, in the investments included in its underlying index. The underlying index seeks to employ a systematic investment process designed to identify opportunities in companies whose equity securities trade in developed markets, including the U.S., and which are involved in announced mergers, acquisitions and other buyout-related transactions. The fund is non-diversified. **Top Holdings:** Recv Xlv Short Ms   Payb Xlv Short Ms   Payb Xlk Short Ms   Recv Xlk Short Ms   Celgene Corp

SPDR® SSGA US Large Cap Low Volatility Index ETF　　　　B　BUY

Ticker	Traded On	NAV	Total Assets ($)	Dividend Yield (TTM)	Turnover Ratio	Expense Ratio
LGLV	NYSE Arca		$881,915,966	1.81	32	0.12

Ratings
Reward	B
Risk	C+
Recent Upgrade/Downgrade	Up

Fund Information
Fund Type	Exchange Traded Funds
Category	US Equity Large Cap Blend
Sub-Category	Large Blend
Prospectus Objective	Income
Inception Date	Feb-13
Open to New Investments	Y

Prices
Price (as of 9/30/2019)	111.48
52-Week High	112.40
52-Week Low	84.44

Total Returns (%)
3-Month	6-Month	1-Year	3-Year	5-Year
2.74	10.85	16.96	52.52	83.95

3-Year Standard Deviation	9.74
Effective Duration	

Valuation
Premium/Discount (1-Year Average)	0.11

Company Information
Provider	SPDR State Street Global Advisors
Manager/Tenure	Michael J. Feehily (6), Karl A. Schneider (4), Juan Acevedo (0)
Website	http://www.spdrs.com
Address	SPDR State Street Global Advisors State Street Financial Center, 1 Lincoln Street Boston MA 02111-2900 United States
Phone Number	617-786-3000

PERFORMANCE

Ratings History
Date	Overall Rating	Risk Rating	Reward Rating
Q3-19	B	C+	B
Q4-18	C	C-	C
Q4-17	B+	A+	B-
Q4-16	C	C-	B-
Q4-15	C	C-	C

Asset & Performance History
Date	NAV	1-Year Total Return
2018	88.93	0.54
2017	90.27	17.82
2016	80.05	11.25
2015	73.84	2.36
2014	74.34	16.65
2013	68.38	

Total Assets: $881,915,966
Asset Allocation
Asset	%
Cash	0%
Stocks	100%
US Stocks	97%
Bonds	0%
US Bonds	0%
Other	0%

Services Offered:

Investment Strategy: The investment seeks to provide investment results that, before fees and expenses, correspond generally to the total return performance of the SSGA US Large Cap Low Volatility Index. The fund generally invests substantially all, but at least 80%, of its total assets in the securities comprising the index. The index is designed to measure the performance of the stocks of U.S. large capitalization companies that exhibit low volatility. Volatility is a statistical measurement of the magnitude of movements in a stock's price over time. The fund is non-diversified. **Top Holdings:** Republic Services Inc Class A Chubb Ltd Berkshire Hathaway Inc B CME Group Inc Class A Marsh & McLennan Companies Inc

---

Invesco BulletShares 2021 High Yield Corporate Bond ETF　　　　C+　HOLD

Ticker	Traded On	NAV	Total Assets ($)	Dividend Yield (TTM)	Turnover Ratio	Expense Ratio
BSJL	NYSE Arca	24.55	$878,959,357	5.16	14	0.42

Ratings
Reward	C
Risk	C+
Recent Upgrade/Downgrade	

Fund Information
Fund Type	Exchange Traded Funds
Category	US Fixed Income
Sub-Category	High Yield Bond
Prospectus Objective	Corp Bond-High Yld
Inception Date	Sep-14
Open to New Investments	Y

Prices
Price (as of 9/30/2019)	24.63
52-Week High	24.89
52-Week Low	23.39

Total Returns (%)
3-Month	6-Month	1-Year	3-Year	5-Year
0.77	2.12	4.50	15.85	27.00

3-Year Standard Deviation	2.77
Effective Duration	1.41

Valuation
Premium/Discount (1-Year Average)	0.14

Company Information
Provider	Invesco
Manager/Tenure	Jeremy Neisewander (3), Peter Hubbard (1), Jeffrey W. Kernagis (1), 1 other
Website	http://www.invesco.com/us
Address	Invesco 11 Greenway Plaza, Ste. 2500 Houston TX 77046 United States
Phone Number	800-659-1005

PERFORMANCE

Ratings History
Date	Overall Rating	Risk Rating	Reward Rating
Q3-19	C+	C+	C
Q4-18	C	C+	C
Q4-17	B-	B	C+
Q4-16	C-	C-	C-
Q4-15	U		

Asset & Performance History
Date	NAV	1-Year Total Return
2018	23.71	0.01
2017	24.88	5.54
2016	24.67	13.81
2015	22.84	-1.48
2014	24.35	
2013		

Total Assets: $878,959,357
Asset Allocation
Asset	%
Cash	6%
Stocks	0%
US Stocks	0%
Bonds	94%
US Bonds	84%
Other	0%

Services Offered:

Investment Strategy: The investment seeks to track the investment results (before fees and expenses) of the Nasdaq BulletShares® USD High Yield Corporate Bond 2021 Index (the "underlying index"). The fund generally will invest at least 80% of its total assets in securities that comprise the underlying index. The underlying index seeks to measure the performance of a portfolio of U.S. dollar-denominated high yield corporate bonds (commonly known as "junk bonds") with maturities or, in some cases, "effective maturities" in the year 2021 (collectively, "2021 Bonds"). The fund is non-diversified. **Top Holdings:** Sprint Corporation 7.25% T-Mobile USA, Inc. 6.5% DISH DBS Corporation 6.75% Bombardier Inc. 8.75% Meredith Corp 6.88%

Invesco High Yield Equity Dividend Achievers™ ETF

C   HOLD

Ticker	Traded On	NAV	Total Assets ($)	Dividend Yield (TTM)	Turnover Ratio	Expense Ratio
PEY	NAS CM	18.31	$876,335,044	3.8	50	0.53

Ratings

Reward	C
Risk	C
Recent Upgrade/Downgrade	Down

Fund Information

Fund Type	Exchange Traded Funds
Category	US Equity Mid Cap
Sub-Category	Mid-Cap Value
Prospectus Objective	Growth & Inc
Inception Date	Dec-04
Open to New Investments	Y

Prices

Price (as of 9/30/2019)	18.31
52-Week High	18.58
52-Week Low	15.14

Total Returns (%)

3-Month	6-Month	1-Year	3-Year	5-Year
1.85	3.68	6.43	28.88	77.84

3-Year Standard Deviation	12.37
Effective Duration	

Valuation

Premium/Discount (1-Year Average)	-0.01

Company Information

Provider	Invesco
Manager/Tenure	Peter Hubbard (12), Michael Jeanette (11), Tony Seisser (5)
Website	http://www.invesco.com/us
Address	Invesco 11 Greenway Plaza, Ste. 2500 Houston TX 77046 United States
Phone Number	800-659-1005

PERFORMANCE

Ratings History

Date	Overall Rating	Risk Rating	Reward Rating
Q3-19	C	C	C
Q4-18	C	C+	C
Q4-17	B+	A	B
Q4-16	B	C+	B+
Q4-15	B-	C+	B-

Asset & Performance History

Date	NAV	1-Year Total Return
2018	15.85	-7.35
2017	17.8	8.64
2016	16.94	31.56
2015	13.34	2.44
2014	13.48	17.84
2013	11.85	30.4

Total Assets: $876,335,044

Asset Allocation

Asset	%
Cash	0%
Stocks	100%
US Stocks	100%
Bonds	0%
US Bonds	0%
Other	0%

Services Offered:

Investment Strategy: The investment seeks to track the investment results (before fees and expenses) of the NASDAQ US Dividend Achievers™ 50 Index (the "underlying index"). The fund generally will invest at least 90% of its total assets in the securities that comprise the underlying index. Strictly in accordance with its guidelines and mandated procedures, Nasdaq, Inc. includes common stocks in the underlying index that have a consistent record of dividend increases, principally on the basis of dividend yield and consistent growth in dividends. **Top Holdings:** Vector Group Ltd AT&T Inc Lazard Ltd Shs A ONEOK Inc Altria Group Inc

iShares MSCI Spain Capped ETF

C-   HOLD

Ticker	Traded On	NAV	Total Assets ($)	Dividend Yield (TTM)	Turnover Ratio	Expense Ratio
EWP	NYSE Arca	27.84	$860,295,887	3.29	21	0.47

Ratings

Reward	D+
Risk	C
Recent Upgrade/Downgrade	Down

Fund Information

Fund Type	Exchange Traded Funds
Category	Europe Equity Large Cap
Sub-Category	Miscellaneous Region
Prospectus Objective	Europe Stock
Inception Date	Mar-96
Open to New Investments	Y

Prices

Price (as of 9/30/2019)	27.84
52-Week High	30.05
52-Week Low	26.11

Total Returns (%)

3-Month	6-Month	1-Year	3-Year	5-Year
-4.13	-2.49	-3.10	14.70	-13.65

3-Year Standard Deviation	17.03
Effective Duration	

Valuation

Premium/Discount (1-Year Average)	-0.12

Company Information

Provider	iShares
Manager/Tenure	Diane Hsiung (11), Greg Savage (11), Jennifer Hsui (6), 3 others
Website	http://www.ishares.com
Address	iShares 400 Howard Street San Francisco CA 94105 United States
Phone Number	800-474-2737

PERFORMANCE

Ratings History

Date	Overall Rating	Risk Rating	Reward Rating
Q3-19	C-	C	D+
Q4-18	D+	D+	C-
Q4-17	C	C	C
Q4-16	D	D	D
Q4-15	C	C	C

Asset & Performance History

Date	NAV	1-Year Total Return
2018	26.96	-15.07
2017	32.85	26.96
2016	26.58	-2.17
2015	28.45	-15.84
2014	34.99	-4.68
2013	38.33	34.26

Total Assets: $860,295,887

Asset Allocation

Asset	%
Cash	0%
Stocks	100%
US Stocks	0%
Bonds	0%
US Bonds	0%
Other	0%

Services Offered: CashInvestment Plan

Investment Strategy: The investment seeks to track the investment results of the MSCI Spain 25/50 Index. The fund will at all times invest at least 80% of its assets in the securities of its underlying index and in depositary receipts representing securities in its underlying index. The underlying index is a free float-adjusted market capitalization-weighted index with a capping methodology applied to issuer weights so that no single issuer of a component exceeds 25% of the underlying index weight, and all issuers with a weight above 5% do not cumulatively exceed 50% of the underlying index weight. The fund is non-diversified. **Top Holdings:** Iberdrola SA Banco Santander SA Telefonica SA Banco Bilbao Vizcaya Argentaria SA Industria De Diseno Textil SA

Invesco BulletShares 2023 Corporate Bond ETF   C+   HOLD

Ticker	Traded On	NAV	Total Assets ($)	Dividend Yield (TTM)	Turnover Ratio	Expense Ratio
BSCN	NYSE Arca	21.22	$859,455,336	3.02	0	0.1

Ratings
Reward	C+
Risk	C+
Recent Upgrade/Downgrade	

Fund Information
Fund Type	Exchange Traded Funds
Category	US Fixed Income
Sub-Category	Target Maturity
Prospectus Objective	Corp Bond - Gen
Inception Date	Sep-14
Open to New Investments	Y

Prices
Price (as of 9/30/2019)	21.29
52-Week High	21.40
52-Week Low	20.00

Total Returns (%)
3-Month	6-Month	1-Year	3-Year	5-Year
1.56	3.74	8.45	9.12	21.85

3-Year Standard Deviation	2.92
Effective Duration	3.49

Valuation
Premium/Discount (1-Year Average)	0.28

Company Information
Provider	Invesco
Manager/Tenure	Jeremy Neisewander (3), Peter Hubbard (1), Jeffrey W. Kernagis (1), 1 other
Website	http://www.invesco.com/us
Address	Invesco 11 Greenway Plaza, Ste. 2500 Houston TX 77046 United States
Phone Number	800-659-1005

PERFORMANCE

Ratings History
Date	Overall Rating	Risk Rating	Reward Rating
Q3-19	C+	C+	C+
Q4-18	C	C+	C-
Q4-17	B	A	C
Q4-16	D+	C-	D+
Q4-15	U		

Asset & Performance History
Date	NAV	1-Year Total Return
2018	20.13	-0.35
2017	20.79	4.41
2016	20.43	6.01
2015	19.86	0.67
2014	20.32	
2013		

Total Assets: $859,455,336

Asset Allocation
Asset	%
Cash	1%
Stocks	0%
US Stocks	0%
Bonds	98%
US Bonds	85%
Other	0%

Services Offered:

Investment Strategy: The investment seeks to track the investment results (before fees and expenses) of the Nasdaq BulletShares® USD Corporate Bond 2023 Index (the "underlying index"). The fund generally will invest at least 80% of its total assets in securities that comprise the underlying index. The underlying index seeks to measure the performance of a portfolio of U.S. dollar-denominated investment grade corporate bonds with maturities or, in some cases, "effective maturities" in the year 2023 (collectively, "2023 Bonds"). The fund is non-diversified. **Top Holdings:** CVS Health Corp 3.7% Apple Inc. 2.4% Verizon Communications Inc. 5.15% Bank of America Corporation 3.3% Wells Fargo & Company 3.07%

---

iShares Global Energy ETF   C-   HOLD

Ticker	Traded On	NAV	Total Assets ($)	Dividend Yield (TTM)	Turnover Ratio	Expense Ratio
IXC	NYSE Arca	30.60	$858,460,610	3.98	6	0.46

Ratings
Reward	C-
Risk	C-
Recent Upgrade/Downgrade	

Fund Information
Fund Type	Exchange Traded Funds
Category	Energy Sector Equity
Sub-Category	Equity Energy
Prospectus Objective	Natl Res
Inception Date	Nov-01
Open to New Investments	Y

Prices
Price (as of 9/30/2019)	30.56
52-Week High	38.52
52-Week Low	27.97

Total Returns (%)
3-Month	6-Month	1-Year	3-Year	5-Year
-5.99	-8.34	-16.72	2.99	-16.55

3-Year Standard Deviation	17.56
Effective Duration	

Valuation
Premium/Discount (1-Year Average)	-0.12

Company Information
Provider	iShares
Manager/Tenure	Greg Savage (11), Jennifer Hsui (7), Alan Mason (3), 2 others
Website	http://www.ishares.com
Address	iShares 400 Howard Street San Francisco CA 94105 United States
Phone Number	800-474-2737

PERFORMANCE

Ratings History
Date	Overall Rating	Risk Rating	Reward Rating
Q3-19	C-	C-	C-
Q4-18	C	C	C
Q4-17	C	C	C
Q4-16	C-	D	C
Q4-15	D+	D+	D+

Asset & Performance History
Date	NAV	1-Year Total Return
2018	29.43	-14.59
2017	35.55	5.45
2016	34.83	28.03
2015	28.02	-22.09
2014	37.2	-11.6
2013	43.2	16.23

Total Assets: $858,460,610

Asset Allocation
Asset	%
Cash	0%
Stocks	100%
US Stocks	51%
Bonds	0%
US Bonds	0%
Other	0%

Services Offered: CashInvestment Plan

Investment Strategy: The investment seeks to track the S&P Global 1200 Energy IndexTM. The fund generally invests at least 90% of its assets in securities of the underlying index and in depositary receipts representing securities of the underlying index. It may invest the remainder of its assets in certain futures, options and swap contracts, cash and cash equivalents, as well as in securities not included in the underlying index. The index measures the performance of companies that the index provider deems to be part of the energy sector of the economy and that the index provider believes are important to global markets. The fund is non-diversified. **Top Holdings:** Exxon Mobil Corp Chevron Corp Total SA BP PLC Royal Dutch Shell PLC Class A

iShares Global Consumer Staples ETF   C   HOLD

Ticker	Traded On	NAV	Total Assets ($)	Dividend Yield (TTM)	Turnover Ratio	Expense Ratio
KXI	NYSE Arca	54.76	$856,935,918	2.4	7	0.46

Ratings
Reward   C
Risk   C-
Recent Upgrade/Downgrade

Fund Information
Fund Type   Exchange Traded Funds
Category   Consumer Goods & Svcs
Sub-Category   Consumer Defensive
Prospectus Objective   Unaligned
Inception Date   Sep-06
Open to New Investments   Y

Prices
Price (as of 9/30/2019)   54.82
52-Week High   55.27
52-Week Low   44.53

Total Returns (%)

3-Month	6-Month	1-Year	3-Year	5-Year
3.94	7.31	11.78	18.54	41.46

3-Year Standard Deviation   10.64
Effective Duration

Valuation
Premium/Discount (1-Year Average)   0.01

Company Information
Provider   iShares
Manager/Tenure   Greg Savage (11), Jennifer Hsui (7),
                  Alan Mason (3), 2 others
Website   http://www.ishares.com
Address   iShares 400 Howard Street San
                  Francisco CA 94105 United States
Phone Number   800-474-2737

PERFORMANCE

Ratings History

Date	Overall Rating	Risk Rating	Reward Rating
Q3-19	C	C-	C
Q4-18	C-	C-	C-
Q4-17	B-	B	C+
Q4-16	C	C	C+
Q4-15	C	C	C

Asset & Performance History

Date	NAV	1-Year Total Return
2018	46.08	-10.59
2017	53.04	17.37
2016	46.19	1.34
2015	46.61	6.11
2014	44.91	6.73
2013	43.06	19.93

Total Assets: $856,935,918
Asset Allocation

Asset	%
Cash	1%
Stocks	99%
US Stocks	53%
Bonds	0%
US Bonds	0%
Other	0%

Services Offered:

Investment Strategy: The investment seeks to track the S&P Global 1200 Consumer Staples (Sector) Capped IndexTM. The fund generally invests at least 90% of its assets in securities of the underlying index and in depositary receipts representing securities of the underlying index. It may invest the remainder of its assets in certain futures, options and swap contracts, cash and cash equivalents, as well as in securities not included in the underlying index. The index measures the performance of global equities in the consumer staples sector. **Top Holdings:** Nestle SA Procter & Gamble Co Coca-Cola Co Walmart Inc PepsiCo Inc

---

SPDR® Bloomberg Barclays Emerging Markets Local Bond ETF   C   HOLD

Ticker	Traded On	NAV	Total Assets ($)	Dividend Yield (TTM)	Turnover Ratio	Expense Ratio
EBND	NYSE Arca		$847,737,226	3.85	43	0.3

Ratings
Reward   C
Risk   C+
Recent Upgrade/Downgrade

Fund Information
Fund Type   Exchange Traded Funds
Category   Emerging Mkts Fixed Inc
Sub-Category   Emerging-Markets Local-Currency Bond
Prospectus Objective   Worldwide Bond
Inception Date   Feb-11
Open to New Investments   Y

Prices
Price (as of 9/30/2019)   27.21
52-Week High   28.15
52-Week Low   25.85

Total Returns (%)

3-Month	6-Month	1-Year	3-Year	5-Year
-0.93	3.17	8.87	5.71	1.08

3-Year Standard Deviation   8.55
Effective Duration   6.41

Valuation
Premium/Discount (1-Year Average)   0.20

Company Information
Provider   SPDR State Street Global Advisors
Manager/Tenure   Abhishek Kumar (8), Peter Spano (4),
                  Jonathan Camissar (0), 1 other
Website   http://www.spdrs.com
Address   SPDR State Street Global Advisors
                  State Street Financial Center, 1
                  Lincoln Street Boston MA 02111-2900
                  United States
Phone Number   617-786-3000

PERFORMANCE

Ratings History

Date	Overall Rating	Risk Rating	Reward Rating
Q3-19	C	C+	C
Q4-18	C-	C-	C-
Q4-17	C	C	C
Q4-16	D+	C-	D+
Q4-15	D	D	D

Asset & Performance History

Date	NAV	1-Year Total Return
2018	26.43	-6.58
2017	29.61	13.03
2016	26.59	7.09
2015	24.83	-11.97
2014	28.21	-4
2013	29.45	-5.89

Total Assets: $847,737,226
Asset Allocation

Asset	%
Cash	1%
Stocks	0%
US Stocks	0%
Bonds	99%
US Bonds	1%
Other	0%

Services Offered:

Investment Strategy: The investment seeks to provide investment results that correspond generally to the price and yield performance of the Bloomberg Barclays EM Local Currency Government Diversified Index. The fund generally invests substantially all, but at least 80%, of its total assets in the securities comprising the index or in securities that the Sub-Adviser determines have economic characteristics that are substantially identical to the economic characteristics of the securities that comprise the index. The index is designed to measure the performance of the fixed-rate local currency sovereign debt of emerging market countries. The fund is non-diversified. **Top Holdings:** Brazil (Federative Republic) 10% Brazil Federative Rep 10% Letra Tesouro Nacional Bills 01/22 0.00000 Philippine Government Sr Unsecured 07/31 8 Poland (Republic of) 2.5%

Schwab 1000 ETF   C   HOLD

Ticker	Traded On	NAV	Total Assets ($)	Dividend Yield (TTM)	Turnover Ratio	Expense Ratio
SCHK	NYSE Arca	29.17	$846,074,863	1.74		0.05

Ratings
Reward   C
Risk   C+
Recent Upgrade/Downgrade

Fund Information
Fund Type   Exchange Traded Funds
Category   US Equity Large Cap Blend
Sub-Category   Large Blend
Prospectus Objective   Growth & Inc
Inception Date   Oct-17
Open to New Investments   Y

Prices
Price (as of 9/30/2019)   29.16
52-Week High   29.75
52-Week Low   23.02

Total Returns (%)

3-Month	6-Month	1-Year	3-Year	5-Year
0.67	4.57	3.57		

3-Year Standard Deviation
Effective Duration

Valuation
Premium/Discount (1-Year Average)   -0.02

Company Information
Provider   Schwab ETFs
Manager/Tenure   Christopher Bliss (1), Ferian Juwono
                  (1), Sabya Sinha (1), 1 other
Website   http://www.schwabfunds.com
Address   Schwab ETFs United States
Phone Number   800-435-4000

PERFORMANCE

Ratings History

Date	Overall Rating	Risk Rating	Reward Rating
Q3-19	C	C+	C
Q4-18	C-	C	D+
Q4-17	U		
Q4-16			
Q4-15			

Asset & Performance History

Date	NAV	1-Year Total Return
2018	24.53	-4.89
2017	26.22	
2016		
2015		
2014		
2013		

Total Assets: $846,074,863
Asset Allocation

Asset	%
Cash	0%
Stocks	100%
US Stocks	99%
Bonds	0%
US Bonds	0%
Other	0%

Services Offered:

Investment Strategy: The investment seeks to track as closely as possible, before fees and expenses, the total return of the Schwab 1000 Index®. It is the fund's policy that under normal circumstances it will invest at least 90% of its net assets (including, for this purpose, any borrowings for investment purposes) in stocks included in the index. The Schwab 1000 Index is a float-adjusted market capitalization weighted index that includes the 1,000 largest stocks of publicly traded companies in the United States, with size being determined by market capitalization (total market value of all shares outstanding). **Top Holdings:** Microsoft Corp   Apple Inc   Amazon.com Inc   Facebook Inc A   Berkshire Hathaway Inc B

First Trust Mid Cap Core AlphaDEX® Fund   C-   HOLD

Ticker	Traded On	NAV	Total Assets ($)	Dividend Yield (TTM)	Turnover Ratio	Expense Ratio
FNX	NAS CM	67.48	$843,446,657	1.12	114	0.62

Ratings
Reward   C
Risk   C-
Recent Upgrade/Downgrade   Down

Fund Information
Fund Type   Exchange Traded Funds
Category   US Equity Mid Cap
Sub-Category   Mid-Cap Blend
Prospectus Objective   Growth
Inception Date   May-07
Open to New Investments   Y

Prices
Price (as of 9/30/2019)   67.54
52-Week High   70.98
52-Week Low   54.08

Total Returns (%)

3-Month	6-Month	1-Year	3-Year	5-Year
-2.13	-0.02	-3.81	31.72	43.59

3-Year Standard Deviation   16.35
Effective Duration

Valuation
Premium/Discount (1-Year Average)   -0.01

Company Information
Provider   First Trust
Manager/Tenure   Jon C. Erickson (12), Daniel J.
                  Lindquist (12), David G. McGarel (12),
                  3 others
Website   http://www.ftportfolios.com/
Address   First Trust 120 E. Liberty Drive, Suite
                  400 Wheaton IL 60187 United States
Phone Number   800-621-1675

PERFORMANCE

Ratings History

Date	Overall Rating	Risk Rating	Reward Rating
Q3-19	C-	C-	C
Q4-18	C-	C-	C-
Q4-17	B	B	B
Q4-16	C	C-	C+
Q4-15	C	C+	C

Asset & Performance History

Date	NAV	1-Year Total Return
2018	57.83	-11.11
2017	65.65	17.62
2016	56.35	18.67
2015	48.03	-8.1
2014	52.79	5.55
2013	50.4	37.46

Total Assets: $843,446,657
Asset Allocation

Asset	%
Cash	0%
Stocks	100%
US Stocks	100%
Bonds	0%
US Bonds	0%
Other	0%

Services Offered:

Investment Strategy: The investment seeks investment results that correspond generally to the price and yield (before the fund's fees and expenses) of an equity index called the Nasdaq AlphaDEX® Mid Cap Core Index. The fund will normally invest at least 90% of its net assets (including investment borrowings) in common stocks that comprise the index. The index is designed to select stocks from the NASDAQ US 600 Mid Cap Index (the "base index") that may generate positive alpha, or risk-adjusted returns, relative to traditional indices through the use of the AlphaDEX® selection methodology. **Top Holdings:** Roku Inc Class A   NovoCure Ltd   Alteryx Inc Class A   FTI Consulting Inc   Insulet Corp

First Trust Rising Dividend Achievers ETF

C+   **HOLD**

Ticker	Traded On	NAV	Total Assets ($)	Dividend Yield (TTM)	Turnover Ratio	Expense Ratio
RDVY	NAS CM	31.82	$832,154,496	1.67	40	0.5

Ratings
Reward   C+
Risk   C+
Recent Upgrade/Downgrade

Fund Information
Fund Type   Exchange Traded Funds
Category   US Equity Large Cap Value
Sub-Category   Large Value
Prospectus Objective   Income
Inception Date   Jan-14
Open to New Investments Y

Prices
Price (as of 9/30/2019)   31.85
52-Week High   32.57
52-Week Low   24.76

Total Returns (%)

3-Month	6-Month	1-Year	3-Year	5-Year
1.81	5.45	2.57	50.38	68.61

3-Year Standard Deviation   15.94
Effective Duration

Valuation
Premium/Discount (1-Year Average)   0.04

Company Information
Provider   First Trust
Manager/Tenure   Jon C. Erickson (5), Daniel J. Lindquist (5), David G. McGarel (5), 3 others
Website   http://www.ftportfolios.com/
Address   First Trust 120 E. Liberty Drive, Suite 400 Wheaton IL 60187 United States
Phone Number   800-621-1675

Ratings History

Date	Overall Rating	Risk Rating	Reward Rating
Q3-19	C+	C+	C+
Q4-18	C	C+	C
Q4-17	B	B	B+
Q4-16	C	C-	C+
Q4-15	D+	C-	C

Asset & Performance History

Date	NAV	1-Year Total Return
2018	26.53	-9.72
2017	29.84	22.56
2016	24.67	21.88
2015	20.73	-2.88
2014	21.79	11.5
2013		

Total Assets: $832,154,496
Asset Allocation

Asset	%
Cash	0%
Stocks	100%
US Stocks	98%
Bonds	0%
US Bonds	0%
Other	0%

Services Offered:

Investment Strategy: The investment seeks investment results that correspond generally to the price and yield (before fees and expenses) of the NASDAQ US Rising Dividend Achievers Index. The fund will normally invest at least 90% of its net assets (including investment borrowings) in the common stock and depositary receipts that comprise the index. The index is designed to provide access to a diversified portfolio of small, mid and large capitalization companies with a history of raising their dividends while exhibiting the characteristics to continue to do so in the future by including companies with strong cash balances, low debt and increasing earnings. **Top Holdings:** KLA Corp Teradyne Inc Lam Research Corp Applied Materials Inc Amgen Inc

Xtrackers MSCI Europe Hedged Equity ETF

C+   **HOLD**

Ticker	Traded On	NAV	Total Assets ($)	Dividend Yield (TTM)	Turnover Ratio	Expense Ratio
DBEU	NYSE Arca	29.82	$829,026,481	3.28	7	0.45

Ratings
Reward   C
Risk   C+
Recent Upgrade/Downgrade

Fund Information
Fund Type   Exchange Traded Funds
Category   Europe Equity Large Cap
Sub-Category   Europe Stock
Prospectus Objective   Europe Stock
Inception Date   Oct-13
Open to New Investments Y

Prices
Price (as of 9/30/2019)   29.83
52-Week High   29.83
52-Week Low   24.49

Total Returns (%)

3-Month	6-Month	1-Year	3-Year	5-Year
1.70	6.52	7.71	33.61	43.78

3-Year Standard Deviation   10.12
Effective Duration

Valuation
Premium/Discount (1-Year Average)   0.03

Company Information
Provider   DWS
Manager/Tenure   Patrick Dwyer (2), Bryan Richards (2), Shlomo Bassous (1)
Website   http://dws.com
Address   DWS 210 West 10th Street Kansas City MO 64105-1614 United States
Phone Number

Ratings History

Date	Overall Rating	Risk Rating	Reward Rating
Q3-19	C+	C+	C
Q4-18	C	C+	D+
Q4-17	B	B	B-
Q4-16	C	C	C
Q4-15	C-	C+	C-

Asset & Performance History

Date	NAV	1-Year Total Return
2018	25.24	-8.75
2017	28.5	14.61
2016	25.44	8.14
2015	25.97	4.2
2014	26.21	4.45
2013	26.2	

Total Assets: $829,026,481
Asset Allocation

Asset	%
Cash	2%
Stocks	98%
US Stocks	2%
Bonds	0%
US Bonds	0%
Other	0%

Services Offered:

Investment Strategy: The investment seeks investment results that correspond generally to the performance, before fees and expenses, of the MSCI Europe US Dollar Hedged Index. The fund, using a "passive" or indexing investment approach, seeks investment results that correspond generally to the performance, of the underlying index, which is designed to track the performance of the developed markets in Europe, while mitigating exposure to fluctuations between the value of the U.S. dollar and the currencies of the countries included in the underlying index. It will invest at least 80% of its total assets in component securities of the underlying index. **Top Holdings:** Nestle SA Roche Holding AG Dividend Right Cert. Novartis AG HSBC Holdings PLC BP PLC

Invesco S&P 500® Top 50 ETF   C+   HOLD

Ticker	Traded On	NAV	Total Assets ($)	Dividend Yield (TTM)	Turnover Ratio	Expense Ratio
XLG	NYSE Arca	212.29	$828,096,881	1.8	8	0.2

Ratings
Reward   B-
Risk   C
Recent Upgrade/Downgrade   Up

Fund Information
Fund Type   Exchange Traded Funds
Category   US Equity Large Cap Blend
Sub-Category   Large Blend
Prospectus Objective   Growth
Inception Date   May-05
Open to New Investments   Y

Prices
Price (as of 9/30/2019)   212.44
52-Week High   217.27
52-Week Low   167.99

Total Returns (%)

3-Month	6-Month	1-Year	3-Year	5-Year
0.63	4.20	2.89	47.10	71.92

3-Year Standard Deviation   12.2
Effective Duration

Valuation
Premium/Discount (1-Year Average)   0.02

Company Information
Provider   Invesco
Manager/Tenure   Peter Hubbard (1), Michael Jeanette (1), Tony Seisser (1)
Website   http://www.invesco.com/us
Address   Invesco 11 Greenway Plaza, Ste. 2500 Houston TX 77046 United States
Phone Number   800-659-1005

PERFORMANCE

Ratings History

Date	Overall Rating	Risk Rating	Reward Rating
Q3-19	C+	C	B-
Q4-18	C	C	C+
Q4-17	B	B+	B
Q4-16	B-	C	B
Q4-15	C+	C	C+

Asset & Performance History

Date	NAV	1-Year Total Return
2018	179.73	-3.48
2017	189.75	23.05
2016	157.39	10.49
2015	144.63	4.23
2014	141.75	11.41
2013	129.85	28.78

Total Assets: $828,096,881
Asset Allocation

Asset	%
Cash	0%
Stocks	100%
US Stocks	100%
Bonds	0%
US Bonds	0%
Other	0%

Services Offered:

Investment Strategy: The investment seeks to track the investment results (before fees and expenses) of the S&P 500® Top 50 Index (the "underlying index"). The fund generally will invest at least 90% of its total assets in the securities that comprise the underlying index. The index provider compiles, maintains and calculates the underlying index, which consists of the 50 largest members of the S&P 500® Index by float-adjusted market capitalization. The underlying index's components are weighted by float-adjusted market capitalization. The fund is non-diversified. **Top Holdings:** Microsoft Corp Apple Inc Amazon.com Inc Facebook Inc A Berkshire Hathaway Inc B

IQ Hedge Multi-Strategy Tracker ETF   C   HOLD

Ticker	Traded On	NAV	Total Assets ($)	Dividend Yield (TTM)	Turnover Ratio	Expense Ratio
QAI	NYSE Arca	30.44	$826,374,163	1.8		0.8

Ratings
Reward   C
Risk   C-
Recent Upgrade/Downgrade

Fund Information
Fund Type   Exchange Traded Funds
Category   Multialternative
Sub-Category   Multialternative
Prospectus Objective   Growth
Inception Date   Mar-09
Open to New Investments   Y

Prices
Price (as of 9/30/2019)   30.42
52-Week High   30.69
52-Week Low   28.81

Total Returns (%)

3-Month	6-Month	1-Year	3-Year	5-Year
-0.27	0.95	0.96	5.82	7.13

3-Year Standard Deviation   3.7
Effective Duration   3.66

Valuation
Premium/Discount (1-Year Average)   -0.04

Company Information
Provider   IndexIQ
Manager/Tenure   Greg Barrato (8), James Harrison (1)
Website   http://www.indexiq.com
Address   IndexIQ 800 Westchester Avenue, Suite N-611 Rye Brook NY 10573 United States
Phone Number   888-934-0777

PERFORMANCE

Ratings History

Date	Overall Rating	Risk Rating	Reward Rating
Q3-19	C	C-	C
Q4-18	C-	C	D+
Q4-17	B-	B+	C
Q4-16	C-	C	D+
Q4-15	C	C+	C

Asset & Performance History

Date	NAV	1-Year Total Return
2018	28.92	-3.21
2017	30.45	6.24
2016	28.66	0.7
2015	28.46	-2.53
2014	29.34	2.77
2013	28.93	5.15

Total Assets: $826,374,163
Asset Allocation

Asset	%
Cash	22%
Stocks	28%
US Stocks	5%
Bonds	47%
US Bonds	38%
Other	2%

Services Offered:

Investment Strategy: The investment seeks investment results that correspond generally to the price and yield performance of its underlying index, the IQ Hedge Multi-Strategy Index. The fund is a "fund of funds" which means it invests, under normal circumstances, at least 80% of its net assets, plus the amount of any borrowings for investment purposes, in the investments included in its underlying index, which includes underlying funds. The underlying index consists of a number of components ("underlying index Components") selected in accordance with IndexIQ's rules-based methodology of such underlying index. **Top Holdings:** iShares Short Treasury Bond ETF SPDR® Blmbg Barclays 1-3 Mth T-Bill ETF iShares Floating Rate Bond ETF iShares iBoxx $ Invmt Grade Corp Bd ETF Vanguard FTSE All-Wld ex-US SmCp ETF

iShares iBonds Dec 2023 Term Corporate ETF   C+   HOLD

Ticker	Traded On	NAV	Total Assets ($)	Dividend Yield (TTM)	Turnover Ratio	Expense Ratio
IBDO	NYSE Arca	25.53	$824,528,021	3.03	8	0.1

Ratings

Reward	C+
Risk	C+
Recent Upgrade/Downgrade	

Fund Information

Fund Type	Exchange Traded Funds
Category	US Fixed Income
Sub-Category	Target Maturity
Prospectus Objective	Corp Bond - Gen
Inception Date	Mar-15
Open to New Investments	Y

Prices

Price (as of 9/30/2019)	25.60
52-Week High	25.69
52-Week Low	23.99

Total Returns (%)

3-Month	6-Month	1-Year	3-Year	5-Year
1.46	4.29	8.69	9.42	

3-Year Standard Deviation	2.88
Effective Duration	3.39

Valuation

Premium/Discount (1-Year Average)	0.22

Company Information

Provider	iShares
Manager/Tenure	James Mauro (4), Scott Radell (4)
Website	http://www.ishares.com
Address	iShares 400 Howard Street San Francisco CA 94105 United States
Phone Number	800-474-2737

PERFORMANCE

Ratings History

Date	Overall Rating	Risk Rating	Reward Rating
Q3-19	C+	C+	C+
Q4-18	C-	C-	C-
Q4-17	B-	A-	C
Q4-16	D+	C-	D+
Q4-15	U		

Asset & Performance History

Date	NAV	1-Year Total Return
2018	24.17	-0.2
2017	24.98	4.5
2016	24.58	5.82
2015	23.93	
2014		
2013		

Total Assets: $824,528,021

Asset Allocation

Asset	%
Cash	0%
Stocks	0%
US Stocks	0%
Bonds	97%
US Bonds	84%
Other	0%

Services Offered:

Investment Strategy: The investment seeks to track the investment results of the Bloomberg Barclays December 2023 Maturity Corporate Index which composed of U.S. dollar-denominated, investment-grade corporate bonds maturing in 2023. The fund generally will invest at least 90% of its assets in the component securities of the underlying index. The underlying index is composed of U.S. dollar-denominated, taxable, investment-grade corporate bonds scheduled to mature after December 31, 2022 and before December 16, 2023. **Top Holdings:** CVS Health Corp 3.7% Apple Inc. 2.4% Bank of America Corporation 3.3% Wells Fargo & Company 3.07% Dell International L.L.C. and EMC Corporation 5.45%

iShares Edge MSCI Intl Quality Factor ETF   C+   HOLD

Ticker	Traded On	NAV	Total Assets ($)	Dividend Yield (TTM)	Turnover Ratio	Expense Ratio
IQLT	NYSE Arca	29.66	$815,604,166	2.26	29	0.3

Ratings

Reward	C+
Risk	C+
Recent Upgrade/Downgrade	Up

Fund Information

Fund Type	Exchange Traded Funds
Category	Global Equity Large Cap
Sub-Category	Foreign Large Blend
Prospectus Objective	World Stock
Inception Date	Jan-15
Open to New Investments	Y

Prices

Price (as of 9/30/2019)	29.68
52-Week High	30.57
52-Week Low	24.90

Total Returns (%)

3-Month	6-Month	1-Year	3-Year	5-Year
-1.95	2.78	2.85	25.56	

3-Year Standard Deviation	11.03
Effective Duration	

Valuation

Premium/Discount (1-Year Average)	0.11

Company Information

Provider	iShares
Manager/Tenure	Diane Hsiung (4), Jennifer Hsui (4), Greg Savage (4), 3 others
Website	http://www.ishares.com
Address	iShares 400 Howard Street San Francisco CA 94105 United States
Phone Number	800-474-2737

PERFORMANCE

Ratings History

Date	Overall Rating	Risk Rating	Reward Rating
Q3-19	C+	C+	C+
Q4-18	D+	C-	D+
Q4-17	C+	B-	C+
Q4-16	D	D	D+
Q4-15	U		

Asset & Performance History

Date	NAV	1-Year Total Return
2018	25.8	-10.86
2017	29.68	24.08
2016	24.52	0.6
2015	25.08	
2014		
2013		

Total Assets: $815,604,166

Asset Allocation

Asset	%
Cash	1%
Stocks	99%
US Stocks	1%
Bonds	0%
US Bonds	0%
Other	0%

Services Offered:

Investment Strategy: The investment seeks to track the investment results of the MSCI World ex USA Sector Neutral Quality Index. The fund generally will invest at least 90% of its assets in the component securities of the underlying index and in investments that have economic characteristics that are substantially identical to the component securities of the underlying index. The index measures the performance of international developed large- and mid-capitalization stocks exhibiting relatively higher quality characteristics as identified through three fundamental variables: return on equity, earnings variability and debt-to-equity. **Top Holdings:** Nestle SA Roche Holding AG Dividend Right Cert. AIA Group Ltd Allianz SE Total SA

iShares Morningstar Large-Cap ETF   C   HOLD

Ticker	Traded On	NAV	Total Assets ($)	Dividend Yield (TTM)	Turnover Ratio	Expense Ratio
JKD	NYSE Arca	167.94	$814,510,510	2.47	38	0.2

Ratings
Reward   C+
Risk   C
Recent Upgrade/Downgrade

Fund Information
Fund Type	Exchange Traded Funds
Category	US Equity Large Cap Blend
Sub-Category	Large Blend
Prospectus Objective	Growth
Inception Date	Jun-04
Open to New Investments	Y

Prices
Price (as of 9/30/2019)	167.94
52-Week High	170.80
52-Week Low	133.93

Total Returns (%)
3-Month	6-Month	1-Year	3-Year	5-Year
1.39	5.41	1.77	39.78	64.48

3-Year Standard Deviation   12.18
Effective Duration

Valuation
Premium/Discount (1-Year Average)   0.00

Company Information
Provider	iShares
Manager/Tenure	Greg Savage (11), Jennifer Hsui (7), Alan Mason (3), 2 others
Website	http://www.ishares.com
Address	iShares 400 Howard Street San Francisco CA 94105 United States
Phone Number	800-474-2737

PERFORMANCE

Ratings History

Date	Overall Rating	Risk Rating	Reward Rating
Q3-19	C	C	C+
Q4-18	C	C-	C
Q4-17	B	B	B
Q4-16	B-	C	B
Q4-15	C+	C	C+

Asset & Performance History

Date	NAV	1-Year Total Return
2018	142.58	-8.39
2017	158.79	22.11
2016	132.56	13.58
2015	119.15	-1.12
2014	123.46	16.84
2013	107.75	34.13

Total Assets: $814,510,510
Asset Allocation

Asset	%
Cash	0%
Stocks	100%
US Stocks	100%
Bonds	0%
US Bonds	0%
Other	0%

Services Offered:

Investment Strategy: The investment seeks to track the investment results of the Morningstar® Large Core IndexSM composed of large-capitalization U.S. equities. The fund generally invests at least 90% of its assets in securities of the underlying index and in depositary receipts representing securities of the underlying index. The underlying index measures the performance of stocks issued by large-capitalization companies that have exhibited average "growth" and "value" characteristics as determined by Morningstar, Inc.'s ("Morningstar" or the "index provider") proprietary index methodology. **Top Holdings:** Apple Inc Berkshire Hathaway Inc B Johnson & Johnson The Home Depot Inc Bank of America Corporation

iShares U.S. Healthcare Providers ETF   B-   BUY

Ticker	Traded On	NAV	Total Assets ($)	Dividend Yield (TTM)	Turnover Ratio	Expense Ratio
IHF	NYSE Arca	161.69	$808,431,460	4.36	48	0.43

Ratings
Reward   B
Risk   C
Recent Upgrade/Downgrade   Up

Fund Information
Fund Type	Exchange Traded Funds
Category	Healthcare Sector Equity
Sub-Category	Health
Prospectus Objective	Health
Inception Date	May-06
Open to New Investments	Y

Prices
Price (as of 9/30/2019)	161.70
52-Week High	201.83
52-Week Low	151.11

Total Returns (%)
3-Month	6-Month	1-Year	3-Year	5-Year
-5.16	-3.67	-15.67	36.57	61.78

3-Year Standard Deviation   16.58
Effective Duration

Valuation
Premium/Discount (1-Year Average)   0.00

Company Information
Provider	iShares
Manager/Tenure	Greg Savage (11), Jennifer Hsui (7), Alan Mason (3), 2 others
Website	http://www.ishares.com
Address	iShares 400 Howard Street San Francisco CA 94105 United States
Phone Number	800-474-2737

PERFORMANCE

Ratings History

Date	Overall Rating	Risk Rating	Reward Rating
Q3-19	B-	C	B
Q4-18	B	C+	B
Q4-17	B	B	B-
Q4-16	B-	C+	B
Q4-15	B+	B	B+

Asset & Performance History

Date	NAV	1-Year Total Return
2018	165.15	9.6
2017	156.76	25.48
2016	125.18	0.9
2015	124.38	5.3
2014	118.35	27.21
2013	93.22	36.71

Total Assets: $808,431,460
Asset Allocation

Asset	%
Cash	0%
Stocks	100%
US Stocks	100%
Bonds	0%
US Bonds	0%
Other	0%

Services Offered:

Investment Strategy: The investment seeks to track the investment results of the Dow Jones U.S. Select Health Care Providers Index composed of U.S. equities in the healthcare providers sector. The fund generally invests at least 90% of its assets in securities of the underlying index and in depositary receipts representing securities of the underlying index. The underlying index measures the performance of the healthcare providers sector of the U.S. equity market. The fund may invest the remainder of its assets in certain futures, options and swap contracts, cash and cash equivalents. It is non-diversified. **Top Holdings:** UnitedHealth Group Inc Anthem Inc CVS Health Corp Humana Inc Laboratory Corp of America Holdings

JPMorgan Diversified Return U.S. Equity ETF

C   **HOLD**

Ticker	Traded On	NAV	Total Assets ($)	Dividend Yield (TTM)	Turnover Ratio	Expense Ratio
JPUS	NYSE Arca	75.90	$804,488,690	1.95	32	0.19

Ratings
Reward	C
Risk	C-
Recent Upgrade/Downgrade	

Fund Information
Fund Type	Exchange Traded Funds
Category	US Equity Large Cap Blend
Sub-Category	Large Blend
Prospectus Objective	Growth & Inc
Inception Date	Sep-15
Open to New Investments	Y

Prices
Price (as of 9/30/2019)	75.92
52-Week High	76.66
52-Week Low	61.37

Total Returns (%)
3-Month	6-Month	1-Year	3-Year	5-Year
1.38	3.86	3.97	37.22	

3-Year Standard Deviation	11.44
Effective Duration	

Valuation
Premium/Discount (1-Year Average)	0.02

Company Information
Provider	JPMorgan
Manager/Tenure	Jonathan Msika (2), Yazann Romahi (2), Joe Staines (2), 1 other
Website	http://www.jpmorganfunds.com
Address	JPMorgan 270 Park Avenue New York NY 10017-2070 United States
Phone Number	800-480-4111

PERFORMANCE

Ratings History
Date	Overall Rating	Risk Rating	Reward Rating
Q3-19	C	C-	C
Q4-18	C-	C-	C-
Q4-17	C	B	C+
Q4-16	D	C-	D+
Q4-15			

Asset & Performance History
Date	NAV	1-Year Total Return
2018	64.88	-6.02
2017	70.46	20.6
2016	59.15	12.08
2015	53.18	
2014		
2013		

Total Assets: $804,488,690

Asset Allocation
Asset	%
Cash	0%
Stocks	100%
US Stocks	99%
Bonds	0%
US Bonds	0%
Other	0%

Services Offered:

Investment Strategy: The investment seeks investment results that closely correspond, before fees and expenses, to the performance of the JP Morgan Diversified Factor US Equity Index. The fund will invest at least 80% of its net assets in securities included in the underlying index. The underlying index is comprised of U.S. equity securities selected to represent a diversified set of factor characteristics: value, momentum, and quality. The fund's securities are large- and mid-cap equity securities of U.S. companies, including common stock, preferred stock and real estate investment trusts (REITs). **Top Holdings:** L3Harris Technologies Inc Fidelity National Information Services Inc Starbucks Corp Zoetis Inc Class A The Estee Lauder Companies Inc Class A

ETFMG Alternative Harvest ETF

D+   **SELL**

Ticker	Traded On	NAV	Total Assets ($)	Dividend Yield (TTM)	Turnover Ratio	Expense Ratio
MJ	NYSE Arca		$800,954,402	4.66	97	0.75

Ratings
Reward	D+
Risk	D
Recent Upgrade/Downgrade	Down

Fund Information
Fund Type	Exchange Traded Funds
Category	Misc
Sub-Category	Miscellaneous Sector
Prospectus Objective	Unaligned
Inception Date	Dec-15
Open to New Investments	Y

Prices
Price (as of 9/30/2019)	20.76
52-Week High	42.48
52-Week Low	20.76

Total Returns (%)
3-Month	6-Month	1-Year	3-Year	5-Year
-31.93	-40.12	-43.79	-11.92	

3-Year Standard Deviation	40.3
Effective Duration	

Valuation
Premium/Discount (1-Year Average)	0.13

Company Information
Provider	ETFMG
Manager/Tenure	Samuel R. Masucci (1), Devin Ryder (1), Donal Bishnoi (0), 1 other
Website	http://www.etfmg.com
Address	ETFMG 30 Maple Street, Suite 2 NJ United States
Phone Number	

PERFORMANCE

Ratings History
Date	Overall Rating	Risk Rating	Reward Rating
Q3-19	D+	D	D+
Q4-18	C	C	C-
Q4-17	C	B	C-
Q4-16	D	D	D
Q4-15			

Asset & Performance History
Date	NAV	1-Year Total Return
2018	24.87	-23
2017	32.46	29.91
2016	24.18	9.65
2015	23.57	
2014		
2013		

Total Assets: $800,954,402

Asset Allocation
Asset	%
Cash	0%
Stocks	100%
US Stocks	27%
Bonds	0%
US Bonds	0%
Other	0%

Services Offered:

Investment Strategy: The investment seeks to provide investment results that, before fees and expenses, correspond generally to the total return performance of the Prime Alternative Harvest Index. The fund will invest at least 80% of its total assets, exclusive of collateral held from securities lending, in the component securities of the index and in ADRs and GDRs based on the component securities in the index. The index is concentrated in the Pharmaceuticals and Tobacco industries and tracks the performance of the exchange-listed common stock (or corresponding ADRs or GDRs) of companies across the globe. The fund is non-diversified. **Top Holdings:** Aurora Cannabis Inc GW Pharmaceuticals PLC ADR Cronos Group Inc Canopy Growth Corp Tilray Inc

WisdomTree U.S. Dividend ex-Financials Fund   C   HOLD

Ticker	Traded On	NAV	Total Assets ($)	Dividend Yield (TTM)	Turnover Ratio	Expense Ratio
DTN	NYSE Arca	87.39	$799,595,716	3.38	32	0.38

Ratings
Reward   C
Risk   C-
Recent Upgrade/Downgrade

Fund Information
Fund Type	Exchange Traded Funds
Category	US Equity Large Cap Value
Sub-Category	Large Value
Prospectus Objective	Growth & Inc
Inception Date	Jun-06
Open to New Investments	Y

Prices
Price (as of 9/30/2019)	87.43
52-Week High	91.27
52-Week Low	73.26

Total Returns (%)

3-Month	6-Month	1-Year	3-Year	5-Year
2.11	3.01	-0.30	23.61	43.16

3-Year Standard Deviation   12.68
Effective Duration

Valuation
Premium/Discount (1-Year Average)   0.01

Company Information
Provider	WisdomTree
Manager/Tenure	Richard A. Brown (11), Thomas J. Durante (11), Karen Q. Wong (11)
Website	http://www.wisdomtree.com
Address	WisdomTree 245 Park Avenue, 35th floor New York NY 10167 United States
Phone Number	866-909-9473

PERFORMANCE

Ratings History

Date	Overall Rating	Risk Rating	Reward Rating
Q3-19	C	C-	C
Q4-18	C	C-	C
Q4-17	B-	B	B-
Q4-16	C+	C-	B
Q4-15	C	C-	C

Asset & Performance History

Date	NAV	1-Year Total Return
2018	77.04	-9.39
2017	88.33	13.78
2016	80.25	18.1
2015	70.26	-5.23
2014	76.63	15.06
2013	68.77	27.64

Total Assets: $799,595,716
Asset Allocation

Asset	%
Cash	0%
Stocks	100%
US Stocks	100%
Bonds	0%
US Bonds	0%
Other	0%

Services Offered:

Investment Strategy: The investment seeks to track the price and yield performance, before fees and expenses, of the WisdomTree U.S. Dividend ex-Financials Index. The fund normally invests at least 95% of its total assets (exclusive of collateral held from securities lending) in component securities of the index and investments that have economic characteristics that are substantially identical to the economic characteristics of such component securities. The index is comprised of the 10 highest dividend-yielding companies in each sector, selected from the three hundred largest companies by market value in the WisdomTree U.S. Dividend Index. The fund is non-diversified. **Top Holdings:** CenturyLink Inc AT&T Inc General Electric Co Targa Resources Corp Ford Motor Co

WisdomTree U.S. SmallCap Earnings Fund   C-   HOLD

Ticker	Traded On	NAV	Total Assets ($)	Dividend Yield (TTM)	Turnover Ratio	Expense Ratio
EES	NYSE Arca	35.65	$798,628,374	1.47	45	0.38

Ratings
Reward   C-
Risk   C-
Recent Upgrade/Downgrade

Fund Information
Fund Type	Exchange Traded Funds
Category	US Equity Small Cap
Sub-Category	Small Blend
Prospectus Objective	Small Company
Inception Date	Feb-07
Open to New Investments	Y

Prices
Price (as of 9/30/2019)	35.60
52-Week High	39.39
52-Week Low	30.28

Total Returns (%)

3-Month	6-Month	1-Year	3-Year	5-Year
-0.35	-2.04	-7.90	30.67	51.70

3-Year Standard Deviation   19.34
Effective Duration

Valuation
Premium/Discount (1-Year Average)   0.04

Company Information
Provider	WisdomTree
Manager/Tenure	Richard A. Brown (11), Thomas J. Durante (11), Karen Q. Wong (11)
Website	http://www.wisdomtree.com
Address	WisdomTree 245 Park Avenue, 35th floor New York NY 10167 United States
Phone Number	866-909-9473

PERFORMANCE

Ratings History

Date	Overall Rating	Risk Rating	Reward Rating
Q3-19	C-	C-	C-
Q4-18	C-	C-	C-
Q4-17	B+	B	A-
Q4-16	C	D+	B-
Q4-15	C	C-	C

Asset & Performance History

Date	NAV	1-Year Total Return
2018	32.02	-9.96
2017	36.14	12.56
2016	32.43	29.95
2015	25.25	-7.08
2014	27.53	2.19
2013	27.22	45.41

Total Assets: $798,628,374
Asset Allocation

Asset	%
Cash	0%
Stocks	100%
US Stocks	99%
Bonds	0%
US Bonds	0%
Other	0%

Services Offered:

Investment Strategy: The investment seeks to track the price and yield performance, before fees and expenses, of the WisdomTree U.S. SmallCap Index. Under normal circumstances, at least 95% of the fund's total assets (exclusive of collateral held from securities lending) will be invested in component securities of the index and investments that have economic characteristics that are substantially identical to the economic characteristics of such component securities. The index is a fundamentally weighted index that is comprised of earnings-generating companies within the small-capitalization segment of the U.S. stock market. The fund is non-diversified. **Top Holdings:** Lithia Motors Inc Class A KB Home Taylor Morrison Home Corp Class A Meritage Homes Corp Dana Inc

Legg Mason Low Volatility High Dividend ETF

C   HOLD

Ticker	Traded On	NAV	Total Assets ($)	Dividend Yield (TTM)	Turnover Ratio	Expense Ratio
LVHD	NAS CM	33.56	$790,246,428	2.66	44	0.27

Ratings

Reward	C+
Risk	C
Recent Upgrade/Downgrade	

Fund Information

Fund Type	Exchange Traded Funds
Category	US Equity Large Cap Value
Sub-Category	Large Value
Prospectus Objective	Income
Inception Date	Dec-15
Open to New Investments	Y

Prices

Price (as of 9/30/2019)	33.59
52-Week High	33.59
52-Week Low	27.85

Total Returns (%)

3-Month	6-Month	1-Year	3-Year	5-Year
4.73	6.40	12.82	32.98	

3-Year Standard Deviation	9.06
Effective Duration	

Valuation

Premium/Discount (1-Year Average)	0.03

Company Information

Provider	Legg Mason
Manager/Tenure	Michael J. LaBella (3), Russell Shtern (3), Robert Y. Wang (3)
Website	http://www.leggmason.com
Address	Legg Mason/Western 100 International Drive Baltimore MD 21202 United States
Phone Number	877-721-1926

PERFORMANCE

Ratings History

Date	Overall Rating	Risk Rating	Reward Rating
Q3-19	C	C	C+
Q4-18	C	C	C+
Q4-17	C-	B+	C-
Q4-16	D-	C	C
Q4-15			

Asset & Performance History

Date	NAV	1-Year Total Return
2018	28.76	-5.17
2017	31.47	13.96
2016	28.54	17.49
2015	24.74	
2014		
2013		

Total Assets: $790,246,428

Asset Allocation

Asset	%
Cash	1%
Stocks	99%
US Stocks	99%
Bonds	0%
US Bonds	0%
Other	0%

Services Offered:

Investment Strategy: The investment seeks to track the investment results of the QS Low Volatility High Dividend Index (the "underlying index"). The fund will invest at least 80% of its net assets, plus borrowings for investment purposes, if any, in securities that compose the underlying index. The underlying index is composed of equity securities of U.S. companies with relatively high yield and low price and earnings volatility. **Top Holdings:** Crown Castle International Corp   Procter & Gamble Co   PepsiCo Inc   Merck & Co Inc   American Electric Power Co Inc

---

WisdomTree International Equity Fund

C-   HOLD

Ticker	Traded On	NAV	Total Assets ($)	Dividend Yield (TTM)	Turnover Ratio	Expense Ratio
DWM	NYSE Arca	49.75	$788,478,761	3.68	15	0.48

Ratings

Reward	C-
Risk	C-
Recent Upgrade/Downgrade	

Fund Information

Fund Type	Exchange Traded Funds
Category	Global Equity Large Cap
Sub-Category	Foreign Large Value
Prospectus Objective	Foreign Stock
Inception Date	Jun-06
Open to New Investments	Y

Prices

Price (as of 9/30/2019)	49.72
52-Week High	53.25
52-Week Low	44.98

Total Returns (%)

3-Month	6-Month	1-Year	3-Year	5-Year
-2.44	-0.36	-2.97	17.48	13.97

3-Year Standard Deviation	11.11
Effective Duration	

Valuation

Premium/Discount (1-Year Average)	-0.12

Company Information

Provider	WisdomTree
Manager/Tenure	Richard A. Brown (11), Thomas J. Durante (11), Karen Q. Wong (11)
Website	http://www.wisdomtree.com
Address	WisdomTree 245 Park Avenue, 35th floor New York NY 10167 United States
Phone Number	866-909-9473

PERFORMANCE

Ratings History

Date	Overall Rating	Risk Rating	Reward Rating
Q3-19	C-	C-	C-
Q4-18	D+	C-	D+
Q4-17	B-	B-	B-
Q4-16	D+	C-	D+
Q4-15	C-	C-	C-

Asset & Performance History

Date	NAV	1-Year Total Return
2018	46.62	-13.55
2017	55.82	23.45
2016	46.67	2.89
2015	46.95	-2.6
2014	49.8	-3.52
2013	53.9	21.74

Total Assets: $788,478,761

Asset Allocation

Asset	%
Cash	0%
Stocks	100%
US Stocks	1%
Bonds	0%
US Bonds	0%
Other	0%

Services Offered:

Investment Strategy: The investment seeks to track the price and yield performance, before fees and expenses, of the WisdomTree International Equity Index. At least 95% of the fund's total assets (exclusive of collateral held from securities lending) will be invested in component securities of the index and investments that have economic characteristics that are substantially identical to the economic characteristics of such component securities. The index is a fundamentally weighted index that is comprised of companies in the industrialized world, excluding Canada and the United States, that pay regular cash dividends. It is non-diversified. **Top Holdings:** Nestle SA   China Mobile Ltd   HSBC Holdings PLC   BP PLC   Novartis AG

SPDR® S&P International Small Cap ETF   D+   SELL

Ticker	Traded On	NAV	Total Assets ($)	Dividend Yield (TTM)	Turnover Ratio	Expense Ratio
GWX	NYSE Arca		$786,805,497	3.92	29	0.4

Ratings
Reward   D
Risk   C
Recent Upgrade/Downgrade   Down

Fund Information
Fund Type	Exchange Traded Funds
Category	Globa Eq Mid/Small Cap
Sub-Category	Foreign Small/Mid Blend
Prospectus Objective	Foreign Stock
Inception Date	Apr-07
Open to New Investments	Y

Prices
Price (as of 9/30/2019)	29.39
52-Week High	34.40
52-Week Low	26.70

Total Returns (%)
3-Month	6-Month	1-Year	3-Year	5-Year
-1.72	-2.55	-10.79	7.95	19.61

3-Year Standard Deviation   12.1
Effective Duration

Valuation
Premium/Discount (1-Year Average)   -0.14

Company Information
Provider	SPDR State Street Global Advisors
Manager/Tenure	Michael J. Feehily (8), Karl A. Schneider (4), Teddy Wong (2)
Website	http://www.spdrs.com
Address	SPDR State Street Global Advisors State Street Financial Center, 1 Lincoln Street Boston MA 02111-2900 United States
Phone Number	617-786-3000

PERFORMANCE

| Date | 1/1/18 | 4/11/18 | 7/22/18 | 11/4/18 | 2/15/19 | 6/18/19 | 9/29/19 |

Ratings History
Date	Overall Rating	Risk Rating	Reward Rating
Q3-19	D+	C	D
Q4-18	D+	C-	D+
Q4-17	B+	B	B+
Q4-16	C	C-	C
Q4-15	C	C+	C

Asset & Performance History
Date	NAV	1-Year Total Return
2018	27.92	-19.11
2017	35.53	28.33
2016	29.17	6.57
2015	28.36	5.67
2014	27.56	-6.05
2013	33.29	21.82

Total Assets: $786,805,497
Asset Allocation
Asset	%
Cash	1%
Stocks	99%
US Stocks	1%
Bonds	0%
US Bonds	0%
Other	0%

Services Offered:

Investment Strategy: The investment seeks investment results that, before fees and expenses, correspond generally to the total return performance of the S&P Developed Ex-U.S. under USD2 Billion Index. The fund generally invests substantially all, but at least 80%, of its total assets in the securities comprising the index and in depositary receipts based on securities comprising the index. The index is a market capitalization weighted index designed to define and measure the investable universe of publicly traded small-cap companies, as defined by the index, domiciled in developed countries outside the United States. It is non-diversified. **Top Holdings:** Wihlborgs Fastigheter AB   Amarin Corp PLC ADR   Barco NV   Premier Investment Co   NIPPON REIT Investment Corp

iShares Micro-Cap ETF   C-   HOLD

Ticker	Traded On	NAV	Total Assets ($)	Dividend Yield (TTM)	Turnover Ratio	Expense Ratio
IWC	NYSE Arca	88.14	$784,477,187	1.16	25	0.6

Ratings
Reward   D+
Risk   C-
Recent Upgrade/Downgrade

Fund Information
Fund Type	Exchange Traded Funds
Category	US Equity Small Cap
Sub-Category	Small Blend
Prospectus Objective	Growth
Inception Date	Aug-05
Open to New Investments	Y

Prices
Price (as of 9/30/2019)	88.15
52-Week High	104.35
52-Week Low	77.77

Total Returns (%)
3-Month	6-Month	1-Year	3-Year	5-Year
-5.57	-5.21	-14.71	16.52	36.85

3-Year Standard Deviation   18.02
Effective Duration

Valuation
Premium/Discount (1-Year Average)   -0.02

Company Information
Provider	iShares
Manager/Tenure	Greg Savage (11), Jennifer Hsui (7), Alan Mason (3), 2 others
Website	http://www.ishares.com
Address	iShares 400 Howard Street San Francisco CA 94105 United States
Phone Number	800-474-2737

PERFORMANCE

| Date | 12/26/17 | 4/5/18 | 7/16/18 | 10/30/18 | 2/11/19 | 6/17/19 | 9/30/19 |

Ratings History
Date	Overall Rating	Risk Rating	Reward Rating
Q3-19	C-	C-	D+
Q4-18	C-	C-	C-
Q4-17	B+	B	A-
Q4-16	C	C-	B-
Q4-15	C	C-	C

Asset & Performance History
Date	NAV	1-Year Total Return
2018	82.37	-13.07
2017	95.57	12.72
2016	85.76	20.53
2015	72.1	-5.04
2014	77.02	3.53
2013	75.24	45.38

Total Assets: $784,477,187
Asset Allocation
Asset	%
Cash	0%
Stocks	100%
US Stocks	99%
Bonds	0%
US Bonds	0%
Other	0%

Services Offered:

Investment Strategy: The investment seeks to track the investment results of the Russell Microcap Index, which measures the performance of the microcap sector of the U.S. equity market. The fund generally invests at least 90% of its assets in securities of the underlying index and in depositary receipts representing securities of the underlying index. It may invest the remainder of its assets in certain futures, options and swap contracts, cash and cash equivalents, as well as in securities not included in the underlying index, but which the advisor believes will help the fund track the underlying index. **Top Holdings:** Independence Realty Trust Inc   Perficient Inc   CSW Industrials Inc   Middlesex Water Co   M/I Homes Inc

SPDR® S&P International Dividend ETF   C+   HOLD

Ticker	Traded On	NAV	Total Assets ($)	Dividend Yield (TTM)	Turnover Ratio	Expense Ratio
DWX	NYSE Arca		$781,555,436	4.34	47	0.45

Ratings
Reward	C+
Risk	C+
Recent Upgrade/Downgrade	Up

Fund Information
Fund Type	Exchange Traded Funds
Category	Global Equity Large Cap
Sub-Category	Foreign Large Value
Prospectus Objective	Foreign Stock
Inception Date	Feb-08
Open to New Investments	Y

Prices
Price (as of 9/30/2019)	38.95
52-Week High	39.99
52-Week Low	33.98

Total Returns (%)
3-Month	6-Month	1-Year	3-Year	5-Year
0.06	4.46	7.62	22.47	6.72

3-Year Standard Deviation	8.9
Effective Duration	

Valuation
Premium/Discount (1-Year Average)	-0.14

Company Information
Provider	SPDR State Street Global Advisors
Manager/Tenure	Michael J. Feehily (8), Karl A. Schneider (4), Ted Janowsky (2)
Website	http://www.spdrs.com
Address	SPDR State Street Global Advisors State Street Financial Center, 1 Lincoln Street Boston MA 02111-2900 United States
Phone Number	617-786-3000

PERFORMANCE

Ratings History
Date	Overall Rating	Risk Rating	Reward Rating
Q3-19	C+	C+	C+
Q4-18	C-	C-	C-
Q4-17	C	C	C+
Q4-16	D+	D+	D+
Q4-15	D+	D+	D+

Asset & Performance History
Date	NAV	1-Year Total Return
2018	34.95	-11.19
2017	41.25	18.43
2016	36.24	12.84
2015	33.62	-16.59
2014	42.42	-5.44
2013	47.3	7.65

Total Assets: $781,555,436

Asset Allocation
Asset	%
Cash	0%
Stocks	100%
US Stocks	0%
Bonds	0%
US Bonds	0%
Other	0%

Services Offered:

Investment Strategy: The investment seeks to provide investment results that, before fees and expenses, correspond generally to the total return performance of the S&P International Dividend Opportunities® Index. The fund generally invests substantially all, but at least 80%, of its total assets in the securities comprising the index and in depositary receipts based on securities comprising the index. The index is designed to measure the performance of 100 high-yielding international common stocks. The fund is non-diversified. **Top Holdings:** EDP - Energias de Portugal SA   BCE Inc   Eni SpA   Orange SA   Enagas SA

ProShares Ultra Financials   C   HOLD

Ticker	Traded On	NAV	Total Assets ($)	Dividend Yield (TTM)	Turnover Ratio	Expense Ratio
UYG	NYSE Arca	46.92	$779,318,552	1.05	10	0.95

Ratings
Reward	C+
Risk	C-
Recent Upgrade/Downgrade	

Fund Information
Fund Type	Exchange Traded Funds
Category	Trading Tools
Sub-Category	Trading--Leveraged Equity
Prospectus Objective	Financial
Inception Date	Jan-07
Open to New Investments	Y

Prices
Price (as of 9/30/2019)	46.90
52-Week High	48.06
52-Week Low	29.07

Total Returns (%)
3-Month	6-Month	1-Year	3-Year	5-Year
2.86	13.77	9.82	99.06	133.14

3-Year Standard Deviation	27.5
Effective Duration	

Valuation
Premium/Discount (1-Year Average)	-0.10

Company Information
Provider	ProShares
Manager/Tenure	Michael Neches (6), Tarak Davé (1)
Website	http://www.proshares.com
Address	ProShares 7501 Wisconsin Avenue, Suite 1000 Bethesda MD 20814 United States
Phone Number	866-776-5125

PERFORMANCE

Ratings History
Date	Overall Rating	Risk Rating	Reward Rating
Q3-19	C	C-	C+
Q4-18	C	C-	C
Q4-17	B+	C+	A+
Q4-16	C	C-	C+
Q4-15	C+	C	B-

Asset & Performance History
Date	NAV	1-Year Total Return
2018	32.63	-22.52
2017	42.59	39.28
2016	30.77	31.18
2015	23.67	-4.06
2014	24.85	27.39
2013	19.63	74.3

Total Assets: $779,318,552

Asset Allocation
Asset	%
Cash	-100%
Stocks	200%
US Stocks	197%
Bonds	0%
US Bonds	0%
Other	1%

Services Offered:

Investment Strategy: The investment seeks daily investment results, before fees and expenses, that correspond to two times (2x) the daily performance of the Dow Jones U.S. Financials℠ Index. The fund invests in financial instruments that ProShare Advisors believes, in combination, should produce daily returns consistent with the fund's investment objective. The index seeks to measure the performance of certain companies in the financial services sector of the U.S. equity market. The fund is non-diversified. **Top Holdings:** Dj U.S. Financials Index Swap Citibank Na   Dj U.S. Financials Index Swap Ubs Ag   Dj U.S. Financials Index Swap Societe Generale   Ishares U.S. Financials (Iyf) Swap Goldman Sachs International   Dj U.S. Financials Index Swap Bnp Paribas

---

Fidelity® Total Bond ETF

C+   HOLD

Ticker	Traded On	NAV	Total Assets ($)	Dividend Yield (TTM)	Turnover Ratio	Expense Ratio
FBND	NYSE Arca	51.61	$774,302,257	2.92	91	0.36

Ratings
Reward	C+
Risk	C+
Recent Upgrade/Downgrade	Up

Fund Information
Fund Type	Exchange Traded Funds
Category	US Fixed Income
Sub-Category	Intermediate Core-Plus Bond
Prospectus Objective	Income
Inception Date	Oct-14
Open to New Investments	Y

Prices
Price (as of 9/30/2019)	51.70
52-Week High	52.16
52-Week Low	47.95

Total Returns (%)
3-Month	6-Month	1-Year	3-Year	5-Year
2.00	5.40	9.80	10.40	19.22

3-Year Standard Deviation	2.98
Effective Duration	5.25

Valuation
Premium/Discount (1-Year Average)	0.22

Company Information
Provider	Fidelity Investments
Manager/Tenure	Michael Foggin (4), Ford E. O'Neil (4), Michael Plage (4), 2 others
Website	http://www.institutional.fidelity.com
Address	Fidelity Investments 82 Devonshire Street Boston MA 2109 United States
Phone Number	617-563-7000

PERFORMANCE

Ratings History
Date	Overall Rating	Risk Rating	Reward Rating
Q3-19	C+	C+	C+
Q4-18	C-	C-	D+
Q4-17	C+	B	C
Q4-16	D+	C-	D+
Q4-15	U		

Asset & Performance History
Date	NAV	1-Year Total Return
2018	48.35	-0.66
2017	50.12	4.07
2016	49.41	6.64
2015	47.67	-1.43
2014	49.92	
2013		

Total Assets: $774,302,257
Asset Allocation
Asset	%
Cash	3%
Stocks	0%
US Stocks	0%
Bonds	96%
US Bonds	89%
Other	0%

Services Offered:

Investment Strategy: The investment seeks a high level of current income. Normally, the fund invests at least 80% of assets in debt securities of all types and repurchase agreements for those securities. It uses the Bloomberg Barclays U.S. Universal Bond Index as a guide in allocating assets across the investment-grade, high yield, and emerging market asset classes. The fund invests up to 20% of assets in lower-quality debt securities. It is managed to have similar overall interest rate risk to the index. **Top Holdings:** United States Treasury Bonds 3% United States Treasury Notes 2.5% United States Treasury Notes 2% United States Treasury Notes 1.88% United States Treasury Notes 3.12%

VictoryShares US 500 Volatility Wtd ETF

C   HOLD

Ticker	Traded On	NAV	Total Assets ($)	Dividend Yield (TTM)	Turnover Ratio	Expense Ratio
CFA	NAS CM	52.93	$770,169,538	1.39	46	0.35

Ratings
Reward	C
Risk	C-
Recent Upgrade/Downgrade	

Fund Information
Fund Type	Exchange Traded Funds
Category	US Equity Large Cap Blend
Sub-Category	Large Blend
Prospectus Objective	Income
Inception Date	Jul-14
Open to New Investments	Y

Prices
Price (as of 9/30/2019)	52.93
52-Week High	53.83
52-Week Low	41.41

Total Returns (%)
3-Month	6-Month	1-Year	3-Year	5-Year
0.54	4.90	3.98	42.71	66.62

3-Year Standard Deviation	12.96
Effective Duration	

Valuation
Premium/Discount (1-Year Average)	0.00

Company Information
Provider	VictoryShares
Manager/Tenure	Mannik Dhillon (1)
Website	http://www.VictorySharesLiterature.com
Address	Victory Shares 4249 Easton Way, Suite 400 Columbus OH 43219 United States
Phone Number	

PERFORMANCE

Ratings History
Date	Overall Rating	Risk Rating	Reward Rating
Q3-19	C	C-	C
Q4-18	C-	C-	C-
Q4-17	B	B	B
Q4-16	C	C-	C
Q4-15	D	D+	D

Asset & Performance History
Date	NAV	1-Year Total Return
2018	43.96	-8.61
2017	48.76	22.38
2016	40.34	13.84
2015	35.78	-0.51
2014	36.43	
2013		

Total Assets: $770,169,538
Asset Allocation
Asset	%
Cash	0%
Stocks	100%
US Stocks	99%
Bonds	0%
US Bonds	0%
Other	0%

Services Offered:

Investment Strategy: The investment seeks to provide investment results that track the performance of the Nasdaq Victory US Large Cap 500 Volatility Weighted Index before fees and expenses. The fund seeks to achieve its investment objective by investing, under normal market conditions, at least 80% of its net assets directly or indirectly in the securities included in the Nasdaq Victory US Large Cap 500 Volatility Weighted Index, an unmanaged, volatility weighted index maintained exclusively by the index provider. The index identifies the 500 largest U.S. stocks by market capitalization measured at the time the index's constituent securities are determined. **Top Holdings:** S&P 500 Emini Fut Sep19 The Hershey Co Republic Services Inc Class A WR Berkley Corp Waste Management Inc

Invesco BulletShares 2019 High Yield Corporate Bond ETF   C+   HOLD

Ticker	Traded On	NAV	Total Assets ($)	Dividend Yield (TTM)	Turnover Ratio	Expense Ratio
BSJJ	NYSE Arca	23.95	$768,755,257	4.09	25	0.42

Ratings
Reward   C
Risk   C+
Recent Upgrade/Downgrade

Fund Information
Fund Type   Exchange Traded Funds
Category   US Fixed Income
Sub-Category   High Yield Bond
Prospectus Objective   Corp Bond-High Yld
Inception Date   Sep-13
Open to New Investments   Y

Prices
Price (as of 9/30/2019)   23.92
52-Week High   24.27
52-Week Low   23.46

Total Returns (%)

3-Month	6-Month	1-Year	3-Year	5-Year
0.70	1.47	2.88	12.97	17.37

3-Year Standard Deviation   1.58
Effective Duration   0.17

Valuation
Premium/Discount (1-Year Average)   -0.12

Company Information
Provider   Invesco
Manager/Tenure   Jeremy Neisewander (3), Peter
                    Hubbard (1), Jeffrey W. Kernagis (1), 1
                    other
Website   http://www.invesco.com/us
Address   Invesco 11 Greenway Plaza, Ste. 2500
                    Houston TX 77046 United States
Phone Number   800-659-1005

PERFORMANCE

Ratings History

Date	Overall Rating	Risk Rating	Reward Rating
Q3-19	C+	C+	C
Q4-18	C	C+	C
Q4-17	C+	B	C
Q4-16	C	C+	C
Q4-15	D+	C-	D

Asset & Performance History

Date	NAV	1-Year Total Return
2018	23.7	1.55
2017	24.33	5.64
2016	24.08	11.04
2015	22.79	-3.74
2014	24.86	0.82
2013	25.74	

Total Assets: $768,755,257
Asset Allocation

Asset	%
Cash	63%
Stocks	0%
US Stocks	0%
Bonds	37%
US Bonds	36%
Other	0%

Services Offered:

Investment Strategy: The investment seeks to track the investment results (before fees and expenses) of the Nasdaq BulletShares® USD High Yield Corporate Bond 2019 Index (the "underlying index"). The fund generally will invest at least 80% of its total assets in securities that comprise the underlying index. The underlying index seeks to measure the performance of a portfolio of U.S. dollar-denominated high yield corporate bonds (commonly known as "junk bonds") with maturities or, in some cases, "effective maturities" in the year 2019 (collectively, "2019 Bonds"). The fund is non-diversified. **Top Holdings:** Solera, LLC / Solera Finance, Inc. 10.5%   Clear Channel Worldwide Holdings Inc. 6.5%   T-Mobile USA, Inc. 6.38%   Dell International L.L.C. and EMC Corporation 5.88%   Centene Corporation 5.62%

Invesco CEF Income Composite ETF   C+   HOLD

Ticker	Traded On	NAV	Total Assets ($)	Dividend Yield (TTM)	Turnover Ratio	Expense Ratio
PCEF	NYSE Arca	22.58	$765,556,033	7.23		2.25

Ratings
Reward   C+
Risk   C+
Recent Upgrade/Downgrade

Fund Information
Fund Type   Exchange Traded Funds
Category   Cautious Allocation
Sub-Category   Allocation--15% to 30% Equity
Prospectus Objective   Income
Inception Date   Feb-10
Open to New Investments   Y

Prices
Price (as of 9/30/2019)   22.61
52-Week High   22.85
52-Week Low   19.45

Total Returns (%)

3-Month	6-Month	1-Year	3-Year	5-Year
1.37	5.07	6.61	23.22	36.45

3-Year Standard Deviation   8.32
Effective Duration   4.00

Valuation
Premium/Discount (1-Year Average)   0.06

Company Information
Provider   Invesco
Manager/Tenure   Peter Hubbard (9), Michael Jeanette
                    (9), Tony Seisser (5)
Website   http://www.invesco.com/us
Address   Invesco 11 Greenway Plaza, Ste. 2500
                    Houston TX 77046 United States
Phone Number   800-659-1005

PERFORMANCE

Ratings History

Date	Overall Rating	Risk Rating	Reward Rating
Q3-19	C+	C+	C+
Q4-18	C	C+	D+
Q4-17	B-	B	B-
Q4-16	C	C-	C
Q4-15	C	C+	C-

Asset & Performance History

Date	NAV	1-Year Total Return
2018	20.2	-8.89
2017	23.87	14.18
2016	22.44	14.08
2015	21.31	-1.56
2014	23.6	5.12
2013	24.25	4.22

Total Assets: $765,556,033
Asset Allocation

Asset	%
Cash	-2%
Stocks	29%
US Stocks	21%
Bonds	68%
US Bonds	46%
Other	-5%

Services Offered:

Investment Strategy: The investment seeks to track the investment results (before fees and expenses) of the S-Network Composite Closed-End Fund IndexSM. The fund generally invests at least 90% of its total assets in securities of U.S.-listed closed-end funds that comprise the underlying index. It is a "fund of funds," as it invests its assets in the common shares of funds included in the underlying index rather than in individual securities (the "underlying funds"). **Top Holdings:** EV Tax-Mgd Gbl Div Equity Income   EV Limited Duration Income   BlackRock Enhanced Equity Div   BlackRock Credit Allocation Inc   Nuveen Pref & Income Securities Fund

ProShares Large Cap Core Plus   C   HOLD

Ticker	Traded On	NAV	Total Assets ($)	Dividend Yield (TTM)	Turnover Ratio	Expense Ratio
CSM	BATS	70.89	$762,044,114	1.51	52	0.45

Ratings
Reward	C
Risk	C-
Recent Upgrade/Downgrade	

Fund Information
Fund Type	Exchange Traded Funds
Category	US Equity Large Cap Blend
Sub-Category	Large Blend
Prospectus Objective	Growth
Inception Date	Jul-09
Open to New Investments	Y

Prices
Price (as of 9/30/2019)	70.93
52-Week High	72.35
52-Week Low	57.18

Total Returns (%)
3-Month	6-Month	1-Year	3-Year	5-Year
0.20	3.06	-0.39	40.35	61.63

3-Year Standard Deviation	12.47
Effective Duration	

Valuation
Premium/Discount (1-Year Average)	0.03

Company Information
Provider	ProShares
Manager/Tenure	Michael Neches (6), Tarak Davé (1)
Website	http://www.proshares.com
Address	ProShares 7501 Wisconsin Avenue, Suite 1000 Bethesda MD 20814 United States
Phone Number	866-776-5125

PERFORMANCE

Ratings History
Date	Overall Rating	Risk Rating	Reward Rating
Q3-19	C	C-	C
Q4-18	C-	C-	C-
Q4-17	B	B	B
Q4-16	B-	C+	B
Q4-15	C	C-	C

Asset & Performance History
Date	NAV	1-Year Total Return
2018	60.64	-7.83
2017	66.73	22.5
2016	55.23	13.78
2015	49.31	-0.45
2014	50.38	16.12
2013	44.02	35.78

Total Assets: $762,044,114
Asset Allocation
Asset	%
Cash	0%
Stocks	100%
US Stocks	99%
Bonds	0%
US Bonds	0%
Other	0%

Services Offered:

Investment Strategy: The investment seeks investment results, before fees and expenses, that track the performance of the Credit Suisse 130/30 Large Cap Index (the "index"). The fund invests in financial instruments that ProShare Advisors believes, in combination, should track the performance of the index. The index is designed to replicate an investment strategy that establishes either long or short positions in the stocks of 500 leading large-cap U.S. companies (the "Universe") by applying a rules-based ranking and weighting methodology. The fund is non-diversified. **Top Holdings:** Credit Suisse 130/30 Large Cap Long Sub-Index Swap Societe Generale Credit Suisse 130/30 Large Cap Short Sub-Index Swap Ubs Ag Credit Suisse 130/30 Large Cap Long Sub-Index Swap Ubs Ag Credit Suisse 130/30 Large Cap Short Sub-Index Swap Goldman Sachs Internati Credit Suisse 130/30 Large Cap Short Sub-Index Swap Societe Generale

VictoryShares US 500 Enhanced Volatility Wtd ETF   C-   HOLD

Ticker	Traded On	NAV	Total Assets ($)	Dividend Yield (TTM)	Turnover Ratio	Expense Ratio
CFO	NAS CM	49.33	$754,781,395	1.5	116	0.35

Ratings
Reward	C
Risk	C-
Recent Upgrade/Downgrade	

Fund Information
Fund Type	Exchange Traded Funds
Category	US Equity Large Cap Blend
Sub-Category	Large Blend
Prospectus Objective	Income
Inception Date	Jul-14
Open to New Investments	Y

Prices
Price (as of 9/30/2019)	49.34
52-Week High	51.62
52-Week Low	41.40

Total Returns (%)
3-Month	6-Month	1-Year	3-Year	5-Year
0.54	4.91	-2.90	33.25	55.28

3-Year Standard Deviation	12.02
Effective Duration	

Valuation
Premium/Discount (1-Year Average)	-0.04

Company Information
Provider	VictoryShares
Manager/Tenure	Mannik Dhillon (1)
Website	http://www.VictorySharesLiterature.com
Address	Victory Shares 4249 Easton Way, Suite 400 Columbus OH 43219 United States
Phone Number	

PERFORMANCE

Ratings History
Date	Overall Rating	Risk Rating	Reward Rating
Q3-19	C-	C-	C
Q4-18	C	C+	C-
Q4-17	B	B	B
Q4-16	C	C-	C
Q4-15	D	C-	D

Asset & Performance History
Date	NAV	1-Year Total Return
2018	43.93	-8.61
2017	48.72	22.39
2016	40.32	13.87
2015	35.75	-0.55
2014	36.42	
2013		

Total Assets: $754,781,395
Asset Allocation
Asset	%
Cash	0%
Stocks	100%
US Stocks	99%
Bonds	0%
US Bonds	0%
Other	0%

Services Offered:

Investment Strategy: The investment seeks to provide investment results that track the performance of the Nasdaq Victory US Large Cap 500 Long/Cash Volatility Weighted Index before fees and expenses. The fund seeks to achieve its investment objective by investing, under normal market conditions, at least 80% of its assets directly or indirectly in the securities included in the Nasdaq Victory US Large Cap 500 Long/Cash Volatility Weighted Index, an unmanaged, volatility weighted index maintained exclusively by the index provider. The index identifies the 500 largest U.S. stocks by market capitalization measured at the time the index's constituent securities are determined. **Top Holdings:** S&P 500 Emini Fut Sep19 The Hershey Co Republic Services Inc Class A WR Berkley Corp Waste Management Inc

Invesco Fundamental High Yield® Corporate Bond ETF   C+   HOLD

Ticker	Traded On	NAV	Total Assets ($)	Dividend Yield (TTM)	Turnover Ratio	Expense Ratio
PHB	NYSE Arca	19.03	$753,572,845	4.12		0.5

Ratings
Reward	C+
Risk	C+
Recent Upgrade/Downgrade	

Fund Information
Fund Type	Exchange Traded Funds
Category	US Fixed Income
Sub-Category	High Yield Bond
Prospectus Objective	Corp Bond-High Yld
Inception Date	Nov-07
Open to New Investments	Y

Prices
Price (as of 9/30/2019)	19.03
52-Week High	19.16
52-Week Low	17.49

Total Returns (%)
3-Month	6-Month	1-Year	3-Year	5-Year
1.28	3.82	6.89	14.68	23.82

3-Year Standard Deviation	3.55
Effective Duration	3.20

Valuation
Premium/Discount (1-Year Average)	-0.12

Company Information
Provider	Invesco
Manager/Tenure	Philip Fang (11), Peter Hubbard (11), Jeffrey W. Kernagis (11), 2 others
Website	http://www.invesco.com/us
Address	Invesco 11 Greenway Plaza, Ste. 2500 Houston TX 77046 United States
Phone Number	800-659-1005

PERFORMANCE

Ratings History
Date	Overall Rating	Risk Rating	Reward Rating
Q3-19	C+	C+	C+
Q4-18	C	C+	C
Q4-17	B-	B	C+
Q4-16	C+	C+	C
Q4-15	C	C+	C-

Asset & Performance History
Date	NAV	1-Year Total Return
2018	17.72	-2.37
2017	18.94	5.11
2016	18.78	12.78
2015	17.46	-2.62
2014	18.74	1.83
2013	19.22	4.3

Total Assets: $753,572,845
Asset Allocation
Asset	%
Cash	1%
Stocks	0%
US Stocks	0%
Bonds	99%
US Bonds	99%
Other	0%

Services Offered:

Investment Strategy: The investment seeks to track the investment results (before fees and expenses) of the RAFI® Bonds U.S. High Yield 1-10 Index (the "underlying index"). The fund generally will invest at least 80% of its total assets in securities that comprise the underlying index. The underlying index is comprised of U.S. dollar-denominated high-yield corporate bonds that are SEC-registered securities or Rule 144A securities with registration rights (issued after July 31, 2013) and whose issuers are public companies listed on a major U.S. stock exchange. **Top Holdings:** EMC Corporation 3.38% United Airlines Holdings Inc 4.25% Genworth Financial Inc. 7.62% Western Digital Corp. 4.75% Centene Corporation 6.12%

Invesco Dynamic Large Cap Growth ETF   C+   HOLD

Ticker	Traded On	NAV	Total Assets ($)	Dividend Yield (TTM)	Turnover Ratio	Expense Ratio
PWB	NYSE Arca	48.36	$752,025,297	0.86		0.55

Ratings
Reward	B-
Risk	C
Recent Upgrade/Downgrade	Up

Fund Information
Fund Type	Exchange Traded Funds
Category	US Equity Large Cap Growth
Sub-Category	Large Growth
Prospectus Objective	Growth
Inception Date	Mar-05
Open to New Investments	Y

Prices
Price (as of 9/30/2019)	48.34
52-Week High	50.26
52-Week Low	38.42

Total Returns (%)
3-Month	6-Month	1-Year	3-Year	5-Year
-0.59	1.28	0.53	56.20	86.40

3-Year Standard Deviation	12.81
Effective Duration	

Valuation
Premium/Discount (1-Year Average)	-0.02

Company Information
Provider	Invesco
Manager/Tenure	Peter Hubbard (12), Michael Jeanette (11), Tony Seisser (5)
Website	http://www.invesco.com/us
Address	Invesco 11 Greenway Plaza, Ste. 2500 Houston TX 77046 United States
Phone Number	800-659-1005

PERFORMANCE

Ratings History
Date	Overall Rating	Risk Rating	Reward Rating
Q3-19	C+	C	B-
Q4-18	C	C	C+
Q4-17	A-	B	A
Q4-16	C+	C	B
Q4-15	B-	C	B

Asset & Performance History
Date	NAV	1-Year Total Return
2018	41.49	1.06
2017	41.44	30.54
2016	31.93	2.93
2015	31.28	7.78
2014	29.22	13.5
2013	25.86	37.32

Total Assets: $752,025,297
Asset Allocation
Asset	%
Cash	0%
Stocks	100%
US Stocks	99%
Bonds	0%
US Bonds	0%
Other	0%

Services Offered:

Investment Strategy: The investment seeks to track the investment results (before fees and expenses) of the Dynamic Large Cap Growth IntellidexSM Index. The fund generally will invest at least 90% of its total assets in the securities that comprise the underlying intellidex. The underlying intellidex is composed of large-capitalization U.S. growth stocks that the Intellidex Provider includes principally on the basis of their capital appreciation potential. **Top Holdings:** Costco Wholesale Corp Visa Inc Class A Accenture PLC Class A Abbott Laboratories Mastercard Inc A

Direxion Daily Technology Bull 3X Shares　　　　C　HOLD

Ticker	Traded On	NAV	Total Assets ($)	Dividend Yield (TTM)	Turnover Ratio	Expense Ratio
TECL	NYSE Arca	166.84	$750,788,013	0.3	41	1.08

Ratings
Reward　　　　　　　　　　　　　　　B-
Risk　　　　　　　　　　　　　　　　D+
Recent Upgrade/Downgrade

Fund Information
Fund Type　　　　　　Exchange Traded Funds
Category　　　　　　　　　　Trading Tools
Sub-Category　　　Trading--Leveraged Equity
Prospectus Objective　　　　　　Technology
Inception Date　　　　　　　　　　Dec-08
Open to New Investments　　　　　　　Y

Prices
Price (as of 9/30/2019)　　　　　　166.79
52-Week High　　　　　　　　　　187.10
52-Week Low　　　　　　　　　　　68.96

Total Returns (%)

3-Month	6-Month	1-Year	3-Year	5-Year
0.80	15.55	-1.30	245.84	459.17

3-Year Standard Deviation　　　　　46.94
Effective Duration

Valuation
Premium/Discount (1-Year Average)　　-0.04

Company Information
Provider　　　　Direxion Funds
Manager/Tenure　Paul Brigandi (10), Tony Ng (4)
Website　　　　http://www.direxionfunds.com
Address　　　　Direxion Funds 1301 Avenue Of The
　　　　　　　　Americas (6th Avenue) New York NY
　　　　　　　　10019 United States
Phone Number　646-572-3390

PERFORMANCE

Ratings History

Date	Overall Rating	Risk Rating	Reward Rating
Q3-19	C	D+	B-
Q4-18	C	C-	C
Q4-17	B+	C+	A
Q4-16	C+	C-	B
Q4-15	C	C+	C

Asset & Performance History

Date	NAV	1-Year Total Return
2018	84.92	-24.04
2017	112.09	124.97
2016	49.87	36.89
2015	36.43	4.77
2014	34.77	52.13
2013	22.86	88.02

Total Assets: $750,788,013

Asset Allocation

Asset	%
Cash	4%
Stocks	96%
US Stocks	96%
Bonds	0%
US Bonds	0%
Other	0%

Services Offered:

Investment Strategy: The investment seeks daily investment results, before fees and expenses, of 300% of the daily performance of the Technology Select Sector Index. The fund invests at least 80% of its net assets (plus borrowing for investment purposes) in financial instruments, such as swap agreements, and securities of the index, ETFs that track the index and other financial instruments that provide daily leveraged exposure to the index or ETFs that track the index. The index includes domestic companies from the technology sector. It is non-diversified. **Top Holdings:** Technology Select Sector SPDR® ETF　Technology Select Sector　Technology Select Sector Technology Select Sector　Technology Select Sector

---

iShares India 50 ETF　　　　C　HOLD

Ticker	Traded On	NAV	Total Assets ($)	Dividend Yield (TTM)	Turnover Ratio	Expense Ratio
INDY	NAS CM	36.62	$748,953,367	0.98	24	0.94

Ratings
Reward　　　　　　　　　　　　　　　C-
Risk　　　　　　　　　　　　　　　　C+
Recent Upgrade/Downgrade　　　　　　Down

Fund Information
Fund Type　　　　　　Exchange Traded Funds
Category　　　　　　　　　　India Equity
Sub-Category　　　　　　　　　India Equity
Prospectus Objective　　　　　　Foreign Stock
Inception Date　　　　　　　　　　Nov-09
Open to New Investments　　　　　　　Y

Prices
Price (as of 9/30/2019)　　　　　　36.70
52-Week High　　　　　　　　　　39.47
52-Week Low　　　　　　　　　　　31.33

Total Returns (%)

3-Month	6-Month	1-Year	3-Year	5-Year
-5.54	-3.20	7.88	25.59	27.36

3-Year Standard Deviation　　　　　16.14
Effective Duration

Valuation
Premium/Discount (1-Year Average)　　0.03

Company Information
Provider　　　　iShares
Manager/Tenure　Greg Savage (9), Jennifer Hsui (7),
　　　　　　　　Alan Mason (3), 2 others
Website　　　　http://www.ishares.com
Address　　　　iShares 400 Howard Street San
　　　　　　　　Francisco CA 94105 United States
Phone Number　800-474-2737

PERFORMANCE

Ratings History

Date	Overall Rating	Risk Rating	Reward Rating
Q3-19	C	C+	C-
Q4-18	C-	C	D+
Q4-17	B-	C	B
Q4-16	C	C	C
Q4-15	C	C+	C

Asset & Performance History

Date	NAV	1-Year Total Return
2018	35.29	-4.48
2017	37.15	35.31
2016	27.53	0.73
2015	27.46	-7.82
2014	29.95	28.84
2013	23.37	-4.69

Total Assets: $748,953,367

Asset Allocation

Asset	%
Cash	0%
Stocks	100%
US Stocks	0%
Bonds	0%
US Bonds	0%
Other	0%

Services Offered:

Investment Strategy: The investment seeks to track the investment results of the Nifty 50 IndexTM composed of 50 of the largest Indian equities. The Subsidiary and the fund will collectively invest at least 90% of the fund's assets in the component securities of the underlying index and in investments that have economic characteristics that are substantially identical to the component securities of the underlying index. The underlying index measures the equity performance of the top 50 companies by free float market capitalization whose equity securities trade in the Indian securities markets. The fund is non-diversified. **Top Holdings:** Reliance Industries Ltd　HDFC Bank Ltd Housing Development Finance Corp Ltd　Infosys Ltd　ICICI Bank Ltd

iShares Currency Hedged MSCI Eurozone ETF   C   HOLD

Ticker	Traded On	NAV	Total Assets ($)	Dividend Yield (TTM)	Turnover Ratio	Expense Ratio
HEZU	NYSE Arca	30.92	$748,262,836	2.91	11	0.5

Ratings
Reward   C
Risk   C+
Recent Upgrade/Downgrade

Fund Information
Fund Type   Exchange Traded Funds
Category   Europe Equity Large Cap
Sub-Category   Europe Stock
Prospectus Objective   Europe Stock
Inception Date   Jul-14
Open to New Investments   Y

Prices
Price (as of 9/30/2019)   30.92
52-Week High   31.03
52-Week Low   25.39

Total Returns (%)

3-Month	6-Month	1-Year	3-Year	5-Year
2.14	6.39	7.07	35.33	44.87

3-Year Standard Deviation   12.13
Effective Duration

Valuation
Premium/Discount (1-Year Average)   -0.02

Company Information
Provider   iShares
Manager/Tenure   Diane Hsiung (5), Jennifer Hsui (5), Orlando Montalvo (5), 2 others
Website   http://www.ishares.com
Address   iShares 400 Howard Street San Francisco CA 94105 United States
Phone Number   800-474-2737

PERFORMANCE

Ratings History

Date	Overall Rating	Risk Rating	Reward Rating
Q3-19	C	C+	C
Q4-18	C-	C	D+
Q4-17	B	B	B
Q4-16	C	C+	C-
Q4-15	D	C+	D

Asset & Performance History

Date	NAV	1-Year Total Return
2018	25.96	-10.68
2017	29.82	14.27
2016	26.61	6.7
2015	25.83	8.15
2014	24.49	
2013		

Total Assets: $748,262,836
Asset Allocation

Asset	%
Cash	1%
Stocks	99%
US Stocks	3%
Bonds	0%
US Bonds	0%
Other	0%

Services Offered:

Investment Strategy: The investment seeks to track the investment results of the MSCI EMU 100% Hedged to USD Index. The fund generally will invest at least 90% of its assets in the component securities (including indirect investments through the underlying fund) and other instruments of the underlying index and in investments that have economic characteristics that are substantially identical to the component securities of the underlying index. The index is an equity benchmark for the Economic and Monetary Union countries with the currency risk inherent in the securities included in the underlying index hedged to the U.S. dollar on a monthly basis. **Top Holdings:** Total SA   SAP SE   LVMH Moet Hennessy Louis Vuitton SE   Sanofi SA   ASML Holding NV

Vanguard Russell 2000 Growth Index Fund ETF Shares   C-   HOLD

Ticker	Traded On	NAV	Total Assets ($)	Dividend Yield (TTM)	Turnover Ratio	Expense Ratio
VTWG	NAS CM	140.13	$746,037,948	0.72	35	0.2

Ratings
Reward   C
Risk   D+
Recent Upgrade/Downgrade   Down

Fund Information
Fund Type   Exchange Traded Funds
Category   US Equity Small Cap
Sub-Category   Small Growth
Prospectus Objective   Small Company
Inception Date   Sep-10
Open to New Investments   Y

Prices
Price (as of 9/30/2019)   140.10
52-Week High   153.71
52-Week Low   114.04

Total Returns (%)

3-Month	6-Month	1-Year	3-Year	5-Year
-4.56	-2.64	-8.54	31.84	53.94

3-Year Standard Deviation   17.47
Effective Duration

Valuation
Premium/Discount (1-Year Average)   -0.01

Company Information
Provider   Vanguard
Manager/Tenure   Walter Nejman (4), Michael A. Johnson (3)
Website   http://www.vanguard.com
Address   Vanguard 100 Vanguard Boulevard Malvern PA 19355 United States
Phone Number   877-662-7447

PERFORMANCE

Ratings History

Date	Overall Rating	Risk Rating	Reward Rating
Q3-19	C-	D+	C
Q4-18	C-	C-	C-
Q4-17	B+	B	A-
Q4-16	C	D+	B-
Q4-15	C	C-	C+

Asset & Performance History

Date	NAV	1-Year Total Return
2018	120.76	-10.28
2017	135.43	22.62
2016	111.66	10.56
2015	101.26	-1.35
2014	103.38	5.64
2013	98.46	43.3

Total Assets: $746,037,948
Asset Allocation

Asset	%
Cash	3%
Stocks	97%
US Stocks	96%
Bonds	0%
US Bonds	0%
Other	0%

Services Offered:

Investment Strategy: The investment seeks to track the performance of a benchmark index that measures the investment return of small-capitalization growth stocks in the United States. The fund employs an indexing investment approach designed to track the performance of the Russell 2000® Growth Index. The index is designed to measure the performance of small-capitalization growth stocks in the United States. The advisor attempts to replicate the target index by investing all, or substantially all, of its assets in the stocks that make up the index, holding each stock in approximately the same proportion as its weighting in the index. **Top Holdings:** NovoCure Ltd   Haemonetics Corp   HealthEquity Inc   Chegg Inc   Science Applications International Corp

ETFMG Prime Mobile Payments ETF

B   BUY

Ticker	Traded On	NAV		Total Assets ($)	Dividend Yield (TTM)	Turnover Ratio	Expense Ratio
IPAY	NYSE Arca	46.60		$743,193,432	0.1	16	0.75

Ratings

Reward	B+
Risk	C
Recent Upgrade/Downgrade	

Fund Information

Fund Type	Exchange Traded Funds
Category	Equity Misc
Sub-Category	Miscellaneous Sector
Prospectus Objective	Growth & Inc
Inception Date	Jul-15
Open to New Investments	Y

Prices

Price (as of 9/30/2019)	46.61
52-Week High	50.00
52-Week Low	32.45

Total Returns (%)

3-Month	6-Month	1-Year	3-Year	5-Year
-1.15	7.07	9.11	88.23	

3-Year Standard Deviation	14.76
Effective Duration	

Valuation

Premium/Discount (1-Year Average)	0.03

Company Information

Provider	ETFMG
Manager/Tenure	Samuel R. Masucci (1), Devin Ryder (1), Donal Bishnoi (0), 1 other
Website	http://www.etfmg.com
Address	ETFMG 30 Maple Street, Suite 2 NJ United States
Phone Number	

PERFORMANCE

Ratings History

Date	Overall Rating	Risk Rating	Reward Rating
Q3-19	B	C	B+
Q4-18	B-	C+	B
Q4-17	C	B	B-
Q4-16	D	C	B-
Q4-15	U		

Asset & Performance History

Date	NAV	1-Year Total Return
2018	35.02	1.33
2017	34.8	36.87
2016	25.43	3.42
2015	24.55	
2014		
2013		

Total Assets: $743,193,432

Asset Allocation

Asset	%
Cash	1%
Stocks	99%
US Stocks	70%
Bonds	0%
US Bonds	0%
Other	0%

Services Offered:

Investment Strategy: The investment seeks to provide investment results that correspond generally to the Prime Mobile Payments Index. The fund invests at least 80% of its total assets in the component securities of the index and in ADRs and GDRs based on the component securities in the index. The index tracks the performance of the exchange-listed equity securities of companies across the globe that (i) engage in providing payment processing services or applications, (ii) provide payment solutions, (iii) build or provide payment industry architecture, infrastructure or software, or (iv) provide services as a credit card network. The fund is non-diversified. **Top Holdings:** Fidelity National Information Services Inc   Fiserv Inc   Mastercard Inc A   Visa Inc Class A   American Express Co

FlexShares International Quality Dividend Index Fund

C   HOLD

Ticker	Traded On	NAV		Total Assets ($)	Dividend Yield (TTM)	Turnover Ratio	Expense Ratio
IQDF	NYSE Arca	22.27		$739,369,090	5.08	71	0.47

Ratings

Reward	D+
Risk	C+
Recent Upgrade/Downgrade	

Fund Information

Fund Type	Exchange Traded Funds
Category	Global Equity Large Cap
Sub-Category	Foreign Large Value
Prospectus Objective	World Stock
Inception Date	Apr-13
Open to New Investments	Y

Prices

Price (as of 9/30/2019)	22.28
52-Week High	24.11
52-Week Low	20.28

Total Returns (%)

3-Month	6-Month	1-Year	3-Year	5-Year
-2.65	-1.04	-2.83	13.09	5.00

3-Year Standard Deviation	11.62
Effective Duration	

Valuation

Premium/Discount (1-Year Average)	-0.03

Company Information

Provider	Flexshares Trust
Manager/Tenure	Robert Anstine (5), Brendan Sullivan (3)
Website	http://www.flexshares.com
Address	50 South LaSalle Street Chicago, Illinois 60603 Chicago Illinois 60603 United States
Phone Number	855-353-9383

PERFORMANCE

Ratings History

Date	Overall Rating	Risk Rating	Reward Rating
Q3-19	C	C+	D+
Q4-18	D+	D+	C-
Q4-17	C+	C	C+
Q4-16	D+	C-	D
Q4-15	C-	C-	D+

Asset & Performance History

Date	NAV	1-Year Total Return
2018	21.1	-16.94
2017	26.75	23.59
2016	22.53	7.75
2015	21.72	-9.53
2014	24.95	-3.66
2013	26.93	

Total Assets: $739,369,090

Asset Allocation

Asset	%
Cash	1%
Stocks	99%
US Stocks	0%
Bonds	0%
US Bonds	0%
Other	0%

Services Offered:

Investment Strategy: The investment seeks investment results that correspond generally to the price and yield performance, before fees and expenses, of the Northern Trust International Quality Dividend IndexSM. The fund will invest at least 80% of its total assets in the securities of the index and in ADRs and GDRs based on the securities in the index. The index is designed to provide exposure to a high-quality, income-oriented portfolio of international equity securities issued by non-U.S.-based companies, with an emphasis on long-term capital growth and a targeted overall volatility similar to that of the Northern Trust International Large Cap IndexSM. **Top Holdings:** GlaxoSmithKline PLC   Unilever NV   Royal Bank of Canada   BP PLC   Allianz SE

ProShares Russell 2000 Dividend Growers ETF   C   HOLD

Ticker	Traded On	NAV	Total Assets ($)	Dividend Yield (TTM)	Turnover Ratio	Expense Ratio
SMDV	BATS	59.30	$730,021,832	2.06	26	0.4

Ratings
Reward   C
Risk   C-
Recent Upgrade/Downgrade

Fund Information
Fund Type	Exchange Traded Funds
Category	US Equity Small Cap
Sub-Category	Small Blend
Prospectus Objective	Growth
Inception Date	Feb-15
Open to New Investments	Y

Prices
Price (as of 9/30/2019)	59.36
52-Week High	60.75
52-Week Low	51.72

Total Returns (%)
3-Month	6-Month	1-Year	3-Year	5-Year
0.94	2.72	4.02	31.60	

3-Year Standard Deviation   12.77
Effective Duration

Valuation
Premium/Discount (1-Year Average)   0.04

Company Information
Provider	ProShares
Manager/Tenure	Michael Neches (4), Devin Sullivan (1)
Website	http://www.proshares.com
Address	ProShares 7501 Wisconsin Avenue, Suite 1000 Bethesda MD 20814 United States
Phone Number	866-776-5125

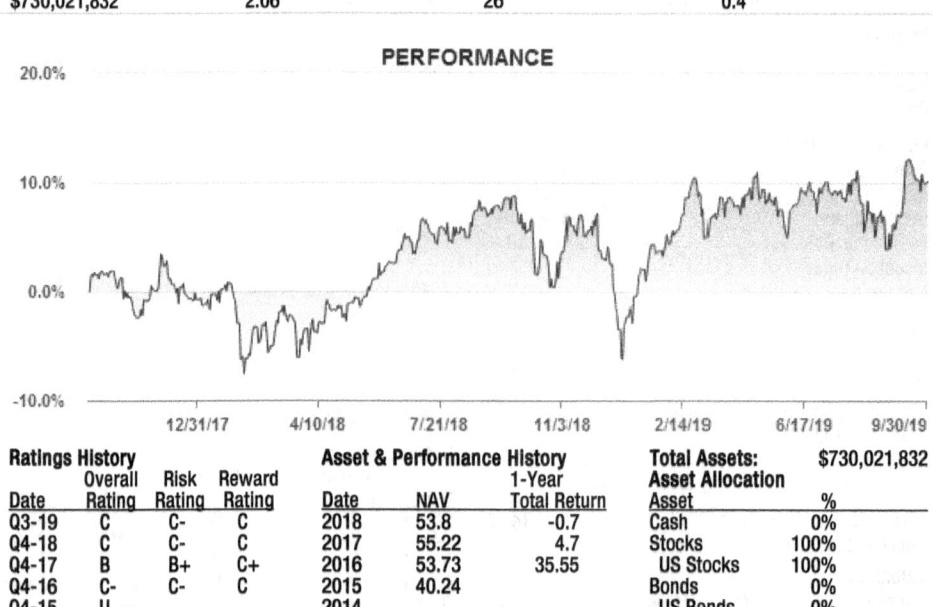

PERFORMANCE

Ratings History
Date	Overall Rating	Risk Rating	Reward Rating
Q3-19	C	C-	C
Q4-18	C	C-	C
Q4-17	B	B+	C+
Q4-16	C-	C-	C
Q4-15	U		

Asset & Performance History
Date	NAV	1-Year Total Return
2018	53.8	-0.7
2017	55.22	4.7
2016	53.73	35.55
2015	40.24	
2014		
2013		

Total Assets: $730,021,832
Asset Allocation
Asset	%
Cash	0%
Stocks	100%
US Stocks	100%
Bonds	0%
US Bonds	0%
Other	0%

Services Offered:

Investment Strategy: The investment seeks investment results, before fees and expenses, that track the performance of the Russell 2000 Dividend Growth Index (the "index"). Under normal circumstances, the fund will invest at least 80% of its total assets in component securities (i.e., securities of the index and comparable securities that have economic characteristics that are substantially identical to the economic characteristics of the securities of the index). The index contains a minimum of 40 stocks, which are equally weighted, and no single sector is allowed to comprise more than 30% of the index weight. **Top Holdings:** American States Water Co Utah Medical Products Inc   J&J Snack Foods Corp   Vector Group Ltd   Lindsay Corp

---

Principal Active Global Dividend Income ETF   C   HOLD

Ticker	Traded On	NAV	Total Assets ($)	Dividend Yield (TTM)	Turnover Ratio	Expense Ratio
GDVD	BATS	27.89	$729,445,485	3.07	32	0.58

Ratings
Reward   C
Risk   D+
Recent Upgrade/Downgrade   Up

Fund Information
Fund Type	Exchange Traded Funds
Category	Global Equity Large Cap
Sub-Category	World Large Stock
Prospectus Objective	Growth & Inc
Inception Date	May-17
Open to New Investments	Y

Prices
Price (as of 9/30/2019)	28.08
52-Week High	28.37
52-Week Low	23.59

Total Returns (%)
3-Month	6-Month	1-Year	3-Year	5-Year
0.99	4.40	2.89		

3-Year Standard Deviation
Effective Duration

Valuation
Premium/Discount (1-Year Average)   0.40

Company Information
Provider	Principal Funds
Manager/Tenure	Daniel R. Coleman (2), Paul S. Kim (2), Cliff Remily (2), 1 other
Website	http://www.principalfunds.com
Address	Principal Funds 430 W 7th St, Ste 219971 Kansas City MO 64105-1407 United States
Phone Number	800-787-1621

PERFORMANCE

Ratings History
Date	Overall Rating	Risk Rating	Reward Rating
Q3-19	C	D+	C
Q4-18	D+	D+	D+
Q4-17	U		
Q4-16			
Q4-15			

Asset & Performance History
Date	NAV	1-Year Total Return
2018	24.3	-10.35
2017	27.84	
2016		
2015		
2014		
2013		

Total Assets: $729,445,485
Asset Allocation
Asset	%
Cash	1%
Stocks	99%
US Stocks	42%
Bonds	0%
US Bonds	0%
Other	0%

Services Offered:

Investment Strategy: The investment seeks current income and long-term growth of income and capital. The fund is an actively managed ETF that seeks to achieve its investment objective by investing, under normal circumstances, at least 80% of its net assets, plus any borrowings for investment purposes, in dividend-paying equity securities at the time of purchase. It invests in equity securities of small, medium and large market capitalization companies and in growth and value stocks. **Top Holdings:** Taiwan Semiconductor Manufacturing Co Ltd ADR   Microsoft Corp   Apple Inc   JPMorgan Chase & Co   Roche Holding AG Dividend Right Cert.

PIMCO 1-5 Year U.S. TIPS Index Exchange-Traded Fund   C   HOLD

Ticker	Traded On	NAV	Total Assets ($)	Dividend Yield (TTM)	Turnover Ratio	Expense Ratio
STPZ	NYSE Arca	52.42	$727,064,283	1.25	36	0.2

Ratings

Reward	C
Risk	C-
Recent Upgrade/Downgrade	

Fund Information

Fund Type	Exchange Traded Funds
Category	US Fixed Income
Sub-Category	Inflation-Protected Bond
Prospectus Objective	Govt Bond - Treasury
Inception Date	Aug-09
Open to New Investments	Y

Prices

Price (as of 9/30/2019)	52.42
52-Week High	52.67
52-Week Low	50.72

Total Returns (%)

3-Month	6-Month	1-Year	3-Year	5-Year
0.28	2.07	3.50	4.23	5.26

3-Year Standard Deviation	1.32
Effective Duration	2.93

Valuation

Premium/Discount (1-Year Average)	0.00

Company Information

Provider	PIMCO
Manager/Tenure	Matthew P. Dorsten (3), Mitchell Handa (0), Graham A. Rennison (0)
Website	http://www.pimco.com
Address	PIMCO 840 Newport Center Drive, Suite 100 Newport Beach CA 92660 United States
Phone Number	866-746-2602

PERFORMANCE

Ratings History

Date	Overall Rating	Risk Rating	Reward Rating
Q3-19	C	C-	C
Q4-18	C-	C-	C-
Q4-17	C	C+	C
Q4-16	C	C-	C
Q4-15	D+	C-	D

Asset & Performance History

Date	NAV	1-Year Total Return
2018	50.85	0.18
2017	51.97	0.64
2016	52.42	2.95
2015	51.23	-0.44
2014	51.71	-1.32
2013	52.84	-2.12

Total Assets: $727,064,283

Asset Allocation

Asset	%
Cash	0%
Stocks	0%
US Stocks	0%
Bonds	100%
US Bonds	100%
Other	0%

Services Offered:

Investment Strategy: The investment seeks to provide total return that closely corresponds, before fees and expenses, to the total return of the ICE BofAML 1-5 Year US Inflation-Linked Treasury Index. The fund invests at least 80% of its total assets (exclusive of collateral held from securities lending) in the component securities of the ICE BofAML 1-5 Year US Inflation-Linked Treasury Index (the "underlying index"). The underlying index is an unmanaged index comprised of Treasury Inflation-Protected Securities ("TIPS") with a maturity of at least 1 year and less than 5 years. **Top Holdings:** United States Treasury Notes 0.12%   United States Treasury Notes 0.38%   United States Treasury Notes 0.12%   United States Treasury Notes 0.62%   United States Treasury Notes 1.12%

iShares S&P GSCI Commodity-Indexed Trust   C-   HOLD

Ticker	Traded On	NAV	Total Assets ($)	Dividend Yield (TTM)	Turnover Ratio	Expense Ratio
GSG	NYSE Arca	15.03	$725,794,535	0	0	0.75

Ratings

Reward	D+
Risk	C-
Recent Upgrade/Downgrade	

Fund Information

Fund Type	Exchange Traded Funds
Category	Commodities Broad Basket
Sub-Category	Commodities Broad Basket
Prospectus Objective	Unaligned
Inception Date	Jul-06
Open to New Investments	Y

Prices

Price (as of 9/30/2019)	15.05
52-Week High	18.72
52-Week Low	13.86

Total Returns (%)

3-Month	6-Month	1-Year	3-Year	5-Year
-4.38	-7.16	-18.71	1.55	-48.99

3-Year Standard Deviation	14.8
Effective Duration	

Valuation

Premium/Discount (1-Year Average)	-0.11

Company Information

Provider	iShares
Manager/Tenure	Management Team (13)
Website	http://www.ishares.com
Address	iShares 400 Howard Street San Francisco CA 94105 United States
Phone Number	800-474-2737

PERFORMANCE

Ratings History

Date	Overall Rating	Risk Rating	Reward Rating
Q3-19	C-	C-	D+
Q4-18	C-	C	C-
Q4-17	D	D	D+
Q4-16	D-	D	D-
Q4-15	D-	D	D-

Asset & Performance History

Date	NAV	1-Year Total Return
2018	13.99	-14.27
2017	16.32	4.48
2016	15.62	9.92
2015	14.21	-33.47
2014	21.36	-33.6
2013	32.17	-2.04

Total Assets: $725,794,535

Asset Allocation

Asset	%
Cash	73%
Stocks	0%
US Stocks	0%
Bonds	27%
US Bonds	27%
Other	0%

Services Offered:

Investment Strategy: The investment seeks investment results, through the Trust's investment in the Investing Pool, that correspond generally, but are not necessarily identical, to the performance of the S&P GSCI™ Total Return Index, before the payment of expenses and liabilities of the Trust and the Investing Pool. The Investing Pool holds long positions in CERFs, which are futures contracts listed on the CME, whose settlement at expiration is based on the value of the S&P GSCI-ER, at that time. The Investing Pool also earns interest on the assets used to collateralize its holdings of CERFs. **Top Holdings:** United States Treasury Bills 0%   United States Treasury Bills 0%   United States Treasury Bills 0%   United States Treasury Bills 0%   United States Treasury Bills 0%

Direxion Daily Small Cap Bull 3X Shares   D+   SELL

Ticker	Traded On	NAV	Total Assets ($)	Dividend Yield (TTM)	Turnover Ratio	Expense Ratio
TNA	NYSE Arca	55.71	$724,174,409	0.54	51	1.14

Ratings
Reward   C-
Risk   D+
Recent Upgrade/Downgrade   Down

Fund Information
Fund Type   Exchange Traded Funds
Category   Trading Tools
Sub-Category   Trading--Leveraged Equity
Prospectus Objective   Small Company
Inception Date   Nov-08
Open to New Investments   Y

Prices
Price (as of 9/30/2019)   55.67
52-Week High   85.79
52-Week Low   35.43

Total Returns (%)

3-Month	6-Month	1-Year	3-Year	5-Year
-11.46	-11.46	-34.59	40.26	86.23

3-Year Standard Deviation   51.89
Effective Duration

Valuation
Premium/Discount (1-Year Average)   -0.09

Company Information
Provider   Direxion Funds
Manager/Tenure   Paul Brigandi (10), Tony Ng (4)
Website   http://www.direxionfunds.com
Address   Direxion Funds 1301 Avenue Of The Americas (6th Avenue) New York NY 10019 United States
Phone Number   646-572-3390

PERFORMANCE

Ratings History

Date	Overall Rating	Risk Rating	Reward Rating
Q3-19	D+	D+	C-
Q4-18	C-	D+	C
Q4-17	B	C-	A+
Q4-16	C	D+	C+
Q4-15	C	C+	C

Asset & Performance History

Date	NAV	1-Year Total Return
2018	42.19	-39.94
2017	70.26	39.58
2016	50.41	57.95
2015	31.92	-21.09
2014	40.45	5.02
2013	38.76	151.22

Total Assets: $724,174,409
Asset Allocation

Asset	%
Cash	26%
Stocks	74%
US Stocks	73%
Bonds	0%
US Bonds	0%
Other	0%

Services Offered:

Investment Strategy: The investment seeks daily investment results, before fees and expenses, of 300% of the daily performance of the Russell 2000® Index. The fund invests at least 80% of its net assets in financial instruments, such as swap agreements, and securities of the index, ETFs that track the index and other financial instruments that provide daily leveraged exposure to the index or ETFs that track the index. The index measures the performance of approximately 2,000 small-capitalization companies in the Russell 3000® Index, based on a combination of their market capitalization and current index membership. The fund is non-diversified. **Top Holdings:** iShares Russell 2000 ETF   Russ 2000 Indx Small Swap   Russ 2000 Indx Small Swap   Russ 2000 Indx Small Swap   Russ 2000 Indx Small Swap

---

iShares MSCI Saudi Arabia ETF   C   HOLD

Ticker	Traded On	NAV	Total Assets ($)	Dividend Yield (TTM)	Turnover Ratio	Expense Ratio
KSA	NYSE Arca	30.35	$722,392,270	2.45	20	0.74

Ratings
Reward   C-
Risk   C+
Recent Upgrade/Downgrade   Down

Fund Information
Fund Type   Exchange Traded Funds
Category   Equity Misc
Sub-Category   Miscellaneous Region
Prospectus Objective   Growth
Inception Date   Sep-15
Open to New Investments   Y

Prices
Price (as of 9/30/2019)   30.48
52-Week High   35.65
52-Week Low   27.31

Total Returns (%)

3-Month	6-Month	1-Year	3-Year	5-Year
-8.28	-7.79	3.33	61.21	

3-Year Standard Deviation   16.59
Effective Duration

Valuation
Premium/Discount (1-Year Average)   0.29

Company Information
Provider   iShares
Manager/Tenure   Diane Hsiung (4), Jennifer Hsui (4), Greg Savage (4), 3 others
Website   http://www.ishares.com
Address   iShares 400 Howard Street San Francisco CA 94105 United States
Phone Number   800-474-2737

PERFORMANCE

Ratings History

Date	Overall Rating	Risk Rating	Reward Rating
Q3-19	C	C+	C-
Q4-18	C-	C-	C-
Q4-17	C	C+	C-
Q4-16	D	D+	D+
Q4-15			

Asset & Performance History

Date	NAV	1-Year Total Return
2018	28.87	15.29
2017	25.65	5.14
2016	24.98	9.23
2015	23.63	
2014		
2013		

Total Assets: $722,392,270
Asset Allocation

Asset	%
Cash	0%
Stocks	100%
US Stocks	0%
Bonds	0%
US Bonds	0%
Other	0%

Services Offered:

Investment Strategy: The investment seeks to track the investment results of the MSCI Saudi Arabia IMI 25/50 Index. The fund generally will invest at least 90% of its assets in the component securities of the index and in investments that have economic characteristics that are substantially identical to the component securities of the index. The index is a free float-adjusted market capitalization-weighted index with a capping methodology applied to issuer weights so that no single issuer of a component exceeds 25% of the index weight, and all issuers with a weight above 5% do not cumulatively exceed 50% of the index weight. The fund is non-diversified. **Top Holdings:** Saudi Basic Industries Corp   Al Rajhi Bank   The National Commercial Bank   Saudi Telecom Co   Riyad Bank

Fidelity® MSCI Consumer Discretionary Index ETF   C+   HOLD

Ticker	Traded On	NAV	Total Assets ($)	Dividend Yield (TTM)	Turnover Ratio	Expense Ratio
FDIS	NYSE Arca	45.80	$721,342,696	1.2	25	0.08

Ratings
Reward	B-
Risk	C-
Recent Upgrade/Downgrade	Up

Fund Information
Fund Type	Exchange Traded Funds
Category	Consumer Goods & Svcs
Sub-Category	Consumer Cyclical
Prospectus Objective	Unaligned
Inception Date	Oct-13
Open to New Investments	Y

Prices
Price (as of 9/30/2019)	45.75
52-Week High	47.66
52-Week Low	35.51

Total Returns (%)
3-Month	6-Month	1-Year	3-Year	5-Year
-0.33	3.80	2.20	51.10	84.19

3-Year Standard Deviation   14.51
Effective Duration

Valuation
Premium/Discount (1-Year Average)   -0.02

Company Information
Provider	Fidelity Investments
Manager/Tenure	Jennifer Hsui (5), Greg Savage (5), Alan Mason (3), 2 others
Website	http://www.institutional.fidelity.com
Address	Fidelity Investments 82 Devonshire Street Boston MA 2109 United States
Phone Number	617-563-7000

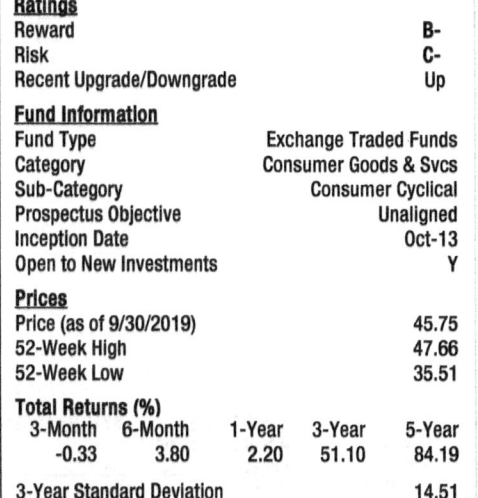

PERFORMANCE

Ratings History
Date	Overall Rating	Risk Rating	Reward Rating
Q3-19	C+	C-	B-
Q4-18	C	C	C+
Q4-17	B	A-	B
Q4-16	C+	C+	C+
Q4-15	C-	C+	C

Asset & Performance History
Date	NAV	1-Year Total Return
2018	38.32	-0.73
2017	39.07	22.78
2016	32.17	6.62
2015	30.67	6.4
2014	29.19	9.29
2013	26.99	

Total Assets: $721,342,696
Asset Allocation
Asset	%
Cash	0%
Stocks	100%
US Stocks	98%
Bonds	0%
US Bonds	0%
Other	0%

Services Offered:

Investment Strategy: The investment seeks to provide investment returns that correspond, before fees and expenses, generally to the performance of the MSCI USA IMI Consumer Discretionary Index. The fund invests at least 80% of assets in securities included in the fund's underlying index. The fund's underlying index is the MSCI USA IMI Consumer Discretionary Index, which represents the performance of the consumer discretionary sector in the U.S. equity market. It may or may not hold all of the securities in the MSCI USA IMI Consumer Discretionary Index. The fund is non-diversified. **Top Holdings:** Amazon.com Inc   The Home Depot Inc   McDonald's Corp   Starbucks Corp   Nike Inc B

Invesco International Dividend Achievers ETF   C   HOLD

Ticker	Traded On	NAV	Total Assets ($)	Dividend Yield (TTM)	Turnover Ratio	Expense Ratio
PID	NAS CM	16.06	$719,572,885	3.86	47	0.54

Ratings
Reward	C
Risk	C+
Recent Upgrade/Downgrade	Down

Fund Information
Fund Type	Exchange Traded Funds
Category	Global Equity Large Cap
Sub-Category	Foreign Large Value
Prospectus Objective	Foreign Stock
Inception Date	Sep-05
Open to New Investments	Y

Prices
Price (as of 9/30/2019)	16.04
52-Week High	16.80
52-Week Low	13.74

Total Returns (%)
3-Month	6-Month	1-Year	3-Year	5-Year
-1.25	2.75	5.20	22.35	5.73

3-Year Standard Deviation   11.51
Effective Duration

Valuation
Premium/Discount (1-Year Average)   -0.08

Company Information
Provider	Invesco
Manager/Tenure	Peter Hubbard (12), Michael Jeanette (11), Tony Seisser (5)
Website	http://www.invesco.com/us
Address	Invesco 11 Greenway Plaza, Ste. 2500 Houston TX 77046 United States
Phone Number	800-659-1005

PERFORMANCE

Ratings History
Date	Overall Rating	Risk Rating	Reward Rating
Q3-19	C	C+	C
Q4-18	C	C	C-
Q4-17	C	C	C
Q4-16	D+	D+	D+
Q4-15	C-	C-	C-

Asset & Performance History
Date	NAV	1-Year Total Return
2018	14.17	-11.08
2017	16.52	19.03
2016	14.39	9.92
2015	13.62	-19.09
2014	17.51	-1.14
2013	18.39	18.71

Total Assets: $719,572,885
Asset Allocation
Asset	%
Cash	0%
Stocks	100%
US Stocks	9%
Bonds	0%
US Bonds	0%
Other	0%

Services Offered:

Investment Strategy: The investment seeks to track the investment results (before fees and expenses) of the NASDAQ International Dividend AchieversTM Index. The fund generally will invest at least 90% of its total assets in the securities that comprise the underlying index. The underlying index is composed of Global Depositary Receipts ("GDRs") and American Depositary Receipts ("ADRs") that are listed on the London Stock Exchange ("LSE") or the London International Exchange, in addition to ADRs and non-U.S. common or ordinary stocks traded on NYSE, NASDAQ or NYSE American. **Top Holdings:** Vodafone Group PLC ADR   Severstal PAO GDR   Novolipetsk Steel PJSC GDR   Brookfield Property Partners LP   WPP PLC ADR

WisdomTree U.S. Total Dividend Fund
C   HOLD

Ticker	Traded On	NAV	Total Assets ($)	Dividend Yield (TTM)	Turnover Ratio	Expense Ratio
DTD	NYSE Arca	99.07	$718,273,952	2.57	11	0.28

Ratings
Reward	C
Risk	C-
Recent Upgrade/Downgrade	

Fund Information
Fund Type	Exchange Traded Funds
Category	US Equity Large Cap Value
Sub-Category	Large Value
Prospectus Objective	Growth & Inc
Inception Date	Jun-06
Open to New Investments	Y

Prices
Price (as of 9/30/2019)	99.11
52-Week High	99.68
52-Week Low	79.60

Total Returns (%)
3-Month	6-Month	1-Year	3-Year	5-Year
2.13	5.01	5.80	37.46	61.18

3-Year Standard Deviation	11.65
Effective Duration	

Valuation
Premium/Discount (1-Year Average)	-0.01

Company Information
Provider	WisdomTree
Manager/Tenure	Richard A. Brown (11), Thomas J. Durante (11), Karen Q. Wong (11)
Website	http://www.wisdomtree.com
Address	WisdomTree 245 Park Avenue, 35th floor New York NY 10167 United States
Phone Number	866-909-9473

PERFORMANCE

Ratings History

Date	Overall Rating	Risk Rating	Reward Rating
Q3-19	C	C-	C
Q4-18	C	C-	C
Q4-17	B-	B	B-
Q4-16	C+	C-	B
Q4-15	C	C	C

Asset & Performance History

Date	NAV	1-Year Total Return
2018	84.56	-6.35
2017	92.8	17.26
2016	81.18	16.58
2015	71.63	-1.31
2014	74.62	14.06
2013	67.11	28.02

Total Assets: $718,273,952

Asset Allocation

Asset	%
Cash	0%
Stocks	100%
US Stocks	100%
Bonds	0%
US Bonds	0%
Other	0%

Services Offered:

Investment Strategy: The investment seeks to track the price and yield performance, before fees and expenses, of the WisdomTree U.S. Dividend Index. The fund invests at least 95% of its total assets (exclusive of collateral held from securities lending) in the component securities of the index and investments that have economic characteristics that are substantially identical to the economic characteristics of such component securities. The index is a fundamentally-weighted index that is comprised of U.S. companies listed on a U.S. stock market that pay regular cash dividends. The fund is non-diversified. **Top Holdings:** Microsoft Corp Apple Inc AT&T Inc Exxon Mobil Corp JPMorgan Chase & Co

---

SPDR S&P® North American Natural Resources ETF
C-   HOLD

Ticker	Traded On	NAV	Total Assets ($)	Dividend Yield (TTM)	Turnover Ratio	Expense Ratio
NANR	NYSE Arca		$717,553,676	2.05	20	0.35

Ratings
Reward	C
Risk	C-
Recent Upgrade/Downgrade	

Fund Information
Fund Type	Exchange Traded Funds
Category	Natural Resources
Sub-Category	Natural Resources
Prospectus Objective	Natl Res
Inception Date	Dec-15
Open to New Investments	Y

Prices
Price (as of 9/30/2019)	31.40
52-Week High	34.85
52-Week Low	27.82

Total Returns (%)
3-Month	6-Month	1-Year	3-Year	5-Year
-2.97	-2.78	-6.63	1.51	

3-Year Standard Deviation	15.79
Effective Duration	

Valuation
Premium/Discount (1-Year Average)	-0.04

Company Information
Provider	SPDR State Street Global Advisors
Manager/Tenure	Michael J. Feehily (3), Karl A. Schneider (3), Emiliano Rabinovich (2)
Website	http://www.spdrs.com
Address	SPDR State Street Global Advisors State Street Financial Center, 1 Lincoln Street Boston MA 02111-2900 United States
Phone Number	617-786-3000

PERFORMANCE

Ratings History

Date	Overall Rating	Risk Rating	Reward Rating
Q3-19	C-	C-	C
Q4-18	C-	D+	C
Q4-17	C	B	D+
Q4-16	D	B+	D+
Q4-15		D+	D+

Asset & Performance History

Date	NAV	1-Year Total Return
2018	29.06	-16.5
2017	35.44	7.98
2016	33.48	34.59
2015	25.06	
2014		
2013		

Total Assets: $717,553,676

Asset Allocation

Asset	%
Cash	0%
Stocks	100%
US Stocks	63%
Bonds	0%
US Bonds	0%
Other	0%

Services Offered:

Investment Strategy: The investment seeks to track the performance of the S&P BMI North American Natural Resources Index. The fund generally invests substantially all, but at least 80%, of its total assets in the securities comprising the index. The index comprises publicly traded large- and mid-capitalization U.S. and Canadian companies in the natural resources and commodities businesses that meet certain investability requirements and are classified within the sub-industries of one of three natural resources categories: energy, metals & mining or agriculture. The fund is non-diversified. **Top Holdings:** Barrick Gold Corp Chevron Corp Newmont Goldcorp Corp Exxon Mobil Corp Nutrien Ltd

---

First Trust Multi-Asset Diversified Income Index Fund   C   HOLD

Ticker	Traded On	NAV	Total Assets ($)	Dividend Yield (TTM)	Turnover Ratio	Expense Ratio
MDIV	NAS CM	18.43	$715,978,516	6.08	84	0.71

Ratings
Reward   C
Risk   C-
Recent Upgrade/Downgrade

Fund Information
Fund Type   Exchange Traded Funds
Category   Moderate Allocation
Sub-Category   Allocation--50% to 70% Equity
Prospectus Objective   Income
Inception Date   Aug-12
Open to New Investments   Y

Prices
Price (as of 9/30/2019)   18.43
52-Week High   18.75
52-Week Low   16.21

Total Returns (%)

3-Month	6-Month	1-Year	3-Year	5-Year
1.04	2.55	5.63	16.95	17.65

3-Year Standard Deviation   8.17
Effective Duration   1.90

Valuation
Premium/Discount (1-Year Average)   0.07

Company Information
Provider   First Trust
Manager/Tenure   Jon C. Erickson (7), Daniel J. Lindquist (7), David G. McGarel (7), 3 others
Website   http://www.ftportfolios.com/
Address   First Trust 120 E. Liberty Drive, Suite 400 Wheaton IL 60187 United States
Phone Number   800-621-1675

PERFORMANCE

Ratings History

Date	Overall Rating	Risk Rating	Reward Rating
Q3-19	C	C-	C
Q4-18	C	C+	C-
Q4-17	C+	C+	C
Q4-16	C	C	C-
Q4-15	C	C+	D+

Asset & Performance History

Date	NAV	1-Year Total Return
2018	16.84	-5.75
2017	19.02	5.47
2016	19.14	11.25
2015	18.36	-7.48
2014	21.23	7.92
2013	20.81	10.86

Total Assets: $715,978,516

Asset Allocation

Asset	%
Cash	2%
Stocks	60%
US Stocks	56%
Bonds	19%
US Bonds	18%
Other	0%

Services Offered:

Investment Strategy: The investment seeks investment results that correspond generally to the price and yield (before the fund's fees and expenses) of an index called the NASDAQ US Multi-Asset Diversified Income IndexSM. The fund will normally invest at least 90% of its net assets (including investment borrowings) in the common stocks and/or depositary receipts, REITs, preferred securities, MLPs and ETF that comprise the index. The index is designed to provide exposure to five asset segments, each selected to result in a consistent and high yield for the index. These five asset segments are: equity securities, REITs, preferred securities, MLPs and high yield corporate bonds. **Top Holdings:** First Trust Tactical High Yield ETF   New York Mortgage Trust Inc   New Residential Investment Corp   Chimera Investment Corp   USA Compression Partners LP

ProShares S&P MidCap 400 Dividend Aristocrats ETF   C   HOLD

Ticker	Traded On	NAV	Total Assets ($)	Dividend Yield (TTM)	Turnover Ratio	Expense Ratio
REGL	BATS	58.07	$711,891,960	1.89	32	0.4

Ratings
Reward   C
Risk   C-
Recent Upgrade/Downgrade

Fund Information
Fund Type   Exchange Traded Funds
Category   US Equity Mid Cap
Sub-Category   Mid-Cap Blend
Prospectus Objective   Growth
Inception Date   Feb-15
Open to New Investments   Y

Prices
Price (as of 9/30/2019)   58.08
52-Week High   59.54
52-Week Low   49.63

Total Returns (%)

3-Month	6-Month	1-Year	3-Year	5-Year
-0.20	3.26	4.83	32.16	

3-Year Standard Deviation   11.62
Effective Duration

Valuation
Premium/Discount (1-Year Average)   0.03

Company Information
Provider   ProShares
Manager/Tenure   Michael Neches (4), Devin Sullivan (1)
Website   http://www.proshares.com
Address   ProShares 7501 Wisconsin Avenue, Suite 1000 Bethesda MD 20814 United States
Phone Number   866-776-5125

PERFORMANCE

Ratings History

Date	Overall Rating	Risk Rating	Reward Rating
Q3-19	C	C-	C
Q4-18	C	C-	C
Q4-17	B-	B	C+
Q4-16	C-	C	C
Q4-15	U		

Asset & Performance History

Date	NAV	1-Year Total Return
2018	51.74	-3.15
2017	54.5	10.22
2016	50.29	29.96
2015	39.2	
2014		
2013		

Total Assets: $711,891,960

Asset Allocation

Asset	%
Cash	0%
Stocks	100%
US Stocks	100%
Bonds	0%
US Bonds	0%
Other	0%

Services Offered:

Investment Strategy: The investment seeks investment results, before fees and expenses, that track the performance of the S&P MidCap 400® Dividend Aristocrats Index (the "index"). Under normal circumstances, the fund will invest at least 80% of its total assets in component securities (i.e., securities of the index and comparable securities that have economic characteristics that are substantially identical to the economic characteristics of the securities of the index). The index contains a minimum of 40 stocks which are equally weighted. No single sector is allowed to comprise more than 30% of the index weight. **Top Holdings:** West Pharmaceutical Services Inc   Royal Gold Inc   Omega Healthcare Investors Inc   Aqua America Inc   National Retail Properties Inc

iShares Morningstar Mid-Cap ETF   C   HOLD

Ticker	Traded On	NAV	Total Assets ($)	Dividend Yield (TTM)	Turnover Ratio	Expense Ratio
JKG	NYSE Arca	197.73	$711,825,024	1.39	60	0.25

Ratings
Reward   C
Risk   D+
Recent Upgrade/Downgrade

Fund Information
Fund Type	Exchange Traded Funds
Category	US Equity Mid Cap
Sub-Category	Mid-Cap Blend
Prospectus Objective	Growth
Inception Date	Jun-04
Open to New Investments	Y

Prices
Price (as of 9/30/2019)	197.77
52-Week High	200.59
52-Week Low	152.72

Total Returns (%)
3-Month	6-Month	1-Year	3-Year	5-Year
1.75	4.43	6.19	34.21	56.35

3-Year Standard Deviation   13.88
Effective Duration

Valuation
Premium/Discount (1-Year Average)   0.05

Company Information
Provider	iShares
Manager/Tenure	Greg Savage (11), Jennifer Hsui (7), Alan Mason (3), 2 others
Website	http://www.ishares.com
Address	iShares 400 Howard Street San Francisco CA 94105 United States
Phone Number	800-474-2737

PERFORMANCE

Ratings History
Date	Overall Rating	Risk Rating	Reward Rating
Q3-19	C	D+	C
Q4-18	C-	D+	C
Q4-17	B	B+	B
Q4-16	C+	C-	B-
Q4-15	C	C-	C

Asset & Performance History
Date	NAV	1-Year Total Return
2018	161.81	-11.41
2017	185.63	19.57
2016	157.42	12.13
2015	143.01	-1.6
2014	147.45	15.63
2013	129.37	32.47

Total Assets: $711,825,024
Asset Allocation
Asset	%
Cash	0%
Stocks	100%
US Stocks	98%
Bonds	0%
US Bonds	0%
Other	0%

Services Offered:

Investment Strategy: The investment seeks to track the investment results of the Morningstar® Mid Core IndexSM composed of mid-capitalization U.S. equities. The fund generally invests at least 90% of its assets in securities of the underlying index and in depositary receipts representing securities of the underlying index. The underlying index measures the performance of stocks issued by mid-capitalization companies that have exhibited average "growth" and "value" characteristics as determined by Morningstar, Inc.'s ("Morningstar" or the "index provider") proprietary index methodology. **Top Holdings:** L3Harris Technologies Inc   Newmont Goldcorp Corp   Motorola Solutions Inc   AutoZone Inc   Ball Corp

---

VanEck Vectors Preferred Securities ex Financials ETF   C+   HOLD

Ticker	Traded On	NAV	Total Assets ($)	Dividend Yield (TTM)	Turnover Ratio	Expense Ratio
PFXF	NYSE Arca	20.25	$706,565,581	5.32	31	0.41

Ratings
Reward   C+
Risk   C+
Recent Upgrade/Downgrade

Fund Information
Fund Type	Exchange Traded Funds
Category	US Fixed Income
Sub-Category	Preferred Stock
Prospectus Objective	Income
Inception Date	Jul-12
Open to New Investments	Y

Prices
Price (as of 9/30/2019)	20.30
52-Week High	20.30
52-Week Low	17.35

Total Returns (%)
3-Month	6-Month	1-Year	3-Year	5-Year
4.10	6.47	11.22	17.07	32.79

3-Year Standard Deviation   6.5
Effective Duration

Valuation
Premium/Discount (1-Year Average)   0.14

Company Information
Provider	VanEck
Manager/Tenure	Hao-Hung (Peter) Liao (7), Guo Hua (Jason) Jin (1)
Website	http://www.vaneck.com
Address	Van Eck Associates Corporation 666 Third Avenue New York NY 10017 United States
Phone Number	800-826-1115

PERFORMANCE

Ratings History
Date	Overall Rating	Risk Rating	Reward Rating
Q3-19	C+	C+	C+
Q4-18	C	C+	C-
Q4-17	B-	B+	C+
Q4-16	C	C+	C
Q4-15	C	C-	C

Asset & Performance History
Date	NAV	1-Year Total Return
2018	17.7	-4.78
2017	19.63	7.98
2016	19.27	5.74
2015	19.27	-0.25
2014	20.46	14.78
2013	18.92	-1.44

Total Assets: $706,565,581
Asset Allocation
Asset	%
Cash	0%
Stocks	8%
US Stocks	8%
Bonds	0%
US Bonds	0%
Other	3%

Services Offered:

Investment Strategy: The investment seeks to replicate as closely as possible, before fees and expenses, the price and yield performance of the Wells Fargo® Hybrid and Preferred Securities ex Financials Index (the "Preferred Securities Index"). The fund normally invests at least 80% of its total assets in securities that comprise the fund's benchmark index. The index is comprised of convertible or exchangeable and non-convertible preferred securities listed on U.S. exchanges. The fund is non-diversified. **Top Holdings:** Becton, Dickinson and Co Pfd   Sempra Energy 6% PRF CONVERT 15/01/2021 USD 100   NextEra Energy Inc Unit   Dominion Engy   AT&T Inc 0%

Direxion Daily Junior Gold Miners Index Bull 3X Shares   C   HOLD

Ticker	Traded On	NAV	Total Assets ($)	Dividend Yield (TTM)	Turnover Ratio	Expense Ratio
JNUG	NYSE Arca	56.83	$698,906,479	0.44	116	1.17

Ratings
Reward	B
Risk	D
Recent Upgrade/Downgrade	Up

Fund Information
Fund Type	Exchange Traded Funds
Category	Trading Tools
Sub-Category	Trading--Leveraged Equity
Prospectus Objective	Prec Metals
Inception Date	Oct-13
Open to New Investments	Y

Prices
Price (as of 9/30/2019)	57.14
52-Week High	100.56
52-Week Low	6.23

Total Returns (%)
3-Month	6-Month	1-Year	3-Year	5-Year
10.75	533.52	668.56	-17.46	-75.27

3-Year Standard Deviation	85.63
Effective Duration	

Valuation
Premium/Discount (1-Year Average)	0.21

Company Information
Provider	Direxion Funds
Manager/Tenure	Paul Brigandi (5), Tony Ng (4)
Website	http://www.direxionfunds.com
Address	Direxion Funds 1301 Avenue Of The Americas (6th Avenue) New York NY 10019 United States
Phone Number	646-572-3390

PERFORMANCE

Ratings History
Date	Overall Rating	Risk Rating	Reward Rating
Q3-19	C	D	B
Q4-18	E+	D-	E+
Q4-17	D-	D-	D
Q4-16	D	D	D+
Q4-15	D-	E+	D-

Asset & Performance History
Date	NAV	1-Year Total Return
2018	9.2	-48.22
2017	17.78	-19.66
2016	22.2	117.82
2015	12.45	-74.34
2014	48.54	-83.96
2013	314.8	

Total Assets: $698,906,479
Asset Allocation
Asset	%
Cash	46%
Stocks	42%
US Stocks	1%
Bonds	0%
US Bonds	0%
Other	12%

Services Offered:

Investment Strategy: The investment seeks daily investment results, before fees and expenses, of 300% of the daily performance of the MVIS Global Junior Gold Miners Index. The fund invests at least 80% of its net assets (plus borrowing for investment purposes) in financial instruments, such as swap agreements, and securities of the index, ETFs that track the index and other financial instruments that provide daily leveraged exposure to the index or ETFs that track the index. The index includes companies from markets that are freely investable to foreign investors, including "emerging markets," as that term is defined by the index provider. It is non-diversified. **Top Holdings:** VanEck Vectors Junior Gold Miners ETF   Ve Vectors Jr Gld Miners   Ve Vectors Jr Gld Miners   Ve Vectors Jr Gld Miners   Ve Vectors Jr Gld Miners

---

Aberdeen Standard Physical Platinum Shares ETF   D+   SELL

Ticker	Traded On	NAV	Total Assets ($)	Dividend Yield (TTM)	Turnover Ratio	Expense Ratio
PPLT	NYSE Arca	84.88	$696,031,836	0		0.6

Ratings
Reward	D+
Risk	D+
Recent Upgrade/Downgrade	Up

Fund Information
Fund Type	Exchange Traded Funds
Category	Commodities Specified
Sub-Category	Commodities Precious Metals
Prospectus Objective	Prec Metals
Inception Date	Jan-10
Open to New Investments	Y

Prices
Price (as of 9/30/2019)	83.47
52-Week High	93.15
52-Week Low	74.32

Total Returns (%)
3-Month	6-Month	1-Year	3-Year	5-Year
6.60	5.19	9.49	-14.51	-31.61

3-Year Standard Deviation	17.11
Effective Duration	

Valuation
Premium/Discount (1-Year Average)	-0.12

Company Information
Provider	Aberdeen Standard Investments
Manager/Tenure	Management Team (9)
Website	http://www.aberdeenstandardetfs.us
Address	Aberdeen Standard Investments 405 Lexington Avenue New York NY 10174 United States
Phone Number	212-918-4954

PERFORMANCE

Ratings History
Date	Overall Rating	Risk Rating	Reward Rating
Q3-19	D+	D+	D+
Q4-18	D	D	D
Q4-17	D	D	D
Q4-16	D	D	D
Q4-15	D-	D-	D-

Asset & Performance History
Date	NAV	1-Year Total Return
2018	75.22	-14.86
2017	88.36	1.59
2016	86.97	3.39
2015	84.12	-28.36
2014	117.43	-11.43
2013	132.59	-11.36

Total Assets: $696,031,836
Asset Allocation
Asset	%
Cash	0%
Stocks	0%
US Stocks	0%
Bonds	0%
US Bonds	0%
Other	100%

Services Offered:

Investment Strategy: The investment seeks to reflect the performance of the price of physical platinum, less the expenses of the Trust's operations.
The fund designed for investors who want a cost-effective and convenient way to invest in platinum with minimal credit risk. Advantages of investing in the Shares include Ease and Flexibility of Investment, Expenses, Minimal Credit Risk. **Top Holdings:** Physical Platinum Bullion

Invesco S&P 500® Equal Weight Health Care ETF   C   HOLD

Ticker	Traded On	NAV	Total Assets ($)	Dividend Yield (TTM)	Turnover Ratio	Expense Ratio
RYH	NYSE Arca	196.04	$695,929,023	0.61		0.4

Ratings
Reward	C
Risk	C-
Recent Upgrade/Downgrade	

Fund Information
Fund Type	Exchange Traded Funds
Category	Healthcare Sector Equity
Sub-Category	Health
Prospectus Objective	Health
Inception Date	Nov-06
Open to New Investments	Y

Prices
Price (as of 9/30/2019)	195.97
52-Week High	206.12
52-Week Low	165.92

Total Returns (%)
3-Month	6-Month	1-Year	3-Year	5-Year
-3.71	-0.88	-4.38	28.18	57.17

3-Year Standard Deviation	15.05
Effective Duration	

Valuation
Premium/Discount (1-Year Average)	-0.03

Company Information
Provider	Invesco
Manager/Tenure	Peter Hubbard (1), Michael Jeanette (1), Tony Seisser (1)
Website	http://www.invesco.com/us
Address	Invesco 11 Greenway Plaza, Ste. 2500 Houston TX 77046 United States
Phone Number	800-659-1005

PERFORMANCE

Ratings History
Date	Overall Rating	Risk Rating	Reward Rating
Q3-19	C	C-	C
Q4-18	C	C-	C
Q4-17	B	B	B-
Q4-16	C	C-	C
Q4-15	C+	C	B-

Asset & Performance History
Date	NAV	1-Year Total Return
2018	177.68	-0.33
2017	179.18	24.01
2016	145.92	-4.98
2015	153.51	8.2
2014	142.55	29.79
2013	110.35	40.75

Total Assets: $695,929,023
Asset Allocation
Asset	%
Cash	0%
Stocks	100%
US Stocks	99%
Bonds	0%
US Bonds	0%
Other	0%

Services Offered:

Investment Strategy: The investment seeks to track the investment results (before fees and expenses) of the S&P 500® Equal Weight Health Care Index (the "underlying index"). The fund generally will invest at least 90% of its total assets in the securities that comprise the underlying index. The underlying index is composed of all of the components of the S&P 500® Health Care Index, an index that contains the common stocks of all companies included in the S&P 500® Index that are classified as members of the health care sector, as defined according to the Global Industry Classification Standard ("GICS"). The fund is non-diversified. **Top Holdings:** Allergan PLC Edwards Lifesciences Corp   Zimmer Biomet Holdings Inc   Amgen Inc   ResMed Inc

---

VanEck Vectors Agribusiness ETF   C+   HOLD

Ticker	Traded On	NAV	Total Assets ($)	Dividend Yield (TTM)	Turnover Ratio	Expense Ratio
MOO	NYSE Arca	65.87	$691,652,696	1.46	16	0.54

Ratings
Reward	B-
Risk	C-
Recent Upgrade/Downgrade	Up

Fund Information
Fund Type	Exchange Traded Funds
Category	Natural Resources
Sub-Category	Natural Resources
Prospectus Objective	Unaligned
Inception Date	Aug-07
Open to New Investments	Y

Prices
Price (as of 9/30/2019)	65.86
52-Week High	67.52
52-Week Low	54.16

Total Returns (%)
3-Month	6-Month	1-Year	3-Year	5-Year
-1.81	4.55	1.84	39.01	41.41

3-Year Standard Deviation	11.78
Effective Duration	

Valuation
Premium/Discount (1-Year Average)	-0.14

Company Information
Provider	VanEck
Manager/Tenure	Hao-Hung (Peter) Liao (12), Guo Hua (Jason) Jin (1)
Website	http://www.vaneck.com
Address	Van Eck Associates Corporation 666 Third Avenue New York NY 10017 United States
Phone Number	800-826-1115

PERFORMANCE

Ratings History
Date	Overall Rating	Risk Rating	Reward Rating
Q3-19	C+	C-	B-
Q4-18	C	C-	C
Q4-17	B-	B-	B-
Q4-16	C	C	C
Q4-15	C+	C+	C+

Asset & Performance History
Date	NAV	1-Year Total Return
2018	57.11	-5.87
2017	61.63	21.68
2016	51.38	12.75
2015	46.55	-8.9
2014	52.59	-0.34
2013	54.44	4.82

Total Assets: $691,652,696
Asset Allocation
Asset	%
Cash	0%
Stocks	100%
US Stocks	54%
Bonds	0%
US Bonds	0%
Other	0%

Services Offered:

Investment Strategy: The investment seeks to replicate as closely as possible, before fees and expenses, the price and yield performance of the MVIS® Global Agribusiness Index. The fund normally invests at least 80% of its total assets in securities that comprise the fund's benchmark index. The index includes equity securities of companies that generate at least 50% of their revenues from agri-chemicals, animal health and fertilizers, seeds and traits, from farm/irrigation equipment and farm machinery, aquaculture and fishing, livestock, cultivation and plantations and trading of agricultural products. It is non-diversified. **Top Holdings:** Bayer AG   Zoetis Inc Class A Deere & Co   Nutrien Ltd   Tyson Foods Inc Class A

iShares ESG MSCI EM ETF   C   HOLD

Ticker	Traded On	NAV	Total Assets ($)	Dividend Yield (TTM)	Turnover Ratio	Expense Ratio
ESGE	NAS CM	32.58	$684,153,170	2.1	45	0.25

Ratings
Reward   C
Risk   C
Recent Upgrade/Downgrade

Fund Information
Fund Type   Exchange Traded Funds
Category   Global Emerg Mkts Equity
Sub-Category   Diversified Emerging Mkts
Prospectus Objective   Div Emerg Mkts
Inception Date   Jun-16
Open to New Investments   Y

Prices
Price (as of 9/30/2019)   32.53
52-Week High   35.40
52-Week Low   29.80

Total Returns (%)

3-Month	6-Month	1-Year	3-Year	5-Year
-4.82	-4.28	-0.31	20.32	

3-Year Standard Deviation   14
Effective Duration

Valuation
Premium/Discount (1-Year Average)   0.15

Company Information
Provider   iShares
Manager/Tenure   Diane Hsiung (3), Jennifer Hsui (3), Alan Mason (3), 3 others
Website   http://www.ishares.com
Address   iShares 400 Howard Street San Francisco CA 94105 United States
Phone Number   800-474-2737

Ratings History

Date	Overall Rating	Risk Rating	Reward Rating
Q3-19	C	C	C
Q4-18	D+	D	D+
Q4-17	D	B-	C
Q4-16	U		
Q4-15			

Asset & Performance History

Date	NAV	1-Year Total Return
2018	30.88	-14.31
2017	36.8	37.88
2016	27.23	
2015		
2014		
2013		

Total Assets: $684,153,170

Asset Allocation

Asset	%
Cash	0%
Stocks	100%
US Stocks	0%
Bonds	0%
US Bonds	0%
Other	0%

Services Offered:

Investment Strategy: The investment seeks to track the investment results of the MSCI Emerging Markets Extended ESG Focus Index. The fund generally will invest at least 90% of its assets in the component securities of the underlying index and in investments that have economic characteristics that are substantially identical to the component securities of the underlying index. The index is an optimized equity index designed to reflect the equity performance of companies that have favorable ESG characteristics, while exhibiting risk and return characteristics similar to those of the MSCI Market Cap Weighted Index (the "parent index"). **Top Holdings:** Tencent Holdings Ltd Taiwan Semiconductor Manufacturing Co Ltd Alibaba Group Holding Ltd ADR Samsung Electronics Co Ltd Naspers Ltd Class N

SPDR® S&P Homebuilders ETF   B-   BUY

Ticker	Traded On	NAV	Total Assets ($)	Dividend Yield (TTM)	Turnover Ratio	Expense Ratio
XHB	NYSE Arca		$680,805,782	1	32	0.35

Ratings
Reward   B
Risk   C
Recent Upgrade/Downgrade   Up

Fund Information
Fund Type   Exchange Traded Funds
Category   Consumer Goods & Svcs
Sub-Category   Consumer Cyclical
Prospectus Objective   Real Estate
Inception Date   Jan-06
Open to New Investments   Y

Prices
Price (as of 9/30/2019)   44.08
52-Week High   44.08
52-Week Low   30.74

Total Returns (%)

3-Month	6-Month	1-Year	3-Year	5-Year
3.83	12.36	15.00	31.93	52.98

3-Year Standard Deviation   17.38
Effective Duration

Valuation
Premium/Discount (1-Year Average)   -0.01

Company Information
Provider   SPDR State Street Global Advisors
Manager/Tenure   Michael J. Feehily (7), Karl A. Schneider (4), Raymond V. Donofrio (2)
Website   http://www.spdrs.com
Address   SPDR State Street Global Advisors State Street Financial Center, 1 Lincoln Street Boston MA 02111-2900 United States
Phone Number   617-786-3000

Ratings History

Date	Overall Rating	Risk Rating	Reward Rating
Q3-19	B-	C	B
Q4-18	C	D+	B-
Q4-17	B+	B	A-
Q4-16	B-	C	B
Q4-15	B+	B	A-

Asset & Performance History

Date	NAV	1-Year Total Return
2018	32.52	-25.64
2017	44.22	31.65
2016	33.86	-0.28
2015	34.17	0.59
2014	34.13	3.15
2013	33.27	25.5

Total Assets: $680,805,782

Asset Allocation

Asset	%
Cash	0%
Stocks	100%
US Stocks	100%
Bonds	0%
US Bonds	0%
Other	0%

Services Offered: Dividend Investment Plan, CashInvestment Plan

Investment Strategy: The investment seeks to provide investment results that, before fees and expenses, correspond generally to the total return performance of an index derived from the homebuilding segment of a U.S. total market composite index. In seeking to track the performance of the S&P Homebuilders Select Industry Index (the "index"), the fund employs a sampling strategy. It generally invests substantially all, but at least 80%, of its total assets in the securities comprising the index. The index represents the homebuilders segment of the S&P Total Market Index ("S&P TMI"). The fund is non-diversified. **Top Holdings:** Lowe's Companies Inc The Home Depot Inc D.R. Horton Inc Williams-Sonoma Inc Johnson Controls International PLC

First Trust Developed Markets Ex-US AlphaDEX® Fund

C-   HOLD

Ticker	Traded On	NAV		Total Assets ($)	Dividend Yield (TTM)	Turnover Ratio	Expense Ratio
FDT	NAS CM	52.34		$680,508,902	2.23	109	0.8

Ratings

Reward	D+
Risk	C
Recent Upgrade/Downgrade	

Fund Information

Fund Type	Exchange Traded Funds
Category	Global Equity Large Cap
Sub-Category	Foreign Large Blend
Prospectus Objective	Foreign Stock
Inception Date	Apr-11
Open to New Investments	Y

Prices

Price (as of 9/30/2019)	52.34
52-Week High	59.64
52-Week Low	47.63

Total Returns (%)

3-Month	6-Month	1-Year	3-Year	5-Year
-2.99	-3.40	-10.21	12.58	17.16

3-Year Standard Deviation	13.5
Effective Duration	

Valuation

Premium/Discount (1-Year Average)	-0.09

Company Information

Provider	First Trust
Manager/Tenure	Jon C. Erickson (8), Daniel J. Lindquist (8), David G. McGarel (8), 3 others
Website	http://www.ftportfolios.com/
Address	First Trust 120 E. Liberty Drive, Suite 400 Wheaton IL 60187 United States
Phone Number	800-621-1675

PERFORMANCE

12/31/17   4/10/18   7/21/18   11/3/18   2/14/19   6/17/19   9/30/19

Ratings History

Date	Overall Rating	Risk Rating	Reward Rating
Q3-19	C-	C	D+
Q4-18	D+	C-	D+
Q4-17	B	B	B+
Q4-16	C-	C-	C-
Q4-15	C-	C-	C-

Asset & Performance History

Date	NAV	1-Year Total Return
2018	49.24	-19.52
2017	62.31	33.58
2016	47.43	3.56
2015	46.63	0.63
2014	47.14	-5.97
2013	50.96	18.41

Total Assets: $680,508,902

Asset Allocation

Asset	%
Cash	1%
Stocks	99%
US Stocks	1%
Bonds	0%
US Bonds	0%
Other	0%

Services Offered:

Investment Strategy: The investment seeks results that correspond generally to the price and yield (before the fund's fees and expenses) of an equity index called the NASDAQ AlphaDEX® Developed Markets Ex-US Index. The fund will normally invest at least 90% of its net assets (including investment borrowings) in the common stocks and depositary receipts that comprise the index. The index is designed to select stocks from the NASDAQ Developed Markets Ex-US Index that may generate positive alpha, or risk-adjusted returns, relative to traditional indices through the use of the AlphaDEX® selection methodology. **Top Holdings:** Shopify Inc A   Afterpay Touch Group Ltd   Air Canada Class B   Magellan Financial Group Ltd   Cogeco Communications Inc

iShares MSCI World ETF

C   HOLD

Ticker	Traded On	NAV		Total Assets ($)	Dividend Yield (TTM)	Turnover Ratio	Expense Ratio
URTH	NYSE Arca	91.71		$678,625,950	2.15	3	0.24

Ratings

Reward	C
Risk	C-
Recent Upgrade/Downgrade	

Fund Information

Fund Type	Exchange Traded Funds
Category	Global Equity Large Cap
Sub-Category	World Large Stock
Prospectus Objective	World Stock
Inception Date	Jan-12
Open to New Investments	Y

Prices

Price (as of 9/30/2019)	91.78
52-Week High	93.05
52-Week Low	75.04

Total Returns (%)

3-Month	6-Month	1-Year	3-Year	5-Year
0.01	3.51	1.99	34.89	44.87

3-Year Standard Deviation	11.3
Effective Duration	

Valuation

Premium/Discount (1-Year Average)	0.06

Company Information

Provider	iShares
Manager/Tenure	Diane Hsiung (7), Greg Savage (7), Jennifer Hsui (6), 3 others
Website	http://www.ishares.com
Address	iShares 400 Howard Street San Francisco CA 94105 United States
Phone Number	800-474-2737

PERFORMANCE

12/28/17   4/7/18   7/18/18   10/31/18   2/11/19   6/16/19   9/30/19

Ratings History

Date	Overall Rating	Risk Rating	Reward Rating
Q3-19	C	C-	C
Q4-18	C	C+	C-
Q4-17	B-	B-	B-
Q4-16	C	C-	C+
Q4-15	C	C+	C

Asset & Performance History

Date	NAV	1-Year Total Return
2018	78.82	-8.44
2017	87.88	22.5
2016	73.16	7.83
2015	69.34	-0.62
2014	71.38	4.9
2013	69.63	26.74

Total Assets: $678,625,950

Asset Allocation

Asset	%
Cash	1%
Stocks	100%
US Stocks	63%
Bonds	0%
US Bonds	0%
Other	0%

Services Offered:

Investment Strategy: The investment seeks to track the investment results of the MSCI World Index. The fund generally will invest at least 90% of its assets in the component securities of the underlying index and in investments that have economic characteristics that are substantially identical to the component securities of the underlying index. The index is designed to measure the performance of equity securities in the top 85% of equity market capitalization, as calculated by the index provider, in certain developed market countries. **Top Holdings:** Microsoft Corp   Apple Inc   Amazon.com Inc   Facebook Inc A   Alphabet Inc Class C

iShares MSCI Mexico Capped ETF

D   SELL

Ticker	Traded On	NAV	Total Assets ($)	Dividend Yield (TTM)	Turnover Ratio	Expense Ratio
EWW	NYSE Arca	42.66	$678,353,194	2.94	7	0.47

Ratings
Reward	D
Risk	C-
Recent Upgrade/Downgrade	

Fund Information
Fund Type	Exchange Traded Funds
Category	Mexico Equity
Sub-Category	Miscellaneous Region
Prospectus Objective	Foreign Stock
Inception Date	Mar-96
Open to New Investments	Y

Prices
Price (as of 9/30/2019)	42.72
52-Week High	51.61
52-Week Low	37.76

Total Returns (%)
3-Month	6-Month	1-Year	3-Year	5-Year
-3.02	-2.24	-15.06	-6.03	-29.60

3-Year Standard Deviation	22.24
Effective Duration	

Valuation
Premium/Discount (1-Year Average)	-0.12

Company Information
Provider	iShares
Manager/Tenure	Diane Hsiung (11), Greg Savage (11), Jennifer Hsui (6), 3 others
Website	http://www.ishares.com
Address	iShares 400 Howard Street San Francisco CA 94105 United States
Phone Number	800-474-2737

PERFORMANCE

Ratings History
Date	Overall Rating	Risk Rating	Reward Rating
Q3-19	D	C-	D
Q4-18	D	D	D
Q4-17	D+	D+	D+
Q4-16	D	D	D+
Q4-15	D	D	D

Asset & Performance History
Date	NAV	1-Year Total Return
2018	41.2	-14.93
2017	49.52	14.25
2016	44.27	-10.1
2015	50.05	-14.29
2014	59.68	-10.13
2013	67.23	-1.47

Total Assets: $678,353,194

Asset Allocation
Asset	%
Cash	0%
Stocks	100%
US Stocks	0%
Bonds	0%
US Bonds	0%
Other	0%

Services Offered: CashInvestment Plan

Investment Strategy: The investment seeks to track the investment results of the MSCI Mexico IMI 25/50 Index. The fund will at all times invest at least 80% of its assets in the securities of its underlying index and in depositary receipts representing securities in its underlying index. The underlying index is a free float-adjusted market capitalization-weighted index with a capping methodology applied to issuer weights so that no single issuer of a component exceeds 25% of the underlying index weight, and all issuers with a weight above 5% do not cumulatively exceed 50% of the underlying index weight. The fund is non-diversified. **Top Holdings:** America Movil SAB de CV Class L   Fomento Economico Mexicano SAB de CV Units (1 Series B, 4 Series D)   Wal - Mart de Mexico SAB de CV Class V   Grupo Financiero Banorte SAB de CV Class O   Grupo Mexico SAB de CV

---

iShares iBonds Dec 2019 Term Corporate ETF

C   HOLD

Ticker	Traded On	NAV	Total Assets ($)	Dividend Yield (TTM)	Turnover Ratio	Expense Ratio
IBDK	NYSE Arca	24.87	$677,718,075	2.26	5	0.1

Ratings
Reward	C
Risk	C+
Recent Upgrade/Downgrade	

Fund Information
Fund Type	Exchange Traded Funds
Category	US Fixed Income
Sub-Category	Short-Term Bond
Prospectus Objective	Corp Bond - Gen
Inception Date	Mar-15
Open to New Investments	Y

Prices
Price (as of 9/30/2019)	24.85
52-Week High	24.87
52-Week Low	24.73

Total Returns (%)
3-Month	6-Month	1-Year	3-Year	5-Year
0.57	1.21	2.64	5.38	

3-Year Standard Deviation	0.66
Effective Duration	

Valuation
Premium/Discount (1-Year Average)	0.05

Company Information
Provider	iShares
Manager/Tenure	James Mauro (4), Scott Radell (4)
Website	http://www.ishares.com
Address	iShares 400 Howard Street San Francisco CA 94105 United States
Phone Number	800-474-2737

PERFORMANCE

Ratings History
Date	Overall Rating	Risk Rating	Reward Rating
Q3-19	C	C+	C
Q4-18	C	C+	C
Q4-17	B-	A	C
Q4-16	D+	C-	D+
Q4-15	U		

Asset & Performance History
Date	NAV	1-Year Total Return
2018	24.74	1.82
2017	24.81	1.79
2016	24.81	3.19
2015	24.51	
2014		
2013		

Total Assets: $677,718,075

Asset Allocation
Asset	%
Cash	99%
Stocks	0%
US Stocks	0%
Bonds	0%
US Bonds	0%
Other	0%

Services Offered:

Investment Strategy: The investment seeks to track the investment results of the Bloomberg Barclays December 2019 Maturity Corporate Index which composed of U.S. dollar-denominated, investment-grade corporate bonds maturing in 2019. The fund generally will invest at least 90% of its assets in the component securities of the underlying index. The underlying index includes U.S. dollar-denominated, investment-grade securities publicly issued by U.S. and non-U.S. corporate issuers that have $300 million or more of outstanding face value at the time of inclusion. **Top Holdings:** Wells Fargo Bank, National Association 2.15%   Goldman Sachs Group, Inc. 2.3% Barclays PLC 2.75%   Kinder Morgan, Inc. 3.05%   Costco Wholesale Corporation 1.7%

First Trust NASDAQ-100 Equal Weighted Index Fund

C   HOLD

Ticker	Traded On	NAV	Total Assets ($)	Dividend Yield (TTM)	Turnover Ratio	Expense Ratio
QQEW	NAS CM	66.33	$673,250,140	0.55	27	0.6

Ratings
Reward	C+
Risk	C-
Recent Upgrade/Downgrade	Down

Fund Information
Fund Type	Exchange Traded Funds
Category	US Equity Large Cap Growth
Sub-Category	Large Growth
Prospectus Objective	Growth
Inception Date	Apr-06
Open to New Investments	Y

Prices
Price (as of 9/30/2019)	66.35
52-Week High	69.62
52-Week Low	51.19

Total Returns (%)
3-Month	6-Month	1-Year	3-Year	5-Year
-1.73	1.86	5.07	47.35	74.18

3-Year Standard Deviation	14.78
Effective Duration	

Valuation
Premium/Discount (1-Year Average)	-0.02

Company Information
Provider	First Trust
Manager/Tenure	Jon C. Erickson (13), Daniel J. Lindquist (13), David G. McGarel (13), 3 others
Website	http://www.ftportfolios.com/
Address	First Trust 120 E. Liberty Drive, Suite 400 Wheaton IL 60187 United States
Phone Number	800-621-1675

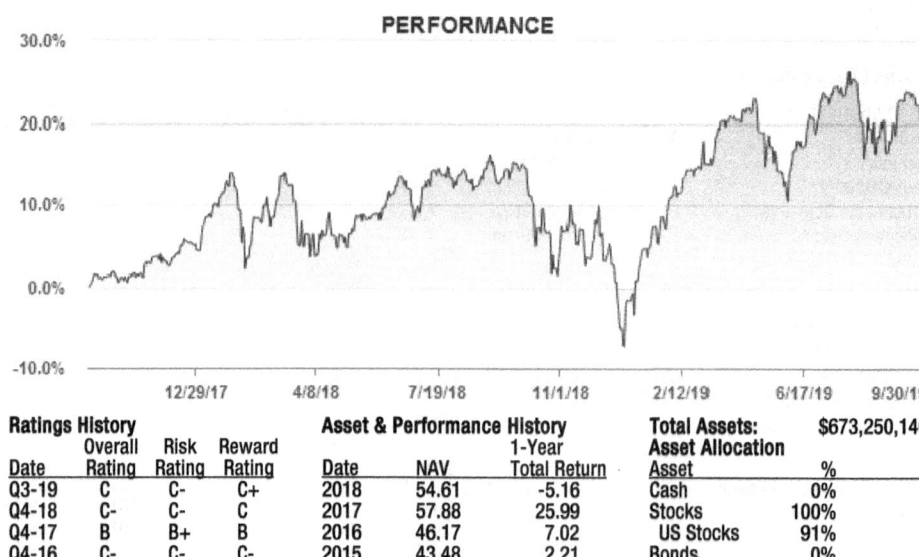

PERFORMANCE

Ratings History
Date	Overall Rating	Risk Rating	Reward Rating
Q3-19	C	C-	C+
Q4-18	C-	C-	C
Q4-17	B	B+	B
Q4-16	C-	C-	C-
Q4-15	C+	C+	C

Asset & Performance History
Date	NAV	1-Year Total Return
2018	54.61	-5.16
2017	57.88	25.99
2016	46.17	7.02
2015	43.48	2.21
2014	42.8	19.12
2013	36.34	39.95

Total Assets: $673,250,140
Asset Allocation
Asset	%
Cash	0%
Stocks	100%
US Stocks	91%
Bonds	0%
US Bonds	0%
Other	0%

Services Offered:

Investment Strategy: The investment seeks investment results that correspond generally to the price and yield (before the fund's fees and expenses) of an equity index called the NASDAQ-100 Equal Weighted IndexSM. The fund will normally invest at least 90% of its net assets (including investment borrowings) in the common stocks and depositary receipts that comprise the index. The index is the equal-weighted version of the NASDAQ-100 Index® which includes 100 of the largest U.S. and international non-financial companies listed on Nasdaq based on market capitalization. **Top Holdings:** Western Digital Corp Micron Technology Inc KLA Corp JB Hunt Transport Services Inc Fiserv Inc

---

Invesco S&P Global Water Index ETF

C   HOLD

Ticker	Traded On	NAV	Total Assets ($)	Dividend Yield (TTM)	Turnover Ratio	Expense Ratio
CGW	NYSE Arca	38.20	$670,865,630	1.74		0.62

Ratings
Reward	B-
Risk	C-
Recent Upgrade/Downgrade	

Fund Information
Fund Type	Exchange Traded Funds
Category	Equity Misc
Sub-Category	Miscellaneous Sector
Prospectus Objective	Natl Res
Inception Date	May-07
Open to New Investments	Y

Prices
Price (as of 9/30/2019)	38.26
52-Week High	38.26
52-Week Low	29.76

Total Returns (%)
3-Month	6-Month	1-Year	3-Year	5-Year
1.92	7.18	11.82	31.11	52.96

3-Year Standard Deviation	11.61
Effective Duration	

Valuation
Premium/Discount (1-Year Average)	0.00

Company Information
Provider	Invesco
Manager/Tenure	Peter Hubbard (1), Michael Jeanette (1), Tony Seisser (1)
Website	http://www.invesco.com/us
Address	Invesco 11 Greenway Plaza, Ste. 2500 Houston TX 77046 United States
Phone Number	800-659-1005

PERFORMANCE

Ratings History
Date	Overall Rating	Risk Rating	Reward Rating
Q3-19	C	C-	B-
Q4-18	C-	C-	C-
Q4-17	B	B+	B
Q4-16	C	C-	C
Q4-15	C	C-	C

Asset & Performance History
Date	NAV	1-Year Total Return
2018	31.23	-10.01
2017	35.48	26.76
2016	28.48	5.55
2015	27.14	-1.81
2014	28.1	3.86
2013	27.53	26.21

Total Assets: $670,865,630
Asset Allocation
Asset	%
Cash	0%
Stocks	100%
US Stocks	49%
Bonds	0%
US Bonds	0%
Other	0%

Services Offered:

Investment Strategy: The investment seeks to track the investment results (before fees and expenses) of the S&P Global Water Index (the "underlying index"). The fund generally will invest at least 90% of its total assets in the securities that comprise the underlying index, as well as ADRs and GDRs that represent securities in the underlying index. Strictly in accordance with its guidelines and mandated procedures, the index provider compiles, maintains, and calculates the underlying index, which is designed to measure the performance of approximately 50 of the largest global companies in water-related businesses. The fund is non-diversified. **Top Holdings:** American Water Works Co Inc Xylem Inc Geberit AG Danaher Corp IDEX Corp

VictoryShares US EQ Income Enhanced Volatility Wtd ETF   C   HOLD

Ticker	Traded On	NAV	Total Assets ($)	Dividend Yield (TTM)	Turnover Ratio	Expense Ratio
CDC	NAS CM	46.52	$662,943,268	3.07	143	0.35

Ratings
Reward	C
Risk	C-
Recent Upgrade/Downgrade	

Fund Information
Fund Type	Exchange Traded Funds
Category	US Equity Large Cap Value
Sub-Category	Large Value
Prospectus Objective	Income
Inception Date	Jul-14
Open to New Investments	Y

Prices
Price (as of 9/30/2019)	46.53
52-Week High	47.77
52-Week Low	40.65

Total Returns (%)
3-Month	6-Month	1-Year	3-Year	5-Year
2.23	4.95	1.45	28.66	57.84

3-Year Standard Deviation	10.7
Effective Duration	

Valuation
Premium/Discount (1-Year Average)	-0.04

Company Information
Provider	VictoryShares
Manager/Tenure	Mannik Dhillon (1)
Website	http://www.VictorySharesLiterature.com
Address	Victory Shares 4249 Easton Way, Suite 400 Columbus OH 43219 United States
Phone Number	

PERFORMANCE

Ratings History
Date	Overall Rating	Risk Rating	Reward Rating
Q3-19	C	C-	C
Q4-18	C	C-	C
Q4-17	B	B+	B
Q4-16	C	C-	B-
Q4-15	D	C	D+

Asset & Performance History
Date	NAV	1-Year Total Return
2018	42.47	-5.52
2017	46.38	15.73
2016	41.28	19.77
2015	35.37	-0.52
2014	36.69	
2013		

Total Assets: $662,943,268
Asset Allocation
Asset	%
Cash	1%
Stocks	99%
US Stocks	99%
Bonds	0%
US Bonds	0%
Other	0%

Services Offered:

Investment Strategy: The investment seeks to provide investment results that track the performance of the Nasdaq Victory US Large Cap High Dividend 100 Long/Cash Volatility Weighted Index before fees and expenses. The fund seeks to achieve its investment objective by investing, under normal market conditions, at least 80% of its assets directly or indirectly in the securities included in the Nasdaq Victory US Large Cap 100 High Dividend Long/Cash Volatility Weighted Index. The index identifies the 100 highest dividend yielding stocks in the Nasdaq Victory US Large Cap 500 Volatility Weighted Index. **Top Holdings:** WEC Energy Group Inc The Western Union Co Eversource Energy Xcel Energy Inc Evergy Inc

---

iShares MSCI Russia Capped ETF   B   BUY

Ticker	Traded On	NAV	Total Assets ($)	Dividend Yield (TTM)	Turnover Ratio	Expense Ratio
ERUS	NYSE Arca	38.98	$658,807,248	5.2	32	0.59

Ratings
Reward	B
Risk	C+
Recent Upgrade/Downgrade	

Fund Information
Fund Type	Exchange Traded Funds
Category	Equity Misc
Sub-Category	Miscellaneous Region
Prospectus Objective	Foreign Stock
Inception Date	Nov-10
Open to New Investments	Y

Prices
Price (as of 9/30/2019)	38.90
52-Week High	40.76
52-Week Low	30.59

Total Returns (%)
3-Month	6-Month	1-Year	3-Year	5-Year
-2.57	13.06	17.20	52.80	41.18

3-Year Standard Deviation	18.63
Effective Duration	

Valuation
Premium/Discount (1-Year Average)	-0.23

Company Information
Provider	iShares
Manager/Tenure	Diane Hsiung (8), Greg Savage (8), Jennifer Hsui (6), 3 others
Website	http://www.ishares.com
Address	iShares 400 Howard Street San Francisco CA 94105 United States
Phone Number	800-474-2737

PERFORMANCE

Ratings History
Date	Overall Rating	Risk Rating	Reward Rating
Q3-19	B	C+	B
Q4-18	C+	C+	C+
Q4-17	B	C	A-
Q4-16	C-	D+	C-
Q4-15	D	D	D

Asset & Performance History
Date	NAV	1-Year Total Return
2018	30.96	-3.66
2017	33.61	4.5
2016	33.42	53.94
2015	22.28	3.36
2014	22.38	-44.95
2013	43.12	-3.21

Total Assets: $658,807,248
Asset Allocation
Asset	%
Cash	0%
Stocks	100%
US Stocks	0%
Bonds	0%
US Bonds	0%
Other	0%

Services Offered:

Investment Strategy: The investment seeks to track the investment results of the MSCI Russia 25/50 Index. The fund generally will invest at least 90% of its assets in the component securities of the underlying index and in investments that have economic characteristics that are substantially identical to the component securities of the underlying index. The index is designed to measure the performance of equity securities listed on stock exchanges in Russia. The fund is non-diversified. **Top Holdings:** Gazprom PJSC PJSC Lukoil Sberbank of Russia PJSC Mining and Metallurgical Company NORILSK NICKEL PJSC Tatneft PJSC

ProShares UltraPro Short S&P500

D   **SELL**

Ticker	Traded On	NAV	Total Assets ($)	Dividend Yield (TTM)	Turnover Ratio	Expense Ratio
SPXU	NYSE Arca	25.99	$652,276,421	2.18	0	0.91

Ratings
Reward	E+
Risk	D
Recent Upgrade/Downgrade	

Fund Information
Fund Type	Exchange Traded Funds
Category	Trading Tools
Sub-Category	Trading--Inverse Equity
Prospectus Objective	Growth
Inception Date	Jun-09
Open to New Investments	Y

Prices
Price (as of 9/30/2019)	25.98
52-Week High	57.55
52-Week Low	25.26

Total Returns (%)
3-Month	6-Month	1-Year	3-Year	5-Year
-3.82	-13.83	-17.13	-71.06	-85.81

3-Year Standard Deviation	35.54
Effective Duration	

Valuation
Premium/Discount (1-Year Average)	0.09

Company Information
Provider	ProShares
Manager/Tenure	Michael Neches (6), Devin Sullivan (1)
Website	http://www.proshares.com
Address	ProShares 7501 Wisconsin Avenue, Suite 1000 Bethesda MD 20814 United States
Phone Number	866-776-5125

PERFORMANCE

Ratings History
Date	Overall Rating	Risk Rating	Reward Rating
Q3-19	D	D	E+
Q4-18	D	D-	D-
Q4-17	E+	E+	E+
Q4-16	D	E+	D-
Q4-15	D-	E+	E+

Asset & Performance History
Date	NAV	1-Year Total Return
2018	46.62	3.75
2017	45.68	-44.2
2016	81.96	-35.28
2015	126.64	-16.79
2014	152.2	-36.96
2013	241.44	-60.04

Total Assets: $652,276,421
Asset Allocation
Asset	%
Cash	260%
Stocks	-172%
US Stocks	-170%
Bonds	12%
US Bonds	12%
Other	0%

Services Offered:

Investment Strategy: The investment seeks daily investment results before fees and expenses that correspond to three times the inverse (-3x) of the daily performance of the S&P 500® Index. The fund invests in financial instruments that ProShare Advisors believes, in combination, should produce daily returns consistent with the fund's investment objective. The index is a measure of large-cap U.S. stock market performance. The fund is non-diversified. **Top Holdings:** S&P 500 Index Swap Ubs Ag S&P 500 Index Swap Bnp Paribas S&P 500 Index Swap Citibank Na S&P 500 Index Swap Societe Generale S&P 500 Index Swap Goldman Sachs International

---

PIMCO Investment Grade Corporate Bond Index Exchange-Traded Fund

B-   **BUY**

Ticker	Traded On	NAV	Total Assets ($)	Dividend Yield (TTM)	Turnover Ratio	Expense Ratio
CORP	NYSE Arca	109.71	$650,574,809	3.29	27	0.2

Ratings
Reward	B-
Risk	C+
Recent Upgrade/Downgrade	Up

Fund Information
Fund Type	Exchange Traded Funds
Category	US Fixed Income
Sub-Category	Corporate Bond
Prospectus Objective	Corp Bond - High Quality
Inception Date	Sep-10
Open to New Investments	Y

Prices
Price (as of 9/30/2019)	109.72
52-Week High	110.62
52-Week Low	97.96

Total Returns (%)
3-Month	6-Month	1-Year	3-Year	5-Year
3.38	8.68	13.35	13.93	25.35

3-Year Standard Deviation	4.2
Effective Duration	7.12

Valuation
Premium/Discount (1-Year Average)	-0.05

Company Information
Provider	PIMCO
Manager/Tenure	Matthew P. Dorsten (3), Mitchell Handa (0), Graham A. Rennison (0)
Website	http://www.pimco.com
Address	PIMCO 840 Newport Center Drive, Suite 100 Newport Beach CA 92660 United States
Phone Number	866-746-2602

PERFORMANCE

Ratings History
Date	Overall Rating	Risk Rating	Reward Rating
Q3-19	B-	C+	B-
Q4-18	C-	C-	D+
Q4-17	B-	B+	C
Q4-16	C	C-	C
Q4-15	C	C-	C

Asset & Performance History
Date	NAV	1-Year Total Return
2018	99.11	-2.7
2017	105.43	6.38
2016	102.24	6.17
2015	99.11	-0.46
2014	102.66	7.43
2013	99.02	-1.62

Total Assets: $650,574,809
Asset Allocation
Asset	%
Cash	-8%
Stocks	0%
US Stocks	0%
Bonds	105%
US Bonds	81%
Other	0%

Services Offered:

Investment Strategy: The investment seeks to provide total return that closely corresponds, before fees and expenses, to the total return of the ICE BofAML US Corporate Index. The fund invests at least 80% of its total assets (exclusive of collateral held from securities lending) in the component securities of the ICE BofAML US Corporate Index (the "underlying index"). The underlying index is an unmanaged index comprised of U.S. dollar denominated investment grade corporate debt securities publicly issued in the U.S. domestic market with at least one year remaining term to final maturity. **Top Holdings:** Cdx Ig32 10y Ice Fin Fut Us 2yr Cbt 12/31/19 Cdx Ig32 5y Ice Fin Fut Us 30yr Cbt 12/19/19 Fin Fut Us Ultra 30yr Cbt 12/19/19

PGIM Ultra Short Bond ETF   C   HOLD

Ticker	Traded On	NAV	Total Assets ($)	Dividend Yield (TTM)	Turnover Ratio	Expense Ratio
PULS	NYSE Arca	50.19	$647,416,892	2.69	145	0.15

Ratings

Reward	C-
Risk	C+
Recent Upgrade/Downgrade	Up

Fund Information

Fund Type	Exchange Traded Funds
Category	US Fixed Income
Sub-Category	Ultrashort Bond
Prospectus Objective	Growth & Inc
Inception Date	Apr-18
Open to New Investments	Y

Prices

Price (as of 9/30/2019)	50.19
52-Week High	50.19
52-Week Low	49.89

Total Returns (%)

3-Month	6-Month	1-Year	3-Year	5-Year
0.72	1.49	2.90		

3-Year Standard Deviation	
Effective Duration	0.20

Valuation

Premium/Discount (1-Year Average)	0.01

Company Information

Provider	PGIM Funds (Prudential)
Manager/Tenure	Joseph D'Angelo (1), Douglas G. Smith (1)
Website	http://www.pgiminvestments.com
Address	PGIM Funds (Prudential) PO Box 9658 Providence RI 02940 United States
Phone Number	800-225-1852

PERFORMANCE

Ratings History

Date	Overall Rating	Risk Rating	Reward Rating
Q3-19	C	C+	C-
Q4-18	U		
Q4-17			
Q4-16			
Q4-15			

Asset & Performance History

Date	NAV	1-Year Total Return
2018	49.9	
2017		
2016		
2015		
2014		
2013		

Total Assets: $647,416,892

Asset Allocation

Asset	%
Cash	20%
Stocks	0%
US Stocks	0%
Bonds	79%
US Bonds	61%
Other	1%

Services Offered:

Investment Strategy: The investment seeks total return through a combination of current income and capital appreciation, consistent with preservation of capital. The fund invests primarily in a portfolio of investment grade, U.S. dollar denominated short-term fixed, variable and floating rate debt instruments. Under normal market conditions, it invests at least 80% of its investable assets in bonds with varying maturities. Although the fund may invest in instruments of any duration or maturity, it normally will seek to maintain a weighted average portfolio duration of one year or less and a weighted average maturity of three years or less. **Top Holdings:** Irs P02.85rus3m 03/11/21 Citcl Fixed   Irs Rus3mp02.85 03/11/21 Citcl Float   Irs P02.71rus3m 07/18/20 Citcl Fixed Irs Rus3mp02.71 07/18/20 Citcl Float   Irs P02.80rus3m 11/02/20 Citcl Fixed

---

SPDR® Portfolio Long Term Corporate Bond ETF   B   BUY

Ticker	Traded On	NAV	Total Assets ($)	Dividend Yield (TTM)	Turnover Ratio	Expense Ratio
SPLB	NYSE Arca		$641,085,661	3.86	18	0.07

Ratings

Reward	B
Risk	C+
Recent Upgrade/Downgrade	Up

Fund Information

Fund Type	Exchange Traded Funds
Category	US Fixed Income
Sub-Category	Long-Term Bond
Prospectus Objective	Corp Bond - Gen
Inception Date	Mar-09
Open to New Investments	Y

Prices

Price (as of 9/30/2019)	30.09
52-Week High	30.71
52-Week Low	24.89

Total Returns (%)

3-Month	6-Month	1-Year	3-Year	5-Year
5.56	13.97	19.98	20.21	39.59

3-Year Standard Deviation	7.71
Effective Duration	14.58

Valuation

Premium/Discount (1-Year Average)	0.13

Company Information

Provider	SPDR State Street Global Advisors
Manager/Tenure	Kyle Kelly (6), Christopher DiStefano (4), Frank Miethe (2)
Website	http://www.spdrs.com
Address	SPDR State Street Global Advisors State Street Financial Center, 1 Lincoln Street Boston MA 02111-2900 United States
Phone Number	617-786-3000

PERFORMANCE

Ratings History

Date	Overall Rating	Risk Rating	Reward Rating
Q3-19	B	C+	B
Q4-18	C-	C	D+
Q4-17	B	B	B-
Q4-16	C	C-	C
Q4-15	C	C	C-

Asset & Performance History

Date	NAV	1-Year Total Return
2018	25.3	-7.43
2017	28.55	11.79
2016	26.54	10.87
2015	24.96	-4.53
2014	27.34	15.61
2013	24.71	-5.9

Total Assets: $641,085,661

Asset Allocation

Asset	%
Cash	1%
Stocks	0%
US Stocks	0%
Bonds	99%
US Bonds	89%
Other	0%

Services Offered:

Investment Strategy: The investment seeks to provide investment results that, before fees and expenses, correspond generally to the price and yield performance of the Bloomberg Barclays U.S. Long Term Corporate Bond Index. The fund generally invests substantially all, but at least 80%, of its total assets in the securities comprising the index or in securities that the Adviser determines have economic characteristics that are substantially identical to the economic characteristics of the securities that comprise the index. The index is designed to measure the performance of U.S. corporate bonds that have a maturity of greater than or equal to 10 years. The fund is non-diversified. **Top Holdings:** Anheuser-Busch Companies LLC / Anheuser-Busch InBev Worldwide Inc 4.9%   CVS Health Corp 5.05%   Verizon Communications Inc. 4.02%   GE Capital International Funding Company Unlimited Company 4.42%   Goldman Sachs Group, Inc. 6.75%

JPMorgan BetaBuilders MSCI U.S. REIT ETF   C   HOLD

Ticker	Traded On	NAV	Total Assets ($)	Dividend Yield (TTM)	Turnover Ratio	Expense Ratio
BBRE	BATS	90.15	$640,043,559	2.07	5	0.11

Ratings
Reward   C
Risk   C-
Recent Upgrade/Downgrade   Up

Fund Information
Fund Type   Exchange Traded Funds
Category   Real Estate Sector Equity
Sub-Category   Real Estate
Prospectus Objective   Real Estate
Inception Date   Jun-18
Open to New Investments Y

Prices
Price (as of 9/30/2019)   90.07
52-Week High   90.29
52-Week Low   69.49

Total Returns (%)

3-Month	6-Month	1-Year	3-Year	5-Year
7.90	8.82	19.38		

3-Year Standard Deviation
Effective Duration

Valuation
Premium/Discount (1-Year Average)   -0.01

Company Information
Provider   JPMorgan
Manager/Tenure Nicholas D'Eramo (1), Oliver Furby (1), Alex Hamilton (1), 1 other
Website   http://www.jpmorganfunds.com
Address   JPMorgan 270 Park Avenue New York NY 10017-2070 United States
Phone Number   800-480-4111

PERFORMANCE

Ratings History

Date	Overall Rating	Risk Rating	Reward Rating
Q3-19	C	C-	C
Q4-18	U		
Q4-17			
Q4-16			
Q4-15			

Asset & Performance History

Date	NAV	1-Year Total Return
2018	72.16	
2017		
2016		
2015		
2014		
2013		

Total Assets: $640,043,559
Asset Allocation

Asset	%
Cash	0%
Stocks	100%
US Stocks	100%
Bonds	0%
US Bonds	0%
Other	0%

Services Offered:

Investment Strategy: The investment seeks results that closely correspond, before fees and expenses, to the performance of the MSCI US REIT Index. The fund will invest at least 80% of its assets in securities included in the underlying index. The underlying index is a free-float adjusted market-cap weighted index designed to measure the performance of U.S. equity real estate investment trust (REIT) securities. The fund may invest up to 20% of its assets in exchange-traded futures to seek performance that corresponds to the underlying index. **Top Holdings:** Prologis Inc Equinix Inc Simon Property Group Inc Public Storage Welltower Inc

ProShares UltraShort 20+ Year Treasury   D   SELL

Ticker	Traded On	NAV	Total Assets ($)	Dividend Yield (TTM)	Turnover Ratio	Expense Ratio
TBT	NYSE Arca	24.41	$639,762,335	2.36		0.9

Ratings
Reward   D-
Risk   D
Recent Upgrade/Downgrade

Fund Information
Fund Type   Exchange Traded Funds
Category   Trading Tools
Sub-Category   Trading--Inverse Debt
Prospectus Objective   Govt Bond - Treasury
Inception Date   Apr-08
Open to New Investments Y

Prices
Price (as of 9/30/2019)   24.36
52-Week High   41.62
52-Week Low   23.13

Total Returns (%)

3-Month	6-Month	1-Year	3-Year	5-Year
-15.84	-25.62	-35.75	-21.08	-53.99

3-Year Standard Deviation   22.79
Effective Duration

Valuation
Premium/Discount (1-Year Average)   -0.26

Company Information
Provider   ProShares
Manager/Tenure Michelle Liu (11), Alexander V. Ilyasov (0)
Website   http://www.proshares.com
Address   ProShares 7501 Wisconsin Avenue, Suite 1000 Bethesda MD 20814 United States
Phone Number   866-776-5125

PERFORMANCE

Ratings History

Date	Overall Rating	Risk Rating	Reward Rating
Q3-19	D	D	D-
Q4-18	C	C	D+
Q4-17	D	D	D
Q4-16	D	D-	D
Q4-15	D	D	D

Asset & Performance History

Date	NAV	1-Year Total Return
2018	35.36	5.85
2017	33.72	-16.82
2016	40.54	-7.77
2015	43.96	-5.42
2014	46.48	-41.39
2013	79.31	26.55

Total Assets: $639,762,335
Asset Allocation

Asset	%
Cash	178%
Stocks	0%
US Stocks	0%
Bonds	15%
US Bonds	15%
Other	-93%

Services Offered:

Investment Strategy: The investment seeks daily investment results, before fees and expenses, that correspond to two times the inverse (-2x) of the daily performance of the ICE U.S. Treasury 20+ Year Bond Index. The fund invests in financial instruments that ProShare Advisors believes, in combination, should produce daily returns consistent with the fund's investment objective. The index includes publicly-issued U.S. Treasury securities that have a remaining maturity greater than or equal to twenty years and have $300 million or more of outstanding face value, excluding amounts held by the Federal Reserve. The fund is non-diversified. **Top Holdings:** Ice 20+ Year U.S. Treasury Index Swap Goldman Sachs International Ice 20+ Year U.S. Treasury Index Swap Bank Of America Na Ice 20+ Year U.S. Treasury Index Swap Citibank Na Ice 20+ Year U.S. Treasury Index Swap Societe Generale United States Treasury Bills

Pacer Trendpilot™ US Mid Cap ETF   C-   HOLD

Ticker	Traded On	NAV	Total Assets ($)	Dividend Yield (TTM)	Turnover Ratio	Expense Ratio
PTMC	BATS	29.16	$635,618,108	0.94	405	0.6

Ratings
Reward   C-
Risk   C-
Recent Upgrade/Downgrade

Fund Information
Fund Type   Exchange Traded Funds
Category   US Equity Mid Cap
Sub-Category   Mid-Cap Blend
Prospectus Objective   Growth
Inception Date   Jun-15
Open to New Investments   Y

Prices
Price (as of 9/30/2019)   29.18
52-Week High   33.09
52-Week Low   27.72

Total Returns (%)

3-Month	6-Month	1-Year	3-Year	5-Year
-0.35	-3.96	-11.02	16.90	

3-Year Standard Deviation   10.07
Effective Duration

Valuation
Premium/Discount (1-Year Average)   0.01

Company Information
Provider   Pacer
Manager/Tenure   Bruce Kavanaugh (4), Michael Mack (4)
Website   http://www.paceretfs.com
Address   Pacer 16 Industrial Blvd, Suite 201 Paoli PA 19301 United States
Phone Number

PERFORMANCE

Ratings History

Date	Overall Rating	Risk Rating	Reward Rating
Q3-19	C-	C-	C-
Q4-18	C-	C-	C-
Q4-17	C	B	C+
Q4-16	D	C-	C-
Q4-15	U		

Asset & Performance History

Date	NAV	1-Year Total Return
2018	30.84	0.06
2017	31.09	17.57
2016	26.62	15.99
2015	23.18	
2014		
2013		

Total Assets: $635,618,108

Asset Allocation

Asset	%
Cash	0%
Stocks	100%
US Stocks	100%
Bonds	0%
US Bonds	0%
Other	0%

Services Offered:

Investment Strategy: The investment seeks to track the total return performance, before fees and expenses, of the Pacer Trendpilot US Mid Cap Index. The fund invests at least 80% of its total assets (exclusive of collateral held from securities lending) in the component securities of the index. The index implements a systematic trend-following strategy that directs exposure (i) 100% to the S&P MidCap 400® Index, (ii) 50% to the S&P MidCap 400 and 50% to 3-Month U.S. Treasury bills, or (iii) 100% to 3-Month U.S. Treasury bills, depending on the relative performance of the S&P MidCap 400 and its 200-business day historical simple moving average. **Top Holdings:** iShares Core S&P Mid-Cap ETF   MarketAxess Holdings Inc   Steris PLC   Leidos Holdings Inc   NVR Inc

---

Fidelity® MSCI Consumer Staples Index ETF   B-   BUY

Ticker	Traded On	NAV	Total Assets ($)	Dividend Yield (TTM)	Turnover Ratio	Expense Ratio
FSTA	NYSE Arca	36.59	$634,819,232	2.5	30	0.08

Ratings
Reward   B
Risk   C
Recent Upgrade/Downgrade   Up

Fund Information
Fund Type   Exchange Traded Funds
Category   Consumer Goods & Svcs
Sub-Category   Consumer Defensive
Prospectus Objective   Unaligned
Inception Date   Oct-13
Open to New Investments   Y

Prices
Price (as of 9/30/2019)   36.61
52-Week High   36.73
52-Week Low   29.30

Total Returns (%)

3-Month	6-Month	1-Year	3-Year	5-Year
5.47	9.73	15.62	24.08	53.86

3-Year Standard Deviation   11.65
Effective Duration

Valuation
Premium/Discount (1-Year Average)   0.05

Company Information
Provider   Fidelity Investments
Manager/Tenure   Jennifer Hsui (5), Greg Savage (5), Alan Mason (3), 2 others
Website   http://www.institutional.fidelity.com
Address   Fidelity Investments 82 Devonshire Street Boston MA 2109 United States
Phone Number   617-563-7000

PERFORMANCE

Ratings History

Date	Overall Rating	Risk Rating	Reward Rating
Q3-19	B-	C	B
Q4-18	C+	C	B
Q4-17	B	A-	C+
Q4-16	B-	C	B
Q4-15	C-	B-	B

Asset & Performance History

Date	NAV	1-Year Total Return
2018	30.52	-8.29
2017	34.26	12.5
2016	31.21	5.9
2015	30.21	5.65
2014	29.45	15.75
2013	26.06	

Total Assets: $634,819,232

Asset Allocation

Asset	%
Cash	0%
Stocks	100%
US Stocks	100%
Bonds	0%
US Bonds	0%
Other	0%

Services Offered:

Investment Strategy: The investment seeks to provide investment returns that correspond, before fees and expenses, generally to the performance of the MSCI USA IMI Consumer Staples Index. The fund invests at least 80% of assets in securities included in the fund's underlying index. The fund's underlying index is the MSCI USA IMI Consumer Staples Index, which represents the performance of the consumer staples sector in the U.S. equity market. It may or may not hold all of the securities in the MSCI USA IMI Consumer Staples Index. The fund is non-diversified. **Top Holdings:** Procter & Gamble Co   Coca-Cola Co   PepsiCo Inc   Walmart Inc   Costco Wholesale Corp

Vanguard ESG U.S. Stock ETF   C-   HOLD

Ticker	Traded On	NAV	Total Assets ($)	Dividend Yield (TTM)	Turnover Ratio	Expense Ratio
ESGV	BATS	51.83	$631,030,250	1.17		0.12

Ratings
Reward   D+
Risk   C-
Recent Upgrade/Downgrade

Fund Information
Fund Type   Exchange Traded Funds
Category   US Equity Large Cap Blend
Sub-Category   Large Blend
Prospectus Objective   Growth & Inc
Inception Date   Sep-18
Open to New Investments   Y

Prices
Price (as of 9/30/2019)   51.91
52-Week High   53.06
52-Week Low   40.33

Total Returns (%)

3-Month	6-Month	1-Year	3-Year	5-Year
0.87	5.21	4.55		

3-Year Standard Deviation
Effective Duration

Valuation
Premium/Discount (1-Year Average)   0.07

Company Information
Provider   Vanguard
Manager/Tenure   William A. Coleman (1), Gerard C.
                   O'Reilly (1)
Website   http://www.vanguard.com
Address   Vanguard 100 Vanguard Boulevard
                   Malvern PA 19355 United States
Phone Number   877-662-7447

PERFORMANCE

Ratings History

Date	Overall Rating	Risk Rating	Reward Rating
Q3-19	C-	C-	D+
Q4-18	U		
Q4-17			
Q4-16			
Q4-15			

Asset & Performance History

Date	NAV	1-Year Total Return
2018	42.6	
2017		
2016		
2015		
2014		
2013		

Total Assets: $631,030,250

Asset Allocation

Asset	%
Cash	0%
Stocks	100%
US Stocks	98%
Bonds	0%
US Bonds	0%
Other	0%

Services Offered:

Investment Strategy: The investment seeks to track the performance of the FTSE US All Cap Choice Index. The adviser attempts to replicate the target index by investing all, or substantially all, of its assets in the stocks that make up the index, holding each stock in approximately the same proportion as its weighting in the index. The index, which is market-capitalization weighted, is composed of large-, mid-, and small-cap stocks of companies located in the United States and is screened for certain environmental, social, and corporate governance (ESG) criteria by the index sponsor, which is independent of Vanguard. **Top Holdings:** Microsoft Corp Apple Inc Amazon.com Inc JPMorgan Chase & Co Alphabet Inc Class C

SPDR® Portfolio Mortgage Backed Bond ETF   C   HOLD

Ticker	Traded On	NAV	Total Assets ($)	Dividend Yield (TTM)	Turnover Ratio	Expense Ratio
SPMB	NYSE Arca		$624,352,727	3.32	245	0.06

Ratings
Reward   C+
Risk   C-
Recent Upgrade/Downgrade

Fund Information
Fund Type   Exchange Traded Funds
Category   US Fixed Income
Sub-Category   Intermediate Government
Prospectus Objective   Govt Bond - Mortgage
Inception Date   Jan-09
Open to New Investments   Y

Prices
Price (as of 9/30/2019)   26.27
52-Week High   26.34
52-Week Low   24.78

Total Returns (%)

3-Month	6-Month	1-Year	3-Year	5-Year
1.31	3.56	7.76	6.43	13.55

3-Year Standard Deviation   2.5
Effective Duration   2.38

Valuation
Premium/Discount (1-Year Average)   0.13

Company Information
Provider   SPDR State Street Global Advisors
Manager/Tenure   Marc DiCosimo (5), Michael Przygoda
                   (4), Nicholas Fischer (0)
Website   http://www.spdrs.com
Address   SPDR State Street Global Advisors
                   State Street Financial Center, 1
                   Lincoln Street Boston MA 02111-2900
                   United States
Phone Number   617-786-3000

PERFORMANCE

Ratings History

Date	Overall Rating	Risk Rating	Reward Rating
Q3-19	C	C-	C+
Q4-18	D+	C-	D+
Q4-17	C+	B+	C
Q4-16	C	C-	C
Q4-15	C	C-	C

Asset & Performance History

Date	NAV	1-Year Total Return
2018	25.41	0.87
2017	26.05	1.93
2016	26.29	1.19
2015	26.73	1.21
2014	27.21	5.92
2013	26.61	-1.58

Total Assets: $624,352,727

Asset Allocation

Asset	%
Cash	8%
Stocks	0%
US Stocks	0%
Bonds	92%
US Bonds	92%
Other	0%

Services Offered:

Investment Strategy: The investment seeks to provide investment results that, before fees and expenses, correspond generally to the price and yield performance of the Bloomberg Barclays U.S. MBS Index. The fund generally invests substantially all, but at least 80%, of its total assets in the securities comprising the index or in securities that the Adviser determines have economic characteristics that are substantially identical to the economic characteristics of the securities that comprise the index. The index is designed to measure the performance of the U.S. agency mortgage pass-through segment of the U.S. investment grade bond market. The fund is non-diversified. **Top Holdings:** Federal National Mortgage Association 3.5% Government National Mortgage Association 3.5% Government National Mortgage Association 3.5% Government National Mortgage Association 4% Federal National Mortgage Association 4%

iShares U.S. Energy ETF

D+   **SELL**

Ticker	Traded On	NAV	Total Assets ($)	Dividend Yield (TTM)	Turnover Ratio	Expense Ratio
IYE	NYSE Arca	31.75	$619,123,751	3.29	6	0.42

Ratings

Reward	D+
Risk	D+
Recent Upgrade/Downgrade	

Fund Information

Fund Type	Exchange Traded Funds
Category	Energy Sector Equity
Sub-Category	Equity Energy
Prospectus Objective	Natl Res
Inception Date	Jun-00
Open to New Investments	Y

Prices

Price (as of 9/30/2019)	31.76
52-Week High	43.05
52-Week Low	29.27

Total Returns (%)

3-Month	6-Month	1-Year	3-Year	5-Year
-7.13	-10.38	-23.01	-11.58	-28.05

3-Year Standard Deviation	21.19
Effective Duration	

Valuation

Premium/Discount (1-Year Average)	-0.02

Company Information

Provider	iShares
Manager/Tenure	Greg Savage (11), Jennifer Hsui (7), Alan Mason (3), 2 others
Website	http://www.ishares.com
Address	iShares 400 Howard Street San Francisco CA 94105 United States
Phone Number	800-474-2737

PERFORMANCE

Ratings History

Date	Overall Rating	Risk Rating	Reward Rating
Q3-19	D+	D+	D+
Q4-18	C	C-	C
Q4-17	C-	C	D+
Q4-16	C-	D	C
Q4-15	C	C	C+

Asset & Performance History

Date	NAV	1-Year Total Return
2018	31.17	-19.2
2017	39.59	-1.94
2016	41.54	25.6
2015	33.85	-22.21
2014	44.82	-9.64
2013	50.5	25.7

Total Assets: $619,123,751

Asset Allocation

Asset	%
Cash	0%
Stocks	100%
US Stocks	99%
Bonds	0%
US Bonds	0%
Other	0%

Services Offered: CashInvestment Plan

Investment Strategy: The investment seeks to track the investment results of the Dow Jones U.S. Oil & Gas Index composed of U.S. equities in the energy sector. The fund generally invests at least 90% of its assets in securities of the underlying index and in depositary receipts representing securities of the underlying index. The underlying index measures the performance of the oil and gas sector of the U.S. equity market. The fund is non-diversified.
Top Holdings: Exxon Mobil Corp Chevron Corp ConocoPhillips Schlumberger Ltd EOG Resources Inc

GraniteShares Gold Trust

D-   **SELL**

Ticker	Traded On	NAV	Total Assets ($)	Dividend Yield (TTM)	Turnover Ratio	Expense Ratio
BAR	NYSE Arca	14.80	$611,789,964	0		0.17

Ratings

Reward	D-
Risk	D-
Recent Upgrade/Downgrade	

Fund Information

Fund Type	Exchange Traded Funds
Category	Commodities Specified
Sub-Category	Commodities Precious Metals
Prospectus Objective	Prec Metals
Inception Date	Aug-17
Open to New Investments	Y

Prices

Price (as of 9/30/2019)	14.71
52-Week High	133.77
52-Week Low	12.67

Total Returns (%)

3-Month	6-Month	1-Year	3-Year	5-Year
6.80	14.72	-87.53		

3-Year Standard Deviation	
Effective Duration	

Valuation

Premium/Discount (1-Year Average)	-0.11

Company Information

Provider	Graniteshares
Manager/Tenure	Management Team (2)
Website	http://www.graniteshares.com
Address	Graniteshares 30 Vesey Street, 9th Floor New York New York 10007 United States
Phone Number	

PERFORMANCE

Ratings History

Date	Overall Rating	Risk Rating	Reward Rating
Q3-19	D-	D-	D-
Q4-18	D	D+	D
Q4-17	U		
Q4-16			
Q4-15			

Asset & Performance History

Date	NAV	1-Year Total Return
2018	127.83	-1.33
2017	129.56	
2016		
2015		
2014		
2013		

Total Assets: $611,789,964

Asset Allocation

Asset	%
Cash	0%
Stocks	0%
US Stocks	0%
Bonds	0%
US Bonds	0%
Other	100%

Services Offered:

Investment Strategy: The investment seeks to reflect generally the performance of the price of gold. The Shares are intended to constitute a simple and cost-effective means of making an investment similar to an investment in gold. **Top Holdings:** Physical Gold Bullion

iShares MSCI Europe Financials ETF   D+   SELL

Ticker	Traded On	NAV	Total Assets ($)	Dividend Yield (TTM)	Turnover Ratio	Expense Ratio
EUFN	NAS CM	17.60	$610,859,192	5.57	5	0.48

Ratings

Reward	D
Risk	C
Recent Upgrade/Downgrade	Down

Fund Information

Fund Type	Exchange Traded Funds
Category	Financials Sector Equity
Sub-Category	Financial
Prospectus Objective	Financial
Inception Date	Jan-10
Open to New Investments	Y

Prices

Price (as of 9/30/2019)	17.60
52-Week High	20.14
52-Week Low	16.08

Total Returns (%)

3-Month	6-Month	1-Year	3-Year	5-Year
-3.56	-1.26	-7.91	17.13	-7.73

3-Year Standard Deviation	17.4
Effective Duration	

Valuation

Premium/Discount (1-Year Average)	-0.13

Company Information

Provider	iShares
Manager/Tenure	Diane Hsiung (9), Greg Savage (9), Jennifer Hsui (6), 3 others
Website	http://www.ishares.com
Address	iShares 400 Howard Street San Francisco CA 94105 United States
Phone Number	800-474-2737

PERFORMANCE

Ratings History

Date	Overall Rating	Risk Rating	Reward Rating
Q3-19	D+	C	D
Q4-18	D+	C	D+
Q4-17	C+	C	B-
Q4-16	D+	D	D+
Q4-15	C	C+	C-

Asset & Performance History

Date	NAV	1-Year Total Return
2018	16.99	-23.18
2017	23.38	27.16
2016	18.99	-3.11
2015	20.44	-5.01
2014	22.22	-7.86
2013	24.86	30.48

Total Assets: $610,859,192

Asset Allocation

Asset	%
Cash	1%
Stocks	99%
US Stocks	1%
Bonds	0%
US Bonds	0%
Other	0%

Services Offered:

Investment Strategy: The investment seeks to track the investment results of the MSCI Europe Financials Index composed of developed market European equities in the financials sector. The fund generally will invest at least 90% of its assets in the component securities of the underlying index and in investments that have economic characteristics that are substantially identical to the component securities of the underlying index. The index is a free float-adjusted market capitalization-weighted index designed to measure the combined equity market performance of the financials sector of developed market countries in Europe. **Top Holdings:** HSBC Holdings PLC Allianz SE Banco Santander SA Zurich Insurance Group AG BNP Paribas

---

Invesco BulletShares 2024 Corporate Bond ETF   C+   HOLD

Ticker	Traded On	NAV	Total Assets ($)	Dividend Yield (TTM)	Turnover Ratio	Expense Ratio
BSCO	NYSE Arca	21.35	$608,340,053	3.22	2	0.1

Ratings

Reward	C+
Risk	C+
Recent Upgrade/Downgrade	

Fund Information

Fund Type	Exchange Traded Funds
Category	US Fixed Income
Sub-Category	Target Maturity
Prospectus Objective	Corp Bond - Gen
Inception Date	Sep-14
Open to New Investments	Y

Prices

Price (as of 9/30/2019)	21.43
52-Week High	21.54
52-Week Low	19.77

Total Returns (%)

3-Month	6-Month	1-Year	3-Year	5-Year
1.64	5.23	10.26	10.69	23.94

3-Year Standard Deviation	3.44
Effective Duration	4.37

Valuation

Premium/Discount (1-Year Average)	0.27

Company Information

Provider	Invesco
Manager/Tenure	Jeremy Neisewander (3), Peter Hubbard (1), Jeffrey W. Kernagis (1), 1 other
Website	http://www.invesco.com/us
Address	Invesco 11 Greenway Plaza, Ste. 2500 Houston TX 77046 United States
Phone Number	800-659-1005

PERFORMANCE

Ratings History

Date	Overall Rating	Risk Rating	Reward Rating
Q3-19	C+	C+	C+
Q4-18	C-	C-	C-
Q4-17	B	A	C
Q4-16	D+	C-	D+
Q4-15	U		

Asset & Performance History

Date	NAV	1-Year Total Return
2018	19.93	-1.06
2017	20.8	5.56
2016	20.34	6.02
2015	19.77	0.62
2014	20.3	
2013		

Total Assets: $608,340,053

Asset Allocation

Asset	%
Cash	0%
Stocks	0%
US Stocks	0%
Bonds	100%
US Bonds	86%
Other	0%

Services Offered:

Investment Strategy: The investment seeks to track the investment results (before fees and expenses) of the Nasdaq BulletShares® USD Corporate Bond 2024 Index (the "underlying index"). The fund generally will invest at least 80% of its total assets in securities that comprise the underlying index. The underlying index seeks to measure the performance of a portfolio of U.S. dollar-denominated investment grade corporate bonds with maturities or, in some cases, "effective maturities" in the year 2024 (collectively, "2024 Bonds"). The fund is non-diversified. **Top Holdings:** JPMorgan Chase & Co. 3.88% Morgan Stanley 3.88% Bank of America Corporation 4.2% Morgan Stanley 3.7% Goldman Sachs Group, Inc. 4%

iShares Emerging Markets Dividend ETF   C   HOLD

Ticker	Traded On	NAV	Total Assets ($)	Dividend Yield (TTM)	Turnover Ratio	Expense Ratio
DVYE	NYSE Arca	37.42	$606,135,655	6.35	69	0.49

Ratings
Reward	C
Risk	C+
Recent Upgrade/Downgrade	Down

Fund Information
Fund Type	Exchange Traded Funds
Category	Global Emerg Mkts Equity
Sub-Category	Diversified Emerging Mkts
Prospectus Objective	Div Emerg Mkts
Inception Date	Feb-12
Open to New Investments	Y

Prices
Price (as of 9/30/2019)	37.42
52-Week High	42.09
52-Week Low	36.59

Total Returns (%)
3-Month	6-Month	1-Year	3-Year	5-Year
-6.75	-4.10	1.64	23.06	7.89

3-Year Standard Deviation	12.42
Effective Duration	

Valuation
Premium/Discount (1-Year Average)	0.03

Company Information
Provider	iShares
Manager/Tenure	Greg Savage (7), Jennifer Hsui (7), Alan Mason (3), 2 others
Website	http://www.ishares.com
Address	iShares 400 Howard Street San Francisco CA 94105 United States
Phone Number	800-474-2737

PERFORMANCE

Ratings History
Date	Overall Rating	Risk Rating	Reward Rating
Q3-19	C	C+	C
Q4-18	C	C+	C-
Q4-17	C	C	C
Q4-16	D+	D+	D+
Q4-15	D	D	D

Asset & Performance History
Date	NAV	1-Year Total Return
2018	37.48	-5.41
2017	41.83	25.7
2016	34.95	20.28
2015	30.43	-23.77
2014	42.15	-9.2
2013	48.31	-9.51

Total Assets: $606,135,655
Asset Allocation
Asset	%
Cash	1%
Stocks	99%
US Stocks	0%
Bonds	0%
US Bonds	0%
Other	0%

Services Offered:

Investment Strategy: The investment seeks to track the investment results of the Dow Jones Emerging Markets Select Dividend Index composed of relatively high dividend paying equities in emerging markets. The fund generally will invest at least 90% of its assets in the component securities of the index and in investments that have economic characteristics that are substantially identical to the component securities of the index. The index measures the performance of 100 leading dividend-paying emerging-market companies, selected by dividend yield subject to screening and buffering criteria. **Top Holdings:** Severstal PAO Nanya Technology Corp Magnitogorsk Iron & Steel Works PJSC Jasmine International PCL DR Astral Foods Ltd

---

Direxion Daily Semiconductor Bull 3X Shares   C+   HOLD

Ticker	Traded On	NAV	Total Assets ($)	Dividend Yield (TTM)	Turnover Ratio	Expense Ratio
SOXL	NYSE Arca	170.23	$604,328,634	0.61	101	0.99

Ratings
Reward	B
Risk	C-
Recent Upgrade/Downgrade	Up

Fund Information
Fund Type	Exchange Traded Funds
Category	Trading Tools
Sub-Category	Trading--Leveraged Equity
Prospectus Objective	Technology
Inception Date	Mar-10
Open to New Investments	Y

Prices
Price (as of 9/30/2019)	170.22
52-Week High	200.88
52-Week Low	67.08

Total Returns (%)
3-Month	6-Month	1-Year	3-Year	5-Year
6.50	15.59	10.17	275.19	585.65

3-Year Standard Deviation	67.33
Effective Duration	

Valuation
Premium/Discount (1-Year Average)	-0.03

Company Information
Provider	Direxion Funds
Manager/Tenure	Paul Brigandi (9), Tony Ng (4)
Website	http://www.direxionfunds.com
Address	Direxion Funds 1301 Avenue Of The Americas (6th Avenue) New York NY 10019 United States
Phone Number	646-572-3390

PERFORMANCE

Ratings History
Date	Overall Rating	Risk Rating	Reward Rating
Q3-19	C+	C-	B
Q4-18	C	D+	C
Q4-17	B	D+	A-
Q4-16	C	D+	C+
Q4-15	C	C	C

Asset & Performance History
Date	NAV	1-Year Total Return
2018	83.4	-38.94
2017	137.76	141.54
2016	57.08	123.29
2015	26.75	-20.72
2014	33.74	96.15
2013	17.2	155.13

Total Assets: $604,328,634
Asset Allocation
Asset	%
Cash	-7%
Stocks	107%
US Stocks	93%
Bonds	0%
US Bonds	0%
Other	0%

Services Offered:

Investment Strategy: The investment seeks daily investment results, before fees and expenses, of 300% of the daily performance of the PHLX Semiconductor Sector Index. The fund, under normal circumstances, invests at least 80% of its net assets (plus borrowing for investment purposes) in financial instruments, such as swap agreements, and securities of the index, ETFs that track the index and other financial instruments that provide daily leveraged exposure to the index or ETFs that track the index. The index measures the performance of domestic companies engaged in the design, distribution, manufacture and sale of semiconductors. The fund is non-diversified. **Top Holdings:** Phila Semiconductor Index Phila Semiconductor Index Phila Semiconductor Index Qualcomm Inc NVIDIA Corp

Hartford Total Return Bond ETF

C- HOLD

Ticker	Traded On	NAV	Total Assets ($)	Dividend Yield (TTM)	Turnover Ratio	Expense Ratio
HTRB	NYSE Arca	41.45	$601,047,425	3.16	54	0.29

Ratings
Reward	C-
Risk	D+
Recent Upgrade/Downgrade	Up

Fund Information
Fund Type	Exchange Traded Funds
Category	US Fixed Income
Sub-Category	Intermediate Core-Plus Bond
Prospectus Objective	Income
Inception Date	Sep-17
Open to New Investments	Y

Prices
Price (as of 9/30/2019)	41.47
52-Week High	41.94
52-Week Low	38.34

Total Returns (%)
3-Month	6-Month	1-Year	3-Year	5-Year
2.45	6.03	10.27		

3-Year Standard Deviation	
Effective Duration	

Valuation
Premium/Discount (1-Year Average)	0.11

Company Information
Provider	Hartford Funds
Manager/Tenure	Robert D. Burn (2), Campe Goodman (2), Joseph F. Marvan (2)
Website	http://www.hartfordfunds.com
Address	690 Lee Road Wayne PA 19087 United States
Phone Number	800-456-7526

PERFORMANCE

Ratings History
Date	Overall Rating	Risk Rating	Reward Rating
Q3-19	C-	D+	C-
Q4-18	D+	C	D
Q4-17	U		
Q4-16			
Q4-15			

Asset & Performance History
Date	NAV	1-Year Total Return
2018	38.72	-0.79
2017	39.96	
2016		
2015		
2014		
2013		

Total Assets: $601,047,425
Asset Allocation
Asset	%
Cash	5%
Stocks	0%
US Stocks	0%
Bonds	94%
US Bonds	86%
Other	0%

Services Offered:

Investment Strategy: The investment seeks a competitive total return, with income as a secondary objective. The fund invests at least 80% of its net assets in bonds that the sub-adviser considers to be attractive from a total return perspective along with current income. It may invest up to 20% of its net assets in securities rated below investment grade (also known as "junk bonds"). The fund may invest up to 40% of its net assets in debt securities of foreign issuers, including from emerging markets, and up to 20% of its net assets in non-dollar securities. **Top Holdings:** US 10 Year Ultra Future Dec19 Federal National Mortgage Association 3.5% Federal National Mortgage Association 3% United States Treasury Bonds 3.62% Government National Mortgage Association 3%

VanEck Vectors Oil Services ETF

D+ SELL

Ticker	Traded On	NAV	Total Assets ($)	Dividend Yield (TTM)	Turnover Ratio	Expense Ratio
OIH	NYSE Arca	11.76	$597,944,858	2.54	22	0.35

Ratings
Reward	C-
Risk	D
Recent Upgrade/Downgrade	Up

Fund Information
Fund Type	Exchange Traded Funds
Category	Energy Sector Equity
Sub-Category	Equity Energy
Prospectus Objective	Natl Res
Inception Date	Dec-11
Open to New Investments	Y

Prices
Price (as of 9/30/2019)	11.75
52-Week High	26.02
52-Week Low	10.89

Total Returns (%)
3-Month	6-Month	1-Year	3-Year	5-Year
-21.02	-33.78	-52.83	-57.17	-72.74

3-Year Standard Deviation	35.88
Effective Duration	

Valuation
Premium/Discount (1-Year Average)	0.00

Company Information
Provider	VanEck
Manager/Tenure	Hao-Hung (Peter) Liao (7), Guo Hua (Jason) Jin (1)
Website	http://www.vaneck.com
Address	Van Eck Associates Corporation 666 Third Avenue New York NY 10017 United States
Phone Number	800-826-1115

PERFORMANCE

Ratings History
Date	Overall Rating	Risk Rating	Reward Rating
Q3-19	D+	D	C-
Q4-18	C-	D	C
Q4-17	D	D	D
Q4-16	D+	D	C-
Q4-15	C	C	C+

Asset & Performance History
Date	NAV	1-Year Total Return
2018	14.03	-44.58
2017	26.02	-19.82
2016	33.36	27.92
2015	26.44	-24.51
2014	35.89	-23.63
2013	48.1	25.92

Total Assets: $597,944,858
Asset Allocation
Asset	%
Cash	0%
Stocks	100%
US Stocks	87%
Bonds	0%
US Bonds	0%
Other	0%

Services Offered:

Investment Strategy: The investment seeks to replicate as closely as possible, before fees and expenses, the price and yield performance of the MVIS® US Listed Oil Services 25 Index. The fund normally invests at least 80% of its total assets in securities that comprise the fund's benchmark index. The index includes common stocks and depositary receipts of U.S. exchange-listed companies in the oil services sector. Such companies may include small- and medium-capitalization companies and foreign companies that are listed on a U.S. exchange. The fund is non-diversified. **Top Holdings:** Schlumberger Ltd Halliburton Co TechnipFMC PLC National Oilwell Varco Inc Baker Hughes, a GE Co Class A

ProShares Ultra VIX Short-Term Futures ETF   **D   SELL**

Ticker	Traded On	NAV	Total Assets ($)	Dividend Yield (TTM)	Turnover Ratio	Expense Ratio
UVXY	NYSE Arca		$597,083,473	0		1.65

Ratings
Reward   D
Risk   D
Recent Upgrade/Downgrade

Fund Information
Fund Type	Exchange Traded Funds
Category	Alternative Misc
Sub-Category	Volatility
Prospectus Objective	Growth
Inception Date	Oct-11
Open to New Investments	Y

Prices
Price (as of 9/30/2019)	26.04
52-Week High	88.08
52-Week Low	23.61

Total Returns (%)
3-Month	6-Month	1-Year	3-Year	5-Year
-5.54	-27.75	-24.83	-91.94	-99.81

3-Year Standard Deviation   87.06
Effective Duration

Valuation
Premium/Discount (1-Year Average)   0.50

Company Information
Provider	ProShares
Manager/Tenure	Management Team (8)
Website	http://www.proshares.com
Address	ProShares 7501 Wisconsin Avenue, Suite 1000 Bethesda MD 20814 United States
Phone Number	866-776-5125

PERFORMANCE

Ratings History				Asset & Performance History			Total Assets:	$597,083,473
Date	Overall Rating	Risk Rating	Reward Rating	Date	NAV	1-Year Total Return	Asset Allocation	
							Asset	%
Q3-19	D	D	D	2018	81.46	738.37	Cash	-50%
Q4-18	C-	D	C	2017	10.34	-94.05	Stocks	150%
Q4-17	E	E	E-	2016	173.92	-93.8	US Stocks	150%
Q4-16	E+	D-	E-	2015	2,808.49	-77.61	Bonds	0%
Q4-15	E	E+	E	2014	12,546.68	-62.59	US Bonds	0%
				2013	33,541.68	-91.67	Other	0%

Services Offered:

Investment Strategy: The investment seeks daily investment results, before fees and expenses, that correspond to one and one-half times (1.5x) the performance of the S&P 500 VIX Short-Term Futures Index for a single day. The index seeks to offer exposure to market volatility through publicly traded futures markets and is designed to measure the implied volatility of the S&P 500 over 30 days in the future. **Top Holdings:** Cboe Vix Future 09/18/2019 (Uxu9)   Cboe Vix Future 10/16/2019 (Uxv9)   Ipath Series-B S&P 500 Vix Sht-Term Fut Swap - Gs   S&P 500 Vix Short-Term Futures Index Swap ¿ Deutsche Bank Ag   S&P 500 Vix Short-Term Futures Index Swap - Deutsche Bank

---

iShares iBonds Dec 2024 Term Corporate ETF   **C   HOLD**

Ticker	Traded On	NAV	Total Assets ($)	Dividend Yield (TTM)	Turnover Ratio	Expense Ratio
IBDP	NYSE Arca	25.61	$596,743,028	3.21	6	0.1

Ratings
Reward   C+
Risk   C-
Recent Upgrade/Downgrade

Fund Information
Fund Type	Exchange Traded Funds
Category	US Fixed Income
Sub-Category	Target Maturity
Prospectus Objective	Corp Bond - Gen
Inception Date	Mar-15
Open to New Investments	Y

Prices
Price (as of 9/30/2019)	25.69
52-Week High	25.80
52-Week Low	23.69

Total Returns (%)
3-Month	6-Month	1-Year	3-Year	5-Year
1.65	5.32	10.20	10.94	

3-Year Standard Deviation   3.37
Effective Duration

Valuation
Premium/Discount (1-Year Average)   0.27

Company Information
Provider	iShares
Manager/Tenure	James Mauro (4), Scott Radell (4)
Website	http://www.ishares.com
Address	iShares 400 Howard Street San Francisco CA 94105 United States
Phone Number	800-474-2737

PERFORMANCE

Ratings History				Asset & Performance History			Total Assets:	$596,743,028
Date	Overall Rating	Risk Rating	Reward Rating	Date	NAV	1-Year Total Return	Asset Allocation	
							Asset	%
Q3-19	C	C-	C+	2018	23.88	-1.08	Cash	0%
Q4-18	C-	C-	C-	2017	24.96	5.35	Stocks	0%
Q4-17	B-	B+	C	2016	24.41	6.02	US Stocks	0%
Q4-16	D+	C-	D+	2015	23.77		Bonds	97%
Q4-15	U			2014			US Bonds	85%
				2013			Other	0%

Services Offered:

Investment Strategy: The investment seeks to track the investment results of the Bloomberg Barclays December 2024 Maturity Corporate Index which composed of U.S. dollar-denominated, investment-grade corporate bonds maturing in 2024. The fund generally will invest at least 90% of its assets in the component securities of the underlying index. The underlying index is composed of U.S. dollar-denominated, taxable, investment-grade corporate bonds scheduled to mature after December 31, 2023 and before December 16, 2024. **Top Holdings:** Bank of America Corporation 4.2%   Morgan Stanley 3.7%   Credit Suisse AG New York Branch 3.63%   Goldman Sachs Group, Inc. 4%   Morgan Stanley 3.88%

iShares Morningstar Mid-Cap Growth ETF   C   HOLD

Ticker	Traded On	NAV	Total Assets ($)	Dividend Yield (TTM)	Turnover Ratio	Expense Ratio
JKH	NYSE Arca	243.40	$596,332,616	0.24	30	0.3

Ratings
Reward   C+
Risk   C-
Recent Upgrade/Downgrade   Down

Fund Information
Fund Type   Exchange Traded Funds
Category   US Equity Mid Cap
Sub-Category   Mid-Cap Growth
Prospectus Objective   Growth
Inception Date   Jun-04
Open to New Investments   Y

Prices
Price (as of 9/30/2019)   243.43
52-Week High   259.55
52-Week Low   180.97

Total Returns (%)

3-Month	6-Month	1-Year	3-Year	5-Year
-3.96	2.57	4.19	51.68	70.84

3-Year Standard Deviation   14.51
Effective Duration

Valuation
Premium/Discount (1-Year Average)   0.03

Company Information
Provider   iShares
Manager/Tenure   Greg Savage (11), Jennifer Hsui (7), Alan Mason (3), 2 others
Website   http://www.ishares.com
Address   iShares 400 Howard Street San Francisco CA 94105 United States
Phone Number   800-474-2737

PERFORMANCE

Ratings History

Date	Overall Rating	Risk Rating	Reward Rating
Q3-19	C	C-	C+
Q4-18	C-	D+	C
Q4-17	B	C+	B
Q4-16	C	D+	C+
Q4-15	C	D+	C

Asset & Performance History

Date	NAV	1-Year Total Return
2018	194.56	-3.38
2017	202.03	25.37
2016	161.93	6.25
2015	153.2	-0.93
2014	155.23	9.53
2013	142.6	33.83

Total Assets: $596,332,616

Asset Allocation

Asset	%
Cash	0%
Stocks	100%
US Stocks	99%
Bonds	0%
US Bonds	0%
Other	0%

Services Offered:

Investment Strategy: The investment seeks to track the investment results of the Morningstar® US Mid Growth IndexSM composed of mid-capitalization U.S. equities that exhibit growth characteristics. The fund generally invests at least 90% of its assets in securities of the underlying index and in depositary receipts representing securities of the underlying index. The underlying index measures the performance of stocks issued by mid-capitalization companies that have exhibited above-average "growth" characteristics as determined by Morningstar, Inc.'s ("Morningstar" or the "index provider") proprietary index methodology. **Top Holdings:** SBA Communications Corp   Hilton Worldwide Holdings Inc   MercadoLibre Inc   Verisk Analytics Inc   TransDigm Group Inc

---

Global X MLP & Energy Infrastructure ETF   C   HOLD

Ticker	Traded On	NAV	Total Assets ($)	Dividend Yield (TTM)	Turnover Ratio	Expense Ratio
MLPX	NYSE Arca	12.28	$593,915,246	5.78	26	0.45

Ratings
Reward   C+
Risk   C-
Recent Upgrade/Downgrade

Fund Information
Fund Type   Exchange Traded Funds
Category   Energy Sector Equity
Sub-Category   Energy Limited Partnership
Prospectus Objective   Growth & Inc
Inception Date   Aug-13
Open to New Investments   Y

Prices
Price (as of 9/30/2019)   12.30
52-Week High   13.70
52-Week Low   10.40

Total Returns (%)

3-Month	6-Month	1-Year	3-Year	5-Year
-4.03	-5.05	-4.86	-5.19	-20.74

3-Year Standard Deviation   17.46
Effective Duration

Valuation
Premium/Discount (1-Year Average)   -0.36

Company Information
Provider   Global X Funds
Manager/Tenure   Chang Kim (5), Nam To (1), Wayne Xie (0), 1 other
Website   http://www.globalxfunds.com
Address   Global X Funds 600 Lexington Avenue, 20th Floor New York NY 10022 United States
Phone Number   888-493-8631

PERFORMANCE

Ratings History

Date	Overall Rating	Risk Rating	Reward Rating
Q3-19	C	C-	C+
Q4-18	C	D+	B-
Q4-17	D	D	D+
Q4-16	C	D	C+
Q4-15	C-	C	B

Asset & Performance History

Date	NAV	1-Year Total Return
2018	10.93	-15.31
2017	13.57	-4.75
2016	14.86	36.17
2015	11.62	-35.23
2014	18.56	16.53
2013	16.28	

Total Assets: $593,915,246

Asset Allocation

Asset	%
Cash	0%
Stocks	100%
US Stocks	76%
Bonds	0%
US Bonds	0%
Other	0%

Services Offered:

Investment Strategy: The investment seeks to provide investment results that correspond generally to the price and yield performance, before fees and expenses, of the Solactive MLP & Energy Infrastructure Index. The fund invests at least 80% of its total assets in the securities of the index. It also invests at least 80% of its total assets in securities of master limited partnerships and energy infrastructure corporations. The fund's 80% investment policies are non-fundamental and require 60 days' prior written notice to shareholders before they can be changed. The index tracks the performance of midstream energy infrastructure MLPs and corporations. It is non-diversified. **Top Holdings:** TC Energy Corp   Kinder Morgan Inc Class P   Enbridge Inc   ONEOK Inc   Williams Companies Inc

iPath® Bloomberg Commodity Index Total Return(SM) ETN　　　　D　　SELL

Ticker	Traded On	NAV	Total Assets ($)	Dividend Yield (TTM)	Turnover Ratio	Expense Ratio
DJP	NYSE Arca		$588,978,446	0	0	0.7

Ratings
Reward	D
Risk	D+
Recent Upgrade/Downgrade	

Fund Information
Fund Type	Exchange Traded Funds
Category	Commodities Broad Basket
Sub-Category	Commodities Broad Basket
Prospectus Objective	Natl Res
Inception Date	Jun-06
Open to New Investments	Y

Prices
Price (as of 9/30/2019)	21.80
52-Week High	24.59
52-Week Low	21.13

Total Returns (%)
3-Month	6-Month	1-Year	3-Year	5-Year
-0.66	-3.92	-9.04	-6.68	-36.02

3-Year Standard Deviation	9.2
Effective Duration	

Valuation
Premium/Discount (1-Year Average)	-0.08

Company Information
Provider	Milleis Investissements Funds
Manager/Tenure	No Manager (13)
Website	
Address	2-4, rue Eugène Ruppert L-2453 Luxembourg Luxembourg L-2453 Luxembourg
Phone Number	

PERFORMANCE

Ratings History
Date	Overall Rating	Risk Rating	Reward Rating
Q3-19	D	D+	D
Q4-18	D+	C-	D
Q4-17	D+	D	D+
Q4-16	D	D	D
Q4-15	D-	D	D-

Asset & Performance History
Date	NAV	1-Year Total Return
2018	21.41	-12.51
2017	24.48	0.34
2016	24.19	13.64
2015	21.48	-27.81
2014	29.75	-19.04
2013	36.75	-10.81

Total Assets: $588,978,446
Asset Allocation
Asset	%
Cash	%
Stocks	%
US Stocks	%
Bonds	%
US Bonds	%
Other	%

Services Offered:

Investment Strategy: The investment seeks to provide investors with exposure to the Dow Jones-UBS Commodity Index Total ReturnService Mark.
The Dow Jones-UBS Commodity Index Total ReturnService Mark (the "index") reflects the returns that are potentially available through an unleveraged investment in the futures contracts on physical commodities comprising the index plus the rate of interest that could be earned on cash collateral invested in specified Treasury Bills. The index is a rolling index rebalancing annually. **Top Holdings:**

Vident International Equity Fund™　　　　D+　　SELL

Ticker	Traded On	NAV	Total Assets ($)	Dividend Yield (TTM)	Turnover Ratio	Expense Ratio
VIDI	NYSE Arca	23.45	$586,337,293	2.89	66	0.61

Ratings
Reward	D+
Risk	C-
Recent Upgrade/Downgrade	Down

Fund Information
Fund Type	Exchange Traded Funds
Category	Global Equity Large Cap
Sub-Category	Foreign Large Value
Prospectus Objective	Foreign Stock
Inception Date	Oct-13
Open to New Investments	Y

Prices
Price (as of 9/30/2019)	23.41
52-Week High	25.56
52-Week Low	22.04

Total Returns (%)
3-Month	6-Month	1-Year	3-Year	5-Year
-3.72	-3.04	-5.58	15.34	8.17

3-Year Standard Deviation	13.14
Effective Duration	

Valuation
Premium/Discount (1-Year Average)	-0.10

Company Information
Provider	Vident Financial
Manager/Tenure	Denise M. Krisko (4), Rafael Zayas (2)
Website	http://www.videntfinancial.com
Address	Vident Financial 201 17th Street, Suite 300 Atlanta GA 30363 United States
Phone Number	800-617-0004

PERFORMANCE

Ratings History
Date	Overall Rating	Risk Rating	Reward Rating
Q3-19	D+	C-	D+
Q4-18	C-	C-	C-
Q4-17	B-	C+	B
Q4-16	D+	C-	D+
Q4-15	D	D+	D

Asset & Performance History
Date	NAV	1-Year Total Return
2018	22.66	-17.3
2017	28.11	32.86
2016	21.66	7.88
2015	20.36	-10.76
2014	23.29	-2.15
2013	24.34	

Total Assets: $586,337,293
Asset Allocation
Asset	%
Cash	0%
Stocks	100%
US Stocks	2%
Bonds	0%
US Bonds	0%
Other	0%

Services Offered:

Investment Strategy: The investment seeks to track the performance, before fees and expenses, of the Vident Core International Equity Index™. The advisor attempts to invest all, or substantially all, of its assets in the common stocks that make up the underlying index. The underlying index is a rules-based, systematic strategy index comprised of equity securities of issuers in developed and emerging markets outside of the United States.
Top Holdings: Sino Biopharmaceutical Ltd　Qualicorp Consultoria E Corretora De Seguros SA　Lite-On Technology Corp　ICA Gruppen AB　Sugi Holdings Co Ltd

First Trust Emerging Markets AlphaDEX® Fund
C   HOLD

Ticker	Traded On	NAV	Total Assets ($)	Dividend Yield (TTM)	Turnover Ratio	Expense Ratio
FEM	NAS CM	23.73	$584,946,057	3.61	103	0.8

Ratings
Reward   C
Risk   C+
Recent Upgrade/Downgrade

Fund Information
Fund Type   Exchange Traded Funds
Category   Global Emerg Mkts Equity
Sub-Category   Diversified Emerging Mkts
Prospectus Objective   Div Emerg Mkts
Inception Date   Apr-11
Open to New Investments   Y

Prices
Price (as of 9/30/2019)   23.54
52-Week High   25.79
52-Week Low   22.37

Total Returns (%)

3-Month	6-Month	1-Year	3-Year	5-Year
-4.16	-3.06	-2.43	26.50	17.16

3-Year Standard Deviation   15.19
Effective Duration

Valuation
Premium/Discount (1-Year Average)   0.07

Company Information
Provider   First Trust
Manager/Tenure   Jon C. Erickson (8), Daniel J. Lindquist (8), David G. McGarel (8), 3 others
Website   http://www.ftportfolios.com/
Address   First Trust 120 E. Liberty Drive, Suite 400 Wheaton IL 60187 United States
Phone Number   800-621-1675

PERFORMANCE

Ratings History

Date	Overall Rating	Risk Rating	Reward Rating
Q3-19	C	C+	C
Q4-18	C-	C	C-
Q4-17	B	C+	B+
Q4-16	D+	C-	D+
Q4-15	D	D+	D

Asset & Performance History

Date	NAV	1-Year Total Return
2018	22.8	-15.44
2017	27.84	39.47
2016	20.5	15.84
2015	18.1	-13.13
2014	21.53	-10.03
2013	24.55	-3.34

Total Assets: $584,946,057
Asset Allocation

Asset	%
Cash	2%
Stocks	98%
US Stocks	0%
Bonds	0%
US Bonds	0%
Other	0%

Services Offered:

Investment Strategy: The investment seeks investment results that correspond generally to the price and yield (before the fund's fees and expenses) of an equity index called the NASDAQ AlphaDEX® Emerging Markets Index. The fund will normally invest at least 90% of its net assets (including investment borrowings) in the common stocks and depositary receipts that comprise the index. The index is designed to select stocks from the NASDAQ Emerging Markets Index (the "base index") that may generate positive alpha, or risk-adjusted returns, relative to traditional indices through the use of the AlphaDEX® selection methodology. **Top Holdings:** JBS SA   Li Ning Co Ltd   Impala Platinum Holdings Ltd   Yihai International Holdings Ltd   Brilliance China Automotive Holdings Ltd

iShares Agency Bond ETF
C   HOLD

Ticker	Traded On	NAV	Total Assets ($)	Dividend Yield (TTM)	Turnover Ratio	Expense Ratio
AGZ	NYSE Arca	116.48	$582,411,395	2.37	69	0.2

Ratings
Reward   C
Risk   C-
Recent Upgrade/Downgrade

Fund Information
Fund Type   Exchange Traded Funds
Category   US Fixed Income
Sub-Category   Short Government
Prospectus Objective   Govt Bond - Gen
Inception Date   Nov-08
Open to New Investments   Y

Prices
Price (as of 9/30/2019)   116.54
52-Week High   117.35
52-Week Low   109.93

Total Returns (%)

3-Month	6-Month	1-Year	3-Year	5-Year
1.82	4.23	7.89	7.05	12.61

3-Year Standard Deviation   2.39
Effective Duration

Valuation
Premium/Discount (1-Year Average)   0.10

Company Information
Provider   iShares
Manager/Tenure   Scott Radell (9), James Mauro (8)
Website   http://www.ishares.com
Address   iShares 400 Howard Street San Francisco CA 94105 United States
Phone Number   800-474-2737

PERFORMANCE

Ratings History

Date	Overall Rating	Risk Rating	Reward Rating
Q3-19	C	C-	C
Q4-18	C-	C-	C-
Q4-17	C+	B	C
Q4-16	C	C-	C
Q4-15	C	C-	C

Asset & Performance History

Date	NAV	1-Year Total Return
2018	111.88	1.33
2017	112.83	1.68
2016	112.55	1.3
2015	112.78	1
2014	113.11	3.55
2013	110.7	-1.31

Total Assets: $582,411,395
Asset Allocation

Asset	%
Cash	1%
Stocks	0%
US Stocks	0%
Bonds	99%
US Bonds	84%
Other	0%

Services Offered:

Investment Strategy: The investment seeks to track the investment results of the Bloomberg Barclays U.S. Agency Bond Index. The underlying index measures the performance of the agency sector of the U.S. government bond market and is comprised of investment-grade U.S. dollar-denominated publicly-issued government agency bonds or debentures. The fund generally will invest at least 90% of its assets in the component securities of the underlying index. **Top Holdings:** Federal National Mortgage Association 2.88% Tennessee Valley Authority 5.88% Israel (State Of) 5.5% Federal Home Loan Banks 2.88% Iraq (Republic Of) 2.15%

iShares Residential Real Estate Capped ETF   B-   BUY

Ticker	Traded On	NAV	Total Assets ($)	Dividend Yield (TTM)	Turnover Ratio	Expense Ratio
REZ	NYSE Arca	79.43	$575,853,900	2.63	10	0.48

Ratings
Reward   B
Risk   C
Recent Upgrade/Downgrade   Up

Fund Information
Fund Type   Exchange Traded Funds
Category   Real Estate Sector Equity
Sub-Category   Real Estate
Prospectus Objective   Real Estate
Inception Date   May-07
Open to New Investments   Y

Prices
Price (as of 9/30/2019)   79.47
52-Week High   80.58
52-Week Low   59.92

Total Returns (%)

3-Month	6-Month	1-Year	3-Year	5-Year
9.90	14.18	31.54	35.93	86.80

3-Year Standard Deviation   13.84
Effective Duration

Valuation
Premium/Discount (1-Year Average)   0.04

Company Information
Provider   iShares
Manager/Tenure   Greg Savage (11), Jennifer Hsui (7),
                    Alan Mason (3), 2 others
Website   http://www.ishares.com
Address   iShares 400 Howard Street San
                    Francisco CA 94105 United States
Phone Number   800-474-2737

PERFORMANCE

Ratings History

Date	Overall Rating	Risk Rating	Reward Rating
Q3-19	B-	C	B
Q4-18	C+	C	B
Q4-17	C+	B	C
Q4-16	B-	C	B
Q4-15	B	C+	B+

Asset & Performance History

Date	NAV	1-Year Total Return
2018	62.39	4.09
2017	62.2	3.82
2016	62.02	3.29
2015	63.39	11.32
2014	58.88	35.02
2013	45.14	-3.53

Total Assets: $575,853,900
Asset Allocation

Asset	%
Cash	1%
Stocks	99%
US Stocks	99%
Bonds	0%
US Bonds	0%
Other	0%

Services Offered:

Investment Strategy: The investment seeks to track the investment results of the FTSE NAREIT All Residential Capped Index composed of U.S. residential, healthcare and self-storage real estate equities. The fund generally will invest at least 90% of its assets in the component securities of the underlying index and may invest up to 10% of its assets in certain futures, options and swap contracts, cash and cash equivalents. The underlying index measures the performance of the residential apartments, manufactured homes, healthcare and self-storage real estate sectors of the U.S. equity market. The fund is non-diversified. **Top Holdings:** Public Storage Welltower Inc Equity Residential AvalonBay Communities Inc Ventas Inc

---

Invesco Russell 1000 Equal Weight ETF   C   HOLD

Ticker	Traded On	NAV	Total Assets ($)	Dividend Yield (TTM)	Turnover Ratio	Expense Ratio
EQAL	NYSE Arca	32.05	$570,522,064	1.52		0.2

Ratings
Reward   C
Risk   C-
Recent Upgrade/Downgrade

Fund Information
Fund Type   Exchange Traded Funds
Category   US Equity Mid Cap
Sub-Category   Mid-Cap Blend
Prospectus Objective   Growth
Inception Date   Dec-14
Open to New Investments

Prices
Price (as of 9/30/2019)   32.07
52-Week High   33.16
52-Week Low   26.31

Total Returns (%)

3-Month	6-Month	1-Year	3-Year	5-Year
-1.76	-0.54	-1.64	27.90	

3-Year Standard Deviation   13.51
Effective Duration

Valuation
Premium/Discount (1-Year Average)   0.03

Company Information
Provider   Invesco
Manager/Tenure   Peter Hubbard (4), Michael Jeanette
                    (4), Tony Seisser (4)
Website   http://www.invesco.com/us
Address   Invesco 11 Greenway Plaza, Ste. 2500
                    Houston TX 77046 United States
Phone Number   800-659-1005

PERFORMANCE

Ratings History

Date	Overall Rating	Risk Rating	Reward Rating
Q3-19	C	C-	C
Q4-18	C-	C-	C-
Q4-17	C+	B-	C+
Q4-16	C-	C-	C-
Q4-15	U		

Asset & Performance History

Date	NAV	1-Year Total Return
2018	27.92	-8.9
2017	31.11	17.18
2016	26.88	16.06
2015	23.54	-4.2
2014	24.97	
2013		

Total Assets: $570,522,064
Asset Allocation

Asset	%
Cash	0%
Stocks	100%
US Stocks	99%
Bonds	0%
US Bonds	0%
Other	0%

Services Offered:

Investment Strategy: The investment seeks to track the investment results (before fees and expenses) of the Russell 1000® Equal Weight Index (the "underlying index"). The fund generally will invest at least 90% of its total assets in the securities that comprise the underlying index. The underlying index is designed to measure the performance of approximately 1000 equally-weighted securities. The underlying index is comprised of all of the securities in the Russell 1000® Index, which is composed of approximately 1,000 of the largest securities within the Russell 3000® Index. **Top Holdings:** Pilgrims Pride Corp Edison International WEC Energy Group Inc Valvoline Inc Tyson Foods Inc Class A

ProShares Short QQQ   D   SELL

Ticker	Traded On	NAV	Total Assets ($)	Dividend Yield (TTM)	Turnover Ratio	Expense Ratio
PSQ	NYSE Arca	27.73	$570,288,208	1.64		0.95

Ratings
Reward   D-
Risk   D-
Recent Upgrade/Downgrade

Fund Information
Fund Type   Exchange Traded Funds
Category   Trading Tools
Sub-Category   Trading--Inverse Equity
Prospectus Objective   Growth
Inception Date   Jun-06
Open to New Investments   Y

Prices
Price (as of 9/30/2019)   27.74
52-Week High   37.20
52-Week Low   27.04

Total Returns (%)

3-Month	6-Month	1-Year	3-Year	5-Year
-0.01	-3.63	-3.60	-40.36	-55.65

3-Year Standard Deviation   14.47
Effective Duration

Valuation
Premium/Discount (1-Year Average)   0.01

Company Information
Provider   ProShares
Manager/Tenure   Michael Neches (6), Devin Sullivan (1)
Website   http://www.proshares.com
Address   ProShares 7501 Wisconsin Avenue,
                             Suite 1000 Bethesda MD 20814
                             United States
Phone Number   866-776-5125

PERFORMANCE

Ratings History

Date	Overall Rating	Risk Rating	Reward Rating
Q3-19	D	D-	D-
Q4-18	D	D-	D
Q4-17	D-	D-	D-
Q4-16	D	D-	D
Q4-15	D	D-	D-

Asset & Performance History

Date	NAV	1-Year Total Return
2018	34.45	-2.2
2017	35.59	-24.8
2016	47.34	-9.34
2015	52.22	-12.26
2014	59.52	-18.42
2013	72.96	-28.66

Total Assets: $570,288,208
Asset Allocation

Asset	%
Cash	147%
Stocks	-58%
US Stocks	-57%
Bonds	12%
US Bonds	12%
Other	0%

Services Offered:

Investment Strategy: The investment seeks daily investment results before fees and expenses that correspond to the inverse (-1x) of the daily performance of the NASDAQ-100 Index®. The fund invests in financial instruments that ProShare Advisors believes, in combination, should produce daily returns consistent with the fund's investment objective. The index includes 100 of the largest domestic and international non-financial companies listed on The Nasdaq Stock Market based on market capitalization. The fund is non-diversified. **Top Holdings:** Nasdaq 100 Index Swap Societe Generale   Nasdaq 100 Index Swap Bnp Paribas   Nasdaq 100 Index Swap Credit Suisse International   Nasdaq 100 Index Swap Bank Of America Na   Nasdaq 100 Index Swap Citibank Na

---

Pacer Trendpilot™ 100 ETF   C+   HOLD

Ticker	Traded On	NAV	Total Assets ($)	Dividend Yield (TTM)	Turnover Ratio	Expense Ratio
PTNQ	BATS	35.94	$569,611,681	0.41	107	0.65

Ratings
Reward   B-
Risk   C
Recent Upgrade/Downgrade   Up

Fund Information
Fund Type   Exchange Traded Funds
Category   US Equity Large Cap Growth
Sub-Category   Large Growth
Prospectus Objective   Growth
Inception Date   Jun-15
Open to New Investments   Y

Prices
Price (as of 9/30/2019)   35.92
52-Week High   37.17
52-Week Low   31.83

Total Returns (%)

3-Month	6-Month	1-Year	3-Year	5-Year
-0.14	4.00	-0.18	58.00	

3-Year Standard Deviation   12.93
Effective Duration

Valuation
Premium/Discount (1-Year Average)   0.06

Company Information
Provider   Pacer
Manager/Tenure   Bruce Kavanaugh (4), Michael Mack
                             (4)
Website   http://www.paceretfs.com
Address   Pacer 16 Industrial Blvd, Suite 201
                             Paoli PA 19301 United States
Phone Number

PERFORMANCE

Ratings History

Date	Overall Rating	Risk Rating	Reward Rating
Q3-19	C+	C	B-
Q4-18	C	C	C+
Q4-17	C	B-	C+
Q4-16	D	C-	C
Q4-15	U		

Asset & Performance History

Date	NAV	1-Year Total Return
2018	32.67	8.83
2017	30.15	32.08
2016	22.9	-4.01
2015	23.9	
2014		
2013		

Total Assets: $569,611,681
Asset Allocation

Asset	%
Cash	0%
Stocks	100%
US Stocks	98%
Bonds	0%
US Bonds	0%
Other	0%

Services Offered:

Investment Strategy: The investment seeks to track the total return performance, before fees and expenses, of the Pacer NASDAQ-100 Trendpilot Index. The fund invests at least 80% of its total assets (exclusive of collateral held from securities lending) in the component securities of the index. The index implements a systematic trend-following strategy that directs exposure (i) 100% to the NASDAQ-100® Index, (ii) 50% to the NASDAQ-100 and 50% to 3-Month U.S. Treasury bills, or (iii) 100% to 3-Month U.S. Treasury bills, depending on the relative performance of the NASDAQ-100 and its 200-business day historical simple moving average. It is non-diversified. **Top Holdings:** Microsoft Corp   Apple Inc   Amazon.com Inc   Facebook Inc A   Alphabet Inc Class C

iShares Core Conservative Allocation ETF   C   HOLD

Ticker	Traded On	NAV	Total Assets ($)	Dividend Yield (TTM)	Turnover Ratio	Expense Ratio
AOK	NYSE Arca	35.64	$568,487,825	2.73	3	0.25

Ratings
Reward   C+
Risk   C-
Recent Upgrade/Downgrade

Fund Information
Fund Type	Exchange Traded Funds
Category	Cautious Allocation
Sub-Category	Allocation--30% to 50% Equity
Prospectus Objective	Asset Allocation
Inception Date	Nov-08
Open to New Investments	Y

Prices
Price (as of 9/30/2019)	35.66
52-Week High	35.73
52-Week Low	32.37

Total Returns (%)
3-Month	6-Month	1-Year	3-Year	5-Year
0.93	4.64	7.27	15.99	24.44

3-Year Standard Deviation	4.08
Effective Duration	

Valuation
Premium/Discount (1-Year Average)	0.03

Company Information
Provider	iShares
Manager/Tenure	Diane Hsiung (10), Greg Savage (10), Jennifer Hsui (6), 3 others
Website	http://www.ishares.com
Address	iShares 400 Howard Street San Francisco CA 94105 United States
Phone Number	800-474-2737

PERFORMANCE

Ratings History
Date	Overall Rating	Risk Rating	Reward Rating
Q3-19	C	C-	C+
Q4-18	C	C+	C-
Q4-17	B	A-	C+
Q4-16	C	C-	C
Q4-15	C	C-	C

Asset & Performance History
Date	NAV	1-Year Total Return
2018	32.74	-3.31
2017	34.6	9.61
2016	32.51	5.13
2015	31.59	-1.13
2014	32.59	3.94
2013	32.01	6.64

Total Assets: $568,487,825
Asset Allocation
Asset	%
Cash	1%
Stocks	29%
US Stocks	16%
Bonds	69%
US Bonds	50%
Other	0%

Services Offered:
Investment Strategy: The investment seeks to track the investment results of the S&P Target Risk Conservative Index composed of a portfolio of underlying equity and fixed income funds intended to represent a conservative target risk allocation strategy. The fund is a fund of funds and seeks its investment objective by investing primarily in other iShares Underlying Funds that themselves seek investment results corresponding to their own respective underlying indexes. It generally will invest at least 90% of its assets in the component securities of the underlying index. The index measures the performance of the S&P Dow Jones Indices LLC proprietary allocation model. **Top Holdings:** United States Treasury Notes 2.5% United States Treasury Notes 2.63% Microsoft Corp United States Treasury Notes 2% Apple Inc

---

First Trust Small Cap Core AlphaDEX® Fund   C-   HOLD

Ticker	Traded On	NAV	Total Assets ($)	Dividend Yield (TTM)	Turnover Ratio	Expense Ratio
FYX	NAS CM	60.08	$567,754,687	1.1	117	0.66

Ratings
Reward   C-
Risk   C-
Recent Upgrade/Downgrade

Fund Information
Fund Type	Exchange Traded Funds
Category	US Equity Small Cap
Sub-Category	Small Blend
Prospectus Objective	Small Company
Inception Date	May-07
Open to New Investments	Y

Prices
Price (as of 9/30/2019)	60.07
52-Week High	68.02
52-Week Low	50.98

Total Returns (%)
3-Month	6-Month	1-Year	3-Year	5-Year
-2.26	-3.07	-10.61	24.06	42.34

3-Year Standard Deviation	18.52
Effective Duration	

Valuation
Premium/Discount (1-Year Average)	-0.02

Company Information
Provider	First Trust
Manager/Tenure	Jon C. Erickson (12), Daniel J. Lindquist (12), David G. McGarel (12), 3 others
Website	http://www.ftportfolios.com/
Address	First Trust 120 E. Liberty Drive, Suite 400 Wheaton IL 60187 United States
Phone Number	800-621-1675

PERFORMANCE

Ratings History
Date	Overall Rating	Risk Rating	Reward Rating
Q3-19	C-	C-	C-
Q4-18	C-	C-	C-
Q4-17	B	B-	B+
Q4-16	C	C-	C+
Q4-15	C	C+	C

Asset & Performance History
Date	NAV	1-Year Total Return
2018	54.33	-10.27
2017	61.13	14.45
2016	53.75	22.71
2015	44.24	-8.91
2014	48.97	1.31
2013	48.62	43.15

Total Assets: $567,754,687
Asset Allocation
Asset	%
Cash	0%
Stocks	100%
US Stocks	99%
Bonds	0%
US Bonds	0%
Other	0%

Services Offered:
Investment Strategy: The investment seeks investment results that correspond generally to the price and yield (before the fund's fees and expenses) of an equity index called the Nasdaq AlphaDEX® Small Cap Core Index. The fund will normally invest at least 90% of its net assets (including investment borrowings) in common stocks that comprise the index. The index is designed to select stocks from the NASDAQ US 700 Small Cap Index (the "base index") that may generate positive alpha, or risk-adjusted returns, relative to traditional indices through the use of the AlphaDEX® selection methodology. **Top Holdings:** Shake Shack Inc A Arrowhead Pharmaceuticals Inc Meritage Homes Corp Medpace Holdings Inc BMC Stock Holdings Inc

SPDR® S&P Health Care Equipment ETF   C   HOLD

Ticker	Traded On	NAV	Total Assets ($)	Dividend Yield (TTM)	Turnover Ratio	Expense Ratio
XHE	NYSE Arca		$566,481,395	0.11	32	0.35

Ratings
Reward   C
Risk   C-
Recent Upgrade/Downgrade

Fund Information
Fund Type   Exchange Traded Funds
Category   Healthcare Sector Equity
Sub-Category   Health
Prospectus Objective   Health
Inception Date   Jan-11
Open to New Investments   Y

Prices
Price (as of 9/30/2019)   78.07
52-Week High   86.98
52-Week Low   64.44

Total Returns (%)

3-Month	6-Month	1-Year	3-Year	5-Year
-5.78	-3.77	-11.00	50.57	127.61

3-Year Standard Deviation   17.6
Effective Duration

Valuation
Premium/Discount (1-Year Average)   -0.01

Company Information
Provider   SPDR State Street Global Advisors
Manager/Tenure Michael J. Feehily (7), Karl A.
              Schneider (4), Kala O'Donnell (2)
Website   http://www.spdrs.com
Address   SPDR State Street Global Advisors
              State Street Financial Center, 1
              Lincoln Street Boston MA 02111-2900
              United States
Phone Number 617-786-3000

PERFORMANCE

Ratings History

Date	Overall Rating	Risk Rating	Reward Rating
Q3-19	C	C-	C
Q4-18	C	C+	C
Q4-17	A-	B+	A-
Q4-16	C	C-	B-
Q4-15	C	C-	C+

Asset & Performance History

Date	NAV	1-Year Total Return
2018	70.12	9.28
2017	64.22	29.99
2016	49.79	11.71
2015	44.28	9.09
2014	43.59	16.25
2013	38.19	36.31

Total Assets: $566,481,395
Asset Allocation

Asset	%
Cash	-1%
Stocks	101%
US Stocks	101%
Bonds	0%
US Bonds	0%
Other	0%

Services Offered:

Investment Strategy: The investment seeks to provide investment results that, before fees and expenses, correspond generally to the total return performance of an index derived from the health care equipment and supplies segment of a U.S. total market composite index. In seeking to track the performance of the S&P Health Care Equipment Select Industry Index (the "index"), the fund employs a sampling strategy. It generally invests substantially all, but at least 80%, of its total assets in the securities comprising the index. The index represents the health care equipment segment of the S&P Total Market Index ("S&P TMI"). The fund is non-diversified. **Top Holdings:** Insulet Corp Nevro Corp Globus Medical Inc Class A Conmed Corp Cardiovascular Systems Inc

SPDR® Russell 1000 Low Volatility Focus ETF   C   HOLD

Ticker	Traded On	NAV	Total Assets ($)	Dividend Yield (TTM)	Turnover Ratio	Expense Ratio
ONEV	NYSE Arca		$562,551,370	1.81	33	0.2

Ratings
Reward   C+
Risk   C-
Recent Upgrade/Downgrade

Fund Information
Fund Type   Exchange Traded Funds
Category   US Equity Mid Cap
Sub-Category   Mid-Cap Blend
Prospectus Objective   Growth & Inc
Inception Date   Dec-15
Open to New Investments   Y

Prices
Price (as of 9/30/2019)   81.55
52-Week High   82.36
52-Week Low   64.20

Total Returns (%)

3-Month	6-Month	1-Year	3-Year	5-Year
1.09	6.35	8.38	41.52	

3-Year Standard Deviation   11.76
Effective Duration

Valuation
Premium/Discount (1-Year Average)   0.02

Company Information
Provider   SPDR State Street Global Advisors
Manager/Tenure Michael J. Feehily (3), Karl A.
              Schneider (3), Emiliano Rabinovich (2)
Website   http://www.spdrs.com
Address   SPDR State Street Global Advisors
              State Street Financial Center, 1
              Lincoln Street Boston MA 02111-2900
              United States
Phone Number 617-786-3000

PERFORMANCE

Ratings History

Date	Overall Rating	Risk Rating	Reward Rating
Q3-19	C	C-	C+
Q4-18	C-	D+	C-
Q4-17	C	B+	C-
Q4-16	D	D+	D+
Q4-15			

Asset & Performance History

Date	NAV	1-Year Total Return
2018	67.54	-4.98
2017	72.53	17.9
2016	65.85	15.94
2015	58.97	
2014		
2013		

Total Assets: $562,551,370
Asset Allocation

Asset	%
Cash	0%
Stocks	100%
US Stocks	99%
Bonds	0%
US Bonds	0%
Other	0%

Services Offered:

Investment Strategy: The investment seeks to provide investment results that, before fees and expenses, correspond generally to the total return performance of the Russell 1000 Low Volatility Focused Factor Index. Under normal market conditions, the fund generally invests substantially all, but at least 80%, of its total assets in the securities comprising the index. The index is designed to reflect the performance of a segment of large-capitalization U.S. equity securities demonstrating a combination of core factors (high value, high quality, and low size characteristics), with a focus factor comprising low volatility characteristics. The fund is non-diversified. **Top Holdings:** HP Inc Genuine Parts Co CDW Corp Phillips 66 The Western Union Co

Invesco S&P MidCap Momentum ETF   C   HOLD

Ticker	Traded On	NAV		Total Assets ($)	Dividend Yield (TTM)	Turnover Ratio	Expense Ratio
XMMO	NYSE Arca	58.26		$559,254,592	0.43		0.39

Ratings
Reward	C+
Risk	C-
Recent Upgrade/Downgrade	Down

Fund Information
Fund Type	Exchange Traded Funds
Category	US Equity Mid Cap
Sub-Category	Mid-Cap Growth
Prospectus Objective	Growth
Inception Date	Mar-05
Open to New Investments	Y

Prices
Price (as of 9/30/2019)	58.27
52-Week High	60.28
52-Week Low	41.61

Total Returns (%)
3-Month	6-Month	1-Year	3-Year	5-Year
-0.93	2.24	8.14	85.52	98.98

3-Year Standard Deviation	17.16
Effective Duration	

Valuation
Premium/Discount (1-Year Average)	-0.01

Company Information
Provider	Invesco
Manager/Tenure	Peter Hubbard (12), Michael Jeanette (11), Tony Seisser (5)
Website	http://www.invesco.com/us
Address	Invesco 11 Greenway Plaza, Ste. 2500 Houston TX 77046 United States
Phone Number	800-659-1005

PERFORMANCE

Ratings History
Date	Overall Rating	Risk Rating	Reward Rating
Q3-19	C	C-	C+
Q4-18	C	C-	C
Q4-17	B	B	A-
Q4-16	C	D+	C
Q4-15	C	C-	C

Asset & Performance History
Date	NAV	1-Year Total Return
2018	45.15	6.81
2017	42.35	36.52
2016	31.1	4.42
2015	29.85	-4.27
2014	31.37	9.35
2013	29.05	27.34

Total Assets: $559,254,592
Asset Allocation
Asset	%
Cash	0%
Stocks	100%
US Stocks	100%
Bonds	0%
US Bonds	0%
Other	0%

Services Offered:

Investment Strategy: The investment seeks to track the investment results (before fees and expenses) of the S&P MidCap 400® Momentum Index (the "underlying index"). The fund generally will invest at least 90% of its total assets in the securities that comprise the underlying index. Strictly in accordance with its guidelines and mandated procedures, the index provider compiles, maintains and calculates the underlying index, which is composed of constituents of the S&P MidCap 400® Index that have the highest "momentum score." **Top Holdings:** Steris PLC Omega Healthcare Investors Inc National Retail Properties Inc OGE Energy Corp Medical Properties Trust Inc

FlexShares iBoxx 5-Year Target Duration TIPS Index Fund   C   HOLD

Ticker	Traded On	NAV		Total Assets ($)	Dividend Yield (TTM)	Turnover Ratio	Expense Ratio
TDTF	NYSE Arca	25.48		$557,985,538	1.74	65	0.18

Ratings
Reward	C+
Risk	C-
Recent Upgrade/Downgrade	

Fund Information
Fund Type	Exchange Traded Funds
Category	US Fixed Income
Sub-Category	Inflation-Protected Bond
Prospectus Objective	Govt Bond - Treasury
Inception Date	Sep-11
Open to New Investments	Y

Prices
Price (as of 9/30/2019)	25.53
52-Week High	25.87
52-Week Low	23.80

Total Returns (%)
3-Month	6-Month	1-Year	3-Year	5-Year
0.87	4.05	7.25	6.70	10.78

3-Year Standard Deviation	2.86
Effective Duration	

Valuation
Premium/Discount (1-Year Average)	0.02

Company Information
Provider	Flexshares Trust
Manager/Tenure	Michael R. Chico (8), Brandon P. Ferguson (8), Daniel J. Personette (8)
Website	http://www.flexshares.com
Address	50 South LaSalle Street Chicago, Illinois 60603 Chicago Illinois 60603 United States
Phone Number	855-353-9383

PERFORMANCE

Ratings History
Date	Overall Rating	Risk Rating	Reward Rating
Q3-19	C	C-	C+
Q4-18	C-	C	D
Q4-17	C	B-	C
Q4-16	C	C-	C
Q4-15	D+	C-	D

Asset & Performance History
Date	NAV	1-Year Total Return
2018	24.09	-0.87
2017	24.93	1.78
2016	24.99	4.22
2015	24.34	-0.17
2014	24.43	-0.48
2013	24.85	-5.02

Total Assets: $557,985,538
Asset Allocation
Asset	%
Cash	0%
Stocks	0%
US Stocks	0%
Bonds	100%
US Bonds	100%
Other	0%

Services Offered:

Investment Strategy: The investment seeks to provide investment results that, before fees and expenses, correspond generally to the price and yield performance of the iBoxx 5-Year Target Duration TIPS Index. Under normal circumstances, the fund will invest at least 80% of its total assets (exclusive of collateral held from securities lending) in the securities of the underlying index. The underlying index reflects the performance of a selection of inflation protected public obligations of the U.S. Treasury, commonly known as "TIPS," with a targeted average modified adjusted duration, as defined by the underlying index, of approximately five years. The fund is non-diversified. **Top Holdings:** United States Treasury Notes 0.62% United States Treasury Notes 0.38% United States Treasury Notes 0.12% United States Treasury Notes 0.62% United States Treasury Notes 0.62%

iShares North American Natural Resources ETF   D+   SELL

Ticker	Traded On	NAV	Total Assets ($)	Dividend Yield (TTM)	Turnover Ratio	Expense Ratio
IGE	BATS	29.07	$555,324,916	2.84	12	0.46

Ratings
Reward	D+
Risk	D+
Recent Upgrade/Downgrade	Up

Fund Information
Fund Type	Exchange Traded Funds
Category	Natural Resources
Sub-Category	Natural Resources
Prospectus Objective	Natl Res
Inception Date	Oct-01
Open to New Investments	Y

Prices
Price (as of 9/30/2019)	29.08
52-Week High	36.70
52-Week Low	25.63

Total Returns (%)
3-Month	6-Month	1-Year	3-Year	5-Year
-4.60	-6.07	-17.83	-9.59	-25.70

3-Year Standard Deviation	19.12
Effective Duration	

Valuation
Premium/Discount (1-Year Average)	-0.02

Company Information
Provider	iShares
Manager/Tenure	Greg Savage (11), Jennifer Hsui (6), Alan Mason (3), 2 others
Website	http://www.ishares.com
Address	iShares 400 Howard Street San Francisco CA 94105 United States
Phone Number	800-474-2737

PERFORMANCE

Ratings History
Date	Overall Rating	Risk Rating	Reward Rating
Q3-19	D+	D+	D+
Q4-18	C-	C-	C-
Q4-17	C-	C	C-
Q4-16	C-	D+	C-
Q4-15	C-	D+	C-

Asset & Performance History
Date	NAV	1-Year Total Return
2018	27.2	-21.44
2017	35.41	0.71
2016	35.96	30.12
2015	28.14	-24.51
2014	38.3	-10.21
2013	43.35	15.89

Total Assets: $555,324,916
Asset Allocation
Asset	%
Cash	0%
Stocks	100%
US Stocks	76%
Bonds	0%
US Bonds	0%
Other	0%

Services Offered: CashInvestment Plan

Investment Strategy: The investment seeks to track the investment results of the S&P North American Natural Resources Index composed of North American equities in the natural resources sector. The fund generally invests at least 90% of its assets in securities of the underlying index and in depositary receipts representing securities of the underlying index. The underlying index measures the performance of U.S.-traded stocks of natural resource-related companies in the U.S. and Canada. **Top Holdings:** Chevron Corp Exxon Mobil Corp Enbridge Inc ConocoPhillips TC Energy Corp

---

Invesco Treasury Collateral ETF   C-   HOLD

Ticker	Traded On	NAV	Total Assets ($)	Dividend Yield (TTM)	Turnover Ratio	Expense Ratio
CLTL	NYSE Arca	105.57	$551,097,131	2.3		0.08

Ratings
Reward	C
Risk	C-
Recent Upgrade/Downgrade	

Fund Information
Fund Type	Exchange Traded Funds
Category	US Fixed Income
Sub-Category	Ultrashort Bond
Prospectus Objective	Govt Bond - Treasury
Inception Date	Jan-17
Open to New Investments	Y

Prices
Price (as of 9/30/2019)	105.58
52-Week High	105.76
52-Week Low	105.37

Total Returns (%)
3-Month	6-Month	1-Year	3-Year	5-Year
0.53	1.22	2.46		

3-Year Standard Deviation	
Effective Duration	

Valuation
Premium/Discount (1-Year Average)	0.02

Company Information
Provider	Invesco
Manager/Tenure	Laurie F. Brignac (2), Peter Hubbard (2), Jeffrey W. Kernagis (2), 3 others
Website	http://www.invesco.com/us
Address	Invesco 11 Greenway Plaza, Ste. 2500 Houston TX 77046 United States
Phone Number	800-659-1005

PERFORMANCE

Ratings History
Date	Overall Rating	Risk Rating	Reward Rating
Q3-19	C-	C-	C
Q4-18	D+	C-	D+
Q4-17	D-	B-	D
Q4-16			
Q4-15			

Asset & Performance History
Date	NAV	1-Year Total Return
2018	105.44	1.8
2017	105.33	0.67
2016		
2015		
2014		
2013		

Total Assets: $551,097,131
Asset Allocation
Asset	%
Cash	40%
Stocks	0%
US Stocks	0%
Bonds	60%
US Bonds	60%
Other	0%

Services Offered:

Investment Strategy: The investment seeks to track the investment results (before fees and expenses) of the ICE U.S. Treasury Short Bond Index. The fund generally will invest at least 80% of its total assets in the components of the index. The index is designed to measure the performance of U.S. Treasury Obligations with a maximum remaining maturity of 12 months. "U.S. Treasury Obligations" refer to securities issued or guaranteed by the U.S. Treasury where the payment of principal and interest is backed by the full faith and credit of the U.S. government. They include U.S. Treasury notes, bills and bonds. It is non-diversified. **Top Holdings:** United States Treasury Notes 3.62% United States Treasury Bills 0% United States Treasury Notes 1.25% United States Treasury Notes 1.38% United States Treasury Notes 1.38%

iShares J.P. Morgan EM Local Currency Bond ETF   C-   HOLD

Ticker	Traded On	NAV	Total Assets ($)	Dividend Yield (TTM)	Turnover Ratio	Expense Ratio
LEMB	NYSE Arca	44.42	$550,788,275	3.35	51	0.3

Ratings
Reward	C-
Risk	C
Recent Upgrade/Downgrade	

Fund Information
Fund Type	Exchange Traded Funds
Category	Emerging Mkts Fixed Inc
Sub-Category	Emerging-Markets Local-Currency Bond
Prospectus Objective	Worldwide Bond
Inception Date	Oct-11
Open to New Investments	Y

Prices
Price (as of 9/30/2019)	44.21
52-Week High	46.98
52-Week Low	42.53

Total Returns (%)
3-Month	6-Month	1-Year	3-Year	5-Year
-3.87	0.54	6.77	0.34	-3.82

3-Year Standard Deviation	10.36
Effective Duration	5.09

Valuation
Premium/Discount (1-Year Average)	0.12

Company Information
Provider	iShares
Manager/Tenure	James Mauro (7), Scott Radell (7)
Website	http://www.ishares.com
Address	iShares 400 Howard Street San Francisco CA 94105 United States
Phone Number	800-474-2737

PERFORMANCE

Ratings History
Date	Overall Rating	Risk Rating	Reward Rating
Q3-19	C-	C	C-
Q4-18	D+	D+	D
Q4-17	C	C	C
Q4-16	D+	C-	D+
Q4-15	D	D	D

Asset & Performance History
Date	NAV	1-Year Total Return
2018	42.96	-7.64
2017	48.15	12.31
2016	42.87	7.01
2015	40.06	-11.76
2014	45.66	-4.04
2013	48.88	-4.91

Total Assets: $550,788,275
Asset Allocation
Asset	%
Cash	2%
Stocks	0%
US Stocks	0%
Bonds	98%
US Bonds	0%
Other	0%

Services Offered:

Investment Strategy: The investment seeks to track the investment results of the J.P. Morgan GBI-EM Global Diversified 15% Cap 4.5% Floor Index composed of local currency denominated, emerging market sovereign bonds. The fund generally will invest at least 90% of its assets in the component securities of the underlying index and may invest up to 10% of its assets in certain futures, options and swap contracts, cash and cash equivalents, including shares of money market funds advised by BFA or its affiliates. The index tracks the performance of local currency-denominated sovereign bond markets of emerging market countries. The fund is non-diversified. **Top Holdings:** Uruguay (Republic of) 9.88% Dominican Republic 9.75% Dominican Republic 8.9% Philippines (Republic Of) 6.25% Brazil (Federative Republic) 10%

KraneShares Bosera MSCI China A ETF   C   HOLD

Ticker	Traded On	NAV	Total Assets ($)	Dividend Yield (TTM)	Turnover Ratio	Expense Ratio
KBA	NYSE Arca	30.01	$550,746,129	1.71	106	0.6

Ratings
Reward	C
Risk	C
Recent Upgrade/Downgrade	

Fund Information
Fund Type	Exchange Traded Funds
Category	Greater China Equity
Sub-Category	China Region
Prospectus Objective	Pacific Stock
Inception Date	Mar-14
Open to New Investments	Y

Prices
Price (as of 9/30/2019)	29.96
52-Week High	34.06
52-Week Low	24.20

Total Returns (%)
3-Month	6-Month	1-Year	3-Year	5-Year
-5.74	-5.86	8.18	11.58	22.58

3-Year Standard Deviation	18.72
Effective Duration	

Valuation
Premium/Discount (1-Year Average)	-0.01

Company Information
Provider	KraneShares
Manager/Tenure	Qiong Wan (3)
Website	http://www.kraneshares.com
Address	1350 Avenue of the Americas Second Floor New York NY 10019 United States
Phone Number	855-857-2638

PERFORMANCE

Ratings History
Date	Overall Rating	Risk Rating	Reward Rating
Q3-19	C	C	C
Q4-18	D	D	D
Q4-17	B-	C-	B+
Q4-16	D+	D	C-
Q4-15	D	C-	C

Asset & Performance History
Date	NAV	1-Year Total Return
2018	24.58	-26.76
2017	34.59	28.63
2016	27.16	-19.36
2015	35.31	-3
2014	46.74	
2013		

Total Assets: $550,746,129
Asset Allocation
Asset	%
Cash	0%
Stocks	100%
US Stocks	0%
Bonds	0%
US Bonds	0%
Other	0%

Services Offered:

Investment Strategy: The investment seeks to provide investment results that, before fees and expenses, correspond to the price and yield performance of the MSCI China A Index (USD) (the "underlying index"). Under normal circumstances, the fund will invest at least 80% of its total assets in securities of the underlying index and depositary receipts representing such securities. The underlying index reflects the large- and mid-cap Chinese renminbi-denominated equity securities listed on the Shenzhen or Shanghai Stock Exchanges ("A Shares") that are accessible through the Shanghai-Hong Kong Stock Connect or Shenzhen-Hong Kong Stock Connect programs. **Top Holdings:** Kweichow Moutai Co Ltd Ping An Insurance (Group) Co. of China Ltd China Merchants Bank Co Ltd Wuliangye Yibin Co Ltd China Yangtze Power Co Ltd

Invesco BulletShares 2022 High Yield Corporate Bond ETF

C+   HOLD

Ticker	Traded On	NAV	Total Assets ($)	Dividend Yield (TTM)	Turnover Ratio	Expense Ratio
BSJM	NYSE Arca	24.31	$547,080,479	5.48	17	0.42

Ratings

Reward	C
Risk	C+
Recent Upgrade/Downgrade	

Fund Information

Fund Type	Exchange Traded Funds
Category	US Fixed Income
Sub-Category	High Yield Bond
Prospectus Objective	Corp Bond-High Yld
Inception Date	Sep-14
Open to New Investments	Y

Prices

Price (as of 9/30/2019)	24.37
52-Week High	24.68
52-Week Low	22.88

Total Returns (%)

3-Month	6-Month	1-Year	3-Year	5-Year
0.57	2.36	4.21	14.69	27.30

3-Year Standard Deviation	3.5
Effective Duration	1.67

Valuation

Premium/Discount (1-Year Average)	0.14

Company Information

Provider	Invesco
Manager/Tenure	Jeremy Neisewander (3), Peter Hubbard (1), Jeffrey W. Kernagis (1), 1 other
Website	http://www.invesco.com/us
Address	Invesco 11 Greenway Plaza, Ste. 2500 Houston TX 77046 United States
Phone Number	800-659-1005

PERFORMANCE

Ratings History

Date	Overall Rating	Risk Rating	Reward Rating
Q3-19	C+	C+	C
Q4-18	C	C+	C
Q4-17	B	B+	C+
Q4-16	C-	C-	C-
Q4-15	U		

Asset & Performance History

Date	NAV	1-Year Total Return
2018	23.29	-1.38
2017	24.9	5.33
2016	24.95	15.87
2015	22.67	-2.32
2014	24.39	
2013		

Total Assets: $547,080,479

Asset Allocation

Asset	%
Cash	4%
Stocks	0%
US Stocks	0%
Bonds	96%
US Bonds	82%
Other	0%

Services Offered:

Investment Strategy: The investment seeks to track the investment results (before fees and expenses) of the Nasdaq BulletShares® USD High Yield Corporate Bond 2022 Index (the "underlying index"). The fund generally will invest at least 80% of its total assets in securities that comprise the underlying index. The underlying index seeks to measure the performance of a portfolio of U.S. dollar-denominated high yield corporate bonds (commonly known as "junk bonds") with maturities or, in some cases, "effective maturities" in the year 2022 (collectively, "2022 Bonds"). The fund is non-diversified. **Top Holdings:** Tenet Healthcare Corporation 8.12% Sprint Communications, Inc. 6% HCA Inc. 7.5% Nielsen Finance LLC/Nielsen Finance Co 5% DISH DBS Corporation 5.88%

PIMCO RAFI Dynamic Multi-Factor Emerging Markets Equity ETF

C-   HOLD

Ticker	Traded On	NAV	Total Assets ($)	Dividend Yield (TTM)	Turnover Ratio	Expense Ratio
MFEM	NYSE Arca	23.04	$546,477,303	3.3	43	0.49

Ratings

Reward	D+
Risk	C-
Recent Upgrade/Downgrade	Up

Fund Information

Fund Type	Exchange Traded Funds
Category	Global Emerg Mkts Equity
Sub-Category	Diversified Emerging Mkts
Prospectus Objective	Div Emerg Mkts
Inception Date	Aug-17
Open to New Investments	Y

Prices

Price (as of 9/30/2019)	22.93
52-Week High	24.23
52-Week Low	21.67

Total Returns (%)

3-Month	6-Month	1-Year	3-Year	5-Year
-4.87	-2.55	-2.07		

3-Year Standard Deviation	
Effective Duration	

Valuation

Premium/Discount (1-Year Average)	-0.06

Company Information

Provider	PIMCO
Manager/Tenure	Thomas C. Seto (2)
Website	http://www.pimco.com
Address	PIMCO 840 Newport Center Drive, Suite 100 Newport Beach CA 92660 United States
Phone Number	866-746-2602

PERFORMANCE

Ratings History

Date	Overall Rating	Risk Rating	Reward Rating
Q3-19	C-	C-	D+
Q4-18	D	D	D
Q4-17	U		
Q4-16			
Q4-15			

Asset & Performance History

Date	NAV	1-Year Total Return
2018	22.07	-12.73
2017	26.03	
2016		
2015		
2014		
2013		

Total Assets: $546,477,303

Asset Allocation

Asset	%
Cash	1%
Stocks	99%
US Stocks	0%
Bonds	0%
US Bonds	0%
Other	0%

Services Offered:

Investment Strategy: The investment seeks to track the investment results of the RAFI Dynamic Multi-Factor Emerging Markets Index. The fund seeks to achieve its investment objective by investing at least 80% of its total assets (exclusive of collateral held from securities lending) in the component securities of the RAFI Dynamic Multi-Factor Emerging Markets Index. The underlying index is constructed by RAFI Indices, LLC using a rules-based approach to construct factor portfolios within the underlying index. The underlying index consists of "factor portfolios," each of which emphasizes one of the following factors: value, low volatility, quality and momentum. **Top Holdings:** Infosys Ltd ADR Gazprom PJSC Vale SA ADR Taiwan Semiconductor Manufacturing Co Ltd ADR Hyundai Motor Co

---

VelocityShares 3x Long Natural Gas ETN Linked to the S&P GSCI® Natural Gas Index ER   E+   SELL

Ticker	Traded On	NAV		Total Assets ($)	Dividend Yield (TTM)	Turnover Ratio	Expense Ratio
UGAZ	NYSE Arca	14.64		$540,282,250	0		1.65

Ratings
Reward	E
Risk	D-
Recent Upgrade/Downgrade	

Fund Information
Fund Type	Exchange Traded Funds
Category	Trading Tools
Sub-Category	Trading--Leveraged Commodities
Prospectus Objective	Natl Res
Inception Date	Feb-12
Open to New Investments	Y

Prices
Price (as of 9/30/2019)	14.59
52-Week High	253.10
52-Week Low	11.64

Total Returns (%)
3-Month	6-Month	1-Year	3-Year	5-Year
-5.05	-51.52	-80.93	-95.97	-99.92

3-Year Standard Deviation	97.03
Effective Duration	

Valuation
Premium/Discount (1-Year Average)	0.87

Company Information
Provider	Credit Suisse AG
Manager/Tenure	Management Team (7)
Website	
Address	Kilmore House Park Lane Dublin Ireland
Phone Number	

PERFORMANCE

Ratings History
Date	Overall Rating	Risk Rating	Reward Rating
Q3-19	E+	D-	E
Q4-18	D	D	D
Q4-17	C-	D	C
Q4-16	E+	D-	E
Q4-15	E+	E+	E

Asset & Performance History
Date	NAV	1-Year Total Return
2018	38.61	-47.12
2017	73.04	44.62
2016	455.6	-7.96
2015	617.5	-87.06
2014	4,775.00	-81.82
2013	26,275.00	-3.31

Total Assets: $540,282,250

Asset Allocation
Asset	%
Cash	%
Stocks	%
US Stocks	%
Bonds	%
US Bonds	%
Other	%

Services Offered:

Investment Strategy: The investment seeks to replicate, net of expenses, three times the performance of the S&P GSCI Natural Gas Index ER. The index comprises futures contracts on a single commodity and is calculated according to the methodology of the S&P GSCI Index. **Top Holdings:**

O'Shares FTSE U.S. Quality Dividend ETF   C   HOLD

Ticker	Traded On	NAV		Total Assets ($)	Dividend Yield (TTM)	Turnover Ratio	Expense Ratio
OUSA	NYSE Arca	34.75		$538,577,253	2.49	15	0.48

Ratings
Reward	C+
Risk	C
Recent Upgrade/Downgrade	

Fund Information
Fund Type	Exchange Traded Funds
Category	US Equity Large Cap Value
Sub-Category	Large Value
Prospectus Objective	Growth
Inception Date	Jul-15
Open to New Investments	Y

Prices
Price (as of 9/30/2019)	34.75
52-Week High	35.07
52-Week Low	28.55

Total Returns (%)
3-Month	6-Month	1-Year	3-Year	5-Year
2.10	4.55	8.43	37.03	

3-Year Standard Deviation	10.46
Effective Duration	

Valuation
Premium/Discount (1-Year Average)	0.02

Company Information
Provider	O'Shares Investments
Manager/Tenure	William H. DeRoche (4), Philip Lee (4), Josh Belko (0)
Website	http://www.oshares.com
Address	O'Shares Investments 60 State Street, Suite 700 Boston MA 02109 United States
Phone Number	617-855-7670

PERFORMANCE

Ratings History
Date	Overall Rating	Risk Rating	Reward Rating
Q3-19	C	C	C+
Q4-18	C	C+	C
Q4-17	C	B+	C+
Q4-16	D	C	C
Q4-15	U		

Asset & Performance History
Date	NAV	1-Year Total Return
2018	30	-3.43
2017	31.87	18.78
2016	27.45	12.3
2015	25.03	
2014		
2013		

Total Assets: $538,577,253

Asset Allocation
Asset	%
Cash	0%
Stocks	100%
US Stocks	99%
Bonds	0%
US Bonds	0%
Other	0%

Services Offered:

Investment Strategy: The investment seeks to track the performance (before fees and expenses) of the FTSE USA Qual/Vol/Yield Factor 5% Capped Index (the "target index"). The target index is designed to reflect the performance of publicly-listed large capitalization and mid-capitalization dividend-paying issuers in the United States exhibiting high quality, low volatility and high dividend yields, as determined by FTSE-Russell (the "index provider"). Under normal market conditions, the fund will invest at least 80% of its total assets in the components of the target index. **Top Holdings:** Procter & Gamble Co   Exxon Mobil Corp   Johnson & Johnson   Cisco Systems Inc   The Home Depot Inc

Invesco KBW Bank ETF

B- **BUY**

Ticker	Traded On	NAV	Total Assets ($)	Dividend Yield (TTM)	Turnover Ratio	Expense Ratio
KBWB	NAS CM	51.51	$535,714,958	2.56		0.35

Ratings
Reward   B
Risk   C
Recent Upgrade/Downgrade   Up

Fund Information
Fund Type   Exchange Traded Funds
Category   Financials Sector Equity
Sub-Category   Financial
Prospectus Objective   Financial
Inception Date   Nov-11
Open to New Investments

Prices
Price (as of 9/30/2019)   51.52
52-Week High   55.36
52-Week Low   41.50

Total Returns (%)

3-Month	6-Month	1-Year	3-Year	5-Year
1.73	5.27	-2.16	49.98	55.78

3-Year Standard Deviation   22.75
Effective Duration

Valuation
Premium/Discount (1-Year Average)   -0.04

Company Information
Provider   Invesco
Manager/Tenure   Peter Hubbard (7), Michael Jeanette (7), Tony Seisser (5)
Website   http://www.invesco.com/us
Address   Invesco 11 Greenway Plaza, Ste. 2500 Houston TX 77046 United States
Phone Number   800-659-1005

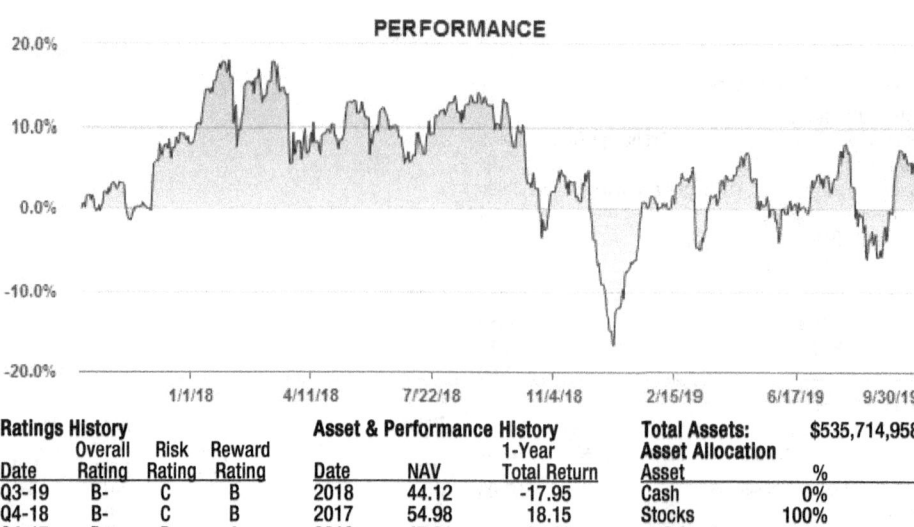

PERFORMANCE

Ratings History

Date	Overall Rating	Risk Rating	Reward Rating
Q3-19	B-	C	B
Q4-18	B-	C	B
Q4-17	B+	B-	A
Q4-16	B	C	B+
Q4-15	A-	A-	B+

Asset & Performance History

Date	NAV	1-Year Total Return
2018	44.12	-17.95
2017	54.98	18.15
2016	47.21	28.03
2015	37.57	0.13
2014	38.1	8.97
2013	35.51	37.25

Total Assets: $535,714,958

Asset Allocation

Asset	%
Cash	0%
Stocks	100%
US Stocks	100%
Bonds	0%
US Bonds	0%
Other	0%

Services Offered:

Investment Strategy: The investment seeks to track the investment results (before fees and expenses) of the KBW Nasdaq Bank Index (the "underlying index"). The fund generally will invest at least 90% of its total assets in the securities that comprise the underlying index. The underlying index is a modified-market capitalization-weighted index of companies primarily engaged in U.S. banking activities, as determined by the index provider. The underlying index is designed to track the performance of large national U.S. money centers, regional banks, and thrift institutions that are publicly traded in the U.S. The fund is non-diversified. **Top Holdings:** US Bancorp Wells Fargo & Co JPMorgan Chase & Co Citigroup Inc Bank of America Corporation

---

iShares Treasury Floating Rate Bond ETF

C **HOLD**

Ticker	Traded On	NAV	Total Assets ($)	Dividend Yield (TTM)	Turnover Ratio	Expense Ratio
TFLO	NYSE Arca	50.27	$532,912,540	2.12	17	0.15

Ratings
Reward   C
Risk   C-
Recent Upgrade/Downgrade   Up

Fund Information
Fund Type   Exchange Traded Funds
Category   US Fixed Income
Sub-Category   Short Government
Prospectus Objective   Govt Bond - Treasury
Inception Date   Feb-14
Open to New Investments   Y

Prices
Price (as of 9/30/2019)   50.28
52-Week High   50.38
52-Week Low   50.20

Total Returns (%)

3-Month	6-Month	1-Year	3-Year	5-Year
0.45	1.01	2.08	4.50	4.91

3-Year Standard Deviation   0.2
Effective Duration

Valuation
Premium/Discount (1-Year Average)   0.03

Company Information
Provider   iShares
Manager/Tenure   James Mauro (5), Scott Radell (5)
Website   http://www.ishares.com
Address   iShares 400 Howard Street San Francisco CA 94105 United States
Phone Number   800-474-2737

PERFORMANCE

Ratings History

Date	Overall Rating	Risk Rating	Reward Rating
Q3-19	C	C-	C
Q4-18	C	C+	C-
Q4-17	C	B-	C-
Q4-16	C-	D+	C-
Q4-15	D	D+	D+

Asset & Performance History

Date	NAV	1-Year Total Return
2018	50.24	1.82
2017	50.16	0.71
2016	50.14	0.46
2015	50.06	0.1
2014	50.08	
2013		

Total Assets: $532,912,540

Asset Allocation

Asset	%
Cash	1%
Stocks	0%
US Stocks	0%
Bonds	99%
US Bonds	99%
Other	0%

Services Offered:

Investment Strategy: The investment seeks to track the investment results of the Bloomberg Barclays U.S. Treasury Floating Rate Index, which is composed of U.S. Treasury floating rate bonds. The fund generally will invest at least 90% of its assets in the component securities of the underlying index and may invest up to 10% of its assets in certain futures, options and swap contracts, cash and cash equivalents. The underlying index is a market capitalization-weighted index that measures the performance of floating rate public obligations of the U.S. Treasury. **Top Holdings:** United States Treasury Notes 2.07% United States Treasury Notes 2% United States Treasury Notes 2% United States Treasury Notes 1.99% United States Treasury Notes 2.1%

First Trust Dow Jones Global Select Dividend Index Fund   C   HOLD

Ticker	Traded On	NAV	Total Assets ($)	Dividend Yield (TTM)	Turnover Ratio	Expense Ratio
FGD	NYSE Arca	22.90	$532,317,397	6.14	31	0.58

Ratings
Reward	D+
Risk	C+
Recent Upgrade/Downgrade	Up

Fund Information
Fund Type	Exchange Traded Funds
Category	Global Equity Large Cap
Sub-Category	Foreign Large Value
Prospectus Objective	World Stock
Inception Date	Nov-07
Open to New Investments	Y

Prices
Price (as of 9/30/2019)	22.93
52-Week High	25.14
52-Week Low	21.06

Total Returns (%)
3-Month	6-Month	1-Year	3-Year	5-Year
0.64	0.87	-3.00	13.08	10.76

3-Year Standard Deviation	11.31
Effective Duration	

Valuation
Premium/Discount (1-Year Average)	0.15

Company Information
Provider	First Trust
Manager/Tenure	Jon C. Erickson (11), Daniel J. Lindquist (11), David G. McGarel (11), 3 others
Website	http://www.ftportfolios.com/
Address	First Trust 120 E. Liberty Drive, Suite 400 Wheaton IL 60187 United States
Phone Number	800-621-1675

PERFORMANCE

Ratings History

Date	Overall Rating	Risk Rating	Reward Rating
Q3-19	C	C+	D+
Q4-18	D+	C-	D+
Q4-17	C+	C	C+
Q4-16	C-	C-	C-
Q4-15	C-	C-	C

Asset & Performance History

Date	NAV	1-Year Total Return
2018	21.89	-12.4
2017	26.36	17.66
2016	23.36	11.77
2015	21.84	-10.17
2014	25.47	-0.73
2013	26.91	17.97

Total Assets: $532,317,397
Asset Allocation

Asset	%
Cash	0%
Stocks	100%
US Stocks	11%
Bonds	0%
US Bonds	0%
Other	0%

Services Offered:

Investment Strategy: The investment seeks investment results that correspond generally to the price and yield (before the fund's fees and expenses) of an equity index called the Dow Jones Global Select Dividend IndexSM. The fund will normally invest at least 90% of its net assets (including investment borrowings) in the common stocks and depositary receipts that comprise the index. The index is an indicated annual dividend yield weighted index of 100 stocks selected from the developed-market portion of the Dow Jones World IndexSM. **Top Holdings:** Harvey Norman Holdings Ltd Standard Life Aberdeen PLC Azimut Holding SPA CSR Ltd BE Semiconductor Industries NV

Global X SuperDividend™ U.S. ETF   C   HOLD

Ticker	Traded On	NAV	Total Assets ($)	Dividend Yield (TTM)	Turnover Ratio	Expense Ratio
DIV	NYSE Arca	23.57	$527,970,497	7.35	33	0.45

Ratings
Reward	C
Risk	C+
Recent Upgrade/Downgrade	

Fund Information
Fund Type	Exchange Traded Funds
Category	US Equity Mid Cap
Sub-Category	Mid-Cap Value
Prospectus Objective	Income
Inception Date	Mar-13
Open to New Investments	Y

Prices
Price (as of 9/30/2019)	23.57
52-Week High	25.33
52-Week Low	21.69

Total Returns (%)
3-Month	6-Month	1-Year	3-Year	5-Year
6.75	2.08	0.52	15.65	14.01

3-Year Standard Deviation	9.65
Effective Duration	

Valuation
Premium/Discount (1-Year Average)	0.01

Company Information
Provider	Global X Funds
Manager/Tenure	Chang Kim (5), Nam To (1), Wayne Xie (0), 1 other
Website	http://www.globalxfunds.com
Address	Global X Funds 600 Lexington Avenue, 20th Floor New York NY 10022 United States
Phone Number	888-493-8631

PERFORMANCE

Ratings History

Date	Overall Rating	Risk Rating	Reward Rating
Q3-19	C	C+	C
Q4-18	C	C-	C
Q4-17	C+	C+	C+
Q4-16	C	C-	C
Q4-15	C	C-	C

Asset & Performance History

Date	NAV	1-Year Total Return
2018	22.37	-6.66
2017	25.57	9.71
2016	24.74	10.75
2015	23.92	-10.52
2014	28.85	17.45
2013	25.93	

Total Assets: $527,970,497
Asset Allocation

Asset	%
Cash	0%
Stocks	100%
US Stocks	100%
Bonds	0%
US Bonds	0%
Other	0%

Services Offered:

Investment Strategy: The investment seeks to provide investment results that correspond generally to the price and yield performance, before fees and expenses, of the Indxx SuperDividend® U.S. Low Volatility Index ("underlying index"). The fund invests at least 80% of its total assets in the securities of the underlying index. The underlying index tracks the performance of 50 equally-weighted common stocks, including Master Limited Partnerships ("MLPs") and Real Estate Investment Trusts ("REITs") that rank among the highest dividend yielding equity securities in the United States. **Top Holdings:** Pattern Energy Group Inc Class A National CineMedia Inc Compass Diversified Holdings Southern Co Ship Finance International Ltd

Global X U.S. Preferred ETF   C   HOLD

Ticker	Traded On	NAV	Total Assets ($)	Dividend Yield (TTM)	Turnover Ratio	Expense Ratio
PFFD	BATS	25.06	$527,565,740	5.5	43	0.23

Ratings

Reward	C-
Risk	C+
Recent Upgrade/Downgrade	Up

Fund Information

Fund Type	Exchange Traded Funds
Category	US Fixed Income
Sub-Category	Preferred Stock
Prospectus Objective	Growth & Inc
Inception Date	Sep-17
Open to New Investments	Y

Prices

Price (as of 9/30/2019)	25.09
52-Week High	25.09
52-Week Low	22.14

Total Returns (%)

3-Month	6-Month	1-Year	3-Year	5-Year
3.97	6.33	10.66		

3-Year Standard Deviation

Effective Duration

Valuation

Premium/Discount (1-Year Average)	0.23

Company Information

Provider	Global X Funds
Manager/Tenure	Chang Kim (2), Nam To (1), Wayne Xie (0), 1 other
Website	http://www.globalxfunds.com
Address	Global X Funds 600 Lexington Avenue, 20th Floor New York NY 10022 United States
Phone Number	888-493-8631

PERFORMANCE

Ratings History

Date	Overall Rating	Risk Rating	Reward Rating
Q3-19	C	C+	C-
Q4-18	D+	C	D
Q4-17	U		
Q4-16			
Q4-15			

Asset & Performance History

Date	NAV	1-Year Total Return
2018	22.46	-4.41
2017	24.79	
2016		
2015		
2014		
2013		

Total Assets: $527,565,740

Asset Allocation

Asset	%
Cash	0%
Stocks	3%
US Stocks	2%
Bonds	0%
US Bonds	0%
Other	0%

Services Offered:

Investment Strategy: The investment seeks to provide investment results that correspond generally to the price and yield performance, before fees and expenses, of the ICE BofAML Diversified Core U.S. Preferred Securities Index. The fund invests at least 80% of its total assets in the securities of its underlying index. It also invests at least 80% of its total assets in preferred securities that are domiciled in, principally traded in or whose revenues are primarily from the U.S. The underlying index is designed to track the broad-based performance of the U.S. preferred securities market. It is non-diversified. **Top Holdings:** Wells Fargo & Co 7 1/2 % Non Cum Perp Conv Pfd Shs -A- Series -L- Bank of America Corporation 7 1/4 % Non-Cum Perp Conv Pfd Shs Series -L- GMAC Capital Trust I Pfd Secs 2011-15.2.40 Gtd Series 2 Crown Castle International Corp Cum Conv Pfd Registered Shs Series -A- Citigroup Capital XIII Floating Rate Trust Pfd Secs Registered 2010-30.10.4

SPDR® S&P Emerging Markets Small Cap ETF   C   HOLD

Ticker	Traded On	NAV	Total Assets ($)	Dividend Yield (TTM)	Turnover Ratio	Expense Ratio
EWX	NYSE Arca		$521,972,584	3.01	24	0.65

Ratings

Reward	D+
Risk	C
Recent Upgrade/Downgrade	Up

Fund Information

Fund Type	Exchange Traded Funds
Category	Global Emerg Mkts Equity
Sub-Category	Diversified Emerging Mkts
Prospectus Objective	Div Emerg Mkts
Inception Date	May-08
Open to New Investments	Y

Prices

Price (as of 9/30/2019)	43.44
52-Week High	45.72
52-Week Low	40.07

Total Returns (%)

3-Month	6-Month	1-Year	3-Year	5-Year
-2.45	-2.54	0.13	11.08	3.70

3-Year Standard Deviation   12.09

Effective Duration

Valuation

Premium/Discount (1-Year Average)	-0.10

Company Information

Provider	SPDR State Street Global Advisors
Manager/Tenure	Michael J. Feehily (8), Karl A. Schneider (4), Amy Cheng (2)
Website	http://www.spdrs.com
Address	SPDR State Street Global Advisors State Street Financial Center, 1 Lincoln Street Boston MA 02111-2900 United States
Phone Number	617-786-3000

PERFORMANCE

Ratings History

Date	Overall Rating	Risk Rating	Reward Rating
Q3-19	C	C	D+
Q4-18	D+	D+	C-
Q4-17	C+	C	B-
Q4-16	D+	C-	D+
Q4-15	D+	D+	D+

Asset & Performance History

Date	NAV	1-Year Total Return
2018	40.96	-18.48
2017	51.81	32.07
2016	40.19	8.1
2015	37.9	-12.21
2014	44.45	-1.5
2013	46.35	2.51

Total Assets: $521,972,584

Asset Allocation

Asset	%
Cash	1%
Stocks	98%
US Stocks	0%
Bonds	0%
US Bonds	0%
Other	0%

Services Offered:

Investment Strategy: The investment seeks investment results that, before fees and expenses, correspond generally to the total return performance of the S&P Emerging Markets Under USD2 Billion Index. The fund generally invests substantially all, but at least 80%, of its total assets in the securities comprising the index and in depositary receipts based on securities comprising the index. The index is a float-adjusted market capitalization weighted index designed to represent the small capitalization segment of emerging countries included in the S&P Global BMI. The fund is non-diversified. **Top Holdings:** Impala Platinum Holdings Ltd Accton Technology Corp BR Malls Participacoes SA Sibanye-Stillwater Yduqs Part Common Stock

Invesco NASDAQ Internet ETF   C+   HOLD

Ticker	Traded On	NAV	Total Assets ($)	Dividend Yield (TTM)	Turnover Ratio	Expense Ratio
PNQI	NAS CM	130.01	$520,059,520	0		0.62

Ratings
Reward	B
Risk	C-
Recent Upgrade/Downgrade	Up

Fund Information
Fund Type	Exchange Traded Funds
Category	Technology Sector Equity
Sub-Category	Technology
Prospectus Objective	Technology
Inception Date	Jun-08
Open to New Investments	Y

Prices
Price (as of 9/30/2019)	130.06
52-Week High	144.17
52-Week Low	102.97

Total Returns (%)
3-Month	6-Month	1-Year	3-Year	5-Year
-6.49	-5.03	-2.91	48.44	94.35

3-Year Standard Deviation	18.83
Effective Duration	

Valuation
Premium/Discount (1-Year Average)	0.01

Company Information
Provider	Invesco
Manager/Tenure	Peter Hubbard (11), Michael Jeanette (11), Tony Seisser (5)
Website	http://www.invesco.com/us
Address	Invesco 11 Greenway Plaza, Ste. 2500 Houston TX 77046 United States
Phone Number	800-659-1005

PERFORMANCE

Ratings History
Date	Overall Rating	Risk Rating	Reward Rating
Q3-19	C+	C-	B
Q4-18	C+	C-	B
Q4-17	B+	B	A-
Q4-16	C+	C-	B
Q4-15	B-	C	B

Asset & Performance History
Date	NAV	1-Year Total Return
2018	109.84	-5.02
2017	115.65	39.94
2016	82.66	3.17
2015	80.12	19.36
2014	67.12	-1.61
2013	68.22	64.78

Total Assets: $520,059,520

Asset Allocation
Asset	%
Cash	0%
Stocks	100%
US Stocks	73%
Bonds	0%
US Bonds	0%
Other	0%

Services Offered:

Investment Strategy: The investment seeks to track the investment results (before fees and expenses) of the NASDAQ Internet IndexSM. The fund generally will invest at least 90% of its total assets in the securities that comprise the underlying index. The underlying index is designed to track the performance of the largest and most liquid U.S.-listed companies engaged in Internet-related businesses that are listed on the New York Stock Exchange ("NYSE"), NYSE American, Cboe Exchange ("Cboe") or The Nasdaq Stock Market ("Nasdaq"). The fund is non-diversified. **Top Holdings:** Alibaba Group Holding Ltd ADR Alphabet Inc Class C Facebook Inc A Amazon.com Inc Netflix Inc

---

WisdomTree Europe SmallCap Dividend Fund   D+   SELL

Ticker	Traded On	NAV	Total Assets ($)	Dividend Yield (TTM)	Turnover Ratio	Expense Ratio
DFE	NYSE Arca	56.10	$518,888,646	3.91	52	0.58

Ratings
Reward	D
Risk	C-
Recent Upgrade/Downgrade	Down

Fund Information
Fund Type	Exchange Traded Funds
Category	Europe Equity Large Cap
Sub-Category	Europe Stock
Prospectus Objective	Europe Stock
Inception Date	Jun-06
Open to New Investments	Y

Prices
Price (as of 9/30/2019)	55.91
52-Week High	63.45
52-Week Low	51.32

Total Returns (%)
3-Month	6-Month	1-Year	3-Year	5-Year
-3.97	-2.63	-8.39	12.73	27.31

3-Year Standard Deviation	13.63
Effective Duration	

Valuation
Premium/Discount (1-Year Average)	-0.24

Company Information
Provider	WisdomTree
Manager/Tenure	Richard A. Brown (11), Thomas J. Durante (11), Karen Q. Wong (11)
Website	http://www.wisdomtree.com
Address	WisdomTree 245 Park Avenue, 35th floor New York NY 10167 United States
Phone Number	866-909-9473

PERFORMANCE

Ratings History
Date	Overall Rating	Risk Rating	Reward Rating
Q3-19	D+	C-	D
Q4-18	D+	D+	D+
Q4-17	B+	A-	B+
Q4-16	C	C-	C
Q4-15	C	C+	C

Asset & Performance History
Date	NAV	1-Year Total Return
2018	53.42	-21.43
2017	70.84	32.46
2016	54.95	1.56
2015	56.29	10.96
2014	52.1	-6.33
2013	57.1	47.17

Total Assets: $518,888,646

Asset Allocation
Asset	%
Cash	0%
Stocks	100%
US Stocks	0%
Bonds	0%
US Bonds	0%
Other	0%

Services Offered:

Investment Strategy: The investment seeks to track the price and yield performance, before fees and expenses, of the WisdomTree Europe SmallCap Dividend Index. Under normal circumstances, at least 95% of the fund's total assets (exclusive of collateral held from securities lending) will be invested in component securities of the index and investments that have economic characteristics that are substantially identical to the economic characteristics of such component securities. The index is a fundamentally weighted index that is comprised of the small-capitalization segment of the European dividend-paying market. The fund is non-diversified. **Top Holdings:** Bpost SA de Droit Public BE Semiconductor Industries NV ADR Deutsche Pfandbriefbank AG Siltronic AG Elkem ASA Ordinary Shares

John Hancock Multifactor Small Cap ETF

D+   SELL

Ticker	Traded On	NAV	Total Assets ($)	Dividend Yield (TTM)	Turnover Ratio	Expense Ratio
JHSC	NYSE Arca	26.13	$518,722,578	0.86	33	0.5

Ratings
Reward	D
Risk	C-
Recent Upgrade/Downgrade	

Fund Information
Fund Type	Exchange Traded Funds
Category	US Equity Small Cap
Sub-Category	Small Blend
Prospectus Objective	Small Company
Inception Date	Nov-17
Open to New Investments	Y

Prices
Price (as of 9/30/2019)	26.15
52-Week High	27.70
52-Week Low	21.34

Total Returns (%)
3-Month	6-Month	1-Year	3-Year	5-Year
-1.21	0.17	-4.67		

3-Year Standard Deviation	
Effective Duration	

Valuation
Premium/Discount (1-Year Average)	0.04

Company Information
Provider	John Hancock
Manager/Tenure	Joel P. Schneider (1), Lukas J. Smart (1), Joseph F. Hohn (1)
Website	http://jhinvestments.com
Address	601 Congress Street, Boston MA 02210 United States
Phone Number	800-225-5913

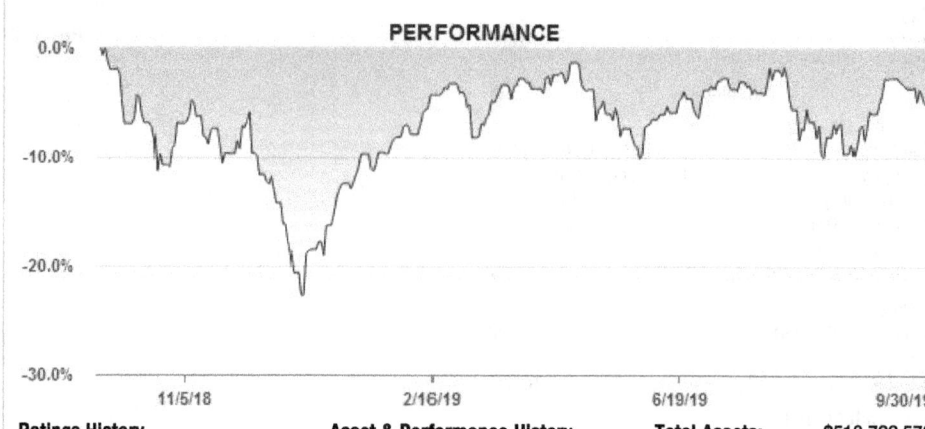

PERFORMANCE

Ratings History
Date	Overall Rating	Risk Rating	Reward Rating
Q3-19	D+	C-	D
Q4-18	D	D	D
Q4-17	U		
Q4-16			
Q4-15			

Asset & Performance History
Date	NAV	1-Year Total Return
2018	22.63	-12.12
2017	26.01	
2016		
2015		
2014		
2013		

Total Assets: $518,722,578

Asset Allocation
Asset	%
Cash	7%
Stocks	93%
US Stocks	93%
Bonds	0%
US Bonds	0%
Other	0%

Services Offered:

Investment Strategy: The investment seeks to provide investment results that closely correspond, before fees and expenses, to the performance of the John Hancock Dimensional Small Cap Index (the index). The fund normally invests at least 80% of its net assets (plus any borrowings for investment purposes) in securities that compose the fund's index. The index is designed to comprise a subset of securities in the U.S. Universe issued by companies whose market capitalizations are smaller than the 750th largest U.S. company but excluding the smallest 4% of U.S. companies at the time of reconstitution. **Top Holdings:** ITT Inc   EMCOR Group Inc   The Hanover Insurance Group Inc   Haemonetics Corp   Genesee & Wyoming Inc Class A

iShares Commodities Select Strategy ETF

C-   HOLD

Ticker	Traded On	NAV	Total Assets ($)	Dividend Yield (TTM)	Turnover Ratio	Expense Ratio
COMT	NAS CM	31.55	$517,456,395	9.84	167	0.48

Ratings
Reward	C-
Risk	C
Recent Upgrade/Downgrade	Down

Fund Information
Fund Type	Exchange Traded Funds
Category	Commodities Broad Basket
Sub-Category	Commodities Broad Basket
Prospectus Objective	Growth & Inc
Inception Date	Oct-14
Open to New Investments	Y

Prices
Price (as of 9/30/2019)	31.54
52-Week High	39.93
52-Week Low	29.85

Total Returns (%)
3-Month	6-Month	1-Year	3-Year	5-Year
-3.78	-5.59	-12.02	13.62	

3-Year Standard Deviation	11.02
Effective Duration	

Valuation
Premium/Discount (1-Year Average)	-0.18

Company Information
Provider	iShares
Manager/Tenure	Greg Savage (4), Robert Shimell (4), Alan Mason (3), 2 others
Website	http://www.ishares.com
Address	iShares 400 Howard Street San Francisco CA 94105 United States
Phone Number	800-474-2737

PERFORMANCE

Ratings History
Date	Overall Rating	Risk Rating	Reward Rating
Q3-19	C-	C	C-
Q4-18	C	C+	C-
Q4-17	C	C	C
Q4-16	D+	D	D+
Q4-15	U		

Asset & Performance History
Date	NAV	1-Year Total Return
2018	30.48	-6.59
2017	36.34	6.9
2016	34.28	21.22
2015	28.44	-30.37
2014	41.31	
2013		

Total Assets: $517,456,395

Asset Allocation
Asset	%
Cash	67%
Stocks	30%
US Stocks	19%
Bonds	2%
US Bonds	2%
Other	0%

Services Offered:

Investment Strategy: The investment seeks total return by providing investors with broad commodity exposure. The fund seeks to achieve its investment objective by investing in a combination of exchange-traded commodity futures contracts, exchange-traded options on commodity-related futures contracts and exchange-cleared commodity-related swaps (together, "Commodity-Linked Investments") and equity securities of issuers engaged in a commodities-related business ("Commodity-Related Equities"), thereby obtaining exposure to the commodities markets. It is an actively managed exchange-traded fund ("ETF") that does not seek to replicate the performance of a specified index. **Top Holdings:** United States Treasury Bills 0%   Exxon Mobil Corp   Chevron Corp   Ecolab Inc   DuPont de Nemours Inc

First Trust Europe AlphaDEX® Fund   C-   HOLD

Ticker	Traded On	NAV	Total Assets ($)	Dividend Yield (TTM)	Turnover Ratio	Expense Ratio
FEP	NAS CM	34.42	$514,565,524	2.32	99	0.8

Ratings
Reward   C-
Risk   C-
Recent Upgrade/Downgrade

Fund Information
Fund Type   Exchange Traded Funds
Category   Europe Equity Large Cap
Sub-Category   Europe Stock
Prospectus Objective   Foreign Stock
Inception Date   Apr-11
Open to New Investments   Y

Prices
Price (as of 9/30/2019)   34.37
52-Week High   38.17
52-Week Low   30.01

Total Returns (%)

3-Month	6-Month	1-Year	3-Year	5-Year
-2.18	-0.53	-7.92	23.72	26.33

3-Year Standard Deviation   14.62
Effective Duration

Valuation
Premium/Discount (1-Year Average)   -0.11

Company Information
Provider   First Trust
Manager/Tenure Jon C. Erickson (8), Daniel J. Lindquist (8), David G. McGarel (8), 3 others
Website   http://www.ftportfolios.com/
Address   First Trust 120 E. Liberty Drive, Suite 400 Wheaton IL 60187 United States
Phone Number   800-621-1675

PERFORMANCE

Ratings History

Date	Overall Rating	Risk Rating	Reward Rating
Q3-19	C-	C-	C-
Q4-18	D+	C-	D+
Q4-17	B+	B	A-
Q4-16	D+	C-	D
Q4-15	C	C+	C-

Asset & Performance History

Date	NAV	1-Year Total Return
2018	31.11	-18.66
2017	39.07	35.68
2016	29.32	1.23
2015	29.61	2.46
2014	29.5	-8.91
2013	33.1	31.33

Total Assets: $514,565,524
Asset Allocation

Asset	%
Cash	1%
Stocks	99%
US Stocks	2%
Bonds	0%
US Bonds	0%
Other	0%

Services Offered:

Investment Strategy: The investment seeks investment results that correspond generally to the price and yield (before the fund's fees and expenses) of an equity index called the NASDAQ AlphaDEX® Europe Index (the "index"). The fund will normally invest at least 90% of its net assets (including investment borrowings) in the common stocks and depositary receipts that comprise the index. The index is designed to select stocks from the NASDAQ Europe Index (the "base index") that may generate positive alpha, or risk-adjusted returns, relative to traditional indices through the use of the AlphaDEX® selection methodology. **Top Holdings:** Puma SE ICA Gruppen AB Fabege AB JD Sports Fashion PLC Alten

---

iShares Transportation Average ETF   B-   BUY

Ticker	Traded On	NAV	Total Assets ($)	Dividend Yield (TTM)	Turnover Ratio	Expense Ratio
IYT	BATS	186.17	$511,968,947	1.31	17	0.42

Ratings
Reward   B
Risk   C
Recent Upgrade/Downgrade   Up

Fund Information
Fund Type   Exchange Traded Funds
Category   Industrials Sector Equity
Sub-Category   Industrials
Prospectus Objective   Unaligned
Inception Date   Oct-03
Open to New Investments   Y

Prices
Price (as of 9/30/2019)   186.14
52-Week High   205.13
52-Week Low   155.39

Total Returns (%)

3-Month	6-Month	1-Year	3-Year	5-Year
-1.09	-2.05	-7.99	32.74	33.95

3-Year Standard Deviation   19.21
Effective Duration

Valuation
Premium/Discount (1-Year Average)   -0.01

Company Information
Provider   iShares
Manager/Tenure Greg Savage (11), Jennifer Hsui (7), Alan Mason (3), 2 others
Website   http://www.ishares.com
Address   iShares 400 Howard Street San Francisco CA 94105 United States
Phone Number   800-474-2737

PERFORMANCE

Ratings History

Date	Overall Rating	Risk Rating	Reward Rating
Q3-19	B-	C	B
Q4-18	B	C	B+
Q4-17	C+	C+	B-
Q4-16	B-	C	B
Q4-15	B	B-	B+

Asset & Performance History

Date	NAV	1-Year Total Return
2018	164.99	-12.82
2017	191.53	18.93
2016	162.7	22.05
2015	134.74	-16.88
2014	164.04	25.32
2013	131.91	41.18

Total Assets: $511,968,947
Asset Allocation

Asset	%
Cash	0%
Stocks	100%
US Stocks	100%
Bonds	0%
US Bonds	0%
Other	0%

Services Offered: CashInvestment Plan

Investment Strategy: The investment seeks to track the investment results of the Dow Jones Transportation Average Index composed of U.S. equities in the transportation sector. The fund generally invests at least 90% of its assets in securities of the underlying index and in depositary receipts representing securities of the underlying index. The underlying index measures the performance of large, well-known companies within the transportation sector of the U.S. equity market. The fund is non-diversified. **Top Holdings:** Norfolk Southern Corp Union Pacific Corp FedEx Corp Kansas City Southern United Parcel Service Inc Class B

iShares Morningstar Large-Cap Value ETF   C   HOLD

Ticker	Traded On	NAV	Total Assets ($)	Dividend Yield (TTM)	Turnover Ratio	Expense Ratio
JKF	NYSE Arca	110.44	$508,010,002	2.76	24	0.25

Ratings
Reward	C+
Risk	C-
Recent Upgrade/Downgrade	

Fund Information
Fund Type	Exchange Traded Funds
Category	US Equity Large Cap Value
Sub-Category	Large Value
Prospectus Objective	Growth
Inception Date	Jun-04
Open to New Investments	Y

Prices
Price (as of 9/30/2019)	110.45
52-Week High	111.53
52-Week Low	91.27

Total Returns (%)
3-Month	6-Month	1-Year	3-Year	5-Year
2.50	5.03	5.48	35.92	52.39

3-Year Standard Deviation	12.16
Effective Duration	

Valuation
Premium/Discount (1-Year Average)	0.00

Company Information
Provider	iShares
Manager/Tenure	Greg Savage (11), Jennifer Hsui (7), Alan Mason (3), 2 others
Website	http://www.ishares.com
Address	iShares 400 Howard Street San Francisco CA 94105 United States
Phone Number	800-474-2737

PERFORMANCE

Ratings History
Date	Overall Rating	Risk Rating	Reward Rating
Q3-19	C	C-	C+
Q4-18	C	C-	C
Q4-17	B	B	B
Q4-16	C+	C-	B
Q4-15	C	C	C+

Asset & Performance History
Date	NAV	1-Year Total Return
2018	96.31	-6.1
2017	105.45	14.81
2016	94.14	18.54
2015	81.79	-1.55
2014	85.61	8.93
2013	80.56	28.53

Total Assets: $508,010,002
Asset Allocation
Asset	%
Cash	0%
Stocks	100%
US Stocks	99%
Bonds	0%
US Bonds	0%
Other	0%

Services Offered:

Investment Strategy: The investment seeks to track the investment results of the Morningstar® Large Value IndexSM composed of large-capitalization U.S. equities that exhibit value characteristics. The fund generally invests at least 90% of its assets in securities of the underlying index and in depositary receipts representing securities of the underlying index. The underlying index measures the performance of stocks issued by large-capitalization companies that have exhibited above-average "value" characteristics as determined by Morningstar, Inc.'s ("Morningstar" or the "index provider") proprietary index methodology. **Top Holdings:** JPMorgan Chase & Co Procter & Gamble Co Exxon Mobil Corp AT&T Inc Verizon Communications Inc

iShares MSCI Singapore Capped ETF   C   HOLD

Ticker	Traded On	NAV	Total Assets ($)	Dividend Yield (TTM)	Turnover Ratio	Expense Ratio
EWS	NYSE Arca	23.13	$507,724,337	3.87	26	0.47

Ratings
Reward	C
Risk	C+
Recent Upgrade/Downgrade	

Fund Information
Fund Type	Exchange Traded Funds
Category	Asia ex-Japan Equity
Sub-Category	Miscellaneous Region
Prospectus Objective	Pacific Stock
Inception Date	Mar-96
Open to New Investments	Y

Prices
Price (as of 9/30/2019)	23.20
52-Week High	25.34
52-Week Low	21.69

Total Returns (%)
3-Month	6-Month	1-Year	3-Year	5-Year
-7.44	-1.50	-0.93	21.75	4.76

3-Year Standard Deviation	15.93
Effective Duration	

Valuation
Premium/Discount (1-Year Average)	0.02

Company Information
Provider	iShares
Manager/Tenure	Diane Hsiung (11), Greg Savage (11), Jennifer Hsui (6), 3 others
Website	http://www.ishares.com
Address	iShares 400 Howard Street San Francisco CA 94105 United States
Phone Number	800-474-2737

PERFORMANCE

Ratings History
Date	Overall Rating	Risk Rating	Reward Rating
Q3-19	C	C+	C
Q4-18	C-	C	C-
Q4-17	C+	C	C+
Q4-16	D	D+	D
Q4-15	D+	D+	D+

Asset & Performance History
Date	NAV	1-Year Total Return
2018	22.21	-11
2017	25.97	33.81
2016	20.11	1.11
2015	20.66	-17.94
2014	26.16	2.91
2013	26.28	0.95

Total Assets: $507,724,337
Asset Allocation
Asset	%
Cash	1%
Stocks	99%
US Stocks	0%
Bonds	0%
US Bonds	0%
Other	0%

Services Offered: CashInvestment Plan

Investment Strategy: The investment seeks to track the investment results of the MSCI Singapore 25/50 Index. The fund will at all times invest at least 80% of its assets in the securities of its underlying index and in depositary receipts representing securities in its underlying index. The index is designed to measure the performance of the large- and mid-cap segments of the Singapore market. A capping methodology is applied that limits the weight of any single component to a maximum of 25% of the underlying index. The fund is non-diversified. **Top Holdings:** DBS Group Holdings Ltd Oversea-Chinese Banking Corp Ltd United Overseas Bank Ltd Singapore Telecommunications Ltd Keppel Corp Ltd

Main Sector Rotation ETF   C-   HOLD

Ticker	Traded On	NAV	Total Assets ($)	Dividend Yield (TTM)	Turnover Ratio	Expense Ratio
SECT	BATS		$507,033,904	1.49	61	0.83

Ratings
Reward	C-
Risk	C-
Recent Upgrade/Downgrade	

Fund Information
Fund Type	Exchange Traded Funds
Category	US Equity Large Cap Blend
Sub-Category	Large Blend
Prospectus Objective	Growth & Inc
Inception Date	Sep-17
Open to New Investments	Y

Prices
Price (as of 9/30/2019)	29.09
52-Week High	29.40
52-Week Low	23.31

Total Returns (%)
3-Month	6-Month	1-Year	3-Year	5-Year
-0.18	3.57	1.16		

3-Year Standard Deviation	
Effective Duration	

Valuation
Premium/Discount (1-Year Average)	0.08

Company Information
Provider	Main Management ETFs
Manager/Tenure	Kim D. Arthur (2), James W. Concidine (2), J. Richard Fredericks (2)
Website	http://www.mainmgtetfs.com
Address	Main Management ETFs 601 California Street, Suite 620 San Francisco CA 94108 United States
Phone Number	

PERFORMANCE

Ratings History

Date	Overall Rating	Risk Rating	Reward Rating
Q3-19	C-	C-	C-
Q4-18	D+	D+	D+
Q4-17	U		
Q4-16			
Q4-15			

Asset & Performance History

Date	NAV	1-Year Total Return
2018	24.4	-9.3
2017	27.33	
2016		
2015		
2014		
2013		

Total Assets: $507,033,904

Asset Allocation

Asset	%
Cash	13%
Stocks	87%
US Stocks	83%
Bonds	0%
US Bonds	0%
Other	0%

Services Offered:

Investment Strategy: The investment seeks to outperform the S&P 500 in rising markets while limiting losses during periods of decline. The fund utilizes a "fund of funds" structure to invest in sector based equity ETFs. It seeks to achieve its objective through dynamic sector rotation. The Adviser focuses its research primarily on sector selection by carefully reviewing the sector, industry, and sub-industries in the fund's portfolio. The Adviser chooses sectors it believes are undervalued and poised to respond favorably to financial market catalysts. The fund will sell a security when it achieves its target price and is, in the opinion of the Adviser, no longer undervalued. **Top Holdings:** Technology Select Sector SPDR® ETF   Financial Select Sector SPDR® ETF   Vanguard Consumer Staples ETF   SPDR® S&P Bank ETF   iShares US Home Construction ETF

Global X Silver Miners ETF   D+   SELL

Ticker	Traded On	NAV	Total Assets ($)	Dividend Yield (TTM)	Turnover Ratio	Expense Ratio
SIL	NYSE Arca	28.25	$505,543,518	1.42	26	0.65

Ratings
Reward	C-
Risk	D
Recent Upgrade/Downgrade	Up

Fund Information
Fund Type	Exchange Traded Funds
Category	Prec Metals
Sub-Category	Equity Precious Metals
Prospectus Objective	Prec Metals
Inception Date	Apr-10
Open to New Investments	Y

Prices
Price (as of 9/30/2019)	28.11
52-Week High	32.22
52-Week Low	21.98

Total Returns (%)
3-Month	6-Month	1-Year	3-Year	5-Year
8.44	8.34	19.18	-33.49	-5.97

3-Year Standard Deviation	24.6
Effective Duration	

Valuation
Premium/Discount (1-Year Average)	-0.07

Company Information
Provider	Global X Funds
Manager/Tenure	Chang Kim (5), Nam To (1), Wayne Xie (0), 1 other
Website	http://www.globalxfunds.com
Address	Global X Funds 600 Lexington Avenue, 20th Floor New York NY 10022 United States
Phone Number	888-493-8631

PERFORMANCE

Ratings History

Date	Overall Rating	Risk Rating	Reward Rating
Q3-19	D+	D	C-
Q4-18	D	D	D+
Q4-17	C-	D	C
Q4-16	C-	D	C
Q4-15	D	D	D

Asset & Performance History

Date	NAV	1-Year Total Return
2018	24.98	-23.6
2017	32.7	1.03
2016	32.37	80.33
2015	18.56	-33.08
2014	27.84	-16.93
2013	33.54	-50.31

Total Assets: $505,543,518

Asset Allocation

Asset	%
Cash	0%
Stocks	100%
US Stocks	8%
Bonds	0%
US Bonds	0%
Other	0%

Services Offered:

Investment Strategy: The investment seeks to provide investment results that correspond generally to the price and yield performance, before fees and expenses, of the Solactive Global Silver Miners Total Return Index. The fund invests at least 80% of its total assets in the securities of the underlying index and in American Depositary Receipts ("ADRs") and Global Depositary Receipts ("GDRs") based on the securities in the underlying index. The underlying index is designed to measure broad-based equity market performance of global companies involved in the silver mining industry. The fund is non-diversified. **Top Holdings:** Pan American Silver Corp Polymetal International PLC Wheaton Precious Metals Corp Korea Zinc Co Ltd First Majestic Silver Corp

John Hancock Multifactor Developed International ETF

C-   HOLD

Ticker	Traded On	NAV	Total Assets ($)	Dividend Yield (TTM)	Turnover Ratio	Expense Ratio
JHMD	NYSE Arca	27.88	$501,827,494	2.35	17	0.45

Ratings

Reward	C-
Risk	C-
Recent Upgrade/Downgrade	

Fund Information

Fund Type	Exchange Traded Funds
Category	Global Equity Large Cap
Sub-Category	Foreign Large Blend
Prospectus Objective	Foreign Stock
Inception Date	Dec-16
Open to New Investments	Y

Prices

Price (as of 9/30/2019)	27.83
52-Week High	29.49
52-Week Low	24.81

Total Returns (%)

3-Month	6-Month	1-Year	3-Year	5-Year
-1.79	0.29	-2.85		

3-Year Standard Deviation	
Effective Duration	

Valuation

Premium/Discount (1-Year Average)	-0.07

Company Information

Provider	John Hancock
Manager/Tenure	Joel P. Schneider (2), Lukas J. Smart (2), Joseph F. Hohn (1)
Website	http://jhinvestments.com
Address	601 Congress Street, Boston MA 02210 United States
Phone Number	800-225-5913

PERFORMANCE

Ratings History

Date	Overall Rating	Risk Rating	Reward Rating
Q3-19	C-	C-	C-
Q4-18	D	D+	D
Q4-17	D-	A	D+
Q4-16			
Q4-15			

Asset & Performance History

Date	NAV	1-Year Total Return
2018	25.61	-13.92
2017	30.31	25.15
2016	24.8	
2015		
2014		
2013		

Total Assets: $501,827,494

Asset Allocation

Asset	%
Cash	2%
Stocks	98%
US Stocks	2%
Bonds	0%
US Bonds	0%
Other	0%

Services Offered:

Investment Strategy: The investment seeks to provide investment results that closely correspond, before fees and expenses, to the performance of the John Hancock Dimensional Developed International Index. The fund normally invests at least 80% of its net assets (plus any borrowings for investment purposes) in securities included in the fund's index, in depositary receipts representing securities included in the fund's index and in underlying stocks in respect of depositary receipts included in the fund's index. The index is designed to comprise a subset of securities associated with developed markets outside the U.S. and Canada. **Top Holdings:** BP PLC Nestle SA Toyota Motor Corp Novartis AG Roche Holding AG Dividend Right Cert.

Vident Core U.S. Equity Fund™

C-   HOLD

Ticker	Traded On	NAV	Total Assets ($)	Dividend Yield (TTM)	Turnover Ratio	Expense Ratio
VUSE	NYSE Arca	30.97	$498,559,960	1.62	63	0.5

Ratings

Reward	C-
Risk	C-
Recent Upgrade/Downgrade	

Fund Information

Fund Type	Exchange Traded Funds
Category	US Equity Mid Cap
Sub-Category	Mid-Cap Value
Prospectus Objective	Growth & Inc
Inception Date	Jan-14
Open to New Investments	Y

Prices

Price (as of 9/30/2019)	30.98
52-Week High	34.24
52-Week Low	26.41

Total Returns (%)

3-Month	6-Month	1-Year	3-Year	5-Year
-1.82	-0.88	-8.13	20.39	32.43

3-Year Standard Deviation	15.98
Effective Duration	

Valuation

Premium/Discount (1-Year Average)	-0.03

Company Information

Provider	Vident Financial
Manager/Tenure	Denise M. Krisko (4), Austin Wen (0)
Website	http://www.videntfinancial.com
Address	Vident Financial 201 17th Street, Suite 300 Atlanta GA 30363 United States
Phone Number	800-617-0004

PERFORMANCE

Ratings History

Date	Overall Rating	Risk Rating	Reward Rating
Q3-19	C-	C-	C-
Q4-18	C-	C-	C-
Q4-17	B	B	B
Q4-16	C	C-	C
Q4-15	D+	C-	D+

Asset & Performance History

Date	NAV	1-Year Total Return
2018	28.05	-14.73
2017	33.36	16.4
2016	29.01	18.25
2015	24.78	-6.04
2014	26.81	
2013		

Total Assets: $498,559,960

Asset Allocation

Asset	%
Cash	0%
Stocks	100%
US Stocks	100%
Bonds	0%
US Bonds	0%
Other	0%

Services Offered:

Investment Strategy: The investment seeks to track the performance, before fees and expenses, of the Vident Core U.S. Stock Index™ (the "index"). Under normal circumstances, at least 80% of the fund's total assets (exclusive of collateral held from securities lending) will be invested in the component securities of the index and investments that have economic characteristics that are substantially identical to the economic characteristics of such component securities. The underlying index is a rules-based, systematic strategy index comprised of equity securities of issuers domiciled and traded in the United States. **Top Holdings:** Target Corp Tyson Foods Inc Class A Pilgrims Pride Corp Vistra Energy Corp Cirrus Logic Inc

Invesco China Technology ETF   D+   SELL

Ticker	Traded On	NAV	Total Assets ($)	Dividend Yield (TTM)	Turnover Ratio	Expense Ratio
CQQQ	NYSE Arca	45.91	$498,092,339	0.37		0.7

Ratings
Reward	D+
Risk	C-
Recent Upgrade/Downgrade	Down

Fund Information
Fund Type	Exchange Traded Funds
Category	Greater China Equity
Sub-Category	China Region
Prospectus Objective	Technology
Inception Date	Dec-09
Open to New Investments	Y

Prices
Price (as of 9/30/2019)	45.76
52-Week High	51.96
52-Week Low	37.92

Total Returns (%)
3-Month	6-Month	1-Year	3-Year	5-Year
-0.92	-8.32	-3.87	16.66	37.90

3-Year Standard Deviation	23.09
Effective Duration	

Valuation
Premium/Discount (1-Year Average)	-0.02

Company Information
Provider	Invesco
Manager/Tenure	Peter Hubbard (1), Michael Jeanette (1), Tony Seisser (1)
Website	http://www.invesco.com/us
Address	Invesco 11 Greenway Plaza, Ste. 2500 Houston TX 77046 United States
Phone Number	800-659-1005

PERFORMANCE

Ratings History
Date	Overall Rating	Risk Rating	Reward Rating
Q3-19	D+	C-	D+
Q4-18	D+	D	C-
Q4-17	B+	C	A+
Q4-16	C-	C-	C-
Q4-15	C	C-	C

Asset & Performance History
Date	NAV	1-Year Total Return
2018	39.72	-34.4
2017	60.55	72.8
2016	35.59	0.01
2015	36.21	6.74
2014	34.51	0.18
2013	34.79	59.71

Total Assets: $498,092,339
Asset Allocation
Asset	%
Cash	0%
Stocks	100%
US Stocks	0%
Bonds	0%
US Bonds	0%
Other	0%

Services Offered:

Investment Strategy: The investment seeks to track the investment results (before fees and expenses) of the FTSE China Incl A 25% Technology Capped Index. The fund generally will invest at least 90% of its total assets in the securities (including ADRs and GDRs) that comprise the underlying index. Strictly in accordance with its guidelines and mandated procedures, the index provider compiles, maintains, and calculates the underlying index. The underlying index may include China A-shares, B-shares, H-shares, N-shares, Red Chip shares, P-chip shares and S-chip shares. The fund is non-diversified. **Top Holdings:** Alibaba Group Holding Ltd ADR Tencent Holdings Ltd Meituan Dianping Baidu Inc ADR Sunny Optical Technology (Group) Co Ltd

---

iShares U.S. Telecommunications ETF   B-   BUY

Ticker	Traded On	NAV	Total Assets ($)	Dividend Yield (TTM)	Turnover Ratio	Expense Ratio
IYZ	BATS	29.21	$496,515,441	1.69	35	0.42

Ratings
Reward	B
Risk	C
Recent Upgrade/Downgrade	Up

Fund Information
Fund Type	Exchange Traded Funds
Category	Communications Sector Equity
Sub-Category	Communications
Prospectus Objective	Comm
Inception Date	May-00
Open to New Investments	Y

Prices
Price (as of 9/30/2019)	29.20
52-Week High	31.04
52-Week Low	24.71

Total Returns (%)
3-Month	6-Month	1-Year	3-Year	5-Year
-0.55	-1.91	0.29	-2.18	12.13

3-Year Standard Deviation	14.65
Effective Duration	

Valuation
Premium/Discount (1-Year Average)	-0.05

Company Information
Provider	iShares
Manager/Tenure	Greg Savage (11), Jennifer Hsui (7), Alan Mason (3), 2 others
Website	http://www.ishares.com
Address	iShares 400 Howard Street San Francisco CA 94105 United States
Phone Number	800-474-2737

PERFORMANCE

Ratings History
Date	Overall Rating	Risk Rating	Reward Rating
Q3-19	B-	C	B
Q4-18	C+	C-	B
Q4-17	C-	C-	D+
Q4-16	C	D+	B-
Q4-15	C+	C	B-

Asset & Performance History
Date	NAV	1-Year Total Return
2018	26.34	-8.54
2017	29.39	-11.58
2016	34.38	22.14
2015	28.84	0.47
2014	29.26	0.51
2013	29.76	26.24

Total Assets: $496,515,441
Asset Allocation
Asset	%
Cash	0%
Stocks	100%
US Stocks	96%
Bonds	0%
US Bonds	0%
Other	0%

Services Offered: CashInvestment Plan

Investment Strategy: The investment seeks to track the investment results of the Dow Jones U.S. Select Telecommunications Index. The fund generally invests at least 90% of its assets in securities of the underlying index and in depositary receipts representing securities of the underlying index. The underlying index measures the performance of the telecommunications sector of the U.S. equity market and may include large-, mid- or small-capitalization companies. The fund is non-diversified. **Top Holdings:** Verizon Communications Inc Cisco Systems Inc Motorola Solutions Inc AT&T Inc T-Mobile US Inc

Invesco Dynamic Software ETF

C+ HOLD

Ticker	Traded On	NAV	Total Assets ($)	Dividend Yield (TTM)	Turnover Ratio	Expense Ratio
PSJ	NYSE Arca	93.06	$493,237,848	0	157	0.58

Ratings
Reward	B
Risk	C
Recent Upgrade/Downgrade	Down

Fund Information
Fund Type	Exchange Traded Funds
Category	Technology Sector Equity
Sub-Category	Technology
Prospectus Objective	Technology
Inception Date	Jun-05
Open to New Investments	Y

Prices
Price (as of 9/30/2019)	93.08
52-Week High	104.07
52-Week Low	68.31

Total Returns (%)
3-Month	6-Month	1-Year	3-Year	5-Year
-3.95	0.97	8.18	91.93	167.51

3-Year Standard Deviation	17.87
Effective Duration	

Valuation
Premium/Discount (1-Year Average)	0.01

Company Information
Provider	Invesco
Manager/Tenure	Peter Hubbard (12), Michael Jeanette (11), Tony Seisser (5)
Website	http://www.invesco.com/us
Address	Invesco 11 Greenway Plaza, Ste. 2500 Houston TX 77046 United States
Phone Number	800-659-1005

PERFORMANCE

Ratings History
Date	Overall Rating	Risk Rating	Reward Rating
Q3-19	C+	C	B
Q4-18	C	C-	C+
Q4-17	A-	B+	A
Q4-16	C-	C-	C-
Q4-15	B-	C	B

Asset & Performance History
Date	NAV	1-Year Total Return
2018	73.98	16.63
2017	63.43	34.47
2016	47.17	11.62
2015	42.27	7.08
2014	39.53	9.51
2013	36.13	33.12

Total Assets: $493,237,848

Asset Allocation
Asset	%
Cash	0%
Stocks	100%
US Stocks	97%
Bonds	0%
US Bonds	0%
Other	0%

Services Offered:

Investment Strategy: The investment seeks to track the investment results (before fees and expenses) of the Dynamic Software IntellidexSM Index. The fund generally will invest at least 90% of its total assets in the securities that comprise the underlying intellidex. The underlying intellidex was composed of common stocks of U.S. software companies. These companies are principally engaged in the research, design, production or distribution of products or processes that relate to software applications and systems and information-based services. The fund is non-diversified. **Top Holdings:** Synopsys Inc Intuit Inc Microsoft Corp Atlassian Corporation PLC A Veeva Systems Inc Class A

---

iShares iBonds Dec 2025 Term Corporate ETF

C HOLD

Ticker	Traded On	NAV	Total Assets ($)	Dividend Yield (TTM)	Turnover Ratio	Expense Ratio
IBDQ	NYSE Arca	25.80	$492,854,046	3.29	5	0.1

Ratings
Reward	B-
Risk	C-
Recent Upgrade/Downgrade	

Fund Information
Fund Type	Exchange Traded Funds
Category	US Fixed Income
Sub-Category	Target Maturity
Prospectus Objective	Corp Bond - Gen
Inception Date	Mar-15
Open to New Investments	Y

Prices
Price (as of 9/30/2019)	25.88
52-Week High	26.02
52-Week Low	23.51

Total Returns (%)
3-Month	6-Month	1-Year	3-Year	5-Year
1.92	6.21	11.83	12.03	

3-Year Standard Deviation	3.87
Effective Duration	

Valuation
Premium/Discount (1-Year Average)	0.22

Company Information
Provider	iShares
Manager/Tenure	James Mauro (4), Scott Radell (4)
Website	http://www.ishares.com
Address	iShares 400 Howard Street San Francisco CA 94105 United States
Phone Number	800-474-2737

PERFORMANCE

Ratings History
Date	Overall Rating	Risk Rating	Reward Rating
Q3-19	C	C-	B-
Q4-18	C-	C-	D+
Q4-17	B-	B+	C
Q4-16	D+	C-	D+
Q4-15	U		

Asset & Performance History
Date	NAV	1-Year Total Return
2018	23.68	-1.69
2017	24.94	5.7
2016	24.34	5.91
2015	23.76	
2014		
2013		

Total Assets: $492,854,046

Asset Allocation
Asset	%
Cash	1%
Stocks	0%
US Stocks	0%
Bonds	98%
US Bonds	90%
Other	0%

Services Offered:

Investment Strategy: The investment seeks to track the investment results of the Bloomberg Barclays December 2025 Maturity Corporate Index which composed of U.S. dollar-denominated, investment-grade corporate bonds maturing in 2025. The fund generally will invest at least 90% of its assets in the component securities of the underlying index. The underlying index is composed of U.S. dollar-denominated, taxable, investment-grade corporate bonds scheduled to mature after December 31, 2024 and before December 16, 2025. **Top Holdings:** AT&T Inc 3.4% Charter Communications Operating, LLC/Charter Communications Operating Capi CVS Health Corp 4.1% Visa Inc 3.15% AbbVie Inc. 3.6%

Goldman Sachs Access Investment Grade Corporate Bond ETF

C HOLD

Ticker	Traded On	NAV	Total Assets ($)	Dividend Yield (TTM)	Turnover Ratio	Expense Ratio
GIGB	NYSE Arca	52.39	$489,838,042	3.24	22	0.14

Ratings
Reward	C
Risk	C-
Recent Upgrade/Downgrade	Up

Fund Information
Fund Type	Exchange Traded Funds
Category	Canada Fixed Income
Sub-Category	Corporate Bond
Prospectus Objective	Corp Bond - Gen
Inception Date	Jun-17
Open to New Investments	Y

Prices
Price (as of 9/30/2019)	52.41
52-Week High	52.95
52-Week Low	46.80

Total Returns (%)
3-Month	6-Month	1-Year	3-Year	5-Year
2.95	7.96	13.03		

3-Year Standard Deviation
Effective Duration

Valuation
Premium/Discount (1-Year Average)	0.05

Company Information
Provider	Goldman Sachs
Manager/Tenure	Jason Singer (2), David Westbrook (1)
Website	http://www.gsamfunds.com
Address	Goldman Sachs 200 West Stree New York NY 10282 United States
Phone Number	800-526-7384

PERFORMANCE

Ratings History
Date	Overall Rating	Risk Rating	Reward Rating
Q3-19	C	C-	C
Q4-18	D	C-	D
Q4-17	U		
Q4-16			
Q4-15			

Asset & Performance History
Date	NAV	1-Year Total Return
2018	47.26	-3.12
2017	50.24	
2016		
2015		
2014		
2013		

Total Assets: $489,838,042

Asset Allocation
Asset	%
Cash	0%
Stocks	0%
US Stocks	0%
Bonds	97%
US Bonds	82%
Other	0%

Services Offered:

Investment Strategy: The investment seeks to provide investment results that closely correspond, before fees and expenses, to the performance of the FTSE Goldman Sachs Investment Grade Corporate Bond Index (the "index"). The fund seeks to achieve its investment objective by investing at least 80% of its assets (exclusive of collateral held from securities lending) in securities included in its underlying index. The index is a rules-based index that is designed to measure the performance of investment grade, corporate bonds denominated in U.S. dollars ("USD") that meet certain liquidity and fundamental screening criteria. **Top Holdings:** Anheuser-Busch Companies LLC / Anheuser-Busch InBev Worldwide Inc 4.9% BP Capital Markets plc 3.56% Berkshire Hathaway Inc. 3.12% Apple Inc. 2.1% JPMorgan Chase & Co. 3.88%

---

iShares MSCI Frontier 100 ETF

C HOLD

Ticker	Traded On	NAV	Total Assets ($)	Dividend Yield (TTM)	Turnover Ratio	Expense Ratio
FM	NYSE Arca	28.49	$488,523,536	3.9	35	0.81

Ratings
Reward	C
Risk	C
Recent Upgrade/Downgrade	

Fund Information
Fund Type	Exchange Traded Funds
Category	Global Emerg Mkts Equity
Sub-Category	Diversified Emerging Mkts
Prospectus Objective	Div Emerg Mkts
Inception Date	Sep-12
Open to New Investments	Y

Prices
Price (as of 9/30/2019)	28.14
52-Week High	30.49
52-Week Low	26.01

Total Returns (%)
3-Month	6-Month	1-Year	3-Year	5-Year
-3.12	1.63	4.83	24.47	-5.93

3-Year Standard Deviation	11.66
Effective Duration	

Valuation
Premium/Discount (1-Year Average)	-0.34

Company Information
Provider	iShares
Manager/Tenure	Diane Hsiung (7), Jennifer Hsui (7), Greg Savage (7), 3 others
Website	http://www.ishares.com
Address	iShares 400 Howard Street San Francisco CA 94105 United States
Phone Number	800-474-2737

PERFORMANCE

Ratings History
Date	Overall Rating	Risk Rating	Reward Rating
Q3-19	C	C	C
Q4-18	D+	D+	C-
Q4-17	C+	C	C+
Q4-16	D	D+	D
Q4-15	D+	C-	D+

Asset & Performance History
Date	NAV	1-Year Total Return
2018	26.49	-17.45
2017	33.36	33.66
2016	25.5	3.46
2015	25.18	-15.31
2014	30.46	4.04
2013	33.12	25.6

Total Assets: $488,523,536

Asset Allocation
Asset	%
Cash	1%
Stocks	99%
US Stocks	0%
Bonds	0%
US Bonds	0%
Other	0%

Services Offered:

Investment Strategy: The investment seeks to track the investment results of the MSCI Frontier Markets 100 Index. The fund generally will invest at least 90% of its assets in the component securities of the underlying index and in investments that have economic characteristics that are substantially identical to the component securities of the underlying index. The index is designed to measure equity market performance of frontier markets while putting stronger emphasis on tradability compared to the MSCI Frontier Markets IMI (the parent index). **Top Holdings:** National Bank of Kuwait SAK Ahli United Bank BSC Kuwait Finance House KSC Maroc Telecom SA Safaricom PLC

Direxion Daily S&P 500® Bear 3X Shares   D   SELL

Ticker	Traded On	NAV	Total Assets ($)	Dividend Yield (TTM)	Turnover Ratio	Expense Ratio
SPXS	NYSE Arca	17.18	$482,728,636	1.72	1	1.08

Ratings

Reward	E+
Risk	D
Recent Upgrade/Downgrade	

Fund Information

Fund Type	Exchange Traded Funds
Category	Trading Tools
Sub-Category	Trading--Inverse Equity
Prospectus Objective	Growth
Inception Date	Nov-08
Open to New Investments	Y

Prices

Price (as of 9/30/2019)	17.15
52-Week High	38.16
52-Week Low	16.66

Total Returns (%)

3-Month	6-Month	1-Year	3-Year	5-Year
-3.94	-14.13	-17.76	-71.50	-86.39

3-Year Standard Deviation	35.52
Effective Duration	

Valuation

Premium/Discount (1-Year Average)	0.03

Company Information

Provider	Direxion Funds
Manager/Tenure	Paul Brigandi (10), Tony Ng (4)
Website	http://www.direxionfunds.com
Address	Direxion Funds 1301 Avenue Of The Americas (6th Avenue) New York NY 10019 United States
Phone Number	646-572-3390

PERFORMANCE

Ratings History

Date	Overall Rating	Risk Rating	Reward Rating
Q3-19	D	D	E+
Q4-18	D	D-	D-
Q4-17	E+	E+	E+
Q4-16	D	E+	D-
Q4-15	D-	E+	E+

Asset & Performance History

Date	NAV	1-Year Total Return
2018	30.92	3.39
2017	30.1	-44.46
2016	54.2	-35.89
2015	84.55	-18.07
2014	103.2	-37.99
2013	166.45	-60.62

Total Assets: $482,728,636

Asset Allocation

Asset	%
Cash	114%
Stocks	-14%
US Stocks	0%
Bonds	0%
US Bonds	0%
Other	0%

Services Offered:

Investment Strategy: The investment seeks daily investment results, before fees and expenses, of 300% of the inverse (or opposite) of the daily performance of the S&P 500® Index. The fund, under normal circumstances, invests in swap agreements, futures contracts, short positions or other financial instruments that, in combination, provide inverse (opposite) or short leveraged exposure to the index equal to at least 80% of the fund's net assets (plus borrowing for investment purposes). The index is a float-adjusted, market capitalization-weighted index. The fund is non-diversified. **Top Holdings:** S&P 500 Index Swap S&P 500 Index Swap S&P 500 Index Swap S&P 500 Index Swap S&P 500 Index Swap

---

iShares U.S. Consumer Goods ETF   C+   HOLD

Ticker	Traded On	NAV	Total Assets ($)	Dividend Yield (TTM)	Turnover Ratio	Expense Ratio
IYK	NYSE Arca	126.46	$480,562,748	2.21	4	0.42

Ratings

Reward	B
Risk	C
Recent Upgrade/Downgrade	Up

Fund Information

Fund Type	Exchange Traded Funds
Category	Consumer Goods & Svcs
Sub-Category	Consumer Defensive
Prospectus Objective	Unaligned
Inception Date	Jun-00
Open to New Investments	Y

Prices

Price (as of 9/30/2019)	126.49
52-Week High	126.90
52-Week Low	102.26

Total Returns (%)

3-Month	6-Month	1-Year	3-Year	5-Year
4.05	6.85	8.78	19.06	44.54

3-Year Standard Deviation	11.76
Effective Duration	

Valuation

Premium/Discount (1-Year Average)	0.03

Company Information

Provider	iShares
Manager/Tenure	Greg Savage (11), Jennifer Hsui (7), Alan Mason (3), 2 others
Website	http://www.ishares.com
Address	iShares 400 Howard Street San Francisco CA 94105 United States
Phone Number	800-474-2737

PERFORMANCE

Ratings History

Date	Overall Rating	Risk Rating	Reward Rating
Q3-19	C+	C	B
Q4-18	C	C-	C
Q4-17	B	A	C+
Q4-16	C	C	C+
Q4-15	C+	C	B-

Asset & Performance History

Date	NAV	1-Year Total Return
2018	106.51	-13.72
2017	126.67	16.52
2016	110.68	4.87
2015	108.3	5.61
2014	104.77	11.61
2013	95.67	29.92

Total Assets: $480,562,748

Asset Allocation

Asset	%
Cash	0%
Stocks	100%
US Stocks	99%
Bonds	0%
US Bonds	0%
Other	0%

Services Offered: CashInvestment Plan

Investment Strategy: The investment seeks to track the investment results of the Dow Jones U.S. Consumer Goods Index composed of U.S. equities in the consumer goods sector. The fund generally invests at least 90% of its assets in securities of the underlying index and in depositary receipts representing securities of the underlying index. The underlying index measures the performance of the consumer goods sector of the U.S. equity market. The fund may invest the remainder of its assets in certain futures, options and swap contracts, cash and cash equivalents. It is non-diversified. **Top Holdings:** Procter & Gamble Co Coca-Cola Co PepsiCo Inc Philip Morris International Inc Nike Inc B

---

iShares MSCI ACWI Low Carbon Target ETF   C   HOLD

Ticker	Traded On	NAV	Total Assets ($)	Dividend Yield (TTM)	Turnover Ratio	Expense Ratio
CRBN	NYSE Arca	120.05	$480,196,425	2.24	14	0.2

Ratings
Reward	C
Risk	D+
Recent Upgrade/Downgrade	

Fund Information
Fund Type	Exchange Traded Funds
Category	Global Equity Large Cap
Sub-Category	World Large Stock
Prospectus Objective	World Stock
Inception Date	Dec-14
Open to New Investments	Y

Prices
Price (as of 9/30/2019)	120.16
52-Week High	122.22
52-Week Low	99.00

Total Returns (%)
3-Month	6-Month	1-Year	3-Year	5-Year
-0.39	3.11	2.24	32.45	

3-Year Standard Deviation	11.32
Effective Duration	

Valuation
Premium/Discount (1-Year Average)	0.02

Company Information
Provider	iShares
Manager/Tenure	Diane Hsiung (4), Jennifer Hsui (4), Greg Savage (4), 3 others
Website	http://www.ishares.com
Address	iShares 400 Howard Street San Francisco CA 94105 United States
Phone Number	800-474-2737

PERFORMANCE

Ratings History
Date	Overall Rating	Risk Rating	Reward Rating
Q3-19	C	D+	C
Q4-18	C-	C-	C-
Q4-17	C+	B-	C+
Q4-16	C-	C-	D+
Q4-15	U		

Asset & Performance History
Date	NAV	1-Year Total Return
2018	103.66	-9.38
2017	117.1	23.71
2016	96.7	7.63
2015	91.94	-1.34
2014	95.04	
2013		

Total Assets: $480,196,425
Asset Allocation
Asset	%
Cash	0%
Stocks	100%
US Stocks	55%
Bonds	0%
US Bonds	0%
Other	0%

Services Offered:

Investment Strategy: The investment seeks to track the investment results of the MSCI ACWI Low Carbon Target Index. The fund generally will invest at least 90% of its assets in the component securities of the underlying index and in investments that have economic characteristics that are substantially identical to the component securities of the underlying index. The underlying index is designed to address two dimensions of carbon exposure - carbon emissions and potential carbon emissions from fossil fuel reserves. **Top Holdings:** Microsoft Corp Apple Inc Amazon.com Inc Facebook Inc A Alphabet Inc A

VictoryShares USAA MSCI USA Value Momentum ETF   D+   SELL

Ticker	Traded On	NAV	Total Assets ($)	Dividend Yield (TTM)	Turnover Ratio	Expense Ratio
ULVM	NYSE Arca	51.25	$479,176,451	1.85	84	0.2

Ratings
Reward	D+
Risk	D+
Recent Upgrade/Downgrade	

Fund Information
Fund Type	Exchange Traded Funds
Category	US Equity Large Cap Blend
Sub-Category	Large Blend
Prospectus Objective	Growth & Inc
Inception Date	Oct-17
Open to New Investments	Y

Prices
Price (as of 9/30/2019)	51.28
52-Week High	53.73
52-Week Low	42.49

Total Returns (%)
3-Month	6-Month	1-Year	3-Year	5-Year
-0.17	1.96	-2.44		

3-Year Standard Deviation	
Effective Duration	

Valuation
Premium/Discount (1-Year Average)	0.14

Company Information
Provider	VictoryShares
Manager/Tenure	Lance Humphrey (1), Wasif A. Latif (1), Mannik Dhillon (0)
Website	http://www.VictorySharesLiterature.com
Address	Victory Shares 4249 Easton Way, Suite 400 Columbus OH 43219 United States
Phone Number	

PERFORMANCE

Ratings History
Date	Overall Rating	Risk Rating	Reward Rating
Q3-19	D+	D+	D+
Q4-18	D	D	D
Q4-17	U		
Q4-16			
Q4-15			

Asset & Performance History
Date	NAV	1-Year Total Return
2018	44.99	-12.1
2017	51.94	
2016		
2015		
2014		
2013		

Total Assets: $479,176,451
Asset Allocation
Asset	%
Cash	0%
Stocks	100%
US Stocks	98%
Bonds	0%
US Bonds	0%
Other	0%

Services Offered:

Investment Strategy: The investment seeks to provide investment results that closely correspond, before fees and expenses, to the performance of the MSCI USA Select Value Momentum Blend Index. Under normal circumstances, the fund seeks to achieve its investment objective by investing at least 80% of its net assets in securities in the index. The index is designed to deliver exposure to equity securities of large- and mid-capitalization U.S. issuers that have higher exposure to value and momentum factors within the MSCI USA Index (the "parent index") while also maintaining moderate index turnover and lower realized volatility than traditional capitalization weighted indexes. **Top Holdings:** Republic Services Inc Class A WR Berkley Corp Waste Management Inc Equity Lifestyle Properties Inc Procter & Gamble Co

VanEck Vectors Investment Grade Floating Rate ETF C HOLD

Ticker	Traded On	NAV	Total Assets ($)	Dividend Yield (TTM)	Turnover Ratio	Expense Ratio
FLTR	NYSE Arca	25.26	$477,380,381	3.15	30	0.14

Ratings
Reward C
Risk C+
Recent Upgrade/Downgrade

Fund Information
Fund Type — Exchange Traded Funds
Category — US Fixed Income
Sub-Category — Ultrashort Bond
Prospectus Objective — Income
Inception Date — Apr-11
Open to New Investments — Y

Prices
Price (as of 9/30/2019) 25.24
52-Week High 25.28
52-Week Low 24.68

Total Returns (%)

3-Month	6-Month	1-Year	3-Year	5-Year
0.87	1.98	3.01	8.65	9.79

3-Year Standard Deviation 1.08
Effective Duration 0.05

Valuation
Premium/Discount (1-Year Average) -0.06

Company Information
Provider VanEck
Manager/Tenure Francis G. Rodilosso (7)
Website http://www.vaneck.com
Address Van Eck Associates Corporation 666 Third Avenue New York NY 10017 United States
Phone Number 800-826-1115

PERFORMANCE

Ratings History

Date	Overall Rating	Risk Rating	Reward Rating
Q3-19	C	C+	C
Q4-18	C	C+	C-
Q4-17	B-	A-	C
Q4-16	C-	D+	C
Q4-15	C	C-	C

Asset & Performance History

Date	NAV	1-Year Total Return
2018	24.75	0.36
2017	25.24	2.84
2016	24.96	2.11
2015	24.73	0.01
2014	24.9	0.41
2013	24.96	1.62

Total Assets: $477,380,381
Asset Allocation

Asset	%
Cash	0%
Stocks	0%
US Stocks	0%
Bonds	98%
US Bonds	65%
Other	0%

Services Offered:

Investment Strategy: The investment seeks to replicate as closely as possible, before fees and expenses, the price and yield performance of the MVIS® US Investment Grade Floating Rate Index (the "Floating Rate Index"). The fund normally invests at least 80% of its total assets in securities that comprise the fund's benchmark index. The index is comprised of U.S. dollar-denominated floating rate notes issued by corporate entities or similar commercial entities that are public reporting companies in the United States and rated investment grade. The fund is non-diversified. **Top Holdings:** AT&T Inc 3.62% Goldman Sachs Group, Inc. 2.9% Morgan Stanley 3.68% HSBC Holdings plc 3.12% Morgan Stanley 3.21%

Invesco S&P 500® Equal Weight Consumer Staples ETF B- BUY

Ticker	Traded On	NAV	Total Assets ($)	Dividend Yield (TTM)	Turnover Ratio	Expense Ratio
RHS	NYSE Arca	140.32	$477,075,458	2.29		0.4

Ratings
Reward B
Risk C
Recent Upgrade/Downgrade Up

Fund Information
Fund Type — Exchange Traded Funds
Category — Consumer Goods & Svcs
Sub-Category — Consumer Defensive
Prospectus Objective — Unaligned
Inception Date — Nov-06
Open to New Investments — Y

Prices
Price (as of 9/30/2019) 140.40
52-Week High 140.40
52-Week Low 112.22

Total Returns (%)

3-Month	6-Month	1-Year	3-Year	5-Year
5.44	8.57	12.35	22.17	60.64

3-Year Standard Deviation 11.93
Effective Duration

Valuation
Premium/Discount (1-Year Average) -0.04

Company Information
Provider Invesco
Manager/Tenure Peter Hubbard (1), Michael Jeanette (1), Tony Seisser (1)
Website http://www.invesco.com/us
Address Invesco 11 Greenway Plaza, Ste. 2500 Houston TX 77046 United States
Phone Number 800-659-1005

PERFORMANCE

Ratings History

Date	Overall Rating	Risk Rating	Reward Rating
Q3-19	B-	C	B
Q4-18	C+	C	B
Q4-17	B	A-	C+
Q4-16	C	C	C+
Q4-15	B	C	B+

Asset & Performance History

Date	NAV	1-Year Total Return
2018	116.47	-10.72
2017	133.52	13.6
2016	119.44	4.3
2015	115.93	13.1
2014	104.45	17.92
2013	90.22	32.55

Total Assets: $477,075,458
Asset Allocation

Asset	%
Cash	0%
Stocks	100%
US Stocks	100%
Bonds	0%
US Bonds	0%
Other	0%

Services Offered:

Investment Strategy: The investment seeks to track the investment results (before fees and expenses) of the S&P 500® Equal Weight Consumer Staples Index (the "underlying index"). The fund generally will invest at least 90% of its total assets in the securities that comprise the underlying index. The underlying index is composed of all of the components of the S&P 500® Consumer Staples Index, an index that contains the common stocks of all companies included in the S&P 500® Index that are classified as members of the consumer staples sector, as defined according to the Global Industry Classification Standard ("GICS"). The fund is non-diversified. **Top Holdings:** The Hershey Co Lamb Weston Holdings Inc Tyson Foods Inc Class A Costco Wholesale Corp The Estee Lauder Companies Inc Class A

iShares Morningstar Mid-Cap Value ETF

C HOLD

Ticker	Traded On	NAV	Total Assets ($)	Dividend Yield (TTM)	Turnover Ratio	Expense Ratio
JKI	NAS CM	160.66	$473,933,796	2.46	35	0.3

Ratings

Reward	C
Risk	D+
Recent Upgrade/Downgrade	

Fund Information

Fund Type	Exchange Traded Funds
Category	US Equity Mid Cap
Sub-Category	Mid-Cap Value
Prospectus Objective	Growth
Inception Date	Jun-04
Open to New Investments	Y

Prices

Price (as of 9/30/2019)	160.99
52-Week High	162.69
52-Week Low	132.21

Total Returns (%)

3-Month	6-Month	1-Year	3-Year	5-Year
2.05	3.29	2.15	28.20	52.20

3-Year Standard Deviation	14
Effective Duration	

Valuation

Premium/Discount (1-Year Average)	0.02

Company Information

Provider	iShares
Manager/Tenure	Greg Savage (11), Jennifer Hsui (7), Alan Mason (3), 2 others
Website	http://www.ishares.com
Address	iShares 400 Howard Street San Francisco CA 94105 United States
Phone Number	800-474-2737

PERFORMANCE

Ratings History

Date	Overall Rating	Risk Rating	Reward Rating
Q3-19	C	D+	C
Q4-18	C-	D+	C
Q4-17	B	B	B
Q4-16	C	C-	C
Q4-15	C	D+	C

Asset & Performance History

Date	NAV	1-Year Total Return
2018	139.05	-10.76
2017	159.53	12.69
2016	144.39	24.76
2015	118.41	-2.8
2014	124.58	11.13
2013	114.35	41.72

Total Assets: $473,933,796

Asset Allocation

Asset	%
Cash	0%
Stocks	100%
US Stocks	97%
Bonds	0%
US Bonds	0%
Other	0%

Services Offered:

Investment Strategy: The investment seeks to track the investment results of the Morningstar® US Mid Value IndexSM composed of mid-capitalization U.S. equities that exhibit value characteristics. The fund generally invests at least 90% of its assets in securities of the underlying index and in depositary receipts representing securities of the underlying index. The underlying index measures the performance of stocks issued by mid-capitalization companies that have exhibited "value" characteristics as determined by Morningstar, Inc.'s ("Morningstar" or the "index provider") proprietary index methodology. **Top Holdings:** WEC Energy Group Inc Zimmer Biomet Holdings Inc Tyson Foods Inc Class A Ventas Inc McKesson Corp

---

WisdomTree International Hedged Quality Dividend Growth Fund

C HOLD

Ticker	Traded On	NAV	Total Assets ($)	Dividend Yield (TTM)	Turnover Ratio	Expense Ratio
IHDG	NYSE Arca	33.48	$473,749,353	1.57	56	0.58

Ratings

Reward	C+
Risk	C-
Recent Upgrade/Downgrade	

Fund Information

Fund Type	Exchange Traded Funds
Category	Global Equity Large Cap
Sub-Category	Foreign Large Growth
Prospectus Objective	Growth
Inception Date	May-14
Open to New Investments	Y

Prices

Price (as of 9/30/2019)	33.62
52-Week High	33.71
52-Week Low	26.92

Total Returns (%)

3-Month	6-Month	1-Year	3-Year	5-Year
1.40	4.83	5.61	31.70	51.95

3-Year Standard Deviation	10.55
Effective Duration	

Valuation

Premium/Discount (1-Year Average)	0.03

Company Information

Provider	WisdomTree
Manager/Tenure	Richard A. Brown (5), Thomas J. Durante (5), Karen Q. Wong (5)
Website	http://www.wisdomtree.com
Address	WisdomTree 245 Park Avenue, 35th floor New York NY 10167 United States
Phone Number	866-909-9473

PERFORMANCE

Ratings History

Date	Overall Rating	Risk Rating	Reward Rating
Q3-19	C	C-	C+
Q4-18	D+	C-	D+
Q4-17	B+	A-	B
Q4-16	C	C-	C
Q4-15	D	C+	C-

Asset & Performance History

Date	NAV	1-Year Total Return
2018	27.9	-11.69
2017	31.66	21.43
2016	26.43	1.67
2015	26.51	12.53
2014	24.28	
2013		

Total Assets: $473,749,353

Asset Allocation

Asset	%
Cash	0%
Stocks	100%
US Stocks	1%
Bonds	0%
US Bonds	0%
Other	0%

Services Offered:

Investment Strategy: The investment seeks to track the price and yield performance of the WisdomTree International Hedged Quality Dividend Growth Index. The fund will invest at least 80% of its total assets in component securities of the index and investments that have economic characteristics that are substantially identical to the economic characteristics of such component securities. The index consists of dividend-paying common stocks with growth characteristics of companies in the industrialized world, excluding Canada and the U.S., while at the same time neutralizing exposure to fluctuations of the value of foreign currencies relative to the USD. It is non-diversified. **Top Holdings:** Industria De Diseno Textil SA Unilever NV British American Tobacco PLC Novo Nordisk A/S B Rio Tinto PLC

Vident Core U.S. Bond Strategy ETF™

C   HOLD

Ticker	Traded On	NAV	Total Assets ($)	Dividend Yield (TTM)	Turnover Ratio	Expense Ratio
VBND	NYSE Arca	50.86	$473,028,069	3.08	324	0.43

Ratings

Reward	C+
Risk	C-
Recent Upgrade/Downgrade	

Fund Information

Fund Type	Exchange Traded Funds
Category	US Fixed Income
Sub-Category	Intermediate Core-Plus Bond
Prospectus Objective	Growth & Inc
Inception Date	Oct-14
Open to New Investments	Y

Prices

Price (as of 9/30/2019)	50.83
52-Week High	51.26
52-Week Low	46.86

Total Returns (%)

3-Month	6-Month	1-Year	3-Year	5-Year
2.32	5.66	10.68	7.43	

3-Year Standard Deviation	3.46
Effective Duration	

Valuation

Premium/Discount (1-Year Average)	-0.10

Company Information

Provider	Vident Financial
Manager/Tenure	Jim Iredale (4), Denise M. Krisko (4)
Website	http://www.videntfinancial.com
Address	Vident Financial 201 17th Street, Suite 300 Atlanta GA 30363 United States
Phone Number	800-617-0004

PERFORMANCE

Ratings History

Date	Overall Rating	Risk Rating	Reward Rating
Q3-19	C	C-	C+
Q4-18	D+	C-	D
Q4-17	C	B-	C-
Q4-16	D+	C-	D+
Q4-15	U		

Asset & Performance History

Date	NAV	1-Year Total Return
2018	47.43	-0.77
2017	49.16	2.82
2016	48.77	2.25
2015	49.12	0.38
2014	49.66	
2013		

Total Assets: $473,028,069

Asset Allocation

Asset	%
Cash	9%
Stocks	0%
US Stocks	0%
Bonds	91%
US Bonds	91%
Other	0%

Services Offered:

Investment Strategy: The investment seeks to track the performance, before fees and expenses, of the Vident Core U.S. Bond Index™. Under normal circumstances, at least 80% of the fund's total assets (exclusive of collateral held from securities lending) will be invested in the component securities of the index and investments that have economic characteristics that are substantially identical to the economic characteristics of such component securities (such as TBA securities). The index seeks to improve the overall mix of credit quality, interest rate and yield as compared to traditional U.S. core bond indices. **Top Holdings:** United States Treasury Bonds 8% Federal National Mortgage Association 4% Federal National Mortgage Association 3.5% Federal National Mortgage Association 4.5% United States Treasury Notes 2%

Direxion Daily S&P Biotech Bull 3X Shares

D   SELL

Ticker	Traded On	NAV	Total Assets ($)	Dividend Yield (TTM)	Turnover Ratio	Expense Ratio
LABU	NYSE Arca	30.89	$471,468,534	0.82	510	1.12

Ratings

Reward	D
Risk	D+
Recent Upgrade/Downgrade	Down

Fund Information

Fund Type	Exchange Traded Funds
Category	Trading Tools
Sub-Category	Trading--Leveraged Equity
Prospectus Objective	Technology
Inception Date	May-15
Open to New Investments	Y

Prices

Price (as of 9/30/2019)	30.90
52-Week High	90.09
52-Week Low	25.21

Total Returns (%)

3-Month	6-Month	1-Year	3-Year	5-Year
-39.49	-47.97	-65.07	-36.07	

3-Year Standard Deviation	80.38
Effective Duration	

Valuation

Premium/Discount (1-Year Average)	-0.07

Company Information

Provider	Direxion Funds
Manager/Tenure	Paul Brigandi (4), Tony Ng (4)
Website	http://www.direxionfunds.com
Address	Direxion Funds 1301 Avenue Of The Americas (6th Avenue) New York NY 10019 United States
Phone Number	646-572-3390

PERFORMANCE

Ratings History

Date	Overall Rating	Risk Rating	Reward Rating
Q3-19	D	D+	D
Q4-18	D	D	D
Q4-17	C-	D+	C
Q4-16	D	D-	D
Q4-15	U		

Asset & Performance History

Date	NAV	1-Year Total Return
2018	33.03	-57.27
2017	77.65	148.69
2016	31.28	-63.02
2015	84.6	
2014		
2013		

Total Assets: $471,468,534

Asset Allocation

Asset	%
Cash	40%
Stocks	60%
US Stocks	60%
Bonds	0%
US Bonds	0%
Other	0%

Services Offered:

Investment Strategy: The investment seeks daily investment results, before fees and expenses, of 300% of the daily performance of the S&P Biotechnology Select Industry Index ("index"). The fund invests at least 80% of its net assets (plus borrowing for investment purposes) in financial instruments and securities of the index, exchange-traded funds ("ETFs") that track the index and other financial instruments that provide daily leveraged exposure to the index or ETFs that track the index. The index is designed to measure the performance of the biotechnology sub-industry based on the Global Industry Classification Standards ("GICS"). The fund is non-diversified. **Top Holdings:** S&P Biotechnology Select S&P Biotechnology Select Industry USD Ligand Pharmaceuticals Inc Exact Sciences Corp Celgene Corp

SPDR® MSCI USA StrategicFactors ETF

C   HOLD

Ticker	Traded On	NAV	Total Assets ($)	Dividend Yield (TTM)	Turnover Ratio	Expense Ratio
QUS	NYSE Arca		$471,036,622	1.85	18	0.15

Ratings
Reward	B-
Risk	C-
Recent Upgrade/Downgrade	Down

Fund Information
Fund Type	Exchange Traded Funds
Category	US Equity Large Cap Blend
Sub-Category	Large Blend
Prospectus Objective	Growth & Inc
Inception Date	Apr-15
Open to New Investments	Y

Prices
Price (as of 9/30/2019)	88.76
52-Week High	89.27
52-Week Low	69.01

Total Returns (%)
3-Month	6-Month	1-Year	3-Year	5-Year
1.69	6.11	7.70	47.89	

3-Year Standard Deviation	11.17
Effective Duration	

Valuation
Premium/Discount (1-Year Average)	0.05

Company Information
Provider	SPDR State Street Global Advisors
Manager/Tenure	Michael J. Feehily (4), Karl A. Schneider (4), John Law (0)
Website	http://www.spdrs.com
Address	SPDR State Street Global Advisors State Street Financial Center, 1 Lincoln Street Boston MA 02111-2900 United States
Phone Number	617-786-3000

PERFORMANCE

Ratings History
Date	Overall Rating	Risk Rating	Reward Rating
Q3-19	C	C-	B-
Q4-18	C	C-	C
Q4-17	B-	B+	C+
Q4-16	D+	D+	C-
Q4-15	U		

Asset & Performance History
Date	NAV	1-Year Total Return
2018	72.93	-3.18
2017	76.92	21.17
2016	64.75	11.79
2015	59.18	
2014		
2013		

Total Assets: $471,036,622

Asset Allocation
Asset	%
Cash	0%
Stocks	100%
US Stocks	99%
Bonds	0%
US Bonds	0%
Other	0%

Services Offered:

Investment Strategy: The investment seeks to track the performance of the MSCI USA Factor Mix A-Series Capped Index. The fund invests at least 80%, of its total assets in the securities comprising the index. The index is designed to measure the equity market performance of large-and mid-cap companies across the U.S. equity market. It aims to represent the performance of a combination of three factors: value, quality, and low volatility. It is an equal weighted combination of the following three MSCI Factor Indices in a single composite index: the MSCI USA Value Weighted Index, the MSCI USA Quality Index, and the MSCI USA Minimum Volatility Index. The fund is non-diversified. **Top Holdings:** Apple Inc Microsoft Corp Johnson & Johnson Visa Inc Class A Mastercard Inc A

First Trust Water ETF

B-   BUY

Ticker	Traded On	NAV	Total Assets ($)	Dividend Yield (TTM)	Turnover Ratio	Expense Ratio
FIW	NYSE Arca	56.12	$468,607,744	0.67	11	0.55

Ratings
Reward	B
Risk	C
Recent Upgrade/Downgrade	Up

Fund Information
Fund Type	Exchange Traded Funds
Category	Industrials Sector Equity
Sub-Category	Miscellaneous Sector
Prospectus Objective	Natl Res
Inception Date	May-07
Open to New Investments	Y

Prices
Price (as of 9/30/2019)	56.11
52-Week High	56.69
52-Week Low	41.46

Total Returns (%)
3-Month	6-Month	1-Year	3-Year	5-Year
2.35	9.21	11.80	52.97	87.06

3-Year Standard Deviation	14.99
Effective Duration	

Valuation
Premium/Discount (1-Year Average)	0.03

Company Information
Provider	First Trust
Manager/Tenure	Jon C. Erickson (12), Daniel J. Lindquist (12), David G. McGarel (12), 3 others
Website	http://www.ftportfolios.com/
Address	First Trust 120 E. Liberty Drive, Suite 400 Wheaton IL 60187 United States
Phone Number	800-621-1675

PERFORMANCE

Ratings History
Date	Overall Rating	Risk Rating	Reward Rating
Q3-19	B-	C	B
Q4-18	C+	C	B
Q4-17	B+	C+	A
Q4-16	C+	C-	B
Q4-15	B-	C+	B-

Asset & Performance History
Date	NAV	1-Year Total Return
2018	43.96	-8.88
2017	48.58	24.25
2016	39.6	32.21
2015	30.12	-9.81
2014	33.65	0.35
2013	33.78	30.91

Total Assets: $468,607,744

Asset Allocation
Asset	%
Cash	0%
Stocks	100%
US Stocks	98%
Bonds	0%
US Bonds	0%
Other	0%

Services Offered:

Investment Strategy: The investment seeks investment results that correspond generally to the price and yield (before the fund's fees and expenses) of an equity index called the ISE Clean Edge Water Index. The fund will normally invest at least 90% of its net assets (including investment borrowings) in the common stocks and depositary receipts that comprise the index. The index is designed to track the performance of small, mid and large capitalization companies that derive a substantial portion of their revenues from the potable water and wastewater industry, according to Clean Edge. **Top Holdings:** IDEXX Laboratories Inc American Water Works Co Ecolab Inc Tetra Tech Inc IDEX Corp

First Trust Dorsey Wright Dynamic Focus 5 ETF

C- **HOLD**

Ticker	Traded On	NAV	Total Assets ($)	Dividend Yield (TTM)	Turnover Ratio	Expense Ratio
FVC	NAS CM	26.46	$468,253,074	0.76	42	0.89

Ratings
Reward	C
Risk	C-
Recent Upgrade/Downgrade	Down

Fund Information
Fund Type	Exchange Traded Funds
Category	US Equity Mid Cap
Sub-Category	Large Blend
Prospectus Objective	Growth & Inc
Inception Date	Mar-16
Open to New Investments	Y

Prices
Price (as of 9/30/2019)	26.43
52-Week High	28.70
52-Week Low	21.74

Total Returns (%)
3-Month	6-Month	1-Year	3-Year	5-Year
-1.83	-1.29	-7.03	26.70	

3-Year Standard Deviation	13.91
Effective Duration	

Valuation
Premium/Discount (1-Year Average)	-0.11

Company Information
Provider	First Trust
Manager/Tenure	Jon C. Erickson (3), Daniel J. Lindquist (3), David G. McGarel (3), 3 others
Website	http://www.ftportfolios.com/
Address	First Trust 120 E. Liberty Drive, Suite 400 Wheaton IL 60187 United States
Phone Number	800-621-1675

PERFORMANCE

Ratings History
Date	Overall Rating	Risk Rating	Reward Rating
Q3-19	C-	C-	C
Q4-18	C-	C-	C-
Q4-17	D+	B+	C
Q4-16	U		
Q4-15			

Asset & Performance History
Date	NAV	1-Year Total Return
2018	23.55	-8.05
2017	25.67	19.83
2016	21.56	
2015		
2014		
2013		

Total Assets: $468,253,074

Asset Allocation
Asset	%
Cash	40%
Stocks	60%
US Stocks	58%
Bonds	0%
US Bonds	0%
Other	0%

Services Offered:

Investment Strategy: The investment seeks investment results that correspond to the price and yield of an index called the Dorsey Wright Dynamic Focus Five Index. The fund will normally invest at least 80% of its net assets in the ETFs and cash equivalents that comprise the index. The index is designed to provide targeted exposure to the five First Trust sector and industry-based ETFs that the index determines offer the greatest potential to outperform the other First Trust sector and industry-based ETFs and that satisfy certain trading volume and liquidity requirements. It is non-diversified. **Top Holdings:** First Trust Utilities AlphaDEX® ETF First Trust Technology AlphaDEX® ETF First Trust NASDAQ-100-Tech Sector ETF First Trust Dow Jones Internet ETF First Trust NYSE Arca Biotech ETF

VanEck Vectors Vietnam ETF

C- **HOLD**

Ticker	Traded On	NAV	Total Assets ($)	Dividend Yield (TTM)	Turnover Ratio	Expense Ratio
VNM	NYSE Arca	16.46	$467,365,117	0.87	49	0.68

Ratings
Reward	C-
Risk	C
Recent Upgrade/Downgrade	Down

Fund Information
Fund Type	Exchange Traded Funds
Category	Asia ex-Japan Equity
Sub-Category	Miscellaneous Region
Prospectus Objective	Growth
Inception Date	Aug-09
Open to New Investments	Y

Prices
Price (as of 9/30/2019)	16.31
52-Week High	17.18
52-Week Low	14.48

Total Returns (%)
3-Month	6-Month	1-Year	3-Year	5-Year
1.10	-1.96	-0.69	12.82	-17.54

3-Year Standard Deviation	15.49
Effective Duration	

Valuation
Premium/Discount (1-Year Average)	0.21

Company Information
Provider	VanEck
Manager/Tenure	Hao-Hung (Peter) Liao (10), Guo Hua (Jason) Jin (1)
Website	http://www.vaneck.com
Address	Van Eck Associates Corporation 666 Third Avenue New York NY 10017 United States
Phone Number	800-826-1115

PERFORMANCE

Ratings History
Date	Overall Rating	Risk Rating	Reward Rating
Q3-19	C-	C	C-
Q4-18	C-	C-	C-
Q4-17	C	C	C
Q4-16	D	D	D
Q4-15	D+	D	D+

Asset & Performance History
Date	NAV	1-Year Total Return
2018	14.84	-14.13
2017	17.45	36.15
2016	12.97	-10.09
2015	14.78	-18.57
2014	18.84	3.89
2013	18.63	12.69

Total Assets: $467,365,117

Asset Allocation
Asset	%
Cash	0%
Stocks	100%
US Stocks	1%
Bonds	0%
US Bonds	0%
Other	0%

Services Offered: Automatic Investment Plan, Retirement Investment

Investment Strategy: The investment seeks to replicate as closely as possible, before fees and expenses, the price and yield performance of the MVIS® Vietnam Index. The fund normally invests at least 80% of its total assets in securities that comprise the fund's benchmark index. The index includes securities of Vietnamese companies. A company is generally considered to be a Vietnamese company if it is incorporated in Vietnam or is incorporated outside of Vietnam but has at least 50% of its revenues/related assets in Vietnam. It is non-diversified. **Top Holdings:** Vingroup JSC Vietnam Dairy Products JSC Vinhomes JSC Joint Stock Commercial Bank for Foreign Trade of Vietnam No Va Land Investment Group Corp

iShares Russell Top 200 Value ETF   C   HOLD

Ticker	Traded On	NAV	Total Assets ($)	Dividend Yield (TTM)	Turnover Ratio	Expense Ratio
IWX	NYSE Arca	54.76	$459,977,131	2.51	14	0.2

Ratings

Reward	C
Risk	C-
Recent Upgrade/Downgrade	

Fund Information

Fund Type	Exchange Traded Funds
Category	US Equity Large Cap Value
Sub-Category	Large Value
Prospectus Objective	Growth
Inception Date	Sep-09
Open to New Investments	Y

Prices

Price (as of 9/30/2019)	54.78
52-Week High	55.72
52-Week Low	44.99

Total Returns (%)

3-Month	6-Month	1-Year	3-Year	5-Year
0.74	4.31	4.39	33.16	46.96

3-Year Standard Deviation	12.05
Effective Duration	

Valuation

Premium/Discount (1-Year Average)	0.04

Company Information

Provider	iShares
Manager/Tenure	Greg Savage (10), Jennifer Hsui (7), Alan Mason (3), 2 others
Website	http://www.ishares.com
Address	iShares 400 Howard Street San Francisco CA 94105 United States
Phone Number	800-474-2737

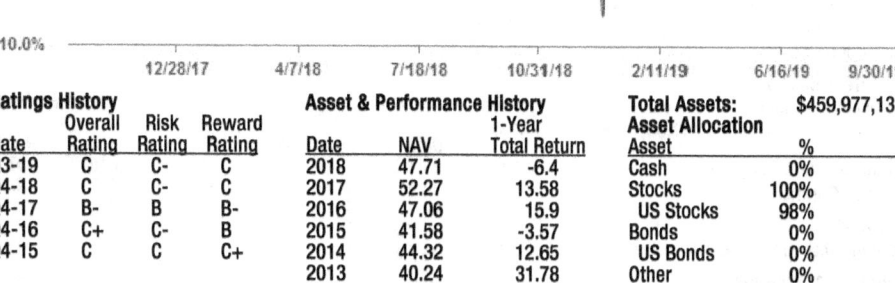

PERFORMANCE

Ratings History

Date	Overall Rating	Risk Rating	Reward Rating
Q3-19	C	C-	C
Q4-18	C	C-	C
Q4-17	B-	B	B-
Q4-16	C+	C-	B
Q4-15	C	C	C+

Asset & Performance History

Date	NAV	1-Year Total Return
2018	47.71	-6.4
2017	52.27	13.58
2016	47.06	15.9
2015	41.58	-3.57
2014	44.32	12.65
2013	40.24	31.78

Total Assets: $459,977,131

Asset Allocation

Asset	%
Cash	0%
Stocks	100%
US Stocks	98%
Bonds	0%
US Bonds	0%
Other	0%

Services Offered:

Investment Strategy: The investment seeks to track the investment results of the Russell Top 200 Value Index, which measures the performance of the largest capitalization value sector of the U.S. equity market. The fund generally will invest at least 90% of its assets in the component securities of the underlying index and may invest up to 10% of its assets in certain futures, options and swap contracts, cash and cash equivalents, including shares of money market funds advised by BFA or its affiliates, as well as in securities not included in the underlying index, but which BFA believes will help the fund track the underlying index. **Top Holdings:** Berkshire Hathaway Inc B JPMorgan Chase & Co Exxon Mobil Corp Johnson & Johnson Procter & Gamble Co

---

Global X Lithium & Battery Tech ETF   D   SELL

Ticker	Traded On	NAV	Total Assets ($)	Dividend Yield (TTM)	Turnover Ratio	Expense Ratio
LIT	NYSE Arca	24.48	$457,092,174	3.68	16	0.75

Ratings

Reward	D
Risk	D
Recent Upgrade/Downgrade	Down

Fund Information

Fund Type	Exchange Traded Funds
Category	Natural Resources
Sub-Category	Natural Resources
Prospectus Objective	Unaligned
Inception Date	Jul-10
Open to New Investments	Y

Prices

Price (as of 9/30/2019)	24.37
52-Week High	33.25
52-Week Low	22.61

Total Returns (%)

3-Month	6-Month	1-Year	3-Year	5-Year
-6.49	-14.65	-23.57	9.15	8.86

3-Year Standard Deviation	19.61
Effective Duration	

Valuation

Premium/Discount (1-Year Average)	-0.26

Company Information

Provider	Global X Funds
Manager/Tenure	Chang Kim (5), Nam To (1), Wayne Xie (0), 1 other
Website	http://www.globalxfunds.com
Address	Global X Funds 600 Lexington Avenue, 20th Floor New York NY 10022 United States
Phone Number	888-493-8631

PERFORMANCE

Ratings History

Date	Overall Rating	Risk Rating	Reward Rating
Q3-19	D	D	D
Q4-18	C	C-	C
Q4-17	B+	C	A+
Q4-16	C-	D+	C-
Q4-15	D	D	D

Asset & Performance History

Date	NAV	1-Year Total Return
2018	27.17	-29.84
2017	38.73	63.36
2016	24.48	23.55
2015	20.24	-10.07
2014	22.56	-12.85
2013	26.16	-9.06

Total Assets: $457,092,174

Asset Allocation

Asset	%
Cash	0%
Stocks	100%
US Stocks	34%
Bonds	0%
US Bonds	0%
Other	0%

Services Offered:

Investment Strategy: The investment seeks to provide investment results that correspond generally to the price and yield performance, before fees and expenses, of the Solactive Global Lithium Index. The fund invests at least 80% of its total assets in the securities of the underlying index and in American Depositary Receipts ("ADRs") and Global Depositary Receipts ("GDRs") based on the securities in the underlying index. The underlying index is designed to measure broad-based equity market performance of global companies involved in the lithium industry. The fund is non-diversified. **Top Holdings:** Albemarle Corp Sociedad Quimica Y Minera De Chile SA ADR LG Chem Ltd Simplo Technology Co Ltd Samsung SDI Co Ltd

Invesco S&P SmallCap Health Care ETF   C   HOLD

Ticker	Traded On	NAV	Total Assets ($)	Dividend Yield (TTM)	Turnover Ratio	Expense Ratio
PSCH	NAS CM	113.51	$454,026,151	0		0.29

Ratings
Reward   C
Risk   C-
Recent Upgrade/Downgrade   Up

Fund Information
Fund Type   Exchange Traded Funds
Category   Healthcare Sector Equity
Sub-Category   Health
Prospectus Objective   Health
Inception Date   Apr-10
Open to New Investments

Prices
Price (as of 9/30/2019)   113.47
52-Week High   138.29
52-Week Low   100.46

Total Returns (%)

3-Month	6-Month	1-Year	3-Year	5-Year
-4.05	-1.82	-17.89	53.33	113.97

3-Year Standard Deviation   21.24
Effective Duration

Valuation
Premium/Discount (1-Year Average)   -0.09

Company Information
Provider   Invesco
Manager/Tenure   Peter Hubbard (9), Michael Jeanette (9), Tony Seisser (5)
Website   http://www.invesco.com/us
Address   Invesco 11 Greenway Plaza, Ste. 2500 Houston TX 77046 United States
Phone Number   800-659-1005

PERFORMANCE

Ratings History

Date	Overall Rating	Risk Rating	Reward Rating
Q3-19	C	C-	C
Q4-18	C	C-	C+
Q4-17	A-	B+	A
Q4-16	C	C-	B-
Q4-15	C	C	C+

Asset & Performance History

Date	NAV	1-Year Total Return
2018	107.89	9.69
2017	98.36	34.42
2016	73.17	1.94
2015	71.79	20.29
2014	59.68	11.02
2013	55.1	55.57

Total Assets: $454,026,151
Asset Allocation

Asset	%
Cash	0%
Stocks	100%
US Stocks	100%
Bonds	0%
US Bonds	0%
Other	0%

Services Offered:

Investment Strategy: The investment seeks to track the investment results (before fees and expenses) of the S&P SmallCap 600® Capped Health Care Index (the "underlying index"). The fund generally will invest at least 90% of its total assets in the securities of small-capitalization U.S. healthcare companies that comprise the underlying index. These companies are principally engaged in the business of providing healthcare-related products, facilities and services, including biotechnology, pharmaceuticals, medical technology and supplies. **Top Holdings:** Repligen Corp   Neogen Corp   LHC Group Inc   Arrowhead Pharmaceuticals Inc   HMS Holdings Corp

First Trust Dorsey Wright International Focus 5 ETF   C   HOLD

Ticker	Traded On	NAV	Total Assets ($)	Dividend Yield (TTM)	Turnover Ratio	Expense Ratio
IFV	NAS CM	19.06	$453,716,699	1.93	0	1.03

Ratings
Reward   D+
Risk   C+
Recent Upgrade/Downgrade

Fund Information
Fund Type   Exchange Traded Funds
Category   Global Equity Large Cap
Sub-Category   Foreign Large Blend
Prospectus Objective   Growth & Inc
Inception Date   Jul-14
Open to New Investments   Y

Prices
Price (as of 9/30/2019)   19.03
52-Week High   20.34
52-Week Low   16.87

Total Returns (%)

3-Month	6-Month	1-Year	3-Year	5-Year
-3.35	-0.99	-4.35	13.94	11.82

3-Year Standard Deviation   14.36
Effective Duration

Valuation
Premium/Discount (1-Year Average)   -0.08

Company Information
Provider   First Trust
Manager/Tenure   Jon C. Erickson (5), Daniel J. Lindquist (5), David G. McGarel (5), 3 others
Website   http://www.ftportfolios.com/
Address   First Trust 120 E. Liberty Drive, Suite 400 Wheaton IL 60187 United States
Phone Number   800-621-1675

PERFORMANCE

Ratings History

Date	Overall Rating	Risk Rating	Reward Rating
Q3-19	C	C+	D+
Q4-18	D+	D+	D+
Q4-17	B	B-	B
Q4-16	D+	C-	D
Q4-15	D	C-	D

Asset & Performance History

Date	NAV	1-Year Total Return
2018	17.46	-20.25
2017	22.25	32.26
2016	17.07	-3.76
2015	17.93	0.27
2014	18.16	
2013		

Total Assets: $453,716,699
Asset Allocation

Asset	%
Cash	0%
Stocks	100%
US Stocks	1%
Bonds	0%
US Bonds	0%
Other	0%

Services Offered:

Investment Strategy: The investment seeks investment results that correspond generally to the price and yield (before fees and expenses) of an index called the Dorsey Wright International Focus Five Index. The fund will normally invest at least 90% of its net assets (including investment borrowings) in the ETFs that comprise the index. The index is designed to provide targeted exposure to the five First Trust country/region-based ETFs that the index provider believes offer the greatest potential to outperform the other ETFs in the selection universe. It is non-diversified. **Top Holdings:** First Trust Brazil AlphaDEX® ETF   First Trust Switzerland AlphaDEX® ETF   First Trust BICK ETF   First Trust Dev Mkts Ex-US AlphaDEX® ETF   First Trust Germany AlphaDEX® ETF

WisdomTree Emerging Markets ex-State-Owned Enterprises Fund　　　　C　　HOLD

Ticker	Traded On	NAV	Total Assets ($)	Dividend Yield (TTM)	Turnover Ratio	Expense Ratio
XSOE	NYSE Arca	27.57	$452,219,896	2.13	24	0.32

Ratings
Reward　　　　　　　　　　　C-
Risk　　　　　　　　　　　　C
Recent Upgrade/Downgrade　　Up

Fund Information
Fund Type　　　　　　Exchange Traded Funds
Category　　　　　　Global Emerg Mkts Equity
Sub-Category　　　　Diversified Emerging Mkts
Prospectus Objective　　Div Emerg Mkts
Inception Date　　　　　　Dec-14
Open to New Investments　　Y

Prices
Price (as of 9/30/2019)　　27.65
52-Week High　　　　　　30.16
52-Week Low　　　　　　24.50

Total Returns (%)

3-Month	6-Month	1-Year	3-Year	5-Year
-3.64	-3.78	-0.06	23.77	

3-Year Standard Deviation　　15.16
Effective Duration

Valuation
Premium/Discount (1-Year Average)　　0.21

Company Information
Provider　　　　WisdomTree
Manager/Tenure　Richard A. Brown (4), Thomas J. Durante (4), Karen Q. Wong (4)
Website　　　　http://www.wisdomtree.com
Address　　　　WisdomTree 245 Park Avenue, 35th floor New York NY 10167 United States
Phone Number　866-909-9473

PERFORMANCE

Ratings History

Date	Overall Rating	Risk Rating	Reward Rating
Q3-19	C	C	C-
Q4-18	C-	C-	C-
Q4-17	C+	C	B-
Q4-16	D+	D+	D+
Q4-15	U		

Asset & Performance History

Date	NAV	1-Year Total Return
2018	25.55	-18.62
2017	31.85	46.5
2016	21.89	7.38
2015	20.67	-12.28
2014	24.38	
2013		

Total Assets: $452,219,896
Asset Allocation

Asset	%
Cash	0%
Stocks	100%
US Stocks	1%
Bonds	0%
US Bonds	0%
Other	0%

Services Offered:

Investment Strategy: The investment seeks to track the price and yield performance, before fees and expenses, of the WisdomTree Emerging Markets ex-State-Owned Enterprises Index (the "index"). Under normal circumstances, at least 80% of the fund's total assets will be invested in component securities of the index and investments that have economic characteristics that are substantially identical to the economic characteristics of such component securities. The index is a modified float-adjusted market cap weighted index that consists of common stocks in emerging markets, excluding common stocks of "state-owned enterprises." The fund is non-diversified. **Top Holdings:** Tencent Holdings Ltd　Alibaba Group Holding Ltd ADR　Samsung Electronics Co Ltd　Taiwan Semiconductor Manufacturing Co Ltd　Naspers Ltd Class N

iShares MSCI Thailand Capped ETF　　　　　　　　　　　　　C+　　HOLD

Ticker	Traded On	NAV	Total Assets ($)	Dividend Yield (TTM)	Turnover Ratio	Expense Ratio
THD	NYSE Arca	89.30	$450,963,462	2.29	10	0.59

Ratings
Reward　　　　　　　　　　　C+
Risk　　　　　　　　　　　　C+
Recent Upgrade/Downgrade　　Up

Fund Information
Fund Type　　　　　　Exchange Traded Funds
Category　　　　　　Thailand Equity
Sub-Category　　　　Miscellaneous Region
Prospectus Objective　　Pacific Stock
Inception Date　　　　　　Mar-08
Open to New Investments　　Y

Prices
Price (as of 9/30/2019)　　88.70
52-Week High　　　　　　96.22
52-Week Low　　　　　　81.75

Total Returns (%)

3-Month	6-Month	1-Year	3-Year	5-Year
-7.02	2.07	-3.43	32.05	21.19

3-Year Standard Deviation　　15.04
Effective Duration

Valuation
Premium/Discount (1-Year Average)　　0.00

Company Information
Provider　　　　iShares
Manager/Tenure　Diane Hsiung (11), Greg Savage (11), Jennifer Hsui (6), 3 others
Website　　　　http://www.ishares.com
Address　　　　iShares 400 Howard Street San Francisco CA 94105 United States
Phone Number　800-474-2737

PERFORMANCE

Ratings History

Date	Overall Rating	Risk Rating	Reward Rating
Q3-19	C+	C+	C+
Q4-18	C	C+	C
Q4-17	B	C	B
Q4-16	C-	C-	C-
Q4-15	D	D	D

Asset & Performance History

Date	NAV	1-Year Total Return
2018	82.24	-8.76
2017	92.43	30.96
2016	72.31	25.65
2015	59.14	-21.13
2014	77.24	18
2013	67.01	-14.98

Total Assets: $450,963,462
Asset Allocation

Asset	%
Cash	0%
Stocks	100%
US Stocks	0%
Bonds	0%
US Bonds	0%
Other	0%

Services Offered:

Investment Strategy: The investment seeks to track the investment results of the MSCI Thailand IMI 25/50 Index. The fund generally will invest at least 90% of its assets in the component securities of the index and in investments that have economic characteristics that are substantially identical to the component securities of the underlying index. The index consists of stocks traded primarily on the Stock Exchange of Thailand. A capping methodology is applied to issuer weights so that no single issuer of a component exceeds 25% of the index weight, and all issuers with weight above 5% do not cumulatively exceed 50% of the index weight. It is non-diversified. **Top Holdings:** Ptt PCL DR　CP All PCL DR　Siam Cement PCL Units Non-Voting Depository Receipt　Airports Of Thailand PLC DR　Advanced Info Service PCL DR

SPDR® FTSE International Government Inflation-Protected Bond ETF   C   HOLD

Ticker	Traded On	NAV	Total Assets ($)	Dividend Yield (TTM)	Turnover Ratio	Expense Ratio
WIP	NYSE Arca		$450,056,168	1.75	37	0.5

Ratings
Reward	C+
Risk	C-
Recent Upgrade/Downgrade	Up

Fund Information
Fund Type	Exchange Traded Funds
Category	Global Fixed Income
Sub-Category	World Bond
Prospectus Objective	Worldwide Bond
Inception Date	Mar-08
Open to New Investments	Y

Prices
Price (as of 9/30/2019)	54.71
52-Week High	55.72
52-Week Low	51.61

Total Returns (%)
3-Month	6-Month	1-Year	3-Year	5-Year
0.47	3.69	7.76	5.85	3.84

3-Year Standard Deviation	7.04
Effective Duration	12.33

Valuation
Premium/Discount (1-Year Average)	-0.02

Company Information
Provider	SPDR State Street Global Advisors
Manager/Tenure	Cynthia Moy (4), James Kramer (2), Orhan Imer (1)
Website	http://www.spdrs.com
Address	SPDR State Street Global Advisors State Street Financial Center, 1 Lincoln Street Boston MA 02111-2900 United States
Phone Number	617-786-3000

PERFORMANCE

Ratings History
Date	Overall Rating	Risk Rating	Reward Rating
Q3-19	C	C-	C+
Q4-18	C-	C-	D+
Q4-17	C	C+	C
Q4-16	D+	C-	D
Q4-15	D	D+	D

Asset & Performance History
Date	NAV	1-Year Total Return
2018	52.12	-5.9
2017	57.58	10.4
2016	52.58	4.76
2015	50.64	-10.43
2014	57.18	-0.36
2013	58.79	-4.82

Total Assets: $450,056,168
Asset Allocation
Asset	%
Cash	0%
Stocks	0%
US Stocks	0%
Bonds	99%
US Bonds	0%
Other	0%

Services Offered:

Investment Strategy: The investment seeks to provide investment results that, before fees and expenses, correspond generally to the price and yield performance of the FTSE International Inflation-Linked Securities Select Index. The fund generally invests substantially all, but at least 80%, of its total assets in the securities comprising the index or in securities that the Adviser determines have economic characteristics. The index is designed to measure the total return performance of inflation-linked bonds outside the United States with fixed-rate coupon payments that are linked to an inflation index. It is non-diversified. **Top Holdings:** Deutschland I/L Bond Bonds Regs 04/26 0.1 United Kingdom of Great Britain and Northern Ireland 0.12% United Kingdom of Great Britain and Northern Ireland 0.62% Brazil (Federative Republic) 6% Deutschland I/L Bond Bonds Regs 04/30 0.5

iShares MSCI Indonesia ETF   C-   HOLD

Ticker	Traded On	NAV	Total Assets ($)	Dividend Yield (TTM)	Turnover Ratio	Expense Ratio
EIDO	NYSE Arca	24.55	$448,104,981	1.87	7	0.59

Ratings
Reward	C
Risk	D+
Recent Upgrade/Downgrade	

Fund Information
Fund Type	Exchange Traded Funds
Category	Asia ex-Japan Equity
Sub-Category	Miscellaneous Region
Prospectus Objective	Pacific Stock
Inception Date	May-10
Open to New Investments	Y

Prices
Price (as of 9/30/2019)	24.47
52-Week High	27.69
52-Week Low	20.88

Total Returns (%)
3-Month	6-Month	1-Year	3-Year	5-Year
-6.08	-3.32	8.78	-1.43	-3.21

3-Year Standard Deviation	16.23
Effective Duration	

Valuation
Premium/Discount (1-Year Average)	-0.20

Company Information
Provider	iShares
Manager/Tenure	Diane Hsiung (9), Greg Savage (9), Jennifer Hsui (6), 3 others
Website	http://www.ishares.com
Address	iShares 400 Howard Street San Francisco CA 94105 United States
Phone Number	800-474-2737

PERFORMANCE

Ratings History
Date	Overall Rating	Risk Rating	Reward Rating
Q3-19	C-	D+	C
Q4-18	D+	D+	D+
Q4-17	C	C-	C
Q4-16	C-	D+	C
Q4-15	D	D	D

Asset & Performance History
Date	NAV	1-Year Total Return
2018	24.89	-10.57
2017	28.39	18.43
2016	24.29	16.82
2015	21.04	-22.02
2014	27.39	24.05
2013	22.39	-24.77

Total Assets: $448,104,981
Asset Allocation
Asset	%
Cash	0%
Stocks	100%
US Stocks	0%
Bonds	0%
US Bonds	0%
Other	0%

Services Offered:

Investment Strategy: The investment seeks to track the investment results of the MSCI Indonesia IMI 25/50 Index. The fund generally will invest at least 90% of its assets in the component securities of the underlying index and in investments that have economic characteristics that are substantially identical to the component securities of the underlying index. The index is sponsored by MSCI Inc., which is independent of the fund and BFA. The index Provider determines the composition and relative weightings of the securities in the index and publishes information regarding the market value of the index. The fund is non-diversified. **Top Holdings:** PT Bank Central Asia Tbk Bank Rakyat Indonesia (Persero) Tbk Class B PT Telekomunikasi Indonesia (Persero) Tbk Class B PT Astra International Tbk PT Bank Mandiri (Persero) Tbk

Aberdeen Standard Physical Precious Metals Basket Shares ETF   C   HOLD

Ticker	Traded On	NAV	Total Assets ($)	Dividend Yield (TTM)	Turnover Ratio	Expense Ratio
GLTR	NYSE Arca	73.14	$442,494,290	0		0.6

Ratings

Reward	C+
Risk	C-
Recent Upgrade/Downgrade	

Fund Information

Fund Type	Exchange Traded Funds
Category	Commodities Specified
Sub-Category	Commodities Precious Metals
Prospectus Objective	Prec Metals
Inception Date	Oct-10
Open to New Investments	Y

Prices

Price (as of 9/30/2019)	72.58
52-Week High	77.41
52-Week Low	58.39

Total Returns (%)

3-Month	6-Month	1-Year	3-Year	5-Year
8.28	14.49	25.21	9.18	15.27

3-Year Standard Deviation	11.67
Effective Duration	

Valuation

Premium/Discount (1-Year Average)	-0.19

Company Information

Provider	Aberdeen Standard Investments
Manager/Tenure	Management Team (8)
Website	http://www.aberdeenstandardetfs.us
Address	Aberdeen Standard Investments 405 Lexington Avenue New York NY 10174 United States
Phone Number	212-918-4954

PERFORMANCE

Ratings History

Date	Overall Rating	Risk Rating	Reward Rating
Q3-19	C	C-	C+
Q4-18	D+	D+	D
Q4-17	C-	C-	C-
Q4-16	D+	D+	C-
Q4-15	D-	D-	D-

Asset & Performance History

Date	NAV	1-Year Total Return
2018	63.03	-2.48
2017	64.63	11.21
2016	58.11	11.36
2015	52.18	-15.28
2014	61.6	-6.54
2013	65.91	-28.29

Total Assets: $442,494,290

Asset Allocation

Asset	%
Cash	0%
Stocks	0%
US Stocks	0%
Bonds	0%
US Bonds	0%
Other	100%

Services Offered:

Investment Strategy: The investment objective of the Trust is for the Shares to reflect the performance of the price of physical gold, silver, platinum and palladium in the proportions held by the Trust, less the expenses of the Trust's operations.
The Shares are designed for investors who want a cost-effective and convenient way to invest in a basket of Bullion with minimal credit risk. **Top Holdings:** Physical Gold Bullion Physical Silver Bullion Physical Palladium Bullion Physical Platinum Bullion

---

FlexShares Quality Dividend Defensive Index Fund   C   HOLD

Ticker	Traded On	NAV	Total Assets ($)	Dividend Yield (TTM)	Turnover Ratio	Expense Ratio
QDEF	NYSE Arca	45.68	$440,801,217	2.41	94	0.37

Ratings

Reward	C+
Risk	C-
Recent Upgrade/Downgrade	

Fund Information

Fund Type	Exchange Traded Funds
Category	US Equity Large Cap Value
Sub-Category	Large Value
Prospectus Objective	Income
Inception Date	Dec-12
Open to New Investments	Y

Prices

Price (as of 9/30/2019)	45.72
52-Week High	46.96
52-Week Low	37.31

Total Returns (%)

3-Month	6-Month	1-Year	3-Year	5-Year
1.68	2.71	4.30	37.97	63.50

3-Year Standard Deviation	11.33
Effective Duration	

Valuation

Premium/Discount (1-Year Average)	0.07

Company Information

Provider	Flexshares Trust
Manager/Tenure	Robert Anstine (5), Brendan Sullivan (3)
Website	http://www.flexshares.com
Address	50 South LaSalle Street Chicago, Illinois 60603 Chicago Illinois 60603 United States
Phone Number	855-353-9383

PERFORMANCE

Ratings History

Date	Overall Rating	Risk Rating	Reward Rating
Q3-19	C	C-	C+
Q4-18	C	C-	C
Q4-17	B-	B	B-
Q4-16	C+	C-	B
Q4-15	C	C	C

Asset & Performance History

Date	NAV	1-Year Total Return
2018	39.47	-7.96
2017	44.05	16.94
2016	38.75	15.39
2015	34.61	-0.19
2014	35.71	13.41
2013	32.32	32.29

Total Assets: $440,801,217

Asset Allocation

Asset	%
Cash	2%
Stocks	98%
US Stocks	98%
Bonds	0%
US Bonds	0%
Other	0%

Services Offered:

Investment Strategy: The investment seeks investment results that correspond generally to the price and yield performance, before fees and expenses, of the Northern Trust Quality Dividend Defensive IndexSM. The fund will invest at least 80% of its total assets (exclusive of collateral held from securities lending) in the securities of the underlying index. The underlying index is designed to provide exposure to a high-quality, income-oriented portfolio of U.S. equity securities, with an emphasis on long-term capital growth and a targeted overall volatility that is lower than that of the Northern Trust 1250 IndexSM. **Top Holdings:** Johnson & Johnson Microsoft Corp Cisco Systems Inc Wells Fargo & Co Apple Inc

SPDR® S&P Emerging Asia Pacific ETF

C-   HOLD

Ticker	Traded On	NAV	Total Assets ($)	Dividend Yield (TTM)	Turnover Ratio	Expense Ratio
GMF	NYSE Arca		$440,251,401	2.19	5	0.49

Ratings
Reward	C-
Risk	C-
Recent Upgrade/Downgrade	

Fund Information
Fund Type	Exchange Traded Funds
Category	Asia ex-Japan Equity
Sub-Category	Pacific/Asia ex-Japan Stk
Prospectus Objective	Pacific Stock
Inception Date	Mar-07
Open to New Investments	Y

Prices
Price (as of 9/30/2019)	93.45
52-Week High	101.85
52-Week Low	84.71

Total Returns (%)
3-Month	6-Month	1-Year	3-Year	5-Year
-3.88	-5.22	-1.51	21.95	25.68

3-Year Standard Deviation	13.96
Effective Duration	

Valuation
Premium/Discount (1-Year Average)	0.03

Company Information
Provider	SPDR State Street Global Advisors
Manager/Tenure	Michael J. Feehily (8), Karl A. Schneider (4), Teddy Wong (2)
Website	http://www.spdrs.com
Address	SPDR State Street Global Advisors State Street Financial Center, 1 Lincoln Street Boston MA 02111-2900 United States
Phone Number	617-786-3000

PERFORMANCE

Ratings History
Date	Overall Rating	Risk Rating	Reward Rating
Q3-19	C-	C-	C-
Q4-18	C-	C-	C-
Q4-17	B	C+	A-
Q4-16	C	C-	C
Q4-15	C	C+	C

Asset & Performance History
Date	NAV	1-Year Total Return
2018	88.13	-13.66
2017	104.32	40.14
2016	75.79	4.1
2015	74.29	-7.85
2014	83.61	10.62
2013	76.78	2.79

Total Assets: $440,251,401
Asset Allocation
Asset	%
Cash	0%
Stocks	100%
US Stocks	1%
Bonds	0%
US Bonds	0%
Other	0%

Services Offered:

Investment Strategy: The investment seeks to provide investment results that, before fees and expenses, correspond generally to the total return performance of the S&P Asia Pacific Emerging BMI Index based upon the emerging markets of the Asia Pacific region. The fund generally invests substantially all, but at least 80%, of its total assets in the securities comprising the index and in depositary receipts (including ADRs or GDRs) based on securities comprising the index. The index is a market capitalization weighted index designed to define and measure the investable universe of publicly traded companies domiciled in emerging Asian Pacific markets. The fund is non-diversified. **Top Holdings:** Tencent Holdings Ltd Alibaba Group Holding Ltd ADR Taiwan Semiconductor Manufacturing Co Ltd ADR China Construction Bank Corp Class H Reliance Industries Ltd ADR

---

iShares New York Muni Bond ETF

C   HOLD

Ticker	Traded On	NAV	Total Assets ($)	Dividend Yield (TTM)	Turnover Ratio	Expense Ratio
NYF	NYSE Arca	57.09	$439,575,640	2.3	19	0.25

Ratings
Reward	C+
Risk	C-
Recent Upgrade/Downgrade	

Fund Information
Fund Type	Exchange Traded Funds
Category	US Muni Fixed Inc
Sub-Category	Muni New York Intermediate
Prospectus Objective	Muni Bond - Single State
Inception Date	Oct-07
Open to New Investments	Y

Prices
Price (as of 9/30/2019)	57.22
52-Week High	57.88
52-Week Low	53.49

Total Returns (%)
3-Month	6-Month	1-Year	3-Year	5-Year
1.31	3.53	7.95	7.88	16.46

3-Year Standard Deviation	3.31
Effective Duration	

Valuation
Premium/Discount (1-Year Average)	0.23

Company Information
Provider	iShares
Manager/Tenure	Scott Radell (9), James Mauro (8)
Website	http://www.ishares.com
Address	iShares 400 Howard Street San Francisco CA 94105 United States
Phone Number	800-474-2737

PERFORMANCE

Ratings History
Date	Overall Rating	Risk Rating	Reward Rating
Q3-19	C	C-	C+
Q4-18	C-	C-	C-
Q4-17	B-	B+	C
Q4-16	C	D+	C
Q4-15	C	D+	C

Asset & Performance History
Date	NAV	1-Year Total Return
2018	54.55	0.56
2017	55.61	4.37
2016	54.62	0.12
2015	55.85	3.23
2014	55.54	8.62
2013	52.61	-2.62

Total Assets: $439,575,640
Asset Allocation
Asset	%
Cash	3%
Stocks	0%
US Stocks	0%
Bonds	97%
US Bonds	97%
Other	0%

Services Offered:

Investment Strategy: The investment seeks to track the investment results of the S&P New York AMT-Free Municipal Bond IndexTM. The fund generally will invest at least 90% of its assets in the component securities of the underlying index and may invest up to 10% of its assets in certain futures, options and swap contracts, cash and cash equivalents. The index measures the performance of the investment-grade segment of the New York municipal bond market. The fund is non-diversified. **Top Holdings:** SUFFOLK CNTY N Y WTR AUTH WTRWKS REV 4% SALES TAX ASSET RECEIVABLE CORP N Y 5% NEW YORK ST TWY AUTH GEN REV JR INDBT OBLIGS 5.25% NEW YORK N Y CITY MUN WTR FIN AUTH WTR & SWR SYS REV 5% NEW YORK ST 4.25%

Invesco Solar ETF   B-   BUY

Ticker	Traded On	NAV	Total Assets ($)	Dividend Yield (TTM)	Turnover Ratio	Expense Ratio
TAN	NYSE Arca	29.46	$438,590,825	0.44	54	0.7

Ratings
Reward	B
Risk	C
Recent Upgrade/Downgrade	Up

Fund Information
Fund Type	Exchange Traded Funds
Category	Technology Sector Equity
Sub-Category	Miscellaneous Sector
Prospectus Objective	Natl Res
Inception Date	Apr-08
Open to New Investments	Y

Prices
Price (as of 9/30/2019)	29.37
52-Week High	32.30
52-Week Low	17.70

Total Returns (%)
3-Month	6-Month	1-Year	3-Year	5-Year
3.11	24.61	42.71	57.30	-17.32

3-Year Standard Deviation	25.43
Effective Duration	

Valuation
Premium/Discount (1-Year Average)	-0.08

Company Information
Provider	Invesco
Manager/Tenure	Peter Hubbard (1), Michael Jeanette (1), Tony Seisser (1)
Website	http://www.invesco.com/us
Address	Invesco 11 Greenway Plaza, Ste. 2500 Houston TX 77046 United States
Phone Number	800-659-1005

PERFORMANCE

Ratings History

Date	Overall Rating	Risk Rating	Reward Rating
Q3-19	B-	C	B
Q4-18	D+	D	D+
Q4-17	C-	D+	C-
Q4-16	D	D-	D
Q4-15	C	C-	C

Asset & Performance History

Date	NAV	1-Year Total Return
2018	18.61	-25.76
2017	25.07	53.1
2016	16.55	-42.7
2015	30.61	-9.37
2014	34.3	-0.71
2013	35.2	129.94

Total Assets: $438,590,825
Asset Allocation

Asset	%
Cash	0%
Stocks	100%
US Stocks	46%
Bonds	0%
US Bonds	0%
Other	0%

Services Offered:

Investment Strategy: The investment seeks to track the investment results (before fees and expenses) of the MAC Global Solar Energy Index (the "underlying index"). The fund will invest at least 90% of its total assets in the securities (including ADRs and GDRs) that comprise the underlying index. The underlying index is designed to provide exposure to companies listed on exchanges in developed markets that derive a significant amount of their revenues from the following business segments of the solar industry: solar power equipment producers including ancillary or enabling products; etc. The fund is non-diversified. **Top Holdings:** SolarEdge Technologies Inc Enphase Energy Inc First Solar Inc Xinyi Solar Holdings Ltd SunPower Corp

---

Vanguard ESG International Stock ETF   D+   SELL

Ticker	Traded On	NAV	Total Assets ($)	Dividend Yield (TTM)	Turnover Ratio	Expense Ratio
VSGX	BATS	49.11	$437,079,000	2.04		0.15

Ratings
Reward	D+
Risk	C-
Recent Upgrade/Downgrade	

Fund Information
Fund Type	Exchange Traded Funds
Category	Global Equity Large Cap
Sub-Category	Foreign Large Blend
Prospectus Objective	Foreign Stock
Inception Date	Sep-18
Open to New Investments	Y

Prices
Price (as of 9/30/2019)	49.28
52-Week High	50.77
52-Week Low	43.28

Total Returns (%)
3-Month	6-Month	1-Year	3-Year	5-Year
-1.36	2.38	-0.69		

3-Year Standard Deviation	
Effective Duration	

Valuation
Premium/Discount (1-Year Average)	0.34

Company Information
Provider	Vanguard
Manager/Tenure	Christine D. Franquin (1), Scott E. Geiger (1)
Website	http://www.vanguard.com
Address	Vanguard 100 Vanguard Boulevard Malvern PA 19355 United States
Phone Number	877-662-7447

PERFORMANCE

Ratings History

Date	Overall Rating	Risk Rating	Reward Rating
Q3-19	D+	C-	D+
Q4-18	U		
Q4-17			
Q4-16			
Q4-15			

Asset & Performance History

Date	NAV	1-Year Total Return
2018	44.26	
2017		
2016		
2015		
2014		
2013		

Total Assets: $437,079,000
Asset Allocation

Asset	%
Cash	3%
Stocks	97%
US Stocks	1%
Bonds	0%
US Bonds	0%
Other	0%

Services Offered:

Investment Strategy: The investment seeks to track the performance of the FTSE Global All Cap ex US Choice Index. The fund invests by sampling the index, meaning that it holds a broadly diversified collection of securities that, in the aggregate, approximates the full index in terms of key characteristics. The index, which is market-capitalization weighted, is composed of large-, mid-, and small-cap stocks of companies in developed and emerging markets, excluding the United States, and is screened for certain environmental, social, and corporate governance (ESG) criteria by the index sponsor, which is independent of Vanguard. **Top Holdings:** Nestle SA Taiwan Semiconductor Manufacturing Co Ltd Samsung Electronics Co Ltd Alibaba Group Holding Ltd ADR Toyota Motor Corp

Fidelity® MSCI Industrials Index ETF

C   **HOLD**

Ticker	Traded On	NAV	Total Assets ($)	Dividend Yield (TTM)	Turnover Ratio	Expense Ratio
FIDU	NYSE Arca	39.86	$436,507,065	1.78	5	0.08

Ratings
Reward   C+
Risk   C-
Recent Upgrade/Downgrade

Fund Information
Fund Type	Exchange Traded Funds
Category	Industrials Sector Equity
Sub-Category	Industrials
Prospectus Objective	Unaligned
Inception Date	Oct-13
Open to New Investments	Y

Prices
Price (as of 9/30/2019)	39.86
52-Week High	40.69
52-Week Low	30.66

Total Returns (%)
3-Month	6-Month	1-Year	3-Year	5-Year
0.45	3.15	0.52	39.18	62.92

3-Year Standard Deviation	16.77
Effective Duration	

Valuation
Premium/Discount (1-Year Average)	-0.02

Company Information
Provider	Fidelity Investments
Manager/Tenure	Jennifer Hsui (5), Greg Savage (5), Alan Mason (3), 2 others
Website	http://www.institutional.fidelity.com
Address	Fidelity Investments 82 Devonshire Street Boston MA 2109 United States
Phone Number	617-563-7000

PERFORMANCE

Ratings History
Date	Overall Rating	Risk Rating	Reward Rating
Q3-19	C	C-	C+
Q4-18	C	C	C+
Q4-17	B	B-	A-
Q4-16	C	C	C+
Q4-15	C-	C+	C

Asset & Performance History
Date	NAV	1-Year Total Return
2018	32.74	-13.81
2017	38.67	22.1
2016	32.23	20.66
2015	27.18	-3.63
2014	28.76	6.51
2013	27.43	

Total Assets: $436,507,065

Asset Allocation
Asset	%
Cash	0%
Stocks	100%
US Stocks	99%
Bonds	0%
US Bonds	0%
Other	0%

Services Offered:

Investment Strategy: The investment seeks to provide investment returns that correspond, before fees and expenses, generally to the performance of the MSCI USA IMI Industrials Index. The fund invests at least 80% of assets in securities included in the fund's underlying index. The fund's underlying index is the MSCI USA IMI Industrials Index, which represents the performance of the industrial sector in the U.S. equity market. It may or may not hold all of the securities in the MSCI USA IMI Industrials Index. **Top Holdings:** Boeing Co   Honeywell International Inc   Union Pacific Corp   United Technologies Corp   Lockheed Martin Corp

---

Fidelity® MSCI Communication Services Index ETF

B-   **BUY**

Ticker	Traded On	NAV	Total Assets ($)	Dividend Yield (TTM)	Turnover Ratio	Expense Ratio
FCOM	NYSE Arca	33.06	$434,732,600	1.04	82	0.08

Ratings
Reward   B
Risk   C
Recent Upgrade/Downgrade   Up

Fund Information
Fund Type	Exchange Traded Funds
Category	Communications Sector Equity
Sub-Category	Communications
Prospectus Objective	Comm
Inception Date	Oct-13
Open to New Investments	Y

Prices
Price (as of 9/30/2019)	33.07
52-Week High	35.04
52-Week Low	26.75

Total Returns (%)
3-Month	6-Month	1-Year	3-Year	5-Year
-0.85	2.67	6.28	22.65	49.48

3-Year Standard Deviation	13.93
Effective Duration	

Valuation
Premium/Discount (1-Year Average)	0.05

Company Information
Provider	Fidelity Investments
Manager/Tenure	Jennifer Hsui (5), Greg Savage (5), Alan Mason (3), 2 others
Website	http://www.institutional.fidelity.com
Address	Fidelity Investments 82 Devonshire Street Boston MA 2109 United States
Phone Number	617-563-7000

PERFORMANCE

Ratings History
Date	Overall Rating	Risk Rating	Reward Rating
Q3-19	B-	C	B
Q4-18	C+	C-	B
Q4-17	B-	B	C
Q4-16	B-	C-	B
Q4-15	C-	C	B-

Asset & Performance History
Date	NAV	1-Year Total Return
2018	28.43	-5.44
2017	30.88	-0.53
2016	32.08	23.17
2015	26.68	3.26
2014	26.6	6.39
2013	25.69	

Total Assets: $434,732,600

Asset Allocation
Asset	%
Cash	0%
Stocks	100%
US Stocks	99%
Bonds	0%
US Bonds	0%
Other	0%

Services Offered:

Investment Strategy: The investment seeks to provide investment returns that correspond, before fees and expenses, generally to the performance of the MSCI USA IMI Communication Services 25/50 Index. The fund invests at least 80% of assets in securities included in the fund's underlying index. The fund's underlying index is the MSCI USA IMI Communication Services 25/50 Index, which represents the performance of the communication services sector in the U.S. equity market. It may or may not hold all of the securities in the MSCI USA IMI Communication Services 25/50 Index. The fund is non-diversified. **Top Holdings:** Facebook Inc A   Alphabet Inc Class C   Alphabet Inc A   The Walt Disney Co   Comcast Corp Class A

SPDR® Russell 1000 Momentum Focus ETF   C-   HOLD

Ticker	Traded On	NAV	Total Assets ($)	Dividend Yield (TTM)	Turnover Ratio	Expense Ratio
ONEO	NYSE Arca		$431,660,651	1.61	40	0.2

Ratings
Reward	C
Risk	D
Recent Upgrade/Downgrade	Down

Fund Information
Fund Type	Exchange Traded Funds
Category	US Equity Mid Cap
Sub-Category	Mid-Cap Blend
Prospectus Objective	Growth & Inc
Inception Date	Dec-15
Open to New Investments	Y

Prices
Price (as of 9/30/2019)	73.55
52-Week High	76.15
52-Week Low	59.44

Total Returns (%)
3-Month	6-Month	1-Year	3-Year	5-Year
-0.09	2.35	-2.04	30.35	

3-Year Standard Deviation	13.22
Effective Duration	

Valuation
Premium/Discount (1-Year Average)	-0.02

Company Information
Provider	SPDR State Street Global Advisors
Manager/Tenure	Michael J. Feehily (3), Karl A. Schneider (3), Emiliano Rabinovich (2)
Website	http://www.spdrs.com
Address	SPDR State Street Global Advisors State Street Financial Center, 1 Lincoln Street Boston MA 02111-2900 United States
Phone Number	617-786-3000

PERFORMANCE

| 12/31/17 | 4/10/18 | 7/21/18 | 11/3/18 | 2/14/19 | 6/16/19 | 9/29/19 |

Ratings History
Date	Overall Rating	Risk Rating	Reward Rating
Q3-19	C-	D	C
Q4-18	C-	D+	C-
Q4-17	C	B+	C
Q4-16	D	D+	D+
Q4-15			

Asset & Performance History
Date	NAV	1-Year Total Return
2018	62.92	-11.97
2017	72.58	20.75
2016	64.84	12.47
2015	58.75	
2014		
2013		

Total Assets: $431,660,651

Asset Allocation
Asset	%
Cash	0%
Stocks	100%
US Stocks	99%
Bonds	0%
US Bonds	0%
Other	0%

Services Offered:

Investment Strategy: The investment seeks to provide investment results that, before fees and expenses, correspond generally to the total return performance of the Russell 1000 Momentum Focused Factor Index. Under normal market conditions, the fund generally invests substantially all, but at least 80%, of its total assets in the securities comprising the index. The index is designed to reflect the performance of a segment of large-capitalization U.S. equity securities demonstrating a combination of core factors (high value, high quality, and low size characteristics), with a focus factor comprising high momentum characteristics. The fund is non-diversified. **Top Holdings:** Lam Research Corp Cummins Inc Dollar General Corp Medical Properties Trust Inc Southwest Airlines Co

---

Direxion Daily Gold Miners Index Bear 3X Shares   D-   SELL

Ticker	Traded On	NAV	Total Assets ($)	Dividend Yield (TTM)	Turnover Ratio	Expense Ratio
DUST	NYSE Arca	8.28	$431,506,251	1.81	0	1.05

Ratings
Reward	E
Risk	D-
Recent Upgrade/Downgrade	Down

Fund Information
Fund Type	Exchange Traded Funds
Category	Trading Tools
Sub-Category	Trading--Inverse Equity
Prospectus Objective	Prec Metals
Inception Date	Dec-10
Open to New Investments	Y

Prices
Price (as of 9/30/2019)	8.23
52-Week High	39.82
52-Week Low	5.69

Total Returns (%)
3-Month	6-Month	1-Year	3-Year	5-Year
-34.22	-56.53	-78.55	-75.19	-99.40

3-Year Standard Deviation	71.17
Effective Duration	

Valuation
Premium/Discount (1-Year Average)	-0.12

Company Information
Provider	Direxion Funds
Manager/Tenure	Paul Brigandi (8), Tony Ng (4)
Website	http://www.direxionfunds.com
Address	Direxion Funds 1301 Avenue Of The Americas (6th Avenue) New York NY 10019 United States
Phone Number	646-572-3390

PERFORMANCE

| 12/30/17 | 4/9/18 | 7/21/18 | 11/3/18 | 2/14/19 | 6/17/19 | 9/30/19 |

Ratings History
Date	Overall Rating	Risk Rating	Reward Rating
Q3-19	D-	D-	E
Q4-18	D+	D	D
Q4-17	E+	D-	E+
Q4-16	D-	D-	E+
Q4-15	C	D	C-

Asset & Performance History
Date	NAV	1-Year Total Return
2018	22.95	-2.92
2017	23.71	-50.92
2016	48.31	-94.12
2015	822	-33.49
2014	1,236.00	-43.98
2013	2,206.50	181.35

Total Assets: $431,506,251

Asset Allocation
Asset	%
Cash	129%
Stocks	-15%
US Stocks	-2%
Bonds	0%
US Bonds	0%
Other	-15%

Services Offered:

Investment Strategy: The investment seeks daily investment results before fees and expenses of 300% of the inverse of the daily performance of the NYSE Arca Gold Miners Index. The fund invests in swap agreements, futures contracts, short positions or other financial instruments that, in combination, provide inverse or short leveraged exposure to the index equal to at least 80% of the fund's net assets. The index is a modified market capitalization weighted index comprised of publicly traded companies that operate globally in both developed and emerging markets, and are involved primarily in mining for gold and, to a lesser extent, in mining for silver. It is non-diversified. **Top Holdings:** Ve Vectors Gld Miners Ve Vectors Gld Miners Ve Vectors Gld Miners Ve Vectors Gld Miners Ve Vectors Gld Miners

iShares Aaa - A Rated Corporate Bond ETF   C   HOLD

Ticker	Traded On	NAV	Total Assets ($)	Dividend Yield (TTM)	Turnover Ratio	Expense Ratio
QLTA	NYSE Arca	54.68	$429,272,598	3.01	15	0.15

Ratings
Reward   C+
Risk   C-
Recent Upgrade/Downgrade

Fund Information
Fund Type   Exchange Traded Funds
Category   US Fixed Income
Sub-Category   Corporate Bond
Prospectus Objective   Corp Bond - High Quality
Inception Date   Feb-12
Open to New Investments   Y

Prices
Price (as of 9/30/2019)   54.81
52-Week High   55.45
52-Week Low   49.32

Total Returns (%)

3-Month	6-Month	1-Year	3-Year	5-Year
2.83	7.34	12.18	11.64	22.50

3-Year Standard Deviation   4.08
Effective Duration

Valuation
Premium/Discount (1-Year Average)   0.21

Company Information
Provider   iShares
Manager/Tenure   James Mauro (7), Scott Radell (7)
Website   http://www.ishares.com
Address   iShares 400 Howard Street San
                            Francisco CA 94105 United States
Phone Number   800-474-2737

PERFORMANCE

Ratings History

Date	Overall Rating	Risk Rating	Reward Rating
Q3-19	C	C-	C+
Q4-18	D+	C-	D+
Q4-17	B	A	C
Q4-16	C	D+	C
Q4-15	C	C-	C

Asset & Performance History

Date	NAV	1-Year Total Return
2018	50	-2.29
2017	52.77	5.23
2016	51.4	4.24
2015	50.58	0.74
2014	51.7	6.5
2013	49.69	-2.19

Total Assets: $429,272,598
Asset Allocation

Asset	%
Cash	0%
Stocks	0%
US Stocks	0%
Bonds	97%
US Bonds	81%
Other	0%

Services Offered:

Investment Strategy: The investment seeks to track the investment results of the Bloomberg Barclays U.S. Corporate Aaa - A Capped Index. The fund generally will invest at least 90% of its assets in the component securities of the underlying index and may invest up to 10% of its assets in certain futures, options and swap contracts, cash and cash equivalents. The underlying index is a subset of the Bloomberg Barclays U.S. Corporate Index, which measures the performance of the Aaa - A rated range of the fixed-rate, U.S. dollar-denominated taxable, corporate bond market. **Top Holdings:** Apple Inc. 2.4% Wells Fargo & Company 3.5% Bank of America Corporation 4.27% Morgan Stanley 2.75% JPMorgan Chase & Co. 4.63%

Vanguard S&P Small-Cap 600 Value Index Fund ETF Shares   C-   HOLD

Ticker	Traded On	NAV	Total Assets ($)	Dividend Yield (TTM)	Turnover Ratio	Expense Ratio
VIOV	NYSE Arca	129.71	$429,212,273	1.62	34	0.2

Ratings
Reward   C-
Risk   D+
Recent Upgrade/Downgrade

Fund Information
Fund Type   Exchange Traded Funds
Category   US Equity Small Cap
Sub-Category   Small Value
Prospectus Objective   Growth & Inc
Inception Date   Sep-10
Open to New Investments   Y

Prices
Price (as of 9/30/2019)   129.65
52-Week High   141.95
52-Week Low   107.15

Total Returns (%)

3-Month	6-Month	1-Year	3-Year	5-Year
1.21	0.98	-7.13	26.20	51.12

3-Year Standard Deviation   18.97
Effective Duration

Valuation
Premium/Discount (1-Year Average)   0.01

Company Information
Provider   Vanguard
Manager/Tenure   William A. Coleman (5), Donald M.
                            Butler (3)
Website   http://www.vanguard.com
Address   Vanguard 100 Vanguard Boulevard
                            Malvern PA 19355 United States
Phone Number   877-662-7447

PERFORMANCE

Ratings History

Date	Overall Rating	Risk Rating	Reward Rating
Q3-19	C-	D+	C-
Q4-18	C-	C-	C-
Q4-17	B+	B	A-
Q4-16	C	C-	C
Q4-15	C	D+	C

Asset & Performance History

Date	NAV	1-Year Total Return
2018	113.17	-13.16
2017	132.29	11.76
2016	120.45	30.07
2015	93.11	-6.83
2014	101.28	7.3
2013	95.59	39.67

Total Assets: $429,212,273
Asset Allocation

Asset	%
Cash	1%
Stocks	99%
US Stocks	98%
Bonds	0%
US Bonds	0%
Other	0%

Services Offered:

Investment Strategy: The investment seeks to track the performance of a benchmark index that measures the investment return of small-capitalization value stocks in the United States. The fund employs an indexing investment approach designed to track the performance of the S&P SmallCap 600® Value Index, which represents the value companies, as determined by the index sponsor, of the S&P SmallCap 600 Index. The Advisor attempts to replicate the target index by investing all, or substantially all, of its assets in the stocks that make up the index, holding each stock in approximately the same proportion as its weighting in the index. **Top Holdings:** Darling Ingredients Inc South Jersey Industries Inc SkyWest Inc Lithia Motors Inc Class A ABM Industries Inc

iShares MSCI Emerging Markets Asia ETF   D+   SELL

Ticker	Traded On	NAV	Total Assets ($)	Dividend Yield (TTM)	Turnover Ratio	Expense Ratio
EEMA	NAS CM	64.03	$428,968,413	2.02	33	0.5

Ratings
Reward	D+
Risk	C-
Recent Upgrade/Downgrade	Down

Fund Information
Fund Type	Exchange Traded Funds
Category	Asia ex-Japan Equity
Sub-Category	Pacific/Asia ex-Japan Stk
Prospectus Objective	Pacific Stock
Inception Date	Feb-12
Open to New Investments	Y

Prices
Price (as of 9/30/2019)	63.74
52-Week High	70.17
52-Week Low	58.61

Total Returns (%)
3-Month	6-Month	1-Year	3-Year	5-Year
-4.30	-5.56	-4.10	18.71	20.62

3-Year Standard Deviation	14.66
Effective Duration	

Valuation
Premium/Discount (1-Year Average)	-0.08

Company Information
Provider	iShares
Manager/Tenure	Diane Hsiung (7), Greg Savage (7), Jennifer Hsui (6), 3 others
Website	http://www.ishares.com
Address	iShares 400 Howard Street San Francisco CA 94105 United States
Phone Number	800-474-2737

PERFORMANCE

Ratings History
Date	Overall Rating	Risk Rating	Reward Rating
Q3-19	D+	C-	D+
Q4-18	C-	C-	C-
Q4-17	B	C+	A
Q4-16	C-	C-	C-
Q4-15	C-	C-	C-

Asset & Performance History
Date	NAV	1-Year Total Return
2018	60.97	-15.53
2017	73.7	41.93
2016	52.87	5.59
2015	50.95	-9.82
2014	57.81	4.2
2013	56.24	1.97

Total Assets: $428,968,413
Asset Allocation
Asset	%
Cash	0%
Stocks	100%
US Stocks	0%
Bonds	0%
US Bonds	0%
Other	0%

Services Offered:

Investment Strategy: The investment seeks to track the investment results of the MSCI EM Asia Custom Capped Index. The fund generally will invest at least 90% of its assets in the component securities of the underlying index and in investments that have economic characteristics that are substantially identical to the component securities of the underlying index. The underlying index is designed to measure equity market performance in the emerging market countries of Asia. It may include large- or mid-capitalization companies. **Top Holdings:** Alibaba Group Holding Ltd ADR   Tencent Holdings Ltd   Samsung Electronics Co Ltd   Taiwan Semiconductor Manufacturing Co Ltd   China Construction Bank Corp Class H

SPDR® Russell 1000® Yield Focus ETF   C   HOLD

Ticker	Traded On	NAV	Total Assets ($)	Dividend Yield (TTM)	Turnover Ratio	Expense Ratio
ONEY	NYSE Arca		$427,417,823	3.29	42	0.2

Ratings
Reward	C
Risk	D+
Recent Upgrade/Downgrade	

Fund Information
Fund Type	Exchange Traded Funds
Category	US Equity Mid Cap
Sub-Category	Mid-Cap Value
Prospectus Objective	Growth & Inc
Inception Date	Dec-15
Open to New Investments	Y

Prices
Price (as of 9/30/2019)	70.70
52-Week High	72.88
52-Week Low	59.15

Total Returns (%)
3-Month	6-Month	1-Year	3-Year	5-Year
-0.17	1.97	0.86	30.20	

3-Year Standard Deviation	13.69
Effective Duration	

Valuation
Premium/Discount (1-Year Average)	0.06

Company Information
Provider	SPDR State Street Global Advisors
Manager/Tenure	Michael J. Feehily (3), Karl A. Schneider (3), John Law (1)
Website	http://www.spdrs.com
Address	SPDR State Street Global Advisors State Street Financial Center, 1 Lincoln Street Boston MA 02111-2900 United States
Phone Number	617-786-3000

PERFORMANCE

Ratings History
Date	Overall Rating	Risk Rating	Reward Rating
Q3-19	C	D+	C
Q4-18	C-	D+	C-
Q4-17	C	B+	C-
Q4-16	D	D	D+
Q4-15			

Asset & Performance History
Date	NAV	1-Year Total Return
2018	62.09	-7.95
2017	69.79	15.28
2016	67.23	23.1
2015	58.18	
2014		
2013		

Total Assets: $427,417,823
Asset Allocation
Asset	%
Cash	0%
Stocks	100%
US Stocks	99%
Bonds	0%
US Bonds	0%
Other	0%

Services Offered:

Investment Strategy: The investment seeks to provide investment results that, before fees and expenses, correspond generally to the total return performance of the Russell 1000 Yield Focused Factor Index. Under normal market conditions, the fund generally invests substantially all, but at least 80%, of its total assets in the securities comprising the index. The index is designed to reflect the performance of a segment of large-capitalization U.S. equity securities demonstrating a combination of core factors (high value, high quality, and low size characteristics), with a focus factor comprising high yield characteristics (the "Factor Characteristics"). It is non-diversified. **Top Holdings:** HP Inc   Valero Energy Corp   Phillips 66   Lam Research Corp   Occidental Petroleum Corp

WisdomTree Japan SmallCap Dividend Fund
D+   **SELL**

Ticker	Traded On	NAV	Total Assets ($)	Dividend Yield (TTM)	Turnover Ratio	Expense Ratio
DFJ	NYSE Arca	68.17	$426,065,893	2.1	42	0.58

Ratings
Reward   D+
Risk   C-
Recent Upgrade/Downgrade   Down

Fund Information
Fund Type	Exchange Traded Funds
Category	Japan Equity
Sub-Category	Japan Stock
Prospectus Objective	Pacific Stock
Inception Date	Jun-06
Open to New Investments	Y

Prices
Price (as of 9/30/2019)	68.77
52-Week High	77.64
52-Week Low	60.90

Total Returns (%)

3-Month	6-Month	1-Year	3-Year	5-Year
1.03	-0.11	-9.54	17.88	44.74

3-Year Standard Deviation	11.34
Effective Duration	

Valuation
Premium/Discount (1-Year Average)	-0.21

Company Information
Provider	WisdomTree
Manager/Tenure	Richard A. Brown (11), Thomas J. Durante (11), Karen Q. Wong (11)
Website	http://www.wisdomtree.com
Address	WisdomTree 245 Park Avenue, 35th floor New York NY 10167 United States
Phone Number	866-909-9473

Ratings History

Date	Overall Rating	Risk Rating	Reward Rating
Q3-19	D+	C-	D+
Q4-18	C-	C	D+
Q4-17	A-	B	A
Q4-16	C	C-	C+
Q4-15	C+	C-	B

Asset & Performance History

Date	NAV	1-Year Total Return
2018	65.09	-17.61
2017	80.4	31.6
2016	62.14	11.04
2015	56.99	17.68
2014	49.03	-1.53
2013	50.57	20.08

Total Assets: $426,065,893
Asset Allocation

Asset	%
Cash	0%
Stocks	100%
US Stocks	0%
Bonds	0%
US Bonds	0%
Other	0%

Services Offered:

Investment Strategy: The investment seeks to track the price and yield performance, before fees and expenses, of the WisdomTree Japan SmallCap Dividend Index. Under normal circumstances, at least 95% of the fund's total assets (exclusive of collateral held from securities lending) will be invested in component securities of the index and investments that have economic characteristics that are substantially identical to the economic characteristics of such component securities. The index is comprised of dividend-paying small capitalization companies in Japan. The fund is non-diversified. **Top Holdings:** HASEKO Corp Matsui Securities Co Ltd Aozora Bank Ltd Mitsubishi Gas Chemical Co Inc Sumitomo Rubber Industries Ltd

Direxion Daily MSCI Brazil Bull 3X Shares
D   **SELL**

Ticker	Traded On	NAV	Total Assets ($)	Dividend Yield (TTM)	Turnover Ratio	Expense Ratio
BRZU	NYSE Arca	27.44	$424,091,896	1.26	133	1.36

Ratings
Reward   D+
Risk   D
Recent Upgrade/Downgrade

Fund Information
Fund Type	Exchange Traded Funds
Category	Trading Tools
Sub-Category	Trading--Leveraged Equity
Prospectus Objective	Foreign Stock
Inception Date	Apr-13
Open to New Investments	Y

Prices
Price (as of 9/30/2019)	27.42
52-Week High	40.87
52-Week Low	18.55

Total Returns (%)

3-Month	6-Month	1-Year	3-Year	5-Year
-17.46	-7.12	49.53	-17.64	-81.25

3-Year Standard Deviation	89.89
Effective Duration	

Valuation
Premium/Discount (1-Year Average)	-0.05

Company Information
Provider	Direxion Funds
Manager/Tenure	Paul Brigandi (6), Tony Ng (4)
Website	http://www.direxionfunds.com
Address	Direxion Funds 1301 Avenue Of The Americas (6th Avenue) New York NY 10019 United States
Phone Number	646-572-3390

Ratings History

Date	Overall Rating	Risk Rating	Reward Rating
Q3-19	D	D	D+
Q4-18	D+	D	C-
Q4-17	C-	D	C
Q4-16	D	D	D+
Q4-15	D-	D-	D-

Asset & Performance History

Date	NAV	1-Year Total Return
2018	25.03	-37.21
2017	40.36	31.19
2016	31.02	168.34
2015	11.56	-86.92
2014	88.4	-56.43
2013	202.9	

Total Assets: $424,091,896
Asset Allocation

Asset	%
Cash	36%
Stocks	64%
US Stocks	0%
Bonds	0%
US Bonds	0%
Other	0%

Services Offered:

Investment Strategy: The investment seeks daily investment results, before fees and expenses, of 300% of the daily performance of the MSCI Brazil 25/50 Index. The fund invests at least 80% of its net assets in financial instruments, such as swap agreements, and securities of the index, ETFs that track the index and other financial instruments that provide daily leveraged exposure to the index or ETFs that track the index. The index is designed to measure the performance of the large- and mid-capitalization segments of the Brazilian equity market, covering approximately 85% of the free float-adjusted market capitalization of Brazilian issuers. It is non-diversified. **Top Holdings:** iShares MSCI Brazil Capped ETF Msci Brazil Index Swap Msci Brazil Index Swap Msci Brazil Index Swap Msci Brazil Index Swap

Fidelity® MSCI Energy Index ETF

D+   **SELL**

Ticker	Traded On	NAV	Total Assets ($)	Dividend Yield (TTM)	Turnover Ratio	Expense Ratio
FENY	NYSE Arca	15.74	$420,376,128	3.58	6	0.08

Ratings
Reward	D+
Risk	D
Recent Upgrade/Downgrade	

Fund Information
Fund Type	Exchange Traded Funds
Category	Energy Sector Equity
Sub-Category	Equity Energy
Prospectus Objective	Natl Res
Inception Date	Oct-13
Open to New Investments	Y

Prices
Price (as of 9/30/2019)	15.74
52-Week High	21.82
52-Week Low	14.63

Total Returns (%)
3-Month	6-Month	1-Year	3-Year	5-Year
-7.81	-12.58	-24.44	-13.25	-29.83

3-Year Standard Deviation	21.63
Effective Duration	

Valuation
Premium/Discount (1-Year Average)	0.00

Company Information
Provider	Fidelity Investments
Manager/Tenure	Jennifer Hsui (5), Greg Savage (5), Alan Mason (3), 2 others
Website	http://www.institutional.fidelity.com
Address	Fidelity Investments 82 Devonshire Street Boston MA 2109 United States
Phone Number	617-563-7000

PERFORMANCE

Ratings History
Date	Overall Rating	Risk Rating	Reward Rating
Q3-19	D+	D	D+
Q4-18	C	C-	C
Q4-17	C-	C	D+
Q4-16	C-	D	C
Q4-15	C-	C	C

Asset & Performance History
Date	NAV	1-Year Total Return
2018	15.61	-19.95
2017	20.03	-2.43
2016	21.18	27.02
2015	17.1	-23
2014	22.81	-9.79
2013	25.71	

Total Assets: $420,376,128
Asset Allocation
Asset	%
Cash	0%
Stocks	100%
US Stocks	99%
Bonds	0%
US Bonds	0%
Other	0%

Services Offered:

Investment Strategy: The investment seeks to provide investment returns that correspond, generally to the performance of the MSCI USA IMI Energy Index. The fund invests at least 80% of assets in securities included in the fund's underlying index. The fund's underlying index is the MSCI USA IMI Energy Index, which represents the performance of the energy sector in the U.S. equity market. It may or may not hold all of the securities in the MSCI USA IMI Energy Index. The fund is non-diversified. **Top Holdings:** Exxon Mobil Corp Chevron Corp ConocoPhillips Schlumberger Ltd Phillips 66

---

iShares Edge MSCI Multifactor Emerging Markets ETF

D+   **SELL**

Ticker	Traded On	NAV	Total Assets ($)	Dividend Yield (TTM)	Turnover Ratio	Expense Ratio
EMGF	BATS	40.99	$418,124,340	2.88	39	0.45

Ratings
Reward	D+
Risk	C-
Recent Upgrade/Downgrade	Down

Fund Information
Fund Type	Exchange Traded Funds
Category	Global Emerg Mkts Equity
Sub-Category	Diversified Emerging Mkts
Prospectus Objective	Div Emerg Mkts
Inception Date	Dec-15
Open to New Investments	Y

Prices
Price (as of 9/30/2019)	40.88
52-Week High	43.96
52-Week Low	37.92

Total Returns (%)
3-Month	6-Month	1-Year	3-Year	5-Year
-3.05	-3.80	-2.71	15.92	

3-Year Standard Deviation	13.87
Effective Duration	

Valuation
Premium/Discount (1-Year Average)	0.07

Company Information
Provider	iShares
Manager/Tenure	Diane Hsiung (3), Jennifer Hsui (3), Greg Savage (3), 3 others
Website	http://www.ishares.com
Address	iShares 400 Howard Street San Francisco CA 94105 United States
Phone Number	800-474-2737

PERFORMANCE

Ratings History
Date	Overall Rating	Risk Rating	Reward Rating
Q3-19	D+	C-	D+
Q4-18	D+	D+	D+
Q4-17	C-	B+	C
Q4-16	D-	D+	D
Q4-15			

Asset & Performance History
Date	NAV	1-Year Total Return
2018	39.03	-18.64
2017	49.21	40.42
2016	35.78	9.21
2015	33.44	
2014		
2013		

Total Assets: $418,124,340
Asset Allocation
Asset	%
Cash	1%
Stocks	99%
US Stocks	1%
Bonds	0%
US Bonds	0%
Other	0%

Services Offered:

Investment Strategy: The investment seeks to track the investment results of the MSCI Emerging Markets Diversified Multiple-Factor Index. The underlying index is designed to select equity securities from the MSCI Emerging Markets Index that have high exposure to four investment style factors: value, quality, momentum and low size, while maintaining a level of risk similar to that of the parent index. The fund generally will invest at least 90% of its assets in the component securities of the underlying index and in investments that have economic characteristics that are substantially identical to the component securities of the underlying index. **Top Holdings:** China Mobile Ltd Tencent Holdings Ltd SK Hynix Inc Itausa Investimentos ITAU SA Participating Preferred Alibaba Group Holding Ltd ADR

SPDR® S&P Metals and Mining ETF

C   HOLD

Ticker	Traded On	NAV	Total Assets ($)	Dividend Yield (TTM)	Turnover Ratio	Expense Ratio
XME	NYSE Arca		$414,956,395	2.66	28	0.35

Ratings
Reward	C
Risk	D
Recent Upgrade/Downgrade	Up

Fund Information
Fund Type	Exchange Traded Funds
Category	Natural Resources
Sub-Category	Natural Resources
Prospectus Objective	Natl Res
Inception Date	Jun-06
Open to New Investments	Y

Prices
Price (as of 9/30/2019)	25.45
52-Week High	34.49
52-Week Low	24.40

Total Returns (%)
3-Month	6-Month	1-Year	3-Year	5-Year
-8.62	-13.58	-23.34	2.16	-23.23

3-Year Standard Deviation	27.66
Effective Duration	

Valuation
Premium/Discount (1-Year Average)	-0.05

Company Information
Provider	SPDR State Street Global Advisors
Manager/Tenure	Michael J. Feehily (7), Karl A. Schneider (4), Raymond V. Donofrio (2)
Website	http://www.spdrs.com
Address	SPDR State Street Global Advisors State Street Financial Center, 1 Lincoln Street Boston MA 02111-2900 United States
Phone Number	617-786-3000

PERFORMANCE

Ratings History
Date	Overall Rating	Risk Rating	Reward Rating
Q3-19	C	D	C
Q4-18	C	D+	C+
Q4-17	C	D+	C+
Q4-16	C	D+	C
Q4-15	C	C-	C

Asset & Performance History
Date	NAV	1-Year Total Return
2018	26.22	-26.16
2017	36.12	20.22
2016	30.44	110.82
2015	14.95	-50.51
2014	30.86	-25.26
2013	42.07	-5.4

Total Assets: $414,956,395
Asset Allocation
Asset	%
Cash	0%
Stocks	100%
US Stocks	98%
Bonds	0%
US Bonds	0%
Other	0%

Services Offered:

Investment Strategy: The investment seeks to provide investment results that, before fees and expenses, correspond generally to the total return performance of an index derived from the metals and mining segment of a U.S. total market composite index. In seeking to track the performance of the S&P Metals & Mining Select Industry Index (the "index"), the fund employs a sampling strategy. It generally invests substantially all, but at least 80%, of its total assets in the securities comprising the index. The index represents the metals and mining segment of the S&P Total Market Index ("S&P TMI"). The fund is non-diversified. **Top Holdings:** Coeur Mining Inc Royal Gold Inc Newmont Goldcorp Corp Reliance Steel & Aluminum Co AK Steel Holding Corp

Vanguard Russell 2000 Value Index Fund ETF Shares

C-   HOLD

Ticker	Traded On	NAV	Total Assets ($)	Dividend Yield (TTM)	Turnover Ratio	Expense Ratio
VTWV	NAS CM	104.02	$414,007,803	1.77	30	0.2

Ratings
Reward	C-
Risk	C-
Recent Upgrade/Downgrade	Up

Fund Information
Fund Type	Exchange Traded Funds
Category	US Equity Small Cap
Sub-Category	Small Value
Prospectus Objective	Small Company
Inception Date	Sep-10
Open to New Investments	Y

Prices
Price (as of 9/30/2019)	104.61
52-Week High	114.43
52-Week Low	88.80

Total Returns (%)
3-Month	6-Month	1-Year	3-Year	5-Year
-0.55	-0.53	-7.10	20.78	40.75

3-Year Standard Deviation	17.66
Effective Duration	

Valuation
Premium/Discount (1-Year Average)	0.06

Company Information
Provider	Vanguard
Manager/Tenure	Walter Nejman (4), Michael A. Johnson (3)
Website	http://www.vanguard.com
Address	Vanguard 100 Vanguard Boulevard Malvern PA 19355 United States
Phone Number	877-662-7447

PERFORMANCE

Ratings History
Date	Overall Rating	Risk Rating	Reward Rating
Q3-19	C-	C-	C-
Q4-18	C-	D+	C-
Q4-17	B	B	B+
Q4-16	D+	D+	D+
Q4-15	C	D+	C

Asset & Performance History
Date	NAV	1-Year Total Return
2018	92.92	-13.35
2017	109.12	8.25
2016	102.97	30.55
2015	79.67	-7.58
2014	87.97	4.07
2013	85.98	34.26

Total Assets: $414,007,803
Asset Allocation
Asset	%
Cash	1%
Stocks	99%
US Stocks	98%
Bonds	0%
US Bonds	0%
Other	0%

Services Offered:

Investment Strategy: The investment seeks to track the performance of a benchmark index that measures the investment return of small-capitalization value stocks in the United States. The fund employs an indexing investment approach designed to track the performance of the Russell 2000® Value Index. The index is designed to measure the performance of small-capitalization value stocks in the United States. The advisor attempts to replicate the target index by investing all, or substantially all, of its assets in the stocks that make up the index, holding each stock in approximately the same proportion as its weighting in the index. **Top Holdings:** Portland General Electric Co Radian Group Inc ONE Gas Inc Black Hills Corp ALLETE Inc

SPDR® S&P Emerging Markets Dividend ETF   C   HOLD

Ticker	Traded On	NAV	Total Assets ($)	Dividend Yield (TTM)	Turnover Ratio	Expense Ratio
EDIV	NYSE Arca		$410,833,365	4.17	55	0.49

Ratings
Reward   C
Risk   C-
Recent Upgrade/Downgrade

Fund Information
Fund Type   Exchange Traded Funds
Category   Global Emerg Mkts Equity
Sub-Category   Diversified Emerging Mkts
Prospectus Objective   Div Emerg Mkts
Inception Date   Feb-11
Open to New Investments   Y

Prices
Price (as of 9/30/2019)   29.84
52-Week High   33.14
52-Week Low   27.94

Total Returns (%)

3-Month	6-Month	1-Year	3-Year	5-Year
-6.92	-3.47	1.27	21.98	0.00

3-Year Standard Deviation   13.91
Effective Duration

Valuation
Premium/Discount (1-Year Average)   -0.14

Company Information
Provider   SPDR State Street Global Advisors
Manager/Tenure   Michael J. Feehily (8), Karl A.
                 Schneider (4), Olga Winner (0)
Website   http://www.spdrs.com
Address   SPDR State Street Global Advisors
                 State Street Financial Center, 1
                 Lincoln Street Boston MA 02111-2900
                 United States
Phone Number   617-786-3000

PERFORMANCE

Ratings History

Date	Overall Rating	Risk Rating	Reward Rating
Q3-19	C	C-	C
Q4-18	C-	C-	C-
Q4-17	C	C	C
Q4-16	D	D	D
Q4-15	D	D	D

Asset & Performance History

Date	NAV	1-Year Total Return
2018	29.96	-6.46
2017	33.07	27.96
2016	26.68	16.9
2015	23.98	-27.03
2014	34.29	-8.21
2013	38.99	-11.87

Total Assets: $410,833,365
Asset Allocation

Asset	%
Cash	0%
Stocks	100%
US Stocks	0%
Bonds	0%
US Bonds	0%
Other	0%

Services Offered:

Investment Strategy: The investment seeks investment results that, before fees and expenses, correspond generally to the total return performance of the S&P Emerging Markets Dividend Opportunities Index. The fund generally invests substantially all, but at least 80%, of its total assets in the securities comprising the index and in depositary receipts based on securities comprising the index. The index is designed to measure the performance of 100 high-yielding emerging market common stocks. The fund is non-diversified. **Top Holdings:** Taiwan Semiconductor Manufacturing Co Ltd ADR   Ptt PCL DR   China Mobile Ltd   China Resources Land Ltd   PTT Exploration & Production PCL DR

DeltaShares S&P 500 Managed Risk ETF   C   HOLD

Ticker	Traded On	NAV	Total Assets ($)	Dividend Yield (TTM)	Turnover Ratio	Expense Ratio
DMRL	NYSE Arca	56.92	$409,825,321	1.74	430	0.35

Ratings
Reward   C
Risk   D+
Recent Upgrade/Downgrade   Up

Fund Information
Fund Type   Exchange Traded Funds
Category   US Equity Large Cap Blend
Sub-Category   Large Blend
Prospectus Objective   Growth
Inception Date   Jul-17
Open to New Investments   Y

Prices
Price (as of 9/30/2019)   56.80
52-Week High   58.50
52-Week Low   49.51

Total Returns (%)

3-Month	6-Month	1-Year	3-Year	5-Year
-0.36	3.14	0.09		

3-Year Standard Deviation
Effective Duration

Valuation
Premium/Discount (1-Year Average)   -0.03

Company Information
Provider   DeltaShares
Manager/Tenure   Blake Graves (2), Charles Lowery (2),
                 Louis Ng (2)
Website   http://www.deltashares.com
Address   DeltaShares United States
Phone Number

PERFORMANCE

Ratings History

Date	Overall Rating	Risk Rating	Reward Rating
Q3-19	C	D+	C
Q4-18	D+	D+	D+
Q4-17	U		
Q4-16			
Q4-15			

Asset & Performance History

Date	NAV	1-Year Total Return
2018	51.23	-4.16
2017	54.1	
2016		
2015		
2014		
2013		

Total Assets: $409,825,321
Asset Allocation

Asset	%
Cash	1%
Stocks	69%
US Stocks	68%
Bonds	30%
US Bonds	30%
Other	0%

Services Offered:

Investment Strategy: The investment seeks to track the investment results, before fees and expenses, of the S&P 500 Managed Risk 2.0 Index. Under normal market conditions, the fund invests a substantial portion, but at least 80%, of its assets, exclusive of collateral held from securities lending, in securities comprising the S&P 500 Managed Risk 2.0 Index. The underlying index seeks to achieve these objectives by allocating weightings among the S&P 500 Index, the S&P U.S. Treasury Bond Current 5-Year Index and the S&P U.S. Treasury Bill 0-3 Month Index. The fund is non-diversified. **Top Holdings:** Microsoft Corp   Apple Inc   Amazon.com Inc   Facebook Inc A   Berkshire Hathaway Inc B

ProShares UltraPro Dow30   C+   HOLD

Ticker	Traded On	NAV	Total Assets ($)	Dividend Yield (TTM)	Turnover Ratio	Expense Ratio
UDOW	NYSE Arca	105.01	$409,540,682	0.64	2	0.95

Ratings

Reward	B-
Risk	C-
Recent Upgrade/Downgrade	Up

Fund Information

Fund Type	Exchange Traded Funds
Category	Trading Tools
Sub-Category	Trading--Leveraged Equity
Prospectus Objective	Growth
Inception Date	Feb-10
Open to New Investments	Y

Prices

Price (as of 9/30/2019)	105.16
52-Week High	113.73
52-Week Low	59.11

Total Returns (%)

3-Month	6-Month	1-Year	3-Year	5-Year
0.85	5.20	-5.11	185.08	261.02

3-Year Standard Deviation	38.05
Effective Duration	

Valuation

Premium/Discount (1-Year Average)	-0.05

Company Information

Provider	ProShares
Manager/Tenure	Michael Neches (6), Devin Sullivan (1)
Website	http://www.proshares.com
Address	ProShares 7501 Wisconsin Avenue, Suite 1000 Bethesda MD 20814 United States
Phone Number	866-776-5125

PERFORMANCE

Ratings History

Date	Overall Rating	Risk Rating	Reward Rating
Q3-19	C+	C-	B-
Q4-18	C	C	C
Q4-17	B	C	A
Q4-16	C	C	C+
Q4-15	C+	C+	C

Asset & Performance History

Date	NAV	1-Year Total Return
2018	71.37	-23.51
2017	93.9	98.87
2016	47.29	47.02
2015	32.28	-8.35
2014	35.3	25.7
2013	28.22	106.69

Total Assets: $409,540,682

Asset Allocation

Asset	%
Cash	-200%
Stocks	300%
US Stocks	300%
Bonds	0%
US Bonds	0%
Other	0%

Services Offered:

Investment Strategy: The investment seeks daily investment results, before fees and expenses, that correspond to three times (3x) the daily performance of the Dow Jones Industrial Average®. The fund invests in financial instruments that ProShare Advisors believes, in combination, should produce daily returns consistent with the fund's investment objective. The index is a price-weighted index and includes 30 large-cap, "blue-chip" U.S. stocks, excluding utility and transportation companies. The fund is non-diversified. **Top Holdings:** Dj Industrial Average Swap Societe Generale Dj Industrial Average Swap Goldman Sachs International Dj Industrial Average Index Swap Bnp Paribas Dj Industrial Average Swap Bank Of America, Na Dj Industrial Average Swap Credit Suisse International

---

PIMCO Enhanced Low Duration Active Exchange-Traded Fund   C   HOLD

Ticker	Traded On	NAV	Total Assets ($)	Dividend Yield (TTM)	Turnover Ratio	Expense Ratio
LDUR	NYSE Arca	100.33	$409,360,293	3.06	1,613	1.02

Ratings

Reward	C
Risk	C-
Recent Upgrade/Downgrade	

Fund Information

Fund Type	Exchange Traded Funds
Category	US Fixed Income
Sub-Category	Short-Term Bond
Prospectus Objective	Income
Inception Date	Jan-14
Open to New Investments	Y

Prices

Price (as of 9/30/2019)	100.35
52-Week High	100.53
52-Week Low	98.55

Total Returns (%)

3-Month	6-Month	1-Year	3-Year	5-Year
0.90	2.12	3.86	7.25	12.49

3-Year Standard Deviation	0.69
Effective Duration	1.33

Valuation

Premium/Discount (1-Year Average)	0.05

Company Information

Provider	PIMCO
Manager/Tenure	Jerome M. Schneider (5), David Braun (2), Sonali Pier (0)
Website	http://www.pimco.com
Address	PIMCO 840 Newport Center Drive, Suite 100 Newport Beach CA 92660 United States
Phone Number	866-746-2602

PERFORMANCE

Ratings History

Date	Overall Rating	Risk Rating	Reward Rating
Q3-19	C	C-	C
Q4-18	C	C-	C
Q4-17	B	A+	C
Q4-16	C-	D+	C
Q4-15	D+	D+	C-

Asset & Performance History

Date	NAV	1-Year Total Return
2018	98.65	1.33
2017	100.32	2.14
2016	100.27	2.83
2015	99.33	2.04
2014	100.2	
2013		

Total Assets: $409,360,293

Asset Allocation

Asset	%
Cash	-28%
Stocks	0%
US Stocks	0%
Bonds	120%
US Bonds	82%
Other	7%

Services Offered:

Investment Strategy: The investment seeks maximum total return, consistent with preservation of capital and prudent investment management. The fund seeks to achieve its investment objective by investing at least 80% of its net assets in a diversified portfolio of Fixed Income Instruments of varying maturities, which may be represented by forwards or derivatives such as options, futures contracts, or swap agreements. It invests primarily in investment grade debt securities, but may invest up to 15% of its total assets in high yield securities, as rated by Moody's, S&P or Fitch, or, if unrated, as determined by PIMCO. **Top Holdings:** Fin Fut Us 2yr Cbt 12/31/19 Cdx Ig32 5y Ice Fin Fut Us 5yr Cbt 12/31/19 Irs Usd 3.00000 06/19/19-7y Cme Fin Fut Us 10yr Cbt 12/19/19

Global X FinTech ETF   C+   HOLD

Ticker	Traded On	NAV	Total Assets ($)	Dividend Yield (TTM)	Turnover Ratio	Expense Ratio
FINX	NAS CM	28.80	$404,581,077	0.01	21	0.68

Ratings

Reward	B-
Risk	C
Recent Upgrade/Downgrade	

Fund Information

Fund Type	Exchange Traded Funds
Category	Technology Sector Equity
Sub-Category	Technology
Prospectus Objective	Technology
Inception Date	Sep-16
Open to New Investments	Y

Prices

Price (as of 9/30/2019)	28.77
52-Week High	31.23
52-Week Low	20.71

Total Returns (%)

3-Month	6-Month	1-Year	3-Year	5-Year
-2.40	2.74	0.85	88.44	

3-Year Standard Deviation	18.18
Effective Duration	

Valuation

Premium/Discount (1-Year Average)	-0.01

Company Information

Provider	Global X Funds
Manager/Tenure	Chang Kim (3), Nam To (1), Wayne Xie (0), 1 other
Website	http://www.globalxfunds.com
Address	Global X Funds 600 Lexington Avenue, 20th Floor New York NY 10022 United States
Phone Number	888-493-8631

PERFORMANCE

Ratings History

Date	Overall Rating	Risk Rating	Reward Rating
Q3-19	C+	C	B-
Q4-18	C+	C	B-
Q4-17	D	B	C
Q4-16	U		
Q4-15			

Asset & Performance History

Date	NAV	1-Year Total Return
2018	22.16	1.38
2017	21.86	50.56
2016	14.52	
2015		
2014		
2013		

Total Assets: $404,581,077

Asset Allocation

Asset	%
Cash	0%
Stocks	100%
US Stocks	61%
Bonds	0%
US Bonds	0%
Other	0%

Services Offered:

Investment Strategy: The investment seeks to provide investment results that correspond generally to the price and yield performance, before fees and expenses, of the Indxx Global Fintech Thematic Index. The fund invests at least 80% of its total assets in the securities of the underlying index. The underlying index is designed to provide exposure to exchange-listed companies in developed markets that provide financial technology products and services, including companies involved in mobile payments, peer-to-peer (P2P) and marketplace lending, financial analytics software and alternative currencies, as defined by the index provider. The fund is non-diversified. **Top Holdings:** Fiserv Inc Fidelity National Information Services Inc Intuit Inc PagSeguro Digital Ltd Class A Adyen NV

iShares MSCI Malaysia ETF   D+   SELL

Ticker	Traded On	NAV	Total Assets ($)	Dividend Yield (TTM)	Turnover Ratio	Expense Ratio
EWM	NYSE Arca	27.85	$401,078,502	3.68	63	0.47

Ratings

Reward	D
Risk	C-
Recent Upgrade/Downgrade	Down

Fund Information

Fund Type	Exchange Traded Funds
Category	Asia ex-Japan Equity
Sub-Category	Miscellaneous Region
Prospectus Objective	Pacific Stock
Inception Date	Mar-96
Open to New Investments	Y

Prices

Price (as of 9/30/2019)	27.85
52-Week High	32.50
52-Week Low	27.64

Total Returns (%)

3-Month	6-Month	1-Year	3-Year	5-Year
-6.94	-4.60	-10.67	1.18	-24.35

3-Year Standard Deviation	11.83
Effective Duration	

Valuation

Premium/Discount (1-Year Average)	-0.06

Company Information

Provider	iShares
Manager/Tenure	Diane Hsiung (11), Greg Savage (11), Jennifer Hsui (6), 3 others
Website	http://www.ishares.com
Address	iShares 400 Howard Street San Francisco CA 94105 United States
Phone Number	800-474-2737

PERFORMANCE

Ratings History

Date	Overall Rating	Risk Rating	Reward Rating
Q3-19	D+	C-	D
Q4-18	C-	D+	C-
Q4-17	C-	D+	C
Q4-16	D	D	D
Q4-15	D	D	D

Asset & Performance History

Date	NAV	1-Year Total Return
2018	29.92	-6.27
2017	33.14	24.51
2016	28.17	-3.95
2015	31.04	-20.35
2014	54	-10.64
2013	62.76	7.08

Total Assets: $401,078,502

Asset Allocation

Asset	%
Cash	1%
Stocks	99%
US Stocks	0%
Bonds	0%
US Bonds	0%
Other	0%

Services Offered: CashInvestment Plan

Investment Strategy: The investment seeks to track the investment results of the MSCI Malaysia Index. The fund will at all times invest at least 90% of its assets in the securities of its underlying index and in depositary receipts representing securities in its underlying index. The underlying index consists of stocks traded primarily on the Kuala Lumpur Stock Exchange. It may include large- or mid-capitalization companies. The fund is non-diversified. **Top Holdings:** Public Bank Bhd Tenaga Nasional Bhd Malayan Banking Bhd CIMB Group Holdings Bhd Petronas Chemicals Group Bhd

Invesco S&P 500® Equal Weight Utilities ETF

B-   **BUY**

Ticker	Traded On	NAV	Total Assets ($)	Dividend Yield (TTM)	Turnover Ratio	Expense Ratio
RYU	NYSE Arca	106.66	$399,956,465	2.45		0.4

Ratings

Reward	B
Risk	C
Recent Upgrade/Downgrade	

Fund Information

Fund Type	Exchange Traded Funds
Category	Utilities Sector Equity
Sub-Category	Utilities
Prospectus Objective	Utility
Inception Date	Nov-06
Open to New Investments	Y

Prices

Price (as of 9/30/2019)	106.64
52-Week High	107.12
52-Week Low	86.44

Total Returns (%)

3-Month	6-Month	1-Year	3-Year	5-Year
8.99	12.44	25.20	44.00	74.37

3-Year Standard Deviation	9.29
Effective Duration	

Valuation

Premium/Discount (1-Year Average)	0.01

Company Information

Provider	Invesco
Manager/Tenure	Peter Hubbard (1), Michael Jeanette (1), Tony Seisser (1)
Website	http://www.invesco.com/us
Address	Invesco 11 Greenway Plaza, Ste. 2500 Houston TX 77046 United States
Phone Number	800-659-1005

PERFORMANCE

Ratings History

Date	Overall Rating	Risk Rating	Reward Rating
Q3-19	B-	C	B
Q4-18	B-	C	B
Q4-17	B	B	B
Q4-16	C	C	C+
Q4-15	B-	C	B

Asset & Performance History

Date	NAV	1-Year Total Return
2018	88.83	6.95
2017	85.81	9.01
2016	80.8	14.67
2015	72.37	-4.02
2014	78.58	28.03
2013	63.32	13.33

Total Assets: $399,956,465

Asset Allocation

Asset	%
Cash	0%
Stocks	100%
US Stocks	100%
Bonds	0%
US Bonds	0%
Other	0%

Services Offered:

Investment Strategy: The investment seeks to track the investment results (before fees and expenses) of the S&P 500® Equal Weight Utilities Plus Index. The fund generally will invest at least 90% of its total assets in the securities that comprise the underlying index. The underlying index is composed of all of the components of the S&P 500® Utilities Plus Index, an index that contains the common stocks of all companies included in the S&P 500® Index that are classified as members of the utilities sector, as defined according to the Global Industry Classification Standard ("GICS"). It is non-diversified. **Top Holdings:** Edison International WEC Energy Group Inc Entergy Corp American Water Works Co Inc CMS Energy Corp

---

SPDR® S&P Global Infrastructure ETF

C   **HOLD**

Ticker	Traded On	NAV	Total Assets ($)	Dividend Yield (TTM)	Turnover Ratio	Expense Ratio
GII	NYSE Arca		$399,855,363	3.14	21	0.4

Ratings

Reward	C+
Risk	C-
Recent Upgrade/Downgrade	Down

Fund Information

Fund Type	Exchange Traded Funds
Category	Infrastructure Sector Equity
Sub-Category	Infrastructure
Prospectus Objective	Utility
Inception Date	Jan-07
Open to New Investments	Y

Prices

Price (as of 9/30/2019)	53.40
52-Week High	53.92
52-Week Low	43.84

Total Returns (%)

3-Month	6-Month	1-Year	3-Year	5-Year
0.92	5.37	13.61	23.38	28.20

3-Year Standard Deviation	10.24
Effective Duration	

Valuation

Premium/Discount (1-Year Average)	0.08

Company Information

Provider	SPDR State Street Global Advisors
Manager/Tenure	Michael J. Feehily (8), Karl A. Schneider (4), Michael Finocchi (2)
Website	http://www.spdrs.com
Address	SPDR State Street Global Advisors State Street Financial Center, 1 Lincoln Street Boston MA 02111-2900 United States
Phone Number	617-786-3000

PERFORMANCE

Ratings History

Date	Overall Rating	Risk Rating	Reward Rating
Q3-19	C	C-	C+
Q4-18	C-	C-	C-
Q4-17	C+	C+	C+
Q4-16	C-	C-	C
Q4-15	C	C-	C

Asset & Performance History

Date	NAV	1-Year Total Return
2018	45.13	-10.05
2017	51.8	19.34
2016	44.89	11.35
2015	41.46	-11.79
2014	48.6	12.25
2013	44.63	17.35

Total Assets: $399,855,363

Asset Allocation

Asset	%
Cash	0%
Stocks	100%
US Stocks	41%
Bonds	0%
US Bonds	0%
Other	0%

Services Offered:

Investment Strategy: The investment seeks investment results that, before fees and expenses, correspond generally to the total return performance of the S&P Global Infrastructure Index. The fund generally invests substantially all, but at least 80%, of its total assets in the securities comprising the index and in depositary receipts based on securities comprising the index. The index is comprised of 75 of the largest publicly listed infrastructure companies that meet specific investability requirements. The fund is non-diversified. **Top Holdings:** Transurban Group NextEra Energy Inc Aena SME SA Atlantia SpA Enbridge Inc Common Stock

FlexShares Morningstar Emerging Markets Factor Tilt Index Fund

D+ SELL

Ticker	Traded On	NAV	Total Assets ($)	Dividend Yield (TTM)	Turnover Ratio	Expense Ratio
TLTE	NYSE Arca	48.66	$399,038,472	2.99	49	0.59

Ratings
Reward	D
Risk	C-
Recent Upgrade/Downgrade	Down

Fund Information
Fund Type	Exchange Traded Funds
Category	Global Emerg Mkts Equity
Sub-Category	Diversified Emerging Mkts
Prospectus Objective	Div Emerg Mkts
Inception Date	Sep-12
Open to New Investments	Y

Prices
Price (as of 9/30/2019)	48.23
52-Week High	55.13
52-Week Low	46.27

Total Returns (%)
3-Month	6-Month	1-Year	3-Year	5-Year
-6.09	-7.00	-4.43	11.53	7.34

3-Year Standard Deviation	13.48
Effective Duration	

Valuation
Premium/Discount (1-Year Average)	-0.40

Company Information
Provider	Flexshares Trust
Manager/Tenure	Robert Anstine (5), Brendan Sullivan (3)
Website	http://www.flexshares.com
Address	50 South LaSalle Street Chicago, Illinois 60603 Chicago Illinois 60603 United States
Phone Number	855-353-9383

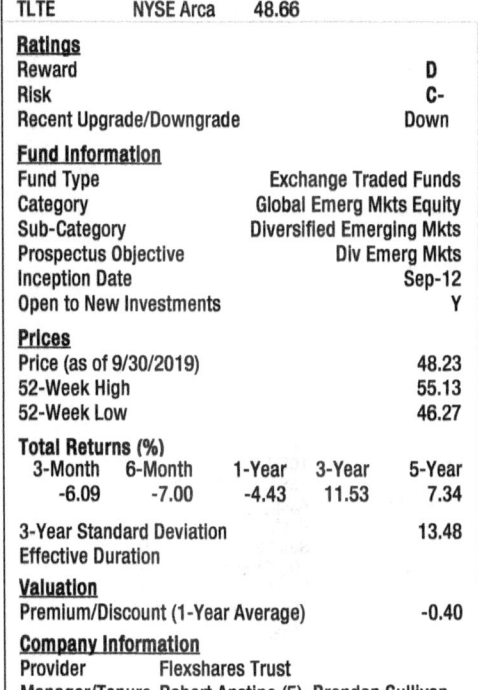

PERFORMANCE

Ratings History
Date	Overall Rating	Risk Rating	Reward Rating
Q3-19	D+	C-	D
Q4-18	C-	C-	C-
Q4-17	B-	C	B
Q4-16	D+	D+	D+
Q4-15	D+	D+	D+

Asset & Performance History
Date	NAV	1-Year Total Return
2018	48.38	-16.12
2017	59.28	32.36
2016	45.79	12.03
2015	41.83	-12.96
2014	49.02	-2.12
2013	51.11	-2.54

Total Assets: $399,038,472

Asset Allocation
Asset	%
Cash	0%
Stocks	100%
US Stocks	0%
Bonds	0%
US Bonds	0%
Other	0%

Services Offered:

Investment Strategy: The investment seeks investment results that correspond generally to the price and yield performance, before fees and expenses, of the Morningstar® Emerging Markets Factor Tilt IndexSM. The fund will invest at least 80% of its total assets (exclusive of collateral held from securities lending) in the securities of the underlying index and in ADRs and GDRs based on the securities in the underlying index. The underlying index reflects the performance of a selection of equity securities designed to provide broad exposure to the global emerging equities markets, with increased exposure (or a "tilt") to small-capitalization stocks and value stocks.
Top Holdings: Samsung Electronics Co Ltd   Tencent Holdings Ltd   Alibaba Group Holding Ltd ADR   China Construction Bank Corp Class H   Taiwan Semiconductor Manufacturing Co Ltd

iShares Convertible Bond ETF

C HOLD

Ticker	Traded On	NAV	Total Assets ($)	Dividend Yield (TTM)	Turnover Ratio	Expense Ratio
ICVT	BATS	58.10	$397,992,224	3.45	29	0.2

Ratings
Reward	C
Risk	C-
Recent Upgrade/Downgrade	

Fund Information
Fund Type	Exchange Traded Funds
Category	Convertibles
Sub-Category	Convertibles
Prospectus Objective	Convertible Bond
Inception Date	Jun-15
Open to New Investments	Y

Prices
Price (as of 9/30/2019)	58.14
52-Week High	61.42
52-Week Low	50.03

Total Returns (%)
3-Month	6-Month	1-Year	3-Year	5-Year
-2.73	0.50	2.06	32.97	

3-Year Standard Deviation	9.36
Effective Duration	1.83

Valuation
Premium/Discount (1-Year Average)	0.19

Company Information
Provider	iShares
Manager/Tenure	James Mauro (4), Scott Radell (4)
Website	http://www.ishares.com
Address	iShares 400 Howard Street San Francisco CA 94105 United States
Phone Number	800-474-2737

PERFORMANCE

Ratings History
Date	Overall Rating	Risk Rating	Reward Rating
Q3-19	C	C-	C
Q4-18	C-	C-	C-
Q4-17	C	B	C+
Q4-16	D	D+	C-
Q4-15	U		

Asset & Performance History
Date	NAV	1-Year Total Return
2018	52.05	-1.85
2017	54.91	15.19
2016	48.75	11.13
2015	45.29	
2014		
2013		

Total Assets: $397,992,224

Asset Allocation
Asset	%
Cash	0%
Stocks	0%
US Stocks	0%
Bonds	0%
US Bonds	0%
Other	0%

Services Offered:

Investment Strategy: The investment seeks to track the investment results of the Bloomberg Barclays U.S. Convertible Cash Pay Bond > $250MM Index (the "underlying index"). The fund generally will invest at least 90% of its assets in the component securities of the underlying index and may invest up to 10% of its assets in certain futures, options and swap contracts, cash and cash equivalents, as well as in securities not included in the underlying index. The underlying index is a subset of the Bloomberg Barclays U.S. Convertibles: Cash Pay Bonds Index, which measures the performance of the U.S. dollar-denominated convertibles market. **Top Holdings:** Advanced Micro Devices, Inc. 2.13%   DISH Network Corporation 3.38%   Microchip Technology Incorporated 1.63% Microchip Technology Incorporated 1.63%   CAESARS ENTERTAINMENT CORP 5%

iShares CMBS ETF   C   HOLD

Ticker	Traded On	NAV	Total Assets ($)	Dividend Yield (TTM)	Turnover Ratio	Expense Ratio
CMBS	NYSE Arca	53.37	$397,628,472	2.68	13	0.25

Ratings
Reward   C+
Risk   C-
Recent Upgrade/Downgrade

Fund Information
Fund Type   Exchange Traded Funds
Category   US Fixed Income
Sub-Category   Intermediate Core Bond
Prospectus Objective   Growth
Inception Date   Feb-12
Open to New Investments   Y

Prices
Price (as of 9/30/2019)   53.47
52-Week High   54.19
52-Week Low   49.03

Total Returns (%)

3-Month	6-Month	1-Year	3-Year	5-Year
2.00	5.51	10.34	9.04	17.76

3-Year Standard Deviation   3.19
Effective Duration

Valuation
Premium/Discount (1-Year Average)   0.15

Company Information
Provider   iShares
Manager/Tenure   James Mauro (7), Scott Radell (7)
Website   http://www.ishares.com
Address   iShares 400 Howard Street San Francisco CA 94105 United States
Phone Number   800-474-2737

PERFORMANCE

Ratings History

Date	Overall Rating	Risk Rating	Reward Rating
Q3-19	C	C-	C+
Q4-18	C-	C-	D+
Q4-17	B-	A-	C
Q4-16	C	C+	C
Q4-15	C	C-	C

Asset & Performance History

Date	NAV	1-Year Total Return
2018	50.14	0.59
2017	51.22	2.85
2016	50.95	3.04
2015	50.57	0.6
2014	51.42	3.47
2013	50.77	0.02

Total Assets: $397,628,472

Asset Allocation

Asset	%
Cash	0%
Stocks	0%
US Stocks	0%
Bonds	99%
US Bonds	99%
Other	0%

Services Offered:

Investment Strategy: The investment seeks to track the investment results of the Bloomberg Barclays U.S. CMBS (ERISA Only) Index. The index measures the performance of investment-grade commercial mortgage-backed securities ("CMBS"), which are classes of securities (known as "certificates") that represent interests in "pools" of commercial mortgages. The fund generally will invest at least 90% of its assets in the component securities of the underlying index and may invest up to 10% of its assets in certain futures, options and swap contracts, cash and cash equivalents. **Top Holdings:** Fhms_k089 A2   FHLMC Pc Prepay Prm 30 3.43%   FHLMC Pc Prepay Prm 30 3.3%   Federal Home Loan Mortgage Corporation 4.06%   Federal Home Loan Mortgage Corporation 3.31%

WisdomTree International LargeCap Dividend Fund   C   HOLD

Ticker	Traded On	NAV	Total Assets ($)	Dividend Yield (TTM)	Turnover Ratio	Expense Ratio
DOL	NYSE Arca	45.92	$397,247,108	3.69	14	0.48

Ratings
Reward   C
Risk   C-
Recent Upgrade/Downgrade   Up

Fund Information
Fund Type   Exchange Traded Funds
Category   Global Equity Large Cap
Sub-Category   Foreign Large Value
Prospectus Objective   Foreign Stock
Inception Date   Jun-06
Open to New Investments   Y

Prices
Price (as of 9/30/2019)   45.95
52-Week High   48.29
52-Week Low   41.44

Total Returns (%)

3-Month	6-Month	1-Year	3-Year	5-Year
-2.17	0.37	-1.39	18.32	10.63

3-Year Standard Deviation   11.11
Effective Duration

Valuation
Premium/Discount (1-Year Average)   -0.03

Company Information
Provider   WisdomTree
Manager/Tenure   Richard A. Brown (11), Thomas J. Durante (11), Karen Q. Wong (11)
Website   http://www.wisdomtree.com
Address   WisdomTree 245 Park Avenue, 35th floor New York NY 10167 United States
Phone Number   866-909-9473

PERFORMANCE

Ratings History

Date	Overall Rating	Risk Rating	Reward Rating
Q3-19	C	C-	C
Q4-18	D+	C-	D+
Q4-17	C+	B-	C+
Q4-16	D+	C-	D
Q4-15	C-	C-	C-

Asset & Performance History

Date	NAV	1-Year Total Return
2018	42.74	-12.49
2017	50.64	21.54
2016	43.08	2.8
2015	43.44	-4.82
2014	47.18	-4.23
2013	51.57	20.74

Total Assets: $397,247,108

Asset Allocation

Asset	%
Cash	0%
Stocks	100%
US Stocks	1%
Bonds	0%
US Bonds	0%
Other	0%

Services Offered:

Investment Strategy: The investment seeks to track the price and yield performance, before fees and expenses, of the WisdomTree International LargeCap Dividend Index. The fund normally invests at least 95% of its total assets (exclusive of collateral held from securities lending) in component securities of the index and investments that have economic characteristics that are substantially identical to the economic characteristics of such component securities. The index is a fundamentally weighted index that is comprised of the large-capitalization segment of the dividend-paying market in the industrialized world outside the U.S. and Canada. The fund is non-diversified. **Top Holdings:** Nestle SA   China Mobile Ltd   BP PLC   Royal Dutch Shell PLC Class A   HSBC Holdings PLC

ARK Genomic Revolution Multi-Sector ETF   D+   SELL

Ticker	Traded On	NAV	Total Assets ($)	Dividend Yield (TTM)	Turnover Ratio	Expense Ratio
ARKG	NYSE Arca	29.55	$396,065,696	0	64	0.75

Ratings
Reward	D+
Risk	D
Recent Upgrade/Downgrade	Down

Fund Information
Fund Type	Exchange Traded Funds
Category	Healthcare Sector Equity
Sub-Category	Health
Prospectus Objective	Unaligned
Inception Date	Oct-14
Open to New Investments	Y

Prices
Price (as of 9/30/2019)	29.52
52-Week High	35.25
52-Week Low	22.36

Total Returns (%)
3-Month	6-Month	1-Year	3-Year	5-Year
-14.29	-10.31	-6.97	53.57	

3-Year Standard Deviation	32.48
Effective Duration	

Valuation
Premium/Discount (1-Year Average)	0.03

Company Information
Provider	ARK ETF Trust
Manager/Tenure	Catherine D. Wood (4)
Website	http://www.ark-funds.com
Address	ARK ETF Trust 155 West 19th Street, 5th Floor New York New York 10011 United States
Phone Number	212-426-7040

PERFORMANCE

Ratings History
Date	Overall Rating	Risk Rating	Reward Rating
Q3-19	D+	D	D+
Q4-18	D+	D	D+
Q4-17	C	C	C
Q4-16	D+	D	C-
Q4-15	U		

Asset & Performance History
Date	NAV	1-Year Total Return
2018	24.04	-0.55
2017	24.38	44.61
2016	16.99	-18.35
2015	20.81	-1.51
2014	21.13	
2013		

Total Assets: $396,065,696
Asset Allocation
Asset	%
Cash	0%
Stocks	100%
US Stocks	86%
Bonds	0%
US Bonds	0%
Other	0%

Services Offered:

Investment Strategy: The investment seeks long-term growth of capital. The fund is an actively-managed exchange-traded fund ("ETF") that will invest under normal circumstances primarily (at least 80% of its assets) in domestic and foreign equity securities of companies across multiple sectors, including healthcare, information technology, materials, energy and consumer discretionary, that are relevant to the fund's investment theme of the genomics revolution ("Genomics Revolution Companies"). It is non-diversified. **Top Holdings:** Illumina Inc Invitae Corp Intellia Therapeutics Inc CRISPR Therapeutics AG Editas Medicine Inc

---

UBS ETRACS Monthly Pay 2xLeveraged Mortgage REIT ETN   C   HOLD

Ticker	Traded On	NAV	Total Assets ($)	Dividend Yield (TTM)	Turnover Ratio	Expense Ratio
MORL	NYSE Arca	13.08	$395,657,438	21.9		0.4

Ratings
Reward	C
Risk	C+
Recent Upgrade/Downgrade	

Fund Information
Fund Type	Exchange Traded Funds
Category	Trading Tools
Sub-Category	Trading--Leveraged Equity
Prospectus Objective	Real Estate
Inception Date	Oct-12
Open to New Investments	Y

Prices
Price (as of 9/30/2019)	13.80
52-Week High	15.70
52-Week Low	11.70

Total Returns (%)
3-Month	6-Month	1-Year	3-Year	5-Year
2.38	-0.46	3.90	52.02	84.68

3-Year Standard Deviation	25.6
Effective Duration	

Valuation
Premium/Discount (1-Year Average)	4.80

Company Information
Provider	UBS Group AG
Manager/Tenure	No Manager (6)
Website	http://www.ubs.com
Address	Bahnhofstrasse 45 Zürich 8098 Switzerland
Phone Number	412-037-1952

PERFORMANCE

Ratings History
Date	Overall Rating	Risk Rating	Reward Rating
Q3-19	C	C+	C
Q4-18	C	C+	C
Q4-17	B	C	B+
Q4-16	C	C-	B-
Q4-15	C-	D+	C-

Asset & Performance History
Date	NAV	1-Year Total Return
2018	12.54	-12.25
2017	17.61	38.04
2016	15.55	47.29
2015	13.25	-20.5
2014	20.86	35.77
2013	18.93	-3.21

Total Assets: $395,657,438
Asset Allocation
Asset	%
Cash	%
Stocks	%
US Stocks	%
Bonds	%
US Bonds	%
Other	%

Services Offered:

Investment Strategy: The investment seeks to link to the Market Vectors® Global Mortgage REITs Index. The index tracks the overall performance of publicly-traded mortgage REITs that derive at least 50% of their revenues from mortgage-related activities. The Securities are senior unsecured debt securities issued by UBS AG (UBS). The Securities provide a monthly compounded two times leveraged long exposure to the performance of the index, reduced by the Accrued Fees. **Top Holdings:**

Fidelity® High Dividend ETF

C   **HOLD**

Ticker	Traded On	NAV		Total Assets ($)	Dividend Yield (TTM)	Turnover Ratio	Expense Ratio
FDVV	NYSE Arca	30.16		$395,142,582	4.22	50	0.29

Ratings
Reward	C
Risk	C-
Recent Upgrade/Downgrade	

Fund Information
Fund Type	Exchange Traded Funds
Category	US Equity Large Cap Value
Sub-Category	Large Value
Prospectus Objective	Growth & Inc
Inception Date	Sep-16
Open to New Investments	Y

Prices
Price (as of 9/30/2019)	30.20
52-Week High	30.83
52-Week Low	26.00

Total Returns (%)
3-Month	6-Month	1-Year	3-Year	5-Year
2.06	2.00	2.67	33.84	

3-Year Standard Deviation	11.07
Effective Duration	

Valuation
Premium/Discount (1-Year Average)	0.09

Company Information
Provider	Fidelity Investments
Manager/Tenure	Louis Bottari (3), Deane Gyllenhaal (3), Peter Matthew (3), 3 others
Website	http://www.institutional.fidelity.com
Address	Fidelity Investments 82 Devonshire Street Boston MA 2109 United States
Phone Number	617-563-7000

PERFORMANCE

Ratings History
Date	Overall Rating	Risk Rating	Reward Rating
Q3-19	C	C-	C
Q4-18	C	C-	C
Q4-17	D	B	C-
Q4-16	U		
Q4-15			

Asset & Performance History
Date	NAV	1-Year Total Return
2018	27.33	-0.93
2017	28.66	13.76
2016	26.15	
2015		
2014		
2013		

Total Assets: $395,142,582

Asset Allocation
Asset	%
Cash	0%
Stocks	100%
US Stocks	94%
Bonds	0%
US Bonds	0%
Other	0%

Services Offered:

Investment Strategy: The investment seeks to provide investment returns that correspond, before fees and expenses, generally to the performance of the Fidelity High Dividend Index. The fund normally invests at least 80% of assets in securities included in the underlying index and in depository receipts representing securities included in the underlying index. The underlying index is designed to reflect the performance of stocks of large and mid-capitalization high-dividend-paying companies that are expected to continue to pay and grow their dividends. **Top Holdings:** Microsoft Corp Procter & Gamble Co Apple Inc JPMorgan Chase & Co PepsiCo Inc

---

Aberdeen Standard Physical Silver Shares ETF

C-   **HOLD**

Ticker	Traded On	NAV		Total Assets ($)	Dividend Yield (TTM)	Turnover Ratio	Expense Ratio
SIVR	NYSE Arca	16.73		$394,103,951	0	4	0.3

Ratings
Reward	C-
Risk	C
Recent Upgrade/Downgrade	Up

Fund Information
Fund Type	Exchange Traded Funds
Category	Commodities Specified
Sub-Category	Commodities Precious Metals
Prospectus Objective	Prec Metals
Inception Date	Jul-09
Open to New Investments	Y

Prices
Price (as of 9/30/2019)	16.52
52-Week High	19.03
52-Week Low	13.61

Total Returns (%)
3-Month	6-Month	1-Year	3-Year	5-Year
12.98	14.32	18.23	-11.62	-0.24

3-Year Standard Deviation	15.77
Effective Duration	

Valuation
Premium/Discount (1-Year Average)	-0.33

Company Information
Provider	Aberdeen Standard Investments
Manager/Tenure	Management Team (10)
Website	http://www.aberdeenstandardetfs.us
Address	Aberdeen Standard Investments 405 Lexington Avenue New York NY 10174 United States
Phone Number	212-918-4954

PERFORMANCE

Ratings History
Date	Overall Rating	Risk Rating	Reward Rating
Q3-19	C-	C	C-
Q4-18	D	D	D-
Q4-17	D+	D+	D+
Q4-16	D+	D	C-
Q4-15	D-	E+	D-

Asset & Performance History
Date	NAV	1-Year Total Return
2018	15.03	-8.57
2017	16.44	3.53
2016	15.88	17.15
2015	13.56	-13.72
2014	15.71	-18.34
2013	19.24	-35.08

Total Assets: $394,103,951

Asset Allocation
Asset	%
Cash	0%
Stocks	0%
US Stocks	0%
Bonds	0%
US Bonds	0%
Other	100%

Services Offered:

Investment Strategy: The investment seeks to replicate, net of expenses, the price of silver bullion. The shares are backed by physical allocated silver bullion held by the custodian. All physical silver held conforms to the London Bullion Market Association's rules for good delivery. **Top Holdings:** Physical Silver Bullion

---

Invesco Variable Rate Investment Grade ETF   C   HOLD

Ticker	Traded On	NAV	Total Assets ($)	Dividend Yield (TTM)	Turnover Ratio	Expense Ratio
VRIG	NAS CM	24.91	$393,576,254	3.22	26	0.3

Ratings
Reward	C
Risk	C-
Recent Upgrade/Downgrade	Up

Fund Information
Fund Type	Exchange Traded Funds
Category	US Fixed Income
Sub-Category	Ultrashort Bond
Prospectus Objective	Income
Inception Date	Sep-16
Open to New Investments	Y

Prices
Price (as of 9/30/2019)	24.89
52-Week High	25.12
52-Week Low	24.60

Total Returns (%)
3-Month	6-Month	1-Year	3-Year	5-Year
0.80	1.68	2.57	8.08	

3-Year Standard Deviation	0.76
Effective Duration	-0.05

Valuation
Premium/Discount (1-Year Average)	-0.09

Company Information
Provider	Invesco
Manager/Tenure	Philip Armstrong (3), Peter Hubbard (3), Jeffrey W. Kernagis (3), 3 others
Website	http://www.invesco.com/us
Address	Invesco 11 Greenway Plaza, Ste. 2500 Houston TX 77046 United States
Phone Number	800-659-1005

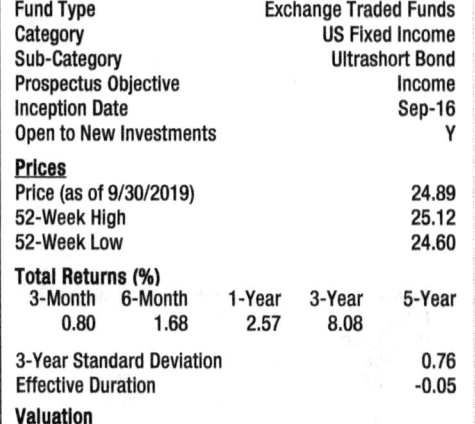

PERFORMANCE

Ratings History
Date	Overall Rating	Risk Rating	Reward Rating
Q3-19	C	C-	C
Q4-18	C	C+	C-
Q4-17	D	A-	D+
Q4-16	U		
Q4-15			

Asset & Performance History
Date	NAV	1-Year Total Return
2018	24.71	1.03
2017	25.16	3.04
2016	24.99	
2015		
2014		
2013		

Total Assets: $393,576,254
Asset Allocation
Asset	%
Cash	3%
Stocks	0%
US Stocks	0%
Bonds	94%
US Bonds	81%
Other	0%

Services Offered:

Investment Strategy: The investment seeks to generate current income while maintaining low portfolio duration as a primary objective and capital appreciation as a secondary objective. The fund invests at least 80% of its net assets (plus any borrowings for investment purposes) in a portfolio of investment-grade, variable rate or floating rate debt securities. At least 80% of its net assets (plus any borrowings for investment purposes) will be invested in Variable Rate Instruments that are, at the time of purchase, investment grade (or in affiliated ETFs that invest primarily in any or all of the foregoing securities). It is non-diversified. **Top Holdings:** United States Treasury Notes 2.1% United States Treasury Notes 2.07% Federal Home Loan Mortgage Corporation 3.5% Invesco Variable Rate Preferred ETF Federal National Mortgage Association 5.15%

iShares U.S. Regional Banks ETF   B-   BUY

Ticker	Traded On	NAV	Total Assets ($)	Dividend Yield (TTM)	Turnover Ratio	Expense Ratio
IAT	NYSE Arca	46.55	$391,011,051	2.63	10	0.42

Ratings
Reward	B
Risk	C
Recent Upgrade/Downgrade	Up

Fund Information
Fund Type	Exchange Traded Funds
Category	Financials Sector Equity
Sub-Category	Financial
Prospectus Objective	Financial
Inception Date	May-06
Open to New Investments	Y

Prices
Price (as of 9/30/2019)	46.56
52-Week High	49.96
52-Week Low	37.63

Total Returns (%)
3-Month	6-Month	1-Year	3-Year	5-Year
1.26	5.58	-1.86	40.65	56.93

3-Year Standard Deviation	22.82
Effective Duration	

Valuation
Premium/Discount (1-Year Average)	-0.04

Company Information
Provider	iShares
Manager/Tenure	Greg Savage (11), Jennifer Hsui (7), Alan Mason (3), 2 others
Website	http://www.ishares.com
Address	iShares 400 Howard Street San Francisco CA 94105 United States
Phone Number	800-474-2737

PERFORMANCE

Ratings History
Date	Overall Rating	Risk Rating	Reward Rating
Q3-19	B-	C	B
Q4-18	B-	C	B
Q4-17	B+	B-	A
Q4-16	B	C+	B+
Q4-15	B+	B+	B+

Asset & Performance History
Date	NAV	1-Year Total Return
2018	39.86	-17.38
2017	49.29	10.53
2016	45.33	32.18
2015	34.96	1.73
2014	34.97	7.58
2013	33.06	37.59

Total Assets: $391,011,051
Asset Allocation
Asset	%
Cash	0%
Stocks	100%
US Stocks	99%
Bonds	0%
US Bonds	0%
Other	0%

Services Offered:

Investment Strategy: The investment seeks to track the investment results of the Dow Jones U.S. Select Regional Banks Index. The fund generally invests at least 90% of its assets in securities of the index and in depositary receipts representing securities of the index. The underlying index measures the performance of the regional bank sector of the U.S. equity market and is a subset of the Dow Jones U.S. Bank Index. The fund is non-diversified. **Top Holdings:** US Bancorp PNC Financial Services Group Inc BB&T Corp SunTrust Banks Inc M&T Bank Corp

iShares Edge MSCI USA Size Factor ETF
C   HOLD

Ticker	Traded On	NAV	Total Assets ($)	Dividend Yield (TTM)	Turnover Ratio	Expense Ratio
SIZE	NYSE Arca	90.81	$390,467,562	1.59	30	0.15

Ratings
Reward   C
Risk   C-
Recent Upgrade/Downgrade

Fund Information
Fund Type	Exchange Traded Funds
Category	US Equity Large Cap Blend
Sub-Category	Large Blend
Prospectus Objective	Growth
Inception Date	Apr-13
Open to New Investments	Y

Prices
Price (as of 9/30/2019)	90.78
52-Week High	93.23
52-Week Low	72.15

Total Returns (%)

3-Month	6-Month	1-Year	3-Year	5-Year
-0.44	2.75	5.05	37.80	64.52

3-Year Standard Deviation	12.96
Effective Duration	

Valuation
Premium/Discount (1-Year Average)	0.06

Company Information
Provider	iShares
Manager/Tenure	Diane Hsiung (6), Jennifer Hsui (6), Greg Savage (6), 3 others
Website	http://www.ishares.com
Address	iShares 400 Howard Street San Francisco CA 94105 United States
Phone Number	800-474-2737

PERFORMANCE

Ratings History

Date	Overall Rating	Risk Rating	Reward Rating
Q3-19	C	C-	C
Q4-18	C-	C-	C-
Q4-17	B-	B	B-
Q4-16	D+	D+	D+
Q4-15	C	D+	C

Asset & Performance History

Date	NAV	1-Year Total Return
2018	76.57	-6.58
2017	83.75	18.87
2016	71.65	13.32
2015	64.48	0.36
2014	65.51	15.77
2013	57.65	

Total Assets: $390,467,562
Asset Allocation

Asset	%
Cash	0%
Stocks	100%
US Stocks	98%
Bonds	0%
US Bonds	0%
Other	0%

Services Offered:

Investment Strategy: The investment seeks to track the investment results of the MSCI USA Low Size Index. The fund generally will invest at least 90% of its assets in the component securities of the underlying index and may invest up to 10% of its assets in certain futures, options and swap contracts, cash and cash equivalents, including shares of money market funds advised by BFA or its affiliates, as well as in securities not included in the underlying index, but which BFA believes will help the fund track the underlying index. The index is based on a traditional market capitalization-weighted parent index, the MSCI USA Index (the "parent index"). **Top Holdings:** Fiserv Inc   Salesforce.com Inc   L3Harris Technologies Inc   Fidelity National Information Services Inc   DexCom Inc

---

SPDR® S&P 500 Fossil Fuel Reserves Free ETF
C   HOLD

Ticker	Traded On	NAV	Total Assets ($)	Dividend Yield (TTM)	Turnover Ratio	Expense Ratio
SPYX	NYSE Arca		$388,441,971	1.67	6	0.2

Ratings
Reward   C+
Risk   C-
Recent Upgrade/Downgrade

Fund Information
Fund Type	Exchange Traded Funds
Category	US Equity Large Cap Blend
Sub-Category	Large Blend
Prospectus Objective	Growth & Inc
Inception Date	Nov-15
Open to New Investments	Y

Prices
Price (as of 9/30/2019)	72.65
52-Week High	73.80
52-Week Low	57.18

Total Returns (%)

3-Month	6-Month	1-Year	3-Year	5-Year
0.64	4.75	3.81	46.69	

3-Year Standard Deviation	12.24
Effective Duration	

Valuation
Premium/Discount (1-Year Average)	0.01

Company Information
Provider	SPDR State Street Global Advisors
Manager/Tenure	Michael J. Feehily (3), Karl A. Schneider (3), John Law (0)
Website	http://www.spdrs.com
Address	SPDR State Street Global Advisors State Street Financial Center, 1 Lincoln Street Boston MA 02111-2900 United States
Phone Number	617-786-3000

PERFORMANCE

Ratings History

Date	Overall Rating	Risk Rating	Reward Rating
Q3-19	C	C-	C+
Q4-18	C	C-	C
Q4-17	C	B+	C
Q4-16	D	D+	D+
Q4-15			

Asset & Performance History

Date	NAV	1-Year Total Return
2018	60.74	-4.32
2017	64.65	22.87
2016	53.56	10.91
2015	49.27	
2014		
2013		

Total Assets: $388,441,971
Asset Allocation

Asset	%
Cash	0%
Stocks	100%
US Stocks	99%
Bonds	0%
US Bonds	0%
Other	0%

Services Offered:

Investment Strategy: The investment seeks to provide investment results that, before fees and expenses, correspond generally to the total return performance of the S&P 500 Fossil Fuel Free Index. Normally, the fund generally invests substantially all, but at least 80%, of its total assets in the securities comprising the index. In addition, it may invest in equity securities that are not included in the index, cash and cash equivalents or money market instruments. The index is designed to measure the performance of companies in the S&P 500 Index that do not own fossil fuel reserves. The fund is non-diversified. **Top Holdings:** Microsoft Corp   Apple Inc   Amazon.com Inc   Facebook Inc A   Berkshire Hathaway Inc B

iShares Global Utilities ETF

C+ **HOLD**

Ticker	Traded On	NAV
JXI	NYSE Arca	58.32

Total Assets ($)	Dividend Yield (TTM)	Turnover Ratio	Expense Ratio
$387,812,341	3.04	8	0.46

Ratings

Reward	B
Risk	C
Recent Upgrade/Downgrade	Down

Fund Information

Fund Type	Exchange Traded Funds
Category	Utilities Sector Equity
Sub-Category	Utilities
Prospectus Objective	Utility
Inception Date	Sep-06
Open to New Investments	Y

Prices

Price (as of 9/30/2019)	58.35
52-Week High	58.45
52-Week Low	48.15

Total Returns (%)

3-Month	6-Month	1-Year	3-Year	5-Year
7.18	10.45	22.62	37.03	46.72

3-Year Standard Deviation	10.3
Effective Duration	

Valuation

Premium/Discount (1-Year Average)	0.02

Company Information

Provider	iShares
Manager/Tenure	Greg Savage (11), Jennifer Hsui (7), Alan Mason (3), 2 others
Website	http://www.ishares.com
Address	iShares 400 Howard Street San Francisco CA 94105 United States
Phone Number	800-474-2737

PERFORMANCE

Ratings History

Date	Overall Rating	Risk Rating	Reward Rating
Q3-19	C+	C	B
Q4-18	C	C	C
Q4-17	C+	B-	C+
Q4-16	C	C-	C
Q4-15	C	C-	C

Asset & Performance History

Date	NAV	1-Year Total Return
2018	49.07	2.02
2017	49.64	14.73
2016	44.83	6.07
2015	44.23	-6.72
2014	49.2	15.61
2013	44.07	12.77

Total Assets: $387,812,341

Asset Allocation

Asset	%
Cash	0%
Stocks	100%
US Stocks	62%
Bonds	0%
US Bonds	0%
Other	0%

Services Offered:

Investment Strategy: The investment seeks to track the investment results of the S&P Global 1200 Utilities IndexTM. The fund generally invests at least 90% of its assets in securities of the underlying index and in depositary receipts representing securities of the underlying index. It may invest the remainder of its assets in certain futures, options and swap contracts, cash and cash equivalents, as well as in securities not included in the underlying index. A significant portion of the underlying index is represented by securities of companies in the utilities industry or sector. **Top Holdings:** NextEra Energy Inc Duke Energy Corp Iberdrola SA Dominion Energy Inc Southern Co

---

iShares Morningstar Small-Cap Value ETF

D+ **SELL**

Ticker	Traded On	NAV
JKL	NYSE Arca	133.70

Total Assets ($)	Dividend Yield (TTM)	Turnover Ratio	Expense Ratio
$387,729,096	2.46	48	0.3

Ratings

Reward	D+
Risk	D+
Recent Upgrade/Downgrade	

Fund Information

Fund Type	Exchange Traded Funds
Category	US Equity Small Cap
Sub-Category	Small Value
Prospectus Objective	Small Company
Inception Date	Jun-04
Open to New Investments	Y

Prices

Price (as of 9/30/2019)	133.73
52-Week High	152.91
52-Week Low	117.04

Total Returns (%)

3-Month	6-Month	1-Year	3-Year	5-Year
-2.01	-3.46	-10.12	9.96	27.90

3-Year Standard Deviation	18.17
Effective Duration	

Valuation

Premium/Discount (1-Year Average)	0.04

Company Information

Provider	iShares
Manager/Tenure	Greg Savage (11), Jennifer Hsui (7), Alan Mason (3), 2 others
Website	http://www.ishares.com
Address	iShares 400 Howard Street San Francisco CA 94105 United States
Phone Number	800-474-2737

PERFORMANCE

Ratings History

Date	Overall Rating	Risk Rating	Reward Rating
Q3-19	D+	D+	D+
Q4-18	C-	D+	C-
Q4-17	B	B-	B
Q4-16	D+	D+	C-
Q4-15	C	C-	C

Asset & Performance History

Date	NAV	1-Year Total Return
2018	123.36	-16.79
2017	151.46	8.08
2016	142.73	27.82
2015	114.73	-8.77
2014	128.89	9.8
2013	120.28	35.35

Total Assets: $387,729,096

Asset Allocation

Asset	%
Cash	0%
Stocks	100%
US Stocks	96%
Bonds	0%
US Bonds	0%
Other	0%

Services Offered:

Investment Strategy: The investment seeks to track the investment results of the Morningstar® US Small Value IndexSM composed of small-capitalization U.S. equities that exhibit value characteristics. The fund generally invests at least 90% of its assets in securities of the underlying index and in depositary receipts representing securities of the underlying index. The underlying index measures the performance of stocks issued by small-capitalization companies that have exhibited "value" characteristics as determined by Morningstar, Inc.'s ("Morningstar" or the "index provider") proprietary index methodology. **Top Holdings:** Amcor PLC Ordinary Shares TCF Financial Corp The Hanover Insurance Group Inc Williams-Sonoma Inc Axis Capital Holdings Ltd

Vanguard S&P Small-Cap 600 Growth Index Fund ETF Shares   C-   HOLD

Ticker	Traded On	NAV	Total Assets ($)	Dividend Yield (TTM)	Turnover Ratio	Expense Ratio
VIOG	NYSE Arca	153.37	$387,259,250	1.02	37	0.2

Ratings
Reward   C
Risk   D+
Recent Upgrade/Downgrade

Fund Information
Fund Type   Exchange Traded Funds
Category   US Equity Small Cap
Sub-Category   Small Growth
Prospectus Objective   Growth & Inc
Inception Date   Sep-10
Open to New Investments Y

Prices
Price (as of 9/30/2019)   153.42
52-Week High   170.64
52-Week Low   129.95

Total Returns (%)

3-Month	6-Month	1-Year	3-Year	5-Year
-2.29	-0.62	-10.68	33.80	66.66

3-Year Standard Deviation   17.56
Effective Duration

Valuation
Premium/Discount (1-Year Average)   -0.05

Company Information
Provider   Vanguard
Manager/Tenure William A. Coleman (5), Donald M.
                Butler (3)
Website   http://www.vanguard.com
Address   Vanguard 100 Vanguard Boulevard
                Malvern PA 19355 United States
Phone Number   877-662-7447

PERFORMANCE

Ratings History

Date	Overall Rating	Risk Rating	Reward Rating
Q3-19	C-	D+	C
Q4-18	C-	C-	C
Q4-17	A-	B+	A
Q4-16	C-	D+	C
Q4-15	C	D+	C+

Asset & Performance History

Date	NAV	1-Year Total Return
2018	137.84	-4.81
2017	145.79	15.07
2016	128.4	20.72
2015	106.31	2.57
2014	104.72	3.63
2013	101.78	42.42

Total Assets: $387,259,250
Asset Allocation

Asset	%
Cash	1%
Stocks	99%
US Stocks	97%
Bonds	0%
US Bonds	0%
Other	0%

Services Offered:

Investment Strategy: The investment seeks to track the performance of a benchmark index that measures the investment return of small-capitalization growth stocks in the United States. The fund employs an indexing investment approach designed to track the performance of the S&P SmallCap 600® Growth Index, which represents the growth companies, as determined by the index sponsor, of the S&P SmallCap 600 Index. The Advisor attempts to replicate the target index by investing all, or substantially all, of its assets in the stocks that make up the index, holding each stock in approximately the same proportion as its weighting in the index. **Top Holdings:** FirstCash Inc Repligen Corp Strategic Education Inc Neogen Corp Exponent Inc

---

Invesco DB Agriculture Fund   D   SELL

Ticker	Traded On	NAV	Total Assets ($)	Dividend Yield (TTM)	Turnover Ratio	Expense Ratio
DBA	NYSE Arca	15.86	$383,906,573	1.13		0.85

Ratings
Reward   D-
Risk   D
Recent Upgrade/Downgrade

Fund Information
Fund Type   Exchange Traded Funds
Category   Commodities Specified
Sub-Category   Commodities Agriculture
Prospectus Objective   Natl Res
Inception Date   Jan-07
Open to New Investments Y

Prices
Price (as of 9/30/2019)   15.86
52-Week High   17.77
52-Week Low   14.84

Total Returns (%)

3-Month	6-Month	1-Year	3-Year	5-Year
-4.23	-4.34	-5.82	-19.95	-37.52

3-Year Standard Deviation   9.48
Effective Duration

Valuation
Premium/Discount (1-Year Average)   -0.07

Company Information
Provider   Invesco
Manager/Tenure Management Team (12)
Website   http://www.invesco.com/us
Address   Invesco 11 Greenway Plaza, Ste. 2500
                Houston TX 77046 United States
Phone Number   800-659-1005

PERFORMANCE

Ratings History

Date	Overall Rating	Risk Rating	Reward Rating
Q3-19	D	D	D-
Q4-18	D	D	D
Q4-17	D	D	D
Q4-16	D	D	D
Q4-15	D	D	D

Asset & Performance History

Date	NAV	1-Year Total Return
2018	16.94	-8.74
2017	18.76	-6.16
2016	19.98	-3.02
2015	20.67	-16.75
2014	24.83	2.26
2013	24.28	-13.17

Total Assets: $383,906,573
Asset Allocation

Asset	%
Cash	41%
Stocks	0%
US Stocks	0%
Bonds	8%
US Bonds	8%
Other	50%

Services Offered:

Investment Strategy: The investment seeks to track changes, whether positive or negative, in the level of the DBIQ Diversified Agriculture Index Excess Return™ (the "index") over time, plus the excess, if any, of the sum of the fund's Treasury Income, Money Market Income and T-Bill ETF Income, over the expenses of the fund. The index, which is comprised of one or more underlying commodities ("index commodities"), is intended to reflect the agricultural sector. The fund pursues its investment objective by investing in a portfolio of exchange-traded futures. **Top Holdings:** United States Treasury Bills 0% Invesco Treasury Collateral ETF Corn Future Sep20 Soybean Future Nov19 Live Cattle Futr Oct19

iShares International Developed Real Estate ETF   C   HOLD

Ticker	Traded On	NAV	Total Assets ($)	Dividend Yield (TTM)	Turnover Ratio	Expense Ratio
IFGL	NAS CM	29.73	$383,481,702	4.92	8	0.48

Ratings
Reward   C
Risk   C-
Recent Upgrade/Downgrade   Down

Fund Information
Fund Type   Exchange Traded Funds
Category   Real Estate Sector Equity
Sub-Category   Global Real Estate
Prospectus Objective   Real Estate
Inception Date   Nov-07
Open to New Investments   Y

Prices
Price (as of 9/30/2019)   29.67
52-Week High   30.55
52-Week Low   26.69

Total Returns (%)

3-Month	6-Month	1-Year	3-Year	5-Year
1.14	0.45	9.02	17.99	26.61

3-Year Standard Deviation   10.66
Effective Duration

Valuation
Premium/Discount (1-Year Average)   -0.11

Company Information
Provider   iShares
Manager/Tenure   Greg Savage (11), Jennifer Hsui (7),
                  Alan Mason (3), 2 others
Website   http://www.ishares.com
Address   iShares 400 Howard Street San
                  Francisco CA 94105 United States
Phone Number   800-474-2737

PERFORMANCE

Ratings History

Date	Overall Rating	Risk Rating	Reward Rating
Q3-19	C	C-	C
Q4-18	C	C	C-
Q4-17	B-	B-	C+
Q4-16	C-	C	C-
Q4-15	C	C+	C-

Asset & Performance History

Date	NAV	1-Year Total Return
2018	26.96	-6.68
2017	30.02	19.88
2016	26.33	1.07
2015	28.03	-4.02
2014	30.23	2.38
2013	30.57	5.29

Total Assets: $383,481,702
Asset Allocation

Asset	%
Cash	1%
Stocks	98%
US Stocks	0%
Bonds	0%
US Bonds	0%
Other	2%

Services Offered:

Investment Strategy: The investment seeks to track the investment results of the FTSE EPRA/NAREIT Developed ex-U.S. Index composed of real estate equities in developed non-U.S. markets. The fund generally will invest at least 90% of its assets in the component securities of the underlying index and in investments that have economic characteristics that are substantially identical to the component securities of the underlying index. The underlying index measures the stock performance of companies engaged in the ownership and development of real estate markets in developed countries (except for the United States) as defined by FTSE EPRA/NAREIT. **Top Holdings:** Vonovia SE Link Real Estate Investment Trust Mitsubishi Estate Co Ltd Mitsui Fudosan Co Ltd Sun Hung Kai Properties Ltd

---

iShares Morningstar Multi-Asset Income ETF   C   HOLD

Ticker	Traded On	NAV	Total Assets ($)	Dividend Yield (TTM)	Turnover Ratio	Expense Ratio
IYLD	BATS	24.97	$382,048,105	5.21	50	0.59

Ratings
Reward   C+
Risk   C-
Recent Upgrade/Downgrade

Fund Information
Fund Type   Exchange Traded Funds
Category   Cautious Allocation
Sub-Category   Allocation--30% to 50% Equity
Prospectus Objective   Multi-Asset Global
Inception Date   Apr-12
Open to New Investments   Y

Prices
Price (as of 9/30/2019)   24.97
52-Week High   25.17
52-Week Low   23.02

Total Returns (%)

3-Month	6-Month	1-Year	3-Year	5-Year
-0.37	3.17	6.52	14.73	23.87

3-Year Standard Deviation   5.8
Effective Duration

Valuation
Premium/Discount (1-Year Average)   0.06

Company Information
Provider   iShares
Manager/Tenure   James Mauro (7), Scott Radell (7)
Website   http://www.ishares.com
Address   iShares 400 Howard Street San
                  Francisco CA 94105 United States
Phone Number   800-474-2737

PERFORMANCE

Ratings History

Date	Overall Rating	Risk Rating	Reward Rating
Q3-19	C	C-	C+
Q4-18	C-	C-	D+
Q4-17	B-	B	C+
Q4-16	C	C-	C
Q4-15	C-	C-	C-

Asset & Performance History

Date	NAV	1-Year Total Return
2018	23.25	-4.75
2017	25.79	10.86
2016	24.28	9.79
2015	23.21	-4.76
2014	25.62	10.16
2013	24.75	0.56

Total Assets: $382,048,105
Asset Allocation

Asset	%
Cash	1%
Stocks	36%
US Stocks	18%
Bonds	58%
US Bonds	29%
Other	0%

Services Offered:

Investment Strategy: The investment seeks to track the investment results of the Morningstar® Multi-Asset High Income IndexSM. The fund generally will invest at least 90% of its assets in the component securities of the underlying index and may invest up to 10% of its assets in certain futures, options and swap contracts, cash and cash equivalents. The index is broadly diversified and seeks to deliver high current income while maintaining long-term capital appreciation. The fund is a fund-of-funds and invests primarily in the securities of the underlying funds that themselves seek investment results corresponding to their own underlying indexes. **Top Holdings:** Annaly Capital Management Inc AGNC Investment Corp Starwood Property Trust Inc New Residential Investment Corp Two Harbors Investment Corp

Invesco S&P MidCap 400® Pure Growth ETF

C- HOLD

Ticker	Traded On	NAV	Total Assets ($)	Dividend Yield (TTM)	Turnover Ratio	Expense Ratio
RFG	NYSE Arca	141.41	$381,797,322	0.74		0.35

Ratings
Reward	C-
Risk	D+
Recent Upgrade/Downgrade	Up

Fund Information
Fund Type	Exchange Traded Funds
Category	US Equity Mid Cap
Sub-Category	Mid-Cap Growth
Prospectus Objective	Growth
Inception Date	Mar-06
Open to New Investments	Y

Prices
Price (as of 9/30/2019)	141.36
52-Week High	163.24
52-Week Low	124.17

Total Returns (%)
3-Month	6-Month	1-Year	3-Year	5-Year
-4.65	-7.13	-12.78	15.58	21.51

3-Year Standard Deviation	16.19
Effective Duration	

Valuation
Premium/Discount (1-Year Average)	0.07

Company Information
Provider	Invesco
Manager/Tenure	Peter Hubbard (1), Michael Jeanette (1), Tony Seisser (1)
Website	http://www.invesco.com/us
Address	Invesco 11 Greenway Plaza, Ste. 2500 Houston TX 77046 United States
Phone Number	800-659-1005

PERFORMANCE

Ratings History
Date	Overall Rating	Risk Rating	Reward Rating
Q3-19	C-	D+	C-
Q4-18	C-	D+	C
Q4-17	B	B	B-
Q4-16	C-	D+	C
Q4-15	B-	C	B

Asset & Performance History
Date	NAV	1-Year Total Return
2018	131.89	-13.76
2017	153.93	20.51
2016	128.84	3.56
2015	124.11	2.45
2014	121.84	-0.33
2013	122.96	35.72

Total Assets: $381,797,322

Asset Allocation
Asset	%
Cash	0%
Stocks	100%
US Stocks	100%
Bonds	0%
US Bonds	0%
Other	0%

Services Offered:

Investment Strategy: The investment seeks to track the investment results (before fees and expenses) of the S&P MidCap 400® Pure Growth Index (the "underlying index"). The fund generally will invest at least 90% of its total assets in the securities that comprise the underlying index. The underlying index is composed of a subset of securities from the S&P MidCap 400® Index that exhibit strong growth characteristics, as measured using the following three factors: three-year sales per share growth, three-year ratio of earnings per share change to price per share, and momentum (the 12-month percentage change in price). The fund is non-diversified. **Top Holdings:** Churchill Downs Inc Eldorado Resorts Inc Amedisys Inc Globus Medical Inc Class A Primerica Inc

iShares MSCI Chile Capped ETF

D SELL

Ticker	Traded On	NAV	Total Assets ($)	Dividend Yield (TTM)	Turnover Ratio	Expense Ratio
ECH	BATS	37.41	$375,963,831	2.17	54	0.59

Ratings
Reward	D
Risk	D
Recent Upgrade/Downgrade	Down

Fund Information
Fund Type	Exchange Traded Funds
Category	Equity Misc
Sub-Category	Miscellaneous Region
Prospectus Objective	Foreign Stock
Inception Date	Nov-07
Open to New Investments	Y

Prices
Price (as of 9/30/2019)	37.44
52-Week High	47.51
52-Week Low	34.44

Total Returns (%)
3-Month	6-Month	1-Year	3-Year	5-Year
-8.37	-13.05	-16.37	7.75	-1.67

3-Year Standard Deviation	22.56
Effective Duration	

Valuation
Premium/Discount (1-Year Average)	-0.22

Company Information
Provider	iShares
Manager/Tenure	Diane Hsiung (11), Greg Savage (11), Jennifer Hsui (6), 3 others
Website	http://www.ishares.com
Address	iShares 400 Howard Street San Francisco CA 94105 United States
Phone Number	800-474-2737

PERFORMANCE

Ratings History
Date	Overall Rating	Risk Rating	Reward Rating
Q3-19	D	D	D
Q4-18	C-	C-	C-
Q4-17	B	C	B+
Q4-16	D+	D+	D+
Q4-15	D-	D-	D-

Asset & Performance History
Date	NAV	1-Year Total Return
2018	41.58	-19.13
2017	52.49	42.59
2016	37.45	17.78
2015	32.4	-18.04
2014	40.26	-12.72
2013	46.84	-23.86

Total Assets: $375,963,831

Asset Allocation
Asset	%
Cash	0%
Stocks	100%
US Stocks	0%
Bonds	0%
US Bonds	0%
Other	0%

Services Offered:

Investment Strategy: The investment seeks to track the investment results of the MSCI Chile IMI 25/50 Index. The fund generally will invest at least 90% of its assets in the component securities of the underlying index and in investments that have economic characteristics that are substantially identical to the component securities of the underlying index. The underlying index is a free float-adjusted market capitalization index that is designed to measure broad-based equity market performance in Chile. The fund is non-diversified. **Top Holdings:** Enel Americas SA Banco De Chile Banco Santander Chile Falabella SA Empresas COPEC SA

First Trust Consumer Staples AlphaDEX® Fund

C   **HOLD**

Ticker	Traded On	NAV	Total Assets ($)	Dividend Yield (TTM)	Turnover Ratio	Expense Ratio
FXG	NYSE Arca	48.32	$372,071,764	1.48	90	0.64

Ratings
Reward   B-
Risk   C-
Recent Upgrade/Downgrade

Fund Information
Fund Type	Exchange Traded Funds
Category	Consumer Goods & Svcs
Sub-Category	Consumer Defensive
Prospectus Objective	Unaligned
Inception Date	May-07
Open to New Investments	Y

Prices
Price (as of 9/30/2019)	48.32
52-Week High	48.81
52-Week Low	40.68

Total Returns (%)
3-Month	6-Month	1-Year	3-Year	5-Year
5.78	6.34	5.18	9.32	35.82

3-Year Standard Deviation   12.24
Effective Duration

Valuation
Premium/Discount (1-Year Average)   0.00

Company Information
Provider	First Trust
Manager/Tenure	Jon C. Erickson (12), Daniel J. Lindquist (12), David G. McGarel (12), 3 others
Website	http://www.ftportfolios.com/
Address	First Trust 120 E. Liberty Drive, Suite 400 Wheaton IL 60187 United States
Phone Number	800-621-1675

PERFORMANCE

Ratings History

Date	Overall Rating	Risk Rating	Reward Rating
Q3-19	C	C-	B-
Q4-18	C+	C-	B
Q4-17	B-	B+	C+
Q4-16	B-	C	B
Q4-15	B+	B	A-

Asset & Performance History

Date	NAV	1-Year Total Return
2018	42.2	-11.43
2017	48.64	7.8
2016	45.75	4.72
2015	44.43	6.13
2014	42.57	21.04
2013	35.64	41.94

Total Assets: $372,071,764
Asset Allocation

Asset	%
Cash	0%
Stocks	100%
US Stocks	100%
Bonds	0%
US Bonds	0%
Other	0%

Services Offered:

Investment Strategy: The investment seeks investment results that correspond generally to the price and yield (before the fund's fees and expenses) of an equity index called the StrataQuant® Consumer Staples Index. The fund will normally invest at least 90% of its net assets (including investment borrowings) in common stocks that comprise the index. The index is a modified equal-dollar weighted index designed by IDI to objectively identify and select stocks from the Russell 1000® Index in the consumer staples sector that may generate positive alpha relative to traditional passive-style indices through the use of the AlphaDEX® selection methodology. The fund is non-diversified. **Top Holdings:** Pilgrims Pride Corp Casey's General Stores Inc The Kroger Co Archer-Daniels Midland Co Walgreens Boots Alliance Inc

---

Principal U.S. Small-Cap Multi-Factor Index ETF

C-   **HOLD**

Ticker	Traded On	NAV	Total Assets ($)	Dividend Yield (TTM)	Turnover Ratio	Expense Ratio
PSC	NAS CM	30.63	$370,676,123	1.33	82	0.38

Ratings
Reward   D+
Risk   C-
Recent Upgrade/Downgrade   Up

Fund Information
Fund Type	Exchange Traded Funds
Category	US Equity Small Cap
Sub-Category	Small Blend
Prospectus Objective	Small Company
Inception Date	Sep-16
Open to New Investments	Y

Prices
Price (as of 9/30/2019)	30.73
52-Week High	34.90
52-Week Low	26.04

Total Returns (%)
3-Month	6-Month	1-Year	3-Year	5-Year
-2.41	-1.94	-10.56	25.76	

3-Year Standard Deviation   17.3
Effective Duration

Valuation
Premium/Discount (1-Year Average)   0.10

Company Information
Provider	Principal Funds
Manager/Tenure	Paul S. Kim (3), Mark R. Nebelung (3), Jeffrey A. Schwarte (3)
Website	http://www.principalfunds.com
Address	Principal Funds 430 W 7th St, Ste 219971 Kansas City MO 64105-1407 United States
Phone Number	800-787-1621

PERFORMANCE

Ratings History

Date	Overall Rating	Risk Rating	Reward Rating
Q3-19	C-	C-	D+
Q4-18	C-	C-	C-
Q4-17	D	B	C
Q4-16	U		
Q4-15			

Asset & Performance History

Date	NAV	1-Year Total Return
2018	27.78	-9.22
2017	30.97	13.4
2016	27.59	
2015		
2014		
2013		

Total Assets: $370,676,123
Asset Allocation

Asset	%
Cash	0%
Stocks	100%
US Stocks	99%
Bonds	0%
US Bonds	0%
Other	0%

Services Offered:

Investment Strategy: The investment seeks investment results that closely correspond, before expenses, to the performance of the Nasdaq U.S. Small Cap Select Leaders Index. The fund invests at least 80% of its net assets, plus any borrowings for investment purposes, in equity securities of companies that compose the index. The index uses a quantitative model designed to identify equity securities (including growth and value stock) of small-capitalization companies in the Nasdaq US Small Cap Index (the "parent index") that exhibit potential for high degrees of sustainable shareholder yield, pricing power and strong momentum, while adjusting for liquidity and quality. **Top Holdings:** Alteryx Inc Class A Aerojet Rocketdyne Holdings Inc Legg Mason Inc-LeggMason RETAIL Five9 Inc KBR Inc

InfraCap MLP ETF
C   **HOLD**

Ticker	Traded On	NAV	Total Assets ($)	Dividend Yield (TTM)	Turnover Ratio	Expense Ratio
AMZA	NYSE Arca	4.91	$370,373,417	21.38	255	2.4

Ratings

Reward	C+
Risk	D+
Recent Upgrade/Downgrade	Up

Fund Information

Fund Type	Exchange Traded Funds
Category	Energy Sector Equity
Sub-Category	Energy Limited Partnership
Prospectus Objective	Growth & Inc
Inception Date	Oct-14
Open to New Investments	Y

Prices

Price (as of 9/30/2019)	4.93
52-Week High	7.64
52-Week Low	4.57

Total Returns (%)

3-Month	6-Month	1-Year	3-Year	5-Year
-7.84	-10.98	-22.41	-21.61	-52.86

3-Year Standard Deviation	22.04
Effective Duration	

Valuation

Premium/Discount (1-Year Average)	0.02

Company Information

Provider	Virtus
Manager/Tenure	Jay D. Hatfield (5), Edward F. Ryan (5)
Website	http://www.virtus.com
Address	Virtus Opportunities Trust 101 Munson Street Greenfield MA 1301 United States
Phone Number	800-243-1574

PERFORMANCE

Ratings History

Date	Overall Rating	Risk Rating	Reward Rating
Q3-19	C	D+	C+
Q4-18	C	D+	C+
Q4-17	D	D	D
Q4-16	D	D	D
Q4-15	U		

Asset & Performance History

Date	NAV	1-Year Total Return
2018	5.1	-25.19
2017	8.58	-6.59
2016	11.26	24.62
2015	11.09	-45.85
2014	22.81	
2013		

Total Assets: $370,373,417

Asset Allocation

Asset	%
Cash	-32%
Stocks	132%
US Stocks	130%
Bonds	0%
US Bonds	0%
Other	0%

Services Offered:

Investment Strategy: The investment seeks total return primarily through investments in equity securities of publicly traded master limited partnerships and limited liability companies taxed as partnerships ("MLPs"). Under normal market conditions, the fund will invest not less than 80% of its net assets (plus the amount of any borrowings for investment purposes) in equity securities of MLPs in the energy infrastructure sector. It is non-diversified. **Top Holdings:** Energy Transfer LP MPLX LP Partnership Units Plains All American Pipeline LP Enterprise Products Partners LP Western Midstream Partners LP

Invesco S&P SmallCap 600 Revenue ETF
D+   **SELL**

Ticker	Traded On	NAV	Total Assets ($)	Dividend Yield (TTM)	Turnover Ratio	Expense Ratio
RWJ	NYSE Arca	63.76	$369,913,236	1.21	39	0.39

Ratings

Reward	D
Risk	C-
Recent Upgrade/Downgrade	Down

Fund Information

Fund Type	Exchange Traded Funds
Category	US Equity Small Cap
Sub-Category	Small Value
Prospectus Objective	Small Company
Inception Date	Feb-08
Open to New Investments	Y

Prices

Price (as of 9/30/2019)	63.73
52-Week High	74.25
52-Week Low	54.53

Total Returns (%)

3-Month	6-Month	1-Year	3-Year	5-Year
0.98	-3.75	-12.87	10.99	31.01

3-Year Standard Deviation	21.98
Effective Duration	

Valuation

Premium/Discount (1-Year Average)	-0.04

Company Information

Provider	Invesco
Manager/Tenure	Peter Hubbard (0), Michael Jeanette (0), Tony Seisser (0)
Website	http://www.invesco.com/us
Address	Invesco 11 Greenway Plaza, Ste. 2500 Houston TX 77046 United States
Phone Number	800-659-1005

PERFORMANCE

Ratings History

Date	Overall Rating	Risk Rating	Reward Rating
Q3-19	D+	C-	D
Q4-18	C-	C-	C-
Q4-17	B	C+	B
Q4-16	C-	C-	C-
Q4-15	C	C-	C

Asset & Performance History

Date	NAV	1-Year Total Return
2018	57.44	-16.87
2017	69.95	5.16
2016	67.14	30.52
2015	51.8	-8.5
2014	57.01	6.3
2013	53.85	45.52

Total Assets: $369,913,236

Asset Allocation

Asset	%
Cash	0%
Stocks	100%
US Stocks	98%
Bonds	0%
US Bonds	0%
Other	0%

Services Offered:

Investment Strategy: The investment seeks to track the investment results (before fees and expenses) of the S&P SmallCap 600® Revenue-Weighted Index. The fund will invest at least 90% of its total assets in the securities that comprise the index. The index is constructed using a rules-based methodology that re-weights the constituent securities of the S&P SmallCap 600® Index (the "parent index"), an index comprised of common stocks of 600 small-cap companies that generally represents the small-cap universe of the U.S. equity market, according to the revenue earned by the companies in the parent index, subject to a maximum 5% per company weighting. The fund is non-diversified. **Top Holdings:** Owens & Minor Inc Core-Mark Holding Co Inc United Natural Foods Inc Lithia Motors Inc Class A Community Health Systems Inc

ELEMENTS Linked to the Rogers International Commodity Index - Total Return   C-   HOLD

Ticker	Traded On	NAV	Total Assets ($)	Dividend Yield (TTM)	Turnover Ratio	Expense Ratio
RJI	NYSE Arca		$368,249,200	0		0.75

Ratings
Reward	D+
Risk	C-
Recent Upgrade/Downgrade	

Fund Information
Fund Type	Exchange Traded Funds
Category	Commodities Broad Basket
Sub-Category	Commodities Broad Basket
Prospectus Objective	Natl Res
Inception Date	Oct-07
Open to New Investments	Y

Prices
Price (as of 9/30/2019)	5.08
52-Week High	5.76
52-Week Low	4.87

Total Returns (%)
3-Month	6-Month	1-Year	3-Year	5-Year
-1.81	-4.29	-10.00	2.60	-31.78

3-Year Standard Deviation	9.43
Effective Duration	

Valuation
Premium/Discount (1-Year Average)	0.00

Company Information
Provider	ELEMENTS
Manager/Tenure	No Manager (11)
Website	http://www.elementsetn.com
Address	ELEMENTS United States
Phone Number	212-449-2957

PERFORMANCE

Ratings History
Date	Overall Rating	Risk Rating	Reward Rating
Q3-19	C-	C-	D+
Q4-18	C-	C	C-
Q4-17	C-	D+	C-
Q4-16	D	D	D
Q4-15	D-	D	D-

Asset & Performance History
Date	NAV	1-Year Total Return
2018	4.88	-9.62
2017	5.4	3.46
2016	5.19	11.37
2015	4.59	-27.14
2014	6.3	-22.79
2013	8.16	-5.33

Total Assets: $368,249,200

Asset Allocation
Asset	%
Cash	%
Stocks	%
US Stocks	%
Bonds	%
US Bonds	%
Other	%

Services Offered:

Investment Strategy: The investment seeks to replicate, net of expenses, the Rogers International Commodity Index – Total Return index.
The index represents the value of a basket of 35 commodity futures contracts. **Top Holdings:**

FlexShares Global Quality Real Estate Index Fund   C   HOLD

Ticker	Traded On	NAV	Total Assets ($)	Dividend Yield (TTM)	Turnover Ratio	Expense Ratio
GQRE	NYSE Arca	65.14	$368,026,141	2.77	61	0.45

Ratings
Reward	C
Risk	C-
Recent Upgrade/Downgrade	

Fund Information
Fund Type	Exchange Traded Funds
Category	Real Estate Sector Equity
Sub-Category	Global Real Estate
Prospectus Objective	Real Estate
Inception Date	Nov-13
Open to New Investments	Y

Prices
Price (as of 9/30/2019)	65.17
52-Week High	65.50
52-Week Low	53.78

Total Returns (%)
3-Month	6-Month	1-Year	3-Year	5-Year
3.41	3.37	9.84	18.28	45.37

3-Year Standard Deviation	10.86
Effective Duration	

Valuation
Premium/Discount (1-Year Average)	0.15

Company Information
Provider	Flexshares Trust
Manager/Tenure	Robert Anstine (5), Brendan Sullivan (3)
Website	http://www.flexshares.com
Address	50 South LaSalle Street Chicago, Illinois 60603 Chicago Illinois 60603 United States
Phone Number	855-353-9383

PERFORMANCE

Ratings History
Date	Overall Rating	Risk Rating	Reward Rating
Q3-19	C	C-	C
Q4-18	D+	D+	C-
Q4-17	B	B	B-
Q4-16	C	C-	C
Q4-15	D+	C-	C-

Asset & Performance History
Date	NAV	1-Year Total Return
2018	55.36	-9.06
2017	62.74	13.42
2016	56.44	3.96
2015	56.55	3.49
2014	55.92	17
2013	49.08	

Total Assets: $368,026,141

Asset Allocation
Asset	%
Cash	1%
Stocks	99%
US Stocks	60%
Bonds	0%
US Bonds	0%
Other	1%

Services Offered:

Investment Strategy: The investment seeks investment results that correspond generally to the price and yield performance, before fees and expenses, of the Northern Trust Global Quality Real Estate IndexSM. The fund normally will invest at least 80% of its total assets (exclusive of collateral held from securities lending) in the securities of the index and in ADRs and GDRs based on the securities in the index. The index is designed to measure the performance of companies that exhibit certain quality, valuation and momentum characteristics within a universe of publicly-traded equity securities of U.S. and non-U.S. REITs and real estate companies. The fund is non-diversified. **Top Holdings:** Prologis Inc Equity Residential AvalonBay Communities Inc Link Real Estate Investment Trust Essex Property Trust Inc

Xtrackers MSCI Japan Hedged Equity ETF

C   **HOLD**

Ticker	Traded On	NAV	Total Assets ($)	Dividend Yield (TTM)	Turnover Ratio	Expense Ratio
DBJP	NYSE Arca	39.52	$367,588,723	3.78	15	0.45

Ratings
Reward	C-
Risk	C
Recent Upgrade/Downgrade	

Fund Information
Fund Type	Exchange Traded Funds
Category	Japan Equity
Sub-Category	Japan Stock
Prospectus Objective	Pacific Stock
Inception Date	Jun-11
Open to New Investments	Y

Prices
Price (as of 9/30/2019)	39.82
52-Week High	45.08
52-Week Low	35.24

Total Returns (%)
3-Month	6-Month	1-Year	3-Year	5-Year
1.75	1.09	-7.91	31.98	30.82

3-Year Standard Deviation	13.21
Effective Duration	

Valuation
Premium/Discount (1-Year Average)	-0.09

Company Information
Provider	DWS
Manager/Tenure	Patrick Dwyer (2), Bryan Richards (2), Shlomo Bassous (1)
Website	http://dws.com
Address	DWS 210 West 10th Street Kansas City MO 64105-1614 United States
Phone Number	

PERFORMANCE

Ratings History
Date	Overall Rating	Risk Rating	Reward Rating
Q3-19	C	C	C-
Q4-18	C	C+	C-
Q4-17	B	B-	A-
Q4-16	C	C	C-
Q4-15	B-	C+	B-

Asset & Performance History
Date	NAV	1-Year Total Return
2018	36.63	-14.01
2017	44.08	20.82
2016	37.34	-2
2015	38.6	9.07
2014	37.36	7.79
2013	38.32	51.68

Total Assets: $367,588,723
Asset Allocation
Asset	%
Cash	5%
Stocks	96%
US Stocks	0%
Bonds	-1%
US Bonds	-1%
Other	0%

Services Offered:

Investment Strategy: The investment seeks investment results that correspond generally to the performance, of the MSCI Japan US Dollar Hedged Index. The fund, using a "passive" or indexing investment approach, seeks investment results that correspond generally to the performance, of the underlying index, which is designed to track the performance of the Japanese equity market while mitigating exposure to fluctuations between the value of the U.S. dollar and the Japanese yen. It will invest at least 80% of its total assets in component securities (including depositary receipts in respect of such securities) of the underlying index. **Top Holdings:** Toyota Motor Corp SoftBank Group Corp Sony Corp TOPIX Index Future Sept19 Mitsubishi UFJ Financial Group Inc

---

SPDR® NYSE Technology ETF

C   **HOLD**

Ticker	Traded On	NAV	Total Assets ($)	Dividend Yield (TTM)	Turnover Ratio	Expense Ratio
XNTK	NYSE Arca		$363,572,765	0.61	10	0.35

Ratings
Reward	B-
Risk	C-
Recent Upgrade/Downgrade	

Fund Information
Fund Type	Exchange Traded Funds
Category	Technology Sector Equity
Sub-Category	Technology
Prospectus Objective	Technology
Inception Date	Sep-00
Open to New Investments	Y

Prices
Price (as of 9/30/2019)	72.75
52-Week High	94.96
52-Week Low	54.51

Total Returns (%)
3-Month	6-Month	1-Year	3-Year	5-Year
-2.49	-0.33	0.00	61.90	103.96

3-Year Standard Deviation	16.79
Effective Duration	

Valuation
Premium/Discount (1-Year Average)	0.01

Company Information
Provider	SPDR State Street Global Advisors
Manager/Tenure	Michael J. Feehily (7), Karl A. Schneider (4), Kathleen Morgan (0)
Website	http://www.spdrs.com
Address	SPDR State Street Global Advisors State Street Financial Center, 1 Lincoln Street Boston MA 02111-2900 United States
Phone Number	617-786-3000

PERFORMANCE

Ratings History
Date	Overall Rating	Risk Rating	Reward Rating
Q3-19	C	C-	B-
Q4-18	C+	C	B
Q4-17	A-	B	A+
Q4-16	C	C	C+
Q4-15	C+	C	B-

Asset & Performance History
Date	NAV	1-Year Total Return
2018	59.56	-6.25
2017	83.77	40.25
2016	60.53	12.91
2015	53.88	7.76
2014	50.48	13.38
2013	44.93	33.21

Total Assets: $363,572,765
Asset Allocation
Asset	%
Cash	0%
Stocks	100%
US Stocks	86%
Bonds	0%
US Bonds	0%
Other	0%

Services Offered: Dividend Investment Plan, CashInvestment Plan

Investment Strategy: The investment seeks to provide investment results that, before fees and expenses, correspond generally to the total return performance of the NYSE Technology Index that tracks the performance of publicly traded technology companies. The fund generally invests substantially all, but at least 80%, of its total assets in the securities comprising the index. It may invest in equity securities that are not included in the index, cash and cash equivalents or money market instruments, such as repurchase agreements and money market funds. The index is composed of 35 leading U.S.-listed technology-related companies. The fund is non-diversified. **Top Holdings:** ServiceNow Inc Applied Materials Inc Twitter Inc Intuit Inc Micron Technology Inc

EMQQ The Emerging Markets Internet & Ecommerce ETF   C-   HOLD

Ticker	Traded On	NAV	Total Assets ($)	Dividend Yield (TTM)	Turnover Ratio	Expense Ratio
EMQQ	NYSE Arca	31.33	$360,248,415	0	33	0.86

Ratings

Reward	C-
Risk	C-
Recent Upgrade/Downgrade	

Fund Information

Fund Type	Exchange Traded Funds
Category	Global Emerg Mkts Equity
Sub-Category	Diversified Emerging Mkts
Prospectus Objective	Div Emerg Mkts
Inception Date	Nov-14
Open to New Investments	Y

Prices

Price (as of 9/30/2019)	31.20
52-Week High	35.27
52-Week Low	26.09

Total Returns (%)

3-Month	6-Month	1-Year	3-Year	5-Year
-3.77	-6.58	-1.60	17.91	

3-Year Standard Deviation	21.93
Effective Duration	

Valuation

Premium/Discount (1-Year Average)	-0.12

Company Information

Provider	EMQQ
Manager/Tenure	Dustin Lewellyn (4), Anand Desai (3), Ernesto Tong (3)
Website	http://www.emqqetf.com
Address	EMQQ 1 Freedom Valley Drive Oaks PA 19456 United States
Phone Number	855-888-9892

PERFORMANCE

Ratings History

Date	Overall Rating	Risk Rating	Reward Rating
Q3-19	C-	C-	C-
Q4-18	C-	D	C
Q4-17	B-	C	B
Q4-16	C	D+	C
Q4-15	U		

Asset & Performance History

Date	NAV	1-Year Total Return
2018	26.89	-29.21
2017	37.99	67.16
2016	22.94	-2.97
2015	23.82	5.2
2014	22.66	
2013		

Total Assets: $360,248,415

Asset Allocation

Asset	%
Cash	0%
Stocks	100%
US Stocks	0%
Bonds	0%
US Bonds	0%
Other	0%

Services Offered:

Investment Strategy: The investment seeks to provide investment results that, before fees and expenses, correspond generally to the price and yield performance of EMQQ The Emerging Markets Internet & Ecommerce IndexTM (the "index"). The fund will normally invest at least 80% of its total assets in securities of the index or in depositary receipts representing securities of the index. The index is designed to measure the performance of an investable universe of publicly-traded, emerging market internet and ecommerce companies. The fund is non-diversified. **Top Holdings:** Alibaba Group Holding Ltd ADR Tencent Holdings Ltd Pinduoduo Inc ADR Naspers Ltd Class N MercadoLibre Inc

---

Barclays ETN+ Select MLP ETN   D+   SELL

Ticker	Traded On	NAV	Total Assets ($)	Dividend Yield (TTM)	Turnover Ratio	Expense Ratio
ATMP	BATS	18.45	$359,080,929	6.42		0.95

Ratings

Reward	D
Risk	C-
Recent Upgrade/Downgrade	Down

Fund Information

Fund Type	Exchange Traded Funds
Category	Energy Sector Equity
Sub-Category	Energy Limited Partnership
Prospectus Objective	Growth
Inception Date	Mar-13
Open to New Investments	Y

Prices

Price (as of 9/30/2019)	18.36
52-Week High	21.27
52-Week Low	16.98

Total Returns (%)

3-Month	6-Month	1-Year	3-Year	5-Year
-6.81	-7.64	-5.77	-6.09	-24.39

3-Year Standard Deviation	16.18
Effective Duration	

Valuation

Premium/Discount (1-Year Average)	-0.20

Company Information

Provider	Milleis Investissements Funds
Manager/Tenure	No Manager (6)
Website	
Address	2-4, rue Eugène Ruppert L-2453 Luxembourg Luxembourg L-2453 Luxembourg
Phone Number	

PERFORMANCE

Ratings History

Date	Overall Rating	Risk Rating	Reward Rating
Q3-19	D+	C-	D
Q4-18	C-	C-	D+
Q4-17	D	D	D+
Q4-16	C-	D+	C-
Q4-15	D+	D+	D+

Asset & Performance History

Date	NAV	1-Year Total Return
2018	17.49	-10.85
2017	20.77	-6.66
2016	23.44	38.12
2015	18.56	-36.79
2014	30.79	16.59
2013	27.37	

Total Assets: $359,080,929

Asset Allocation

Asset	%
Cash	%
Stocks	%
US Stocks	%
Bonds	%
US Bonds	%
Other	%

Services Offered:

Investment Strategy: The investment seeks to replicate, net of expenses, the Atlantic Trust Select MLP Index. The index seeks to capture returns that may be available from investing in a basket of direct or indirect interests in master limited partnerships ("MLPs"), limited liability companies ("LLCs") and corporations (collectively, "MLP Interests") that are selected pursuant to the Atlantic Trust Select MLP Strategy. **Top Holdings:**

iShares Global Clean Energy ETF

C+   HOLD

Ticker	Traded On	NAV	Total Assets ($)	Dividend Yield (TTM)	Turnover Ratio	Expense Ratio
ICLN	NAS CM	10.88	$357,872,749	1.68	42	0.46

Ratings
Reward   B-
Risk   C
Recent Upgrade/Downgrade

Fund Information
Fund Type   Exchange Traded Funds
Category   Utilities Sector Equity
Sub-Category   Miscellaneous Sector
Prospectus Objective   Natl Res
Inception Date   Jun-08
Open to New Investments   Y

Prices
Price (as of 9/30/2019)   10.90
52-Week High   11.39
52-Week Low   7.91

Total Returns (%)

3-Month	6-Month	1-Year	3-Year	5-Year
2.35	11.63	29.82	29.67	17.48

3-Year Standard Deviation   16.68
Effective Duration

Valuation
Premium/Discount (1-Year Average)   0.13

Company Information
Provider   iShares
Manager/Tenure   Greg Savage (11), Jennifer Hsui (7),
                  Alan Mason (3), 2 others
Website   http://www.ishares.com
Address   iShares 400 Howard Street San
                  Francisco CA 94105 United States
Phone Number   800-474-2737

PERFORMANCE

Ratings History

Date	Overall Rating	Risk Rating	Reward Rating
Q3-19	C+	C	B-
Q4-18	C-	C-	C-
Q4-17	C	C	C-
Q4-16	D	D	D
Q4-15	C-	C-	C-

Asset & Performance History

Date	NAV	1-Year Total Return
2018	8.27	-8.61
2017	9.29	20.47
2016	7.92	-15.95
2015	9.78	2.76
2014	9.72	-3.92
2013	10.39	49.01

Total Assets: $357,872,749

Asset Allocation

Asset	%
Cash	1%
Stocks	99%
US Stocks	38%
Bonds	0%
US Bonds	0%
Other	0%

Services Offered:

Investment Strategy: The investment seeks to track the S&P Global Clean Energy IndexTM. The fund generally invests at least 90% of its assets in the component securities of the index and in investments that have economic characteristics that are substantially identical to the component securities and may invest up to 10% of its assets in certain futures, options and swap contracts, cash and cash equivalents, as well as in securities not included in the index. The index is designed to track the performance of approximately 30 of what are will be the most liquid and tradable securities of global companies involved in clean energy related businesses. The fund is non-diversified. **Top Holdings:** SolarEdge Technologies Inc Ormat Technologies Inc Contact Energy Ltd Meridian Energy Ltd Verbund AG

ARK Web x.0 ETF

C   HOLD

Ticker	Traded On	NAV	Total Assets ($)	Dividend Yield (TTM)	Turnover Ratio	Expense Ratio
ARKW	NYSE Arca	48.65	$357,545,487	0		0.75

Ratings
Reward   C+
Risk   D+
Recent Upgrade/Downgrade   Down

Fund Information
Fund Type   Exchange Traded Funds
Category   Technology Sector Equity
Sub-Category   Technology
Prospectus Objective   Technology
Inception Date   Sep-14
Open to New Investments   Y

Prices
Price (as of 9/30/2019)   48.67
52-Week High   58.05
52-Week Low   40.89

Total Returns (%)

3-Month	6-Month	1-Year	3-Year	5-Year
-7.31	-7.72	-5.24	119.24	194.15

3-Year Standard Deviation   21.99
Effective Duration

Valuation
Premium/Discount (1-Year Average)   0.01

Company Information
Provider   ARK ETF Trust
Manager/Tenure   Catherine D. Wood (5)
Website   http://www.ark-funds.com
Address   ARK ETF Trust 155 West 19th Street,
                  5th Floor New York New York 10011
                  United States
Phone Number   212-426-7040

PERFORMANCE

Ratings History

Date	Overall Rating	Risk Rating	Reward Rating
Q3-19	C	D+	C+
Q4-18	C	C-	C+
Q4-17	B	B	B
Q4-16	C	D+	C
Q4-15	U		

Asset & Performance History

Date	NAV	1-Year Total Return
2018	42.45	-6.34
2017	45.97	87.17
2016	25.06	8.72
2015	23.05	15.28
2014	20.45	
2013		

Total Assets: $357,545,487

Asset Allocation

Asset	%
Cash	0%
Stocks	98%
US Stocks	84%
Bonds	0%
US Bonds	0%
Other	1%

Services Offered:

Investment Strategy: The investment seeks long-term growth of capital. The fund is an actively-managed exchange-traded fund ("ETF") that will invest under normal circumstances primarily (at least 80% of its assets) in domestic and foreign equity securities of companies that are relevant to the fund's investment theme of Web x.0. Under normal circumstances, substantially all of the fund's assets will be invested in equity securities, including common stocks, partnership interests, business trust shares and other equity investments or ownership interests in business enterprises. The fund is non-diversified. **Top Holdings:** Tesla Inc Square Inc A NVIDIA Corp Twitter Inc Tencent Holdings Ltd ADR

iShares MSCI South Africa ETF   D+   SELL

Ticker	Traded On	NAV	Total Assets ($)	Dividend Yield (TTM)	Turnover Ratio	Expense Ratio
EZA	NYSE Arca	47.53	$356,482,632	5.01	15	0.59

Ratings
Reward	D
Risk	D+
Recent Upgrade/Downgrade	Down

Fund Information
Fund Type	Exchange Traded Funds
Category	Equity Misc
Sub-Category	Miscellaneous Region
Prospectus Objective	Foreign Stock
Inception Date	Feb-03
Open to New Investments	Y

Prices
Price (as of 9/30/2019)	47.45
52-Week High	58.17
52-Week Low	45.52

Total Returns (%)
3-Month	6-Month	1-Year	3-Year	5-Year
-13.44	-10.20	-7.40	-6.81	-12.96

3-Year Standard Deviation	20.91
Effective Duration	

Valuation
Premium/Discount (1-Year Average)	-0.17

Company Information
Provider	iShares
Manager/Tenure	Diane Hsiung (11), Greg Savage (11), Jennifer Hsui (6), 3 others
Website	http://www.ishares.com
Address	iShares 400 Howard Street San Francisco CA 94105 United States
Phone Number	800-474-2737

PERFORMANCE

Ratings History

Date	Overall Rating	Risk Rating	Reward Rating
Q3-19	D+	D+	D
Q4-18	D	D	D+
Q4-17	C	C	C+
Q4-16	D+	D	D+
Q4-15	D+	D+	C-

Asset & Performance History

Date	NAV	1-Year Total Return
2018	50.97	-24.58
2017	70.11	34.77
2016	52.94	17.24
2015	47.02	-25.92
2014	65.15	4.55
2013	63.71	-6.81

Total Assets: $356,482,632

Asset Allocation

Asset	%
Cash	0%
Stocks	100%
US Stocks	0%
Bonds	0%
US Bonds	0%
Other	0%

Services Offered:

Investment Strategy: The investment seeks to track the investment results of the MSCI South Africa 25/50 Index. The fund normally invests at least 95% of its total assets in the securities of its underlying index and in depositary receipts representing securities in its underlying index. The underlying index uses a capping methodology to limit the weight of any single component to a maximum of 25% of the underlying index. The underlying index may include large- or mid-capitalization companies. The fund is non-diversified. **Top Holdings:** Naspers Ltd Class N Standard Bank Group Ltd Firstrand Ltd MTN Group Ltd Sasol Ltd

---

Invesco Dynamic Pharmaceuticals ETF   C   HOLD

Ticker	Traded On	NAV	Total Assets ($)	Dividend Yield (TTM)	Turnover Ratio	Expense Ratio
PJP	NYSE Arca	56.71	$354,415,429	1.24	81	0.56

Ratings
Reward	C+
Risk	C-
Recent Upgrade/Downgrade	Up

Fund Information
Fund Type	Exchange Traded Funds
Category	Healthcare Sector Equity
Sub-Category	Health
Prospectus Objective	Health
Inception Date	Jun-05
Open to New Investments	Y

Prices
Price (as of 9/30/2019)	56.66
52-Week High	72.73
52-Week Low	55.49

Total Returns (%)
3-Month	6-Month	1-Year	3-Year	5-Year
-6.40	-12.66	-20.77	-5.57	0.80

3-Year Standard Deviation	17.54
Effective Duration	

Valuation
Premium/Discount (1-Year Average)	-0.07

Company Information
Provider	Invesco
Manager/Tenure	Peter Hubbard (12), Michael Jeanette (11), Tony Seisser (5)
Website	http://www.invesco.com/us
Address	Invesco 11 Greenway Plaza, Ste. 2500 Houston TX 77046 United States
Phone Number	800-659-1005

PERFORMANCE

Ratings History

Date	Overall Rating	Risk Rating	Reward Rating
Q3-19	C	C-	C+
Q4-18	C	D+	B-
Q4-17	C	C	C
Q4-16	C	D+	B-
Q4-15	B	B-	B

Asset & Performance History

Date	NAV	1-Year Total Return
2018	62.4	-1.69
2017	64.18	15.31
2016	56.03	-19.24
2015	69.98	11.05
2014	66.48	28.1
2013	53.45	55.6

Total Assets: $354,415,429

Asset Allocation

Asset	%
Cash	0%
Stocks	100%
US Stocks	94%
Bonds	0%
US Bonds	0%
Other	0%

Services Offered:

Investment Strategy: The investment seeks to track the investment results (before fees and expenses) of the Dynamic Pharmaceutical IntellidexSM Index. The fund generally will invest at least 90% of its total assets in the securities that comprise the underlying intellidex. The underlying intellidex was composed of common stocks of U.S. pharmaceutical companies. These companies are engaged principally in the research, development, manufacture, sale or distribution of pharmaceuticals and drugs of all types. The fund is non-diversified. **Top Holdings:** Amgen Inc Abbott Laboratories Merck & Co Inc Gilead Sciences Inc Johnson & Johnson

iShares iBonds Dec 2026 Term Corporate ETF   C   HOLD

Ticker	Traded On	NAV	Total Assets ($)	Dividend Yield (TTM)	Turnover Ratio	Expense Ratio
IBDR	NYSE Arca	25.36	$353,779,597	3.34	3	0.1

Ratings
Reward	C
Risk	C+
Recent Upgrade/Downgrade	

Fund Information
Fund Type	Exchange Traded Funds
Category	US Fixed Income
Sub-Category	Target Maturity
Prospectus Objective	Corp Bond - Gen
Inception Date	Sep-16
Open to New Investments	Y

Prices
Price (as of 9/30/2019)	25.47
52-Week High	25.68
52-Week Low	22.85

Total Returns (%)
3-Month	6-Month	1-Year	3-Year	5-Year
2.36	7.31	13.10	11.66	

3-Year Standard Deviation	4.36
Effective Duration	

Valuation
Premium/Discount (1-Year Average)	0.31

Company Information
Provider	iShares
Manager/Tenure	James Mauro (3), Scott Radell (3)
Website	http://www.ishares.com
Address	iShares 400 Howard Street San Francisco CA 94105 United States
Phone Number	800-474-2737

PERFORMANCE

Ratings History
Date	Overall Rating	Risk Rating	Reward Rating
Q3-19	C	C+	C
Q4-18	D+	C-	D+
Q4-17	D	B	D+
Q4-16	U		
Q4-15			

Asset & Performance History
Date	NAV	1-Year Total Return
2018	23.04	-2.3
2017	24.43	5.68
2016	23.84	
2015		
2014		
2013		

Total Assets: $353,779,597

Asset Allocation
Asset	%
Cash	0%
Stocks	0%
US Stocks	0%
Bonds	97%
US Bonds	86%
Other	0%

Services Offered:

Investment Strategy: The investment seeks to track the investment results of the Bloomberg Barclays December 2026 Maturity Corporate Index composed of U.S. dollar-denominated, investment-grade corporate bonds maturing in 2026. The fund generally will invest at least 90% of its assets in the component securities of the underlying index, and may invest up to 10% of its assets in certain futures, options and swap contracts, cash and cash equivalents. The index includes U.S. dollar-denominated, investment-grade securities publicly issued by U.S. and non-U.S. corporate issuers that have $300 million or more of outstanding face value at the time of inclusion. It is non-diversified. **Top Holdings:** Dell International L.L.C. and EMC Corporation 6.02% Wells Fargo & Company 3% Microsoft Corporation 2.4% Apple Inc. 3.25% Wells Fargo & Company 3%

PIMCO 25+ Year Zero Coupon U.S. Treasury Index Exchange-Traded Fund   C   HOLD

Ticker	Traded On	NAV	Total Assets ($)	Dividend Yield (TTM)	Turnover Ratio	Expense Ratio
ZROZ	NYSE Arca	144.52	$349,735,538	2.16	21	0.15

Ratings
Reward	C
Risk	C-
Recent Upgrade/Downgrade	

Fund Information
Fund Type	Exchange Traded Funds
Category	US Fixed Income
Sub-Category	Long Government
Prospectus Objective	Govt Bond - Treasury
Inception Date	Oct-09
Open to New Investments	Y

Prices
Price (as of 9/30/2019)	144.61
52-Week High	151.72
52-Week Low	100.48

Total Returns (%)
3-Month	6-Month	1-Year	3-Year	5-Year
13.75	24.85	38.09	16.04	52.83

3-Year Standard Deviation	18.34
Effective Duration	27.48

Valuation
Premium/Discount (1-Year Average)	0.12

Company Information
Provider	PIMCO
Manager/Tenure	Matthew P. Dorsten (3), Mitchell Handa (0), Graham A. Rennison (0)
Website	http://www.pimco.com
Address	PIMCO 840 Newport Center Drive, Suite 100 Newport Beach CA 92660 United States
Phone Number	866-746-2602

PERFORMANCE

Ratings History
Date	Overall Rating	Risk Rating	Reward Rating
Q3-19	C	C-	C
Q4-18	D+	D+	D
Q4-17	C	C	C
Q4-16	C	C-	C
Q4-15	C	D+	C

Asset & Performance History
Date	NAV	1-Year Total Return
2018	112.45	-4.28
2017	120.96	14.06
2016	108.88	1.61
2015	110.24	-4.94
2014	119.36	49.35
2013	82.35	-21.94

Total Assets: $349,735,538

Asset Allocation
Asset	%
Cash	0%
Stocks	0%
US Stocks	0%
Bonds	100%
US Bonds	100%
Other	0%

Services Offered:

Investment Strategy: The investment seeks to provide total return that closely corresponds, before fees and expenses, to the total return of the ICE BofAML Long US Treasury Principal STRIPS Index. The fund invests at least 80% of its total assets (exclusive of collateral held from securities lending) in the component securities of the ICE BofAML Long US Treasury Principal STRIPS Index (the "underlying index"). The underlying index is an unmanaged index comprised of long maturity Separate Trading of Registered Interest and Principal of Securities ("STRIPS") representing the final principal payment of U.S. Treasury bonds. **Top Holdings:** U.S. Treasury Bond Stripped Principal Payment 0% U.S. Treasury Bond Stripped Principal Payment 0% U.S. Treasury Bond Stripped Principal Payment 0% U.S. Treasury Bond Stripped Principal Payment 0% U.S. Treasury Bond Stripped Principal Payment 0%

Invesco California AMT-Free Municipal Bond ETF　　　　　　　C　　HOLD

Ticker	Traded On	NAV	Total Assets ($)	Dividend Yield (TTM)	Turnover Ratio	Expense Ratio
PWZ	NYSE Arca	27.34	$348,530,111	2.45		0.28

Ratings
Reward	C+
Risk	C-
Recent Upgrade/Downgrade	

Fund Information
Fund Type	Exchange Traded Funds
Category	US Muni Fixed Inc
Sub-Category	Muni California Long
Prospectus Objective	Muni Bond - Single State
Inception Date	Oct-07
Open to New Investments	Y

Prices
Price (as of 9/30/2019)	27.35
52-Week High	27.69
52-Week Low	25.05

Total Returns (%)
3-Month	6-Month	1-Year	3-Year	5-Year
2.34	5.20	9.81	11.24	23.40

3-Year Standard Deviation	4.35
Effective Duration	8.86

Valuation
Premium/Discount (1-Year Average)	-0.03

Company Information
Provider	Invesco
Manager/Tenure	Philip Fang (11), Peter Hubbard (11), Jeffrey W. Kernagis (11), 2 others
Website	http://www.invesco.com/us
Address	Invesco 11 Greenway Plaza, Ste. 2500 Houston TX 77046 United States
Phone Number	800-659-1005

PERFORMANCE

Ratings History
Date	Overall Rating	Risk Rating	Reward Rating
Q3-19	C	C-	C+
Q4-18	C	C+	C-
Q4-17	B-	B+	C
Q4-16	C	C-	C
Q4-15	C	C-	C+

Asset & Performance History
Date	NAV	1-Year Total Return
2018	25.76	0.39
2017	26.32	6.65
2016	25.31	0.86
2015	25.8	4.15
2014	25.58	14.01
2013	23.34	-4.1

Total Assets: $348,530,111
Asset Allocation
Asset	%
Cash	1%
Stocks	0%
US Stocks	0%
Bonds	99%
US Bonds	99%
Other	0%

Services Offered:

Investment Strategy: The investment seeks to track the investment results (before fees and expenses) of the ICE BofAML California Long-Term Core Plus Municipal Securities Index. The fund generally will invest at least 80% of its total assets in municipal securities that comprise the underlying index and that also are exempt from the federal AMT. The underlying index is composed of U.S. dollar-denominated, investment grade, tax-exempt debt publicly issued by California or any U.S. territory or their political subdivisions, in the U.S. domestic market with a term of at least 15 years remaining to final maturity. It is non-diversified. **Top Holdings:** SAN DIEGO CALIF UNI SCH DIST 5% CALIFORNIA HEALTH FACS FING AUTH REV 5% SAN FRANCISCO CALIF CITY & CNTY ARPTS COMMN INTL ARPT REV 5% SACRAMENTO CALIF TRANSIENT OCCUPANCY TAX REV 5% LOS ANGELES CNTY CALIF FACS INC LEASE REV 5%

iShares MSCI Turkey ETF　　　　　　　　　　　　　　　　D　　SELL

Ticker	Traded On	NAV	Total Assets ($)	Dividend Yield (TTM)	Turnover Ratio	Expense Ratio
TUR	NAS CM	26.77	$348,042,201	2.5	7	0.59

Ratings
Reward	D+
Risk	D
Recent Upgrade/Downgrade	

Fund Information
Fund Type	Exchange Traded Funds
Category	Equity Misc
Sub-Category	Miscellaneous Region
Prospectus Objective	Foreign Stock
Inception Date	Mar-08
Open to New Investments	Y

Prices
Price (as of 9/30/2019)	26.72
52-Week High	28.97
52-Week Low	20.24

Total Returns (%)
3-Month	6-Month	1-Year	3-Year	5-Year
5.60	10.94	15.54	-22.53	-36.83

3-Year Standard Deviation	34.7
Effective Duration	

Valuation
Premium/Discount (1-Year Average)	0.00

Company Information
Provider	iShares
Manager/Tenure	Diane Hsiung (11), Greg Savage (11), Jennifer Hsui (6), 3 others
Website	http://www.ishares.com
Address	iShares 400 Howard Street San Francisco CA 94105 United States
Phone Number	800-474-2737

PERFORMANCE

Ratings History
Date	Overall Rating	Risk Rating	Reward Rating
Q3-19	D	D	D+
Q4-18	D-	D	D-
Q4-17	D+	D	C-
Q4-16	D	D	D
Q4-15	D	D	D

Asset & Performance History
Date	NAV	1-Year Total Return
2018	24.68	-41.41
2017	43.61	37.44
2016	32.62	-8.28
2015	36.42	-31.46
2014	54.41	16.71
2013	47.36	-26.76

Total Assets: $348,042,201
Asset Allocation
Asset	%
Cash	0%
Stocks	100%
US Stocks	0%
Bonds	0%
US Bonds	0%
Other	0%

Services Offered:

Investment Strategy: The investment seeks to track the investment results of the MSCI Turkey IMI 25/50 Index. The fund generally will invest at least 90% of its assets in the component securities of the underlying index and in investments that have economic characteristics that are substantially identical to the component securities of the underlying index. The underlying index consists of stocks traded primarily on the Istanbul Stock Exchange (ISE). The fund is non-diversified. **Top Holdings:** Turkiye Garanti Bankasi AS Bim Birlesik Magazalar AS Akbank TAS Tupras-Turkiye Petrol Rafineleri AS Koc Holding AS

ProShares Ultra Dow30   C+   HOLD

Ticker	Traded On	NAV	Total Assets ($)	Dividend Yield (TTM)	Turnover Ratio	Expense Ratio
DDM	NYSE Arca	49.60	$347,205,657	0.57	35	0.95

Ratings
Reward   B-
Risk   C
Recent Upgrade/Downgrade

Fund Information
Fund Type   Exchange Traded Funds
Category   Trading Tools
Sub-Category   Trading--Leveraged Equity
Prospectus Objective   Growth
Inception Date   Jun-06
Open to New Investments   Y

Prices
Price (as of 9/30/2019)   49.59
52-Week High   51.35
52-Week Low   33.20

Total Returns (%)

3-Month	6-Month	1-Year	3-Year	5-Year
1.24	4.59	-0.53	113.70	161.26

3-Year Standard Deviation   25.09
Effective Duration

Valuation
Premium/Discount (1-Year Average)   -0.02

Company Information
Provider   ProShares
Manager/Tenure   Michael Neches (6), Devin Sullivan (1)
Website   http://www.proshares.com
Address   ProShares 7501 Wisconsin Avenue, Suite 1000 Bethesda MD 20814 United States
Phone Number   866-776-5125

PERFORMANCE

Ratings History

Date	Overall Rating	Risk Rating	Reward Rating
Q3-19	C+	C	B-
Q4-18	C+	C+	C
Q4-17	B+	C	A+
Q4-16	B	C+	B+
Q4-15	B-	B-	C+

Asset & Performance History

Date	NAV	1-Year Total Return
2018	37.76	-13.35
2017	43.92	59.38
2016	27.79	31.3
2015	21.44	-3.26
2014	22.44	17.93
2013	19.19	63.8

Total Assets: $347,205,657
Asset Allocation

Asset	%
Cash	-100%
Stocks	83%
US Stocks	83%
Bonds	0%
US Bonds	0%
Other	117%

Services Offered:

Investment Strategy: The investment seeks daily investment results, before fees and expenses, that correspond to two times (2x) the daily performance of the Dow Jones Industrial Average® Index. The fund invests in financial instruments that ProShare Advisors believes, in combination, should produce daily returns consistent with the fund's investment objective. The index is a price-weighted index and includes 30 large-cap, "blue-chip" U.S. stocks, excluding utility and transportation companies. The fund is non-diversified. **Top Holdings:** Dj Industrial Average Swap Citibank Na Spdr Dow Jones Industrial Average (Dia) Swap Goldman Sachs International Dj Industrial Average Swap Societe Generale Spdr Dow Jones Industrial Average (Dia) Swap Morgan Stanley & Co. Internati Boeing Co

---

Direxion Daily Small Cap Bear 3X Shares   B-   BUY

Ticker	Traded On	NAV	Total Assets ($)	Dividend Yield (TTM)	Turnover Ratio	Expense Ratio
TZA	NYSE Arca	46.93	$346,854,638	0.82	0	1.11

Ratings
Reward   B
Risk   D+
Recent Upgrade/Downgrade   Up

Fund Information
Fund Type   Exchange Traded Funds
Category   Trading Tools
Sub-Category   Trading--Inverse Equity
Prospectus Objective   Small Company
Inception Date   Nov-08
Open to New Investments   Y

Prices
Price (as of 9/30/2019)   46.99
52-Week High   55.00
52-Week Low   8.48

Total Returns (%)

3-Month	6-Month	1-Year	3-Year	5-Year
4.02	392.40	438.26	77.22	-32.80

3-Year Standard Deviation   51.52
Effective Duration

Valuation
Premium/Discount (1-Year Average)   0.06

Company Information
Provider   Direxion Funds
Manager/Tenure   Paul Brigandi (10), Tony Ng (4)
Website   http://www.direxionfunds.com
Address   Direxion Funds 1301 Avenue Of The Americas (6th Avenue) New York NY 10019 United States
Phone Number   646-572-3390

PERFORMANCE

Ratings History

Date	Overall Rating	Risk Rating	Reward Rating
Q3-19	B-	D+	B
Q4-18	D	D	D-
Q4-17	E+	E+	E+
Q4-16	D	D-	E+
Q4-15	D-	E+	E+

Asset & Performance History

Date	NAV	1-Year Total Return
2018	15.2	24.79
2017	12.28	-38.35
2016	19.92	-55.53
2015	44.8	-6.82
2014	48.08	-29.12
2013	67.84	-68.61

Total Assets: $346,854,638
Asset Allocation

Asset	%
Cash	115%
Stocks	-15%
US Stocks	-15%
Bonds	0%
US Bonds	0%
Other	0%

Services Offered:

Investment Strategy: The investment seeks daily investment results, before fees and expenses, of 300% of the inverse (or opposite) of the daily performance of the Russell 2000® Index. The fund invests in swap agreements, futures contracts, short positions or other financial instruments that, in combination, provide inverse (opposite) or short leveraged exposure to the index equal to at least 80% of the fund's net assets (plus borrowing for investment purposes). The index measures the performance of approximately 2,000 small-capitalization companies in the Russell 3000® Index, based on a combination of their market capitalization and current index membership. It is non-diversified. **Top Holdings:** Russ 2000 Indx Small Swap Russ 2000 Indx Small Swap Russ 2000 Indx Small Swap Russ 2000 Indx Small Swap Russ 2000 Indx Small Swap

---

ProShares Ultra Technology   C+   HOLD

Ticker	Traded On	NAV	Total Assets ($)	Dividend Yield (TTM)	Turnover Ratio	Expense Ratio
ROM	NYSE Arca	123.31	$345,275,295	0.23	14	0.95

Ratings
Reward	B
Risk	C
Recent Upgrade/Downgrade	Up

Fund Information
Fund Type	Exchange Traded Funds
Category	Trading Tools
Sub-Category	Trading--Leveraged Equity
Prospectus Objective	Technology
Inception Date	Jan-07
Open to New Investments	Y

Prices
Price (as of 9/30/2019)	123.27
52-Week High	133.94
52-Week Low	68.54

Total Returns (%)
3-Month	6-Month	1-Year	3-Year	5-Year
1.74	8.52	2.16	159.88	262.39

3-Year Standard Deviation	32.56
Effective Duration	

Valuation
Premium/Discount (1-Year Average)	-0.04

Company Information
Provider	ProShares
Manager/Tenure	Michael Neches (6), Tarak Davé (1)
Website	http://www.proshares.com
Address	ProShares 7501 Wisconsin Avenue, Suite 1000 Bethesda MD 20814 United States
Phone Number	866-776-5125

PERFORMANCE

Ratings History

Date	Overall Rating	Risk Rating	Reward Rating
Q3-19	C+	C	B
Q4-18	C+	C	C+
Q4-17	A-	B-	A+
Q4-16	C	D+	B-
Q4-15	C	C	C

Asset & Performance History

Date	NAV	1-Year Total Return
2018	78.86	-10.04
2017	87.9	81.2
2016	48.55	24.37
2015	39.13	2.88
2014	38.08	38.86
2013	27.49	55.88

Total Assets: $345,275,295

Asset Allocation

Asset	%
Cash	-100%
Stocks	101%
US Stocks	100%
Bonds	0%
US Bonds	0%
Other	99%

Services Offered:

Investment Strategy: The investment seeks daily investment results that correspond to two times (2x) the daily performance of the Dow Jones U.S. TechnologySM Index. The fund invests in financial instruments that ProShare Advisors believes, in combination, should produce daily returns consistent with the fund's investment objective. The index measures the performance of certain companies in the technology sector of the U.S. equity market. Component companies include, among others, those involved in computers and office equipment, software, communications technology, semiconductors, diversified technology services and Internet services. The fund is non-diversified. **Top Holdings:** Dj U.S. Technology Index Swap Goldman Sachs International   Dj U.S. Technology Index Swap Citibank Na   Dj U.S. Technology Index Swap Ubs Ag   Microsoft Corp   Ishares U.S. Technology (Iyw) Swap Goldman Sachs International

Fidelity® Dividend ETF for Rising Rates   C   HOLD

Ticker	Traded On	NAV	Total Assets ($)	Dividend Yield (TTM)	Turnover Ratio	Expense Ratio
FDRR	NYSE Arca	32.28	$343,739,418	3.54	35	0.29

Ratings
Reward	C
Risk	C-
Recent Upgrade/Downgrade	

Fund Information
Fund Type	Exchange Traded Funds
Category	US Equity Large Cap Value
Sub-Category	Large Value
Prospectus Objective	Growth & Inc
Inception Date	Sep-16
Open to New Investments	Y

Prices
Price (as of 9/30/2019)	32.26
52-Week High	32.81
52-Week Low	27.18

Total Returns (%)
3-Month	6-Month	1-Year	3-Year	5-Year
1.20	2.90	3.18	38.86	

3-Year Standard Deviation	11.68
Effective Duration	

Valuation
Premium/Discount (1-Year Average)	-0.05

Company Information
Provider	Fidelity Investments
Manager/Tenure	Louis Bottari (3), Deane Gyllenhaal (3), Peter Matthew (3), 3 others
Website	http://www.institutional.fidelity.com
Address	Fidelity Investments 82 Devonshire Street Boston MA 2109 United States
Phone Number	617-563-7000

PERFORMANCE

Ratings History

Date	Overall Rating	Risk Rating	Reward Rating
Q3-19	C	C-	C
Q4-18	C	C+	C
Q4-17	D	B+	C
Q4-16	U		
Q4-15			

Asset & Performance History

Date	NAV	1-Year Total Return
2018	28.75	-3.23
2017	30.61	19.51
2016	26.41	
2015		
2014		
2013		

Total Assets: $343,739,418

Asset Allocation

Asset	%
Cash	0%
Stocks	100%
US Stocks	95%
Bonds	0%
US Bonds	0%
Other	0%

Services Offered:

Investment Strategy: The investment seeks to provide investment returns that correspond, before fees and expenses, generally to the performance of the Fidelity Dividend Index for Rising Rates. The fund normally invests at least 80% of assets in securities included in the underlying index and in depository receipts representing securities included in the underlying index. The underlying index is designed to reflect the performance of stocks of large and mid-capitalization dividend-paying companies that are expected to continue to pay and grow their dividends and have a positive correlation of returns to increasing 10-year U.S. Treasury yields. **Top Holdings:** Microsoft Corp   Apple Inc   Johnson & Johnson   JPMorgan Chase & Co   Merck & Co Inc

Tortoise North American Pipeline Fund   C   HOLD

Ticker	Traded On	NAV	Total Assets ($)	Dividend Yield (TTM)	Turnover Ratio	Expense Ratio
TPYP	NYSE Arca	23.37	$343,581,719	4.17	16	0.4

Ratings
Reward   C+
Risk   C-
Recent Upgrade/Downgrade

Fund Information
Fund Type   Exchange Traded Funds
Category   Energy Sector Equity
Sub-Category   Energy Limited Partnership
Prospectus Objective   Unaligned
Inception Date   Jun-15
Open to New Investments   Y

Prices
Price (as of 9/30/2019)   23.40
52-Week High   24.58
52-Week Low   19.22

Total Returns (%)

3-Month	6-Month	1-Year	3-Year	5-Year
-1.18	-0.61	3.16	11.57	

3-Year Standard Deviation   14.42
Effective Duration

Valuation
Premium/Discount (1-Year Average)   0.03

Company Information
Provider   Tortoise Capital Advisors
Manager/Tenure   Matthew Weglarz (4)
Website   http://www.tortoiseadvisors.com/
Address   Tortoise Capital Advisors 11550 Ash Street, Suite 300 Leawood KS 66211 United States
Phone Number   866-362-9331

PERFORMANCE

Ratings History

Date	Overall Rating	Risk Rating	Reward Rating
Q3-19	C	C-	C+
Q4-18	C	C	C
Q4-17	C	C	C
Q4-16	D	D+	C+
Q4-15	U		

Asset & Performance History

Date	NAV	1-Year Total Return
2018	19.92	-10.85
2017	23.29	2.15
2016	23.66	40.05
2015	17.87	
2014		
2013		

Total Assets: $343,581,719
Asset Allocation

Asset	%
Cash	0%
Stocks	100%
US Stocks	71%
Bonds	0%
US Bonds	0%
Other	0%

Services Offered:

Investment Strategy: The investment seeks investment results that correspond (before fees and expenses) generally to the price and distribution rate (total return) performance of the Tortoise North American Pipeline IndexSM (the "underlying index"). The fund will normally invest at least 80% of its total assets in securities that comprise the underlying index (or depository receipts based on such securities). The underlying index is a proprietary rules-based, capitalization weighted, float adjusted index designed to track the overall performance of equity securities of North American Pipeline Companies. The fund is non-diversified. **Top Holdings:** ONEOK Inc TC Energy Corp   Kinder Morgan Inc Class P   Enbridge Inc   Williams Companies Inc

---

VictoryShares US Large Cap High Div Volatility Wtd ETF   C   HOLD

Ticker	Traded On	NAV	Total Assets ($)	Dividend Yield (TTM)	Turnover Ratio	Expense Ratio
CDL	NAS CM	48.02	$343,336,913	2.98	66	0.35

Ratings
Reward   C
Risk   C-
Recent Upgrade/Downgrade

Fund Information
Fund Type   Exchange Traded Funds
Category   US Equity Large Cap Value
Sub-Category   Large Value
Prospectus Objective   Growth
Inception Date   Jul-15
Open to New Investments   Y

Prices
Price (as of 9/30/2019)   48.02
52-Week High   48.20
52-Week Low   39.56

Total Returns (%)

3-Month	6-Month	1-Year	3-Year	5-Year
2.24	4.95	7.52	36.36	

3-Year Standard Deviation   11.44
Effective Duration

Valuation
Premium/Discount (1-Year Average)   0.06

Company Information
Provider   VictoryShares
Manager/Tenure   Mannik Dhillon (1)
Website   http://www.VictorySharesLiterature.com
Address   Victory Shares 4249 Easton Way, Suite 400 Columbus OH 43219 United States
Phone Number

PERFORMANCE

Ratings History

Date	Overall Rating	Risk Rating	Reward Rating
Q3-19	C	C-	C
Q4-18	C	C-	C
Q4-17	C	B+	C+
Q4-16	D	C-	C
Q4-15	U		

Asset & Performance History

Date	NAV	1-Year Total Return
2018	41.36	-5.54
2017	45.16	15.74
2016	40.22	19.84
2015	34.43	
2014		
2013		

Total Assets: $343,336,913
Asset Allocation

Asset	%
Cash	1%
Stocks	99%
US Stocks	99%
Bonds	0%
US Bonds	0%
Other	0%

Services Offered:

Investment Strategy: The investment seeks to provide investment results that track the performance of the Nasdaq Victory US Large Cap High Dividend 100 Volatility Weighted Index. The fund seeks to achieve its investment objective by investing at least 80% of its assets directly or indirectly in the securities included in the Nasdaq Victory US Large Cap High Dividend 100 Volatility Weighted Index. The index universe begins with the stocks included in the Nasdaq Victory US Large Cap 500 Volatility Weighted Index, a volatility weighted index comprised of the 500 largest U.S. companies by market capitalization with positive earnings in each of the four most recent quarters. **Top Holdings:** WEC Energy Group Inc   The Western Union Co   Eversource Energy   Xcel Energy Inc   Evergy Inc

JPMorgan Diversified Return Emerging Markets Equity ETF

C   HOLD

Ticker	Traded On	NAV	Total Assets ($)	Dividend Yield (TTM)	Turnover Ratio	Expense Ratio
JPEM	NYSE Arca	52.70	$342,535,733	2.88	53	0.45

Ratings

Reward	C
Risk	C-
Recent Upgrade/Downgrade	Up

Fund Information

Fund Type	Exchange Traded Funds
Category	Global Emerg Mkts Equity
Sub-Category	Diversified Emerging Mkts
Prospectus Objective	Div Emerg Mkts
Inception Date	Jan-15
Open to New Investments	Y

Prices

Price (as of 9/30/2019)	52.45
52-Week High	56.56
52-Week Low	49.44

Total Returns (%)

3-Month	6-Month	1-Year	3-Year	5-Year
-4.53	-1.78	0.07	18.59	

3-Year Standard Deviation	12
Effective Duration	

Valuation

Premium/Discount (1-Year Average)	0.09

Company Information

Provider	JPMorgan
Manager/Tenure	Kartik Aiyar (2), Yazann Romahi (2), Joe Staines (2)
Website	http://www.jpmorganfunds.com
Address	JPMorgan 270 Park Avenue New York NY 10017-2070 United States
Phone Number	800-480-4111

PERFORMANCE

Ratings History

Date	Overall Rating	Risk Rating	Reward Rating
Q3-19	C	C-	C
Q4-18	C-	C-	C-
Q4-17	C+	C	C+
Q4-16	D+	C-	D+
Q4-15	U		

Asset & Performance History

Date	NAV	1-Year Total Return
2018	50.58	-10.55
2017	58.06	28.83
2016	46.05	13.3
2015	41.18	-15.04
2014		
2013		

Total Assets: $342,535,733

Asset Allocation

Asset	%
Cash	0%
Stocks	100%
US Stocks	0%
Bonds	0%
US Bonds	0%
Other	0%

Services Offered:

Investment Strategy: The investment seeks investment results that closely correspond, before fees and expenses, to the performance of the JP Morgan Diversified Factor Emerging Markets Equity Index. The fund will invest at least 80% of its assets in securities included in the underlying index. "Assets" means net assets, plus the amount of borrowing for investment purposes. The underlying index is comprised of equity securities from emerging markets selected to represent a diversified set of factor characteristics. **Top Holdings:** Naspers Ltd Class N   China Mobile Ltd   PJSC Lukoil   Gazprom PJSC   Vale SA

---

iShares iBonds Sep 2020 Term Muni Bond ETF

C   HOLD

Ticker	Traded On	NAV	Total Assets ($)	Dividend Yield (TTM)	Turnover Ratio	Expense Ratio
IBMI	NYSE Arca	25.54	$340,990,157	1.23	0	0.18

Ratings

Reward	C
Risk	C-
Recent Upgrade/Downgrade	Up

Fund Information

Fund Type	Exchange Traded Funds
Category	US Muni Fixed Inc
Sub-Category	Muni Target Maturity
Prospectus Objective	Muni Bond - Natl
Inception Date	Aug-14
Open to New Investments	Y

Prices

Price (as of 9/30/2019)	25.53
52-Week High	25.61
52-Week Low	25.17

Total Returns (%)

3-Month	6-Month	1-Year	3-Year	5-Year
0.24	0.85	2.37	2.54	7.67

3-Year Standard Deviation	1.78
Effective Duration	

Valuation

Premium/Discount (1-Year Average)	0.04

Company Information

Provider	iShares
Manager/Tenure	James Mauro (5), Scott Radell (5)
Website	http://www.ishares.com
Address	iShares 400 Howard Street San Francisco CA 94105 United States
Phone Number	800-474-2737

PERFORMANCE

Ratings History

Date	Overall Rating	Risk Rating	Reward Rating
Q3-19	C	C-	C
Q4-18	C-	C-	C-
Q4-17	C	C+	C
Q4-16	C-	C-	C-
Q4-15	D-	C-	D+

Asset & Performance History

Date	NAV	1-Year Total Return
2018	25.35	1.35
2017	25.31	1.48
2016	25.2	0.02
2015	25.48	2.75
2014	25.1	
2013		

Total Assets: $340,990,157

Asset Allocation

Asset	%
Cash	0%
Stocks	0%
US Stocks	0%
Bonds	100%
US Bonds	100%
Other	0%

Services Offered:

Investment Strategy: The investment seeks to track the investment results of the S&P AMT-Free Municipal Series 2020 IndexTM. The fund generally will invest at least 90% of its assets in the component securities of the underlying index, and may invest up to 10% of its assets in certain futures, options and swap contracts, cash and cash equivalents, as well as in securities not included in the underlying index, but which the advisor believes will help the fund track the underlying index. The underlying index measures the performance of investment-grade, non-callable U.S. municipal bonds maturing in 2020. **Top Holdings:** CALIFORNIA ST 5%   MASSACHUSETTS ST 5%   WISCONSIN ST CLEAN WTR REV 5%   HONOLULU HAWAII CITY & CNTY 5%   CHARLOTTE N C WTR & SWR SYS REV 5%

SPDR® Bloomberg Barclays 1-10 Year TIPS ETF   C   HOLD

Ticker	Traded On	NAV	Total Assets ($)	Dividend Yield (TTM)	Turnover Ratio	Expense Ratio
TIPX	NYSE Arca		$340,031,207	2.59	20	0.15

Ratings
Reward   C
Risk   C-
Recent Upgrade/Downgrade

Fund Information
Fund Type   Exchange Traded Funds
Category   US Fixed Income
Sub-Category   Inflation-Protected Bond
Prospectus Objective   Govt Bond - Treasury
Inception Date   May-13
Open to New Investments   Y

Prices
Price (as of 9/30/2019)   19.57
52-Week High   19.76
52-Week Low   18.75

Total Returns (%)

3-Month	6-Month	1-Year	3-Year	5-Year
0.84	3.47	5.88	5.70	9.54

3-Year Standard Deviation   2.32
Effective Duration   5.23

Valuation
Premium/Discount (1-Year Average)   0.03

Company Information
Provider   SPDR State Street Global Advisors
Manager/Tenure Cynthia Moy (4), James Kramer (2),
                Orhan Imer (1)
Website   http://www.spdrs.com
Address   SPDR State Street Global Advisors
                State Street Financial Center, 1
                Lincoln Street Boston MA 02111-2900
                United States
Phone Number   617-786-3000

PERFORMANCE

Ratings History

Date	Overall Rating	Risk Rating	Reward Rating
Q3-19	C	C-	C
Q4-18	C-	C-	D+
Q4-17	C	C	C
Q4-16	C-	D+	C
Q4-15	D+	D+	D+

Asset & Performance History

Date	NAV	1-Year Total Return
2018	18.85	-0.42
2017	19.29	0.85
2016	19.49	3.82
2015	18.97	-0.66
2014	19.11	0.73
2013	19.25	

Total Assets: $340,031,207
Asset Allocation

Asset	%
Cash	0%
Stocks	0%
US Stocks	0%
Bonds	100%
US Bonds	100%
Other	0%

Services Offered:

Investment Strategy: The investment seeks to provide investment results that correspond generally to the price and yield performance of the Bloomberg Barclays 1-10 Year U.S. Government Inflation-Linked Bond Index that tracks the 1-10 year inflation protected sector of the United States Treasury market. Under normal market conditions, the fund generally invests substantially all, but at least 80%, of its total assets in the securities comprising the index or in securities that the Adviser determines have economic characteristics that are substantially identical to the economic characteristics of the securities that comprise the index. The fund is non-diversified. **Top Holdings:** United States Treasury Notes 0.12% United States Treasury Notes 0.62% United States Treasury Notes 0.62% United States Treasury Notes 0.12% United States Treasury Notes 0.62%

VictoryShares USAA MSCI International Value Momentum ETF   D   SELL

Ticker	Traded On	NAV	Total Assets ($)	Dividend Yield (TTM)	Turnover Ratio	Expense Ratio
UIVM	NYSE Arca	44.40	$337,419,478	2.82	65	0.35

Ratings
Reward   D
Risk   D+
Recent Upgrade/Downgrade

Fund Information
Fund Type   Exchange Traded Funds
Category   Global Equity Large Cap
Sub-Category   Foreign Large Value
Prospectus Objective   Growth & Inc
Inception Date   Oct-17
Open to New Investments   Y

Prices
Price (as of 9/30/2019)   44.59
52-Week High   49.09
52-Week Low   40.20

Total Returns (%)

3-Month	6-Month	1-Year	3-Year	5-Year
-2.05	-1.70	-6.15		

3-Year Standard Deviation
Effective Duration

Valuation
Premium/Discount (1-Year Average)   0.20

Company Information
Provider   VictoryShares
Manager/Tenure Lance Humphrey (1), Wasif A. Latif (1),
                Mannik Dhillon (0)
Website   http://www.VictorySharesLiterature.com
Address   Victory Shares 4249 Easton Way,
                Suite 400 Columbus OH 43219 United
                States
Phone Number

PERFORMANCE

Ratings History

Date	Overall Rating	Risk Rating	Reward Rating
Q3-19	D	D+	D
Q4-18	D	D	D
Q4-17	U		
Q4-16			
Q4-15			

Asset & Performance History

Date	NAV	1-Year Total Return
2018	41.43	-17.44
2017	51.42	
2016		
2015		
2014		
2013		

Total Assets: $337,419,478
Asset Allocation

Asset	%
Cash	1%
Stocks	99%
US Stocks	3%
Bonds	0%
US Bonds	0%
Other	0%

Services Offered:

Investment Strategy: The investment seeks to provide investment results that correspond to the MSCI World ex USA Select Value Momentum Blend Index. The fund seeks to achieve its investment objective by investing at least 80% of its net assets in securities in the index, depositary receipts on securities in the index, and securities underlying depositary receipts in the index. The index is designed to deliver exposure to equity market performance in non-U.S. markets and provide higher exposure to value and momentum factors within the MSCI World ex USA Index while also maintaining moderate index turnover and lower realized volatility than traditional capitalization weighted indexes. **Top Holdings:** Nestle SA Emera, Inc. ASX Ltd CapitaLand Mall Trust HKT Trust and HKT Ltd

Innovator IBD® 50 ETF   C   HOLD

Ticker	Traded On	NAV	Total Assets ($)	Dividend Yield (TTM)	Turnover Ratio	Expense Ratio
FFTY	NYSE	32.27	$337,191,754	0	719	0.8

Ratings

Reward	C+
Risk	C
Recent Upgrade/Downgrade	

Fund Information

Fund Type	Exchange Traded Funds
Category	US Equity Mid Cap
Sub-Category	Mid-Cap Growth
Prospectus Objective	Growth
Inception Date	Apr-15
Open to New Investments	Y

Prices

Price (as of 9/30/2019)	32.27
52-Week High	38.07
52-Week Low	25.43

Total Returns (%)

3-Month	6-Month	1-Year	3-Year	5-Year
-6.97	-4.47	-15.17	37.42	

3-Year Standard Deviation	20.1
Effective Duration	

Valuation

Premium/Discount (1-Year Average)	-0.04

Company Information

Provider	Innovator ETFs
Manager/Tenure	Anand Desai (1), Dustin Lewellyn (1), Ernesto Tong (1)
Website	http://innovatoretfs.com/
Address	Innovator ETFs 120 N Hale Street, Suite 200 Wheaton IL 60187 United States
Phone Number	800-208-5212

PERFORMANCE

Ratings History

Date	Overall Rating	Risk Rating	Reward Rating
Q3-19	C	C	C+
Q4-18	C	C	C+
Q4-17	C+	C	B-
Q4-16	D+	C-	C
Q4-15	U		

Asset & Performance History

Date	NAV	1-Year Total Return
2018	27.65	-16.62
2017	33.16	37.31
2016	24.19	8.6
2015	22.17	
2014		
2013		

Total Assets: $337,191,754

Asset Allocation

Asset	%
Cash	0%
Stocks	100%
US Stocks	84%
Bonds	0%
US Bonds	0%
Other	0%

Services Offered:

Investment Strategy: The investment seeks to track, before fees and expenses, the performance of the IBD® 50 Index (the "index"). The fund will normally invest at least 80% of its net assets (including investment borrowings) in securities that comprise the index. The IBD® 50 Index is a weekly, rules-based, computer-generated stock index compiled and published by Investor's Business Daily® ("IBD" or the "index provider") that seeks to identify the current top 50 growth stocks. **Top Holdings:** Kirkland Lake Gold Ltd   MasTec Inc   Heico Corp   Paylocity Holding Corp   Paycom Software Inc

---

iShares Currency Hedged MSCI Japan ETF   C   HOLD

Ticker	Traded On	NAV	Total Assets ($)	Dividend Yield (TTM)	Turnover Ratio	Expense Ratio
HEWJ	NYSE Arca	31.22	$337,164,072	2.04	9	0.48

Ratings

Reward	C-
Risk	C
Recent Upgrade/Downgrade	

Fund Information

Fund Type	Exchange Traded Funds
Category	Japan Equity
Sub-Category	Japan Stock
Prospectus Objective	Pacific Stock
Inception Date	Jan-14
Open to New Investments	Y

Prices

Price (as of 9/30/2019)	31.16
52-Week High	34.61
52-Week Low	27.38

Total Returns (%)

3-Month	6-Month	1-Year	3-Year	5-Year
2.70	1.32	-7.84	32.65	35.55

3-Year Standard Deviation	14.41
Effective Duration	

Valuation

Premium/Discount (1-Year Average)	0.03

Company Information

Provider	iShares
Manager/Tenure	Diane Hsiung (5), Jennifer Hsui (5), Orlando Montalvo (5), 2 others
Website	http://www.ishares.com
Address	iShares 400 Howard Street San Francisco CA 94105 United States
Phone Number	800-474-2737

PERFORMANCE

Ratings History

Date	Overall Rating	Risk Rating	Reward Rating
Q3-19	C	C	C-
Q4-18	C	C+	C-
Q4-17	B	B-	A-
Q4-16	C	C	C-
Q4-15	D+	C+	C

Asset & Performance History

Date	NAV	1-Year Total Return
2018	28.02	-15.28
2017	33.36	21.5
2016	27.81	-0.93
2015	28.66	9.04
2014	27.1	
2013		

Total Assets: $337,164,072

Asset Allocation

Asset	%
Cash	1%
Stocks	99%
US Stocks	0%
Bonds	0%
US Bonds	0%
Other	0%

Services Offered:

Investment Strategy: The investment seeks to track the investment results of the MSCI Japan 100% Hedged to USD Index. The fund generally will invest at least 90% of its assets in the component securities (including indirect investments through the underlying fund) and other instruments of the underlying index and in investments that have economic characteristics that are substantially identical to the component securities of the underlying index. The index consists of stocks traded primarily on the Tokyo Stock Exchange with the currency risk inherent in the securities included in the underlying index hedged to the U.S. dollar on a monthly basis. **Top Holdings:** Toyota Motor Corp   SoftBank Group Corp   Sony Corp   Mitsubishi UFJ Financial Group Inc   Keyence Corp

PIMCO Intermediate Municipal Bond Active Exchange-Traded Fund   C   HOLD

Ticker	Traded On	NAV	Total Assets ($)	Dividend Yield (TTM)	Turnover Ratio	Expense Ratio
MUNI	NYSE Arca	55.18	$337,124,790	2.51	39	0.35

Ratings
Reward   C+
Risk   C-
Recent Upgrade/Downgrade

Fund Information
Fund Type	Exchange Traded Funds
Category	US Muni Fixed Inc
Sub-Category	Muni National Interm
Prospectus Objective	Muni Bond - Natl
Inception Date	Nov-09
Open to New Investments	Y

Prices
Price (as of 9/30/2019)	55.30
52-Week High	55.79
52-Week Low	51.81

Total Returns (%)
3-Month	6-Month	1-Year	3-Year	5-Year
1.32	3.60	7.91	8.35	15.89

3-Year Standard Deviation	3.04
Effective Duration	4.61

Valuation
Premium/Discount (1-Year Average)	0.12

Company Information
Provider	PIMCO
Manager/Tenure	Julie P. Callahan (4), David Hammer (3)
Website	http://www.pimco.com
Address	PIMCO 840 Newport Center Drive, Suite 100 Newport Beach CA 92660 United States
Phone Number	866-746-2602

PERFORMANCE

Ratings History
Date	Overall Rating	Risk Rating	Reward Rating
Q3-19	C	C-	C+
Q4-18	C-	C-	C-
Q4-17	B-	B+	C
Q4-16	C	C-	C
Q4-15	C	C-	C

Asset & Performance History
Date	NAV	1-Year Total Return
2018	52.76	1.11
2017	53.54	4.54
2016	52.45	-0.19
2015	53.77	2.58
2014	53.59	5.32
2013	51.87	-2.32

Total Assets: $337,124,790
Asset Allocation
Asset	%
Cash	6%
Stocks	0%
US Stocks	0%
Bonds	94%
US Bonds	94%
Other	0%

Services Offered:

Investment Strategy: The investment seeks attractive tax-exempt income, consistent with preservation of capital. The fund invests at least 80% of its assets in a diversified portfolio of debt securities whose interest is, in the opinion of bond counsel for the issuer at the time of issuance, exempt from federal income tax ("Municipal Bonds"). It may invest 25% or more of its total assets in Municipal Bonds that finance similar projects, such as those relating to education, health care, housing, transportation, and utilities, and 25% or more of its total assets in industrial development bonds. **Top Holdings:** TOBACCO SETTLEMENT FING CORP RHODE IS 5%   CHICAGO ILL MIDWAY ARPT REV 5%   NEW YORK N Y CITY TRANSITIONAL FIN AUTH REV 5%   DETROIT MICH CITY SCH DIST 6% CONNECTICUT ST 5%

SPDR® S&P Semiconductor ETF   B-   BUY

Ticker	Traded On	NAV	Total Assets ($)	Dividend Yield (TTM)	Turnover Ratio	Expense Ratio
XSD	NYSE Arca		$336,968,345	0.66	32	0.35

Ratings
Reward   B
Risk   C-
Recent Upgrade/Downgrade

Fund Information
Fund Type	Exchange Traded Funds
Category	Technology Sector Equity
Sub-Category	Technology
Prospectus Objective	Technology
Inception Date	Jan-06
Open to New Investments	Y

Prices
Price (as of 9/30/2019)	89.82
52-Week High	94.32
52-Week Low	60.13

Total Returns (%)
3-Month	6-Month	1-Year	3-Year	5-Year
3.07	11.35	19.16	72.03	152.33

3-Year Standard Deviation	22.91
Effective Duration	

Valuation
Premium/Discount (1-Year Average)	0.00

Company Information
Provider	SPDR State Street Global Advisors
Manager/Tenure	Michael J. Feehily (7), Karl A. Schneider (4), Kala O'Donnell (2)
Website	http://www.spdrs.com
Address	SPDR State Street Global Advisors State Street Financial Center, 1 Lincoln Street Boston MA 02111-2900 United States
Phone Number	617-786-3000

PERFORMANCE

Ratings History
Date	Overall Rating	Risk Rating	Reward Rating
Q3-19	B-	C-	B
Q4-18	C	C-	B-
Q4-17	A-	B	A+
Q4-16	C	C-	C
Q4-15	C	C	C+

Asset & Performance History
Date	NAV	1-Year Total Return
2018	64.74	-6.25
2017	69.79	25.23
2016	56.08	29.08
2015	43.71	10.29
2014	39.86	30.97
2013	30.59	36.31

Total Assets: $336,968,345
Asset Allocation
Asset	%
Cash	0%
Stocks	100%
US Stocks	97%
Bonds	0%
US Bonds	0%
Other	0%

Services Offered: Dividend Investment Plan, Cash Investment Plan

Investment Strategy: The investment seeks to provide investment results that, before fees and expenses, correspond generally to the total return performance of an index derived from the semiconductor segment of a U.S. total market composite index. In seeking to track the performance of the S&P Semiconductor Select Industry Index (the "index"), the fund employs a sampling strategy. It generally invests substantially all, but at least 80%, of its total assets in the securities comprising the index. The index represents the semiconductors segment of the S&P Total Market Index ("S&P TMI"). The fund is non-diversified. **Top Holdings:** Lattice Semiconductor Corp   Micron Technology Inc   Cirrus Logic Inc   Inphi Corp   Monolithic Power Systems Inc

Franklin LibertyQ Emerging Markets ETF

C-   HOLD

Ticker	Traded On	NAV	Total Assets ($)	Dividend Yield (TTM)	Turnover Ratio	Expense Ratio
FLQE	NYSE Arca	29.00	$336,440,637	3.72	52	0.45

Ratings
Reward	C-
Risk	D+
Recent Upgrade/Downgrade	

Fund Information
Fund Type	Exchange Traded Funds
Category	Global Emerg Mkts Equity
Sub-Category	Diversified Emerging Mkts
Prospectus Objective	Growth & Inc
Inception Date	Jun-16
Open to New Investments	Y

Prices
Price (as of 9/30/2019)	28.94
52-Week High	30.62
52-Week Low	27.40

Total Returns (%)
3-Month	6-Month	1-Year	3-Year	5-Year
-3.52	-2.41	-1.96	12.01	

3-Year Standard Deviation	11.15
Effective Duration	

Valuation
Premium/Discount (1-Year Average)	-0.05

Company Information
Provider	Franklin Templeton Investments
Manager/Tenure	Dina Ting (3), Louis Hsu (1)
Website	http://www.franklintempleton.com
Address	Franklin Templeton Investments One Franklin Parkway, Building 970, 1st Floor San Mateo CA 94403 United States
Phone Number	650-312-2000

PERFORMANCE

Ratings History
Date	Overall Rating	Risk Rating	Reward Rating
Q3-19	C-	D+	C-
Q4-18	D+	C-	D+
Q4-17	D+	B-	C
Q4-16	U		
Q4-15			

Asset & Performance History
Date	NAV	1-Year Total Return
2018	28.16	-11.72
2017	33.12	28.36
2016	26.51	
2015		
2014		
2013		

Total Assets: $336,440,637

Asset Allocation
Asset	%
Cash	0%
Stocks	100%
US Stocks	0%
Bonds	0%
US Bonds	0%
Other	0%

Services Offered:

Investment Strategy: The investment seeks to provide investment results that closely correspond, before fees and expenses, to the performance of the LibertyQ Emerging Markets Index. The fund invests at least 80% of its assets in the component securities of the index and in depositary receipts representing such securities. The index seeks to achieve a lower level of risk and higher risk-adjusted performance than the MSCI Emerging Markets Index over the long term by applying a multi-factor selection process. **Top Holdings:** PT Telekomunikasi Indonesia (Persero) Tbk Class B   Advanced Info Service PCL DR   Mining and Metallurgical Company NORILSK NICKEL PJSC ANTA Sports Products Ltd   Gazprom PJSC

Invesco S&P MidCap 400 Revenue ETF

C-   HOLD

Ticker	Traded On	NAV	Total Assets ($)	Dividend Yield (TTM)	Turnover Ratio	Expense Ratio
RWK	NYSE Arca	59.52	$336,358,577	1.12	33	0.39

Ratings
Reward	C-
Risk	C-
Recent Upgrade/Downgrade	Down

Fund Information
Fund Type	Exchange Traded Funds
Category	US Equity Mid Cap
Sub-Category	Mid-Cap Value
Prospectus Objective	Growth
Inception Date	Feb-08
Open to New Investments	Y

Prices
Price (as of 9/30/2019)	59.54
52-Week High	62.82
52-Week Low	48.52

Total Returns (%)
3-Month	6-Month	1-Year	3-Year	5-Year
-2.13	-0.88	-3.44	22.78	41.09

3-Year Standard Deviation	18.6
Effective Duration	

Valuation
Premium/Discount (1-Year Average)	-0.05

Company Information
Provider	Invesco
Manager/Tenure	Peter Hubbard (0), Michael Jeanette (0), Tony Seisser (0)
Website	http://www.invesco.com/us
Address	Invesco 11 Greenway Plaza, Ste. 2500 Houston TX 77046 United States
Phone Number	800-659-1005

PERFORMANCE

Ratings History
Date	Overall Rating	Risk Rating	Reward Rating
Q3-19	C-	C-	C-
Q4-18	C-	C-	C-
Q4-17	B	B	B
Q4-16	C+	C-	B
Q4-15	C	C	C

Asset & Performance History
Date	NAV	1-Year Total Return
2018	51.27	-14.49
2017	60.61	12.87
2016	54.11	21.56
2015	45.13	-5.78
2014	48.32	9.47
2013	44.6	40.6

Total Assets: $336,358,577

Asset Allocation
Asset	%
Cash	0%
Stocks	100%
US Stocks	100%
Bonds	0%
US Bonds	0%
Other	0%

Services Offered:

Investment Strategy: The investment seeks to track the investment results (before fees and expenses) of the S&P MidCap 400® Revenue-Weighted Index. The fund generally will invest at least 90% of its total assets in the securities that comprise the index. The index is constructed using a rules-based methodology that re-weights the constituent securities of the S&P MidCap 400® Index (the "parent index"), an index comprised of common stocks of 400 mid-cap companies that generally represents the mid-cap universe of the U.S. equity market, according to the revenue earned by the companies in the parent index, subject to a maximum 5% per company weighting. The fund is non-diversified. **Top Holdings:** World Fuel Services Corp   Tech Data Corp   Arrow Electronics Inc   PBF Energy Inc Class A   Jabil Inc

ProShares Short VIX Short-Term Futures ETF   C   HOLD

Ticker	Traded On	NAV	Total Assets ($)	Dividend Yield (TTM)	Turnover Ratio	Expense Ratio
SVXY	NYSE Arca		$336,183,112	0		1.38

Ratings
Reward	C
Risk	D+
Recent Upgrade/Downgrade	

Fund Information
Fund Type	Exchange Traded Funds
Category	Alternative Misc
Sub-Category	Volatility
Prospectus Objective	Growth
Inception Date	Oct-11
Open to New Investments	Y

Prices
Price (as of 9/30/2019)	53.41
52-Week High	59.50
52-Week Low	41.30

Total Returns (%)
3-Month	6-Month	1-Year	3-Year	5-Year
-4.86	-0.32	-11.02	45.19	40.91

3-Year Standard Deviation	64.14
Effective Duration	

Valuation
Premium/Discount (1-Year Average)	-0.19

Company Information
Provider	ProShares
Manager/Tenure	Management Team (8)
Website	http://www.proshares.com
Address	ProShares 7501 Wisconsin Avenue, Suite 1000 Bethesda MD 20814 United States
Phone Number	866-776-5125

PERFORMANCE

Ratings History
Date	Overall Rating	Risk Rating	Reward Rating
Q3-19	C	D+	C
Q4-18	C-	D	C-
Q4-17	B	D+	A+
Q4-16	C	D+	C
Q4-15	C+	D+	C+

Asset & Performance History
Date	NAV	1-Year Total Return
2018	42.36	-67.37
2017	127.32	179.11
2016	45.62	79.53
2015	25.41	-17.24
2014	30.7	-9.02
2013	33.75	104.05

Total Assets: $336,183,112

Asset Allocation
Asset	%
Cash	150%
Stocks	-50%
US Stocks	-50%
Bonds	0%
US Bonds	0%
Other	0%

Services Offered:

Investment Strategy: The investment seeks daily investment results, before fees and expenses, that correspond to one-half the inverse (-0.5x) of the performance of the S&P 500 VIX Short-Term Futures Index for a single day. The index seeks to offer exposure to market volatility through publicly traded futures markets and is designed to measure the implied volatility of the S&P 500 over 30 days in the future. **Top Holdings:** Cboe Vix Future 09/18/2019 (Uxu9) Cboe Vix Future 10/16/2019 (Uxv9)

Global X MSCI Greece ETF   C+   HOLD

Ticker	Traded On	NAV	Total Assets ($)	Dividend Yield (TTM)	Turnover Ratio	Expense Ratio
GREK	NYSE Arca	9.36	$335,957,707	2.23	16	0.59

Ratings
Reward	B
Risk	C
Recent Upgrade/Downgrade	Up

Fund Information
Fund Type	Exchange Traded Funds
Category	Europe Equity Mid/Small Cap
Sub-Category	Miscellaneous Region
Prospectus Objective	Foreign Stock
Inception Date	Dec-11
Open to New Investments	Y

Prices
Price (as of 9/30/2019)	9.33
52-Week High	9.95
52-Week Low	6.79

Total Returns (%)
3-Month	6-Month	1-Year	3-Year	5-Year
-3.00	14.09	15.88	40.13	-44.18

3-Year Standard Deviation	22.72
Effective Duration	

Valuation
Premium/Discount (1-Year Average)	-0.26

Company Information
Provider	Global X Funds
Manager/Tenure	Chang Kim (5), Nam To (1), Wayne Xie (0), 1 other
Website	http://www.globalxfunds.com
Address	Global X Funds 600 Lexington Avenue, 20th Floor New York NY 10022 United States
Phone Number	888-493-8631

PERFORMANCE

Ratings History
Date	Overall Rating	Risk Rating	Reward Rating
Q3-19	C+	C	B
Q4-18	D	D	D
Q4-17	D+	D	D+
Q4-16	D	D-	D
Q4-15	D-	D-	D-

Asset & Performance History
Date	NAV	1-Year Total Return
2018	6.96	-31.56
2017	10.17	32.18
2016	7.86	-1.16
2015	8.11	-39.33
2014	13.57	-38.18
2013	22.16	26.92

Total Assets: $335,957,707

Asset Allocation
Asset	%
Cash	0%
Stocks	100%
US Stocks	2%
Bonds	0%
US Bonds	0%
Other	0%

Services Offered:

Investment Strategy: The investment seeks to provide investment results that correspond generally to the price and yield performance, before fees and expenses, of the MSCI All Greece Select 25/50 Index. The fund invests at least 80% of its total assets in the securities of the underlying index and in American Depositary Receipts ("ADRs") and Global Depositary Receipts ("GDRs") based on the securities in the underlying index. The underlying index is designed to represent the performance of the broad Greece equity universe. The fund is non-diversified. **Top Holdings:** Hellenic Telecommunication Organization SA Alpha Bank AE Eurobank Ergasias SA Greek Organisation of Football Prognostics SA National Bank of Greece SA

Xtrackers MSCI EAFE High Dividend Yield Equity ETF

C   HOLD

Ticker	Traded On	NAV	Total Assets ($)	Dividend Yield (TTM)	Turnover Ratio	Expense Ratio
HDEF	NYSE Arca	22.67	$335,555,859	5.27	20	0.2

Ratings

Reward	C
Risk	C+
Recent Upgrade/Downgrade	Up

Fund Information

Fund Type	Exchange Traded Funds
Category	Global Equity Large Cap
Sub-Category	Foreign Large Value
Prospectus Objective	Growth & Inc
Inception Date	Aug-15
Open to New Investments	Y

Prices

Price (as of 9/30/2019)	22.71
52-Week High	23.45
52-Week Low	20.25

Total Returns (%)

3-Month	6-Month	1-Year	3-Year	5-Year
-0.53	1.66	2.20	13.66	

3-Year Standard Deviation	10.69
Effective Duration	

Valuation

Premium/Discount (1-Year Average)	0.06

Company Information

Provider	DWS
Manager/Tenure	Patrick Dwyer (2), Bryan Richards (2), Shlomo Bassous (1)
Website	http://dws.com
Address	DWS 210 West 10th Street Kansas City MO 64105-1614 United States
Phone Number	

PERFORMANCE

Ratings History

Date	Overall Rating	Risk Rating	Reward Rating
Q3-19	C	C+	C
Q4-18	C-	C-	D+
Q4-17	C	B	C+
Q4-16	D	D+	C-
Q4-15	U		

Asset & Performance History

Date	NAV	1-Year Total Return
2018	20.71	-13.48
2017	24.67	9.83
2016	23.24	11.58
2015	22.92	
2014		
2013		

Total Assets: $335,555,859

Asset Allocation

Asset	%
Cash	0%
Stocks	100%
US Stocks	0%
Bonds	0%
US Bonds	0%
Other	0%

Services Offered:

Investment Strategy: The investment seeks investment results that correspond generally to the performance, before fees and expenses, of the MSCI EAFE High Dividend Yield Index. The fund will invest at least 80% of its total assets (but typically far more) in component securities of the underlying index. The underlying index is designed to reflect the performance of equities in its parent index, the MSCI EAFE Index, with higher dividend income and quality characteristics than average dividend yields of equities in the parent index, where such higher dividend income and quality characteristics are both sustainable and persistent. It is non-diversified. **Top Holdings:** AstraZeneca PLC GlaxoSmithKline PLC Sanofi SA Allianz SE Total SA

---

iShares Emerging Markets High Yield Bond ETF

C   HOLD

Ticker	Traded On	NAV	Total Assets ($)	Dividend Yield (TTM)	Turnover Ratio	Expense Ratio
EMHY	BATS	46.43	$331,983,415	7.06	19	0.5

Ratings

Reward	C+
Risk	C-
Recent Upgrade/Downgrade	

Fund Information

Fund Type	Exchange Traded Funds
Category	Emerging Mkts Fixed Inc
Sub-Category	Emerging Markets Bond
Prospectus Objective	Corp Bond-High Yld
Inception Date	Apr-12
Open to New Investments	Y

Prices

Price (as of 9/30/2019)	46.49
52-Week High	48.10
52-Week Low	44.09

Total Returns (%)

3-Month	6-Month	1-Year	3-Year	5-Year
-1.54	2.14	8.36	10.03	25.38

3-Year Standard Deviation	6.81
Effective Duration	

Valuation

Premium/Discount (1-Year Average)	0.34

Company Information

Provider	iShares
Manager/Tenure	James Mauro (7), Scott Radell (7)
Website	http://www.ishares.com
Address	iShares 400 Howard Street San Francisco CA 94105 United States
Phone Number	800-474-2737

PERFORMANCE

Ratings History

Date	Overall Rating	Risk Rating	Reward Rating
Q3-19	C	C-	C+
Q4-18	C-	C-	C-
Q4-17	B	A	C+
Q4-16	C	C-	C
Q4-15	C-	C-	C-

Asset & Performance History

Date	NAV	1-Year Total Return
2018	44.3	-5.1
2017	49.85	8.65
2016	48.35	14.71
2015	44.98	1.77
2014	47.26	2.06
2013	49.15	-5.47

Total Assets: $331,983,415

Asset Allocation

Asset	%
Cash	1%
Stocks	0%
US Stocks	0%
Bonds	99%
US Bonds	1%
Other	0%

Services Offered:

Investment Strategy: The investment seeks to track the investment results of the Morningstar® Emerging Markets High Yield Bond IndexSM. The fund generally will invest at least 90% of its assets in the component securities of the underlying index and may invest up to 10% of its assets in certain futures, options and swap contracts, cash and cash equivalents, including shares of money market funds advised by BFA or its affiliates. The index tracks the performance of the below-investment-grade U.S. dollar-denominated emerging market sovereign and corporate high yield bond market. The fund is non-diversified. **Top Holdings:** Petroleos Mexicanos 6.75% Petroleos Mexicanos 6.5% Petrobras Global Finance B.V. 6% Petroleos Mexicanos 6.5% Brazil (Federative Republic) 4.25%

Invesco KBW Premium Yield Equity REIT ETF

C HOLD

Ticker	Traded On	NAV	Total Assets ($)	Dividend Yield (TTM)	Turnover Ratio	Expense Ratio
KBWY	NAS CM	31.26	$331,360,791	6.16		0.35

Ratings
Reward C+
Risk D+
Recent Upgrade/Downgrade Up

Fund Information
Fund Type Exchange Traded Funds
Category Real Estate Sector Equity
Sub-Category Real Estate
Prospectus Objective Real Estate
Inception Date Dec-10
Open to New Investments

Prices
Price (as of 9/30/2019) 31.23
52-Week High 33.29
52-Week Low 26.11

Total Returns (%)

3-Month	6-Month	1-Year	3-Year	5-Year
6.48	4.17	0.21	7.45	40.53

3-Year Standard Deviation 19.31
Effective Duration

Valuation
Premium/Discount (1-Year Average) -0.01

Company Information
Provider Invesco
Manager/Tenure Peter Hubbard (8), Michael Jeanette (8), Tony Seisser (5)
Website http://www.invesco.com/us
Address Invesco 11 Greenway Plaza, Ste. 2500 Houston TX 77046 United States
Phone Number 800-659-1005

PERFORMANCE

Ratings History

Date	Overall Rating	Risk Rating	Reward Rating
Q3-19	C	D+	C+
Q4-18	C	D+	B-
Q4-17	C+	B-	C
Q4-16	C	D+	B-
Q4-15	B-	C	B

Asset & Performance History

Date	NAV	1-Year Total Return
2018	26.97	-18.04
2017	35.38	0.85
2016	37.59	33.04
2015	30.41	-8.17
2014	34.94	23.85
2013	29.66	10.28

Total Assets: $331,360,791

Asset Allocation

Asset	%
Cash	0%
Stocks	100%
US Stocks	97%
Bonds	0%
US Bonds	0%
Other	0%

Services Offered:

Investment Strategy: The investment seeks to track the investment results (before fees and expenses) of the KBW Nasdaq Premium Yield Equity REIT Index (the "underlying index"). The fund generally will invest at least 90% of its total assets in the securities that comprise the underlying index. The underlying index is a modified-dividend yield-weighted index of domestic equity real estate investment trusts ("REITs") of small- and mid-capitalization, as determined by the index provider. The underlying index is designed to track the performance of small- and mid-capitalization equity REITs that have competitive dividend yields and are publicly-traded in the U.S. **Top Holdings:** Washington Prime Group Inc Global Net Lease Inc Sabra Health Care REIT Inc Office Properties Income Trust Pennsylvania Real Estate Investment Trust

Invesco DB US Dollar Index Bullish Fund

C+ HOLD

Ticker	Traded On	NAV	Total Assets ($)	Dividend Yield (TTM)	Turnover Ratio	Expense Ratio
UUP	NYSE Arca	27.09	$330,464,067	1.02		0.75

Ratings
Reward C
Risk C+
Recent Upgrade/Downgrade

Fund Information
Fund Type Exchange Traded Funds
Category Currency
Sub-Category Multicurrency
Prospectus Objective Growth & Inc
Inception Date Feb-07
Open to New Investments Y

Prices
Price (as of 9/30/2019) 27.10
52-Week High 27.10
52-Week Low 25.19

Total Returns (%)

3-Month	6-Month	1-Year	3-Year	5-Year
3.53	4.12	8.21	11.10	19.85

3-Year Standard Deviation 5.75
Effective Duration

Valuation
Premium/Discount (1-Year Average) -0.03

Company Information
Provider Invesco
Manager/Tenure Management Team (12)
Website http://www.invesco.com/us
Address Invesco 11 Greenway Plaza, Ste. 2500 Houston TX 77046 United States
Phone Number 800-659-1005

PERFORMANCE

Ratings History

Date	Overall Rating	Risk Rating	Reward Rating
Q3-19	C+	C+	C
Q4-18	C	C+	C
Q4-17	D+	C	D+
Q4-16	C+	C+	C+
Q4-15	C+	C+	C

Asset & Performance History

Date	NAV	1-Year Total Return
2018	25.48	6.29
2017	24	-9.05
2016	26.43	3.91
2015	25.65	6.96
2014	23.98	11.43
2013	21.52	-1.33

Total Assets: $330,464,067

Asset Allocation

Asset	%
Cash	89%
Stocks	0%
US Stocks	0%
Bonds	11%
US Bonds	11%
Other	0%

Services Offered:

Investment Strategy: The investment seeks to establish long positions in ICE U.S. Dollar Index futures contracts with a view to tracking the changes, whether positive or negative, in the level of the Deutsche Bank Long USD Currency Portfolio Index — Excess ReturnTM over time, plus the excess, if any, of the sum of the fund's Treasury Income, Money Market Income and T-Bill ETF Income over the expenses of the fund.
The fund invests in futures contracts in an attempt to track its index. The index is calculated to reflect the changes in market value over time, whether positive or negative, of long positions in DX Contracts. **Top Holdings:** United States Treasury Bills 0% Invesco Treasury Collateral ETF United States Treasury Bills 0% United States Treasury Bills 0% United States Treasury Bills 0%

Invesco S&P Emerging Markets Low Volatility ETF   C   HOLD

Ticker	Traded On	NAV	Total Assets ($)	Dividend Yield (TTM)	Turnover Ratio	Expense Ratio
EELV	NYSE Arca	22.80	$329,451,398	4.89	125	0.29

Ratings
Reward	C
Risk	C-
Recent Upgrade/Downgrade	Up

Fund Information
Fund Type	Exchange Traded Funds
Category	Global Emerg Mkts Equity
Sub-Category	Diversified Emerging Mkts
Prospectus Objective	Div Emerg Mkts
Inception Date	Jan-12
Open to New Investments	

Prices
Price (as of 9/30/2019)	22.74
52-Week High	24.92
52-Week Low	22.22

Total Returns (%)
3-Month	6-Month	1-Year	3-Year	5-Year
-5.17	-3.18	-4.27	14.74	-0.17

3-Year Standard Deviation	11.07
Effective Duration	

Valuation
Premium/Discount (1-Year Average)	0.03

Company Information
Provider	Invesco
Manager/Tenure	Peter Hubbard (7), Michael Jeanette (4), Tony Seisser (4)
Website	http://www.invesco.com/us
Address	Invesco 11 Greenway Plaza, Ste. 2500 Houston TX 77046 United States
Phone Number	800-659-1005

PERFORMANCE

Ratings History
Date	Overall Rating	Risk Rating	Reward Rating
Q3-19	C	C-	C
Q4-18	C-	C-	C-
Q4-17	C	C	C
Q4-16	D	D+	D
Q4-15	D	D	D

Asset & Performance History
Date	NAV	1-Year Total Return
2018	22.77	-5.7
2017	25.44	24.53
2016	21.05	4.72
2015	20.55	-17.54
2014	25.51	-4.53
2013	27.56	-1.15

Total Assets: $329,451,398
Asset Allocation
Asset	%
Cash	0%
Stocks	100%
US Stocks	0%
Bonds	0%
US Bonds	0%
Other	0%

Services Offered:

Investment Strategy: The investment seeks to track the investment results (before fees and expenses) of the S&P BMI Emerging Markets Low Volatility IndexTM (the "underlying index"). The fund will invest at least 90% of its total assets in the securities of companies that comprise the underlying index. S&P Dow Jones Indices LLC ("S&P DJI" or the "index provider") compiles, maintains and calculates the underlying index, which is designed to measure the performance of 200 of the least volatile stocks of the S&P Emerging Plus LargeMidCap Index. **Top Holdings:** Nestle Malaysia Bhd   Kuala Lumpur Kepong Bhd   Hua Nan Financial Holdings Co Ltd   Taiwan Cooperative Financial Holding Co Ltd   First Financial Holding Co Ltd

---

ProShares Short Russell2000   D+   SELL

Ticker	Traded On	NAV	Total Assets ($)	Dividend Yield (TTM)	Turnover Ratio	Expense Ratio
RWM	NYSE Arca	40.60	$327,491,169	1.39	0	0.95

Ratings
Reward	D
Risk	D
Recent Upgrade/Downgrade	

Fund Information
Fund Type	Exchange Traded Funds
Category	Trading Tools
Sub-Category	Trading--Inverse Equity
Prospectus Objective	Small Company
Inception Date	Jan-07
Open to New Investments	Y

Prices
Price (as of 9/30/2019)	40.63
52-Week High	49.87
52-Week Low	38.23

Total Returns (%)
3-Month	6-Month	1-Year	3-Year	5-Year
2.59	1.63	7.63	-22.82	-40.44

3-Year Standard Deviation	17.21
Effective Duration	

Valuation
Premium/Discount (1-Year Average)	0.02

Company Information
Provider	ProShares
Manager/Tenure	Michael Neches (6), Devin Sullivan (1)
Website	http://www.proshares.com
Address	ProShares 7501 Wisconsin Avenue, Suite 1000 Bethesda MD 20814 United States
Phone Number	866-776-5125

PERFORMANCE

Ratings History
Date	Overall Rating	Risk Rating	Reward Rating
Q3-19	D+	D	D
Q4-18	D	D	D
Q4-17	D-	D-	D-
Q4-16	D	D	D
Q4-15	D	D-	D

Asset & Performance History
Date	NAV	1-Year Total Return
2018	46.69	11.5
2017	42.29	-13.61
2016	48.99	-21.04
2015	62.05	0.4
2014	61.8	-8.41
2013	67.48	-30.57

Total Assets: $327,491,169
Asset Allocation
Asset	%
Cash	149%
Stocks	-60%
US Stocks	-60%
Bonds	11%
US Bonds	11%
Other	0%

Services Offered:

Investment Strategy: The investment seeks daily investment results that correspond to the inverse (-1x) of the daily performance of the Russell 2000® Index. The fund invests in financial instruments that ProShare Advisors believes, in combination, should produce daily returns consistent with the fund's investment objective. It is a float-adjusted, market capitalization-weighted index containing approximately 2000 of the smallest companies in the Russell 3000® Index or approximately 8% of the total market capitalization of the Russell 3000® Index, which in turn represents approximately 98% of the investable U.S. equity market. The fund is non-diversified. **Top Holdings:** Russell 2000 Index Swap Bank Of America Na   Russell 2000 Index Swap Goldman Sachs International   Russell 2000 Index Swap Bnp Paribas   Russell 2000 Index Swap Societe Generale   E-mini Russell 2000 Index Futures

iShares Edge MSCI Min Vol USA Small-Cap ETF

C   **HOLD**

Ticker	Traded On	NAV	Total Assets ($)	Dividend Yield (TTM)	Turnover Ratio	Expense Ratio
SMMV	BATS	34.26	$325,451,274	1.5	48	0.2

Ratings
Reward	C
Risk	C+
Recent Upgrade/Downgrade	

Fund Information
Fund Type	Exchange Traded Funds
Category	US Equity Small Cap
Sub-Category	Small Blend
Prospectus Objective	Small Company
Inception Date	Sep-16
Open to New Investments	Y

Prices
Price (as of 9/30/2019)	34.33
52-Week High	34.72
52-Week Low	27.82

Total Returns (%)
3-Month	6-Month	1-Year	3-Year	5-Year
2.86	6.64	7.39	46.69	

3-Year Standard Deviation	9.87
Effective Duration	

Valuation
Premium/Discount (1-Year Average)	0.16

Company Information
Provider	iShares
Manager/Tenure	Diane Hsiung (3), Jennifer Hsui (3), Alan Mason (3), 3 others
Website	http://www.ishares.com
Address	iShares 400 Howard Street San Francisco CA 94105 United States
Phone Number	800-474-2737

PERFORMANCE

Ratings History
Date	Overall Rating	Risk Rating	Reward Rating
Q3-19	C	C+	C
Q4-18	C-	C-	C-
Q4-17	D	B+	C
Q4-16	U		
Q4-15			

Asset & Performance History
Date	NAV	1-Year Total Return
2018	29	1.48
2017	29.05	13.94
2016	25.93	
2015		
2014		
2013		

Total Assets: $325,451,274

Asset Allocation
Asset	%
Cash	0%
Stocks	100%
US Stocks	99%
Bonds	0%
US Bonds	0%
Other	0%

Services Offered:

Investment Strategy: The investment seeks to track the investment results of the MSCI USA Small Cap Minimum Volatility (USD) Index. The fund generally will invest at least 90% of its assets in the component securities of the underlying index. The index has been developed by MSCI Inc. (the "index provider" or "MSCI") to measure the performance of small-capitalization U.S. equities that in the aggregate have lower volatility characteristics relative to the small-capitalization U.S. equity market. The manager uses a "passive" or indexing approach to try to achieve the fund's investment objective. It is non-diversified. **Top Holdings:** Royal Gold Inc Brown & Brown Inc Bright Horizons Family Solutions Inc Equity Commonwealth Blackstone Mortgage Trust Inc A

Global X SuperDividend® REIT ETF

B-   **BUY**

Ticker	Traded On	NAV	Total Assets ($)	Dividend Yield (TTM)	Turnover Ratio	Expense Ratio
SRET	NAS CM	14.99	$324,475,083	7.9	42	0.59

Ratings
Reward	B-
Risk	C+
Recent Upgrade/Downgrade	Up

Fund Information
Fund Type	Exchange Traded Funds
Category	Real Estate Sector Equity
Sub-Category	Real Estate
Prospectus Objective	Real Estate
Inception Date	Mar-15
Open to New Investments	Y

Prices
Price (as of 9/30/2019)	15.04
52-Week High	15.24
52-Week Low	13.25

Total Returns (%)
3-Month	6-Month	1-Year	3-Year	5-Year
3.39	3.22	7.88	25.84	

3-Year Standard Deviation	12.02
Effective Duration	

Valuation
Premium/Discount (1-Year Average)	0.18

Company Information
Provider	Global X Funds
Manager/Tenure	Chang Kim (4), Nam To (1), Wayne Xie (0), 1 other
Website	http://www.globalxfunds.com
Address	Global X Funds 600 Lexington Avenue, 20th Floor New York NY 10022 United States
Phone Number	888-493-8631

PERFORMANCE

Ratings History
Date	Overall Rating	Risk Rating	Reward Rating
Q3-19	B-	C+	B-
Q4-18	C+	C	B
Q4-17	C+	B-	C+
Q4-16	D+	C-	B-
Q4-15	U		

Asset & Performance History
Date	NAV	1-Year Total Return
2018	13.59	-5.14
2017	15.5	17.8
2016	14.3	23.72
2015	12.55	
2014		
2013		

Total Assets: $324,475,083

Asset Allocation
Asset	%
Cash	0%
Stocks	100%
US Stocks	87%
Bonds	0%
US Bonds	0%
Other	0%

Services Offered:

Investment Strategy: The investment seeks investment results that correspond generally to the price and yield performance, before fees and expenses, of the Solactive Global SuperDividend® REIT Index. The fund invests at least 80% of its total assets in the securities of the underlying index and in American Depositary Receipts ("ADRs") and Global Depositary Receipts ("GDRs") based on the securities in the underlying index. The underlying index tracks the performance of REITs that rank among the highest yielding REITs globally, as determined by Solactive AG, the provider of the underlying index. **Top Holdings:** Independence Realty Trust Inc VEREIT Inc Class A Stockland Corp Ltd Arbor Realty Trust Inc Starwood Property Trust Inc

First Trust Consumer Discretionary AlphaDEX® Fund   C   HOLD

Ticker	Traded On	NAV	Total Assets ($)	Dividend Yield (TTM)	Turnover Ratio	Expense Ratio
FXD	NYSE Arca	42.04	$323,684,154	1.03	97	0.64

Ratings

Reward	C
Risk	C-
Recent Upgrade/Downgrade	

Fund Information

Fund Type	Exchange Traded Funds
Category	Consumer Goods & Svcs
Sub-Category	Consumer Cyclical
Prospectus Objective	Unaligned
Inception Date	May-07
Open to New Investments	Y

Prices

Price (as of 9/30/2019)	42.05
52-Week High	44.45
52-Week Low	34.86

Total Returns (%)

3-Month	6-Month	1-Year	3-Year	5-Year
-1.70	-0.63	-1.61	22.80	38.43

3-Year Standard Deviation	14.76
Effective Duration	

Valuation

Premium/Discount (1-Year Average)	-0.02

Company Information

Provider	First Trust
Manager/Tenure	Jon C. Erickson (12), Daniel J. Lindquist (12), David G. McGarel (12), 3 others
Website	http://www.ftportfolios.com/
Address	First Trust 120 E. Liberty Drive, Suite 400 Wheaton IL 60187 United States
Phone Number	800-621-1675

PERFORMANCE

Ratings History	Overall Rating	Risk Rating	Reward Rating
Date			
Q3-19	C	C-	C
Q4-18	C	C+	C
Q4-17	B-	B	C+
Q4-16	C+	C+	C+
Q4-15	C+	C+	C

Asset & Performance History		1-Year
Date	NAV	Total Return
2018	36.89	-11.43
2017	42.06	19.75
2016	35.48	5.12
2015	34.11	-3.81
2014	35.77	11.63
2013	32.22	42.99

Total Assets: $323,684,154

Asset Allocation

Asset	%
Cash	0%
Stocks	100%
US Stocks	97%
Bonds	0%
US Bonds	0%
Other	0%

Services Offered:

Investment Strategy: The investment seeks investment results that correspond generally to the price and yield (before the fund's fees and expenses) of an equity index called the StrataQuant® Consumer Discretionary Index. The fund will normally invest at least 90% of its net assets (including investment borrowings) in common stocks that comprise the index. The index is a modified equal-dollar weighted index designed by IDI to objectively identify and select stocks from the Russell 1000® Index in the consumer discretionary sector that may generate positive alpha relative to traditional passive-style indices through the use of the AlphaDEX® selection methodology. **Top Holdings:** Roku Inc Class A Carvana Co Class A The Trade Desk Inc A PulteGroup Inc Lennar Corp

---

VictoryShares USAA Core Intermediate-Term Bond ETF   C-   HOLD

Ticker	Traded On	NAV	Total Assets ($)	Dividend Yield (TTM)	Turnover Ratio	Expense Ratio
UITB	NYSE Arca	52.06	$322,774,927	2.98	10	0.4

Ratings

Reward	C-
Risk	C-
Recent Upgrade/Downgrade	

Fund Information

Fund Type	Exchange Traded Funds
Category	US Fixed Income
Sub-Category	Intermediate Core-Plus Bond
Prospectus Objective	Income
Inception Date	Oct-17
Open to New Investments	Y

Prices

Price (as of 9/30/2019)	52.12
52-Week High	52.75
52-Week Low	47.60

Total Returns (%)

3-Month	6-Month	1-Year	3-Year	5-Year
2.51	6.66	11.58		

3-Year Standard Deviation	
Effective Duration	6.17

Valuation

Premium/Discount (1-Year Average)	0.06

Company Information

Provider	VictoryShares
Manager/Tenure	Julianne Bass (1), Kurt Daum (1), Brian W. Smith (1), 3 others
Website	http://www.VictorySharesLiterature.com
Address	Victory Shares 4249 Easton Way, Suite 400 Columbus OH 43219 United States
Phone Number	

PERFORMANCE

Ratings History	Overall Rating	Risk Rating	Reward Rating
Date			
Q3-19	C-	C-	C-
Q4-18	D+	C-	D+
Q4-17	U		
Q4-16			
Q4-15			

Asset & Performance History		1-Year
Date	NAV	Total Return
2018	48.14	-0.88
2017	50.03	
2016		
2015		
2014		
2013		

Total Assets: $322,774,927

Asset Allocation

Asset	%
Cash	2%
Stocks	0%
US Stocks	0%
Bonds	95%
US Bonds	84%
Other	0%

Services Offered:

Investment Strategy: The investment seeks high current income without undue risk to principal. Under normal circumstances, the fund invests at least 80% of its net assets (plus any borrowings for investment purposes, exclusive of collateral held from securities lending) in debt securities and in derivatives and other instruments that have economic characteristics similar to such securities. The fund may not invest more than 20% of fixed-income securities (by weight of all fixed-income securities in the portfolio) in non-agency, non-government sponsored entities (GSEs), or privately issued mortgage- or asset-backed securities. **Top Holdings:** United States Treasury Notes 2% United States Treasury Bonds 3% United States Treasury Notes 2.38% United States Treasury Notes 2.88% United States Treasury Bonds 2.88%

ProShares UltraShort QQQ

D   SELL

Ticker	Traded On	NAV	Total Assets ($)	Dividend Yield (TTM)	Turnover Ratio	Expense Ratio
QID	NYSE Arca	30.04	$321,249,688	2.46	0	0.95

Ratings
Reward   E+
Risk   D-
Recent Upgrade/Downgrade

Fund Information
Fund Type   Exchange Traded Funds
Category   Trading Tools
Sub-Category   Trading--Inverse Equity
Prospectus Objective   Growth
Inception Date   Jul-06
Open to New Investments   Y

Prices
Price (as of 9/30/2019)   30.03
52-Week High   55.66
52-Week Low   28.74

Total Returns (%)

3-Month	6-Month	1-Year	3-Year	5-Year
-1.12	-9.16	-12.79	-68.01	-83.07

3-Year Standard Deviation   28.39
Effective Duration

Valuation
Premium/Discount (1-Year Average)   0.03

Company Information
Provider   ProShares
Manager/Tenure Michael Neches (6), Devin Sullivan (1)
Website   http://www.proshares.com
Address   ProShares 7501 Wisconsin Avenue,
                Suite 1000 Bethesda MD 20814
                United States
Phone Number   866-776-5125

PERFORMANCE

Ratings History

Date	Overall Rating	Risk Rating	Reward Rating
Q3-19	D	D-	E+
Q4-18	D	D-	D-
Q4-17	E+	E+	E+
Q4-16	D	D-	D-
Q4-15	D-	E+	E+

Asset & Performance History

Date	NAV	1-Year Total Return
2018	47.57	-9.91
2017	53.64	-44.03
2016	95.92	-19.34
2015	118.92	-24.73
2014	158	-34.12
2013	239.84	-49.4

Total Assets: $321,249,688

Asset Allocation

Asset	%
Cash	192%
Stocks	-105%
US Stocks	-102%
Bonds	13%
US Bonds	13%
Other	0%

Services Offered:

Investment Strategy: The investment seeks daily investment results, before fees and expenses, that correspond to two times the inverse (-2x) of the daily performance of the NASDAQ-100 Index®. The fund invests in financial instruments that ProShare Advisors believes, in combination, should produce daily returns consistent with the fund's investment objective. The index includes 100 of the largest domestic and international non-financial companies listed on The Nasdaq Stock Market based on market capitalization. The fund is non-diversified. **Top Holdings:** Nasdaq 100 Index Swap Bank Of America, Na Nasdaq 100 Index Swap Societe Generale Nasdaq 100 Index Swap Credit Suisse International Nasdaq 100 Index Swap Citibank, N.A. Nasdaq 100 Index Swap Bnp Paribas

---

iShares iBonds Dec 2022 Term Muni Bond ETF

C   HOLD

Ticker	Traded On	NAV	Total Assets ($)	Dividend Yield (TTM)	Turnover Ratio	Expense Ratio
IBMK	NYSE Arca	26.10	$321,063,387	1.53	0	0.18

Ratings
Reward   C
Risk   C-
Recent Upgrade/Downgrade

Fund Information
Fund Type   Exchange Traded Funds
Category   US Muni Fixed Inc
Sub-Category   Muni Target Maturity
Prospectus Objective   Muni Bond - Natl
Inception Date   Sep-15
Open to New Investments   Y

Prices
Price (as of 9/30/2019)   26.14
52-Week High   26.33
52-Week Low   25.21

Total Returns (%)

3-Month	6-Month	1-Year	3-Year	5-Year
0.35	1.57	4.42	3.56	

3-Year Standard Deviation   3.12
Effective Duration

Valuation
Premium/Discount (1-Year Average)   0.07

Company Information
Provider   iShares
Manager/Tenure James Mauro (4), Scott Radell (4)
Website   http://www.ishares.com
Address   iShares 400 Howard Street San
                Francisco CA 94105 United States
Phone Number   800-474-2737

PERFORMANCE

Ratings History

Date	Overall Rating	Risk Rating	Reward Rating
Q3-19	C	C-	C
Q4-18	C-	C-	C-
Q4-17	C	C	C-
Q4-16	D	C-	D+
Q4-15			

Asset & Performance History

Date	NAV	1-Year Total Return
2018	25.58	1.25
2017	25.65	2.86
2016	25.27	-0.07
2015	25.62	
2014		
2013		

Total Assets: $321,063,387

Asset Allocation

Asset	%
Cash	0%
Stocks	0%
US Stocks	0%
Bonds	100%
US Bonds	100%
Other	0%

Services Offered:

Investment Strategy: The investment seeks to track the investment results of the S&P AMT-Free Municipal Series Dec 2022 IndexTM, which measures the performance of investment-grade, non-callable U.S. municipal bonds maturing in 2022. The fund generally will invest at least 90% of its assets in the component securities of the underlying index, and may invest up to 10% of its assets in certain futures, options and swap contracts, cash and cash equivalents, including shares of money market funds advised by BFA or its affiliates, as well as in securities not included in the underlying index, but which BFA believes will help the fund track the underlying index. **Top Holdings:** GUILFORD CNTY N C 5% WISCONSIN ST TRANSN REV 5% NEW JERSEY ST TPK AUTH TPK REV 5% HONOLULU HAWAII CITY & CNTY 5% WISCONSIN ST TRANSN REV 5%

SPDR® MSCI EAFE StrategicFactors ETF   C   HOLD

Ticker	Traded On	NAV	Total Assets ($)	Dividend Yield (TTM)	Turnover Ratio	Expense Ratio
QEFA	NYSE Arca		$320,537,757	3.16	6	0.3

Ratings
Reward   C
Risk   C-
Recent Upgrade/Downgrade

Fund Information
Fund Type   Exchange Traded Funds
Category   Global Equity Large Cap
Sub-Category   Foreign Large Blend
Prospectus Objective   World Stock
Inception Date   Jun-14
Open to New Investments   Y

Prices
Price (as of 9/30/2019)   63.05
52-Week High   64.34
52-Week Low   54.70

Total Returns (%)

3-Month	6-Month	1-Year	3-Year	5-Year
-0.30	2.73	2.09	22.74	25.72

3-Year Standard Deviation   9.92
Effective Duration

Valuation
Premium/Discount (1-Year Average)   0.09

Company Information
Provider   SPDR State Street Global Advisors
Manager/Tenure Michael J. Feehily (5), Karl A.
                Schneider (4), Lisa Hobart (0)
Website   http://www.spdrs.com
Address   SPDR State Street Global Advisors
                State Street Financial Center, 1
                Lincoln Street Boston MA 02111-2900
                United States
Phone Number   617-786-3000

PERFORMANCE

Ratings History

Date	Overall Rating	Risk Rating	Reward Rating
Q3-19	C	C-	C
Q4-18	D+	C-	D+
Q4-17	B	B	B
Q4-16	D+	D+	C-
Q4-15	D	D+	D+

Asset & Performance History

Date	NAV	1-Year Total Return
2018	56.52	-10.22
2017	64.89	23.89
2016	53.66	0.32
2015	54.59	1.76
2014	55.19	
2013		

Total Assets: $320,537,757

Asset Allocation

Asset	%
Cash	1%
Stocks	99%
US Stocks	2%
Bonds	0%
US Bonds	0%
Other	0%

Services Offered:

Investment Strategy: The investment seeks to track the performance of the MSCI EAFE Factor Mix A-Series Index. The fund generally invests substantially all, but at least 80%, of its total assets in the securities comprising the index and in depositary receipts based on securities comprising the index. The index captures large- and mid-cap representation across 21 developed market Europe, Australasia, and Far East countries and aims to represent the performance of value, low volatility, and quality factor strategies. The fund is non-diversified. **Top Holdings:** Nestle SA   Roche Holding AG Dividend Right Cert.   Diageo PLC   AstraZeneca PLC   Novo Nordisk A/S B

UBS ETRACS Alerian MLP Index ETN   D   SELL

Ticker	Traded On	NAV	Total Assets ($)	Dividend Yield (TTM)	Turnover Ratio	Expense Ratio
AMU	NYSE Arca	14.66	$319,531,320	7.75		0.8

Ratings
Reward   D
Risk   C-
Recent Upgrade/Downgrade   Down

Fund Information
Fund Type   Exchange Traded Funds
Category   Energy Sector Equity
Sub-Category   Energy Limited Partnership
Prospectus Objective   Income
Inception Date   Jul-12
Open to New Investments   Y

Prices
Price (as of 9/30/2019)   14.67
52-Week High   17.68
52-Week Low   13.39

Total Returns (%)

3-Month	6-Month	1-Year	3-Year	5-Year
-5.22	-6.20	-10.71	-8.98	-37.64

3-Year Standard Deviation   16.9
Effective Duration

Valuation
Premium/Discount (1-Year Average)   -0.05

Company Information
Provider   UBS Group AG
Manager/Tenure No Manager (7)
Website   http://www.ubs.com
Address   Bahnhofstrasse 45 Zürich 8098
                Switzerland
Phone Number   412-037-1952

PERFORMANCE

Ratings History

Date	Overall Rating	Risk Rating	Reward Rating
Q3-19	D	C-	D
Q4-18	D+	C-	D+
Q4-17	D	D	D
Q4-16	D	D	D
Q4-15	D	D	D

Asset & Performance History

Date	NAV	1-Year Total Return
2018	14.02	-13.03
2017	17.31	-6.57
2016	19.89	17.2
2015	18.24	-32.92
2014	28.92	3.82
2013	29.19	26.51

Total Assets: $319,531,320

Asset Allocation

Asset	%
Cash	%
Stocks	%
US Stocks	%
Bonds	%
US Bonds	%
Other	%

Services Offered:

Investment Strategy: The investment seeks to replicate, net of expenses, the Alerian MLP Index.
The index measures the performance of 50 prominent energy master limited partnerships. It constituents earn the majority of their cash flow from the transportation, storage, processing or production of energy commodities. The Alerian MLP Index is calculated, maintained and published by S&P in consultation with the index sponsor. **Top Holdings:**

iShares MSCI USA Equal Weighted ETF   C   HOLD

Ticker	Traded On	NAV	Total Assets ($)	Dividend Yield (TTM)	Turnover Ratio	Expense Ratio
EUSA	NYSE Arca	59.61	$318,916,925	1.55	23	0.15

Ratings
Reward   C
Risk   C-
Recent Upgrade/Downgrade

Fund Information
Fund Type   Exchange Traded Funds
Category   US Equity Large Cap Blend
Sub-Category   Large Blend
Prospectus Objective   Growth
Inception Date   May-10
Open to New Investments   Y

Prices
Price (as of 9/30/2019)   59.64
52-Week High   60.88
52-Week Low   47.02

Total Returns (%)
3-Month	6-Month	1-Year	3-Year	5-Year
0.10	3.39	2.85	36.34	56.21

3-Year Standard Deviation   13.38
Effective Duration

Valuation
Premium/Discount (1-Year Average)   0.00

Company Information
Provider   iShares
Manager/Tenure   Diane Hsiung (9), Greg Savage (9), Jennifer Hsui (6), 3 others
Website   http://www.ishares.com
Address   iShares 400 Howard Street San Francisco CA 94105 United States
Phone Number   800-474-2737

PERFORMANCE

Ratings History
Date	Overall Rating	Risk Rating	Reward Rating
Q3-19	C	C-	C
Q4-18	C-	C-	C-
Q4-17	B-	B-	B-
Q4-16	C+	D+	B
Q4-15	C	C-	C

Asset & Performance History
Date	NAV	1-Year Total Return
2018	50	-8.23
2017	55.44	19.09
2016	47.3	14.07
2015	42.16	-2.17
2014	44.04	13.19
2013	39.69	32.38

Total Assets: $318,916,925
Asset Allocation
Asset	%
Cash	0%
Stocks	100%
US Stocks	98%
Bonds	0%
US Bonds	0%
Other	0%

Services Offered:

Investment Strategy: The investment seeks to track the investment results of the MSCI USA Equal Weighted Index. The fund generally will invest at least 90% of its assets in the component securities of the underlying index and may invest up to 10% of its assets in certain futures, options and swap contracts, cash and cash equivalents. The index is an equally-weighted securities index that measures the performance of equity securities in the top 85% by market capitalization of equity securities listed on stock exchanges in the United States and which represents an alternative weighting scheme to its market capitalization-weighted parent index, the MSCI USA Index. **Top Holdings:** Target Corp Lowe's Companies Inc Burlington Stores Inc Roku Inc Class A Keysight Technologies Inc

---

VanEck Vectors Biotech ETF   C   HOLD

Ticker	Traded On	NAV	Total Assets ($)	Dividend Yield (TTM)	Turnover Ratio	Expense Ratio
BBH	NAS CM	118.04	$318,299,087	0.47	30	0.35

Ratings
Reward   C
Risk   D+
Recent Upgrade/Downgrade

Fund Information
Fund Type   Exchange Traded Funds
Category   Healthcare Sector Equity
Sub-Category   Health
Prospectus Objective   Unaligned
Inception Date   Dec-11
Open to New Investments   Y

Prices
Price (as of 9/30/2019)   117.98
52-Week High   135.09
52-Week Low   103.76

Total Returns (%)
3-Month	6-Month	1-Year	3-Year	5-Year
-9.17	-8.72	-12.29	3.81	15.02

3-Year Standard Deviation   20.38
Effective Duration

Valuation
Premium/Discount (1-Year Average)   -0.07

Company Information
Provider   VanEck
Manager/Tenure   Hao-Hung (Peter) Liao (7), Guo Hua (Jason) Jin (1)
Website   http://www.vaneck.com
Address   Van Eck Associates Corporation 666 Third Avenue New York NY 10017 United States
Phone Number   800-826-1115

PERFORMANCE

Ratings History
Date	Overall Rating	Risk Rating	Reward Rating
Q3-19	C	D+	C
Q4-18	C	D+	C
Q4-17	C	C+	C
Q4-16	C	D+	B-
Q4-15	B	B-	B

Asset & Performance History
Date	NAV	1-Year Total Return
2018	111.33	-10.21
2017	124.62	16.63
2016	107.43	-15.03
2015	126.82	10.2
2014	115.39	30.35
2013	88.52	65.49

Total Assets: $318,299,087
Asset Allocation
Asset	%
Cash	0%
Stocks	100%
US Stocks	95%
Bonds	0%
US Bonds	0%
Other	0%

Services Offered:

Investment Strategy: The investment seeks to replicate as closely as possible, before fees and expenses, the price and yield performance of the MVIS® US Listed Biotech 25 Index. The fund normally invests at least 80% of its total assets in securities that comprise the fund's benchmark index. The Biotech Index includes common stocks and depositary receipts of U.S. exchange-listed companies in the biotechnology industry. Such companies may include medium-capitalization companies and foreign companies that are listed on a U.S. exchange. It is non-diversified. **Top Holdings:** Amgen Inc Gilead Sciences Inc Celgene Corp Allergan PLC IQVIA Holdings Inc

iShares Edge MSCI Intl Value Factor ETF   C-   HOLD

Ticker	Traded On	NAV	Total Assets ($)	Dividend Yield (TTM)	Turnover Ratio	Expense Ratio
IVLU	NYSE Arca	22.77	$316,478,195	3.44	20	0.3

Ratings

Reward	D
Risk	C
Recent Upgrade/Downgrade	

Fund Information

Fund Type	Exchange Traded Funds
Category	Global Equity Large Cap
Sub-Category	Foreign Large Value
Prospectus Objective	Foreign Stock
Inception Date	Jun-15
Open to New Investments	Y

Prices

Price (as of 9/30/2019)	22.79
52-Week High	25.50
52-Week Low	21.17

Total Returns (%)

3-Month	6-Month	1-Year	3-Year	5-Year
-2.02	-3.15	-7.10	15.81	

3-Year Standard Deviation	11.84
Effective Duration	

Valuation

Premium/Discount (1-Year Average)	0.05

Company Information

Provider	iShares
Manager/Tenure	Diane Hsiung (4), Jennifer Hsui (4), Greg Savage (4), 3 others
Website	http://www.ishares.com
Address	iShares 400 Howard Street San Francisco CA 94105 United States
Phone Number	800-474-2737

PERFORMANCE

Ratings History

Date	Overall Rating	Risk Rating	Reward Rating
Q3-19	C-	C	D
Q4-18	D+	C-	D+
Q4-17	C	C+	C+
Q4-16	D	D+	D
Q4-15	U		

Asset & Performance History

Date	NAV	1-Year Total Return
2018	21.94	-14.71
2017	26.4	23.1
2016	22.1	3.12
2015	22	
2014		
2013		

Total Assets: $316,478,195

Asset Allocation

Asset	%
Cash	1%
Stocks	99%
US Stocks	3%
Bonds	0%
US Bonds	0%
Other	0%

Services Offered:

Investment Strategy: The investment seeks to track the investment results of the MSCI World ex USA Enhanced Value Index. The fund generally will invest at least 90% of its assets in the component securities of the underlying index and in investments that have economic characteristics that are substantially identical to the component securities of the underlying index and may invest up to 10% of its assets in certain futures, options and swap contracts, cash and cash equivalents as well as in securities not included in the underlying index. The index is based on a traditional market capitalization-weighted parent index, the MSCI World ex USA Index. **Top Holdings:** Novartis AG British American Tobacco PLC Sanofi SA Toyota Motor Corp Bayer AG

Invesco BulletShares 2025 Corporate Bond ETF   C+   HOLD

Ticker	Traded On	NAV	Total Assets ($)	Dividend Yield (TTM)	Turnover Ratio	Expense Ratio
BSCP	NYSE Arca	21.31	$316,449,343	3.23	1	0.1

Ratings

Reward	C+
Risk	C+
Recent Upgrade/Downgrade	

Fund Information

Fund Type	Exchange Traded Funds
Category	US Fixed Income
Sub-Category	Target Maturity
Prospectus Objective	Corp Bond - Gen
Inception Date	Oct-15
Open to New Investments	Y

Prices

Price (as of 9/30/2019)	21.37
52-Week High	21.51
52-Week Low	19.40

Total Returns (%)

3-Month	6-Month	1-Year	3-Year	5-Year
1.97	5.76	11.71	11.08	

3-Year Standard Deviation	4.02
Effective Duration	5.14

Valuation

Premium/Discount (1-Year Average)	0.25

Company Information

Provider	Invesco
Manager/Tenure	Jeremy Neisewander (3), Peter Hubbard (1), Jeffrey W. Kernagis (1), 1 other
Website	http://www.invesco.com/us
Address	Invesco 11 Greenway Plaza, Ste. 2500 Houston TX 77046 United States
Phone Number	800-659-1005

PERFORMANCE

Ratings History

Date	Overall Rating	Risk Rating	Reward Rating
Q3-19	C+	C+	C+
Q4-18	C-	C-	D+
Q4-17	C	B	C
Q4-16	D	C-	D
Q4-15			

Asset & Performance History

Date	NAV	1-Year Total Return
2018	19.59	-1.9
2017	20.63	5.82
2016	20.11	5.13
2015	19.68	
2014		
2013		

Total Assets: $316,449,343

Asset Allocation

Asset	%
Cash	0%
Stocks	0%
US Stocks	0%
Bonds	99%
US Bonds	91%
Other	0%

Services Offered:

Investment Strategy: The investment seeks to track the investment results (before fees and expenses) of the Nasdaq BulletShares® USD Corporate Bond 2025 Index (the "underlying index"). The fund generally will invest at least 80% of its total assets in securities that comprise the underlying index. The underlying index seeks to measure the performance of a portfolio of U.S. dollar-denominated investment grade corporate bonds with maturities or, in some cases, "effective maturities" in the year 2025 (collectively, "2025 Bonds"). The fund is non-diversified. **Top Holdings:** AT&T Inc 3.4% CVS Health Corp 4.1% Charter Communications Operating, LLC/Charter Communications Operating Capi Medtronic, Inc. 3.5% Visa Inc 3.15%

Direxion Daily FTSE China Bull 3X Shares D SELL

Ticker	Traded On	NAV	Total Assets ($)	Dividend Yield (TTM)	Turnover Ratio	Expense Ratio
YINN	NYSE Arca	16.50	$315,902,587	1.36	158	1.52

Ratings
Reward   D
Risk   D
Recent Upgrade/Downgrade   Down

Fund Information
Fund Type	Exchange Traded Funds
Category	Trading Tools
Sub-Category	Trading--Leveraged Equity
Prospectus Objective	Pacific Stock
Inception Date	Dec-09
Open to New Investments	Y

Prices
Price (as of 9/30/2019)	16.48
52-Week High	26.74
52-Week Low	14.25

Total Returns (%)
3-Month	6-Month	1-Year	3-Year	5-Year
-25.94	-34.43	-30.94	-11.29	-35.69

3-Year Standard Deviation   56.61
Effective Duration

Valuation
Premium/Discount (1-Year Average)   0.02

Company Information
Provider	Direxion Funds
Manager/Tenure	Paul Brigandi (9), Tony Ng (4)
Website	http://www.direxionfunds.com
Address	Direxion Funds 1301 Avenue Of The Americas (6th Avenue) New York NY 10019 United States
Phone Number	646-572-3390

PERFORMANCE

Ratings History
Date	Overall Rating	Risk Rating	Reward Rating
Q3-19	D	D	D
Q4-18	D+	D+	D+
Q4-17	B-	D+	B+
Q4-16	D	D	D
Q4-15	C-	D+	C

Asset & Performance History
Date	NAV	1-Year Total Return
2018	17.42	-48.5
2017	34.1	130.19
2016	14.99	-15.45
2015	17.73	-50.44
2014	35.78	19.21
2013	30.08	60.42

Total Assets: $315,902,587
Asset Allocation
Asset	%
Cash	52%
Stocks	48%
US Stocks	0%
Bonds	0%
US Bonds	0%
Other	0%

Services Offered:

Investment Strategy: The investment seeks daily investment results, before fees and expenses, of 300% of the daily performance of the FTSE China 50 Index. The fund, under normal circumstances, invests at least 80% of its net assets (plus borrowing for investment purposes) in financial instruments, such as swap agreements, and securities of the index, exchange-traded funds ("ETFs") that track the index and other financial instruments that provide daily leveraged exposure to the index or ETFs that track the index. The index consists of the 50 largest and most liquid public Chinese companies currently trading on the Hong Kong Stock Exchange ("SEHK"). The fund is non-diversified. **Top Holdings:** iShares China Large-Cap ETF Ishares China Largecap iShares China Largecap iShares China Large Cap ETF USD Dist Ishares China Largecap

---

iShares Core 10+ Year USD Bond ETF C HOLD

Ticker	Traded On	NAV	Total Assets ($)	Dividend Yield (TTM)	Turnover Ratio	Expense Ratio
ILTB	NYSE Arca	69.29	$315,259,144	3.52	10	0.06

Ratings
Reward   B-
Risk   C-
Recent Upgrade/Downgrade

Fund Information
Fund Type	Exchange Traded Funds
Category	US Fixed Income
Sub-Category	Long-Term Bond
Prospectus Objective	Growth
Inception Date	Dec-09
Open to New Investments	Y

Prices
Price (as of 9/30/2019)	69.36
52-Week High	71.13
52-Week Low	57.00

Total Returns (%)
3-Month	6-Month	1-Year	3-Year	5-Year
6.34	14.07	21.53	17.83	37.56

3-Year Standard Deviation   8.27
Effective Duration

Valuation
Premium/Discount (1-Year Average)   0.23

Company Information
Provider	iShares
Manager/Tenure	Scott Radell (9), James Mauro (8)
Website	http://www.ishares.com
Address	iShares 400 Howard Street San Francisco CA 94105 United States
Phone Number	800-474-2737

PERFORMANCE

Ratings History
Date	Overall Rating	Risk Rating	Reward Rating
Q3-19	C	C-	B-
Q4-18	D+	C-	D
Q4-17	B-	B	C+
Q4-16	C	C-	C
Q4-15	C	C-	C

Asset & Performance History
Date	NAV	1-Year Total Return
2018	58.86	-4.99
2017	64.53	10.61
2016	60.58	7.63
2015	58.49	-2.96
2014	62.75	17.83
2013	55.32	-8.72

Total Assets: $315,259,144
Asset Allocation
Asset	%
Cash	1%
Stocks	0%
US Stocks	0%
Bonds	99%
US Bonds	83%
Other	0%

Services Offered:

Investment Strategy: The investment seeks to track the investment results of the Bloomberg Barclays U.S. Universal 10+ Year Index (the "underlying index"). The underlying index measures the performance of U.S. dollar-denominated taxable bonds that are rated either investment-grade or high yield with remaining maturities greater than ten years. The fund generally will invest at least 90% of its assets in the component securities of the underlying index and may invest up to 10% of its assets in certain futures, options and swap contracts, cash and cash equivalents, as well as in securities not included in the underlying index. **Top Holdings:** United States Treasury Bonds 3% United States Treasury Bonds 2.5% United States Treasury Bonds 3% United States Treasury Bonds 3% United States Treasury Bonds 2.88%

Invesco FTSE RAFI Developed Markets ex-U.S. Small-Mid ETF   D+   SELL

Ticker	Traded On	NAV	Total Assets ($)	Dividend Yield (TTM)	Turnover Ratio	Expense Ratio
PDN	NYSE Arca	29.44	$314,999,333	2.54	21	0.49

Ratings
Reward   D+
Risk   C-
Recent Upgrade/Downgrade   Down

Fund Information
Fund Type   Exchange Traded Funds
Category   Globa Eq Mid/Small Cap
Sub-Category   Foreign Small/Mid Value
Prospectus Objective   Foreign Stock
Inception Date   Sep-07
Open to New Investments

Prices
Price (as of 9/30/2019)   29.47
52-Week High   32.71
52-Week Low   26.23

Total Returns (%)

3-Month	6-Month	1-Year	3-Year	5-Year
-1.71	-0.94	-7.50	13.79	22.52

3-Year Standard Deviation   11.65
Effective Duration

Valuation
Premium/Discount (1-Year Average)   -0.20

Company Information
Provider   Invesco
Manager/Tenure   Peter Hubbard (12), Michael Jeanette
                  (4), Tony Seisser (4)
Website   http://www.invesco.com/us
Address   Invesco 11 Greenway Plaza, Ste. 2500
                  Houston TX 77046 United States
Phone Number   800-659-1005

PERFORMANCE

Ratings History

Date	Overall Rating	Risk Rating	Reward Rating
Q3-19	D+	C-	D+
Q4-18	C-	C-	D+
Q4-17	B+	B	B+
Q4-16	C	C-	C
Q4-15	C-	C-	C-

Asset & Performance History

Date	NAV	1-Year Total Return
2018	27.66	-17.71
2017	34.26	29.35
2016	27.17	6.37
2015	26.11	3.6
2014	25.71	-4.55
2013	27.44	20.83

Total Assets: $314,999,333
Asset Allocation

Asset	%
Cash	0%
Stocks	100%
US Stocks	1%
Bonds	0%
US Bonds	0%
Other	0%

Services Offered:

Investment Strategy: The investment seeks to track the investment results (before fees and expenses) of the FTSE RAFI TM Developed ex U.S. Mid-Small 1500 Index (the "underlying index"). The fund generally will invest at least 90% of its total assets in the securities that comprise the underlying index, as well as American depositary receipts ("ADRs") and global depositary receipts ("GDRs") that represent securities in the underlying index. The underlying index is comprised of securities of small-and mid-capitalization companies that are classified as "developed" within the country classification definition of FTSE, excluding the United States. **Top Holdings:** Eldorado Gold Corp Hitachi Chemical Co Ltd Leo Palace21 Corp IWG PLC Nomura Research Institute Ltd

Invesco DWA Technology Momentum ETF   C   HOLD

Ticker	Traded On	NAV	Total Assets ($)	Dividend Yield (TTM)	Turnover Ratio	Expense Ratio
PTF	NAS CM	68.58	$312,025,094	0		0.6

Ratings
Reward   B-
Risk   D+
Recent Upgrade/Downgrade   Down

Fund Information
Fund Type   Exchange Traded Funds
Category   Technology Sector Equity
Sub-Category   Technology
Prospectus Objective   Technology
Inception Date   Oct-06
Open to New Investments   Y

Prices
Price (as of 9/30/2019)   68.59
52-Week High   80.31
52-Week Low   48.33

Total Returns (%)

3-Month	6-Month	1-Year	3-Year	5-Year
-6.79	0.49	5.49	65.89	105.27

3-Year Standard Deviation   21.01
Effective Duration

Valuation
Premium/Discount (1-Year Average)   -0.09

Company Information
Provider   Invesco
Manager/Tenure   Peter Hubbard (12), Michael Jeanette
                  (11), Tony Seisser (5)
Website   http://www.invesco.com/us
Address   Invesco 11 Greenway Plaza, Ste. 2500
                  Houston TX 77046 United States
Phone Number   800-659-1005

PERFORMANCE

Ratings History

Date	Overall Rating	Risk Rating	Reward Rating
Q3-19	C	D+	B-
Q4-18	C	C-	C
Q4-17	B+	B	A
Q4-16	C-	C-	C-
Q4-15	B-	C+	B-

Asset & Performance History

Date	NAV	1-Year Total Return
2018	52.94	0.98
2017	52.46	31.14
2016	40.02	1.09
2015	39.69	3.38
2014	38.39	9.06
2013	35.44	34.62

Total Assets: $312,025,094
Asset Allocation

Asset	%
Cash	0%
Stocks	100%
US Stocks	100%
Bonds	0%
US Bonds	0%
Other	0%

Services Offered:

Investment Strategy: The investment seeks to track the investment results (before fees and expenses) of the Dorsey Wright® Technology Technical Leaders Index (the "underlying index"). The fund generally will invest at least 90% of its total assets in the securities that comprise the underlying index. The underlying index is composed of at least 30 securities of companies in the technology sector that have powerful relative strength or "momentum" characteristics. **Top Holdings:** Enphase Energy Inc Paycom Software Inc Alteryx Inc Class A RingCentral Inc Class A Match Group Inc

iShares MSCI Global Gold Miners ETF

C   HOLD

Ticker	Traded On	NAV		Total Assets ($)	Dividend Yield (TTM)	Turnover Ratio	Expense Ratio
RING	NAS CM	21.72		$309,469,299	0.86	4	0.39

Ratings

Reward	C
Risk	C-
Recent Upgrade/Downgrade	Up

Fund Information

Fund Type	Exchange Traded Funds
Category	Prec Metals
Sub-Category	Equity Precious Metals
Prospectus Objective	Prec Metals
Inception Date	Jan-12
Open to New Investments	Y

Prices

Price (as of 9/30/2019)	21.53
52-Week High	24.66
52-Week Low	14.21

Total Returns (%)

3-Month	6-Month	1-Year	3-Year	5-Year
7.73	26.52	52.94	1.16	25.56

3-Year Standard Deviation	26.13
Effective Duration	

Valuation

Premium/Discount (1-Year Average)	-0.25

Company Information

Provider	iShares
Manager/Tenure	Diane Hsiung (7), Greg Savage (7), Jennifer Hsui (6), 3 others
Website	http://www.ishares.com
Address	iShares 400 Howard Street San Francisco CA 94105 United States
Phone Number	800-474-2737

PERFORMANCE

Ratings History

Date	Overall Rating	Risk Rating	Reward Rating
Q3-19	C	C-	C
Q4-18	D	D	D+
Q4-17	D+	D	C-
Q4-16	C-	D	C
Q4-15	D-	D-	D-

Asset & Performance History

Date	NAV	1-Year Total Return
2018	16.19	-13.57
2017	18.86	9
2016	17.38	62.47
2015	10.86	-26.61
2014	14.92	-16.87
2013	18.08	-52.16

Total Assets: $309,469,299

Asset Allocation

Asset	%
Cash	0%
Stocks	100%
US Stocks	19%
Bonds	0%
US Bonds	0%
Other	0%

Services Offered:

Investment Strategy: The investment seeks to track the investment results of the MSCI ACWI Select Gold Miners Investable Market Index. The fund generally will invest at least 90% of its assets in the component securities of the underlying index and in investments that have economic characteristics that are substantially identical to the component securities of the underlying index. The index measures the combined performance of equity securities of companies primarily engaged in the business of gold mining in both developed and emerging markets. The fund is non-diversified. **Top Holdings:** Barrick Gold Corp   Newmont Goldcorp Corp   Newcrest Mining Ltd   Anglogold Ashanti Ltd   Kirkland Lake Gold Ltd

---

iShares U.S. Pharmaceuticals ETF

C+   HOLD

Ticker	Traded On	NAV		Total Assets ($)	Dividend Yield (TTM)	Turnover Ratio	Expense Ratio
IHE	NYSE Arca	139.81		$307,582,713	1.48	51	0.42

Ratings

Reward	B-
Risk	C-
Recent Upgrade/Downgrade	Up

Fund Information

Fund Type	Exchange Traded Funds
Category	Healthcare Sector Equity
Sub-Category	Health
Prospectus Objective	Health
Inception Date	May-06
Open to New Investments	Y

Prices

Price (as of 9/30/2019)	139.85
52-Week High	167.62
52-Week Low	132.01

Total Returns (%)

3-Month	6-Month	1-Year	3-Year	5-Year
-7.70	-8.71	-14.45	-2.76	7.56

3-Year Standard Deviation	15.33
Effective Duration	

Valuation

Premium/Discount (1-Year Average)	0.01

Company Information

Provider	iShares
Manager/Tenure	Greg Savage (11), Jennifer Hsui (7), Alan Mason (3), 2 others
Website	http://www.ishares.com
Address	iShares 400 Howard Street San Francisco CA 94105 United States
Phone Number	800-474-2737

PERFORMANCE

Ratings History

Date	Overall Rating	Risk Rating	Reward Rating
Q3-19	C+	C-	B-
Q4-18	C	C-	C+
Q4-17	C	C	C
Q4-16	C	D+	C+
Q4-15	C+	C	B-

Asset & Performance History

Date	NAV	1-Year Total Return
2018	140.74	-7.67
2017	154.21	10.65
2016	141.26	-11.72
2015	161.48	8.81
2014	151.23	29.74
2013	118.1	40.52

Total Assets: $307,582,713

Asset Allocation

Asset	%
Cash	0%
Stocks	100%
US Stocks	96%
Bonds	0%
US Bonds	0%
Other	0%

Services Offered:

Investment Strategy: The investment seeks to track the investment results of the Dow Jones U.S. Select Pharmaceuticals Index. The fund generally invests at least 90% of its assets in securities of the underlying index and in depositary receipts representing securities of the underlying index. The underlying index measures the performance of the pharmaceuticals sector of the U.S. equity market. The underlying index includes pharmaceutical companies such as manufacturers of prescription or over-the-counter drugs or vaccines, but excludes producers of vitamins. The fund is non-diversified. **Top Holdings:**   Johnson & Johnson   Pfizer Inc Allergan PLC   Zoetis Inc Class A   Merck & Co Inc

Hartford Multifactor US Equity ETF   C   HOLD

Ticker	Traded On	NAV	Total Assets ($)	Dividend Yield (TTM)	Turnover Ratio	Expense Ratio
ROUS	NYSE Arca	32.20	$307,491,269	2.03	36	0.19

Ratings
Reward   C
Risk   C-
Recent Upgrade/Downgrade

Fund Information
Fund Type   Exchange Traded Funds
Category   US Equity Large Cap Blend
Sub-Category   Large Value
Prospectus Objective   Growth
Inception Date   Feb-15
Open to New Investments   Y

Prices
Price (as of 9/30/2019)   32.22
52-Week High   33.06
52-Week Low   26.23

Total Returns (%)

3-Month	6-Month	1-Year	3-Year	5-Year
1.61	3.93	-0.23	39.12	

3-Year Standard Deviation   13.67
Effective Duration

Valuation
Premium/Discount (1-Year Average)   0.08

Company Information
Provider   Hartford Funds
Manager/Tenure   Richard A. Brown (4), Thomas J.
                    Durante (4), Karen Q. Wong (4)
Website   http://www.hartfordfunds.com
Address   690 Lee Road Wayne PA 19087 United
                    States
Phone Number   800-456-7526

PERFORMANCE

Ratings History

Date	Overall Rating	Risk Rating	Reward Rating
Q3-19	C	C-	C
Q4-18	C-	C-	C-
Q4-17	B-	B-	C+
Q4-16	D+	D+	C-
Q4-15	U		

Asset & Performance History

Date	NAV	1-Year Total Return
2018	27.84	-8.97
2017	31.12	22.58
2016	25.82	11.36
2015	23.68	
2014		
2013		

Total Assets: $307,491,269
Asset Allocation

Asset	%
Cash	1%
Stocks	99%
US Stocks	98%
Bonds	0%
US Bonds	0%
Other	0%

Services Offered:

Investment Strategy: The investment seeks to provide investment results that, before fees and expenses, correspond to the total return performance of the Hartford Multifactor Large Cap Index. Under normal conditions, the fund will invest at least 80% of its net assets (plus the amount of borrowings for investment purposes) in equity securities of issuers of U.S. companies. The index methodology seeks to enhance return potential through multifactor stock selection while applying a comprehensive risk framework to overall index construction. **Top Holdings:** Sprint Corp Registered Shs Series -1- Micron Technology Inc HP Inc VMware Inc United Airlines Holdings Inc

---

First Trust Industrials/Producer Durables AlphaDEX® Fund   C+   HOLD

Ticker	Traded On	NAV	Total Assets ($)	Dividend Yield (TTM)	Turnover Ratio	Expense Ratio
FXR	NYSE Arca	41.81	$307,300,617	0.99	79	0.62

Ratings
Reward   C+
Risk   C+
Recent Upgrade/Downgrade   Up

Fund Information
Fund Type   Exchange Traded Funds
Category   Industrials Sector Equity
Sub-Category   Industrials
Prospectus Objective   Unaligned
Inception Date   May-07
Open to New Investments   Y

Prices
Price (as of 9/30/2019)   41.82
52-Week High   43.36
52-Week Low   32.01

Total Returns (%)

3-Month	6-Month	1-Year	3-Year	5-Year
-1.45	3.29	-0.01	45.30	51.28

3-Year Standard Deviation   18.54
Effective Duration

Valuation
Premium/Discount (1-Year Average)   -0.04

Company Information
Provider   First Trust
Manager/Tenure   Jon C. Erickson (12), Daniel J.
                    Lindquist (12), David G. McGarel (12),
                    3 others
Website   http://www.ftportfolios.com/
Address   First Trust 120 E. Liberty Drive, Suite
                    400 Wheaton IL 60187 United States
Phone Number   800-621-1675

PERFORMANCE

Ratings History

Date	Overall Rating	Risk Rating	Reward Rating
Q3-19	C+	C+	C+
Q4-18	C	C+	C
Q4-17	B	C+	A-
Q4-16	C+	C	B-
Q4-15	C+	C+	C

Asset & Performance History

Date	NAV	1-Year Total Return
2018	34.11	-15.02
2017	40.57	24.14
2016	32.88	26.75
2015	26.09	-13.44
2014	30.33	8.13
2013	28.36	46.46

Total Assets: $307,300,617
Asset Allocation

Asset	%
Cash	0%
Stocks	100%
US Stocks	98%
Bonds	0%
US Bonds	0%
Other	0%

Services Offered:

Investment Strategy: The investment seeks investment results that correspond generally to the price and yield (before the fund's fees and expenses) of an equity index called the StrataQuant® Industrials Index. The fund will normally invest at least 90% of its net assets (including investment borrowings) in common stocks that comprise the index. The index is a modified equal-dollar weighted index designed by IDI to objectively identify and select stocks from the Russell 1000® Index in the industrials and producer durables sectors that may generate positive alpha relative to traditional passive-style indices through the use of the AlphaDEX® selection methodology. **Top Holdings:** Northrop Grumman Corp Booz Allen Hamilton Holding Corp Class A CoStar Group Inc Heico Corp Genpact Ltd

Invesco Dividend Achievers™ ETF   C+   HOLD

Ticker	Traded On	NAV	Total Assets ($)	Dividend Yield (TTM)	Turnover Ratio	Expense Ratio
PFM	NAS CM	29.55	$307,292,234	1.93	13	0.54

Ratings
Reward   B-
Risk   C
Recent Upgrade/Downgrade   Up

Fund Information
Fund Type   Exchange Traded Funds
Category   US Equity Large Cap Value
Sub-Category   Large Value
Prospectus Objective   Equity-Income
Inception Date   Sep-05
Open to New Investments   Y

Prices
Price (as of 9/30/2019)   29.56
52-Week High   29.84
52-Week Low   23.52

Total Returns (%)

3-Month	6-Month	1-Year	3-Year	5-Year
3.12	7.18	9.06	39.15	60.16

3-Year Standard Deviation   10.91
Effective Duration

Valuation
Premium/Discount (1-Year Average)   0.05

Company Information
Provider   Invesco
Manager/Tenure   Peter Hubbard (12), Michael Jeanette (11), Tony Seisser (5)
Website   http://www.invesco.com/us
Address   Invesco 11 Greenway Plaza, Ste. 2500 Houston TX 77046 United States
Phone Number   800-659-1005

PERFORMANCE

Ratings History

Date	Overall Rating	Risk Rating	Reward Rating
Q3-19	C+	C	B-
Q4-18	C	C-	C
Q4-17	B	B	B-
Q4-16	C+	C-	B-
Q4-15	C	C	C+

Asset & Performance History

Date	NAV	1-Year Total Return
2018	24.71	-4.4
2017	26.42	17.35
2016	22.92	14.64
2015	20.52	-3.13
2014	21.69	11.12
2013	19.91	25.63

Total Assets: $307,292,234

Asset Allocation

Asset	%
Cash	0%
Stocks	100%
US Stocks	99%
Bonds	0%
US Bonds	0%
Other	0%

Services Offered:

Investment Strategy: The investment seeks to track the investment results (before fees and expenses) of the NASDAQ US Broad Dividend Achievers™ Index. The fund generally will invest at least 90% of its total assets in the securities that comprise the underlying index. Strictly in accordance with its guidelines and mandated procedures, Nasdaq, Inc. ("Nasdaq" or the "index provider") includes common stock in the underlying index pursuant to a proprietary selection methodology that identifies a universe of "Dividend Achievers™." **Top Holdings:** Microsoft Corp   Walmart Inc   Johnson & Johnson   Visa Inc Class A   Procter & Gamble Co

VanEck Vectors Emerging Markets High Yield Bond ETF   C   HOLD

Ticker	Traded On	NAV	Total Assets ($)	Dividend Yield (TTM)	Turnover Ratio	Expense Ratio
HYEM	NYSE Arca	23.17	$305,780,773	6.16	27	0.4

Ratings
Reward   C
Risk   C-
Recent Upgrade/Downgrade   Down

Fund Information
Fund Type   Exchange Traded Funds
Category   Emerging Mkts Fixed Inc
Sub-Category   Emerging Markets Bond
Prospectus Objective   Corp Bond-High Yld
Inception Date   May-12
Open to New Investments   Y

Prices
Price (as of 9/30/2019)   23.18
52-Week High   23.93
52-Week Low   22.23

Total Returns (%)

3-Month	6-Month	1-Year	3-Year	5-Year
-0.98	2.35	7.27	12.46	24.60

3-Year Standard Deviation   5.01
Effective Duration   3.52

Valuation
Premium/Discount (1-Year Average)   0.25

Company Information
Provider   VanEck
Manager/Tenure   Francis G. Rodilosso (7)
Website   http://www.vaneck.com
Address   Van Eck Associates Corporation 666 Third Avenue New York NY 10017 United States
Phone Number   800-826-1115

PERFORMANCE

Ratings History

Date	Overall Rating	Risk Rating	Reward Rating
Q3-19	C	C-	C
Q4-18	C	C+	C-
Q4-17	B	B+	C+
Q4-16	C	C-	C+
Q4-15	C	C+	C-

Asset & Performance History

Date	NAV	1-Year Total Return
2018	22.37	-4.01
2017	24.5	7.98
2016	24.05	15.12
2015	22.27	2.95
2014	23.25	-2.21
2013	25.28	0.37

Total Assets: $305,780,773

Asset Allocation

Asset	%
Cash	1%
Stocks	0%
US Stocks	0%
Bonds	99%
US Bonds	13%
Other	0%

Services Offered:

Investment Strategy: The investment seeks to replicate as closely as possible, before fees and expenses, the price and yield performance of the ICE BofAML Diversified High Yield US Emerging Markets Corporate Plus Index. The fund normally invests at least 80% of its total assets in securities that comprise the fund's benchmark index. The index is comprised of U.S. dollar denominated bonds issued by non-sovereign emerging market issuers that have a below investment grade rating and that are issued in the major domestic and Eurobond markets. **Top Holdings:** Southern Gas Corridor 6.88%   DAE Funding LLC 13%   SB Capital SA 5.12%   ABJA Investment Co. Pte. Ltd. 5.95%   Yapi Ve Kredi Bankasi A.S. 5.5%

Invesco S&P SmallCap Information Technology ETF   C   HOLD

Ticker	Traded On	NAV	Total Assets ($)	Dividend Yield (TTM)	Turnover Ratio	Expense Ratio
PSCT	NAS CM	86.11	$305,704,467	0.27		0.29

Ratings
Reward   C
Risk   C-
Recent Upgrade/Downgrade

Fund Information
Fund Type	Exchange Traded Funds
Category	Technology Sector Equity
Sub-Category	Technology
Prospectus Objective	Technology
Inception Date	Apr-10
Open to New Investments	

Prices
Price (as of 9/30/2019)	85.80
52-Week High	88.72
52-Week Low	64.05

Total Returns (%)
3-Month	6-Month	1-Year	3-Year	5-Year
2.32	5.21	3.99	36.99	98.11

3-Year Standard Deviation	19.17
Effective Duration	

Valuation
Premium/Discount (1-Year Average)	-0.16

Company Information
Provider	Invesco
Manager/Tenure	Peter Hubbard (9), Michael Jeanette (9), Tony Seisser (5)
Website	http://www.invesco.com/us
Address	Invesco 11 Greenway Plaza, Ste. 2500 Houston TX 77046 United States
Phone Number	800-659-1005

PERFORMANCE

Ratings History

Date	Overall Rating	Risk Rating	Reward Rating
Q3-19	C	C-	C
Q4-18	C-	C-	C-
Q4-17	B+	A-	B
Q4-16	C+	C-	B-
Q4-15	C	C	C

Asset & Performance History

Date	NAV	1-Year Total Return
2018	69.2	-9.13
2017	76.47	10.11
2016	69.58	33.46
2015	52.27	4.33
2014	50.17	12.97
2013	44.47	44.44

Total Assets: $305,704,467
Asset Allocation

Asset	%
Cash	1%
Stocks	99%
US Stocks	95%
Bonds	0%
US Bonds	0%
Other	0%

Services Offered:

Investment Strategy: The investment seeks to track the investment results (before fees and expenses) of the S&P SmallCap 600® Capped Information Technology Index (the "underlying index"). The fund generally will invest at least 90% of its total assets in the securities of small-capitalization U.S. information technology companies that comprise the underlying index. These companies are principally engaged in the business of providing information technology-related products and services, including computer hardware and software, Internet, electronics and semiconductors, and communication technologies. **Top Holdings:** SolarEdge Technologies Inc Cabot Microelectronics Corp Viavi Solutions Inc Qualys Inc Finisar Corp

VelocityShares 3x Long Crude Oil ETNs linked to the S&P GSCI® Crude Oil Index ER New   D   SELL

Ticker	Traded On	NAV	Total Assets ($)	Dividend Yield (TTM)	Turnover Ratio	Expense Ratio
UWT	NYSE Arca	10.23	$305,367,320	0		1.5

Ratings
Reward   D
Risk   D
Recent Upgrade/Downgrade

Fund Information
Fund Type	Exchange Traded Funds
Category	Trading Tools
Sub-Category	Trading--Leveraged Commodities
Prospectus Objective	Growth & Inc
Inception Date	Dec-16
Open to New Investments	Y

Prices
Price (as of 9/30/2019)	10.37
52-Week High	49.34
52-Week Low	8.22

Total Returns (%)
3-Month	6-Month	1-Year	3-Year	5-Year
-34.37	-47.20	-78.56		

3-Year Standard Deviation	
Effective Duration	

Valuation
Premium/Discount (1-Year Average)	-0.33

Company Information
Provider	Credit Suisse AG
Manager/Tenure	No Manager (2)
Website	
Address	Kilmore House Park Lane Dublin Ireland
Phone Number	

PERFORMANCE

Ratings History

Date	Overall Rating	Risk Rating	Reward Rating
Q3-19	D	D	D
Q4-18	D	D	D+
Q4-17	D	D	D+
Q4-16			
Q4-15			

Asset & Performance History

Date	NAV	1-Year Total Return
2018	8.67	-65.15
2017	24.87	-12.7
2016	27.61	
2015		
2014		
2013		

Total Assets: $305,367,320
Asset Allocation

Asset	%
Cash	%
Stocks	%
US Stocks	%
Bonds	%
US Bonds	%
Other	%

Services Offered:

Investment Strategy: The investment seeks to replicate, net of expenses, three times of the S&P GSCI® Crude Oil Index ER.
The index tracks a hypothetical position in the nearest-to-expiration NYMEX light sweet crude oil futures contract, which is rolled each month into the futures contract expiring in the next month. The value of the index fluctuates with changes in the price of the relevant NYMEX light sweet crude oil futures contracts. **Top Holdings:**

Invesco DWA SmallCap Momentum ETF   C-   HOLD

Ticker	Traded On	NAV	Total Assets ($)	Dividend Yield (TTM)	Turnover Ratio	Expense Ratio
DWAS	NAS CM	50.05	$302,790,542	0.03		0.6

Ratings
Reward   C
Risk   C-
Recent Upgrade/Downgrade   Down

Fund Information
Fund Type   Exchange Traded Funds
Category   US Equity Small Cap
Sub-Category   Small Growth
Prospectus Objective   Small Company
Inception Date   Jul-12
Open to New Investments

Prices
Price (as of 9/30/2019)   50.04
52-Week High   56.36
52-Week Low   40.08

Total Returns (%)

3-Month	6-Month	1-Year	3-Year	5-Year
-7.82	-1.21	-11.11	31.02	44.32

3-Year Standard Deviation   19.37
Effective Duration

Valuation
Premium/Discount (1-Year Average)   -0.08

Company Information
Provider   Invesco
Manager/Tenure   Peter Hubbard (7), Michael Jeanette (7), Tony Seisser (5)
Website   http://www.invesco.com/us
Address   Invesco 11 Greenway Plaza, Ste. 2500 Houston TX 77046 United States
Phone Number   800-659-1005

PERFORMANCE

Ratings History

Date	Overall Rating	Risk Rating	Reward Rating
Q3-19	C-	C-	C
Q4-18	C-	C-	C-
Q4-17	B	B-	B+
Q4-16	C-	C-	C
Q4-15	C	C-	C

Asset & Performance History

Date	NAV	1-Year Total Return
2018	43.66	-10.18
2017	48.63	20.58
2016	40.41	7.88
2015	37.66	-3.33
2014	39.03	-1.64
2013	39.7	49.19

Total Assets: $302,790,542
Asset Allocation

Asset	%
Cash	0%
Stocks	100%
US Stocks	99%
Bonds	0%
US Bonds	0%
Other	0%

Services Offered:

Investment Strategy: The investment seeks to track the investment results (before fees and expenses) of the Dorsey Wright® SmallCap Technical Leaders Index (the "underlying index"). The fund generally will invest at least 90% of its total assets in the securities of small-capitalization companies that comprise the underlying index. The index provider selects securities pursuant to its proprietary selection methodology for inclusion in the underlying index, which is designed to identify securities that demonstrate powerful relative strength characteristics. **Top Holdings:** Arrowhead Pharmaceuticals Inc   PaySign Inc   Five9 Inc   CryoPort Inc   Casella Waste Systems Inc Class A

SPDR® Bloomberg Barclays Short Term International Treasury Bond ETF   D+   SELL

Ticker	Traded On	NAV	Total Assets ($)	Dividend Yield (TTM)	Turnover Ratio	Expense Ratio
BWZ	NYSE Arca		$302,232,829	1.32	66	0.35

Ratings
Reward   D+
Risk   C-
Recent Upgrade/Downgrade

Fund Information
Fund Type   Exchange Traded Funds
Category   Global Fixed Income
Sub-Category   World Bond
Prospectus Objective   Worldwide Bond
Inception Date   Jan-09
Open to New Investments   Y

Prices
Price (as of 9/30/2019)   30.29
52-Week High   31.16
52-Week Low   30.28

Total Returns (%)

3-Month	6-Month	1-Year	3-Year	5-Year
-1.99	-0.80	-1.22	-2.77	-9.15

3-Year Standard Deviation   5.53
Effective Duration   1.87

Valuation
Premium/Discount (1-Year Average)   0.02

Company Information
Provider   SPDR State Street Global Advisors
Manager/Tenure   Joanna Madden (4), James Kramer (2), Orhan Imer (1)
Website   http://www.spdrs.com
Address   SPDR State Street Global Advisors State Street Financial Center, 1 Lincoln Street Boston MA 02111-2900 United States
Phone Number   617-786-3000

PERFORMANCE

Ratings History

Date	Overall Rating	Risk Rating	Reward Rating
Q3-19	D+	C-	D+
Q4-18	C-	C-	D+
Q4-17	C	C	C-
Q4-16	D+	D+	D
Q4-15	D	D+	D

Asset & Performance History

Date	NAV	1-Year Total Return
2018	30.74	-3.16
2017	32.09	9.55
2016	29.31	-1.9
2015	29.76	-7.44
2014	32.17	-9.83
2013	35.75	-2.34

Total Assets: $302,232,829
Asset Allocation

Asset	%
Cash	1%
Stocks	0%
US Stocks	0%
Bonds	99%
US Bonds	0%
Other	0%

Services Offered:

Investment Strategy: The investment seeks to provide investment results that correspond generally to the Bloomberg Barclays 1-3 Year Global Treasury ex-US Capped Index. The fund invests substantially all, but at least 80%, of its total assets in the securities comprising the index or in securities that the Adviser determines have economic characteristics that are substantially identical to the economic characteristics of the securities that comprise the index. The index is designed to measure the performance of fixed-rate local currency sovereign debt of investment grade countries outside the United States that have remaining maturities of 1-3 years. The fund is non-diversified. **Top Holdings:** The Republic of Korea 2%   Japan (5 Year Issue) Sr Unsecured 06/21 0.1   Japan (5 Year Issue) Sr Unsecured 12/21 0.1   Japan (5 Year Issue) Sr Unsecured 09/21 0.1   Japan(Govt Of) 0.1%

ProShares Ultra Bloomberg Crude Oil   D+   SELL

Ticker	Traded On	NAV	Total Assets ($)	Dividend Yield (TTM)	Turnover Ratio	Expense Ratio
UCO	NYSE Arca		$301,560,573	0	0	0.95

Ratings

Reward	D
Risk	D+
Recent Upgrade/Downgrade	

Fund Information

Fund Type	Exchange Traded Funds
Category	Trading Tools
Sub-Category	Trading--Leveraged Commodities
Prospectus Objective	Natl Res
Inception Date	Nov-08
Open to New Investments	Y

Prices

Price (as of 9/30/2019)	16.22
52-Week High	38.61
52-Week Low	12.43

Total Returns (%)

3-Month	6-Month	1-Year	3-Year	5-Year
-14.14	-23.73	-54.44	-18.14	-94.28

3-Year Standard Deviation	54
Effective Duration	

Valuation

Premium/Discount (1-Year Average)	-0.20

Company Information

Provider	ProShares
Manager/Tenure	Management Team (10)
Website	http://www.proshares.com
Address	ProShares 7501 Wisconsin Avenue, Suite 1000 Bethesda MD 20814 United States
Phone Number	866-776-5125

PERFORMANCE

Ratings History

Date	Overall Rating	Risk Rating	Reward Rating
Q3-19	D+	D+	D
Q4-18	D+	D	D+
Q4-17	D	D	D
Q4-16	E+	D-	E
Q4-15	E+	D-	E+

Asset & Performance History

Date	NAV	1-Year Total Return
2018	13.06	-45.11
2017	23.67	1.41
2016	23.34	-7.23
2015	25.15	-75.21
2014	101.49	-68.37
2013	320.87	9.16

Total Assets: $301,560,573
Asset Allocation

Asset	%
Cash	-100%
Stocks	0%
US Stocks	0%
Bonds	0%
US Bonds	0%
Other	200%

Services Offered:

Investment Strategy: The investment seeks daily investment results, before fees and expenses, that correspond to two times (2x) the daily performance of the Bloomberg WTI Crude Oil SubindexSM.
The fund seeks to meet its investment objective by investing, under normal market conditions, in futures contracts for WTI sweet, light crude oil listed on the NYMEX, ICE Futures U.S. or other U.S. exchanges and listed options on such contracts. It will not invest directly in oil. **Top Holdings:** Bloomberg Wti Crude Oil Subindex Swap - Citibank N   Crude Oil Oct19   Bloomberg Wti Crude Oil Subindex Swap - Rbc   Bloomberg Wti Crude Oil Subindex Swap - Ubs Ag   Bloomberg Wti Crude Oil Subindex Swap - Gs

WisdomTree U.S. Earnings 500 Fund   C   HOLD

Ticker	Traded On	NAV	Total Assets ($)	Dividend Yield (TTM)	Turnover Ratio	Expense Ratio
EPS	NYSE Arca	33.52	$299,976,160	1.86	14	0.08

Ratings

Reward	C+
Risk	C-
Recent Upgrade/Downgrade	

Fund Information

Fund Type	Exchange Traded Funds
Category	US Equity Large Cap Blend
Sub-Category	Large Blend
Prospectus Objective	Growth & Inc
Inception Date	Feb-07
Open to New Investments	Y

Prices

Price (as of 9/30/2019)	33.54
52-Week High	34.14
52-Week Low	26.55

Total Returns (%)

3-Month	6-Month	1-Year	3-Year	5-Year
1.63	5.12	4.53	46.29	63.27

3-Year Standard Deviation	12.79
Effective Duration	

Valuation

Premium/Discount (1-Year Average)	0.03

Company Information

Provider	WisdomTree
Manager/Tenure	Richard A. Brown (11), Thomas J. Durante (11), Karen Q. Wong (11)
Website	http://www.wisdomtree.com
Address	WisdomTree 245 Park Avenue, 35th floor New York NY 10167 United States
Phone Number	866-909-9473

PERFORMANCE

Ratings History

Date	Overall Rating	Risk Rating	Reward Rating
Q3-19	C	C-	C+
Q4-18	C	C-	C
Q4-17	B	B-	B
Q4-16	C+	D+	B
Q4-15	C	C-	C

Asset & Performance History

Date	NAV	1-Year Total Return
2018	28.19	-7.31
2017	30.99	22.54
2016	25.73	13.87
2015	23.08	-1.65
2014	23.97	13.48
2013	21.49	32.56

Total Assets: $299,976,160
Asset Allocation

Asset	%
Cash	0%
Stocks	100%
US Stocks	100%
Bonds	0%
US Bonds	0%
Other	0%

Services Offered:

Investment Strategy: The investment seeks to track the price and yield performance, before fees and expenses, of the WisdomTree U.S. LargeCap Index. Under normal circumstances, at least 95% of the fund's total assets (exclusive of collateral held from securities lending) will be invested in component securities of the index and investments that have economic characteristics that are substantially identical to the economic characteristics of such component securities. The index is a fundamentally weighted index that is comprised of earnings-generating companies within the large-capitalization segment of the U.S. Stock Market. The fund is non-diversified. **Top Holdings:** Apple Inc   Microsoft Corp   Berkshire Hathaway Inc B   Alphabet Inc A   JPMorgan Chase & Co

ProShares VIX Short-Term Futures ETF

D- **SELL**

Ticker	Traded On	NAV	Total Assets ($)	Dividend Yield (TTM)	Turnover Ratio	Expense Ratio
VIXY	NYSE Arca		$299,371,289	0		0.87

Ratings
Reward ... E+
Risk ... D
Recent Upgrade/Downgrade

Fund Information
Fund Type ... Exchange Traded Funds
Category ... Alternative Misc
Sub-Category ... Volatility
Prospectus Objective ... Growth
Inception Date ... Jan-11
Open to New Investments ... Y

Prices
Price (as of 9/30/2019) ... 19.52
52-Week High ... 40.68
52-Week Low ... 17.70

Total Returns (%)
3-Month	6-Month	1-Year	3-Year	5-Year
-0.27	-14.61	-7.56	-82.38	-95.17

3-Year Standard Deviation ... 58.83
Effective Duration

Valuation
Premium/Discount (1-Year Average) ... 0.35

Company Information
Provider ... ProShares
Manager/Tenure ... Management Team (8)
Website ... http://www.proshares.com
Address ... ProShares 7501 Wisconsin Avenue, Suite 1000 Bethesda MD 20814 United States
Phone Number ... 866-776-5125

PERFORMANCE

Ratings History
Date	Overall Rating	Risk Rating	Reward Rating
Q3-19	D-	D	E+
Q4-18	D-	D	E+
Q4-17	E	E+	E
Q4-16	E+	D-	E
Q4-15	E+	E+	E+

Asset & Performance History
Date	NAV	1-Year Total Return
2018	38.58	72.11
2017	23.34	-72.48
2016	84.86	-67.96
2015	264.87	-36.73
2014	418.65	-26.65
2013	570.81	-65.99

Total Assets: $299,371,289
Asset Allocation
Asset	%
Cash	0%
Stocks	100%
US Stocks	100%
Bonds	0%
US Bonds	0%
Other	0%

Services Offered:

Investment Strategy: The investment seeks investment results, before fees and expenses, that over time, match the performance of the S&P 500 VIX Short-Term Futures Index for a single day.
The index seeks to offer exposure to market volatility through publicly traded futures markets and is designed to measure the implied volatility of the S&P 500 over 30 days in the future. **Top Holdings:** Cboe Vix Future 09/18/2019 (Uxu9) Cboe Vix Future 10/16/2019 (Uxv9)

Invesco DWA Utilities Momentum ETF

B- **BUY**

Ticker	Traded On	NAV	Total Assets ($)	Dividend Yield (TTM)	Turnover Ratio	Expense Ratio
PUI	NAS CM	34.99	$297,400,583	1.56		0.6

Ratings
Reward ... B
Risk ... C+
Recent Upgrade/Downgrade

Fund Information
Fund Type ... Exchange Traded Funds
Category ... Utilities Sector Equity
Sub-Category ... Utilities
Prospectus Objective ... Utility
Inception Date ... Oct-05
Open to New Investments ... Y

Prices
Price (as of 9/30/2019) ... 35.02
52-Week High ... 35.16
52-Week Low ... 28.07

Total Returns (%)
3-Month	6-Month	1-Year	3-Year	5-Year
8.36	10.27	24.66	46.47	81.91

3-Year Standard Deviation ... 10.86
Effective Duration

Valuation
Premium/Discount (1-Year Average) ... 0.09

Company Information
Provider ... Invesco
Manager/Tenure ... Peter Hubbard (12), Michael Jeanette (11), Tony Seisser (5)
Website ... http://www.invesco.com/us
Address ... Invesco 11 Greenway Plaza, Ste. 2500 Houston TX 77046 United States
Phone Number ... 800-659-1005

PERFORMANCE

Ratings History
Date	Overall Rating	Risk Rating	Reward Rating
Q3-19	B-	C+	B
Q4-18	B	C+	B
Q4-17	B-	B	B-
Q4-16	B-	C	B
Q4-15	B	C+	B

Asset & Performance History
Date	NAV	1-Year Total Return
2018	28.91	6.1
2017	27.79	11.64
2016	25.63	19.07
2015	22.25	-2.98
2014	23.61	16.92
2013	20.64	21.93

Total Assets: $297,400,583
Asset Allocation
Asset	%
Cash	0%
Stocks	100%
US Stocks	100%
Bonds	0%
US Bonds	0%
Other	0%

Services Offered:

Investment Strategy: The investment seeks to track the investment results (before fees and expenses) of the Dorsey Wright® Utilities Technical Leaders Index (the "underlying index"). The fund generally will invest at least 90% of its total assets in the securities that comprise the underlying index. The underlying index is composed of at least 30 securities of companies in the utilities sector that have powerful relative strength or "momentum" characteristics. **Top Holdings:** WEC Energy Group Inc NextEra Energy Inc CMS Energy Corp Entergy Corp Atmos Energy Corp

---

Fidelity® Low Volatility Factor ETF   C   HOLD

Ticker	Traded On	NAV	Total Assets ($)	Dividend Yield (TTM)	Turnover Ratio	Expense Ratio
FDLO	NYSE Arca	36.69	$297,165,631	1.57	36	0.29

Ratings
Reward   C
Risk   C-
Recent Upgrade/Downgrade

Fund Information
Fund Type   Exchange Traded Funds
Category   US Equity Large Cap Blend
Sub-Category   Large Blend
Prospectus Objective   Growth & Inc
Inception Date   Sep-16
Open to New Investments   Y

Prices
Price (as of 9/30/2019)   36.72
52-Week High   37.11
52-Week Low   28.31

Total Returns (%)

3-Month	6-Month	1-Year	3-Year	5-Year
2.63	7.85	10.68	53.09	

3-Year Standard Deviation   10.09
Effective Duration

Valuation
Premium/Discount (1-Year Average)   0.00

Company Information
Provider   Fidelity Investments
Manager/Tenure   Louis Bottari (3), Deane Gyllenhaal (3), Peter Matthew (3), 3 others
Website   http://www.institutional.fidelity.com
Address   Fidelity Investments 82 Devonshire Street Boston MA 2109 United States
Phone Number   617-563-7000

PERFORMANCE

Ratings History

Date	Overall Rating	Risk Rating	Reward Rating
Q3-19	C	C-	C
Q4-18	C	C-	C
Q4-17	D	B+	C
Q4-16	U		
Q4-15			

Asset & Performance History

Date	NAV	1-Year Total Return
2018	30.15	0.53
2017	30.49	19.95
2016	25.86	
2015		
2014		
2013		

Total Assets: $297,165,631

Asset Allocation

Asset	%
Cash	0%
Stocks	100%
US Stocks	98%
Bonds	0%
US Bonds	0%
Other	0%

Services Offered:

Investment Strategy: The investment seeks to provide investment returns that correspond, before fees and expenses, generally to the performance of the Fidelity U.S. Low Volatility Factor Index. The fund normally invests at least 80% of assets in securities included in the Fidelity U.S. Low Volatility Factor Index, which is designed to reflect the performance of stocks of large and mid-capitalization U.S. companies with lower volatility than the broader market. It may lend securities to earn income for the fund. **Top Holdings:** Microsoft Corp   Alphabet Inc A   Berkshire Hathaway Inc B   Johnson & Johnson   Visa Inc Class A

Direxion Daily Energy Bull 3X Shares   D-   SELL

Ticker	Traded On	NAV	Total Assets ($)	Dividend Yield (TTM)	Turnover Ratio	Expense Ratio
ERX	NYSE Arca	15.59	$293,894,686	1.8	56	1.09

Ratings
Reward   D-
Risk   D
Recent Upgrade/Downgrade   Down

Fund Information
Fund Type   Exchange Traded Funds
Category   Trading Tools
Sub-Category   Trading--Leveraged Equity
Prospectus Objective   Natl Res
Inception Date   Nov-08
Open to New Investments   Y

Prices
Price (as of 9/30/2019)   15.58
52-Week High   40.44
52-Week Low   12.78

Total Returns (%)

3-Month	6-Month	1-Year	3-Year	5-Year
-21.94	-33.76	-59.36	-51.54	-82.09

3-Year Standard Deviation   61.74
Effective Duration

Valuation
Premium/Discount (1-Year Average)   -0.08

Company Information
Provider   Direxion Funds
Manager/Tenure   Paul Brigandi (10), Tony Ng (4)
Website   http://www.direxionfunds.com
Address   Direxion Funds 1301 Avenue Of The Americas (6th Avenue) New York NY 10019 United States
Phone Number   646-572-3390

PERFORMANCE

Ratings History

Date	Overall Rating	Risk Rating	Reward Rating
Q3-19	D-	D	D-
Q4-18	D	D	D
Q4-17	D	D+	D
Q4-16	D	D	D+
Q4-15	D	D	D

Asset & Performance History

Date	NAV	1-Year Total Return
2018	15.15	-55.83
2017	34.85	-11.7
2016	39.87	69.8
2015	23.48	-61.16
2014	60.46	-32.7
2013	89.84	84.89

Total Assets: $293,894,686

Asset Allocation

Asset	%
Cash	42%
Stocks	58%
US Stocks	57%
Bonds	0%
US Bonds	0%
Other	0%

Services Offered:

Investment Strategy: The investment seeks daily investment results, before fees and expenses, of 300% of the daily performance of the Energy Select Sector Index. The fund invests at least 80% of its net assets (plus borrowing for investment purposes) in financial instruments and securities of the index, ETFs that track the index and other financial instruments that provide daily leveraged exposure to the index or ETFs that track the index. The index is provided by S&P Dow Jones Indices and includes domestic companies from the energy sector which includes the following industries: oil, gas and consumable fuels; and energy equipment and services. The fund is non-diversified. **Top Holdings:** Energy Select Sector SPDR® ETF   Energy Select Sector   Energy Select Sector   Energy Select Sector   Energy Select Sector

First Trust STOXX® European Select Dividend Index Fund

C   HOLD

Ticker	Traded On	NAV	Total Assets ($)	Dividend Yield (TTM)	Turnover Ratio	Expense Ratio
FDD	NYSE Arca	12.75	$293,835,262	5.16	35	0.57

Ratings
Reward   C
Risk   C+
Recent Upgrade/Downgrade

Fund Information
Fund Type	Exchange Traded Funds
Category	Europe Equity Large Cap
Sub-Category	Europe Stock
Prospectus Objective	Europe Stock
Inception Date	Aug-07
Open to New Investments	Y

Prices
Price (as of 9/30/2019)	12.74
52-Week High	13.32
52-Week Low	11.69

Total Returns (%)
3-Month	6-Month	1-Year	3-Year	5-Year
2.80	2.95	2.88	22.76	18.83

3-Year Standard Deviation	11.34
Effective Duration	

Valuation
Premium/Discount (1-Year Average)	-0.05

Company Information
Provider	First Trust
Manager/Tenure	Jon C. Erickson (12), Daniel J. Lindquist (12), David G. McGarel (12), 3 others
Website	http://www.ftportfolios.com/
Address	First Trust 120 E. Liberty Drive, Suite 400 Wheaton IL 60187 United States
Phone Number	800-621-1675

PERFORMANCE

Ratings History
Date	Overall Rating	Risk Rating	Reward Rating
Q3-19	C	C+	C
Q4-18	C-	C	D+
Q4-17	B-	B	C+
Q4-16	D+	C-	D+
Q4-15	C	C+	C

Asset & Performance History
Date	NAV	1-Year Total Return
2018	11.98	-8.8
2017	13.75	19.05
2016	11.89	2.45
2015	12.17	-3.33
2014	13.11	-0.1
2013	13.64	17.19

Total Assets: $293,835,262

Asset Allocation
Asset	%
Cash	0%
Stocks	100%
US Stocks	0%
Bonds	0%
US Bonds	0%
Other	0%

Services Offered:

Investment Strategy: The investment seeks investment results that correspond generally to the price and yield (before the fund's fees and expenses) of an equity index called the STOXX® Europe Select Dividend 30 Index. The fund will normally invest at least 90% of its net assets (including investment borrowings) in the common stocks and depositary receipts that comprise the index. The index consists of 30 high dividend-yielding securities selected from the STOXX® Europe 600 Index. In addition, a security must be issued by a company with a non-negative five-year dividend-per-share growth rate and a dividend-to-earnings ratio of 60% or less. **Top Holdings:** SSE PLC Intesa Sanpaolo GlaxoSmithKline PLC Swiss Prime Site AG Royal Dutch Shell PLC B

---

iShares iBonds Dec 2021 Term Muni Bond ETF

C   HOLD

Ticker	Traded On	NAV	Total Assets ($)	Dividend Yield (TTM)	Turnover Ratio	Expense Ratio
IBMJ	NYSE Arca	25.76	$293,625,598	1.42	0	0.18

Ratings
Reward   C
Risk   C-
Recent Upgrade/Downgrade

Fund Information
Fund Type	Exchange Traded Funds
Category	US Muni Fixed Inc
Sub-Category	Muni Target Maturity
Prospectus Objective	Muni Bond - Natl
Inception Date	Sep-15
Open to New Investments	Y

Prices
Price (as of 9/30/2019)	25.78
52-Week High	25.89
52-Week Low	25.19

Total Returns (%)
3-Month	6-Month	1-Year	3-Year	5-Year
0.31	1.24	3.37	3.02	

3-Year Standard Deviation	2.48
Effective Duration	

Valuation
Premium/Discount (1-Year Average)	0.05

Company Information
Provider	iShares
Manager/Tenure	James Mauro (4), Scott Radell (4)
Website	http://www.ishares.com
Address	iShares 400 Howard Street San Francisco CA 94105 United States
Phone Number	800-474-2737

PERFORMANCE

Ratings History
Date	Overall Rating	Risk Rating	Reward Rating
Q3-19	C	C-	C
Q4-18	C-	C-	C-
Q4-17	C	C	C-
Q4-16	D	C-	D+
Q4-15			

Asset & Performance History
Date	NAV	1-Year Total Return
2018	25.42	1.35
2017	25.42	2.07
2016	25.19	-0.07
2015	25.51	
2014		
2013		

Total Assets: $293,625,598

Asset Allocation
Asset	%
Cash	0%
Stocks	0%
US Stocks	0%
Bonds	100%
US Bonds	100%
Other	0%

Services Offered:

Investment Strategy: The investment seeks to track the investment results of the S&P AMT-Free Municipal Series Dec 2021 IndexTM, which measures the performance of investment-grade, non-callable U.S. municipal bonds maturing in 2021. The fund generally will invest at least 90% of its assets in the component securities of the underlying index, and may invest up to 10% of its assets in certain futures, options and swap contracts, cash and cash equivalents, including shares of money market funds advised by BFA or its affiliates, as well as in securities not included in the underlying index, but which BFA believes will help the fund track the underlying index. **Top Holdings:** OHIO STATE 5% MARYLAND ST DEPT TRANSN CONS TRANSN 5% ARLINGTON CNTY VA 4% VIRGINIA COMMWLTH TRANSN BRD TRANSN REV 5% NORTH TEX TWY AUTH REV 5.25%

Invesco S&P 500 BuyWrite ETF   C   HOLD

Ticker	Traded On	NAV	Total Assets ($)	Dividend Yield (TTM)	Turnover Ratio	Expense Ratio
PBP	NYSE Arca	21.65	$291,161,637	1.48	15	0.49

Ratings

Reward	C
Risk	C-
Recent Upgrade/Downgrade	

Fund Information

Fund Type	Exchange Traded Funds
Category	Long/Short Equity
Sub-Category	Options-based
Prospectus Objective	Growth
Inception Date	Dec-07
Open to New Investments	Y

Prices

Price (as of 9/30/2019)	21.65
52-Week High	22.76
52-Week Low	19.12

Total Returns (%)

3-Month	6-Month	1-Year	3-Year	5-Year
-0.13	3.21	-1.67	20.34	30.54

3-Year Standard Deviation	7.93
Effective Duration	

Valuation

Premium/Discount (1-Year Average)	0.10

Company Information

Provider	Invesco
Manager/Tenure	Peter Hubbard (11), Theodore Samulowitz (6), Michael Jeanette (6), 2 others
Website	http://www.invesco.com/us
Address	Invesco 11 Greenway Plaza, Ste. 2500 Houston TX 77046 United States
Phone Number	800-659-1005

PERFORMANCE

Ratings History

Date	Overall Rating	Risk Rating	Reward Rating
Q3-19	C	C-	C
Q4-18	C	C+	C
Q4-17	B	B+	C+
Q4-16	C	C-	B-
Q4-15	C+	C+	C+

Asset & Performance History

Date	NAV	1-Year Total Return
2018	19.8	-5.26
2017	21.43	11.5
2016	21.22	6.21
2015	20.5	4.44
2014	20.66	4.83
2013	20.68	12.39

Total Assets: $291,161,637

Asset Allocation

Asset	%
Cash	0%
Stocks	100%
US Stocks	99%
Bonds	0%
US Bonds	0%
Other	0%

Services Offered:

Investment Strategy: The investment seeks to track the investment results (before fees and expenses) of the CBOE S&P 500 BuyWrite IndexSM. The fund generally will invest at least 90% of its total assets in the securities that comprise the underlying index and will write (sell) call options thereon. The underlying index is a total return benchmark index that is designed to track the performance of a hypothetical "buy-write" strategy on the S&P 500® Index. **Top Holdings:** Microsoft Corp Apple Inc Amazon.com Inc Facebook Inc A Berkshire Hathaway Inc B

First Trust Mid Cap Growth AlphaDEX® Fund   C   HOLD

Ticker	Traded On	NAV	Total Assets ($)	Dividend Yield (TTM)	Turnover Ratio	Expense Ratio
FNY	NAS CM	44.73	$290,728,837	0.1	144	0.7

Ratings

Reward	C
Risk	C-
Recent Upgrade/Downgrade	

Fund Information

Fund Type	Exchange Traded Funds
Category	US Equity Mid Cap
Sub-Category	Mid-Cap Growth
Prospectus Objective	Growth
Inception Date	Apr-11
Open to New Investments	Y

Prices

Price (as of 9/30/2019)	44.75
52-Week High	47.28
52-Week Low	33.42

Total Returns (%)

3-Month	6-Month	1-Year	3-Year	5-Year
-2.02	2.57	-2.18	45.76	67.39

3-Year Standard Deviation	16.62
Effective Duration	

Valuation

Premium/Discount (1-Year Average)	-0.01

Company Information

Provider	First Trust
Manager/Tenure	Jon C. Erickson (8), Daniel J. Lindquist (8), David G. McGarel (8), 3 others
Website	http://www.ftportfolios.com/
Address	First Trust 120 E. Liberty Drive, Suite 400 Wheaton IL 60187 United States
Phone Number	800-621-1675

PERFORMANCE

Ratings History

Date	Overall Rating	Risk Rating	Reward Rating
Q3-19	C	C-	C
Q4-18	C-	C-	C
Q4-17	B	B-	A-
Q4-16	C	C-	C+
Q4-15	C	C	C+

Asset & Performance History

Date	NAV	1-Year Total Return
2018	36.24	-7.35
2017	39.14	24.92
2016	31.4	9.42
2015	28.87	-1.19
2014	29.35	4.98
2013	28.02	36.64

Total Assets: $290,728,837

Asset Allocation

Asset	%
Cash	0%
Stocks	100%
US Stocks	100%
Bonds	0%
US Bonds	0%
Other	0%

Services Offered:

Investment Strategy: The investment seeks investment results that correspond generally to the price and yield (before the fund's fees and expenses) of an equity index called the Nasdaq AlphaDEX® Mid Cap Growth Index. The fund will normally invest at least 90% of its net assets (including investment borrowings) in common stocks that comprise the index. The index is designed to select growth stocks from the NASDAQ US 600 Mid Cap Index (the "base index") that may generate positive alpha, or risk-adjusted returns, relative to traditional indices through the use of the AlphaDEX® selection methodology. **Top Holdings:** Roku Inc Class A NovoCure Ltd Alteryx Inc Class A FTI Consulting Inc Insulet Corp

Deep Value ETF   C   HOLD

Ticker	Traded On	NAV	Total Assets ($)	Dividend Yield (TTM)	Turnover Ratio	Expense Ratio
DVP	NYSE Arca	30.60	$290,727,811	2.81	126	0.59

Ratings
Reward	B-
Risk	D
Recent Upgrade/Downgrade	Up

Fund Information
Fund Type	Exchange Traded Funds
Category	US Equity Mid Cap
Sub-Category	Mid-Cap Value
Prospectus Objective	Growth & Inc
Inception Date	Sep-14
Open to New Investments	Y

Prices
Price (as of 9/30/2019)	30.63
52-Week High	35.13
52-Week Low	27.93

Total Returns (%)
3-Month	6-Month	1-Year	3-Year	5-Year
-1.96	-6.07	-10.32	31.68	47.25

3-Year Standard Deviation	18.71
Effective Duration	

Valuation
Premium/Discount (1-Year Average)	0.01

Company Information
Provider	TWM FUNDS
Manager/Tenure	Andrew Serowik (0), Travis E. Trampe (0)
Website	http://www.twmfunds.com/
Address	Tiedemann New York City United States
Phone Number	

PERFORMANCE

Ratings History
Date	Overall Rating	Risk Rating	Reward Rating
Q3-19	C	D	B-
Q4-18	C	D	B
Q4-17	C+	C	C+
Q4-16	C	D	C+
Q4-15	U		

Asset & Performance History
Date	NAV	1-Year Total Return
2018	30.2	-5.48
2017	32.77	27.29
2016	26.3	24.86
2015	21.83	-10.22
2014	25.24	
2013		

Total Assets: $290,727,811
Asset Allocation
Asset	%
Cash	0%
Stocks	100%
US Stocks	100%
Bonds	0%
US Bonds	0%
Other	0%

Services Offered:

Investment Strategy: The investment seeks to track the price and total return performance, before fees and expenses, of the Deep Value Index. The index is composed of the common stock of typically 20 companies included in the S&P 500® Index that have been selected through a proprietary ranking system developed by the fund's index provider, that evaluates the earnings and cash flows of each company to create a final universe of companies that are deeply undervalued as compared to the S&P 500® Index overall. Under normal circumstances, at least 80% of the fund's total assets will be invested in the component securities of the index. It is non-diversified. **Top Holdings:** Western Digital Corp   Viacom Inc B   CVS Health Corp   Seagate Technology PLC   H&R Block Inc

---

ProShares Investment Grade—Interest Rate Hedged   C   HOLD

Ticker	Traded On	NAV	Total Assets ($)	Dividend Yield (TTM)	Turnover Ratio	Expense Ratio
IGHG	BATS	74.55	$287,012,165	3.89	22	0.3

Ratings
Reward	C
Risk	C-
Recent Upgrade/Downgrade	

Fund Information
Fund Type	Exchange Traded Funds
Category	Fixed Income Misc
Sub-Category	Nontraditional Bond
Prospectus Objective	Worldwide Bond
Inception Date	Nov-13
Open to New Investments	Y

Prices
Price (as of 9/30/2019)	74.55
52-Week High	75.82
52-Week Low	70.32

Total Returns (%)
3-Month	6-Month	1-Year	3-Year	5-Year
-0.01	2.30	2.32	12.16	12.19

3-Year Standard Deviation	4.84
Effective Duration	

Valuation
Premium/Discount (1-Year Average)	0.01

Company Information
Provider	ProShares
Manager/Tenure	Benjamin McAbee (3), Alexander V. Ilyasov (0)
Website	http://www.proshares.com
Address	ProShares 7501 Wisconsin Avenue, Suite 1000 Bethesda MD 20814 United States
Phone Number	866-776-5125

PERFORMANCE

Ratings History
Date	Overall Rating	Risk Rating	Reward Rating
Q3-19	C	C-	C
Q4-18	C-	C-	C-
Q4-17	B-	B	C
Q4-16	C-	C-	C
Q4-15	D	C-	D

Asset & Performance History
Date	NAV	1-Year Total Return
2018	71	-4.73
2017	77.18	5.63
2016	75.59	7.26
2015	72.99	-2.16
2014	77.3	-1.92
2013	81.59	

Total Assets: $287,012,165
Asset Allocation
Asset	%
Cash	102%
Stocks	0%
US Stocks	0%
Bonds	-6%
US Bonds	-34%
Other	0%

Services Offered:

Investment Strategy: The investment seeks investment results, before fees and expenses, that track the performance of the FTSE Corporate Investment Grade (Treasury Rate-Hedged) Index (the "index"). The index is comprised of (a) long positions in USD-denominated investment grade corporate bonds issued by both U.S. and foreign domiciled companies; and (b) short positions in U.S. Treasury notes or bonds ("Treasury Securities") of, in aggregate, approximate equivalent duration to the investment grade bonds. The fund will invest at least 80% of its total assets in component securities (i.e., securities of the index) and invest at least 80% of its total assets in investment grade bonds. **Top Holdings:** U.S. Treasury Bond Dec19   US Ultra Bond (CBT) Dec19   US 10 Year Note (CBT) Dec19   Goldman Sachs Group, Inc.   Pfizer Inc.

Schwab Fundamental U.S. Broad Market Index ETF

C **HOLD**

Ticker	Traded On	NAV	Total Assets ($)	Dividend Yield (TTM)	Turnover Ratio	Expense Ratio
FNDB	NYSE Arca	39.13	$285,652,520	2.19	11	0.25

Ratings
Reward	C
Risk	C-
Recent Upgrade/Downgrade	

Fund Information
Fund Type	Exchange Traded Funds
Category	US Equity Large Cap Value
Sub-Category	Large Value
Prospectus Objective	Growth & Inc
Inception Date	Aug-13
Open to New Investments	Y

Prices
Price (as of 9/30/2019)	39.13
52-Week High	39.77
52-Week Low	31.73

Total Returns (%)
3-Month	6-Month	1-Year	3-Year	5-Year
1.06	3.86	1.06	35.32	53.38

3-Year Standard Deviation	13.04
Effective Duration	

Valuation
Premium/Discount (1-Year Average)	-0.01

Company Information
Provider	Schwab ETFs
Manager/Tenure	Christopher Bliss (2), Ferian Juwono (2), Sabya Sinha (2), 1 other
Website	http://www.schwabfunds.com
Address	Schwab ETFs United States
Phone Number	800-435-4000

Ratings History
Date	Overall Rating	Risk Rating	Reward Rating
Q3-19	C	C-	C
Q4-18	C	C-	C
Q4-17	B	B	B-
Q4-16	C+	C-	B
Q4-15	C-	C-	C-

Asset & Performance History
Date	NAV	1-Year Total Return
2018	33.64	-7.64
2017	37.22	16.76
2016	32.56	16.96
2015	28.46	-3.07
2014	30.03	11.93
2013	27.29	

Total Assets: $285,652,520
Asset Allocation
Asset	%
Cash	0%
Stocks	100%
US Stocks	98%
Bonds	0%
US Bonds	0%
Other	0%

Services Offered:

Investment Strategy: The investment seeks to track as closely as possible, before fees and expenses, the total return of the Russell RAFI™ US Index. The fund will invest at least 90% of its net assets (including, for this purpose, any borrowings for investment purposes) in stocks included in the index. The index measures the performance of the constituent companies by fundamental overall company scores (scores), which are created using as the universe the U.S. companies in the FTSE Global Total Cap Index (the parent index). It may invest up to 10% of its net assets in securities not included in the index. **Top Holdings:** Apple Inc Exxon Mobil Corp AT&T Inc Microsoft Corp Chevron Corp

---

iShares MSCI India Small-Cap ETF

D **SELL**

Ticker	Traded On	NAV	Total Assets ($)	Dividend Yield (TTM)	Turnover Ratio	Expense Ratio
SMIN	BATS	34.86	$282,364,138	0.61	49	0.77

Ratings
Reward	D
Risk	D+
Recent Upgrade/Downgrade	Down

Fund Information
Fund Type	Exchange Traded Funds
Category	India Equity
Sub-Category	India Equity
Prospectus Objective	Small Company
Inception Date	Feb-12
Open to New Investments	Y

Prices
Price (as of 9/30/2019)	35.16
52-Week High	40.98
52-Week Low	32.20

Total Returns (%)
3-Month	6-Month	1-Year	3-Year	5-Year
-10.17	-13.42	-3.74	0.04	17.73

3-Year Standard Deviation	22.04
Effective Duration	

Valuation
Premium/Discount (1-Year Average)	0.20

Company Information
Provider	iShares
Manager/Tenure	Diane Hsiung (7), Greg Savage (7), Jennifer Hsui (6), 3 others
Website	http://www.ishares.com
Address	iShares 400 Howard Street San Francisco CA 94105 United States
Phone Number	800-474-2737

PERFORMANCE

Ratings History
Date	Overall Rating	Risk Rating	Reward Rating
Q3-19	D	D+	D
Q4-18	D+	D	D+
Q4-17	B+	B-	A+
Q4-16	C+	C-	B
Q4-15	C	C-	C

Asset & Performance History
Date	NAV	1-Year Total Return
2018	38.73	-25.43
2017	52.71	61.77
2016	32.88	-0.41
2015	33.79	2.01
2014	33.43	56.27
2013	21.47	-15.49

Total Assets: $282,364,138
Asset Allocation
Asset	%
Cash	0%
Stocks	100%
US Stocks	0%
Bonds	0%
US Bonds	0%
Other	0%

Services Offered:

Investment Strategy: The investment seeks to track the investment results of the MSCI India Small Cap Index. The fund generally will collectively invest at least 90% of its assets in the component securities of the underlying index and in investments that have economic characteristics that are substantially identical to the component securities of the underlying index. The index is designed to measure the performance of equity securities of small-capitalization companies whose market capitalization, as calculated by the index provider, represents the bottom 14% of companies in the Indian securities market. **Top Holdings:** Apollo Hospitals Enterprise Ltd Info Edge (India) Ltd The Federal Bank Ltd RBL Bank Ltd AU Small Finance Bank Ltd

Invesco KBW High Dividend Yield Financial ETF   C   HOLD

Ticker	Traded On	NAV	Total Assets ($)	Dividend Yield (TTM)	Turnover Ratio	Expense Ratio
KBWD	NAS CM	20.85	$281,467,005	8.76		2.42

Ratings
Reward	C
Risk	D+
Recent Upgrade/Downgrade	

Fund Information
Fund Type	Exchange Traded Funds
Category	Financials Sector Equity
Sub-Category	Financial
Prospectus Objective	Financial
Inception Date	Dec-10
Open to New Investments	

Prices
Price (as of 9/30/2019)	20.88
52-Week High	22.70
52-Week Low	18.90

Total Returns (%)

3-Month	6-Month	1-Year	3-Year	5-Year
-0.86	-0.85	0.19	22.58	29.45

3-Year Standard Deviation	15.49
Effective Duration	

Valuation
Premium/Discount (1-Year Average)	0.00

Company Information
Provider	Invesco
Manager/Tenure	Peter Hubbard (8), Michael Jeanette (8), Tony Seisser (5)
Website	http://www.invesco.com/us
Address	Invesco 11 Greenway Plaza, Ste. 2500 Houston TX 77046 United States
Phone Number	800-659-1005

PERFORMANCE

Ratings History

Date	Overall Rating	Risk Rating	Reward Rating
Q3-19	C	D+	C
Q4-18	C	C-	B-
Q4-17	B-	C+	B-
Q4-16	C	C-	C+
Q4-15	C	C-	C

Asset & Performance History

Date	NAV	1-Year Total Return
2018	19.81	-8.77
2017	23.6	11.92
2016	23	20.61
2015	20.99	-10.19
2014	25.26	8.23
2013	25.35	18.2

Total Assets: $281,467,005

Asset Allocation

Asset	%
Cash	-1%
Stocks	101%
US Stocks	101%
Bonds	0%
US Bonds	0%
Other	0%

Services Offered:

Investment Strategy: The investment seeks to track the investment results (before fees and expenses) of the KBW Nasdaq Financial Sector Dividend Yield Index (the "underlying index"). The fund generally will invest at least 90% of its total assets in the securities that comprise the underlying index. The underlying index is a modified-dividend yield-weighted index of companies principally engaged in the business of providing financial services and products, as determined by the index provider. The underlying index is designed to track the performance of financial companies with competitive dividend yields that are publicly-traded in the U.S. **Top Holdings:** Two Harbors Investment Corp   Orchid Island Capital Inc   New York Mortgage Trust Inc   Annaly Capital Management Inc   BGC Partners Inc Class A

Direxion Daily 20+ Year Treasury Bull 3X Shares   C   HOLD

Ticker	Traded On	NAV	Total Assets ($)	Dividend Yield (TTM)	Turnover Ratio	Expense Ratio
TMF	NYSE Arca	30.67	$280,622,157	0.95	1	1.09

Ratings
Reward	C
Risk	D+
Recent Upgrade/Downgrade	Up

Fund Information
Fund Type	Exchange Traded Funds
Category	Trading Tools
Sub-Category	Trading--Leveraged Debt
Prospectus Objective	Govt Bond - Treasury
Inception Date	Apr-09
Open to New Investments	Y

Prices
Price (as of 9/30/2019)	30.63
52-Week High	34.12
52-Week Low	15.21

Total Returns (%)

3-Month	6-Month	1-Year	3-Year	5-Year
24.00	48.76	83.13	14.05	78.75

3-Year Standard Deviation	36.75
Effective Duration	17.32

Valuation
Premium/Discount (1-Year Average)	0.04

Company Information
Provider	Direxion Funds
Manager/Tenure	Paul Brigandi (10), Tony Ng (4)
Website	http://www.direxionfunds.com
Address	Direxion Funds 1301 Avenue Of The Americas (6th Avenue) New York NY 10019 United States
Phone Number	646-572-3390

PERFORMANCE

Ratings History

Date	Overall Rating	Risk Rating	Reward Rating
Q3-19	C	D+	C
Q4-18	D	D	D
Q4-17	C-	D+	C
Q4-16	C	D+	C
Q4-15	C-	D	C

Asset & Performance History

Date	NAV	1-Year Total Return
2018	19.22	-12.06
2017	22.2	23.16
2016	18.1	-3.6
2015	18.78	-12.57
2014	21.48	100.81
2013	10.7	-40.53

Total Assets: $280,622,157

Asset Allocation

Asset	%
Cash	18%
Stocks	0%
US Stocks	0%
Bonds	82%
US Bonds	82%
Other	0%

Services Offered:

Investment Strategy: The investment seeks daily investment results, before fees and expenses, of 300% of the daily performance of the ICE U.S. Treasury 20+ Year Bond Index. The fund, under normal circumstances, invests at least 80% of its net assets (plus borrowing for investment purposes) in financial instruments and securities of the index, ETFs that track the index and other financial instruments that provide daily leveraged exposure to the index or ETFs that track the index. The index is a market value weighted index that includes publicly issued U.S. Treasury securities that have a remaining maturity of greater than 20 years. The fund is non-diversified. **Top Holdings:** iShares 20+ Year Treasury Bond ETF   20+ Yr Treas Bd Idx Swap   20+ Yr Treas Bd Idx Swap   20+ Yr Treas Bd Idx Swap   20+ Yr Treas Bd Idx Swap

VelocityShares 3x Long Silver ETN Linked to the S&P GSCI® Silver Index ER   B   BUY

Ticker	Traded On	NAV	Total Assets ($)	Dividend Yield (TTM)	Turnover Ratio	Expense Ratio
USLV	NAS CM	82.34	$278,667,025	0		1.65

Ratings
Reward	A-
Risk	D+
Recent Upgrade/Downgrade	Up

Fund Information
Fund Type	Exchange Traded Funds
Category	Trading Tools
Sub-Category	Trading--Leveraged Commodities
Prospectus Objective	Prec Metals
Inception Date	Oct-11
Open to New Investments	Y

Prices
Price (as of 9/30/2019)	83.51
52-Week High	132.23
52-Week Low	54.70

Total Returns (%)
3-Month	6-Month	1-Year	3-Year	5-Year
29.16	25.22	30.35	275.82	194.18

3-Year Standard Deviation	52.64
Effective Duration	

Valuation
Premium/Discount (1-Year Average)	0.02

Company Information
Provider	Credit Suisse AG
Manager/Tenure	Management Team (7)
Website	
Address	Kilmore House Park Lane Dublin Ireland
Phone Number	

PERFORMANCE

Ratings History
Date	Overall Rating	Risk Rating	Reward Rating
Q3-19	B	D+	A-
Q4-18	B-	D+	A-
Q4-17	D-	D-	D-
Q4-16	D	D-	D
Q4-15	E	E+	E

Asset & Performance History
Date	NAV	1-Year Total Return
2018	74.1	521.72
2017	11.92	-4.04
2016	11.44	21.31
2015	9.76	-47.55
2014	18.61	-58.52
2013	44.87	-82.54

Total Assets: $278,667,025
Asset Allocation
Asset	%
Cash	%
Stocks	%
US Stocks	%
Bonds	%
US Bonds	%
Other	%

Services Offered:

Investment Strategy: The investment seeks to replicate, net of expenses, three times the S&P GSCI Silver index ER.
The index comprises futures contracts on a single commodity. The fluctuations in the values of it are intended generally to correlate with changes in the price of silver in global markets. **Top Holdings:**

SPDR® S&P Global Dividend ETF   C   HOLD

Ticker	Traded On	NAV	Total Assets ($)	Dividend Yield (TTM)	Turnover Ratio	Expense Ratio
WDIV	NYSE Arca		$276,688,217	4.54	39	0.4

Ratings
Reward	C
Risk	C-
Recent Upgrade/Downgrade	

Fund Information
Fund Type	Exchange Traded Funds
Category	Global Equity Large Cap
Sub-Category	World Large Stock
Prospectus Objective	Growth & Inc
Inception Date	May-13
Open to New Investments	Y

Prices
Price (as of 9/30/2019)	67.52
52-Week High	68.57
52-Week Low	60.00

Total Returns (%)
3-Month	6-Month	1-Year	3-Year	5-Year
0.82	3.02	4.15	20.13	28.92

3-Year Standard Deviation	10.09
Effective Duration	

Valuation
Premium/Discount (1-Year Average)	0.05

Company Information
Provider	SPDR State Street Global Advisors
Manager/Tenure	Michael J. Feehily (6), Karl A. Schneider (4), Amy Scofield (2)
Website	http://www.spdrs.com
Address	SPDR State Street Global Advisors State Street Financial Center, 1 Lincoln Street Boston MA 02111-2900 United States
Phone Number	617-786-3000

PERFORMANCE

Ratings History
Date	Overall Rating	Risk Rating	Reward Rating
Q3-19	C	C-	C
Q4-18	C-	C-	C-
Q4-17	B-	B-	B-
Q4-16	C	C-	C
Q4-15	D+	D+	D

Asset & Performance History
Date	NAV	1-Year Total Return
2018	61.87	-8.85
2017	70.76	18.83
2016	61.85	12.38
2015	56.94	-7.94
2014	64.78	4.67
2013	64.77	

Total Assets: $276,688,217
Asset Allocation
Asset	%
Cash	0%
Stocks	100%
US Stocks	21%
Bonds	0%
US Bonds	0%
Other	0%

Services Offered:

Investment Strategy: The investment seeks to provide investment results that, before fees and expenses, correspond generally to the total return of the S&P Global Dividend Aristocrats Index. The fund generally invests substantially all, but at least 80%, of its total assets in the securities comprising the index and in depositary receipts based on securities comprising the index. The index is designed to measure the performance of high dividend-yield companies included in the S&P Global BMI that have followed a managed-dividends policy of increasing or stable dividends for at least ten consecutive years. The fund is non-diversified. **Top Holdings:** Hennes & Mauritz AB B   Greene King PLC   AT&T Inc   IGM Financial Inc   WPP PLC

Invesco Zacks Mid-Cap ETF

C   HOLD

Ticker	Traded On	NAV	Total Assets ($)	Dividend Yield (TTM)	Turnover Ratio	Expense Ratio
CZA	NYSE Arca	72.79	$276,619,431	1.03		0.76

Ratings
Reward	C+
Risk	C-
Recent Upgrade/Downgrade	

Fund Information
Fund Type	Exchange Traded Funds
Category	US Equity Mid Cap
Sub-Category	Mid-Cap Blend
Prospectus Objective	Growth
Inception Date	Apr-07
Open to New Investments	Y

Prices
Price (as of 9/30/2019)	72.82
52-Week High	73.51
52-Week Low	56.31

Total Returns (%)
3-Month	6-Month	1-Year	3-Year	5-Year
0.91	5.47	7.97	42.98	63.02

3-Year Standard Deviation	12.51
Effective Duration	

Valuation
Premium/Discount (1-Year Average)	0.03

Company Information
Provider	Invesco
Manager/Tenure	Peter Hubbard (1), Michael Jeanette (1), Tony Seisser (1)
Website	http://www.invesco.com/us
Address	Invesco 11 Greenway Plaza, Ste. 2500 Houston TX 77046 United States
Phone Number	800-659-1005

PERFORMANCE

Ratings History
Date	Overall Rating	Risk Rating	Reward Rating
Q3-19	C	C-	C+
Q4-18	C	C-	C
Q4-17	B	B-	B
Q4-16	C+	D+	B
Q4-15	C	C	C

Asset & Performance History
Date	NAV	1-Year Total Return
2018	58.98	-8.75
2017	65.5	22.03
2016	54.42	15.17
2015	47.87	-1.78
2014	49.4	9.49
2013	45.45	35.99

Total Assets: $276,619,431
Asset Allocation
Asset	%
Cash	0%
Stocks	100%
US Stocks	88%
Bonds	0%
US Bonds	0%
Other	0%

Services Offered:

Investment Strategy: The investment seeks to track the investment results (before fees and expenses) of the Zacks Mid-Cap Core Index (the "underlying index"). The fund generally will invest at least 90% of its total assets in the securities that comprise the underlying index, as well as American depositary receipts ("ADRs") that represent securities in the underlying index. The underlying index is composed of 100 securities that Zacks selects from a universe of mid-capitalization securities including common stocks, master limited partnerships ("MLPs"), ADRs, real estate investment trusts ("REITs") and business development companies ("BDCs"). The fund is non-diversified. **Top Holdings:** IHS Markit Ltd Discover Financial Services Willis Towers Watson PLC Royal Caribbean Cruises Ltd Parker Hannifin Corp

---

Principal Active Income ETF

C   HOLD

Ticker	Traded On	NAV	Total Assets ($)	Dividend Yield (TTM)	Turnover Ratio	Expense Ratio
YLD	NYSE Arca	40.10	$271,643,531	5.7	32	0.49

Ratings
Reward	C
Risk	C-
Recent Upgrade/Downgrade	

Fund Information
Fund Type	Exchange Traded Funds
Category	Cautious Allocation
Sub-Category	Allocation--30% to 50% Equity
Prospectus Objective	Income
Inception Date	Jul-15
Open to New Investments	Y

Prices
Price (as of 9/30/2019)	40.20
52-Week High	41.05
52-Week Low	37.39

Total Returns (%)
3-Month	6-Month	1-Year	3-Year	5-Year
1.49	3.23	4.89	16.85	

3-Year Standard Deviation	5.19
Effective Duration	3.59

Valuation
Premium/Discount (1-Year Average)	0.44

Company Information
Provider	Principal Funds
Manager/Tenure	Charles D. Averill (4), Todd A. Jablonski (4), Paul S. Kim (4), 2 others
Website	http://www.principalfunds.com
Address	Principal Funds 430 W 7th St, Ste 219971 Kansas City MO 64105-1407 United States
Phone Number	800-787-1621

PERFORMANCE

Ratings History
Date	Overall Rating	Risk Rating	Reward Rating
Q3-19	C	C-	C
Q4-18	C-	D+	C-
Q4-17	C	B	C
Q4-16	D	D+	C-
Q4-15	U		

Asset & Performance History
Date	NAV	1-Year Total Return
2018	37.22	-4.87
2017	41.2	8.32
2016	40.32	16.21
2015	36.35	
2014		
2013		

Total Assets: $271,643,531
Asset Allocation
Asset	%
Cash	3%
Stocks	20%
US Stocks	19%
Bonds	66%
US Bonds	64%
Other	0%

Services Offered:

Investment Strategy: The investment seeks to provide current income. The fund is an actively managed exchange-traded fund ("ETF") that seeks to achieve its investment objective by investing, under normal circumstances, its assets in investment grade and non-investment grade fixed income securities (commonly known as "junk bonds") and in equity securities. The fund's Sub-Advisors, actively and tactically allocates the fund's assets among fixed income securities and equity securities in an effort to take advantage of changing economic conditions that the Advisor believes favors one asset class over another. **Top Holdings:** PPL Capital Funding Inc. 4.99% Waste Pro USA Inc 5.5% Mobile Mini, Inc. 5.88% Hologic Inc 4.62% JPMorgan Chase & Co Pfd

SPDR® SSGA Gender Diversity Index ETF   C+   HOLD

Ticker	Traded On	NAV	Total Assets ($)	Dividend Yield (TTM)	Turnover Ratio	Expense Ratio
SHE	NYSE Arca		$271,537,046	1.91	53	0.2

Ratings

Reward	B-
Risk	C
Recent Upgrade/Downgrade	Up

Fund Information

Fund Type	Exchange Traded Funds
Category	US Equity Large Cap Blend
Sub-Category	Large Blend
Prospectus Objective	Growth & Inc
Inception Date	Mar-16
Open to New Investments	Y

Prices

Price (as of 9/30/2019)	73.47
52-Week High	76.68
52-Week Low	60.07

Total Returns (%)

3-Month	6-Month	1-Year	3-Year	5-Year
-1.11	2.95	1.96	37.34	

3-Year Standard Deviation	11.59
Effective Duration	

Valuation

Premium/Discount (1-Year Average)	0.06

Company Information

Provider	SPDR State Street Global Advisors
Manager/Tenure	Lynn Blake (3), Melissa Kapitulik (3), Amy Cheng (2)
Website	http://www.spdrs.com
Address	SPDR State Street Global Advisors State Street Financial Center, 1 Lincoln Street Boston MA 02111-2900 United States
Phone Number	617-786-3000

PERFORMANCE

Ratings History

Date	Overall Rating	Risk Rating	Reward Rating
Q3-19	C+	C	B-
Q4-18	C	C-	C
Q4-17	C-	B+	C
Q4-16	U		
Q4-15			

Asset & Performance History

Date	NAV	1-Year Total Return
2018	63.69	-1.59
2017	70.72	19.67
2016	62.35	
2015		
2014		
2013		

Total Assets: $271,537,046

Asset Allocation

Asset	%
Cash	0%
Stocks	100%
US Stocks	99%
Bonds	0%
US Bonds	0%
Other	0%

Services Offered:

Investment Strategy: The investment seeks to provide investment results that, before fees and expenses, correspond generally to the total return performance of the SSGA Gender Diversity Index, which tracks U.S. companies that are leaders in advancing women through gender diversity on their boards of directors and in management. Under normal market conditions, the fund generally invests substantially all, but at least 80%, of its total assets in the securities comprising the index. In addition, it may invest in equity securities that are not included in the index, cash and cash equivalents or money market instruments. The fund is non-diversified. **Top Holdings:** Visa Inc Class A The Home Depot Inc Wells Fargo & Co Johnson & Johnson PayPal Holdings Inc

iShares Edge MSCI Multifactor USA Small-Cap ETF   C-   HOLD

Ticker	Traded On	NAV	Total Assets ($)	Dividend Yield (TTM)	Turnover Ratio	Expense Ratio
SMLF	NYSE Arca	39.87	$271,093,266	1.29	45	0.3

Ratings

Reward	C-
Risk	C-
Recent Upgrade/Downgrade	

Fund Information

Fund Type	Exchange Traded Funds
Category	US Equity Small Cap
Sub-Category	Small Blend
Prospectus Objective	Small Company
Inception Date	Apr-15
Open to New Investments	Y

Prices

Price (as of 9/30/2019)	39.89
52-Week High	43.15
52-Week Low	33.54

Total Returns (%)

3-Month	6-Month	1-Year	3-Year	5-Year
-1.00	-1.07	-6.18	29.68	

3-Year Standard Deviation	16.67
Effective Duration	

Valuation

Premium/Discount (1-Year Average)	0.09

Company Information

Provider	iShares
Manager/Tenure	Diane Hsiung (4), Jennifer Hsui (4), Greg Savage (4), 3 others
Website	http://www.ishares.com
Address	iShares 400 Howard Street San Francisco CA 94105 United States
Phone Number	800-474-2737

PERFORMANCE

Ratings History

Date	Overall Rating	Risk Rating	Reward Rating
Q3-19	C-	C-	C-
Q4-18	C-	C-	C-
Q4-17	B-	B	C+
Q4-16	D+	D+	C-
Q4-15	U		

Asset & Performance History

Date	NAV	1-Year Total Return
2018	35.75	-8.16
2017	39.34	12.06
2016	35.45	22.49
2015	29.19	
2014		
2013		

Total Assets: $271,093,266

Asset Allocation

Asset	%
Cash	0%
Stocks	100%
US Stocks	98%
Bonds	0%
US Bonds	0%
Other	0%

Services Offered:

Investment Strategy: The investment seeks to track the investment results of the MSCI USA Small Cap Diversified Multiple-Factor Index. The fund generally will invest at least 90% of its assets in the component securities of the underlying index and may invest up to 10% of its assets in certain futures, options and swap contracts, cash and cash equivalents. The underlying index is designed to select equity securities from the MSCI USA Small Cap Index (the "parent index") that have high exposure to four investment style factors: value, quality, momentum and low size, while maintaining a level of risk similar to that of the parent index. **Top Holdings:** Teradyne Inc Aspen Technology Inc Masimo Corp Medical Properties Trust Inc Chemed Corp

SPDR® MSCI Emerging Markets StrategicFactors ETF   C-   HOLD

Ticker	Traded On	NAV	Total Assets ($)	Dividend Yield (TTM)	Turnover Ratio	Expense Ratio
QEMM	NYSE Arca		$268,866,174	2.97	30	0.3

Ratings
Reward   C
Risk   D+
Recent Upgrade/Downgrade

Fund Information
Fund Type	Exchange Traded Funds
Category	Global Emerg Mkts Equity
Sub-Category	Diversified Emerging Mkts
Prospectus Objective	World Stock
Inception Date	Jun-14
Open to New Investments	Y

Prices
Price (as of 9/30/2019)	57.36
52-Week High	60.98
52-Week Low	52.90

Total Returns (%)
3-Month	6-Month	1-Year	3-Year	5-Year
-3.14	-2.73	-0.51	15.12	8.23

3-Year Standard Deviation   11.96
Effective Duration

Valuation
Premium/Discount (1-Year Average)   -0.03

Company Information
Provider	SPDR State Street Global Advisors
Manager/Tenure	Michael J. Feehily (5), Karl A. Schneider (4), John Law (0)
Website	http://www.spdrs.com
Address	SPDR State Street Global Advisors State Street Financial Center, 1 Lincoln Street Boston MA 02111-2900 United States
Phone Number	617-786-3000

PERFORMANCE

Ratings History

Date	Overall Rating	Risk Rating	Reward Rating
Q3-19	C-	D+	C
Q4-18	D+	D+	C-
Q4-17	C+	C	C+
Q4-16	D+	D+	D+
Q4-15	D	D	D

Asset & Performance History

Date	NAV	1-Year Total Return
2018	54.8	-12.1
2017	64.08	30.21
2016	50.33	9.39
2015	46.96	-14.53
2014	56.05	
2013		

Total Assets: $268,866,174
Asset Allocation

Asset	%
Cash	1%
Stocks	99%
US Stocks	0%
Bonds	0%
US Bonds	0%
Other	0%

Services Offered:

Investment Strategy: The investment seeks to track the performance of the MSCI Emerging Markets (EM) Factor Mix A-Series Index. The fund generally invests substantially all, but at least 80%, of its total assets in the securities comprising the index and in depositary receipts based on securities comprising the index. The index captures large- and mid-cap representation across 24 emerging markets countries and aims to represent the performance of value, low volatility, and quality factor strategies. The fund is non-diversified. **Top Holdings:** Taiwan Semiconductor Manufacturing Co Ltd   Samsung Electronics Co Ltd   SK Hynix Inc   Tencent Holdings Ltd   Tata Consultancy Services Ltd

iShares MSCI Poland ETF   D+   SELL

Ticker	Traded On	NAV	Total Assets ($)	Dividend Yield (TTM)	Turnover Ratio	Expense Ratio
EPOL	NYSE Arca	20.67	$268,772,217	1.71	7	0.63

Ratings
Reward   D
Risk   C
Recent Upgrade/Downgrade   Down

Fund Information
Fund Type	Exchange Traded Funds
Category	Europe Equity Mid/Small Cap
Sub-Category	Miscellaneous Region
Prospectus Objective	Europe Stock
Inception Date	May-10
Open to New Investments	Y

Prices
Price (as of 9/30/2019)	20.64
52-Week High	24.40
52-Week Low	20.01

Total Returns (%)
3-Month	6-Month	1-Year	3-Year	5-Year
-12.60	-10.70	-11.98	20.80	-18.22

3-Year Standard Deviation   20.78
Effective Duration

Valuation
Premium/Discount (1-Year Average)   -0.06

Company Information
Provider	iShares
Manager/Tenure	Diane Hsiung (9), Greg Savage (9), Jennifer Hsui (6), 3 others
Website	http://www.ishares.com
Address	iShares 400 Howard Street San Francisco CA 94105 United States
Phone Number	800-474-2737

PERFORMANCE

Ratings History

Date	Overall Rating	Risk Rating	Reward Rating
Q3-19	D+	C	D
Q4-18	C-	C-	C-
Q4-17	C	C	C+
Q4-16	D	D	D
Q4-15	D	D	D

Asset & Performance History

Date	NAV	1-Year Total Return
2018	22.99	-14.3
2017	27.21	52.69
2016	18.17	2.75
2015	18.07	-23.26
2014	24.08	-15.33
2013	29.35	4.62

Total Assets: $268,772,217
Asset Allocation

Asset	%
Cash	0%
Stocks	100%
US Stocks	0%
Bonds	0%
US Bonds	0%
Other	0%

Services Offered:

Investment Strategy: The investment seeks to track the investment results of the MSCI Poland IMI 25/50 Index. The fund generally will invest at least 90% of its assets in the component securities of the index and in investments that have economic characteristics that are substantially identical to the component securities of the index and may invest up to 10% of its assets in certain futures, options and swap contracts, cash and cash equivalents. The index is a free float-adjusted market capitalization-weighted index designed to measure the performance of equity securities listed on stock exchanges in Poland. The fund is non-diversified. **Top Holdings:** PKO Bank Polski SA Polski Koncern Naftowy ORLEN SA   Powszechny Zaklad Ubezpieczen SA   Bank Polska Kasa Opieki SA   CD Projekt SA

SPDR® SSGA US Small Cap Low Volatility Index ETF C HOLD

Ticker	Traded On	NAV	Total Assets ($)	Dividend Yield (TTM)	Turnover Ratio	Expense Ratio
SMLV	NYSE Arca		$267,917,220	2.81	34	0.12

Ratings
Reward C
Risk C-
Recent Upgrade/Downgrade

Fund Information
Fund Type Exchange Traded Funds
Category US Equity Small Cap
Sub-Category Small Blend
Prospectus Objective Income
Inception Date Feb-13
Open to New Investments Y

Prices
Price (as of 9/30/2019) 95.07
52-Week High 96.95
52-Week Low 79.55

Total Returns (%)

3-Month	6-Month	1-Year	3-Year	5-Year
2.29	4.39	2.16	33.30	66.05

3-Year Standard Deviation 14.6
Effective Duration

Valuation
Premium/Discount (1-Year Average) 0.00

Company Information
Provider SPDR State Street Global Advisors
Manager/Tenure Michael J. Feehily (6), Karl A. Schneider (4), John Law (0)
Website http://www.spdrs.com
Address SPDR State Street Global Advisors State Street Financial Center, 1 Lincoln Street Boston MA 02111-2900 United States
Phone Number 617-786-3000

PERFORMANCE

Ratings History

Date	Overall Rating	Risk Rating	Reward Rating
Q3-19	C	C-	C
Q4-18	C-	D+	C-
Q4-17	B+	B+	B+
Q4-16	C	C-	C+
Q4-15	C	C-	C

Asset & Performance History

Date	NAV	1-Year Total Return
2018	83.16	-6.01
2017	91.09	5.21
2016	93.49	30.65
2015	73.99	-1.86
2014	77.4	12.58
2013	70.76	

Total Assets: $267,917,220
Asset Allocation

Asset	%
Cash	0%
Stocks	100%
US Stocks	97%
Bonds	0%
US Bonds	0%
Other	0%

Services Offered:

Investment Strategy: The investment seeks to provide investment results that, before fees and expenses, correspond generally to the total return performance of the SSGA US Small Cap Low Volatility Index. The fund generally invests substantially all, but at least 80%, of its total assets in the securities comprising the index. The index is designed to measure the performance of the stocks of U.S. small capitalization companies that exhibit low volatility. Volatility is a statistical measurement of the magnitude of movements in a stock's price over time. The fund is non-diversified. **Top Holdings:** Apollo Commercial Real Estate Finance Inc White Mountains Insurance Group Ltd MFA Financial Inc Meridian Bancorp Inc Capitol Federal Financial Inc

FlexShares Ready Access Variable Income Fund C HOLD

Ticker	Traded On	NAV	Total Assets ($)	Dividend Yield (TTM)	Turnover Ratio	Expense Ratio
RAVI	NYSE Arca	75.84	$267,347,925	2.61	131	0.25

Ratings
Reward C
Risk C-
Recent Upgrade/Downgrade

Fund Information
Fund Type Exchange Traded Funds
Category US Fixed Income
Sub-Category Ultrashort Bond
Prospectus Objective Income
Inception Date Oct-12
Open to New Investments Y

Prices
Price (as of 9/30/2019) 75.83
52-Week High 75.92
52-Week Low 74.89

Total Returns (%)

3-Month	6-Month	1-Year	3-Year	5-Year
0.69	1.63	3.05	6.09	7.70

3-Year Standard Deviation 0.41
Effective Duration 0.57

Valuation
Premium/Discount (1-Year Average) 0.00

Company Information
Provider Flexshares Trust
Manager/Tenure Bilal Memon (6), Peter Yi (6)
Website http://www.flexshares.com
Address 50 South LaSalle Street Chicago, Illinois 60603 Chicago Illinois 60603 United States
Phone Number 855-353-9383

PERFORMANCE

Ratings History

Date	Overall Rating	Risk Rating	Reward Rating
Q3-19	C	C-	C
Q4-18	C-	C-	C
Q4-17	C+	B+	C
Q4-16	C	C-	C
Q4-15	C	C-	C

Asset & Performance History

Date	NAV	1-Year Total Return
2018	75.09	1.82
2017	75.39	1.29
2016	75.38	1.21
2015	75.16	0.38
2014	75.36	0.72
2013	75.32	0.9

Total Assets: $267,347,925
Asset Allocation

Asset	%
Cash	11%
Stocks	0%
US Stocks	0%
Bonds	85%
US Bonds	69%
Other	0%

Services Offered:

Investment Strategy: The investment seeks maximum current income consistent with the preservation of capital and liquidity. The fund seeks to achieve its investment objective by investing at least 80% of its total assets in a non-diversified portfolio of fixed-income instruments, including bonds, debt securities and other similar instruments issued by U.S. and non-U.S. public and private sector entities. The dollar-weighted average portfolio maturity of the fund is normally not expected to exceed two years. It may invest up to 20% of its total assets in fixed-income securities and instruments of issuers in emerging markets. The fund is non-diversified. **Top Holdings:** Bank of America, N.A. 2.59% Gilead Sciences, Inc. 2.35% Volkswagen Group of America Finance HLLC 2.95% Prudential Financial, Inc. 4.5% Intel Corporation 2.45%

Global X S&P 500® Catholic Values ETF

C   HOLD

Ticker	Traded On	NAV	Total Assets ($)	Dividend Yield (TTM)	Turnover Ratio	Expense Ratio
CATH	NAS CM	36.43	$265,903,141	2.23	4	0.29

Ratings

Reward	C+
Risk	C-
Recent Upgrade/Downgrade	

Fund Information

Fund Type	Exchange Traded Funds
Category	US Equity Large Cap Blend
Sub-Category	Large Blend
Prospectus Objective	Growth & Inc
Inception Date	Apr-16
Open to New Investments	Y

Prices

Price (as of 9/30/2019)	36.46
52-Week High	36.95
52-Week Low	29.28

Total Returns (%)

3-Month	6-Month	1-Year	3-Year	5-Year
0.91	4.42	3.03	44.97	

3-Year Standard Deviation	12.41
Effective Duration	

Valuation

Premium/Discount (1-Year Average)	0.15

Company Information

Provider	Global X Funds
Manager/Tenure	Chang Kim (3), Nam To (1), Wayne Xie (0), 1 other
Website	http://www.globalxfunds.com
Address	Global X Funds 600 Lexington Avenue, 20th Floor New York NY 10022 United States
Phone Number	888-493-8631

PERFORMANCE

Ratings History

Date	Overall Rating	Risk Rating	Reward Rating
Q3-19	C	C-	C+
Q4-18	C-	C-	C
Q4-17	D+	B+	C
Q4-16	U		
Q4-15			

Asset & Performance History

Date	NAV	1-Year Total Return
2018	30.57	-5.09
2017	32.81	22.47
2016	27.12	
2015		
2014		
2013		

Total Assets: $265,903,141

Asset Allocation

Asset	%
Cash	0%
Stocks	100%
US Stocks	99%
Bonds	0%
US Bonds	0%
Other	0%

Services Offered:

Investment Strategy: The investment seeks investment results that correspond generally to the price and yield performance, of the S&P 500® Catholic Values Index. The fund invests at least 80% of its total assets in the securities of the underlying index. The underlying index is based on the S&P 500® Index, and generally comprises approximately 500 or less U.S. listed common stocks. From this starting universe, constituents are screened to exclude companies involved in activities which are perceived to be inconsistent with Catholic values as outlined in the Socially Responsible Investment Guidelines of the United States Conference of Catholic Bishops. **Top Holdings:** Microsoft Corp   Apple Inc   Amazon.com Inc   Coca-Cola Co   Facebook Inc A

SPDR® S&P Retail ETF

D+   SELL

Ticker	Traded On	NAV	Total Assets ($)	Dividend Yield (TTM)	Turnover Ratio	Expense Ratio
XRT	NYSE Arca		$265,331,324	1.59	45	0.35

Ratings

Reward	D+
Risk	D+
Recent Upgrade/Downgrade	Down

Fund Information

Fund Type	Exchange Traded Funds
Category	Consumer Goods & Svcs
Sub-Category	Consumer Cyclical
Prospectus Objective	Unaligned
Inception Date	Jun-06
Open to New Investments	Y

Prices

Price (as of 9/30/2019)	42.43
52-Week High	50.72
52-Week Low	37.81

Total Returns (%)

3-Month	6-Month	1-Year	3-Year	5-Year
-0.58	-6.49	-15.74	0.91	5.20

3-Year Standard Deviation	18.7
Effective Duration	

Valuation

Premium/Discount (1-Year Average)	-0.03

Company Information

Provider	SPDR State Street Global Advisors
Manager/Tenure	Michael J. Feehily (7), Karl A. Schneider (4), Ted Janowsky (2)
Website	http://www.spdrs.com
Address	SPDR State Street Global Advisors State Street Financial Center, 1 Lincoln Street Boston MA 02111-2900 United States
Phone Number	617-786-3000

PERFORMANCE

Ratings History

Date	Overall Rating	Risk Rating	Reward Rating
Q3-19	D+	D+	D+
Q4-18	C-	C-	C-
Q4-17	D+	C	D
Q4-16	C	C	C
Q4-15	C+	C+	C

Asset & Performance History

Date	NAV	1-Year Total Return
2018	41.01	-8.01
2017	45.19	4.16
2016	44.1	2.97
2015	43.28	-8.8
2014	48.02	9.92
2013	44.04	42.16

Total Assets: $265,331,324

Asset Allocation

Asset	%
Cash	2%
Stocks	99%
US Stocks	99%
Bonds	0%
US Bonds	0%
Other	0%

Services Offered:

Investment Strategy: The investment seeks to provide investment results that, before fees and expenses, correspond generally to the total return performance of an index derived from the retail segment of a U.S. total market composite index. In seeking to track the performance of the S&P Retail Select Industry Index (the "Index"), the fund employs a sampling strategy. It generally invests substantially all, but at least 80%, of its total assets in the securities comprising the index. The index represents the retail segment of the S&P Total Market Index ("S&P TMI"). The fund is non-diversified. **Top Holdings:** Stamps.com Inc   Carvana Co Class A   Guess? Inc   Target Corp   Burlington Stores Inc

iShares Global Financials ETF   C   HOLD

Ticker	Traded On	NAV	Total Assets ($)	Dividend Yield (TTM)	Turnover Ratio	Expense Ratio
IXG	NYSE Arca	63.88	$261,915,266	2.8	7	0.46

Ratings
Reward	C
Risk	C-
Recent Upgrade/Downgrade	Up

Fund Information
Fund Type	Exchange Traded Funds
Category	Financials Sector Equity
Sub-Category	Financial
Prospectus Objective	Financial
Inception Date	Nov-01
Open to New Investments	Y

Prices
Price (as of 9/30/2019)	64.05
52-Week High	66.25
52-Week Low	54.20

Total Returns (%)
3-Month	6-Month	1-Year	3-Year	5-Year
-1.05	3.49	-0.37	35.23	30.12

3-Year Standard Deviation	14.56
Effective Duration	

Valuation
Premium/Discount (1-Year Average)	-0.03

Company Information
Provider	iShares
Manager/Tenure	Greg Savage (11), Jennifer Hsui (7), Alan Mason (3), 2 others
Website	http://www.ishares.com
Address	iShares 400 Howard Street San Francisco CA 94105 United States
Phone Number	800-474-2737

PERFORMANCE

Ratings History
Date	Overall Rating	Risk Rating	Reward Rating
Q3-19	C	C-	C
Q4-18	C	C	C-
Q4-17	B	B-	B
Q4-16	C-	C-	C
Q4-15	C	C+	C

Asset & Performance History
Date	NAV	1-Year Total Return
2018	57.02	-15.97
2017	69.82	23.42
2016	57.86	12.26
2015	52.81	-4.39
2014	56.71	3.42
2013	56.13	27.03

Total Assets: $261,915,266
Asset Allocation
Asset	%
Cash	1%
Stocks	99%
US Stocks	47%
Bonds	0%
US Bonds	0%
Other	0%

Services Offered: CashInvestment Plan

Investment Strategy: The investment seeks to track the investment results of the S&P Global 1200 Financials IndexTM. The fund generally invests at least 90% of its assets in securities of the underlying index and in depositary receipts representing securities of the underlying index. It may invest the remainder of its assets in certain futures, options and swap contracts, cash and cash equivalents, as well as in securities not included in the underlying index. The index measures the performance of companies that the index provider deems to be part of the financial sector of the economy and that the index provider believes are important to global markets. **Top Holdings:** Berkshire Hathaway Inc B   JPMorgan Chase & Co   Bank of America Corporation   Wells Fargo & Co   Citigroup Inc

Highland/iBoxx Senior Loan ETF   C   HOLD

Ticker	Traded On	NAV	Total Assets ($)	Dividend Yield (TTM)	Turnover Ratio	Expense Ratio
SNLN	NAS CM	17.44	$261,565,935	5.18	186	0.55

Ratings
Reward	C
Risk	C+
Recent Upgrade/Downgrade	

Fund Information
Fund Type	Exchange Traded Funds
Category	US Fixed Income
Sub-Category	Bank Loan
Prospectus Objective	Income
Inception Date	Nov-12
Open to New Investments	Y

Prices
Price (as of 9/30/2019)	17.45
52-Week High	18.27
52-Week Low	17.10

Total Returns (%)
3-Month	6-Month	1-Year	3-Year	5-Year
0.53	1.48	0.52	8.07	12.26

3-Year Standard Deviation	3.18
Effective Duration	

Valuation
Premium/Discount (1-Year Average)	0.02

Company Information
Provider	Highland Funds
Manager/Tenure	Jon Poglitsch (1)
Website	http://www.highlandfunds.com
Address	Highland Funds 200 Crescent Court, Suite 700 Dallas TX 75201 United States
Phone Number	877-665-1287

PERFORMANCE

Ratings History
Date	Overall Rating	Risk Rating	Reward Rating
Q3-19	C	C+	C
Q4-18	C	C+	C-
Q4-17	B-	B+	C
Q4-16	C	C+	C
Q4-15	C	C+	C-

Asset & Performance History
Date	NAV	1-Year Total Return
2018	17.16	-1.11
2017	18.2	1.82
2016	18.73	8.41
2015	18.06	-2.25
2014	19.26	0.71
2013	19.96	5.34

Total Assets: $261,565,935
Asset Allocation
Asset	%
Cash	22%
Stocks	0%
US Stocks	0%
Bonds	78%
US Bonds	73%
Other	0%

Services Offered:

Investment Strategy: The investment seeks to provide investment results that, before fees and expenses, correspond generally to the price and yield performance of the Markit iBoxx USD Liquid Leveraged Loan Index. The fund will, under normal circumstances, invest at least 80% of its assets (the "80% basket") in component securities of the underlying index. The underlying index is a subset of the Markit iBoxx USD Leveraged Loan Index. "Leveraged Loans" are loans to companies that typically already have a high amount of debt and are often characterized by lower credit ratings or higher interest rates. It is non-diversified. **Top Holdings:** Financial & Risk Us   Charter Communications Op   Envision Healthcare Corp   Bausch Health Term Loan   Scientific Games Int'l

SPDR® SSgA Global Allocation ETF   C   HOLD

Ticker	Traded On	NAV	Total Assets ($)	Dividend Yield (TTM)	Turnover Ratio	Expense Ratio
GAL	NYSE Arca		$259,977,393	2.74	71	0.35

Ratings
Reward   C
Risk   D+
Recent Upgrade/Downgrade

Fund Information
Fund Type	Exchange Traded Funds
Category	Moderate Allocation
Sub-Category	Allocation--50% to 70% Equity
Prospectus Objective	Growth
Inception Date	Apr-12
Open to New Investments	Y

Prices
Price (as of 9/30/2019)	38.59
52-Week High	38.98
52-Week Low	33.88

Total Returns (%)
3-Month	6-Month	1-Year	3-Year	5-Year
0.72	2.99	2.75	22.52	28.11

3-Year Standard Deviation	8.24
Effective Duration	5.50

Valuation
Premium/Discount (1-Year Average)	-0.02

Company Information
Provider	SPDR State Street Global Advisors
Manager/Tenure	Michael O. Martel (4), Jeremiah K. Holly (1)
Website	http://www.spdrs.com
Address	SPDR State Street Global Advisors State Street Financial Center, 1 Lincoln Street Boston MA 02111-2900 United States
Phone Number	617-786-3000

PERFORMANCE

Ratings History
Date	Overall Rating	Risk Rating	Reward Rating
Q3-19	C	D+	C
Q4-18	C-	C-	C-
Q4-17	B	B+	C+
Q4-16	C-	C-	C
Q4-15	C	C-	C

Asset & Performance History
Date	NAV	1-Year Total Return
2018	34.64	-7.25
2017	38.22	18.42
2016	33.05	3.2
2015	32.8	-2.28
2014	34.61	5.19
2013	34.01	12.7

Total Assets: $259,977,393
Asset Allocation
Asset	%
Cash	9%
Stocks	60%
US Stocks	38%
Bonds	28%
US Bonds	22%
Other	0%

Services Offered:

Investment Strategy: The investment seeks to provide capital appreciation. The Adviser primarily invests the assets of the fund among exchange traded products ("ETPs") that provide balanced exposure to domestic and international debt and equity securities. The fund typically allocates approximately 60% of its assets to equity securities, though this percentage can vary based on the Adviser's tactical decisions. **Top Holdings:** SPDR® S&P 500 ETF SPDR® Portfolio Developed Wld ex-US ETF SPDR® Blmbg Barclays High Yield Bd ETF SPDR® Dow Jones REIT ETF Invesco DB Gold

---

ProShares Short 20+ Year Treasury   D   SELL

Ticker	Traded On	NAV	Total Assets ($)	Dividend Yield (TTM)	Turnover Ratio	Expense Ratio
TBF	NYSE Arca	18.78	$258,227,619	1.82	0	0.92

Ratings
Reward   D
Risk   D
Recent Upgrade/Downgrade   Down

Fund Information
Fund Type	Exchange Traded Funds
Category	Trading Tools
Sub-Category	Trading--Inverse Debt
Prospectus Objective	Govt Bond - Treasury
Inception Date	Aug-09
Open to New Investments	Y

Prices
Price (as of 9/30/2019)	18.77
52-Week High	24.42
52-Week Low	18.29

Total Returns (%)
3-Month	6-Month	1-Year	3-Year	5-Year
-7.85	-13.11	-18.83	-8.96	-29.63

3-Year Standard Deviation	11.5
Effective Duration	

Valuation
Premium/Discount (1-Year Average)	-0.13

Company Information
Provider	ProShares
Manager/Tenure	Michelle Liu (10), Alexander V. Ilyasov (0)
Website	http://www.proshares.com
Address	ProShares 7501 Wisconsin Avenue, Suite 1000 Bethesda MD 20814 United States
Phone Number	866-776-5125

PERFORMANCE

Ratings History
Date	Overall Rating	Risk Rating	Reward Rating
Q3-19	D	D	D
Q4-18	C	C	D+
Q4-17	D	D+	D
Q4-16	D	D	D
Q4-15	D+	D+	D

Asset & Performance History
Date	NAV	1-Year Total Return
2018	22.49	3.81
2017	21.85	-8.42
2016	23.86	-3.47
2015	24.72	-1.9
2014	25.2	-23.42
2013	32.91	12.78

Total Assets: $258,227,619
Asset Allocation
Asset	%
Cash	139%
Stocks	0%
US Stocks	0%
Bonds	13%
US Bonds	13%
Other	-52%

Services Offered:

Investment Strategy: The investment seeks daily investment results, before fees and expenses, that correspond to the inverse (-1x) of the daily performance of the ICE U.S. Treasury 20+ Year Bond Index. The fund invests in financial instruments that ProShare Advisors believes, in combination, should produce daily returns consistent with the fund's investment objective. The index includes publicly- issued U.S. Treasury securities that have a remaining maturity greater than or equal to twenty years and have $300 million or more of outstanding face value, excluding amounts held by the Federal Reserve. The fund is non-diversified. **Top Holdings:** Ice 20+ Year U.S. Treasury Index Swap Societe Generale Ice 20+ Year U.S. Treasury Index Swap Citibank Na United States Treasury Bills United States Treasury Bills United States Treasury Bills

United States Natural Gas Fund, LP   D-   SELL

Ticker	Traded On	NAV	Total Assets ($)	Dividend Yield (TTM)	Turnover Ratio	Expense Ratio
UNG	NYSE Arca	19.93	$256,831,687	0		1.28

Ratings
Reward	D-
Risk	D
Recent Upgrade/Downgrade	Down

Fund Information
Fund Type	Exchange Traded Funds
Category	Commodities Specified
Sub-Category	Commodities Energy
Prospectus Objective	Natl Res
Inception Date	Apr-07
Open to New Investments	Y

Prices
Price (as of 9/30/2019)	19.93
52-Week High	39.32
52-Week Low	18.10

Total Returns (%)
3-Month	6-Month	1-Year	3-Year	5-Year
2.32	-16.32	-22.06	-40.14	-76.90

3-Year Standard Deviation	38.7
Effective Duration	

Valuation
Premium/Discount (1-Year Average)	0.31

Company Information
Provider	USCF Investments
Manager/Tenure	Management Team (12)
Website	http://www.uscfinvestments.com
Address	USCF 1290 Broadway, Suite 1100 Denver CO 80203 United States
Phone Number	

PERFORMANCE

Ratings History
Date	Overall Rating	Risk Rating	Reward Rating
Q3-19	D-	D	D-
Q4-18	D+	D+	D+
Q4-17	D-	E+	D-
Q4-16	D-	D-	D-
Q4-15	D-	D-	D-

Asset & Performance History
Date	NAV	1-Year Total Return
2018	24.35	4.34
2017	23.34	-37.22
2016	37.18	6.96
2015	34.76	-40.59
2014	58.5	-28.98
2013	82.38	9.13

Total Assets: $256,831,687
Asset Allocation
Asset	%
Cash	28%
Stocks	0%
US Stocks	0%
Bonds	24%
US Bonds	24%
Other	48%

Services Offered:

Investment Strategy: The investment seeks to reflect the daily changes in percentage terms of the price of natural gas delivered at the Henry Hub, Louisiana, as measured by the daily changes in the price of a specified short-term futures contract.
The fund invests primarily in futures contracts for natural gas that are traded on the NYMEX, ICE Futures Europe and ICE Futures U.S. (together, "ICE Futures") or other U.S. and foreign exchanges. The Benchmark Futures Contract is the futures contract on natural gas as traded on the New York Mercantile Exchange that is the near month contract to expire, except when the near month contract is within two weeks of expiration. **Top Holdings:** Natural Gas _TAS Oct19   United States Treasury Bills   United States Treasury Bills   United States Treasury Bills   United States Treasury Bills

WisdomTree International MidCap Dividend Fund   C-   HOLD

Ticker	Traded On	NAV	Total Assets ($)	Dividend Yield (TTM)	Turnover Ratio	Expense Ratio
DIM	NYSE Arca	60.37	$256,572,585	3.51	28	0.58

Ratings
Reward	D+
Risk	C-
Recent Upgrade/Downgrade	

Fund Information
Fund Type	Exchange Traded Funds
Category	Globa Eq Mid/Small Cap
Sub-Category	Foreign Small/Mid Value
Prospectus Objective	Foreign Stock
Inception Date	Jun-06
Open to New Investments	Y

Prices
Price (as of 9/30/2019)	60.31
52-Week High	65.57
52-Week Low	54.86

Total Returns (%)
3-Month	6-Month	1-Year	3-Year	5-Year
-2.58	-1.33	-4.65	17.81	23.93

3-Year Standard Deviation	11.38
Effective Duration	

Valuation
Premium/Discount (1-Year Average)	-0.20

Company Information
Provider	WisdomTree
Manager/Tenure	Richard A. Brown (11), Thomas J. Durante (11), Karen Q. Wong (11)
Website	http://www.wisdomtree.com
Address	WisdomTree 245 Park Avenue, 35th floor New York NY 10167 United States
Phone Number	866-909-9473

PERFORMANCE

Ratings History
Date	Overall Rating	Risk Rating	Reward Rating
Q3-19	C-	C-	D+
Q4-18	D+	C-	D+
Q4-17	B	B	B
Q4-16	C-	D+	C-
Q4-15	C	C-	C

Asset & Performance History
Date	NAV	1-Year Total Return
2018	57.01	-15.07
2017	69.1	28.07
2016	55.44	2.23
2015	55.85	2.37
2014	56.02	-1.29
2013	58.61	21.97

Total Assets: $256,572,585
Asset Allocation
Asset	%
Cash	0%
Stocks	100%
US Stocks	1%
Bonds	0%
US Bonds	0%
Other	0%

Services Offered:

Investment Strategy: The investment seeks to track the price and yield performance, before fees and expenses, of the WisdomTree International MidCap Dividend Index. The fund normally invests at least 95% of its total assets (exclusive of collateral held from securities lending) in component securities of the index and investments that have economic characteristics that are substantially identical to the economic characteristics of such component securities. The index is a fundamentally weighted index that is comprised of the mid-capitalization segment of the dividend-paying market in the industrialized world outside the U.S. and Canada. The fund is non-diversified. **Top Holdings:** SSE PLC   Natixis   EVRAZ PLC   Danske Bank A/S   Persimmon PLC

WisdomTree Dynamic Currency Hedged International Equity Fund | C | HOLD

Ticker	Traded On	NAV	Total Assets ($)	Dividend Yield (TTM)	Turnover Ratio	Expense Ratio
DDWM	BATS	28.82	$256,476,174	3.56	26	0.35

Ratings
Reward   C
Risk   C-
Recent Upgrade/Downgrade

Fund Information
Fund Type	Exchange Traded Funds
Category	Global Equity Large Cap
Sub-Category	Foreign Large Value
Prospectus Objective	Foreign Stock
Inception Date	Jan-16
Open to New Investments	Y

Prices
Price (as of 9/30/2019)	28.82
52-Week High	29.62
52-Week Low	25.36

Total Returns (%)
3-Month	6-Month	1-Year	3-Year	5-Year
-0.26	2.43	1.14	25.94	

3-Year Standard Deviation   9.86
Effective Duration

Valuation
Premium/Discount (1-Year Average)   0.10

Company Information
Provider	WisdomTree
Manager/Tenure	Richard A. Brown (3), Thomas J. Durante (3), Karen Q. Wong (3)
Website	http://www.wisdomtree.com
Address	WisdomTree 245 Park Avenue, 35th floor New York NY 10167 United States
Phone Number	866-909-9473

PERFORMANCE

Ratings History
Date	Overall Rating	Risk Rating	Reward Rating
Q3-19	C	C-	C
Q4-18	D+	C-	D+
Q4-17	C-	B+	C
Q4-16	D-	C-	D+
Q4-15			

Asset & Performance History
Date	NAV	1-Year Total Return
2018	26.08	-11.05
2017	30.51	18.53
2016	26.48	14.5
2015		
2014		
2013		

Total Assets: $256,476,174
Asset Allocation
Asset	%
Cash	0%
Stocks	100%
US Stocks	1%
Bonds	0%
US Bonds	0%
Other	0%

Services Offered:
Investment Strategy: The investment seeks to track the WisdomTree Dynamic Currency Hedged International Equity Index. The fund will invest at least 80% of its total assets in component securities of the index and investments that have economic characteristics that are substantially identical to the economic characteristics of such component securities. The index is a dividend weighted index designed to provide exposure to equity securities in the industrialized world, excluding Canada and the United States, while at the same time dynamically hedging currency exposure to fluctuations between the value of the applicable foreign currencies and the USD. The fund is non-diversified. **Top Holdings:** Nestle SA   China Mobile Ltd   HSBC Holdings PLC   BP PLC   Novartis AG

First Trust RiverFront Dynamic Developed International ETF | C- | HOLD

Ticker	Traded On	NAV	Total Assets ($)	Dividend Yield (TTM)	Turnover Ratio	Expense Ratio
RFDI	NAS CM	55.65	$256,006,125	2.67		0.83

Ratings
Reward   D+
Risk   C-
Recent Upgrade/Downgrade

Fund Information
Fund Type	Exchange Traded Funds
Category	Global Equity Large Cap
Sub-Category	Foreign Large Blend
Prospectus Objective	Growth
Inception Date	Apr-16
Open to New Investments	Y

Prices
Price (as of 9/30/2019)	55.69
52-Week High	61.99
52-Week Low	49.45

Total Returns (%)
3-Month	6-Month	1-Year	3-Year	5-Year
-2.28	-0.49	-7.50	14.37	

3-Year Standard Deviation   12.21
Effective Duration

Valuation
Premium/Discount (1-Year Average)   -0.19

Company Information
Provider	First Trust
Manager/Tenure	Adam Grossman (3), Scott Hays (3), Chris Konstantinos (3), 1 other
Website	http://www.ftportfolios.com/
Address	First Trust 120 E. Liberty Drive, Suite 400 Wheaton IL 60187 United States
Phone Number	800-621-1675

PERFORMANCE

Ratings History
Date	Overall Rating	Risk Rating	Reward Rating
Q3-19	C-	C-	D+
Q4-18	D+	C-	D+
Q4-17	D+	B+	C
Q4-16	U		
Q4-15			

Asset & Performance History
Date	NAV	1-Year Total Return
2018	51.6	-17.6
2017	64.03	24.93
2016	52.13	
2015		
2014		
2013		

Total Assets: $256,006,125
Asset Allocation
Asset	%
Cash	0%
Stocks	100%
US Stocks	2%
Bonds	0%
US Bonds	0%
Other	0%

Services Offered:
Investment Strategy: The investment seeks capital appreciation. The fund will seek to achieve its investment objective by investing at least 80% of its net assets in a portfolio of equity securities of developed market companies, including through investments in common stock, depositary receipts, and common and preferred shares of real estate investment trusts ("REITs"), and forward foreign currency exchange contracts and currency spot transactions used to hedge the fund's exposure to the currencies in which the equity securities of such developed market companies are denominated. It is non-diversified. **Top Holdings:** Nestle SA   Novartis AG   Roche Holding AG Dividend Right Cert.   BP PLC   SAP SE

Invesco S&P 500® Equal Weight Financials ETF   C   HOLD

Ticker	Traded On	NAV	Total Assets ($)	Dividend Yield (TTM)	Turnover Ratio	Expense Ratio
RYF	NYSE Arca	43.64	$255,276,061	2.16		0.4

Ratings
Reward   C
Risk   C-
Recent Upgrade/Downgrade

Fund Information
Fund Type	Exchange Traded Funds
Category	Financials Sector Equity
Sub-Category	Financial
Prospectus Objective	Financial
Inception Date	Nov-06
Open to New Investments	Y

Prices
Price (as of 9/30/2019)	43.65
52-Week High	45.22
52-Week Low	34.13

Total Returns (%)
3-Month	6-Month	1-Year	3-Year	5-Year
-0.05	9.32	3.61	47.20	66.41

3-Year Standard Deviation	17.25
Effective Duration	

Valuation
Premium/Discount (1-Year Average)	-0.02

Company Information
Provider	Invesco
Manager/Tenure	Peter Hubbard (1), Michael Jeanette (1), Tony Seisser (1)
Website	http://www.invesco.com/us
Address	Invesco 11 Greenway Plaza, Ste. 2500 Houston TX 77046 United States
Phone Number	800-659-1005

Ratings History

Date	Overall Rating	Risk Rating	Reward Rating
Q3-19	C	C-	C
Q4-18	C-	C-	C
Q4-17	A-	B	A
Q4-16	C	C-	C
Q4-15	C	C	C+

Asset & Performance History

Date	NAV	1-Year Total Return
2018	36.36	-15.62
2017	44.06	22.32
2016	36.83	-14.75
2015	30.13	-1.19
2014	31.16	14.63
2013	27.65	37.73

Total Assets: $255,276,061
Asset Allocation

Asset	%
Cash	0%
Stocks	100%
US Stocks	98%
Bonds	0%
US Bonds	0%
Other	0%

Services Offered:

Investment Strategy: The investment seeks to track the investment results (before fees and expenses) of the S&P 500® Equal Weight Financials Index (the "underlying index"). The fund generally will invest at least 90% of its total assets in the securities that comprise the underlying index. The underlying index is composed of all of the components of the S&P 500® Financials Index, an index that contains the common stocks of all companies included in the S&P 500® Index that are classified as members of the financials sector, as defined according to the Global Industry Classification Standard ("GICS"). The fund is non-diversified. **Top Holdings:** MarketAxess Holdings Inc Assurant Inc S&P Global Inc Moody's Corporation Cboe Global Markets Inc

---

iShares Global Comm Services ETF   C   HOLD

Ticker	Traded On	NAV	Total Assets ($)	Dividend Yield (TTM)	Turnover Ratio	Expense Ratio
IXP	NYSE Arca	57.32	$255,092,056	3.07	79	0.46

Ratings
Reward   C+
Risk   C
Recent Upgrade/Downgrade

Fund Information
Fund Type	Exchange Traded Funds
Category	Communications Sector Equity
Sub-Category	Communications
Prospectus Objective	Comm
Inception Date	Nov-01
Open to New Investments	Y

Prices
Price (as of 9/30/2019)	57.28
52-Week High	60.35
52-Week Low	48.09

Total Returns (%)
3-Month	6-Month	1-Year	3-Year	5-Year
-0.43	2.38	2.19	3.80	10.37

3-Year Standard Deviation	12.95
Effective Duration	

Valuation
Premium/Discount (1-Year Average)	-0.05

Company Information
Provider	iShares
Manager/Tenure	Greg Savage (11), Jennifer Hsui (7), Alan Mason (3), 2 others
Website	http://www.ishares.com
Address	iShares 400 Howard Street San Francisco CA 94105 United States
Phone Number	800-474-2737

Ratings History

Date	Overall Rating	Risk Rating	Reward Rating
Q3-19	C	C	C+
Q4-18	C	C-	C
Q4-17	C	C	C
Q4-16	C	C-	B-
Q4-15	C	C-	C

Asset & Performance History

Date	NAV	1-Year Total Return
2018	50.33	-13.54
2017	60.62	6.38
2016	58.96	5.59
2015	58.05	-0.3
2014	60.43	-0.7
2013	68.22	24.43

Total Assets: $255,092,056
Asset Allocation

Asset	%
Cash	0%
Stocks	100%
US Stocks	67%
Bonds	0%
US Bonds	0%
Other	0%

Services Offered: CashInvestment Plan

Investment Strategy: The investment seeks to track the investment results of the S&P Global 1200 Communication Services 4.5/22.5/45 Capped IndexTM. The fund invests at least 90% of its assets in securities of the index and in depositary receipts representing securities of the index. It may invest the remainder of its assets in certain futures, options and swap contracts, cash and cash equivalents, as well as in securities not included in the index. The index is designed to measure the performance of global equities in the communication services sector. The fund is non-diversified. **Top Holdings:** Facebook Inc A Alphabet Inc Class C Alphabet Inc A The Walt Disney Co Tencent Holdings Ltd

VelocityShares 3x Inverse Crude Oil ETNs linked to the S&P GSCI® Crude Oil Index ER New   D   SELL

Ticker	Traded On	NAV	Total Assets ($)	Dividend Yield (TTM)	Turnover Ratio	Expense Ratio
DWT	NYSE Arca	5.60	$255,071,572	0		1.5

Ratings
Reward	D-
Risk	D
Recent Upgrade/Downgrade	

Fund Information
Fund Type	Exchange Traded Funds
Category	Trading Tools
Sub-Category	Trading--Inverse Commodities
Prospectus Objective	Growth & Inc
Inception Date	Dec-16
Open to New Investments	Y

Prices
Price (as of 9/30/2019)	5.52
52-Week High	19.42
52-Week Low	3.91

Total Returns (%)
3-Month	6-Month	1-Year	3-Year	5-Year
-10.22	-9.98	15.75		

3-Year Standard Deviation	
Effective Duration	

Valuation
Premium/Discount (1-Year Average)	0.26

Company Information
Provider	Credit Suisse AG
Manager/Tenure	No Manager (2)
Website	
Address	Kilmore House Park Lane Dublin Ireland
Phone Number	

PERFORMANCE

Ratings History
Date	Overall Rating	Risk Rating	Reward Rating
Q3-19	D	D	D-
Q4-18	D	D	D
Q4-17	D	D-	D
Q4-16			
Q4-15			

Asset & Performance History
Date	NAV	1-Year Total Return
2018	16.38	18.25
2017	13.85	-35.01
2016	22.01	
2015		
2014		
2013		

Total Assets: $255,071,572

Asset Allocation
Asset	%
Cash	%
Stocks	%
US Stocks	%
Bonds	%
US Bonds	%
Other	%

Services Offered:

Investment Strategy: The investment seeks to replicate, net of expenses, three times the opposite (inverse) of the S&P GSCI® Crude Oil Index ER.
The index tracks a hypothetical position in the nearest-to-expiration NYMEX light sweet crude oil futures contract, which is rolled each month into the futures contract expiring in the next month. The value of the index fluctuates with changes in the price of the relevant NYMEX light sweet crude oil futures contracts. **Top Holdings:**

Invesco Defensive Equity ETF   C   HOLD

Ticker	Traded On	NAV	Total Assets ($)	Dividend Yield (TTM)	Turnover Ratio	Expense Ratio
DEF	NYSE Arca	54.18	$254,636,642	1.13	136	0.59

Ratings
Reward	B-
Risk	C-
Recent Upgrade/Downgrade	Down

Fund Information
Fund Type	Exchange Traded Funds
Category	US Equity Large Cap Blend
Sub-Category	Large Blend
Prospectus Objective	Growth
Inception Date	Dec-06
Open to New Investments	Y

Prices
Price (as of 9/30/2019)	54.20
52-Week High	54.45
52-Week Low	41.71

Total Returns (%)
3-Month	6-Month	1-Year	3-Year	5-Year
1.68	7.50	9.78	46.59	62.01

3-Year Standard Deviation	10.97
Effective Duration	

Valuation
Premium/Discount (1-Year Average)	0.03

Company Information
Provider	Invesco
Manager/Tenure	Peter Hubbard (1), Michael Jeanette (1), Tony Seisser (1)
Website	http://www.invesco.com/us
Address	Invesco 11 Greenway Plaza, Ste. 2500 Houston TX 77046 United States
Phone Number	800-659-1005

PERFORMANCE

Ratings History
Date	Overall Rating	Risk Rating	Reward Rating
Q3-19	C	C-	B-
Q4-18	C	C-	C
Q4-17	B-	C+	B-
Q4-16	C	D+	C+
Q4-15	C	C-	C

Asset & Performance History
Date	NAV	1-Year Total Return
2018	44	-3.73
2017	46.38	20.91
2016	38.91	14.08
2015	34.82	-4.5
2014	37.66	12.82
2013	34.22	22.64

Total Assets: $254,636,642

Asset Allocation
Asset	%
Cash	0%
Stocks	100%
US Stocks	99%
Bonds	0%
US Bonds	0%
Other	0%

Services Offered:

Investment Strategy: The investment seeks to track the investment results (before fees and expenses) of the Invesco Defensive Equity Index (the "underlying index"). The fund generally will invest at least 80% of its total assets in the securities that comprise the underlying index. The underlying index is comprised of a subset of securities from the S&P 500® Index (the "S&P 500"). The fund will concentrate its investments in securities of issuers in any one industry or group of industries only to the extent that the underlying index reflects a concentration in that industry or group of industries. The fund is non-diversified. **Top Holdings:** Ball Corp Fiserv Inc Amgen Inc ResMed Inc S&P Global Inc

---

Invesco S&P 500 GARP ETF   C   HOLD

Ticker	Traded On	NAV	Total Assets ($)	Dividend Yield (TTM)	Turnover Ratio	Expense Ratio
SPGP	NYSE Arca	56.40	$253,815,089	0.98		0.35

Ratings
Reward   C+
Risk   C-
Recent Upgrade/Downgrade

Fund Information
Fund Type   Exchange Traded Funds
Category   US Equity Large Cap Growth
Sub-Category   Large Growth
Prospectus Objective   Growth
Inception Date   Jun-11
Open to New Investments   Y

Prices
Price (as of 9/30/2019)   56.42
52-Week High   58.76
52-Week Low   42.07

Total Returns (%)

3-Month	6-Month	1-Year	3-Year	5-Year
-0.32	4.88	4.22	71.63	89.08

3-Year Standard Deviation   14.41
Effective Duration

Valuation
Premium/Discount (1-Year Average)   -0.10

Company Information
Provider   Invesco
Manager/Tenure   Peter Hubbard (8), Michael Jeanette (8), Tony Seisser (5)
Website   http://www.invesco.com/us
Address   Invesco 11 Greenway Plaza, Ste. 2500 Houston TX 77046 United States
Phone Number   800-659-1005

PERFORMANCE

Ratings History

Date	Overall Rating	Risk Rating	Reward Rating
Q3-19	C	C-	C+
Q4-18	C	C	C+
Q4-17	A-	A-	A
Q4-16	C	C-	B-
Q4-15	B-	C	B

Asset & Performance History

Date	NAV	1-Year Total Return
2018	45.76	1.8
2017	45.36	35.82
2016	33.64	-0.49
2015	34.11	6.18
2014	32.49	15.95
2013	28.46	29.42

Total Assets: $253,815,089

Asset Allocation

Asset	%
Cash	0%
Stocks	100%
US Stocks	100%
Bonds	0%
US Bonds	0%
Other	0%

Services Offered:

Investment Strategy: The investment seeks to track the investment results (before fees and expenses) of the S&P 500® GARP Index (the "underlying index"). The fund generally will invest at least 90% of its total assets in the securities that comprise the underlying index. Strictly in accordance with its guidelines and mandated procedures, the index provider compiles, maintains and calculates the underlying index, which is designed to track the performance of approximately 75 growth stocks in the S&P 500® Index that exhibit quality characteristics and have attractive valuation. **Top Holdings:** NVIDIA Corp Micron Technology Inc Lam Research Corp Facebook Inc A Applied Materials Inc

---

Invesco CurrencyShares® Euro Currency Trust   D   SELL

Ticker	Traded On	NAV	Total Assets ($)	Dividend Yield (TTM)	Turnover Ratio	Expense Ratio
FXE	NYSE Arca	103.56	$253,724,741	0	0	0.4

Ratings
Reward   D
Risk   C-
Recent Upgrade/Downgrade   Down

Fund Information
Fund Type   Exchange Traded Funds
Category   Currency
Sub-Category   Single Currency
Prospectus Objective   Worldwide Bond
Inception Date   Dec-05
Open to New Investments   Y

Prices
Price (as of 9/30/2019)   103.56
52-Week High   110.99
52-Week Low   103.56

Total Returns (%)

3-Month	6-Month	1-Year	3-Year	5-Year
-3.92	-3.23	-6.89	-5.31	-16.58

3-Year Standard Deviation   6.37
Effective Duration

Valuation
Premium/Discount (1-Year Average)   -0.07

Company Information
Provider   Invesco
Manager/Tenure   Management Team (13)
Website   http://www.invesco.com/us
Address   Invesco 11 Greenway Plaza, Ste. 2500 Houston TX 77046 United States
Phone Number   800-659-1005

PERFORMANCE

Ratings History

Date	Overall Rating	Risk Rating	Reward Rating
Q3-19	D	C-	D
Q4-18	C-	C	D+
Q4-17	C	C+	C
Q4-16	D	D	D
Q4-15	D	D	D

Asset & Performance History

Date	NAV	1-Year Total Return
2018	109.25	-5.56
2017	115.69	12.93
2016	102.45	-3.66
2015	106.34	-10.74
2014	119.14	-12.53
2013	136.22	4.1

Total Assets: $253,724,741

Asset Allocation

Asset	%
Cash	100%
Stocks	0%
US Stocks	0%
Bonds	0%
US Bonds	0%
Other	0%

Services Offered:

Investment Strategy: The investment objective of the Trust is for the Shares to reflect the price in USD of the Euro. The Shares are intended to provide institutional and retail investors with a simple, cost-effective means of gaining investment benefits similar to those of holding euro. **Top Holdings:**

ProShares UltraPro Short Dow30   C   HOLD

Ticker	Traded On	NAV	Total Assets ($)	Dividend Yield (TTM)	Turnover Ratio	Expense Ratio
SDOW	NYSE Arca	46.23	$253,513,040	2.38		0.95

Ratings
Reward   C
Risk   D+
Recent Upgrade/Downgrade

Fund Information
Fund Type	Exchange Traded Funds
Category	Trading Tools
Sub-Category	Trading--Inverse Equity
Prospectus Objective	Growth
Inception Date	Feb-10
Open to New Investments	Y

Prices
Price (as of 9/30/2019)	46.16
52-Week High	61.56
52-Week Low	13.45

Total Returns (%)
3-Month	6-Month	1-Year	3-Year	5-Year
-5.00	-10.89	236.24	-10.44	-53.74

3-Year Standard Deviation   35.43
Effective Duration

Valuation
Premium/Discount (1-Year Average)   0.02

Company Information
Provider	ProShares
Manager/Tenure	Michael Neches (6), Devin Sullivan (1)
Website	http://www.proshares.com
Address	ProShares 7501 Wisconsin Avenue, Suite 1000 Bethesda MD 20814 United States
Phone Number	866-776-5125

PERFORMANCE

Ratings History
Date	Overall Rating	Risk Rating	Reward Rating
Q3-19	C	D+	C
Q4-18	D-	D-	E+
Q4-17	E+	E+	E+
Q4-16	D	D-	D-
Q4-15	D	E+	D-

Asset & Performance History
Date	NAV	1-Year Total Return
2018	19.2	-0.69
2017	19.59	-52.17
2016	41	-42.18
2015	70.92	-13.84
2014	82.32	-30.14
2013	117.84	-56.94

Total Assets: $253,513,040

Asset Allocation
Asset	%
Cash	251%
Stocks	-164%
US Stocks	-164%
Bonds	12%
US Bonds	12%
Other	0%

Services Offered:

Investment Strategy: The investment seeks daily investment results, before fees and expenses, that correspond to three times the inverse (-3x) of the daily performance of the Dow Jones Industrial Average® Index. The fund invests in financial instruments that ProShare Advisors believes, in combination, should produce daily returns consistent with the fund's investment objective. The index is a price-weighted index and includes 30 large-cap, "blue-chip" U.S. stocks, excluding utility and transportation companies. The fund is non-diversified. **Top Holdings:** Dj Industrial Average Swap Societe Generale   Dj Industrial Average Swap Bank Of America, Na   Dj Industrial Average Swap Morgan Stanley & Co. International Plc   Dj Industrial Average Swap Ubs Ag   Dj Industrial Average Swap Credit Suisse International

---

iShares Russell Top 200 ETF   C   HOLD

Ticker	Traded On	NAV	Total Assets ($)	Dividend Yield (TTM)	Turnover Ratio	Expense Ratio
IWL	NYSE Arca	68.90	$251,499,920	1.9	5	0.15

Ratings
Reward   C+
Risk   C-
Recent Upgrade/Downgrade

Fund Information
Fund Type	Exchange Traded Funds
Category	US Equity Large Cap Blend
Sub-Category	Large Blend
Prospectus Objective	Growth
Inception Date	Sep-09
Open to New Investments	Y

Prices
Price (as of 9/30/2019)	68.93
52-Week High	70.25
52-Week Low	54.65

Total Returns (%)
3-Month	6-Month	1-Year	3-Year	5-Year
0.91	4.85	3.45	48.19	71.12

3-Year Standard Deviation   12.07
Effective Duration

Valuation
Premium/Discount (1-Year Average)   0.02

Company Information
Provider	iShares
Manager/Tenure	Greg Savage (10), Jennifer Hsui (7), Alan Mason (3), 2 others
Website	http://www.ishares.com
Address	iShares 400 Howard Street San Francisco CA 94105 United States
Phone Number	800-474-2737

PERFORMANCE

Ratings History
Date	Overall Rating	Risk Rating	Reward Rating
Q3-19	C	C-	C+
Q4-18	C	C-	C
Q4-17	B	B+	B
Q4-16	C+	C-	B
Q4-15	C	C-	C

Asset & Performance History
Date	NAV	1-Year Total Return
2018	58.34	-3.2
2017	61.37	22.78
2016	50.9	11.14
2015	46.75	2.21
2014	46.74	13.02
2013	42.09	32.17

Total Assets: $251,499,920

Asset Allocation
Asset	%
Cash	0%
Stocks	100%
US Stocks	99%
Bonds	0%
US Bonds	0%
Other	0%

Services Offered:

Investment Strategy: The investment seeks to track the investment results of the Russell Top 200® Index, which measures the performance of the largest capitalization sector of the U.S. equity market. The fund generally will invest at least 90% of its assets in the component securities of the underlying index and may invest up to 10% of its assets in certain futures, options and swap contracts, cash and cash equivalents, including shares of money market funds advised by the advisor or its affiliates, as well as in securities not included in the underlying index, but which the advisor believes will help the fund track the underlying index. **Top Holdings:** Microsoft Corp Apple Inc   Amazon.com Inc   Facebook Inc A   Berkshire Hathaway Inc B

Invesco DB Oil Fund

C-   HOLD

Ticker	Traded On	NAV	Total Assets ($)	Dividend Yield (TTM)	Turnover Ratio	Expense Ratio
DBO	NYSE Arca	9.41	$250,379,867	1.43		0.75

Ratings
Reward	D+
Risk	C-
Recent Upgrade/Downgrade	

Fund Information
Fund Type	Exchange Traded Funds
Category	Commodities Specified
Sub-Category	Commodities Energy
Prospectus Objective	Natl Res
Inception Date	Jan-07
Open to New Investments	Y

Prices
Price (as of 9/30/2019)	9.46
52-Week High	14.02
52-Week Low	8.12

Total Returns (%)
3-Month	6-Month	1-Year	3-Year	5-Year
-8.06	-11.84	-30.93	7.15	-64.31

3-Year Standard Deviation	25.38
Effective Duration	

Valuation
Premium/Discount (1-Year Average)	-0.17

Company Information
Provider	Invesco
Manager/Tenure	Management Team (12)
Website	http://www.invesco.com/us
Address	Invesco 11 Greenway Plaza, Ste. 2500 Houston TX 77046 United States
Phone Number	800-659-1005

PERFORMANCE

Ratings History
Date	Overall Rating	Risk Rating	Reward Rating
Q3-19	C-	C-	D+
Q4-18	C-	C-	C-
Q4-17	D	D	D+
Q4-16	D-	D-	D-
Q4-15	D-	D-	D-

Asset & Performance History
Date	NAV	1-Year Total Return
2018	8.38	-17.88
2017	10.21	4.41
2016	9.67	8.25
2015	9.07	-41.52
2014	15.51	-43.97
2013	27.69	6.55

Total Assets: $250,379,867
Asset Allocation
Asset	%
Cash	50%
Stocks	0%
US Stocks	0%
Bonds	1%
US Bonds	1%
Other	49%

Services Offered:

Investment Strategy: The investment seeks to track the DBIQ Optimum Yield Crude Oil Index Excess Return™ (DBIQ-OY CL ER™), which is intended to reflect the changes in market value of crude oil. The single index Commodity consists of Light, Sweet Crude Oil (WTI). The fund invests in futures contracts in an attempt to track its corresponding index. **Top Holdings:** Wti Crude Future Mar20   United States Treasury Bills 0%   Invesco Treasury Collateral ETF   Invesco Treasury Collateral ETF   Invesco Treasury Collateral ETF

United States Commodity Index Fund, LP

D   SELL

Ticker	Traded On	NAV	Total Assets ($)	Dividend Yield (TTM)	Turnover Ratio	Expense Ratio
USCI	NYSE Arca	35.83	$249,038,340	0		1.03

Ratings
Reward	D
Risk	D
Recent Upgrade/Downgrade	

Fund Information
Fund Type	Exchange Traded Funds
Category	Commodities Broad Basket
Sub-Category	Commodities Broad Basket
Prospectus Objective	Natl Res
Inception Date	Aug-10
Open to New Investments	Y

Prices
Price (as of 9/30/2019)	35.83
52-Week High	43.11
52-Week Low	34.69

Total Returns (%)
3-Month	6-Month	1-Year	3-Year	5-Year
-2.43	-8.29	-16.43	-13.66	-34.81

3-Year Standard Deviation	8.57
Effective Duration	

Valuation
Premium/Discount (1-Year Average)	-0.14

Company Information
Provider	USCF Investments
Manager/Tenure	Management Team (9)
Website	http://www.uscfinvestments.com
Address	USCF 1290 Broadway, Suite 1100 Denver CO 80203 United States
Phone Number	

PERFORMANCE

Ratings History
Date	Overall Rating	Risk Rating	Reward Rating
Q3-19	D	D	D
Q4-18	D+	C-	D
Q4-17	D	D+	D
Q4-16	D	D	D
Q4-15	D	D	D

Asset & Performance History
Date	NAV	1-Year Total Return
2018	37.49	-11.73
2017	42.48	6.14
2016	40.02	-1.22
2015	40.52	-16.01
2014	48.24	-13.95
2013	56.06	-4.1

Total Assets: $249,038,340
Asset Allocation
Asset	%
Cash	39%
Stocks	0%
US Stocks	0%
Bonds	11%
US Bonds	11%
Other	49%

Services Offered:

Investment Strategy: The investment seeks the daily changes in percentage terms of its shares' per share net asset value ("NAV") to reflect the daily changes in percentage terms of the SummerHaven Dynamic Commodity Index Total ReturnSM (the "SDCI"), plus interest earned on USCI's collateral holdings, less USCI's expenses. The fund seeks to achieve its investment objective by investing to the fullest extent possible in the Benchmark Component Futures Contracts. The SDCI is designed to reflect the performance of a diversified group of commodities. **Top Holdings:** United States Treasury Bills   Future Contract On Lme Nickel Future Nov19   Future Contract On Silver Future Dec19   Gold 100 oz Dec19   Future Contract On Lme Lead Future Oct19

Invesco BulletShares 2023 High Yield Corporate Bond ETF   C   HOLD

Ticker	Traded On	NAV	Total Assets ($)	Dividend Yield (TTM)	Turnover Ratio	Expense Ratio
BSJN	NYSE Arca	25.94	$249,035,649	5.64	6	0.42

Ratings

Reward	C
Risk	C-
Recent Upgrade/Downgrade	

Fund Information

Fund Type	Exchange Traded Funds
Category	US Fixed Income
Sub-Category	High Yield Bond
Prospectus Objective	Corp Bond-High Yld
Inception Date	Oct-15
Open to New Investments	Y

Prices

Price (as of 9/30/2019)	26.07
52-Week High	26.29
52-Week Low	24.23

Total Returns (%)

3-Month	6-Month	1-Year	3-Year	5-Year
0.77	2.77	4.63	15.38	

3-Year Standard Deviation	3.9
Effective Duration	2.08

Valuation

Premium/Discount (1-Year Average)	0.14

Company Information

Provider	Invesco
Manager/Tenure	Jeremy Neisewander (3), Peter Hubbard (1), Jeffrey W. Kernagis (1), 1 other
Website	http://www.invesco.com/us
Address	Invesco 11 Greenway Plaza, Ste. 2500 Houston TX 77046 United States
Phone Number	800-659-1005

PERFORMANCE

Ratings History

Date	Overall Rating	Risk Rating	Reward Rating
Q3-19	C	C-	C
Q4-18	C-	C-	C-
Q4-17	C	B	C
Q4-16	D	D+	D+
Q4-15			

Asset & Performance History

Date	NAV	1-Year Total Return
2018	24.63	-1.35
2017	26.33	5.55
2016	26.35	12.6
2015	24.56	
2014		
2013		

Total Assets: $249,035,649

Asset Allocation

Asset	%
Cash	1%
Stocks	0%
US Stocks	0%
Bonds	98%
US Bonds	81%
Other	0%

Services Offered:

Investment Strategy: The investment seeks to track the investment results (before fees and expenses) of the Nasdaq BulletShares® USD High Yield Corporate Bond 2023 Index (the "underlying index"). The fund generally will invest at least 80% of its total assets in securities that comprise the underlying index. The underlying index seeks to measure the performance of a portfolio of U.S. dollar-denominated high yield corporate bonds (commonly known as "junk bonds") with maturities or, in some cases, "effective maturities" in the year 2023 (collectively, "2023 Bonds"). The fund is non-diversified. **Top Holdings:** Sprint Corporation 7.88% Community Health Systems Incorporated 6.25% Bausch Health Companies Inc 5.88% Altice Financing S.A. 6.62% Intelsat Jackson Holdings, Ltd. 5.5%

PIMCO 15+ Year U.S. TIPS Index Exchange-Traded Fund   C   HOLD

Ticker	Traded On	NAV	Total Assets ($)	Dividend Yield (TTM)	Turnover Ratio	Expense Ratio
LTPZ	NYSE Arca	73.53	$247,804,435	1.45	6	0.2

Ratings

Reward	C+
Risk	C-
Recent Upgrade/Downgrade	

Fund Information

Fund Type	Exchange Traded Funds
Category	US Fixed Income
Sub-Category	Inflation-Protected Bond
Prospectus Objective	Govt Bond - Treasury
Inception Date	Sep-09
Open to New Investments	Y

Prices

Price (as of 9/30/2019)	73.53
52-Week High	76.75
52-Week Low	60.38

Total Returns (%)

3-Month	6-Month	1-Year	3-Year	5-Year
6.96	12.58	16.65	11.08	24.13

3-Year Standard Deviation	9.55
Effective Duration	21.42

Valuation

Premium/Discount (1-Year Average)	0.02

Company Information

Provider	PIMCO
Manager/Tenure	Matthew P. Dorsten (3), Mitchell Handa (0), Graham A. Rennison (0)
Website	http://www.pimco.com
Address	PIMCO 840 Newport Center Drive, Suite 100 Newport Beach CA 92660 United States
Phone Number	866-746-2602

PERFORMANCE

Ratings History

Date	Overall Rating	Risk Rating	Reward Rating
Q3-19	C	C-	C+
Q4-18	D+	C-	D
Q4-17	C+	B-	C
Q4-16	C	C-	C
Q4-15	D+	D+	D+

Asset & Performance History

Date	NAV	1-Year Total Return
2018	62.33	-7.38
2017	69.45	9.44
2016	64.95	8.84
2015	60.65	-8.73
2014	66.91	19.31
2013	57.11	-19.54

Total Assets: $247,804,435

Asset Allocation

Asset	%
Cash	0%
Stocks	0%
US Stocks	0%
Bonds	100%
US Bonds	100%
Other	0%

Services Offered:

Investment Strategy: The investment seeks to provide total return that closely corresponds, before fees and expenses, to the total return of the ICE BofAML 15+ Year US Inflation-Linked Treasury Index. The fund invests at least 80% of its total assets (exclusive of collateral held from securities lending) in the component securities of the ICE BofAML 15+ Year US Inflation-Linked Treasury Index (the "underlying index"). The underlying index is an unmanaged index comprised of Treasury Inflation-Protected Securities ("TIPS") with a maturity of at least 15 years. **Top Holdings:** United States Treasury Bonds 2.12% United States Treasury Bonds 1.38% United States Treasury Bonds 0.75% United States Treasury Bonds 0.75% United States Treasury Bonds 0.62%

First Trust Small Cap Growth AlphaDEX® Fund   C-   HOLD

Ticker	Traded On	NAV	Total Assets ($)	Dividend Yield (TTM)	Turnover Ratio	Expense Ratio
FYC	NAS CM	43.90	$245,834,927	0.12	152	0.7

Ratings
Reward	C
Risk	C-
Recent Upgrade/Downgrade	Down

Fund Information
Fund Type	Exchange Traded Funds
Category	US Equity Small Cap
Sub-Category	Small Growth
Prospectus Objective	Small Company
Inception Date	Apr-11
Open to New Investments	Y

Prices
Price (as of 9/30/2019)	43.87
52-Week High	51.51
52-Week Low	37.33

Total Returns (%)
3-Month	6-Month	1-Year	3-Year	5-Year
-6.01	-5.32	-14.50	30.56	63.05

3-Year Standard Deviation	18.39
Effective Duration	

Valuation
Premium/Discount (1-Year Average)	-0.02

Company Information
Provider	First Trust
Manager/Tenure	Jon C. Erickson (8), Daniel J. Lindquist (8), David G. McGarel (8), 3 others
Website	http://www.ftportfolios.com/
Address	First Trust 120 E. Liberty Drive, Suite 400 Wheaton IL 60187 United States
Phone Number	800-621-1675

PERFORMANCE

Ratings History
Date	Overall Rating	Risk Rating	Reward Rating
Q3-19	C-	C-	C
Q4-18	C-	C-	C
Q4-17	B+	B	A
Q4-16	C+	C-	B
Q4-15	C+	C-	B-

Asset & Performance History
Date	NAV	1-Year Total Return
2018	40.16	-5.6
2017	42.58	23.19
2016	34.6	13.91
2015	30.47	1.78
2014	30	-1.64
2013	30.51	42.93

Total Assets: $245,834,927
Asset Allocation
Asset	%
Cash	0%
Stocks	100%
US Stocks	98%
Bonds	0%
US Bonds	0%
Other	0%

Services Offered:

Investment Strategy: The investment seeks investment results that correspond generally to the price and yield (before the fund's fees and expenses) of an equity index called the Nasdaq AlphaDEX® Small Cap Growth Index. The fund will normally invest at least 90% of its net assets (including investment borrowings) in common stocks that comprise the index. The index is designed to select growth stocks from the NASDAQ US 700 Small Cap Index (the "base index") that may generate positive alpha, or risk-adjusted returns, relative to traditional indices through the use of the AlphaDEX® selection methodology. **Top Holdings:** Shake Shack Inc A Lattice Semiconductor Corp Arrowhead Pharmaceuticals Inc Medpace Holdings Inc Q2 Holdings Inc

---

Nuveen Enhanced Yield U.S. Aggregate Bond ETF   C   HOLD

Ticker	Traded On	NAV	Total Assets ($)	Dividend Yield (TTM)	Turnover Ratio	Expense Ratio
NUAG	NYSE Arca	24.84	$243,464,248	3.51	167	0.2

Ratings
Reward	C
Risk	C-
Recent Upgrade/Downgrade	Up

Fund Information
Fund Type	Exchange Traded Funds
Category	US Fixed Income
Sub-Category	Intermediate Core Bond
Prospectus Objective	Corp Bond - Gen
Inception Date	Sep-16
Open to New Investments	Y

Prices
Price (as of 9/30/2019)	24.89
52-Week High	25.09
52-Week Low	22.81

Total Returns (%)
3-Month	6-Month	1-Year	3-Year	5-Year
2.60	6.37	10.20	9.23	

3-Year Standard Deviation	3.44
Effective Duration	5.99

Valuation
Premium/Discount (1-Year Average)	-0.10

Company Information
Provider	Nuveen
Manager/Tenure	Lijun (Kevin) Chen (3), Yong (Mark) Zheng (1)
Website	http://www.nuveen.com
Address	Nuveen Investment Trust John Nuveen & Co. Inc. Chicago IL 60606 United States
Phone Number	312-917-8146

PERFORMANCE

Ratings History
Date	Overall Rating	Risk Rating	Reward Rating
Q3-19	C	C-	C
Q4-18	D+	D+	D+
Q4-17	D	B	D+
Q4-16	U		
Q4-15			

Asset & Performance History
Date	NAV	1-Year Total Return
2018	23.19	-1.86
2017	24.43	3.67
2016	24.25	
2015		
2014		
2013		

Total Assets: $243,464,248
Asset Allocation
Asset	%
Cash	0%
Stocks	0%
US Stocks	0%
Bonds	99%
US Bonds	94%
Other	0%

Services Offered:

Investment Strategy: The investment seeks to track the investment results, before fees and expenses, of the ICE BofAML Enhanced Yield US Broad Bond Index (the "index"). Under normal market conditions, the fund invests at least 80% of its assets, exclusive of collateral held from securities lending, in component securities of the index. The index consists of U.S. dollar-denominated, investment grade taxable debt securities with fixed rate coupons that have at least one year to final maturity. **Top Holdings:** United States Treasury Notes 2.63% Federal National Mortgage Association 3% United States Treasury Notes 2% Federal National Mortgage Association 3% United States Treasury Notes 2.38%

First Trust Horizon Managed Volatility Domestic ETF

C   HOLD

Ticker	Traded On	NAV	Total Assets (s)	Dividend Yield (TTM)	Turnover Ratio	Expense Ratio
HUSV	NYSE Arca	27.50	$243,412,475	1.45	147	0.7

Ratings

Reward	C
Risk	C-
Recent Upgrade/Downgrade	

Fund Information

Fund Type	Exchange Traded Funds
Category	US Equity Large Cap Blend
Sub-Category	Large Blend
Prospectus Objective	Growth
Inception Date	Aug-16
Open to New Investments	Y

Prices

Price (as of 9/30/2019)	27.54
52-Week High	27.65
52-Week Low	21.11

Total Returns (%)

3-Month	6-Month	1-Year	3-Year	5-Year
3.67	10.21	16.17	45.04	

3-Year Standard Deviation	9.37
Effective Duration	

Valuation

Premium/Discount (1-Year Average)	0.10

Company Information

Provider	First Trust
Manager/Tenure	Steven Clark (3), Michael Dickson (3), Scott E. Ladner (3)
Website	http://www.ftportfolios.com/
Address	First Trust 120 E. Liberty Drive, Suite 400 Wheaton IL 60187 United States
Phone Number	800-621-1675

PERFORMANCE

Ratings History

Date	Overall Rating	Risk Rating	Reward Rating
Q3-19	C	C-	C
Q4-18	C	C-	C
Q4-17	D	B	C-
Q4-16	U		
Q4-15			

Asset & Performance History

Date	NAV	1-Year Total Return
2018	22.21	-2.1
2017	23.01	16.16
2016	20.08	
2015		
2014		
2013		

Total Assets: $243,412,475

Asset Allocation

Asset	%
Cash	0%
Stocks	100%
US Stocks	96%
Bonds	0%
US Bonds	0%
Other	0%

Services Offered:

Investment Strategy: The investment seeks to provide capital appreciation. The fund seeks to achieve its investment objective by investing at least 80% of its net assets in common stocks of domestic companies listed and traded on U.S. national securities exchanges that the sub-advisor believes exhibit low future expected volatility. To implement this strategy, the sub-advisor employs volatility forecasting models to forecast future expected volatility. The strategy is largely quantitative and rules-based, but also includes multiple parameters over which the sub-advisor may exercise discretion in connection with its active management of the fund. The fund is non-diversified. **Top Holdings:** Citrix Systems Inc Waste Management Inc PepsiCo Inc Yum Brands Inc AvalonBay Communities Inc

FormulaFolios Tactical Income ETF

C   HOLD

Ticker	Traded On	NAV	Total Assets (s)	Dividend Yield (TTM)	Turnover Ratio	Expense Ratio
FFTI	BATS		$242,536,711	3.19	135	1.04

Ratings

Reward	C
Risk	C-
Recent Upgrade/Downgrade	Up

Fund Information

Fund Type	Exchange Traded Funds
Category	US Fixed Income
Sub-Category	Multisector Bond
Prospectus Objective	Multisector Bond
Inception Date	Jun-17
Open to New Investments	Y

Prices

Price (as of 9/30/2019)	25.01
52-Week High	25.21
52-Week Low	22.89

Total Returns (%)

3-Month	6-Month	1-Year	3-Year	5-Year
2.40	5.81	7.05		

3-Year Standard Deviation	
Effective Duration	5.22

Valuation

Premium/Discount (1-Year Average)	-0.02

Company Information

Provider	FormulaFolioFunds
Manager/Tenure	Derek Prusa (2), Jason Wenk (2)
Website	
Address	89 Ionia NW, Suite 600 Grand Rapids, MI 49503 United States
Phone Number	

PERFORMANCE

Ratings History

Date	Overall Rating	Risk Rating	Reward Rating
Q3-19	C	C-	C
Q4-18	D	C-	D
Q4-17	U		
Q4-16			
Q4-15			

Asset & Performance History

Date	NAV	1-Year Total Return
2018	23.15	-3.76
2017	24.93	
2016		
2015		
2014		
2013		

Total Assets: $242,536,711

Asset Allocation

Asset	%
Cash	3%
Stocks	0%
US Stocks	0%
Bonds	91%
US Bonds	83%
Other	0%

Services Offered:

Investment Strategy: The investment seeks to provide income. The fund seeks to achieve its investment objective by investing through other exchange traded funds ("ETFs") in foreign and domestic fixed income securities. The fixed income securities in which the ETFs will invest are U.S. Treasuries, investment grade U.S. bonds, high-yield U.S. bonds, U.S. aggregate bond, municipal bonds and international government bonds of any maturity and duration. The adviser uses its proprietary investment model to rank 5 major fixed income asset classes based on the strongest combination of yield spread and price momentum. **Top Holdings:** iShares iBoxx $ High Yield Corp Bd ETF SPDR® Blmbg Barclays High Yield Bd ETF iShares 20+ Year Treasury Bond ETF iShares iBoxx $ Invmt Grade Corp Bd ETF iShares 7-10 Year Treasury Bond ETF

Invesco RAFI™ Strategic Developed ex-US ETF   D+   SELL

Ticker	Traded On	NAV	Total Assets ($)	Dividend Yield (TTM)	Turnover Ratio	Expense Ratio
ISDX	NAS CM	24.59	$240,959,958	2.73		0.23

Ratings
Reward	D+
Risk	C-
Recent Upgrade/Downgrade	

Fund Information
Fund Type	Exchange Traded Funds
Category	Global Equity Large Cap
Sub-Category	Foreign Large Blend
Prospectus Objective	Growth
Inception Date	Sep-18
Open to New Investments	Y

Prices
Price (as of 9/30/2019)	24.57
52-Week High	27.06
52-Week Low	22.25

Total Returns (%)
3-Month	6-Month	1-Year	3-Year	5-Year
-1.47	0.48	-1.92		

3-Year Standard Deviation	
Effective Duration	

Valuation
Premium/Discount (1-Year Average)	0.14

Company Information
Provider	Invesco
Manager/Tenure	Peter Hubbard (1), Michael Jeanette (1), Tony Seisser (1)
Website	http://www.invesco.com/us
Address	Invesco 11 Greenway Plaza, Ste. 2500 Houston TX 77046 United States
Phone Number	800-659-1005

PERFORMANCE

(chart: y-axis from 0.0% to -20.0%; x-axis 11/4/18, 2/15/19, 6/17/19, 9/30/19)

Ratings History
Date	Overall Rating	Risk Rating	Reward Rating
Q3-19	D+	C-	D+
Q4-18	U		
Q4-17			
Q4-16			
Q4-15			

Asset & Performance History
Date	NAV	1-Year Total Return
2018	22.37	
2017		
2016		
2015		
2014		
2013		

Total Assets: $240,959,958
Asset Allocation
Asset	%
Cash	0%
Stocks	100%
US Stocks	4%
Bonds	0%
US Bonds	0%
Other	0%

Services Offered:

Investment Strategy: The investment seeks to track the investment results (before fees and expenses) of the Invesco Strategic Developed ex-US Index (the "underlying index"). The fund generally will invest at least 80% of its total assets in securities that comprise the underlying index and American depositary receipts ("ADRs") and global depositary receipts ("GDRs") that are based on securities in the underlying index. The underlying index is designed to measure the performance of equity securities issued by higher quality, large-business-sized companies located in countries designated as developed market countries (excluding the U.S.). The fund is non-diversified. **Top Holdings:** Samsung Electronics Co Ltd BP PLC Nestle SA Royal Dutch Shell PLC Class A Total SA

ProShares Short Dow30   D   SELL

Ticker	Traded On	NAV	Total Assets ($)	Dividend Yield (TTM)	Turnover Ratio	Expense Ratio
DOG	NYSE Arca	52.48	$240,031,170	1.53	0	0.95

Ratings
Reward	D-
Risk	D
Recent Upgrade/Downgrade	

Fund Information
Fund Type	Exchange Traded Funds
Category	Trading Tools
Sub-Category	Trading--Inverse Equity
Prospectus Objective	Growth
Inception Date	Jun-06
Open to New Investments	Y

Prices
Price (as of 9/30/2019)	52.46
52-Week High	65.91
52-Week Low	51.97

Total Returns (%)
3-Month	6-Month	1-Year	3-Year	5-Year
-0.98	-2.54	-2.14	-35.38	-46.44

3-Year Standard Deviation	12.17
Effective Duration	

Valuation
Premium/Discount (1-Year Average)	0.02

Company Information
Provider	ProShares
Manager/Tenure	Michael Neches (6), Devin Sullivan (1)
Website	http://www.proshares.com
Address	ProShares 7501 Wisconsin Avenue, Suite 1000 Bethesda MD 20814 United States
Phone Number	866-776-5125

PERFORMANCE

(chart: y-axis from 10.0% to -30.0%; x-axis 12/31/17, 4/10/18, 7/21/18, 11/3/18, 2/14/19, 6/17/19, 9/30/19)

Ratings History
Date	Overall Rating	Risk Rating	Reward Rating
Q3-19	D	D	D-
Q4-18	D	D-	D
Q4-17	D-	D-	D-
Q4-16	D	D	D
Q4-15	D	D	D

Asset & Performance History
Date	NAV	1-Year Total Return
2018	61.33	3.48
2017	59.8	-21.49
2016	76.2	-15.67
2015	90.36	-3.04
2014	93.2	-10.72
2013	104.4	-24.19

Total Assets: $240,031,170
Asset Allocation
Asset	%
Cash	146%
Stocks	-58%
US Stocks	-58%
Bonds	12%
US Bonds	12%
Other	0%

Services Offered:

Investment Strategy: The investment seeks daily investment results, before fees and expenses, that correspond to the inverse (-1x) of the daily performance of the Dow Jones Industrial Average®. The fund invests in financial instruments that ProShare Advisors believes, in combination, should produce daily returns consistent with the fund's investment objective. The index is a price-weighted index and includes 30 large-cap, "blue-chip" U.S. stocks, excluding utility and transportation companies. The fund is non-diversified. **Top Holdings:** Dj Industrial Average Swap Goldman Sachs International Dj Industrial Average Swap Credit Suisse International Dj Industrial Average Swap Societe Generale Dj Industrial Average Index Swap Bnp Paribas Dj Industrial Average Swap Bank Of America Na

Pacer US Cash Cows 100 ETF
C- HOLD

Ticker	Traded On	NAV	Total Assets ($)	Dividend Yield (TTM)	Turnover Ratio	Expense Ratio
COWZ	BATS	28.83	$239,294,524	1.91	122	0.49

Ratings
Reward   C-
Risk   C-
Recent Upgrade/Downgrade

Fund Information
Fund Type	Exchange Traded Funds
Category	US Equity Large Cap Blend
Sub-Category	Large Value
Prospectus Objective	Growth & Inc
Inception Date	Dec-16
Open to New Investments	Y

Prices
Price (as of 9/30/2019)	28.79
52-Week High	30.88
52-Week Low	24.24

Total Returns (%)
3-Month	6-Month	1-Year	3-Year	5-Year
-0.22	-0.85	-4.56		

3-Year Standard Deviation
Effective Duration

Valuation
Premium/Discount (1-Year Average)   0.03

Company Information
Provider	Pacer
Manager/Tenure	Bruce Kavanaugh (2), Michael Mack (2)
Website	http://www.paceretfs.com
Address	Pacer 16 Industrial Blvd, Suite 201 Paoli PA 19301 United States
Phone Number	

PERFORMANCE

Ratings History

Date	Overall Rating	Risk Rating	Reward Rating
Q3-19	C-	C-	C-
Q4-18	C-	C-	C-
Q4-17	D-	B+	D+
Q4-16			
Q4-15			

Asset & Performance History

Date	NAV	1-Year Total Return
2018	25.77	-9.3
2017	28.85	19.54
2016	24.64	
2015		
2014		
2013		

Total Assets: $239,294,524
Asset Allocation
Asset	%
Cash	0%
Stocks	100%
US Stocks	100%
Bonds	0%
US Bonds	0%
Other	0%

Services Offered:

Investment Strategy: The investment seeks to track the total return performance, before fees and expenses, of the Pacer US Cash Cows 100 Index (the "index"). Under normal circumstances, at least 80% of the fund's total assets (exclusive of collateral held from securities lending) will be invested in the component securities of the index. The index uses an objective, rules-based methodology to provide exposure to large and mid-capitalization U.S. companies with high free cash flow yields. Companies with high free cash flow yields are commonly referred to as "cash cows". The fund is non-diversified. **Top Holdings:** Micron Technology Inc Allergan PLC Amgen Inc Starbucks Corp Applied Materials Inc

---

Columbia Emerging Markets Consumer ETF
D SELL

Ticker	Traded On	NAV	Total Assets ($)	Dividend Yield (TTM)	Turnover Ratio	Expense Ratio
ECON	NYSE Arca	22.04	$239,097,628	0.91	61	0.59

Ratings
Reward   D
Risk   D+
Recent Upgrade/Downgrade   Down

Fund Information
Fund Type	Exchange Traded Funds
Category	Global Emerg Mkts Equity
Sub-Category	Diversified Emerging Mkts
Prospectus Objective	Unaligned
Inception Date	Sep-10
Open to New Investments	Y

Prices
Price (as of 9/30/2019)	21.94
52-Week High	23.34
52-Week Low	19.79

Total Returns (%)
3-Month	6-Month	1-Year	3-Year	5-Year
-4.21	-3.67	-0.32	-8.71	-11.24

3-Year Standard Deviation   14.19
Effective Duration

Valuation
Premium/Discount (1-Year Average)   -0.26

Company Information
Provider	Columbia
Manager/Tenure	Christopher Lo (3)
Website	http://www.columbiathreadneedleus.com
Address	Liberty Financial Funds P.O. Box 8081 Boston MA 02266-8081 United States
Phone Number	800-345-6611

PERFORMANCE

Ratings History

Date	Overall Rating	Risk Rating	Reward Rating
Q3-19	D	D+	D
Q4-18	D	D	D
Q4-17	C	C	C
Q4-16	D+	D+	D+
Q4-15	C-	C-	C-

Asset & Performance History

Date	NAV	1-Year Total Return
2018	20.46	-26.72
2017	28.2	26.86
2016	22.31	4.95
2015	21.42	-15.12
2014	25.51	-2.84
2013	26.57	1.66

Total Assets: $239,097,628
Asset Allocation
Asset	%
Cash	0%
Stocks	100%
US Stocks	0%
Bonds	0%
US Bonds	0%
Other	0%

Services Offered:

Investment Strategy: The investment seeks investment results that correspond (before fees and expenses) to the price and yield performance of the Dow Jones Emerging Markets Consumer Titans TM Index. The fund will invest at least 80% of its net assets in securities of Emerging Markets Consumer companies which comprise the index and the advisor generally expects to be substantially invested at such times with at least 95% of its net assets invested in these securities. It is non-diversified. **Top Holdings:** Alibaba Group Holding Ltd ADR Tencent Holdings Ltd Hindustan Unilever Ltd China Mobile Ltd Chunghwa Telecom Co Ltd

Amplify Online Retail ETF   C   HOLD

Ticker	Traded On	NAV	Total Assets ($)	Dividend Yield (TTM)	Turnover Ratio	Expense Ratio
IBUY	NAS CM	46.80	$238,657,259	0	17	0.65

Ratings
Reward   C+
Risk   D+
Recent Upgrade/Downgrade

Fund Information
Fund Type   Exchange Traded Funds
Category   Consumer Goods & Svcs
Sub-Category   Consumer Cyclical
Prospectus Objective   Growth & Inc
Inception Date   Apr-16
Open to New Investments   Y

Prices
Price (as of 9/30/2019)   46.76
52-Week High   51.93
52-Week Low   37.41

Total Returns (%)

3-Month	6-Month	1-Year	3-Year	5-Year
-5.50	-5.27	-9.29	69.85	

3-Year Standard Deviation   20.87
Effective Duration

Valuation
Premium/Discount (1-Year Average)   -0.09

Company Information
Provider   Amplifyetfs
Manager/Tenure   Anand Desai (3), Dustin Lewellyn (3), Ernesto Tong (3)
Website   http://www.amplifyetfs.com
Address   3250 Lacey Road, Suite 130 Downers Grove Downers Grove IL 60515 United States
Phone Number   630-487-2530

PERFORMANCE

Ratings History

Date	Overall Rating	Risk Rating	Reward Rating
Q3-19	C	D+	C+
Q4-18	C	C-	C+
Q4-17	D+	B+	C
Q4-16	U		
Q4-15			

Asset & Performance History

Date	NAV	1-Year Total Return
2018	40.19	-1.56
2017	40.83	50.16
2016	27.19	
2015		
2014		
2013		

Total Assets: $238,657,259

Asset Allocation

Asset	%
Cash	4%
Stocks	96%
US Stocks	74%
Bonds	0%
US Bonds	0%
Other	0%

Services Offered:

Investment Strategy: The investment seeks investment results that generally correspond (before fees and expenses) to the price and yield of the EQM Online Retail Index. The fund will invest at least 80% of its total assets in global equity securities that comprise the index, which will primarily include common stocks and/or depositary receipts, such as ADRs and GDRs. The index seeks to measure the performance of global equity securities of publicly traded companies with significant revenue from the online retail business. The index methodology is designed to result in a portfolio that has the potential for capital appreciation. The fund is non-diversified. **Top Holdings:** Stamps.com Inc Carvana Co Class A Shutterfly Inc A Overstock.com Inc Copart Inc

---

WisdomTree Interest Rate Hedged High Yield Bond Fund   C   HOLD

Ticker	Traded On	NAV	Total Assets ($)	Dividend Yield (TTM)	Turnover Ratio	Expense Ratio
HYZD	NAS CM	23.15	$238,397,546	5.57	60	0.43

Ratings
Reward   C
Risk   C-
Recent Upgrade/Downgrade

Fund Information
Fund Type   Exchange Traded Funds
Category   Fixed Income Misc
Sub-Category   Nontraditional Bond
Prospectus Objective   Corp Bond-High Yld
Inception Date   Dec-13
Open to New Investments   Y

Prices
Price (as of 9/30/2019)   23.01
52-Week High   24.26
52-Week Low   22.16

Total Returns (%)

3-Month	6-Month	1-Year	3-Year	5-Year
0.38	1.04	1.08	15.39	20.99

3-Year Standard Deviation   3.57
Effective Duration   -0.09

Valuation
Premium/Discount (1-Year Average)   -0.34

Company Information
Provider   WisdomTree
Manager/Tenure   Paul L. Benson (3), Stephanie Shu (3)
Website   http://www.wisdomtree.com
Address   WisdomTree 245 Park Avenue, 35th floor New York NY 10167 United States
Phone Number   866-909-9473

PERFORMANCE

Ratings History

Date	Overall Rating	Risk Rating	Reward Rating
Q3-19	C	C-	C
Q4-18	C	C+	C-
Q4-17	C+	B	C+
Q4-16	C-	D+	C
Q4-15	D	C-	D

Asset & Performance History

Date	NAV	1-Year Total Return
2018	22.63	-0.72
2017	24.02	6.44
2016	23.72	13.58
2015	21.91	-5.32
2014	24.11	-0.47
2013	25.1	

Total Assets: $238,397,546

Asset Allocation

Asset	%
Cash	73%
Stocks	0%
US Stocks	0%
Bonds	27%
US Bonds	14%
Other	0%

Services Offered:

Investment Strategy: The investment seeks to track the price and yield performance of the ICE BofA Merrill Lynch 0-5 Year U.S. High Yield Constrained, Zero Duration Index. The index is designed to provide long exposure to the ICE BofA Merrill Lynch 0-5 Year U.S. High Yield Constrained Index while seeking to manage interest rate risk through the use of short positions in U.S. Treasury securities. Normally, at least 80% of the fund's total assets will be invested in the component securities of the index and investments that have economic characteristics that are substantially identical to the economic characteristics of such component securities. It is non-diversified. **Top Holdings:** Us 2yr Note (Cbt) Dec19 Xcbt 20191231 Us 5yr Note (Cbt) Dec19 Xcbt 20191231 Sprint Corporation 7.88% Community Health Systems Incorporated 6.25% Tenet Healthcare Corporation 8.13%

iShares U.S. Broker-Dealers & Securities Exchanges ETF   B-   BUY

Ticker	Traded On	NAV	Total Assets ($)	Dividend Yield (TTM)	Turnover Ratio	Expense Ratio
IAI	NYSE Arca	64.32	$237,990,584	1.63	27	0.42

Ratings
Reward   B
Risk   C
Recent Upgrade/Downgrade   Up

Fund Information
Fund Type   Exchange Traded Funds
Category   Financials Sector Equity
Sub-Category   Financial
Prospectus Objective   Financial
Inception Date   May-06
Open to New Investments   Y

Prices
Price (as of 9/30/2019)   64.31
52-Week High   66.75
52-Week Low   52.67

Total Returns (%)

3-Month	6-Month	1-Year	3-Year	5-Year
1.22	7.61	4.94	62.54	79.31

3-Year Standard Deviation   16.39
Effective Duration

Valuation
Premium/Discount (1-Year Average)   -0.01

Company Information
Provider   iShares
Manager/Tenure   Greg Savage (11), Jennifer Hsui (7),
                    Alan Mason (3), 2 others
Website   http://www.ishares.com
Address   iShares 400 Howard Street San
                    Francisco CA 94105 United States
Phone Number   800-474-2737

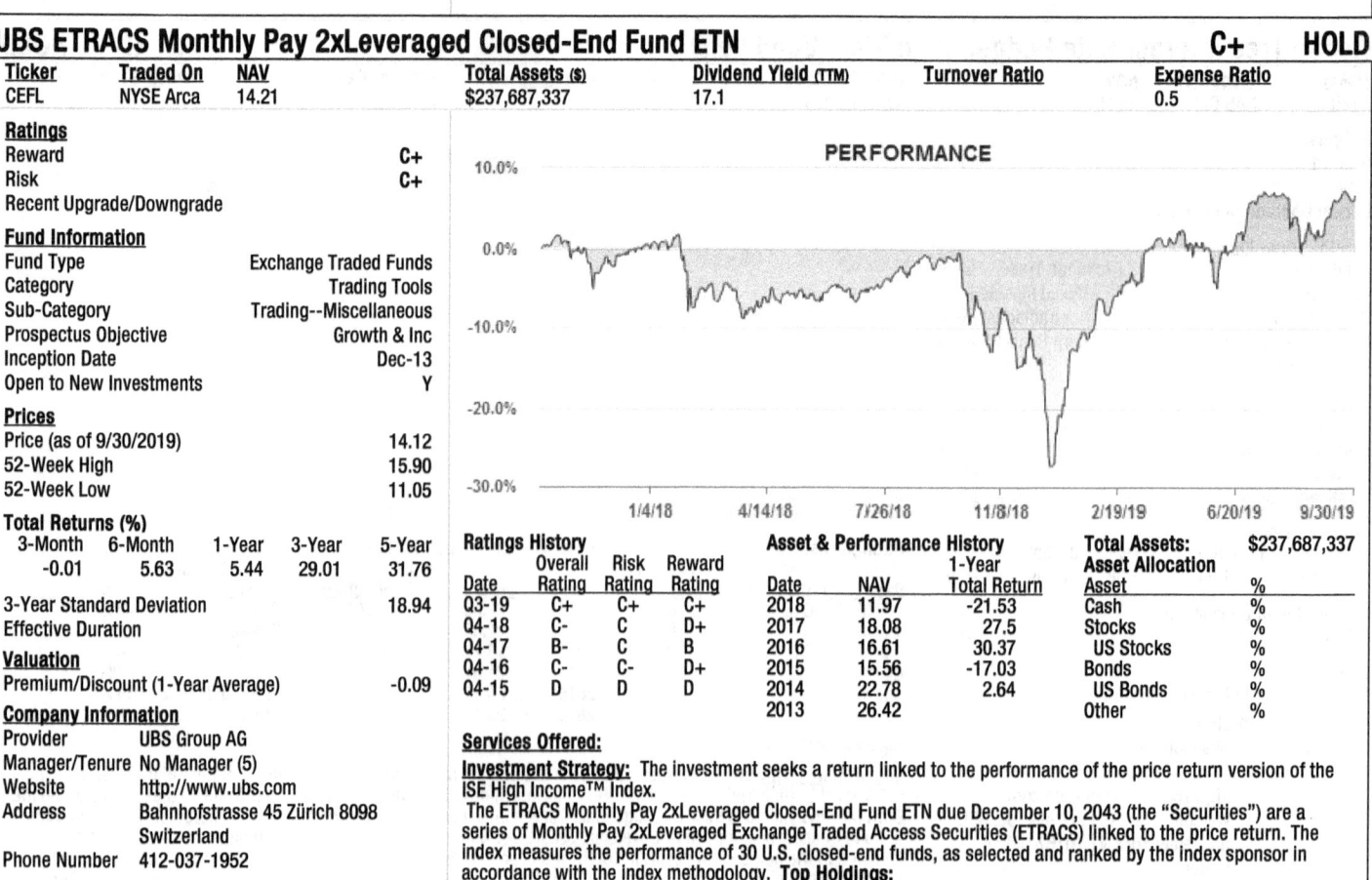

Ratings History

Date	Overall Rating	Risk Rating	Reward Rating
Q3-19	B-	C	B
Q4-18	B-	C	B
Q4-17	A-	B	A
Q4-16	B-	C	B
Q4-15	B	B+	B

Asset & Performance History

Date	NAV	1-Year Total Return
2018	56.08	-9.29
2017	62.72	28.78
2016	49.47	21.73
2015	41.38	-1.59
2014	42.6	11.6
2013	38.63	65.61

Total Assets: $237,990,584
Asset Allocation

Asset	%
Cash	0%
Stocks	100%
US Stocks	100%
Bonds	0%
US Bonds	0%
Other	0%

Services Offered:

Investment Strategy: The investment seeks to track the investment results of the Dow Jones U.S. Select Investment Services Index composed of U.S. equities in the investment services sector. The fund generally invests at least 90% of its assets in securities of the underlying index and in depositary receipts representing securities of the underlying index. The underlying index measures the performance of the investment services sector of the U.S. equity market. The fund may invest the remainder of its assets in certain futures, options and swap contracts, cash and cash equivalents. It is non-diversified. **Top Holdings:** CME Group Inc Class A   Goldman Sachs Group Inc   Morgan Stanley   MarketAxess Holdings Inc   Cboe Global Markets Inc

---

UBS ETRACS Monthly Pay 2xLeveraged Closed-End Fund ETN   C+   HOLD

Ticker	Traded On	NAV	Total Assets ($)	Dividend Yield (TTM)	Turnover Ratio	Expense Ratio
CEFL	NYSE Arca	14.21	$237,687,337	17.1		0.5

Ratings
Reward   C+
Risk   C+
Recent Upgrade/Downgrade

Fund Information
Fund Type   Exchange Traded Funds
Category   Trading Tools
Sub-Category   Trading--Miscellaneous
Prospectus Objective   Growth & Inc
Inception Date   Dec-13
Open to New Investments   Y

Prices
Price (as of 9/30/2019)   14.12
52-Week High   15.90
52-Week Low   11.05

Total Returns (%)

3-Month	6-Month	1-Year	3-Year	5-Year
-0.01	5.63	5.44	29.01	31.76

3-Year Standard Deviation   18.94
Effective Duration

Valuation
Premium/Discount (1-Year Average)   -0.09

Company Information
Provider   UBS Group AG
Manager/Tenure   No Manager (5)
Website   http://www.ubs.com
Address   Bahnhofstrasse 45 Zürich 8098
                    Switzerland
Phone Number   412-037-1952

Ratings History

Date	Overall Rating	Risk Rating	Reward Rating
Q3-19	C+	C+	C+
Q4-18	C-	C	D+
Q4-17	B-	C	B
Q4-16	C-	C-	D+
Q4-15	D	D	D

Asset & Performance History

Date	NAV	1-Year Total Return
2018	11.97	-21.53
2017	18.08	27.5
2016	16.61	30.37
2015	15.56	-17.03
2014	22.78	2.64
2013	26.42	

Total Assets: $237,687,337
Asset Allocation

Asset	%
Cash	%
Stocks	%
US Stocks	%
Bonds	%
US Bonds	%
Other	%

Services Offered:

Investment Strategy: The investment seeks a return linked to the performance of the price return version of the ISE High Income™ Index.
The ETRACS Monthly Pay 2xLeveraged Closed-End Fund ETN due December 10, 2043 (the "Securities") are a series of Monthly Pay 2xLeveraged Exchange Traded Access Securities (ETRACS) linked to the price return. The index measures the performance of 30 U.S. closed-end funds, as selected and ranked by the index sponsor in accordance with the index methodology. **Top Holdings:**

Aberdeen Standard Physical Palladium Shares ETF   B-   BUY

Ticker	Traded On	NAV	Total Assets ($)	Dividend Yield (TTM)	Turnover Ratio	Expense Ratio
PALL	NYSE Arca	157.88	$236,820,588	0		0.6

Ratings
Reward	B+
Risk	C-
Recent Upgrade/Downgrade	Up

Fund Information
Fund Type	Exchange Traded Funds
Category	Commodities Specified
Sub-Category	Commodities Precious Metals
Prospectus Objective	Prec Metals
Inception Date	Jan-10
Open to New Investments	Y

Prices
Price (as of 9/30/2019)	159.19
52-Week High	159.25
52-Week Low	99.98

Total Returns (%)
3-Month	6-Month	1-Year	3-Year	5-Year
7.69	20.06	58.02	127.70	110.68

3-Year Standard Deviation	26.26
Effective Duration	

Valuation
Premium/Discount (1-Year Average)	-0.62

Company Information
Provider	Aberdeen Standard Investments
Manager/Tenure	Management Team (9)
Website	http://www.aberdeenstandardetfs.us
Address	Aberdeen Standard Investments 405 Lexington Avenue New York NY 10174 United States
Phone Number	212-918-4954

PERFORMANCE

Ratings History
Date	Overall Rating	Risk Rating	Reward Rating
Q3-19	B-	C-	B+
Q4-18	B-	C-	B+
Q4-17	B	C	A
Q4-16	D+	C-	D+
Q4-15	D	D	D

Asset & Performance History
Date	NAV	1-Year Total Return
2018	119.66	18.88
2017	100.65	55.27
2016	64.82	22.84
2015	52.77	-31.86
2014	77.44	11.56
2013	69.42	1.1

Total Assets: $236,820,588

Asset Allocation
Asset	%
Cash	0%
Stocks	0%
US Stocks	0%
Bonds	0%
US Bonds	0%
Other	100%

Services Offered:

Investment Strategy: The investment seeks to reflect the performance of the price of physical palladium, less the expenses of the Trust's operations.
The fund is designed for investors who want a cost-effective and convenient way to invest in palladium with minimal credit risk. **Top Holdings:** Physical Palladium Bullion Physical Gold Bullion

---

Amplify High Income ETF   C   HOLD

Ticker	Traded On	NAV	Total Assets ($)	Dividend Yield (TTM)	Turnover Ratio	Expense Ratio
YYY	NYSE Arca	17.79	$236,557,139	8.77	40	2.28

Ratings
Reward	C+
Risk	C-
Recent Upgrade/Downgrade	

Fund Information
Fund Type	Exchange Traded Funds
Category	Moderate Allocation
Sub-Category	Tactical Allocation
Prospectus Objective	Income
Inception Date	Jun-12
Open to New Investments	Y

Prices
Price (as of 9/30/2019)	17.80
52-Week High	18.43
52-Week Low	15.44

Total Returns (%)
3-Month	6-Month	1-Year	3-Year	5-Year
1.19	4.59	5.92	19.52	22.89

3-Year Standard Deviation	9.49
Effective Duration	4.98

Valuation
Premium/Discount (1-Year Average)	0.06

Company Information
Provider	YieldShares
Manager/Tenure	Denise M. Krisko (4), Austin Wen (0)
Website	http://www.yieldshares.com
Address	YieldShares 10900 Hefner Pointe Drive, Suite 207 Oklahoma OK 73120 United States
Phone Number	

PERFORMANCE

Ratings History
Date	Overall Rating	Risk Rating	Reward Rating
Q3-19	C	C-	C+
Q4-18	D+	C-	D+
Q4-17	C+	C+	C+
Q4-16	C-	C-	C-
Q4-15	D+	C-	D+

Asset & Performance History
Date	NAV	1-Year Total Return
2018	16.09	-9.96
2017	19.49	14.02
2016	18.55	15.42
2015	17.84	-8.3
2014	21.44	1.07
2013	23.16	8.42

Total Assets: $236,557,139

Asset Allocation
Asset	%
Cash	-4%
Stocks	25%
US Stocks	20%
Bonds	79%
US Bonds	50%
Other	-9%

Services Offered:

Investment Strategy: The investment seeks to provide investment results that, before fees and expenses, correspond generally to the price and yield performance of the ISE High Income™ Index (the "Index"). The fund will normally invest at least 80% of its total assets in securities of the index. Because the index is comprised of securities issued by other investment companies, the fund operates in a manner that is commonly referred to as a "fund of funds," meaning that it invests its assets in shares of funds included in the index. The index seeks to measure the performance of the top 30 U.S. exchange-listed closed-end funds. **Top Holdings:** Nuveen Pref & Income Securities Fund   First Trust Inter Dur Pref & Income Fund   Brookfield Real Assets Income Fund Inc.   DoubleLine Income Solutions   Western Asset High Inc Fund II

iShares Morningstar Small-Cap ETF   C-   HOLD

Ticker	Traded On	NAV	Total Assets ($)	Dividend Yield (TTM)	Turnover Ratio	Expense Ratio
JKJ	NYSE Arca	175.14	$236,434,604	1.3	67	0.25

Ratings

Reward   C
Risk   D+
Recent Upgrade/Downgrade

Fund Information

Fund Type	Exchange Traded Funds
Category	US Equity Small Cap
Sub-Category	Small Blend
Prospectus Objective	Small Company
Inception Date	Jun-04
Open to New Investments	Y

Prices

Price (as of 9/30/2019)	175.07
52-Week High	179.26
52-Week Low	139.81

Total Returns (%)

3-Month	6-Month	1-Year	3-Year	5-Year
0.21	2.88	-0.25	26.17	47.95

3-Year Standard Deviation	16.16
Effective Duration	

Valuation

Premium/Discount (1-Year Average)	0.09

Company Information

Provider	iShares
Manager/Tenure	Greg Savage (11), Jennifer Hsui (7), Alan Mason (3), 2 others
Website	http://www.ishares.com
Address	iShares 400 Howard Street San Francisco CA 94105 United States
Phone Number	800-474-2737

PERFORMANCE

Ratings History

Date	Overall Rating	Risk Rating	Reward Rating
Q3-19	C-	D+	C
Q4-18	C-	D+	C-
Q4-17	B	B	B
Q4-16	C-	D+	C-
Q4-15	C	D+	C

Asset & Performance History

Date	NAV	1-Year Total Return
2018	148.04	-13.8
2017	174.16	13.01
2016	156.15	23.42
2015	128.72	-5.58
2014	138.15	8.31
2013	129.09	36.06

Total Assets: $236,434,604

Asset Allocation

Asset	%
Cash	0%
Stocks	100%
US Stocks	99%
Bonds	0%
US Bonds	0%
Other	0%

Services Offered:

Investment Strategy: The investment seeks to track the investment results of the Morningstar® US Small Core IndexSM composed of small-capitalization U.S. equities. The fund generally invests at least 90% of its assets in securities of the underlying index and in depositary receipts representing securities of the underlying index. The underlying index measures the performance of stocks issued by small-capitalization companies that have exhibited average "growth" and "value" characteristics as determined by Morningstar, Inc.'s ("Morningstar" or the "index provider") proprietary index methodology. **Top Holdings:** Genesee & Wyoming Inc Class A Casey's General Stores Inc CACI International Inc Class A Curtiss-Wright Corp Horizon Therapeutics PLC

VanEck Vectors Short High-Yield Municipal Index ETF   C   HOLD

Ticker	Traded On	NAV	Total Assets ($)	Dividend Yield (TTM)	Turnover Ratio	Expense Ratio
SHYD	BATS	25.14	$236,307,189	3.19	22	0.35

Ratings

Reward   C+
Risk   C-
Recent Upgrade/Downgrade

Fund Information

Fund Type	Exchange Traded Funds
Category	US Muni Fixed Inc
Sub-Category	High Yield Muni
Prospectus Objective	Muni Bond - Natl
Inception Date	Jan-14
Open to New Investments	Y

Prices

Price (as of 9/30/2019)	25.18
52-Week High	25.37
52-Week Low	23.89

Total Returns (%)

3-Month	6-Month	1-Year	3-Year	5-Year
1.37	3.47	6.68	9.44	15.62

3-Year Standard Deviation	3.16
Effective Duration	4.33

Valuation

Premium/Discount (1-Year Average)	0.08

Company Information

Provider	VanEck
Manager/Tenure	James T. Colby (5)
Website	http://www.vaneck.com
Address	Van Eck Associates Corporation 666 Third Avenue New York NY 10017 United States
Phone Number	800-826-1115

PERFORMANCE

Ratings History

Date	Overall Rating	Risk Rating	Reward Rating
Q3-19	C	C-	C+
Q4-18	C-	C-	C
Q4-17	C+	B	C
Q4-16	C-	C-	C-
Q4-15	D+	C-	D+

Asset & Performance History

Date	NAV	1-Year Total Return
2018	24.18	2.16
2017	24.36	5.52
2016	23.81	-1.86
2015	24.96	1.47
2014	25.39	
2013		

Total Assets: $236,307,189

Asset Allocation

Asset	%
Cash	0%
Stocks	0%
US Stocks	0%
Bonds	100%
US Bonds	95%
Other	0%

Services Offered:

Investment Strategy: The investment seeks to replicate as closely as possible, before fees and expenses, the price and yield performance of the Bloomberg Barclays Municipal High Yield Short Duration Index. The fund normally invests at least 80% of its total assets in securities that comprise the benchmark index. The index is composed of publicly traded municipal bonds that cover the U.S. dollar denominated high yield short-term tax-exempt bond market. **Top Holdings:** FLORIDA DEV FIN CORP SURFACE TRANSN FAC REV 6.5% BUCKEYE OHIO TOB SETTLEMENT FING AUTH 5.12% FLORIDA DEV FIN CORP SURFACE TRANSN FAC REV 6.25% BUCKEYE OHIO TOB SETTLEMENT FING AUTH 5.88% FLORIDA DEV FIN CORP SURFACE TRANSN FAC REV 6.37%

WisdomTree International High Dividend Fund   C-   HOLD

Ticker	Traded On	NAV	Total Assets ($)	Dividend Yield (TTM)	Turnover Ratio	Expense Ratio
DTH	NYSE Arca	39.11	$234,630,640	4.5	24	0.58

Ratings
Reward   C-
Risk   C-
Recent Upgrade/Downgrade

Fund Information
Fund Type   Exchange Traded Funds
Category   Global Equity Large Cap
Sub-Category   Foreign Large Value
Prospectus Objective   Foreign Stock
Inception Date   Jun-06
Open to New Investments   Y

Prices
Price (as of 9/30/2019)   39.02
52-Week High   41.71
52-Week Low   36.10

Total Returns (%)
3-Month	6-Month	1-Year	3-Year	5-Year
-2.79	-1.18	-2.24	16.31	6.67

3-Year Standard Deviation   11.31
Effective Duration

Valuation
Premium/Discount (1-Year Average)   -0.21

Company Information
Provider   WisdomTree
Manager/Tenure   Richard A. Brown (11), Thomas J. Durante (11), Karen Q. Wong (11)
Website   http://www.wisdomtree.com
Address   WisdomTree 245 Park Avenue, 35th floor New York NY 10167 United States
Phone Number   866-909-9473

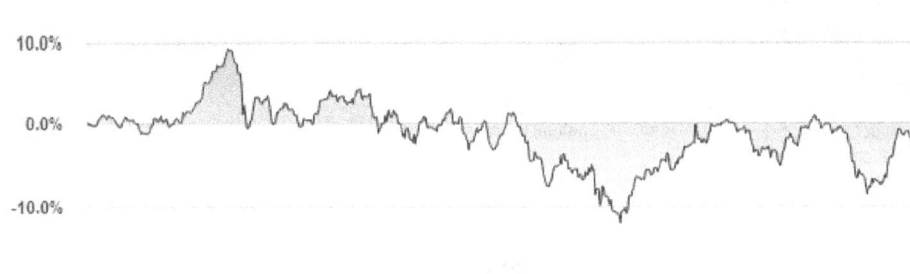

PERFORMANCE

Ratings History
Date	Overall Rating	Risk Rating	Reward Rating
Q3-19	C-	C-	C-
Q4-18	D+	C-	D+
Q4-17	C+	C	C+
Q4-16	D+	C-	D+
Q4-15	C	C-	C

Asset & Performance History
Date	NAV	1-Year Total Return
2018	37.25	-12.56
2017	44.42	20.31
2016	38.38	5.11
2015	38.07	-6.99
2014	42.57	-4.46
2013	47.01	23.15

Total Assets: $234,630,640
Asset Allocation
Asset	%
Cash	0%
Stocks	100%
US Stocks	0%
Bonds	0%
US Bonds	0%
Other	0%

Services Offered:

Investment Strategy: The investment seeks to track the price and yield performance, before fees and expenses, of the WisdomTree International High Dividend Index. Under normal circumstances, at least 95% of the fund's total assets (exclusive of collateral held from securities lending) will be invested in component securities of the index and investments that have economic characteristics that are substantially identical to the economic characteristics of such component securities. The index is a fundamentally weighted index that is comprised of companies with high dividend yields selected from the WisdomTree International Equity Index. The fund is non-diversified. **Top Holdings:** China Mobile Ltd BP PLC Royal Dutch Shell PLC Class A Total SA British American Tobacco PLC

iShares MSCI Italy Capped ETF   C   HOLD

Ticker	Traded On	NAV	Total Assets ($)	Dividend Yield (TTM)	Turnover Ratio	Expense Ratio
EWI	NYSE Arca	27.54	$233,395,689	4.48	10	0.47

Ratings
Reward   C
Risk   C+
Recent Upgrade/Downgrade

Fund Information
Fund Type   Exchange Traded Funds
Category   Europe Equity Large Cap
Sub-Category   Miscellaneous Region
Prospectus Objective   Europe Stock
Inception Date   Mar-96
Open to New Investments   Y

Prices
Price (as of 9/30/2019)   27.57
52-Week High   28.59
52-Week Low   23.28

Total Returns (%)
3-Month	6-Month	1-Year	3-Year	5-Year
0.36	1.92	4.84	39.13	4.22

3-Year Standard Deviation   19.52
Effective Duration

Valuation
Premium/Discount (1-Year Average)   -0.07

Company Information
Provider   iShares
Manager/Tenure   Diane Hsiung (11), Greg Savage (11), Jennifer Hsui (6), 3 others
Website   http://www.ishares.com
Address   iShares 400 Howard Street San Francisco CA 94105 United States
Phone Number   800-474-2737

PERFORMANCE

Ratings History
Date	Overall Rating	Risk Rating	Reward Rating
Q3-19	C	C+	C
Q4-18	D+	D	D+
Q4-17	C+	C	B
Q4-16	D	D	D
Q4-15	C	C	C

Asset & Performance History
Date	NAV	1-Year Total Return
2018	24.15	-17.51
2017	30.49	28.46
2016	24.3	-9.4
2015	27.84	4
2014	27.32	-9.83
2013	30.94	20.93

Total Assets: $233,395,689
Asset Allocation
Asset	%
Cash	0%
Stocks	100%
US Stocks	4%
Bonds	0%
US Bonds	0%
Other	0%

Services Offered: CashInvestment Plan

Investment Strategy: The investment seeks to track the investment results of the MSCI Italy 25/50 Index. The fund will at all times invest at least 80% of its assets in the securities of its underlying index and in depositary receipts representing securities in its underlying index. The underlying index is a free float-adjusted market capitalization-weighted index with a capping methodology applied to issuer weights so that no single issuer of a component exceeds 25% of the underlying index weight, and all issuers with a weight above 5% do not cumulatively exceed 50% of the underlying index weight. The fund is non-diversified. **Top Holdings:** Enel SpA Eni SpA Intesa Sanpaolo UniCredit SpA Assicurazioni Generali

Franklin Liberty Investment Grade Corporate ETF   C   HOLD

Ticker	Traded On	NAV	Total Assets ($)	Dividend Yield (TTM)	Turnover Ratio	Expense Ratio
FLCO	NYSE Arca	25.57	$232,717,000	2.9	22	0.35

Ratings
Reward   C
Risk   D+
Recent Upgrade/Downgrade   Up

Fund Information
Fund Type   Exchange Traded Funds
Category   US Fixed Income
Sub-Category   Corporate Bond
Prospectus Objective   Corp Bond - Gen
Inception Date   Oct-16
Open to New Investments   Y

Prices
Price (as of 9/30/2019)   25.61
52-Week High   25.90
52-Week Low   22.86

Total Returns (%)

3-Month	6-Month	1-Year	3-Year	5-Year
2.51	7.75	12.18	16.56	

3-Year Standard Deviation
Effective Duration   7.83

Valuation
Premium/Discount (1-Year Average)   0.07

Company Information
Provider   Franklin Templeton Investments
Manager/Tenure   Marc Kremer (2), Shawn Lyons (2)
Website   http://www.franklintempleton.com
Address   Franklin Templeton Investments One
                    Franklin Parkway, Building 970, 1st
                    Floor San Mateo CA 94403 United
                    States
Phone Number   650-312-2000

PERFORMANCE

Ratings History

Date	Overall Rating	Risk Rating	Reward Rating
Q3-19	C	D+	C
Q4-18	D	D	D+
Q4-17	D	B	D+
Q4-16	U		
Q4-15			

Asset & Performance History

Date	NAV	1-Year Total Return
2018	23.11	-3.06
2017	24.76	6.11
2016	24.13	
2015		
2014		
2013		

Total Assets: $232,717,000
Asset Allocation

Asset	%
Cash	2%
Stocks	0%
US Stocks	0%
Bonds	96%
US Bonds	70%
Other	0%

Services Offered:

Investment Strategy: The investment seeks a high level of current income as is consistent with prudent investing, while seeking preservation of capital. Under normal market conditions, the fund invests at least 80% of its net assets in investment grade corporate debt securities and investments. It invests primarily in U.S. dollar denominated corporate debt securities issued by U.S. and foreign companies. The fund may invest in debt securities of any maturity or duration. The fund's focus on the credit quality of its portfolio is intended to reduce credit risk and help to preserve the fund's capital. **Top Holdings:** Us 10yr Note (Cbt)sep19 Xcbt 20190919 U.S. Treasury Bond Dec19 Bank of America Corporation 4.18% Morgan Stanley 3.59% Credit Suisse Group Funding (Guernsey) Limited 3.8%

VelocityShares 3x Inverse Natural Gas ETN Linked to the S&P GSCI® Natural Gas Index ER   C+   HOLD

Ticker	Traded On	NAV	Total Assets ($)	Dividend Yield (TTM)	Turnover Ratio	Expense Ratio
DGAZ	NYSE Arca	135.49	$231,603,205	0		1.65

Ratings
Reward   B
Risk   D
Recent Upgrade/Downgrade   Down

Fund Information
Fund Type   Exchange Traded Funds
Category   Trading Tools
Sub-Category   Trading--Inverse Commodities
Prospectus Objective   Natl Res
Inception Date   Feb-12
Open to New Investments   Y

Prices
Price (as of 9/30/2019)   136.05
52-Week High   337.40
52-Week Low   47.88

Total Returns (%)

3-Month	6-Month	1-Year	3-Year	5-Year
-19.85	31.47	-60.35	340.60	598.38

3-Year Standard Deviation   121.65
Effective Duration

Valuation
Premium/Discount (1-Year Average)   -0.85

Company Information
Provider   Credit Suisse AG
Manager/Tenure   Management Team (7)
Website
Address   Kilmore House Park Lane Dublin
                    Ireland
Phone Number

PERFORMANCE

Ratings History

Date	Overall Rating	Risk Rating	Reward Rating
Q3-19	C+	D	B
Q4-18	C+	D+	B
Q4-17	C	D+	C+
Q4-16	C-	D	C-
Q4-15	C-	D-	C-

Asset & Performance History

Date	NAV	1-Year Total Return
2018	123.89	348.31
2017	27.64	98.56
2016	15.4	-80.51
2015	62	48.68
2014	41.7	-7.33
2013	45	-56.6

Total Assets: $231,603,205
Asset Allocation

Asset	%
Cash	%
Stocks	%
US Stocks	%
Bonds	%
US Bonds	%
Other	%

Services Offered:

Investment Strategy: The investment seeks to replicate, net of expenses, three times the opposite (inverse) of this GSCI Natural Gas Index ER.
The index comprises futures contracts on a single commodity and is calculated according to the methodology of the S&P GSCI Index. **Top Holdings:**

Invesco Global Short Term High Yield Bond ETF   C   HOLD

Ticker	Traded On	NAV	Total Assets ($)	Dividend Yield (TTM)	Turnover Ratio	Expense Ratio
PGHY	NYSE Arca	22.89	$231,220,528	5.29	42	0.35

Ratings
Reward	C
Risk	C-
Recent Upgrade/Downgrade	

Fund Information
Fund Type	Exchange Traded Funds
Category	Global Fixed Income
Sub-Category	High Yield Bond
Prospectus Objective	Worldwide Bond
Inception Date	Jun-13
Open to New Investments	Y

Prices
Price (as of 9/30/2019)	22.91
52-Week High	23.36
52-Week Low	22.65

Total Returns (%)
3-Month	6-Month	1-Year	3-Year	5-Year
0.02	1.35	3.26	11.27	23.92

3-Year Standard Deviation	1.74
Effective Duration	1.15

Valuation
Premium/Discount (1-Year Average)	0.00

Company Information
Provider	Invesco
Manager/Tenure	Philip Fang (6), Peter Hubbard (6), Gary Jones (6), 2 others
Website	http://www.invesco.com/us
Address	Invesco 11 Greenway Plaza, Ste. 2500 Houston TX 77046 United States
Phone Number	800-659-1005

PERFORMANCE

Ratings History
Date	Overall Rating	Risk Rating	Reward Rating
Q3-19	C	C-	C
Q4-18	C	C-	C
Q4-17	B	A-	C+
Q4-16	C	C-	C+
Q4-15	D+	C-	D

Asset & Performance History
Date	NAV	1-Year Total Return
2018	22.82	0.61
2017	23.91	3.87
2016	24.3	12.48
2015	23.04	3.03
2014	23.39	-2.03
2013	24.9	

Total Assets: $231,220,528
Asset Allocation
Asset	%
Cash	10%
Stocks	0%
US Stocks	0%
Bonds	90%
US Bonds	40%
Other	0%

Services Offered:

Investment Strategy: The investment seeks to track the investment results (before fees and expenses) of the DB Global Short Maturity High Yield Bond Index. The fund invests at least 80% of its total assets in U.S. and foreign short-term, non-investment grade bonds that comprise the index. The index provider selects such bonds issued by corporations, as well as sovereign, sub-sovereign or quasi-government entities, from a universe of eligible securities that: are denominated in USD; are rated below investment grade; have not been marked as defaulted by any rating agency; have 3 years or less to maturity; have a minimum amount outstanding of $250 million; and have a fixed coupon. **Top Holdings:** Studio City Company Limited 5.88% Guitar Center Escrow Issuer Inc 9.5% Hughes Satellite Systems Corporation 7.62% Tahoe Group Global Co Ltd 7.88% Banco BTG Pactual S.A. Cayman Islands Branch 4%

IQ Chaikin U.S. Small Cap ETF   D+   SELL

Ticker	Traded On	NAV	Total Assets ($)	Dividend Yield (TTM)	Turnover Ratio	Expense Ratio
CSML	NAS CM	25.12	$229,810,032	1.4		0.35

Ratings
Reward	D+
Risk	C-
Recent Upgrade/Downgrade	Up

Fund Information
Fund Type	Exchange Traded Funds
Category	US Equity Small Cap
Sub-Category	Small Blend
Prospectus Objective	Small Company
Inception Date	May-17
Open to New Investments	Y

Prices
Price (as of 9/30/2019)	25.13
52-Week High	27.90
52-Week Low	21.19

Total Returns (%)
3-Month	6-Month	1-Year	3-Year	5-Year
0.62	0.41	-8.45		

3-Year Standard Deviation	
Effective Duration	

Valuation
Premium/Discount (1-Year Average)	-0.01

Company Information
Provider	IndexIQ
Manager/Tenure	Greg Barrato (2), James Harrison (1)
Website	http://www.indexiq.com
Address	IndexIQ 800 Westchester Avenue, Suite N-611 Rye Brook NY 10573 United States
Phone Number	888-934-0777

PERFORMANCE

Ratings History
Date	Overall Rating	Risk Rating	Reward Rating
Q3-19	D+	C-	D+
Q4-18	D	D	D
Q4-17	U		
Q4-16			
Q4-15			

Asset & Performance History
Date	NAV	1-Year Total Return
2018	22.36	-19.51
2017	28.01	
2016		
2015		
2014		
2013		

Total Assets: $229,810,032
Asset Allocation
Asset	%
Cash	0%
Stocks	100%
US Stocks	98%
Bonds	0%
US Bonds	0%
Other	0%

Services Offered:

Investment Strategy: The investment seeks investment results that track (before fees and expenses) the price and yield performance of its underlying index, the Nasdaq Chaikin Power US Small Cap Index. The fund invests at least 80% of the value of its assets (net assets plus the amount of any borrowings for investment purposes) in securities of small-capitalization U.S. issuers. The underlying index applies the Chaikin Power Gauge®, a quantitative multi-factor model that seeks to identify securities that are expected to outperform peers, to select securities from the Nasdaq US 1500 Index. **Top Holdings:** GMS Inc SunPower Corp Meta Financial Group Inc Vectrus Inc iStar Inc

IQ Chaikin U.S. Large Cap ETF   D+   SELL

Ticker	Traded On	NAV	Total Assets ($)	Dividend Yield (TTM)	Turnover Ratio	Expense Ratio
CLRG	NAS CM	24.93	$228,097,640	2.11		0.25

Ratings
Reward   D+
Risk   D+
Recent Upgrade/Downgrade

Fund Information
Fund Type   Exchange Traded Funds
Category   US Equity Large Cap Blend
Sub-Category   Large Value
Prospectus Objective   Growth & Inc
Inception Date   Dec-17
Open to New Investments   Y

Prices
Price (as of 9/30/2019)   24.97
52-Week High   27.28
52-Week Low   20.41

Total Returns (%)

3-Month	6-Month	1-Year	3-Year	5-Year
0.72	4.83	-2.51		

3-Year Standard Deviation
Effective Duration

Valuation
Premium/Discount (1-Year Average)   -0.14

Company Information
Provider   IndexIQ
Manager/Tenure Greg Barrato (1), James Harrison (1)
Website   http://www.indexiq.com
Address   IndexIQ 800 Westchester Avenue, Suite N-611 Rye Brook NY 10573 United States
Phone Number   888-934-0777

PERFORMANCE

Ratings History

Date	Overall Rating	Risk Rating	Reward Rating
Q3-19	D+	D+	D+
Q4-18	D+	D	D+
Q4-17	U		
Q4-16			
Q4-15			

Asset & Performance History

Date	NAV	1-Year Total Return
2018	21.48	-13.1
2017	25.17	
2016		
2015		
2014		
2013		

Total Assets: $228,097,640

Asset Allocation

Asset	%
Cash	0%
Stocks	100%
US Stocks	100%
Bonds	0%
US Bonds	0%
Other	0%

Services Offered:

Investment Strategy: The investment seeks investment results that track (before fees and expenses) the price and yield performance of the Nasdaq Chaikin Power US Large Cap Index (the "underlying index"). The underlying index is an equally weighted index of large-capitalization securities. The fund generally will invest in all of the securities that comprise its underlying index in proportion to their weightings in the underlying index. It invests, under normal circumstances, at least 80% of the value of its assets (net assets plus the amount of any borrowings for investment purposes) in securities of large-capitalization U.S. issuers. **Top Holdings:** Starbucks Corp IDEXX Laboratories Inc Motorola Solutions Inc TransDigm Group Inc Applied Materials Inc

First Trust Long/Short Equity ETF   C   HOLD

Ticker	Traded On	NAV	Total Assets ($)	Dividend Yield (TTM)	Turnover Ratio	Expense Ratio
FTLS	NYSE Arca	40.96	$227,302,278	1.03	249	1.59

Ratings
Reward   C+
Risk   C-
Recent Upgrade/Downgrade

Fund Information
Fund Type   Exchange Traded Funds
Category   Long/Short Equity
Sub-Category   Long-Short Equity
Prospectus Objective   Growth
Inception Date   Sep-14
Open to New Investments   Y

Prices
Price (as of 9/30/2019)   41.00
52-Week High   41.27
52-Week Low   35.84

Total Returns (%)

3-Month	6-Month	1-Year	3-Year	5-Year
1.35	4.41	2.31	26.97	45.22

3-Year Standard Deviation   7.86
Effective Duration

Valuation
Premium/Discount (1-Year Average)   0.02

Company Information
Provider   First Trust
Manager/Tenure John W. Gambla (5), Rob A. Guttschow (5)
Website   http://www.ftportfolios.com/
Address   First Trust 120 E. Liberty Drive, Suite 400 Wheaton IL 60187 United States
Phone Number   800-621-1675

PERFORMANCE

Ratings History

Date	Overall Rating	Risk Rating	Reward Rating
Q3-19	C	C-	C+
Q4-18	C	C-	C
Q4-17	B	A+	C+
Q4-16	C	C-	C
Q4-15	U		

Asset & Performance History

Date	NAV	1-Year Total Return
2018	37.04	-4.79
2017	39.23	14.09
2016	34.54	6.82
2015	32.68	5.17
2014	31.22	
2013		

Total Assets: $227,302,278

Asset Allocation

Asset	%
Cash	35%
Stocks	65%
US Stocks	51%
Bonds	0%
US Bonds	0%
Other	0%

Services Offered:

Investment Strategy: The investment seeks to provide investors with long-term total return. Under normal conditions, the fund will expose at least 80% of its net assets (including investment borrowings) to U.S. exchange-listed equity securities and/or U.S. exchange-traded funds ("ETFs") that provide exposure to U.S. exchange-listed equity securities. It pursues its investment objective by establishing long and short positions in its portfolio of U.S. exchange-listed equity securities and ETFs. The fund may invest up to 20% of its net assets (including investment borrowings) in U.S. exchange-listed equity index futures contracts. **Top Holdings:** SPDR® S&P 500 ETF JPMorgan Chase & Co Microsoft Corp Apple Inc Old Republic International Corp

iShares iBonds Dec 2027 Term Corporate ETF   C-   HOLD

Ticker	Traded On	NAV	Total Assets ($)	Dividend Yield (TTM)	Turnover Ratio	Expense Ratio
IBDS	NYSE Arca	25.82	$227,183,709	3.41	5	0.1

Ratings
Reward   C-
Risk   C-
Recent Upgrade/Downgrade

Fund Information
Fund Type	Exchange Traded Funds
Category	US Fixed Income
Sub-Category	Target Maturity
Prospectus Objective	Corp Bond - Gen
Inception Date	Sep-17
Open to New Investments	Y

Prices
Price (as of 9/30/2019)	25.92
52-Week High	26.19
52-Week Low	23.05

Total Returns (%)
3-Month	6-Month	1-Year	3-Year	5-Year
2.61	8.02	13.88		

3-Year Standard Deviation
Effective Duration

Valuation
Premium/Discount (1-Year Average)   0.36

Company Information
Provider	iShares
Manager/Tenure	James Mauro (2), Scott Radell (2)
Website	http://www.ishares.com
Address	iShares 400 Howard Street San Francisco CA 94105 United States
Phone Number	800-474-2737

PERFORMANCE

Ratings History
Date	Overall Rating	Risk Rating	Reward Rating
Q3-19	C-	C-	C-
Q4-18	D	C-	D
Q4-17	U		
Q4-16			
Q4-15			

Asset & Performance History
Date	NAV	1-Year Total Return
2018	23.26	-2.74
2017	24.8	
2016		
2015		
2014		
2013		

Total Assets: $227,183,709
Asset Allocation
Asset	%
Cash	0%
Stocks	0%
US Stocks	0%
Bonds	99%
US Bonds	88%
Other	0%

Services Offered:

Investment Strategy: The investment seeks to meet its investment objective generally by investing in individual securities which satisfy the criteria of the Bloomberg Barclays December 2027 Maturity Corporate Index. The fund generally will invest at least 90% of its assets in the component securities of the underlying index, except during the last months of the fund's operations, and may invest up to 10% of its assets in certain futures, options and swap contracts, cash and cash equivalents, including shares of money market funds. The index is composed of U.S. dollar-denominated, investment-grade corporate bonds maturing in 2027. The fund is non-diversified. **Top Holdings:** Broadcom Corporation/Broadcom Cayman Finance Ltd 3.88% Microsoft Corporation 3.3% Citigroup Inc. 4.45% Amazon.com, Inc. 3.15% Verizon Communications Inc. 4.12%

---

iShares MSCI Philippines ETF   D+   SELL

Ticker	Traded On	NAV	Total Assets ($)	Dividend Yield (TTM)	Turnover Ratio	Expense Ratio
EPHE	NYSE Arca	33.74	$222,714,548	0.76	8	0.59

Ratings
Reward   D
Risk   D+
Recent Upgrade/Downgrade

Fund Information
Fund Type	Exchange Traded Funds
Category	Asia ex-Japan Equity
Sub-Category	Miscellaneous Region
Prospectus Objective	Pacific Stock
Inception Date	Sep-10
Open to New Investments	Y

Prices
Price (as of 9/30/2019)	33.45
52-Week High	37.08
52-Week Low	28.20

Total Returns (%)
3-Month	6-Month	1-Year	3-Year	5-Year
-5.99	-0.40	13.16	-7.01	-8.88

3-Year Standard Deviation   14.24
Effective Duration

Valuation
Premium/Discount (1-Year Average)   -0.08

Company Information
Provider	iShares
Manager/Tenure	Diane Hsiung (9), Greg Savage (9), Jennifer Hsui (6), 3 others
Website	http://www.ishares.com
Address	iShares 400 Howard Street San Francisco CA 94105 United States
Phone Number	800-474-2737

PERFORMANCE

Ratings History
Date	Overall Rating	Risk Rating	Reward Rating
Q3-19	D+	D+	D
Q4-18	D	D	D
Q4-17	C	C-	C
Q4-16	C-	C-	D+
Q4-15	C	C	C

Asset & Performance History
Date	NAV	1-Year Total Return
2018	31.9	-17.44
2017	38.82	20.87
2016	32.24	-5.17
2015	34.22	-10.44
2014	38.57	25.18
2013	31.12	-7.92

Total Assets: $222,714,548
Asset Allocation
Asset	%
Cash	0%
Stocks	100%
US Stocks	0%
Bonds	0%
US Bonds	0%
Other	0%

Services Offered:

Investment Strategy: The investment seeks to track the investment results of the MSCI Philippines Investable Market Index (IMI). The fund generally will invest at least 90% of its assets in the component securities of the underlying index and in investments that have economic characteristics that are substantially identical to the component securities of the underlying index. The index is a free float-adjusted market capitalization-weighted index designed to measure the performance of the Philippine equity markets. The fund is non-diversified. **Top Holdings:** SM Prime Holdings Inc Ayala Land Inc BDO Unibank Inc Ayala Corporation SM Investments Corp

VanEck Vectors BDC Income ETF

B- **BUY**

Ticker	Traded On	NAV	Total Assets ($)	Dividend Yield (TTM)	Turnover Ratio	Expense Ratio
BIZD	NYSE Arca	16.83	$221,327,099	9.45	13	9.62

Ratings

Reward	B
Risk	C
Recent Upgrade/Downgrade	Up

Fund Information

Fund Type	Exchange Traded Funds
Category	Financials Sector Equity
Sub-Category	Financial
Prospectus Objective	Income
Inception Date	Feb-13
Open to New Investments	Y

Prices

Price (as of 9/30/2019)	16.86
52-Week High	16.99
52-Week Low	14.04

Total Returns (%)

3-Month	6-Month	1-Year	3-Year	5-Year
3.56	7.01	8.86	24.16	34.98

3-Year Standard Deviation	13.31
Effective Duration	

Valuation

Premium/Discount (1-Year Average)	-0.08

Company Information

Provider	VanEck
Manager/Tenure	Hao-Hung (Peter) Liao (6), Guo Hua (Jason) Jin (1)
Website	http://www.vaneck.com
Address	Van Eck Associates Corporation 666 Third Avenue New York NY 10017 United States
Phone Number	800-826-1115

PERFORMANCE

Ratings History

Date	Overall Rating	Risk Rating	Reward Rating
Q3-19	B-	C	B
Q4-18	C+	C-	B
Q4-17	C	C+	C
Q4-16	C	C-	C+
Q4-15	D+	C-	D+

Asset & Performance History

Date	NAV	1-Year Total Return
2018	14.22	-5.53
2017	16.57	0.04
2016	18.03	25.35
2015	15.73	-4.45
2014	17.92	-7.29
2013	20.9	

Total Assets: $221,327,099

Asset Allocation

Asset	%
Cash	1%
Stocks	98%
US Stocks	98%
Bonds	0%
US Bonds	0%
Other	2%

Services Offered:

Investment Strategy: The investment seeks to replicate as closely as possible, before fees and expenses, the price and yield performance of the MVIS® US Business Development Companies Index. The fund normally invests at least 80% of its total assets in securities that comprise the fund's benchmark index. The index is comprised of BDCs. BDCs are vehicles whose principal business is to invest in, lend capital to or provide services to privately-held companies or thinly traded U.S. public companies. **Top Holdings:** Ares Capital Corp FS KKR Capital Corp Main Street Capital Corp Prospect Capital Corp Hercules Capital Inc

---

iPath® S&P GSCI® Crude Oil Total Return Index ETN

D **SELL**

Ticker	Traded On	NAV	Total Assets ($)	Dividend Yield (TTM)	Turnover Ratio	Expense Ratio
OILNF	NYSE Arca		$220,527,935	2.53	0	0.75

Ratings

Reward	C-
Risk	E
Recent Upgrade/Downgrade	

Fund Information

Fund Type	Exchange Traded Funds
Category	Commodities Specified
Sub-Category	Commodities Energy
Prospectus Objective	Natl Res
Inception Date	Aug-06
Open to New Investments	Y

Prices

Price (as of 9/30/2019)	9.26
52-Week High	9.49
52-Week Low	9.16

Total Returns (%)

3-Month	6-Month	1-Year	3-Year	5-Year
-5.96	-10.72	-31.76	9.94	-71.53

3-Year Standard Deviation	37.97
Effective Duration	

Valuation

Premium/Discount (1-Year Average)	49.19

Company Information

Provider	Milleis Investissements Funds
Manager/Tenure	No Manager (13)
Website	
Address	2-4, rue Eugène Ruppert L-2453 Luxembourg Luxembourg L-2453 Luxembourg
Phone Number	

PERFORMANCE

Ratings History

Date	Overall Rating	Risk Rating	Reward Rating
Q3-19	D	E	C-
Q4-18	D	E	D+
Q4-17	D	D	D+
Q4-16	D-	D-	D-
Q4-15	D-	D-	D-

Asset & Performance History

Date	NAV	1-Year Total Return
2018	4.7	-28.64
2017	6.59	3.1
2016	6.3	11.92
2015	5.73	-53.41
2014	12.29	-46.68
2013	23.06	5.61

Total Assets: $220,527,935

Asset Allocation

Asset	%
Cash	%
Stocks	%
US Stocks	%
Bonds	%
US Bonds	%
Other	%

Services Offered:

Investment Strategy: The investment seeks to provide with exposure to the S&P GSCI® Crude Oil Total Return Index.
The S&P GSCI® Crude Oil Total Return Index (the "index") is a sub-index of the S&P GSCI® Commodity Index. The index reflects the returns that are potentially available through an unleveraged investment in the West Texas Intermediate (WTI) crude oil futures contract. **Top Holdings:**

Invesco CurrencyShares® Japanese Yen Trust   C   HOLD

Ticker	Traded On	NAV	Total Assets ($)	Dividend Yield (TTM)	Turnover Ratio	Expense Ratio
FXY	NYSE Arca	88.02	$220,041,281	0	0	0.4

Ratings

Reward	C
Risk	C
Recent Upgrade/Downgrade	Up

Fund Information

Fund Type	Exchange Traded Funds
Category	Currency
Sub-Category	Single Currency
Prospectus Objective	Worldwide Bond
Inception Date	Feb-07
Open to New Investments	Y

Prices

Price (as of 9/30/2019)	87.95
52-Week High	90.37
52-Week Low	83.60

Total Returns (%)

3-Month	6-Month	1-Year	3-Year	5-Year
0.10	2.63	4.56	-7.70	-0.96

3-Year Standard Deviation	7.8
Effective Duration	

Valuation

Premium/Discount (1-Year Average)	-0.03

Company Information

Provider	Invesco
Manager/Tenure	Management Team (12)
Website	http://www.invesco.com/us
Address	Invesco 11 Greenway Plaza, Ste. 2500 Houston TX 77046 United States
Phone Number	800-659-1005

PERFORMANCE

Ratings History

Date	Overall Rating	Risk Rating	Reward Rating
Q3-19	C	C	C
Q4-18	D+	C-	D
Q4-17	C-	C	D+
Q4-16	C-	C-	C-
Q4-15	D-	D-	D

Asset & Performance History

Date	NAV	1-Year Total Return
2018	87.03	2.16
2017	85.19	3.02
2016	82.69	2.65
2015	80.55	-0.73
2014	81.15	-12.68
2013	92.94	-18.06

Total Assets: $220,041,281
Asset Allocation

Asset	%
Cash	100%
Stocks	0%
US Stocks	0%
Bonds	0%
US Bonds	0%
Other	0%

Services Offered:

Investment Strategy: The investment seeks to track the price of the Japanese Yen, net of trust expenses. The fund seeks to reflect the price in USD of the Japanese Yen. The sponsor believes that, for many investors, the shares represent a cost-effective investment relative to traditional means of investing in the foreign exchange market. **Top Holdings:**

Davis Select Worldwide ETF   C   HOLD

Ticker	Traded On	NAV	Total Assets ($)	Dividend Yield (TTM)	Turnover Ratio	Expense Ratio
DWLD	NAS CM	22.89	$219,754,434	1.3	36	0.64

Ratings

Reward	C
Risk	C-
Recent Upgrade/Downgrade	Up

Fund Information

Fund Type	Exchange Traded Funds
Category	Global Equity Large Cap
Sub-Category	World Large Stock
Prospectus Objective	World Stock
Inception Date	Jan-17
Open to New Investments	Y

Prices

Price (as of 9/30/2019)	22.86
52-Week High	25.56
52-Week Low	19.34

Total Returns (%)

3-Month	6-Month	1-Year	3-Year	5-Year
-3.42	-3.02	-6.67		

3-Year Standard Deviation	
Effective Duration	

Valuation

Premium/Discount (1-Year Average)	0.05

Company Information

Provider	Davis ETFs
Manager/Tenure	Danton Goei (2)
Website	
Address	c/o Davis Selected Advisers, L.P. 2949 E. Elvira Rd., Ste. 101 Tucson Arizona 85756 United States
Phone Number	800-279-0279

PERFORMANCE

Ratings History

Date	Overall Rating	Risk Rating	Reward Rating
Q3-19	C	C-	C
Q4-18	D+	D	C-
Q4-17	D-	B+	D+
Q4-16			
Q4-15			

Asset & Performance History

Date	NAV	1-Year Total Return
2018	19.6	-22.09
2017	26.2	31.16
2016		
2015		
2014		
2013		

Total Assets: $219,754,434
Asset Allocation

Asset	%
Cash	0%
Stocks	100%
US Stocks	52%
Bonds	0%
US Bonds	0%
Other	0%

Services Offered:

Investment Strategy: The investment seeks long-term growth of capital. The fund's investment adviser, uses the Davis Investment Discipline to invest the fund's portfolio principally in common stocks issued by both United States and foreign companies, including countries with developed or emerging markets. It will invest significantly in issuers (i) organized or located outside of the U.S.; (ii) whose primary trading market is located outside the U.S.; or (iii) doing a substantial amount of business outside the U.S., which the adviser considers to be a company that derives at least 50% of its revenue from business outside the U.S. or has at least 50% of its assets outside the U.S. **Top Holdings:** New Oriental Education & Technology Group Inc ADR   Alphabet Inc Class C   Amazon.com Inc   Alibaba Group Holding Ltd ADR   JD.com Inc ADR

ALPS International Sector Dividend Dogs ETF

C   **HOLD**

Ticker	Traded On	NAV	Total Assets ($)	Dividend Yield (TTM)	Turnover Ratio	Expense Ratio
IDOG	NYSE Arca	25.94	$217,919,712	4.42	72	0.5

Ratings

Reward	C
Risk	C-
Recent Upgrade/Downgrade	Up

Fund Information

Fund Type	Exchange Traded Funds
Category	Global Equity Large Cap
Sub-Category	Foreign Large Value
Prospectus Objective	Growth
Inception Date	Jun-13
Open to New Investments	Y

Prices

Price (as of 9/30/2019)	25.91
52-Week High	26.88
52-Week Low	23.10

Total Returns (%)

3-Month	6-Month	1-Year	3-Year	5-Year
0.05	0.54	1.22	21.40	12.21

3-Year Standard Deviation	11.24
Effective Duration	

Valuation

Premium/Discount (1-Year Average)	-0.06

Company Information

Provider	ALPS
Manager/Tenure	Ryan Mischker (4), Andrew Hicks (3)
Website	http://www.alpsfunds.com
Address	ALPS 1290 Broadway, Suite 1100 Denver CO 80203 United States
Phone Number	866-759-5679

PERFORMANCE

Ratings History

Date	Overall Rating	Risk Rating	Reward Rating
Q3-19	C	C-	C
Q4-18	D+	C-	D+
Q4-17	B-	B-	B-
Q4-16	D+	C-	D+
Q4-15	D	C-	D

Asset & Performance History

Date	NAV	1-Year Total Return
2018	23.96	-13.08
2017	28.7	25.82
2016	23.63	3.93
2015	23.67	-6.23
2014	26.22	-5.99
2013	29.03	

Total Assets: $217,919,712

Asset Allocation

Asset	%
Cash	1%
Stocks	99%
US Stocks	2%
Bonds	0%
US Bonds	0%
Other	0%

Services Offered:

Investment Strategy: The investment seeks investment results that replicate as closely as possible, before fees and expenses, the performance of the S-Network® International Sector Dividend Dogs Index. The fund seeks investment results that replicate as closely as possible, before fees and expenses, the performance of the underlying index. The underlying index is a rules-based index intended to give investors a means of tracking the overall performance of the highest dividend paying stocks (i.e. "Dividend Dogs") in the S-Network Developed Markets (ex NA) Index. **Top Holdings:** Tokyo Electron Ltd Bayer AG Hennes & Mauritz AB B Vodafone Group PLC Subaru Corp

---

iShares Global Timber & Forestry ETF

D+   **SELL**

Ticker	Traded On	NAV	Total Assets ($)	Dividend Yield (TTM)	Turnover Ratio	Expense Ratio
WOOD	NAS CM	58.46	$217,469,873	3.3	18	0.46

Ratings

Reward	D+
Risk	D+
Recent Upgrade/Downgrade	Down

Fund Information

Fund Type	Exchange Traded Funds
Category	Natural Resources
Sub-Category	Natural Resources
Prospectus Objective	Natl Res
Inception Date	Jun-08
Open to New Investments	Y

Prices

Price (as of 9/30/2019)	58.64
52-Week High	75.21
52-Week Low	52.98

Total Returns (%)

3-Month	6-Month	1-Year	3-Year	5-Year
-3.19	-8.49	-19.77	24.42	31.63

3-Year Standard Deviation	19.18
Effective Duration	

Valuation

Premium/Discount (1-Year Average)	-0.12

Company Information

Provider	iShares
Manager/Tenure	Greg Savage (11), Jennifer Hsui (7), Alan Mason (3), 2 others
Website	http://www.ishares.com
Address	iShares 400 Howard Street San Francisco CA 94105 United States
Phone Number	800-474-2737

PERFORMANCE

Ratings History

Date	Overall Rating	Risk Rating	Reward Rating
Q3-19	D+	D+	D+
Q4-18	C-	D+	C
Q4-17	B	C	A
Q4-16	C	C-	C+
Q4-15	C	C	C

Asset & Performance History

Date	NAV	1-Year Total Return
2018	57.23	-17.56
2017	71.12	34.28
2016	53.68	13.34
2015	48.23	-7.25
2014	53.01	2.21
2013	52.76	19.95

Total Assets: $217,469,873

Asset Allocation

Asset	%
Cash	1%
Stocks	100%
US Stocks	37%
Bonds	0%
US Bonds	0%
Other	0%

Services Offered:

Investment Strategy: The investment seeks to track the investment results of the S&P Global Timber & Forestry Index™. The fund generally will invest at least 90% of its assets in the component securities of the underlying index and in investments that have economic characteristics that are substantially identical to the component securities and may invest up to 10% of its assets in certain futures, options and swap contracts, cash and cash equivalents. The index is comprised of approximately 25 of the largest publicly-traded companies engaged in the ownership, management or upstream supply chain of forests and timberlands. The fund is non-diversified. **Top Holdings:** Weyerhaeuser Co Svenska Cellulosa AB B Rayonier Inc PotlatchDeltic Corp West Fraser Timber Co.Ltd

ProShares Ultra Silver   C-   HOLD

Ticker	Traded On	NAV	Total Assets ($)	Dividend Yield (TTM)	Turnover Ratio	Expense Ratio
AGQ	NYSE Arca		$216,021,008	0	0	0.95

Ratings
Reward	C-
Risk	D+
Recent Upgrade/Downgrade	Up

Fund Information
Fund Type	Exchange Traded Funds
Category	Trading Tools
Sub-Category	Trading--Leveraged Commodities
Prospectus Objective	Prec Metals
Inception Date	Dec-08
Open to New Investments	Y

Prices
Price (as of 9/30/2019)	29.48
52-Week High	39.66
52-Week Low	21.75

Total Returns (%)
3-Month	6-Month	1-Year	3-Year	5-Year
30.63	28.82	32.53	-35.62	-32.02

3-Year Standard Deviation	31.28
Effective Duration	

Valuation
Premium/Discount (1-Year Average)	-0.14

Company Information
Provider	ProShares
Manager/Tenure	Management Team (10)
Website	http://www.proshares.com
Address	ProShares 7501 Wisconsin Avenue, Suite 1000 Bethesda MD 20814 United States
Phone Number	866-776-5125

PERFORMANCE

Ratings History
Date	Overall Rating	Risk Rating	Reward Rating
Q3-19	C-	D+	C-
Q4-18	D-	D-	D-
Q4-17	D	D	D
Q4-16	D	D-	D+
Q4-15	E+	E+	E+

Asset & Performance History
Date	NAV	1-Year Total Return
2018	26.39	-23
2017	33.56	0.33
2016	33.44	23.56
2015	27.06	-31.24
2014	39.37	-37.83
2013	63.33	-63.15

Total Assets: $216,021,008
Asset Allocation
Asset	%
Cash	-100%
Stocks	163%
US Stocks	163%
Bonds	0%
US Bonds	0%
Other	37%

Services Offered:

Investment Strategy: The investment seeks daily investment results, before fees and expenses, that correspond to two times (2x) the daily performance of the Bloomberg Silver SubindexSM.
The fund seeks to meet its investment objective by investing, under normal market conditions, in any one of, or combinations of, Financial Instruments (including swap agreements, futures contracts and forward contracts) based on the benchmark. The types and mix of Financial Instruments in which the fund invest may vary daily at the discretion of the Sponsor. It will not invest directly in any commodity. **Top Holdings:** Bloomberg Silver Subindex Swap - Citibank Na Bloomberg Silver Subindex Swap - Ubs Ag Bloomberg Silver Subindex Swap - Goldman Sachs Silver Future 12/27/2019 (Siz9) London Silver Price Forward - Societe Generale

iShares Global Consumer Discretionary ETF   C   HOLD

Ticker	Traded On	NAV	Total Assets ($)	Dividend Yield (TTM)	Turnover Ratio	Expense Ratio
RXI	NYSE Arca	119.72	$215,488,361	1.57	30	0.46

Ratings
Reward	C+
Risk	C-
Recent Upgrade/Downgrade	

Fund Information
Fund Type	Exchange Traded Funds
Category	Consumer Goods & Svcs
Sub-Category	Consumer Cyclical
Prospectus Objective	Unaligned
Inception Date	Sep-06
Open to New Investments	Y

Prices
Price (as of 9/30/2019)	119.88
52-Week High	122.34
52-Week Low	94.89

Total Returns (%)
3-Month	6-Month	1-Year	3-Year	5-Year
0.17	5.31	1.40	40.35	61.23

3-Year Standard Deviation	13.37
Effective Duration	

Valuation
Premium/Discount (1-Year Average)	-0.06

Company Information
Provider	iShares
Manager/Tenure	Greg Savage (11), Jennifer Hsui (7), Alan Mason (3), 2 others
Website	http://www.ishares.com
Address	iShares 400 Howard Street San Francisco CA 94105 United States
Phone Number	800-474-2737

PERFORMANCE

Ratings History
Date	Overall Rating	Risk Rating	Reward Rating
Q3-19	C	C-	C+
Q4-18	C	C-	C
Q4-17	B	A-	B
Q4-16	C	C-	B-
Q4-15	C	C	C+

Asset & Performance History
Date	NAV	1-Year Total Return
2018	100.91	-6.19
2017	109.29	22.61
2016	90.32	2.94
2015	89.32	5.62
2014	85.53	3.77
2013	83.86	38.44

Total Assets: $215,488,361
Asset Allocation
Asset	%
Cash	0%
Stocks	100%
US Stocks	56%
Bonds	0%
US Bonds	0%
Other	0%

Services Offered:

Investment Strategy: The investment seeks to track the S&P Global 1200 Consumer Discretionary (Sector) Capped IndexTM. The fund generally invests at least 90% of its assets in securities of the underlying index and in depositary receipts representing securities of the underlying index. The underlying index is designed to measure the performance of global equities in the consumer discretionary sector. The underlying index uses a capping methodology to limit the weight of the securities of any single issuer (as determined by S&P Dow Jones Indices LLC (the "index provider" or "SPDJI")) to a maximum of 10% of the underlying index. **Top Holdings:** Amazon.com Inc The Home Depot Inc Toyota Motor Corp McDonald's Corp Starbucks Corp

SPDR® S&P Software & Services ETF   C   HOLD

Ticker	Traded On	NAV	Total Assets ($)	Dividend Yield (TTM)	Turnover Ratio	Expense Ratio
XSW	NYSE Arca		$214,612,327	0.22	47	0.35

Ratings
Reward	C
Risk	C-
Recent Upgrade/Downgrade	Down

Fund Information
Fund Type	Exchange Traded Funds
Category	Technology Sector Equity
Sub-Category	Technology
Prospectus Objective	Technology
Inception Date	Sep-11
Open to New Investments	Y

Prices
Price (as of 9/30/2019)	93.36
52-Week High	101.79
52-Week Low	70.06

Total Returns (%)
3-Month	6-Month	1-Year	3-Year	5-Year
-4.73	-2.98	3.28	68.42	120.05

3-Year Standard Deviation	16.11
Effective Duration	

Valuation
Premium/Discount (1-Year Average)	-0.06

Company Information
Provider	SPDR State Street Global Advisors
Manager/Tenure	Michael J. Feehily (8), Karl A. Schneider (4), Melissa Kapitulik (0)
Website	http://www.spdrs.com
Address	SPDR State Street Global Advisors State Street Financial Center, 1 Lincoln Street Boston MA 02111-2900 United States
Phone Number	617-786-3000

PERFORMANCE

Ratings History
Date	Overall Rating	Risk Rating	Reward Rating
Q3-19	C	C-	C
Q4-18	C	C-	C
Q4-17	A-	B	A
Q4-16	C	D+	C
Q4-15	C	D+	C+

Asset & Performance History
Date	NAV	1-Year Total Return
2018	75.13	8.89
2017	69.2	27.58
2016	54.5	9.41
2015	50.26	7.39
2014	47.05	4.56
2013	45.25	47.84

Total Assets: $214,612,327
Asset Allocation
Asset	%
Cash	0%
Stocks	100%
US Stocks	99%
Bonds	0%
US Bonds	0%
Other	0%

Services Offered:

Investment Strategy: The investment seeks to provide investment results that, before fees and expenses, correspond generally to the total return performance of an index derived from the computer software segment of a U.S. total market composite index. In seeking to track the performance of the S&P Software & Services Select Industry Index (the "index"), the fund employs a sampling strategy. It generally invests substantially all, but at least 80%, of its total assets in the securities comprising the index. The index represents the software and services segment of the S&P Total Market Index ("S&P TMI"). The fund is non-diversified. **Top Holdings:** Appian Corp A Carbon Black Inc LivePerson Inc Pivotal Software Inc Alteryx Inc Class A

Direxion Daily Semiconductor Bear 3X Shares   C   HOLD

Ticker	Traded On	NAV	Total Assets ($)	Dividend Yield (TTM)	Turnover Ratio	Expense Ratio
SOXS	NYSE Arca	37.69	$214,256,806	2	0	1.08

Ratings
Reward	C+
Risk	D
Recent Upgrade/Downgrade	Up

Fund Information
Fund Type	Exchange Traded Funds
Category	Trading Tools
Sub-Category	Trading--Inverse Equity
Prospectus Objective	Technology
Inception Date	Mar-10
Open to New Investments	Y

Prices
Price (as of 9/30/2019)	37.73
52-Week High	53.24
52-Week Low	4.39

Total Returns (%)
3-Month	6-Month	1-Year	3-Year	5-Year
-20.34	518.80	292.37	-48.65	-90.52

3-Year Standard Deviation	67.83
Effective Duration	

Valuation
Premium/Discount (1-Year Average)	0.05

Company Information
Provider	Direxion Funds
Manager/Tenure	Paul Brigandi (9), Tony Ng (4)
Website	http://www.direxionfunds.com
Address	Direxion Funds 1301 Avenue Of The Americas (6th Avenue) New York NY 10019 United States
Phone Number	646-572-3390

PERFORMANCE

Ratings History
Date	Overall Rating	Risk Rating	Reward Rating
Q3-19	C	D	C+
Q4-18	D	D-	E+
Q4-17	E	E+	E
Q4-16	D-	D-	E
Q4-15	D-	E+	D-

Asset & Performance History
Date	NAV	1-Year Total Return
2018	13.16	-19.62
2017	16.51	-69.36
2016	53.9	-73.19
2015	201.05	-25.09
2014	268.4	-64.36
2013	753.2	-71.48

Total Assets: $214,256,806
Asset Allocation
Asset	%
Cash	124%
Stocks	-24%
US Stocks	-24%
Bonds	0%
US Bonds	0%
Other	0%

Services Offered:

Investment Strategy: The investment seeks daily investment results, before fees and expenses, of 300% of the inverse (or opposite) of the daily performance of the PHLX Semiconductor Sector Index. The fund, under normal circumstances, invests in swap agreements, futures contracts, short positions or other financial instruments that, in combination, provide inverse (opposite) or short leveraged exposure to the index equal to at least 80% of the fund's net assets (plus borrowing for investment purposes). The index measures the performance of domestic companies engaged in the design, distribution, manufacture and sale of semiconductors. The fund is non-diversified. **Top Holdings:** Phila Semiconductor Index Phila Semiconductor Index Phila Semiconductor Index Phila Semiconductor Index Fidelity Institutional Go

iShares Morningstar Small-Cap Growth ETF

C- HOLD

Ticker	Traded On	NAV	Total Assets ($)	Dividend Yield (TTM)	Turnover Ratio	Expense Ratio
JKK	NYSE Arca	194.72	$214,191,457	0.26	55	0.3

Ratings

Reward	C
Risk	D+
Recent Upgrade/Downgrade	Down

Fund Information

Fund Type	Exchange Traded Funds
Category	US Equity Small Cap
Sub-Category	Small Growth
Prospectus Objective	Small Company
Inception Date	Jun-04
Open to New Investments	Y

Prices

Price (as of 9/30/2019)	194.66
52-Week High	210.36
52-Week Low	154.61

Total Returns (%)

3-Month	6-Month	1-Year	3-Year	5-Year
-4.90	-2.93	-6.98	37.80	62.28

3-Year Standard Deviation	17.34
Effective Duration	

Valuation

Premium/Discount (1-Year Average)	-0.06

Company Information

Provider	iShares
Manager/Tenure	Greg Savage (11), Jennifer Hsui (7), Alan Mason (3), 2 others
Website	http://www.ishares.com
Address	iShares 400 Howard Street San Francisco CA 94105 United States
Phone Number	800-474-2737

PERFORMANCE

Ratings History

Date	Overall Rating	Risk Rating	Reward Rating
Q3-19	C-	D+	C
Q4-18	C-	D+	C-
Q4-17	B+	B	A-
Q4-16	C	D+	C+
Q4-15	C	D+	C

Asset & Performance History

Date	NAV	1-Year Total Return
2018	166.99	-5.79
2017	177.88	23.48
2016	144.88	9.47
2015	133.95	-0.03
2014	134.83	2.36
2013	132.47	41.9

Total Assets: $214,191,457

Asset Allocation

Asset	%
Cash	0%
Stocks	100%
US Stocks	99%
Bonds	0%
US Bonds	0%
Other	0%

Services Offered:

Investment Strategy: The investment seeks to track the investment results of the Morningstar® US Small Growth IndexSM composed of small-capitalization U.S. equities that exhibit growth characteristics. The fund generally invests at least 90% of its assets in securities of the underlying index and in depositary receipts representing securities of the underlying index. The underlying index measures the performance of stocks issued by small-capitalization companies that have exhibited above-average "growth" characteristics as determined by Morningstar, Inc.'s ("Morningstar" or the "index provider") proprietary index methodology. **Top Holdings:** Roku Inc Class A Haemonetics Corp Alteryx Inc Class A NovoCure Ltd Entegris Inc

---

Invesco Dynamic Biotechnology & Genome ETF

C HOLD

Ticker	Traded On	NAV	Total Assets ($)	Dividend Yield (TTM)	Turnover Ratio	Expense Ratio
PBE	NYSE Arca	47.42	$213,384,017	0	117	0.57

Ratings

Reward	C+
Risk	D+
Recent Upgrade/Downgrade	

Fund Information

Fund Type	Exchange Traded Funds
Category	Healthcare Sector Equity
Sub-Category	Health
Prospectus Objective	Health
Inception Date	Jun-05
Open to New Investments	Y

Prices

Price (as of 9/30/2019)	47.37
52-Week High	58.75
52-Week Low	43.44

Total Returns (%)

3-Month	6-Month	1-Year	3-Year	5-Year
-11.92	-14.14	-19.36	14.03	5.51

3-Year Standard Deviation	22.44
Effective Duration	

Valuation

Premium/Discount (1-Year Average)	-0.05

Company Information

Provider	Invesco
Manager/Tenure	Peter Hubbard (12), Michael Jeanette (11), Tony Seisser (5)
Website	http://www.invesco.com/us
Address	Invesco 11 Greenway Plaza, Ste. 2500 Houston TX 77046 United States
Phone Number	800-659-1005

PERFORMANCE

Ratings History

Date	Overall Rating	Risk Rating	Reward Rating
Q3-19	C	D+	C+
Q4-18	C	D+	C+
Q4-17	C-	C	D+
Q4-16	C-	D	C
Q4-15	C+	C	B-

Asset & Performance History

Date	NAV	1-Year Total Return
2018	47.29	0.23
2017	47.18	22.42
2016	38.78	-23.02
2015	50.56	2
2014	50.1	36.39
2013	36.96	61.67

Total Assets: $213,384,017

Asset Allocation

Asset	%
Cash	0%
Stocks	100%
US Stocks	100%
Bonds	0%
US Bonds	0%
Other	0%

Services Offered:

Investment Strategy: The investment seeks to track the investment results (before fees and expenses) of the Dynamic Biotech & Genome IntellidexSM Index. The fund generally will invest at least 90% of its total assets in securities that comprise the underlying intellidex. The underlying intellidex was composed of common stocks of U.S. biotechnology and genome companies. These companies are engaged principally in the research, development, manufacture and marketing and distribution of various biotechnological products, services and processes, etc. It is non-diversified. **Top Holdings:** Amgen Inc Vertex Pharmaceuticals Inc Incyte Corp Celgene Corp Ionis Pharmaceuticals Inc

First Trust Institutional Preferred Securities and Income ETF

C-   HOLD

Ticker	Traded On	NAV	Total Assets ($)	Dividend Yield (TTM)	Turnover Ratio	Expense Ratio
FPEI	NYSE Arca	19.63	$212,945,418	5.29		0.85

Ratings
Reward	C-
Risk	C-
Recent Upgrade/Downgrade	

Fund Information
Fund Type	Exchange Traded Funds
Category	US Fixed Income
Sub-Category	Preferred Stock
Prospectus Objective	Growth & Inc
Inception Date	Aug-17
Open to New Investments	Y

Prices
Price (as of 9/30/2019)	19.62
52-Week High	19.74
52-Week Low	18.05

Total Returns (%)
3-Month	6-Month	1-Year	3-Year	5-Year
2.63	6.28	8.58		

3-Year Standard Deviation	
Effective Duration	3.72

Valuation
Premium/Discount (1-Year Average)	0.27

Company Information
Provider	First Trust
Manager/Tenure	Scott T. Fleming (2), Robert Wolf (2)
Website	http://www.ftportfolios.com/
Address	First Trust 120 E. Liberty Drive, Suite 400 Wheaton IL 60187 United States
Phone Number	800-621-1675

PERFORMANCE

Ratings History
Date	Overall Rating	Risk Rating	Reward Rating
Q3-19	C-	C-	C-
Q4-18	D	C-	D
Q4-17	U		
Q4-16			
Q4-15			

Asset & Performance History
Date	NAV	1-Year Total Return
2018	18	-5.37
2017	20.11	
2016		
2015		
2014		
2013		

Total Assets: $212,945,418

Asset Allocation
Asset	%
Cash	3%
Stocks	0%
US Stocks	0%
Bonds	55%
US Bonds	34%
Other	0%

Services Offered:

Investment Strategy: The investment seeks total return and to provide current income. The fund invests at least 80% of its net assets (including investment borrowings) in institutional preferred securities and income-producing debt securities ("Income Securities"). Preferred securities are a type of equity security that have preference over common stock in the payment of distributions and the liquidation of a company's assets, but are generally junior to all forms of the company's debt, including both senior and subordinated debt. The fund's investments in preferred securities will primarily be in institutional preferred securities. It is non-diversified. **Top Holdings:** EMERA INCORPORATED 6.75% NiSource Inc. 5.65% Enbridge Incorporation 6% Aercap Global Aviation Trust 6.5% The Hartford Financial Services Group, Inc. 4.28%

Vanguard Total Corporate Bond ETF ETF Shares

C-   HOLD

Ticker	Traded On	NAV	Total Assets ($)	Dividend Yield (TTM)	Turnover Ratio	Expense Ratio
VTC	NAS CM	88.44	$212,256,000	3.36	4	0.07

Ratings
Reward	C-
Risk	C-
Recent Upgrade/Downgrade	

Fund Information
Fund Type	Exchange Traded Funds
Category	US Fixed Income
Sub-Category	Corporate Bond
Prospectus Objective	Corp Bond - Gen
Inception Date	Nov-17
Open to New Investments	Y

Prices
Price (as of 9/30/2019)	88.46
52-Week High	89.51
52-Week Low	79.04

Total Returns (%)
3-Month	6-Month	1-Year	3-Year	5-Year
2.81	8.00	13.07		

3-Year Standard Deviation	
Effective Duration	7.48

Valuation
Premium/Discount (1-Year Average)	0.06

Company Information
Provider	Vanguard
Manager/Tenure	Joshua C. Barrickman (1)
Website	http://www.vanguard.com
Address	Vanguard 100 Vanguard Boulevard Malvern PA 19355 United States
Phone Number	877-662-7447

PERFORMANCE

Ratings History
Date	Overall Rating	Risk Rating	Reward Rating
Q3-19	C-	C-	C-
Q4-18	D+	D+	D+
Q4-17	U		
Q4-16			
Q4-15			

Asset & Performance History
Date	NAV	1-Year Total Return
2018	79.82	-2.69
2017	84.94	
2016		
2015		
2014		
2013		

Total Assets: $212,256,000

Asset Allocation
Asset	%
Cash	1%
Stocks	0%
US Stocks	0%
Bonds	97%
US Bonds	85%
Other	0%

Services Offered:

Investment Strategy: The investment seeks to track the performance of a broad, market-weighted corporate bond index. The fund is a fund of funds and employs an indexing investment approach designed to track the performance of the Bloomberg Barclays U.S. Corporate Bond Index, which measures the investment-grade, fixed-rate, taxable corporate bond market. The index includes U.S. dollar-denominated securities that are publicly issued by industrial, utility, and financial issuers. **Top Holdings:** Vanguard Short-Term Corporate Bond ETF Vanguard Long-Term Corporate Bd ETF Vanguard Interm-Term Corp Bd ETF

SPDR® SSgA Ultra Short Term Bond ETF   C   HOLD

Ticker	Traded On	NAV	Total Assets ($)	Dividend Yield (TTM)	Turnover Ratio	Expense Ratio
ULST	NYSE Arca		$212,179,258	2.53	100	0.2

Ratings
Reward	C
Risk	C-
Recent Upgrade/Downgrade	

Fund Information
Fund Type	Exchange Traded Funds
Category	US Fixed Income
Sub-Category	Ultrashort Bond
Prospectus Objective	Growth & Inc
Inception Date	Oct-13
Open to New Investments	Y

Prices
Price (as of 9/30/2019)	40.43
52-Week High	40.45
52-Week Low	40.10

Total Returns (%)
3-Month	6-Month	1-Year	3-Year	5-Year
0.66	1.49	2.81	6.18	7.60

3-Year Standard Deviation	0.29
Effective Duration	0.26

Valuation
Premium/Discount (1-Year Average)	0.04

Company Information
Provider	SPDR State Street Global Advisors
Manager/Tenure	James F. Palmieri (0), John Mele (0)
Website	http://www.spdrs.com
Address	SPDR State Street Global Advisors State Street Financial Center, 1 Lincoln Street Boston MA 02111-2900 United States
Phone Number	617-786-3000

PERFORMANCE

Ratings History
Date	Overall Rating	Risk Rating	Reward Rating
Q3-19	C	C-	C
Q4-18	C-	C-	C
Q4-17	C+	B+	C
Q4-16	C-	D+	C
Q4-15	D+	D+	D+

Asset & Performance History
Date	NAV	1-Year Total Return
2018	40.13	2.1
2017	40.22	1.39
2016	40.15	1.52
2015	39.92	0.11
2014	40.02	0.28
2013	40.04	

Total Assets: $212,179,258
Asset Allocation
Asset	%
Cash	7%
Stocks	0%
US Stocks	0%
Bonds	93%
US Bonds	72%
Other	0%

Services Offered:

Investment Strategy: The investment seeks to provide current income consistent with preservation of capital and daily liquidity through short duration high quality investments. The Adviser invests, under normal circumstances, at least 80% of the fund's net assets (plus the amount of borrowings for investment purposes) in a diversified portfolio of U.S. dollar-denominated investment-grade fixed income securities. The fund may also invest in exchange traded products ("ETPs"). It is non-diversified. **Top Holdings:** Nissan Master Owne 2.52% Evergreen Credit Card Trust 2.68% AT&T Inc 3.27% General Motors Financial Company Inc 3.64% Dupont De Nemours Inc 4.2%

WisdomTree CBOE S&P 500 PutWrite Strategy Fund   C-   HOLD

Ticker	Traded On	NAV	Total Assets ($)	Dividend Yield (TTM)	Turnover Ratio	Expense Ratio
PUTW	NYSE Arca	27.69	$210,435,777	0.85	0	0.38

Ratings
Reward	C-
Risk	C-
Recent Upgrade/Downgrade	

Fund Information
Fund Type	Exchange Traded Funds
Category	Long/Short Equity
Sub-Category	Options-based
Prospectus Objective	Growth
Inception Date	Feb-16
Open to New Investments	Y

Prices
Price (as of 9/30/2019)	27.63
52-Week High	30.73
52-Week Low	24.52

Total Returns (%)
3-Month	6-Month	1-Year	3-Year	5-Year
-0.21	2.34	-4.25	14.67	

3-Year Standard Deviation	7.91
Effective Duration	

Valuation
Premium/Discount (1-Year Average)	-0.10

Company Information
Provider	WisdomTree
Manager/Tenure	Vassilis Dagioglu (3), James H. Stavena (3)
Website	http://www.wisdomtree.com
Address	WisdomTree 245 Park Avenue, 35th floor New York NY 10167 United States
Phone Number	866-909-9473

PERFORMANCE

Ratings History
Date	Overall Rating	Risk Rating	Reward Rating
Q3-19	C-	C-	C-
Q4-18	C-	C-	C-
Q4-17	C-	A	C-
Q4-16	U		
Q4-15			

Asset & Performance History
Date	NAV	1-Year Total Return
2018	25.57	-4.81
2017	29.05	10.29
2016	27.27	11.13
2015		
2014		
2013		

Total Assets: $210,435,777
Asset Allocation
Asset	%
Cash	102%
Stocks	-2%
US Stocks	-2%
Bonds	0%
US Bonds	0%
Other	0%

Services Offered:

Investment Strategy: The investment seeks to track the price and yield performance, before fees and expenses, of the CBOE S&P 500 PutWrite Index (the "index"). Under normal circumstances, at least 80% of the fund's total assets will be invested in component securities of the index and investments that have economic characteristics that are substantially identical to the economic characteristics of such component securities. The index tracks the value of a cash-secured put option sales strategy, which consists of selling (or "writing") S&P 500 Index put options ("SPX Puts") and investing the sale proceeds in one- and three-month Treasury bills. The fund is non-diversified. **Top Holdings:** S+p 500 Index Sep19 2890 Put

Direxion NASDAQ-100® Equal Weighted Index Shares

C   HOLD

Ticker	Traded On	NAV	Total Assets ($)	Dividend Yield (TTM)	Turnover Ratio	Expense Ratio
QQQE	NYSE Arca	49.42	$210,035,380	0.77	27	0.35

Ratings

Reward   C+
Risk   C-
Recent Upgrade/Downgrade

Fund Information

Fund Type	Exchange Traded Funds
Category	US Equity Large Cap Growth
Sub-Category	Large Growth
Prospectus Objective	Growth
Inception Date	Mar-12
Open to New Investments	Y

Prices

Price (as of 9/30/2019)	49.41
52-Week High	51.83
52-Week Low	38.25

Total Returns (%)

3-Month	6-Month	1-Year	3-Year	5-Year
-1.66	1.99	5.36	48.47	76.36

3-Year Standard Deviation   14.77
Effective Duration

Valuation

Premium/Discount (1-Year Average)   -0.04

Company Information

Provider	Direxion Funds
Manager/Tenure	Paul Brigandi (7), Tony Ng (4)
Website	http://www.direxionfunds.com
Address	Direxion Funds 1301 Avenue Of The Americas (6th Avenue) New York NY 10019 United States
Phone Number	646-572-3390

PERFORMANCE

Ratings History

Date	Overall Rating	Risk Rating	Reward Rating
Q3-19	C	C-	C+
Q4-18	C	C-	C
Q4-17	B	B+	B
Q4-16	C-	C-	C-
Q4-15	C	C-	C+

Asset & Performance History

Date	NAV	1-Year Total Return
2018	40.69	-4.92
2017	43.11	26.28
2016	34.37	7.24
2015	32.45	2.52
2014	31.83	19.36
2013	27.07	40.23

Total Assets: $210,035,380

Asset Allocation

Asset	%
Cash	0%
Stocks	100%
US Stocks	91%
Bonds	0%
US Bonds	0%
Other	0%

Services Offered:

Investment Strategy: The investment seeks investment results before fees and expenses that track the NASDAQ-100® Equal Weighted Index. The fund, under normal circumstances, invests at least 80% of its assets in the securities that comprise the index. The index is the equal weighted version of the NASDAQ-100 Index® which includes approximately 100 of the largest domestic and international non-financial companies listed on the NASDAQ® Stock Market based on market capitalization. The fund is non-diversified. **Top Holdings:** Qualcomm Inc Align Technology Inc Wynn Resorts Ltd Lululemon Athletica Inc Advanced Micro Devices Inc

---

First Trust TCW Unconstrained Plus Bond ETF

C-   HOLD

Ticker	Traded On	NAV	Total Assets ($)	Dividend Yield (TTM)	Turnover Ratio	Expense Ratio
UCON	NYSE Arca	25.76	$209,927,972	3.12	70	0.75

Ratings

Reward   C-
Risk   C-
Recent Upgrade/Downgrade   Up

Fund Information

Fund Type	Exchange Traded Funds
Category	Fixed Income Misc
Sub-Category	Nontraditional Bond
Prospectus Objective	Multisector Bond
Inception Date	Jun-18
Open to New Investments	Y

Prices

Price (as of 9/30/2019)	25.78
52-Week High	25.91
52-Week Low	24.78

Total Returns (%)

3-Month	6-Month	1-Year	3-Year	5-Year
0.93	3.24	5.67		

3-Year Standard Deviation
Effective Duration   1.80

Valuation

Premium/Discount (1-Year Average)   0.04

Company Information

Provider	First Trust
Manager/Tenure	Stephen M. Kane (1), Laird R. Landmann (1), Tad Rivelle (1), 1 other
Website	http://www.ftportfolios.com/
Address	First Trust 120 E. Liberty Drive, Suite 400 Wheaton IL 60187 United States
Phone Number	800-621-1675

PERFORMANCE

Ratings History

Date	Overall Rating	Risk Rating	Reward Rating
Q3-19	C-	C-	C-
Q4-18	U		
Q4-17			
Q4-16			
Q4-15			

Asset & Performance History

Date	NAV	1-Year Total Return
2018	24.94	
2017		
2016		
2015		
2014		
2013		

Total Assets: $209,927,972

Asset Allocation

Asset	%
Cash	7%
Stocks	0%
US Stocks	0%
Bonds	92%
US Bonds	83%
Other	0%

Services Offered:

Investment Strategy: The investment seeks to maximize long-term total return. Under normal market conditions, the fund invests at least 80% of its net assets (including investment borrowings) in a portfolio of fixed income securities. Its average portfolio duration will vary from between 0 to 10 years. The fund may invest a significant portion of its assets in securitized investment products, including up to 50% in each of ABS, RMBS and CMBS. It may also utilize listed and over-the-counter ("OTC") traded derivatives instruments for duration/yield curve management and/or hedging purposes. The fund is non-diversified. **Top Holdings:** US 10 Year Ultra Future Dec19 US Ultra Bond (CBT) Dec19 Us 5yr Note (Cbt) Dec19 Morgan Stanley 3.7% GE Capital International Funding Company Unlimited Company 4.42%

Invesco Zacks Multi-Asset Income ETF   C   HOLD

Ticker	Traded On	NAV	Total Assets ($)	Dividend Yield (TTM)	Turnover Ratio	Expense Ratio
CVY	NYSE Arca	22.32	$209,793,660	3.31		0.97

Ratings
Reward   C
Risk   C-
Recent Upgrade/Downgrade

Fund Information
Fund Type   Exchange Traded Funds
Category   Aggressive Allocation
Sub-Category   Allocation--85%+ Equity
Prospectus Objective   Multi-Asset Global
Inception Date   Sep-06
Open to New Investments   Y

Prices
Price (as of 9/30/2019)   22.28
52-Week High   22.88
52-Week Low   18.31

Total Returns (%)

3-Month	6-Month	1-Year	3-Year	5-Year
1.22	3.56	4.34	29.54	16.31

3-Year Standard Deviation   12.91
Effective Duration   4.82

Valuation
Premium/Discount (1-Year Average)   -0.15

Company Information
Provider   Invesco
Manager/Tenure   Peter Hubbard (1), Michael Jeanette (1), Tony Seisser (1)
Website   http://www.invesco.com/us
Address   Invesco 11 Greenway Plaza, Ste. 2500 Houston TX 77046 United States
Phone Number   800-659-1005

PERFORMANCE

Ratings History

Date	Overall Rating	Risk Rating	Reward Rating
Q3-19	C	C-	C
Q4-18	C-	C-	C-
Q4-17	C+	C	C+
Q4-16	C-	C-	D+
Q4-15	C-	C-	C-

Asset & Performance History

Date	NAV	1-Year Total Return
2018	19.25	-10.42
2017	22.37	15.55
2016	20.19	16.31
2015	18.21	-14.16
2014	22.37	-4.2
2013	24.74	19.62

Total Assets: $209,793,660
Asset Allocation

Asset	%
Cash	0%
Stocks	82%
US Stocks	70%
Bonds	8%
US Bonds	5%
Other	-1%

Services Offered:

Investment Strategy: The investment seeks to track the investment results (before fees and expenses) of the Zacks Multi-Asset Income Index (the "underlying index"). The fund generally will invest at least 90% of its total assets in the securities that comprise the underlying index, as well as American depositary receipts ("ADRs") that represent securities in the underlying index. The underlying index is composed of securities that Zacks selects from a universe of domestic and international companies listed on major U.S. exchanges. The fund is non-diversified. **Top Holdings:** Western Digital Corp Deluxe Corp OneMain Holdings Inc Wells Fargo & Co 7 1/2 % Non Cum Perp Conv Pfd Shs -A- Series -L- GrafTech International Ltd

---

Pacer Global Cash Cows Dividend ETF   C   HOLD

Ticker	Traded On	NAV	Total Assets ($)	Dividend Yield (TTM)	Turnover Ratio	Expense Ratio
GCOW	BATS	29.70	$209,416,446	4.35	74	0.6

Ratings
Reward   C
Risk   C-
Recent Upgrade/Downgrade

Fund Information
Fund Type   Exchange Traded Funds
Category   Global Equity Large Cap
Sub-Category   World Large Stock
Prospectus Objective   Growth & Inc
Inception Date   Feb-16
Open to New Investments   Y

Prices
Price (as of 9/30/2019)   29.69
52-Week High   31.52
52-Week Low   26.95

Total Returns (%)

3-Month	6-Month	1-Year	3-Year	5-Year
-1.54	-1.46	-0.11	19.56	

3-Year Standard Deviation   11.07
Effective Duration

Valuation
Premium/Discount (1-Year Average)   0.07

Company Information
Provider   Pacer
Manager/Tenure   Bruce Kavanaugh (3), Michael Mack (3)
Website   http://www.paceretfs.com
Address   Pacer 16 Industrial Blvd, Suite 201 Paoli PA 19301 United States
Phone Number

PERFORMANCE

Ratings History

Date	Overall Rating	Risk Rating	Reward Rating
Q3-19	C	C-	C
Q4-18	C-	C-	C-
Q4-17	C-	B	C-
Q4-16	U		
Q4-15			

Asset & Performance History

Date	NAV	1-Year Total Return
2018	27.99	-7.56
2017	31.42	20.62
2016	26.82	
2015		
2014		
2013		

Total Assets: $209,416,446
Asset Allocation

Asset	%
Cash	0%
Stocks	100%
US Stocks	28%
Bonds	0%
US Bonds	0%
Other	0%

Services Offered:

Investment Strategy: The investment seeks to track the total return performance, before fees and expenses, of the Pacer Global Cash Cows Dividend Index. Under normal circumstances, the fund will invest at least 80% of its total assets (exclusive of collateral held from securities lending) in the components of the index and investments that have economic characteristics that are substantially identical to the economic characteristics of such component securities (e.g., depositary receipts). The index uses an objective, rules-based methodology to provide exposure to global companies with high dividend yields backed by a high free cash flow yield. **Top Holdings:** Bayer AG ADR United Parcel Service Inc Class B AT&T Inc NTT DOCOMO Inc Vodafone Group PLC ADR

Xtrackers Russell 1000 Comprehensive Factor ETF   C   HOLD

Ticker	Traded On	NAV	Total Assets ($)	Dividend Yield (TTM)	Turnover Ratio	Expense Ratio
DEUS	NYSE Arca	34.47	$208,532,544	1.67	45	0.17

Ratings

Reward	C
Risk	C-
Recent Upgrade/Downgrade	

Fund Information

Fund Type	Exchange Traded Funds
Category	US Equity Mid Cap
Sub-Category	Mid-Cap Blend
Prospectus Objective	Growth & Inc
Inception Date	Nov-15
Open to New Investments	Y

Prices

Price (as of 9/30/2019)	34.49
52-Week High	34.81
52-Week Low	27.13

Total Returns (%)

3-Month	6-Month	1-Year	3-Year	5-Year
1.61	5.84	4.58	37.83	

3-Year Standard Deviation	12.08
Effective Duration	

Valuation

Premium/Discount (1-Year Average)	0.01

Company Information

Provider	DWS
Manager/Tenure	Bryan Richards (3), Patrick Dwyer (3), Shlomo Bassous (1)
Website	http://dws.com
Address	DWS 210 West 10th Street Kansas City MO 64105-1614 United States
Phone Number	

PERFORMANCE

Ratings History

Date	Overall Rating	Risk Rating	Reward Rating
Q3-19	C	C-	C
Q4-18	C-	C-	C-
Q4-17	C	B+	C
Q4-16	D	C-	D+
Q4-15			

Asset & Performance History

Date	NAV	1-Year Total Return
2018	28.71	-9.59
2017	31.97	19.92
2016	27.03	12.79
2015	24.64	
2014		
2013		

Total Assets: $208,532,544

Asset Allocation

Asset	%
Cash	1%
Stocks	99%
US Stocks	99%
Bonds	0%
US Bonds	0%
Other	0%

Services Offered:

Investment Strategy: The investment seeks investment results that correspond generally to the performance, before fees and expenses, of the Russell 1000 Comprehensive Factor Index. The fund, using a "passive" or indexing investment approach, seeks investment results that correspond generally to the performance of the underlying index, which is designed to track the equity market performance of companies in the United States selected on the investment style criteria ("factors") of value, momentum, quality, low volatility and size. It will invest at least 80% of its total assets (but typically far more) in component securities of the underlying index. **Top Holdings:** CDW Corp Lam Research Corp Cummins Inc Dollar General Corp Darden Restaurants Inc

---

iShares Short Maturity Municipal Bond ETF   C   HOLD

Ticker	Traded On	NAV	Total Assets ($)	Dividend Yield (TTM)	Turnover Ratio	Expense Ratio
MEAR	BATS	50.10	$207,920,446	1.57	221	0.25

Ratings

Reward	C
Risk	C-
Recent Upgrade/Downgrade	Up

Fund Information

Fund Type	Exchange Traded Funds
Category	US Muni Fixed Inc
Sub-Category	Muni National Short
Prospectus Objective	Muni Bond - Natl
Inception Date	Mar-15
Open to New Investments	Y

Prices

Price (as of 9/30/2019)	50.14
52-Week High	50.30
52-Week Low	49.74

Total Returns (%)

3-Month	6-Month	1-Year	3-Year	5-Year
0.33	1.07	2.07	3.97	

3-Year Standard Deviation	0.48
Effective Duration	

Valuation

Premium/Discount (1-Year Average)	0.04

Company Information

Provider	iShares
Manager/Tenure	Scott Radell (4), Kristi Manidis (0), Kevin A. Schiatta (0)
Website	http://www.ishares.com
Address	iShares 400 Howard Street San Francisco CA 94105 United States
Phone Number	800-474-2737

PERFORMANCE

Ratings History

Date	Overall Rating	Risk Rating	Reward Rating
Q3-19	C	C-	C
Q4-18	C-	C-	C-
Q4-17	C	B-	C
Q4-16	D+	D+	D+
Q4-15	U		

Asset & Performance History

Date	NAV	1-Year Total Return
2018	49.88	1.44
2017	49.78	0.97
2016	49.8	0.59
2015	49.91	
2014		
2013		

Total Assets: $207,920,446

Asset Allocation

Asset	%
Cash	11%
Stocks	0%
US Stocks	0%
Bonds	89%
US Bonds	89%
Other	0%

Services Offered:

Investment Strategy: The investment seeks to maximize tax-free current income. The fund normally invests at least 80% of its net assets in municipal securities such that the interest on each bond is exempt from U.S. federal income taxes and the federal alternative minimum tax ("AMT"). It primarily invests in U.S. dollar-denominated investment-grade short-term fixed- and floating-rate municipal securities with remaining maturities of five years or less, such as municipal bonds, municipal notes and variable rate demand obligations, as well as money market instruments and registered investment companies. The fund is an actively managed exchange-traded fund ("ETF"). **Top Holdings:** MIZUHO FLOATER / RESIDUAL TR VAR STS 1.5% TEXAS ST 1.47% BURLINGTON KANS ENVIRONMENTAL IMPT REV 1.6% NASSAU CNTY N Y 4% NEW YORK N Y CITY MUN WTR FIN AUTH WTR & SWR SYS REV 1.52%

Franklin FTSE Japan ETF   D+   SELL

Ticker	Traded On	NAV	Total Assets ($)	Dividend Yield (TTM)	Turnover Ratio	Expense Ratio
FLJP	NYSE Arca	24.75	$207,864,248	2.15	4	0.09

Ratings
Reward   D
Risk   C-
Recent Upgrade/Downgrade   Up

Fund Information
Fund Type   Exchange Traded Funds
Category   Japan Equity
Sub-Category   Japan Stock
Prospectus Objective   Foreign Stock
Inception Date   Nov-17
Open to New Investments Y

Prices
Price (as of 9/30/2019)   24.94
52-Week High   26.94
52-Week Low   21.71

Total Returns (%)

3-Month	6-Month	1-Year	3-Year	5-Year
1.47	2.51	-5.21		

3-Year Standard Deviation
Effective Duration

Valuation
Premium/Discount (1-Year Average)   -0.09

Company Information
Provider   Franklin Templeton Investments
Manager/Tenure   Louis Hsu (1), Dina Ting (1)
Website   http://www.franklintempleton.com
Address   Franklin Templeton Investments One
                  Franklin Parkway, Building 970, 1st
                  Floor San Mateo CA 94403 United
                  States
Phone Number   650-312-2000

PERFORMANCE

Ratings History

Date	Overall Rating	Risk Rating	Reward Rating
Q3-19	D+	C-	D
Q4-18	D	D	D
Q4-17	U		
Q4-16			
Q4-15			

Asset & Performance History

Date	NAV	1-Year Total Return
2018	22.66	-13.1
2017	26.45	
2016		
2015		
2014		
2013		

Total Assets: $207,864,248

Asset Allocation

Asset	%
Cash	0%
Stocks	100%
US Stocks	0%
Bonds	0%
US Bonds	0%
Other	0%

Services Offered:

Investment Strategy: The investment seeks to provide investment results that closely correspond, before fees and expenses, to the performance of the FTSE Japan RIC Capped Index (the FTSE Japan Capped Index). Under normal market conditions, the fund invests at least 80% of its assets in the component securities of the FTSE Japan Capped Index and in depositary receipts representing such securities. The FTSE Japan Capped Index is based on the FTSE Japan Index and is designed to measure the performance of Japanese large- and mid-capitalization stocks. **Top Holdings:** Toyota Motor Corp SoftBank Group Corp Sony Corp Mitsubishi UFJ Financial Group Inc Keyence Corp

---

iShares MSCI Sweden ETF   C-   HOLD

Ticker	Traded On	NAV	Total Assets ($)	Dividend Yield (TTM)	Turnover Ratio	Expense Ratio
EWD	NYSE Arca	29.42	$207,406,403	3.28	5	0.53

Ratings
Reward   D+
Risk   C+
Recent Upgrade/Downgrade   Down

Fund Information
Fund Type   Exchange Traded Funds
Category   Europe Equity Large Cap
Sub-Category   Miscellaneous Region
Prospectus Objective   Europe Stock
Inception Date   Mar-96
Open to New Investments Y

Prices
Price (as of 9/30/2019)   29.45
52-Week High   32.72
52-Week Low   26.79

Total Returns (%)

3-Month	6-Month	1-Year	3-Year	5-Year
-5.49	-1.70	-7.20	12.85	9.17

3-Year Standard Deviation   15.36
Effective Duration

Valuation
Premium/Discount (1-Year Average)   -0.06

Company Information
Provider   iShares
Manager/Tenure   Diane Hsiung (11), Greg Savage (11),
                  Jennifer Hsui (6), 3 others
Website   http://www.ishares.com
Address   iShares 400 Howard Street San
                  Francisco CA 94105 United States
Phone Number   800-474-2737

PERFORMANCE

Ratings History

Date	Overall Rating	Risk Rating	Reward Rating
Q3-19	C-	C+	D+
Q4-18	C-	C-	C-
Q4-17	C+	B-	C
Q4-16	D	D+	D
Q4-15	C	C+	C-

Asset & Performance History

Date	NAV	1-Year Total Return
2018	28.17	-13.22
2017	34.01	21.94
2016	28.81	1.25
2015	29.58	-3.71
2014	31.83	-7.43
2013	35.64	24.66

Total Assets: $207,406,403

Asset Allocation

Asset	%
Cash	2%
Stocks	98%
US Stocks	0%
Bonds	0%
US Bonds	0%
Other	0%

Services Offered: CashInvestment Plan

Investment Strategy: The investment seeks to track the investment results of the MSCI Sweden 25/50 Index. The fund will at all times invest at least 80% of its assets in the securities of its underlying index and in depositary receipts representing securities in its underlying index. The underlying index is designed to measure the performance of the large- and mid-cap segments of the Swedish market. A capping methodology is applied that limits the weight of any single component to a maximum of 25% of the underlying index. The fund is non-diversified. **Top Holdings:** Telefonaktiebolaget L M Ericsson Class B Volvo AB B Investor AB B Assa Abloy AB B Nordea Bank Abp

WisdomTree Managed Futures Strategy Fund   D+   SELL

Ticker	Traded On	NAV	Total Assets ($)	Dividend Yield (TTM)	Turnover Ratio	Expense Ratio
WTMF	NYSE Arca	38.05	$207,372,706	3.66	0	0.65

Ratings
Reward	D+
Risk	C-
Recent Upgrade/Downgrade	

Fund Information
Fund Type	Exchange Traded Funds
Category	Alternative Misc
Sub-Category	Managed Futures
Prospectus Objective	Growth & Inc
Inception Date	Jan-11
Open to New Investments	Y

Prices
Price (as of 9/30/2019)	38.06
52-Week High	41.16
52-Week Low	37.68

Total Returns (%)
3-Month	6-Month	1-Year	3-Year	5-Year
0.85	-2.20	-3.57	-6.35	-9.64

3-Year Standard Deviation	4.48
Effective Duration	

Valuation
Premium/Discount (1-Year Average)	-0.04

Company Information
Provider	WisdomTree
Manager/Tenure	Vassilis Dagioglu (8), James H. Stavena (8)
Website	http://www.wisdomtree.com
Address	WisdomTree 245 Park Avenue, 35th floor New York NY 10167 United States
Phone Number	866-909-9473

PERFORMANCE

(graph: 12/31/17, 4/10/18, 7/21/18, 11/3/18, 2/14/19, 6/17/19, 9/30/19; scale -2.5% to 7.5%)

Ratings History

Date	Overall Rating	Risk Rating	Reward Rating
Q3-19	D+	C-	D+
Q4-18	D+	C-	D+
Q4-17	D	C-	D
Q4-16	D+	C-	D+
Q4-15	C-	C-	C-

Asset & Performance History

Date	NAV	1-Year Total Return
2018	38.79	0.32
2017	40.05	-3.21
2016	41.38	-1
2015	41.8	-4.06
2014	43.58	5.07
2013	41.47	2.75

Total Assets: $207,372,706
Asset Allocation

Asset	%
Cash	112%
Stocks	0%
US Stocks	0%
Bonds	39%
US Bonds	39%
Other	-51%

Services Offered:

Investment Strategy: The investment seeks to provide investors with positive total returns in rising or falling markets. The fund normally invests at least 80% of its net assets, plus the amount of any borrowings for investment purposes, in "managed futures". It is an actively managed exchange traded fund ("ETF") that seeks to achieve positive total returns in rising or falling markets that are not directly correlated to broad market equity or fixed income returns. The fund is managed using a quantitative, rules-based strategy designed to provide returns that correspond to the performance of the WisdomTree Managed Futures Index. It is non-diversified. **Top Holdings:** Wt Cayman Managed Futures Mutual Funds Coffee \'c\' Future Dec19 Ifus 20191218 US 10 Year Note (CBT) Dec19 Silver Future Dec19 Xcec 20191227 Soybean Future Nov19 Xcbt 20191114

iShares U.S. Oil & Gas Exploration & Production ETF   C   HOLD

Ticker	Traded On	NAV	Total Assets ($)	Dividend Yield (TTM)	Turnover Ratio	Expense Ratio
IEO	BATS	50.99	$206,516,747	2.08	12	0.42

Ratings
Reward	B-
Risk	D
Recent Upgrade/Downgrade	Up

Fund Information
Fund Type	Exchange Traded Funds
Category	Energy Sector Equity
Sub-Category	Equity Energy
Prospectus Objective	Natl Res
Inception Date	May-06
Open to New Investments	Y

Prices
Price (as of 9/30/2019)	51.00
52-Week High	78.42
52-Week Low	46.40

Total Returns (%)
3-Month	6-Month	1-Year	3-Year	5-Year
-8.90	-12.62	-32.59	-13.73	-35.64

3-Year Standard Deviation	25.81
Effective Duration	

Valuation
Premium/Discount (1-Year Average)	-0.02

Company Information
Provider	iShares
Manager/Tenure	Greg Savage (11), Jennifer Hsui (7), Alan Mason (3), 2 others
Website	http://www.ishares.com
Address	iShares 400 Howard Street San Francisco CA 94105 United States
Phone Number	800-474-2737

PERFORMANCE

(graph: 12/27/17, 4/6/18, 7/17/18, 10/30/18, 2/10/19, 6/15/19, 9/30/19; scale -40.0% to 40.0%)

Ratings History

Date	Overall Rating	Risk Rating	Reward Rating
Q3-19	C	D	B-
Q4-18	C+	C-	B
Q4-17	D+	D+	D+
Q4-16	D+	D	C-
Q4-15	C+	C+	C+

Asset & Performance History

Date	NAV	1-Year Total Return
2018	51.66	-19.36
2017	64.95	0.29
2016	65.45	25.09
2015	52.91	-24.59
2014	71.38	-12.27
2013	82.27	30.63

Total Assets: $206,516,747
Asset Allocation

Asset	%
Cash	0%
Stocks	100%
US Stocks	99%
Bonds	0%
US Bonds	0%
Other	0%

Services Offered:

Investment Strategy: The investment seeks to track the investment results of the Dow Jones U.S. Select Oil Exploration & Production Index composed of U.S. equities in the oil and gas exploration and production sector. The fund generally invests at least 90% of its assets in securities of the underlying index and in depositary receipts representing securities of the underlying index. The underlying index measures the performance of the oil exploration and production sector of the U.S. equity market. The fund is non-diversified. **Top Holdings:** ConocoPhillips EOG Resources Inc Phillips 66 Valero Energy Corp Marathon Petroleum Corp

Invesco DWA Consumer Staples Momentum ETF   B-   BUY

Ticker	Traded On	NAV	Total Assets ($)	Dividend Yield (TTM)	Turnover Ratio	Expense Ratio
PSL	NAS CM	72.08	$205,430,503	0.53		0.6

Ratings
Reward	B
Risk	C
Recent Upgrade/Downgrade	Up

Fund Information
Fund Type	Exchange Traded Funds
Category	Consumer Goods & Svcs
Sub-Category	Consumer Defensive
Prospectus Objective	Unaligned
Inception Date	Oct-06
Open to New Investments	Y

Prices
Price (as of 9/30/2019)	72.10
52-Week High	75.95
52-Week Low	62.43

Total Returns (%)
3-Month	6-Month	1-Year	3-Year	5-Year
-0.11	2.06	1.60	31.14	63.06

3-Year Standard Deviation	9.74
Effective Duration	

Valuation
Premium/Discount (1-Year Average)	-0.02

Company Information
Provider	Invesco
Manager/Tenure	Peter Hubbard (12), Michael Jeanette (11), Tony Seisser (5)
Website	http://www.invesco.com/us
Address	Invesco 11 Greenway Plaza, Ste. 2500 Houston TX 77046 United States
Phone Number	800-659-1005

PERFORMANCE

Ratings History

Date	Overall Rating	Risk Rating	Reward Rating
Q3-19	B-	C	B
Q4-18	B-	C	B
Q4-17	B	B	B
Q4-16	B	C+	B
Q4-15	B+	B	A

Asset & Performance History

Date	NAV	1-Year Total Return
2018	65.44	1.51
2017	64.93	21.4
2016	53.68	-3.49
2015	56.77	13.48
2014	50.64	15.77
2013	44.19	34.53

Total Assets: $205,430,503
Asset Allocation

Asset	%
Cash	0%
Stocks	100%
US Stocks	100%
Bonds	0%
US Bonds	0%
Other	0%

Services Offered:

Investment Strategy: The investment seeks to track the investment results (before fees and expenses) of the Dorsey Wright® Consumer Staples Technical Leaders Index (the "underlying index"). The fund generally will invest at least 90% of its total assets in the securities that comprise the underlying index. The underlying index is composed of at least 30 securities of companies in the consumer staples sector that have powerful relative strength or "momentum" characteristics. **Top Holdings:** Tyson Foods Inc Class A   Boston Beer Co Inc Class A   Church & Dwight Co Inc   Chegg Inc   Constellation Brands Inc A

Invesco Global Listed Private Equity ETF   C   HOLD

Ticker	Traded On	NAV	Total Assets ($)	Dividend Yield (TTM)	Turnover Ratio	Expense Ratio
PSP	NYSE Arca	11.81	$204,957,396	3.26	64	1.78

Ratings
Reward	C
Risk	C+
Recent Upgrade/Downgrade	

Fund Information
Fund Type	Exchange Traded Funds
Category	Financials Sector Equity
Sub-Category	World Small/Mid Stock
Prospectus Objective	Growth
Inception Date	Oct-06
Open to New Investments	Y

Prices
Price (as of 9/30/2019)	11.82
52-Week High	12.34
52-Week Low	9.72

Total Returns (%)
3-Month	6-Month	1-Year	3-Year	5-Year
-0.12	4.92	-1.27	32.57	46.33

3-Year Standard Deviation	13.91
Effective Duration	

Valuation
Premium/Discount (1-Year Average)	-0.10

Company Information
Provider	Invesco
Manager/Tenure	Peter Hubbard (12), Michael Jeanette (4), Tony Seisser (4)
Website	http://www.invesco.com/us
Address	Invesco 11 Greenway Plaza, Ste. 2500 Houston TX 77046 United States
Phone Number	800-659-1005

PERFORMANCE

Ratings History

Date	Overall Rating	Risk Rating	Reward Rating
Q3-19	C	C+	C
Q4-18	C-	C-	D+
Q4-17	B	C+	B
Q4-16	C	C-	C
Q4-15	C+	C+	C

Asset & Performance History

Date	NAV	1-Year Total Return
2018	10.04	-14.91
2017	12.46	23.9
2016	11.13	10.31
2015	10.53	1.14
2014	11.01	-3.58
2013	11.97	37.1

Total Assets: $204,957,396
Asset Allocation

Asset	%
Cash	6%
Stocks	86%
US Stocks	40%
Bonds	0%
US Bonds	0%
Other	7%

Services Offered:

Investment Strategy: The investment seeks to track the investment results (before fees and expenses) of the Red Rocks Global Listed Private Equity Index. The fund generally will invest at least 90% of its total assets in securities (including American depositary receipts ("ADRs") and global depositary receipts ("GDRs")) that comprise the underlying index. The underlying index is composed of securities, ADRs and GDRs of 40 to 75 private equity companies, including business development companies ("BDCs"), master limited partnerships ("MLPs") and other vehicles. **Top Holdings:** IAC/InterActiveCorp   3i Ord   Partners Group Holding AG   Melrose Industries PLC   Blackstone Group Inc

iShares MSCI Global Metals & Mining Producers ETF   C   HOLD

Ticker	Traded On	NAV	Total Assets ($)	Dividend Yield (TTM)	Turnover Ratio	Expense Ratio
PICK	BATS	26.72	$203,060,958	6.34	14	0.39

Ratings
Reward   C-
Risk   C
Recent Upgrade/Downgrade

Fund Information
Fund Type   Exchange Traded Funds
Category   Prec Metals
Sub-Category   Equity Precious Metals
Prospectus Objective   Prec Metals
Inception Date   Jan-12
Open to New Investments   Y

Prices
Price (as of 9/30/2019)   26.62
52-Week High   32.95
52-Week Low   24.56

Total Returns (%)

3-Month	6-Month	1-Year	3-Year	5-Year
-12.45	-14.16	-12.66	28.39	-6.30

3-Year Standard Deviation   21.78
Effective Duration

Valuation
Premium/Discount (1-Year Average)   -0.27

Company Information
Provider   iShares
Manager/Tenure   Diane Hsiung (7), Greg Savage (7), Jennifer Hsui (6), 3 others
Website   http://www.ishares.com
Address   iShares 400 Howard Street San Francisco CA 94105 United States
Phone Number   800-474-2737

PERFORMANCE

Ratings History

Date	Overall Rating	Risk Rating	Reward Rating
Q3-19	C	C	C-
Q4-18	C	C	C-
Q4-17	C+	C-	B
Q4-16	C-	D+	C-
Q4-15	D-	D	D-

Asset & Performance History

Date	NAV	1-Year Total Return
2018	27.05	-18.5
2017	34.67	37.14
2016	26.02	57.16
2015	16.76	-40.25
2014	31.08	-19.45
2013	39.64	-7.53

Total Assets: $203,060,958

Asset Allocation

Asset	%
Cash	1%
Stocks	99%
US Stocks	13%
Bonds	0%
US Bonds	0%
Other	0%

Services Offered:

Investment Strategy: The investment seeks to track the investment results of the MSCI ACWI Select Metals & Mining Producers ex Gold and Silver Investable Market Index. The fund generally will invest at least 90% of its assets in the component securities of the index and in investments that have economic characteristics that are substantially identical to the component securities of the index. The index composed of global equities of companies primarily engaged in mining, extraction or production of diversified metals, excluding gold and silver. The fund is non-diversified. **Top Holdings:** BHP Group Ltd Rio Tinto PLC BHP Group PLC Vale SA Glencore PLC

Invesco S&P SmallCap 600® Pure Growth ETF   C-   HOLD

Ticker	Traded On	NAV	Total Assets ($)	Dividend Yield (TTM)	Turnover Ratio	Expense Ratio
RZG	NYSE Arca	106.70	$202,733,644	0.67		0.35

Ratings
Reward   C-
Risk   D+
Recent Upgrade/Downgrade   Up

Fund Information
Fund Type   Exchange Traded Funds
Category   US Equity Small Cap
Sub-Category   Small Growth
Prospectus Objective   Small Company
Inception Date   Mar-06
Open to New Investments   Y

Prices
Price (as of 9/30/2019)   106.66
52-Week High   131.68
52-Week Low   98.06

Total Returns (%)

3-Month	6-Month	1-Year	3-Year	5-Year
-4.19	-6.15	-18.46	21.75	47.70

3-Year Standard Deviation   19.46
Effective Duration

Valuation
Premium/Discount (1-Year Average)   -0.10

Company Information
Provider   Invesco
Manager/Tenure   Peter Hubbard (1), Michael Jeanette (1), Tony Seisser (1)
Website   http://www.invesco.com/us
Address   Invesco 11 Greenway Plaza, Ste. 2500 Houston TX 77046 United States
Phone Number   800-659-1005

PERFORMANCE

Ratings History

Date	Overall Rating	Risk Rating	Reward Rating
Q3-19	C-	D+	C-
Q4-18	C-	D+	C
Q4-17	A-	B	A
Q4-16	D+	D+	D+
Q4-15	C	C	B-

Asset & Performance History

Date	NAV	1-Year Total Return
2018	104.25	-7.74
2017	113.47	18.4
2016	96.73	19.33
2015	80.82	0.88
2014	80.64	1.44
2013	79.78	43.44

Total Assets: $202,733,644

Asset Allocation

Asset	%
Cash	0%
Stocks	100%
US Stocks	96%
Bonds	0%
US Bonds	0%
Other	0%

Services Offered:

Investment Strategy: The investment seeks to track the investment results (before fees and expenses) of the S&P SmallCap 600® Pure Growth Index (the "underlying index"). The fund generally will invest at least 90% of its total assets in the securities that comprise the underlying index. The underlying index is composed of a subset of securities from the S&P SmallCap 600® Index that exhibit strong growth characteristics, as measured using the following three factors: three-year sales per share growth, three-year ratio of earnings per share change to price per share, and momentum (the 12-month percentage change in price). The fund is non-diversified. **Top Holdings:** Avon Products Inc Shake Shack Inc A NeoGenomics Inc Medpace Holdings Inc Perficient Inc

iShares Government/Credit Bond ETF   C   HOLD

Ticker	Traded On	NAV	Total Assets ($)	Dividend Yield (TTM)	Turnover Ratio	Expense Ratio
GBF	NYSE Arca	118.83	$202,015,367	2.52	24	0.2

Ratings

Reward .... C+
Risk .... D+
Recent Upgrade/Downgrade

Fund Information

Fund Type	Exchange Traded Funds
Category	US Fixed Income
Sub-Category	Intermediate Core Bond
Prospectus Objective	Income
Inception Date	Jan-07
Open to New Investments	Y

Prices

Price (as of 9/30/2019)	119.02
52-Week High	120.25
52-Week Low	108.16

Total Returns (%)

3-Month	6-Month	1-Year	3-Year	5-Year
2.72	6.62	11.26	9.25	17.79

3-Year Standard Deviation	3.78
Effective Duration	

Valuation

Premium/Discount (1-Year Average)	0.08

Company Information

Provider	iShares
Manager/Tenure	Scott Radell (9), James Mauro (8)
Website	http://www.ishares.com
Address	iShares 400 Howard Street San Francisco CA 94105 United States
Phone Number	800-474-2737

PERFORMANCE

Ratings History

Date	Overall Rating	Risk Rating	Reward Rating
Q3-19	C	D+	C+
Q4-18	D+	D+	D
Q4-17	B-	B+	C
Q4-16	C-	D+	C
Q4-15	C	C-	C

Asset & Performance History

Date	NAV	1-Year Total Return
2018	110.29	-0.6
2017	113.88	3.53
2016	112.24	2.76
2015	111.47	0.05
2014	113.68	5.81
2013	109.73	-2.55

Total Assets: $202,015,367

Asset Allocation

Asset	%
Cash	1%
Stocks	0%
US Stocks	0%
Bonds	98%
US Bonds	89%
Other	0%

Services Offered:

Investment Strategy: The investment seeks to track the investment results of the Bloomberg Barclays U.S. Government/Credit Bond Index (the "underlying index"). The underlying index measures the performance of U.S. dollar-denominated U.S. Treasury bonds, government-related bonds and investment-grade U.S. corporate bonds that have a remaining maturity of greater than or equal to one year. The fund generally invests at least 90% of its assets in securities of the underlying index. It may invest the remainder of its assets in certain futures, options and swap contracts, cash and cash equivalents, as well as in securities not included in the underlying index. **Top Holdings:** United States Treasury Notes 2% United States Treasury Notes 2% United States Treasury Notes 1.38% United States Treasury Bonds 3.38% United States Treasury Notes 1.5%

---

iShares iBonds Dec 2023 Term Muni Bond ETF   C   HOLD

Ticker	Traded On	NAV	Total Assets ($)	Dividend Yield (TTM)	Turnover Ratio	Expense Ratio
IBML	BATS	25.72	$201,911,787	1.7	0	0.18

Ratings

Reward C
Risk .... C-
Recent Upgrade/Downgrade ...... Up

Fund Information

Fund Type	Exchange Traded Funds
Category	US Muni Fixed Inc
Sub-Category	Muni Target Maturity
Prospectus Objective	Muni Bond - Natl
Inception Date	Apr-17
Open to New Investments	Y

Prices

Price (as of 9/30/2019)	25.76
52-Week High	26.04
52-Week Low	24.60

Total Returns (%)

3-Month	6-Month	1-Year	3-Year	5-Year
0.42	1.93	5.58		

3-Year Standard Deviation	
Effective Duration	

Valuation

Premium/Discount (1-Year Average)	0.11

Company Information

Provider	iShares
Manager/Tenure	James Mauro (2), Scott Radell (2)
Website	http://www.ishares.com
Address	iShares 400 Howard Street San Francisco CA 94105 United States
Phone Number	800-474-2737

PERFORMANCE

Ratings History

Date	Overall Rating	Risk Rating	Reward Rating
Q3-19	C	C-	C
Q4-18	D+	C-	D
Q4-17	U		
Q4-16			
Q4-15			

Asset & Performance History

Date	NAV	1-Year Total Return
2018	25.05	1.2
2017	25.17	
2016		
2015		
2014		
2013		

Total Assets: $201,911,787

Asset Allocation

Asset	%
Cash	0%
Stocks	0%
US Stocks	0%
Bonds	100%
US Bonds	100%
Other	0%

Services Offered:

Investment Strategy: The investment seeks to track the investment results of the S&P AMT-Free Municipal Series Dec 2023 IndexTM composed of investment-grade U.S. municipal bonds maturing after December 31, 2022 and before December 2, 2023. The fund generally will invest at least 90% of its assets in the component securities of the index, and may invest up to 10% of its assets in certain futures, options and swap contracts, cash and cash equivalents. The index includes municipal bonds primarily from issuers that are state or local governments or agencies such that the interest on the bonds is exempt from U.S. federal income taxes. The fund is non-diversified. **Top Holdings:** WISCONSIN ST 5%   SALT LAKE CNTY UTAH EXCISE TAX RD REV 5%   CALIFORNIA ST 5% UNIVERSITY CALIF REVS 5%   METROPOLITAN GOVT NASHVILLE & DAVIDSON CNTY TENN 5%

Invesco DWA Developed Markets Momentum ETF

C-   **HOLD**

Ticker	Traded On	NAV	Total Assets ($)	Dividend Yield (TTM)	Turnover Ratio	Expense Ratio
PIZ	NAS CM	26.44	$200,954,640	1.34	94	0.8

Ratings
Reward	C-
Risk	C-
Recent Upgrade/Downgrade	

Fund Information
Fund Type	Exchange Traded Funds
Category	Global Equity Large Cap
Sub-Category	Foreign Large Growth
Prospectus Objective	Foreign Stock
Inception Date	Dec-07
Open to New Investments	

Prices
Price (as of 9/30/2019)	26.38
52-Week High	27.60
52-Week Low	22.12

Total Returns (%)
3-Month	6-Month	1-Year	3-Year	5-Year
-2.40	2.61	-2.62	16.41	16.89

3-Year Standard Deviation	12.76
Effective Duration	

Valuation
Premium/Discount (1-Year Average)	-0.15

Company Information
Provider	Invesco
Manager/Tenure	Peter Hubbard (11), Michael Jeanette (4), Tony Seisser (4)
Website	http://www.invesco.com/us
Address	Invesco 11 Greenway Plaza, Ste. 2500 Houston TX 77046 United States
Phone Number	800-659-1005

PERFORMANCE

Ratings History
Date	Overall Rating	Risk Rating	Reward Rating
Q3-19	C-	C-	C-
Q4-18	D+	D+	D+
Q4-17	B-	B	B-
Q4-16	D	D+	D
Q4-15	C	C+	C-

Asset & Performance History
Date	NAV	1-Year Total Return
2018	23.03	-16.17
2017	27.72	30.7
2016	21.5	-7.99
2015	23.87	-0.15
2014	24.16	-6.64
2013	26.27	36.13

Total Assets: $200,954,640
Asset Allocation
Asset	%
Cash	0%
Stocks	100%
US Stocks	1%
Bonds	0%
US Bonds	0%
Other	0%

Services Offered:

Investment Strategy: The investment seeks to track the investment results (before fees and expenses) of the Dorsey Wright® Developed Markets Technical Leaders Index (the "underlying index"). The fund will invest at least 90% of its total assets in the securities that comprise the underlying index. The underlying index is comprised of equity securities of large capitalization companies based in countries with developed economies, excluding the United States. **Top Holdings:** Ramsay Health Care Ltd Constellation Software Inc Kirkland Lake Gold Ltd Magellan Financial Group Ltd KONE Oyj Class B

Davis Select U.S. Equity ETF

C+   **HOLD**

Ticker	Traded On	NAV	Total Assets ($)	Dividend Yield (TTM)	Turnover Ratio	Expense Ratio
DUSA	NAS CM	23.83	$200,148,184	1.41	28	0.63

Ratings
Reward	B
Risk	C
Recent Upgrade/Downgrade	Up

Fund Information
Fund Type	Exchange Traded Funds
Category	US Equity Large Cap Blend
Sub-Category	Large Blend
Prospectus Objective	Growth
Inception Date	Jan-17
Open to New Investments	Y

Prices
Price (as of 9/30/2019)	23.85
52-Week High	25.36
52-Week Low	19.43

Total Returns (%)
3-Month	6-Month	1-Year	3-Year	5-Year
0.38	3.81	-3.37		

3-Year Standard Deviation	
Effective Duration	

Valuation
Premium/Discount (1-Year Average)	0.10

Company Information
Provider	Davis ETFs
Manager/Tenure	Christopher Cullom Davis (2), Danton Goei (2)
Website	
Address	c/o Davis Selected Advisers, L.P. 2949 E. Elvira Rd., Ste. 101 Tucson Arizona 85756 United States
Phone Number	800-279-0279

PERFORMANCE

Ratings History
Date	Overall Rating	Risk Rating	Reward Rating
Q3-19	C+	C	B
Q4-18	C+	C	B-
Q4-17	D-	B+	D+
Q4-16			
Q4-15			

Asset & Performance History
Date	NAV	1-Year Total Return
2018	20.03	-11.57
2017	23.28	18.19
2016		
2015		
2014		
2013		

Total Assets: $200,148,184
Asset Allocation
Asset	%
Cash	0%
Stocks	100%
US Stocks	85%
Bonds	0%
US Bonds	0%
Other	0%

Services Offered:

Investment Strategy: The investment seeks long-term capital growth and capital preservation. Under normal market conditions, the fund will invest at least 80% of its net assets plus any borrowings for investment purposes in equity securities issued by U.S. companies. The fund's portfolio generally contains between 15 and 35 companies. It may invest a portion of its assets in financial services companies. The fund may also invest in mid- and small-capitalization companies, which the manager considers to be those companies with less than $10 billion in market capitalization. It may invest up to 20% of net assets in non-U.S. companies. The fund is non-diversified. **Top Holdings:** Alphabet Inc Class C Berkshire Hathaway Inc B Amazon.com Inc United Technologies Corp New Oriental Education & Technology Group Inc ADR

IQ 50 Percent Hedged FTSE International ETF   C   HOLD

Ticker	Traded On	NAV	Total Assets ($)	Dividend Yield (TTM)	Turnover Ratio	Expense Ratio
HFXI	NYSE Arca	20.31	$199,037,155	4.46		0.2

Ratings

Reward	C
Risk	C-
Recent Upgrade/Downgrade	

Fund Information

Fund Type	Exchange Traded Funds
Category	Global Equity Large Cap
Sub-Category	Foreign Large Blend
Prospectus Objective	World Stock
Inception Date	Jul-15
Open to New Investments	Y

Prices

Price (as of 9/30/2019)	20.34
52-Week High	21.10
52-Week Low	17.88

Total Returns (%)

3-Month	6-Month	1-Year	3-Year	5-Year
-0.24	2.67	0.60	26.38	

3-Year Standard Deviation	10.31
Effective Duration	

Valuation

Premium/Discount (1-Year Average)	0.02

Company Information

Provider	IndexIQ
Manager/Tenure	Greg Barrato (4), James Harrison (1)
Website	http://www.indexiq.com
Address	IndexIQ 800 Westchester Avenue, Suite N-611 Rye Brook NY 10573 United States
Phone Number	888-934-0777

PERFORMANCE

Ratings History

Date	Overall Rating	Risk Rating	Reward Rating
Q3-19	C	C-	C
Q4-18	C-	C	D+
Q4-17	C	B-	C+
Q4-16	D	C-	D+
Q4-15	U		

Asset & Performance History

Date	NAV	1-Year Total Return
2018	18.25	-13.26
2017	21.56	21.68
2016	18.2	3.5
2015	18.21	
2014		
2013		

Total Assets: $199,037,155

Asset Allocation

Asset	%
Cash	0%
Stocks	100%
US Stocks	1%
Bonds	0%
US Bonds	0%
Other	0%

Services Offered:

Investment Strategy: The investment seeks investment results that correspond generally to the price and yield performance of its underlying index, the FTSE Developed ex North America 50% Hedged to USD Index (the "underlying index"). The underlying index is an equity benchmark of international stocks from developed markets, with approximately half of the currency exposure of the securities included in the underlying index "hedged" against the U.S. dollar on a monthly basis. The fund invests, under normal circumstances, at least 80% of its net assets, plus the amount of any borrowings for investment purposes, in the securities and other instruments included in its underlying index. **Top Holdings:** Nestle SA Novartis AG Roche Holding AG Dividend Right Cert. Samsung Electronics Co Ltd Toyota Motor Corp

Global X SuperIncome™ Preferred ETF   C   HOLD

Ticker	Traded On	NAV	Total Assets ($)	Dividend Yield (TTM)	Turnover Ratio	Expense Ratio
SPFF	NYSE Arca	11.74	$197,807,698	6.39	105	0.58

Ratings

Reward	C
Risk	C-
Recent Upgrade/Downgrade	Up

Fund Information

Fund Type	Exchange Traded Funds
Category	US Fixed Income
Sub-Category	Preferred Stock
Prospectus Objective	Equity-Income
Inception Date	Jul-12
Open to New Investments	Y

Prices

Price (as of 9/30/2019)	11.74
52-Week High	11.86
52-Week Low	10.92

Total Returns (%)

3-Month	6-Month	1-Year	3-Year	5-Year
2.55	3.68	5.55	7.28	11.81

3-Year Standard Deviation	4.25
Effective Duration	

Valuation

Premium/Discount (1-Year Average)	0.13

Company Information

Provider	Global X Funds
Manager/Tenure	Chang Kim (5), Nam To (1), Wayne Xie (0), 1 other
Website	http://www.globalxfunds.com
Address	Global X Funds 600 Lexington Avenue, 20th Floor New York NY 10022 United States
Phone Number	888-493-8631

PERFORMANCE

Ratings History

Date	Overall Rating	Risk Rating	Reward Rating
Q3-19	C	C-	C
Q4-18	D+	C-	D+
Q4-17	C	C	C
Q4-16	C-	C-	C
Q4-15	C	C+	C-

Asset & Performance History

Date	NAV	1-Year Total Return
2018	11.06	-2.62
2017	12.2	2.29
2016	12.78	3.72
2015	13.19	-2.66
2014	14.54	6.87
2013	14.54	5

Total Assets: $197,807,698

Asset Allocation

Asset	%
Cash	0%
Stocks	5%
US Stocks	0%
Bonds	0%
US Bonds	0%
Other	0%

Services Offered:

Investment Strategy: The investment seeks investment results that correspond generally to the price and yield performance, before fees and expenses, of the S&P Enhanced Yield North American Preferred Stock Index ("underlying index"). The fund will invest at least 80% of its total assets in the securities of the underlying index and in American Depositary Receipts ("ADRs") and Global Depositary Receipts ("GDRs") based on the securities in the underlying index. The underlying index tracks the performance of the highest-yielding preferred securities in the United States and Canada. **Top Holdings:** GMAC Capital Trust I Pfd Secs 2011-15.2.40 Gtd Series 2 HSBC Holdings PLC ADR US Bancorp Shs Repr 1/1000th Non Cum Perp Pfd Shs Series-F VEREIT Inc 6 7/10 % Cum Red Pfd Shs Series -F- Deutsche Bank Conting Cp-8 05 PC Tr Pfd Secs 08-Without Fixed Maturity Pfd

VanEck Vectors AMT-Free Short Municipal Index ETF

C HOLD

Ticker	Traded On	NAV	Total Assets ($)	Dividend Yield (TTM)	Turnover Ratio	Expense Ratio
SMB	BATS	17.73	$197,671,405	1.57	33	0.2

Ratings
Reward — C
Risk — C-
Recent Upgrade/Downgrade

Fund Information
Fund Type — Exchange Traded Funds
Category — US Muni Fixed Inc
Sub-Category — Muni National Short
Prospectus Objective — Muni Bond - Natl
Inception Date — Feb-08
Open to New Investments — Y

Prices
Price (as of 9/30/2019) — 17.70
52-Week High — 17.88
52-Week Low — 17.09

Total Returns (%)

3-Month	6-Month	1-Year	3-Year	5-Year
0.43	1.75	4.59	4.92	7.20

3-Year Standard Deviation — 1.93
Effective Duration — 3.02

Valuation
Premium/Discount (1-Year Average) — -0.11

Company Information
Provider — VanEck
Manager/Tenure — James T. Colby (11)
Website — http://www.vaneck.com
Address — Van Eck Associates Corporation 666 Third Avenue New York NY 10017 United States
Phone Number — 800-826-1115

PERFORMANCE

Ratings History

Date	Overall Rating	Risk Rating	Reward Rating
Q3-19	C	C-	C
Q4-18	C-	C-	D+
Q4-17	C	C	C
Q4-16	C	C+	C-
Q4-15	C	C-	C

Asset & Performance History

Date	NAV	1-Year Total Return
2018	17.34	1.42
2017	17.35	1.68
2016	17.27	-0.44
2015	17.54	1.13
2014	17.54	1.33
2013	17.52	0.35

Total Assets: $197,671,405
Asset Allocation

Asset	%
Cash	0%
Stocks	0%
US Stocks	0%
Bonds	100%
US Bonds	100%
Other	0%

Services Offered:

Investment Strategy: The investment seeks to replicate as closely as possible, before fees and expenses, the price and yield performance of the Bloomberg Barclays AMT-Free Short Continuous Municipal Index. The fund normally invests at least 80% of its total assets in fixed income securities that comprise the index. The index is comprised of publicly traded municipal bonds that cover the U.S. dollar denominated short-term tax-exempt bond market. **Top Holdings:** MARYLAND ST 5% CITIZENS PPTY INS CORP FLA 5% CALIFORNIA ST PUB WKS BRD LEASE REV 5% FLORIDA ST BRD ED PUB ED 5% GEORGIA ST 5%

VanEck Vectors Mortgage REIT Income ETF

C HOLD

Ticker	Traded On	NAV	Total Assets ($)	Dividend Yield (TTM)	Turnover Ratio	Expense Ratio
MORT	NYSE Arca	23.31	$196,982,731	7.22	35	0.42

Ratings
Reward — C+
Risk — C
Recent Upgrade/Downgrade

Fund Information
Fund Type — Exchange Traded Funds
Category — Real Estate Sector Equity
Sub-Category — Real Estate
Prospectus Objective — Real Estate
Inception Date — Aug-11
Open to New Investments — Y

Prices
Price (as of 9/30/2019) — 23.28
52-Week High — 23.77
52-Week Low — 21.00

Total Returns (%)

3-Month	6-Month	1-Year	3-Year	5-Year
2.19	1.51	5.22	30.92	47.36

3-Year Standard Deviation — 12.95
Effective Duration —

Valuation
Premium/Discount (1-Year Average) — -0.02

Company Information
Provider — VanEck
Manager/Tenure — Hao-Hung (Peter) Liao (8), Guo Hua (Jason) Jin (1)
Website — http://www.vaneck.com
Address — Van Eck Associates Corporation 666 Third Avenue New York NY 10017 United States
Phone Number — 800-826-1115

PERFORMANCE

Ratings History

Date	Overall Rating	Risk Rating	Reward Rating
Q3-19	C	C	C+
Q4-18	C+	C	B-
Q4-17	B-	C+	B-
Q4-16	C	C-	B-
Q4-15	C	C	B-

Asset & Performance History

Date	NAV	1-Year Total Return
2018	21.28	-4.45
2017	24.04	18.53
2016	21.9	22.61
2015	19.44	-10.06
2014	23.66	17.93
2013	22.13	0.99

Total Assets: $196,982,731
Asset Allocation

Asset	%
Cash	0%
Stocks	100%
US Stocks	100%
Bonds	0%
US Bonds	0%
Other	0%

Services Offered:

Investment Strategy: The investment seeks to replicate as closely as possible, before fees and expenses, the price and yield performance of the MVIS® US Mortgage REITs Index (the "Mortgage REITs Index"). The fund normally invests at least 80% of its total assets in securities that comprise the fund's benchmark index. The Mortgage REITs Index may include small-, medium- and large-capitalization companies. The fund is non-diversified. **Top Holdings:** Annaly Capital Management Inc AGNC Investment Corp Starwood Property Trust Inc New Residential Investment Corp Two Harbors Investment Corp

iShares MSCI Emerging Markets Small-Cap ETF   D+   SELL

Ticker	Traded On	NAV	Total Assets ($)	Dividend Yield (TTM)	Turnover Ratio	Expense Ratio
EEMS	NYSE Arca	42.34	$196,901,915	2.69	39	0.67

Ratings
Reward	D
Risk	C-
Recent Upgrade/Downgrade	Down

Fund Information
Fund Type	Exchange Traded Funds
Category	Global Emerg Mkts Equity
Sub-Category	Diversified Emerging Mkts
Prospectus Objective	Div Emerg Mkts
Inception Date	Aug-11
Open to New Investments	Y

Prices
Price (as of 9/30/2019)	42.11
52-Week High	46.29
52-Week Low	39.95

Total Returns (%)
3-Month	6-Month	1-Year	3-Year	5-Year
-5.34	-6.65	-5.34	4.32	-1.06

3-Year Standard Deviation	12.96
Effective Duration	

Valuation
Premium/Discount (1-Year Average)	-0.31

Company Information
Provider	iShares
Manager/Tenure	Diane Hsiung (8), Greg Savage (8), Jennifer Hsui (6), 3 others
Website	http://www.ishares.com
Address	iShares 400 Howard Street San Francisco CA 94105 United States
Phone Number	800-474-2737

PERFORMANCE

Ratings History
Date	Overall Rating	Risk Rating	Reward Rating
Q3-19	D+	C-	D
Q4-18	D+	D+	D+
Q4-17	B-	C+	B-
Q4-16	D+	C-	D+
Q4-15	C-	C-	C-

Asset & Performance History
Date	NAV	1-Year Total Return
2018	42.04	-18.19
2017	52.89	33.96
2016	40.53	1.78
2015	40.83	-7.58
2014	45.16	-0.33
2013	46.53	0.96

Total Assets: $196,901,915
Asset Allocation
Asset	%
Cash	0%
Stocks	100%
US Stocks	0%
Bonds	0%
US Bonds	0%
Other	0%

Services Offered:

Investment Strategy: The investment seeks to track the investment results of the MSCI Emerging Markets Small Cap Index. The fund generally will invest at least 90% of its assets in the component securities of the underlying index and in investments that have economic characteristics that are substantially identical to the component securities of the underlying index. The index is designed to measure the performance of equity securities of small-capitalization companies whose market capitalization represents the bottom 14% of companies in emerging market countries, as measured by market capitalization. **Top Holdings:** Impala Platinum Holdings Ltd   Azul SA Participating Preferred   Sibanye-Stillwater   Accton Technology Corp   Estacio Participacoes SA

First Trust IndXX NextG ETF   C   HOLD

Ticker	Traded On	NAV	Total Assets ($)	Dividend Yield (TTM)	Turnover Ratio	Expense Ratio
NXTG	NAS CM	50.26	$196,015,254	0.48	80	0.7

Ratings
Reward	C
Risk	C-
Recent Upgrade/Downgrade	Up

Fund Information
Fund Type	Exchange Traded Funds
Category	Technology Sector Equity
Sub-Category	Technology
Prospectus Objective	Technology
Inception Date	Feb-11
Open to New Investments	Y

Prices
Price (as of 9/30/2019)	50.33
52-Week High	51.53
52-Week Low	41.69

Total Returns (%)
3-Month	6-Month	1-Year	3-Year	5-Year
1.41	2.15	2.35	26.11	46.70

3-Year Standard Deviation	13.86
Effective Duration	

Valuation
Premium/Discount (1-Year Average)	-0.05

Company Information
Provider	First Trust
Manager/Tenure	Jon C. Erickson (8), Daniel J. Lindquist (8), David G. McGarel (8), 3 others
Website	http://www.ftportfolios.com/
Address	First Trust 120 E. Liberty Drive, Suite 400 Wheaton IL 60187 United States
Phone Number	800-621-1675

PERFORMANCE

Ratings History
Date	Overall Rating	Risk Rating	Reward Rating
Q3-19	C	C-	C
Q4-18	C-	D+	C-
Q4-17	B+	B	A-
Q4-16	D+	D	C-
Q4-15	C	C-	C

Asset & Performance History
Date	NAV	1-Year Total Return
2018	43.01	-16.81
2017	52.28	29.09
2016	41.18	14.7
2015	36.36	-2.99
2014	37.89	14.56
2013	33.44	33.65

Total Assets: $196,015,254
Asset Allocation
Asset	%
Cash	0%
Stocks	100%
US Stocks	49%
Bonds	0%
US Bonds	0%
Other	0%

Services Offered:

Investment Strategy: The investment seeks investment results that correspond generally to the price and yield (before the fund's fees and expenses) of an equity index called the Indxx 5G & NextG Thematic Index. The fund will normally invest at least 90% of its net assets (including investment borrowings) in the common stocks and depositary receipts that comprise the index. The index is designed to track the performance of companies that have devoted, or have committed to devote, material resources to the research, development and application of fifth generation ("5G") and next generation digital cellular technologies as they emerge. **Top Holdings:** Win Semiconductors Corp   Micron Technology Inc   CyrusOne Inc   MediaTek Inc   Lumentum Holdings Inc

Global X Uranium ETF

D   SELL

Ticker	Traded On	NAV	Total Assets ($)	Dividend Yield (TTM)	Turnover Ratio	Expense Ratio
URA	NYSE Arca	11.08	$194,884,416	1.4	54	0.69

Ratings
Reward	D
Risk	D
Recent Upgrade/Downgrade	

Fund Information
Fund Type	Exchange Traded Funds
Category	Natural Resources
Sub-Category	Natural Resources
Prospectus Objective	Unaligned
Inception Date	Nov-10
Open to New Investments	Y

Prices
Price (as of 9/30/2019)	11.00
52-Week High	13.58
52-Week Low	10.01

Total Returns (%)
3-Month	6-Month	1-Year	3-Year	5-Year
-8.80	-12.35	-16.73	-5.45	-48.52

3-Year Standard Deviation	32.13
Effective Duration	

Valuation
Premium/Discount (1-Year Average)	-0.68

Company Information
Provider	Global X Funds
Manager/Tenure	Chang Kim (5), Nam To (1), Wayne Xie (0), 1 other
Website	http://www.globalxfunds.com
Address	Global X Funds 600 Lexington Avenue, 20th Floor New York NY 10022 United States
Phone Number	888-493-8631

PERFORMANCE

Ratings History
Date	Overall Rating	Risk Rating	Reward Rating
Q3-19	D	D	D
Q4-18	D	D	D
Q4-17	D+	D	C
Q4-16	D	D	D
Q4-15	D+	D+	D+

Asset & Performance History
Date	NAV	1-Year Total Return
2018	11.82	-20.51
2017	14.87	19.04
2016	12.75	-2.69
2015	14.09	-36.63
2014	22.68	-22.33
2013	30.46	-21.58

Total Assets: $194,884,416
Asset Allocation
Asset	%
Cash	0%
Stocks	100%
US Stocks	5%
Bonds	0%
US Bonds	0%
Other	0%

Services Offered:

Investment Strategy: The investment seeks to provide investment results that correspond generally to the price and yield performance, before fees and expenses, of the Solactive Global Uranium & Nuclear Components Total Return Index. The fund invests at least 80% of its total assets in the securities of the underlying index and in American Depository Receipts ("ADRs") and Global Depository Receipts ("GDRs") based on the securities in the underlying index. The underlying index is designed to measure broad based equity market performance of global companies involved in the uranium industry. The fund is non-diversified. **Top Holdings:** Cameco Corp Uranium Participation Corp NexGen Energy Ltd Barrick Gold Corp ITOCHU Corp

---

Direxion Daily S&P Oil & Gas Exp. & Prod. Bull 3X Shares

E+   SELL

Ticker	Traded On	NAV	Total Assets ($)	Dividend Yield (TTM)	Turnover Ratio	Expense Ratio
GUSH	NYSE Arca	3.30	$194,567,130	1.77	119	1.17

Ratings
Reward	E+
Risk	D
Recent Upgrade/Downgrade	Down

Fund Information
Fund Type	Exchange Traded Funds
Category	Trading Tools
Sub-Category	Trading--Leveraged Equity
Prospectus Objective	Natl Res
Inception Date	May-15
Open to New Investments	Y

Prices
Price (as of 9/30/2019)	3.32
52-Week High	43.24
52-Week Low	2.78

Total Returns (%)
3-Month	6-Month	1-Year	3-Year	5-Year
-52.85	-71.32	-91.82	-92.33	

3-Year Standard Deviation	88.3
Effective Duration	

Valuation
Premium/Discount (1-Year Average)	0.21

Company Information
Provider	Direxion Funds
Manager/Tenure	Paul Brigandi (4), Tony Ng (4)
Website	http://www.direxionfunds.com
Address	Direxion Funds 1301 Avenue Of The Americas (6th Avenue) New York NY 10019 United States
Phone Number	646-572-3390

PERFORMANCE

Ratings History
Date	Overall Rating	Risk Rating	Reward Rating
Q3-19	E+	D	E+
Q4-18	D	D	D
Q4-17	D	D	D
Q4-16	D	D	D
Q4-15	U		

Asset & Performance History
Date	NAV	1-Year Total Return
2018	7.79	-73.46
2017	30.3	-40.18
2016	50.66	57.58
2015	33.15	
2014		
2013		

Total Assets: $194,567,130
Asset Allocation
Asset	%
Cash	47%
Stocks	53%
US Stocks	52%
Bonds	0%
US Bonds	0%
Other	0%

Services Offered:

Investment Strategy: The investment seeks daily investment results, of 300% of the daily performance of the S&P Oil & Gas Exploration & Production Select Industry Index. The fund, under normal circumstances, invests at least 80% of its net assets (plus borrowing for investment purposes) in financial instruments and securities of the index, ETFs that track the index and other financial instruments that provide daily leveraged exposure to the index or ETFs that track the index. The index is designed to measure the performance of a sub-industry or group of sub-industries determined based on the Global Industry Classification Standards. The fund is non-diversified. **Top Holdings:** S&P Oil & Gas Exploration S&P Oil & Gas Exploration Anadarko Petroleum Corp Pioneer Natural Resources Co Noble Energy Inc

JPMorgan Global Bond Opportunities ETF   C   HOLD

Ticker	Traded On	NAV	Total Assets ($)	Dividend Yield (TTM)	Turnover Ratio	Expense Ratio
JPGB	BATS	51.02	$193,862,739	5.31	73	0.55

Ratings
Reward   C
Risk   C-
Recent Upgrade/Downgrade   Up

Fund Information
Fund Type   Exchange Traded Funds
Category   US Fixed Income
Sub-Category   Multisector Bond
Prospectus Objective   Worldwide Bond
Inception Date   Apr-17
Open to New Investments   Y

Prices
Price (as of 9/30/2019)   51.12
52-Week High   51.53
52-Week Low   47.26

Total Returns (%)

3-Month	6-Month	1-Year	3-Year	5-Year
1.49	4.70	7.76		

3-Year Standard Deviation
Effective Duration   4.30

Valuation
Premium/Discount (1-Year Average)   0.08

Company Information
Provider   JPMorgan
Manager/Tenure   Robert Michele (2), Iain T. Stealey (2)
Website   http://www.jpmorganfunds.com
Address   JPMorgan 270 Park Avenue New York NY 10017-2070 United States
Phone Number   800-480-4111

PERFORMANCE

Ratings History

Date	Overall Rating	Risk Rating	Reward Rating
Q3-19	C	C-	C
Q4-18	D+	C-	D
Q4-17	U		
Q4-16			
Q4-15			

Asset & Performance History

Date	NAV	1-Year Total Return
2018	47.34	-4.41
2017	50.93	
2016		
2015		
2014		
2013		

Total Assets: $193,862,739
Asset Allocation

Asset	%
Cash	7%
Stocks	0%
US Stocks	0%
Bonds	90%
US Bonds	45%
Other	0%

Services Offered:

Investment Strategy: The investment seeks to provide total return. Under normal circumstances, the fund will invest at least 80% of its assets in bonds. It will invest at least 40% of its assets in countries other than the United States. The fund may invest in developed or emerging markets. It generally invests at least 25% of its assets in securities that, at the time of purchase are rated investment grade or the unrated equivalent. "Assets" means net assets plus the amount of borrowings for investment purposes. The fund may also use currency related transactions involving currency derivatives as part of its primary investment strategy. **Top Holdings:** Canada (Government of) 2.25% Portugal (Republic Of) 2.88% Spain (Kingdom of) 2.15% Republic of South Africa 6.5% Fnma Pass-Thru I 3.5%

Fidelity® MSCI Materials Index ETF   C+   HOLD

Ticker	Traded On	NAV	Total Assets ($)	Dividend Yield (TTM)	Turnover Ratio	Expense Ratio
FMAT	NYSE Arca	32.34	$192,412,677	2.01	12	0.08

Ratings
Reward   B-
Risk   C
Recent Upgrade/Downgrade   Up

Fund Information
Fund Type   Exchange Traded Funds
Category   Natural Resources
Sub-Category   Natural Resources
Prospectus Objective   Natl Res
Inception Date   Oct-13
Open to New Investments   Y

Prices
Price (as of 9/30/2019)   32.33
52-Week High   33.91
52-Week Low   26.67

Total Returns (%)

3-Month	6-Month	1-Year	3-Year	5-Year
-1.57	2.17	-2.34	24.60	30.65

3-Year Standard Deviation   15.67
Effective Duration

Valuation
Premium/Discount (1-Year Average)   -0.02

Company Information
Provider   Fidelity Investments
Manager/Tenure   Jennifer Hsui (5), Greg Savage (5), Alan Mason (3), 2 others
Website   http://www.institutional.fidelity.com
Address   Fidelity Investments 82 Devonshire Street Boston MA 2109 United States
Phone Number   617-563-7000

PERFORMANCE

Ratings History

Date	Overall Rating	Risk Rating	Reward Rating
Q3-19	C+	C	B-
Q4-18	C	C-	C
Q4-17	B	C+	B+
Q4-16	C	C-	C+
Q4-15	C-	C	C-

Asset & Performance History

Date	NAV	1-Year Total Return
2018	28.37	-17.4
2017	35.02	23.41
2016	28.85	21.46
2015	24.21	-10.21
2014	27.52	5.75
2013	26.45	

Total Assets: $192,412,677
Asset Allocation

Asset	%
Cash	0%
Stocks	100%
US Stocks	86%
Bonds	0%
US Bonds	0%
Other	0%

Services Offered:

Investment Strategy: The investment seeks to provide investment returns that correspond, before fees and expenses, generally to the performance of the MSCI USA IMI Materials Index. The fund invests at least 80% of assets in securities included in the fund's underlying index. The fund's underlying index is the MSCI USA IMI Materials Index, which represents the performance of the materials sector in the U.S. equity market. It may or may not hold all of the securities in the MSCI USA IMI Materials Index. The fund is non-diversified. **Top Holdings:** Linde PLC Ecolab Inc DuPont de Nemours Inc Air Products & Chemicals Inc Sherwin-Williams Co

VanEck Vectors AMT-Free Long Municipal Index ETF   C   HOLD

Ticker	Traded On	NAV	Total Assets ($)	Dividend Yield (TTM)	Turnover Ratio	Expense Ratio
MLN	BATS	21.14	$192,390,915	2.82	22	0.24

Ratings
Reward   B-
Risk   C-
Recent Upgrade/Downgrade

Fund Information
Fund Type   Exchange Traded Funds
Category   US Muni Fixed Inc
Sub-Category   Muni National Long
Prospectus Objective   Muni Bond - Natl
Inception Date   Jan-08
Open to New Investments   Y

Prices
Price (as of 9/30/2019)   21.15
52-Week High   21.46
52-Week Low   18.91

Total Returns (%)

3-Month	6-Month	1-Year	3-Year	5-Year
2.44	5.82	11.68	11.32	26.15

3-Year Standard Deviation   5.36
Effective Duration   8.01

Valuation
Premium/Discount (1-Year Average)   -0.08

Company Information
Provider   VanEck
Manager/Tenure   James T. Colby (11)
Website   http://www.vaneck.com
Address   Van Eck Associates Corporation 666
                    Third Avenue New York NY 10017
                    United States
Phone Number   800-826-1115

PERFORMANCE

Ratings History

Date	Overall Rating	Risk Rating	Reward Rating
Q3-19	C	C-	B-
Q4-18	D+	C-	D+
Q4-17	B-	B	C
Q4-16	C	C-	C
Q4-15	C	C-	C

Asset & Performance History

Date	NAV	1-Year Total Return
2018	19.62	-0.98
2017	20.38	8.55
2016	19.34	0.16
2015	19.9	4.16
2014	19.77	15.69
2013	17.77	-8.18

Total Assets: $192,390,915

Asset Allocation

Asset	%
Cash	0%
Stocks	0%
US Stocks	0%
Bonds	100%
US Bonds	100%
Other	0%

Services Offered:

Investment Strategy: The investment seeks to replicate as closely as possible, before fees and expenses, the price and yield performance of the Bloomberg Barclays AMT-Free Long Continuous Municipal Index. The fund normally invests at least 80% of its total assets in fixed income securities that comprise the index. The index is comprised of publicly traded municipal bonds that cover the U.S. dollar denominated long-term tax-exempt bond market. **Top Holdings:** PENNSYLVANIA ST TPK COMMN TPK REV 5% HUDSON YDS INFRASTRUCTURE CORP N Y SECOND INDENTURE REV 5% NEW YORK ST MTG AGY HOMEOWNER MTG REV 3.62% PENNSYLVANIA ST CTFS PARTN 4% CALIFORNIA ST 5%

Invesco Cleantech™ ETF   C   HOLD

Ticker	Traded On	NAV	Total Assets ($)	Dividend Yield (TTM)	Turnover Ratio	Expense Ratio
PZD	NYSE Arca	44.53	$191,471,493	0.46	21	0.68

Ratings
Reward   C
Risk   D+
Recent Upgrade/Downgrade

Fund Information
Fund Type   Exchange Traded Funds
Category   Industrials Sector Equity
Sub-Category   Miscellaneous Sector
Prospectus Objective   Technology
Inception Date   Oct-06
Open to New Investments   Y

Prices
Price (as of 9/30/2019)   44.61
52-Week High   46.01
52-Week Low   35.15

Total Returns (%)

3-Month	6-Month	1-Year	3-Year	5-Year
-2.90	4.35	3.84	37.63	59.60

3-Year Standard Deviation   15.99
Effective Duration

Valuation
Premium/Discount (1-Year Average)   0.12

Company Information
Provider   Invesco
Manager/Tenure   Peter Hubbard (12), Michael Jeanette
                    (6), Tony Seisser (4)
Website   http://www.invesco.com/us
Address   Invesco 11 Greenway Plaza, Ste. 2500
                    Houston TX 77046 United States
Phone Number   800-659-1005

PERFORMANCE

Ratings History

Date	Overall Rating	Risk Rating	Reward Rating
Q3-19	C	D+	C
Q4-18	C-	D+	C-
Q4-17	A-	B	A
Q4-16	C	D+	B-
Q4-15	C-	D+	C

Asset & Performance History

Date	NAV	1-Year Total Return
2018	36.89	-12.34
2017	42.31	30.26
2016	32.79	12.86
2015	29.37	2.59
2014	28.85	-8.1
2013	31.63	37.72

Total Assets: $191,471,493

Asset Allocation

Asset	%
Cash	0%
Stocks	100%
US Stocks	58%
Bonds	0%
US Bonds	0%
Other	0%

Services Offered:

Investment Strategy: The investment seeks to track the investment results (before fees and expenses) of The Cleantech IndexTM. The fund generally will invest at least 90% of its total assets in the securities that comprise the underlying index, which is designed to track the performance of publicly traded clean technology (or "cleantech") companies. Cleantech considers a company to be a cleantech company when it derives at least 50% of its revenues or operating profits from cleantech businesses. **Top Holdings:** Johnson Controls International PLC Ansys Inc Eurofins Scientific SE Roper Technologies Inc Hexcel Corp

First Trust SSI Strategic Convertible Securities ETF   C   HOLD

Ticker	Traded On	NAV	Total Assets ($)	Dividend Yield (TTM)	Turnover Ratio	Expense Ratio
FCVT	NAS CM	31.12	$191,396,114	1.58	71	0.95

Ratings
Reward   C+
Risk   C-
Recent Upgrade/Downgrade

Fund Information
Fund Type   Exchange Traded Funds
Category   Convertibles
Sub-Category   Convertibles
Prospectus Objective   Convertible Bond
Inception Date   Nov-15
Open to New Investments   Y

Prices
Price (as of 9/30/2019)   31.20
52-Week High   32.22
52-Week Low   26.47

Total Returns (%)

3-Month	6-Month	1-Year	3-Year	5-Year
-1.21	2.69	3.30	28.46	

3-Year Standard Deviation   8.74
Effective Duration   2.18

Valuation
Premium/Discount (1-Year Average)   -0.06

Company Information
Provider   First Trust
Manager/Tenure   George M. Douglas (3), Florian Eitner
                    (3), Ethan Ganz (3), 2 others
Website   http://www.ftportfolios.com/
Address   First Trust 120 E. Liberty Drive, Suite
                    400 Wheaton IL 60187 United States
Phone Number   800-621-1675

PERFORMANCE

Ratings History

Date	Overall Rating	Risk Rating	Reward Rating
Q3-19	C	C-	C+
Q4-18	C-	C-	C-
Q4-17	C	B+	C-
Q4-16	D	C-	D+
Q4-15			

Asset & Performance History

Date	NAV	1-Year Total Return
2018	27.65	-1.54
2017	28.58	12.78
2016	25.72	6.78
2015	24.56	
2014		
2013		

Total Assets: $191,396,114
Asset Allocation

Asset	%
Cash	1%
Stocks	3%
US Stocks	3%
Bonds	0%
US Bonds	0%
Other	1%

Services Offered:

Investment Strategy: The investment seeks total return. Under normal market conditions, the fund seeks to achieve its investment objective by investing at least 80% of its net assets (including investment borrowings) in a portfolio of U.S. and non-U.S. convertible securities. In general, convertible securities combine the investment characteristics of bonds and common stocks and typically consist of debt securities or preferred securities that may be converted or exchanged within a specified period of time into a certain amount of common stock or other equity security of the same or a different issuer. The fund is non-diversified. **Top Holdings:** Wells Fargo & Co 7 1/2 % Non Cum Perp Conv Pfd Shs -A- Series -L- Bank of America Corporation 7 1/4 % Non-Cum Perp Conv Pfd Shs Series -L- Microchip Technology Incorporated 1.63% Akamai Technologies, Inc. 0.13% Advanced Micro Devices, Inc. 2.13%

UBS ETRACS 2xLeveraged Long Wells Fargo Business Development Company Index ETN   C   HOLD

Ticker	Traded On	NAV	Total Assets ($)	Dividend Yield (TTM)	Turnover Ratio	Expense Ratio
BDCL	NYSE Arca	14.68	$191,136,204	15.51		0.85

Ratings
Reward   C
Risk   C-
Recent Upgrade/Downgrade

Fund Information
Fund Type   Exchange Traded Funds
Category   Trading Tools
Sub-Category   Trading--Leveraged Equity
Prospectus Objective   Growth
Inception Date   May-11
Open to New Investments   Y

Prices
Price (as of 9/30/2019)   14.70
52-Week High   16.03
52-Week Low   11.01

Total Returns (%)

3-Month	6-Month	1-Year	3-Year	5-Year
5.77	10.68	7.74	27.32	40.95

3-Year Standard Deviation   26.23
Effective Duration

Valuation
Premium/Discount (1-Year Average)   0.06

Company Information
Provider   UBS Group AG
Manager/Tenure   No Manager (8)
Website   http://www.ubs.com
Address   Bahnhofstrasse 45 Zürich 8098
                    Switzerland
Phone Number   412-037-1952

PERFORMANCE

Ratings History

Date	Overall Rating	Risk Rating	Reward Rating
Q3-19	C	C-	C
Q4-18	C	C	C-
Q4-17	C	C	C
Q4-16	C	C-	C+
Q4-15	C-	C-	C-

Asset & Performance History

Date	NAV	1-Year Total Return
2018	11.59	-16.36
2017	16.25	-1.88
2016	19.7	48.65
2015	15.84	-10.88
2014	21.15	-16.77
2013	29.64	31.57

Total Assets: $191,136,204
Asset Allocation

Asset	%
Cash	%
Stocks	%
US Stocks	%
Bonds	%
US Bonds	%
Other	%

Services Offered:

Investment Strategy: The investment seeks to replicate, net of expenses, twice the performance of the Wells Fargo Business Development Company Index.
 The index is a float adjusted, capitalization-weighted index that is intended to measure the performance of all Business Development Companies ("BDC") that are listed on the New York Stock Exchange or NASDAQ and satisfy specified market capitalization and other eligibility requirements. The BDC business model is to lend to small and midsized companies at high yield equivalent rates while also at times taking equity stakes in such companies. **Top Holdings:**

DeltaShares S&P International Managed Risk ETF   D+   SELL

Ticker	Traded On	NAV	Total Assets ($)	Dividend Yield (TTM)	Turnover Ratio	Expense Ratio
DMRI	NYSE Arca	48.27	$190,663,870	2.85	189	0.5

Ratings
Reward	C-
Risk	D
Recent Upgrade/Downgrade	Up

Fund Information
Fund Type	Exchange Traded Funds
Category	Global Equity Large Cap
Sub-Category	Foreign Large Blend
Prospectus Objective	Foreign Stock
Inception Date	Jul-17
Open to New Investments	Y

Prices
Price (as of 9/30/2019)	48.24
52-Week High	51.19
52-Week Low	44.43

Total Returns (%)
3-Month	6-Month	1-Year	3-Year	5-Year
-1.51	1.24	-2.27		

3-Year Standard Deviation	
Effective Duration	

Valuation
Premium/Discount (1-Year Average)	0.34

Company Information
Provider	DeltaShares
Manager/Tenure	Blake Graves (2), Charles Lowery (2), Louis Ng (2)
Website	http://www.deltashares.com
Address	DeltaShares United States
Phone Number	

PERFORMANCE

Ratings History
Date	Overall Rating	Risk Rating	Reward Rating
Q3-19	D+	D	C-
Q4-18	D	D	D
Q4-17	U		
Q4-16			
Q4-15			

Asset & Performance History
Date	NAV	1-Year Total Return
2018	44.94	-13.3
2017	53.13	
2016		
2015		
2014		
2013		

Total Assets: $190,663,870
Asset Allocation
Asset	%
Cash	1%
Stocks	99%
US Stocks	2%
Bonds	0%
US Bonds	0%
Other	0%

Services Offered:

Investment Strategy: The investment seeks to track the investment results, before fees and expenses, of the S&P EPAC Ex. Korea LargeMidCap Managed Risk 2.0 Index. Under normal market conditions, the fund invests a substantial portion, but at least 80%, of its assets, exclusive of collateral held from securities lending, in securities comprising the underlying index. The underlying index seeks to achieve these objectives by allocating weightings among the S&P EPAC Ex. Korea LargeMidCap Index, the S&P U.S. Treasury Bond Current 5-Year Index and the S&P U.S. Treasury Bill 0-3 Month Index. The fund is non-diversified. **Top Holdings:** Nestle SA Novartis AG mini MSCI EAFE Index Futures Sept19 Roche Holding AG Dividend Right Cert. Toyota Motor Corp

---

WisdomTree Emerging Markets Local Debt Fund   C   HOLD

Ticker	Traded On	NAV	Total Assets ($)	Dividend Yield (TTM)	Turnover Ratio	Expense Ratio
ELD	NYSE Arca	34.57	$190,152,857	5.18	44	0.55

Ratings
Reward	C+
Risk	C-
Recent Upgrade/Downgrade	Up

Fund Information
Fund Type	Exchange Traded Funds
Category	Emerging Mkts Fixed Inc
Sub-Category	Emerging-Markets Local-Currency Bond
Prospectus Objective	Income
Inception Date	Aug-10
Open to New Investments	Y

Prices
Price (as of 9/30/2019)	34.41
52-Week High	36.25
52-Week Low	32.28

Total Returns (%)
3-Month	6-Month	1-Year	3-Year	5-Year
-1.55	3.08	10.68	5.96	-0.26

3-Year Standard Deviation	9.27
Effective Duration	5.00

Valuation
Premium/Discount (1-Year Average)	-0.06

Company Information
Provider	WisdomTree
Manager/Tenure	Stephanie Shu (9), Paul L. Benson (3)
Website	http://www.wisdomtree.com
Address	WisdomTree 245 Park Avenue, 35th floor New York NY 10167 United States
Phone Number	866-909-9473

PERFORMANCE

Ratings History
Date	Overall Rating	Risk Rating	Reward Rating
Q3-19	C	C-	C+
Q4-18	D+	C-	D+
Q4-17	C	C	C
Q4-16	D+	C-	D+
Q4-15	D	D	D

Asset & Performance History
Date	NAV	1-Year Total Return
2018	33.49	-7.71
2017	38.52	12.46
2016	35.91	9.9
2015	34.28	-13.64
2014	41.73	-5.43
2013	45.91	-10.38

Total Assets: $190,152,857
Asset Allocation
Asset	%
Cash	7%
Stocks	0%
US Stocks	0%
Bonds	93%
US Bonds	0%
Other	0%

Services Offered:

Investment Strategy: The investment seeks a high level of total return consisting of both income and capital appreciation. The fund seeks to achieve its investment objective through investment in bonds and other debt instruments denominated in the local currencies of emerging market countries. Under normal circumstances, it will invest at least 80% of its net assets, plus the amount of any borrowings for investment purposes, in Local Debt. The Advisor attempts to maintain an aggregate portfolio duration of between two and ten years under normal market conditions. The fund is non-diversified. **Top Holdings:** Brazil (Federative Republic) 10% Brazil (Federative Republic) 10% Nota Do Tesouro Nacional Notes 01/25 10 Indonesia(Rep Of) 8.75% Nota Do Tesouro Nacional Notes 01/27 10

UBS ETRACS Monthly Pay 2xLeveraged Mortgage REIT ETN Series B   C   HOLD

Ticker	Traded On	NAV	Total Assets ($)	Dividend Yield (TTM)	Turnover Ratio	Expense Ratio
MRRL	NYSE Arca	13.08	$189,675,950	21.9		0.4

Ratings

Reward	C
Risk	C+
Recent Upgrade/Downgrade	

Fund Information

Fund Type	Exchange Traded Funds
Category	Trading Tools
Sub-Category	Trading--Leveraged Equity
Prospectus Objective	Real Estate
Inception Date	Oct-15
Open to New Investments	Y

Prices

Price (as of 9/30/2019)	13.13
52-Week High	15.46
52-Week Low	11.53

Total Returns (%)

3-Month	6-Month	1-Year	3-Year	5-Year
2.38	-0.46	3.90	52.02	

3-Year Standard Deviation	25.51
Effective Duration	

Valuation

Premium/Discount (1-Year Average)	0.02

Company Information

Provider	UBS Group AG
Manager/Tenure	No Manager (3)
Website	http://www.ubs.com
Address	Bahnhofstrasse 45 Zürich 8098 Switzerland
Phone Number	412-037-1952

PERFORMANCE

Ratings History

Date	Overall Rating	Risk Rating	Reward Rating
Q3-19	C	C+	C
Q4-18	C-	C-	C-
Q4-17	C	B-	C
Q4-16	D	D+	D+
Q4-15			

Asset & Performance History

Date	NAV	1-Year Total Return
2018	12.54	-12.25
2017	17.61	38.04
2016	15.55	47.29
2015	13.25	
2014		
2013		

Total Assets: $189,675,950

Asset Allocation

Asset	%
Cash	%
Stocks	%
US Stocks	%
Bonds	%
US Bonds	%
Other	%

Services Offered:

Investment Strategy: The investment seeks a return linked to the Market Vectors® Global Mortgage REITs Index. The ETRACS Monthly Pay 2xLeveraged Mortgage REIT ETN Series B due October 16, 2042 is a series of Monthly Pay 2xLeveraged ETRACS. The index tracks the overall performance of publicly-traded mortgage REITs that derive at least 50% of their revenues from mortgage-related activities. The Securities are senior unsecured debt securities issued by UBS AG. The Securities are two times leveraged with respect to the index, and, as a result, will benefit from two times any positive, but will be exposed to two times any negative, compounded monthly performance of the index. **Top Holdings:**

Invesco S&P 500® Equal Weight Industrials ETF   C   HOLD

Ticker	Traded On	NAV	Total Assets ($)	Dividend Yield (TTM)	Turnover Ratio	Expense Ratio
RGI	NYSE Arca	126.41	$189,618,683	1.52		0.4

Ratings

Reward	C+
Risk	C-
Recent Upgrade/Downgrade	

Fund Information

Fund Type	Exchange Traded Funds
Category	Industrials Sector Equity
Sub-Category	Industrials
Prospectus Objective	Unaligned
Inception Date	Nov-06
Open to New Investments	Y

Prices

Price (as of 9/30/2019)	126.46
52-Week High	129.26
52-Week Low	96.98

Total Returns (%)

3-Month	6-Month	1-Year	3-Year	5-Year
0.27	3.80	1.66	41.16	62.34

3-Year Standard Deviation	17.24
Effective Duration	

Valuation

Premium/Discount (1-Year Average)	-0.04

Company Information

Provider	Invesco
Manager/Tenure	Peter Hubbard (1), Michael Jeanette (1), Tony Seisser (1)
Website	http://www.invesco.com/us
Address	Invesco 11 Greenway Plaza, Ste. 2500 Houston TX 77046 United States
Phone Number	800-659-1005

PERFORMANCE

Ratings History

Date	Overall Rating	Risk Rating	Reward Rating
Q3-19	C	C-	C+
Q4-18	C	C-	C
Q4-17	B+	B	A-
Q4-16	B-	C-	B
Q4-15	C	C-	C

Asset & Performance History

Date	NAV	1-Year Total Return
2018	103.4	-12.98
2017	120.47	22.99
2016	99.08	20.94
2015	82.75	-6.85
2014	90.15	11.58
2013	81.87	39.47

Total Assets: $189,618,683

Asset Allocation

Asset	%
Cash	0%
Stocks	100%
US Stocks	100%
Bonds	0%
US Bonds	0%
Other	0%

Services Offered:

Investment Strategy: The investment seeks to track the investment results (before fees and expenses) of the S&P 500® Equal Weight Industrials Index (the "underlying index"). The fund generally will invest at least 90% of its total assets in the securities that comprise the underlying index. The underlying index is composed of all of the components of the S&P 500® Industrials Index, an index that contains the common stocks of all companies included in the S&P 500® Index that are classified as members of the industrials sector, as defined according to the Global Industry Classification Standard ("GICS"). The fund is non-diversified. **Top Holdings:** JB Hunt Transport Services Inc   Northrop Grumman Corp   United Parcel Service Inc Class B   TransDigm Group Inc   Jacobs Engineering Group Inc

Invesco Global Water ETF   C   HOLD

Ticker	Traded On	NAV	Total Assets ($)	Dividend Yield (TTM)	Turnover Ratio	Expense Ratio
PIO	NAS CM	27.94	$188,584,287	1.49	34	0.75

Ratings
Reward   C+
Risk   C-
Recent Upgrade/Downgrade

Fund Information
Fund Type   Exchange Traded Funds
Category   Equity Misc
Sub-Category   Miscellaneous Sector
Prospectus Objective   Natl Res
Inception Date   Jun-07
Open to New Investments

Prices
Price (as of 9/30/2019)   27.88
52-Week High   28.36
52-Week Low   22.13

Total Returns (%)

3-Month	6-Month	1-Year	3-Year	5-Year
-0.10	3.70	9.93	31.07	33.17

3-Year Standard Deviation   12.33
Effective Duration

Valuation
Premium/Discount (1-Year Average)   -0.26

Company Information
Provider   Invesco
Manager/Tenure   Peter Hubbard (12), Michael Jeanette (4), Tony Seisser (4)
Website   http://www.invesco.com/us
Address   Invesco 11 Greenway Plaza, Ste. 2500 Houston TX 77046 United States
Phone Number   800-659-1005

PERFORMANCE

Ratings History

Date	Overall Rating	Risk Rating	Reward Rating
Q3-19	C	C-	C+
Q4-18	C-	C-	C
Q4-17	C+	B-	C+
Q4-16	C-	C-	C-
Q4-15	C	C	C

Asset & Performance History

Date	NAV	1-Year Total Return
2018	23.19	-9.37
2017	26.07	26.17
2016	20.88	0.91
2015	20.99	-7.62
2014	23.07	1.87
2013	22.95	29.15

Total Assets: $188,584,287

Asset Allocation

Asset	%
Cash	0%
Stocks	100%
US Stocks	51%
Bonds	0%
US Bonds	0%
Other	0%

Services Offered: Wire Redemption

Investment Strategy: The investment seeks to track the investment results (before fees and expenses) of the Nasdaq OMX Global Water IndexSM (the "underlying index"). The fund generally will invest at least 90% of its total assets in the securities that comprise the underlying index, as well as ADRs and GDRs that are based on the securities in the underlying index. The underlying index may be comprised of common stocks, ordinary shares, depositary receipts, depositary shares, Dutch certificates, shares of beneficial interest, stapled securities and tracking stocks and also may include companies in emerging market countries. It is non-diversified. **Top Holdings:** Ecolab Inc Danaher Corp Pentair PLC Geberit AG Ferguson PLC

iShares Global Industrials ETF   C   HOLD

Ticker	Traded On	NAV	Total Assets ($)	Dividend Yield (TTM)	Turnover Ratio	Expense Ratio
EXI	NYSE Arca	91.27	$187,098,711	1.88	5	0.46

Ratings
Reward   C
Risk   C-
Recent Upgrade/Downgrade

Fund Information
Fund Type   Exchange Traded Funds
Category   Industrials Sector Equity
Sub-Category   Industrials
Prospectus Objective   World Stock
Inception Date   Sep-06
Open to New Investments   Y

Prices
Price (as of 9/30/2019)   91.33
52-Week High   94.16
52-Week Low   73.93

Total Returns (%)

3-Month	6-Month	1-Year	3-Year	5-Year
-0.79	2.24	-0.90	30.63	44.69

3-Year Standard Deviation   13.92
Effective Duration

Valuation
Premium/Discount (1-Year Average)   -0.03

Company Information
Provider   iShares
Manager/Tenure   Greg Savage (11), Jennifer Hsui (7), Alan Mason (3), 2 others
Website   http://www.ishares.com
Address   iShares 400 Howard Street San Francisco CA 94105 United States
Phone Number   800-474-2737

PERFORMANCE

Ratings History

Date	Overall Rating	Risk Rating	Reward Rating
Q3-19	C	C-	C
Q4-18	C-	C-	C-
Q4-17	B	B-	B
Q4-16	C	C-	C+
Q4-15	C	C	C

Asset & Performance History

Date	NAV	1-Year Total Return
2018	77.91	-14.31
2017	92.77	24.88
2016	75.45	13
2015	67.98	-2.17
2014	70.81	1.66
2013	70.97	31.97

Total Assets: $187,098,711

Asset Allocation

Asset	%
Cash	0%
Stocks	100%
US Stocks	54%
Bonds	0%
US Bonds	0%
Other	0%

Services Offered:

Investment Strategy: The investment seeks to track the investment results of the S&P Global 1200 Industrials IndexTM. The fund generally invests at least 90% of its assets in securities of the underlying index and in depositary receipts representing securities of the underlying index. It may invest the remainder of its assets in certain futures, options and swap contracts, cash and cash equivalents, as well as in securities not included in the underlying index. The index measures the performance of companies that the index provider deems to be part of the industrials sector of the economy and that the index provider believes are important to global markets. **Top Holdings:** Boeing Co Honeywell International Inc Union Pacific Corp United Technologies Corp Lockheed Martin Corp

SPDR® Portfolio Europe ETF   C   HOLD

Ticker	Traded On	NAV	Total Assets ($)	Dividend Yield (TTM)	Turnover Ratio	Expense Ratio
SPEU	NYSE Arca		$186,499,874	3.5	5	0.09

Ratings

Reward	C
Risk	C-
Recent Upgrade/Downgrade	

Fund Information

Fund Type	Exchange Traded Funds
Category	Europe Equity Large Cap
Sub-Category	Europe Stock
Prospectus Objective	Europe Stock
Inception Date	Oct-02
Open to New Investments	Y

Prices

Price (as of 9/30/2019)	33.25
52-Week High	34.78
52-Week Low	28.95

Total Returns (%)

3-Month	6-Month	1-Year	3-Year	5-Year
-2.31	2.01	2.55	21.65	7.33

3-Year Standard Deviation	12.42
Effective Duration	

Valuation

Premium/Discount (1-Year Average)	-0.09

Company Information

Provider	SPDR State Street Global Advisors
Manager/Tenure	Michael J. Feehily (8), Karl A. Schneider (4), Mark Krivitsky (2)
Website	http://www.spdrs.com
Address	SPDR State Street Global Advisors State Street Financial Center, 1 Lincoln Street Boston MA 02111-2900 United States
Phone Number	617-786-3000

PERFORMANCE

Ratings History

Date	Overall Rating	Risk Rating	Reward Rating
Q3-19	C	C-	C
Q4-18	D+	C-	D+
Q4-17	C+	B-	C+
Q4-16	D+	D+	D+
Q4-15	C-	C-	C-

Asset & Performance History

Date	NAV	1-Year Total Return
2018	29.83	-14.34
2017	36.09	23.66
2016	30.07	-4.21
2015	31.93	-4.37
2014	34.51	-6.68
2013	39	22.36

Total Assets: $186,499,874

Asset Allocation

Asset	%
Cash	1%
Stocks	99%
US Stocks	2%
Bonds	0%
US Bonds	0%
Other	0%

Services Offered: Dividend Investment Plan

Investment Strategy: The investment seeks to provide investment results that, before fees and expenses, correspond generally to the total return performance of the STOXX Europe Total Market Index. Under normal market conditions, the fund generally invests substantially all, but at least 80%, of its total assets in the securities comprising the index. It employs a sampling strategy, which means that the fund is not required to purchase all of the securities represented in the index. The index is a free-float market capitalization weighted index designed to provide a broad representation of publicly traded Western European companies. The fund is non-diversified. **Top Holdings:** Nestle SA Novartis AG Roche Holding AG Dividend Right Cert. HSBC Holdings PLC Total SA

First Trust S&P REIT Index Fund   C   HOLD

Ticker	Traded On	NAV	Total Assets ($)	Dividend Yield (TTM)	Turnover Ratio	Expense Ratio
FRI	NYSE Arca	26.60	$184,841,044	2.6	10	0.5

Ratings

Reward	C+
Risk	C-
Recent Upgrade/Downgrade	

Fund Information

Fund Type	Exchange Traded Funds
Category	Real Estate Sector Equity
Sub-Category	Real Estate
Prospectus Objective	Real Estate
Inception Date	May-07
Open to New Investments	Y

Prices

Price (as of 9/30/2019)	26.62
52-Week High	26.64
52-Week Low	20.79

Total Returns (%)

3-Month	6-Month	1-Year	3-Year	5-Year
7.60	7.93	18.22	20.37	55.90

3-Year Standard Deviation	12.96
Effective Duration	

Valuation

Premium/Discount (1-Year Average)	0.03

Company Information

Provider	First Trust
Manager/Tenure	Jon C. Erickson (12), Daniel J. Lindquist (12), David G. McGarel (12), 3 others
Website	http://www.ftportfolios.com/
Address	First Trust 120 E. Liberty Drive, Suite 400 Wheaton IL 60187 United States
Phone Number	800-621-1675

PERFORMANCE

Ratings History

Date	Overall Rating	Risk Rating	Reward Rating
Q3-19	C	C-	C+
Q4-18	C	C-	C
Q4-17	B-	B	C+
Q4-16	C+	C	C+
Q4-15	C	C	C+

Asset & Performance History

Date	NAV	1-Year Total Return
2018	21.63	-4.23
2017	23.28	3.81
2016	23.07	8
2015	22.07	1.96
2014	22.24	29.57
2013	17.54	1.83

Total Assets: $184,841,044

Asset Allocation

Asset	%
Cash	0%
Stocks	100%
US Stocks	100%
Bonds	0%
US Bonds	0%
Other	0%

Services Offered:

Investment Strategy: The investment seeks investment results that correspond generally to the price and yield (before the fund's fees and expenses) of an equity index called the S&P United States REIT Index. The fund will normally invest at least 90% of its net assets (including investment borrowings) in the real estate investment trusts ("REITs") that comprise the index. The index seeks to measure the performance of publicly-traded traded REITs domiciled in the United States that meet certain eligibility requirements. **Top Holdings:** Prologis Inc Simon Property Group Inc Public Storage Welltower Inc Equity Residential

Motley Fool 100 Index ETF   C   HOLD

Ticker	Traded On	NAV	Total Assets ($)	Dividend Yield (TTM)	Turnover Ratio	Expense Ratio
TMFC	BATS	22.46	$184,755,775	0.51	10	0.5

Ratings
Reward   C+
Risk   C
Recent Upgrade/Downgrade   Up

Fund Information
Fund Type   Exchange Traded Funds
Category   US Equity Large Cap Growth
Sub-Category   Large Growth
Prospectus Objective   Growth & Inc
Inception Date   Jan-18
Open to New Investments   Y

Prices
Price (as of 9/30/2019)   22.46
52-Week High   23.23
52-Week Low   17.54

Total Returns (%)

3-Month	6-Month	1-Year	3-Year	5-Year
-0.32	4.06	1.65		

3-Year Standard Deviation
Effective Duration

Valuation
Premium/Discount (1-Year Average)   -0.08

Company Information
Provider   Motley Fool
Manager/Tenure   Anthony L. Arsta (1), Bryan C. Hinmon (1)
Website   http://www.foolfunds.com
Address   Motley Fool 2000 Duke Street, Suite 175 Alexandria VA 22314 United States
Phone Number

PERFORMANCE

11/2/18   2/13/19   6/17/19   9/30/19

Ratings History

Date	Overall Rating	Risk Rating	Reward Rating
Q3-19	C	C	C+
Q4-18	U		
Q4-17			
Q4-16			
Q4-15			

Asset & Performance History

Date	NAV	1-Year Total Return
2018	18.69	
2017		
2016		
2015		
2014		
2013		

Total Assets: $184,755,775
Asset Allocation

Asset	%
Cash	0%
Stocks	100%
US Stocks	100%
Bonds	0%
US Bonds	0%
Other	0%

Services Offered:

Investment Strategy: The investment seeks investment results that correspond (before fees and expenses) generally to the total return performance of the Motley Fool 100 Index (the "index"). Under normal circumstances, at least 80% of the fund's total assets (exclusive of any collateral held from securities lending) will be invested in the component securities of the index. The index was established by The Motley Fool in 2017 and is a proprietary, rules-based index designed to track the performance of the 100 largest, most liquid U.S. companies that have been recommended by The Motley Fool's analysts and newsletters. The fund is non-diversified. **Top Holdings:** Microsoft Corp Apple Inc Amazon.com Inc Alphabet Inc Class C Facebook Inc A

SPDR® S&P Pharmaceuticals ETF   C   HOLD

Ticker	Traded On	NAV	Total Assets ($)	Dividend Yield (TTM)	Turnover Ratio	Expense Ratio
XPH	NYSE Arca		$183,483,242	1.62	42	0.35

Ratings
Reward   C
Risk   D+
Recent Upgrade/Downgrade   Up

Fund Information
Fund Type   Exchange Traded Funds
Category   Healthcare Sector Equity
Sub-Category   Health
Prospectus Objective   Health
Inception Date   Jun-06
Open to New Investments   Y

Prices
Price (as of 9/30/2019)   35.59
52-Week High   47.26
52-Week Low   34.77

Total Returns (%)

3-Month	6-Month	1-Year	3-Year	5-Year
-10.35	-13.15	-22.68	-16.85	-21.72

3-Year Standard Deviation   20.28
Effective Duration

Valuation
Premium/Discount (1-Year Average)   -0.01

Company Information
Provider   SPDR State Street Global Advisors
Manager/Tenure   Michael J. Feehily (7), Karl A. Schneider (4), Keith Richardson (2)
Website   http://www.spdrs.com
Address   SPDR State Street Global Advisors State Street Financial Center, 1 Lincoln Street Boston MA 02111-2900 United States
Phone Number   617-786-3000

PERFORMANCE

1/4/18   4/14/18   7/25/18   11/7/18   2/17/19   6/16/19   9/29/19

Ratings History

Date	Overall Rating	Risk Rating	Reward Rating
Q3-19	C	D+	C
Q4-18	C	D+	C
Q4-17	D+	D+	D+
Q4-16	C	D+	C
Q4-15	C	C	C+

Asset & Performance History

Date	NAV	1-Year Total Return
2018	36.67	-14.7
2017	43.49	12.05
2016	39.08	-24.97
2015	51.21	1.61
2014	54	29.52
2013	43.98	60.69

Total Assets: $183,483,242
Asset Allocation

Asset	%
Cash	0%
Stocks	100%
US Stocks	95%
Bonds	0%
US Bonds	0%
Other	0%

Services Offered:

Investment Strategy: The investment seeks to provide investment results that, before fees and expenses, correspond generally to the total return performance of an index derived from the pharmaceuticals segment of a U.S. total market composite index. In seeking to track the performance of the S&P Pharmaceuticals Select Industry Index (the "index"), the fund employs a sampling strategy. It generally invests substantially all, but at least 80%, of its total assets in the securities comprising the index. The index represents the pharmaceuticals segment of the S&P Total Market Index ("S&P TMI"). The fund is non-diversified. **Top Holdings:** Allergan PLC Horizon Therapeutics PLC Mylan NV Zoetis Inc Class A Perrigo Co PLC

Invesco S&P SmallCap 600® Pure Value ETF   D+   SELL

Ticker	Traded On	NAV	Total Assets ($)	Dividend Yield (TTM)	Turnover Ratio	Expense Ratio
RZV	NYSE Arca	64.14	$182,801,574	1.22		0.35

Ratings
Reward	D+
Risk	D+
Recent Upgrade/Downgrade	

Fund Information
Fund Type	Exchange Traded Funds
Category	US Equity Small Cap
Sub-Category	Small Value
Prospectus Objective	Small Company
Inception Date	Mar-06
Open to New Investments	Y

Prices
Price (as of 9/30/2019)	64.11
52-Week High	75.60
52-Week Low	55.11

Total Returns (%)
3-Month	6-Month	1-Year	3-Year	5-Year
2.65	-3.65	-14.12	5.91	17.57

3-Year Standard Deviation	24.23
Effective Duration	

Valuation
Premium/Discount (1-Year Average)	0.00

Company Information
Provider	Invesco
Manager/Tenure	Peter Hubbard (1), Michael Jeanette (1), Tony Seisser (1)
Website	http://www.invesco.com/us
Address	Invesco 11 Greenway Plaza, Ste. 2500 Houston TX 77046 United States
Phone Number	800-659-1005

PERFORMANCE

Ratings History
Date	Overall Rating	Risk Rating	Reward Rating
Q3-19	D+	D+	D+
Q4-18	C-	C-	C-
Q4-17	B-	C	B
Q4-16	C	C-	B-
Q4-15	C	C-	C

Asset & Performance History
Date	NAV	1-Year Total Return
2018	57.81	-19.52
2017	73.03	0.87
2016	73.02	34.26
2015	54.95	-12.45
2014	63.47	2.66
2013	62.25	45.1

Total Assets: $182,801,574
Asset Allocation
Asset	%
Cash	0%
Stocks	100%
US Stocks	99%
Bonds	0%
US Bonds	0%
Other	0%

Services Offered:

Investment Strategy: The investment seeks to track the investment results (before fees and expenses) of the S&P SmallCap 600® Pure Value Index (the "underlying index"). The fund generally will invest at least 90% of its total assets in the securities that comprise the underlying index. The underlying index is composed of a subset of securities from the S&P SmallCap 600® Index that exhibit strong value characteristics, as measured using the following three factors: book value to price ratio, earnings to price ratio, and sales to price ratio. The fund is non-diversified. **Top Holdings:** Sonic Automotive Inc Class A   M/I Homes Inc   GMS Inc   William Lyon Homes Meritage Homes Corp

---

Direxion Daily Financial Bear 3X Shares   C+   HOLD

Ticker	Traded On	NAV	Total Assets ($)	Dividend Yield (TTM)	Turnover Ratio	Expense Ratio
FAZ	NYSE Arca	34.65	$182,680,231	0.99	0	1.07

Ratings
Reward	B-
Risk	D+
Recent Upgrade/Downgrade	Up

Fund Information
Fund Type	Exchange Traded Funds
Category	Trading Tools
Sub-Category	Trading--Inverse Equity
Prospectus Objective	Financial
Inception Date	Nov-08
Open to New Investments	Y

Prices
Price (as of 9/30/2019)	34.61
52-Week High	41.82
52-Week Low	7.64

Total Returns (%)
3-Month	6-Month	1-Year	3-Year	5-Year
-7.41	285.80	258.55	10.13	-49.15

3-Year Standard Deviation	38.15
Effective Duration	

Valuation
Premium/Discount (1-Year Average)	0.07

Company Information
Provider	Direxion Funds
Manager/Tenure	Paul Brigandi (10), Tony Ng (4)
Website	http://www.direxionfunds.com
Address	Direxion Funds 1301 Avenue Of The Americas (6th Avenue) New York NY 10019 United States
Phone Number	646-572-3390

PERFORMANCE

Ratings History
Date	Overall Rating	Risk Rating	Reward Rating
Q3-19	C+	D+	B-
Q4-18	D	D	D-
Q4-17	E+	E+	E+
Q4-16	D-	D-	E+
Q4-15	D-	E+	E+

Asset & Performance History
Date	NAV	1-Year Total Return
2018	13.56	16.26
2017	11.74	-46.09
2016	21.78	-47.08
2015	41.16	-19.04
2014	50.84	-40.91
2013	86.04	-64.41

Total Assets: $182,680,231
Asset Allocation
Asset	%
Cash	109%
Stocks	-9%
US Stocks	-9%
Bonds	0%
US Bonds	0%
Other	0%

Services Offered:

Investment Strategy: The investment seeks daily investment results, before fees and expenses, of 300% of the inverse (or opposite) of the daily performance of the Russell 1000® Financial Services Index. The fund invests in swap agreements, futures contracts, short positions or other financial instruments that, in combination, provide inverse or short leveraged exposure to the index equal to at least 80% of the fund's net assets (plus borrowing for investment purposes). The index is a subset of the Russell 1000® Index that measures the performance of the securities classified in the financial services sector of the large-capitalization U.S. equity market. It is non-diversified. **Top Holdings:** Russ 1000 Finan Indx Swap   Russ 1000 Finan Indx Swap   Russ 1000 Finan Indx Swap Russ 1000 Finan Indx Swap   Russ 1000 Finan Indx Swap

iShares Global Materials ETF

C   HOLD

Ticker	Traded On	NAV	Total Assets ($)	Dividend Yield (TTM)	Turnover Ratio	Expense Ratio
MXI	NYSE Arca	62.77	$182,046,315	3.84	11	0.46

Ratings

Reward   C
Risk   C-
Recent Upgrade/Downgrade

Fund Information

Fund Type	Exchange Traded Funds
Category	Natural Resources
Sub-Category	Natural Resources
Prospectus Objective	Natl Res
Inception Date	Sep-06
Open to New Investments	Y

Prices

Price (as of 9/30/2019)	62.72
52-Week High	68.02
52-Week Low	54.93

Total Returns (%)

3-Month	6-Month	1-Year	3-Year	5-Year
-4.38	-1.43	-3.72	26.87	20.61

3-Year Standard Deviation	13.8
Effective Duration	

Valuation

Premium/Discount (1-Year Average)	-0.14

Company Information

Provider	iShares
Manager/Tenure	Greg Savage (11), Jennifer Hsui (7), Alan Mason (3), 2 others
Website	http://www.ishares.com
Address	iShares 400 Howard Street San Francisco CA 94105 United States
Phone Number	800-474-2737

PERFORMANCE

Ratings History

Date	Overall Rating	Risk Rating	Reward Rating
Q3-19	C	C-	C
Q4-18	D+	D+	C-
Q4-17	B-	C	B
Q4-16	C-	C-	C-
Q4-15	D+	D+	D+

Asset & Performance History

Date	NAV	1-Year Total Return
2018	57.52	-15.79
2017	70.06	29.55
2016	55.15	23.51
2015	45.28	-16.83
2014	56.19	-7.73
2013	62.21	2.92

Total Assets: $182,046,315

Asset Allocation

Asset	%
Cash	0%
Stocks	100%
US Stocks	34%
Bonds	0%
US Bonds	0%
Other	0%

Services Offered:

Investment Strategy: The investment seeks to track the investment results of the S&P Global 1200 Materials IndexTM. The fund generally invests at least 90% of its assets in securities of the underlying index and in depositary receipts representing securities of the underlying index. It may invest the remainder of its assets in certain futures, options and swap contracts, cash and cash equivalents, as well as in securities not included in the underlying index. The index measures the performance of companies that the index provider deems to be part of the materials sector of the economy and that the index provider believes are important to global markets. **Top Holdings:** Linde PLC BHP Group Ltd Basf SE Air Liquide SA Rio Tinto PLC

---

iShares Edge MSCI Intl Momentum Factor ETF

C   HOLD

Ticker	Traded On	NAV	Total Assets ($)	Dividend Yield (TTM)	Turnover Ratio	Expense Ratio
IMTM	NYSE Arca	29.32	$181,768,644	2.33	105	0.3

Ratings

Reward   C
Risk   C-
Recent Upgrade/Downgrade   Up

Fund Information

Fund Type	Exchange Traded Funds
Category	Global Equity Large Cap
Sub-Category	Foreign Large Growth
Prospectus Objective	World Stock
Inception Date	Jan-15
Open to New Investments	Y

Prices

Price (as of 9/30/2019)	29.38
52-Week High	30.71
52-Week Low	24.83

Total Returns (%)

3-Month	6-Month	1-Year	3-Year	5-Year
-1.17	3.45	-1.69	19.53	

3-Year Standard Deviation	11.34
Effective Duration	

Valuation

Premium/Discount (1-Year Average)	0.08

Company Information

Provider	iShares
Manager/Tenure	Diane Hsiung (4), Jennifer Hsui (4), Greg Savage (4), 3 others
Website	http://www.ishares.com
Address	iShares 400 Howard Street San Francisco CA 94105 United States
Phone Number	800-474-2737

PERFORMANCE

Ratings History

Date	Overall Rating	Risk Rating	Reward Rating
Q3-19	C	C-	C
Q4-18	C-	C-	D+
Q4-17	C+	C+	C+
Q4-16	D+	D+	D+
Q4-15	U		

Asset & Performance History

Date	NAV	1-Year Total Return
2018	25.68	-13.96
2017	30.49	25.5
2016	24.79	0.59
2015	25.32	
2014		
2013		

Total Assets: $181,768,644

Asset Allocation

Asset	%
Cash	0%
Stocks	100%
US Stocks	2%
Bonds	0%
US Bonds	0%
Other	0%

Services Offered:

Investment Strategy: The investment seeks to track the investment results of the MSCI World ex USA Momentum Index that measures the performance of international developed large- and mid-capitalization stocks exhibiting relatively higher momentum characteristics. The fund will invest at least 90% of its assets in the component securities of the index and in investments that have economic characteristics that are substantially identical to the component securities of the index. The index consists of stocks exhibiting relatively higher momentum characteristics than the traditional market capitalization-weighted parent index, the MSCI World ex USA Index. **Top Holdings:** Nestle SA Roche Holding AG Dividend Right Cert. Novartis AG SAP SE LVMH Moet Hennessy Louis Vuitton SE

Direxion Daily Junior Gold Miners Index Bear 3X Shares   D-   SELL

Ticker	Traded On	NAV	Total Assets ($)	Dividend Yield (TTM)	Turnover Ratio	Expense Ratio
JDST	NYSE Arca	17.80	$181,359,086	2.1	0	1.09

Ratings
Reward	E
Risk	D-
Recent Upgrade/Downgrade	Down

Fund Information
Fund Type	Exchange Traded Funds
Category	Trading Tools
Sub-Category	Trading--Inverse Equity
Prospectus Objective	Prec Metals
Inception Date	Oct-13
Open to New Investments	Y

Prices
Price (as of 9/30/2019)	17.75
52-Week High	85.34
52-Week Low	11.99

Total Returns (%)
3-Month	6-Month	1-Year	3-Year	5-Year
-40.76	-57.78	-77.06	-81.26	-99.86

3-Year Standard Deviation	76.25
Effective Duration	

Valuation
Premium/Discount (1-Year Average)	-0.24

Company Information
Provider	Direxion Funds
Manager/Tenure	Paul Brigandi (5), Tony Ng (4)
Website	http://www.direxionfunds.com
Address	Direxion Funds 1301 Avenue Of The Americas (6th Avenue) New York NY 10019 United States
Phone Number	646-572-3390

PERFORMANCE

Ratings History
Date	Overall Rating	Risk Rating	Reward Rating
Q3-19	D-	D-	E
Q4-18	D	D	D
Q4-17	E+	D-	E+
Q4-16	D-	D-	E+
Q4-15	D	D-	D

Asset & Performance History
Date	NAV	1-Year Total Return
2018	50.4	-1.45
2017	51.37	-63.85
2016	142.12	-97.6
2015	5,944.00	-52.7
2014	12,568.00	-74.24
2013	51,360.00	

Total Assets: $181,359,086
Asset Allocation
Asset	%
Cash	126%
Stocks	-11%
US Stocks	0%
Bonds	0%
US Bonds	0%
Other	-15%

Services Offered:

Investment Strategy: The investment seeks daily investment results, before fees and expenses, of 300% of the inverse (or opposite) of the daily performance of the MVIS Global Junior Gold Miners Index. The fund invests in swap agreements, futures contracts, short positions or other financial instruments that, in combination, provide inverse (opposite) or short leveraged exposure to the index equal to at least 80% of the fund's net assets (plus borrowing for investment purposes). The index tracks the performance of foreign and domestic micro-, small- and mid-capitalization companies. The fund is non-diversified. **Top Holdings:** Ve Vectors Jr Gld Miners Ve Vectors Jr Gld Miners Ve Vectors Jr Gld Miners Ve Vectors Jr Gld Miners Ve Vectors Jr Gld Miners

---

Direxion Daily MSCI Emerging Markets Bull 3X Shares   D+   SELL

Ticker	Traded On	NAV	Total Assets ($)	Dividend Yield (TTM)	Turnover Ratio	Expense Ratio
EDC	NYSE Arca	65.17	$181,271,433	1.34	136	1.47

Ratings
Reward	D
Risk	D+
Recent Upgrade/Downgrade	

Fund Information
Fund Type	Exchange Traded Funds
Category	Trading Tools
Sub-Category	Trading--Leveraged Equity
Prospectus Objective	Div Emerg Mkts
Inception Date	Dec-08
Open to New Investments	Y

Prices
Price (as of 9/30/2019)	65.02
52-Week High	88.89
52-Week Low	56.33

Total Returns (%)
3-Month	6-Month	1-Year	3-Year	5-Year
-19.48	-21.67	-22.38	2.58	-34.25

3-Year Standard Deviation	46.19
Effective Duration	

Valuation
Premium/Discount (1-Year Average)	-0.01

Company Information
Provider	Direxion Funds
Manager/Tenure	Paul Brigandi (10), Tony Ng (4)
Website	http://www.direxionfunds.com
Address	Direxion Funds 1301 Avenue Of The Americas (6th Avenue) New York NY 10019 United States
Phone Number	646-572-3390

PERFORMANCE

Ratings History
Date	Overall Rating	Risk Rating	Reward Rating
Q3-19	D+	D+	D
Q4-18	D+	D	C-
Q4-17	B-	D+	A-
Q4-16	D	D	D
Q4-15	D	D	D-

Asset & Performance History
Date	NAV	1-Year Total Return
2018	62.73	-49.96
2017	125.81	138.8
2016	52.83	14.74
2015	46.04	-49.91
2014	91.92	-19.76
2013	114.56	-21.53

Total Assets: $181,271,433
Asset Allocation
Asset	%
Cash	55%
Stocks	45%
US Stocks	-3%
Bonds	0%
US Bonds	0%
Other	0%

Services Offered:

Investment Strategy: The investment seeks daily investment results, before fees and expenses, of 300% of the daily performance of the MSCI Emerging Markets IndexSM. The fund invests at least 80% of its net assets (plus borrowing for investment purposes) in financial instruments, such as swap agreements, and securities of the index, ETFs that track the index and other financial instruments that provide daily leveraged exposure to the index or ETFs that track the index. The index is designed to represent the performance of large- and mid-capitalizations securities across 24 emerging market countries. The fund is non-diversified. **Top Holdings:** iShares MSCI Emerging Markets ETF Msci Emerg Mkts Idx Swap Msci Emerg Mkts Idx Swap Msci Emerg Mkts Idx Swap Msci Emerg Mkts Idx Swap

JPMorgan Diversified Return U.S. Mid Cap Equity ETF   C   HOLD

Ticker	Traded On	NAV	Total Assets ($)	Dividend Yield (TTM)	Turnover Ratio	Expense Ratio
JPME	NYSE Arca	66.76	$180,249,428	1.6	35	0.24

Ratings
Reward   C
Risk   D+
Recent Upgrade/Downgrade

Fund Information
Fund Type   Exchange Traded Funds
Category   US Equity Mid Cap
Sub-Category   Mid-Cap Blend
Prospectus Objective   Growth
Inception Date   May-16
Open to New Investments   Y

Prices
Price (as of 9/30/2019)   66.81
52-Week High   67.86
52-Week Low   54.16

Total Returns (%)

3-Month	6-Month	1-Year	3-Year	5-Year
0.33	2.45	1.40	32.24	

3-Year Standard Deviation   12.38
Effective Duration

Valuation
Premium/Discount (1-Year Average)   0.04

Company Information
Provider   JPMorgan
Manager/Tenure   Jonathan Msika (2), Yazann Romahi
                  (2), Joe Staines (2), 1 other
Website   http://www.jpmorganfunds.com
Address   JPMorgan 270 Park Avenue New York
                  NY 10017-2070 United States
Phone Number   800-480-4111

PERFORMANCE

Ratings History

Date	Overall Rating	Risk Rating	Reward Rating
Q3-19	C	D+	C
Q4-18	C-	C-	C-
Q4-17	D+	B+	C
Q4-16	U		
Q4-15			

Asset & Performance History

Date	NAV	1-Year Total Return
2018	57.35	-8.42
2017	63.67	19.06
2016	54.1	
2015		
2014		
2013		

Total Assets: $180,249,428
Asset Allocation

Asset	%
Cash	0%
Stocks	100%
US Stocks	99%
Bonds	0%
US Bonds	0%
Other	0%

Services Offered:

Investment Strategy: The investment seeks investment results that closely correspond, before fees and expenses, to the performance of the JP Morgan Diversified Factor US Mid Cap Equity Index. The fund will invest at least 80% of its net assets in securities included in the underlying index. The underlying index is comprised of U.S. equity securities selected to represent a diversified set of factor characteristics: value, momentum, and quality.
Top Holdings: L3Harris Technologies Inc Royal Gold Inc Fiserv Inc Teleflex Inc West Pharmaceutical Services Inc

---

Sprott Gold Miners ETF   C   HOLD

Ticker	Traded On	NAV	Total Assets ($)	Dividend Yield (TTM)	Turnover Ratio	Expense Ratio
SGDM	NYSE Arca	22.95	$180,169,381	0.38	82	0.5

Ratings
Reward   C
Risk   C-
Recent Upgrade/Downgrade   Up

Fund Information
Fund Type   Exchange Traded Funds
Category   Prec Metals
Sub-Category   Equity Precious Metals
Prospectus Objective   Prec Metals
Inception Date   Jul-14
Open to New Investments   Y

Prices
Price (as of 9/30/2019)   22.90
52-Week High   26.40
52-Week Low   14.90

Total Returns (%)

3-Month	6-Month	1-Year	3-Year	5-Year
8.33	23.74	47.77	-3.65	19.52

3-Year Standard Deviation   27.6
Effective Duration

Valuation
Premium/Discount (1-Year Average)   -0.09

Company Information
Provider   Sprott
Manager/Tenure   Ryan Mischker (4), Andrew Hicks (3)
Website   http://www.sprottetfs.com
Address   Sprott United States
Phone Number

PERFORMANCE

Ratings History

Date	Overall Rating	Risk Rating	Reward Rating
Q3-19	C	C-	C
Q4-18	C	D	C
Q4-17	D+	D	C-
Q4-16	C-	D	C
Q4-15	D	C-	C

Asset & Performance History

Date	NAV	1-Year Total Return
2018	17.53	-14.99
2017	20.73	10.98
2016	18.78	47.65
2015	12.72	-26.41
2014	17.54	
2013		

Total Assets: $180,169,381
Asset Allocation

Asset	%
Cash	0%
Stocks	100%
US Stocks	20%
Bonds	0%
US Bonds	0%
Other	0%

Services Offered:

Investment Strategy: The investment seeks results that correspond (before fees and expenses) to the performance of the Solactive Gold Miners Custom Factors Index. The underlying index aims to track the performance of gold companies located in the U.S. and Canada who common stocks or American Depository Receipts ("ADRs") are traded on the Toronto Stock Exchange, the New York Stock Exchange and NASDAQ. The fund will normally invest at least 90% of its net assets in securities that comprise the index. The fund is non-diversified.
Top Holdings: Barrick Gold Corp Newmont Goldcorp Corp Franco-Nevada Corp Kirkland Lake Gold Ltd Royal Gold Inc

iShares Currency Hedged MSCI Emerging Markets ETF   C-   HOLD

Ticker	Traded On	NAV	Total Assets ($)	Dividend Yield (TTM)	Turnover Ratio	Expense Ratio
HEEM	BATS	24.64	$179,897,313	2.44	7	0.67

Ratings
Reward   C
Risk   C-
Recent Upgrade/Downgrade

Fund Information
Fund Type   Exchange Traded Funds
Category   Global Emerg Mkts Equity
Sub-Category   Diversified Emerging Mkts
Prospectus Objective   Div Emerg Mkts
Inception Date   Sep-14
Open to New Investments   Y

Prices
Price (as of 9/30/2019)   24.62
52-Week High   26.35
52-Week Low   22.74

Total Returns (%)

3-Month	6-Month	1-Year	3-Year	5-Year
-3.90	-3.60	-0.67	19.15	21.04

3-Year Standard Deviation   12.15
Effective Duration

Valuation
Premium/Discount (1-Year Average)   -0.05

Company Information
Provider   iShares
Manager/Tenure   Diane Hsiung (5), Jennifer Hsui (5), Orlando Montalvo (5), 2 others
Website   http://www.ishares.com
Address   iShares 400 Howard Street San Francisco CA 94105 United States
Phone Number   800-474-2737

PERFORMANCE

Ratings History

Date	Overall Rating	Risk Rating	Reward Rating
Q3-19	C-	C-	C
Q4-18	C-	C	C-
Q4-17	C+	C	C+
Q4-16	D+	C-	D+
Q4-15	U		

Asset & Performance History

Date	NAV	1-Year Total Return
2018	23.08	-12.3
2017	26.51	27.99
2016	21.15	8.02
2015	19.95	-10.02
2014	23.52	
2013		

Total Assets: $179,897,313

Asset Allocation

Asset	%
Cash	1%
Stocks	99%
US Stocks	0%
Bonds	0%
US Bonds	0%
Other	0%

Services Offered:

Investment Strategy: The investment seeks to track the investment results of the MSCI Emerging Markets 100% Hedged to USD Index. The fund generally will invest at least 90% of its assets in the component securities (including indirect investments through the underlying fund) and other instruments of the underlying index and in investments that have economic characteristics that are substantially identical to the component securities of the underlying index. The index is an equity benchmark for global emerging markets stock performance with the currency risk inherent in the securities included in the index hedged to the U.S. dollar on a monthly basis. **Top Holdings:** Alibaba Group Holding Ltd ADR Tencent Holdings Ltd Taiwan Semiconductor Manufacturing Co Ltd Samsung Electronics Co Ltd Naspers Ltd Class N

Invesco WilderHill Clean Energy ETF   C+   HOLD

Ticker	Traded On	NAV	Total Assets ($)	Dividend Yield (TTM)	Turnover Ratio	Expense Ratio
PBW	NYSE Arca	29.14	$179,761,870	1.47	40	0.7

Ratings
Reward   B
Risk   C-
Recent Upgrade/Downgrade   Up

Fund Information
Fund Type   Exchange Traded Funds
Category   Technology Sector Equity
Sub-Category   Miscellaneous Sector
Prospectus Objective   Natl Res
Inception Date   Mar-05
Open to New Investments   Y

Prices
Price (as of 9/30/2019)   29.17
52-Week High   31.46
52-Week Low   20.12

Total Returns (%)

3-Month	6-Month	1-Year	3-Year	5-Year
-2.64	8.35	19.14	58.08	4.29

3-Year Standard Deviation   19.76
Effective Duration

Valuation
Premium/Discount (1-Year Average)   -0.01

Company Information
Provider   Invesco
Manager/Tenure   Peter Hubbard (12), Michael Jeanette (11), Tony Seisser (5)
Website   http://www.invesco.com/us
Address   Invesco 11 Greenway Plaza, Ste. 2500 Houston TX 77046 United States
Phone Number   800-659-1005

PERFORMANCE

Ratings History

Date	Overall Rating	Risk Rating	Reward Rating
Q3-19	C+	C-	B
Q4-18	C	D+	C+
Q4-17	C	C	C
Q4-16	C-	D	C
Q4-15	C-	C-	C

Asset & Performance History

Date	NAV	1-Year Total Return
2018	21.41	-13.71
2017	25.27	39.78
2016	18.35	-20.74
2015	23.75	-8.58
2014	26.35	-15.29
2013	31.9	59.83

Total Assets: $179,761,870

Asset Allocation

Asset	%
Cash	0%
Stocks	100%
US Stocks	84%
Bonds	0%
US Bonds	0%
Other	0%

Services Offered:

Investment Strategy: The investment seeks to track the investment results (before fees and expenses) of the WilderHill Clean Energy Index (the "underlying index"). The fund generally will invest at least 90% of its total assets in the securities that comprise the underlying index. The underlying index is composed of stocks of publicly traded companies in the United States that are engaged in the business of the advancement of cleaner energy and conservation. Stocks are included in the underlying index based on the index provider's evaluation that such companies will substantially benefit from a societal transition toward the use of cleaner energy and conservation. **Top Holdings:** Enphase Energy Inc SolarEdge Technologies Inc SunPower Corp Itron Inc TerraForm Power Inc Class A

First Trust Multi Cap Growth AlphaDEX® Fund

C   HOLD

Ticker	Traded On	NAV	Total Assets ($)	Dividend Yield (TTM)	Turnover Ratio	Expense Ratio
FAD	NAS CM	73.26	$179,489,508	0.38	130	0.69

Ratings
Reward   C
Risk   D+
Recent Upgrade/Downgrade

Fund Information
Fund Type   Exchange Traded Funds
Category   US Equity Mid Cap
Sub-Category   Mid-Cap Growth
Prospectus Objective   Growth
Inception Date   May-07
Open to New Investments   Y

Prices
Price (as of 9/30/2019)   73.30
52-Week High   76.90
52-Week Low   56.57

Total Returns (%)

3-Month	6-Month	1-Year	3-Year	5-Year
-2.38	1.49	-3.77	40.25	67.13

3-Year Standard Deviation   15.21
Effective Duration

Valuation
Premium/Discount (1-Year Average)   0.01

Company Information
Provider   First Trust
Manager/Tenure   Jon C. Erickson (12), Daniel J.
                  Lindquist (12), David G. McGarel (12),
                  3 others
Website   http://www.ftportfolios.com/
Address   First Trust 120 E. Liberty Drive, Suite
                  400 Wheaton IL 60187 United States
Phone Number   800-621-1675

PERFORMANCE

Ratings History

Date	Overall Rating	Risk Rating	Reward Rating
Q3-19	C	D+	C
Q4-18	C-	C-	C-
Q4-17	A-	B+	A-
Q4-16	C	C-	B-
Q4-15	C	C-	B-

Asset & Performance History

Date	NAV	1-Year Total Return
2018	61.15	-6.22
2017	65.33	24.68
2016	52.52	6.82
2015	49.48	2.09
2014	48.66	8.28
2013	45.14	38.4

Total Assets: $179,489,508
Asset Allocation

Asset	%
Cash	0%
Stocks	100%
US Stocks	100%
Bonds	0%
US Bonds	0%
Other	0%

Services Offered:

Investment Strategy: The investment seeks investment results that correspond generally to the price and yield (before the fund's fees and expenses) of the Nasdaq AlphaDEX® Multi Cap Growth Index. The fund will normally invest at least 90% of its net assets (including investment borrowings) in common stocks that comprise the index. The index is designed to select growth stocks from the NASDAQ US 500 Large Cap Index, NASDAQ US 600 Mid Cap Index and NASDAQ US 700 Small Cap Index that may generate positive alpha, or risk-adjusted returns, relative to traditional indices through the use of the AlphaDEX® selection methodology. **Top Holdings:** Altice USA Inc Class A Starbucks Corp TransDigm Group Inc Chipotle Mexican Grill Inc Class A Ball Corp

---

Invesco Dynamic Semiconductors ETF

B-   BUY

Ticker	Traded On	NAV	Total Assets ($)	Dividend Yield (TTM)	Turnover Ratio	Expense Ratio
PSI	NYSE Arca	57.85	$179,338,358	0.69	98	0.58

Ratings
Reward   B
Risk   C-
Recent Upgrade/Downgrade   Up

Fund Information
Fund Type   Exchange Traded Funds
Category   Technology Sector Equity
Sub-Category   Technology
Prospectus Objective   Technology
Inception Date   Jun-05
Open to New Investments   Y

Prices
Price (as of 9/30/2019)   57.81
52-Week High   60.29
52-Week Low   41.12

Total Returns (%)

3-Month	6-Month	1-Year	3-Year	5-Year
4.12	7.04	9.89	80.11	168.39

3-Year Standard Deviation   24.78
Effective Duration

Valuation
Premium/Discount (1-Year Average)   -0.05

Company Information
Provider   Invesco
Manager/Tenure   Peter Hubbard (12), Michael Jeanette
                  (11), Tony Seisser (5)
Website   http://www.invesco.com/us
Address   Invesco 11 Greenway Plaza, Ste. 2500
                  Houston TX 77046 United States
Phone Number   800-659-1005

PERFORMANCE

Ratings History

Date	Overall Rating	Risk Rating	Reward Rating
Q3-19	B-	C-	B
Q4-18	C+	C-	B
Q4-17	A-	B	A+
Q4-16	C	C	C+
Q4-15	B	B-	B

Asset & Performance History

Date	NAV	1-Year Total Return
2018	44.46	-11.19
2017	50.44	40.03
2016	36.1	44.44
2015	25.18	-0.78
2014	25.42	36.98
2013	18.9	31.57

Total Assets: $179,338,358
Asset Allocation

Asset	%
Cash	0%
Stocks	100%
US Stocks	94%
Bonds	0%
US Bonds	0%
Other	0%

Services Offered:

Investment Strategy: The investment seeks to track the investment results (before fees and expenses) of the Dynamic Semiconductor IntellidexSM Index. The fund generally will invest at least 90% of its total assets in the securities that comprise the underlying intellidex. The underlying intellidex was composed of common stocks of U.S. semiconductor companies. These companies are principally engaged in the manufacture of semiconductors. The fund is non-diversified. **Top Holdings:** Micron Technology Inc Applied Materials Inc Texas Instruments Inc Qualcomm Inc NXP Semiconductors NV

AdvisorShares Ranger Equity Bear ETF   D   SELL

Ticker	Traded On	NAV	Total Assets ($)	Dividend Yield (TTM)	Turnover Ratio	Expense Ratio
HDGE	NYSE Arca	6.57	$179,201,895	0		2.72

Ratings

Reward	D
Risk	D
Recent Upgrade/Downgrade	

Fund Information

Fund Type	Exchange Traded Funds
Category	Alternative Misc
Sub-Category	Bear Market
Prospectus Objective	Growth
Inception Date	Jan-11
Open to New Investments	Y

Prices

Price (as of 9/30/2019)	6.58
52-Week High	8.97
52-Week Low	6.24

Total Returns (%)

3-Month	6-Month	1-Year	3-Year	5-Year
2.95	-2.66	-11.69	-31.63	-45.65

3-Year Standard Deviation	16.8
Effective Duration	0.69

Valuation

Premium/Discount (1-Year Average)	0.05

Company Information

Provider	AdvisorShares
Manager/Tenure	John Del Vecchio (8), Brad H. Lamensdorf (8)
Website	http://www.advisorshares.com
Address	AdvisorShares 2 Bethesda Metro Center, Suite 1330 Bethesda MD 20814 United States
Phone Number	877-843-3831

PERFORMANCE

Ratings History

Date	Overall Rating	Risk Rating	Reward Rating
Q3-19	D	D	D
Q4-18	D+	D+	D
Q4-17	D-	D-	D-
Q4-16	D+	D+	D
Q4-15	D	D	D

Asset & Performance History

Date	NAV	1-Year Total Return
2018	8.43	7.11
2017	7.87	-15.01
2016	9.26	-13.86
2015	10.75	-6.27
2014	11.47	-10.18
2013	12.77	-30.29

Total Assets: $179,201,895

Asset Allocation

Asset	%
Cash	121%
Stocks	-98%
US Stocks	-87%
Bonds	76%
US Bonds	72%
Other	0%

Services Offered:

Investment Strategy: The investment seeks capital appreciation through short sales of domestically traded equity securities. The Sub-Advisor seeks to achieve the fund's investment objective by short selling a portfolio of liquid mid- and large-cap U.S. exchange-traded equity securities, ETFs, ETNs and other exchange-traded products. The fund invests at least 80% of its net assets, plus any borrowings for investment purposes, in short positions in equity securities. The Sub-Advisor implements a bottom-up, fundamental, research driven security selection process. **Top Holdings:** AdvisorShares Sage Core Reserves ETF   Blackrock Federal Fd 30 Instl   Brunswick Corp   Snap-on Inc   Guess? Inc

---

VanEck Vectors Rare Earth/Strategic Metals ETF   D   SELL

Ticker	Traded On	NAV	Total Assets ($)	Dividend Yield (TTM)	Turnover Ratio	Expense Ratio
REMX	NYSE Arca	12.69	$178,569,421	13.28	68	0.59

Ratings

Reward	D
Risk	D
Recent Upgrade/Downgrade	

Fund Information

Fund Type	Exchange Traded Funds
Category	Prec Metals
Sub-Category	Equity Precious Metals
Prospectus Objective	Natl Res
Inception Date	Oct-10
Open to New Investments	Y

Prices

Price (as of 9/30/2019)	12.63
52-Week High	20.28
52-Week Low	11.95

Total Returns (%)

3-Month	6-Month	1-Year	3-Year	5-Year
-16.78	-21.18	-29.83	-6.77	-45.45

3-Year Standard Deviation	28.02
Effective Duration	

Valuation

Premium/Discount (1-Year Average)	-0.18

Company Information

Provider	VanEck
Manager/Tenure	Hao-Hung (Peter) Liao (8), Guo Hua (Jason) Jin (1)
Website	http://www.vaneck.com
Address	Van Eck Associates Corporation 666 Third Avenue New York NY 10017 United States
Phone Number	800-826-1115

PERFORMANCE

Ratings History

Date	Overall Rating	Risk Rating	Reward Rating
Q3-19	D	D	D
Q4-18	D+	D	C-
Q4-17	C+	D+	B
Q4-16	D	D	D
Q4-15	D-	E+	D-

Asset & Performance History

Date	NAV	1-Year Total Return
2018	13.56	-48.31
2017	29.75	81.55
2016	16.9	26.3
2015	13.68	-43.59
2014	25.49	-28.06
2013	35.98	-31.84

Total Assets: $178,569,421

Asset Allocation

Asset	%
Cash	0%
Stocks	100%
US Stocks	13%
Bonds	0%
US Bonds	0%
Other	0%

Services Offered:

Investment Strategy: The investment seeks to replicate as closely as possible, before fees and expenses, the price and yield performance of the MVIS® Global Rare Earth/Strategic Metals Index. The fund normally invests at least 80% of its total assets in securities that comprise the fund's benchmark index. The index includes companies primarily engaged in a variety of activities that are related to the producing, refining and recycling of rare earth and strategic metals and minerals. It is non-diversified. **Top Holdings:** Zhejiang Huayou Cobalt Co Ltd   China Molybdenum Co Ltd Class A   China Northern Rare Earth (Group) High-Tech Co Ltd   Xiamen Tungsten Co Ltd   Lynas Corp Ltd

Goldman Sachs Equal Weight U.S. Large Cap Equity ETF

C-   HOLD

Ticker	Traded On	NAV	Total Assets ($)	Dividend Yield (TTM)	Turnover Ratio	Expense Ratio
GSEW	BATS	47.30	$177,370,057	1.58	34	0.09

Ratings
Reward	C-
Risk	C-
Recent Upgrade/Downgrade	

Fund Information
Fund Type	Exchange Traded Funds
Category	US Equity Large Cap Blend
Sub-Category	Large Blend
Prospectus Objective	Growth & Inc
Inception Date	Sep-17
Open to New Investments	Y

Prices
Price (as of 9/30/2019)	47.34
52-Week High	48.16
52-Week Low	37.41

Total Returns (%)
3-Month	6-Month	1-Year	3-Year	5-Year
0.51	4.40	4.19		

3-Year Standard Deviation	
Effective Duration	

Valuation
Premium/Discount (1-Year Average)	0.01

Company Information
Provider	Goldman Sachs
Manager/Tenure	Raj Garigipati (2), Jamie McGregor (2)
Website	http://www.gsamfunds.com
Address	Goldman Sachs 200 West Stree New York NY 10282 United States
Phone Number	800-526-7384

PERFORMANCE

Ratings History

Date	Overall Rating	Risk Rating	Reward Rating
Q3-19	C-	C-	C-
Q4-18	D+	C-	D+
Q4-17	U		
Q4-16			
Q4-15			

Asset & Performance History

Date	NAV	1-Year Total Return
2018	39.58	-7.28
2017	43.31	
2016		
2015		
2014		
2013		

Total Assets: $177,370,057

Asset Allocation

Asset	%
Cash	0%
Stocks	100%
US Stocks	99%
Bonds	0%
US Bonds	0%
Other	0%

Services Offered:

Investment Strategy: The investment seeks to provide investment results that closely correspond, before fees and expenses, to the performance of the Solactive US Large Cap Equal Weight Index (GTR). The fund seeks to achieve its investment objective by investing at least 80% of its assets (exclusive of collateral held from securities lending) in securities included in its underlying index. The index consists of equity securities of large capitalization U.S. issuers. The index is an equal-weight version of the Solactive US Large Cap Index, a market capitalization-weighted index that includes equity securities of approximately 500 of the largest U.S. companies. **Top Holdings:** Target Corp   Kontoor Brands Inc   DexCom Inc   Dollar General Corp   Burlington Stores Inc

Barclays ETN+ Shiller Capet ETN

C   HOLD

Ticker	Traded On	NAV	Total Assets ($)	Dividend Yield (TTM)	Turnover Ratio	Expense Ratio
CAPE	NYSE Arca		$176,756,580	0		0.45

Ratings
Reward	C+
Risk	D+
Recent Upgrade/Downgrade	

Fund Information
Fund Type	Exchange Traded Funds
Category	US Equity Large Cap Value
Sub-Category	Large Value
Prospectus Objective	Growth
Inception Date	Oct-12
Open to New Investments	Y

Prices
Price (as of 9/30/2019)	137.41
52-Week High	142.13
52-Week Low	106.83

Total Returns (%)
3-Month	6-Month	1-Year	3-Year	5-Year
-0.45	3.62	2.27	47.63	86.87

3-Year Standard Deviation	13
Effective Duration	

Valuation
Premium/Discount (1-Year Average)	-0.03

Company Information
Provider	Milleis Investissements Funds
Manager/Tenure	No Manager (6)
Website	
Address	2-4, rue Eugène Ruppert L-2453 Luxembourg Luxembourg L-2453 Luxembourg
Phone Number	

PERFORMANCE

Ratings History

Date	Overall Rating	Risk Rating	Reward Rating
Q3-19	C	D+	C+
Q4-18	C-	D+	C
Q4-17	B	B+	B
Q4-16	C	D+	C
Q4-15	C	D+	C

Asset & Performance History

Date	NAV	1-Year Total Return
2018	112.24	-3.4
2017	116.2	20.7
2016	96.12	18.29
2015	80.97	4.7
2014	77.33	15.02
2013	67.23	32.88

Total Assets: $176,756,580

Asset Allocation

Asset	%
Cash	%
Stocks	%
US Stocks	%
Bonds	%
US Bonds	%
Other	%

Services Offered:

Investment Strategy: The investment seeks to replicate, net of expenses, the Shiller Barclays CAPETM US Core Sector Index.

The index seeks to provide a notional long exposure to the top four relatively undervalued U.S. equity sectors that also exhibit relatively strong price momentum. It incorporates the CAPE (Cyclically Adjusted Price Earnings) ratio to assess equity market valuations of nine sectors on a monthly basis and to identify the relatively undervalued sectors represented in the S&P 500®. **Top Holdings:**

Columbia Diversified Fixed Income Allocation ETF

C-   HOLD

Ticker	Traded On	NAV	Total Assets ($)	Dividend Yield (TTM)	Turnover Ratio	Expense Ratio
DIAL	NYSE Arca	20.72	$176,096,739	3.46	140	0.28

Ratings

Reward	C-
Risk	C-
Recent Upgrade/Downgrade	

Fund Information

Fund Type	Exchange Traded Funds
Category	US Fixed Income
Sub-Category	Multisector Bond
Prospectus Objective	Growth & Inc
Inception Date	Oct-17
Open to New Investments	Y

Prices

Price (as of 9/30/2019)	20.80
52-Week High	20.90
52-Week Low	18.78

Total Returns (%)

3-Month	6-Month	1-Year	3-Year	5-Year
2.44	6.45	12.05		

3-Year Standard Deviation

Effective Duration

Valuation

Premium/Discount (1-Year Average)	0.11

Company Information

Provider	Columbia
Manager/Tenure	David Janssen (1), Gene R. Tannuzzo (1)
Website	http://www.columbiathreadneedleus.com
Address	Liberty Financial Funds P.O. Box 8081 Boston MA 02266-8081 United States
Phone Number	800-345-6611

PERFORMANCE

Ratings History

Date	Overall Rating	Risk Rating	Reward Rating
Q3-19	C-	C-	C-
Q4-18	D	C-	D
Q4-17	U		
Q4-16			
Q4-15			

Asset & Performance History

Date	NAV	1-Year Total Return
2018	18.91	-1.53
2017	19.89	
2016		
2015		
2014		
2013		

Total Assets: $176,096,739

Asset Allocation

Asset	%
Cash	11%
Stocks	0%
US Stocks	0%
Bonds	88%
US Bonds	56%
Other	0%

Services Offered:

Investment Strategy: The investment seeks investment results that closely correspond to the performance of the Beta Advantage® Multi-Sector Bond Index. The fund invests at least 80% of its assets in securities within the index or in securities, that have economic characteristics that are substantially the same as the economic characteristics of the securities within the index. The index reflects a rules-based multi-sector strategic beta approach to measuring the performance of the debt market through representation of six sectors of the debt market in the index, each focused on yield, quality, and liquidity of the particular eligible universe. **Top Holdings:** United States Treasury Bills 0% Federal National Mortgage Association 4% Federal National Mortgage Association 3.5% Federal National Mortgage Association 4.5% United States Treasury Bonds 3.75%

Global X Adaptive U.S. Factor ETF

C-   HOLD

Ticker	Traded On	NAV	Total Assets ($)	Dividend Yield (TTM)	Turnover Ratio	Expense Ratio
AUSF	NYSE Arca	25.07	$175,520,153	3.97	29	0.27

Ratings

Reward	D+
Risk	C-
Recent Upgrade/Downgrade	

Fund Information

Fund Type	Exchange Traded Funds
Category	US Equity Large Cap Value
Sub-Category	Large Value
Prospectus Objective	Growth
Inception Date	Aug-18
Open to New Investments	Y

Prices

Price (as of 9/30/2019)	25.10
52-Week High	25.31
52-Week Low	21.22

Total Returns (%)

3-Month	6-Month	1-Year	3-Year	5-Year
2.13	4.59	4.73		

3-Year Standard Deviation

Effective Duration

Valuation

Premium/Discount (1-Year Average)	0.13

Company Information

Provider	Global X Funds
Manager/Tenure	Chang Kim (1), Nam To (1), Wayne Xie (0), 1 other
Website	http://www.globalxfunds.com
Address	Global X Funds 600 Lexington Avenue, 20th Floor New York NY 10022 United States
Phone Number	888-493-8631

PERFORMANCE

Ratings History

Date	Overall Rating	Risk Rating	Reward Rating
Q3-19	C-	C-	D+
Q4-18	U		
Q4-17			
Q4-16			
Q4-15			

Asset & Performance History

Date	NAV	1-Year Total Return
2018	22.09	
2017		
2016		
2015		
2014		
2013		

Total Assets: $175,520,153

Asset Allocation

Asset	%
Cash	0%
Stocks	100%
US Stocks	98%
Bonds	0%
US Bonds	0%
Other	0%

Services Offered:

Investment Strategy: The investment seeks to provide investment results that correspond generally to the price and yield performance, before fees and expenses, of the Adaptive Wealth Strategies U.S. Factor Index (the "index"). The fund invests at least 80% of its total assets in the securities of the index. Its 80% investment policy is non-fundamental and requires 60 days prior written notice to shareholders before it can be changed. The index is designed to dynamically allocate across three sub-indices that provide exposure to U.S. equities that exhibit characteristics of one of three primary factors: value, momentum and low volatility. The fund is non-diversified. **Top Holdings:** Starwood Property Trust Inc Tribune Media Co A Blackstone Mortgage Trust Inc A MFA Financial Inc Equity Commonwealth

iShares US & Intl High Yield Corp Bond ETF   C   HOLD

Ticker	Traded On	NAV	Total Assets ($)	Dividend Yield (TTM)	Turnover Ratio	Expense Ratio
GHYG	BATS	48.73	$175,421,507	5.51	20	0.4

Ratings
Reward   C+
Risk   C-
Recent Upgrade/Downgrade

Fund Information
Fund Type   Exchange Traded Funds
Category   Global Fixed Income
Sub-Category   High Yield Bond
Prospectus Objective   Corp Bond-High Yld
Inception Date   Apr-12
Open to New Investments   Y

Prices
Price (as of 9/30/2019)   48.79
52-Week High   49.41
52-Week Low   45.07

Total Returns (%)

3-Month	6-Month	1-Year	3-Year	5-Year
0.06	2.56	4.31	15.53	19.73

3-Year Standard Deviation   4.58
Effective Duration

Valuation
Premium/Discount (1-Year Average)   0.22

Company Information
Provider   iShares
Manager/Tenure   James Mauro (7), Scott Radell (7)
Website   http://www.ishares.com
Address   iShares 400 Howard Street San Francisco CA 94105 United States
Phone Number   800-474-2737

PERFORMANCE

Ratings History

Date	Overall Rating	Risk Rating	Reward Rating
Q3-19	C	C-	C+
Q4-18	C-	C-	C-
Q4-17	C+	B-	C+
Q4-16	C-	D+	C
Q4-15	C-	D+	C-

Asset & Performance History

Date	NAV	1-Year Total Return
2018	46	-3.67
2017	50.36	8.37
2016	48.17	12.29
2015	44.96	-6.4
2014	50.21	-0.66
2013	53.34	7.78

Total Assets: $175,421,507

Asset Allocation

Asset	%
Cash	1%
Stocks	0%
US Stocks	0%
Bonds	99%
US Bonds	66%
Other	0%

Services Offered:

Investment Strategy: The investment seeks to track the investment results of the Markit iBoxx Global Developed Markets High Yield Index. The fund generally will invest at least 90% of its assets in the component securities of the underlying index and may invest up to 10% of its assets in certain futures, options and swap contracts, cash and cash equivalents, including shares of money market funds advised by BFA or its affiliates. The index is a rules-based index consisting of high yield corporate bonds denominated in U.S. dollars, euros, British pounds sterling and Canadian dollars. **Top Holdings:** ALTICE FRANCE S.A 7.38% Sprint Corporation 7.88% TransDigm, Inc. 6.25% Altice Financing S.A. 7.5% CCO Holdings, LLC/ CCO Holdings Capital Corp. 5.13%

ProShares UltraShort Dow30   D   SELL

Ticker	Traded On	NAV	Total Assets ($)	Dividend Yield (TTM)	Turnover Ratio	Expense Ratio
DXD	NYSE Arca	25.58	$174,043,984	1.77	0	0.95

Ratings
Reward   D-
Risk   D-
Recent Upgrade/Downgrade

Fund Information
Fund Type   Exchange Traded Funds
Category   Trading Tools
Sub-Category   Trading--Inverse Equity
Prospectus Objective   Growth
Inception Date   Jul-06
Open to New Investments   Y

Prices
Price (as of 9/30/2019)   25.55
52-Week High   40.95
52-Week Low   25.08

Total Returns (%)

3-Month	6-Month	1-Year	3-Year	5-Year
-2.76	-6.49	-8.17	-61.06	-73.92

3-Year Standard Deviation   23.98
Effective Duration

Valuation
Premium/Discount (1-Year Average)   0.02

Company Information
Provider   ProShares
Manager/Tenure   Michael Neches (6), Devin Sullivan (1)
Website   http://www.proshares.com
Address   ProShares 7501 Wisconsin Avenue, Suite 1000 Bethesda MD 20814 United States
Phone Number   866-776-5125

PERFORMANCE

Ratings History

Date	Overall Rating	Risk Rating	Reward Rating
Q3-19	D	D-	D-
Q4-18	D	D-	D-
Q4-17	E+	E+	E+
Q4-16	D	D-	D-
Q4-15	D	D-	D

Asset & Performance History

Date	NAV	1-Year Total Return
2018	35.41	2.78
2017	34.88	-38.55
2016	56.84	-29.54
2015	80.68	-7.39
2014	87.12	-20.56
2013	109.68	-42.64

Total Assets: $174,043,984

Asset Allocation

Asset	%
Cash	204%
Stocks	-115%
US Stocks	-115%
Bonds	12%
US Bonds	12%
Other	0%

Services Offered:

Investment Strategy: The investment seeks daily investment results, before fees and expenses, that correspond to two times the inverse (-2x) of the daily performance of the Dow Jones Industrial Average® Index. The fund invests in financial instruments that ProShare Advisors believes, in combination, should produce daily returns consistent with the fund's investment objective. The index is a price-weighted index and includes 30 large-cap, "blue-chip" U.S. stocks, excluding utility and transportation companies. The fund is non-diversified. **Top Holdings:** Dj Industrial Average Index Swap Bnp Paribas Dj Industrial Average Swap Bank Of America, Na Dj Industrial Average Swap Societe Generale Dj Industrial Average Swap Goldman Sachs International Dj Industrial Average Swap Citibank, N.A.

iShares GNMA Bond ETF   C   HOLD

Ticker	Traded On	NAV	Total Assets ($)	Dividend Yield (TTM)	Turnover Ratio	Expense Ratio
GNMA	NAS CM	50.28	$173,455,088	2.7	834	0.15

Ratings
Reward	C
Risk	C-
Recent Upgrade/Downgrade	

Fund Information
Fund Type	Exchange Traded Funds
Category	US Fixed Income
Sub-Category	Intermediate Government
Prospectus Objective	Govt Bond - Mortgage
Inception Date	Feb-12
Open to New Investments	Y

Prices
Price (as of 9/30/2019)	50.31
52-Week High	50.45
52-Week Low	47.32

Total Returns (%)
3-Month	6-Month	1-Year	3-Year	5-Year
1.18	3.50	7.40	6.10	11.75

3-Year Standard Deviation	2.4
Effective Duration	

Valuation
Premium/Discount (1-Year Average)	0.05

Company Information
Provider	iShares
Manager/Tenure	James Mauro (7), Scott Radell (7)
Website	http://www.ishares.com
Address	iShares 400 Howard Street San Francisco CA 94105 United States
Phone Number	800-474-2737

PERFORMANCE

Ratings History
Date	Overall Rating	Risk Rating	Reward Rating
Q3-19	C	C-	C
Q4-18	D+	C-	D
Q4-17	C+	B+	C
Q4-16	C	C-	C
Q4-15	C	C-	C

Asset & Performance History
Date	NAV	1-Year Total Return
2018	48.68	0.68
2017	49.54	1.7
2016	49.76	1.32
2015	50.03	0.98
2014	50.29	5.98
2013	48.04	-2.77

Total Assets: $173,455,088

Asset Allocation
Asset	%
Cash	8%
Stocks	0%
US Stocks	0%
Bonds	92%
US Bonds	92%
Other	0%

Services Offered:

Investment Strategy: The investment seeks to track the investment results of the Bloomberg Barclays U.S. GNMA Bond Index. The fund generally will invest at least 90% of its assets in the component securities of the underlying index and in investments that have economic characteristics that are substantially identical to the component securities of the underlying index. The underlying index includes fixed-rate mortgage pass-through securities issued by GNMA that have 30- or 15-year maturities. The index measures the performance of mortgage-backed pass-through securities issued by GNMA. **Top Holdings:** Gnma2 30yr 2016 Production Gnma2 30yr 2016 Production Gnma2 30yr 2017 Production Gnma 30yr 4% Fico <660 2015 Gnma2 30yr 2018 Production

---

Vanguard Total World Bond ETF   D+   SELL

Ticker	Traded On	NAV	Total Assets ($)	Dividend Yield (TTM)	Turnover Ratio	Expense Ratio
BNDW	NAS CM	80.44	$172,946,000	2.79		0.09

Ratings
Reward	D+
Risk	C-
Recent Upgrade/Downgrade	

Fund Information
Fund Type	Exchange Traded Funds
Category	Global Fixed Income
Sub-Category	World Bond-USD Hedged
Prospectus Objective	Worldwide Bond
Inception Date	Sep-18
Open to New Investments	Y

Prices
Price (as of 9/30/2019)	80.43
52-Week High	81.08
52-Week Low	74.05

Total Returns (%)
3-Month	6-Month	1-Year	3-Year	5-Year
2.62	6.12	11.02		

3-Year Standard Deviation	
Effective Duration	7.13

Valuation
Premium/Discount (1-Year Average)	0.05

Company Information
Provider	Vanguard
Manager/Tenure	Joshua C. Barrickman (1)
Website	http://www.vanguard.com
Address	Vanguard 100 Vanguard Boulevard Malvern PA 19355 United States
Phone Number	877-662-7447

PERFORMANCE

Ratings History
Date	Overall Rating	Risk Rating	Reward Rating
Q3-19	D+	C-	D+
Q4-18	U		
Q4-17			
Q4-16			
Q4-15			

Asset & Performance History
Date	NAV	1-Year Total Return
2018	74.63	
2017		
2016		
2015		
2014		
2013		

Total Assets: $172,946,000

Asset Allocation
Asset	%
Cash	1%
Stocks	0%
US Stocks	0%
Bonds	98%
US Bonds	45%
Other	0%

Services Offered:

Investment Strategy: The investment seeks to track the performance of the Bloomberg Barclays Global Aggregate Float Adjusted Composite Index that measures the investment return of investment-grade U.S. bonds and investment-grade non-U.S. dollar-denominated bonds. The advisor intends to obtain its exposure to the bonds held in the index by investing all, or substantially all, of its assets in two Vanguard bond index ETFs (underlying funds), rather than in individual securities held in the index. The index is designed to track the market capitalized weights of the global investment-grade bond market. **Top Holdings:** Vanguard Total International Bond ETF Vanguard Total Bond Market ETF

ProShares Ultra Nasdaq Biotechnology

D+   **SELL**

Ticker	Traded On	NAV	Total Assets ($)	Dividend Yield (TTM)	Turnover Ratio	Expense Ratio
BIB	NAS CM	42.58	$172,430,263	0	31	0.95

Ratings
Reward	D+
Risk	D+
Recent Upgrade/Downgrade	

Fund Information
Fund Type	Exchange Traded Funds
Category	Trading Tools
Sub-Category	Trading--Leveraged Equity
Prospectus Objective	Technology
Inception Date	Apr-10
Open to New Investments	Y

Prices
Price (as of 9/30/2019)	42.53
52-Week High	68.95
52-Week Low	36.42

Total Returns (%)
3-Month	6-Month	1-Year	3-Year	5-Year
-18.80	-23.36	-37.93	-12.20	-15.59

3-Year Standard Deviation	41.97
Effective Duration	

Valuation
Premium/Discount (1-Year Average)	-0.08

Company Information
Provider	ProShares
Manager/Tenure	Michael Neches (6), Tarak Davé (1)
Website	http://www.proshares.com
Address	ProShares 7501 Wisconsin Avenue, Suite 1000 Bethesda MD 20814 United States
Phone Number	866-776-5125

PERFORMANCE

Ratings History
Date	Overall Rating	Risk Rating	Reward Rating
Q3-19	D+	D+	D+
Q4-18	D+	D+	D+
Q4-17	D+	D+	D+
Q4-16	C-	D+	C-
Q4-15	B-	C+	B

Asset & Performance History
Date	NAV	1-Year Total Return
2018	42.41	-24.36
2017	56.07	40.73
2016	39.84	-44.22
2015	71.43	13.79
2014	62.77	66.69
2013	37.66	160.13

Total Assets: $172,430,263

Asset Allocation
Asset	%
Cash	-100%
Stocks	182%
US Stocks	172%
Bonds	0%
US Bonds	0%
Other	18%

Services Offered:

Investment Strategy: The investment seeks daily investment results that correspond to two times (2x) the daily performance of the Nasdaq Biotechnology Index®. The fund invests in financial instruments that ProShare Advisors believes, in combination, should produce daily returns consistent with the fund's investment objective. The index is a modified capitalization weighted index that includes securities of Nasdaq listed companies that are classified as either biotechnology or pharmaceutical. The fund is non-diversified. **Top Holdings:** Nasdaq Biotechnology Index Swap Ubs Ag   Nasdaq Biotechnology Index Swap Bank Of America Na   Nasdaq Biotechnology Index Swap Societe Generale   Ishares Biotech (Ibb) Swap Goldman Sachs International   Nasdaq Biotechnology Index Swap Citibank Na

---

VictoryShares USAA MSCI Emerging Markets Value Momentum ETF

D   **SELL**

Ticker	Traded On	NAV	Total Assets ($)	Dividend Yield (TTM)	Turnover Ratio	Expense Ratio
UEVM	NYSE Arca	42.01	$172,229,595	2.21	58	0.45

Ratings
Reward	D
Risk	D
Recent Upgrade/Downgrade	

Fund Information
Fund Type	Exchange Traded Funds
Category	Global Emerg Mkts Equity
Sub-Category	Diversified Emerging Mkts
Prospectus Objective	Div Emerg Mkts
Inception Date	Oct-17
Open to New Investments	Y

Prices
Price (as of 9/30/2019)	42.09
52-Week High	46.24
52-Week Low	39.95

Total Returns (%)
3-Month	6-Month	1-Year	3-Year	5-Year
-6.24	-6.40	-6.66		

3-Year Standard Deviation	
Effective Duration	

Valuation
Premium/Discount (1-Year Average)	0.25

Company Information
Provider	VictoryShares
Manager/Tenure	Lance Humphrey (1), Wasif A. Latif (1), Mannik Dhillon (0)
Website	http://www.VictorySharesLiterature.com
Address	Victory Shares 4249 Easton Way, Suite 400 Columbus OH 43219 United States
Phone Number	

PERFORMANCE

Ratings History
Date	Overall Rating	Risk Rating	Reward Rating
Q3-19	D	D	D
Q4-18	D	D	D
Q4-17	U		
Q4-16			
Q4-15			

Asset & Performance History
Date	NAV	1-Year Total Return
2018	41.76	-16.62
2017	51.19	
2016		
2015		
2014		
2013		

Total Assets: $172,229,595

Asset Allocation
Asset	%
Cash	1%
Stocks	99%
US Stocks	0%
Bonds	0%
US Bonds	0%
Other	0%

Services Offered:

Investment Strategy: The investment seeks to provide investment results that correspond to the MSCI Emerging Markets Select Value Momentum Blend Index. The fund seeks to achieve by investing at least 80% of its net assets in securities in the index, depositary receipts on securities in the index, and securities underlying depositary receipts in the index. The index is designed to deliver exposure to equity market performance in the global emerging markets and provide higher exposure to value and momentum factors within the MSCI Emerging Markets Index while also maintaining moderate index turnover and lower realized volatility than traditional capitalization weighted indexes. **Top Holdings:** Mini Msci Em Mk Fut Sep19   Taiwan Cooperative Financial Holding Co Ltd   Taiwan Business Bank   PPB Group Bhd   Ratch Group PCL

Invesco Golden Dragon China ETF   C   HOLD

Ticker	Traded On	NAV	Total Assets ($)	Dividend Yield (TTM)	Turnover Ratio	Expense Ratio
PGJ	NAS CM	35.75	$171,592,092	0.2	36	0.7

Ratings
Reward	C+
Risk	D+
Recent Upgrade/Downgrade	Up

Fund Information
Fund Type	Exchange Traded Funds
Category	Greater China Equity
Sub-Category	China Region
Prospectus Objective	Pacific Stock
Inception Date	Dec-04
Open to New Investments	Y

Prices
Price (as of 9/30/2019)	35.61
52-Week High	42.73
52-Week Low	30.68

Total Returns (%)
3-Month	6-Month	1-Year	3-Year	5-Year
-6.61	-13.91	-6.67	12.48	28.65

3-Year Standard Deviation	24.38
Effective Duration	

Valuation
Premium/Discount (1-Year Average)	-0.16

Company Information
Provider	Invesco
Manager/Tenure	Peter Hubbard (12), Michael Jeanette (11), Tony Seisser (4)
Website	http://www.invesco.com/us
Address	Invesco 11 Greenway Plaza, Ste. 2500 Houston TX 77046 United States
Phone Number	800-659-1005

PERFORMANCE

Ratings History
Date	Overall Rating	Risk Rating	Reward Rating
Q3-19	C	D+	C+
Q4-18	C	D	B-
Q4-17	B+	C+	A+
Q4-16	C	D+	B
Q4-15	B-	C	B

Asset & Performance History
Date	NAV	1-Year Total Return
2018	31.62	-29.15
2017	44.74	59.96
2016	28.57	-11.35
2015	32.85	18.23
2014	27.89	-7.27
2013	30.33	59.64

Total Assets: $171,592,092

Asset Allocation
Asset	%
Cash	0%
Stocks	100%
US Stocks	0%
Bonds	0%
US Bonds	0%
Other	0%

Services Offered:

Investment Strategy: The investment seeks to track the investment results (before fees and expenses) of the NASDAQ Golden Dragon China Index. The fund generally will invest at least 90% of its total assets in the securities that comprise the underlying index. The underlying index is composed of securities of U.S. exchange-listed companies that are headquartered or incorporated in the People's Republic of China. The fund is non-diversified. **Top Holdings:** Alibaba Group Holding Ltd ADR   JD.com Inc ADR   NetEase Inc ADR   Baidu Inc ADR   Ctrip.com International Ltd ADR

VanEck Merk Gold Trust   C   HOLD

Ticker	Traded On	NAV	Total Assets ($)	Dividend Yield (TTM)	Turnover Ratio	Expense Ratio
OUNZ	NYSE Arca	14.54	$171,506,703	0		0.4

Ratings
Reward	C+
Risk	C-
Recent Upgrade/Downgrade	Up

Fund Information
Fund Type	Exchange Traded Funds
Category	Commodities Specified
Sub-Category	Commodities Precious Metals
Prospectus Objective	Prec Metals
Inception Date	May-14
Open to New Investments	Y

Prices
Price (as of 9/30/2019)	14.42
52-Week High	15.23
52-Week Low	11.66

Total Returns (%)
3-Month	6-Month	1-Year	3-Year	5-Year
6.75	14.66	24.41	10.99	19.70

3-Year Standard Deviation	11.15
Effective Duration	

Valuation
Premium/Discount (1-Year Average)	-0.15

Company Information
Provider	Merk Funds
Manager/Tenure	Management Team (5)
Website	http://www.merkfund.com
Address	Merk Funds P.O. Box 588 Portland ME 4112 United States
Phone Number	866-637-5386

PERFORMANCE

Ratings History
Date	Overall Rating	Risk Rating	Reward Rating
Q3-19	C	C-	C+
Q4-18	D+	C-	D
Q4-17	C-	C-	C-
Q4-16	C-	C-	C-
Q4-15	D	D	D

Asset & Performance History
Date	NAV	1-Year Total Return
2018	12.58	-1.54
2017	12.78	12.21
2016	11.47	7.67
2015	10.55	-11.78
2014	11.96	
2013		

Total Assets: $171,506,703

Asset Allocation
Asset	%
Cash	0%
Stocks	0%
US Stocks	0%
Bonds	0%
US Bonds	0%
Other	100%

Services Offered:

Investment Strategy: The Trust's primary objective is to provide investors with an opportunity to invest in gold through the shares and be able to take delivery of physical gold in exchange for those shares. The Trust's secondary objective is for the shares to reflect the performance of the price of gold less the expenses of the Trust's operations. Each share represents a fractional undivided beneficial interest in the Trust's net assets. The Trust's assets consist principally of gold held on the Trust's behalf in financial institutions for safekeeping. **Top Holdings:** Gold Oz.

Invesco 1-30 Laddered Treasury ETF

C   HOLD

Ticker	Traded On	NAV	Total Assets ($)	Dividend Yield (TTM)	Turnover Ratio	Expense Ratio
PLW	NAS CM	35.54	$170,575,669	1.93		0.25

Ratings
Reward	C
Risk	C+
Recent Upgrade/Downgrade	

Fund Information
Fund Type	Exchange Traded Funds
Category	US Fixed Income
Sub-Category	Long Government
Prospectus Objective	Govt Bond - Treasury
Inception Date	Oct-07
Open to New Investments	Y

Prices
Price (as of 9/30/2019)	35.57
52-Week High	36.39
52-Week Low	30.35

Total Returns (%)
3-Month	6-Month	1-Year	3-Year	5-Year
5.08	10.28	17.34	9.06	24.11

3-Year Standard Deviation	7.27
Effective Duration	11.09

Valuation
Premium/Discount (1-Year Average)	0.08

Company Information
Provider	Invesco
Manager/Tenure	Philip Fang (11), Peter Hubbard (11), Jeffrey W. Kernagis (11), 2 others
Website	http://www.invesco.com/us
Address	Invesco 11 Greenway Plaza, Ste. 2500 Houston TX 77046 United States
Phone Number	800-659-1005

PERFORMANCE

Ratings History
Date	Overall Rating	Risk Rating	Reward Rating
Q3-19	C	C+	C
Q4-18	D+	C-	D
Q4-17	C	C	C
Q4-16	C	C-	C
Q4-15	C	C+	C

Asset & Performance History
Date	NAV	1-Year Total Return
2018	31.94	-0.37
2017	32.77	4.64
2016	31.96	0.99
2015	32.25	0.11
2014	32.9	14.73
2013	29.38	-8.16

Total Assets: $170,575,669
Asset Allocation
Asset	%
Cash	0%
Stocks	0%
US Stocks	0%
Bonds	100%
US Bonds	100%
Other	0%

Services Offered:

Investment Strategy: The investment seeks to track the investment results (before fees and expenses) of the Ryan/NASDAQ U.S. 1-30 Year Treasury Laddered Index (the "underlying index"). The fund generally invests at least 80% of its total assets in U.S. Treasury securities that comprise the underlying index. The index seeks to maintain a continuous maturity laddered portfolio of securities, meaning that securities holdings are scheduled to mature in a proportional, annual sequential pattern. Nasdaq, Inc. (the "index provider") allows a six-month maturity deviation if securities with a desired maturity date are not available. **Top Holdings:** United States Treasury Bonds 4.5% United States Treasury Bonds 5.38% United States Treasury Bonds 3% United States Treasury Bonds 3% United States Treasury Bonds 2.5%

Invesco DB Gold Fund

C   HOLD

Ticker	Traded On	NAV	Total Assets ($)	Dividend Yield (TTM)	Turnover Ratio	Expense Ratio
DGL	NYSE Arca	44.77	$170,124,611	1.29	0	0.75

Ratings
Reward	C
Risk	C-
Recent Upgrade/Downgrade	Up

Fund Information
Fund Type	Exchange Traded Funds
Category	Commodities Specified
Sub-Category	Commodities Precious Metals
Prospectus Objective	Prec Metals
Inception Date	Jan-07
Open to New Investments	Y

Prices
Price (as of 9/30/2019)	44.96
52-Week High	47.45
52-Week Low	37.34

Total Returns (%)
3-Month	6-Month	1-Year	3-Year	5-Year
5.61	13.13	21.75	6.95	12.73

3-Year Standard Deviation	10.94
Effective Duration	

Valuation
Premium/Discount (1-Year Average)	0.01

Company Information
Provider	Invesco
Manager/Tenure	Management Team (12)
Website	http://www.invesco.com/us
Address	Invesco 11 Greenway Plaza, Ste. 2500 Houston TX 77046 United States
Phone Number	800-659-1005

PERFORMANCE

Ratings History
Date	Overall Rating	Risk Rating	Reward Rating
Q3-19	C	C-	C
Q4-18	D+	D+	D
Q4-17	C-	C-	C-
Q4-16	D+	D+	C-
Q4-15	D	D	D

Asset & Performance History
Date	NAV	1-Year Total Return
2018	39.42	-5.04
2017	41.51	10.53
2016	37.04	7.37
2015	34.69	-11.45
2014	39.17	-2.87
2013	40.33	-29.77

Total Assets: $170,124,611
Asset Allocation
Asset	%
Cash	47%
Stocks	0%
US Stocks	0%
Bonds	3%
US Bonds	3%
Other	0%

Services Offered:

Investment Strategy: The investment seeks to track the DBIQ Optimum Yield Gold Index Excess Return™ (DBIQ-OY GC ER™), which is intended to reflect the changes in market value of gold.
The single index Commodity consists of Gold. The fund invests in futures contracts in an attempt to track its corresponding index. **Top Holdings:** GOLDMAN SACHS FINANCE CORP INTERNATIONAL LTD 0% United States Treasury Bills 0% United States Treasury Bills 0% United States Treasury Bills 0% United States Treasury Bills 0%

Invesco S&P 500® ex-Rate Sensitive Low Volatility ETF   C+   HOLD

Ticker	Traded On	NAV	Total Assets ($)	Dividend Yield (TTM)	Turnover Ratio	Expense Ratio
XRLV	NYSE Arca	39.45	$169,621,914	1.68		0.25

Ratings
Reward   B-
Risk   C-
Recent Upgrade/Downgrade

Fund Information
Fund Type	Exchange Traded Funds
Category	US Equity Large Cap Blend
Sub-Category	Large Blend
Prospectus Objective	Growth
Inception Date	Apr-15
Open to New Investments	

Prices
Price (as of 9/30/2019)	39.42
52-Week High	39.69
52-Week Low	30.55

Total Returns (%)
3-Month	6-Month	1-Year	3-Year	5-Year
1.78	8.21	10.73	49.68	

3-Year Standard Deviation	11.03
Effective Duration	

Valuation
Premium/Discount (1-Year Average)	0.05

Company Information
Provider	Invesco
Manager/Tenure	Peter Hubbard (4), Michael Jeanette (4), Tony Seisser (4)
Website	http://www.invesco.com/us
Address	Invesco 11 Greenway Plaza, Ste. 2500 Houston TX 77046 United States
Phone Number	800-659-1005

PERFORMANCE

Ratings History

Date	Overall Rating	Risk Rating	Reward Rating
Q3-19	C+	C-	B-
Q4-18	C	C-	C
Q4-17	B-	B+	C+
Q4-16	D+	C-	C-
Q4-15	U		

Asset & Performance History

Date	NAV	1-Year Total Return
2018	32.33	-2.83
2017	33.83	22.99
2016	27.93	11.54
2015	25.49	
2014		
2013		

Total Assets: $169,621,914

Asset Allocation

Asset	%
Cash	0%
Stocks	100%
US Stocks	99%
Bonds	0%
US Bonds	0%
Other	0%

Services Offered:

Investment Strategy: The investment seeks to track the investment results (before fees and expenses) of the S&P 500 Low Volatility Rate Response Index (the "underlying index"). The fund generally will invest at least 90% of its total assets in the securities that comprise the underlying index. The underlying index is designed to provide exposure to the 100 constituents of the S&P 500® Index that exhibit both low volatility and low interest rate risk. The underlying index is designed to include stocks exhibiting low volatility characteristics, after removing stocks that historically have performed poorly in rising interest rate environments. **Top Holdings:** Republic Services Inc Class A Waste Management Inc Mondelez International Inc Class A Yum Brands Inc McDonald's Corp

---

VelocityShares 3x Long Gold ETN Linked to the S&P GSCI® Gold Index ER   B   BUY

Ticker	Traded On	NAV	Total Assets ($)	Dividend Yield (TTM)	Turnover Ratio	Expense Ratio
UGLD	NAS CM	130.76	$169,540,817	0		1.35

Ratings
Reward   A-
Risk   C-
Recent Upgrade/Downgrade   Up

Fund Information
Fund Type	Exchange Traded Funds
Category	Trading Tools
Sub-Category	Trading--Leveraged Commodities
Prospectus Objective	Prec Metals
Inception Date	Oct-11
Open to New Investments	Y

Prices
Price (as of 9/30/2019)	132.67
52-Week High	157.03
52-Week Low	77.90

Total Returns (%)
3-Month	6-Month	1-Year	3-Year	5-Year
14.59	38.67	67.91	916.04	940.29

3-Year Standard Deviation	33.25
Effective Duration	

Valuation
Premium/Discount (1-Year Average)	0.05

Company Information
Provider	Credit Suisse AG
Manager/Tenure	Management Team (7)
Website	
Address	Kilmore House Park Lane Dublin Ireland
Phone Number	

PERFORMANCE

Ratings History

Date	Overall Rating	Risk Rating	Reward Rating
Q3-19	B	C-	A-
Q4-18	B	D+	A-
Q4-17	D+	D	C-
Q4-16	D	D	D+
Q4-15	E+	D-	E+

Asset & Performance History

Date	NAV	1-Year Total Return
2018	94.74	742.64
2017	11.24	28.67
2016	8.36	15.48
2015	7.37	-34.6
2014	11.27	-11.95
2013	12.8	-69.52

Total Assets: $169,540,817

Asset Allocation

Asset	%
Cash	%
Stocks	%
US Stocks	%
Bonds	%
US Bonds	%
Other	%

Services Offered:

Investment Strategy: The investment seeks to replicate, net of expenses, three times the S&P GSCI Gold index ER. The index comprises futures contracts on a single commodity. The fluctuations in the values of it are intended generally to correlate with changes in the price of gold in global markets. **Top Holdings:**

ClearBridge Large Cap Growth ESG ETF

C+   HOLD

Ticker	Traded On	NAV	Total Assets ($)	Dividend Yield (TTM)	Turnover Ratio	Expense Ratio
LRGE	NAS CM	34.75	$168,526,654	0.46	20	0.6

Ratings
Reward   B-
Risk   C
Recent Upgrade/Downgrade   Up

Fund Information
Fund Type   Exchange Traded Funds
Category   US Equity Large Cap Growth
Sub-Category   Large Growth
Prospectus Objective   Growth
Inception Date   May-17
Open to New Investments   Y

Prices
Price (as of 9/30/2019)   34.79
52-Week High   36.31
52-Week Low   27.10

Total Returns (%)

3-Month	6-Month	1-Year	3-Year	5-Year
-1.22	3.45	4.07		

3-Year Standard Deviation
Effective Duration

Valuation
Premium/Discount (1-Year Average)   -0.20

Company Information
Provider   Legg Mason
Manager/Tenure   Peter Bourbeau (2), Mary Jane McQuillen (2), Margaret B. Vitrano (2)
Website   http://www.leggmason.com
Address   Legg Mason/Western 100 International Drive Baltimore MD 21202 United States
Phone Number   877-721-1926

PERFORMANCE

Ratings History

Date	Overall Rating	Risk Rating	Reward Rating
Q3-19	C+	C	B-
Q4-18	C	C-	C
Q4-17	U		
Q4-16			
Q4-15			

Asset & Performance History

Date	NAV	1-Year Total Return
2018	28.86	-0.18
2017	29.24	
2016		
2015		
2014		
2013		

Total Assets: $168,526,654
Asset Allocation

Asset	%
Cash	2%
Stocks	98%
US Stocks	96%
Bonds	0%
US Bonds	0%
Other	0%

Services Offered:

Investment Strategy: The investment seeks long-term capital appreciation through investing in large-capitalization companies with the potential for high future earnings growth. Under normal circumstances, the fund seeks to meet its investment objective by investing at least 80% of its net assets, plus borrowings for investment purposes, if any, in equity securities or other instruments with similar economic characteristics of U.S. companies with large market capitalizations that meet its financial and environmental, social and governance ("ESG") criteria. **Top Holdings:** Amazon.com Inc   Microsoft Corp   Facebook Inc A   Visa Inc Class A   The Walt Disney Co

---

SPDR® Portfolio MSCI Global Stock Market ETF

C   HOLD

Ticker	Traded On	NAV	Total Assets ($)	Dividend Yield (TTM)	Turnover Ratio	Expense Ratio
SPGM	NYSE Arca		$167,886,365	2.03	4	0.09

Ratings
Reward   C
Risk   C-
Recent Upgrade/Downgrade

Fund Information
Fund Type   Exchange Traded Funds
Category   Global Equity Large Cap
Sub-Category   World Large Stock
Prospectus Objective   World Stock
Inception Date   Feb-12
Open to New Investments   Y

Prices
Price (as of 9/30/2019)   39.91
52-Week High   81.46
52-Week Low   37.90

Total Returns (%)

3-Month	6-Month	1-Year	3-Year	5-Year
-50.41	-48.99	-49.77	-34.21	-29.70

3-Year Standard Deviation   11.43
Effective Duration

Valuation
Premium/Discount (1-Year Average)   0.01

Company Information
Provider   SPDR State Street Global Advisors
Manager/Tenure   Michael J. Feehily (7), Karl A. Schneider (4), Keith Richardson (0)
Website   http://www.spdrs.com
Address   SPDR State Street Global Advisors State Street Financial Center, 1 Lincoln Street Boston MA 02111-2900 United States
Phone Number   617-786-3000

PERFORMANCE

Ratings History

Date	Overall Rating	Risk Rating	Reward Rating
Q3-19	C	C-	C
Q4-18	C-	C-	C-
Q4-17	B-	B-	B-
Q4-16	C	D+	C+
Q4-15	C	D+	C

Asset & Performance History

Date	NAV	1-Year Total Return
2018	69.82	-9.54
2017	78.6	23.98
2016	64.92	8.83
2015	60.8	-1.68
2014	64.1	5.7
2013	61.97	23.45

Total Assets: $167,886,365
Asset Allocation

Asset	%
Cash	0%
Stocks	100%
US Stocks	56%
Bonds	0%
US Bonds	0%
Other	0%

Services Offered:

Investment Strategy: The investment seeks to provide investment results that, before fees and expenses, correspond generally to the total return performance of the MSCI ACWI IMI Index. The fund generally invests substantially all, but at least 80%, of its total assets in the securities comprising the index and in depositary receipts based on securities comprising the index. The index is a free float-adjusted market capitalization-weighted index that is designed to measure the combined equity market performance of developed and emerging markets. It is non-diversified. **Top Holdings:** Microsoft Corp   Apple Inc   Amazon.com Inc   Visa Inc Class A   Alphabet Inc A

iShares MSCI Peru ETF

C- HOLD

Ticker	Traded On	NAV
EPU	NYSE Arca	34.92

Total Assets ($)	Dividend Yield (TTM)	Turnover Ratio	Expense Ratio
$165,876,164	2.36	11	0.59

Ratings

Reward	C-
Risk	C-
Recent Upgrade/Downgrade	

Fund Information

Fund Type	Exchange Traded Funds
Category	Equity Misc
Sub-Category	Miscellaneous Region
Prospectus Objective	Foreign Stock
Inception Date	Jun-09
Open to New Investments	Y

Prices

Price (as of 9/30/2019)	35.06
52-Week High	40.04
52-Week Low	32.84

Total Returns (%)

3-Month	6-Month	1-Year	3-Year	5-Year
-6.02	-9.45	-3.63	13.66	12.70

3-Year Standard Deviation	13.88
Effective Duration	

Valuation

Premium/Discount (1-Year Average)	0.03

Company Information

Provider	iShares
Manager/Tenure	Diane Hsiung (10), Greg Savage (10), Jennifer Hsui (6), 3 others
Website	http://www.ishares.com
Address	iShares 400 Howard Street San Francisco CA 94105 United States
Phone Number	800-474-2737

PERFORMANCE

Ratings History

Date	Overall Rating	Risk Rating	Reward Rating
Q3-19	C-	C-	C-
Q4-18	C-	C-	C
Q4-17	B	C	A
Q4-16	C-	D+	C
Q4-15	D	D	D

Asset & Performance History

Date	NAV	1-Year Total Return
2018	35.49	-12.18
2017	40.98	30.34
2016	32.63	61.55
2015	20.38	-36.12
2014	32.4	-1.33
2013	33.35	-25.83

Total Assets: $165,876,164

Asset Allocation

Asset	%
Cash	0%
Stocks	100%
US Stocks	11%
Bonds	0%
US Bonds	0%
Other	0%

Services Offered:

Investment Strategy: The investment seeks to track the investment results of the MSCI All Peru Capped Index. The fund generally will invest at least 90% of its assets in the component securities of the underlying index and in investments that have economic characteristics that are substantially identical to the component securities of the underlying index. The index is an index composed of Peruvian equities. The fund is non-diversified. **Top Holdings:** Credicorp Ltd Buenaventura Mining Co Inc ADR Southern Copper Corp InRetail Peru Corp Alicorp SA

SPDR® Bloomberg Barclays International Corporate Bond ETF

C HOLD

Ticker	Traded On	NAV
IBND	NYSE Arca	

Total Assets ($)	Dividend Yield (TTM)	Turnover Ratio	Expense Ratio
$165,671,442	0.48	16	0.5

Ratings

Reward	C
Risk	C-
Recent Upgrade/Downgrade	Up

Fund Information

Fund Type	Exchange Traded Funds
Category	Global Fixed Income
Sub-Category	World Bond
Prospectus Objective	Worldwide Bond
Inception Date	May-10
Open to New Investments	Y

Prices

Price (as of 9/30/2019)	33.30
52-Week High	34.34
52-Week Low	32.28

Total Returns (%)

3-Month	6-Month	1-Year	3-Year	5-Year
-2.16	0.34	0.06	1.16	-4.11

3-Year Standard Deviation	6.83
Effective Duration	5.74

Valuation

Premium/Discount (1-Year Average)	0.15

Company Information

Provider	SPDR State Street Global Advisors
Manager/Tenure	Peter Spano (4), Richard Darby-Dowman (3), Paul Brown (3)
Website	http://www.spdrs.com
Address	SPDR State Street Global Advisors State Street Financial Center, 1 Lincoln Street Boston MA 02111-2900 United States
Phone Number	617-786-3000

PERFORMANCE

Ratings History

Date	Overall Rating	Risk Rating	Reward Rating
Q3-19	C	C-	C
Q4-18	D+	C-	D+
Q4-17	C	C+	C
Q4-16	D+	C-	D
Q4-15	D+	D+	D

Asset & Performance History

Date	NAV	1-Year Total Return
2018	32.72	-6.32
2017	35.19	14.76
2016	30.77	-0.01
2015	30.78	-10.28
2014	34.31	-4.48
2013	36.49	5.08

Total Assets: $165,671,442

Asset Allocation

Asset	%
Cash	0%
Stocks	0%
US Stocks	0%
Bonds	99%
US Bonds	28%
Other	0%

Services Offered:

Investment Strategy: The investment seeks to provide investment results that correspond generally to the price and yield performance of the Bloomberg Barclays Global Aggregate ex-USD >$1B: Corporate Bond Index. The fund invests substantially all, but at least 80%, of its total assets in the securities comprising the index or in securities that the Adviser determines have economic characteristics that are substantially identical to the economic characteristics of the securities that comprise the index. The index is designed to be a broad based measure of the global investment grade, fixed rate, fixed income corporate markets outside the United States. It is non-diversified. **Top Holdings:** Anheuser-Busch InBev N.V./S.A. 2.75% Deutsche Bank Ag Sr Unsecured Regs 03/25 1.125 Panasonic Corp 0.47% Sanofi 0.5% Orange 8.12%

Perth Mint Physical Gold ETF

D+ **SELL**

Ticker	Traded On	NAV	Total Assets ($)	Dividend Yield (TTM)	Turnover Ratio	Expense Ratio
AAAU	NYSE Arca	14.82	$164,533,116	0		0.18

Ratings

Reward	D+
Risk	C-
Recent Upgrade/Downgrade	

Fund Information

Fund Type	Exchange Traded Funds
Category	Commodities Specified
Sub-Category	Commodities Precious Metals
Prospectus Objective	Prec Metals
Inception Date	Jul-18
Open to New Investments	Y

Prices

Price (as of 9/30/2019)	14.72
52-Week High	15.52
52-Week Low	11.86

Total Returns (%)

3-Month	6-Month	1-Year	3-Year	5-Year
6.77	14.70	24.64		

3-Year Standard Deviation	
Effective Duration	

Valuation

Premium/Discount (1-Year Average)	-0.10

Company Information

Provider	Exchange Traded Concepts
Manager/Tenure	Management Team (1)
Website	
Address	10900 Hefner Pointe Drive, Suite 207, Oklahoma City, Oklahoma 73120 Oklahoma City United States
Phone Number	

PERFORMANCE

Ratings History

Date	Overall Rating	Risk Rating	Reward Rating
Q3-19	D+	C-	D+
Q4-18	U		
Q4-17			
Q4-16			
Q4-15			

Asset & Performance History

Date	NAV	1-Year Total Return
2018	12.81	
2017		
2016		
2015		
2014		
2013		

Total Assets: $164,533,116

Asset Allocation

Asset	%
Cash	0%
Stocks	0%
US Stocks	0%
Bonds	0%
US Bonds	0%
Other	100%

Services Offered:

Investment Strategy: The investment seeks to provide investors with an opportunity to invest in gold through shares, and have the gold securely stored by the Custodial Sponsor; reflecting the performance of the price of gold less the expenses of the trust's operations is the secondary consideration.
The trust holds London Bars and Physical Gold of other specifications without numismatic value. It receives gold deposited by Authorized Participants in exchange for the creation of Baskets and delivers gold to Authorized Participants in exchange for Baskets surrendered to it for redemption. **Top Holdings:** Gold Oz.

First Trust Global Tactical Commodity Strategy Fund

D **SELL**

Ticker	Traded On	NAV	Total Assets ($)	Dividend Yield (TTM)	Turnover Ratio	Expense Ratio
FTGC	NAS CM	18.13	$164,153,740	0.6	0	0.95

Ratings

Reward	D
Risk	D+
Recent Upgrade/Downgrade	

Fund Information

Fund Type	Exchange Traded Funds
Category	Commodities Broad Basket
Sub-Category	Commodities Broad Basket
Prospectus Objective	Growth & Inc
Inception Date	Oct-13
Open to New Investments	Y

Prices

Price (as of 9/30/2019)	18.15
52-Week High	20.24
52-Week Low	17.70

Total Returns (%)

3-Month	6-Month	1-Year	3-Year	5-Year
-2.13	-3.61	-8.89	-10.35	-36.84

3-Year Standard Deviation	7.26
Effective Duration	

Valuation

Premium/Discount (1-Year Average)	-0.09

Company Information

Provider	First Trust
Manager/Tenure	John W. Gambla (5), Rob A. Guttschow (5)
Website	http://www.ftportfolios.com/
Address	First Trust 120 E. Liberty Drive, Suite 400 Wheaton IL 60187 United States
Phone Number	800-621-1675

PERFORMANCE

Ratings History

Date	Overall Rating	Risk Rating	Reward Rating
Q3-19	D	D+	D
Q4-18	D	D+	D
Q4-17	D	D+	D
Q4-16	D	D	D
Q4-15	D	D	D

Asset & Performance History

Date	NAV	1-Year Total Return
2018	17.92	-12.98
2017	20.75	2.84
2016	20.43	0.52
2015	20.32	-22.55
2014	26.24	-11.88
2013	29.78	

Total Assets: $164,153,740

Asset Allocation

Asset	%
Cash	85%
Stocks	0%
US Stocks	0%
Bonds	0%
US Bonds	0%
Other	15%

Services Offered:

Investment Strategy: The investment seeks to provide total return by providing investors with commodity exposure while seeking a relatively stable risk profile. The fund is an actively managed exchange-traded fund ("ETF") that seeks to achieve attractive risk adjusted return by investing in commodity futures contracts and exchange-traded commodity linked instruments (collectively, "Commodities Instruments") through a wholly-owned subsidiary of the fund organized under the laws of the Cayman Islands (the "Subsidiary"). The advisor expects to gain exposure to these investments exclusively by investing in the Subsidiary. **Top Holdings:** Ft Cayman Subsidiary Ii United States Treasury Bills United States Treasury Bills United States Treasury Bills

JPMorgan High Yield Research Enhanced ETF   C   HOLD

Ticker	Traded On	NAV	Total Assets ($)	Dividend Yield (TTM)	Turnover Ratio	Expense Ratio
JPHY	BATS	51.17	$163,748,638	4.94	23	0.24

Ratings
Reward	C
Risk	C-
Recent Upgrade/Downgrade	

Fund Information
Fund Type	Exchange Traded Funds
Category	US Fixed Income
Sub-Category	High Yield Bond
Prospectus Objective	Corp Bond-High Yld
Inception Date	Sep-16
Open to New Investments	Y

Prices
Price (as of 9/30/2019)	51.33
52-Week High	51.83
52-Week Low	47.14

Total Returns (%)
3-Month	6-Month	1-Year	3-Year	5-Year
1.01	3.85	7.42	17.18	

3-Year Standard Deviation	4.08
Effective Duration	3.51

Valuation
Premium/Discount (1-Year Average)	0.20

Company Information
Provider	JPMorgan
Manager/Tenure	Bhupinder Bahra (3), Frederick Bourgoin (3), William J. Morgan (3), 2 others
Website	http://www.jpmorganfunds.com
Address	JPMorgan 270 Park Avenue New York NY 10017-2070 United States
Phone Number	800-480-4111

PERFORMANCE

Ratings History
Date	Overall Rating	Risk Rating	Reward Rating
Q3-19	C	C-	C
Q4-18	C-	C-	C-
Q4-17	D	B	D+
Q4-16	U		
Q4-15			

Asset & Performance History
Date	NAV	1-Year Total Return
2018	47.3	-2.53
2017	50.94	6.11
2016	50.38	
2015		
2014		
2013		

Total Assets: $163,748,638

Asset Allocation
Asset	%
Cash	4%
Stocks	0%
US Stocks	0%
Bonds	96%
US Bonds	82%
Other	0%

Services Offered:

Investment Strategy: The investment seeks a high level of income; capital appreciation is a secondary objective. The fund invests primarily in high yield, high risk debt securities. Under normal circumstances, it invests at least 80% of its assets in high yield securities. For purposes of this policy, "assets" means net assets plus the amount of borrowings for investment purposes. The fund may invest up to 100% of its total assets in below investment grade or unrated securities. **Top Holdings:** ALTICE FRANCE S.A 7.38% Sprint Corporation 7.88% TransDigm, Inc. 6.25% Bausch Health Companies Inc 6.12% CCO Holdings, LLC/ CCO Holdings Capital Corp. 5.12%

---

iShares MSCI China A ETF   C   HOLD

Ticker	Traded On	NAV	Total Assets ($)	Dividend Yield (TTM)	Turnover Ratio	Expense Ratio
CNYA	BATS	27.65	$163,154,497	0.65	44	0.65

Ratings
Reward	C
Risk	C-
Recent Upgrade/Downgrade	Up

Fund Information
Fund Type	Exchange Traded Funds
Category	Greater China Equity
Sub-Category	China Region
Prospectus Objective	Pacific Stock
Inception Date	Jun-16
Open to New Investments	Y

Prices
Price (as of 9/30/2019)	27.71
52-Week High	31.33
52-Week Low	22.38

Total Returns (%)
3-Month	6-Month	1-Year	3-Year	5-Year
-5.76	-7.75	9.04	14.04	

3-Year Standard Deviation	18.24
Effective Duration	

Valuation
Premium/Discount (1-Year Average)	0.48

Company Information
Provider	iShares
Manager/Tenure	Diane Hsiung (3), Jennifer Hsui (3), Alan Mason (3), 3 others
Website	http://www.ishares.com
Address	iShares 400 Howard Street San Francisco CA 94105 United States
Phone Number	800-474-2737

PERFORMANCE

Ratings History
Date	Overall Rating	Risk Rating	Reward Rating
Q3-19	C	C-	C
Q4-18	D	D	D
Q4-17	D+	B	C
Q4-16	U		
Q4-15			

Asset & Performance History
Date	NAV	1-Year Total Return
2018	22.61	-26.26
2017	31.81	29.15
2016	24.89	
2015		
2014		
2013		

Total Assets: $163,154,497

Asset Allocation
Asset	%
Cash	0%
Stocks	100%
US Stocks	0%
Bonds	0%
US Bonds	0%
Other	0%

Services Offered:

Investment Strategy: The investment seeks to track the investment results of the MSCI China A Inclusion Index composed of domestic Chinese equities that trade on the Shanghai or Shenzhen Stock Exchange. The fund generally will invest at least 90% of its assets in the component securities of the index and in investments that have economic characteristics that are substantially identical to the component securities of the index. The index is designed to measure the equity market performance in the People's Republic of China, as represented by "A-shares" that are accessible through the Shanghai Connect or the Shenzhen-Hong Kong Stock Connect program. **Top Holdings:** Kweichow Moutai Co Ltd Ping An Insurance (Group) Co. of China Ltd China Merchants Bank Co Ltd Wuliangye Yibin Co Ltd China Yangtze Power Co Ltd

Invesco DWA Emerging Markets Momentum ETF   C-   HOLD

Ticker	Traded On	NAV	Total Assets ($)	Dividend Yield (TTM)	Turnover Ratio	Expense Ratio
PIE	NAS CM	17.59	$162,700,099	2.35	163	0.9

Ratings
Reward   C-
Risk   C-
Recent Upgrade/Downgrade

Fund Information
Fund Type   Exchange Traded Funds
Category   Global Emerg Mkts Equity
Sub-Category   Diversified Emerging Mkts
Prospectus Objective   Div Emerg Mkts
Inception Date   Dec-07
Open to New Investments

Prices
Price (as of 9/30/2019)   17.50
52-Week High   18.16
52-Week Low   15.34

Total Returns (%)

3-Month	6-Month	1-Year	3-Year	5-Year
-0.55	4.03	0.74	16.17	3.52

3-Year Standard Deviation   13.56
Effective Duration

Valuation
Premium/Discount (1-Year Average)   -0.34

Company Information
Provider   Invesco
Manager/Tenure   Peter Hubbard (11), Michael Jeanette (4), Tony Seisser (4)
Website   http://www.invesco.com/us
Address   Invesco 11 Greenway Plaza, Ste. 2500 Houston TX 77046 United States
Phone Number   800-659-1005

PERFORMANCE

Ratings History

Date	Overall Rating	Risk Rating	Reward Rating
Q3-19	C-	C-	C-
Q4-18	D+	C-	D+
Q4-17	C+	C	B-
Q4-16	D+	D+	D
Q4-15	D+	C-	D

Asset & Performance History

Date	NAV	1-Year Total Return
2018	15.67	-21.24
2017	20.49	39.48
2016	14.94	0.15
2015	15.13	-13.99
2014	17.73	-1.97
2013	18.18	-0.08

Total Assets: $162,700,099

Asset Allocation

Asset	%
Cash	0%
Stocks	100%
US Stocks	2%
Bonds	0%
US Bonds	0%
Other	0%

Services Offered:

Investment Strategy: The investment seeks to track the investment results (before fees and expenses) of the Dorsey Wright® Emerging Markets Technical Leaders Index (the "underlying index"). The fund will invest at least 90% of its total assets in the securities that comprise the underlying index. The underlying index is comprised of equity securities of large capitalization companies based in emerging market countries. **Top Holdings:** Magazine Luiza SA   CP All PCL DR   Yihai International Holdings Ltd   ANTA Sports Products Ltd   Tencent Holdings Ltd

---

iShares MSCI BRIC ETF   C-   HOLD

Ticker	Traded On	NAV	Total Assets ($)	Dividend Yield (TTM)	Turnover Ratio	Expense Ratio
BKF	NYSE Arca	40.65	$162,603,444	2.17	22	0.67

Ratings
Reward   C
Risk   C-
Recent Upgrade/Downgrade   Down

Fund Information
Fund Type   Exchange Traded Funds
Category   Global Emerg Mkts Equity
Sub-Category   Diversified Emerging Mkts
Prospectus Objective   Foreign Stock
Inception Date   Nov-07
Open to New Investments   Y

Prices
Price (as of 9/30/2019)   40.45
52-Week High   44.29
52-Week Low   36.50

Total Returns (%)

3-Month	6-Month	1-Year	3-Year	5-Year
-5.33	-5.95	2.77	26.42	22.16

3-Year Standard Deviation   15.36
Effective Duration

Valuation
Premium/Discount (1-Year Average)   -0.22

Company Information
Provider   iShares
Manager/Tenure   Diane Hsiung (11), Greg Savage (11), Jennifer Hsui (6), 3 others
Website   http://www.ishares.com
Address   iShares 400 Howard Street San Francisco CA 94105 United States
Phone Number   800-474-2737

PERFORMANCE

Ratings History

Date	Overall Rating	Risk Rating	Reward Rating
Q3-19	C-	C-	C
Q4-18	C-	C-	C-
Q4-17	B	C+	A
Q4-16	D+	C-	D+
Q4-15	D+	D+	C-

Asset & Performance History

Date	NAV	1-Year Total Return
2018	37.81	-13.57
2017	44.73	40.83
2016	32.27	11.28
2015	29.54	-13.62
2014	35.18	-3.49
2013	37.54	-4.25

Total Assets: $162,603,444

Asset Allocation

Asset	%
Cash	1%
Stocks	99%
US Stocks	0%
Bonds	0%
US Bonds	0%
Other	0%

Services Offered:

Investment Strategy: The investment seeks to track the investment results of the MSCI BRIC Index. The fund generally will invest at least 90% of its assets in the component securities of the underlying index and in investments that have economic characteristics that are substantially identical to the component securities of the underlying index. The index is a free float-adjusted market capitalization index that is designed to measure the combined equity market performance in Brazil, Russia, India and China ("BRIC"). **Top Holdings:** Alibaba Group Holding Ltd ADR   Tencent Holdings Ltd   China Construction Bank Corp Class H   Ping An Insurance (Group) Co. of China Ltd Class H   China Mobile Ltd

ALPS Equal Sector Weight ETF   C   HOLD

Ticker	Traded On	NAV	Total Assets ($)	Dividend Yield (TTM)	Turnover Ratio	Expense Ratio
EQL	NYSE Arca	75.61	$162,562,386	2.07	14	0.28

Ratings

Reward	C
Risk	D+
Recent Upgrade/Downgrade	

Fund Information

Fund Type	Exchange Traded Funds
Category	US Equity Large Cap Blend
Sub-Category	Large Blend
Prospectus Objective	Growth
Inception Date	Jul-09
Open to New Investments	Y

Prices

Price (as of 9/30/2019)	75.60
52-Week High	76.51
52-Week Low	60.34

Total Returns (%)

3-Month	6-Month	1-Year	3-Year	5-Year
1.50	5.01	5.64	37.79	57.22

3-Year Standard Deviation	11.24
Effective Duration	

Valuation

Premium/Discount (1-Year Average)	-0.02

Company Information

Provider	ALPS
Manager/Tenure	Ryan Mischker (4), Andrew Hicks (3)
Website	http://www.alpsfunds.com
Address	ALPS 1290 Broadway, Suite 1100
	Denver CO 80203 United States
Phone Number	866-759-5679

PERFORMANCE

Ratings History

Date	Overall Rating	Risk Rating	Reward Rating
Q3-19	C	D+	C
Q4-18	C-	D+	C-
Q4-17	B-	B	B-
Q4-16	C	D+	B-
Q4-15	C	D+	C

Asset & Performance History

Date	NAV	1-Year Total Return
2018	63.9	-6
2017	69.53	18.13
2016	60.09	12.63
2015	54.65	-1.67
2014	56.73	13.04
2013	51.06	30.17

Total Assets: $162,562,386

Asset Allocation

Asset	%
Cash	0%
Stocks	100%
US Stocks	98%
Bonds	0%
US Bonds	0%
Other	0%

Services Offered:

Investment Strategy: The investment seeks investment results that replicate as closely as possible, before fees and expenses, the performance of the NYSE Select Sector Equal Weight Index (the "underlying index"). In order to track the underlying index, the fund will use a "fund of funds" approach, and seek to achieve its investment objective by investing at least 90% of its total assets in the shares of the Underlying Sector ETFs. The underlying index is an index of ETFs comprised of all active Select Sector SPDR® ETFs in an equal weighted portfolio. It is non-diversified. **Top Holdings:** Real Estate Select Sector SPDR® Consumer Staples Select Sector SPDR® ETF Utilities Select Sector SPDR® ETF Technology Select Sector SPDR® ETF Communication Services Sel Sect SPDR®ETF

RiverFront Strategic Income Fund   C   HOLD

Ticker	Traded On	NAV	Total Assets ($)	Dividend Yield (TTM)	Turnover Ratio	Expense Ratio
RIGS	NYSE Arca	24.70	$161,812,185	4.17	35	0.48

Ratings

Reward	C
Risk	C-
Recent Upgrade/Downgrade	

Fund Information

Fund Type	Exchange Traded Funds
Category	Global Fixed Income
Sub-Category	World Bond
Prospectus Objective	Income
Inception Date	Oct-13
Open to New Investments	Y

Prices

Price (as of 9/30/2019)	24.84
52-Week High	24.94
52-Week Low	23.90

Total Returns (%)

3-Month	6-Month	1-Year	3-Year	5-Year
0.97	2.40	4.81	11.15	22.74

3-Year Standard Deviation	1.74
Effective Duration	

Valuation

Premium/Discount (1-Year Average)	0.19

Company Information

Provider	ALPS
Manager/Tenure	Tim Anderson (5), Rob Glownia (3)
Website	http://www.alpsfunds.com
Address	ALPS 1290 Broadway, Suite 1100
	Denver CO 80203 United States
Phone Number	866-759-5679

PERFORMANCE

Ratings History

Date	Overall Rating	Risk Rating	Reward Rating
Q3-19	C	C-	C
Q4-18	C	C-	C
Q4-17	B-	B	C+
Q4-16	C	C-	C
Q4-15	C-	C-	D+

Asset & Performance History

Date	NAV	1-Year Total Return
2018	24.05	-0.04
2017	25.16	4.68
2016	25.12	8.79
2015	24.16	0.6
2014	24.87	3.06
2013	24.93	

Total Assets: $161,812,185

Asset Allocation

Asset	%
Cash	14%
Stocks	0%
US Stocks	0%
Bonds	87%
US Bonds	78%
Other	0%

Services Offered:

Investment Strategy: The investment seeks total return, with an emphasis on income as the source of that total return. The fund seeks to achieve its investment objective by investing in a global portfolio of fixed income securities of various maturities, ratings and currency denominations. The fund utilizes various investment strategies in a broad array of fixed income sectors. The fund may purchase fixed income securities issued by U.S. or foreign corporations or financial institutions, including debt securities of all types and maturities, convertible securities and preferred stocks. **Top Holdings:** Sprint Communications, Inc. 7% CIT Group, Inc. 5% Park Aerospace Holdings Limited 5.25% Wesco Distribution, Inc. 5.38% Cablevision Systems Corporation 8%

iShares Currency Hedged MSCI Germany ETF

C   **HOLD**

Ticker	Traded On	NAV	Total Assets ($)	Dividend Yield (TTM)	Turnover Ratio	Expense Ratio
HEWG	NAS CM	27.12	$161,393,147	2.68	11	0.53

Ratings
Reward   C
Risk   C+
Recent Upgrade/Downgrade

Fund Information
Fund Type	Exchange Traded Funds
Category	Equity Misc
Sub-Category	Miscellaneous Region
Prospectus Objective	Foreign Stock
Inception Date	Jan-14
Open to New Investments	Y

Prices
Price (as of 9/30/2019)	27.13
52-Week High	28.03
52-Week Low	22.95

Total Returns (%)
3-Month	6-Month	1-Year	3-Year	5-Year
-0.27	5.66	1.35	21.85	36.40

3-Year Standard Deviation	12.74
Effective Duration	

Valuation
Premium/Discount (1-Year Average)	-0.01

Company Information
Provider	iShares
Manager/Tenure	Diane Hsiung (5), Jennifer Hsui (5), Orlando Montalvo (5), 2 others
Website	http://www.ishares.com
Address	iShares 400 Howard Street San Francisco CA 94105 United States
Phone Number	800-474-2737

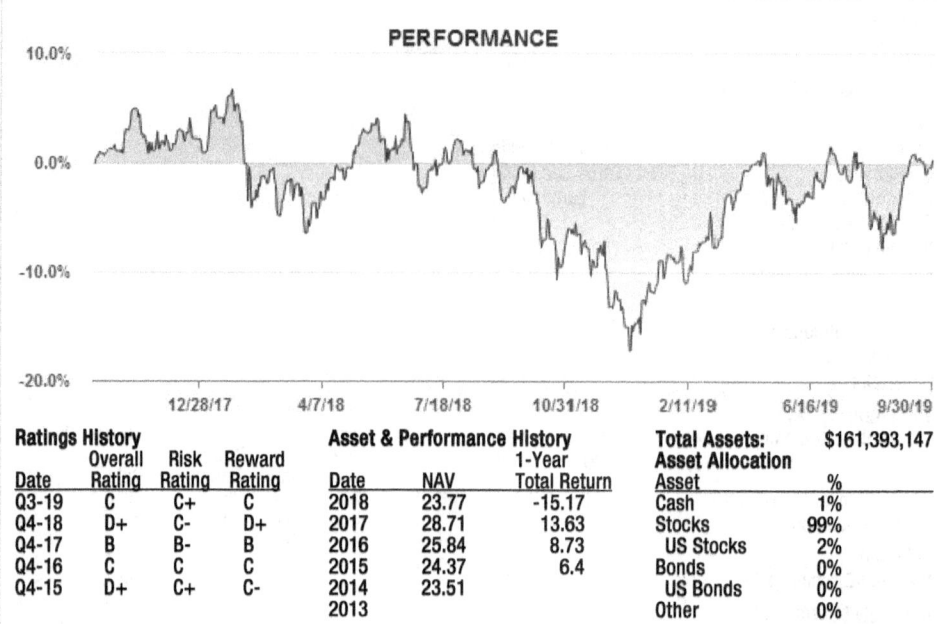

PERFORMANCE

Ratings History
Date	Overall Rating	Risk Rating	Reward Rating
Q3-19	C	C+	C
Q4-18	D+	C-	D+
Q4-17	B	B-	B
Q4-16	C	C	C
Q4-15	D+	C+	C-

Asset & Performance History
Date	NAV	1-Year Total Return
2018	23.77	-15.17
2017	28.71	13.63
2016	25.84	8.73
2015	24.37	6.4
2014	23.51	
2013		

Total Assets: $161,393,147
Asset Allocation
Asset	%
Cash	1%
Stocks	99%
US Stocks	2%
Bonds	0%
US Bonds	0%
Other	0%

Services Offered:

Investment Strategy: The investment seeks to track the investment results of the MSCI Germany 100% Hedged to USD Index. The fund generally will invest at least 90% of its assets in the component securities (including indirect investments through the underlying fund) and other instruments of the underlying index and in investments that have economic characteristics that are substantially identical to the component securities of the underlying index. The index consists of stocks traded primarily on the Frankfurt Stock Exchange with the currency risk inherent in the securities included in the underlying index hedged to the U.S. dollar on a monthly basis. **Top Holdings:** SAP SE Allianz SE Siemens AG Bayer AG Basf SE

---

iShares MSCI New Zealand ETF

C+   **HOLD**

Ticker	Traded On	NAV	Total Assets ($)	Dividend Yield (TTM)	Turnover Ratio	Expense Ratio
ENZL	NAS CM	52.05	$161,342,080	3.06	14	0.47

Ratings
Reward   B
Risk   C-
Recent Upgrade/Downgrade   Down

Fund Information
Fund Type	Exchange Traded Funds
Category	Australia & New Zealand Equity
Sub-Category	Miscellaneous Region
Prospectus Objective	Pacific Stock
Inception Date	Sep-10
Open to New Investments	Y

Prices
Price (as of 9/30/2019)	51.87
52-Week High	55.85
52-Week Low	43.93

Total Returns (%)
3-Month	6-Month	1-Year	3-Year	5-Year
-2.08	0.91	10.26	26.04	65.82

3-Year Standard Deviation	13.48
Effective Duration	

Valuation
Premium/Discount (1-Year Average)	-0.10

Company Information
Provider	iShares
Manager/Tenure	Diane Hsiung (9), Greg Savage (9), Jennifer Hsui (6), 3 others
Website	http://www.ishares.com
Address	iShares 400 Howard Street San Francisco CA 94105 United States
Phone Number	800-474-2737

PERFORMANCE

Ratings History
Date	Overall Rating	Risk Rating	Reward Rating
Q3-19	C+	C-	B
Q4-18	C-	C-	C-
Q4-17	C+	C	C+
Q4-16	C	C-	C
Q4-15	C-	D+	C

Asset & Performance History
Date	NAV	1-Year Total Return
2018	46.15	-0.22
2017	47.88	23.9
2016	40.12	11
2015	37.87	-1.28
2014	40.11	13.03
2013	37.32	13.8

Total Assets: $161,342,080
Asset Allocation
Asset	%
Cash	1%
Stocks	99%
US Stocks	0%
Bonds	0%
US Bonds	0%
Other	0%

Services Offered:

Investment Strategy: The investment seeks to track the investment results of the MSCI New Zealand IMI 25/50 Index. The fund generally will invest at least 90% of its assets in the component securities of the underlying index and in investments that have economic characteristics that are substantially identical to the component securities of the underlying index. The index is a free float-adjusted market capitalization-weighted index designed to measure the performance of equity securities in the top 99% by market capitalization of equity securities listed on stock exchanges in New Zealand. The fund is non-diversified. **Top Holdings:** The a2 Milk Co Ltd Fisher & Paykel Healthcare Corp Ltd Auckland International Airport Ltd Spark New Zealand Ltd Meridian Energy Ltd

---

ALPS Medical Breakthroughs ETF   C-   HOLD

Ticker	Traded On	NAV	Total Assets ($)	Dividend Yield (TTM)	Turnover Ratio	Expense Ratio
SBIO	NYSE Arca	31.60	$161,176,909	2.48	48	0.5

Ratings

Reward	C-
Risk	D+
Recent Upgrade/Downgrade	Down

Fund Information

Fund Type	Exchange Traded Funds
Category	Healthcare Sector Equity
Sub-Category	Health
Prospectus Objective	Health
Inception Date	Dec-14
Open to New Investments	Y

Prices

Price (as of 9/30/2019)	31.56
52-Week High	38.40
52-Week Low	25.86

Total Returns (%)

3-Month	6-Month	1-Year	3-Year	5-Year
-13.84	-12.08	-15.18	26.88	

3-Year Standard Deviation	26.94
Effective Duration	

Valuation

Premium/Discount (1-Year Average)	-0.07

Company Information

Provider	ALPS
Manager/Tenure	Ryan Mischker (4), Andrew Hicks (3)
Website	http://www.alpsfunds.com
Address	ALPS 1290 Broadway, Suite 1100
	Denver CO 80203 United States
Phone Number	866-759-5679

PERFORMANCE

Ratings History

Date	Overall Rating	Risk Rating	Reward Rating
Q3-19	C-	D+	C-
Q4-18	C-	D+	C-
Q4-17	C	C	C
Q4-16	D	D	D
Q4-15	U		

Asset & Performance History

Date	NAV	1-Year Total Return
2018	28.23	-11.19
2017	32.7	44.98
2016	22.96	-27.65
2015	31.74	28.07
2014	24.78	
2013		

Total Assets: $161,176,909

Asset Allocation

Asset	%
Cash	0%
Stocks	100%
US Stocks	92%
Bonds	0%
US Bonds	0%
Other	0%

Services Offered:

Investment Strategy: The investment seeks investment results that correspond (before fees and expenses) generally to the performance of its underlying index, the S-Network® Medical Breakthroughs Index. The fund employs a "passive management" - or indexing - investment approach designed to track the performance of the underlying index. It will normally invest at least 80% of its net assets in securities that comprise the underlying index. The underlying index is comprised of small- and mid-cap stocks of biotechnology companies that have one or more drugs in either Phase II or Phase III of the U.S. Food and Drug Administration clinical trials. **Top Holdings:** ACADIA Pharmaceuticals Inc   FibroGen Inc   Allakos Inc   MorphoSys AG ADR   United Therapeutics Corp

---

VanEck Vectors CEF Municipal Income ETF   C   HOLD

Ticker	Traded On	NAV	Total Assets ($)	Dividend Yield (TTM)	Turnover Ratio	Expense Ratio
XMPT	BATS	27.60	$160,094,152	4.16	13	1.86

Ratings

Reward	C+
Risk	C-
Recent Upgrade/Downgrade	

Fund Information

Fund Type	Exchange Traded Funds
Category	US Muni Fixed Inc
Sub-Category	Muni National Long
Prospectus Objective	Muni Bond - Natl
Inception Date	Jul-11
Open to New Investments	Y

Prices

Price (as of 9/30/2019)	27.60
52-Week High	27.96
52-Week Low	23.37

Total Returns (%)

3-Month	6-Month	1-Year	3-Year	5-Year
3.75	8.04	17.07	10.68	37.19

3-Year Standard Deviation	8.03
Effective Duration	7.94

Valuation

Premium/Discount (1-Year Average)	0.00

Company Information

Provider	VanEck
Manager/Tenure	Hao-Hung (Peter) Liao (8), Guo Hua (Jason) Jin (1)
Website	http://www.vaneck.com
Address	Van Eck Associates Corporation 666 Third Avenue New York NY 10017 United States
Phone Number	800-826-1115

PERFORMANCE

Ratings History

Date	Overall Rating	Risk Rating	Reward Rating
Q3-19	C	C-	C+
Q4-18	D+	C-	D
Q4-17	C+	B	C
Q4-16	C	C-	C
Q4-15	C-	D+	C

Asset & Performance History

Date	NAV	1-Year Total Return
2018	23.89	-6.31
2017	26.65	8.26
2016	25.83	1.56
2015	26.73	7.7
2014	26.19	18.57
2013	23.37	-12.93

Total Assets: $160,094,152

Asset Allocation

Asset	%
Cash	-5%
Stocks	0%
US Stocks	0%
Bonds	107%
US Bonds	105%
Other	-1%

Services Offered:

Investment Strategy: The investment seeks to replicate as closely as possible, before fees and expenses, the price and yield performance of the S-Network Municipal Bond Closed-End Fund IndexSM (the "CEFMX Index"). The fund normally invests at least 80% of its total assets in investments the income from which is exempt from U.S. federal income tax (other than federal alternative minimum tax). It normally invests at least 80% of its total assets in securities of issuers that comprise the fund's benchmark index. The CEFMX Index is comprised of shares of U.S.-listed closed-end funds. **Top Holdings:** Nuveen AMT-Free Muni Credit Inc   Nuveen Quality Muni Income Fund   Nuveen AMT-Free Quality Muni Inc   BlackRock Municipal 2030 Target Term   Nuveen Municipal Credit Income

iShares J.P. Morgan EM Corporate Bond ETF   C   HOLD

Ticker	Traded On	NAV	Total Assets ($)	Dividend Yield (TTM)	Turnover Ratio	Expense Ratio
CEMB	BATS	51.09	$155,810,166	4.42	16	0.5

Ratings
Reward   B-
Risk   C-
Recent Upgrade/Downgrade

Fund Information
Fund Type   Exchange Traded Funds
Category   Emerging Mkts Fixed Inc
Sub-Category   Emerging Markets Bond
Prospectus Objective   Income
Inception Date   Apr-12
Open to New Investments   Y

Prices
Price (as of 9/30/2019)   51.19
52-Week High   51.29
52-Week Low   47.04

Total Returns (%)

3-Month	6-Month	1-Year	3-Year	5-Year
1.69	5.42	10.88	14.55	24.86

3-Year Standard Deviation   3.66
Effective Duration

Valuation
Premium/Discount (1-Year Average)   0.38

Company Information
Provider   iShares
Manager/Tenure   James Mauro (7), Scott Radell (7)
Website   http://www.ishares.com
Address   iShares 400 Howard Street San
                    Francisco CA 94105 United States
Phone Number   800-474-2737

PERFORMANCE

Ratings History

Date	Overall Rating	Risk Rating	Reward Rating
Q3-19	C	C-	B-
Q4-18	D+	D+	C-
Q4-17	B	B+	C+
Q4-16	C	D+	C
Q4-15	C-	D+	C-

Asset & Performance History

Date	NAV	1-Year Total Return
2018	47.34	-2.82
2017	50.99	7.57
2016	49.23	10.93
2015	46.33	-0.59
2014	48.76	2.61
2013	49.5	-3.16

Total Assets: $155,810,166
Asset Allocation

Asset	%
Cash	1%
Stocks	0%
US Stocks	0%
Bonds	97%
US Bonds	3%
Other	0%

Services Offered:

Investment Strategy: The investment seeks to track the investment results of the J.P. Morgan CEMBI Broad Diversified Core Index composed of U.S. dollar-denominated, emerging market corporate bonds. The fund generally will invest at least 90% of its assets in the component securities of the underlying index and may invest up to 10% of its assets in certain futures, options and swap contracts, cash and cash equivalents. The index tracks the performance of the U.S. dollar-denominated emerging market corporate bond market. **Top Holdings:** CK Hutchison International (16) Limited 2.75% Ecopetrol S.A. 5.88% Ecopetrol S.A. 5.88% Sands China Ltd 5.4% Dp World Plc 6.85%

WisdomTree International Dividend ex-Financials Fund   C   HOLD

Ticker	Traded On	NAV	Total Assets ($)	Dividend Yield (TTM)	Turnover Ratio	Expense Ratio
DOO	NYSE Arca	40.35	$155,355,631	4.29	41	0.58

Ratings
Reward   C
Risk   C-
Recent Upgrade/Downgrade   Up

Fund Information
Fund Type   Exchange Traded Funds
Category   Global Equity Large Cap
Sub-Category   Foreign Large Value
Prospectus Objective   Foreign Stock
Inception Date   Jun-06
Open to New Investments   Y

Prices
Price (as of 9/30/2019)   40.38
52-Week High   42.06
52-Week Low   36.91

Total Returns (%)

3-Month	6-Month	1-Year	3-Year	5-Year
-1.35	-0.14	0.23	17.17	6.36

3-Year Standard Deviation   10.83
Effective Duration

Valuation
Premium/Discount (1-Year Average)   -0.19

Company Information
Provider   WisdomTree
Manager/Tenure   Richard A. Brown (11), Thomas J.
                    Durante (11), Karen Q. Wong (11)
Website   http://www.wisdomtree.com
Address   WisdomTree 245 Park Avenue, 35th
                    floor New York NY 10167 United
                    States
Phone Number   866-909-9473

PERFORMANCE

Ratings History

Date	Overall Rating	Risk Rating	Reward Rating
Q3-19	C	C-	C
Q4-18	D+	D+	D+
Q4-17	C+	C+	C+
Q4-16	D	D+	D
Q4-15	C-	C-	C

Asset & Performance History

Date	NAV	1-Year Total Return
2018	37.97	-9.35
2017	43.53	20.01
2016	37.67	2.04
2015	38.38	-8.26
2014	43.46	-4.08
2013	47.43	19.67

Total Assets: $155,355,631
Asset Allocation

Asset	%
Cash	0%
Stocks	100%
US Stocks	1%
Bonds	0%
US Bonds	0%
Other	0%

Services Offered:

Investment Strategy: The investment seeks to track the price and yield performance, before fees and expenses, of the WisdomTree International Dividend ex-Financials Index. Under normal circumstances, at least 95% of the fund's total assets (exclusive of collateral held from securities lending) will be invested in component securities of the index and investments that have economic characteristics that are substantially identical to the economic characteristics of such component securities. The index is a fundamentally weighted index that is comprised of high dividend-yielding international common stocks outside the financial sector. The fund is non-diversified. **Top Holdings:** Imperial Brands PLC SSE PLC EVRAZ PLC Hennes & Mauritz AB B Vodafone Group PLC

Invesco CurrencyShares® British Pound Sterling Trust　　　　　　　D　　SELL

Ticker	Traded On	NAV	Total Assets ($)	Dividend Yield (TTM)	Turnover Ratio	Expense Ratio
FXB	NYSE Arca	119.49	$155,338,536	0	0	0.4

Ratings
Reward	D
Risk	C-
Recent Upgrade/Downgrade	Down

Fund Information
Fund Type	Exchange Traded Funds
Category	Currency
Sub-Category	Single Currency
Prospectus Objective	Worldwide Bond
Inception Date	Jun-06
Open to New Investments	Y

Prices
Price (as of 9/30/2019)	119.25
52-Week High	129.05
52-Week Low	116.66

Total Returns (%)
3-Month	6-Month	1-Year	3-Year	5-Year
-2.60	-6.27	-5.54	-5.81	-24.97

3-Year Standard Deviation	8.12
Effective Duration	

Valuation
Premium/Discount (1-Year Average)	-0.13

Company Information
Provider	Invesco
Manager/Tenure	Management Team (13)
Website	http://www.invesco.com/us
Address	Invesco 11 Greenway Plaza, Ste. 2500 Houston TX 77046 United States
Phone Number	800-659-1005

PERFORMANCE

Ratings History
Date	Overall Rating	Risk Rating	Reward Rating
Q3-19	D	C-	D
Q4-18	D	D+	D
Q4-17	D+	D+	D+
Q4-16	D	D	D
Q4-15	D+	C-	D+

Asset & Performance History
Date	NAV	1-Year Total Return
2018	123.54	-6.04
2017	131.49	9.05
2016	120.57	-16.45
2015	144.31	-5.77
2014	153.15	-6.17
2013	163.24	1.54

Total Assets: $155,338,536

Asset Allocation
Asset	%
Cash	100%
Stocks	0%
US Stocks	0%
Bonds	0%
US Bonds	0%
Other	0%

Services Offered:

Investment Strategy: The investment seeks to reflect the price in USD of the British Pound Sterling. The shares are intended to provide institutional and retail investors with a simple, cost-effective means of gaining investment benefits similar to those of holding British Pounds Sterling. **Top Holdings:**

ProShares Ultra Russell2000　　　　　　　　　　　　C-　　HOLD

Ticker	Traded On	NAV	Total Assets ($)	Dividend Yield (TTM)	Turnover Ratio	Expense Ratio
UWM	NYSE Arca	64.56	$154,955,963	0.68	41	0.95

Ratings
Reward	C-
Risk	C-
Recent Upgrade/Downgrade	

Fund Information
Fund Type	Exchange Traded Funds
Category	Trading Tools
Sub-Category	Trading--Leveraged Equity
Prospectus Objective	Small Company
Inception Date	Jan-07
Open to New Investments	Y

Prices
Price (as of 9/30/2019)	64.47
52-Week High	82.19
52-Week Low	46.50

Total Returns (%)
3-Month	6-Month	1-Year	3-Year	5-Year
-6.73	-5.92	-20.84	37.40	77.90

3-Year Standard Deviation	34.5
Effective Duration	

Valuation
Premium/Discount (1-Year Average)	-0.08

Company Information
Provider	ProShares
Manager/Tenure	Michael Neches (6), Devin Sullivan (1)
Website	http://www.proshares.com
Address	ProShares 7501 Wisconsin Avenue, Suite 1000 Bethesda MD 20814 United States
Phone Number	866-776-5125

PERFORMANCE

Ratings History
Date	Overall Rating	Risk Rating	Reward Rating
Q3-19	C-	C-	C-
Q4-18	C	C-	C
Q4-17	B+	C	A+
Q4-16	C	C-	C+
Q4-15	C	C+	C

Asset & Performance History
Date	NAV	1-Year Total Return
2018	52.23	-25.75
2017	70.62	27.04
2016	55.65	40.71
2015	39.67	-11.99
2014	45.18	6.03
2013	42.65	87.02

Total Assets: $154,955,963

Asset Allocation
Asset	%
Cash	-100%
Stocks	200%
US Stocks	198%
Bonds	0%
US Bonds	0%
Other	0%

Services Offered:

Investment Strategy: The investment seeks daily investment results that correspond to two times (2x) the daily performance of the Russell 2000® Index. The fund invests in financial instruments that ProShare Advisors believes, in combination, should produce daily returns consistent with the fund's investment objective. The index is a float-adjusted, market capitalization-weighted index containing approximately 2000 of the smallest companies in the Russell 3000® Index or approximately 8% of the total market capitalization of the Russell 3000® Index, which in turn represents approximately 98% of the investable U.S. equity market. It is non-diversified. **Top Holdings:** Russell 2000 Index Swap Citibank Na　Russell 2000 Index Swap Societe Generale　Russell 2000 Index Swap Goldman Sachs International　E-mini Russell 2000 Index Futures　Russell 2000 Index Swap Morgan Stanley & Co. International Plc

Nuveen ESG Small-Cap ETF   C-   HOLD

Ticker	Traded On	NAV	Total Assets ($)	Dividend Yield (TTM)	Turnover Ratio	Expense Ratio
NUSC	BATS	29.23	$154,918,614	0.9	54	0.4

Ratings
Reward   C-
Risk   C-
Recent Upgrade/Downgrade   Down

Fund Information
Fund Type   Exchange Traded Funds
Category   US Equity Small Cap
Sub-Category   Small Blend
Prospectus Objective   Small Company
Inception Date   Dec-16
Open to New Investments   Y

Prices
Price (as of 9/30/2019)   29.28
52-Week High   31.28
52-Week Low   24.25

Total Returns (%)

3-Month	6-Month	1-Year	3-Year	5-Year
-1.57	0.56	-2.74		

3-Year Standard Deviation
Effective Duration

Valuation
Premium/Discount (1-Year Average)   0.07

Company Information
Provider   Nuveen
Manager/Tenure   Philip James(Jim) Campagna (2), Lei Liao (2)
Website   http://www.nuveen.com
Address   Nuveen Investment Trust John Nuveen & Co. Inc. Chicago IL 60606 United States
Phone Number   312-917-8146

PERFORMANCE

Ratings History

Date	Overall Rating	Risk Rating	Reward Rating
Q3-19	C-	C-	C-
Q4-18	D+	C-	D+
Q4-17	D	B+	D+
Q4-16			
Q4-15			

Asset & Performance History

Date	NAV	1-Year Total Return
2018	24.8	-10.23
2017	28.43	15.87
2016	24.61	
2015		
2014		
2013		

Total Assets: $154,918,614

Asset Allocation

Asset	%
Cash	0%
Stocks	100%
US Stocks	99%
Bonds	0%
US Bonds	0%
Other	0%

Services Offered:

Investment Strategy: The investment seeks to track the investment results, before fees and expenses, of the TIAA ESG USA Small-Cap Index (the "index"). Under normal market conditions, the fund invests at least 80% of the sum of its net assets and the amount of any borrowings for investment purposes in component securities of the index. The index is comprised of equity securities issued by small-capitalization companies listed on U.S. exchanges that meet certain environmental, social, and governance ("ESG") criteria. **Top Holdings:** Booz Allen Hamilton Holding Corp Class A Brown & Brown Inc Service Corp International First American Financial Corp Starwood Property Trust Inc

---

VictoryShares US Multi-Factor Minimum Volatility ETF   C   HOLD

Ticker	Traded On	NAV	Total Assets ($)	Dividend Yield (TTM)	Turnover Ratio	Expense Ratio
VSMV	NAS CM	31.90	$154,732,417	2.09	34	0.35

Ratings
Reward   B-
Risk   C-
Recent Upgrade/Downgrade   Up

Fund Information
Fund Type   Exchange Traded Funds
Category   US Equity Large Cap Blend
Sub-Category   Large Value
Prospectus Objective   Growth & Inc
Inception Date   Jun-17
Open to New Investments   Y

Prices
Price (as of 9/30/2019)   31.94
52-Week High   31.99
52-Week Low   25.31

Total Returns (%)

3-Month	6-Month	1-Year	3-Year	5-Year
3.37	8.92	7.93		

3-Year Standard Deviation
Effective Duration

Valuation
Premium/Discount (1-Year Average)   0.16

Company Information
Provider   VictoryShares
Manager/Tenure   Mannik Dhillon (2)
Website   http://www.VictorySharesLiterature.com
Address   Victory Shares 4249 Easton Way, Suite 400 Columbus OH 43219 United States
Phone Number

PERFORMANCE

Ratings History

Date	Overall Rating	Risk Rating	Reward Rating
Q3-19	C	C-	B-
Q4-18	C	C	C
Q4-17	U		
Q4-16			
Q4-15			

Asset & Performance History

Date	NAV	1-Year Total Return
2018	26.73	-0.24
2017	27.42	
2016		
2015		
2014		
2013		

Total Assets: $154,732,417

Asset Allocation

Asset	%
Cash	0%
Stocks	100%
US Stocks	100%
Bonds	0%
US Bonds	0%
Other	0%

Services Offered:

Investment Strategy: The investment seeks to provide investment results that track the performance of the Nasdaq Victory US Multi-Factor Minimum Volatility Index before fees and expenses. The fund seeks to achieve its investment objective by investing, under normal market conditions, at least 80% of its assets in securities included in the Nasdaq Victory US Multi-Factor Minimum Volatility Index (the "index"). The index utilizes a rules-based approach designed to generate investment returns with less volatility than the broader U.S. market. **Top Holdings:** Microsoft Corp Apple Inc Procter & Gamble Co Johnson & Johnson Lockheed Martin Corp

Aberdeen Standard Bloomberg All Commodity Strategy K-1 Free ETF   D+   SELL

Ticker	Traded On	NAV	Total Assets ($)	Dividend Yield (TTM)	Turnover Ratio	Expense Ratio
BCI	NYSE Arca	22.02	$154,113,201	1.1		0.25

Ratings
Reward	D
Risk	C-
Recent Upgrade/Downgrade	

Fund Information
Fund Type	Exchange Traded Funds
Category	Commodities Broad Basket
Sub-Category	Commodities Broad Basket
Prospectus Objective	Growth & Inc
Inception Date	Mar-17
Open to New Investments	Y

Prices
Price (as of 9/30/2019)	22.03
52-Week High	24.61
52-Week Low	21.46

Total Returns (%)
3-Month	6-Month	1-Year	3-Year	5-Year
-0.05	-2.71	-8.15		

3-Year Standard Deviation	
Effective Duration	

Valuation
Premium/Discount (1-Year Average)	-0.03

Company Information
Provider	Aberdeen Standard Investments
Manager/Tenure	Denise M. Krisko (2), Austin Wen (0)
Website	http://www.aberdeenstandardetfs.us
Address	Aberdeen Standard Investments 405 Lexington Avenue New York NY 10174 United States
Phone Number	212-918-4954

PERFORMANCE

Ratings History
Date	Overall Rating	Risk Rating	Reward Rating
Q3-19	D+	C-	D
Q4-18	D+	C	D
Q4-17	U		
Q4-16			
Q4-15			

Asset & Performance History
Date	NAV	1-Year Total Return
2018	21.38	-8.12
2017	24.48	
2016		
2015		
2014		
2013		

Total Assets: $154,113,201
Asset Allocation
Asset	%
Cash	80%
Stocks	20%
US Stocks	1%
Bonds	1%
US Bonds	0%
Other	0%

Services Offered:

Investment Strategy: The investment seeks to provide total return through actively managed exposure to the Bloomberg Commodity Index Total ReturnSM (the "index"). The fund is an actively managed exchange-traded fund ("ETF") that is not required to track the index or invest in all of the index's components. However, it will generally seek to hold similar interests to those included in the index and will seek exposure to many of the commodities included in the index under the same futures rolling schedule as the index. It is non-diversified. **Top Holdings:** United States Treasury Bills Aberdeen Frontier Markets Investment Ord United States Treasury Bills United States Treasury Bills United States Treasury Bills

---

Invesco S&P MidCap 400® Pure Value ETF   C-   HOLD

Ticker	Traded On	NAV	Total Assets ($)	Dividend Yield (TTM)	Turnover Ratio	Expense Ratio
RFV	NYSE Arca	63.83	$153,229,818	1.51		0.35

Ratings
Reward	C-
Risk	C-
Recent Upgrade/Downgrade	Up

Fund Information
Fund Type	Exchange Traded Funds
Category	US Equity Small Cap
Sub-Category	Small Value
Prospectus Objective	Growth
Inception Date	Mar-06
Open to New Investments	Y

Prices
Price (as of 9/30/2019)	63.81
52-Week High	71.62
52-Week Low	53.74

Total Returns (%)
3-Month	6-Month	1-Year	3-Year	5-Year
-4.29	-4.62	-9.02	19.79	36.15

3-Year Standard Deviation	22.18
Effective Duration	

Valuation
Premium/Discount (1-Year Average)	-0.06

Company Information
Provider	Invesco
Manager/Tenure	Peter Hubbard (1), Michael Jeanette (1), Tony Seisser (1)
Website	http://www.invesco.com/us
Address	Invesco 11 Greenway Plaza, Ste. 2500 Houston TX 77046 United States
Phone Number	800-659-1005

PERFORMANCE

Ratings History
Date	Overall Rating	Risk Rating	Reward Rating
Q3-19	C-	C-	C-
Q4-18	C-	D+	C
Q4-17	B	B-	B+
Q4-16	C+	C-	B
Q4-15	C	C-	C

Asset & Performance History
Date	NAV	1-Year Total Return
2018	56.59	-17.95
2017	69.79	14.63
2016	61.71	30.54
2015	47.64	-10.79
2014	54.3	8.35
2013	50.73	38.28

Total Assets: $153,229,818
Asset Allocation
Asset	%
Cash	0%
Stocks	100%
US Stocks	99%
Bonds	0%
US Bonds	0%
Other	0%

Services Offered:

Investment Strategy: The investment seeks to track the investment results (before fees and expenses) of the S&P MidCap 400® Pure Value Index (the "underlying index"). The fund generally will invest at least 90% of its total assets in the securities that comprise the underlying index. The underlying index is composed of a subset of securities from the S&P MidCap 400® Index that exhibit strong value characteristics, as measured using the following three factors: book value to price ratio, earnings to price ratio, and sales to price ratio. The fund is non-diversified. **Top Holdings:** KB Home World Fuel Services Corp AutoNation Inc Legg Mason Inc-LeggMason RETAIL AECOM

iShares iBonds Mar 2020 Term Corporate ETF   C   HOLD

Ticker	Traded On	NAV	Total Assets ($)	Dividend Yield (TTM)	Turnover Ratio	Expense Ratio
IBDC	NYSE Arca	26.10	$152,711,505	2.32	5	0.1

Ratings
Reward   C
Risk   C-
Recent Upgrade/Downgrade

Fund Information
Fund Type   Exchange Traded Funds
Category   US Fixed Income
Sub-Category   Short-Term Bond
Prospectus Objective   Corp Bond - Gen
Inception Date   Jul-13
Open to New Investments   Y

Prices
Price (as of 9/30/2019)   26.15
52-Week High   26.15
52-Week Low   25.85

Total Returns (%)

3-Month	6-Month	1-Year	3-Year	5-Year
0.58	1.37	2.99	5.45	12.03

3-Year Standard Deviation   0.84
Effective Duration

Valuation
Premium/Discount (1-Year Average)   0.09

Company Information
Provider   iShares
Manager/Tenure James Mauro (6), Scott Radell (6)
Website   http://www.ishares.com
Address   iShares 400 Howard Street San
                 Francisco CA 94105 United States
Phone Number   800-474-2737

PERFORMANCE

Ratings History

Date	Overall Rating	Risk Rating	Reward Rating
Q3-19	C	C-	C
Q4-18	C	C-	C
Q4-17	B	A+	C
Q4-16	C	D+	C
Q4-15	D+	D+	C-

Asset & Performance History

Date	NAV	1-Year Total Return
2018	25.89	1.6
2017	26.04	1.95
2016	26.04	3.48
2015	25.72	1.49
2014	25.92	4.78
2013	25.39	

Total Assets: $152,711,505
Asset Allocation

Asset	%
Cash	57%
Stocks	0%
US Stocks	0%
Bonds	43%
US Bonds	34%
Other	0%

Services Offered:

Investment Strategy: The investment seeks to track the investment results of the Bloomberg Barclays 2020 Maturity Corporate Index composed of U.S. dollar-denominated, investment-grade corporate bonds maturing after March 31, 2019 and before April 1, 2020. The fund generally will invest at least 90% of its assets in the component securities (including indirect investments through an underlying fund) of the index, except during the last months of the fund's operations. The index includes U.S. dollar-denominated, investment-grade securities publicly issued by U.S. and non-U.S. corporate issuers that have $300 million or more of outstanding face value at the time of inclusion. **Top Holdings:** JPMorgan Chase & Co. 2.25% Allergan Funding SCS 3% BP Capital Markets plc 2.31% Wells Fargo & Company 2.15% Goldman Sachs Group, Inc. 5.38%

Fidelity® Value Factor ETF   C   HOLD

Ticker	Traded On	NAV	Total Assets ($)	Dividend Yield (TTM)	Turnover Ratio	Expense Ratio
FVAL	NYSE Arca	34.29	$152,573,571	2	31	0.29

Ratings
Reward   C
Risk   C-
Recent Upgrade/Downgrade

Fund Information
Fund Type   Exchange Traded Funds
Category   US Equity Large Cap Value
Sub-Category   Large Value
Prospectus Objective   Growth & Inc
Inception Date   Sep-16
Open to New Investments   Y

Prices
Price (as of 9/30/2019)   34.35
52-Week High   35.11
52-Week Low   28.19

Total Returns (%)

3-Month	6-Month	1-Year	3-Year	5-Year
0.59	2.96	0.10	42.65	

3-Year Standard Deviation   13.52
Effective Duration

Valuation
Premium/Discount (1-Year Average)   -0.04

Company Information
Provider   Fidelity Investments
Manager/Tenure Louis Bottari (3), Deane Gyllenhaal (3),
                 Peter Matthew (3), 3 others
Website   http://www.institutional.fidelity.com
Address   Fidelity Investments 82 Devonshire
                 Street Boston MA 2109 United States
Phone Number   617-563-7000

PERFORMANCE

Ratings History

Date	Overall Rating	Risk Rating	Reward Rating
Q3-19	C	C-	C
Q4-18	C	C-	C
Q4-17	D	B+	C
Q4-16	U		
Q4-15			

Asset & Performance History

Date	NAV	1-Year Total Return
2018	29.88	-7.07
2017	32.77	21.89
2016	27.36	
2015		
2014		
2013		

Total Assets: $152,573,571
Asset Allocation

Asset	%
Cash	0%
Stocks	100%
US Stocks	99%
Bonds	0%
US Bonds	0%
Other	0%

Services Offered:

Investment Strategy: The investment seeks to provide investment returns that correspond, before fees and expenses, generally to the performance of the Fidelity U.S. Value Factor Index. The fund normally invests at least 80% of assets in securities included in the Fidelity U.S. Value Factor Index, which is designed to reflect the performance of stocks of large and mid-capitalization U.S. companies that have attractive valuations. It may lend securities to earn income for the fund. **Top Holdings:** Microsoft Corp Apple Inc Amazon.com Inc Alphabet Inc A Johnson & Johnson

Invesco Raymond James SB-1 Equity ETF   D+   SELL

Ticker	Traded On	NAV	Total Assets ($)	Dividend Yield (TTM)	Turnover Ratio	Expense Ratio
RYJ	NYSE Arca	42.53	$151,952,762	1.23		0.82

Ratings
Reward	C-
Risk	D+
Recent Upgrade/Downgrade	Down

Fund Information
Fund Type	Exchange Traded Funds
Category	US Equity Mid Cap
Sub-Category	Mid-Cap Growth
Prospectus Objective	Growth
Inception Date	May-06
Open to New Investments	Y

Prices
Price (as of 9/30/2019)	42.56
52-Week High	48.36
52-Week Low	34.27

Total Returns (%)
3-Month	6-Month	1-Year	3-Year	5-Year
-5.80	-4.03	-10.42	19.96	33.90

3-Year Standard Deviation	18.41
Effective Duration	

Valuation
Premium/Discount (1-Year Average)	0.04

Company Information
Provider	Invesco
Manager/Tenure	Peter Hubbard (1), Michael Jeanette (1), Tony Seisser (1)
Website	http://www.invesco.com/us
Address	Invesco 11 Greenway Plaza, Ste. 2500 Houston TX 77046 United States
Phone Number	800-659-1005

PERFORMANCE

Ratings History
Date	Overall Rating	Risk Rating	Reward Rating
Q3-19	D+	D+	C-
Q4-18	C-	D+	C-
Q4-17	B	B	B
Q4-16	C	D+	B-
Q4-15	C	C-	C

Asset & Performance History
Date	NAV	1-Year Total Return
2018	36.19	-16.59
2017	43.39	13.29
2016	38.39	19.5
2015	32.56	-6.17
2014	35.02	4.65
2013	33.55	43.37

Total Assets: $151,952,762
Asset Allocation
Asset	%
Cash	0%
Stocks	100%
US Stocks	96%
Bonds	0%
US Bonds	0%
Other	0%

Services Offered:

Investment Strategy: The investment seeks to track the investment results (before fees and expenses) of the Raymond James SB-1 Equity Index (the "underlying index"). The fund generally will invest at least 90% of its total assets in the securities that comprise the underlying index. Strictly in accordance with its guidelines and mandated procedures, the index provider compiles, maintains, and calculates the underlying index, which is comprised of U.S.-listed equity securities that are rated Strong Buy 1 ("SB-1") by an affiliate of the index provider. The fund is non-diversified. **Top Holdings:** GMS Inc   SRC Energy Inc   Flexion Therapeutics Inc   Construction Partners Inc Class A   Dollar General Corp

---

Aptus Defined Risk ETF   D+   SELL

Ticker	Traded On	NAV	Total Assets ($)	Dividend Yield (TTM)	Turnover Ratio	Expense Ratio
DRSK	BATS	27.38	$151,931,125	1.66		0.76

Ratings
Reward	D+
Risk	C-
Recent Upgrade/Downgrade	

Fund Information
Fund Type	Exchange Traded Funds
Category	Long/Short Equity
Sub-Category	Options-based
Prospectus Objective	Growth & Inc
Inception Date	Aug-18
Open to New Investments	Y

Prices
Price (as of 9/30/2019)	27.39
52-Week High	28.03
52-Week Low	24.82

Total Returns (%)
3-Month	6-Month	1-Year	3-Year	5-Year
0.94	5.65	13.23		

3-Year Standard Deviation	
Effective Duration	

Valuation
Premium/Discount (1-Year Average)	0.13

Company Information
Provider	Aptus Capital Advisors
Manager/Tenure	John D. Gardner (1), Beckham D. Wyrick (1)
Website	
Address	407 Johnson Avenue, Fairhope, Alabama 36532 United States
Phone Number	

PERFORMANCE

Ratings History
Date	Overall Rating	Risk Rating	Reward Rating
Q3-19	D+	C-	D+
Q4-18	U		
Q4-17			
Q4-16			
Q4-15			

Asset & Performance History
Date	NAV	1-Year Total Return
2018	24.88	
2017		
2016		
2015		
2014		
2013		

Total Assets: $151,931,125
Asset Allocation
Asset	%
Cash	1%
Stocks	4%
US Stocks	4%
Bonds	93%
US Bonds	80%
Other	0%

Services Offered:

Investment Strategy: The investment seeks current income and capital appreciation. The fund is an actively-managed exchange-traded fund ("ETF") that seeks to achieve its objective through a hybrid fixed income and equity strategy. It typically invests approximately 90% to 95% of its assets to obtain exposure to investment-grade corporate bonds (the "Fixed Income Strategy") and invests the remainder of its assets to obtain exposure to large capitalization U.S. stocks, while limiting downside risk (the "Equity Strategy"). **Top Holdings:** iShares iBonds Dec 2026 Term Corp ETF   iShares iBonds Dec 2025 Term Corp ETF   iShares iBonds Dec 2024 Term Corp ETF   iShares iBonds Dec 2023 Term Corp ETF   iShares iBonds Dec 2022 Term Corp ETF

ProShares Ultra Real Estate   C   HOLD

Ticker	Traded On	NAV	Total Assets ($)	Dividend Yield (TTM)	Turnover Ratio	Expense Ratio
URE	NYSE Arca	87.56	$151,798,916	1.09	6	0.95

Ratings
Reward   C+
Risk   C-
Recent Upgrade/Downgrade

Fund Information
Fund Type   Exchange Traded Funds
Category   Trading Tools
Sub-Category   Trading--Leveraged Equity
Prospectus Objective   Real Estate
Inception Date   Jan-07
Open to New Investments   Y

Prices
Price (as of 9/30/2019)   87.44
52-Week High   88.11
52-Week Low   52.35

Total Returns (%)

3-Month	6-Month	1-Year	3-Year	5-Year
14.08	16.03	38.30	46.61	117.83

3-Year Standard Deviation   24.46
Effective Duration

Valuation
Premium/Discount (1-Year Average)   -0.09

Company Information
Provider   ProShares
Manager/Tenure   Michael Neches (6), Tarak Davé (1)
Website   http://www.proshares.com
Address   ProShares 7501 Wisconsin Avenue, Suite 1000 Bethesda MD 20814 United States
Phone Number   866-776-5125

PERFORMANCE

Ratings History

Date	Overall Rating	Risk Rating	Reward Rating
Q3-19	C	C-	C+
Q4-18	C-	C-	C-
Q4-17	B	C+	B
Q4-16	C	C-	C
Q4-15	C	C	C

Asset & Performance History

Date	NAV	1-Year Total Return
2018	56.17	-13.52
2017	65.91	16.57
2016	57.08	10.38
2015	52.23	-0.19
2014	52.77	57.63
2013	33.96	-0.76

Total Assets: $151,798,916
Asset Allocation

Asset	%
Cash	-100%
Stocks	103%
US Stocks	103%
Bonds	0%
US Bonds	0%
Other	97%

Services Offered:

Investment Strategy: The investment seeks daily investment results, before fees and expenses, that correspond to two times (2x) the daily performance of the Dow Jones U.S. Real EstateSM Index. The fund invests in financial instruments that ProShare Advisors believes, in combination, should produce daily returns consistent with the fund's investment objective. The index seeks to measure the performance of certain companies in the real estate sector of the U.S. equity market. Component companies include, among others, real estate holding and development and real estate services companies and real estate investment trusts ("REITs"). The fund is non-diversified. **Top Holdings:** Dj U.S. Real Estate Index Swap Goldman Sachs International   Ishares U.S. Real Estate (lyr) Swap Bank Of America Na   Dj U.S. Real Estate Index Swap Credit Suisse International   Dj U.S. Real Estate Index Swap Bank Of America Na   Ishares U.S. Real Estate (lyr) Swap Goldman Sachs International

ARK Industrial Innovation ETF   C   HOLD

Ticker	Traded On	NAV	Total Assets ($)	Dividend Yield (TTM)	Turnover Ratio	Expense Ratio
ARKQ	NYSE Arca	31.70	$150,593,227	0		0.75

Ratings
Reward   C+
Risk   D+
Recent Upgrade/Downgrade   Up

Fund Information
Fund Type   Exchange Traded Funds
Category   Technology Sector Equity
Sub-Category   Technology
Prospectus Objective   Unaligned
Inception Date   Sep-14
Open to New Investments   Y

Prices
Price (as of 9/30/2019)   31.70
52-Week High   36.56
52-Week Low   28.43

Total Returns (%)

3-Month	6-Month	1-Year	3-Year	5-Year
-6.21	-9.03	-9.31	48.02	68.65

3-Year Standard Deviation   21.94
Effective Duration

Valuation
Premium/Discount (1-Year Average)   -0.02

Company Information
Provider   ARK ETF Trust
Manager/Tenure   Catherine D. Wood (5)
Website   http://www.ark-funds.com
Address   ARK ETF Trust 155 West 19th Street, 5th Floor New York New York 10011 United States
Phone Number   212-426-7040

PERFORMANCE

Ratings History

Date	Overall Rating	Risk Rating	Reward Rating
Q3-19	C	D+	C+
Q4-18	C	D+	C+
Q4-17	B-	C	B
Q4-16	C	D+	C+
Q4-15	U		

Asset & Performance History

Date	NAV	1-Year Total Return
2018	29.52	-10.16
2017	32.86	50.22
2016	21.89	14.72
2015	19.08	-2.26
2014	19.71	
2013		

Total Assets: $150,593,227
Asset Allocation

Asset	%
Cash	1%
Stocks	99%
US Stocks	67%
Bonds	0%
US Bonds	0%
Other	0%

Services Offered:

Investment Strategy: The investment seeks long-term growth of capital. The fund is an actively-managed exchange-traded fund that will invest under normal circumstances primarily (at least 80% of its assets) in domestic and foreign equity securities of companies that are relevant to the fund's investment theme of industrial innovation. Substantially all of the fund's assets will be invested in equity securities, including common stocks, partnership interests, business trust shares and other equity investments or ownership interests in business enterprises. The advisor currently intends to use only ADRs when purchasing foreign securities. The fund is non-diversified. **Top Holdings:** Tesla Inc   Stratasys Ltd   NVIDIA Corp   Materialise NV ADR   Proto Labs Inc

Xtrackers High Beta High Yield Bond ETF   D+   SELL

Ticker	Traded On	NAV	Total Assets ($)	Dividend Yield (TTM)	Turnover Ratio	Expense Ratio
HYUP	NYSE Arca	48.42	$150,104,674	6.84		0.2

Ratings
Reward   C-
Risk   D
Recent Upgrade/Downgrade

Fund Information
Fund Type   Exchange Traded Funds
Category   US Fixed Income
Sub-Category   High Yield Bond
Prospectus Objective   Corp Bond-High Yld
Inception Date   Jan-18
Open to New Investments   Y

Prices
Price (as of 9/30/2019)   48.43
52-Week High   49.35
52-Week Low   44.26

Total Returns (%)

3-Month	6-Month	1-Year	3-Year	5-Year
0.44	3.62	5.51		

3-Year Standard Deviation
Effective Duration   3.66

Valuation
Premium/Discount (1-Year Average)   -0.18

Company Information
Provider   DWS
Manager/Tenure   Alexander Bridgeforth (1), Tanuj Dora
                 (1), Brandon Matsui (1), 1 other
Website   http://dws.com
Address   DWS 210 West 10th Street Kansas
                 City MO 64105-1614 United States
Phone Number

PERFORMANCE

Ratings History

Date	Overall Rating	Risk Rating	Reward Rating
Q3-19	D+	D	C-
Q4-18	U		
Q4-17			
Q4-16			
Q4-15			

Asset & Performance History

Date	NAV	1-Year Total Return
2018	45.07	
2017		
2016		
2015		
2014		
2013		

Total Assets: $150,104,674
Asset Allocation

Asset	%
Cash	1%
Stocks	0%
US Stocks	0%
Bonds	99%
US Bonds	77%
Other	0%

Services Offered:

Investment Strategy: The investment seeks investment results that correspond generally to the performance, before fees and expenses, of the Solactive USD High Yield Corporates Total Market High Beta Index (the "underlying index"). The fund will invest at least 80% of its total assets, (but typically far more) in component securities of the underlying index. The underlying index is designed to track the performance of the segment of the U.S. dollar denominated high yield corporate bond market that exhibits higher overall beta to the broader high yield corporate fixed income market. The fund is non-diversified. **Top Holdings:** ALTICE FRANCE S.A 7.38% Sprint Corporation 7.12% Sprint Corporation 7.88% CCO Holdings, LLC/ CCO Holdings Capital Corp. 5.12% Teva Pharmaceutical Finance Netherlands III B.V. 2.2%

Inspire Global Hope ETF   C   HOLD

Ticker	Traded On	NAV	Total Assets ($)	Dividend Yield (TTM)	Turnover Ratio	Expense Ratio
BLES	NYSE Arca		$150,024,682	2.1		0.61

Ratings
Reward   C
Risk   C-
Recent Upgrade/Downgrade

Fund Information
Fund Type   Exchange Traded Funds
Category   Global Equity Large Cap
Sub-Category   World Large Stock
Prospectus Objective   Growth
Inception Date   Feb-17
Open to New Investments   Y

Prices
Price (as of 9/30/2019)   27.76
52-Week High   28.95
52-Week Low   23.44

Total Returns (%)

3-Month	6-Month	1-Year	3-Year	5-Year
-1.45	0.56	0.86		

3-Year Standard Deviation
Effective Duration

Valuation
Premium/Discount (1-Year Average)   0.19

Company Information
Provider   Inspire
Manager/Tenure   Darrell Jayroe (2), Robert Netzly (2)
Website
Address   Inspire 650 San Benito Street, Suite
                 130 Hollister CA 95023 United States
Phone Number

PERFORMANCE

Ratings History

Date	Overall Rating	Risk Rating	Reward Rating
Q3-19	C	C-	C
Q4-18	D	D+	D
Q4-17	U		
Q4-16			
Q4-15			

Asset & Performance History

Date	NAV	1-Year Total Return
2018	24.31	-12.74
2017	28.29	
2016		
2015		
2014		
2013		

Total Assets: $150,024,682
Asset Allocation

Asset	%
Cash	1%
Stocks	99%
US Stocks	52%
Bonds	0%
US Bonds	0%
Other	0%

Services Offered:

Investment Strategy: The investment seeks to replicate investment results that generally correspond to the Inspire Global Hope Large Cap Index. The fund will invest at least 80% of its total assets in the component securities of the index. The index provider selects foreign and domestic equity securities included in the Russell 1,000 Index, MSCI EAFE Index, and MSCI Emerging Markets Large Cap Index using the index provider's Inspire Impact Score®, a proprietary selection methodology that is designed to assign a score to a particular security based on the security's alignment with biblical values and the positive impact that company has on the world through various ESG criterion. **Top Holdings:** Pioneer Food Group Ltd Western Digital Corp KLA Corp Lendlease Group Pandora A/S

Fidelity® Quality Factor ETF

C   HOLD

Ticker	Traded On	NAV	Total Assets ($)	Dividend Yield (TTM)	Turnover Ratio	Expense Ratio
FQAL	NYSE Arca	35.02	$148,842,266	1.65	29	0.29

Ratings
Reward   C
Risk   C-
Recent Upgrade/Downgrade

Fund Information
Fund Type	Exchange Traded Funds
Category	US Equity Large Cap Blend
Sub-Category	Large Growth
Prospectus Objective	Growth & Inc
Inception Date	Sep-16
Open to New Investments	Y

Prices
Price (as of 9/30/2019)	35.04
52-Week High	35.80
52-Week Low	28.26

Total Returns (%)
3-Month	6-Month	1-Year	3-Year	5-Year
0.57	3.35	2.56	44.18	

3-Year Standard Deviation   11.57
Effective Duration

Valuation
Premium/Discount (1-Year Average)   0.00

Company Information
Provider	Fidelity Investments
Manager/Tenure	Louis Bottari (3), Deane Gyllenhaal (3), Peter Matthew (3), 3 others
Website	http://www.institutional.fidelity.com
Address	Fidelity Investments 82 Devonshire Street Boston MA 2109 United States
Phone Number	617-563-7000

PERFORMANCE

Ratings History
Date	Overall Rating	Risk Rating	Reward Rating
Q3-19	C	C-	C
Q4-18	C	C-	C
Q4-17	D	B	C
Q4-16	U		
Q4-15			

Asset & Performance History
Date	NAV	1-Year Total Return
2018	30.05	-3.72
2017	31.72	22.81
2016	26.26	
2015		
2014		
2013		

Total Assets: $148,842,266

Asset Allocation
Asset	%
Cash	0%
Stocks	100%
US Stocks	100%
Bonds	0%
US Bonds	0%
Other	0%

Services Offered:

Investment Strategy: The investment seeks to provide investment returns that correspond, before fees and expenses, generally to the performance of the Fidelity U.S. Quality Factor Index. The fund normally invests at least 80% of assets in securities included in the Fidelity U.S. Quality Factor Index, which is designed to reflect the performance of stocks of large and mid-capitalization U.S. companies with a higher quality profile than the broader market. It may lend securities to earn income for the fund. **Top Holdings:** Microsoft Corp Apple Inc Alphabet Inc A Johnson & Johnson Facebook Inc A

Invesco International BuyBack Achievers™ ETF

D+   SELL

Ticker	Traded On	NAV	Total Assets ($)	Dividend Yield (TTM)	Turnover Ratio	Expense Ratio
IPKW	NAS CM	30.97	$148,668,587	3.02	121	0.55

Ratings
Reward   D+
Risk   C-
Recent Upgrade/Downgrade   Down

Fund Information
Fund Type	Exchange Traded Funds
Category	Global Equity Large Cap
Sub-Category	Foreign Large Blend
Prospectus Objective	Growth
Inception Date	Feb-14
Open to New Investments	

Prices
Price (as of 9/30/2019)	30.99
52-Week High	34.44
52-Week Low	28.19

Total Returns (%)
3-Month	6-Month	1-Year	3-Year	5-Year
-2.52	-1.77	-7.12	16.36	38.44

3-Year Standard Deviation   13.56
Effective Duration

Valuation
Premium/Discount (1-Year Average)   -0.19

Company Information
Provider	Invesco
Manager/Tenure	Peter Hubbard (5), Michael Jeanette (4), Tony Seisser (4)
Website	http://www.invesco.com/us
Address	Invesco 11 Greenway Plaza, Ste. 2500 Houston TX 77046 United States
Phone Number	800-659-1005

PERFORMANCE

Ratings History
Date	Overall Rating	Risk Rating	Reward Rating
Q3-19	D+	C-	D+
Q4-18	D+	D+	D+
Q4-17	A-	B	A
Q4-16	C	C-	C
Q4-15	D	C-	C-

Asset & Performance History
Date	NAV	1-Year Total Return
2018	28.98	-20.97
2017	37.51	33.57
2016	28.36	11.79
2015	26.13	6.74
2014	24.79	
2013		

Total Assets: $148,668,587

Asset Allocation
Asset	%
Cash	0%
Stocks	100%
US Stocks	9%
Bonds	0%
US Bonds	0%
Other	0%

Services Offered:

Investment Strategy: The investment seeks to track the investment results (before fees and expenses) of the Nasdaq International BuyBack Achievers™ Index (the "underlying index"). The fund generally will invest at least 90% of its total assets in securities that comprise the underlying index. Strictly in accordance with its guidelines and mandated procedures, Nasdaq, Inc. ("Nasdaq" or the "index provider") compiles, maintains, and calculates the underlying index, which is comprised of the securities of foreign companies that are classified as "International BuyBack Achievers™" pursuant to the index provider's proprietary selection methodology. It is non-diversified. **Top Holdings:** Yahoo Japan Corp NTT DOCOMO Inc Thomson Reuters Corp Koninklijke Ahold Delhaize NV Magna International Inc Class A

Invesco Dynamic Market ETF   C   HOLD

Ticker	Traded On	NAV	Total Assets ($)	Dividend Yield (TTM)	Turnover Ratio	Expense Ratio
PWC	NYSE Arca	94.85	$147,017,612	0.96	240	0.59

Ratings

Reward	C
Risk	C-
Recent Upgrade/Downgrade	Up

Fund Information

Fund Type	Exchange Traded Funds
Category	US Equity Mid Cap
Sub-Category	Mid-Cap Blend
Prospectus Objective	Growth
Inception Date	May-03
Open to New Investments	Y

Prices

Price (as of 9/30/2019)	94.91
52-Week High	106.09
52-Week Low	83.08

Total Returns (%)

3-Month	6-Month	1-Year	3-Year	5-Year
-4.29	-2.13	-9.59	30.65	44.03

3-Year Standard Deviation	13.31
Effective Duration	

Valuation

Premium/Discount (1-Year Average)	-0.05

Company Information

Provider	Invesco
Manager/Tenure	Peter Hubbard (12), Michael Jeanette (11), Tony Seisser (5)
Website	http://www.invesco.com/us
Address	Invesco 11 Greenway Plaza, Ste. 2500 Houston TX 77046 United States
Phone Number	800-659-1005

PERFORMANCE

Ratings History

Date	Overall Rating	Risk Rating	Reward Rating
Q3-19	C	C-	C
Q4-18	C	C-	C
Q4-17	B	B-	B+
Q4-16	C+	C-	B
Q4-15	C+	C	B-

Asset & Performance History

Date	NAV	1-Year Total Return
2018	88.15	-5.84
2017	94.86	19.53
2016	80.81	12.85
2015	72.65	-0.52
2014	73.77	8.95
2013	68.27	40.74

Total Assets: $147,017,612
Asset Allocation

Asset	%
Cash	0%
Stocks	100%
US Stocks	95%
Bonds	0%
US Bonds	0%
Other	0%

Services Offered:

Investment Strategy: The investment seeks to track the investment results (before fees and expenses) of the Dynamic Market IntellidexSM Index. The fund generally will invest at least 90% of its total assets in the securities that comprise the underlying intellidex. The underlying intellidex was composed of 100 U.S. stocks that the intellidex provider, strictly in accordance with its guidelines and mandated procedures, included pursuant to a proprietary selection methodology. Stocks are selected from the top of each sector and size category in a manner designed to produce an index with sector and size dispersion similar to the overall broad market. **Top Holdings:** Charter Communications Inc A   Comcast Corp Class A   CDW Corp   Cadence Design Systems Inc   Procter & Gamble Co

Xtrackers Low Beta High Yield Bond ETF   C-   HOLD

Ticker	Traded On	NAV	Total Assets ($)	Dividend Yield (TTM)	Turnover Ratio	Expense Ratio
HYDW	NYSE Arca	50.52	$146,494,414	4.53		0.2

Ratings

Reward	C-
Risk	D+
Recent Upgrade/Downgrade	Up

Fund Information

Fund Type	Exchange Traded Funds
Category	US Fixed Income
Sub-Category	High Yield Bond
Prospectus Objective	Corp Bond-High Yld
Inception Date	Jan-18
Open to New Investments	Y

Prices

Price (as of 9/30/2019)	50.58
52-Week High	50.61
52-Week Low	46.81

Total Returns (%)

3-Month	6-Month	1-Year	3-Year	5-Year
1.40	3.76	7.55		

3-Year Standard Deviation	
Effective Duration	2.42

Valuation

Premium/Discount (1-Year Average)	-0.08

Company Information

Provider	DWS
Manager/Tenure	Alexander Bridgeforth (1), Tanuj Dora (1), Brandon Matsui (1), 1 other
Website	http://dws.com
Address	DWS 210 West 10th Street Kansas City MO 64105-1614 United States
Phone Number	

PERFORMANCE

Ratings History

Date	Overall Rating	Risk Rating	Reward Rating
Q3-19	C-	D+	C-
Q4-18	U		
Q4-17			
Q4-16			
Q4-15			

Asset & Performance History

Date	NAV	1-Year Total Return
2018	47.39	
2017		
2016		
2015		
2014		
2013		

Total Assets: $146,494,414
Asset Allocation

Asset	%
Cash	1%
Stocks	0%
US Stocks	0%
Bonds	99%
US Bonds	89%
Other	0%

Services Offered:

Investment Strategy: The investment seeks investment results that correspond generally to the performance, before fees and expenses, of the Solactive USD High Yield Corporates Total Market Low Beta Index (the "underlying index"). The fund will invest at least 80% of its total assets, (but typically far more) in component securities of the underlying index. The underlying index is designed to track the performance of the segment of the U.S. dollar denominated high yield corporate bond market that exhibits lower overall beta to the broader high yield corporate fixed income market. The fund is non-diversified. **Top Holdings:** TransDigm, Inc. 6.25%   Reynolds Group Issuer LLC. 5.75%   HCA Inc. 5.38%   CCO Holdings, LLC/ CCO Holdings Capital Corp. 5.75%   Sprint Corporation 7.25%

Cambria Global Value ETF

C   HOLD

Ticker	Traded On	NAV	Total Assets ($)	Dividend Yield (TTM)	Turnover Ratio	Expense Ratio
GVAL	BATS	22.40	$145,593,523	2.75		0.69

Ratings
Reward	C
Risk	C-
Recent Upgrade/Downgrade	Up

Fund Information
Fund Type	Exchange Traded Funds
Category	Globa Eq Mid/Small Cap
Sub-Category	Foreign Small/Mid Value
Prospectus Objective	Div Emerg Mkts
Inception Date	Mar-14
Open to New Investments	Y

Prices
Price (as of 9/30/2019)	22.36
52-Week High	24.08
52-Week Low	20.97

Total Returns (%)
3-Month	6-Month	1-Year	3-Year	5-Year
-5.40	0.00	-1.19	26.18	14.89

3-Year Standard Deviation	14.12
Effective Duration	

Valuation
Premium/Discount (1-Year Average)	-0.19

Company Information
Provider	CAMBRIA ETF TRUST
Manager/Tenure	Mebane T. Faber (5)
Website	http://www.cambriafunds.com
Address	CAMBRIA ETF TRUST 2711 Centreville Road Suite 400 Wilmington, DE 19808 Wilmington DE 19808 United States
Phone Number	310-683-5500

PERFORMANCE

Ratings History
Date	Overall Rating	Risk Rating	Reward Rating
Q3-19	C	C-	C
Q4-18	C-	C-	C-
Q4-17	B-	B-	B-
Q4-16	D+	C-	D+
Q4-15	D	D	D

Asset & Performance History
Date	NAV	1-Year Total Return
2018	21.12	-13.46
2017	25.5	28.75
2016	20.23	16.14
2015	17.92	-7.43
2014	19.73	
2013		

Total Assets: $145,593,523

Asset Allocation
Asset	%
Cash	1%
Stocks	99%
US Stocks	0%
Bonds	0%
US Bonds	0%
Other	0%

Services Offered:

Investment Strategy: The investment seeks investment results that correspond (before fees and expenses) generally to the price and yield performance of its underlying index, the Cambria Global Value Index (the "underlying index"). Under normal market conditions, the fund will invest at least 80% of its total assets in the components of the underlying index and in depositary receipts representing components of the underlying index. The underlying index is comprised of equity securities of issuers located in developed and emerging countries, as well as exchange-traded funds composed of issuers located in such countries. **Top Holdings:** Corticeira Amorim SGPS SA   JBS SA   Motor Oil (Hellas) Corinth Refineries SA   Gazprom Neft PJSC   Enel SpA

First Trust NASDAQ® ABA Community Bank Index Fund

C-   HOLD

Ticker	Traded On	NAV	Total Assets ($)	Dividend Yield (TTM)	Turnover Ratio	Expense Ratio
QABA	NAS CM	47.71	$145,517,140	2.31	11	0.6

Ratings
Reward	C-
Risk	C-
Recent Upgrade/Downgrade	Up

Fund Information
Fund Type	Exchange Traded Funds
Category	Financials Sector Equity
Sub-Category	Financial
Prospectus Objective	Financial
Inception Date	Jun-09
Open to New Investments	Y

Prices
Price (as of 9/30/2019)	47.89
52-Week High	53.74
52-Week Low	41.05

Total Returns (%)
3-Month	6-Month	1-Year	3-Year	5-Year
-0.33	1.82	-7.28	21.44	54.13

3-Year Standard Deviation	22.02
Effective Duration	

Valuation
Premium/Discount (1-Year Average)	0.00

Company Information
Provider	First Trust
Manager/Tenure	Jon C. Erickson (10), Daniel J. Lindquist (10), David G. McGarel (10), 3 others
Website	http://www.ftportfolios.com/
Address	First Trust 120 E. Liberty Drive, Suite 400 Wheaton IL 60187 United States
Phone Number	800-621-1675

PERFORMANCE

Ratings History
Date	Overall Rating	Risk Rating	Reward Rating
Q3-19	C-	C-	C-
Q4-18	C-	C-	C-
Q4-17	B+	B	A
Q4-16	C	C-	C+
Q4-15	C	C	C+

Asset & Performance History
Date	NAV	1-Year Total Return
2018	43.16	-16.17
2017	52.34	0.57
2016	52.81	37.57
2015	38.94	7.88
2014	36.61	2.72
2013	36.11	42.91

Total Assets: $145,517,140

Asset Allocation
Asset	%
Cash	0%
Stocks	100%
US Stocks	98%
Bonds	0%
US Bonds	0%
Other	0%

Services Offered:

Investment Strategy: The investment seeks investment results that correspond generally to the price and yield (before the fund's fees and expenses) of an equity index called the NASDAQ OMX® ABA Community Bank IndexSM. The fund will normally invest at least 90% of its net assets (including investment borrowings) in the common stocks that comprise the index. The index is designed to track the performance of small, mid and large capitalization companies that comprise the community banking industry. **Top Holdings:** Commerce Bancshares Inc   TCF Financial Corp   East West Bancorp Inc   BOK Financial Corp   Popular Inc

Hartford Municipal Opportunities ETF   C-   HOLD

Ticker	Traded On	NAV	Total Assets ($)	Dividend Yield (TTM)	Turnover Ratio	Expense Ratio
HMOP	NYSE Arca	41.92	$144,607,320	2.43	32	0.29

Ratings
Reward   C-
Risk   D+
Recent Upgrade/Downgrade

Fund Information
Fund Type   Exchange Traded Funds
Category   US Muni Fixed Inc
Sub-Category   Muni National Interm
Prospectus Objective   Growth & Inc
Inception Date   Dec-17
Open to New Investments   Y

Prices
Price (as of 9/30/2019)   41.91
52-Week High   42.47
52-Week Low   39.08

Total Returns (%)
3-Month	6-Month	1-Year	3-Year	5-Year
1.56	4.10	9.07		

3-Year Standard Deviation
Effective Duration

Valuation
Premium/Discount (1-Year Average)   0.06

Company Information
Provider   Hartford Funds
Manager/Tenure   Timothy D. Haney (1), Brad W. Libby (1)
Website   http://www.hartfordfunds.com
Address   690 Lee Road Wayne PA 19087 United States
Phone Number   800-456-7526

PERFORMANCE

Ratings History
Date	Overall Rating	Risk Rating	Reward Rating
Q3-19	C-	D+	C-
Q4-18	D	D	D+
Q4-17	U		
Q4-16			
Q4-15			

Asset & Performance History
Date	NAV	1-Year Total Return
2018	39.84	1.44
2017	40.18	
2016		
2015		
2014		
2013		

Total Assets: $144,607,320

Asset Allocation
Asset	%
Cash	2%
Stocks	0%
US Stocks	0%
Bonds	98%
US Bonds	97%
Other	0%

Services Offered:

Investment Strategy: The investment seeks to provide current income that is generally exempt from federal income taxes and long-term total return. The fund invests in investment grade and non-investment grade municipal securities (known as "junk bonds") that the sub-adviser considers to be attractive from a yield perspective while considering total return. At least 80% of the fund's net assets must be invested in municipal securities, and up to 35% of its net assets may be invested in non-investment grade municipal securities. The fund may invest in securities of any maturity or duration. **Top Holdings:** NEW YORK N Y CITY TRANSITIONAL FIN AUTH REV 5% BUCKEYE OHIO TOB SETTLEMENT FING AUTH 5.88% NEW YORK N Y CITY MUN WTR FIN AUTH WTR & SWR SYS REV 1.39% ALABAMA ST PORT AUTH DOCKS FACS REV 5% JEA FLA ELEC SYS REV 5%

---

iShares MSCI Netherlands ETF   C+   HOLD

Ticker	Traded On	NAV	Total Assets ($)	Dividend Yield (TTM)	Turnover Ratio	Expense Ratio
EWN	NYSE Arca	31.35	$144,214,575	2.75	14	0.47

Ratings
Reward   C
Risk   C+
Recent Upgrade/Downgrade   Up

Fund Information
Fund Type   Exchange Traded Funds
Category   Europe Equity Large Cap
Sub-Category   Miscellaneous Region
Prospectus Objective   Europe Stock
Inception Date   Mar-96
Open to New Investments   Y

Prices
Price (as of 9/30/2019)   31.36
52-Week High   31.98
52-Week Low   25.35

Total Returns (%)
3-Month	6-Month	1-Year	3-Year	5-Year
0.70	6.42	6.55	34.91	46.58

3-Year Standard Deviation   13.83
Effective Duration

Valuation
Premium/Discount (1-Year Average)   -0.07

Company Information
Provider   iShares
Manager/Tenure   Diane Hsiung (11), Greg Savage (11), Jennifer Hsui (6), 3 others
Website   http://www.ishares.com
Address   iShares 400 Howard Street San Francisco CA 94105 United States
Phone Number   800-474-2737

PERFORMANCE

Ratings History
Date	Overall Rating	Risk Rating	Reward Rating
Q3-19	C+	C+	C
Q4-18	C-	C-	C-
Q4-17	B	B	B+
Q4-16	C	C	C
Q4-15	C+	C+	C

Asset & Performance History
Date	NAV	1-Year Total Return
2018	26.42	-14.99
2017	31.74	33.4
2016	24.22	3.91
2015	23.95	1.33
2014	24.06	-4.73
2013	25.81	30.14

Total Assets: $144,214,575

Asset Allocation
Asset	%
Cash	0%
Stocks	100%
US Stocks	13%
Bonds	0%
US Bonds	0%
Other	0%

Services Offered: Cash Investment Plan

Investment Strategy: The investment seeks to track the investment results of the MSCI Netherlands IMI 25/50 Index. The fund will at all times invest at least 80% of its assets in the securities of its underlying index and in depositary receipts representing securities in its underlying index. The underlying index uses a capping methodology to limit the weight of any single component to a maximum of 25% of the underlying index. The underlying index may include large-, mid- or small- capitalization companies. The fund is non-diversified. **Top Holdings:** ASML Holding NV Unilever NV Royal Philips NV ING Groep NV Koninklijke Ahold Delhaize NV

Janus Henderson Mortgage-Backed Securities ETF   D+   SELL

Ticker	Traded On	NAV	Total Assets ($)	Dividend Yield (TTM)	Turnover Ratio	Expense Ratio
JMBS	NYSE Arca	52.40	$144,100,968	2.65	91	0.35

Ratings
Reward   D+
Risk   C-
Recent Upgrade/Downgrade

Fund Information
Fund Type	Exchange Traded Funds
Category	US Fixed Income
Sub-Category	Intermediate Government
Prospectus Objective	Convertible Bond
Inception Date	Sep-18
Open to New Investments	Y

Prices
Price (as of 9/30/2019)	52.45
52-Week High	52.49
52-Week Low	49.20

Total Returns (%)
3-Month	6-Month	1-Year	3-Year	5-Year
1.50	3.83	8.16		

3-Year Standard Deviation
Effective Duration

Valuation
Premium/Discount (1-Year Average)   0.03

Company Information
Provider   Janus Henderson
Manager/Tenure   Nick Childs (1), John P. Kerschner (1)
Website   http://janushenderson.com
Address   Janus 151 Detroit Street Denver CO
                  80206 United States
Phone Number   877-335-2687

PERFORMANCE

Ratings History
Date	Overall Rating	Risk Rating	Reward Rating
Q3-19	D+	C-	D+
Q4-18	U		
Q4-17			
Q4-16			
Q4-15			

Asset & Performance History
Date	NAV	1-Year Total Return
2018	50.38	
2017		
2016		
2015		
2014		
2013		

Total Assets: $144,100,968
Asset Allocation
Asset	%
Cash	2%
Stocks	0%
US Stocks	0%
Bonds	98%
US Bonds	98%
Other	0%

Services Offered:

Investment Strategy: The investment seeks a high level of total return consisting of income and capital appreciation. The fund seeks to achieve its investment objective by investing mainly in mortgage-related instruments. Under normal circumstances, it will invest at least 80%, and often times substantially all, of its net assets (plus any borrowings for investment purposes) in a portfolio of mortgage-related fixed income instruments of varying maturities. Additionally, the fund may invest in derivatives. **Top Holdings:** Government National Mortgage Association 3% Government National Mortgage Association 4% Federal National Mortgage Association 3.5% Government National Mortgage Association 3.5% Federal National Mortgage Association 4%

Davis Select Financial ETF   C+   HOLD

Ticker	Traded On	NAV	Total Assets ($)	Dividend Yield (TTM)	Turnover Ratio	Expense Ratio
DFNL	NAS CM	23.76	$143,769,891	1.79	20	0.64

Ratings
Reward   B-
Risk   C
Recent Upgrade/Downgrade   Up

Fund Information
Fund Type	Exchange Traded Funds
Category	Financials Sector Equity
Sub-Category	Financial
Prospectus Objective	Financial
Inception Date	Jan-17
Open to New Investments	Y

Prices
Price (as of 9/30/2019)	23.77
52-Week High	24.89
52-Week Low	20.12

Total Returns (%)
3-Month	6-Month	1-Year	3-Year	5-Year
0.99	5.43	-0.69		

3-Year Standard Deviation
Effective Duration

Valuation
Premium/Discount (1-Year Average)   -0.04

Company Information
Provider   Davis ETFs
Manager/Tenure   Christopher Cullom Davis (2), Pierce
                  Crosbie (0)
Website
Address   c/o Davis Selected Advisers, L.P. 2949
                  E. Elvira Rd., Ste. 101 Tucson Arizona
                  85756 United States
Phone Number   800-279-0279

PERFORMANCE

Ratings History
Date	Overall Rating	Risk Rating	Reward Rating
Q3-19	C+	C	B-
Q4-18	C+	C	B-
Q4-17	D-	B+	D+
Q4-16			
Q4-15			

Asset & Performance History
Date	NAV	1-Year Total Return
2018	20.64	-10.79
2017	23.87	21.81
2016		
2015		
2014		
2013		

Total Assets: $143,769,891
Asset Allocation
Asset	%
Cash	0%
Stocks	100%
US Stocks	83%
Bonds	0%
US Bonds	0%
Other	0%

Services Offered:

Investment Strategy: The investment seeks long-term growth of capital. The fund's investment adviser, uses the Davis Investment Discipline to invest, under normal market conditions, at least 80% of its net assets plus any borrowings for investment purposes in securities issued by companies principally engaged in the financial services sector. The fund's portfolio generally contains between 15 and 35 companies. It invests, principally, in common stocks. The fund may invest in large, medium or small companies without regard to market capitalization and may invest in issuers in foreign countries, including countries with developed or emerging markets. It is non-diversified. **Top Holdings:** US Bancorp Capital One Financial Corp Berkshire Hathaway Inc B American Express Co Markel Corp

Invesco CurrencyShares® Swiss Franc Trust

D+ SELL

Ticker	Traded On	NAV	Total Assets ($)	Dividend Yield (TTM)	Turnover Ratio	Expense Ratio
FXF	NYSE Arca	92.72	$143,713,029	0	0	0.4

Ratings
Reward	D+
Risk	C-
Recent Upgrade/Downgrade	Up

Fund Information
Fund Type	Exchange Traded Funds
Category	Currency
Sub-Category	Single Currency
Prospectus Objective	Worldwide Bond
Inception Date	Jun-06
Open to New Investments	Y

Prices
Price (as of 9/30/2019)	92.62
52-Week High	95.74
52-Week Low	90.99

Total Returns (%)
3-Month	6-Month	1-Year	3-Year	5-Year
-1.54	-0.54	-3.17	-6.10	-9.06

3-Year Standard Deviation	6.5
Effective Duration	

Valuation
Premium/Discount (1-Year Average)	-0.07

Company Information
Provider	Invesco
Manager/Tenure	Management Team (13)
Website	http://www.invesco.com/us
Address	Invesco 11 Greenway Plaza, Ste. 2500 Houston TX 77046 United States
Phone Number	800-659-1005

PERFORMANCE

Ratings History
Date	Overall Rating	Risk Rating	Reward Rating
Q3-19	D+	C-	D+
Q4-18	D	C-	D
Q4-17	D+	C-	D
Q4-16	D	D+	D
Q4-15	D+	C-	D

Asset & Performance History
Date	NAV	1-Year Total Return
2018	94.6	-2.28
2017	96.81	3.08
2016	93.91	-2.64
2015	96.47	-1.77
2014	98.2	-10.85
2013	110.16	2.51

Total Assets: $143,713,029

Asset Allocation
Asset	%
Cash	100%
Stocks	0%
US Stocks	0%
Bonds	0%
US Bonds	0%
Other	0%

Services Offered:

Investment Strategy: The investment seeks to track the price of the Swiss Franc, net of trust expenses. The fund seeks to reflect the price of the Swiss Franc. The sponsor believes that, for many investors, the shares represent a cost-effective investment relative to traditional means of investing in the foreign exchange market.
Top Holdings:

IQ Global Resources ETF

C- HOLD

Ticker	Traded On	NAV	Total Assets ($)	Dividend Yield (TTM)	Turnover Ratio	Expense Ratio
GRES	NYSE Arca	26.57	$143,478,033	0.73		0.77

Ratings
Reward	C
Risk	D+
Recent Upgrade/Downgrade	

Fund Information
Fund Type	Exchange Traded Funds
Category	Natural Resources
Sub-Category	Natural Resources
Prospectus Objective	World Stock
Inception Date	Oct-09
Open to New Investments	Y

Prices
Price (as of 9/30/2019)	26.52
52-Week High	27.96
52-Week Low	25.05

Total Returns (%)
3-Month	6-Month	1-Year	3-Year	5-Year
-3.03	-3.70	-2.15	3.74	1.42

3-Year Standard Deviation	8.95
Effective Duration	

Valuation
Premium/Discount (1-Year Average)	-0.24

Company Information
Provider	IndexIQ
Manager/Tenure	Greg Barrato (8), James Harrison (1)
Website	http://www.indexiq.com
Address	IndexIQ 800 Westchester Avenue, Suite N-611 Rye Brook NY 10573 United States
Phone Number	888-934-0777

PERFORMANCE

Ratings History
Date	Overall Rating	Risk Rating	Reward Rating
Q3-19	C-	D+	C
Q4-18	C-	C-	D+
Q4-17	C	C	C+
Q4-16	D+	C-	D+
Q4-15	D	D	D

Asset & Performance History
Date	NAV	1-Year Total Return
2018	25.39	-10.23
2017	28.5	13.36
2016	25.14	20.17
2015	21	-19.37
2014	26.74	-5.12
2013	28.55	-3.28

Total Assets: $143,478,033

Asset Allocation
Asset	%
Cash	0%
Stocks	91%
US Stocks	30%
Bonds	0%
US Bonds	0%
Other	0%

Services Offered:

Investment Strategy: The investment seeks investment results that correspond generally to the price and yield performance of its underlying index, the IQ Global Resources Index. The fund invests at least 80% of its net assets, in the investments included in its underlying index. The underlying index seeks to employ a systematic investment process designed to identify opportunities in markets exhibiting trending or momentum characteristics across commodity asset classes, represented by companies that operate in commodity-specific market segments and whose equity securities trade in developed markets, including the U.S. The fund is non-diversified. **Top Holdings:** Payb Spdr S&P500 Etf Trus   Payb Ishares Msci Eafe Index Fund Swap   Drey Inst Pref Gov Mm Inst 6546   Recv Spdr S&P 500 Etf Trus   Recv Ishares Msci Eafe Index Fund Swap

iShares MSCI Kokusai ETF
C   HOLD

Ticker	Traded On	NAV	Total Assets ($)	Dividend Yield (TTM)	Turnover Ratio	Expense Ratio
TOK	NYSE Arca	68.21	$143,246,052	2.2	4	0.25

Ratings

Reward	C
Risk	D+
Recent Upgrade/Downgrade	

Fund Information

Fund Type	Exchange Traded Funds
Category	Global Equity Large Cap
Sub-Category	World Large Stock
Prospectus Objective	World Stock
Inception Date	Dec-07
Open to New Investments	Y

Prices

Price (as of 9/30/2019)	68.45
52-Week High	69.26
52-Week Low	55.44

Total Returns (%)

3-Month	6-Month	1-Year	3-Year	5-Year
-0.20	3.50	2.42	36.06	45.76

3-Year Standard Deviation	11.53
Effective Duration	

Valuation

Premium/Discount (1-Year Average)	-0.04

Company Information

Provider	iShares
Manager/Tenure	Diane Hsiung (11), Greg Savage (11), Jennifer Hsui (6), 3 others
Website	http://www.ishares.com
Address	iShares 400 Howard Street San Francisco CA 94105 United States
Phone Number	800-474-2737

PERFORMANCE

Ratings History

Date	Overall Rating	Risk Rating	Reward Rating
Q3-19	C	D+	C
Q4-18	C-	D+	C-
Q4-17	B-	B-	B-
Q4-16	C	D+	C+
Q4-15	C	D+	C

Asset & Performance History

Date	NAV	1-Year Total Return
2018	58.37	-8.11
2017	65.15	22.5
2016	54.63	8.31
2015	51.76	-1.54
2014	54.12	5.98
2013	52.42	26.87

Total Assets: $143,246,052

Asset Allocation

Asset	%
Cash	1%
Stocks	99%
US Stocks	68%
Bonds	0%
US Bonds	0%
Other	0%

Services Offered:

Investment Strategy: The investment seeks to track the investment results of the MSCI Kokusai Index composed of developed market equities, excluding Japan. The fund generally will invest at least 90% of its assets in the component securities of the underlying index and in investments that have economic characteristics that are substantially identical to the component securities of the underlying index. The index is designed to measure equity market performance in those countries that MSCI Inc. (the "index provider" or "MSCI") has classified as having developed economies, excluding Japan ("DEEJ"). **Top Holdings:** Microsoft Corp Apple Inc Amazon.com Inc Facebook Inc A Alphabet Inc Class C

Barron's 400 ETF
C-   HOLD

Ticker	Traded On	NAV	Total Assets ($)	Dividend Yield (TTM)	Turnover Ratio	Expense Ratio
BFOR	NYSE Arca	39.77	$143,153,821	0.84	88	0.66

Ratings

Reward	C-
Risk	C-
Recent Upgrade/Downgrade	Up

Fund Information

Fund Type	Exchange Traded Funds
Category	US Equity Mid Cap
Sub-Category	Mid-Cap Growth
Prospectus Objective	Growth
Inception Date	Jun-13
Open to New Investments	Y

Prices

Price (as of 9/30/2019)	39.78
52-Week High	44.89
52-Week Low	33.40

Total Returns (%)

3-Month	6-Month	1-Year	3-Year	5-Year
-2.31	-2.47	-10.34	26.00	39.08

3-Year Standard Deviation	16.9
Effective Duration	

Valuation

Premium/Discount (1-Year Average)	-0.05

Company Information

Provider	ALPS ETF
Manager/Tenure	Ryan Mischker (4), Andrew Hicks (3)
Website	http://www.alpsfunds.com
Address	ALPS ETF PO Box 328 Denver CO 80201-0328 United States
Phone Number	855-724-0450

PERFORMANCE

Ratings History

Date	Overall Rating	Risk Rating	Reward Rating
Q3-19	C-	C-	C-
Q4-18	C-	D+	C-
Q4-17	B	B	B+
Q4-16	C	D+	C+
Q4-15	C-	C-	C-

Asset & Performance History

Date	NAV	1-Year Total Return
2018	35.52	-13.43
2017	41.43	18.93
2016	35.04	17.41
2015	30.07	-3.74
2014	31.51	6.27
2013	29.86	

Total Assets: $143,153,821

Asset Allocation

Asset	%
Cash	0%
Stocks	100%
US Stocks	98%
Bonds	0%
US Bonds	0%
Other	0%

Services Offered:

Investment Strategy: The investment seeks investment results that correspond generally, before fees and expenses, to the performance of the Barron's 400SM Index (the "underlying index"). The underlying index is a rules-based index intended to give investors a means of tracking the overall performance of high performing equity securities of U.S. companies. The fund will invest at least 80% of its total assets in the equity securities which comprise the underlying index. **Top Holdings:** TCF Financial Corp Meta Financial Group Inc Match Group Inc Medpace Holdings Inc Meritage Homes Corp

JPMorgan Diversified Return Global Equity ETF   C   HOLD

Ticker	Traded On	NAV	Total Assets ($)	Dividend Yield (TTM)	Turnover Ratio	Expense Ratio
JPGE	NYSE Arca	59.33	$142,382,543	2.74	29	0.38

Ratings
Reward   C
Risk   C-
Recent Upgrade/Downgrade

Fund Information
Fund Type	Exchange Traded Funds
Category	Global Equity Large Cap
Sub-Category	World Large Stock
Prospectus Objective	Growth & Inc
Inception Date	Jun-14
Open to New Investments	Y

Prices
Price (as of 9/30/2019)	59.26
52-Week High	61.42
52-Week Low	52.65

Total Returns (%)
3-Month	6-Month	1-Year	3-Year	5-Year
-0.38	0.73	-0.69	20.87	35.79

3-Year Standard Deviation   10.24
Effective Duration

Valuation
Premium/Discount (1-Year Average)   -0.07

Company Information
Provider	JPMorgan
Manager/Tenure	Kartik Aiyar (2), Wei (Victor) Li (2), Yazann Romahi (2), 1 other
Website	http://www.jpmorganfunds.com
Address	JPMorgan 270 Park Avenue New York NY 10017-2070 United States
Phone Number	800-480-4111

PERFORMANCE

Ratings History
Date	Overall Rating	Risk Rating	Reward Rating
Q3-19	C	C-	C
Q4-18	C-	C-	D+
Q4-17	B	B+	B-
Q4-16	C-	D+	C
Q4-15	D	D+	D

Asset & Performance History
Date	NAV	1-Year Total Return
2018	54.49	-10.33
2017	62.18	24.41
2016	50.74	5.79
2015	49.03	3.51
2014	48.29	
2013		

Total Assets: $142,382,543
Asset Allocation
Asset	%
Cash	0%
Stocks	100%
US Stocks	23%
Bonds	0%
US Bonds	0%
Other	0%

Services Offered:

Investment Strategy: The investment seeks investment results that closely correspond, before fees and expenses, to the performance of the JP Morgan Diversified Factor Global Developed Equity Index. The index is comprised of equity securities across developed global markets selected to represent a diversified set of factor characteristics: value, price momentum and quality. The fund will invest at least 80% of its assets in securities included in the index. **Top Holdings:** L3Harris Technologies Inc   Advantest Corp   Daiichi Sankyo Co Ltd   Starbucks Corp   Hikari Tsushin Inc

---

First Trust Emerging Markets Local Currency Bond ETF   C   HOLD

Ticker	Traded On	NAV	Total Assets ($)	Dividend Yield (TTM)	Turnover Ratio	Expense Ratio
FEMB	NAS CM	37.94	$142,265,193	5.07	61	0.85

Ratings
Reward   C
Risk   C-
Recent Upgrade/Downgrade   Up

Fund Information
Fund Type	Exchange Traded Funds
Category	Emerging Mkts Fixed Inc
Sub-Category	Emerging-Markets Local-Currency Bond
Prospectus Objective	Div Emerg Mkts
Inception Date	Nov-14
Open to New Investments	Y

Prices
Price (as of 9/30/2019)	38.05
52-Week High	39.95
52-Week Low	35.97

Total Returns (%)
3-Month	6-Month	1-Year	3-Year	5-Year
-1.21	2.70	9.30	5.30	

3-Year Standard Deviation   9.2
Effective Duration   5.34

Valuation
Premium/Discount (1-Year Average)   0.18

Company Information
Provider	First Trust
Manager/Tenure	Leonardo Da Costa (4), Derek Fulton (4), Anthony Beevers (0)
Website	http://www.ftportfolios.com/
Address	First Trust 120 E. Liberty Drive, Suite 400 Wheaton IL 60187 United States
Phone Number	800-621-1675

PERFORMANCE

Ratings History
Date	Overall Rating	Risk Rating	Reward Rating
Q3-19	C	C-	C
Q4-18	D+	D+	D+
Q4-17	C	C	C
Q4-16	D+	D+	D+
Q4-15	U		

Asset & Performance History
Date	NAV	1-Year Total Return
2018	37.02	-7.22
2017	42.18	12.61
2016	39.92	7.73
2015	39.21	-14.68
2014	48.05	
2013		

Total Assets: $142,265,193
Asset Allocation
Asset	%
Cash	7%
Stocks	0%
US Stocks	0%
Bonds	93%
US Bonds	0%
Other	0%

Services Offered:

Investment Strategy: The investment seeks maximum total return and current income. Under normal market conditions, the fund seeks to achieve its investment objective by investing at least 80% of its net assets (including investment borrowings) in bonds, notes and bills issued or guaranteed by entities incorporated or domiciled in emerging market countries (collectively, "Bonds") that are denominated in the local currency of the issuer. It is non-diversified. **Top Holdings:** Israel (State Of) 2.25%   Republic of South Africa 8.88%   The Republic of Peru 6.95%   Republic of South Africa 6.25%   International Finance Corporation 6.3%

Invesco S&P 500® Equal Weight Materials ETF

C+   HOLD

Ticker	Traded On	NAV	Total Assets ($)	Dividend Yield (TTM)	Turnover Ratio	Expense Ratio
RTM	NYSE Arca	109.05	$141,766,410	2		0.4

Ratings
Reward	B
Risk	C
Recent Upgrade/Downgrade	Up

Fund Information
Fund Type	Exchange Traded Funds
Category	Natural Resources
Sub-Category	Natural Resources
Prospectus Objective	Unaligned
Inception Date	Nov-06
Open to New Investments	Y

Prices
Price (as of 9/30/2019)	108.95
52-Week High	111.94
52-Week Low	88.78

Total Returns (%)
3-Month	6-Month	1-Year	3-Year	5-Year
-0.93	2.54	1.69	32.18	44.64

3-Year Standard Deviation	15.36
Effective Duration	

Valuation
Premium/Discount (1-Year Average)	-0.02

Company Information
Provider	Invesco
Manager/Tenure	Peter Hubbard (1), Michael Jeanette (1), Tony Seisser (1)
Website	http://www.invesco.com/us
Address	Invesco 11 Greenway Plaza, Ste. 2500 Houston TX 77046 United States
Phone Number	800-659-1005

PERFORMANCE

Ratings History
Date	Overall Rating	Risk Rating	Reward Rating
Q3-19	C+	C	B
Q4-18	C+	C-	B
Q4-17	B+	B-	A
Q4-16	C+	C-	B-
Q4-15	B	C+	B

Asset & Performance History
Date	NAV	1-Year Total Return
2018	94.6	-14.52
2017	112.57	24.89
2016	91.05	21.48
2015	76.11	-7.9
2014	83.88	6.65
2013	79.8	24.66

Total Assets: $141,766,410
Asset Allocation
Asset	%
Cash	0%
Stocks	100%
US Stocks	93%
Bonds	0%
US Bonds	0%
Other	0%

Services Offered:

Investment Strategy: The investment seeks to track the investment results (before fees and expenses) of the S&P 500® Equal Weight Materials Index (the "underlying index"). The fund generally will invest at least 90% of its total assets in the securities that comprise the underlying index. The underlying index is composed of all of the components of the S&P 500® Materials Index, an index that contains the common stocks of all companies included in the S&P 500® Index that are classified as members of the materials sector, as defined according to the Global Industry Classification Standard ("GICS"). The fund is non-diversified. **Top Holdings:** Ball Corp Corteva Inc Martin Marietta Materials Inc Sherwin-Williams Co Newmont Goldcorp Corp

---

iShares Edge U.S. Fixed Income Balanced Risk ETF

C   HOLD

Ticker	Traded On	NAV	Total Assets ($)	Dividend Yield (TTM)	Turnover Ratio	Expense Ratio
FIBR	BATS	101.24	$141,733,450	3.52	633	0.25

Ratings
Reward	C+
Risk	D+
Recent Upgrade/Downgrade	

Fund Information
Fund Type	Exchange Traded Funds
Category	Fixed Income Misc
Sub-Category	Intermediate Core-Plus Bond
Prospectus Objective	Income
Inception Date	Feb-15
Open to New Investments	Y

Prices
Price (as of 9/30/2019)	101.32
52-Week High	101.63
52-Week Low	94.77

Total Returns (%)
3-Month	6-Month	1-Year	3-Year	5-Year
1.10	3.86	8.07	10.24	

3-Year Standard Deviation	2.61
Effective Duration	

Valuation
Premium/Discount (1-Year Average)	0.10

Company Information
Provider	iShares
Manager/Tenure	James Mauro (4), Scott Radell (4)
Website	http://www.ishares.com
Address	iShares 400 Howard Street San Francisco CA 94105 United States
Phone Number	800-474-2737

PERFORMANCE

Ratings History
Date	Overall Rating	Risk Rating	Reward Rating
Q3-19	C	D+	C+
Q4-18	D+	D+	C-
Q4-17	C+	B	C
Q4-16	D+	D+	D+
Q4-15	U		

Asset & Performance History
Date	NAV	1-Year Total Return
2018	95.45	-1.01
2017	99.93	3.84
2016	98.91	5.31
2015	96.69	
2014		
2013		

Total Assets: $141,733,450
Asset Allocation
Asset	%
Cash	-23%
Stocks	0%
US Stocks	0%
Bonds	121%
US Bonds	112%
Other	0%

Services Offered:

Investment Strategy: The investment seeks to track the investment results of the Bloomberg Barclays U.S. Fixed Income Balanced Risk Index. The underlying index measures the performance of the corporate and mortgage portion of the Bloomberg Barclays U.S. Universal Index while targeting an equal allocation between interest rate and credit spread risk. The fund generally will invest at least 90% of its assets in the component securities of the underlying index and in investments that have economic characteristics that are substantially identical to the component securities of the underlying index. It is non-diversified. **Top Holdings:** Fhlmc Umbs 30yr Federal National Mortgage Association 3.5% Bank of America Corporation 3% Gnma2 30yr 2017 Production Government National Mortgage Association 3.5%

VanEck Vectors Pharmaceutical ETF   C   HOLD

Ticker	Traded On	NAV	Total Assets ($)	Dividend Yield (TTM)	Turnover Ratio	Expense Ratio
PPH	NAS CM	56.93	$141,660,424	1.95	18	0.36

Ratings
Reward	C+
Risk	C-
Recent Upgrade/Downgrade	Up

Fund Information
Fund Type	Exchange Traded Funds
Category	Healthcare Sector Equity
Sub-Category	Health
Prospectus Objective	Health
Inception Date	Dec-11
Open to New Investments	Y

Prices
Price (as of 9/30/2019)	56.99
52-Week High	64.52
52-Week Low	52.66

Total Returns (%)
3-Month	6-Month	1-Year	3-Year	5-Year
-3.21	-5.49	-9.78	4.86	-0.38

3-Year Standard Deviation	15.33
Effective Duration	

Valuation
Premium/Discount (1-Year Average)	-0.02

Company Information
Provider	VanEck
Manager/Tenure	Hao-Hung (Peter) Liao (7), Guo Hua (Jason) Jin (1)
Website	http://www.vaneck.com
Address	Van Eck Associates Corporation 666 Third Avenue New York NY 10017 United States
Phone Number	800-826-1115

PERFORMANCE

Ratings History
Date	Overall Rating	Risk Rating	Reward Rating
Q3-19	C	C-	C+
Q4-18	C	C-	C+
Q4-17	D+	C-	D+
Q4-16	C	D+	C+
Q4-15	B	C+	B

Asset & Performance History
Date	NAV	1-Year Total Return
2018	55.02	-5.52
2017	59.34	15.37
2016	52.47	-17.76
2015	65.24	3.41
2014	64.27	23.07
2013	53.16	36.82

Total Assets: $141,660,424
Asset Allocation
Asset	%
Cash	0%
Stocks	100%
US Stocks	57%
Bonds	0%
US Bonds	0%
Other	0%

Services Offered:

Investment Strategy: The investment seeks to replicate as closely as possible, before fees and expenses, the price and yield performance of the MVIS® US Listed Pharmaceutical 25 Index. The fund normally invests at least 80% of its total assets in securities that comprise the fund's benchmark index. The index includes common stocks and depositary receipts of U.S. exchange-listed companies in the pharmaceutical industry. Such companies may include medium-capitalization companies and foreign companies that are listed on a U.S. exchange. It is non-diversified. **Top Holdings:** AstraZeneca PLC ADR Merck & Co Inc GlaxoSmithKline PLC ADR Mylan NV Zoetis Inc Class A

Invesco DWA Healthcare Momentum ETF   C   HOLD

Ticker	Traded On	NAV	Total Assets ($)	Dividend Yield (TTM)	Turnover Ratio	Expense Ratio
PTH	NAS CM	78.25	$140,844,775	0		0.6

Ratings
Reward	C
Risk	C-
Recent Upgrade/Downgrade	

Fund Information
Fund Type	Exchange Traded Funds
Category	Healthcare Sector Equity
Sub-Category	Health
Prospectus Objective	Health
Inception Date	Oct-06
Open to New Investments	Y

Prices
Price (as of 9/30/2019)	78.22
52-Week High	97.20
52-Week Low	64.96

Total Returns (%)
3-Month	6-Month	1-Year	3-Year	5-Year
-11.49	-0.89	-19.47	48.62	60.51

3-Year Standard Deviation	25
Effective Duration	

Valuation
Premium/Discount (1-Year Average)	-0.08

Company Information
Provider	Invesco
Manager/Tenure	Peter Hubbard (12), Michael Jeanette (11), Tony Seisser (5)
Website	http://www.invesco.com/us
Address	Invesco 11 Greenway Plaza, Ste. 2500 Houston TX 77046 United States
Phone Number	800-659-1005

PERFORMANCE

Ratings History
Date	Overall Rating	Risk Rating	Reward Rating
Q3-19	C	C-	C
Q4-18	C	C-	C
Q4-17	B	C	A-
Q4-16	C-	D+	C-
Q4-15	C+	C	B

Asset & Performance History
Date	NAV	1-Year Total Return
2018	71.48	-0.86
2017	72.1	50.11
2016	48.03	-12.91
2015	55.15	2.28
2014	53.92	13.75
2013	47.4	44.08

Total Assets: $140,844,775
Asset Allocation
Asset	%
Cash	0%
Stocks	100%
US Stocks	100%
Bonds	0%
US Bonds	0%
Other	0%

Services Offered:

Investment Strategy: The investment seeks to track the investment results (before fees and expenses) of the Dorsey Wright® Healthcare Technical Leaders Index (the "underlying index"). The fund generally will invest at least 90% of its total assets in the securities that comprise the underlying index. The underlying index is composed of at least 30 securities of companies in the healthcare sector that have powerful relative strength or "momentum" characteristics. **Top Holdings:** Exact Sciences Corp Mirati Therapeutics Inc NovoCure Ltd Masimo Corp Insulet Corp

High Yield ETF   C   HOLD

Ticker	Traded On	NAV	Total Assets ($)	Dividend Yield (TTM)	Turnover Ratio	Expense Ratio
HYLD	NYSE Arca	34.11	$139,851,418	7.51	74	1.25

Ratings
Reward C
Risk C-
Recent Upgrade/Downgrade

Fund Information
Fund Type Exchange Traded Funds
Category US Fixed Income
Sub-Category High Yield Bond
Prospectus Objective Income
Inception Date Nov-10
Open to New Investments Y

Prices
Price (as of 9/30/2019) 33.88
52-Week High 36.72
52-Week Low 33.65

Total Returns (%)

3-Month	6-Month	1-Year	3-Year	5-Year
0.03	1.36	0.16	20.30	0.57

3-Year Standard Deviation 3.68
Effective Duration

Valuation
Premium/Discount (1-Year Average) -0.41

Company Information
Provider Peritus
Manager/Tenure Michael DePalma (1), Michael Ning (1), Barry Boland (0), 2 others
Website http://www.hyldetf.com
Address Peritus 10900 Hefner Pointe Drive, Suite 207 Oklahoma City OK 73120 United States
Phone Number

Ratings History

Date	Overall Rating	Risk Rating	Reward Rating
Q3-19	C	C-	C
Q4-18	C-	C-	C-
Q4-17	C	C+	C
Q4-16	D+	C-	D+
Q4-15	D+	C-	D

Asset & Performance History

Date	NAV	1-Year Total Return
2018	33.93	-0.29
2017	36.63	8.63
2016	36.19	17.21
2015	33.08	-13.87
2014	42.09	-11.61
2013	51.67	12.12

Total Assets: $139,851,418
Asset Allocation

Asset	%
Cash	6%
Stocks	0%
US Stocks	0%
Bonds	94%
US Bonds	69%
Other	0%

Services Offered:

Investment Strategy: The investment seeks high current income with a secondary goal of capital appreciation. The Sub-Advisor seeks to achieve the fund's investment objective by selecting a focused portfolio of high-yield debt securities, which include senior and subordinated corporate debt obligations (such as loans, bonds, debentures, notes and commercial paper). The fund does not have any portfolio maturity limitation and may invest its assets in instruments with short-term, medium-term or long-term maturities. It invests at least 80% of its net assets (plus any borrowings for investment purposes) in high-yield debt securities. **Top Holdings:** Osum Production 08/01/22 Term Loan Compass Group Diversified Holdings LLC 8% Techniplas, LLC. 10% LEE Enterprises Inc 9.5% Global Ship Lease Inc 9.88%

First Trust Nasdaq Bank ETF   B-   BUY

Ticker	Traded On	NAV	Total Assets ($)	Dividend Yield (TTM)	Turnover Ratio	Expense Ratio
FTXO	NAS CM	25.59	$139,476,462	3.78	87	0.6

Ratings
Reward B
Risk C
Recent Upgrade/Downgrade Up

Fund Information
Fund Type Exchange Traded Funds
Category Financials Sector Equity
Sub-Category Financial
Prospectus Objective Financial
Inception Date Sep-16
Open to New Investments Y

Prices
Price (as of 9/30/2019) 25.59
52-Week High 28.52
52-Week Low 21.01

Total Returns (%)

3-Month	6-Month	1-Year	3-Year	5-Year
0.78	3.52	-4.17	35.51	

3-Year Standard Deviation 23.03
Effective Duration

Valuation
Premium/Discount (1-Year Average) -0.04

Company Information
Provider First Trust
Manager/Tenure Jon C. Erickson (3), Daniel J. Lindquist (3), David G. McGarel (3), 3 others
Website http://www.ftportfolios.com/
Address First Trust 120 E. Liberty Drive, Suite 400 Wheaton IL 60187 United States
Phone Number 800-621-1675

Ratings History

Date	Overall Rating	Risk Rating	Reward Rating
Q3-19	B-	C	B
Q4-18	B-	C	B
Q4-17	D	B	C
Q4-16	U		
Q4-15			

Asset & Performance History

Date	NAV	1-Year Total Return
2018	22.28	-21.57
2017	29.32	13.95
2016	26.02	
2015		
2014		
2013		

Total Assets: $139,476,462
Asset Allocation

Asset	%
Cash	1%
Stocks	99%
US Stocks	99%
Bonds	0%
US Bonds	0%
Other	0%

Services Offered:

Investment Strategy: The investment seeks investment results that correspond generally to the price and yield (before the fund's fees and expenses) of an equity index called the Nasdaq US Smart Banks Index. The fund will normally invest at least 90% of its net assets (including investment borrowings) in the common stocks and depository receipts that comprise the underlying index. The index is designed to provide exposure to U.S. companies comprising the banking sector that have been selected based upon their liquidity and weighted based upon their cumulative score on three investing factors: volatility, value and growth. The fund is non-diversified. **Top Holdings:** US Bancorp JPMorgan Chase & Co Citigroup Inc PNC Financial Services Group Inc Fifth Third Bancorp

First Trust Dow Jones Select MicroCap Index Fund   C-   HOLD

Ticker	Traded On	NAV	Total Assets ($)	Dividend Yield (TTM)	Turnover Ratio	Expense Ratio
FDM	NYSE Arca	45.65	$139,467,929	1.72	75	0.6

Ratings
Reward	C
Risk	C-
Recent Upgrade/Downgrade	Up

Fund Information
Fund Type	Exchange Traded Funds
Category	US Equity Small Cap
Sub-Category	Small Value
Prospectus Objective	Growth
Inception Date	Sep-05
Open to New Investments	Y

Prices
Price (as of 9/30/2019)	45.70
52-Week High	50.54
52-Week Low	38.71

Total Returns (%)
3-Month	6-Month	1-Year	3-Year	5-Year
1.33	1.80	-8.06	30.39	65.47

3-Year Standard Deviation	18.72
Effective Duration	

Valuation
Premium/Discount (1-Year Average)	-0.01

Company Information
Provider	First Trust
Manager/Tenure	Jon C. Erickson (14), Daniel J. Lindquist (14), David G. McGarel (14), 3 others
Website	http://www.ftportfolios.com/
Address	First Trust 120 E. Liberty Drive, Suite 400 Wheaton IL 60187 United States
Phone Number	800-621-1675

PERFORMANCE

Ratings History
Date	Overall Rating	Risk Rating	Reward Rating
Q3-19	C-	C-	C
Q4-18	C-	C-	C-
Q4-17	A-	B+	A
Q4-16	C	D+	C+
Q4-15	C	D+	C+

Asset & Performance History
Date	NAV	1-Year Total Return
2018	40.76	-12.69
2017	47.21	8.46
2016	43.98	35.45
2015	32.92	0.54
2014	33.21	3.08
2013	32.47	43.33

Total Assets: $139,467,929
Asset Allocation
Asset	%
Cash	1%
Stocks	99%
US Stocks	99%
Bonds	0%
US Bonds	0%
Other	0%

Services Offered:

Investment Strategy: The investment seeks investment results that correspond generally to the price and yield (before the fund's fees and expenses) of an equity index called the Dow Jones Select MicroCap Index(SM). The fund will normally invest at least 90% of its net assets (including investment borrowings) in the common stocks that comprise the index. The index is designed to measure the performance of micro-cap stocks issued by U.S. companies that are comparatively liquid and have strong fundamentals relative to the micro-cap segment as a whole. **Top Holdings:** Photronics Inc Barrett Business Services Inc Kimball International Inc Class B Tower International Inc Myers Industries Inc

Fidelity® Momentum Factor ETF   C   HOLD

Ticker	Traded On	NAV	Total Assets ($)	Dividend Yield (TTM)	Turnover Ratio	Expense Ratio
FDMO	NYSE Arca	34.98	$138,160,313	1.2	133	0.29

Ratings
Reward	C
Risk	C-
Recent Upgrade/Downgrade	

Fund Information
Fund Type	Exchange Traded Funds
Category	US Equity Large Cap Growth
Sub-Category	Large Growth
Prospectus Objective	Growth & Inc
Inception Date	Sep-16
Open to New Investments	Y

Prices
Price (as of 9/30/2019)	35.00
52-Week High	36.62
52-Week Low	27.72

Total Returns (%)
3-Month	6-Month	1-Year	3-Year	5-Year
-1.83	3.15	-0.20	42.56	

3-Year Standard Deviation	12.42
Effective Duration	

Valuation
Premium/Discount (1-Year Average)	0.03

Company Information
Provider	Fidelity Investments
Manager/Tenure	Louis Bottari (3), Deane Gyllenhaal (3), Peter Matthew (3), 3 others
Website	http://www.institutional.fidelity.com
Address	Fidelity Investments 82 Devonshire Street Boston MA 2109 United States
Phone Number	617-563-7000

PERFORMANCE

Ratings History
Date	Overall Rating	Risk Rating	Reward Rating
Q3-19	C	C-	C
Q4-18	C	C-	C
Q4-17	D	B	C
Q4-16	U		
Q4-15			

Asset & Performance History
Date	NAV	1-Year Total Return
2018	29.71	-3.71
2017	31.21	23.71
2016	25.53	
2015		
2014		
2013		

Total Assets: $138,160,313
Asset Allocation
Asset	%
Cash	0%
Stocks	100%
US Stocks	99%
Bonds	0%
US Bonds	0%
Other	0%

Services Offered:

Investment Strategy: The investment seeks to provide investment returns that correspond, before fees and expenses, generally to the performance of the Fidelity U.S. Momentum Factor Index. The fund normally invests at least 80% of assets in securities included in the Fidelity U.S. Momentum Factor Index, which is designed to reflect the performance of stocks of large and mid-capitalization U.S. companies that exhibit positive momentum signals. It may lend securities to earn income for the fund. **Top Holdings:** Microsoft Corp Amazon.com Inc Facebook Inc A Berkshire Hathaway Inc B Johnson & Johnson

C-Tracks Exchange-Traded Notes Miller/Howard Strategic Dividend Reinvestor   D   SELL

Ticker	Traded On	NAV	Total Assets ($)	Dividend Yield (TTM)	Turnover Ratio	Expense Ratio
DIVC	NYSE Arca	34.34	$137,378,000	0		0.7

Ratings
Reward	C-
Risk	E+
Recent Upgrade/Downgrade	Down

Fund Information
Fund Type	Exchange Traded Funds
Category	US Equity Large Cap Value
Sub-Category	Large Value
Prospectus Objective	Income
Inception Date	Sep-14
Open to New Investments	Y

Prices
Price (as of 9/30/2019)	34.34
52-Week High	36.39
52-Week Low	29.19

Total Returns (%)
3-Month	6-Month	1-Year	3-Year	5-Year
-0.77	-1.13	-5.62	29.50	44.48

3-Year Standard Deviation	17.54
Effective Duration	

Valuation
Premium/Discount (1-Year Average)	0.00

Company Information
Provider	Citigroup
Manager/Tenure	No Manager (5)
Website	
Address	Citigroup 388 Greenwich Street New York NULL NULL United States
Phone Number	

PERFORMANCE

Ratings History
Date	Overall Rating	Risk Rating	Reward Rating
Q3-19	D	E+	C-
Q4-18	D	E+	C-
Q4-17	B	B-	B
Q4-16	D+	D	C-
Q4-15	U		

Asset & Performance History
Date	NAV	1-Year Total Return
2018	30.76	-12.12
2017	35	16.39
2016	30.07	20.42
2015	24.97	-2.38
2014	25.58	
2013		

Total Assets: $137,378,000
Asset Allocation
Asset	%
Cash	%
Stocks	%
US Stocks	%
Bonds	%
US Bonds	%
Other	%

Services Offered:

Investment Strategy: The investment seeks to provide exposure to the performance of the Miller/Howard Strategic Dividend Index Total Return.
The C-Tracks Exchange-Traded Notes Miller/Howard Strategic Dividend Reinvestor, are unsecured senior debt securities. The index is designed to track the performance of 30 equally weighted stocks traded on U.S. exchanges selected quarterly pursuant to rules based upon certain quantitative fundamental factors, including dividend yield, expected growth of dividend yield, market valuation relative to book value, return on invested capital relative to price-to-earnings ratio and trailing 26-week stock price momentum. **Top Holdings:**

Innovator Lunt Low Vol/High Beta Tactical ETF   C   HOLD

Ticker	Traded On	NAV	Total Assets ($)	Dividend Yield (TTM)	Turnover Ratio	Expense Ratio
LVHB	BATS	36.81	$136,194,483	1.89	667	0.52

Ratings
Reward	C
Risk	C-
Recent Upgrade/Downgrade	

Fund Information
Fund Type	Exchange Traded Funds
Category	US Equity Large Cap Blend
Sub-Category	Large Value
Prospectus Objective	Growth & Inc
Inception Date	Oct-16
Open to New Investments	Y

Prices
Price (as of 9/30/2019)	36.82
52-Week High	37.03
52-Week Low	28.29

Total Returns (%)
3-Month	6-Month	1-Year	3-Year	5-Year
5.24	11.32	19.78	46.03	

3-Year Standard Deviation	
Effective Duration	

Valuation
Premium/Discount (1-Year Average)	-0.03

Company Information
Provider	Innovator ETFs
Manager/Tenure	Anand Desai (1), Dustin Lewellyn (1), Ernesto Tong (1)
Website	http://innovatoretfs.com/
Address	Innovator ETFs 120 N Hale Street, Suite 200 Wheaton IL 60187 United States
Phone Number	800-208-5212

PERFORMANCE

Ratings History
Date	Overall Rating	Risk Rating	Reward Rating
Q3-19	C	C-	C
Q4-18	C-	D+	C-
Q4-17	D	B	C
Q4-16	U		
Q4-15			

Asset & Performance History
Date	NAV	1-Year Total Return
2018	29.69	-7.58
2017	32.35	15.84
2016	28.38	
2015		
2014		
2013		

Total Assets: $136,194,483
Asset Allocation
Asset	%
Cash	0%
Stocks	100%
US Stocks	99%
Bonds	0%
US Bonds	0%
Other	0%

Services Offered:

Investment Strategy: The investment seeks investment results that generally correspond (before fees and expenses) to the price and yield of the Lunt Capital U.S. Large Cap Equity Rotation Index. The fund generally invests at least 80% of its net assets (including investment borrowing) in the common stocks that comprise the index. The index utilizes the index provider's proprietary relative strength methodology to rotate between the holdings of one of two sub-indices, the S&P 500 Low Volatility Index and the S&P 500 High Beta Index, that seek to identify the 100 components of the S&P 500 Index that most strongly exhibit a particular trait. The fund is non-diversified. **Top Holdings:** Coca-Cola Co   Duke Energy Corp   Exelon Corp   WEC Energy Group Inc   Republic Services Inc Class A

Global X U.S. Infrastructure Development ETF   C   HOLD

Ticker	Traded On	NAV	Total Assets ($)	Dividend Yield (TTM)	Turnover Ratio	Expense Ratio
PAVE	BATS	16.19	$135,995,441	1.05	7	0.47

Ratings

Reward	C
Risk	C-
Recent Upgrade/Downgrade	Up

Fund Information

Fund Type	Exchange Traded Funds
Category	Infrastructure Sector Equity
Sub-Category	Infrastructure
Prospectus Objective	Utility
Inception Date	Mar-17
Open to New Investments	Y

Prices

Price (as of 9/30/2019)	16.17
52-Week High	17.23
52-Week Low	12.79

Total Returns (%)

3-Month	6-Month	1-Year	3-Year	5-Year
-1.58	1.59	-4.85		

3-Year Standard Deviation	
Effective Duration	

Valuation

Premium/Discount (1-Year Average)	-0.01

Company Information

Provider	Global X Funds
Manager/Tenure	Chang Kim (2), Nam To (1), Wayne Xie (0), 1 other
Website	http://www.globalxfunds.com
Address	Global X Funds 600 Lexington Avenue, 20th Floor New York NY 10022 United States
Phone Number	888-493-8631

PERFORMANCE

Ratings History

Date	Overall Rating	Risk Rating	Reward Rating
Q3-19	C	C-	C
Q4-18	C	C-	C
Q4-17	U		
Q4-16			
Q4-15			

Asset & Performance History

Date	NAV	1-Year Total Return
2018	13.5	-18.62
2017	16.72	
2016		
2015		
2014		
2013		

Total Assets: $135,995,441

Asset Allocation

Asset	%
Cash	0%
Stocks	100%
US Stocks	100%
Bonds	0%
US Bonds	0%
Other	0%

Services Offered:

Investment Strategy: The investment seeks to provide investment results that correspond generally to the price and yield performance, of the Indxx U.S. Infrastructure Development Index. The fund invests at least 80% of its total assets in the securities of the underlying index. The underlying index is designed to measure the performance of U.S. listed companies that provide exposure to domestic infrastructure development, including companies involved in construction and engineering; production of infrastructure raw materials, composites and products; industrial transportation; and producers/distributors of heavy construction equipment. It is non-diversified. **Top Holdings:** Vulcan Materials Co   Martin Marietta Materials Inc   Eaton Corp PLC   Kansas City Southern   Jacobs Engineering Group Inc

---

ProShares UltraShort Euro   C+   HOLD

Ticker	Traded On	NAV	Total Assets ($)	Dividend Yield (TTM)	Turnover Ratio	Expense Ratio
EUO	NYSE Arca		$135,893,180	0	0	0.95

Ratings

Reward	C+
Risk	C-
Recent Upgrade/Downgrade	

Fund Information

Fund Type	Exchange Traded Funds
Category	Trading Tools
Sub-Category	Trading--Miscellaneous
Prospectus Objective	Worldwide Bond
Inception Date	Nov-08
Open to New Investments	Y

Prices

Price (as of 9/30/2019)	28.03
52-Week High	28.03
52-Week Low	23.39

Total Returns (%)

3-Month	6-Month	1-Year	3-Year	5-Year
7.89	8.14	18.62	16.91	39.15

3-Year Standard Deviation	12.79
Effective Duration	

Valuation

Premium/Discount (1-Year Average)	-0.06

Company Information

Provider	ProShares
Manager/Tenure	Management Team (10)
Website	http://www.proshares.com
Address	ProShares 7501 Wisconsin Avenue, Suite 1000 Bethesda MD 20814 United States
Phone Number	866-776-5125

PERFORMANCE

Ratings History

Date	Overall Rating	Risk Rating	Reward Rating
Q3-19	C+	C-	C+
Q4-18	C	C	D+
Q4-17	D	D	D
Q4-16	B	C+	B-
Q4-15	C+	C	C

Asset & Performance History

Date	NAV	1-Year Total Return
2018	24.27	14.6
2017	21.21	-21.68
2016	27.09	6.04
2015	25.54	18.27
2014	21.59	26.57
2013	17.06	-10.28

Total Assets: $135,893,180

Asset Allocation

Asset	%
Cash	100%
Stocks	0%
US Stocks	0%
Bonds	0%
US Bonds	0%
Other	0%

Services Offered:

Investment Strategy: The investment seeks daily investment results, before fees and expenses, that correspond to two times the inverse (-2x) of the daily performance of the U.S. Dollar price of the Euro. The fund seeks to meet its investment objective, under normal market conditions, by obtaining short exposures to its benchmark through futures contracts on its underlying currency. It will not invest directly in any currency. **Top Holdings:**

Invesco India ETF   D+   SELL

Ticker	Traded On	NAV	Total Assets ($)	Dividend Yield (TTM)	Turnover Ratio	Expense Ratio
PIN	NYSE Arca	24.22	$135,606,379	1.14	27	0.82

Ratings

Reward	D+
Risk	C-
Recent Upgrade/Downgrade	Down

Fund Information

Fund Type	Exchange Traded Funds
Category	India Equity
Sub-Category	India Equity
Prospectus Objective	Foreign Stock
Inception Date	Mar-08
Open to New Investments	Y

Prices

Price (as of 9/30/2019)	24.22
52-Week High	25.96
52-Week Low	21.45

Total Returns (%)

3-Month	6-Month	1-Year	3-Year	5-Year
-4.94	-5.09	1.83	19.68	16.84

3-Year Standard Deviation	15.86
Effective Duration	

Valuation

Premium/Discount (1-Year Average)	-0.20

Company Information

Provider	Invesco
Manager/Tenure	Peter Hubbard (11), Michael Jeanette (4), Tony Seisser (4)
Website	http://www.invesco.com/us
Address	Invesco 11 Greenway Plaza, Ste. 2500 Houston TX 77046 United States
Phone Number	800-659-1005

PERFORMANCE

Ratings History

Date	Overall Rating	Risk Rating	Reward Rating
Q3-19	D+	C-	D+
Q4-18	D+	C-	D+
Q4-17	B-	C	B
Q4-16	C	C	C
Q4-15	C	C+	C

Asset & Performance History

Date	NAV	1-Year Total Return
2018	24.08	-8.09
2017	26.46	37.11
2016	19.52	0.11
2015	19.73	-5.91
2014	21.09	21.89
2013	17.48	-4.14

Total Assets: $135,606,379

Asset Allocation

Asset	%
Cash	0%
Stocks	100%
US Stocks	0%
Bonds	0%
US Bonds	0%
Other	0%

Services Offered:

Investment Strategy: The investment seeks to track the investment results (before fees and expenses) of the FTSE India Quality and Yield Select Index (the "underlying index"). The fund seeks to achieve its investment objective by investing at least 90% of its total assets in the securities that comprise the underlying index, as well as ADRs and GDRs that represent securities in the underlying index. The underlying index is a modified-market capitalization-weighted index of equity securities that are traded on the National Stock Exchange of India. The fund is non-diversified. **Top Holdings:** Reliance Industries Ltd Infosys Ltd Housing Development Finance Corp Ltd Hindustan Unilever Ltd Axis Bank Ltd

PIMCO RAFI Dynamic Multi-Factor U.S. Equity ETF   C-   HOLD

Ticker	Traded On	NAV	Total Assets ($)	Dividend Yield (TTM)	Turnover Ratio	Expense Ratio
MFUS	NYSE Arca	29.99	$135,575,420	1.95	40	0.29

Ratings

Reward	C-
Risk	C-
Recent Upgrade/Downgrade	Up

Fund Information

Fund Type	Exchange Traded Funds
Category	US Equity Large Cap Blend
Sub-Category	Large Blend
Prospectus Objective	Growth & Inc
Inception Date	Aug-17
Open to New Investments	Y

Prices

Price (as of 9/30/2019)	30.03
52-Week High	30.13
52-Week Low	24.14

Total Returns (%)

3-Month	6-Month	1-Year	3-Year	5-Year
2.63	5.88	2.20		

3-Year Standard Deviation	
Effective Duration	

Valuation

Premium/Discount (1-Year Average)	0.09

Company Information

Provider	PIMCO
Manager/Tenure	Thomas C. Seto (2)
Website	http://www.pimco.com
Address	PIMCO 840 Newport Center Drive, Suite 100 Newport Beach CA 92660 United States
Phone Number	866-746-2602

PERFORMANCE

Ratings History

Date	Overall Rating	Risk Rating	Reward Rating
Q3-19	C-	C-	C-
Q4-18	D+	D+	D+
Q4-17	U		
Q4-16			
Q4-15			

Asset & Performance History

Date	NAV	1-Year Total Return
2018	25.21	-6.58
2017	27.5	
2016		
2015		
2014		
2013		

Total Assets: $135,575,420

Asset Allocation

Asset	%
Cash	7%
Stocks	93%
US Stocks	92%
Bonds	0%
US Bonds	0%
Other	0%

Services Offered:

Investment Strategy: The investment seeks to track the investment results of the RAFI Dynamic Multi-Factor U.S. Index. The fund seeks to achieve its investment objective by investing at least 80% of its total assets (exclusive of collateral held from securities lending) in the component securities of the RAFI Dynamic Multi-Factor U.S. Index. The underlying index is constructed by RAFI Indices, LLC (the "index provider") using a rules-based approach to construct factor portfolios within the underlying index. The underlying index consists of "factor portfolios," each of which emphasizes one of the following factors: value, low volatility, quality, momentum and size. **Top Holdings:** Procter & Gamble Co Verizon Communications Inc Walmart Inc Johnson & Johnson Coca-Cola Co

RiverFront Dynamic Core Income ETF   C   HOLD

Ticker	Traded On	NAV	Total Assets ($)	Dividend Yield (TTM)	Turnover Ratio	Expense Ratio
RFCI	NYSE Arca	25.29	$135,308,315	2.79	15	0.53

Ratings
Reward	C+
Risk	C-
Recent Upgrade/Downgrade	Up

Fund Information
Fund Type	Exchange Traded Funds
Category	US Fixed Income
Sub-Category	Intermediate Core-Plus Bond
Prospectus Objective	Income
Inception Date	Jun-16
Open to New Investments	Y

Prices
Price (as of 9/30/2019)	25.24
52-Week High	25.49
52-Week Low	23.48

Total Returns (%)
3-Month	6-Month	1-Year	3-Year	5-Year
2.21	5.28	9.30	8.35	

3-Year Standard Deviation	3.1
Effective Duration	

Valuation
Premium/Discount (1-Year Average)	-0.01

Company Information
Provider	ALPS
Manager/Tenure	Tim Anderson (3), Rob Glownia (3)
Website	http://www.alpsfunds.com
Address	ALPS 1290 Broadway, Suite 1100 Denver CO 80203 United States
Phone Number	866-759-5679

PERFORMANCE

Ratings History

Date	Overall Rating	Risk Rating	Reward Rating
Q3-19	C	C-	C+
Q4-18	D+	C-	D+
Q4-17	D+	B-	D+
Q4-16	U		
Q4-15			

Asset & Performance History

Date	NAV	1-Year Total Return
2018	23.78	-0.76
2017	24.63	3.27
2016	24.34	
2015		
2014		
2013		

Total Assets: $135,308,315

Asset Allocation

Asset	%
Cash	15%
Stocks	0%
US Stocks	0%
Bonds	84%
US Bonds	76%
Other	0%

Services Offered:

Investment Strategy: The investment seeks total return, with an emphasis on income as the source of that total return. The fund invests in a global portfolio of fixed income securities of various maturities, ratings and currency denominations. It may purchase fixed income securities issued by U.S. or foreign corporations or financial institutions, including debt securities of all types and maturities, convertible securities and preferred stocks. The fund is non-diversified. **Top Holdings:** United States Treasury Notes 2.75% United States Treasury Notes 3% United States Treasury Notes 2.88% U.S. Treasury Bond Stripped Principal Payment 0% U.S. Treasury Bond Stripped Principal Payment 0%

ProShares Ultra MidCap400   C-   HOLD

Ticker	Traded On	NAV	Total Assets ($)	Dividend Yield (TTM)	Turnover Ratio	Expense Ratio
MVV	NYSE Arca	39.95	$134,822,137	0.68	31	0.95

Ratings
Reward	C
Risk	C-
Recent Upgrade/Downgrade	Down

Fund Information
Fund Type	Exchange Traded Funds
Category	Trading Tools
Sub-Category	Trading--Leveraged Equity
Prospectus Objective	Growth
Inception Date	Jun-06
Open to New Investments	Y

Prices
Price (as of 9/30/2019)	39.95
52-Week High	44.78
52-Week Low	27.06

Total Returns (%)
3-Month	6-Month	1-Year	3-Year	5-Year
-2.51	-0.12	-10.10	47.30	91.18

3-Year Standard Deviation	30.58
Effective Duration	

Valuation
Premium/Discount (1-Year Average)	0.07

Company Information
Provider	ProShares
Manager/Tenure	Michael Neches (6), Devin Sullivan (1)
Website	http://www.proshares.com
Address	ProShares 7501 Wisconsin Avenue, Suite 1000 Bethesda MD 20814 United States
Phone Number	866-776-5125

PERFORMANCE

Ratings History

Date	Overall Rating	Risk Rating	Reward Rating
Q3-19	C-	C-	C
Q4-18	C	C	C
Q4-17	B+	C+	A+
Q4-16	C	C-	C
Q4-15	C	C+	C

Asset & Performance History

Date	NAV	1-Year Total Return
2018	30.3	-25.65
2017	40.97	30.7
2016	31.42	39.86
2015	22.57	-7.81
2014	24.53	15.91
2013	21.16	71.39

Total Assets: $134,822,137

Asset Allocation

Asset	%
Cash	-100%
Stocks	200%
US Stocks	200%
Bonds	0%
US Bonds	0%
Other	0%

Services Offered:

Investment Strategy: The investment seeks daily investment results, before fees and expenses, that correspond to two times (2x) the daily performance of the S&P MidCap 400®. The fund invests in financial instruments that ProShare Advisors believes, in combination, should produce daily returns consistent with the fund's investment objective. The index is a float-adjusted, market capitalization-weighted index of 400 U.S. operating companies and real estate investment trusts selected through a process that factors in criteria such as liquidity, price, market capitalization and financial viability. The fund is non-diversified. **Top Holdings:** S&P Midcap 400 Index Swap Ubs Ag S&P Midcap 400 Index Swap Societe Generale S&P Midcap 400 Index Swap Goldman Sachs International Spdr S&P Midcap 400 (Mdy) Swap Goldman Sachs International S&P Midcap 400 Index Swap Credit Suisse International

Invesco BulletShares 2026 Corporate Bond ETF   C   HOLD

Ticker	Traded On	NAV	Total Assets ($)	Dividend Yield (TTM)	Turnover Ratio	Expense Ratio
BSCQ	NYSE Arca	20.41	$134,705,264	3.24	0	0.1

Ratings
Reward   C
Risk   C-
Recent Upgrade/Downgrade

Fund Information
Fund Type	Exchange Traded Funds
Category	US Fixed Income
Sub-Category	Target Maturity
Prospectus Objective	Corp Bond - Gen
Inception Date	Sep-16
Open to New Investments	Y

Prices
Price (as of 9/30/2019)	20.45
52-Week High	20.67
52-Week Low	18.38

Total Returns (%)
3-Month	6-Month	1-Year	3-Year	5-Year
2.41	6.76	13.14	11.36	

3-Year Standard Deviation	4.38
Effective Duration	6.03

Valuation
Premium/Discount (1-Year Average)	0.26

Company Information
Provider	Invesco
Manager/Tenure	Jeremy Neisewander (3), Peter Hubbard (1), Jeffrey W. Kernagis (1), 1 other
Website	http://www.invesco.com/us
Address	Invesco 11 Greenway Plaza, Ste. 2500 Houston TX 77046 United States
Phone Number	800-659-1005

PERFORMANCE

Ratings History

Date	Overall Rating	Risk Rating	Reward Rating
Q3-19	C	C-	C
Q4-18	D+	C-	D+
Q4-17	D	B	D+
Q4-16	U		
Q4-15			

Asset & Performance History

Date	NAV	1-Year Total Return
2018	18.55	-2.38
2017	19.64	5.51
2016	19.15	
2015		
2014		
2013		

Total Assets: $134,705,264
Asset Allocation

Asset	%
Cash	0%
Stocks	0%
US Stocks	0%
Bonds	100%
US Bonds	88%
Other	0%

Services Offered:

Investment Strategy: The investment seeks to track the investment results (before fees and expenses) of the Nasdaq BulletShares® USD Corporate Bond 2026 Index (the "underlying index"). The fund generally will invest at least 80% of its total assets in securities that comprise the underlying index. The underlying index seeks to measure the performance of a portfolio of U.S. dollar-denominated investment grade corporate bonds with maturities or, in some cases, "effective maturities" in the year 2026 (collectively, "2026 Bonds"). The fund is non-diversified. **Top Holdings:** Anheuser-Busch InBev Finance Inc. 3.65% Microsoft Corporation 2.4% Wells Fargo & Company 3% Wells Fargo & Company 3% Apple Inc. 3.25%

iShares MSCI Europe Small-Cap ETF   D+   SELL

Ticker	Traded On	NAV	Total Assets ($)	Dividend Yield (TTM)	Turnover Ratio	Expense Ratio
IEUS	NAS CM	48.92	$134,524,528	4.49	17	0.4

Ratings
Reward   D+
Risk   C-
Recent Upgrade/Downgrade   Down

Fund Information
Fund Type	Exchange Traded Funds
Category	Europe Equity Large Cap
Sub-Category	Europe Stock
Prospectus Objective	Small Company
Inception Date	Nov-07
Open to New Investments	Y

Prices
Price (as of 9/30/2019)	48.74
52-Week High	55.55
52-Week Low	43.21

Total Returns (%)
3-Month	6-Month	1-Year	3-Year	5-Year
-3.09	-1.34	-8.03	18.03	32.63

3-Year Standard Deviation	14.18
Effective Duration	

Valuation
Premium/Discount (1-Year Average)	-0.29

Company Information
Provider	iShares
Manager/Tenure	Diane Hsiung (11), Greg Savage (11), Jennifer Hsui (6), 3 others
Website	http://www.ishares.com
Address	iShares 400 Howard Street San Francisco CA 94105 United States
Phone Number	800-474-2737

PERFORMANCE

Ratings History

Date	Overall Rating	Risk Rating	Reward Rating
Q3-19	D+	C-	D+
Q4-18	D+	C-	D+
Q4-17	B+	B	A-
Q4-16	C-	C-	C
Q4-15	C	D+	C

Asset & Performance History

Date	NAV	1-Year Total Return
2018	45.12	-19.82
2017	57.85	35.27
2016	43.75	-1.78
2015	45.64	10.85
2014	42.01	-3.04
2013	44.32	27.34

Total Assets: $134,524,528
Asset Allocation

Asset	%
Cash	0%
Stocks	98%
US Stocks	3%
Bonds	0%
US Bonds	0%
Other	1%

Services Offered:

Investment Strategy: The investment seeks to track the investment results of the MSCI Europe Small Cap Index composed of small-capitalization developed market equities in Europe. The fund generally will invest at least 90% of its assets in the component securities of the underlying index and in investments that have economic characteristics that are substantially identical to the component securities of the underlying index. The index is a free float-adjusted, market capitalization-weighted index that captures small-capitalization representation across the 15 developed market countries in Europe. **Top Holdings:** LEG Immobilien AG Galapagos NV Logitech International SA Scout24 AG Just Eat PLC

iShares Fallen Angels USD Bond ETF   C   HOLD

Ticker	Traded On	NAV	Total Assets ($)	Dividend Yield (TTM)	Turnover Ratio	Expense Ratio
FALN	NAS CM	26.54	$134,019,178	5.66	29	0.25

Ratings

Reward	C+
Risk	C-
Recent Upgrade/Downgrade	

Fund Information

Fund Type	Exchange Traded Funds
Category	US Fixed Income
Sub-Category	High Yield Bond
Prospectus Objective	Corp Bond-High Yld
Inception Date	Jun-16
Open to New Investments	Y

Prices

Price (as of 9/30/2019)	26.77
52-Week High	26.99
52-Week Low	24.12

Total Returns (%)

3-Month	6-Month	1-Year	3-Year	5-Year
1.39	4.18	5.92	20.05	

3-Year Standard Deviation	4.84
Effective Duration	

Valuation

Premium/Discount (1-Year Average)	0.43

Company Information

Provider	iShares
Manager/Tenure	James Mauro (3), Scott Radell (3)
Website	http://www.ishares.com
Address	iShares 400 Howard Street San Francisco CA 94105 United States
Phone Number	800-474-2737

PERFORMANCE

Ratings History

Date	Overall Rating	Risk Rating	Reward Rating
Q3-19	C	C-	C+
Q4-18	C-	C-	C-
Q4-17	D+	A-	C-
Q4-16	U		
Q4-15			

Asset & Performance History

Date	NAV	1-Year Total Return
2018	24.47	-4.36
2017	27.05	8.88
2016	26.54	
2015		
2014		
2013		

Total Assets: $134,019,178

Asset Allocation

Asset	%
Cash	2%
Stocks	1%
US Stocks	0%
Bonds	97%
US Bonds	78%
Other	0%

Services Offered:

Investment Strategy: The investment seeks to track the investment results of the Bloomberg Barclays US High Yield Fallen Angel 3% Capped Index composed of U.S. dollar-denominated, high yield corporate bonds that were previously rated investment grade. The fund generally will invest at least 90% of its assets in the component securities of the index and may invest up to 10% of its assets in certain futures, options and swap contracts, cash and cash equivalents. The index is designed to reflect the performance of U.S. dollar denominated, high yield corporate bonds that were previously rated investment grade. **Top Holdings:** Intesa Sanpaolo S.p.A. 5.02% Sprint Capital Corporation 6.88% Deutsche Bank AG New York Branch 4.3% Sprint Capital Corporation 8.75% Deutsche Bank AG New York Branch 4.5%

Knowledge Leaders Developed World ETF   C-   HOLD

Ticker	Traded On	NAV	Total Assets ($)	Dividend Yield (TTM)	Turnover Ratio	Expense Ratio
KLDW	NYSE Arca	33.70	$133,117,622	0.85	18	0.75

Ratings

Reward	C
Risk	C-
Recent Upgrade/Downgrade	

Fund Information

Fund Type	Exchange Traded Funds
Category	Global Equity Large Cap
Sub-Category	World Large Stock
Prospectus Objective	Growth & Inc
Inception Date	Jul-15
Open to New Investments	Y

Prices

Price (as of 9/30/2019)	33.74
52-Week High	35.01
52-Week Low	27.85

Total Returns (%)

3-Month	6-Month	1-Year	3-Year	5-Year
-0.08	1.78	-2.32	26.66	

3-Year Standard Deviation	12.01
Effective Duration	

Valuation

Premium/Discount (1-Year Average)	-0.05

Company Information

Provider	Knowledge Leaders Capital
Manager/Tenure	Andrew Serowik (0), Travis E. Trampe (0)
Website	http://www.knowledgeleadersfunds.com
Address	Knowledge Leaders Capital 370 17th Street, Suite 4930 Denver CO 80202 United States

PERFORMANCE

Ratings History

Date	Overall Rating	Risk Rating	Reward Rating
Q3-19	C-	C-	C
Q4-18	C-	C-	C-
Q4-17	C	B+	C+
Q4-16	D	D+	D+
Q4-15	U		

Asset & Performance History

Date	NAV	1-Year Total Return
2018	29.26	-11.43
2017	33.37	27.61
2016	26.33	7.04
2015	24.76	
2014		
2013		

Total Assets: $133,117,622

Asset Allocation

Asset	%
Cash	0%
Stocks	100%
US Stocks	32%
Bonds	0%
US Bonds	0%
Other	0%

Services Offered:

Investment Strategy: The investment seeks to provide investment results that, before fees and expenses, correspond generally to the total return performance of the Knowledge Leaders Developed World Index. The fund will normally invest at least 80% of its total assets in securities of the index. The index is designed to measure the performance of issuers in developed markets countries that are considered to be "Knowledge Leaders," as defined and determined by the index provider, based on a proprietary selection model developed by the index provider and incorporated into the index methodology. The fund is non-diversified. **Top Holdings:** Daiichi Sankyo Co Ltd Nomura Research Institute Ltd Hitachi High-Technologies Corp Shin-Etsu Chemical Co Ltd Synopsys Inc

First Trust Horizon Managed Volatility Developed International ETF

C HOLD

Ticker	Traded On	NAV		Total Assets ($)	Dividend Yield (TTM)	Turnover Ratio	Expense Ratio
HDMV	NYSE Arca	33.21		$132,844,025	2.86	99	0.8

Ratings

Reward	C
Risk	C-
Recent Upgrade/Downgrade	

Fund Information

Fund Type	Exchange Traded Funds
Category	Global Equity Large Cap
Sub-Category	Foreign Large Blend
Prospectus Objective	Growth
Inception Date	Aug-16
Open to New Investments	Y

Prices

Price (as of 9/30/2019)	33.28
52-Week High	34.35
52-Week Low	29.97

Total Returns (%)

3-Month	6-Month	1-Year	3-Year	5-Year
-0.68	1.95	2.71	21.20	

3-Year Standard Deviation	9.32
Effective Duration	

Valuation

Premium/Discount (1-Year Average)	0.44

Company Information

Provider	First Trust
Manager/Tenure	Steven Clark (3), Michael Dickson (3), Scott E. Ladner (3)
Website	http://www.ftportfolios.com/
Address	First Trust 120 E. Liberty Drive, Suite 400 Wheaton IL 60187 United States
Phone Number	800-621-1675

PERFORMANCE

Ratings History

Date	Overall Rating	Risk Rating	Reward Rating
Q3-19	C	C-	C
Q4-18	D+	D+	D+
Q4-17	D	B-	C
Q4-16	U		
Q4-15			

Asset & Performance History

Date	NAV	1-Year Total Return
2018	30.81	-7.69
2017	34.15	27.17
2016	27.78	
2015		
2014		
2013		

Total Assets: $132,844,025

Asset Allocation

Asset	%
Cash	1%
Stocks	99%
US Stocks	1%
Bonds	0%
US Bonds	0%
Other	0%

Services Offered:

Investment Strategy: The investment seeks to provide capital appreciation. Under normal market conditions, the fund seeks to achieve its investment objective by investing at least 80% of its net assets (including investment borrowings) in common stocks and depositary receipts of developed market companies listed and traded on non-U.S. exchanges that the Sub-Advisor believes exhibit low future expected volatility. Under normal market conditions, it will invest in at least three countries and at least 40% of its net assets in countries other than the United States. It is non-diversified. **Top Holdings:** Deutsche Telekom AG Swisscom AG Swiss Prime Site AG Nestle SA Singapore Airlines Ltd

---

First Trust Emerging Markets Small Cap AlphaDEX® Fund

C- HOLD

Ticker	Traded On	NAV		Total Assets ($)	Dividend Yield (TTM)	Turnover Ratio	Expense Ratio
FEMS	NAS CM	34.43		$132,550,121	4.35	126	0.8

Ratings

Reward	C-
Risk	C-
Recent Upgrade/Downgrade	

Fund Information

Fund Type	Exchange Traded Funds
Category	Global Emerg Mkts Equity
Sub-Category	Diversified Emerging Mkts
Prospectus Objective	Div Emerg Mkts
Inception Date	Feb-12
Open to New Investments	Y

Prices

Price (as of 9/30/2019)	34.07
52-Week High	36.82
52-Week Low	31.64

Total Returns (%)

3-Month	6-Month	1-Year	3-Year	5-Year
-1.54	-1.90	-1.37	18.10	13.87

3-Year Standard Deviation	16.87
Effective Duration	

Valuation

Premium/Discount (1-Year Average)	-0.58

Company Information

Provider	First Trust
Manager/Tenure	Jon C. Erickson (7), Daniel J. Lindquist (7), David G. McGarel (7), 3 others
Website	http://www.ftportfolios.com/
Address	First Trust 120 E. Liberty Drive, Suite 400 Wheaton IL 60187 United States
Phone Number	800-621-1675

PERFORMANCE

Ratings History

Date	Overall Rating	Risk Rating	Reward Rating
Q3-19	C-	C-	C-
Q4-18	C-	D+	C-
Q4-17	B	C+	B+
Q4-16	C-	C-	C-
Q4-15	C-	C-	C-

Asset & Performance History

Date	NAV	1-Year Total Return
2018	32.45	-21.47
2017	43.02	46.6
2016	30.42	13.53
2015	27.43	-13.41
2014	32.64	-4.91
2013	35.44	5.65

Total Assets: $132,550,121

Asset Allocation

Asset	%
Cash	2%
Stocks	98%
US Stocks	0%
Bonds	0%
US Bonds	0%
Other	0%

Services Offered:

Investment Strategy: The investment seeks investment results that correspond generally to the price and yield (before the fund's fees and expenses) of an equity index called the NASDAQ AlphaDEX® Emerging Markets Small Cap Index. The fund will normally invest at least 90% of its net assets (including investment borrowings) in the common stocks and depositary receipts that comprise the index. The index is designed to select stocks from the NASDAQ Emerging Markets Index (the "base index") that may generate positive alpha, or risk-adjusted returns, relative to traditional indices through the use of the AlphaDEX® selection methodology. **Top Holdings:** Pegasus Hava Tasimaciligi AS Kasen International Holdings Ltd Taiwan Surface Mounting Technology Corp Bosideng International Holdings Ltd Cia Paranaense De Energia Copel Participating Preferred

Fidelity® Corporate Bond ETF

C HOLD

Ticker	Traded On	NAV	Total Assets ($)	Dividend Yield (TTM)	Turnover Ratio	Expense Ratio
FCOR	NYSE Arca	52.82	$132,048,761	3.23	81	0.36

Ratings
Reward **B-**
Risk **C-**
Recent Upgrade/Downgrade

Fund Information
Fund Type	Exchange Traded Funds
Category	US Fixed Income
Sub-Category	Corporate Bond
Prospectus Objective	Corp Bond - Gen
Inception Date	Oct-14
Open to New Investments	Y

Prices
Price (as of 9/30/2019)	53.00
52-Week High	53.63
52-Week Low	47.14

Total Returns (%)
3-Month	6-Month	1-Year	3-Year	5-Year
2.94	7.97	12.93	13.91	24.11

3-Year Standard Deviation 4.13
Effective Duration 7.49

Valuation
Premium/Discount (1-Year Average) 0.19

Company Information
Provider	Fidelity Investments
Manager/Tenure	Michael Plage (4), David Prothro (4), Matthew Bartlett (2)
Website	http://www.institutional.fidelity.com
Address	Fidelity Investments 82 Devonshire Street Boston MA 2109 United States
Phone Number	617-563-7000

PERFORMANCE

Ratings History
Date	Overall Rating	Risk Rating	Reward Rating
Q3-19	C	C-	B-
Q4-18	D+	D+	D+
Q4-17	C+	B	C
Q4-16	D+	D+	D+
Q4-15	U		

Asset & Performance History
Date	NAV	1-Year Total Return
2018	47.57	-2.92
2017	50.79	5.99
2016	49.3	7.52
2015	47.26	-2.24
2014	50.16	
2013		

Total Assets: $132,048,761

Asset Allocation
Asset	%
Cash	3%
Stocks	0%
US Stocks	0%
Bonds	94%
US Bonds	81%
Other	0%

Services Offered:

Investment Strategy: The investment seeks a high level of current income. Normally, the fund invests at least 80% of its assets in investment-grade corporate bonds and other corporate debt securities and repurchase agreements for those securities. It is managed to have similar overall interest rate risk to the Bloomberg Barclays U.S. Credit Bond Index. The fund invests in lower-quality debt securities. **Top Holdings:** United States Treasury Bonds 2.5% Bank of America Corporation 2.82% Micron Technology Inc. 4.64% CLECO CORPORATE HOLDINGS LLC 3.74% Park Aerospace Holdings Limited 5.25%

JPMorgan Diversified Return U.S. Small Cap Equity ETF

C HOLD

Ticker	Traded On	NAV	Total Assets ($)	Dividend Yield (TTM)	Turnover Ratio	Expense Ratio
JPSE	NYSE Arca	30.29	$131,767,234	1.25	30	0.29

Ratings
Reward **C-**
Risk **C+**
Recent Upgrade/Downgrade

Fund Information
Fund Type	Exchange Traded Funds
Category	US Equity Small Cap
Sub-Category	Small Blend
Prospectus Objective	Small Company
Inception Date	Nov-16
Open to New Investments	Y

Prices
Price (as of 9/30/2019)	30.30
52-Week High	32.29
52-Week Low	25.38

Total Returns (%)
3-Month	6-Month	1-Year	3-Year	5-Year
-1.61	-0.26	-4.62		

3-Year Standard Deviation
Effective Duration

Valuation
Premium/Discount (1-Year Average) 0.04

Company Information
Provider	JPMorgan
Manager/Tenure	Jonathan Msika (2), Yazann Romahi (2), Joe Staines (2), 1 other
Website	http://www.jpmorganfunds.com
Address	JPMorgan 270 Park Avenue New York NY 10017-2070 United States
Phone Number	800-480-4111

PERFORMANCE

Ratings History
Date	Overall Rating	Risk Rating	Reward Rating
Q3-19	C	C+	C-
Q4-18	D+	C-	D+
Q4-17	D	B+	D+
Q4-16	U		
Q4-15			

Asset & Performance History
Date	NAV	1-Year Total Return
2018	26.89	-8.13
2017	29.59	14.38
2016	26.06	
2015		
2014		
2013		

Total Assets: $131,767,234

Asset Allocation
Asset	%
Cash	1%
Stocks	99%
US Stocks	98%
Bonds	0%
US Bonds	0%
Other	0%

Services Offered:

Investment Strategy: The investment seeks investment results that closely correspond, before fees and expenses, to the performance of the JP Morgan Diversified Factor US Small Cap Equity Index. The fund will invest at least 80% of its assets in securities included in the underlying index. "Assets" means net assets, plus the amount of borrowing for investment purposes. The underlying index is comprised of U.S. equity securities selected to represent a diversified set of factor characteristics. The rules based proprietary multi-factor selection process utilizes the following characteristics: value, momentum and quality. **Top Holdings:** El Paso Electric Co Ormat Technologies Inc American States Water Co Fox Factory Holding Corp California Water Service Group

First Trust Switzerland AlphaDEX® Fund   C-   HOLD

Ticker	Traded On	NAV	Total Assets ($)	Dividend Yield (TTM)	Turnover Ratio	Expense Ratio
FSZ	NAS CM	48.70	$131,494,621	2.23	65	0.8

Ratings
Reward   C
Risk   C-
Recent Upgrade/Downgrade

Fund Information
Fund Type   Exchange Traded Funds
Category   Europe Equity Large Cap
Sub-Category   Miscellaneous Region
Prospectus Objective Europe Stock
Inception Date   Feb-12
Open to New Investments   Y

Prices
Price (as of 9/30/2019)   48.65
52-Week High   51.43
52-Week Low   42.24

Total Returns (%)

3-Month	6-Month	1-Year	3-Year	5-Year
-4.31	1.77	-2.21	25.31	37.54

3-Year Standard Deviation   12.37
Effective Duration

Valuation
Premium/Discount (1-Year Average) -0.08

Company Information
Provider   First Trust
Manager/Tenure   Jon C. Erickson (7), Daniel J. Lindquist
                  (7), David G. McGarel (7), 3 others
Website   http://www.ftportfolios.com/
Address   First Trust 120 E. Liberty Drive, Suite
                  400 Wheaton IL 60187 United States
Phone Number   800-621-1675

PERFORMANCE

Ratings History

Date	Overall Rating	Risk Rating	Reward Rating
Q3-19	C-	C-	C
Q4-18	D+	C-	D+
Q4-17	B	B+	B
Q4-16	C-	D+	C
Q4-15	C-	C-	C-

Asset & Performance History

Date	NAV	1-Year Total Return
2018	43.89	-15.12
2017	52.73	31.27
2016	40.82	4.2
2015	39.97	6.01
2014	38.09	-5.04
2013	40.79	28.9

Total Assets: $131,494,621

Asset Allocation

Asset	%
Cash	0%
Stocks	100%
US Stocks	0%
Bonds	0%
US Bonds	0%
Other	0%

Services Offered:

Investment Strategy: The investment seeks investment results that correspond generally to the price and yield (before the fund's fees and expenses) of an equity index called the NASDAQ AlphaDEX® Switzerland Index. The fund will normally invest at least 90% of its net assets (including investment borrowings) in the common stocks and depositary receipts that comprise the index. The index is designed to select stocks from the NASDAQ Switzerland Index (the "base index") that may generate positive alpha, or risk-adjusted returns, relative to traditional indices through the use of the AlphaDEX® selection methodology. **Top Holdings:** BKW AG LafargeHolcim Ltd Swiss Life Holding AG The Swatch Group AG Bearer Shares Temenos AG

First Trust Dorsey Wright Momentum & Low Volatility ETF   C   HOLD

Ticker	Traded On	NAV	Total Assets ($)	Dividend Yield (TTM)	Turnover Ratio	Expense Ratio
DVOL	NAS CM	22.81	$131,168,687	1.21	0	0.6

Ratings
Reward   C
Risk   B-
Recent Upgrade/Downgrade

Fund Information
Fund Type   Exchange Traded Funds
Category   US Equity Large Cap Blend
Sub-Category   Large Blend
Prospectus Objective Growth & Inc
Inception Date   Sep-18
Open to New Investments   Y

Prices
Price (as of 9/30/2019)   22.82
52-Week High   22.91
52-Week Low   17.33

Total Returns (%)

3-Month	6-Month	1-Year	3-Year	5-Year
6.04	12.00	16.09		

3-Year Standard Deviation
Effective Duration

Valuation
Premium/Discount (1-Year Average) -0.01

Company Information
Provider   First Trust
Manager/Tenure   Jon C. Erickson (1), Daniel J. Lindquist
                  (1), David G. McGarel (1), 3 others
Website   http://www.ftportfolios.com/
Address   First Trust 120 E. Liberty Drive, Suite
                  400 Wheaton IL 60187 United States
Phone Number   800-621-1675

PERFORMANCE

Ratings History

Date	Overall Rating	Risk Rating	Reward Rating
Q3-19	C	B-	C
Q4-18	U		
Q4-17			
Q4-16			
Q4-15			

Asset & Performance History

Date	NAV	1-Year Total Return
2018	18.05	
2017		
2016		
2015		
2014		
2013		

Total Assets: $131,168,687

Asset Allocation

Asset	%
Cash	0%
Stocks	100%
US Stocks	100%
Bonds	0%
US Bonds	0%
Other	0%

Services Offered:

Investment Strategy: The investment seeks investment results that correspond generally to the price and yield (before the fund's fees and expenses) of an index called the Dorsey Wright Momentum Plus Low Volatility Index (the "index"). Under normal conditions, the fund will invest at least 90% of its net assets (including investment borrowings) in the equity securities that comprise the index. The index is a rules-based equity index designed to track the overall performance of the 50 stocks comprising the NASDAQ US Large Mid Index that exhibit the lowest levels of volatility while still maintaining high levels of "relative strength." The fund is non-diversified. **Top Holdings:** Republic Services Inc Class A Blackstone Mortgage Trust Inc A WEC Energy Group Inc Chimera Investment Corp WR Berkley Corp

Invesco DWA Industrials Momentum ETF   B   BUY

Ticker	Traded On	NAV	Total Assets ($)	Dividend Yield (TTM)	Turnover Ratio	Expense Ratio
PRN	NAS CM	65.55	$131,102,482	0.43		0.6

Ratings
Reward   B
Risk   C
Recent Upgrade/Downgrade   Up

Fund Information
Fund Type   Exchange Traded Funds
Category   Industrials Sector Equity
Sub-Category   Industrials
Prospectus Objective   Unaligned
Inception Date   Oct-06
Open to New Investments   Y

Prices
Price (as of 9/30/2019)   65.57
52-Week High   69.69
52-Week Low   47.61

Total Returns (%)
3-Month	6-Month	1-Year	3-Year	5-Year
-2.06	5.76	2.98	37.24	50.48

3-Year Standard Deviation   16.06
Effective Duration

Valuation
Premium/Discount (1-Year Average)   -0.15

Company Information
Provider   Invesco
Manager/Tenure   Peter Hubbard (12), Michael Jeanette (11), Tony Seisser (5)
Website   http://www.invesco.com/us
Address   Invesco 11 Greenway Plaza, Ste. 2500 Houston TX 77046 United States
Phone Number   800-659-1005

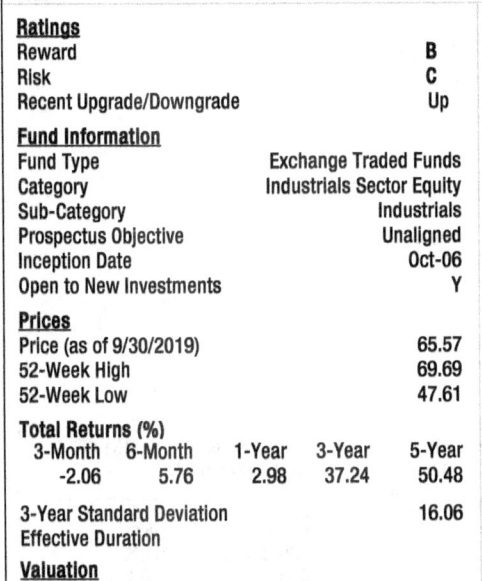

PERFORMANCE

Ratings History
Date	Overall Rating	Risk Rating	Reward Rating
Q3-19	B	C	B
Q4-18	C	C-	C
Q4-17	B	B	B+
Q4-16	C	C-	B-
Q4-15	C+	C	B-

Asset & Performance History
Date	NAV	1-Year Total Return
2018	51.22	-15.54
2017	60.81	22.48
2016	49.97	13.05
2015	44.46	-5.7
2014	47.35	-0.42
2013	47.72	48.82

Total Assets: $131,102,482
Asset Allocation
Asset	%
Cash	0%
Stocks	100%
US Stocks	100%
Bonds	0%
US Bonds	0%
Other	0%

Services Offered:

Investment Strategy: The investment seeks to track the investment results (before fees and expenses) of the Dorsey Wright® Industrials Technical Leaders Index (the "underlying index"). The fund generally will invest at least 90% of its total assets in the securities that comprise the underlying index. The underlying index is composed of at least 30 securities of companies in the industrials sector that have powerful relative strength or "momentum" characteristics. **Top Holdings:** Heico Corp TransDigm Group Inc Sherwin-Williams Co Lockheed Martin Corp Fair Isaac Corp

---

Goldman Sachs JUST U.S. Large Cap Equity ETF   C-   HOLD

Ticker	Traded On	NAV	Total Assets ($)	Dividend Yield (TTM)	Turnover Ratio	Expense Ratio
JUST	NYSE Arca	42.63	$131,073,896	2.03	2	0.2

Ratings
Reward   C
Risk   D+
Recent Upgrade/Downgrade   Up

Fund Information
Fund Type   Exchange Traded Funds
Category   US Equity Large Cap Blend
Sub-Category   Large Blend
Prospectus Objective   Growth & Inc
Inception Date   Jun-18
Open to New Investments   Y

Prices
Price (as of 9/30/2019)   42.65
52-Week High   43.44
52-Week Low   33.79

Total Returns (%)
3-Month	6-Month	1-Year	3-Year	5-Year
0.92	5.03	3.09		

3-Year Standard Deviation
Effective Duration

Valuation
Premium/Discount (1-Year Average)   0.01

Company Information
Provider   Goldman Sachs
Manager/Tenure   Raj Garigipati (1), Jamie McGregor (1)
Website   http://www.gsamfunds.com
Address   Goldman Sachs 200 West Stree New York NY 10282 United States
Phone Number   800-526-7384

PERFORMANCE

Ratings History
Date	Overall Rating	Risk Rating	Reward Rating
Q3-19	C-	D+	C
Q4-18	U		
Q4-17			
Q4-16			
Q4-15			

Asset & Performance History
Date	NAV	1-Year Total Return
2018	35.94	
2017		
2016		
2015		
2014		
2013		

Total Assets: $131,073,896
Asset Allocation
Asset	%
Cash	0%
Stocks	100%
US Stocks	100%
Bonds	0%
US Bonds	0%
Other	0%

Services Offered:

Investment Strategy: The investment seeks to provide investment results that closely correspond, before fees and expenses, to the performance of the JUST US Large Cap Diversified Index. The fund seeks to achieve its investment objective by investing at least 80% of its assets in securities included in its underlying index, in depositary receipts representing securities included in its underlying index and in underlying stocks in respect of depositary receipts included in its underlying index. The index is designed to deliver exposure to equity securities of large capitalization U.S. issuers that engage in "just business behavior" based on rankings produced by the index provider. **Top Holdings:** Microsoft Corp Apple Inc Amazon.com Inc JPMorgan Chase & Co Facebook Inc A

VictoryShares Dividend Accelerator ETF   C   HOLD

Ticker	Traded On	NAV	Total Assets ($)	Dividend Yield (TTM)	Turnover Ratio	Expense Ratio
VSDA	NAS CM	34.04	$131,037,070	1.42	62	0.35

Ratings
Reward   C+
Risk   C-
Recent Upgrade/Downgrade

Fund Information
Fund Type   Exchange Traded Funds
Category   US Equity Large Cap Value
Sub-Category   Large Blend
Prospectus Objective   Equity-Income
Inception Date   Apr-17
Open to New Investments   Y

Prices
Price (as of 9/30/2019)   34.07
52-Week High   34.66
52-Week Low   26.21

Total Returns (%)

3-Month	6-Month	1-Year	3-Year	5-Year
3.32	7.80	11.47		

3-Year Standard Deviation
Effective Duration

Valuation
Premium/Discount (1-Year Average)   -0.05

Company Information
Provider   VictoryShares
Manager/Tenure   Mannik Dhillon (2)
Website   http://www.VictorySharesLiterature.com
Address   Victory Shares 4249 Easton Way,
                    Suite 400 Columbus OH 43219 United
                    States
Phone Number

PERFORMANCE

Ratings History

Date	Overall Rating	Risk Rating	Reward Rating
Q3-19	C	C-	C+
Q4-18	C-	C-	C-
Q4-17	U		
Q4-16			
Q4-15			

Asset & Performance History

Date	NAV	1-Year Total Return
2018	27.68	-0.69
2017	28.33	
2016		
2015		
2014		
2013		

Total Assets: $131,037,070

Asset Allocation

Asset	%
Cash	0%
Stocks	100%
US Stocks	100%
Bonds	0%
US Bonds	0%
Other	0%

Services Offered:

Investment Strategy: The investment seeks to provide investment results that track the performance of the Nasdaq Victory Dividend Accelerator Index before fees and expenses. The fund seeks to achieve its investment objective by investing, under normal market conditions, at least 80% of its assets in securities included in the Nasdaq Victory Dividend Accelerator Index (the "index"). The index utilizes a rules-based approach designed to identify dividend paying stocks with a higher likelihood of future dividend growth. **Top Holdings:** Raytheon Co Paychex Inc Morningstar Inc Target Corp Procter & Gamble Co

Invesco DB Precious Metals Fund   C   HOLD

Ticker	Traded On	NAV	Total Assets ($)	Dividend Yield (TTM)	Turnover Ratio	Expense Ratio
DBP	NYSE Arca	40.78	$130,498,451	1.1		0.75

Ratings
Reward   C
Risk   C-
Recent Upgrade/Downgrade   Up

Fund Information
Fund Type   Exchange Traded Funds
Category   Commodities Specified
Sub-Category   Commodities Precious Metals
Prospectus Objective   Prec Metals
Inception Date   Jan-07
Open to New Investments   Y

Prices
Price (as of 9/30/2019)   40.98
52-Week High   43.96
52-Week Low   34.26

Total Returns (%)

3-Month	6-Month	1-Year	3-Year	5-Year
6.75	12.71	20.40	2.01	8.10

3-Year Standard Deviation   11.68
Effective Duration

Valuation
Premium/Discount (1-Year Average)   -0.03

Company Information
Provider   Invesco
Manager/Tenure   Management Team (12)
Website   http://www.invesco.com/us
Address   Invesco 11 Greenway Plaza, Ste. 2500
                    Houston TX 77046 United States
Phone Number   800-659-1005

PERFORMANCE

Ratings History

Date	Overall Rating	Risk Rating	Reward Rating
Q3-19	C	C-	C
Q4-18	D	D+	D
Q4-17	C-	C-	C-
Q4-16	D+	D+	C-
Q4-15	D-	D-	D-

Asset & Performance History

Date	NAV	1-Year Total Return
2018	36.29	-6.17
2017	38.68	8.96
2016	34.93	8.95
2015	32.28	-11.78
2014	36.59	-6.58
2013	39.17	-31.39

Total Assets: $130,498,451

Asset Allocation

Asset	%
Cash	48%
Stocks	0%
US Stocks	0%
Bonds	1%
US Bonds	1%
Other	10%

Services Offered:

Investment Strategy: The investment seeks to track the DBIQ Optimum Yield Precious Metals Index Excess Return™ (DBIQ-OY Precious Metals ER™), which is intended to reflect the precious metals sector.
The index Commodities consist of Gold and Silver. The fund invests in futures contracts in an attempt to track its corresponding index. **Top Holdings:** Gold 100 Oz Futr Feb20 United States Treasury Bills 0% Silver Future May20 United States Treasury Bills 0%

Fidelity® Limited Term Bond ETF   C   HOLD

Ticker	Traded On	NAV	Total Assets ($)	Dividend Yield (TTM)	Turnover Ratio	Expense Ratio
FLTB	NYSE Arca	50.92	$129,858,132	2.73	113	0.36

Ratings
Reward   C+
Risk   C-
Recent Upgrade/Downgrade

Fund Information
Fund Type   Exchange Traded Funds
Category   US Fixed Income
Sub-Category   Short-Term Bond
Prospectus Objective   Income
Inception Date   Oct-14
Open to New Investments   Y

Prices
Price (as of 9/30/2019)   50.94
52-Week High   51.20
52-Week Low   49.01

Total Returns (%)

3-Month	6-Month	1-Year	3-Year	5-Year
1.15	3.18	6.29	7.18	12.23

3-Year Standard Deviation   1.52
Effective Duration   2.60

Valuation
Premium/Discount (1-Year Average)   0.05

Company Information
Provider   Fidelity Investments
Manager/Tenure   Robert Galusza (4), David Prothro (4),
                      David DeBiase (0)
Website   http://www.institutional.fidelity.com
Address   Fidelity Investments 82 Devonshire
                      Street Boston MA 2109 United States
Phone Number   617-563-7000

PERFORMANCE

Ratings History

Date	Overall Rating	Risk Rating	Reward Rating
Q3-19	C	C-	C+
Q4-18	C-	C-	C-
Q4-17	C+	A-	C
Q4-16	C-	C-	D+
Q4-15	U		

Asset & Performance History

Date	NAV	1-Year Total Return
2018	49.29	0.87
2017	50.1	1.84
2016	50.07	2.28
2015	49.72	1.26
2014	49.9	
2013		

Total Assets: $129,858,132
Asset Allocation

Asset	%
Cash	1%
Stocks	0%
US Stocks	0%
Bonds	97%
US Bonds	88%
Other	0%

Services Offered:

Investment Strategy: The investment seeks to provide a high rate of income. The fund normally invests at least 80% of assets in investment-grade debt securities (those of medium and high quality) of all types and repurchase agreements for those securities. It is managed to have similar overall interest rate risk to the Fidelity Limited Term Composite Index. Normally, the fund maintains a dollar-weighted average maturity between two and five years. **Top Holdings:** United States Treasury Notes 1.62% United States Treasury Notes 2.38% JPMorgan Chase & Co. 2.55% United States Treasury Notes 2.12% United States Treasury Notes 1.88%

---

iShares ESG 1-5 Year USD Corporate Bond ETF   C   HOLD

Ticker	Traded On	NAV	Total Assets ($)	Dividend Yield (TTM)	Turnover Ratio	Expense Ratio
SUSB	NAS CM	25.38	$129,433,485	2.83	29	0.12

Ratings
Reward   C
Risk   C-
Recent Upgrade/Downgrade   Up

Fund Information
Fund Type   Exchange Traded Funds
Category   US Fixed Income
Sub-Category   Short-Term Bond
Prospectus Objective   Corp Bond - Gen
Inception Date   Jul-17
Open to New Investments   Y

Prices
Price (as of 9/30/2019)   25.45
52-Week High   25.53
52-Week Low   24.33

Total Returns (%)

3-Month	6-Month	1-Year	3-Year	5-Year
1.19	3.40	6.81		

3-Year Standard Deviation
Effective Duration

Valuation
Premium/Discount (1-Year Average)   0.29

Company Information
Provider   iShares
Manager/Tenure   James Mauro (2), Scott Radell (2)
Website   http://www.ishares.com
Address   iShares 400 Howard Street San
                      Francisco CA 94105 United States
Phone Number   800-474-2737

PERFORMANCE

Ratings History

Date	Overall Rating	Risk Rating	Reward Rating
Q3-19	C	C-	C
Q4-18	D+	C-	D
Q4-17	U		
Q4-16			
Q4-15			

Asset & Performance History

Date	NAV	1-Year Total Return
2018	24.42	0.83
2017	24.86	
2016		
2015		
2014		
2013		

Total Assets: $129,433,485
Asset Allocation

Asset	%
Cash	3%
Stocks	0%
US Stocks	0%
Bonds	94%
US Bonds	73%
Other	0%

Services Offered:

Investment Strategy: The investment seeks to track the investment results of the Bloomberg Barclays MSCI US Corporate 1-5 Year ESG Focus Index. The fund generally will invest at least 90% of its assets in the component securities of the underlying index and may invest up to 10% of its assets in certain futures, options and swap contracts, cash and cash equivalents. The index has been developed by Bloomberg Barclays Capital Inc. with environmental, social and governance ("ESG") rating inputs from MSCI ESG Research LLC pursuant to an agreement between MSCI ESG Research and Bloomberg Index Services Limited, a subsidiary of Bloomberg Barclays. The fund is non-diversified. **Top Holdings:** Banco Bilbao Vizcaya Argentaria, S.A. 3% Bunge Limited Finance Corp. 3% 3M Company 1.63% Rockwell Collins Incorporated 2.8% Baker Hughes a GE company LLC and Baker Hughes Co-Obligor Inc 2.77%

RiverFront Dynamic US Dividend Advantage ETF   C   HOLD

Ticker	Traded On	NAV	Total Assets ($)	Dividend Yield (TTM)	Turnover Ratio	Expense Ratio
RFDA	NYSE Arca	32.72	$129,233,442	2.03	96	0.52

Ratings
Reward   C
Risk   C-
Recent Upgrade/Downgrade

Fund Information
Fund Type	Exchange Traded Funds
Category	US Equity Large Cap Blend
Sub-Category	Large Value
Prospectus Objective	Growth & Inc
Inception Date	Jun-16
Open to New Investments	Y

Prices
Price (as of 9/30/2019)	32.73
52-Week High	33.34
52-Week Low	26.47

Total Returns (%)
3-Month	6-Month	1-Year	3-Year	5-Year
1.15	1.66	0.31	34.04	

3-Year Standard Deviation	13.3
Effective Duration	

Valuation
Premium/Discount (1-Year Average)	0.02

Company Information
Provider	ALPS
Manager/Tenure	Adam Grossman (3), Scott Hays (3), Chris Konstantinos (3), 1 other
Website	http://www.alpsfunds.com
Address	ALPS 1290 Broadway, Suite 1100 Denver CO 80203 United States
Phone Number	866-759-5679

PERFORMANCE

Ratings History
Date	Overall Rating	Risk Rating	Reward Rating
Q3-19	C	C-	C
Q4-18	C-	C-	C-
Q4-17	D+	B+	C
Q4-16	U		
Q4-15			

Asset & Performance History
Date	NAV	1-Year Total Return
2018	28.18	-8.89
2017	31.61	19.76
2016	26.95	
2015		
2014		
2013		

Total Assets: $129,233,442
Asset Allocation
Asset	%
Cash	0%
Stocks	100%
US Stocks	100%
Bonds	0%
US Bonds	0%
Other	0%

Services Offered:

Investment Strategy: The investment seeks to provide capital appreciation and dividend income. The fund invests at least 65% of its net assets in a portfolio of equity securities of publicly traded U.S. companies with the potential for dividend income. Equity securities include common stocks and common or preferred shares of real estate investment trusts. The fund may invest in small-, mid- and large-capitalization companies. It is non-diversified. **Top Holdings:** Microsoft Corp Apple Inc Amazon.com Inc JPMorgan Chase & Co Chevron Corp

---

SPDR® DoubleLine Short Duration Total Return Tactical ETF   C   HOLD

Ticker	Traded On	NAV	Total Assets ($)	Dividend Yield (TTM)	Turnover Ratio	Expense Ratio
STOT	BATS		$128,832,292	2.67	62	0.45

Ratings
Reward   C
Risk   C-
Recent Upgrade/Downgrade   Up

Fund Information
Fund Type	Exchange Traded Funds
Category	US Fixed Income
Sub-Category	Short-Term Bond
Prospectus Objective	Income
Inception Date	Apr-16
Open to New Investments	Y

Prices
Price (as of 9/30/2019)	49.67
52-Week High	49.77
52-Week Low	48.39

Total Returns (%)
3-Month	6-Month	1-Year	3-Year	5-Year
0.72	2.30	4.56	5.87	

3-Year Standard Deviation	1.09
Effective Duration	1.30

Valuation
Premium/Discount (1-Year Average)	0.16

Company Information
Provider	SPDR State Street Global Advisors
Manager/Tenure	Philip A. Barach (3), Jeffrey E. Gundlach (3), Jeffrey J. Sherman (3)
Website	http://www.spdrs.com
Address	SPDR State Street Global Advisors State Street Financial Center, 1 Lincoln Street Boston MA 02111-2900 United States
Phone Number	617-786-3000

PERFORMANCE

Ratings History
Date	Overall Rating	Risk Rating	Reward Rating
Q3-19	C	C-	C
Q4-18	C-	D+	C-
Q4-17	D+	B-	D+
Q4-16	U		
Q4-15			

Asset & Performance History
Date	NAV	1-Year Total Return
2018	48.61	1.16
2017	49.27	1.62
2016	49.43	
2015		
2014		
2013		

Total Assets: $128,832,292
Asset Allocation
Asset	%
Cash	20%
Stocks	0%
US Stocks	0%
Bonds	80%
US Bonds	69%
Other	0%

Services Offered:

Investment Strategy: The investment seeks to maximize current income with a dollar-weighted average effective duration between one and three years. Under normal circumstances, the fund will invest at least 80% of its net assets in a diversified portfolio of fixed income securities of any credit quality. Fixed income securities in which the fund principally invests are defined as securities issued or guaranteed by the U.S. government or its agencies, instrumentalities or sponsored corporations; TIPS; municipal bonds (the fund may invest up to 20% of its portfolio in municipal bonds); asset-backed securities; etc. **Top Holdings:** United States Treasury Notes 2.25% United States Treasury Bills 0% United States Treasury Notes 1.62% United States Treasury Notes 2.25% Federal Home Loan Mortgage Corporation 2.71%

SPDR® S&P Oil & Gas Equipment & Services ETF   D+   SELL

Ticker	Traded On	NAV	Total Assets ($)	Dividend Yield (TTM)	Turnover Ratio	Expense Ratio
XES	NYSE Arca		$128,679,878	1.28	34	0.35

Ratings
Reward	D+
Risk	D
Recent Upgrade/Downgrade	Up

Fund Information
Fund Type	Exchange Traded Funds
Category	Energy Sector Equity
Sub-Category	Equity Energy
Prospectus Objective	Natl Res
Inception Date	Jun-06
Open to New Investments	Y

Prices
Price (as of 9/30/2019)	7.24
52-Week High	17.45
52-Week Low	6.85

Total Returns (%)
3-Month	6-Month	1-Year	3-Year	5-Year
-24.61	-36.36	-56.34	-60.30	-80.57

3-Year Standard Deviation	40.8
Effective Duration	

Valuation
Premium/Discount (1-Year Average)	0.00

Company Information
Provider	SPDR State Street Global Advisors
Manager/Tenure	Michael J. Feehily (7), Karl A. Schneider (4), Melissa Kapitulik (0)
Website	http://www.spdrs.com
Address	SPDR State Street Global Advisors State Street Financial Center, 1 Lincoln Street Boston MA 02111-2900 United States
Phone Number	617-786-3000

PERFORMANCE

Ratings History
Date	Overall Rating	Risk Rating	Reward Rating
Q3-19	D+	D	D+
Q4-18	D+	D	C-
Q4-17	D	D	D
Q4-16	D	D	D+
Q4-15	D	D	D

Asset & Performance History
Date	NAV	1-Year Total Return
2018	9	-47.04
2017	17.13	-21.87
2016	22.33	29.35
2015	17.55	-36.53
2014	28.22	-34.65
2013	43.69	26.99

Total Assets: $128,679,878
Asset Allocation
Asset	%
Cash	0%
Stocks	100%
US Stocks	91%
Bonds	0%
US Bonds	0%
Other	0%

Services Offered:

Investment Strategy: The investment seeks to provide investment results that, before fees and expenses, correspond generally to the total return performance of an index derived from the oil and gas equipment and services segment of a U.S. total market composite index. In seeking to track the performance of the S&P Oil & Gas Equipment & Services Select Industry Index, the fund employs a sampling strategy. It generally invests substantially all, but at least 80%, of its total assets in the securities comprising the index. The index represents the oil and gas equipment and services segment of the S&P Total Market Index ("S&P TMI"). The fund is non-diversified. **Top Holdings:** TechnipFMC PLC National Oilwell Varco Inc US Silica Holdings Inc Baker Hughes, a GE Co Class A Schlumberger Ltd

---

Inspire Corporate Bond Impact ETF   C   HOLD

Ticker	Traded On	NAV	Total Assets ($)	Dividend Yield (TTM)	Turnover Ratio	Expense Ratio
IBD	NYSE Arca		$128,343,846	2.46		0.61

Ratings
Reward	C
Risk	C-
Recent Upgrade/Downgrade	Up

Fund Information
Fund Type	Exchange Traded Funds
Category	US Fixed Income
Sub-Category	Corporate Bond
Prospectus Objective	Corp Bond - Gen
Inception Date	Jul-17
Open to New Investments	Y

Prices
Price (as of 9/30/2019)	25.68
52-Week High	25.98
52-Week Low	24.16

Total Returns (%)
3-Month	6-Month	1-Year	3-Year	5-Year
1.45	4.30	8.21		

3-Year Standard Deviation	
Effective Duration	

Valuation
Premium/Discount (1-Year Average)	0.28

Company Information
Provider	Inspire
Manager/Tenure	Darrell Jayroe (2), Robert Netzly (2)
Website	
Address	Inspire 650 San Benito Street, Suite 130 Hollister CA 95023 United States
Phone Number	

PERFORMANCE

Ratings History
Date	Overall Rating	Risk Rating	Reward Rating
Q3-19	C	C-	C
Q4-18	D	D+	D
Q4-17	U		
Q4-16			
Q4-15			

Asset & Performance History
Date	NAV	1-Year Total Return
2018	24.35	-0.23
2017	24.94	
2016		
2015		
2014		
2013		

Total Assets: $128,343,846
Asset Allocation
Asset	%
Cash	5%
Stocks	0%
US Stocks	0%
Bonds	95%
US Bonds	93%
Other	0%

Services Offered:

Investment Strategy: The investment seeks to replicate investment results that generally correspond to the Inspire Corporate Bond Impact Index. The fund generally will invest at least 80% of its total assets in the component securities of the index. The index provider selects domestic corporate bonds issued by companies that have market capitalizations of $5 billion or more and are included in the S&P 500 Investment Grade Corporate Bond Index using the Inspire Impact Score®, a proprietary selection methodology that is designed to assign a score to a particular security based on the security's alignment with biblical values and the positive impact that company has on the world. **Top Holdings:** Globe Life Inc 4.55% Union Pacific Corporation 3.95% Roper Technologies Inc 3.8% Nasdaq Inc 3.85% Cboe Global Markets Inc 3.65%

ClearBridge All Cap Growth ETF   C   HOLD

Ticker	Traded On	NAV	Total Assets ($)	Dividend Yield (TTM)	Turnover Ratio	Expense Ratio
CACG	NAS CM	31.66	$128,220,999	0.57	15	0.53

Ratings
Reward	C+
Risk	C-
Recent Upgrade/Downgrade	Up

Fund Information
Fund Type	Exchange Traded Funds
Category	US Equity Large Cap Growth
Sub-Category	Large Growth
Prospectus Objective	Growth
Inception Date	May-17
Open to New Investments	Y

Prices
Price (as of 9/30/2019)	31.66
52-Week High	33.01
52-Week Low	25.40

Total Returns (%)
3-Month	6-Month	1-Year	3-Year	5-Year
-1.12	2.69	1.42		

3-Year Standard Deviation
Effective Duration

Valuation
Premium/Discount (1-Year Average)	0.07

Company Information
Provider	Legg Mason
Manager/Tenure	Evan Bauman (2), Peter Bourbeau (2), Richard A. Freeman (2), 1 other
Website	http://www.leggmason.com
Address	Legg Mason/Western 100 International Drive Baltimore MD 21202 United States
Phone Number	877-721-1926

PERFORMANCE

Ratings History

Date	Overall Rating	Risk Rating	Reward Rating
Q3-19	C	C-	C+
Q4-18	C-	C-	C-
Q4-17	U		
Q4-16			
Q4-15			

Asset & Performance History

Date	NAV	1-Year Total Return
2018	26.82	-2.92
2017	27.79	
2016		
2015		
2014		
2013		

Total Assets: $128,220,999

Asset Allocation

Asset	%
Cash	4%
Stocks	96%
US Stocks	91%
Bonds	0%
US Bonds	0%
Other	0%

Services Offered:

Investment Strategy: The investment seeks to achieve long-term capital appreciation. The fund seeks to invest in a diversified portfolio of large, medium and small capitalization stocks that have the potential for above-average long-term earnings and/or cash flow growth. The fund's subadviser uses a bottom-up investment process that seeks to find inefficiently priced companies with strong fundamentals, incentive-driven management teams, dominant positions in niche markets and/or goods and services that are in high customer demand. **Top Holdings:** UnitedHealth Group Inc Comcast Corp Class A Amazon.com Inc Microsoft Corp Facebook Inc A

Fidelity® Low Duration Bond Factor ETF   C-   HOLD

Ticker	Traded On	NAV	Total Assets ($)	Dividend Yield (TTM)	Turnover Ratio	Expense Ratio
FLDR	NYSE Arca	50.67	$127,948,227	2.63		0.15

Ratings
Reward	C-
Risk	C-
Recent Upgrade/Downgrade	Up

Fund Information
Fund Type	Exchange Traded Funds
Category	US Fixed Income
Sub-Category	Ultrashort Bond
Prospectus Objective	Growth & Inc
Inception Date	Jun-18
Open to New Investments	Y

Prices
Price (as of 9/30/2019)	50.72
52-Week High	50.84
52-Week Low	49.79

Total Returns (%)
3-Month	6-Month	1-Year	3-Year	5-Year
0.97	2.26	4.02		

3-Year Standard Deviation
Effective Duration	0.93

Valuation
Premium/Discount (1-Year Average)	0.14

Company Information
Provider	Fidelity Investments
Manager/Tenure	Brandon Bettencourt (1), Jay Small (1)
Website	http://www.institutional.fidelity.com
Address	Fidelity Investments 82 Devonshire Street Boston MA 2109 United States
Phone Number	617-563-7000

PERFORMANCE

Ratings History

Date	Overall Rating	Risk Rating	Reward Rating
Q3-19	C-	C-	C-
Q4-18	U		
Q4-17			
Q4-16			
Q4-15			

Asset & Performance History

Date	NAV	1-Year Total Return
2018	49.75	
2017		
2016		
2015		
2014		
2013		

Total Assets: $127,948,227

Asset Allocation

Asset	%
Cash	2%
Stocks	0%
US Stocks	0%
Bonds	96%
US Bonds	70%
Other	0%

Services Offered:

Investment Strategy: The investment seeks to provide investment returns that correspond, before fees and expenses, generally to the performance of the Fidelity Low Duration Investment Grade Factor Index. The fund normally invests at least 80% of assets in securities included in the index. The index is designed to optimize the balance of interest rate risk and credit risk such that both returns and risk measures may be improved relative to traditional U.S. investment grade floating rate note indices. The index is comprised solely of U.S. investment grade floating rate notes and U.S. Treasury notes. **Top Holdings:** United States Treasury Notes 2.62% National Australia Bank Limited 2.66% U.S. Bank National Association 2.53% Morgan Stanley 2.73% HSBC Holdings plc 2.72%

SPDR® SSgA Income Allocation ETF   C   HOLD

Ticker	Traded On	NAV	Total Assets ($)	Dividend Yield (TTM)	Turnover Ratio	Expense Ratio
INKM	NYSE Arca		$127,571,657	4.86	71	0.5

Ratings
Reward   C+
Risk   C-
Recent Upgrade/Downgrade

Fund Information
Fund Type	Exchange Traded Funds
Category	Moderate Allocation
Sub-Category	Allocation--30% to 50% Equity
Prospectus Objective	Income
Inception Date	Apr-12
Open to New Investments	Y

Prices
Price (as of 9/30/2019)	33.76
52-Week High	34.02
52-Week Low	30.39

Total Returns (%)
3-Month	6-Month	1-Year	3-Year	5-Year
2.14	4.99	9.20	19.55	27.59

3-Year Standard Deviation	6.01
Effective Duration	9.35

Valuation
Premium/Discount (1-Year Average)	0.01

Company Information
Provider	SPDR State Street Global Advisors
Manager/Tenure	Jeremiah K. Holly (7), Michael O. Martel (4)
Website	http://www.spdrs.com
Address	SPDR State Street Global Advisors State Street Financial Center, 1 Lincoln Street Boston MA 02111-2900 United States
Phone Number	617-786-3000

PERFORMANCE

Ratings History

Date	Overall Rating	Risk Rating	Reward Rating
Q3-19	C	C-	C+
Q4-18	C-	D+	C-
Q4-17	B-	B	C+
Q4-16	C-	D+	C
Q4-15	C-	C-	C

Asset & Performance History

Date	NAV	1-Year Total Return
2018	30.6	-5.24
2017	33.6	13.65
2016	30.51	6.63
2015	29.58	-4.65
2014	32.08	8.43
2013	30.62	3.04

Total Assets: $127,571,657

Asset Allocation
Asset	%
Cash	3%
Stocks	36%
US Stocks	29%
Bonds	51%
US Bonds	40%
Other	0%

Services Offered:

Investment Strategy: The investment seeks to provide total return by focusing on investments in income and yield-generating assets. The Adviser primarily invests the assets of the fund among ETPs that provide exposure to five primary asset classes: (i) domestic and international equity securities; (ii) domestic and international investment-grade and high yield debt securities; (iii) hybrid equity/debt securities; (iv) first lien senior secured floating rate bank loans, commonly referred to as "Senior Loans"; and (v) REITs, including equity REITs and mortgage REITs. **Top Holdings:** SPDR® Portfolio S&P 500 High Div ETF SPDR® Blmbg Barclays High Yield Bd ETF SPDR® Portfolio Long Term Treasury ETF SPDR® Blackstone / GSO Senior Loan ETF SPDR® Blmbg Barclays Em Mkts Lcl Bd ETF

WisdomTree China ex-State-Owned Enterprises Fund   C-   HOLD

Ticker	Traded On	NAV	Total Assets ($)	Dividend Yield (TTM)	Turnover Ratio	Expense Ratio
CXSE	NAS CM	71.44	$126,806,266	1.22	35	0.32

Ratings
Reward   C-
Risk   C-
Recent Upgrade/Downgrade

Fund Information
Fund Type	Exchange Traded Funds
Category	Greater China Equity
Sub-Category	China Region
Prospectus Objective	Pacific Stock
Inception Date	Sep-12
Open to New Investments	Y

Prices
Price (as of 9/30/2019)	71.09
52-Week High	82.08
52-Week Low	58.75

Total Returns (%)
3-Month	6-Month	1-Year	3-Year	5-Year
-4.50	-8.95	1.17	41.13	47.32

3-Year Standard Deviation	21.34
Effective Duration	

Valuation
Premium/Discount (1-Year Average)	-0.05

Company Information
Provider	WisdomTree
Manager/Tenure	Richard A. Brown (5), Thomas J. Durante (5), Karen Q. Wong (5)
Website	http://www.wisdomtree.com
Address	WisdomTree 245 Park Avenue, 35th floor New York NY 10167 United States
Phone Number	866-909-9473

PERFORMANCE

Ratings History

Date	Overall Rating	Risk Rating	Reward Rating
Q3-19	C-	C-	C-
Q4-18	C-	D+	C-
Q4-17	B+	C+	A+
Q4-16	C-	D	C
Q4-15	C-	D+	C

Asset & Performance History

Date	NAV	1-Year Total Return
2018	61.37	-27.92
2017	86.16	78.03
2016	48.82	-1.19
2015	50.08	-1.43
2014	52.07	1.64
2013	52.41	-1.1

Total Assets: $126,806,266

Asset Allocation
Asset	%
Cash	0%
Stocks	100%
US Stocks	2%
Bonds	0%
US Bonds	0%
Other	0%

Services Offered:

Investment Strategy: The investment seeks to track the price and yield performance, before fees and expenses, of the WisdomTree China ex-State-Owned Enterprises Index. Under normal circumstances, at least 80% of the fund's total assets (exclusive of collateral held from securities lending) will be invested in component securities of the index and investments that have economic characteristics that are substantially identical to the economic characteristics of such component securities. The index is a modified float-adjusted market cap weighted index that consists of common stocks in China, excluding common stocks of "state-owned enterprises." The fund is non-diversified. **Top Holdings:** Alibaba Group Holding Ltd ADR Tencent Holdings Ltd Ping An Insurance (Group) Co. of China Ltd Ping An Insurance (Group) Co. of China Ltd Class H Baidu Inc ADR

Global X Social Media ETF   C   HOLD

Ticker	Traded On	NAV	Total Assets ($)	Dividend Yield (TTM)	Turnover Ratio	Expense Ratio
SOCL	NAS CM	32.06	$126,646,509	0	21	0.65

Ratings
Reward   C
Risk   C-
Recent Upgrade/Downgrade

Fund Information
Fund Type	Exchange Traded Funds
Category	Technology Sector Equity
Sub-Category	Technology
Prospectus Objective	Technology
Inception Date	Nov-11
Open to New Investments	Y

Prices
Price (as of 9/30/2019)	31.93
52-Week High	34.60
52-Week Low	26.60

Total Returns (%)
3-Month	6-Month	1-Year	3-Year	5-Year
-1.80	-1.17	0.75	29.74	72.90

3-Year Standard Deviation   18.64
Effective Duration

Valuation
Premium/Discount (1-Year Average)   -0.23

Company Information
Provider	Global X Funds
Manager/Tenure	Chang Kim (5), Nam To (1), Wayne Xie (0), 1 other
Website	http://www.globalxfunds.com
Address	Global X Funds 600 Lexington Avenue, 20th Floor New York NY 10022 United States
Phone Number	888-493-8631

PERFORMANCE

Ratings History
Date	Overall Rating	Risk Rating	Reward Rating
Q3-19	C	C-	C
Q4-18	C-	C-	C
Q4-17	A-	B-	A+
Q4-16	C+	C-	B
Q4-15	C	C-	C+

Asset & Performance History
Date	NAV	1-Year Total Return
2018	27.74	-16.04
2017	33.04	54.71
2016	21.67	8.7
2015	19.97	10.21
2014	18.12	-14.44
2013	21.19	64.39

Total Assets: $126,646,509

Asset Allocation
Asset	%
Cash	0%
Stocks	100%
US Stocks	49%
Bonds	0%
US Bonds	0%
Other	0%

Services Offered:

Investment Strategy: The investment seeks to provide investment results that correspond generally to the price and yield performance, before fees and expenses, of the Solactive Social Media Total Return Index. The fund will invest at least 80% of its total assets in the securities of the underlying index and in American Depositary Receipts and Global Depositary Receipts based on the securities in the underlying index. The underlying index tracks the equity performance of the largest and most liquid companies involved in the social media industry, including companies that provide social networking, file sharing, and other web-based media applications. The fund is non-diversified. **Top Holdings:** Twitter Inc Facebook Inc A Tencent Holdings Ltd NAVER Corp IAC/InterActiveCorp

iShares Yield Optimized Bond ETF   C   HOLD

Ticker	Traded On	NAV	Total Assets ($)	Dividend Yield (TTM)	Turnover Ratio	Expense Ratio
BYLD	NYSE Arca	25.58	$126,624,226	4.05	48	0.2

Ratings
Reward   B-
Risk   C-
Recent Upgrade/Downgrade

Fund Information
Fund Type	Exchange Traded Funds
Category	US Fixed Income
Sub-Category	Intermediate Core-Plus Bond
Prospectus Objective	Income
Inception Date	Apr-14
Open to New Investments	Y

Prices
Price (as of 9/30/2019)	25.59
52-Week High	25.76
52-Week Low	23.53

Total Returns (%)
3-Month	6-Month	1-Year	3-Year	5-Year
1.69	5.85	10.46	13.19	20.68

3-Year Standard Deviation   3.25
Effective Duration

Valuation
Premium/Discount (1-Year Average)   0.01

Company Information
Provider	iShares
Manager/Tenure	James Mauro (5), Scott Radell (5)
Website	http://www.ishares.com
Address	iShares 400 Howard Street San Francisco CA 94105 United States
Phone Number	800-474-2737

PERFORMANCE

Ratings History
Date	Overall Rating	Risk Rating	Reward Rating
Q3-19	C	C-	B-
Q4-18	C-	C-	C-
Q4-17	B-	A-	C
Q4-16	C-	D+	C-
Q4-15	D	D+	D+

Asset & Performance History
Date	NAV	1-Year Total Return
2018	23.64	-1.85
2017	24.98	4.91
2016	24.59	5.26
2015	24.1	-0.95
2014	25.14	
2013		

Total Assets: $126,624,226

Asset Allocation
Asset	%
Cash	2%
Stocks	0%
US Stocks	0%
Bonds	97%
US Bonds	73%
Other	0%

Services Offered:

Investment Strategy: The investment seeks to track the investment results of the Morningstar® U.S. Bond Market Yield-Optimized IndexSM. The fund invests primarily in underlying funds that themselves seek investment results corresponding to their own underlying indexes. It also invests in a combination of other ETFs (including other iShares ETFs), cash and cash equivalents, including shares of money market funds advised by BFA or its affiliates. The index is a broadly diversified fixed income index that seeks to deliver current income. It will invest at least 90% of its assets in the component securities (including indirect investments through the underlying funds) of the index. **Top Holdings:** United States Treasury Notes 2.25% United States Treasury Notes 1.88% United States Treasury Notes 2.13% United States Treasury Notes 2.5% United States Treasury Notes 2.5%

Invesco S&P 500® Equal Weight Energy ETF   C-   HOLD

Ticker	Traded On	NAV	Total Assets ($)	Dividend Yield (TTM)	Turnover Ratio	Expense Ratio
RYE	NYSE Arca	44.41	$126,575,205	2.34	31	0.4

Ratings
Reward   C
Risk   D
Recent Upgrade/Downgrade   Up

Fund Information
Fund Type   Exchange Traded Funds
Category   Energy Sector Equity
Sub-Category   Equity Energy
Prospectus Objective   Natl Res
Inception Date   Nov-06
Open to New Investments   Y

Prices
Price (as of 9/30/2019)   44.38
52-Week High   63.78
52-Week Low   40.29

Total Returns (%)

3-Month	6-Month	1-Year	3-Year	5-Year
-8.20	-12.54	-27.75	-21.10	-38.22

3-Year Standard Deviation   25.36
Effective Duration

Valuation
Premium/Discount (1-Year Average)   -0.01

Company Information
Provider   Invesco
Manager/Tenure   Peter Hubbard (1), Michael Jeanette (1), Tony Seisser (1)
Website   http://www.invesco.com/us
Address   Invesco 11 Greenway Plaza, Ste. 2500 Houston TX 77046 United States
Phone Number   800-659-1005

PERFORMANCE

Ratings History

Date	Overall Rating	Risk Rating	Reward Rating
Q3-19	C-	D	C
Q4-18	C	D+	C+
Q4-17	D+	D+	D+
Q4-16	C-	D+	C-
Q4-15	C-	D+	C-

Asset & Performance History

Date	NAV	1-Year Total Return
2018	43.18	-24.45
2017	58.18	-6.49
2016	64.05	40.65
2015	47.09	-28.69
2014	67.58	-14.89
2013	80.71	26.62

Total Assets: $126,575,205
Asset Allocation

Asset	%
Cash	0%
Stocks	100%
US Stocks	97%
Bonds	0%
US Bonds	0%
Other	0%

Services Offered:

Investment Strategy: The investment seeks to track the investment results (before fees and expenses) of the S&P 500® Equal Weight Energy Index (the "underlying index"). The fund generally will invest at least 90% of its total assets in the securities that comprise the underlying index. The underlying index is composed of all of the components of the S&P 500® Energy Index, an index that contains the common stocks of all companies included in the S&P 500® Index that are classified as members of the energy sector, as defined according to the Global Industry Classification Standard ("GICS"). The fund is non-diversified. **Top Holdings:** Phillips 66   Noble Energy Inc   ONEOK Inc   HollyFrontier Corp   Hess Corp

---

Direxion Daily Healthcare Bull 3X Shares   C-   HOLD

Ticker	Traded On	NAV	Total Assets ($)	Dividend Yield (TTM)	Turnover Ratio	Expense Ratio
CURE	NYSE Arca	50.62	$126,540,347	0.85	43	1.08

Ratings
Reward   C
Risk   C-
Recent Upgrade/Downgrade   Down

Fund Information
Fund Type   Exchange Traded Funds
Category   Trading Tools
Sub-Category   Trading--Leveraged Equity
Prospectus Objective   Health
Inception Date   Jun-11
Open to New Investments   Y

Prices
Price (as of 9/30/2019)   50.59
52-Week High   67.75
52-Week Low   39.11

Total Returns (%)

3-Month	6-Month	1-Year	3-Year	5-Year
-10.99	-9.07	-24.51	60.74	105.11

3-Year Standard Deviation   40.3
Effective Duration

Valuation
Premium/Discount (1-Year Average)   -0.11

Company Information
Provider   Direxion Funds
Manager/Tenure   Paul Brigandi (8), Tony Ng (4)
Website   http://www.direxionfunds.com
Address   Direxion Funds 1301 Avenue Of The Americas (6th Avenue) New York NY 10019 United States
Phone Number   646-572-3390

PERFORMANCE

Ratings History

Date	Overall Rating	Risk Rating	Reward Rating
Q3-19	C-	C-	C
Q4-18	C	C	C
Q4-17	B	C	A+
Q4-16	C-	D+	C-
Q4-15	B	C+	B

Asset & Performance History

Date	NAV	1-Year Total Return
2018	47.62	2.91
2017	46.58	69.25
2016	27.57	-17.43
2015	33.39	7.57
2014	31.04	79.98
2013	17.25	162.39

Total Assets: $126,540,347
Asset Allocation

Asset	%
Cash	29%
Stocks	71%
US Stocks	71%
Bonds	0%
US Bonds	0%
Other	0%

Services Offered:

Investment Strategy: The investment seeks daily investment results, before fees and expenses, of 300% of the daily performance of the Health Care Select Sector Index. The fund invests at least 80% of its net assets in financial instruments and securities of the index, ETFs that track the index and other financial instruments that provide daily leveraged exposure to the index or ETFs that track the index. The index includes domestic companies from the healthcare sector, which includes the following industries: pharmaceuticals; health care equipment and supplies; health care providers and services; biotechnology; life sciences tools and services; and etc. It is non-diversified. **Top Holdings:** Health Care Select Sector SPDR® ETF   Health Care Sel Sec Index   Health Care Sel Sec Index   Health Care Sel Sec Index   Health Care Sel Sec Index

Invesco MSCI Global Timber ETF   D+   SELL

Ticker	Traded On	NAV	Total Assets ($)	Dividend Yield (TTM)	Turnover Ratio	Expense Ratio
CUT	NYSE Arca	26.03	$126,244,171	3.17		0.55

Ratings
Reward	D+
Risk	C-
Recent Upgrade/Downgrade	Down

Fund Information
Fund Type	Exchange Traded Funds
Category	Natural Resources
Sub-Category	Natural Resources
Prospectus Objective	Natl Res
Inception Date	Nov-07
Open to New Investments	Y

Prices
Price (as of 9/30/2019)	26.02
52-Week High	32.03
52-Week Low	23.21

Total Returns (%)
3-Month	6-Month	1-Year	3-Year	5-Year
-4.75	-7.03	-16.01	12.27	24.77

3-Year Standard Deviation	16.53
Effective Duration	

Valuation
Premium/Discount (1-Year Average)	-0.12

Company Information
Provider	Invesco
Manager/Tenure	Peter Hubbard (1), Michael Jeanette (1), Tony Seisser (1)
Website	http://www.invesco.com/us
Address	Invesco 11 Greenway Plaza, Ste. 2500 Houston TX 77046 United States
Phone Number	800-659-1005

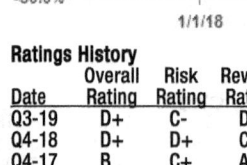

PERFORMANCE

Ratings History
Date	Overall Rating	Risk Rating	Reward Rating
Q3-19	D+	C-	D+
Q4-18	D+	D+	C-
Q4-17	B	C+	A-
Q4-16	C	C-	C+
Q4-15	C	C-	C

Asset & Performance History
Date	NAV	1-Year Total Return
2018	24.2	-21.1
2017	31.76	29.18
2016	24.86	6.92
2015	23.69	-1.17
2014	24.33	-2.79
2013	25.73	28.73

Total Assets: $126,244,171
Asset Allocation
Asset	%
Cash	0%
Stocks	100%
US Stocks	43%
Bonds	0%
US Bonds	0%
Other	0%

Services Offered:

Investment Strategy: The investment seeks to track the investment results (before fees and expenses) of the MSCI ACWI IMI Timber Select Capped Index (the underlying index). The fund generally will invest at least 90% of its total assets in the securities that comprise the underlying index, as well as American depositary receipts ("ADRs") and global depositary receipts ("GDRs") that represent securities in the underlying index. The underlying index is comprised of equity securities of companies that are primarily engaged in the ownership and management of forests and timberlands and the production of finished products that use timber as a raw material. The fund is non-diversified. **Top Holdings:** UPM-Kymmene Oyj Mondi PLC Weyerhaeuser Co Avery Dennison Corp International Paper Co

---

Invesco S&P 500® High Beta ETF   C   HOLD

Ticker	Traded On	NAV	Total Assets ($)	Dividend Yield (TTM)	Turnover Ratio	Expense Ratio
SPHB	NYSE Arca	41.32	$126,034,998	1.4		0.25

Ratings
Reward	C
Risk	C+
Recent Upgrade/Downgrade	

Fund Information
Fund Type	Exchange Traded Funds
Category	US Equity Large Cap Blend
Sub-Category	Large Blend
Prospectus Objective	Growth
Inception Date	May-11
Open to New Investments	

Prices
Price (as of 9/30/2019)	41.34
52-Week High	45.16
52-Week Low	32.76

Total Returns (%)
3-Month	6-Month	1-Year	3-Year	5-Year
-4.20	-1.93	-6.94	31.72	36.38

3-Year Standard Deviation	19.67
Effective Duration	

Valuation
Premium/Discount (1-Year Average)	-0.01

Company Information
Provider	Invesco
Manager/Tenure	Peter Hubbard (8), Michael Jeanette (8), Tony Seisser (5)
Website	http://www.invesco.com/us
Address	Invesco 11 Greenway Plaza, Ste. 2500 Houston TX 77046 United States
Phone Number	800-659-1005

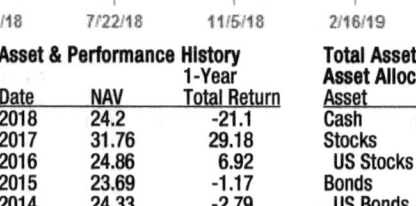

PERFORMANCE

Ratings History
Date	Overall Rating	Risk Rating	Reward Rating
Q3-19	C	C+	C
Q4-18	C-	C-	C
Q4-17	B	C	B+
Q4-16	C+	C	B
Q4-15	C+	C+	C

Asset & Performance History
Date	NAV	1-Year Total Return
2018	35.29	-15.43
2017	42.44	17.77
2016	36.57	26.11
2015	29.29	-12.77
2014	34.12	12.72
2013	30.58	40.81

Total Assets: $126,034,998
Asset Allocation
Asset	%
Cash	0%
Stocks	100%
US Stocks	98%
Bonds	0%
US Bonds	0%
Other	0%

Services Offered:

Investment Strategy: The investment seeks to track the investment results (before fees and expenses) of the S&P 500® High Beta Index (the "underlying index"). The fund generally will invest at least 90% of its total assets in the securities that comprise the underlying index. Strictly in accordance with its guidelines and mandated procedures, S&P DJI selects 100 securities from the S&P 500® Index for inclusion in the underlying index that have the highest sensitivity to market movements, or "beta," over the past 12 months as determined by the index provider. **Top Holdings:** NVIDIA Corp Advanced Micro Devices Inc Micron Technology Inc Salesforce.com Inc Twitter Inc

First Trust Germany AlphaDEX® Fund   D+   SELL

Ticker	Traded On	NAV	Total Assets ($)	Dividend Yield (TTM)	Turnover Ratio	Expense Ratio
FGM	NAS CM	39.93	$125,770,411	2.4	81	0.8

Ratings

Reward	D
Risk	C-
Recent Upgrade/Downgrade	Down

Fund Information

Fund Type	Exchange Traded Funds
Category	Europe Equity Large Cap
Sub-Category	Miscellaneous Region
Prospectus Objective	Europe Stock
Inception Date	Feb-12
Open to New Investments	Y

Prices

Price (as of 9/30/2019)	39.93
52-Week High	46.52
52-Week Low	36.33

Total Returns (%)

3-Month	6-Month	1-Year	3-Year	5-Year
-4.09	-2.19	-12.38	13.44	25.59

3-Year Standard Deviation	15.97
Effective Duration	

Valuation

Premium/Discount (1-Year Average)	0.02

Company Information

Provider	First Trust
Manager/Tenure	Jon C. Erickson (7), Daniel J. Lindquist (7), David G. McGarel (7), 3 others
Website	http://www.ftportfolios.com/
Address	First Trust 120 E. Liberty Drive, Suite 400 Wheaton IL 60187 United States
Phone Number	800-621-1675

PERFORMANCE

Ratings History

Date	Overall Rating	Risk Rating	Reward Rating
Q3-19	D+	C-	D
Q4-18	D+	D+	D+
Q4-17	A-	B	A
Q4-16	C-	D+	C-
Q4-15	C-	C-	C-

Asset & Performance History

Date	NAV	1-Year Total Return
2018	37.57	-25.41
2017	51.26	43.94
2016	36.47	1.68
2015	36.37	1.9
2014	36.07	-11.59
2013	41.48	26.63

Total Assets: $125,770,411
Asset Allocation

Asset	%
Cash	0%
Stocks	100%
US Stocks	2%
Bonds	0%
US Bonds	0%
Other	0%

Services Offered:

Investment Strategy: The investment seeks investment results that correspond generally to the price and yield (before the fund's fees and expenses) of an equity index called the NASDAQ AlphaDEX® Germany Index. The fund will normally invest at least 90% of its net assets (including investment borrowings) in the common stocks and depositary receipts that comprise the index. The index is designed to select stocks from the NASDAQ Germany Index (the "base index") that may generate positive alpha, or risk-adjusted returns, relative to traditional indices through the use of the AlphaDEX® selection methodology. **Top Holdings:** Aroundtown SA Stroeer SE & Co KGaA Porsche Automobil Holding SE Participating Preferred Talanx AG Puma SE

iShares Interest Rate Hedged Corporate Bond ETF   C   HOLD

Ticker	Traded On	NAV	Total Assets ($)	Dividend Yield (TTM)	Turnover Ratio	Expense Ratio
LQDH	NYSE Arca	93.01	$125,565,605	3.34	2	0.25

Ratings

Reward	C
Risk	C-
Recent Upgrade/Downgrade	

Fund Information

Fund Type	Exchange Traded Funds
Category	US Fixed Income
Sub-Category	Corporate Bond
Prospectus Objective	Growth & Inc
Inception Date	May-14
Open to New Investments	Y

Prices

Price (as of 9/30/2019)	92.97
52-Week High	97.25
52-Week Low	90.21

Total Returns (%)

3-Month	6-Month	1-Year	3-Year	5-Year
-1.12	0.82	0.79	11.61	10.83

3-Year Standard Deviation	3.75
Effective Duration	

Valuation

Premium/Discount (1-Year Average)	-0.05

Company Information

Provider	iShares
Manager/Tenure	James Mauro (5), Scott Radell (5)
Website	http://www.ishares.com
Address	iShares 400 Howard Street San Francisco CA 94105 United States
Phone Number	800-474-2737

PERFORMANCE

Ratings History

Date	Overall Rating	Risk Rating	Reward Rating
Q3-19	C	C-	C
Q4-18	C-	C-	C-
Q4-17	C+	B	C+
Q4-16	C-	D+	C-
Q4-15	D	D+	D+

Asset & Performance History

Date	NAV	1-Year Total Return
2018	90.86	-2.07
2017	97.13	6.16
2016	93.73	5.21
2015	91.24	-2.38
2014	96.23	
2013		

Total Assets: $125,565,605
Asset Allocation

Asset	%
Cash	1%
Stocks	0%
US Stocks	0%
Bonds	96%
US Bonds	84%
Other	0%

Services Offered:

Investment Strategy: The investment seeks to mitigate the interest rate risk of a portfolio composed of U.S. dollar-denominated, investment-grade corporate bonds. The fund seeks to invest, at least 80% of its net assets in U.S. dollar-denominated investment-grade corporate bonds, in one or more underlying funds that principally invest in investment-grade bonds. It is an actively managed exchange-traded fund that does not seek to replicate the performance of a specified index. **Top Holdings:** GE Capital International Funding Company Unlimited Company 4.42% Anheuser-Busch Companies LLC / Anheuser-Busch InBev Worldwide Inc 4.9% CVS Health Corp 4.3% CVS Health Corp 5.05% Verizon Communications Inc. 4.33%

VanEck Vectors India Small-Cap Index ETF

D-   SELL

Ticker	Traded On	NAV	Total Assets ($)	Dividend Yield (TTM)	Turnover Ratio	Expense Ratio
SCIF	NYSE Arca	32.36	$125,412,788	0.15	39	0.83

Ratings
Reward	D-
Risk	D
Recent Upgrade/Downgrade	Down

Fund Information
Fund Type	Exchange Traded Funds
Category	India Equity
Sub-Category	India Equity
Prospectus Objective	Small Company
Inception Date	Aug-10
Open to New Investments	Y

Prices
Price (as of 9/30/2019)	32.60
52-Week High	44.62
52-Week Low	29.73

Total Returns (%)
3-Month	6-Month	1-Year	3-Year	5-Year
-15.68	-27.08	-17.95	-28.97	-22.51

3-Year Standard Deviation	26.33
Effective Duration	

Valuation
Premium/Discount (1-Year Average)	-0.09

Company Information
Provider	VanEck
Manager/Tenure	Hao-Hung (Peter) Liao (9), Guo Hua (Jason) Jin (1)
Website	http://www.vaneck.com
Address	Van Eck Associates Corporation 666 Third Avenue New York NY 10017 United States
Phone Number	800-826-1115

PERFORMANCE

Ratings History
Date	Overall Rating	Risk Rating	Reward Rating
Q3-19	D-	D	D-
Q4-18	D	D	D
Q4-17	B+	C+	A
Q4-16	C+	C-	B
Q4-15	C	C-	C

Asset & Performance History
Date	NAV	1-Year Total Return
2018	42.36	-37.99
2017	68.4	66.89
2016	41.03	-4.73
2015	43.66	1.12
2014	44.53	43.64
2013	31.31	-28.77

Total Assets: $125,412,788
Asset Allocation
Asset	%
Cash	1%
Stocks	49%
US Stocks	1%
Bonds	0%
US Bonds	0%
Other	49%

Services Offered: Automatic Investment Plan, Retirement Investment

Investment Strategy: The investment seeks to replicate as closely as possible, before fees and expenses, the price and yield performance of the MVIS® India Small-Cap Index. The fund invests substantially all of its assets in the Subsidiary, a wholly-owned subsidiary located in the Republic of Mauritius. The Subsidiary in turn will normally invest at least 80% of its total assets in securities that comprise the fund's benchmark index, and depositary receipts based on the securities in the fund's benchmark index. The index includes Indian small-capitalization companies selected on the basis of their relative market capitalizations. **Top Holdings:** India Small Cap Mauritius NIIT Technologies Ltd Ipca Laboratories Ltd PVR Ltd DCB Bank Ltd

---

RiverFront Dynamic US Flex-Cap ETF

C   HOLD

Ticker	Traded On	NAV	Total Assets ($)	Dividend Yield (TTM)	Turnover Ratio	Expense Ratio
RFFC	NYSE Arca	32.99	$125,345,223	1.51	152	0.52

Ratings
Reward	C
Risk	C-
Recent Upgrade/Downgrade	

Fund Information
Fund Type	Exchange Traded Funds
Category	US Equity Large Cap Blend
Sub-Category	Large Blend
Prospectus Objective	Growth
Inception Date	Jun-16
Open to New Investments	Y

Prices
Price (as of 9/30/2019)	32.98
52-Week High	36.06
52-Week Low	27.40

Total Returns (%)
3-Month	6-Month	1-Year	3-Year	5-Year
-1.45	-0.44	-6.92	31.95	

3-Year Standard Deviation	14.82
Effective Duration	

Valuation
Premium/Discount (1-Year Average)	-0.06

Company Information
Provider	ALPS
Manager/Tenure	Adam Grossman (3), Scott Hays (3), Chris Konstantinos (3), 1 other
Website	http://www.alpsfunds.com
Address	ALPS 1290 Broadway, Suite 1100 Denver CO 80203 United States
Phone Number	866-759-5679

PERFORMANCE

Ratings History
Date	Overall Rating	Risk Rating	Reward Rating
Q3-19	C	C-	C
Q4-18	C-	C-	C
Q4-17	D+	B+	C
Q4-16	U		
Q4-15			

Asset & Performance History
Date	NAV	1-Year Total Return
2018	29.15	-9.66
2017	32.66	20.81
2016	27.31	
2015		
2014		
2013		

Total Assets: $125,345,223
Asset Allocation
Asset	%
Cash	0%
Stocks	100%
US Stocks	99%
Bonds	0%
US Bonds	0%
Other	0%

Services Offered:

Investment Strategy: The investment seeks to provide capital appreciation. The fund invests at least 65% of its net assets in a portfolio of equity securities of publicly traded U.S. companies. Equity securities include common stocks and common or preferred shares of real estate investment trusts. The fund may invest in small-, mid- and large-capitalization companies. It is non-diversified. **Top Holdings:** Microsoft Corp Apple Inc Amazon.com Inc Facebook Inc A Alphabet Inc Class C

Invesco BLDRS Emerging Markets 50 ADR Index Fund   C   HOLD

Ticker	Traded On	NAV	Total Assets ($)	Dividend Yield (TTM)	Turnover Ratio	Expense Ratio
ADRE	NAS CM	38.53	$125,225,044	1.64	10	0.3

Ratings
Reward	B-
Risk	D+
Recent Upgrade/Downgrade	Up

Fund Information
Fund Type	Exchange Traded Funds
Category	Global Emerg Mkts Equity
Sub-Category	Diversified Emerging Mkts
Prospectus Objective	Div Emerg Mkts
Inception Date	Nov-02
Open to New Investments	Y

Prices
Price (as of 9/30/2019)	38.42
52-Week High	42.47
52-Week Low	34.99

Total Returns (%)
3-Month	6-Month	1-Year	3-Year	5-Year
-4.77	-6.24	-3.75	16.96	11.68

3-Year Standard Deviation	16.76
Effective Duration	

Valuation
Premium/Discount (1-Year Average)	-0.14

Company Information
Provider	Invesco
Manager/Tenure	Management Team (16)
Website	http://www.invesco.com/us
Address	Invesco 11 Greenway Plaza, Ste. 2500
	Houston TX 77046 United States
Phone Number	800-659-1005

PERFORMANCE

Ratings History

Date	Overall Rating	Risk Rating	Reward Rating
Q3-19	C	D+	B-
Q4-18	C	D+	B-
Q4-17	C+	C	B-
Q4-16	C-	D+	C
Q4-15	C+	C	B-

Asset & Performance History

Date	NAV	1-Year Total Return
2018	36.2	-14
2017	42.92	35.34
2016	32.24	12.61
2015	29.13	-15.99
2014	35.58	-2.22
2013	37.2	-4.96

Total Assets: $125,225,044

Asset Allocation

Asset	%
Cash	1%
Stocks	99%
US Stocks	0%
Bonds	0%
US Bonds	0%
Other	0%

Services Offered:

Investment Strategy: The investment seeks to provide investment results that correspond generally, before fees and expenses, to the price and yield performance of the Bank of New York Mellon Emerging Markets 50 ADR Index. The fund typically invests substantially all of its assets in the securities that make up the index. The index is intended to give investors a benchmark for tracking the price and yield performance of Emerging Markets Depositary Receipts. the fund is non-diversified. **Top Holdings:** Alibaba Group Holding Ltd ADR Taiwan Semiconductor Manufacturing Co Ltd ADR HDFC Bank Ltd ADR China Mobile Ltd ADR Infosys Ltd ADR

Direxion Daily 20+ Year Treasury Bear 3X Shares   D   SELL

Ticker	Traded On	NAV	Total Assets ($)	Dividend Yield (TTM)	Turnover Ratio	Expense Ratio
TMV	NYSE Arca	10.39	$124,675,145	2.15	0	1.02

Ratings
Reward	D-
Risk	D
Recent Upgrade/Downgrade	

Fund Information
Fund Type	Exchange Traded Funds
Category	Trading Tools
Sub-Category	Trading--Inverse Debt
Prospectus Objective	Govt Bond - Treasury
Inception Date	Apr-09
Open to New Investments	Y

Prices
Price (as of 9/30/2019)	10.39
52-Week High	23.66
52-Week Low	9.60

Total Returns (%)
3-Month	6-Month	1-Year	3-Year	5-Year
-23.53	-37.16	-50.65	-35.96	-73.74

3-Year Standard Deviation	34.38
Effective Duration	

Valuation
Premium/Discount (1-Year Average)	-0.10

Company Information
Provider	Direxion Funds
Manager/Tenure	Paul Brigandi (10), Tony Ng (4)
Website	http://www.direxionfunds.com
Address	Direxion Funds 1301 Avenue Of The
	Americas (6th Avenue) New York NY
	10019 United States
Phone Number	646-572-3390

PERFORMANCE

Ratings History

Date	Overall Rating	Risk Rating	Reward Rating
Q3-19	D	D	D-
Q4-18	C-	D+	D+
Q4-17	D	D	D
Q4-16	D	D-	D
Q4-15	D	D	D-

Asset & Performance History

Date	NAV	1-Year Total Return
2018	18.43	5.67
2017	17.54	-26.79
2016	23.96	-14.06
2015	27.88	-12.27
2014	31.78	-57.15
2013	74.17	37.45

Total Assets: $124,675,145

Asset Allocation

Asset	%
Cash	117%
Stocks	0%
US Stocks	0%
Bonds	-17%
US Bonds	-17%
Other	0%

Services Offered:

Investment Strategy: The investment seeks daily investment results before fees and expenses of 300% of the inverse (or opposite) of the daily performance of the ICE U.S. Treasury 20+ Year Bond Index. The fund, under normal circumstances, invests in swap agreements, futures contracts, short positions or other financial instruments that, in combination, provide inverse (opposite) or short leveraged exposure to the index equal to at least 80% of the fund's net assets (plus borrowing for investment purposes). The index is a market value weighted index that includes publicly issued U.S. Treasury securities that have a remaining maturity of greater than 20 years. It is non-diversified. **Top Holdings:** 20+ Yr Treas Bd Idx Swap 20+ Yr Treas Bd Idx Swap 20+ Yr Treas Bd Idx Swap 20+ Yr Treas Bd Idx Swap 20+ Yr Treas Bd Idx Swap

PPTY – U.S. Diversified Real Estate ETF   C   HOLD

Ticker	Traded On	NAV	Total Assets ($)	Dividend Yield (TTM)	Turnover Ratio	Expense Ratio
PPTY	NYSE Arca	32.65	$124,072,748	2.29		0.53

Ratings
Reward	C
Risk	C-
Recent Upgrade/Downgrade	Up

Fund Information
Fund Type	Exchange Traded Funds
Category	Real Estate Sector Equity
Sub-Category	Real Estate
Prospectus Objective	Real Estate
Inception Date	Mar-18
Open to New Investments	Y

Prices
Price (as of 9/30/2019)	32.66
52-Week High	32.69
52-Week Low	24.89

Total Returns (%)
3-Month	6-Month	1-Year	3-Year	5-Year
7.01	9.42	21.13		

3-Year Standard Deviation	
Effective Duration	

Valuation
Premium/Discount (1-Year Average)	-0.01

Company Information
Provider	PPTY
Manager/Tenure	Denise M. Krisko (1), Austin Wen (1)
Website	http://https://pptyetf.com
Address	US United States
Phone Number	

PERFORMANCE

Ratings History
Date	Overall Rating	Risk Rating	Reward Rating
Q3-19	C	C-	C
Q4-18	U		
Q4-17			
Q4-16			
Q4-15			

Asset & Performance History
Date	NAV	1-Year Total Return
2018	25.88	
2017		
2016		
2015		
2014		
2013		

Total Assets: $124,072,748

Asset Allocation
Asset	%
Cash	0%
Stocks	100%
US Stocks	100%
Bonds	0%
US Bonds	0%
Other	0%

Services Offered:

Investment Strategy: The investment seeks to track the performance, before fees and expenses, of the USREX – U.S. Diversified Real Estate Index™. Under normal circumstances, at least 80% of the fund's total assets (exclusive of any collateral held from securities lending) will be invested in the component securities of the index. The index was developed in 2017 by the fund's index provider and the parent company of the fund's investment adviser and sub-adviser, and uses a rules-based methodology to provide diversified exposure to the liquid U.S. real estate market. **Top Holdings:** AvalonBay Communities Inc Prologis Inc Equity Residential Equinix Inc Mid-America Apartment Communities Inc

Pacer Trendpilot™ European Index ETF   C-   HOLD

Ticker	Traded On	NAV	Total Assets ($)	Dividend Yield (TTM)	Turnover Ratio	Expense Ratio
PTEU	BATS	26.36	$123,871,370	1.77	396	0.65

Ratings
Reward	C-
Risk	C-
Recent Upgrade/Downgrade	

Fund Information
Fund Type	Exchange Traded Funds
Category	Europe Equity Large Cap
Sub-Category	Europe Stock
Prospectus Objective	Growth & Inc
Inception Date	Dec-15
Open to New Investments	Y

Prices
Price (as of 9/30/2019)	26.40
52-Week High	27.08
52-Week Low	24.59

Total Returns (%)
3-Month	6-Month	1-Year	3-Year	5-Year
-1.93	2.16	1.33	14.25	

3-Year Standard Deviation	12.5
Effective Duration	

Valuation
Premium/Discount (1-Year Average)	-0.04

Company Information
Provider	Pacer
Manager/Tenure	Bruce Kavanaugh (3), Michael Mack (3)
Website	http://www.paceretfs.com
Address	Pacer 16 Industrial Blvd, Suite 201 Paoli PA 19301 United States
Phone Number	

PERFORMANCE

Ratings History
Date	Overall Rating	Risk Rating	Reward Rating
Q3-19	C-	C-	C-
Q4-18	D+	D+	D+
Q4-17	C-	C+	C
Q4-16	D-	D	D
Q4-15			

Asset & Performance History
Date	NAV	1-Year Total Return
2018	25.06	-15.97
2017	30.38	28.04
2016	23.87	-5.2
2015	25	
2014		
2013		

Total Assets: $123,871,370

Asset Allocation
Asset	%
Cash	0%
Stocks	100%
US Stocks	2%
Bonds	0%
US Bonds	0%
Other	0%

Services Offered:

Investment Strategy: The investment seeks to track the total return performance of the Pacer Trendpilot European Index. Normally the fund will invest at least 80% of its total assets in the component securities of the index and investments that have economic characteristics that are substantially identical to the economic characteristics of such component securities. The index uses an objective, rules-based methodology to implement a systematic trend-following strategy that directs exposure (i) 100% to the FTSE Eurozone Index, (ii) 50% to the FTSE Eurozone Index and 50% to 3-Month U.S. Treasury bills, or (iii) 100% to 3-Month U.S. Treasury bills. It is non-diversified. **Top Holdings:** Total SA ADR SAP SE ADR LVMH Moet Hennessy Louis Vuitton SE Sanofi SA ADR Unilever NV

Cambria Shareholder Yield ETF   C-   HOLD

Ticker	Traded On	NAV	Total Assets ($)	Dividend Yield (TTM)	Turnover Ratio	Expense Ratio
SYLD	BATS	36.35	$123,586,226	2.15		0.59

Ratings

Reward	C
Risk	D+
Recent Upgrade/Downgrade	

Fund Information

Fund Type	Exchange Traded Funds
Category	US Equity Mid Cap
Sub-Category	Mid-Cap Value
Prospectus Objective	Growth & Inc
Inception Date	May-13
Open to New Investments	Y

Prices

Price (as of 9/30/2019)	36.41
52-Week High	39.44
52-Week Low	30.75

Total Returns (%)

3-Month	6-Month	1-Year	3-Year	5-Year
0.63	0.22	-5.68	28.59	44.55

3-Year Standard Deviation	16.1
Effective Duration	

Valuation

Premium/Discount (1-Year Average)	-0.02

Company Information

Provider	CAMBRIA ETF TRUST
Manager/Tenure	Mebane T. Faber (6)
Website	http://www.cambriafunds.com
Address	CAMBRIA ETF TRUST 2711 Centreville Road Suite 400 Wilmington, DE 19808 Wilmington DE 19808 United States
Phone Number	310-683-5500

PERFORMANCE

Ratings History

Date	Overall Rating	Risk Rating	Reward Rating
Q3-19	C-	D+	C
Q4-18	C-	C-	C
Q4-17	B	B+	B
Q4-16	C	D+	B-
Q4-15	C	C	C

Asset & Performance History

Date	NAV	1-Year Total Return
2018	32.48	-13.36
2017	38.33	19.73
2016	32.53	15.25
2015	28.82	-1.25
2014	31.2	11.08
2013	29.32	

Total Assets: $123,586,226

Asset Allocation

Asset	%
Cash	1%
Stocks	99%
US Stocks	99%
Bonds	0%
US Bonds	0%
Other	0%

Services Offered:

Investment Strategy: The investment seeks investment results that correspond (before fees and expenses) generally to the price and yield performance of the Cambria Shareholder Yield Index (the "underlying index"). Under normal market conditions, the fund will invest at least 80% of its total assets in the components of the underlying index. The underlying index is comprised of equity securities issued by U.S.-based issuers. The adviser considers an issuer to be U.S.-based if it is domiciled or incorporated or has substantial business activity in the United States. **Top Holdings:** Texas Instruments Inc The Home Depot Inc Apple Inc Meritage Homes Corp Allstate Corp

---

iShares International Developed Property ETF   C   HOLD

Ticker	Traded On	NAV	Total Assets ($)	Dividend Yield (TTM)	Turnover Ratio	Expense Ratio
WPS	NYSE Arca	38.58	$123,452,828	4.22	9	0.48

Ratings

Reward	C
Risk	C-
Recent Upgrade/Downgrade	

Fund Information

Fund Type	Exchange Traded Funds
Category	Real Estate Sector Equity
Sub-Category	Global Real Estate
Prospectus Objective	Real Estate
Inception Date	Jul-07
Open to New Investments	Y

Prices

Price (as of 9/30/2019)	38.50
52-Week High	39.08
52-Week Low	34.00

Total Returns (%)

3-Month	6-Month	1-Year	3-Year	5-Year
1.65	1.17	9.19	17.84	30.41

3-Year Standard Deviation	10.33
Effective Duration	

Valuation

Premium/Discount (1-Year Average)	-0.11

Company Information

Provider	iShares
Manager/Tenure	Greg Savage (11), Jennifer Hsui (7), Alan Mason (3), 2 others
Website	http://www.ishares.com
Address	iShares 400 Howard Street San Francisco CA 94105 United States
Phone Number	800-474-2737

PERFORMANCE

Ratings History

Date	Overall Rating	Risk Rating	Reward Rating
Q3-19	C	C-	C
Q4-18	D+	C-	D+
Q4-17	B	B	B-
Q4-16	C-	C-	C
Q4-15	C-	D+	C

Asset & Performance History

Date	NAV	1-Year Total Return
2018	34.61	-8.89
2017	39.59	22.07
2016	33.91	1.37
2015	35.32	-0.81
2014	36.72	3.17
2013	37	7.59

Total Assets: $123,452,828

Asset Allocation

Asset	%
Cash	1%
Stocks	98%
US Stocks	0%
Bonds	0%
US Bonds	0%
Other	1%

Services Offered:

Investment Strategy: The investment seeks to track the investment results of the S&P Developed ex-U.S. Property IndexTM. The fund generally invests at least 90% of its assets in the component securities of the index and in investments that have economic characteristics that are substantially identical to the component securities and may invest up to 10% of its assets in certain futures, options and swap contracts, cash and cash equivalents. The index is a free float-adjusted, market capitalization-weighted index that defines and measures the investable universe of publicly-traded property companies domiciled in developed countries outside of the U.S. **Top Holdings:** Vonovia SE Mitsubishi Estate Co Ltd Link Real Estate Investment Trust Mitsui Fudosan Co Ltd Sun Hung Kai Properties Ltd

SPDR® S&P Transportation ETF

C   HOLD

Ticker	Traded On	NAV	Total Assets ($)	Dividend Yield (TTM)	Turnover Ratio	Expense Ratio
XTN	NYSE Arca		$123,347,766	1.21	18	0.35

Ratings
Reward	C
Risk	C-
Recent Upgrade/Downgrade	Up

Fund Information
Fund Type	Exchange Traded Funds
Category	Industrials Sector Equity
Sub-Category	Industrials
Prospectus Objective	Utility
Inception Date	Jan-11
Open to New Investments	Y

Prices
Price (as of 9/30/2019)	61.03
52-Week High	66.70
52-Week Low	50.73

Total Returns (%)
3-Month	6-Month	1-Year	3-Year	5-Year
-0.51	-0.65	-7.71	32.28	36.91

3-Year Standard Deviation	20.98
Effective Duration	

Valuation
Premium/Discount (1-Year Average)	-0.05

Company Information
Provider	SPDR State Street Global Advisors
Manager/Tenure	Michael J. Feehily (7), Karl A. Schneider (4), Michael Finocchi (2)
Website	http://www.spdrs.com
Address	SPDR State Street Global Advisors State Street Financial Center, 1 Lincoln Street Boston MA 02111-2900 United States
Phone Number	617-786-3000

PERFORMANCE

Ratings History
Date	Overall Rating	Risk Rating	Reward Rating
Q3-19	C	C-	C
Q4-18	C	C-	C
Q4-17	B	C+	B+
Q4-16	C+	C-	B
Q4-15	C	C	C+

Asset & Performance History
Date	NAV	1-Year Total Return
2018	53.63	-17
2017	65.18	21.63
2016	53.97	27.29
2015	42.84	-20.19
2014	54.21	33.78
2013	40.7	52.01

Total Assets: $123,347,766
Asset Allocation
Asset	%
Cash	0%
Stocks	100%
US Stocks	100%
Bonds	0%
US Bonds	0%
Other	0%

Services Offered:
Investment Strategy: The investment seeks to provide investment results that, before fees and expenses, correspond generally to the total return performance of an index derived from the transportation segment of a U.S. total market composite index. In seeking to track the performance of the S&P Transportation Select Industry Index (the "index"), the fund employs a sampling strategy. It generally invests substantially all, but at least 80%, of its total assets in the securities comprising the index. The index represents the transportation segment of the S&P Total Market Index ("S&P TMI"). The fund is non-diversified. **Top Holdings:** XPO Logistics Inc   JB Hunt Transport Services Inc   United Parcel Service Inc Class B   Genesee & Wyoming Inc Class A   Saia Inc

Principal Investment Grade Corporate Active ETF

D+   SELL

Ticker	Traded On	NAV	Total Assets ($)	Dividend Yield (TTM)	Turnover Ratio	Expense Ratio
IG	NYSE Arca	26.74	$123,020,562	3.7	93	0.26

Ratings
Reward	C-
Risk	D
Recent Upgrade/Downgrade	

Fund Information
Fund Type	Exchange Traded Funds
Category	US Fixed Income
Sub-Category	Corporate Bond
Prospectus Objective	Corp Bond - Gen
Inception Date	Apr-18
Open to New Investments	Y

Prices
Price (as of 9/30/2019)	26.81
52-Week High	27.12
52-Week Low	23.97

Total Returns (%)
3-Month	6-Month	1-Year	3-Year	5-Year
3.11	8.56	13.80		

3-Year Standard Deviation	
Effective Duration	7.80

Valuation
Premium/Discount (1-Year Average)	0.36

Company Information
Provider	Principal Funds
Manager/Tenure	John R. Friedl (1), Paul S. Kim (1), Daniela Spassova (1), 1 other
Website	http://www.principalfunds.com
Address	Principal Funds 430 W 7th St, Ste 219971 Kansas City MO 64105-1407 United States
Phone Number	800-787-1621

PERFORMANCE

Ratings History
Date	Overall Rating	Risk Rating	Reward Rating
Q3-19	D+	D	C-
Q4-18	U		
Q4-17			
Q4-16			
Q4-15			

Asset & Performance History
Date	NAV	1-Year Total Return
2018	24	
2017		
2016		
2015		
2014		
2013		

Total Assets: $123,020,562
Asset Allocation
Asset	%
Cash	2%
Stocks	0%
US Stocks	0%
Bonds	97%
US Bonds	90%
Other	0%

Services Offered:
Investment Strategy: The investment seeks to provide current income and, as a secondary objective, capital appreciation. The fund is an actively managed exchange-traded fund ("ETF") that seeks to achieve its investment objective by investing, under normal circumstances, at least 80% of its net assets, plus any borrowings for investment purposes, in investment grade corporate bonds and other fixed income securities at the time of purchase. "Investment grade" securities are rated BBB- or higher by S&P Global Ratings ("S&P Global") or Baa3 or higher by Moody's Investors Service, Inc. ("Moody's") or, if unrated, of comparable quality in the opinion of those selecting such investments. **Top Holdings:** Skandinaviska Enskilda Jr Subordina Regs 11/49 Var   XLIT Ltd. 4.45%   TIAA Asset Management Finance Company, LLC 4.12%   Royal Bank of Scotland Group plc 5.12%   Synchrony Bank 3%

Direxion Daily CSI 300 China A Share Bull 2X Shares   D+   SELL

Ticker	Traded On	NAV	Total Assets ($)	Dividend Yield (TTM)	Turnover Ratio	Expense Ratio
CHAU	NYSE Arca	20.33	$122,972,572	0.72	339	1.15

Ratings

Reward	D+
Risk	D+
Recent Upgrade/Downgrade	Down

Fund Information

Fund Type	Exchange Traded Funds
Category	Trading Tools
Sub-Category	Trading--Leveraged Equity
Prospectus Objective	Growth
Inception Date	Apr-15
Open to New Investments	Y

Prices

Price (as of 9/30/2019)	20.26
52-Week High	27.64
52-Week Low	13.90

Total Returns (%)

3-Month	6-Month	1-Year	3-Year	5-Year
-14.38	-21.11	6.43	11.47	

3-Year Standard Deviation	40.04
Effective Duration	

Valuation

Premium/Discount (1-Year Average)	-0.02

Company Information

Provider	Direxion Funds
Manager/Tenure	Paul Brigandi (4), Tony Ng (4)
Website	http://www.direxionfunds.com
Address	Direxion Funds 1301 Avenue Of The Americas (6th Avenue) New York NY 10019 United States
Phone Number	646-572-3390

PERFORMANCE

Ratings History

Date	Overall Rating	Risk Rating	Reward Rating
Q3-19	D+	D+	D+
Q4-18	D	D	D-
Q4-17	C	D+	B-
Q4-16	D	D	D
Q4-15	U		

Asset & Performance History

Date	NAV	1-Year Total Return
2018	14.41	-51.17
2017	29.73	75.29
2016	16.96	-26.73
2015	23.15	
2014		
2013		

Total Assets: $122,972,572
Asset Allocation

Asset	%
Cash	59%
Stocks	41%
US Stocks	0%
Bonds	0%
US Bonds	0%
Other	0%

Services Offered:

Investment Strategy: The investment seeks daily investment results, before fees and expenses, of 200% of the daily performance of the CSI 300 Index. The fund invests at least 80% of its net assets (plus borrowing for investment purposes) in financial instruments, such as swap agreements, and securities of the index, ETFs that track the index and other financial instruments that provide daily leveraged exposure to the index or to ETFs that track the index. The index is a modified free-float market capitalization weighted index comprised of the largest and most liquid stocks in the Chinese A-share market. The fund is non-diversified. **Top Holdings:** Xtrackers Harvest CSI 300 China A ETF   Deutsche X-Trck Harv Swp   Deutsche X-Trck Harv Swp   Deutsche X-Trck Harv Swp Deutsche X-Trck Harv Swp

---

TrimTabs All Cap U.S. Free-Cash-Flow ETF   C   HOLD

Ticker	Traded On	NAV	Total Assets ($)	Dividend Yield (TTM)	Turnover Ratio	Expense Ratio
TTAC	BATS	37.14	$122,578,037	0.52	49	0.59

Ratings

Reward	C
Risk	D+
Recent Upgrade/Downgrade	

Fund Information

Fund Type	Exchange Traded Funds
Category	US Equity Large Cap Blend
Sub-Category	Mid-Cap Growth
Prospectus Objective	Growth & Inc
Inception Date	Sep-16
Open to New Investments	Y

Prices

Price (as of 9/30/2019)	37.16
52-Week High	38.32
52-Week Low	29.75

Total Returns (%)

3-Month	6-Month	1-Year	3-Year	5-Year
-1.17	3.39	-1.72	49.01	

3-Year Standard Deviation	13.44
Effective Duration	

Valuation

Premium/Discount (1-Year Average)	-0.01

Company Information

Provider	TrimTabs
Manager/Tenure	Ted M. Theodore (3), Janet F. Johnston (1)
Website	http://www.trimtabsfunds.com
Address	TrimTabs 1350 Avenue of the Americas, Suite 248 New York NY 10019 United States
Phone Number	

PERFORMANCE

Ratings History

Date	Overall Rating	Risk Rating	Reward Rating
Q3-19	C	D+	C
Q4-18	C-	C-	C
Q4-17	D	B	C
Q4-16	U		
Q4-15			

Asset & Performance History

Date	NAV	1-Year Total Return
2018	31.48	-5.99
2017	33.7	25.59
2016	26.94	
2015		
2014		
2013		

Total Assets: $122,578,037
Asset Allocation

Asset	%
Cash	1%
Stocks	99%
US Stocks	97%
Bonds	0%
US Bonds	0%
Other	0%

Services Offered:

Investment Strategy: The investment seeks to generate long-term returns in excess of the total return of the Russell 3000® Index (the "index"), with less volatility than the index. The fund is an actively managed ETF. It seeks to achieve its investment objective by investing in stocks with liquidity and fundamental characteristics that the adviser believes are historically associated with superior long-term performance. Based on extensive historical research, the adviser designed the following quantitative stock selection rules to make allocation decisions and seek to protect against dramatic over- or under-weighting of individual securities in the fund's portfolio. **Top Holdings:** Match Group Inc   Zoetis Inc Class A   Chemed Corp   Costco Wholesale Corp   Aspen Technology Inc

ProShares MSCI EAFE Dividend Growers ETF   C-   HOLD

Ticker	Traded On	NAV	Total Assets ($)	Dividend Yield (TTM)	Turnover Ratio	Expense Ratio
EFAD	BATS	37.31	$122,375,864	2.05	31	0.5

Ratings
Reward   C
Risk   C-
Recent Upgrade/Downgrade

Fund Information
Fund Type   Exchange Traded Funds
Category   Global Equity Large Cap
Sub-Category   Foreign Large Growth
Prospectus Objective   Equity-Income
Inception Date   Aug-14
Open to New Investments   Y

Prices
Price (as of 9/30/2019)   37.32
52-Week High   38.23
52-Week Low   32.66

Total Returns (%)

3-Month	6-Month	1-Year	3-Year	5-Year
-0.10	2.15	-0.20	14.20	9.99

3-Year Standard Deviation   10.94
Effective Duration

Valuation
Premium/Discount (1-Year Average)   -0.07

Company Information
Provider   ProShares
Manager/Tenure   Scott Hanson (3), Ryan Dofflemeyer (0)
Website   http://www.proshares.com
Address   ProShares 7501 Wisconsin Avenue, Suite 1000 Bethesda MD 20814 United States
Phone Number   866-776-5125

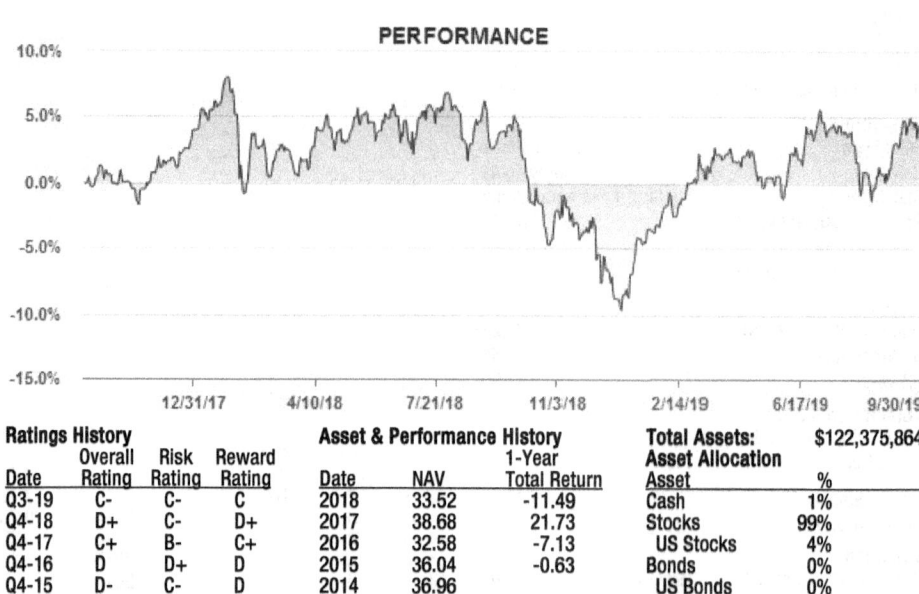

Ratings History

Date	Overall Rating	Risk Rating	Reward Rating
Q3-19	C-	C-	C
Q4-18	D+	C-	D+
Q4-17	C+	B-	C+
Q4-16	D	D+	D
Q4-15	D-	C-	D

Asset & Performance History

Date	NAV	1-Year Total Return
2018	33.52	-11.49
2017	38.68	21.73
2016	32.58	-7.13
2015	36.04	-0.63
2014	36.96	
2013		

Total Assets: $122,375,864
Asset Allocation

Asset	%
Cash	1%
Stocks	99%
US Stocks	4%
Bonds	0%
US Bonds	0%
Other	0%

Services Offered:

Investment Strategy: The investment seeks investment results, before fees and expenses, that track the performance of the MSCI EAFE Dividend Masters Index (the "index"). The index, constructed and maintained by MSCI, targets companies that are currently members of the MSCI EAFE Index ("MSCI EAFE") and have increased dividend payments each year for at least 10 years. The index contains a minimum of 40 stocks, which are equally weighted. Under normal circumstances, the fund will invest at least 80% of its total assets in component securities. **Top Holdings:** Ashtead Group PLC Sundrug Co Ltd L'Oreal SA Sysmex Corp Flutter Entertainment PLC

Invesco S&P SmallCap Financials ETF   C   HOLD

Ticker	Traded On	NAV	Total Assets ($)	Dividend Yield (TTM)	Turnover Ratio	Expense Ratio
PSCF	NAS CM	54.26	$122,079,819	3		0.29

Ratings
Reward   C
Risk   C-
Recent Upgrade/Downgrade

Fund Information
Fund Type   Exchange Traded Funds
Category   Financials Sector Equity
Sub-Category   Financial
Prospectus Objective   Financial
Inception Date   Apr-10
Open to New Investments

Prices
Price (as of 9/30/2019)   54.37
52-Week High   56.75
52-Week Low   46.25

Total Returns (%)

3-Month	6-Month	1-Year	3-Year	5-Year
1.08	3.67	0.78	32.85	69.35

3-Year Standard Deviation   17.25
Effective Duration

Valuation
Premium/Discount (1-Year Average)   -0.04

Company Information
Provider   Invesco
Manager/Tenure   Peter Hubbard (9), Michael Jeanette (9), Tony Seisser (5)
Website   http://www.invesco.com/us
Address   Invesco 11 Greenway Plaza, Ste. 2500 Houston TX 77046 United States
Phone Number   800-659-1005

Ratings History

Date	Overall Rating	Risk Rating	Reward Rating
Q3-19	C	C-	C
Q4-18	C-	D+	C
Q4-17	A-	B	A
Q4-16	C	C-	C+
Q4-15	C+	C-	B

Asset & Performance History

Date	NAV	1-Year Total Return
2018	48.11	-8.81
2017	54.28	6.28
2016	52.25	32.06
2015	40.74	0.07
2014	41.68	7.96
2013	39.59	31.45

Total Assets: $122,079,819
Asset Allocation

Asset	%
Cash	0%
Stocks	100%
US Stocks	98%
Bonds	0%
US Bonds	0%
Other	0%

Services Offered:

Investment Strategy: The investment seeks to track the investment results (before fees and expenses) of the S&P SmallCap 600® Capped Financials & Real Estate Index (the "underlying index"). The fund generally will invest at least 90% of its total assets in the securities, which may include real estate investment trusts ("REITs"), of small-capitalization U.S. financial service companies that comprise the underlying index. These companies are principally engaged in the business of providing financial services and products, including banking, investment services, insurance and real estate finance services. **Top Holdings:** Selective Insurance Group Inc FirstCash Inc RLI Corp Glacier Bancorp Inc Community Bank System Inc

Davis Select International ETF
D+   SELL

Ticker	Traded On	NAV	Total Assets ($)	Dividend Yield (TTM)	Turnover Ratio	Expense Ratio
DINT	NAS CM	17.38	$121,640,344	0.36	17	0.75

Ratings
Reward	D
Risk	D+
Recent Upgrade/Downgrade	Up

Fund Information
Fund Type	Exchange Traded Funds
Category	Global Equity Large Cap
Sub-Category	Foreign Large Blend
Prospectus Objective	Growth
Inception Date	Mar-18
Open to New Investments	Y

Prices
Price (as of 9/30/2019)	17.40
52-Week High	18.91
52-Week Low	14.59

Total Returns (%)
3-Month	6-Month	1-Year	3-Year	5-Year
-3.46	-4.36	-3.51		

3-Year Standard Deviation	
Effective Duration	

Valuation
Premium/Discount (1-Year Average)	0.26

Company Information
Provider	Davis ETFs
Manager/Tenure	Danton Goei (1)
Website	
Address	c/o Davis Selected Advisers, L.P. 2949 E. Elvira Rd., Ste. 101 Tucson Arizona 85756 United States
Phone Number	800-279-0279

PERFORMANCE

Ratings History
Date	Overall Rating	Risk Rating	Reward Rating
Q3-19	D+	D+	D
Q4-18	U		
Q4-17			
Q4-16			
Q4-15			

Asset & Performance History
Date	NAV	1-Year Total Return
2018	15.09	
2017		
2016		
2015		
2014		
2013		

Total Assets: $121,640,344

Asset Allocation
Asset	%
Cash	0%
Stocks	100%
US Stocks	8%
Bonds	0%
US Bonds	0%
Other	0%

Services Offered:

Investment Strategy: The investment seeks long-term growth of capital. The fund's investment adviser uses the Davis Investment Discipline to invest the fund's portfolio principally in common stocks (including indirect holdings of common stock through depositary receipts) issued by foreign companies, including countries with developed or emerging markets. The fund may invest in large, medium or small companies without regard to market capitalization. **Top Holdings:** New Oriental Education & Technology Group Inc ADR Alibaba Group Holding Ltd ADR Naspers Ltd Class N Sul America SA JD.com Inc ADR

First Trust Materials AlphaDEX® Fund
C-   HOLD

Ticker	Traded On	NAV	Total Assets ($)	Dividend Yield (TTM)	Turnover Ratio	Expense Ratio
FXZ	NYSE Arca	37.25	$121,064,358	1.62	82	0.64

Ratings
Reward	C
Risk	C-
Recent Upgrade/Downgrade	

Fund Information
Fund Type	Exchange Traded Funds
Category	Natural Resources
Sub-Category	Natural Resources
Prospectus Objective	Unaligned
Inception Date	May-07
Open to New Investments	Y

Prices
Price (as of 9/30/2019)	37.24
52-Week High	41.59
52-Week Low	31.50

Total Returns (%)
3-Month	6-Month	1-Year	3-Year	5-Year
-3.59	-3.01	-8.80	13.24	26.82

3-Year Standard Deviation	18.81
Effective Duration	

Valuation
Premium/Discount (1-Year Average)	-0.02

Company Information
Provider	First Trust
Manager/Tenure	Jon C. Erickson (12), Daniel J. Lindquist (12), David G. McGarel (12), 3 others
Website	http://www.ftportfolios.com/
Address	First Trust 120 E. Liberty Drive, Suite 400 Wheaton IL 60187 United States
Phone Number	800-621-1675

PERFORMANCE

Ratings History
Date	Overall Rating	Risk Rating	Reward Rating
Q3-19	C-	C-	C
Q4-18	C	C-	C
Q4-17	B	C+	A
Q4-16	B-	C	B
Q4-15	C	C	C

Asset & Performance History
Date	NAV	1-Year Total Return
2018	33.54	-22.55
2017	43.83	23.68
2016	35.83	29.17
2015	28.09	-9.85
2014	31.54	-0.98
2013	32.39	26.73

Total Assets: $121,064,358

Asset Allocation
Asset	%
Cash	0%
Stocks	100%
US Stocks	99%
Bonds	0%
US Bonds	0%
Other	0%

Services Offered:

Investment Strategy: The investment seeks investment results that correspond generally to the price and yield (before the fund's fees and expenses) of an equity index called the StrataQuant® Materials Index. The fund will normally invest at least 90% of its net assets (including investment borrowings) in common stocks that comprise the index. The index is a modified equal-dollar weighted index designed by IDI to objectively identify and select stocks from the Russell 1000® Index in the materials and processing sector that may generate positive alpha relative to traditional passive-style indices through the use of the AlphaDEX® selection methodology. **Top Holdings:** Crown Holdings Inc The Scotts Miracle Gro Co A Reliance Steel & Aluminum Co WestRock Co A Steel Dynamics Inc

WisdomTree U.S. SmallCap Quality Dividend Growth Fund

C-   **HOLD**

Ticker	Traded On	NAV	Total Assets ($)	Dividend Yield (TTM)	Turnover Ratio	Expense Ratio
DGRS	NAS CM	35.55	$120,869,675	2.61	42	0.38

Ratings
Reward	C
Risk	D+
Recent Upgrade/Downgrade	

Fund Information
Fund Type	Exchange Traded Funds
Category	US Equity Small Cap
Sub-Category	Small Blend
Prospectus Objective	Small Company
Inception Date	Jul-13
Open to New Investments	Y

Prices
Price (as of 9/30/2019)	35.58
52-Week High	37.24
52-Week Low	29.46

Total Returns (%)
3-Month	6-Month	1-Year	3-Year	5-Year
0.69	2.10	-1.91	23.79	50.97

3-Year Standard Deviation	17.91
Effective Duration	

Valuation
Premium/Discount (1-Year Average)	0.10

Company Information
Provider	WisdomTree
Manager/Tenure	Richard A. Brown (6), Thomas J. Durante (6), Karen Q. Wong (6)
Website	http://www.wisdomtree.com
Address	WisdomTree 245 Park Avenue, 35th floor New York NY 10167 United States
Phone Number	866-909-9473

PERFORMANCE

Ratings History
Date	Overall Rating	Risk Rating	Reward Rating
Q3-19	C-	D+	C
Q4-18	C-	C-	C
Q4-17	B	B	B+
Q4-16	C-	C-	C
Q4-15	C-	D+	C-

Asset & Performance History
Date	NAV	1-Year Total Return
2018	31.15	-10.29
2017	35.55	7.09
2016	33.94	30.08
2015	26.53	-7.02
2014	29.23	4.36
2013	28.61	

Total Assets: $120,869,675
Asset Allocation
Asset	%
Cash	0%
Stocks	100%
US Stocks	100%
Bonds	0%
US Bonds	0%
Other	0%

Services Offered:

Investment Strategy: The investment seeks to track the price and yield performance, before fees and expenses, of the WisdomTree U.S. SmallCap Quality Dividend Growth Index. The index is a fundamentally weighted index that consists of the small-capitalization segment of dividend-paying U.S. common stocks with growth characteristics. Under normal circumstances, at least 80% of the fund's total assets (exclusive of collateral held from securities lending) will be invested in component securities of the index and investments that have economic characteristics that are substantially identical to the economic characteristics of such component securities. It is non-diversified.
Top Holdings: Brookfield Property REIT Inc   Artisan Partners Asset Management Inc   PotlatchDeltic Corp   M.D.C. Holdings Inc   Cohen & Steers Inc

---

Credit Suisse X-Links Monthly Pay 2xLeveraged Mortgage REIT ETN

C   **HOLD**

Ticker	Traded On	NAV	Total Assets ($)	Dividend Yield (TTM)	Turnover Ratio	Expense Ratio
REML	NYSE Arca		$120,597,750	22.01		0.5

Ratings
Reward	C
Risk	C-
Recent Upgrade/Downgrade	Up

Fund Information
Fund Type	Exchange Traded Funds
Category	Trading Tools
Sub-Category	Trading--Leveraged Equity
Prospectus Objective	Real Estate
Inception Date	Jul-16
Open to New Investments	Y

Prices
Price (as of 9/30/2019)	23.02
52-Week High	26.92
52-Week Low	20.20

Total Returns (%)
3-Month	6-Month	1-Year	3-Year	5-Year
1.42	-1.51	5.03	53.14	

3-Year Standard Deviation	25.33
Effective Duration	

Valuation
Premium/Discount (1-Year Average)	0.25

Company Information
Provider	Credit Suisse AG
Manager/Tenure	No Manager (3)
Website	
Address	Kilmore House Park Lane Dublin Ireland
Phone Number	

PERFORMANCE

Ratings History
Date	Overall Rating	Risk Rating	Reward Rating
Q3-19	C	C-	C
Q4-18	C-	C-	C-
Q4-17	D	B	C
Q4-16	U		
Q4-15			

Asset & Performance History
Date	NAV	1-Year Total Return
2018	22.95	-7.56
2017	30.36	37.8
2016	26.83	
2015		
2014		
2013		

Total Assets: $120,597,750
Asset Allocation
Asset	%
Cash	%
Stocks	%
US Stocks	%
Bonds	%
US Bonds	%
Other	%

Services Offered:

Investment Strategy: The investment seeks to provide a monthly compounded 2x leveraged long exposure to the price return version of the FTSE NAREIT All Mortgage Capped Index (the "index").
The index measures the composite performance of tax-qualified U.S. mortgage real estate investment trusts ("Mortgage REITs") with more than 50% of total assets invested in mortgage loans or mortgage-backed securities secured by interests in real property that are listed on the New York Stock Exchange, the NYSE Arca or the NASDAQ National Market List (the "index constituents"). **Top Holdings:**

Pacer Benchmark Data & Infrastructure Real Estate SCTR ETF   B-   BUY

Ticker	Traded On	NAV	Total Assets ($)	Dividend Yield (TTM)	Turnover Ratio	Expense Ratio
SRVR	NYSE Arca	32.15	$120,576,022	1.63	27	0.6

Ratings
Reward	B+
Risk	C-
Recent Upgrade/Downgrade	Up

Fund Information
Fund Type	Exchange Traded Funds
Category	Real Estate Sector Equity
Sub-Category	Real Estate
Prospectus Objective	Growth & Inc
Inception Date	May-18
Open to New Investments	Y

Prices
Price (as of 9/30/2019)	32.20
52-Week High	32.66
52-Week Low	22.35

Total Returns (%)
3-Month	6-Month	1-Year	3-Year	5-Year
9.44	14.95	26.28		

3-Year Standard Deviation	
Effective Duration	

Valuation
Premium/Discount (1-Year Average)	0.02

Company Information
Provider	Pacer
Manager/Tenure	Bruce Kavanaugh (1), Michael Mack (1)
Website	http://www.paceretfs.com
Address	Pacer 16 Industrial Blvd, Suite 201 Paoli PA 19301 United States
Phone Number	

PERFORMANCE

Ratings History
Date	Overall Rating	Risk Rating	Reward Rating
Q3-19	B-	C-	B+
Q4-18	U		
Q4-17			
Q4-16			
Q4-15			

Asset & Performance History
Date	NAV	1-Year Total Return
2018	23.42	
2017		
2016		
2015		
2014		
2013		

Total Assets: $120,576,022

Asset Allocation
Asset	%
Cash	0%
Stocks	100%
US Stocks	95%
Bonds	0%
US Bonds	0%
Other	0%

Services Offered:

Investment Strategy: The investment seeks to track the total return performance, before fees and expenses, of the Benchmark Data & Infrastructure Real Estate SCTR Index (the "index"). Under normal circumstances, at least 80% of the fund's total assets (exclusive of collateral held from securities lending) will be invested in the component securities of the index. The index is generally composed of the U.S.-listed equity securities of companies that derive at least 85% of their earnings or revenues from real estate operations in the data and infrastructure real estate sectors ("Eligible Companies"). The fund is non-diversified. **Top Holdings:** Equinix Inc Crown Castle International Corp American Tower Corp CyrusOne Inc SBA Communications Corp

---

Invesco RAFI™ Strategic US ETF   C-   HOLD

Ticker	Traded On	NAV	Total Assets ($)	Dividend Yield (TTM)	Turnover Ratio	Expense Ratio
IUS	NAS CM	25.53	$119,984,867	2.03		0.19

Ratings
Reward	D+
Risk	C-
Recent Upgrade/Downgrade	

Fund Information
Fund Type	Exchange Traded Funds
Category	US Equity Large Cap Blend
Sub-Category	Large Blend
Prospectus Objective	Growth
Inception Date	Sep-18
Open to New Investments	Y

Prices
Price (as of 9/30/2019)	25.53
52-Week High	26.08
52-Week Low	21.65

Total Returns (%)
3-Month	6-Month	1-Year	3-Year	5-Year
0.83	4.28	2.66		

3-Year Standard Deviation	
Effective Duration	

Valuation
Premium/Discount (1-Year Average)	-0.91

Company Information
Provider	Invesco
Manager/Tenure	Peter Hubbard (1), Michael Jeanette (1), Tony Seisser (1)
Website	http://www.invesco.com/us
Address	Invesco 11 Greenway Plaza, Ste. 2500 Houston TX 77046 United States
Phone Number	800-659-1005

PERFORMANCE

Ratings History
Date	Overall Rating	Risk Rating	Reward Rating
Q3-19	C-	C-	D+
Q4-18	U		
Q4-17			
Q4-16			
Q4-15			

Asset & Performance History
Date	NAV	1-Year Total Return
2018	21.92	
2017		
2016		
2015		
2014		
2013		

Total Assets: $119,984,867

Asset Allocation
Asset	%
Cash	0%
Stocks	100%
US Stocks	100%
Bonds	0%
US Bonds	0%
Other	0%

Services Offered:

Investment Strategy: The investment seeks to track the investment results (before fees and expenses) of the Invesco Strategic US Index (the "underlying index"). The fund generally will invest at least 80% of its total assets in securities that comprise the underlying index. It generally invests in all of the securities comprising its underlying index in proportion to their weightings in the underlying index. The underlying index is designed to measure the performance of equity securities issued by higher quality, large-business-sized companies designated as U.S. companies. The fund is non-diversified. **Top Holdings:** Apple Inc Berkshire Hathaway Inc B AT&T Inc Microsoft Corp Exxon Mobil Corp

Nationwide Risk-Based International Equity ETF | D SELL

Ticker	Traded On	NAV	Total Assets ($)	Dividend Yield (TTM)	Turnover Ratio	Expense Ratio
RBIN	NYSE Arca	25.22	$119,170,699	2.64		0.42

Ratings
Reward   D+
Risk   D
Recent Upgrade/Downgrade   Up

Fund Information
Fund Type   Exchange Traded Funds
Category   Global Equity Large Cap
Sub-Category   Foreign Large Blend
Prospectus Objective   Foreign Stock
Inception Date   Sep-17
Open to New Investments Y

Prices
Price (as of 9/30/2019) 25.23
52-Week High   26.05
52-Week Low   22.56

Total Returns (%)

3-Month	6-Month	1-Year	3-Year	5-Year
0.31	1.11	-0.13		

3-Year Standard Deviation
Effective Duration

Valuation
Premium/Discount (1-Year Average)   0.05

Company Information
Provider   Nationwide
Manager/Tenure   Denise M. Krisko (2), Rafael Zayas (2)
Website   http://www.nationwide.com/mutualfunds
Address   Nationwide One Nationwide Plaza
                 Columbus OH 43215 United States
Phone Number   800-848-0920

PERFORMANCE

Ratings History

Date	Overall Rating	Risk Rating	Reward Rating
Q3-19	D	D	D+
Q4-18	D	D	D
Q4-17	U		
Q4-16			
Q4-15			

Asset & Performance History

Date	NAV	1-Year Total Return
2018	22.8	-11.91
2017	25.88	
2016		
2015		
2014		
2013		

Total Assets: $119,170,699

Asset Allocation

Asset	%
Cash	0%
Stocks	100%
US Stocks	2%
Bonds	0%
US Bonds	0%
Other	0%

Services Offered:

Investment Strategy: The investment seeks to track the total return performance, before fees and expenses, of the Rothschild & Co Risk-Based International Index. At least 80% of its total assets will be invested in the component securities of the index. The index is a rules-based, equal risk-weighted index that is designed to provide exposure to large capitalization companies in developed markets outside the U.S. and Canada with lower volatility, reduced maximum drawdown, and an improved Sharpe ratio as compared to traditional, market capitalization weighted approaches. **Top Holdings:** Deutsche Wohnen SE   NTT DOCOMO Inc   Vonovia SE   KDDI Corp   Compass Group PLC

iShares Interest Rate Hedged High Yield Bond ETF | C HOLD

Ticker	Traded On	NAV	Total Assets ($)	Dividend Yield (TTM)	Turnover Ratio	Expense Ratio
HYGH	NYSE Arca	88.21	$119,088,532	6.01	0	0.53

Ratings
Reward   C
Risk   C-
Recent Upgrade/Downgrade

Fund Information
Fund Type   Exchange Traded Funds
Category   US Fixed Income
Sub-Category   High Yield Bond
Prospectus Objective   Corp Bond-High Yld
Inception Date   May-14
Open to New Investments Y

Prices
Price (as of 9/30/2019) 88.20
52-Week High   92.71
52-Week Low   84.17

Total Returns (%)

3-Month	6-Month	1-Year	3-Year	5-Year
0.02	0.88	1.00	17.57	18.28

3-Year Standard Deviation   5.06
Effective Duration

Valuation
Premium/Discount (1-Year Average)   -0.04

Company Information
Provider   iShares
Manager/Tenure   James Mauro (5), Scott Radell (5)
Website   http://www.ishares.com
Address   iShares 400 Howard Street San
                 Francisco CA 94105 United States
Phone Number   800-474-2737

PERFORMANCE

Ratings History

Date	Overall Rating	Risk Rating	Reward Rating
Q3-19	C	C-	C
Q4-18	C-	C-	C-
Q4-17	C+	B-	C+
Q4-16	C-	D+	C
Q4-15	D	D+	D+

Asset & Performance History

Date	NAV	1-Year Total Return
2018	84.83	-1.83
2017	90.93	6.53
2016	89.53	12.93
2015	83.19	-6.32
2014	93.65	
2013		

Total Assets: $119,088,532

Asset Allocation

Asset	%
Cash	3%
Stocks	0%
US Stocks	0%
Bonds	97%
US Bonds	82%
Other	0%

Services Offered:

Investment Strategy: The investment seeks to mitigate the interest rate risk of a portfolio composed of U.S. dollar-denominated, high yield corporate bonds. The fund seeks to achieve its investment objective by investing, under normal circumstances, at least 80% of its net assets in U.S. dollar-denominated high yield bonds, in one or more underlying funds that principally invest in high yield bonds. It may also invest in other interest rate futures contracts, including but not limited to, Eurodollar and Federal Funds futures. **Top Holdings:** ALTICE FRANCE S.A 7.38%   Sprint Corporation 7.88%   TransDigm, Inc. 6.25%   CCO Holdings, LLC/ CCO Holdings Capital Corp. 5.13% Bausch Health Companies Inc 6.13%

Invesco DB Base Metals Fund

D   SELL

Ticker	Traded On	NAV	Total Assets ($)	Dividend Yield (TTM)	Turnover Ratio	Expense Ratio
DBB	NYSE Arca	14.82	$118,598,687	0	0	0.75

Ratings
Reward	D
Risk	D+
Recent Upgrade/Downgrade	Down

Fund Information
Fund Type	Exchange Traded Funds
Category	Commodities Specified
Sub-Category	Commodities Industrial Metals
Prospectus Objective	Prec Metals
Inception Date	Jan-07
Open to New Investments	Y

Prices
Price (as of 9/30/2019)	14.77
52-Week High	17.30
52-Week Low	14.45

Total Returns (%)
3-Month	6-Month	1-Year	3-Year	5-Year
-3.60	-13.05	-10.47	7.20	-10.45

3-Year Standard Deviation	15.12
Effective Duration	

Valuation
Premium/Discount (1-Year Average)	-0.14

Company Information
Provider	Invesco
Manager/Tenure	Management Team (12)
Website	http://www.invesco.com/us
Address	Invesco 11 Greenway Plaza, Ste. 2500 Houston TX 77046 United States
Phone Number	800-659-1005

PERFORMANCE

Ratings History
Date	Overall Rating	Risk Rating	Reward Rating
Q3-19	D	D+	D
Q4-18	C-	C-	C-
Q4-17	C+	C	B
Q4-16	C-	C-	C-
Q4-15	D	D	D

Asset & Performance History
Date	NAV	1-Year Total Return
2018	15.44	-20.37
2017	19.39	31.91
2016	14.95	22.98
2015	11.87	-25.74
2014	15.99	-4.7
2013	16.78	-12.31

Total Assets: $118,598,687
Asset Allocation
Asset	%
Cash	48%
Stocks	0%
US Stocks	0%
Bonds	4%
US Bonds	4%
Other	48%

Services Offered:

Investment Strategy: The investment seeks to track the DBIQ Optimum Yield Industrial Metals Index Excess Return™ (DBIQ-OY Industrial Metals ER™), which is intended to reflect the base metals sector. The index Commodities consist of Aluminum, Zinc and Copper – Grade A. The fund invests in futures contracts in an attempt to track its corresponding index. **Top Holdings:** Lme Pri Alum Futr Oct19   United States Treasury Bills 0%   Lme Copper Future Sep19   Lme Copper Future Sep19   Lme Zinc Future Sep19

Invesco S&P Spin-Off ETF

C   HOLD

Ticker	Traded On	NAV	Total Assets ($)	Dividend Yield (TTM)	Turnover Ratio	Expense Ratio
CSD	NYSE Arca	46.45	$118,443,279	0.91	49	0.62

Ratings
Reward	C+
Risk	C-
Recent Upgrade/Downgrade	Up

Fund Information
Fund Type	Exchange Traded Funds
Category	US Equity Mid Cap
Sub-Category	Mid-Cap Blend
Prospectus Objective	Growth
Inception Date	Dec-06
Open to New Investments	Y

Prices
Price (as of 9/30/2019)	46.44
52-Week High	54.88
52-Week Low	39.90

Total Returns (%)
3-Month	6-Month	1-Year	3-Year	5-Year
-7.30	-9.59	-14.16	11.86	12.04

3-Year Standard Deviation	17.49
Effective Duration	

Valuation
Premium/Discount (1-Year Average)	-0.03

Company Information
Provider	Invesco
Manager/Tenure	Peter Hubbard (1), Michael Jeanette (1), Tony Seisser (1)
Website	http://www.invesco.com/us
Address	Invesco 11 Greenway Plaza, Ste. 2500 Houston TX 77046 United States
Phone Number	800-659-1005

PERFORMANCE

Ratings History
Date	Overall Rating	Risk Rating	Reward Rating
Q3-19	C	C-	C+
Q4-18	C	C-	B-
Q4-17	C+	C	B-
Q4-16	B-	C	B
Q4-15	C	C-	C+

Asset & Performance History
Date	NAV	1-Year Total Return
2018	42.37	-17.83
2017	52.11	21.15
2016	43.4	14.18
2015	38.46	-12.09
2014	44.87	1.37
2013	44.98	51.83

Total Assets: $118,443,279
Asset Allocation
Asset	%
Cash	0%
Stocks	100%
US Stocks	98%
Bonds	0%
US Bonds	0%
Other	0%

Services Offered:

Investment Strategy: The investment seeks to track the investment results (before the fund's fees and expenses) of the S&P U.S. Spin-Off Index (the "underlying index"). The fund generally will invest at least 90% of its total assets in the securities that comprise the underlying index. The underlying index is designed to measure the performance of U.S. companies that have been spun off from a parent company within the past four years. The fund is non-diversified. **Top Holdings:** Hewlett Packard Enterprise Co   Fortive Corp   Corteva Inc   Dow Inc   Synchrony Financial

WisdomTree U.S. Multifactor Fund

C   HOLD

Ticker	Traded On	NAV		Total Assets ($)	Dividend Yield (TTM)	Turnover Ratio	Expense Ratio
USMF	BATS	30.35		$118,369,897	1.53	179	0.28

Ratings

Reward	C
Risk	C-
Recent Upgrade/Downgrade	Up

Fund Information

Fund Type	Exchange Traded Funds
Category	US Equity Large Cap Blend
Sub-Category	Large Blend
Prospectus Objective	Growth & Inc
Inception Date	Jun-17
Open to New Investments	Y

Prices

Price (as of 9/30/2019)	30.34
52-Week High	30.91
52-Week Low	24.84

Total Returns (%)

3-Month	6-Month	1-Year	3-Year	5-Year
0.76	4.72	0.95		

3-Year Standard Deviation	
Effective Duration	

Valuation

Premium/Discount (1-Year Average)	0.04

Company Information

Provider	WisdomTree
Manager/Tenure	Richard A. Brown (2), Thomas J. Durante (2), Karen Q. Wong (2)
Website	http://www.wisdomtree.com
Address	WisdomTree 245 Park Avenue, 35th floor New York NY 10167 United States
Phone Number	866-909-9473

PERFORMANCE

Ratings History

Date	Overall Rating	Risk Rating	Reward Rating
Q3-19	C	C-	C
Q4-18	C-	C-	D+
Q4-17	U		
Q4-16			
Q4-15			

Asset & Performance History

Date	NAV	1-Year Total Return
2018	26.16	-4.24
2017	27.7	
2016		
2015		
2014		
2013		

Total Assets: $118,369,897

Asset Allocation

Asset	%
Cash	0%
Stocks	100%
US Stocks	100%
Bonds	0%
US Bonds	0%
Other	0%

Services Offered:

Investment Strategy: The investment seeks to track the price and yield performance, before fees and expenses, of the WisdomTree U.S. Multifactor Index. Under normal circumstances, at least 80% of the fund's total assets will be invested in component securities of the index and investments that have economic characteristics that are substantially identical to the economic characteristics of such component securities. The index is generally comprised of 200 U.S. companies with the highest composite scores based on two fundamental factors (value and quality measures) and two technical factors (momentum and correlation). The fund is non-diversified. **Top Holdings:** The Western Union Co   Booz Allen Hamilton Holding Corp Class A   Maximus Inc   Fidelity National Information Services Inc   Citrix Systems Inc

Invesco KBW Property & Casualty Insurance ETF

B   BUY

Ticker	Traded On	NAV		Total Assets ($)	Dividend Yield (TTM)	Turnover Ratio	Expense Ratio
KBWP	NAS CM	73.82		$118,108,142	1.95		0.35

Ratings

Reward	B
Risk	C+
Recent Upgrade/Downgrade	Up

Fund Information

Fund Type	Exchange Traded Funds
Category	Financials Sector Equity
Sub-Category	Financial
Prospectus Objective	Growth
Inception Date	Dec-10
Open to New Investments	

Prices

Price (as of 9/30/2019)	73.94
52-Week High	74.04
52-Week Low	53.39

Total Returns (%)

3-Month	6-Month	1-Year	3-Year	5-Year
4.56	19.12	20.07	56.60	111.54

3-Year Standard Deviation	11.4
Effective Duration	

Valuation

Premium/Discount (1-Year Average)	0.03

Company Information

Provider	Invesco
Manager/Tenure	Peter Hubbard (8), Michael Jeanette (8), Tony Seisser (5)
Website	http://www.invesco.com/us
Address	Invesco 11 Greenway Plaza, Ste. 2500 Houston TX 77046 United States
Phone Number	800-659-1005

PERFORMANCE

Ratings History

Date	Overall Rating	Risk Rating	Reward Rating
Q3-19	B	C+	B
Q4-18	B-	C	B
Q4-17	B+	A	B
Q4-16	B	B	A-
Q4-15	B	C	A-

Asset & Performance History

Date	NAV	1-Year Total Return
2018	56.92	-2.24
2017	59.42	8.96
2016	55.59	19.09
2015	47.76	14.24
2014	42.4	11.25
2013	39.22	33.88

Total Assets: $118,108,142

Asset Allocation

Asset	%
Cash	0%
Stocks	100%
US Stocks	92%
Bonds	0%
US Bonds	0%
Other	0%

Services Offered:

Investment Strategy: The investment seeks to track the investment results (before fees and expenses) of the KBW Nasdaq Property & Casualty Index (the "underlying index"). The fund generally will invest at least 90% of its total assets in the securities that comprise the underlying index. The underlying index is a modified-market capitalization-weighted index of companies primarily engaged in U.S. property and casualty insurance activities, as determined by the index provider. The fund is non-diversified. **Top Holdings:** Chubb Ltd   Allstate Corp   American International Group Inc   The Travelers Companies Inc   Progressive Corp

Cambria Global Momentum ETF　　　　　　　　　　　　　　　　C-　　HOLD

Ticker	Traded On	NAV	Total Assets ($)	Dividend Yield (TTM)	Turnover Ratio	Expense Ratio
GMOM	BATS	25.38	$117,995,006	2.62		0.94

Ratings

Reward	C-
Risk	D+
Recent Upgrade/Downgrade	

Fund Information

Fund Type	Exchange Traded Funds
Category	Moderate Allocation
Sub-Category	World Allocation
Prospectus Objective	Growth & Inc
Inception Date	Nov-14
Open to New Investments	Y

Prices

Price (as of 9/30/2019)	25.36
52-Week High	26.85
52-Week Low	24.22

Total Returns (%)

3-Month	6-Month	1-Year	3-Year	5-Year
1.45	2.51	-2.74	15.03	

3-Year Standard Deviation	7.49
Effective Duration	9.99

Valuation

Premium/Discount (1-Year Average)	-0.08

Company Information

Provider	CAMBRIA ETF TRUST
Manager/Tenure	Mebane T. Faber (4)
Website	http://www.cambriafunds.com
Address	CAMBRIA ETF TRUST 2711 Centreville Road Suite 400 Wilmington, DE 19808 Wilmington DE 19808 United States
Phone Number	310-683-5500

PERFORMANCE

Ratings History

Date	Overall Rating	Risk Rating	Reward Rating
Q3-19	C-	D+	C-
Q4-18	D+	C-	D+
Q4-17	C+	C+	C+
Q4-16	D+	C-	D+
Q4-15	U		

Asset & Performance History

Date	NAV	1-Year Total Return
2018	24.45	-8.72
2017	27.28	20.59
2016	23.12	4.3
2015	22.56	-8.51
2014	25.1	
2013		

Total Assets: $117,995,006

Asset Allocation

Asset	%
Cash	5%
Stocks	42%
US Stocks	26%
Bonds	50%
US Bonds	32%
Other	3%

Services Offered:

Investment Strategy: The investment seeks to preserve and grow capital from investments in the U.S. and foreign equity, fixed income, commodity and currency markets, independent of market direction. The fund is considered a "fund of funds" that seeks to achieve its investment objective by primarily investing in other exchange-traded funds and other exchange traded products including, but not limited to, exchange-traded notes, exchange traded currency trusts, closed-end funds, and real estate investment trusts that offer diversified exposure, including inverse exposure, to global regions, countries, styles and sectors. **Top Holdings:** iShares 7-10 Year Treasury Bond ETF iShares 20+ Year Treasury Bond ETF iShares Residential Real Estate Capd ETF Invesco DB Precious Metals iShares iBoxx $ Invmt Grade Corp Bd ETF

Xtrackers International Real Estate ETF　　　　　　　　　　　　C　　HOLD

Ticker	Traded On	NAV	Total Assets ($)	Dividend Yield (TTM)	Turnover Ratio	Expense Ratio
HAUZ	NYSE Arca	28.73	$117,779,703	2.05	43	0.1

Ratings

Reward	C
Risk	C-
Recent Upgrade/Downgrade	

Fund Information

Fund Type	Exchange Traded Funds
Category	Asia ex-Japan Equity
Sub-Category	Pacific/Asia ex-Japan Stk
Prospectus Objective	Pacific Stock
Inception Date	Oct-13
Open to New Investments	Y

Prices

Price (as of 9/30/2019)	28.74
52-Week High	29.14
52-Week Low	24.80

Total Returns (%)

3-Month	6-Month	1-Year	3-Year	5-Year
0.41	0.97	4.70	28.75	33.56

3-Year Standard Deviation	9.94
Effective Duration	

Valuation

Premium/Discount (1-Year Average)	0.05

Company Information

Provider	DWS
Manager/Tenure	Patrick Dwyer (2), Bryan Richards (2), Shlomo Bassous (1)
Website	http://dws.com
Address	DWS 210 West 10th Street Kansas City MO 64105-1614 United States
Phone Number	

PERFORMANCE

Ratings History

Date	Overall Rating	Risk Rating	Reward Rating
Q3-19	C	C-	C
Q4-18	D	D	D+
Q4-17	B	B-	A-
Q4-16	D+	D	C-
Q4-15	D+	D+	D+

Asset & Performance History

Date	NAV	1-Year Total Return
2018	25.35	-11.04
2017	28.95	28.58
2016	23.11	6.02
2015	22.28	-5.29
2014	25.65	4.16
2013	25.88	

Total Assets: $117,779,703

Asset Allocation

Asset	%
Cash	1%
Stocks	99%
US Stocks	0%
Bonds	0%
US Bonds	0%
Other	1%

Services Offered:

Investment Strategy: The investment seeks investment results that correspond generally to the performance, of the iSTOXX Developed and Emerging Markets ex USA PK VN Real Estate Index (the "underlying index"). The fund, using a "passive" or indexing investment approach, seeks investment results that correspond generally to the performance, of the underlying index, which is a free-float capitalization weighted index that provides exposure to publicly traded real estate securities in countries outside the United States, excluding Pakistan and Vietnam. It will invest at least 80% of its total assets in component securities of the underlying index. **Top Holdings:** Mitsubishi Estate Co Ltd Link Real Estate Investment Trust Vonovia SE Mitsui Fudosan Co Ltd Sun Hung Kai Properties Ltd

ProShares High Yield—Interest Rate Hedged   C   HOLD

Ticker	Traded On	NAV	Total Assets ($)	Dividend Yield (TTM)	Turnover Ratio	Expense Ratio
HYHG	BATS	64.40	$117,527,861	6.35	49	0.5

Ratings
Reward   C
Risk   D+
Recent Upgrade/Downgrade

Fund Information
Fund Type   Exchange Traded Funds
Category   Fixed Income Misc
Sub-Category   Nontraditional Bond
Prospectus Objective   Income
Inception Date   May-13
Open to New Investments   Y

Prices
Price (as of 9/30/2019)   64.55
52-Week High   68.33
52-Week Low   61.54

Total Returns (%)

3-Month	6-Month	1-Year	3-Year	5-Year
-0.49	0.38	0.01	15.72	12.22

3-Year Standard Deviation   5.74
Effective Duration

Valuation
Premium/Discount (1-Year Average)   0.04

Company Information
Provider   ProShares
Manager/Tenure Benjamin McAbee (3), Alexander V.
                Ilyasov (0)
Website   http://www.proshares.com
Address   ProShares 7501 Wisconsin Avenue,
                Suite 1000 Bethesda MD 20814
                United States
Phone Number   866-776-5125

PERFORMANCE

Ratings History

Date	Overall Rating	Risk Rating	Reward Rating
Q3-19	C	D+	C
Q4-18	C-	C-	C-
Q4-17	C+	C+	C
Q4-16	D+	D+	C-
Q4-15	D+	C-	D+

Asset & Performance History

Date	NAV	1-Year Total Return
2018	62.09	-2.82
2017	67.41	4.42
2016	68.19	14.6
2015	63	-9.51
2014	73.73	-2.5
2013	79.65	

Total Assets: $117,527,861
Asset Allocation

Asset	%
Cash	57%
Stocks	0%
US Stocks	0%
Bonds	43%
US Bonds	30%
Other	0%

Services Offered:

Investment Strategy: The investment seeks investment results, before fees and expenses, that track the performance of the FTSE High Yield (Treasury Rate-Hedged) Index (the "index"). Under normal circumstances, the fund will invest at least 80% of its total assets in high-yield bonds included in the index. The index is comprised of (a) long positions in U.S. dollar-denominated high yield corporate bonds ("high yield bonds") and (b) short positions in U.S. Treasury notes or bonds ("Treasury Securities") of, in aggregate, approximate equivalent duration to the high yield bonds. **Top Holdings:** Us 5yr Note Future 12/31/2019 (Fvz8) Us 2yr Note Future 12/31/2019 (Tuz9) US 10 Year Note (CBT) Dec19 TransDigm, Inc. Sprint Corporation

---

iShares MSCI Israel Capped ETF   C   HOLD

Ticker	Traded On	NAV	Total Assets ($)	Dividend Yield (TTM)	Turnover Ratio	Expense Ratio
EIS	NYSE Arca	54.63	$117,452,994	0.45	6	0.59

Ratings
Reward   C
Risk   C-
Recent Upgrade/Downgrade   Up

Fund Information
Fund Type   Exchange Traded Funds
Category   Equity Misc
Sub-Category   Miscellaneous Region
Prospectus Objective   Foreign Stock
Inception Date   Mar-08
Open to New Investments   Y

Prices
Price (as of 9/30/2019)   54.60
52-Week High   56.84
52-Week Low   46.52

Total Returns (%)

3-Month	6-Month	1-Year	3-Year	5-Year
-0.10	0.24	-1.78	17.83	16.62

3-Year Standard Deviation   15.74
Effective Duration

Valuation
Premium/Discount (1-Year Average)   -0.05

Company Information
Provider   iShares
Manager/Tenure Diane Hsiung (11), Greg Savage (11),
                Jennifer Hsui (6), 3 others
Website   http://www.ishares.com
Address   iShares 400 Howard Street San
                Francisco CA 94105 United States
Phone Number   800-474-2737

PERFORMANCE

Ratings History

Date	Overall Rating	Risk Rating	Reward Rating
Q3-19	C	C-	C
Q4-18	C-	C-	C
Q4-17	C-	C	C-
Q4-16	C-	C-	C-
Q4-15	B	C+	B+

Asset & Performance History

Date	NAV	1-Year Total Return
2018	48.54	-4.98
2017	51.5	13.08
2016	46.47	-4.08
2015	49.31	7.13
2014	47.18	-0.66
2013	48.34	18.27

Total Assets: $117,452,994
Asset Allocation

Asset	%
Cash	0%
Stocks	100%
US Stocks	17%
Bonds	0%
US Bonds	0%
Other	0%

Services Offered:

Investment Strategy: The investment seeks to track the investment results of the MSCI Israel Capped Investable Market Index (IMI). The fund generally will invest at least 90% of its assets in the component securities of the underlying index and in investments that have economic characteristics that are substantially identical to the component securities of the underlying index. The index is a free float-adjusted market capitalization index designed to measure broad-based equity market performance in Israel. The fund is non-diversified. **Top Holdings:** Check Point Software Technologies Ltd Bank Leumi Le-Israel BM NICE Ltd Bank Hapoalim BM Teva Pharmaceutical Industries Ltd ADR

Nationwide Risk-Based U.S. Equity ETF   D+   SELL

Ticker	Traded On	NAV	Total Assets ($)	Dividend Yield (TTM)	Turnover Ratio	Expense Ratio
RBUS	NYSE Arca	29.81	$117,022,080	2.01		0.3

Ratings
Reward   C-
Risk   D
Recent Upgrade/Downgrade   Up

Fund Information
Fund Type	Exchange Traded Funds
Category	US Equity Large Cap Blend
Sub-Category	Large Blend
Prospectus Objective	Growth
Inception Date	Sep-17
Open to New Investments	Y

Prices
Price (as of 9/30/2019)	29.82
52-Week High	29.85
52-Week Low	23.93

Total Returns (%)
3-Month	6-Month	1-Year	3-Year	5-Year
3.01	8.46	9.62		

3-Year Standard Deviation
Effective Duration

Valuation
Premium/Discount (1-Year Average)   -0.03

Company Information
Provider	Nationwide
Manager/Tenure	Denise M. Krisko (2), Austin Wen (2)
Website	http://www.nationwide.com/mutualfunds
Address	Nationwide One Nationwide Plaza
	Columbus OH 43215 United States
Phone Number	800-848-0920

PERFORMANCE

Ratings History
Date	Overall Rating	Risk Rating	Reward Rating
Q3-19	D+	D	C-
Q4-18	D	D	D+
Q4-17	U		
Q4-16			
Q4-15			

Asset & Performance History
Date	NAV	1-Year Total Return
2018	24.44	-3.94
2017	26.07	
2016		
2015		
2014		
2013		

Total Assets: $117,022,080
Asset Allocation
Asset	%
Cash	0%
Stocks	100%
US Stocks	97%
Bonds	0%
US Bonds	0%
Other	0%

Services Offered:

Investment Strategy: The investment seeks to track the total return performance, before fees and expenses, of the Rothschild & Co Risk-Based US Index (the "index"). The advisor attempts to invest all, or substantially all, of its assets in the component securities that make up the index. Normally, at least 80% of the fund's total assets will be invested in the component securities of the index. The index is a rules-based, equal risk-weighted index that is designed to provide exposure to U.S.-listed large capitalization companies with lower volatility, reduced maximum drawdown, and an improved Sharpe ratio as compared to traditional, market capitalization weighted approaches.
Top Holdings: Newmont Goldcorp Corp Evergy Inc AutoZone Inc Duke Energy Corp WEC Energy Group Inc

---

Invesco Total Return Bond ETF   C+   HOLD

Ticker	Traded On	NAV	Total Assets ($)	Dividend Yield (TTM)	Turnover Ratio	Expense Ratio
GTO	NYSE Arca	54.26	$116,665,332	2.91		0.51

Ratings
Reward   B-
Risk   C-
Recent Upgrade/Downgrade   Up

Fund Information
Fund Type	Exchange Traded Funds
Category	US Fixed Income
Sub-Category	Intermediate Core-Plus Bond
Prospectus Objective	Corp Bond - Gen
Inception Date	Feb-16
Open to New Investments	Y

Prices
Price (as of 9/30/2019)	54.27
52-Week High	54.87
52-Week Low	50.00

Total Returns (%)
3-Month	6-Month	1-Year	3-Year	5-Year
2.64	6.65	10.61	16.06	

3-Year Standard Deviation   3.04
Effective Duration   5.66

Valuation
Premium/Discount (1-Year Average)   0.01

Company Information
Provider	Invesco
Manager/Tenure	Matthew Brill (1), Chuck Burge (1),
	Michael Hyman (1)
Website	http://www.invesco.com/us
Address	Invesco 11 Greenway Plaza, Ste. 2500
	Houston TX 77046 United States
Phone Number	800-659-1005

PERFORMANCE

Ratings History
Date	Overall Rating	Risk Rating	Reward Rating
Q3-19	C+	C-	B-
Q4-18	C-	D+	C-
Q4-17	C-	A-	D+
Q4-16	U		
Q4-15			

Asset & Performance History
Date	NAV	1-Year Total Return
2018	50.13	-1.71
2017	52.68	6.33
2016	50.7	
2015		
2014		
2013		

Total Assets: $116,665,332
Asset Allocation
Asset	%
Cash	4%
Stocks	0%
US Stocks	0%
Bonds	94%
US Bonds	85%
Other	0%

Services Offered:

Investment Strategy: The investment seeks maximum total return, comprised of income and capital appreciation. The fund will normally invest in a portfolio of fixed income instruments of varying maturities and of any credit quality. It will normally invest at least 80% of its net assets (plus any borrowings for investment purposes) in fixed income instruments, which may be represented by certain derivative instruments, and also include exchange-traded funds ("ETFs") and closed-end funds ("CEFs") that invest substantially all of their assets in fixed income instruments (which may include ETFs and CEFs affiliated with the fund). The fund is non-diversified. **Top Holdings:** US 10 Year Ultra Future Dec19 United States Treasury Notes 1.75% United States Treasury Bonds 2.88% Us 5yr Note (Cbt) Dec19 United States Treasury Notes 1.5%

First Trust BICK Index Fund

D+   SELL

Ticker	Traded On	NAV	Total Assets ($)	Dividend Yield (TTM)	Turnover Ratio	Expense Ratio
BICK	NAS CM	25.61	$116,503,243	1.57	65	0.64

Ratings
Reward   D
Risk   C-
Recent Upgrade/Downgrade   Down

Fund Information
Fund Type   Exchange Traded Funds
Category   Global Emerg Mkts Equity
Sub-Category   Diversified Emerging Mkts
Prospectus Objective   Foreign Stock
Inception Date   Apr-10
Open to New Investments   Y

Prices
Price (as of 9/30/2019)   25.36
52-Week High   27.92
52-Week Low   23.64

PERFORMANCE

Total Returns (%)

3-Month	6-Month	1-Year	3-Year	5-Year
-5.15	-7.20	-1.57	16.39	12.13

3-Year Standard Deviation   14.25
Effective Duration

Valuation
Premium/Discount (1-Year Average)   -0.32

Company Information
Provider   First Trust
Manager/Tenure   Jon C. Erickson (9), Daniel J. Lindquist
                   (9), David G. McGarel (9), 3 others
Website   http://www.ftportfolios.com/
Address   First Trust 120 E. Liberty Drive, Suite
                   400 Wheaton IL 60187 United States
Phone Number   800-621-1675

Ratings History

Date	Overall Rating	Risk Rating	Reward Rating
Q3-19	D+	C-	D
Q4-18	C-	C-	C-
Q4-17	B	C	B
Q4-16	D	D	D+
Q4-15	D+	D	C-

Asset & Performance History

Date	NAV	1-Year Total Return
2018	24.78	-15.89
2017	30.01	37.97
2016	21.98	16.65
2015	19.09	-18.47
2014	23.79	-2.54
2013	24.85	-0.16

Total Assets: $116,503,243
Asset Allocation

Asset	%
Cash	0%
Stocks	100%
US Stocks	4%
Bonds	0%
US Bonds	0%
Other	0%

Services Offered:

Investment Strategy: The investment seeks investment results that correspond generally to the price and yield (before the fund's fees and expenses) of an equity index called the ISE BICKTM. The fund will normally invest at least 90% of its net assets (including investment borrowings) in the common stocks and depositary receipts that comprise the index. The index is designed to provide a benchmark for investors interested in tracking some of the largest and most liquid public companies that are domiciled in Brazil, India, China (including Hong Kong) and South Korea that are accessible for investment by U.S. investors. **Top Holdings:** Infosys Ltd ADR WNS (Holdings) Ltd ADR Pinduoduo Inc ADR MakeMyTrip Ltd Yatra Online Inc

iShares MSCI Brazil Small-Cap ETF

B   BUY

Ticker	Traded On	NAV	Total Assets ($)	Dividend Yield (TTM)	Turnover Ratio	Expense Ratio
EWZS	NAS CM	17.14	$115,705,325	3.48	67	0.59

Ratings
Reward   B+
Risk   C
Recent Upgrade/Downgrade   Up

Fund Information
Fund Type   Exchange Traded Funds
Category   Latin America Equity
Sub-Category   Latin America Stock
Prospectus Objective   Foreign Stock
Inception Date   Sep-10
Open to New Investments   Y

Prices
Price (as of 9/30/2019)   17.21
52-Week High   18.65
52-Week Low   11.78

PERFORMANCE

Total Returns (%)

3-Month	6-Month	1-Year	3-Year	5-Year
1.24	11.54	53.12	67.66	22.24

3-Year Standard Deviation   30.24
Effective Duration

Valuation
Premium/Discount (1-Year Average)   -0.16

Company Information
Provider   iShares
Manager/Tenure   Diane Hsiung (9), Greg Savage (9),
                   Jennifer Hsui (6), 3 others
Website   http://www.ishares.com
Address   iShares 400 Howard Street San
                   Francisco CA 94105 United States
Phone Number   800-474-2737

Ratings History

Date	Overall Rating	Risk Rating	Reward Rating
Q3-19	B	C	B+
Q4-18	C-	D+	C
Q4-17	C	D+	C+
Q4-16	D+	D+	D+
Q4-15	E+	D-	E+

Asset & Performance History

Date	NAV	1-Year Total Return
2018	14.36	-7.17
2017	16.28	51.13
2016	11.19	64.81
2015	7.06	-49.35
2014	14.37	-25.77
2013	19.85	-26.52

Total Assets: $115,705,325
Asset Allocation

Asset	%
Cash	0%
Stocks	100%
US Stocks	0%
Bonds	0%
US Bonds	0%
Other	0%

Services Offered:

Investment Strategy: The investment seeks to track the investment results of the MSCI Brazil Small Cap Index. The fund generally will invest at least 90% of its assets in the component securities of the underlying index and in investments that have economic characteristics that are substantially identical to the component securities of the underlying index. The index is a free float-adjusted market capitalization-weighted index designed to measure the performance of equity securities in the bottom 14% by market capitalization of equity securities listed on stock exchanges in Brazil. **Top Holdings:** Azul SA Participating Preferred Totvs SA Estacio Participacoes SA Via Varejo SA CVC Brasil Operadora e Agencia de Viagens SA

Invesco CurrencyShares® Canadian Dollar Trust   C-   HOLD

Ticker	Traded On	NAV		Total Assets ($)	Dividend Yield (TTM)	Turnover Ratio	Expense Ratio
FXC	NYSE Arca	74.54		$115,539,713	0.76	0	0.4

Ratings

Reward	D+
Risk	C-
Recent Upgrade/Downgrade	Up

Fund Information

Fund Type	Exchange Traded Funds
Category	Currency
Sub-Category	Single Currency
Prospectus Objective	Worldwide Bond
Inception Date	Jun-06
Open to New Investments	Y

Prices

Price (as of 9/30/2019)	74.51
52-Week High	77.02
52-Week Low	72.20

Total Returns (%)

3-Month	6-Month	1-Year	3-Year	5-Year
-0.85	1.29	-1.62	0.03	-15.25

3-Year Standard Deviation	6.98
Effective Duration	

Valuation

Premium/Discount (1-Year Average)	-0.08

Company Information

Provider	Invesco
Manager/Tenure	Management Team (13)
Website	http://www.invesco.com/us
Address	Invesco 11 Greenway Plaza, Ste. 2500
	Houston TX 77046 United States
Phone Number	800-659-1005

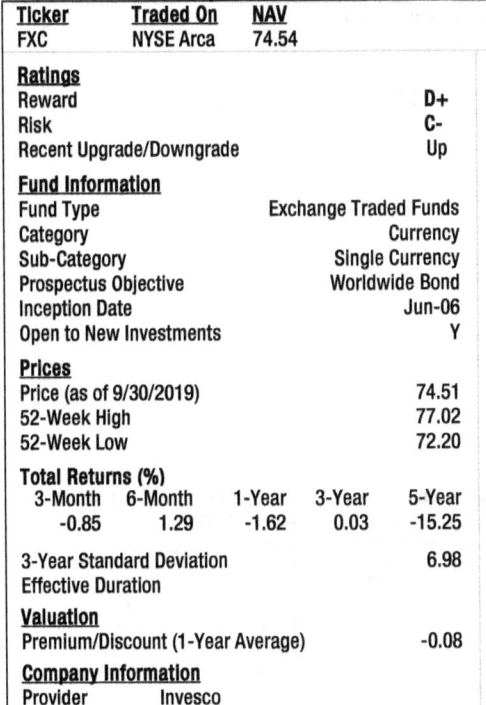

PERFORMANCE

Ratings History

Date	Overall Rating	Risk Rating	Reward Rating
Q3-19	C-	C-	D+
Q4-18	D+	C-	D+
Q4-17	C-	C	D+
Q4-16	D	D+	D
Q4-15	D	D	D

Asset & Performance History

Date	NAV	1-Year Total Return
2018	72.26	-7.88
2017	78.73	6.85
2016	73.7	3.18
2015	71.42	-16.79
2014	85.86	-8.06
2013	93.61	-6.09

Total Assets: $115,539,713

Asset Allocation

Asset	%
Cash	100%
Stocks	0%
US Stocks	0%
Bonds	0%
US Bonds	0%
Other	0%

Services Offered:

Investment Strategy: The investment seeks to track the price of the Canadian Dollar, net of trust expenses. The fund seeks to reflect the price of the Canadian Dollar. The sponsor believes that, for many investors, the shares represent a cost-effective investment relative to traditional means of investing in the foreign exchange market. **Top Holdings:**

Invesco Active U.S. Real Estate Fund   C+   HOLD

Ticker	Traded On	NAV		Total Assets ($)	Dividend Yield (TTM)	Turnover Ratio	Expense Ratio
PSR	NYSE Arca	95.84		$115,008,633	2.48	92	0.35

Ratings

Reward	B-
Risk	C-
Recent Upgrade/Downgrade	Up

Fund Information

Fund Type	Exchange Traded Funds
Category	Real Estate Sector Equity
Sub-Category	Real Estate
Prospectus Objective	Real Estate
Inception Date	Nov-08
Open to New Investments	Y

Prices

Price (as of 9/30/2019)	95.80
52-Week High	96.82
52-Week Low	73.52

Total Returns (%)

3-Month	6-Month	1-Year	3-Year	5-Year
7.73	9.45	22.09	29.28	67.90

3-Year Standard Deviation	11.96
Effective Duration	

Valuation

Premium/Discount (1-Year Average)	0.07

Company Information

Provider	Invesco
Manager/Tenure	Mark D. Blackburn (10), Paul S. Curbo (10), Joe V. Rodriguez (10), 3 others
Website	http://www.invesco.com/us
Address	Invesco 11 Greenway Plaza, Ste. 2500
	Houston TX 77046 United States
Phone Number	800-659-1005

PERFORMANCE

Ratings History

Date	Overall Rating	Risk Rating	Reward Rating
Q3-19	C+	C-	B-
Q4-18	C	C-	C
Q4-17	B	B+	B-
Q4-16	C+	C-	B
Q4-15	B-	C	B

Asset & Performance History

Date	NAV	1-Year Total Return
2018	76.16	-4.59
2017	81.94	9.35
2016	75.03	7.29
2015	72.43	2.47
2014	72.99	30.1
2013	56.85	0.93

Total Assets: $115,008,633

Asset Allocation

Asset	%
Cash	0%
Stocks	100%
US Stocks	100%
Bonds	0%
US Bonds	0%
Other	0%

Services Offered:

Investment Strategy: The investment seeks high total return through growth of capital and current income. The fund invests normally at least 80% of its assets in securities of companies that are principally engaged in the U.S. real estate industry and included within the FTSE NAREIT All Equity REITs Index. It also may invest in real estate operating companies ("REOCs"), as well as securities of other companies principally engaged in the U.S. real estate industry. REOCs are similar to REITs, except that REOCs reinvest their earnings into the business, rather than distributing them to unitholders like REITs. **Top Holdings:** American Tower Corp   Crown Castle International Corp   Prologis Inc   Simon Property Group Inc   Equinix Inc

SPDR® Dorsey Wright Fixed Income Allocation ETF   C-   HOLD

Ticker	Traded On	NAV	Total Assets ($)	Dividend Yield (TTM)	Turnover Ratio	Expense Ratio
DWFI	NAS CM		$114,814,088	4.26	104	0.6

Ratings
Reward	C
Risk	C-
Recent Upgrade/Downgrade	Up

Fund Information
Fund Type	Exchange Traded Funds
Category	Cautious Allocation
Sub-Category	Allocation--15% to 30% Equity
Prospectus Objective	Growth & Inc
Inception Date	Jun-16
Open to New Investments	Y

Prices
Price (as of 9/30/2019)	23.55
52-Week High	23.86
52-Week Low	22.07

Total Returns (%)
3-Month	6-Month	1-Year	3-Year	5-Year
1.26	3.86	4.66	4.04	

3-Year Standard Deviation	5
Effective Duration	8.09

Valuation
Premium/Discount (1-Year Average)	-0.01

Company Information
Provider   SPDR State Street Global Advisors
Manager/Tenure   Michael J. Feehily (3), Karl A.
                  Schneider (3), Raymond V. Donofrio (2)
Website   http://www.spdrs.com
Address   SPDR State Street Global Advisors
                  State Street Financial Center, 1
                  Lincoln Street Boston MA 02111-2900
                  United States
Phone Number   617-786-3000

PERFORMANCE

Ratings History
Date	Overall Rating	Risk Rating	Reward Rating
Q3-19	C-	C-	C
Q4-18	D+	C-	D+
Q4-17	D+	B	D+
Q4-16	U		
Q4-15			

Asset & Performance History
Date	NAV	1-Year Total Return
2018	22.24	-8.69
2017	25.24	8.92
2016	24.3	
2015		
2014		
2013		

Total Assets: $114,814,088
Asset Allocation
Asset	%
Cash	0%
Stocks	0%
US Stocks	0%
Bonds	99%
US Bonds	91%
Other	0%

Services Offered:

Investment Strategy: The investment seeks to provide investment results that, before fees and expenses, correspond generally to the price and yield performance of the Dorsey Wright Fixed Income Allocation Index. The index is comprised of exchange-traded funds advised by SSGA Funds Management, Inc. The selection universe for the index includes U.S.-listed fixed income ETFs advised by SSGA FM or its affiliates that are designed to target exposure to fixed income securities. The fund invests at least 80%, of its total assets in securities comprising the index. It is non-diversified. **Top Holdings:** SPDR® Portfolio Long Term Treasury ETF SPDR® Blmbg Barclays High Yield Bd ETF SPDR® Portfolio Interm Term Corp Bd ETF SPDR® Nuveen Blmbg Barclays Muni Bd ETF Ssi Us Gov Money Market Class State Street Inst Us Gov

AI Powered Equity ETF   C-   HOLD

Ticker	Traded On	NAV	Total Assets ($)	Dividend Yield (TTM)	Turnover Ratio	Expense Ratio
AIEQ	NYSE Arca	26.19	$114,573,018	0.61		0.77

Ratings
Reward	C-
Risk	C-
Recent Upgrade/Downgrade	

Fund Information
Fund Type	Exchange Traded Funds
Category	US Equity Large Cap Growth
Sub-Category	Large Growth
Prospectus Objective	Growth & Inc
Inception Date	Oct-17
Open to New Investments	Y

Prices
Price (as of 9/30/2019)	26.14
52-Week High	29.46
52-Week Low	20.35

Total Returns (%)
3-Month	6-Month	1-Year	3-Year	5-Year
-1.36	0.05	-2.10		

3-Year Standard Deviation	
Effective Duration	

Valuation
Premium/Discount (1-Year Average)	-0.10

Company Information
Provider   ETFMG
Manager/Tenure   Samuel R. Masucci (1), Devin Ryder
                  (1), Donal Bishnoi (0), 1 other
Website   http://www.etfmg.com
Address   ETFMG 30 Maple Street, Suite 2 NJ
                  United States
Phone Number

PERFORMANCE

Ratings History
Date	Overall Rating	Risk Rating	Reward Rating
Q3-19	C-	C-	C-
Q4-18	D+	D+	D+
Q4-17	U		
Q4-16			
Q4-15			

Asset & Performance History
Date	NAV	1-Year Total Return
2018	21.87	-7.28
2017	25.87	
2016		
2015		
2014		
2013		

Total Assets: $114,573,018
Asset Allocation
Asset	%
Cash	2%
Stocks	98%
US Stocks	96%
Bonds	0%
US Bonds	0%
Other	0%

Services Offered:

Investment Strategy: The investment seeks capital appreciation. The fund is actively managed and invests primarily in equity securities listed on a U.S. exchange based on the results of a proprietary, quantitative model (the "EquBot Model") developed by EquBot LLC ("EquBot") that runs on the IBM Watson™ platform. EquBot, the fund's sub-adviser, is a technology based company focused on applying artificial intelligence ("AI") based solutions to investment analyses. The fund is non-diversified. **Top Holdings:** Alphabet Inc A Intuit Inc Amazon.com Inc Martin Marietta Materials Inc SS&C Technologies Holdings Inc

IQ Enhanced Core Plus Bond U.S. ETF   C   HOLD

Ticker	Traded On	NAV	Total Assets ($)	Dividend Yield (TTM)	Turnover Ratio	Expense Ratio
AGGP	NYSE Arca	19.71	$114,324,540	2.84		0.33

Ratings
Reward	C
Risk	C-
Recent Upgrade/Downgrade	Up

Fund Information
Fund Type	Exchange Traded Funds
Category	US Fixed Income
Sub-Category	Intermediate Core-Plus Bond
Prospectus Objective	Income
Inception Date	May-16
Open to New Investments	Y

Prices
Price (as of 9/30/2019)	19.70
52-Week High	19.84
52-Week Low	18.74

Total Returns (%)
3-Month	6-Month	1-Year	3-Year	5-Year
1.82	4.38	6.07	5.96	

3-Year Standard Deviation	2.86
Effective Duration	5.55

Valuation
Premium/Discount (1-Year Average)	-0.09

Company Information
Provider	IndexIQ
Manager/Tenure	Greg Barrato (3), James Harrison (1)
Website	http://www.indexiq.com
Address	IndexIQ 800 Westchester Avenue, Suite N-611 Rye Brook NY 10573 United States
Phone Number	888-934-0777

PERFORMANCE

Ratings History

Date	Overall Rating	Risk Rating	Reward Rating
Q3-19	C	C-	C
Q4-18	D+	C-	D+
Q4-17	D+	B	D+
Q4-16	U		
Q4-15			

Asset & Performance History

Date	NAV	1-Year Total Return
2018	18.93	-2.31
2017	19.96	4.27
2016	19.73	
2015		
2014		
2013		

Total Assets: $114,324,540

Asset Allocation
Asset	%
Cash	2%
Stocks	0%
US Stocks	0%
Bonds	96%
US Bonds	90%
Other	0%

Services Offered:

Investment Strategy: The investment seeks to track the price and yield performance of its underlying index, the IQ Enhanced Core Plus Bond U.S. Index. The fund is a "fund of funds" which means it invests, under normal circumstances, at least 80% of its net assets, plus the amount of any borrowings for investment purposes, in the investments included in its underlying index, which includes underlying funds. The underlying index seeks to outperform the U.S. dollar-denominated taxable fixed income universe by using a combination of short- and long-term momentum to overweight and underweight various sectors of the investment grade and high yield fixed income securities market. **Top Holdings:** iShares MBS ETF Vanguard Mortgage-Backed Secs ETF Vanguard Short-Term Corporate Bond ETF Vanguard Long-Term Corporate Bd ETF Vanguard Interm-Term Corp Bd ETF

PIMCO Short Term Municipal Bond Active Exchange-Traded Fund   C   HOLD

Ticker	Traded On	NAV	Total Assets ($)	Dividend Yield (TTM)	Turnover Ratio	Expense Ratio
SMMU	NYSE Arca	50.57	$114,298,347	1.88	49	0.35

Ratings
Reward	C
Risk	C-
Recent Upgrade/Downgrade	

Fund Information
Fund Type	Exchange Traded Funds
Category	US Muni Fixed Inc
Sub-Category	Muni National Short
Prospectus Objective	Muni Bond - Natl
Inception Date	Feb-10
Open to New Investments	Y

Prices
Price (as of 9/30/2019)	50.65
52-Week High	50.98
52-Week Low	49.50

Total Returns (%)
3-Month	6-Month	1-Year	3-Year	5-Year
0.52	1.56	3.66	5.03	6.90

3-Year Standard Deviation	1.22
Effective Duration	1.86

Valuation
Premium/Discount (1-Year Average)	0.08

Company Information
Provider	PIMCO
Manager/Tenure	Julie P. Callahan (5), David Hammer (4)
Website	http://www.pimco.com
Address	PIMCO 840 Newport Center Drive, Suite 100 Newport Beach CA 92660 United States
Phone Number	866-746-2602

PERFORMANCE

Ratings History

Date	Overall Rating	Risk Rating	Reward Rating
Q3-19	C	C-	C
Q4-18	C-	D+	C-
Q4-17	C	B-	C
Q4-16	C-	C-	C
Q4-15	C-	D+	C

Asset & Performance History

Date	NAV	1-Year Total Return
2018	49.8	1.37
2017	49.98	1.98
2016	49.7	-0.23
2015	50.33	0.88
2014	50.33	0.82
2013	50.25	0.31

Total Assets: $114,298,347

Asset Allocation
Asset	%
Cash	15%
Stocks	0%
US Stocks	0%
Bonds	85%
US Bonds	85%
Other	0%

Services Offered:

Investment Strategy: The investment seeks attractive tax-exempt income, consistent with preservation of capital. The fund invests at least 80% of its assets in a diversified portfolio of debt securities whose interest is, in the opinion of bond counsel for the issuer at the time of issuance, exempt from federal income tax ("Municipal Bonds"). Municipal Bonds generally are issued by or on behalf of states and local governments and their agencies, authorities and other instrumentalities. It may only invest in U.S. dollar-denominated investment grade debt securities, rated Baa or higher. **Top Holdings:** WEBER CNTY UTAH HOSP REV 1.39% SOUTHEASTERN PA TRANSN AUTH REV 5% CONNECTICUT ST SPL TAX OBLIG REV 5% LEE MEM HEALTH SYS FLA HOSP REV 5% METROPOLITAN TRANSN AUTH N Y REV 5%

Hartford Short Duration ETF

C-   HOLD

Ticker	Traded On	NAV	Total Assets ($)	Dividend Yield (TTM)	Turnover Ratio	Expense Ratio
HSRT	BATS	40.82	$114,287,148	3.38	28	0.29

Ratings
Reward	C-
Risk	D+
Recent Upgrade/Downgrade	Up

Fund Information
Fund Type	Exchange Traded Funds
Category	US Fixed Income
Sub-Category	Short-Term Bond
Prospectus Objective	Growth & Inc
Inception Date	May-18
Open to New Investments	Y

Prices
Price (as of 9/30/2019)	40.83
52-Week High	41.02
52-Week Low	39.56

Total Returns (%)
3-Month	6-Month	1-Year	3-Year	5-Year
1.14	2.94	5.52		

3-Year Standard Deviation	
Effective Duration	

Valuation
Premium/Discount (1-Year Average)	0.05

Company Information
Provider	Hartford Funds
Manager/Tenure	Timothy E. Smith (1)
Website	http://www.hartfordfunds.com
Address	690 Lee Road Wayne PA 19087 United States
Phone Number	800-456-7526

PERFORMANCE

Ratings History
Date	Overall Rating	Risk Rating	Reward Rating
Q3-19	C-	D+	C-
Q4-18	U		
Q4-17			
Q4-16			
Q4-15			

Asset & Performance History
Date	NAV	1-Year Total Return
2018	39.59	
2017		
2016		
2015		
2014		
2013		

Total Assets: $114,287,148

Asset Allocation
Asset	%
Cash	4%
Stocks	0%
US Stocks	0%
Bonds	95%
US Bonds	79%
Other	0%

Services Offered:

Investment Strategy: The investment seeks to provide current income and long-term total return. The fund seeks to achieve its investment objective by investing in securities that considered to be attractive giving consideration to both yield and total return. It normally invests in investment grade securities. The fund may invest up to 35% of its net assets in non-investment grade fixed income securities (also referred to as "junk bonds"). It may also invest up to 35% of its net assets in bank loans or loan participation interests in secured or unsecured variable, fixed or floating rate loans to U.S. and foreign corporations, partnerships and other entities ("bank loans"). **Top Holdings:** Us 2yr Note (Cbt) Dec19 Xcbt 20191231   Us 5yr Note (Cbt) Dec19 Xcbt 20191231   US 10 Year Note (CBT) Dec19 Federal National Mortgage Association 3.5%   Federal National Mortgage Association 3.25%

WisdomTree Continuous Commodity Index Fund

D   SELL

Ticker	Traded On	NAV	Total Assets ($)	Dividend Yield (TTM)	Turnover Ratio	Expense Ratio
GCC	NYSE Arca	17.56	$114,116,511	0		0.75

Ratings
Reward	D
Risk	D+
Recent Upgrade/Downgrade	

Fund Information
Fund Type	Exchange Traded Funds
Category	Commodities Broad Basket
Sub-Category	Commodities Broad Basket
Prospectus Objective	Natl Res
Inception Date	Jan-08
Open to New Investments	Y

Prices
Price (as of 9/30/2019)	17.54
52-Week High	18.76
52-Week Low	16.84

Total Returns (%)
3-Month	6-Month	1-Year	3-Year	5-Year
-1.51	-3.16	-3.69	-10.02	-29.25

3-Year Standard Deviation	6.16
Effective Duration	

Valuation
Premium/Discount (1-Year Average)	-0.10

Company Information
Provider	WisdomTree
Manager/Tenure	Management Team (11)
Website	http://www.wisdomtree.com
Address	WisdomTree 245 Park Avenue, 35th floor New York NY 10167 United States
Phone Number	866-909-9473

PERFORMANCE

Ratings History
Date	Overall Rating	Risk Rating	Reward Rating
Q3-19	D	D+	D
Q4-18	D	C-	D
Q4-17	D	D+	D
Q4-16	D	D	D
Q4-15	D	D	D

Asset & Performance History
Date	NAV	1-Year Total Return
2018	17.5	-9.09
2017	19.25	-0.53
2016	19.35	4.27
2015	18.56	-18.63
2014	22.81	-11.24
2013	25.7	-10.91

Total Assets: $114,116,511

Asset Allocation
Asset	%
Cash	50%
Stocks	0%
US Stocks	0%
Bonds	1%
US Bonds	0%
Other	48%

Services Offered:

Investment Strategy: The investment seeks, through its investment in the master fund, to reflect the performance of the index, over time, less the expenses of the fund and the master fund's overall operations.
The master fund invests in a portfolio of index commodities, as well as holding cash and United States Treasury securities and other high credit quality short-term fixed income securities for deposit with the master fund's Commodity Broker as margin. The Continuous Commodity Total Return Index is a broad based commodity index that reflects the price movement of 17 exchange-traded futures contracts. **Top Holdings:** Platinum Apr20   Sugar 11 (World) May20 Ifus 20200430   Platinum Jan20   Sugar 11 (World) Mar20 Ifus 20200228   Lean Hogs Future Apr20 Xcme 20200415

ProShares DJ Brookfield Global Infrastructure ETF   C   HOLD

Ticker	Traded On	NAV	Total Assets ($)	Dividend Yield (TTM)	Turnover Ratio	Expense Ratio
TOLZ	NYSE Arca	45.53	$113,358,361	3.07	14	0.46

Ratings
Reward   B-
Risk   C-
Recent Upgrade/Downgrade

Fund Information
Fund Type   Exchange Traded Funds
Category   Infrastructure Sector Equity
Sub-Category   Infrastructure
Prospectus Objective   Utility
Inception Date   Mar-14
Open to New Investments   Y

Prices
Price (as of 9/30/2019)   45.55
52-Week High   46.15
52-Week Low   37.16

Total Returns (%)

3-Month	6-Month	1-Year	3-Year	5-Year
2.03	5.41	12.74	21.81	23.87

3-Year Standard Deviation   9.93
Effective Duration

Valuation
Premium/Discount (1-Year Average)   0.08

Company Information
Provider   ProShares
Manager/Tenure   Scott Hanson (3), Ryan Dofflemeyer
                  (0)
Website   http://www.proshares.com
Address   ProShares 7501 Wisconsin Avenue,
                  Suite 1000 Bethesda MD 20814
                  United States
Phone Number   866-776-5125

PERFORMANCE

Ratings History

Date	Overall Rating	Risk Rating	Reward Rating
Q3-19	C	C-	B-
Q4-18	C-	C-	C-
Q4-17	C	C+	C
Q4-16	D+	D+	C-
Q4-15	D	D+	D

Asset & Performance History

Date	NAV	1-Year Total Return
2018	38.12	-7.97
2017	42.87	13.18
2016	39.16	11.84
2015	36.06	-13.91
2014	43.71	
2013		

Total Assets: $113,358,361
Asset Allocation

Asset	%
Cash	0%
Stocks	99%
US Stocks	50%
Bonds	0%
US Bonds	0%
Other	0%

Services Offered:

Investment Strategy: The investment seeks investment results, before fees and expenses, that track the performance of the Dow Jones Brookfield Global Infrastructure Composite Index (the "index"). The index consists of companies domiciled globally that qualify as "pure-play" infrastructure companies-companies whose primary business is the ownership and operation of infrastructure assets, activities that generally generate long-term stable cash flows. Under normal circumstances, the fund will invest at least 80% of its total assets in component securities. **Top Holdings:** American Tower Corp Enbridge Inc Vinci SA Crown Castle International Corp TC Energy Corp

---

First Trust NASDAQ® Clean Edge® Green Energy Index Fund   C   HOLD

Ticker	Traded On	NAV	Total Assets ($)	Dividend Yield (TTM)	Turnover Ratio	Expense Ratio
QCLN	NAS CM	21.38	$113,329,994	1.24	45	0.6

Ratings
Reward   B-
Risk   D+
Recent Upgrade/Downgrade

Fund Information
Fund Type   Exchange Traded Funds
Category   Technology Sector Equity
Sub-Category   Miscellaneous Sector
Prospectus Objective   Technology
Inception Date   Feb-07
Open to New Investments   Y

Prices
Price (as of 9/30/2019)   21.41
52-Week High   22.53
52-Week Low   16.31

Total Returns (%)

3-Month	6-Month	1-Year	3-Year	5-Year
0.28	5.01	9.02	44.91	20.32

3-Year Standard Deviation   16.76
Effective Duration

Valuation
Premium/Discount (1-Year Average)   -0.01

Company Information
Provider   First Trust
Manager/Tenure   Daniel J. Lindquist (12), David G.
                  McGarel (12), Roger F. Testin (12), 3
                  others
Website   http://www.ftportfolios.com/
Address   First Trust 120 E. Liberty Drive, Suite
                  400 Wheaton IL 60187 United States
Phone Number   800-621-1675

PERFORMANCE

Ratings History

Date	Overall Rating	Risk Rating	Reward Rating
Q3-19	C	D+	B-
Q4-18	C	D+	C+
Q4-17	C+	C	B-
Q4-16	C	D+	C+
Q4-15	C	C	C+

Asset & Performance History

Date	NAV	1-Year Total Return
2018	17.63	-12.23
2017	20.28	31.73
2016	15.47	-2.1
2015	16.01	-6.44
2014	17.23	-3.04
2013	17.9	89.81

Total Assets: $113,329,994
Asset Allocation

Asset	%
Cash	0%
Stocks	100%
US Stocks	93%
Bonds	0%
US Bonds	0%
Other	0%

Services Offered:

Investment Strategy: The investment seeks investment results that correspond generally to the price and yield (before the fund's fees and expenses) of an equity index called the NASDAQ® Clean Edge® Green Energy IndexSM. The fund will normally invest at least 90% of its net assets (including investment borrowings) in the common stocks and depositary receipts that comprise the index. The index is designed to track the performance of small, mid and large capitalization clean energy companies that are publicly traded in the United States. It is non-diversified. **Top Holdings:** Tesla Inc Universal Display Corp ON Semiconductor Corp Hexcel Corp Albemarle Corp

First Trust Latin America AlphaDEX® Fund

C HOLD

Ticker	Traded On	NAV	Total Assets ($)	Dividend Yield (TTM)	Turnover Ratio	Expense Ratio
FLN	NAS CM	20.37	$113,044,158	2.75	158	0.8

Ratings

Reward	C+
Risk	C-
Recent Upgrade/Downgrade	

Fund Information

Fund Type	Exchange Traded Funds
Category	Latin America Equity
Sub-Category	Latin America Stock
Prospectus Objective	Foreign Stock
Inception Date	Apr-11
Open to New Investments	Y

Prices

Price (as of 9/30/2019)	20.42
52-Week High	21.76
52-Week Low	17.71

Total Returns (%)

3-Month	6-Month	1-Year	3-Year	5-Year
-1.63	2.82	12.84	32.11	14.04

3-Year Standard Deviation	21.33
Effective Duration	

Valuation

Premium/Discount (1-Year Average)	-0.17

Company Information

Provider	First Trust
Manager/Tenure	Jon C. Erickson (8), Daniel J. Lindquist (8), David G. McGarel (8), 3 others
Website	http://www.ftportfolios.com/
Address	First Trust 120 E. Liberty Drive, Suite 400 Wheaton IL 60187 United States
Phone Number	800-621-1675

PERFORMANCE

Ratings History

Date	Overall Rating	Risk Rating	Reward Rating
Q3-19	C	C-	C+
Q4-18	C-	D+	C-
Q4-17	C	C	C
Q4-16	D+	D+	D+
Q4-15	D	D	D-

Asset & Performance History

Date	NAV	1-Year Total Return
2018	18.33	-7.42
2017	20.43	20.61
2016	18.74	42.74
2015	13.28	-29.03
2014	19.09	-15.84
2013	23.43	-10.07

Total Assets: $113,044,158

Asset Allocation

Asset	%
Cash	1%
Stocks	99%
US Stocks	0%
Bonds	0%
US Bonds	0%
Other	0%

Services Offered:

Investment Strategy: The investment seeks investment results that correspond generally to the price and yield (before the fund's fees and expenses) of an equity index called the NASDAQ AlphaDEX® Latin America Index. The fund will normally invest at least 90% of its net assets (including investment borrowings) in the common stocks and depositary receipts that comprise the index. The index is designed to select stocks from the NASDAQ Latin America Index (the "base index") that may generate positive alpha, or risk-adjusted returns, relative to traditional indices through the use of the AlphaDEX® selection methodology. **Top Holdings:** JBS SA Cia de Transmissao de Energia Eletrica Paulista Participating Preferred Centrais Eletricas Brasileiras SA Participating Preferred Natura Cosmeticos SA Telefonica Brasil SA Participating Preferred

Direxion All Cap Insider Sentiment Shares

C HOLD

Ticker	Traded On	NAV	Total Assets ($)	Dividend Yield (TTM)	Turnover Ratio	Expense Ratio
KNOW	NYSE Arca	38.27	$112,916,069	2.38	919	0.59

Ratings

Reward	C
Risk	C-
Recent Upgrade/Downgrade	Up

Fund Information

Fund Type	Exchange Traded Funds
Category	US Equity Mid Cap
Sub-Category	Mid-Cap Blend
Prospectus Objective	Balanced
Inception Date	Dec-11
Open to New Investments	Y

Prices

Price (as of 9/30/2019)	38.28
52-Week High	41.07
52-Week Low	32.19

Total Returns (%)

3-Month	6-Month	1-Year	3-Year	5-Year
-1.85	-0.67	-4.54	23.28	46.90

3-Year Standard Deviation	15.38
Effective Duration	

Valuation

Premium/Discount (1-Year Average)	-0.09

Company Information

Provider	Direxion Funds
Manager/Tenure	Paul Brigandi (7), Tony Ng (4)
Website	http://www.direxionfunds.com
Address	Direxion Funds 1301 Avenue Of The Americas (6th Avenue) New York NY 10019 United States
Phone Number	646-572-3390

PERFORMANCE

Ratings History

Date	Overall Rating	Risk Rating	Reward Rating
Q3-19	C	C-	C
Q4-18	C-	C-	C
Q4-17	B+	A-	B
Q4-16	C-	D+	C-
Q4-15	C	C	C

Asset & Performance History

Date	NAV	1-Year Total Return
2018	33.77	-14.78
2017	41.4	16.43
2016	38.31	14.3
2015	35.46	3.44
2014	34.52	17.96
2013	29.62	36.24

Total Assets: $112,916,069

Asset Allocation

Asset	%
Cash	0%
Stocks	100%
US Stocks	99%
Bonds	0%
US Bonds	0%
Other	0%

Services Offered:

Investment Strategy: The investment seeks investment results before fees and expenses that track the Sabrient Multi-Cap Insider/Analyst Quant-Weighted Index. The fund, under normal circumstances, invests at least 80% of its assets in the securities that comprise the index. The index is composed of a mix of U.S. large-capitalization, mid-capitalization, and small-capitalization companies that are listed on the New York Stock Exchange ("NYSE") and the NASDAQ Stock Exchange ("NASDAQ") and selected by Sabrient Systems LLC using a quantitative methodology. The fund is non-diversified. **Top Holdings:** Mercury General Corp Berkshire Hills Bancorp Inc The Hartford Financial Services Group Inc United Community Banks Inc Aflac Inc

Xtrackers Russell 1000 US QARP ETF   C-   HOLD

Ticker	Traded On	NAV	Total Assets ($)	Dividend Yield (TTM)	Turnover Ratio	Expense Ratio
QARP	NYSE Arca	27.51	$112,782,034	1.81		0.19

Ratings

Reward	C
Risk	D+
Recent Upgrade/Downgrade	Up

Fund Information

Fund Type	Exchange Traded Funds
Category	US Equity Large Cap Blend
Sub-Category	Large Blend
Prospectus Objective	Growth & Inc
Inception Date	Apr-18
Open to New Investments	Y

Prices

Price (as of 9/30/2019)	27.54
52-Week High	28.07
52-Week Low	22.66

Total Returns (%)

3-Month	6-Month	1-Year	3-Year	5-Year
1.53	3.77	2.22		

3-Year Standard Deviation
Effective Duration

Valuation

Premium/Discount (1-Year Average)	-0.05

Company Information

Provider	DWS
Manager/Tenure	Shlomo Bassous (1), Patrick Dwyer (1), Bryan Richards (1)
Website	http://dws.com
Address	DWS 210 West 10th Street Kansas City MO 64105-1614 United States
Phone Number	

PERFORMANCE

Ratings History

Date	Overall Rating	Risk Rating	Reward Rating
Q3-19	C-	D+	C
Q4-18	U		
Q4-17			
Q4-16			
Q4-15			

Asset & Performance History

Date	NAV	1-Year Total Return
2018	23.51	
2017		
2016		
2015		
2014		
2013		

Total Assets: $112,782,034

Asset Allocation

Asset	%
Cash	3%
Stocks	97%
US Stocks	96%
Bonds	0%
US Bonds	0%
Other	0%

Services Offered:

Investment Strategy: The investment seeks investment results that correspond generally to the performance, before fees and expenses, of the Russell 1000 2Qual/Val 5% Capped Factor Index (the "underlying index"). The fund will invest at least 80% of its total assets (but typically far more) in component securities of the underlying index. The underlying index is designed to track the equity market performance of companies in the United States selected on the investment style criteria ("factors") of quality and value. The fund is non-diversified. **Top Holdings:** Apple Inc S&P500 Emini Fut Sep19 Exxon Mobil Corp Intel Corp Facebook Inc A

Invesco Dynamic Building & Construction ETF   B   BUY

Ticker	Traded On	NAV	Total Assets ($)	Dividend Yield (TTM)	Turnover Ratio	Expense Ratio
PKB	NYSE Arca	32.66	$112,691,705	0.42	148	0.6

Ratings

Reward	B+
Risk	C
Recent Upgrade/Downgrade	Up

Fund Information

Fund Type	Exchange Traded Funds
Category	Industrials Sector Equity
Sub-Category	Industrials
Prospectus Objective	Unaligned
Inception Date	Oct-05
Open to New Investments	Y

Prices

Price (as of 9/30/2019)	32.64
52-Week High	32.64
52-Week Low	22.38

Total Returns (%)

3-Month	6-Month	1-Year	3-Year	5-Year
5.13	16.67	10.82	27.84	62.31

3-Year Standard Deviation   19.16
Effective Duration

Valuation

Premium/Discount (1-Year Average)	-0.04

Company Information

Provider	Invesco
Manager/Tenure	Peter Hubbard (12), Michael Jeanette (11), Tony Seisser (5)
Website	http://www.invesco.com/us
Address	Invesco 11 Greenway Plaza, Ste. 2500 Houston TX 77046 United States
Phone Number	800-659-1005

PERFORMANCE

Ratings History

Date	Overall Rating	Risk Rating	Reward Rating
Q3-19	B	C	B+
Q4-18	C+	C-	B
Q4-17	A-	B+	A
Q4-16	B-	C	B
Q4-15	B+	B-	A-

Asset & Performance History

Date	NAV	1-Year Total Return
2018	23.83	-30.87
2017	34.64	24.43
2016	27.89	17.71
2015	23.77	10.42
2014	21.55	-3.57
2013	22.37	28.93

Total Assets: $112,691,705

Asset Allocation

Asset	%
Cash	0%
Stocks	100%
US Stocks	100%
Bonds	0%
US Bonds	0%
Other	0%

Services Offered:

Investment Strategy: The investment seeks to track the investment results (before fees and expenses) of the Dynamic Building & Construction IntellidexSM Index. The fund generally will invest at least 90% of its total assets in the securities that comprise the underlying intellidex. The underlying intellidex was composed of common stocks of U.S. building and construction companies. These companies are engaged primarily in providing construction and related engineering services for building and remodeling residential properties, commercial or industrial buildings, etc. It is non-diversified. **Top Holdings:** Martin Marietta Materials Inc The Home Depot Inc Jacobs Engineering Group Inc NVR Inc Johnson Controls International PLC

Columbia India Consumer ETF   D+   SELL

Ticker	Traded On	NAV	Total Assets ($)	Dividend Yield (TTM)	Turnover Ratio	Expense Ratio
INCO	NYSE Arca	41.43	$111,869,818	0.13	15	0.75

Ratings
Reward   D
Risk   D+
Recent Upgrade/Downgrade   Down

Fund Information
Fund Type   Exchange Traded Funds
Category   India Equity
Sub-Category   India Equity
Prospectus Objective   Unaligned
Inception Date   Aug-11
Open to New Investments   Y

Prices
Price (as of 9/30/2019)   41.34
52-Week High   44.75
52-Week Low   36.58

Total Returns (%)

3-Month	6-Month	1-Year	3-Year	5-Year
-0.38	-1.73	0.70	15.33	34.98

3-Year Standard Deviation   18.24
Effective Duration

Valuation
Premium/Discount (1-Year Average)   -0.18

Company Information
Provider   Columbia
Manager/Tenure   Christopher Lo (3)
Website   http://www.columbiathreadneedleus.com
Address   Liberty Financial Funds P.O. Box 8081
     Boston MA 02266-8081 United States
Phone Number   800-345-6611

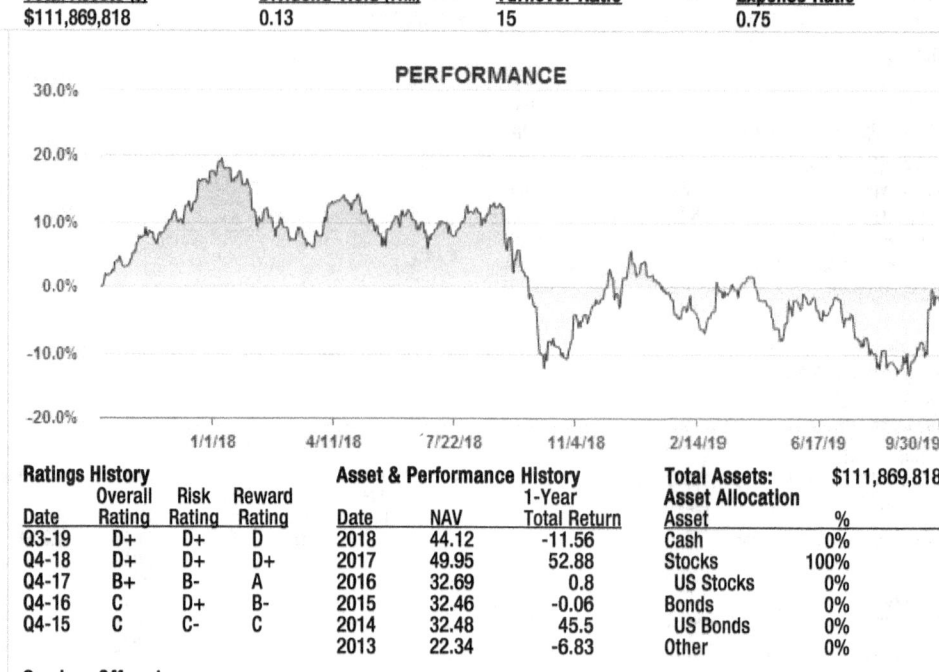

PERFORMANCE

Ratings History

Date	Overall Rating	Risk Rating	Reward Rating
Q3-19	D+	D+	D
Q4-18	D+	D+	D+
Q4-17	B+	B-	A
Q4-16	C	D+	B-
Q4-15	C	C-	C

Asset & Performance History

Date	NAV	1-Year Total Return
2018	44.12	-11.56
2017	49.95	52.88
2016	32.69	0.8
2015	32.46	-0.06
2014	32.48	45.5
2013	22.34	-6.83

Total Assets: $111,869,818
Asset Allocation

Asset	%
Cash	0%
Stocks	100%
US Stocks	0%
Bonds	0%
US Bonds	0%
Other	0%

Services Offered:

Investment Strategy: The investment seeks investment results that correspond to the price and yield performance of the Indxx India Consumer Index. The fund will invest at least 80% of its net assets in Indian consumer companies included in the index and the advisor generally expects to be substantially invested at such times, with at least 95% of its net assets invested in these securities. The index is a maximum 30-stock free-float adjusted market capitalization-weighted index designed to measure the market performance of companies in the consumer industry in India, as defined by Indxx's proprietary methodology. It is non-diversified. **Top Holdings:** Nestle India Ltd   Hindustan Unilever Ltd   Titan Co Ltd   Dabur India Ltd   Britannia Industries Ltd

---

iShares Edge MSCI Multifactor Global ETF   C   HOLD

Ticker	Traded On	NAV	Total Assets ($)	Dividend Yield (TTM)	Turnover Ratio	Expense Ratio
ACWF	NYSE Arca	29.03	$111,770,496	2.22	43	0.35

Ratings
Reward   C
Risk   C-
Recent Upgrade/Downgrade   Up

Fund Information
Fund Type   Exchange Traded Funds
Category   Global Equity Large Cap
Sub-Category   World Large Stock
Prospectus Objective   Growth & Inc
Inooption Date   Apr-15
Open to New Investments   Y

Prices
Price (as of 9/30/2019)   29.00
52-Week High   30.77
52-Week Low   24.98

Total Returns (%)

3-Month	6-Month	1-Year	3-Year	5-Year
-1.49	-0.29	-3.09	28.45	

3-Year Standard Deviation   12.56
Effective Duration

Valuation
Premium/Discount (1-Year Average)   0.01

Company Information
Provider   iShares
Manager/Tenure   Diane Hsiung (4), Jennifer Hsui (4),
     Greg Savage (4), 3 others
Website   http://www.ishares.com
Address   iShares 400 Howard Street San
     Francisco CA 94105 United States
Phone Number   800-474-2737

PERFORMANCE

Ratings History

Date	Overall Rating	Risk Rating	Reward Rating
Q3-19	C	C-	C
Q4-18	C-	C-	C-
Q4-17	B-	B-	C+
Q4-16	D+	D	C-
Q4-15	U		

Asset & Performance History

Date	NAV	1-Year Total Return
2018	25.97	-13.38
2017	30.35	29.62
2016	23.9	5.12
2015	23.19	
2014		
2013		

Total Assets: $111,770,496
Asset Allocation

Asset	%
Cash	0%
Stocks	100%
US Stocks	59%
Bonds	0%
US Bonds	0%
Other	0%

Services Offered:

Investment Strategy: The investment seeks to track the investment results of the MSCI ACWI Diversified Multiple-Factor Index. The fund generally will invest at least 90% of its assets in the component securities of the underlying index and in investments that have economic characteristics that are substantially identical to the component securities of the underlying index. The underlying index is designed to contain equity securities from the MSCI ACWI Index (the "parent index") that have high exposure to four investment style factors: value, quality, momentum and low size, while maintaining a level of risk similar to that of the parent index. **Top Holdings:** Intel Corp Accenture PLC Class A   Intuit Inc   Anthem Inc   China Construction Bank Corp Class H

iShares U.S. Insurance ETF   C+   HOLD

Ticker	Traded On	NAV		Total Assets ($)	Dividend Yield (TTM)	Turnover Ratio	Expense Ratio
IAK	NYSE Arca	72.02		$111,626,790	1.84	17	0.43

Ratings

Reward	B
Risk	C
Recent Upgrade/Downgrade	Up

Fund Information

Fund Type	Exchange Traded Funds
Category	Financials Sector Equity
Sub-Category	Financial
Prospectus Objective	Financial
Inception Date	May-06
Open to New Investments	Y

Prices

Price (as of 9/30/2019)	72.04
52-Week High	72.90
52-Week Low	54.51

Total Returns (%)

3-Month	6-Month	1-Year	3-Year	5-Year
0.96	12.36	11.44	44.24	70.18

3-Year Standard Deviation	13.46
Effective Duration	

Valuation

Premium/Discount (1-Year Average)	-0.07

Company Information

Provider	iShares
Manager/Tenure	Greg Savage (11), Jennifer Hsui (7), Alan Mason (3), 2 others
Website	http://www.ishares.com
Address	iShares 400 Howard Street San Francisco CA 94105 United States
Phone Number	800-474-2737

PERFORMANCE

Ratings History

Date	Overall Rating	Risk Rating	Reward Rating
Q3-19	C+	C	B
Q4-18	C	C-	C
Q4-17	B+	A-	B+
Q4-16	C	C-	C
Q4-15	B+	B+	B+

Asset & Performance History

Date	NAV	1-Year Total Return
2018	57.97	-11.05
2017	66.59	14.1
2016	59.36	18.36
2015	51.1	3.94
2014	49.98	7.33
2013	47.33	45.17

Total Assets: $111,626,790

Asset Allocation

Asset	%
Cash	0%
Stocks	100%
US Stocks	88%
Bonds	0%
US Bonds	0%
Other	0%

Services Offered:

Investment Strategy: The investment seeks to track the investment results of the Dow Jones U.S. Select Insurance Index composed of U.S. equities in the insurance sector. The fund generally invests at least 90% of its assets in securities of the underlying index and in depositary receipts representing securities of the underlying index. The underlying index measures the performance of the insurance sector of the U.S. equity market. The fund is non-diversified. **Top Holdings:** Chubb Ltd   American International Group Inc   Progressive Corp   MetLife Inc   Aflac Inc

---

ProShares Ultra Gold   C   HOLD

Ticker	Traded On	NAV		Total Assets ($)	Dividend Yield (TTM)	Turnover Ratio	Expense Ratio
UGL	NYSE Arca			$109,334,454	0	0	0.95

Ratings

Reward	C
Risk	C
Recent Upgrade/Downgrade	Up

Fund Information

Fund Type	Exchange Traded Funds
Category	Trading Tools
Sub-Category	Trading--Leveraged Commodities
Prospectus Objective	Prec Metals
Inception Date	Dec-08
Open to New Investments	Y

Prices

Price (as of 9/30/2019)	46.94
52-Week High	52.55
52-Week Low	32.56

Total Returns (%)

3-Month	6-Month	1-Year	3-Year	5-Year
15.19	31.32	49.40	9.60	18.48

3-Year Standard Deviation	22.5
Effective Duration	

Valuation

Premium/Discount (1-Year Average)	0.07

Company Information

Provider	ProShares
Manager/Tenure	Management Team (10)
Website	http://www.proshares.com
Address	ProShares 7501 Wisconsin Avenue, Suite 1000 Bethesda MD 20814 United States
Phone Number	866-776-5125

PERFORMANCE

Ratings History

Date	Overall Rating	Risk Rating	Reward Rating
Q3-19	C	C	C
Q4-18	D	D	D
Q4-17	D+	D	C-
Q4-16	D+	D	C-
Q4-15	D-	D-	D-

Asset & Performance History

Date	NAV	1-Year Total Return
2018	37.12	-6.87
2017	39.88	21.19
2016	32.9	10.68
2015	29.73	-25.68
2014	40	-3.04
2013	41.26	-50.74

Total Assets: $109,334,454

Asset Allocation

Asset	%
Cash	-100%
Stocks	138%
US Stocks	138%
Bonds	0%
US Bonds	0%
Other	63%

Services Offered:

Investment Strategy: The investment seeks daily investment results, before fees and expenses, that correspond to two times (2x) the daily performance of the Bloomberg Gold SubindexSM.
The fund seeks to meet its investment objective by investing, under normal market conditions, in any one of, or combinations of, Financial Instruments (including swap agreements, futures contracts and forward contracts) based on the benchmark. The types and mix of Financial Instruments in which the fund invest may vary daily at the discretion of the Sponsor. It will not invest directly in any commodity. **Top Holdings:** Gold 100 oz Dec19 Bloomberg Gold Subindex Swap - Citibank Na   Bloomberg Gold Subindex Swap - Ubs Ag   Bloomberg Gold Subindex Swap - Goldman Sachs   Gold 100 Oz Future 12/27/2018 (Gcz8)

Invesco Russell 1000 Low Beta Equal Weight ETF

C   HOLD

Ticker	Traded On	NAV	Total Assets ($)	Dividend Yield (TTM)	Turnover Ratio	Expense Ratio
USLB	NAS CM	33.60	$109,189,469	1.74		0.35

Ratings

Reward	C
Risk	D+
Recent Upgrade/Downgrade	

Fund Information

Fund Type	Exchange Traded Funds
Category	US Equity Mid Cap
Sub-Category	Mid-Cap Blend
Prospectus Objective	Growth & Inc
Inception Date	Nov-15
Open to New Investments	

Prices

Price (as of 9/30/2019)	33.59
52-Week High	33.88
52-Week Low	27.11

Total Returns (%)

3-Month	6-Month	1-Year	3-Year	5-Year
2.22	5.48	4.32	33.30	

3-Year Standard Deviation	11.36
Effective Duration	

Valuation

Premium/Discount (1-Year Average)	-0.15

Company Information

Provider	Invesco
Manager/Tenure	Peter Hubbard (3), Michael Jeanette (3), Tony Seisser (3)
Website	http://www.invesco.com/us
Address	Invesco 11 Greenway Plaza, Ste. 2500 Houston TX 77046 United States
Phone Number	800-659-1005

PERFORMANCE

Ratings History

Date	Overall Rating	Risk Rating	Reward Rating
Q3-19	C	D+	C
Q4-18	C-	D+	C-
Q4-17	C	B+	C-
Q4-16	D	C-	D+
Q4-15			

Asset & Performance History

Date	NAV	1-Year Total Return
2018	28.32	-7.37
2017	31.06	16.29
2016	27.11	11.2
2015	24.63	
2014		
2013		

Total Assets: $109,189,469

Asset Allocation

Asset	%
Cash	0%
Stocks	100%
US Stocks	99%
Bonds	0%
US Bonds	0%
Other	0%

Services Offered:

Investment Strategy: The investment seeks to track the investment results (before fees and expenses) of the Russell 1000® Low Beta Equal Weight Index (the "underlying index"). The fund generally will invest at least 90% of its total assets in the securities that comprise the underlying index. The underlying index is comprised of securities in the Russell 1000® Index that exhibit low beta characteristics. The underlying index is a subset of the Russell 1000, which is designed to measure the performance of the large-cap segment of the U.S. equity market and consists of the stocks of the largest 1,000 U.S. companies, by capitalization. **Top Holdings:** L3Harris Technologies Inc   Royal Gold Inc   Insulet Corp   Switch Inc Class A   Casey's General Stores Inc

---

Invesco International Corporate Bond ETF

C   HOLD

Ticker	Traded On	NAV	Total Assets ($)	Dividend Yield (TTM)	Turnover Ratio	Expense Ratio
PICB	NYSE Arca	26.26	$108,985,576	1.52	12	0.5

Ratings

Reward	C
Risk	C-
Recent Upgrade/Downgrade	Up

Fund Information

Fund Type	Exchange Traded Funds
Category	Global Fixed Income
Sub-Category	World Bond
Prospectus Objective	Worldwide Bond
Inception Date	Jun-10
Open to New Investments	Y

Prices

Price (as of 9/30/2019)	26.20
52-Week High	26.70
52-Week Low	24.84

Total Returns (%)

3-Month	6-Month	1-Year	3-Year	5-Year
-1.07	1.04	2.92	3.30	-0.62

3-Year Standard Deviation	7.08
Effective Duration	7.01

Valuation

Premium/Discount (1-Year Average)	-0.21

Company Information

Provider	Invesco
Manager/Tenure	Philip Fang (9), Peter Hubbard (9), Jeffrey W. Kernagis (9), 2 others
Website	http://www.invesco.com/us
Address	Invesco 11 Greenway Plaza, Ste. 2500 Houston TX 77046 United States
Phone Number	800-659-1005

PERFORMANCE

Ratings History

Date	Overall Rating	Risk Rating	Reward Rating
Q3-19	C	C-	C
Q4-18	D+	C-	D+
Q4-17	C	C+	C
Q4-16	D+	C-	D
Q4-15	D+	C-	D+

Asset & Performance History

Date	NAV	1-Year Total Return
2018	25.14	-7.39
2017	27.59	14.19
2016	24.54	-0.43
2015	25.17	-9.39
2014	28.42	-0.92
2013	29.42	2.27

Total Assets: $108,985,576

Asset Allocation

Asset	%
Cash	1%
Stocks	0%
US Stocks	0%
Bonds	97%
US Bonds	1%
Other	0%

Services Offered:

Investment Strategy: The investment seeks to track the investment results (before fees and expenses) of the S&P International Corporate Bond Index® (the "underlying index"). The fund generally will invest at least 80% of its total assets in investment grade corporate bonds that comprise the underlying index. The underlying index measures the performance of investment grade corporate bonds issued in the following currencies of Group of Ten countries, excluding the U.S. Dollar (USD): Australian Dollar (AUD), British Pound (GBP), Canadian Dollar (CAD), Euro (EUR), Japanese Yen (JPY), New Zealand Dollar (NZD), Norwegian Krone (NOK), Swedish Krona (SEK) and Swiss Franc (SFR). **Top Holdings:** Electricite de France SA 6%   Electricite de France SA 6.12%   ENEL Finance International N.V. 5.75%   Electricite de France SA 5.5%   Engie 5%

ProShares Short High Yield　　　　　　　　　　　　　　　D　　SELL

Ticker	Traded On	NAV	Total Assets ($)	Dividend Yield (TTM)	Turnover Ratio	Expense Ratio
SJB	NYSE Arca	21.15	$108,907,378	1.28		0.95

Ratings
Reward	D
Risk	D+
Recent Upgrade/Downgrade	

Fund Information
Fund Type	Exchange Traded Funds
Category	Trading Tools
Sub-Category	Trading--Inverse Debt
Prospectus Objective	Corp Bond-High Yld
Inception Date	Mar-11
Open to New Investments	Y

Prices
Price (as of 9/30/2019)	21.13
52-Week High	24.12
52-Week Low	21.10

Total Returns (%)
3-Month	6-Month	1-Year	3-Year	5-Year
-0.98	-2.77	-4.66	-14.05	-23.20

3-Year Standard Deviation　　4.42
Effective Duration

Valuation
Premium/Discount (1-Year Average)　　-0.01

Company Information
Provider	ProShares
Manager/Tenure	Benjamin McAbee (3), Alexander V. Ilyasov (0)
Website	http://www.proshares.com
Address	ProShares 7501 Wisconsin Avenue, Suite 1000 Bethesda MD 20814 United States
Phone Number	866-776-5125

PERFORMANCE

Ratings History
Date	Overall Rating	Risk Rating	Reward Rating
Q3-19	D	D+	D
Q4-18	D+	D+	D
Q4-17	D	D+	D
Q4-16	D+	D	D
Q4-15	D+	D+	D

Asset & Performance History
Date	NAV	1-Year Total Return
2018	23.53	2.47
2017	23.13	-6.28
2016	24.68	-13.85
2015	28.65	2.24
2014	28.02	-4.75
2013	29.42	-8.57

Total Assets: $108,907,378
Asset Allocation
Asset	%
Cash	155%
Stocks	0%
US Stocks	0%
Bonds	6%
US Bonds	6%
Other	-61%

Services Offered:

Investment Strategy: The investment seeks daily investment results that correspond to the inverse (-1x) of the daily performance of the Markit iBoxx $ Liquid High Yield Index. The fund invests in financial instruments that ProShare Advisors believes, in combination, should produce daily returns consistent with the fund's investment objective. The index is a market-value weighted index designed to provide a balanced representation of U.S. dollar denominated high yield corporate bonds for sale within the U.S. by means of including the most liquid high yield corporate bonds available as determined by a set of transparent and objective index rules. The fund is non-diversified. **Top Holdings:** Markit Iboxx $ Liquid High Yield Index (Hyg) Swap Goldman Sachs Internation　Markit Iboxx $ Liquid High Yield Index (Hyg) Swap Citibank Na　Markit Iboxx $ Liquid High Yield Index (Hyg) Swap Credit Suisse (Internatio　United States Treasury Bills　United States Treasury Bills

First Trust Brazil AlphaDEX® Fund　　　　　　　　　　　B-　　BUY

Ticker	Traded On	NAV	Total Assets ($)	Dividend Yield (TTM)	Turnover Ratio	Expense Ratio
FBZ	NAS CM	15.89	$108,875,991	2.77	128	0.8

Ratings
Reward	B
Risk	C-
Recent Upgrade/Downgrade	Up

Fund Information
Fund Type	Exchange Traded Funds
Category	Latin America Equity
Sub-Category	Latin America Stock
Prospectus Objective	Foreign Stock
Inception Date	Apr-11
Open to New Investments	Y

Prices
Price (as of 9/30/2019)	15.82
52-Week High	17.29
52-Week Low	11.39

Total Returns (%)
3-Month	6-Month	1-Year	3-Year	5-Year
0.69	9.67	45.70	53.07	26.59

3-Year Standard Deviation　　27.51
Effective Duration

Valuation
Premium/Discount (1-Year Average)　　-0.29

Company Information
Provider	First Trust
Manager/Tenure	Jon C. Erickson (8), Daniel J. Lindquist (8), David G. McGarel (8), 3 others
Website	http://www.ftportfolios.com/
Address	First Trust 120 E. Liberty Drive, Suite 400 Wheaton IL 60187 United States
Phone Number	800-621-1675

PERFORMANCE

Ratings History
Date	Overall Rating	Risk Rating	Reward Rating
Q3-19	B-	C-	B
Q4-18	C	C-	C
Q4-17	C	C-	C
Q4-16	D+	D+	D+
Q4-15	D-	D-	D-

Asset & Performance History
Date	NAV	1-Year Total Return
2018	13.37	-1.12
2017	15.51	21.01
2016	13.93	59.84
2015	8.87	-41.76
2014	15.65	-16.42
2013	19.45	-14.69

Total Assets: $108,875,991
Asset Allocation
Asset	%
Cash	0%
Stocks	100%
US Stocks	0%
Bonds	0%
US Bonds	0%
Other	0%

Services Offered:

Investment Strategy: The investment seeks investment results that correspond generally to the price and yield (before the fund's fees and expenses) of an equity index called the NASDAQ AlphaDEX® Brazil Index. The fund will normally invest at least 90% of its net assets (including investment borrowings) in the common stocks and depositary receipts that comprise the index. The index is designed to select stocks from the NASDAQ Brazil Index (the "base index") that may generate positive alpha, or risk-adjusted returns, relative to traditional indices through the use of the AlphaDEX® selection methodology. **Top Holdings:** JBS SA　Centrais Eletricas Brasileiras SA Participating Preferred　Sul America SA　Telefonica Brasil SA Participating Preferred　Cia Paranaense De Energia Copel Participating Preferred

WBI BullBear Global Income ETF

C   HOLD

Ticker	Traded On	NAV	Total Assets ($)	Dividend Yield (TTM)	Turnover Ratio	Expense Ratio
WBII	NYSE Arca	25.60	$108,798,974	3.62	686	1.28

Ratings
Reward   B-
Risk   C-
Recent Upgrade/Downgrade

Fund Information
Fund Type   Exchange Traded Funds
Category   US Fixed Income
Sub-Category   Multisector Bond
Prospectus Objective   Income
Inception Date   Aug-14
Open to New Investments   Y

Prices
Price (as of 9/30/2019)   25.56
52-Week High   25.76
52-Week Low   23.26

Total Returns (%)

3-Month	6-Month	1-Year	3-Year	5-Year
2.50	5.92	10.59	10.87	16.76

3-Year Standard Deviation   3.63
Effective Duration   5.19

Valuation
Premium/Discount (1-Year Average)   -0.13

Company Information
Provider   WBI Investments
Manager/Tenure   Donald R. Schreiber (5), Steven Van
                 Solkema (0)
Website   http://www.wbishares.com
Address   34 Sycamore Ave Suite 1-E Little
                      Silver NJ 07739 United States
Phone Number   732-842-4920

PERFORMANCE

Ratings History

Date	Overall Rating	Risk Rating	Reward Rating
Q3-19	C	C-	B-
Q4-18	C-	C-	D+
Q4-17	B-	A-	C
Q4-16	C-	C-	C-
Q4-15	D-	C-	D+

Asset & Performance History

Date	NAV	1-Year Total Return
2018	24.08	-1.45
2017	25.4	4.19
2016	24.83	2.59
2015	24.53	-0.69
2014	25.13	
2013		

Total Assets: $108,798,974
Asset Allocation

Asset	%
Cash	2%
Stocks	0%
US Stocks	0%
Bonds	98%
US Bonds	85%
Other	0%

Services Offered:

Investment Strategy: The investment seeks current income with the potential for long-term capital appreciation, while also seeking to protect principal during unfavorable market conditions. Under normal market conditions, the fund will invest at least 80% of its net assets, plus the amount of any borrowings for investment purposes, in income-producing debt and equity securities of foreign and domestic issuers, including the securities of foreign and domestic corporate and government entities. **Top Holdings:** Xtrackers USD High Yield Corp Bd ETF iShares Broad USD High Yield Corp Bd ETF SPDR® Blmbg Barclays High Yield Bd ETF Vanguard Extended Duration Trs ETF iShares 7-10 Year Treasury Bond ETF

MicroSectors™ FANG+™ Index 3X Leveraged ETN

D   SELL

Ticker	Traded On	NAV	Total Assets ($)	Dividend Yield (TTM)	Turnover Ratio	Expense Ratio
FNGU	NYSE Arca	33.94	$108,618,432	0		0.95

Ratings
Reward   D
Risk   D
Recent Upgrade/Downgrade

Fund Information
Fund Type   Exchange Traded Funds
Category   Trading Tools
Sub-Category   Trading--Leveraged Equity
Prospectus Objective   Growth & Inc
Inception Date   Jan-18
Open to New Investments   Y

Prices
Price (as of 9/30/2019)   33.55
52-Week High   65.43
52-Week Low   22.61

Total Returns (%)

3-Month	6-Month	1-Year	3-Year	5-Year
-10.59	-20.52	-45.42		

3-Year Standard Deviation
Effective Duration

Valuation
Premium/Discount (1-Year Average)   -0.02

Company Information
Provider   BMO Capital Markets Corp.
Manager/Tenure   No Manager (1)
Website
Address   3 Times Square New York, NY 10036
                      New York NY 10036 United States
Phone Number

PERFORMANCE

Ratings History

Date	Overall Rating	Risk Rating	Reward Rating
Q3-19	D	D	D
Q4-18	U		
Q4-17			
Q4-16			
Q4-15			

Asset & Performance History

Date	NAV	1-Year Total Return
2018	27.6	
2017		
2016		
2015		
2014		
2013		

Total Assets: $108,618,432
Asset Allocation

Asset	%
Cash	%
Stocks	%
US Stocks	%
Bonds	%
US Bonds	%
Other	%

Services Offered:

Investment Strategy: The investment seeks return linked to a three times leveraged participation in the daily performance of the NYSE FANG+™ Index, total return (the "index").
The notes are intended to be daily trading tools for sophisticated investors to manage daily trading risks as part of an overall diversified portfolio. The index is an equal-dollar weighted index designed to represent a segment of the technology and consumer discretionary sectors consisting of highly-traded growth stocks of technology and tech-enabled companies. **Top Holdings:**

AdvisorShares Sage Core Reserves ETF   C   HOLD

Ticker	Traded On	NAV	Total Assets ($)	Dividend Yield (TTM)	Turnover Ratio	Expense Ratio
HOLD	NYSE Arca	99.77	$107,248,540	2.31		0.35

Ratings

Reward	C
Risk	C-
Recent Upgrade/Downgrade	Up

Fund Information

Fund Type	Exchange Traded Funds
Category	US Fixed Income
Sub-Category	Ultrashort Bond
Prospectus Objective	Income
Inception Date	Jan-14
Open to New Investments	Y

Prices

Price (as of 9/30/2019)	99.74
52-Week High	99.90
52-Week Low	99.09

Total Returns (%)

3-Month	6-Month	1-Year	3-Year	5-Year
0.67	1.47	2.76	5.76	6.87

3-Year Standard Deviation	0.32
Effective Duration	0.68

Valuation

Premium/Discount (1-Year Average)	0.00

Company Information

Provider	AdvisorShares
Manager/Tenure	Mark Cordes MacQueen (5), Thomas Hideo Urano (5)
Website	http://www.advisorshares.com
Address	AdvisorShares 2 Bethesda Metro Center, Suite 1330 Bethesda MD 20814 United States
Phone Number	877-843-3831

PERFORMANCE

Ratings History

Date	Overall Rating	Risk Rating	Reward Rating
Q3-19	C	C-	C
Q4-18	C-	D+	C
Q4-17	C+	B	C
Q4-16	C-	D+	C
Q4-15	D	D	D+

Asset & Performance History

Date	NAV	1-Year Total Return
2018	99.09	1.75
2017	99.3	1.27
2016	99.33	1.29
2015	99.02	0.2
2014	99.2	
2013		

Total Assets: $107,248,540

Asset Allocation

Asset	%
Cash	6%
Stocks	0%
US Stocks	0%
Bonds	94%
US Bonds	88%
Other	0%

Services Offered:

Investment Strategy: The investment seeks to preserve capital while maximizing income. Sage Advisory Services, Ltd. Co. (the "Sub-Advisor") seeks to achieve the fund's investment objective by investing in a variety of fixed income securities, including bonds, forwards and instruments issued by U.S. and foreign issuers. It will invest in U.S. dollar-denominated investment grade debt securities, including mortgage- or asset-backed securities, rated Baa- or higher by Moody's Investors Service, Inc. ("Moody's"), or equivalently rated by Standard & Poor's Ratings Services ("S&P") or Fitch, Inc. ("Fitch"), or, if unrated, determined by the Sub-Advisor to be of comparable quality. **Top Holdings:** Us 2yr Note (Cbt) Dec19 Us 5yr Note (Cbt) Dec19 United States Treasury Notes 1.38% EMC Corporation 2.65% American Express Credit Account Master Trust 2.04%

iShares MSCI Japan Small-Cap ETF   C-   HOLD

Ticker	Traded On	NAV	Total Assets ($)	Dividend Yield (TTM)	Turnover Ratio	Expense Ratio
SCJ	NYSE Arca	71.25	$106,875,522	2.41	9	0.47

Ratings

Reward	C-
Risk	C-
Recent Upgrade/Downgrade	

Fund Information

Fund Type	Exchange Traded Funds
Category	Japan Equity
Sub-Category	Japan Stock
Prospectus Objective	Pacific Stock
Inception Date	Dec-07
Open to New Investments	Y

Prices

Price (as of 9/30/2019)	71.84
52-Week High	78.48
52-Week Low	61.80

Total Returns (%)

3-Month	6-Month	1-Year	3-Year	5-Year
1.98	1.80	-6.07	18.40	45.28

3-Year Standard Deviation	11.31
Effective Duration	

Valuation

Premium/Discount (1-Year Average)	-0.18

Company Information

Provider	iShares
Manager/Tenure	Diane Hsiung (11), Greg Savage (11), Jennifer Hsui (6), 3 others
Website	http://www.ishares.com
Address	iShares 400 Howard Street San Francisco CA 94105 United States
Phone Number	800-474-2737

PERFORMANCE

Ratings History

Date	Overall Rating	Risk Rating	Reward Rating
Q3-19	C-	C-	C-
Q4-18	C-	C-	D+
Q4-17	A	A	A
Q4-16	B	C+	B
Q4-15	C+	C+	C+

Asset & Performance History

Date	NAV	1-Year Total Return
2018	65.82	-16.35
2017	79.73	30.92
2016	61.85	7.6
2015	59.08	14.85
2014	52.23	-1.01
2013	53.97	25.52

Total Assets: $106,875,522

Asset Allocation

Asset	%
Cash	1%
Stocks	99%
US Stocks	0%
Bonds	0%
US Bonds	0%
Other	0%

Services Offered:

Investment Strategy: The investment seeks to track the investment results of the MSCI Japan Small Cap Index. The fund generally will invest at least 90% of its assets in the component securities of the underlying index and in investments that have economic characteristics that are substantially identical to the component securities of the underlying index. The index is designed to measure the performance of equity securities of small-capitalization companies in Japan. **Top Holdings:** Orix Jreit Inc GLP J-REIT Advance Residence Investment Corp TIS Inc Nihon M&A Center Inc

JPMorgan Diversified Alternative ETF

D+   **SELL**

Ticker	Traded On	NAV	Total Assets ($)	Dividend Yield (TTM)	Turnover Ratio	Expense Ratio
JPHF	NYSE Arca	25.05	$106,442,417	0	145	0.85

Ratings

Reward	D+
Risk	C-
Recent Upgrade/Downgrade	

Fund Information

Fund Type	Exchange Traded Funds
Category	Multialternative
Sub-Category	Multialternative
Prospectus Objective	Asset Allocation
Inception Date	Sep-16
Open to New Investments	Y

Prices

Price (as of 9/30/2019)	24.95
52-Week High	25.09
52-Week Low	23.72

Total Returns (%)

3-Month	6-Month	1-Year	3-Year	5-Year
1.54	0.12	0.44	-0.10	

3-Year Standard Deviation	4.54
Effective Duration	

Valuation

Premium/Discount (1-Year Average)	-0.22

Company Information

Provider	JPMorgan
Manager/Tenure	Wei (Victor) Li (3), Yazann Romahi (3), Alistair Lowe (0)
Website	http://www.jpmorganfunds.com
Address	JPMorgan 270 Park Avenue New York NY 10017-2070 United States
Phone Number	800-480-4111

PERFORMANCE

Ratings History

Date	Overall Rating	Risk Rating	Reward Rating
Q3-19	D+	C-	D+
Q4-18	D	C-	D
Q4-17	D	B+	D+
Q4-16	U		
Q4-15			

Asset & Performance History

Date	NAV	1-Year Total Return
2018	24.04	-7.82
2017	26.08	2.11
2016	25.54	
2015		
2014		
2013		

Total Assets: $106,442,417

Asset Allocation

Asset	%
Cash	34%
Stocks	51%
US Stocks	48%
Bonds	2%
US Bonds	0%
Other	14%

Services Offered:

Investment Strategy: The investment seeks to provide long-term total return. The fund will seek to achieve its investment objective by allocating assets across several different investment strategies, including traditional and alternative investment strategies, such as those utilized by certain hedge funds. The strategies identified by the adviser for the fund fall into the following broad categories: Equity Long/Short, Event Driven and Macro/Managed Futures strategies. The fund will invest its assets based on a systematic investment process for securities selection and asset allocation. **Top Holdings:** Tribune Media Co A   Spark Therapeutics Inc   Danaher Corp   SunTrust Banks Inc   Unizo Holdings Co Ltd

---

iShares iBonds Dec 2028 Term Corporate ETF

D+   **SELL**

Ticker	Traded On	NAV	Total Assets ($)	Dividend Yield (TTM)	Turnover Ratio	Expense Ratio
IBDT	NYSE Arca	27.63	$106,384,340	3.71	0	0.1

Ratings

Reward	D+
Risk	C-
Recent Upgrade/Downgrade	

Fund Information

Fund Type	Exchange Traded Funds
Category	US Fixed Income
Sub-Category	Target Maturity
Prospectus Objective	Corp Bond - Gen
Inception Date	Sep-18
Open to New Investments	Y

Prices

Price (as of 9/30/2019)	27.75
52-Week High	28.06
52-Week Low	24.64

Total Returns (%)

3-Month	6-Month	1-Year	3-Year	5-Year
2.86	8.57	14.70		

3-Year Standard Deviation	
Effective Duration	

Valuation

Premium/Discount (1-Year Average)	0.47

Company Information

Provider	iShares
Manager/Tenure	James Mauro (1), Scott Radell (1)
Website	http://www.ishares.com
Address	iShares 400 Howard Street San Francisco CA 94105 United States
Phone Number	800-474-2737

PERFORMANCE

Ratings History

Date	Overall Rating	Risk Rating	Reward Rating
Q3-19	D+	C-	D+
Q4-18	U		
Q4-17			
Q4-16			
Q4-15			

Asset & Performance History

Date	NAV	1-Year Total Return
2018	24.79	
2017		
2016		
2015		
2014		
2013		

Total Assets: $106,384,340

Asset Allocation

Asset	%
Cash	0%
Stocks	0%
US Stocks	0%
Bonds	98%
US Bonds	85%
Other	0%

Services Offered:

Investment Strategy: The investment seeks to track the investment results of the Bloomberg Barclays December 2028 Maturity Corporate Index composed of U.S. dollar-denominated, investment-grade corporate bonds maturing in 2028. The fund generally will invest at least 90% of its assets in the component securities of the index, except during the last months of its operations. The index consists of U.S. dollar-denominated, investment-grade securities publicly issued by U.S. and non-U.S. corporate issuers that have $300 million or more of outstanding face value at the time of inclusion. The fund is non-diversified. **Top Holdings:** CVS Health Corp 4.3%   Verizon Communications Inc. 4.33%   Comcast Corporation 4.15%   Cigna Holding Company 4.38%   United Technologies Corporation 4.13%

Nationwide Maximum Diversification U.S. Core Equity ETF   C-   HOLD

Ticker	Traded On	NAV	Total Assets ($)	Dividend Yield (TTM)	Turnover Ratio	Expense Ratio
MXDU	NYSE Arca	29.41	$105,887,056	1.43		0.34

Ratings
Reward	C-
Risk	D+
Recent Upgrade/Downgrade	Up

Fund Information
Fund Type	Exchange Traded Funds
Category	US Equity Large Cap Blend
Sub-Category	Large Blend
Prospectus Objective	Growth
Inception Date	Sep-17
Open to New Investments	Y

Prices
Price (as of 9/30/2019)	29.43
52-Week High	29.83
52-Week Low	23.92

Total Returns (%)
3-Month	6-Month	1-Year	3-Year	5-Year
0.81	4.51	1.51		

3-Year Standard Deviation
Effective Duration

Valuation
Premium/Discount (1-Year Average)	-0.22

Company Information
Provider	Nationwide
Manager/Tenure	Denise M. Krisko (2), Austin Wen (2)
Website	http://www.nationwide.com/mutualfunds
Address	Nationwide One Nationwide Plaza Columbus OH 43215 United States
Phone Number	800-848-0920

PERFORMANCE

Ratings History
Date	Overall Rating	Risk Rating	Reward Rating
Q3-19	C-	D+	C-
Q4-18	D+	D+	D+
Q4-17	U		
Q4-16			
Q4-15			

Asset & Performance History
Date	NAV	1-Year Total Return
2018	24.86	-4.37
2017	26.44	
2016		
2015		
2014		
2013		

Total Assets: $105,887,056
Asset Allocation
Asset	%
Cash	0%
Stocks	100%
US Stocks	98%
Bonds	0%
US Bonds	0%
Other	0%

Services Offered:

Investment Strategy: The investment seeks to track the total return performance, before fees and expenses, of the TOBAM Maximum Diversification USA Index (the "index"). The advisor attempts to invest all, or substantially all, of its assets in the component securities that make up the index. Normally, at least 80% of the fund's total assets will be invested in the component securities of the index. The index is a rules-based index that is designed to create a more diversified equity portfolio of the common and preferred stock of large and mid-capitalization U.S. companies relative to traditional market capitalization weighted benchmarks. **Top Holdings:** Chipotle Mexican Grill Inc Class A Newmont Goldcorp Corp Facebook Inc A Consolidated Edison Inc AutoZone Inc

Innovator S&P 500 Power Buffer ETF — July   D+   SELL

Ticker	Traded On	NAV	Total Assets ($)	Dividend Yield (TTM)	Turnover Ratio	Expense Ratio
PJUL	BATS	26.11	$105,731,737	0		0.79

Ratings
Reward	D+
Risk	C-
Recent Upgrade/Downgrade	

Fund Information
Fund Type	Exchange Traded Funds
Category	Long/Short Equity
Sub-Category	Options-based
Prospectus Objective	Growth
Inception Date	Aug-18
Open to New Investments	Y

Prices
Price (as of 9/30/2019)	26.08
52-Week High	26.21
52-Week Low	23.30

Total Returns (%)
3-Month	6-Month	1-Year	3-Year	5-Year
0.92	2.36	1.91		

3-Year Standard Deviation
Effective Duration

Valuation
Premium/Discount (1-Year Average)	0.20

Company Information
Provider	Innovator ETFs
Manager/Tenure	Robert T Cummings (1), Daniel S Hare (1), Hayley M Peppers (1)
Website	http://innovatoretfs.com/
Address	Innovator ETFs 120 N Hale Street, Suite 200 Wheaton IL 60187 United States
Phone Number	800-208-5212

PERFORMANCE

Ratings History
Date	Overall Rating	Risk Rating	Reward Rating
Q3-19	D+	C-	D+
Q4-18	U		
Q4-17			
Q4-16			
Q4-15			

Asset & Performance History
Date	NAV	1-Year Total Return
2018	23.95	
2017		
2016		
2015		
2014		
2013		

Total Assets: $105,731,737
Asset Allocation
Asset	%
Cash	4%
Stocks	96%
US Stocks	95%
Bonds	0%
US Bonds	0%
Other	0%

Services Offered:

Investment Strategy: The investment seeks to provide investors with returns that match those of the S&P 500 Price Index. The fund invests at least 80% of its net assets in FLexible EXchange® Options ("FLEX Options") that reference the S&P 500 Price Return Index. FLEX Options are exchange-traded options contracts with uniquely customizable terms. The S&P 500 Price Index is a large-cap, market-weighted, U.S. equities index that tracks the price (excluding dividends) of the 500 leading companies in leading industries. The fund is non-diversified. **Top Holdings:** Option on S&P 500 PR Option on S&P 500 PR Option on S&P 500 PR Option on S&P 500 PR Option on CBOE Mini-Spx Index Xsp

JPMorgan U.S. Quality Factor ETF   C   HOLD

Ticker	Traded On	NAV	Total Assets ($)	Dividend Yield (TTM)	Turnover Ratio	Expense Ratio
JQUA	NYSE Arca	29.37	$105,716,487	1.73		0.12

Ratings
Reward   C
Risk   C-
Recent Upgrade/Downgrade   Up

Fund Information
Fund Type	Exchange Traded Funds
Category	US Equity Large Cap Blend
Sub-Category	Large Blend
Prospectus Objective	Growth & Inc
Inception Date	Nov-17
Open to New Investments	Y

Prices
Price (as of 9/30/2019)	29.39
52-Week High	29.78
52-Week Low	23.43

Total Returns (%)
3-Month	6-Month	1-Year	3-Year	5-Year
1.41	4.05	5.49		

3-Year Standard Deviation
Effective Duration

Valuation
Premium/Discount (1-Year Average)   -0.02

Company Information
Provider	JPMorgan
Manager/Tenure	Aijaz Hussain (1), Jonathan Msika (1), Yazann Romahi (1), 2 others
Website	http://www.jpmorganfunds.com
Address	JPMorgan 270 Park Avenue New York NY 10017-2070 United States
Phone Number	800-480-4111

PERFORMANCE

10.0% / 0.0% / -10.0% / -20.0% — 11/3/18, 2/14/19, 6/16/19, 9/30/19

Ratings History
Date	Overall Rating	Risk Rating	Reward Rating
Q3-19	C	C-	C
Q4-18	D+	C-	D+
Q4-17	U		
Q4-16			
Q4-15			

Asset & Performance History
Date	NAV	1-Year Total Return
2018	24.91	-1.9
2017	25.91	
2016		
2015		
2014		
2013		

Total Assets: $105,716,487
Asset Allocation
Asset	%
Cash	0%
Stocks	100%
US Stocks	99%
Bonds	0%
US Bonds	0%
Other	0%

Services Offered:

Investment Strategy: The investment seeks investment results that closely correspond, before fees and expenses, to the performance of the JP Morgan US Quality Factor Index. The fund will invest at least 80% of its assets in securities included in the underlying index. "Assets" means net assets, plus the amount of borrowing for investment purposes. The underlying index is comprised of U.S. equity securities selected to represent quality factor characteristics. **Top Holdings:** Apple Inc Visa Inc Class A Microsoft Corp The Home Depot Inc Mastercard Inc A

VictoryShares USAA MSCI USA Small Cap Value Momentum ETF   D   SELL

Ticker	Traded On	NAV	Total Assets ($)	Dividend Yield (TTM)	Turnover Ratio	Expense Ratio
USVM	NYSE Arca	50.19	$105,404,650	2	17	0.25

Ratings
Reward   D
Risk   D+
Recent Upgrade/Downgrade

Fund Information
Fund Type	Exchange Traded Funds
Category	US Equity Small Cap
Sub-Category	Small Blend
Prospectus Objective	Small Company
Inception Date	Oct-17
Open to New Investments	Y

Prices
Price (as of 9/30/2019)	50.22
52-Week High	54.99
52-Week Low	42.68

Total Returns (%)
3-Month	6-Month	1-Year	3-Year	5-Year
-1.48	-1.52	-6.79		

3-Year Standard Deviation
Effective Duration

Valuation
Premium/Discount (1-Year Average)   0.08

Company Information
Provider	VictoryShares
Manager/Tenure	Lance Humphrey (1), Wasif A. Latif (1), Mannik Dhillon (0)
Website	http://www.VictorySharesLiterature.com
Address	Victory Shares 4249 Easton Way, Suite 400 Columbus OH 43219 United States
Phone Number	

PERFORMANCE

20.0% / 10.0% / 0.0% / -10.0% / -20.0% — 12/31/17, 4/10/18, 7/21/18, 11/3/18, 2/14/19, 6/17/19, 9/30/19

Ratings History
Date	Overall Rating	Risk Rating	Reward Rating
Q3-19	D	D+	D
Q4-18	D	D	D
Q4-17	U		
Q4-16			
Q4-15			

Asset & Performance History
Date	NAV	1-Year Total Return
2018	45.4	-9.26
2017	50.67	
2016		
2015		
2014		
2013		

Total Assets: $105,404,650
Asset Allocation
Asset	%
Cash	1%
Stocks	99%
US Stocks	97%
Bonds	0%
US Bonds	0%
Other	0%

Services Offered:

Investment Strategy: The investment seeks to provide investment results that closely correspond, before fees and expenses, to the performance of the MSCI USA Small Cap Select Value Momentum Blend Index. Under normal circumstances, the fund seeks to achieve its investment objective by investing at least 80% of its net assets in securities in the index. The index is designed to deliver exposure to equity securities of small-capitalization U.S. issuers that have higher exposure to value and momentum factors within the MSCI USA Small Cap Index while also maintaining moderate Index turnover and lower realized volatility than traditional capitalization weighted indexes. **Top Holdings:** Russ 2000 Idx Fut Sep19 Blackstone Mortgage Trust Inc A Hawaiian Electric Industries Inc Apollo Commercial Real Estate Finance Inc PS Business Parks Inc

ELEMENTS Linked to the Rogers International Commodity Index - Agriculture Total Return   D   SELL

Ticker	Traded On	NAV	Total Assets ($)	Dividend Yield (TTM)	Turnover Ratio	Expense Ratio
RJA	NYSE Arca		$104,508,288	0	0	0.75

Ratings

Reward	D-
Risk	D
Recent Upgrade/Downgrade	

Fund Information

Fund Type	Exchange Traded Funds
Category	Commodities Specified
Sub-Category	Commodities Agriculture
Prospectus Objective	Natl Res
Inception Date	Oct-07
Open to New Investments	Y

Prices

Price (as of 9/30/2019)	5.25
52-Week High	5.94
52-Week Low	4.97

Total Returns (%)

3-Month	6-Month	1-Year	3-Year	5-Year
-6.72	-6.40	-9.51	-16.23	-25.60

3-Year Standard Deviation	9.45
Effective Duration	

Valuation

Premium/Discount (1-Year Average)	0.00

Company Information

Provider	ELEMENTS
Manager/Tenure	No Manager (11)
Website	http://www.elementsetn.com
Address	ELEMENTS United States
Phone Number	212-449-2957

PERFORMANCE

Ratings History

Date	Overall Rating	Risk Rating	Reward Rating
Q3-19	D	D	D-
Q4-18	D	D	D
Q4-17	D	D	D
Q4-16	D	D	D
Q4-15	D	D	D

Asset & Performance History

Date	NAV	1-Year Total Return
2018	5.61	-6.5
2017	6	-4.59
2016	6.31	0.63
2015	6.27	-15.04
2014	7.38	-7.63
2013	7.99	-11.9

Total Assets: $104,508,288
Asset Allocation

Asset	%
Cash	%
Stocks	%
US Stocks	%
Bonds	%
US Bonds	%
Other	%

Services Offered:

Investment Strategy: The investment seeks to replicate, net of expenses, the Rogers International Commodity Index – Agriculture Total Return index.
The index represents the value of a basket of 20 agricultural commodity futures contracts. **Top Holdings:**

JPMorgan U.S. Minimum Volatility ETF   C-   HOLD

Ticker	Traded On	NAV	Total Assets ($)	Dividend Yield (TTM)	Turnover Ratio	Expense Ratio
JMIN	NYSE Arca	30.16	$104,055,531	1.72		0.12

Ratings

Reward	C
Risk	C-
Recent Upgrade/Downgrade	

Fund Information

Fund Type	Exchange Traded Funds
Category	US Equity Large Cap Blend
Sub-Category	Large Blend
Prospectus Objective	Growth & Inc
Inception Date	Nov-17
Open to New Investments	Y

Prices

Price (as of 9/30/2019)	30.19
52-Week High	30.28
52-Week Low	23.72

Total Returns (%)

3-Month	6-Month	1-Year	3-Year	5-Year
3.62	8.42	12.58		

3-Year Standard Deviation	
Effective Duration	

Valuation

Premium/Discount (1-Year Average)	-0.06

Company Information

Provider	JPMorgan
Manager/Tenure	Aijaz Hussain (1), Jonathan Msika (1), Yazann Romahi (1), 2 others
Website	http://www.jpmorganfunds.com
Address	JPMorgan 270 Park Avenue New York NY 10017-2070 United States
Phone Number	800-480-4111

PERFORMANCE

Ratings History

Date	Overall Rating	Risk Rating	Reward Rating
Q3-19	C-	C-	C
Q4-18	D	D+	D
Q4-17	U		
Q4-16			
Q4-15			

Asset & Performance History

Date	NAV	1-Year Total Return
2018	24.93	-0.89
2017	25.75	
2016		
2015		
2014		
2013		

Total Assets: $104,055,531
Asset Allocation

Asset	%
Cash	0%
Stocks	100%
US Stocks	98%
Bonds	0%
US Bonds	0%
Other	0%

Services Offered:

Investment Strategy: The investment seeks investment results that closely correspond, before fees and expenses, to the performance of the JP Morgan US Minimum Volatility Index. The fund will invest at least 80% of its assets in securities included in the underlying index. "Assets" means net assets, plus the amount of borrowing for investment purposes. The underlying index measures the performance of U.S. equity securities selected using a rules-based process that is designed so the underlying index targets lower volatility than the Russell 1000 Index. **Top Holdings:** Zoetis Inc Class A   Costco Wholesale Corp   Target Corp   Teleflex Inc   ResMed Inc

ClearShares OCIO ETF

C-   HOLD

Ticker	Traded On	NAV	Total Assets ($)	Dividend Yield (TTM)	Turnover Ratio	Expense Ratio
OCIO	NYSE Arca	26.97	$103,827,466	1.14	28	0.67

Ratings

Reward	C
Risk	D+
Recent Upgrade/Downgrade	Up

Fund Information

Fund Type	Exchange Traded Funds
Category	Moderate Allocation
Sub-Category	Allocation--50% to 70% Equity
Prospectus Objective	Growth & Inc
Inception Date	Jun-17
Open to New Investments	Y

Prices

Price (as of 9/30/2019)	26.97
52-Week High	27.12
52-Week Low	23.77

Total Returns (%)

3-Month	6-Month	1-Year	3-Year	5-Year
0.30	2.64	1.87		

3-Year Standard Deviation	
Effective Duration	4.94

Valuation

Premium/Discount (1-Year Average)	-0.01

Company Information

Provider	ClearShares
Manager/Tenure	Eric J Blasberg (2), Jonathan M Chesshire (2), Mark N Hong (2)
Website	http://www.clear-shares.com
Address	ClearShares United States
Phone Number	

PERFORMANCE

Ratings History

Date	Overall Rating	Risk Rating	Reward Rating
Q3-19	C-	D+	C
Q4-18	D	D	D+
Q4-17	U		
Q4-16			
Q4-15			

Asset & Performance History

Date	NAV	1-Year Total Return
2018	24.03	-7.52
2017	26.55	
2016		
2015		
2014		
2013		

Total Assets: $103,827,466

Asset Allocation

Asset	%
Cash	7%
Stocks	61%
US Stocks	38%
Bonds	32%
US Bonds	28%
Other	0%

Services Offered:

Investment Strategy: The investment seeks to outperform a traditional 60/40 mix of global equity and fixed-income investments. The fund is expected to typically invest approximately 40% to 70% of its total assets in underlying funds that principally invest in equity securities of any market capitalization. It is expected to typically invest approximately 20% to 50% of its total assets in underlying funds that principally invest in debt obligations. **Top Holdings:** iShares Core US Aggregate Bond ETF   Vanguard Total Bond Market ETF   Vanguard Total Stock Market ETF   iShares Core S&P 500 ETF   Vanguard S&P 500 ETF

VanEck Vectors International High Yield Bond ETF

C   HOLD

Ticker	Traded On	NAV	Total Assets ($)	Dividend Yield (TTM)	Turnover Ratio	Expense Ratio
IHY	NYSE Arca	24.51	$102,942,565	4.83	32	0.4

Ratings

Reward	C+
Risk	C-
Recent Upgrade/Downgrade	

Fund Information

Fund Type	Exchange Traded Funds
Category	Global Fixed Income
Sub-Category	High Yield Bond
Prospectus Objective	Corp Bond-High Yld
Inception Date	Apr-12
Open to New Investments	Y

Prices

Price (as of 9/30/2019)	24.46
52-Week High	24.93
52-Week Low	23.30

Total Returns (%)

3-Month	6-Month	1-Year	3-Year	5-Year
-0.38	2.44	5.23	14.00	18.61

3-Year Standard Deviation	4.81
Effective Duration	3.32

Valuation

Premium/Discount (1-Year Average)	-0.26

Company Information

Provider	VanEck
Manager/Tenure	Francis G. Rodilosso (7)
Website	http://www.vaneck.com
Address	Van Eck Associates Corporation 666 Third Avenue New York NY 10017 United States
Phone Number	800-826-1115

PERFORMANCE

Ratings History

Date	Overall Rating	Risk Rating	Reward Rating
Q3-19	C	C-	C+
Q4-18	C-	C-	C-
Q4-17	B-	B	C+
Q4-16	C-	C-	C
Q4-15	C-	C-	C-

Asset & Performance History

Date	NAV	1-Year Total Return
2018	23.39	-4.96
2017	25.64	11.6
2016	24.02	11.22
2015	22.73	-3.58
2014	24.89	-3.28
2013	27.12	7.63

Total Assets: $102,942,565

Asset Allocation

Asset	%
Cash	0%
Stocks	0%
US Stocks	0%
Bonds	99%
US Bonds	3%
Other	0%

Services Offered:

Investment Strategy: The investment seeks to replicate as closely as possible, before fees and expenses, the price and yield performance of the ICE BofAML Global ex-US Issuers High Yield Constrained Index. The fund normally invests at least 80% of its total assets in securities that comprise the fund's benchmark index. The index is comprised of below investment grade bonds issued by corporations located throughout the world (which may include emerging market countries) excluding the United States denominated in Euros, U.S. dollars, Canadian dollars or pound sterling and issued in the major domestic or Eurobond markets. **Top Holdings:** ALTICE FRANCE S.A 7.38%   Banco do Brasil S.A. (Grand Cayman Branch) 3.88%   Softbank Group Corp 6%   Softbank Group Corp 6.25%   China Evergrande Group 8.75%

AdvisorShares Dorsey Wright ADR ETF   C   HOLD

Ticker	Traded On	NAV	Total Assets ($)	Dividend Yield (TTM)	Turnover Ratio	Expense Ratio
AADR	NYSE Arca	47.84	$102,862,100	0.66		0.88

Ratings
Reward	C
Risk	C-
Recent Upgrade/Downgrade	Up

Fund Information
Fund Type	Exchange Traded Funds
Category	Global Equity Large Cap
Sub-Category	Foreign Large Growth
Prospectus Objective	Growth
Inception Date	Jul-10
Open to New Investments	Y

Prices
Price (as of 9/30/2019)	47.67
52-Week High	53.70
52-Week Low	38.43

Total Returns (%)
3-Month	6-Month	1-Year	3-Year	5-Year
-4.15	4.81	-10.56	20.65	35.09

3-Year Standard Deviation	17.53
Effective Duration	

Valuation
Premium/Discount (1-Year Average)	-0.17

Company Information
Provider	AdvisorShares
Manager/Tenure	John G. Lewis (3)
Website	http://www.advisorshares.com
Address	AdvisorShares 2 Bethesda Metro Center, Suite 1330 Bethesda MD 20814 United States
Phone Number	877-843-3831

PERFORMANCE

Ratings History
Date	Overall Rating	Risk Rating	Reward Rating
Q3-19	C	C-	C
Q4-18	C	D+	C
Q4-17	A-	B+	A+
Q4-16	C	D+	C+
Q4-15	C	D+	C

Asset & Performance History
Date	NAV	1-Year Total Return
2018	40.18	-31.18
2017	58.71	46.92
2016	40.31	5.57
2015	38.41	4.38
2014	37.1	-0.83
2013	37.59	20.87

Total Assets: $102,862,100
Asset Allocation
Asset	%
Cash	0%
Stocks	100%
US Stocks	14%
Bonds	0%
US Bonds	0%
Other	0%

Services Offered:

Investment Strategy: The investment seeks long-term capital appreciation above international benchmarks such as the BNY Mellon Classic ADR Index, the fund's primary benchmark, and the MSCI EAFE Index, the fund's secondary benchmark. The fund seeks to achieve the fund's investment objective by selecting primarily a portfolio of U.S.-traded securities of non-U.S. organizations, most often American Depositary Receipts ("ADRs"). It will invest at least 80% of its total assets in ADRs and in securities that have economic characteristics similar to ADRs. **Top Holdings:** NICE Ltd ADR   Galapagos NV ADR   Anglogold Ashanti Ltd ADR   MercadoLibre Inc   Airbus SE ADR

Amplify Transformational Data Sharing ETF   D+   SELL

Ticker	Traded On	NAV	Total Assets ($)	Dividend Yield (TTM)	Turnover Ratio	Expense Ratio
BLOK	NYSE Arca	17.93	$102,192,638	1.07	44	0.7

Ratings
Reward	D
Risk	C-
Recent Upgrade/Downgrade	Up

Fund Information
Fund Type	Exchange Traded Funds
Category	Technology Sector Equity
Sub-Category	Technology
Prospectus Objective	Technology
Inception Date	Jan-18
Open to New Investments	Y

Prices
Price (as of 9/30/2019)	17.94
52-Week High	20.39
52-Week Low	14.46

Total Returns (%)
3-Month	6-Month	1-Year	3-Year	5-Year
-2.51	0.66	-10.91		

3-Year Standard Deviation	
Effective Duration	

Valuation
Premium/Discount (1-Year Average)	-0.25

Company Information
Provider	Amplifyetfs
Manager/Tenure	Charles A. Ragauss (1), Michael Venuto (1)
Website	http://www.amplifyetfs.com
Address	3250 Lacey Road, Suite 130 Downers Grove Downers Grove IL 60515 United States
Phone Number	630-487-2530

PERFORMANCE

Ratings History
Date	Overall Rating	Risk Rating	Reward Rating
Q3-19	D+	C-	D
Q4-18	U		
Q4-17			
Q4-16			
Q4-15			

Asset & Performance History
Date	NAV	1-Year Total Return
2018	14.88	
2017		
2016		
2015		
2014		
2013		

Total Assets: $102,192,638
Asset Allocation
Asset	%
Cash	0%
Stocks	100%
US Stocks	44%
Bonds	0%
US Bonds	0%
Other	0%

Services Offered:

Investment Strategy: The investment seeks to provide investors with total return. The fund is an actively managed ETF that seeks to provide total return by investing at least 80% of its net assets (including investment borrowings) in the equity securities of companies actively involved in the development and utilization of transformational data sharing technologies. It may invest in non-U.S. equity securities, including depositary receipts. The fund is non-diversified. **Top Holdings:** GMO internet Inc   Digital Garage Inc   Kakao Corp   Opera Ltd ADR   Overstock.com Inc

Xtrackers MSCI All World ex U.S. Hedged Equity ETF

C   HOLD

Ticker	Traded On	NAV	Total Assets ($)	Dividend Yield (TTM)	Turnover Ratio	Expense Ratio
DBAW	NYSE Arca	27.61	$102,170,377	3.21	13	0.4

Ratings
Reward	C
Risk	D+
Recent Upgrade/Downgrade	

Fund Information
Fund Type	Exchange Traded Funds
Category	Global Equity Large Cap
Sub-Category	Foreign Large Blend
Prospectus Objective	World Stock
Inception Date	Jan-14
Open to New Investments	Y

Prices
Price (as of 9/30/2019)	27.61
52-Week High	28.14
52-Week Low	23.68

Total Returns (%)
3-Month	6-Month	1-Year	3-Year	5-Year
0.07	2.47	2.77	28.76	33.08

3-Year Standard Deviation	9.43
Effective Duration	

Valuation
Premium/Discount (1-Year Average)	-0.10

Company Information
Provider	DWS
Manager/Tenure	Patrick Dwyer (2), Bryan Richards (2), Shlomo Bassous (1)
Website	http://dws.com
Address	DWS 210 West 10th Street Kansas City MO 64105-1614 United States
Phone Number	

PERFORMANCE

Ratings History
Date	Overall Rating	Risk Rating	Reward Rating
Q3-19	C	D+	C
Q4-18	D+	C-	D+
Q4-17	B-	C+	B
Q4-16	C-	C-	C
Q4-15	D+	C-	C-

Asset & Performance History
Date	NAV	1-Year Total Return
2018	24.43	-9.7
2017	27.74	18.49
2016	24	6.43
2015	23.03	0.33
2014	24.22	
2013		

Total Assets: $102,170,377
Asset Allocation
Asset	%
Cash	3%
Stocks	97%
US Stocks	1%
Bonds	0%
US Bonds	0%
Other	0%

Services Offered:

Investment Strategy: The investment seeks investment results that correspond generally to the performance, of the MSCI ACWI ex USA US Dollar Hedged Index. The fund, using a "passive" or indexing investment approach, seeks investment results that correspond generally to the performance, of the underlying index, which is designed to track the performance of equity securities in developed and emerging stock markets while mitigating exposure to fluctuations between the value of the USD and the currencies of the countries included in the underlying index. It will invest at least 80% of its total assets in component securities of the underlying index. **Top Holdings:** Msci Eafe Sep19 Nestle SA Alibaba Group Holding Ltd ADR Tencent Holdings Ltd Taiwan Semiconductor Manufacturing Co Ltd

---

AGFiQ U.S. Market Neutral Anti-Beta Fund

C   HOLD

Ticker	Traded On	NAV	Total Assets ($)	Dividend Yield (TTM)	Turnover Ratio	Expense Ratio
BTAL	NYSE Arca	23.66	$101,720,323	0.36	341	0.76

Ratings
Reward	C
Risk	C+
Recent Upgrade/Downgrade	

Fund Information
Fund Type	Exchange Traded Funds
Category	Market Neutral
Sub-Category	Market Neutral
Prospectus Objective	Growth & Inc
Inception Date	Sep-11
Open to New Investments	Y

Prices
Price (as of 9/30/2019)	23.70
52-Week High	24.63
52-Week Low	19.92

Total Returns (%)
3-Month	6-Month	1-Year	3-Year	5-Year
8.35	11.10	17.84	12.79	20.56

3-Year Standard Deviation	11.29
Effective Duration	

Valuation
Premium/Discount (1-Year Average)	0.26

Company Information
Provider	AGFiQ
Manager/Tenure	William H. DeRoche (8), Philip Lee (6), Josh Belko (1)
Website	http://www.agfiq.com
Address	53 State Street Suite 1308 Boston MA 02109 United States
Phone Number	617-292-9801

PERFORMANCE

Ratings History
Date	Overall Rating	Risk Rating	Reward Rating
Q3-19	C	C+	C
Q4-18	C	C-	C
Q4-17	D	D+	D
Q4-16	C-	D+	C
Q4-15	D+	C-	D+

Asset & Performance History
Date	NAV	1-Year Total Return
2018	21.98	15.05
2017	19.18	-2.77
2016	19.73	-4.7
2015	20.71	3.2
2014	20.06	4.37
2013	19.22	-11.47

Total Assets: $101,720,323
Asset Allocation
Asset	%
Cash	102%
Stocks	-2%
US Stocks	-3%
Bonds	0%
US Bonds	0%
Other	0%

Services Offered:

Investment Strategy: The investment seeks performance results that correspond to the price and yield performance, before fees and expenses, of the Dow Jones U.S. Thematic Market Neutral Anti-Beta Index. The fund invests at least 80% of its net assets in common stock of the long positions in the underlying index and sells short at least 80% of the short positions in the underlying index. The underlying index is a long/short market neutral index that is dollar-neutral. As such, it identifies long and short securities positions of approximately equal dollar amounts. **Top Holdings:** Dow Jones Thematic L Anti-B Royal Gold Inc NVR Inc Generac Holdings Inc Micron Technology Inc

First Trust Energy AlphaDEX® Fund   C-   HOLD

Ticker	Traded On	NAV	Total Assets ($)	Dividend Yield (TTM)	Turnover Ratio	Expense Ratio
FXN	NYSE Arca	9.82	$101,616,128	1.82	99	0.63

Ratings
Reward	C
Risk	D
Recent Upgrade/Downgrade	Up

Fund Information
Fund Type	Exchange Traded Funds
Category	Energy Sector Equity
Sub-Category	Equity Energy
Prospectus Objective	Natl Res
Inception Date	May-07
Open to New Investments	Y

Prices
Price (as of 9/30/2019)	9.81
52-Week High	18.18
52-Week Low	8.94

Total Returns (%)
3-Month	6-Month	1-Year	3-Year	5-Year
-13.84	-24.47	-43.88	-33.86	-58.28

3-Year Standard Deviation	27.65
Effective Duration	

Valuation
Premium/Discount (1-Year Average)	-0.05

Company Information
Provider	First Trust
Manager/Tenure	Jon C. Erickson (12), Daniel J. Lindquist (12), David G. McGarel (12), 3 others
Website	http://www.ftportfolios.com/
Address	First Trust 120 E. Liberty Drive, Suite 400 Wheaton IL 60187 United States
Phone Number	800-621-1675

PERFORMANCE

Ratings History
Date	Overall Rating	Risk Rating	Reward Rating
Q3-19	C-	D	C
Q4-18	C	D+	C
Q4-17	D	D	D
Q4-16	D	D	D+
Q4-15	D+	D	C-

Asset & Performance History
Date	NAV	1-Year Total Return
2018	11.53	-24.64
2017	15.48	-5.08
2016	16.52	20.46
2015	13.87	-32.41
2014	20.91	-16.01
2013	25.26	28.66

Total Assets: $101,616,128
Asset Allocation
Asset	%
Cash	0%
Stocks	100%
US Stocks	100%
Bonds	0%
US Bonds	0%
Other	0%

Services Offered:

Investment Strategy: The investment seeks results that correspond generally to the price and yield (before the fund's fees and expenses) of an equity index called the StrataQuant® Energy Index. The fund will normally invest at least 90% of its net assets (including investment borrowings) in common stocks that comprise the index. The index is a modified equal-dollar weighted index designed by IDI to objectively identify and select stocks from the Russell 1000® Index in the energy sector that may generate positive alpha relative to traditional passive-style indices through the use of the AlphaDEX® selection methodology. **Top Holdings:** Phillips 66 Occidental Petroleum Corp HollyFrontier Corp Marathon Oil Corp ConocoPhillips

---

SPDR® SSgA Multi-Asset Real Return ETF   C-   HOLD

Ticker	Traded On	NAV	Total Assets ($)	Dividend Yield (TTM)	Turnover Ratio	Expense Ratio
RLY	NYSE Arca		$101,105,899	2.84	28	0.5

Ratings
Reward	C-
Risk	C-
Recent Upgrade/Downgrade	

Fund Information
Fund Type	Exchange Traded Funds
Category	Moderate Allocation
Sub-Category	Allocation--50% to 70% Equity
Prospectus Objective	Growth & Inc
Inception Date	Apr-12
Open to New Investments	Y

Prices
Price (as of 9/30/2019)	24.74
52-Week High	26.72
52-Week Low	22.58

Total Returns (%)
3-Month	6-Month	1-Year	3-Year	5-Year
-1.23	-0.95	-4.38	8.08	-3.33

3-Year Standard Deviation	9.43
Effective Duration	9.53

Valuation
Premium/Discount (1-Year Average)	-0.06

Company Information
Provider	SPDR State Street Global Advisors
Manager/Tenure	Robert Guiliano (7), John A. Gulino (7), Michael O. Martel (4)
Website	http://www.spdrs.com
Address	SPDR State Street Global Advisors State Street Financial Center, 1 Lincoln Street Boston MA 02111-2900 United States
Phone Number	617-786-3000

PERFORMANCE

Ratings History
Date	Overall Rating	Risk Rating	Reward Rating
Q3-19	C-	C-	C-
Q4-18	C-	C-	C-
Q4-17	C	C	C
Q4-16	D+	D+	D
Q4-15	D	D	D

Asset & Performance History
Date	NAV	1-Year Total Return
2018	22.87	-11.06
2017	26.37	10.24
2016	24.39	12.04
2015	22.23	-15.24
2014	26.66	-6.54
2013	29.02	-3.06

Total Assets: $101,105,899
Asset Allocation
Asset	%
Cash	9%
Stocks	55%
US Stocks	26%
Bonds	30%
US Bonds	26%
Other	4%

Services Offered:

Investment Strategy: The investment seeks to achieve real return consisting of capital appreciation and current income. Under normal circumstances, the Adviser invests at least 80% of the net assets of the fund among ETPs that provide exposure to the following primary asset classes: (i) inflation protected securities issued by the United States government, its agencies and/or instrumentalities, as well as inflation protected securities issued by foreign governments, agencies, and/or instrumentalities; (ii) domestic and international real estate securities; (iii) commodities; and (iv) publicly-traded companies in natural resources and/or commodities businesses. **Top Holdings:** SPDR® S&P Global Natural Resources ETF Invesco Optm Yd Dvrs Cdty Stra No K1 ETF SPDR® Blmbg Barclays TIPS ETF SPDR® Dow Jones REIT ETF SPDR® Dow Jones International RelEst ETF

WisdomTree Global ex-US Real Estate Fund

C- HOLD

Ticker	Traded On	NAV	Total Assets ($)	Dividend Yield (TTM)	Turnover Ratio	Expense Ratio
DRW	NYSE Arca	29.30	$101,072,054	6.49	17	0.58

Ratings
Reward	C
Risk	D+
Recent Upgrade/Downgrade	Down

Fund Information
Fund Type	Exchange Traded Funds
Category	Real Estate Sector Equity
Sub-Category	Global Real Estate
Prospectus Objective	Real Estate
Inception Date	Jun-07
Open to New Investments	Y

Prices
Price (as of 9/30/2019)	29.27
52-Week High	32.57
52-Week Low	27.14

Total Returns (%)
3-Month	6-Month	1-Year	3-Year	5-Year
-2.93	-4.56	6.29	24.86	38.28

3-Year Standard Deviation	12.74
Effective Duration	

Valuation
Premium/Discount (1-Year Average)	-0.15

Company Information
Provider	WisdomTree
Manager/Tenure	Richard A. Brown (11), Thomas J. Durante (11), Karen Q. Wong (11)
Website	http://www.wisdomtree.com
Address	WisdomTree 245 Park Avenue, 35th floor New York NY 10167 United States
Phone Number	866-909-9473

PERFORMANCE

Ratings History
Date	Overall Rating	Risk Rating	Reward Rating
Q3-19	C-	D+	C
Q4-18	C-	C-	D+
Q4-17	B	B-	A-
Q4-16	C-	D+	C
Q4-15	C-	D+	C

Asset & Performance History
Date	NAV	1-Year Total Return
2018	27.83	-10.97
2017	32.56	36.51
2016	25.49	2.38
2015	26.35	-2.73
2014	28.32	8.78
2013	27.41	-2.87

Total Assets: $101,072,054
Asset Allocation
Asset	%
Cash	0%
Stocks	99%
US Stocks	0%
Bonds	0%
US Bonds	0%
Other	1%

Services Offered:

Investment Strategy: The investment seeks to track the price and yield performance, before fees and expenses, of the WisdomTree Global ex-U.S. Real Estate Index. Under normal circumstances, at least 95% of the fund's total assets will be invested in component securities of the index and investments that have economic characteristics that are substantially identical to the economic characteristics of such component securities. The index is a fundamentally weighted index that is comprised of companies from developed and emerging markets outside of the United States that are classified as being part of the "Global Real Estate" sector. The fund is non-diversified. **Top Holdings:** Sun Hung Kai Properties Ltd   Henderson Land Development Co Ltd   Unibail-Rodamco-Westfield Link Real Estate Investment Trust   Scentre Group

Cambria Core Equity ETF

C HOLD

Ticker	Traded On	NAV	Total Assets ($)	Dividend Yield (TTM)	Turnover Ratio	Expense Ratio
CCOR	NYSE Arca	27.24	$100,782,476	0.61		1.23

Ratings
Reward	C+
Risk	C
Recent Upgrade/Downgrade	Up

Fund Information
Fund Type	Exchange Traded Funds
Category	Long/Short Equity
Sub-Category	Options-based
Prospectus Objective	Growth & Inc
Inception Date	May-17
Open to New Investments	Y

Prices
Price (as of 9/30/2019)	27.28
52-Week High	28.02
52-Week Low	25.11

Total Returns (%)
3-Month	6-Month	1-Year	3-Year	5-Year
0.54	1.63	8.41		

3-Year Standard Deviation	
Effective Duration	

Valuation
Premium/Discount (1-Year Average)	-0.05

Company Information
Provider	CAMBRIA ETF TRUST
Manager/Tenure	Mebane T. Faber (2), David C. Pursell (2)
Website	http://www.cambriafunds.com
Address	CAMBRIA ETF TRUST 2711 Centreville Road Suite 400 Wilmington, DE 19808 Wilmington DE 19808 United States
Phone Number	310-683-5500

PERFORMANCE

Ratings History
Date	Overall Rating	Risk Rating	Reward Rating
Q3-19	C	C	C+
Q4-18	C-	C-	C-
Q4-17	U		
Q4-16			
Q4-15			

Asset & Performance History
Date	NAV	1-Year Total Return
2018	26.63	4.86
2017	25.81	
2016		
2015		
2014		
2013		

Total Assets: $100,782,476
Asset Allocation
Asset	%
Cash	2%
Stocks	98%
US Stocks	96%
Bonds	0%
US Bonds	0%
Other	0%

Services Offered:

Investment Strategy: The investment seeks capital appreciation and capital preservation with a low correlation to the broader U.S. equity market. Under normal market conditions, at least 80% of the value of the fund's net assets (plus borrowings for investment purposes) will be invested in equity securities. It invests primarily in U.S. equity securities that tend to offer current dividends. The fund focuses on high-quality companies that have prospects for long-term total returns as a result of their ability to grow earnings and their willingness to increase dividends over time. **Top Holdings:** Dollar General Corp   Starbucks Corp   L3Harris Technologies Inc   CME Group Inc Class A Lockheed Martin Corp

O'Shares FTSE Russell Small Cap Quality Dividend ETF　　　　　　　　C　　HOLD

Ticker	Traded On	NAV	Total Assets ($)	Dividend Yield (TTM)	Turnover Ratio	Expense Ratio
OUSM	NYSE Arca	27.87	$100,460,422	2.12	52	0.48

Ratings

Reward	C
Risk	C-
Recent Upgrade/Downgrade	Up

Fund Information

Fund Type	Exchange Traded Funds
Category	US Equity Small Cap
Sub-Category	Small Blend
Prospectus Objective	Small Company
Inception Date	Dec-16
Open to New Investments	Y

Prices

Price (as of 9/30/2019)	27.88
52-Week High	28.38
52-Week Low	22.48

Total Returns (%)

3-Month	6-Month	1-Year	3-Year	5-Year
1.58	5.98	1.28		

3-Year Standard Deviation	
Effective Duration	

Valuation

Premium/Discount (1-Year Average)	0.01

Company Information

Provider	O'Shares Investments
Manager/Tenure	Denise M. Krisko (2), Austin Wen (0)
Website	http://www.oshares.com
Address	O'Shares Investments 60 State Street, Suite 700 Boston MA 02109 United States
Phone Number	617-855-7670

PERFORMANCE

Ratings History

Date	Overall Rating	Risk Rating	Reward Rating
Q3-19	C	C-	C
Q4-18	C-	C-	D+
Q4-17	D-	B+	D+
Q4-16			
Q4-15			

Asset & Performance History

Date	NAV	1-Year Total Return
2018	23.67	-10.29
2017	27.01	10.08
2016	24.95	
2015		
2014		
2013		

Total Assets: $100,460,422

Asset Allocation

Asset	%
Cash	0%
Stocks	100%
US Stocks	100%
Bonds	0%
US Bonds	0%
Other	0%

Services Offered:

Investment Strategy: The investment seeks to track the performance (before fees and expenses) of the FTSE USA Small Cap ex Real Estate 2Qual/Vol/Yield 3% Capped Factor Index. Under normal market conditions, the fund will invest at least 80% of its total assets in the components of the index. The index is constructed using a proprietary, rules-based methodology designed to select equity securities from the FTSE USA Small Cap Index that have exposure to the following three factors: 1) quality, 2) low volatility and 3) yield. **Top Holdings:** Leidos Holdings Inc Eaton Vance Corp Lazard Ltd Shs A Teradyne Inc OGE Energy Corp

---

ETFMG Prime Junior Silver ETF　　　　　　　　　　　　　　　　　C-　　HOLD

Ticker	Traded On	NAV	Total Assets ($)	Dividend Yield (TTM)	Turnover Ratio	Expense Ratio
SILJ	NYSE Arca	9.45	$100,118,936	1.52	36	0.69

Ratings

Reward	C-
Risk	D+
Recent Upgrade/Downgrade	Up

Fund Information

Fund Type	Exchange Traded Funds
Category	Prec Metals
Sub-Category	Equity Precious Metals
Prospectus Objective	Prec Metals
Inception Date	Nov-12
Open to New Investments	Y

Prices

Price (as of 9/30/2019)	9.46
52-Week High	11.39
52-Week Low	6.80

Total Returns (%)

3-Month	6-Month	1-Year	3-Year	5-Year
11.81	8.66	10.71	-37.91	-0.42

3-Year Standard Deviation	31.05
Effective Duration	

Valuation

Premium/Discount (1-Year Average)	0.01

Company Information

Provider	ETFMG
Manager/Tenure	Samuel R. Masucci (1), Devin Ryder (1), Donal Bishnoi (0), 1 other
Website	http://www.etfmg.com
Address	ETFMG 30 Maple Street, Suite 2 NJ United States
Phone Number	

PERFORMANCE

Ratings History

Date	Overall Rating	Risk Rating	Reward Rating
Q3-19	C-	D+	C-
Q4-18	D+	D	C-
Q4-17	C-	D+	C
Q4-16	D+	D	C-
Q4-15	D+	D+	D+

Asset & Performance History

Date	NAV	1-Year Total Return
2018	8.01	-28.45
2017	11.38	-5.56
2016	12.05	152.32
2015	5.05	-37.84
2014	8.32	-11.2
2013	9.37	-53.05

Total Assets: $100,118,936

Asset Allocation

Asset	%
Cash	0%
Stocks	100%
US Stocks	16%
Bonds	0%
US Bonds	0%
Other	0%

Services Offered:

Investment Strategy: The investment seeks investment results that, before fees and expenses, correspond generally to the price and yield performance of the Prime Junior Silver Miners & Explorers Index. The fund invests at least 80% of its total assets in the component securities of the index and in ADRs and GDRs based on the component securities in the index. The index tracks the performance of the equity securities (or corresponding American Depositary Receipts ("ADRs") or Global Depositary Receipts ("GDRs")) of small-capitalization companies actively engaged in silver refining, mining, or exploration ("Junior Silver Companies"). The fund is non-diversified.
Top Holdings: First Majestic Silver Corp Pan American Silver Corp Hochschild Mining PLC MAG Silver Corp Yamana Gold Inc

iShares JPX-Nikkei 400 ETF

C-   HOLD

Ticker	Traded On	NAV	Total Assets ($)	Dividend Yield (TTM)	Turnover Ratio	Expense Ratio
JPXN	NYSE Arca	60.49	$99,807,772	1.56	11	0.48

Ratings
Reward   C-
Risk   C-
Recent Upgrade/Downgrade

Fund Information
Fund Type	Exchange Traded Funds
Category	Japan Equity
Sub-Category	Japan Stock
Prospectus Objective	Pacific Stock
Inception Date	Oct-01
Open to New Investments	Y

Prices
Price (as of 9/30/2019)	61.12
52-Week High	65.34
52-Week Low	52.64

Total Returns (%)
3-Month	6-Month	1-Year	3-Year	5-Year
1.64	2.55	-5.14	17.90	30.23

3-Year Standard Deviation   10.51
Effective Duration

Valuation
Premium/Discount (1-Year Average)   -0.19

Company Information
Provider	iShares
Manager/Tenure	Greg Savage (11), Jennifer Hsui (7), Alan Mason (3), 2 others
Website	http://www.ishares.com
Address	iShares 400 Howard Street San Francisco CA 94105 United States
Phone Number	800-474-2737

PERFORMANCE

Ratings History
Date	Overall Rating	Risk Rating	Reward Rating
Q3-19	C-	C-	C-
Q4-18	D+	D+	D+
Q4-17	B+	B	A-
Q4-16	C	D+	B-
Q4-15	C	D+	C

Asset & Performance History
Date	NAV	1-Year Total Return
2018	55.03	-13.94
2017	64.89	24
2016	53.15	2.07
2015	53.16	10.63
2014	48.67	-5.28
2013	52.09	26.03

Total Assets: $99,807,772
Asset Allocation
Asset	%
Cash	1%
Stocks	99%
US Stocks	0%
Bonds	0%
US Bonds	0%
Other	0%

Services Offered: CashInvestment Plan

Investment Strategy: The investment seeks to track the investment results of the JPX-Nikkei Index 400 composed of Japanese equities. The fund generally invests at least 90% of its assets in securities of the underlying index and in depositary receipts representing securities of the underlying index. The underlying index may include large-, mid- or small-capitalization companies. The currency of the component securities of the underlying index is the Japanese yen ("JPY"). **Top Holdings:** Sony Corp   Toyota Motor Corp   Nippon Telegraph & Telephone Corp Mitsubishi UFJ Financial Group Inc   Keyence Corp

---

Global X Scientific Beta US ETF

C   HOLD

Ticker	Traded On	NAV	Total Assets ($)	Dividend Yield (TTM)	Turnover Ratio	Expense Ratio
SCIU	NYSE Arca	33.70	$99,404,962	2.71	39	0.19

Ratings
Reward   C+
Risk   D+
Recent Upgrade/Downgrade

Fund Information
Fund Type	Exchange Traded Funds
Category	US Equity Large Cap Blend
Sub-Category	Large Blend
Prospectus Objective	Growth
Inception Date	May-15
Open to New Investments	Y

Prices
Price (as of 9/30/2019)	33.70
52-Week High	33.86
52-Week Low	27.01

Total Returns (%)
3-Month	6-Month	1-Year	3-Year	5-Year
1.90	6.07	4.88	37.62	

3-Year Standard Deviation   11.46
Effective Duration

Valuation
Premium/Discount (1-Year Average)   0.04

Company Information
Provider	Global X Funds
Manager/Tenure	Chang Kim (4), Nam To (1), Wayne Xie (0), 1 other
Website	http://www.globalxfunds.com
Address	Global X Funds 600 Lexington Avenue, 20th Floor New York NY 10022 United States
Phone Number	888-493-8631

PERFORMANCE

Ratings History
Date	Overall Rating	Risk Rating	Reward Rating
Q3-19	C	D+	C+
Q4-18	C-	C-	C-
Q4-17	B-	B	C+
Q4-16	D+	D+	C-
Q4-15	U		

Asset & Performance History
Date	NAV	1-Year Total Return
2018	27.91	-7.35
2017	30.83	18.81
2016	26.33	10.76
2015	24.08	
2014		
2013		

Total Assets: $99,404,962
Asset Allocation
Asset	%
Cash	0%
Stocks	100%
US Stocks	99%
Bonds	0%
US Bonds	0%
Other	0%

Services Offered:

Investment Strategy: The investment seeks investment results that correspond generally to the price and yield performance, before fees and expenses, of the Scientific Beta United States Multi-Beta Multi-Strategy Four-Factor Equal Risk Contribution (ERC) Index. The fund invests at least 80% of its total assets in the securities of the underlying index. The underlying index generally comprises approximately 500 or less U.S. listed common stocks selected based on a proprietary methodology developed by EDHEC Risk Institute Asia Ltd. **Top Holdings:** Duke Energy Corp   Dominion Energy Inc   Southern Co   CME Group Inc Class A   Entergy Corp

Pacer WealthShield ETF   D+   SELL

Ticker	Traded On	NAV	Total Assets ($)	Dividend Yield (TTM)	Turnover Ratio	Expense Ratio
PWS	BATS	22.94	$98,637,159	1.57	542	0.6

Ratings
Reward   D
Risk   C-
Recent Upgrade/Downgrade

Fund Information
Fund Type   Exchange Traded Funds
Category   Moderate Allocation
Sub-Category   Allocation--50% to 70% Equity
Prospectus Objective   Growth & Inc
Inception Date   Dec-17
Open to New Investments   Y

Prices
Price (as of 9/30/2019)   22.95
52-Week High   26.83
52-Week Low   22.02

Total Returns (%)

3-Month	6-Month	1-Year	3-Year	5-Year
-5.78	-5.18	-13.15		

3-Year Standard Deviation
Effective Duration

Valuation
Premium/Discount (1-Year Average)   -0.03

Company Information
Provider   Pacer
Manager/Tenure Bruce Kavanaugh (1), Michael Mack (1)
Website   http://www.paceretfs.com
Address   Pacer 16 Industrial Blvd, Suite 201
                          Paoli PA 19301 United States
Phone Number

PERFORMANCE

Ratings History

Date	Overall Rating	Risk Rating	Reward Rating
Q3-19	D+	C-	D
Q4-18	D+	D+	D+
Q4-17	U		
Q4-16			
Q4-15			

Asset & Performance History

Date	NAV	1-Year Total Return
2018	24.14	-2.88
2017	25.13	
2016		
2015		
2014		
2013		

Total Assets: $98,637,159
Asset Allocation

Asset	%
Cash	0%
Stocks	0%
US Stocks	0%
Bonds	100%
US Bonds	100%
Other	0%

Services Offered:

Investment Strategy: The investment seeks to track the total return performance, before fees and expenses, of the Pacer WealthShield Index. Under normal circumstances, at least 80% of the fund's total assets (exclusive of collateral held from securities lending) will be invested in (i) the component securities of the index or (ii) ETFs that seek to track the performance of some or all of the component securities of the index in the same approximate weight as such component securities. The index utilizes a systematic risk management strategy that directs the index's exposure to U.S. equity securities, U.S. Treasury securities, or a mix of each. The fund is non-diversified.
Top Holdings: Amazon.com Inc Microsoft Corp Apple Inc The Home Depot Inc Boeing Co

iPath® MSCI India Index(SM) ETN   D+   SELL

Ticker	Traded On	NAV	Total Assets ($)	Dividend Yield (TTM)	Turnover Ratio	Expense Ratio
INPTF	OTC BB		$98,376,874	0.3	0	0.89

Ratings
Reward   D+
Risk   D+
Recent Upgrade/Downgrade   Down

Fund Information
Fund Type   Exchange Traded Funds
Category   India Equity
Sub-Category   India Equity
Prospectus Objective   Foreign Stock
Inception Date   Dec-06
Open to New Investments   Y

Prices
Price (as of 9/30/2019)   82.30
52-Week High   89.00
52-Week Low   69.81

Total Returns (%)

3-Month	6-Month	1-Year	3-Year	5-Year
-5.09	-4.86	5.10	20.66	18.29

3-Year Standard Deviation   18.04
Effective Duration

Valuation
Premium/Discount (1-Year Average)   -1.39

Company Information
Provider   Milleis Investissements Funds
Manager/Tenure No Manager (12)
Website
Address   2-4, rue Eugène Ruppert L-2453
                    Luxembourg Luxembourg L-2453
                    Luxembourg
Phone Number

PERFORMANCE

Ratings History

Date	Overall Rating	Risk Rating	Reward Rating
Q3-19	D+	D+	D+
Q4-18	D+	D+	D+
Q4-17	B-	C	B
Q4-16	C-	D+	C
Q4-15	C	C-	C

Asset & Performance History

Date	NAV	1-Year Total Return
2018	80.79	-9.04
2017	88.82	41.43
2016	62.96	-2.78
2015	64.58	-7.45
2014	69.78	24.36
2013	56.11	-4.93

Total Assets: $98,376,874
Asset Allocation

Asset	%
Cash	%
Stocks	%
US Stocks	%
Bonds	%
US Bonds	%
Other	%

Services Offered:

Investment Strategy: The investment seeks to track the performance, before fees and expenses, of the MSCI India Total Return Index.
The index is a free float-adjusted market capitalization index that is designed to measure the market performance of Indian securities. It is currently comprised of the top 68 companies by market capitalization listed on the Nation Stock Exchange of India. **Top Holdings:**

ProShares Ultra Health Care

C   HOLD

Ticker	Traded On	NAV	Total Assets ($)	Dividend Yield (TTM)	Turnover Ratio	Expense Ratio
RXL	NYSE Arca	98.28	$98,275,888	0.34	11	0.95

Ratings
Reward	C+
Risk	C-
Recent Upgrade/Downgrade	

Fund Information
Fund Type	Exchange Traded Funds
Category	Trading Tools
Sub-Category	Trading--Leveraged Equity
Prospectus Objective	Health
Inception Date	Jan-07
Open to New Investments	Y

Prices
Price (as of 9/30/2019)	98.21
52-Week High	117.11
52-Week Low	80.30

Total Returns (%)
3-Month	6-Month	1-Year	3-Year	5-Year
-7.70	-6.26	-15.77	51.03	89.95

3-Year Standard Deviation	27.2
Effective Duration	

Valuation
Premium/Discount (1-Year Average)	-0.09

Company Information
Provider	ProShares
Manager/Tenure	Michael Neches (6), Tarak Davé (1)
Website	http://www.proshares.com
Address	ProShares 7501 Wisconsin Avenue, Suite 1000 Bethesda MD 20814 United States
Phone Number	866-776-5125

PERFORMANCE

Ratings History

Date	Overall Rating	Risk Rating	Reward Rating
Q3-19	C	C-	C+
Q4-18	C	C-	C
Q4-17	B+	C+	A
Q4-16	C	D+	C
Q4-15	B-	C	B

Asset & Performance History

Date	NAV	1-Year Total Return
2018	91.97	5.39
2017	87.54	46.01
2016	60.02	-8.93
2015	65.99	7.96
2014	61.7	52.07
2013	40.67	94.55

Total Assets: $98,275,888
Asset Allocation

Asset	%
Cash	-100%
Stocks	98%
US Stocks	98%
Bonds	0%
US Bonds	0%
Other	102%

Services Offered:

Investment Strategy: The investment seeks daily investment results, before fees and expenses, that correspond to two times (2x) the daily performance of the Dow Jones U.S. Health CareSM Index. The fund invests in financial instruments that ProShare Advisors believes, in combination, should produce daily returns consistent with the fund's investment objective. The index measures the performance of certain companies in the healthcare sector of the U.S. equity market. Component companies include, among others, health care providers, biotechnology companies, medical supplies, advanced medical devices and pharmaceuticals. The fund is non-diversified. **Top Holdings:** Dj U.S. Health Care Index Swap Goldman Sachs International   Dj U.S. Health Care Index Swap Ubs Ag   Dj U.S. Health Care Index Swap Societe Generale   Ishares U.S. Healthcare (Iyh) Swap Goldman Sachs International   Ishares U.S. Healthcare (Iyh) Swap Morgan Stanley & Co. International Plc

GS Connect S&P GSCI Enhanced Commodity Total Return ETN

D+   SELL

Ticker	Traded On	NAV	Total Assets ($)	Dividend Yield (TTM)	Turnover Ratio	Expense Ratio
GSC	NYSE Arca		$98,256,000	0	0	1.25

Ratings
Reward	D+
Risk	D+
Recent Upgrade/Downgrade	

Fund Information
Fund Type	Exchange Traded Funds
Category	Commodities Broad Basket
Sub-Category	Commodities Broad Basket
Prospectus Objective	Natl Res
Inception Date	Jul-07
Open to New Investments	Y

Prices
Price (as of 9/30/2019)	21.83
52-Week High	30.97
52-Week Low	17.93

Total Returns (%)
3-Month	6-Month	1-Year	3-Year	5-Year
2.93		-17.81	1.87	-51.48

3-Year Standard Deviation	20.65
Effective Duration	

Valuation
Premium/Discount (1-Year Average)	0.00

Company Information
Provider	Goldman Sachs
Manager/Tenure	No Manager (12)
Website	http://www.gsamfunds.com
Address	Goldman Sachs 200 West Stree New York NY 10282 United States
Phone Number	800-526-7384

PERFORMANCE

Ratings History

Date	Overall Rating	Risk Rating	Reward Rating
Q3-19	D+	D+	D+
Q4-18	D+	D	C-
Q4-17	D	D	D+
Q4-16	D	D	D-
Q4-15	D-	D-	D-

Asset & Performance History

Date	NAV	1-Year Total Return
2018	17.93	-25.35
2017	23.98	2.33
2016	23.31	16.69
2015	20.08	-34.05
2014	30.45	-35.01
2013	46.86	-1.92

Total Assets: $98,256,000
Asset Allocation

Asset	%
Cash	%
Stocks	%
US Stocks	%
Bonds	%
US Bonds	%
Other	%

Services Offered:

Investment Strategy: The investment seeks to replicates, net of expenses, the S&P GSCI Enhanced Commodity Total Return Strategy Index.
The index reflects the total returns that are potentially available through an unleveraged investment in the same futures contracts as are included in the S&P GSCI. **Top Holdings:**

ProShares UltraShort Russell2000

D+ SELL

Ticker	Traded On	NAV	Total Assets ($)	Dividend Yield (TTM)	Turnover Ratio	Expense Ratio
TWM	NYSE Arca	15.19	$98,089,502	1.38	0	0.95

Ratings

Reward	D
Risk	D
Recent Upgrade/Downgrade	Up

Fund Information

Fund Type	Exchange Traded Funds
Category	Trading Tools
Sub-Category	Trading--Inverse Equity
Prospectus Objective	Small Company
Inception Date	Jan-07
Open to New Investments	Y

Prices

Price (as of 9/30/2019)	15.19
52-Week High	23.50
52-Week Low	14.04

Total Returns (%)

3-Month	6-Month	1-Year	3-Year	5-Year
3.96	0.88	9.48	-46.12	-69.40

3-Year Standard Deviation	34.33
Effective Duration	

Valuation

Premium/Discount (1-Year Average)	0.02

Company Information

Provider	ProShares
Manager/Tenure	Michael Neches (6), Devin Sullivan (1)
Website	http://www.proshares.com
Address	ProShares 7501 Wisconsin Avenue, Suite 1000 Bethesda MD 20814 United States
Phone Number	866-776-5125

PERFORMANCE

Ratings History

Date	Overall Rating	Risk Rating	Reward Rating
Q3-19	D+	D	D
Q4-18	D	D	D-
Q4-17	E+	E+	E+
Q4-16	D	D	D-
Q4-15	D	E+	D-

Asset & Performance History

Date	NAV	1-Year Total Return
2018	20.58	18.95
2017	17.46	-26.51
2016	23.77	-39.39
2015	39.22	-1.03
2014	39.63	-17.57
2013	48.08	-52.5

Total Assets: $98,089,502

Asset Allocation

Asset	%
Cash	216%
Stocks	-122%
US Stocks	-122%
Bonds	6%
US Bonds	6%
Other	0%

Services Offered:

Investment Strategy: The investment seeks daily investment results that correspond to two times the inverse (-2x) of the daily performance of the Russell 2000® Index. The fund invests in financial instruments that ProShare Advisors believes, in combination, should produce daily returns consistent with the fund's investment objective. The index is a measure of small-cap U.S. stock market performance. The fund is non-diversified. **Top Holdings:** Russell 2000 Index Swap Societe Generale Russell 2000 Index Swap Bnp Paribas Russell 2000 Index Swap Citibank Na Russell 2000 Index Swap Morgan Stanley & Co. International Plc Russell 2000 Index Swap Bank Of America Na

Invesco BulletShares 2024 High Yield Corporate Bond ETF

C HOLD

Ticker	Traded On	NAV	Total Assets ($)	Dividend Yield (TTM)	Turnover Ratio	Expense Ratio
BSJO	NYSE Arca	25.11	$97,912,098	5.44	8	0.42

Ratings

Reward	C
Risk	C-
Recent Upgrade/Downgrade	

Fund Information

Fund Type	Exchange Traded Funds
Category	US Fixed Income
Sub-Category	High Yield Bond
Prospectus Objective	Corp Bond-High Yld
Inception Date	Sep-16
Open to New Investments	Y

Prices

Price (as of 9/30/2019)	25.22
52-Week High	25.42
52-Week Low	23.03

Total Returns (%)

3-Month	6-Month	1-Year	3-Year	5-Year
0.82	3.80	6.80	16.05	

3-Year Standard Deviation	4.22
Effective Duration	2.39

Valuation

Premium/Discount (1-Year Average)	0.21

Company Information

Provider	Invesco
Manager/Tenure	Jeremy Neisewander (3), Peter Hubbard (1), Jeffrey W. Kernagis (1), 1 other
Website	http://www.invesco.com/us
Address	Invesco 11 Greenway Plaza, Ste. 2500 Houston TX 77046 United States
Phone Number	800-659-1005

PERFORMANCE

Ratings History

Date	Overall Rating	Risk Rating	Reward Rating
Q3-19	C	C-	C
Q4-18	D+	D+	D+
Q4-17	D	B	D+
Q4-16	U		
Q4-15			

Asset & Performance History

Date	NAV	1-Year Total Return
2018	23.4	-3.19
2017	25.47	6.47
2016	25.04	
2015		
2014		
2013		

Total Assets: $97,912,098

Asset Allocation

Asset	%
Cash	1%
Stocks	0%
US Stocks	0%
Bonds	99%
US Bonds	87%
Other	0%

Services Offered:

Investment Strategy: The investment seeks to track the investment results (before fees and expenses) of the Nasdaq BulletShares® USD High Yield Corporate Bond 2024 Index (the "underlying index"). The fund generally will invest at least 80% of its total assets in securities that comprise the underlying index. The underlying index seeks to measure the performance of a portfolio of U.S. dollar-denominated high yield corporate bonds (commonly known as "junk bonds") with maturities or, in some cases, "effective maturities" in the year 2024 (collectively, "2024 Bonds"). The fund is non-diversified. **Top Holdings:** Sprint Corporation 7.12% Bausch Health Companies Inc 7% CSC Holdings, LLC 6.5% DISH DBS Corporation 5.88% Tenet Healthcare Corporation 4.62%

Invesco CurrencyShares® Australian Dollar Trust — D   SELL

Ticker	Traded On	NAV	Total Assets ($)	Dividend Yield (TTM)	Turnover Ratio	Expense Ratio
FXA	NYSE Arca	67.44	$97,789,125	0.82	0	0.4

Ratings
Reward	D
Risk	C-
Recent Upgrade/Downgrade	

Fund Information
Fund Type	Exchange Traded Funds
Category	Currency
Sub-Category	Single Currency
Prospectus Objective	Worldwide Bond
Inception Date	Jun-06
Open to New Investments	Y

Prices
Price (as of 9/30/2019)	67.51
52-Week High	73.59
52-Week Low	67.25

Total Returns (%)
3-Month	6-Month	1-Year	3-Year	5-Year
-3.15	-5.10	-6.24	-9.67	-18.48

3-Year Standard Deviation	7.96
Effective Duration	

Valuation
Premium/Discount (1-Year Average)	-0.12

Company Information
Provider	Invesco
Manager/Tenure	Management Team (13)
Website	http://www.invesco.com/us
Address	Invesco 11 Greenway Plaza, Ste. 2500 Houston TX 77046 United States
Phone Number	800-659-1005

PERFORMANCE

Ratings History
Date	Overall Rating	Risk Rating	Reward Rating
Q3-19	D	C-	D
Q4-18	D+	C-	D
Q4-17	C-	C	D+
Q4-16	D+	C-	D
Q4-15	D	D	D

Asset & Performance History
Date	NAV	1-Year Total Return
2018	70.45	-9.13
2017	78.25	8.89
2016	72.47	0.47
2015	72.84	-9.83
2014	81.98	-6.83
2013	89.6	-12.16

Total Assets: $97,789,125
Asset Allocation
Asset	%
Cash	100%
Stocks	0%
US Stocks	0%
Bonds	0%
US Bonds	0%
Other	0%

Services Offered:

Investment Strategy: The investment objective of the fund is for the Shares to reflect the price in USD of the Australian Dollar.
The Shares are intended to provide institutional and retail investors with a simple, cost-effective means of gaining investment benefits similar to those of holding Australian Dollars. The costs of purchasing Shares should not exceed the costs associated with purchasing any other publicly-traded equity securities. **Top Holdings:**

Goldman Sachs ActiveBeta® U.S. Small Cap Equity ETF — D+   SELL

Ticker	Traded On	NAV	Total Assets ($)	Dividend Yield (TTM)	Turnover Ratio	Expense Ratio
GSSC	NYSE Arca	43.82	$96,398,899	1.25	27	0.2

Ratings
Reward	C-
Risk	D+
Recent Upgrade/Downgrade	Up

Fund Information
Fund Type	Exchange Traded Funds
Category	US Equity Small Cap
Sub-Category	Small Blend
Prospectus Objective	Growth
Inception Date	Jun-17
Open to New Investments	Y

Prices
Price (as of 9/30/2019)	43.79
52-Week High	47.65
52-Week Low	36.76

Total Returns (%)
3-Month	6-Month	1-Year	3-Year	5-Year
-1.09	0.20	-6.41		

3-Year Standard Deviation	
Effective Duration	

Valuation
Premium/Discount (1-Year Average)	0.08

Company Information
Provider	Goldman Sachs
Manager/Tenure	Raj Garigipati (2), Jamie McGregor (2)
Website	http://www.gsamfunds.com
Address	Goldman Sachs 200 West Stree New York NY 10282 United States
Phone Number	800-526-7384

PERFORMANCE

Ratings History
Date	Overall Rating	Risk Rating	Reward Rating
Q3-19	D+	D+	C-
Q4-18	D+	C-	D+
Q4-17	U		
Q4-16			
Q4-15			

Asset & Performance History
Date	NAV	1-Year Total Return
2018	38.89	-8.71
2017	43.08	
2016		
2015		
2014		
2013		

Total Assets: $96,398,899
Asset Allocation
Asset	%
Cash	0%
Stocks	100%
US Stocks	99%
Bonds	0%
US Bonds	0%
Other	0%

Services Offered:

Investment Strategy: The investment seeks to provide investment results that closely correspond, before fees and expenses, to the performance of the Goldman Sachs ActiveBeta® U.S. Small Cap Equity Index. The fund invests at least 80% of its assets in securities included in its index. The index is designed to deliver exposure to equity securities of small capitalization U.S. issuers. The index is constructed using the patented ActiveBeta® Portfolio Construction Methodology, which was developed to provide exposure to the "factors" that are commonly tied to a stock's outperformance relative to market returns. These factors include value, momentum, quality and low volatility. **Top Holdings:** Haemonetics Corp Trex Co Inc Amedisys Inc Genomic Health Inc Boston Beer Co Inc Class A

Janus Henderson Small/Mid Cap Growth Alpha ETF   C   HOLD

Ticker	Traded On	NAV	Total Assets ($)	Dividend Yield (TTM)	Turnover Ratio	Expense Ratio
JSMD	NAS CM	43.73	$96,296,485	0.43	79	0.35

Ratings
Reward	C+
Risk	D+
Recent Upgrade/Downgrade	

Fund Information
Fund Type	Exchange Traded Funds
Category	US Equity Mid Cap
Sub-Category	Mid-Cap Growth
Prospectus Objective	Growth
Inception Date	Feb-16
Open to New Investments	Y

Prices
Price (as of 9/30/2019)	43.77
52-Week High	46.38
52-Week Low	34.41

Total Returns (%)
3-Month	6-Month	1-Year	3-Year	5-Year
-3.63	-0.04	-3.45	49.61	

3-Year Standard Deviation	17.06
Effective Duration	

Valuation
Premium/Discount (1-Year Average)	0.00

Company Information
Provider	Janus Henderson
Manager/Tenure	Benjamin Wang (3), Scott M Weiner (3)
Website	http://janushenderson.com
Address	Janus 151 Detroit Street Denver CO 80206 United States
Phone Number	877-335-2687

PERFORMANCE

Ratings History
Date	Overall Rating	Risk Rating	Reward Rating
Q3-19	C	D+	C+
Q4-18	C-	D+	C
Q4-17	C-	B+	C
Q4-16	U		
Q4-15			

Asset & Performance History
Date	NAV	1-Year Total Return
2018	36.97	-3.82
2017	38.68	23.83
2016	31.3	
2015		
2014		
2013		

Total Assets: $96,296,485
Asset Allocation
Asset	%
Cash	0%
Stocks	100%
US Stocks	100%
Bonds	0%
US Bonds	0%
Other	0%

Services Offered:

Investment Strategy: The investment seeks investment results that correspond generally, to the performance of its underlying index, the Janus Henderson Small/Mid Cap Growth Alpha Index. The fund pursues its investment objective by normally investing at least 80% of its net assets in the securities that comprise the underlying index. The underlying index is composed of common stocks of small- and medium-sized companies that are included in the Solactive Small/Mid Cap Index, a universe of 2,500 small- and medium-sized capitalization stocks. **Top Holdings:** Paycom Software Inc   Masimo Corp   Jazz Pharmaceuticals PLC   Westlake Chemical Corp   Heico Corp

VictoryShares Developed Enhanced Volatility Wtd ETF   C-   HOLD

Ticker	Traded On	NAV	Total Assets ($)	Dividend Yield (TTM)	Turnover Ratio	Expense Ratio
CIZ	NAS CM	31.41	$95,806,349	3.01	154	0.45

Ratings
Reward	C-
Risk	C-
Recent Upgrade/Downgrade	

Fund Information
Fund Type	Exchange Traded Funds
Category	Global Equity Large Cap
Sub-Category	Foreign Large Blend
Prospectus Objective	Income
Inception Date	Sep-14
Open to New Investments	Y

Prices
Price (as of 9/30/2019)	31.33
52-Week High	34.13
52-Week Low	29.68

Total Returns (%)
3-Month	6-Month	1-Year	3-Year	5-Year
-1.89	0.24	-5.17	13.24	0.37

3-Year Standard Deviation	9.53
Effective Duration	

Valuation
Premium/Discount (1-Year Average)	-0.29

Company Information
Provider	VictoryShares
Manager/Tenure	Mannik Dhillon (1)
Website	http://www.VictorySharesLiterature.com
Address	Victory Shares 4249 Easton Way, Suite 400 Columbus OH 43219 United States
Phone Number	

PERFORMANCE

Ratings History
Date	Overall Rating	Risk Rating	Reward Rating
Q3-19	C-	C-	C-
Q4-18	D+	C-	D+
Q4-17	C	C+	C
Q4-16	D	D	D
Q4-15	U		

Asset & Performance History
Date	NAV	1-Year Total Return
2018	30.87	-9.46
2017	34.96	25.66
2016	28.34	-8.73
2015	31.42	-6.64
2014	34.23	
2013		

Total Assets: $95,806,349
Asset Allocation
Asset	%
Cash	0%
Stocks	100%
US Stocks	2%
Bonds	0%
US Bonds	0%
Other	0%

Services Offered:

Investment Strategy: The investment seeks to track the performance of the Nasdaq Victory International 500 Long/Cash Volatility Weighted Index before fees and expenses. The fund seeks to achieve its investment objective by investing, under normal market conditions, at least 80% of its assets directly or indirectly in the securities included in the Nasdaq Victory International 500 Long/Cash Volatility Weighted Index, an unmanaged, volatility weighted index maintained exclusively by the index provider. The index identifies the 500 largest foreign companies by market capitalization measured at the time the index's constituent securities are determined. **Top Holdings:** Mini Msci Eafe Fut Sep19   National Bank of Canada   TELUS Corp   Fortis Inc   Power Assets Holdings Ltd

Global X Internet of Things ETF

C HOLD

Ticker	Traded On	NAV	Total Assets ($)	Dividend Yield (TTM)	Turnover Ratio	Expense Ratio
SNSR	NAS CM	20.37	$95,748,268	1.39	17	0.68

Ratings

Reward	C+
Risk	C-
Recent Upgrade/Downgrade	Up

Fund Information

Fund Type	Exchange Traded Funds
Category	Technology Sector Equity
Sub-Category	Technology
Prospectus Objective	Technology
Inception Date	Sep-16
Open to New Investments	Y

Prices

Price (as of 9/30/2019)	20.40
52-Week High	20.76
52-Week Low	15.40

Total Returns (%)

3-Month	6-Month	1-Year	3-Year	5-Year
1.49	10.14	2.57	35.09	

3-Year Standard Deviation	18.13
Effective Duration	

Valuation

Premium/Discount (1-Year Average)	-0.02

Company Information

Provider	Global X Funds
Manager/Tenure	Chang Kim (3), Nam To (1), Wayne Xie (0), 1 other
Website	http://www.globalxfunds.com
Address	Global X Funds 600 Lexington Avenue, 20th Floor New York NY 10022 United States
Phone Number	888-493-8631

PERFORMANCE

Ratings History

Date	Overall Rating	Risk Rating	Reward Rating
Q3-19	C	C-	C+
Q4-18	C	C-	C
Q4-17	D	B	C
Q4-16	U		
Q4-15			

Asset & Performance History

Date	NAV	1-Year Total Return
2018	16.19	-16.44
2017	19.62	26.7
2016	15.57	
2015		
2014		
2013		

Total Assets: $95,748,268

Asset Allocation

Asset	%
Cash	0%
Stocks	100%
US Stocks	61%
Bonds	0%
US Bonds	0%
Other	0%

Services Offered:

Investment Strategy: The investment seeks to provide investment results that correspond generally to the price and yield performance, before fees and expenses, of the Indxx Global Internet of Things Thematic Index. The fund invests at least 80% of its total assets in the securities of the underlying index. The underlying index is designed to provide exposure to exchange-listed companies in developed markets that facilitate the Internet of Things industry, including companies involved in wearable technology, home automation, connected automotive technology, sensors, networking infrastructure/software, smart metering and energy control devices. The fund is non-diversified. **Top Holdings:** DexCom Inc STMicroelectronics NV Cypress Semiconductor Corp Garmin Ltd Skyworks Solutions Inc

JPMorgan U.S. Momentum Factor ETF

C- HOLD

Ticker	Traded On	NAV	Total Assets ($)	Dividend Yield (TTM)	Turnover Ratio	Expense Ratio
JMOM	NYSE Arca	28.84	$95,188,380	1.04		0.12

Ratings

Reward	C
Risk	D+
Recent Upgrade/Downgrade	Up

Fund Information

Fund Type	Exchange Traded Funds
Category	US Equity Large Cap Growth
Sub-Category	Large Growth
Prospectus Objective	Growth & Inc
Inception Date	Nov-17
Open to New Investments	Y

Prices

Price (as of 9/30/2019)	28.87
52-Week High	29.79
52-Week Low	22.40

Total Returns (%)

3-Month	6-Month	1-Year	3-Year	5-Year
-0.41	4.35	1.85		

3-Year Standard Deviation	
Effective Duration	

Valuation

Premium/Discount (1-Year Average)	0.07

Company Information

Provider	JPMorgan
Manager/Tenure	Aijaz Hussain (1), Jonathan Msika (1), Yazann Romahi (1), 2 others
Website	http://www.jpmorganfunds.com
Address	JPMorgan 270 Park Avenue New York NY 10017-2070 United States
Phone Number	800-480-4111

PERFORMANCE

Ratings History

Date	Overall Rating	Risk Rating	Reward Rating
Q3-19	C-	D+	C
Q4-18	D	D	D+
Q4-17	U		
Q4-16			
Q4-15			

Asset & Performance History

Date	NAV	1-Year Total Return
2018	24	-5.04
2017	25.6	
2016		
2015		
2014		
2013		

Total Assets: $95,188,380

Asset Allocation

Asset	%
Cash	0%
Stocks	100%
US Stocks	99%
Bonds	0%
US Bonds	0%
Other	0%

Services Offered:

Investment Strategy: The investment seeks investment results that closely correspond, before fees and expenses, to the performance of the JP Morgan US Momentum Factor Index. The fund will invest at least 80% of its assets in securities included in the underlying index. "Assets" means net assets, plus the amount of borrowing for investment purposes. The underlying index is comprised of U.S. equity securities selected to represent positive momentum factor characteristics. **Top Holdings:** Visa Inc Class A Microsoft Corp Berkshire Hathaway Inc B Mastercard Inc A The Home Depot Inc

ProShares UltraShort Bloomberg Crude Oil   D+   SELL

Ticker	Traded On	NAV	Total Assets ($)	Dividend Yield (TTM)	Turnover Ratio	Expense Ratio
SCO	NYSE Arca		$94,921,353	0	0	0.95

Ratings
Reward	D
Risk	D
Recent Upgrade/Downgrade	Up

Fund Information
Fund Type	Exchange Traded Funds
Category	Trading Tools
Sub-Category	Trading--Inverse Commodities
Prospectus Objective	Natl Res
Inception Date	Nov-08
Open to New Investments	Y

Prices
Price (as of 9/30/2019)	16.24
52-Week High	33.13
52-Week Low	12.52

Total Returns (%)
3-Month	6-Month	1-Year	3-Year	5-Year
-6.75	-4.30	19.88	-61.53	-0.08

3-Year Standard Deviation	57.57
Effective Duration	

Valuation
Premium/Discount (1-Year Average)	0.19

Company Information
Provider	ProShares
Manager/Tenure	Management Team (10)
Website	http://www.proshares.com
Address	ProShares 7501 Wisconsin Avenue, Suite 1000 Bethesda MD 20814 United States
Phone Number	866-776-5125

PERFORMANCE

Ratings History

Date	Overall Rating	Risk Rating	Reward Rating
Q3-19	D+	D	D
Q4-18	D	D	D-
Q4-17	D	D	D+
Q4-16	C	D+	C-
Q4-15	B-	D+	B

Asset & Performance History

Date	NAV	1-Year Total Return
2018	29.79	23.16
2017	24.31	-23.29
2016	31.7	-52.4
2015	66.6	70.82
2014	38.99	145.77
2013	15.86	-21.27

Total Assets: $94,921,353

Asset Allocation

Asset	%
Cash	300%
Stocks	0%
US Stocks	0%
Bonds	0%
US Bonds	0%
Other	-200%

Services Offered:

Investment Strategy: The investment seeks daily investment results, before fees and expenses, that correspond to two times the inverse (-2x) of the daily performance of the Bloomberg WTI Crude Oil SubindexSM. The fund seeks to meet its investment objective by investing, under normal market conditions, in futures contracts for WTI sweet, light crude oil listed on the NYMEX, ICE Futures U.S. or other U.S. exchanges and listed options on such contracts. It will not invest directly in oil. **Top Holdings:** Crude Oil Oct19 Bloomberg Wti Crude Oil Subindex Swap - Citibank Bloomberg Wti Crude Oil Subindex Swap - Gs Bloomberg Wti Crude Oil Subindex Swap - Ubs Ag Bloomberg Wti Crude Oil Subindex Swap - Rbc

---

WisdomTree International Quality Dividend Growth Fund   C-   HOLD

Ticker	Traded On	NAV	Total Assets ($)	Dividend Yield (TTM)	Turnover Ratio	Expense Ratio
IQDG	BATS	28.72	$94,789,976	2.18	55	0.38

Ratings
Reward	C
Risk	C-
Recent Upgrade/Downgrade	

Fund Information
Fund Type	Exchange Traded Funds
Category	Global Equity Large Cap
Sub-Category	Foreign Large Growth
Prospectus Objective	Growth & Inc
Inception Date	Apr-16
Open to New Investments	Y

Prices
Price (as of 9/30/2019)	28.79
52-Week High	29.78
52-Week Low	24.23

Total Returns (%)
3-Month	6-Month	1-Year	3-Year	5-Year
-1.65	0.86	-0.59	19.33	

3-Year Standard Deviation	12.58
Effective Duration	

Valuation
Premium/Discount (1-Year Average)	0.21

Company Information
Provider	WisdomTree
Manager/Tenure	Richard A. Brown (3), Thomas J. Durante (3), Karen Q. Wong (3)
Website	http://www.wisdomtree.com
Address	WisdomTree 245 Park Avenue, 35th floor New York NY 10167 United States
Phone Number	866-909-9473

PERFORMANCE

Ratings History

Date	Overall Rating	Risk Rating	Reward Rating
Q3-19	C-	C-	C
Q4-18	D+	C-	D+
Q4-17	D+	B-	C
Q4-16	U		
Q4-15			

Asset & Performance History

Date	NAV	1-Year Total Return
2018	25.1	-17.05
2017	30.79	31.39
2016	23.87	
2015		
2014		
2013		

Total Assets: $94,789,976

Asset Allocation

Asset	%
Cash	0%
Stocks	100%
US Stocks	1%
Bonds	0%
US Bonds	0%
Other	0%

Services Offered:

Investment Strategy: The investment seeks to track the price and yield performance, before fees and expenses, of the WisdomTree International Quality Dividend Growth Index. Under normal circumstances, at least 80% of the fund's total assets (exclusive of collateral held from securities lending) will be invested in component securities of the index and investments that have economic characteristics that are substantially identical to the economic characteristics of such component securities. The index consists of dividend-paying common stocks with growth characteristics of companies in the industrialized world, excluding Canada and the United States. The fund is non-diversified. **Top Holdings:** Industria De Diseno Textil SA Unilever NV British American Tobacco PLC Novo Nordisk A/S B Rio Tinto PLC

FlexShares Credit-Scored US Corporate Bond Index Fund
C   HOLD

Ticker	Traded On	NAV	Total Assets ($)	Dividend Yield (TTM)	Turnover Ratio	Expense Ratio
SKOR	NAS CM	52.38	$94,283,332	3.01	76	0.22

Ratings
Reward	C+
Risk	D+
Recent Upgrade/Downgrade	

Fund Information
Fund Type	Exchange Traded Funds
Category	US Fixed Income
Sub-Category	Corporate Bond
Prospectus Objective	Corp Bond - Gen
Inception Date	Nov-14
Open to New Investments	Y

Prices
Price (as of 9/30/2019)	52.30
52-Week High	52.77
52-Week Low	48.38

Total Returns (%)
3-Month	6-Month	1-Year	3-Year	5-Year
1.81	5.56	10.41	9.86	

3-Year Standard Deviation	3.03
Effective Duration	4.81

Valuation
Premium/Discount (1-Year Average)	0.04

Company Information
Provider	Flexshares Trust
Manager/Tenure	Bradley Camden (4), Michael T. Doyle (4), Brandon P. Ferguson (4)
Website	http://www.flexshares.com
Address	50 South LaSalle Street Chicago, Illinois 60603 Chicago Illinois 60603 United States
Phone Number	855-353-9383

PERFORMANCE

Ratings History

Date	Overall Rating	Risk Rating	Reward Rating
Q3-19	C	D+	C+
Q4-18	C-	C-	D+
Q4-17	C+	B+	C
Q4-16	D+	D+	D+
Q4-15	U		

Asset & Performance History

Date	NAV	1-Year Total Return
2018	48.81	-0.82
2017	50.63	3.3
2016	50.03	2.6
2015	49.79	1.64
2014	50.09	
2013		

Total Assets: $94,283,332
Asset Allocation

Asset	%
Cash	0%
Stocks	0%
US Stocks	0%
Bonds	96%
US Bonds	83%
Other	0%

Services Offered:

Investment Strategy: The investment seeks the price and yield performance, before fees and expenses, of the Northern Trust Credit-Scored US Corporate Bond IndexSM. The fund generally will invest under normal circumstances at least 80% of its total assets (exclusive of collateral held from securities lending) in the securities of its underlying index. The underlying index is designed to outperform the parent index on a risk-adjusted basis, as measured by a combination of yield return and price appreciation. Securities included in the underlying index are component securities of the Parent Index. The fund is non-diversified. **Top Holdings:** Morgan Stanley 2.75% Goldman Sachs Group, Inc. 5.75% Morgan Stanley 3.77% TransCanada Pipelines Limited 2.5% Capital One Financial Corporation 3.2%

DB Gold Double Long ETN
C   HOLD

Ticker	Traded On	NAV	Total Assets ($)	Dividend Yield (TTM)	Turnover Ratio	Expense Ratio
DGP	NYSE Arca		$94,240,335	0	0	0.75

Ratings
Reward	C
Risk	C-
Recent Upgrade/Downgrade	Up

Fund Information
Fund Type	Exchange Traded Funds
Category	Trading Tools
Sub-Category	Trading--Leveraged Commodities
Prospectus Objective	Prec Metals
Inception Date	Feb-08
Open to New Investments	Y

Prices
Price (as of 9/30/2019)	29.25
52-Week High	32.59
52-Week Low	20.17

Total Returns (%)
3-Month	6-Month	1-Year	3-Year	5-Year
15.74	31.42	50.54	13.35	22.44

3-Year Standard Deviation	21.79
Effective Duration	

Valuation
Premium/Discount (1-Year Average)	1.26

Company Information
Provider	Deutsche Bank AG
Manager/Tenure	No Manager (11)
Website	
Address	Theodor-Heuss-Allee 72 Frankfurt am Main 60486 Germany
Phone Number	

PERFORMANCE

Ratings History

Date	Overall Rating	Risk Rating	Reward Rating
Q3-19	C	C-	C
Q4-18	D	D	D
Q4-17	D+	D	C-
Q4-16	D+	D	C-
Q4-15	D-	D-	D-

Asset & Performance History

Date	NAV	1-Year Total Return
2018	23.07	-8.29
2017	25.16	21.35
2016	20.13	11.97
2015	18.18	-22.79
2014	23.55	-6.01
2013	25.06	-51.96

Total Assets: $94,240,335
Asset Allocation

Asset	%
Cash	%
Stocks	%
US Stocks	%
Bonds	%
US Bonds	%
Other	%

Services Offered:

Investment Strategy: The investment seeks to replicate, net of expenses, twice the daily performance of the Deutsche Bank Liquid Commodity index - Optimum Yield Gold Excess Return.
The index is intended to reflect changes in the market value of certain gold futures contracts and is comprised of a single unfunded gold futures contract. **Top Holdings:**

Direxion Daily S&P Biotech Bear 3X Shares
D SELL

Ticker	Traded On	NAV	Total Assets ($)	Dividend Yield (TTM)	Turnover Ratio	Expense Ratio
LABD	NYSE Arca	25.39	$93,546,700	1.32	0	1.11

Ratings
Reward	E+
Risk	D
Recent Upgrade/Downgrade	Up

Fund Information
Fund Type	Exchange Traded Funds
Category	Trading Tools
Sub-Category	Trading--Inverse Equity
Prospectus Objective	Technology
Inception Date	May-15
Open to New Investments	Y

Prices
Price (as of 9/30/2019)	25.32
52-Week High	59.28
52-Week Low	16.49

Total Returns (%)
3-Month	6-Month	1-Year	3-Year	5-Year
43.35	38.57	0.69	-85.06	

3-Year Standard Deviation	82.14
Effective Duration	

Valuation
Premium/Discount (1-Year Average)	0.05

Company Information
Provider	Direxion Funds
Manager/Tenure	Paul Brigandi (4), Tony Ng (4)
Website	http://www.direxionfunds.com
Address	Direxion Funds 1301 Avenue Of The Americas (6th Avenue) New York NY 10019 United States
Phone Number	646-572-3390

PERFORMANCE

Ratings History
Date	Overall Rating	Risk Rating	Reward Rating
Q3-19	D	D	E+
Q4-18	D	D	E+
Q4-17	D-	D-	E+
Q4-16	D	D-	D-
Q4-15	U		

Asset & Performance History
Date	NAV	1-Year Total Return
2018	42.5	-7.45
2017	46.2	-75.63
2016	189.6	-39.05
2015	311.1	
2014		
2013		

Total Assets: $93,546,700
Asset Allocation
Asset	%
Cash	106%
Stocks	-6%
US Stocks	-6%
Bonds	0%
US Bonds	0%
Other	0%

Services Offered:

Investment Strategy: The investment seeks daily investment results, before fees and expenses, of 300% of the inverse of the daily performance of the S&P Biotechnology Select Industry Index. The fund, under normal circumstances, invests in swap agreements, futures contracts, short positions or other financial instruments that, in combination, provide inverse (opposite) or short leveraged exposure to the index equal to at least 80% of the fund's net assets (plus borrowing for investment purposes). The index is designed to measure the performance of the biotechnology sub-industry based on the Global Industry Classification Standards ("GICS"). The fund is non-diversified. **Top Holdings:** S&P Biotechnology Select S&P Biotechnology Select S&P Biotechnology Select Industry USD S&P Biotechnology Select S&P Biotechnology Select

---

First Trust NASDAQ-100 Ex-Technology Sector Index Fund
C HOLD

Ticker	Traded On	NAV	Total Assets ($)	Dividend Yield (TTM)	Turnover Ratio	Expense Ratio
QQXT	NAS CM	53.43	$93,500,105	0.42	26	0.6

Ratings
Reward	C
Risk	D+
Recent Upgrade/Downgrade	

Fund Information
Fund Type	Exchange Traded Funds
Category	US Equity Large Cap Growth
Sub-Category	Large Growth
Prospectus Objective	Growth
Inception Date	Feb-07
Open to New Investments	Y

Prices
Price (as of 9/30/2019)	53.39
52-Week High	55.77
52-Week Low	43.14

Total Returns (%)
3-Month	6-Month	1-Year	3-Year	5-Year
-2.98	0.37	1.29	33.47	49.48

3-Year Standard Deviation	14.05
Effective Duration	

Valuation
Premium/Discount (1-Year Average)	0.05

Company Information
Provider	First Trust
Manager/Tenure	Jon C. Erickson (12), Daniel J. Lindquist (12), David G. McGarel (12), 3 others
Website	http://www.ftportfolios.com/
Address	First Trust 120 E. Liberty Drive, Suite 400 Wheaton IL 60187 United States
Phone Number	800-621-1675

PERFORMANCE

Ratings History
Date	Overall Rating	Risk Rating	Reward Rating
Q3-19	C	D+	C
Q4-18	C-	D+	C
Q4-17	B-	B	C+
Q4-16	C	D+	C+
Q4-15	C	C	C+

Asset & Performance History
Date	NAV	1-Year Total Return
2018	45.66	-5.58
2017	48.53	20.4
2016	40.44	-2.13
2015	41.45	4.74
2014	39.73	15.35
2013	34.77	41.24

Total Assets: $93,500,105
Asset Allocation
Asset	%
Cash	0%
Stocks	100%
US Stocks	92%
Bonds	0%
US Bonds	0%
Other	0%

Services Offered:

Investment Strategy: The investment seeks investment results that correspond generally to the price and yield (before the fund's fees and expenses) of an equity index called the NASDAQ-100 Ex-Tech Sector IndexSM. The fund will normally invest at least 90% of its net assets (including investment borrowings) in the common stocks and depositary receipts that comprise the index. The index is an equal-weighted index composed of the securities comprising the NASDAQ-100 Index® that are not classified as "technology" according to the Industry Classification Benchmark ("ICB") classification system. **Top Holdings:** JB Hunt Transport Services Inc Fiserv Inc Take-Two Interactive Software Inc Starbucks Corp Cintas Corp

Inspire Small/Mid Cap Impact ETF   C-   HOLD

Ticker	Traded On	NAV	Total Assets ($)	Dividend Yield (TTM)	Turnover Ratio	Expense Ratio
ISMD	NYSE Arca		$93,474,333	1.24		0.61

Ratings
Reward	D+
Risk	C-
Recent Upgrade/Downgrade	

Fund Information
Fund Type	Exchange Traded Funds
Category	US Equity Mid Cap
Sub-Category	Small Blend
Prospectus Objective	Growth
Inception Date	Feb-17
Open to New Investments	Y

Prices
Price (as of 9/30/2019)	26.33
52-Week High	29.18
52-Week Low	21.59

Total Returns (%)
3-Month	6-Month	1-Year	3-Year	5-Year
-1.19	-0.90	-6.69		

3-Year Standard Deviation	
Effective Duration	

Valuation
Premium/Discount (1-Year Average)	-0.07

Company Information
Provider	Inspire
Manager/Tenure	Darrell Jayroe (2), Robert Netzly (2)
Website	
Address	Inspire 650 San Benito Street, Suite 130 Hollister CA 95023 United States
Phone Number	

PERFORMANCE

Ratings History
Date	Overall Rating	Risk Rating	Reward Rating
Q3-19	C-	C-	D+
Q4-18	D+	C-	D+
Q4-17	U		
Q4-16			
Q4-15			

Asset & Performance History
Date	NAV	1-Year Total Return
2018	22.94	-10.56
2017	26.33	
2016		
2015		
2014		
2013		

Total Assets: $93,474,333
Asset Allocation
Asset	%
Cash	1%
Stocks	99%
US Stocks	98%
Bonds	0%
US Bonds	0%
Other	0%

Services Offered:

Investment Strategy: The investment seeks to replicate investment results that generally correspond to the Inspire Small/Mid Cap Impact Index. The fund generally will invest at least 80% of its total assets in the component securities. The index provider selects domestic small and mid capitalization equity securities included in the Russell 2,000 Index and S&P 400 Index using the Inspire Impact Score®, a proprietary selection methodology that is designed to assign a score to a particular security based on the security's alignment with biblical values and the positive impact that company has on the world through various environmental, social and governance criterion.
Top Holdings: Stamps.com Inc Shake Shack Inc A Saia Inc Genomic Health Inc Cambrex Corp

---

iShares iBonds Dec 2024 Term Muni Bond ETF   C-   HOLD

Ticker	Traded On	NAV	Total Assets ($)	Dividend Yield (TTM)	Turnover Ratio	Expense Ratio
IBMM	BATS	26.30	$93,366,146	1.83	0	0.18

Ratings
Reward	C-
Risk	C-
Recent Upgrade/Downgrade	

Fund Information
Fund Type	Exchange Traded Funds
Category	US Muni Fixed Inc
Sub-Category	Muni Target Maturity
Prospectus Objective	Growth & Inc
Inception Date	Mar-18
Open to New Investments	Y

Prices
Price (as of 9/30/2019)	26.32
52-Week High	26.67
52-Week Low	24.83

Total Returns (%)
3-Month	6-Month	1-Year	3-Year	5-Year
0.58	2.43	7.15		

3-Year Standard Deviation	
Effective Duration	

Valuation
Premium/Discount (1-Year Average)	0.09

Company Information
Provider	iShares
Manager/Tenure	James Mauro (1), Scott Radell (1)
Website	http://www.ishares.com
Address	iShares 400 Howard Street San Francisco CA 94105 United States
Phone Number	800-474-2737

PERFORMANCE

Ratings History
Date	Overall Rating	Risk Rating	Reward Rating
Q3-19	C-	C-	C-
Q4-18	U		
Q4-17			
Q4-16			
Q4-15			

Asset & Performance History
Date	NAV	1-Year Total Return
2018	25.4	
2017		
2016		
2015		
2014		
2013		

Total Assets: $93,366,146
Asset Allocation
Asset	%
Cash	0%
Stocks	0%
US Stocks	0%
Bonds	100%
US Bonds	100%
Other	0%

Services Offered:

Investment Strategy: The investment seeks to track the investment results of S&P AMT-Free Municipal Series Dec 2024 IndexTM. The fund generally will invest at least 90% of its assets in the component securities of the underlying index. The index measures the performance of investment-grade (as determined by the index provider), non-callable U.S. municipal bonds maturing in 2024. It includes municipal bonds primarily from issuers that are state or local governments or agencies such that the interest on the bonds is exempt from U.S. federal income taxes. The fund is non-diversified. **Top Holdings:** CALIFORNIA ST 5% MARYLAND ST 5% SAN DIEGO CALIF UNI SCH DIST 0% NEW YORK ST DORM AUTH SALES TAX REV ST SUPPORTED DEBT 5% GUILFORD CNTY N C 5%

WBI Power Factor™ High Dividend ETF　　　　　　　　　　C　　HOLD

Ticker	Traded On	NAV	Total Assets ($)	Dividend Yield (TTM)	Turnover Ratio	Expense Ratio
WBIY	NYSE Arca	24.47	$92,996,468	4.89	163	0.7

Ratings
Reward	B-
Risk	D+
Recent Upgrade/Downgrade	Up

Fund Information
Fund Type	Exchange Traded Funds
Category	US Equity Large Cap Value
Sub-Category	Large Value
Prospectus Objective	Equity-Income
Inception Date	Dec-16
Open to New Investments	Y

Prices
Price (as of 9/30/2019)	24.44
52-Week High	26.96
52-Week Low	21.81

Total Returns (%)
3-Month	6-Month	1-Year	3-Year	5-Year
0.35	0.24	-3.51		

3-Year Standard Deviation	
Effective Duration	

Valuation
Premium/Discount (1-Year Average)	-0.05

Company Information
Provider	WBI Investments
Manager/Tenure	Donald R. Schreiber (2), Steven Van Solkema (0)
Website	http://www.wbishares.com
Address	34 Sycamore Ave Suite 1-E Little Silver NJ 07739 United States
Phone Number	732-842-4920

PERFORMANCE

Ratings History
Date	Overall Rating	Risk Rating	Reward Rating
Q3-19	C	D+	B-
Q4-18	C	D+	C+
Q4-17	D-	B	D+
Q4-16			
Q4-15			

Asset & Performance History
Date	NAV	1-Year Total Return
2018	22.24	-12.65
2017	26.49	14.1
2016	24.65	
2015		
2014		
2013		

Total Assets: $92,996,468
Asset Allocation
Asset	%
Cash	1%
Stocks	99%
US Stocks	94%
Bonds	0%
US Bonds	0%
Other	0%

Services Offered:

Investment Strategy: The investment seeks to provide investment results that correspond to the price and yield of its underlying index, the Solactive Power FactorTM High Dividend Index. Under normal circumstances the fund will invest at least 80% of its total assets in the securities of the underlying index. The underlying index is designed to select securities from the Solactive US Broad Market Index that exhibit certain yield and fundamental value characteristics. The parent index includes large, mid- and small-cap securities listed in the U.S., including approximately the 3,000 largest U.S. companies that are selected and weighted according to free float market capitalization. **Top Holdings:** AT&T Inc　Seagate Technology PLC　Verizon Communications Inc　AbbVie Inc　Ford Motor Co

First Trust Chindia ETF　　　　　　　　　　　　　　　　C-　　HOLD

Ticker	Traded On	NAV	Total Assets ($)	Dividend Yield (TTM)	Turnover Ratio	Expense Ratio
FNI	NYSE Arca	34.29	$92,594,058	0.76	22	0.59

Ratings
Reward	C-
Risk	C-
Recent Upgrade/Downgrade	

Fund Information
Fund Type	Exchange Traded Funds
Category	Equity Misc
Sub-Category	Miscellaneous Region
Prospectus Objective	Pacific Stock
Inception Date	May-07
Open to New Investments	Y

Prices
Price (as of 9/30/2019)	34.35
52-Week High	38.48
52-Week Low	29.74

Total Returns (%)
3-Month	6-Month	1-Year	3-Year	5-Year
-6.03	-9.25	0.47	18.03	25.54

3-Year Standard Deviation	17.68
Effective Duration	

Valuation
Premium/Discount (1-Year Average)	-0.02

Company Information
Provider	First Trust
Manager/Tenure	Jon C. Erickson (12), Daniel J. Lindquist (12), David G. McGarel (12), 3 others
Website	http://www.ftportfolios.com/
Address	First Trust 120 E. Liberty Drive, Suite 400 Wheaton IL 60187 United States
Phone Number	800-621-1675

PERFORMANCE

Ratings History
Date	Overall Rating	Risk Rating	Reward Rating
Q3-19	C-	C-	C-
Q4-18	C	D+	C+
Q4-17	B	C	A-
Q4-16	C	D+	B-
Q4-15	C+	C	B-

Asset & Performance History
Date	NAV	1-Year Total Return
2018	30.93	-20.71
2017	39.57	47.34
2016	27.39	-2.15
2015	28.36	-0.32
2014	28.63	2.37
2013	28.22	35.83

Total Assets: $92,594,058
Asset Allocation
Asset	%
Cash	0%
Stocks	100%
US Stocks	2%
Bonds	0%
US Bonds	0%
Other	0%

Services Offered:

Investment Strategy: The investment seeks investment results that correspond generally to the price and yield (before the fund's fees and expenses) of an equity index called the ISE ChindiaTM Index. The fund will normally invest at least 90% of its net assets (including investment borrowings) in the common stocks and depositary receipts that comprise the index. The index is a modified market capitalization-weighted index designed to track the performance of U.S.-listed securities issued by small, mid and large capitalization companies domiciled in China or India. It is non-diversified. **Top Holdings:** JD.com Inc ADR　Alibaba Group Holding Ltd ADR　Infosys Ltd ADR　Pinduoduo Inc ADR　Baidu Inc ADR

iShares MSCI Global Silver Miners ETF   C-   HOLD

Ticker	Traded On	NAV	Total Assets ($)	Dividend Yield (TTM)	Turnover Ratio	Expense Ratio
SLVP	BATS	9.64	$92,528,106	0.88	19	0.39

Ratings
Reward	C-
Risk	D+
Recent Upgrade/Downgrade	Up

Fund Information
Fund Type	Exchange Traded Funds
Category	Prec Metals
Sub-Category	Equity Precious Metals
Prospectus Objective	Prec Metals
Inception Date	Jan-12
Open to New Investments	Y

Prices
Price (as of 9/30/2019)	9.67
52-Week High	11.35
52-Week Low	7.32

Total Returns (%)
3-Month	6-Month	1-Year	3-Year	5-Year
4.66	8.66	18.60	-28.81	3.26

3-Year Standard Deviation	26.58
Effective Duration	

Valuation
Premium/Discount (1-Year Average)	0.25

Company Information
Provider	iShares
Manager/Tenure	Diane Hsiung (7), Greg Savage (7), Jennifer Hsui (6), 3 others
Website	http://www.ishares.com
Address	iShares 400 Howard Street San Francisco CA 94105 United States
Phone Number	800-474-2737

PERFORMANCE

Ratings History
Date	Overall Rating	Risk Rating	Reward Rating
Q3-19	C-	D+	C-
Q4-18	D+	D	C-
Q4-17	C-	D	C
Q4-16	C-	D	C
Q4-15	D	D	D

Asset & Performance History
Date	NAV	1-Year Total Return
2018	8.32	-22.28
2017	10.83	3.73
2016	10.53	92
2015	5.62	-35.67
2014	8.78	-14.47
2013	10.48	-51.38

Total Assets: $92,528,106
Asset Allocation
Asset	%
Cash	0%
Stocks	100%
US Stocks	7%
Bonds	0%
US Bonds	0%
Other	0%

Services Offered:

Investment Strategy: The investment seeks to track the investment results of the MSCI ACWI Select Silver Miners Investable Market Index. The fund generally will invest at least 90% of its assets in the component securities of the underlying index and in investments that have economic characteristics that are substantially identical to the component securities of the underlying index. The index measures the combined performance of equity securities of companies primarily engaged in the business of silver mining in both developed and emerging markets. The fund is non-diversified. **Top Holdings:** Wheaton Precious Metals Corp Pan American Silver Corp Buenaventura Mining Co Inc ADR First Majestic Silver Corp Eldorado Gold Corp

---

DeltaShares S&P 400 Managed Risk ETF   D   SELL

Ticker	Traded On	NAV	Total Assets ($)	Dividend Yield (TTM)	Turnover Ratio	Expense Ratio
DMRM	NYSE Arca	51.40	$92,522,397	1.36	435	0.45

Ratings
Reward	D+
Risk	D
Recent Upgrade/Downgrade	

Fund Information
Fund Type	Exchange Traded Funds
Category	US Equity Mid Cap
Sub-Category	Mid-Cap Blend
Prospectus Objective	Growth
Inception Date	Jul-17
Open to New Investments	Y

Prices
Price (as of 9/30/2019)	51.59
52-Week High	55.88
52-Week Low	47.01

Total Returns (%)
3-Month	6-Month	1-Year	3-Year	5-Year
-2.00	-0.28	-6.17		

3-Year Standard Deviation	
Effective Duration	

Valuation
Premium/Discount (1-Year Average)	0.00

Company Information
Provider	DeltaShares
Manager/Tenure	Blake Graves (2), Charles Lowery (2), Louis Ng (2)
Website	http://www.deltashares.com
Address	DeltaShares United States
Phone Number	

PERFORMANCE

Ratings History
Date	Overall Rating	Risk Rating	Reward Rating
Q3-19	D	D	D+
Q4-18	D	D	D+
Q4-17	U		
Q4-16			
Q4-15			

Asset & Performance History
Date	NAV	1-Year Total Return
2018	48.3	-9.18
2017	53.88	
2016		
2015		
2014		
2013		

Total Assets: $92,522,397
Asset Allocation
Asset	%
Cash	1%
Stocks	55%
US Stocks	55%
Bonds	44%
US Bonds	44%
Other	0%

Services Offered:

Investment Strategy: The investment seeks to track the investment results, before fees and expenses, of the S&P 400 Managed Risk 2.0 Index. Under normal market conditions, the fund invests a substantial portion, but at least 80%, of its assets, exclusive of collateral held from securities lending, in securities comprising the S&P 400 Managed Risk 2.0 Index. The underlying index seeks to achieve these objectives by allocating weightings among the S&P MidCap 400 Index, the S&P U.S. Treasury Bond Current 5-Year Index and the S&P U.S. Treasury Bill 0-3 Month Index. The fund is non-diversified. **Top Holdings:** S+p Mid 400 Emini Sep19 Xcme 20190920 IDEX Corp Steris PLC Leidos Holdings Inc Zebra Technologies Corp

Alpha Architect U.S. Quantitative Value ETF   C   HOLD

Ticker	Traded On	NAV	Total Assets ($)	Dividend Yield (TTM)	Turnover Ratio	Expense Ratio
QVAL	BATS	27.86	$91,941,425	1.93	46	0.49

Ratings
Reward	C
Risk	D+
Recent Upgrade/Downgrade	Up

Fund Information
Fund Type	Exchange Traded Funds
Category	US Equity Mid Cap
Sub-Category	Mid-Cap Value
Prospectus Objective	Growth & Inc
Inception Date	Oct-14
Open to New Investments	Y

Prices
Price (as of 9/30/2019)	27.86
52-Week High	30.92
52-Week Low	23.89

Total Returns (%)
3-Month	6-Month	1-Year	3-Year	5-Year
-1.13	-3.45	-8.16	25.77	

3-Year Standard Deviation	19.69
Effective Duration	

Valuation
Premium/Discount (1-Year Average)	0.07

Company Information
Provider	Alpha Architect
Manager/Tenure	Tao Wang (4)
Website	http://www.alphaarchitect.com/funds
Address	Alpha Architect 213 Foxcroft Road Broomall PA 19008 United States
Phone Number	

PERFORMANCE

Ratings History
Date	Overall Rating	Risk Rating	Reward Rating
Q3-19	C	D+	C
Q4-18	C	C-	C
Q4-17	C+	C	C+
Q4-16	C-	C-	C
Q4-15	U		

Asset & Performance History
Date	NAV	1-Year Total Return
2018	25.18	-16.55
2017	30.61	24.98
2016	24.79	12.59
2015	22.16	-13.39
2014	25.91	
2013		

Total Assets: $91,941,425
Asset Allocation
Asset	%
Cash	0%
Stocks	100%
US Stocks	97%
Bonds	0%
US Bonds	0%
Other	0%

Services Offered:

Investment Strategy: The investment seeks to track the total return performance, before fees and expenses, of the Alpha Architect Quantitative Value Index. The fund will normally invest at least 80% of its total assets in the component securities of the index. The index uses a 5-step, quantitative, rules-based methodology to identify a portfolio of approximately 40-50 undervalued U.S. equity securities with the potential for capital appreciation. **Top Holdings:** Micron Technology Inc   Applied Materials Inc   Lam Research Corp   Seagate Technology PLC HollyFrontier Corp

---

Teucrium Corn Fund   D   SELL

Ticker	Traded On	NAV	Total Assets ($)	Dividend Yield (TTM)	Turnover Ratio	Expense Ratio
CORN	NYSE Arca	15.22	$90,963,563	0		1.11

Ratings
Reward	D
Risk	D
Recent Upgrade/Downgrade	

Fund Information
Fund Type	Exchange Traded Funds
Category	Commodities Specified
Sub-Category	Commodities Agriculture
Prospectus Objective	Unaligned
Inception Date	Jun-10
Open to New Investments	Y

Prices
Price (as of 9/30/2019)	15.18
52-Week High	17.41
52-Week Low	14.30

Total Returns (%)
3-Month	6-Month	1-Year	3-Year	5-Year
-5.65	-1.12	-6.13	-18.63	-33.36

3-Year Standard Deviation	12.16
Effective Duration	

Valuation
Premium/Discount (1-Year Average)	-0.09

Company Information
Provider	Teucrium
Manager/Tenure	Management Team (9)
Website	http://www.teucriumcornfund.com
Address	Teucrium Three Main Street Suite 215 Burlington VT 05401 United States
Phone Number	802-540-0019

PERFORMANCE

Ratings History
Date	Overall Rating	Risk Rating	Reward Rating
Q3-19	D	D	D
Q4-18	D	D	D
Q4-17	D-	D-	D
Q4-16	D-	D-	D-
Q4-15	D-	D-	D-

Asset & Performance History
Date	NAV	1-Year Total Return
2018	16.11	-3.83
2017	16.75	-10.76
2016	18.77	-12.07
2015	21.24	-20.19
2014	26.62	-13.14
2013	30.64	-30.88

Total Assets: $90,963,563
Asset Allocation
Asset	%
Cash	-3%
Stocks	0%
US Stocks	0%
Bonds	0%
US Bonds	0%
Other	103%

Services Offered:

Investment Strategy: The investment seeks to have the daily changes in percentage terms of the shares' NAV reflect the daily changes in percentage terms of a weighted average of the closing settlement prices for three futures contracts for corn that are traded on the Chicago Board of Trade.
The fund invests under normal market conditions in Benchmark Component Futures Contracts or, in certain circumstances, in other Corn Futures Contracts traded on the CBOT or on foreign exchanges. **Top Holdings:** C Z0 Cbot Corn Futures Dec 2020   C Z9 Cbot Corn Futures Dec 2019   C H0 Cbot Corn Futures Mar 2020

VictoryShares US Small Cap High Div Volatility Wtd ETF   C   HOLD

Ticker	Traded On	NAV	Total Assets ($)	Dividend Yield (TTM)	Turnover Ratio	Expense Ratio
CSB	NAS CM	44.35	$90,916,295	3.22	83	0.35

Ratings
Reward	C
Risk	C-
Recent Upgrade/Downgrade	Up

Fund Information
Fund Type	Exchange Traded Funds
Category	US Equity Small Cap
Sub-Category	Small Value
Prospectus Objective	Small Company
Inception Date	Jul-15
Open to New Investments	Y

Prices
Price (as of 9/30/2019)	44.43
52-Week High	46.64
52-Week Low	38.78

Total Returns (%)
3-Month	6-Month	1-Year	3-Year	5-Year
0.91	1.51	-1.45	32.71	

3-Year Standard Deviation	15.76
Effective Duration	

Valuation
Premium/Discount (1-Year Average)	0.19

Company Information
Provider	VictoryShares
Manager/Tenure	Mannik Dhillon (1)
Website	http://www.VictorySharesLiterature.com
Address	Victory Shares 4249 Easton Way, Suite 400 Columbus OH 43219 United States
Phone Number	

PERFORMANCE

Ratings History
Date	Overall Rating	Risk Rating	Reward Rating
Q3-19	C	C-	C
Q4-18	C-	D+	C
Q4-17	C	B+	C+
Q4-16	D	D+	C
Q4-15	U		

Asset & Performance History
Date	NAV	1-Year Total Return
2018	40.13	-7.05
2017	44.57	10.92
2016	41.58	29.18
2015	32.84	
2014		
2013		

Total Assets: $90,916,295
Asset Allocation
Asset	%
Cash	1%
Stocks	99%
US Stocks	99%
Bonds	0%
US Bonds	0%
Other	0%

Services Offered:

Investment Strategy: The investment seeks to provide investment results that track the performance of the Nasdaq Victory US Small Cap High Dividend 100 Volatility Weighted Index. The fund seeks to achieve its investment objective by investing, under normal market conditions, at least 80% of its assets directly or indirectly in the securities included in the Nasdaq Victory US Small Cap High Dividend 100 Volatility Weighted Index, an unmanaged, volatility weighted index maintained exclusively by the index provider. The index identifies the 100 highest dividend yielding stocks in the Nasdaq Victory US Small Cap 500 Volatility Weighted Index. **Top Holdings:** Four Corners Property Trust Inc   Safety Insurance Group Inc   Cohen & Steers Inc   James River Group Holdings Ltd   MGE Energy Inc

---

WisdomTree Yield Enhanced U.S. Short-Term Aggregate Bond Fund   C   HOLD

Ticker	Traded On	NAV	Total Assets ($)	Dividend Yield (TTM)	Turnover Ratio	Expense Ratio
SHAG	BATS	50.40	$90,721,992	2.79	177	0.12

Ratings
Reward	C
Risk	C-
Recent Upgrade/Downgrade	Up

Fund Information
Fund Type	Exchange Traded Funds
Category	US Fixed Income
Sub-Category	Short-Term Bond
Prospectus Objective	Growth & Inc
Inception Date	May-17
Open to New Investments	Y

Prices
Price (as of 9/30/2019)	50.38
52-Week High	50.66
52-Week Low	48.47

Total Returns (%)
3-Month	6-Month	1-Year	3-Year	5-Year
1.10	3.22	6.48		

3-Year Standard Deviation	
Effective Duration	2.68

Valuation
Premium/Discount (1-Year Average)	0.09

Company Information
Provider	WisdomTree
Manager/Tenure	Sean Banai (2), Dave Goodson (2), Bob Kase (2), 2 others
Website	http://www.wisdomtree.com
Address	WisdomTree 245 Park Avenue, 35th floor New York NY 10167 United States
Phone Number	866-909-9473

PERFORMANCE

Ratings History
Date	Overall Rating	Risk Rating	Reward Rating
Q3-19	C	C-	C
Q4-18	D	D+	D
Q4-17	U		
Q4-16			
Q4-15			

Asset & Performance History
Date	NAV	1-Year Total Return
2018	48.81	0.89
2017	49.64	
2016		
2015		
2014		
2013		

Total Assets: $90,721,992
Asset Allocation
Asset	%
Cash	3%
Stocks	0%
US Stocks	0%
Bonds	96%
US Bonds	88%
Other	0%

Services Offered:

Investment Strategy: The investment seeks to track the price and yield performance, before fees and expenses, of the Bloomberg Barclays U.S. Short Aggregate Enhanced Yield Index (the "index"). Under normal circumstances, at least 80% of the fund's total assets will be invested in component securities of the index and investments that have economic characteristics that are substantially identical to the economic characteristics of such component securities. The index is designed to broadly capture the short-term U.S. investment grade, fixed income securities market while seeking to enhance yield within desired risk parameters and constraints. The fund is non-diversified. **Top Holdings:** United States Treasury Notes 2.13%   United States Treasury Notes 2%   United States Treasury Notes 2.5%   United States Treasury Notes 2.25%   United States Treasury Notes 2.88%

WisdomTree Global High Dividend Fund

C   HOLD

Ticker	Traded On	NAV	Total Assets ($)	Dividend Yield (TTM)	Turnover Ratio	Expense Ratio
DEW	NYSE Arca	46.08	$89,854,266	3.88	19	0.58

Ratings
Reward	C
Risk	D+
Recent Upgrade/Downgrade	

Fund Information
Fund Type	Exchange Traded Funds
Category	Global Equity Large Cap
Sub-Category	World Large Stock
Prospectus Objective	Equity-Income
Inception Date	Jun-06
Open to New Investments	Y

Prices
Price (as of 9/30/2019)	46.00
52-Week High	47.09
52-Week Low	40.24

Total Returns (%)
3-Month	6-Month	1-Year	3-Year	5-Year
0.05	1.22	2.35	20.85	20.49

3-Year Standard Deviation	10.23
Effective Duration	

Valuation
Premium/Discount (1-Year Average)	-0.10

Company Information
Provider	WisdomTree
Manager/Tenure	Richard A. Brown (11), Thomas J. Durante (11), Karen Q. Wong (11)
Website	http://www.wisdomtree.com
Address	WisdomTree 245 Park Avenue, 35th floor New York NY 10167 United States
Phone Number	866-909-9473

PERFORMANCE

Ratings History
Date	Overall Rating	Risk Rating	Reward Rating
Q3-19	C	D+	C
Q4-18	C-	C-	C-
Q4-17	C+	C+	C+
Q4-16	C-	D+	C
Q4-15	C-	C-	C-

Asset & Performance History
Date	NAV	1-Year Total Return
2018	41.96	-9.83
2017	48.37	15.24
2016	43.39	14.05
2015	39.41	-7.1
2014	44.16	-2.19
2013	47.3	14.87

Total Assets: $89,854,266
Asset Allocation
Asset	%
Cash	0%
Stocks	100%
US Stocks	58%
Bonds	0%
US Bonds	0%
Other	0%

Services Offered:

Investment Strategy: The investment seeks to track the price and yield performance of the WisdomTree Global High Dividend Index. The fund will invest at least 95% of its total assets in component securities of the index and investments that have economic characteristics that are substantially identical to the economic characteristics of such component securities. The index is a fundamentally weighted index that is comprised of high dividend-yielding companies selected from the WisdomTree Global Dividend Index, which defines the dividend-paying universe of companies in the U.S., developed countries and emerging markets throughout the world. The fund is non-diversified. **Top Holdings:** AT&T Inc Exxon Mobil Corp Procter & Gamble Co Verizon Communications Inc Chevron Corp

SPDR® Global Dow ETF

C   HOLD

Ticker	Traded On	NAV	Total Assets ($)	Dividend Yield (TTM)	Turnover Ratio	Expense Ratio
DGT	NYSE Arca		$89,736,011	2.91	11	0.5

Ratings
Reward	C
Risk	D+
Recent Upgrade/Downgrade	

Fund Information
Fund Type	Exchange Traded Funds
Category	Global Equity Large Cap
Sub-Category	World Large Stock
Prospectus Objective	World Stock
Inception Date	Sep-00
Open to New Investments	Y

Prices
Price (as of 9/30/2019)	83.40
52-Week High	86.69
52-Week Low	72.28

Total Returns (%)
3-Month	6-Month	1-Year	3-Year	5-Year
-1.81	0.73	-0.73	31.58	33.91

3-Year Standard Deviation	11.76
Effective Duration	

Valuation
Premium/Discount (1-Year Average)	-0.16

Company Information
Provider	SPDR State Street Global Advisors
Manager/Tenure	Michael J. Feehily (7), Karl A. Schneider (4), Kathleen Morgan (0)
Website	http://www.spdrs.com
Address	SPDR State Street Global Advisors State Street Financial Center, 1 Lincoln Street Boston MA 02111-2900 United States
Phone Number	617-786-3000

PERFORMANCE

Ratings History
Date	Overall Rating	Risk Rating	Reward Rating
Q3-19	C	D+	C
Q4-18	C-	D+	C-
Q4-17	B-	C+	B-
Q4-16	C	D+	C
Q4-15	C	D+	C

Asset & Performance History
Date	NAV	1-Year Total Return
2018	75.68	-9.2
2017	85.29	24.47
2016	69.98	10.04
2015	64.69	-4.41
2014	69.22	2.82
2013	69.09	26.95

Total Assets: $89,736,011
Asset Allocation
Asset	%
Cash	0%
Stocks	100%
US Stocks	48%
Bonds	0%
US Bonds	0%
Other	0%

Services Offered: Dividend Investment Plan, CashInvestment Plan

Investment Strategy: The investment seeks to provide investment results that, before fees and expenses, correspond generally to the total return performance of the Global Dow that tracks the performance of multinational blue-chip issuers. The fund generally invests substantially all, but at least 80%, of its total assets in the securities comprising the index. The index is made up of 150 companies from around the world. It may purchase a subset of the securities in the index in an effort to hold a portfolio of securities with generally the same risk and return characteristics of the index. The fund is non-diversified. **Top Holdings:** Starbucks Corp Gazprom PJSC ADR Procter & Gamble Co MTN Group Ltd McDonald's Corp

C-Tracks Exchange-Traded Notes Based on the Performance of the Miller/Howard MLP Fundamental Index   D

Ticker	Traded On	NAV	Total Assets ($)	Dividend Yield (TTM)	Turnover Ratio	Expense Ratio
MLPC	NYSE Arca	12.76	$89,317,200	6.22		0.95

Ratings

Reward	D
Risk	D
Recent Upgrade/Downgrade	Down

Fund Information

Fund Type	Exchange Traded Funds
Category	Energy Sector Equity
Sub-Category	Energy Limited Partnership
Prospectus Objective	Growth
Inception Date	Sep-13
Open to New Investments	Y

Prices

Price (as of 9/30/2019)	12.76
52-Week High	15.12
52-Week Low	11.82

Total Returns (%)

3-Month	6-Month	1-Year	3-Year	5-Year
-6.46	-5.49	-11.10	-10.02	-43.96

3-Year Standard Deviation	17.64
Effective Duration	

Valuation

Premium/Discount (1-Year Average)	0.00

Company Information

Provider	Citigroup
Manager/Tenure	No Manager (6)
Website	
Address	Citigroup 388 Greenwich Street New York NULL NULL United States
Phone Number	

PERFORMANCE

Ratings History

Date	Overall Rating	Risk Rating	Reward Rating
Q3-19	D	D	D
Q4-18	D	D+	D
Q4-17	D	D	D+
Q4-16	D	D	D
Q4-15	D	D	D

Asset & Performance History

Date	NAV	1-Year Total Return
2018	12.05	-18
2017	15.22	-5.08
2016	16.7	14.78
2015	15.46	-35.53
2014	25.5	1.99
2013	26.2	

Total Assets: $89,317,200

Asset Allocation

Asset	%
Cash	%
Stocks	%
US Stocks	%
Bonds	%
US Bonds	%
Other	%

Services Offered:

Investment Strategy: The investment seeks a return that based on the Performance of the Miller/Howard MLP Fundamental Index (the "index"), which the adviser refer to as the C-Tracks, are unsecured senior debt securities issued by Citigroup Inc.
The index is designed to measure the performance of 25 energy master limited partnerships ("MLPs") selected quarterly by a methodology that is based upon certain quantitative fundamental factors of publicly traded MLPs, including distribution growth, estimated capital expenditures and distribution coverage. **Top Holdings:**

---

iShares Edge Investment Grade Enhanced Bond ETF   C   HOLD

Ticker	Traded On	NAV	Total Assets ($)	Dividend Yield (TTM)	Turnover Ratio	Expense Ratio
IGEB	BATS	52.51	$89,268,407	3.51	63	

Ratings

Reward	C
Risk	C-
Recent Upgrade/Downgrade	Up

Fund Information

Fund Type	Exchange Traded Funds
Category	US Fixed Income
Sub-Category	Corporate Bond
Prospectus Objective	Corp Bond - Gen
Inception Date	Jul-17
Open to New Investments	Y

Prices

Price (as of 9/30/2019)	52.76
52-Week High	53.08
52-Week Low	46.87

Total Returns (%)

3-Month	6-Month	1-Year	3-Year	5-Year
3.18	8.69	14.03		

3-Year Standard Deviation	
Effective Duration	

Valuation

Premium/Discount (1-Year Average)	0.28

Company Information

Provider	iShares
Manager/Tenure	James Mauro (2), Scott Radell (2)
Website	http://www.ishares.com
Address	iShares 400 Howard Street San Francisco CA 94105 United States
Phone Number	800-474-2737

PERFORMANCE

Ratings History

Date	Overall Rating	Risk Rating	Reward Rating
Q3-19	C	C-	C
Q4-18	D	C-	D
Q4-17	U		
Q4-16			
Q4-15			

Asset & Performance History

Date	NAV	1-Year Total Return
2018	47.14	-3.06
2017	50.39	
2016		
2015		
2014		
2013		

Total Assets: $89,268,407

Asset Allocation

Asset	%
Cash	1%
Stocks	0%
US Stocks	0%
Bonds	98%
US Bonds	89%
Other	0%

Services Offered:

Investment Strategy: The investment seeks to track the investment results of the BlackRock Investment Grade Enhanced Bond Index. The fund will invest at least 80% of its assets in the component securities of the underlying index and may invest up to 20% of its assets in certain index futures, options, options on index futures, swap contracts or other derivatives, as related to its underlying index, cash and cash equivalents, other investment companies, as well as in securities and other instruments not included in the underlying index. The index consists of U.S. dollar-denominated, investment-grade corporate bonds. **Top Holdings:** Citigroup Inc. 3.7% B.A.T. Capital Corporation 3.56% JPMorgan Chase & Co. 3.2% HSBC Holdings plc 3.9% Kinder Morgan, Inc. 5.3%

Invesco Fundamental Investment Grade Corporate Bond ETF   C   HOLD

Ticker	Traded On	NAV	Total Assets ($)	Dividend Yield (TTM)	Turnover Ratio	Expense Ratio
PFIG	NYSE Arca	26.19	$89,052,445	2.92		0.22

Ratings
Reward	C+
Risk	C-
Recent Upgrade/Downgrade	

Fund Information
Fund Type	Exchange Traded Funds
Category	US Fixed Income
Sub-Category	Corporate Bond
Prospectus Objective	Corp Bond - Gen
Inception Date	Sep-11
Open to New Investments	Y

Prices
Price (as of 9/30/2019)	26.19
52-Week High	26.38
52-Week Low	24.40

Total Returns (%)
3-Month	6-Month	1-Year	3-Year	5-Year
1.79	5.21	9.56	9.38	17.60

3-Year Standard Deviation	2.77
Effective Duration	4.48

Valuation
Premium/Discount (1-Year Average)	0.06

Company Information
Provider	Invesco
Manager/Tenure	Philip Fang (8), Peter Hubbard (8), Jeffrey W. Kernagis (8), 2 others
Website	http://www.invesco.com/us
Address	Invesco 11 Greenway Plaza, Ste. 2500 Houston TX 77046 United States
Phone Number	800-659-1005

PERFORMANCE

Ratings History
Date	Overall Rating	Risk Rating	Reward Rating
Q3-19	C	C-	C+
Q4-18	C-	C-	D+
Q4-17	B	A	C
Q4-16	C	C-	C
Q4-15	C	D+	C

Asset & Performance History
Date	NAV	1-Year Total Return
2018	24.64	-0.59
2017	25.51	3.46
2016	25.29	4.02
2015	24.94	0.75
2014	25.39	4.6
2013	24.86	-1.06

Total Assets: $89,052,445
Asset Allocation
Asset	%
Cash	1%
Stocks	0%
US Stocks	0%
Bonds	99%
US Bonds	98%
Other	0%

Services Offered:

Investment Strategy: The investment seeks to track the investment results (before fees and expenses) of the RAFI® Bonds U.S. Investment Grade 1-10 Index (the "underlying index"). The fund generally will invest at least 80% of its total assets in the securities that comprise the underlying index. The underlying index is comprised of U.S. dollar-denominated investment grade corporate bonds which are SEC-registered securities or Rule 144A securities with registration rights (issued after July 31, 2013) and whose issuers are public companies listed on a major U.S. stock exchange. **Top Holdings:** JPMorgan Chase & Co. 2.95% Apple Inc. 3.25% Wells Fargo & Company 3% Exxon Mobil Corporation 3.04% WALMART INC 3.7%

First Trust Strategic Income ETF   C   HOLD

Ticker	Traded On	NAV	Total Assets ($)	Dividend Yield (TTM)	Turnover Ratio	Expense Ratio
FDIV	NAS CM	50.81	$88,922,577	4.17	113	0.87

Ratings
Reward	C+
Risk	D+
Recent Upgrade/Downgrade	

Fund Information
Fund Type	Exchange Traded Funds
Category	Cautious Allocation
Sub-Category	Allocation--30% to 50% Equity
Prospectus Objective	Income
Inception Date	Aug-14
Open to New Investments	Y

Prices
Price (as of 9/30/2019)	50.81
52-Week High	51.84
52-Week Low	45.32

Total Returns (%)
3-Month	6-Month	1-Year	3-Year	5-Year
1.74	3.98	7.92	15.24	27.02

3-Year Standard Deviation	5.71
Effective Duration	3.62

Valuation
Premium/Discount (1-Year Average)	-0.01

Company Information
Provider	First Trust
Manager/Tenure	Richard Bernstein (5), Jeremiah Charles (5), Jon C. Erickson (5), 20 others
Website	http://www.ftportfolios.com/
Address	First Trust 120 E. Liberty Drive, Suite 400 Wheaton IL 60187 United States
Phone Number	800-621-1675

PERFORMANCE

Ratings History
Date	Overall Rating	Risk Rating	Reward Rating
Q3-19	C	D+	C+
Q4-18	C-	C-	C-
Q4-17	B-	B	C+
Q4-16	C-	D+	C
Q4-15	D-	D+	D

Asset & Performance History
Date	NAV	1-Year Total Return
2018	46.35	-4.05
2017	51.13	6.47
2016	49.9	11.71
2015	46.46	-4.38
2014	50.54	
2013		

Total Assets: $88,922,577
Asset Allocation
Asset	%
Cash	3%
Stocks	37%
US Stocks	33%
Bonds	50%
US Bonds	33%
Other	0%

Services Offered:

Investment Strategy: The investment seeks risk-adjusted income; capital appreciation is the secondary objective. The fund is a multi-manager, multi-strategy actively managed ETF. Its investment categories will be: (i) high yield corporate bonds, and first lien senior secured floating rate bank loans; (ii) mortgage-related investments; (iii) preferred securities; (iv) international sovereign bonds; (v) equity securities of Energy Infrastructure Companies, certain of which are referred to as master limited partnerships; and (vi) dividend paying U.S. exchange-traded equity securities of companies and depositary receipts. It is non-diversified. **Top Holdings:** First Trust Tactical High Yield ETF First Trust Preferred Sec & Inc ETF First Trust Emerging Mkts Lcl Ccy Bd ETF iShares MBS ETF First Trust Instl Pref Secs and Inc ETF

VictoryShares International High Div Volatility Wtd ETF

C-   HOLD

Ticker	Traded On	NAV	Total Assets ($)	Dividend Yield (TTM)	Turnover Ratio	Expense Ratio
CID	NAS CM	31.66	$88,658,998	5.01	76	0.45

Ratings
Reward   C-
Risk   D+
Recent Upgrade/Downgrade

Fund Information
Fund Type   Exchange Traded Funds
Category   Global Equity Large Cap
Sub-Category   Foreign Large Value
Prospectus Objective   Foreign Stock
Inception Date   Aug-15
Open to New Investments   Y

Prices
Price (as of 9/30/2019)   31.77
52-Week High   33.74
52-Week Low   29.45

Total Returns (%)

3-Month	6-Month	1-Year	3-Year	5-Year
-1.51	0.00	0.28	12.68	

3-Year Standard Deviation   10.2
Effective Duration

Valuation
Premium/Discount (1-Year Average)   0.44

Company Information
Provider   VictoryShares
Manager/Tenure   Mannik Dhillon (1)
Website   http://www.VictorySharesLiterature.com
Address   Victory Shares 4249 Easton Way,
                   Suite 400 Columbus OH 43219 United
                   States
Phone Number

PERFORMANCE

Ratings History

Date	Overall Rating	Risk Rating	Reward Rating
Q3-19	C-	D+	C-
Q4-18	D+	D+	D+
Q4-17	C	B	C
Q4-16	D	D+	D
Q4-15	U		

Asset & Performance History

Date	NAV	1-Year Total Return
2018	29.9	-13.28
2017	36.05	19.55
2016	31.29	-0.26
2015	32.27	
2014		
2013		

Total Assets: $88,658,998
Asset Allocation

Asset	%
Cash	0%
Stocks	100%
US Stocks	1%
Bonds	0%
US Bonds	0%
Other	0%

Services Offered:

Investment Strategy: The investment seeks to provide investment results that track the performance of the Nasdaq Victory International High Dividend 100 Volatility Weighted Index. The fund seeks to achieve its investment objective by investing, under normal market conditions, at least 80% of its assets directly or indirectly in the securities included in the Nasdaq Victory International High Dividend 100 Volatility Weighted Index, an unmanaged, volatility weighted index maintained exclusively by the index provider. The index identifies the 100 highest dividend yielding stocks in the Nasdaq Victory International 500 Volatility Weighted Index. **Top Holdings:** TELUS Corp Emera, Inc. BCE Inc Hydro One Ltd Power Assets Holdings Ltd

VanEck Vectors Low Carbon Energy ETF

C   HOLD

Ticker	Traded On	NAV	Total Assets ($)	Dividend Yield (TTM)	Turnover Ratio	Expense Ratio
SMOG	NYSE Arca	63.95	$88,455,696	0.53	31	0.63

Ratings
Reward   C+
Risk   C-
Recent Upgrade/Downgrade

Fund Information
Fund Type   Exchange Traded Funds
Category   Equity Misc
Sub-Category   Miscellaneous Sector
Prospectus Objective   Natl Res
Inception Date   May-07
Open to New Investments   Y

Prices
Price (as of 9/30/2019)   64.01
52-Week High   67.90
52-Week Low   51.82

Total Returns (%)

3-Month	6-Month	1-Year	3-Year	5-Year
-3.31	0.50	9.77	24.20	15.41

3-Year Standard Deviation   16.61
Effective Duration

Valuation
Premium/Discount (1-Year Average)   -0.19

Company Information
Provider   VanEck
Manager/Tenure   Hao-Hung (Peter) Liao (12), Guo Hua
                  (Jason) Jin (1)
Website   http://www.vaneck.com
Address   Van Eck Associates Corporation 666
                 Third Avenue New York NY 10017
                 United States
Phone Number   800-826-1115

PERFORMANCE

Ratings History

Date	Overall Rating	Risk Rating	Reward Rating
Q3-19	C	C-	C+
Q4-18	C-	D+	C-
Q4-17	C+	B-	C+
Q4-16	D+	D+	D+
Q4-15	C-	D+	C-

Asset & Performance History

Date	NAV	1-Year Total Return
2018	55.1	-8.96
2017	60.94	21.89
2016	50.62	-5.24
2015	54.57	1.45
2014	54.09	-3.04
2013	55.9	69.71

Total Assets: $88,455,696
Asset Allocation

Asset	%
Cash	0%
Stocks	100%
US Stocks	68%
Bonds	0%
US Bonds	0%
Other	0%

Services Offered:

Investment Strategy: The investment seeks to replicate as closely as possible, before fees and expenses, the price and yield performance of the Ardour Global IndexSM (Extra Liquid). The fund normally invests at least 80% of its total assets in stocks of low carbon energy companies. Such companies may include small- and medium-capitalization companies and foreign issuers. "Low carbon energy companies" refers to companies primarily engaged in alternative energy, including renewable energy, alternative fuels and related enabling technologies (such as advanced batteries). It is non-diversified. **Top Holdings:** Tesla Inc Microchip Technology Inc Eaton Corp PLC AMETEK Inc Vestas Wind Systems A/S

ALPS Clean Energy ETF   C   HOLD

Ticker	Traded On	NAV	Total Assets ($)	Dividend Yield (TTM)	Turnover Ratio	Expense Ratio
ACES	BATS	30.84	$87,903,174	1.76	9	0.65

Ratings
Reward	C
Risk	D+
Recent Upgrade/Downgrade	Up

Fund Information
Fund Type	Exchange Traded Funds
Category	Energy Sector Equity
Sub-Category	Equity Energy
Prospectus Objective	Growth & Inc
Inception Date	Jun-18
Open to New Investments	Y

Prices
Price (as of 9/30/2019)	30.97
52-Week High	32.11
52-Week Low	21.36

Total Returns (%)
3-Month	6-Month	1-Year	3-Year	5-Year
3.79	14.35	23.09		

3-Year Standard Deviation	
Effective Duration	

Valuation
Premium/Discount (1-Year Average)	0.30

Company Information
Provider	ALPS
Manager/Tenure	Andrew Hicks (1), Ryan Mischker (1)
Website	http://www.alpsfunds.com
Address	ALPS 1290 Broadway, Suite 1100 Denver CO 80203 United States
Phone Number	866-759-5679

PERFORMANCE

Ratings History
Date	Overall Rating	Risk Rating	Reward Rating
Q3-19	C	D+	C
Q4-18	U		
Q4-17			
Q4-16			
Q4-15			

Asset & Performance History
Date	NAV	1-Year Total Return
2018	22.68	
2017		
2016		
2015		
2014		
2013		

Total Assets: $87,903,174

Asset Allocation
Asset	%
Cash	0%
Stocks	100%
US Stocks	84%
Bonds	0%
US Bonds	0%
Other	0%

Services Offered:

Investment Strategy: The investment seeks investment results that correspond (before fees and expenses) generally to the performance of its underlying index, the CIBC Atlas Clean Energy Index (ticker symbol NACEX) (the "underlying index"). The fund will invest at least 80% of its net assets in securities that comprise the underlying index. The underlying index utilizes a rules-based methodology developed by CIBC National Trust Company (the "index provider"), which is designed to provide exposure to a diverse set of U.S. and Canadian companies involved in the clean energy sector including renewables and clean technology. The fund is non-diversified. **Top Holdings:** Enphase Energy Inc   Universal Display Corp   Pattern Energy Group Inc Class A   Ormat Technologies Inc   Itron Inc

SPDR® Portfolio Corporate Bond ETF   C   HOLD

Ticker	Traded On	NAV	Total Assets ($)	Dividend Yield (TTM)	Turnover Ratio	Expense Ratio
SPBO	NYSE Arca		$87,685,409	3.53	29	0.06

Ratings
Reward	B-
Risk	D+
Recent Upgrade/Downgrade	

Fund Information
Fund Type	Exchange Traded Funds
Category	US Fixed Income
Sub-Category	Corporate Bond
Prospectus Objective	Growth
Inception Date	Apr-11
Open to New Investments	Y

Prices
Price (as of 9/30/2019)	33.83
52-Week High	34.21
52-Week Low	30.11

Total Returns (%)
3-Month	6-Month	1-Year	3-Year	5-Year
3.07	8.19	13.31	14.01	23.91

3-Year Standard Deviation	4.06
Effective Duration	7.90

Valuation
Premium/Discount (1-Year Average)	0.21

Company Information
Provider	SPDR State Street Global Advisors
Manager/Tenure	Kyle Kelly (6), Christopher DiStefano (4), Michael J. Brunell (0)
Website	http://www.spdrs.com
Address	SPDR State Street Global Advisors State Street Financial Center, 1 Lincoln Street Boston MA 02111-2900 United States
Phone Number	617-786-3000

PERFORMANCE

Ratings History
Date	Overall Rating	Risk Rating	Reward Rating
Q3-19	C	D+	B-
Q4-18	D+	D+	D+
Q4-17	B-	B+	C
Q4-16	C	C-	C
Q4-15	C-	D+	C

Asset & Performance History
Date	NAV	1-Year Total Return
2018	30.49	-2.31
2017	32.34	5.52
2016	31.55	5.4
2015	30.86	-1.07
2014	32.14	7.06
2013	31.01	-1.23

Total Assets: $87,685,409

Asset Allocation
Asset	%
Cash	0%
Stocks	0%
US Stocks	0%
Bonds	98%
US Bonds	87%
Other	0%

Services Offered:

Investment Strategy: The investment seeks investment results that, before fees and expenses, correspond generally to the price and yield performance of an index that tracks the Bloomberg Barclays US Corporate Bond Index. The fund generally invests substantially all, but at least 80%, of its total assets in the securities comprising the index or in securities that the Adviser determines have economic characteristics that are substantially identical to the economic characteristics of the securities that comprise the index. The index is designed to measure the performance of the investment grade corporate bond market. It is non-diversified. **Top Holdings:** CVS Health Corp 4.78%   Apple Inc. 2.7%   Bank of America Corporation 3.5%   Goldman Sachs Group, Inc. 3%   AT&T Inc 4.75%

UBS ETRACS Linked to the Wells Fargo Business Development Company Index ETN   C   HOLD

Ticker	Traded On	NAV	Total Assets ($)	Dividend Yield (TTM)	Turnover Ratio	Expense Ratio
BDCS	NYSE Arca	20.13	$87,647,859	8.53		0.85

Ratings

Reward	C
Risk	C-
Recent Upgrade/Downgrade	

Fund Information

Fund Type	Exchange Traded Funds
Category	Financials Sector Equity
Sub-Category	Financial
Prospectus Objective	Growth
Inception Date	Apr-11
Open to New Investments	Y

Prices

Price (as of 9/30/2019)	20.16
52-Week High	20.67
52-Week Low	17.15

Total Returns (%)

3-Month	6-Month	1-Year	3-Year	5-Year
3.06	5.82	6.34	17.80	26.30

3-Year Standard Deviation	13.21
Effective Duration	

Valuation

Premium/Discount (1-Year Average)	-0.02

Company Information

Provider	UBS Group AG
Manager/Tenure	No Manager (8)
Website	http://www.ubs.com
Address	Bahnhofstrasse 45 Zürich 8098 Switzerland
Phone Number	412-037-1952

PERFORMANCE

Ratings History

Date	Overall Rating	Risk Rating	Reward Rating
Q3-19	C	C-	C
Q4-18	C-	C-	C-
Q4-17	C	C+	C
Q4-16	C	C-	C
Q4-15	C-	C-	C-

Asset & Performance History

Date	NAV	1-Year Total Return
2018	17.69	-6.95
2017	20.71	-0.16
2016	22.66	23.09
2015	20.1	-4.75
2014	22.89	-8.26
2013	26.85	15.06

Total Assets: $87,647,859

Asset Allocation

Asset	%
Cash	%
Stocks	%
US Stocks	%
Bonds	%
US Bonds	%
Other	%

Services Offered:

Investment Strategy: The investment seeks to replicate, net of expenses, the performance of the Wells Fargo Business Development Company Index.
The index is a float adjusted, capitalization-weighted index that is intended to measure the performance of all Business Development Companies ("BDC") that are listed on the New York Stock Exchange or NASDAQ and satisfy specified market capitalization and other eligibility requirements. The BDC business model is to lend to small and midsized companies at high yield equivalent rates while also at times taking equity stakes in such companies. **Top Holdings:**

WisdomTree U.S. Total Earnings Fund   C   HOLD

Ticker	Traded On	NAV	Total Assets ($)	Dividend Yield (TTM)	Turnover Ratio	Expense Ratio
EXT	NYSE Arca	33.89	$86,419,070	2.05	22	0.28

Ratings

Reward	C
Risk	D+
Recent Upgrade/Downgrade	

Fund Information

Fund Type	Exchange Traded Funds
Category	US Equity Large Cap Blend
Sub-Category	Large Blend
Prospectus Objective	Growth & Inc
Inception Date	Feb-07
Open to New Investments	Y

Prices

Price (as of 9/30/2019)	33.90
52-Week High	34.53
52-Week Low	26.85

Total Returns (%)

3-Month	6-Month	1-Year	3-Year	5-Year
1.23	4.48	3.49	44.23	61.24

3-Year Standard Deviation	13.06
Effective Duration	

Valuation

Premium/Discount (1-Year Average)	-0.01

Company Information

Provider	WisdomTree
Manager/Tenure	Richard A. Brown (11), Thomas J. Durante (11), Karen Q. Wong (11)
Website	http://www.wisdomtree.com
Address	WisdomTree 245 Park Avenue, 35th floor New York NY 10167 United States
Phone Number	866-909-9473

PERFORMANCE

Ratings History

Date	Overall Rating	Risk Rating	Reward Rating
Q3-19	C	D+	C
Q4-18	C	C-	C
Q4-17	B	B-	B
Q4-16	C+	D+	B
Q4-15	C	C-	C

Asset & Performance History

Date	NAV	1-Year Total Return
2018	28.54	-7.79
2017	31.8	21.71
2016	26.58	14.75
2015	23.64	-2.07
2014	24.67	12.58
2013	22.27	33.66

Total Assets: $86,419,070

Asset Allocation

Asset	%
Cash	0%
Stocks	100%
US Stocks	100%
Bonds	0%
US Bonds	0%
Other	0%

Services Offered:

Investment Strategy: The investment seeks to track the price and yield performance, before fees and expenses, of the WisdomTree U.S. Total Market Index. Under normal circumstances, at least 95% of the fund's total assets (exclusive of collateral held from securities lending) will be invested in component securities of the index and investments that have economic characteristics that are substantially identical to the economic characteristics of such component securities. The index is a fundamentally weighted index that is comprised of earnings-generating companies within the broad U.S. stock market. The fund is non-diversified. **Top Holdings:** Apple Inc Microsoft Corp Berkshire Hathaway Inc B Alphabet Inc A JPMorgan Chase & Co

---

iShares Core 5-10 Year USD Bond ETF   C   HOLD

Ticker	Traded On	NAV	Total Assets ($)	Dividend Yield (TTM)	Turnover Ratio	Expense Ratio
IMTB	NYSE Arca	50.66	$86,122,216	3.05	481	0.06

Ratings
Reward	C
Risk	C-
Recent Upgrade/Downgrade	Up

Fund Information
Fund Type	Exchange Traded Funds
Category	US Fixed Income
Sub-Category	Intermediate Core-Plus Bond
Prospectus Objective	Income
Inception Date	Nov-16
Open to New Investments	Y

Prices
Price (as of 9/30/2019)	50.75
52-Week High	51.08
52-Week Low	46.97

Total Returns (%)
3-Month	6-Month	1-Year	3-Year	5-Year
1.73	4.89	9.83	10.13	

3-Year Standard Deviation
Effective Duration

Valuation
Premium/Discount (1-Year Average)	0.28

Company Information
Provider	iShares
Manager/Tenure	James Mauro (2), Scott Radell (2)
Website	http://www.ishares.com
Address	iShares 400 Howard Street San Francisco CA 94105 United States
Phone Number	800-474-2737

PERFORMANCE

Ratings History
Date	Overall Rating	Risk Rating	Reward Rating
Q3-19	C	C-	C
Q4-18	D	D+	D
Q4-17	D	A-	D+
Q4-16	U		
Q4-15			

Asset & Performance History
Date	NAV	1-Year Total Return
2018	47.82	0.06
2017	49.27	3.88
2016	48.76	
2015		
2014		
2013		

Total Assets: $86,122,216
Asset Allocation
Asset	%
Cash	1%
Stocks	0%
US Stocks	0%
Bonds	98%
US Bonds	90%
Other	0%

Services Offered:

Investment Strategy: The investment seeks to track the investment results of the Bloomberg Barclays U.S. Universal 5-10 Year Index. The fund generally will invest at least 90% of its assets in the component securities of the underlying index and may invest up to 10% of its assets in certain futures, options and swap contracts, cash and cash equivalents, including shares of money market funds advised by BFA or its affiliates. The index measures the performance of U.S. dollar-denominated taxable bonds that are rated either investment-grade or high yield with remaining effective maturities between five and ten years. It is non-diversified. **Top Holdings:** Gnma2 30yr 2017 Production Fnma Pass-Thru I 3% Gnma2 30yr 2012 Production United States Treasury Notes 2.25% United States Treasury Notes 2.88%

Direxion Daily MSCI India Bull 3x Shares   D+   SELL

Ticker	Traded On	NAV	Total Assets ($)	Dividend Yield (TTM)	Turnover Ratio	Expense Ratio
INDL	NYSE Arca	61.39	$85,929,064	0.93	59	1.38

Ratings
Reward	D
Risk	D+
Recent Upgrade/Downgrade	Down

Fund Information
Fund Type	Exchange Traded Funds
Category	Trading Tools
Sub-Category	Trading--Leveraged Equity
Prospectus Objective	Foreign Stock
Inception Date	Mar-10
Open to New Investments	Y

Prices
Price (as of 9/30/2019)	61.35
52-Week High	81.14
52-Week Low	46.97

Total Returns (%)
3-Month	6-Month	1-Year	3-Year	5-Year
-20.49	-21.55	-5.51	6.14	-28.47

3-Year Standard Deviation 49.85
Effective Duration

Valuation
Premium/Discount (1-Year Average)	-0.21

Company Information
Provider	Direxion Funds
Manager/Tenure	Paul Brigandi (9), Tony Ng (4)
Website	http://www.direxionfunds.com
Address	Direxion Funds 1301 Avenue Of The Americas (6th Avenue) New York NY 10019 United States
Phone Number	646-572-3390

PERFORMANCE

Ratings History
Date	Overall Rating	Risk Rating	Reward Rating
Q3-19	D+	D+	D
Q4-18	D+	D	D+
Q4-17	C	D+	B-
Q4-16	D	D	D+
Q4-15	C-	D+	C

Asset & Performance History
Date	NAV	1-Year Total Return
2018	67.54	-33.91
2017	102.39	128.21
2016	45.01	-15.9
2015	53.52	-33.33
2014	80.28	46.07
2013	54.96	-31.74

Total Assets: $85,929,064
Asset Allocation
Asset	%
Cash	59%
Stocks	41%
US Stocks	0%
Bonds	0%
US Bonds	0%
Other	0%

Services Offered:

Investment Strategy: The investment seeks daily investment results, before fees and expenses, of 300% of the daily performance of the MSCI India Index. The fund, under normal circumstances, invests at least 80% of its net assets in financial instruments, such as swap agreements, and securities of the index, ETFs that track the index and other financial instruments that provide daily leveraged exposure to the index or ETFs that track the index. The index is designed to measure the performance of the large- and mid-capitalization segments of the Indian equity market, covering approximately 85% of the Indian equity universe. The fund is non-diversified. **Top Holdings:** iShares MSCI India ETF Ishares Msci India Etf iShares MSCI India ETF Ishares Msci India Etf Dreyfus Govt Cm Inst 289

Invesco S&P MidCap 400® Equal Weight ETF   C-   HOLD

Ticker	Traded On	NAV	Total Assets ($)	Dividend Yield (TTM)	Turnover Ratio	Expense Ratio
EWMC	NYSE Arca	63.33	$85,495,202	1.33		0.4

Ratings
Reward   C-
Risk   D+
Recent Upgrade/Downgrade

Fund Information
Fund Type	Exchange Traded Funds
Category	US Equity Mid Cap
Sub-Category	Mid-Cap Blend
Prospectus Objective	Growth
Inception Date	Dec-10
Open to New Investments	Y

Prices
Price (as of 9/30/2019)	63.31
52-Week High	67.70
52-Week Low	52.58

Total Returns (%)
3-Month	6-Month	1-Year	3-Year	5-Year
-1.82	-1.45	-5.06	23.82	39.01

3-Year Standard Deviation   16.64
Effective Duration

Valuation
Premium/Discount (1-Year Average)   -0.07

Company Information
Provider	Invesco
Manager/Tenure	Peter Hubbard (1), Michael Jeanette (1), Tony Seisser (1)
Website	http://www.invesco.com/us
Address	Invesco 11 Greenway Plaza, Ste. 2500 Houston TX 77046 United States
Phone Number	800-659-1005

PERFORMANCE

Ratings History
Date	Overall Rating	Risk Rating	Reward Rating
Q3-19	C-	D+	C-
Q4-18	C-	D+	C-
Q4-17	B	B	B
Q4-16	D+	D+	D+
Q4-15	C	C-	C

Asset & Performance History
Date	NAV	1-Year Total Return
2018	55.72	-12.26
2017	64.35	13.56
2016	57.4	22.53
2015	47.4	-5.13
2014	50.65	9.93
2013	46.67	35.06

Total Assets: $85,495,202
Asset Allocation
Asset	%
Cash	0%
Stocks	100%
US Stocks	100%
Bonds	0%
US Bonds	0%
Other	0%

Services Offered:

Investment Strategy: The investment seeks to track the investment results (before fees and expenses) of the S&P MidCap 400® Equal Weight Index (the "underlying index"). The fund generally will invest at least 90% of its total assets in the securities that comprise the underlying index. The underlying index consists of all of the components of the S&P MidCap 400® Index, a broad-based index of approximately 400 securities that measures the mid-cap segment of the U.S. equity market. The fund is non-diversified. **Top Holdings:** Sothebys Class A Limited Voting Weight Watchers International Inc Genworth Financial Inc Royal Gold Inc Cirrus Logic Inc

---

SPDR® MSCI EAFE Fossil Fuel Free ETF   C-   HOLD

Ticker	Traded On	NAV	Total Assets ($)	Dividend Yield (TTM)	Turnover Ratio	Expense Ratio
EFAX	NYSE Arca		$84,176,987	2.87	5	0.2

Ratings
Reward   C-
Risk   D+
Recent Upgrade/Downgrade   Up

Fund Information
Fund Type	Exchange Traded Funds
Category	Global Equity Large Cap
Sub-Category	Foreign Large Blend
Prospectus Objective	Growth & Inc
Inception Date	Oct-16
Open to New Investments	Y

Prices
Price (as of 9/30/2019)	67.83
52-Week High	70.26
52-Week Low	58.71

Total Returns (%)
3-Month	6-Month	1-Year	3-Year	5-Year
-0.70	2.58	-0.20	23.71	

3-Year Standard Deviation
Effective Duration

Valuation
Premium/Discount (1-Year Average)   0.07

Company Information
Provider	SPDR State Street Global Advisors
Manager/Tenure	Michael J. Feehily (2), Karl A. Schneider (2), John Law (1)
Website	http://www.spdrs.com
Address	SPDR State Street Global Advisors State Street Financial Center, 1 Lincoln Street Boston MA 02111-2900 United States
Phone Number	617-786-3000

PERFORMANCE

Ratings History
Date	Overall Rating	Risk Rating	Reward Rating
Q3-19	C-	D+	C-
Q4-18	D	D	D
Q4-17	D	A	D+
Q4-16	U		
Q4-15			

Asset & Performance History
Date	NAV	1-Year Total Return
2018	60.53	-14.35
2017	72.65	24.69
2016	60.06	
2015		
2014		
2013		

Total Assets: $84,176,987
Asset Allocation
Asset	%
Cash	0%
Stocks	100%
US Stocks	2%
Bonds	0%
US Bonds	0%
Other	0%

Services Offered:

Investment Strategy: The investment seeks to provide investment results that, before fees and expenses, correspond generally to the total return performance of the MSCI EAFE ex Fossil Fuels Index. Under normal market conditions, the fund generally invests substantially all, but at least 80%, of its total assets in the securities comprising the index and in depositary receipts based on securities comprising the index. The index is designed to measure the performance of companies in the MSCI EAFE Index that are "fossil fuel reserves free," which are defined as companies that do not own fossil fuel reserves. The fund is non-diversified. **Top Holdings:** Nestle SA Novartis AG Roche Holding AG Dividend Right Cert. Toyota Motor Corp HSBC Holdings PLC

Principal Spectrum Preferred Securities Active ETF   C   HOLD

Ticker	Traded On	NAV	Total Assets ($)	Dividend Yield (TTM)	Turnover Ratio	Expense Ratio
PREF	BATS	99.03	$84,173,266	5	28	0.55

Ratings

Reward	C
Risk	D+
Recent Upgrade/Downgrade	Up

Fund Information

Fund Type	Exchange Traded Funds
Category	US Fixed Income
Sub-Category	Preferred Stock
Prospectus Objective	Equity-Income
Inception Date	Jul-17
Open to New Investments	Y

Prices

Price (as of 9/30/2019)	99.55
52-Week High	99.55
52-Week Low	89.67

Total Returns (%)

3-Month	6-Month	1-Year	3-Year	5-Year
3.34	7.07	10.19		

3-Year Standard Deviation	
Effective Duration	5.03

Valuation

Premium/Discount (1-Year Average)	0.52

Company Information

Provider	Principal Funds
Manager/Tenure	Roberto Giangregorio (2), L. Phillip Jacoby (2), Paul S. Kim (2), 3 others
Website	http://www.principalfunds.com
Address	Principal Funds 430 W 7th St, Ste 219971 Kansas City MO 64105-1407 United States
Phone Number	800-787-1621

PERFORMANCE

Ratings History

Date	Overall Rating	Risk Rating	Reward Rating
Q3-19	C	D+	C
Q4-18	D	D+	D
Q4-17	U		
Q4-16			
Q4-15			

Asset & Performance History

Date	NAV	1-Year Total Return
2018	89.28	-6.09
2017	99.67	
2016		
2015		
2014		
2013		

Total Assets: $84,173,266
Asset Allocation

Asset	%
Cash	2%
Stocks	0%
US Stocks	0%
Bonds	83%
US Bonds	46%
Other	0%

Services Offered:

Investment Strategy: The investment seeks to provide current income. Under normal circumstances, the fund invests at least 80% of its net assets, plus any borrowings for investment purposes, in preferred securities at the time of purchase. Examples of preferred securities include preferred stock, certain depositary receipts, and various types of junior subordinated debt (such debt generally includes the contractual ability to defer payment of interest without accelerating an immediate default event). It concentrates its investments (invests more than 25% of its net assets) in securities in the financial services (i.e., banking, insurance and commercial finance) industry. **Top Holdings:** AXA 6.38%   Cloverie Plc Secd Mtn FRN 5.62%   Sumitomo Life Insurance Company 6.5%   HSBC Capital Funding Dollar I L.P. 10.18%   BNP Paribas 7.2%

FlexShares STOXX Global ESG Impact Index Fund   C   HOLD

Ticker	Traded On	NAV	Total Assets ($)	Dividend Yield (TTM)	Turnover Ratio	Expense Ratio
ESGG	BATS	98.99	$84,141,973	2.03	78	0.42

Ratings

Reward	C
Risk	D+
Recent Upgrade/Downgrade	

Fund Information

Fund Type	Exchange Traded Funds
Category	Global Equity Large Cap
Sub-Category	World Large Stock
Prospectus Objective	Growth & Inc
Inception Date	Jul-16
Open to New Investments	Y

Prices

Price (as of 9/30/2019)	99.37
52-Week High	100.93
52-Week Low	80.43

Total Returns (%)

3-Month	6-Month	1-Year	3-Year	5-Year
0.25	4.48	1.83	36.69	

3-Year Standard Deviation	11.35
Effective Duration	

Valuation

Premium/Discount (1-Year Average)	0.26

Company Information

Provider	Flexshares Trust
Manager/Tenure	Robert Anstine (3), Brendan Sullivan (3)
Website	http://www.flexshares.com
Address	50 South LaSalle Street Chicago, Illinois 60603 Chicago Illinois 60603 United States
Phone Number	855-353-9383

PERFORMANCE

Ratings History

Date	Overall Rating	Risk Rating	Reward Rating
Q3-19	C	D+	C
Q4-18	C-	D+	C
Q4-17	D	B	C
Q4-16	U		
Q4-15			

Asset & Performance History

Date	NAV	1-Year Total Return
2018	85.05	-8.49
2017	94.75	23.86
2016	77.92	
2015		
2014		
2013		

Total Assets: $84,141,973
Asset Allocation

Asset	%
Cash	1%
Stocks	99%
US Stocks	59%
Bonds	0%
US Bonds	0%
Other	0%

Services Offered:

Investment Strategy: The investment seeks investment results that correspond generally to the price and yield performance, before fees and expenses, of the STOXX® Global ESG Impact Index. The fund will invest at least 80% of its total assets (exclusive of collateral held from securities lending) in the securities of the index and in ADRs and GDRs based on the securities in the index. The index is an optimized index designed to provide broad market exposure that is tilted toward global companies that score better with respect to a small set of ESG characteristics and to provide the potential for attractive risk-adjusted performance relative to the STOXX® Global 1800 Index. **Top Holdings:** Apple Inc   Microsoft Corp   Amazon.com Inc   Facebook Inc A   Alphabet Inc Class C

VictoryShares International Volatility Wtd ETF

D+   SELL

Ticker	Traded On	NAV	Total Assets ($)	Dividend Yield (TTM)	Turnover Ratio	Expense Ratio
CIL	NAS CM	37.35	$84,035,509	2.89	53	0.45

Ratings
Reward	C
Risk	D
Recent Upgrade/Downgrade	Down

Fund Information
Fund Type	Exchange Traded Funds
Category	Global Equity Large Cap
Sub-Category	Foreign Large Blend
Prospectus Objective	Foreign Stock
Inception Date	Aug-15
Open to New Investments	Y

Prices
Price (as of 9/30/2019)	37.30
52-Week High	40.21
52-Week Low	33.54

Total Returns (%)
3-Month	6-Month	1-Year	3-Year	5-Year
-1.73	0.37	-2.57	19.02	

3-Year Standard Deviation	10.77
Effective Duration	

Valuation
Premium/Discount (1-Year Average)	0.33

Company Information
Provider	VictoryShares
Manager/Tenure	Mannik Dhillon (1)
Website	http://www.VictorySharesLiterature.com
Address	Victory Shares 4249 Easton Way, Suite 400 Columbus OH 43219 United States
Phone Number	

PERFORMANCE

Ratings History
Date	Overall Rating	Risk Rating	Reward Rating
Q3-19	D+	D	C
Q4-18	D+	D+	D+
Q4-17	C	B	C+
Q4-16	D	D	D+
Q4-15	U		

Asset & Performance History
Date	NAV	1-Year Total Return
2018	34.22	-13.27
2017	40.46	26.91
2016	32.63	-1.77
2015	33.68	
2014		
2013		

Total Assets: $84,035,509
Asset Allocation
Asset	%
Cash	0%
Stocks	100%
US Stocks	2%
Bonds	0%
US Bonds	0%
Other	0%

Services Offered:

Investment Strategy: The investment seeks to provide investment results that track the performance of the Nasdaq Victory International 500 Volatility Weighted Index before fees and expenses. The fund seeks to achieve its investment objective by investing, under normal market conditions, at least 80% of its assets directly or indirectly in the securities included in the Nasdaq Victory International 500 Volatility Weighted Index, an unmanaged, volatility weighted index maintained exclusively by the index provider. The index identifies the 500 largest foreign companies by market capitalization measured at the time the index's constituent securities are determined. **Top Holdings:** Mini Msci Eafe Fut Sep19 National Bank of Canada TELUS Corp Fortis Inc Emera, Inc.

WisdomTree Europe Hedged SmallCap Equity Fund

C   HOLD

Ticker	Traded On	NAV	Total Assets ($)	Dividend Yield (TTM)	Turnover Ratio	Expense Ratio
EUSC	NYSE Arca	30.40	$83,595,971	2.93	37	0.58

Ratings
Reward	C
Risk	D+
Recent Upgrade/Downgrade	Up

Fund Information
Fund Type	Exchange Traded Funds
Category	Europe Equity Large Cap
Sub-Category	Europe Stock
Prospectus Objective	Small Company
Inception Date	Mar-15
Open to New Investments	Y

Prices
Price (as of 9/30/2019)	30.33
52-Week High	31.54
52-Week Low	25.52

Total Returns (%)
3-Month	6-Month	1-Year	3-Year	5-Year
0.19	2.64	2.90	34.01	

3-Year Standard Deviation	12.31
Effective Duration	

Valuation
Premium/Discount (1-Year Average)	-0.18

Company Information
Provider	WisdomTree
Manager/Tenure	Richard A. Brown (4), Thomas J. Durante (4), Karen Q. Wong (4)
Website	http://www.wisdomtree.com
Address	WisdomTree 245 Park Avenue, 35th floor New York NY 10167 United States
Phone Number	866-909-9473

PERFORMANCE

Ratings History
Date	Overall Rating	Risk Rating	Reward Rating
Q3-19	C	D+	C
Q4-18	D+	C-	D+
Q4-17	B-	B-	C+
Q4-16	D+	C-	D+
Q4-15	U		

Asset & Performance History
Date	NAV	1-Year Total Return
2018	26.5	-13.41
2017	31.23	22.3
2016	25.92	7.85
2015	24.69	
2014		
2013		

Total Assets: $83,595,971
Asset Allocation
Asset	%
Cash	0%
Stocks	100%
US Stocks	1%
Bonds	0%
US Bonds	0%
Other	0%

Services Offered:

Investment Strategy: The investment seeks to track the price and yield performance, before fees and expenses, of the WisdomTree Europe Hedged SmallCap Equity Index. Under normal circumstances, at least 80% of the fund's total assets will be invested in component securities of the index and investments that have economic characteristics that are substantially identical to the economic characteristics of such component securities. The index is a dividend weighted index designed to provide exposure to small cap equity securities within Europe, while at the same time neutralizing exposure to fluctuations between the value of the euro and the U.S. dollar. The fund is non-diversified. **Top Holdings:** Banca Mediolanum Eutelsat Communications A2A SpA Metro Ag (New) ProSiebenSat 1 Media SE

Invesco S&P 500® Equal Weight Consumer Discretionary ETF   C   HOLD

Ticker	Traded On	NAV	Total Assets ($)	Dividend Yield (TTM)	Turnover Ratio	Expense Ratio
RCD	NYSE Arca	104.46	$83,569,004	1.74		0.4

Ratings

Reward	C
Risk	D+
Recent Upgrade/Downgrade	

Fund Information

Fund Type	Exchange Traded Funds
Category	Consumer Goods & Svcs
Sub-Category	Consumer Cyclical
Prospectus Objective	Unaligned
Inception Date	Nov-06
Open to New Investments	Y

Prices

Price (as of 9/30/2019)	104.48
52-Week High	109.19
52-Week Low	84.82

Total Returns (%)

3-Month	6-Month	1-Year	3-Year	5-Year
-0.33	0.21	0.43	25.83	41.69

3-Year Standard Deviation	15.41
Effective Duration	

Valuation

Premium/Discount (1-Year Average)	0.02

Company Information

Provider	Invesco
Manager/Tenure	Peter Hubbard (1), Michael Jeanette (1), Tony Seisser (1)
Website	http://www.invesco.com/us
Address	Invesco 11 Greenway Plaza, Ste. 2500 Houston TX 77046 United States
Phone Number	800-659-1005

PERFORMANCE

Ratings History

Date	Overall Rating	Risk Rating	Reward Rating
Q3-19	C	D+	C
Q4-18	C-	D+	C
Q4-17	B-	B	C+
Q4-16	C	D+	B-
Q4-15	C	C	C

Asset & Performance History

Date	NAV	1-Year Total Return
2018	89.92	-8.48
2017	99.8	14.67
2016	88.37	5.54
2015	84.73	-2.86
2014	88.38	11.33
2013	80.28	43.18

Total Assets: $83,569,004

Asset Allocation

Asset	%
Cash	0%
Stocks	100%
US Stocks	97%
Bonds	0%
US Bonds	0%
Other	0%

Services Offered:

Investment Strategy: The investment seeks to track the investment results (before fees and expenses) of the S&P 500® Equal Weight Consumer Discretionary Index (the "underlying index"). The fund generally will invest at least 90% of its total assets in the securities that comprise the underlying index. The underlying index is composed of all of the components of the S&P 500® Consumer Discretionary Index, an index that contains the common stocks of all companies included in the S&P 500® Index that are classified as members of the consumer discretionary sector, as defined according to the Global Industry Classification Standard ("GICS"). The fund is non-diversified.
Top Holdings: Target Corp Dollar General Corp Starbucks Corp Newell Brands Inc Chipotle Mexican Grill Inc Class A

VictoryShares USAA Core Short-Term Bond ETF   C-   HOLD

Ticker	Traded On	NAV	Total Assets ($)	Dividend Yield (TTM)	Turnover Ratio	Expense Ratio
USTB	NYSE Arca	50.56	$83,421,960	2.67	22	0.35

Ratings

Reward	C-
Risk	D+
Recent Upgrade/Downgrade	Up

Fund Information

Fund Type	Exchange Traded Funds
Category	US Fixed Income
Sub-Category	Short-Term Bond
Prospectus Objective	Income
Inception Date	Oct-17
Open to New Investments	Y

Prices

Price (as of 9/30/2019)	50.63
52-Week High	50.81
52-Week Low	49.24

Total Returns (%)

3-Month	6-Month	1-Year	3-Year	5-Year
0.92	2.47	5.15		

3-Year Standard Deviation	
Effective Duration	1.69

Valuation

Premium/Discount (1-Year Average)	0.10

Company Information

Provider	VictoryShares
Manager/Tenure	Julianne Bass (1), Kurt Daum (1), Brian W. Smith (1), 3 others
Website	http://www.VictorySharesLiterature.com
Address	Victory Shares 4249 Easton Way, Suite 400 Columbus OH 43219 United States
Phone Number	

PERFORMANCE

Ratings History

Date	Overall Rating	Risk Rating	Reward Rating
Q3-19	C-	D+	C-
Q4-18	D+	D+	D
Q4-17	U		
Q4-16			
Q4-15			

Asset & Performance History

Date	NAV	1-Year Total Return
2018	49.47	1.43
2017	49.92	
2016		
2015		
2014		
2013		

Total Assets: $83,421,960

Asset Allocation

Asset	%
Cash	7%
Stocks	0%
US Stocks	0%
Bonds	93%
US Bonds	82%
Other	0%

Services Offered:

Investment Strategy: The investment seeks high current income consistent with preservation of principal. Under normal circumstances, the fund invests at least 80% of its net assets in debt securities and in derivatives and other instruments that have economic characteristics similar to such securities. It primarily invests in securities that have a dollar-weighted average portfolio maturity of three years or less. The fund may not invest more than 20% of fixed-income securities in non-agency, non-government sponsored entities (GSEs), or privately issued mortgage- or asset-backed securities. **Top Holdings:** United States Treasury Notes 1.12% United States Treasury Notes 1.25% United States Treasury Notes 1.88% Carmax Auto Owner Trust 2.22% United States Treasury Notes 1.62%

ETFMG Video Game Tech ETF
C- HOLD

Ticker	Traded On	NAV	Total Assets ($)	Dividend Yield (TTM)	Turnover Ratio	Expense Ratio
GAMR	NYSE Arca	41.50	$82,997,559	1.56	42	0.75

Ratings
Reward   D+
Risk   C-
Recent Upgrade/Downgrade

Fund Information
Fund Type   Exchange Traded Funds
Category   Technology Sector Equity
Sub-Category   Technology
Prospectus Objective   Technology
Inception Date   Mar-16
Open to New Investments Y

Prices
Price (as of 9/30/2019) 41.53
52-Week High   47.60
52-Week Low   37.44

Total Returns (%)

3-Month	6-Month	1-Year	3-Year	5-Year
-2.78	-6.16	-11.40	32.42	

3-Year Standard Deviation   17.8
Effective Duration

Valuation
Premium/Discount (1-Year Average)   -0.22

Company Information
Provider   ETFMG
Manager/Tenure Samuel R. Masucci (1), Devin Ryder (1), Donal Bishnoi (0), 1 other
Website   http://www.etfmg.com
Address   ETFMG 30 Maple Street, Suite 2 NJ United States
Phone Number

PERFORMANCE

Ratings History

Date	Overall Rating	Risk Rating	Reward Rating
Q3-19	C-	C-	D+
Q4-18	D+	C-	D+
Q4-17	C-	B+	C
Q4-16	U		
Q4-15			

Asset & Performance History

Date	NAV	1-Year Total Return
2018	39.19	-16.89
2017	47.77	59.89
2016	30.02	
2015		
2014		
2013		

Total Assets: $82,997,559

Asset Allocation

Asset	%
Cash	1%
Stocks	99%
US Stocks	30%
Bonds	0%
US Bonds	0%
Other	0%

Services Offered:

Investment Strategy: The investment seeks to provide investment results that, before fees and expenses, correspond generally to the price and yield performance of the EEFund Video Game Tech Index. The index tracks the performance of the common stock of exchange-listed companies across the globe that are actively engaged in a business activity supporting or utilizing the video gaming industry. The fund normally invests at least 80% of its total assets, exclusive of collateral held from securities lending, in securities, ADRs, or GDRs of Video Gaming Companies. It is non-diversified. **Top Holdings:** Capcom Co Ltd   Square Enix Holdings Co Ltd   Take-Two Interactive Software Inc   CD Projekt SA   NCsoft Corp

---

iShares Edge MSCI Multifactor Intl Small-Cap ETF
C- HOLD

Ticker	Traded On	NAV	Total Assets ($)	Dividend Yield (TTM)	Turnover Ratio	Expense Ratio
ISCF	NYSE Arca	28.62	$82,988,075	2.27	45	0.4

Ratings
Reward   C-
Risk   C-
Recent Upgrade/Downgrade

Fund Information
Fund Type   Exchange Traded Funds
Category   Globa Eq Mid/Small Cap
Sub-Category   Foreign Small/Mid Blend
Prospectus Objective   Small Company
Inception Date   Apr-15
Open to New Investments Y

Prices
Price (as of 9/30/2019) 28.58
52-Week High   31.52
52-Week Low   24.74

Total Returns (%)

3-Month	6-Month	1-Year	3-Year	5-Year
-1.78	0.19	-6.49	19.87	

3-Year Standard Deviation   12.22
Effective Duration

Valuation
Premium/Discount (1-Year Average)   0.05

Company Information
Provider   iShares
Manager/Tenure Diane Hsiung (4), Jennifer Hsui (4), Greg Savage (4), 3 others
Website   http://www.ishares.com
Address   iShares 400 Howard Street San Francisco CA 94105 United States
Phone Number   800-474-2737

PERFORMANCE

Ratings History

Date	Overall Rating	Risk Rating	Reward Rating
Q3-19	C-	C-	C-
Q4-18	D+	C-	D+
Q4-17	B-	B	C+
Q4-16	D+	D+	D+
Q4-15	U		

Asset & Performance History

Date	NAV	1-Year Total Return
2018	25.92	-18.18
2017	32.29	36.23
2016	24.21	0.01
2015	24.91	
2014		
2013		

Total Assets: $82,988,075

Asset Allocation

Asset	%
Cash	1%
Stocks	99%
US Stocks	3%
Bonds	0%
US Bonds	0%
Other	1%

Services Offered:

Investment Strategy: The investment seeks to track the investment results of the MSCI World ex USA Small Cap Diversified Multiple-Factor Index. The fund generally will invest at least 90% of its assets in the component securities of the underlying index and in investments that have economic characteristics that are substantially identical to the component securities of the underlying index. The underlying index is designed to select equity securities from the MSCI World ex USA Small Cap Index that have high exposure to four investment style factors: value, quality, momentum and low size, while maintaining a level of risk similar to that of the parent index. **Top Holdings:** Logitech International SA   GN Store Nord A/S   Northern Star Resources Ltd   ASR Nederland NV   Euronext NV

SPDR® MSCI ACWI Low Carbon Target ETF　　　　　　　　　　　　　C　　HOLD

Ticker	Traded On	NAV	Total Assets ($)	Dividend Yield (TTM)	Turnover Ratio	Expense Ratio
LOWC	NYSE Arca		$82,838,341	2.2	17	0.2

Ratings
Reward　　　　　　　　　C
Risk　　　　　　　　　　D+
Recent Upgrade/Downgrade

Fund Information
Fund Type	Exchange Traded Funds
Category	Global Equity Large Cap
Sub-Category	World Large Stock
Prospectus Objective	World Stock
Inception Date	Nov-14
Open to New Investments	Y

Prices
Price (as of 9/30/2019)	92.15
52-Week High	93.67
52-Week Low	75.73

Total Returns (%)
3-Month	6-Month	1-Year	3-Year	5-Year
-0.47	2.93	1.97	32.01	

3-Year Standard Deviation	11.32
Effective Duration	

Valuation
Premium/Discount (1-Year Average)　　0.13

Company Information
Provider	SPDR State Street Global Advisors
Manager/Tenure	Michael J. Feehily (4), Karl A. Schneider (4), Thomas Coleman (0)
Website	http://www.spdrs.com
Address	SPDR State Street Global Advisors State Street Financial Center, 1 Lincoln Street Boston MA 02111-2900 United States
Phone Number	617-786-3000

PERFORMANCE

Ratings History

Date	Overall Rating	Risk Rating	Reward Rating
Q3-19	C	D+	C
Q4-18	C-	D+	C-
Q4-17	C+	B-	C+
Q4-16	D+	D	C-
Q4-15	U		

Asset & Performance History

Date	NAV	1-Year Total Return
2018	79.49	-9.45
2017	89.92	23.62
2016	74.43	7.71
2015	70.56	-1.52
2014	73.32	
2013		

Total Assets: $82,838,341

Asset Allocation

Asset	%
Cash	0%
Stocks	100%
US Stocks	55%
Bonds	0%
US Bonds	0%
Other	0%

Services Offered:

Investment Strategy: The investment seeks to provide investment results that, before fees and expenses, correspond generally to the total return performance of the MSCI ACWI Low Carbon Target Index. The fund generally invests substantially all, but at least 80%, of its total assets in the securities comprising the index and in depositary receipts based on securities comprising the index. The index is designed to address two dimensions of carbon exposure - carbon emissions and fossil fuel reserves, expressed as potential emissions. The fund is non-diversified. **Top Holdings:** Microsoft Corp Apple Inc Amazon.com Inc Facebook Inc A Alphabet Inc A

Nuveen ESG Large-Cap Value ETF　　　　　　　　　　　　　　　　C　　HOLD

Ticker	Traded On	NAV	Total Assets ($)	Dividend Yield (TTM)	Turnover Ratio	Expense Ratio
NULV	BATS	31.22	$82,726,957	1.8	59	0.35

Ratings
Reward　　　　　　　　　C+
Risk　　　　　　　　　　C
Recent Upgrade/Downgrade

Fund Information
Fund Type	Exchange Traded Funds
Category	US Equity Large Cap Value
Sub-Category	Large Value
Prospectus Objective	Growth
Inception Date	Dec-16
Open to New Investments	Y

Prices
Price (as of 9/30/2019)	31.25
52-Week High	31.38
52-Week Low	25.77

Total Returns (%)
3-Month	6-Month	1-Year	3-Year	5-Year
2.68	5.33	6.89		

3-Year Standard Deviation	
Effective Duration	

Valuation
Premium/Discount (1-Year Average)　　0.05

Company Information
Provider	Nuveen
Manager/Tenure	Philip James(Jim) Campagna (2), Lei Liao (2)
Website	http://www.nuveen.com
Address	Nuveen Investment Trust John Nuveen & Co. Inc. Chicago IL 60606 United States
Phone Number	312-917-8146

PERFORMANCE

Ratings History

Date	Overall Rating	Risk Rating	Reward Rating
Q3-19	C	C	C+
Q4-18	C-	C-	C-
Q4-17	D	A-	D+
Q4-16			
Q4-15			

Asset & Performance History

Date	NAV	1-Year Total Return
2018	26.25	-6.48
2017	28.51	15.39
2016	24.78	
2015		
2014		
2013		

Total Assets: $82,726,957

Asset Allocation

Asset	%
Cash	0%
Stocks	100%
US Stocks	97%
Bonds	0%
US Bonds	0%
Other	0%

Services Offered:

Investment Strategy: The investment seeks to track the investment results, before fees and expenses, of the TIAA ESG USA Large-Cap Value Index (the "index"). Under normal market conditions, the fund invests at least 80% of the sum of its net assets and the amount of any borrowings for investment purposes in component securities of the index. The index is comprised of equity securities issued by large capitalization companies listed on U.S. exchanges that meet certain environmental, social, and governance ("ESG") criteria. **Top Holdings:** Procter & Gamble Co The Walt Disney Co Verizon Communications Inc Merck & Co Inc Coca-Cola Co

VanEck Vectors Brazil Small-Cap ETF   C+   HOLD

Ticker	Traded On	NAV	Total Assets ($)	Dividend Yield (TTM)	Turnover Ratio	Expense Ratio
BRF	NYSE Arca	23.30	$82,718,993	2.48	45	0.6

Ratings
Reward   B
Risk   C-
Recent Upgrade/Downgrade   Up

Fund Information
Fund Type   Exchange Traded Funds
Category   Latin America Equity
Sub-Category   Latin America Stock
Prospectus Objective   Growth
Inception Date   May-09
Open to New Investments   Y

Prices
Price (as of 9/30/2019)   23.19
52-Week High   25.57
52-Week Low   16.67

Total Returns (%)

3-Month	6-Month	1-Year	3-Year	5-Year
-2.18	6.78	43.52	54.14	11.75

3-Year Standard Deviation   27.47
Effective Duration

Valuation
Premium/Discount (1-Year Average)   -0.17

Company Information
Provider   VanEck
Manager/Tenure   Hao-Hung (Peter) Liao (10), Guo Hua (Jason) Jin (1)
Website   http://www.vaneck.com
Address   Van Eck Associates Corporation 666 Third Avenue New York NY 10017 United States
Phone Number   800-826-1115

PERFORMANCE

Ratings History

Date	Overall Rating	Risk Rating	Reward Rating
Q3-19	C+	C-	B
Q4-18	C-	D+	C
Q4-17	C	D+	C+
Q4-16	D+	D+	D+
Q4-15	E+	E+	E+

Asset & Performance History

Date	NAV	1-Year Total Return
2018	20.09	-11.79
2017	23.33	51.75
2016	16.1	61.17
2015	10.44	-48.87
2014	21.23	-25.21
2013	29.61	-28.52

Total Assets: $82,718,993
Asset Allocation

Asset	%
Cash	0%
Stocks	100%
US Stocks	0%
Bonds	0%
US Bonds	0%
Other	0%

Services Offered: Automatic Investment Plan, Retirement Investment

Investment Strategy: The investment seeks to replicate as closely as possible, before fees and expenses, the price and yield performance of the MVIS® Brazil Small-Cap Index. The fund normally invests at least 80% of its total assets in securities that comprise the fund's benchmark index. The index includes securities of Brazilian small-capitalization companies. A company is generally considered to be a Brazilian company if it is incorporated in Brazil or is incorporated outside of Brazil but has at least 50% of its revenues/related assets in Brazil. **Top Holdings:** Transmissora Alianca de Energia Eletrica SA Unit Totvs SA CIA Saneamento Do Parana-SANEPAR Units (1 Ord Share & 4 Pref Shares) RHI Magnesita NV Ordinary Shares CVC Brasil Operadora e Agencia de Viagens SA

VanEck Vectors Morningstar International Moat ETF   D+   SELL

Ticker	Traded On	NAV	Total Assets ($)	Dividend Yield (TTM)	Turnover Ratio	Expense Ratio
MOTI	NYSE Arca	30.57	$82,550,223	3.46	112	0.57

Ratings
Reward   D+
Risk   D+
Recent Upgrade/Downgrade   Down

Fund Information
Fund Type   Exchange Traded Funds
Category   Global Equity Large Cap
Sub-Category   Foreign Large Blend
Prospectus Objective   Foreign Stock
Inception Date   Jul-15
Open to New Investments   Y

Prices
Price (as of 9/30/2019)   30.50
52-Week High   33.10
52-Week Low   27.71

Total Returns (%)

3-Month	6-Month	1-Year	3-Year	5-Year
-2.05	-3.38	-4.21	20.17	

3-Year Standard Deviation   13.1
Effective Duration

Valuation
Premium/Discount (1-Year Average)   -0.01

Company Information
Provider   VanEck
Manager/Tenure   Hao-Hung (Peter) Liao (4), Guo Hua (Jason) Jin (1)
Website   http://www.vaneck.com
Address   Van Eck Associates Corporation 666 Third Avenue New York NY 10017 United States
Phone Number   800-826-1115

PERFORMANCE

Ratings History

Date	Overall Rating	Risk Rating	Reward Rating
Q3-19	D+	D+	D+
Q4-18	C-	C-	C-
Q4-17	C	B	C
Q4-16	D	C-	D+
Q4-15	U		

Asset & Performance History

Date	NAV	1-Year Total Return
2018	28.48	-13.17
2017	34.1	26.03
2016	27.85	5.11
2015	26.85	
2014		
2013		

Total Assets: $82,550,223
Asset Allocation

Asset	%
Cash	0%
Stocks	100%
US Stocks	0%
Bonds	0%
US Bonds	0%
Other	0%

Services Offered:

Investment Strategy: The investment seeks to replicate as closely as possible, before fees and expenses, the price and yield performance of the Morningstar® Global ex-US Moat Focus IndexSM. The fund normally invests at least 80% of its total assets in securities that comprise the fund's benchmark index. The index is comprised of securities issued by companies that Morningstar, Inc. ("Morningstar") determines have sustainable competitive advantages based on a proprietary methodology that considers quantitative and qualitative factors ("wide and narrow moat companies"). **Top Holdings:** LINE Corp Grifols SA A Meggitt PLC KDDI Corp Yum China Holdings Inc

First Trust Multi Cap Value AlphaDEX® Fund   D+   SELL

Ticker	Traded On	NAV	Total Assets ($)	Dividend Yield (TTM)	Turnover Ratio	Expense Ratio
FAB	NAS CM	53.24	$82,518,029	1.94	96	0.71

Ratings

Reward	C-
Risk	D+
Recent Upgrade/Downgrade	

Fund Information

Fund Type	Exchange Traded Funds
Category	US Equity Mid Cap
Sub-Category	Mid-Cap Value
Prospectus Objective	Growth
Inception Date	May-07
Open to New Investments	Y

Prices

Price (as of 9/30/2019)	53.40
52-Week High	57.35
52-Week Low	45.89

Total Returns (%)

3-Month	6-Month	1-Year	3-Year	5-Year
-1.21	-1.70	-4.93	23.05	29.78

3-Year Standard Deviation	16.6
Effective Duration	

Valuation

Premium/Discount (1-Year Average)	-0.13

Company Information

Provider	First Trust
Manager/Tenure	Jon C. Erickson (12), Daniel J. Lindquist (12), David G. McGarel (12), 3 others
Website	http://www.ftportfolios.com/
Address	First Trust 120 E. Liberty Drive, Suite 400 Wheaton IL 60187 United States
Phone Number	800-621-1675

PERFORMANCE

Ratings History

Date	Overall Rating	Risk Rating	Reward Rating
Q3-19	D+	D+	C-
Q4-18	C-	D+	C-
Q4-17	B-	B-	B
Q4-16	C	D+	C+
Q4-15	C	C-	C

Asset & Performance History

Date	NAV	1-Year Total Return
2018	47.94	-13.97
2017	56.71	14.11
2016	50.45	25.84
2015	40.71	-12.46
2014	47.22	7.86
2013	44.4	37.02

Total Assets: $82,518,029

Asset Allocation

Asset	%
Cash	0%
Stocks	100%
US Stocks	99%
Bonds	0%
US Bonds	0%
Other	0%

Services Offered:

Investment Strategy: The investment seeks investment results that correspond generally to the price and yield (before the fund's fees and expenses) of the Nasdaq AlphaDEX® Multi Cap Value Index. The fund will normally invest at least 90% of its net assets (including investment borrowings) in common stocks that comprise the index. The index is designed to select value stocks from the NASDAQ US 500 Large Cap Index, NASDAQ US 600 Mid Cap Index and NASDAQ US 700 Small Cap Index that may generate positive alpha, or risk-adjusted returns, relative to traditional indices through the use of the AlphaDEX® selection methodology. **Top Holdings:** Micron Technology Inc   D.R. Horton Inc   The Kroger Co   Lennar Corp   AT&T Inc

ProShares UltraPro Russell2000   D+   SELL

Ticker	Traded On	NAV	Total Assets ($)	Dividend Yield (TTM)	Turnover Ratio	Expense Ratio
URTY	NYSE Arca	65.90	$82,380,018	0.26	24	0.95

Ratings

Reward	C-
Risk	D+
Recent Upgrade/Downgrade	Down

Fund Information

Fund Type	Exchange Traded Funds
Category	Trading Tools
Sub-Category	Trading--Leveraged Equity
Prospectus Objective	Small Company
Inception Date	Feb-10
Open to New Investments	Y

Prices

Price (as of 9/30/2019)	65.83
52-Week High	100.94
52-Week Low	41.91

Total Returns (%)

3-Month	6-Month	1-Year	3-Year	5-Year
-11.31	-11.29	-34.42	41.20	89.86

3-Year Standard Deviation	51.84
Effective Duration	

Valuation

Premium/Discount (1-Year Average)	-0.07

Company Information

Provider	ProShares
Manager/Tenure	Michael Neches (6), Devin Sullivan (1)
Website	http://www.proshares.com
Address	ProShares 7501 Wisconsin Avenue, Suite 1000 Bethesda MD 20814 United States
Phone Number	866-776-5125

PERFORMANCE

Ratings History

Date	Overall Rating	Risk Rating	Reward Rating
Q3-19	D+	D+	C-
Q4-18	C-	D+	C
Q4-17	B	C-	A+
Q4-16	C	D+	C+
Q4-15	C	C	C

Asset & Performance History

Date	NAV	1-Year Total Return
2018	49.75	-39.52
2017	82.5	39.75
2016	59.03	58.74
2015	37.2	-20.59
2014	46.84	5.6
2013	44.36	148.2

Total Assets: $82,380,018

Asset Allocation

Asset	%
Cash	-200%
Stocks	300%
US Stocks	297%
Bonds	0%
US Bonds	0%
Other	0%

Services Offered:

Investment Strategy: The investment seeks daily investment results that correspond to three times (3x) the daily performance of the Russell 2000® Index. The fund invests in financial instruments that ProShare Advisors believes, in combination, should produce daily returns consistent with the fund's investment objective. The index is a measure of small-cap U.S. stock market performance. The fund is non-diversified. **Top Holdings:** Russell 2000 Index Swap Bnp Paribas   Russell 2000 Index Swap Morgan Stanley & Co. International Plc   Russell 2000 Index Swap Credit Suisse International   Russell 2000 Index Swap Ubs Ag   Russell 2000 Index Swap Goldman Sachs International

SPDR® S&P Health Care Services ETF   C   HOLD

Ticker	Traded On	NAV	Total Assets ($)	Dividend Yield (TTM)	Turnover Ratio	Expense Ratio
XHS	NYSE Arca		$82,325,208	0.34	35	0.35

Ratings

Reward	C
Risk	D+
Recent Upgrade/Downgrade	Up

Fund Information

Fund Type	Exchange Traded Funds
Category	Healthcare Sector Equity
Sub-Category	Health
Prospectus Objective	Health
Inception Date	Sep-11
Open to New Investments	Y

Prices

Price (as of 9/30/2019)	62.30
52-Week High	76.46
52-Week Low	59.72

Total Returns (%)

3-Month	6-Month	1-Year	3-Year	5-Year
-7.07	-4.11	-18.58	12.87	24.33

3-Year Standard Deviation	18.72
Effective Duration	

Valuation

Premium/Discount (1-Year Average)	-0.02

Company Information

Provider	SPDR State Street Global Advisors
Manager/Tenure	Michael J. Feehily (7), Karl A. Schneider (4), Raymond V. Donofrio (0)
Website	http://www.spdrs.com
Address	SPDR State Street Global Advisors State Street Financial Center, 1 Lincoln Street Boston MA 02111-2900 United States
Phone Number	617-786-3000

PERFORMANCE

Ratings History

Date	Overall Rating	Risk Rating	Reward Rating
Q3-19	C	D+	C
Q4-18	C	C-	C
Q4-17	C	C	C-
Q4-16	C	C-	C
Q4-15	C	C	C+

Asset & Performance History

Date	NAV	1-Year Total Return
2018	62.75	2.61
2017	61.34	17.12
2016	52.49	-8.37
2015	57.34	3.22
2014	56.07	25.28
2013	45.29	37.16

Total Assets: $82,325,208

Asset Allocation

Asset	%
Cash	3%
Stocks	97%
US Stocks	97%
Bonds	0%
US Bonds	0%
Other	0%

Services Offered:

Investment Strategy: The investment seeks to provide investment results that, before fees and expenses, correspond generally to the total return performance of an index derived from the health care providers and services segment of a U.S. total market composite index. In seeking to track the performance of the S&P Health Care Services Select Industry Index (the "index"), the fund employs a sampling strategy. It generally invests substantially all, but at least 80%, of its total assets in the securities comprising the index. The index represents the health care services segment of the S&P Total Market Index ("S&P TMI"). The fund is non-diversified. **Top Holdings:** Brookdale Senior Living Inc Chemed Corp Universal Health Services Inc Class B DaVita Inc AMN Healthcare Services Inc

WBI BullBear Yield 1000 ETF   C   HOLD

Ticker	Traded On	NAV	Total Assets ($)	Dividend Yield (TTM)	Turnover Ratio	Expense Ratio
WBIG	NYSE Arca	23.77	$82,021,023	2.16	610	1.04

Ratings

Reward	C
Risk	C
Recent Upgrade/Downgrade	Up

Fund Information

Fund Type	Exchange Traded Funds
Category	US Equity Large Cap Blend
Sub-Category	Large Blend
Prospectus Objective	Growth & Inc
Inception Date	Aug-14
Open to New Investments	Y

Prices

Price (as of 9/30/2019)	23.78
52-Week High	26.94
52-Week Low	22.95

Total Returns (%)

3-Month	6-Month	1-Year	3-Year	5-Year
-1.26	-2.84	-9.66	24.97	3.59

3-Year Standard Deviation	10.75
Effective Duration	

Valuation

Premium/Discount (1-Year Average)	-0.13

Company Information

Provider	WBI Investments
Manager/Tenure	Donald R. Schreiber (5), Steven Van Solkema (0)
Website	http://www.wbishares.com
Address	34 Sycamore Ave Suite 1-E Little Silver NJ 07739 United States
Phone Number	732-842-4920

PERFORMANCE

Ratings History

Date	Overall Rating	Risk Rating	Reward Rating
Q3-19	C	C	C
Q4-18	C	C	C
Q4-17	C+	C	C+
Q4-16	C-	C-	C
Q4-15	D-	C+	B-

Asset & Performance History

Date	NAV	1-Year Total Return
2018	23.46	-7.98
2017	25.83	24.99
2016	20.93	-2.44
2015	21.61	-10.52
2014	24.46	
2013		

Total Assets: $82,021,023

Asset Allocation

Asset	%
Cash	1%
Stocks	99%
US Stocks	99%
Bonds	0%
US Bonds	0%
Other	0%

Services Offered:

Investment Strategy: The investment seeks long-term capital appreciation and the potential for current income, while also seeking to protect principal during unfavorable market conditions. The fund will seek to invest in the dividend-paying equity securities of large capitalization domestic and foreign companies that WBI Investments, Inc., the sub-advisor ("Sub-Advisor") to the fund and an affiliate of Millington Securities Inc., the advisor ("Advisor"), believes display attractive dividend payment prospects, and in other tactical investment opportunities. It may invest up to 50% of its net assets in the securities of issuers in emerging markets. **Top Holdings:** AT&T Inc Target Corp Amgen Inc Lockheed Martin Corp Intuit Inc

iShares U.S. Oil Equipment & Services ETF   D+   SELL

Ticker	Traded On	NAV	Total Assets ($)	Dividend Yield (TTM)	Turnover Ratio	Expense Ratio
IEZ	NYSE Arca	17.61	$81,891,404	2.43	35	0.42

Ratings
Reward	C
Risk	D
Recent Upgrade/Downgrade	Up

Fund Information
Fund Type	Exchange Traded Funds
Category	Energy Sector Equity
Sub-Category	Equity Energy
Prospectus Objective	Natl Res
Inception Date	May-06
Open to New Investments	Y

Prices
Price (as of 9/30/2019)	17.61
52-Week High	36.99
52-Week Low	16.32

Total Returns (%)
3-Month	6-Month	1-Year	3-Year	5-Year
-18.59	-31.42	-50.19	-52.51	-69.87

3-Year Standard Deviation	35.6
Effective Duration	

Valuation
Premium/Discount (1-Year Average)	0.01

Company Information
Provider	iShares
Manager/Tenure	Greg Savage (11), Jennifer Hsui (7), Alan Mason (3), 2 others
Website	http://www.ishares.com
Address	iShares 400 Howard Street San Francisco CA 94105 United States
Phone Number	800-474-2737

PERFORMANCE

Ratings History
Date	Overall Rating	Risk Rating	Reward Rating
Q3-19	D+	D	C
Q4-18	D+	D	C
Q4-17	D	D	D
Q4-16	D+	D	C-
Q4-15	D+	D+	C-

Asset & Performance History
Date	NAV	1-Year Total Return
2018	20.4	-42.48
2017	35.9	-18.19
2016	45.43	28.35
2015	35.78	-26.97
2014	49.99	-21.93
2013	64.89	28.16

Total Assets: $81,891,404
Asset Allocation
Asset	%
Cash	0%
Stocks	100%
US Stocks	94%
Bonds	0%
US Bonds	0%
Other	0%

Services Offered:

Investment Strategy: The investment seeks to track the investment results of the Dow Jones U.S. Select Oil Equipment & Services Index. The fund generally invests at least 90% of its assets in securities of the underlying index and in depositary receipts representing securities of the underlying index. The underlying fund measures the performance of the oil equipment and services sector of the U.S. equity market and includes companies that are suppliers of equipment or services to oil fields and offshore platforms, such as drilling, exploration, seismic information services and platform construction. The fund is non-diversified. **Top Holdings:** Schlumberger Ltd Halliburton Co Baker Hughes, a GE Co Class A TechnipFMC PLC National Oilwell Varco Inc

---

Invesco Dow Jones Industrial Average Dividend ETF   B-   BUY

Ticker	Traded On	NAV	Total Assets ($)	Dividend Yield (TTM)	Turnover Ratio	Expense Ratio
DJD	NYSE Arca	37.22	$81,876,769	2.75	20	0.07

Ratings
Reward	B
Risk	C
Recent Upgrade/Downgrade	Up

Fund Information
Fund Type	Exchange Traded Funds
Category	US Equity Large Cap Value
Sub-Category	Large Value
Prospectus Objective	Growth & Inc
Inception Date	Dec-15
Open to New Investments	Y

Prices
Price (as of 9/30/2019)	37.23
52-Week High	38.05
52-Week Low	31.25

Total Returns (%)
3-Month	6-Month	1-Year	3-Year	5-Year
0.57	2.64	5.46	47.98	

3-Year Standard Deviation	11.22
Effective Duration	

Valuation
Premium/Discount (1-Year Average)	0.11

Company Information
Provider	Invesco
Manager/Tenure	Peter Hubbard (1), Michael Jeanette (1), Tony Seisser (1)
Website	http://www.invesco.com/us
Address	Invesco 11 Greenway Plaza, Ste. 2500 Houston TX 77046 United States
Phone Number	800-659-1005

PERFORMANCE

Ratings History
Date	Overall Rating	Risk Rating	Reward Rating
Q3-19	B-	C	B
Q4-18	C+	C	B
Q4-17	C-	B+	C
Q4-16	D-	C	B
Q4-15			

Asset & Performance History
Date	NAV	1-Year Total Return
2018	33.17	0.11
2017	34.02	21.75
2016	28.82	16.26
2015	25.3	
2014		
2013		

Total Assets: $81,876,769
Asset Allocation
Asset	%
Cash	0%
Stocks	100%
US Stocks	100%
Bonds	0%
US Bonds	0%
Other	0%

Services Offered:

Investment Strategy: The investment seeks to track the investment results (before fees and expenses) of the Dow Jones Industrial Average Yield Weighted (the "underlying index"). The fund will generally invest at least 90% of its total assets in the securities that comprise the underlying index. The underlying index is designed to provide exposure to dividend-paying equity securities of companies included in the Dow Jones Industrial Average™, which is a price-weighted index of 30 U.S. companies that meet certain size, listing and liquidity requirements. The fund is non-diversified. **Top Holdings:** International Business Machines Corp Verizon Communications Inc Coca-Cola Co Chevron Corp The Home Depot Inc

Direxion Daily FTSE China Bear 3X Shares

D **SELL**

Ticker	Traded On	NAV	Total Assets ($)	Dividend Yield (TTM)	Turnover Ratio	Expense Ratio
YANG	NYSE Arca	55.41	$81,855,444	0.98	0	1.08

Ratings
Reward   D-
Risk   D
Recent Upgrade/Downgrade

Fund Information
Fund Type	Exchange Traded Funds
Category	Trading Tools
Sub-Category	Trading--Inverse Equity
Prospectus Objective	Pacific Stock
Inception Date	Dec-09
Open to New Investments	Y

Prices
Price (as of 9/30/2019)	55.28
52-Week High	77.18
52-Week Low	39.69

Total Returns (%)
3-Month	6-Month	1-Year	3-Year	5-Year
26.18	26.03	-0.76	-60.83	-87.41

3-Year Standard Deviation	53.22
Effective Duration	

Valuation
Premium/Discount (1-Year Average)	-0.10

Company Information
Provider	Direxion Funds
Manager/Tenure	Paul Brigandi (9), Tony Ng (4)
Website	http://www.direxionfunds.com
Address	Direxion Funds 1301 Avenue Of The Americas (6th Avenue) New York NY 10019 United States
Phone Number	646-572-3390

PERFORMANCE

Ratings History

Date	Overall Rating	Risk Rating	Reward Rating
Q3-19	D	D	D-
Q4-18	D	D	D-
Q4-17	E+	D-	E+
Q4-16	D	D	E+
Q4-15	D-	D-	E+

Asset & Performance History

Date	NAV	1-Year Total Return
2018	66.66	12.95
2017	59.2	-64.94
2016	168.9	-31.84
2015	247.83	-13.04
2014	285	-45.63
2013	524.25	-59.55

Total Assets: $81,855,444
Asset Allocation

Asset	%
Cash	105%
Stocks	-5%
US Stocks	0%
Bonds	0%
US Bonds	0%
Other	0%

Services Offered:

Investment Strategy: The investment seeks daily investment results, before fees and expenses, of 300% of the inverse (or opposite) of the daily performance of the FTSE China 50 Index. The fund, under normal circumstances, invests in swap agreements, futures contracts, short positions or other financial instruments that, in combination, provide inverse (opposite) or short leveraged exposure to the index equal to at least 80% of the fund's net assets (plus borrowing for investment purposes). The index consists of the 50 largest and most liquid public Chinese companies currently trading on the Hong Kong Stock Exchange ("SEHK"). The fund is non-diversified. **Top Holdings:** Ishares China Largecap Ishares China Largecap iShares China Large Cap ETF USD Dist Ishares China Largecap Goldman Finl Sq Trsry Ins

---

First Trust RiverFront Dynamic Emerging Markets ETF

D+ **SELL**

Ticker	Traded On	NAV	Total Assets ($)	Dividend Yield (TTM)	Turnover Ratio	Expense Ratio
RFEM	NAS CM	58.22	$81,508,903	2.35		0.95

Ratings
Reward   D
Risk   D+
Recent Upgrade/Downgrade

Fund Information
Fund Type	Exchange Traded Funds
Category	Global Emerg Mkts Equity
Sub-Category	Diversified Emerging Mkts
Prospectus Objective	Div Emerg Mkts
Inception Date	Jun-16
Open to New Investments	Y

Prices
Price (as of 9/30/2019)	57.79
52-Week High	65.11
52-Week Low	54.25

Total Returns (%)
3-Month	6-Month	1-Year	3-Year	5-Year
-5.46	-6.29	-4.60	12.13	

3-Year Standard Deviation	15.12
Effective Duration	

Valuation
Premium/Discount (1-Year Average)	-0.12

Company Information
Provider	First Trust
Manager/Tenure	Adam Grossman (3), Scott Hays (3), Chris Konstantinos (3), 1 other
Website	http://www.ftportfolios.com/
Address	First Trust 120 E. Liberty Drive, Suite 400 Wheaton IL 60187 United States
Phone Number	800-621-1675

PERFORMANCE

Ratings History

Date	Overall Rating	Risk Rating	Reward Rating
Q3-19	D+	D+	D
Q4-18	D+	D	D+
Q4-17	D+	B	C
Q4-16	U		
Q4-15			

Asset & Performance History

Date	NAV	1-Year Total Return
2018	56.34	-18.07
2017	70.25	35.57
2016	52.71	
2015		
2014		
2013		

Total Assets: $81,508,903
Asset Allocation

Asset	%
Cash	1%
Stocks	99%
US Stocks	0%
Bonds	0%
US Bonds	0%
Other	0%

Services Offered:

Investment Strategy: The investment seeks to provide capital appreciation. The fund invests at least 80% of its net assets (including investment borrowings) in a portfolio of equity securities of emerging market companies, including through investments in common stock, depositary receipts, and common and preferred shares of real estate investment trusts, and forward foreign currency exchange contracts and currency spot transactions used to hedge the fund's exposure to the currencies in which the equity securities of such emerging market companies are denominated. The fund may invest in small, mid and large capitalization companies. It is non-diversified. **Top Holdings:** Alibaba Group Holding Ltd ADR Tencent Holdings Ltd Samsung Electronics Co Ltd Taiwan Semiconductor Manufacturing Co Ltd Naspers Ltd Class N

iPath® Series B S&P GSCI® Crude Oil Total Return Index ETN   D-   SELL

Ticker	Traded On	NAV	Total Assets ($)	Dividend Yield (TTM)	Turnover Ratio	Expense Ratio
OIL	NYSE Arca		$81,499,509	0		0.75

Ratings
Reward	D-
Risk	D
Recent Upgrade/Downgrade	Down

Fund Information
Fund Type	Exchange Traded Funds
Category	Commodities Specified
Sub-Category	Commodities Energy
Prospectus Objective	Natl Res
Inception Date	Nov-16
Open to New Investments	Y

Prices
Price (as of 9/30/2019)	11.11
52-Week High	79.07
52-Week Low	10.65

Total Returns (%)
3-Month	6-Month	1-Year	3-Year	5-Year
-80.98	-81.78	-85.31		

3-Year Standard Deviation	
Effective Duration	

Valuation
Premium/Discount (1-Year Average)	-0.11

Company Information
Provider	Milleis Investissements Funds
Manager/Tenure	No Manager (2)
Website	
Address	2-4, rue Eugène Ruppert L-2453 Luxembourg Luxembourg L-2453 Luxembourg
Phone Number	

PERFORMANCE

Ratings History
Date	Overall Rating	Risk Rating	Reward Rating
Q3-19	D-	D	D-
Q4-18	D+	D	D+
Q4-17	D	C-	D+
Q4-16	U		
Q4-15			

Asset & Performance History
Date	NAV	1-Year Total Return
2018	46.91	-21
2017	59.38	2.53
2016	57.3	
2015		
2014		
2013		

Total Assets: $81,499,509
Asset Allocation
Asset	%
Cash	%
Stocks	%
US Stocks	%
Bonds	%
US Bonds	%
Other	%

Services Offered:

Investment Strategy: The investment seeks to provide investors with exposure to the performance of the S&P GSCI® Crude Oil Total Return Index.
The underlying index is a sub-index of the S&P GSCI® Commodity Index and reflects the excess returns that are potentially available through an unleveraged investment in the commodities futures contracts comprising the Index, plus the Treasury Bill rate of interest that could be earned on funds committed to the trading of the underlying futures contracts. **Top Holdings:**

WisdomTree Interest Rate Hedged U.S. Aggregate Bond Fund   C   HOLD

Ticker	Traded On	NAV	Total Assets ($)	Dividend Yield (TTM)	Turnover Ratio	Expense Ratio
AGZD	NAS CM	47.74	$81,158,456	2.9	81	0.23

Ratings
Reward	C
Risk	D+
Recent Upgrade/Downgrade	

Fund Information
Fund Type	Exchange Traded Funds
Category	Fixed Income Misc
Sub-Category	Nontraditional Bond
Prospectus Objective	Growth & Inc
Inception Date	Dec-13
Open to New Investments	Y

Prices
Price (as of 9/30/2019)	47.80
52-Week High	48.00
52-Week Low	47.23

Total Returns (%)
3-Month	6-Month	1-Year	3-Year	5-Year
0.80	1.62	2.61	7.52	7.22

3-Year Standard Deviation	0.97
Effective Duration	0.12

Valuation
Premium/Discount (1-Year Average)	0.05

Company Information
Provider	WisdomTree
Manager/Tenure	Paul L. Benson (3), Stephanie Shu (3)
Website	http://www.wisdomtree.com
Address	WisdomTree 245 Park Avenue, 35th floor New York NY 10167 United States
Phone Number	866-909-9473

PERFORMANCE

Ratings History
Date	Overall Rating	Risk Rating	Reward Rating
Q3-19	C	D+	C
Q4-18	C-	C-	C
Q4-17	C+	B+	C
Q4-16	C-	D+	C-
Q4-15	D+	C-	D

Asset & Performance History
Date	NAV	1-Year Total Return
2018	47.24	0.58
2017	48.2	2.55
2016	48.12	1.87
2015	48	-1.13
2014	49.36	0.12
2013	50.13	

Total Assets: $81,158,456
Asset Allocation
Asset	%
Cash	101%
Stocks	0%
US Stocks	0%
Bonds	-1%
US Bonds	-8%
Other	0%

Services Offered:

Investment Strategy: The investment seeks to track the price and yield performance, before fees and expenses, of the Bloomberg Barclays Rate Hedged U.S. Aggregate Bond Index, Zero Duration (the "index"). The index is designed to provide long exposure to the Bloomberg Barclays U.S. Aggregate Bond Index while seeking to manage interest rate risk through the use of short positions in U.S. Treasury securities. The fund normally invests at least 80% of its total assets in the component securities of the index and investments that have economic characteristics that are substantially identical to the economic characteristics of such component securities. It is non-diversified. **Top Holdings:** Us 5yr Note (Cbt) Dec19 Xcbt 20191231   Us 2yr Note (Cbt) Dec19 Xcbt 20191231 US 10 Year Ultra Future Dec19   US Ultra Bond (CBT) Dec19   United States Treasury Bonds 2.5%

Alpha Architect Value Momentum Trend ETF   D   SELL

Ticker	Traded On	NAV	Total Assets ($)	Dividend Yield (TTM)	Turnover Ratio	Expense Ratio
VMOT	BATS	23.52	$81,152,314	0.52	44	0.8

Ratings
Reward   D
Risk   D+
Recent Upgrade/Downgrade

Fund Information
Fund Type   Exchange Traded Funds
Category   Long/Short Equity
Sub-Category   Long-Short Equity
Prospectus Objective   Growth & Inc
Inception Date   May-17
Open to New Investments   Y

Prices
Price (as of 9/30/2019)   23.51
52-Week High   28.96
52-Week Low   22.87

Total Returns (%)

3-Month	6-Month	1-Year	3-Year	5-Year
-2.02	-5.48	-18.41		

3-Year Standard Deviation
Effective Duration

Valuation
Premium/Discount (1-Year Average)   -0.01

Company Information
Provider   Alpha Architect
Manager/Tenure   Tao Wang (2)
Website   http://www.alphaarchitect.com/funds
Address   Alpha Architect 213 Foxcroft Road
     Broomall PA 19008 United States
Phone Number

PERFORMANCE

Ratings History

Date	Overall Rating	Risk Rating	Reward Rating
Q3-19	D	D+	D
Q4-18	D	D	D
Q4-17	U		
Q4-16			
Q4-15			

Asset & Performance History

Date	NAV	1-Year Total Return
2018	24.23	-15.69
2017	28.97	
2016		
2015		
2014		
2013		

Total Assets: $81,152,314
Asset Allocation

Asset	%
Cash	27%
Stocks	73%
US Stocks	44%
Bonds	0%
US Bonds	0%
Other	0%

Services Offered:

Investment Strategy: The investment seeks to track the total return performance, before fees and expenses, of the Alpha Architect Value Momentum Trend Index. Under normal circumstances, at least 80% of the fund's total assets (exclusive of collateral held from securities lending) will be invested in the component securities of the index and other instruments of the index. The index will be composed primarily of the other ETFs advised by the Adviser. Currently, there are four Alpha Architect ETFs, which invest in either domestic or international equity securities, and employ either a "momentum" or a "value" investment strategy. The fund is non-diversified. **Top Holdings:** Alpha Architect Intl Quant Momt ETF   iShares MSCI EAFE ETF   Alpha Architect Intl Quant Val ETF   Alpha Architect US Quantitative Momt ETF   Alpha Architect US Quantitative Val ETF

First Trust Japan AlphaDEX® Fund   D   SELL

Ticker	Traded On	NAV	Total Assets ($)	Dividend Yield (TTM)	Turnover Ratio	Expense Ratio
FJP	NAS CM	47.56	$80,845,937	1.97	90	0.8

Ratings
Reward   D
Risk   D+
Recent Upgrade/Downgrade   Down

Fund Information
Fund Type   Exchange Traded Funds
Category   Japan Equity
Sub-Category   Japan Stock
Prospectus Objective   Pacific Stock
Inception Date   Apr-11
Open to New Investments   Y

Prices
Price (as of 9/30/2019)   47.87
52-Week High   57.97
52-Week Low   44.61

Total Returns (%)

3-Month	6-Month	1-Year	3-Year	5-Year
-2.30	-4.24	-15.73	1.28	11.08

3-Year Standard Deviation   11.76
Effective Duration

Valuation
Premium/Discount (1-Year Average)   -0.17

Company Information
Provider   First Trust
Manager/Tenure   Jon C. Erickson (8), Daniel J. Lindquist
     (8), David G. McGarel (8), 3 others
Website   http://www.ftportfolios.com/
Address   First Trust 120 E. Liberty Drive, Suite
     400 Wheaton IL 60187 United States
Phone Number   800-621-1675

PERFORMANCE

Ratings History

Date	Overall Rating	Risk Rating	Reward Rating
Q3-19	D	D+	D
Q4-18	D+	C-	D+
Q4-17	B+	B	A-
Q4-16	C	C-	C
Q4-15	C	C+	C

Asset & Performance History

Date	NAV	1-Year Total Return
2018	48.55	-17.67
2017	59.8	26.69
2016	47.85	2.92
2015	47.18	5.71
2014	44.99	-1.23
2013	46.02	30.68

Total Assets: $80,845,937
Asset Allocation

Asset	%
Cash	0%
Stocks	100%
US Stocks	0%
Bonds	0%
US Bonds	0%
Other	0%

Services Offered:

Investment Strategy: The investment seeks investment results that correspond generally to the price and yield (before the fund's fees and expenses) of an equity index called the NASDAQ AlphaDEX® Japan Index. The fund will normally invest at least 90% of its net assets (including investment borrowings) in the common stocks and depositary receipts that comprise the index. The index is designed to select stocks from the NASDAQ Japan Index (the "base index") that may generate positive alpha, or risk-adjusted returns, relative to traditional indices through the use of the AlphaDEX® selection methodology. **Top Holdings:** Advantest Corp   NEC Corp   ITOCHU Corp   Hitachi High-Technologies Corp   SUMCO Corp

Goldman Sachs Hedge Industry VIP ETF   C   HOLD

Ticker	Traded On	NAV	Total Assets ($)	Dividend Yield (TTM)	Turnover Ratio	Expense Ratio
GVIP	NYSE Arca	55.61	$80,635,704	1	1	0.45

Ratings
Reward	C
Risk	D+
Recent Upgrade/Downgrade	

Fund Information
Fund Type	Exchange Traded Funds
Category	US Equity Large Cap Blend
Sub-Category	Large Growth
Prospectus Objective	Growth & Inc
Inception Date	Nov-16
Open to New Investments	Y

Prices
Price (as of 9/30/2019)	55.67
52-Week High	60.03
52-Week Low	46.00

Total Returns (%)
3-Month	6-Month	1-Year	3-Year	5-Year
-5.48	-2.69	-3.45	43.44	

3-Year Standard Deviation	
Effective Duration	

Valuation
Premium/Discount (1-Year Average)	0.01

Company Information
Provider	Goldman Sachs
Manager/Tenure	Raj Garigipati (2), Jamie McGregor (2)
Website	http://www.gsamfunds.com
Address	Goldman Sachs 200 West Stree New York NY 10282 United States
Phone Number	800-526-7384

PERFORMANCE

Ratings History
Date	Overall Rating	Risk Rating	Reward Rating
Q3-19	C	D+	C
Q4-18	C-	C-	C-
Q4-17	D	A-	D+
Q4-16	U		
Q4-15			

Asset & Performance History
Date	NAV	1-Year Total Return
2018	49.17	-6.66
2017	52.9	25.72
2016	42.34	
2015		
2014		
2013		

Total Assets: $80,635,704

Asset Allocation
Asset	%
Cash	0%
Stocks	100%
US Stocks	96%
Bonds	0%
US Bonds	0%
Other	0%

Services Offered:

Investment Strategy: The investment seeks to provide investment results that closely correspond, before fees and expenses, to the performance of the Goldman Sachs Hedge Fund VIP IndexTM. The fund seeks to achieve its investment objective by investing at least 80% of its assets in securities included in its underlying index, in depositary receipts representing securities included in its underlying index and in underlying stocks in respect of depositary receipts included in its underlying index. The index is designed to deliver exposure to equity securities whose performance is expected to influence the long portfolios of hedge funds. **Top Holdings:** Vistra Energy Corp Salesforce.com Inc   Charter Communications Inc A   Alibaba Group Holding Ltd ADR   Micron Technology Inc

---

Alpha Architect International Quantitative Value ETF   D+   SELL

Ticker	Traded On	NAV	Total Assets ($)	Dividend Yield (TTM)	Turnover Ratio	Expense Ratio
IVAL	BATS	26.76	$80,294,165	2.83	30	0.59

Ratings
Reward	D
Risk	D+
Recent Upgrade/Downgrade	

Fund Information
Fund Type	Exchange Traded Funds
Category	Global Equity Large Cap
Sub-Category	Foreign Large Value
Prospectus Objective	Growth & Inc
Inception Date	Dec-14
Open to New Investments	Y

Prices
Price (as of 9/30/2019)	26.90
52-Week High	30.84
52-Week Low	24.27

Total Returns (%)
3-Month	6-Month	1-Year	3-Year	5-Year
-1.56	-4.11	-10.11	16.89	

3-Year Standard Deviation	15.15
Effective Duration	

Valuation
Premium/Discount (1-Year Average)	-0.10

Company Information
Provider	Alpha Architect
Manager/Tenure	Tao Wang (4)
Website	http://www.alphaarchitect.com/funds
Address	Alpha Architect 213 Foxcroft Road Broomall PA 19008 United States
Phone Number	

PERFORMANCE

Ratings History
Date	Overall Rating	Risk Rating	Reward Rating
Q3-19	D+	D+	D
Q4-18	D+	D+	D+
Q4-17	C+	C	C+
Q4-16	D+	D+	D+
Q4-15	U		

Asset & Performance History
Date	NAV	1-Year Total Return
2018	25.18	-21.62
2017	32.95	30.33
2016	25.74	8.51
2015	24.11	-3.32
2014	25.37	
2013		

Total Assets: $80,294,165

Asset Allocation
Asset	%
Cash	0%
Stocks	100%
US Stocks	0%
Bonds	0%
US Bonds	0%
Other	0%

Services Offered:

Investment Strategy: The investment seeks to track the total return performance, before fees and expenses, of the Alpha Architect International Quantitative Value Index. The fund normally will invest at least 80% of its total assets in the component securities of the index and investments that have economic characteristics that are substantially identical to the economic characteristics of such component securities. The index uses a 5-step, quantitative, rules-based methodology to identify a portfolio of approximately 40-50 undervalued U.S. equity securities with the potential for capital appreciation. **Top Holdings:** Advantest Corp   Hitachi High-Technologies Corp   JB Hi Fi Ltd   Sony Corp   NTT DOCOMO Inc

First Trust BuyWrite Income ETF   C   HOLD

Ticker	Traded On	NAV	Total Assets ($)	Dividend Yield (TTM)	Turnover Ratio	Expense Ratio
FTHI	NAS CM	22.43	$80,154,046	4.28	239	0.85

Ratings
Reward   C
Risk   C-
Recent Upgrade/Downgrade

Fund Information
Fund Type   Exchange Traded Funds
Category   Long/Short Equity
Sub-Category   Options-based
Prospectus Objective   Income
Inception Date   Jan-14
Open to New Investments   Y

Prices
Price (as of 9/30/2019)   22.49
52-Week High   23.32
52-Week Low   19.24

Total Returns (%)

3-Month	6-Month	1-Year	3-Year	5-Year
0.67	5.04	1.02	24.06	40.30

3-Year Standard Deviation   9.68
Effective Duration

Valuation
Premium/Discount (1-Year Average)   0.02

Company Information
Provider   First Trust
Manager/Tenure   John W. Gambla (5), Rob A. Guttschow (5)
Website   http://www.ftportfolios.com/
Address   First Trust 120 E. Liberty Drive, Suite 400 Wheaton IL 60187 United States
Phone Number   800-621-1675

PERFORMANCE

Ratings History

Date	Overall Rating	Risk Rating	Reward Rating
Q3-19	C	C-	C
Q4-18	C-	D+	C
Q4-17	B	A	B-
Q4-16	C	C-	C+
Q4-15	D+	C	C

Asset & Performance History

Date	NAV	1-Year Total Return
2018	20.28	-9.1
2017	23.29	13.92
2016	21.33	12.21
2015	19.92	2.07
2014	20.49	7.03
2013		

Total Assets: $80,154,046
Asset Allocation

Asset	%
Cash	1%
Stocks	99%
US Stocks	98%
Bonds	0%
US Bonds	0%
Other	0%

Services Offered:

Investment Strategy: The investment seeks current income; capital appreciation is a secondary objective. The fund will pursue its objectives by investing in equity securities listed on U.S. exchanges and by utilizing an "option strategy" consisting of writing (selling) U.S. exchange-traded covered call options on the Standard & Poor's 500® Index (the "index"). The call options written by the fund will be a laddered portfolio of call options with expirations of less than one year, written at-the-money to slightly out-of-the-money. The fund is non-diversified. **Top Holdings:** Alphabet Inc A Microsoft Corp Johnson & Johnson The Home Depot Inc Apple Inc

---

Invesco S&P SmallCap Momentum ETF   C   HOLD

Ticker	Traded On	NAV	Total Assets ($)	Dividend Yield (TTM)	Turnover Ratio	Expense Ratio
XSMO	NYSE Arca	37.27	$80,139,757	0.43		0.39

Ratings
Reward   C
Risk   D+
Recent Upgrade/Downgrade

Fund Information
Fund Type   Exchange Traded Funds
Category   US Equity Small Cap
Sub-Category   Small Growth
Prospectus Objective   Growth
Inception Date   Mar-05
Open to New Investments   Y

Prices
Price (as of 9/30/2019)   37.27
52-Week High   39.03
52-Week Low   28.65

Total Returns (%)

3-Month	6-Month	1-Year	3-Year	5-Year
-0.58	2.46	-4.27	44.83	65.03

3-Year Standard Deviation   17.46
Effective Duration

Valuation
Premium/Discount (1-Year Average)   -0.03

Company Information
Provider   Invesco
Manager/Tenure   Peter Hubbard (12), Michael Jeanette (11), Tony Seisser (5)
Website   http://www.invesco.com/us
Address   Invesco 11 Greenway Plaza, Ste. 2500 Houston TX 77046 United States
Phone Number   800-659-1005

PERFORMANCE

Ratings History

Date	Overall Rating	Risk Rating	Reward Rating
Q3-19	C	D+	C
Q4-18	C-	C-	C
Q4-17	B	B	B+
Q4-16	C	D+	C+
Q4-15	C	D+	C+

Asset & Performance History

Date	NAV	1-Year Total Return
2018	30.93	-2.88
2017	32.03	23.42
2016	26.03	7.16
2015	24.37	0.32
2014	24.37	4.53
2013	23.62	32.33

Total Assets: $80,139,757
Asset Allocation

Asset	%
Cash	1%
Stocks	99%
US Stocks	97%
Bonds	0%
US Bonds	0%
Other	0%

Services Offered:

Investment Strategy: The investment seeks to track the investment results (before fees and expenses) of the S&P SmallCap 600 Momentum Index (the "underlying index"). The fund generally will invest at least 90% of its total assets in the securities that comprise the underlying index. Strictly in accordance with its guidelines and mandated procedures, the index provider compiles, maintains and calculates the underlying index, which is composed of constituents of the S&P SmallCap 600® that have the highest "momentum score." **Top Holdings:** LHC Group Inc FTI Consulting Inc Repligen Corp HMS Holdings Corp Exponent Inc

Invesco New York AMT-Free Municipal Bond ETF   C   HOLD

Ticker	Traded On	NAV	Total Assets ($)	Dividend Yield (TTM)	Turnover Ratio	Expense Ratio
PZT	NYSE Arca	25.41	$80,041,814	2.75		0.28

Ratings

Reward	C+
Risk	C-
Recent Upgrade/Downgrade	

Fund Information

Fund Type	Exchange Traded Funds
Category	US Muni Fixed Inc
Sub-Category	Muni New York Long
Prospectus Objective	Muni Bond - Single State
Inception Date	Oct-07
Open to New Investments	Y

Prices

Price (as of 9/30/2019)	25.44
52-Week High	25.78
52-Week Low	23.24

Total Returns (%)

3-Month	6-Month	1-Year	3-Year	5-Year
2.15	5.10	10.23	11.00	22.18

3-Year Standard Deviation	3.91
Effective Duration	7.98

Valuation

Premium/Discount (1-Year Average)	-0.07

Company Information

Provider	Invesco
Manager/Tenure	Philip Fang (11), Peter Hubbard (11), Jeffrey W. Kernagis (11), 2 others
Website	http://www.invesco.com/us
Address	Invesco 11 Greenway Plaza, Ste. 2500 Houston TX 77046 United States
Phone Number	800-659-1005

PERFORMANCE

Ratings History

Date	Overall Rating	Risk Rating	Reward Rating
Q3-19	C	C-	C+
Q4-18	C-	C-	D+
Q4-17	B-	B+	C
Q4-16	C	D+	C
Q4-15	C	D+	C

Asset & Performance History

Date	NAV	1-Year Total Return
2018	23.92	0.23
2017	24.58	5.82
2016	23.93	1.06
2015	24.46	3.81
2014	24.38	14.41
2013	22.15	-6.29

Total Assets: $80,041,814

Asset Allocation

Asset	%
Cash	4%
Stocks	0%
US Stocks	0%
Bonds	96%
US Bonds	95%
Other	0%

Services Offered:

Investment Strategy: The investment seeks to track the investment results (before fees and expenses) of the ICE BofAML New York Long-Term Core Plus Municipal Securities Index (the "underlying index"). The fund generally will invest at least 80% of its total assets in municipal securities that comprise the underlying index and that also are exempt from the federal alternative minimum tax. The index is composed of U.S. dollar-denominated, investment grade, tax-exempt debt publicly issued by New York or any U.S. territory or their political subdivisions, in the U.S. domestic market with a term of at least 15 years remaining to final maturity. It is non-diversified. **Top Holdings:** UTILITY DEBT SECURITIZATION AUTH N Y 5%   NEW YORK N Y CITY INDL DEV AGY REV 6.5%   NEW YORK N Y 1.33% NEW YORK ST DORM AUTH REVS NON ST SUPPORTED DEBT 5%   BROOKLYN ARENA LOC DEV CORP N Y PILOT REV 5%

iShares iBonds Mar 2020 Term Corporate ex-Financials ETF   C   HOLD

Ticker	Traded On	NAV	Total Assets ($)	Dividend Yield (TTM)	Turnover Ratio	Expense Ratio
IBCD	NYSE Arca	24.60	$79,947,734	2	5	0.1

Ratings

Reward	C
Risk	C-
Recent Upgrade/Downgrade	Up

Fund Information

Fund Type	Exchange Traded Funds
Category	US Fixed Income
Sub-Category	Short-Term Bond
Prospectus Objective	Corp Bond - High Quality
Inception Date	Apr-13
Open to New Investments	Y

Prices

Price (as of 9/30/2019)	24.61
52-Week High	24.62
52-Week Low	24.32

Total Returns (%)

3-Month	6-Month	1-Year	3-Year	5-Year
0.59	1.36	2.90	4.72	10.85

3-Year Standard Deviation	0.86
Effective Duration	

Valuation

Premium/Discount (1-Year Average)	0.07

Company Information

Provider	iShares
Manager/Tenure	James Mauro (6), Scott Radell (6)
Website	http://www.ishares.com
Address	iShares 400 Howard Street San Francisco CA 94105 United States
Phone Number	800-474-2737

PERFORMANCE

Ratings History

Date	Overall Rating	Risk Rating	Reward Rating
Q3-19	C	C-	C
Q4-18	C-	D+	C
Q4-17	B	A+	C
Q4-16	C	D+	C
Q4-15	D+	D	C

Asset & Performance History

Date	NAV	1-Year Total Return
2018	24.37	1.5
2017	24.47	1.63
2016	24.49	3.01
2015	24.25	1.54
2014	24.4	4.43
2013	23.87	

Total Assets: $79,947,734

Asset Allocation

Asset	%
Cash	62%
Stocks	0%
US Stocks	0%
Bonds	38%
US Bonds	33%
Other	0%

Services Offered:

Investment Strategy: The investment seeks to track the investment results of the Bloomberg Barclays 2020 Maturity High Quality Corporate Index which is composed of U.S. dollar-denominated, investment-grade corporate bonds, excluding financials, maturing after March 31, 2019 and before April 1, 2020. The fund generally will invest at least 90% of its assets in the component securities of the underlying index, and may invest up to 10% of its assets in certain futures, options and swap contracts, cash and cash equivalents, as well as in securities not included in the underlying index. **Top Holdings:** Comcast Corporation 5.15% Pepsico Inc 4.5% Exxon Mobil Corporation 1.91% Novartis Capital Corporation 1.8% Microsoft Corporation 1.85%

Nuveen ESG Large-Cap Growth ETF
C   HOLD

Ticker	Traded On	NAV	Total Assets ($)	Dividend Yield (TTM)	Turnover Ratio	Expense Ratio
NULG	BATS	38.04	$79,887,156	0.61	65	0.35

Ratings
Reward	C+
Risk	C
Recent Upgrade/Downgrade	

Fund Information
Fund Type	Exchange Traded Funds
Category	US Equity Large Cap Growth
Sub-Category	Large Growth
Prospectus Objective	Growth
Inception Date	Dec-16
Open to New Investments	Y

Prices
Price (as of 9/30/2019)	38.09
52-Week High	38.78
52-Week Low	29.07

Total Returns (%)
3-Month	6-Month	1-Year	3-Year	5-Year
1.39	6.69	5.23		

3-Year Standard Deviation	
Effective Duration	

Valuation
Premium/Discount (1-Year Average)	0.07

Company Information
Provider	Nuveen
Manager/Tenure	Philip James(Jim) Campagna (2), Lei Liao (2)
Website	http://www.nuveen.com
Address	Nuveen Investment Trust John Nuveen & Co. Inc. Chicago IL 60606 United States
Phone Number	312-917-8146

PERFORMANCE

Ratings History
Date	Overall Rating	Risk Rating	Reward Rating
Q3-19	C	C	C+
Q4-18	C-	C-	C
Q4-17	D	A-	D+
Q4-16			
Q4-15			

Asset & Performance History
Date	NAV	1-Year Total Return
2018	30.06	-0.15
2017	31.01	24.9
2016	24.91	
2015		
2014		
2013		

Total Assets: $79,887,156
Asset Allocation
Asset	%
Cash	0%
Stocks	100%
US Stocks	98%
Bonds	0%
US Bonds	0%
Other	0%

Services Offered:

Investment Strategy: The investment seeks to track the investment results, before fees and expenses, of the TIAA ESG USA Large-Cap Growth Index (the "index"). Under normal market conditions, the fund invests at least 80% of the sum of its net assets and the amount of any borrowings for investment purposes in component securities of the index. The index is comprised of equity securities issued by large capitalization companies listed on U.S. exchanges that meet certain environmental, social, and governance ("ESG") criteria. **Top Holdings:** Microsoft Corp Alphabet Inc Class C Mastercard Inc A The Home Depot Inc Alphabet Inc A

---

iShares North American Tech-Multimedia Networking ETF
C   HOLD

Ticker	Traded On	NAV	Total Assets ($)	Dividend Yield (TTM)	Turnover Ratio	Expense Ratio
IGN	NYSE Arca	53.19	$79,784,186	0.38	29	0.46

Ratings
Reward	B-
Risk	C-
Recent Upgrade/Downgrade	Up

Fund Information
Fund Type	Exchange Traded Funds
Category	Technology Sector Equity
Sub-Category	Technology
Prospectus Objective	Technology
Inception Date	Jul-01
Open to New Investments	Y

Prices
Price (as of 9/30/2019)	53.19
52-Week High	60.69
52-Week Low	44.15

Total Returns (%)
3-Month	6-Month	1-Year	3-Year	5-Year
-3.35	-7.38	-1.50	32.02	62.20

3-Year Standard Deviation	18.03
Effective Duration	

Valuation
Premium/Discount (1-Year Average)	-0.03

Company Information
Provider	iShares
Manager/Tenure	Greg Savage (11), Jennifer Hsui (6), Alan Mason (3), 2 others
Website	http://www.ishares.com
Address	iShares 400 Howard Street San Francisco CA 94105 United States
Phone Number	800-474-2737

PERFORMANCE

Ratings History
Date	Overall Rating	Risk Rating	Reward Rating
Q3-19	C	C-	B-
Q4-18	C	D+	B-
Q4-17	B	B	B
Q4-16	B-	C-	B
Q4-15	B-	C+	B

Asset & Performance History
Date	NAV	1-Year Total Return
2018	47.4	-0.93
2017	48.13	10.97
2016	43.63	19.42
2015	36.85	-0.07
2014	37.14	15.54
2013	32.31	15.13

Total Assets: $79,784,186
Asset Allocation
Asset	%
Cash	0%
Stocks	100%
US Stocks	100%
Bonds	0%
US Bonds	0%
Other	0%

Services Offered: CashInvestment Plan

Investment Strategy: The investment seeks to track the investment results of the S&P North American Technology Multimedia Networking Index composed of North American equities in the multimedia and networking technology sectors. The fund generally invests at least 90% of its assets in securities of the underlying index and in depositary receipts representing securities of the underlying index. The underlying index measures the performance of U.S.-traded stocks of communication equipment companies in the U.S. and Canada. The fund is non-diversified. **Top Holdings:** Motorola Solutions Inc Arista Networks Inc F5 Networks Inc Juniper Networks Inc Cisco Systems Inc

---

Vanguard U.S. Multifactor ETF Shares   D   SELL

Ticker	Traded On	NAV	Total Assets ($)	Dividend Yield (TTM)	Turnover Ratio	Expense Ratio
VFMF	BATS	75.62	$79,401,000	1.68	64	0.18

Ratings

Reward	D
Risk	D+
Recent Upgrade/Downgrade	

Fund Information

Fund Type	Exchange Traded Funds
Category	US Equity Mid Cap
Sub-Category	Mid-Cap Blend
Prospectus Objective	Growth
Inception Date	Feb-18
Open to New Investments	Y

Prices

Price (as of 9/30/2019)	75.64
52-Week High	82.00
52-Week Low	63.72

Total Returns (%)

3-Month	6-Month	1-Year	3-Year	5-Year
-0.66	0.43	-6.23		

3-Year Standard Deviation	
Effective Duration	

Valuation

Premium/Discount (1-Year Average)	-0.01

Company Information

Provider	Vanguard
Manager/Tenure	Antonio Picca (1)
Website	http://www.vanguard.com
Address	Vanguard 100 Vanguard Boulevard Malvern PA 19355 United States
Phone Number	877-662-7447

PERFORMANCE

Ratings History

Date	Overall Rating	Risk Rating	Reward Rating
Q3-19	D	D+	D
Q4-18	U		
Q4-17			
Q4-16			
Q4-15			

Asset & Performance History

Date	NAV	1-Year Total Return
2018	67.21	
2017		
2016		
2015		
2014		
2013		

Total Assets: $79,401,000
Asset Allocation

Asset	%
Cash	0%
Stocks	100%
US Stocks	98%
Bonds	0%
US Bonds	0%
Other	0%

Services Offered:

Investment Strategy: The investment seeks to provide long-term capital appreciation. The fund invests primarily in U.S. common stocks with the potential to generate higher returns relative to the broad U.S. equity market by investing in stocks with relatively strong recent performance, strong fundamentals, and low prices relative to fundamentals as determined by the advisor. Under normal circumstances, at least 80% of its assets will be invested in securities issued by U.S. companies. **Top Holdings:** Merck & Co Inc HCA Healthcare Inc JPMorgan Chase & Co Starbucks Corp Intel Corp

---

ProShares UltraPro 3x Crude Oil ETF   D   SELL

Ticker	Traded On	NAV	Total Assets ($)	Dividend Yield (TTM)	Turnover Ratio	Expense Ratio
OILU	NYSE Arca		$79,388,839	0		0.49

Ratings

Reward	D
Risk	D+
Recent Upgrade/Downgrade	

Fund Information

Fund Type	Exchange Traded Funds
Category	Trading Tools
Sub-Category	Trading--Leveraged Commodities
Prospectus Objective	Growth & Inc
Inception Date	Mar-17
Open to New Investments	Y

Prices

Price (as of 9/30/2019)	15.62
52-Week High	73.04
52-Week Low	12.37

Total Returns (%)

3-Month	6-Month	1-Year	3-Year	5-Year
-26.45	-40.82	-75.78		

3-Year Standard Deviation	
Effective Duration	

Valuation

Premium/Discount (1-Year Average)	-0.32

Company Information

Provider	ProShares
Manager/Tenure	Management Team (2)
Website	http://www.proshares.com
Address	ProShares 7501 Wisconsin Avenue, Suite 1000 Bethesda MD 20814 United States
Phone Number	866-776-5125

PERFORMANCE

Ratings History

Date	Overall Rating	Risk Rating	Reward Rating
Q3-19	D	D+	D
Q4-18	D+	D	D+
Q4-17	U		
Q4-16			
Q4-15			

Asset & Performance History

Date	NAV	1-Year Total Return
2018	13.08	-65.64
2017	37.79	
2016		
2015		
2014		
2013		

Total Assets: $79,388,839
Asset Allocation

Asset	%
Cash	-200%
Stocks	0%
US Stocks	0%
Bonds	0%
US Bonds	0%
Other	300%

Services Offered:

Investment Strategy: The investment seeks daily investment results, before fees and expenses, that correspond to three times (3x) the daily performance of the Bloomberg WTI Crude Oil SubindexSM.
The fund seeks to meet its investment objective by investing, under normal market conditions, in futures contracts for WTI sweet, light crude oil listed on the NYMEX, ICE Futures U.S. or other U.S. exchanges and listed options on such contracts. **Top Holdings:** Crude Oil Oct19

iShares iBonds Mar 2023 Term Corporate ETF   C   HOLD

Ticker	Traded On	NAV	Total Assets ($)	Dividend Yield (TTM)	Turnover Ratio	Expense Ratio
IBDD	NYSE Arca	26.82	$79,128,930	2.85	3	0.1

Ratings
Reward	C+
Risk	D+
Recent Upgrade/Downgrade	

Fund Information
Fund Type	Exchange Traded Funds
Category	US Fixed Income
Sub-Category	Target Maturity
Prospectus Objective	Corp Bond - Gen
Inception Date	Jul-13
Open to New Investments	Y

Prices
Price (as of 9/30/2019)	26.86
52-Week High	26.97
52-Week Low	25.36

Total Returns (%)
3-Month	6-Month	1-Year	3-Year	5-Year
1.25	3.65	7.64	8.14	19.03

3-Year Standard Deviation	2.62
Effective Duration	

Valuation
Premium/Discount (1-Year Average)	0.13

Company Information
Provider	iShares
Manager/Tenure	James Mauro (6), Scott Radell (6)
Website	http://www.ishares.com
Address	iShares 400 Howard Street San Francisco CA 94105 United States
Phone Number	800-474-2737

PERFORMANCE

Ratings History
Date	Overall Rating	Risk Rating	Reward Rating
Q3-19	C	D+	C+
Q4-18	D+	D+	C-
Q4-17	B	A	C
Q4-16	C	D+	C
Q4-15	D	D	D+

Asset & Performance History
Date	NAV	1-Year Total Return
2018	25.57	-0.09
2017	26.38	3.76
2016	26.11	5.54
2015	25.47	0.64
2014	26.1	8.55
2013	24.84	

Total Assets: $79,128,930

Asset Allocation
Asset	%
Cash	2%
Stocks	0%
US Stocks	0%
Bonds	96%
US Bonds	84%
Other	0%

Services Offered:

Investment Strategy: The investment seeks to track the investment results of Bloomberg Barclays 2023 Maturity Corporate Index which composed of U.S. dollar-denominated, investment-grade corporate bonds maturing after March 31, 2022 and before April 1, 2023. The fund generally will invest at least 90% of its assets in the component securities (including indirect investments through an underlying fund) of the underlying index, and may invest up to 10% of its assets in certain futures, options and swap contracts, cash and cash equivalents, as well as in securities not included in the underlying index. **Top Holdings:** Bank of America Corporation 3.3% Anheuser-Busch InBev Finance Inc. 3.3% Goldman Sachs Group, Inc. 3.63% CVS Health Corp 3.7% Wells Fargo & Company 2.63%

SPDR® Portfolio High Yield Bond ETF   C   HOLD

Ticker	Traded On	NAV	Total Assets ($)	Dividend Yield (TTM)	Turnover Ratio	Expense Ratio
SPHY	NYSE Arca		$78,332,152	5.2	75	0.15

Ratings
Reward	C+
Risk	C-
Recent Upgrade/Downgrade	

Fund Information
Fund Type	Exchange Traded Funds
Category	US Fixed Income
Sub-Category	Corporate Bond
Prospectus Objective	Corp Bond-High Yld
Inception Date	Jun-12
Open to New Investments	Y

Prices
Price (as of 9/30/2019)	26.18
52-Week High	26.22
52-Week Low	24.47

Total Returns (%)
3-Month	6-Month	1-Year	3-Year	5-Year
1.16	3.59	8.00	12.99	24.53

3-Year Standard Deviation	3.55
Effective Duration	2.95

Valuation
Premium/Discount (1-Year Average)	0.09

Company Information
Provider	SPDR State Street Global Advisors
Manager/Tenure	Michael J. Brunell (7), Kyle Kelly (6), Bradley J. Sullivan (3)
Website	http://www.spdrs.com
Address	SPDR State Street Global Advisors State Street Financial Center, 1 Lincoln Street Boston MA 02111-2900 United States
Phone Number	617-786-3000

PERFORMANCE

Ratings History
Date	Overall Rating	Risk Rating	Reward Rating
Q3-19	C	C-	C+
Q4-18	D+	D+	C-
Q4-17	B-	B+	C+
Q4-16	C	D+	C
Q4-15	C-	D+	C-

Asset & Performance History
Date	NAV	1-Year Total Return
2018	24.62	-2.8
2017	26.36	5.83
2016	25.86	10.42
2015	24.45	-1.94
2014	25.97	6.04
2013	25.47	1.06

Total Assets: $78,332,152

Asset Allocation
Asset	%
Cash	1%
Stocks	0%
US Stocks	0%
Bonds	99%
US Bonds	85%
Other	0%

Services Offered:

Investment Strategy: The investment seeks to provide investment results that, before fees and expenses, correspond generally to the price and yield performance of ICE BofAML US High Yield Index. The fund invests substantially all, but at least 80%, of its total assets in the securities comprising the index or in securities that the Adviser determines have economic characteristics that are substantially identical to the economic characteristics of the securities that comprise the index. The index is designed to measure the performance of U.S. dollar denominated below investment grade corporate debt publicly issued in the U.S. domestic market. The fund is non-diversified. **Top Holdings:** CCO Holdings, LLC/ CCO Holdings Capital Corp. 5.75% ALTICE FRANCE S.A 7.38% Sprint Corporation 7.88% CSC Holdings, LLC 6.62% Community Health Systems Incorporated 6.25%

United States Brent Oil Fund, LP

C-   **HOLD**

Ticker	Traded On	NAV		Total Assets ($)	Dividend Yield (TTM)	Turnover Ratio	Expense Ratio
BNO	NYSE Arca	18.09		$76,902,878	0		0.9

Ratings

Reward	C-
Risk	C-
Recent Upgrade/Downgrade	

Fund Information

Fund Type	Exchange Traded Funds
Category	Commodities Specified
Sub-Category	Commodities Energy
Prospectus Objective	Natl Res
Inception Date	Jun-10
Open to New Investments	Y

Prices

Price (as of 9/30/2019)	18.15
52-Week High	24.21
52-Week Low	14.70

Total Returns (%)

3-Month	6-Month	1-Year	3-Year	5-Year
-5.89	-7.79	-24.32	24.05	-51.76

3-Year Standard Deviation	25.74
Effective Duration	

Valuation

Premium/Discount (1-Year Average)	-0.21

Company Information

Provider	USCF Investments
Manager/Tenure	Management Team (9)
Website	http://www.uscfinvestments.com
Address	USCF 1290 Broadway, Suite 1100 Denver CO 80203 United States
Phone Number	

PERFORMANCE

Ratings History

Date	Overall Rating	Risk Rating	Reward Rating
Q3-19	C-	C-	C-
Q4-18	C-	C-	C-
Q4-17	C-	D+	C
Q4-16	D-	D	D-
Q4-15	D-	D-	D-

Asset & Performance History

Date	NAV	1-Year Total Return
2018	15.18	-16.51
2017	18.18	15.82
2016	15.7	28.45
2015	12.22	-45.42
2014	22.39	-48.89
2013	43.81	6.92

Total Assets: $76,902,878
Asset Allocation

Asset	%
Cash	33%
Stocks	0%
US Stocks	0%
Bonds	18%
US Bonds	18%
Other	49%

Services Offered:

Investment Strategy: The investment seeks the daily changes in percentage terms of its shares' per share net asset value ("NAV") to reflect the daily changes in percentage terms of the spot price of Brent crude oil. The Benchmark Futures Contract is the futures contract on Brent crude oil as traded on the Ice Futures Europe Exchange that is the near month contract to expire, except when the near month contract is within two weeks of expiration, in which case it will be measured by the futures contract that is the next month contract to expire. **Top Holdings:** Future Contract On Brent Crude Futr Nov19 United States Treasury Bills United States Treasury Bills United States Treasury Bills United States Treasury Bills

---

Inspire 100 ETF

C-   **HOLD**

Ticker	Traded On	NAV		Total Assets ($)	Dividend Yield (TTM)	Turnover Ratio	Expense Ratio
BIBL	NYSE Arca			$76,592,366	1.13		0.35

Ratings

Reward	C-
Risk	C-
Recent Upgrade/Downgrade	

Fund Information

Fund Type	Exchange Traded Funds
Category	US Equity Large Cap Blend
Sub-Category	Large Growth
Prospectus Objective	Growth & Inc
Inception Date	Oct-17
Open to New Investments	Y

Prices

Price (as of 9/30/2019)	27.91
52-Week High	28.33
52-Week Low	22.55

Total Returns (%)

3-Month	6-Month	1-Year	3-Year	5-Year
-0.28	0.94	-0.35		

3-Year Standard Deviation	
Effective Duration	

Valuation

Premium/Discount (1-Year Average)	0.12

Company Information

Provider	Inspire
Manager/Tenure	Darrell Jayroe (1), Robert Netzly (1)
Website	
Address	Inspire 650 San Benito Street, Suite 130 Hollister CA 95023 United States
Phone Number	

PERFORMANCE

Ratings History

Date	Overall Rating	Risk Rating	Reward Rating
Q3-19	C-	C-	C-
Q4-18	C-	D+	C-
Q4-17	U		
Q4-16			
Q4-15			

Asset & Performance History

Date	NAV	1-Year Total Return
2018	23.81	-7.36
2017	26.06	
2016		
2015		
2014		
2013		

Total Assets: $76,592,366
Asset Allocation

Asset	%
Cash	1%
Stocks	99%
US Stocks	98%
Bonds	0%
US Bonds	0%
Other	0%

Services Offered:

Investment Strategy: The investment seeks to replicate investment results that generally correspond, before fees and expenses, to the performance of the Inspire 100 Index. The fund generally will invest at least 80% of its total assets in the component securities of the Inspire 100 Index. The index provider selects domestic large capitalization equity securities using the index provider's Inspire Impact Score®, a proprietary selection methodology that is designed to assign a score to a particular security based on the security's alignment with biblical values and the positive impact that company has on the world through various environmental, social and governance criterion. **Top Holdings:** Danaher Corp Union Pacific Corp Honeywell International Inc NVIDIA Corp NextEra Energy Inc

Goldman Sachs Access High Yield Corporate Bond ETF

C-   HOLD

Ticker	Traded On	NAV	Total Assets ($)	Dividend Yield (TTM)	Turnover Ratio	Expense Ratio
GHYB	NYSE Arca	49.38	$76,534,338	5.65	69	0.34

Ratings

Reward	C-
Risk	C-
Recent Upgrade/Downgrade	

Fund Information

Fund Type	Exchange Traded Funds
Category	US Fixed Income
Sub-Category	High Yield Bond
Prospectus Objective	Corp Bond-High Yld
Inception Date	Sep-17
Open to New Investments	Y

Prices

Price (as of 9/30/2019)	49.35
52-Week High	49.58
52-Week Low	45.28

Total Returns (%)

3-Month	6-Month	1-Year	3-Year	5-Year
1.07	3.51	6.73		

3-Year Standard Deviation	
Effective Duration	

Valuation

Premium/Discount (1-Year Average)	-0.23

Company Information

Provider	Goldman Sachs
Manager/Tenure	Jason Singer (2), David Westbrook (1)
Website	http://www.gsamfunds.com
Address	Goldman Sachs 200 West Stree New York NY 10282 United States
Phone Number	800-526-7384

PERFORMANCE

Ratings History

Date	Overall Rating	Risk Rating	Reward Rating
Q3-19	C-	C-	C-
Q4-18	D+	D+	D+
Q4-17	U		
Q4-16			
Q4-15			

Asset & Performance History

Date	NAV	1-Year Total Return
2018	46.06	-2.26
2017	49.67	
2016		
2015		
2014		
2013		

Total Assets: $76,534,338

Asset Allocation

Asset	%
Cash	1%
Stocks	0%
US Stocks	0%
Bonds	99%
US Bonds	90%
Other	0%

Services Offered:

Investment Strategy: The investment seeks to provide investment results that closely correspond, before fees and expenses, to the performance of the FTSE Goldman Sachs High Yield Corporate Bond Index (the "index"). The fund seeks to achieve its investment objective by investing at least 80% of its assets (exclusive of collateral held from securities lending) in securities included in its underlying index. The index is a rules-based index that is designed to measure the performance of high yield corporate bonds denominated in U.S. dollars ("USD") that meet certain liquidity and fundamental screening criteria. **Top Holdings:** TransDigm, Inc. 6.25% Tenet Healthcare Corporation 4.62% Post Holdings Inc. 5.75% Centene Escrow I Corporation 5.38% CCO Holdings, LLC/ CCO Holdings Capital Corp. 5.12%

Global X MSCI Norway ETF

C-   HOLD

Ticker	Traded On	NAV	Total Assets ($)	Dividend Yield (TTM)	Turnover Ratio	Expense Ratio
NORW	NYSE Arca	11.67	$76,408,908	7.75	10	0.5

Ratings

Reward	C-
Risk	C-
Recent Upgrade/Downgrade	

Fund Information

Fund Type	Exchange Traded Funds
Category	Equity Misc
Sub-Category	Miscellaneous Region
Prospectus Objective	Europe Stock
Inception Date	Nov-10
Open to New Investments	Y

Prices

Price (as of 9/30/2019)	11.62
52-Week High	15.32
52-Week Low	10.83

Total Returns (%)

3-Month	6-Month	1-Year	3-Year	5-Year
-5.81	-5.30	-17.58	20.06	-8.56

3-Year Standard Deviation	14.93
Effective Duration	

Valuation

Premium/Discount (1-Year Average)	-0.36

Company Information

Provider	Global X Funds
Manager/Tenure	Chang Kim (5), Nam To (1), Wayne Xie (0), 1 other
Website	http://www.globalxfunds.com
Address	Global X Funds 600 Lexington Avenue, 20th Floor New York NY 10022 United States
Phone Number	888-493-8631

PERFORMANCE

Ratings History

Date	Overall Rating	Risk Rating	Reward Rating
Q3-19	C-	C-	C-
Q4-18	C	C+	C
Q4-17	C	C	C
Q4-16	D+	D	D+
Q4-15	D	D	D

Asset & Performance History

Date	NAV	1-Year Total Return
2018	11.54	-8.38
2017	13.19	22.03
2016	11.12	17.63
2015	9.73	-15.72
2014	11.98	-22.84
2013	16.59	12.79

Total Assets: $76,408,908

Asset Allocation

Asset	%
Cash	0%
Stocks	100%
US Stocks	1%
Bonds	0%
US Bonds	0%
Other	0%

Services Offered:

Investment Strategy: The investment seeks investment results that correspond generally to the price and yield performance, before fees and expenses, of the MSCI Norway IMI 25/50 Index. The fund invests at least 80% of its total assets in the securities of the underlying index and in American Depositary Receipts ("ADRs") and Global Depositary Receipts ("GDRs") based on the securities in the underlying index. The underlying index is designed to represent the performance of the broad Norway equity universe. The fund is non-diversified. **Top Holdings:** Equinor ASA DNB ASA Telenor ASA Mowi ASA Yara International ASA

FlexShares International Quality Dividend Defensive Index Fund   D+   SELL

Ticker	Traded On	NAV	Total Assets ($)	Dividend Yield (TTM)	Turnover Ratio	Expense Ratio
IQDE	NYSE Arca	21.15	$76,148,773	5.28	69	0.47

Ratings
Reward   D+
Risk   C-
Recent Upgrade/Downgrade   Down

Fund Information
Fund Type   Exchange Traded Funds
Category   Global Equity Large Cap
Sub-Category   Foreign Large Value
Prospectus Objective   World Stock
Inception Date   Apr-13
Open to New Investments   Y

Prices
Price (as of 9/30/2019)   21.20
52-Week High   22.94
52-Week Low   19.98

Total Returns (%)

3-Month	6-Month	1-Year	3-Year	5-Year
-2.97	-1.87	-2.93	7.98	2.37

3-Year Standard Deviation   10.76
Effective Duration

Valuation
Premium/Discount (1-Year Average)   -0.05

Company Information
Provider   Flexshares Trust
Manager/Tenure   Robert Anstine (5), Brendan Sullivan (3)
Website   http://www.flexshares.com
Address   50 South LaSalle Street Chicago, Illinois 60603 Chicago Illinois 60603 United States
Phone Number   855-353-9383

PERFORMANCE

Ratings History

Date	Overall Rating	Risk Rating	Reward Rating
Q3-19	D+	C-	D+
Q4-18	C-	C-	C-
Q4-17	C+	C+	C+
Q4-16	D+	D+	D+
Q4-15	D+	D+	D+

Asset & Performance History

Date	NAV	1-Year Total Return
2018	20.38	-16.12
2017	25.44	21.68
2016	21.9	6.5
2015	21.33	-8.61
2014	24.41	-3.91
2013	26.34	

Total Assets: $76,148,773
Asset Allocation

Asset	%
Cash	1%
Stocks	99%
US Stocks	0%
Bonds	0%
US Bonds	0%
Other	0%

Services Offered:

Investment Strategy: The investment seeks investment results that correspond generally to the price and yield performance, before fees and expenses, of the Northern Trust International Quality Dividend Defensive IndexSM. The fund will invest at least 80% of its total assets in the securities of the index and in ADRs and GDRs based on the securities in the index. The index is designed to provide exposure to a high-quality, income-oriented portfolio of international equity securities issued by non-U.S.-based companies, with an emphasis on long-term capital growth and a targeted overall volatility that is lower than that of the Northern Trust International Large Cap IndexSM. **Top Holdings:** GlaxoSmithKline PLC Nestle SA Royal Bank of Canada Enel SpA BP PLC

Innovator S&P 500 Buffer ETF – July   D+   SELL

Ticker	Traded On	NAV	Total Assets ($)	Dividend Yield (TTM)	Turnover Ratio	Expense Ratio
BJUL	BATS	26.21	$75,994,694	0		0.79

Ratings
Reward   D+
Risk   C-
Recent Upgrade/Downgrade

Fund Information
Fund Type   Exchange Traded Funds
Category   Long/Short Equity
Sub-Category   Options-based
Prospectus Objective   Growth
Inception Date   Aug-18
Open to New Investments   Y

Prices
Price (as of 9/30/2019)   26.15
52-Week High   26.40
52-Week Low   22.50

Total Returns (%)

3-Month	6-Month	1-Year	3-Year	5-Year
1.00	2.52	1.97		

3-Year Standard Deviation
Effective Duration

Valuation
Premium/Discount (1-Year Average)   0.09

Company Information
Provider   Innovator ETFs
Manager/Tenure   Robert T Cummings (1), Daniel S Hare (1), Hayley M Peppers (1)
Website   http://innovatoretfs.com/
Address   Innovator ETFs 120 N Hale Street, Suite 200 Wheaton IL 60187 United States
Phone Number   800-208-5212

PERFORMANCE

Ratings History

Date	Overall Rating	Risk Rating	Reward Rating
Q3-19	D+	C-	D+
Q4-18	U		
Q4-17			
Q4-16			
Q4-15			

Asset & Performance History

Date	NAV	1-Year Total Return
2018	23.47	
2017		
2016		
2015		
2014		
2013		

Total Assets: $75,994,694
Asset Allocation

Asset	%
Cash	4%
Stocks	96%
US Stocks	95%
Bonds	0%
US Bonds	0%
Other	0%

Services Offered:

Investment Strategy: The investment seeks to provide investors with returns that match those of the S&P 500 Price Index. The fund invests at least 80% of its net assets in FLexible EXchange® Options ("FLEX Options") that reference the S&P 500 Price Return Index ("S&P 500 Price Index"). FLEX Options are exchange-traded options contracts with uniquely customizable terms. The fund's investment sub-adviser has constructed a portfolio principally composed of seven FLEX Options on the S&P 500 Price Index that are each set to expire on the last day of the Outcome Period. The fund is non-diversified. **Top Holdings:** Option on S&P 500 PR Option on S&P 500 PR Option on S&P 500 PR Option on CBOE Mini-Spx Index Xsp Option on S&P 500 PR

Invesco BulletShares 2025 High Yield Corporate Bond ETF   C-   HOLD

Ticker	Traded On	NAV	Total Assets ($)	Dividend Yield (TTM)	Turnover Ratio	Expense Ratio
BSJP	NYSE Arca	24.46	$75,830,479	5.71	9	0.42

Ratings
Reward	C-
Risk	C-
Recent Upgrade/Downgrade	

Fund Information
Fund Type	Exchange Traded Funds
Category	US Fixed Income
Sub-Category	High Yield Bond
Prospectus Objective	Corp Bond-High Yld
Inception Date	Sep-17
Open to New Investments	Y

Prices
Price (as of 9/30/2019)	24.53
52-Week High	24.73
52-Week Low	21.97

Total Returns (%)
3-Month	6-Month	1-Year	3-Year	5-Year
1.39	4.42	6.48		

3-Year Standard Deviation	
Effective Duration	3.33

Valuation
Premium/Discount (1-Year Average)	0.11

Company Information
Provider	Invesco
Manager/Tenure	Jeremy Neisewander (2), Peter Hubbard (1), Jeffrey W. Kernagis (1), 1 other
Website	http://www.invesco.com/us
Address	Invesco 11 Greenway Plaza, Ste. 2500 Houston TX 77046 United States
Phone Number	800-659-1005

PERFORMANCE

Ratings History
Date	Overall Rating	Risk Rating	Reward Rating
Q3-19	C-	C-	C-
Q4-18	D+	D+	D+
Q4-17	U		
Q4-16			
Q4-15			

Asset & Performance History
Date	NAV	1-Year Total Return
2018	22.37	-5.42
2017	24.8	
2016		
2015		
2014		
2013		

Total Assets: $75,830,479
Asset Allocation
Asset	%
Cash	0%
Stocks	0%
US Stocks	0%
Bonds	100%
US Bonds	83%
Other	0%

Services Offered:

Investment Strategy: The investment seeks to track the investment results (before fees and expenses) of the Nasdaq BulletShares® USD High Yield Corporate Bond 2025 Index (the "underlying index"). The fund generally will invest at least 80% of its total assets in securities that comprise the underlying index. The underlying index seeks to measure the performance of a portfolio of U.S. dollar-denominated high yield corporate bonds (commonly known as "junk bonds") with maturities or, in some cases, "effective maturities" in the year 2025 (collectively, "2025 Bonds"). The fund is non-diversified. **Top Holdings:** Bausch Health Companies Inc 6.12% HCA Inc. 5.38% 1011778 B.C. Unlimited Liability Company / New Red Finance, Inc. 5% AVANTOR INC 9% Bausch Health Companies Inc 5.5%

Global X Millennials Thematic ETF   C+   HOLD

Ticker	Traded On	NAV	Total Assets ($)	Dividend Yield (TTM)	Turnover Ratio	Expense Ratio
MILN	NAS CM	24.84	$75,758,529	0.4	11	0.5

Ratings
Reward	B-
Risk	C
Recent Upgrade/Downgrade	Up

Fund Information
Fund Type	Exchange Traded Funds
Category	US Equity Large Cap Growth
Sub-Category	Large Growth
Prospectus Objective	Growth & Inc
Inception Date	May-16
Open to New Investments	Y

Prices
Price (as of 9/30/2019)	24.82
52-Week High	26.14
52-Week Low	18.58

Total Returns (%)
3-Month	6-Month	1-Year	3-Year	5-Year
-0.56	3.93	5.93	58.63	

3-Year Standard Deviation	13.99
Effective Duration	

Valuation
Premium/Discount (1-Year Average)	0.03

Company Information
Provider	Global X Funds
Manager/Tenure	Chang Kim (3), Nam To (1), Wayne Xie (0), 1 other
Website	http://www.globalxfunds.com
Address	Global X Funds 600 Lexington Avenue, 20th Floor New York NY 10022 United States
Phone Number	888-493-8631

PERFORMANCE

Ratings History
Date	Overall Rating	Risk Rating	Reward Rating
Q3-19	C+	C	B-
Q4-18	C	C-	C
Q4-17	D+	B+	C
Q4-16	U		
Q4-15			

Asset & Performance History
Date	NAV	1-Year Total Return
2018	19.73	3.06
2017	19.22	23.58
2016	15.59	
2015		
2014		
2013		

Total Assets: $75,758,529
Asset Allocation
Asset	%
Cash	0%
Stocks	100%
US Stocks	99%
Bonds	0%
US Bonds	0%
Other	0%

Services Offered:

Investment Strategy: The investment seeks to provide investment results that correspond generally to the price and yield performance, before fees and expenses, of the Indxx Millennials Thematic Index. The fund invests more than 80% of its total assets in the securities of the underlying index. The underlying index is designed to measure the performance of U.S. listed companies that provide exposure to the millennial generation, (collectively, "Millennial Companies"), as defined by the index provider. The millennial generation refers to the demographic in the U.S. with birth years ranging from 1980 to 2000. The fund is non-diversified. **Top Holdings:** Starbucks Corp Fiserv Inc Costco Wholesale Corp The Walt Disney Co The Home Depot Inc

WisdomTree Global ex-U.S. Quality Dividend Growth Fund   C   HOLD

Ticker	Traded On	NAV	Total Assets ($)	Dividend Yield (TTM)	Turnover Ratio	Expense Ratio
DNL	NYSE Arca	58.18	$75,638,106	2.02	60	0.58

Ratings
Reward	C
Risk	C-
Recent Upgrade/Downgrade	

Fund Information
Fund Type	Exchange Traded Funds
Category	Global Equity Large Cap
Sub-Category	Foreign Large Growth
Prospectus Objective	Foreign Stock
Inception Date	Jun-06
Open to New Investments	Y

Prices
Price (as of 9/30/2019)	58.22
52-Week High	59.24
52-Week Low	47.65

Total Returns (%)
3-Month	6-Month	1-Year	3-Year	5-Year
0.60	4.89	3.71	26.49	28.63

3-Year Standard Deviation	11.88
Effective Duration	

Valuation
Premium/Discount (1-Year Average)	-0.02

Company Information
Provider	WisdomTree
Manager/Tenure	Richard A. Brown (11), Thomas J. Durante (11), Karen Q. Wong (11)
Website	http://www.wisdomtree.com
Address	WisdomTree 245 Park Avenue, 35th floor New York NY 10167 United States
Phone Number	866-909-9473

PERFORMANCE

Ratings History
Date	Overall Rating	Risk Rating	Reward Rating
Q3-19	C	C-	C
Q4-18	C-	C-	D+
Q4-17	B	B-	B
Q4-16	D+	D+	D+
Q4-15	D+	D+	C-

Asset & Performance History
Date	NAV	1-Year Total Return
2018	49.47	-14.25
2017	59.01	29.53
2016	46.48	5.11
2015	45.3	-7.01
2014	49.61	-0.12
2013	50.81	0.09

Total Assets: $75,638,106
Asset Allocation
Asset	%
Cash	0%
Stocks	100%
US Stocks	1%
Bonds	0%
US Bonds	0%
Other	0%

Services Offered:

Investment Strategy: The investment seeks to track the price and yield performance, before fees and expenses, of the WisdomTree Global ex-U.S. Quality Dividend Growth Index. Under normal circumstances, at least 95% of the fund's total assets (exclusive of collateral held from securities lending) will be invested in component securities of the index and investments that have economic characteristics that are substantially identical to the economic characteristics of such component securities. The index is a fundamentally weighted index that consists of dividend-paying global ex-U.S. common stocks with growth characteristics. The fund is non-diversified. **Top Holdings:** British American Tobacco PLC Telenor ASA Tokyo Electron Ltd Atlas Copco AB A CSL Ltd

ProShares Short MSCI Emerging Markets   C-   HOLD

Ticker	Traded On	NAV	Total Assets ($)	Dividend Yield (TTM)	Turnover Ratio	Expense Ratio
EUM	NYSE Arca	19.14	$75,622,370	1.66	0	0.95

Ratings
Reward	D+
Risk	D+
Recent Upgrade/Downgrade	Up

Fund Information
Fund Type	Exchange Traded Funds
Category	Trading Tools
Sub-Category	Trading--Inverse Equity
Prospectus Objective	Div Emerg Mkts
Inception Date	Oct-07
Open to New Investments	Y

Prices
Price (as of 9/30/2019)	19.14
52-Week High	21.51
52-Week Low	17.79

Total Returns (%)
3-Month	6-Month	1-Year	3-Year	5-Year
6.23	5.99	1.64	-18.29	-25.10

3-Year Standard Deviation	14.7
Effective Duration	

Valuation
Premium/Discount (1-Year Average)	-0.02

Company Information
Provider	ProShares
Manager/Tenure	Scott Hanson (3), Ryan Dofflemeyer (0)
Website	http://www.proshares.com
Address	ProShares 7501 Wisconsin Avenue, Suite 1000 Bethesda MD 20814 United States
Phone Number	866-776-5125

PERFORMANCE

Ratings History
Date	Overall Rating	Risk Rating	Reward Rating
Q3-19	C-	D+	D+
Q4-18	C-	D+	D+
Q4-17	D-	D	D-
Q4-16	D	D	D
Q4-15	C	C	C

Asset & Performance History
Date	NAV	1-Year Total Return
2018	20.39	14.6
2017	17.95	-28.08
2016	24.96	-15.27
2015	29.46	11.97
2014	26.31	-0.11
2013	26.34	-1.23

Total Assets: $75,622,370
Asset Allocation
Asset	%
Cash	154%
Stocks	-61%
US Stocks	-61%
Bonds	7%
US Bonds	7%
Other	0%

Services Offered:

Investment Strategy: The investment seeks daily investment results, before fees and expenses, that correspond to the inverse (-1x) of the daily performance of the MSCI Emerging Markets Index®. The fund invests in financial instruments that ProShare Advisors believes, in combination, should produce daily returns consistent with the fund's investment objective. The index includes 85% of the free float-adjusted market capitalization in emerging market countries. The fund is non-diversified. **Top Holdings:** Ishares Msci Emerging Markets (Eem) Swap Citibank Na Ishares Msci Emerging Markets (Eem) Swap Bank Of America Na Ishares Msci Emerging Markets (Eem) Swap Ubs Ag Ishares Msci Emerging Markets (Eem) Swap Societe Generale United States Treasury Bills

First Trust Natural Gas ETF

D+   SELL

Ticker	Traded On	NAV	Total Assets ($)	Dividend Yield (TTM)	Turnover Ratio	Expense Ratio
FCG	NYSE Arca	11.45	$75,534,215	2.12	47	0.6

Ratings

Reward	C
Risk	D
Recent Upgrade/Downgrade	Up

Fund Information

Fund Type	Exchange Traded Funds
Category	Energy Sector Equity
Sub-Category	Equity Energy
Prospectus Objective	Natl Res
Inception Date	May-07
Open to New Investments	Y

Prices

Price (as of 9/30/2019)	11.46
52-Week High	23.18
52-Week Low	10.66

Total Returns (%)

3-Month	6-Month	1-Year	3-Year	5-Year
-20.61	-33.76	-48.63	-54.65	-85.45

3-Year Standard Deviation	26.95
Effective Duration	

Valuation

Premium/Discount (1-Year Average)	0.02

Company Information

Provider	First Trust
Manager/Tenure	Jon C. Erickson (12), Daniel J. Lindquist (12), David G. McGarel (12), 3 others
Website	http://www.ftportfolios.com/
Address	First Trust 120 E. Liberty Drive, Suite 400 Wheaton IL 60187 United States
Phone Number	800-621-1675

PERFORMANCE

Ratings History

Date	Overall Rating	Risk Rating	Reward Rating
Q3-19	D+	D	C
Q4-18	C-	D	C
Q4-17	D	D-	D
Q4-16	D	D	D+
Q4-15	C-	C-	C

Asset & Performance History

Date	NAV	1-Year Total Return
2018	14.69	-34.76
2017	22.75	-11.43
2016	26.15	19.47
2015	22.3	-59.13
2014	56.1	-42.02
2013	97.65	25.12

Total Assets: $75,534,215

Asset Allocation

Asset	%
Cash	1%
Stocks	99%
US Stocks	85%
Bonds	0%
US Bonds	0%
Other	0%

Services Offered:

Investment Strategy: The investment seeks investment results that correspond generally to the price and yield (before the fund's fees and expenses) of an equity index called the ISE-Revere Natural Gas™ Index. The fund will normally invest at least 90% of its net assets (including investment borrowings) in the common stocks, depositary receipts and MLP units that comprise the index. The index is designed to track the performance of mid and large capitalization companies that derive a substantial portion of their revenues from midstream activities and/or the exploration and production of natural gas. **Top Holdings:** Noble Energy Inc PDC Energy Inc Matador Resources Co Devon Energy Corp Encana Corp

First Trust Global Wind Energy ETF

C   HOLD

Ticker	Traded On	NAV	Total Assets ($)	Dividend Yield (TTM)	Turnover Ratio	Expense Ratio
FAN	NYSE Arca	13.13	$75,501,845	2.34	22	0.6

Ratings

Reward	C
Risk	C-
Recent Upgrade/Downgrade	

Fund Information

Fund Type	Exchange Traded Funds
Category	Utilities Sector Equity
Sub-Category	Miscellaneous Sector
Prospectus Objective	Natl Res
Inception Date	Jun-08
Open to New Investments	Y

Prices

Price (as of 9/30/2019)	13.16
52-Week High	13.73
52-Week Low	11.09

Total Returns (%)

3-Month	6-Month	1-Year	3-Year	5-Year
-1.59	1.44	8.52	11.04	35.35

3-Year Standard Deviation	14.96
Effective Duration	

Valuation

Premium/Discount (1-Year Average)	-0.01

Company Information

Provider	First Trust
Manager/Tenure	Jon C. Erickson (11), Daniel J. Lindquist (11), David G. McGarel (11), 3 others
Website	http://www.ftportfolios.com/
Address	First Trust 120 E. Liberty Drive, Suite 400 Wheaton IL 60187 United States
Phone Number	800-621-1675

PERFORMANCE

Ratings History

Date	Overall Rating	Risk Rating	Reward Rating
Q3-19	C	C-	C
Q4-18	C-	C-	C-
Q4-17	B-	B+	C
Q4-16	C	C-	C
Q4-15	C	C-	C

Asset & Performance History

Date	NAV	1-Year Total Return
2018	11.51	-11.12
2017	13.27	16.28
2016	11.72	4.31
2015	11.37	13.21
2014	10.28	-6.62
2013	11.27	64.53

Total Assets: $75,501,845

Asset Allocation

Asset	%
Cash	0%
Stocks	96%
US Stocks	18%
Bonds	0%
US Bonds	0%
Other	4%

Services Offered:

Investment Strategy: The investment seeks investment results that correspond generally to the price and yield of an equity index called the ISE Clean Edge Global Wind Energy™ Index. The fund will normally invest at least 90% of its net assets (including investment borrowings) in the common stocks and depositary receipts that comprise the index. The index provides a benchmark for investors interested in tracking public companies throughout the world that are active in the wind energy industry. In order to be eligible for inclusion in the index, a security must be issued by a company that is actively engaged in some aspect of the wind energy industry. The fund is non-diversified. **Top Holdings:** Orsted A/S Siemens Gamesa Renewable Energy SA Vestas Wind Systems A/S Northland Power Inc Pattern Energy Group Inc Class A

VelocityShares Daily Inverse VIX Medium-Term ETN   C-   HOLD

Ticker	Traded On	NAV	Total Assets ($)	Dividend Yield (TTM)	Turnover Ratio	Expense Ratio
ZIV	NAS CM	66.25	$75,395,474	0		1.35

Ratings
Reward   D+
Risk   C-
Recent Upgrade/Downgrade   Down

Fund Information
Fund Type   Exchange Traded Funds
Category   Alternative Misc
Sub-Category   Volatility
Prospectus Objective   Growth
Inception Date   Nov-10
Open to New Investments   Y

Prices
Price (as of 9/30/2019)   65.66
52-Week High   80.87
52-Week Low   59.10

Total Returns (%)

3-Month	6-Month	1-Year	3-Year	5-Year
-11.80	-11.60	-17.75	51.39	54.14

3-Year Standard Deviation   27.97
Effective Duration

Valuation
Premium/Discount (1-Year Average)   -0.18

Company Information
Provider   Credit Suisse AG
Manager/Tenure   Management Team (8)
Website
Address   Kilmore House Park Lane Dublin Ireland
Phone Number

PERFORMANCE

Ratings History

Date	Overall Rating	Risk Rating	Reward Rating
Q3-19	C-	C-	D+
Q4-18	C	C-	C-
Q4-17	B+	C	A+
Q4-16	C	C-	C-
Q4-15	C+	C-	C+

Asset & Performance History

Date	NAV	1-Year Total Return
2018	60.57	-31.31
2017	88.17	88.67
2016	46.77	12.89
2015	41.58	-0.85
2014	41.94	8.59
2013	38.62	64.83

Total Assets: $75,395,474
Asset Allocation

Asset	%
Cash	%
Stocks	%
US Stocks	%
Bonds	%
US Bonds	%
Other	%

Services Offered:

Investment Strategy: The investment seeks to replicate, net of expenses, the inverse of the daily performance of the S&P 500 VIX Mid-Term Futures index.
The index was designed to provide investors with exposure to one or more maturities of futures contracts on the VIX, which reflects implied volatility of the S&P 500 Index at various points along the volatility forward curve. The calculation of the VIX is based on prices of put and call options on the S&P 500 Index. The ETNs are linked to the daily inverse return of the index and do not represent an investment in the inverse of the VIX. **Top Holdings:**

Virtus InfraCap U.S. Preferred Stock ETF   C-   HOLD

Ticker	Traded On	NAV	Total Assets ($)	Dividend Yield (TTM)	Turnover Ratio	Expense Ratio
PFFA	NYSE Arca	26.31	$74,970,109	8.67		2.13

Ratings
Reward   C-
Risk   C-
Recent Upgrade/Downgrade   Up

Fund Information
Fund Type   Exchange Traded Funds
Category   US Fixed Income
Sub-Category   Preferred Stock
Prospectus Objective   Income
Inception Date   May-18
Open to New Investments   Y

Prices
Price (as of 9/30/2019)   26.34
52-Week High   26.43
52-Week Low   21.26

Total Returns (%)

3-Month	6-Month	1-Year	3-Year	5-Year
4.99	8.83	13.80		

3-Year Standard Deviation
Effective Duration

Valuation
Premium/Discount (1-Year Average)   0.40

Company Information
Provider   Virtus
Manager/Tenure   Jay D. Hatfield (1), Edward F. Ryan (1)
Website   http://www.virtus.com
Address   Virtus Opportunities Trust 101 Munson Street Greenfield MA 1301 United States
Phone Number   800-243-1574

PERFORMANCE

Ratings History

Date	Overall Rating	Risk Rating	Reward Rating
Q3-19	C-	C-	C-
Q4-18	U		
Q4-17			
Q4-16			
Q4-15			

Asset & Performance History

Date	NAV	1-Year Total Return
2018	22.07	
2017		
2016		
2015		
2014		
2013		

Total Assets: $74,970,109
Asset Allocation

Asset	%
Cash	-18%
Stocks	9%
US Stocks	9%
Bonds	-8%
US Bonds	-8%
Other	0%

Services Offered:

Investment Strategy: The investment seeks current income and, secondarily, capital appreciation. Under normal market conditions, the fund will invest not less than 80% of its net assets (plus the amount of any borrowings for investment purposes) in U.S. preferred stock, and in derivatives and other instruments that have economic characteristics similar to such investments. The Sub-Adviser actively manages the fund's assets pursuant to a variety of quantitative, qualitative and relative valuation factors. The fund is non-diversified. **Top Holdings:** National General Holdings Corp Deposit Repr 1/40th Non-Cum Pfd Series B   Annaly Capital Management Inc FXDFR PRF PERPETUAL USD 25 - Ser G   EPR Properties 5.70% PRF PERPETUAL USD 25 - Ser G   iShares US Real Estate ETF   SCE Trust VI 0%

Invesco BulletShares 2027 Corporate Bond ETF

C- HOLD

Ticker	Traded On	NAV	Total Assets ($)	Dividend Yield (TTM)	Turnover Ratio	Expense Ratio
BSCR	NYSE Arca	20.81	$74,900,208	3.43	0	0.1

Ratings

Reward	C-
Risk	C-
Recent Upgrade/Downgrade	

Fund Information

Fund Type	Exchange Traded Funds
Category	US Fixed Income
Sub-Category	Target Maturity
Prospectus Objective	Corp Bond - Gen
Inception Date	Sep-17
Open to New Investments	Y

Prices

Price (as of 9/30/2019)	20.87
52-Week High	21.12
52-Week Low	18.58

Total Returns (%)

3-Month	6-Month	1-Year	3-Year	5-Year
2.67	7.43	13.94		

3-Year Standard Deviation	
Effective Duration	6.65

Valuation

Premium/Discount (1-Year Average)	0.26

Company Information

Provider	Invesco
Manager/Tenure	Jeremy Neisewander (2), Peter Hubbard (1), Jeffrey W. Kernagis (1), 1 other
Website	http://www.invesco.com/us
Address	Invesco 11 Greenway Plaza, Ste. 2500 Houston TX 77046 United States
Phone Number	800-659-1005

PERFORMANCE

Ratings History

Date	Overall Rating	Risk Rating	Reward Rating
Q3-19	C-	C-	C-
Q4-18	D	C-	D
Q4-17	U		
Q4-16			
Q4-15			

Asset & Performance History

Date	NAV	1-Year Total Return
2018	18.78	-2.89
2017	19.99	
2016		
2015		
2014		
2013		

Total Assets: $74,900,208

Asset Allocation

Asset	%
Cash	0%
Stocks	0%
US Stocks	0%
Bonds	99%
US Bonds	89%
Other	0%

Services Offered:

Investment Strategy: The investment seeks to track the investment results (before fees and expenses) of the Nasdaq BulletShares® USD Corporate Bond 2027 Index (the "underlying index"). The fund generally will invest at least 80% of its total assets in securities that comprise the underlying index. The underlying index seeks to measure the performance of a portfolio of U.S. dollar-denominated investment grade corporate bonds with maturities or, in some cases, "effective maturities" in the year 2027 (collectively, "2027 Bonds"). The fund is non-diversified. **Top Holdings:** Broadcom Corporation/Broadcom Cayman Finance Ltd 3.88% Microsoft Corporation 3.3% Citigroup Inc. 4.45% Amazon.com, Inc. 3.15% Verizon Communications Inc. 4.12%

Invesco S&P SmallCap Value with Momentum ETF

C- HOLD

Ticker	Traded On	NAV	Total Assets ($)	Dividend Yield (TTM)	Turnover Ratio	Expense Ratio
XSVM	NYSE Arca	30.54	$74,816,635	1.69		0.39

Ratings

Reward	C-
Risk	D+
Recent Upgrade/Downgrade	Up

Fund Information

Fund Type	Exchange Traded Funds
Category	US Equity Small Cap
Sub-Category	Small Value
Prospectus Objective	Growth
Inception Date	Mar-05
Open to New Investments	Y

Prices

Price (as of 9/30/2019)	30.53
52-Week High	32.29
52-Week Low	25.28

Total Returns (%)

3-Month	6-Month	1-Year	3-Year	5-Year
4.33	2.41	-3.17	24.07	45.92

3-Year Standard Deviation	19.16
Effective Duration	

Valuation

Premium/Discount (1-Year Average)	-0.18

Company Information

Provider	Invesco
Manager/Tenure	Peter Hubbard (12), Michael Jeanette (11), Tony Seisser (5)
Website	http://www.invesco.com/us
Address	Invesco 11 Greenway Plaza, Ste. 2500 Houston TX 77046 United States
Phone Number	800-659-1005

PERFORMANCE

Ratings History

Date	Overall Rating	Risk Rating	Reward Rating
Q3-19	C-	D+	C-
Q4-18	C-	D+	C-
Q4-17	B	B-	B
Q4-16	C-	D+	C-
Q4-15	C	D+	C

Asset & Performance History

Date	NAV	1-Year Total Return
2018	26.42	-11.81
2017	30.66	3.16
2016	30.3	35.52
2015	22.93	-8.84
2014	25.81	5.22
2013	24.86	44.14

Total Assets: $74,816,635

Asset Allocation

Asset	%
Cash	1%
Stocks	99%
US Stocks	97%
Bonds	0%
US Bonds	0%
Other	0%

Services Offered:

Investment Strategy: The investment seeks to track the investment results (before fees and expenses) of the S&P SmallCap 600 High Momentum Value Index (the "underlying index"). The fund generally will invest at least 90% of its total assets in the securities that comprise the underlying index. Strictly in accordance with its guidelines and mandated procedures, the index provider compiles, maintains and calculates the underlying index, which is designed to track the performance of approximately 120 stocks in the S&P SmallCap 600® Index that have the highest "value" and "momentum" scores. **Top Holdings:** Vitamin Shoppe Inc Sonic Automotive Inc Class A INTL FCStone Inc SpartanNash Co Era Group Inc

Anfield Capital Diversified Alternatives ETF

C-   HOLD

Ticker	Traded On	NAV	Total Assets ($)	Dividend Yield (TTM)	Turnover Ratio	Expense Ratio
DALT	BATS		$74,680,710	3.59	50	3.23

Ratings
Reward	C-
Risk	C-
Recent Upgrade/Downgrade	

Fund Information
Fund Type	Exchange Traded Funds
Category	Multialternative
Sub-Category	Multialternative
Prospectus Objective	Growth & Inc
Inception Date	Sep-17
Open to New Investments	Y

Prices
Price (as of 9/30/2019)	10.24
52-Week High	10.48
52-Week Low	8.53

Total Returns (%)
3-Month	6-Month	1-Year	3-Year	5-Year
0.35	2.78	1.43		

3-Year Standard Deviation	
Effective Duration	

Valuation
Premium/Discount (1-Year Average)	-0.01

Company Information
Provider	Regents Park Funds, LLC
Manager/Tenure	Peter Van de Zilver (2), David Young (2)
Website	
Address	Regents Park Funds, LLC 4041 MacArthur Blvd., Suite 155 Newport Beach CA 92660 United States
Phone Number	

PERFORMANCE

Ratings History
Date	Overall Rating	Risk Rating	Reward Rating
Q3-19	C-	C-	C-
Q4-18	D+	C-	D+
Q4-17	U		
Q4-16			
Q4-15			

Asset & Performance History
Date	NAV	1-Year Total Return
2018	8.97	-9.22
2017	10.18	
2016		
2015		
2014		
2013		

Total Assets: $74,680,710
Asset Allocation
Asset	%
Cash	2%
Stocks	64%
US Stocks	58%
Bonds	14%
US Bonds	11%
Other	0%

Services Offered:

Investment Strategy: The investment seeks to provide capital growth and income. The fund is an actively managed exchange traded fund ("ETF") that is a fund of funds. It seeks to achieve its investment objective by investing primarily in alternative asset classes and securities that represent sectors, market segments or asset classes that do not represent the general investment universe. The fund will implement this strategy primarily through investments in unaffiliated ETFs, closed-end funds ("CEFs"), business development companies ("BDCs") and real estate investment trusts ("REITs"). **Top Holdings:** iShares Preferred&Income Securities ETF   Ares Capital Corp   E-mini S&P 500 Sept19   Oxford Lane Capital Corp   Main Street Capital Corp

---

iShares International Dividend Growth ETF

C   HOLD

Ticker	Traded On	NAV	Total Assets ($)	Dividend Yield (TTM)	Turnover Ratio	Expense Ratio
IGRO	BATS	55.11	$74,393,289	2.88	34	0.22

Ratings
Reward	C
Risk	D+
Recent Upgrade/Downgrade	Up

Fund Information
Fund Type	Exchange Traded Funds
Category	Global Equity Large Cap
Sub-Category	Foreign Large Blend
Prospectus Objective	Equity-Income
Inception Date	May-16
Open to New Investments	Y

Prices
Price (as of 9/30/2019)	55.36
52-Week High	56.34
52-Week Low	48.08

Total Returns (%)
3-Month	6-Month	1-Year	3-Year	5-Year
-0.49	3.30	1.28	20.15	

3-Year Standard Deviation	11.41
Effective Duration	

Valuation
Premium/Discount (1-Year Average)	0.30

Company Information
Provider	iShares
Manager/Tenure	Jennifer Hsui (3), Alan Mason (3), Greg Savage (3), 2 others
Website	http://www.ishares.com
Address	iShares 400 Howard Street San Francisco CA 94105 United States
Phone Number	800-474-2737

PERFORMANCE

Ratings History
Date	Overall Rating	Risk Rating	Reward Rating
Q3-19	C	D+	C
Q4-18	D+	D+	D+
Q4-17	D+	B	C
Q4-16	U		
Q4-15			

Asset & Performance History
Date	NAV	1-Year Total Return
2018	49.1	-13.11
2017	58.05	23.71
2016	48.18	
2015		
2014		
2013		

Total Assets: $74,393,289
Asset Allocation
Asset	%
Cash	1%
Stocks	99%
US Stocks	2%
Bonds	0%
US Bonds	0%
Other	0%

Services Offered:

Investment Strategy: The investment seeks to track the investment results of the Morningstar® Global ex-US Dividend Growth IndexSM. The fund generally will invest at least 90% of its assets in the component securities of the underlying index and in investments that have economic characteristics that are substantially identical to the component securities of the underlying index and may invest up to 10% of its assets in certain futures, options and swap contracts, cash and cash equivalents. The index is a dividend dollars weighted index that seeks to measure the performance of international equities selected based on a consistent history of growing dividends. **Top Holdings:** Nestle SA   Novartis AG   Roche Holding AG Dividend Right Cert.   Taiwan Semiconductor Manufacturing Co Ltd   Samsung Electronics Co Ltd

Global X Conscious Companies ETF

C HOLD

Ticker	Traded On	NAV	Total Assets ($)	Dividend Yield (TTM)	Turnover Ratio	Expense Ratio
KRMA	NAS CM	22.07	$73,922,077	2.27	36	0.43

Ratings
Reward	C
Risk	C-
Recent Upgrade/Downgrade	

Fund Information
Fund Type	Exchange Traded Funds
Category	US Equity Large Cap Blend
Sub-Category	Large Blend
Prospectus Objective	Growth & Inc
Inception Date	Jul-16
Open to New Investments	Y

Prices
Price (as of 9/30/2019)	22.16
52-Week High	22.47
52-Week Low	17.71

Total Returns (%)
3-Month	6-Month	1-Year	3-Year	5-Year
0.50	4.27	6.32	48.90	

3-Year Standard Deviation	12.69
Effective Duration	

Valuation
Premium/Discount (1-Year Average)	0.10

Company Information
Provider	Global X Funds
Manager/Tenure	Chang Kim (3), Nam To (1), Wayne Xie (0), 1 other
Website	http://www.globalxfunds.com
Address	Global X Funds 600 Lexington Avenue, 20th Floor New York NY 10022 United States
Phone Number	888-493-8631

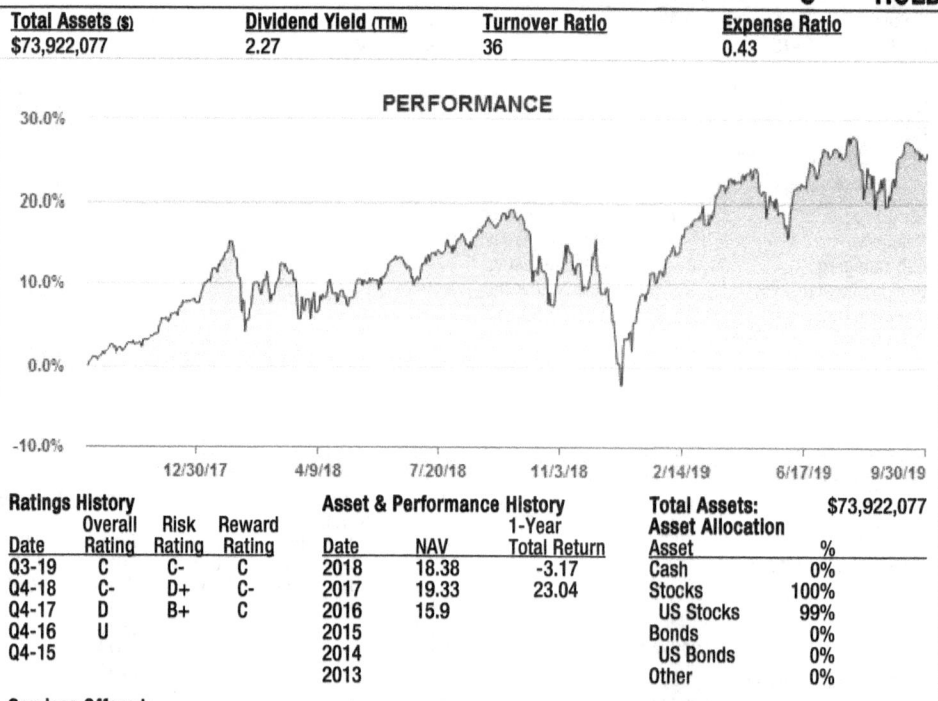

PERFORMANCE

Ratings History
Date	Overall Rating	Risk Rating	Reward Rating
Q3-19	C	C-	C
Q4-18	C-	D+	C-
Q4-17	D	B+	C
Q4-16	U		
Q4-15			

Asset & Performance History
Date	NAV	1-Year Total Return
2018	18.38	-3.17
2017	19.33	23.04
2016	15.9	
2015		
2014		
2013		

Total Assets: $73,922,077
Asset Allocation
Asset	%
Cash	0%
Stocks	100%
US Stocks	99%
Bonds	0%
US Bonds	0%
Other	0%

Services Offered:

Investment Strategy: The investment seeks to provide investment results that correspond generally to the price and yield performance, before fees and expenses, of the Concinnity Conscious Companies Index. The fund invests at least 80% of its total assets in the securities of the underlying index. The underlying index is designed to provide exposure to companies listed in the U.S. that operate their businesses in a sustainable and responsible manner, as measured by their ability to achieve positive outcomes that are consistent with a multi-stakeholder operating system ("MsOS"), as defined by the provider of the underlying index. **Top Holdings:** Amgen Inc American Water Works Co Inc WEC Energy Group Inc Bristol-Myers Squibb Company Campbell Soup Co

---

Invesco Dynamic Food & Beverage ETF

B- BUY

Ticker	Traded On	NAV	Total Assets ($)	Dividend Yield (TTM)	Turnover Ratio	Expense Ratio
PBJ	NYSE Arca	35.17	$73,851,139	1.09	122	0.63

Ratings
Reward	B
Risk	C
Recent Upgrade/Downgrade	Up

Fund Information
Fund Type	Exchange Traded Funds
Category	Consumer Goods & Svcs
Sub-Category	Consumer Defensive
Prospectus Objective	Unaligned
Inception Date	Jun-05
Open to New Investments	Y

Prices
Price (as of 9/30/2019)	35.18
52-Week High	35.65
52-Week Low	28.60

Total Returns (%)
3-Month	6-Month	1-Year	3-Year	5-Year
4.90	6.88	10.38	10.93	33.30

3-Year Standard Deviation	11.28
Effective Duration	

Valuation
Premium/Discount (1-Year Average)	-0.02

Company Information
Provider	Invesco
Manager/Tenure	Peter Hubbard (12), Michael Jeanette (11), Tony Seisser (5)
Website	http://www.invesco.com/us
Address	Invesco 11 Greenway Plaza, Ste. 2500 Houston TX 77046 United States
Phone Number	800-659-1005

PERFORMANCE

Ratings History
Date	Overall Rating	Risk Rating	Reward Rating
Q3-19	B-	C	B
Q4-18	B-	C	B
Q4-17	B-	B	C
Q4-16	B	C+	B
Q4-15	B	B	B+

Asset & Performance History
Date	NAV	1-Year Total Return
2018	29.8	-10.77
2017	33.84	1.57
2016	33.56	5.91
2015	32.19	6.82
2014	30.51	17.37
2013	26.36	33.38

Total Assets: $73,851,139
Asset Allocation
Asset	%
Cash	0%
Stocks	100%
US Stocks	94%
Bonds	0%
US Bonds	0%
Other	0%

Services Offered:

Investment Strategy: The investment seeks to track the investment results (before fees and expenses) of the Dynamic Food & Beverage IntellidexSM Index. The fund generally will invest at least 90% of its total assets in the securities that comprise the underlying intellidex. The underlying intellidex was composed of common stocks of U.S. food and beverage companies. These companies are engaged principally in the manufacture, sale or distribution of food and beverage products, agricultural products and products related to the development of new food technologies. The fund is non-diversified. **Top Holdings:** Starbucks Corp The Hershey Co Tyson Foods Inc Class A Yum Brands Inc Coca-Cola Co

BlueStar Israel Technology ETF   C   HOLD

Ticker	Traded On	NAV	Total Assets ($)	Dividend Yield (TTM)	Turnover Ratio	Expense Ratio
ITEQ	NYSE Arca	39.92	$73,845,912	0.26	11	0.75

Ratings
Reward	B-
Risk	C-
Recent Upgrade/Downgrade	Down

Fund Information
Fund Type	Exchange Traded Funds
Category	Technology Sector Equity
Sub-Category	Technology
Prospectus Objective	Technology
Inception Date	Nov-15
Open to New Investments	Y

Prices
Price (as of 9/30/2019)	39.86
52-Week High	42.64
52-Week Low	29.60

Total Returns (%)

3-Month	6-Month	1-Year	3-Year	5-Year
1.92	6.09	11.97	58.00	

3-Year Standard Deviation	13.71
Effective Duration	

Valuation
Premium/Discount (1-Year Average)	0.04

Company Information
Provider	ETFMG
Manager/Tenure	Samuel R. Masucci (1), Devin Ryder (1), Donal Bishnoi (0), 1 other
Website	http://www.etfmg.com
Address	ETFMG 30 Maple Street, Suite 2 NJ United States
Phone Number	

PERFORMANCE

Ratings History

Date	Overall Rating	Risk Rating	Reward Rating
Q3-19	C	C-	B-
Q4-18	C	C-	C+
Q4-17	C	B	C
Q4-16	D	C-	C
Q4-15			

Asset & Performance History

Date	NAV	1-Year Total Return
2018	31.46	-0.17
2017	31.61	27.74
2016	24.88	3.66
2015	24.07	
2014		
2013		

Total Assets: $73,845,912

Asset Allocation

Asset	%
Cash	0%
Stocks	100%
US Stocks	58%
Bonds	0%
US Bonds	0%
Other	0%

Services Offered:

Investment Strategy: The investment seeks to provide investment results that correspond generally to the total return performance of the BlueStar Israel Global Technology Index™ ("BIGITech™"). The fund will invest at least 80% of its total assets in the component securities of the index and in depositary receipts representing such securities. As a result, normally the fund will invest at least 80% of its total assets in Israeli technology companies. BIGITech™ was created in 2013 by BlueStar Global Investors LLC d/b/a BlueStar Indexes® and tracks the performance of exchange-listed Israeli technology operating companies. It is non-diversified. **Top Holdings:** NovoCure Ltd NICE Ltd Amdocs Ltd Wix.com Ltd Check Point Software Technologies Ltd

---

Xtrackers Municipal Infrastructure Revenue Bond ETF   C   HOLD

Ticker	Traded On	NAV	Total Assets ($)	Dividend Yield (TTM)	Turnover Ratio	Expense Ratio
RVNU	NYSE Arca	28.22	$73,379,760	2.66	25	0.15

Ratings
Reward	B-
Risk	D+
Recent Upgrade/Downgrade	

Fund Information
Fund Type	Exchange Traded Funds
Category	US Muni Fixed Inc
Sub-Category	Muni National Long
Prospectus Objective	Muni Bond - Natl
Inception Date	Jun-13
Open to New Investments	Y

Prices
Price (as of 9/30/2019)	28.27
52-Week High	28.61
52-Week Low	25.58

Total Returns (%)

3-Month	6-Month	1-Year	3-Year	5-Year
2.42	5.67	11.13	11.30	26.69

3-Year Standard Deviation	4.87
Effective Duration	9.79

Valuation
Premium/Discount (1-Year Average)	0.09

Company Information
Provider	DWS
Manager/Tenure	Alexander Bridgeforth (2), Tanuj Dora (2), Brandon Matsui (2), 1 other
Website	http://dws.com
Address	DWS 210 West 10th Street Kansas City MO 64105-1614 United States
Phone Number	

PERFORMANCE

Ratings History

Date	Overall Rating	Risk Rating	Reward Rating
Q3-19	C	D+	B-
Q4-18	D+	D+	C-
Q4-17	B-	B	C
Q4-16	C	C-	C
Q4-15	C-	D+	C

Asset & Performance History

Date	NAV	1-Year Total Return
2018	26.22	-0.46
2017	27.08	7.29
2016	25.89	1.18
2015	26.26	4.94
2014	25.8	15.02
2013	23.18	

Total Assets: $73,379,760

Asset Allocation

Asset	%
Cash	0%
Stocks	0%
US Stocks	0%
Bonds	100%
US Bonds	99%
Other	0%

Services Offered:

Investment Strategy: The investment seeks investment results that correspond generally to the performance, before fees and expenses, of the Solactive Municipal Infrastructure Revenue Bond Index (the "underlying index"). The fund will invest at least 80% of its total assets (but typically far more) in instruments that comprise the underlying index. The underlying index is comprised of tax-exempt municipal securities issued by states, cities, counties, districts, their respective agencies, and other tax-exempt issuers. **Top Holdings:** NORTH TEX TWY AUTH REV 5% NEW JERSEY ST TPK AUTH TPK REV 5% NEW YORK N Y CITY MUN WTR FIN AUTH WTR & SWR SYS REV 5% PORT AUTH N Y & N J 5% ILLINOIS ST TOLL HWY AUTH TOLL HIGHWAY REV 5%

Fidelity® High Yield Factor ETF   C-   HOLD

Ticker	Traded On	NAV	Total Assets ($)	Dividend Yield (TTM)	Turnover Ratio	Expense Ratio
FDHY	NYSE Arca	52.38	$73,329,171	4.7		0.45

Ratings

Reward	C-
Risk	C-
Recent Upgrade/Downgrade	Up

Fund Information

Fund Type	Exchange Traded Funds
Category	US Fixed Income
Sub-Category	High Yield Bond
Prospectus Objective	Corp Bond-High Yld
Inception Date	Jun-18
Open to New Investments	Y

Prices

Price (as of 9/30/2019)	52.70
52-Week High	53.05
52-Week Low	47.35

Total Returns (%)

3-Month	6-Month	1-Year	3-Year	5-Year
2.12	5.61	9.24		

3-Year Standard Deviation	
Effective Duration	

Valuation

Premium/Discount (1-Year Average)	0.60

Company Information

Provider	Fidelity Investments
Manager/Tenure	Michael Cheng (1), Michael Weaver (1), Alexandre Karam (0)
Website	http://www.institutional.fidelity.com
Address	Fidelity Investments 82 Devonshire Street Boston MA 2109 United States
Phone Number	617-563-7000

PERFORMANCE

Ratings History

Date	Overall Rating	Risk Rating	Reward Rating
Q3-19	C-	C-	C-
Q4-18	U		
Q4-17			
Q4-16			
Q4-15			

Asset & Performance History

Date	NAV	1-Year Total Return
2018	47.51	
2017		
2016		
2015		
2014		
2013		

Total Assets: $73,329,171

Asset Allocation

Asset	%
Cash	7%
Stocks	0%
US Stocks	0%
Bonds	92%
US Bonds	74%
Other	0%

Services Offered:

Investment Strategy: The investment seeks a high level of income. The fund normally invests at least 80% of its assets in debt securities rated below investment grade (also referred to as high yield debt securities or junk bonds). It uses the ICE BofAML BB-B US High Yield Constrained Index as a guide in structuring the fund and selecting its investments as it relates to credit quality distribution and risk characteristics. The fund normally invests primarily in securities rated BB or B by S&P, Ba or B by Moody's, comparably rated by at least one nationally recognized credit rating agency, or, if unrated, considered by FMRC to be of comparable quality. **Top Holdings:** CCO Holdings, LLC/ CCO Holdings Capital Corp. 5.38% MPT Operating Partnership LP / MPT Finance Corporation 4.62% Go Daddy Operating Company LLC and GD Finance Co Inc 5.25% 1011778 B.C. Unlimited Liability Company / New Red Finance, Inc. 5% TransDigm, Inc. 6.25%

Xtrackers FTSE Developed ex US Comprehensive Factor ETF   C-   HOLD

Ticker	Traded On	NAV	Total Assets ($)	Dividend Yield (TTM)	Turnover Ratio	Expense Ratio
DEEF	NYSE Arca	27.02	$72,955,630	3.49	45	0.24

Ratings

Reward	C-
Risk	C-
Recent Upgrade/Downgrade	

Fund Information

Fund Type	Exchange Traded Funds
Category	Global Equity Large Cap
Sub-Category	Foreign Large Blend
Prospectus Objective	Foreign Stock
Inception Date	Nov-15
Open to New Investments	Y

Prices

Price (as of 9/30/2019)	27.03
52-Week High	28.70
52-Week Low	24.42

Total Returns (%)

3-Month	6-Month	1-Year	3-Year	5-Year
-1.05	-0.12	-2.27	16.81	

3-Year Standard Deviation	10.31
Effective Duration	

Valuation

Premium/Discount (1-Year Average)	-0.14

Company Information

Provider	DWS
Manager/Tenure	Bryan Richards (3), Patrick Dwyer (3), Shlomo Bassous (1)
Website	http://www.dws.com
Address	DWS 210 West 10th Street Kansas City MO 64105-1614 United States
Phone Number	

PERFORMANCE

Ratings History

Date	Overall Rating	Risk Rating	Reward Rating
Q3-19	C-	C-	C-
Q4-18	D+	C-	D+
Q4-17	C	B+	C
Q4-16	D	C-	D
Q4-15			

Asset & Performance History

Date	NAV	1-Year Total Return
2018	25.18	-13.93
2017	29.88	27.58
2016	24.08	1.3
2015	24.78	
2014		
2013		

Total Assets: $72,955,630

Asset Allocation

Asset	%
Cash	0%
Stocks	100%
US Stocks	2%
Bonds	0%
US Bonds	0%
Other	0%

Services Offered:

Investment Strategy: The investment seeks investment results that correspond generally to the performance, before fees and expenses, of the FTSE Developed ex US Comprehensive Factor Index. The fund will normally invest at least 80% of its net assets, plus the amount of any borrowings for investment purposes, in equity securities of issuers from developed markets countries other than the United States. The index is designed to track the equity market performance of companies in developed countries selected on the investment style criteria of value, momentum, quality, low volatility and size. **Top Holdings:** Link Real Estate Investment Trust Dexus GPT Group Mirvac Group Koninklijke Ahold Delhaize NV

iPath® Series B Bloomberg Coffee Subindex Total Return ETN   D   SELL

Ticker	Traded On	NAV	Total Assets ($)	Dividend Yield (TTM)	Turnover Ratio	Expense Ratio
JO	NYSE Arca		$72,905,202	0		0.45

Ratings
Reward	D
Risk	D-
Recent Upgrade/Downgrade	Up

Fund Information
Fund Type	Exchange Traded Funds
Category	Commodities Broad Basket
Sub-Category	Commodities Broad Basket
Prospectus Objective	Growth & Inc
Inception Date	Jan-18
Open to New Investments	Y

Prices
Price (as of 9/30/2019)	33.43
52-Week High	46.23
52-Week Low	30.92

Total Returns (%)
3-Month	6-Month	1-Year	3-Year	5-Year
-12.16	1.31	-13.37		

3-Year Standard Deviation	
Effective Duration	

Valuation
Premium/Discount (1-Year Average)	-0.10

Company Information
Provider	Milleis Investissements Funds
Manager/Tenure	No Manager (1)
Website	
Address	2-4, rue Eugène Ruppert L-2453 Luxembourg Luxembourg L-2453 Luxembourg
Phone Number	

PERFORMANCE

Ratings History
Date	Overall Rating	Risk Rating	Reward Rating
Q3-19	D	D-	D
Q4-18	U		
Q4-17			
Q4-16			
Q4-15			

Asset & Performance History
Date	NAV	1-Year Total Return
2018	37.16	
2017		
2016		
2015		
2014		
2013		

Total Assets: $72,905,202

Asset Allocation
Asset	%
Cash	%
Stocks	%
US Stocks	%
Bonds	%
US Bonds	%
Other	%

Services Offered:

Investment Strategy: The investment seeks return linked to the performance of the Bloomberg Coffee Subindex Total ReturnSM.
The ETN offers exposure to futures contracts and not direct exposure to the physical commodities. The index is composed of one or more futures contracts on the relevant commodity (the "index components") and is intended to reflect the returns that are potentially available through (1) an unleveraged investment in those contracts plus (2) the rate of interest that could be earned on cash collateral invested in specified Treasury Bills. **Top Holdings:**

---

iShares Currency Hedged MSCI ACWI ex U.S. ETF   C   HOLD

Ticker	Traded On	NAV	Total Assets ($)	Dividend Yield (TTM)	Turnover Ratio	Expense Ratio
HAWX	NYSE Arca	26.97	$72,806,500	2.47	7	0.35

Ratings
Reward	C
Risk	D+
Recent Upgrade/Downgrade	

Fund Information
Fund Type	Exchange Traded Funds
Category	Global Equity Large Cap
Sub-Category	Foreign Large Blend
Prospectus Objective	Growth & Inc
Inception Date	Jun-15
Open to New Investments	Y

Prices
Price (as of 9/30/2019)	26.96
52-Week High	27.36
52-Week Low	23.30

Total Returns (%)
3-Month	6-Month	1-Year	3-Year	5-Year
0.19	2.55	3.24	29.75	

3-Year Standard Deviation	9.46
Effective Duration	

Valuation
Premium/Discount (1-Year Average)	0.01

Company Information
Provider	iShares
Manager/Tenure	Diane Hsiung (4), Jennifer Hsui (4), Orlando Montalvo (4), 2 others
Website	http://www.ishares.com
Address	iShares 400 Howard Street San Francisco CA 94105 United States
Phone Number	800-474-2737

PERFORMANCE

Ratings History
Date	Overall Rating	Risk Rating	Reward Rating
Q3-19	C	D+	C
Q4-18	D+	D+	D+
Q4-17	C	B-	C+
Q4-16	D	D	D+
Q4-15	U		

Asset & Performance History
Date	NAV	1-Year Total Return
2018	23.74	-9.98
2017	26.76	18.66
2016	23.12	7.32
2015	22.12	
2014		
2013		

Total Assets: $72,806,500

Asset Allocation
Asset	%
Cash	1%
Stocks	99%
US Stocks	1%
Bonds	0%
US Bonds	0%
Other	0%

Services Offered:

Investment Strategy: The investment seeks to track the investment results of the MSCI ACWI ex USA 100% Hedged to USD Index composed of large- and mid-capitalization developed and emerging equities, excluding the U.S., while mitigating exposure to fluctuations between the value of the component currencies and the U.S. dollar. The fund generally will invest at least 90% of its assets in the component securities (including indirect investments through the underlying fund) and other instruments of the index and in investments that have economic characteristics that are substantially identical to the component securities of the index. **Top Holdings:** Nestle SA Alibaba Group Holding Ltd ADR Tencent Holdings Ltd Taiwan Semiconductor Manufacturing Co Ltd Novartis AG

AdvisorShares Newfleet Multi-Sector Income ETF   C   HOLD

Ticker	Traded On	NAV	Total Assets ($)	Dividend Yield (TTM)	Turnover Ratio	Expense Ratio
MINC	NYSE Arca	48.52	$72,781,140	2.94		0.69

Ratings
Reward	C
Risk	D+
Recent Upgrade/Downgrade	

Fund Information
Fund Type	Exchange Traded Funds
Category	US Fixed Income
Sub-Category	Short-Term Bond
Prospectus Objective	Income
Inception Date	Mar-13
Open to New Investments	Y

Prices
Price (as of 9/30/2019)	48.52
52-Week High	48.66
52-Week Low	47.16

Total Returns (%)
3-Month	6-Month	1-Year	3-Year	5-Year
0.93	2.50	4.39	7.52	12.52

3-Year Standard Deviation	0.99
Effective Duration	1.62

Valuation
Premium/Discount (1-Year Average)	-0.07

Company Information
Provider	AdvisorShares
Manager/Tenure	David L. Albrycht (6), Benjamin L. Caron (0)
Website	http://www.advisorshares.com
Address	AdvisorShares 2 Bethesda Metro Center, Suite 1330 Bethesda MD 20814 United States
Phone Number	877-843-3831

PERFORMANCE

Ratings History

Date	Overall Rating	Risk Rating	Reward Rating
Q3-19	C	D+	C
Q4-18	C-	C-	C-
Q4-17	B	A+	C
Q4-16	C	C-	C
Q4-15	C	C-	C

Asset & Performance History

Date	NAV	1-Year Total Return
2018	47.37	0.53
2017	48.46	2.3
2016	48.57	3.24
2015	48.35	1.27
2014	49.07	2.11
2013	49.42	

Total Assets: $72,781,140

Asset Allocation

Asset	%
Cash	2%
Stocks	0%
US Stocks	0%
Bonds	98%
US Bonds	93%
Other	0%

Services Offered:

Investment Strategy: The investment seeks to provide current income consistent with preservation of capital, while limiting fluctuations in net asset value ("NAV") due to changes in interest rates. The Sub-Advisor applies a time-tested approach and extensive credit research to capitalize on opportunities across undervalued areas of the bond markets. The fund principally invests in investment-grade securities, which are securities with credit ratings within the four highest rating categories of a nationally recognized statistical rating organization or, if unrated, those securities that the Sub-Advisor determines to be of comparable quality. **Top Holdings:** United States Treasury Notes 1.75% Morgan Stanley 3.68% SBA Tower Trust 3.17% SBA Tower Trust 2.88% GLS AUTO RECEIVABLES TRUST 2.98%

ERShares Entrepreneur 30 ETF   C+   HOLD

Ticker	Traded On	NAV	Total Assets ($)	Dividend Yield (TTM)	Turnover Ratio	Expense Ratio
ENTR	NYSE Arca	16.84	$72,402,535	0.16		0.49

Ratings
Reward	B
Risk	C-
Recent Upgrade/Downgrade	Up

Fund Information
Fund Type	Exchange Traded Funds
Category	US Equity Large Cap Growth
Sub-Category	Large Growth
Prospectus Objective	Growth & Inc
Inception Date	Nov-17
Open to New Investments	Y

Prices
Price (as of 9/30/2019)	16.84
52-Week High	18.72
52-Week Low	13.02

Total Returns (%)
3-Month	6-Month	1-Year	3-Year	5-Year
-4.91	-3.10	-6.47		

3-Year Standard Deviation	
Effective Duration	

Valuation
Premium/Discount (1-Year Average)	-0.06

Company Information
Provider	EntrepreneurShares
Manager/Tenure	Joel M. Shulman (1)
Website	http://www.ershares.com
Address	EntrepreneurShares 175 Federal Street, Suite #875 Boston MA 02110 United States
Phone Number	

PERFORMANCE

Ratings History

Date	Overall Rating	Risk Rating	Reward Rating
Q3-19	C+	C-	B
Q4-18	C+	C-	B
Q4-17	U		
Q4-16			
Q4-15			

Asset & Performance History

Date	NAV	1-Year Total Return
2018	14.04	-1.66
2017	15.26	
2016		
2015		
2014		
2013		

Total Assets: $72,402,535

Asset Allocation

Asset	%
Cash	1%
Stocks	99%
US Stocks	99%
Bonds	0%
US Bonds	0%
Other	0%

Services Offered:

Investment Strategy: The investment seeks investment results that correspond (before fees and expenses) generally to the performance of its underlying index, the Entrepreneur 30 Index. Under normal circumstances, the fund will invest at least 80% of its net assets, plus any borrowings for investment purposes, in securities of companies included in the Entrepreneur 30 Index. The index comprises 30 U.S. Companies with the highest market capitalizations and composite scores based on six criteria. The fund is non-diversified. **Top Holdings:** Alphabet Inc A Amazon.com Inc Facebook Inc A Salesforce.com Inc NVIDIA Corp

---

Strategy Shares US Market Rotation Strategy ETF   C-   HOLD

Ticker	Traded On	NAV	Total Assets ($)	Dividend Yield (TTM)	Turnover Ratio	Expense Ratio
HUSE	NYSE Arca	33.55	$72,142,303	0.17		1.2

Ratings
Reward	C-
Risk	C-
Recent Upgrade/Downgrade	

Fund Information
Fund Type	Exchange Traded Funds
Category	US Equity Large Cap Blend
Sub-Category	Large Blend
Prospectus Objective	Growth
Inception Date	Jul-12
Open to New Investments	Y

Prices
Price (as of 9/30/2019)	33.60
52-Week High	40.86
52-Week Low	32.94

Total Returns (%)
3-Month	6-Month	1-Year	3-Year	5-Year
-4.47	-4.55	-15.19	6.74	20.11

3-Year Standard Deviation	9.47
Effective Duration	

Valuation
Premium/Discount (1-Year Average)	-0.12

Company Information
Provider	Strategy shares
Manager/Tenure	Matthew B. Tuttle (3)
Website	
Address	Strategy shares United States
Phone Number	

PERFORMANCE

Ratings History
Date	Overall Rating	Risk Rating	Reward Rating
Q3-19	C-	C-	C-
Q4-18	C-	C-	C
Q4-17	B	A	C+
Q4-16	C	D+	B-
Q4-15	C-	D	C

Asset & Performance History
Date	NAV	1-Year Total Return
2018	33.56	-9.56
2017	38.25	13.27
2016	36.1	6.62
2015	37.35	2.49
2014	37.39	12
2013	35.02	33.64

Total Assets: $72,142,303
Asset Allocation
Asset	%
Cash	8%
Stocks	86%
US Stocks	84%
Bonds	0%
US Bonds	0%
Other	6%

Services Offered:

Investment Strategy: The investment seeks capital appreciation. Under normal circumstances, at least 80% of the fund's net assets, plus any borrowings for investment purposes, will be invested in securities of U.S. companies and/or the U.S. government, or in other investment companies that principally invest in such securities. It will invest in companies within each of the large-cap, mid-cap and small-cap U.S. equity segments (each a "Market Segment"). **Top Holdings:** VelocityShares Daily 2x VIX ST ETN ProShares Short VIX Short-Term Futures S&P Global Inc Fiserv Inc Fidelity National Information Services Inc

---

First Trust Municipal High Income ETF   C-   HOLD

Ticker	Traded On	NAV	Total Assets ($)	Dividend Yield (TTM)	Turnover Ratio	Expense Ratio
FMHI	NAS CM	53.05	$71,614,099	3.37	71	0.55

Ratings
Reward	C-
Risk	D+
Recent Upgrade/Downgrade	Up

Fund Information
Fund Type	Exchange Traded Funds
Category	US Muni Fixed Inc
Sub-Category	High Yield Muni
Prospectus Objective	Muni Bond - Natl
Inception Date	Nov-17
Open to New Investments	Y

Prices
Price (as of 9/30/2019)	53.25
52-Week High	53.60
52-Week Low	49.43

Total Returns (%)
3-Month	6-Month	1-Year	3-Year	5-Year
2.38	5.44	9.76		

3-Year Standard Deviation	
Effective Duration	6.04

Valuation
Premium/Discount (1-Year Average)	0.25

Company Information
Provider	First Trust
Manager/Tenure	J. Thomas Futrell (1), Johnathan N. Wilhelm (1)
Website	http://www.ftportfolios.com/
Address	First Trust 120 E. Liberty Drive, Suite 400 Wheaton IL 60187 United States
Phone Number	800-621-1675

PERFORMANCE

Ratings History
Date	Overall Rating	Risk Rating	Reward Rating
Q3-19	C-	D+	C-
Q4-18	D+	D+	D+
Q4-17	U		
Q4-16			
Q4-15			

Asset & Performance History
Date	NAV	1-Year Total Return
2018	49.86	2.03
2017	50.58	
2016		
2015		
2014		
2013		

Total Assets: $71,614,099
Asset Allocation
Asset	%
Cash	3%
Stocks	0%
US Stocks	0%
Bonds	97%
US Bonds	94%
Other	0%

Services Offered:

Investment Strategy: The investment seeks to provide federally tax-exempt income, and its secondary objective will be long-term capital appreciation. Under normal market conditions, the fund seeks to achieve its investment objectives by investing at least 80% of its net assets (including investment borrowings) in municipal debt securities that pay interest that is exempt from regular federal income taxes. Municipal securities are generally issued by or on behalf of states, territories or possessions of the U.S. and the District of Columbia and their political subdivisions, agencies, authorities and other instrumentalities. The fund is non-diversified. **Top Holdings:** US 10 Year Ultra Future Sept19 OHIO ST AIR QUALITY DEV AUTH REV 3.25% FLORIDA DEV FIN CORP SURFACE TRANSN FAC REV 6.5% Future Contract On Us 10yr Note (Cbt)sep19 CAPITAL CITY ECONOMIC DEV AUTH CONN PKG & ENERGY FEE REV 1.51%

ProShares Ultra Oil & Gas   D   SELL

Ticker	Traded On	NAV	Total Assets ($)	Dividend Yield (TTM)	Turnover Ratio	Expense Ratio
DIG	NYSE Arca	23.60	$71,401,907	2.7	14	0.95

Ratings
Reward	D+
Risk	D
Recent Upgrade/Downgrade	

Fund Information
Fund Type	Exchange Traded Funds
Category	Trading Tools
Sub-Category	Trading--Leveraged Equity
Prospectus Objective	Natl Res
Inception Date	Jan-07
Open to New Investments	Y

Prices
Price (as of 9/30/2019)	23.63
52-Week High	45.75
52-Week Low	20.84

Total Returns (%)
3-Month	6-Month	1-Year	3-Year	5-Year
-15.56	-24.78	-45.85	-35.10	-63.42

3-Year Standard Deviation	42.27
Effective Duration	

Valuation
Premium/Discount (1-Year Average)	0.02

Company Information
Provider	ProShares
Manager/Tenure	Michael Neches (6), Tarak Davé (1)
Website	http://www.proshares.com
Address	ProShares 7501 Wisconsin Avenue, Suite 1000 Bethesda MD 20814 United States
Phone Number	866-776-5125

PERFORMANCE

Ratings History

Date	Overall Rating	Risk Rating	Reward Rating
Q3-19	D	D	D+
Q4-18	C-	D	C-
Q4-17	D+	D+	D+
Q4-16	D+	D	D+
Q4-15	D+	D+	C-

Asset & Performance History

Date	NAV	1-Year Total Return
2018	23.35	-40.03
2017	39.55	-7.25
2016	43.49	47.2
2015	29.94	-43.93
2014	53.98	-21.95
2013	69.64	53.13

Total Assets: $71,401,907

Asset Allocation

Asset	%
Cash	-101%
Stocks	107%
US Stocks	106%
Bonds	0%
US Bonds	0%
Other	93%

Services Offered:

Investment Strategy: The investment seeks daily investment results that correspond to two times (2x) the daily performance of the Dow Jones U.S. Oil & GasSM Index. The fund invests in financial instruments that ProShare Advisors believes, in combination, should produce daily returns consistent with the fund's investment objective. The index measures the performance of certain companies in the oil and gas sector of the U.S. equity market. Component companies include, among others, exploration and production, integrated oil and gas, oil equipment and services, pipelines, renewable energy equipment companies and alternative fuel producers. The fund is non-diversified. **Top Holdings:** Dj U.S. Oil & Gas Index Swap Bank Of America Na Exxon Mobil Corp Dj U.S. Oil & Gas Index Swap Societe Generale Chevron Corp Ishares U.S. Energy (Iye) Swap Goldman Sachs International

VanEck Vectors Retail ETF   B-   BUY

Ticker	Traded On	NAV	Total Assets ($)	Dividend Yield (TTM)	Turnover Ratio	Expense Ratio
RTH	NYSE Arca	114.49	$71,156,086	0.86	16	0.35

Ratings
Reward	B+
Risk	C
Recent Upgrade/Downgrade	Up

Fund Information
Fund Type	Exchange Traded Funds
Category	Consumer Goods & Svcs
Sub-Category	Consumer Cyclical
Prospectus Objective	Unaligned
Inception Date	Dec-11
Open to New Investments	Y

Prices
Price (as of 9/30/2019)	114.47
52-Week High	116.89
52-Week Low	87.33

Total Returns (%)
3-Month	6-Month	1-Year	3-Year	5-Year
4.23	8.23	3.87	53.35	98.97

3-Year Standard Deviation	15.28
Effective Duration	

Valuation
Premium/Discount (1-Year Average)	-0.01

Company Information
Provider	VanEck
Manager/Tenure	Hao-Hung (Peter) Liao (7), Guo Hua (Jason) Jin (1)
Website	http://www.vaneck.com
Address	Van Eck Associates Corporation 666 Third Avenue New York NY 10017 United States
Phone Number	800-826-1115

PERFORMANCE

Ratings History

Date	Overall Rating	Risk Rating	Reward Rating
Q3-19	B-	C	B+
Q4-18	C+	C-	B
Q4-17	B+	A	B
Q4-16	C+	C-	B
Q4-15	B	C+	B+

Asset & Performance History

Date	NAV	1-Year Total Return
2018	93.97	3.76
2017	91.31	22.22
2016	75.88	-0.6
2015	77.71	10.84
2014	71.7	18.31
2013	60.85	40.48

Total Assets: $71,156,086

Asset Allocation

Asset	%
Cash	0%
Stocks	100%
US Stocks	98%
Bonds	0%
US Bonds	0%
Other	0%

Services Offered:

Investment Strategy: The investment seeks to replicate as closely as possible, before fees and expenses, the price and yield performance of the MVIS® US Listed Retail 25 Index. The fund normally invests at least 80% of its total assets in securities that comprise the fund's benchmark index. To be initially eligible for the index, companies must generate at least 50% of their revenues from retail. Retail includes companies engaged primarily in retail distribution; wholesalers; online, direct mail and TV retailers; multi-line retailers; specialty retailers; and food and other staples retailers. The fund is non-diversified. **Top Holdings:** Amazon.com Inc The Home Depot Inc Walmart Inc Lowe's Companies Inc Costco Wholesale Corp

ProShares UltraPro 3x Short Crude Oil ETF   D   SELL

Ticker	Traded On	NAV	Total Assets ($)	Dividend Yield (TTM)	Turnover Ratio	Expense Ratio
OILD	NYSE Arca		$71,083,504	0		0.49

Ratings
Reward	D-
Risk	D
Recent Upgrade/Downgrade	

Fund Information
Fund Type	Exchange Traded Funds
Category	Trading Tools
Sub-Category	Trading--Inverse Commodities
Prospectus Objective	Growth & Inc
Inception Date	Mar-17
Open to New Investments	Y

Prices
Price (as of 9/30/2019)	16.80
52-Week High	59.09
52-Week Low	11.91

Total Returns (%)
3-Month	6-Month	1-Year	3-Year	5-Year
-19.15	-18.98	3.03		

3-Year Standard Deviation	
Effective Duration	

Valuation
Premium/Discount (1-Year Average)	0.33

Company Information
Provider	ProShares
Manager/Tenure	Management Team (2)
Website	http://www.proshares.com
Address	ProShares 7501 Wisconsin Avenue, Suite 1000 Bethesda MD 20814 United States
Phone Number	866-776-5125

PERFORMANCE

Ratings History

Date	Overall Rating	Risk Rating	Reward Rating
Q3-19	D	D	D-
Q4-18	D	D	D
Q4-17	U		
Q4-16			
Q4-15			

Asset & Performance History

Date	NAV	1-Year Total Return
2018	49.79	18.56
2017	42.33	
2016		
2015		
2014		
2013		

Total Assets: $71,083,504

Asset Allocation
Asset	%
Cash	400%
Stocks	0%
US Stocks	0%
Bonds	0%
US Bonds	0%
Other	-300%

Services Offered:

Investment Strategy: The investment seeks daily investment results, before fees and expenses, that correspond to three times (3x) the daily performance of the Bloomberg WTI Crude Oil SubindexSM.
The underlying index reflects the performance of the price of West Texas Intermediate sweet, light crude oil futures contracts traded on the NYMEX. The fund seeks to meet its investment objective by investing, under normal market conditions, in futures contracts for WTI sweet, light crude oil listed on the NYMEX, ICE Futures U.S. or other U.S. exchanges and listed options on such contracts. **Top Holdings:** Crude Oil Oct19

Invesco S&P 500® Momentum ETF   C+   HOLD

Ticker	Traded On	NAV	Total Assets ($)	Dividend Yield (TTM)	Turnover Ratio	Expense Ratio
SPMO	NYSE Arca	40.56	$70,979,413	1.3		0.13

Ratings
Reward	B-
Risk	C
Recent Upgrade/Downgrade	Up

Fund Information
Fund Type	Exchange Traded Funds
Category	US Equity Large Cap Growth
Sub-Category	Large Growth
Prospectus Objective	Growth
Inception Date	Oct-15
Open to New Investments	

Prices
Price (as of 9/30/2019)	40.59
52-Week High	41.76
52-Week Low	31.20

Total Returns (%)
3-Month	6-Month	1-Year	3-Year	5-Year
-0.04	3.40	0.69	55.39	

3-Year Standard Deviation	12.85
Effective Duration	

Valuation
Premium/Discount (1-Year Average)	0.02

Company Information
Provider	Invesco
Manager/Tenure	Peter Hubbard (3), Michael Jeanette (3), Tony Seisser (3)
Website	http://www.invesco.com/us
Address	Invesco 11 Greenway Plaza, Ste. 2500 Houston TX 77046 United States
Phone Number	800-659-1005

PERFORMANCE

Ratings History

Date	Overall Rating	Risk Rating	Reward Rating
Q3-19	C+	C	B-
Q4-18	C	C	C+
Q4-17	C	B	C+
Q4-16	D	D+	C
Q4-15			

Asset & Performance History

Date	NAV	1-Year Total Return
2018	33.79	-0.14
2017	34.18	27.88
2016	26.95	5.43
2015	26.07	
2014		
2013		

Total Assets: $70,979,413

Asset Allocation
Asset	%
Cash	0%
Stocks	100%
US Stocks	100%
Bonds	0%
US Bonds	0%
Other	0%

Services Offered:

Investment Strategy: The investment seeks to track the investment results (before fees and expenses) of the S&P 500 Momentum Index (the "underlying index"). The fund generally will invest at least 90% of its total assets in the securities that comprise the underlying index. The underlying index is designed to track the performance of approximately 100 stocks in the S&P 500® Index that have the highest "momentum score." In general, momentum is the tendency of an investment to exhibit persistence in its relative performance; a "momentum style" of investing emphasizes investing in securities that have had better recent performance compared to other securities. It is non-diversified. **Top Holdings:** Amazon.com Inc Merck & Co Inc Procter & Gamble Co Mastercard Inc A Pfizer Inc

Invesco Investment Grade Defensive ETF   D+   SELL

Ticker	Traded On	NAV	Total Assets ($)	Dividend Yield (TTM)	Turnover Ratio	Expense Ratio
IIGD	NYSE Arca	26.21	$70,770,434	2.85		0.13

Ratings
Reward	D+
Risk	D+
Recent Upgrade/Downgrade	

Fund Information
Fund Type	Exchange Traded Funds
Category	US Fixed Income
Sub-Category	Short-Term Bond
Prospectus Objective	Corp Bond - Gen
Inception Date	Jul-18
Open to New Investments	Y

Prices
Price (as of 9/30/2019)	26.30
52-Week High	26.41
52-Week Low	24.88

Total Returns (%)
3-Month	6-Month	1-Year	3-Year	5-Year
1.57	4.20	7.96		

3-Year Standard Deviation	
Effective Duration	3.58

Valuation
Premium/Discount (1-Year Average)	0.18

Company Information
Provider	Invesco
Manager/Tenure	Peter Hubbard (1), Jeffrey W. Kernagis (1), Greg Meisenger (1), 2 others
Website	http://www.invesco.com/us
Address	Invesco 11 Greenway Plaza, Ste. 2500 Houston TX 77046 United States
Phone Number	800-659-1005

PERFORMANCE (chart: 10.0%, 7.5%, 5.0%, 2.5%, 0.0%, -2.5%; dates 11/5/18, 2/15/19, 6/17/19, 9/30/19)

Ratings History
Date	Overall Rating	Risk Rating	Reward Rating
Q3-19	D+	D+	D+
Q4-18	U		
Q4-17			
Q4-16			
Q4-15			

Asset & Performance History
Date	NAV	1-Year Total Return
2018	25.03	
2017		
2016		
2015		
2014		
2013		

Total Assets: $70,770,434

Asset Allocation
Asset	%
Cash	0%
Stocks	0%
US Stocks	0%
Bonds	100%
US Bonds	99%
Other	0%

Services Offered:

Investment Strategy: The investment seeks to track the investment results (before fees and expenses) of the Invesco Investment Grade Defensive Index (the "underlying index"). The fund generally will invest at least 80% of its total assets in securities that comprise the underlying index. The underlying index is designed to provide exposure to U.S. investment grade bonds having the highest "quality scores" (within the eligible universe of U.S. investment grade bonds) as determined by the index provider. The fund is non-diversified. **Top Holdings:** Caterpillar Financial Services Corporation 1.7% SunTrust Banks, Inc. 2.7% Wells Fargo Bank, National Association 3.55% Pfizer Inc. 3% American Express Company 2.5%

First Trust Dorsey Wright DALI 1 ETF   D+   SELL

Ticker	Traded On	NAV	Total Assets ($)	Dividend Yield (TTM)	Turnover Ratio	Expense Ratio
DALI	NAS CM	19.86	$70,500,729	0.26	34	0.91

Ratings
Reward	D
Risk	D+
Recent Upgrade/Downgrade	

Fund Information
Fund Type	Exchange Traded Funds
Category	Aggressive Allocation
Sub-Category	World Allocation
Prospectus Objective	Growth & Inc
Inception Date	May-18
Open to New Investments	Y

Prices
Price (as of 9/30/2019)	19.89
52-Week High	21.03
52-Week Low	16.00

Total Returns (%)
3-Month	6-Month	1-Year	3-Year	5-Year
-3.24	-1.87	-5.02		

3-Year Standard Deviation	
Effective Duration	

Valuation
Premium/Discount (1-Year Average)	-0.03

Company Information
Provider	First Trust
Manager/Tenure	Jon C. Erickson (1), Daniel J. Lindquist (1), David G. McGarel (1), 3 others
Website	http://www.ftportfolios.com/
Address	First Trust 120 E. Liberty Drive, Suite 400 Wheaton IL 60187 United States
Phone Number	800-621-1675

PERFORMANCE (chart: 10.0%, 0.0%, -10.0%, -20.0%, -30.0%; dates 11/3/18, 2/14/19, 6/17/19, 9/30/19)

Ratings History
Date	Overall Rating	Risk Rating	Reward Rating
Q3-19	D+	D+	D
Q4-18	U		
Q4-17			
Q4-16			
Q4-15			

Asset & Performance History
Date	NAV	1-Year Total Return
2018	17.03	
2017		
2016		
2015		
2014		
2013		

Total Assets: $70,500,729

Asset Allocation
Asset	%
Cash	0%
Stocks	100%
US Stocks	98%
Bonds	0%
US Bonds	0%
Other	0%

Services Offered:

Investment Strategy: The investment seeks investment results that correspond generally to the price and yield (before the fund's fees and expenses) of an index called the Nasdaq Dorsey Wright DALI 1 Index. Under normal conditions, the fund will invest at least 90% of its net assets (including investment borrowings) in the equity securities that comprise the index. The index has been designed based upon the principle that the asset class exhibiting the highest levels of "relative strength," based on current prices, will be the asset class with the best performance over the near term. It is non-diversified. **Top Holdings:** First Trust Large Cap Gr AlphaDEX® ETF First Trust Small Cap Gr AlphaDEX® ETF First Trust Utilities AlphaDEX® ETF First Trust Technology AlphaDEX® ETF First Trust NASDAQ-100-Tech Sector ETF

Invesco Insider Sentiment ETF   C   HOLD

Ticker	Traded On	NAV	Total Assets ($)	Dividend Yield (TTM)	Turnover Ratio	Expense Ratio
NFO	NYSE Arca	70.14	$70,196,767	0.84	116	0.66

Ratings
Reward   B-
Risk   D+
Recent Upgrade/Downgrade

Fund Information
Fund Type   Exchange Traded Funds
Category   US Equity Mid Cap
Sub-Category   Mid-Cap Blend
Prospectus Objective   Growth
Inception Date   Sep-06
Open to New Investments   Y

Prices
Price (as of 9/30/2019)   70.14
52-Week High   70.91
52-Week Low   53.28

PERFORMANCE

Total Returns (%)

3-Month	6-Month	1-Year	3-Year	5-Year
1.12	6.87	6.57	46.60	63.56

3-Year Standard Deviation   11.3
Effective Duration

Valuation
Premium/Discount (1-Year Average)   -0.01

Company Information
Provider   Invesco
Manager/Tenure   Peter Hubbard (1), Michael Jeanette
                  (1), Tony Seisser (1)
Website   http://www.invesco.com/us
Address   Invesco 11 Greenway Plaza, Ste. 2500
                  Houston TX 77046 United States
Phone Number   800-659-1005

Ratings History

Date	Overall Rating	Risk Rating	Reward Rating
Q3-19	C	D+	B-
Q4-18	C-	D+	C
Q4-17	B	B	B
Q4-16	C	D+	C+
Q4-15	C	C	C

Asset & Performance History

Date	NAV	1-Year Total Return
2018	56.63	-7.35
2017	61.8	27.96
2016	49.08	7.36
2015	46.45	-3.73
2014	48.99	5.89
2013	46.81	35.38

Total Assets: $70,196,767
Asset Allocation

Asset	%
Cash	0%
Stocks	100%
US Stocks	100%
Bonds	0%
US Bonds	0%
Other	0%

Services Offered:

Investment Strategy: The investment seeks to track the investment results (before fees and expenses) of the Nasdaq US Insider Sentiment Index. The fund will invest at least 90% of its total assets in the securities that comprise the underlying index and depositary receipts representing common stocks included in the underlying index (or underlying securities representing depositary receipts included in the underlying index). The companies eligible for the underlying index are derived from its starting universe, the Nasdaq US Large Mid Cap Index, which is designed to track the performance of mid- to large-capitalization U.S. companies. The fund is non-diversified.
Top Holdings: Okta Inc A   Match Group Inc   Dollar General Corp   Fair Isaac Corp   Zoetis Inc Class A

ProShares Ultra Semiconductors   B-   BUY

Ticker	Traded On	NAV	Total Assets ($)	Dividend Yield (TTM)	Turnover Ratio	Expense Ratio
USD	NYSE Arca	45.07	$69,863,329	0.97	38	0.95

Ratings
Reward   B
Risk   C
Recent Upgrade/Downgrade   Up

Fund Information
Fund Type   Exchange Traded Funds
Category   Trading Tools
Sub-Category   Trading--Leveraged Equity
Prospectus Objective   Technology
Inception Date   Jan-07
Open to New Investments   Y

Prices
Price (as of 9/30/2019)   45.01
52-Week High   52.31
52-Week Low   25.73

PERFORMANCE

Total Returns (%)

3-Month	6-Month	1-Year	3-Year	5-Year
4.51	4.28	0.81	123.66	254.14

3-Year Standard Deviation   43.16
Effective Duration

Valuation
Premium/Discount (1-Year Average)   -0.14

Company Information
Provider   ProShares
Manager/Tenure   Michael Neches (6), Tarak Davé (1)
Website   http://www.proshares.com
Address   ProShares 7501 Wisconsin Avenue,
                  Suite 1000 Bethesda MD 20814
                  United States
Phone Number   866-776-5125

Ratings History

Date	Overall Rating	Risk Rating	Reward Rating
Q3-19	B-	C	B
Q4-18	C	C-	C
Q4-17	B	C	A-
Q4-16	C+	C-	B
Q4-15	C	C	C+

Asset & Performance History

Date	NAV	1-Year Total Return
2018	29.77	-26.27
2017	40.68	80.92
2016	22.58	58.14
2015	14.36	-8.32
2014	15.73	78.02
2013	8.92	77.91

Total Assets: $69,863,329
Asset Allocation

Asset	%
Cash	-99%
Stocks	83%
US Stocks	81%
Bonds	0%
US Bonds	0%
Other	117%

Services Offered:

Investment Strategy: The investment seeks daily investment results that correspond to two times (2x) the daily performance of the Dow Jones U.S. SemiconductorsSM Index. The fund invests in financial instruments that ProShare Advisors believes, in combination, should produce daily returns consistent with the fund's investment objective. The index measures the performance of certain companies in the semiconductor sub-sector of the U.S. equity market. Component companies are engaged in the production of semiconductors and other integrated chips, as well as other related products such as semiconductor capital equipment and mother-boards. The fund is non-diversified. **Top Holdings:** Dj U.S. Semiconductors Index Swap Societe Generale   Dj U.S. Semiconductors Index Swap Ubs Ag   Intel Corp   Texas Instruments Inc   Broadcom Inc

UBS ETRACS 2xMonthly Leveraged Alerian MLP Infrastructure Index ETN SeriesB   D   SELL

Ticker	Traded On	NAV	Total Assets ($)	Dividend Yield (TTM)	Turnover Ratio	Expense Ratio
MLPQ	NYSE Arca	24.57	$69,293,604	17.83		0.85

Ratings
Reward   D
Risk   D+
Recent Upgrade/Downgrade

Fund Information
Fund Type	Exchange Traded Funds
Category	Trading Tools
Sub-Category	Trading--Leveraged Equity
Prospectus Objective	Growth & Inc
Inception Date	Feb-16
Open to New Investments	Y

Prices
Price (as of 9/30/2019)	24.65
52-Week High	36.91
52-Week Low	21.00

Total Returns (%)

3-Month	6-Month	1-Year	3-Year	5-Year
-11.40	-13.60	-22.61	-30.11	

3-Year Standard Deviation	33.17
Effective Duration	

Valuation
Premium/Discount (1-Year Average)	0.20

Company Information
Provider	UBS Group AG
Manager/Tenure	No Manager (3)
Website	http://www.ubs.com
Address	Bahnhofstrasse 45 Zürich 8098 Switzerland
Phone Number	412-037-1952

PERFORMANCE

Ratings History

Date	Overall Rating	Risk Rating	Reward Rating
Q3-19	D	D+	D
Q4-18	D	D	D
Q4-17	D	D	D
Q4-16	U		
Q4-15			

Asset & Performance History

Date	NAV	1-Year Total Return
2018	23.33	-28.16
2017	37.66	-19.42
2016	53.92	
2015		
2014		
2013		

Total Assets: $69,293,604
Asset Allocation

Asset	%
Cash	%
Stocks	%
US Stocks	%
Bonds	%
US Bonds	%
Other	%

Services Offered:

Investment Strategy: The investment seeks to provide two times leveraged long exposure to the compounded monthly performance of the Alerian MLP Infrastructure Index (the "index").
The index, comprising 22 energy infrastructure master limited partnerships, is a subset of the Alerian MLP Infrastructure Index. The index constituent securities earn the majority of their cash flow from the transportation, storage, and processing of energy commodities. **Top Holdings:**

Vanguard U.S. Minimum Volatility ETF ETF Shares   C-   HOLD

Ticker	Traded On	NAV	Total Assets ($)	Dividend Yield (TTM)	Turnover Ratio	Expense Ratio
VFMV	BATS	89.21	$69,137,750	2.49	5	0.13

Ratings
Reward   C
Risk   D+
Recent Upgrade/Downgrade   Up

Fund Information
Fund Type	Exchange Traded Funds
Category	US Equity Mid Cap
Sub-Category	Mid-Cap Blend
Prospectus Objective	Growth
Inception Date	Feb-18
Open to New Investments	Y

Prices
Price (as of 9/30/2019)	89.25
52-Week High	90.11
52-Week Low	70.84

Total Returns (%)

3-Month	6-Month	1-Year	3-Year	5-Year
3.56	8.79	8.19		

3-Year Standard Deviation	
Effective Duration	

Valuation
Premium/Discount (1-Year Average)	0.02

Company Information
Provider	Vanguard
Manager/Tenure	Antonio Picca (1)
Website	http://www.vanguard.com
Address	Vanguard 100 Vanguard Boulevard Malvern PA 19355 United States
Phone Number	877-662-7447

PERFORMANCE

Ratings History

Date	Overall Rating	Risk Rating	Reward Rating
Q3-19	C-	D+	C
Q4-18	U		
Q4-17			
Q4-16			
Q4-15			

Asset & Performance History

Date	NAV	1-Year Total Return
2018	73.73	
2017		
2016		
2015		
2014		
2013		

Total Assets: $69,137,750
Asset Allocation

Asset	%
Cash	0%
Stocks	100%
US Stocks	99%
Bonds	0%
US Bonds	0%
Other	0%

Services Offered:

Investment Strategy: The investment seeks to provide long-term capital appreciation with lower volatility relative to the broad U.S. equity market. The fund invests primarily in a group of U.S. common stocks that together are deemed by the advisor to have the potential to generate lower volatility relative to the broad U.S. equity market. The portfolio will include a diverse mix of companies representing many different market sectors and industry groups. Under normal circumstances, at least 80% of the fund's assets will be invested in securities issued by U.S. companies. **Top Holdings:** Republic Services Inc Class A Equity Commonwealth Royal Gold Inc Redwood Trust Inc Yum Brands Inc

ProShares UltraPro Short Russell2000   D+   SELL

Ticker	Traded On	NAV	Total Assets ($)	Dividend Yield (TTM)	Turnover Ratio	Expense Ratio
SRTY	NYSE Arca	24.12	$69,061,891	1.73		0.95

Ratings
Reward   D
Risk   D
Recent Upgrade/Downgrade   Up

Fund Information
Fund Type   Exchange Traded Funds
Category   Trading Tools
Sub-Category   Trading--Inverse Equity
Prospectus Objective   Small Company
Inception Date   Feb-10
Open to New Investments   Y

Prices
Price (as of 9/30/2019)   24.16
52-Week High   48.34
52-Week Low   21.62

Total Returns (%)

3-Month	6-Month	1-Year	3-Year	5-Year
4.47	-1.46	7.10	-65.05	-86.35

3-Year Standard Deviation   51.42
Effective Duration

Valuation
Premium/Discount (1-Year Average)   0.11

Company Information
Provider   ProShares
Manager/Tenure   Michael Neches (6), Devin Sullivan (1)
Website   http://www.proshares.com
Address   ProShares 7501 Wisconsin Avenue,
                    Suite 1000 Bethesda MD 20814
                    United States
Phone Number   866-776-5125

PERFORMANCE

Ratings History

Date	Overall Rating	Risk Rating	Reward Rating
Q3-19	D+	D	D
Q4-18	D	D	D-
Q4-17	E+	E+	E+
Q4-16	D	D-	E+
Q4-15	D-	E+	E+

Asset & Performance History

Date	NAV	1-Year Total Return
2018	39.5	23.14
2017	32.38	-38.41
2016	52.6	-54.98
2015	116.84	-5.4
2014	123.52	-27.98
2013	171.52	-68.21

Total Assets: $69,061,891
Asset Allocation

Asset	%
Cash	251%
Stocks	-163%
US Stocks	-163%
Bonds	11%
US Bonds	11%
Other	0%

Services Offered:

Investment Strategy: The investment seeks daily investment results that correspond to three times the inverse (-3x) of the daily performance of the Russell 2000® Index. The fund invests in financial instruments that ProShare Advisors believes, in combination, should produce daily returns consistent with the fund's investment objective. The index is a measure of small-cap U.S. stock market performance. The fund is non-diversified. **Top Holdings:** Russell 2000 Index Swap Societe Generale   Russell 2000 Index Swap Citibank Na   Russell 2000 Index Swap Ubs Ag   Russell 2000 Index Swap Morgan Stanley & Co. International Plc   Russell 2000 Index Swap Bank Of America Na

Hartford Multifactor Emerging Markets ETF   C-   HOLD

Ticker	Traded On	NAV	Total Assets ($)	Dividend Yield (TTM)	Turnover Ratio	Expense Ratio
ROAM	NYSE Arca	22.20	$68,823,296	2.73	25	0.44

Ratings
Reward   C
Risk   C-
Recent Upgrade/Downgrade

Fund Information
Fund Type   Exchange Traded Funds
Category   Global Emerg Mkts Equity
Sub-Category   Diversified Emerging Mkts
Prospectus Objective   Div Emerg Mkts
Inception Date   Feb-15
Open to New Investments   Y

Prices
Price (as of 9/30/2019)   22.04
52-Week High   24.39
52-Week Low   21.30

Total Returns (%)

3-Month	6-Month	1-Year	3-Year	5-Year
-6.60	-4.65	-1.70	9.52	

3-Year Standard Deviation   13.1
Effective Duration

Valuation
Premium/Discount (1-Year Average)   -0.24

Company Information
Provider   Hartford Funds
Manager/Tenure   Richard A. Brown (4), Thomas J.
                    Durante (4), Karen Q. Wong (4)
Website   http://www.hartfordfunds.com
Address   690 Lee Road Wayne PA 19087 United
                    States
Phone Number   800-456-7526

PERFORMANCE

Ratings History

Date	Overall Rating	Risk Rating	Reward Rating
Q3-19	C-	C-	C
Q4-18	C-	C-	C-
Q4-17	C	C	C+
Q4-16	D+	D+	D+
Q4-15	U		

Asset & Performance History

Date	NAV	1-Year Total Return
2018	22.17	-11.61
2017	25.71	28.21
2016	20.45	8.2
2015	19.26	
2014		
2013		

Total Assets: $68,823,296
Asset Allocation

Asset	%
Cash	0%
Stocks	100%
US Stocks	0%
Bonds	0%
US Bonds	0%
Other	0%

Services Offered:

Investment Strategy: The investment seeks to provide investment results that, before fees and expenses, correspond to the total return performance of the Hartford Multifactor Emerging Markets Equity Index. The fund generally invests at least 80% of its assets in securities of the index and in depositary receipts (such as American Depositary Receipts ("ADRs"), Global Depositary Receipts ("GDRs") and European Depositary Receipts ("EDRs") representing securities of the index. The index is designed to balance risks and opportunities within equity markets of emerging economies while emphasizing constituents exhibiting a favorable combination of factor characteristics. **Top Holdings:** Infosys Ltd ADR   Telefonica Brasil SA Participating Preferred   Dr Reddy's Laboratories Ltd ADR   ICICI Bank Ltd ADR   HDFC Bank Ltd ADR

SPDR® MSCI Emerging Markets Fossil Fuel Free ETF

D+   SELL

Ticker	Traded On	NAV	Total Assets ($)	Dividend Yield (TTM)	Turnover Ratio	Expense Ratio
EEMX	NYSE Arca		$68,734,262	2.11	8	0.3

Ratings
Reward   D+
Risk   D+
Recent Upgrade/Downgrade

Fund Information
Fund Type   Exchange Traded Funds
Category   Global Emerg Mkts Equity
Sub-Category   Diversified Emerging Mkts
Prospectus Objective   Growth & Inc
Inception Date   Oct-16
Open to New Investments   Y

Prices
Price (as of 9/30/2019)   59.81
52-Week High   64.86
52-Week Low   55.74

Total Returns (%)

3-Month	6-Month	1-Year	3-Year	5-Year
-5.20	-4.80	-2.47	16.59	

3-Year Standard Deviation
Effective Duration

Valuation
Premium/Discount (1-Year Average)   -0.11

Company Information
Provider   SPDR State Street Global Advisors
Manager/Tenure   Michael J. Feehily (2), Karl A.
                 Schneider (2), Kala O'Donnell (2)
Website   http://www.spdrs.com
Address   SPDR State Street Global Advisors
                 State Street Financial Center, 1
                 Lincoln Street Boston MA 02111-2900
                 United States
Phone Number   617-786-3000

PERFORMANCE

Ratings History

Date	Overall Rating	Risk Rating	Reward Rating
Q3-19	D+	D+	D+
Q4-18	D	D	D
Q4-17	D	B+	D+
Q4-16	U		
Q4-15			

Asset & Performance History

Date	NAV	1-Year Total Return
2018	57.06	-15.86
2017	69.4	38.37
2016	51.49	
2015		
2014		
2013		

Total Assets: $68,734,262
Asset Allocation

Asset	%
Cash	0%
Stocks	99%
US Stocks	0%
Bonds	0%
US Bonds	0%
Other	0%

Services Offered:

Investment Strategy: The investment seeks to provide investment results that, before fees and expenses, correspond generally to the total return performance of the MSCI Emerging Markets ex Fossil Fuels Index. Under normal market conditions, the fund generally invests substantially all, but at least 80%, of its total assets in the securities comprising the index and in depositary receipts based on securities comprising the index. The index is designed to measure the performance of companies in the MSCI Emerging Markets Index that are "fossil fuel reserves free," which are defined as companies that do not own fossil fuel reserves. The fund is non-diversified.
Top Holdings: Tencent Holdings Ltd Alibaba Group Holding Ltd ADR Taiwan Semiconductor Manufacturing Co Ltd Samsung Electronics Co Ltd Naspers Ltd Class N

SPDR® DoubleLine® Emerging Markets Fixed Income ETF

C   HOLD

Ticker	Traded On	NAV	Total Assets ($)	Dividend Yield (TTM)	Turnover Ratio	Expense Ratio
EMTL	BATS		$68,324,272	3.98	37	0.65

Ratings
Reward   B-
Risk   D+
Recent Upgrade/Downgrade

Fund Information
Fund Type   Exchange Traded Funds
Category   Emerging Mkts Fixed Inc
Sub-Category   Emerging Markets Bond
Prospectus Objective   Income
Inception Date   Apr-16
Open to New Investments   Y

Prices
Price (as of 9/30/2019)   50.68
52-Week High   51.43
52-Week Low   47.34

Total Returns (%)

3-Month	6-Month	1-Year	3-Year	5-Year
0.09	4.09	9.02	14.21	

3-Year Standard Deviation   3.28
Effective Duration   4.80

Valuation
Premium/Discount (1-Year Average)   0.21

Company Information
Provider   SPDR State Street Global Advisors
Manager/Tenure   Mark W. Christensen (3), Su Fei Koo
                 (3), Luz M. Padilla (3)
Website   http://www.spdrs.com
Address   SPDR State Street Global Advisors
                 State Street Financial Center, 1
                 Lincoln Street Boston MA 02111-2900
                 United States
Phone Number   617-786-3000

PERFORMANCE

Ratings History

Date	Overall Rating	Risk Rating	Reward Rating
Q3-19	C	D+	B-
Q4-18	D+	C-	D+
Q4-17	D+	A	D+
Q4-16	U		
Q4-15			

Asset & Performance History

Date	NAV	1-Year Total Return
2018	47.6	-1.93
2017	50.17	7.6
2016	48.61	
2015		
2014		
2013		

Total Assets: $68,324,272
Asset Allocation

Asset	%
Cash	4%
Stocks	0%
US Stocks	0%
Bonds	96%
US Bonds	2%
Other	0%

Services Offered:

Investment Strategy: The investment seeks to provide high total return from current income and capital appreciation. Under normal circumstances, the fund will invest at least 80% of its net assets (plus the amount of borrowings for investment purposes) in emerging market fixed income securities. Fixed income securities are defined as fixed income securities issued or guaranteed by foreign corporations or foreign governments; corporate or government bonds; sovereign debt; structured securities; foreign currency transactions; certain derivatives; preferred securities; zero coupon bonds; credit-linked notes; pass through notes; bank loans; and perpetual maturity bonds. **Top Holdings:** Cometa Energia SA DE CV 6.38% DBS Group Holdings Ltd 3.6% Perusahaan Listrik Negara PT 5.5% PT Pertamina (Persero) 4.88% Syngenta Finance N.V. 5.68%

Global X MSCI Colombia ETF　　　　　　　　　　　　　　　　　　　　　D+　　SELL

Ticker	Traded On	NAV	Total Assets ($)	Dividend Yield (TTM)	Turnover Ratio	Expense Ratio
GXG	NYSE Arca	8.95	$68,289,224	4.35	39	0.61

Ratings
Reward　　　　　　　D+
Risk　　　　　　　　C-
Recent Upgrade/Downgrade　　Down

Fund Information
Fund Type　　　　Exchange Traded Funds
Category　　　　　Equity Misc
Sub-Category　　　Miscellaneous Region
Prospectus Objective　Foreign Stock
Inception Date　　Feb-09
Open to New Investments　Y

Prices
Price (as of 9/30/2019)　8.95
52-Week High　　10.24
52-Week Low　　7.75

Total Returns (%)

3-Month	6-Month	1-Year	3-Year	5-Year
-5.09	-7.18	-6.49	2.57	-43.51

3-Year Standard Deviation　19.95
Effective Duration

Valuation
Premium/Discount (1-Year Average)　-0.42

Company Information
Provider　Global X Funds
Manager/Tenure　Chang Kim (5), Nam To (1), Wayne Xie (0), 1 other
Website　http://www.globalxfunds.com
Address　Global X Funds 600 Lexington Avenue, 20th Floor New York NY 10022 United States
Phone Number　888-493-8631

PERFORMANCE

Ratings History

Date	Overall Rating	Risk Rating	Reward Rating
Q3-19	D+	C-	D+
Q4-18	D+	D	D+
Q4-17	D+	D	C-
Q4-16	D	D	D
Q4-15	D-	D	D-

Asset & Performance History

Date	NAV	1-Year Total Return
2018	7.87	-19.26
2017	10.04	12.34
2016	9.1	23.64
2015	7.47	-41.26
2014	12.92	-26.45
2013	18.13	-14.41

Total Assets: $68,289,224
Asset Allocation

Asset	%
Cash	0%
Stocks	99%
US Stocks	1%
Bonds	0%
US Bonds	0%
Other	0%

Services Offered:

Investment Strategy: The investment seeks to provide investment results that correspond generally to the price and yield performance, before fees and expenses, of the MSCI All Colombia Select 25/50 Index. The fund invests at least 80% of its total assets in the securities of the underlying index and in American Depositary Receipts ("ADRs") and Global Depositary Receipts ("GDRs") based on the securities in the underlying index. It also invests at least 80% of its total assets in securities of companies that are economically tied to Colombia. The underlying index is designed to represent the performance of the broad Colombia equity universe. The fund is non-diversified. **Top Holdings:** BanColombia SA ADR　Ecopetrol SA ADR　Grupo de Inversiones Suramericana SA　BanColombia SA Interconexion Electrica SA ESP

Direxion Daily Russia Bull 3X Shares　　　　　　　　　　　　　　　　　　C　　HOLD

Ticker	Traded On	NAV	Total Assets ($)	Dividend Yield (TTM)	Turnover Ratio	Expense Ratio
RUSL	NYSE Arca	46.48	$68,229,631	1.96	93	1.36

Ratings
Reward　　　　　　　C+
Risk　　　　　　　　D+
Recent Upgrade/Downgrade

Fund Information
Fund Type　　　　Exchange Traded Funds
Category　　　　　Trading Tools
Sub-Category　　　Trading--Leveraged Equity
Prospectus Objective　Foreign Stock
Inception Date　　May-11
Open to New Investments　Y

Prices
Price (as of 9/30/2019)　46.44
52-Week High　　57.10
52-Week Low　　28.52

Total Returns (%)

3-Month	6-Month	1-Year	3-Year	5-Year
-16.16	17.95	8.71	38.74	-62.56

3-Year Standard Deviation　56.75
Effective Duration

Valuation
Premium/Discount (1-Year Average)　0.02

Company Information
Provider　Direxion Funds
Manager/Tenure　Paul Brigandi (8), Tony Ng (4)
Website　http://www.direxionfunds.com
Address　Direxion Funds 1301 Avenue Of The Americas (6th Avenue) New York NY 10019 United States
Phone Number　646-572-3390

PERFORMANCE

Ratings History

Date	Overall Rating	Risk Rating	Reward Rating
Q3-19	C	D+	C+
Q4-18	D+	D+	D+
Q4-17	C	D+	C+
Q4-16	D	D	D+
Q4-15	E+	D-	E

Asset & Performance History

Date	NAV	1-Year Total Return
2018	29.82	-40.05
2017	50.35	0.4
2016	50.68	126.22
2015	22.4	-31.99
2014	32.94	-91.15
2013	372.6	-15.96

Total Assets: $68,229,631
Asset Allocation

Asset	%
Cash	72%
Stocks	29%
US Stocks	0%
Bonds	0%
US Bonds	0%
Other	-1%

Services Offered:

Investment Strategy: The investment seeks daily investment results, before fees and expenses, of 300% of the daily performance of the MVIS Russia Index. The fund invests at least 80% of its net assets in financial instruments and securities of the index, ETFs that track the index and other financial instruments that provide daily leveraged exposure to the index or ETFs that track the index. The index is intended to represent the overall performance of publically traded companies that are domiciled and primarily listed on an exchange in Russia or that are not Russian companies, but nonetheless generate at least 50% of their revenues in Russia. It is non-diversified. **Top Holdings:** VanEck Vectors Russia ETF　Mrkt Vectors Russia Swap　Mrkt Vectors Russia Swap　Market Vectors Russia Etf Swap　Mrkt Vectors Russia Swap

ALPS Disruptive Technologies ETF   C-   HOLD

Ticker	Traded On	NAV	Total Assets ($)	Dividend Yield (TTM)	Turnover Ratio	Expense Ratio
DTEC	BATS	28.99	$68,114,722	0.27	33	0.5

Ratings
Reward   C-
Risk   C-
Recent Upgrade/Downgrade

Fund Information
Fund Type   Exchange Traded Funds
Category   Technology Sector Equity
Sub-Category   Technology
Prospectus Objective   Growth
Inception Date   Dec-17
Open to New Investments   Y

Prices
Price (as of 9/30/2019)   29.07
52-Week High   31.11
52-Week Low   22.47

Total Returns (%)

3-Month	6-Month	1-Year	3-Year	5-Year
-5.37	-1.02	-1.35		

3-Year Standard Deviation
Effective Duration

Valuation
Premium/Discount (1-Year Average)   0.10

Company Information
Provider   ALPS
Manager/Tenure   Andrew Hicks (1), Ryan Mischker (1)
Website   http://www.alpsfunds.com
Address   ALPS 1290 Broadway, Suite 1100
                  Denver CO 80203 United States
Phone Number   866-759-5679

PERFORMANCE chart (11/3/18 to 9/30/19), range -30.0% to 10.0%

Ratings History

Date	Overall Rating	Risk Rating	Reward Rating
Q3-19	C-	C-	C-
Q4-18	D	D	D
Q4-17			
Q4-16			
Q4-15			

Asset & Performance History

Date	NAV	1-Year Total Return
2018	24.06	-3.28
2017	24.96	
2016		
2015		
2014		
2013		

Total Assets: $68,114,722
Asset Allocation

Asset	%
Cash	0%
Stocks	100%
US Stocks	65%
Bonds	0%
US Bonds	0%
Other	0%

Services Offered:

Investment Strategy: The investment seeks investment results that correspond (before fees and expenses) generally to the performance of the Indxx Disruptive Technologies Index (the "underlying index"). The fund will invest at least 80% of its net assets in securities that comprise the underlying index. The underlying index is designed to identify the companies using disruptive technologies in each of ten thematic areas: Healthcare Innovation, Internet of Things, Clean Energy and Smart Grid, Cloud Computing, Data and Analytics, FinTech, Robotics and Artificial Intelligence, Cybersecurity, 3D Printing, and Mobile Payments. The fund is non-diversified. **Top Holdings:** Fiserv Inc   Netgear Inc   SLM Solutions Group AG   Symantec Corp   DexCom Inc

---

GraniteShares Bloomberg Commodity Broad Strategy No K-1 ETF   D+   SELL

Ticker	Traded On	NAV	Total Assets ($)	Dividend Yield (TTM)	Turnover Ratio	Expense Ratio
COMB	NYSE Arca	23.53	$67,118,776	0.94		0.25

Ratings
Reward   D
Risk   C-
Recent Upgrade/Downgrade   Up

Fund Information
Fund Type   Exchange Traded Funds
Category   Commodities Broad Basket
Sub-Category   Commodities Broad Basket
Prospectus Objective   Growth & Inc
Inception Date   May-17
Open to New Investments   Y

Prices
Price (as of 9/30/2019)   23.52
52-Week High   26.31
52-Week Low   22.97

Total Returns (%)

3-Month	6-Month	1-Year	3-Year	5-Year
-1.15	-3.86	-8.15		

3-Year Standard Deviation
Effective Duration

Valuation
Premium/Discount (1-Year Average)   -0.09

Company Information
Provider   Graniteshares
Manager/Tenure   Benoît Autier (2), Jeff Klearman (2)
Website   http://www.graniteshares.com
Address   Graniteshares 30 Vesey Street, 9th
                  Floor New York New York 10007
                  United States
Phone Number

PERFORMANCE chart (12/20/17 to 9/30/19), range -10.0% to 10.0%

Ratings History

Date	Overall Rating	Risk Rating	Reward Rating
Q3-19	D+	C-	D
Q4-18	D+	C-	D
Q4-17	U		
Q4-16			
Q4-15			

Asset & Performance History

Date	NAV	1-Year Total Return
2018	22.87	-11.8
2017	26.18	
2016		
2015		
2014		
2013		

Total Assets: $67,118,776
Asset Allocation

Asset	%
Cash	100%
Stocks	0%
US Stocks	0%
Bonds	0%
US Bonds	0%
Other	0%

Services Offered:

Investment Strategy: The investment seeks to provide long-term capital appreciation, primarily through exposure to commodity futures markets. The fund is an actively managed ETF that seeks to provide long-term capital appreciation, primarily through exposure to commodity futures markets. While the fund generally will seek exposure to the commodity futures markets included in the Bloomberg Commodity Index, it is not an index tracking ETF and will seek to improve its performance, in part through a cash management strategy consisting of investments in investment grade fixed income securities. The fund is non-diversified. **Top Holdings:** GraniteShares S&PGSCI CmdtyBrdStrNoK1ETF   United States Treasury Bills 0%   United States Treasury Bills 0%   United States Treasury Bills 0%   United States Treasury Bills 0%

First Trust RBA American Industrial RenaissanceTM ETF   C   HOLD

Ticker	Traded On	NAV	Total Assets ($)	Dividend Yield (TTM)	Turnover Ratio	Expense Ratio
AIRR	NAS CM	26.76	$66,899,527	0.21	35	0.7

Ratings
Reward   C+
Risk   C-
Recent Upgrade/Downgrade   Up

Fund Information
Fund Type   Exchange Traded Funds
Category   Industrials Sector Equity
Sub-Category   Industrials
Prospectus Objective   Growth & Inc
Inception Date   Mar-14
Open to New Investments   Y

Prices
Price (as of 9/30/2019)   26.86
52-Week High   27.74
52-Week Low   20.46

Total Returns (%)

3-Month	6-Month	1-Year	3-Year	5-Year
0.98	7.52	-2.64	31.60	50.71

3-Year Standard Deviation   21.52
Effective Duration

Valuation
Premium/Discount (1-Year Average)   0.06

Company Information
Provider   First Trust
Manager/Tenure   Jon C. Erickson (5), Daniel J. Lindquist
                    (5), David G. McGarel (5), 3 others
Website   http://www.ftportfolios.com/
Address   First Trust 120 E. Liberty Drive, Suite
                    400 Wheaton IL 60187 United States
Phone Number   800-621-1675

PERFORMANCE

Ratings History

Date	Overall Rating	Risk Rating	Reward Rating
Q3-19	C	C-	C+
Q4-18	C+	C-	B-
Q4-17	B+	C+	A
Q4-16	C+	C-	B
Q4-15	D	C	C

Asset & Performance History

Date	NAV	1-Year Total Return
2018	21.73	-20.45
2017	27.42	16.33
2016	23.64	43.33
2015	16.51	-9.47
2014	18.32	
2013		

Total Assets: $66,899,527
Asset Allocation

Asset	%
Cash	0%
Stocks	100%
US Stocks	100%
Bonds	0%
US Bonds	0%
Other	0%

Services Offered:

Investment Strategy: The investment seeks investment results that correspond generally to the price and yield (before the fund's fees and expenses) of an index called the Richard Bernstein Advisors American Industrial Renaissance® Index (the "index"). The fund will normally invest at least 90% of its net assets (including investment borrowings) in the equity securities that comprise the index. The index is designed to measure the performance of small and mid cap U.S. companies in the industrial and community banking sectors. **Top Holdings:** MasTec Inc Atkore International Group Inc SPX Corp Federal Signal Corp Generac Holdings Inc

---

American Century Diversified Corporate Bond ETF   C-   HOLD

Ticker	Traded On	NAV	Total Assets ($)	Dividend Yield (TTM)	Turnover Ratio	Expense Ratio
KORP	NYSE Arca	51.13	$66,577,078	2.99	38	0.29

Ratings
Reward   C-
Risk   D+
Recent Upgrade/Downgrade   Up

Fund Information
Fund Type   Exchange Traded Funds
Category   US Fixed Income
Sub-Category   Corporate Bond
Prospectus Objective   Govt Bond - Gen
Inception Date   Jan-18
Open to New Investments   Y

Prices
Price (as of 9/30/2019)   51.34
52-Week High   51.59
52-Week Low   47.83

Total Returns (%)

3-Month	6-Month	1-Year	3-Year	5-Year
1.62	4.80	8.60		

3-Year Standard Deviation
Effective Duration   4.25

Valuation
Premium/Discount (1-Year Average)   0.36

Company Information
Provider   American Century Investments
Manager/Tenure   Gavin Fleischman (1), Jeffrey L.
                    Houston (1), Le Tran (1), 2 others
Website   http://www.americancentury.com
Address   American Century Investments P.O.
                    Box 419200,4500 Main Street Kansas
                    City, MO 64141 United States
Phone Number   800-444-4015

PERFORMANCE

Ratings History

Date	Overall Rating	Risk Rating	Reward Rating
Q3-19	C-	D+	C-
Q4-18	U		
Q4-17			
Q4-16			
Q4-15			

Asset & Performance History

Date	NAV	1-Year Total Return
2018	47.94	
2017		
2016		
2015		
2014		
2013		

Total Assets: $66,577,078
Asset Allocation

Asset	%
Cash	2%
Stocks	0%
US Stocks	0%
Bonds	98%
US Bonds	90%
Other	0%

Services Offered:

Investment Strategy: The investment seeks to provide current income. The portfolio managers will invest at least 80% of the fund's net assets, plus any borrowings for investment purposes, in corporate debt securities and corporate debt investments. Under normal market conditions, the weighted average duration of the fund's portfolio is expected to be between three and seven years. **Top Holdings:** US 10 Year Note (CBT) Dec19 Bp9fdcsr4 Cds Usd P F 5.00000 Markit Cdx Na Ig Ice Ccp Bp9fdcsr4 Cds Usd R V 00mevent 2i65brrt9 Ice Ccp Bank of America Corporation 3% JPMorgan Chase & Co. 3.38%

IQ U.S. Real Estate Small Cap ETF

C   HOLD

Ticker	Traded On	NAV	Total Assets ($)	Dividend Yield (TTM)	Turnover Ratio	Expense Ratio
ROOF	NYSE Arca	25.59	$66,539,062	6.17		0.7

Ratings
Reward	C
Risk	D+
Recent Upgrade/Downgrade	

Fund Information
Fund Type	Exchange Traded Funds
Category	Real Estate Sector Equity
Sub-Category	Real Estate
Prospectus Objective	Real Estate
Inception Date	Jun-11
Open to New Investments	Y

Prices
Price (as of 9/30/2019)	25.62
52-Week High	25.82
52-Week Low	21.68

Total Returns (%)

3-Month	6-Month	1-Year	3-Year	5-Year
5.17	4.55	6.11	11.81	37.87

3-Year Standard Deviation	15.17
Effective Duration	

Valuation
Premium/Discount (1-Year Average)	0.02

Company Information
Provider	IndexIQ
Manager/Tenure	Greg Barrato (8), James Harrison (1)
Website	http://www.indexiq.com
Address	IndexIQ 800 Westchester Avenue, Suite N-611 Rye Brook NY 10573 United States
Phone Number	888-934-0777

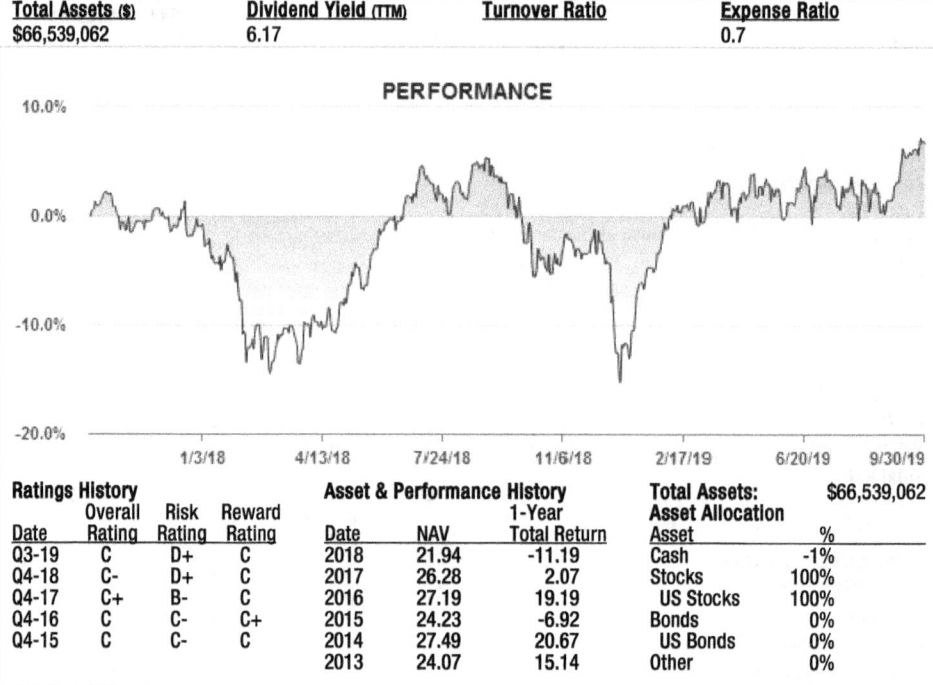

PERFORMANCE

Ratings History

Date	Overall Rating	Risk Rating	Reward Rating
Q3-19	C	D+	C
Q4-18	C-	D+	C
Q4-17	C+	B-	C
Q4-16	C	C-	C+
Q4-15	C	C-	C

Asset & Performance History

Date	NAV	1-Year Total Return
2018	21.94	-11.19
2017	26.28	2.07
2016	27.19	19.19
2015	24.23	-6.92
2014	27.49	20.67
2013	24.07	15.14

Total Assets: $66,539,062

Asset Allocation

Asset	%
Cash	-1%
Stocks	100%
US Stocks	100%
Bonds	0%
US Bonds	0%
Other	0%

Services Offered:

Investment Strategy: The investment seeks investment results that correspond generally to the price and yield performance of its underlying index, the IQ U.S. Real Estate Small Cap Index. The fund invests at least 80% of its net assets, plus the amount of any borrowings for investment purposes, in the investments included in its index. The index is a rules based, modified capitalization weighted, float adjusted index intended to give investors a means of tracking the overall performance of the small capitalization sector of publicly traded companies domiciled and primarily listed on an exchange in the U.S. and that invest in real estate. The fund is non-diversified. **Top Holdings:** Stag Industrial Inc Physicians Realty Trust Terreno Realty Corp Apollo Commercial Real Estate Finance Inc Agree Realty Corp

UBS ETRACS CMCI Total Return ETN

D+   SELL

Ticker	Traded On	NAV	Total Assets ($)	Dividend Yield (TTM)	Turnover Ratio	Expense Ratio
UCI	NYSE Arca	14.06	$66,472,139	0	0	0.55

Ratings
Reward	D+
Risk	C-
Recent Upgrade/Downgrade	Down

Fund Information
Fund Type	Exchange Traded Funds
Category	Commodities Broad Basket
Sub-Category	Commodities Broad Basket
Prospectus Objective	Natl Res
Inception Date	Apr-08
Open to New Investments	Y

Prices
Price (as of 9/30/2019)	14.05
52-Week High	15.85
52-Week Low	13.50

Total Returns (%)

3-Month	6-Month	1-Year	3-Year	5-Year
-3.10	-6.37	-9.57	4.17	-26.24

3-Year Standard Deviation	10.16
Effective Duration	

Valuation
Premium/Discount (1-Year Average)	-0.18

Company Information
Provider	UBS Group AG
Manager/Tenure	No Manager (11)
Website	http://www.ubs.com
Address	Bahnhofstrasse 45 Zürich 8098 Switzerland
Phone Number	412-037-1952

PERFORMANCE

Ratings History

Date	Overall Rating	Risk Rating	Reward Rating
Q3-19	D+	C-	D+
Q4-18	C-	C-	C-
Q4-17	C-	D+	C
Q4-16	D	D	D+
Q4-15	D-	D	D-

Asset & Performance History

Date	NAV	1-Year Total Return
2018	13.56	-11.59
2017	15.34	7.96
2016	14.19	17.28
2015	12.1	-26.01
2014	16.35	-19.97
2013	20.43	-7.26

Total Assets: $66,472,139

Asset Allocation

Asset	%
Cash	%
Stocks	%
US Stocks	%
Bonds	%
US Bonds	%
Other	%

Services Offered:

Investment Strategy: The investment seeks to track the price and performance yield, before fees and expenses, of the UBS Bloomberg Constant Maturity Commodity index.
The fund is designed to be a diversified benchmark for commodities as an asset class. The index is comprised of 28 futures contracts with up to five different maturities for each individual commodity. **Top Holdings:**

Direxion Daily MSCI Emerging Markets Bear 3X Shares   D   SELL

Ticker	Traded On	NAV	Total Assets ($)	Dividend Yield (TTM)	Turnover Ratio	Expense Ratio
EDZ	NYSE Arca	47.64	$66,466,729	1.22	0	1.09

Ratings
Reward	D-
Risk	D
Recent Upgrade/Downgrade	

Fund Information
Fund Type	Exchange Traded Funds
Category	Trading Tools
Sub-Category	Trading--Inverse Equity
Prospectus Objective	Div Emerg Mkts
Inception Date	Dec-08
Open to New Investments	Y

Prices
Price (as of 9/30/2019)	47.69
52-Week High	70.95
52-Week Low	39.09

Total Returns (%)
3-Month	6-Month	1-Year	3-Year	5-Year
17.45	8.99	-5.42	-57.19	-73.83

3-Year Standard Deviation	42.74
Effective Duration	

Valuation
Premium/Discount (1-Year Average)	0.01

Company Information
Provider	Direxion Funds
Manager/Tenure	Paul Brigandi (10), Tony Ng (4)
Website	http://www.direxionfunds.com
Address	Direxion Funds 1301 Avenue Of The Americas (6th Avenue) New York NY 10019 United States
Phone Number	646-572-3390

PERFORMANCE

Ratings History
Date	Overall Rating	Risk Rating	Reward Rating
Q3-19	D	D	D-
Q4-18	D+	D	D
Q4-17	E+	D-	E+
Q4-16	D	D	D-
Q4-15	C	D+	C-

Asset & Performance History
Date	NAV	1-Year Total Return
2018	59.8	32.61
2017	45.25	-64.18
2016	126.35	-46.16
2015	234.7	25.34
2014	187.25	-6.3
2013	199.85	-11.27

Total Assets: $66,466,729
Asset Allocation
Asset	%
Cash	105%
Stocks	-5%
US Stocks	-5%
Bonds	0%
US Bonds	0%
Other	0%

Services Offered:

Investment Strategy: The investment seeks daily investment results, before fees and expenses, of 300% of the inverse of the daily performance of the MSCI Emerging Markets IndexSM. The fund invests in swap agreements, futures contracts, short positions or other financial instruments that, in combination, provide inverse or short leveraged exposure to the index equal to at least 80% of the fund's net assets (plus borrowing for investment purposes). The index is a free float-adjusted market capitalization weighted index that is designed to represent the performance of large- and mid-capitalizations securities across 24 emerging market countries. The fund is non-diversified. **Top Holdings:** Msci Emerg Mkts Idx Swap   Msci Emerg Mkts Idx Swap   Msci Emerg Mkts Idx Swap   Msci Emerg Mkts Idx Swap   Msci Emerg Mkts Idx Swap

Cambria Tail Risk ETF   D+   SELL

Ticker	Traded On	NAV	Total Assets ($)	Dividend Yield (TTM)	Turnover Ratio	Expense Ratio
TAIL	BATS	20.36	$66,157,393	1.53		0.59

Ratings
Reward	D+
Risk	D+
Recent Upgrade/Downgrade	Up

Fund Information
Fund Type	Exchange Traded Funds
Category	Alternative Misc
Sub-Category	Bear Market
Prospectus Objective	Growth & Inc
Inception Date	Apr-17
Open to New Investments	Y

Prices
Price (as of 9/30/2019)	20.40
52-Week High	24.70
52-Week Low	19.79

Total Returns (%)
3-Month	6-Month	1-Year	3-Year	5-Year
1.17	1.91	3.87		

3-Year Standard Deviation	
Effective Duration	

Valuation
Premium/Discount (1-Year Average)	0.20

Company Information
Provider	CAMBRIA ETF TRUST
Manager/Tenure	Mebane T. Faber (2)
Website	http://www.cambriafunds.com
Address	CAMBRIA ETF TRUST 2711 Centreville Road Suite 400 Wilmington, DE 19808 Wilmington DE 19808 United States
Phone Number	310-683-5500

PERFORMANCE

Ratings History
Date	Overall Rating	Risk Rating	Reward Rating
Q3-19	D+	D+	D+
Q4-18	D	D	D
Q4-17	U		
Q4-16			
Q4-15			

Asset & Performance History
Date	NAV	1-Year Total Return
2018	22.76	2.33
2017	22.6	
2016		
2015		
2014		
2013		

Total Assets: $66,157,393
Asset Allocation
Asset	%
Cash	2%
Stocks	4%
US Stocks	4%
Bonds	94%
US Bonds	94%
Other	0%

Services Offered:

Investment Strategy: The investment seeks to provide income and capital appreciation from investments in the U.S. market while protecting against significant downside risk. The fund is actively managed and seeks to achieve its investment objective by investing in cash and U.S. government bonds, and utilizing a put option strategy to manage the risk of a significant negative movement in the value of domestic equities. The adviser intends to spend approximately one percent of the fund's total assets per month to purchase put options. **Top Holdings:** United States Treasury Notes 2.25%   Spx Us 06/19/20 P2600   Spx Us 03/20/20 P2600   Spx Us 03/20/20 P2700   Spx Us 06/19/20 P2700

WisdomTree Emerging Markets Quality Dividend Growth Fund

C-   HOLD

Ticker	Traded On	NAV	Total Assets ($)	Dividend Yield (TTM)	Turnover Ratio	Expense Ratio
DGRE	NAS CM	23.60	$66,078,424	2.84	81	0.32

Ratings
Reward   C-
Risk   C-
Recent Upgrade/Downgrade

Fund Information
Fund Type	Exchange Traded Funds
Category	Global Emerg Mkts Equity
Sub-Category	Diversified Emerging Mkts
Prospectus Objective	Div Emerg Mkts
Inception Date	Aug-13
Open to New Investments	Y

Prices
Price (as of 9/30/2019)	23.44
52-Week High	25.68
52-Week Low	21.16

Total Returns (%)
3-Month	6-Month	1-Year	3-Year	5-Year
-3.61	-3.80	0.80	12.20	6.00

3-Year Standard Deviation	12.93
Effective Duration	

Valuation
Premium/Discount (1-Year Average)	0.02

Company Information
Provider	WisdomTree
Manager/Tenure	Richard A. Brown (6), Thomas J. Durante (6), Karen Q. Wong (6)
Website	http://www.wisdomtree.com
Address	WisdomTree 245 Park Avenue, 35th floor New York NY 10167 United States
Phone Number	866-909-9473

PERFORMANCE

Ratings History
Date	Overall Rating	Risk Rating	Reward Rating
Q3-19	C-	C-	C-
Q4-18	C-	C-	C-
Q4-17	C+	C	B-
Q4-16	D+	D+	D+
Q4-15	D	D	D

Asset & Performance History
Date	NAV	1-Year Total Return
2018	22.37	-15.19
2017	27.05	29.9
2016	21.3	11.12
2015	19.66	-16.86
2014	24.3	1.21
2013	24.57	

Total Assets: $66,078,424
Asset Allocation
Asset	%
Cash	0%
Stocks	100%
US Stocks	0%
Bonds	0%
US Bonds	0%
Other	0%

Services Offered:

Investment Strategy: The investment seeks income and capital appreciation. The fund seeks to achieve its investment objective by investing primarily in emerging market dividend-paying common stocks with growth characteristics. The adviser, using a disciplined model-based process focused on a long-term approach to investing, seeks to identify dividend-paying companies with strong corporate profitability and sustainable growth characteristics. The fund is non-diversified. **Top Holdings:** Tencent Holdings Ltd Taiwan Semiconductor Manufacturing Co Ltd Samsung Electronics Co Ltd Ping An Insurance (Group) Co. of China Ltd Class H Reliance Industries Ltd

---

iShares 1-3 Year International Treasury Bond ETF

D   SELL

Ticker	Traded On	NAV	Total Assets ($)	Dividend Yield (TTM)	Turnover Ratio	Expense Ratio
ISHG	NAS CM	77.73	$66,068,476	1.84	47	0.35

Ratings
Reward   D
Risk   D+
Recent Upgrade/Downgrade

Fund Information
Fund Type	Exchange Traded Funds
Category	Global Fixed Income
Sub-Category	World Bond
Prospectus Objective	Worldwide Bond
Inception Date	Jan-09
Open to New Investments	Y

Prices
Price (as of 9/30/2019)	77.68
52-Week High	81.56
52-Week Low	77.68

Total Returns (%)
3-Month	6-Month	1-Year	3-Year	5-Year
-2.52	-1.44	-2.64	-4.36	-10.55

3-Year Standard Deviation	5.72
Effective Duration	

Valuation
Premium/Discount (1-Year Average)	-0.08

Company Information
Provider	iShares
Manager/Tenure	Scott Radell (9), James Mauro (8)
Website	http://www.ishares.com
Address	iShares 400 Howard Street San Francisco CA 94105 United States
Phone Number	800-474-2737

PERFORMANCE

Ratings History
Date	Overall Rating	Risk Rating	Reward Rating
Q3-19	D	D+	D
Q4-18	D+	D+	D+
Q4-17	C	C	C-
Q4-16	D	D+	D
Q4-15	D	D	D

Asset & Performance History
Date	NAV	1-Year Total Return
2018	79.69	-3.67
2017	84.23	9.51
2016	76.91	-1.22
2015	77.86	-7.49
2014	84.24	-10.88
2013	94.9	-1.92

Total Assets: $66,068,476
Asset Allocation
Asset	%
Cash	5%
Stocks	0%
US Stocks	0%
Bonds	95%
US Bonds	0%
Other	0%

Services Offered:

Investment Strategy: The investment seeks to track the investment results of the S&P International Sovereign Ex-U.S. 1-3 Year Bond Index. The fund will invest at least 90% of its assets in the component securities of the index and may invest up to 10% of its assets in certain futures, options and swap contracts, cash and cash equivalents. The index is a broad, diverse, market value-weighted index designed to measure the performance of bonds denominated in local currencies and issued by foreign governments in developed market countries outside the U.S. that have a remaining maturity of greater than one year and less than or equal to three years. The fund is non-diversified. **Top Holdings:** Japan (Government Of) 0.1% Japan (Government Of) 0.1% Japan (Government Of) 1% Japan (Government Of) 0.1% Austria (Republic of) 3.5%

Invesco DWA Tactical Sector Rotation ETF   C   HOLD

Ticker	Traded On	NAV		Total Assets ($)	Dividend Yield (TTM)	Turnover Ratio	Expense Ratio
DWTR	NAS CM	31.40		$65,940,531	0.56		0.75

Ratings
Reward   C
Risk   D+
Recent Upgrade/Downgrade

Fund Information
Fund Type	Exchange Traded Funds
Category	US Equity Mid Cap
Sub-Category	Mid-Cap Growth
Prospectus Objective	Growth & Inc
Inception Date	Oct-15
Open to New Investments	Y

Prices
Price (as of 9/30/2019)	31.38
52-Week High	32.98
52-Week Low	22.70

Total Returns (%)
3-Month	6-Month	1-Year	3-Year	5-Year
0.28	6.02	0.86	26.80	

3-Year Standard Deviation	15.7
Effective Duration	

Valuation
Premium/Discount (1-Year Average)	-0.15

Company Information
Provider	Invesco
Manager/Tenure	Peter Hubbard (3), Michael Jeanette (3), Tony Seisser (3)
Website	http://www.invesco.com/us
Address	Invesco 11 Greenway Plaza, Ste. 2500 Houston TX 77046 United States
Phone Number	800-659-1005

PERFORMANCE

Ratings History

Date	Overall Rating	Risk Rating	Reward Rating
Q3-19	C	D+	C
Q4-18	C-	C-	C-
Q4-17	C	B-	C
Q4-16	D	C-	D
Q4-15			

Asset & Performance History

Date	NAV	1-Year Total Return
2018	24.7	-12.61
2017	28.28	16.68
2016	24.36	-2.84
2015	25.18	
2014		
2013		

Total Assets: $65,940,531

Asset Allocation

Asset	%
Cash	0%
Stocks	100%
US Stocks	99%
Bonds	0%
US Bonds	0%
Other	0%

Services Offered:

Investment Strategy: The investment seeks to track the investment results (before fees and expenses) of the Dorsey Wright® Sector 4 Index (the "underlying index"). The fund generally will invest at least 90% of its total assets in the securities that comprise the underlying index. It is a "fund of funds," meaning that it invests its assets in the shares of other exchange-traded funds ("ETFs") eligible for inclusion in the underlying index. The underlying index seeks to gain exposure to the sectors of the U.S. equity markets that display the strongest relative strength, as evaluated on a monthly basis. The fund is non-diversified. **Top Holdings:** Invesco DWA Utilities Momentum ETF Invesco DWA Technology Momentum ETF Invesco DWA Financial Momentum ETF Invesco DWA Industrials Momentum ETF

Reality Shares Nasdaq NexGen Economy ETF   C-   HOLD

Ticker	Traded On	NAV		Total Assets ($)	Dividend Yield (TTM)	Turnover Ratio	Expense Ratio
BLCN	NAS CM	23.11		$65,863,244	1.55		0.68

Ratings
Reward   C-
Risk   D+
Recent Upgrade/Downgrade   Up

Fund Information
Fund Type	Exchange Traded Funds
Category	Technology Sector Equity
Sub-Category	Technology
Prospectus Objective	Growth
Inception Date	Jan-18
Open to New Investments	Y

Prices
Price (as of 9/30/2019)	23.05
52-Week High	24.04
52-Week Low	18.83

Total Returns (%)
3-Month	6-Month	1-Year	3-Year	5-Year
-1.41	0.96	-1.11		

3-Year Standard Deviation	
Effective Duration	

Valuation
Premium/Discount (1-Year Average)	-0.29

Company Information
Provider	Reality Shares ETF Trust
Manager/Tenure	Eric Ervin (1)
Website	http://www.realityshares.com
Address	Reality Shares ETF Trust 402 West Broadway, Suite 2800 San Diego CA 92101 United States
Phone Number	619-487-1445

PERFORMANCE

Ratings History

Date	Overall Rating	Risk Rating	Reward Rating
Q3-19	C-	D+	C-
Q4-18	U		
Q4-17			
Q4-16			
Q4-15			

Asset & Performance History

Date	NAV	1-Year Total Return
2018	19.56	
2017		
2016		
2015		
2014		
2013		

Total Assets: $65,863,244

Asset Allocation

Asset	%
Cash	1%
Stocks	99%
US Stocks	47%
Bonds	0%
US Bonds	0%
Other	0%

Services Offered:

Investment Strategy: The investment seeks long-term growth by tracking the investment returns, before fees and expenses, of the Reality Shares Nasdaq Blockchain Economy Index (the "index"). Under normal circumstances, at least 80% of the fund's assets, other than collateral held from securities lending, if any, will be invested in component securities of the index. The index is designed to measure the returns of companies that are committing material resources to developing, researching, supporting, innovating or utilizing blockchain technology for their proprietary use or for use by others ("Blockchain Companies"). The fund is non-diversified. **Top Holdings:** Accenture PLC Class A Advanced Micro Devices Inc Microsoft Corp SAP SE ADR Digital Garage Inc

VanEck Vectors® NDR CMG Long/Flat Allocation ETF   C-   HOLD

Ticker	Traded On	NAV	Total Assets ($)	Dividend Yield (TTM)	Turnover Ratio	Expense Ratio
LFEQ	NYSE Arca	28.02	$65,850,561	0.94	28	0.6

Ratings
Reward   C-
Risk   C-
Recent Upgrade/Downgrade

Fund Information
Fund Type   Exchange Traded Funds
Category   US Equity Large Cap Blend
Sub-Category   Large Blend
Prospectus Objective   Growth & Inc
Inception Date   Oct-17
Open to New Investments   Y

Prices
Price (as of 9/30/2019)   28.03
52-Week High   28.40
52-Week Low   23.52

Total Returns (%)

3-Month	6-Month	1-Year	3-Year	5-Year
0.75	4.55	-0.06		

3-Year Standard Deviation
Effective Duration

Valuation
Premium/Discount (1-Year Average)   0.04

Company Information
Provider   VanEck
Manager/Tenure   Hao-Hung (Peter) Liao (1), Guo Hua
                  (Jason) Jin (1)
Website   http://www.vaneck.com
Address   Van Eck Associates Corporation 666
                  Third Avenue New York NY 10017
                  United States
Phone Number   800-826-1115

PERFORMANCE

Ratings History

Date	Overall Rating	Risk Rating	Reward Rating
Q3-19	C-	C-	C-
Q4-18	D+	C-	D+
Q4-17	U		
Q4-16			
Q4-15			

Asset & Performance History

Date	NAV	1-Year Total Return
2018	24.69	-4.98
2017	26.23	
2016		
2015		
2014		
2013		

Total Assets: $65,850,561
Asset Allocation

Asset	%
Cash	0%
Stocks	100%
US Stocks	99%
Bonds	0%
US Bonds	0%
Other	0%

Services Offered:

Investment Strategy: The investment seeks to replicate as closely as possible, the price and yield performance of the Ned Davis Research CMG US Large Cap Long/Flat Index. The fund normally invests at least 80% of its total assets in securities that track and/or comprise the fund's benchmark index. The index is a rules-based index that follows a proprietary model developed by Ned Davis Research, Inc. in conjunction with CMG Capital Management Group, Inc. To help limit potential loss associated with adverse market conditions, the model produces trade signals that dictate the index's equity allocation ranging from 100% fully invested to 100% in cash. It is non-diversified. **Top Holdings:** Vanguard S&P 500 ETF Meta Financial Group Inc

Franklin FTSE Europe ETF   D+   SELL

Ticker	Traded On	NAV	Total Assets ($)	Dividend Yield (TTM)	Turnover Ratio	Expense Ratio
FLEE	NYSE Arca	23.51	$65,824,810	2.51	6	0.09

Ratings
Reward   D+
Risk   D+
Recent Upgrade/Downgrade

Fund Information
Fund Type   Exchange Traded Funds
Category   Europe Equity Large Cap
Sub-Category   Europe Stock
Prospectus Objective   Foreign Stock
Inception Date   Nov-17
Open to New Investments   Y

Prices
Price (as of 9/30/2019)   23.47
52-Week High   24.42
52-Week Low   20.33

Total Returns (%)

3-Month	6-Month	1-Year	3-Year	5-Year
-2.00	1.45	-0.71		

3-Year Standard Deviation
Effective Duration

Valuation
Premium/Discount (1-Year Average)   -0.05

Company Information
Provider   Franklin Templeton Investments
Manager/Tenure   Louis Hsu (1), Dina Ting (1)
Website   http://www.franklintempleton.com
Address   Franklin Templeton Investments One
                  Franklin Parkway, Building 970, 1st
                  Floor San Mateo CA 94403 United
                  States
Phone Number   650-312-2000

PERFORMANCE

Ratings History

Date	Overall Rating	Risk Rating	Reward Rating
Q3-19	D+	D+	D+
Q4-18	D	D	D
Q4-17	U		
Q4-16			
Q4-15			

Asset & Performance History

Date	NAV	1-Year Total Return
2018	20.96	-14.8
2017	25.47	
2016		
2015		
2014		
2013		

Total Assets: $65,824,810
Asset Allocation

Asset	%
Cash	0%
Stocks	100%
US Stocks	2%
Bonds	0%
US Bonds	0%
Other	0%

Services Offered:

Investment Strategy: The investment seeks to provide investment results that closely correspond, before fees and expenses, to the performance of the FTSE Developed Europe RIC Capped Index (the FTSE Developed Europe Capped Index). Under normal market conditions, the fund invests at least 80% of its assets in the component securities of the FTSE Developed Europe Capped Index and in depositary receipts representing such securities. The FTSE Developed Europe Capped Index is based on the FTSE Developed Europe Index and is designed to measure the performance of large- and mid-capitalization stocks from developed European countries. **Top Holdings:** Nestle SA Novartis AG Roche Holding AG Dividend Right Cert. HSBC Holdings PLC Royal Dutch Shell PLC Class A

JPMorgan USD Emerging Markets Sovereign Bond ETF   C-   HOLD

Ticker	Traded On	NAV	Total Assets ($)	Dividend Yield (TTM)	Turnover Ratio	Expense Ratio
JPMB	NYSE Arca	50.50	$65,645,191	4.64	28	0.39

Ratings

Reward	C-
Risk	D+
Recent Upgrade/Downgrade	Up

Fund Information

Fund Type	Exchange Traded Funds
Category	Emerging Mkts Fixed Inc
Sub-Category	Emerging Markets Bond
Prospectus Objective	Div Emerg Mkts
Inception Date	Jan-18
Open to New Investments	Y

Prices

Price (as of 9/30/2019)	50.61
52-Week High	51.48
52-Week Low	44.79

Total Returns (%)

3-Month	6-Month	1-Year	3-Year	5-Year
1.97	7.20	13.64		

3-Year Standard Deviation	
Effective Duration	7.35

Valuation

Premium/Discount (1-Year Average)	0.30

Company Information

Provider	JPMorgan
Manager/Tenure	Eric J Isenberg (1), Naveen Kumar (1), Niels Schuehle (1)
Website	http://www.jpmorganfunds.com
Address	JPMorgan 270 Park Avenue New York NY 10017-2070 United States
Phone Number	800-480-4111

PERFORMANCE

Ratings History

Date	Overall Rating	Risk Rating	Reward Rating
Q3-19	C-	D+	C-
Q4-18	U		
Q4-17			
Q4-16			
Q4-15			

Asset & Performance History

Date	NAV	1-Year Total Return
2018	45.4	
2017		
2016		
2015		
2014		
2013		

Total Assets: $65,645,191

Asset Allocation

Asset	%
Cash	1%
Stocks	0%
US Stocks	0%
Bonds	99%
US Bonds	0%
Other	0%

Services Offered:

Investment Strategy: The investment seeks investment results that closely correspond, before fees and expenses, to the performance of the JPMorgan Emerging Markets Risk-Aware Bond Index. The fund will invest at least 80% of its assets in securities included in the underlying index. The underlying index is comprised of liquid, U.S. dollar-denominated sovereign and quasi-sovereign fixed and floating rate debt securities from emerging markets selected using a rules-based methodology that was developed and is owned by the adviser. The fund is non-diversified. **Top Holdings:** Republic of Ecuador 7.95% Brazil (Federative Republic) 5.62% Republic of Ecuador 9.65% Democratic Socialist Republic of Sri Lanka 6.85% Egypt (Arab Republic of) 8.5%

Reality Shares DIVS ETF   C-   HOLD

Ticker	Traded On	NAV	Total Assets ($)	Dividend Yield (TTM)	Turnover Ratio	Expense Ratio
DIVY	NYSE Arca	26.20	$65,610,149	0.92	0	0.85

Ratings

Reward	C-
Risk	D+
Recent Upgrade/Downgrade	

Fund Information

Fund Type	Exchange Traded Funds
Category	Multialternative
Sub-Category	Multialternative
Prospectus Objective	Growth
Inception Date	Dec-14
Open to New Investments	Y

Prices

Price (as of 9/30/2019)	26.11
52-Week High	27.12
52-Week Low	24.84

Total Returns (%)

3-Month	6-Month	1-Year	3-Year	5-Year
-0.83	-1.05	-2.25	9.89	

3-Year Standard Deviation	5.18
Effective Duration	

Valuation

Premium/Discount (1-Year Average)	-0.15

Company Information

Provider	Reality Shares ETF Trust
Manager/Tenure	Eric Ervin (4)
Website	http://www.realityshares.com
Address	Reality Shares ETF Trust 402 West Broadway, Suite 2800 San Diego CA 92101 United States
Phone Number	619-487-1445

PERFORMANCE

Ratings History

Date	Overall Rating	Risk Rating	Reward Rating
Q3-19	C-	D+	C-
Q4-18	C-	C-	C-
Q4-17	B-	B+	C
Q4-16	D+	D+	D+
Q4-15	U		

Asset & Performance History

Date	NAV	1-Year Total Return
2018	25.23	-2.7
2017	26.18	4.63
2016	25.23	8.05
2015	23.35	2.24
2014	23.29	
2013		

Total Assets: $65,610,149

Asset Allocation

Asset	%
Cash	13%
Stocks	6%
US Stocks	6%
Bonds	85%
US Bonds	85%
Other	-4%

Services Offered:

Investment Strategy: The investment seeks to produce long-term capital appreciation. The fund's principal investment strategy is designed to provide exposure to the aggregate value of ordinary dividends expected to be paid on a portfolio of large capitalization equity securities listed for trading in the U.S. ("Large Cap Securities"). The fund may use a variety of investment strategies to achieve this objective. Under normal circumstances, it generally invests in a combination of dividend swaps, dividend futures and forwards on indexes of Large Cap Securities ("Large Cap Securities Indexes"). The fund is non-diversified. **Top Holdings:** Payb Bnppspx D21dvdswap Recv Bnppspx D21dvdswap United States Treasury Bills 0% United States Treasury Bills 0% Payb Bnppspx D22dvdswap

IQ S&P High Yield Low Volatility Bond ETF   C   HOLD

Ticker	Traded On	NAV	Total Assets ($)	Dividend Yield (TTM)	Turnover Ratio	Expense Ratio
HYLV	NYSE Arca	25.23	$65,586,305	4.38		0.4

Ratings

Reward	C
Risk	C-
Recent Upgrade/Downgrade	Up

Fund Information

Fund Type	Exchange Traded Funds
Category	US Fixed Income
Sub-Category	High Yield Bond
Prospectus Objective	Corp Bond-High Yld
Inception Date	Feb-17
Open to New Investments	Y

Prices

Price (as of 9/30/2019)	25.32
52-Week High	25.44
52-Week Low	23.07

Total Returns (%)

3-Month	6-Month	1-Year	3-Year	5-Year
1.70	4.63	8.27		

3-Year Standard Deviation	
Effective Duration	

Valuation

Premium/Discount (1-Year Average)	0.10

Company Information

Provider	IndexIQ
Manager/Tenure	Scott Dolph (2), Dan C. Roberts (2), Alexandra Wilson-Elizondo (2)
Website	http://www.indexiq.com
Address	IndexIQ 800 Westchester Avenue, Suite N-611 Rye Brook NY 10573 United States
Phone Number	888-934-0777

PERFORMANCE

Ratings History

Date	Overall Rating	Risk Rating	Reward Rating
Q3-19	C	C-	C
Q4-18	D	D+	D
Q4-17	U		
Q4-16			
Q4-15			

Asset & Performance History

Date	NAV	1-Year Total Return
2018	23.29	-3.38
2017	25.07	
2016		
2015		
2014		
2013		

Total Assets: $65,586,305

Asset Allocation

Asset	%
Cash	0%
Stocks	0%
US Stocks	0%
Bonds	100%
US Bonds	88%
Other	0%

Services Offered:

Investment Strategy: The investment seeks investment results that track (before fees and expenses) the price and yield performance of its underlying index, the S&P U.S. High Yield Low Volatility Corporate Bond Index. The fund uses a "Representative Sampling" strategy in seeking to track the performance of the underlying index. The underlying index is comprised of U.S. dollar denominated high yield corporate bonds that have been selected in accordance with a rules-based methodology that seeks to identify securities that, in the aggregate, are expected to have lower volatility relative to the broad U.S. dollar denominated high yield corporate bond market. **Top Holdings:** Sprint Corporation 7.88% TransDigm, Inc. 6.25% Blackrock Treasury Trust Instl 62 Sprint Corporation 7.12% 1011778 B.C. Unlimited Liability Company / New Red Finance, Inc. 5%

Invesco DWA Financial Momentum ETF   B   BUY

Ticker	Traded On	NAV	Total Assets ($)	Dividend Yield (TTM)	Turnover Ratio	Expense Ratio
PFI	NAS CM	37.36	$65,382,803	1.09		0.6

Ratings

Reward	B+
Risk	C
Recent Upgrade/Downgrade	Up

Fund Information

Fund Type	Exchange Traded Funds
Category	Financials Sector Equity
Sub-Category	Financial
Prospectus Objective	Financial
Inception Date	Oct-06
Open to New Investments	Y

Prices

Price (as of 9/30/2019)	37.43
52-Week High	38.84
52-Week Low	27.13

Total Returns (%)

3-Month	6-Month	1-Year	3-Year	5-Year
-0.12	11.15	11.21	27.03	42.63

3-Year Standard Deviation	14
Effective Duration	

Valuation

Premium/Discount (1-Year Average)	-0.05

Company Information

Provider	Invesco
Manager/Tenure	Peter Hubbard (12), Michael Jeanette (11), Tony Seisser (5)
Website	http://www.invesco.com/us
Address	Invesco 11 Greenway Plaza, Ste. 2500 Houston TX 77046 United States
Phone Number	800-659-1005

PERFORMANCE

Ratings History

Date	Overall Rating	Risk Rating	Reward Rating
Q3-19	B	C	B+
Q4-18	C	C-	C
Q4-17	B	B+	C+
Q4-16	C	C-	B-
Q4-15	B-	C	B

Asset & Performance History

Date	NAV	1-Year Total Return
2018	28.67	-16.66
2017	35	14.82
2016	30.6	2.16
2015	30.61	1.13
2014	30.71	6.22
2013	29.24	40.25

Total Assets: $65,382,803

Asset Allocation

Asset	%
Cash	0%
Stocks	100%
US Stocks	97%
Bonds	0%
US Bonds	0%
Other	0%

Services Offered:

Investment Strategy: The investment seeks to track the investment results (before fees and expenses) of the Dorsey Wright® Financials Technical Leaders Index (the "underlying index"). The fund generally will invest at least 90% of its total assets in the securities that comprise the underlying index. The underlying index is composed of at least 30 securities of companies in the financials sector that have powerful relative strength or "momentum" characteristics. **Top Holdings:** MarketAxess Holdings Inc Crown Castle International Corp Mastercard Inc A Extra Space Storage Inc UDR Inc

VictoryShares US Discovery Enhanced Volatility Wtd ETF   D   SELL

Ticker	Traded On	NAV	Total Assets ($)	Dividend Yield (TTM)	Turnover Ratio	Expense Ratio
CSF	NAS CM	36.26	$65,265,901	1.79	398	0.35

Ratings
Reward   D
Risk   D+
Recent Upgrade/Downgrade   Down

Fund Information
Fund Type   Exchange Traded Funds
Category   US Equity Small Cap
Sub-Category   Small Blend
Prospectus Objective   Income
Inception Date   Jul-14
Open to New Investments   Y

Prices
Price (as of 9/30/2019)   36.29
52-Week High   47.82
52-Week Low   35.33

Total Returns (%)

3-Month	6-Month	1-Year	3-Year	5-Year
-3.79	-8.63	-22.78	5.03	12.67

3-Year Standard Deviation   15.64
Effective Duration

Valuation
Premium/Discount (1-Year Average)   0.07

Company Information
Provider   VictoryShares
Manager/Tenure   Mannik Dhillon (1)
Website   http://www.VictorySharesLiterature.com
Address   Victory Shares 4249 Easton Way,
                   Suite 400 Columbus OH 43219 United
                   States
Phone Number

PERFORMANCE

Ratings History

Date	Overall Rating	Risk Rating	Reward Rating
Q3-19	D	D+	D
Q4-18	C-	C-	C-
Q4-17	B	B	B
Q4-16	C-	D+	C
Q4-15	D-	D+	D

Asset & Performance History

Date	NAV	1-Year Total Return
2018	39.45	-11.27
2017	44.99	12.09
2016	40.59	17.75
2015	34.49	-8.29
2014	38	
2013		

Total Assets: $65,265,901
Asset Allocation

Asset	%
Cash	73%
Stocks	27%
US Stocks	27%
Bonds	0%
US Bonds	0%
Other	0%

Services Offered:

Investment Strategy: The investment seeks investment results that match the performance of the Nasdaq Victory US Small Cap 500 Long/Cash Volatility Weighted Index before fees and expenses. The fund seeks to achieve its investment objective by investing, under normal market conditions, at least 80% of its assets directly or indirectly in the securities included in the Nasdaq Victory US Small Cap 500 Long/Cash Volatility Weighted Index. The index identifies the 500 largest U.S. companies with market capitalizations of less than $3 billion measured at the time the index's constituent securities are determined. **Top Holdings:** Russ 2000 Idx Fut Sep19 American States Water Co Capitol Federal Financial Inc Tootsie Roll Industries Inc UniFirst Corp

---

VanEck Vectors Natural Resources ETF   C   HOLD

Ticker	Traded On	NAV	Total Assets ($)	Dividend Yield (TTM)	Turnover Ratio	Expense Ratio
HAP	NYSE Arca	35.25	$65,215,274	2.6	23	0.5

Ratings
Reward   C
Risk   D+
Recent Upgrade/Downgrade   Up

Fund Information
Fund Type   Exchange Traded Funds
Category   Natural Resources
Sub-Category   Natural Resources
Prospectus Objective   Natl Res
Inception Date   Aug-08
Open to New Investments   Y

Prices
Price (as of 9/30/2019)   35.20
52-Week High   38.05
52-Week Low   30.80

Total Returns (%)

3-Month	6-Month	1-Year	3-Year	5-Year
-4.18	-2.51	-4.22	18.93	8.76

3-Year Standard Deviation   13.04
Effective Duration

Valuation
Premium/Discount (1-Year Average)   -0.14

Company Information
Provider   VanEck
Manager/Tenure   Hao-Hung (Peter) Liao (11), Guo Hua
                   (Jason) Jin (1)
Website   http://www.vaneck.com
Address   Van Eck Associates Corporation 666
                   Third Avenue New York NY 10017
                   United States
Phone Number   800-826-1115

PERFORMANCE

Ratings History

Date	Overall Rating	Risk Rating	Reward Rating
Q3-19	C	D+	C
Q4-18	C-	D+	C
Q4-17	C+	C	C+
Q4-16	C-	D+	C-
Q4-15	D+	D+	D+

Asset & Performance History

Date	NAV	1-Year Total Return
2018	32.2	-10.67
2017	37.09	17.17
2016	32.31	24.93
2015	26.38	-19.39
2014	33.73	-7.7
2013	37.46	6.58

Total Assets: $65,215,274
Asset Allocation

Asset	%
Cash	0%
Stocks	100%
US Stocks	46%
Bonds	0%
US Bonds	0%
Other	0%

Services Offered:

Investment Strategy: The investment seeks to replicate as closely as possible, before fees and expenses, the price and yield performance of the VanEck® Natural Resources Index. The fund normally invests at least 80% of its total assets in securities that comprise the fund's benchmark index. The index is comprised of publicly traded companies engaged (derive greater than 50% of revenues from applicable sources) in the production and distribution of commodities and commodity-related products and services in the following sectors: 1) Agriculture; 2) Alternatives (Water & Alternative Energy); 3) Base and Industrial Metals; 4) Energy; 5) Forest Products; and 6) Precious Metals. **Top Holdings:** Deere & Co Nutrien Ltd Tyson Foods Inc Class A Exxon Mobil Corp Archer-Daniels Midland Co

Invesco S&P 500® Enhanced Value ETF   C   HOLD

Ticker	Traded On	NAV	Total Assets ($)	Dividend Yield (TTM)	Turnover Ratio	Expense Ratio
SPVU	NYSE Arca	35.08	$64,895,090	2.44		0.13

Ratings
Reward   C+
Risk   D+
Recent Upgrade/Downgrade

Fund Information
Fund Type   Exchange Traded Funds
Category   US Equity Large Cap Value
Sub-Category   Large Value
Prospectus Objective   Growth
Inception Date   Oct-15
Open to New Investments

Prices
Price (as of 9/30/2019)   35.10
52-Week High   36.28
52-Week Low   29.09

Total Returns (%)

3-Month	6-Month	1-Year	3-Year	5-Year
0.40	4.14	1.72	43.20	

3-Year Standard Deviation   16.32
Effective Duration

Valuation
Premium/Discount (1-Year Average)   0.11

Company Information
Provider   Invesco
Manager/Tenure   Peter Hubbard (3), Michael Jeanette (3), Tony Seisser (3)
Website   http://www.invesco.com/us
Address   Invesco 11 Greenway Plaza, Ste. 2500 Houston TX 77046 United States
Phone Number   800-659-1005

PERFORMANCE

Ratings History

Date	Overall Rating	Risk Rating	Reward Rating
Q3-19	C	D+	C+
Q4-18	C	D+	C
Q4-17	C	B	C+
Q4-16	D	D	C
Q4-15			

Asset & Performance History

Date	NAV	1-Year Total Return
2018	30.78	-9.26
2017	34.71	18.8
2016	29.93	20.02
2015	25.25	
2014		
2013		

Total Assets: $64,895,090
Asset Allocation

Asset	%
Cash	0%
Stocks	100%
US Stocks	99%
Bonds	0%
US Bonds	0%
Other	0%

Services Offered:

Investment Strategy: The investment seeks to track the investment results (before fees and expenses) of the S&P 500 Enhanced Value Index (the "underlying index"). The fund generally will invest at least 90% of its total assets in the securities that comprise the underlying index. The underlying index is designed to track the performance of approximately 100 stocks in the S&P 500® Index that have the highest "value score," which the index provider calculates based on fundamental ratios of a company's stock. A value stock tends to trade at a lower price relative to such fundamentals and thus may be considered undervalued by investors. **Top Holdings:** AT&T Inc Wells Fargo & Co Bank of America Corporation Citigroup Inc CVS Health Corp

---

FormulaFolios Hedged Growth ETF   D+   SELL

Ticker	Traded On	NAV	Total Assets ($)	Dividend Yield (TTM)	Turnover Ratio	Expense Ratio
FFHG	BATS		$64,870,518	0.58	666	1.19

Ratings
Reward   D+
Risk   C-
Recent Upgrade/Downgrade

Fund Information
Fund Type   Exchange Traded Funds
Category   Long/Short Equity
Sub-Category   Long-Short Equity
Prospectus Objective   Growth
Inception Date   Jun-17
Open to New Investments   Y

Prices
Price (as of 9/30/2019)   25.96
52-Week High   29.50
52-Week Low   24.91

Total Returns (%)

3-Month	6-Month	1-Year	3-Year	5-Year
-4.20	-5.28	-10.52		

3-Year Standard Deviation
Effective Duration

Valuation
Premium/Discount (1-Year Average)   -0.11

Company Information
Provider   FormulaFolioFunds
Manager/Tenure   Derek Prusa (2), Jason Wenk (2)
Website
Address   89 Ionia NW, Suite 600 Grand Rapids, MI 49503 United States
Phone Number

PERFORMANCE

Ratings History

Date	Overall Rating	Risk Rating	Reward Rating
Q3-19	D+	C-	D+
Q4-18	D+	D+	D+
Q4-17	U		
Q4-16			
Q4-15			

Asset & Performance History

Date	NAV	1-Year Total Return
2018	26.01	-5.41
2017	27.58	
2016		
2015		
2014		
2013		

Total Assets: $64,870,518
Asset Allocation

Asset	%
Cash	-12%
Stocks	112%
US Stocks	111%
Bonds	0%
US Bonds	0%
Other	0%

Services Offered:

Investment Strategy: The investment seeks to provide capital growth. The fund seeks to achieve its investment objective by investing primarily in domestic equity securities of any market capitalization and U.S. Treasuries through other unaffiliated ETFs (including leveraged ETFs and inverse ETFs). The adviser allocates the fund's assets equally between two proprietary investment models. The adviser's first investment model identifies trends in the equity markets. The adviser's second investment model uses two sub-strategies. **Top Holdings:** Health Care Select Sector SPDR® ETF Vanguard Short-Term Treasury ETF SPDR® Portfolio Short Term Treasury ETF iShares 1-3 Year Treasury Bond ETF iShares Core S&P Small-Cap ETF

Strategy Shares EcoLogical Strategy ETF　　　　　　　　　　　　　C　　HOLD

Ticker	Traded On	NAV	Total Assets ($)	Dividend Yield (TTM)	Turnover Ratio	Expense Ratio
HECO	NYSE Arca	41.14	$64,800,533	0.27		1.07

Ratings
Reward　　　　　　　　　　　　　　　　C+
Risk　　　　　　　　　　　　　　　　　C-
Recent Upgrade/Downgrade

Fund Information
Fund Type	Exchange Traded Funds
Category	Equity Misc
Sub-Category	Miscellaneous Sector
Prospectus Objective	Growth
Inception Date	Jun-12
Open to New Investments	Y

Prices
Price (as of 9/30/2019)	41.19
52-Week High	44.31
52-Week Low	38.80

Total Returns (%)
3-Month	6-Month	1-Year	3-Year	5-Year
-1.01	1.53	-5.17	30.02	46.59

3-Year Standard Deviation　　　　　　9.3
Effective Duration

Valuation
Premium/Discount (1-Year Average)　　-0.07

Company Information
Provider	Strategy shares
Manager/Tenure	Matthew B. Tuttle (1)
Website	
Address	Strategy shares United States
Phone Number	

PERFORMANCE

Ratings History

Date	Overall Rating	Risk Rating	Reward Rating
Q3-19	C	C-	C+
Q4-18	C	C-	C
Q4-17	B-	B	B-
Q4-16	D+	D+	D+
Q4-15	C	D	C

Asset & Performance History

Date	NAV	1-Year Total Return
2018	39.31	-3.27
2017	41.47	20.85
2016	36.34	12.05
2015	35.48	0.95
2014	36.61	7.95
2013	34.34	29.57

Total Assets: $64,800,533
Asset Allocation

Asset	%
Cash	26%
Stocks	71%
US Stocks	71%
Bonds	0%
US Bonds	0%
Other	3%

Services Offered:

Investment Strategy: The investment seeks capital appreciation. The fund is an actively managed exchange-traded fund ("ETF") and, under normal conditions, will invest at least 80% of its net assets (plus borrowings for investment purposes), directly or indirectly through mutual funds and ETFs, in the equity and fixed income securities of ecologically-focused companies and/or green bonds. It may also invest up to 20% of its net assets in cash and cash equivalents including U.S. government securities. The fund may invest in domestic and foreign securities of companies of any market capitalization. **Top Holdings:** The Home Depot Inc　Synopsys Inc　Intuit Inc　IDEXX Laboratories Inc　Costco Wholesale Corp

---

Invesco KBW Regional Banking ETF　　　　　　　　　　　　　　C-　　HOLD

Ticker	Traded On	NAV	Total Assets ($)	Dividend Yield (TTM)	Turnover Ratio	Expense Ratio
KBWR	NAS CM	49.63	$64,517,804	2.55		0.35

Ratings
Reward　　　　　　　　　　　　　　　　C
Risk　　　　　　　　　　　　　　　　　D+
Recent Upgrade/Downgrade　　　　　　Up

Fund Information
Fund Type	Exchange Traded Funds
Category	Financials Sector Equity
Sub-Category	Financial
Prospectus Objective	Financial
Inception Date	Nov-11
Open to New Investments	

Prices
Price (as of 9/30/2019)	49.78
52-Week High	56.50
52-Week Low	42.37

Total Returns (%)
3-Month	6-Month	1-Year	3-Year	5-Year
-1.11	0.24	-7.54	21.13	51.54

3-Year Standard Deviation　　　　　　23.69
Effective Duration

Valuation
Premium/Discount (1-Year Average)　　0.07

Company Information
Provider	Invesco
Manager/Tenure	Peter Hubbard (7), Michael Jeanette (7), Tony Seisser (5)
Website	http://www.invesco.com/us
Address	Invesco 11 Greenway Plaza, Ste. 2500 Houston TX 77046 United States
Phone Number	800-659-1005

PERFORMANCE

Ratings History

Date	Overall Rating	Risk Rating	Reward Rating
Q3-19	C-	D+	C
Q4-18	C-	C-	C
Q4-17	B	C+	A-
Q4-16	C	C-	C+
Q4-15	B-	C	B

Asset & Performance History

Date	NAV	1-Year Total Return
2018	44.89	-17.77
2017	55.76	1.36
2016	55.91	38.5
2015	41.11	5.52
2014	39.71	2.04
2013	39.63	46.31

Total Assets: $64,517,804
Asset Allocation

Asset	%
Cash	0%
Stocks	100%
US Stocks	98%
Bonds	0%
US Bonds	0%
Other	0%

Services Offered:

Investment Strategy: The investment seeks to track the investment results (before fees and expenses) of the KBW Nasdaq Regional Banking Index (the "underlying index"). The fund generally will invest at least 90% of its total assets in the securities that comprise the underlying index. The underlying index is a modified-market capitalization-weighted index comprised of companies primarily engaged in U.S. regional banking activities, as determined by the index provider. The underlying index is designed to track the performance of U.S. regional banking and thrift companies that are publicly-traded in the U.S. **Top Holdings:** TCF Financial Corp　Signature Bank　Commerce Bancshares Inc　East West Bancorp Inc　Cullen/Frost Bankers Inc

Alerian Energy Infrastructure ETF   C-   HOLD

Ticker	Traded On	NAV	Total Assets ($)	Dividend Yield (TTM)	Turnover Ratio	Expense Ratio
ENFR	NYSE Arca	20.71	$64,205,676	5.05	73	0.65

Ratings
Reward   C
Risk   C-
Recent Upgrade/Downgrade

Fund Information
Fund Type	Exchange Traded Funds
Category	Energy Sector Equity
Sub-Category	Energy Limited Partnership
Prospectus Objective	Natl Res
Inception Date	Oct-13
Open to New Investments	Y

Prices
Price (as of 9/30/2019)	20.73
52-Week High	22.66
52-Week Low	17.34

Total Returns (%)

3-Month	6-Month	1-Year	3-Year	5-Year
-2.82	-3.74	-3.22	-0.01	-17.09

3-Year Standard Deviation	16.27
Effective Duration	

Valuation
Premium/Discount (1-Year Average)	-0.03

Company Information
Provider	ALPS
Manager/Tenure	Ryan Mischker (4), Andrew Hicks (3)
Website	http://www.alpsfunds.com
Address	ALPS 1290 Broadway, Suite 1100
	Denver CO 80203 United States
Phone Number	866-759-5679

PERFORMANCE

Ratings History

Date	Overall Rating	Risk Rating	Reward Rating
Q3-19	C-	C-	C
Q4-18	C	D+	C+
Q4-17	C-	D+	C
Q4-16	C	D	B-
Q4-15	C-	C	B

Asset & Performance History

Date	NAV	1-Year Total Return
2018	18.21	-18.31
2017	23.09	-0.02
2016	23.8	42
2015	17.41	-37.31
2014	28.47	12.68
2013	25.81	

Total Assets: $64,205,676
Asset Allocation

Asset	%
Cash	0%
Stocks	100%
US Stocks	67%
Bonds	0%
US Bonds	0%
Other	0%

Services Offered:

Investment Strategy: The investment seeks investment results that correspond (before fees and expenses) generally to the price and yield performance of its underlying index, the Alerian Midstream Energy Select Index. The underlying index is a composite of North American energy infrastructure companies engaged midstream activities involving energy commodities including gathering and processing, liquefaction, pipeline transportation, rail terminaling, and storage (also known as "midstream energy businesses"). The fund will normally invest at least 90% of its total assets in securities that comprise the underlying index. It is non-diversified. **Top Holdings:** Enbridge Inc Transcanada Enterprise Products Partners LP Kinder Morgan Inc Class P Energy Transfer LP

JPMorgan U.S. Value Factor ETF   C-   HOLD

Ticker	Traded On	NAV	Total Assets ($)	Dividend Yield (TTM)	Turnover Ratio	Expense Ratio
JVAL	NYSE Arca	26.71	$64,115,618	2.38		0.12

Ratings
Reward   C-
Risk   C-
Recent Upgrade/Downgrade   Up

Fund Information
Fund Type	Exchange Traded Funds
Category	US Equity Large Cap Value
Sub-Category	Large Value
Prospectus Objective	Growth & Inc
Inception Date	Nov-17
Open to New Investments	Y

Prices
Price (as of 9/30/2019)	26.74
52-Week High	27.33
52-Week Low	21.96

Total Returns (%)

3-Month	6-Month	1-Year	3-Year	5-Year
0.54	2.77	1.86		

3-Year Standard Deviation	
Effective Duration	

Valuation
Premium/Discount (1-Year Average)	0.06

Company Information
Provider	JPMorgan
Manager/Tenure	Aijaz Hussain (1), Jonathan Msika (1),
	Yazann Romahi (1), 2 others
Website	http://www.jpmorganfunds.com
Address	JPMorgan 270 Park Avenue New York
	NY 10017-2070 United States
Phone Number	800-480-4111

PERFORMANCE

Ratings History

Date	Overall Rating	Risk Rating	Reward Rating
Q3-19	C-	C-	C-
Q4-18	D+	D+	D+
Q4-17	U		
Q4-16			
Q4-15			

Asset & Performance History

Date	NAV	1-Year Total Return
2018	23.22	-8.58
2017	26.02	
2016		
2015		
2014		
2013		

Total Assets: $64,115,618
Asset Allocation

Asset	%
Cash	0%
Stocks	100%
US Stocks	99%
Bonds	0%
US Bonds	0%
Other	0%

Services Offered:

Investment Strategy: The investment seeks investment results that closely correspond, before fees and expenses, to the performance of the JP Morgan US Value Factor Index. The fund will invest at least 80% of its assets in securities included in the underlying index. "Assets" means net assets, plus the amount of borrowing for investment purposes. The underlying index is comprised of U.S. equity securities selected to represent value factor characteristics. **Top Holdings:** Apple Inc Microsoft Corp Procter & Gamble Co The Walt Disney Co Wells Fargo & Co

iShares MSCI United Kingdom Small-Cap ETF   D+   SELL

Ticker	Traded On	NAV	Total Assets ($)	Dividend Yield (TTM)	Turnover Ratio	Expense Ratio
EWUS	BATS	37.65	$64,006,088	2.8	20	0.59

Ratings

Reward	D+
Risk	D+
Recent Upgrade/Downgrade	

PERFORMANCE

Fund Information

Fund Type	Exchange Traded Funds
Category	Equity Misc
Sub-Category	Miscellaneous Region
Prospectus Objective	Europe Stock
Inception Date	Jan-12
Open to New Investments	Y

Prices

Price (as of 9/30/2019)	37.58
52-Week High	41.97
52-Week Low	32.68

Total Returns (%)

3-Month	6-Month	1-Year	3-Year	5-Year
-1.25	-3.06	-7.65	13.74	15.45

3-Year Standard Deviation	15.11
Effective Duration	

Valuation

Premium/Discount (1-Year Average)	-0.37

Company Information

Provider	iShares
Manager/Tenure	Diane Hsiung (7), Greg Savage (7), Jennifer Hsui (6), 3 others
Website	http://www.ishares.com
Address	iShares 400 Howard Street San Francisco CA 94105 United States
Phone Number	800-474-2737

Ratings History

Date	Overall Rating	Risk Rating	Reward Rating
Q3-19	D+	D+	D+
Q4-18	D+	D	D+
Q4-17	B	C	B+
Q4-16	D	D+	D
Q4-15	C	D+	B

Asset & Performance History

Date	NAV	1-Year Total Return
2018	33.89	-20.46
2017	43.94	31.6
2016	34.33	-10.89
2015	39.69	7.85
2014	37.82	-6.28
2013	41.71	38.31

Total Assets: $64,006,088

Asset Allocation

Asset	%
Cash	1%
Stocks	97%
US Stocks	2%
Bonds	0%
US Bonds	0%
Other	2%

Services Offered:

Investment Strategy: The investment seeks to track the investment results of the MSCI United Kingdom Small Cap Index. The fund generally will invest at least 90% of its assets in the component securities of the underlying index and in investments that have economic characteristics that are substantially identical to the component securities of the underlying index. The index is designed to measure the performance of equity securities of small-capitalization companies whose market capitalization, as calculated by the index provider, represents the bottom 14% of the United Kingdom securities market. **Top Holdings:** Just Eat PLC Rightmove PLC Smith (DS) PLC Hiscox Ltd Intermediate Capital Group PLC

Aptus Behavioral Momentum ETF   B-   BUY

Ticker	Traded On	NAV	Total Assets ($)	Dividend Yield (TTM)	Turnover Ratio	Expense Ratio
BEMO	BATS	30.48	$64,004,703	0.8	321	0.81

Ratings

Reward	B
Risk	C
Recent Upgrade/Downgrade	Up

PERFORMANCE

Fund Information

Fund Type	Exchange Traded Funds
Category	US Equity Large Cap Blend
Sub-Category	Large Growth
Prospectus Objective	Growth & Inc
Inception Date	Jun-16
Open to New Investments	Y

Prices

Price (as of 9/30/2019)	30.48
52-Week High	37.07
52-Week Low	28.10

Total Returns (%)

3-Month	6-Month	1-Year	3-Year	5-Year
-0.41	3.48	-17.04	21.66	

3-Year Standard Deviation	15.39
Effective Duration	

Valuation

Premium/Discount (1-Year Average)	-0.01

Company Information

Provider	Aptus Capital Advisors
Manager/Tenure	John D. Gardner (2), Beckham D. Wyrick (2)
Website	
Address	407 Johnson Avenue, Fairhope, Alabama 36532 United States
Phone Number	

Ratings History

Date	Overall Rating	Risk Rating	Reward Rating
Q3-19	B-	C	B
Q4-18	B-	C	B
Q4-17	D+	B	C
Q4-16	U		
Q4-15			

Asset & Performance History

Date	NAV	1-Year Total Return
2018	28.26	-5.88
2017	30.28	17.28
2016	25.9	
2015		
2014		
2013		

Total Assets: $64,004,703

Asset Allocation

Asset	%
Cash	0%
Stocks	100%
US Stocks	100%
Bonds	0%
US Bonds	0%
Other	0%

Services Offered:

Investment Strategy: The investment seeks to track the performance, before fees and expenses, of the Aptus Behavioral Momentum Index. The index uses an objective, rules-based methodology to implement a systematic trend-following strategy that directs 100% of its exposure to either equity exposure or treasure exposure. The fund invests at least 80% of its total assets in the component securities of the index. The fund generally may invest up to 20% of its total assets (exclusive of any collateral held from securities lending) in securities or other investments not included in the index, but which the Adviser believes will help the fund track the index. **Top Holdings:** Ball Corp Veeva Systems Inc Class A Tyson Foods Inc Class A Edwards Lifesciences Corp TransDigm Group Inc

IQ Enhanced Core Bond U.S. ETF

C   HOLD

Ticker	Traded On	NAV	Total Assets ($)	Dividend Yield (TTM)	Turnover Ratio	Expense Ratio
AGGE	NYSE Arca	19.38	$63,960,588	2.6		0.28

Ratings

Reward	C
Risk	C-
Recent Upgrade/Downgrade	Up

Fund Information

Fund Type	Exchange Traded Funds
Category	US Fixed Income
Sub-Category	Intermediate Core Bond
Prospectus Objective	Income
Inception Date	May-16
Open to New Investments	Y

Prices

Price (as of 9/30/2019)	19.38
52-Week High	19.51
52-Week Low	18.31

Total Returns (%)

3-Month	6-Month	1-Year	3-Year	5-Year
1.79	4.51	7.52	2.86	

3-Year Standard Deviation	3.17
Effective Duration	5.55

Valuation

Premium/Discount (1-Year Average)	-0.03

Company Information

Provider	IndexIQ
Manager/Tenure	Greg Barrato (3), James Harrison (1)
Website	http://www.indexiq.com
Address	IndexIQ 800 Westchester Avenue, Suite N-611 Rye Brook NY 10573 United States
Phone Number	888-934-0777

PERFORMANCE

Ratings History

Date	Overall Rating	Risk Rating	Reward Rating
Q3-19	C	C-	C
Q4-18	D+	C-	D
Q4-17	D+	C+	D+
Q4-16	U		
Q4-15			

Asset & Performance History

Date	NAV	1-Year Total Return
2018	18.6	-2.57
2017	19.59	2.5
2016	19.54	
2015		
2014		
2013		

Total Assets: $63,960,588

Asset Allocation

Asset	%
Cash	2%
Stocks	0%
US Stocks	0%
Bonds	97%
US Bonds	90%
Other	0%

Services Offered:

Investment Strategy: The investment seeks to track (before fees and expenses) the price and yield performance of its underlying index, the IQ Enhanced Core Bond U.S. Index. The fund is a "fund of funds" which means it invests, under normal circumstances, at least 80% of its net assets, plus the amount of any borrowings for investment purposes, in the investments included in its underlying index. The underlying index seeks to outperform the U.S. dollar-denominated taxable fixed income universe by using a combination of short- and long-term momentum to overweight and underweight various sectors of the investment grade U.S. fixed income securities market. **Top Holdings:** iShares MBS ETF Vanguard Mortgage-Backed Secs ETF Vanguard Short-Term Corporate Bond ETF Vanguard Long-Term Corporate Bd ETF Vanguard Interm-Term Corp Bd ETF

Aptus Fortified Value ETF

C-   HOLD

Ticker	Traded On	NAV	Total Assets ($)	Dividend Yield (TTM)	Turnover Ratio	Expense Ratio
FTVA	BATS	26.10	$63,938,427	0.3	51	0.79

Ratings

Reward	C-
Risk	C-
Recent Upgrade/Downgrade	Up

Fund Information

Fund Type	Exchange Traded Funds
Category	Long/Short Equity
Sub-Category	Options-based
Prospectus Objective	Growth & Inc
Inception Date	Oct-17
Open to New Investments	Y

Prices

Price (as of 9/30/2019)	26.10
52-Week High	29.01
52-Week Low	23.23

Total Returns (%)

3-Month	6-Month	1-Year	3-Year	5-Year
-0.55	-2.20	-8.91		

3-Year Standard Deviation	
Effective Duration	

Valuation

Premium/Discount (1-Year Average)	-0.01

Company Information

Provider	Aptus Capital Advisors
Manager/Tenure	John D. Gardner (1), Beckham D. Wyrick (1)
Website	
Address	407 Johnson Avenue, Fairhope, Alabama 36532 United States
Phone Number	

PERFORMANCE

Ratings History

Date	Overall Rating	Risk Rating	Reward Rating
Q3-19	C-	C-	C-
Q4-18	D+	D	C-
Q4-17	U		
Q4-16			
Q4-15			

Asset & Performance History

Date	NAV	1-Year Total Return
2018	23.73	-12.13
2017	27.1	
2016		
2015		
2014		
2013		

Total Assets: $63,938,427

Asset Allocation

Asset	%
Cash	0%
Stocks	100%
US Stocks	96%
Bonds	0%
US Bonds	0%
Other	0%

Services Offered:

Investment Strategy: The investment seeks to track the performance, before fees and expenses, of the Aptus Fortified Value Index (the "index"). Under normal circumstances, at least 80% of the fund's total assets (exclusive of any collateral held from securities lending) will be invested in the component securities of the index. The index is a rules-based, equal-weighted index that is designed to gain exposure to 50 of the most undervalued U.S.-listed common stocks and real estate investment trusts ("REITs"), while hedging against significant U.S. equity market declines when the market is overvalued. The fund is non-diversified. **Top Holdings:** KLA Corp Amgen Inc Teradyne Inc Gentex Corp Lam Research Corp

VanEck Vectors ChinaAMC CSI 300 ETF   C-   HOLD

Ticker	Traded On	NAV	Total Assets ($)	Dividend Yield (TTM)	Turnover Ratio	Expense Ratio
PEK	NYSE Arca	38.86	$62,182,298	0.75	34	0.6

Ratings
Reward	C-
Risk	D+
Recent Upgrade/Downgrade	

Fund Information
Fund Type	Exchange Traded Funds
Category	Greater China Equity
Sub-Category	China Region
Prospectus Objective	Pacific Stock
Inception Date	Oct-10
Open to New Investments	Y

Prices
Price (as of 9/30/2019)	38.53
52-Week High	43.99
52-Week Low	31.34

Total Returns (%)
3-Month	6-Month	1-Year	3-Year	5-Year
-6.27	-8.97	7.83	11.73	37.59

3-Year Standard Deviation	19.38
Effective Duration	

Valuation
Premium/Discount (1-Year Average)	-0.07

Company Information
Provider	VanEck
Manager/Tenure	Hao-Hung (Peter) Liao (8), Leo Fan (4), Guo Hua (Jason) Jin (1)
Website	http://www.vaneck.com
Address	Van Eck Associates Corporation 666 Third Avenue New York NY 10017 United States
Phone Number	800-826-1115

PERFORMANCE

Ratings History
Date	Overall Rating	Risk Rating	Reward Rating
Q3-19	C-	D+	C-
Q4-18	D	D	D
Q4-17	B	C	A-
Q4-16	C-	D+	C
Q4-15	C	C	C+

Asset & Performance History
Date	NAV	1-Year Total Return
2018	31.58	-33.78
2017	48.37	31.89
2016	37.08	-16.16
2015	44.76	0.1
2014	46.06	49.1
2013	30.89	-4.71

Total Assets: $62,182,298

Asset Allocation
Asset	%
Cash	0%
Stocks	100%
US Stocks	0%
Bonds	0%
US Bonds	0%
Other	0%

Services Offered:

Investment Strategy: The investment seeks to replicate as closely as possible, before fees and expenses, the price and yield performance of the CSI 300 Index. The fund normally invests at least 80% of its total assets in securities that comprise the fund's benchmark index and/or in investments that have economic characteristics that are substantially identical to the economic characteristics of the securities that comprise its benchmark index. The index is comprised of the largest and most liquid stocks in the Chinese A-share market. **Top Holdings:** Ping An Insurance (Group) Co. of China Ltd Kweichow Moutai Co Ltd China Merchants Bank Co Ltd Wuliangye Yibin Co Ltd Gree Electric Appliances Inc of Zhuhai

---

Invesco Dynamic Networking ETF   C+   HOLD

Ticker	Traded On	NAV	Total Assets ($)	Dividend Yield (TTM)	Turnover Ratio	Expense Ratio
PXQ	NYSE Arca	56.35	$61,980,668	1.09	98	0.63

Ratings
Reward	B
Risk	C
Recent Upgrade/Downgrade	Up

Fund Information
Fund Type	Exchange Traded Funds
Category	Technology Sector Equity
Sub-Category	Technology
Prospectus Objective	Technology
Inception Date	Jun-05
Open to New Investments	Y

Prices
Price (as of 9/30/2019)	56.33
52-Week High	63.15
52-Week Low	45.28

Total Returns (%)
3-Month	6-Month	1-Year	3-Year	5-Year
-4.56	-5.21	-0.46	43.83	81.98

3-Year Standard Deviation	17.08
Effective Duration	

Valuation
Premium/Discount (1-Year Average)	-0.02

Company Information
Provider	Invesco
Manager/Tenure	Peter Hubbard (12), Michael Jeanette (11), Tony Seisser (5)
Website	http://www.invesco.com/us
Address	Invesco 11 Greenway Plaza, Ste. 2500 Houston TX 77046 United States
Phone Number	800-659-1005

PERFORMANCE

Ratings History
Date	Overall Rating	Risk Rating	Reward Rating
Q3-19	C+	C	B
Q4-18	C	D+	B-
Q4-17	B	B	B
Q4-16	C	C-	C
Q4-15	C+	C	B

Asset & Performance History
Date	NAV	1-Year Total Return
2018	48.44	6.36
2017	46.09	14.89
2016	40.39	17.82
2015	34.46	-0.94
2014	34.79	10.19
2013	31.57	25.05

Total Assets: $61,980,668

Asset Allocation
Asset	%
Cash	0%
Stocks	100%
US Stocks	97%
Bonds	0%
US Bonds	0%
Other	0%

Services Offered:

Investment Strategy: The investment seeks to track the investment results (before fees and expenses) of the Dynamic Networking IntellidexSM Index. The fund generally will invest at least 90% of its total assets in securities that comprise the underlying intellidex. The underlying intellidex was composed of common stocks of U.S. networking companies. These companies are principally engaged in the development, manufacture, sale or distribution of products, services or technologies that support the flow of electronic information, including voice, data, images and commercial transactions. It is non-diversified. **Top Holdings:** Motorola Solutions Inc Apple Inc Qualcomm Inc Amphenol Corp Class A Check Point Software Technologies Ltd

Nuveen ESG U.S. Aggregate Bond ETF   C-   HOLD

Ticker	Traded On	NAV	Total Assets ($)	Dividend Yield (TTM)	Turnover Ratio	Expense Ratio
NUBD	NYSE Arca	25.73	$61,760,766	2.61	27	0.2

Ratings
Reward   C-
Risk   C-
Recent Upgrade/Downgrade

Fund Information
Fund Type   Exchange Traded Funds
Category   US Fixed Income
Sub-Category   Intermediate Core Bond
Prospectus Objective   Growth & Inc
Inception Date   Sep-17
Open to New Investments   Y

Prices
Price (as of 9/30/2019)   25.72
52-Week High   26.00
52-Week Low   23.73

Total Returns (%)

3-Month	6-Month	1-Year	3-Year	5-Year
2.25	5.57	10.09		

3-Year Standard Deviation
Effective Duration   5.43

Valuation
Premium/Discount (1-Year Average)   0.10

Company Information
Provider   Nuveen
Manager/Tenure   Lijun (Kevin) Chen (2), Yong (Mark)
                    Zheng (1)
Website   http://www.nuveen.com
Address   Nuveen Investment Trust John
                    Nuveen & Co. Inc. Chicago IL 60606
                    United States
Phone Number   312-917-8146

PERFORMANCE

Ratings History

Date	Overall Rating	Risk Rating	Reward Rating
Q3-19	C-	C-	C-
Q4-18	D	D+	D
Q4-17	U		
Q4-16			
Q4-15			

Asset & Performance History

Date	NAV	1-Year Total Return
2018	24.22	-0.26
2017	24.93	
2016		
2015		
2014		
2013		

Total Assets: $61,760,766

Asset Allocation

Asset	%
Cash	2%
Stocks	0%
US Stocks	0%
Bonds	98%
US Bonds	89%
Other	0%

Services Offered:

Investment Strategy: The investment seeks to track the investment results, before fees and expenses, of the Bloomberg Barclays MSCI US Aggregate ESG Select Index (the "index"). Under normal market conditions, the fund invests at least 80% of the sum of its net assets and the amount of any borrowings for investment purposes in component securities of the index. The index utilizes certain environmental, social, and governance ("ESG") criteria to select from the securities included in the Bloomberg Barclays US Aggregate Bond Index (the "base index"), which is designed to broadly capture the U.S. investment grade, taxable fixed income market. **Top Holdings:** Federal National Mortgage Association 3% United States Treasury Notes 2% Federal National Mortgage Association 3.5% United States Treasury Bonds 2.75% Government National Mortgage Association 3.5%

iShares Interest Rate Hedged Long-Term Corporate Bond ETF   C   HOLD

Ticker	Traded On	NAV	Total Assets ($)	Dividend Yield (TTM)	Turnover Ratio	Expense Ratio
IGBH	NYSE Arca	24.17	$61,629,008	3.99	5	0.16

Ratings
Reward   C
Risk   C-
Recent Upgrade/Downgrade

Fund Information
Fund Type   Exchange Traded Funds
Category   US Fixed Income
Sub-Category   Corporate Bond
Prospectus Objective   Growth & Inc
Inception Date   Jul-15
Open to New Investments   Y

Prices
Price (as of 9/30/2019)   24.11
52-Week High   26.37
52-Week Low   23.80

Total Returns (%)

3-Month	6-Month	1-Year	3-Year	5-Year
-2.31	-0.62	-2.53	13.88	

3-Year Standard Deviation   5.86
Effective Duration

Valuation
Premium/Discount (1-Year Average)   -0.06

Company Information
Provider   iShares
Manager/Tenure   James Mauro (4), Scott Radell (4)
Website   http://www.ishares.com
Address   iShares 400 Howard Street San
                    Francisco CA 94105 United States
Phone Number   800-474-2737

PERFORMANCE

Ratings History

Date	Overall Rating	Risk Rating	Reward Rating
Q3-19	C	C-	C
Q4-18	C-	C-	C-
Q4-17	C	B	C
Q4-16	D	D+	D+
Q4-15	U		

Asset & Performance History

Date	NAV	1-Year Total Return
2018	23.97	-3.34
2017	26.26	9.66
2016	24.67	6.98
2015	23.7	
2014		
2013		

Total Assets: $61,629,008

Asset Allocation

Asset	%
Cash	11%
Stocks	0%
US Stocks	0%
Bonds	89%
US Bonds	75%
Other	0%

Services Offered:

Investment Strategy: The investment seeks to mitigate the interest rate risk of a portfolio composed of U.S. dollar-denominated investment-grade corporate bonds with remaining maturities greater than ten years. The fund invests at least 80% of its net assets in U.S. dollar-denominated investment-grade corporate bonds with remaining maturities greater than ten years, in one or more underlying funds that principally invest in U.S. dollar-denominated investment-grade corporate bonds. **Top Holdings:** GE Capital International Funding Company Unlimited Company 4.42% Anheuser-Busch Companies LLC / Anheuser-Busch InBev Worldwide Inc 4.9% Goldman Sachs Group, Inc. 6.75% CVS Health Corp 5.05% Anheuser-Busch Companies LLC / Anheuser-Busch InBev Worldwide Inc 4.7%

Nuveen ESG International Developed Markets Equity ETF   C-   HOLD

Ticker	Traded On	NAV	Total Assets ($)	Dividend Yield (TTM)	Turnover Ratio	Expense Ratio
NUDM	BATS	25.66	$61,574,921	2.14	56	0.4

Ratings
Reward   C
Risk   D+
Recent Upgrade/Downgrade   Up

Fund Information
Fund Type — Exchange Traded Funds
Category — Global Equity Large Cap
Sub-Category — Foreign Large Blend
Prospectus Objective — World Stock
Inception Date — Jun-17
Open to New Investments — Y

Prices
Price (as of 9/30/2019) — 25.84
52-Week High — 26.35
52-Week Low — 22.15

Total Returns (%)
3-Month	6-Month	1-Year	3-Year	5-Year
-0.31	4.73	0.49		

3-Year Standard Deviation
Effective Duration

Valuation
Premium/Discount (1-Year Average) — 0.26

Company Information
Provider — Nuveen
Manager/Tenure — Philip James(Jim) Campagna (2), Lei Liao (2)
Website — http://www.nuveen.com
Address — Nuveen Investment Trust John Nuveen & Co. Inc. Chicago IL 60606 United States
Phone Number — 312-917-8146

PERFORMANCE

Ratings History
Date	Overall Rating	Risk Rating	Reward Rating
Q3-19	C-	D+	C
Q4-18	D	D	D
Q4-17	U		
Q4-16			
Q4-15			

Asset & Performance History
Date	NAV	1-Year Total Return
2018	22.36	-16.7
2017	26.85	
2016		
2015		
2014		
2013		

Total Assets: $61,574,921

Asset Allocation
Asset	%
Cash	1%
Stocks	100%
US Stocks	1%
Bonds	0%
US Bonds	0%
Other	0%

Services Offered:
Investment Strategy: The investment seeks to track the investment results, before fees and expenses, of the TIAA ESG International Developed Markets Equity Index (the "index"). In seeking to track the investment results of the index, the advisor attempts to replicate the index by investing all, or substantially all, of its assets in the securities represented in the index in approximately the same proportions as the index. The index identifies equity securities from the base index that satisfy certain ESG criteria, based on ESG performance data collected by MSCI ESG Research, Inc. **Top Holdings:** Nestle SA   Roche Holding AG Dividend Right Cert.   AstraZeneca PLC   Sony Corp L'Oreal SA

First Trust Nasdaq Artificial Intelligence and Robotics ETF   C-   HOLD

Ticker	Traded On	NAV	Total Assets ($)	Dividend Yield (TTM)	Turnover Ratio	Expense Ratio
ROBT	NAS CM	31.51	$61,443,155	0.44	67	0.65

Ratings
Reward   C-
Risk   C-
Recent Upgrade/Downgrade

Fund Information
Fund Type — Exchange Traded Funds
Category — Technology Sector Equity
Sub-Category — Technology
Prospectus Objective — Technology
Inception Date — Feb-18
Open to New Investments — Y

Prices
Price (as of 9/30/2019) — 31.61
52-Week High — 33.88
52-Week Low — 24.55

Total Returns (%)
3-Month	6-Month	1-Year	3-Year	5-Year
-5.52	-1.78	-1.37		

3-Year Standard Deviation
Effective Duration

Valuation
Premium/Discount (1-Year Average) — 0.20

Company Information
Provider — First Trust
Manager/Tenure — Jon C. Erickson (1), Daniel J. Lindquist (1), David G. McGarel (1), 3 others
Website — http://www.ftportfolios.com/
Address — First Trust 120 E. Liberty Drive, Suite 400 Wheaton IL 60187 United States
Phone Number — 800-621-1675

PERFORMANCE

Ratings History
Date	Overall Rating	Risk Rating	Reward Rating
Q3-19	C-	C-	C-
Q4-18	U		
Q4-17			
Q4-16			
Q4-15			

Asset & Performance History
Date	NAV	1-Year Total Return
2018	25.79	
2017		
2016		
2015		
2014		
2013		

Total Assets: $61,443,155

Asset Allocation
Asset	%
Cash	0%
Stocks	100%
US Stocks	50%
Bonds	0%
US Bonds	0%
Other	0%

Services Offered:
Investment Strategy: The investment seeks investment results that correspond generally to the price and yield (before the fund's fees and expenses) of an index called the Nasdaq CTA Artificial Intelligence and Robotics IndexSM (the "index"). The fund will normally invest at least 90% of its net assets (including investment borrowings) in common stocks and depositary receipts that comprise the index. The index is designed to track the performance of companies engaged in the artificial intelligence ("AI") and robotics segments of the technology, industrial and other economic sectors. The fund is non-diversified. **Top Holdings:** Appian Corp A   Ambarella Inc Pros Holdings Inc   Gentex Corp   CoreLogic Inc

Invesco S&P High Income Infrastructure ETF

C   HOLD

Ticker	Traded On	NAV	Total Assets ($)	Dividend Yield (TTM)	Turnover Ratio	Expense Ratio
GHII	NYSE Arca	27.26	$61,337,545	4.05	45	0.45

Ratings
Reward   C
Risk   D+
Recent Upgrade/Downgrade

Fund Information
Fund Type	Exchange Traded Funds
Category	Infrastructure Sector Equity
Sub-Category	Infrastructure
Prospectus Objective	Equity-Income
Inception Date	Feb-15
Open to New Investments	Y

Prices
Price (as of 9/30/2019)	27.21
52-Week High	27.53
52-Week Low	22.90

Total Returns (%)
3-Month	6-Month	1-Year	3-Year	5-Year
2.73	4.86	8.83	20.81	

3-Year Standard Deviation	11.49
Effective Duration	

Valuation
Premium/Discount (1-Year Average)	-0.07

Company Information
Provider	Invesco
Manager/Tenure	Peter Hubbard (1), Michael Jeanette (1), Tony Seisser (1)
Website	http://www.invesco.com/us
Address	Invesco 11 Greenway Plaza, Ste. 2500 Houston TX 77046 United States
Phone Number	800-659-1005

PERFORMANCE

Ratings History
Date	Overall Rating	Risk Rating	Reward Rating
Q3-19	C	D+	C
Q4-18	C-	D+	C-
Q4-17	C	C+	C
Q4-16	D+	D+	C-
Q4-15	U		

Asset & Performance History
Date	NAV	1-Year Total Return
2018	23.47	-11.2
2017	27.43	13.03
2016	25.94	26.65
2015	21.43	
2014		
2013		

Total Assets: $61,337,545

Asset Allocation
Asset	%
Cash	0%
Stocks	100%
US Stocks	33%
Bonds	0%
US Bonds	0%
Other	0%

Services Offered:

Investment Strategy: The investment seeks to track the investment results (before fees and expenses) of the S&P High Income Infrastructure Index (the "underlying index"). The fund will invest at least 90% of its total assets in the securities that comprise the underlying index, as well as American depositary receipts ("ADRs") and global depositary receipts ("GDRs") that represent securities in the underlying index. The underlying index is designed to measure the performance of 50 high-yielding global equity securities of companies that engage in various infrastructure-related sub-industries. The fund is non-diversified. **Top Holdings:** Inter Pipeline Ltd   Macquarie Infrastructure Corp   Targa Resources Corp   Semgroup Corp   Enbridge Inc

---

iShares MSCI USA Small-Cap ESG Optimized ETF

D+   SELL

Ticker	Traded On	NAV	Total Assets ($)	Dividend Yield (TTM)	Turnover Ratio	Expense Ratio
ESML	BATS	26.64	$61,266,685	1.15	15	0.17

Ratings
Reward   D
Risk   C-
Recent Upgrade/Downgrade

Fund Information
Fund Type	Exchange Traded Funds
Category	US Equity Small Cap
Sub-Category	Small Blend
Prospectus Objective	Growth & Inc
Inception Date	Apr-18
Open to New Investments	Y

Prices
Price (as of 9/30/2019)	26.70
52-Week High	27.89
52-Week Low	21.37

Total Returns (%)
3-Month	6-Month	1-Year	3-Year	5-Year
-1.34	0.48	-3.11		

3-Year Standard Deviation	
Effective Duration	

Valuation
Premium/Discount (1-Year Average)	0.15

Company Information
Provider	iShares
Manager/Tenure	Diane Hsiung (1), Jennifer Hsui (1), Alan Mason (1), 3 others
Website	http://www.ishares.com
Address	iShares 400 Howard Street San Francisco CA 94105 United States
Phone Number	800-474-2737

PERFORMANCE

Ratings History
Date	Overall Rating	Risk Rating	Reward Rating
Q3-19	D+	C-	D
Q4-18	U		
Q4-17			
Q4-16			
Q4-15			

Asset & Performance History
Date	NAV	1-Year Total Return
2018	22.72	
2017		
2016		
2015		
2014		
2013		

Total Assets: $61,266,685

Asset Allocation
Asset	%
Cash	0%
Stocks	100%
US Stocks	99%
Bonds	0%
US Bonds	0%
Other	0%

Services Offered:

Investment Strategy: The investment seeks to track the investment results of the MSCI USA Small Cap Extended ESG Focus Index. The fund generally will invest at least 90% of its assets in the component securities of the underlying index and may invest up to 10% of its assets in certain futures, options and swap contracts, cash and cash equivalents. The underlying index is an optimized equity index designed to produce investment results comparable to the MSCI USA Small Cap Index (the "parent index"), while reflecting a higher allocation than that of the parent index to U.S. small-capitalization companies with favorable ESG profiles. It is non-diversified. **Top Holdings:** Bright Horizons Family Solutions Inc   Douglas Emmett Inc   Kilroy Realty Corp   West Pharmaceutical Services Inc   VICI Properties Inc Ordinary Shares

iShares MSCI Global Impact ETF   C   HOLD

Ticker	Traded On	NAV	Total Assets ($)	Dividend Yield (TTM)	Turnover Ratio	Expense Ratio
SDG	NAS CM	58.29	$61,200,702	1.8	36	0.49

Ratings
Reward	C
Risk	D+
Recent Upgrade/Downgrade	Up

Fund Information
Fund Type	Exchange Traded Funds
Category	Global Equity Large Cap
Sub-Category	World Large Stock
Prospectus Objective	Growth & Inc
Inception Date	Apr-16
Open to New Investments	Y

Prices
Price (as of 9/30/2019)	58.38
52-Week High	60.34
52-Week Low	51.40

Total Returns (%)
3-Month	6-Month	1-Year	3-Year	5-Year
0.44	-0.97	2.50	25.46	

3-Year Standard Deviation	11.2
Effective Duration	

Valuation
Premium/Discount (1-Year Average)	0.30

Company Information
Provider	iShares
Manager/Tenure	Diane Hsiung (3), Jennifer Hsui (3), Alan Mason (3), 3 others
Website	http://www.ishares.com
Address	iShares 400 Howard Street San Francisco CA 94105 United States
Phone Number	800-474-2737

PERFORMANCE

Ratings History

Date	Overall Rating	Risk Rating	Reward Rating
Q3-19	C	D+	C
Q4-18	D+	D+	D+
Q4-17	D+	B	C
Q4-16	U		
Q4-15			

Asset & Performance History

Date	NAV	1-Year Total Return
2018	53.05	-7.55
2017	58.74	26.92
2016	47.52	
2015		
2014		
2013		

Total Assets: $61,200,702

Asset Allocation

Asset	%
Cash	0%
Stocks	100%
US Stocks	36%
Bonds	0%
US Bonds	0%
Other	0%

Services Offered:

Investment Strategy: The investment seeks to track the performance of the MSCI ACWI Sustainable Impact Index. The fund generally will invest at least 90% of its assets in the component securities of the underlying index and in investments that have economic characteristics that are substantially identical to the component securities of the underlying index. The index is an index composed of positive impact companies that derive a majority of their revenue from products and services that address at least one of the world's major social and environmental challenges as identified by the United Nations Sustainable Development Goals. **Top Holdings:** Umicore SA Johnson Matthey PLC East Japan Railway Co Procter & Gamble Co Tesla Inc

iShares ESG USD Corporate Bond ETF   C   HOLD

Ticker	Traded On	NAV	Total Assets ($)	Dividend Yield (TTM)	Turnover Ratio	Expense Ratio
SUSC	NAS CM	26.32	$60,534,704	3.18	20	0.18

Ratings
Reward	C
Risk	C-
Recent Upgrade/Downgrade	Up

Fund Information
Fund Type	Exchange Traded Funds
Category	US Fixed Income
Sub-Category	Corporate Bond
Prospectus Objective	Corp Bond - Gen
Inception Date	Jul-17
Open to New Investments	Y

Prices
Price (as of 9/30/2019)	26.29
52-Week High	26.68
52-Week Low	23.63

Total Returns (%)
3-Month	6-Month	1-Year	3-Year	5-Year
3.06	8.14	13.07		

3-Year Standard Deviation	
Effective Duration	

Valuation
Premium/Discount (1-Year Average)	0.32

Company Information
Provider	iShares
Manager/Tenure	James Mauro (2), Scott Radell (2)
Website	http://www.ishares.com
Address	iShares 400 Howard Street San Francisco CA 94105 United States
Phone Number	800-474-2737

PERFORMANCE

Ratings History

Date	Overall Rating	Risk Rating	Reward Rating
Q3-19	C	C-	C
Q4-18	D	D+	D
Q4-17	U		
Q4-16			
Q4-15			

Asset & Performance History

Date	NAV	1-Year Total Return
2018	23.77	-2.78
2017	25.27	
2016		
2015		
2014		
2013		

Total Assets: $60,534,704

Asset Allocation

Asset	%
Cash	1%
Stocks	0%
US Stocks	0%
Bonds	97%
US Bonds	83%
Other	0%

Services Offered:

Investment Strategy: The investment seeks to track the investment results of the Bloomberg Barclays MSCI US Corporate ESG Focus Index. The fund generally will invest at least 90% of its assets in the component securities of the underlying index and may invest up to 10% of its assets in certain futures, options and swap contracts, cash and cash equivalents. The index has been developed by Bloomberg Barclays Capital Inc. with environmental, social and governance ("ESG") rating inputs from MSCI ESG Research LLC ("MSCI ESG Research") pursuant to an agreement between MSCI ESG Research and Bloomberg Index Services Limited, a subsidiary of Bloomberg Barclays. The fund is non-diversified. **Top Holdings:** Compass Bank 2.88% Cummins Inc. 3.65% Orange S.A. 4.13% Baker Hughes a GE company LLC and Baker Hughes Co-Obligor Inc 2.77% Commonwealth Bank Australia New York Branch 2.55%

Cambria Global Asset Allocation ETF   C   HOLD

Ticker	Traded On	NAV	Total Assets ($)	Dividend Yield (TTM)	Turnover Ratio	Expense Ratio
GAA	BATS	26.89	$60,506,179	3.03		0.34

Ratings
Reward   C
Risk   D+
Recent Upgrade/Downgrade

Fund Information
Fund Type	Exchange Traded Funds
Category	Cautious Allocation
Sub-Category	World Allocation
Prospectus Objective	Asset Allocation
Inception Date	Dec-14
Open to New Investments	Y

Prices
Price (as of 9/30/2019)	26.92
52-Week High	27.39
52-Week Low	24.59

Total Returns (%)
3-Month	6-Month	1-Year	3-Year	5-Year
-0.36	2.18	3.42	16.78	

3-Year Standard Deviation	6.28
Effective Duration	7.54

Valuation
Premium/Discount (1-Year Average)	0.01

Company Information
Provider	CAMBRIA ETF TRUST
Manager/Tenure	Mebane T. Faber (4)
Website	http://www.cambriafunds.com
Address	CAMBRIA ETF TRUST 2711 Centreville Road Suite 400 Wilmington, DE 19808 Wilmington DE 19808 United States
Phone Number	310-683-5500

PERFORMANCE

Ratings History	Overall Rating	Risk Rating	Reward Rating
Date			
Q3-19	C	D+	C
Q4-18	D+	D+	D+
Q4-17	B-	B	C
Q4-16	D+	D+	D+
Q4-15	U		

Asset & Performance History		1-Year
Date	NAV	Total Return
2018	24.85	-6.84
2017	27.45	15.21
2016	24.41	8.64
2015	23.11	-3.86
2014	24.63	
2013		

Total Assets: $60,506,179
Asset Allocation
Asset	%
Cash	6%
Stocks	44%
US Stocks	21%
Bonds	48%
US Bonds	29%
Other	2%

Services Offered:

Investment Strategy: The investment seeks income and capital appreciation. Under normal market conditions, the fund invests at least 80% of its total assets in affiliated and unaffiliated exchange-traded funds ("ETFs") and other exchange-traded products ("ETPs") (collectively, "underlying vehicles") that provide exposure to various (i) investment asset classes, including equity and fixed income securities, real estate, commodities, and currencies, and (ii) factors such as value, momentum, and trend investing. **Top Holdings:** Cambria Emerging Shareholder Yield ETF Vanguard Total Bond Market ETF Cambria Sovereign Bond ETF Invesco Optm Yd Dvrs Cdty Stra No K1 ETF Cambria Shareholder Yield ETF

Invesco S&P 100 Equal Weight ETF   C   HOLD

Ticker	Traded On	NAV	Total Assets ($)	Dividend Yield (TTM)	Turnover Ratio	Expense Ratio
EQWL	NYSE Arca	57.16	$60,014,454	2.11		0.25

Ratings
Reward   C+
Risk   D+
Recent Upgrade/Downgrade

Fund Information
Fund Type	Exchange Traded Funds
Category	US Equity Large Cap Blend
Sub-Category	Large Blend
Prospectus Objective	Growth
Inception Date	Dec-06
Open to New Investments	Y

Prices
Price (as of 9/30/2019)	57.16
52-Week High	58.22
52-Week Low	45.99

Total Returns (%)
3-Month	6-Month	1-Year	3-Year	5-Year
0.88	4.21	3.78	45.71	65.42

3-Year Standard Deviation	12.1
Effective Duration	

Valuation
Premium/Discount (1-Year Average)	-0.13

Company Information
Provider	Invesco
Manager/Tenure	Peter Hubbard (12), Michael Jeanette (11), Tony Seisser (5)
Website	http://www.invesco.com/us
Address	Invesco 11 Greenway Plaza, Ste. 2500 Houston TX 77046 United States
Phone Number	800-659-1005

PERFORMANCE

Ratings History	Overall Rating	Risk Rating	Reward Rating
Date			
Q3-19	C	D+	C+
Q4-18	C-	D+	C
Q4-17	B	B-	B
Q4-16	D+	D+	D+
Q4-15	C	D+	C

Asset & Performance History		1-Year
Date	NAV	Total Return
2018	48.74	-5.67
2017	52.77	23.66
2016	43.25	13.78
2015	38.81	-1.76
2014	40.31	14.08
2013	35.98	35.63

Total Assets: $60,014,454
Asset Allocation
Asset	%
Cash	0%
Stocks	100%
US Stocks	100%
Bonds	0%
US Bonds	0%
Other	0%

Services Offered:

Investment Strategy: The investment seeks to track the investment results (before fees and expenses) of the S&P 100® Equal Weight Index. The fund generally will invest at least 90% of its total assets in the securities that comprise the underlying index. Strictly in accordance with its guidelines and mandated procedures, the index provider compiles, maintains and calculates the underlying index, which is an equal-weighted version of the S&P 100® Index. **Top Holdings:** Allergan PLC Target Corp Amgen Inc United Parcel Service Inc Class B Starbucks Corp

Global X MSCI Argentina ETF   C-   HOLD

Ticker	Traded On	NAV	Total Assets ($)	Dividend Yield (TTM)	Turnover Ratio	Expense Ratio
ARGT	NYSE Arca	22.86	$59,998,391	2.44	34	0.59

Ratings

Reward	C
Risk	D
Recent Upgrade/Downgrade	

Fund Information

Fund Type	Exchange Traded Funds
Category	Equity Misc
Sub-Category	Miscellaneous Region
Prospectus Objective	Foreign Stock
Inception Date	Mar-11
Open to New Investments	Y

Prices

Price (as of 9/30/2019)	22.81
52-Week High	33.89
52-Week Low	21.88

Total Returns (%)

3-Month	6-Month	1-Year	3-Year	5-Year
-29.79	-17.52	-12.45	-0.97	15.41

3-Year Standard Deviation	30.36
Effective Duration	

Valuation

Premium/Discount (1-Year Average)	-0.18

Company Information

Provider	Global X Funds
Manager/Tenure	Chang Kim (5), Nam To (1), Wayne Xie (0), 1 other
Website	http://www.globalxfunds.com
Address	Global X Funds 600 Lexington Avenue, 20th Floor New York NY 10022 United States
Phone Number	888-493-8631

PERFORMANCE

Ratings History

Date	Overall Rating	Risk Rating	Reward Rating
Q3-19	C-	D	C
Q4-18	C-	D	C
Q4-17	B+	C+	A+
Q4-16	C	D+	B-
Q4-15	B-	C+	B-

Asset & Performance History

Date	NAV	1-Year Total Return
2018	23.58	-33.38
2017	35.4	53.86
2016	23.12	28.91
2015	18	-3.66
2014	18.85	-2.88
2013	19.5	13.67

Total Assets: $59,998,391

Asset Allocation

Asset	%
Cash	0%
Stocks	100%
US Stocks	9%
Bonds	0%
US Bonds	0%
Other	0%

Services Offered:

Investment Strategy: The investment seeks to provide investment results that correspond generally to the price and yield performance, before fees and expenses, of the MSCI All Argentina 25/50 Index. The fund invests at least 80% of its total assets in the securities of the underlying index and in American Depositary Receipts ("ADRs") and Global Depositary Receipts ("GDRs") based on the securities in the underlying index. The underlying index is designed to represent the performance of the broad Argentina equity universe, while including a minimum number of constituents. The fund is non-diversified. **Top Holdings:** MercadoLibre Inc Tenaris SA Globant SA YPF SA ADR Pan American Silver Corp

SPDR® FactSet Innovative Technology ETF   C   HOLD

Ticker	Traded On	NAV	Total Assets ($)	Dividend Yield (TTM)	Turnover Ratio	Expense Ratio
XITK	NYSE Arca		$59,896,971	0.1	43	0.45

Ratings

Reward	C
Risk	D+
Recent Upgrade/Downgrade	

Fund Information

Fund Type	Exchange Traded Funds
Category	Technology Sector Equity
Sub-Category	Technology
Prospectus Objective	Technology
Inception Date	Jan-16
Open to New Investments	Y

Prices

Price (as of 9/30/2019)	99.83
52-Week High	112.48
52-Week Low	76.98

Total Returns (%)

3-Month	6-Month	1-Year	3-Year	5-Year
-7.32	-6.52	-1.37	65.63	

3-Year Standard Deviation	19.31
Effective Duration	

Valuation

Premium/Discount (1-Year Average)	0.00

Company Information

Provider	SPDR State Street Global Advisors
Manager/Tenure	Michael J. Feehily (3), Karl A. Schneider (3), Michael Finocchi (2)
Website	http://www.spdrs.com
Address	SPDR State Street Global Advisors State Street Financial Center, 1 Lincoln Street Boston MA 02111-2900 United States
Phone Number	617-786-3000

PERFORMANCE

Ratings History

Date	Overall Rating	Risk Rating	Reward Rating
Q3-19	C	D+	C
Q4-18	C-	C-	C
Q4-17	C-	B+	C
Q4-16	D-	D+	D+
Q4-15			

Asset & Performance History

Date	NAV	1-Year Total Return
2018	82.95	8.37
2017	77.78	35.55
2016	58.37	19.97
2015		
2014		
2013		

Total Assets: $59,896,971

Asset Allocation

Asset	%
Cash	0%
Stocks	100%
US Stocks	88%
Bonds	0%
US Bonds	0%
Other	0%

Services Offered:

Investment Strategy: The investment seeks to provide investment results that, before fees and expenses, correspond generally to the total return performance of the FactSet Innovative Technology Index. The index is designed to represent the performance of U.S.-listed stock and American Depository Receipts of Technology companies and Technology-related companies within the most innovative segments of the Technology sector and Electronic Media sub-sector of the Media sector, as defined by FactSet Research Systems, Inc. The fund generally invests substantially all, but at least 80%, of its total assets in the securities comprising the index. It is non-diversified. **Top Holdings:** Roku Inc Class A Shopify Inc A Snap Inc Class A Appian Corp A Alteryx Inc Class A

AdvisorShares DoubleLine Value Equity ETF

C   HOLD

Ticker	Traded On	NAV	Total Assets ($)	Dividend Yield (TTM)	Turnover Ratio	Expense Ratio
DBLV	NYSE Arca	69.73	$59,268,244	1.06		0.9

Ratings
Reward	C+
Risk	C-
Recent Upgrade/Downgrade	Up

Fund Information
Fund Type	Exchange Traded Funds
Category	US Equity Mid Cap
Sub-Category	Mid-Cap Value
Prospectus Objective	Growth
Inception Date	Oct-11
Open to New Investments	Y

Prices
Price (as of 9/30/2019)	69.44
52-Week High	70.92
52-Week Low	56.67

Total Returns (%)
3-Month	6-Month	1-Year	3-Year	5-Year
1.84	5.40	0.70	23.24	42.98

3-Year Standard Deviation	12.82
Effective Duration	

Valuation
Premium/Discount (1-Year Average)	-0.31

Company Information
Provider	AdvisorShares
Manager/Tenure	Emidio Checcone (0), Brian C. Ear (0)
Website	http://www.advisorshares.com
Address	AdvisorShares 2 Bethesda Metro Center, Suite 1330 Bethesda MD 20814 United States
Phone Number	877-843-3831

PERFORMANCE

Ratings History
Date	Overall Rating	Risk Rating	Reward Rating
Q3-19	C	C-	C+
Q4-18	C-	D+	C
Q4-17	B	B	B
Q4-16	C-	D+	C-
Q4-15	C	C	C

Asset & Performance History
Date	NAV	1-Year Total Return
2018	59.26	-15.78
2017	71.25	12.72
2016	63.62	18.94
2015	54.09	-1.49
2014	55.33	14.88
2013	48.45	42.41

Total Assets: $59,268,244

Asset Allocation
Asset	%
Cash	3%
Stocks	97%
US Stocks	83%
Bonds	0%
US Bonds	0%
Other	0%

Services Offered:

Investment Strategy: The investment seeks to generate long-term capital appreciation. The fund is an actively managed exchange-traded fund that seeks to achieve its investment objective by primarily investing in the broad U.S. equity market. It invests in stocks with liquidity and fundamental characteristics that are historically associated with superior long-term performance. The fund invests at least 80% of its net assets (plus any borrowings for investment purposes) in equity securities. **Top Holdings:** American Tower Corp Verizon Communications Inc Chevron Corp Microsoft Corp Philip Morris International Inc

---

Invesco DWA NASDAQ Momentum ETF

C-   HOLD

Ticker	Traded On	NAV	Total Assets ($)	Dividend Yield (TTM)	Turnover Ratio	Expense Ratio
DWAQ	NAS CM	107.69	$59,229,978	0		0.6

Ratings
Reward	C
Risk	D+
Recent Upgrade/Downgrade	

Fund Information
Fund Type	Exchange Traded Funds
Category	US Equity Mid Cap
Sub-Category	Mid-Cap Growth
Prospectus Objective	Growth
Inception Date	May-03
Open to New Investments	Y

Prices
Price (as of 9/30/2019)	107.72
52-Week High	123.33
52-Week Low	80.71

Total Returns (%)
3-Month	6-Month	1-Year	3-Year	5-Year
-9.63	-2.14	-6.15	40.34	65.77

3-Year Standard Deviation	18.89
Effective Duration	

Valuation
Premium/Discount (1-Year Average)	0.12

Company Information
Provider	Invesco
Manager/Tenure	Peter Hubbard (12), Michael Jeanette (11), Tony Seisser (5)
Website	http://www.invesco.com/us
Address	Invesco 11 Greenway Plaza, Ste. 2500 Houston TX 77046 United States
Phone Number	800-659-1005

PERFORMANCE

Ratings History
Date	Overall Rating	Risk Rating	Reward Rating
Q3-19	C-	D+	C
Q4-18	C-	D+	C
Q4-17	B+	C+	A
Q4-16	C	D+	B-
Q4-15	C-	C-	C-

Asset & Performance History
Date	NAV	1-Year Total Return
2018	88.34	-13.46
2017	102.08	30.98
2016	78.01	5.52
2015	74.06	3.81
2014	71.39	3.03
2013	69.29	43.43

Total Assets: $59,229,978

Asset Allocation
Asset	%
Cash	0%
Stocks	100%
US Stocks	98%
Bonds	0%
US Bonds	0%
Other	0%

Services Offered:

Investment Strategy: The investment seeks to track the investment results (before fees and expenses) of the Dorsey Wright® NASDAQ Technical Leaders Index. The fund generally will invest at least 90% of its total assets in the securities that comprise the underlying index. The underlying index is composed of approximately 100 securities from an eligible universe of approximately 1,000 of the largest capitalization companies whose securities are included within the NASDAQ US Benchmark Index, except U.S.-listed American depositary receipts ("ADRs") or foreign securities that trade on The Nasdaq Stock Market. **Top Holdings:** Tandem Diabetes Care Inc NovoCure Ltd Exact Sciences Corp Five9 Inc Intuit Inc

FormulaFolios Tactical Growth ETF

C-   HOLD

Ticker	Traded On	NAV	Total Assets ($)	Dividend Yield (TTM)	Turnover Ratio	Expense Ratio
FFTG	BATS		$59,222,009	1.4	92	1.02

Ratings
Reward	C-
Risk	C-
Recent Upgrade/Downgrade	Up

Fund Information
Fund Type	Exchange Traded Funds
Category	Moderate Allocation
Sub-Category	Tactical Allocation
Prospectus Objective	Growth
Inception Date	Oct-17
Open to New Investments	Y

Prices
Price (as of 9/30/2019)	26.33
52-Week High	27.12
52-Week Low	21.11

Total Returns (%)
3-Month	6-Month	1-Year	3-Year	5-Year
5.31	9.90	7.47		

3-Year Standard Deviation
Effective Duration

Valuation
Premium/Discount (1-Year Average)	0.03

Company Information
Provider	FormulaFolioFunds
Manager/Tenure	Derek Prusa (1), Jason Wenk (1)
Website	
Address	89 Ionia NW, Suite 600 Grand Rapids, MI 49503 United States
Phone Number	

PERFORMANCE

Ratings History
Date	Overall Rating	Risk Rating	Reward Rating
Q3-19	C-	C-	C-
Q4-18	D	D	D
Q4-17	U		
Q4-16			
Q4-15			

Asset & Performance History
Date	NAV	1-Year Total Return
2018	21.99	-12.44
2017	25.53	
2016		
2015		
2014		
2013		

Total Assets: $59,222,009
Asset Allocation
Asset	%
Cash	11%
Stocks	79%
US Stocks	67%
Bonds	1%
US Bonds	1%
Other	0%

Services Offered:

Investment Strategy: The investment seeks long-term total return. The fund is an actively managed exchange traded fund ("ETF") that is a fund of funds. It seeks to achieve its investment objective by investing primarily in foreign and domestic growth-oriented equity securities of any market capitalization, domestic investment grade fixed income securities (bonds) of any maturity or duration, domestic real estate investment trusts ("REITs"), and commodities (gold) securities through unaffiliated ETFs. **Top Holdings:** Vanguard Total Stock Market ETF Invesco DB Gold iShares US Real Estate ETF Vanguard Real Estate ETF VanEck Vectors Gold Miners ETF

WisdomTree Japan Hedged SmallCap Equity Fund

D+   SELL

Ticker	Traded On	NAV	Total Assets ($)	Dividend Yield (TTM)	Turnover Ratio	Expense Ratio
DXJS	NAS CM	39.10	$58,644,736	1.14	38	0.58

Ratings
Reward	D+
Risk	C-
Recent Upgrade/Downgrade	Down

Fund Information
Fund Type	Exchange Traded Funds
Category	Japan Equity
Sub-Category	Japan Stock
Prospectus Objective	Pacific Stock
Inception Date	Jun-13
Open to New Investments	Y

Prices
Price (as of 9/30/2019)	39.35
52-Week High	45.59
52-Week Low	35.05

Total Returns (%)
3-Month	6-Month	1-Year	3-Year	5-Year
1.14	-2.00	-12.38	32.91	48.52

3-Year Standard Deviation	14.41
Effective Duration	

Valuation
Premium/Discount (1-Year Average)	-0.23

Company Information
Provider	WisdomTree
Manager/Tenure	Richard A. Brown (6), Thomas J. Durante (6), Karen Q. Wong (6)
Website	http://www.wisdomtree.com
Address	WisdomTree 245 Park Avenue, 35th floor New York NY 10167 United States
Phone Number	866-909-9473

PERFORMANCE

Ratings History
Date	Overall Rating	Risk Rating	Reward Rating
Q3-19	D+	C-	D+
Q4-18	C-	C-	D+
Q4-17	A-	B	A
Q4-16	C	C-	C
Q4-15	C	C-	C

Asset & Performance History
Date	NAV	1-Year Total Return
2018	37.29	-17.82
2017	46.17	29.46
2016	36.28	6.26
2015	34.6	17.34
2014	30.55	10.71
2013	30.01	

Total Assets: $58,644,736
Asset Allocation
Asset	%
Cash	0%
Stocks	100%
US Stocks	0%
Bonds	0%
US Bonds	0%
Other	0%

Services Offered:

Investment Strategy: The investment seeks to track the price and yield performance, before fees and expenses, of the WisdomTree Japan Hedged SmallCap Equity Index. The fund normally invests at least 80% of its total assets in component securities of the index and investments that have economic characteristics that are substantially identical to the economic characteristics of such component securities. The index is a dividend weighted index designed to provide exposure to Japanese equity markets while at the same time neutralizing exposure to fluctuations of the value of the Japanese yen relative to the U.S. dollar. The fund is non-diversified. **Top Holdings:** HASEKO Corp Matsui Securities Co Ltd Aozora Bank Ltd Mitsubishi Gas Chemical Co Inc Sumitomo Rubber Industries Ltd

WBI BullBear Rising Income 1000 ETF

B   **BUY**

Ticker	Traded On	NAV	Total Assets ($)	Dividend Yield (TTM)	Turnover Ratio	Expense Ratio
WBIE	NYSE Arca	27.19	$58,463,232	0.9	512	1.05

Ratings
Reward	B
Risk	C
Recent Upgrade/Downgrade	Up

Fund Information
Fund Type	Exchange Traded Funds
Category	US Equity Large Cap Growth
Sub-Category	Large Growth
Prospectus Objective	Growth & Inc
Inception Date	Aug-14
Open to New Investments	Y

Prices
Price (as of 9/30/2019)	27.19
52-Week High	28.12
52-Week Low	24.97

Total Returns (%)
3-Month	6-Month	1-Year	3-Year	5-Year
1.19	4.08	-2.18	28.90	16.87

3-Year Standard Deviation	10.79
Effective Duration	

Valuation
Premium/Discount (1-Year Average)	-0.05

Company Information
Provider	WBI Investments
Manager/Tenure	Donald R. Schreiber (5), Steven Van Solkema (0)
Website	http://www.wbishares.com
Address	34 Sycamore Ave Suite 1-E Little Silver NJ 07739 United States
Phone Number	732-842-4920

PERFORMANCE

Ratings History
Date	Overall Rating	Risk Rating	Reward Rating
Q3-19	B	C	B
Q4-18	C	C	C
Q4-17	C+	C+	C
Q4-16	C	C	B
Q4-15	D-	B-	B

Asset & Performance History
Date	NAV	1-Year Total Return
2018	24.99	-2.86
2017	25.97	16.55
2016	22.4	-2.67
2015	23.04	-7.29
2014	25.09	
2013		

Total Assets: $58,463,232
Asset Allocation
Asset	%
Cash	1%
Stocks	99%
US Stocks	99%
Bonds	0%
US Bonds	0%
Other	0%

Services Offered:

Investment Strategy: The investment seeks long-term capital appreciation and the potential for current income, while also seeking to protect principal during unfavorable market conditions. The fund will seek to invest in the equity securities of large capitalization domestic and foreign companies. These securities will be selected on the basis of the Sub-Advisor's proprietary selection process ("Selection Process"). Cash and cash equivalents are some of the investment opportunities evaluated by the Selection Process. It may invest up to 50% of its net assets in the securities of issuers in emerging markets. **Top Holdings:** Tyson Foods Inc Class A Motorola Solutions Inc Northrop Grumman Corp Amgen Inc NextEra Energy Inc

---

American Customer Satisfaction ETF

C   **HOLD**

Ticker	Traded On	NAV	Total Assets ($)	Dividend Yield (TTM)	Turnover Ratio	Expense Ratio
ACSI	BATS	34.12	$57,998,915	1.34	72	0.66

Ratings
Reward	C+
Risk	C-
Recent Upgrade/Downgrade	

Fund Information
Fund Type	Exchange Traded Funds
Category	US Equity Large Cap Blend
Sub-Category	Large Blend
Prospectus Objective	Growth & Inc
Inception Date	Oct-16
Open to New Investments	Y

Prices
Price (as of 9/30/2019)	34.11
52-Week High	34.96
52-Week Low	27.89

Total Returns (%)
3-Month	6-Month	1-Year	3-Year	5-Year
0.95	3.59	2.23	41.97	

3-Year Standard Deviation	
Effective Duration	

Valuation
Premium/Discount (1-Year Average)	-0.04

Company Information
Provider	Exponential ETFs
Manager/Tenure	Charles A. Ragauss (2), Qiao Duan (0)
Website	http://https://exponentialetfs.com/
Address	Exponential ETFs United States
Phone Number	

PERFORMANCE

Ratings History
Date	Overall Rating	Risk Rating	Reward Rating
Q3-19	C	C-	C+
Q4-18	C-	C-	C-
Q4-17	D	A-	D+
Q4-16	U		
Q4-15			

Asset & Performance History
Date	NAV	1-Year Total Return
2018	28.98	-4.41
2017	30.8	15.52
2016	26.98	
2015		
2014		
2013		

Total Assets: $57,998,915
Asset Allocation
Asset	%
Cash	0%
Stocks	100%
US Stocks	100%
Bonds	0%
US Bonds	0%
Other	0%

Services Offered:

Investment Strategy: The investment seeks to track the performance of the American Customer Satisfaction Investable Index. Under normal circumstances, at least 80% of the fund's total assets will be invested in the component securities of the index. Construction of the index begins with over 350 ACSI Companies across 43 industries and 10 economic sectors. The initial universe is then screened to eliminate companies whose stock is not principally listed on a U.S. exchange, whose stock does not meet minimum liquidity requirements, or whose ACSI Score falls below its respective industry average. The remaining companies are included in the index. **Top Holdings:** Apple Inc The Hershey Co Netflix Inc CenterPoint Energy Inc Amazon.com Inc

Nuveen ESG Mid-Cap Value ETF   C   HOLD

Ticker	Traded On	NAV	Total Assets ($)	Dividend Yield (TTM)	Turnover Ratio	Expense Ratio
NUMV	BATS	28.99	$57,971,572	2.1	69	0.4

Ratings
Reward	C
Risk	C-
Recent Upgrade/Downgrade	Up

Fund Information
Fund Type	Exchange Traded Funds
Category	US Equity Mid Cap
Sub-Category	Mid-Cap Value
Prospectus Objective	Growth
Inception Date	Dec-16
Open to New Investments	Y

Prices
Price (as of 9/30/2019)	29.04
52-Week High	29.26
52-Week Low	23.56

Total Returns (%)
3-Month	6-Month	1-Year	3-Year	5-Year
1.31	4.78	5.33		

3-Year Standard Deviation	
Effective Duration	

Valuation
Premium/Discount (1-Year Average)	0.03

Company Information
Provider	Nuveen
Manager/Tenure	Philip James(Jim) Campagna (2), Lei Liao (2)
Website	http://www.nuveen.com
Address	Nuveen Investment Trust John Nuveen & Co. Inc. Chicago IL 60606 United States
Phone Number	312-917-8146

PERFORMANCE

Ratings History
Date	Overall Rating	Risk Rating	Reward Rating
Q3-19	C	C-	C
Q4-18	D+	D+	C-
Q4-17	D	B+	D+
Q4-16			
Q4-15			

Asset & Performance History
Date	NAV	1-Year Total Return
2018	23.91	-13.66
2017	28.09	14.29
2016	24.61	
2015		
2014		
2013		

Total Assets: $57,971,572
Asset Allocation
Asset	%
Cash	5%
Stocks	95%
US Stocks	90%
Bonds	0%
US Bonds	0%
Other	0%

Services Offered:

Investment Strategy: The investment seeks to track the investment results, before fees and expenses, of the TIAA ESG USA Mid-Cap Value Index (the "index"). Under normal market conditions, the fund invests at least 80% of the sum of its net assets and the amount of any borrowings for investment purposes in component securities of the index. The index is comprised of equity securities issued by mid-capitalization companies listed on U.S. exchanges that meet certain environmental, social, and governance ("ESG") criteria. **Top Holdings:** Eversource Energy CMS Energy Corp Arthur J. Gallagher & Co HCP Inc Arch Capital Group Ltd

---

Invesco BRIC ETF   C   HOLD

Ticker	Traded On	NAV	Total Assets ($)	Dividend Yield (TTM)	Turnover Ratio	Expense Ratio
EEB	NYSE Arca	35.07	$57,888,609	2.82		0.64

Ratings
Reward	C
Risk	D+
Recent Upgrade/Downgrade	

Fund Information
Fund Type	Exchange Traded Funds
Category	Global Emerg Mkts Equity
Sub-Category	Diversified Emerging Mkts
Prospectus Objective	Growth
Inception Date	Sep-06
Open to New Investments	Y

Prices
Price (as of 9/30/2019)	35.04
52-Week High	37.82
52-Week Low	31.24

Total Returns (%)
3-Month	6-Month	1-Year	3-Year	5-Year
-7.04	-5.92	2.16	26.74	17.76

3-Year Standard Deviation	15.05
Effective Duration	

Valuation
Premium/Discount (1-Year Average)	-0.03

Company Information
Provider	Invesco
Manager/Tenure	Peter Hubbard (1), Michael Jeanette (1), Tony Seisser (1)
Website	http://www.invesco.com/us
Address	Invesco 11 Greenway Plaza, Ste. 2500 Houston TX 77046 United States
Phone Number	800-659-1005

PERFORMANCE

Ratings History
Date	Overall Rating	Risk Rating	Reward Rating
Q3-19	C	D+	C
Q4-18	C-	D+	C-
Q4-17	B-	C	B
Q4-16	C-	C-	C-
Q4-15	D	D	D

Asset & Performance History
Date	NAV	1-Year Total Return
2018	31.99	-14.35
2017	37.35	31.29
2016	28.84	20.12
2015	24.36	-13.92
2014	28.85	-13.67
2013	34.61	-1.47

Total Assets: $57,888,609
Asset Allocation
Asset	%
Cash	0%
Stocks	100%
US Stocks	0%
Bonds	0%
US Bonds	0%
Other	0%

Services Offered:

Investment Strategy: The investment seeks to track the investment results (before fees and expenses) of the S&P/BNY Mellon BRIC Select DR Index (USD). The fund generally will invest at least 90% of its total assets in the securities that comprise the underlying index. Strictly in accordance with its guidelines and mandated procedures, the index provider compiles, maintains, and calculates the underlying index, which is composed of American depositary receipts ("ADRs") and global depositary receipts ("GDRs") that represent securities of companies domiciled in Brazil, Russia, India and China and, when appropriate, China H-shares. It is non-diversified. **Top Holdings:** Alibaba Group Holding Ltd ADR China Mobile Ltd Gazprom PJSC ADR Itau Unibanco Holding SA ADR Sberbank of Russia PJSC ADR

Invesco Frontier Markets ETF   C-   HOLD

Ticker	Traded On	NAV	Total Assets ($)	Dividend Yield (TTM)	Turnover Ratio	Expense Ratio
FRN	NYSE Arca	13.81	$57,878,227	1.72		0.7

Ratings
Reward   C
Risk   C-
Recent Upgrade/Downgrade

Fund Information
Fund Type   Exchange Traded Funds
Category   Global Emerg Mkts Equity
Sub-Category   Diversified Emerging Mkts
Prospectus Objective   Div Emerg Mkts
Inception Date   Jun-08
Open to New Investments   Y

Prices
Price (as of 9/30/2019)   13.63
52-Week High   14.79
52-Week Low   12.00

Total Returns (%)

3-Month	6-Month	1-Year	3-Year	5-Year
-5.21	-0.36	5.55	27.70	-2.56

3-Year Standard Deviation   12.96
Effective Duration

Valuation
Premium/Discount (1-Year Average)   -0.23

Company Information
Provider   Invesco
Manager/Tenure   Peter Hubbard (1), Michael Jeanette (1), Tony Seisser (1)
Website   http://www.invesco.com/us
Address   Invesco 11 Greenway Plaza, Ste. 2500 Houston TX 77046 United States
Phone Number   800-659-1005

PERFORMANCE

Ratings History

Date	Overall Rating	Risk Rating	Reward Rating
Q3-19	C-	C-	C
Q4-18	C-	D+	C-
Q4-17	C+	C	B-
Q4-16	D+	D	D+
Q4-15	D	D	D

Asset & Performance History

Date	NAV	1-Year Total Return
2018	12.24	-16.06
2017	14.87	33.08
2016	11.61	11.87
2015	10.78	-20.79
2014	13.87	-12.73
2013	16.39	-13.32

Total Assets: $57,878,227

Asset Allocation

Asset	%
Cash	0%
Stocks	100%
US Stocks	7%
Bonds	0%
US Bonds	0%
Other	0%

Services Offered:

Investment Strategy: The investment seeks to track the investment results (before fees and expenses) of the S&P/BNY Mellon New Frontier Index (USD) (the "underlying index"). The fund generally will invest at least 90% of its total assets in the securities that comprise the underlying index. The underlying index is comprised of liquid American depositary receipts ("ADRs") listed on a U.S. exchange, global depositary receipts ("GDRs") traded on the London Stock Exchange, and ordinary share classes of equity securities listed on exchanges in Frontier Market countries that meet certain trading volume and free-float market capitalization criteria. The fund is non-diversified. **Top Holdings:** MercadoLibre Inc   National Bank of Kuwait SAK   Copa Holdings SA Class A   Safaricom PLC   Guaranty Trust Bank PLC

Invesco FTSE International Low Beta Equal Weight ETF   C-   HOLD

Ticker	Traded On	NAV	Total Assets ($)	Dividend Yield (TTM)	Turnover Ratio	Expense Ratio
IDLB	NAS CM	27.47	$57,684,322	3.15	50	0.45

Ratings
Reward   C-
Risk   C-
Recent Upgrade/Downgrade

Fund Information
Fund Type   Exchange Traded Funds
Category   Global Equity Large Cap
Sub-Category   Foreign Large Blend
Prospectus Objective   Growth & Inc
Inception Date   Nov-15
Open to New Investments

Prices
Price (as of 9/30/2019)   27.43
52-Week High   29.45
52-Week Low   25.28

Total Returns (%)

3-Month	6-Month	1-Year	3-Year	5-Year
-1.85	-1.01	-3.77	16.09	

3-Year Standard Deviation   10.32
Effective Duration

Valuation
Premium/Discount (1-Year Average)   -0.35

Company Information
Provider   Invesco
Manager/Tenure   Peter Hubbard (3), Michael Jeanette (3), Tony Seisser (3)
Website   http://www.invesco.com/us
Address   Invesco 11 Greenway Plaza, Ste. 2500 Houston TX 77046 United States
Phone Number   800-659-1005

PERFORMANCE

Ratings History

Date	Overall Rating	Risk Rating	Reward Rating
Q3-19	C-	C-	C-
Q4-18	D+	D+	D+
Q4-17	C	B+	C
Q4-16	D	C-	D
Q4-15			

Asset & Performance History

Date	NAV	1-Year Total Return
2018	25.9	-12.55
2017	30.28	27.2
2016	24.49	0.83
2015	24.6	
2014		
2013		

Total Assets: $57,684,322

Asset Allocation

Asset	%
Cash	0%
Stocks	100%
US Stocks	1%
Bonds	0%
US Bonds	0%
Other	0%

Services Offered:

Investment Strategy: The investment seeks to track the investment results (before fees and expenses) of the FTSE Developed ex-U.S. Low Beta Equal Weight Index (the "underlying index"). The fund generally will invest at least 90% of its total assets in the securities that comprise the underlying index. Strictly in accordance with its guidelines and mandated procedures, the index provider compiles, maintains and calculates the underlying index, which is designed to provide exposure to constituents of the FTSE Developed ex US Index that exhibit low beta characteristics. **Top Holdings:** BANDAI NAMCO Holdings Inc   GrandVision NV   London Stock Exchange Group PLC   Newcrest Mining Ltd   Welcia Holdings Co Ltd

WBI BullBear Value 1000 ETF   C   HOLD

Ticker	Traded On	NAV	Total Assets ($)	Dividend Yield (TTM)	Turnover Ratio	Expense Ratio
WBIF	NYSE Arca	26.82	$57,672,107	1.07	567	1.05

Ratings
Reward	C
Risk	C-
Recent Upgrade/Downgrade	Up

Fund Information
Fund Type	Exchange Traded Funds
Category	US Equity Large Cap Blend
Sub-Category	Large Blend
Prospectus Objective	Growth & Inc
Inception Date	Aug-14
Open to New Investments	Y

Prices
Price (as of 9/30/2019)	26.86
52-Week High	30.79
52-Week Low	26.31

Total Returns (%)
3-Month	6-Month	1-Year	3-Year	5-Year
-1.60	-4.11	-11.87	26.35	15.86

3-Year Standard Deviation	11.34
Effective Duration	

Valuation
Premium/Discount (1-Year Average)	-0.03

Company Information
Provider	WBI Investments
Manager/Tenure	Donald R. Schreiber (5), Steven Van Solkema (0)
Website	http://www.wbishares.com
Address	34 Sycamore Ave Suite 1-E Little Silver NJ 07739 United States
Phone Number	732-842-4920

Ratings History
Date	Overall Rating	Risk Rating	Reward Rating
Q3-19	C	C-	C
Q4-18	C	C-	C
Q4-17	C+	C+	C+
Q4-16	C	C	B
Q4-15	D-	B-	B

Asset & Performance History
Date	NAV	1-Year Total Return
2018	27.35	-4.14
2017	28.82	18.84
2016	24.45	7.51
2015	22.78	-4.66
2014	24.09	
2013		

Total Assets: $57,672,107
Asset Allocation
Asset	%
Cash	1%
Stocks	99%
US Stocks	94%
Bonds	0%
US Bonds	0%
Other	0%

Services Offered:

Investment Strategy: The investment seeks long-term capital appreciation and the potential for current income, while also seeking to protect principal during unfavorable market conditions. The fund will seek to invest in the equity securities of large capitalization domestic and foreign companies. These securities will be selected on the basis of the Sub-Advisor's proprietary selection process ("Selection Process"). Cash and cash equivalents are considered some of the investment opportunities evaluated by Selection Process. It may invest up to 50% of its net assets in the securities of issuers in emerging markets. **Top Holdings:** NXP Semiconductors NV Bristol-Myers Squibb Company Verizon Communications Inc Texas Instruments Inc S&P Global Inc

John Hancock Multifactor Technology ETF   C   HOLD

Ticker	Traded On	NAV	Total Assets ($)	Dividend Yield (TTM)	Turnover Ratio	Expense Ratio
JHMT	NYSE Arca	50.00	$57,496,504	0.95	27	0.4

Ratings
Reward	B-
Risk	C-
Recent Upgrade/Downgrade	

Fund Information
Fund Type	Exchange Traded Funds
Category	Technology Sector Equity
Sub-Category	Technology
Prospectus Objective	Technology
Inception Date	Sep-15
Open to New Investments	Y

Prices
Price (as of 9/30/2019)	50.01
52-Week High	52.66
52-Week Low	36.84

Total Returns (%)
3-Month	6-Month	1-Year	3-Year	5-Year
-0.15	3.58	6.17	68.30	

3-Year Standard Deviation	16.24
Effective Duration	

Valuation
Premium/Discount (1-Year Average)	-0.05

Company Information
Provider	John Hancock
Manager/Tenure	Joel P. Schneider (4), Lukas J. Smart (4), Joseph F. Hohn (1)
Website	http://jhinvestments.com
Address	601 Congress Street, Boston MA 02210 United States
Phone Number	800-225-5913

Ratings History
Date	Overall Rating	Risk Rating	Reward Rating
Q3-19	C	C-	B-
Q4-18	C	D+	C
Q4-17	C	B	B-
Q4-16	D	C-	C
Q4-15			

Asset & Performance History
Date	NAV	1-Year Total Return
2018	39.54	-2.75
2017	41.04	34.52
2016	30.73	16.29
2015	26.8	
2014		
2013		

Total Assets: $57,496,504
Asset Allocation
Asset	%
Cash	3%
Stocks	97%
US Stocks	95%
Bonds	0%
US Bonds	0%
Other	0%

Services Offered:

Investment Strategy: The investment seeks to provide investment results that closely correspond, before fees and expenses, to the performance of the John Hancock Dimensional Technology Index. The fund normally invests at least 80% of its net assets (plus any borrowings for investment purposes) in securities that compose the fund's index. The index is designed to comprise securities in the technology sector within the U.S. Universe whose market capitalizations are larger than that of the 1001st largest U.S. company at the time of reconstitution. The fund is non-diversified. **Top Holdings:** Microsoft Corp Apple Inc Intel Corp Cisco Systems Inc Oracle Corp

Invesco VRDO Tax-Free Weekly ETF

C-   HOLD

Ticker	Traded On	NAV	Total Assets ($)	Dividend Yield (TTM)	Turnover Ratio	Expense Ratio
PVI	NYSE Arca	24.93	$57,338,435	1.24	0	0.25

Ratings

Reward	C
Risk	C-
Recent Upgrade/Downgrade	

Fund Information

Fund Type	Exchange Traded Funds
Category	US Muni Fixed Inc
Sub-Category	Muni National Short
Prospectus Objective	Muni Bond - Natl
Inception Date	Nov-07
Open to New Investments	Y

Prices

Price (as of 9/30/2019)	24.91
52-Week High	24.99
52-Week Low	24.87

Total Returns (%)

3-Month	6-Month	1-Year	3-Year	5-Year
0.25	0.58	1.24	2.74	2.61

3-Year Standard Deviation	0.11
Effective Duration	0.00

Valuation

Premium/Discount (1-Year Average)	-0.06

Company Information

Provider	Invesco
Manager/Tenure	Philip Fang (11), Peter Hubbard (11), Jeffrey W. Kernagis (11), 2 others
Website	http://www.invesco.com/us
Address	Invesco 11 Greenway Plaza, Ste. 2500 Houston TX 77046 United States
Phone Number	800-659-1005

PERFORMANCE

Ratings History

Date	Overall Rating	Risk Rating	Reward Rating
Q3-19	C-	C-	C
Q4-18	C-	D+	C-
Q4-17	C	C+	C-
Q4-16	D+	C-	D+
Q4-15	D+	C-	D

Asset & Performance History

Date	NAV	1-Year Total Return
2018	24.93	1.1
2017	24.94	0.6
2016	24.93	0.17
2015	24.92	-0.15
2014	24.96	-0.11
2013	24.99	-0.01

Total Assets: $57,338,435

Asset Allocation

Asset	%
Cash	5%
Stocks	0%
US Stocks	0%
Bonds	96%
US Bonds	96%
Other	0%

Services Offered:

Investment Strategy: The investment seeks to track the investment results (before fees and expenses) of the Bloomberg U.S. Municipal AMT-Free Weekly VRDO Index (the "underlying index"). The fund generally will invest at least 80% of its total assets in variable rate demand obligation bonds that are exempt from federal income tax with interest rates that reset weekly, which comprise the underlying index, which is comprised of municipal securities issued in the primary market as VRDOs. **Top Holdings:** BAY AREA TOLL AUTH CALIF TOLL BRDG REV 1.12% ARIZONA HEALTH FACS AUTH REV 1.39% CALIFORNIA STATEWIDE CMNTYS DEV AUTH REV 1.25% CLARK CNTY NEV ARPT REV 1.35% FLORIDA KEYS AQUEDUCT AUTH WTR REV 1.35%

Franklin Liberty Senior Loan ETF

D+   SELL

Ticker	Traded On	NAV	Total Assets ($)	Dividend Yield (TTM)	Turnover Ratio	Expense Ratio
FLBL	BATS	24.89	$57,255,122	4.09	11	0.45

Ratings

Reward	C-
Risk	D+
Recent Upgrade/Downgrade	Up

Fund Information

Fund Type	Exchange Traded Funds
Category	US Fixed Income
Sub-Category	Bank Loan
Prospectus Objective	Income
Inception Date	May-18
Open to New Investments	Y

Prices

Price (as of 9/30/2019)	25.00
52-Week High	25.35
52-Week Low	24.26

Total Returns (%)

3-Month	6-Month	1-Year	3-Year	5-Year
1.01	2.20	2.89		

3-Year Standard Deviation	
Effective Duration	

Valuation

Premium/Discount (1-Year Average)	0.27

Company Information

Provider	Franklin Templeton Investments
Manager/Tenure	Justin G. Ma (1), Reema Agarwal (0), Margaret Chiu (0)
Website	http://www.franklintempleton.com
Address	Franklin Templeton Investments One Franklin Parkway, Building 970, 1st Floor San Mateo CA 94403 United States
Phone Number	650-312-2000

PERFORMANCE

Ratings History

Date	Overall Rating	Risk Rating	Reward Rating
Q3-19	D+	D+	C-
Q4-18	U		
Q4-17			
Q4-16			
Q4-15			

Asset & Performance History

Date	NAV	1-Year Total Return
2018	24.19	
2017		
2016		
2015		
2014		
2013		

Total Assets: $57,255,122

Asset Allocation

Asset	%
Cash	9%
Stocks	0%
US Stocks	0%
Bonds	91%
US Bonds	91%
Other	0%

Services Offered:

Investment Strategy: The investment seeks high level of current income; the secondary goal is preservation of capital. Under normal market conditions, the fund invests at least 80% of its net assets in senior loans and investments that provide exposure to senior loans. Senior loans include loans referred to as leveraged loans, bank loans and/or floating rate loans. The fund invests predominantly in income-producing senior floating interest rate corporate loans made to or issued by U.S. companies, non-U.S. entities and U.S. subsidiaries of non-U.S. entities. **Top Holdings:** AMGH HLDG CORP TERM LOAN Davita Inc 2019 Term Loan B ASURION LLC TERM LOAN B 6 COMMSCOPE INC TERM LOAN B MICHAELS STORES INC TERM LOAN

iShares MSCI Ireland ETF   D+   SELL

Ticker	Traded On	NAV		Total Assets ($)	Dividend Yield (TTM)	Turnover Ratio	Expense Ratio
EIRL	NYSE Arca	40.81		$57,134,446	1.65	20	0.47

Ratings
Reward   D+
Risk   D+
Recent Upgrade/Downgrade   Down

Fund Information
Fund Type   Exchange Traded Funds
Category   Equity Misc
Sub-Category   Miscellaneous Region
Prospectus Objective   Europe Stock
Inception Date   May-10
Open to New Investments   Y

Prices
Price (as of 9/30/2019)   40.96
52-Week High   44.70
52-Week Low   36.16

Total Returns (%)

3-Month	6-Month	1-Year	3-Year	5-Year
-2.99	-1.34	-7.35	11.83	29.92

3-Year Standard Deviation   12.32
Effective Duration

Valuation
Premium/Discount (1-Year Average)   0.01

Company Information
Provider   iShares
Manager/Tenure   Diane Hsiung (9), Greg Savage (9), Jennifer Hsui (6), 3 others
Website   http://www.ishares.com
Address   iShares 400 Howard Street San Francisco CA 94105 United States
Phone Number   800-474-2737

PERFORMANCE

Ratings History

Date	Overall Rating	Risk Rating	Reward Rating
Q3-19	D+	D+	D+
Q4-18	D+	D+	D+
Q4-17	B+	B	A-
Q4-16	C	C-	C
Q4-15	C+	C-	B

Asset & Performance History

Date	NAV	1-Year Total Return
2018	37.24	-20.98
2017	47.73	28.57
2016	37.69	-6.95
2015	41.04	19.94
2014	34.82	1.14
2013	35.2	46.75

Total Assets: $57,134,446
Asset Allocation

Asset	%
Cash	0%
Stocks	97%
US Stocks	52%
Bonds	0%
US Bonds	0%
Other	3%

Services Offered:

Investment Strategy: The investment seeks to track the investment results of the MSCI All Ireland Capped Index. The fund generally will invest at least 90% of its assets in the component securities of the underlying index and in investments that have economic characteristics that are substantially identical to the component securities of the underlying index. The index is a free float-adjusted market capitalization-weighted index that aims to reflect the performance of Irish equities securities of companies. The fund is non-diversified. **Top Holdings:** CRH PLC   Kerry Group PLC Class A   Bank of Ireland Group PLC   Smurfit Kappa Group PLC   Flutter Entertainment PLC

Invesco S&P SmallCap Industrials ETF   C   HOLD

Ticker	Traded On	NAV		Total Assets ($)	Dividend Yield (TTM)	Turnover Ratio	Expense Ratio
PSCI	NAS CM	67.20		$57,124,230	0.63		0.29

Ratings
Reward   C
Risk   D+
Recent Upgrade/Downgrade   Up

Fund Information
Fund Type   Exchange Traded Funds
Category   Industrials Sector Equity
Sub-Category   Industrials
Prospectus Objective   Unaligned
Inception Date   Apr-10
Open to New Investments

Prices
Price (as of 9/30/2019)   67.16
52-Week High   71.96
52-Week Low   52.49

Total Returns (%)

3-Month	6-Month	1-Year	3-Year	5-Year
0.68	5.63	-6.01	38.27	71.48

3-Year Standard Deviation   20.68
Effective Duration

Valuation
Premium/Discount (1-Year Average)   -0.11

Company Information
Provider   Invesco
Manager/Tenure   Peter Hubbard (9), Michael Jeanette (9), Tony Seisser (5)
Website   http://www.invesco.com/us
Address   Invesco 11 Greenway Plaza, Ste. 2500 Houston TX 77046 United States
Phone Number   800-659-1005

PERFORMANCE

Ratings History

Date	Overall Rating	Risk Rating	Reward Rating
Q3-19	C	D+	C
Q4-18	C-	D+	C
Q4-17	A-	B	A
Q4-16	C	C-	C
Q4-15	C	C-	C

Asset & Performance History

Date	NAV	1-Year Total Return
2018	56.02	-12.39
2017	64.32	17.08
2016	55.36	29.18
2015	43.2	-5.55
2014	46.19	2.35
2013	45.51	41.41

Total Assets: $57,124,230
Asset Allocation

Asset	%
Cash	0%
Stocks	100%
US Stocks	100%
Bonds	0%
US Bonds	0%
Other	0%

Services Offered:

Investment Strategy: The investment seeks to track the investment results (before fees and expenses) of the S&P SmallCap 600® Capped Industrials Index (the "underlying index"). The fund generally will invest at least 90% of its total assets in the securities of small-capitalization U.S. industrial companies that comprise the underlying index. These companies are principally engaged in the business of providing industrial products and services, including engineering, heavy machinery, construction, electrical equipment, aerospace and defense and general manufacturing. **Top Holdings:** Mercury Systems Inc   FTI Consulting Inc   Aerojet Rocketdyne Holdings Inc   Exponent Inc   John Bean Technologies Corp

Sprott Junior Gold Miners ETF

C- **HOLD**

Ticker	Traded On	NAV	Total Assets ($)	Dividend Yield (TTM)	Turnover Ratio	Expense Ratio
SGDJ	NYSE Arca	30.82	$57,017,053	0	37	0.5

Ratings
Reward	C-
Risk	C-
Recent Upgrade/Downgrade	Up

Fund Information
Fund Type	Exchange Traded Funds
Category	Prec Metals
Sub-Category	Equity Precious Metals
Prospectus Objective	Prec Metals
Inception Date	Mar-15
Open to New Investments	Y

Prices
Price (as of 9/30/2019)	30.64
52-Week High	36.25
52-Week Low	21.48

Total Returns (%)
3-Month	6-Month	1-Year	3-Year	5-Year
3.83	14.76	28.05	-23.57	

3-Year Standard Deviation	27.29
Effective Duration	

Valuation
Premium/Discount (1-Year Average)	-0.30

Company Information
Provider	Sprott
Manager/Tenure	Ryan Mischker (4), Andrew Hicks (3)
Website	http://www.sprottetfs.com
Address	Sprott United States
Phone Number	

PERFORMANCE

Ratings History
Date	Overall Rating	Risk Rating	Reward Rating
Q3-19	C-	C-	C-
Q4-18	D	D	D
Q4-17	C-	C-	C-
Q4-16	D+	D+	C
Q4-15	U		

Asset & Performance History
Date	NAV	1-Year Total Return
2018	24.88	-25.66
2017	33.47	5.52
2016	31.76	67.25
2015	19.37	
2014		
2013		

Total Assets: $57,017,053
Asset Allocation
Asset	%
Cash	0%
Stocks	100%
US Stocks	0%
Bonds	0%
US Bonds	0%
Other	0%

Services Offered:

Investment Strategy: The investment seeks investment results that correspond (before fees and expenses) to the performance of its underlying index, the Solactive Junior Gold Miners Index. The fund will invest at least 90% of its net assets in securities that comprise the underlying index. The underlying index aims to track the performance of "junior" gold companies primarily located in the U.S., Canada and Australia whose common stock, American Depository Receipts ("ADRs") or Global Depository Receipts ("GDRs") are traded on a regulated stock exchange in the form of shares tradeable for foreign investors without any restrictions. It is non-diversified. **Top Holdings:** Centamin PLC   PT Aneka Tambang (Persero) Tbk   Koza Altin Izletmeleri AS   Lundin Gold Inc   Saracen Mineral Holdings Ltd

---

Direxion Daily Aerospace & Defense Bull 3X Shares Direxion Daily Aerospace

C **HOLD**

Ticker	Traded On	NAV	Total Assets ($)	Dividend Yield (TTM)	Turnover Ratio	Expense Ratio
DFEN	NYSE Arca	59.83	$56,837,561	0.58	39	0.98

Ratings
Reward	C+
Risk	C-
Recent Upgrade/Downgrade	Up

Fund Information
Fund Type	Exchange Traded Funds
Category	Trading Tools
Sub-Category	Trading--Leveraged Equity
Prospectus Objective	Unaligned
Inception Date	May-17
Open to New Investments	Y

Prices
Price (as of 9/30/2019)	59.81
52-Week High	64.85
52-Week Low	24.66

Total Returns (%)
3-Month	6-Month	1-Year	3-Year	5-Year
15.81	26.73	-4.05		

3-Year Standard Deviation	
Effective Duration	

Valuation
Premium/Discount (1-Year Average)	-0.01

Company Information
Provider	Direxion Funds
Manager/Tenure	Paul Brigandi (2), Tony Ng (2)
Website	http://www.direxionfunds.com
Address	Direxion Funds 1301 Avenue Of The Americas (6th Avenue) New York NY 10019 United States
Phone Number	646-572-3390

PERFORMANCE

Ratings History
Date	Overall Rating	Risk Rating	Reward Rating
Q3-19	C	C-	C+
Q4-18	C	C	C
Q4-17	U		
Q4-16			
Q4-15			

Asset & Performance History
Date	NAV	1-Year Total Return
2018	29.67	-32.7
2017	44.41	
2016		
2015		
2014		
2013		

Total Assets: $56,837,561
Asset Allocation
Asset	%
Cash	7%
Stocks	93%
US Stocks	93%
Bonds	0%
US Bonds	0%
Other	0%

Services Offered:

Investment Strategy: The investment seeks daily investment results, before fees and expenses, of 300% of the daily performance of the Dow Jones U.S. Select Aerospace & Defense Index. The fund invests at least 80% of its net assets (plus borrowing for investment purposes) in financial instruments, such as swap agreements, and securities of the index, ETFs that track the index and other financial instruments that provide daily leveraged exposure to the index or ETFs that track the index. The index attempts to measure the performance of the aerospace and defense industry of the U.S. equity market. The fund is non-diversified. **Top Holdings:** Dow Jon Us A & D Indx Sw   Boeing Co   United Technologies Corp   Lockheed Martin Corp   Dow Jon Us A & D Indx Sw

---

Franklin Liberty U.S. Low Volatility ETF   C   HOLD

Ticker	Traded On	NAV	Total Assets ($)	Dividend Yield (TTM)	Turnover Ratio	Expense Ratio
FLLV	NYSE Arca	36.59	$56,716,038	1.27	47	0.29

Ratings
Reward   C
Risk   D+
Recent Upgrade/Downgrade

PERFORMANCE

Fund Information
Fund Type	Exchange Traded Funds
Category	US Equity Large Cap Blend
Sub-Category	Large Blend
Prospectus Objective	Growth
Inception Date	Sep-16
Open to New Investments	Y

Prices
Price (as of 9/30/2019)	36.61
52-Week High	37.08
52-Week Low	27.74

Total Returns (%)
3-Month	6-Month	1-Year	3-Year	5-Year
2.41	8.64	13.34	52.71	

3-Year Standard Deviation   10.55
Effective Duration

Valuation
Premium/Discount (1-Year Average)   0.07

Company Information
Provider	Franklin Templeton Investments
Manager/Tenure	Todd Brighton (3)
Website	http://www.franklintempleton.com
Address	Franklin Templeton Investments One Franklin Parkway, Building 970, 1st Floor San Mateo CA 94403 United States
Phone Number	650-312-2000

Ratings History
Date	Overall Rating	Risk Rating	Reward Rating
Q3-19	C	D+	C
Q4-18	C-	D+	C
Q4-17	D	B	C
Q4-16	U		
Q4-15			

Asset & Performance History
Date	NAV	1-Year Total Return
2018	29.34	-0.4
2017	30.24	19.82
2016	25.62	
2015		
2014		
2013		

Total Assets: $56,716,038
Asset Allocation
Asset	%
Cash	1%
Stocks	99%
US Stocks	96%
Bonds	0%
US Bonds	0%
Other	0%

Services Offered:

Investment Strategy: The investment seeks capital appreciation with an emphasis on lower volatility. The fund invests at least 80% of its net assets in U.S. investments. It invests primarily in equity securities (principally common stocks) of U.S. companies. The fund seeks capital appreciation while providing a lower level of volatility than the broader equity market as measured by the Russell 1000 Index. It may invest a portion of its assets in mid-capitalization companies. **Top Holdings:** Fiserv Inc   Texas Instruments Inc   Synopsys Inc   Intuit Inc   Mastercard Inc A

IQ MacKay Shields Municipal Insured ETF   C-   HOLD

Ticker	Traded On	NAV	Total Assets ($)	Dividend Yield (TTM)	Turnover Ratio	Expense Ratio
MMIN	NYSE Arca	26.34	$56,629,730	2.51		0.31

Ratings
Reward   C-
Risk   C-
Recent Upgrade/Downgrade   Up

PERFORMANCE

Fund Information
Fund Type	Exchange Traded Funds
Category	US Muni Fixed Inc
Sub-Category	Muni National Interm
Prospectus Objective	Muni Bond - Natl
Inception Date	Oct-17
Open to New Investments	Y

Prices
Price (as of 9/30/2019)	26.38
52-Week High	26.67
52-Week Low	24.32

Total Returns (%)
3-Month	6-Month	1-Year	3-Year	5-Year
1.79	4.38	9.55		

3-Year Standard Deviation
Effective Duration

Valuation
Premium/Discount (1-Year Average)   0.08

Company Information
Provider	IndexIQ
Manager/Tenure	Robert A. DiMella (1), David M. Dowden (1), John Lawlor (1), 4 others
Website	http://www.indexiq.com
Address	IndexIQ 800 Westchester Avenue, Suite N-611 Rye Brook NY 10573 United States
Phone Number	888-934-0777

Ratings History
Date	Overall Rating	Risk Rating	Reward Rating
Q3-19	C-	C-	C-
Q4-18	D	D	D+
Q4-17	U		
Q4-16			
Q4-15			

Asset & Performance History
Date	NAV	1-Year Total Return
2018	24.97	1.58
2017	25.25	
2016		
2015		
2014		
2013		

Total Assets: $56,629,730
Asset Allocation
Asset	%
Cash	2%
Stocks	0%
US Stocks	0%
Bonds	98%
US Bonds	96%
Other	0%

Services Offered:

Investment Strategy: The investment seeks current income exempt from federal income tax. The fund is an actively managed ETF and thus does not seek to replicate the performance of a specific index. Instead, it uses an active management strategy to meet its investment objective. The fund, under normal circumstances, invests at least 80% of its assets (net assets plus borrowings for investment purposes) in: (i) debt securities whose interest is, in the opinion of bond counsel for the issuer at the time of issuance, exempt from federal income tax ("Municipal Bonds"); and (ii) debt securities covered by an insurance policy guaranteeing the payment of principal and interest. **Top Holdings:** DETROIT MICH SEW DISP REV 5.5%   ABAG FIN AUTH FOR NONPROFIT CORPS CALIF REV 5%   FORT LUPTON COLO WTR SYS REV 5%   ROBERTSON CNTY TEX 4%   DEARBORN MICH SCH DIST 5%

Global X Guru™ Index ETF

C   HOLD

Ticker	Traded On	NAV	Total Assets ($)	Dividend Yield (TTM)	Turnover Ratio	Expense Ratio
GURU	NYSE Arca	33.23	$56,482,703	0.64	113	0.75

Ratings

Reward	C+
Risk	D+
Recent Upgrade/Downgrade	

Fund Information

Fund Type	Exchange Traded Funds
Category	US Equity Large Cap Growth
Sub-Category	Large Growth
Prospectus Objective	Income
Inception Date	Jun-12
Open to New Investments	Y

Prices

Price (as of 9/30/2019)	33.22
52-Week High	34.56
52-Week Low	26.14

Total Returns (%)

3-Month	6-Month	1-Year	3-Year	5-Year
-1.56	2.85	3.07	43.77	33.03

3-Year Standard Deviation	14.44
Effective Duration	

Valuation

Premium/Discount (1-Year Average)	0.06

Company Information

Provider	Global X Funds
Manager/Tenure	Chang Kim (5), Nam To (1), Wayne Xie (0), 1 other
Website	http://www.globalxfunds.com
Address	Global X Funds 600 Lexington Avenue, 20th Floor New York NY 10022 United States
Phone Number	888-493-8631

PERFORMANCE

Ratings History

Date	Overall Rating	Risk Rating	Reward Rating
Q3-19	C	D+	C+
Q4-18	C-	D+	C
Q4-17	C+	C	C+
Q4-16	C-	C-	C-
Q4-15	C	C	C

Asset & Performance History

Date	NAV	1-Year Total Return
2018	27.45	-7.35
2017	29.63	23.8
2016	24.06	3.8
2015	23.23	-10.81
2014	26.17	3.33
2013	25.59	46.98

Total Assets: $56,482,703

Asset Allocation

Asset	%
Cash	0%
Stocks	100%
US Stocks	86%
Bonds	0%
US Bonds	0%
Other	0%

Services Offered:

Investment Strategy: The investment seeks investment results that correspond generally to the price and yield performance, before fees and expenses, of the Solactive Guru Index ("underlying index"). The fund invests at least 80% of its total assets in the securities of the underlying index and in American Depositary Receipts ("ADRs") and Global Depositary Receipts ("GDRs") based on the securities in the underlying index. The underlying index is comprised of the top U.S. listed equity positions reported on Form 13F by a select group of entities characterized as hedge funds. **Top Holdings:** Grupo Televisa SAB ADR Spirit AeroSystems Holdings Inc Class A Vistra Energy Corp XPO Logistics Inc Charter Communications Inc A

First Trust FTSE EPRA/NAREIT Developed Markets Real Estate Index Fund

C   HOLD

Ticker	Traded On	NAV	Total Assets ($)	Dividend Yield (TTM)	Turnover Ratio	Expense Ratio
FFR	NYSE Arca	49.44	$56,435,841	2.89	9	0.6

Ratings

Reward	C
Risk	D+
Recent Upgrade/Downgrade	

Fund Information

Fund Type	Exchange Traded Funds
Category	Real Estate Sector Equity
Sub-Category	Global Real Estate
Prospectus Objective	Real Estate
Inception Date	Aug-07
Open to New Investments	Y

Prices

Price (as of 9/30/2019)	49.58
52-Week High	49.58
52-Week Low	40.92

Total Returns (%)

3-Month	6-Month	1-Year	3-Year	5-Year
4.64	4.37	13.85	18.53	40.71

3-Year Standard Deviation	10.68
Effective Duration	

Valuation

Premium/Discount (1-Year Average)	-0.04

Company Information

Provider	First Trust
Manager/Tenure	Jon C. Erickson (12), Daniel J. Lindquist (12), David G. McGarel (12), 3 others
Website	http://www.ftportfolios.com/
Address	First Trust 120 E. Liberty Drive, Suite 400 Wheaton IL 60187 United States
Phone Number	800-621-1675

PERFORMANCE

Ratings History

Date	Overall Rating	Risk Rating	Reward Rating
Q3-19	C	D+	C
Q4-18	C-	D+	C-
Q4-17	B-	B	C+
Q4-16	C	D+	C
Q4-15	C	D+	C

Asset & Performance History

Date	NAV	1-Year Total Return
2018	41.95	-5.15
2017	45.66	10.6
2016	42.58	4.43
2015	42.45	-0.66
2014	43.49	14.72
2013	39.19	3.01

Total Assets: $56,435,841

Asset Allocation

Asset	%
Cash	0%
Stocks	99%
US Stocks	56%
Bonds	0%
US Bonds	0%
Other	1%

Services Offered:

Investment Strategy: The investment seeks investment results that correspond generally to the price and yield (before the fund's fees and expenses) of an equity index called the FTSE EPRA/NAREIT Developed Index. The fund will normally invest at least 90% of its net assets (including investment borrowings) in the common stocks and depositary receipts that comprise the index. The index is modified market cap weighted based on free float market capitalization and includes the securities of real estate companies or REITs that are publicly traded on an official stock exchange located in North America, Europe or Asia and provides an audited annual report in English. **Top Holdings:** Prologis Inc Simon Property Group Inc Public Storage Welltower Inc Equity Residential

---

Alpha Architect International Quantitative Momentum ETF   D+   SELL

Ticker	Traded On	NAV
IMOM	BATS	25.63

Total Assets ($)	Dividend Yield (TTM)	Turnover Ratio	Expense Ratio
$56,387,979	1.36	119	0.59

Ratings
Reward	D+
Risk	D+
Recent Upgrade/Downgrade	

Fund Information
Fund Type	Exchange Traded Funds
Category	Global Equity Large Cap
Sub-Category	Foreign Large Growth
Prospectus Objective	Growth & Inc
Inception Date	Dec-15
Open to New Investments	Y

Prices
Price (as of 9/30/2019)	25.62
52-Week High	28.77
52-Week Low	22.43

Total Returns (%)
3-Month	6-Month	1-Year	3-Year	5-Year
-2.05	-0.11	-9.15	2.03	

3-Year Standard Deviation	13.7
Effective Duration	

Valuation
Premium/Discount (1-Year Average)	0.03

Company Information
Provider	Alpha Architect
Manager/Tenure	Tao Wang (3)
Website	http://www.alphaarchitect.com/funds
Address	Alpha Architect 213 Foxcroft Road Broomall PA 19008 United States
Phone Number	

PERFORMANCE

Ratings History
Date	Overall Rating	Risk Rating	Reward Rating
Q3-19	D+	D+	D+
Q4-18	D	D	D+
Q4-17	C-	C+	C
Q4-16	D-	D+	D
Q4-15			

Asset & Performance History
Date	NAV	1-Year Total Return
2018	23.31	-22.13
2017	30.14	33.15
2016	22.91	-10.59
2015	25.5	
2014		
2013		

Total Assets: $56,387,979

Asset Allocation
Asset	%
Cash	1%
Stocks	99%
US Stocks	3%
Bonds	0%
US Bonds	0%
Other	0%

Services Offered:

Investment Strategy: The investment seeks to track the total return performance, before fees and expenses, of the Alpha Architect International Quantitative Momentum Index. The fund will normally invest at least 80% of its total assets in the component securities of the index and investments that have economic characteristics that are substantially identical to the economic characteristics of such component securities. The index uses a 5-step, quantitative, rules-based methodology to identify a portfolio of approximately 40-50 non-U.S. equity securities with positive momentum. **Top Holdings:** WiseTech Global Ltd   Beach Energy Ltd   Afterpay Touch Group Ltd   ICA Gruppen AB   Ferrovial SA

Arrow Reserve Capital Management ETF   D+   SELL

Ticker	Traded On	NAV
ARCM	BATS	

Total Assets ($)	Dividend Yield (TTM)	Turnover Ratio	Expense Ratio
$56,152,149	2.39	33	0.42

Ratings
Reward	C
Risk	D
Recent Upgrade/Downgrade	Down

Fund Information
Fund Type	Exchange Traded Funds
Category	US Fixed Income
Sub-Category	Ultrashort Bond
Prospectus Objective	Growth & Inc
Inception Date	Mar-17
Open to New Investments	Y

Prices
Price (as of 9/30/2019)	100.22
52-Week High	100.73
52-Week Low	99.63

Total Returns (%)
3-Month	6-Month	1-Year	3-Year	5-Year
0.50	1.16	2.36		

3-Year Standard Deviation	
Effective Duration	

Valuation
Premium/Discount (1-Year Average)	-0.02

Company Information
Provider	ArrowShares
Manager/Tenure	Joseph Barrato (2), Steven Boyd (2), Adam Cohn (2), 3 others
Website	http://www.ArrowShares.com
Address	c/o Gemini Fund Services, LLC 17605 Wright Street, Suite 2 Omaha NE 68130 United States
Phone Number	877-277-6933

PERFORMANCE

Ratings History
Date	Overall Rating	Risk Rating	Reward Rating
Q3-19	D+	D	C
Q4-18	D	D	D+
Q4-17	U		
Q4-16			
Q4-15			

Asset & Performance History
Date	NAV	1-Year Total Return
2018	99.72	1.57
2017	100.05	
2016		
2015		
2014		
2013		

Total Assets: $56,152,149

Asset Allocation
Asset	%
Cash	30%
Stocks	0%
US Stocks	0%
Bonds	70%
US Bonds	67%
Other	0%

Services Offered:

Investment Strategy: The investment seeks to preserve capital while maximizing current income. The fund invests in a variety of domestic fixed income securities. It will invest in fixed income instruments with a dollar-weighted average effective maturity of 0 to 2 years issued by U.S. Dollar-denominated issuers, including mortgage- or asset-backed securities, rated Baa- or higher by Moody's, or equivalently rated by S&P or Fitch, or, if unrated, determined by the Sub-Advisor. It may also invest in interest rate futures and forwards. The Sub-Advisor attempts to maximize income by identifying securities that offer an acceptable yield for a given level of credit risk and maturity. **Top Holdings:** United States Treasury Notes 2.1% Medtronic, Inc. 3.21% MARTIN MARIETTA MATERIALS INC 2.89% Citigroup Inc. 3.13% General Dynamics Corporation 2.47%

Invesco DB Energy Fund   C-   HOLD

Ticker	Traded On	NAV	Total Assets ($)	Dividend Yield (TTM)	Turnover Ratio	Expense Ratio
DBE	NYSE Arca	13.34	$56,047,815	1.56		0.75

Ratings
Reward   D+
Risk   C-
Recent Upgrade/Downgrade

Fund Information
Fund Type   Exchange Traded Funds
Category   Commodities Specified
Sub-Category   Commodities Energy
Prospectus Objective   Natl Res
Inception Date   Jan-07
Open to New Investments   Y

Prices
Price (as of 9/30/2019)   13.38
52-Week High   18.74
52-Week Low   12.16

Total Returns (%)

3-Month	6-Month	1-Year	3-Year	5-Year
-7.19	-10.49	-26.87	9.16	-49.20

3-Year Standard Deviation   21.17
Effective Duration

Valuation
Premium/Discount (1-Year Average)   -0.15

Company Information
Provider   Invesco
Manager/Tenure   Management Team (12)
Website   http://www.invesco.com/us
Address   Invesco 11 Greenway Plaza, Ste. 2500
   Houston TX 77046 United States
Phone Number   800-659-1005

PERFORMANCE

Ratings History

Date	Overall Rating	Risk Rating	Reward Rating
Q3-19	C-	C-	D+
Q4-18	C	C	C-
Q4-17	C-	D+	C
Q4-16	D	D	D
Q4-15	D-	D-	D-

Asset & Performance History

Date	NAV	1-Year Total Return
2018	12.33	-14.06
2017	14.59	5.08
2016	13.8	25.69
2015	11.15	-34.87
2014	17.13	-41.27
2013	29.16	4.21

Total Assets: $56,047,815

Asset Allocation

Asset	%
Cash	34%
Stocks	0%
US Stocks	0%
Bonds	15%
US Bonds	15%
Other	50%

Services Offered:

Investment Strategy: The investment seeks to track the DBIQ Optimum Yield Energy Index Excess Return™, which is intended to reflect the changes in market value of the energy sector.
The index Commodities consist of Light, Sweet Crude Oil (WTI), Heating Oil, Brent Crude Oil, RBOB Gasoline and Natural Gas. The fund invests in futures contracts in an attempt to track its index. **Top Holdings:** United States Treasury Bills 0% Invesco Treasury Collateral ETF Gasoline Rbob Fut Jan20 Ny Harb Ulsd Fut Jun20 Wti Crude Future Mar20

---

iShares MSCI Austria Capped ETF   D+   SELL

Ticker	Traded On	NAV	Total Assets ($)	Dividend Yield (TTM)	Turnover Ratio	Expense Ratio
EWO	NYSE Arca	19.30	$55,959,580	4.04	19	0.47

Ratings
Reward   D+
Risk   C-
Recent Upgrade/Downgrade   Down

Fund Information
Fund Type   Exchange Traded Funds
Category   Europe Equity Mid/Small Cap
Sub-Category   Miscellaneous Region
Prospectus Objective   Europe Stock
Inception Date   Mar-96
Open to New Investments   Y

Prices
Price (as of 9/30/2019)   19.26
52-Week High   22.99
52-Week Low   17.50

Total Returns (%)

3-Month	6-Month	1-Year	3-Year	5-Year
-3.54	-1.68	-12.54	29.04	36.19

3-Year Standard Deviation   16.59
Effective Duration

Valuation
Premium/Discount (1-Year Average)   -0.22

Company Information
Provider   iShares
Manager/Tenure   Diane Hsiung (11), Greg Savage (11),
   Jennifer Hsui (6), 3 others
Website   http://www.ishares.com
Address   iShares 400 Howard Street San
   Francisco CA 94105 United States
Phone Number   800-474-2737

PERFORMANCE

Ratings History

Date	Overall Rating	Risk Rating	Reward Rating
Q3-19	D+	C-	D+
Q4-18	C-	C-	C-
Q4-17	B+	B-	A+
Q4-16	C-	C-	C-
Q4-15	C-	C-	C-

Asset & Performance History

Date	NAV	1-Year Total Return
2018	18.32	-23.19
2017	24.69	52.53
2016	16.56	7.07
2015	15.8	4.9
2014	15.28	-20.07
2013	19.73	13.24

Total Assets: $55,959,580

Asset Allocation

Asset	%
Cash	2%
Stocks	98%
US Stocks	0%
Bonds	0%
US Bonds	0%
Other	0%

Services Offered: CashInvestment Plan

Investment Strategy: The investment seeks to track the investment results of the MSCI Austria IMI 25/50 Index. The fund generally invests at least 90% of its assets in the securities of its underlying index and in depositary receipts representing securities in the index. The index is a free float-adjusted market capitalization-weighted index with a capping methodology applied to issuer weights so that no single issuer of a component exceeds 25% of the index weight, and all issuers with a weight above 5% do not cumulatively exceed 50% of the index weight. The fund is non-diversified. **Top Holdings:** Erste Group Bank AG. Omv AG Verbund AG voestalpine AG Immofinanz AG

Vanguard U.S. Value Factor ETF ETF Shares

D **SELL**

Ticker	Traded On	NAV	Total Assets ($)	Dividend Yield (TTM)	Turnover Ratio	Expense Ratio
VFVA	BATS	72.19	$55,947,250	2.17	16	0.13

Ratings
Reward	D
Risk	C-
Recent Upgrade/Downgrade	

Fund Information
Fund Type	Exchange Traded Funds
Category	US Equity Mid Cap
Sub-Category	Mid-Cap Value
Prospectus Objective	Growth
Inception Date	Feb-18
Open to New Investments	Y

Prices
Price (as of 9/30/2019)	72.24
52-Week High	80.01
52-Week Low	60.57

Total Returns (%)
3-Month	6-Month	1-Year	3-Year	5-Year
-0.48	-0.97	-7.26		

3-Year Standard Deviation	
Effective Duration	

Valuation
Premium/Discount (1-Year Average)	0.06

Company Information
Provider	Vanguard
Manager/Tenure	Antonio Picca (1)
Website	http://www.vanguard.com
Address	Vanguard 100 Vanguard Boulevard Malvern PA 19355 United States
Phone Number	877-662-7447

PERFORMANCE

Ratings History
Date	Overall Rating	Risk Rating	Reward Rating
Q3-19	D	C-	D
Q4-18	U		
Q4-17			
Q4-16			
Q4-15			

Asset & Performance History
Date	NAV	1-Year Total Return
2018	63.74	
2017		
2016		
2015		
2014		
2013		

Total Assets: $55,947,250

Asset Allocation
Asset	%
Cash	0%
Stocks	100%
US Stocks	97%
Bonds	0%
US Bonds	0%
Other	0%

Services Offered:

Investment Strategy: The investment seeks to provide long-term capital appreciation by investing in stocks with relatively lower share prices relative to fundamental values as determined by the advisor. The fund invests primarily in U.S. common stocks with the potential to generate higher returns relative to the broad U.S. equity market by investing in stocks with relatively lower share prices relative to fundamental values as determined by the advisor. Under normal circumstances, at least 80% of the fund's assets will be invested in securities issued by U.S. companies. **Top Holdings:** Micron Technology Inc Ford Motor Co AT&T Inc Marathon Petroleum Corp Delta Air Lines Inc

---

IQ Real Return ETF

C- **HOLD**

Ticker	Traded On	NAV	Total Assets ($)	Dividend Yield (TTM)	Turnover Ratio	Expense Ratio
CPI	NYSE Arca	27.97	$55,943,677	1.24		0.44

Ratings
Reward	C
Risk	D+
Recent Upgrade/Downgrade	

Fund Information
Fund Type	Exchange Traded Funds
Category	Moderate Allocation
Sub-Category	Tactical Allocation
Prospectus Objective	Growth & Inc
Inception Date	Oct-09
Open to New Investments	Y

Prices
Price (as of 9/30/2019)	27.95
52-Week High	28.16
52-Week Low	26.47

Total Returns (%)
3-Month	6-Month	1-Year	3-Year	5-Year
0.20	1.17	1.06	6.23	8.48

3-Year Standard Deviation	2.9
Effective Duration	

Valuation
Premium/Discount (1-Year Average)	-0.08

Company Information
Provider	IndexIQ
Manager/Tenure	Greg Barrato (8), James Harrison (1)
Website	http://www.indexiq.com
Address	IndexIQ 800 Westchester Avenue, Suite N-611 Rye Brook NY 10573 United States
Phone Number	888-934-0777

PERFORMANCE

Ratings History
Date	Overall Rating	Risk Rating	Reward Rating
Q3-19	C-	D+	C
Q4-18	D+	D+	C-
Q4-17	B-	A	C
Q4-16	C-	D+	C
Q4-15	C-	D+	C

Asset & Performance History
Date	NAV	1-Year Total Return
2018	26.62	-1.78
2017	27.46	3.05
2016	26.93	1.69
2015	26.48	0.01
2014	26.48	2.13
2013	25.95	-1.37

Total Assets: $55,943,677

Asset Allocation
Asset	%
Cash	42%
Stocks	11%
US Stocks	10%
Bonds	42%
US Bonds	36%
Other	3%

Services Offered:

Investment Strategy: The investment seeks investment results that correspond generally to the price and yield performance of its underlying index, the IQ Real Return Index. The fund is a "fund of funds" which means it invests, under normal circumstances, at least 80% of its net assets, plus the amount of any borrowings for investment purposes, in the investments included in its underlying index, which includes underlying funds. The underlying index consists of a number of components ("underlying index components") selected in accordance with the rules-based methodology of such underlying index. **Top Holdings:** PIMCO Enhanced Short Maturity Active ETF iShares Short Treasury Bond ETF SPDR® Blmbg Barclays 1-3 Mth T-Bill ETF SPDR® S&P 500 ETF Invesco DB Oil

FormulaFolios Smart Growth ETF　　　　　　　　　　　　　　　　　　　　　　C-　HOLD

Ticker	Traded On	NAV	Total Assets ($)	Dividend Yield (TTM)	Turnover Ratio	Expense Ratio
FFSG	BATS		$55,732,314	1.58	0	0.7

Ratings
Reward	D+
Risk	C-
Recent Upgrade/Downgrade	Up

Fund Information
Fund Type	Exchange Traded Funds
Category	Aggressive Allocation
Sub-Category	Allocation--85%+ Equity
Prospectus Objective	Growth
Inception Date	Oct-17
Open to New Investments	Y

Prices
Price (as of 9/30/2019)	26.54
52-Week High	26.97
52-Week Low	21.78

Total Returns (%)
3-Month	6-Month	1-Year	3-Year	5-Year
-0.28	1.77	-0.07		

3-Year Standard Deviation	
Effective Duration	

Valuation
Premium/Discount (1-Year Average)	0.06

Company Information
Provider	FormulaFolioFunds
Manager/Tenure	Derek Prusa (1), Jason Wenk (1)
Website	
Address	89 Ionia NW, Suite 600 Grand Rapids, MI 49503 United States
Phone Number	

PERFORMANCE

Ratings History

Date	Overall Rating	Risk Rating	Reward Rating
Q3-19	C-	C-	D+
Q4-18	D	D	D
Q4-17	U		
Q4-16			
Q4-15			

Asset & Performance History

Date	NAV	1-Year Total Return
2018	22.93	-9.29
2017	25.69	
2016		
2015		
2014		
2013		

Total Assets: $55,732,314
Asset Allocation

Asset	%
Cash	1%
Stocks	99%
US Stocks	77%
Bonds	0%
US Bonds	0%
Other	0%

Services Offered:

Investment Strategy: The investment seeks to provide capital growth. The fund seeks to achieve its investment objective by investing through other unaffiliated ETFs primarily in domestic and foreign growth-oriented equity securities of any market capitalization and U.S. Treasuries or other cash equivalents. It is generally 100% invested in growth-oriented equity ETFs when the adviser's investment models indicate a bullish trend for the equity market, and is generally 50% invested in growth-oriented equity ETFs and 50% invested in U.S. treasuries and/or U.S. short-term bonds to hedge risk when the adviser's models indicate a bearish trend for the equity markets. **Top Holdings:** iShares Core S&P 500 ETF iShares Core S&P Mid-Cap ETF iShares Core S&P Small-Cap ETF iShares Core MSCI EAFE ETF iShares US Real Estate ETF

Alpha Architect U.S. Quantitative Momentum ETF　　　　　　　　　　　　　C　HOLD

Ticker	Traded On	NAV	Total Assets ($)	Dividend Yield (TTM)	Turnover Ratio	Expense Ratio
QMOM	BATS	30.02	$55,543,680	0.05	91	0.49

Ratings
Reward	C
Risk	D+
Recent Upgrade/Downgrade	

Fund Information
Fund Type	Exchange Traded Funds
Category	US Equity Mid Cap
Sub-Category	Mid-Cap Growth
Prospectus Objective	Growth & Inc
Inception Date	Dec-15
Open to New Investments	Y

Prices
Price (as of 9/30/2019)	30.02
52-Week High	33.70
52-Week Low	23.31

Total Returns (%)
3-Month	6-Month	1-Year	3-Year	5-Year
-5.24	1.21	-11.01	22.69	

3-Year Standard Deviation	18.04
Effective Duration	

Valuation
Premium/Discount (1-Year Average)	0.00

Company Information
Provider	Alpha Architect
Manager/Tenure	Tao Wang (3)
Website	http://www.alphaarchitect.com/funds
Address	Alpha Architect 213 Foxcroft Road Broomall PA 19008 United States
Phone Number	

PERFORMANCE

Ratings History

Date	Overall Rating	Risk Rating	Reward Rating
Q3-19	C	D+	C
Q4-18	C-	D+	C
Q4-17	C	B	C-
Q4-16	D	C-	C-
Q4-15			

Asset & Performance History

Date	NAV	1-Year Total Return
2018	25.3	-11.03
2017	28.45	15.62
2016	24.64	5.19
2015	23.52	
2014		
2013		

Total Assets: $55,543,680
Asset Allocation

Asset	%
Cash	0%
Stocks	100%
US Stocks	96%
Bonds	0%
US Bonds	0%
Other	0%

Services Offered:

Investment Strategy: The investment seeks to track the total return performance, before fees and expenses, of the Alpha Architect Quantitative Momentum Index. The fund will normally invest at least 80% of its total assets in the component securities of the index. The index uses a 5-step, quantitative, rules-based methodology to identify a portfolio of approximately 40-50 U.S. equity securities with positive momentum, as described below. A "momentum" style of investing emphasizes investing in securities that have had higher recent total return performance compared to other securities. **Top Holdings:** VMware Inc Erie Indemnity Co Class A Danaher Corp Federated Investors Inc Class B Keysight Technologies Inc

FlexShares® High Yield Value-Scored Bond Index Fund   D+   SELL

Ticker	Traded On	NAV	Total Assets ($)	Dividend Yield (TTM)	Turnover Ratio	Expense Ratio
HYGV	NYSE Arca	48.28	$55,518,266	9.42	18	0.37

Ratings
Reward   D+
Risk   C-
Recent Upgrade/Downgrade

Fund Information
Fund Type	Exchange Traded Funds
Category	US Fixed Income
Sub-Category	High Yield Bond
Prospectus Objective	Corp Bond-High Yld
Inception Date	Jul-18
Open to New Investments	Y

Prices
Price (as of 9/30/2019)	48.42
52-Week High	49.91
52-Week Low	44.70

Total Returns (%)
3-Month	6-Month	1-Year	3-Year	5-Year
1.21	3.71	5.41		

3-Year Standard Deviation
Effective Duration   3.28

Valuation
Premium/Discount (1-Year Average)   0.07

Company Information
Provider	Flexshares Trust
Manager/Tenure	Bradley Camden (1), Brandon P. Ferguson (1)
Website	http://www.flexshares.com
Address	50 South LaSalle Street Chicago, Illinois 60603 Chicago Illinois 60603 United States
Phone Number	855-353-9383

PERFORMANCE

Ratings History

Date	Overall Rating	Risk Rating	Reward Rating
Q3-19	D+	C-	D+
Q4-18	U		
Q4-17			
Q4-16			
Q4-15			

Asset & Performance History

Date	NAV	1-Year Total Return
2018	45.49	
2017		
2016		
2015		
2014		
2013		

Total Assets: $55,518,266
Asset Allocation

Asset	%
Cash	0%
Stocks	0%
US Stocks	0%
Bonds	99%
US Bonds	85%
Other	0%

Services Offered:

Investment Strategy: The investment seeks investment results that correspond generally to the price and yield performance, before fees and expenses, of the Northern Trust High Yield Value-Scored US Corporate Bond IndexSM (the underlying index). The fund generally will invest at least 80% of its total assets (exclusive of collateral held from securities lending) in the securities of its underlying index. The underlying index reflects the performance of a broad universe of U.S.-dollar denominated high yield corporate bonds that seeks a higher yield than the overall high yield corporate bond market, as represented by the Northern Trust High Yield US Corporate Bond IndexSM.
Top Holdings: Sprint Capital Corporation 6.88% TransDigm, Inc. 6.38% T-Mobile USA, Inc. 6.5% Financial & Risk US Holdings Inc 8.25% Bausch Health Companies Inc 6.12%

Arrow Dow Jones Global Yield ETF   C-   HOLD

Ticker	Traded On	NAV	Total Assets ($)	Dividend Yield (TTM)	Turnover Ratio	Expense Ratio
GYLD	NYSE Arca		$55,427,470	7.99	69	0.75

Ratings
Reward   C-
Risk   C-
Recent Upgrade/Downgrade   Down

Fund Information
Fund Type	Exchange Traded Funds
Category	Moderate Allocation
Sub-Category	World Allocation
Prospectus Objective	Growth & Inc
Inception Date	May-12
Open to New Investments	Y

Prices
Price (as of 9/30/2019)	15.96
52-Week High	17.43
52-Week Low	14.88

Total Returns (%)
3-Month	6-Month	1-Year	3-Year	5-Year
-0.40	-0.91	-0.88	4.21	-11.37

3-Year Standard Deviation   9.34
Effective Duration

Valuation
Premium/Discount (1-Year Average)   -0.94

Company Information
Provider	ArrowShares
Manager/Tenure	William E. Flaig (7), Joseph Barrato (5), Jonathan S. Guyer (5)
Website	http://www.ArrowShares.com
Address	c/o Gemini Fund Services, LLC 17605 Wright Street, Suite 2 Omaha NE 68130 United States
Phone Number	877-277-6933

PERFORMANCE

Ratings History

Date	Overall Rating	Risk Rating	Reward Rating
Q3-19	C-	C-	C-
Q4-18	D+	C-	D+
Q4-17	C-	C-	C
Q4-16	D+	D+	D
Q4-15	C-	D+	C-

Asset & Performance History

Date	NAV	1-Year Total Return
2018	15.42	-9.35
2017	18.27	5.84
2016	18.44	13.85
2015	17.46	-21.3
2014	24.05	-1.1
2013	26.12	8.03

Total Assets: $55,427,470
Asset Allocation

Asset	%
Cash	0%
Stocks	61%
US Stocks	28%
Bonds	39%
US Bonds	18%
Other	0%

Services Offered:

Investment Strategy: The investment seeks investment results that generally correspond, before fees and expenses, to the price and yield performance of the Dow Jones Global Composite Yield Index (the "underlying index"). The fund uses a "passive" or "indexing" investment approach to seek to track the price and yield performance of the underlying index. It invests at least 80% of its total assets in the component securities of the underlying index (or depositary receipts representing those securities). The underlying index seeks to identify the 150 highest yielding investable securities in the world within three "asset classes." **Top Holdings:** Republic of South Africa 6.25% Republic of Colombia 6.12% Indonesia (Republic of) 3.5% Turkey (Republic of) 6% Chemtrade Logistics Income Fund

First Trust Small Cap Value AlphaDEX® Fund   C-   HOLD

Ticker	Traded On	NAV	Total Assets ($)	Dividend Yield (TTM)	Turnover Ratio	Expense Ratio
FYT	NAS CM	34.58	$55,333,124	1.75	120	0.76

Ratings
Reward   D+
Risk   C-
Recent Upgrade/Downgrade   Up

Fund Information
Fund Type   Exchange Traded Funds
Category   US Equity Small Cap
Sub-Category   Small Value
Prospectus Objective   Small Company
Inception Date   Apr-11
Open to New Investments   Y

Prices
Price (as of 9/30/2019)   34.63
52-Week High   38.38
52-Week Low   29.75

Total Returns (%)

3-Month	6-Month	1-Year	3-Year	5-Year
0.41	-2.30	-8.38	17.12	25.31

3-Year Standard Deviation   20.06
Effective Duration

Valuation
Premium/Discount (1-Year Average)   0.06

Company Information
Provider   First Trust
Manager/Tenure   Jon C. Erickson (8), Daniel J. Lindquist (8), David G. McGarel (8), 3 others
Website   http://www.ftportfolios.com/
Address   First Trust 120 E. Liberty Drive, Suite 400 Wheaton IL 60187 United States
Phone Number   800-621-1675

PERFORMANCE

Ratings History

Date	Overall Rating	Risk Rating	Reward Rating
Q3-19	C-	C-	D+
Q4-18	C-	C-	C-
Q4-17	B-	C+	B-
Q4-16	C	C-	C
Q4-15	C	C-	C

Asset & Performance History

Date	NAV	1-Year Total Return
2018	31.08	-14.53
2017	36.93	7.36
2016	34.82	30.14
2015	27.09	-16.67
2014	32.79	3.75
2013	31.88	43.5

Total Assets: $55,333,124

Asset Allocation

Asset	%
Cash	0%
Stocks	100%
US Stocks	100%
Bonds	0%
US Bonds	0%
Other	0%

Services Offered:

Investment Strategy: The investment seeks investment results that correspond generally to the price and yield (before the fund's fees and expenses) of an equity index called the Nasdaq AlphaDEX® Small Cap Value Index. The fund will normally invest at least 90% of its net assets (including investment borrowings) in common stocks that comprise the index. The index is designed to select value stocks from the NASDAQ US 700 Small Cap Index (the "base index") that may generate positive alpha, or risk-adjusted returns, relative to traditional indices through the use of the AlphaDEX® selection methodology. **Top Holdings:** Meritage Homes Corp   BMC Stock Holdings Inc   Avaya Holdings Corp   Amkor Technology Inc   ACCO Brands Corp

---

Invesco Dynamic Leisure and Entertainment ETF   B-   BUY

Ticker	Traded On	NAV	Total Assets ($)	Dividend Yield (TTM)	Turnover Ratio	Expense Ratio
PEJ	NYSE Arca	42.56	$55,323,979	0.42	207	0.63

Ratings
Reward   B
Risk   C
Recent Upgrade/Downgrade   Up

Fund Information
Fund Type   Exchange Traded Funds
Category   Consumer Goods & Svcs
Sub-Category   Consumer Cyclical
Prospectus Objective   Unaligned
Inception Date   Jun-05
Open to New Investments   Y

Prices
Price (as of 9/30/2019)   42.55
52-Week High   46.42
52-Week Low   38.07

Total Returns (%)

3-Month	6-Month	1-Year	3-Year	5-Year
-2.13	-1.33	-7.99	22.06	34.66

3-Year Standard Deviation   13.41
Effective Duration

Valuation
Premium/Discount (1-Year Average)   0.02

Company Information
Provider   Invesco
Manager/Tenure   Peter Hubbard (12), Michael Jeanette (11), Tony Seisser (5)
Website   http://www.invesco.com/us
Address   Invesco 11 Greenway Plaza, Ste. 2500 Houston TX 77046 United States
Phone Number   800-659-1005

PERFORMANCE

Ratings History

Date	Overall Rating	Risk Rating	Reward Rating
Q3-19	B-	C	B
Q4-18	C+	C-	B
Q4-17	B	B+	B-
Q4-16	C	C	C
Q4-15	B	B-	B+

Asset & Performance History

Date	NAV	1-Year Total Return
2018	39.86	-8.93
2017	44.08	10.88
2016	40.04	9.7
2015	36.77	3.71
2014	35.63	5.13
2013	34.07	49.21

Total Assets: $55,323,979

Asset Allocation

Asset	%
Cash	0%
Stocks	100%
US Stocks	92%
Bonds	0%
US Bonds	0%
Other	0%

Services Offered:

Investment Strategy: The investment seeks to track the investment results (before fees and expenses) of the Dynamic Leisure & Entertainment IntellidexSM Index. The fund generally will invest at least 90% of its total assets in the securities that comprise the underlying intellidex. The underlying intellidex was composed of common stocks of U.S. leisure and entertainment companies. These companies are engaged principally in the design, production or distribution of goods or services in the leisure and entertainment industries. The fund is non-diversified. **Top Holdings:** Starbucks Corp   Chipotle Mexican Grill Inc Class A   Yum Brands Inc   Expedia Group Inc   The Walt Disney Co

Nuveen Short-Term REIT ETF   B-   BUY

Ticker	Traded On	NAV	Total Assets ($)	Dividend Yield (TTM)	Turnover Ratio	Expense Ratio
NURE	BATS	30.73	$55,308,575	3.27	16	0.35

Ratings
Reward	B
Risk	C
Recent Upgrade/Downgrade	Up

Fund Information
Fund Type	Exchange Traded Funds
Category	Real Estate Sector Equity
Sub-Category	Real Estate
Prospectus Objective	Real Estate
Inception Date	Dec-16
Open to New Investments	Y

Prices
Price (as of 9/30/2019)	30.76
52-Week High	30.90
52-Week Low	24.37

Total Returns (%)
3-Month	6-Month	1-Year	3-Year	5-Year
6.78	9.04	18.62		

3-Year Standard Deviation
Effective Duration

Valuation
Premium/Discount (1-Year Average)	0.03

Company Information
Provider	Nuveen
Manager/Tenure	Philip James(Jim) Campagna (2), Lei Liao (2)
Website	http://www.nuveen.com
Address	Nuveen Investment Trust John Nuveen & Co. Inc. Chicago IL 60606 United States
Phone Number	312-917-8146

PERFORMANCE

Ratings History
Date	Overall Rating	Risk Rating	Reward Rating
Q3-19	B-	C	B
Q4-18	B-	C	B
Q4-17	D-	B+	D+
Q4-16			
Q4-15			

Asset & Performance History
Date	NAV	1-Year Total Return
2018	25.05	-2.09
2017	26.35	7.07
2016	25.49	
2015		
2014		
2013		

Total Assets: $55,308,575
Asset Allocation
Asset	%
Cash	8%
Stocks	92%
US Stocks	92%
Bonds	0%
US Bonds	0%
Other	0%

Services Offered:

Investment Strategy: The investment seeks to track the investment results of the Dow Jones U.S. Select Short-Term REIT Index. The fund invests at least 80% of the sum of its net assets and the amount of any borrowings for investment purposes in REITs. The index is a subset of the Dow Jones U.S. Select REIT Index, which generally includes equity REITs traded on a national securities exchange in the U.S. that derive at least 75% of their total revenue from the ownership and operation of real estate assets and that have a minimum total market capitalization of $200 million at the time of their inclusion. It is non-diversified. **Top Holdings:** Invitation Homes Inc Sun Communities Inc Extra Space Storage Inc Equity Lifestyle Properties Inc Public Storage

Invesco DWA Basic Materials Momentum ETF   C-   HOLD

Ticker	Traded On	NAV	Total Assets ($)	Dividend Yield (TTM)	Turnover Ratio	Expense Ratio
PYZ	NAS CM	58.21	$55,296,294	1.4	89	0.6

Ratings
Reward	C
Risk	C-
Recent Upgrade/Downgrade	Up

Fund Information
Fund Type	Exchange Traded Funds
Category	Natural Resources
Sub-Category	Natural Resources
Prospectus Objective	Unaligned
Inception Date	Oct-06
Open to New Investments	Y

Prices
Price (as of 9/30/2019)	58.19
52-Week High	69.15
52-Week Low	50.28

Total Returns (%)
3-Month	6-Month	1-Year	3-Year	5-Year
-3.77	-2.49	-14.29	3.59	14.67

3-Year Standard Deviation	19.28
Effective Duration	

Valuation
Premium/Discount (1-Year Average)	-0.13

Company Information
Provider	Invesco
Manager/Tenure	Peter Hubbard (12), Michael Jeanette (11), Tony Seisser (5)
Website	http://www.invesco.com/us
Address	Invesco 11 Greenway Plaza, Ste. 2500 Houston TX 77046 United States
Phone Number	800-659-1005

PERFORMANCE

Ratings History
Date	Overall Rating	Risk Rating	Reward Rating
Q3-19	C-	C-	C
Q4-18	C	D+	C
Q4-17	B	C	A-
Q4-16	C+	C	B
Q4-15	B	B-	B

Asset & Performance History
Date	NAV	1-Year Total Return
2018	53.48	-23.31
2017	70.46	19.43
2016	59.33	23.33
2015	48.64	-6.1
2014	52.45	3.88
2013	50.99	27.71

Total Assets: $55,296,294
Asset Allocation
Asset	%
Cash	0%
Stocks	100%
US Stocks	100%
Bonds	0%
US Bonds	0%
Other	0%

Services Offered:

Investment Strategy: The investment seeks to track the investment results (before fees and expenses) of the Dorsey Wright® Basic Materials Technical Leaders Index (the "underlying index"). The fund generally will invest at least 90% of its total assets in the securities that comprise the underlying index. The underlying index is composed of at least 30 securities of companies in the basic materials sector that have powerful relative strength or "momentum" characteristics. **Top Holdings:** FMC Corp Ecolab Inc Air Products & Chemicals Inc Ashland Global Holdings Inc Avery Dennison Corp

iShares MSCI Qatar ETF   C-   HOLD

Ticker	Traded On	NAV	Total Assets ($)	Dividend Yield (TTM)	Turnover Ratio	Expense Ratio
QAT	NAS CM	17.82	$55,247,379	4.24	58	0.59

Ratings

Reward	C
Risk	D+
Recent Upgrade/Downgrade	

Fund Information

Fund Type	Exchange Traded Funds
Category	Equity Misc
Sub-Category	Miscellaneous Region
Prospectus Objective	Foreign Stock
Inception Date	Apr-14
Open to New Investments	Y

Prices

Price (as of 9/30/2019)	17.56
52-Week High	19.86
52-Week Low	16.29

Total Returns (%)

3-Month	6-Month	1-Year	3-Year	5-Year
-1.81	-0.31	5.08	4.94	-17.08

3-Year Standard Deviation	17.47
Effective Duration	

Valuation

Premium/Discount (1-Year Average)	-0.45

Company Information

Provider	iShares
Manager/Tenure	Diane Hsiung (5), Jennifer Hsui (5), Greg Savage (5), 3 others
Website	http://www.ishares.com
Address	iShares 400 Howard Street San Francisco CA 94105 United States
Phone Number	800-474-2737

PERFORMANCE

Ratings History

Date	Overall Rating	Risk Rating	Reward Rating
Q3-19	C-	D+	C
Q4-18	C	C-	C
Q4-17	D-	D	D-
Q4-16	D	D	D
Q4-15	D	D	D

Asset & Performance History

Date	NAV	1-Year Total Return
2018	18.59	22.57
2017	15.94	-13.82
2016	19.25	3.66
2015	19.25	-15.37
2014	23.62	
2013		

Total Assets: $55,247,379

Asset Allocation

Asset	%
Cash	0%
Stocks	100%
US Stocks	0%
Bonds	0%
US Bonds	0%
Other	0%

Services Offered:

Investment Strategy: The investment seeks to track the investment results of the MSCI All Qatar Capped Index. The fund will invest at least 90% of its assets in the component securities of the index and in investments that have economic characteristics that are substantially identical to the component securities of the index. The index, which is designed to measure the equity market in Qatar, is a free float-adjusted market capitalization-weighted index with a capping methodology applied to issuer weights. The fund is non-diversified. **Top Holdings:** Qatar National Bank SAQ Industries Qatar QSC Qatar Islamic Bank QPSC Masraf Al Rayan QSC Mesaieed Petrochemical Holding Company QSC

Direxion Daily Homebuilders & Supplies Bull 3X Shares   C   HOLD

Ticker	Traded On	NAV	Total Assets ($)	Dividend Yield (TTM)	Turnover Ratio	Expense Ratio
NAIL	NYSE Arca	64.82	$55,098,111	0.27	38	0.99

Ratings

Reward	C
Risk	D+
Recent Upgrade/Downgrade	Up

Fund Information

Fund Type	Exchange Traded Funds
Category	Trading Tools
Sub-Category	Trading--Leveraged Equity
Prospectus Objective	Unaligned
Inception Date	Aug-15
Open to New Investments	Y

Prices

Price (as of 9/30/2019)	64.88
52-Week High	64.88
52-Week Low	20.86

Total Returns (%)

3-Month	6-Month	1-Year	3-Year	5-Year
38.90	70.85	54.92	152.59	

3-Year Standard Deviation	58.39
Effective Duration	

Valuation

Premium/Discount (1-Year Average)	-0.05

Company Information

Provider	Direxion Funds
Manager/Tenure	Paul Brigandi (4), Tony Ng (4)
Website	http://www.direxionfunds.com
Address	Direxion Funds 1301 Avenue Of The Americas (6th Avenue) New York NY 10019 United States
Phone Number	646-572-3390

PERFORMANCE

Ratings History

Date	Overall Rating	Risk Rating	Reward Rating
Q3-19	C	D+	C
Q4-18	C-	D+	C
Q4-17	C	C	B+
Q4-16	D	D	D
Q4-15	U		

Asset & Performance History

Date	NAV	1-Year Total Return
2018	24.07	-73.87
2017	92.41	266.11
2016	25.29	-10
2015	28.1	
2014		
2013		

Total Assets: $55,098,111

Asset Allocation

Asset	%
Cash	22%
Stocks	78%
US Stocks	78%
Bonds	0%
US Bonds	0%
Other	0%

Services Offered:

Investment Strategy: The investment seeks daily investment results of 300% of the daily performance of the Dow Jones U.S. Select Home Construction Index. The fund invests at least 80% of its net assets in financial instruments and securities of the index, ETFs that track the index and other financial instruments that provide daily leveraged exposure to the index or ETFs that track the index. The index measures U.S. companies in the home construction sector that provide a wide range of products and services related to homebuilding, including home construction and producers, sellers and suppliers of building materials, furnishings and fixtures and etc. It is non-diversified. **Top Holdings:** Dow Jones U.S Select Home D.R. Horton Inc Lennar Corp NVR Inc Dow Jones U.S Select Home

---

Invesco China Small Cap ETF
D+ **SELL**

Ticker	Traded On	NAV	Total Assets ($)	Dividend Yield (TTM)	Turnover Ratio	Expense Ratio
HAO	NYSE Arca	23.85	$54,858,909	5.01		0.75

Ratings
Reward	D+
Risk	C-
Recent Upgrade/Downgrade	Down

Fund Information
Fund Type	Exchange Traded Funds
Category	Greater China Equity
Sub-Category	China Region
Prospectus Objective	Pacific Stock
Inception Date	Jan-08
Open to New Investments	Y

Prices
Price (as of 9/30/2019)	23.70
52-Week High	27.79
52-Week Low	21.99

Total Returns (%)
3-Month	6-Month	1-Year	3-Year	5-Year
-7.30	-11.37	-6.16	9.41	9.85

3-Year Standard Deviation	17.25
Effective Duration	

Valuation
Premium/Discount (1-Year Average)	-0.25

Company Information
Provider	Invesco
Manager/Tenure	Peter Hubbard (1), Michael Jeanette (1), Tony Seisser (1)
Website	http://www.invesco.com/us
Address	Invesco 11 Greenway Plaza, Ste. 2500 Houston TX 77046 United States
Phone Number	800-659-1005

PERFORMANCE

Ratings History

Date	Overall Rating	Risk Rating	Reward Rating
Q3-19	D+	C-	D+
Q4-18	D+	D+	D+
Q4-17	B	C	B+
Q4-16	C-	C-	C-
Q4-15	C	C+	C

Asset & Performance History

Date	NAV	1-Year Total Return
2018	22.32	-25.07
2017	29.79	37.36
2016	22.61	-5.28
2015	24.42	-2.01
2014	25.88	0.38
2013	26.38	15.01

Total Assets: $54,858,909

Asset Allocation

Asset	%
Cash	0%
Stocks	100%
US Stocks	0%
Bonds	0%
US Bonds	0%
Other	0%

Services Offered:

Investment Strategy: The investment seeks to track the investment results (before fees and expenses) of the AlphaShares China Small Cap Index (the "underlying index"). The fund generally will invest at least 90% of its total assets in the securities (including American depositary receipts ("ADRs") and global depositary receipts ("GDRs")) that comprise the underlying index. The underlying index is comprised of equity securities of publicly-traded mainland China companies of small capitalization. The fund is non-diversified. **Top Holdings:** Li Ning Co Ltd GDS Holdings Ltd ADR Tsingtao Brewery Co Ltd Class H Yihai International Holdings Ltd Genscript Biotech Corp Class H

First Trust Dorsey Wright People's Portfolio ETF
C **HOLD**

Ticker	Traded On	NAV	Total Assets ($)	Dividend Yield (TTM)	Turnover Ratio	Expense Ratio
DWPP	NAS CM	31.09	$54,410,983	1.26	32	0.6

Ratings
Reward	C
Risk	C-
Recent Upgrade/Downgrade	

Fund Information
Fund Type	Exchange Traded Funds
Category	Long/Short Equity
Sub-Category	Long-Short Equity
Prospectus Objective	Growth & Inc
Inception Date	Aug-12
Open to New Investments	Y

Prices
Price (as of 9/30/2019)	31.08
52-Week High	31.82
52-Week Low	24.51

Total Returns (%)
3-Month	6-Month	1-Year	3-Year	5-Year
0.01	3.80	3.65	36.46	41.40

3-Year Standard Deviation	12.59
Effective Duration	

Valuation
Premium/Discount (1-Year Average)	0.01

Company Information
Provider	First Trust
Manager/Tenure	Jon C. Erickson (7), Daniel J. Lindquist (7), David G. McGarel (7), 3 others
Website	http://www.ftportfolios.com/
Address	First Trust 120 E. Liberty Drive, Suite 400 Wheaton IL 60187 United States
Phone Number	800-621-1675

PERFORMANCE

Ratings History

Date	Overall Rating	Risk Rating	Reward Rating
Q3-19	C	C-	C
Q4-18	C-	D+	C-
Q4-17	B-	B-	C+
Q4-16	D+	D	C
Q4-15	C-	D	C

Asset & Performance History

Date	NAV	1-Year Total Return
2018	25.96	-8.27
2017	28.64	21.76
2016	23.79	0.49
2015	24.07	-5.89
2014	25.97	15.21
2013	22.86	19

Total Assets: $54,410,983

Asset Allocation

Asset	%
Cash	0%
Stocks	100%
US Stocks	99%
Bonds	0%
US Bonds	0%
Other	0%

Services Offered:

Investment Strategy: The investment seeks results that correspond generally to an index called the Nasdaq Dorsey Wright People's Portfolio Index. The fund will normally invest at least 80% of its total assets (including investment borrowings) in the common stocks or U.S. Treasury Bills ("T-Bills") that comprise the index. The index is a modified market-capitalization weighted index designed to tactically allocate exposure to one of three indices: (i) Nasdaq US 500 Large Cap Index; (ii) Nasdaq US 500 Large Cap Equal Weight Index; or (iii) Nasdaq US T-Bill Index (each, an "underlying index"), based on daily relative strength readings. **Top Holdings:** Western Digital Corp Micron Technology Inc KLA Corp Altice USA Inc Class A Target Corp

Nuveen ESG Emerging Markets Equity ETF   D+   SELL

Ticker	Traded On	NAV	Total Assets ($)	Dividend Yield (TTM)	Turnover Ratio	Expense Ratio
NUEM	BATS	24.67	$54,274,514	1.98	65	0.45

Ratings
Reward	D+
Risk	D+
Recent Upgrade/Downgrade	Up

Fund Information
Fund Type	Exchange Traded Funds
Category	Global Emerg Mkts Equity
Sub-Category	Diversified Emerging Mkts
Prospectus Objective	Div Emerg Mkts
Inception Date	Jun-17
Open to New Investments	Y

Prices
Price (as of 9/30/2019)	24.90
52-Week High	27.10
52-Week Low	23.23

Total Returns (%)
3-Month	6-Month	1-Year	3-Year	5-Year
-5.98	-6.32	-3.51		

3-Year Standard Deviation	
Effective Duration	

Valuation
Premium/Discount (1-Year Average)	0.77

Company Information
Provider	Nuveen
Manager/Tenure	Philip James(Jim) Campagna (2), Lei Liao (2)
Website	http://www.nuveen.com
Address	Nuveen Investment Trust John Nuveen & Co. Inc. Chicago IL 60606 United States
Phone Number	312-917-8146

PERFORMANCE

Ratings History
Date	Overall Rating	Risk Rating	Reward Rating
Q3-19	D+	D+	D+
Q4-18	D	D	D
Q4-17	U		
Q4-16			
Q4-15			

Asset & Performance History
Date	NAV	1-Year Total Return
2018	23.8	-18.43
2017	29.18	
2016		
2015		
2014		
2013		

Total Assets: $54,274,514
Asset Allocation
Asset	%
Cash	0%
Stocks	100%
US Stocks	1%
Bonds	0%
US Bonds	0%
Other	0%

Services Offered:

Investment Strategy: The investment seeks to track the investment results, before fees and expenses, of the TIAA ESG Emerging Markets Equity Index (the "index"). In seeking to track the investment results of the index, the advisor attempts to replicate the index by investing all, or substantially all, of its assets in the securities represented in the index in approximately the same proportions as the index. The index identifies equity securities from the base index that satisfy certain ESG criteria, based on ESG performance data collected by MSCI ESG Research, Inc. **Top Holdings:** Tencent Holdings Ltd Alibaba Group Holding Ltd ADR Taiwan Semiconductor Manufacturing Co Ltd Naspers Ltd Class N Itau Unibanco Holding SA Participating Preferred

---

VanEck Vectors Israel ETF   C   HOLD

Ticker	Traded On	NAV	Total Assets ($)	Dividend Yield (TTM)	Turnover Ratio	Expense Ratio
ISRA	NYSE Arca	32.85	$54,196,038	0.63	23	0.6

Ratings
Reward	C
Risk	D+
Recent Upgrade/Downgrade	

Fund Information
Fund Type	Exchange Traded Funds
Category	Equity Misc
Sub-Category	Miscellaneous Region
Prospectus Objective	Growth
Inception Date	Jun-13
Open to New Investments	Y

Prices
Price (as of 9/30/2019)	32.89
52-Week High	33.90
52-Week Low	26.75

Total Returns (%)
3-Month	6-Month	1-Year	3-Year	5-Year
1.01	3.13	0.05	22.29	15.51

3-Year Standard Deviation	14.2
Effective Duration	

Valuation
Premium/Discount (1-Year Average)	0.06

Company Information
Provider	VanEck
Manager/Tenure	Hao-Hung (Peter) Liao (6), Guo Hua (Jason) Jin (1)
Website	http://www.vaneck.com
Address	Van Eck Associates Corporation 666 Third Avenue New York NY 10017 United States
Phone Number	800-826-1115

PERFORMANCE

Ratings History
Date	Overall Rating	Risk Rating	Reward Rating
Q3-19	C	D+	C
Q4-18	C-	D+	C
Q4-17	C	C	C
Q4-16	D+	D+	D+
Q4-15	C-	C-	C-

Asset & Performance History
Date	NAV	1-Year Total Return
2018	28.05	-6.96
2017	30.37	14.94
2016	26.84	-5.29
2015	28.8	-1.29
2014	29.56	0.84
2013	30.04	

Total Assets: $54,196,038
Asset Allocation
Asset	%
Cash	0%
Stocks	100%
US Stocks	36%
Bonds	0%
US Bonds	0%
Other	0%

Services Offered: Automatic Investment Plan, Retirement Investment

Investment Strategy: The investment seeks to replicate as closely as possible, before fees and expenses, the price and yield performance of the BlueStar Israel Global Index®. The fund normally invests at least 80% of its total assets in securities that comprise the fund's benchmark index. The index is comprised of equity securities, which may include depositary receipts, of publicly traded companies that are generally considered by BlueStar Global Investors, LLC to be Israeli companies. It may also utilize depositary receipts to seek performance that corresponds to the fund's benchmark index. The fund is non-diversified. **Top Holdings:** Check Point Software Technologies Ltd Bank Leumi Le-Israel BM NICE Ltd Amdocs Ltd Bank Hapoalim BM

Invesco S&P 500 Value with Momentum ETF　　　　　　　　　　　C　HOLD

Ticker	Traded On	NAV	Total Assets ($)	Dividend Yield (TTM)	Turnover Ratio	Expense Ratio
SPVM	NYSE Arca	40.10	$54,130,294	2.57		0.39

Ratings
Reward	C
Risk	D+
Recent Upgrade/Downgrade	

Fund Information
Fund Type	Exchange Traded Funds
Category	US Equity Large Cap Value
Sub-Category	Large Value
Prospectus Objective	Growth
Inception Date	Jun-11
Open to New Investments	Y

Prices
Price (as of 9/30/2019)	40.09
52-Week High	41.21
52-Week Low	32.62

Total Returns (%)
3-Month	6-Month	1-Year	3-Year	5-Year
-0.39	4.46	5.30	37.37	53.88

3-Year Standard Deviation	12.93
Effective Duration	

Valuation
Premium/Discount (1-Year Average)	0.08

Company Information
Provider	Invesco
Manager/Tenure	Peter Hubbard (8), Michael Jeanette (8), Tony Seisser (5)
Website	http://www.invesco.com/us
Address	Invesco 11 Greenway Plaza, Ste. 2500 Houston TX 77046 United States
Phone Number	800-659-1005

PERFORMANCE

Ratings History
Date	Overall Rating	Risk Rating	Reward Rating
Q3-19	C	D+	C
Q4-18	C	C-	C
Q4-17	B	B	B
Q4-16	C+	D+	B
Q4-15	C	C	C+

Asset & Performance History
Date	NAV	1-Year Total Return
2018	34.19	-8.59
2017	38.49	13.98
2016	34.36	23.88
2015	28.58	-5.19
2014	30.95	10.46
2013	28.58	33

Total Assets: $54,130,294
Asset Allocation
Asset	%
Cash	0%
Stocks	100%
US Stocks	99%
Bonds	0%
US Bonds	0%
Other	0%

Services Offered:

Investment Strategy: The investment seeks to track the investment results (before fees and expenses) of the S&P 500® High Momentum Value Index (the "underlying index"). The fund generally will invest at least 90% of its total assets in the securities that comprise the underlying index. Strictly in accordance with its guidelines and mandated procedures, the index provider compiles, maintains and calculates the underlying index, which is designed to track the performance of approximately 100 stocks in the S&P 500® Index that have the highest "value" and "momentum" scores. **Top Holdings:** General Motors Co　The Kroger Co　Archer-Daniels Midland Co　Kohl's Corp Capital One Financial Corp

---

iPath® Pure Beta Broad Commodity ETN　　　　　　　　　　　D+　SELL

Ticker	Traded On	NAV	Total Assets ($)	Dividend Yield (TTM)	Turnover Ratio	Expense Ratio
BCM	NYSE Arca		$53,735,748	0		0.6

Ratings
Reward	D+
Risk	D+
Recent Upgrade/Downgrade	

Fund Information
Fund Type	Exchange Traded Funds
Category	Commodities Broad Basket
Sub-Category	Commodities Broad Basket
Prospectus Objective	Natl Res
Inception Date	Apr-11
Open to New Investments	Y

Prices
Price (as of 9/30/2019)	27.21
52-Week High	30.49
52-Week Low	25.68

Total Returns (%)
3-Month	6-Month	1-Year	3-Year	5-Year
-0.67	-2.46	-8.26	3.91	-24.88

3-Year Standard Deviation	9.8
Effective Duration	

Valuation
Premium/Discount (1-Year Average)	-0.10

Company Information
Provider	Milleis Investissements Funds
Manager/Tenure	Management Team (8)
Website	
Address	2-4, rue Eugène Ruppert L-2453 Luxembourg Luxembourg L-2453 Luxembourg
Phone Number	

PERFORMANCE

Ratings History
Date	Overall Rating	Risk Rating	Reward Rating
Q3-19	D+	D+	D+
Q4-18	D+	D+	C-
Q4-17	C-	D+	C
Q4-16	D	D	D
Q4-15	D-	D	D-

Asset & Performance History
Date	NAV	1-Year Total Return
2018	25.78	-11.92
2017	29.27	6.75
2016	27.26	15.62
2015	23.65	-25.71
2014	31.83	-19.38
2013	39.49	-9.97

Total Assets: $53,735,748
Asset Allocation
Asset	%
Cash	%
Stocks	%
US Stocks	%
Bonds	%
US Bonds	%
Other	%

Services Offered:

Investment Strategy: The investment seeks to provide investors with exposure to the Barclays Commodity Index Pure Beta Total Return.
The Barclays Commodity Index Pure Beta Total Return (the "index") is comprised of a basket of exchange traded futures contracts and reflects the returns that are potentially available through an unleveraged investment in the futures contracts on certain physical commodities. For each commodity, the index may roll into one of a number of futures contracts with varying expiration dates, as selected using the Barclays Pure Beta Series 2 Methodology.
Top Holdings:

SPDR® S&P Telecom ETF

C   HOLD

Ticker	Traded On	NAV	Total Assets ($)	Dividend Yield (TTM)	Turnover Ratio	Expense Ratio
XTL	NYSE Arca		$53,679,864	1.01	35	0.35

Ratings

Reward	C+
Risk	C-
Recent Upgrade/Downgrade	Up

Fund Information

Fund Type	Exchange Traded Funds
Category	Communications Sector Equity
Sub-Category	Communications
Prospectus Objective	Comm
Inception Date	Jan-11
Open to New Investments	Y

Prices

Price (as of 9/30/2019)	67.13
52-Week High	75.71
52-Week Low	58.72

Total Returns (%)

3-Month	6-Month	1-Year	3-Year	5-Year
-2.00	-6.38	-9.90	6.89	30.76

3-Year Standard Deviation	15.15
Effective Duration	

Valuation

Premium/Discount (1-Year Average)	-0.05

Company Information

Provider	SPDR State Street Global Advisors
Manager/Tenure	Michael J. Feehily (7), Karl A. Schneider (4), Michael Finocchi (2)
Website	http://www.spdrs.com
Address	SPDR State Street Global Advisors State Street Financial Center, 1 Lincoln Street Boston MA 02111-2900 United States
Phone Number	617-786-3000

PERFORMANCE

Ratings History

Date	Overall Rating	Risk Rating	Reward Rating
Q3-19	C	C-	C+
Q4-18	C	C-	C
Q4-17	C+	B-	C
Q4-16	C	D+	C
Q4-15	C	C	C

Asset & Performance History

Date	NAV	1-Year Total Return
2018	63.08	-6.03
2017	68.26	0.44
2016	69.35	25.49
2015	55.95	-1.68
2014	57.69	4.57
2013	55.74	23.21

Total Assets: $53,679,864

Asset Allocation

Asset	%
Cash	-3%
Stocks	103%
US Stocks	103%
Bonds	0%
US Bonds	0%
Other	0%

Services Offered:

Investment Strategy: The investment seeks to provide investment results that, before fees and expenses, correspond generally to the total return performance of an index derived from the telecommunications segment of a U.S. total market composite index. In seeking to track the performance of the S&P Telecom Select Industry Index (the "index"), the fund employs a sampling strategy. It generally invests substantially all, but at least 80%, of its total assets in the securities comprising the index. The index represents the telecommunications segment of the S&P Total Market Index ("S&P TMI"). The fund is non-diversified. **Top Holdings:** Acacia Communications Inc Infinera Corp Lumentum Holdings Inc Vonage Holdings Corp Motorola Solutions Inc

Etho Climate Leadership U.S. ETF

C   HOLD

Ticker	Traded On	NAV	Total Assets ($)	Dividend Yield (TTM)	Turnover Ratio	Expense Ratio
ETHO	NYSE Arca	39.58	$53,430,639	0.84	19	0.45

Ratings

Reward	C+
Risk	D+
Recent Upgrade/Downgrade	

Fund Information

Fund Type	Exchange Traded Funds
Category	US Equity Mid Cap
Sub-Category	Mid-Cap Growth
Prospectus Objective	Growth & Inc
Inception Date	Nov-15
Open to New Investments	Y

Prices

Price (as of 9/30/2019)	39.58
52-Week High	40.20
52-Week Low	30.11

Total Returns (%)

3-Month	6-Month	1-Year	3-Year	5-Year
0.65	5.59	6.86	51.23	

3-Year Standard Deviation	13.7
Effective Duration	

Valuation

Premium/Discount (1-Year Average)	0.03

Company Information

Provider	ETFMG
Manager/Tenure	Samuel R. Masucci (1), Devin Ryder (1), Donal Bishnoi (0), 1 other
Website	http://www.etfmg.com
Address	ETFMG 30 Maple Street, Suite 2 NJ United States
Phone Number	

PERFORMANCE

Ratings History

Date	Overall Rating	Risk Rating	Reward Rating
Q3-19	C	D+	C+
Q4-18	C-	D+	C-
Q4-17	C	B+	C
Q4-16	D	D+	D+
Q4-15			

Asset & Performance History

Date	NAV	1-Year Total Return
2018	32.04	-4.51
2017	33.84	24.54
2016	27.63	12.67
2015	24.6	
2014		
2013		

Total Assets: $53,430,639

Asset Allocation

Asset	%
Cash	1%
Stocks	99%
US Stocks	98%
Bonds	0%
US Bonds	0%
Other	0%

Services Offered:

Investment Strategy: The investment seeks to provide investment results that, before fees and expenses, correspond generally to the total return performance of the Etho Climate Leadership Index - US (the "index"). The index tracks the performance of the equity securities of a diversified set of U.S. companies that are leaders in their industry with respect to their carbon impact. "Carbon impact" calculated based on the total greenhouse gas ("GHG") emissions from a company's operations, fuel use, supply chain, and business activities, divided by the company's market capitalization. The fund will invest at least 80% of its total assets in the component securities of the index. **Top Holdings:** SunPower Corp Cypress Semiconductor Corp Itron Inc DexCom Inc TopBuild Corp

Cohen & Steers Global Realty Majors ETF   C   HOLD

Ticker	Traded On	NAV	Total Assets ($)	Dividend Yield (TTM)	Turnover Ratio	Expense Ratio
GRI	NYSE Arca	48.57	$53,424,618	2.88	14	0.55

Ratings
Reward   C+
Risk   D+
Recent Upgrade/Downgrade

Fund Information
Fund Type   Exchange Traded Funds
Category   Real Estate Sector Equity
Sub-Category   Global Real Estate
Prospectus Objective   Real Estate
Inception Date   May-08
Open to New Investments   Y

Prices
Price (as of 9/30/2019)   48.59
52-Week High   48.83
52-Week Low   40.34

Total Returns (%)

3-Month	6-Month	1-Year	3-Year	5-Year
3.48	3.34	15.08	19.11	40.34

3-Year Standard Deviation   10.62
Effective Duration

Valuation
Premium/Discount (1-Year Average)   -0.15

Company Information
Provider   ALPS
Manager/Tenure   Ryan Mischker (4), Andrew Hicks (3)
Website   http://www.alpsfunds.com
Address   ALPS 1290 Broadway, Suite 1100
                         Denver CO 80203 United States
Phone Number   866-759-5679

PERFORMANCE

Ratings History

Date	Overall Rating	Risk Rating	Reward Rating
Q3-19	C	D+	C+
Q4-18	C-	D+	C
Q4-17	B-	B	C+
Q4-16	C	D+	C
Q4-15	C	D+	C

Asset & Performance History

Date	NAV	1-Year Total Return
2018	41.48	-4.84
2017	44.91	11.08
2016	41.94	0.01
2015	42.68	1.11
2014	43.65	14.81
2013	39.17	1.35

Total Assets: $53,424,618
Asset Allocation

Asset	%
Cash	0%
Stocks	100%
US Stocks	59%
Bonds	0%
US Bonds	0%
Other	0%

Services Offered:

Investment Strategy: The investment seeks investment results that correspond generally to the performance, before the fund's fees and expenses, of an index called the Cohen & Steers Global Realty Majors Index. The fund will normally invest at least 90% of its total assets in common stocks and other equity securities (which may include ADRs, ADSs and GDRs) that comprise the underlying index. The underlying index consists of the largest and most liquid securities within the global real estate universe that the index provider believes are likely to lead the global securitization of real estate. **Top Holdings:** American Tower Corp   Equinix Inc   Prologis Inc   Public Storage   Simon Property Group Inc

---

WBI BullBear Quality 1000 ETF   B-   BUY

Ticker	Traded On	NAV	Total Assets ($)	Dividend Yield (TTM)	Turnover Ratio	Expense Ratio
WBIL	NYSE Arca	26.69	$53,388,923	0.66	477	1.07

Ratings
Reward   B
Risk   C
Recent Upgrade/Downgrade   Up

Fund Information
Fund Type   Exchange Traded Funds
Category   US Equity Large Cap Blend
Sub-Category   Large Blend
Prospectus Objective   Growth & Inc
Inception Date   Aug-14
Open to New Investments   Y

Prices
Price (as of 9/30/2019)   26.68
52-Week High   28.27
52-Week Low   24.58

Total Returns (%)

3-Month	6-Month	1-Year	3-Year	5-Year
-2.31	0.95	-5.07	27.81	12.09

3-Year Standard Deviation   11.51
Effective Duration

Valuation
Premium/Discount (1-Year Average)   -0.06

Company Information
Provider   WBI Investments
Manager/Tenure   Donald R. Schreiber (5), Steven Van
                 Solkema (0)
Website   http://www.wbishares.com
Address   34 Sycamore Ave Suite 1-E Little
                         Silver NJ 07739 United States
Phone Number   732-842-4920

PERFORMANCE

Ratings History

Date	Overall Rating	Risk Rating	Reward Rating
Q3-19	B-	C	B
Q4-18	C	C-	C
Q4-17	C+	C+	C+
Q4-16	C	C	B
Q4-15	D-	B-	B

Asset & Performance History

Date	NAV	1-Year Total Return
2018	24.63	-9.39
2017	27.41	19
2016	23.24	4.05
2015	22.42	-7.14
2014	24.19	
2013		

Total Assets: $53,388,923
Asset Allocation

Asset	%
Cash	1%
Stocks	99%
US Stocks	99%
Bonds	0%
US Bonds	0%
Other	0%

Services Offered:

Investment Strategy: The investment seeks long-term capital appreciation and the potential for current income, while also seeking to protect principal during unfavorable market conditions. The fund will seek to invest in the equity securities of large capitalization domestic and foreign companies that WBI Investments, Inc., the sub-advisor ("Sub-Advisor") to the fund and an affiliate of Millington Securities Inc., the advisor ("Advisor"), believes display an attractive financial condition and prospects for ongoing financial stability, and in other tactical investment opportunities. It may invest up to 50% of its net assets in the securities of issuers in emerging markets. **Top Holdings:** Target Corp   Texas Instruments Inc   PayPal Holdings Inc   Hormel Foods Corp   S&P Global Inc

Direxion Daily Technology Bear 3X Shares   D-   SELL

Ticker	Traded On	NAV	Total Assets ($)	Dividend Yield (TTM)	Turnover Ratio	Expense Ratio
TECS	NYSE Arca	10.86	$53,224,998	1.74	0	1.1

Ratings
Reward   E+
Risk   D-
Recent Upgrade/Downgrade

Fund Information
Fund Type   Exchange Traded Funds
Category   Trading Tools
Sub-Category   Trading--Inverse Equity
Prospectus Objective   Technology
Inception Date   Dec-08
Open to New Investments   Y

Prices
Price (as of 9/30/2019)   10.85
52-Week High   35.20
52-Week Low   10.52

PERFORMANCE

Total Returns (%)

3-Month	6-Month	1-Year	3-Year	5-Year
-9.39	-29.05	-39.04	-88.32	-96.06

3-Year Standard Deviation   42.05
Effective Duration

Valuation
Premium/Discount (1-Year Average)   0.07

Company Information
Provider   Direxion Funds
Manager/Tenure   Paul Brigandi (10), Tony Ng (4)
Website   http://www.direxionfunds.com
Address   Direxion Funds 1301 Avenue Of The
                  Americas (6th Avenue) New York NY
                  10019 United States
Phone Number   646-572-3390

Ratings History

Date	Overall Rating	Risk Rating	Reward Rating
Q3-19	D-	D-	E+
Q4-18	D-	D-	E+
Q4-17	E+	E+	E
Q4-16	D-	E+	E+
Q4-15	D-	E+	E+

Asset & Performance History

Date	NAV	1-Year Total Return
2018	27.69	-19.51
2017	34.6	-60.7
2016	88.05	-43.35
2015	155.45	-31.39
2014	226.6	-45.89
2013	418.8	-55.11

Total Assets: $53,224,998

Asset Allocation

Asset	%
Cash	116%
Stocks	-16%
US Stocks	-16%
Bonds	0%
US Bonds	0%
Other	0%

Services Offered:

Investment Strategy: The investment seeks daily investment results, before fees and expenses, of 300% of the inverse (or opposite) of the daily performance of the Technology Select Sector Index. The fund, under normal circumstances, invests in swap agreements, futures contracts, short positions or other financial instruments that, in combination, provide inverse (opposite) or short leveraged exposure to the index equal to at least 80% of the fund's net assets (plus borrowing for investment purposes). The index is provided by S&P Dow Jones Indices (the "index provider") and includes domestic companies from the technology sector. It is non-diversified. **Top Holdings:** Technology Select Sector Technology Select Sector Technology Select Sector Technology Select Sector Goldman Fini Sq Trsry Ins

PIMCO Broad U.S. TIPS Index Exchange-Traded Fund   C   HOLD

Ticker	Traded On	NAV	Total Assets ($)	Dividend Yield (TTM)	Turnover Ratio	Expense Ratio
TIPZ	NYSE Arca	60.02	$52,819,155	1.23	9	0.21

Ratings
Reward   C+
Risk   D+
Recent Upgrade/Downgrade

Fund Information
Fund Type   Exchange Traded Funds
Category   US Fixed Income
Sub-Category   Inflation-Protected Bond
Prospectus Objective   Govt Bond - Treasury
Inception Date   Sep-09
Open to New Investments   Y

Prices
Price (as of 9/30/2019)   60.04
52-Week High   61.03
52-Week Low   55.39

PERFORMANCE

Total Returns (%)

3-Month	6-Month	1-Year	3-Year	5-Year
1.82	4.99	7.78	6.48	11.79

3-Year Standard Deviation   3.53
Effective Duration   7.96

Valuation
Premium/Discount (1-Year Average)   0.02

Company Information
Provider   PIMCO
Manager/Tenure   Matthew P. Dorsten (3), Mitchell
                  Handa (0), Graham A. Rennison (0)
Website   http://www.pimco.com
Address   PIMCO 840 Newport Center Drive,
                  Suite 100 Newport Beach CA 92660
                  United States
Phone Number   866-746-2602

Ratings History

Date	Overall Rating	Risk Rating	Reward Rating
Q3-19	C	D+	C+
Q4-18	D+	D+	D
Q4-17	C	B-	C
Q4-16	C-	C-	C
Q4-15	D+	C-	D+

Asset & Performance History

Date	NAV	1-Year Total Return
2018	55.96	-1.72
2017	58.31	3.22
2016	57.46	4.61
2015	55.36	-2.12
2014	56.87	4.37
2013	55.07	-9.41

Total Assets: $52,819,155

Asset Allocation

Asset	%
Cash	1%
Stocks	0%
US Stocks	0%
Bonds	99%
US Bonds	99%
Other	0%

Services Offered:

Investment Strategy: The investment seeks to provide total return that closely corresponds, before fees and expenses, to the total return of the ICE BofAML US Inflation-Linked Treasury Index. The fund invests at least 80% of its total assets (exclusive of collateral held from securities lending) in the component securities of the ICE BofAML US Inflation-Linked Treasury Index (the "underlying index"). The underlying index is an unmanaged index comprised of Treasury Inflation-Protected Securities ("TIPS"). **Top Holdings:** United States Treasury Notes 0.62% United States Treasury Bonds 1.75% United States Treasury Bonds 2.38% United States Treasury Notes 0.12% United States Treasury Bonds 2.5%

Invesco Multi-Factor Core Plus fixed Income ETF   D   SELL

Ticker	Traded On	NAV	Total Assets ($)	Dividend Yield (TTM)	Turnover Ratio	Expense Ratio
IMFP	NYSE Arca	26.40	$52,803,814	3.63		0.16

Ratings
Reward   D+
Risk   D
Recent Upgrade/Downgrade

Fund Information
Fund Type	Exchange Traded Funds
Category	US Fixed Income
Sub-Category	Intermediate Core-Plus Bond
Prospectus Objective	Multisector Bond
Inception Date	Jul-18
Open to New Investments	Y

Prices
Price (as of 9/30/2019)	26.48
52-Week High	26.66
52-Week Low	24.70

Total Returns (%)
3-Month	6-Month	1-Year	3-Year	5-Year
2.17	5.33	9.87		

3-Year Standard Deviation
Effective Duration   4.60

Valuation
Premium/Discount (1-Year Average)   0.11

Company Information
Provider	Invesco
Manager/Tenure	Peter Hubbard (1), Jeffrey W. Kernagis (1), Greg Meisenger (1), 2 others
Website	http://www.invesco.com/us
Address	Invesco 11 Greenway Plaza, Ste. 2500 Houston TX 77046 United States
Phone Number	800-659-1005

PERFORMANCE

15.0%
10.0%
5.0%
0.0%
-5.0%
   11/5/18   2/15/19   6/17/19   9/30/19

Ratings History

Date	Overall Rating	Risk Rating	Reward Rating
Q3-19	D	D	D+
Q4-18	U		
Q4-17			
Q4-16			
Q4-15			

Asset & Performance History

Date	NAV	1-Year Total Return
2018	24.9	
2017		
2016		
2015		
2014		
2013		

Total Assets: $52,803,814
Asset Allocation

Asset	%
Cash	0%
Stocks	0%
US Stocks	0%
Bonds	100%
US Bonds	89%
Other	0%

Services Offered:

Investment Strategy: The investment seeks to track the investment results (before fees and expenses) of the Invesco Multi-Factor Core Plus Index (the "underlying index"). The fund generally will invest at least 80% of its total assets in securities that comprise the underlying index. The underlying index is designed to provide multi-factor exposure to fixed income securities. The fund is non-diversified. **Top Holdings:** Fnma Pass-Thru I 4.5% Federal National Mortgage Association 4% Federal National Mortgage Association 3.5% Federal National Mortgage Association 4% Federal National Mortgage Association 4%

ProShares UltraShort 7-10 Year Treasury   D   SELL

Ticker	Traded On	NAV	Total Assets ($)	Dividend Yield (TTM)	Turnover Ratio	Expense Ratio
PST	NYSE Arca	18.50	$52,737,167	1.86	0	0.95

Ratings
Reward   D
Risk   D
Recent Upgrade/Downgrade   Down

Fund Information
Fund Type	Exchange Traded Funds
Category	Trading Tools
Sub-Category	Trading--Inverse Debt
Prospectus Objective	Govt Bond - Treasury
Inception Date	Apr-08
Open to New Investments	Y

Prices
Price (as of 9/30/2019)	18.49
52-Week High	23.88
52-Week Low	17.97

Total Returns (%)
3-Month	6-Month	1-Year	3-Year	5-Year
-4.83	-11.40	-19.54	-6.30	-27.75

3-Year Standard Deviation   10.32
Effective Duration

Valuation
Premium/Discount (1-Year Average)   -0.14

Company Information
Provider	ProShares
Manager/Tenure	Michelle Liu (11), Alexander V. Ilyasov (0)
Website	http://www.proshares.com
Address	ProShares 7501 Wisconsin Avenue, Suite 1000 Bethesda MD 20814 United States
Phone Number	866-776-5125

PERFORMANCE

20.0%
10.0%
0.0%
-10.0%
-20.0%
  12/31/17   4/10/18   7/21/18   11/3/18   2/14/19   6/17/19   9/30/19

Ratings History

Date	Overall Rating	Risk Rating	Reward Rating
Q3-19	D	D	D
Q4-18	C	C-	C-
Q4-17	D+	C-	D+
Q4-16	D	D	D
Q4-15	D+	D+	D

Asset & Performance History

Date	NAV	1-Year Total Return
2018	21.84	1.85
2017	21.58	-4.13
2016	22.51	-3.43
2015	23.31	-6
2014	24.8	-17.93
2013	30.22	10.05

Total Assets: $52,737,167
Asset Allocation

Asset	%
Cash	200%
Stocks	0%
US Stocks	0%
Bonds	6%
US Bonds	6%
Other	-106%

Services Offered:

Investment Strategy: The investment seeks daily investment results that correspond to two times the inverse (-2x) of the daily performance of the ICE U.S. Treasury 7-10 Year Bond Index. The fund invests in financial instruments that ProShare Advisors believes, in combination, should produce daily returns consistent with the fund's investment objective. The index includes publicly-issued U.S. Treasury securities that have a remaining maturity of greater than or equal to seven years and less than or equal to ten years and have $300 million or more of outstanding face value, excluding amounts held by the Federal Reserve. The fund is non-diversified. **Top Holdings:** Ice 7-10 Year U.S. Treasury Index Swap Societe Generale United States Treasury Bills United States Treasury Bills United States Treasury Bills United States Treasury Bills

VanEck Vectors Africa Index ETF

D   SELL

Ticker	Traded On	NAV		Total Assets ($)	Dividend Yield (TTM)	Turnover Ratio	Expense Ratio
AFK	NYSE Arca	20.26		$52,674,834	1.66	23	0.78

Ratings

Reward	D
Risk	D+
Recent Upgrade/Downgrade	Down

Fund Information

Fund Type	Exchange Traded Funds
Category	Equity Misc
Sub-Category	Miscellaneous Region
Prospectus Objective	Growth
Inception Date	Jul-08
Open to New Investments	Y

Prices

Price (as of 9/30/2019)	19.95
52-Week High	22.55
52-Week Low	19.22

Total Returns (%)

3-Month	6-Month	1-Year	3-Year	5-Year
-8.86	-7.90	-4.99	3.84	-27.54

3-Year Standard Deviation	14.73
Effective Duration	

Valuation

Premium/Discount (1-Year Average)	-0.82

Company Information

Provider	VanEck
Manager/Tenure	Hao-Hung (Peter) Liao (11), Guo Hua (Jason) Jin (1)
Website	http://www.vaneck.com
Address	Van Eck Associates Corporation 666 Third Avenue New York NY 10017 United States
Phone Number	800-826-1115

PERFORMANCE

Ratings History

Date	Overall Rating	Risk Rating	Reward Rating
Q3-19	D	D+	D
Q4-18	D+	D	D+
Q4-17	C	C	C
Q4-16	D	D	D
Q4-15	D	D	D

Asset & Performance History

Date	NAV	1-Year Total Return
2018	20.08	-17.22
2017	24.81	26.06
2016	20.09	13.97
2015	18.11	-29.38
2014	26.2	-12.79
2013	30.93	3.28

Total Assets: $52,674,834

Asset Allocation

Asset	%
Cash	0%
Stocks	100%
US Stocks	0%
Bonds	0%
US Bonds	0%
Other	0%

Services Offered: Automatic Investment Plan, Retirement Investment

Investment Strategy: The investment seeks to replicate as closely as possible, before fees and expenses, the price and yield performance of the MVIS® GDP Africa Index. The fund normally invests at least 80% of its total assets in securities that comprise the fund's benchmark index. The index includes local listings of companies that are incorporated in Africa and listings of companies incorporated outside of Africa but that have at least 50% of their revenues/related assets in Africa. **Top Holdings:** Naspers Ltd Class N Safaricom PLC Attijariwafa Bank SA Guaranty Trust Bank PLC Commercial International Bank (Egypt) SAE GDR

Direxion Daily MSCI Real Estate Bull 3X Shares

C   HOLD

Ticker	Traded On	NAV		Total Assets ($)	Dividend Yield (TTM)	Turnover Ratio	Expense Ratio
DRN	NYSE Arca	30.09		$52,650,534	1.63	149	1.04

Ratings

Reward	C
Risk	C-
Recent Upgrade/Downgrade	

Fund Information

Fund Type	Exchange Traded Funds
Category	Trading Tools
Sub-Category	Trading--Leveraged Equity
Prospectus Objective	Real Estate
Inception Date	Jul-09
Open to New Investments	Y

Prices

Price (as of 9/30/2019)	30.09
52-Week High	30.45
52-Week Low	15.11

Total Returns (%)

3-Month	6-Month	1-Year	3-Year	5-Year
19.94	19.23	45.11	30.49	134.47

3-Year Standard Deviation	39.54
Effective Duration	

Valuation

Premium/Discount (1-Year Average)	0.00

Company Information

Provider	Direxion Funds
Manager/Tenure	Paul Brigandi (10), Tony Ng (4)
Website	http://www.direxionfunds.com
Address	Direxion Funds 1301 Avenue Of The Americas (6th Avenue) New York NY 10019 United States
Phone Number	646-572-3390

PERFORMANCE

Ratings History

Date	Overall Rating	Risk Rating	Reward Rating
Q3-19	C	C-	C
Q4-18	C-	C-	C-
Q4-17	C+	C-	B
Q4-16	C	D+	C
Q4-15	C	D+	C

Asset & Performance History

Date	NAV	1-Year Total Return
2018	16.67	-25.02
2017	22.84	7.71
2016	21.4	13.31
2015	18.89	-4.34
2014	19.74	108.41
2013	9.47	-2.35

Total Assets: $52,650,534

Asset Allocation

Asset	%
Cash	29%
Stocks	71%
US Stocks	71%
Bonds	0%
US Bonds	0%
Other	0%

Services Offered:

Investment Strategy: The investment seeks daily investment results of 300% of the daily performance of the MSCI US IMI Real Estate 25/50 Index. The fund invests at least 80% of its net assets (plus borrowing for investment purposes) in financial instruments, such as swap agreements, and securities of the index, ETFs that track the index and other financial instruments that provide daily leveraged exposure to the index or ETFs that track the index. The index is designed to measure the performance of the large-, mid- and small-capitalization segments of the U.S. equity universe that are classified in the real estate sector as per the GICS. It is non-diversified. **Top Holdings:** Simon Property Group Inc Prologis Inc Equinix Inc Msci Us Reit Index Swap Public Storage

---

Nuveen ESG Mid-Cap Growth ETF   C   HOLD

Ticker	Traded On	NAV	Total Assets ($)	Dividend Yield (TTM)	Turnover Ratio	Expense Ratio
NUMG	BATS	32.69	$52,308,913	0.17	60	0.4

Ratings
Reward	C+
Risk	D+
Recent Upgrade/Downgrade	

Fund Information
Fund Type	Exchange Traded Funds
Category	US Equity Mid Cap
Sub-Category	Mid-Cap Growth
Prospectus Objective	Growth
Inception Date	Dec-16
Open to New Investments	Y

Prices
Price (as of 9/30/2019)	32.73
52-Week High	34.60
52-Week Low	25.46

Total Returns (%)
3-Month	6-Month	1-Year	3-Year	5-Year
-3.69	2.98	1.02		

3-Year Standard Deviation

Effective Duration

Valuation
Premium/Discount (1-Year Average)	0.10

Company Information
Provider	Nuveen
Manager/Tenure	Philip James(Jim) Campagna (2), Lei Liao (2)
Website	http://www.nuveen.com
Address	Nuveen Investment Trust John Nuveen & Co. Inc. Chicago IL 60606 United States
Phone Number	312-917-8146

PERFORMANCE

Ratings History
Date	Overall Rating	Risk Rating	Reward Rating
Q3-19	C	D+	C+
Q4-18	D+	D+	C-
Q4-17	D	B+	D+
Q4-16			
Q4-15			

Asset & Performance History
Date	NAV	1-Year Total Return
2018	26.3	-5.4
2017	29.19	19.5
2016	24.53	
2015		
2014		
2013		

Total Assets: $52,308,913

Asset Allocation
Asset	%
Cash	0%
Stocks	100%
US Stocks	98%
Bonds	0%
US Bonds	0%
Other	0%

Services Offered:

Investment Strategy: The investment seeks to track the investment results, before fees and expenses, of the TIAA ESG USA Mid-Cap Growth Index (the "index"). Under normal market conditions, the fund invests at least 80% of the sum of its net assets and the amount of any borrowings for investment purposes in component securities of the index. The index is comprised of equity securities issued by mid-capitalization companies listed on U.S. exchanges that meet certain environmental, social, and governance ("ESG") criteria. **Top Holdings:** SBA Communications Corp Ball Corp IDEXX Laboratories Inc Cintas Corp ResMed Inc

First Trust Mid Cap Value AlphaDEX® Fund   D+   SELL

Ticker	Traded On	NAV	Total Assets ($)	Dividend Yield (TTM)	Turnover Ratio	Expense Ratio
FNK	NAS CM	33.55	$52,003,039	1.81	113	0.7

Ratings
Reward	C-
Risk	D+
Recent Upgrade/Downgrade	

Fund Information
Fund Type	Exchange Traded Funds
Category	US Equity Small Cap
Sub-Category	Small Value
Prospectus Objective	Growth
Inception Date	Apr-11
Open to New Investments	Y

Prices
Price (as of 9/30/2019)	33.62
52-Week High	36.67
52-Week Low	29.15

Total Returns (%)
3-Month	6-Month	1-Year	3-Year	5-Year
-2.62	-3.45	-6.39	18.45	23.69

3-Year Standard Deviation   17.7

Effective Duration

Valuation
Premium/Discount (1-Year Average)	0.03

Company Information
Provider	First Trust
Manager/Tenure	Jon C. Erickson (8), Daniel J. Lindquist (8), David G. McGarel (8), 3 others
Website	http://www.ftportfolios.com/
Address	First Trust 120 E. Liberty Drive, Suite 400 Wheaton IL 60187 United States
Phone Number	800-621-1675

PERFORMANCE

Ratings History
Date	Overall Rating	Risk Rating	Reward Rating
Q3-19	D+	D+	C-
Q4-18	C-	D+	C-
Q4-17	B-	B-	B-
Q4-16	C	C-	C
Q4-15	C	D+	C

Asset & Performance History
Date	NAV	1-Year Total Return
2018	30.47	-14.47
2017	36.19	11.46
2016	32.95	26.28
2015	26.49	-13.12
2014	30.9	5.56
2013	29.59	37.86

Total Assets: $52,003,039

Asset Allocation
Asset	%
Cash	0%
Stocks	100%
US Stocks	99%
Bonds	0%
US Bonds	0%
Other	0%

Services Offered:

Investment Strategy: The investment seeks results that correspond generally to the price and yield (before the fund's fees and expenses) of an equity index called the Nasdaq AlphaDEX® Mid Cap Value Index. The fund will normally invest at least 90% of its net assets (including investment borrowings) in common stocks that comprise the index. The index is designed to select value stocks from the NASDAQ US 600 Mid Cap Index (the "base index") that may generate positive alpha, or risk-adjusted returns, relative to traditional indices through the use of the AlphaDEX® selection methodology. **Top Holdings:** OneMain Holdings Inc PulteGroup Inc Reliance Steel & Aluminum Co Urban Outfitters Inc Knight-Swift Transportation Holdings Inc A

SPDR® S&P 1500 Momentum Tilt ETF   C   HOLD

Ticker	Traded On	NAV	Total Assets ($)	Dividend Yield (TTM)	Turnover Ratio	Expense Ratio
MMTM	NYSE Arca		$51,902,149	1.55	58	0.12

Ratings
Reward   C+
Risk   D+
Recent Upgrade/Downgrade

Fund Information
Fund Type   Exchange Traded Funds
Category   US Equity Large Cap Blend
Sub-Category   Large Blend
Prospectus Objective   Growth
Inception Date   Oct-12
Open to New Investments   Y

Prices
Price (as of 9/30/2019)   129.84
52-Week High   131.53
52-Week Low   100.85

Total Returns (%)

3-Month	6-Month	1-Year	3-Year	5-Year
0.44	4.70	1.81	46.96	68.87

3-Year Standard Deviation   12.4
Effective Duration

Valuation
Premium/Discount (1-Year Average)   0.09

Company Information
Provider   SPDR State Street Global Advisors
Manager/Tenure   Michael J. Feehily (6), Karl A. Schneider (4), John Law (1)
Website   http://www.spdrs.com
Address   SPDR State Street Global Advisors State Street Financial Center, 1 Lincoln Street Boston MA 02111-2900 United States
Phone Number   617-786-3000

PERFORMANCE

Ratings History

Date	Overall Rating	Risk Rating	Reward Rating
Q3-19	C	D+	C+
Q4-18	C-	D+	C
Q4-17	B	B+	B
Q4-16	D	D	D+
Q4-15	C	C-	C

Asset & Performance History

Date	NAV	1-Year Total Return
2018	108.05	-3.83
2017	114.07	23.71
2016	93.75	8.51
2015	88.17	2.98
2014	87.1	12.24
2013	78.86	33.23

Total Assets: $51,902,149

Asset Allocation

Asset	%
Cash	0%
Stocks	100%
US Stocks	99%
Bonds	0%
US Bonds	0%
Other	0%

Services Offered:

Investment Strategy: The investment seeks investment results that, before fees and expenses, correspond generally to the total return performance of the S&P 1500 Positive Momentum Tilt Index. The fund generally invests substantially all, but at least 80%, of its total assets in the securities comprising the index. The index applies an alternative weighting methodology to the S&P Composite 1500 Index so that stocks with relatively high momentum are overweight relative to the S&P Composite 1500 Index and stocks with relatively low momentum are underweight. The fund is non-diversified. **Top Holdings:** Microsoft Corp Apple Inc Amazon.com Inc Procter & Gamble Co Visa Inc Class A

ProShares Ultra 7-10 Year Treasury   C   HOLD

Ticker	Traded On	NAV	Total Assets ($)	Dividend Yield (TTM)	Turnover Ratio	Expense Ratio
UST	NYSE Arca	64.74	$51,795,044	1.48	188	0.95

Ratings
Reward   C
Risk   C-
Recent Upgrade/Downgrade   Up

Fund Information
Fund Type   Exchange Traded Funds
Category   Trading Tools
Sub-Category   Trading--Leveraged Debt
Prospectus Objective   Govt Bond - Treasury
Inception Date   Jan-10
Open to New Investments   Y

Prices
Price (as of 9/30/2019)   64.75
52-Week High   67.13
52-Week Low   51.24

Total Returns (%)

3-Month	6-Month	1-Year	3-Year	5-Year
5.15	13.43	25.74	6.17	27.64

3-Year Standard Deviation   10.48
Effective Duration

Valuation
Premium/Discount (1-Year Average)   0.10

Company Information
Provider   ProShares
Manager/Tenure   Michelle Liu (9), Alexander V. Ilyasov (0)
Website   http://www.proshares.com
Address   ProShares 7501 Wisconsin Avenue, Suite 1000 Bethesda MD 20814 United States
Phone Number   866-776-5125

PERFORMANCE

Ratings History

Date	Overall Rating	Risk Rating	Reward Rating
Q3-19	C	C-	C
Q4-18	D	C-	D
Q4-17	C-	C	C-
Q4-16	C	C-	C
Q4-15	C	C-	C

Asset & Performance History

Date	NAV	1-Year Total Return
2018	55.67	-1.29
2017	57.41	3.11
2016	56.14	0.5
2015	56.2	1.92
2014	55.55	17.4
2013	49.79	-12.67

Total Assets: $51,795,044

Asset Allocation

Asset	%
Cash	-100%
Stocks	0%
US Stocks	0%
Bonds	57%
US Bonds	57%
Other	143%

Services Offered:

Investment Strategy: The investment seeks daily investment results that correspond to two times (2x) the daily performance of the ICE U.S. Treasury 7-10 Year Bond Index. The fund invests in financial instruments that ProShare Advisors believes, in combination, should produce daily returns consistent with the fund's investment objective. The index includes publicly- issued U.S. Treasury securities that have a remaining maturity of greater than or equal to seven years and less than or equal to ten years and have $300 million or more of outstanding face value, excluding amounts held by the Federal Reserve. The fund is non-diversified. **Top Holdings:** Ice 7-10 Year U.S. Treasury Index Swap Citibank Na Ice 7-10 Year U.S. Treasury Index Swap Goldman Sachs International United States Treasury Notes United States Treasury Notes United States Treasury Notes

United States 12 Month Oil Fund, LP   C-   HOLD

Ticker	Traded On	NAV	Total Assets ($)	Dividend Yield (TTM)	Turnover Ratio	Expense Ratio
USL	NYSE Arca	20.16	$51,413,917	0	50	0.82

Ratings
Reward   C-
Risk   C-
Recent Upgrade/Downgrade

Fund Information
Fund Type   Exchange Traded Funds
Category   Commodities Specified
Sub-Category   Commodities Energy
Prospectus Objective   Natl Res
Inception Date   Dec-07
Open to New Investments   Y

Prices
Price (as of 9/30/2019)   20.18
52-Week High   28.28
52-Week Low   17.20

Total Returns (%)

3-Month	6-Month	1-Year	3-Year	5-Year
-8.50	-12.17	-27.85	7.50	-51.45

3-Year Standard Deviation   24.85
Effective Duration

Valuation
Premium/Discount (1-Year Average)   -0.21

Company Information
Provider   USCF Investments
Manager/Tenure   Management Team (11)
Website   http://www.uscfinvestments.com
Address   USCF 1290 Broadway, Suite 1100
Denver CO 80203 United States
Phone Number

PERFORMANCE

Ratings History

Date	Overall Rating	Risk Rating	Reward Rating
Q3-19	C-	C-	C-
Q4-18	C-	C-	C-
Q4-17	D+	D	D+
Q4-16	D	D	D
Q4-15	D-	D-	D-

Asset & Performance History

Date	NAV	1-Year Total Return
2018	17.82	-15.31
2017	21.05	3.24
2016	20.39	19.94
2015	17	-36.09
2014	26.59	-37.9
2013	42.83	7.59

Total Assets: $51,413,917
Asset Allocation

Asset	%
Cash	34%
Stocks	0%
US Stocks	0%
Bonds	17%
US Bonds	17%
Other	48%

Services Offered:

Investment Strategy: The investment seeks to reflect the daily changes in percentage terms of the spot price of light, sweet crude oil delivered to Cushing, Oklahoma, as measured by the daily changes in the average of the prices of specified short-term futures contracts on light, sweet crude oil called the "Benchmark Oil Futures Contracts.
The fund invests investing primarily in futures contracts for light, sweet crude oil, other types of crude oil, diesel-heating oil, gasoline, natural gas, and other petroleum-based fuels. The Benchmark Oil Futures Contracts are the futures contracts on light, sweet crude oil as traded on the New York Mercantile Exchange. **Top Holdings:** Future Contract On Wti Crude Future Oct19   Future Contract On Wti Crude Future Dec19   Future Contract On Wti Crude Future Nov19   Future Contract On Wti Crude Future Jan20   Future Contract On Wti Crude Future Mar20

FlexShares STOXX US ESG Impact Index Fund   C   HOLD

Ticker	Traded On	NAV	Total Assets ($)	Dividend Yield (TTM)	Turnover Ratio	Expense Ratio
ESG	BATS	70.89	$51,396,829	1.55	78	0.32

Ratings
Reward   C+
Risk   C-
Recent Upgrade/Downgrade

Fund Information
Fund Type   Exchange Traded Funds
Category   US Equity Large Cap Blend
Sub-Category   Large Blend
Prospectus Objective   Growth & Inc
Inception Date   Jul-16
Open to New Investments   Y

Prices
Price (as of 9/30/2019)   70.93
52-Week High   72.43
52-Week Low   56.27

Total Returns (%)

3-Month	6-Month	1-Year	3-Year	5-Year
1.05	5.34	4.10	46.83	

3-Year Standard Deviation   12.1
Effective Duration

Valuation
Premium/Discount (1-Year Average)   0.05

Company Information
Provider   Flexshares Trust
Manager/Tenure   Robert Anstine (3), Brendan Sullivan (3)
Website   http://www.flexshares.com
Address   50 South LaSalle Street Chicago, Illinois 60603 Chicago Illinois 60603 United States
Phone Number   855-353-9383

PERFORMANCE

Ratings History

Date	Overall Rating	Risk Rating	Reward Rating
Q3-19	C	C-	C+
Q4-18	C-	D+	C
Q4-17	D	A-	C
Q4-16	U		
Q4-15			

Asset & Performance History

Date	NAV	1-Year Total Return
2018	59.62	-3.56
2017	62.82	21.37
2016	52.61	
2015		
2014		
2013		

Total Assets: $51,396,829
Asset Allocation

Asset	%
Cash	1%
Stocks	99%
US Stocks	99%
Bonds	0%
US Bonds	0%
Other	0%

Services Offered:

Investment Strategy: The investment seeks investment results that correspond generally to the price and yield performance, before fees and expenses, of the STOXX® USA ESG Impact Index. The fund will invest at least 80% of its total assets (exclusive of collateral held from securities lending) in the securities of the underlying index. The underlying index is an optimized index designed to provide broad market exposure that is tilted toward U.S. companies that score better with respect to a small set of ESG characteristics and to provide the potential for attractive risk-adjusted performance relative to the STOXX® USA 900 Index, as determined by the index provider. **Top Holdings:** Apple Inc   Microsoft Corp   Amazon.com Inc   Facebook Inc A   Alphabet Inc Class C

Direxion Zacks MLP High Income Index Shares   C   HOLD

Ticker	Traded On	NAV	Total Assets ($)	Dividend Yield (TTM)	Turnover Ratio	Expense Ratio
ZMLP	NYSE Arca	12.53	$51,362,453	12.77	115	0.65

Ratings
Reward	C+
Risk	D
Recent Upgrade/Downgrade	Up

Fund Information
Fund Type	Exchange Traded Funds
Category	Energy Sector Equity
Sub-Category	Energy Limited Partnership
Prospectus Objective	Income
Inception Date	Jan-14
Open to New Investments	Y

Prices
Price (as of 9/30/2019)	12.55
52-Week High	15.73
52-Week Low	11.78

Total Returns (%)
3-Month	6-Month	1-Year	3-Year	5-Year
-4.71	-2.77	-9.71	-8.10	-49.84

3-Year Standard Deviation	17.9
Effective Duration	

Valuation
Premium/Discount (1-Year Average)	0.00

Company Information
Provider	Direxion Funds
Manager/Tenure	Paul Brigandi (5), Tony Ng (4)
Website	http://www.direxionfunds.com
Address	Direxion Funds 1301 Avenue Of The Americas (6th Avenue) New York NY 10019 United States
Phone Number	646-572-3390

PERFORMANCE

Ratings History

Date	Overall Rating	Risk Rating	Reward Rating
Q3-19	C	D	C+
Q4-18	C	D	B-
Q4-17	D	D	D
Q4-16	C	D	C+
Q4-15	D+	C-	C+

Asset & Performance History

Date	NAV	1-Year Total Return
2018	11.9	-16.81
2017	16.03	-6.77
2016	18.91	22.82
2015	17.45	-41.88
2014	33.16	
2013		

Total Assets: $51,362,453

Asset Allocation
Asset	%
Cash	0%
Stocks	100%
US Stocks	96%
Bonds	0%
US Bonds	0%
Other	0%

Services Offered:

Investment Strategy: The investment seeks investment results, before fees and expenses, that track the price and yield performance of the Zacks MLP High Income Index. The fund, under normal circumstances, invests at least 80% of its net assets in the securities that comprise the index. The index is comprised of 25 securities selected from a universe of master limited partnerships ("MLPs") listed on U.S. exchanges. The fund is non-diversified. **Top Holdings:** NGL Energy Partners LP AmeriGas Partners LP Crestwood Equity Partners LP Teekay LNG Partners LP USA Compression Partners LP

Legg Mason International Low Volatility High Dividend ETF   C-   HOLD

Ticker	Traded On	NAV	Total Assets ($)	Dividend Yield (TTM)	Turnover Ratio	Expense Ratio
LVHI	BATS	26.60	$51,063,754	4.17	41	0.4

Ratings
Reward	C
Risk	D+
Recent Upgrade/Downgrade	

Fund Information
Fund Type	Exchange Traded Funds
Category	Global Equity Large Cap
Sub-Category	Foreign Large Value
Prospectus Objective	Growth & Inc
Inception Date	Jul-16
Open to New Investments	Y

Prices
Price (as of 9/30/2019)	26.73
52-Week High	27.11
52-Week Low	24.04

Total Returns (%)
3-Month	6-Month	1-Year	3-Year	5-Year
2.26	4.42	7.24	26.69	

3-Year Standard Deviation	8.61
Effective Duration	

Valuation
Premium/Discount (1-Year Average)	0.36

Company Information
Provider	Legg Mason
Manager/Tenure	Michael J. LaBella (3), Russell Shtern (3)
Website	http://www.leggmason.com
Address	Legg Mason/Western 100 International Drive Baltimore MD 21202 United States
Phone Number	877-721-1926

PERFORMANCE

Ratings History

Date	Overall Rating	Risk Rating	Reward Rating
Q3-19	C-	D+	C
Q4-18	D+	D+	D+
Q4-17	D	B+	C-
Q4-16	U		
Q4-15			

Asset & Performance History

Date	NAV	1-Year Total Return
2018	24.04	-9.7
2017	28.13	11.69
2016	26.07	
2015		
2014		
2013		

Total Assets: $51,063,754

Asset Allocation
Asset	%
Cash	2%
Stocks	98%
US Stocks	0%
Bonds	0%
US Bonds	0%
Other	0%

Services Offered:

Investment Strategy: The investment seeks to track the investment results of the QS International Low Volatility High Dividend Hedged Index. The fund will invest at least 80% of its net assets, plus borrowings for investment purposes, if any, in securities that compose its underlying index. The underlying index seeks to provide more stable income through investments in stocks of profitable companies in developed markets outside of the United States with relatively high dividend yields or anticipated dividend yields and lower price and earnings volatility, while mitigating exposure to exchange-rate fluctuations between the USD and other international currencies. **Top Holdings:** Iberdrola SA Enel SpA Swisscom AG NTT DOCOMO Inc BCE Inc

ELEMENTS Dogs of the Dow Linked to the Dow Jones High Yield Select 10 Total Return Index | D+ | SELL

Ticker	Traded On	NAV	Total Assets ($)	Dividend Yield (TTM)	Turnover Ratio	Expense Ratio
DOD	NYSE Arca		$51,043,500	0	0	0.75

Ratings
Reward	C
Risk	E+
Recent Upgrade/Downgrade	Down

Fund Information
Fund Type	Exchange Traded Funds
Category	US Equity Large Cap Value
Sub-Category	Large Value
Prospectus Objective	Growth
Inception Date	Nov-07
Open to New Investments	Y

Prices
Price (as of 9/30/2019)	25.65
52-Week High	26.78
52-Week Low	21.22

Total Returns (%)
3-Month	6-Month	1-Year	3-Year	5-Year
0.00	0.76	4.79	41.47	69.08

3-Year Standard Deviation	14.35
Effective Duration	

Valuation
Premium/Discount (1-Year Average)	0.00

Company Information
Provider	ELEMENTS
Manager/Tenure	No Manager (11)
Website	http://www.elementsetn.com
Address	ELEMENTS United States
Phone Number	212-449-2957

PERFORMANCE

Ratings History
Date	Overall Rating	Risk Rating	Reward Rating
Q3-19	D+	E+	C
Q4-18	C	D+	B
Q4-17	A-	B	A
Q4-16	C	C-	C
Q4-15	C	D+	C

Asset & Performance History
Date	NAV	1-Year Total Return
2018	22.98	-9.99
2017	25.53	27.41
2016	18.63	18.21
2015	15.65	2.69
2014	15.24	10.03
2013	13.85	33.94

Total Assets: $51,043,500
Asset Allocation
Asset	%
Cash	%
Stocks	%
US Stocks	%
Bonds	%
US Bonds	%
Other	%

Services Offered:

Investment Strategy: The investment seeks to replicate, net of expenses, the Dow Jones High Yield Select 10 Total Return Index. The index tracks the stocks with the highest dividend yield in Dow Jones Industrial Average. **Top Holdings:**

PIMCO 1-3 Year U.S. Treasury Index Exchange-Traded Fund | C | HOLD

Ticker	Traded On	NAV	Total Assets ($)	Dividend Yield (TTM)	Turnover Ratio	Expense Ratio
TUZ	NYSE Arca	50.92	$51,024,336	2.03	54	0.16

Ratings
Reward	C
Risk	D+
Recent Upgrade/Downgrade	Up

Fund Information
Fund Type	Exchange Traded Funds
Category	US Fixed Income
Sub-Category	Short Government
Prospectus Objective	Govt Bond - Treasury
Inception Date	Jun-09
Open to New Investments	Y

Prices
Price (as of 9/30/2019)	50.93
52-Week High	51.08
52-Week Low	49.70

Total Returns (%)
3-Month	6-Month	1-Year	3-Year	5-Year
0.59	2.20	4.19	4.15	5.84

3-Year Standard Deviation	0.99
Effective Duration	1.87

Valuation
Premium/Discount (1-Year Average)	-0.01

Company Information
Provider	PIMCO
Manager/Tenure	Matthew P. Dorsten (3), Mitchell Handa (0), Graham A. Rennison (0)
Website	http://www.pimco.com
Address	PIMCO 840 Newport Center Drive, Suite 100 Newport Beach CA 92660 United States
Phone Number	866-746-2602

PERFORMANCE

Ratings History
Date	Overall Rating	Risk Rating	Reward Rating
Q3-19	C	D+	C
Q4-18	C-	D+	C-
Q4-17	C	C	C-
Q4-16	C	C-	C
Q4-15	C	C-	C

Asset & Performance History
Date	NAV	1-Year Total Return
2018	50.15	1.42
2017	50.3	0.26
2016	50.67	0.71
2015	50.74	0.41
2014	50.84	0.49
2013	50.85	0.26

Total Assets: $51,024,336
Asset Allocation
Asset	%
Cash	1%
Stocks	0%
US Stocks	0%
Bonds	99%
US Bonds	99%
Other	0%

Services Offered:

Investment Strategy: The investment seeks total return that closely corresponds, before fees and expenses, to the total return of the ICE BofAML 1-3 Year US Treasury Index. The fund invests at least 80% of its total assets (exclusive of collateral held from securities lending) in the component securities of the ICE BofAML 1-3 Year US Treasury Index (the "underlying index"). The underlying index is an unmanaged index comprised of U.S. dollar denominated sovereign debt securities publicly issued by the U.S. Treasury having a maturity of at least 1 year and less than 3 years. **Top Holdings:** United States Treasury Notes 2.38% United States Treasury Notes 2.12% United States Treasury Notes 3.12% United States Treasury Notes 3.62% United States Treasury Notes 2.62%

FlexShares US Quality Large Cap Index Fund   C   HOLD

Ticker	Traded On	NAV	Total Assets ($)	Dividend Yield (TTM)	Turnover Ratio	Expense Ratio
QLC	BATS	33.99	$50,990,017	2.11	94	0.32

Ratings
Reward   C
Risk   C-
Recent Upgrade/Downgrade

Fund Information
Fund Type	Exchange Traded Funds
Category	US Equity Large Cap Value
Sub-Category	Large Value
Prospectus Objective	Growth
Inception Date	Sep-15
Open to New Investments	Y

Prices
Price (as of 9/30/2019)	34.01
52-Week High	35.98
52-Week Low	28.41

Total Returns (%)
3-Month	6-Month	1-Year	3-Year	5-Year
0.47	1.15	-3.05	33.84	

3-Year Standard Deviation   12.9
Effective Duration

Valuation
Premium/Discount (1-Year Average)   0.01

Company Information
Provider	Flexshares Trust
Manager/Tenure	Robert Anstine (4), Brendan Sullivan (3)
Website	http://www.flexshares.com
Address	50 South LaSalle Street Chicago, Illinois 60603 Chicago Illinois 60603 United States
Phone Number	855-353-9383

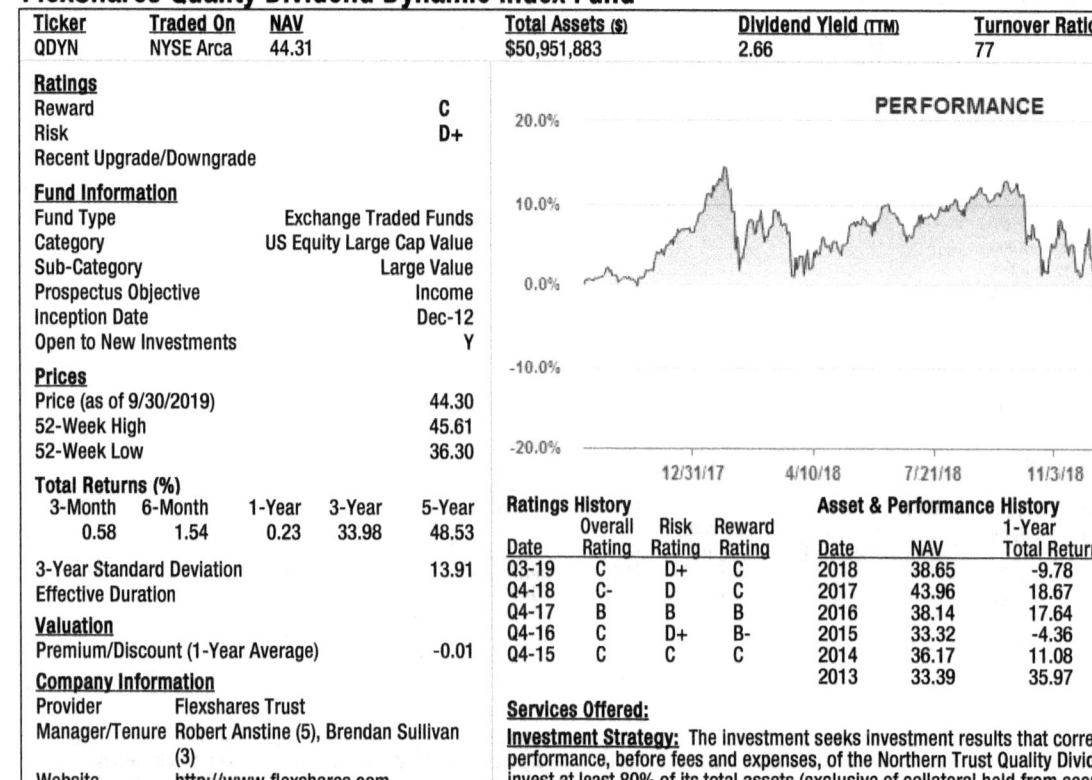

PERFORMANCE

Ratings History				Asset & Performance History			Total Assets:	$50,990,017
Date	Overall Rating	Risk Rating	Reward Rating	Date	NAV	1-Year Total Return	Asset Allocation Asset	%
Q3-19	C	C-	C	2018	30.28	-7.51	Cash	0%
Q4-18	C	C-	C	2017	33.3	21.32	Stocks	100%
Q4-17	C	B	C+	2016	27.83	8.23	US Stocks	99%
Q4-16	D	D+	C-	2015	25.93		Bonds	0%
Q4-15				2014			US Bonds	0%
				2013			Other	0%

Services Offered:
Investment Strategy: The investment seeks investment results that correspond generally to the price and yield performance, before fees and expenses, of the Northern Trust Quality Large Cap IndexSM. The fund generally will invest under normal circumstances at least 80% of its total assets (exclusive of collateral held from securities lending) in the securities of its underlying index. The underlying index is designed to measure the performance of companies that exhibit certain quality, valuation and momentum characteristics within a universe of publicly-traded U.S. large capitalization equity securities. **Top Holdings:** Apple Inc Microsoft Corp The Home Depot Inc Johnson & Johnson Verizon Communications Inc

FlexShares Quality Dividend Dynamic Index Fund   C   HOLD

Ticker	Traded On	NAV	Total Assets ($)	Dividend Yield (TTM)	Turnover Ratio	Expense Ratio
QDYN	NYSE Arca	44.31	$50,951,883	2.66	77	0.37

Ratings
Reward   C
Risk   D+
Recent Upgrade/Downgrade

Fund Information
Fund Type	Exchange Traded Funds
Category	US Equity Large Cap Value
Sub-Category	Large Value
Prospectus Objective	Income
Inception Date	Dec-12
Open to New Investments	Y

Prices
Price (as of 9/30/2019)	44.30
52-Week High	45.61
52-Week Low	36.30

Total Returns (%)
3-Month	6-Month	1-Year	3-Year	5-Year
0.58	1.54	0.23	33.98	48.53

3-Year Standard Deviation   13.91
Effective Duration

Valuation
Premium/Discount (1-Year Average)   -0.01

Company Information
Provider	Flexshares Trust
Manager/Tenure	Robert Anstine (5), Brendan Sullivan (3)
Website	http://www.flexshares.com
Address	50 South LaSalle Street Chicago, Illinois 60603 Chicago Illinois 60603 United States
Phone Number	855-353-9383

PERFORMANCE

Ratings History				Asset & Performance History			Total Assets:	$50,951,883
Date	Overall Rating	Risk Rating	Reward Rating	Date	NAV	1-Year Total Return	Asset Allocation Asset	%
Q3-19	C	D+	C	2018	38.65	-9.78	Cash	1%
Q4-18	C-	D	C	2017	43.96	18.67	Stocks	99%
Q4-17	B	B	B	2016	38.14	17.64	US Stocks	98%
Q4-16	C	D+	B-	2015	33.32	-4.36	Bonds	0%
Q4-15	C	C	C	2014	36.17	11.08	US Bonds	0%
				2013	33.39	35.97	Other	0%

Services Offered:
Investment Strategy: The investment seeks investment results that correspond generally to the price and yield performance, before fees and expenses, of the Northern Trust Quality Dividend Dynamic IndexSM. The fund will invest at least 80% of its total assets (exclusive of collateral held from securities lending) in the securities of the index. The underlying index is designed to provide exposure to a high-quality, income-oriented portfolio of U.S. equity securities, with an emphasis on long-term capital growth and a targeted overall volatility that is greater than that of the Northern Trust 1250 IndexSM. It may also invest up to 20% of its assets in cash and cash equivalents. **Top Holdings:** Apple Inc Microsoft Corp The Home Depot Inc JPMorgan Chase & Co Cisco Systems Inc

VanEck Vectors Steel ETF   C   HOLD

Ticker	Traded On	NAV	Total Assets ($)	Dividend Yield (TTM)	Turnover Ratio	Expense Ratio
SLX	NYSE Arca	33.91	$50,869,129	6.43	16	0.56

Ratings
Reward	B-
Risk	D+
Recent Upgrade/Downgrade	Up

Fund Information
Fund Type	Exchange Traded Funds
Category	Natural Resources
Sub-Category	Natural Resources
Prospectus Objective	Unaligned
Inception Date	Oct-06
Open to New Investments	Y

Prices
Price (as of 9/30/2019)	33.90
52-Week High	46.56
52-Week Low	30.97

Total Returns (%)
3-Month	6-Month	1-Year	3-Year	5-Year
-14.15	-17.93	-21.86	20.72	-6.55

3-Year Standard Deviation	25.15
Effective Duration	

Valuation
Premium/Discount (1-Year Average)	-0.03

Company Information
Provider	VanEck
Manager/Tenure	Hao-Hung (Peter) Liao (12), Guo Hua (Jason) Jin (1)
Website	http://www.vaneck.com
Address	Van Eck Associates Corporation 666 Third Avenue New York NY 10017 United States
Phone Number	800-826-1115

PERFORMANCE

Ratings History
Date	Overall Rating	Risk Rating	Reward Rating
Q3-19	C	D+	B-
Q4-18	C+	C-	B
Q4-17	B-	D+	B
Q4-16	C	D	C
Q4-15	C	C-	C

Asset & Performance History
Date	NAV	1-Year Total Return
2018	34.87	-20.08
2017	45.74	24.07
2016	37.82	95.78
2015	19.52	-41.89
2014	35.45	-26.38
2013	49.76	3.93

Total Assets: $50,869,129

Asset Allocation
Asset	%
Cash	0%
Stocks	100%
US Stocks	46%
Bonds	0%
US Bonds	0%
Other	0%

Services Offered:

Investment Strategy: The investment seeks to replicate as closely as possible, before fees and expenses, the price and yield performance of the NYSE® Arca Steel Indexä. The fund normally invests at least 80% of its total assets in common stocks and depositary receipts of companies involved in the steel sector. Such companies may include small- and medium-capitalization companies and foreign and emerging market issuers. It may concentrate its investments in a particular industry or group of industries to the extent that the Steel Index concentrates in an industry or group of industries. The fund is non-diversified. **Top Holdings:** Rio Tinto PLC ADR   Vale SA ADR   Ternium SA ADR   Vedanta Ltd ADR   Reliance Steel & Aluminum Co

---

JPMorgan Managed Futures Strategy ETF   D+   SELL

Ticker	Traded On	NAV	Total Assets ($)	Dividend Yield (TTM)	Turnover Ratio	Expense Ratio
JPMF	NYSE Arca	25.38	$50,756,131	0.65		0.59

Ratings
Reward	C-
Risk	D+
Recent Upgrade/Downgrade	

Fund Information
Fund Type	Exchange Traded Funds
Category	Alternative Misc
Sub-Category	Managed Futures
Prospectus Objective	Growth & Inc
Inception Date	Dec-17
Open to New Investments	Y

Prices
Price (as of 9/30/2019)	25.46
52-Week High	26.00
52-Week Low	22.97

Total Returns (%)
3-Month	6-Month	1-Year	3-Year	5-Year
4.01	5.18	5.78		

3-Year Standard Deviation	
Effective Duration	

Valuation
Premium/Discount (1-Year Average)	-0.13

Company Information
Provider	JPMorgan
Manager/Tenure	Wei (Victor) Li (1), Yazann Romahi (1), Joe Staines (1), 1 other
Website	http://www.jpmorganfunds.com
Address	JPMorgan 270 Park Avenue New York NY 10017-2070 United States
Phone Number	800-480-4111

PERFORMANCE

Ratings History
Date	Overall Rating	Risk Rating	Reward Rating
Q3-19	D+	D+	C-
Q4-18	D	D+	D
Q4-17	U		
Q4-16			
Q4-15			

Asset & Performance History
Date	NAV	1-Year Total Return
2018	23.42	-5.7
2017	25.01	
2016		
2015		
2014		
2013		

Total Assets: $50,756,131

Asset Allocation
Asset	%
Cash	94%
Stocks	0%
US Stocks	0%
Bonds	-1%
US Bonds	0%
Other	7%

Services Offered:

Investment Strategy: The investment seeks to provide long-term total return. The fund will generally invest its assets globally to gain exposure, either directly or through the use of derivatives, to equity securities (across market capitalizations) in developed markets, debt securities (including below investment grade or high yield securities), commodities and currencies (including in emerging markets). It may invest in fixed income securities of any average weighted maturity or duration. The fund may use both long and short positions (achieved primarily through the use of derivative instruments). It is non-diversified. **Top Holdings:** Managed Futures Fund Cs Ltd   Australian 10 Year Treasury Bond Future Sept19   Euro BUND Future Sept19   Euro BUXL 30Y Bond Sept19   Euro BUND Future Sept19

WisdomTree Emerging Markets Dividend Fund   C-   HOLD

Ticker	Traded On	NAV	Total Assets ($)	Dividend Yield (TTM)	Turnover Ratio	Expense Ratio
DVEM	BATS	29.80	$50,653,089	3.67	26	0.32

PERFORMANCE

Ratings
Reward	C
Risk	D+
Recent Upgrade/Downgrade	

Fund Information
Fund Type	Exchange Traded Funds
Category	Global Emerg Mkts Equity
Sub-Category	Diversified Emerging Mkts
Prospectus Objective	Div Emerg Mkts
Inception Date	Apr-16
Open to New Investments	Y

Prices
Price (as of 9/30/2019)	29.97
52-Week High	32.62
52-Week Low	28.00

Total Returns (%)
3-Month	6-Month	1-Year	3-Year	5-Year
-4.20	-2.98	-1.61	20.89	

3-Year Standard Deviation	12.89
Effective Duration	

Valuation
Premium/Discount (1-Year Average)	0.29

Company Information
Provider	WisdomTree
Manager/Tenure	Richard A. Brown (3), Thomas J. Durante (3), Karen Q. Wong (3)
Website	http://www.wisdomtree.com
Address	WisdomTree 245 Park Avenue, 35th floor New York NY 10167 United States
Phone Number	866-909-9473

Ratings History
Date	Overall Rating	Risk Rating	Reward Rating
Q3-19	C-	D+	C
Q4-18	D+	D+	D+
Q4-17	D+	B+	C
Q4-16	U		
Q4-15			

Asset & Performance History
Date	NAV	1-Year Total Return
2018	28.62	-10.69
2017	33.11	27.49
2016	26.67	
2015		
2014		
2013		

Total Assets: $50,653,089
Asset Allocation
Asset	%
Cash	0%
Stocks	100%
US Stocks	0%
Bonds	0%
US Bonds	0%
Other	0%

Services Offered:

Investment Strategy: The investment seeks to track the price and yield performance, before fees and expenses, of the WisdomTree Emerging Markets Dividend Index (the "index"). Under normal circumstances, at least 80% of the fund's total assets (exclusive of collateral held from securities lending) will be invested in component securities of the index and investments that have economic characteristics that are substantially identical to the economic characteristics of such component securities. The index is a dividend weighted index that consists of emerging market dividend-paying common stocks. The fund is non-diversified. **Top Holdings:** Samsung Electronics Co Ltd Taiwan Semiconductor Manufacturing Co Ltd China Construction Bank Corp Class H Gazprom PJSC ADR China Mobile Ltd

---

UBS ETRACS Bloomberg Commodity Index Total Return ETN   D   SELL

Ticker	Traded On	NAV	Total Assets ($)	Dividend Yield (TTM)	Turnover Ratio	Expense Ratio
DJCI	NYSE Arca	14.51	$50,620,397	0	0	0.5

PERFORMANCE

Ratings
Reward	D
Risk	D+
Recent Upgrade/Downgrade	

Fund Information
Fund Type	Exchange Traded Funds
Category	Commodities Broad Basket
Sub-Category	Commodities Broad Basket
Prospectus Objective	Natl Res
Inception Date	Oct-09
Open to New Investments	Y

Prices
Price (as of 9/30/2019)	14.53
52-Week High	16.16
52-Week Low	13.96

Total Returns (%)
3-Month	6-Month	1-Year	3-Year	5-Year
-1.30	-4.23	-8.84	-6.25	-33.86

3-Year Standard Deviation	8.46
Effective Duration	

Valuation
Premium/Discount (1-Year Average)	-0.02

Company Information
Provider	UBS Group AG
Manager/Tenure	No Manager (9)
Website	http://www.ubs.com
Address	Bahnhofstrasse 45 Zürich 8098 Switzerland
Phone Number	412-037-1952

Ratings History
Date	Overall Rating	Risk Rating	Reward Rating
Q3-19	D	D+	D
Q4-18	D+	C-	D+
Q4-17	D+	D	C-
Q4-16	D	D	D
Q4-15	D-	D	D-

Asset & Performance History
Date	NAV	1-Year Total Return
2018	14.1	-12.42
2017	16.1	0.52
2016	15.89	11.84
2015	14.21	-26
2014	19.2	-17.93
2013	23.4	-10.16

Total Assets: $50,620,397
Asset Allocation
Asset	%
Cash	%
Stocks	%
US Stocks	%
Bonds	%
US Bonds	%
Other	%

Services Offered:

Investment Strategy: The investment seeks to replicate, net of expenses, the DJ-UBS Commodity Index Total Return Index.
The index measures the collateralized returns from a basket of 19 commodity futures contracts representing the energy, precious metals, industrial metals, grains, softs and livestock sectors. In addition, the index is rebalanced once a year to ensure that no commodity sector may constitute more than 33% of the index as of the date of such rebalancing. **Top Holdings:**

First Trust California Municipal High Income ETF   C   HOLD

Ticker	Traded On	NAV		Total Assets ($)	Dividend Yield (TTM)	Turnover Ratio	Expense Ratio
FCAL	NAS CM	53.20		$50,543,217	2.8	69	0.5

Ratings
Reward   C
Risk   C-
Recent Upgrade/Downgrade   Up

Fund Information
Fund Type   Exchange Traded Funds
Category   US Muni Fixed Inc
Sub-Category   Muni California Intermediate
Prospectus Objective   Muni Bond - Natl
Inception Date   Jun-17
Open to New Investments   Y

Prices
Price (as of 9/30/2019)   53.25
52-Week High   53.78
52-Week Low   49.04

Total Returns (%)

3-Month	6-Month	1-Year	3-Year	5-Year
2.30	5.38	9.91		

3-Year Standard Deviation
Effective Duration   6.11

Valuation
Premium/Discount (1-Year Average)   0.13

Company Information
Provider   First Trust
Manager/Tenure   J. Thomas Futrell (2), Johnathan N. Wilhelm (2)
Website   http://www.ftportfolios.com/
Address   First Trust 120 E. Liberty Drive, Suite 400 Wheaton IL 60187 United States
Phone Number   800-621-1675

PERFORMANCE

Ratings History

Date	Overall Rating	Risk Rating	Reward Rating
Q3-19	C	C-	C
Q4-18	D+	D+	D+
Q4-17	U		
Q4-16			
Q4-15			

Asset & Performance History

Date	NAV	1-Year Total Return
2018	49.98	1.09
2017	50.94	
2016		
2015		
2014		
2013		

Total Assets: $50,543,217

Asset Allocation

Asset	%
Cash	7%
Stocks	0%
US Stocks	0%
Bonds	93%
US Bonds	91%
Other	0%

Services Offered:

Investment Strategy: The investment seeks to provide current income that is exempt from regular federal income taxes and California income taxes, and its secondary objective is long-term capital appreciation. The fund seeks to achieve its investment objectives by investing at least 80% of its net assets (including investment borrowings) in municipal debt securities that pay interest that is exempt from regular federal income taxes and California income taxes. It will invest no more than 50% of its net assets in Municipal Securities that are, at the time of investment, not investment grade, commonly referred to as "high yield" or "junk" bonds. The fund is non-diversified. **Top Holdings:** LOS ANGELES CALIF HBR DEPT REV 5% ORANGE CNTY CALIF APT DEV REV 1.4% CALIFORNIA HEALTH FACS FING AUTH REV 1.33% US 10 Year Ultra Future Sept19 EL DORADO CALIF IRR DIST REV 4%

Teucrium Wheat   D   SELL

Ticker	Traded On	NAV		Total Assets ($)	Dividend Yield (TTM)	Turnover Ratio	Expense Ratio
WEAT	NYSE Arca	5.31		$50,469,334	0		1

Ratings
Reward   D
Risk   D
Recent Upgrade/Downgrade   Up

Fund Information
Fund Type   Exchange Traded Funds
Category   Commodities Specified
Sub-Category   Commodities Agriculture
Prospectus Objective   Unaligned
Inception Date   Sep-11
Open to New Investments   Y

Prices
Price (as of 9/30/2019)   5.30
52-Week High   6.43
52-Week Low   4.88

Total Returns (%)

3-Month	6-Month	1-Year	3-Year	5-Year
-5.88	-0.68	-15.31	-26.11	-51.17

3-Year Standard Deviation   22.4
Effective Duration

Valuation
Premium/Discount (1-Year Average)   -0.03

Company Information
Provider   Teucrium
Manager/Tenure   Management Team (8)
Website   http://www.teucriumcornfund.com
Address   Teucrium Three Main Street Suite 215 Burlington VT 05401 United States
Phone Number   802-540-0019

PERFORMANCE

Ratings History

Date	Overall Rating	Risk Rating	Reward Rating
Q3-19	D	D	D
Q4-18	D	D	D
Q4-17	D-	E+	D-
Q4-16	D-	E+	D-
Q4-15	D-	D-	D-

Asset & Performance History

Date	NAV	1-Year Total Return
2018	5.95	-0.73
2017	5.99	-13.06
2016	6.89	-25.13
2015	9.15	-28.07
2014	12.72	-14.26
2013	14.84	-30.18

Total Assets: $50,469,334

Asset Allocation

Asset	%
Cash	-2%
Stocks	0%
US Stocks	0%
Bonds	0%
US Bonds	0%
Other	102%

Services Offered:

Investment Strategy: The investment seeks to have the daily changes in percentage terms of the shares' NAV reflect the daily changes in percentage terms of a weighted average of the closing settlement prices for three futures contracts for wheat that are traded on the Chicago Board of Trade.
The fund seeks to achieve its investment objective by investing under normal market conditions in Benchmark Component Futures Contracts or, in certain circumstances, in other Wheat Futures Contracts traded on the CBOT or on foreign exchanges. **Top Holdings:** W Z0 Cbot Wheat Futures Dec 2020 W Z9 Cbot Wheat Futures Dec 2019 W H0 Cbot Wheat Futures Mar 2020

Invesco S&P SmallCap Utilities & Communication Services ETF

C+   HOLD

Ticker	Traded On	NAV	Total Assets ($)	Dividend Yield (TTM)	Turnover Ratio	Expense Ratio
PSCU	NAS CM	52.74	$50,100,586	2.07		0.29

Ratings

Reward	B-
Risk	C-
Recent Upgrade/Downgrade	Up

Fund Information

Fund Type	Exchange Traded Funds
Category	Utilities Sector Equity
Sub-Category	Utilities
Prospectus Objective	Utility
Inception Date	Apr-10
Open to New Investments	

Prices

Price (as of 9/30/2019)	52.72
52-Week High	58.05
52-Week Low	46.95

Total Returns (%)

3-Month	6-Month	1-Year	3-Year	5-Year
3.12	-1.11	-5.60	28.66	84.71

3-Year Standard Deviation	13.34
Effective Duration	

Valuation

Premium/Discount (1-Year Average)	-0.02

Company Information

Provider	Invesco
Manager/Tenure	Peter Hubbard (9), Michael Jeanette (9), Tony Seisser (5)
Website	http://www.invesco.com/us
Address	Invesco 11 Greenway Plaza, Ste. 2500 Houston TX 77046 United States
Phone Number	800-659-1005

PERFORMANCE

Ratings History

Date	Overall Rating	Risk Rating	Reward Rating
Q3-19	C+	C-	B-
Q4-18	C+	C-	B-
Q4-17	A-	A-	B+
Q4-16	B-	C	B
Q4-15	B-	C	B-

Asset & Performance History

Date	NAV	1-Year Total Return
2018	49.27	-4.46
2017	52.72	11.91
2016	47.96	20.43
2015	41.14	7.04
2014	39.67	16.55
2013	34.94	20.35

Total Assets: $50,100,586

Asset Allocation

Asset	%
Cash	0%
Stocks	100%
US Stocks	100%
Bonds	0%
US Bonds	0%
Other	0%

Services Offered:

Investment Strategy: The investment seeks to track the investment results (before fees and expenses) of the S&P SmallCap 600® Capped Utilities & Communication Services Index (the "underlying index"). The fund generally will invest at least 90% of its total assets in the securities of small-capitalization U.S. utility companies and companies in the communication services sector that comprise the underlying index. These companies are principally engaged in providing either energy, water, electric or natural gas utilities. The fund is non-diversified. **Top Holdings:** American States Water Co   Avista Corp   South Jersey Industries Inc   El Paso Electric Co   Gannett Co Inc

---

Invesco S&P MidCap Value with Momentum ETF

C   HOLD

Ticker	Traded On	NAV	Total Assets ($)	Dividend Yield (TTM)	Turnover Ratio	Expense Ratio
XMVM	NYSE Arca	32.31	$50,084,312	2.27		0.39

Ratings

Reward	C
Risk	D+
Recent Upgrade/Downgrade	

Fund Information

Fund Type	Exchange Traded Funds
Category	US Equity Mid Cap
Sub-Category	Mid-Cap Value
Prospectus Objective	Growth
Inception Date	Mar-05
Open to New Investments	Y

Prices

Price (as of 9/30/2019)	32.37
52-Week High	33.12
52-Week Low	26.32

Total Returns (%)

3-Month	6-Month	1-Year	3-Year	5-Year
-1.24	2.77	6.29	21.09	41.86

3-Year Standard Deviation	14.15
Effective Duration	

Valuation

Premium/Discount (1-Year Average)	-0.09

Company Information

Provider	Invesco
Manager/Tenure	Peter Hubbard (12), Michael Jeanette (11), Tony Seisser (5)
Website	http://www.invesco.com/us
Address	Invesco 11 Greenway Plaza, Ste. 2500 Houston TX 77046 United States
Phone Number	800-659-1005

PERFORMANCE

Ratings History

Date	Overall Rating	Risk Rating	Reward Rating
Q3-19	C	D+	C
Q4-18	C-	D+	C-
Q4-17	B-	B-	C+
Q4-16	C-	D+	C-
Q4-15	C	D+	C

Asset & Performance History

Date	NAV	1-Year Total Return
2018	27.56	-9.66
2017	31.34	3.05
2016	31.1	28.49
2015	24.79	-7.23
2014	27.41	12.17
2013	24.82	40.59

Total Assets: $50,084,312

Asset Allocation

Asset	%
Cash	0%
Stocks	100%
US Stocks	100%
Bonds	0%
US Bonds	0%
Other	0%

Services Offered:

Investment Strategy: The investment seeks to track the investment results (before fees and expenses) of the S&P MidCap 400® High Momentum Value Index (the "underlying index"). The fund generally will invest at least 90% of its total assets in the securities that comprise the underlying index. Strictly in accordance with its guidelines and mandated procedures, the index provider compiles, maintains and calculates the underlying index, which is designed to track the performance of approximately 80 stocks in the S&P MidCap 400® Index that have the highest "value" and "momentum" scores. **Top Holdings:** Genworth Financial Inc   AutoNation Inc   World Fuel Services Corp   Arrow Electronics Inc   PBF Energy Inc Class A

Section IV:
100 Largest Exchange-Traded Funds

Investment Ratings and analysis of the 100 Largest Exchange-Traded Funds. Funds are listed in order by their asset size.

Section IV: Contents

This section contains Weiss Investment Ratings, key rating factors, and summary financial data for the 100 Largest Exchange-Traded Funds. If your priority is to stick with large funds because you believe that the size of the fund matters then these funds should be looked at. In this listing of the 100 largest funds you can also be assured that the Weiss Exchange-Traded Fund Rating is just as important as for the smallest fund. Funds are listed in order by their asset size.

Fund Name
Describes the fund's assets, regions of investments and investment strategies. Many funds have similar names, so you want to make sure the fund you look up is really the one you are interested in evaluating.

MARKET

Ticker Symbol
An arrangement of characters (usually letters) representing a particular security listed on an exchange or otherwise traded publicly. When a company issues securities to the public marketplace, it selects an available ticker symbol for its securities which investors use to place trade orders. Every listed security has a unique ticker symbol, facilitating the vast array of trade orders that flow through the financial markets every day.

Traded On (Exchange)
The stock exchange on which the fund is listed. The core function of a stock exchange is to ensure fair and orderly trading, as well as efficient dissemination of price information. Exchanges such as: NYSE (New York Stock Exchange), AMEX (American Stock Exchange), NNM (NASDAQ National Market), and NASQ (NASDAQ Small Cap) give companies, governments and other groups a platform to sell securities to the investing public. NASDAQ is abbreviated as NAS.

RATINGS

Overall Rating
The Weiss rating measured on a scale from A to E based on each fund's risk and performance. See the preceding section, "What Our Ratings Mean," for an explanation of each letter grade rating.

Reward Rating
This is based on the total return over a period of up to five years, including net asset value and price growth. The total return figure is stated net of the expenses and fees charged by the fund. Based on proprietary modeling the individual components of the risk and reward ratings are calculated and weighted and the final rating is generated.

Risk Rating
This is includes the risk ratings of component stocks where applicable and also includes the financial stability of the fund, turnover where applicable, together with the level of volatility as measured by the fund's daily returns over a period of up to five years. Funds with greater stability are considered less risky and receive a higher risk rating. Funds with greater volatility are considered riskier, and will receive a lower risk rating. In addition to considering the fund's

volatility, the risk rating also considers an assessment of the valuation and quality of a fund's holdings.

Recent Upgrade/Downgrade
An "Up" or "Down" indicates that the Weiss Exchange-Traded Fund rating has changed since the publication of the last print edition. If a fund has had a rating change since June 30, 2019, the change is identified with an "Up" or "Down."

PRICE

Price
The price at which the fund is traded on a regular trading day. Prices in this guide are listed as of September 30, 2019.

TOTAL RETURNS & PERFORMANCE

Total Assets (MIL)
The total of all assets listed on the institution's balance sheet. This figure primarily consists of loans, investments, and fixed assets. Total Assets are displayed in millions.

1-Year Total Return
The rate of return on an investment over one year that includes interest, capital gains, dividends and distributions realized.

3-Year Total Return
The rate of return on an investment over three years that includes interest, capital gains, dividends and distributions realized.

5-Year Total Return
The rate of return on an investment over five years that includes interest, capital gains, dividends and distributions realized.

Dividend Yield (TTM)
Trailing twelve months dividends paid out relative to the share price. Expressed as a percentage and measures how much cash flow an investor is getting for each invested dollar. **Trailing Twelve Months (TTM)** is a representation of a fund's financial performance over the most recent 12 months. TTM uses the latest available financial data from a company's interim, quarterly or annual reports.

VALUATION

Premium/Discount 1-Year Average
The annual average premium or discount of the market price to the NAV (Net Asset Value), expressed as a percentage of the NAV. This value provides a year-by-year picture a fund's trading status. A negative number indicates that, on average, the fund's shares sold at a discount to NAV, and a positive number indicates the shares sold at a premium. If the number shown is –10.00, for example, the shares sold at an average 10% discount to NAV during the listed time-period.

Fund Name	Ticker Symbol	Traded On	Overall Rating	Reward Rating	Risk Rating	Recent Up/ Downgrade	Price as of 9/30/2019	Total Assets (MIL)	1-Year Total Return	3-Year Total Return	5-Year Total Return	Dividend Yield (TTM)	Premium/ Discount 1-Year Avg
Vanguard S&P 500 ETF	VOO	NYSE Arca	B-	C+	B		272.60	493,907	3.87	45.66	69.21	1.99	-0.03
Vanguard Total International Stock Index Fund ETF Shares	VXUS	NAS CM	C	C	C+		51.66	384,493	-1.60	19.35	18.16	3.05	0.11
SPDR® S&P 500 ETF	SPY	NYSE Arca	B-	C+	B		296.77	273,532	3.28	44.59	65.58	1.85	-0.05
Vanguard Total Bond Market Index Fund ETF Shares	BND	NAS CM	B-	C+	B		84.43	241,309	10.59	8.92	17.29	2.74	0.05
iShares Core S&P 500 ETF	IVV	NYSE Arca	B-	C+	B		298.52	186,488	3.84	45.65	69.14	2.06	-0.01
Vanguard Total International Bond Index Fund ETF Shares	BNDX	NAS CM	B-	B-	C+	Up	58.83	140,100	11.36	12.93	24.95	2.85	0.16
Vanguard FTSE Developed Markets Index Fund ETF Shares	VEA	NYSE Arca	C	C	B		41.08	114,321	-2.12	20.08	20.87	3.13	0.05
Vanguard Mid-Cap Index Fund ETF Shares	VO	NYSE Arca	C+	C	C+		167.60	105,404	3.91	35.57	57.62	1.4	0.01
Vanguard Growth Index Fund ETF Shares	VUG	NYSE Arca	B-	B-	C+	Up	166.28	92,060	4.25	53.67	80.40	1.06	-0.03
Vanguard FTSE Emerging Markets Index Fund ETF Shares	VWO	NYSE Arca	C	C	C+		40.26	83,541	1.25	16.73	11.87	2.82	0.04
Vanguard Value Index Fund ETF Shares	VTV	NYSE Arca	C+	C	C+		111.62	82,529	3.14	38.50	58.22	2.51	-0.01
Invesco QQQ Trust	QQQ	NAS CM	B-	B-	B-		188.81	74,717	2.31	63.28	103.88	0.82	-0.02
Vanguard Real Estate Index Fund ETF Shares	VNQ	NYSE Arca	B-	C+	B-	Up	93.25	69,465	20.97	22.70	60.39	3.12	-0.01
Vanguard Extended Market Index Fund ETF Shares	VXF	NYSE Arca	C	C	C+		116.33	69,318	-2.95	32.94	52.77	1.26	0.01
iShares Core U.S. Aggregate Bond ETF	AGG	NYSE Arca	B-	C+	B		113.17	66,025	10.35	8.90	17.24	2.71	0.06
iShares Core MSCI EAFE ETF	IEFA	BATS	C	C	B		61.07	65,004	-1.64	21.25	21.62	3.2	0.00
iShares MSCI EAFE ETF	EFA	NYSE Arca	C	C	B		65.21	58,937	-1.22	20.52	18.06	3.1	-0.08
iShares Core MSCI Emerging Markets ETF	IEMG	NYSE Arca	C	C-	C+		49.02	54,218	-2.23	17.40	11.91	2.74	-0.02
iShares Core S&P Mid-Cap ETF	IJH	NYSE Arca	C	C	C+		193.23	49,539	-1.79	30.64	54.71	1.5	-0.01
Vanguard Short-Term Bond Index Fund ETF Shares	BSV	NYSE Arca	C+	C	C+	Up	80.79	48,183	6.00	5.94	9.84	2.23	0.04
Vanguard Dividend Appreciation Index Fund ETF Shares	VIG	NYSE Arca	B-	B	C+		119.58	47,776	9.16	50.41	71.36	1.77	-0.01
iShares Russell 1000 Growth ETF	IWF	NYSE Arca	C+	B-	C+	Down	159.63	44,890	3.26	58.83	88.51	1.06	-0.04
iShares Core S&P Small-Cap ETF	IJR	NYSE Arca	C	C-	C		77.84	44,003	-8.02	25.20	55.48	1.44	0.00
SPDR® Gold Shares	GLD	NYSE Arca	C+	C+	C+	Up	138.87	43,959	24.39	10.97	19.68	0	-0.11
iShares Russell 2000 ETF	IWM	NYSE Arca	C	C-	C+		151.34	43,616	-7.67	26.69	50.52	1.29	-0.05
iShares Russell 1000 Value ETF	IWD	NYSE Arca	C+	C	C+	Up	128.26	39,502	3.53	30.39	46.12	2.35	-0.03
Vanguard FTSE All-World ex-US Index Fund ETF Shares	VEU	NYSE Arca	C	C	B		49.90	37,889	-1.18	20.06	17.10	3.07	0.00
iShares iBoxx $ Investment Grade Corporate Bond ETF	LQD	NYSE Arca	B-	B-	B		127.48	36,121	14.99	14.75	26.90	3.35	0.09
iShares Edge MSCI Min Vol USA ETF	USMV	BATS	B	B	A-	Down	64.10	35,010	14.68	49.72	89.73	1.84	-0.05
Vanguard High Dividend Yield Index Fund ETF Shares	VYM	NYSE Arca	C+	C	C+		88.73	34,794	4.59	34.72	55.87	3.16	0.01
Vanguard Intermediate-Term Bond Index Fund ETF Shares	BIV	NYSE Arca	C+	C+	C+	Up	88.00	34,291	12.60	9.54	20.43	2.74	0.07
Vanguard Sh-Term Inflation-Prot Securities Ind ETF Shares	VTIP	NAS CM	C	C	C+		49.05	31,193	3.45	4.89	6.20	1.97	0.07
Vanguard Short-Term Corporate Bond Index Fund ETF Shares	VCSH	NAS CM	C+	C+	C+		81.05	30,932	6.66	8.43	14.06	2.84	0.09
Vanguard Intermediate-Term Corp Bond Ind Fund ETF Shares	VCIT	NAS CM	C+	B-	C+		91.24	26,893	12.99	12.77	25.80	3.42	0.18
iShares MSCI Emerging Markets ETF	EEM	NYSE Arca	C	C-	C+		40.87	25,089	-2.46	16.95	9.92	2.19	-0.04
Vanguard Small-Cap Growth Index Fund ETF Shares	VBK	NYSE Arca	C+	C	C+		182.04	23,785	-0.88	41.57	61.72	0.62	-0.02
Vanguard Information Technology Index Fund ETF Shares	VGT	NYSE Arca	B-	B	C+	Down	215.55	23,769	6.46	83.56	128.70	1.26	-0.02
Vanguard Large-Cap Index Fund ETF Shares	VV	NYSE Arca	C+	C+	C+		136.33	23,362	3.31	44.96	65.42	1.88	-0.01
iShares S&P 500 Growth ETF	IVW	NYSE Arca	C+	C+	C+	Down	180.03	23,323	2.77	54.21	83.88	1.37	-0.03
iShares Core S&P Total U.S. Stock Market ETF	ITOT	NYSE Arca	C+	C+	C+		67.07	22,811	2.68	43.46	67.01	1.98	-0.04
Financial Select Sector SPDR® Fund	XLF	NYSE Arca	B-	C+	B-	Up	28.00	22,702	3.54	53.43	63.90	2.01	-0.03
iShares Short Treasury Bond ETF	SHV	NAS CM	C	C	C+		110.62	21,314	2.42	4.36	4.71	2.22	0.02
SPDR® Dow Jones Industrial Average ETF	DIA	NYSE Arca	B	B	C+	Up	269.18	21,223	3.70	56.62	76.57	2.15	0.00
iShares TIPS Bond ETF	TIP	NYSE Arca	C+	C+	C+	Up	116.29	20,420	7.12	6.38	11.26	1.85	0.06
iShares Russell 1000 ETF	IWB	NYSE Arca	C+	C+	C+		164.54	20,403	3.46	44.44	66.86	1.84	-0.03
iShares Russell Mid-Cap ETF	IWR	NYSE Arca	D	D	D	Up	55.95	20,009	3.43	-66.23	-61.10	1.43	-0.01
Vanguard Mid-Cap Value Index Fund ETF Shares	VOE	NYSE Arca	C	C	C+		113.00	19,610	2.02	28.55	49.05	2.12	-0.01
SPDR® S&P MidCap 400 ETF	MDY	NYSE Arca	C	C	C+		352.47	19,100	-1.94	29.80	53.08	1.38	0.00
SPDR® S&P Dividend ETF	SDY	NYSE Arca	C+	C	C+		102.60	18,915	7.17	34.85	69.45	2.45	-0.02
iShares 7-10 Year Treasury Bond ETF	IEF	NAS CM	C+	C	B-	Up	112.47	18,869	14.01	7.03	18.93	2.21	0.07
iShares MBS ETF	MBB	NAS CM	C+	C+	C+	Up	108.30	18,818	7.86	6.69	13.41	2.77	0.03
Schwab International Equity ETF™	SCHF	NYSE Arca	C	C	B		31.86	18,690	-1.59	20.74	18.50	3.54	0.10

Fund Name	MARKET			RATINGS				PRICE	TOTAL RETURNS & PERFORMANCE				VALUATION	
	Ticker Symbol	Traded On	Overall Rating	Reward Rating	Risk Rating	Recent Up/ Downgrade		Price as of 9/30/2019	Total Assets (MIL)	1-Year Total Return	3-Year Total Return	5-Year Total Return	Dividend Yield (TTM)	Premium/ Discount 1-Year Avg
iShares 20+ Year Treasury Bond ETF	TLT	NAS CM	C+	C	B-	Up		143.08	18,504	25.73	12.48	37.15	2.24	0.16
Schwab U.S. Large-Cap ETF™	SCHX	NYSE Arca	C+	C+	C+			70.93	18,300	3.72	45.58	68.42	1.9	-0.01
Vanguard FTSE Europe Index Fund ETF Shares	VGK	NYSE Arca	C	C	B-			53.61	18,214	-1.34	21.30	15.54	3.54	-0.02
iShares iBoxx $ High Yield Corporate Bond ETF	HYG	NYSE Arca	B	C+	A			87.17	17,978	6.14	17.19	23.69	5.29	0.15
iShares 1-3 Year Treasury Bond ETF	SHY	NAS CM	C	C	C+			84.82	17,773	4.26	4.22	5.98	2.11	0.04
iShares Select Dividend ETF	DVY	NAS CM	C	C	C+	Down		101.95	17,744	5.69	31.52	64.33	3.4	-0.02
Vanguard Total World Stock Index Fund ETF Shares	VT	NYSE Arca	C	C	C+			74.82	16,872	0.61	31.49	39.32	2.35	-0.04
iShares Preferred and Income Securities ETF	PFF	NAS CM	B	C+	A-	Up		37.53	16,568	7.35	12.53	26.69	5.56	0.17
iShares Gold Trust	IAU	NYSE Arca	C+	C+	C+	Up		14.10	16,353	24.57	11.48	20.57	0	-0.10
iShares Core MSCI Total International Stock ETF	IXUS	NAS CM	C	C	C+			57.76	16,192	-1.61	20.19	18.23	2.82	0.09
Invesco S&P 500® Equal Weight ETF	RSP	NYSE Arca	C	C	C+	Down		108.08	15,852	3.17	35.91	56.80	1.87	-0.03
iShares S&P 500 Value ETF	IVE	NYSE Arca	C+	C	C+	Up		119.14	15,747	4.97	34.66	50.84	2.3	-0.01
Schwab U.S. Broad Market ETF™	SCHB	NYSE Arca	C+	C+	C+			71.02	15,109	2.76	43.58	66.27	1.88	-0.01
iShares J.P. Morgan USD Emerging Markets Bond ETF	EMB	NAS CM	B-	B-	B-			113.35	14,869	11.53	12.24	28.19	5.45	0.30
iShares National Muni Bond ETF	MUB	NYSE Arca	C+	C+	C+			114.10	14,198	8.35	8.63	17.07	2.46	0.05
Vanguard Mid-Cap Growth Index Fund ETF Shares	VOT	NYSE Arca	C+	C+	C+			148.11	14,142	4.39	41.58	59.78	0.75	-0.02
Consumer Staples Select Sector SPDR® Fund	XLP	NYSE Arca	B-	B	C	Up		61.42	14,061	16.67	24.73	54.82	2.55	-0.02
Consumer Discretionary Select Sector SPDR® Fund	XLY	NYSE Arca	B	B+	C			120.70	14,001	3.80	55.86	92.75	1.3	-0.01
iShares U.S. Treasury Bond ETF	GOVT	BATS	C+	C	B			26.33	13,877	10.53	6.52	14.33	1.98	0.02
iShares Short-Term Corporate Bond ETF	IGSB	NAS CM	D-	D-	D	Down		53.67	12,902	6.78	-45.73	-44.22	3.06	0.07
Invesco S&P 500® Low Volatility ETF	SPLV	NYSE Arca	B	B	A-	Down		57.90	12,816	19.75	48.88	86.14	2	-0.01
PIMCO Enhanced Short Maturity Active Exchange-Traded Fund	MINT	NYSE Arca	C	C	C+			101.73	12,788	2.87	6.80	8.97	2.7	-0.01
Vanguard Long-Term Bond Index Fund ETF Shares	BLV	NYSE Arca	C+	C+	C+			102.67	12,668	22.64	17.27	36.99	3.33	0.12
iShares Edge MSCI Min Vol EAFE ETF	EFAV	BATS	C+	C+	C+	Up		73.28	11,982	3.94	19.67	36.06	2.95	0.06
iShares Edge MSCI USA Quality Factor ETF	QUAL	BATS	C+	C+	C+			92.40	11,734	3.73	44.68	72.38	1.72	0.00
iShares MSCI Japan ETF	EWJ	NYSE Arca	C	C-	C+			56.74	11,507	-4.82	18.55	29.80	1.59	-0.12
Vanguard Mortgage-Backed Securities Index Fund ETF Shares	VMBS	NAS CM	C+	C+	C+	Up		53.26	11,416	7.42	6.58	13.72	2.9	0.08
Utilities Select Sector SPDR® Fund	XLU	NYSE Arca	B	B	B-			64.74	11,403	27.07	45.74	81.83	2.88	-0.01
VanEck Vectors Gold Miners ETF	GDX	NYSE Arca	C	C	C-	Up		26.71	11,268	45.52	3.30	29.34	0.39	-0.10
iShares Russell Mid-Cap Value ETF	IWS	NYSE Arca	C	C	C+			89.70	10,979	1.73	24.65	44.23	1.99	-0.01
iShares Russell Mid-Cap Growth ETF	IWP	NYSE Arca	C+	C+	C+	Down		141.35	10,758	5.49	49.10	70.41	0.6	-0.01
iShares MSCI ACWI ETF	ACWI	NAS CM	B-	C	B			73.75	10,677	1.34	33.15	41.16	2.1	0.00
Schwab U.S. Dividend Equity ETF™	SCHD	NYSE Arca	B-	B	C	Up		54.78	10,335	6.42	41.48	66.81	3.04	-0.03
iShares Edge MSCI USA Momentum Factor ETF	MTUM	BATS	B-	B	C+	Up		119.25	10,222	1.28	60.39	98.99	1.46	0.00
SPDR® Bloomberg Barclays High Yield Bond ETF	JNK	NYSE Arca	A+	A+	A			108.74	10,168	218.82	252.02	262.72	5.59	0.09
Vanguard Health Care Index Fund ETF Shares	VHT	NYSE Arca	C+	C+	C+			167.68	10,016	-5.92	31.23	54.03	2.1	0.00
iShares Floating Rate Bond ETF	FLOT	BATS	C	C	C+			50.97	9,885	2.80	6.94	8.05	2.88	0.02
Industrial Select Sector SPDR® Fund	XLI	NYSE Arca	C+	C+	C+			77.63	9,810	0.14	40.89	61.57	2.02	-0.02
iShares MSCI EAFE Small-Cap ETF	SCZ	NAS CM	C	C-	C+			57.23	9,332	-5.80	18.62	34.71	2.83	-0.05
iShares 3-7 Year Treasury Bond ETF	IEI	NAS CM	C	C	C+			126.80	9,126	8.82	5.69	12.75	2.08	0.05
JPMorgan Ultra-Short Income ETF	JPST	BATS	C	C	C+			50.43	8,810	3.00			2.65	0.06
iShares Russell 2000 Growth ETF	IWO	NYSE Arca	C	C	C+			192.73	8,746	-8.24	32.42	57.76	0.72	-0.06
iShares Core Dividend Growth ETF	DGRO	NYSE Arca	C+	C+	C+			39.14	8,645	7.90	51.93	78.06	2.29	0.02
SPDR® Bloomberg Barclays 1-3 Month T-Bill ETF	BIL	NYSE Arca	C	C	B-			91.59	8,603	2.18	4.11	4.06	2.16	0.01
Schwab U.S. TIPS ETF™	SCHP	NYSE Arca	C+	C+	C+	Up		56.76	8,441	7.23	6.57	11.63	1.86	0.02
iShares MSCI Brazil Capped ETF	EWZ	NYSE Arca	C	C+	C			42.13	8,411	28.28	34.50	11.95	2.64	-0.12
iShares Intermediate-Term Corporate Bond ETF	IGIB	NAS CM	D	D	D			57.92	8,297	13.34	-43.00	-39.30	3.65	0.08
Alerian MLP ETF	AMLP	NYSE Arca	C	B-	D+	Up		9.14	8,260	-8.85	-9.19	-28.28	8.43	0.00

Section V:
Best One-Year Return BUY Rated Exchange-Traded Funds

Investment Ratings and analysis of the Best One-Year Return BUY Rated Exchange-Traded Funds.   Funds are listed in order by their one-year returns and overall rating.

Section V: Contents

This section contains Weiss Investment Ratings, key rating factors, and summary financial data for the Best One-Year Return BUY Rated Exchange-Traded Funds. Funds are listed in order by their one-year returns and overall rating.

Fund Name
Describes the fund's assets, regions of investments and investment strategies. Many funds have similar names, so you want to make sure the fund you look up is really the one you are interested in evaluating.

MARKET

Ticker Symbol
An arrangement of characters (usually letters) representing a particular security listed on an exchange or otherwise traded publicly. When a company issues securities to the public marketplace, it selects an available ticker symbol for its securities which investors use to place trade orders. Every listed security has a unique ticker symbol, facilitating the vast array of trade orders that flow through the financial markets every day.

Traded On (Exchange)
The stock exchange on which the fund is listed. The core function of a stock exchange is to ensure fair and orderly trading, as well as efficient dissemination of price information. Exchanges such as: NYSE (New York Stock Exchange), AMEX (American Stock Exchange), NNM (NASDAQ National Market), and NASQ (NASDAQ Small Cap) give companies, governments and other groups a platform to sell securities to the investing public. NASDAQ is abbreviated as NAS.

RATINGS

Overall Rating
The Weiss rating measured on a scale from A to E based on each fund's risk and performance. See the preceding section, "What Our Ratings Mean," for an explanation of each letter grade rating.

Reward Rating
This is based on the total return over a period of up to five years, including net asset value and price growth. The total return figure is stated net of the expenses and fees charged by the fund. Based on proprietary modeling the individual components of the risk and reward ratings are calculated and weighted and the final rating is generated.

Risk Rating
This is includes the risk ratings of component stocks where applicable and also includes the financial stability of the fund, turnover where applicable, together with the level of volatility as measured by the fund's daily returns over a period of up to five years. Funds with greater stability are considered less risky and receive a higher risk rating. Funds with greater volatility are considered riskier, and will receive a lower risk rating. In addition to considering the fund's volatility, the risk rating also considers an assessment of the valuation and quality of a fund's holdings.

Recent Upgrade/Downgrade

An "Up" or "Down" indicates that the Weiss Exchange-Traded Fund rating has changed since the publication of the last print edition. If a fund has had a rating change since June 30, 2019, the change is identified with an "Up" or "Down."

PRICE

Price

The price at which the fund is traded on a regular trading day. Prices in this guide are listed as of September 30, 2019.

TOTAL RETURNS & PERFORMANCE

Total Assets (MIL)

The total of all assets listed on the institution's balance sheet. This figure primarily consists of loans, investments, and fixed assets. Total Assets are displayed in millions.

1-Year Total Return

The rate of return on an investment over one year that includes interest, capital gains, dividends and distributions realized.

3-Year Total Return

The rate of return on an investment over three years that includes interest, capital gains, dividends and distributions realized.

5-Year Total Return

The rate of return on an investment over five years that includes interest, capital gains, dividends and distributions realized.

Dividend Yield (TTM)

Trailing twelve months dividends paid out relative to the share price. Expressed as a percentage and measures how much cash flow an investor is getting for each invested dollar. **Trailing Twelve Months (TTM)** is a representation of a fund's financial performance over the most recent 12 months. TTM uses the latest available financial data from a company's interim, quarterly or annual reports.

VALUATION

Premium/Discount 1-Year Average

The annual average premium or discount of the market price to the NAV (Net Asset Value), expressed as a percentage of the NAV. This value provides a year-by-year picture a fund's trading status. A negative number indicates that, on average, the fund's shares sold at a discount to NAV, and a positive number indicates the shares sold at a premium. If the number shown is –10.00, for example, the shares sold at an average 10% discount to NAV during the listed time-period.

Fund Name	Ticker Symbol	Traded On	Overall Rating	Reward Rating	Risk Rating	Recent Up/ Downgrade	Price as of 9/30/2019	Total Assets (MIL)	1-Year Total Return	3-Year Total Return	5-Year Total Return	Dividend Yield (TTM)	Premium/ Discount 1-Year Avg
SPDR® Bloomberg Barclays High Yield Bond ETF	JNK	NYSE Arca	A+	A+	A		108.74	10,168	218.82	252.02	262.72	5.59	0.09
iShares Cohen & Steers REIT ETF	ICF	BATS	B-	B+	C	Up	120.02	2,417	23.93	26.09	67.53	2.34	-0.02
iShares U.S. Home Construction ETF	ITB	BATS	B-	B+	C	Up	43.31	1,264	23.78	59.45	98.79	0.52	-0.02
SPDR® S&P Semiconductor ETF	XSD	NYSE Arca	B-	B	C-		89.82	337.0	19.16	72.03	152.33	0.66	0.00
iShares PHLX Semiconductor ETF	SOXX	NAS CM	B-	B+	C	Up	211.41	1,756	15.51	94.03	167.08	1.22	-0.01
SPDR® S&P Homebuilders ETF	XHB	NYSE Arca	B-	B	C	Up	44.08	680.8	15.00	31.93	52.98	1	-0.01
VanEck Vectors Semiconductor ETF	SMH	NYSE Arca	B-	B	C	Up	119.13	1,361	13.83	78.97	156.51	1.37	0.05
SPDR® S&P Insurance ETF	KIE	NYSE Arca	B-	B-	C+		35.23	898.7	12.57	50.04	83.05	1.68	-0.03
VanEck Vectors AMT-Free Intermediate Municipal Index ETF	ITM	BATS	B	B	C+		50.31	1,892	10.15	119.13	140.24	2.22	-0.11
VanEck Vectors J.P. Morgan EM Local Currency Bond ETF	EMLC	NYSE Arca	B-	B	C+		33.00	4,798	7.90	108.53	94.33	6.44	-0.18
VanEck Vectors High-Yield Municipal Index ETF	HYD	BATS	B	B	C+		64.43	3,054	7.68	127.72	161.80	4.17	-0.06
iShares Global Tech ETF	IXN	NYSE Arca	B-	B	C	Up	184.97	2,805	6.06	72.17	116.09	1.03	-0.03
iShares U.S. Broker-Dealers & Securities Exchanges ETF	IAI	NYSE Arca	B-	B	C	Up	64.31	238.0	4.94	62.54	79.31	1.63	-0.01
iShares U.S. Aerospace & Defense ETF	ITA	BATS	B-	B	C	Up	224.70	5,496	4.60	79.77	125.14	0.9	-0.02
iShares U.S. Financial Services ETF	IYG	NYSE Arca	B	B	C	Up	136.43	1,193	3.91	62.69	73.07	1.75	-0.01
iShares Expanded Tech-Software Sector ETF	IGV	BATS	B-	B	C		211.88	2,553	3.81	87.15	152.65	0.13	-0.02
Financial Select Sector SPDR® Fund	XLF	NYSE Arca	B-	C+	B-	Up	28.00	22,702	3.54	53.43	63.90	2.01	-0.03

Section VI:
Best Low Expense Exchange-Traded Funds

Investment Ratings and analysis of the Best Low Expense Exchange-Traded Funds. Funds are listed in order by their expense ratios and overall rating.

Section VI: Contents

This section contains Weiss Investment Ratings, key rating factors, and summary financial data for the Best Low Expense Exchange-Traded Funds. Funds are listed in order by their expense ratios and overall rating.

Fund Name
Describes the fund's assets, regions of investments and investment strategies. Many funds have similar names, so you want to make sure the fund you look up is really the one you are interested in evaluating.

MARKET

Ticker Symbol
An arrangement of characters (usually letters) representing a particular security listed on an exchange or otherwise traded publicly. When a company issues securities to the public marketplace, it selects an available ticker symbol for its securities which investors use to place trade orders. Every listed security has a unique ticker symbol, facilitating the vast array of trade orders that flow through the financial markets every day.

Traded On (Exchange)
The stock exchange on which the fund is listed. The core function of a stock exchange is to ensure fair and orderly trading, as well as efficient dissemination of price information. Exchanges such as: NYSE (New York Stock Exchange), AMEX (American Stock Exchange), NNM (NASDAQ National Market), and NASQ (NASDAQ Small Cap) give companies, governments and other groups a platform to sell securities to the investing public. NASDAQ is abbreviated as NAS.

RATINGS

Overall Rating
The Weiss rating measured on a scale from A to E based on each fund's risk and performance. See the preceding section, "What Our Ratings Mean," for an explanation of each letter grade rating.

Reward Rating
This is based on the total return over a period of up to five years, including net asset value and price growth. The total return figure is stated net of the expenses and fees charged by the fund. Based on proprietary modeling the individual components of the risk and reward ratings are calculated and weighted and the final rating is generated.

Risk Rating
This is includes the risk ratings of component stocks where applicable and also includes the financial stability of the fund, turnover where applicable, together with the level of volatility as measured by the fund's daily returns over a period of up to five years. Funds with greater stability are considered less risky and receive a higher risk rating. Funds with greater volatility are considered riskier, and will receive a lower risk rating. In addition to considering the fund's volatility, the risk rating also considers an assessment of the valuation and quality of a fund's holdings.

Recent Upgrade/Downgrade

An "Up" or "Down" indicates that the Weiss Exchange-Traded Fund rating has changed since the publication of the last print edition. If a fund has had a rating change since June 30, 2019, the change is identified with an "Up" or "Down."

PRICE

Price

The price at which the fund is traded on a regular trading day. Prices in this guide are listed as of September 30, 2019.

TOTAL RETURNS & PERFORMANCE

1-Year Total Return

The rate of return on an investment over one year that includes interest, capital gains, dividends and distributions realized.

3-Year Total Return

The rate of return on an investment over three years that includes interest, capital gains, dividends and distributions realized.

5-Year Total Return

The rate of return on an investment over five years that includes interest, capital gains, dividends and distributions realized.

Dividend Yield (TTM)

Trailing twelve months dividends paid out relative to the share price. Expressed as a percentage and measures how much cash flow an investor is getting for each invested dollar. **Trailing Twelve Months (TTM)** is a representation of a fund's financial performance over the most recent 12 months. TTM uses the latest available financial data from a company's interim, quarterly or annual reports.

Expense Ratio

A measure of what it costs an investment company to operate an exchange-traded fund. An expense ratio is determined through an annual calculation, where a fund's operating expenses are divided by the average dollar value of its assets under management. Operating expenses may include money spent on administration and management of the fund, advertising, etc. An expense ratio of 1 percent per annum means that each year 1 percent of the fund's total assets will be used to cover expenses.

VALUATION

Premium/Discount 1-Year Average

The annual average premium or discount of the market price to the NAV (Net Asset Value), expressed as a percentage of the NAV. This value provides a year-by-year picture a fund's trading status. A negative number indicates that, on average, the fund's shares sold at a discount to NAV, and a positive number indicates the shares sold at a premium. If the number shown is –10.00, for example, the shares sold at an average 10% discount to NAV during the listed time-period.

Fund Name	Ticker Symbol	Traded On	Overall Rating	Reward Rating	Risk Rating	Recent Up/Downgrade	Price as of 9/30/2019	1-Year Total Return	3-Year Total Return	5-Year Total Return	Dividend Yield (TTM)	Expense Ratio	Premium/Discount 1-Year Avg
Vanguard S&P 500 ETF	VOO	NYSE Arca	B-	C+	B		272.60	3.87	45.66	69.21	1.99	0.03	-0.03
iShares Core S&P 500 ETF	IVV	NYSE Arca	B-	C+	B		298.52	3.84	45.65	69.14	2.06	0.04	-0.01
Vanguard Growth Index Fund ETF Shares	VUG	NYSE Arca	B-	B-	C+	Up	166.28	4.25	53.67	80.40	1.06	0.04	-0.03
Vanguard Dividend Appreciation Index Fund ETF Shares	VIG	NYSE Arca	B-	B	C+		119.58	9.16	50.41	71.36	1.77	0.06	-0.01
SPDR® Portfolio Long Term Corporate Bond ETF	SPLB	NYSE Arca	B	B	C+	Up	30.09	19.98	20.21	39.59	3.86	0.07	0.13
Vanguard Mega Cap Growth Index Fund ETF Shares	MGK	NYSE Arca	B-	B	C+	Up	132.66	2.88	55.40	80.04	0.47	0.07	-0.01
Fidelity® MSCI Utilities Index ETF	FUTY	NYSE Arca	B-	B	C+	Down	42.49	25.93	47.17	83.80	2.66	0.08	0.03
Fidelity® MSCI Information Technology Index ETF	FTEC	NYSE Arca	B-	B	C+	Down	63.77	7.13	80.60	129.18	1.17	0.08	-0.03
SPDR® S&P 500 ETF	SPY	NYSE Arca	B-	C+	B		296.77	3.28	44.59	65.58	1.85	0.09	-0.05
Vanguard Utilities Index Fund ETF Shares	VPU	NYSE Arca	B	B	C+		143.65	25.87	47.41	84.91	2.81	0.1	-0.01
Vanguard Information Technology Index Fund ETF Shares	VGT	NYSE Arca	B-	B	C+	Down	215.55	6.46	83.56	128.70	1.26	0.1	-0.02
Vanguard Consumer Staples Index Fund ETF Shares	VDC	NYSE Arca	B-	B	C	Up	156.56	14.38	23.11	52.68	2.51	0.1	0.00
Utilities Select Sector SPDR® Fund	XLU	NYSE Arca	B	B	B-		64.74	27.07	45.74	81.83	2.88	0.13	-0.01
Consumer Staples Select Sector SPDR® Fund	XLP	NYSE Arca	B-	B	C	Up	61.42	16.67	24.73	54.82	2.55	0.13	-0.02
Financial Select Sector SPDR® Fund	XLF	NYSE Arca	B-	C+	B-	Up	28.00	3.54	53.43	63.90	2.01	0.13	-0.03
SPDR® Dow Jones Industrial Average ETF	DIA	NYSE Arca	B	B	C+	Up	269.18	3.70	56.62	76.57	2.15	0.17	0.00
Invesco QQQ Trust	QQQ	NAS CM	B-	B-	B-		188.81	2.31	63.28	103.88	0.82	0.2	-0.02
VanEck Vectors AMT-Free Intermediate Municipal Index ETF	ITM	BATS	B	B	C+		50.31	10.15	119.13	140.24	2.22	0.24	-0.11
iShares Cohen & Steers REIT ETF	ICF	BATS	B-	B+	C	Up	120.02	23.93	26.09	67.53	2.34	0.34	-0.02
VanEck Vectors Retail ETF	RTH	NYSE Arca	B-	B+	C	Up	114.47	3.87	53.35	98.97	0.86	0.35	-0.01
Invesco S&P 500® Equal Weight Utilities ETF	RYU	NYSE Arca	B-	B	C		106.64	25.20	44.00	74.37	2.45	0.4	0.01
Invesco S&P 500® Equal Weight Consumer Staples ETF	RHS	NYSE Arca	B-	B	C	Up	140.40	12.35	22.17	60.64	2.29	0.4	-0.04
iShares U.S. Technology ETF	IYW	NYSE Arca	B	B+	C+	Up	204.21	6.04	76.29	117.12	0.8	0.42	-0.01
iShares U.S. Financial Services ETF	IYG	NYSE Arca	B	B	C	Up	136.43	3.91	62.69	73.07	1.75	0.42	-0.01
iShares U.S. Real Estate ETF	IYR	NYSE Arca	B-	B-	B-		93.54	20.99	29.09	62.70	2.59	0.42	0.01
iShares U.S. Home Construction ETF	ITB	BATS	B-	B+	C	Up	43.31	23.78	59.45	98.79	0.52	0.42	-0.02
iShares U.S. Utilities ETF	IDU	NYSE Arca	B-	B	C		162.85	25.32	44.87	80.39	2.56	0.42	-0.01
iShares Expanded Tech-Software Sector ETF	IGV	BATS	B-	B	C		211.88	3.81	87.15	152.65	0.13	0.46	-0.02
iShares Global Tech ETF	IXN	NYSE Arca	B-	B	C	Up	184.97	6.06	72.17	116.09	1.03	0.46	-0.03
iShares MSCI Switzerland ETF	EWL	NYSE Arca	B-	B	C+	Down	37.70	10.47	31.85	31.05	1.99	0.47	0.03
iShares Residential Real Estate Capped ETF	REZ	NYSE Arca	B-	B	C	Up	79.47	31.54	35.93	86.80	2.63	0.48	0.04

Section VII:
BUY Rated Exchange-Traded Funds by Category

Investment Ratings and analysis for BUY Rated Exchange-Traded Funds by Category. Within Category, funds are listed in alphabetical order.

Section VII: Contents

This section contains Weiss Investment Ratings, key rating factors, and summary financial data for BUY Rated Exchange-Traded Funds by Category. Within category, funds are listed in alphabetical order.

Fund Name
Describes the fund's assets, regions of investments and investment strategies. Many funds have similar names, so you want to make sure the fund you look up is really the one you are interested in evaluating.

MARKET

Ticker Symbol
An arrangement of characters (usually letters) representing a particular security listed on an exchange or otherwise traded publicly. When a company issues securities to the public marketplace, it selects an available ticker symbol for its securities which investors use to place trade orders. Every listed security has a unique ticker symbol, facilitating the vast array of trade orders that flow through the financial markets every day.

Traded On (Exchange)
The stock exchange on which the fund is listed. The core function of a stock exchange is to ensure fair and orderly trading, as well as efficient dissemination of price information. Exchanges such as: NYSE (New York Stock Exchange), AMEX (American Stock Exchange), NNM (NASDAQ National Market), and NASQ (NASDAQ Small Cap) give companies, governments and other groups a platform to sell securities to the investing public. NASDAQ is abbreviated as NAS.

RATINGS

Overall Rating
The Weiss rating measured on a scale from A to E based on each fund's risk and performance. See the preceding section, "What Our Ratings Mean," for an explanation of each letter grade rating.

Reward Rating
This is based on the total return over a period of up to five years, including net asset value and price growth. The total return figure is stated net of the expenses and fees charged by the fund. Based on proprietary modeling the individual components of the risk and reward ratings are calculated and weighted and the final rating is generated.

Risk Rating
This is includes the risk ratings of component stocks where applicable and also includes the financial stability of the fund, turnover where applicable, together with the level of volatility as measured by the fund's daily returns over a period of up to five years. Funds with greater stability are considered less risky and receive a higher risk rating. Funds with greater volatility are considered riskier, and will receive a lower risk rating. In addition to considering the fund's volatility, the risk rating also considers an assessment of the valuation and quality of a fund's holdings.

Recent Upgrade/Downgrade

An "Up" or "Down" indicates that the Weiss Exchange-Traded Fund rating has changed since the publication of the last print edition. If a fund has had a rating change since June 30, 2019, the change is identified with an "Up" or "Down."

PRICE

Price

The price at which the fund is traded on a regular trading day. Prices in this guide are listed as of September 30, 2019.

TOTAL RETURNS & PERFORMANCE

Total Assets (MIL)

The total of all assets listed on the institution's balance sheet. This figure primarily consists of loans, investments, and fixed assets. Total Assets are displayed in millions.

1-Year Total Return

The rate of return on an investment over one year that includes interest, capital gains, dividends and distributions realized.

3-Year Total Return

The rate of return on an investment over three years that includes interest, capital gains, dividends and distributions realized.

5-Year Total Return

The rate of return on an investment over five years that includes interest, capital gains, dividends and distributions realized.

Dividend Yield (TTM)

Trailing twelve months dividends paid out relative to the share price. Expressed as a percentage and measures how much cash flow an investor is getting for each invested dollar. **Trailing Twelve Months (TTM)** is a representation of a fund's financial performance over the most recent 12 months. TTM uses the latest available financial data from a company's interim, quarterly or annual reports.

VALUATION

Premium/Discount 1-Year Average

The annual average premium or discount of the market price to the NAV (Net Asset Value), expressed as a percentage of the NAV. This value provides a year-by-year picture a fund's trading status. A negative number indicates that, on average, the fund's shares sold at a discount to NAV, and a positive number indicates the shares sold at a premium. If the number shown is –10.00, for example, the shares sold at an average 10% discount to NAV during the listed time-period.

Category: Commodities Specified

Fund Name	Ticker Symbol	Traded On	Overall Rating	Reward Rating	Risk Rating	Recent Up/Downgrade	Price as of 9/30/2019	Total Assets (MIL)	1-Year Total Return	3-Year Total Return	5-Year Total Return	Dividend Yield (TTM)	Premium/Discount 1-Year Avg
Aberdeen Standard Physical Palladium Shares ETF	PALL	NYSE Arca	B-	B+	C-	Up	159.19	236.8	58.02	127.70	110.68	0	-0.62

Category: Communications Sector Equity

Fund Name	Ticker Symbol	Traded On	Overall Rating	Reward Rating	Risk Rating	Recent Up/Downgrade	Price as of 9/30/2019	Total Assets (MIL)	1-Year Total Return	3-Year Total Return	5-Year Total Return	Dividend Yield (TTM)	Premium/Discount 1-Year Avg
Communication Services Select Sector SPDR® Fund	XLC	NYSE Arca	B-	B	C	Up	49.52	5,879	1.98			0.92	-0.01
Fidelity® MSCI Communication Services Index ETF	FCOM	NYSE Arca	B-	B	C	Up	33.07	434.7	6.28	22.65	49.48	1.04	0.05
iShares U.S. Telecommunications ETF	IYZ	BATS	B-	B	C	Up	29.20	496.5	0.29	-2.18	12.13	1.69	-0.05
Vanguard Communication Services Index Fund ETF Shares	VOX	NYSE Arca	B-	B	C	Up	86.70	2,134	0.67	-1.30	16.25	0.93	-0.01

Category: Consumer Goods & Services

Fund Name	Ticker Symbol	Traded On	Overall Rating	Reward Rating	Risk Rating	Recent Up/Downgrade	Price as of 9/30/2019	Total Assets (MIL)	1-Year Total Return	3-Year Total Return	5-Year Total Return	Dividend Yield (TTM)	Premium/Discount 1-Year Avg
Consumer Discretionary Select Sector SPDR® Fund	XLY	NYSE Arca	B	B+	C		120.70	14,001	3.80	55.86	92.75	1.3	-0.01
Consumer Staples Select Sector SPDR® Fund	XLP	NYSE Arca	B-	B	C	Up	61.42	14,061	16.67	24.73	54.82	2.55	-0.02
Fidelity® MSCI Consumer Staples Index ETF	FSTA	NYSE Arca	B-	B	C	Up	36.61	634.8	15.62	24.08	53.86	2.5	0.05
First Trust Nasdaq Food & Beverage ETF	FTXG	NAS CM	B-	B	C	Up	21.25	5.3	11.75	10.21		1.32	-0.28
First Trust Nasdaq Retail ETF	FTXD	NAS CM	B-	B	C	Up	23.36	8.2	-3.24	21.80		1.25	-0.12
Invesco DWA Consumer Cyclicals Momentum ETF	PEZ	NAS CM	B-	B	C	Up	52.75	31.7	-10.71	26.13	35.50	0.1	-0.02
Invesco DWA Consumer Staples Momentum ETF	PSL	NAS CM	B-	B	C	Up	72.10	205.4	1.60	31.14	63.06	0.53	-0.02
Invesco Dynamic Food & Beverage ETF	PBJ	NYSE Arca	B-	B	C	Up	35.18	73.9	10.38	10.93	33.30	1.09	-0.02
Invesco Dynamic Leisure and Entertainment ETF	PEJ	NYSE Arca	B-	B	C	Up	42.55	55.3	-7.99	22.06	34.66	0.42	0.02
Invesco Dynamic Retail ETF	PMR	NYSE Arca	B-	B	C-	Up	39.23	7.8	-2.78	15.38	25.92	0.68	-0.04
Invesco S&P 500® Equal Weight Consumer Staples ETF	RHS	NYSE Arca	B-	B	C	Up	140.40	477.1	12.35	22.17	60.64	2.29	-0.04
iShares Evolved U.S. Consumer Staples ETF	IECS	BATS	B-	B	C	Up	28.01	8.4	16.10			2.55	0.04
iShares U.S. Home Construction ETF	ITB	BATS	B-	B+	C	Up	43.31	1,264	23.78	59.45	98.79	0.52	-0.02
John Hancock Multifactor Consumer Staples ETF	JHMS	NYSE Arca	B-	B	C	Up	29.14	30.3	12.01	21.11		2.6	0.02
SPDR® S&P Homebuilders ETF	XHB	NYSE Arca	B-	B	C	Up	44.08	680.8	15.00	31.93	52.98	1	-0.01
VanEck Vectors Retail ETF	RTH	NYSE Arca	B-	B+	C	Up	114.47	71.2	3.87	53.35	98.97	0.86	-0.01
Vanguard Consumer Staples Index Fund ETF Shares	VDC	NYSE Arca	B-	B	C	Up	156.56	6,131	14.38	23.11	52.68	2.51	0.00

Category: Emerging Markets Fixed Income

Fund Name	Ticker Symbol	Traded On	Overall Rating	Reward Rating	Risk Rating	Recent Up/Downgrade	Price as of 9/30/2019	Total Assets (MIL)	1-Year Total Return	3-Year Total Return	5-Year Total Return	Dividend Yield (TTM)	Premium/Discount 1-Year Avg
iShares J.P. Morgan USD Emerging Markets Bond ETF	EMB	NAS CM	B-	B-	B-		113.35	14,869	11.53	12.24	28.19	5.45	0.30
VanEck Vectors J.P. Morgan EM Local Currency Bond ETF	EMLC	NYSE Arca	B-	B	C+		33.00	4,798	7.90	108.53	94.33	6.44	-0.18
Vanguard Emerg Mkts Govt Bond Ind Fund ETF Shares	VWOB	NAS CM	B-	B	C+		80.60	1,789	11.47	13.66	28.84	4.54	0.36

Category: Equity Miscellaneous

Fund Name	Ticker Symbol	Traded On	Overall Rating	Reward Rating	Risk Rating	Recent Up/Downgrade	Price as of 9/30/2019	Total Assets (MIL)	1-Year Total Return	3-Year Total Return	5-Year Total Return	Dividend Yield (TTM)	Premium/Discount 1-Year Avg
ETFMG Prime Mobile Payments ETF	IPAY	NYSE Arca	B	B+	C		46.61	743.2	9.11	88.23		0.1	0.03
iShares MSCI Russia Capped ETF	ERUS	NYSE Arca	B	B	C+		38.90	658.8	17.20	52.80	41.18	5.2	-0.23
VanEck Vectors Russia ETF	RSX	NYSE Arca	B	B	B-		22.81	1,173	10.85	36.52	24.12	4.23	-0.24

Category: Europe Equity Large Cap

Fund Name	Ticker Symbol	Traded On	Overall Rating	Reward Rating	Risk Rating	Recent Up/ Downgrade	Price as of 9/30/2019	Total Assets (MIL)	1-Year Total Return	3-Year Total Return	5-Year Total Return	Dividend Yield (TTM)	Premium/ Discount 1-Year Avg
iShares MSCI Switzerland ETF	EWL	NYSE Arca	B-	B	C+	Down	37.70	1,026	10.47	31.85	31.05	1.99	0.03

Category: Financials Sector Equity

Fund Name	Ticker Symbol	Traded On	Overall Rating	Reward Rating	Risk Rating	Recent Up/ Downgrade	Price as of 9/30/2019	Total Assets (MIL)	1-Year Total Return	3-Year Total Return	5-Year Total Return	Dividend Yield (TTM)	Premium/ Discount 1-Year Avg
Financial Select Sector SPDR® Fund	XLF	NYSE Arca	B-	C+	B-	Up	28.00	22,702	3.54	53.43	63.90	2.01	-0.03
First Trust Nasdaq Bank ETF	FTXO	NAS CM	B-	B	C	Up	25.59	139.5	-4.17	35.51		3.78	-0.04
Invesco DWA Financial Momentum ETF	PFI	NAS CM	B	B+	C	Up	37.43	65.4	11.21	27.03	42.63	1.09	-0.05
Invesco KBW Bank ETF	KBWB	NAS CM	B-	B	C	Up	51.52	535.7	-2.16	49.98	55.78	2.56	-0.04
Invesco KBW Property & Casualty Insurance ETF	KBWP	NAS CM	B	B	C+	Up	73.94	118.1	20.07	56.60	111.54	1.95	0.03
iShares U.S. Broker-Dealers & Securities Exchanges ETF	IAI	NYSE Arca	B-	B	C	Up	64.31	238.0	4.94	62.54	79.31	1.63	-0.01
iShares U.S. Financial Services ETF	IYG	NYSE Arca	B	B	C	Up	136.43	1,193	3.91	62.69	73.07	1.75	-0.01
iShares U.S. Regional Banks ETF	IAT	NYSE Arca	B-	B	C	Up	46.56	391.0	-1.86	40.65	56.93	2.63	-0.04
SPDR® S&P Insurance ETF	KIE	NYSE Arca	B-	B-	C+		35.23	898.7	12.57	50.04	83.05	1.68	-0.03
VanEck Vectors BDC Income ETF	BIZD	NYSE Arca	B-	B	C	Up	16.86	221.3	8.86	24.16	34.98	9.45	-0.08

Category: Global Equity Large Cap

Fund Name	Ticker Symbol	Traded On	Overall Rating	Reward Rating	Risk Rating	Recent Up/ Downgrade	Price as of 9/30/2019	Total Assets (MIL)	1-Year Total Return	3-Year Total Return	5-Year Total Return	Dividend Yield (TTM)	Premium/ Discount 1-Year Avg
iShares Edge MSCI Min Vol Global ETF	ACWV	BATS	B-	B-	C+		94.75	5,477	10.18	33.43	59.78	2.13	0.06
iShares MSCI ACWI ETF	ACWI	NAS CM	B-	C	B		73.75	10,677	1.34	33.15	41.16	2.1	0.00

Category: Global Fixed Income

Fund Name	Ticker Symbol	Traded On	Overall Rating	Reward Rating	Risk Rating	Recent Up/ Downgrade	Price as of 9/30/2019	Total Assets (MIL)	1-Year Total Return	3-Year Total Return	5-Year Total Return	Dividend Yield (TTM)	Premium/ Discount 1-Year Avg
iShares Core International Aggregate Bond ETF	IAGG	BATS	B-	B-	C+	Up	55.79	1,790	11.63	13.16		4.16	0.23
Vanguard Total International Bond Index Fund ETF Shares	BNDX	NAS CM	B-	B-	C+	Up	58.83	140,100	11.36	12.93	24.95	2.85	0.16

Category: Healthcare Sector Equity

Fund Name	Ticker Symbol	Traded On	Overall Rating	Reward Rating	Risk Rating	Recent Up/ Downgrade	Price as of 9/30/2019	Total Assets (MIL)	1-Year Total Return	3-Year Total Return	5-Year Total Return	Dividend Yield (TTM)	Premium/ Discount 1-Year Avg
iShares U.S. Healthcare Providers ETF	IHF	NYSE Arca	B-	B	C	Up	161.70	808.4	-15.67	36.57	61.78	4.36	0.00
iShares U.S. Medical Devices ETF	IHI	NYSE Arca	B	B+	C+	Up	247.24	4,268	9.05	72.08	156.02	0.3	0.01

Category: Industrials Sector Equity

Fund Name	Ticker Symbol	Traded On	Overall Rating	Reward Rating	Risk Rating	Recent Up/ Downgrade	Price as of 9/30/2019	Total Assets (MIL)	1-Year Total Return	3-Year Total Return	5-Year Total Return	Dividend Yield (TTM)	Premium/ Discount 1-Year Avg
First Trust Nasdaq Transportation ETF	FTXR	NAS CM	B-	B	C	Up	23.08	2.3	-7.57	17.52		1.53	0.13
First Trust Water ETF	FIW	NYSE Arca	B-	B	C	Up	56.11	468.6	11.80	52.97	87.06	0.67	0.03
Invesco Aerospace & Defense ETF	PPA	NYSE Arca	B	B+	C	Up	67.70	1,087	11.04	80.30	126.50	0.95	0.00
Invesco DWA Industrials Momentum ETF	PRN	NAS CM	B	B	C	Up	65.57	131.1	2.98	37.24	50.48	0.43	-0.15
Invesco Dynamic Building & Construction ETF	PKB	NYSE Arca	B	B+	C	Up	32.64	112.7	10.82	27.84	62.31	0.42	-0.04
Invesco Water Resources ETF	PHO	NAS CM	B-	B	C		36.60	1,017	16.20	51.08	54.08	0.47	0.00
iShares Transportation Average ETF	IYT	BATS	B-	B	C	Up	186.14	512.0	-7.99	32.74	33.95	1.31	-0.01
iShares U.S. Aerospace & Defense ETF	ITA	BATS	B-	B	C	Up	224.70	5,496	4.60	79.77	125.14	0.9	-0.02
VanEck Vectors Environmental Services ETF	EVX	NYSE Arca	B-	B	C	Up	104.43	36.5	9.05	52.67	71.96	0.31	0.10

Category: Latin America Equity

Fund Name	Ticker Symbol	Traded On	Overall Rating	Reward Rating	Risk Rating	Recent Up/Downgrade	Price as of 9/30/2019	Total Assets (MIL)	1-Year Total Return	3-Year Total Return	5-Year Total Return	Dividend Yield (TTM)	Premium/ Discount 1-Year Avg
First Trust Brazil AlphaDEX® Fund	FBZ	NAS CM	B-	B	C-	Up	15.82	108.9	45.70	53.07	26.59	2.77	-0.29
iShares MSCI Brazil Small-Cap ETF	EWZS	NAS CM	B	B+	C	Up	17.21	115.7	53.12	67.66	22.24	3.48	-0.16

Category: Long/Short Equity

Fund Name	Ticker Symbol	Traded On	Overall Rating	Reward Rating	Risk Rating	Recent Up/Downgrade	Price as of 9/30/2019	Total Assets (MIL)	1-Year Total Return	3-Year Total Return	5-Year Total Return	Dividend Yield (TTM)	Premium/ Discount 1-Year Avg
Amplify CWP Enhanced Dividend Income ETF	DIVO	BATS	B-	B	C	Up	30.48	19.8	7.15			5.23	0.01

Category: Moderate Allocation

Fund Name	Ticker Symbol	Traded On	Overall Rating	Reward Rating	Risk Rating	Recent Up/Downgrade	Price as of 9/30/2019	Total Assets (MIL)	1-Year Total Return	3-Year Total Return	5-Year Total Return	Dividend Yield (TTM)	Premium/ Discount 1-Year Avg
Eaton Vance Global Income Builder NextShares™	EVGBC	NAS CM	B-	C	B+	Up	9.73	6.1	3.06	23.56		11.33	0.00

Category: Natural Resources

Fund Name	Ticker Symbol	Traded On	Overall Rating	Reward Rating	Risk Rating	Recent Up/Downgrade	Price as of 9/30/2019	Total Assets (MIL)	1-Year Total Return	3-Year Total Return	5-Year Total Return	Dividend Yield (TTM)	Premium/ Discount 1-Year Avg
Materials Select Sector SPDR® Fund	XLB	NYSE Arca	B-	B	C	Up	58.20	4,245	0.83	28.34	28.82	2.06	-0.01

Category: Real Estate Sector Equity

Fund Name	Ticker Symbol	Traded On	Overall Rating	Reward Rating	Risk Rating	Recent Up/Downgrade	Price as of 9/30/2019	Total Assets (MIL)	1-Year Total Return	3-Year Total Return	5-Year Total Return	Dividend Yield (TTM)	Premium/ Discount 1-Year Avg
Global X SuperDividend® REIT ETF	SRET	NAS CM	B-	B-	C+	Up	15.04	324.5	7.88	25.84		7.9	0.18
Invesco S&P 500® Equal Weight Real Estate ETF	EWRE	NYSE Arca	B-	B	C	Up	31.84	46.2	20.96	27.41		2.68	0.06
iShares Cohen & Steers REIT ETF	ICF	BATS	B-	B+	C	Up	120.02	2,417	23.93	26.09	67.53	2.34	-0.02
iShares Residential Real Estate Capped ETF	REZ	NYSE Arca	B-	B	C	Up	79.47	575.9	31.54	35.93	86.80	2.63	0.04
iShares U.S. Real Estate ETF	IYR	NYSE Arca	B-	B-	B-		93.54	5,005	20.99	29.09	62.70	2.59	0.01
Nuveen Short-Term REIT ETF	NURE	BATS	B-	B	C	Up	30.76	55.3	18.62			3.27	0.03
Pacer Benchmark Data & Infrastructure Real Estate SCTR ETF	SRVR	NYSE Arca	B-	B+	C-	Up	32.20	120.6	26.28			1.63	0.02
Pacer Benchmark Industrial Real Estate SCTR ETF	INDS	NYSE Arca	B	B+	C	Up	32.41	24.3	32.75			1.88	0.13
The Real Estate Select Sector SPDR Fund	XLRE	NYSE Arca	B	B+	C-	Up	39.34	3,902	25.33	33.59		2.89	-0.03
Vanguard Real Estate Index Fund ETF Shares	VNQ	NYSE Arca	B-	C+	B-	Up	93.25	69,465	20.97	22.70	60.39	3.12	-0.01

Category: Technology Sector Equity

Fund Name	Ticker Symbol	Traded On	Overall Rating	Reward Rating	Risk Rating	Recent Up/Downgrade	Price as of 9/30/2019	Total Assets (MIL)	1-Year Total Return	3-Year Total Return	5-Year Total Return	Dividend Yield (TTM)	Premium/ Discount 1-Year Avg
Fidelity® MSCI Information Technology Index ETF	FTEC	NYSE Arca	B-	B	C+	Down	63.77	2,556	7.13	80.60	129.18	1.17	-0.03
First Trust Nasdaq Semiconductor ETF	FTXL	NAS CM	B-	B+	C	Up	34.70	31.2	15.07	71.58		0.95	0.05
First Trust NASDAQ Technology Dividend Index Fund	TDIV	NAS CM	B-	B	C	Up	40.11	1,011	7.01	47.14	71.05	2.41	0.02
Innovation Shares NextGen Protocol ETF	KOIN	NYSE Arca	B-	B	C	Up	26.81	10.1	0.72			0.8	-0.15
Invesco Dynamic Semiconductors ETF	PSI	NYSE Arca	B-	B	C-	Up	57.81	179.3	9.89	80.11	168.39	0.69	-0.05
Invesco Solar ETF	TAN	NYSE Arca	B-	B	C	Up	29.37	438.6	42.71	57.30	-17.32	0.44	-0.08
iShares Expanded Tech-Software Sector ETF	IGV	BATS	B-	B	C		211.88	2,553	3.81	87.15	152.65	0.13	-0.02
iShares Global Tech ETF	IXN	NYSE Arca	B-	B	C	Up	184.97	2,805	6.06	72.17	116.09	1.03	-0.03

Category: Technology
Sector Equity (con't)

Fund Name	Ticker Symbol	Traded On	Overall Rating	Reward Rating	Risk Rating	Recent Up/ Downgrade	Price as of 9/30/2019	Total Assets (MIL)	1-Year Total Return	3-Year Total Return	5-Year Total Return	Dividend Yield (TTM)	Premium/ Discount 1-Year Avg
iShares PHLX Semiconductor ETF	SOXX	NAS CM	B-	B+	C	Up	211.41	1,756	15.51	94.03	167.08	1.22	-0.01
iShares U.S. Technology ETF	IYW	NYSE Arca	B	B+	C+	Up	204.21	4,126	6.04	76.29	117.12	0.8	-0.01
SPDR® S&P Semiconductor ETF	XSD	NYSE Arca	B-	B	C-		89.82	337.0	19.16	72.03	152.33	0.66	0.00
VanEck Vectors Semiconductor ETF	SMH	NYSE Arca	B-	B	C	Up	119.13	1,361	13.83	78.97	156.51	1.37	0.05
Vanguard Information Technology Index Fund ETF Shares	VGT	NYSE Arca	B-	B	C+	Down	215.55	23,769	6.46	83.56	128.70	1.26	-0.02

Category: Trading Tools

Fund Name	Ticker Symbol	Traded On	Overall Rating	Reward Rating	Risk Rating	Recent Up/ Downgrade	Price as of 9/30/2019	Total Assets (MIL)	1-Year Total Return	3-Year Total Return	5-Year Total Return	Dividend Yield (TTM)	Premium/ Discount 1-Year Avg
Direxion Daily Mid Cap Bear 3X Shares	MIDZ	NYSE Arca	B-	B	D+	Up	50.60	3.2	372.08	83.16	-20.43	0.75	-0.17
Direxion Daily MSCI Real Estate Bear 3X Shares	DRV	NYSE Arca	B	A	D+	Up	26.56	16.0	179.40	120.24	-33.05	0.95	-0.02
Direxion Daily S&P Oil & Gas Exp. & Prod. Bear 3X Shares	DRIP	NYSE Arca	B	A-	D	Up	78.50	39.8	1,399.15	299.54		0.61	-0.06
Direxion Daily Small Cap Bear 3X Shares	TZA	NYSE Arca	B-	B	D+	Up	46.99	346.9	438.26	77.22	-32.80	0.82	0.06
Grayscale Bitcoin Trust	GBTC	OTC BB	B	A+	D+	Up	10.59	1,925	20.39	1,154.20	1,795.68	0	24.90
ProShares Ultra Semiconductors	USD	NYSE Arca	B-	B	C	Up	45.01	69.9	0.81	123.66	254.14	0.97	-0.14
ProShares Ultra Utilities	UPW	NYSE Arca	B-	B	D+	Up	70.29	35.1	49.25	85.97	169.34	0.65	0.11
VelocityShares 3x Long Gold ETN - S&P GSCI® Gold Ind ER	UGLD	NAS CM	B	A-	C-	Up	132.67	169.5	67.91	916.04	940.29	0	0.05
VelocityShares 3x Long Silver ETN - S&P GSCI® Silver Ind E	USLV	NAS CM	B	A-	D+	Up	83.51	278.7	30.35	275.82	194.18	0	0.02

Category: US Equity
Large Cap Blend

Fund Name	Ticker Symbol	Traded On	Overall Rating	Reward Rating	Risk Rating	Recent Up/ Downgrade	Price as of 9/30/2019	Total Assets (MIL)	1-Year Total Return	3-Year Total Return	5-Year Total Return	Dividend Yield (TTM)	Premium/ Discount 1-Year Avg
AdvisorShares Focused Equity ETF	CWS	NYSE Arca	B	B	C	Up	35.22	17.6	4.63	41.04		0.63	0.40
Aptus Behavioral Momentum ETF	BEMO	BATS	B-	B	C	Up	30.48	64.0	-17.04	21.66		0.8	-0.01
First Trust Capital Strength ETF	FTCS	NAS CM	B-	B-	C+	Up	56.78	2,863	3.86	46.96	74.18	1.39	0.01
Invesco S&P 500® Quality ETF	SPHQ	NYSE Arca	B-	B-	C+	Up	33.54	1,492	3.62	40.54	72.42	1.56	-0.03
iShares Core S&P 500 ETF	IVV	NYSE Arca	B-	C+	B		298.52	186,488	3.84	45.65	69.14	2.06	-0.01
iShares Edge MSCI Min Vol USA ETF	USMV	BATS	B	B	A-	Down	64.10	35,010	14.68	49.72	89.73	1.84	-0.05
SPDR® S&P 500 ETF	SPY	NYSE Arca	B-	C+	B		296.77	273,532	3.28	44.59	65.58	1.85	-0.05
SPDR® SSGA US Large Cap Low Volatility Index ETF	LGLV	NYSE Arca	B	B	C+	Up	111.48	881.9	16.96	52.52	83.95	1.81	0.11
Vanguard Dividend Appreciation Index Fund ETF Shares	VIG	NYSE Arca	B-	B	C+		119.58	47,776	9.16	50.41	71.36	1.77	-0.01
Vanguard S&P 500 ETF	VOO	NYSE Arca	B-	C+	B		272.60	493,907	3.87	45.66	69.21	1.99	-0.03
Vesper U.S. Large Cap Short-Term Reversal Strategy ETF	UTRN	NYSE Arca	B-	B	C		26.31	31.5	7.07			0.58	0.08
WBI BullBear Quality 1000 ETF	WBIL	NYSE Arca	B-	B	C	Up	26.68	53.4	-5.07	27.81	12.09	0.66	-0.06

Category: US Equity
Large Cap Growth

Fund Name	Ticker Symbol	Traded On	Overall Rating	Reward Rating	Risk Rating	Recent Up/ Downgrade	Price as of 9/30/2019	Total Assets (MIL)	1-Year Total Return	3-Year Total Return	5-Year Total Return	Dividend Yield (TTM)	Premium/ Discount 1-Year Avg
Invesco QQQ Trust	QQQ	NAS CM	B-	B-	B-		188.81	74,717	2.31	63.28	103.88	0.82	-0.02
iShares Edge MSCI USA Momentum Factor ETF	MTUM	BATS	B-	B	C+	Up	119.25	10,222	1.28	60.39	98.99	1.46	0.00
Ivy Focused Growth NextShares™	IVFGC	NAS CM	B	A-	C	Up	20.54	14.3	9.82			0.17	0.00
SPDR® MFS Systematic Growth Equity ETF	SYG	NYSE Arca	B-	B	C	Up	81.40	37.4	-4.79	35.60	63.61	1.13	-0.01
Vanguard Growth Index Fund ETF Shares	VUG	NYSE Arca	B-	B-	C+	Up	166.28	92,060	4.25	53.67	80.40	1.06	-0.03
Vanguard Mega Cap Growth Index Fund ETF Shares	MGK	NYSE Arca	B-	B	C+	Up	132.66	4,508	2.88	55.40	80.04	0.47	-0.01
WBI BullBear Rising Income 1000 ETF	WBIE	NYSE Arca	B	B	C		27.19	58.5	-2.18	28.90	16.87	0.9	-0.05

Category: US Equity
Large Cap Value

Fund Name	Ticker Symbol	Traded On	Overall Rating	Reward Rating	Risk Rating	Recent Up/ Downgrade	Price as of 9/30/2019	Total Assets (MIL)	1-Year Total Return	3-Year Total Return	5-Year Total Return	Dividend Yield (TTM)	Premium/ Discount 1-Year Avg
First Trust Dow 30 Equal Weight ETF	EDOW	NYSE Arca	B-	B	C	Up	24.52	49.0	5.19			1.77	-0.01
Invesco Dow Jones Industrial Average Dividend ETF	DJD	NYSE Arca	B-	B	C	Up	37.23	81.9	5.46	47.98		2.75	0.11
Invesco S&P 500® Low Volatility ETF	SPLV	NYSE Arca	B	B	A-	Down	57.90	12,816	19.75	48.88	86.14	2	-0.01
iShares Core High Dividend ETF	HDV	NYSE Arca	B-	B	C	Up	94.16	7,409	7.01	28.45	50.78	3.33	-0.01
Schwab U.S. Dividend Equity ETF™	SCHD	NYSE Arca	B-	B	C	Up	54.78	10,335	6.42	41.48	66.81	3.04	-0.03
SPDR® Dow Jones Industrial Average ETF	DIA	NYSE Arca	B	B	C+	Up	269.18	21,223	3.70	56.62	76.57	2.15	0.00
SPDR® MFS Systematic Core Equity ETF	SYE	NYSE Arca	B-	B	C	Up	82.41	35.4	2.03	43.54	69.34	1.67	-0.05

Category: US Equity Mid Cap

Fund Name	Ticker Symbol	Traded On	Overall Rating	Reward Rating	Risk Rating	Recent Up/ Downgrade	Price as of 9/30/2019	Total Assets (MIL)	1-Year Total Return	3-Year Total Return	5-Year Total Return	Dividend Yield (TTM)	Premium/ Discount 1-Year Avg
Invesco DWA Momentum ETF	PDP	NAS CM	B-	B-	C+	Up	60.90	1,706	2.86	45.18	60.78	0.26	-0.02
WBI BullBear Rising Income 2000 ETF	WBIA	NYSE Arca	B-	B	C	Up	21.53	7.5	-10.44	1.11	-9.81	0.85	-0.02

Category: US Fixed Income

Fund Name	Ticker Symbol	Traded On	Overall Rating	Reward Rating	Risk Rating	Recent Up/ Downgrade	Price as of 9/30/2019	Total Assets (MIL)	1-Year Total Return	3-Year Total Return	5-Year Total Return	Dividend Yield (TTM)	Premium/ Discount 1-Year Avg
First Trust Preferred Securities and Income ETF	FPE	NYSE Arca	B-	B-	C+		19.73	4,425	9.47	19.68	38.94	5.55	0.12
Invesco Taxable Municipal Bond ETF	BAB	NYSE Arca	B-	B-	C+	Up	32.40	1,306	15.29	16.61	34.23	3.79	0.21
iShares Core U.S. Aggregate Bond ETF	AGG	NYSE Arca	B-	C+	B		113.17	66,025	10.35	8.90	17.24	2.71	0.06
iShares iBoxx $ High Yield Corporate Bond ETF	HYG	NYSE Arca	B	C+	A		87.17	17,978	6.14	17.19	23.69	5.29	0.15
iShares iBoxx $ Investment Grade Corporate Bond ETF	LQD	NYSE Arca	B-	B-	B		127.48	36,121	14.99	14.75	26.90	3.35	0.09
iShares Long-Term Corporate Bond ETF	IGLB	NYSE Arca	B-	B	C+		66.63	1,734	20.05	19.85	36.16	3.92	0.21
iShares Preferred and Income Securities ETF	PFF	NAS CM	B	C+	A-	Up	37.53	16,568	7.35	12.53	26.69	5.56	0.17
PIMCO Investment Grade Corp Bond Ind ETF	CORP	NYSE Arca	B-	B-	C+	Up	109.72	650.6	13.35	13.93	25.35	3.29	-0.05
SPDR® Bloomberg Barclays High Yield Bond ETF	JNK	NYSE Arca	A+	A+	A		108.74	10,168	218.82	252.02	262.72	5.59	0.09
SPDR® Bloomberg Barclays Short Term High Yield Bond ETF	SJNK	NYSE Arca	B-	C	B	Down	27.01	3,301	3.47	15.66	19.16	5.69	0.11
SPDR® Portfolio Long Term Corporate Bond ETF	SPLB	NYSE Arca	B	B	C+	Up	30.09	641.1	19.98	20.21	39.59	3.86	0.13
Vanguard Long-Term Corporate Bond Index Fund ETF Shares	VCLT	NAS CM	B-	B	C+		101.14	4,732	19.93	20.12	39.51	3.88	0.22
Vanguard Total Bond Market Index Fund ETF Shares	BND	NAS CM	B-	C+	B		84.43	241,309	10.59	8.92	17.29	2.74	0.05

Category: US Municipal
Fixed Income

Fund Name	Ticker Symbol	Traded On	Overall Rating	Reward Rating	Risk Rating	Recent Up/ Downgrade	Price as of 9/30/2019	Total Assets (MIL)	1-Year Total Return	3-Year Total Return	5-Year Total Return	Dividend Yield (TTM)	Premium/ Discount 1-Year Avg
Eaton Vance TABS 5-to-15 Year Ladder Muni Bond NextShares™	EVLMC	NAS CM	B-	C+	B		10.47	7.3	8.40	8.58		2.18	0.00
VanEck Vectors AMT-Free Intermediate Municipal Index ETF	ITM	BATS	B	B	C+		50.31	1,892	10.15	119.13	140.24	2.22	-0.11
VanEck Vectors High-Yield Municipal Index ETF	HYD	BATS	B	B	C+		64.43	3,054	7.68	127.72	161.80	4.17	-0.06

Category: Utilities
Sector Equity

Fund Name	Ticker Symbol	Traded On	Overall Rating	Reward Rating	Risk Rating	Recent Up/ Downgrade	Price as of 9/30/2019	Total Assets (MIL)	1-Year Total Return	3-Year Total Return	5-Year Total Return	Dividend Yield (TTM)	Premium/ Discount 1-Year Avg
Fidelity® MSCI Utilities Index ETF	FUTY	NYSE Arca	B-	B	C+	Down	42.49	896.0	25.93	47.17	83.80	2.66	0.03
First Trust Utilities AlphaDEX® Fund	FXU	NYSE Arca	B-	B-	C+	Up	29.65	1,308	10.34	24.70	52.98	2.49	-0.01
Invesco DWA Utilities Momentum ETF	PUI	NAS CM	B-	B	C+		35.02	297.4	24.66	46.47	81.91	1.56	0.09
Invesco S&P 500® Equal Weight Utilities ETF	RYU	NYSE Arca	B-	B	C		106.64	400.0	25.20	44.00	74.37	2.45	0.01

Category: Utilities Sector Equity (con't) Fund Name	MARKET		RATINGS				PRICE	TOTAL RETURNS & PERFORMANCE				VALUATION	
	Ticker Symbol	Traded On	Overall Rating	Reward Rating	Risk Rating	Recent Up/ Downgrade	Price as of 9/30/2019	Total Assets (MIL)	1-Year Total Return	3-Year Total Return	5-Year Total Return	Dividend Yield (TTM)	Premium/ Discount 1-Year Avg
iShares U.S. Utilities ETF	IDU	NYSE Arca	B-	B	C		162.85	952.8	25.32	44.87	80.39	2.56	-0.01
Utilities Select Sector SPDR® Fund	XLU	NYSE Arca	B	B	B-		64.74	11,403	27.07	45.74	81.83	2.88	-0.01
Vanguard Utilities Index Fund ETF Shares	VPU	NYSE Arca	B	B	C+		143.65	5,717	25.87	47.41	84.91	2.81	-0.01
Virtus Reaves Utilities ETF	UTES	NYSE Arca	B-	B	C+	Up	41.83	27.1	26.63	48.62		1.82	0.12

Appendix:

Glossary

This section contains an explanation of the fields of data used throughout this guide.

1-Year Total Return
The rate of return on an investment over one year that includes interest, capital gains, dividends and distributions realized.

3-Year Total Return
The rate of return on an investment over three years that includes interest, capital gains, dividends and distributions realized.

3-Month Total Return
The rate of return on an investment over three months that includes interest, capital gains, dividends and distributions realized.

3-Year Standard Deviation
A statistical measurement of dispersion about an average, which depicts how widely the returns varied over the past three years. Investors use the standard deviation of historical performance to try to predict the range of returns that are most likely for a given fund. When a fund has a high standard deviation, the predicted range of performance is wide, implying greater volatility. Standard deviation is most appropriate for measuring risk if it is for a fund that is an investor's only holding. The figure cannot be combined for more than one fund because the standard deviation for a portfolio of multiple funds is a function of not only the individual standard deviations, but also of the degree of correlation among the funds' returns. If a fund's returns follow a normal distribution, then approximately 68 percent of the time they will fall within one standard deviation of the mean return for the fund, and 95 percent of the time within two standard deviations.

5-Year Total Return
The rate of return on an investment over five years that includes interest, capital gains, dividends and distributions realized.

52-Week High
The highest price that a fund has achieved during the previous 52 weeks.

52-Week Low
The lowest price that a fund has achieved during the previous 52 weeks.

6-Month Total Return
The rate of return on an investment over six months that includes interest, capital gains, dividends and distributions realized.

Address
The company's street address.

Asset & Performance History
Indicates the fund's **NAV (Net Asset Value)** and **1-Year Total Return** for the previous 6 years.

Asset Allocation
Indicates the percentage of assets in each category. Used as an investment strategy that attempts to balance risk versus reward by adjusting the percentage of each asset in an investment portfolio according to the investor's risk tolerance, goals and investment time frame. Allocation percentages may not add up to 100%. Negative values reflect short positions. See Cash, Stocks, US Stocks, Bonds, US Bonds, Other)

Bonds (%)
The percentage of the fund's assets invested in bonds. A bond is an unsecured debt security issued by companies, municipalities, states and sovereign governments to raise funds. When a company issues a bond it borrows money from the bondholder to boost the business, in exchange the bondholder receives the principal amount back plus the interest on the determined maturity date.

BUY-HOLD-SELL Indicator
Funds that are rated in the A or B range are, in our opinion, a potential BUY. Funds in the C range will indicate a HOLD status. Funds in the D or E range will indicate a SELL status.

Cash (%)
The percentage of the fund's assets invested in short-term obligations, usually less than 90 days, that provide a return in the form of interest payments. This type of investment generally offers a low return compared to other investments but has a low risk level.

Category
Identifies funds according to their actual investment styles as measured by their portfolio holdings. This categorization allows investors to spread their money around in a mix of funds with a variety of risk and return characteristics.

Dividend Yield (TTM)
Trailing twelve months dividends paid out relative to the share price. Expressed as a percentage and measures how much cash flow an investor is getting for each invested dollar. **Trailing Twelve Months** (TTM) is a representation of a fund's financial performance over the most recent 12 months. TTM uses the latest available financial data from a company's interim, quarterly or annual reports.

Effective Duration
Effective duration for all long fixed income positions in a portfolio. This value gives a better estimation of how the price of bonds with embedded options, which are common in many exchange-traded funds, will change as a result of changes in interest rates. Effective duration takes into account expected mortgage prepayment or the likelihood that embedded options will be exercised if a fund holds futures, other derivative securities, or other funds as assets, the aggregate effective duration should include the weighted impact of those exposures.

Expense Ratio
A measure of what it costs an investment company to operate an exchange-traded fund. An expense ratio is determined through an annual calculation, where a fund's operating expenses are divided by the average dollar value of its assets under management. Operating expenses may include money spent on administration and management of the fund, advertising, etc. An expense ratio of 1 percent per annum means that each year 1 percent of the fund's total assets will be used to cover expenses.

Fund Name
Describes the fund's assets, regions of investments and investment strategies. Many funds have similar names, so you want to make sure the fund you look up is really the one you are interested in evaluating.

Inception Date
The date on which the fund began its operations. The commencement date indicates when a fund began investing in the market. Many investors prefer funds with longer operating histories. Funds with longer histories have longer track records and can thereby provide investors with a more long-standing picture of their performance.

Institutional Only
This indicates if the fund is offered to institutional clients only (pension funds, mutual funds, money managers, insurance companies, investment banks, commercial trusts, endowment funds, hedge funds, and some hedge fund investors). See **Services Offered**.

Investment Strategy
A set of rules, behaviors or procedures, designed to guide an investor's selection of an investment portfolio. Individuals have different profit objectives, and their individual skills make different tactics and strategies appropriate.

Manager/Tenure (Years)
The name of the manager and the number of years spent managing the fund.

NAV (Net Asset Value)
A fund's price per share. The value is calculated by dividing the total value of all the securities in the portfolio, less any liabilities, by the number of fund shares outstanding.

Open to New Investments
Indicates whether the fund accepts investments from those who are not existing investors. A "Y" in this column identifies that the fund accepts new investors. No data in this column indicates that the fund is closed to new investors. The fund may be closed to new investors because the fund's asset base is getting too large to effectively execute its investing style. Although, the fund may be closed, in most cases, existing investors are able to add to their holdings.

Other (%)
The percentage of the fund's assets invested in other financial instruments. See **Asset Allocation**.

Overall Rating
The Weiss rating measured on a scale from A to E based on each fund's risk and performance. See the preceding section, "What Our Ratings Mean," for an explanation of each letter grade rating.

Performance Chart
A graphical representation of the fund's total returns over the past year.

Phone Exchange
This indicates that investors can move money between different funds within the same fund family over the phone. See **Services Offered**.

Phone Number
The company's phone number.

Premium/Discount 1-Year Average
The annual average premium or discount of the market price to the NAV (Net Asset Value), expressed as a percentage of the NAV. This value provides a year-by-year picture a fund's trading status. A negative number indicates that, on average, the fund's shares sold at a discount to NAV, and a positive number indicates the shares sold at a premium. If the number shown is –10.00, for example, the shares sold at an average 10% discount to NAV during the listed time-period.

Price
The price at which the fund is traded on a regular trading day. Prices in this guide are listed as of September 30, 2019.

Prospectus Objective
Gives a general idea of a fund's overall investment approach and goals.

Provider
The legal company that issues the fund.

Ratings History
Indicates the fund's Overall, Risk and Reward Ratings for the previous four years. Ratings are listed as of September 30, 2019 (Q3-19), December 31, 2018 (Q4-18), December 31, 2017 (Q4-17), December 31, 2016 (Q4-16), and December 31, 2015 (Q4-15).
See **Overall Rating, Risk Rating, Reward Rating**.

Recent Upgrade/Downgrade
An "Up" or "Down" indicates that the Weiss Exchange-Traded Fund rating has changed since the publication of the last print edition. If a fund has had a rating change since June 30, 2019, the change is identified with an "Up" or "Down."

Reward Rating

This is based on the total return over a period of up to five years, including net asset value and price growth. The total return figure is stated net of the expenses and fees charged by the fund. Based on proprietary modeling the individual components of the risk and reward ratings are calculated and weighted and the final rating is generated.

Risk Rating

This is includes the risk ratings of component stocks where applicable and also includes the financial stability of the fund, turnover where applicable, together with the level of volatility as measured by the fund's daily returns over a period of up to five years. Funds with greater stability are considered less risky and receive a higher risk rating. Funds with greater volatility are considered riskier, and will receive a lower risk rating. In addition to considering the fund's volatility, the risk rating also considers an assessment of the valuation and quality of a fund's holdings.

Services Offered

Services offered by the fund provider. Such services can include:

Systematic Withdrawal Plan

A plan offered by exchange-traded funds that pays specific amounts to shareholders at predetermined intervals.

Institutional Only

This indicates if the fund is offered to institutional clients only (pension funds, mutual funds, money managers, insurance companies, investment banks, commercial trusts, endowment funds, hedge funds, and some hedge fund investors).

Phone Exchange

This indicates that investors can move money between different funds within the same fund family over the phone.

Wire Redemption

This indicates whether or not investors can redeem electronically.

Qualified Investment

Under a qualified plan, an investor may invest in the variable annuity with pretax dollars through an employee pension plan, such as a 401(k) or 403(b). Money builds up on a tax-deferred basis, and when the qualified investor makes a withdrawal or annuitizes, all contributions received are taxable income.

Stocks (%)

The percentage of the fund's assets invested in stock. See **Asset Allocation**.

Sub-Category

A subdivision of funds, usually with common characteristics as the category.

Systematic Withdrawal Plan
A plan offered by exchange-traded funds that pays specific amounts to shareholders at predetermined intervals. See **Services Offered**.

Ticker Symbol
An arrangement of characters (usually letters) representing a particular security listed on an exchange or otherwise traded publicly. When a company issues securities to the public marketplace, it selects an available ticker symbol for its securities which investors use to place trade orders. Every listed security has a unique ticker symbol, facilitating the vast array of trade orders that flow through the financial markets every day.

Top Holdings
The highest amount of publicly traded assets held by a fund. These publicly traded assets may include company stock, mutual funds or other investment vehicles.

Total Returns (%)
See 3-Month Total Return, 6-Month Total Return, 1-Year Total Return, 3-Year Total Return, 5-Year Total Return.

Traded On (Exchange)
The stock exchange on which the fund is listed. The core function of a stock exchange is to ensure fair and orderly trading, as well as efficient dissemination of price information. Exchanges such as: NYSE (New York Stock Exchange), AMEX (American Stock Exchange), NNM (NASDAQ National Market), and NASQ (NASDAQ Small Cap) give companies, governments and other groups a platform to sell securities to the investing public. NASDAQ is abbreviated as NAS.

Turnover Ratio
The percentage of an exchange-traded fund or other investment vehicle's holdings that have been replaced with other holdings in a given year. Generally, low turnover ratio is favorable, because high turnover equates to higher brokerage transaction fees, which reduce fund returns.

US Bonds %
The percentage of the fund's assets invested in U.S. bonds. See **Asset Allocation**.

US Stocks %
The percentage of the fund's assets invested in U.S. stock. See **Asset Allocation**.

Website
The company's web address.

Wire Redemption
This indicates whether or not investors can redeem electronically. See **Services Offered**.

This section lists all of the Providers in Section I: Index of Exchange-Traded Funds. Address, Telephone and Website are provided where available.

AAM
AAM 18925 Base Camp Road Monument CO 80132
United States
800-617-0004
http://www.aamlive.com/publicsite/mutual-funds

Aberdeen Standard Investments
Aberdeen Standard Investments 405 Lexington Avenue
New York NY 10174 United States
212-918-4954
http://www.aberdeenstandardetfs.us

Acquirers Funds
21515 Hawthorne Boulevard, Suite 200 PMB#82,
Torrance, United States

AdvisorShares
AdvisorShares 2 Bethesda Metro Center, Suite 1330
Bethesda MD 20814 United States
877-843-3831
http://www.advisorshares.com

Affinity
Affinity 18111 Von Karman Ave., Suite 550 Irvine CA
92612 United States
http://www.affinityinvestment.com

AGFiQ
53 State Street Suite 1308 Boston MA 02109 United
States
617-292-9801
http://www.agfiq.com

Alpha Architect
Alpha Architect 213 Foxcroft Road Broomall PA 19008
United States
http://www.alphaarchitect.com/funds

AlphaClone
AlphaClone One Market Street Spear Tower, 36th Floor
San Francisco CA 94105 United States
415-967-2532
http://www.alphaclonefunds.com

AlphaMark
AlphaMark Funds PO Box 46707 Cincinatti OH 45246-
0707 United States
866-420-3350
http://www.alphamarkfunds.com

ALPS
ALPS 1290 Broadway, Suite 1100 Denver CO 80203
United States
866-759-5679
http://www.alpsfunds.com

ALPS ETF
ALPS ETF PO Box 328 Denver CO 80201-0328 United
States
855-724-0450
http://www.alpsfunds.com

American Century Investments
American Century Investments P.O. Box 419200,4500
Main Street Kansas City, MO 64141 United States
800-444-4015
http://www.americancentury.com

Amplifyetfs
3250 Lacey Road, Suite 130 Downers Grove Downers
Grove IL 60515 United States
630-487-2530
http://www.amplifyetfs.com

Aptus Capital Advisors
407 Johnson Avenue, Fairhope, Alabama 36532 United
States

ARK ETF Trust
ARK ETF Trust 155 West 19th Street, 5th Floor New York
New York 10011 United States
212-426-7040
http://www.ark-funds.com

ArrowShares
c/o Gemini Fund Services, LLC 17605 Wright Street,
Suite 2 Omaha NE 68130 United States
877-277-6933
http://www.ArrowShares.com

Aware
Aware United States

BlackRock
BlackRock Funds Providence RI 02940-8019 United
States
800-441-7762
http://www.blackrock.com

BMO Capital Markets
BMO Capital Markets United States
http://https://www.bmocm.com/

BMO Capital Markets Corp.
3 Times Square New York, NY 10036 New York NY
10036 United States

BOON
BOON P.O. Box 701 Milwaukee WI 53201-0701 United
States
800-617-0004
http://www.tboonetf.com

Cadence Capital Management
Cadence Capital Management 265 Franklin Street
Boston MA 02109 United States
617-367-7400

CAMBRIA ETF TRUST
CAMBRIA ETF TRUST 2711 Centreville Road Suite 400
Wilmington, DE 19808 Wilmington DE 19808 United
States
310-683-5500
http://www.cambriafunds.com

CBOE Vest
CBOE Vest 8730 Stony Point Parkway, Suite 205
Richmond VA 23235 United States
855-505-8378
http://www.cboevestfunds.com

Change Finance
Change Finance United States
http://www.changefinanceetf.com

Citigroup
Citigroup 388 Greenwich Street New York NULL NULL
United States

ClearShares
ClearShares United States
http://www.clear-shares.com

Columbia
Liberty Financial Funds P.O. Box 8081 Boston MA
02266-8081 United States
800-345-6611
http://www.columbiathreadneedleus.com

Credit Suisse AG
Kilmore House Park Lane Dublin Ireland

CSOP Asset Management
2801-2803, Two Exchange Square 8 Connaught Place
Central, Hong Kong Hong Kong
http://www.csopasset.us/en-us/product/etf/a50

Cushing ETFs
Cushing ETFs United States
http://www.cushingetfs.com

Davis ETFs
c/o Davis Selected Advisers, L.P. 2949 E. Elvira Rd., Ste.
101 Tucson Arizona 85756 United States
800-279-0279

Defiance ETFs
450 West 42nd Street New York New York United States

DeltaShares
DeltaShares United States
http://www.deltashares.com

Deutsche Asset Management
Deutsche Asset & Wealth Management 345 Park Avenue
New York NY 10154 United States
844-851-4255
http://www.deutsche-etfs.com

Deutsche Bank AG
Theodor-Heuss-Allee 72 Frankfurt am Main 60486
Germany

Deutsche Bank AG
Taunusanlage 12 Frankfurt 60325 Germany
496-991-000
http://www.deutsche-bank.de

Direxion Funds
Direxion Funds 1301 Avenue Of The Americas (6th
Avenue) New York NY 10019 United States
646-572-3390
http://www.direxionfunds.com

Distillate Capital Partners
53 West Jackson Blvd, Suite 530 Chicago, IL 60604
Chicago Illinois 60604 United States
http://distillatecapital.com/about

DWS
DWS 210 West 10th Street Kansas City MO 64105-1614
United States
http://dws.com

Eaton Vance
P.O. Boc 43027 Providence RI 02940-3027 United
States

ELEMENTS
ELEMENTS United States
212-449-2957
http://www.elementsetn.com

EMQQ
EMQQ 1 Freedom Valley Drive Oaks PA 19456 United
States
855-888-9892
http://www.emqqetf.com

EntrepreneurShares
EntrepreneurShares 175 Federal Street, Suite #875
Boston MA 02110 United States
http://www.ershares.com

Equbot
Equbot 450 Townsend St San Francisco United States
650-451-5497
http://www.equbotetf.com

ETFMG
ETFMG 30 Maple Street, Suite 2 NJ United States
http://www.etfmg.com

EVENT SHARES
EVENT SHARES 260 Newport Center Drive Newport
Beach CA 92660 United States
877-539-1510
http://www.EventSharesFunds.com

Exchange Traded Concepts
10900 Hefner Pointe Drive, Suite 207, Oklahoma City,
Oklahoma 73120 Oklahoma City United States

Exponential ETFs
Exponential ETFs United States
http://https://exponentialetfs.com/

Fidelity Investments
Fidelity Investments 82 Devonshire Street Boston MA
2109 United States
617-563-7000
http://www.institutional.fidelity.com

First Trust
First Trust 120 E. Liberty Drive, Suite 400 Wheaton IL
60187 United States
800-621-1675
http://www.ftportfolios.com/

Flexshares Trust
50 South LaSalle Street Chicago, Illinois 60603 Chicago
Illinois 60603 United States
855-353-9383
http://www.flexshares.com

FormulaFolioFunds
89 Ionia NW, Suite 600 Grand Rapids, MI 49503 United
States

Franklin Templeton Investments
Franklin Templeton Investments One Franklin Parkway,
Building 970, 1st Floor San Mateo CA 94403 United
States
650-312-2000
http://www.franklintempleton.com

Gabelli
Gabelli 1 Corporate Center Rye NY NY United States
914-921-5135
http://www.gabelli.com

Gadsden
Gadsden Eight Tower Bridge, 161 Washington Street,
Suite 580 Conshohocken PA 19428 United States

Global X Funds
Global X Funds 600 Lexington Avenue, 20th Floor New
York NY 10022 United States
888-493-8631
http://www.globalxfunds.com

Goldman Sachs
Goldman Sachs 200 West Stree New York NY 10282
United States
800-526-7384
http://www.gsamfunds.com

Graniteshares
Graniteshares 30 Vesey Street, 9th Floor New York New
York 10007 United States
http://www.graniteshares.com

Grayscale
Grayscale 636 Avenue of the Americas New York New
York 10011 United States
212-668-5920
http://grayscale.co/bitcoin-investment-trust/#overview

Hartford Funds
690 Lee Road Wayne PA 19087 United States
800-456-7526
http://www.hartfordfunds.com

Highland Funds
Highland Funds 200 Crescent Court, Suite 700 Dallas TX
75201 United States
877-665-1287
http://www.highlandfunds.com

Hoya Capital Real Estate
137 Rowayton Avenue Suite 430 Rowayton CT 06853
United States

Hull Tactical Funds
Hull Tactical Funds United States
http://www.hulltacticalfunds.com

iM Global Partner (US)
iM Global Partner 300 Barr Harbor Drive, Suite 720
Conshohocken PA United States
888-898-1041
http://www.imglobalpartner.com

Impact Shares
DALLAS, TEXAS United States
http://https://www.impactshares.org.

IndexIQ
IndexIQ 800 Westchester Avenue, Suite N-611 Rye
Brook NY 10573 United States
888-934-0777
http://www.indexiq.com

Innovation Shares
Innovation Shares 10900 Hefner Pointe Drive, Suite 207
Oklahoma City OK 73120 United States
833-466-6383
http://www.innovationshares.com

Innovator ETFs
Innovator ETFs 120 N Hale Street, Suite 200 Wheaton IL 60187 United States
800-208-5212
http://innovatoretfs.com/

InsightShares
InsightShares 10900 Hefner Pointe Drive, Suite 207 Oklahoma City OK 73120 United States
833-627-2417
http://www.insightshares.com

Inspire
Inspire 650 San Benito Street, Suite 130 Hollister CA 95023 United States

Invesco
Invesco 11 Greenway Plaza, Ste. 2500 Houston TX 77046 United States
800-659-1005
http://www.invesco.com/us

iShares
iShares 400 Howard Street San Francisco CA 94105 United States
800-474-2737
http://www.ishares.com

Ivy Funds
Ivy Funds Inc 6300 Lamar Ave Overland Park KS 66202 United States
http://www.ivyfunds.com

Janus Henderson
Janus 151 Detroit Street Denver CO 80206 United States
877-335-2687
http://janushenderson.com

John Hancock
601 Congress Street, Boston MA 02210 United States
800-225-5913
http://jhinvestments.com

JPMorgan
JPMorgan One Beacon Street Boston MA 02108 United States

JPMorgan
JPMorgan 270 Park Avenue New York NY 10017-2070 United States
800-480-4111
http://www.jpmorganfunds.com

JPMorgan Chase Financial Company LLC
383 Madison Avenue Floor 21 NY NY 10179 United States

Knowledge Leaders Capital
Knowledge Leaders Capital 370 17th Street, Suite 4930 Denver CO 80202 United States
303-763-1810
http://www.knowledgeleadersfunds.com

KraneShares
1350 Avenue of the Americas Second Floor New York NY 10019 United States
855-857-2638
http://www.kraneshares.com

Legg Mason
Legg Mason/Western 100 International Drive Baltimore MD 21202 United States
877-721-1926
http://www.leggmason.com

Little Harbor Advisers, LLC
Little Harbor Advisers, LLC 30 Doaks Lane Marblehead MA 01945 United States
781-639-3000

Loncar Investments
Loncar Investments United States
http://www.LoncarFunds.com

Main Management ETFs
Main Management ETFs 601 California Street, Suite 620 San Francisco CA 94108 United States
http://www.mainmgtetfs.com

Market Vectors
MARKET VECTORS 335 MADISON AVENUE - 19TH FLOOR New York NY 10017 United States
888-658-8287
http://www.marketvectorsetfs.com

M-CAM
513 East Main Street, #2014, Charlottesville, Virginia, 22903 United States

Merk Funds
Merk Funds P.O. Box 588 Portland ME 4112 United States
866-637-5386
http://www.merkfund.com

Metaurus
Metaurus 589 Fifth Avenue, Suite 808 New York NY 10017 United States
212-634-4250
http://https://www.metaurus.com/

Microsectors
44 Post Road West Westport, CT 06680 United States
203-557-6201

Milleis Investissements Funds
2-4, rue Eugène Ruppert L-2453 Luxembourg Luxembourg L-2453 Luxembourg

Motley Fool
Motley Fool 2000 Duke Street, Suite 175 Alexandria VA 22314 United States
http://www.foolfunds.com

Nationwide
Nationwide One Nationwide Plaza Columbus OH 43215
United States
800-848-0920
http://www.nationwide.com/mutualfunds

Natixis Funds
Natixis Funds 399 Boylston Street Boston MA 02116
United States
800-862-4863
http://NGAM.natixis.com

Nuveen
Nuveen Investment Trust John Nuveen & Co. Inc.
Chicago IL 60606 United States
312-917-8146
http://www.nuveen.com

O'Shares Investments
O'Shares Investments 60 State Street, Suite 700 Boston
MA 02109 United States
617-855-7670
http://www.oshares.com

Pacer
Pacer 16 Industrial Blvd, Suite 201 Paoli PA 19301
United States
http://www.paceretfs.com

Peritus
Peritus 10900 Hefner Pointe Drive, Suite 207 Oklahoma
City OK 73120 United States
http://www.hyldetf.com

PGIM Funds (Prudential)
PGIM Funds (Prudential) PO Box 9658 Providence RI
02940 United States
800-225-1852
http://www.pgiminvestments.com

PIMCO
PIMCO 840 Newport Center Drive, Suite 100 Newport
Beach CA 92660 United States
866-746-2602
http://www.pimco.com

Point Bridge Capital
Point Bridge Capital P.O. Box 701 Milwaukee WI 53201-
0701 United States
800-617-0004
http://www.investpolitically.com

PPTY
US United States
http://https://pptyetf.com

Premise Capital
300 East 5th Avenue Suite 265 Naperville IL 60563
United States
630-596-9911
http://www.premisecapital.com

Principal Funds
Principal Funds 430 W 7th St, Ste 219971 Kansas City
MO 64105-1407 United States
800-787-1621
http://www.principalfunds.com

Procure ETF Trust II
Procure ETF Trust II Robert Tull 16 Firebush Road
Levittown PA 19056 United States

ProShares
ProShares 7501 Wisconsin Avenue, Suite 1000 Bethesda
MD 20814 United States
866-776-5125
http://www.proshares.com

Reality Shares
Reality Shares 402 W Broadway, 28th Floor San Diego
CA 92101 United States
http://www.realityshares.com

Reality Shares ETF Trust
Reality Shares ETF Trust 402 West Broadway, Suite
2800 San Diego CA 92101 United States
619-487-1445
http://www.realityshares.com

Redwood
Redwood United States
http://www.redwoodmutualfund.com

Regents Park Funds, LLC
Regents Park Funds, LLC 4041 MacArthur Blvd., Suite
155 Newport Beach CA 92660 United States

Renaissance Capital
Renaissance Capital United States
866-486-6645
http://www.renaissancecapital.com

Robo Global
Robo Global United States
http://www.roboglobaletfs.com

Roundhill Financial
575 5th Avenue, 14th Floor New York United States

RYZZ Capital Management
9260 E. Raintree Drive Suite 100 Scottsdale AZ 85260
United States

SABA ETF
SABA ETF United States
212-542-4644
http://www.sabaetf.com

Sage
Sage Life Assurance of America Inc 969 High Ridge
Road, Suite 200 Stamford CT 6905 United States

Salt Financial
79 Madison Avenue, 8th Floor, New York New York
10016 United States
http://www.saltfinancial.com

Schwab ETFs
Schwab ETFs United States
800-435-4000
http://www.schwabfunds.com

Sofi
Sofi United States

SPDR State Street Global Advisors
SPDR State Street Global Advisors State Street Financial
Center, 1 Lincoln Street Boston MA 02111-2900 United
States
617-786-3000
http://www.spdrs.com

Spinnaker ETF Trust
116 South Franklin Street P. O. Box 69 Rocky Mount NC
27802 United States
252-972-9922

Sprott
Sprott United States
http://www.sprottetfs.com

Strategy shares
Strategy shares United States

Syntax
Syntax 110 East 59th Street, 31st Floor New York NY
10022 United States
212-880-0200
http://www.syntaxadvisors.com

Teucrium
Teucrium Three Main Street Suite 215 Burlington VT
05401 United States
802-540-0019
http://www.teucriumcornfund.com

Timothy Plan
Timothy Plan 1055 Maitland Center Commons Maitland
FL 32759 United States
800-662-0201
http://www.timothyplan.com

Tortoise Capital Advisors
Tortoise Capital Advisors 11550 Ash Street, Suite 300
Leawood KS 66211 United States
866-362-9331
http://www.tortoiseadvisors.com/

TrimTabs
TrimTabs 1350 Avenue of the Americas, Suite 248 New
York NY 10019 United States
http://www.trimtabsfunds.com

TWM FUNDS
Tiedemann New York City United States
http://www.twmfunds.com/

U.S. Global Investors
U.S. Global Investors P.O. Box 781234 San Antonio TX
78278-1234 United States
800-873-8637
http://www.usfunds.com

UBS
UBS Global Asset Management (Americas) Inc. 1285
Avenue of the Americas New York 10019 United States
800-647-1568
http://www.ubs.com/

UBS Group AG
Bahnhofstrasse 45 Zürich 8098 Switzerland
412-037-1952
http://www.ubs.com

USAI ETF
USAI ETF P.O. Box 701 Milwaukee WI 53201-0701
United States
800-617-0004
http://www.usaietf.com

USCF Investments
USCF 1290 Broadway, Suite 1100 Denver CO 80203
United States
http://www.uscfinvestments.com

Validea
Validea 363 Ridgewood Road 06107 United States
http://www.valideafunds.com

VanEck
Van Eck Associates Corporation 666 Third Avenue New
York NY 10017 United States
800-826-1115
http://www.vaneck.com

Vanguard
Vanguard 100 Vanguard Boulevard Malvern PA 19355
United States
877-662-7447
http://www.vanguard.com

VelocityShares
VelocityShares 17 Old Kings Highway South United
States
203-992-4301
http://www.janusindices.com

VictoryShares
Victory Shares 4249 Easton Way, Suite 400 Columbus
OH 43219 United States
http://www.VictorySharesLiterature.com

Vident Financial
Vident Financial 201 17th Street, Suite 300 Atlanta GA
30363 United States
800-617-0004
http://www.videntfinancial.com

Virtus
Virtus Opportunities Trust 101 Munson Street Greenfield
MA 1301 United States
800-243-1574
http://www.virtus.com

WBI Investments
34 Sycamore Ave Suite 1-E Little Silver NJ 07739 United
States
732-842-4920
http://www.wbishares.com

Wealthn LLC
Wealthn LLC 3532 Muirwood Drive Newtown PA 19073
United States

weatherstorm
weatherstorm United States

WisdomTree
WisdomTree 245 Park Avenue, 35th floor New York NY
10167 United States
866-909-9473
http://www.wisdomtree.com

YieldShares
YieldShares 10900 Hefner Pointe Drive, Suite 207
Oklahoma OK 73120 United States
http://www.yieldshares.com

Weiss Ratings Investment Series

Weiss Ratings Investment Research Guide to Stock Mutual Funds

Weiss Ratings Investment Research Guide to Stock Mutual Funds provides immediate access to Weiss' Buy-Hold-Sell Investment Ratings, key rating factors, and summary financial data for 20,000 stock mutual funds—more than any other ratings publication. This easy-to-use guide provides understandable, accurate investment ratings so investors can make informed decisions about their investment selections.

- Index of Stock Mutual Funds – with data on 20,000 funds
- Expanded Analysis of 100 Largest Stock Mutual Funds
- Best All-Around Stock Mutual Funds
- Consistent Return BUY Stock Mutual Funds
- High Performance Stock Mutual Funds
- Low Volatility Stock Mutual Funds
- BUY Rated Stock Mutual Funds by Category

Annual Subscription of 4 Quarterly Issues: $549 | Single Issue: $279

Weiss Ratings Investment Research Guide to Bond & Money Market Mutual Funds

Weiss Ratings Investment Research Guide to Bond & Money Market Mutual Funds offers readers a one-stop source for important, up-to-date financial data and easy-to-use Weiss Investment Ratings for 8,000 bond and money market mutual funds. Weiss Ratings takes the guesswork out of investment research, providing consumers and investors with understandable information and proven investment ratings.

- Index of Bond & Money Market Mutual Funds – over 8,000 funds
- Analysis of 100 Largest Bond & Money Market Mutual Funds
- Best All-Around Bond & Money Market Mutual Funds
- High Performance Bond & Money Market Mutual Funds
- Low Volatility Bond & Money Market Mutual Funds
- BUY Rated Bond & Money Market Mutual Funds by Category

Annual Subscription of 4 Quarterly Issues: $549 | Single Issue: $279

Weiss Ratings Investment Research Guide to Stocks

Taking into account the thousands of stock options available, it is no surprise that consumers need assistance. It is a complex subject and consumers want unbiased, independent guidance in helping them find a path to investing that is focused on their needs. *Weiss Ratings Investment Research Guide to Stocks* gives investors and consumers independent, unbiased data on which stocks to consider and those that should be avoided.

- Index of Stocks – over 11,000 U.S. traded stocks are listed
- Best Performing Stocks
- High Yield BUYs
- Stocks with High Volatility
- Undervalued Stocks by Sector
- BUY Rated Stocks by Sector
- Expanded Analysis of All A Rated Stocks

Annual Subscription of 4 Quarterly Issues: $549 | Single Issue: $279

GET YOUR RATINGS ONLINE!

Designed for both the beginner and the seasoned investor, Financial Ratings Series Online provides the accurate, independent information you need to make INFORMED DECISIONS about your finances, including insurance, Medicare, banking and investment options.

"An excellent financial tool that will certainly get an enormous amount of use anywhere it's available, this rates a strong overall ten. Recommended for public and academic libraries." –Library Journal

This must-have resource provides accurate, unbiased, easy-to-use guidance on:

- How to Find the Safest **Bank** or **Credit Union** in your area
- How to Avoid the Weakest **Insurance Companies**... and How to Find the Best Ones
- How to Pick the Best **Medicare Supplement Insurance Plan** and Pick Providers with the Lowest Premiums
- How to Find the Best **Mutual Funds**... and Make Sure your Retirement Funds are Safe
- How to Pick the Best-Performing **Stocks**
- How to Navigate the **Tough Decisions** in a wide variety of Healthcare and Insurance topics
- Get the Facts on How to Best **Manage your Finances**

All powered by the independent, unbiased ratings that Weiss Ratings and Grey House Publishing have been providing for years!

Selected by *Library Journal* as one of the Best Databases for 2018!

This new online database gives library patrons more tools, more power and more flexibility than ever before!

When your library subscribes to the online database, using your library card, you can:

- Get independent, unbiased ratings of over **63,000** stocks, funds, insurers and financial institutions
- Create your own **Screeners** to compare companies or investments using criteria that are important to you
- **Compare** companies or investments side by side
- Create your own **Personal Account** to store and manage your own **Watchlists**, get email updates of upgrades or downgrades, customize your home page, and log in from anywhere.
- See current **Stock Quotes** & **Live News** Feeds
- Read **Articles** on timely investment, banking and insurance topics

Visit the reference desk at your local library and ask for Weiss Ratings!

https://greyhouse.weissratings.com